THE GUINNESS ENCYCLOPEDIA

GUINNESS PUBLISHING

First published 1990

Reprinted 1990, 1992 (with updates and corrections),
1993 (with updates and corrections)

© Guinness Publishing Ltd., 1990

Published in Great Britain by Guinness Publishing Ltd.,
33 London Road, Enfield, Middlesex

Colour origination by Bright Arts (HK) Ltd., Hong Kong
Printed and bound in Italy by New Interlitho SpA, Milan

'Guinness' is a registered trademark of
Guinness Publishing Ltd.

British Library Cataloguing in Publication Data:
The Guinness encyclopedia.
1. Encyclopaedias in English
032

ISBN 0-85112-740-1

Editor
Ian Crofton

Deputy Editors
Clive Carpenter
Ben Dupré
Richard Milbank
Sian Mills

Editorial Systems Assistant
Tina Persaud

Design
David Roberts
Amanda Sedge
Jon Lucas

Picture Editor
Alex Goldberg

Picture Assistants
Muriel Ling
Julie O'Leary

Illustrators
Peter Harper
Robert and Rhoda Burns
Edward Q. Botchway
Pat Gibbon
The Maltings Partnership
Matthew Hillier FSCD
Peter Bull
Chris Forsey
Mike Long (Design Associates)
Ad Vantage
Kevin Williamson
Suzanne Alexander

Index
Ann Hall

INTRODUCTION

The Guinness Encyclopedia is a completely new kind of single-volume encyclopedia. All other single-volume encyclopedias are arranged as A-to-Z listings, and so only give isolated snippets of information – useful for looking up a quick reference or checking a fact, but unable to present the reader with a complete overview of a subject.

The word *encyclopedia* is derived from the Greek for 'general education', and it is a general introduction to all the main fields of knowledge that *The Guinness Encyclopedia* aims to provide. This aim is achieved by a thematic rather than an alphabetical arrangement: the world of knowledge is divided into twelve main sections – the physical sciences, animals and plants, history, the visual arts, and so on. Each section is then subdivided into a series of in-depth articles on key topics, each presented on a self-contained double-page spread. In this way, the Encyclopedia does not just list facts – it explains them, and puts them in context.

An equally important aim of *The Guinness Encyclopedia* is to provide stimulation and interest – to embody the excitement of acquiring knowledge. To this end, the text is combined with a vast number of full-colour illustrations – photographs, paintings, maps, diagrams, pie charts and graphs – all of which have been chosen for their ability to convey additional information.

Because *The Guinness Encyclopedia* is not just a source of facts, many of the sections will merit careful study. This is particularly so in the physical sciences, mathematics, economics and philosophy; the articles dealing with these subjects attempt to give an idea of their underlying principles, together with a flavour of the latest advances. Hence the reader will find information on matters – such as quantum physics, infinity, and logic – that are rarely covered in schools, but which are of fundamental importance.

The Sections of the Encyclopedia

The Guinness Encyclopedia is a network of knowledge, around which readers will soon find their way. To start with, a quick glance through the Contents on the following pages will show the main sections of the Encyclopedia and what subjects fall under which heading.

The first section, **The Nature of the Universe**, deals with the physical sciences – astronomy, physics and chemistry – together with mathematics. The earth sciences – geology and physical geography – are dealt with under **The Restless Earth**, while the life sciences are covered under **The Living Planet** and **The Human Organism**. The former section is concerned with broad biological topics such as classification, evolution, behaviour, ecosystems and agriculture, and also provides extensive details of the main animal and plant groups. The latter section, focused on the human being, deals with anatomy and physiology, psychology, and medicine.

The way human beings organize themselves is reviewed under **The World Today**, which not only includes sociology, politics and economics, but also discusses a range of important contemporary issues, such as the women's movement, nuclear disarmament, and threats to the environment. **Technology and Industry** is concerned both with how things work – from nuclear power stations to jet aircraft – and with how they are made. Although the emphasis is on the latest developments, historical perspectives – including details of key inventors – are also given.

A History of the World gives a broad overview of world history, from prehistoric times to the present. As with the sections on the arts – **The Visual Arts**, **Music and Dance** and **Language and Literature** – the emphasis is on Europe and America, although coverage is also given of non-Western history and traditions. Further details on the history of each of the world's countries will be found under **The Countries of the World** section (see below). **Religion and Philosophy** discusses how human beings have attempted to make sense of profound issues outside the scope of science. As well as covering the main religious traditions of the world, the section also looks at those elements that different religions have in common. The pages on philosophy start by defining the subject and listing major philosophers, and then proceed to examine various central philosophical issues.

The last section of the Encyclopedia, **The Countries of the World**, differs from the other sections in that it is an alphabetical listing of all the world's sovereign states. The flag and a map of each state are included, together with basic statistics and details of government, geography, economy and history.

How to use the Encyclopedia

In the body of the Encyclopedia itself, the pages have colour-coded flashes at the top to indicate to which main section they belong. The reader will quickly become familiar with these colours and be able to flick from section to section with ease.

Each topic within every main section is contained within a double-page spread, and on each spread there is a 'See Also' box to guide the reader to related spreads in the same section or elsewhere. There are also cross-references within the text itself to guide the reader to other pages where further relevant details will be found. Each time a technical term is introduced, it is either *italicized* and defined on the spot, or a cross-reference is given to a page where a definition will be found.

In highly interrelated subjects such as physics, cross-referencing is particularly important, as the full understanding of one concept may well depend on the understanding of other concepts dealt with elsewhere. For example, a fuller understanding of light – which is principally dealt with under 'Optics' – will be gained if the reader also refers to the spreads on 'Wave Theory' and 'Electromagnetism'; those spreads are also important to the understanding of 'Quantum Theory' and 'Atoms and Subatomic Particles'.

In addition to consulting the Contents, using the colour codes and following up cross-references, a final invaluable tool in finding one's way around the Encyclopedia is the index, in which every key concept, idea, object, institution, person and place mentioned in the Encyclopedia is listed, together with a page reference. Where there are numerous page references, the index entry is subdivided to indicate which aspect of the entry is dealt with on which page.

Acknowledgements

A vast number of people have been involved in the planning and building of this Encyclopedia. They include writers, advisers, editors, designers, illustrators, picture researchers and many others, and they – together with all those agencies, museums, galleries and individuals who supplied pictures for use in the Encyclopedia – are listed on the following pages. To all those who have contributed in whatever capacity, Guinness Publishing wish to extend their sincere thanks.

Ian Crofton
Editor

CONTENTS

1. THE NATURE OF THE UNIVERSE

The Universe and Cosmology 4
Time 6
Stars and Galaxies 8
The Sun and the Solar System 10
The Inner Planets 12
The Outer Planets 14
The History of Astronomy 16
Space Exploration 18
Motion and Force 20
Forces affecting Solids and Fluids 22
Thermodynamics 24
Quantum Theory and Relativity 26
Wave Theory 28
Acoustics 30
Optics 32
Electromagnetism 34
Electricity in Action 36
Atoms and Subatomic Particles 38
What is Chemistry? 40
Elements and the Periodic Table 42
Chemical Bonds 44
Chemical Reactions 46
Small Molecules 48
Metals 50
Natural Compounds 52
Man-made Products 54
Chemicals in Everyday Life 56
The Scientific Method 58
The History of Science 60
Mathematics and its Applications 62
Number Systems and Algebra 64
Sets and Paradoxes 66
Correspondence, Counting and Infinity 68
Functions, Graphs and Change 70
Probability: Chance and Choice 72

2. THE RESTLESS EARTH

The Earth's Structure and Atmosphere 76
Plate Tectonics 78
Earthquakes 80
Volcanoes 82
The Formation of Rocks 84
Mountains 86
Caves 88
Ice 90
Deserts 92
Rivers and Lakes 94
Coasts 96
Islands 98
The Oceans 100
Weather 102
Climatic and Vegetation Regions 104

3. THE LIVING PLANET

The Classification of Life 108
The Beginnings of Life 110
Evolution 112
Genetics and Inheritance 114
Plant Physiology 116
Non-flowering Plants 118
Flowering Plants 120
Primitive Animals 122
Arthropods 1: Crustaceans, Myriapods and Arachnids 124
Arthropods 2: Insects 126
Fishes 128
Amphibians 130
Dinosaurs 132
Reptiles 134
Birds of the Sea and Air 136
Birds of the Land and Water 138
Early Mammals 140
Monotremes and Marsupials 142
Edentates, Pangolins and the Aardvark 144
Bats 146
Insectivores 148
Rodents, Lagomorphs and Hyraxes 150
Carnivores 1: Cats, Civets, Hyenas 152
Carnivores 2: Dogs, Bears, Raccoons, Weasels 154
Elephants and Perissodactyls: Horses, Rhinos, Tapirs 156
Artiodactyls 1: Pigs, Peccaries, Hippos, Camels 158
Artiodactyls 2: Deer, Giraffes, Bovids, etc. 160
Marine Mammals 162
Primates 164
Animal Communication 166
Territory, Mating, Social Organization 168
Migration 170
How Animals Move 172
Parasitism and Symbiosis 174
The Biosphere 176
Ecosystems: Aquatic 178
Ecosystems: Coniferous and Temperate Forests 180
Ecosystems: Tropical Forests 182
Ecosystems: Grasslands 184
Ecosystems: Extreme 186
Arable Farming 188
Livestock Farming 190
Forestry 192
Fishing 194
Food Processing 196

4. THE HUMAN ORGANISM

Physical Evolution 200
Reproduction 202
Physical Development 204
How People Move 206
Food, Diet and Digestion 208
Respiration and Circulation 210
The Immune System 212
Glands and Hormones 214
Touch, Taste and Smell 216
Seeing and Hearing 218
The Nervous System 220
The Brain 222
Perception 224
The Power of Speech 226
Body Language 228
Learning, Creativity and Intelligence 230
Sleep and Dreams 232
Mental Disorders 234
Non-Infectious Diseases 236
Infectious Diseases 238
Surgery 240
Medical Technology 242
Preventing Disease 244
Drug Abuse 246
The History of Medicine 248
Alternative Medicine 250

5. THE WORLD TODAY

Age Roles and Rites of Passage 254
The Family 256
Social Stratification and Divisions 258
Education 260
Deviance, Crime and Law Enforcement 262
The Law: Criminal and Civil 264
Government and the People 266
Political Theories of the Left 268
Political Theories of the Right 270
Economic Systems 272
Microeconomics 274
Macroeconomics 276
Trade 278
From Raw Material to the Consumer 280
Business Organization and Accounting 282
International Organizations 1: The United Nations 284
International Organizations 2 286
Nuclear Armament and Disarmament 288
Civil and Human Rights 290
The Women's Movement 292
Youth Movements 294
Population and Hunger 296
The Third World and the Developed World 298
Threats to the Environment 300

6. TECHNOLOGY AND INDUSTRY

Energy 1: Coal, Oil and Nuclear 304
Energy 2: Other Sources 306
Engines 308
Oil and Gas 310
Mining, Minerals and Metals 312
Iron and Steel 314
Rubber and Plastics 316
Textiles 318
Chemicals and Biotechnology 320
Printing 322
Photography and Film 324
Radio, Television and Video 326
Hi-fi 328
Telecommunications 330
Seeing the Invisible 332
Computers 334
Artificial Intelligence 336
Building Construction 338
Civil Engineering 340
Ships 1: Development 342
Ships 2: The Modern Ship 344

CONTENTS

Railways 346
Aircraft 1: Development 348
Aircraft 2: How Aircraft Work 350
The Motorcar 1: Development 352
The Motorcar 2: How Cars Work 354
Weaponry 356

7. A HISTORY OF THE WORLD

Discovering the Past 360
Human Prehistory 362
The Ancient Near East 364
Ancient Egypt 366
Minoans and Mycenaeans 368
Archaic and Classical Greece 370
Alexander the Great and the 372
    Hellenistic World
The Celts 374
The Rise of Rome 376
The Roman Empire 378
The Decline of Rome 380
China to the Colonial Age 382
India and Southeast Asia to the 384
    Colonial Age
Japan to the 20th Century 386
Africa, Australasia and Oceania to the 388
    Colonial Age
Pre-Columbian America 390
The Rise of Islam 392
The Successors of Rome 394
The Invasions 396
Christianity Resurgent 398
The Hundred Years War 400
Crisis in Europe 402
Medieval and Renaissance Economy, 404
    Society and Exploration
Medieval and Renaissance Culture 406
The Reformation 408
The Spanish and Portuguese Empires 410
The Rise of Britain 412
Louis XIV 414
European Empires in the 17th and 416
    18th Centuries
The Enlightenment 418
The Industrial and Agricultural 420
    Revolutions
The Birth of the USA 422
The French Revolution 424
The Revolutionary and Napoleonic 426
    Wars

Nationalism in Europe 428
The Expansion of the USA 430
The Peak of Empire 432
Industrial Society 434
World War I 436
The Russian Revolutions 438
The Postwar Settlement 440
The Growth of Totalitarianism 442
World War II 444
China in the 20th Century 446
Decolonization 448
The Cold War 450
The Wars in Vietnam 452
The Middle East 454

8. RELIGION AND PHILOSOPHY

What is Religion? 458
Religions of the Ancient Near East 460
The Primal Religions: Ancient Europe 462
The Primal Religions: Modern Times 464
The Religions of India 466
Buddhism 468
Religions of China and Japan 470
Judaism 472
Christianity: Belief and Practice 474
World Christianity 476
Islam 478
Worship, Prayer and Pilgrimage 480
Sacred Space, Sacred Time 482
Good and Evil 484
What is Philosophy? 486
Knowledge and Reality 488
Mind and Body 490
Ethics 492
Logic and Argument 494
The Philosophy of Language 496

9. THE VISUAL ARTS

Art Techniques 1: Painting and 500
    Drawing
Art Techniques 2: Sculpture and 502
    Printmaking
Prehistoric Art 504
Art of the Ancient Near East and 506
    Egypt
Greek and Roman Art 508

Islamic Art 510
The Arts of Southern Asia, Australasia 512
    and Oceania
Chinese and Japanese Art 514
Native American and African Art 516
Early Medieval and Byzantine Art 518
Gothic Painting and Sculpture 520
Gothic Architecture 522
The Early Renaissance 524
Early Netherlandish and German Art 526
The High Renaissance and Mannerism 528
The Baroque and Classicism 530
The Dutch School 532
Rococo and Neoclassicism 534
Romanticism 536
Architecture and the Applied Arts in 538
    the 19th Century
Realism 540
Impressionism 542
Post-Impressionism and Fauvism 544
Symbolism, Secession and 546
    Expressionism
Cubism and Abstraction 548
Dada and Surrealism 550
Architecture and the Applied Arts in 552
    the 20th Century
Movements in Art since 1945 554
Photography as Art 556
The Silent Cinema 558
Hollywood 560
World Cinema 562
How a Film is Made 564

10. MUSIC AND DANCE

What is Music? 568
Plainsong and Polyphony 570
Music of the Baroque 572
The Classical Period 574
Music of the Romantics 576
Modernists and Others 578
The New Music 580
The Symphony Orchestra and its 582
    Instruments
Opera 584
Folk Music 586
Popular Music in the 20th Century 588
Music from around the World 590
The World of Dance 592
Folk and Social Dancing 594

Classical Ballet 596
Modern Dance 598

11. LANGUAGE AND LITERATURE

The World's Languages 602
Writing Systems 604
The Story of English 606
How Language Works 608
The Language of Signs 610
The Making of Myths 612
Classical Literature 614
The Literature of Asia 616
Medieval Epic and Romance 618
Medieval Tales 620
Renaissance Theatre 622
Renaissance Poetry 624
Classicism in Literature 626
The Beginnings of the Novel 628
Romanticism in Europe 630
The British Romantics 632
Realism and Naturalism 634
The Novel in 19th-Century Britain 636
American Literature of the 638
    19th Century
Symbolism, Aestheticism and 640
    Modernism
Experimental Theatre 642
Modern Drama in Britain and the USA 644
Modern Poetry in English 646
The Modern Novel 648
Popular Literature 650
Literary Theory and 652
    Literary Criticism
Journalism 654

12. THE COUNTRIES OF THE WORLD

An A-Z of all the world's countries. 656
    Basic facts, plus details on government,
    geography economy and history.

INDEX 740

PICTURE ACKNOWLEDGEMENTS

The Publishers would like to thank the following for
permission to reproduce pictures in the Encyclopedia:

The Albertina Collection
Allsport (UK) Ltd.
Alte Pinakothek (Munich)
The Alton Telegraph (Illinois)
Ancient Art & Architecture Collection
Archiv für Kunst und Geschichte
Art Directors Photo Library
The Art Institute of Chicago
Artists Rights Society, Inc.
Ashmolean Museum (Oxford)
Aspect Picture Library
The Associated Press
Austin Rover Group Ltd.
Austrian Institute (London)
De Beers
Bell Laboratories
Bibliothèque Nationale (Paris)
Bildarchiv Paysan
Bildarchiv Preussischer Kulturbesitz
Bodleian Library (Oxford)
The Bridgeman Art Library
British Coal
British Museum
BP International Ltd.
Chemical Design Ltd. (Oxford)
Christie's
Bruce Coleman
Colorphoto Hinz (Basel)
Colorific Photo Library
Courtauld Institute (London)
DACS
Daimler-Benz Aktiengesellschaft
Demart Pro Arte BV
Derby Art Gallery
Zoe Dominic/Catherine Ashmore
Professor Ronald Draper
Dr Roland Emson
E T Archive
Mary Evans Picture Library
Explorer/FPG
Fine Art Photographic Library
Ford Motor Company
Werner Forman Archive
Galleria degli Uffizi (Florence)
Galleria Nazionale delle Marche (Urbino)
Gamma Presse Images
Giraudon
The Robert Harding Picture Library
Hoa-Qui
The Hulton Picture Company
Idemitsu Museum (Tokyo)
Images Colour Library
Imperial War Museum
INCAFO Editorial (Barcelona)
Jacana Press Agency
Japan Information Centre
The Kobal Collection Kunsthaus (Zürich)

Simon McBride Photographic Library
The Mansell Collection
The Metropolitan Museum of Art (New
    York)
Motor-Presse International (Stuttgart)
Musée Carnavalet (Paris)
Musée d'Art et d'Histoire (Geneva)
Musée des Beaux-Arts (Dijon)
Musée et Château de Chantilly (Musée
    Condé)
Musée National des Arts Africains et
    Océaniens (Paris)
Musée Guimet (Paris)
Musée d'Art Moderne (Paris)
Musée National de l'Automobile,
    (Mulhouse)
Musée d'Orsay (Paris)
Musée du Louvre
Musée Gustave Moreau (Paris)
Musée National d'Art Moderne (Paris)
Musée Saint-Denis (Reims)
Museo Archeologico Nazionale (Naples)
Museo del Prado (Madrid)
Museu Nacional de Arte Antiga (Lisbon)
Museum of London
The Museum of Modern Art (New York)
Museum of the Moving Image (London)
Mykonos Museum (Greece)
N A S A
Nasjonalgalleriet (Oslo)
National Archaeological Museum (Athens)
National Film Archive (London)
National Galerie (Berlin)
National Gallery (London)
National Gallery of Ireland
National Maritime Museum (Haifa)
National Motor Museum (Beaulieu)
National Museum (Ljubljana)
National Museum (Naples)
National Palace Museum (Taipei)
National Portrait Gallery (London)
National Power
Natural History Museum (London)
Öffentliche Kunstsammlung (Basel)
Österreichische Galerie (Vienna)
Oxford University Press
Photo Researchers, Inc.
Planet Earth Pictures
Popperfoto
Redferns
The Research House
Réunion des Musées Nationaux (Paris)
Rex Features
David Roberts
The Royal Collection
Royal Commonwealth Society
Royal Ontario Museum (Canada)

Saatchi Collection
Scala
Schiller-Nationalmuseum (Marbach)
Science Photo Library
Scottish National Portrait Gallery
Silvestris Fotoservice
SPADEM
Spectrum Colour Library
Staatsgalerie (Stuttgart)
Städelsches Kunstinstitut und Städtische
    Galerie (Frankfurt)
Statens Konstmueer (Stockholm)
Succession H. Matisse
Sun Newspaper
Sygma
Syndication International
Tate Gallery (London)
Michael J.H. Taylor
Telegraph Colour Library
Texas Children's Hospital
Topham Picture Source
United States Navy
Van Gogh Museum (Amsterdam)
VG-Bild-Kunst
Michael Vickers
Victoria & Albert Museum (London)
Vienna Classical Art Collection
Virginia Museum of Fine Arts
Gerry Wooldridge Photography
Yale University Art Gallery
Zefa Picture Library

The Publishers would like to express
special appreciation to the following
individuals who have assisted us with
the illustrations:

Ronald Sheridan
Jurgen Raible
Hannelore Schmidt
James Clift
Catherine Ashmore
Veronique Doutaz
Françoise Rachelle
Catherine Terk
Marie-Hélène Cambos
Gary Fisk
Françoise Mestre
Joëlle Pichon
Debra Rahn
Isobel Volf
Maria Storey
Anne Jones
Billie Love

The table on page 655 from Roland
Barthes' *S/Z* is reproduced by per-
mission of Les Editions du Seuil,
Paris.

UNITS OF MEASUREMENT

SI units – Système Internationale d'Unités – are the most widely used units of measurement and are used universally for scientific and most technical purposes. SI is the modern form of the metric system, which is based on the metre as a unit of length and the kilogram as a unit of weight, and was first adopted in France in 1799. Other systems of units commonly employed include the British imperial system and the related US customary units.

In the SI system there are seven *base units*, which relate to fundamental standards of length, mass, time, etc. Additionally, there are two geometrical *supplementary units*. The base units may be combined to form *derived units*; for example, the SI units of length and time may be combined to form units of acceleration or velocity. Further details on the more commonly used units will be found in the sections on physics and chemistry (pp. 20–57).

SI Base Units

Quantity	SI unit	symbol
Length	metre	m
Mass	kilogram	kg
Time	second	s
Electric current	ampere	A
Thermodynamic temperature	kelvin	K
Luminous intensity	candela	cd
Amount of substance	mole	mol

SI Supplementary Units

Quantity	SI unit	symbol
Plane angle	radian	rad
Solid angle	steradian	sr

Named SI Derived Units

Quantity	SI unit	symbol
Frequency	hertz	Hz
Force	newton	N
Pressure	pascal	Pa
Energy	joule	J
Power	watt	W
Temperature	degree Celsius	°C
Electric charge	coulomb	C
Potential difference	volt	V
Electric resistance	ohm	Ω
Electric conductance	siemens	S
Electric capacitance	farad	F
Inductance	henry	H
Magnetic flux	weber	Wb
Magnetic flux density	tesla	T
Luminous flux	lumen	lm
Illumination	lux	lx
Radiation activity	becquerel	Bq
Radiation absorbed dose	gray	Gy

Additional SI Derived Units

Quantity	SI unit	symbol
Area	square metre	m^2
Volume	cubic metre	m^3
Velocity	metres per second	$m\,s^{-1}$
Acceleration	metres per second per second	$m\,s^{-2}$
Density	kilograms per cubic metre	$kg\,m^{-3}$
Mass rate of flow	kilograms per second	$kg\,s^{-1}$
Volume rate of flow	cubic metres per second	$m^3\,s^{-1}$

Multiples and Submultiples

SI units are used in decimal *multiples* and *submultiples* of both the base units and derived units, for example 1 kilogram is divided into 1000 milligrams.

Submultiple	prefix	symbol
$\times 10^{-18}$	atto-	a
$\times 10^{-15}$	femto-	f
$\times 10^{-12}$	pico-	p
$\times 10^{-9}$	nano-	n
$\times 10^{-6}$	micro-	μ
$\times 10^{-3}$	milli-	m
$\times 10^{-2}$	centi-	c
$\times 10^{-1}$	deci-	d

Multiple	prefix	symbol
$\times 10$	deca-	da
$\times 10^2$	hecto-	h
$\times 10^3$	kilo-	k
$\times 10^6$	mega-	M
$\times 10^9$	giga-	G
$\times 10^{12}$	tera-	T
$\times 10^{15}$	peta-	P
$\times 10^{18}$	exa-	E

Metric Conversions

Length

1 mm	= 0.039 37 in
1 cm (10 mm)	= 0.393 700 78 in
1 m (100 cm)	= 3.280 840 ft (1 foot = 12 inches)
1 m	= 1.093 61 yd (1 yard = 3 feet)
1 km (1000 m)	= 0.621 371 1 mi (1 mile = 1760 yards)

Area

1 cm^2	= 0.155 sq in
1 m^2 (10 000 cm^2)	= 10.763 9 sq ft (144 sq in = 1 sq ft)
	= 1.195 99 sq yd (9 sq ft = 1 sq yd)
1 hectare (10 000 m^2)	= 2.471 05 acres (4840 sq yd = 1 acre)
1 km^2	= 0.386 1 sq mi (640 acres = 1 sq mi)

Mass

1 gram	= 0.035 274 ounces (avoirdupois)
1 kilogram (1000 grams)	= 2.204 62 lb (16 oz = 1 pound)
1 tonne (1000 kg)	= 0.984 206 5 tons (imperial) (2240 lb = 1 ton)
	= 0.8786 tons (US) (2000 lb = 1 US ton)

Volume

1 cm^3	= 0.061 02 cubic in
1 dm^3 (1000 cm^3/1 litre)	= 61.023 cubic in
1 m^3 (1000 dm^3)	= 35.314 cubic ft

THE
GUINNESS
ENCYCLOPEDIA

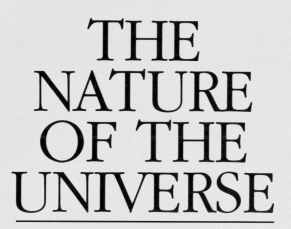

THE NATURE OF THE UNIVERSE

'The most incomprehensible
thing about the world
is that it is comprehensible.'

Albert Einstein

The Universe and Cosmology

The study of the universe, its overall structure and origin, is known as _cosmology_. In the 17th century, the universe was thought to be static, infinite and unchanging. Modern cosmology can be traced back to the 1920s when the American astronomer Edwin Hubble, using observations made by Vesto Slipher in 1912, showed that the space between galaxies is increasing and the universe is therefore expanding.

SEE ALSO

- TIME p. 6
- STARS AND GALAXIES p. 8
- THE HISTORY OF ASTRONOMY p. 16
- NEWTON AND FORCE p. 20
- QUANTUM THEORY AND RELATIVITY p. 26
- WAVE THEORY p. 28
- OPTICS p. 32
- ATOMS AND SUBATOMIC PARTICLES p. 38

There are several theories describing the origin and future of the universe. Among these, the big-bang theory is the most widely accepted. Opinions differ, however, as to the future of the universe. Some think that it will continue to expand for ever, whereas others believe that it will eventually end by collapsing in on itself in a big crunch.

The big bang

The universe is thought to have originated between 15 000 and 20 000 million years ago in a cataclysmic event known as the _big bang_. Theoretical models of the big bang suggest that events in the early history of the universe occurred very rapidly.

At the beginning of time, the universe comprised a mixture of different subatomic particles, including electrons, positrons, neutrinos and antineutrinos (see p. 38), together with photons of radiation.

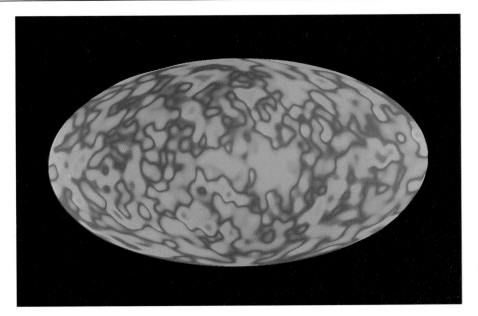

Echoes of the early universe. This microwave map of the whole sky was created using data from the Cosmic Background Explorer (COBE) satellite. It shows minute variations (between blue and pink) in the cosmic microwave radiation some 300 000 years after the big bang, and may explain the origin of the 'lumpiness' of the universe.

The temperature was 100 000 million °C (180 000 million °F) and its density 4000 million times that of water.

One second later, the temperature has dropped to 10 000 million °C (18 000 million °F). Matter is spreading out and the density of the universe has fallen to 400 000 times that of water. Heavier particles, protons and neutrons, begin to form.

Fourteen seconds later the temperature has dropped to 3000 million °C (5400 million °F). Oppositely charged positrons and electrons are annihilating each other and liberating energy. Stable nuclei of helium consisting of two protons and two neutrons begin to form.

Three minutes after the creation of the universe, the temperature has fallen to 900 million °C (1620 million °F). This is cool enough for deuterium nuclei consisting of one proton and one neutron to form.

Thirty minutes later, the temperature is 300 million °C (540 million °F). Very few of the original particles remain, most of the electrons and protons having been annihilated by their antiparticles, positrons and antiprotons. Many of the remaining protons and neutrons have combined to form hydrogen and helium nuclei and the density of the universe is about one tenth that of water. Expansion of the universe continues and the hydrogen and helium begins to form into stars and galaxies (see p. 8).

The Copernican universe. Nikolaus Copernicus (1473–1543) correctly argued that the planets orbit the Sun, but he mistakenly thought the Sun was at the centre of the universe. In fact the universe has no centre.

ASTRONOMICAL DISTANCES

The *light year* is a unit used to measure great distances, and is equal to the distance travelled by light in one year. Light (in a vacuum) travels at 300 000 km/sec (186 000 mi/sec), and so a light year is approximately 9 461 000 million km (5 875 000 million mi).

Distances to nearby stars can be measured by the *parallax method*. Any object, when viewed from two different vantage points, will appear to move against a background of more distant objects. This apparent change in position is called the *parallax*, and is measured as an angle. Thus if a nearby star is viewed from the Earth at intervals of six months, the Earth will have moved from one side of its orbit to the other and the star will seem to move against the background of more distant stars. The diameter of the Earth's orbit is known, so the distance of the star can be calculated.

The parallax method leads to the definition of the *parsec*, which is the distance at which an object would exhibit a parallax of one second of arc (i.e. $^1/_{3600}$ of a degree). One parsec is 3.26 light years, so with the exception of the Sun, no stars are as close as one parsec.

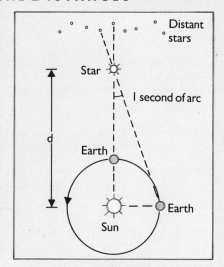

Definition of the parsec. If the change in angle between the two observations of the star is 1 second of arc, then d = 1 parsec (equivalent to 3.26 light years). In fact, no star is as close to the Solar System as 1 parsec. Note that the angle in the diagram has been exaggerated for the sake of clarity.

The 3 K microwave background

Astronomers can detect an 'echo' from the big bang in the form of microwave radiation. The existence of the microwave background was predicted by George Gamow in 1948 and found by Penzias and Wilson in 1965. The radiation has a maximum intensity at a wavelength of 2.5 mm (0.1 in) and represents a temperature of 3 K (− 270 °C or − 454 °F). In the vicinity of the Solar System, the radiation appears to have equal intensity in all directions.

The apparent uniformity of the background radiation provided a problem for big-bang theorists, in that it posed the question of how the universe became as irregular ('lumpy') as it is, with clusters of galaxies in some areas, and empty space in others. A possible answer came in 1992, when data from the COBE satellite (see photo) showed minute differences in temperature (+ and − 0.27 millikelvins) in the background radiation. These have been interpreted as evidence of infinitesimal density fluctuations, which in turn would have led to local gravitational effects in the expanding fireball. With the beginnings of gravitational instability in certain regions, matter would begin to coalesce, eventually giving rise to protogalaxies.

Red shift

In 1868, the English amateur astronomer Sir William Huggins (1824–1910) noticed that lines in the spectra of certain stars were displaced towards the red end of the spectrum. Huggins realized that this was due to the Doppler effect, which had been discovered in 1842 (see p. 30). Just as the noise from a moving vehicle will appear to change pitch as it passes, the colour of light from a star will change in wavelength as the star moves towards us, or away from us. Stars moving away from the Earth have their light moved towards the red end of the spectrum (*red shift*), while those moving towards us exhibit a shift towards the blue end.

Hubble's law

In 1929, Edwin Hubble (1889–1953) – who also worked on the classification of galaxies (see p. 8) – analysed the red shifts of a number of galaxies. He found that the speed at which a galaxy is moving away from us is proportional to its distance – i.e. the more distant a galaxy, the faster it is receding. This principle was formulated as Hubble's law, which can be written in the form: speed = H × distance, where H is the *Hubble constant*.

Various values for the Hubble constant have been proposed, but the generally accepted value is 56 km (35 mi) per second per megaparsec (a megaparsec is 3.26 million light years; see box). Thus a galaxy that is receding from the Earth at 56 km/sec will be 326 000 light years distant.

The future of the universe

At present the universe is still expanding, but whether or not this will continue for ever depends upon the amount of matter it contains. One possible ending for the universe is the *big crunch*. The galaxies and other matter may be moving apart, but their motion is restrained by their mutual gravitational attraction. If there is sufficient matter in the universe, gravity will eventually win and begin pulling the galaxies together again, causing the universe to experience a reverse of the big bang – the big crunch.

What will follow the big crunch is hard to imagine. One possibility is that a new universe will come into being, perhaps containing completely different types of particles from our present universe. The *cyclic theory* suggests that the universe may continue alternately to expand and collapse.

However, it may be that there is not enough matter in the universe for the big crunch to happen. If this is the case, the universe will continue to expand for ever. Although this means there may never be an 'edge' to the universe, there is bound to be an end to the observable universe. Hubble's law states that the speed of recession of a galaxy is proportional to its distance. A galaxy which is far enough away to be travelling at the speed of light will no longer be visible and this will therefore mark the end of the universe we can see. The end of the observable universe lies at a distance of between 15 000 and 20 000 million light years.

The steady-state theory

Another cosmological model, which is no longer generally accepted, is the *steady-state theory*. This supposes that the universe has always existed and will always continue to exist.

The theory was first proposed in 1948 by a group of Cambridge astronomers and popularized by Sir Fred Hoyle (1915–). However, among many other objections, the theory offers no satisfactory explanation for the 3 K microwave background radiation.   GE

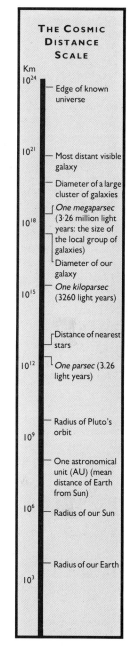

THE COSMIC DISTANCE SCALE

Km

10^{24} — Edge of known universe

10^{21} — Most distant visible galaxy
— Diameter of a large cluster of galaxies

10^{18} ⎰ One megaparsec (3·26 million light years: the size of the local group of galaxies)
— Diameter of our galaxy
— One kiloparsec (3260 light years)

10^{15}
— Distance of nearest stars
⎱ One parsec (3.26 light years)

10^{12}

10^9 — Radius of Pluto's orbit

— One astronomical unit (AU) (mean distance of Earth from Sun)

10^6 — Radius of our Sun

— Radius of our Earth

10^3

The expanding universe . The speed (indicated by the length of arrow) at which a galaxy is moving away from the observer becomes greater the further the galaxy is from the observer. Wherever the observer is in the universe, all other galaxies are seen to be receding.

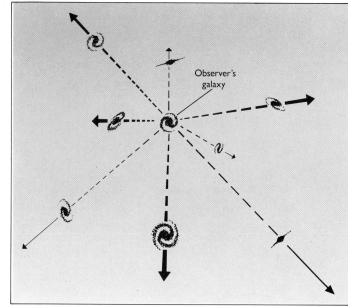

Observer's galaxy

Time

Time forms the basis of many scientific laws, but time itself is very difficult to define. Time, like distance, separates objects and events and for this reason can be regarded as the fourth dimension. However, time cannot be measured directly. We must make do with measuring the way in which the passage of time affects things.

Time always moves forwards. This is demonstrated by the fact that there are many processes that once done cannot be undone. Although we measure time as if it passes at a regular rate, time can appear to move at different rates depending upon what one is doing. Someone enjoying themselves may find that time appears to pass very quickly. Conversely, a person labouring at a monotonous job may find that time appears to pass slowly. This is known as *subjective time*.

Time systems

The Earth's orbit is not circular but elliptical, so the Sun does not appear to move against the stars at a constant speed. Most everyday time systems are therefore based on a hypothetical 'mean Sun', which is taken to travel at a constant speed equal to the average speed of the actual Sun.

A *day* is the time taken for the Earth to turn once on its axis. A *sidereal day* is reckoned with reference to the stars and is the time taken between successive passes of the observer's meridian by the same star. (The *meridian* is an imaginary line from due north to due south running through a point directly above the observer.) One sidereal day is 23 hours 56 minutes 4 seconds. A *solar day* is calculated with respect to the mean Sun. The mean solar day is 24 hours long.

A *year* is the time taken for the Earth to complete one orbit of the Sun. The Earth's true revolution period is 365 days 6 hours 9 minutes 10 seconds, and this is known as a *sidereal year*. However, the direction in which the Earth's axis points is changing due to an effect known as *precession*. The north celestial pole now lies near the star Polaris in the constellation Ursa Minor, thus Polaris is also known as the Pole Star. By the year AD 14 000, the Earth's axis will point in a different direction and the bright star Vega in Lyra will be near the pole. This effect also means that the position of the Sun's apparent path across the sky is changing with respect to the stars. A *tropical year* compensates for the effects of precession and is 365 days 5 hours 48 minutes 45 seconds long. It is the tropical year which is used as the basis for developing a calendar.

The SI unit of time is the *second*, which was originally defined as $1/_{86\,400}$ of the mean solar day. However, as we have seen, the Earth is not a very good timekeeper, so scientists no longer use it to define the fundamental unit of time. The

An Aztec calendar stone. In the inner circle are the symbols of the twenty Aztec days, each of which was associated with a particular god. The Aztec year of 365 days was made up of 18 months of 20 days each, with an additional 5 unlucky days. At the centre of this stone, which weighs around 25 tonnes, is the date on which the Aztecs believed the world would be destroyed by an earthquake, together with the dates on which they believed similar destructions had occurred.

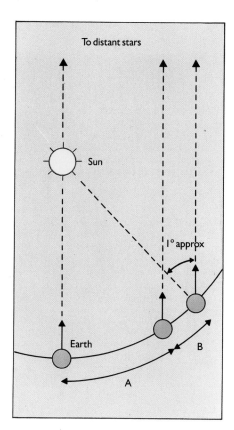

Sidereal and solar days. In travelling through distance A the Earth rotates once in relation to more distant stars, so completing one *sidereal day* (23 hours 56 minutes 4 seconds). To complete a *mean solar day*, with the Sun in the same position in the sky as it was 24 hours before, the Earth has to turn approximately 1° more, and in so doing travels the additional distance B. (Diagram not to scale.)

second is now defined as the duration of 9 192 631 770 periods of the radiation corresponding to the transition between the two hyperfine levels of the ground state of a caesium-133 atom.

Greenwich Mean Time (GMT) is the local time at Greenwich, England. The *Greenwich Meridian* is the line of 0° longitude which passes through Greenwich Observatory. The mean Sun crosses the Greenwich Meridian at midday GMT. Also known as *Universal Time* (UT), GMT is used as a standard reference time throughout the world. *Sidereal time* literally means 'star time'. It is reckoned with reference to the stars and not the Sun.

Calendars

The Earth takes 365.2422 days to complete one orbit of the Sun, which makes planning a calendar rather difficult, as the extra 0.2422 days per year have to be accounted for. The first person to attempt to do this was Julius Caesar (100–44 BC), who commissioned the astronomer Sosigenes to produce what became known as the *Julian calendar*. In order to compensate for the errors that had accumulated over previous years, Caesar decreed that the first year of his new calendar would be 445 days long. Thus 46 BC became known as 'The Year of Confusion'. Julius Caesar also introduced the idea of *leap years* to compensate for the extra 0.2422 days per

year. However, the original Julian calendar had a leap year every third year – 0.0911 days or 2 hours 11 minutes too much.

The calendar was further refined by the Emperor Augustus (63 BC–AD 14), who in 8 BC revised the frequency to one leap year every fourth year. This gives an 'extra' 0.2500 days per year and reduces the error to 0.0078 days (i.e. 11 minutes) per year. By the 14th century, the extra 11 minutes per year had accumulated to a total error of 10 days. Pope Gregory XIII (1572–85) therefore introduced the *Gregorian calendar*, decreeing that 4 October 1582 should be followed by 15 October. He also decided that the century years would not be leap years, unless divisible by 400. Thus, for example, 1800 and 1900 were not leap years, but 2000 will be. The Gregorian calendar allows an extra 0.2425 days per year and is in error by just 0.0003 days per year. It will therefore be many centuries before the calendar will need to be revised again.

When Britain and its colonies, long antagonistic to anything emanating from Rome, eventually adopted the Gregorian calendar in 1752, riots broke out with mobs chanting, 'Give us back our eleven days!' Russia did not adopt the Gregorian calendar until after the 1917 Revolution, by which time there was a 13-day lag. This explains why the October Revolution (25 October 1917) is now commemorated in November (7 November).

The Muslim calendar has either 354 or 355 days in a year. The Jewish calendar employs a year that varies from a minimum of 353 days to a maximum of 385 days. The Chinese used to have a calendar based on a 60-year cycle. Although it was banned in China in 1930, the Chinese calendar is still used in parts of Southeast Asia.

Measuring time

The earliest device for measuring time was the *sundial*, which can be traced back to the Middle East c. 3500 BC. A sundial comprises a rod or plate called a *gnomon* that casts a shadow on a disc; where the shadow points indicates the position of the Sun and hence the time of day.

Mechanical clocks, driven by falling weights, appeared in the 14th century, and the first *mechanical watches*, driven by a coiled mainspring, in the 16th century. The first *pendulum clock* was invented by Christiaan Huygens (1629–95), a Dutch physicist, in the middle of the 17th century.

Pendulum clocks could not be used on board ships owing to the vessel's motion. In 1714 the British Longitude Board offered a prize for the development of a *marine chronometer*, as being able to tell the time accurately is vital to navigation. Fourteen years later the English clockmaker John Harrison (1693–1776) set to work on the problem, producing his first marine chronometer in 1735.

The first *quartz clock*, operated by the vibrations of a quartz crystal when an electrical voltage is applied, appeared in 1929. The quartz clock is accurate to within one second in ten years. This was followed in 1948 by the *atomic clock*, which depends on the natural vibrations of atoms. The most accurate modern atomic clocks are accurate to one second in 1.7 million years. GE

SEE ALSO

● THE UNIVERSE AND COSMOLOGY p. 4
● THE SUN AND THE SOLAR SYSTEM p. 10
● THE INNER PLANETS p. 12
● QUANTUM THEORY AND RELATIVITY p. 26
● THE REVOLUTIONARY CALENDAR p. 425

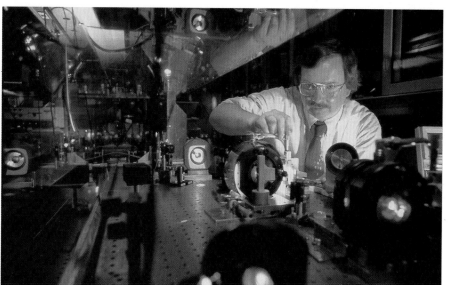

The equipment responsible for creating the shortest 'slice' of time ever – a pulse of light from a laser lasting only 30 femtoseconds. A femtosecond is 10^{-15} seconds (0.000000000000001 or a millionth billionth of a second). Scientists use such pulses of light as 'stopwatches' to study subtle physical and chemical changes, such as how electrons move in semiconductor materials. In one second, a pulse of light can travel almost to the Moon, but in 30 femtoseconds it travels no further than one third of the thickness of a human hair.

Stars and Galaxies

A galaxy is a system of many thousands of millions of stars, together with interstellar gas and dust. Many galaxies are spiral in shape, while others can be spherical, elliptical or irregular. Telescopes have revealed the existence of about 1000 million galaxies, although apart from our own galaxy, only three can be clearly seen with the naked eye.

Stars – of which our Sun is an example – are accretions of gas that radiate energy produced by nuclear-fusion reactions. They range in mass from about 0.06 to 100 solar masses, one solar mass being equivalent to the mass of the Sun. The properties of a star and the manner in which it evolves depend principally on its mass.

Stars are formed within clouds of dust and gas called *nebulae*. Patches of gas and dust inside a nebula collapse under gravity forming dark regions called protostars. As the protostars continue to collapse, they become denser and hotter. Eventually, they may become hot enough for nuclear-fusion reactions to start and thus turn into stars.

Galaxies

The American astronomer Edwin Hubble (see also pp. 4–5) devised a system for classifying galaxies that is still in use. He grouped galaxies into three basic categories: elliptical, spiral and irregular. *Elliptical galaxies* range from the spherical EO type to the very flattened E7. *Spiral galaxies* are labelled Sa, Sb or Sc, depending upon how tightly wound the arms are. Some spirals appear to have their arms coming from the ends of a central bar and these *barred spirals* are designated SBa, SBb or SBc. *Irregular galaxies* are those whose shape is neither spiral nor elliptical.

Sometimes known as the *Milky Way*, our own galaxy – 'the Galaxy' – contains about 10 000 million stars. It is an ordinary spiral galaxy and the Sun is situated in one of the spiral arms. The diameter of the Galaxy is about 100 000 light years and the Sun is some 30 000 light years from the centre. The nearest star to the Sun, Proxima Centauri, is 4.2 light years distant. The Galaxy is rotating and the Sun takes 225 million years to complete one revolution. This is sometimes called a *cosmic year*.

Some galaxies are extremely active and emit vast amounts of radiation. One such galaxy is the powerful radio source Centaurus A. *Quasars* are very distant and immensely bright objects, which are thought to represent the nuclei of active galaxies. They may be powered by massive central black holes (see below). The most

Two interacting galaxies (right), named NGC 5216 and NGC 5218. On ordinary optical photographs the two galaxies appear to be completely different systems, but on this photograph taken by a charge-coupled device a 'rope of stars' is revealed linking the two. The thin 'rope' consists of stars torn out of the two galaxies by their gravitational pull on each other. The colours in this photograph show levels of brightness, with the background sky coloured pink.

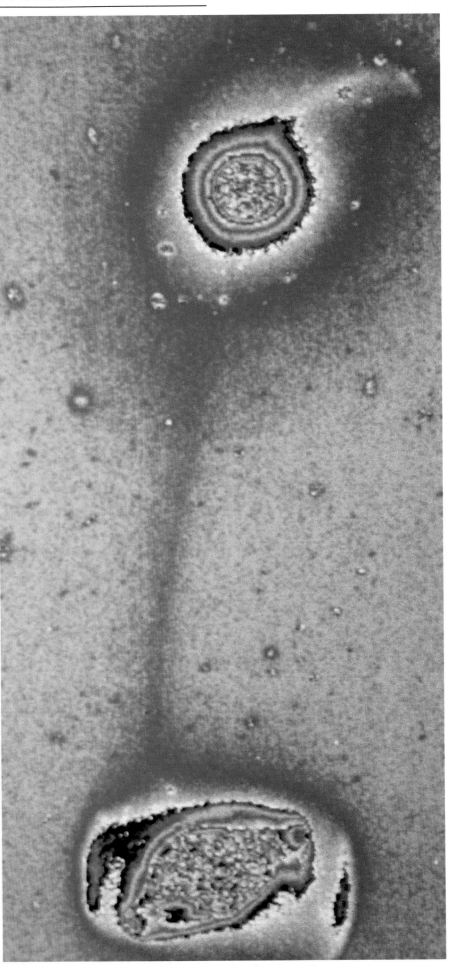

distant quasar yet detected, PKS 2000–330, is 13 000 million light years from the Earth.

Binary, multiple and variable stars

The majority of stars – over 75% – are members of binary or multiple star systems. *Binary stars* consist of two stars each orbiting around their common centre of gravity. An *eclipsing binary* can occur where one component of the system periodically obscures, and is obscured by, the other (as seen from Earth). This leads to a reduction in the light intensity seen from Earth – which is how binary stars were first discovered. Some stars are actually complex *multiple stars*. For example, the 'star' Castor in the constellation of Gemini has six individual components.

Most stars are of constant brightness, but some – *variable stars* – brighten and fade. The variability can be caused by a line-of-sight effect, as in eclipsing binaries (see above). In other cases, changes in the star itself cause periodic increases and reductions of energy output. Variable stars can have periods ranging from a few hours to several years.

Magnitude

Magnitude is a measure of a star's 'brightness'. *Apparent magnitude* indicates how bright a star appears to the naked eye. Paradoxically, the lower the magnitude the brighter the star. Magnitude is measured on a logarithmic scale, taking as its basis the fact that a difference of 5 in magnitude is equivalent to a factor of 100 in brightness. On this basis, a star of magnitude +1 is 2.512 times brighter than a star of +2, 2.512^2 (= 6.310) times brighter than a star of +3, and 2.512^5 (= 100) times brighter than a star of +6.

The limit of naked-eye visibility depends upon how clear the sky is, but the faintest stars that can be seen on a really clear

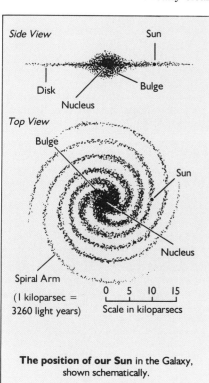

Side View

Sun

Disk

Bulge

Nucleus

Top View

Bulge

Sun

Nucleus

Spiral Arm

(1 kiloparsec = 3260 light years)

0   5   10   15

Scale in kiloparsecs

The position of our Sun in the Galaxy, shown schematically.

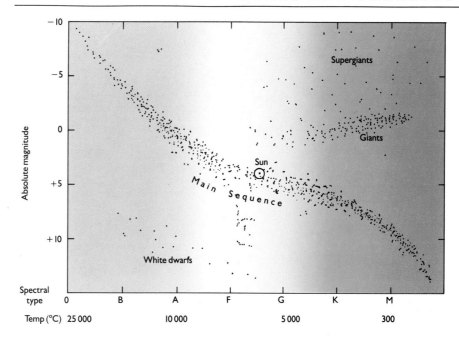

Supergiants

Giants

Sun

Main Sequence

White dwarfs

Absolute magnitude

−10

−5

0

+5

+10

Spectral type   O   B   A   F   G   K   M

Temp (°C)   25 000   10 000   5 000   300

SEE ALSO

● THE UNIVERSE AND COSMOLOGY p. 4
● THE SUN AND THE SOLAR SYSTEM p. 10
● THE HISTORY OF ASTRONOMY p. 16
● ENERGY: COAL, OIL AND NUCLEAR p. 304

The Hertzsprung-Russell Diagram for classifying stars.

The relative sizes (below) of different types of stars. Typical red giants are 100 times the size of the Sun, which in turn is 100 times the size of a white dwarf. White dwarfs are 1000 times larger than neutron stars, which typically have a diameter of 10–20 km (6–12 mi). Red supergiants may be 5 times larger than a typical red giant.

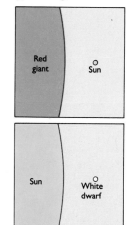

Red giant

Sun

Sun

White dwarf

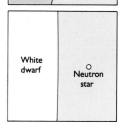

White dwarf

Neutron star

night are about magnitude +6. The world's largest telescopes can detect objects as faint as magnitude +27. Very bright objects can have negative magnitudes: the planet Venus can reach −4.4, the full Moon −12.0 and the Sun −26.8.

The nearer a star is, the brighter it will appear. Different stars lie at different distances, so apparent magnitude does not measure the true brightness of a star. *Absolute magnitude* compensates for a star's distance by calculating its apparent magnitude if it were placed at a distance of 32.6 light years (= 10 parsecs, see p. 5). For example, Sirius is a nearby star and has an apparent magnitude of −1.5. However, its absolute magnitude is +1.3. The Sun has an absolute magnitude of +4.8.

Colour and temperature

The colour of a star gives an indication of its temperature. Hot stars are blue, while cool stars are red. Stars are grouped into *spectral types* according to their temperatures.

Type	Colour	Temperature	
		(°C)	(°F)
O	Blue	25 000–40 000	45 000–75 000
B	Blue	11 000–25 000	20 800–45 000
A	Blue-white	7500–11 000	13 500–20 000
F	White	6000–7500	10 800–13 500
G	Yellow	5000–6000	9000–10 800
K	Orange	3500–5000	6300–9000
M	Red	3000–3500	5400–6300

Each spectral type is further subdivided on a scale 0–9. The Sun is classified as G2.

The Hertzsprung-Russell diagram

Stars can be arranged on a diagram that plots their absolute magnitudes against their spectral types. This is known as a *Hertzsprung-Russell diagram*, after the Danish astronomer Ejnar Hertzsprung (1873–1967) and Henry Norris Russell (1877–1957), an American. Most stars fit

into a diagonal band (called the *main sequence*) across the diagram.

Stellar evolution and black holes

The manner in which a star evolves depends upon its mass. Protostars with mass less then 0.06 of the Sun will never become hot enough for nuclear reactions to start. Those with mass between 0.06 and 1.4 solar masses quickly move on to the main sequence and can remain there for at least 10 000 million years. When the available hydrogen is used up, the core contracts, which increases its temperature to 100 million °C (180 million °F). This produces conditions in which helium can begin a fusion reaction and the star expands to become a *red giant*. Finally, the outer layers of the star are expelled, forming a *planetary nebula*. The core then shrinks to become a small *white dwarf* star.

Stars of between 1.4 and 4.2 solar masses evolve more quickly and die younger. They remain on the main sequence for about one million years before the red giant phase begins. The temperature continues to increase as even heavier elements are synthesized until iron is produced at the temperature of 700 million °C (1260 million °F). The star is then disrupted in a huge *supernova* explosion producing a vast expanding cloud of dust and gas. At the centre of the cloud a small *neutron star* will remain. This rotates very rapidly and is incredibly dense: 1 cm³ (0.061 cu in) of neutron-star material has a mass of about 250 million tonnes (tons).

The evolution of more massive stars is stranger still. They may end their lives by producing a *black hole* – an object so dense that not even light can escape. The only means of detecting a black hole is by observing its gravitational effects on other objects. The X-ray source Cygnus X-1 may comprise a giant star and a black hole. Material would be pulled away from the star by the black hole and heated – giving off X-rays as it is pulled in.   GE

The Sun and the Solar System

The Sun, the principal source of light and heat for planet Earth, is a very ordinary star, situated near the edge of a spiral arm about 30 000 light years from the centre of the Galaxy. The Sun is the centre of the Solar System, which includes at least nine major planets and their satellites, together with interplanetary material and thousands of minor planets, comets and meteoroids.

The Sun mainly consists of the gases hydrogen and helium. At its centre is a vast nuclear reactor whose temperature is at least 14 million °C (25 million °F). The Sun produces energy by nuclear fusion (see p. 39), a process in which hydrogen is converted into helium.

The Sun is losing mass at a rate of 4 million tonnes (tons) per second, but its total mass is 2×10^{27} tonnes (tons), which is 330 000 times that of the Earth and 745 times that of all the planets put together. The diameter of the Sun is 1 392 000 km (863 000 mi) – 109 times greater than that of the Earth – and its volume is 1 300 000 times that of the Earth.

The Sun's surface and atmosphere

When the image of the Sun is projected through a telescope, dark patches, called *sunspots*, can often be seen. Although they look black, sunspots are actually quite bright – they only appear dark by contrast with the surrounding brighter areas. Sunspots are about 2000 °C (3600 °F) cooler than other parts of the Sun's surface. The number of sunspots that can be seen on the Sun varies over an 11-year cycle. At the maximum of the cycle it is possible to see many sunspot groups, whereas at the minimum of the cycle no spots may be seen for several days.

The bright surface of the Sun is called the *photosphere*. A closer view of the photosphere shows that it consists of millions of granules, each of which is several hundred kilometres in diameter. The surface of the Sun is constantly changing its appearance, with individual granules persisting for about 10 minutes. Rising up from the photosphere are huge jets of gas called *spicules*. These can reach 15 000 km (9000 mi) in diameter, but last for just a few minutes.

The part of the Sun that lies above the photosphere is called the *chromosphere*. It is red in colour and consists mainly of hydrogen gas. It is normally impossible to see with the naked eye, owing to the proximity of the much brighter photosphere. However, during a total eclipse of the Sun, when the photosphere is obscured by the Moon, the chromosphere can be seen.

Masses of glowing hydrogen called *prominences* are sometimes ejected from the chromosphere. These penetrate the outermost part of the Sun's atmosphere. Prominences average 100 000 km (60 000 mi) in length. There are two types of prominences – active and quiescent. *Active prominences* are violent and short-lived phenomena, whereas *quiescent prominences* are much calmer and may persist for several weeks.

The outermost layer of the solar atmosphere is the *corona*, which consists of thin hydrogen gas at high temperature. *Solar flares* are another category of brilliant outbursts in the solar atmosphere. They are often associated with sunspot groups and can reach maximum brightness in just a few minutes. They are essentially magnetic phenomena and send out large amounts of charged particles and radiation.

The solar wind and aurorae

The Sun is constantly sending out a stream of charged particles into space. This is known as the *solar wind*. The strength of the solar wind is not constant, but changes with the activity of the Sun. Near the peak of the sunspot cycle, the solar wind is at its strongest.

The Earth has a strong magnetic field, which traps ionized particles from the solar wind in the upper atmosphere. These regions are the *Van Allen Zones*,

The surface of the Sun, seen here in a false-colour extreme ultra-violet image, taken by the Skylab space station in 1973. At the top a huge solar prominence – some 500 000 km (300 000 mi) in height – leaps up through the Sun's atmosphere.

0
Sun
Mercury
Venus
Earth
Mars
Jupiter
1000 (620)
Saturn
2000 (1240)
Uranus
3000 (1860)

COMETS

Comets can best be described as 'dirty snowballs'. They are thought to originate in a region known as the *Oort Cloud*, about one light year from the Sun.

Sometimes comets are perturbed from the Oort Cloud and swing in towards the Sun. The gravitational attraction of a planet may trap a comet into a closed but highly elliptical orbit, which will periodically bring it close to the Sun. The best-known example is *Halley's Comet*, which has a period of 76 years. Halley's Comet is named in honour of the English astronomer Edmond Halley (1656–1742), who successfully predicted the comet's return in 1758.

Other comets may reach open parabolic or hyperbolic orbits. These will swing past the Sun just once and then be lost from the Solar System for ever.

Comets may have on occasion collided with the Earth. On 30 June 1908 a great explosion occurred in the sparsely populated Tunguska area of Siberia, flattening trees over a wide area. The object that caused this enormous devastation may have been the nucleus of a small comet, rather than a meteorite, which would have left a crater.

Halley's Comet, photographed in 1910. Comets probably consist of a small nucleus of ice and dust. When a comet approaches the Sun, part of the nucleus vaporizes to form a luminous cloud (the *coma*) and the tail, which always points away from the Sun. Although the nucleus may only be a few km in diameter, comas may have diameters up to 1 million km (620 000 mi).

The aurora borealis or 'northern lights' flickers in the night sky above Manitoba, Canada. Aurorae are caused by collisions between charged particles in the solar wind and gas molecules in the Earth's atmosphere, and are particularly common around the peak of the sunspot cycle.

two belts which extend from 1000 to 5000 km (620 to 3100 mi) and from 15 000 to 25 000 km (9300 to 15 500 mi) above the equator.

The solar wind also interacts with the Earth's magnetic field to produce brilliant displays of light called *aurorae* – the *aurora borealis* (or 'northern lights') in the northern hemisphere and the *aurora australis* in the southern. Aurorae are formed by the charged particles in the solar wind interacting with gases in the Earth's atmosphere at a height of about 100 km (60 mi), causing them to emit visible light. This can be seen from the ground as an ever-changing pattern of white or multicoloured lights. The charged particles are attracted towards the Earth's magnetic poles and aurorae are therefore best seen from high latitudes. The most spectacular displays occur about 24 hours after major solar-flare activity.

The Solar System

The Solar System consists of the Sun together with a large number of bodies and matter that is gravitationally bound to it. These include the planets, their satellites, minor planets, comets, meteoroids and interplanetary gas and dust.

There are nine known planets, all going round the Sun in elliptical orbits. In order of mean distance from the Sun, the planets are Mercury, Venus, Earth, Mars, Jupiter, Saturn, Uranus, Neptune and Pluto (see pp. 12–15). Of these, Pluto has a rather eccentric orbit so that although its average distance from the Sun is greater than that of Neptune, part of its orbit brings it closer to the Sun than Neptune. Thus from 1979 to 1999 Neptune holds the title of the outermost planet. However, in 1992 the discovery was announced of a body even further from the Sun. This body, which has a diameter of 200 km (120 mi), is thought to be an asteroid or comet. It has been designated 1992 QB_1, and its mean distance from the Sun may be as much as 8800 million km (5400 million mi).

The Solar System is generally thought to have formed 4600 million years ago by accretion (cumulative coming together) from the *solar nebula* – a spinning cloud of gas and dust that also gave birth to the Sun. Gravity was the dominant force during the formation of the Solar System, and at some stage nuclei developed within the solar nebula that eventually accreted into the planets we now know. The fact that the planets all orbit the Sun in the same direction is thought to be a relic from the rotation of the original solar nebula. GE

SEE ALSO

- STARS AND GALAXIES p. 8
- THE INNER PLANETS p. 12
- THE OUTER PLANETS p. 14

SUN
Pluto
Mercury
Mars
Venus
Earth
Neptune
Uranus
Saturn
Jupiter

THE SOLAR SYSTEM
The comparative sizes of the planets (above) in order of size, and (left) a scale showing the distances of the planets from the Sun.

4000
(2480)

Neptune

5000
(3100)

Millions of km (mi)

Pluto

The Inner Planets

The four inner members of the Sun's family are relatively small, rocky planets. The Earth is a member of this group and they are therefore often known as the *terrestrial planets*. Despite this initial similarity, the four terrestrial planets are very different worlds. Mercury and Venus are inhospitably hot, whereas for much of the year Mars is bitterly cold.

Until the 1960s, little was known about the Earth's nearest neighbours in space. However, since the advent of the space age, unmanned craft have visited all members of the inner Solar System. *Mariner 10* has flown by Mercury and many different spacecraft have flown by, orbited and landed on Venus and Mars.

Mercury

Mercury's proximity to the Sun makes it a difficult planet to see, as it only appears low in the west after sunset, or low in the east before sunrise. The first telescopic observations were made from Danzig by Johannes Hevelius (1611–87), who saw that the planet shows phases like the Moon.

Following a series of observations beginning in 1881, the Italian Giovanni Schiaparelli (1835–1910) reported markings on the surface of Mercury, leading him to conclude that it had a rotation period of 88 days. We now know that Schiaparelli was wrong. Modern observations have shown that Mercury rotates once every 59 days, which is two thirds as long as a Mercury 'year'. Mercury therefore rotates on its axis three times for every two orbits of the Sun.

Almost all of our information about Mercury comes from *Mariner 10*, the only spacecraft to have visited the planet. The pictures it returned showed a barren, rocky world, covered in craters, some of which are over 200 km (120 mi) in diameter. To all intents and purposes, Mercury does not have an atmosphere: its atmospheric pressure is one thousandth of a millionth of a millionth of the pressure on the Earth.

Venus

Venus is the Earth's nearest neighbour and is often the brightest object in the night sky, apart from the Moon. Like Mercury, Venus can only be seen with the naked eye in the morning or evening. Venus, like Mercury, also shows phases, which binoculars or a small telescope will reveal.

Venus is covered by a dense atmosphere, so telescopes cannot show any surface detail. In 1962 astronomers managed to bounce radio waves off the planet and these showed that Venus was rotating backwards (i.e. in the opposite direction to the Sun and nearly all the other planets) once every 243 days.

Venus's atmosphere is composed mainly

A photomosaic of Mercury (left), made up from photographs taken by *Mariner 10* in 1974. The image has been tinted to approximate the visual appearance of the planet.

The far side of the Moon (right), photographed by *Apollo 11*. The large crater at the top has a diameter of about 80 km (50 mi). The craters on the Moon were formed by meteors striking the surface.

THE INNER PLANETS: BASIC STATISTICS

MERCURY
Diameter: 4880 km / 3032 mi
(0.38 × Earth)
Mass: 0.555 x Earth
Average temperature: 420 °C / 790 °F
(day) −180 °C / −290 °F (night)
Rotation period: 59 Earth days *
Tilt of axis: 2°
Average distance from Sun:
57 900 000 km / 36 000 000 mi
(0.387 x Earth)
Length of year: 88 Earth days
Number of known moons: none
* The length of a solar day (sunrise to sunrise) on Mercury is 176 Earth days.

VENUS
Diameter: 12 103 km / 7520 mi
(0.95 × Earth)
Mass: 0.81 × Earth
Average temperature: 464 °C / 867 °F
Rotation period: 243 Earth days *
Tilt of axis: 178°
Average distance from Sun:
108 200 000 km / 67 200 000 mi
(0.723 × Earth)
Length of year: 225 Earth days
Number of known moons: none
* The length of a solar day on Venus is 116 Earth days.

EARTH
Diameter: 12 756 km / 7921 mi
Mass: 1.00 × Earth
Average temperature: 15 °C / 59 °F
Rotation period: 24 h
Tilt of axis: 23.5°
Average distance from Sun:
149 600 000 km / 92 900 000 mi
Length of year: 365 days
Number of known moons: 1

MARS
Diameter: 6780 km / 4213 mi
(0.53 × Earth)
Mass: 0.11 × Earth
Average temperature: −53 °C / −63 °F
Rotation period: 24 h 37 m
Tilt of axis: 24°
Average distance from Sun:
227 900 000 km / 141 500 000 mi
(1.523 × Earth)
Length of year: 687 Earth days
Number of known moons: 2

A view of the surface of Mars, processed by computer from images sent back by the *Viking* spacecraft and from topographic maps. In the left foreground is the giant Valles Marineris canyon system, which is over 3000 km (1860 mi) long and up to 8 km (5 mi) deep. In the background are the three Tharsis volcanoes. The canyon system was formed by a combination of geological faulting, landslides, and erosion by wind and water.

of carbon dioxide and has clouds of sulphuric acid floating in it. Carbon dioxide acts rather like the glass in a greenhouse, letting in the energy from the Sun, but without allowing much heat to escape. The upper clouds race around the planet once every four days – much faster than the planet itself is turning.

The first spacecraft to transmit from the surface of Venus was the Soviet *Venera 7*, which found a temperature of 470° C (878 °F) and an atmospheric pressure 90 times that on Earth. The later probes, *Veneras 9, 10, 13* and *14*, returned pictures from the surface of Venus.

In 1978, the American *Pioneer-Venus* spacecraft was put into orbit around the planet to start making a map of the surface, using radar to penetrate Venus's thick clouds. This revealed a complex surface with low-lying plains, upland areas, volcanoes and rift valleys. The American *Magellan* spacecraft, launched in 1989, will produce a more detailed radar map of the planet's surface. Mission planners hope to detect features as small as 250 m (820 ft) across and the probe will study 92% of the planet.

The Earth

The Earth is the largest of the inner planets and the only planet able to support life. Its atmosphere consists mainly of nitrogen (78%) and oxygen (21%). Two thirds of its surface is covered by water, which has an average depth of 3700 m (12 140 ft). The land rises above the oceans to an average height of 860 m (2800 ft). More detailed information on the Earth's interior, atmosphere and magnetic field will be found on pp. 76–7.

The Moon

The Moon, which maintains a mean distance from the Earth of 384 400 km

(238 700 mi), is the Earth's largest satellite and has a mass $^1/_{81}$ of that of the Earth. The Moon has a diameter of 3476 km (2159 mi), making it larger than the planet Pluto. The Moon orbits the Earth once every 27.3 days in *synchronous rotation* – i.e. it keeps the same face towards the Earth.

Surface features include craters formed by meteoritic bombardment, mountains and broad plains, which in the past were mistakenly named 'seas' or *maria* (Latin, singular *mare*). The temperature on the lunar surface ranges from − 180 °C (− 292 °F) to + 110 °C (+ 200 °F).

It was not until October 1959 that the Soviet probe *Luna 3* returned the first pictures from the far side of the Moon – which turned out to be much the same as the near side, except for the absence of maria. When men first landed on the Moon in 1969 (see p. 18) they found rocks that were 3700 million years old – as old as some of the oldest rocks found on the Earth.

As seen from the Earth, the Moon passes through a series of *phases* every 27.3 days – waxing from new Moon, through first quarter, to full Moon, then waning to last quarter and new Moon again (see diagram).

Mars

Mars is the fourth planet from the Sun. It is the most hospitable planet other than the Earth, having a thin carbon dioxide atmosphere. Early observers, including Schiaparelli (see above), believed they saw canals and vegetation on Mars, but modern observations have shown that these do not exist.

In 1965 the American *Mariner 4* spacecraft flew by Mars and returned pictures showing a barren, cratered surface, massive extinct volcanoes and deep chasms. The largest volcano on Mars is Olympus Mons, which rises 22 km (14 mi) above the surrounding plains. Later probes, including *Mariner 9* and *Vikings 1* and *2* (the latter two successfully sending back pictures from the planet's surface) revealed other features that may have been caused by running water at some time in the past history of the planet.

Mars has two small satellites, Phobos and Deimos, which were mapped by *Vikings 1*

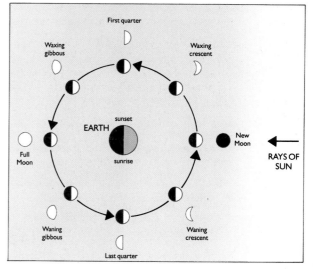

and *2* in 1976. In 1989 Phobos was further studied by the Soviet *Phobos 2*.

The minor planets

The minor planets, sometimes known as *asteroids*, comprise several thousand objects, most of which orbit between Mars and Jupiter (the *asteroid belt*). The largest of the minor planets is Ceres, which has a diameter of 940 km (584 mi). Once thought to be the residue of a planet broken up by the gravitational pull of Jupiter, most astronomers now think that the minor planets represent a class of primitive objects which were 'left over' during the formation of the Solar System, due to Jupiter's disruptive pull.

Meteors and meteorites

The Sun is also orbited by millions of minute particles called *meteoroids*. They are about the size of grains of sand and are therefore too small to be seen in space. When a meteoroid enters the Earth's atmosphere, it is heated by friction and destroyed. As this happens, the air glows, producing the effect we see as a *meteor* or 'shooting star'. Over 40 million meteoroids enter the atmosphere every day.

Larger bodies may survive and reach the Earth intact. These are called *meteorites*. Sometimes a meteorite may produce a crater – one of the best preserved of such craters is in Arizona and measures 1265 m (4150 ft) in diameter. GE

The phases of the Moon. The drawings in the outer circle show how the Moon is viewed from the Earth at its various phases. The Moon goes through the complete cycle of phases every 27.3 days.

SEE ALSO

- TIME p. 6
- THE SUN AND THE SOLAR SYSTEM p. 10
- THE OUTER PLANETS p. 14
- THE HISTORY OF ASTRONOMY p. 16
- SPACE EXPLORATION p. 18
- THE EARTH'S STRUCTURE AND ATMOSPHERE p. 76

The Outer Planets

The outer planets are very different from the inner planets. They are much further away from the Sun and, with the exception of Pluto, are much larger than the inner planets. Jupiter, Saturn, Uranus and Neptune are giant 'gas' planets without solid surfaces.

Much of our knowledge of the outer planets has been gained from the American space probes *Pioneer 10, Pioneer 11, Voyager 1* and *Voyager 2*, the last of which visited Jupiter, Saturn, Uranus and Neptune in turn from 1979 to 1989.

Jupiter

Jupiter is the largest planet in the Solar System. It appears very bright to the naked eye and can outshine everything in the sky except the Sun, the Moon, Venus and (very occasionally) Mars.

Through a telescope, several belts or bands can be seen in Jupiter's atmosphere. The planet's rapid rotation rate of 9 hours 55 minutes throws the equator outwards, producing a distinct 'squashed' appearance. One of the most prominent features is the Great Red Spot, which may have been seen as long ago as 1664. Modern observations of Jupiter have been made by four spacecraft, *Pioneers 10* and *11* and

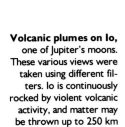

Volcanic plumes on Io, one of Jupiter's moons. These various views were taken using different filters. Io is continuously rocked by violent volcanic activity, and matter may be thrown up to 250 km (155 mi) above the surface.

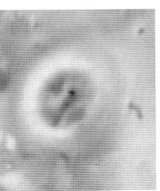
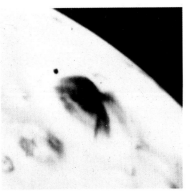

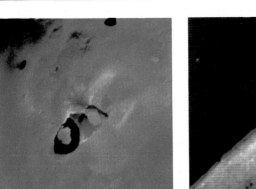
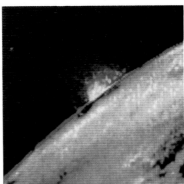

Voyagers 1 and *2*; pictures from these show that the Red Spot is a whirling storm in Jupiter's atmosphere.

At the centre of Jupiter is a rocky core. Above this are layers of metallic hydrogen (i.e. so cold that it is solid) and liquid hydrogen. Jupiter's upper atmosphere is mainly hydrogen and helium, but also contains small amounts of many different gases, including methane, ammonia, ethane, acetylene, water vapour, phosphine, carbon monoxide and germanium tetrahydride.

Jupiter is known to have at least 16 satellites. Four of these, Io, Europa, Ganymede and Callisto, were seen by Galileo (see p. 16) with his early telescope in 1610 and they are often called the 'Galilean Satellites' in his honour. The remaining satellites are small objects – the outermost group revolving around the planet in a retrograde direction. They are probably asteroids that were captured by Jupiter's immense gravitational pull. *Voyager 1* also discovered a very faint ring around Jupiter (see below), which *Voyager 2* was able to study in more detail.

Saturn

The next planet out from the Sun is Saturn, with its magnificent system of rings (see below). In 1610 Galileo became the first person to look at Saturn through a telescope. He saw the rings, but could not understand what they were, at first thinking that Saturn was a 'triple planet'. It was not until 1659 that the Dutch physicist Christiaan Huygens (1629–95) realized Saturn's true nature. Most of our current information about Saturn has come from the three spacecraft that have flown by the planet: *Pioneer 11* in 1979,

Voyager 1 in 1980 and *Voyager 2* in 1981.

If we could cut a slice out of Saturn we would see a small rocky core at the centre. Above this is a region of metallic hydrogen, followed by a deep ocean of liquid hydrogen. The outside layer of the planet is made of hydrogen gas, together with some helium. Tiny amounts of the gases methane, ammonia, ethane and phosphine have also been detected. Saturn has at least 18 satellites, including Titan, which has a dense nitrogen atmosphere.

Uranus

Uranus was discovered in March 1781 by Sir William Herschel (1738–1822), an amateur astronomer born in Germany but living in England. Herschel was making a routine survey of the sky when he came across an object that did not look like a star. At first he thought he had found a comet. The new object was watched carefully over the following months so that its orbit could be calculated. Once this was done, astronomers realized that Herschel had found a new planet.

When the sky is very dark and very clear, Uranus can just be seen with the naked eye. However, the planet is always extremely faint and the observer has to know exactly where to look. A telescope will show Uranus as a small disc. Most of our information about Uranus was sent back by *Voyager 2*, which flew past the planet in January 1986.

One of the strangest things about Uranus is that it orbits the Sun tipped on its side, which means that the calendar on the planet must be very odd indeed. At present the planet's north pole is pointing towards the Sun and anyone above the north pole of Uranus would have been in sunlight since 1966 and will not see the Sun set until 2007. This will be followed by 42 years of darkness while the south pole points towards the Sun. Although the south pole had been in darkness for 20 years, *Voyager 2* found that it is slightly warmer than the north pole – which must give rise to some very peculiar weather.

Uranus has an atmosphere of hydrogen and helium, which surrounds a layer of water, methane and ammonia ices. At the centre of Uranus is a rocky core. Before *Voyager 2* flew past the planet, Uranus was known to have 5 satellites. *Voyager* found 10 more bringing the total to 15.

Uranus also has a system of rings (see below). These were discovered in 1977 when the planet passed between a star and the Earth. Astronomers saw the light from the star flash on and off as each of the rings passed in front of it. Nine rings were eventually detected from Earth, but *Voyager* found two more.

Neptune

Neptune is so distant that it can never be seen with the naked eye and even a small telescope will only show it as a tiny disc. Larger telescopes show that the planet is bluish-green in colour, but very few markings can be seen. Our first good look at Neptune came in August 1989, when the *Voyager 2* spacecraft flew past the planet. *Voyager* revealed Neptune's most prominent feature, the Great Dark Spot. This is

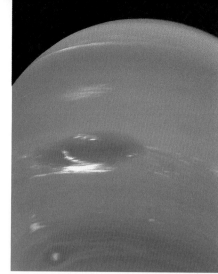

Neptune and its Great Dark Spot photographed through coloured filters by *Voyager 2* in August 1989 from a distance of 6.1 million km (3.8 million mi). The Great Dark Spot is a giant storm system the size of the Earth.

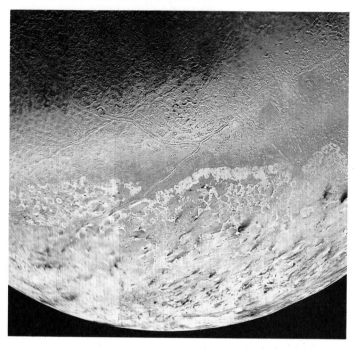

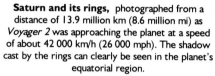

Saturn and its rings, photographed from a distance of 13.9 million km (8.6 million mi) as *Voyager 2* was approaching the planet at a speed of about 42 000 km/h (26 000 mph). The shadow cast by the rings can clearly be seen in the planet's equatorial region.

a massive storm system in the planet's atmosphere and is similar to Jupiter's Great Red Spot. Small wispy white clouds of methane ice can also be seen circling the planet.

The outside layer of Neptune is made of the gases hydrogen and helium. Beneath this comes a layer of ice. The ice is made of frozen methane and ammonia, as well as frozen water. At the centre of the planet is a rocky core.

Neptune was discovered thanks to the mathematical calculations of two men. They were an Englishman, John Couch Adams (1819–92), and Urbain Le Verrier (1811–77) from France. Adams and Le Verrier had been looking at the movements of Uranus and had noticed that it was behaving in a very strange manner. Sometimes it would speed up and move quickly along its orbit, whereas at other times it would slow down. The two men both thought that Uranus was being pulled by the gravity of another planet, so they set out to calculate where the 'hidden planet' must be. Both men worked

on their own, but they eventually arrived at the same answer. Le Verrier sent details of his calculations to the observatory in Berlin. The German astronomers Johann Galle (1812–1910) and Heinrich d'Arrest (1822–75) looked for the planet in September 1846 and found it almost immediately.

Neptune is now known to have eight satellites and a system of four rings (see below). Triton is the largest of Neptune's satellites, with a diameter of 2270 km (1410 mi) – slightly smaller than that of the Earth's Moon. Triton has an atmosphere and its surface is covered with a frozen mixture of nitrogen and methane.

Pluto

Although Pluto is normally the most distant member of the Solar System, it has a highly eccentric orbit that sometimes carries it inside that of Neptune. Thus for 20 years from 1979 to 1999 Neptune is temporarily the most distant planet.

Pluto is a very small, icy planet. Its satellite, Charon, is very large by comparison, having 10% of Pluto's mass – compared to the Moon, which has only 1.2% of the Earth's mass. Together, Pluto and Charon virtually form a twin-planet system. Little is known about the nature of Pluto, but evidence of a thin methane atmosphere has been detected.

Planetary rings

The gas planets Jupiter, Saturn, Uranus and Neptune all possess systems of rings. Of these, Saturn's is by far the most spectacular.

Rings are made from millions of small particles of ice and dust. Rings can have diameters of thousands of kilometres, but they are typically less than one kilometre thick. The mechanics of ring systems are not fully understood, but, especially in the case of Saturn, the ring particles appear to be kept in place by tiny 'shepherd' satellites.   GE

Triton, Neptune's largest moon, photographed by *Voyager 2*. At the bottom is the south polar cap.

SEE ALSO

- THE SUN AND THE SOLAR SYSTEM p. 10
- THE INNER PLANETS p. 12
- THE HISTORY OF ASTRONOMY p. 16
- SPACE EXPLORATION p. 18

THE OUTER PLANETS: BASIC STATISTICS

JUPITER	SATURN	URANUS	NEPTUNE	PLUTO
Diameter: 139 892 km / 86 925 mi (11.0 × Earth)	**Diameter:** 116 000 km / 72 452 mi (9.41 × Earth)	**Diameter:** 50 724 km / 31 519 mi (4.11 × Earth)	**Diameter:** 49 248 km / 30 601 mi (3.87 × Earth)	**Diameter:** 2302 km / 1430 mi (0.09 × Earth)
Mass: 318 × Earth	**Mass:** 95 × Earth	**Mass:** 15 × Earth	**Mass:** 17 × Earth	**Mass:** 0.002 × Earth
Average temperature: −150 °C / −238 °F	**Average temperature:** −180 °C / −292 °F	**Average temperature:** −210 °C / −346 °F	**Average temperature:** −225 °C / −373 °F	**Average temperature:** −220 °C / −364 °F
Rotation period: 9 h 55 m	**Rotation period:** 10 h 39 m	**Rotation period:** 17 h 14 m	**Rotation period:** 16 h 7 m	**Rotation period:** 6 d 9 h
Tilt of axis: 3°	**Tilt of axis:** 27°	**Tilt of axis:** 98°	**Tilt of axis:** 30°	**Tilt of axis:** 117°
Average distance from Sun: 778 300 000 km / 483 300 000 mi (5.202 × Earth)	**Average distance from Sun:** 1 427 000 000 km / 886 000 000 mi (9.538 × Earth)	**Average distance from Sun:** 2 869 600 000 km / 1 782 000 000 mi (19.181 × Earth)	**Average distance from Sun:** 4 496 700 000 km / 2 792 500 000 mi (30.058 × Earth)	**Average distance from Sun:** 5 900 000 000 km / 3 700 000 000 mi (39.44 × Earth)
Length of year: 11.9 Earth years	**Length of year:** 29.5 Earth years	**Length of year:** 84.0 Earth years	**Length of year:** 164.8 Earth years	**Length of year:** 248 Earth years
Number of known moons: 16	**Number of known moons:** 18	**Number of known moons:** 15	**Number of known moons:** 8	**Number of known moons:** 1

The History of Astronomy

Mankind has always been fascinated by the stars. The history of astronomy stretches back in time to the beginnings of civilization. Prehistoric structures such as the stone circles at Stonehenge and Avebury in England are aligned on astronomical principles, so the civilizations that built them must have had some astronomical knowledge. The earliest recorded astronomical observations were made by the Chinese, the Egyptians and the Babylonians, who, however, made no real effort to interpret what they saw.

An astrolabe (above right), from the Assyrian city of Nineveh, dating from the 7th century BC. One of the earliest of astronomical instruments, the astrolabe was used to measure the altitudes of stars and planets.

Many important astronomical observations were made by the Greeks during a period of roughly 800 years from 600 BC to AD 200. No major breakthroughs were then made until the 16th century.

The early astronomers

Thales of Miletus (640–560 BC) was the first of the great Greek philosophers. Though he believed the Earth to be flat, he initiated serious astronomical observation. Thales is accredited with predicting an eclipse in 585 BC. A *solar eclipse* occurs when the Moon passes between the Earth and the Sun, and a *lunar eclipse* is caused by the Moon passing into the Earth's shadow.

The Greek astronomer *Aristarchus of Samos* (c. 310–250 BC) was one of the first people to state that the Earth turns on its axis and orbits the Sun. He attempted to measure the relative distances of the Sun and Moon, arriving at a value of between 18 and 20. Modern measurements have shown that the true value is about 390.

Eratosthenes (276–196 BC) was a librarian in the Greek city of Alexandria in Egypt. He devised an experiment for measuring the circumference of the Earth, based on the observation that the Sun shone directly down a well in Aswan at midday on Midsummer's Day. Eratosthenes found that the angle of the Sun at the same time in Alexandria, 800 km (497 mi) north of Aswan, was about $1/50$ of a circle. He therefore deduced that the distance from Alexandria to Aswan was $1/50$ of the circumference of the Earth, which he calculated to be 40 000 km (24 840 mi). This is in close agreement with the modern value of 40 007 km (24 844 mi).

Claudius Ptolemaeus or *Ptolemy* (c. AD 120–180) was an Alexandrian scholar, whose *Almagest* was regarded as a standard text until the 16th century. In the *Ptolemaic system*, the Earth was stationary at the centre of the Universe, with the

Tycho Brahe (right) (1546–1601), the great Danish astronomer, in his observatory on the island of Hven. Tycho was the last of the great astronomers to rely on the naked eye, and he improved every previous astronomical observation. Among other things he calculated the length of the year to an accuracy of less than one second.

Sun, planets, Moon and stars revolving around it; their paths were small circles, whose centres moved along larger circles.

Nikolaus Copernicus (1473–1543) was a Polish astronomer who argued that the Sun, not the Earth, is at the centre of the Universe. His theories were published in 1543 in the book, *Concerning the Movement of the Heavenly Bodies*. Although Copernicus was correct in believing that the planets orbited the Sun and not the Earth, he mistakenly thought that the Sun marked the centre of the Universe and that the planets moved in perfect circles.

The Danish astronomer *Tycho Brahe* (1546–1601) had intended to become a lawyer, but changed his mind upon wit-

nessing a solar eclipse in 1560. In 1572 he witnessed the supernova in Cassiopeia and wrote a book about it. From 1576 to 1596 he worked at Uraniborg on the Danish island of Hven, compiling an accurate star catalogue.

The German mathematician *Johannes Kepler* (1571–1630) was the first person to show that the planets move around the Sun in elliptical orbits. He was originally an assistant to Tycho Brahe and his work was based on Tycho's observations. Kepler devised three important laws of planetary motion that are still in use today:

1. The motion of a planet around the Sun describes an ellipse, with the Sun at one of the foci (i.e. centres).

2. A line joining the centre of the Sun with the centre of a planet sweeps out equal areas in equal times.

3. The square of a planet's orbital period is proportional to the cube of its mean distance from the Sun.

The Italian *Galileo Galilei* (1564–1642) developed the astronomical telescope and used it to discover the four main satellites of Jupiter. He also observed the stars of the Milky Way and craters on the Moon, and found that the planet Venus showed phases. Galileo's book, *Two Chief Systems of the World*, published in 1632, backed up the theory of a Sun-centred Solar System, but was banned by the Roman Catholic Church as this theory went against Church dogma, which stated that the Earth was the centre of the Universe. He was forced to retract his views by the Inquisition and placed under house arrest.

The laws of motion derived by the English scientist *Sir Isaac Newton* (1642–1727) are fundamental to our understanding of the physical world (see p. 20) and are also of enormous importance to astronomers. Newton's discovery of gravity is also essential to all subsequent astronomical theory.

Several later astronomers are mentioned on previous pages in relation to their particular discoveries.

Early instruments and observations

One of the first astronomical instruments was the *astrolabe*, a circular disc marked off in degrees along its rim, which was used to measure the altitudes of stars and planets.

The *quadrant* was another device for measuring the positions of celestial objects. As its name implies, the quadrant is a 90° arc, together with a pointer for sighting stars. Before the advent of the telescope, astronomers would use astrolabes and quadrants for measuring stellar positions.

One of the earliest good star charts was the *Uranometria*, published by the Bavarian Johann Bayer (1572–1625) in 1603. Bayer introduced the system of identifying individual stars within a constellation by letters of the Greek alphabet.

SEE ALSO
● SPACE EXPLORATION p. 18
● NEWTON AND FORCE p. 20
● QUANTUM THEORY AND RELATIVITY p. 26
● OPTICS p. 32
● THE HISTORY OF SCIENCE p. 60
● SEEING THE INVISIBLE p. 332

IS THERE LIFE ELSEWHERE?

The acronym SETI stands for Search for Extra-Terrestrial Intelligence. The search began in earnest with Project Ozma in 1960, when a 26 m (85 ft) diameter radio telescope at Green Bank, West Virginia, USA, was used to search for signals from the nearby stars Tau Ceti and Epsilon Eridani. Nothing was found. Since Project Ozma, several further attempts have been made to detect radio signals produced by other intelligent civilizations, but without success.

It is possible to represent the probable number of advanced civilizations in the Galaxy by a mathematical equation. This was originally done by Frank Drake of Cornell University in the USA, and the equation thus bears his name.

Drake's equation states that the number (N) of advanced technical civilizations in the Galaxy can be expressed as follows:

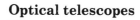

$$N = N_* \times f_p \times n_e \times f_l \times f_i \times f_c \times f_L$$

where:

N_* is the number of stars in the Galaxy;

f_p is the fraction of stars that have planetary systems;

n_e is the number of Earth-like planets in every star system (again, this will be a fraction, in that it is thought that most stars do not have Earth-like planets);

f_l is the fraction of suitable planets on which life actually arises;

f_i is the fraction of inhabited planets on which intelligent life evolves;

f_c is the fraction of planets inhabited by intelligent beings that attempt to communicate; and

f_L is the fraction of the planet's life for which the civilization survives.

A major problem with the Drake equation is that some of the terms are very difficult to estimate. Different estimates can yield wildly different results. These range from mankind being the only intelligent civilization in the Galaxy, to our being one among many millions of intelligent Galactic life forms.

Optical telescopes

The optical telescope was invented by the Dutch spectacle maker, Hans Lippershey (died c. 1619), but its first practical form was developed by Galileo. There are two principal types: *refracting telescopes*, which employ lenses, and *reflecting telescopes*, which use mirrors (see pp. 32–3).

The two largest optical telescopes are at Zelenchuskaya in the USSR, with a 6.0 m (19 ft 8 in) diameter mirror, and the Hale Telescope at Mount Palomar, California, which has a 5.0 m (16 ft 5 in) diameter mirror. Future developments are likely to include telescopes employing several mirrors or a multi-faceted mirror controlled by computer. These would be able to detect far fainter objects than is possible with conventional optical telescopes.

Radio astronomy

In 1931 the American radio engineer Karl Jansky (1905–1949) used an improvised aerial to detect radio emissions from the Milky Way. This marked the beginnings of *radio astronomy*, which has made possible such exciting developments as the discovery of quasars (see p. 8).

The most famous steerable radio telescope is the 75 m (250 ft) diameter Lovell Telescope at Jodrell Bank, England. The world's largest radio telescope, the 300 m (1000 ft) diameter dish at Arecibo in Puerto Rico, is built into a natural hollow in the ground.

Many astronomical bodies also emit gamma rays and X-rays, which can give us information about the physical properties of those bodies. However, these radiations are difficult to study, because they do not pass through the Earth's atmosphere. Most observations are therefore confined to spacecraft.

Modern astronomy now covers the whole of the electromagnetic spectrum (see p. 34), and observations are also being made at infrared, ultraviolet and microwave wavelengths. GE

The Lovell Telescope at Jodrell Bank (near Manchester, England) was the world's first giant-dish radio telescope. Since its construction in 1957, it has provided a vast amount of data from the furthest reaches of space.

Space Exploration

The development of space technology has been remarkably rapid. Less than 10 years after Yuri Gagarin became the first person in space, Neil Armstrong set foot upon the Moon. During the 21st century, space travel is likely to become routine. Permanent space stations will operate in Earth orbit, bases will be built on the Moon and man will begin to explore the planet Mars.

The theory of rocketry was developed at the beginning of the 20th century by the Russian physicist Konstantin Tsiolkovsky (1857–1935). He produced designs for multistage liquid-fuelled rockets decades before such vehicles were actually built. Tsiolkovsky also wrote about space suits, satellites and colonizing the Solar system. The inscription on his tombstone reads 'Mankind will not remain tied to Earth forever.'

The pioneers of rocketry

The first successful liquid-propellant rocket was launched by the American physicist Robert Goddard (1882–1945) in 1926. By the mid-1930s, Goddard had perfected rockets that could travel to an altitude of several kilometres.

Born in Germany, Wernher von Braun (1912–77) helped to develop the V-2 rocket during World War II. He surrendered to the Americans in 1945 and led the team that launched *Explorer 1* in 1958, the first American artificial satellite. He then turned his attention to the Apollo programme, which landed a man on the Moon in 1969.

The first artificial satellites

The first object successfully launched into space was the Soviet *Sputnik 1*, which lifted off on 4 October 1957. The satellite measured temperatures and electron densities, before burning up as it re-entered the atmosphere on 4 January 1958.

The dog Laika became the first living creature in space following her launch aboard *Sputnik 2* on 3 November 1957. Laika spent 10 days in orbit, but died when her oxygen supply was exhausted.

Man in space

The era of manned spaceflight began on 12 April 1961, when the Soviet cosmonaut Yuri Gagarin (1934–68) was launched aboard *Vostok 1*. His spacecraft completed a single orbit of the Earth in a flight lasting 90 minutes. Gagarin landed by parachute, having been ejected from the capsule during its descent.

The USA became the second country to put a man into orbit when John Glenn (1921–) was launched aboard his *Friendship 7* capsule on 20 February 1962.

Following the success of Gagarin's flight, President Kennedy announced that the USA intended to place a man on the Moon by the end of the decade. Thus the Apollo programme was born, which used the massive Saturn V rockets. The project reached a successful climax on 20 July 1969 when Neil Armstrong (1930–) and Edwin 'Buzz' Aldrin (1930–) landed their *Apollo 11* lunar module *Eagle* at the Sea of Tranquillity. The Apollo Moon-landing programme ended in 1972, five more successful missions having landed 10 more men on the Moon.

Space stations

Space stations are primarily used for scientific research, but have also been used to test the ability of humans to endure long periods of weightlessness in preparation for interplanetary flight. The first space station was the Soviet Union's

The Lunar Roving Vehicle or 'moon buggy' in action among the foothills of the Lunar Apennines. The LRV was taken to the Moon by *Apollo 15* in 1971.

Salyut 1, which was launched on 19 April 1971. This was followed by six further stations in the Salyut series, before the larger *Mir* space station was launched on 20 February 1986. Two cosmonauts spent a year aboard *Mir* from 21 December 1987 to 21 December 1988.

The American *Skylab* space station was launched on 14 May 1973 and was subsequently visited by three crews, the last of which stayed for 84 days.

Space shuttles

Unlike earlier spacecraft, space shuttles are reusable. The main vehicle is winged like an aeroplane, but is launched into orbit by booster rockets that are then discarded. The main vehicle can subsequently land like a conventional glider.

The American space shuttle made its debut on 12 April 1981, with the launch of the orbiter *Columbia*. The programme came to an abrupt halt on 28 January 1986, 73 seconds after the 25th shuttle launch. A leak from a rocket booster caused an explosion that destroyed the *Challenger* orbiter and killed its crew of seven. Shuttle operations resumed on 29 September 1988, when *Discovery* was launched on the 26th shuttle mission.

The USSR developed a reusable spacecraft – the VKK (*Vosdushno Kosmicheski Korabl*, 'airborne spacecraft'). The first VKK to be launched was *Buran* ('snowstorm'), which completed two orbits of the Earth on 15 November 1988. Although designed to carry a crew, *Buran's* first flight was unmanned.

Unmanned probes

Much of our knowledge of the Solar System has come from unmanned probes (see pp. 12–15). These have now returned data from every known planet except Pluto. Spacecraft have landed on Venus and Mars and probes are either planned, or on course, to enter orbit around Jupiter and Saturn.

The future

The rocket is the space launcher of the 20th century, but the spaceplane will be the launcher of the 21st century. Spaceplanes will be fully reusable and able to take off as well as land from runways like conventional aeroplanes. One such spaceplane was the British Hotol project, abandoned in 1992 owing to lack of funding. Other designs for spaceplanes are being studied by the USA (the X–30 project), Japan and Germany.

The early years of the 21st century are likely to see a return to the Moon. However, unlike the Apollo missions, the next time human beings venture to the Moon they will be equipped to stay and establish a permanent base. Following the return to the Moon, a manned flight to Mars is likely to be undertaken. The collapse of the Soviet economy and the break up of the USSR (1991) raised doubts concerning further projects, although Russian missions have taken place.   GE

Floating in space (left). On 7 February 1984 Captain Bruce McCandless left the US space shuttle *Challenger* to make the first untethered 'float' in space.

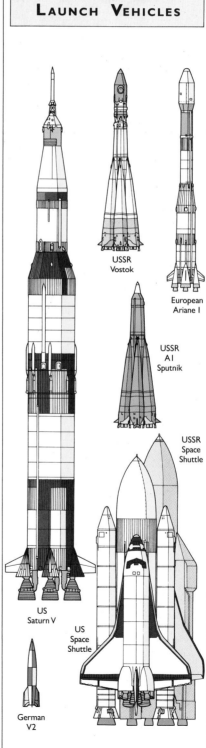

COMPARATIVE SIZES OF VARIOUS LAUNCH VEHICLES

USSR Vostok

European Ariane I

USSR A1 Sputnik

USSR Space Shuttle

US Saturn V

US Space Shuttle

German V2

THE USES OF SPACE TECHNOLOGY

Many artificial satellites are used for communications. *Comsats*, as they are sometimes known, are often placed in *geostationary orbit*, 36 900 km (22 900 mi) above the equator. Satellites in this orbit travel at the same speed as the Earth rotates and thus appear to remain fixed in the sky.

Weather satellites operate either in geostationary orbit, or *polar orbit*. A polar orbit carries a satellite over the North and South Poles, passing over a different strip of the Earth on every orbit. Such satellites can survey the entire planet every 24 hours.

Earth-resources satellites, such as those in the US Landsat series, can be used to prospect for new mineral resources, check the spread of diseases in crops and monitor pollution.

Space provides a good vantage point for astronomers, whose instruments can examine the universe from above the distortions of the atmosphere. The Hubble Space Telescope, launched by space shuttle early in 1990, is designed to detect fainter objects than any telescope on the ground, although it has suffered technical problems.

The movement of a space station cancels out the effect of gravity, making astronauts and their equipment weightless. These conditions can be used for manufacturing new materials such as perfect crystals.

The military also make use of space, both for surveillance and for weapons. Satellites can detect ground detail far more effectively than conventional aircraft. Spy satellites can detect objects as small as individual vehicles and people. The US Strategic Defence Initiative ('Star Wars') programme aims to provide a space-based laser defence system against nuclear weapons (see p. 289). However, many scientists doubt whether an effective system can ever be built and others doubt the wisdom of even trying to do so.

SEE ALSO

● THE INNER PLANETS p. 12
● THE OUTER PLANETS p. 14
● NUCLEAR ARMAMENT AND DISARMAMENT p. 288
● ENGINES p. 308
● SEEING THE INVISIBLE p. 332
● AIRCRAFT pp. 348–51

Motion and Force

Physics is the study of the basic laws that govern matter. ***Mechanics*** is the branch of physics that describes the movement or motion of objects, ranging in scale from a planet to the smallest particle within an atom. Sir Isaac Newton (see box) developed a theory of mechanics that has proved highly successful in describing most types of motion, and his work has been acclaimed as one of the greatest advances in the history of science.

Sir Isaac Newton

The Newtonian approach, although valid for velocities and dimensions within normal experience, has been shown to fail for velocities approaching the speed of light and for dimensions on a subatomic scale. Newton's discoveries are therefore considered to be a special case within a more general theory (see p. 26).

Motion

When a body is in *motion* it can be thought of as moving in space and time. If the body moves from one position to another, the straight line joining its starting point to its finishing point is its *displacement* (see diagram 1). This has both magnitude and direction, and is therefore said to be a *vector quantity*. The motion is *linear*.

The rate at which a body moves, in a straight line or *rectilinearly*, is its *velocity*. Again, this has magnitude and direction and is a vector quantity. In contrast, the *speed*, which has magnitude, but is not considered to be in any particular direction, is a *scalar quantity*. The *average velocity* of the body during this rectilinear motion is defined as the change in displacement divided by the total time taken. Its dimensions are therefore length divided by time, and are given in metres per second (m s^{-1}). The *instantaneous velocity* (the velocity of any instant) at

any point is the rate of change of velocity at that point.

If the body moves with a changing velocity, then the rate of change of the velocity is the *acceleration*. This is defined as the change in velocity in a given time interval. Its dimensions are velocity divided by time, and are given in metres per second per second (m s^{-2}). When a body moves with uniform acceleration (uniformly accelerated motion), the displacement, velocity and acceleration are related. These relationships are described in the *kinematic equations* (see box), sometimes called the *laws of uniformly accelerated motion*. Kinematics is the study of bodies in motion, ignoring masses and forces.

To use the equations to solve a problem in kinematics it is necessary to identify the information given in the problem, then to identify which of the four equations can be manipulated to give the answer required.

Galileo Galilei (1564–1642) was an Italian physicist and astronomer (see also p. 17) who investigated the motion of objects falling freely in air. He believed that all objects falling freely towards the Earth have the same downward acceleration.

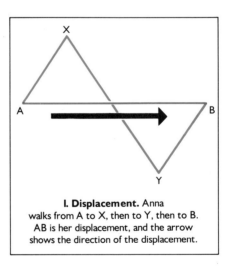

1. Displacement. Anna walks from A to X, then to Y, then to B. AB is her displacement, and the arrow shows the direction of the displacement.

This is called the *acceleration due to gravity* or the *gravitational acceleration*. Near the surface of the Earth it is 9.80 m s^{-2}, but there are small variations in its value depending upon latitude and elevation. In the idealized situation, air resistance is neglected, although in a practical experiment it would have to be considered. In a demonstration on the Moon in August 1971, an American astronaut showed that, under conditions where air resistance was negligible, a feather and a hammer, released at the same time from the same height, would fall side by side. They landed on the lunar surface together.

When real motion is considered, both the magnitude and the direction of the velocity have to be investigated. A golf ball,

THE KINEMATIC EQUATIONS

For a body moving in a straight line with uniformly accelerated motion:

1. $v = u + at$
2. $s = ut + \frac{1}{2}at^2$
3. $v^2 = u^2 + 2as$
4. $s = \frac{1}{2}t(u + v)$

where s = displacement
t = time
u = initial or starting velocity
v = velocity after time t
a = acceleration

hit upwards, will return to the ground. During flight its velocity will change in both magnitude and direction. In this case, instead of average velocity, the *instantaneous velocities* have to be evaluated. The velocity can, at any instant, be considered to be acting in two directions, vertical and horizontal. Then the velocity at that instant can be separated into a *vertical* and a *horizontal component* (see diagram 2). Each component can be considered as being uniformly accelerated rectilinear motion, so the kinematic equations can be applied in each direction. Then the instantaneous velocity and position at any point of the flight can be calculated.

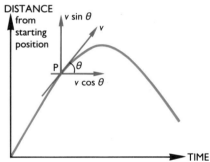

2. Instantaneous velocity v can be expressed as a horizontal component and a vertical component. The velocity at point P is v. It has a horizontal component $v \cos \theta$ and a vertical component $v \sin \theta$ (for explanations of sine, cosine and θ, see pp. 62–3).

Circular motion

If a body moves in a circular path at constant speed its direction of motion (and therefore its velocity) will be changing continuously. Since the velocity is changing, the body must have acceleration, which is also changing continuously. Thus the laws of uniformly accelerated motion do not apply. The acceleration of a body moving in a circular path is called the *centripetal* ('centre-seeking') *acceleration*. This is directed inward, towards the centre of the circle (see diagram 3).

Newton's laws of motion

Newton's laws of motion (see box) state relationships between the acceleration of a body and the forces acting on it. A *force* is something that causes a change in the rate of change of velocity of an object.

SIR ISAAC NEWTON

Sir Isaac Newton was born in a small village in Lincolnshire in 1642. In 1661 he was sent to Trinity College, Cambridge. By 1666, at the age of 24, he had made important discoveries in mathematics (the binomial theorem, differential calculus), optics (theory of colours) and mechanics.

Newton became Professor of Mathematics at Cambridge, and in 1687 he published his *Philosophiae Naturalis Principia Mathematica*, known as the *Principia*. Through careful analysis of the available experimental data and the application of his theory he was able to explain many previously inexplicable phenomena, such as the tides and the precession of the equinoxes. In 1689 and 1701 he represented Cambridge University in Parliament. From 1703 until his death in 1727 he was President of the Royal Society. He was buried in Westminster Abbey.

Newton's *first law* states that a body will remain at rest or travelling in a straight line at constant speed unless it is acted upon by an external force. Notice that the force has to be an external one. In general, a body does not exert a force upon itself.

The tendency of a body to remain at rest or moving with constant velocity is called the *inertia* of the body. The inertia is related to the mass, which is the amount of substance in the body. The unit of mass is the *kilogram* (kg).

Newton's *second law* states that the resultant force exerted on a body is directly proportional to the acceleration produced by the force. The unit of force is the *newton* (N), which is defined as the force that, acting on a body of mass 1 kg, produces an acceleration of 1 m s^{-2}.

The mass of a body is often confused with its weight. The mass is the amount of matter in the body, whereas the *weight* is the gravitational force acting on the body, and varies with location. The unit of weight is the newton (see above). Thus a body will have the same mass on the Moon as on Earth, but its weight on the Moon will be less than on Earth since the gravitational force on the Moon is approximately one sixth of that on Earth. The same person, stepping on a set of compression scales at the bottom of a mountain and then at the top, would weigh less at the top because of the slight decrease in the gravitational force, which results from the slight increase in distance from the centre of the Earth.

Newton expressed his second law by stating that the force acting on a body is equal to the rate of change in its 'quantity of motion', which is now called *momentum*. The momentum of a body is defined as the product of its mass and velocity.

Newton's *third law* states that a single isolated force cannot exist on its own: there is always a resulting 'mirror-image' force. In Newton's words, 'To every action there is always opposed an equal reaction.' This means that, because any two

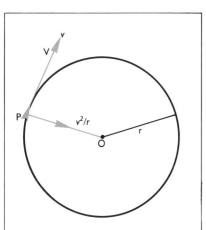

3. Centripetal acceleration. At point P the body is moving with instantaneous velocity *v*. The centripetal acceleration along PO is v^2/r^2 (where *r* is the radius of the circle), and this force prevents the body from moving in a straight line along PV.

NEWTON'S LAWS OF MOTION

1. A body will remain at rest or travelling in a straight line at constant speed unless it is acted upon by an external force.

2. The resultant force exerted on a body is directly proportional to the acceleration produced by the force.

$$F = ma$$

where *F* is the force exerted,
m is the mass of the body
a is the acceleration
v_1 is the initial velocity
v_2 is the final velocity

3. To every action there is an equal and opposite reaction.

masses exert on each other a mutual gravitational attraction, the Earth is always attracted towards a ball as much as the ball is attracted towards the Earth. Because of the huge difference in their sizes, however, the observable result is the downward acceleration of the ball.

The *principle of the conservation of momentum* follows from this third law. This states that, when two bodies interact, the total momentum before impact is the same as the total momentum after impact. Thus the total of the components of momentum in any direction before and after the interaction are equal.

In an *accelerating* or *non-inertial* frame of reference, Newton's second law will not work unless some fictitious force is introduced. For example, passengers on a circus merry-go-round feel as if they are being forced outward when the machine is operating. This is ascribed to a 'centre-fleeing' or 'centrifugal force'. The passengers experience this because they are moving within the system; they are within an accelerating frame of reference (see circular motion, above). To an observer on the ground it appears that the passengers on the ride should fly off at a tangent to the circular motion unless there were a force keeping them aboard. This is the centripetal force and is experienced as the *friction* between each passenger and the seat. If a passenger were to fall off, it would be because the centripetal force was not strong enough, not because the 'centrifugal force' was too great.

THE CONSERVATION OF MOMENTUM

The principle of the conservation of momentum states that when two bodies collide, the total of their momenta before impact is the same as the total after impact:

$$m_1 u_1 + m_2 u_2 = m_1 v_1 + m_2 v_2$$

where m_1, m_2 are the masses
u_1, u_2 are the initial velocities
v_1, v_2 are the resultant velocities of the bodies.

NEWTON'S LAW OF GRAVITATION

Every particle in the universe attracts every other particle with a force that is directly proportional to the product of their masses and inversely proportional to the square of the distance between them.

$$F = G \frac{m_1 m_2}{x^2}$$

where *F* is the force
m_1, m_2 are the masses
x is the distance between the particles.

Gravitation

Gravitational force is one of the four fundamental forces that occur in nature. The others are electromagnetic force (see p. 34), and the strong and the weak nuclear forces (see p. 38). The electromagnetic and weak forces have recently been shown to be part of an electro-weak force.

Gravitational force is the mutual force of attraction between masses. The gravitational force is much weaker than the other forces mentioned above. However, this long-range force should not be thought of as a weak force. An object resting on a table is acted on by the gravitational force of the whole Earth – a significant force. The almost equal force exerted by the table is the result of short-range forces exerted by molecules on its surface.

Newton's *law of gravitation* was first described in his *Philosophiae Naturalis Principia Mathematica* ('The Mathematical Principles of Natural Philosophy'), which he wrote in 1687. Newton used the notion of a *particle*, by which he meant a body so small that its dimensions are negligible compared to other distances. He stated that every particle in the universe attracts every other particle with a force that is directly proportional to the product of their masses and inversely proportional to the square of the distance between them (see box). The constant of proportionality is represented by *G* and is known as the *gravitational constant*. The law is an 'inverse-square law', since the magnitude of the force is inversely proportional to the square of the distance between the masses. A similar inverse-square law applies for the force between two electric charges (see Coulomb's law, p. 34).

Newtonian mechanics were so successful that a mechanistic belief developed in which it was thought that with the knowledge of Newton's laws (and later those of electromagnetism) it would be possible to predict the future of the Universe if the positions, velocities and accelerations of all particles at any one instant were known. Later the quantum theory and the Heisenberg Uncertainty Principle (see p. 26) confounded this belief by predicting the fundamental impossibility of making simultaneous measurements of the position and velocity of a particle with infinite accuracy. AS

SEE ALSO

● THE HISTORY OF ASTRONOMY p. 16
● FORCES AFFECTING SOLIDS AND FLUIDS p. 22
● THERMODYNAMICS p. 24
● QUANTUM THEORY AND RELATIVITY p. 26
● THE HISTORY OF SCIENCE p. 60
● FUNCTIONS, GRAPHS AND CHANGE p. 70

Forces affecting Solids and Fluids

In addition to the fundamental forces (see p. 21), other forces such as frictional, elastic and viscous forces may be encountered. Because of their different natures, solids and fluids appear in some ways to react differently to similar applied forces.

When forces are applied to solids they tend to resist. Friction inhibits displacement, but is overcome after a certain limit. Bodies may be deformed by tensions. Fluids, although lacking definite shape, are held together by internal forces. They exert pressure on the walls of the containing vessel (see pp. 24–5). Fluids – by definition – have a tendency to flow; this may be greater in some substances than in others and is governed by the viscosity of the fluid.

SEE ALSO

● MOTION AND FORCE p. 20
● THERMODYNAMICS p. 24
● HOW CARS WORK p. 354

Statics

Newton's first law (see p. 20), stated for a single particle, can also apply to real bodies that have definite sizes and shapes and consist of many particles. Such a body may be in *equilibrium*, which means it is at rest or moving with constant velocity in a straight line. This means that it is acted on by *zero net force*, and that it has no tendency to rotate.

A body is acted on by zero net force if the total or resultant of all the forces acting on it is zero – i.e. all the forces cancel each other out (see diagram 1). If the body is at rest it is in *static equilibrium*. Studies of such conditions are important in the design of bridges, dams and buildings.

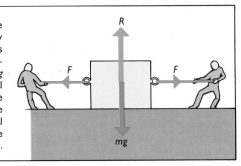

1. Equilibrium. The net force on the body is zero. The mass is balanced by the reaction force: $R = mg$ (mg is the gravitational force acting on the mass). The men are pulling with equal force: $F = F$. The body will not move.

Forces involved in rotation

Torque (or *moment of a force*) measures the tendency of a force to cause the body to rotate. In this case the force causes *angular acceleration*, which is the *rate of change of angular momentum* of the body. Torque is defined as the product of the force acting on a body and the perpendicular distance from the axis of the rotation of the body to the line of action of the force (see diagram 2). Torque has units of force × distance, usually expressed as *newton metres* (N m).

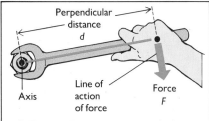

2. Torque. Torque or moment of a force = force x perpendicular distance = Fd.

Torque is increased if either the force or the perpendicular distance is increased. If a wedge is used to keep a door open, it has maximum effect if it is placed on the floor as far from the hinge as possible.

When a body is acted on by two equal and opposite forces, not in the same line, then the result is a *couple*, which has a constant turning moment about any axis perpendicular to the plane in which they act (see diagram 3). When the total or net torque on a body is zero about any axis, the body is in *equilibrium*. A body is in stable equilibrium if a small linear displacement causes a force to act on the body to return it to its previous position, or an angular displacement causes a couple to act to bring it back to its previous position, called the *equilibrium position*.

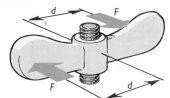

3. A couple. The total turning force acting on the wing nut is 2Fd.

The *centre of mass* of a body is a point, normally within the body, such that the net resultant force produces an acceleration at this point, as though all the mass of the body were concentrated there. For bodies of certain shapes this point may lie outside the object.

If a uniform gravitational field is present, the centre of gravity coincides with the centre of mass. Thus all the weight can be considered to act at this single point. The stability of an object is helped by keeping the centre of gravity as low as possible. A

racing car is low-slung to improve stability (see diagrams 4 and 5).

Friction

Sliding friction occurs when a solid body slides on a rough surface. Its progress is hindered by an interaction of the surface of the solid with the surface it is moving on (see diagram 6). This is called a *kinetic frictional force*.

Another type of friction is called *static friction*. Before the object moves, the resultant force acting on it must be zero. The frictional force acting between the object and the surface on which it rests cannot exceed its limiting value. Thus, when the other forces acting on the object, against friction, exceed this value the object is caused to accelerate. The limiting or maximum value of the frictional force occurs when the stationary object acted on by the resultant force is just about to slip.

Both these types of friction involve interaction with a solid surface. The frictional forces depend on the two contacting surfaces and in particular on the presence of any surface contaminants. The friction between metal surfaces is largely due to adhesion, shearing and deformation within and around the regions of real contact. Energy is dissipated in friction and appears as internal energy, which can be observed as heat (see below). Thus car brakes heat up when used to slow a

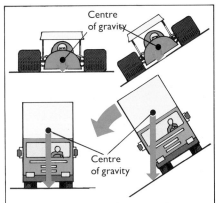

4. Centre of gravity. A racing car has a very low centre of gravity and will remain stable even on a slope. A loaded truck will have a high centre of gravity and will topple over if driven on too steep a slope.

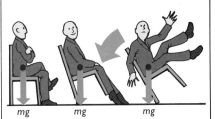

5. Centre of mass. In the left-hand picture the person is in a stable state because the perpendicular through his centre of mass falls between the legs of the chair. In the centre picture, although the chair is tipped, the perpendicular still falls within the safe area between the legs of the chair. In the right-hand picture the perpendicular falls outside the legs of the chair. The person sitting on the chair is in trouble...

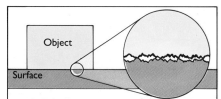

6. Friction. If one were to enlarge a section of two apparently smooth surfaces, roughnesses would become apparent – so explaining why friction occurs between two surfaces.

vehicle. The results of friction may be reduced by the use of lubricants between the surfaces in contact. This is one function of the oil used in car engines. A further type of friction is *rolling friction*, which occurs when a wheel rolls. Energy is dissipated through the system, because of imperfect elasticity (see below). This effect does not depend upon surfaces and is unaffected by lubrication.

Elasticity

Elasticity deals with deformations that disappear when the external applied forces are removed. Most bodies may be deformed by the action of external forces and behave elastically for small deformations.

Strain is a measure of the amount of deformation. *Stress* is a quantity proportional to the force causing the deformation. Its value at any point is given by the magnitude of the force acting at that point divided by the area over which it acts.

It is found that for small stresses the stress is proportional to the strain. The constant of proportionality is called the *elastic modulus* and it varies according to the material and the type of deformation. *Young's modulus* refers to changes in length of a material under the action of an applied force. The *shear modulus* relates to another type of deformation – that of planes in a solid sliding past each other. The third modulus is called the *bulk modulus* and characterizes the behaviour of a substance subject to a uniform volume comparison.

A special example of deformation is the extension or elongation of a spring by an applied force. *Hooke's law*, formulated by the English scientist Robert Hooke (1635–1703), states that, for small forces, the extension is proportional to the applied force. Thus a spring balance will have a uniform scale for the measurement of various weights.

In scientific terms, spring steel – which returns to its initial state readily – is almost *perfectly elastic*. In contrast, a soft rubber ball dropped on hard ground bounces to only about half its initial height, demonstrating *imperfect elasticity*.

Some bodies behave elastically for low values of stress, but above a critical level they behave in a perfectly viscous manner and 'flow' like thick treacle (see below), with irreversible deformation. This is called *plastic flow* (see diagram 7).

Fluids at rest – hydrostatics

Pressure is defined as the perpendicular or normal force per unit area of a plane surface in the fluid, and its unit is the *pascal* (Pa), equivalent to 1 newton per square metre (N m²). At all points in the fluid at the same depth the pressure is the same. The pressure depends only on depth in an enclosed fluid, and is independent of cross-sectional area. In the hydraulic brakes of a car (see diagram 8), a force is applied by the foot pedal to a small piston. The pressure is transmitted via the hydraulic fluid to a larger piston connected to the brake. In this way the force applied to the brake is magnified by comparison with the force applied to the pedal (see diagram 8).

Atmospheric pressure may be measured using a barometer. At sea level, it is equivalent to the weight of a column of mercury about 0.76 m high, which is about 1.01×10^5 Pa. It varies by up to about 5%, depending on the weather systems passing overhead (see p. 102).

The *buoyancy force* was described by the Greek mathematician and physicist Archimedes (287–212 BC). Archimedes' principle states that an object placed in a fluid is buoyed up by a force equal to the weight of fluid displaced by the body (see diagram 9). It was the realization of this principle that – according to legend – prompted Archimedes to leap out of his bath with shouts of '*Eureka! Eureka!*' ('I have found it! I have found it!').

A body with density greater than that of the fluid will sink, because the fluid it displaces weighs less than it does itself. A body with density less than that of the fluid will float. A submarine varies its density by flooding ballast tanks with sea water or emptying them; this enables it to dive or rise to the surface.

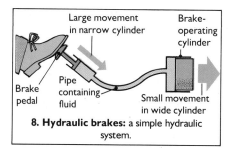

8. Hydraulic brakes: a simple hydraulic system.

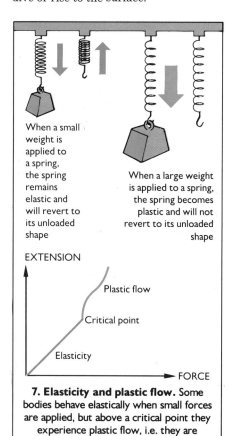

When a small weight is applied to a spring, the spring remains elastic and will revert to its unloaded shape

When a large weight is applied to a spring, the spring becomes plastic and will not revert to its unloaded shape

7. Elasticity and plastic flow. Some bodies behave elastically when small forces are applied, but above a critical point they experience plastic flow, i.e. they are irreversibly extended.

Surface tension

Surface tension occurs at an interface between a liquid and either a gas or a solid. Molecules in a liquid exert forces on other molecules. At the surface there is asymmetry in these forces, resulting in surface tension. Thus falling rainwater coalesces into spherical drops.

Surface tension may be reduced by the presence of a detergent, which acts as a wetting agent, spreading out the liquid over the solid surface. In the human lung, fluid on the alveoli surfaces (see p. 211) contains a detergent to prevent collapse of the lung during breathing; its absence, particularly in babies, is fatal.

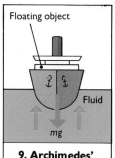

9. Archimedes' principle. Total upward force is equal to the weight of fluid displaced.

AS

Thermo-dynamics

Thermodynamics is the study of heat and temperature. *Heat* is a form of energy, and the *temperature* of a substance is a measure of its internal energy. One fundamental principle in the study of thermodynamics is the *conservation of energy*. This theory was developed in the late 19th century by about a dozen scientists, including James Joule (1818–89), a brewery-owner from the north of England, and Baron Herman von Helmholtz (1821–94), a German physiologist. Although there seemed to be plenty of evidence in the world that energy was not conserved, this important principle was eventually established.

Much of the energy that seems to be lost in typical interactions – such as a box sliding across a floor – is converted into internal energy; in the case of the sliding box, this is the kinetic energy (see below) gained by the atoms and molecules within the box and the floor as they interact and are pulled from their equilibrium positions. The name given to the energy in the form of hidden motion of atoms and molecules is *thermal energy*. Strictly speaking, heat is transferred between two bodies as a result of a change in temperature, although the term 'heat' is commonly used for the thermal energy as well. Processes that turn kinetic energy, which is the organized energy of a moving body, into thermal energy, which is the disorganized energy due to the motion of atoms, include friction and viscosity (see pp. 22–3). In a steam engine, heat is turned into work (see p. 308).

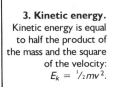

3. Kinetic energy. Kinetic energy is equal to half the product of the mass and the square of the velocity: $E_k = \frac{1}{2}mv^2$.

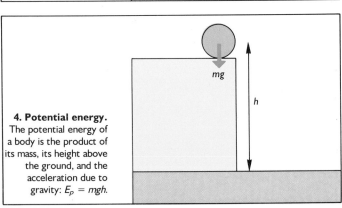

4. Potential energy. The potential energy of a body is the product of its mass, its height above the ground, and the acceleration due to gravity: $E_p = mgh$.

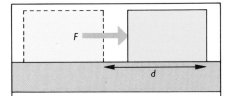

I. Work. Work done on a body by a constant force is the product of the magnitude of the force and the displacement of the body as a result of the action of the force: $W = Fd$.

Work and energy

When a force (see p. 20) acts on a body, causing acceleration in the direction of the force, *work* is done. The work done on a body by a constant force is defined as the product of the magnitude of the force and the consequent displacement of the body in the direction of the force (see diagram 1).

The unit of work is the *joule* (sometimes referred to as the *newton metre*). A joule (J) is defined as the work done on a body when it is displaced 1 metre as the result of the action of a force of 1 newton (see p. 20) acting in the direction of motion:

$$1\,J = 1\,N\,m$$

The result may be expressed more generally (see diagram 2).

Energy is the capacity of a body to do work. The total energy stored in a *closed system* – one in which no external forces are experienced – remains constant, however it may be transformed. This is the principle of *conservation of energy*. It may take the form of mechanical energy (kinetic or potential; see below), electrical energy, chemical energy, or heat energy. There are also other forms of energy, including gravitational, magnetic, the energy of electromagnetic radiation, and the energy of matter.

The *kinetic energy* of a body is the energy it has because it is moving. It is equal to half the product of the mass and the square of the velocity (see diagram 3).

Alternatively, a body may have *potential energy*. In contrast to kinetic energy, which is dependent upon velocity, potential energy is dependent upon position. The gravitational potential energy of a body of mass m at a height h above the ground is mgh, where g is the acceleration due to gravity (see diagram 4). This gravitational potential energy is equal to the work that the Earth's gravitational field will do on the body as it moves to ground level.

Potential energy can be converted into kinetic energy or it can be used to do work. It acts as a store of energy. If a body moves upward against the gravitational force, work is done on it and there is an increase in gravitational potential energy.

Temperature

Temperature is a measure of the internal energy or 'hotness' of a body, not the heat of the body. Thermometers are used to measure temperature. They may be based on the change in volume of a liquid (as in a mercury thermometer), the change in length of a strip of metal (as used in many thermometers), or the change in electrical resistance of a conductor. Other parameters may also be involved in measuring temperature.

The *thermodynamic temperature scale* – also known as the *kelvin scale* or the *ideal gas scale* – is based on a unit called the *kelvin* (K); the scale is used in both practical and theoretical physics. The scale is named after the Scottish physicist William Thomson, later Lord Kelvin (1824–1907), who did important work in thermodynamics and electricity. An *ideal gas* is one that would obey the ideal gas law perfectly (see below and diagram 5). In fact no gas is ideal, but most behave sufficiently closely that the ideal gas law can be used in calculations. At ordinary temperatures and pressures, dry air can be considered as a very good approximation to an ideal gas.

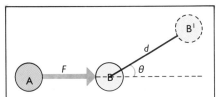

2. Work done. A exerts a force F on B and as a result B moves to position B' with displacement d at angle θ to the line of F. Work $W = Fd\cos\theta$. (For explanations of cosine and θ, see pp. 62–3.)

On the kelvin scale the freezing point of water is 273.15 K (0 °C or 32 °F) and its boiling point is 373.15 K (100 °C or 212 °F): one degree kelvin is equal in magnitude to one degree on the Celsius scale. The temperature of 0 (zero) K is known as *absolute zero*. At this temperature, for an ideal gas, the volume would be infinitely large and the pressure zero.

Heat and internal energy

The molecular energy (kinetic and potential) within a body is called *internal energy*. When this energy is transferred from a place of high energy to one of lower energy, it is described as a flow of heat.

If two bodies of different temperatures are placed in thermal contact with each other, after a time they are found both to be at the same temperature. Energy is transferred from the warmer to the colder body, until both are at a new *equilibrium temperature*. Heat is a form of energy, and heat flow is a transfer of energy resulting from differences in temperature.

The unit of internal energy and heat is the *joule*, as defined above. Units used previously include the *calorie*, which is equivalent to 4.2 joules and is defined as the heat required to raise the temperature of 1 gram of water from 14.5 °C (58.1 °F) to 15.5 °C (59.9 °F). The unit used by nutritionists is actually the *kilocalorie*, or *Calorie* (= 1000 calories).

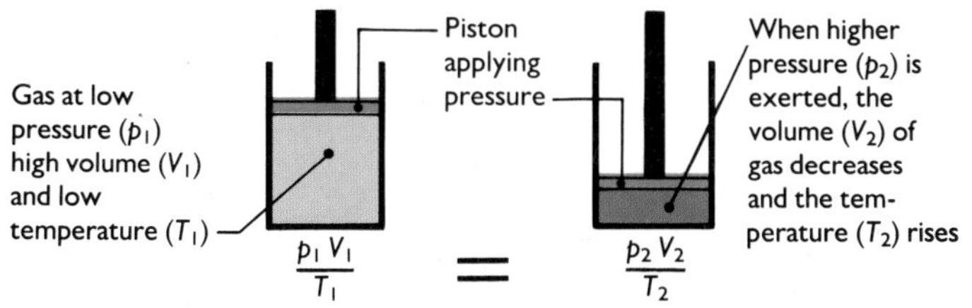
Piston applying pressure
Gas at low pressure (p_1) high volume (V_1) and low temperature (T_1)
When higher pressure (p_2) is exerted, the volume (V_2) of gas decreases and the temperature (T_2) rises
$\frac{p_1 V_1}{T_1} = \frac{p_2 V_2}{T_2}$

5. The ideal gas law. This combines Boyle's law and Charles' law.

The kinetic theory of gases

The kinetic theory of gases takes Newton's laws (see pp. 20–21) and applies them statistically to a group of molecules. It treats a gas as if it were made up of extremely small – dimensionless – particles, all in constant random motion. It is based on an ideal gas.

One conclusion is that the pressure and volume of such a gas are related to the average kinetic energy for each molecule. The kinetic theory explains that pressure in a gas is due to the impact of the molecules on the containing walls around the gas. There is an equation that relates the pressure, temperature and volume of an ideal gas – the *ideal gas law* (see diagram 5).

The temperature of an ideal gas is a measure of the average molecular kinetic energies. At a higher temperature the mean speed of the molecules is increased. For air at room temperature and atmospheric pressure the mean speed is about 500 m s^{-1} (about 1800 km/h or 1100 mph, the velocity of a rifle bullet).

The internal energy of a gas is associated with the motion of its molecules and their potential energy. For a gas that is more complex than one with monatomic (i.e. single-atom) molecules, account has to be taken of energies associated with the rotation and vibration of its molecules, as well as their speed.

A *thermally isolated system* is one that neither receives nor transmits transfer of heat, although the temperature within the system may vary. If mechanical or electrical work is performed on a thermally isolated system, its internal energy increases. James Joule observed the effects of doing measured amounts of work on insulated bodies (thermally isolated systems). He discovered an equivalence relation between the amount of work done *(W)* and the heat gained *(Q)*:

$$W = JQ$$

The constant *J* was described by Joule as the *mechanical equivalent of heat.*

Laws of thermodynamics

The *first law of thermodynamics* is a development of the law of conservation of energy, which states that in any interaction, energy is neither created nor destroyed. The first law states that if, during an interaction, a quantity of heat is absorbed by a body, it is equal to the sum of the increase in internal energy of the body and any external work done by the body.

The increase in internal energy will be made up of an increase in the kinetic energy of the molecules in the body and an increase in their potential energy, since work will have been done against intermolecular forces as the body expands.

The change in internal energy of a body thus depends only on its initial and final states. The change may be the result of an increase in energy in any form – thermal, mechanical, gravitational, etc. Another statement of this law is that it is possible to convert work totally into heat.

The *second law of thermodynamics* states that the converse is not true. There are several ways in which the second law may be stated but, essentially, it means that heat cannot itself flow from a cold object to a hot object. Thus the law shows that certain processes may only operate in one direction.

The second law was established after work by a French engineer, Sadi Carnot (1796–1832), who was trying to build the most efficient engine. His ideal engine – the *Carnot engine* – established an upper limit for the efficiency with which thermal energy could be converted into mechanical energy. Real engines fall short of this ideal efficiency because of losses due to friction and heat conduction (see below). As the temperature of the sink (the place where energy is removed from the system) in a working engine is near room temperature, the amount of work that can be done is restricted by the relatively small temperature difference. This limits the efficiency of most steam engines to about 30–40%. Thus it makes sense to use the vast amounts of waste heat from electrical power stations for heating purposes rather than allow it to be lost in cooling towers.

Entropy

Entropy is a parameter used in statistical mechanics to describe the *disorder* or *chaos* of a system. A highly disordered state is one in which molecules move haphazardly in all directions, with many different velocities. An alternative form of the second law of thermodynamics is that the entropy of the universe never decreases. It follows from this analysis that the universe is moving through increasing disorder towards thermal equilibrium. Therefore the universe cannot have existed for ever, otherwise it would have reached this equilibrium state already.

Latent heat

When heat flows between a body and its surroundings there is usually a change in the temperature of the body, as well as changes in internal energies. This is not so when a change of form occurs, as from solid to liquid or from liquid to gas. This is called a *phase change* and involves a change in the internal energy of the body only.

The amount of heat needed to make the change of phase is called the *hidden* or *latent heat.* To change water at 100 °C (212°F) to water vapour requires nearly seven times as much heat (*latent heat of vaporization*) as to change ice to water (*latent heat of fusion*). This varies for water at different temperatures – more heat is required to change it to water vapour at 80 °C (176 °F), less at 110 °C (230 °F). In each case the attractive forces binding the water molecules together must be loosened or broken.

Latent heat has an important effect on climate (see diagram 6). A similar cycle takes place in a heat pump or refrigerator (see p. 309). AS

—HEAT TRANSFER—

CONDUCTION

Heat conduction occurs when kinetic and molecular energy is passed from one molecule to another. Metals are good conductors of heat because of electrons that transport energy through the material (see p. 51). Air is a poor conductor in comparison. Thus a string vest keeps its wearer warm by trapping air and so preventing the conduction of heat outwards from the body.

CONVECTION

Heat convection results from the motion of the heated substance. Warm air is less dense than cold air and so, according to Archimedes' principle (see p. 23), it rises. Convection is the main mechanism for mixing the atmosphere and diluting pollutants emitted into the air.

RADIATION

Radiation is the third process for heat transfer. All bodies radiate energy in the form of electromagnetic waves (see p. 34). This radiation may pass across a vacuum, and thus the Earth receives energy radiated from the Sun. A body remains at a constant temperature when it both radiates and receives energy at the same rate.

SEE ALSO

- MOTION AND FORCE p. 20
- FORCES AFFECTING SOLIDS AND FLUIDS p. 22
- THE HISTORY OF SCIENCE p. 60
- ENERGY pp. 304–7
- ENGINES p. 308

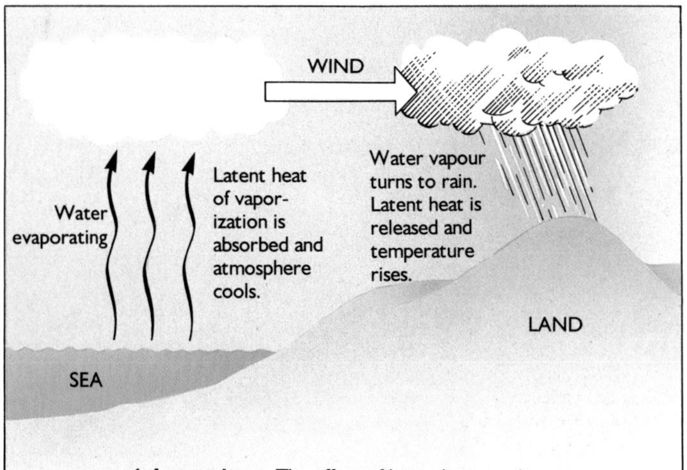
WIND
Water evaporating
Latent heat of vaporization is absorbed and atmosphere cools.
Water vapour turns to rain. Latent heat is released and temperature rises.
LAND
SEA

6. Latent heat. The effect of latent heat on climate.

Quantum Theory and Relativity

Three of the most important theories of the 20th century are the quantum theory and the theories of special and general relativity. When special relativity is combined with the full quantum theory and with electromagnetism (see p. 34), almost all of the physical world is described by it. The most important application is in the theory of subatomic particles (see also pp. 38–9). General relativity is as yet not fully combined with quantum theory and is a theory of gravity and cosmology.

The physical world is not as simple as the theories of Newton supposed (see pp. 20–1), although such views are appropriate simplifications for large objects moving relatively slowly with respect to the observer. Quantum mechanics is the only correct description of effects on an atomic scale, and special relativity must be used when speeds approaching the speed of light, with respect to the observer, are involved.

The development of quantum theory

At the very beginning of the 20th century scientists such as the German physicist Max Planck (1858–1947) discovered that the theories of classical physics were not sufficient to explain certain phenomena on the subatomic scale, particularly in the field of electromagnetic radiation and the study of light waves. Their work

SEE ALSO

● TIME p. 6
● MOTION AND FORCE p. 20
● WAVE THEORY p. 28
● ELECTROMAGNETISM p. 34
● ATOMS AND SUBATOMIC PARTICLES p. 38
● ELEMENTS AND THE PERIODIC TABLE p. 42

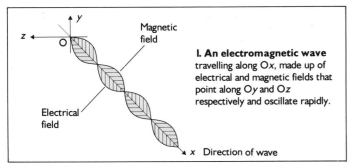

I. An electromagnetic wave travelling along Ox, made up of electrical and magnetic fields that point along Oy and Oz respectively and oscillate rapidly.

DISCRETE VARIABLES

Variables that can only take certain values – such as the number of children in a family, which must be a whole number – are *discrete* variables. Those that can take any value within a range, such as the height of children within a family, are *continuous*. Thus the time as displayed on a digital watch can usually only take discrete values, whilst the time displayed on a watch with hands (an *analogue device*) shows continuous variation.

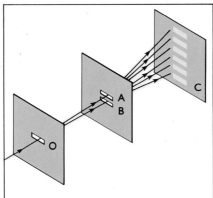

2. Interference. The waves passing through slits A and B and reaching the screen C will be either in phase or out of phase and will either reinforce or cancel each other (see diagrams II and I2, p. 29). The result is a series of light and dark bands on the screen. Reinforcement occurs when the path difference is a whole number of wavelengths.

resulted in the development of the quantum theory, which states that nothing can be measured or observed without disturbing it: the observer can affect the outcome of the effect being measured.

The Scottish physicist James Clerk Maxwell (1831–79) had developed a theory about the electromagnetic wave nature of light (see p. 35), and this was crucial to the development of quantum theory. Maxwell showed that at any point on a beam of light there is a magnetic field and an electric field that are perpendicular to each other and to the direction of the light beam. The fields oscillate millions of times every second, forming a wave pattern (as shown in diagram 1).

Photons

If light is directed onto a piece of metal in a vacuum, electrons (see p. 38) are knocked from the surface of the metal. This is the *photoelectric effect*. For light of a given wavelength, the number of electrons emitted per second increases with the intensity of the light, although the energies of the electrons are independent of the wavelength.

This discovery led the German physicist Albert Einstein (1879–1955) to deduce that the energy in a light beam exists in small discrete packets called *photons* or *quanta* (see box on discrete variables). These can be detected in experiments in which light is allowed to fall on a detector, usually photographic film. This has led to the theory of the *dual nature of light*, which behaves as a wave during interference experiments (see diagram 2 and pp. 28–9) but as a stream of particles during the photoelectric effect. Further work on this phenomenon has led to the acceptance of *wave-particle duality*, which is a fundamental principle in quantum physics. The way a system is described depends upon the apparatus with which it is interacting: light behaves as a wave when it passes through slits in an interference

experiment, but as a stream of particles when it hits a detector (see diagram 3).

Uncertainty

Werner Karl Heisenberg (1901–76), a German physicist, interpreted wave-particle duality differently. He proposed that when a beam of light is directed at a screen with two slits, the interference pattern formed exists only if we do not know which slit the photon passed through. If we make an additional measurement and determine which slit was traversed, we destroy the interference pattern. Heisenberg showed that it was impossible to measure position and momentum simultaneously with infinite accuracy; he expressed his findings in the *uncertainty principle* named after him. This changed the thinking about the precision with which simultaneous measurements of two physical quantities can be made.

Particles

Matter is made up of vast numbers of very small particles (see p. 38). The behaviour of these particles cannot be described by the theories of classical physics, since there is no equivalence to subatomic particles in everyday mechanics. Thus it is not helpful to discuss the behaviour of electrons in atoms in terms of tiny 'planets' orbiting a 'sun'. Louis Victor de Broglie (1892–1987), the French physicist, suggested that if light waves can behave like particles, then particles might in certain circumstances behave like waves. Later experiments confirmed that under appropriate conditions particles can exhibit wave phenomena.

Atomic energy levels

Quantum systems are described by a mathematical equation known as the *Schrödinger equation* after the Austrian physicist Erwin Schrödinger (1887–1961), who first formulated it. In situations as where a negatively charged electron is bound to the positively charged nucleus of an atom (see p. 38), the Schrödinger equation has solutions for only *discrete* or *quantized* allowed values of the energy of the electron (see box on discrete variables). The energy of an electron in an atom cannot take a lower value than the least of the allowed values – the *ground state* – so the electron cannot fall into the

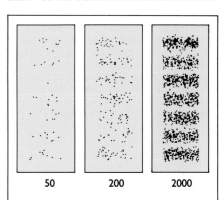

| 50 | 200 | 2000 |

3. The photon nature of light. The results of two-slit interference after the passage of 50, 200 and 2000 photons have passed through. The characteristic pattern is only observed after many photons have passed. The initial results appear random.

nucleus. If an atom, through the interaction of forces on it, is excited into an allowed state of energy that is higher than the ground state, it can emit a photon and jump into the ground state (see diagram 3 on pp. 38–9). The energy of the photon is equal to the difference in energy levels of the two states. The energy of the photon is related to the wavelength of the light wave associated with it – thus light can be emitted by atoms only at particular wavelengths.

Quantum mechanics

Quantum mechanics is the study of the observable behaviour of particles. This includes electromagnetic radiation in all its details (see pp. 34–5). In particular, it is the only appropriate theory for describing the effects that occur on an atomic scale.

Quantum mechanics deals exclusively with what can be observed, and does not attempt to describe what is happening in between measurements. This is not true of classical theories, which are essentially complete descriptions of what is occurring whether or not attempts are made to measure it. In quantum mechanics the experimenter is directly included in the theory. Quantum mechanics predicts all the possible results of making a measurement, but it does not say which one will occur when an experiment is actually carried out. All that can be known is the probability of something being seen. In some experiments one event is very much more likely than any other, therefore most of the time this is what will be found, but sometimes one of the less probable events will occur. It is impossible to predict which will occur; the only way to find out is by making the appropriate measurement. For example, in an isotope of the element americium, 19% of the nuclei decay purely by alpha-particle emission (see p.39) and 81% decay by alpha emission followed by photon emission. For any individual americium nucleus it is not possible to say which decay will occur, only what will be observed on average. In some experiments the same event can occur in different ways. What is measured depends on whether it is known which of the possible paths was taken. Thus any additional knowledge, which can only be gained by making an additional measurement, changes the outcome of the first experiment.

Special relativity

Inertial frames. Physical laws such as Newton's laws of mechanics (see p. 20) are stated with respect to some *frame of reference* that allows physical quantities such as velocity and acceleration to be defined. A frame of reference is called *inertial* if it is unaccelerated and it does not contain a gravitational field.

Einstein's relativity principle. In 1905 Einstein stated that all inertial frames are equally good for carrying out experiments. This assumption, coupled with the evidence that the speed of light (see box) is the same in all frames, led Einstein to develop the theory of special relativity. This theory has been extensively tested using particle accelerators, where electrons or protons travel at speeds within a fraction of 1% of the speed of light. The

masses of such particles measured by an observer in the laboratory in which the particles are travelling are higher than the masses measured by an observer at rest with respect to the particles.

Time. The classical view of time is that if two events take place simultaneously with reference to one frame then they must also occur simultaneously within another frame. In terms of special relativity, however, two events that occur simultaneously in one frame may not be seen as simultaneous in another frame moving relative to the first (see diagram 4). The sequence of cause and effect in related events is not, however, affected. Light plays a special role in synchronizing clocks in different frames because it has the same speed in all frames. In the classical view all observers have the same time scale, whereas in special relativity every inertial observer requires an individual time scale.

Space-time. An important feature of special relativity is that time and space have to be considered as unified and not as two separate things. This means that time is related to the frame of reference in which it is being measured. This is a different view of space to that of Newton.

Length contraction. The equations of special relativity lead to the very simple prediction that the length of a moving body in the direction of its motion measured in another frame is reduced by a factor dependent on its velocity with respect to the observer. What this means is that a car travelling very fast on a motorway would be measured by a stationary observer to be slightly shorter and heavier than usual, although the driver would not determine any difference. The length of a body is greatest when it is measured in a frame travelling *with* the body; as the speed of the body *relative to* the frame of reference approaches the speed of light the measured length approaches zero.

Time dilation. A similar effect happens to moving clocks (which can be any regularly occurring phenomenon, such as the vibration of atoms – the basis of atomic clocks – or the decay of particles). A clock moving with a uniform velocity in one frame is measured as running slow in another frame. Its fastest rate is in its own frame, and at speeds – relative to the observer – approaching the speed of light the clock rate approaches zero.

Paradox of reality? Both of the above effects of length and time contraction have been the inspiration of numerous 'paradoxes' (and some science-fiction writing), and have been criticized on such grounds. But this simply goes to show that our 'common-sense' view of the world is rooted in frames that travel with respect to the observer at tiny speeds compared to that of light, and is just as inappropriate in describing these phenomena as it is in describing the quantum effects of the atomic world. Time dilation has been measured experimentally both with decaying particles and with actual

macroscopic clocks. In all cases the effects predicted by special relativity were encountered.

General relativity

This is an extension of the theory of special relativity to include gravitational fields and accelerating reference frames. Gravitational fields arise because of the distortions of space-time in the vicinity of large masses, and space-time is no longer thought of as having an existence independent of the mass in the universe. Rather, space-time, mass and gravity are interdependent. The concept of 'curved space-time' was put forward by Einstein in his general theory of relativity. The motion of astronomical bodies is controlled by this deformation or curvature of space and time close to large masses. Light is also bent by the gravitational fields of large masses. Light rays have been observed to bend as they pass close to the Sun, so providing experimental verification of Einstein's theories.   PH

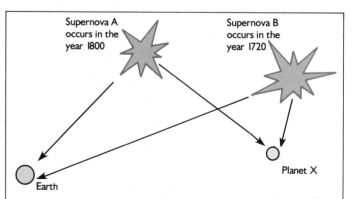

4. Relative time. Supernova A occurs 120 light years from Earth (i.e. light takes 120 years to travel from Supernova A to Earth), and Supernova B is 200 light years from Earth. From Earth the two events are observed simultaneously in 1920, even though Supernova B occurred 80 years before Supernova A. From Planet X, in contrast, the two events are not observed simultaneously. Planet X is only 40 light years from Supernova B, but 150 light years from Supernova A. Therefore, on Planet X, Supernova B is observed in 1760, while Supernova A is not seen until 1950.

Wave Theory

Water waves are a phenomenon that can be seen, and the effects of sound waves are sensed directly by the ear. Some of the waves in the electromagnetic spectrum (see p. 35) can also be sensed by the body: light waves by the eye, and the heating effect of infrared by the skin. There are other electromagnetic waves, however, that cannot be experienced directly through any of the human senses, and even infrared can generally only be observed using specialized detectors (see pp. 332–3).

SEE ALSO

- QUANTUM THEORY AND RELATIVITY p. 26
- ACOUSTICS p. 30
- OPTICS p. 32
- ELECTROMAGNETISM p. 34
- COASTS p. 96
- THE OCEANS p. 100
- MEDICAL TECHNOLOGY p. 242
- RADIO, TELEVISION AND VIDEO p. 326
- SEEING THE INVISIBLE p. 332

Wave phenomena are found in all areas of physics, and similar mathematical equations may be used in each application. Some of the general principles of wave motions are explored here. Special types of wave motion – relating to acoustics and optics – are examined on pp. 30–33, and electromagnetic waves in general are examined on pp. 26–7 and 34–5.

Wave types and characteristics

A *travelling wave* is a disturbance that moves or *propagates* from one point to another. *Mechanical waves* are travelling waves that propagate through a material – as, for example, happens when a metal rod is tapped at one end with a hammer. An initial disturbance at a particular place in a material will cause a force to be exerted on adjacent parts of the material. An *elastic force* (see p. 22) then acts to restore the material to its equilibrium position. In so doing, it compresses the adjacent particles and so the disturbance moves outward from the source. In attempting to return to their original positions, the particles overshoot, so that at a particular point a *rarefaction* (or stretching) follows a *compression* (or squeezing). The passage of the wave is observed as variations in the pressure about the equilibrium position or by the speed of oscillations. This change is described as *oscillatory* (like a pendulum) or *periodic*.

There are two main types of periodic oscillation – *transverse* and *longitudinal* (see diagrams 1 and 2). In transverse waves the vibrations are perpendicular to the direction of travel. In longitudinal waves the vibrations are parallel to the direction of travel. *Sound waves* are alternate compressions and rarefactions

of whatever material through which they are travelling, and the waves are longitudinal.

Water waves (see also p. 100) may be produced by the wind or some other disturbance. The particles move in vertical circles so there are both transverse and longitudinal displacements. The motion causes the familiar wave profile with narrow peaks and broad troughs.

Wave motions transfer energy – for example, sound waves (see p. 30), seismic waves (see pp. 80–1) and water waves (see pp. 96 and 100) transfer mechanical energy. However, energy is lost as the wave passes through a medium. The amplitude (see diagram 3 and below) diminishes and the wave is said to be attenuated (see diagram 4). There are two distinct processes – *spreading* and *absorption*. In many cases there is little or no absorption – electromagnetic radiation from the Sun travels through space without any absorption at all, but planets that are more distant than the Earth receive less radiation because it is spreading over a larger area and so the *intensity* (the ratio

of power to area) decreases according to an inverse-square law. The same applies to sound in the atmosphere. In some cases, however, energy is absorbed in a medium, as, for example, when light enters and exposes a photographic film, or when X-rays enter flesh. For homogeneous radiation, absorption is *exponential*, for example if half the radiation goes through 1 mm of absorber, a quarter would go through 2 mm and an eighth through 3 mm.

The *frequency* (*f*) of the wave motion is defined as the number of complete oscillations or cycles per second (see diagram 5). The unit of frequency is the *hertz* (Hz), named after the German physicist Heinrich Rudolf Hertz (see p. 35): 1 hertz = 1 cycle per second. The *amplitude* is the maximum displacement from the equilibrium position (see diagram 3). The *wavelength* (λ) is the distance between two successive peaks (or troughs) in the wave (see diagram 6). The *speed of propagation* (*v*) of the compressions, or *phase speed* of the wave, is equal to the product of the frequency and the wavelength: $v = f(\lambda)$.

Waves originating from a point source will propagate outwards, in all directions, forming *wavefronts*; these wavefronts will be circular or spherical if propagating through a homogeneous medium. When the distance of a wavefront from the source is great, then it can be considered as a *plane wavefront* (see diagram 7).

Reflection and refraction

Reflection of plane waves at a plane surface are as shown in diagram 8. The angle between the direction of the wavefront and the *normal* (i.e. a line perpendicular to the plane surface) is the angle of incidence (*i*). The angle between the reflected wave and the normal to the plane surface is the angle of reflection (*r*), and these angles *i* and *r* are equal. The behaviour of waves reflected at curved surfaces is shown in diagram 9.

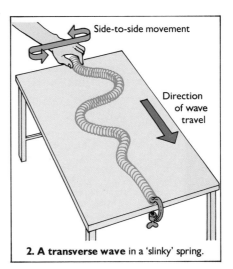

2. A transverse wave in a 'slinky' spring.

Side-to-side movement

Direction of wave travel

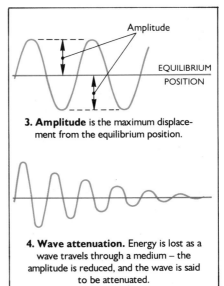

Amplitude

EQUILIBRIUM POSITION

3. Amplitude is the maximum displacement from the equilibrium position.

4. Wave attenuation. Energy is lost as a wave travels through a medium – the amplitude is reduced, and the wave is said to be attenuated.

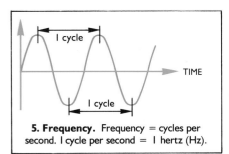

I cycle

TIME

I cycle

5. Frequency. Frequency = cycles per second. I cycle per second = I hertz (Hz).

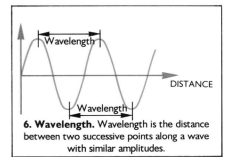

Wavelength

DISTANCE

Wavelength

6. Wavelength. Wavelength is the distance between two successive points along a wave with similar amplitudes.

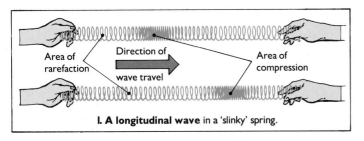

Area of rarefaction

Direction of wave travel

Area of compression

I. A longitudinal wave in a 'slinky' spring.

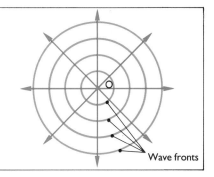

7. Spherical and plane wavefronts. Wavefronts propagating outwards from point source O will be spherical in a three-dimensional context (such as light waves propagating from the Sun) or circular in a two-dimensional context (such as water waves propagating from a dropped pebble). Once far enough from the source, such wavefronts can for most practical purposes be considered as straight lines – plane wavefronts – much in the same way that the curvature of the Earth is not noticeable to someone standing on it.

Wave fronts

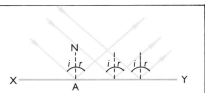

8. Reflection of plane waves at a plane surface. The waves are parallel as they approach XY and after they are reflected. AN is the normal to XY at A. i is the angle of incidence of the wave as it meets XY. The angle of reflection is r, and $i = r$.

9. Waves reflected at a curved surface. Waves behave in the same way as light reflected in a concave mirror. S is the principal focus of the surface A.

If a wave travels from one medium to another, the direction of propagation is changed or 'bent'; the wave is said to be *refracted*. The wave will travel in medium 1 with velocity v, and come upon the surface of medium 2 with angle of incidence i. Then the wave will be refracted, as in diagram 10, and r is the angle of refraction. The new velocity will be v_2, which will be less than v_1 if medium 2 is more dense than medium 1, but greater than v_1 if medium is less dense. The velocities are related by:

$$\frac{v_1}{v_2} = \frac{\sin i}{\sin r}$$

and the ratio of $\sin i / \sin r$ is a constant (see pp. 62–3 for an explanation of sine). This constant is the *refractive index* of medium 2 with respect to medium 1. This relationship was formulated by the Dutch astronomer Willebrord Snell (1591–1626) and is known as *Snell's Law*.

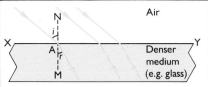

10. Refraction of a plane wavefront. MAN is the normal to XY; i is the angle of incidence; r is the angle of refraction. The waves are parallel after refraction.

Interference

If several waves are travelling through a medium, the resultant at any point and time is the vector sum of the amplitudes of the individual waves. This is known as the *superposition principle*. Two or more waves combining together in this way exhibit the phenomenon of *interference*. If the resultant wave amplitude is greater than those of the individual waves then *constructive interference* is taking place (see diagram 11); if it is less, *destructive interference* occurs (see diagram 12). If two sound waves of slightly different frequencies and equal amplitudes are played together (for example two tuning forks), then the resulting sound has what is called *varying amplitude*. These varying amplitudes are called *beats* and their frequency is the *beat frequency*. This frequency is equal to the difference between the frequencies of the two original notes. Listening for beats is an aid to tuning musical instruments: the closer the beats, the more nearly in tune is the instrument.

Amplitude and frequency modulation

Radio waves can be used to carry sound waves by superimposing the pattern of the sound wave onto the radio wave. This is called *modulation*, and is one of the basic forms of radio transmission. There are two ways of modulating radio waves. *Amplitude modulation* (AM) is the form most commonly used. The amplitude of the radio *carrier wave* is made to vary with the amplitude of the sound signal. For *frequency modulation* (FM) the frequency of the carrier wave is made to vary so that the variations are in step with the changes in amplitude of the sound signal (see diagram 13).

Standing or stationary waves

These are the result of confining waves in a specific region. When a travelling wave, such as a wave propagating along a guitar string towards a bridge, reaches the support, the string must be almost at rest. A force is exerted on the support that then reacts by setting up a reflected wave travelling back along the string. This wave has the same frequency and wavelength as the source wave. At certain frequencies the two waves, travelling in opposite directions, interfere to produce a stationary- or standing-wave pattern. Each pattern or mode of vibration corresponds to a particular frequency.

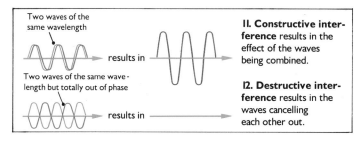

11. Constructive interference results in the effect of the waves being combined.

12. Destructive interference results in the waves cancelling each other out.

The standing wave may be transverse, as on a plucked violin string, or longitudinal, as in the air in an organ pipe. The positions of maximum and minimum amplitude are called *antinodes* and *nodes* respectively (see page 31). At antinodes the interference is constructive. At nodes it is destructive.

If a periodic force is applied to a system with frequency at or near to the *natural frequency* of the system, then the resulting amplitude of vibration is much greater than for other frequencies. These natural frequencies are called *resonant frequencies*. When a driving frequency equals the resonant frequency then maximum amplitude is obtained.

The natural frequency of objects can be used destructively. High winds can cause suspension bridges to reach their natural frequency and vibrate, sometimes resulting in the destruction of the bridge. Soldiers marching in formation need to break step when crossing bridges in case they achieve the natural frequency of the structure and cause it to disintegrate.

Diffraction

Waves will usually proceed in a straight line through a uniform medium. However, when they pass through a slit with width comparable to their wavelength, they spread out, i.e. they are diffracted (see diagram 14). Thus waves are able to bend round corners. For a sound wave of 256 Hz the wavelength is about 1.3 m (4¼ ft), comparable with the dimensions of open doors or windows.

If a beam of light is shone through a wide single slit onto a screen that is close to the slit, then a bright and clear image of the slit is seen. As the slit is narrowed there comes a point where the image does not continue getting thinner. Instead, a diffraction pattern of light and dark fringes is seen.

Huygens' principle was proposed in 1676 by the Dutch physicist Christiaan Huygens (1629–95) to explain the laws of reflection and refraction. He postulated that light was a wave motion. Each point on a wavefront becomes a new or secondary source. The new wavefront is the surface that touches all the wavefronts from the secondary sources. Diffraction describes the interference effects observed between light derived from a continuous portion of a wavefront, such as that at a narrow slit. The work of the British physician and physicist Thomas Young (1773–1829) and others eventually supported Huygens' theory.   AS

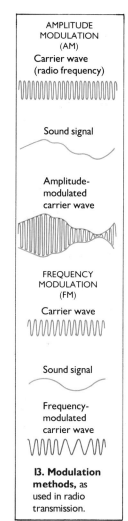

AMPLITUDE MODULATION (AM)

Carrier wave (radio frequency)

Sound signal

Amplitude-modulated carrier wave

FREQUENCY MODULATION (FM)

Carrier wave

Sound signal

Frequency-modulated carrier wave

13. Modulation methods, as used in radio transmission.

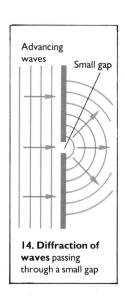

Advancing waves

Small gap

14. Diffraction of waves passing through a small gap

Acoustics

The range of frequencies for which sound waves are audible to humans is from 20 to 20 000 Hz (i.e. vibrations or cycles per second) – the higher the frequency, the higher the pitch. In music, the A above middle C is internationally standardized at 440 Hz (see also pp. 568–9). For orchestral instruments, the frequencies range between 6272 Hz achieved on a handbell, and 16.4 Hz on a sub-contrabass clarinet. On a standard piano (and a violin) the highest note is 4186 Hz. For the organ, the highest frequency is 12 544 Hz and the lowest is 8.12 Hz, using pipes of 1.9 cm (¾ in) and 19.5 m (64 ft) respectively.

Frequencies that are lower than the human audible range are referred to as *infrasonic*, and those above as *ultrasonic*. Many mammals such as dolphins and bats have sensitive hearing in the ultrasonic range, and they use high-pitched squeaks for echolocation (see .pp. 146–7 and 163). Large animals such as whales and elephants use frequencies in the infrasonic range to communicate over long distances. It is thought that migrating birds can detect infrasonic sounds produced by various natural features, and that they use the distinctive sounds produced by particular features as aids to navigation (see p. 171).

The velocity of sound

Sound shares the general characteristics of other wave forms (see pp. 28–9). Sound waves are longitudinal compressions (squeezings) and rarefactions (stretchings) of the medium through which they are travelling, and are produced by a vibrating object.

If a sound wave is travelling in any medium then the pressure variations formed along its path cause strains as a result of the applied stresses. The velocity of the sound is given by the square root of the appropriate elastic modulus (see p. 22) divided by the density.

The velocity of sound – as with the velocity of other types of wave – differs in different media. In still air at 0 °C, the velocity of sound is about 331 m s^{-1} (1191.6 km/h, or 740 mph). If the air temperature rises by 1 °C, then the velocity of sound increases by about 0.6 m s^{-1}. The velocity of sound in a metal such as steel is about 5060 m s^{-1}. Sometimes, in a Western film, someone will put an ear to a railway line to listen for an oncoming train. This works because the sound wave travels much faster through the steel track than through the air.

In the ocean depths the combined effect of salinity, temperature and pressure results in a minimum velocity for sound. The channel that is centred around this minimum velocity at a depth of about 1000–1300 m (3300–4250 ft) allows sound waves, travelling at the minimum velocity, to propagate within it with relatively little loss over large horizontal distances. Signals have been transmitted in this way from Australia to Bermuda.

The fact that the velocity of sound varies in different media is one reason why seismic techniques can be used to probe layers of rock or minerals underground (see diagram 1, and p. 332). Similarly ultrasonic scanning can be used in medicine – for example, in the imaging of a baby in its mother's womb (see pp. 242 and 332). In each case variations in materials are shown up through variations in the time it takes sound waves to travel to the detector.

Refraction of sound

At night the air near the ground is often colder than the air higher up, as the Earth cools after sunset. Thus a sound wave moving upward will be slowly bent back towards the horizontal as it meets warmer layers of air. Eventually it will be reflected back downwards. Under these circumstances sound can be heard over long distances. This phenomenon is explained by Snell's law of refraction (see pp. 28–9); layers of air at different temperatures act as different media through which sound travels at different velocities (see diagram 2).

During World War I the guns at the front in northern France could sometimes be heard in southern England, although not in the intervening area. This was a significant piece of evidence for the existence of the *stratosphere*, that part of the atmosphere above the *troposphere* (the lowest layer); in the middle and upper stratosphere the temperature increases with altitude (see p. 77).

I. Seismic surveying relies on the variation of seismic velocities in different rocks; this causes some layers to reflect the waves more strongly than others.

SEE ALSO

● WAVE THEORY p. 28
● OPTICS p. 32
● EARTHQUAKES p. 80
● SEEING AND HEARING p. 218
● MEDICAL TECHNOLOGY p. 242
● SEEING THE INVISIBLE p. 332
● WHAT IS MUSIC? p. 568

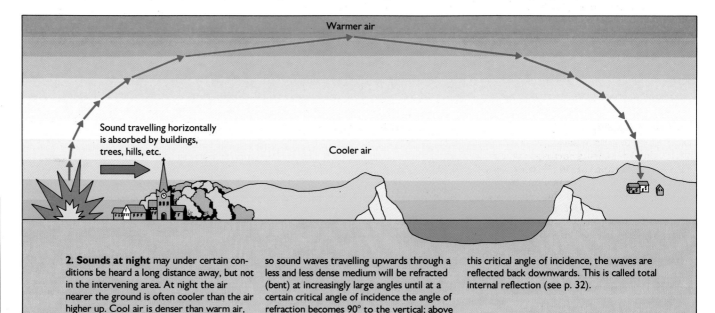

Sound travelling horizontally is absorbed by buildings, trees, hills, etc.

Warmer air

Cooler air

2. Sounds at night may under certain conditions be heard a long distance away, but not in the intervening area. At night the air nearer the ground is often cooler than the air higher up. Cool air is denser than warm air, so sound waves travelling upwards through a less and less dense medium will be refracted (bent) at increasingly large angles until at a certain critical angle of incidence the angle of refraction becomes 90° to the vertical; above this critical angle of incidence, the waves are reflected back downwards. This is called total internal reflection (see p. 32).

The human ear

The ear is an extremely sensitive detector. Its threshold of hearing corresponds to an intensity of sound of 10^{-12} watts per square metre (W m²): this is a measure of the energy impinging on the ear, and is known as the *threshold intensity*. The loudest tolerable sound is about 1 W m². This range is enormous, and so a logarithmic scale, to the base 10, is used. The original unit was the *bel*, named after Alexander Graham Bell (1847–1922), the Scottish inventor of the telephone.

The bel is graduated using a logarithmic scale, but as the bel is rather a large unit,

the *decibel* (db) is more normally used (1 bel = 10 db). If threshold intensity is at 0 db, then a sound at ten times threshold intensity is 10 db, one at a hundred times threshold intensity is 20 db, one at a thousand times threshold intensity is 30 db, and so on. This means that the value of 1 W m² is at 120 db above threshold.

The ear canal resonates slightly to sounds with frequencies of about 3200 Hz. The human ear is most sensitive in the range 2500–4000 Hz. Even then, only about 10% of the population can hear a 0 db sound and then only in the 2500–4000 Hz region. The response of the ear is not linear, i.e. there is no direct relationship with the intensity of the sound it detects. Sensitivity is related to frequency: it decreases strongly at the lowest audible frequencies, but less so at the highest.

The audible range of the normal human ear varies with age. It is usually about 20–20 000 Hz in the mid-teens. For someone 40 years old, the upper limit is more likely to be 12 000–14 000 Hz. At the lower hearing threshold, the pressure fluctuations from the sound wave are about 3×10^{-10} of atmospheric pressure. The eardrum (called the *tympanic membrane*) vibrates at very low velocities – about 10 cm (4 in) per year. This may seem strange, given that it can vibrate at frequencies of up to 20 000 Hz (cycles per second); however, the low velocity is explained by the fact that the detected displacement of the air molecules adjacent to the eardrum each time it moves is less than the typical atomic radius (about 10^{-10} m). The human ear is an astonishingly sensitive detector and so it is not surprising that constant overload will bring deterioration in its performance.

Characteristics of tones

There are three main characteristics of the notes played by musical instruments. *Loudness* would seem to be the most simple, but it is complicated by the non-linear response of the ear (see above). At 100 Hz and 10 000 Hz the hearing threshold is about 40 db compared to the 0 db at 2500–4000 Hz. Thus the concept of loudness is not dependent just on the energy reaching the ear, but also on frequency.

Pitch is closely related to frequency. If the

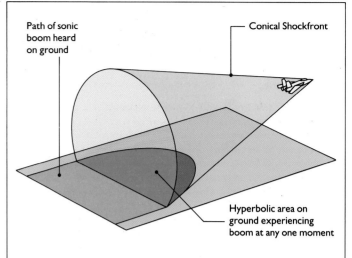

The greater the plane's velocity exceeds the velocity of sound, the narrower the angle of the cone. If an aeroplane is particularly long, a double boom may be heard, as both the front and tail of the plane generate shockfronts.

frequency of vibration is doubled the pitch rises by one octave (see pp. 568–9). In general, the higher the frequency the higher the pitch.

Sounds created by musical instruments are not simple waveforms, but are the result of several waves combining. This complexity results in the *tone quality* or *timbre* of a note played by a particular musical instrument. Even a 'pure' note may contain many waves of different frequencies. These frequencies are *harmonics* or *multiples* of the fundamental or lowest frequency, which has 2 nodes and 1 antinode, and is called the *first harmonic* (see diagram 3, and p. 29). The *second harmonic* has 3 nodes and 2 antinodes. The wavelength is halved and the frequency is doubled. The *third harmonic* has 4 nodes and 3 antinodes. The wavelength is one third of the original wavelength, and the frequency has tripled. Different instruments emphasize different harmonics. Musical synthesizers are able to mimic instruments by mixing the appropriate harmonics electronically at various amplitudes.   AS

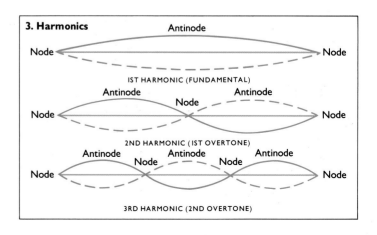

3. Harmonics

Optics

Optics is the branch of physics that deals with the high-frequency electromagnetic waves that we call light. Optics is concerned with the way in which light propagates from sources to detectors via intermediate lenses, mirrors and other modifying elements. The electromagnetic spectrum includes a wide range of waves in addition to light (see pp. 34–5), light being that small part of the spectrum that can be detected by the human eye.

This region, with wavelengths from 700 nanometres (nm; $1 \, nm = 10^{-9} \, m$) in the red region to 400 nm in the violet (see the prism, below), is extended for practical optical systems into the ultraviolet and the mid-infrared regions. For many purposes light can be treated as a classical wave phenomenon (see pp. 28–9), but some effects can only be described by using the full quantum theory (see pp. 26 and 36).

A *beam* of light may be considered to be made up of many *rays*, all travelling outwards from the source. This approach is used in ray diagrams. In geometric simplifications, as in the diagrams used here, rays of light are drawn as straight lines. The wavelength and amplitude of light waves are very short compared to the other dimensions of the systems. The basic concept is very simple: light travels in straight lines unless it is reflected by a mirror or refracted by a lens or prism (see below).

A point source of light emits rays in all directions. For an isolated point source in a vacuum the geometric wavefront will be a sphere (see p. 28). The variation of the speed of light in different materials must be taken into account – the speed of light (as of other electromagnetic waves) in a vacuum is $3 \times 10^8 \, m \, s^{-1}$ (300 000 km or 186 000 miles per second), but it travels more slowly through other media. Light waves have transverse magnetic and electric fields (see p. 26).

Reflection and refraction

Light is reflected and refracted (i.e. bent) in the same way as other waves (see pp. 28–9). Diagram 1 shows a monochromatic (single-colour) beam of light falling or *incident upon* a transparent material such

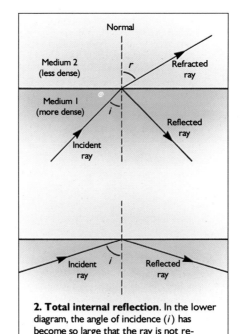

2. Total internal reflection. In the lower diagram, the angle of incidence (i) has become so large that the ray is not refracted but is reflected back into medium I.

as a block of glass. Angle i is the angle of *incidence* of the beam. Part of the beam is reflected at an angle t, the angle of *reflection*; and part is transmitted according to the law of refraction, and r is the angle of *refraction*.

Snell's law of refraction (see also p. 29) can be stated as:

$$n_1 \sin i = n_2 \sin r$$

where n_1 and n_2 are the refractive indices of the materials (the sine of an angle is explained on pp. 62–3). Basically, the *refractive index* of a material determines how much it will refract light.

The refractive index of a material is often expressed relative to another material. If no other material is quoted, the refractive index is assumed to be relative to air. The refractive index of a medium can also be derived as the ratio of the speed of light in a vacuum to the speed of light in the medium. The refractive index for a typical optical glass is 1.6, whereas the refractive index of diamond is about 2.4 in visible light.

The prism

The refractive index of optical glasses is not constant for light of all frequencies. It is greater at the violet end and less at the red end of the spectrum. This means that a beam of light containing a mixture of different frequencies, for example sunlight, will leave a prism with the different frequencies bent by different amounts.

A *prism* is a block of glass with a triangular cross-section; it is used to deviate a beam of light by refraction. A beam of white light will be split into its component monochromatic coloured lights – from red to violet – which will form the familiar rainbow effect. Any light can be split up in this way; the display of separated wave-

lengths is called the *spectrum* of the original beam.

The effect of prisms on light has been well known for many centuries. Newton used this effect, called *dispersion*, to produce and study the spectrum of sunlight. Under the right conditions dispersion occurring in spherical raindrops in the atmosphere produces a rainbow.

Total internal reflection

When light travels from one medium to another less dense medium it is *deviated* or turned away from the *normal* – perpendicular to the interface at the point of incidence. This means the angle of refraction (r) is greater than the angle of incidence (i). When the angle of refraction is less than 90°, some of the incident light will be refracted and some will be reflected. If the angle of incidence increases, the angle of refraction will increase more. It is possible to increase the angle of incidence to such a value that eventually the refracted ray disappears and all the light is reflected. This is known as *total internal reflection* (see diagram 2).

The lens

A lens is a piece of transparent material made in a simple geometric shape. Usually at least one surface is spherical, and often both are. In diagram 3 the features of lenses are described. Under appropriate conditions a lens will produce an image of an object by refraction of light. It does this by bending rays of light from the object.

Some rays are refracted more than others, depending how they arrive at the surface

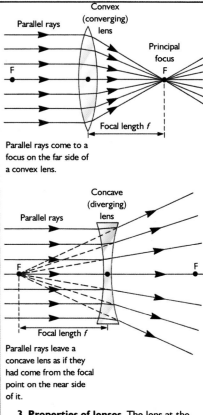

3. Properties of lenses. The lens at the top is *convex* (i.e. it is thicker in the middle), while the one below it is *concave* (i.e. it is thinner in the middle).

Parallel rays come to a focus on the far side of a convex lens.

Parallel rays leave a concave lens as if they had come from the focal point on the near side of it.

SEE ALSO

● THE HISTORY OF
  ASTRONOMY p. 16
● QUANTUM THEORY AND
  RELATIVITY p. 26
● WAVE THEORY p. 28
● ELECTROMAGNETISM p. 34
● ATOMS AND SUBATOMIC
  PARTICLES p. 38
● PHOTOGRAPHY AND FILM
  p. 324
● RADIO, TELEVISION AND
  VIDEO p. 326
● TELECOMMUNICATIONS
  p. 330
● SEEING THE INVISIBLE p. 332

I. Reflection and refraction

of the lens. The lens affects the velocity of the rays, since light travels more slowly in a dense medium such as the lens than in a less dense medium such as air. In this way, the expanding geometric wavefront that is generated by the object is changed into a wavefront which, for a *convex* or *converging lens*, converges to a point behind the lens. If the object is located a long way from the lens (strictly an *infinite* distance, but a star is an excellent approximation for practical purposes) this point is known as the *rear focal point* or *principal focus* of the lens (see diagram 3). Notice that a lens has two principal foci – one on each side. The distance between the optical centre of the lens and the principal focus is the *focal length (f)*. If a point source of light is placed at the principal focus of the convex lens, the rays of light will be refracted to form a parallel beam.

Because of the effects of dispersion (see above), the distance from the lens at which red light and blue light from an object will be focused will be different. This can be demonstrated in the colour fringes that can be seen in simple hand magnifiers (small magnifying glasses). Such fringes are unacceptable in, for example, camera lenses. A lens made from two different types of glass can be made to bring two colours to exactly the same focus with only a very small variation for other frequencies. Such a lens is called *achromatic*. Single-element lenses are, therefore, only used for simple applications. Lenses for cameras, binoculars, telescopes and microscopes are made with many elements, with different curvatures. These lenses are made from glasses with different refractive indices and dispersions. The additional elements allow the lens designer greatly to reduce the faults or *aberrations* of the lens.

Mirrors

Mirrors are reflecting optical elements. Plane mirrors are used to deviate light beams without dispersion or to reverse or invert images. Curved mirrors, which usually have spherical or parabolic surfaces, can form images, and are often used

in illumination systems such as car head-lamps.

Mirrors can be coated with metals such as aluminium or silver, which have high reflectance for visible light (or gold for the infrared). Alternatively, they may be coated with many thin layers of non-metallic materials for very high reflectances over a more restricted range of frequencies. A freshly coated aluminium mirror will reflect about 90% of visible light. Special mirrors, such as those used in lasers (see box), can reflect over 99.7% of the light at one frequency.

Mirrors do not introduce any chromatic aberrations into optical systems. Those with large diameters are also lighter than glass lenses of equivalent size. For these reasons they are always used as the primary reflectors of large astronomical telescopes.

The microscope and the telescope

The *microscope* is a device for making very small objects visible. It was probably invented by a Dutch spectacle-maker, Zacharias Janssen (1580–1638), in 1609.

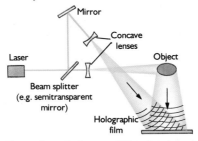
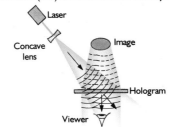
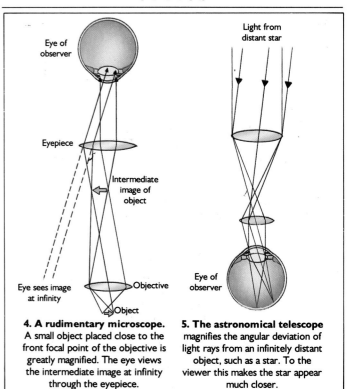

4. A rudimentary microscope. A small object placed close to the front focal point of the objective is greatly magnified. The eye views the intermediate image at infinity through the eyepiece.

5. The astronomical telescope magnifies the angular deviation of light rays from an infinitely distant object, such as a star. To the viewer this makes the star appear much closer.

Essentially, it is an elaboration of the simple magnifying glass. The *objective* – a lens with short focal length – is used to form a highly magnified image of a small object placed close to its focal point (see diagram 4). This can be viewed directly, by means of another lens called the *eyepiece*. It can also be recorded directly on film or viewed via a video camera.

The *telescope* is used to form an enlarged image of an infinitely distant object, and the enlarged image is viewed by the observer by means of an eyepiece (see diagram 5). The term 'infinite' is used relatively in this context: compared with the length of the telescope, the distance of the object can be considered as infinite. Telescopes are often made with reflecting mirrors instead of glass lenses, as large lenses sag under their own weight, thereby introducing distortions into the image. The primary mirror is often a large concave paraboloid.

Fibre optics

Light can be transmitted over great distances by the use of flexible glass fibres. These fibres are usually each less than 1 mm (1/25 in) in diameter, and can be used singly or in bunches. Each fibre consists of a small core surrounded by a layer of 'cladding' glass with a slightly lower refractive index. Certain rays experience total internal reflection (see above), and this, coupled with the very low absorption of modern silica glasses, allows light to travel very long distances with little reduction in intensity. Fibre optics provide the basis of endoscopy, a medical diagnostic technique (see pp. 242–3), and are also used extensively in telecommunications, as light in a fibre optic cable can carry more digital (on or off) signals with less loss of intensity than a copper wire carrying electrical digital signals (see pp. 330–1).   PH

Electro-magnetism

Electromagnetism is the study of effects caused by stationary and moving electric charges. Electricity and magnetism were originally observed separately, but in the 19th century, scientists began to investigate their interaction. This work resulted in a theory that electricity and magnetism were both manifestations of a single force, the electromagnetic force.

The electromagnetic force is one of the fundamental forces of nature, the others being gravitational force (see p. 21) and the strong and weak nuclear forces (see pp. 38–9). Recently the electromagnetic and weak forces have been shown to be manifestations of an electro-weak force. Magnetism has been known about since ancient times, but it was not until the late 18th century that the electric force was identified – by the French physicist Charles Augustin de Coulomb (1736–1806).

Magnetism

Metallic ores with magnetic properties were being used around 500 BC as compasses. It is now known that the Earth itself has magnetic properties (see p. 77). Investigation of the properties of magnetic materials gave birth to the concept of *magnetic fields*, showing the force one magnet exerts on another. These lines of force can be demonstrated by means of small plotting compasses or iron filings (see diagram 1). An important feature of a magnet is that it has two poles, one of which is attracted to the Earth's magnetic north pole (see p. 77), while the other is attracted to the south pole. Conventionally, the north-seeking end of a magnet is called its *north pole*, and the other is the *south pole*. Magnets are identified by the fact that unlike or opposite poles (i.e. north and south) attract each other, while like poles (north and north, or south and south) repel each other.

Magnetic effects are now known to be caused by moving electric charges. Atomic electrons (see pp. 38–9) are in motion, and thus all atoms exhibit magnetic fields.

Static electric charges

In dry weather, a woollen sweater being pulled off over the hair of the wearer may crackle; sparks may even be seen. This is caused by an *electric charge*, which is the result of electrons being pulled from one surface to the other. Objects can gain an electric charge by being rubbed against another material.

SEE ALSO

● STARS AND GALAXIES p. 8
● QUANTUM THEORY AND RELATIVITY p. 26
● WAVE THEORY p. 28
● OPTICS p. 32
● ELECTRICITY IN ACTION p. 36
● ATOMS AND SUBATOMIC PARTICLES p. 38
● THE EARTH'S STRUCTURE p. 76
● MEDICAL TECHNOLOGY p. 242
● RADIO, TELEVISION AND VIDEO p. 326
● SEEING THE INVISIBLE p. 332

Magnetic field lines lines

1. The magnetic field around a bar magnet can be plotted using a small compass, or by scattering iron filings on a sheet of paper placed above it.

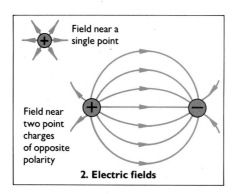

Field near a single point

Field near two point charges of opposite polarity

2. Electric fields

Experiment has shown that there are two types of charge. These are now associated with the negative and positive charges on electrons and protons respectively (see pp. 38–9). Similar electric charges (i.e. two positives, or two negatives) repel each other and unlike charges (i.e. a positive and a negative) attract. (Note that the terms 'positive' and 'negative' are merely conventions for opposite properties.) No smaller charge than that of the electron has been detected (but see quarks, p. 39).

The force of repulsion or attraction is known as the *electric force*. It is described by *Coulomb's law*, an inverse-square law similar to the law for the gravitational force (see p. 21). Coulomb's law states that the attractive or repulsive force (F) between two point (or spherically symmetrical) charges is given by:

$$F = k\frac{Q_1 Q_2}{r^2}$$

where k is a constant, Q_1 and Q_2 are the magnitudes of the charges, and r is the distance between them. The force acts along the direction of r. The unit of charge is called a *coulomb* (C) and is the quantity of electric charge carried past a given point in 1 second by a current of 1 ampere (see below).

Electric field

Arrows can be plotted to show the magnitude and direction of the magnetic force that acts at points around a magnet (see diagram 1), or the electric force that acts on a unit charge at each point. In the latter case, such a map (see diagram 2) would show the distribution of the electric field intensity. It is measured in terms of a force per unit charge, or newtons per coulomb.

In the same way that a mass may have gravitational potential energy because of its position (see p. 24), so a charge can have *electrical potential energy*. This potential per unit charge is measured in *volts* (V), named after the Italian physicist Alessandro Volta (1745–1827). The volt may be defined as follows: if one joule (see p. 24) is required to move 1 coulomb of electric charge between two points, then the *potential difference* between the points is 1 joule per coulomb = 1 volt.

The electrical potential may vary with distance. This change may be measured in volts per metre (V m^{-1}). The Earth's surface is negatively charged with an average electric field over the whole of its surface of about 120 V m^{-1}. In the presence of thunderclouds or where the air is highly polluted the field may be much greater. This field is maintained partially by thunderstorms, which transfer negative charge to the Earth (see diagram 3). Dry air can only allow an electric field of 3 × 10^6 V m^{-1} to build up before there is a sudden breakdown – a lightning flash. If water droplets are present, then the value is lower, perhaps 1 × 10^6 V m^{-1}. (To find out how thunderstorms build up, see pp. 102–3.)

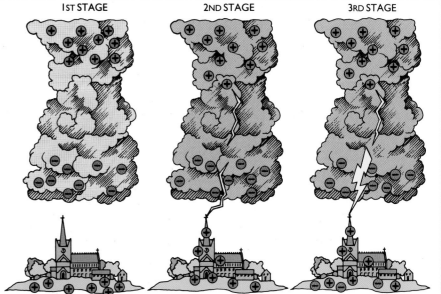

1ST STAGE   2ND STAGE   3RD STAGE

3. How lightning is caused. In the *1st stage*, a net charge collects on top of the cloud, equal in polarity to the charge collecting on the surface of the Earth. A net charge of opposite polarity collects at the base of the cloud. In the *2nd stage*, if the cloud has become very large, discharges start to take place. A 'leader' (invisible to the naked eye) opens an ionized channel through the air – which will allow electricity to follow. In the *3rd stage*, the lightning strikes, following along the path made by the leader.

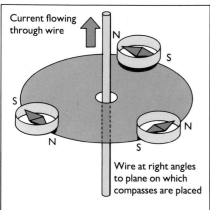

4. Oersted's discovery. When a current flows through a wire, magnetic compasses on a plane at right angles to the wire will be deflected until they are tangential to a circle drawn round the wire.

Current flowing through wire

Wire at right angles to plane on which compasses are placed

Electric current, conductors and insulators

Electric current consists of a flow of electrons (see pp. 38–9), usually through a material but also through a vacuum, as in a cathode-ray tube in a TV set (see pp. 326–7). Current flows when there is a *potential difference* or *voltage* (see above) between two ends of a conductor (see below). Conventional current flows from the positive terminal to the negative terminal. However, electron flow is in fact from negative to positive.

For measurement purposes, an electric current is defined as the rate of flow of charge. The unit of electric current is the *ampere* (A), often abbreviated to amp:

1 ampere = 1 coulomb per second.

The ampere is named after the French physicist André Marie Ampère (1775–1836), who pioneered work on electricity and magnetism.

A material that will allow an electric current to flow through it is a *conductor*. The best conductors are metals. A material that will not allow an electric current to flow is an *insulator*. Effective insulators include rubber, plastic and porcelain. (More information on conductors, semiconductors and insulators will be found on p. 37.)

Electromagnetic fields

In 1820 the Danish physicist Hans Christiaan Oersted (1777–1851) discovered that a copper wire bearing an electric current caused a pivoted magnetic needle to be deflected until it was tangential to a circle drawn around the wire (see diagram 4). This was the first connection to be established between the electrical and magnetic forces. Oersted's work was developed by the Frenchmen Jean-Baptiste Biot (1774–1862) and Félix Savart (1791–1841), who showed that the field strength of a current flowing in a straight wire varied with the distance from the wire. Biot and Savart were able to find a law relating the current in a small part of the conductor to the magnetic field. Ampère, at about the same time, found a more fundamental relationship between the current in a wire and the magnetic field about it.

We now believe that the Earth's magnetic field (see p. 77) is generated by the motion of charged particles in the liquid iron part of the core. This is known as the *dynamo theory*.

From Newton's third law (see p. 21) and Oersted's observation it might be expected that a magnetic field can exert a force on a moving charge. This is observed if a magnet is brought up close to a cathode-ray tube in a TV set. The beam of electrons moving from the cathode to the screen is deflected. The force acts in a direction perpendicular to both the magnetic field and the direction of electron flow. If the magnetic field is perpendicular to the direction of the electrons, then the force has its maximum value. This is the second way in which the electric and magnetic properties are linked.

Electromagnetic induction

The next advance came in 1831, when the English physicist Michael Faraday (1791–1867) found that an electric current could be induced in a wire by another, changing current in a second wire. Faraday published his findings before the US physicist Joseph Henry (1797–1878), who had first made the same discovery. Faraday showed that the magnetic field at the wire had to be changing for an electric current to be produced. This may be done by changing the current in a second wire, by moving a magnet relative to the wire, or by moving the wire relative to a magnet. This last technique is that employed in a dynamo generator, which maintains an electric current when it is driven mechanically (see pp. 36–7). An electric motor (see pp. 36–7) uses the reverse process, being driven by elecricity to provide a mechanical result.

Maxwell's theory

The work of the Scottish physicist James Clerk Maxwell (1831–79) on electromagnetism is of immense importance for physics. It united the separate concepts of electricity and magnetism in terms of a new *electromagnetic force*. Maxwell extended the ideas of Ampère, then in 1864 he proposed that a magnetic field could also be caused by a changing electric field. Thus, when either an electric or magnetic field is changing, a field of the other type is induced. Maxwell predicted that electrical oscillations would generate electromagnetic waves, and he derived a formula giving the speed in terms of electric and magnetic quantities. When these quantities were measured he calculated the speed and found that it was equal to the speed of light in a vacuum (see p. 32). This suggested that light might be electromagnetic in nature – a theory that was later confirmed in various ways. Thus, when an electric current in a wire changes, electromagnetic waves are generated, which will be propagated with a velocity equal to that of light.

The electric and magnetic field components in electromagnetic waves are perpendicular to each other and to the direction of propagation. The existence of electromagnetic waves was demonstrated experimentally in 1887 by the German physicist Heinrich Rudolf Hertz (1857–94) – who also gave his name to the unit of frequency (see p. 280). In his laboratory, Hertz transmitted and detected electromagnetic waves, and he was able to verify that their velocity was close to the speed of light. AS

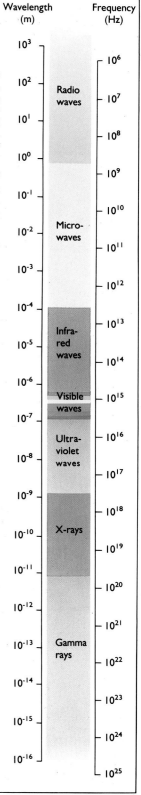

THE ELECTROMAGNETIC SPECTRUM

Prior to Maxwell's discoveries it had been known that light was a wave motion, although the type of wave motion had not been identified. Maxwell was able to show that the oscillations were of the electric and magnetic field. Hertz's waves had a wavelength of about 60 cm; thus they were of much longer wavelength than light waves.

Nowadays we recognize a spectrum of electromagnetic radiation that extends from about 10^{-15} to 10^9 m. It is subdivided into smaller, sometimes overlapping, ranges. The extension of astronomical observations from visible to other electromagnetic wavelengths has revolutionized our knowledge of the universe (see pp. 17 and 332–3).

Radio waves have a large range of wavelengths – from a few millimetres up to several kilometres (see p. 326).

Microwaves are radio waves with shorter wavelengths, between 1 mm and 30 cm. They are used in radar and microwave ovens.

Infrared waves of different wavelengths are radiated by bodies at different temperatures. (Bodies at higher temperatures radiate either visible or ultraviolet waves.) The Earth and its atmosphere, at a mean temperature of 250 K (−23 °C or −9.4 °F) radiates infrared waves with wavelengths centred at about 10 micrometres (μm) or 10^{-5} m (1 μm = 10^{-6} m).

Visible waves have wavelengths of 400–700 nanometres (nm; 1 nm = 10^{-9} m). The peak of the solar radiation (temperature of about 6000 K / 6270 °C / 11 323 °F) is at a wavelength of about 550 nm, where the human eye is at its most sensitive.

Ultraviolet waves have wavelengths from about 380 nm down to 60 nm. The radiation from hotter stars (above 25 000 K / 25 000 °C / 45 000 °F is shifted towards the violet and ultraviolet parts of the spectrum.

X-rays have wavelengths from about 10 nm down to 10^{-4} nm.

Gamma rays have wavelengths less than 10^{-11} m. They are emitted by certain radioactive nuclei and in the course of some nuclear reactions.

Note that the *cosmic rays* continually bombarding the Earth from outer space are not electromagnetic waves, but high-speed protons and x-particles (i.e. nuclei of hydrogen and helium atoms; see pp. 38–9), together with some heavier nuclei.

Wavelength (m)		Frequency (Hz)
10^3		
10^2	Radio waves	10^6
10^1		10^7
10^0		10^8
10^{-1}		10^9
10^{-2}	Micro-waves	10^{10}
10^{-3}		10^{11}
10^{-4}		10^{12}
10^{-5}	Infra-red waves	10^{13}
10^{-6}		10^{14}
10^{-7}	Visible waves	10^{15}
10^{-8}	Ultra-violet waves	10^{16}
10^{-9}		10^{17}
10^{-10}	X-rays	10^{18}
10^{-11}		10^{19}
10^{-12}		10^{20}
10^{-13}	Gamma rays	10^{21}
10^{-14}		10^{22}
10^{-15}		10^{23}
10^{-16}		10^{24}
		10^{25}

Electricity in Action

There have been several key advances in the application of electricity towards developing our civilization. The first two were the dynamo and the electric motor. The dynamo provided a way of producing electricity in large quantities, and the electric motor provided a way of converting electric current into mechanical work.

The evolution of electromagnetic theory (see p. 34) provided the basis for the modern communications industry through radio and television, while the miniaturization of electronic components using semiconductor materials enabled powerful computers to be built for control purposes and to handle large amounts of information.

Batteries and cells

Electric current is the flow of electrons through a conductor (see pp. 34–5). The first source of a steady electric current was demonstrated by the Italian physicist Alessandro Volta (1745–1827) in 1800. His original *voltaic pile* used chemical energy to produce an electric current. The pile consisted of a series of pairs of metal plates (one of silver and one of zinc) piled on top of each other, each pair sandwiching a piece of cloth soaked in a dilute acid solution (see also p.51).

The same principle is still used today (see diagram 1). The plates are called *electrodes* and must be made of dissimilar metals. Alternatively, one may be made of carbon. The positive electrode – the one from which electrons flow inside the cell – is called the *anode*. The negative electrode is the *cathode*. The acid solution is called the *electrolyte* and in a dry cell is absorbed into a paste (see diagram 2).

SEE ALSO

- QUANTUM THEORY AND RELATIVITY p. 26
- ELECTROMAGNETISM p. 34
- ATOMS AND SUBATOMIC PARTICLES p. 38
- METALS p. 50
- MAN-MADE PRODUCTS p. 54
- ENERGY pp. 304–7
- RADIO, TELEVISION AND VIDEO p. 326
- HIFI p. 328
- TELECOMMUNICATIONS p. 330
- COMPUTERS p. 334

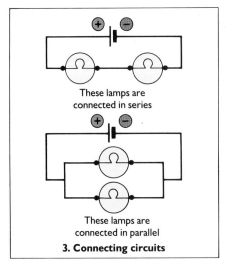

I. A simple cell. The lamp lights but soon goes out because bubbles of hydrogen cling to the copper electrode, thus decreasing the output of the cell. This is known as polarizing. The zinc electrode is eventually eaten away.

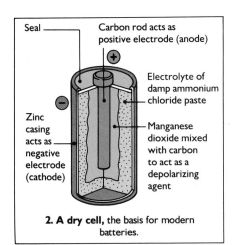

2. A dry cell, the basis for modern batteries.

A single cell can normally produce only a small voltage (see p. 34), but a number of them connected in a series (positive to negative) will give a higher voltage. A series of cells connected in this way is called a *battery*. Some batteries, known as *accumulators*, are designed so that they can be 'recharged' by the passage of an electric current back through them. Similar principles as those used in cells are used in electrolysis and electroplating (see pp. 46–7).

Circuitry

A circuit is a complete conductive path between positive and negative terminals; conventionally current flows from positive to negative, although the direction of electron flow (see pp. 34–5) is actually from negative to positive. When electrical components such as bulbs and switches are joined end to end the arrangement is a *series* connection. When they are connected side by side, this is called *parallel* connection (see diagram 3).

These lamps are connected in series

These lamps are connected in parallel

3. Connecting circuits

Resistance

When an electric current passes through a conductor there is a force that acts to reduce or *resist* the flow. This is called the *resistance* and is dependent upon the nature of the conductor and its dimen-

sions. The unit of resistance is the *ohm* (Ω), named after the German physicist Georg Simon Ohm (1787–1854). He discovered a relationship between the current (I), voltage (V) and resistance (R) in a conductor:

$$V = IR.$$

This is known as Ohm's law.

Power

Power is the rate at which a body or system does work (work and its unit, the joule, are defined on p. 24). The power in an electric conductor is measured in *watts* (W), named after the British engineer James Watt (1736–1819). One watt is one joule per second, or the energy used per second by a current of one amp flowing between two points with a potential difference of one volt (volts and amps are defined on p. 34). In an electric conductor the power (W) is the product of the current (I) and the voltage (V).

Lighting, heating and fuses

A light bulb consists of a glass envelope containing an inert ('noble') gas (see p. 42), usually argon, at low pressure. The bulb has two electrodes connected internally by a *filament* – a fine coiled tungsten wire of high resistance. The passage of a suitable electric current through the filament will raise its temperature sufficiently to make it glow white hot (2500 °C / 4500 °F). The inert gas prevents the filament from evaporating. The efficiency of filament lamps is low. *Gas discharge lamps* are much more efficient. They consist of a glass tube with electrodes sealed into each end. The tube is filled with a gas such as neon, sodium or mercury vapour, which can be *excited* (see discontinuity, pp. 26–7) to emit light by the application of a high voltage to the electrodes.

When electrons pass through a wire they cause the atoms in it to vibrate and generate heat – the greater the resistance, the greater the heat generated. This effect is used in electric heating devices. An electric radiant heater glows red hot. The temperature reached by using a special tough resistance wire is 900 °C (1650 °F). The connecting wires are of low resistance and stay cool.

If a small resistance consisting of wire with a low melting point is connected in a circuit the amount of current that can flow will be limited by that resistance. If too much current flows the resistance will overheat and melt, breaking the circuit. This resistance is called a *fuse* and can be used as a device to protect circuits from current overload.

Alternating current and direct current

There are two types of current electricity. The type produced by a battery is *direct current* (DC), in which there is a constant flow of electrons in one direction. The type used in most electrical appliances is *alternating current* (AC), in which the direction of flow of electrons alternates. The frequency of alternating current can vary over an enormous range. The electric mains operate at 50 Hz (cycles per second) in the UK and Europe, and at 60 Hz in the USA. Most of today's electricity is produced by AC generators. These were developed following Faraday's discovery of the induction of a current in a circuit as a result of a changing magnetic field (see p. 35).

Generators and motors

A *dynamo* (see diagram 4) is an electrical current generator, consisting of a coil that is rotated in a magnetic field by some external means. The source of the rotation may be a turbine in which blades are moved by the passage through them of water, as in a hydroelectric plant, or steam, produced from a boiler heated by nuclear fission or by burning fossil fuels (see pp. 304–7). Wind turbines spin as a result of the passage of air through the large rotors. Different types of generator produce either AC or DC current, while *alternators* (used to charge car batteries) produce AC current that is then rectified to DC current using semiconductor diodes (see below).

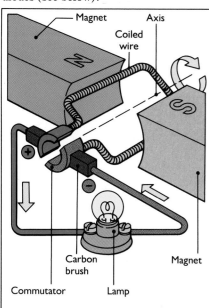

4. A simple generator. As the coiled wire rotates within the magnetic field, an electrical current is induced within the circuit, illuminating the lamp. This simple device shows the basic principle by which all electricity is generated.

An *electric motor* is a similar device to a generator, but works in reverse. An electric current is applied to the coil windings, causing rotation of the *armature*, which consists of a shaft on which are mounted electromagnet windings.

Electron emission

If the filament of a light bulb is heated, the energy of some of the electrons in the filament is greatly increased by thermal motion, although the average increase for all the electrons is very small. If their energy reaches an adequate level, many are able to escape; this process is called *thermionic emission*. If another electrode is put in the evacuated bulb and placed at a higher potential than the filament, this

will act as an anode and will attract electrons towards it. A current will then flow in an external circuit; the device thus formed is called a *diode* (see diagram 5). If a third electrode in the shape of a grid is placed in the tube between the filament and the anode, then the anode current is so sensitive to changes in the grid voltage that the whole device, called a *triode*, can act as an amplifier (see diagram 6).

The *photoelectric effect* occurs when light of a sufficiently high frequency shines onto a metal, causing electrons to be emitted from its surface (see photons and discontinuity, pp. 26–7).

Conductors and semiconductors

A metal consists of an array of positive ions in a 'sea' of free electrons. The electrons move randomly with mean speeds of around 10^6 m s^{-1}. When a potential difference is applied across a metal a small drift velocity is added. The metal atoms are thought to give up one or more electrons, which can then migrate freely through the material. These electrons move in a zigzag manner along a conductor. As a result their typical velocity, called the *drift velocity*, is small, in the order of 10^{-4} m s^{-1}. Thus it would take more than an hour to move one metre. Note that the electric signals that drive the electrons travel with a speed in the order of 10^8 m s^{-1} in some circuits.

This classical picture of electron conduction explains some but not all conduction phenomena. For these a quantum mechanical model is required (see p. 26). This model explains the basis of semiconductors, which now play such an important part in electronics.

Metals are good conductors of electricity because there are always many unoccupied quantum states into which electrons can move. Non-metallic solids and liquids have nearly all their quantum states occupied by electrons, so it is difficult to produce large currents. If the numbers of unoccupied states and of electrons free to move into them are small the material is an *insulator*. If there are more free electrons and unoccupied states the substance is called a *semiconductor*.

Semiconductors have a charge-carrier density that lies between those of conductors and insulators. Two metal-like elements, silicon and germanium, are the two semiconductors used most frequently. These may be 'doped' with an impurity to modify their conduction behaviour – *n*-type doping increases the number of free electrons, *p*-type increases the number of unoccupied states. If the doping results in the charge carriers being negative electrons, then the result is an *n*-type semiconductor. If electron deficiencies or holes are the charge carriers, then the result is a *p*-type semiconductor.

Most semiconductor devices are made from materials that are partly p-type and partly n-type. The boundary between them is known as a *p-n junction*. Such a device, called a *semiconductor diode*, will act as a *rectifier*, a device used to convert alternating current to direct current.

In some materials, such as gallium arsenide, a p-n junction will emit light whenever an electric current passes through it. This device is called a *light-emitting diode*. These are used in digital displays in clocks and radios. The light is emitted when an electron and hole meet at the junction and annihilate each other – they cancel each other out.

Solar cells

The *photovoltaic effect* occurs when light is absorbed by a p-n or n-p junction. Electrons are liberated at the junction by an incident photon and diffuse through the n-type region. The hole drifts through the p-type layer until it recombines with an electron flowing round the external circuit. The first practical photovoltaic device – called a solar cell – was made in 1954. In essence a solar cell is a light-emitting diode acting in reverse – it converts light into electric current, which is the basis of solar power (see p. 306).

Transistors

A transistor consists of semiconductor material in n-p-n or p-n-p form. The middle part is the *base* and the ends are called the *emitter* and *collector*. An *integrated circuit* consists of many transistors, rectifiers or other components embedded in a chip of silicon.

Superconductivity

Superconductivity was discovered by the Dutch physicist Kamerlingh Onnes (1853–1926) in 1911. Below a certain critical temperature, various metals show zero resistance to current flow. Once a current is started in a closed circuit, it keeps flowing as long as the circuit is kept cold. The critical temperature for aluminium is 1.19 K (−272 °C / −457 °F), and similar values hold for other metals. Some alloys have higher critical temperatures. Up to 1986 the highest transition temperature known was about −248 °C (−414 °F). More recently a new class of copper oxide and other materials have shown superconductivity up to at least −148 °C (−234 °F). These developments promise enormous savings in energy (see also p. 55). AS

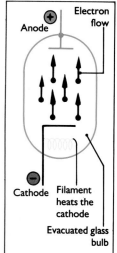

5. A diode. Electrons emitted by the heated cathode flow through the vacuum to the anode. A diode allows passage of electricity in one direction only.

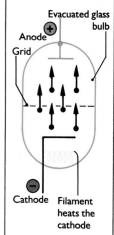

6. A triode. The potential on the grid controls the flow of electrons between cathode and anode. It can act as a switch or an amplifier.

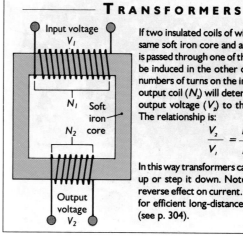

TRANSFORMERS

If two insulated coils of wire are wound on the same soft iron core and an alternating current is passed through one of the coils, a current will be induced in the other coil. The ratio of the numbers of turns on the input coil (N_1) and the output coil (N_2) will determine the ratio of the output voltage (V_2) to the input voltage (V_1). The relationship is:

$$\frac{V_2}{V_1} = \frac{N_2}{N_1}$$

In this way transformers can either step voltage up or step it down. Note that they have the reverse effect on current. This principle is used for efficient long-distance power transmission (see p. 304).

Atoms and Subatomic Particles

Of the fundamental forces that are important in the natural world, the gravitational force (see p. 21) is the dominant long-range force when the motion of planets and other celestial bodies is considered. When the smallest entities are investigated, the other fundamental forces – the electromagnetic force (see p. 34), the *strong force* (which holds together the atomic nucleus) and the *weak force* (which is involved in nuclear decay) – become important.

The word *atom* is derived from an ancient Greek word for a particle of matter so small it cannot be split up. In his atomic theory of 1803, the British chemist John Dalton (1766–1844) defined the atom as the smallest particle of an element (see p. 42) that retained its chemical properties. Various phenomena could be explained using this hypothesis – which still holds good today.

Atomic structure

However, no physical description of the atom was available until after the discovery of the *electron* in 1897 by the British physicist J.J. Thompson (1856–1940). The nuclear atom was proposed by the English physicist Ernest Rutherford (1871–1937) in 1911 (see diagram 1). His model consists of a small but dense central *nucleus*, which is positively charged, orbited by negatively charged electrons. The nucleus contains over

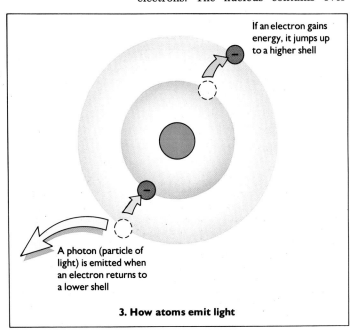

If an electron gains energy, it jumps up to a higher shell

A photon (particle of light) is emitted when an electron returns to a lower shell

3. How atoms emit light

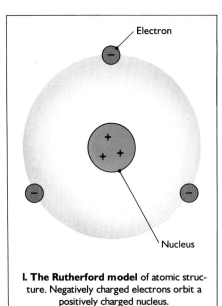

I. The Rutherford model of atomic structure. Negatively charged electrons orbit a positively charged nucleus.

99.9% of the mass of the atom, but its diameter is of the order of 10^{-15} m – compared to the much larger size (about 10^{-10} m) of the atom.

The electron was first recognized by its behaviour as a particle. In 1923 a *wave-particle duality* for atomic particles – analogous to the concept of the wave-particle duality of light (see pp. 26–7) proposed by the French physicist Louis Victor de Broglie (1892–1987) – was put forward. The wavelength of a particle would be equal to the Planck constant (see p. 26) divided by its momentum. As the wavelength is dependent on momentum it can take any value. For an electron the wavelength can be of the order of the atomic diameter. This led to the development of the *electron microscope* (see p. 333). At suitable energy levels the wavelength of electrons and neutrons can be equivalent to the atomic spacing in solids. Thus a crystal can be used as a *diffraction grating* (as for X-rays). This has led to a better understanding of the way in which the electrons orbit the atomic nucleus.

The Danish physicist Niels Bohr (1885–1962) had suggested that electrons were allowed to move in circular orbits or *shells* around the nucleus, but that only certain orbits were *allowable* (see diagram 2). This theory was able to explain many of the features of the spectrum of light emitted by excited hydrogen atoms. The wavelengths of the spectral lines are related to the energy levels of the allowed orbits. The wave theory of the electron provided a reason for the allowed orbits. These would be those whose circumference was a multiple of the electron's wavelength. When Rutherford showed experimentally that an atom must consist of a small nucleus surrounded by electrons, there was a fundamental problem. To avoid collapsing into the nucleus, the electrons would have to move in orbits – as Bohr had proposed. This means that they must have continuous acceleration towards the nucleus. But, according to the electromagnetic theory, an accelerated charge

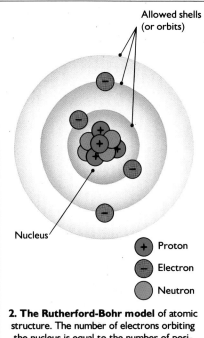

2. The Rutherford-Bohr model of atomic structure. The number of electrons orbiting the nucleus is equal to the number of positively charged protons within the nucleus. The number of electrons within each shell is also limited – no more than 2 in the first shell, 8 in the second, 18 in the third, etc.

must radiate energy, so no permanent orbit could exist. Bohr therefore argued that energy could not be lost continuously but only in quanta (discrete amounts) equivalent to the difference in energies between allowed orbits (see p. 26). Thus light would be emitted when an electron jumps from one allowed level to another of lower energy (see diagram 3).

Nuclear structure

With the exception of the hydrogen atom, which only contains one proton, atomic nuclei contain a mixture of protons and neutrons, collectively known as *nucleons*. The *proton* carries a positive charge, equal in magnitude to that of the negatively charged electron. The *neutron* is of similar size but is electrically neutral. Each has a mass about 1836 times that of the electron (which has a rest mass of 9.11×10^{-31} kg). The protons and neutrons in the atomic nucleus are held tightly together by the *strong nuclear force*, which overcomes the much weaker electromagnetic force of repulsion between positively charged protons.

The mass of a nucleus is always less than the sum of the masses of its constituent nucleons. This is explained using the relationship derived by Einstein (see p. 27). If the nucleus is to be separated into protons and neutrons then the strong nuclear force needs to be overcome and energy has to be supplied to the nucleus – from an external source – to break it up. This energy is called the *binding energy* and is related to the *mass defect* (the difference between the masses of the nucleus and its component parts). Those nuclei with large binding energies per nucleon are most stable; these have about 50–75 nucleons in the nucleus.

Fission and fusion

Nuclear power comes from either of two processes – *fission* and *fusion*, which are both forms of *nuclear reaction*. In the

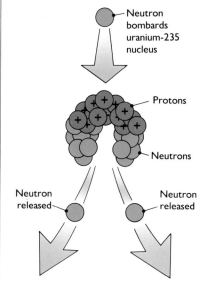

Neutron bombards uranium-235 nucleus

Protons

Neutrons

Neutron released

Neutron released

4. Nuclear fission. A neutron bombards the uranium–235 nucleus, causing it to split and release energy when the strong nuclear force is broken. Two lighter nuclei are formed and these are also radioactive. The neutrons released may bombard and split other nuclei – further fission can take place. A *chain reaction* will be set up if the mass of uranium–235 is above a certain level – the *critical mass*.

fission process (see diagram 4) a large nucleus, such as uranium-235 (^{235}U), splits to form two smaller nuclei that have greater binding energies than the original uranium. Thus energy is given out in the process. Fission is used in nuclear reactors (see p. 304) and in atomic weapons (see p. 288). There are other isotopes (see box) in addition to uranium-235, such as plutonium-239, that give rise to fission. In the fusion process (see diagram 5), two light nuclei fuse together to form two particles, one larger and one smaller than the original nuclei. Usually one of them is sufficiently strongly bound to give a great

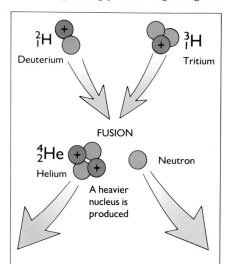

$^2_1$H
Deuterium

$^3_1$H
Tritium

FUSION

$^4_2$He
Helium

Neutron

A heavier nucleus is produced

5. Nuclear fusion occurs when two small nuclei collide and combine, breaking the weak nuclear force and releasing energy. The reaction shown involves nuclei of deuterium and tritium (isotopes of hydrogen) combining to produce helium (a waste product), a neutron, and released energy. This type of reaction releases considerably more energy than a fission process for a given mass of material. However, the neutrons released have to be contained or controlled in some way.

release of energy. The fusion of hydrogen to form helium is a power source in stars such as the Sun (see p. 10), although the solar fusion process differs in detail from the simpler process described. Nuclear fusion is the basis of the hydrogen bomb (see p. 288), and research is continuing into the possible use of fusion in power generation (see p. 305).

Radioactivity

Radiation – either as a spontaneous emission of particles or as an electromagnetic wave – may occur from certain substances. This is *radioactivity*. The three types of radiation are from alpha decay, beta decay and gamma decay.

Alpha (α) decay produces nuclei of helium that each contain two neutrons and two protons. They are called *alpha-particles* and are formed in spontaneous decay of the parent nucleus. Thus uranium-238 decays to thorium-234 with emission of an alpha-particle.

In *beta (β) decay* the emitted particles are either electrons or *positrons* (identical to the electron but with a positive charge). The parent nucleus retains the same number of nucleons but its charge varies by plus or minus 1. In these processes another kind of particle – either a *neutrino* or an *antineutrino* – is produced. The neutrino has no charge (the word means 'little neutral one') and a mass that – if it could be measured at rest – would probably be zero. The *relativistic mass* can, however, be significant, as the speed – with respect to any observer – is that of electromagnetic radiation.

In *gamma (γ) decay* high-energy photons may be produced in a process of radioactive decay if the resultant nucleus jumps from an excited energy state to a lower energy state (see pp. 26–27). The rate at which radioactive decay takes place depends only on the number of radioactive nuclei that are present. Thus the *half-life*, or the time taken for half a given number of radioactive nuclei to decay, is characteristic for that type of nucleus. The isotope carbon-14 has a half-life of 5730 years, and measurement of its decay is used in carbon-dating of organic material (see p. 361). Decay can result in a series of new elements being produced, each of which may in its turn decay until a stable state is achieved.

Nuclear particles

Over 200 elementary particles are now known. They may be divided into two types: hadrons and leptons. *Hadrons* (from the Greek for 'bulky') are heavy particles that are affected by the strong force. *Leptons* (from the Greek for 'small') are generally light particles, such as electrons and neutrinos (see above), that are not subject to the strong force. A further very important distinction is that between *fermions* (Fermi–Dirac particles) and *bosons* (Bose–Einstein particles). Fermions have a permanent existence, whereas bosons can be produced and destroyed freely, provided the laws of conservation of charge and of mechanics are obeyed. Leptons are fermions. Every type of particle is thought to have a companion *antiparticle*, that is, a particle with the same mass but opposite in some other characteristic such as charge. Thus the positron with positive charge is the

antiparticle of the negatively charged electron. Some particles such as the photon may be their own antiparticles. Whilst the leptons are thought to be fundamental particles, the hadrons are thought to be made up of *quarks* (a word borrowed from James Joyce's novel *Finnegans Wake*; see p. 641). Quarks may have fractional electrical charge. It is probable that free quarks do not exist. If three quarks combine, the resulting hadron is called a *baryon*; if a quark and an antiquark combine the result is called a *meson*. A meson is a boson; it is a short-lived particle that jumps between protons and neutrons, thus holding them together. In the same way that Mendeleyev's table of chemical elements (see p. 42) predicted new elements such as gallium and germanium that were subsequently discovered, so a pattern of hadrons may be drawn up based on combinations of different types of quark. This pattern is called the *eight-fold way* – a term borrowed from Buddhism (see p. 469). It predicted the existence of the omega-particle (Ω-particle), the discovery of which in 1963 helped to validate the theory. There are believed to be six types or *flavours* of quark – up, down, charmed, strange, top and bottom. Evidence for the existence of all except the top quark is now available.

Quarks carry electrical charge and another type of charge called *colour*. The force associated with the colour charge binds the quarks together and is thought to be the source of the strong force binding the hadrons together. Thus the colour force is the more fundamental force. The weak force is associated with the radioactive beta-decay of some nuclei. It has been shown – in the theory of the *electroweak* force – that the electromagnetic and weak forces are linked. This theory predicted the existence of the W and Z° particles, which were discovered at the CERN nuclear accelerator at Geneva during 1982–83.

Nuclear accelerators

Accelerators are large machines that accelerate particle beams to very high speeds, so enabling research into particle physics. Electric fields are used to accelerate the particles, either in a straight line (*linear accelerator*) or in a circle (*cyclotron, synchrotron* or *synchrocyclotron*). Powerful magnetic fields are used to guide the beams. Energy levels of the particles may be as high as several hundred giga electronvolts. An electron-volt (eV) is the increase in energy of an electron when it undergoes a rise in potential of 1 volt: $1\ \text{eV} = 1.6 \times 10^{-19}$ joules (J). Nuclear accelerators have provided experimental evidence for the existence of numerous subatomic particles predicted in theory.   AS

SEE ALSO

● QUANTUM THEORY AND RELATIVITY p. 26
● ELECTROMAGNETISM p. 34
● ELEMENTS AND THE PERIODIC TABLE p. 42
● CHEMICAL BONDS p. 44
● NUCLEAR ARMAMENT AND DISARMAMENT p. 288
● ENERGY I p. 304

ISOTOPES AND NUCLEAR NOTATION

It is possible for atoms of the same element to contain equal numbers of protons but different numbers of neutrons in their nuclei – these different atoms are called *isotopes*. Isotopes of an element contain the same nuclear charge, and their chemical properties are identical, but they display different physical properties. An isotope may be represented in various ways, such as uranium-235, U-235 or ^{235}U. A special notation is used to show the numbers of protons and neutrons in a nucleus. $^{226}_{88}$Ra defines a radium nucleus with 88 protons and 138 neutrons, making a total of 226 nucleons. Similarly, $^{14}_{6}$C is a carbon nucleus with 6 protons and 8 neutrons, making a total of 14 nucleons.

What is Chemistry?

Alchemy, from which modern chemistry derives its name, probably had its origins in the region of Khimi, 'the land of black earth', in the Nile Delta. It was here, more than 4000 years ago, that it was first discovered that the action of heat on minerals could result in the isolation of metals and glasses with useful properties – and which could therefore be sold at a profit. The practice of alchemy spread throughout the Arab world and into Asia, gaining from the Chinese the secret of making gunpowder in the process.

One of the aims of alchemy was the transmutation of metals: alchemists strove for a 'philosopher's stone' that could be used to convert easily corrupted 'base' metals such as iron, copper and lead into the 'noble' metal gold, which retained its lustre and its commercial value. They thought that the philosopher's stone would also be the 'elixir' of immortality – that it would confer eternal health on those who possessed it. Much experimentation followed, which – although not leading to the desired ends – led to the development of techniques that formed the basis of modern chemistry.

Alchemy became associated with mystical practices and ideas, but from the 12th century the availability of Arab writings on alchemy gradually led to the study of chemical processes using more rational techniques and ideas – although many of the original aims were retained. Indeed, even Sir Isaac Newton (see p. 20) experimented with the transmutation of base metals into gold – relevant research, given that he was Master of the Royal Mint!

The aims of modern chemistry

In modern chemistry, the philosopher's stone has been replaced by a fundamental belief in the importance of understanding the physical laws that govern the behaviour of atoms and molecules. Such an understanding has resulted in the development of methods for converting cheaply available and naturally occurring minerals, gases and oils into substances that have high commercial or social value.

During the last 150 years this approach has completely transformed our world. The discovery that iron could be made into steel (see p. 314) by chemical means played a major part in the Industrial Revolution. In the 20th century, spectacular increases in the yields of cereals from an acre of farmland can be traced to the discovery in Germany in 1908 that nitrogen from air could be converted into ammonia fertilizers (see p. 320). Similarly, the greater understanding of the structures and reactions of carbon-based (organic) compounds has resulted in products such as medicines and synthetic fibres that affect all our lives (see p. 56).

The evolution of chemistry from small laboratories making new substances in tiny quantities to modern industrial processes producing millions of tonnes of chemicals brings its own problems. The rotten-egg smell of hydrogen sulphide in a school chemistry laboratory may be relatively harmless, but a leakage of a noxious gas, on a proportionate scale, from a chemical plant can represent a major health hazard. There is therefore a twofold responsibility in modern industrial chemistry – not only to produce the chemical products that an affluent society needs in ever-increasing quantities, but to do so in a way that does not lead to major local or global environmental effects.

Elements and molecules

The structure of atoms (see p. 38) serves as a convenient starting point for discussing chemical phenomena. In chemical processes, the nuclei of atoms remain unchanged – shattering at once the alchemist's dream of transmuting elements. The great variety of known chemical compounds results from the different ways in which the electrons of atoms are able to interact either with atoms of the same kind or with atoms of a different kind. In an *element*, all the atoms are of the same kind, but the varying strengths of the interactions between the electrons in different types of atom means that elements have very different properties. For example, helium melts at −272 °C (−458 °F), whereas carbon in the form of diamond has a melting point of 3500 °C (6332 °F). This ability of electrons to interact between atoms is known as *chemical bonding* (for more details, see p. 44).

The elements nitrogen, oxygen, fluorine and chlorine form strong bonds, with two identical atoms linked together. They therefore exist at room temperature as gases, with pairs of linked atoms moving chaotically in space. Two or more atoms linked in this fashion are described as *molecules*, and a shorthand notation is used to describe their chemical identity. The atomic symbol for the element (see p. 43) is used in conjunction with the number of atoms present to define the *chemical formula* of the molecule. The elements described above are therefore designated, respectively, by the formulae N_2, O_2, F_2 and Cl_2.

Other familiar elements, such as sulphur and phosphorus, form additional bonds to like atoms, and their formulae reflect this fact. Thus sulphur forms a ring of eight atoms and is described by the formula S_8 (see p. 45). As the number of atoms in the fundamental unit increases, the element is no longer a gas but becomes a solid with a low melting point; thus sulphur can be extracted from the Earth as a molten fluid (see p. 313).

Most elements do not form discrete molecular entities such as those described

KEY

- Carbon (C)
- Hydrogen (H)
- Oxygen (O)
- Nitrogen (N)
- Bromine (Br)
- Sulphur (S)

Ethanol

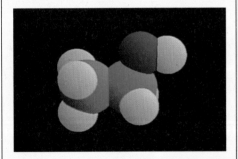

CH_3CH_2OH

The discovery of alcoholic fermentation is lost in the mists of time. Noah's first task after the Flood was to plant a vineyard (Genesis 9.20). The alcohol present in beers, wines and spirits is ethanol (shown above). The art of distilling alcohol from fermented juices represents an important early example of a chemical separation technique.

In 1763 a clergyman in Chipping Norton, England, described the effect of willow bark for the cure of 'agues' (fevers). In Naples in 1838 the first chemical synthesis of salicylic acid was achieved – the precursor of aspirin (acetylsalicylic acid; shown right). Large-scale production of aspirin has continued since 1900; it is still the most widely used analgesic (pain-killer).

Aspirin

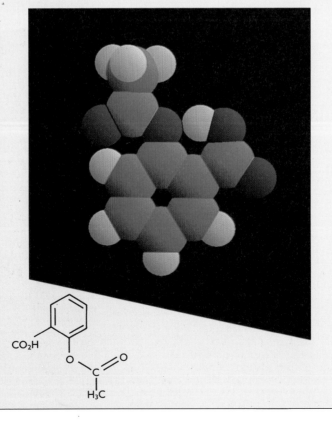

Laughing gas

N – N – O

Nitrous oxide – or laughing gas – is a sweet-smelling, colourless, non-flammable gas, which has been used as an anaesthetic (see pp. 49 and 57). Its popular name is derived from the euphoric initial effects on inhalation; in the early 1800s, the English chemist Sir Humphrey Davy (1778–1829) used to invite his poet friends – Coleridge, Southey and Wordsworth – to experience its effects.

Lacrimatory gases

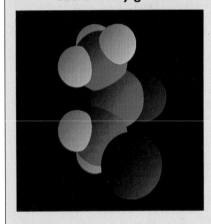

$$H_3C$$
$$C = O$$
$$BrH_2C$$

Molecules such as bromoacetone (above) react with water on the surface of the eye to produce acids that irritate the eye and cause tears to flow. Tear gas is a variant of this molecule.

above, but have structures that are held together by chemical bonds in all directions. Most of the 109 known elements are metals, such as iron and copper, and have *infinite structures* of this kind. Such elements can no longer be given distinct molecular formulae and are therefore represented by the element symbol alone; thus iron, for example, is represented simply as Fe. For a more detailed discussion of the properties of metals, see p. 50.

Chemical compounds

In *chemical compounds*, the atoms of more than one element come together to form either molecules or infinite structures. They are described by formulae similar to those given above for elements. For example, water has a finite structure based on one oxygen atom chemically bonded to two hydrogen atoms and is

denoted by the formula H_2O (see p. 48). Common salt (sodium chloride; NaCl) has sodium (Na) and chlorine (Cl) atoms linked together in an infinite three-dimensional lattice (similar to that formed by potassium chloride; see p. 44).

In a pure chemical compound, all the molecules have the same ratio of different atoms and behave in an identical chemical fashion. Thus a pure sample of water, for example, behaves identically to any other pure sample, however different their origins may be. Furthermore, the same ratios of atoms are retained irrespective of whether the compound is a solid, a liquid or a gas. For example, ice, water and water vapour all have molecules with the constitution H_2O. The transformation of ice into water and then into water vapour by heating is not a chemical reaction, because the identities of the molecules do not change (see latent heat, p. 25).

From the 109 chemical elements now known, more than 2 million chemical compounds have been made during the last 100 years. The chemist views chemistry as a set of molecular building blocks, constructing more and more complex and diverse molecular structures, the variety of which is limited only by his or her imagination. It is important to emphasize that the properties of a chemical compound are unique and not a sum of the properties of the individual elements from which it is made. For example, common salt does not have any properties remotely like those of metallic sodium, which catches fire on contact with water, or chlorine, which is a harmful yellow-green gas.

Although all compounds are unique, they can be classified into broad families based on common chemical properties. Acids, bases, salts, and oxidizing and reducing agents are examples of such families (see pp. 46–7). Classifications reflecting the atoms present are also useful for cataloguing purposes: for example, hydrides, chlorides and oxides indicate compounds containing hydrogen, chlorine and oxygen respectively. Another particularly important classification is that of organic compounds (see p. 52), which contain carbon and are not only important for life processes but make up many modern industrial chemicals such as plastics, paints and artificial fibres (see pp. 56, 316 and 320).

Mixtures

When elements or compounds are mixed together but not chemically bonded, they form a *chemical mixture*. A mixture can be of two solids (e.g. salt and sand), two liquids, two gases or permutations of these. A mixture can be separated into its pure chemical constituents by either chemical or physical means. For example, adding water to the sand–salt mixture dissolves the salt, leaving the sand in a pure state. The salt and water is itself

a mixture described as a *solution*, from which the pure salt can be obtained by boiling off the water.

The modern-day chemist has many other techniques for separating mixtures, such as distillation, chromatography, crystallization and electrolysis. The petrochemical industry is a prime example of how this technology can be used to convert natural gas and crude oil into a range of useful commercial and domestic products (see pp. 311 and 320). DMPM

SEE ALSO

● CHEMISTRY pp. 42–57
● OIL AND GAS p. 310
● IRON AND STEEL p. 314
● RUBBER AND PLASTICS p. 316
● CHEMICALS AND BIO-TECHNOLOGY p. 320

Rotten-smelling molecules

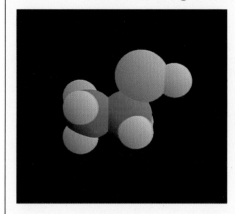

North Sea gas contains methane (see p. 49), which – unlike coal gas – is odourless. Tiny amounts of ethanethiol (left) – an evil-smelling chemical – are therefore added to aid its detection from open taps and gas leaks.

CH_3CH_2SH

Nice-smelling molecules

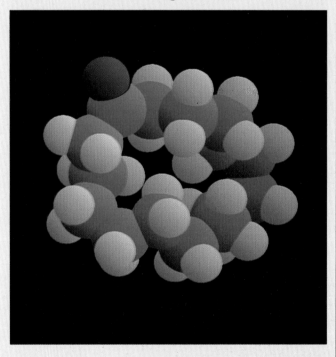

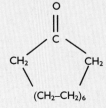

Exaltone (above) was the first synthetic chemical to be used in the manufacture of perfumes. Now a major industry is based on the production and use of chemicals with a wide range of smells. These chemicals obviate the need to extract tiny amounts of chemicals from animals, such as musk from deer and civettone from civets.

Elements and the Periodic Table

The world we see around us is made up of a limited number of chemical elements (see p. 40). In the Earth's crust, there are 82 stable elements and a few unstable (radioactive) ones. Among the stable elements, there are some, such as oxygen and silicon, that are very abundant, while others – the metals ruthenium and rhodium, for example – are extremely rare. Indeed, 98% of the Earth's crust is made up of just eight elements, while the rest account for only 2% (see pie chart).

SEE ALSO

- QUANTUM THEORY AND RELATIVITY p. 26
- ATOMS AND SUBATOMIC PARTICLES p. 38
- CHEMICAL BONDS p. 44
- CHEMICAL REACTIONS p. 46
- METALS p. 50

Each element is associated with a unique number, called its *atomic number*. This figure represents the number of protons (positively charged particles; see p. 38) in the nucleus of each atom of the element. Hydrogen has one proton, so it is the first and lightest of the elements and is placed first in the Periodic Table; helium has two protons, and thus is the second lightest element and is placed second in the Table; and so we continue through each of the elements, establishing their order in the Table according to their atomic numbers.

The atomic number of bismuth is 83, and this number of protons represents the upper limit for a stable nucleus. Beyond 83, all elements are unstable, although their radioactive decay (see p. 39) may be so slow that some of them, such as thorium and uranium, are found in large natural deposits. The largest atomic number so far observed is 109, but only a few atoms of this element have been made artificially, so little is known about it. Its name is unnilennium, meaning 'one-zero-nine'.

Groups and blocks

When an atom is electrically neutral, the number of electrons (negatively charged particles; see p. 38) circling the nucleus is the same as the number of (positive) protons in the nucleus. Thus, for example, an electrically neutral atom of calcium contains 20 protons and 20 electrons. While the atomic number identifies an atom and determines its order in the Periodic Table, it is these electrons surrounding the nucleus that determine how it behaves chemically. Electrons can be thought of as moving around the nucleus in certain fixed orbits or 'shells', the electrons in a particular shell being associated with a particular energy level (see pp. 26 and 38). With regard to an atom's chemical behaviour, it is the elec-

trons in the outer shell that are most important, and it is these that fix the *group position* of the atom in the Table.

The major energy levels are numbered 1, 2, 3, etc., counting outwards from the nucleus. This number is called the *principal quantum number*, and is given the symbol **n**. Each energy level can hold only a certain number of electrons; the further out it is, the more it can accommodate. This capacity is related to the value of **n**: the maximum number of electrons each shell can hold is $2\mathbf{n}^2$. Thus the nearest shell to the nucleus can hold only 2 electrons (2×1^2), the next 8 (2×2^2), then 18, then 32, and so on.

Each principal energy level is divided into smaller sub-levels, called **s**, **p**, **d** and **f**, which hold a maximum of 2, 6, 10 and 14 electrons respectively. The first principal energy level thus contains only the **s** sub-level; the second contains the **s** and **p** sub-levels; and so on. It is these sub-levels that identify the main blocks of the Periodic Table: thus the **s**-block is made up of 2 columns or groups, the **p**-block of 6, the **d**-block of 10, and the **f**-block of 14.

Group position and chemical reactivity

Hydrogen (see also p. 48) has one electron in the first principal energy level, while helium has two – the maximum capacity for this level. The possession of one extra electron may seem a trivial difference, but a world of difference separates hydrogen and helium; hydrogen is very reactive and forms compounds with many other elements; helium combines with nothing. These two elements are rather exceptional in all their chemical behaviour and are given a small section of their own in the Table, above groups 17 and 18 of the **p**-block.

Hydrogen and helium are placed on the far right of the Table so that the latter falls in the same group (group 18) as other elements – the so-called *noble gases* – that have full outer shells. Thus below helium we find neon, another chemically unreactive gas, which has the second principal energy level filled and is said to have an *electron configuration* of 2.8. Just as we find hydrogen, a highly reactive element, immediately to the left of helium, so we find another reactive element – fluorine (configuration 2.7) – to the left of neon. Fluorine (like the other elements in group 17 – the *halogens*) is one electron short of a full outer shell. Fluorine's tendency to combine with other elements in order to achieve a full (and so stable) outer shell (see p. 44) makes it one of the most reactive of all the elements – so reactive that it will even combine with the noble gases krypton and xenon.

The noble gases, with their stable electron arrangement, make a natural break in the arrangement of the Periodic Table. After the **p** sub-shell has been filled, the next electron starts another shell further out from the nucleus. This lone electron makes the elements of group 1 – the *alkali metals* (see p. 50) – highly reactive, because they tend to lose the extra electron

in order to form a full outer shell (see p. 44). They are indeed so reactive that some of them, such as caesium, explode when dropped into water.

The groups of the Periodic Table are numbered 1 to 18, with the **f**-block not included. Members of the same group have the same number of electrons in the outer shell of the atom and consequently behave in a similar manner chemically. This fact is reflected in the composition of their chemical compounds (which can in turn be explained in terms of their oxidation states; see box, p. 51). Thus, for example, the formulae of the chlorides of sodium and potassium in group 1 are NaCl and KCl, while their oxides are Na_2O and K_2O.

As we go from left to right across the Table, we can see particular properties change in a regular fashion. It was this periodic rise and fall in such properties as density and atomic volume that led to the term 'Periodic Table'. In fact, members of the same group often bear only a superficial chemical resemblance to one another. The image and philosophy of the Periodic Table is so powerful, however, that it remains the standard starting point for learning about chemistry.　JEm

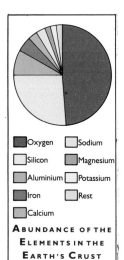

ABUNDANCE OF THE ELEMENTS IN THE EARTH'S CRUST

- Oxygen
- Silicon
- Aluminium
- Iron
- Calcium
- Sodium
- Magnesium
- Potassium
- Rest

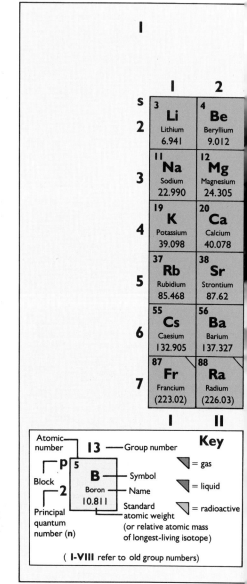

Key

Atomic number — 13 — Group number

P — 5

B

Block — Symbol

Boron — Name

2 — 10.811 — Standard atomic weight (or relative atomic mass of longest-living isotope)

Principal quantum number (n)

▽ = gas
▽ = liquid
▽ = radioactive

(I-VIII refer to old group numbers)

THE HISTORY OF THE PERIODIC TABLE

The discovery of the Periodic Table was made possible by an Italian chemist, Stanislao Cannizzaro (1826–1910), who in 1858 published a list of fixed atomic weights (now known as relative atomic masses) for the 60 elements that were then known. By arranging the elements in order of increasing atomic weight, a curious repetition of chemical properties at regular intervals was revealed. This was noticed in 1864 by the English chemist John Newlands (1838–98), but his 'law of octaves' brought him nothing but ridicule. It was left to the Russian chemist Dmitri Ivanovich Mendeleyev (1834–1907) to make essentially the same discovery five years later. What Mendeleyev did, however, was so much more impressive that he is rightly credited as the true discoverer of the Periodic Table.

While working on his *Principles of Chemistry* in 1869, Mendeleyev wrote the names and some of the main features of the elements on individual cards, to help establish a suitable order in which to discuss their chemistry. It was while arranging this pack of cards in different ways that he stumbled upon the pattern we now recognize as the Periodic Table. Mendeleyev laid out his cards in order of the atomic weights of the

elements, placing together elements that formed similar oxides. By arranging similar elements in columns, he established the arrangement of the Table that has been followed ever since.

Mendeleyev's genius lay in the fact that he recognized that there was an underlying order to the elements – he did not design the Periodic Table, he *discovered* it. If he was right, he knew that there should be places in his table for new elements. He was so confident in his discovery that he predicted the properties of these missing elements – and his predictions were subsequently shown to be accurate. In some cases, Mendeleyev also swapped the order of atomic weights, so that similar elements appeared in the same groups. This apparent anomaly was not explained until 1913, when the theory of isotopes was put forward (see p. 39).

Since 1869, when Mendeleyev published his table, a further 40 elements have been found or produced by nuclear reactions, and the Periodic Table has been redesigned to accommodate them. Mendeleyev lived long enough to learn of the discovery of the electron, but not long enough to know how the arrangement of electrons about the nucleus of the atom explains the structure of the Table.

Dmitri Ivanovich Mendeleyev

THE PERIODIC TABLE OF ELEMENTS

													13	14	15	16	17	18
1s																	1 **H** Hydrogen 1.008	2 **He** Helium 4.003
p **2**													5 **B** Boron 10.811	6 **C** Carbon 12.011	7 **N** Nitrogen 14.007	8 **O** Oxygen 15.999	9 **F** Fluorine 18.998	10 **Ne** Neon 20.180
3			3	4	5	6	7	8	9	10	11	12	13 **Al** Aluminium 26.982	14 **Si** Silicon 28.086	15 **P** Phosphorus 30.974	16 **S** Sulphur 32.066	17 **Cl** Chlorine 35.453	18 **Ar** Argon 39.948
d **3**	21 **Sc** Scandium 44.956	22 **Ti** Titanium 47.88	23 **V** Vanadium 50.942	24 **Cr** Chromium 51.996	25 **Mn** Manganese 54.938	26 **Fe** Iron 55.847	27 **Co** Cobalt 58.933	28 **Ni** Nickel 58.693	29 **Cu** Copper 63.546	30 **Zn** Zinc 65.39		31 **Ga** Gallium 69.723	32 **Ge** Germanium 72.61	33 **As** Arsenic 74.922	34 **Se** Selenium 78.96	35 **Br** Bromine 79.904	36 **Kr** Krypton 83.80
4	39 **Y** Yttrium 88.906	40 **Zr** Zirconium 91.224	41 **Nb** Niobium 92.906	42 **Mo** Molybdenum 95.94	43 **Tc** Technetium (97.907)	44 **Ru** Ruthenium 101.07	45 **Rh** Rhodium 102.906	46 **Pd** Palladium 106.42	47 **Ag** Silver 107.868	48 **Cd** Cadmium 112.411		49 **In** Indium 114.82	50 **Sn** Tin 118.71	51 **Sb** Antimony 121.76	52 **Te** Tellurium 127.60	53 **I** Iodine 126.905	54 **Xe** Xenon 131.29
5	71 **Lu** Lutetium 174.967	72 **Hf** Hafnium 178.49	73 **Ta** Tantalum 180.948	74 **W** Tungsten 183.84	75 **Re** Rhenium 186.207	76 **Os** Osmium 190.23	77 **Ir** Iridium 192.22	78 **Pt** Platinum 195.08	79 **Au** Gold 196.967	80 **Hg** Mercury 200.59		81 **Tl** Thallium 204.383	82 **Pb** Lead 207.2	83 **Bi** Bismuth 208.980	84 **Po** Polonium (208.98)	85 **At** Astatine (209.99)	86 **Rn** Radon (222.02)
6	103 **Lr** Lawrencium (262.11)	104 **Unq** Unnilquadium (261.11)	105 **Unp** Unnilpentium (262.11)	106 **Unh** Unnilhexium (263.12)	107 **Uns** Unnilseptium (262.12)	108 **Uno** Unniloctium (265.13)	109 **Une** Unnilennium (266.14)											

Metals ← → Non-metals

I	II								III	IV	V	VI	VII	VIII

III IV V VI VII VIII

57 **La** Lanthanum 138.906	58 **Ce** Cerium 140.115	59 **Pr** Praseodymium 140.908	60 **Nd** Neodymium 144.24	61 **Pm** Promethium (144.91)	62 **Sm** Samarium 150.36	63 **Eu** Europium 151.965	64 **Gd** Gadolinium 157.25	65 **Tb** Terbium 158.925	66 **Dy** Dysprosium 162.50	67 **Ho** Holmium 164.930	68 **Er** Erbium 167.26	69 **Tm** Thulium 168.934	70 **Yb** Ytterbium 173.04
89 **Ac** Actinium 227.028	90 **Th** Thorium 232.038	91 **Pa** Protactinium 231.036	92 **U** Uranium 238.029	93 **Np** Neptunium (237.048)	94 **Pu** Plutonium (244.06)	95 **Am** Americium (243.06)	96 **Cm** Curium (247.07)	97 **Bk** Berkelium (247.07)	98 **Cf** Californium (251.08)	99 **Es** Einsteinium (252.08)	100 **Fm** Fermium (257.10)	101 **Md** Mendelevium (258.10)	102 **No** Nobelium (259.10)

Chemical Bonds

Although there are only 109 known elements, there are millions of chemical substances found in nature or made artificially. These substances are not simply mixtures of two or more elements: they are specifically determined chemical compounds, formed by combining two or more elements together in a chemical reaction. The chemical 'glue' that holds these compounds together is known as *chemical bonding*.

The properties of compounds vary very widely. Some are highly reactive, others inert; some are solids with high melting points, others are gases. Furthermore, the properties of a compound are generally very different from those of its constituent elements. To understand how and why these differences arise, we need to understand the different types of chemical bond.

Ionic bonding

The atoms of the element neon have a full outer shell of electrons, with the electron configuration 2.8 (see p. 42). This arrangement is very stable and neon is not known to form chemical bonds with any other element. An atom of the element sodium (Na) has one more electron than neon (configuration 2.8.1), while an atom of the element fluorine (F) has one electron less (configuration 2.7). If an electron is transferred from a sodium atom to a fluorine atom, two species are produced with the same stable electron configuration as neon. Unlike neon, however, the species are charged and are known as *ions*. The sodium atom, having lost a (negative) electron, has a net positive charge and is known as a *cation* (written Na^+), while the fluorine atom, having gained an electron, has a net negative charge and is called a fluoride *anion* (written F^-).

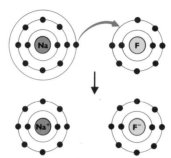

When oppositely charged ions such as Na^+ and F^- are brought together, there is a strong attraction between them; a large amount of energy is released – the same amount of energy as would have to be supplied in order to separate the ions again. This force of attraction is called an *ionic* (or *electrovalent*) bond. The energy released more than compensates for the energy input required to transfer the electron from the sodium atom to the fluorine atom. Overall there is a net release of energy and a solid crystalline compound – sodium fluoride (NaF) – is formed. The structure of a similar ionic compound – potassium chloride (KCl) – is illustrated in the box.

Atoms that have two more electrons than the nearest noble gas (such as magnesium, configuration 2.8.2) or two less (such as oxygen, 2.6) also form ions having the noble-gas configuration by transfer of electrons – in this case Mg^{2+} and O^{2-}. The ionic compound magnesium oxide (MgO; see photo, p. 47) has the same arrangement of ions as NaF, but since the ions in MgO have a greater charge, there is a stronger force between them. Thus more energy must be supplied to overcome this force of attraction, and the melting point of MgO is higher than that of NaF. Although the ions are fixed in position in the solid crystal, they become free to move when the solid is melted. As a liquid, therefore, the compound becomes electrolytic (see pp. 46–7) and is able to conduct electricity.

Many other more complex ionic structures are known. The formula of any ionic compound can be worked out by balancing the charges of its ions. For example, Mg^{2+} and F^- form MgF_2, while Na^+ and O^{2-} form Na_2O.

Covalent bonding

If we bring together two fluorine atoms, each with seven outer electrons (one less than neon), the formation of two ions with the noble-gas configuration is not possible by transfer of electrons. If, however, they share a pair of electrons – one from each atom – then both effectively achieve the noble-gas configuration and a stable molecule results:

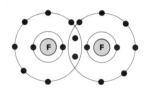

There is a force of attraction between the shared pair of electrons and both positive nuclei, and this is what is known as a *covalent bond*. The stronger the attraction of the nuclei for the shared pair, the stronger the bond.

An atom of oxygen, having two electrons less than neon, must form two covalent bonds to attain a share in eight electrons. For example, a molecule of water (H_2O), consisting of two hydrogen atoms (H) and one oxygen atom (O), has two covalent O–H bonds (see also p. 48). Another way for oxygen to achieve the stable noble-gas configuration is to form two bonds to the same atom. Thus two oxygen atoms bond covalently to one another by sharing two pairs of electrons (see p. 48). This is known as a *double bond*.

Like oxygen, sulphur (S) has six outer electrons and again needs to form two bonds to attain a share in eight electrons. There are two ways in which sulphur atoms join together – either in rings of eight atoms (S_8) or in long chains of many atoms bonded together (see photos). The

---

IONIC COMPOUNDS

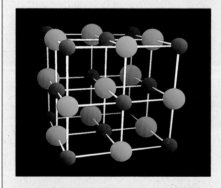

In a crystal of potassium chloride (KCl), each K^+ ion (represented here as a purple sphere) surrounds itself with as many Cl^- ions (green spheres) as there is space for – which turns out to be six; in the same way, each Cl^- ion is surrounded by six K^+ ions. The ions are packed in a regular repeating manner, so that – even though the smallest crystal of KCl contains many millions of ions – it has the same cubic shape as a simple model cube containing just 27 ions.

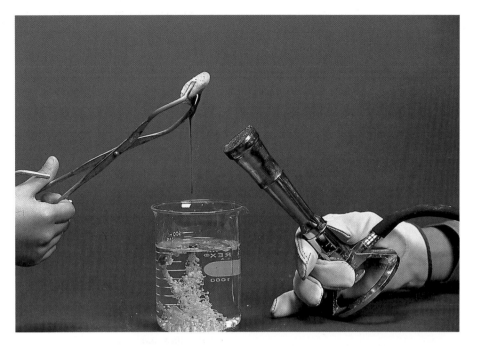

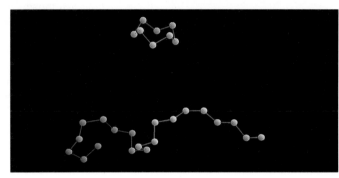

The allotropes of sulphur. One type of sulphur crystal, known as *rhombic sulphur*, contains rings of eight atoms (right, top). When this is melted and poured into water, *plastic sulphur* is formed, containing long tangled zigzag chains of covalently bonded sulphur atoms (right, bottom).

more energy to separate the bromine atoms by breaking the covalent bond between them.

Hydrogen bonds

Some small molecules have much higher melting and boiling points than would be expected on the basis of their size. One such example is water (H_2O), which has about the same mass as a neon atom but has a much higher melting point (see also p. 48). There must therefore be unusually strong intermolecular forces between the water molecules. Although the oxygen and hydrogen atoms share a pair of electrons in a covalent bond, the oxygen atom exerts a stronger 'pull' on these electrons and so becomes electron-rich, leaving the hydrogen atom electron-poor. As a result, there is a force of attraction between hydrogen and oxygen atoms on neighbouring molecules. This is known as *hydrogen bonding*.

As well as accounting for the surprisingly high melting point of water, hydrogen bonding is responsible for the rigid open structure of ice crystals (see photo), and is very important in influencing the structures and properties of biological molecules (see pp. 52–3). Although hydrogen bonds are stronger than van der Waals forces, they are still much weaker than covalent bonds.   DGE

SEE ALSO

● ATOMS AND SUBATOMIC
  PARTICLES p. 38
● WHAT IS CHEMISTRY?
  p. 40
● ELEMENTS AND THE
  PERIODIC TABLE p. 42
● CHEMICAL REACTIONS
  p. 46
● SMALL MOLECULES p. 48
● THE REACTIVITY SERIES
  p. 51

different forms in which elemental sulphur exist are known as *allotropes*; other elements found in allotropic forms include carbon (graphite, diamond and newly discovered buckminsterfullerene) and oxygen (oxygen and ozone; see p. 48).

Atoms of nitrogen (N), containing five outer electrons, need to form three covalent bonds to attain a share in eight electrons. This may be done, for example, by forming one bond to each of three hydrogen atoms, to give ammonia (NH_3; see p. 49). Another possibility is to form all three bonds to a second nitrogen atom, which produces a nitrogen molecule (N_2; see p. 49), containing a *triple covalent bond*.

The carbon atom (C), which has four outer electrons, needs to form four bonds to attain the noble-gas configuration. Thus a carbon atom forms one bond to each of four hydrogen atoms to give methane (CH_4; see table, p. 49). Although carbon is not known to form a quadruple bond to another carbon atom, some other elements, such as the heavy metal rhenium, do form such quadruple bonds. (For more on carbon bonding, see p. 52.)

Giant molecules

Although two carbon atoms do not form a quadruple bond to one another, carbon atoms can combine to form a giant crystal lattice in which each atom is bonded to four others by single covalent bonds. This

is the structure of diamond, one of the allotropes of elemental carbon. Many other elements and compounds exist as giant covalent crystal lattices, including quartz, which is a form of silicon dioxide (SiO_2). Crystals of these substances contain many millions of atoms held together by strong covalent bonds, so that a large amount of energy is needed to break them. Thus these substances all have high melting points and are hard solids.

Intermolecular forces

As we have seen, two neon atoms do not form covalent bonds with one another because of their full outer shells of electrons. There are, however, weak forces of attraction between two neon atoms. We know this because, when neon gas is compressed or cooled, it eventually turns into a liquid in which the atoms are weakly attracted to one another. These weak forces are called *van der Waals forces* and their strength depends on the size of the molecule.

Bromine (Br_2) is made up of large covalently bonded molecules that have much stronger van der Waals forces between them than exist between atoms of neon. Thus at room temperature bromine exists as a mixture of liquid and vapour. However, the forces *between* the bromine molecules are much weaker than covalent bonds, so that – while it is easy to separate the bromine molecules from one another and vaporize the liquid – it requires much

A snowflake, magnified to 20 times its actual size. Hydrogen bonding is responsible for the characteristic hexagonal symmetry of the ice crystals in a snowflake.

Chemical Reactions

Chemical reactions are the means by which new substances are formed from old ones. Among the chemical reactions occurring everywhere around us are the changes that take place when fuels are burnt, the industrial methods by which metals are extracted from their ores, and the processes controlling life itself. Since chemistry is centrally concerned with the means by which substances change, the study of reactions lies at the very heart of the subject.

SEE ALSO

● ELEMENTS AND THE
   PERIODIC TABLE p. 42
● CHEMICAL BONDS p. 44
● METALS p. 50
● NATURAL COMPOUNDS
   p. 52

During a chemical reaction, the atomic constituents of the substances that react together (the *reactants*) are rearranged to produce different substances (the *products*). Thus, for example, in the reaction of potassium (K) with water (H_2O), potassium hydroxide (KOH) and hydrogen gas (H_2) are formed. This information can be represented as a chemical equation. By convention the reactants appear on the left-hand side and the products on the right; letters may also be added after each chemical species to indicate its physical state – s means 'solid', l 'liquid', aq 'aqueous' (solution) and g 'gas':

$$2K(s) + 2H_2O(l) \rightarrow 2KOH(aq) + H_2(g)$$

An essential characteristic of chemical reactions is that there is an exchange of energy between the reacting system and the surroundings. So much heat is liberated during the reaction of potassium and water that the highly inflammable hydrogen gas frequently ignites above the molten metal.

A precipitation reaction. The addition of colourless potassium iodide solution to colourless lead nitrate leads to the formation of an insoluble precipitate of yellow lead iodide; colourless potassium nitrate remains in solution.

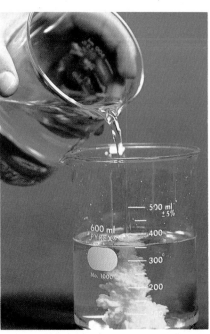

Stoichiometry and the mole concept

According to the *law of constant composition*, matter cannot be created or destroyed during a chemical reaction. Thus in the reaction described above, the number of atoms of potassium, hydrogen and oxygen (calculated by multiplying each element in the equation by the numbers placed before the chemical formula) is the same before and after the reaction, and the equation is said to be balanced. The numerical proportions in which substances combine to form the products of a chemical reaction is described as the reaction *stoichiometry*.

A balanced equation is thus a quantitative statement about the chemical reaction concerned. Such an equation (in conjunction with the mole concept; see below) enables us to predict how much product will be formed from a given mass of reactants. This provides valuable information that can be put to use, for example, in industrial production processes and in the analysis of chemical samples of unknown composition.

A *mole* is a measure of the amount of substance, based on the atomic theory of matter (see p. 38). A mole is defined as the number of carbon atoms in 12 grams of the isotope carbon-12 and has the colossal value of 6.022×10^{23}. Every chemical compound has a fixed *relative molecular mass* or RMM (determined by the relative atomic masses of its constituent elements; see pp. 42–3), so that molar quantities (the number of moles) of any substance can be found using simple arithmetic. (For an industrial application of the mole concept, see box.)

Reactions of acids and bases

According to the Brønsted–Lowry definition, *acids* are substances that tend to donate protons (ionized hydrogen atoms, H^+) to other molecules. For example, gaseous hydrogen chloride (HCl) readily dissolves in water to form hydrochloric acid, by donating a proton to a water molecule:

$$HCl(g) + H_2O(l) \rightarrow H_3O^+(aq) + Cl^-(aq)$$

The products of the reaction are ions (electrically charged species; see p. 44): H_3O^+ (the hydronium ion) and Cl^- (the chloride ion). Many non-metal oxides form acids when dissolved in water; for example, sulphur trioxide gas (SO_3) dissolves in water to form sulphuric acid (H_2SO_4) – the reaction that occurs in the formation of acid rain (see pp. 49 and 300).

By contrast, *bases* are defined as proton acceptors, capable of accepting protons from hydronium ions present in solution. A good example of a Brønsted–Lowry base is the hydroxide ion, $OH^-(aq)$, which reacts with the hydronium ion to produce two molecules of water:

$$H_3O^+(aq) + OH^-(aq) \rightarrow 2H_2O(l)$$

Examples of bases include sodium and potassium hydroxides (NaOH and KOH), which generate aqueous hydroxide ions in solution. Many metal oxides are also basic, such as calcium oxide (CaO; 'lime'),

which reacts violently with water to form calcium hydroxide ($Ca(OH)_2$; 'slaked lime'). Aqueous solutions of bases are known as *alkalis*.

Acids and bases can be detected by their effects on a class of natural dyes called *indicators*. The best-known indicator is *litmus*, a dye derived from lichen, which is turned red by acids and blue by bases.

Acids and bases react together to form compounds known as *salts*, which are neither acidic nor basic. For example, sodium hydroxide reacts with hydrochloric acid to form sodium chloride (common salt):

$$NaOH(aq) + HCl(aq) \rightarrow NaCl(aq) + H_2O(l)$$

The end-points of such *neutralization reactions* can be determined visually by the choice of an appropriate indicator, which changes colour when acid and base are exactly neutralized, i.e. when they have completely reacted. Neutralizations are of great importance in quantitative chemical analysis.

Precipitation reactions

Ionic compounds (see p. 44) that dissolve in water produce *electrolyte* solutions. These consist of ions moving randomly throughout the solution; for example, sodium chloride in aqueous solution contains sodium (Na^+) and chloride (Cl^-) ions. These ions are responsible for the electrical conductivity of electrolytes (see also below).

Silver nitrate ($AgNO_3$) is another ionic solid that dissolves readily in water, producing a colourless solution of aqueous silver (Ag^+) and nitrate (NO_3^-) ions. If solutions of silver nitrate and sodium

chloride are mixed, a white turbidity (cloudiness) instantly forms; this is due to the *precipitation* of fine particles of highly insoluble silver chloride. The precipitate gradually accumulates at the bottom of the vessel, leaving colourless sodium nitrate in solution:

$$NaCl(aq) + AgNO_3(aq) \rightarrow$$
$$AgCl(s) + NaNO_3(aq)$$

The overall reaction is one in which ions are exchanged between partners. It is possible to predict the outcome of such precipitation reactions from a knowledge of the solubilities of the various species involved.

Electron-transfer reactions: oxidation and reduction

Magnesium metal (Mg) burns with an incandescent white flame in air because of a vigorous reaction with oxygen, forming magnesium oxide (see photo):

$$Mg(s) + O_2(g) \rightarrow 2MgO(s)$$

This is an example of the class of reactions known as *oxidations*, which include all combustion processes such as those occurring when fuels burn in air, as well as the reactions that cause metals to corrode in air (see p. 51). The product in this case is an ionic solid, which we could write more specifically as $Mg^{2+}O^{2-}$. During the reaction, magnesium loses two electrons to form the cation Mg^{2+}; the electrons are accepted by oxygen, which becomes the oxide anion O^{2-} (see also p. 44).

The transfer of electrons between chemical species is a common process in many chemical reactions, so the term oxidation has come to possess a wider meaning than that implying solely the addition of oxygen atoms to an element or compound. As in the case of the formation of magnesium oxide, oxidation means the loss of electrons by a compound; the opposite process, *reduction*, implies a gain of electrons. Thus magnesium is said to be oxidized to Mg^{2+}, while oxygen is reduced to O^{2-}; the overall reaction is described as a *redox* process. Many metals are extracted from their ores by reduction reactions (see p. 50).

If an electric current is passed through an electrolyte such as an aqueous solution of copper(II) chloride ($CuCl_2$), a redox process known as *electrolysis* occurs. Positively charged Cu^{2+} ions are attracted to the negative electrode (the cathode; see p. 36), where they take up two electrons each

and are thereby reduced to copper metal, which is deposited on the cathode. At the same time, the negatively charged Cl^- ions are attracted to the positive electrode (the anode), where they give up their extra electrons (i.e. are oxidized) to form chlorine gas. Electrolysis is the basis of *electroplating*, in which a thin layer of metal, such as copper, tin, chromium or silver, is applied as a protective or decorative finish on cheaper or less durable materials (see photo, p. 50). It is also used to purify metals and to extract reactive metals such as aluminium from their ores (see p. 50).

In a *disproportionation* reaction, a single chemical species is simultaneously oxidized and reduced. For example, copper(I) sulphate (Cu_2SO_4) dissolves in water to produce copper metal and copper(II) sulphate:

$$Cu_2SO_4(aq) \rightarrow Cu(s) + CuSO_4(aq)$$

Here one Cu^+ ion is oxidized to Cu^{2+}, while the second is reduced to Cu metal.

Reaction equilibria

All the reactions described so far have gone to completion, i.e. a fixed quantity of reactants is converted into a fixed quantity of products. However, in general such a state of affairs is more the exception than the rule. The end of a reaction occurs when there is no further change in the amount of products formed or reactants destroyed: this is the point at which a reaction is said to reach *equilibrium*. At equilibrium, there may be appreciable amounts of reactants still present. For example, when acetic acid is dissolved in water, it forms a *weak acid*, because at equilibrium there is only a low concentration of hydronium ions:

$$CH_3COOH(l) + H_2O(l) \rightleftharpoons$$
$$CH_3CO_2^-(aq) + H_3O^+(aq)$$

The equilibrium, indicated by the two half-headed arrows, lies in favour of the reactants (in contrast to *strong acids*, such as hydrochloric acid, which are totally dissociated into ions). For the same reason, aqueous ammonia is a *weak base*, because at equilibrium there is a low concentration of hydroxide ions in the solution. Most of the solution consists of unreacted ammonia and water, in contrast to *strong bases*, which consist solely of ions.

The position of equilibrium in a chemical reaction (whether it favours reactants or products) depends in a detailed way on the thermodynamic properties of all the species involved.

Rates of chemical reactions

Very often it is important to know not only where the position of a chemical equilibrium lies but how fast it is reached. A graphic illustration is provided by a mixture of hydrogen gas and oxygen gas at room temperature. If undisturbed, the mixture does not react, but if a spark is passed through the gases, there is a violent explosion leading to the formation of water (see also p. 48). Thus temperature is seen to exert a strong influence on the rate at which a reaction proceeds – the higher the temperature, the faster the reaction.

On the other hand, the same reaction can be made to proceed smoothly at room temperature by the addition of finely divided platinum metal, which acts as a catalyst. A *catalyst* is a substance that is not chemically transformed during a reaction but whose presence serves to accelerate its rate. Catalysts play an extremely important role in many industrial processes, where they allow reactions to be carried out under conditions that would otherwise have to be much more severe.

Another factor influencing the rate of reaction is the intrinsic reactivity – i.e. willingness to undergo chemical reaction – of the chemical species involved. An example is provided by the reactions of the halogens – fluorine, chlorine, bromine and iodine (see p. 42) – with hydrogen gas. The form of the reaction is identical for all the halogens, in each case producing the hydrogen halide (halogen-containing compound). However, the rate of the reaction decreases progressively down the series, fluorine reacting violently and iodine sluggishly at room temperature.

Complex reactions

Many chemical reactions, including those of the halogens with hydrogen gas, are actually much more complicated than their simple chemical equations suggest, and can be very sensitive to the precise conditions existing at the time of the reaction. One of the most fascinating illustrations of this is the Belousov–Zhabotinsky reaction (see photo), which involves a mixture of malonic acid, cerium(III) sulphate, potassium bromate and an iron(II) catalyst (ferroin) in aqueous acid solution. Depending on the conditions used, the reaction can display blue–red oscillations (chemical clock behaviour) and/or spatial patterns (chemical waves), which spread in a regular manner through the solution. The red colour is due to regions in which the reduced form Fe^{2+} predominates, while blue regions consist of oxidized Fe^{3+} ions.

Such remarkable organization, brought about by complex chemical (or biochemical) reactions in which vast numbers of molecules 'beat' in unison, is now recognized to be of fundamental importance for the control and regulation of many processes in living systems. PVC

47

An oxidation reaction: (left) magnesium metal burns in air to produce magnesium oxide. This common and important type of reaction includes combustion processes, the reactions that occur when metals corrode in air, and the biochemical reactions by which we obtain energy from food.

The Belousov–Zhabotinsky reaction (see text): a spectacular example of the complexity of many chemical reactions. The astonishing organization underlying such complex reactions is now recognized to be of crucial importance in the regulation of many processes in living systems.

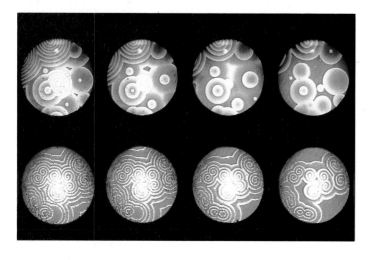

Small Molecules

Although the Earth's atmosphere consists almost entirely of two gases – nitrogen and oxygen – a number of other gases are present at low concentration, together with varying amounts of water vapour. With the exception of the noble gases (see p. 42), most other components of air form part of natural cycles, each remaining in the atmosphere only for a limited time. Not only are these gases of major importance in relation to industrial processes that dominate economies throughout the world, but cyclical processes involving water, oxygen, carbon dioxide and nitrogen – together with solar radiation – are essential to plant and animal life.

SEE ALSO

- WHAT IS CHEMISTRY? p. 40
- CHEMICAL BONDS p. 44
- THE EARTH'S STRUCTURE AND ATMOSPHERE p. 76
- THE HYDROLOGICAL CYCLE p. 95
- WEATHER p. 102
- PLANT PHYSIOLOGY p. 116
- THE BIOSPHERE p. 176
- THREATS TO THE ENVIRONMENT p. 300

Current interest in various atmospheric gases centres on the possible global effects of changes in their atmospheric concentration due to human activities (see also p. 300). Increase in carbon dioxide may upset the heat balance at the Earth's surface, while the use of chlorofluorocarbons (CFCs) might result in depletion of the ozone layer, thereby allowing destructive high-energy solar radiation to reach the Earth's surface.

Although these small molecules are simple in the sense that they are composed of few atoms, their structures and – for those with three or more atoms – their shapes vary (see table). In most cases, their atoms are held together in the molecule by two, four or six electrons, resulting in single, double or triple covalent bonds (see pp. 44–5). Three of these molecules (nitric oxide, nitrogen dioxide and oxygen) are paramagnetic – i.e. attracted to a magnet, like iron – because of the number or arrangement of their electrons.

Hydrogen

Hydrogen (H_2) is the simplest of all stable molecules, consisting of two protons and two electrons. It is a colourless, odourless gas and is lighter than air. The last of these properties led to its use in lifting airships, but this use was discontinued – because of its explosiveness when ignited (see p. 47) – following the *Hindenburg* disaster in 1937 (see p. 348). Most hydrogen is used on the site where it is produced, but it is also transported as compressed gas in steel cylinders and in liquid form at very low temperature.

Water

The total amount of water (H_2O) on Earth is fixed, and most is recycled and re-used (see pp. 95 and 102). The largest reservoirs are the oceans and open seas, followed by glaciers, ice caps and ground water (see pp. 90, 94 and 100). Very little is actually contained within living organisms, although water is a major constituent of most life forms.

Water is one of the most remarkable of all small molecules. On the basis of its molecular weight (18), it should be a gas; its high boiling point (100 °C / 212 °F) is due to the interaction of water molecules with each other (hydrogen bonding; see p. 45), which effectively increases its molecular weight. Water is also unusual in that – as ice – it is less dense than the liquid at the same temperature.

Carbon dioxide and oxygen

Carbon dioxide (CO_2) is a colourless gas with a slight odour and an acid taste. It is available as gas, as liquid and as the white solid known as 'dry ice'. Its cycle in nature is tied to that of oxygen, the relative levels of the two gases in the atmosphere (apart from human activity) being regulated by the photosynthetic activity of plants (see p. 117). It is produced on a vast scale, mostly as a by-product of other processes.

With the ever-increasing input of carbon dioxide to the atmosphere, due largely to the burning of fossil fuels and forests and the manufacture of cement, the natural 'sinks' for carbon dioxide – chiefly photosynthesis and transfer to the oceans – can no longer keep pace with the total input. If this imbalance continues, it is thought that levels will be reached where the infrared-absorbing properties of carbon dioxide will result in a progressive warming of the Earth's atmosphere, accompanied by melting of the polar ice and flooding of what is now dry land – the so-called *greenhouse effect* (see also p. 301). This is perhaps too extreme and pessimistic a view: in the past there have been many warm interglacial periods due to factors not ascribable to human activity.

Oxygen (O_2) is a highly reactive colourless, odourless and tasteless gas. At low temperature, it condenses to a pale blue liquid, slightly denser than water. Oxygen supports burning, causes rusting (see p. 51) and is vital to both plant and animal respiration (see pp. 116 and 210).

Ozone

Ozone (O_3) is a highly toxic, unstable, colourless gas. Its primary importance stems from its formation in the stratosphere (see p. 77). In this layer of the atmosphere, temperature increases with height, principally because of the reaction of high-energy ultraviolet solar radiation with oxygen. This can be expressed in the form of two chemical equations:

$$O_2 + \text{sunlight} \rightarrow 2\,O\ (\text{atoms})$$
$$O_2 + O\ (\text{atom}) \rightarrow O_3$$

Ozone in the stratosphere functions as a very effective filter for high-energy ultraviolet solar radiation. Radiation in this energy range is sufficiently high to break bonds between carbon and other atoms, making it lethal to all forms of life. It is

Molecule	Hydrogen	Water	Oxygen	Ozone	Carbon dioxide	Carbon monoxide
Formula	H_2	H_2O	O_2	O_3	CO_2	CO
Structure						
Concentration in unpolluted air (parts per million)	0.5	Variable	209 400	c. 0.01	c. 315	0.1
Industrial production	Reaction of coal or petroleum with steam in the presence of a catalyst; electrolysis of water	—	Liquefying and distilling air	Ultraviolet irradiation of air; electric discharge through air	By-product of other processes, e.g. burning of fossil fuels, fermentation and calcining limestone	Action of steam on carbonaceous material
Major uses	Synthesis of ammonia and methanol (CH_3OH, the simplest alcohol); removal of impurities such as sulphur-containing compounds from natural gas, oil and coal	Solvent	Steel manufacture; all combustion processes; extensively used in chemical industry, e.g. in conversion of ethylene (ethene, $CH_2{:}CH_2$) to ethylene oxide (see box, p. 321)	Treatment of drinking water; bleach for clay materials	Fire extinguishers; coolant	Fuel; reducing agent in metallurgy; chemical production of e.g. methanol (CH_3OH), acetic acid (CH_3CO_2H) and phosgene ($COCl_2$)

Structure key:
— Single bond
= Double bond
≡ Triple bond
=·= Intermediate between single and double bond
=·≡ Intermediate between double and triple bond

currently thought that the introduction of CFCs (used in sprays and refrigerants) and the related 'halons' (used in fire extinguishers) may contribute to the partial or even total destruction of the ozone layer (see also p. 301). These classes of compounds are highly volatile, chemically very stable and essentially insoluble in water, so that they are not washed out of the atmosphere by rain. When, by normal convection (see p. 25), they reach the stratosphere, they react destructively with ozone.

Carbon monoxide

Carbon monoxide (CO) is a colourless, odourless, toxic gas. The input to the atmosphere due to human activity is about 360 million tonnes (tons) per year, mostly from the incomplete combustion of fossil fuels. The natural input is some 10 times this figure and results from the partial oxidation of biologically produced methane (see table). The background level of 0.1 parts per million (ppm) can rise to 20 ppm at a busy road intersection, and a five-minute cigarette gives an intake of 400 ppm.

Since the atmospheric level of carbon monoxide is not rising significantly, there must be effective sink processes, one being its oxidation in air to carbon dioxide. In addition, there are soil microorganisms that utilize carbon monoxide in photosynthesis.

Nitrogen

Nitrogen (N_2) is a colourless, odourless gas. Although very stable and chemically unreactive, it cycles both naturally and as a result of its use in the chemical industry. The natural cycle (see p. 177) results from the ability of some types of bacteria and blue-green algae (in the presence of sunlight) to 'fix' nitrogen – i.e. to convert it into inorganic nitrogen compounds (ammonium and nitrate salts) that can be assimilated by plants. Since 1913 human activity has increasingly contributed to the cycling of nitrogen, because of the catalytic conversion of nitrogen

into ammonia (used mainly in nitrate fertilizers, see below), which ultimately reverts to nitrogen gas.

Oxides of nitrogen

The presence of nitric oxide (NO) and nitrogen dioxide (NO_2) at high levels in the atmosphere is closely connected with the internal-combustion engine (see pp. 308–9 and 355). At the high temperature reached when petroleum and air ignite, nitrogen and oxygen combine to form nitric oxide, which slowly reacts with more oxygen to form nitrogen dioxide. Most internal-combustion engines also produce some unburnt or partially burnt fuel: in the presence of sunlight, this reacts with nitrogen dioxide by a sequence of fast reactions, forming organic peroxides, which are the harmful constituents of photochemical smog (smoke plus fog).

Ammonia

Ammonia (NH_3) is a colourless gas with a penetrating odour, and is less dense than air. It is highly soluble in water, giving an alkaline solution (see p. 47). World production is of the order of 100 million tonnes (tons) a year, most of which is converted into fertilizers (80%), plastics (9%) and explosives (4%).

Oxides of sulphur

Both sulphur dioxide (SO_2) and sulphur trioxide (SO_3) are pungent-smelling acidic gases, which are produced by volcanic action and – to the extent of some 150 million tonnes (tons) a year – by the burning of fossil fuels and smelting operations.

The level of sulphur dioxide in unpolluted air is 0.002 parts per million (ppm), but in the 1952 London smog the levels rose to 1.54 ppm, accompanied by a dramatic increase in the death rate. In the atmosphere sulphur dioxide is slowly oxidized to sulphur trioxide, reactions that are catalysed by sunlight, water droplets and particulate matter in the air. Ultimately the latter is deposited as dilute sulphuric acid – *acid rain* (see pp. 46 and 300).   FG

Dry ice vaporizing. A colourless gas at room temperature, carbon dioxide becomes a liquid under compression. If the liquid is allowed to expand rapidly to atmospheric pressure, it becomes cooler and freezes to dry ice – a white, snowlike solid. Dry ice sublimes (passes directly into vapour without melting) at -78.5 °C (-109.3 °F); it is used to produce stage fog and as a refrigerant.

Methane	Nitrogen	Nitric oxide	Nitrous oxide	Nitrogen dioxide	Ammonia	Sulphur dioxide	Sulphur trioxide
CH_4	N_2	NO	N_2O	NO_2	NH_3	SO_2	SO_3
1–1.6	780 900	Variable	0.5	c. 0.02	Variable	Variable (c. 0.002)	Variable
—	Liquefying and distilling air	Catalytic oxidation of ammonia	Heating ammonium nitrate (NH_4NO_3)	Oxidation of nitric oxide	Catalytic reaction of nitrogen and hydrogen	Oxidation of sulphur	Oxidation of sulphur dioxide
The main constituent of natural gas (see p. 311); major feedstock for the chemical industry	Synthesis of ammonia; uses due to its inertness, e.g. in metallurgy and in the chemical and food industries	Vital in the chemical industry, as an intermediate in the production of nitric acid (HNO_3)	Anaesthetic (laughing gas; see pp. 41 and 56); propellant in the food industry, e.g. in whipped ice cream	As nitric oxide	Fertilizers; plastics; explosives	Vital in the chemical industry, as an intermediate in the production of sulphuric acid (H_2SO_4)	As sulphur dioxide

Metals

Metals are usually defined by their physical properties, such as strength, hardness, lustre, conduction of heat and electricity, malleability and high melting point. They can also be characterized chemically as elements that dissolve (or whose oxides dissolve) in acids, usually to form positively charged ions (cations; see p. 44). By either definition, more than three quarters of the known elements can be classified as metals. They occupy all but the top right-hand corner of the Periodic Table (see figure), the remainder being non-metals.

A few elements on the borderline, such as germanium, arsenic and antimony, have some of the properties of both metals and non-metals, and are often classed as *metalloids*.

Electrochemistry in industry: (right) copper-plated sheets used for flexible electronic circuitboards are seen being removed from an electroplating bath. The bath is filled with an electrolyte (see pp. 46–7) of copper(II) sulphate solution; the object to be plated acts as the cathode (see p. 36), while the anode is made of copper metal. As an electric current passes through the solution, the copper anode 'dissolves' and copper metal is deposited at the cathode.

Given such a large number of metals, it is not surprising that some of them have rather untypical properties. For instance, mercury is a liquid at room temperature, and – with the exception of lithium – all the alkali metals (see Periodic Table) melt below 100 °C (212 °F). The alkali metals are also quite soft – they can easily be cut with a knife – and extremely reactive: rubidium and caesium cannot be handled in air and may react explosively with water.

Occurrence

Most metals occur naturally as oxides, while some – mostly the heavier ones, such as mercury and lead – occur as sulphides. Only a few – the noble and coinage metals (see Periodic Table) – are found in the metallic state, being chemically the most inert metals. It is their chemical unreactiveness that makes them useful in coinage and jewellery, since they do not corrode (see below).

A few metals do not occur naturally at all, because they are radioactive and have decayed away (see p. 39). Technetium and all the elements with higher atomic numbers than plutonium (Pu, 94; see Periodic Table) are made by the 'modern alchemy' of nuclear reactors or accelerators (see pp. 38–9 and 304–5), while promethium is found only in minute amounts as a product of the spontaneous fission of uranium. The very heaviest elements have been obtained only a few atoms at a time, and are intensely radioactive.

The discovery and extraction of metals

Artificial elements have of course been known only in modern times, since the 1940s or later. The discovery of most other metals was also comparatively recent: with the exception of zinc, platinum and the handful of metals known to the Ancients, all metals have been discovered since 1735. The only metals known in antiquity were copper, silver, gold, iron, tin, mercury and lead. Of these, it was not the most abundant – iron – that was discovered first: the Bronze Age came before the Iron Age. The reason for this is that it is easier to extract the metals used in bronze – copper and tin – from their minerals than it is to extract iron from its ores. The discovery of copper is thought to have been accidental: pieces of the metal ore used in fireplaces came into contact with the hot charcoal, so releasing the metal. Essentially the same process under controlled conditions (*smelting*) is used in modern blast furnaces (see p. 314). Any of the metals from manganese (Mn) to zinc (Zn) in the Periodic Table (see figure) can be obtained by roasting their oxides with coke at temperatures of up to about 1600 °C (2912 °F).

The ores of the lighter, more reactive metals cannot be reduced by carbon at practical temperatures, because their atoms are more strongly bonded in the ore (see box on reactivity). These metals are usually obtained by electrolysis (see pp. 46–7) or by the reaction of their compounds with an even more reactive metal. For instance, the reduction of aluminium oxide with carbon requires a temperature in excess of 2000 °C (3632 °F); so electrolysis of a melt of aluminium oxide in a mixture of cryolite (a double fluoride of aluminium and sodium) and calcium fluoride at about 950 °C (1742 °F) is used. On the other hand, titanium is obtained by converting its oxide into the chloride, which is then reduced with elemental sodium or magnesium (see box, p. 46). These methods are rather expensive, but are justified by the usefulness of the metals obtained, which are both strong and light.

Conductivity

The conduction of heat and electricity (see pp. 25 and 34–7) that characterizes metals is due to their unique type of bonding. The solid metals behave as if they were composed of arrays of positively charged ions, with electrons free to move throughout the crystalline structure of the metal (see below). This results in high

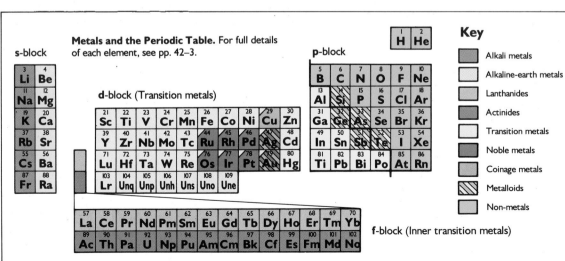

Metals and the Periodic Table. For full details of each element, see pp. 42–3.

s-block

3 Li	4 Be
11 Na	12 Mg
19 K	20 Ca
37 Rb	38 Sr
55 Cs	56 Ba
87 Fr	88 Ra

d-block (Transition metals)

21 Sc	22 Ti	23 V	24 Cr	25 Mn	26 Fe	27 Co	28 Ni	29 Cu	30 Zn
39 Y	40 Zr	41 Nb	42 Mo	43 Tc	44 Ru	45 Rh	46 Pd	47 Ag	48 Cd
71 Lu	72 Hf	73 Ta	74 W	75 Re	76 Os	77 Ir	78 Pt	79 Au	80 Hg
103 Lr	104 Unq	105 Unp	106 Unh	107 Uns	108 Uno	109 Une			

p-block

1 H	2 He

5 B	6 C	7 N	8 O	9 F	10 Ne
13 Al	14 Si	15 P	16 S	17 Cl	18 Ar
31 Ga	32 Ge	33 As	34 Se	35 Br	36 Kr
49 In	50 Sn	51 Sb	52 Te	53 I	54 Xe
81 Ti	82 Pb	83 Bi	84 Po	85 At	86 Rn

Key

- Alkali metals
- Alkaline-earth metals
- Lanthanides
- Actinides
- Transition metals
- Noble metals
- Coinage metals
- Metalloids
- Non-metals

f-block (Inner transition metals)

57 La	58 Ce	59 Pr	60 Nd	61 Pm	62 Sm	63 Eu	64 Gd	65 Tb	66 Dy	67 Ho	68 Er	69 Tm	70 Yb
89 Ac	90 Th	91 Pa	92 U	93 Np	94 Pu	95 Am	96 Cm	97 Bk	98 Cf	99 Es	100 Fm	101 Md	102 No

THE REACTIVITY SERIES

The widely varying reactivity of metals can be related to their positions in the Periodic Table (see figure). The s-block metals are highly reactive, while the transition metals typically become less reactive from left to right across the table, with the noble and coinage metals least reactive of all.

When metals react, they usually lose electrons to form positively charged ions (cations, see p. 44). This charge (also known as the *oxidation state*) is again related to the position of a metal in the Periodic Table. In the s-block, the charge equals the group number, +1 or +2 (e.g. K^+, Mg^{2+}). In the transition metals, variability of oxidation state is the rule: for instance, iron may lose 2 or 3 electrons (Fe^{2+}, Fe^{3+}), and this fact is indicated in the names and formulae of its compounds – iron(II) chloride ($FeCl_2$) and iron(III) chloride ($FeCl_3$).

The reactivity of a metal can thus be explained in terms of its readiness to lose electrons to form cations: potassium (K) readily loses an electron to form a K^+ ion, while gold (Au) is highly unreactive and dissolves only in aqua regia, a fiercely oxidizing mixture of hydrochloric and nitric acids. Metals can be placed in order of reactivity, in a sequence known as the *reactivity series*; for some of the more important metals, the series runs as follows (in order of decreasing reactivity):

K Na Ca Mg Al Zn Fe Pb Cu Hg Ag Au Pt

A metal can be displaced from a solution of one of its salts simply by addition of a metal higher (earlier) in the series. For instance, if zinc metal (Zn) is added to a solution of copper(II) sulphate ($CuSO_4$), the zinc becomes coated by copper metal and the blue colour of the solution fades, as the coloured copper ions in solution are displaced by zinc ions:

$$Zn(s) + Cu^{2+}(aq) + SO_4{}^{2-}(aq) \rightarrow Zn^{2+}(aq) + SO_4{}^{2-}(aq) + Cu(s)$$

The reactivity series also indicates the affinity of a metal for oxygen. As such, it explains the differing susceptibility of metals to corrosion (surface oxidation) and underlies the extraction of metals from their oxides. The more reactive a metal is, the higher the temperature required to reduce its oxide by carbon. In practice, the most reactive metals cannot be economically reduced by carbon, and are therefore obtained by electrolysis or by displacement by an even more reactive metal.

The reactivity series can also be seen as an *electrochemical series*. When two different metals are dipped into an electrolyte solution (see pp. 46–7), a voltage forms between them and the metal higher in the series becomes the anode (positive electrode). The distance between the two metals in the series reflects the size of the voltage produced. Electrochemical reactions of this kind underlie electroplating (see photo) and the operation of electrolytic cells and batteries (see p. 36). Frequently some hydrogen is also produced: such a reaction often occurs in domestic central heating systems, where copper pipes and iron radiators are both in contact with hot water; the 'air' that accumulates in the system is actually hydrogen.

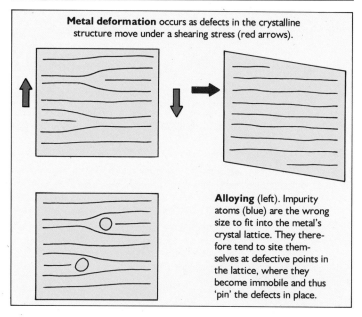

Metal deformation occurs as defects in the crystalline structure move under a shearing stress (red arrows).

Alloying (left). Impurity atoms (blue) are the wrong size to fit into the metal's crystal lattice. They therefore tend to site themselves at defective points in the lattice, where they become immobile and thus 'pin' the defects in place.

electrical conductivity. The conduction of heat can also be seen in terms of the motion of electrons, which becomes faster as temperature rises. Since the electrons are mobile, the heat can be conducted readily through the solid.

The majority of metals are good conductors of electricity, but germanium and tin (in the form stable below 19 °C / 64 °F) are semiconductors (see p. 37).

Mechanical strength

Many metals are used because of their strength. However, most pure metals are actually quite soft. In order to obtain a tough hard metal, something else has to be added. For instance, the earliest useful metal was not copper but bronze, which is copper alloyed with tin. Similarly, iron is never used in the pure state but as some form of steel (see p. 314).

The softness of a pure metal results from a lack of perfection in the crystal framework formed by its atoms (see diagram). Even when the most rigorous conditions are employed, it is impossible to grow any material in perfect crystalline form. There will always be some atoms in the wrong place or missing from their proper place. When solidification occurs fairly rapidly,

as when a molten metal is cooled in a mould, even more defects occur. Under bending or shearing stresses, such defects can move and allow the metal to change shape easily. When the foreign atoms of an alloying element are present, they usually have a different size from those of the host and cannot easily fit into the crystal lattice. They therefore tend to site themselves where the lattice is irregular, i.e. where the defects are. The effect of this is to prevent the defects from moving, and so to increase the rigidity of the metal.

Tarnishing and corrosion

Nearly all metals are prone to surface oxidation, i.e. the surface of the metal reacts with oxygen or other components of the atmosphere (see box on reactivity). The major exceptions are the coinage metals and those of the platinum group (see Periodic Table), and even these react with sulphur compounds (see p. 49) in industrially polluted atmospheres and turn black. All other metals should, in principle, react with moisture and the oxygen in air, yet some corrode badly and others appear to be inert. In fact, they all oxidize, but in many cases a thin layer of oxide adheres firmly to the metal surface

and prevents further reaction. This is the case with aluminium and titanium. On the other hand, iron forms porous oxides that readily break away, allowing corrosion to continue (see photo). Stainless steels are produced by alloying iron with chromium and sometimes also with nickel, which form a protective oxide on the surface; the thickness of this layer is so small that the surface still appears shiny and metallic.

An alternative way of preventing corrosion is essentially electrochemical. Corrosion can be prevented by connecting a metal object to a piece of more reactive metal and completing the circuit through the earth. The more reactive metal becomes the anode (see box on reactivity) and gradually 'dissolves' or degrades. This method is sometimes used for metal tanks that have to stand outdoors: a block of magnesium buried and connected by a wire to the tank slowly oxidizes – it acts as a 'sacrificial' anode. This is also the reason why galvanization works. Contrary to what would be expected, the layer of zinc on the iron needs to be somewhat porous so that water can bring the two metals into electrochemical contact. It is then the zinc that reacts instead of the iron.   RVP

SEE ALSO

● ELECTROMAGNETISM p. 34
● ELECTRICITY IN ACTION p. 36
● ATOMS AND SUBATOMIC PARTICLES p. 38
● ELEMENTS AND THE PERIODIC TABLE p. 42
● CHEMICAL BONDS p. 44
● CHEMICAL REACTIONS p. 46
● MINING, MINERALS AND METALS p. 312
● IRON AND STEEL p. 314
● HUMAN PREHISTORY p. 362

Metal corrosion. A flake of badly corroded car bodywork, magnified and shown in false colour: the rust at the bottom is covered by three coats of original paint and one coat of a later respray. Most metals are prone to corrosion, or surface oxidation; the problem is particularly acute in the case of iron, because it forms porous oxides that break away and allow corrosion to continue.

Natural Compounds

The molecular basis for life processes, which have evolved with such remarkable elegance around carbon as the key element, is beginning to be understood, thanks to the combined triumphs of biological, chemical and physical scientists during the last hundred years.

Alanine

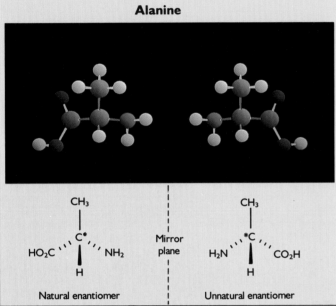

Natural enantiomer   Mirror plane   Unnatural enantiomer

Many organic compounds, such as alanine and limonene, are built up asymmetrically around a central carbon atom and can exist in two mirror-image forms, known as *enantiomers* (see text). In the case of amino acids such as alanine, one enantiomer predominates greatly over the other, the latter having a small role in nature. This apparently superficial difference in form can have a startling effect on the properties of the compound concerned. A trivial but striking example of this is provided by the enantiomers of limonene: one smells strongly of lemons, the other of oranges.

Limonene

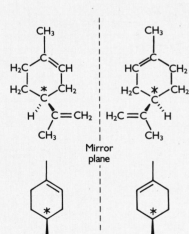

Mirror plane

Structural formulae. Chiral carbon atoms are conventionally indicated by an asterisk (∗). Covalent bonds located in the plane of the paper are represented by lines (—), while bonds orientated (tetrahedrally) above and below this plane are displayed as wedges (▶) and dashes (ııı) respectively.

In simplified structural formulae (such as those given for limonene, below), the junctions and termini of lines, wedges and dashes represent carbon atoms. It is understood that hydrogen atoms complete the tetracovalency requirement around each carbon atom (see text).

Although the chemist can now make synthetically almost any chemical compound that nature produces, the challenge remains to achieve this objective routinely with the efficiency and precision that characterizes the chemistry of living systems.

There is something very special about the chemistry of carbon that has singled it out as the atomic building block from which all naturally occurring compounds in living systems are constructed. The subject that deals with this important area of science, nestling between biology and physics, has become so vast and significant that it has earned recognition as a separate field of scientific investigation. As it was originally thought that such carbon-based compounds could be obtained only from natural sources, this field of study became known as *organic chemistry*.

The unique carbon atom

Carbon's unique feature is the readiness with which it forms bonds both with other carbon atoms and with the atoms of other elements. Having four electrons in its outer shell, a carbon atom requires four more electrons to attain a stable noble-gas configuration (see p. 44). It therefore forms four covalent bonds with other atoms, each of which donates a single electron to each bond. In this way the electronic requirements are satisfied, and a three-dimensional 'tetracovalent' environment is built up around the carbon atom.

Carbon bonds are found both in pure forms of carbon (graphite, diamond and newly discovered buckminsterfullerene) and in association with other atoms in a vast array of compounds. Compounds consisting of just carbon and hydrogen – *hydrocarbons* – are extremely important, notably as the principal constituents of fossil fuels. In addition, carbon readily bonds with many other atoms, including oxygen, nitrogen, sulphur, phosphorus and the halogens, such as chlorine and bromine. Often the covalent bonds between carbon and other atoms are stable enough for us to handle the resulting compounds at room temperature; yet these compounds are not so strongly bonded that they cannot be manipulated by means of well-known chemical reactions.

Functional groups and reactivity

Carbon combines with itself and other atoms to produce open-chain (*acyclic*) and ring (*cyclic*) skeletons, into which are built highly characteristic arrangements of atoms, known as *functional groups* (see table). The diverse but predictable chemical behaviour of the different functional groups is a consequence of their ability either to attract or to repel electrons compared with the rest of the carbon skeleton. The overall effect of the resulting charge distribution is to

FUNCTIONAL GROUPS

A selection of important functional groups. An 'R' indicates a site where another functional group or an atom may be attached.

Alkenes are hydrocarbons that contain one or more carbon double bonds. Alkenes with just one double bond form a series including ethene (ethylene; C_2H_4), propene and butene.

Alcohols. Examples include methanol (CH_3OH) and ethanol (C_2H_5OH; see p. 40).

Ketones. Examples include propanone (acetone; CH_3COCH_3) and MVK (see box, far right).

Aldehydes. An important example is methanal (formaldehyde; $HCOH$), used in the production of formalin (a disinfectant) and of synthetic resins.

Carboxylic acids. As well as occurring in organic acids, such as acetic (ethanoic) acid (CH_3CO_2H; vinegar), this group occurs in all amino acids, including alanine (see box, left).

Amines, together with the carboxylic-acid group, occur in all amino acids.

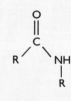

Amides. The most important type of amide bond is that formed in protein synthesis, when the carboxylic-acid group of one amino acid condenses with the amine group of another to give a *peptide bond*.

Thiols. This group is characterized by a strong, disagreeable odour. An example is ethanethiol (see p. 41).

Aromatic compounds. The six-membered ring containing three double bonds is highly stable and is thus a very common characteristic of organic compounds.

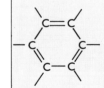

create a molecule in which some regions are slightly negatively charged (*nucleophilic*), and others slightly positively charged (*electrophilic*).

Most organic reactions involve the electrophilic and nucleophilic centres of different molecules coming together as a prelude to the formation of new covalent bonds. An appreciation of how particular compounds behave towards others and of the various mechanisms by which such reactions occur forms the basis of classical organic synthesis. This allows chemists to build up large molecules, containing many different functional groups and with a great diversity of chemical properties, in a controlled and predictable manner.

Chirality and the tetrahedral carbon atom

Alanine (see box, left) is one of the 20 naturally occurring amino acids from which proteins are synthesized in living organisms (see below and p. 114). Amino acids are characterized by their possession of two functional groups – a carboxylic-acid group (CO_2H) and an amine group (NH_2). Different amino acids, often with very different properties, are distinguished by the identity of a third group – a methyl group (CH_3) in the case of alanine.

A more detailed examination of alanine reveals another feature of paramount importance to the modern chemist. The four groups bonded to the central carbon atom are arranged in such a way as to define a tetrahedron in three dimensions. This spatial arrangement (or *configuration*) can exist in two different forms, one the non-superimposable mirror image of the other. They differ as our right hand does to our left, so the central carbon atom is said to be *chiral* (from the Greek for 'hand'), or *asymmetric*. The two different forms are known as *enantiomers*.

The physical consequences of this apparently minor difference can be quite startling. Limonene is a liquid hydrocarbon with one chiral carbon atom, and occurs as two enantiomers (see box, left). While one enantiomer smells strongly of lemons, the other smells strongly of oranges. The different spatial arrangements of the groups and consequently the different overall shapes of the two molecules cause them to interact differently with molecular sensors in our nose, so each initiates a different message that is then sent to our brain.

Molecular recognition of this kind, based upon chirality, is prevalent in the chemistry of the molecules of life. Nucleic acids (DNA, RNA; see photo), polysaccharides (large natural sugar molecules) and proteins, especially enzymes, all discriminate between enantiomers in their respective modes of action. The *enzymes* are nature's catalysts, providing a very efficient environment in which molecules can come together and react. Like other proteins, they are built up from chains of amino acids, joined together in numerous different combinations. The chains twist and coil, so causing the functional groups of different amino acids to come together or 'converge', thereby creating specific regions known as *active sites*. It is at the active site that particular molecules may be held briefly while reactions are performed on them, before being released as new molecules. However, an enzyme is generally very selective about which molecules it will accept; often, only one of a pair of enantiomers will be accepted, the other being the wrong shape to fit comfortably into the active site. In this way, life itself depends vitally upon chirality.

Aspects of design

If a desired compound does not occur naturally, it must be made, or synthesized, by modifying a molecule that already exists. Such a chemical synthesis may involve a number of different steps, and even relatively simple molecules could, in principle, be synthesized in many different ways from many different starting materials. Using their knowledge of chemical reactions, chemists examine several possible routes to a molecule before setting out upon its synthesis. *Retrosynthetic analysis* is a design method in which the desired product is broken down theoretically, or 'disconnected', into smaller and smaller fragments until a convenient starting material is reached (see box, right). It relies upon a knowledge of how different functional groups can be manipulated to build up the desired molecule gradually.

The art of synthetic design has progressed rapidly over the last 30 years. Chemists have learnt to handle and manipulate new families of compounds, and discovered new synthetic transformations that may operate under milder conditions than existing ones or at a much faster rate. This has been coupled with great advances in the methods used to purify and analyse molecules; such methods have

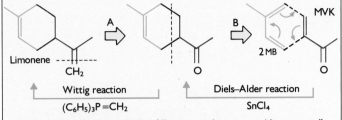

The retrosynthetic analysis of limonene. Limonene is 'disconnected' in two steps (yellow arrows) to the readily available starting materials 2-methyl-butadiene (2MB) and methylvinylketone (MVK). In step A, the CH_2 group is replaced by an oxygen atom; in step B, the six-membered ring is disconnected to 2MB and MVK. The large green arrows indicate the actual synthetic reactions required to transform the two starting materials into limonene; the small green arrows indicate how the six-membered ring is formed in the Diels–Alder reaction.

allowed the structures of molecules to be probed more deeply, thereby revealing how they react together and how a particular molecule may interact with its surroundings. In principle, the expertise already exists to synthesize any molecule, however complex: the only constraint is time. As we learn more and more about the chemicals that exist all around us – and within us – we put ourselves in an increasingly strong position to tackle the many intricate scientific and environmental issues facing mankind as the new century approaches.   SU

DNA

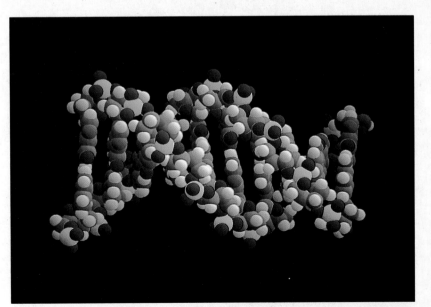

The phosphorus atoms (light blue), each surrounded by four oxygen atoms (red), give a strong sense of the right-handed twist of the sugar–phosphate backbone of this form of DNA (B-DNA). The dark-blue spheres, representing nitrogen atoms, form part of the nucleotide bases that link the two strands of the molecule. Green represents carbon, and white hydrogen.

Nucleic acids – DNA and RNA – are present in all living cells, with the exception of red blood cells. The highly variable sequences of bases allow information relating to the characteristics of the individual cell to be encoded in a molecular fashion. This information controls both the inherited characteristics of the next generation and the life processes of the organism itself. (See also p. 114.)

SEE ALSO

- THE BEGINNINGS OF LIFE p. 110
- GENETICS AND INHERITANCE p. 114
- OIL AND GAS p. 310
- RUBBER AND PLASTICS p. 316
- CHEMICALS AND BIO-TECHNOLOGY p. 320

Man-made Products

Our chemical knowledge of natural compounds will ultimately be dwarfed by that relating to man-made, or unnatural, products. The reason for this is that chemistry is not only the science that deals with molecules, but also an exercise in design and engineering at the molecular level. In so far as chemistry creates its own world, its practice in an abstract form has infinite possibilities.

Synthetic zeolites, which have important applications in the petrochemical industry, and ceramics, which have been found to behave as high-temperature superconductors, are typical examples of man-made products that are totally inorganic in their atomic composition. Likewise, liquid crystals – although based on organic compounds – are for the most part wholly synthetic compounds. Man-made products are also beginning to show promise in other areas, notably as *artificial enzymes*, i.e. tailor-made biological catalysts (see p. 53).

Liquid crystals

Discovered in 1888 by the Austrian botanist Friedrich Reinitzer, liquid crystals have been heralded as the fourth state of matter, occurring at the interface between the solid and the liquid phases. About 5% of crystalline compounds do not simply melt when heated: they form turbid (cloudy) liquids, which may also exhibit marked colour changes as the temperature is raised, before becoming normal liquids. The process is reversible: upon cooling, the liquid passes back through the so-called 'liquid-crystalline'

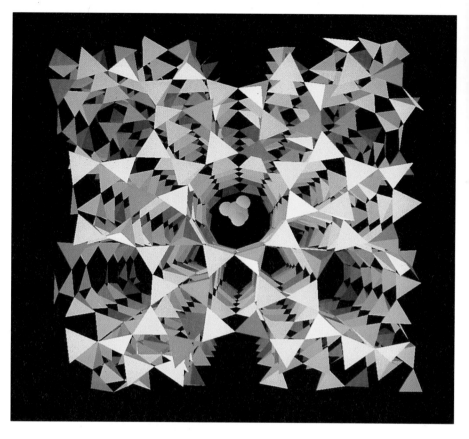

A computer-graphics representation of ZSM-5, with a methane molecule in the central channel. ZSM-5 is just one of a range of synthetic zeolites that have been tailor-made to accomplish specific tasks. The role of zeolites as molecular sieves and size-selective catalysts is due to their distinctive crystalline structure; the tiny channels and cavities are formed from tetrahedrons based on aluminium (red) and silicon (yellow).

state before solidifying again (see box). Generally, it is rod-shaped molecules, such as 4-n-hexyl-4'-cyanobiphenyl, that exhibit liquid-crystal behaviour.

Because of the relatively weak forces between the molecules of a liquid crystal, the interactions between the molecules and hence their relative orientations can be changed not only by temperature and pressure but also by electric and magnetic fields. The effect of temperature on the colour of liquid crystals has led to their use in the detection of tumours that are 'warmer' than surrounding healthy tissue. Their most familiar application is in the liquid-crystal displays (LCDs) used in watches and calculators, where their optical properties are controlled by applying electric fields to change the orientation of the molecules in the liquid crystal.

Synthetic zeolites

Natural zeolites are highly porous crystalline minerals, consisting mainly of silicon, aluminium and oxygen. They are built up of three-dimensional networks of silicate (SiO_4) and aluminate (AlO_4) tetra-

hedrons, arranged in such a way that they form tiny submicroscopic channels (see photo). In the natural state, these channels may hold water molecules; however, if the water is driven off by heat, other molecules of appropriate size can be absorbed.

Because the size of the channels determines the size of the molecules that can enter, zeolites are said to be *size-selective*. This property allows zeolites to be used as *molecular sieves*, which separate mixtures of compounds purely on the basis of their different sizes. For example, the zeolite chabazite contains channels of which the diameter is just 0.39 nanometres – or 0.00000000039 metres; these allow straight-chain hydrocarbons to pass through, while bulkier branched-chain hydrocarbons are retained. Zeolites can also be used as size-selective catalysts, since only molecules of a particular size can enter and undergo chemical reactions.

By altering the ratios of aluminium and silicon, along with conditions under which the zeolites are formed, chemists can fashion synthetic zeolites with different channel sizes and shapes. In this way a new generation of zeolites is being specifically designed to accomplish particular tasks. For instance, the synthetic zeolite ZSM-5 is used to convert toluene ($C_6H_5CH_3$) into benzene (C_6H_6) and para-xylene ($CH_3C_6H_4CH_3$), an intermediate in the production of polyester fibres. The catalytic activity of synthetic zeolites is increasingly being exploited in the pro-

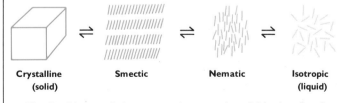

| Crystalline (solid) | Smectic | Nematic | Isotropic (liquid) |

The liquid-crystal phase occurs between the solid (ordered) and liquid (disordered) phases. The intermediate phase may take a number of slightly different forms, of which 'smectic' and 'nematic' are examples. The characteristic orientations of the molecules of a liquid-crystalline substance are due to the long, rod-like shape of the molecules, which allows a weak, long-range order to develop between each molecule and its neighbours. A typical example is 4-n-hexyl-4-cyanobiphenyl:

duction of petroleum (gasoline) to break down large straight-chain hydrocarbon molecules into smaller branched ones that lead to smoother performance in internal-combustion engines.

High-temperature superconductors

The amazing ability of a material to transmit an electrical current without showing any electrical resistance is known as *superconductivity* (see box and p. 37). In 1911 the Dutch physicist Heike Kamerlingh Onnes (1853–1926) discovered that the resistance of mercury falls to zero in liquid helium, which boils at 4.2 K (−268.8 °C / −452 °F). Progress was subsequently made in increasing the transition temperature to the superconducting state, notably by using certain alloys of niobium and titanium, but the major breakthrough came in 1986, when it was announced that a ceramic metal oxide of lanthanum (La), barium (Ba) and copper (Cu) loses its resistance at 30 K (−243 °C/ −405 °F). The frantic research activity that followed this announcement resulted in an oxide in which yttrium (Y) replaces lanthanum, with the formula $YBa_2Cu_3O_7$, which was demonstrated to be superconducting at liquid-nitrogen temperatures, just below 100 K (−173 °C / −279 °F). This material is often referred to as '1-2-3' because of the ratios of the metals involved. Further advances have since increased the transition temperature to around 125 K (−148 °C / −234 °F).

Another remarkable feature of superconducting materials is that within a bulk specimen there is no magnetic field. One important consequence of this is the so-called *Meissner effect* (named after one of its two discoverers), an awe-inspiring phenomenon in which a rotating magnet levitates above a superconductor (see box). Why does this happen? Simply because, when a magnet approaches a superconductor, a supercurrent is induced in the superconductor, which generates a magnetic field of the same polarity as that of the magnet and therefore repels it (see p. 34). Thus a superconductor – which can be viewed as a kind of magnetic mirror – responds electromagnetically to the magnet rotating above it and keeps it levitated.

The discovery of a practical room-temperature superconductor would undoubtedly bring about a major technological revolution. For instance, the transmission of electricity could be achieved effortlessly without energy loss, while the efficiency of computer chips could be greatly enhanced without risk of their burning themselves up. Yet even now in the early 1990s, *magnetic resonance imaging* (see p. 242) is already established in medical practice, using superconducting magnets composed of niobium–titanium alloys and operating at liquid-helium temperatures. Such magnets, again cooled by liquid helium, have also been used in experimental magnetically levitated (maglev) trains (see p. 347). SU

SEE ALSO

- ELECTRICITY IN ACTION p. 36
- NATURAL COMPOUNDS p. 52
- CHEMICALS IN EVERYDAY LIFE p. 56
- RUBBER AND PLASTICS p. 316
- CHEMICALS AND BIO-TECHNOLOGY p. 320

SUPERCONDUCTIVITY

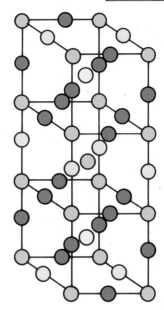

The '1–2–3' compound ($YBa_2Cu_3O_7$) was the first substance shown to become superconducting at liquid-nitrogen temperatures, just below 100 K (−173 °C / −279 °F). The lattice structure of superconductors causes moving electrons to join together in pairs; because the pairs are in the lowest possible energy state (see p. 38), they cannot lose energy and so electrical resistance is reduced to zero.

- ⬤ Yttrium (Y)
- ◯ Barium (Ba)
- ⬤ Copper (Cu)
- ⬤ Oxygen (O)
- ◯ Oxygen vacancy

The Meissner effect: a rotating magnet is seen levitating above a nitrogen-cooled specimen of the superconducting material '1–2–3'. A major technological revolution is expected to follow the discovery of materials that become superconducting at less extreme temperatures. Superconducting magnets cooled by liquid helium have already been used in prototypes of magnetically levitated trains (see p. 347).

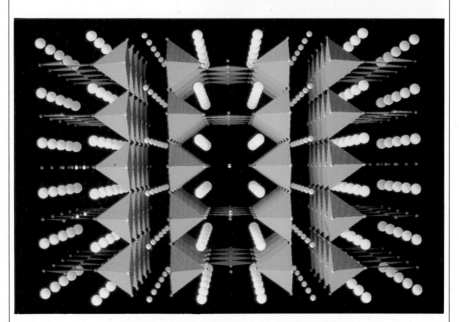

The crystal structure of 1–2–3, as displayed in a computer-graphics image. Copper atoms occur at the centre of layers of copper oxide pyramids (green) and planes (dark blue); oxygen atoms are red, yttrium atoms light blue, and barium atoms yellow.

Chemicals in Everyday Life

We live with chemicals all around us – and we are ourselves a highly complex assembly of chemical compounds. Chemicals are to be found where we live, where we work and as we travel. They influence the way we grow our food, control our environment, and protect our health; they can brighten our lives and enhance the quality of our everyday experiences.

Few people realize the extent to which chemistry supports and pervades many aspects of modern life. Man-made fibres such as nylon and polyester have revolutionized the fashion industry, while computers rely on materials developed through chemistry for their operation. However, most of the chemicals we come into contact with are mixtures, or formulations, rather than pure chemical compounds. In some formulations, the properties of certain chemicals are enhanced by the presence of others. In other products, such as soap powders, particular chemicals may be present simply in order to provide a more convenient medium in which the active chemicals can operate.

Synthetic polymers

One of the most far-reaching influences chemistry has had on our lives in the 20th century has been the introduction of increasingly advanced materials based on *synthetic polymers* (see also pp. 316–17).

Nylon 66

Kevlar

Victrex PEEK

A selection of synthetic polymers. The advent of the synthetic fibre nylon in the 1930s (see p. 317) caused a major revolution in the fashion industry. Technological demands for light, high-strength materials were the driving force behind the production of the latest synthetic polymers, such as Kevlar and Victrex PEEK. The square brackets indicate that the illustrated structure (the monomer unit) recurs again and again to form long polymer chains.

These are materials composed of repeating small molecules, or *monomers*, joined together to make long chains. The way in which these chains interact with one another depends on the monomers from which they are composed, and can differ greatly. This accounts for the wide range of properties that polymers can possess, including flexibility, strength and heat resistance. Demand for improved materials, both for technological and household application, is still increasing, and – although already widespread – there is still a lot more polymer-based technology to come into our lives.

Along with the emergence of excellent new dyes and paints, the fashion and display industries have been revolutionized by the advent of polyester fibres such as Dacron, and polyamide fibres such as Nylon 6 and Nylon 66 (see p. 316). These early synthetic polymers were all composed of moderately flexible chains. More recently, stiff-chain polymers – often incorporating aromatic rings (see p. 52) – have found many applications. Because of their low flammability, high thermal stability and great tensile strength, compounds such as Kevlar and Victrex PEEK (see box) are becoming very widespread; they may be found in an enormous range of products, from electrically heated hair-styling brushes to bullet-proof vests.

Not only has Kevlar a tensile strength higher than that of steel but it also has a strength-to-weight ratio that is six times better. Composite materials containing Kevlar have been used to build the tail sections of jumbo jets; it is transparent to radar, it eliminates corrosion, and its lightness lowers fuel costs. The outstanding mechanical and electrical properties of Victrex PEEK, particularly when employed in fibre-reinforced composites with glass, carbon or Kevlar, are such that it can be used to replace metal alloys to great advantage in many engineering situations. The day of the all-plastic motor car is just around the corner.

Agrochemicals

At the end of the 20th century, the challenge of feeding the world's growing population can only be met with the aid of chemicals produced by the fertilizer industry (see also p. 320). In addition to sunlight, oxygen, carbon dioxide and water, plants require *macro-nutrients* – as well as trace elements – from the soil (see p. 116). By far the most important of these are nitrogen (N), phosphorus (P) and potassium (K). The fertilizer industry provides compounds in which these macro-nutrients are in a form that can be readily used by plants, principally as water-soluble salts: nitrogen as nitrates (NO_3^-) of sodium and potassium, and as ammonium sulphate ((NH_4)$_2SO_4$); phosphorus as phosphates (PO_4^{3-}) and potassium as potash (K_2O). Commercially produced

fertilizers are currently responsible for approximately 50% of Europe's agricultural output.

Pesticides (see also p. 321) have been developed in order to protect crops from predators such as insects (insecticides) and from fungi (fungicides), or simply to prevent them from being overrun by weeds (herbicides). Pesticides have two general modes of action by which they achieve these ends: non-systemically active pesticides do not actually penetrate the plant surface – for this reason they are known as contact killers; systemically active pesticides are taken up by the plant's vascular system and inhibit some life-sustaining process. The latter is more desirable, since the chemical is thereby located within the plant itself and is less prone to being washed away into the surrounding water table, but it is a much more difficult goal to achieve. It is only in the last 50 years that effective systemically active pesticides have proved successful. An example is Glyphosate, a widely used herbicide that kills weeds by inhibiting the biological synthesis of a family of vital amino acids:

Glyphosate

Chemistry in medicine

The enormous influence of pharmaceutical products (see also pp. 243 and 320–1) upon modern medical practice is an illustration of the problem-solving capacity of chemistry. Some of the greatest advances in medicine in the last 150 years have come about as a result of advances in chemical thinking and a growing appreciation of the chemical processes occurring in our bodies. The development of chemistry allowed people not only to isolate the active components in herbal remedies, but to start to synthesize them – and, more importantly, to synthesize closely related analogues that often display even greater activity.

The first advance was the development of *anaesthetic gases*, used to render patients insensitive during surgical operations (see p. 249). The first widely used anaesthetics were chloroform ($CHCl_3$) and ether ($CH_3CH_2OCH_2CH_3$); however, chloroform was discovered to have undesirable side-effects and was replaced by the gas nitrous oxide (N_2O; see pp. 41 and 49) and fluorocarbons. *Antiseptics*, such as phenol (C_6H_5OH), were also introduced to surgery in the 19th century (see p. 249), to prevent bacterial infections. A related category of compounds – *disinfectants* – also kill bacteria and microorganisms, but because of their strength they are only used on non-living objects. Common examples of disinfectants include sodium hypochlorite (NaOCl) and hydrogen peroxide (H_2O_2). Some of these compounds

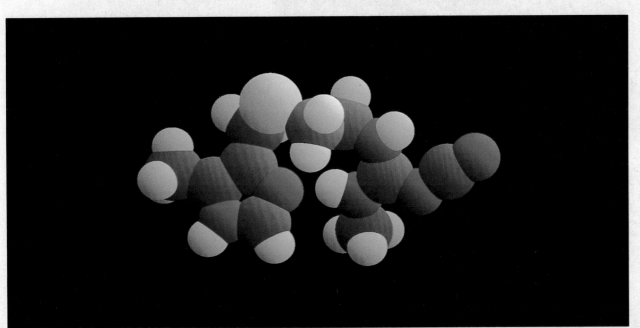

Ampicillin is one of a family of closely related antibiotics – the penicillins. Because of the shape of these drugs, the enzyme in the invading bacterium responsible for cell-wall construction mistakes them for constituents of the cell wall. Once this has occurred, the enzyme cannot continue its work, the wall protecting the cell is left unfinished and the cell can be destroyed by the body's immune system (see p. 212).

have survived, but most have been replaced by more effective and less toxic alternatives.

One of the most important classes of drugs to be discovered are the *antibiotics*. These are drugs that generally work by aiding the body's own defence system, helping the white blood cells to stop bacterial cells from multiplying. The first antibiotic was discovered by chance in 1928 by Alexander Fleming (see pp. 238 and 249). However, it was not until after World War II that the active ingredient – *penicillin* – could be identified and produced in large enough quantities for clinical trials; its success was then immediate. Many different types of penicillin exist, but they all share the same basic structure as ampicillin (see box, left).

Certain medical problems, particularly those associated with heart disease and ulcers, have been aggravated by the stresses imposed by modern life styles. Combating such medical conditions has become a major concern of pharmaceutical companies, and a number of spectacularly successful drugs have recently been produced (see box, below).   SU

SEE ALSO

- WHAT IS CHEMISTRY? p. 40
- NATURAL COMPOUNDS p. 52
- MAN-MADE PRODUCTS p. 54
- MEDICAL TECHNOLOGY p. 242
- THREATS TO THE ENVIRONMENT p. 300
- OIL AND GAS p. 310
- RUBBER AND PLASTICS p. 316
- CHEMICALS AND BIO-TECHNOLOGY p. 320

BETA-BLOCKERS AND ULCER DRUGS

Tagamet (cimetidine)

In 1958 the Scottish pharmacologist James Black (1924–), convinced that the challenge in pharmacology was to reduce the randomness in the game of 'molecular roulette' played by drug companies at the time, applied his unconventional thinking to coronary heart disease. He initiated a search for a compound that would combat the undesired effect of increasing heart rate and muscle tension brought about by adrenaline, the hormone released under panic to prepare the body for 'fight or flight'. The molecules of such a compound, he argued, would have to bind to the so-called beta-adrenergic receptors in the heart and thus block the action of adrenaline molecules, without exhibiting their undesired physiological activity. This led to the synthesis of propanolol (Inderal), which was launched in 1964 and was the first of the *beta-blockers*. Many more have subsequently appeared on the market, and today atenolol (Tenormin) is the most widely prescribed drug for the management of hypertension and coronary heart disease.

In 1964 James Black applied a similar line of reasoning in search of a drug to treat ulcers. Histamine in the body is capable of interacting with two receptor sites – at the H_1 receptor during allergic responses and at the H_2 receptor, causing increased gastric-acid secretion, which in turn leads to ulceration of the stomach and/or the duodenum. The need was to find a drug that would compete successfully for the H_2 receptor without blocking the H_1 receptor, at which the older anti-histamines were known to act. After 12 years and the synthesis of 12 000 compounds at a cost of millions of pounds, the anTAGonist

ciMETidine or 'TAGaMET' was introduced into clinical practice to wide acclaim. By preventing gastric-acid secretion, it proved to be spectacular in healing peptic ulcers, and surgical operations for duodenal ulcers became less and less necessary. Subsequently a team of researchers discovered that a simple modification of cimetidine led to the ulcer drug ranitidine (Zantac), which has fewer side-effects than Tagamet. Not only have these drugs proved to be a blessing for thousands of people with ulcers, but they have also benefited national economies by reducing drastically the numbers of patients requiring hospitalization.

The ulcer drugs Zantac and Tagamet are currently two of the three most important pharmaceutical products, with annual sales throughout the world running at $1500 million and $1000 million respectively. The third, also with annual sales of $1000 million, is Tenormin – one of the descendants of James Black's first beta-blocker.

The Scientific Method

The spectacular successes of the natural sciences from the 17th century onwards have prompted a search for 'the scientific method'. Until the 20th century this was seen as the search for a general set of instructions or recipe for getting scientific results. But nowadays it has become an attempt to describe the general aims of science. Scientific method is now thought of as whatever in practice serves to promote those aims.

Asking what all the various subjects popularly called 'sciences' have in common would yield only platitudes like 'Don't jump to conclusions in the absence of firm evidence.' So attention has focused on clear *paradigms* – or models – of science such as physics. Physical theories are paradigms of *comprehensiveness* because they explain physical processes that vary in scale from the subatomic (about 10^{-15} m or less) to the astronomical (billions of billions of kilometres), and vary in time from about 10^{-24} seconds to billions of years. Furthermore, physical theories yield paradigms of *accurate prediction*. For example, NASA was able to calculate the speed, direction and time of launch needed to send the *Voyager 2* spacecraft, without any later course correction, on a journey of thousands of millions of kilometres passing close to each of the outer planets in turn.

By studying paradigms of science we may hope to answer still controversial questions such as 'Is Freudian psychiatry really scientific?' or 'Can social or historical processes be explained scientifically, as Karl Marx claimed?'

Physics as a paradigm of science

Galileo and Descartes (see p. 60) were the first to insist clearly that science should employ only precise mathematical concepts in its theories. The application of such a theory to physical reality will then be a calculation in applied mathematics. This is the feature that makes physical theories so comprehensive and such precise predictors.

Sir Karl Popper. According to Popper, knowledge is better advanced by scientists attempting to *disprove* theories, rather than trying to prove them.

Newton, for example, needed only four laws to explain the orbits of the moon and planets to the accuracy afforded by available measuring instruments (see p. 20). But those same laws also explain the rate at which a body falls, the motion of a pendulum, and even a simplified version of the relation between the temperature, pressure and volume of a gas. Set out in full the calculations would be very long, because the very same small set of laws are being used to explain such diverse phenomena. Such mathematical calculations are logical, *deductive inferences* (see box). Deductive inferences using *non-*mathematical concepts, on the other hand, cannot in practice be sustained for long without losing their credibility. Hence the central role of mathematics in physics. Theories employing non-mathematical concepts could not achieve such comprehensiveness and precision.

However, not all successful sciences match the paradigm of physics. Darwin's theory of evolution (see p. 112) and Pasteur's germ theory of disease (see pp. 248–9) are examples of theories using non-mathematical concepts. But biologists seek to use quantitative mathematical conceptions wherever they can.

The ideal of science, and the practice

Full comprehensiveness is an ideal yet to be achieved. The two current leading theories, quantum mechanics (which explains atomic processes, see p. 26) and the general theory of relativity (which explains astronomical processes, see p. 26) are mutually inconsistent, although *both* are firmly accepted by all physicists. But comprehensiveness remains an *ideal* of physics, because physicists recognize this inconsistency as a problem requiring resolution.

Surprisingly, a theory can be accepted as true even though it is known to make

The medieval world view is broken.
This l6th-century German woodcut is a symbolic celebration of the attempts of Renaissance astronomers to penetrate appearances and find the mechanisms underlying the universe.

some false predictions. For example, it was well known in the 19th century that Newton's laws could not be squared with the precise orbit of the planet Mercury. However, because Newton's laws were so successful elsewhere, 19th-century physicists regarded Mercury's orbit as an unexplained anomaly that did not shake their belief in Newton's laws. Only after those laws had been superseded by the theory of relativity was the orbit of Mercury regarded as one of the facts that refuted Newton.

The problem of induction

Inductive inferences (see box) were long supposed by philosophers to provide a recipe for *devising* justified theories. Nowadays we know that theories are due more to the creative imagination of the scientist than to inference. Induction has been relegated to the *justification* of theories, once devised, by experiment. Such justification is inductive because the information contained in the conclusion (a *general* theory) goes beyond the information stored in the premises (reports of *particular* observations).

Even this reduced role for induction was rejected by the Scottish philosopher David Hume (1711–76), who argued that inductive inferences give no justification whatever for belief in their conclusions. No matter how many times an experiment has been repeated with a positive result, Hume claims, it does not make a theory probable nor even more likely to be true than false.

However, Hume is making a *logical* not a practical point. He recognizes that in

An experimental biochemical laboratory. Many of the observed phenomena upon which scientists seek to build theories are in the form of specially designed experiments. Such experiments are often used to test a *hypothesis* – a suggested explanation for a collection of known facts. If the experiments confirm the hypothesis, the hypothesis may be elevated to the more certain status of a *theory*. However, such a theory is never – in the strictest sense – a logical conclusion from the observed facts.

DEDUCTIVE AND INDUCTIVE INFERENCES

Here is a simple *deductive* inference. Given the premises

All rabbits are mammals.

All mammals have kidneys.

we *deduce* the conclusion

All rabbits have kidneys.

The defining characteristic of a valid deductive argument is that it is *impossible* for all the premises to be true and the conclusion false, because the information contained in the conclusion is already stored in the premises, taken collectively. Mathematical calculations are deductive inferences.

Here is a simple *inductive* inference. Given the premise

All observed ravens are black.

we *induce* the conclusion

All ravens, whether observed or not, are black.

The defining characteristic of an inductive argument is that the information contained in the conclusion *goes beyond* the information contained in the pre-

mises. Hence it is *possible* for inductive arguments to let us down – for their premises to be true but their conclusions false.

Indeed, inductive inferences have been known to let us down. Once upon a time we were in a position to assert

All observed swans are white.

and hence to induce the conclusion

All swans are white.

But then black swans were discovered in Australia.

Deductive inferences, no matter how long, have been codified and the rules for their validity worked out. Inductive inferences have resisted codification, and their validity is controversial.

***Explanations* of particular experimental results by theories use *deductive* inferences. *Justification* of a theory by experimental results uses *inductive* inferences, although of a kind more complex than the simple example given.**

practice scientists do believe theories that are supported by a wide variety of instances drawn from a large sample. He is not recommending that they change their method, but is claiming that it cannot be *logically* justified.

Sir Karl Popper (1902–   ), the British philosopher, endorses Hume's radical rejection of induction. But Popper claims that science is nonetheless a rational enterprise because the real role of observation and experiment is to *refute* theories, not to confirm them – the contrary beliefs of practising scientists notwithstanding. Popper switches from confirmation to refutation of theories because refutation employs only *deductive inferences* (see box).

Popper's heroic attempt fails to purge induction from science. Popper recognizes that a theory is refuted only by experiments that are indefinitely repeatable. But a belief that an experiment is indefinitely repeatable (the belief needed to refute a theory) is an inductive conclusion from evidence that it has been repeated some number of times.

To what extent science needs induction, and the validity of inductive inferences, remain controversial questions.   JE

SEE ALSO

● THE HISTORY OF ASTRONOMY p. 16
● THE HISTORY OF SCIENCE p. 58
● THE HISTORY OF MEDICINE p. 248
● PHILOSOPHY p. 486–97

The History of Science

If we consider science as the systematic investigation of reality by observation, experimentation and induction (see pp. 58–9), then among early civilizations science did not exist. Certainly discoveries were made, but they were piecemeal. Myth and religion dominated as modes for explaining the world.

This began to change with the speculations of the early Greek philosophers, who excluded supernatural causes from their accounts of reality. By the 3rd century BC Greek science was highly sophisticated and producing theoretical models that have shaped the development of science ever since.

With the fall of Greece to the Roman Empire, science fell from grace. Few important advances were made outside medicine, and the work done was firmly within the Greek traditions and conceptual frameworks.

For several centuries from the fall of Rome in the 5th century AD, science was practically unknown in Western Europe. Islamic culture alone preserved Greek knowledge (see p. 392), and later transmitted it back to the West (see p. 406). Between the 13th and 15th centuries some advances were made in the fields of mech-

anics and optics, while men like Roger Bacon insisted on the importance of personal experience and observation.

The 16th century marked the coming of the so-called 'Scientific Revolution', a period of scientific progress beginning with Copernicus (see p. 16) and culminating with Newton (see pp. 17 and 20). Not only did science break new conceptual ground but it gained enormously in prestige as a result. Science and its trappings became highly fashionable from the later 17th century, and also attracted a great deal of royal and state patronage. The founding of the Académie des Sciences by Louis XIV in France and the Royal Society by Charles II in Britain were landmarks in this trend.

In the course of the 19th century science became professionalized, with clearcut career structures and hierarchies emerging, centred on universities, government

The Alchemist (detail) by the 17th century Dutch painter Adriaen van Ostade. Although the theoretical basis of alchemy was an extraordinary mixture of occult and esoteric ideas, the alchemists of the Middle Ages made many practical chemical discoveries, including alcohol and the mineral acids. (National Gallery, London/Bildarchiv Preussischer Kulturbesitz)

MAJOR DEVELOPMENTS IN SCIENCE

3500–3000 BC
The Sumerians develop metallurgy and the use of a lunar calendar.

3000–2500 BC
Multiplication tables are invented and mathematics used for calculating areas. In Egypt a solar calendar is used.

2500–2000 BC
A superior lunar calendar is used in Babylon. Units of time such as the minute and hour are introduced.

2000–1500 BC
Babylonians use maths to plot planetary positions. The stellar constellations are identified. Simple taxonomies for classifying animals are used.

1500–1000 BC
Mathematics continues to develop. Chemicals are used to make paints and cosmetics.

1000–500 BC
Early Greek philosophers conceive rational theories of the universe. Those of **Thales of Miletus** (640–560 BC; see p. 16) and **Anaximander** (611–547 BC) are notable. Anaximander introduced the concept of infinity into cosmology and believed that life had evolved from the sea. The notion that the world is a sphere is attributed to **Pythagoras** (c. 580–c. 500 BC), who also formulated basic laws of geometry (see pp. 62–3).

500–400 BC
The concept of elementary matter was introduced by **Empedocles of Agrigentum** (c. 490–430 BC), who believed that there are four elements, namely earth, water, fire and air. **Democritus** (c. 460–c. 370 BC) and **Leucippus** (c. 500–450 BC) conceived of matter as consisting of minute invisible particles called atoms (see p. 38).

400–300 BC
The first fully comprehensive cosmology to give a rational account of all physical phenomena was devised by **Aristotle** (384–322 BC; see also p. 486). He divided the universe into two distinct regions. Below the sphere of the Moon was the realm of the four elements and of change and

decay. Above was the realm of a fifth element, the ether, changeless and divine. Each element had its natural place and motion, the ether moving in circles around the Earth, and carrying the stars with it. Aristotle's cosmology and physics ruled until the time of Galileo and Newton. Aristotle did the first systematic work on comparative biology (see p. 108).

300–200 BC
Archimedes of Syracuse (287–212 BC) pioneered the sciences of mechanics and hydrostatics (see pp. 22–3), invented the lever and the Archimedian screw for raising water, and made many contributions to mathematics. Observational astronomy reached its peak with **Aristarchus of Samos** (c. 310–250 BC; see p. 16), who realized that the Earth rotates on its own axis and orbits the Sun. Geography was founded by **Eratosthenes of Cyrene** (276–196 BC; see p. 16), who calculated the circumference of the Earth to within 7 km (4 mi) of the modern value.

200–100 BC
The most accurate ancient star catalogue was constructed by **Hipparchus of Nicaea** (c. 190–120 BC), who also discovered the precession of the equinoxes.

100 BC–AD 100
Little original science was done in these centuries, although Greek astronomy was perfected by **Ptolemy** (Claudius Ptolemaeus, AD 100–170), in whose system the Earth was the centre of the universe (see p. 16), so rejecting the theory of Aristarchus. Greek knowledge was codified by encyclopedists such as **Pliny the Elder** (Gaius Plinius Secundus, AD 23–79). The earliest known alchemical text appeared; alchemy was a mystical forefather of chemistry that sought to transmute base metals into gold and produce the elixir of eternal life.

AD 200–1200
Much of classical learning disappeared from Europe during the so-called 'Dark Ages', but was preserved by Islamic scholars such as **Avicenna** (Ibn Sinna, AD 980–1037) and **Averroës** (ibn-Rushd, 1126–98; see p. 392). From c. 1100 it was transmitted back when Christian scholars such as **Gerard of Cremona** (1145–87) translated Arabic texts into Latin and began to assimilate ancient knowledge.

1200–1300
Albertus Magnus (Count von Böllstadt, c. 1193–1280), a German scholastic philosopher, patron saint of scientists and teacher of Aquinas (see p. 486), worked to reconcile Aristotelian science and philosophy with Christian doctrine. The English friar **Roger Bacon** (c. 1214–92) became a great advocate of experimentation. He did important work in optics and was the first European to describe the manufacture of gunpowder. He was also a great speculator, proposing flying machines and mechanically powered ships and carriages. The man considered by Bacon to be the greatest experimental scientist of his day was the French crusader **Petrus Peregrinus** (active 13th century), who described in detail the use of the magnetic compass in navigation.

1300–1400
The English philosopher **William of Ockham** (c. 1285–1349) propounded the principle (known as *Ockham's razor*) that 'entities are not to be multiplied beyond necessity'. This principle, that the simplest explanation is the best, was adopted by many later scientists, including the French bishop **Nicole d'Oresme** (c. 1325–82), who worked on cosmology and motion. In the latter field, Oresme confirmed the theories of the Merton School at Oxford, and both Oresme and the Mertonians worked on the mathematization of science.

1400–1500
There was little of scientific note in this century, although at the end of the century **Leonardo da Vinci** (1452–1519) began his studies of all kinds of natural phenomena (see p. 525). The discovery of the New World in 1492 contradicted the geographical teachings of Ptolemy, so helping to free science from its psychological dependence on ancient authorities.

1500–1550
Nicholas Copernicus (1473–1543), the Polish astronomer, revived the heliocentric theory, placing the Sun at the centre of the universe (see p. 16). Because this theory threatened the Church's cosmology, Copernicus only circulated it among a few friends. Chemistry was to some extent freed from its alchemical bonds by **Paracelsus** (real name Theophrastus Bombastus von Hohenheim, 1493–1541).

A laboratory (far left) at Giessen University, Germany. In the 19th century this small university became the centre of the world for chemical research. This was largely due to the presence there of Justus von Liebig (1803–73), who did much to establish the new science of organic chemistry.

Marie Curie (1867–1934), the Polish scientist who, with her French husband Pierre (1859–1906) and Henri Becquerel (1852–1908), received the 1903 Nobel Prize for Physics for the discovery of radioactivity. She also received the 1911 Prize for Chemistry for her discovery of the elements radium and polonium.

departments and commercial organizations. This trend continued into the 20th century, which has seen science become highly dependent on technological advances. These have not been lacking.

Modern science is immense and extremely complex. It is virtually impossible to have an informed overview of what science as a whole is up to. This has made many people

regard it with some suspicion. Nevertheless Western civilization is fully committed to a belief in the value of scientific progress as a force for the good of humanity. While some of the world's greatest dangers and horrors have their roots in scientific endeavour, there is some hope that science will also eventually provide viable solutions to them.   BB

SEE ALSO

- ASTRONOMY pp. 4–15
- THE HISTORY OF ASTRONOMY p. 16
- PHYSICS pp. 20–39
- CHEMISTRY pp. 40–57
- THE SCIENTIFIC METHOD p. 59
- MATHEMATICS pp. 62–73
- EARTH SCIENCES pp. 76–105
- LIFE SCIENCES pp. 108–245
- THE HISTORY OF MEDICINE p. 248
- TECHNOLOGY pp. 304–57

1550–1600

The study of terrestrial magnetism was developed by English physician **William Gilbert** (1540–1603), who introduced the concept of magnetic poles (see p. 34). **Tycho Brahe** (1546–1601; see p. 16) produced a very accurate star catalogue, and his assistant **Johann Kepler** (1571–1630; see p. 17) demonstrated that planetary orbits round the Sun are elliptical. The English statesman and philosopher **Sir Francis Bacon** (1561–1626) revived the use of induction in scientific method (see p. 59).

1600–1650

The modern science of mechanics (statics; see pp. 20–3) was founded by **Galileo Galilei** (1564–1642). Galileo formulated laws of motion that conflicted with ancient physics, and tended to support the heliocentric hypothesis (see p. 17). The French philosopher and mathematician **René Descartes** (1596–1650; see also pp. 62, 418 and 486) proposed a radically mechanistic model of the universe that rendered God virtually redundant. He invented coordinate geometry (see p. 70).

1650–1700

The controversy between ancient and modern cosmologies and physics was resolved in the work of Englishman **Sir Isaac Newton** (1643–1727). He formulated the law of universal gravitation and three laws of motion (see pp. 20–1) and made important contributions to optics and calculus (see p. 70). Chemistry continued to be separated from its alchemical roots by the work of men such as the English scientists **Robert Boyle** (1627–1716) and **Robert Hooke** (1635–1703), who studied the chemistry of gases and the nature of respiration and combustion.

1700–1750

This problem was also tackled by the German chemist **Georg Stahl** (1660–1743), who suggested a hypothetical substance called *phlogiston* as the causal agent of combustion.

1750–1800

The Swedish botanist **Carl Linnaeus** (1707–78) introduced his binomial system of biological classification (see p. 108). The phlogiston theory was rendered obsolete with the discovery of oxygen by the English chemist and radical

Joseph Priestley (1733–1804), who also invented soda water. However, it was left to the Frenchman **Antoine Lavoisier** (1743–94) to name oxygen and demonstrate its role in combustion. Lavoisier also formulated the important law of conservation of matter and recognized that air and water are chemical compounds. In geology the Scotsman **James Hutton** (1726–97) introduced the notion that the Earth is millions of years old, denying catastrophes such as Noah's Flood. The Frenchman **Charles Augustin Coulomb** (1736–1806) first identified the electric force (see p. 34). In Italy **Count Alessandro Volta** (1745–1827) made important experiments with electricity (see p. 36), while the Frenchman **André Ampère** (1775–1836) did pioneering work on electricity and magnetism (see pp. 34–5). The concept of 'biology' was established by the Frenchman **Jean-Baptiste Lamarck** (1744–1829), who also set out a theory of evolution (see p. 112).

1800–1850

The conceptual groundwork of modern chemistry was laid by the Englishman **John Dalton** (1766–1844) when he revived atomic theory (see p. 38) and applied it to gases. The Englishman **Michael Faraday** (1791–1867) and the American **Joseph Henry** (1797–1878) separately discovered electromagnetic induction (see pp. 34–5), the basis of electricity generation. Study of the nature of heat was furthered by American-born physicist **Benjamin Thompson** (Count Rumford, 1753–1814), who suggested that it was a form of motion rather than a substance. The English amateur scientist **James Joule** (1818–89) did important work on thermodynamics (see pp. 24–5), discovering the principle of the mechanical equivalent of heat, and helping to develop the principle of the conservation of energy.

1850–1900

Thermodynamics was furthered by the Scottish physicist **William Thomson** (**Lord Kelvin**, 1824–1907). The Russian chemist **Dmitri Mendeleyev** (1834–1907) compiled the first periodic table of chemical elements (see p. 42). The English naturalist **Charles Darwin** (1809–92) revolutionized biology with his theory of evolution by natural selection (see p. 112). The study of genetics was furthered by the Austrian monk **Gregor Mendel**

(1822–84), who demonstrated that inheritance involves dominant and recessive characteristics (see p. 114). The Scottish physicist **James Clerk Maxwell** (1831–79) established the concept of the electromagnetic force (see p. 35), and in 1887 the existence of electromagnetic waves was demonstrated experimentally by the German physicist **Heinrich Rudolf Hertz** (1857–94). At the end of the century another German physicist **Wilhelm Röntgen** (1845–1923) discovered X-rays, a fundamental research tool in physics and a vital diagnostic tool in medicine (see pp. 35, 242 and 332). **Ernest Rutherford** (1871–1937), an English physicist, used X-rays to investigate gases, and discovered alpha, beta and gamma rays (see pp. 38–9 and below).

1900–PRESENT

Mendel's work was developed by the American geneticist **Thomas Hunt Morgan** (1866–1945), the discoverer of chromosomes (see pp. 114–5). After the Canadian bacteriologist **Oswald Avery** (1877–1955) had demonstrated that DNA is responsible for inheritance, the Anglo-American team of **Francis Crick** (1916–), **James Watson** (1928–) and **Maurice Wilkins** (1916–) were able in 1953 to unravel its structure (see p. 114).

The structure of atoms was investigated by Ernest Rutherford, who discovered the atomic nucleus (see p. 38). The German physicist **Albert Einstein** (1879–1955) radically revised classical physics and with his theories of special and general relativity (see p. 27). The German **Max Planck** (1858–1947) formulated quantum theory (see p. 26), which was applied to Rutherford's atom by the Dane **Niels Bohr** (1885–1962), thereby effecting another major revision of classical physics (see p. 38). Understanding of the structure of the atom and the tremendous forces locked into it led to the development of nuclear power and nuclear weapons.

Modern science is dominated by expensive technology and extreme specialization. In physics subatomic particles (see p. 39) continue to be investigated, and are thought to hold the key to understanding the origin and ultimate nature of the universe. In biology, genetic engineering (see pp. 189, 191 and 197) has become feasible and may produce untold benefits – or otherwise.

Mathematics and its Applications

Many people think of mathematics in terms of rules to be learned in order to manipulate symbols or study numbers or shapes in the abstract for their own sake. Mathematical theory does develop in the abstract; it need have no dependence on anything outside itself. The truth of the theory is measured by logic rather than experiment. However, one of its most valuable uses is in describing or modelling processes in the real world, and thus there is constant interaction between pure mathematics and applied mathematics.

Mathematics may be considered as the very general study of the structure of systems. Since the study is unrelated to the physical world, rigorous formal proofs are sought, rather than experimental verifications. Theory is presented in terms of a small number of given truths (known as *axioms*) from which the entire theory can be inferred.

Thus, the aims are for generality in approach and rigour in proof, aims that explain the traditional concern of mathematicians for the unification of seemingly different branches of mathematics. As an example, Descartes showed that geometrical figures could be described in terms of algebra (see p. 70), enabling geometric proofs to be established in terms of arithmetic, so that both generality and rigour were advanced.

Applied mathematics and modelling

There is no sharp boundary between the study of mathematical systems in the abstract (the field of *pure mathematics)* and the study of such systems to make inferences about certain physical systems that are described by the mathematical theory (the field of *applied mathematics*). In principle, any branch of mathematics may turn out to describe some physical, economic, biological, medical, or other system. *Modelling* a physical system consists of seeking a formal mathematical theory that conforms with the properties of the physical system. Often, as for example in computer simulations of space travel, the mathematical theories are very large and complex, but sometimes the model can be quite simple. Sometimes, known mathematics can describe and predict the behaviour of the system; at other times, the modelling can give rise to completely new branches of mathematics.

Applied mathematics encompasses many specialized fields in which the relationships between the experimental findings and the mathematical theories are well established. Although the subject can include the application of statistical theory to such areas as sociology, the term is usually restricted to the application of the methods of advanced calculus, linear algebra and other branches of advanced mathematics to physical and technological processes.

Triangulation, geometry and trigonometry

A simple example of a mathematical model is the representation of a portion of the Earth's surface by a set of interlocking triangles, from the measurement of which maps may be constructed. The triangulation model uses the rules of geometry and trigonometry to derive angles and distances that cannot be measured directly.

SOME EMINENT MATHEMATICIANS

Pythagoras (c. 582–500 BC), Greek philosopher. Born in Samos, he founded a religious community at Croton in southern Italy. The Pythagorean brotherhood saw mystical significance in the idea of number. Popularly remembered today for Pythagoras' theorem (see main text).

Euclid (c. 3rd century BC), Greek mathematician. Euclid devised the first axiomatic treatment of geometry and studied irrational numbers (see p. 65). Until recent times, most elementary geometry textbooks were little more than versions of Euclid's great book.

Archimedes (c. 287–212 BC), Greek mathematician, philosopher and engineer, born in Syracuse, Sicily. His extensions of the work of Euclid especially concerned the surface and volume of the sphere and the study of other solid shapes. His methods anticipated the fundamentals of integral calculus.

Descartes, René (1596-1650), French philosopher, mathematician and military scientist. Descartes sought an axiomatic treatment of all knowledge, and is known for his doctrine that all knowledge can be derived from the one certainty: *Cogito ergo sum* ('I think therefore I am'). One of his major mathematical contributions was the development of analytical geometry, whereby geometrical figures can be described in algebraic terms (see p. 70).

Newton, Sir Isaac (1643–1727), English mathematician, astronomer and physicist. Newton came to be recognized as the most influential scientist of all time. He developed differential calculus (see p. 70) and his treatments of gravity and motion (see pp. 20–1) form the basis of much applied mathematics.

Euler, Leonhard (1707–83), Swiss-born mathematician, who worked mainly in Berlin and St Petersburg. He was particularly famed for being able to perform complex calculations in his head, and so was able to go on working after he went blind. He worked in almost all branches of mathematics and made particular contributions to analytical geometry, trigonometry and calculus, and thus to the unification of mathematics. Euler was responsible for much of modern mathematical notation.

Gauss, Carl Friedrich (1777–1855), German mathematician. He developed the theory of complex numbers (see p. 65). He was director of the astronomical observatory at Göttingen and conducted a survey, based on trigonometric techniques, of the kingdom of Hanover. He published works in many fields, including the application of mathematics to electrostatics and electrodynamics.

Cauchy, Baron Augustin-Louis (1789–1857), French mathematician and physicist. He developed the modern treatment of calculus and also the theory of functions (see pp. 70–1), as well as introducing rigour to much of mathematics. As an engineer he contributed to Napoleon's preparations to invade Britain, and he twice gave up academic posts to serve the exiled Charles X.

Boole, George (1815–64), English mathematician. Despite being largely self-taught, Boole became Professor of Mathematics at Cork University. He laid the foundations of Boolean algebra, which was fundamental to the development of the digital electronic computer (see p. 334).

Cantor, Georg (1845–1918), Russian-born mathematician who spent most of his life in Germany. His most important work was on finite and infinite sets (see p. 68). He was greatly interested in theology and philosophy.

Klein, Christian Felix (1849–1925), German mathematician. Klein introduced a programme for the classification of geometry in terms of group theory. His interest in *topology* (the study of geometric figures that are subjected to deformations) produced the first description of a *Klein bottle* – which has a continuous one-sided surface.

Hilbert, David (1862–1943), German mathematician. In 1901, Hilbert listed 23 major unsolved problems in mathematics, many of which still remain unsolved. His work contributed to the rigour and unity of modern mathematics and to the development of the theory of *computability* (see also p. 69).

Russell, Lord Bertrand (1872–1970), English philosopher and mathematician. Russell did much of the basic work on mathematical logic and the foundations of mathematics. He found the paradox now named after him (see p. 67) in the theory of sets proposed by the German logician Gottlob Frege (1848–1925), and went on to develop the whole of arithmetic in terms of pure logic. He was jailed for his pacifist activities in World War I. In 1950, he was awarded the Nobel Prize for Literature.

Geometry establishes that two triangles each have angles of the same sizes if, and only if, corresponding pairs of sides are in the same proportions.

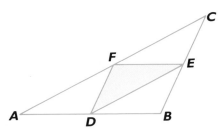

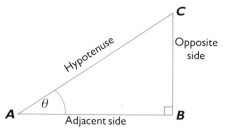

Here D, E and F are the centre-points of sides AB, BC and CA respectively. So, DE is half the length of AC, EF is half the length of AB, and FD is half the length of BC. Thus, the shaded triangle, DEF, is *similar* to the large triangle, and the angles at D, E and F are, respectively, equal to those at C, A and B. Furthermore, the triangles ADF, FEC, DBE and EFD are all *congruent*, i.e. identical in shape and size, and are thus all similar to triangle ABC.

A right-angled triangle is a triangle where one of the angles is 90°. *Pythagoras' theorem* states that, in a right-angled triangle, the square of the length of the *hypotenuse* (the side opposite the right angle) equals the sum of the squares of the lengths of the other two sides. So, in the triangle shown, below, $AC^2 = AB^2 + BC^2$. Trigonometry relies on the recognition that in a right-angled triangle the ratio of the lengths of pairs of sides depends only on the sizes of the two acute angles (i.e. angles less than 90°) of the triangle.

These ratios are given names. For example, the *sine* of an angle is the ratio of the side opposite the given angle to the hypotenuse. The Greek letters θ (*theta*) and ϕ (*phi*) are usually used to denote the angles; thus in the triangle shown we say that the sine of θ, usually written $\sin \theta$, is BC/AC. Similarly, since the *cosine* (cos) of the angle is the ratio of the side adjacent to the given angle to the hypotenuse, $\cos \theta$ is AB/AC. The third basic ratio is the *tangent* (tan), which is the ratio of the opposite to the adjacent side, BC/AB in the example; it is easy to see that $\tan \theta$ must always equal $\sin \theta / \cos \theta$. Pythagoras' theorem can be used to establish some very useful values for sin, cos and tan.

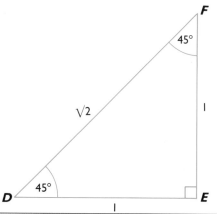

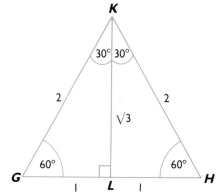

In triangle DEF, $DE = EF = 1$, so the angles at D and F are equal, that is they are each 45° (the internal angles of a triangle add up to 180°). Using Pythagoras' theorem, $DF^2 = 1^2 + 1^2 = 2$, so $DF = \sqrt{2}$. We can therefore conclude:

$$\sin 45° = \frac{1}{\sqrt{2}}$$

$$\cos 45° = \frac{1}{\sqrt{2}}$$

$$\tan 45° = 1$$

In triangle GHK, $GH = HK = KG = 2$, so the angles at G, H and K are equal, that is they are each 60°. Using Pythagoras' theorem, $KL^2 + 1^2 = 2^2$, so $KL = \sqrt{3}$. We therefore have:

$$\sin 60° = \tfrac{1}{2}\sqrt{3} = \cos 30°$$

$$\cos 60° = 1/2 = \sin 30°$$

$$\tan 60° = \sqrt{3}$$

$$\tan 30° = 1/\sqrt{3} \qquad \text{EJB}$$

SEE ALSO

● ASTRONOMY p. 4–19
● PHYSICS p. 20–39
● CHEMISTRY p. 40–57
● THE HISTORY OF SCIENCE p. 60

CHAOS THEORY

From its beginnings, science has been a quest for orderly laws that govern nature. And with each advance it has seemed that some element of disorder has been conquered. Complex dynamical systems, in particular, could be understood and quantified when the calculus was invented (▷ pp. 70–71). But scientists have long recognized that many natural phenomena – the movement of clouds, turbulence in streams or in the rising smoke from a cigarette (▷ box, p. 23), the movement of a leaf in the wind, the patterns of brain waves, disease epidemics or traffic jams – are so inherently disordered and chaotic as to seem to defy any attempt to find governing laws.

As early as 1903, however, the French mathematician Jules Henri Poincaré (1854–1912) – famous for his work on topology – recognized that there are circumstances in which tiny inaccuracies in initial conditions can be multiplied so as to lead to huge differences in the outcome. Poincaré's work was largely forgotten until in 1961 the American meteorologist and mathematician Edward N. Lorenz, working with a crude early computer, set out to produce a mathematical model of how the atmosphere behaves. In the course of this work Lorenz accidentally hit upon the first mathematical system in which small changes in the initial conditions led to overwhelming differences in the outcome. Lorenz showed that this phenomenon made long-range weather prediction almost impossible. His work and the analogies that developed from it attracted the attention of scientists in other fields and led to the development of a new branch of mathematics – chaos theory. One of the most striking of these analogies is known as the 'butterfly effect' – the idea that the air perturbation caused by the movement of a butterfly wing in China can cause a storm a month later in New York.

By the 1970s some scientists and mathematicians, and even some economists, were beginning to investigate disorder and instability. Physiologists were considering patterns of chaos in the action of the heart-patterns that could lead to sudden cardiac arrest; electronic engineers were investigating the sometimes chaotic behaviour of oscillators; ecologists were examining the seemingly random way in which wildlife populations changed; chemists were studying unexpected fluctuations in chemical reactions; and economists were wondering whether some order might be found in random stock-market price fluctuations.

The first indication for an underlying pattern in chaos was found by the American physicist Mitchell Feigenbaum. In 1976 Feigenbaum noticed that when an ordered system starts to break down into chaos, it often does so in accordance with a consistent pattern in which the rate of occurrence of some event suddenly doubles over and over again. This is exactly what happens in *fractal geometry* – in which any part of a figure is a reduced copy of a larger part. Feigenbaum also discovered that at a certain constant number of doublings, the structure acquires a kind of stability. This numerical constant, called Feigenbaum's number, can be applied to a wide range of chaotic systems.

To understand what mathematicians mean by chaos it is best to consider a simple example. Iteration is the mathematical process in which the result of a calculation is applied as the starting point for a repeat of the same process and so on. One might, for instance, take a number and halve it, then take the result and halve that, and so on repeatedly. The set of numbers that result is called the *orbit* of the number. Starting with, say, 16, the orbit would be 8, 4, 2, 1, 1/2, 1/4, 1/8, 1/16... Again, one might perform an iterative process on any number (x) between 0 and 1, the process being 'multiply the product of x and $1 - x$ by 3'. This gives a readily predictable orbit. Surprisingly, iteration for numbers between 0 and 1 using the process 'multiply the product of x and $1 - x$ by 4' produces a chaotic orbit for some numbers and a predictable one for others. Closely related starting values give orbital numbers that are widely different. In other words, the system is sometimes highly sensitive to its starting values, sometimes not. This is characteristic of what mathematicians mean by chaos. Chaos theory attempts to describe how such systems change from predictable to wholly disordered.

Today there is much debate as to whether chaos theory, so far as it goes at present, actually does adequately describe seemingly disordered dynamical systems in nature – whether it really is, as some have claimed, a new mathematical tool of the same order of importance as calculus, or even that it is a discipline to rank in importance with relativity and quantum mechanics. The controversy rages on but the level of interest and the volume of research continue to rise. Major developments, one way or the other, are to be expected soon.

Number Systems and Algebra

The *natural numbers* or *whole numbers* are those we use in counting. We learn these at an early age, perhaps pairing them with our fingers or else learning to chant their names in order: 'one, two, three, four, . . . '. These are both important features of our number system – that these numbers can be used to count sets of objects (see p. 66), and that they form a naturally ordered progression that has a first member, the number 1, but no last member: no matter how big a number you come up with, I can always reply with a bigger one – simply by adding 1.

However, even quite simple arithmetic, as we shall see, cannot be carried out wholly within the natural numbers. Ordinarily we take the principles that govern such systems for granted, yet merely to be able to subtract and divide, for example, requires other, more complex, number systems, such as fractions and negative numbers.

Natural numbers and arithmetic

If I have 3 sheep and you give me 4 more, I can count that I now have 7 sheep, or I can use the operation of *addition* to get the same answer: $3 + 4 = 7$. If I promise to give 5 children 4 sweets each, again I can count out 20 sweets altogether, or I can use the operation of *multiplication*: $5 \times 4 = 20$. Here, we have examples of another principle of natural numbers: any addition or multiplication of natural numbers gives another natural number. Such a system is said to be *closed* under these operations. (A closed system is one where an operation on two of its elements produces another element of that system.)

If I had 3 sheep and when you gave me your sheep I had 7, I can use the operation

SEE ALSO

● SETS AND PARADOXES p. 64
● CORRESPONDENCE, COUNT-ING AND INFINITY p. 68
● COMPUTERS p. 334

LAWS OF ARITHMETIC

Commutative law
for addition: $a + b = b + a$
for multiplication: $a \times b = b \times a$

Associative law
for addition: $(a + b) + c = a + (b + c)$
for multiplication: $(a \times b) \times c = a \times (b \times c)$

Distributive law
for multiplication
over addition: $a \times (b + c) = (a \times b) + (a \times c)$

of *subtraction* to find how many sheep you gave to me: $7 - 3 = 4$. If I distribute 20 sweets equally to 5 children, I can use the operation of *division* to find how many I gave to each: $20 \div 5 = 4$. Subtraction is the *inverse operation* of addition; division is the inverse operation of multiplication. However, the natural numbers are not closed under the operations of subtraction and division, as we shall see later.

In simple algebra, we generalize arithmetic by using letters to stand for unknown numbers whose value is to be discovered, or to stand for numbers in general. Usually letters from the beginning of the alphabet are used in the latter way – for example, to express a general truth about numbers, such as $a + b = b + a$. The letters at the end of the alphabet are generally used to represent unknown numbers. For example, the information about the sheep can be expressed by the *equation*, $3 + x = 7$, where x represents the unknown number of sheep you gave to me. Since the two sides of this equation are equal, they remain equal if we treat them both the same way. If we then subtract 3 from each side we get $x = 7 - 3$, that is $x = 4$. We have *solved the equation*.

Subtraction and the integers

The set of natural numbers is not closed under the operation of subtraction; for example, $3 - 7$ does not give a natural number as an answer. We need a system of numbers that is closed under subtraction. The smallest set of numbers that is closed under subtraction is the set of *integers*, i.e. the set $\{..., -3, -2, -1, 0, 1, 2, 3, ...\}$. Here, the positive integers can be identified with the natural numbers; zero (0) is defined as the result of subtracting any integer from itself; and the negative integers are the result of subtracting the corresponding positive integers from zero (e.g. $-3 = 0 - 3$).

Now, every subtraction has an answer within the number system of integers, that is, the integers are closed under subtraction.

Division and the rational numbers

The integers, however, are still not closed under the operation of division. We can construct a system that is by defining the result of any division, $a \div b$ to be the pair of integers, a and b, written in a notation that clearly distinguishes which divides which. Thus, we write $a \div b$ as the *ratio* or *fraction*, a/b, and we have the system of *rational numbers*.

It is important to note that rational numbers are not identical with their symbols. The same rational number may be represented by many different fractions (in fact, an infinite number of them). For example, 24/8 is the same rational number as 12/4 or 6/2. We adopt the convention of representing them, where possible, by the unique fraction in which there is no *common factor* that can be cancelled out

A prime number is a natural number that has no *proper factors* – that is, which cannot be divided by any natural numbers other than itself and 1. We can find the primes by taking a sequence of numbers such as

1, 2, 3, 4, 5, 6, 7, 8, 9, 10, 11, 12, 13, 14, 15, 16 . . .

and first deleting all the numbers divisible by 2 (excluding 2 itself, which is only divisible by itself and 1), then all those divisible by 3, then (since anything divisible by 4 has already been deleted) all those divisible by 5, and so on.

All non-prime natural numbers must by definition be divisible by other numbers apart from themselves and 1; these other numbers can in turn be repeatedly divided until one is left with a series of prime factors. Hence, all non-prime numbers can be expressed as the product of a series of primes – in fact, for each number, the expression is unique.

The prime numbers have been studied since the days of the ancient Greeks, who knew, for example, that there is no largest prime. Their proof is quite easy to understand: Suppose there is a largest prime, so that all the prime numbers can be listed in order of size. Now consider the number we obtain if we multiply all these primes together, and add 1; call this number N. Clearly N cannot be divided by any of the list of primes without leaving a remainder of 1. But since these are (we are assuming) all the primes, any other number is non-prime and so has prime factors (see above). Therefore it cannot divide N unless its prime factors divide N – but no primes can divide N. Thus N must itself be prime. But it is a bigger prime than what we supposed was the biggest prime, so that supposition has led us to a contradiction and must be false. The largest known prime number (August 1989) is $391582 \times 2^{216193} - 1$, which is a number of 65087 digits.

On the other hand it is not known whether or not there are infinitely many *twin primes*. These are pairs of successive odd numbers that are both prime, like 5 and 7, 11 and 13, or 29 and 31. Another famous conjecture about prime numbers is that of Christian Goldbach (1690–1764), who postulated that every even number is the sum of two prime numbers. It is not known whether this is true or false.

Prime numbers have recently become of great interest to cyptographers: certain codes are based on the result of multiplying two very large primes together, and because even the fastest possible computer would take years to factorize this product, the resulting code is virtually unbreakable.

(thus, 14/21 becomes 2/3, where the factor, 7, has been cancelled out). It should also be noted that decimals are rational numbers, since, for example, $0.5 = 5/10 = 1/2$, and $1.61 = 161/100$.

We do have a problem, however: the

OTHER NUMBER NOTATIONS

The usual notation for numbers is a *decimal place-value system*. This means that there are ten distinct digits (0, 1, 2, 3, 4, 5, 6, 7, 8, 9) and that the position of each digit determines what it contributes to the value of the number. Each position gives a value 10 times as great as the position to its right, so, for example, 7234 can be written as 4 units (4×10^0) on the right, plus 3 tens (3×10^1) plus 2 hundreds (2×10^2) plus 7 thousands (7×10^3). We say that 10 is the *base* of the decimal place-value system.

We can easily construct systems with other bases to suit particular needs. The *binary system* uses only the digits 0 and 1; so it has base 2. This is used in the representation of numbers within computers, since the two numerals correspond to the on and off positions of an electronic switch. In the binary system we count as follows: 1, 10 (= 2 + 0), 11 (= 2 + 1), 100 (= 4 + 0 + 0), 101 (= 4 + 0 + 1), 110 (4 + 2 + 0), 111 (4 + 2 + 1), 1000 (= 8 + 0 + 0 + 0), 1001 (= 8 + 0 + 0 + 1), etc.

Sometimes, especially in computing, it is convenient to use *octal arithmetic* (with base 8) or *hexadecimal arithmetic* (base 16). In base 16, the letters A to F are used as well as the numerals 0 to 9. Obviously it is necessary to know which base is being used, so the base is indicated by a subscript, for example, $31_{10} = 1F_{16} = 37_8 = 11111_2$.

There are many other ways in which numbers systems can vary. Sometimes one can see vestiges of other systems in the numerical terms of a language: in French one counts up to 100 in a mixture of base 10 and base 20; for example, *quatre-vingt-dix* (four times twenty plus ten) equals 90. Even English retains vestiges of base 12, with the words 'eleven' and 'twelve'. The traditional Chinese abacus uses a mixture of base 5 and base 10.

The system of Roman numerals is not a place-value system: the letters have fixed values and are ordered from the largest to the smallest. For example, MDCLXVI = 1000 + 500 + 100 + 50 + 10 + 5 + 1 = 1666. When, however, a letter representing a smaller value precedes a larger, it is subtracted; thus CM = 900, and IX = 9. This makes calculations very difficult, and it has been suggested that the superiority of Eastern mathematics over that of early medieval Europe was a result of the system of Roman numerals.

rationals cannot be closed under division, because of the integer 0. We cannot give value to $a/0$ for any rational number a. This problem, however, cannot be avoided: we have to be content with the fact that the rationals, excluding the integer 0, are closed under division.

Roots and irrational numbers

6^9, which we read as, '6 to the *power* 9' means 6 multiplied by itself 9 times $(6 \times 6 \times 6 \times 6 \times 6 \times 6 \times 6 \times 6 \times 6)$. Generally, a^b, which we read as, 'a to the power b', means a multiplied by itself b times. These are closed operations for the systems of numbers we have so far considered. However, none of these systems guarantees the possibility of the inverse operation, the *extraction of roots*. If $b = a^n$, (where n represents an integer), then a is the nth root of b, written $a = \sqrt[n]{b}$. For example, since $3 \times 3 = 9$, the second or *square root* of 9 (written $\sqrt[2]{9}$ or more usually $\sqrt{9}$) equals 3. To give another example, since $2 \times 2 \times 2 = 8$, the third or *cube root* of 8 (written $\sqrt[3]{8}$) is 2. But none of the systems we have considered is closed under this operation. For example, $\sqrt{2}$, $\sqrt{3}$, and $\sqrt{5}$ cannot be expressed as fractions or as terminating decimals; they are examples of what are called *irrational numbers*. They have exact meaning – for example, by Pythagoras' theorem (see p. 62), $\sqrt{2}$ is the length of the hypotenuse of a right-angled triangle whose other sides are each length 1; $\sqrt{5}$ is the length of the hypotenuse of a right-angled triangle whose other sides have lengths 1 and 2, etc. Obviously, we need to add the irrationals to our number systems to ensure closure under these calculations.

All the systems we have discussed, the natural numbers, the integers, the rational numbers and the irrationals form together the system of *real numbers*.

Imaginary and complex numbers

However, now we have admitted the extraction of roots, we have opened up a new gap in our number system: we have not, as yet, defined the square root of a negative number. At first sight, we may wonder why this omission should be of any great importance, but without the development of a system to include such numbers, many valuable applications to engineering and physics would not be possible. Surprisingly, we need only extend the number system by one new number. Since all negative numbers are positive multiples of -1 (for example, -6 is 6×-1, so that $\sqrt{-6} = \sqrt{6} \times \sqrt{-1}$) we are concerned only with the square root of -1. The square root of -1 is denoted by the letter i, so we have $i^2 = -1$.

Real multiples of i, such as $3i$, $2.7i$, $2i/3$, $i\sqrt{2}$, etc., are called *imaginary numbers*. The sum of a real number and an imaginary number, such as $5 + 3i$, is a *complex number*. It can be shown that every complex number can be expressed uniquely as the sum of its real and imaginary parts.

The rules for using complex numbers are the same as those for real numbers. It can be shown, for example, that

$$(a + ib)(a - ib) = a^2 + b^2.$$

The terms in brackets are thus the factors of $a^2 + b^2$. In fact it turns out that in the complex number system any algebraic expression with integer powers has exactly the same number of factors as the highest power in the expression. This result is so important that it is called the *fundamental theorem of algebra*. EJB

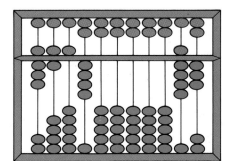

The Chinese abacus usually has two beads representing 5s on each wire above the cross bar, and five beads representing 1s on each wire below the bar. The beads are moved towards the bar. Two numbers are shown here, 8654 on the left and 93 on the right.

LOGARITHMS

Since $a^3 = a \times a \times a$, and $a^2 = a \times a$, then $a^2 \times a^3 = a \times a \times a \times a \times a = a^5$. This is an instance of the general rule for the multiplication of powers of the same base:

$$a^x \times a^y = a^{x+y}.$$

From this it is easy to see that $a^0 = 1$, whence also $a^{-x} = 1/a^x$, and the corresponding rule for division is

$$a^x / a^y = a^{x-y}$$

Similar considerations enable us to give a meaning to a^x even where x is not an integer; for example, since $\sqrt{x} \times \sqrt{x} = x = x^1$, $\sqrt{x}$ must be $x^{1/2}$.

The *logarithm* of a number to a given base is simply the power of that base that is equal to the given number. Tables of *common logarithms*, which use base 10, were used in the days before pocket calculators to assist with complicated multiplications and divisions. For example, it is obviously quite difficult to multiply 135.763 by 4386.734, but it is much easier to add their logarithms, which can be found in a table. Since 135.763 is 10 to the power 2.1327 we find that the logarithm of 135.763 is 2.1327; similarly, since 4386.734 is 10 to the power 3.6421, we find that the logarithm of 4386.734 is 3.6421. We then add these logarithms to find the logarithm of the product of the given numbers. Thus the logarithm of the product is 5.7748, which we can look up in a table of *antilogarithms* to find the answer 595400 (since 10 to the power 5.7748 is 595400). (NB: This is only approximate because the tables are only made up to four figures; the precise answer is 595556.168042.)

A *slide rule* is a mechanical device that applies this principle. You can add two numbers using two ordinary rulers (where the numbers are equally spaced) by placing the zero of one scale against one of the numbers and reading their sum off the other ruler opposite the second number.

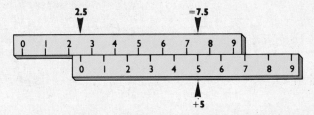

A slide rule has a scale that shows numbers spaced according to their logarithms, so that the same method has the effect of adding the logarithms, so that the number read off as the answer is the product of the two given numbers:

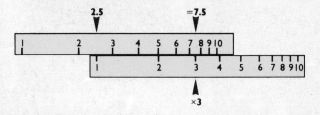

Here, if we place 1 on the lower slide against 2.5 on the top slide, then the number on the top slide opposite any number on the bottom slide is the result of multiplying it by 2.5; for example, 2.5 × 3 = 7.5 as shown.

Sets and Paradoxes

Sets can be considered simply as any collections of objects. However, in the early 20th century, when attempts were made to formalize the properties of sets, contradictions were discovered that have affected mathematical thinking ever since.

A *set* can be specified either by stipulating some property for an object as a condition of *membership* of the set, or by listing the *members* of the set in any order.

Sets are usually indicated by the use of curly brackets {}, known as *braces*. Thus, suppose we are considering a family that has a cat, a rabbit, a horse, a dog, a mouse and a piranha: we could represent the pets fed and looked after by Sue as {cat, rabbit, horse}. In that case {cat, rabbit, horse} = {x: x is a family pet looked after by Sue}. Sets are often

SEE ALSO

● THE SCIENTIFIC METHOD
  p. 58
● CORRESPONDENCE, COUNT-
  ING AND INFINITY p. 68
● COMPUTERS p. 334
● LOGIC p. 494

pictured by drawing a circle around representations of their members, thus:

Family pets fed and looked after by Sue.

Union and intersection

We can use circles to show the relationship between two (or more) sets. Let us suppose that Sue has a brother, Tim, who feeds and looks after the dog and the mouse; he also helps Sue look after the horse. If *S* is the set of pets looked after by Sue and *T* is the set of pets looked after by Tim, we can show their responsibilities like this:

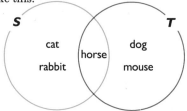

It is easy to see that the set of all the family pets looked after by the children is {cat, rabbit, horse, dog, mouse}. This is

called the *union* of the two sets, and is written $S \cup T$ (we say, '*S* union *T* ').

The two sets have a member in common, the horse. The set of members that belong to both of two given sets is known as their *intersection*; here, it is the set whose only member is the horse. This is written $S \cap T$ = {horse}. This is a set, even though it has only one member (as far as the family's pets are concerned) and we write 'horse $\in$ { horse}', where the symbol '$\in$' means 'is a member of '.

Subsets

Formally, a set is a *subset* of another set if all the members of the first set are members of the other set, that is, one set is contained within another. Thus, among the family's pets, {horse} is a subset of {cat, rabbit, horse, dog, mouse}. If the bigger set is *A* and the subset is *H*, then we write $H \subset A$, to mean that *H* is a *subset* of *A*, or $A \supset H$, to mean that set *A* *contains* set *H*. These could be shown:

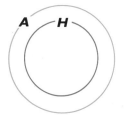

The universal set and complements

Often, we need to know which objects are *not members* of a given set. For example, we might wish to know which pets are not looked after by Sue. If we think of this as the set of all pets not looked after by Sue, this would then include any other pets in the world – which is obviously not what we intended. We are concerned only with the pets looked after by Sue and Tim and their family. A *universal set* contains all the objects being discussed – in this case, all the pets looked after by the whole family. Those pets not looked after by Sue, within the universal set, form what is known as the *relative complement* of the set of her pets. Where *S* is the set of pets looked after by Sue, the complement set is written *C* (*S*) or *S*′. Let us suppose that Sue and Tim's parents look after the only other family pet, a piranha, and that the children are banned from the piranha. The circle for Sue's pets is as before. The rectangle, identified *U*, is the universal set of the family's pets. We can see that the complement of *S* is *S*′ = {dog, mouse, piranha}.

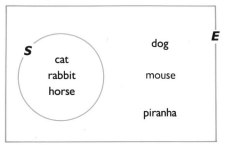

Empty and disjoint sets

The *empty set* (sometimes called the *null*

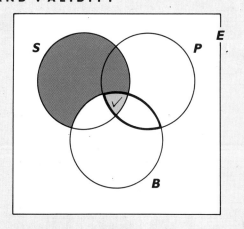

set) has *no members*. It is written {} or ø. If we consider the family's pets, we could write, for example,

{parents' pets} ∩ {Sue's pets} = ø,

meaning the set of pets looked after by both Sue and her parents is the empty set – it has no members.

Disjoint sets have *no members in common.* As the diagram below shows, the set of pets looked after by Sue does not intersect with the set of pets looked after by her parents, *P; S* and *P* have no members in common and their intersection is the empty set. That is, $S \cap P = ø$.

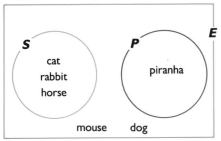

Sets and logic

There is a direct link with *logic* that becomes apparent if we write the formal definitions of union, intersection and complement in set notation:

$S \cup T$ = {*x*: *x* is a member of *S or* a member of T }
$S \cap T$ = {*x*: *x* is a member of *S and* a member of T }
S' = {*x*: *x* is *not* a member of *S* }

These words, 'and', 'or' and 'not', represent what logicians call *truth-functions*. That means that when they are attached to sentences to form more complex sentences, the truth or falsehood of the latter depends only on that of the former. For example, 'John is in London and Mary is in Paris' can only be true if both 'John is in London' and 'Mary is in Paris' are separately true; and in that case, 'John is not in London' must be false. These relations can be shown by the following tables:

P	−P		P	Q	P & Q	P v Q
T	F		T	T	T	T
F	T		T	F	F	T
			F	T	F	T
			F	F	F	F

Here, P and Q stand for any sentences whatever, '−P' is 'not-P', 'P & Q' is read 'P and Q', and 'P v Q' represents 'P or Q'. The tables show every possible combination of values, and can be used to work out tables for more complex formulae. When 'T' represents a positive signal and 'F' the absence of one (sometimes written '1' or '0' respectively), these tables show the outputs from the electronic logic gates of the same names out of which computers are built.

Paradoxes

Although developments from the simple concept of sets – such as have been outlined – seem to work well enough for practical purposes, various paradoxes were discovered when *axioms* for the theory of sets were sought. The German Gottlob Frege (1848–1925) and the Englishman Bertrand Russell (1872–1970) were independently interested in showing that all of mathematics could be reduced to pure logic, and looked to set theory as a link. In 1908, just as Frege was publishing a major work on the subject, Russell discovered, and communicated to Frege, that his axioms generated an important contradiction; this has become known as *Russell's paradox*.

The simplest way of explaining Russell's paradox is by a particular example (a more general account is given in the box). Let us consider a doctor who serves a community. This doctor treats only those in the community who do not treat themselves. Now, if the doctor treats himself, he cannot be included in the set of those who do not treat themselves. If he does not treat himself, then he is included in the set of those he does treat. Either way, there is a contradiction; but there are only two possibilities and we cannot make sense of either of them. There has to be something wrong with the definition itself from which we were able to derive the contradiction. This, and other paradoxes, proved a great blow to mathematical logicians and new philosophies such as intuitionism (see pp. 68–9) grew up partly as a result. EJB

(see pp. 68–9)

VENN DIAGRAMS AND NUMERICAL DATA

Venn diagrams can be used to assist with calculations that involve a subdivided population about which only fragmentary numerical data are available. The story of 'The Thirty-Sixth Man' provides an entertaining example . . .

Vennseta is a spymaster. To his horror, he discovers that three hostile powers, Xylia, Yoravia and Zenobia, have cracked the cover of some of his agents. Unfortunately for Vennseta, the information he has is only fragmentary, but he has to find out which of his agents he can still trust.

Of his 36 operatives, he knows that 21 have been cracked by Xylia, only 4 of whom have been cracked by no other power. He knows that 5 have been uncovered by Zenobia alone and that the cover of 12 has been broken by Xylia and Zenobia. Of those who are known to Yoravia, 9 are also known to Xylia and 7 are also known to Zenobia. His information tells him that 18 are entirely unsuspected by Yoravia.

Wondering whether he has enough data, Vennseta draws one of those diagrams for which he is famed in the world of espionage. *E* is the set of all his espionage operatives. The circles he labels *X, Y* and *Z*, to represent the sets of agents cracked by, respectively, Xylia (*X*), Yoravia (*Y*) and Zenobia (*Z*). He then writes in the numbers to represent the data he has.

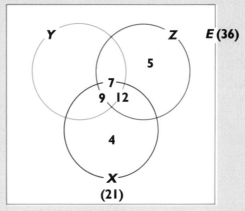

He still has one piece of information that he cannot fit into his diagram, but he is quite sure it will be useful later.

The spymaster decides he can now determine how many of his agents are known to all three powers, by considering the subdivisions of *X*. He adds the 4 who were cracked only by *X*, the 9 also cracked by *Y* and the 12 also cracked by *Z*. He gets a total of 25 agents cracked. But he sees that only 21 have been cracked by *X*, so there are, seemingly, 4 spies too many. He realizes what this means: 4 of the 9 + 12 must have been cracked by both *Y* and *Z*, as well as *X*. He decides to draw another diagram, putting this information into it.

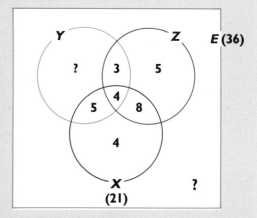

From his second diagram, he sees that 12 − 4 = 8 are not known to *Y*; 9 − 4 = 5 are not known to *Z*; and 7 − 4 = 3 are not known to *X*. The only subsets he has to determine are those agents known only to *Y* and those agents not known to any of the three hostile powers. He marks these sets by question marks.

Vennseta puzzles a while, and then reaches for his one unused piece of information: 18 agents are unsuspected by *Y*. He quickly adds up the agents cracked by *X* and *Z* but outside *Y*: 5 + 8 + 4 = 17. This leaves one agent who is safe from all three powers.

The spymaster is elated; not only have his diagrams, once again, solved his problem for him, but out there in hostile regions there is an agent on whom he can rely, absolutely. He idly scribbles in a 6 as the missing number in *Y*; he writes a large 1 in the rectangle outside the circles. Suddenly he stiffens and turns pale: how on earth can he find out *which* of his agents he can still trust?

RUSSELL'S PARADOX

Obviously, sets in general can be members of other sets; for example, { 1,2} is a member of

$$\{\{0,1\}, \{1,2\}, \{2,3\}\},$$

and that set is a member of the set of three-membered sets, which in turn is a member of the set of large sets (since there are many three-membered sets). More particularly, some sets are members of themselves, like the set of large sets, while others are not members of themselves, like the set of small sets (since there are many small sets).

Let us then consider the set W of all sets that are not members of themselves: is it a member of itself or not? An element of a set must have the property that defines the set, so if W is a member of the set of sets that are not members of themselves, then it can't be a member of itself – but that just means that it can't be a member of W. On the other hand, if W is not a member of itself that just is the property that defines W, so that W must be a member of W – that is, it is a member of itself.

There are only two possibilities: if you think of any entity you like and any set you like, either the thing is in the set or it is not; there is no third possibility. Thus in particular, either W is a member of itself or it is not; yet whichever supposition we make leads straight to the contradiction. This is a deeper problem than the paradox in the text; there we said that although the description of the doctor's contract looks inoffensive, analysis shows it is really self-contradictory. Here there is no such description to reject; W was constructed out of pure logic. So the contradiction can only lie in one place – at the heart of logic itself.

Correspondence, Counting and Infinity

The simplest way of counting a set of objects is to point at them one by one, making sure that none have been missed or repeated, and saying 'one', 'two', 'three', etc., as each object is indicated. These are, in order, the names of the *natural* or *counting numbers* (see p. 64). The number of objects in the set is just the last number counted out in this process.

This fact can be used to define the size of a finite set (i.e. one that can be completely counted off) in a way that our intuition tells us is acceptable. However, when we seek to apply this intuitively satisfactory account to infinite sets, we discover that our intuitions break down, and we are forced to the puzzling conclusion that there must be different sizes of infinity.

Mappings

Sometimes it is useful to compare two sets of objects without actually counting them. For example, a shepherd might check that he has equal numbers of black and white sheep, without using numbers. Even today, cricket umpires drop pebbles or coins into their pockets, corresponding to the number of balls that have been bowled in an over; they do not count them in numbers.

The first set (in the examples, the white sheep, or the umpire's pebbles) is called

the *domain*. The other set (the black sheep, or the balls bowled) is called the *codomain*. A *mapping* associates members of the domain with members of the co-domain.

We shall now move to a different domain, that of friends at a party. For the codomain, we shall consider what snacks they choose to eat. We can show the relation in a *mapping diagram*, where the *mapping arrows* all lead from the domain to the codomain.

Here, we have a *many-to-one relation*, since more than one party-goer (member of the domain) chooses the same snack. The codomain, that is the set of snacks available, is {crisps, nuts, cheese, fruit}. Although fruit was available, none of {Al, Beth, Charles, Dirk, Eve} choose it. The set {crisps, nuts, cheese} is called the *range*.

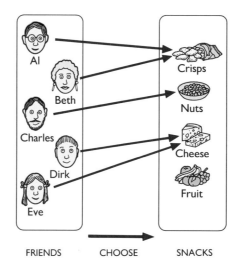

A many-to-one mapping

As the party continues, some of the

friends get bored with the same food. The diagram looks like this:

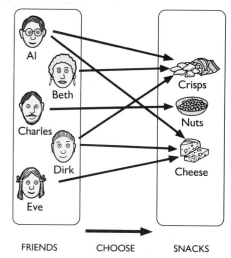

A many-to-many mapping

Many friends choose one snack; at least one friend chooses many snacks; this shows a *many-to-many relation*.

As the hours pass, Beth, Dirk and Eve go home from the party, leaving Al and Charles still nibbling. We see that at least one of the friends (Al) prefers many (crisps and cheese) snacks. The diagram now shows a *one-to-many relation*.

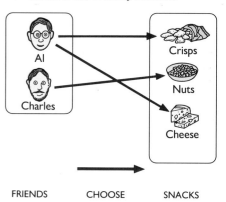

A one-to-many mapping

Correspondence and number

There is one other kind of relation – *one-to-one correspondence*. Let us suppose that Beth, Dirk and Eve decide to have a bedtime drink when they get home. Their preferences are shown in the next diagram, which illustrates a *one-to-one mapping*.

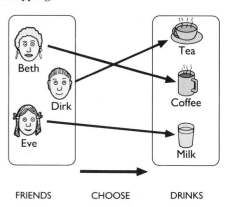

A one-to-one mapping

A scene from Sterne's paradoxical anti-novel *Tristram Shandy* (published 1759–67).

The earlier examples of the shepherd pairing his black and white sheep, and of the cricket umpire pairing pebbles and balls, are also one-to-one relations. One-to-one correspondence forms the foundation of arithmetic. When sets are paired in this way, they are said to be *equivalent*, and two such equivalent sets must have the same number of members. It is possible to prove formally that every set whatsoever is in some family of equivalent sets, and that no set can be in more than one family. Thus, one-to-one correspondence separates out all sets into families of sets that have the same number of members. Two equivalent sets are said to have the same *cardinality*, and this serves to base arithmetic in set theory. So all sets with, for example, seven members, have the same cardinality.

Infinite sets

The sequence of sets, {1}, {1,2}, {1,2,3}, etc., has the property that every *finite set* (i.e. a set with a finite number of members) corresponds to one of them. Thus every set corresponds to a unique set of natural numbers starting with 1 and in their natural order, and the size of the set is given by the largest number in that unique set.

However, a set that does not have a largest member cannot be equivalent to any set that does, and this leads to the idea of an *infinite set* as one that cannot be counted. In particular, the set of all the natural numbers cannot be counted, so it might seem possible to define *infinity* in terms of equivalence to the set of all the natural numbers.

All we need to do to show that two sets are equivalent is to show that their members can be put in one-to-one correspondence. But this immediately gives rise to a puzzle. It is easy to show that the mappings that associate each natural number with its double (and so, each even natural number with its half) are one to one.

Thus, we have shown there are exactly as many *even* natural numbers as there are natural numbers. However, since every natural number is either even or odd and there are as many even numbers as odd, there must be twice as many natural numbers as even natural numbers.

This is only a paradox if we expect that a subset of a set must be smaller than the set itself; but since our idea of an infinite set means that it is possible to list members of the set for ever, we can see why adding extra members at the end does not increase its size. Our intuition that a set must have more members than any of its subsets is false for infinite sets. In fact, the usual definition of an infinite set is that it can be put into one-to-one correspondence with some subset of itself.

Different infinities

One remarkable application of this definition of an infinite set shows that there are no more *rational numbers* (see p. 64) than there are natural numbers. Again, we look for a one-to-one correspondence between the two sets. There are many possible mappings, but the simplest is by first counting the fractions whose numerator and denominator add up to 1, then those for which the total is 2, then those totalling 3, and so on. Within each group, the fractions are put in order of size and any fraction that equals a previously listed fraction is omitted. This results in the rationals being listed in a unique order:

1/1, 1/2, 2/1, 1/3, (2/2), 3/1, 1/4, 2/3, 3/2, 4/1, ...

Obviously, we can calculate both which natural numbers any rational corresponds to, and which rational corresponds to any given natural number, and this is sufficient to prove that there are no more rationals than there are natural numbers:

Rational

Natural number corresponding

It would be wrong, however, to conclude from all this that all infinite sets are equivalent. In fact, it is possible to prove that *real numbers* (the rationals and irrationals together; see pp. 64–5) cannot be counted off in the way that we counted off natural numbers and rationals (see box on Cantor's diagonal theorem). This gave rise, at the end of the 19th century, to new studies of what was called *transfinite arithmetic* (*transfinite* means 'extending beyond the finite'), and attempts were made to prove that the cardinality of the reals is the next transfinite cardinal after that of the integers. In 1963 it was finally shown that this conjecture can neither be proved nor disproved; this is a 'gap' in mathematics itself.

Intuitionism and infinity

The various paradoxes and discoveries about infinity caused much attention to be paid in the late 19th century to the philosophical and logical foundations of mathematics.

One school of thought, called *intuitionism*, blamed the contradictions that became apparent on the assumption that it is possible to complete infinite processes. Intuitionists resolved to ban infinity from mathematics, with the result that statements have to be allowed to be neither true nor false.

As an example, let us consider π. Suppose we define N to be 0 if the sequence 0123456789 occurs in the decimal part of π, and to be 1 if this sequence never occurs. A *classical* mathematician will be prepared to assert that 'N is either 0 or 1' is true, even though, at the time, he or she has no way of knowing it is. An intuitionist claims that, until we are able to prove one result or the other, the statement cannot be said to be either true or false.

SEE ALSO

- NUMBER SYSTEMS AND ALGEBRA p. 64
- SETS AND PARADOXES p. 66
- FUNCTIONS, GRAPHS AND CHANGE p. 70

CANTOR'S DIAGONAL THEOREM

The German mathematician Georg Cantor (see p. 63) was responsible for the development of the whole theory of cardinality outlined in the text.

He proved that every set has a *power set* (set of all its subsets) that is strictly bigger than the given set; that is, the power set cannot be put in one-to-one correspondence with the given set – even in the case of an infinite set. The proof is easiest to understand in terms of the real numbers, by assuming that such a correspondence is possible and then showing that this assumption cannot be true since it leads to a contradiction.

We consider the real numbers between 0 and 1, expressed as decimals (0.47936421 ... is an example), so that each number has an infinite number of digits after the decimal point. Where decimals terminate, we continue the number with zeros. Suppose real numbers can be listed in order, that is put into one-to-one correspondence with the natural numbers. We could then write all the real numbers in this form:

$$0.\ a_1\ a_2\ a_3\ a_4\ ...$$
$$0.\ b_1\ b_2\ b_3\ b_4\ ...$$
$$0.\ c_1\ c_2\ c_3\ c_4\ ...$$

and so on.

Now, we try to construct a new number. We make the first digit after the decimal point differ from a_1, the second digit differ from b_2, the third digit differ from c_3, and so on. Thus, we have constructed a new real number between 0 and 1, but we have constructed it so that it differs from every member of the list of real numbers that we began by supposing was complete: we have derived our contradiction. It follows, therefore, that such a list of the real numbers is *not possible*.

However, the construction required by Cantor's proof requires the completion of an infinite number of steps, and intuitionists therefore claim that the new number is ill-defined; they therefore reject 'Cantor's paradise' of different infinities.

Arithmetic, however, requires that there is no largest integer. The intuitionist resolves this by looking at things in a different way from the classicist. For example, the classicist might think of a distance of 2 units as actually made up of infinitely many steps of length 1 unit, then 1/2 unit, then 1/4 unit, then 1/8 unit, etc. The intuitionist, however, would interpret the result that the infinite series of $1 + 1/2 + 1/4 + 1/8 ... + 1/2^n + ...$ has a sum (in fact 2) to mean that the total of finitely many terms in order can be made as close as we like to 2 by taking sufficiently many – but still finitely many – terms of the series.

EJB

Functions, Graphs and Change

In studying events in real life, we are often concerned with continuous change: a boulder rolling downhill picks up speed; a balloon expands as air is blown into it; our reaction-time slows as we grow older. Processes like these can be represented by a *function*. A function can be represented by a *curve*, so allowing us to picture how a process changes and develops.

Calculus is the branch of mathematics that studies continuous change in terms of the mathematical properties of the functions that represent it, and these results can also be interpreted in geometric terms relating to the graph of the function. Calculus was developed independently by Sir Isaac Newton (see pp. 20 and 63) and Gottfried Wilhelm Leibniz (see p. 486) in the late 17th century. Because their presentation involved paradoxical references to *infinitesimals* (infinitely small quantities), many scientists rejected their 'infidel mathematics', but at the same time there was a considerable dispute about who should have the credit for its discovery.

Functions and mappings

Suppose we go out for a cycle run, and keep up a speed of 15 km/h. Then our distance from home is determined by how long we have been travelling. For example, after half an hour we will have travelled 7.5 km; after an hour 15 km; after 2 hours 30 km, and so on. We can express this relationship by saying that the distance we travelled is a *function* of the time we have been travelling. Here the two quantities, time and distance, might be represented by the *variables* t and d, and the mathematical relationship between them would then be written $d = 15t$. What that means is that for any number of units of time, t, we can work out the number of units of distance travelled, d, by multiplying t by 15.

A function is just a mapping (see p. 68), but the term function is preferred when the domain and codomain are quantities that can be represented by sets of numbers, and especially real numbers (see p. 64). In general, the notation for a function is $y = f(x)$, which indicates that the value of y depends upon the value of x; in that case, y is called the *dependent variable*, and x is called the *independent variable*. The variables are thought of as running through a range of values – for example, if our journey takes a total of 3 hours, the range of t is the *interval* (0,3), and the range of d is the *interval* (0,45).

Cartesian coordinates

The real numbers can be represented geometrically by a line (an *axis*) marked off from the origin (0) using some numerical scale. Any point in a *plane*, a two-dimensional area, can similarly be represented by the pair of numbers that correspond to its respective distances from two such axes, as shown below; these numbers are the *coordinates* of the point. Thus the coordinates of the point P in the diagram below are (1,2):

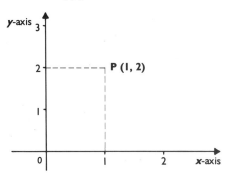

Here the independent and the dependent variables of a function are represented by two lines at right angles (the x-axis and the y-axis) that cross at the origin. The curve representing the function is then the line that passes through the points whose coordinates satisfy the function. For example, the curve of the function $y = x^2$ is the set of pairs, (x, y), of real numbers for which y is the square of x; thus, for example, (2,4), (−1,1), (−2,4), ($\sqrt{2}$,2), etc., are all in the graph of the function. The curve corresponding to this function is shown below.

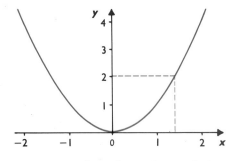

This system of coordinates is named after the French philosopher and mathematician René Descartes (or des Cartes, whence the adjective 'Cartesian'; see pp. 63 and 486).

Graphs and curves

Because a function associates elements of one set with those of another, it defines the set of all pairs of elements, (x,y), in which x is a value of the independent variable and y is the value of the function for the argument x. Another way of expressing this is that any point that *satisfies* the function $y = f(x)$ can be represented by the point $(x, f(x))$. Since a function must be a many-one relation (see p. 68), every such pair has a different first element, so the pairs can be listed in a unique order. The function can then be thought of as moving through the values of the dependent variable as the value of the independent variable increases. This is what is represented by a graph in the Cartesian coordinate system: if we now draw a line joining the points $(x, f(x))$ as x increases, this line passes through all and only the points whose coordinates satisfy the function. Such a line is usually called a *graph*, although mathematicians prefer to use that term for the set of values of the variables, and call the diagram a *curve*. Since this way of representing change and dependency is equivalent to the function itself, curves provide us with a way of visualizing processes of change.

Average rates of change

Let us now consider a different example: suppose I throw a ball straight up in the air; it is slowed down by gravity until it stops and falls back to the ground, falling faster all the time. This is an example of a functional relationship between time (t) and height (h). If this relationship is described, say, by the equation $h = 20t − 5t^2$ then its graph looks like this:

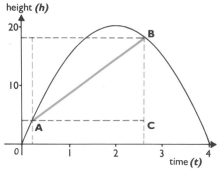

Velocity is defined to be the rate of change of displacement (here height), that is, displacement per unit time. Thus in the form

$$\text{velocity} = \frac{\text{increase of height}}{\text{time taken}}$$

the well known formula for velocity permits the *average* velocity over any time interval to be calculated. In the figure, the average velocity between A and B is therefore the change of height, CB, divided by the change of time, AC. Where the dependent variable (in this case height) is represented by the vertical axis, and the independent variable (time) by the horizontal axis, this average is equivalent to the *gradient* or *slope* of the line joining the points on the curve that correspond to the ends of the interval, as indicated by the bold line above. However, in this case the average clearly conceals more than it reveals, since we know that between $t = $ A and $t = $ C, the ball actually changed direction, so that its upward velocity changed from positive to negative.

Instantaneous rates of change

Similarly if you want to know how fast the Orient Express was travelling as it flashed through the Simplon Tunnel, you obviously get a very poor answer if you divide the whole distance from London to Venice by the total time taken to cover it. You get a better approximation if you measure the distance and time between

Paris and Milan, and a better approximation still if you time the train between the stations at either end of the tunnel. This suggests that if we had accurate enough clocks and measuring tapes we would be able to get closer and closer to a precise answer by timing the train over increasingly shorter distances. Although this still never tells us the speed at any one instant, it suggests that the instantaneous speed is the limit that this sequence of averages tends to as the length of the interval gets smaller.

Let us now return to the example of the ball, and apply this reasoning formally: here the vertical height could be expressed in terms of elapsed time as $h = 20t - 5t^2$; for example, the height after 0.5 second is 8.75 m, and after 1 second is 15 m. Now consider an arbitrary time t after the ball is thrown and take an interval of duration d on either side of it:

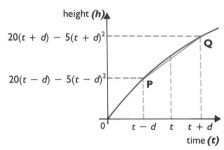

We can see that the average velocity over this distance is the difference between the values of the distance function at the arguments $t + d$ and at $t - d$, divided by the difference between these arguments. This is the slope of the chord PQ, that is

$$\frac{[20(t+d)-5(t+d)^2]-[20(t-d)-5(t-d)^2]}{(t+d)-(t-d)}$$

which simplifies to: $(40d - 20td)/2d = 20 - 10t$. Since this value is independent of d, this remains the average velocity round t no matter how small the interval d becomes, so that we can infer that the instantaneous velocity at time t from the starting point is actually equal to $20 - 10t$.

This, of course, is another function of t, so that the rate of change of a function is another function of the same independent variable. Where the original function was $y = f(x)$, the new function, known as its *derivative*, is written $f'(x)$ or dy/dx (read as 'dy by dx'), where dy and dx represent small *increments* in y and x respectively; here, for example, the derivative of $f(t) = 20t - 5t^2$ is $f'(t) = 20 - 10t$. Similarly, in the expression $y = x^2$, $f(x) = x^2$, and the derivative of $f(x) = x^2$ is

$$\frac{(x+d)^2-(x-d)^2}{(x+d)-(x-d)} = \frac{4xd}{2d} = 2x$$

Derivatives and differentiation

The process of finding the derivative of a function is called *differentiation*, and this branch of mathematics is known as the *differential calculus*. This process can also be interpreted geometrically: as d becomes smaller, the points P and Q come closer together until finally they coincide, at which point the slope has the

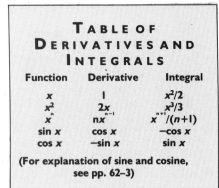

TABLE OF DERIVATIVES AND INTEGRALS

Function	Derivative	Integral
x	1	$x^2/2$
x^2	$2x$	$x^3/3$
x^n	nx^{n-1}	$x^{n+1}/(n+1)$
$\sin x$	$\cos x$	$-\cos x$
$\cos x$	$-\sin x$	$\sin x$

(For explanation of sine and cosine, see pp. 62–3)

value we have calculated, and represents the tangent to the curve.

However, it is not necessary always to work out a derivative either as we have done, or by drawing the graph. Instead, certain general principles apply; for example, as we have seen, the derivative of x^2 with respect to x is $2x$, and we can generalize this to state that the derivative of ax^n with respect to x is anx^{n-1} (see also table).

The derivative of a function can itself be differentiated; for example, acceleration is the rate of change of velocity, and we can repeat the line of reasoning in the previous example to find the derivative of the velocity function with respect to time. This is the *second derivative* of the distance function.

In the previous example, the average acceleration over the interval $(t - d, t + d)$ is

$$\frac{[20-10(t+d)]-[20-10(t-d)]}{(t+d)-(t-d)}$$

which simplifies to the constant -10. It is because acceleration is a second derivative, that is the rate of change of a rate of change, that it is measured in units of distance per second per second. In this case the value -10 approximates to the downward force of gravity, which slows the ball down and returns it to the ground.

Totals and integrals

So far we have been considering how much we can find out about speed if we are given functional information about distance in terms of time. Now consider the converse problem: if we know a train's velocity as a function of time, how can we calculate the total distance it has travelled? Clearly if we knew the average speed, the total distance would be the result of multiplying the overall average speed by the total duration of the journey; and if the journey was undertaken in stages for which we knew separate average speeds and durations, the total distance travelled would be the sum of the distances calculated by this method for each separate stage. However, this formula requires the journey to be broken down into separable stages whose average speeds are known; where we only know the instantaneous speed at any moment expressed as a function of time, it is of no help at all. On the other hand, we can conjecture that we can approximate to the right answer by breaking the whole journey down into more and more, shorter and shorter stages.

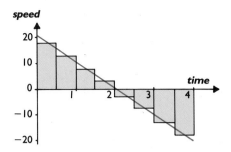

Let us now go back to the previous example: the above figure shows the function derived for the velocity of the ball. The complete duration is divided into equal intervals, and in each we take the speed at the midpoint as an approximation to the average. But this really represents the stepped graph (shaded), rather than the true continuous function. However, if we double the number of intervals and halve the duration of each, we get a better approximation, and carrying on in the same way gives a sequence of better and better approximations whose limit can be thought of as the sum of the areas of infinitely many infinitely thin slices of the area under the graph. The *integral calculus* is the study of such processes, and it enables us to calculate infinite sums that can be expressed in terms of continuous functions.

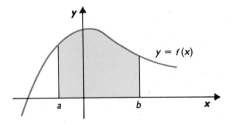

The sum of the value of the function $y = f(x)$ between arbitrary $x = a$ and $x = b$ (the shaded area on the figure) is written $\int_a^b f(x)\,dx$, and is equal to $F(b) - F(a)$, where $F(x)$ is the *indefinite integral* of $f(x)$; this is another continuous function of x, written $\int f(x)\,dx$. For example, in the ball example, the indefinite integral, $\int (20 - 10t)\,dt$, of $y = 20 - 10t$, is $20t - (10/2)t^2 + c$ (where c can be any constant). If we denote this new function $Int(x)$, then the definite integral between a and b is $Int(b) - Int(a)$, that is

$$(20b - 5b^2 + c) - (20a - 5a^2 + c)$$
$$= 5(a^2 - b^2) + 20(b - a).$$

In fact it turns out that this process of *integration* is the inverse of differentiation and it is therefore sometimes called *antidifferentiation*. This means that the indefinite integral of the derivative of a given function, and the derivative of its indefinite integral, are both equal to the given function – a result so important that it is called the *fundamental theorem of calculus*.　　EJB

SEE ALSO

● MOTION AND FORCE p. 20
● MATHEMATICS AND ITS APPLICATIONS p. 62
● SETS AND PARADOXES p. 66
● CORRESPONDENCE, COUNTING AND INFINITY p. 68

Probability:
Chance and Choice

Not all actions and happenings have completely predictable results. Often we know that there is only a limited range of possible outcomes, but we do not know with certainty which of these to expect.

SEE ALSO

● MATHEMATICS AND ITS APPLI-
  CATIONS p. 62
● NUMBER SYSTEMS AND
  ALGEBRA p. 64

Probability theory enables us to describe with mathematical rigour the chance of an action or happening having a particular outcome. We may not, even then, make the right choice, but it will at least be a *justifiable* choice.

Probability and frequency

When we toss a coin or throw a die, we cannot predict which of the sides will land facing upwards – this, after all, is the point of tossing coins and throwing dice. Assuming we accept the fairness of the coin and the way it is tossed, we know it is just as likely to come up heads as tails, and there is no other possible outcome. Similarly, with a fair die, it is just as likely to fall with any of its numbers – from 1 to 6 – upwards, and there are no other possible outcomes. We describe these examples by saying that all the possible *outcomes* are *equiprobable*, and that the *a priori probability* (i.e. the theoretical probability) of a coin coming up heads is 1 in 2 or 1/2, and that of throwing a 6 on a single die is 1 in 6 or 1/6.

On the other hand, *empirical probability* (often called *a posteriori probability*) is based on observation and experiment. Here, the probability of a particular outcome is calculated from the proportion of times it has been observed to have happened before under the same conditions – its *relative frequency*. Thus, if you tossed a coin 10 times and the coin came up heads 3 times, the empirical probability that one of these throws came up heads is 3/10.

The probability scale

When an outcome is certain, it occurs every time: 1 in 1, 2 in 2, etc. Expressing this as a fraction, we say the probability is 1/1, that is, one. When an outcome is impossible, it occurs no times in any number of tests, so we say the probability is zero. For example, when throwing a die, the probability of throwing a number greater than 6 is zero, and the probability of throwing a number between 1 and 6 is one.

Probabilities between certainty and impossibility are expressed as fractions. So if, for example, we know that the 6 sides of a die are equiprobable, and the probability of throwing any of them is 1, the probability of each must be 1/6. Furthermore, if we consider only two possible outcomes, an odd number or an even, the probability of each must be 1/2. The fact that there are three odd outcomes each with probability 1/6, and 1/6 + 1/6 + 1/6 = 1/2, demonstrates, very simply, the *addition rule*: we can add up the individual probabilities of the different possible outcomes in a particular trial to get the combined probability.

Particularly in gaming and gambling, we see *odds* used as a scale for measuring chance. 'Odds' – more formally known as *likelihood ratio* – means the proportion of favourable to unfavourable possibilities, and is a different way of expressing probability. As we have seen, the probability of throwing, say, a 4, with a die is 1/6. Therefore, the probability of not throwing a 4 is 5/6. The 'odds' are thus expressed as 1 to 5 on throwing a 4 (or 5 to 1 against throwing a 4).

The law of large numbers

Suppose we toss a coin 10 times and the outcome is only 3 heads. The probability of a head is 1/2, so why do we not get 5 heads? We try a total of 100 tosses of the coin and the outcome is now, say, 40 heads, the last 6 being all heads. A gambler might back the chance that the 101st toss would fall tails, because, previously, there had been more tails than heads. Another gambler might back heads, because there seemed to be a 'run of heads', which would conform with the so-called 'law of averages'.

However, we know that the probability of a head or a tail at any one toss is 1/2 and a coin cannot remember – it cannot be influenced by what has gone before. Both gamblers are relying on empirical probability where theoretical probability is what matters – both are therefore betting on hope.

There is no 'law of averages'. Experimental and theoretical probability are connected only by the *law of large numbers*, which states that as the number of trials increases, the observed empirical probability comes closer and closer to the theoretical value. Thus in this example it means only that in the *very* long run, the relative frequency settles down towards 1/2.

Rules of probability

If, we wish to find the combined probabi-

Card games offer very many more combinations of possibilities than tossing coins or throwing dice. Some of the odds are staggering: for example, the odds against dealing 13 cards of one suit are 158 753 389 899 to 1, while the odds against a named player receiving a 'perfect hand' consisting of all 13 spades are 653 013 559 599 to 1. The odds against each of four players receiving a complete suit (a 'perfect hand') are in excess of 2×10^{27} to 1.

lity of two independent trials, we use the *multiplication rule*. When we throw a pair of dice, we can consider these as two independent trials – because how one die falls does not affect the other. No matter what the first die shows, the second can show any of its six faces – and there are six ways the first die can fall. So there are $6 \times 6 = 36$ possible outcomes for the ordered pair. Since these are equiprobable, the probability of any particular outcome, say a 1 with the first die and a 4 with the second, is 1/36, which is $1/6 \times 1/6$; that is, we multiply the individual probabilities to get the probability of a particular ordered outcome using the two dice. Since there are six ways of throwing a double, the probability of throwing the same number with two dice is 6/36 = 1/6, whence the probability of throwing different numbers is $1 - 1/6 = 5/6$.

When a third die is thrown, there are now only four available faces differing from those of the first two dice, so that the probability of this showing a third different number is 4/6. Hence, the probability of throwing three different numbers with three dice is $5/6 \times 4/6$. Throwing six dice, the probability of an outcome of six different numbers is $5/6 \times 4/6 \times 3/6 \times 2/6 \times 1/6$, which equals 5/324, or approximately 0.015. Thus we can expect the outcome to occur only once or twice in every hundred trials.

However, if we wish to specify the order beforehand (say, 1, 2, 3, 4, 5, 6 or 6, 4, 2, 5, 3, 1, for example), the probability is 1/6 for the first throw multiplied by 1/6 for the second throw, and so on. With the six dice the probability is therefore $(1/6)^6$ which equals 1/46656, or approximately 0.000021. Thus, we can expect such an outcome only about twice in every 100 000 trials.

It is very important that we correctly define a problem before applying the addition or multiplication rule. Many problems in fact require both. Suppose, for example, we wish to achieve a total of 8 with two dice. This could be from 6 and 2, 5 and 3, or 4 and 4; but there are two other possibilities: 2 and 6, and 5 and 3. That is, there are two ways of throwing a pair of distinct numbers, so that the probability

that one die will show a 6 and the other a 2 is 2/36. Similarly, for a 5 and a 3. But there is only one way of throwing a double, so that the probability of a double 4 is only 1/36. The probability of an outcome of a total of 8 is the sum of these probabilities, that is, 5/36.

Decision-making

Very often we are required to make decisions based on only a little knowledge of the likely circumstances. As examples: a doctor may have to choose between different treatments for a patient with relatively little experimental evidence as to which is more successful; or the directors of a business may have to choose between different advertising strategies on the basis of rival claims about the effectiveness of the different media. In such cases, the decision-makers need ways of measuring the competing strategies against one another. One way of doing this involves calculating the *expected value*.

A simple way to explain this is by considering a hockey or soccer league table, where 2 points are awarded for a win, 1 for a draw, and 0 for a loss. Suppose a particular team in the league decides, at the beginning of the season, that – based on all the available evidence – its probability of winning any match is 1/4 and of drawing is 1/3. Then its probability of losing is $1 - 1/4 - 1/3 = 5/12$. Over a run of 12 matches the team would expect to win 3, draw 4, and lose 5. The points it would expect to gain in 12 average matches would be $(3 \times 2) + (4 \times 1) + (5 \times 0) = 10$ points. Thus the average number of points they can expect in each match is 10/12. This is the expected value.

By calculating an expected value for each course of action available to us, we are able to choose the one that has the best likely outcome. On the basis of only partial knowledge, we are enabled to make a rational choice, even though it may not be the one with the highest probability (see box for an example). EJB

A roulette wheel. On a normal roulette wheel there are 37 compartments numbered from 0 to 36. The probability of, say, 0 winning is 1/37; the odds against 0 winning are 36 to 1. The casino will not usually offer odds better than 35 to 1, so in the long run the casino will make a profit.

SHARING A BIRTHDAY

Suppose we are looking for a pair of people who have the same birthday. What is the smallest number of people, chosen at random, for which there is a better than evens chance of two sharing a birthday? Since, allowing for leap years, there are 366 possible birthdays, many people guess that 183 is the answer. In fact, the answer is 23.

The probability of the second person we ask not matching the birthday of the first, is 365/366. The probability of the third person not matching either of the other two is 364/366. So the chance of three people not sharing the same birthday is 365/366 × 364/366. For *n* people, the chances of them all having different birthdays is, thus, 365/366 ×

364/366 × 363/366 × .... to $n - 1$ terms. We need to find how many terms of this sequence we need to multiply together before their product becomes less than 1/2 – that is, before there is a less than evens chance that this number of people do not include a single pair with the same birthday.

If we work it out, we find that the probability of 22 people having different birthdays is 0.5252, and for 23 people, it is 0.494. Therefore, 23 is the smallest number of people for which there is a better than evens chance of at least one shared birthday. On the other hand, we need 367 to be *certain* that two of them have the same birthday!

THE RESTLESS EARTH

'What happens to us
Is irrelevant to the world's geology
But what happens to the world's geology
Is not irrelevant to us.'

Hugh MacDiarmid

The Earth's Structure and Atmosphere

Moving outwards from the Earth, man has been to the Moon, landed spacecraft on planets, and sent space probes to the outermost reaches of the Solar System. But in the opposite direction the story is very different. Man's direct access to the Earth's interior is limited to the depth of the deepest mine, which is less than 4 km (2.5 mi). The Russians spent most of the 1980s drilling a hole in the crust to a target depth of 15 km (9.3 mi), but in doing so they have penetrated no more than the upper 0.24% of the Earth, the average radius of which is 6371 km (3956 mi).

SEE ALSO

● THE SUN AND THE SOLAR
  SYSTEM p. 10
● THE INNER PLANETS p. 12
● PLATE TECTONICS p. 78
● THE FORMATION OF ROCKS
  p. 84
● THE WEATHER p. 102

Unable to visit the Earth's deep interior or place instruments within it, scientists must explore in more subtle ways. One method is to measure natural phenomena – the magnetic and gravitational fields are the chief examples – at the Earth's surface and interpret the observations in terms of the planet's internal properties. A second approach is to study the Earth

Seismic wave paths through the Earth's interior. Two of the four kinds of seismic waves, P and S waves, travel through the interior of the Earth (see p.80). By measuring the time it takes these waves to reach seismograph stations around the world, scientists can trace the paths the waves take, observe how their velocities vary, and hence determine the Earth's structure.

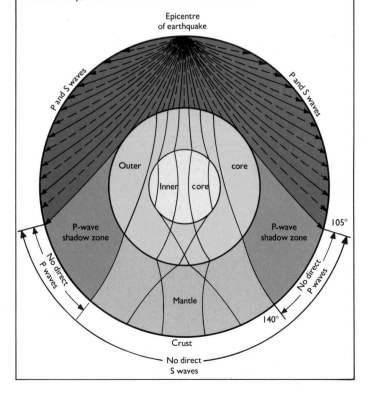

THE INTERIOR OF THE EARTH

ILLUSTRATING ITS VARIOUS LAYERS

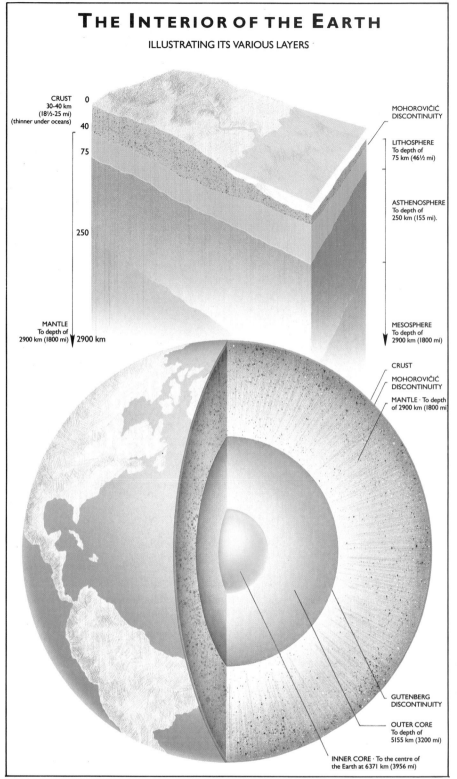

with non-material probes, the most important of which are the seismic waves emitted by earthquakes (see diagram, and also p. 80). As seismic waves pass through the Earth, they undergo sudden changes in direction and velocity at certain depths. These depths mark the major boundaries, or *discontinuities*, that divide the Earth into crust, mantle and core.

The crust

The outermost layer of the Earth, the crust, accounts for only about 0.6% of the planet's volume. The average thickness of the *oceanic crust* is 5–9 km (3–5½ mi) and varies comparatively little throughout the world. By contrast, the *continental crust* has the much higher average thickness of 30–40 km (18½–25 mi) and varies much more. Beneath the central valley of California, for example, the crust is only about 20 km (12½ mi) thick, but beneath parts of major mountain ranges such as the Himalaya it can exceed 80 km (50 mi).

The rocks that form the continental crust are highly varied, including volcanic lava flows, huge blocks of granite, and sediments laid down in shallow water when parts of the continents were inundated by the sea. Despite the diversity of materials, the average composition is roughly that of the rock granite, and the two most common elements (in addition to oxygen) are silicon and aluminium.

The oceanic crust is much more uniform in composition and, apart from a thin covering of sediment, consists largely of the rock basalt, possibly underlain by the rock gabbro (which has the same composition as basalt but is coarser grained). Oxygen apart, the most common elements in the oceanic crust are again silicon and aluminium, but there is markedly more magnesium than in the upper continental crust.

The composition of the lower crust, which cannot be sampled directly, is uncertain, but the predominant rock is probably gabbro. The lower crust is certainly different from the upper crust because seismic waves pass through it at a higher velocity.

The mantle

The mantle extends from the base of the crust to a depth of about 2900 km (1800 mi) and accounts for about 82% of the Earth's volume. The sharp boundary between the crust and the mantle is called the *Mohorovičić discontinuity* (or *Moho* for short) after the Yugoslav seismologist who discovered it in 1909.

The mantle is thought to consist largely of peridotite, a rock that contains high proportions of the elements iron, silicon and magnesium, in addition to oxygen. The mantle is inaccessible, but evidence of its composition comes from surface rocks thought to have originated there. Although mostly solid, the mantle contains a partially molten layer (see below).

The core

The core extends from the base of the mantle to the Earth's centre and accounts for about 17% of the Earth's volume. The discontinuity between the mantle and core is called the *core-mantle boundary* or, sometimes, the *Gutenberg discontinuity*, after the German-American seismologist Beno Gutenberg. The core actually comprises two distinct parts. The *outer core* – which extends down to a depth of about 5155 km (3200 mi) – is liquid. The *inner core* is solid.

The main constituent of the core is iron, although measurements of the Earth's rate of rotation show that the density must be slightly lower than that of pure iron. The core must therefore contain a small proportion (5–20%) of some lighter element – possibly sulphur, silicon, carbon, hydrogen or oxygen.

An alternative view

The division of the Earth into crust, mantle and core is based on the fact that the three zones have different chemical compositions. However, there is another way of looking at the Earth, in terms of its physical state.

In the upper mantle, at depths of 75–250 km (46½–155 mi), the velocity of seismic waves is slightly lower than in the zones just above and below. Scientists believe that this layer of the upper mantle is partially molten, and they have named it the *asthenosphere*. It is this layer that is

the source of volcanic *magma* (molten rock; see p. 82). The rigid layer above the asthenosphere, the *lithosphere*, comprises the crust and uppermost mantle. The solid region of the mantle below the asthenosphere is called the *mesosphere*.

The magnetic field

The Earth has a magnetic field, which is why a compass needle points approximately north at most places on the Earth's surface. But where, and how, is the field generated?

The magnetic field has two parts. Most of it is that of a simple dipole (see p. 34); it is as if a giant bar magnet were placed at the centre of the Earth (although the magnet slopes at 11° to the Earth's axis of rotation). But a small proportion of it is much more complicated and changes very rapidly. This is why a compass needle points in a slightly different direction each year.

The rapid changing indicates that the magnetic field must be produced in a part of the Earth that is fluid, for no solid region could reorganize itself rapidly enough without shaking the planet to pieces. The only liquid zone inside the Earth is the outer core.

This fits in with something else. The only conceivable way in which a magnetic field could be generated within the Earth is by the flow of very large electric currents, and electric currents need a conductor. The Earth's core is the most conductive zone in the whole Earth, because it consists largely of iron. The silicates of the mantle would simply not conduct well enough.

The atmosphere

The atmosphere is easier to investigate than the Earth's interior because it is directly accessible to instruments carried by kites, balloons, aeroplanes and, latterly, rockets and satellites. What these instruments have shown is that traces of the atmosphere extend for thousands of kilometres above the Earth's surface. There is no sharp boundary between the atmosphere and 'interplanetary space'.

The atmosphere may be divided into four layers on the basis of temperature. In the layer closest to the Earth, the *troposphere*,

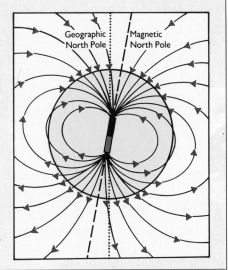

The magnetic field of the Earth (shown here in cross-section) is mainly that of a dipole – it has the same shape as that of a giant bar magnet at the centre of the Earth (although the field is actually produced by motions of liquid iron within the Earth's core).

The lines emerging from the magnet are lines of induction (see p. 34); they show the directions in which magnetic compass needles (red arrows) would point if placed in the field.

Most navigational compasses are mounted on a vertical pin, and so can only move on a horizontal plane. However, if a compass needle is suspended on a thread, it will point downwards towards the Earth (in the northern hemisphere) or upwards (in the southern hemisphere), as well as towards the magnetic north pole.

Geographic North Pole Magnetic North Pole

THE COMPOSITION OF DRY AIR

Constituent	Percentage by volume
Nitrogen (N_2)	78.084
Oxygen (O_2)	20.946
Argon (A)	0.934
Carbon dioxide (CO_2)	0.034
Neon (Ne)	0.00182
Helium (He)	0.000524
Methane (CH_4)	0.00015
Krypton (Kr)	0.000114
Hydrogen (H_2)	0.00005

temperature decreases with altitude to the top of the layer, which on average is at a height of 10–12 km (6–7½ mi), although the thickness of the layer varies from more than 16 km (10 mi) in the tropics to less than 9 km (5½ mi) in polar regions. Most weather phenomena occur in the troposphere (see p. 102).

Above the troposphere lies the *stratosphere*. In the stratosphere the temperature remains more or less constant up to 20 km (12½ mi) and thereafter increases to the top of the layer at 45–50 km (28–31 mi). The reason for the temperature rise is that the stratosphere is the home of the atmosphere's ozone (O_3), and the ozone absorbs dangerous ultraviolet radiation from the Sun, protecting life on Earth in the process (see pp. 300–1). In the next layer, the *mesosphere* (not to be confused with the mesosphere in the deep Earth), temperature again decreases to the top of the layer at 80–85 km (50–53 mi). Above this lies the *thermosphere*, throughout most of which the temperature again rises. The thermosphere fades out over thousands of kilometres, gradually merging with 'space', although the region above about 500 km (310 mi) is sometimes called the *exosphere*.

In the altitude range 80–400 km (50–250 mi) – but the upper limit is very poorly defined – the atoms of oxygen and molecules of nitrogen are electrically charged (ionized). This layer, part of the thermosphere, is known as the *ionosphere*. The ionosphere reflects radio waves and hence makes long-range communications possible. PJS

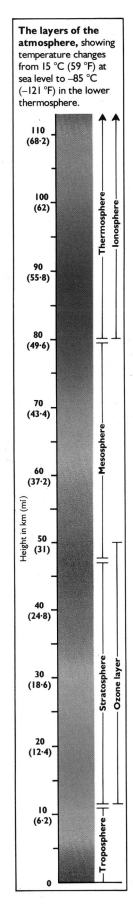

The layers of the atmosphere, showing temperature changes from 15 °C (59 °F) at sea level to –85 °C (–121 °F) in the lower thermosphere.

Height in km (mi)

110 (68·2)
100 (62)
90 (55·8)
80 (49·6)
70 (43·4)
60 (37·2)
50 (31)
40 (24·8)
30 (18·6)
20 (12·4)
10 (6·2)
0

Thermosphere — Ionosphere

Mesosphere

Stratosphere — Ozone layer

Troposphere

Plate Tectonics

Throughout almost the whole of human history, most people have imagined the continents to be fixed in their present positions and the ocean floors to be the oldest and most primitive parts of the Earth. In the space of a few years during the early 1960s, however, both of these assumptions were overthrown in an intellectual revolution. It suddenly became possible to prove that the continents are drifting across the Earth's surface, that the ocean floors are spreading, and that none of the oceanic crust is more than about 200 million years old – less than 5% of the age of the Earth (4600 million years).

Continental drift was not a new idea in the 1960s – it had been proposed by Antonio Snider of Paris in 1858. But it was not taken seriously until, in 1915, the German meteorologist Alfred Wegener (1890–1930) wrote a book drawing together all the scientific evidence for drift then available.

Many of Wegener's arguments are still valid today. He pointed out, for example, that the rocks along the west coast of Africa are very similar to those along the east coast of South America, suggesting that the two continents were once one. He also noted that certain identical fossils are found on continents now separated by thousands of kilometres of ocean. The animals concerned could never have swum so far; so the continents involved must once have been joined.

Wegener proposed that about 200 million years ago there was just one super-continent, which he named Pangaea. Subsequently, Pangaea split into smaller landmasses, which then drifted to their present positions (and are still drifting, at rates of a few centimetres a year). But for over 40 years Wegener's arguments were rejected by most geologists, who could not envisage how solid continents could possibly plough their way through equally solid ocean floor.

The revolution

In the early 1960s scientists managed to prove continental drift by making use of the weak magnetism that many rocks contain (see box). Once this had been done, it was no longer possible to use the problem of *how* drift occurs as a reason for rejecting it. A solution must exist and had to be found. It was not long in coming. Scientists soon realized that continents did not have to plough through ocean floors, because the ocean floors are moving too. Indeed, it is the spreading oceanic lithosphere (see pp. 76–7) that pushes the continents along.

The secret lay in the huge ocean-floor mountain ranges, known as oceanic ridges, discovered by oceanographers during the 1950s. These are now known to

SEE ALSO

● THE EARTH'S STRUCTURE
  AND ATMOSPHERE p. 76
● EARTHQUAKES p. 80
● VOLCANOES p. 82
● THE FORMATION OF ROCKS
  p. 84
● MOUNTAINS p. 86
● ISLANDS p. 98
● THE OCEANS p. 100

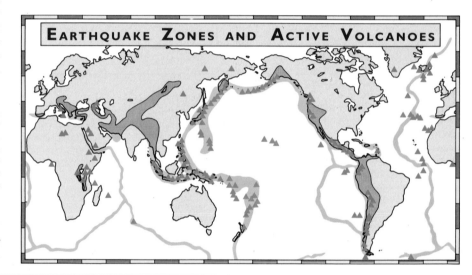

EARTHQUAKE ZONES AND ACTIVE VOLCANOES

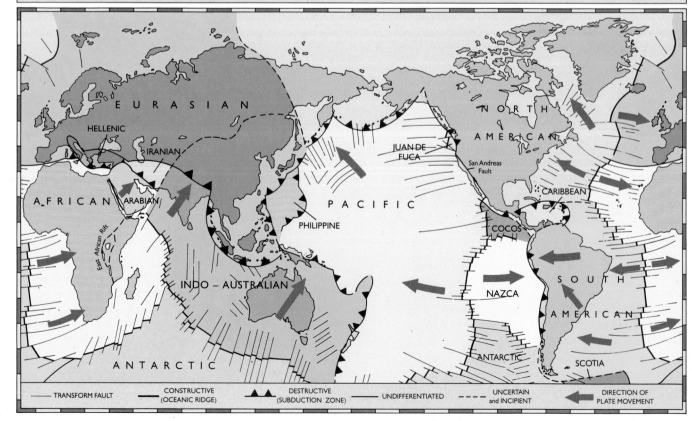

THE EARTH'S TECTONIC PLATES

EURASIAN
HELLENIC
IRANIAN
AFRICAN
ARABIAN
East African Rift
JUAN DE FUCA
San Andreas Fault
NORTH AMERICAN
PACIFIC
PHILIPPINE
CARIBBEAN
COCOS
INDO – AUSTRALIAN
NAZCA
SOUTH AMERICAN
ANTARCTIC
ANTARCTIC
SCOTIA

| ——— TRANSFORM FAULT | ▬▬ CONSTRUCTIVE (OCEANIC RIDGE) | ▲▲ DESTRUCTIVE (SUBDUCTION ZONE) | —— UNDIFFERENTIATED | – – – UNCERTAIN and INCIPIENT | ➤ DIRECTION OF PLATE MOVEMENT |

be the sites at which magma rises from the asthenosphere below (see pp. 76–7), cools, and solidifies to form new oceanic lithosphere (see diagram). Once solid, the lava moves away on each side of the ridge, and more magma rises into the gap to take its place. Oceanic lithosphere is thus being created continuously at oceanic ridges.

But unless the Earth is expanding, lithosphere must also be destroyed at the same rate as it is created. This happens at *subduction zones* (see diagram), most – but not all – of which lie around the margins of the Pacific. As the spreading oceanic lithosphere reaches the edges of the Pacific continents, it is forced down into the Earth's interior where it gradually melts and loses its identity. All the ocean floor is recycled in this way in less than about 200 million years.

Plate tectonics

By the late 1960s, continental drift and ocean-floor spreading had come to be seen as two aspects of a wider phenomenon – plate tectonics.

The Earth's lithosphere (not just the crust) is divided into 15 major *plates* of various sizes. The plates 'float' on the partially molten asthenosphere below, and it is because they are floating that they have the freedom to move horizontally. A few of the plates (for example, the Pacific) are almost completely oceanic, but most include both oceanic and continental lithosphere. There are no completely continental plates.

The boundaries between the plates are of three types (see diagram). The oceanic ridges are known as *constructive plate boundaries*, because they are where new lithosphere is being created. The subduction zones are known as *destructive plate boundaries*, because they are where lithosphere is being consumed by the Earth's interior. Finally, there are *conservative plate boundaries*, also known as *transform faults*, along which lithosphere is neither being created nor destroyed, but where the plate edges are simply sliding past each other. Most transform faults are on the ocean floor, where they offset sections of oceanic ridge, enabling the ridges to adjust to the curvature of the Earth. Occasionally, however, they impinge on land. The notorious San Andreas fault of California is a transform fault.

The plate boundaries are the most tectonically active parts of the Earth – they are where most mountain building, earthquakes and volcanoes occur (see pp. 80–7). The plates floating on the asthenosphere may be regarded as jostling against each other, generating tectonic activity at their margins. However, because plates have destructive and constructive plate boundaries, they are also continuously changing their sizes and shapes.

Not even the continents themselves are immune from change. Running for more than 6400 km (3975 mi) up eastern Africa, from the Zambezi to Syria, is a giant *rift valley*, where a long strip of crust has sunk

PLATE BOUNDARIES

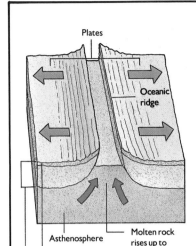
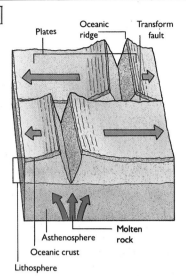

Constructive plate boundary: new lithosphere is formed at oceanic ridges by molten rock rising from the asthenosphere.

Destructive plate boundary: at subduction zones oceanic lithosphere is forced beneath continental lithosphere, descending into the asthenosphere at approximately 45° angle.

Conservative plate boundary: at transform faults, plates slide past each other, with lithosphere being neither created nor destroyed.

HOW CONTINENTAL DRIFT WAS PROVED

Many rocks contain minute magnetic particles, usually oxides of iron and titanium. When a rock forms, these particles become magnetized in the direction of the Earth's magnetic field at the particular site. Using highly sensitive instruments, it is possible to measure this weak magnetism and from it determine the position of the north pole at the time the rock was formed.

Scientists were surprised to discover that for rocks older than a few million years the north poles determined in this way did not lie at the present north pole, and that the older the rocks the greater was the discrepancy. They were even more surprised to find that rocks of the same age from different continents gave ancient north poles in quite different positions.

There can only be one north pole at any given time, however, and that must lie close to the north end of the Earth's rotational axis. The only way of explaining the rock magnetic data, therefore, was to assume that the continents have drifted with respect to both the present north pole and each other.

between more or less parallel faults (see also diagram, p. 85). Many scientists believe that this, the East African Rift, represents an early stage in the break-up of Africa, leading to the creation of a new spreading ocean.   PJS

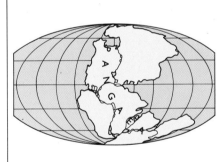

200 million years ago: virtually all the Earth's dry land is contained in Pangaea, the original supercontinent.

110 million years ago: Pangaea has split into two smaller continents, Laurasia and Gondwana, which themselves begin to split up.

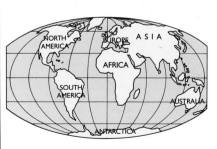

0 million years ago: the continents have assumed their present positions, but are continuing to move (see arrows on main map).

Earthquakes

An earthquake is a sudden release of energy in the Earth's crust or upper mantle. As the planet's tectonic plates (see p. 78) jostle against each other and become distorted, tremendous strain builds up – and from time to time the strain energy is discharged in zones where the rocks are weakest. The result is a sudden violent shock that can have highly destructive effects on the Earth's surface nearby.

The massively destructive power of earthquakes can be seen in this photograph of the Mexico earthquake of 1985, in which nearly 10 000 people died.

The damaging effects of an earthquake are due to the vibrations (*seismic waves*) emitted by the shock (see diagram). For a brief moment the waves shake the ground close to the earthquake, frequently producing permanent effects. Few people are ever killed or injured directly by an earthquake; death and injury are more likely to result from the collapse of buildings caused by the earthquake.

Whether or not there are people or buildings present, earthquakes may cause fissures to appear in the ground, produce changes in the level and tilt of the ground surface, divert rivers and streams, and trigger landslides and avalanches. Undersea earthquakes may also give rise to *tsunami* – huge sea waves that can travel across the oceans for thousands of kilometres, causing devastation when they hit land.

Where earthquakes occur

Most earthquakes take place along the boundaries of the tectonic plates (see p. 78) – along oceanic ridges, transform faults and subduction zones – because this is where the plates interact most intensely, and hence where distortion and strain build-up are greatest (see map, p. 78).

However, not all earthquakes occur along plate margins. In North America, for example, the most damaging earthquakes of historic times have taken place not in California, through which runs a transform fault (the San Andreas fault), but in South Carolina and Missouri, both of which are far from plate margins. The reasons for this are unclear, but earthquakes within the interiors of plates may be due to deep, still active faults remaining from a much earlier phase of plate tectonics. California is still America's most notorious seismic area, however, because it is there that earthquakes are most frequent.

The point at which an earthquake occurs is called the *focus*, or *hypocentre*. The point on the Earth's surface directly above the focus is called the *epicentre*. A world map of epicentres is largely a map of the Earth's plate boundaries (see p. 79).

All earthquake foci lie within about the upper 700 km (435 mi) of the Earth. Within this range, earthquakes are classified as *shallow* (focal depths of 0–70 km / 0–43 mi), *intermediate* (70–300 km / 43–186 mi), or *deep* (below 300 km / 186 mi). There are about three times as many intermediate earthquakes as there are deep ones, and about ten times as many shallow ones. It is the shallow shocks that produce most of the damage at the Earth's surface, for the obvious reason that they are closer to it. Collectively, the shallow earthquakes also release the most energy – about 75% of the total, compared to 3% for deep earthquakes.

Earthquake foci at the various depths are not distributed uniformly along the plate boundaries. Almost all the deep earthquakes, about 90% of the intermediate ones and about 75% of the shallow ones occur along the subduction zones around the Pacific Ocean. Oceanic ridges and transform faults, on the other hand, are generally the sites of shallower and smaller events.

Measuring earthquakes

The size of an earthquake is specified by its *magnitude*, sometimes called the *Richter magnitude* after the American seismologist, Charles Richter, who devised the scale in the 1930s. Magnitude is actually a measure of the size (*amplitude*) of the waves emitted by the earthquake. However, the magnitude scale is logarithmic. This means that each step up the scale represents a ten-fold increase in the amplitude of the emitted waves. Thus the waves from a magnitude-7 earthquake are 10 times bigger than those from a magnitude-6 shock, 100 times bigger than those from a magnitude-5 event, and so on.

Magnitude can also be regarded as a measure of the energy released by an earthquake, because energy is related to wave size. The relationship is such that each division on the magnitude scale represents an approximately thirty-fold difference in energy. Thus a magnitude-7 earthquake releases about 30 times more energy than a magnitude-6 shock and about $30 \times 30 = 900$ times more energy than a magnitude-5 event. This explains why most of the energy released by earthquakes comes from the very few big shocks that occur each year rather than from the million or so smaller earthquakes.

In principle, there is no upper limit to the possible magnitude of earthquakes, although in practice there are no shocks with magnitudes greater than about 9. On the basis of magnitude, earthquakes are classified as *great* (magnitude above 7.5), *major* (6.5–7.5), *large* (5.5–6.5), *moderate* (4.5–5.5) or *small* (below 4.5). Magnitudes may be determined from the amplitudes of either body waves or surface waves,

---

CAN EARTHQUAKES BE PREDICTED?

The short answer to this question is 'no'. Although scientists have managed to predict a few specific earthquakes, they have been quite unable to devise a generally applicable method of prediction.

The Americans, Japanese, Chinese and Russians have been researching into prediction for several decades. They have discovered that before some earthquakes ground level and tilt may change, tide levels may fluctuate, the seismic velocities in nearby rocks may vary, and the local magnetic field may waver. But no one of these applies to all, or even the majority of, earthquakes, and some earthquakes appear to have no early warning signs at all.

The most spectacularly successful prediction was that of

the magnitude-7.3 earthquake at Haicheng, China, in 1975. By mobilizing scientists and many members of the public to observe a large number of natural phenomena, the Chinese were able to predict the location and timing of the event quite accurately. They could thus evacuate the population, reducing deaths from a likely million or so to just 1328. Unfortunately, they have had little success since. In 1976, for example, they failed to forecast the magnitude-7.8 earthquake in Tangshan, and at least 240 000 people died.

In the early 1960s scientists were optimistic enough to suggest that prediction would be possible within a decade or so. Nowadays, however, they will not even guarantee that it will ever be possible.

THE PRINCIPLE OF THE SEISMOMETER

Support moves

Wire flexes

Pen

Rotating drum
records movement
as waves

Heavy weight remains
motionless

Base moves
horizontally

Base attached
to bedrock

Earth moves
horizontally

The seismometer is an instrument for measuring earthquakes. There are two different kinds: one measures horizontal movement, and the other vertical movement.

Spring flexes

Heavy weight
remains
motionless

Pen

Support moves
vertically

Rotating drum moves
vertically, recording
movement as waves

Hinge

Base moves
vertically

Earth moves
vertically

Base attached
to bedrock

night (people asleep in low-rise houses) and whether or not the cities concerned have made any attempt to construct earthquake-resistant buildings.

To specify the size of an earthquake in terms of its effects, an intensity scale is used. In the West (but not in Japan or the former Soviet republics, which use slightly different systems) this is usually the *Modified Mercalli Scale* (see table).

After a big earthquake there is frequently a survey to discover how intensity varies with distance from the epicentre. The intensity is determined at many points (by observing ground effects and questioning local inhabitants), and points with the same intensity are joined by lines to make an intensity 'contour' map, known as an *isoseismal map*. Intensity decreases away from the epicentre. If 'the intensity of the earthquake' is specified, it means the maximum intensity – i.e. that at the epicentre. PJS

SEE ALSO

● THE EARTH'S STRUCTURE
AND ATMOSPHERE p. p. 76
● PLATE TECTONICS p. p. 78
● VOLCANOES p. p. 82
● THE FORMATION OF ROCKS
p. p. 84

whichever happen to be the most convenient.

Earthquake damage

Although magnitude is a fairly accurate scientific measure of the strength of an earthquake, it does not necessarily relate directly to the amount of death and damage that the earthquake causes, because the destructive power of a seismic disturbance depends on more than the quantity of energy released. For example, a magnitude-7 earthquake can, and often does, produce more devastation than a magnitude-8 shock, even though the latter releases about 30 times more energy than the former. This is because as important as the energy are the characteristics of the ground in the epicentral region, the population density there, and the nature of the buildings in the area.

However big an earthquake is, it will cause no damage or death at all if it takes place in an uninhabited wilderness. By contrast, a much smaller earthquake can produce havoc in a major city. Moreover, two earthquakes of the same magnitude may have quite different effects on two more or less identical cities if one of the cities is built on soft sediment (making it very vulnerable to vibrations) and the other on hard rock (less susceptible). The effects of the earthquakes will also depend on such factors as whether the shocks happen during the day (people at work, possibly in high-rise offices) or at

THE MODIFIED MERCALLI SCALE

I Not felt except by a few people under favourable circumstances

II Felt by a few people at rest. Delicately suspended objects swing.

III Felt noticeably indoors. Standing cars may rock.

IV Felt generally indoors, and sleeping people are woken. Cars rocked, windows rattle.

V Felt generally. Some plaster falls and dishes and windows are broken. Pendulum clocks stop.

VI Felt by all – many frightened. Chimneys and plaster damaged. Furniture moved and objects upset.

VII Everyone runs outdoors. Felt in moving cars. Moderate structural damage.

VIII General alarm. Weak structures badly damaged. Walls and furniture fall over. Water level changes in wells.

IX Panic. Weak structures totally destroyed, extensive damage to well-built structures, foundations and underground pipes. Ground fissured and cracked.

X Panic. Only strongest buildings survive. Ground badly cracked. Rails bent, and water slopped over river banks.

XI Panic. Few buildings survive. Broad fissures in ground. Fault scarps formed. Underground pipes out of service.

XII Panic. Total destruction. Waves seen in ground, and lines of sight and level are distorted. Objects thrown in the air.

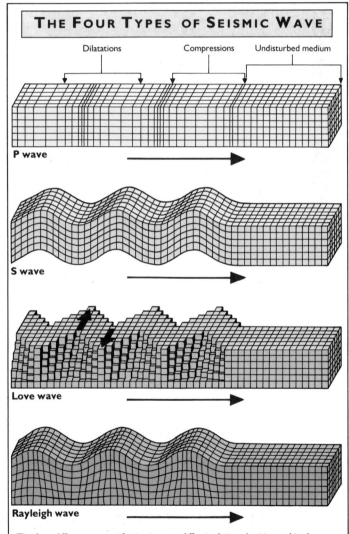

THE FOUR TYPES OF SEISMIC WAVE

Dilatations   Compressions   Undisturbed medium

P wave

S wave

Love wave

Rayleigh wave

The four different types of seismic wave differ in their velocities and in the ways that the Earth's rock particles vibrate as the waves pass through.

P and S waves are known as *body waves*, because they travel through the interior (body) of the Earth (see p.76). Indeed, the body waves emitted by very big earthquakes can be detected by sensitive instruments on the opposite side of the globe.

Love and Rayleigh waves are known as *surface waves*, because they are restricted to the vicinity of the Earth's surface.

Volcanoes

The popular image of a volcano is of a conical structure hurling ash, steam, fire and molten rock from a crater in the top, often with explosive violence. Such volcanoes do indeed exist, but they account for less than 1% of the world's volcanic activity. In fact more than 80% of molten rock, or *magma*, reaching the Earth's surface does so through long fissures in the Earth's outer shell, the lithosphere (see p. 76); this is called *fissure volcanism*. As the most important of such fissures lie along the axes of the oceanic ridges, the bulk of the Earth's volcanism occurs, unseen, on the floors of the oceans.

Volcanism occurs where magma from the Earth's interior is able to force its way through a weak zone in the lithosphere. Because such weaknesses are most likely to occur where the Earth's tectonic plates interact and become distorted, most volcanism occurs in the vicinity of plate boundaries. Continental volcanoes are usually associated with subduction zones and regions in which continents are colliding (see p. 78).

Fountains and rivers of lava erupting from Kilauea-Iki on the island of Hawaii in November 1959. Kilauea is a good example of a cone-shaped volcano with a lake-filled caldera.

SOME MAJOR VOLCANIC ERUPTIONS

SANTORÍNI (THERA)
Height: 584 m (1960 ft)
Location: Cyclades, Greece
Date: c. 1550 BC
A massive explosion virtually destroyed the island, and is thought by some to have contributed to the demise of Minoan civilization on nearby Crete. The disaster may also have given rise to the legend of the lost city of Atlantis.

VESUVIUS
Height: 1280 m (4198 ft)
Location: Bay of Naples, Italy
Date: AD 79
The towns of Pompeii, Herculaneum and Stabiae were completely buried, and thousands died. In 1631 3000 people were killed, since when there have been around 20 major eruptions, the last in 1944.

UNNAMED
Height: unknown
Location: North Island, New Zealand
Date: c. AD 130
Around 30 million tonnes (tons) of pumice were ejected, creating the vast caldera now filled by Lake Taupo. An area of c. 16 000 km^2 (6180 sq mi) was devastated – the most violent of all documented volcanic events.

ETNA
Height: 3308 m (10 853 ft)
Location: Sicily, Italy
Date: 1669
20 000 people were killed, and lava overran the west part of the city of Catania, 28 km (17 mi) from the summit.

KELUD
Height: 1731 m (5679 ft)
Location: Java, Indonesia
Date: 1586
10 000 people killed. Another eruption in 1919 killed 5000 people.

TAMBORA
Height: 2850 m (9350 ft)
Location: Sumbawa, Indonesia
Date: 1815
An estimated 150–180 km^3 (36–43 cu mi) were blasted from the cone, which dropped in height from 4100 m (13 450 ft) to 2850 m (9350 ft) in minutes. About 90 000 people were killed in the explosion and subsequent giant wave, or died later of famine.

KRAKATAU
Height: 813 m (2667 ft)
Location: Krakatau, Indonesia
Date: 1883
163 villages were wiped out and 36 380 people killed by the giant wave caused by this, the greatest volcanic explosion recorded – although possibly only one fifth of the explosion that destroyed Santoríni. Rocks were thrown 55 km (34 mi) into the air, and dust fell 5330 km (3313 mi) away 10 days later. The explosion was heard over one thirteenth of the Earth's surface.

MONT PELÉE
Height: 1397 m (4582 ft)
Location: Martinique, West Indies
Date: 1902
Within three minutes a *nuée ardente* (see main text) destroyed the town of St Pierre, killing all 26 000 inhabitants – except for one, a prisoner who survived in the thick-walled prison.

MOUNT ST HELENS
Height: 2549 m (8360 ft)
Location: Washington State, USA
Date: 1980
66 people were presumed dead and 260 km^2 (100 sq mi) of forest destroyed. Smoke and ash rose to a height of 6000 m (20 000 ft), depositing ash 800 km (440 mi) away.

The ultimate source of most magma is thought to be the partially molten asthenosphere, the layer immediately below the lithosphere. However, beneath the majority of volcanoes there appears to be a reservoir, or *magma chamber*, that acts as a staging post for magma between the asthenosphere and the Earth's surface. Between the magma chamber and the surface there is a narrower passage called a *vent*.

Volcanoes that have long ceased to erupt are said to be *extinct*. Other volcanoes that have been quiet for a very long time but that may erupt again are described as *dormant*, while those that have erupted in historic times are said to be *active*.

Volcanic products

The material in a magma chamber is liquid, but by the time it reaches the Earth's surface it can be liquid, solid or gaseous. Magma contains dissolved *volatiles* such as water and carbon dioxide. As the magma rises towards the surface it experiences a reduction in pressure, and

the volatiles are released, often with explosive force. The explosion then shatters the magma and shoots the pieces into the air. By the time they reach the ground they are often solid, albeit still very hot. Such solid fragments are known as *pyroclasts* or, as a group, *tephra*. In order of increasing particle size, tephra may consist of dust (less than 0.35 mm / $^1/_{70}$ in in diameter), ash (less than 4 mm / $^1/_6$ in), lapilli (less than 32 mm / $1\frac{1}{4}$ in), and bombs or blocks (more than 32 mm / $1\frac{1}{4}$ in). In particularly violent explosions, bombs weighing over 100 tonnes (tons) are known to have been thrown several kilometres. The finer particles can travel much further, however, carried by the wind.

In some explosive eruptions there is no sudden blast but rather a continuous stream of hot gases and rock fragments issuing from the volcanic vent at high velocity for up to several hours. Both types of explosive activity may carry tephra up to a considerable height before they fall back to the surface. In some less violent cases, however, the volcanic frag-

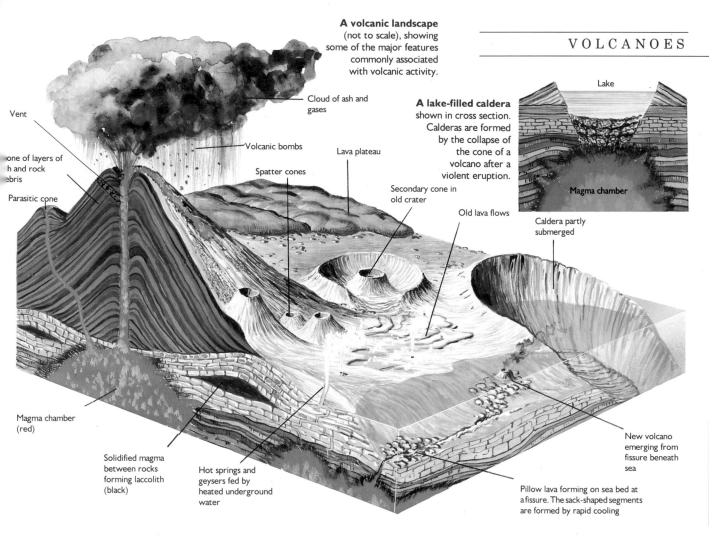

A volcanic landscape (not to scale), showing some of the major features commonly associated with volcanic activity.

Vent

Cloud of ash and gases

Volcanic bombs

Lava plateau

[c]one of layers of [as]h and rock [d]ebris

Spatter cones

Secondary cone in old crater

Parasitic cone

Old lava flows

Magma chamber (red)

Solidified magma between rocks forming laccolith (black)

Hot springs and geysers fed by heated underground water

New volcano emerging from fissure beneath sea

Pillow lava forming on sea bed at a fissure. The sack-shaped segments are formed by rapid cooling

A lake-filled caldera shown in cross section. Calderas are formed by the collapse of the cone of a volcano after a violent eruption.

Lake

Magma chamber

Caldera partly submerged

SEE ALSO

● THE EARTH'S STRUCTURE AND ATMOSPHERE p. 76
● PLATE TECTONICS p. 78
● EARTHQUAKES p. 80
● THE FORMATION OF ROCKS p. 84
● MOUNTAINS p. 86
● ISLANDS p. 98

ments may stay close to the ground where, in deadly association with hot gases, they roll along destroying everything in their path. This is known as a *nuée ardente* (French, 'burning cloud').

Lava

Not all continental volcanic eruptions are explosive. In many there is simply a quiet extrusion of magma. Magma erupted onto the Earth's surface is usually called *lava*, both in its molten state and when it has cooled and solidified into a *lava flow*.

Although flow rates of molten lava are generally quite low, speeds of up to 100 km/h (62 mph) have been observed on occasions; and although most lava solidifies in close proximity to the volcano, some is known to have travelled up to 50 km (31 mi) from the vent.

Lava is usually extruded at temperatures of 800–1200 °C (1450–2200 °F), but as it flows it loses heat to the atmosphere and the ground, thus cooling and solidifying from the outside inwards. As it solidifies, its surface takes on a variety of textures, depending largely on the viscosity of the lava in its molten form.

When the molten lava is highly mobile (that is, a relatively thin fluid, with low viscosity) it acquires, on cooling, a thin plastic surface layer that gets dragged into rope-like folds by the continued flow of the still-molten lava beneath. When finally solid, this is known as a *pahoehoe lava*. With thicker, more viscous and thus

slow-moving lava, cooling leads to a thicker and harder skin that the continued flow of still-molten lava beneath breaks into a fragmented surface. If the surface is very jagged, the solid lava is known as *aa lava*; if the surface is more lumpy, the lava is *block lava*.

When lava is extruded under water, it often acquires an altogether different form. As a result of very rapid cooling by the water, it splits into sack-shaped segments, and so the solid lava is called *pillow lava*.

Volcanic forms

There are three main types of continental volcano. The simplest is the steep cone (a *cinder-cone volcano*) built from layers of tephra ejected from a succession of explosive eruptions. A well-known example is Paricutín, in Mexico, which began erupting in 1943 and in 10 years produced a cone over 460 m (1500 ft) high.

Few volcanoes emit only tephra at every eruption. Many eject tephra on some occasions and extrude lavas on others. The result is a cone with alternating layers of tephra and lava (a *composite volcano*). Well-known examples are Vesuvius and Stromboli (Italy), Etna (Sicily) and Fujiyama (Japan).

Where lava is plentiful and eruptions frequent – through several vents – the result is likely to be a *shield volcano*, a large structure up to tens of kilometres across and with gentle slopes constructed from hundreds to thousands of successive

lava flows. Shield volcanoes are often found in mountain ranges adjacent to subduction zones (for example, the Andes), although Mauna Loa, Hawaii, is also a shield volcano.

Most volcanoes have a *crater* at, or near, the top, resulting from the sinking of solid lava back into the volcanic vent. However, if there has been a particularly violent explosion, or if the top of the volcano has collapsed because the lava has retreated a long way down the vent, a very large basin-shaped depression known as a *caldera* may be formed.

Oceanic volcanoes

About 6% of the Earth's volcanism takes place on the ocean floor away from plate margins. Such volcanoes are called *sea-mounts* if their tops fail to reach the surface, although some build up above sea level. More than 10 000 seamounts have been mapped on the Pacific Ocean floor alone, although most of them are now extinct. Some of these volcanoes are generated by magma derived, as for continental volcanoes, from the asthenosphere. Seamounts originating this way are distributed randomly. However, some oceanic volcanoes are produced by magma that comes not from the asthenosphere but from far deeper. These are *hot-spot volcanoes* (see p. 99). In addition to these oceanic volcanoes, there are two other forms of oceanic volcanism: fissure volcanism (see above), and island-arc volcanism at subduction zones (see pp. 78 and 98).

PJS

The Formation of Rocks

Rock can be one of three types – igneous, sedimentary or metamorphic. *Igneous rock* starts deep in the Earth as molten magma, which then forces its way up through the crust to cool and solidify. *Sedimentary rock* is mostly formed when rock of any type is weathered down into fine particles that are then re-deposited under water and later compacted. *Metamorphic rock* is igneous or sedimentary rock that has been subjected to high pressure and/or temperature, thereby changing its nature.

SEE ALSO

- THE EARTH'S STRUCTURE p. 76
- PLATE TECTONICS p. 78
- VOLCANOES p. 82
- MOUNTAINS p. 86
- CAVES p. 88

The Earth is perpetually recycling its rocks. Material brought to the surface is eroded, transported and ultimately returned to the Earth's interior, where it becomes available to begin the cycle all over again. This series of processes is known as the *rock cycle*, or *geological cycle* (see diagram). The energy to maintain it comes partly from the Sun (to fuel the erosion processes) and partly from the Earth's interior (to generate volcanic activity and uplift).

Igneous rock

Magma – which comes from the Earth's surface via volcanic activity (see p. 82) – comprises a mixture of oxides (compounds with oxygen) and silicates (compounds with silicon and oxygen). When it cools and solidifies, the oxides and silicates produce a complex mixture of mineral crystals. The nature and properties of the crystals in any particular igneous rock depend partly on the composition of the original magma and partly upon the physical conditions under which the magma crystallized. As compositions and conditions vary greatly, there are thousands of different igneous rock types.

Igneous rocks that form on the Earth's surface are known as *extrusive*. Those that form within the crust from magma that never reached the surface are known as *intrusive*. Intrusive rocks cool more slowly because, being surrounded by other rock rather than being open to the air, the heat cannot escape so readily. As a result, the crystals have longer to grow, and the mineral grains are larger (coarser).

Despite the many varieties of igneous rock, just six account for most of the igneous components of the crust. These are *granite*, *diorite* and *gabbro*, which are coarse-grained intrusive rocks, and *rhyolite*, *andesite* and *basalt*, which are fine-grained extrusive rocks.

Most of the lava produced at constructive plate boundaries (see p. 78) is basalt. Both basalt and andesite are generated at destructive plate boundaries (see p. 78), and rhyolite is sometimes also produced. Granite is common in the upper continental crust, and gabbro probably dominates in the lower continental crust (see p. 76).

Sedimentary rock

At least 75% of all sedimentary rock is known as *clastic sedimentary rock*, which means that it is derived from the erosion products of other rocks. All rocks, even those in the most massive of mountain ranges, are ultimately broken down into smaller and smaller fragments. When the particles become small enough they are then transported by water, wind or ice, usually ending up in the ocean. There they fall as sediment to the ocean floor where, under the pressure of subsequent deposits, they are compacted into hard rock. The most common sedimentary rock is *sandstone*.

The remaining 25% of sediment is either chemical or organic. Rivers dissolve minerals out of the rocks through which they pass, and the mineral solutions end up in the oceans. When the oceans reach their saturation limit for the particular mineral concerned, the excess mineral is precipitated out chemically as solid particles, which fall to the ocean floor. The most common chemical sedimentary rock is *limestone* (calcium carbonate – $CaCO_3$).

Not all limestone is precipitated chemically, however. Many ocean organisms extract calcium carbonate from the water to build their shells, and when they die the shells sink to the ocean floor to form sediment in their own right. The most common organic sedimentary rock is again limestone, but there are other organisms that in a similar way generate silica (SiO_2) sediments.

Most sedimentary rocks are a mixture of clastic, chemical and organic, although one type usually predominates.

Metamorphic rock

When igneous or sedimentary rocks are subjected to high temperatures and pressures, especially in the presence of percolating fluids, their internal structures, and sometimes even their mineralogical compositions, may be changed. The processes involved are known collectively as *metamorphism*. The sort of temperatures and pressures required are, respectively, 300 °C (572 °F) and 100 megapascals (equivalent to 100 atmospheres).

The most extreme conditions in the Earth's crust occur at plate boundaries

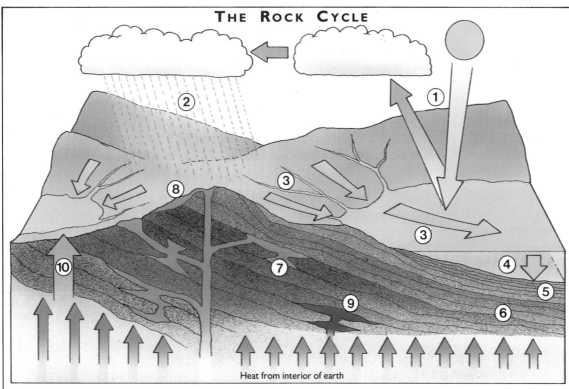

THE ROCK CYCLE

Heat from interior of earth

1. Heat from the Sun causes evaporation. Water vapour rises and condenses into clouds.

2. Water in cloud precipitates as rain or snow.

3. Water erodes rock, and rivers carry away sediment.

4. Rivers deposit sediment as alluvium on flat ground, or transport it to lakes and seas where it settles on the bottom as clay or sand.

5. As sediment builds up, increasing pressure changes lower layers into sedimentary rock.

6. Deeper sedimentary rock is turned into metamorphic rock by pressure from above and heat from below.

7. Magma – molten rock from deep inside the Earth – rises towards the surface. Some is trapped underground and hardens into intrusive igneous rock.

8. Some magma reaches the Earth's surface via volcanoes and fissures as lava and is classified as extrusive igneous rock.

9. Some intrusive igneous rock is forced deeper by the pressure of sedimentation, and is changed into metamorphic rock. This metamorphosis may be assisted by thermal energy from below.

10. Pressure from colliding continental plates pushes all kinds of rock to the surface, and forces them upwards, where they are eroded. The rock cycle begins again.

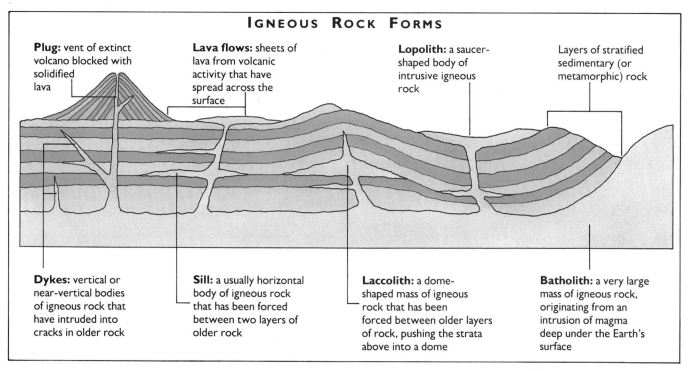

IGNEOUS ROCK FORMS

Plug: vent of extinct volcano blocked with solidified lava

Lava flows: sheets of lava from volcanic activity that have spread across the surface

Lopolith: a saucer-shaped body of intrusive igneous rock

Layers of stratified sedimentary (or metamorphic) rock

Dykes: vertical or near-vertical bodies of igneous rock that have intruded into cracks in older rock

Sill: a usually horizontal body of igneous rock that has been forced between two layers of older rock

Laccolith: a dome-shaped mass of igneous rock that has been forced between older layers of rock, pushing the strata above into a dome

Batholith: a very large mass of igneous rock, originating from an intrusion of magma deep under the Earth's surface

where continents collide (see p. 78). Most metamorphic rocks are thus generated in the roots of mountains. Depending upon temperature and pressure, there are various grades of metamorphism; but in the most intense (high-grade) metamorphism, rock structures, holes and even fossils are so completely obliterated that the original rock type can no longer be identified.

As a result of the realignment of minerals under pressure, many metamorphic rocks are layered, or banded. Sometimes the layering is visible; but even when it is not, it can often be detected by the way that the rock breaks. A common example is *slate,* which easily breaks into thin sheets along the layering.

Not all metamorphic rock is layered, however. Common examples of non-layered metamorphics are *marble,* formed by the metamorphism of limestone, and *quartz-ite,* derived from sandstone.

Faults and folds

As soon as rocks form they not only begin to erode, they are also subject to faulting and folding. The most intense faulting and the most intense folding both occur at plate boundaries, but these pressures are also very common within plates, on scales ranging from centimetres to thousands of kilometres.

Faults are fractures along which opposing blocks of rock are moving or have moved in the past. The surface over which the slippage occurs is called the *fault plane,* and the line along which the fault plane cuts the Earth's surface (if it does; not all faults reach the surface) is known as the *fault trace.*

Faults are classified according to the direction in which the blocks of rock slip. If the movement is basically vertical (up or down the fault plane) the result is a *dip-slip fault,* of which there are two basic types – *normal* and *reverse.* Horizontal

movement gives rise to a *strike-slip fault.* Where there are two parallel faults, the result can be either a *horst* or a *graben* (rift valley).

Folding is the bending of rock without fracturing. The two sides of a fold are called *limbs,* and the surface that bisects the angle between the limbs is known as the *axial plane.* Folds are classified according to the severity of the folding, the shape of the resulting folds, and the angle of the axial plane. There are a few basic types of fold and a great number of variations.   PJS

THE GEOLOGICAL TIME CHART

ERA	PERIOD	EPOCH	BEGAN (Millions of years ago)
CENOZOIC	QUATERNARY	Holocene	0.01
		Pleistocene	1.6
	TERTIARY	Pliocene	5.3
		Miocene	23
		Oligocene	34
		Eocene	53
		Palaeocene	65
MESOZOIC	CRETACEOUS		135
	JURASSIC		205
	TRIASSIC		250
PALAEOZOIC	PERMIAN		300
	CARBONIFEROUS (divided into lower Mississippian and upper Pennsylvanian in USA)		355
	DEVONIAN		410
	SILURIAN		438
	ORDOVICIAN		510
	CAMBRIAN		570
PRECAMBRIAN ERA			4600

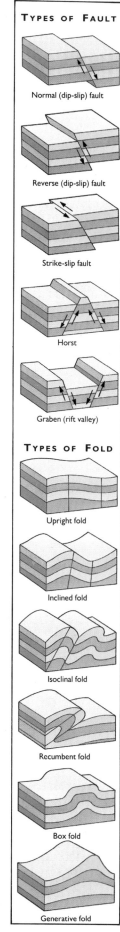

TYPES OF FAULT

Normal (dip-slip) fault

Reverse (dip-slip) fault

Strike-slip fault

Horst

Graben (rift valley)

TYPES OF FOLD

Upright fold

Inclined fold

Isoclinal fold

Recumbent fold

Box fold

Generative fold

Mountains

Mountains and mountain ranges are largely formed by the interaction of mountain-building processes (*orogeny*) and the subsequent erosional processes that tend to destroy them. The distribution of the world's major mountain ranges generally follows those belts of the Earth's landmasses where earthquakes and volcanoes are common. These phenomena are in turn caused by the collision of the moving plates that make up the Earth's lithosphere (see pp. 76–9). Such collisions often result in the margin of one plate being forced upwards, and this process has resulted in the formation of many mountain ranges – although other processes may also play a part in mountain building.

The Earth's largest mountain ranges today – the Alps, Himalaya, Rockies and Andes – are all relatively young, resulting from plate collisions in the last 25 million years or so. Much older ranges include the Scottish Highlands, the Scandinavian mountains and the Appalachians in the USA, which are all around 300–400 million years old. The deeply eroded remnants of even older ranges – up to 3000 million years old – occur in many parts of Africa and Australia.

Fold mountains

The world's largest and most complex continental mountain ranges are the result of the collision of tectonic plates. Mountains formed directly by plate collisions are known as *fold mountains*, because they are conspicuously folded, faulted and otherwise deformed by the huge collision pressures. In some cases the collision is between landmasses. Thus India is pressing into the rest of Asia to form the Himalaya, and Africa is being forced into Europe, producing the Alps. In other cases the collision is between an oceanic plate and a continent. Thus the Pacific plate is spreading towards South America, forcing up the Andes. The Himalaya, the Alps and the Andes are still being formed, but some mountain ranges – for example, the Urals and the Appalachians – are the products of older, long-ceased plate collisions.

Fault-block and upwarped mountains

Other types of mountain exist where plate collisions are at best only marginally involved. In *fault-block mountains* a central block of the Earth's crust has sunk and the adjacent blocks have been forced upwards. Mountains of this type define the Basin and Range Province of the western USA (Nevada and parts of Utah, New Mexico, Arizona and California) and form the Sierra Nevada of California and the Teton Range of Wyoming.

In *upwarped mountains*, on the other hand, a central block has been forced upwards. Examples are the Black Hills of Dakota and the Adirondacks of New York State.

Volcanic mountains

Spectacular mountains may also be built by volcanic action (see also p. 82). For example, Mauna Loa in Hawaii, is, at 10 203 m (33 476 ft), the world's highest mountain if measured from the Pacific Ocean floor, although less than half is above sea level. Much more important than such isolated volcanoes, however, are the oceanic ridges (see pp. 82 and 101), the undersea mountain ranges along which the bulk of the Earth's volcanism takes place. Intense volcanism also occurs where oceanic and continental plates collide. The Andes, for example, owe not a little of their mass to volcanic activity.

The erosion and destruction of isolated continental volcanoes can be a rapid process. Some volcanoes are partially self-destructive – for example, Mount St Helens in the northwest USA, which blasted part of its side out in 1980, or Vesuvius, whose crater top disintegrated in AD 79. Others are completely self-destructive – for example, Krakatau (sometimes incorrectly called Krakatoa), Indonesia, which in 1883 blasted itself entirely out of existence.

Apart from these spectacular episodes, the erosion of volcanoes can be fast, the

The European Alps are relatively young mountains, pushed up by the collision of continental plates within the last 25 million years. This section of the frontier ridge between Switzerland and Italy includes (from left to right) Lyskamm, Castor, Pollux and the Breithorn, whose summits are all over 4000 m (13 120 ft). The action of ice in shaping mountains can be clearly seen, with glaciers gouging out cirques between the ridges of the summits, and carving valleys lower down the slopes.

SEE ALSO

● PLATE TECTONICS p. 78
● VOLCANOES p. 82
● THE FORMATION OF ROCKS p. 84
● ICE p. 90
● THE OCEANS p. 100

Monument Valley, USA. These spectacular sandstone towers have been sculpted by water and trimmed by the wind.

loose ash of which they are partly built being easily transported by runoff of rainwater. In the case of some Andean volcanoes, earth tremors set off avalanches, which tear down into nearby valleys. Such an event occurred in 1970, when an estimated 40 million m³ (52 million cu yd) of rock and ice avalanched off Huascarán in Peru, completely obliterating several towns and villages and killing many thousands of their inhabitants up to 20 km (12 mi) away.

Volcanoes built up in the sea are sometimes easily eroded by wave action, as in the case of Surtsey, which grew out of the sea off Iceland in the 1960s and has largely been worn away now.

On the other hand, volcanoes built of harder rock can persist indefinitely. On the Pacific Ocean floor alone there are tens of thousands of extinct volcanic cones (*seamounts*), and in various parts of the world there are the remains of volcanoes up to hundreds of millions of years old.

Wind and water erosion

As soon as a mountain range starts to rise, the forces of erosion commence operation. Water, wind, ice and vegetation are all agents of erosion, often acting in unison. Mountains are the intermediate result of erosive processes that will ultimately wear everything away to sea level. Young mountain ranges are those which have only been uplifted to somewhere near their present height in the last 25 million years or so, and they tend to be high and jagged. Old mountain ranges are those that have suffered the processes of erosion for hundreds if not thousands of millions of years, and they tend to be lower and more rounded.

The processes of erosion start with weathering of exposed rocks. Rainfall provides water, which reacts chemically with many rocks and minerals. The loose rock fragments are then transported by water down streams into rivers and eventually to the sea, with the more resistant rock masses left upstanding as individual mountains. Mountains that have been worn away by water action alone are generally rounded, with shallow gullies radiating outwards.

Wind sculpture of whole mountain ranges is unusual on its own, but bare and polished surfaces on jagged rocks in desert regions may result from the wind hurling sand grains at rock faces at high speed as, for example, in Death Valley in California and the Hoggar mountains of the central Sahara. Wind sculpture in combination with storm-water runoff (flash floods) can cut canyons into the mountains. At the point where the canyon opens out, the water deposits its sediments in *alluvial fans*, whilst the wind-blown material covers adjacent lowlands with sand dunes.

The action of ice

When water freezes in cracks in rocks, it expands and forces the rocks apart, thus causing erosion of mountain peaks. (In a similar way, vegetation may also contribute to erosion – for example, roots may force open cracks.) As it accumulates, ice, in the form of glaciers (see p. 90), sculpts most high mountain ranges – for example, the Alps, Himalaya, Rockies (particularly in Canada), and the Scandinavian mountains. Many other ranges were sculpted to their present shapes by glaciers during the last Ice Age (some 100 000 to 10 000 years ago), for example, the Scottish Highlands, the US Rockies, much of the Andes, the Caucasus and the Ural Mountains.

Headward erosion by glaciers (i.e. erosion of the slope on which the glacier originates) etches out *corries* (also known as *cirques* or *cwms*) and, when two or three corries impinge, the result may be a pyramidal peak such as the Swiss Matterhorn. The high passes between corries cutting into a range are called *cols*, and gullies leading from them are called *couloirs*. Steep slopes on such mountains often yield avalanches, in which rock and soil, as well as snow and ice, may be swept away.

The lower parts of mountains that either have or have had glaciers tend to be characterized by *terminal moraines*, mounds of ice-borne debris across a valley at the melting limit of the glacier. Moraines may hold back lakes but the meltwater streams eventually breach these and *outwash plains* spread out from the valley mouths.

Thus, as mountain ranges are gradually worn down, it is the more resistant parts that linger longest, giving their present shapes. A peculiarity is that mountains may continue to grow higher as their sides are worn away. The Alps and Himalaya, for example, are still being raised by plate-tectonic processes – Everest is getting higher in spite of the glaciers carving away its sides.   TF

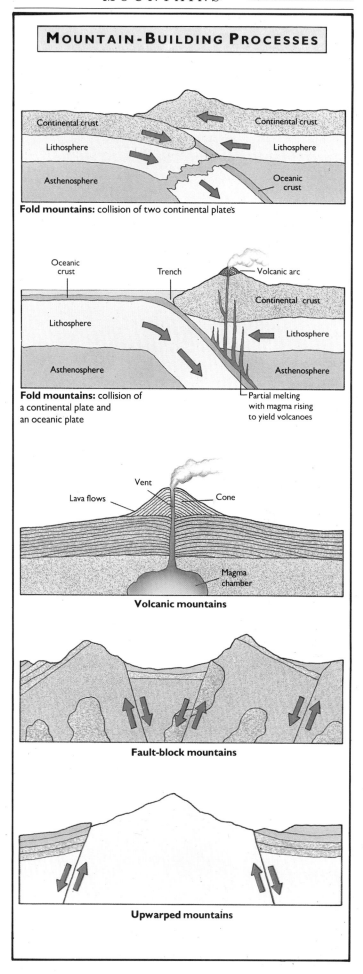

MOUNTAIN-BUILDING PROCESSES

Fold mountains: collision of two continental plates

Continental crust / Lithosphere / Asthenosphere / Continental crust / Lithosphere / Oceanic crust

Fold mountains: collision of a continental plate and an oceanic plate

Oceanic crust / Trench / Volcanic arc / Lithosphere / Continental crust / Asthenosphere / Lithosphere / Asthenosphere / Partial melting with magma rising to yield volcanoes

Volcanic mountains

Vent / Lava flows / Cone / Magma chamber

Fault-block mountains

Upwarped mountains

Caves

Caves are naturally occurring holes in the ground, generally large enough to be entered by humans. They are often linked into complex systems of chambers and passageways, and these systems can extend many kilometres in length, and penetrate deep into the Earth. The entrances of many caves have provided shelter for both animals and humans in the past, and their accumulated remains can tell us much about extinct animal forms and the life of prehistoric man (see pp. 141, 362 and 504). Some caves are also noted for their animal life today: bats, birds, snakes and even crocodiles, in addition to numerous invertebrates, may make their homes in caves.

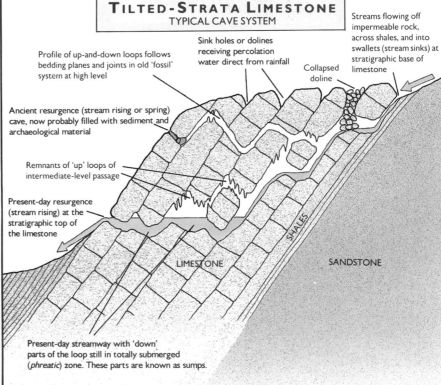

TILTED-STRATA LIMESTONE
TYPICAL CAVE SYSTEM

Streams flowing off impermeable rock, across shales, and into swallets (stream sinks) at stratigraphic base of limestone

Sink holes or dolines receiving percolation water direct from rainfall

Collapsed doline

Profile of up-and-down loops follows bedding planes and joints in old 'fossil' system at high level

Ancient resurgence (stream rising or spring) cave, now probably filled with sediment and archaeological material

Remnants of 'up' loops of intermediate-level passage

Present-day resurgence (stream rising) at the stratigraphic top of the limestone

Present-day streamway with 'down' parts of the loop still in totally submerged (*phreatic*) zone. These parts are known as sumps.

SHALES

LIMESTONE

SANDSTONE

By far the majority of caves occur in limestone areas. This is because of the solubility of limestone in rainwater (H_2O) containing carbon dioxide (CO_2) in solution. This solution is carbonic acid (H_2CO_3), a weak acid that can attack limestone on its own, but its effects are much greater if it is augmented by acids from soil and vegetation. Limestone consists almost entirely of calcium carbonate ($CaCO_3$), which undergoes a reversible reaction with carbonic acid to form calcium bicarbonate – $Ca(HCO_3)_2$ – which is soluble in water. Because the reaction is reversible, if the calcium bicarbonate dissolved in the water reaches excessive proportions then calcium carbonate can be precipitated elsewhere in cave systems as stalactites (see below) or at springs as *tufa* (a soft porous rock), or it can be carried away downstream.

Beimo Cave, China. Flowstone sheets descend from the walls and spread across the floor, while stalactites hang from the ceiling. A massive stalagmite can be seen in the distance.

Cave formation

Not all limestones have caves as some, such as chalk, are mechanically weak and will not support cave roofs. Others have few caves owing to their high porosity, which allows the acidic water to pass through the whole rock mass without concentrating at any particular points. Massive, low-porosity, well-jointed limestones, such as Carboniferous limestone, are the most favourable rock types for caves. Bedding planes and joints (see diagram), together with faults (see p. 84), are weaknesses through which rainwater can percolate, and where its acid can attack the limestone. Prolonged attack may lead to the formation of a cave.

When a limestone mass is first uplifted above sea level it has no caves, but they begin to form as soon as rainwater percolates down joints and bedding planes. Water movement through a limestone mass is very slow at first, but as joints are widened so the flow rates increase. Once the conduits reach a diameter of a few millimetres, free and relatively fast flow is possible. The increased flow rate leads to enhanced solution and erosion of the walls by rock particles, for as the flow increases, sediment grains from overlying rock formations wash in. Once the conduits are large enough for distinct streams to flow through, they are enlarged relatively rapidly to the size of caves.

Free stream flow through caves leads to gradual drainage of the higher parts of the system, with the streams eventually rising at springs near the base of the limestone. Renewed uplift of the limestone may lead to the underground streams finding still lower routes through the rock, and thus the old routes are abandoned.

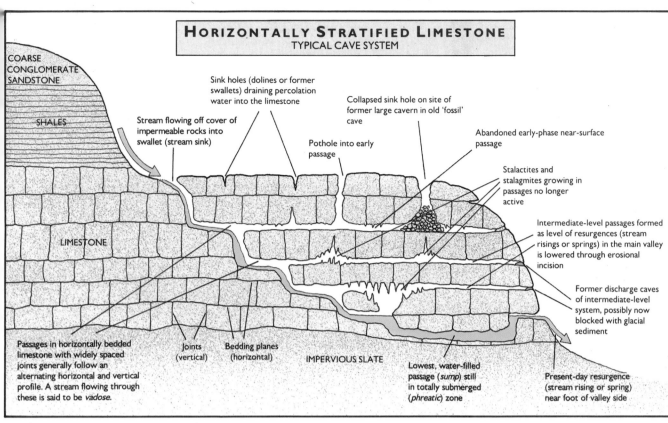

HORIZONTALLY STRATIFIED LIMESTONE
TYPICAL CAVE SYSTEM

COARSE CONGLOMERATE SANDSTONE

SHALES

Stream flowing off cover of impermeable rocks into swallet (stream sink)

Sink holes (dolines or former swallets) draining percolation water into the limestone

Pothole into early passage

Collapsed sink hole on site of former large cavern in old 'fossil' cave

Abandoned early-phase near-surface passage

Stalactites and stalagmites growing in passages no longer active

Intermediate-level passages formed as level of resurgences (stream risings or springs) in the main valley is lowered through erosional incision

LIMESTONE

Former discharge caves of intermediate-level system, possibly now blocked with glacial sediment

Passages in horizontally bedded limestone with widely spaced joints generally follow an alternating horizontal and vertical profile. A stream flowing through these is said to be *vadose*.

Joints (vertical)

Bedding planes (horizontal)

IMPERVIOUS SLATE

Lowest, water-filled passage (*sump*) still in totally submerged (*phreatic*) zone

Present-day resurgence (stream rising or spring) near foot of valley side

SEE ALSO

- THE FORMATION OF ROCKS p. 84
- EARLY MAMMALS p. 140
- HUMAN PREHISTORY p. 362
- PREHISTORIC ART p. 504

Cave types

Cave passages evolve from the totally submerged (*phreatic*) state to the free-flowing stream (*vadose*) state. Each has its own features, and from these it may be possible to work out the cave's history. Very rapid drainage may leave the cave with phreatic features only, most notably passages that are more or less circular in cross section. Free-flowing vadose streams only cut down the floor, giving a trench or canyon-like cross section to the passage. Undermining of the walls may lead to the collapse of parts of the roof and the gradual enlargement of caverns, possibly resulting in openings to the surface known as *potholes*.

Cave entrances may be at the water-inflow (input) end, when they are known as *swallets* or *sinks*, at the water-outflow (resurgence) end, or at intermediate points through collapses or abandoned sinks. The profile of a cave system may show a steady gradient, as is characteristic of vadose caves, or up-and-down loops, typical of phreatic caves in steeply dipping limestones.

Karst landscapes

Limestone landscapes with cave systems are known as *karst landscapes*, named after an area of Croatia and Slovenia. Karst landscapes are typified by a lack of surface streams, the presence of swallets and collapse potholes, dry valleys (which once had streams now flowing underground), resurgences, and bare rock pavements. These *limestone pavements* are dissected into areas known as *clints* by fissures about 50 cm (20 in) wide known as *grikes*, this process being caused by the etching out of joints, often with subsequent glacial smoothing.

Karst landscapes may also have numerous *dolines* (funnel-shaped hollows at joint intersections) and *poljes* (enclosed valleys with internal drainage through caves). Tropical karst is typified by towers and cones formed by intense downward erosion, with 'cockpits' separating cone-shaped hills.

Stalactites and stalagmites

Stalactites and stalagmites (collectively known as *speleothems*) are caused by the precipitation of calcium carbonate from water rich in calcium bicarbonate percolating through the cave roof. Stalactites on the ceiling start as straw-like tubes with drops running down the inside, but as crystals grow inside the tubes they become blocked, and the stalactites thicken. Stalagmites grow where drops fall to the floor.

If drops of lime-saturated water fall into small pools with particles of grit, the latter may become coated with layers of lime and so form *cave pearls*. Other forms of speleothem include *curtain stalactites* along rock edges, *columns* where stalactites have met stalagmites, *flowstone sheets* (rippled sheets of precipitated calcium carbonate) and *helictites*. Helictites consist of clusters of irregular, branching rod-like structures that appear to defy gravity, their growth being fed by capillary flow of water through very narrow tubes.

Many speleothems contain a small proportion of uranium, and measurement of the radioactive decay can give the age of the speleothem. This is one of the few ways of dating cave formation, as stalactite growth rates are much more variable than generally thought.

Non-limestone caves

Caves in rocks other than limestone include a variety of *sea caves* where erosion has etched out weaknesses in the rocks of sea cliffs. *Lava caves* occur in many basalt volcanic areas, such as Iceland, Hawaii, Kenya and Australia. They are generally tubes within lava flows where the molten material has flowed out from beneath the solidified crust. *Fissure caves* occur in a few hard-rock areas where fault zones have been widened by erosion or by mass movement pulling rock masses apart.

Ice caves are of two sorts. First, there are *englacial tubes* through which streams of meltwater run beneath glaciers. Though entirely in ice, they show many of the features of limestone caves, although rapid changes may take place owing to glacier movement. Second, there are caves in high mountain regions where the air within the cave rarely if ever rises above freezing point, so that water percolating in from the surface during the summer freezes into icicles, often very large, and sometimes joining into ice masses underground.   TF

Karst formations in Guilin, China. Karst landscapes are limestone areas with cave systems, dry valleys and underground streams. In places such as China and Southeast Asia such landscapes are characterized by sheer towers and cones, formed by intense downward erosion.

Ice

It has been estimated that over a tenth of the Earth's land surface – some 15 600 000 km² (6 021 000 sq mi) – is permanently covered with ice. Ice is in fact the world's biggest reservoir of fresh water, with over three quarters of the global total contained in ice sheets, ice caps and glaciers. These range in size from the huge Antarctic and Greenland ice sheets to the small glaciers found in high-latitude and high-altitude mountain ranges.

Ice bodies develop where winter snowfall is able to accumulate and persist through the summer. Over time this snow is compressed into an ice body, and such ice bodies may grow to blanket the landscape as an *ice sheet* or *ice cap*. Alternatively, the ice body may grow to form a mass that flows down a slope – a *glacier* – often cutting a valley and eroding rock material that is eventually deposited at a lower altitude as the ice melts.

The formation of ice bodies

Ice bodies develop mainly through the accumulation of snow, or sometimes by the freezing of rain as it hits an ice surface. Obviously, not all the snow that falls is turned into ice – during the northern-hemisphere winter over half the world's land surface and up to one third of the surfaces of the oceans may be blanketed by snow and ice. Most of this snow and ice is only temporary, as the Sun's warmth and energy are able to melt the cover during warm winter days or as winter passes into spring and summer.

In some places, however, the summer warmth is unable to melt all the snowfall of the previous winter. This may be because summer temperatures are rather low, or summer is very short, or because winter snowfall is very high. Where this occurs, snow lies all year round (this snow is sometimes called *firn* or *névé*) and becomes covered by the snow of the next winter. As this process continues from year to year, the snow that is buried becomes compressed and transformed into *glacier ice*.

Latitude and altitude both affect where permanent snow can accumulate. The level that separates permanent snow cover from places where the snow melts in the summer is called the *snowline* or *firnline*. The snowline increases in altitude towards the equator: in polar regions it lies at sea level, in Norway at 1200–1500 m (4000–5000 ft) above sea level, and in the Alps at about 2700 m (9000 ft). Permanent snow and ice can even occur in the tropics close to the equator: in East Africa, for example, the snowline lies at about 4900 m (16 000 ft), so that glaciers are found on Mount Kenya, Kilimanjaro, and the Ruwenzori Mountains.

Ice sheets and ice caps

Ice sheets and ice caps are ice bodies that have grown into domes that blanket an area of land, submerging valleys, hills and mountains. Occasionally, 'islands' of land, called *nunataks*, protrude through the 'sea' of ice. Ice sheets are defined as having an area over 50 000 km² (19 000 sq mi); ice caps are smaller.

The continent of Antarctica is covered by an ice sheet, which rises to about 4200 m (13 800 ft) above sea level and spreads over an area of 12.5 million km² (4.8 million sq mi). Much of Greenland is covered by an ice sheet (1.7 million km² / 660 000 sq mi in area), while ice caps occur in Norway, Canada and Iceland. Together, the Antarctic and Greenland ice sheets account for 94% of the Earth's land area covered by ice bodies.

Sea ice

There is no ice sheet over the North Pole because there is no land there – however, the Arctic Ocean is always frozen and, during the winter, Arctic *sea ice* covers about 12 million km² (4.6 million sq mi).

An area of sea ice that is joined to a coast is called an *ice shelf*. Ice shelves occur in the Arctic, joined to the coasts of northern Canada and Greenland, and in the Antarctic – notably the Ross Ice Shelf, which has an area greater than France. Ocean currents and seasonal melting can cause ice sheets to break up, creating areas of *pack ice* or smaller *ice floes*.

Types of glacier

In comparison to ice sheets and ice caps, glaciers are small, relatively narrow bodies of ice, which flow down slopes. Some Arctic and Antarctic glaciers reach several hundred kilometres in length, but the longest glacier in the European Alps, for example, is only 35 km (22 mi) long.

There are several types of glacier: *outlet glaciers* extend from the edges of ice sheets and ice caps; *valley* or *alpine glaciers* are confined within valleys for

The Antarctic ice sheet (below). This aerial shot shows one of the giant glaciers that travel down from the Trans-antarctic Mountains, with the ice sheet spreading out as far as the eye can see on either side.

THE ICE AGES

During colder periods of the Earth's history, ice sheets, ice caps and glaciers have covered much larger areas of the land surface than they do today. There have been several *ice ages* or *glacial periods* in the past: scientists now believe that there have been between 15 and 22 glacial periods during the last 2 million years.

The last Ice Age ended about 10 000 years ago and, at its height, great ice sheets covered most of Canada and Scandinavia, ice caps covered Highland Scotland, Snowdonia and the English Lake District, and large glaciers extended into southern England. Throughout Europe, the ice extended roughly to the latitude of the English Midlands, the Netherlands and northern Germany, although in North America it extended even further south, into the northern USA. There are no ice bodies (apart from high-mountain glaciers) so far south today, but the landscape still records the presence of ice in the past, in the form of erosion valleys and large volumes of transported sediment.

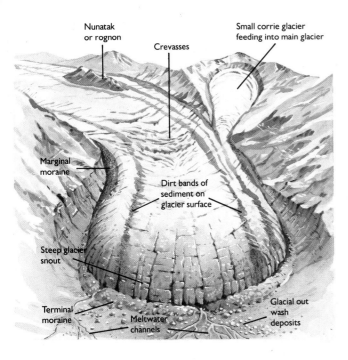

Nunatak or rognon

Crevasses

Small corrie glacier feeding into main glacier

Marginal moraine

Dirt bands of sediment on glacier surface

Steep glacier snout

Terminal moraine

Meltwater channels

Glacial out wash deposits

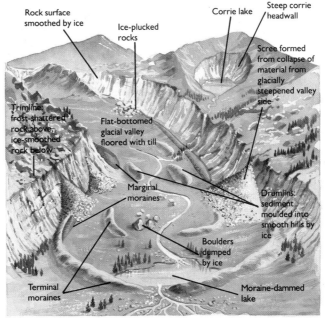

Rock surface smoothed by ice

Ice-plucked rocks

Corrie lake

Steep corrie headwall

Scree formed from collapse of material from glacially steepened valley side

Trimline: frost-shattered rock above, ice-smoothed rock below

Flat-bottomed glacial valley floored with till

Marginal moraines

Drumlins: sediment moulded into smooth hills by ice

Boulders dumped by ice

Terminal moraines

Moraine-dammed lake

Ice shaping a landscape (left), and the same landscape after the glacier has melted (right).

The northeast coast of Greenland (below), photographed by the *Landsat-1* satellite from an altitude of 914 km (568 mi). The ice sheet on the left feeds numerous glaciers that flow down to the sea (right). Here, icebergs break off from the snouts of the glaciers. The sea ice in this photograph includes large floes, together with newer ice in the process of formation.

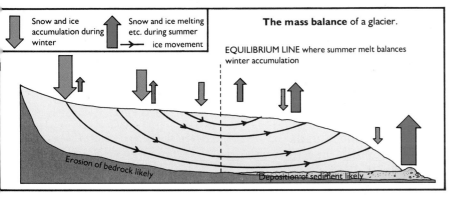

Snow and ice accumulation during winter

Snow and ice melting etc. during summer

ice movement

The mass balance of a glacier.

EQUILIBRIUM LINE where summer melt balances winter accumulation

Erosion of bedrock likely

Deposition of sediment likely

much of their length; and *cirque* (sometimes called *corrie* or *cwm*) *glaciers* are totally confined to a small rock basin and may cover an area of less than 1 km² (⅓ sq mi).

Most glaciers terminate on land, but some – especially those that are outlets of extensive ice sheets or ice caps – may reach the sea. Where this occurs, large blocks of ice may break off the end of the glacier (the *snout*) to form *icebergs*, which are carried away by the tide and ocean currents (see p. 100).

Ice movements

Ice bodies move and flow under the influence of gravity. The movement of frozen water is obviously much slower than when it is in its liquid form. Most glaciers flow at a velocity between 3 and 300 m (10 and 1000 ft) per year. Glaciers on steep slopes may move much faster, and the Quarayaq Glacier, which is supplied with ice from the Greenland Ice Sheet, averages 20–24 m (65–80 ft) per day. Many glaciers experience *surges* – which may last a few days or several years – when flow is extremely rapid, often equivalent to rates of up to 10 km (6 mi) a year.

Glaciers move in two ways. The first, called *glacial sliding*, occurs when the base of a glacier slides over the rock beneath it. The other, called *internal deformation*, involves movements within

the glacier, caused by the stresses resulting from the weight of the ice body itself. Many glaciers flow through the combination of both mechanisms, but in very cold environments, where a glacier may be frozen to its rock bed, internal deformation may account for all the movement that occurs.

At the steeper points in a glacier, deep cracks called *crevasses* will form, usually at right angles to the direction of flow. Where the glacier tumbles over an underlying cliff, an *icefall* will form, characterized by many crevasses and unstable towers of ice called *seracs*. Sometimes a glacier will flow round either side of an area of harder rock known as a *rognon*.

As a glacier flows downhill it will extend the snowline. The area below the snowline will be subject to greater melting than that above it, so the glacier is kept in equilibrium and prevented from growing indefinitely in size (see diagram).

Glaciers and landscape

Glacier ice is a very powerful erosional agent, smoothing rock surfaces and cutting deep valleys. *Fjords* (for example, along the coasts of Norway and Alaska) are U-shaped glacial valleys that become submerged by the sea after the melting of the ice that produced them. U-shaped valleys are classically regarded as glacial features, but they can be formed by other

processes – for example, by rivers in their middle and lower reaches.

A sliding glacier erodes by *plucking* blocks of rock from its bed and by *abrading* rock surfaces, i.e. breaking off small particles and rock fragments. The rock that is eroded is transported by the ice and deposited as the glacier travels down slope and melts. Glacial deposits can form distinct landforms such as *moraines* and *drumlins* (see illustration), or they may simply be deposited as *glacial till*, a blanket of sediment covering the landscape. As glacial ice melts, especially during the summer months, the *meltwater* that emerges from beneath a glacier can carry large quantities of sediment away from the glacier system. DT

SEE ALSO

● MOUNTAINS p. 86
● RIVERS AND LAKES p. 94
● THE OCEANS p. 100
● THE MAKING OF THE WEATHER p. 102
● CLIMATIC AND VEGETATION REGIONS p. 104
● ECOSYSTEMS: EXTREME p. 186

Deserts

Deserts are areas of the world where there is a considerable deficiency of water. The major cause of this aridity is low precipitation, particularly rainfall, but desert areas also frequently experience a great variation in rainfall amounts from year to year. Although deserts are not necessarily hot, many are found in hot climates, which increases the shortage of water because of high rates of evaporation. The lack of water in deserts makes conditions difficult for human, animal and plant life. As a result, living organisms are less common than in wetter areas, with special adaptations necessary in order to allow survival (see p. 186).

A massive sand dune (right) rises above a solitary tree in the Namib Desert of Namibia. Despite the popular image, only a relatively small proportion of the world's deserts are sandy – for example, only 28% of the Sahara is composed of sand dunes and sand plains.

Because water deficiency is the main characteristic of deserts, Arctic and Antarctic areas are sometimes called *polar deserts* because water is not generally available in its liquid form (see p. 90).

What causes deserts?

Many of the world's deserts coincide with areas characterized by stable atmospheric high pressure (see pp. 102–5), conditions that not do not favour rainfall. These subtropical high-pressure belts are responsible for deserts such as the Sahara and Kalahari in Africa and the deserts of Australia and Arabia.

Other deserts – for example, the Gobi Desert in Asia – exist because of their *continentality*, that is, their distance from the sea. This prevents them being reached by moisture-bearing winds from the oceans. This effect may be enhanced by the shape of the landscape: for example, moist air coming in from the sea will precipitate on mountains as rain or snow, and by the time the air has reached the far side of the mountains it will be dry, so forming a *rain-shadow* desert. Such deserts occur, for example, to the north of the Himalaya.

The deserts of the west coasts of southern Africa and South America – the Namib and Atacama Deserts – are affected by the presence of cold ocean currents running along the coast. These cool the air that they come into contact with, so preventing evaporation of moisture from the ocean surface and the formation of rain. At some places in the Atacama Desert, no rain was recorded in the 400 years prior to 1971. The cold ocean water does, however, cause a high frequency of fog, which is the major source of moisture in these extremely dry or *hyper-arid* deserts.

Human activity may also contribute to the creation of new desert areas – a process known as *desertification* (see pp. 186–7).

Desert climates

Some deserts are drier than others. Because of this it is usual for a distinction to be made between *semi-arid* areas, which receive on average 200–500 mm (8–20 in) of rainfall per year; *arid* areas, with an average annual rainfall of 25–200 mm (1–8 in); and *hyper-arid* areas, which are so dry that rainfall may not occur for several years on end. Together, arid and hyper-arid areas form the world's true deserts. Semi-arid areas, which are often on the margins of deserts, cover about 15% of the world's land area, while arid and hyper-arid desert areas respectively cover about 16% and 4%.

Most deserts tend to experience warm or hot summer months, with mean temperatures greater than 20 °C (68 °F), and maximum temperatures sometimes reaching over 50 °C (122 °F) in the hotter deserts. However, temperatures in the winter months can vary widely, because of the range of latitudes in which deserts are found. The deserts formed by the subtropical high-pressure belts generally have the warmest winters; indeed parts of the Arabian Desert do not experience anything that really deserves to be called winter, with the mean temperatures of the coldest month being over 20 °C (68 °F). Some deserts do, however, experience cold winters. Parts of the central Sahara are extremely mountainous, so that high altitudes contribute to low winter temperatures, while the mean temperature of the coldest month in the Gobi Desert falls below –20 °C (–4 °F) owing both to its great distance from the sea and to its high altitude.

THE LANDSCAPES OF FOUR DESERT AREAS
(percentages of total areas)

	Southwest USA	Sahara	Arabia	Australia
Mountains	38.1	43	47	16
Gentle rock slopes	0.7	10	1	14
Alluvial fans	31.4	1	4	} 13
Ephemeral rivers and floodplains	4.8	2	2	
Dry lakes	1.1	1	1	1
Gullied areas	2.6	2	1	0
Sand dunes and sand plains	0.6	28	26	38
Other miscellaneous	20.7	13	18	18

Many deserts also experience very high daily temperature ranges, with hot days and cold nights. This is due to clear, cloudless skies allowing heat to escape, combined with the lower ability of ground without vegetation to absorb heat. A daily temperature range of 55 °C (99 °F) has been recorded in the central Sahara: from 52 °C to –3.3 °C (126 °F to 26 °F).

Desert landscapes

Popular images of deserts paint a picture of vast plains of *sand dunes* without a plant or rock in sight. Although some deserts are composed of huge dunes shaped by the wind, it is by no means the case that all deserts are, or that this type of feature is typical of deserts as a whole.

Nevertheless, the wind can be an important landscaping agent in deserts because of the limited presence of vegetation to protect the ground surface. The wind can erode by *sandblasting* bare rock faces, creating smooth rock faces and upstanding features such as *yardangs* (see illustration). If a sufficient supply of sediment is available, the wind can also transport and deposit sand to form dunes. The sand making up desert dunes often comes from dry river courses and lake beds, or the coast. Rock weathering – which is encouraged by high daily temperature ranges – can also be effective on the bare rock surfaces, adding to the supply of sand-sized material.

Although rainfall is limited in deserts, the lack of vegetation and the high intensity of desert rainstorms does mean that water plays an important part in shaping desert landscapes. Desert river courses, often called *wadis*, can carry large volumes of water and sediment during storms. This can lead to the formation of canyons and heavily gullied areas, called *badlands*, in areas where soft and highly erodable sediments are found. Where mountains are present, highly erosive *flash floods* may occur. The large loads of sediments carried by these floods may be deposited where a river leaves the mountains and passes onto gentler, flatter ground, forming an *alluvial fan*. Over time, the work of wind and water can cause a desert landscape to become dissected. In areas where the bedrock consists of horizontally bedded strata – for example in the desert areas of Arizona and New Mexico in the southwestern USA – this can lead to the development of isolated, flat-topped hills called *mesas* and *buttes* (see illustration). Where the rocks are not stratified in this way, more rounded 'island hills' (sometimes called *inselbergs*) may develop. A famous example is Ayers Rock in Australia.

Plants, animals and people

Plants and animals can survive in deserts if they become specially adapted to the harsh conditions that occur (see p. 186). People, too, have adapted to desert conditions by finding ways of using the water that is available – for example, by living at an *oasis* (a constant spring) or digging wells in the beds of dry rivers to tap water supplies. Today, technology has enabled more people than ever to exist and travel comfortably in deserts, as the cities in the North American deserts testify. However, desert life can remain precarious, and is always prone to the dangers of drought, as the human tragedies in recent years on the southern margins of the Sahara have so clearly demonstrated.   DT

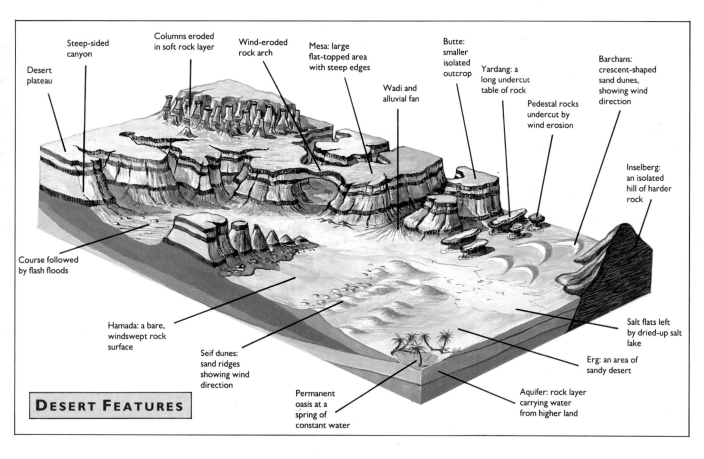

DESERT FEATURES

Desert plateau

Steep-sided canyon

Columns eroded in soft rock layer

Wind-eroded rock arch

Mesa: large flat-topped area with steep edges

Butte: smaller isolated outcrop

Wadi and alluvial fan

Yardang: a long undercut table of rock

Barchans: crescent-shaped sand dunes, showing wind direction

Pedestal rocks undercut by wind erosion

Inselberg: an isolated hill of harder rock

Course followed by flash floods

Hamada: a bare, windswept rock surface

Seif dunes: sand ridges showing wind direction

Permanent oasis at a spring of constant water

Aquifer: rock layer carrying water from higher land

Erg: an area of sandy desert

Salt flats left by dried-up salt lake

SEE ALSO

- MOUNTAINS p. 86
- ICE p. 90
- THE MAKING OF THE WEATHER p. 102
- CLIMATIC AND VEGETATION REGIONS p. 104
- ECOSYSTEMS: EXTREME p. 186

Rivers and Lakes

River source (spring)

Watershed separating neighbouring drainage basins

Meanders in lower course of river, where it crosses flatter ground

Waterfall as stream passes over band of resistant rock

Tributaries

Levées, formed when river deposits sediments and builds up banks

Oxbow lake formed by abandoned meander

Gorge cut by river

Lake

Mud islands in braided section of river

Point bar formed by river depositing sediment on outside of meander

Sea

Delta

Rivers and lakes are the most important bodies of surface water on land masses. A river is a freshwater body confined in a channel that flows down a slope into another river, a lake or the sea, or sometimes into an inland desert. Small, narrow rivers may be called brooks, streams or creeks.

Tributaries of the Amazon from space, showing the numerous meanders typical of rivers flowing over soft, flat ground. In such terrain, rivers frequently change their courses.

A lake is an inland body of water occupying a depression in the Earth's surface. Usually, lakes receive water from rivers, but sometimes only directly from springs. Lakes normally lose water into an outlet or river, but some, called *closed lakes*, have no outlet and lose water only by evaporation – for example, Lake Eyre in Australia and Great Salt Lake in Utah, USA.

Where do rivers get their water from?

Rivers may receive their water from several sources, but all of these are indirectly or directly related to *precipitation* – a collective term for the fall of moisture onto the Earth's surface from the atmosphere. Rain falling on the ground may immediately run down slopes as *overland flow*, becoming concentrated and eventually forming a stream. This tends to occur where the ground surface is *impermeable* (i.e. water cannot pass through it, as is the case with some kinds of rock). It may also occur where the ground is already saturated with water, or when rainfall is very heavy.

Often, however, rivers receive their water from *springs*. This is because rainfall will commonly soak into the ground, to accumulate in the soil or to pass into permeable and porous rocks as *groundwater*. In *permeable* rock, water can pass right through the rock itself, whereas in *porous* rock there are holes and fissures through which water can pass. A deposit of rock containing groundwater is known as an *aquifer*. Springs occur where the top of the aquifer intersects with the ground surface. Groundwater is important as a source for rivers in that it can supply water even when precipitation is not occurring, thereby constantly maintaining river flow.

A third source of water for rivers is the melting of solid precipitation (snow) or snow that has been turned to ice to form a glacier or ice sheet (see p. 90). This is particularly important in high-latitude and mountainous areas.

Perennial, seasonal and ephemeral rivers

Rivers occur in all the world's major environments, even in polar areas and deserts. In temperate areas, such as Western Europe, northeastern USA and New Zealand, and in the wet tropics, enough precipitation tends to fall fairly evenly throughout the year to replenish groundwater constantly, and therefore to allow rivers to flow all year round. These *perennial rivers* do, however, experience seasonal and day-to-day variations in the volume of water they carry (the *flow regime*), due to seasonal fluctuations in precipitation and additional inputs from individual storms.

Some rivers may only flow seasonally, particularly in environments with Mediterranean-type climates, which have a very distinct wet, winter season and a dry summer. Rivers in glaciated areas may also have very seasonal flow regimes. *Glacial meltwater streams*, which receive their water directly from glaciers, usually only flow during the few months in the summer when the ice melts.

In dry desert climates, rivers may not flow for years on end, because of the infrequency of desert storms, and then only for a few days, or even hours. However, when storms do occur these *ephemeral* rivers may flow at great rates, because desert rainfall is often very heavy. This gives them considerable power and the ability to erode and transport large quantities of sediment (see pp. 92–3).

Some deserts do possess perennial rivers. The Nile, for example, despite experiencing a distinctly seasonal flow regime, flows all year round through the Egyptian Desert; likewise, the Colorado River passes through desert areas of the southwestern USA. The reason that these and other rivers can successfully exist in deserts is that their *catchments* (source areas) lie in areas with wetter climates.

River basins

Only some very short rivers are able to flow from a source to the sea without either being joined by others or becoming a *tributary* of a larger river. Most rivers therefore form part of a *drainage network*, occupying a *drainage basin*. In fact, the whole of the Earth's land surface can be divided up into drainage basins, and these basins are separated by areas of relatively high ground called *watersheds*. Some drainage basins occupy only a few square kilometres, but others are enormous – the largest, the Amazon basin, covers over 7 million km² (2.7 million sq mi).

Rivers and landscapes

Rivers are a major force in shaping landscapes. They erode rock and sediment, thereby cutting channels and even valleys and shaping the landscape of upland areas. Such channels may be very shallow, but they may be as deep as the Grand Canyon, which the Colorado River has cut to a depth of up to 1500 m (5000 ft) in places. River valleys are commonly regarded as V-shaped, but in fact their shape can vary according to the position along the river's course, the size of the river, and the rock types in the landscape through which the river passes.

Rivers also transport vast quantities of

material that has been eroded by other agencies – for example, rock-weathering processes, glaciers (see p. 90) and the wind. This sediment may in turn be deposited by the rivers themselves, within river channels or as *flood plains* (see box, p. 93), or carried into lakes or the sea.

The deposition of sediment in a valley to form a flood plain tends to result in a lessening of the gradient of a river channel. A gentler gradient means that a river may cut *meanders* (wandering channels) in the soft flood-plain deposits. Over time, erosion of the river bank of the outside bend of a meander (where flow is fastest) may cause the channel to straighten and the meander to be 'cut off' to form an *oxbow lake*.

Mud islands may form within the channel of a river carrying a particularly large load of sediment, and a pattern of *braided channels* may develop. Where a river with a large load of sediment meets the sea, the loss of river energy can cause sediment to be deposited at the coast, forming a *delta*, as in the cases of the Mississippi and Nile. Over the centuries, deltas – so named because their shape resembles the Greek letter delta ($\triangle$) – can build up large areas of land where once there was sea.

Lakes

Lakes can occur along the course of a river, where it flows into a depression. In some circumstances, a lake can mark the end point of a river course. Such depressions can be *erosional*, formed by the action of glaciers or wind. They may also be *depositional*, formed, for example, by a landslide blocking the course of a river. Finally, they may be *structural*, formed by Earth movements, for example in rift valleys (see pp. 78–9 and 85). Lakes may also be formed behind the terminal moraines of retreating glaciers (see p. 90).

A *volcanic lake*, formed by the accumulation of rainfall in a volcanic crater (see p. 82), may even have no inflowing or outflowing river.

In hot, relatively dry climates, lakes will lose a lot of water through evaporation. This results in the concentration of salts and the lake water becoming saline. The Caspian Sea, Aral Sea and Dead Sea are in fact all saline lakes. These three lakes do have outlets, but lakes that lose as much water through evaporation as they gain from inputs will in fact be *closed*, that is, without an outflow.

Rivers, lakes and people

Rivers and lakes are used by humans for a variety of purposes. Ever since mankind has existed, they have provided water and food. Over time their importance and the diversity of usage have both increased. They have provided water for irrigation and also natural transport routes. In North America, the Mississippi River and the Great Lakes are important routes for the transport of agricultural and industrial produce; in addition, the construction of canals has improved the 'linkages' in the water transport system.

Rivers have been straightened, widened and deepened, and also dammed to create reservoirs and sources of hydroelectricity (see p. 306). Humans have, however, misused rivers and lakes too, by using them to dispose of sewage and industrial waste so endangering natural plant and animal communities (see pp. 300–1).   DT

Niagara Falls. Waterfalls are formed when rivers pass over bands of harder, more resistant rock. The softer rock downstream from the hard rock is more quickly eroded, but even the harder rock is eventually undercut and eroded, and the waterfall gradually moves upstream and decreases in height.

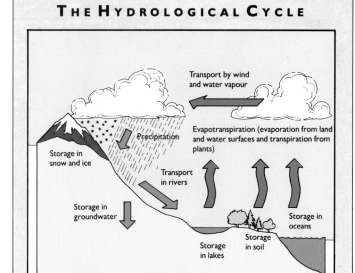

THE HYDROLOGICAL CYCLE

Transport by wind and water vapour

Precipitation

Evapotranspiration (evaporation from land and water surfaces and transpiration from plants)

Storage in snow and ice

Transport in rivers

Storage in groundwater

Storage in oceans

Storage in lakes

Storage in soil

Water exists in three states: liquid, gaseous (water vapour or steam) and solid (snow and ice). It can also pass from one state to another by freezing, melting, condensing and evaporating. New water is not created on the Earth's surface or in its atmosphere; nor is 'old' water lost. Rather, there is a finite amount, and this circulates in what is known as the *hydrological cycle*. Water moves around the cycle both by physically moving and by changing its state, as the diagram shows.

Today, 97% of the water in the hydrological cycle is contained in the world's seas, oceans and saline lakes. The remaining 3% is fresh water. About 75% of all fresh water is contained in glaciers and ice sheets, and just over 24% is groundwater (i.e. underground). The rivers, lakes, soil and atmosphere therefore contain a very small amount (less than 0.5%) of the world's fresh water at any one time.

During glacial periods of the Earth's history (see p. 91), the amount of water contained in ice sheets and glaciers has been greater, and the amount in oceans smaller (see also graph, p. 97).

SEE ALSO

● ICE p. 90
● COASTS p. 96
● THE OCEANS p. 100
● ECOSYSTEMS: AQUATIC p. 178

Coasts

Coasts are where the land meets the sea. The coastline is a zone of landscape activity where new land can be created by the deposition (laying down) of sediment, but also where existing land can be lost through the processes of marine erosion. But what happens where on the coast depends on many factors such as climate, coastal geology, the orientation of the coast to wind and waves, and the history of human activities.

With so many factors affecting the nature of the processes at work on coastlines, it is not surprising that the world's coasts are extremely diverse. In polar regions, the coastline may be protected from the direct impact of the sea by the presence of *ice shelves* (see p. 90), while in many tropical areas the arrival of great volumes of muddy sediments, transported to the sea by rivers, has allowed the development of extensive mangrove swamps that both protect the coast and make human access to the sea difficult. But in other locations the coastline is actively changing and evolving through the direct impact of the sea's energy.

The energy of the sea

Tides and currents (see p. 100–1) contribute some of the sea's energy at the coast, but waves (see p. 100) are the most important factor in shaping the coastline, contributing most of the energy that erodes, transports and deposits sediment. Also important, in areas where winds and waves from one direction dominate, is the sea's ability to transport material along the coast in a preferred direction, by the process known as *longshore drift*.

Waves are generated by the wind in the open sea where water is deep, and are driven onshore by it. The height of waves and the distance between them (the *wave-*

length), together with wave energy, are largely determined by wind strength and the distance, called the *fetch*, over which they have been transported. The fetch can extend for many thousands of kilometres; for example, the predominant westerly winds that affect the coastline of Western Europe can transport waves generated off the east coast of North America. Waves with a long fetch tend to possess considerable energy with which to shape the coast.

As the sea becomes shallower at the coast and waves move onshore, they lose energy and 'break', and water rushes onshore as *swash*. On a sloping beach, the water returns to the sea under the effect of gravity as *backwash*; in some circumstances this can become concentrated in *rip currents*, which are particularly erosive.

An important factor in determining the effect of waves on the coast is whether waves are *destructive* or *constructive*. Destructive waves are relatively high compared to their wavelength, and break with a force that generates a strong, erosive backwash that tends to remove material from a beach. Constructive waves break more gently, pushing material up the beach, building it up.

Beaches

Beaches result from the depositional effects of constructive waves, usually in low-energy coastal environments. They can be made out of fine sediments such as mud and sand, or coarser material such as pebbles, or a combination of all three. The type of material present on any one beach is determined by the type of sediment available to the waves that construct it. This in turn is affected by the *sediment source*, which can be a river bringing sediment to the sea (see pp. 94–5), the ocean floor, or the coast itself, in the form of eroded material transported to the beach by longshore drift.

The type of sediment, wave energy, the tidal range (see p. 100) and the effect of storms will determine beach shape. The upper beach is generally steepest and is affected only by high tides and storm waves. It usually consists of coarse mater-

ial, pushed up the beach by constructive waves, and possesses several parallel ridges (*berms*) produced by successive high tides. At the back of the beach, a *storm ridge* may be present. The lower beach is usually more gentle and consists of finer sediments. On some coasts, the beach is backed by sand dunes, which accumulate from sand that is blown onshore by the wind at low tide.

Longshore drift can result in the growth of a beach along the coast. Where this occurs, and the coastline changes direction, for example at an estuary (river mouth) or bay, the growth of the beach can continue to form a *spit*, a depositional landform that extends out into the sea. A spit can even grow to rejoin the land again, forming a *sand bar* or *barrier beach*. Some bays and estuaries are so sheltered from wave action that beaches do not form. However, if there is a source of fine sediment, such as mud supplied by a river, these sheltered places can see the growth of *tidal salt marshes*, which support types of plants that can withstand the twice daily incursion of salt water during high tides.

Erosional coasts

Erosion occurs where coasts are exposed to waves that have a long fetch, or where strong onshore winds generate high-energy waves over relatively short distances. Erosional coastlines are commonly dominated by cliffs, at the foot of which a *wavecut platform* may be exposed at low tide. This feature represents the seaward remnant of the eroded cliffs. In areas where the cliffs are formed of rocks that are well jointed and susceptible to erosion – for example, chalk, limestone and some sandstones – *sea stacks* (free-standing pinnacles), arches and caves may be formed by the sea's erosive action.

Coastal erosion occurs through *hydraulic action* (the pressure of waves breaking at the foot of the cliff) and by *corrasion* (a process in which sediment in the water is thrown against the rock surface). Erosion at the cliff foot may slow down over time as the wavecut platform widens and is able to absorb the energy of the waves being driven onshore. This can even result in the formation of a beach at the foot of the cliff.

Coastal landscapes

Coastal landscapes are not only determined by the processes of deposition and erosion but also by the nature and structure of the coastal geology. Where the rock structure generally lies parallel to the coast, the processes affecting it will generally be constant along its length, so the coastline will be *concordant*, i.e. relatively straight.

On the other hand, a *discordant* coast

The IJsselmeer (right), in the Netherlands photographed by the Landsat satellite. The freshwater IJsselmeer was created when a dyke (seen here as a thin white line) was built in the 1930s across the mouth of what was then the Zuider Zee, an inlet of the North Sea. Within the dyke, four huge areas of land (*polders*) have been reclaimed – identifiable here by their distinctive, predominantly blue field patterns. Further reclamation is in progress.

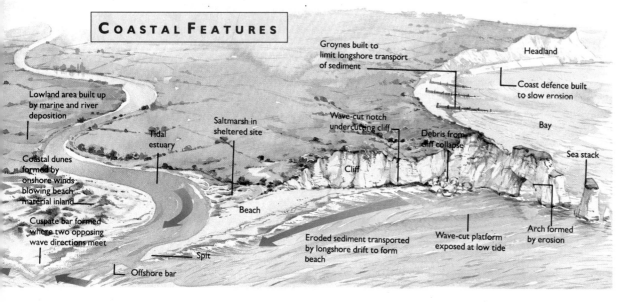

COASTAL FEATURES

Lowland area built up by marine and river deposition

Coastal dunes formed by onshore winds blowing beach material inland

Cuspate bar formed where two opposing wave directions meet

Spit

Offshore bar

Tidal estuary

Saltmarsh in sheltered site

Beach

Eroded sediment transported by longshore drift to form beach

Groynes built to limit longshore transport of sediment

Wave-cut notch undercutting cliff

Cliff

Debris from cliff collapse

Wave-cut platform exposed at low tide

Headland

Coast defence built to slow erosion

Bay

Sea stack

Arch formed by erosion

develops where the rock structure meets the coastline at an angle. This allows the sea to exploit the relative strengths of different rocks, leading to greater erosion of those that are less resistant. A coast characterized by bays and headlands will result and, as the erosion progresses over time, the bays will become more sheltered. These will then become the sites of sediment deposition and beach development.

Humans also affect coastal landscapes. One important way is in the construction of coastal defences, either to reduce the risk of storm flooding in low-lying areas, or in an attempt to control coastal erosion. Sediment deposition and land reclamation can also be influenced by human actions, as in the Netherlands where 2227 km² (860 sq mi) of the Zuider Zee have been reclaimed from the sea.   DT

Surfer's Paradise (below left), a magnificent beach in Queensland, Australia, is a classic example of longshore drift and a river estuary combining to build up a spit parallel to the coast.

SEE ALSO

● ICE p. 90
● RIVERS AND LAKES p. 94
● ISLANDS p. 98
● THE OCEANS p. 100
● ECOSYSTEMS: AQUATIC p. 178

CHANGES IN SEA LEVEL

Throughout geological history, sea level has changed significantly for a number of different reasons. An obvious one is that, during ice ages (see p. 91), water is withdrawn from the oceans to form ice sheets, ice caps and glaciers, causing sea level to fall. However, recent research has indicated that no less important is the fact that during particularly cold periods the ocean water contracts, again resulting in lower sea level. Conversely, when the Earth warms up again the ice melts and the water expands, leading to a rise in sea level.

But not all sea-level changes are caused by climatic effects. For example, at times when the movement of tectonic plates (see p. 78) is particularly vigorous, the increased volume of magma rising at oceanic ridges will displace more ocean water than usual, causing sea level to rise.

The eustatic (worldwide) changes in sea level over the past 60 million years, as proposed by P. R. Vail and colleagues at Exxon. It is thought that falls in sea level have all been relatively abrupt. The details of this curve are not universally agreed by scientists.

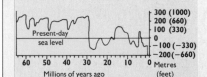

Such worldwide changes in sea level are known as *eustatic* changes. However, there can also be more local changes in sea level, known as *isostatic* changes. The growth of ice on land results in the depression of the Earth's crust beneath the great weight of ice sheets and ice caps, and when the ice melts the crust beneath rises again. The melting of ice caps in North America and Scandinavia at the end of the last Ice Age 10 000 years ago caused the crust to rebound, resulting in coastal areas rising relative to the sea – by as much as 300 m (1000 ft) in Hudson's Bay and the Baltic Sea. Moreover, crustal rebound in some areas can cause subsidence in others by way of compensation. This has occurred in Britain; uplift in Scotland has contributed to the subsidence of the south coast of England.

Rising sea levels can cause coastal areas to become flooded, drowning valleys to form narrow sea inlets called *rias*. Conversely, falling sea levels or rising land can sometimes create *raised beaches*, former beaches stranded high above the present sea level.

Islands

An island is a body of land, smaller than a continent, that is completely surrounded by water. Islands occur in rivers, lakes, and the seas and oceans. They range in size from very small mud and sand islands of only a few square metres, to Greenland, which has an area of 2.2 million km² (840 000 sq mi).

Islands, especially those in seas and oceans, have a range of origins. Islands can develop through *constructional* processes, involving the deposition (laying down) of sediment or the building up of volcanic or organic material. They may also be formed by *erosional* processes that cause an area of land to become separated from the mainland (see also pp. 96–7). Rising sea levels can also lead to the development of islands, by drowning low-lying areas of land and separating higher areas from the main land mass (see also p. 97).

Volcanic islands

When volcanic activity occurs beneath the oceans, it can lead to the growth of islands. This is often closely linked to the movement of the Earth's crustal plates, with island-building (e.g. Iceland) occurring both at constructive plate margins

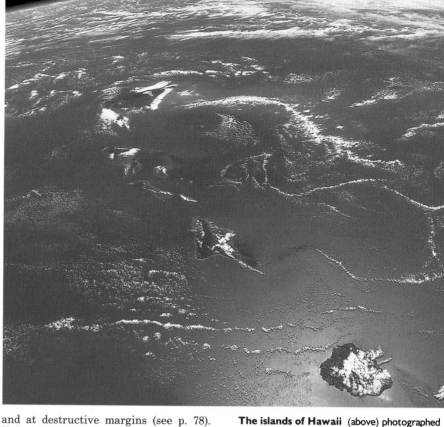

Volcanic activity on Iceland. The island of Iceland started forming about 20 million years ago, and is still growing today. Iceland was largely built up by the slow extrusion of lava at the boundary of a tectonic plate, rather than by violent volcanic eruptions.

and at destructive margins (see p. 78). Volcanic islands (e.g. Hawaii) can also form far from any plate boundary (see hot-spot islands below).

Iceland, situated on the mid-Atlantic ridge, is the largest example of a volcanic island formed at a constructive plate margin. About 100 000 km² (38 600 sq mi) in area, Iceland started forming about 20 million years ago – the age of the oldest

The islands of Hawaii (above) photographed from the space shuttle. The Hawaiian–Emperor island chain was formed as the Pacific plate passed over a 'hot spot' in the Earth's mantle. Periods of volcanic activity arising from this hot spot have created a succession of islands.

rocks on the island. It is still growing in size today, as new material is periodically added, along a line of volcanic activity running from the southwest to the northeast of the island. Much of the volcanic activity responsible for Iceland's growth has not been in the form of spectacular eruptions, but rather as quiet *extrusive fissure eruptions*, involving the outpouring of large quantities of lava from cracks in the Earth's surface, giving rise to *basaltic* rocks.

Spectacular eruptions, have, however, also played their part. For example, in 1963, eruptions occurred off the south coast of Iceland. In the space of a few weeks, ash and lava built up on the sea floor and a new, small island named Surtsey was born.

Island archipelagos

The collision of crustal plates at destructive margins (see p. 78) can generate significant volcanic activity. If this occurs at the edge of a land mass it can cause mountain building, but when the collision zone lies beneath an ocean, island development can result.

Islands that are born in this way do not occur singly, but in chains or archipelagos ('arcs') that parallel the plate boundary. This is well illustrated on the western side of the Pacific Ocean (see map, p. 79). Here thousands of islands – most of them volcanic but some formed by the folding up of the ocean floor – mark the western edge of the Pacific plate. These islands start in the south at New Zealand, run north to the Tongan chain before heading west to New Guinea, and north again through the Philippines, Japan, the

Kurile island chain and finally the Aleutian Islands, which continue to the mainland of North America. The Indonesian archipelago, which extends westwards into the Indian Ocean from the island chains of the west Pacific, is the world's largest archipelago, its 13 000 islands stretching over a distance of 5600 km (3500 mi).

Hot-spot islands

The Hawaiian–Emperor island chain and some other mid-Pacific islands owe their existence to volcanic hot-spot activity. Volcanic activity has erupted through the Pacific plate as it has passed over areas of the Earth's mantle that are particularly active. As the plate has moved, so has the location of volcanic activity and island construction. The Hawaiian–Emperor chain is more than 6000 km (3700 mi) long

and includes more than 100 islands and seamounts (volcanoes that have not reached the ocean surface). The youngest island, which is the furthest east, is Hawaii itself, where volcanic activity is still occurring.

Coral islands

Coral islands and reefs are an important component of warm tropical and subtropical oceans and seas. They are formed from the skeletons of the group of primitive marine organisms known as corals (see box, and also pp. 122–3). Coral islands develop where coral grows up towards the ocean surface from shallow submarine platforms – often volcanic cones. If the cone is totally submerged, then a *coral atoll* will develop – a circular or horseshoe-shaped coral ring that encloses a body of sea water called a *lagoon*.

Upward growth of the coral ceases once sea level has been reached. Coral islands are therefore flat and low, unless a change in sea level has caused their elevation to change.

Sea level and islands

Changes in sea level can cause new islands to appear or existing ones to disappear. During the last Ice Age (see pp. 90–1) eastern Britain was joined to mainland Europe, because sea levels were lower as much of the world's water was frozen in the ice caps and glaciers. As the ice melted and the sea level rose, the North Sea and the Straits of Dover were re-established. By about 8500 years ago Britain was again an island.   DT

SEE ALSO

- PLATE TECTONICS p. 78
- VOLCANOES p. 82
- ICE p. 90
- COASTS p. 96
- THE OCEANS p. 100

CORAL

Coral reefs, coral atolls and coral islands are the largest living structures on Earth, although any one structure will probably contain far more skeletons of dead coral than live individuals. The Great Barrier Reef of northeastern Australia is 2027 km (1260 mi) long. The largest coral atoll is Kwajalein, in the Marshall Islands, of the Pacific Ocean. The 283 km (176 mi) long arc of coral encloses a lagoon that covers 2850 km² (1100 sq mi). The coral body of Christmas Island, in the central Pacific Ocean, has the greatest coral area, covering 323 km² (125 sq mi).

As well as being the largest living bodies, coral reefs are amongst the most diverse and spectacular of natural habitats. In amongst the many species of hard coral – each adapted for slightly different conditions on the reef – are to be found soft coral, sea anemonies and a host of other species. Of these, the myriads of fish are perhaps the most spectacular.

Corals will not survive in fresh water nor in water that is cooler than 20 °C (68 °F). They are therefore restricted to warm tropical and subtropical seas, though living coral reefs do occur around the coast of Bermuda in the Atlantic (latitude 32° N), because of the warming effect of the Gulf Stream. They also require light, so living corals are not usually found in water deeper than about 55 m (180 ft), or in water that contains a lot of sediment.

Corals feed off plankton and also gain food in a symbiotic relationship with small algal cells. Corals reproduce not only sexually but also by budding and by splitting in half, so creating large colonies of genetically identical individuals. During the day, corals appear inactive, with their tentacles retracted, but at night their tentacles extend to feed on the plankton that emerge from crevices in the reef. Many other invertebrates emerge at this time, to feed on plankton and other materials, the threat of predation by fish being largely removed by darkness. Space is at a premium on coral reefs, so individual corals fight each other for the right to grow and reproduce, by using stinging cells, releasing toxic chemicals and even by trying to digest their neighbours.

Coral islands in the Maldives, Indian Ocean. In the distance is a more-or-less totally submerged coral atoll, surrounding a lagoon.

The Oceans

The oceans cover a greater area of the Earth than does the land – 71% or almost three quarters of the Earth's surface. The three major oceans are the Pacific, Atlantic and Indian Oceans. The Pacific is the largest ocean, and covers more than one third of the surface of the Earth. The Arctic Ocean is smaller than the other three and is covered almost entirely by ice (see p. 90). Seas are smaller than the four oceans.

Waves, generated by the wind far out to sea, are the most important factor in shaping the coasts. Tides and currents also play a part.

The depth of the oceans is very small compared with their area. The deepest part, the Mariana Trench in the western Pacific, is only about 11 000 m deep (36 000 ft). However, this is greater than the height of the highest mountain on land, Mount Everest at 8863 m (29 078 ft).

Sea water

Sea water has solid substances dissolved in it. Sodium and chlorine are the most abundant of these (which combine in their solid form to make up sodium chloride – common salt), and together with magnesium, calcium and potassium they make up over 90% of the elements dissolved in sea water. Other elements are present only in very small amounts.

The saltiness, or *salinity*, of sea water depends on the amount of these substances dissolved in it. An average of about 3.5% of the volume of sea water consists of dissolved substances. High evaporation removes more of the pure water, leaving behind the dissolved substances, so the salinity is higher where evaporation is high – particularly if the sea water is also enclosed or cannot mix easily with the sea water of a larger ocean. This occurs, for example, in the Mediterranean and Red Seas. Low values of salinity occur in polar regions, particularly in the summer months when melting ice dilutes the sea water. Low salinity also occurs in seas such as the Baltic, which is linked to the Atlantic Ocean only by a narrow channel and which is fed by a larger number of freshwater rivers.

Most of the water on the Earth, about 94% of it, is in the oceans. More pure water is evaporated from the oceans than is returned as precipitation (rain, snow, etc.), but the volume of water in the oceans remains the same because water is also returned to the oceans from the land by rivers (see p. 94).

Waves

Sea water is rarely still: it is usually moving in waves, tides or currents. Waves are caused by wind blowing across the surface of the ocean. The height of a wave is determined by the wind speed, the time the wind has been blowing, and the distance the wave has travelled over the ocean. The highest wave ever recorded had a height of 34 m (116 ft), although usually they are much smaller. Waves play a very important role in the shaping of coastlines (see p. 100).

Water does not move along with waves. Instead the water changes shape as a wave passes, moving in a roughly circular motion, rising towards a wave crest as it arrives and falling as it passes. This motion can be seen by watching a boat: the boat bobs up and down as the waves move past it but does not move along with the waves (see wave theory, p. 28).

There is another type of wave in the ocean, which is not generated by winds. These are *tsunami*. They are also popularly called *tidal waves*, but this name is quite wrong because they are not caused by tides. Tsunami are due to earthquakes or the eruption of undersea volcanoes. Such events move a large amount of water rapidly, disturbing the sea surface and creating waves that travel away from the area of the earthquake or volcano. Tsunami travel at very high speeds, around 750 km/h (470 mph). However, in the open ocean they cause little damage because their wave height is very low, usually less than 1 m (3¼ ft), but in shallow water they slow down and their height increases to 10 m (33 ft) or more, and they can cause extensive damage when they hit a shore.

Tides

Tides are caused by the gravitational pull of the Moon and the Sun on the Earth, causing the level of the oceans to change. The pull is greatest on the side of the Earth facing the Moon, and this produces a high tide. The pull is weakest on the side away from the Moon, where the sea water rises away from the Moon, and this also gives a high tide.

The Sun is much further away than the Moon, so although it is much larger its effect on tides is less than half that of the

AREA, VOLUME AND AVERAGE DEPTH		Pacific Ocean	Atlantic Ocean (including Arctic Ocean)	Indian Ocean
Area	millions km²	180	106	75
	millions sq mi	70	41	29
Volume	millions km³	724	355	292
	millions cu mi	174	85	70
Average depth	m	3940	3310	3840
	ft	12 930	10 860	12 600

Icebergs (left) are a hazard to shipping as most of their bulk is hidden under water. Icebergs form as parts of the floating ice shelves around Antarctica break off, or as terrestrial glaciers in both the Arctic and Antarctic feed into the sea.

Moon. When both the Moon and the Sun are on the same or opposite sides of the Earth, the pull is greatest, producing very high tides called *spring tides*. Weaker tides, called *neap tides*, occur when the Moon and the Sun form a right angle with the Earth, because the pulls of the two are in different directions. Spring tides occur every 14 days and neap tides half-way between each spring tide.

There are two high tides and two low tides every day in most parts of the Earth, but a few areas have only one high tide and one low tide, or a mixture, with one high tide being much higher than the other.

The *tidal range* (the difference between the high and the low water levels) varies from place to place, from less than 1 m (3¼ ft) in the Mediterranean Sea and Gulf of Mexico to 14.5 m (47½ ft) in the Bay of Fundy on the east coast of Canada.

Currents

The currents near the surface of the oceans, like waves, are driven by the winds. The wind drags the water along with it. Currents move much more slowly than the wind, with speeds of less than 8 km/h (5 mph). They do not flow exactly in the same direction as the wind, but are deflected to one side by the Earth's spin.

There are two main wind systems in each hemisphere. The *trade winds*, between latitudes 0° and 30°, blow from the northeast in the northern hemisphere, and the southeast in the southern. The *westerlies*, between latitudes 30° and 60°, blow from the southwest in the northern hemisphere, and the northwest in the southern. These two wind systems produce a circulating system of currents that flow from equatorial regions to latitudes of about 50° and return to the equator (see map on p. 105).

Currents may have a significant effect on climate. For example, the North Atlantic Drift, flowing from the Caribbean, gives northwest Europe much milder winters than other parts of the world at the same latitude. Conversely, cold currents, such as the Humboldt Current on the Pacific coast of South America, have a cooling effect on climate (see p. 104).

Features of the sea bed

The region of the sea bed closest to land is the *continental margin*, which is divided into the *continental shelf*, the *continental slope* and (sometimes) the *continental rise* (see diagram). The continental shelf is the shallowest – around 130 m (430 ft) deep – and is relatively flat. It is about 100 km (60 mi) wide. The sea water over continental shelves usually has abundant marine life and most fishing is done here. About a quarter of the world's supply of oil and gas comes from the rocks beneath the continental shelves (see p. 310).

Oceanic ridges are vast, rugged, undersea mountain chains often, but not always, at the centre of oceans. On average they are some 1000 km (620 mi) wide and stand up to 3000 m (10 000 ft) above the adjacent ocean basins. They form a more-or-less linked system about 80 000 km (50 000 mi) long, and this system enters all the major oceans. Different parts of it have different names: in the centre and South Atlantic, for example, it is called the Mid-Atlantic Ridge, in the North Atlantic to the southwest of Iceland it is the Reykjanes Ridge, and in the Pacific it is known as the East Pacific Rise. On average, ridge crests lie some 2500 m (8200 ft) below the ocean surface, but there are a few places, such as Iceland, where the rocks have risen above the water surface, forming an island. Oceanic ridges are sites at which new oceanic lithosphere is continuously being created (see p. 78).

Between the ocean ridges and the continental margins there are *abyssal plains*. These are very flat and featureless parts of the sea floor, around 4000 m (13 000 ft) deep. Abyssal plains are broken in some places by *seamounts*, underwater volcanoes that have erupted from the sea floor. Seamounts may rise above the sea surface to form islands, such as Hawaii.

The deepest parts of the oceans are the *ocean trenches*. These are on average about 100 km (62 mi) wide and 7000–8000 m (23 000–26 000 ft) deep, and may be thousands of kilometres long. Trenches occur in two different kinds of location: parallel to the edge of a continent, at the bottom of the continental slope; or in the open ocean, where they are arc-shaped, and are parallel to an island arc. SS

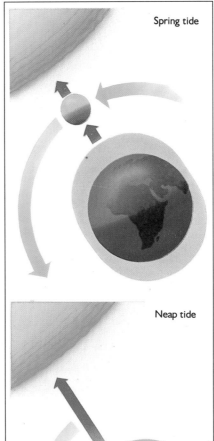
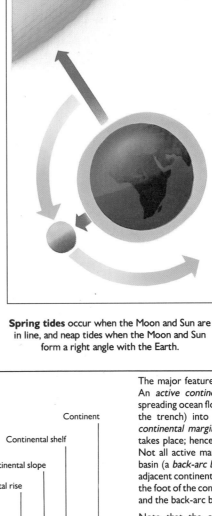

Spring tide

Neap tide

Spring tides occur when the Moon and Sun are in line, and neap tides when the Moon and Sun form a right angle with the Earth.

SEE ALSO
- WAVE THEORY p. 28
- PLATE TECTONICS p. 78
- RIVERS AND LAKES p. 94
- COASTS p. 96
- ISLANDS p. 98
- PRIMITIVE ANIMALS I p. 122
- ARTHROPODS I p. 124
- FISHES p. 128
- MARINE MAMMALS p. 162
- ECOSYSTEMS: AQUATIC p. 178
- FISHING p. 194

MAJOR FEATURES OF THE SEA BED

Continent · Continental shelf · Continental slope · Back-arc basin · Island arc · Trench · Seamounts · Oceanic ridge · Oceanic island · Continental slope · Continental rise · Seamount · Continental shelf · Continent

ACTIVE CONTINENTAL MARGIN (with island arc) · Abyssal plain · Abyssal plain · PASSIVE CONTINENTAL MARGIN

The major features are as described in the text. An *active continental margin* is one at which spreading ocean floor is being subducted (beneath the trench) into the mantle below. A *passive continental margin* is one where no subduction takes place; hence there is no trench (see p.78). Not all active margins have an island arc with a basin (a *back-arc basin*) between the arc and the adjacent continent; in some cases the trench lies at the foot of the continental slope, and the island arc and the back-arc basin are missing.

Note that the cross-section and the features marked on it are not to scale, either in the vertical or horizontal directions. Moreover, the cross-section is a composite of the world's major oceans. A section across the Pacific, for example, would generally have an active margin at each side. Both margins of the Atlantic, by contrast, are passive.

Weather

The weather is the atmospheric conditions we experience at any one time. These can vary rapidly as rain gives way to sunshine or snow starts to melt. Such sudden changes of weather are more common in temperate latitudes than in the tropics.

SEE ALSO

● THE EARTH'S STRUCTURE AND ATMOSPHERE p. 76
● THE HYDROLOGICAL CYCLE p. 95
● CLIMATIC AND VEGETATION REGIONS p. 104

Weather is the result of air movements in the atmosphere (see p. 77). The atmosphere responds to the differences in heat received from the Sun between the warm tropics and the cold poles. The Earth's rotation and the nature of the ground surface – whether it is land or sea, mountain or lowland – will all affect the way the atmosphere moves. Viewed from space, cloud patterns show the way in which this movement takes place to give day-to-day variations called weather.

Atmospheric pressure

In temperate parts of the world, the most important feature of the weather is atmospheric pressure. Atmospheric pressure represents the force exerted by a column of the atmosphere on the Earth's surface (see p. 22). If pressure is measured using a barometer and compared with readings taken elsewhere at the same time, patterns appear showing areas of higher and lower surface pressure.

From a pressure map (see illustration) it is possible to find wind direction. As a rough guide, winds blow parallel to the *isobars* – the lines that link points experiencing the same pressure. In the northern hemisphere, the low pressure lies to the left of the wind direction, while in the southern hemisphere it is to the right. The strength of the wind depends upon the *pressure gradient*. If the pressure gradient is steep, that means that the isobars are close together and winds will be strong.

Temperature

A pressure map can also inform us about other aspects of weather. Temperature is affected by the origin of air. Air blowing from polar latitudes will be cold, while air from tropical latitudes will be warm. Winds blowing from the Atlantic Ocean onto northwest Europe are relatively cool in summer but relatively mild in winter, while winds from the east are very cold in winter but warm in summer. Temperatures will also depend upon how much the Sun is obscured by clouds. However, nocturnal cloud cover helps to retain the daytime warmth.

Clouds and precipitation

Clouds form when air cools so much that it can no longer hold all its water as a vapour. Water droplets then appear, which we see as clouds. To produce a cloud, air needs to rise or be forced to rise. On sunny days, the ground will warm. *Thermals* of warm, moist air may then rise sufficiently to produce clouds. Clouds often develop over hills or mountains where air is forced to rise.

Some clouds, though by no means all, produce *precipitation* (rain, snow, sleet, etc.). To do this, the right sort of conditions have to exist in the cloud. There appear to be two main processes. One method of precipitation formation is through the collision and coalescence of water droplets of different size within the cloud. The rising air that is producing the cloud may be strong enough to carry some of the smaller droplets upwards whilst larger droplets start falling as they become too heavy to be supported by the rising air. Through collision they grow and may become large enough to fall out of the base of the cloud and not be evaporated before reaching the ground.

The other method of precipitation takes place in clouds that consist of a mixture of water droplets and ice crystals. Not all droplets freeze at 0 °C (32 °F) – some remain as droplets down to –38 °C (–36 °F) because they are so small. Under these conditions, water tends to transfer from the droplets onto the larger, already frozen droplets, and these ice crystals may eventually fall out of the cloud. If they reach the ground we get snow. Much more frequently, however, the ice crystals melt as they fall to produce rain. Occasionally, some raindrops get swept into the upper parts of the cloud, where they freeze. Several phases of rising and sinking can produce a hailstone consisting of layers of ice. Hailstones only occur in certain types of cloud when the air is rising very rapidly.

It is in this type of cloud – the *cumulonimbus* cloud – that thunder and lightning may occur. A separation of electrical charge (positive from negative) develops during hail formation. The flash of lightning is a spark of electricity between cloud and Earth or from cloud to cloud resulting from the build-up of charges and potential differences of up to 1000 million volts. The air is heated by the lightning,

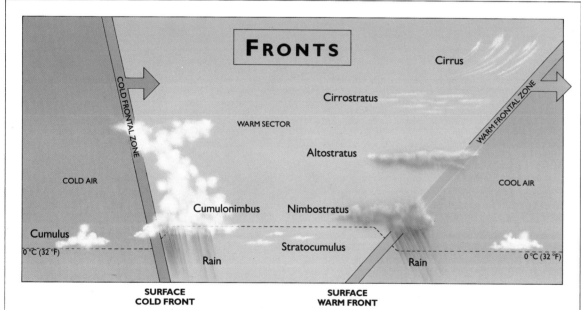

FRONTS

Cirrus

Cirrostratus

COLD FRONTAL ZONE

WARM SECTOR

WARM FRONTAL ZONE

Altostratus

COLD AIR

COOL AIR

Cumulonimbus   Nimbostratus

Cumulus

Stratocumulus

0 °C (32 °F)

Rain   Rain   0 °C (32 °F)

SURFACE COLD FRONT   **SURFACE WARM FRONT**

Both types of occluded front are associated with extensive cloud and rain.

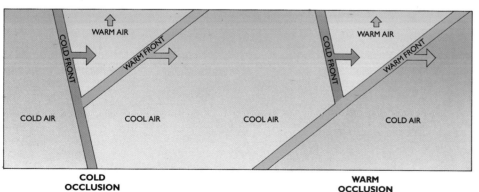

WARM AIR   WARM AIR

COLD FRONT   WARM FRONT   COLD FRONT   WARM FRONT

COLD AIR   COOL AIR   COOL AIR   COLD AIR

COLD OCCLUSION   **WARM OCCLUSION**

Fronts mark boundaries between air of different temperatures. Where warm air is replacing cold air there is a *warm front*. It extends into the atmosphere well ahead of the surface warm front. Clouds are usually associated with the front, as shown in the diagram.

A *cold front* occurs where cold air replaces warm air. The temperature change can be quite sudden – several degrees in

a few minutes. Cumulonimbus clouds often mark the line of the cold front and give a short period of heavy rain.

In many depressions the cold front moves faster than the warm front, gradually squeezing out the warm sector. When this has taken place, there is an *occluded front*. Its precise form depends on whether the air following the original cold front is warmer or cooler than the air ahead of the depression.

and the sudden expansion of the air produces the thunder that we hear.

Cloud types

Clouds are identified on the basis of their appearance and height. The highest clouds are called *cirrus* clouds. They form at heights between 6 and 10 km (3½ and 6 mi), where the temperatures are well below freezing point. They consist of ice crystals, which often tend to be spread out by the strong winds at those levels. Hooked cirrus ('mare's-tails') are usually found ahead of a depression and so indicate imminent rain. When the sheets of ice crystals thicken and cover more of the sky, they are called *cirrostratus* clouds. Middle-level clouds of uniform greyness that totally obscure the Sun are known as *altostratus*. They often follow cirrostratus clouds. As rain approaches, the cloud base lowers to give a sheet of thick cloud called *nimbostratus*, which can give much rain. Where clouds are not able to develop upwards, as in anticyclones, *stratocumulus* clouds may form. These clouds indicate that air has only been able to rise to a certain level before sinking in the clear zones between the clouds. This gives a fish-scale effect ('mackerel sky') if the clouds are relatively high.

The most impressive clouds are those associated with rapidly rising air. If the clouds have not developed very far, they are called *cumulus*. They have sharp outlines, and often resemble cauliflowers. Cumulus clouds can build up to enter the ice-crystal zone or even reach the base of the stratosphere. When this happens they cannot rise further but spread out to produce an anvil-like cloud that is known as *cumulonimbus*. Most give showers, and hail and thunder are possible.

Temperate weather systems

In temperate latitudes, one of the main areas of uplift and cloud formation – and so of rainfall – is the *low-pressure area* or *depression* (also called a *cyclone*). Seen from space, depressions often possess a distinctive spiral or swirl of clouds showing where the air is rising. With depressions the wind blows anticlockwise in the northern hemisphere and clockwise in the southern. Most cloud occurs near frontal surfaces, where temperatures change rapidly. In a typical low-pressure system, a warm front, a cold front, an occluded front and a warm sector are found (see weather map and box on weather fronts). Away from the cloud bands of the depression, showers still occur but become less frequent as pressure rises away from the low-pressure centre.

High-pressure areas or *anticyclones* contain generally sinking and warming air. As a result air does not rise enough for deep cloud to form, so rain is rare. In all temperate land areas, anticyclones can bring hot, sunny weather in summer or cold weather in winter, but they are always dry. Within anticyclones the wind blows clockwise in the northern hemisphere and anticlockwise in the southern.

Tropical weather systems

In the tropics, distinctive pressure patterns are less common. Pressure gradients are usually much weaker than in temperate latitudes, so winds are generally light. One major low-pressure system that is found is the *tropical storm*. It has a number of names, including *hurricane*, *typhoon* and *cyclone*. Tropical storms normally occur in summer or autumn when tropical seas are warmest. At their centre is an area of very low pressure surrounded by strong winds, which can exceed 240 km/h (150 mph) in the worst storms. At the centre or *eye* of the storm, winds are light. Away from the eye sweep vast bands of cloud spiralling like a giant Catherine wheel. Heavy rain falls from these cloud bands and more damage is usually caused by flood water following the heavy rain than from the strong winds.

A less dramatic feature of the tropics is the seasonal change of winds known as the *monsoon*. Over parts of Africa, India, Southeast Asia and northern Australia, the monsoons bring rain during the summer season. The rest of the year is dry with winds blowing in the opposite direction.

PAS

THE BEAUFORT SCALE
FOR MEASURING WIND STRENGTH

Beaufort Number (or wind force)	Description	Speed km/h	Speed mph
0	Calm	less than 1	
1	Light air	1–5	1–3
2	Light breeze	6–11	4–7
3	Gentle breeze	12–19	8–12
4	Moderate breeze	20–29	13–18
5	Fresh breeze	30–39	19–24
6	Strong breeze	40–50	25–31
7	Near gale	51–61	32–38
8	Gale	62–74	39–46
9	Strong gale	75–87	47–54
10	Storm	88–101	55–63
11	Violent storm	102–117	64–73
12	Hurricane	118+	74+

PRESSURE CHARTS

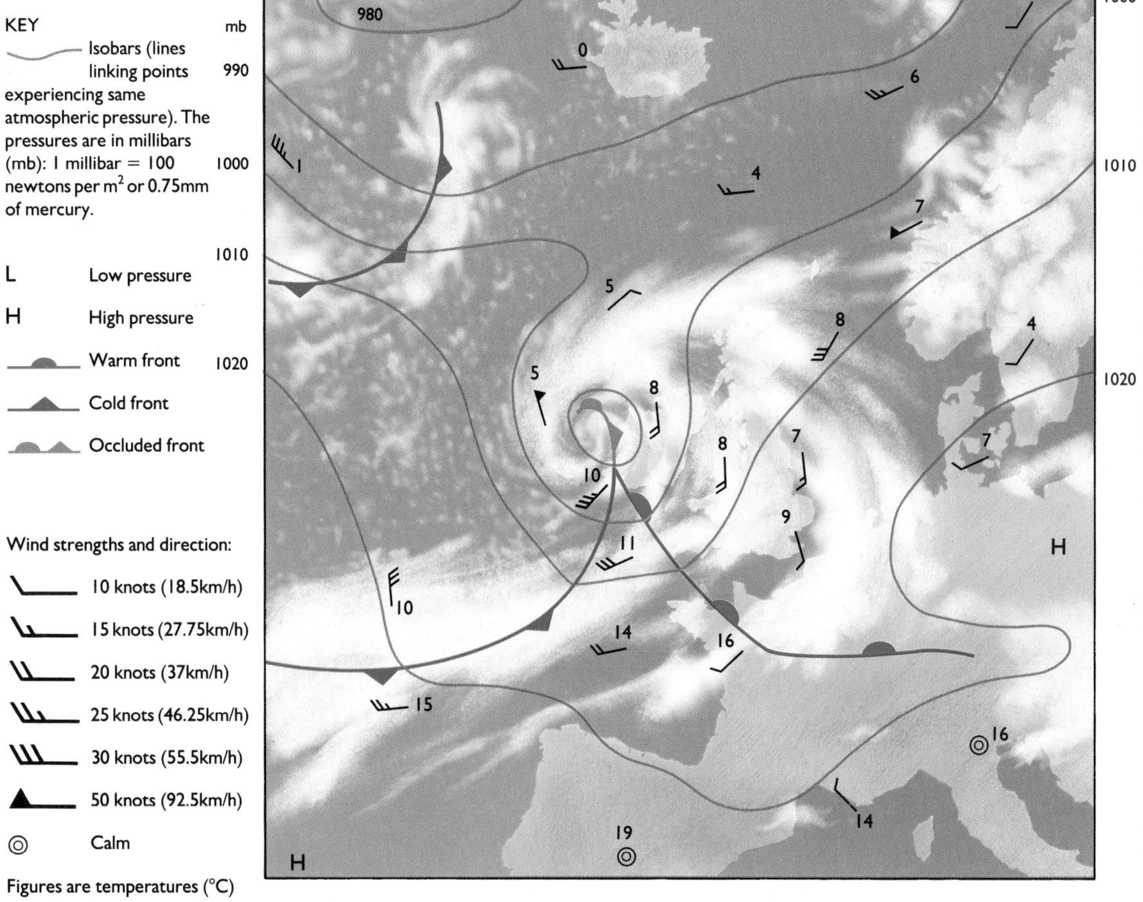
KEY
mb
Isobars (lines linking points experiencing same atmospheric pressure). The pressures are in millibars (mb): 1 millibar = 100 newtons per m² or 0.75mm of mercury.
990
1000
1010
1020
L Low pressure
H High pressure
Warm front
Cold front
Occluded front
Wind strengths and direction:
10 knots (18.5km/h)
15 knots (27.75km/h)
20 knots (37km/h)
25 knots (46.25km/h)
30 knots (55.5km/h)
50 knots (92.5km/h)
Calm
Figures are temperatures (°C)
980
L
L
H
H
mb
1000
1010
1020

Weather forecasters use pressure charts to help them decide what the weather is going to do. The satellite image and superimposed pressure chart show the way in which cloud systems and pressure systems are related. The main areas of thicker cloud are associated with the rising air near the low-pressure centre to the west of Ireland. The centre of the low marks the start of the typical spiral cloud pattern, with the cold front being a distinctive feature sweeping in from the west.

Ahead of the low pressure, high-level ice-crystal clouds cover much of Britain. They are often an indication of approaching rain – which duly fell later in the day. Behind the depression (to its west), the cellular cloud pattern produced by air rising from the relatively warm sea is typical. Occasional showers will fall. Further to the west a band of thicker cloud shows a weak cold front sweeping eastwards giving more frequent showers south of Iceland. Over the Mediterranean, high pressure keeps the skies clear.

Climatic and Vegetation Regions

The average weather condition found in a region is known as its _climate_, and this is based on long-term records, usually 30 years. In contrast, _weather_ is the day-to-day variation in atmospheric conditions. Climate is the weather we might expect in a given area at a particular time, while the weather is the actual condition that prevails.

There are many different climates around the world, from arctic to tropical. Climate has a crucial effect on the kinds of vegetation found in a particular region, although as the maps show, climate and vegetation zones do not always coincide.

SEE ALSO

- THE MAKING OF THE WEATHER p. 102
- NON-FLOWERING PLANTS p. 118
- FLOWERING PLANTS p. 120
- THE BIOSPHERE p. 176
- ECOSYSTEMS p. 178–87

Classification of climate

Climate can be classified in many complex ways. The broadest and most general method is to divide each hemisphere into broad belts or _climatic zones_. The ancient Greeks made the earliest attempts at classifying climate. They recognized a _winterless tropical region_ located in the low latitudes, a _summerless polar region_ where temperatures are usually very low, and an _intermediate_ or _middle-latitude region_, now called the _temperate latitudes_, with cool summers and mild winters.

A simple classification can be based on two climatic elements, namely temperature and precipitation (rain, snow, dew, etc.). When both average temperature and precipitation are known it is possible to classify a particular location into a _climatic type_.

The seasons

Apart from those locations at or very near to the equator, all climatic regions show seasonal variation. Generally, the further away from the equator, the greater the seasonal variation becomes.

Seasons are caused by the annual revolution of the Earth in a slightly elliptical orbit around the Sun, and by the daily rotation of the Earth on its axis. The axis of rotation is inclined at 23.5° from the vertical. The effect of the Earth's rotation and revolution around the Sun is to produce changing day length and varying angles at which the Sun's rays strike the surface of the Earth.

Together these two factors cause a seasonal variation in climate (see diagram).

Twice during each year, on 21 March and 23 September, the Sun's rays are directly overhead at the equator. These two days are the _spring_ and _autumnal equinoxes_. On 21 June the Earth is midway between the equinoxes and the North Pole is inclined at 23.5° towards the Sun; the Sun's rays are overhead at the Tropic of Cancer (latitude 23.5° N) and the _summer solstice_ occurs in the northern hemisphere (and the _winter solstice_ in the southern hemisphere). By 21 December the position is reversed and the Sun is overhead at the Tropic of Capricorn (23.5° S) and the winter solstice occurs in the northern hemisphere (summer solstice in the southern hemisphere).

Controls on climate

Climatic controls include the proximity of land to water, and the effects of elevation, mountain barriers and ocean currents. _Climatic effects_ include the seasonal or daily ranges of temperature and precipitation, together with humidity, winds, etc.

Even though two places may have similar average yearly temperature and precipitation values, or share the same latitude, they can experience different climates. If the climatic controls of the two places are not alike, then neither will be the resulting climatic effects.

As water is slower to heat up than land and slower to cool down, places in the mid-latitudes near the sea will have

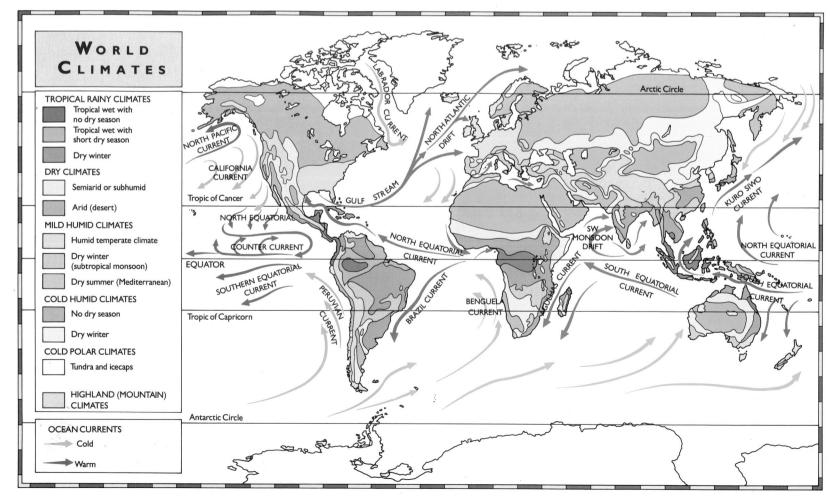

WORLD CLIMATES

TROPICAL RAINY CLIMATES
- Tropical wet with no dry season
- Tropical wet with short dry season
- Dry winter

DRY CLIMATES
- Semiarid or subhumid
- Arid (desert)

MILD HUMID CLIMATES
- Humid temperate climate
- Dry winter (subtropical monsoon)
- Dry summer (Mediterranean)

COLD HUMID CLIMATES
- No dry season
- Dry winter

COLD POLAR CLIMATES
- Tundra and icecaps

- HIGHLAND (MOUNTAIN) CLIMATES

OCEAN CURRENTS
- Cold
- Warm

cooler summers and milder winters than those far from the sea. The former are said to have *maritime climates* while the latter have *continental climates*. Ocean currents can either give a location a milder climate than would be expected at that latitude (for example, the effect of the warm North Atlantic Drift on northwest Europe), or a cooler climate (for example, the effect of the cold Labrador Current on Newfoundland).

Temperature decreases with altitude. High ground may also be wetter, because warm moist air will condense as it rises over a cool land mass, so producing rain or snow. If the rain-bearing winds mostly come from one direction, the land on that side will be wetter than the land on the opposite side, which will be in a *rain shadow*. On the South Island of New Zealand, for example, there is heavy precipitation to the west side of the New Zealand Alps, but on the east side precipitation in places is as low as 330 mm (13 in).

Climate and vegetation

The map showing the world's vegetation regions is complicated by the fact that it attempts to show the original distribution of *natural* vegetation, that is, the vegetation as it was before being greatly altered by human interference such as deforestation and agriculture. Elevation, slope, drainage, soil type, soil depth and climate all influence the vegetation distribution.

Climate is a major factor in determining the type and number of plants (and to a lesser extent animals) that can live in an area. Three main terrestrial ecosystems can be recognized: deserts, grasslands and forests (see pp. 180–87). Precipitation is the element that determines which vegetation type will occur in an area. If the annual precipitation is less than 250 mm (10 in) then deserts usually occur. Grasslands can be found when precipitation is between 250 and 750 mm (10 and 30 in) per annum, while areas that receive more than 750 mm (30 in) rainfall a year are usually covered by forests.

The average temperature and the nature of the seasons in a region are important in that they can determine the type of desert, grassland or forest. Wherever the monthly average temperature exceeds 21 °C (70 °F) then hot deserts, savannah grasslands or tropical forests occur.

In the middle latitudes, the winter temperatures are low enough (one month or more below 5 °C / 41 °F) to cause vegetation to become dormant. In autumn, growth stops, leaves are often shed and the plant survives the unfavourable winter months in a resting or dormant phase. In spring, when temperatures rise, new growth begins. In high latitudes, the winter conditions are such that between four and six months are dark and average temperature falls well below 0 °C (32 °F). The evergreen conifers can survive these conditions but growth is very slow and confined to the short, cool summers. In the highest latitudes, trees disappear and only small, low-growing plants can survive. GJ

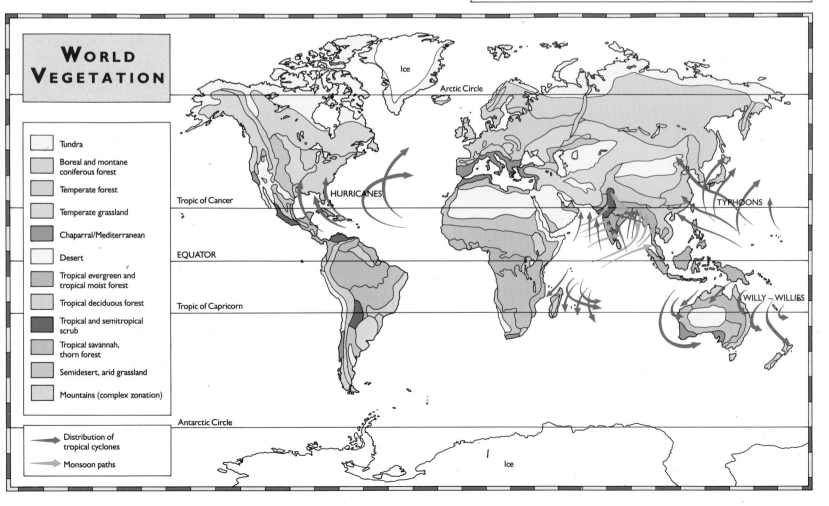

WORLD VEGETATION

Tundra

Boreal and montane coniferous forest

Temperate forest

Temperate grassland

Chaparral/Mediterranean

Desert

Tropical evergreen and tropical moist forest

Tropical deciduous forest

Tropical and semitropical scrub

Tropical savannah, thorn forest

Semidesert, arid grassland

Mountains (complex zonation)

Distribution of tropical cyclones

Monsoon paths

THE LIVING PLANET

'Animals are not brethren, they are
not underlings; they are other
nations, caught with ourselves in
the net of life and time.'

Henry Beston

THE LIVING PLANET

The Classification of Life

The study of biological classification, or *taxonomy*, aims to provide a rational framework in which to organize our knowledge of the great diversity of living and extinct organisms. Today comparative biology seeks to understand the living world by searching for the underlying order that exists in nature.

The foundation of comparative biology as well as the first well-authenticated system of classification goes back to Aristotle (384–322 BC), who believed that members of a species share a common essence and could be grouped together on that basis. However, it was not until the 17th century that the Englishman John

THE CLASSIFICATION OF MAN

Rank		Distinguishing features
Kingdom	Animalia	Nervous system
Subkingdom	Metazoa	Multicellular
Phylum	Chordata	Notochord
Subphylum	Vertebrata	Backbone
No rank available	Gnathostomata	Jaws
	Osteichthyes	Cartilage bone
	Sarcopterygii	Paired appendages with muscular lobes
	Chonata	Internal nares (nostrils)
Superclass	Tetrapoda	Pentadactyl (five-digit) limbs
Class	Mammalia	Hair, sweat and milk glands
Subclass	Eutheria	Placenta
Order	Primates	Fingers with sensitive pads and nails
Family	Hominidae	Upright posture, flat face, large brain
Genus	*Homo*	Bipedality, manual dexterity
Species	*sapiens*	Double-curved spine
Subspecies	*sapiens*	Well-developed chin

Ray (1628–1705) proposed the first *natural classification* – an arrangement based on presumed relationships, rather than an artificial scheme aiming merely to facilitate correct identification of species. In the 18th century the Swedish naturalist Carl Linnaeus (1707–78) produced a rational system of classification based on patterns of similarity between different organisms. Linnaeus developed one of the first comprehensive subordinated schemes of taxonomy – a scheme that places each organism in a group that is itself part of a larger group.

The Linnaean system

The essential feature of Linnaeus's scheme is that it is *binomial*. He gave every distinct type or *species* of organism (e.g. the lion) a two-part (binomial) name (e.g. *Felis leo*) in which the second element identified the individual species, while the first element placed the species in a particular *genus* – a group comprising all those species that showed obvious similarities with one another. For instance, he grouped together all cat-like animals in the genus *Felis* : *Felis leo* – the lion; *Felis tigris* – the tiger; *Felis pardus* – the leopard; and so on. Having thus subordinated each species to a particular genus, he went on to place groups of genera in a higher rank or category called a *family*, then families in *orders*, and so on through *classes, phyla* (or *divisions*, for plants) and finally *kingdoms*. Within this hierarchy, each successive rank is thus more embracing than the last, each containing a greater number of organisms with fewer characteristics in common.

Although Linnaeus's genera and families were for the most part natural, his higher

ranks were of necessity artificial in order to deal with the vast numbers of new organisms being discovered. Linnaeus used his highest taxonomic rank (kingdom) to separate plants and animals, but it is now clear that this simple subdivision is untenable, because certain groups such as archaebacteria and fungi fit into neither category. Nevertheless, the binomial system has remained unchanged to this day and every newly discovered organism is given a Latin or Latinized binomial name.

Another difficulty with the Linnaean system is that it is too simplistic to reflect the complexity of classification that is implied by Darwin's theory of evolution (see p. 112). Since it is generally believed that every organism on this planet has arisen through a unique historical process of descent with modification, it follows that all of them should fall into uncontradicted patterns of groups within groups. Thus, although we shall go on using such terms as family, order and class, we will need to introduce additional ranks as the analysis of the pattern of life is further elucidated. For example, the classification of living organisms illustrated opposite has at least 24 major branching points or divisions, each of which would need to be assigned a separate hierarchical category – 12 of them higher, or more embracing, than that of class.

Modern classification systems

The change from essentially artificial systems of classification, such as that used by Linnaeus, came about as taxonomists realized that there was a natural order underlying all living things; this order was furthermore provided with a theoretical background by Darwin in 1859 (see p. 112). Today's taxonomist endeavours to provide the most natural classification possible by the use of one of the following systems:

Phenetic classification aims to incorporate as much information as possible about organisms, and then groups them together on the basis of their overall similarity. All characteristics are given equal weight and no account is taken of the evolutionary relationships of the groups. This approach is amenable to numerical analysis (*numerical taxonomy*) and may be useful for large groups of simple organisms such as bacteria.

Orthodox (or *phylogenetic*) *classification* provides the basis for most text-book classifications. The system is based on presumed evolutionary relationships, and – as with phenetics – as much information as possible is taken into account. Organisms are grouped by features they share in common and that seem to reflect their common ancestry.

Cladistics is generally believed to be the most precise and natural method of classification, and is used by most progressive taxonomists. The only groups formally recognized are *clades*, each clade being defined by features that are shared by all its members and that are found in members of no other group. These groups may be represented on a branching diagram or *cladogram* (such as the diagrams

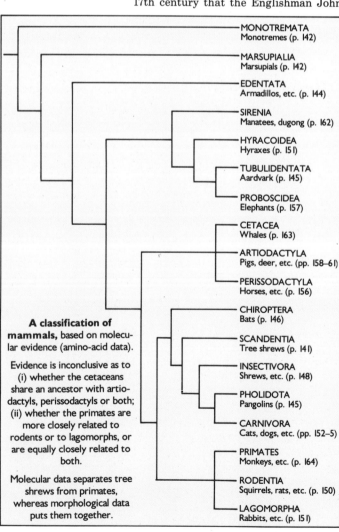

A classification of mammals, based on molecular evidence (amino-acid data).

Evidence is inconclusive as to (i) whether the cetaceans share an ancestor with artiodactyls, perissodactyls or both; (ii) whether the primates are more closely related to rodents or to lagomorphs, or are equally closely related to both.

Molecular data separates tree shrews from primates, whereas morphological data puts them together.

MONOTREMATA
Monotremes (p. 142)

MARSUPIALIA
Marsupials (p. 142)

EDENTATA
Armadillos, etc. (p. 144)

SIRENIA
Manatees, dugong (p. 162)

HYRACOIDEA
Hyraxes (p. 151)

TUBULIDENTATA
Aardvark (p. 145)

PROBOSCIDEA
Elephants (p. 157)

CETACEA
Whales (p. 163)

ARTIODACTYLA
Pigs, deer, etc. (pp. 158–61)

PERISSODACTYLA
Horses, etc. (p. 156)

CHIROPTERA
Bats (p. 146)

SCANDENTIA
Tree shrews (p. 141)

INSECTIVORA
Shrews, etc. (p. 148)

PHOLIDOTA
Pangolins (p. 145)

CARNIVORA
Cats, dogs, etc. (pp. 152–5)

PRIMATES
Monkeys, etc. (p. 164)

RODENTIA
Squirrels, rats, etc. (p. 150)

LAGOMORPHA
Rabbits, etc. (p. 151)

shown here), which shows how particular organisms are grouped together and how the various clades form a hierarchical distribution of groups within groups. In evolutionary terms, a clade is a *monophyletic group* – a group consisting of species descended from a single ancestor and including all the most recent common ancestors of all its members. Thus cladograms can literally be seen as evolutionary trees. However, cladistics may or may not consider the evolutionary history of the organisms concerned.

The evidence used to classify organisms has for the most part been *morphological*, i.e. derived from the study of structural features such as bones and teeth. *Physiological* evidence is also employed but is of limited use. *Embryological* evidence, on the other hand, is of greater importance, since the developmental stages of an embryo may mirror the evolutionary progression by which a species has reached its present form.

More recently, *molecular evidence* has proved to be of paramount importance in solving the more difficult problems of phylogenetic relationship. This kind of evidence has been provided by new techniques such as *DNA hybridization* (by which DNA from different sources can be compared), and sequence analysis of proteins. The analysis of amino-acid sequences in proteins such as cytochrome C and the sequencing of RNA itself give us a means of comparing the very genotypes of different organisms, and hence provide us with the number of nucleotide substitutions in the DNA of the genes (see p. 114). The result is a new and more comprehensive means of comparing the different forms of life on Earth. BG

SEE ALSO

- THE BEGINNINGS OF LIFE p. 110
- EVOLUTION p. 112
- GENETICS AND INHERITANCE p. 114
- PLANT AND ANIMAL GROUPS pp. 118–65
- PHYSICAL EVOLUTION (HUMAN) p. 200

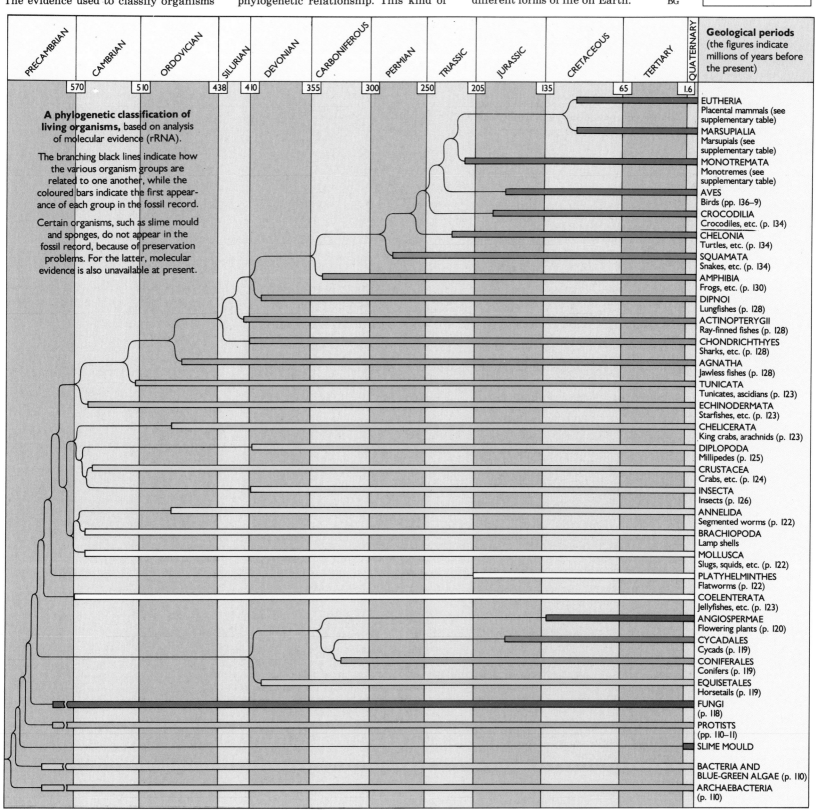

A phylogenetic classification of living organisms, based on analysis of molecular evidence (rRNA).

The branching black lines indicate how the various organism groups are related to one another, while the coloured bars indicate the first appearance of each group in the fossil record.

Certain organisms, such as slime mould and sponges, do not appear in the fossil record, because of preservation problems. For the latter, molecular evidence is also unavailable at present.

Geological periods (the figures indicate millions of years before the present)

PRECAMBRIAN | CAMBRIAN 570 | ORDOVICIAN 510 | SILURIAN 438 | DEVONIAN 410 | CARBONIFEROUS 355 | PERMIAN 300 | TRIASSIC 250 | JURASSIC 205 | CRETACEOUS 135 | TERTIARY 65 | QUATERNARY 1.6

EUTHERIA — Placental mammals (see supplementary table)
MARSUPIALIA — Marsupials (see supplementary table)
MONOTREMATA — Monotremes (see supplementary table)
AVES — Birds (pp. 136–9)
CROCODILIA — Crocodiles, etc. (p. 134)
CHELONIA — Turtles, etc. (p. 134)
SQUAMATA — Snakes, etc. (p. 134)
AMPHIBIA — Frogs, etc. (p. 130)
DIPNOI — Lungfishes (p. 128)
ACTINOPTERYGII — Ray-finned fishes (p. 128)
CHONDRICHTHYES — Sharks, etc. (p. 128)
AGNATHA — Jawless fishes (p. 128)
TUNICATA — Tunicates, ascidians (p. 123)
ECHINODERMATA — Starfishes, etc. (p. 123)
CHELICERATA — King crabs, arachnids (p. 123)
DIPLOPODA — Millipedes (p. 125)
CRUSTACEA — Crabs, etc. (p. 124)
INSECTA — Insects (p. 126)
ANNELIDA — Segmented worms (p. 122)
BRACHIOPODA — Lamp shells
MOLLUSCA — Slugs, squids, etc. (p. 122)
PLATYHELMINTHES — Flatworms (p. 122)
COELENTERATA — Jellyfishes, etc. (p. 123)
ANGIOSPERMAE — Flowering plants (p. 120)
CYCADALES — Cycads (p. 119)
CONIFERALES — Conifers (p. 119)
EQUISETALES — Horsetails (p. 119)
FUNGI (p. 118)
PROTISTS (pp. 110–11)
SLIME MOULD
BACTERIA AND BLUE-GREEN ALGAE (p. 110)
ARCHAEBACTERIA (p. 110)

The Beginnings of Life

Around every star in the universe – of which the Sun is but one – there is a zone, the *ecosphere*, where water could potentially exist as a liquid. Water is the prime requisite for life as we know it. If there is a body of sufficient mass in this zone (i.e. a planet), with a sufficient gravitational force to hold onto water and a gaseous atmosphere, then the conditions for life may be present.

The nature of the original conditions on the Earth can be worked out by considering our neighbouring planets, Venus and Mars, together with the gases that erupt from volcanoes. The major gases produced by volcanoes are carbon dioxide and water vapour – the principal components of the oceans and atmospheres. On Venus it is too hot for water to be liquid,

Stromatolite structures on the coast of Western Australia. These structures are composed of the remains of numerous cyanobacteria (blue-green algae) and may be as much as 2900 million years old. Although these are some of the oldest organic remains to have survived, traces of bacteria have been found in rocks some 900 million years older.

on Mars too cold – but on the Earth it is just right. Other simple compounds such as ammonia (NH_3) and methane (CH_4) are known to be able to combine with carbon dioxide (CO_2) and water (H_2O). This will happen if they are subjected to ultraviolet light (as emitted by the Sun) and if an electrical spark (such as might be provided by lightning) is passed through a mixture of these gases.

From such reactions are formed simple *amino acids*. These are the building blocks of *proteins* – the essential components of living things. The problem of joining up amino acids involves the removal of a molecule of water, but this seems to be achieved under conditions of dry heat – again associated with periods of volcanic activity.

Protein

Protein may be in the form of *enzymes*, which act as catalysts (see p. 47) in various biochemical reactions, or it may take the form of structural materials. Proteins are chains of amino acids, and there is an almost infinite variety of forms that can be synthesized from the 20 different amino acids. The functioning of a protein depends on the way the chain is folded.

Viruses

One of the fundamental aspects of living things is their ability to replicate themselves and pass on instructions to make new individuals from one generation to another. These instructions are contained in a special, complex molecule known as *deoxyribonucleic acid* or *DNA* (see p. 114), which is made up of various organic compounds. DNA has the capacity to replicate itself, and acts as a blueprint for making amino acids, and hence proteins.

The most basic forms of life, the viruses, simply consist of a protein coat protecting a strand of DNA. Viruses are so small (on average about 100 millionths of a millimetre long) that they can only be seen with an electron microscope. Viruses can only reproduce within the cells of other organisms (see diagram). In this way viruses cause many diseases (see p. 238), from the common cold to AIDS.

Bacteria

Because viruses are parasitic upon more complex organisms, it is unlikely that they were the first forms of life, even though they are the simplest. The first evidence of life on Earth comes from minute globules preserved in rocks 3800 million years old. These are believed to be the fossils of primitive bacteria.

Bacteria each consist of a single *cell* – the smallest biological unit able to function independently. The largest bacteria are only a few thousandths of a millimetre long. A typical bacterial cell consists of a cell wall, within which is contained the *protoplasm* (a jelly-like substance) and strings of DNA. A single bacterium reproduces by splitting into two new cells, each one an exact copy of the original. This process can happen as often as once every 15 minutes.

The first bacteria were probably *heterotro-*

phic, i.e. they fed on the organic molecules that were so abundant in the early oceans. As the 'organic soup' was used up, new types of bacteria evolved, the *autotrophs*. Some autotrophs are capable of synthesizing their food from inorganic material, while others use light energy, but not in a way that produces oxygen. Such bacteria are described as *anaerobic* (without air).

About 2900 million years ago a new type of bacteria – known as *cyanobacteria* or *blue-green algae* – evolved. These bacteria had the ability to use light to photosynthesize (see p. 117). The waste product of photosynthesis is oxygen, and oxygen began to accumulate in the ocean waters and in the atmosphere. Whereas oxygen had previously been a poison for all living things it was now exploited by new kinds of bacteria (described as *aerobic*) as a fuel for burning food to obtain energy (see p. 210). Like the most primitive bacteria, these bacteria were heterotrophic, and from them evolved all the higher animals. From the autotrophic bacteria evolved the plants, all of which use photosynthesis. In this way, animals and plants share a common ancestry.

Over the millennia great numbers of specialized bacteria have evolved, some of which survive in even the most adverse conditions of heat and cold. Bacteria play a crucial role in the carbon and nitrogen cycles (see p. 177), and are important in animal digestion (see p. 208). They have also been exploited in various industrial processes such as fermentation and cheese-making (see p. 196). Certain bacteria cause specific diseases (see p. 238), ranging from acne to salmonella to tetanus.

Protists

One of the most remarkable events in the

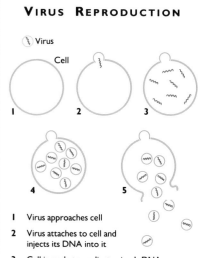

VIRUS REPRODUCTION

Virus

Cell

1   2   3

4   5

1   Virus approaches cell

2   Virus attaches to cell and injects its DNA into it

3   Cell is made to replicate virus's DNA

4   New viruses are formed inside cell

5   The cell bursts and the new viruses are spread out

Viruses, the most basic forms of life, simply consist of a protein coat protecting a strand of DNA. They can only reproduce inside the living cells of other organisms, and the cells are destroyed in the process. This is why viruses cause diseases.

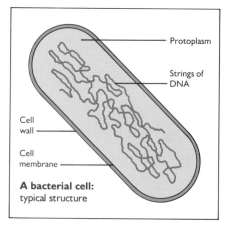

A bacterial cell:
typical structure

Protoplasm

Strings of DNA

Cell wall

Cell membrane

SEE ALSO

● EVOLUTION p. 112
● GENETICS AND INHERITANCE p. 114
● PLANTS pp. 116–21
● PRIMITIVE ANIMALS p. 122
● SYMBIOSIS AND PARASITISM p. 174
● THE BIOSPHERE p. 176
● INFECTIOUS DISEASES p. 238

STRUCTURE OF A TYPICAL EUKARYOTE CELL

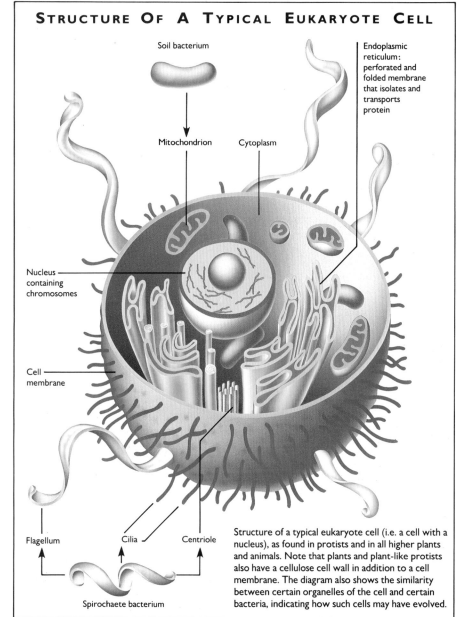

Soil bacterium

Endoplasmic reticulum: perforated and folded membrane that isolates and transports protein

Mitochondrion

Cytoplasm

Nucleus containing chromosomes

Cell membrane

Flagellum

Cilia

Centriole

Spirochaete bacterium

Structure of a typical eukaryote cell (i.e. a cell with a nucleus), as found in protists and in all higher plants and animals. Note that plants and plant-like protists also have a cellulose cell wall in addition to a cell membrane. The diagram also shows the similarity between certain organelles of the cell and certain bacteria, indicating how such cells may have evolved.

history of life on Earth took place about 1500 million years ago. Suddenly the microscopic organisms – although still single-celled – became many times larger than the bacteria that preceded them. This event marked the origin of the protists, some of which are plant-like and others animal-like (the latter also being known as *protozoans*). The smallest protists are one or two thousandths of a millimetre long, while the largest, the *amoeba*, are about 1 mm in length. As with viruses and bacteria, some protists can cause disease (see p. 238).

The protists and all later, more advanced forms of life – fungi, plants and animals – are known as *eukaryotes* (meaning 'true kernel'). This is because the protoplasm in their cells is differentiated into the *cytoplasm* and the *nucleus* (the 'kernel'). The nucleus is a separate part of the cell, surrounded by the cytoplasm, and contains the chromosomes (see p. 114), the structures into which the DNA is organized. In contrast to bacteria, the cells of protists also contain miniature organs, or *organelles*, which perform specialized tasks.

Organelles

One of the most important organelles is the *mitochondrion*, which contains enzymes that break up organic compounds to release energy. The mitochondrion has its own DNA, which is passed on from generation to generation. It also has special structures (*ribosomes*) for the synthesis of proteins. In fact mitochondria are basically similar to soil bacteria, and indeed there is an amoeba, *Pelomyxa*, which does not have any mitochondria at all, but instead contains symbiotic bacteria (see symbiosis, p. 174) exactly like those found in soil.

Perhaps even more remarkable is the fact that in plant-like protists and in plants the organelles that are responsible for photosynthesis also have their own DNA and are hardly distinguishable from blue-green algae. Even more surprising is the detailed structure of the *centrioles* (which organize cell division) and the *flagella* and *cilia* (which are concerned with movement) – all these organelles have an internal strengthening of nine miniature tubes that are indistinguishable from the internal parts of the swimming spirochaete bacteria.

These observations have been explained by proposing that the basic protist single-celled organisms were formed as the result of the cooperative coming together of separate organisms. If this was indeed the case, then one of the most important events in the evolution of life was not the consequence of competition but rather of cooperation.

Sponges

The first sign of cells coming together to form large organisms is in the sponges, a group of marine organisms that first evolved at least 570 million years ago. Sponges may grow up to 1 m (3¼ ft) across, and their structure is supported by skeletal spicules, or (as in the case of bath sponges) by a network of fibres.

Within a sponge there are several types of cell, each of which is capable of functioning independently. Some of the specialized cells are in fact indistinguishable from certain protozoans. If living sponges are disintegrated, the individual cells are capable of coming together to re-form the original colony anew.

The beginnings of sex

The next major breakthrough in the evolution of life came with the development of sex – the exchange of genetic material between two individual organisms. It was this exchange that provided the level of variation upon which natural selection could act (see p. 112).

It is possible that sex may have originated in the engulfing of one organism by another in a kind of cannibalism. An engorged organism with double the genetic material would then divide in two to relieve itself. In time an alternating pattern of single and double units of genetic material would succeed each other, until the situation was reached where the norm would be for the double system. In this system the splitting into a single unit only occurred in the production of the sex cells or *gametes*, which would then come from different parents to combine to form a new individual and so restore the now normal double system (see p. 114). With the advent of sex the pace of evolution accelerated.

BH

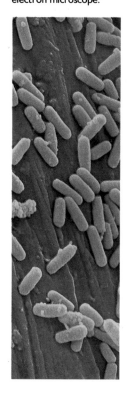

Rod-shaped bacteria on the head of a pin, magnified nearly 3000 times by a false-colour electron microscope.

Evolution

Until the late 18th century it was generally accepted that the living world was the result of a single more-or-less instantaneous creation as outlined in the Bible. However, the discovery of giant bones in Ohio and also in Europe led a Frenchman, Baron Georges Cuvier (1779–1832), to demonstrate that many species preserved as fossils no longer existed – they had become extinct. By the beginning of the 19th century it was acknowledged by many thinkers that there had been worlds before man. Furthermore, it was recognized that the history of life, as recorded by fossils in the geological sequence (see p. 85), portrayed a pattern of change through time. The idea of the evolution or transformation of species was born. The main issue of contention for many scientists was not whether change had taken place but rather concerned the nature of change itself.

Charles Darwin, the British naturalist whose theory of natural selection provided an explanation of how evolution works.

There were two contrasting views on the nature of change. The view held by the Frenchman Jean-Baptiste Lamarck (1744–1829) was that change was gradual. The opposing view was held by Cuvier himself, who believed he detected a pattern of successive catastrophes and sudden replacements. The mechanism of change that Lamarck suggested in 1809 was that organisms during their lifetime develop structures that better enable them to adapt to their environment, and that they pass on these characteristics to their offspring. According to his scheme, the giraffe developed its long neck from its habit of browsing on tall trees.

Charles Darwin

At odds with Lamarck's ideas on the inheritance of acquired characteristics

was the theory of evolutionary change proposed by the British naturalist Charles Darwin (1809–82). Darwin first developed his ideas on a voyage round the world as ship's naturalist on HMS *Beagle* in 1831–36, but he did not outline his theory until 1858, when he presented a paper jointly with Alfred Russel Wallace (1823–1913). He then expanded his theory the following year in his book *On the Origin of Species by Means of Natural Selection*. Predictably, Darwin's theory gave rise to bitter controversy, contradicting as it did the Bible's account of creation. Eventually, however, with the support of such eminent biologists as T. H. Huxley (1825–95), Darwin's theories became widely accepted.

Natural selection

When Darwin embarked on his voyage round the world, like most of his contemporaries he believed in the fixity of species. It was his observations on the pampas of Patagonia that gave rise to his first doubts. Darwin noted that the extinct mammals whose fossilized remains he discovered were clearly directly related to forms still living. When he visited the Galapagos Islands, the British governor pointed out that he could identify the islands to which the giant tortoises belonged from the different patterns on their shells. This was the critical clue that led Darwin to realize that from a common stock a species could change.

Like many of his colleagues Darwin was well aware that the fossil record revealed a history of change – albeit on a broad canvas. Darwin's genius was to suggest a mechanism by means of which such observed changes could have come about. It was a common observation of natural history that more eggs were laid and more offspring produced than ever reached breeding age. Darwin was also familiar with the weeding out of unfavourable strains by animal and plant breeders. However, what Darwin concluded was that in the natural world such weeding out was accomplished without direct intervention by man – the selection was natural. Individual organisms fortuitously better adapted to their environment than others of their species stood a better chance of surviving, and so of passing on their 'desirable' characteristics to the next generation. This process has been called 'the survival of the fittest'. In this way, in the course of numerous generations, new species may arise.

A classic example of natural selection is seen in the peppered moth. Usually about 2% of these normally pale moths are black, but, as they are conspicuous, the birds easily see them and eat them. During the 19th century, industrial towns became heavily polluted with soot, so that all the trees and buildings were blackened. In these conditions the black variety of moth was effectively camouflaged and the proportion of black moths rose to 98% of the population. With the introduction of legislation against air pollution the proportion of black moths began to decline.

Mutation

One of the great problems of the theory of

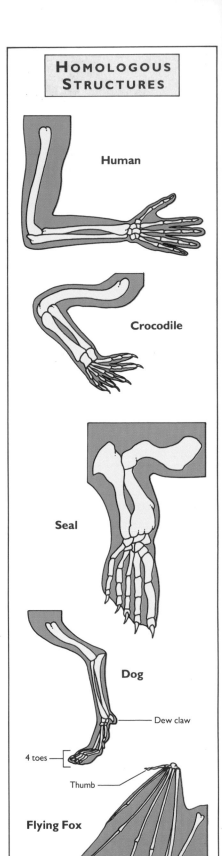

HOMOLOGOUS STRUCTURES

Human

Crocodile

Seal

Dog

Dew claw

4 toes

Thumb

Flying Fox

The forelimbs of five different animals, showing that the pentadactyl (five-digit) limb is common to them all. Such basically similar structures are described as *homologous*, and the existence of homologous structures in different organisms suggests that they have all evolved from a common ancestor.

natural selection is that it does not explain how new changes arise in the first instance. However, once the function of the DNA molecule in inheritance was established (see p. 114), it was discovered that it was very common for an accidental change to occur when DNA replicates itself. Such changes (known as *mutations*) usually have little effect, but in some instances the altered DNA gives rise to protein whose functioning is severely disrupted.

Fortunately most mutations have no effect, but in some cases they are harmful to the individual (see p. 236). However, mutations can also lead to desirable characteristics that enable the individual to survive more effectively than others of its species: examples include the coloration of the peppered moth (see above), and new types of mosquito that are resistant to DDT. Indeed, all present species have probably inherited a whole host of mutations that have occurred among their ancestors.

Mutations can also be used to determine how closely different species may be related. By examining the sequence of amino acids along certain protein chains (see p. 114) and comparing them, it is possible to decide which species are closely or distantly related. An evolutionary tree can then be constructed based upon these molecular similarities.

The speed of evolution

If the unit of selection is the individual then the nature of evolutionary change must of necessity be gradual. The characteristics of the population of a species will be modified as the generations suc-

The rhea (below) and the **ostrich** (right). Although one lives in South America and the other in Africa, both are flightless, with reduced wings, long necks and a flat breastbone. These similarities suggest that they have a common ancestor, although they are sufficiently different to suggest that they evolved in different ways once the continents separated.

ceed one another. This *phyletic gradualism* contrasts with the alternative view, which sees the species as a whole as the unit of selection, i.e. the fittest species survive, while less well-adapted species become extinct. In this case change can be sudden (precipitated, for example, by climatic changes) and the evolutionary process would appear as a series of jumps or *saltations*. In 1972 it was claimed that the fossil record revealed a pattern of periods of little change (equilibrium), interspersed with rapid change. The term *punctuated equilibrium* was coined to describe the inferred process.

Since then a furious debate has taken place between the protagonists. This has had the effect of stimulating a great deal of new research on the fossil record, which appears to have resolved the controversy. The currently accepted theory is known as *punctuated gradualism*. Evolutionary change *is* gradual, but at certain specified times the slow tempo of evolutionary change is punctuated by a fairly rapid speeding up. However, this is still achieved by the normal process (as described by Darwin) of selection of individuals.

Competition versus cooperation

One of the major controversies regarding evolution arose out of the idea that the theory of evolution might apply to human society. In 1888 T.H. Huxley claimed that 'the survival of the fittest' epitomized modern capitalist society. The idea that individual endeavour was the key to success fitted neatly with the notion that selection of the individual was the driving force of evolution. In contrast, Prince Petr Kropotkin (1842–1921), the Russian geographer, geologist and anarchist, insisted that a fundamental trait within a species was mutual cooperation. The features that organisms shared were considered to be of greater significance than individual differences.

By the 1980s the century-old controversy

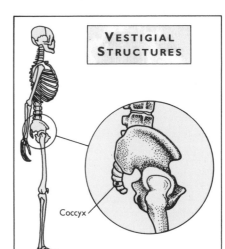

VESTIGIAL STRUCTURES

Coccyx

One piece of evidence that humans and monkeys had a common ancestor is the existence in humans of the coccyx – the bone at the base of the spine. The coccyx is the remains of a tail, and is an example of a *vestigial structure*, i.e. one that no longer functions. In very rare cases humans are actually born with an enlarged stump of a tail. Another example of a vestigial structure is the pair of 'claws' about two thirds of the way down the bodies of certain snakes, which indicates that the ancestors of the snakes may have had hind legs like other reptiles.

SEE ALSO

● THE CLASSIFICATION OF LIFE p. 108
● THE BEGINNINGS OF LIFE p. 110
● GENETICS AND INHERITANCE p. 114
● PHYSICAL EVOLUTION (HUMAN) p. 200

over the relative importance of cooperation and competition seemed to have been resolved. This has been settled by the application of games theory, which seems to have established that for success over generations, selection will favour those individuals with a cooperative nature. As has long been realized in our own species and indeed in our individual personalities, there is an ever-present mixture of both selfish and altruistic traits. It is this inner conflict that provides the driving force of evolution.   BH

Genetics and Inheritance

Although theories of inheritance or heredity were put forward at least as early as the 5th and 4th centuries BC, genetics – the scientific study of inheritance – only truly began in the 18th and 19th centuries. Observations were made of how specific characteristics of plants and animals were passed from one generation to the next, to provide a rational basis for the improvement of crop plants and livestock.

The most significant breakthrough in genetics was made by the Austrian monk Gregor Mendel (1822–84). He observed specific features of the pea plant and counted the number of individuals in which each characteristic appeared through several generations. By concentrating on just a few features and determining what proportion of each generation received them, he was able to demonstrate specific patterns of inheritance. The discrete nature and indepen-

dent segregation of genetic characteristics that he observed became known as Mendel's laws of inheritance, and have been shown to apply to most genetic systems (see box, right).

DNA

By the start of the 20th century it was clear that organisms inherited characteristics by the reassortment and redistribution of many apparently independent factors, but the identity of the material that carried this information was unknown. To code for such a large amount of information, any type of molecule would have to be highly variable, and proteins were thought to be the most likely candidate. In 1944, however, the American microbiologist Oswald T. Avery (1877–1955) demonstrated that the inheritable characteristics of a certain bacterium could be altered by *deoxyribonucleic acid* (DNA) taken up from outside the cell.

To understand how genetic information was encoded required the structure of DNA to be determined. In 1953 the American James Watson (1928–) and the Englishman Francis Crick (1916–) reported that DNA is a large molecule in the shape of a double helix (see box). The genetic code is contained in the sequence of paired *nucleotide bases* that lie in the central region of the molecule, with each *triplet* (or *codon*) of bases specifying a particular amino acid. The complementary pairing of bases on each of the two strands also explains how DNA replication can take place (see below). Incorrect pairing disrupts the structure of the DNA molecule and may be a source of mutation, but is usually recognized and changed by an enzyme correction system.

Genes, the genome and mutation

Mendel discovered that characteristics are passed from generation to generation in the form of discrete units. Once the structure of DNA was established, these units, called *genes*, could be understood at the molecular level. A gene is a linear section of a DNA molecule that includes all the information for the structure of a particular protein or *ribonucleic acid* (RNA) molecule. The sum of all an organism's genetic information is called its *genome*.

A *mutation* occurs when there is a change in the sequence of nucleotide bases in a piece of DNA. Such changes may occur naturally, as bases are added, deleted or exchanged. The rate at which this process (known as *mutagenesis*) takes place may be accelerated by exposure to chemicals or radiation, and mutations may disrupt or prevent the production of proteins, thus disturbing the functioning of the organism as a whole. However, natural mutations passed on from generation to generation may also confer benefits, and are indeed essential to the process of evolution (see p. 112).

Every sequence of nucleotide bases that makes up a single gene is called an *allele*. There are usually several different alleles available for each gene. Thus, if the eye colour of a given organism is dependent

on a single gene, different eye colours will be dictated by various alleles of the gene responsible.

Reading of genes and protein synthesis

The first stage in the process by which cells use genetic information stored in DNA is to make an RNA copy of a gene. This is called *gene transcription*. Most of the RNA copies (known as messenger RNA or mRNA) travel from the nucleus of the cell (where the genes are located) to the *ribosomes* – particles in the cytoplasm (see p. 111) – where proteins are manufactured or *synthesized*. Ribosomes make proteins by joining together amino acids in the sequence dictated by the order of triplet groups in the mRNA. Proteins may become part of the cell structure or they may be enzymes, which catalyse biochemical reactions (see p. 53).

Chromosomes

A *chromosome* consists of several different types of protein tightly associated with a single DNA molecule, and each chromosome carries a large number of genes. Most eukaryotic organisms (organisms with cell nucleuses) have several chromosomes, but bacteria, which do not have a nucleus, have only one.

All the cells of a particular organism have the same number of different chromosomes, but numbers vary widely between different species. There is no clear pattern to this, but plants tend to have fewer different chromosomes than animals. Humans have 23 different chromosomes per cell, but there are two copies of each (called *homologous* chromosomes), making 46 altogether.

DNA replication and cell division

As organisms grow, their body cells divide and multiply. By the time a cell divides, its DNA will have doubled by a process called *DNA replication*. The hydrogen bonds linking the two strands of a DNA molecule break apart, and each strand uses nucleotides present in the nucleus to synthesize a new strand complementary to itself; the result is that two daughter molecules are produced, each identical to the parent molecule. This process is completed just before cells divide, so that each chromosome contains two DNA molecules instead of the usual one. A mechanism called *mitosis* operates during cell division to ensure that each of the daughter cells receives one of the DNA molecules from every chromosome.

Most organisms are *diploid* – like humans, they have two copies of each different chromosome in normal body cells. However, sex cells or *gametes* (sperm and egg cells in most organisms) are *haploid* – they contain only one of each chromosome. Sex cells are produced from body cells by a process called *meiosis*. DNA replication takes place as before mitosis, but an extra stage of chromosome separation results in four sex cells being produced from a single body cell. As sex cells fuse at fertilization, a single diploid cell (called a *zygote*) is created, with the full complement of chromosomes.

Sex chromosomes and recombination

In humans, one of the pairs of chromo-

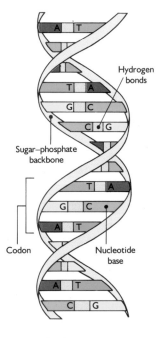

somes – the sex chromosomes – is responsible for determining the sex of an individual, and can have two different forms, X and Y (see also p. 202). Females have a pair made up of two X chromosomes, while a male has an X and a Y. Thus the sex cells of a female always carry an X chromosome, while a male's sex cells may contain either an X or a Y. The sex of a child is therefore determined by the type of chromosome passed on by the father. A similar form of sexual determination is found in most sexually differentiated animals.

In organisms with several different chromosomes, the offspring receive some chromosomes from each parent and so a combination of genes different from either. Genetic diversity is further increased by a process known as *crossing-over*: during meiosis, homologous chromosomes can exchange bits of DNA between themselves, and so move genes into new combinations. However, the closer together genes are on the same chromosome, the more likely it is that they will be inherited together. Sexual interaction therefore greatly accelerates the rate at which genes are moved into new and potentially beneficial combinations; as such it is crucial to the evolutionary development of species (see p. 111).

Dominant and recessive genes

In diploid organisms there are two copies of every gene, one in each member of every chromosome pair (the only exception being the sex chromosomes of the male). When both copies of a particular gene have identical alleles, the individual is said to be *homozygous* for that gene. However, many genes will have different alleles in each copy and the individual is said to be *heterozygous* for such genes. One allele may be *dominant* in that the gene product it codes for is used by the cell in preference to that of the other allele, which is called *recessive*. The outcome of such interactions between the alleles of all the different genes produces the characteristics of an individual, known collectively as the *phenotype*. The entire set of alleles in the genome of an individual is known as its *genotype*.

Molecular genetics and the future

The basis of *genetic engineering* is the use of certain bacterial enzymes that can cut DNA into small fragments. These fragments can be joined together in almost any combination, using a range of other enzymes. This can be done with DNA from any source – for example, human genes can be put into bacterial DNA. Bacteria are easy to grow in large quantities and can make useful products if they contain suitable genes. So human insulin, for example – the hormone that is deficient in diabetics (see p. 214) – can be produced from genetically engineered bacteria.

Except in the case of identical twins, everybody's DNA is significantly different from every other person's. For this reason, the forensic technique known as *genetic fingerprinting* is becoming increasingly important in the identification of criminals. The chance of a wrong identification of a suspect's DNA and DNA extracted from blood or other body tissue found at the scene of the crime are hundreds of millions to one against.

Genetic-engineering techniques can also be used to determine the exact sequence of nucleotide bases in short stretches of DNA. Many genes from different organisms have been sequenced. For some organisms with small genomes (such as viruses), the entire genome sequence has been determined: the HIV I virus that causes AIDS is one example.

A worldwide project to sequence the human genome has begun and will take about 30 years to complete. It will reveal the location of many genes and probably unexpected information about human genetic organization. This type of information is likely to allow *gene-replacement therapy* – the replacement of defective genes with normal copies, to be used in the 21st century to cure many inherited diseases.
PM

SEE ALSO

- NATURAL COMPOUNDS p. 52
- THE BEGINNINGS OF LIFE p. 110
- EVOLUTION p. 112
- PLANTS pp. 116–21
- FARMING pp. 188–91
- FOOD PROCESSING p. 196
- NON-INFECTIOUS DISEASES p. 236
- CHEMICALS AND BIOTECHNOLOGY p. 320

A SINGLE-FACTOR INHERITANCE

The simplicity of Mendel's laws is illustrated by a single-factor inheritance, in which an inheritable characteristic is determined by the action of a pair of dominant and recessive alleles of a single gene.

The coloration of rats is an example of such a characteristic, with the allele for black being dominant over the allele for white. If a homozygous black rat (i.e. with two identical alleles) mates with a homozygous white rat, all the offspring will be heterozygous black – each similar in appearance to the black parent, but with a recessive (and unexpressed) white allele. However, mating between these offspring will result (potentially) in a mixture of black and white rats. The ratio of black rats to white will be on average 3 to 1, any white rat having inherited one recessive white allele from each of its parents.

The same pattern is found in the inheritance of certain human characteristics, including recessive genetic diseases such as cystic fibrosis and sickle-cell anaemia (see p. 236). The inheritance of characteristics dependent on a number of different genes is more complex, but the underlying principle is the same in all genetic interactions.

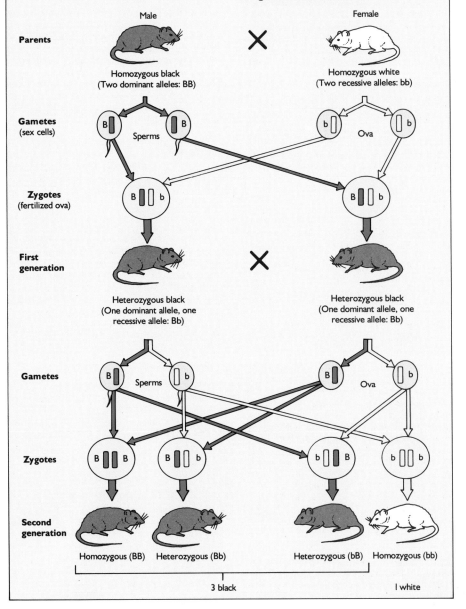

Parents

Male — Homozygous black (Two dominant alleles: BB)
Female — Homozygous white (Two recessive alleles: bb)

Gametes (sex cells) — Sperms (B, B) — Ova (b, b)

Zygotes (fertilized ova) — B b — B b

First generation — Heterozygous black (One dominant allele, one recessive allele: Bb) — Heterozygous black (One dominant allele, one recessive allele: Bb)

Gametes — Sperms (B, b) — Ova (B, b)

Zygotes — B B — B b — b B — b b

Second generation — Homozygous (BB) — Heterozygous (Bb) — Heterozygous (bB) — Homozygous (bb)

3 black — 1 white

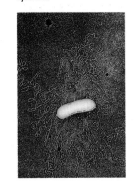

The human-gut parasite *Escherichia coli*, magnified about 10 000 times and shown in false colour. The bacterium has been 'osmotically shocked' by immersion in water, causing the cell to burst and its DNA (here coloured gold) to be ejected.

Plant Physiology

Like all living organisms, plants have to feed, breed and compete. Plants obtain the materials required for growth and development by converting simple inorganic chemicals in their environment – such as carbon dioxide, water and various mineral salts – into the complex organic substances of which they are made. This ability is unique to plants and certain primitive organisms (see pp. 110–11).

Since they are fixed in one spot, plants have also developed special physiological systems of adaptation to their environment, and use environmental cues to regulate almost every facet of their activities – including growth, development and reproduction. Reproduction works in different ways in different plants, and more details are given on pp. 118–21.

How do plants grow?

Plants grow by increasing the number and size of their cells. Unlike animals, where new cells are produced all over the body, new cells in plants are only produced in areas of specialized tissue called *meristems*. The *primary growth* – i.e. increase in length – of plants takes place in meristems situated at the tips of shoots and roots. These tips are called *apices* (singular: *apex*). At the apex of a shoot or root, new cells are produced by the form of cell division known as mitosis (see pp. 114–15). Some of the new cells grow out of the stem apex and develop into leaves.

Slightly behind the apex – in the portions of stem between the youngest leaves, or in the region beginning a few millimetres behind the root tip – the new cells begin to expand, and it is here that the biggest contribution to length increase is made.

Initially the cells expand by taking up water; new protoplasm – the jelly-like substance in cells (see pp. 110–11) – is only made later. It is at this later stage that the cells begin to differentiate into specialized tissues with different functions.

Before a cell can expand, the cell wall (consisting mostly of cellulose) must become stretchable. One factor which regulates this is a substance called *auxin*, one of several hormones that act as growth regulators in plants.

Secondary growth, which involves growth in thickness or girth, occurs after a stem or root has grown in length. The meristem responsible for secondary growth is called the *cambium*, which in woody plants forms a ring of cells between the *xylem* and *phloem* (see diagram). As the cambium cells divide, new xylem is formed on the inside of the cambium, and new phloem on the outside. Both xylem and phloem are found in all plants, and are types of *vascular* tissue (i.e. they are full of conducting cells) used to transport water and nutrients round the plant (see below).

The material for growth

During growth, the substance in a plant obviously increases enormously. Much of a plant's substance is water, but the 'dry' matter is *synthesized* (manufactured) by the plant from relatively simple, inorganic substances taken up from the soil and the air. The most abundant elements in plants are carbon, hydrogen and oxygen. Carbon and oxygen come from carbon dioxide in the air: using the energy of sunlight in the process of *photosynthesis* (see box), the plant converts the carbon dioxide into organic substances, initially the carbohydrate glucose (a simple sugar), and then sucrose (the same chemical as household sugar). The hydrogen is derived from water.

Nitrogen, a key element in proteins (see p. 110), is usually taken up from soil in the form of nitrates. The nitrates are converted into ammonia in the *chloroplasts* – miniature organs in the cells of leaves and stems. Using the glucose made in photosynthesis, the ammonia is then transformed into amino acids, from which proteins are assembled. The addition of artificial fertilizers containing nitrates will enhance plant growth. (See also the nitrogen cycle, pp. 176–7.)

Legumes (peas, beans, clover, etc.) are different from other plants in the way that they obtain nitrogen. On the roots of legumes are nodules containing a certain kind of bacteria, and these bacteria transform (or *fix*) nitrogen from the air via ammonia into organic nitrogenous chemicals, from which the host plant manufactures protein. This is why legumes (such as soyabean) are particularly rich in protein, and why they need no added nitrogenous fertilizer. In fact, when ploughed in, legumes enrich the soil, and are therefore commonly used in four-crop rotation (see pp. 188–9).

Elements such as potassium, iron, sulphur, calcium, magnesium and phosphorus, taken up from the soil, also play an essential role in plant chemistry. Plant

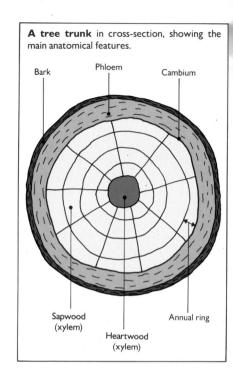

A tree trunk in cross-section, showing the main anatomical features.

Bark — Phloem — Cambium

Sapwood (xylem) — Heartwood (xylem) — Annual ring

cells and organs can now be grown under completely artificial conditions in the laboratory, on media that contain everything that the plant needs. Such techniques provide the cornerstone of plant biotechnology, a rapidly developing field that enables us to manipulate plants to an extent that was unimaginable just ten or twenty years ago.

Transport and utilization of synthesized material

The sucrose from photosynthesis together with certain amino acids are carried around the plant in the phloem (see above) to growing regions where they are needed for building cell walls or making protoplasm.

Relatively massive amounts of sucrose and amino acids are also transported into storage organs such as tubers and into developing seeds, where they are stored as reserves until they are needed for growth and energy when the seeds germinate. Sucrose in a plant is in solution, so for convenience of storage sucrose is converted into starch. When energy is needed, the starch breaks down into soluble sucrose, which can easily be transported round the plant.

Because of their reserves of starch, protein and vegetable oil, seeds are the most important constituents of the diets of many animals and humans – the cereals and pulses (peas, beans, etc.) being widely cultivated examples. Certain tubers and roots (potatoes, carrots, etc.) are similarly nutritious.

Within the plant, energy must be provided to support all kinds of chemical processes. This energy comes from respiration. Respiration in plants involves broadly the same processes as it does in animals, including humans (see pp. 210–11). In plants, oxygen is slowly absorbed from the atmosphere, and is used to oxidize ('burn') compounds such as glucose. The

Cell membrane

Chloroplast containing chlorophyl for photosynthesis

Nucleus containing chromosomes

Starch grain storing food

Cell wall (mainly cellulose and other carbohydrates)

Cytoplasm

Vacuole containing cell sap (a watery solution of various amino acids and sugars)

Mitochondrion where oxidation of food occurs during respiration

A plant cell: typical structure. The protoplasm in plant and animal cells is differentiated into cytoplasm, the nucleus, and other bodies such as mitochondria and chloroplasts.

PHOTOSYNTHESIS

The chemicals in plants that give them their green colour are the *chlorophylls*. The chlorophylls are particularly abundant in leaves, and are contained in *chloroplasts*, which are miniature organs within cells. Chlorophyll strongly absorbs the blue and red regions of the light spectrum, and this ability is used to drive the most important single chemical reaction on Earth. This reaction, which maintains both plant and animal life, is photosynthesis.

In photosynthesis, carbon dioxide that has entered the plant from the air via the stomata (microscopic leaf pores) is transformed into the sugar glucose, and eventually sucrose and starch. This transformation is powered by the energy from sunlight absorbed by the chlorophylls. This is how the plant obtains the organic carbon needed for the synthesis of the materials of which it is composed. As vegetation is the primary food of all animal food chains, it is by photosynthesis that almost all of the carbon enters the living world: hence it sustains life on Earth.

Overall, the chemical reaction of photosynthesis is:

$$\underset{\substack{\text{carbon} \\ \text{dioxide}}}{6CO_2} + \underset{\text{water}}{6H_2O} \xrightarrow{\text{Sunlight}} \underset{\text{glucose}}{C_6H_{12}O_6} + \underset{\text{oxygen}}{6O_2}$$

But this simple equation hides the complex chemical nature of photosynthesis, which comprises a set of reactions involved with the absorption of light (the *light reactions*) and a set that can take place in darkness (the *dark reactions*). The essential feature of the light reactions is that the light energy absorbed by chlorophyll is used to split water molecules into hydrogen and oxygen. The oxygen ultimately released by plants is the source of all oxygen in the atmosphere of this planet.

In the dark reactions carbon dioxide is converted into glucose by a complex cycle of chemical transformations, some of which use the hydrogen generated from water, and the chemical energy that has been produced from light energy.

Because in photosynthesis carbon dioxide is used up and oxygen given out as a waste product – the reverse of plant and animal respiration – the overall effect of plants and animals living together is to keep the levels of carbon dioxide and oxygen in the atmosphere more or less constant. The felling and burning of vast areas of tropical forest, combined with industrial processes that produce vast quantities of carbon dioxide, may contribute to an imbalance in the atmosphere, and hence to the 'greenhouse effect' (see pp. 300-1).

SEE ALSO
- NON-FLOWERING PLANTS p. 118
- FLOWERING PLANTS p. 120
- THE BIOSPHERE p. 176
- ECOSYSTEMS pp. 178–87
- ARABLE FARMING p. 188
- FORESTRY p. 192

PLANTS AND THE ATMOSPHERE

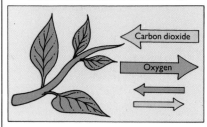

Day: plants absorb more carbon dioxide from the atmosphere by photosynthesis than they give out by respiration. They also give out more oxygen by photosynthesis than they absorb from the atmosphere for respiration.

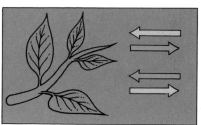

Dawn and dusk: with less light available for photosynthesis, plants give out similar amounts of oxygen and carbon dioxide as they take in.

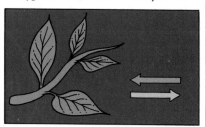

Night: with no light available, photosynthesis ceases. However, respiration continues, with oxygen being absorbed and carbon dioxide being given out.

oxidation occurs in the organelles (miniature organs) called *mitochondria* (see p. 111) that occur in each cell. Carbon dioxide is released back into the atmosphere as the waste product of this reaction.

Water uptake and transport

In terrestrial plants, water is taken up by the roots and moves up the plant in the xylem (see above). Water evaporates from the leaf through microscopic pores, the *stomata*. These pores regulate water loss by opening and closing in response to light, carbon dioxide, and the amount of water within the leaf. When the leaves begin to lose too much water, a hormone, *abscisic acid*, is produced, and this causes the two 'guard' cells surrounding the pore to close it and thus prevent further escape of water vapour.

Plant development and the environment

Many aspects of plant development are governed by the environment. Rates of stem growth, for example, are determined by the brightness of light. By means of a light-absorbing protein, *phytochrome*, present in stems cells, a plant can detect how bright the light is and especially if it is in the shade of other plants. The growth of the stem then increases to carry the leaves into brighter light more suitable for photosynthesis. This ability is important in competition between plants, and may contribute to the phenomenal growth rates exhibited by many trees in dense tropical forests (see pp. 182–3).

Once the plant has reached bright light,

the light affects stems by preventing the cell walls from becoming too stretchable, and this restricts cell expansion and hence limits growth. Curiously, light affects leaf cells differently, and actually increases the stretchability of cell walls: hence, leaves expand in light, providing a larger area to absorb the light needed for photosynthesis.

Phytochrome is so sensitive that in seeds it can detect how deeply they are buried in the soil, or if they are shaded by other plants. This information will determine whether or not the seed germinates – if it is near enough the surface, the young shoot will soon reach the light it needs, but if the seed were to germinate too deeply, the young shoot would die before it reached the light.

Plants can also bend towards light, an ability known as *phototropism*. It is thought that this may work through the redistribution of the growth hormone auxin to the darker side of the stem, which consequently grows more.

Flowering is regulated by the duration of daily light – the *photoperiod*. Some species (e.g. chrysanthemum) form flowers more readily in short days, such as in autumn, while others (e.g. radish) do so in the long days of midsummer. Plants of many species form flowers only after experiencing low temperatures: these so called *biennials* do not flower in their first season, but only after the winter, in their second year. This phenomenon, called *vernalization*, together with the response to photoperiod, explains why different plants flower in different seasons.   MBl

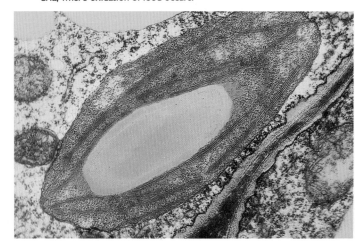

A chloroplast of a leaf cell seen in false colour under an electron microscope. The chloroplast is the green area, and the blue inside it is a starch granule. The strands (*grana*) running through the chloroplast contain the chlorophyll pigments responsible for photosynthesis. The brown line at the right is the cell wall, the yellow area is the vacuole, and the larger red bodies are mitochondria, where oxidation of food occurs.

Non-flowering Plants

The most primitive plants can be divided into two main groups, the first comprising algae and fungi and the second comprising the spore-bearing mosses and liverworts. In all there are about 150 000 different species, the ancestors of which were the first colonizers of the land surface of our planet some 400–500 million years ago. More advanced and larger forms of plant life slowly evolved: the earliest ferns first emerged during the Devonian period, about 400 million years ago, and the conifers more than 300 million years ago during the Carboniferous period.

The primitive plants evolved from the even simpler plant-like protists (see pp. 110–11), which floated at or near the surface of the oceans. These ancestral

forms were washed ashore and gradually developed into forms that were eventually to spread to every land area.

Knowledge of these ancient species is incomplete because the soft plant remains have not made good fossils. In addition, in the 400 million years or so since the primitive plant forms first developed there has been much erosion of older rocks, with consequent loss of fossils.

General characteristics of primitive plants

Primitive plants are usually extremely small in size, growing horizontally rather than vertically. There is little visual difference between the roots, stems or leaves. They lack specialized cells for transporting water and nutrients around the plant and because of this are called *non-vascular plants* (i.e. without veins).

A separate line of evolution in the middle and late Devonian period (410–355 million years ago) produced the first tree-like land plants. These were the ancestors of the present-day horsetails (small herbaceous reed-like plants). Some 400 million years ago they grew to a large size – 10 m (30 ft) tall – and formed the very first forests. Alongside the horsetails were an early form of conifer. They reproduced by means of spores (a primitive feature) but had cells that had many of the characteristics of the later conifers (see below). These trees had an extensive branch system, and leaf-like structures that were to develop into the needle-like leaves of the modern conifer.

The simple bodies of the primitive plants have no means of controlling the loss of water from their cells. They are confined to permanently damp areas such as along river banks, in bogs or in areas of high rainfall. Some have adapted to cope with short, dry spells by becoming dormant. Only the highly specialized lichens have been able to move into the colder, drier areas of the world.

Water plays an essential role in the complex cycle of reproduction. The life history of primitive plants as illustrated by the bryophytes (mosses and liverworts; see below) can be divided into two distinct parts. A 'leafy' green stage culminates in the formation of male and female organs. Sexual reproduction can only occur if moisture is present to wash the male sperm to a female 'egg' (see also p. 114). The second stage comprises a microscopic structure called a *zygote*, which develops into a spore-producing capsule. The spore germinates and grows into the 'leafy' stage.

Fungi

The fungi differ in most respects from all other plants. They form a diverse group numbering 70 000 different species, in-

cluding mushrooms, toadstools, moulds, mildews and rusts. They do not contain chlorophyll and thus cannot photosynthesize (see p. 117).

Fungi contain many thousands of 'cells', but these do not have cell walls. Instead the protoplasm (which is made of chitin and not of cellulose as in other plants) is continuous and contains more than one nucleus (see also p. 111). The main body of a fungus occurs beneath the soil or plant surface and is arranged in branched threads called *hyphae*. These intertwine and grow into a dense mat of white fibres. The visible portion – the toadstool – is a short-lived fruiting body from which new spores are released.

Fungi perform the essential job of decomposing dead plants and animals (see p. 176). Some have become parasitic on plants and animals. Forty species produce disease in humans, from ringworm and athlete's foot to serious lung infections (see p. 238). Damage to stored food products from fungal deterioration amounts to many hundreds of millions of dollars' worth per year. On the positive side, fungi have been developed into essential antibiotic drugs such as penicillin.

Algae

Algae are flat, slimy, green plants that can cling to almost any damp surface. The most primitive forms, the cyanobacteria (or blue-green algae), are often classified as bacteria (see p. 110). Algae are found on the bark of trees, in water, on rocks in hot sulphurous springs, and in soil to a depth of a metre (3 ft) or so. Some have become parasitic on other plants and animals. All algae photosynthesize, and nearly all are unicellular, although many marine forms (the seaweeds) are arranged in long strands or filaments; the Pacific kelp can grow up to 30 m (98 ft) in length. Even unicellular algae show amazing diversity of shape and form, often being decorated with arms or bristles.

Algae have few direct commercial uses for humans, although seaweed is gathered and used as fertilizer in some parts of the world, while in Japan it provides a locally important human food source. In the West, it has been made into food for animals, while in recent years its popularity as a health food has increased. However, algae play a vital role in providing a source of food for many other life forms. They are of great importance in marine food chains, where they form the main food supply of many fish, crustaceans and whales.

Lichen

The lichens are a special group of plants comprising a slow-growing and intimate association (or *symbiosis*; see p. 174) between fungus and alga. In most cases the fungus forms the 'skeleton' on and in which live the algae. Most lichens occur on the surfaces of rocks or tree trunks and are particularly common at higher altitudes. They are used as essential additives for perfumes, and in the manufacture of antibiotics. They were also formerly used as an early form of litmus paper, and their

Lichen in Greenland. Lichen are actually symbiotic associations of certain fungi and algae. They can withstand extreme cold, and therefore can survive at high altitudes and high latitudes. One species has been found below 89° South in Antarctica.

SEE ALSO

- CLIMATIC AND VEGETATION REGIONS p. 104
- THE CLASSIFICATION OF LIFE p. 108
- THE BEGINNINGS OF LIFE p. 110
- PLANT PHYSIOLOGY p. 116
- FLOWERING PLANTS p. 120
- ECOSYSTEMS pp. 178–87
- FORESTRY p. 192

The fly agaric toadstool is a poisonous but only occasionally fatal fungus. Its name derives from its use as a poison on flypaper. The toadstools one sees are only short-lived fruiting bodies; the main bodies of fungi are dense clusters of underground fibres.

Liverworts – with mosses – belong to the group known as bryophytes. There are two main kinds of liverwort: one has a flat liver-like body, while the other has stems and leaves.

The club moss (*Lycopodium*) is not actually a moss, but a primitive vascular plant. It grows true roots, but sexual reproduction relies on the presence of moisture.

Horsetails – another primitive vascular plant – have hollow, segmented stems. Giant tree-like ancestors of the horsetails grew in the Carboniferous period (355–300 million years ago), and their fossilized remains form an important part of many coal seams.

Ferns – like many primitive plants – alternate between asexual and sexual forms. The asexual generation consists of the plants we are familiar with, which produce spores on the underside of their fronds. The spores grow into the sexual generation; this consists of tiny heart-shaped plants, which produce egg and sperm cells.

The cycads, a small order of tropical plants, belong to the same group (the gymnosperms) as the conifers, and are among the oldest seed-bearing plants. Like the conifers, they produce male and female cones, and when the latter are fertilized by windblown sperm cells from the former, seeds are produced.

presence or absence is sometimes used as an indicator of atmospheric pollution.

Mosses and liverworts

This group of primitive plants are called the *bryophytes*. They are small, often inconspicuous plants that grow in dense mats in shaded, damp places. Their smallness of size is due to the lack of strengthening tissues in their stems.

The evolutionary position of bryophytes is unclear as they show features common to both lower and higher plants. Some botanists believe they have developed from green algae. Although living on the land, they are not considered to be true land plants.

The true land plants

Life on land requires some very special modifications to be made to the body of plants. One of the distinguishing features of true land plants is their possession of specialist tissues – xylem and phloem – for the transport of water and synthesized materials (see p. 116). Land plants require strengthening tissue to allow them to grow upright, and they also need to be able to control water loss from their cells. Finally, the embryos of land plants need more protection than water plants.

Plants that show these features are called

vascular plants. They first appeared in the fossil record during the Silurian period (425 million years ago). Members of this group quickly achieved world dominance, and during the Devonian and Carboniferous periods (410–300 million years ago) they formed vast forests that eventually rotted down and were compressed to form the Carboniferous coal measures. Unlike primitive plants, the vascular plants possess true roots, stems and leaves.

Today, few of the ancestral vascular plants remain. Those that do are small but physically tenacious. Examples include the clubmoss and the horsetail. Of the early vascular forms, ferns are now the most numerous, but due to the clearance of land for agriculture and woodland, many have become endangered species.

The seed plants

The earliest forms of vascular plants (such as the fern) showed one important similarity to the non-vascular plants. They retained a complex two-stage life cycle in which one part, the *gametophyte* stage in which fertilization occurred, was totally dependent on water for its success. This was clearly unsuited for life on land.

Only a short time after the first spore-bearing vascular plants appeared in the fossil record there also occurred a dif-

ferent group in which the embryo was contained in a resistant seed that could (if conditions were unfavourable) remain dormant for many years before finally germinating.

The conifers

Seed plants have been traditionally divided into two groups, the less specialized *gymnosperms* and the more advanced *angiosperms* (see p. 120). Fossils of the leaves of the early gymnosperms are so similar to the ferns that at first they were classified as such. Only when their seeds were discovered were they reclassified as seed-bearing plants. Although five different groups of gymnosperms have been recognized, only one group – the conifers – remains of importance today.

The conifers include all the resinous, softwood trees such as pines, spruces, firs and larches. The 'leaves' are evergreen (except in larches) and needle-like, and the reproductive organs are separated into small male cones and larger female cones. Conifers can grow to great heights – over 100 m (328 ft) in the case of sequoias and Douglas firs. They grow in extensive forests in the colder temperate zones (see p. 180), and are of great economic importance as sources of timber (see p. 192). GJ

Flowering Plants

Magnolia bear a strong resemblance to the first flowering plants that appeared some 135 million years ago.

The flowering plants or *angiosperms* are the most advanced and dominant plant forms on the Earth. Some 250 000 different species have been identified. The first true flowering plants appeared in the fossil record during the early Cretaceous period, some 135 million years ago. The angiosperms differ from the gymnosperms (see p. 119) in a number of major ways.

The main difference is the presence of the flower, a specialized part of the plant that develops into a fruit and within which is held one or more well-protected seeds. Other differences include broader leaves that are sometimes highly ornate, and stems that do not contain resin ducts.

Flowering plants occupy every possible habitat apart from snow and ice, hot springs, and the oceans. Apart from these extreme locations, the flowering plants can grow in the driest, wettest, hottest, coldest, most exposed and most sheltered sites on this planet. They show an amazing variety of size and shape, ranging from just 1 mm ($^1/_{25}$ in) for the smallest to about 100 m (328 ft) for the tallest (a eucalyptus tree), while members of the baobab family have attained girths of almost 55 m (180 ft).

The structure of flowering plants

At the base of a flowering plant is a finely branched root system. The roots provide anchorage in the soil, and also collect moisture in which are dissolved the nutrients needed for growth (see p. 116).

From the roots arise either a single, vertical cylindrical stem, or multiple, branched stems. The stem is held erect either by the presence of the fluid within it or by cells that have become strengthened by deposits of lignin (as in woody plants). The stem is strong yet very light and supple. Its purpose is to hold the leaves towards the Sun, thus maximizing the opportunity for photosynthesis (see p. 117). Growing from the junctions between leaves and stem are the flowers.

The flower consists of a series of circular structures. On the outside are the leaf-like *sepals*, which protect the flower at its bud stage. Inside are the *petals*, usually brightly coloured to attract pollinating insects (see box). At the centre of the flower is the *carpel*; this consists of the sticky stalk-like *stigma* and, below it, a slightly swollen area (the *ovary*), within which is the *ovule* containing the egg. Immediately surrounding the stigma are the *stamens*, which consist of a thin stalk with pollen sacs at the end. Each pollen sac ripens to produce millions of tiny pollen grains (the male sperm).

Reproduction

Fertilization occurs when a pollen grain (originating either from the stamens within the plant or transported by wind or an insect from an adjacent flower of the same type) is deposited on the stigma and cuts a channel (the *pollen tube*) down to the ovary. The ovary swells to form a *fruit*, within which is the *seed*, containing an embryo of a new individual.

In addition to sexual reproduction, many kinds of plants can also perform *vegetative reproduction*. This may involve the parent plant sending out side shoots that develop their own leaves and roots, which can then be separated from the parent (for example, grasses, strawberries). Plants such as potatoes can produce several tubers, all of which can give rise to new plants; and a similar method is found in bulbs, corms and rhizomes (see box).

SOME COMMON TYPES OF FLOWERING PLANTS

Annual – a plant that completes its life cycle from germination to death in less than one year (e.g. marigold, zinnia).

Biennial – a plant that completes its life cycle from germination to death in more than one year but less than two. Flowering usually occurs in year two (e.g. foxglove, cabbage, carrot).

Herb or **herbaceous perennial** – a plant lacking woody cells that dies back to the roots at the onset of frost or drought, but that produces new growth on the return of spring or rain (e.g. dock, daisies, dandelion).

Woody perennial – a plant that takes longer than two years to complete its life cycle, and does not die back to its roots (e.g. trees, shrubs, roses).

Bulb – an underground fleshy stem that functions as a food-storage organ. Many spring-flowering plants grow rapidly from bulbs (e.g. daffodil, tulip).

Corm – a swollen underground stem-base with a similar shape and function as a bulb (e.g. crocus).

Rhizome – a horizontally creeping stem (sometimes swollen) that allows the plant to spread over a very wide area (e.g. mint, iris, couch grass).

Tuber – an underground swollen stem tip (e.g. potato) or root (e.g. dahlia) containing large reserves of food.

Classifying the flowering plants

Despite such an amazing variety of species the flowering plants can be divided into just two main botanical groups based upon the structure of the embryo.

The first group (70 000 species) are the *monocotyledons* (abbreviated to monocots), which produce just one seed leaf from the germinating embryo. Examples of monocots include grasses, maize,

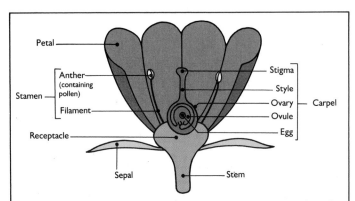

Cross-section of a typical flower showing the stamen containing the pollen (male sperm) and the carpel containing the female egg. The process of fertilization is described in the main text.

Petal
Stamen
Anther (containing pollen)
Filament
Receptacle
Sepal
Stigma
Style
Ovary
Ovule
Egg
Carpel
Stem

wheat, daffodils, irises and palms. The leaves of monocots are generally long and narrow with parallel veins.

Monocots are considered to be more primitive than the larger, second group (180 000 species), the *dicotyledons* (or dicots). These produce new plants with two seed leaves. Examples include oak trees, roses, beans, tomatoes and dandelions. The leaves of dicots are generally more rounded, with branching veins.

A number of very specialized adaptations have taken place that allow certain plants to live upon other plants. Some, such as mistletoe growing on trees, are *parasites* (see p. 174). Others, such as some orchids, use other plants merely for support, and are known as *epiphytes*. Others again have become *carnivorous* and trap insects on their leaves: the insects are then digested and their fluids absorbed. Carnivorous plants (which include sundew, butterwort, Venus flytrap and pitcher plants) tend to have evolved in areas where the soil is poor in nutrients.

The importance of flowering plants

The development of the flowering plants was one of the most significant events in the biological history of this planet. The existence of an advanced plant population that could survive unfavourable climatic events and that produced large quantities of leafy growth provided a superabundance of food for grazing and browsing animals. The dead and decaying vegetation also aided the formation of a thick layer of humus on the soil surface, and this in turn helped retain the nutrients within the soil.

The great variety of vegetation types (see pp. 104 and 178–87) supports an equally varied animal population. Humans are totally dependent on the flowering plants for food (cereals, root crops, pulses, beans, nuts, fruit) or for feeding to domesticated animals. The flowering plants also provide industrial crops (cotton, jute, sisal) and timber, and are increasingly yielding vital medicinal extracts. Some 25% of medicines already contain extracts from the tropical rain forest, a figure thought likely to increase greatly in the future.

Not only are the flowering plants of immense economic value, but, with the non-flowering plants, they are also responsible – via photosynthesis – for stabilizing the carbon dioxide content of the atmosphere. As such they help to maintain the heat balance of the planet.   GJ

Carnivorous plants make up for nutrient-poor soil by trapping and digesting insects. This sundew, which lives in boggy areas, has caught an insect on its sticky hairs. Other forms of carnivorous plant include pitcher plants and Venus flytraps. The former have slippery pitcher-shaped organs into which insects slither, while the latter have hinged leaves that snap shut when an insect touches one of its sensitive trigger hairs.

SEE ALSO

- CLIMATIC AND VEGETATION REGIONS p. 104
- THE CLASSIFICATION OF LIFE p. 108
- PLANT PHYSIOLOGY p. 116
- NON-FLOWERING PLANTS p. 118
- THE BIOSPHERE p. 176
- ECOSYSTEMS pp. 178–87
- ARABLE FARMING p. 188
- FORESTRY p. 192

POLLINATION

A bee pollinating a flower while collecting nectar for honey.

In primitive plants, reproduction is a haphazard event, reliant upon water and wind to propagate the species. In contrast, the flowering plants use the flight of insects to improve the efficiency of their reproduction.

The coloured, scented petals of flowers attract insects. Once inside the bowl-shaped flower, the insect crawls around eating pollen and brushing it off the stamens and onto its body. The insect then visits the flower of another plant, where the pollen from the first plant is brushed onto the stigma, so fertilizing the second flower (see main text).

This achieves the all-important process of *cross-fertilization*, the process whereby genetic material from different plants is exchanged. This ensures the maintenance of vigour within the species, and allows it to produce variants that can colonize new localities. If the male and female organs in the flower reach maturity at different times, cross-fertilization – rather than self-fertilization – is assured.

Many amazing examples of special relationships between flowers and insects have developed. Many flowers produce a sugary fluid called *nectar*, which serves no other purpose than to attract the insects that feed on it. It is a 'reward' to the insects for helping in pollination, and it also appears to stop insects from eating the all-important pollen.

Many flowers, such as foxgloves, violets and rhododendrons, provide 'sign posts' to lead the insect into the flower. Some members of the orchid family have flowers that look like wasps or flies, and this deceives the appropriate insect into attempting to mate with the flower, so pollinating it.

Sometimes plant and insect become totally dependent on each other. The yucca plant of Central America can only be pollinated by the yucca moth. The moth lays its eggs only in the yucca flower and caterpillars can only eat the yucca plant. In this example the plant and the moth are totally dependent upon each other. Extinction of either species would spell doom for the other.

Primitive Animals

One of the most important events in the evolution of life on Earth was the development of multicellular organisms – ranging from simple worms to complex insects and squids – from unicellular animal-like protists (see pp. 110–11). Most groups of primitive multicellular invertebrates are found in very old fossil-bearing rocks, so it is clear that this major breakthrough occurred at least 600 million years ago.

The similarity in mineral composition of animal body fluids and sea water indicates that all groups of primitive animals arose in the sea. One of these groups (the echinoderms) is of particular interest in that they share a common ancestor with the chordates, from which all vertebrates – including man – evolved.

Worms

All *flatworms* (phylum Platyhelminthes) are simple in construction and characterized by a blind-ending gut. The free-living *turbellarians* (class Turbellaria) are small, flattened, leaf-like worms found in aquatic and damp terrestrial habitats, where they have a scavenging or predatory way of life. The *trematodes* (Trematoda), which include the flukes, are external and internal parasitic flat-

Fan worms are sedentary paddle worms that feed by extending their crowns of tentacles into water currents to catch plankton. They withdraw rapidly into their chalky protective tubes if threatened.

worms, with special attachment suckers and a complex life history involving at least two hosts. One trematode is responsible for the debilitating disease Schistosomiasis (see p. 174). The *cestodes* (Cestoda), which include tapeworms, are ribbon-like gut parasites, with a complex hooked head for attachment to their host.

The **nematodes** (phylum Nematoda) – roundworms, eelworms, threadworms and hookworms – are found in soil and in both fresh and salt water. They are important crop pests, causing damage both by consumption of plant tissue and by facilitating the entry of viruses and other diseases into plants. Many have become parasitic in animals, and hookworms are thought to be among the most important causes of human illness. Nematodes are responsible for elephantiasis (see p. 174) and other diseases.

Annelid (or ***segmented***) ***worms*** (phylum Annelida) have long thin bodies with distinct head and tail ends. The body is made up of a series of separate segments, usually having external limbs or hair-like protrusions called *chaetae*. Internally, an extensive body cavity separating the gut from the body wall is a feature distinguishing them from other worms.

Of the three classes of annelids, the marine *paddle worms* (Polychaeta) are the oldest and most diverse. Characterized by a pair of limbs on each segment, most live in or on the sea bed, feeding on all kinds of material. Mobile predatory and scavenging worms have sensory tentacles and retractable jaws, while sedentary forms, such as fan worms (see photo), depend mainly on floating particles.

The *earthworms* and their freshwater relatives (class Oligochaeta) burrow their way through earth, feeding on decaying vegetable matter. They are long thin worms without external structures except retractable chaetae – used as anchors in burrowing (see p. 172) – and a reproductive structure (the *clitellum*). Earthworms are of considerable economic importance because of their role in recycling nutrients in the soil.

The most advanced annelids are the *leeches* (class Hirudinea). They are either predatory or externally parasitic blood-suckers, and have developed suckers at each end of the body. They do not crawl like other worms, but have adopted a looping method of movement (see p. 172). Parasitic leeches have saliva containing an anaesthetic to prevent detection and an anticoagulant so that blood remains fluid and is easily digested.

Except for paddleworms, which are sexually differentiated, all worms are hermaphrodite – every individual has both male and female reproductive organs. Larvae are free-swimming and frequently multiply asexually.

Molluscs

Molluscs (phylum Mollusca) make up a highly varied group of unsegmented animals. Classic mollusc characteristics include a broad locomotory foot, a protective shell, a tongue-like feeding organ (*radula*), and a special respiratory gill (*ctenidium*). Although some or all of these

Many sea-slugs have conspicuous warning coloration, to signal to would-be predators that they are poisonous and best left alone. In this sea slug (*Chromodoris purpurea*) the protrusions at the rear end are branched respiratory gills; those at the front are sensory tentacles.

characteristics are found in all molluscs, each class has specialized very differently. Some molluscs are sexually differentiated, while others are hermaphrodite. Aquatic forms have a free-swimming larva.

Gastropods (class Gastropoda) – land and sea snails and slugs – form the largest group of molluscs and are the most diverse in feeding habit. All gastropods have a foot for walking or swimming and a radula, and most also have an external shell. The radula is a broad tongue in limpets, with iron-hardened teeth to rasp rocks, while in carnivores it has sharp pointed teeth. In the specialized cone shells it is modified into a single harpoon-like weapon armed with a poison gland. Sea slugs are predatory gastropods, which lack shells and are frequently brightly coloured (see photo). Some species transfer to their own backs the stinging cells of the coelenterates upon which they feed.

Bivalves (class Bivalvia), which include cockles, mussels, oysters and clams, are essentially living filter pumps. Enclosed within the two-valved shell are massive gills covered with whip-like projections called *cilia*. The gills pump water through themselves and sieve particles from the water. Most bivalves have a large foot for burrowing into sand or mud, while others glue themselves to rocks. Many are prime targets for predators such as starfish (see photo) and can use the foot to spring away from their assailants. Giant clams – like corals (see below) – have a symbiotic relationship with a certain alga and obtain nutrition from the alga's excess productivity. Such clams may grow to 1 m (39 in) in length – the largest of all living bivalves.

The *cephalopods* (class Cephalopoda), which include squids, cuttlefish (see photo), octopuses and the nautilus, are highly specialized predators. They have well-developed sensory faculties and the ability to change colour instantly. They are also capable of versatile and rapid

movement, and – with their complex brains – even possess powers of learning and memory. Their tentacles have developed from the modified foot, and in the mouth behind the beak is found a classic mollusc radula. The giant squids, which live in deep water and are rarely seen, are the largest invertebrates known, with bodies in excess of 5 m (16 ft) in length.

Despite their sophistication, present-day cephalopods are only the remnant of a previously superabundant group, which in the Cretaceous period (135–65 million years ago) included a vast array of ammonites and belemnites. Competition with fish has since led to a reduction in their numbers.

Coelenterates

Although simple in structure, coelenterates (phylum Coelenterata) form the largest living structures on Earth – the coral barrier reefs of Australia and Belize. All coelenterates have a simple two-layered contractible body wall surrounding a central gut with a single opening. Tentacles bearing stinging cells surround the mouth in corals and sea anemones (class Anthozoa), and form a fringe to the bell of jellyfish (Scyphozoa). Jellyfish are given strength by the jelly between the two cell layers, while corals lay down a rigid basal skeleton, and the related sea whips a skeleton of horny material.

Coelenterates are mostly predatory, capturing prey by means of the tentacles and the batteries of gripping and stinging cells these carry. The stinging cells touch prey and turn inside out, penetrating the

A jellyfish (Cotylorhiza tuberculata) swims in the upper waters of the sea by muscular movements of the bell, feeding on tiny planktonic organisms. The fish hiding beneath the bell derive protection and probably food from the association.

tissues and injecting a neurotoxin – lethal even to humans in the case of some jellyfish. Corals obtain nutrients from symbiosis with an alga, making use of the surplus products of photosynthesis (see p. 117) and providing the algal cells with waste nitrogen.

Many coelenterates exhibit *alternation of generations*. A jellyfish stage (called a *medusa*), at which the animal is free-swimming and reproduces sexually, leads to a sedentary stage (a *polyp*) from which medusae are produced asexually. Sea anemones, corals and hydroids spend most of their lives as polyps, singly or in colonies, whereas jellyfish spend almost all their lives as medusae, swimming by means of pulsations of the bell (see photo), with a very brief polyp phase. (More details on coral and coral reefs can be found on p. 99.)

Echinoderms

Echinoderms (phylum Echinodermata) are characterized as a group by their five-part symmetry, internal skeleton and tube feet, but are otherwise very different. Representatives are found in all marine habitats, from the shallowest waters to the deepest abyssal depths. Echinoderms are sexually differentiated and have free-swimming larvae.

Echinoderms are essentially very simple animals, without some of the organ systems that characterize more complex groups. Yet they are among the most successful of marine animals, and share certain structural and developmental features with vertebrates. Although evolving in very different ways, several obscure groups of marine invertebrates – hemichordates (acorn worms), ascidians (sea squirts) and cephalochordates (lancelets) – are thought to have developed from a single ancestral stock; and it is from this same stock that echinoderms and chordates (the group to which vertebrates belong) are believed to have evolved. For this reason the echinoderms and these other primitive animals have been seen by some as link groups between invertebrates and vertebrates.

Sea lilies (class Crinoidea) are the most primitive echinoderms. Two groups exist today – sedentary stalked sea lilies found exclusively in deep water, and free-living mobile species, which lack a stalk and are found principally in shallow water. Both feed in the same way, by sieving particles

from passing currents with their upward-pointing tube feet. As a large surface area is required for effective filter-feeding, sea lilies have 10, 20 or 40 arms, creating a huge crown, or *calyx*.

Sea urchins (class Echinoidea) are globular, oval or disc-shaped creatures, densely covered with spines – poisonous in some species – and other external structures based on an underlying shell composed largely of calcium carbonate. Some are grazing herbivores, living on hard rocky surfaces, with large spines used in locomotion and defence. Others, with short spines used for burrowing, live in sand and feed on organic debris. The tube feet, arranged in five rows around the shell, are variously used for movement, attachment and sensory perception.

Starfish or *sea stars* (class Asteroidea) have five hollow arms linked to a central disc. Small spines cover the upper surface, while the arm edges are often set with large defensive plates. Most of the tube feet, arranged in five rows and surrounding the central mouth, are used for locomotion and grasping prey, but those near the arm tips are sensory. Starfish are mostly scavengers or predators, and frequently feed on clams (see photo). The gut may be turned inside out over prey, and digestion may take place outside the body. In this way the crown-of-thorns starfish eats large quantities of coral, causing extensive damage to reefs.

Brittle stars or *serpent stars* (class Ophiuroidea) – so called because of their readiness to cast off arms and regrow them – are thin-armed, highly mobile animals with a compact central disc. Found in all marine habitats, often in huge numbers, they are mostly filter-feeders or scavengers.

Sea cucumbers (class Holothuroidea) are worm-like echinoderms that have reduced the internal skeleton to a vestige and become soft and extremely flexible. Found in all marine habitats, they use enlarged branched tube feet around the mouth for feeding, either spreading them out on a surface to pick up particles or extending them in a water current to intercept food. RE

A cuttlefish (*Sepia latimana*) moving over a coral reef (left). Once detected by the large eyes, small fish and crustaceans are seized by two long tentacles, gripped by eight short tentacles around the mouth, and then bitten by the powerful beak. Cuttlefish can change their coloration almost instantly, different patterns being used in sexual display, for concealment or to intimidate.

SEE ALSO

- CORAL AND CORAL ISLANDS p. 99
- HOW ANIMALS MOVE p. 172
- PARASITISM AND SYMBIOSIS p. 174
- ECOSYSTEMS: AQUATIC p. 178
- INFECTIOUS DISEASES p. 238

Common starfish feeding on a dead clam. Live clams are also preyed on, the two valves of their shell being prised apart by the starfish's tube feet.

Arthropods
1. Crustaceans, Myriapods and Arachnids

Arthropods are by far the most diverse and successful of all invertebrates, with close to two million species recognized. All the major groups of the phylum Arthropoda – crustaceans, myriapods, arachnids and insects – share certain fundamental features that have contributed significantly to their success. Their bodies are segmented, with a strong external skeleton (*exoskeleton*) and jointed limbs. The skeleton is formed by a protective layer known as the *cuticle*, which consists largely of a protein called chitin and is often hardened with calcium carbonate. The cuticle is impermeable and mostly rigid, but joints allow flexibility, and thin areas are necessary for respiration and sensory perception.

An arrowhead spider crab searches among the tentacles of a sea anemone, intending to steal any prey that the latter may have captured. This crab well illustrates the jointed nature of arthropod limbs.

The skeleton allows the development of hollow jointed limbs, and muscles attached to either side of joints give arthropod limbs versatility and rapidity of movement. Primitive forms, including some modern-day crustaceans, have a series of many similar limbs down the body, but in advanced forms, such as insects and spiders, limbs are reduced in number and each pair may have a different structure and function. Head limbs are adapted for sensory perception,

defence and food handling; thorax limbs for walking and swimming; and abdominal limbs for respiratory and reproductive functions, such as holding eggs or gripping a partner during reproduction (see insect structure, p. 126).

Most arthropods have large eyes. Insects and crustaceans have compound eyes made up of individual light-sensing components whose combined input to the brain produces a mosaic-like image. Receptors sensitive to chemical stimuli (*chemoreceptors*), as in taste or smell, and vibration receptors are found all over the body, but are concentrated on the antennae and head.

Crustaceans

Crustaceans – the 'insects of the sea' – form a very varied group of arthropods and are extremely abundant throughout the sea. The freshwater species, though numerous, suffer competition from insects and are less abundant. A very few – woodlice and the land crabs (see p. 170) – have successfully adapted to life on land.

The subphylum Crustacea contains some 42 000 species and is divided into 10 classes. The most important of these are Branchiopoda (fairy shrimps); Copepoda (copepods); Cirripedia (barnacles); Decapoda (crabs, shrimps and prawns); Amphipoda (sand hoppers; see p. 170); and Isopoda (woodlice).

The elongated bodies of crustaceans have many segments, each bearing a pair of limbs, and are clearly divided into a head/thorax region and a tail or abdomen. The head/thorax is often covered by a protective shell plate (the *carapace*).

In primitive forms the head segments, bearing the antennae and mouthparts, are followed by a series of similar limbs, often fringed with hairs for food sifting. In more advanced forms the various limbs differ in function and structure – thorax limbs being used for walking and swimming,

A Pacific lobster with its slough. Almost all arthropods can only grow by moulting: the rigid exoskeleton is periodically shed under hormonal control, and the animal expands in size while the new skeleton is still soft. The Pacific lobster is a predatory species, using its powerful claws to crush prey such as clams.

abdominal limbs usually for respiratory purposes and in reproduction. The front limbs of some crustaceans are adapted as claws, for food capture and defence.

Most crustaceans are *unisexual* – male and female are distinct. All crustaceans have the same basic larva – the *nauplius* – but later stages may be different. Eventually a final moult transforms the larva to a juvenile.

Barnacles are highly modified for feeding on marine phytoplankton (tiny planktonic plants). As larvae they resemble other crustaceans, but they later settle on a carefully chosen surface, usually close to other members of the same species, and attach themselves by means of head glands. The animal secretes a protective shell complete with closing lid, from which the thorax limbs, fringed with hairs, are protruded to catch plankton. The success of this way of life can be judged on any rocky seashore.

Copepods are small crustaceans of immense importance in the economy of the sea. They are the principal grazers of marine phytoplankton, and are themselves the food of commercially important fish such as herring. Shrimp-like crustaceans called *krill*, which feed in a similar way to copepods, form the main food source of the whales of the southern oceans. Decline in whale populations has led to a huge build-up of these crustaceans, which are now harvested directly by man as food for domestic animals and as fertilizer.

The *fairy* (or *brine*) *shrimps* live in temporary pools where they escape predation. They are classic primitive crustaceans, with rows of similar limbs used for movement and feeding, and they feed by sieving particles from the water. Water fleas are more advanced forms common in fresh water.

The group known as the *decapods* – so called because they have 10 walking legs – includes most of the many commercially important crustaceans such as crabs, lobsters, shrimps and prawns. It is the most numerous crustacean group with around 10 000 species, and includes the largest crustacean – the giant spider crab, which commonly has a claw span of around 2.5 m (8 ft). Most are scavengers or predators, but the fiddler crabs feed on organic debris.

The claw and leg structure of crabs is often a clue to their way of life. Those that feed on molluscs are slow-moving and heavily armoured, using their strong claws to crack shells. Species that rely on moving prey have claws with serrated edges, and often have limbs specially modified for swimming.

Myriapods

There are four groups of myriapods, totalling some 10 000 species. Their principal characteristic is a body composed of a head and a long trunk with many leg-bearing segments. The various groups are probably not closely related, however, and only two groups are of significance.

Centipedes (class Chilopoda) are secretive predatory animals found throughout the world in damp terrestrial habitats (beneath bark, logs, stones, etc.). They are confined to such habitats by their vulnerability to water loss in dry air. The head has large jaws concealed beneath the modified first pair of legs, which form poison fangs. Following this are 15 or so similar segments with strong walking legs. Nocturnal in habit, they are able to move very quickly, sensing their prey by means of chemoreceptors on the head, and killing with their poison fangs.

Millipedes (class Diplopoda) are herbivorous scavengers found in similar habitats to centipedes. They appear to have two pairs of legs on each segment but in reality these are fused segments, which may number as many as a hundred. They move slowly over the ground, but their legs and movement pattern are suitable for burrowing. Rapid escape from predators is impossible, so millipedes have chemical defences in the form of poisons and are heavily armoured.

Arachnids

The arachnids (class Arachnida) – the largest group of arthropods after the insects, with over 60 000 species – include scorpions (order Xiphosura), ticks and mites (Acari), and spiders (Araneae).

Scorpions were among the earliest terrestrial animals, appearing on land in the Carboniferous period (355 to 300 million years ago). Nocturnal and secretive, they hide under stones or logs by day, and are found in most warm habitats, including deserts. They detect prey with highly sensitive vibration and odour receptors. Waiting for their prey to move into range, they grip it with their massive claws and inject a paralysing venom with the sting in their tail. The venom of some species may cause death in humans. They undertake elaborate courtship rituals culminating in fertilization of the female, who then broods the young.

Ticks and *mites* are economically important as plant and animal parasites, as carriers of disease in both animals and humans, and as food pests. Mites are found in enormous numbers in all environments. Most ticks and mites are tiny – adult mites are often less than 1 mm (¹⁄₂₅ in) in length, although some ticks are larger. Characteristically, they have an oval body with four pairs of limbs, and a mouthpart adapted for biting, sucking or sawing.

Spiders are the most successful group of land-living arthropods – judged by numbers of species – after the insects. They are compact specialist predators, with a body clearly divided into two parts. The front section combining head and thorax bears four pairs of walking legs and two other pairs of limbs. One is a pair of hollow fangs; the

SEE ALSO
- INSECTS p. 126
- ANIMAL COMMUNICATION p. 166
- HOW ANIMALS MOVE p. 172
- PARASITISM AND SYMBIOSIS p. 174

Two millipedes mating. As is the case with most arthropods, male and female millipedes are sexually distinct, and copulation is necessary for fertilization.

other pair is leg-like in females, and a complicated reproductive structure in males. As many as eight large eyes may be seen at the front end.

Spiders feed mainly on insects and have evolved an amazing variety of techniques for capturing their prey. Camouflaged crab spiders, for instance, sit in flowers and ambush visiting insects, while trapdoor spiders leave radiating silken trip lines and rush out from their burrow when an insect stumbles over one.

Silk is used by many spiders to construct a variety of webs to catch different insects: orb webs slung across gaps catch flying insects, while sheet and hammock webs trap insects that crawl or hop onto them. Silk is a protein manufactured in the spider's body, expelled from several gland openings and spun into a multi-strand thread by structures called *spinnerets* on the abdomen.

Spiders are often not particular about their prey, and as the female is usually larger, elaborate rituals are gone through by the male to avoid being eaten and to allow successful mating. Signalling from a distance combined with conspicuous striped body patterns may be necessary to suppress the female's predatory tendencies, while offering a silk-wrapped food item may also be effective.   RE

Sea slaters (centre), a species of marine woodlouse, emerge at night to feed on fragments of seaweed left behind by the receding tide. These amphibious crustaceans are important scavengers on rocky shores throughout the world.

A jumping spider (left). No more than 1 cm (²⁄₅ in) long, jumping spiders are superbly equipped as predators. Provided with excellent sensory ability by their large simple eyes, they leap on prey from a distance, immobilizing it with their massive jaws.

Arthropods
2. Insects

Insects form by far the largest class of animals, accounting for over 80% of all animal species on Earth. There are more insect species than all other animal and plant species put together – well over a million species are recognized, with hundreds of new ones discovered each year. Insects are remarkable in many ways – for their diversity of form, for their dominance of land environments, for their complex social organization, for their ability (unique among invertebrates) to fly. They are also of immense economic importance to man – many insects are animal or plant pests, while others play a central role in crop pollination or in pest control.

Adult insects are instantly recognizable as arthropods (see p. 124). As well as having the usual arthropod characteristics of exoskeleton and jointed limbs, the body is clearly divided into three parts.

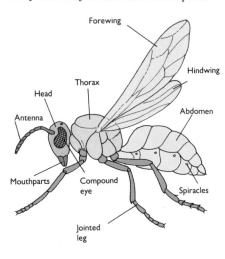

The head houses a large brain; within the thorax, there is a mass of muscles and associated respiratory structures; and the abdomen contains the organ systems responsible for much of digestion, excretion and reproduction. Most variation in insect structure is found in the form of the legs, the wings and the mouthparts, which are all carefully adapted for particular ways of life.

Insects would suffer respiratory problems if they were any larger than they are. Although the African goliath beetle, for instance, may grow to as much as 20 cm (8 in), most insects are small, many species being less than 1 mm (1/25 in). Small size is indeed an advantage to insects, in that individuals are inconspicuous, can find hiding places easily, and can readily satisfy their food requirements.

Classification and reproduction

Two major groups of the class Insecta are recognized – winged insects (Pterygota) and wingless insects (Apterygota). The wingless insects, believed to be the most primitive surviving insects, fall into four orders, familiar examples being silverfish and springtails. There are 24 orders of winged insects, commonly divided by their method of development into the Exopterygota and Endopterygota. These orders are of varying size and importance, 85% of all species belonging to four orders: Coleoptera (beetles); Lepidoptera (butterflies and moths); Diptera (flies); and Hymenoptera (bees, wasps and ants).

Insects develop from egg to adult in two distinct ways. In exopterygote forms, such as cockroaches and grasshoppers, the young live in the same environment and hatch as *nymphs* – miniature adults without reproductive structures. If the insect is a winged form, wing buds are present and grow proportionately larger at each moult. The final moult, in which external reproductive structures appear, transforms the animal to a functional adult. The alternative method, found in endopterygote insects such as bees, butterflies and beetles, involves larval and pupal stages (see illustration).

Insect habitats

Of all invertebrates insects are the most suited to existence on land. This is chiefly due to the nature of the cuticle (the material from which the exoskeleton is made). This is so resistant to water loss that insects can easily exist even in the driest environments, and may also make them resistant to pesticides and disease. Water loss is also minimal in excretion and in respiration, the latter taking place by means of small closable pores or *spiracles* located along the thorax and abdomen. The cuticle has also allowed the evolution of very strong mouthparts, capable of tackling tough terrestrial plants.

Insects have reinvaded water from the land, and – although rare in the sea because of competition from crustaceans – are the predominant invertebrate group in fresh water. Many insects, such as dragonflies and mayflies, live as larvae in water, exploiting the massive food resources of that environment but abandoning the water at metamorphosis, leaving the emerging adult free to feed, fly and mate in the aerial environment. Such larvae are completely aquatic, breathing by means of gills. Other insects, such as water boatmen and pond skaters, are said to be incompletely aquatic: although highly adapted for life in water and spending their whole life there, they have to return to the surface to breathe.

Insect senses

Visual, chemical and auditory sensory abilities are all well developed in insects. They are capable of producing and perceiving sounds in and beyond the range of human hearing. Insects' compound eyes are capable not only of perceiving the environment as we know it, in colour, but also of perceiving polarized light patterns in the sky and using them in navigation. Their colour-range perception is different from that of humans, in that they see

Dragonflies have a two-part life history. The larva lives as an underwater predator before reaching a size at which it undergoes metamorphosis into an adult. Here the young adult is seen emerging from the larval skin, prior to taking to life in the air.

The praying mantis (below) is a voracious predator. Camouflaged in vegetation by its coloration, it waits for passing insects, which it grabs with its penknife-like front legs. Even its mate is not safe: this female is eating a male seized just as he has finished mating with her.

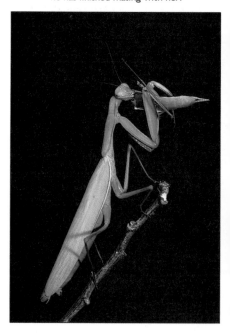

ultraviolet light: plants that seem dull to us may appear bright and colourful to an insect.

Chemical signals are perceived with extraordinary sensitivity by insects, and are used for many purposes. Female moths, for example, release a special chemical called a *pheromone* that can be detected by males over several kilometres at extremely low concentrations (see photo, p. 166). When a bee stings, it produces an alarm pheromone, which causes other bees that receive the chemical to fly rapidly to the source of the pheromone, ready to attack. Another pheromone controls the development of social insects (see below).

SEE ALSO
● FLOWERING PLANTS (POL-LINATION) p. 121
● ARTHROPODS 1 p. 124
● ANIMAL BEHAVIOUR p. 166–75

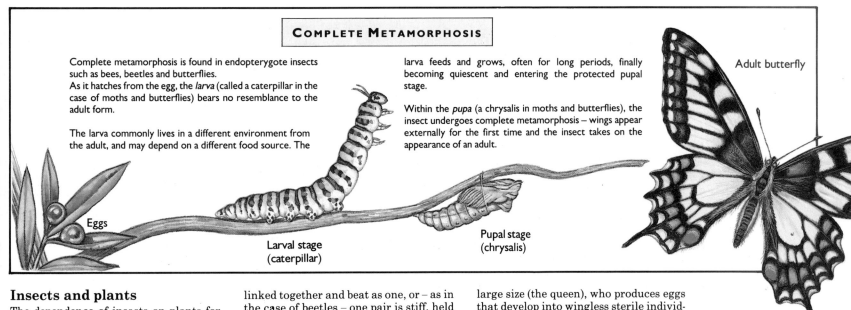

COMPLETE METAMORPHOSIS

Complete metamorphosis is found in endopterygote insects such as bees, beetles and butterflies.

As it hatches from the egg, the *larva* (called a caterpillar in the case of moths and butterflies) bears no resemblance to the adult form.

The larva commonly lives in a different environment from the adult, and may depend on a different food source. The larva feeds and grows, often for long periods, finally becoming quiescent and entering the protected pupal stage.

Within the *pupa* (a chrysalis in moths and butterflies), the insect undergoes complete metamorphosis – wings appear externally for the first time and the insect takes on the appearance of an adult.

Eggs

Larval stage
(caterpillar)

Pupal stage
(chrysalis)

Adult butterfly

Insects and plants

The dependence of insects on plants for food has led over millions of years to a high degree of coevolution, resulting in much interdependence and anatomical modification on both sides. Two thirds of flowering plants are insect-pollinated (see p. 121). Insects such as bees and butterflies have evolved specialized mouthparts to enable them to reach nectar.

Most insects, however, attack plants, which may supplement structural defences with chemical ones. Some produce highly toxic chemicals, others high levels of indigestible material. Insects have responded in various ways, some evolving enzymes to combat the toxic chemicals, others adapting their life history to take advantage of the limited periods when plants are more easily digestible.

Many insects avoid predation by camouflaging themselves, often so that they resemble plant material such as leaves or twigs. Some can change colour to match their background. Not all insects hide, however. Many caterpillars, butterflies, wasps and other insects are brightly coloured and obvious, to warn potential predators that they are dangerous and to be avoided. Other species, harmless in themselves, mimic the coloration of noxious species (see p. 167).

Insect flight

Flight is a major factor in the success of insects. Projections from the thorax, giving hopping insects a gliding ability, became increasingly more mobile and eventually evolved into effective wings – thin layers of chitin, stiffened by tubular veins.

Insect flight is diverse and complex. Every flying insect has two pairs of wings but does not necessarily use both for flight. In primitive insects such as dragonflies, flight is achieved by raising and lowering the two pairs of wings by means of muscles attached to the wings. The wings beat out of phase in such a way as to give maximum efficiency. In more advanced insects, the wings are either linked together and beat as one, or – as in the case of beetles – one pair is stiff, held out as an aerofoil, while the other provides the propulsive force. In flies one pair of wings is reduced to a pair of fast-vibrating knobs that function as gyro-stabilizers. Wing-beat rates vary from a leisurely 300 per minute in some butterflies to an astonishing rate in excess of 50 000 beats per minute in certain tiny midges. In advanced insects the flight muscles are not attached to the wings but to the thorax wall (see p. 173).

Flying is very energy-consuming, and insects in flight have a very high metabolic rate, using large amounts of energy stored in the thorax. Flying can, however, be highly energy-efficient – and has to be for migratory species such as locusts and monarch butterflies (see photo, p. 171). The nature of locust thorax cuticle is such that as much as 90% of the energy exerted in one wing movement is stored by the cuticle and used in the next movement. This property of the body wall allows insects to fly great distances without becoming exhausted.

Flight muscles operate best in warm conditions, and flight is impossible in cold conditions for small insects. Some insects undertake 'pre-flight' exercises to warm up their muscles. Wings beat in an aerodynamically efficient fashion with the correct posture to give maximum effectiveness. The most proficient fliers, such as hover flies, can fly forwards, backwards and hover by subtly altering the way the wings thrust on the air.

Social insects

Two orders of insects – wasps, bees and ants (Hymenoptera) and termites (Isoptera) – exhibit social organization in which closely related individuals live together in large groups. Individuals differ both in function and structure, and cannot survive outside the colony. The development of the colony is controlled by one or more reproductive individuals.

Ants are always social and every colony is founded by a single fertilized female of large size (the queen), who produces eggs that develop into wingless sterile individuals. These workers and soldiers are all female and any males present do not work. Winged males and females develop at appropriate times to leave the nest and found a new generation. Termites behave in a similar way (see photo and p. 169).

Bees and wasps, only some of which are colonial, are similar in some respects to ants: all workers are female and the sole purpose of male bees (known as 'drones') is to mate with the queen. All individuals have wings, and queens are either just a little larger or distinctive only by their behaviour.

Honeybees have a single queen whose role is to lay eggs. The workers that emerge from the eggs have different roles in the function of the colony: they start as cell cleaners; graduate to feeding either larvae or the queen and to building combs; and finally become food foragers. Despite their busy life, workers usually live little more than a month. Many individuals are usually idling in the hive, ready to respond if a large food source is found or if the hive is threatened. Individuals returning to the hive are able to communicate information about a valuable food source (see p. 167).   RE

A termite mound.
Termites and other social insects (ants, bees and wasps) often build large and elaborate structures to house their colonies. The interior of a mound consists of vertical and horizontal tunnels and galleries, and the mound itself provides shelter and protection from predators.

Fishes

Fishes, the vertebrates with the longest ancestry, inhabit the largest ecosystem on Earth – the water. Fishes spend all their life in water, and unlike aquatic mammals, such as whales and dolphins, they are cold-blooded and (with a few exceptions) can only use oxygen if it is dissolved in water.

SEE ALSO

● MIGRATION p. 170
● HOW ANIMALS MOVE p. 172
● ECOSYSTEMS: AQUATIC p. 178
● FISHING p. 194

Modern fishes are extremely diverse in structure, and – although distinguished as a group as aquatic cold-blooded vertebrates – have not attained their present form by following a single evolutionary path. The 22 000 living species of fish are classified in 4 (or sometimes 5) classes, containing a total of more than 40 orders. This division at the class level implies a degree of distinctness among the various fish groups equivalent to that between, say, reptiles and mammals.

The most primitive class, Agnatha, comprises around 60 species of lamprey and hagfish – soft-bodied fishes that lack jaws and are barely vertebrate. All other fishes have jaws and are therefore sometimes grouped together in the superclass Gnathostomata; within this group, two classes are of pre-eminent importance.

The class Chondrichthyes contains nearly 600 species of *cartilaginous fishes*; most of these belong to the predominantly marine subclass Salachii, which includes sharks, skates and rays (sometimes known collectively as *elasmobranches*). The class Osteichthyes (bony fishes) contains over 21 000 species, and is again divided into two unequal subclasses: the small subclass Sarcopterygii (fleshy-finned fishes) contains the coelacanth and the lungfishes; the much larger subclass Actinopterygii (ray-finned fishes) is almost entirely made up of the group known as the *teleosts*. The teleosts are the dominant fishes of the world today, accounting for over 95% of all living species. In terms of diversification, they are the most successful of all vertebrate groups, with more species than all other vertebrates put together. They are widely distributed in fresh and salt water from Arctic to Antarctic regions.

An archerfish shoots a jet of water by sudden compression of the tongue and the gill covers. Its target, an insect, is dislodged and falls into the water, where it is eaten. The archerfish is able to compensate for the bending of images between air and water, and its judgement of distance is enhanced by its slightly forward-pointing eyes.

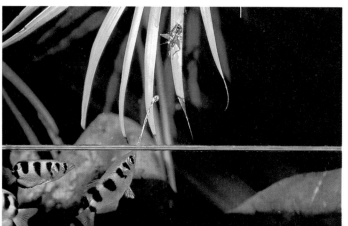

Bony-Fish Structure

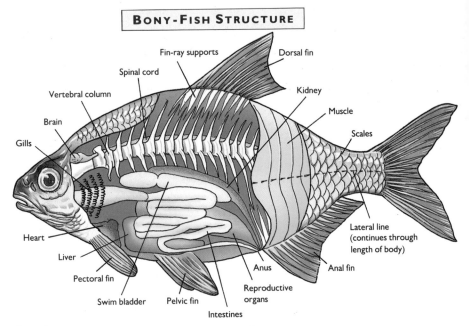

Anatomy

The characteristic adaptations of fishes are related to propulsion through water and extraction of oxygen from water. Typically, fishes have well-muscled paddles called *fins*, and the tail is well developed, to provide power and aid steering (see p. 172). The skin is impermeable to water, and often amply supplied with mucus cells, spines or bony plates for further protection.

In cartilaginous fishes, the skeleton is formed from gristly, partially calcified cartilage, and the body is solidly – almost inflexibly – muscled. Like most other fishes, their body fluids have a lower salt content than that of their environment, and – because they lack the swim bladder or lungs possessed by bony fishes – they must keep moving to maintain their chosen position. Generally their skins are rough and leathery, with many minute toothed scales, and their fins are fleshy. The bodies of rays and skates are flattened, with the mouth and gill slits on the underside, and the eyes and two gill spiracles (modified gill slits) on the upper surface.

Bony fishes have internal skeletons made of true bone. The head and shoulder regions are covered by large bony plates, while the rest of the body is typically covered in iridescent bony scales (see diagram). There is flexibility in both body and tail, and the fins are supported by bony rays, usually movable and often bearing sharp spines. Their pelvic fins are generally well developed. In some species, such as eels, the knife fish and the lungfishes, it is the dorsal or anal fins that provide propulsion.

A few bony fishes have stiffly rayed pectoral fins that can be used as props or stilts. The climbing perch of India and the Asian and African mudskippers are able to move on land, while the bizarre shortnose batfish of the Caribbean – a poor swimmer – crawls over the sea bed on arm-like fins.

The coelacanth, found only off the Comoro Islands near Madagascar, is virtually a living fossil, scarcely changed in 90 million years. It was once thought that its fleshy bone-supported fins were used to walk on the sea bed. In fact these fins are used primarily for balance and for putting on the occasional burst of speed. However, the coelacanth and the related lungfishes move their fins alternately – just like salamanders walking on land – and it is thought that these fins are the precursors of land-vertebrate limbs.

Lampreys and hagfishes lack jaws, but they have rasping horny teeth. Many species attach themselves to other fishes by means of their sucker-like mouths, and feed on their blood and tissues (see photo, p. 174).

Gills and lungs

Almost all fishes take in water through the mouth and expel it to the exterior across their *gills* – internal blood-rich organs that extract oxygen from the water. Jawless and some cartilaginous fishes have visible gill slits on each side of the neck region, while bony fishes have a pair of hard bony flaps (the *opercula*) covering their gill exits. Rays and some sharks that also have spiracles may take in water chiefly through these openings, rather than through the mouth.

Lungs are found in the most primitive bony fishes, but in teleosts they have been transformed into the *swim bladder*, a gas-filled buoyancy aid. Some fishes, typically mud, estuary and swamp dwellers, use the swim bladder in addition to the gills for gas exchange, gulping in air when at the surface. Lungfishes have one or two lungs, which they use when they spend drought periods dormant in their dried-up burrows – an example of aestivation (see p. 171).

Fish senses

Most fishes have large well-developed eyes, with a reflective layer (the *tapetum*) inside the eye and more cells in the retina sensitive to low light than land animals. This allows fishes to make maximum use of light filtering through water or generated by other fishes. The sense of smell is very important for migratory fishes, leading them back to their beach or river of origin (see p. 170).

Fishes can detect magnetic and electrical fields, as well as vibration and sound. Changes in their environment can be sensed by means of specialized organs – mucus-filled pits with sensory hairs – located on the head and within the lateral lines (see diagram). Skates, rays, the South American knife fish and the Nile elephant snout fish all use their sensitivity to electrical fields to help them hunt in muddy waters and at night.

Diet

Some fishes are vegetation-eaters, feeding on fallen fruit, plants or bottom detritus. Most, however, are predatory carnivores, taking crustaceans such as copepods, krill and other shrimps, invertebrates such as jellyfish, and any vertebrates they can catch, including mammals, birds and other fishes. Some fishes are specialized for dealing with their food. The archerfish of Australasia and Southeast Asia shoots jets of water from its mouth to knock insects off vegetation (see photo). The parrotfishes have strong beaked teeth at the front of the mouth and crushing teeth at the back, to scrape algae and coral off the reefs they inhabit. The pacu, related to the carnivorous piranhas, also has crushing teeth, and eats fruit and seeds.

The basking shark is one of the largest fishes, and the whale shark is the biggest of all, sometimes growing to around 18 m (60 ft). Despite their great size, however, they resemble baleen whales in their method of feeding (see p. 163), living on plankton and small fishes, sieved from sea water as it passes across their gills. Their passive feeding behaviour contrasts sharply with the aggression shown by other sharks (see photo) and the active hunting of smaller fishes by barracuda and other ocean fishes such as tuna, swordfish and sailfish.

The life cycle of fishes

The eggs of most bony fishes are fertilized externally – the male sprays the eggs with sperm after they have been laid by the female. Eggs are provided with a supply of yolk and a protective coat. Spawning fishes can gather in huge numbers. At high spring tides, millions of grunion are carried up onto the beaches of the southwestern USA, where eggs and sperm are shed and the fertilized eggs are buried in the sand. The eggs hatch only at the next high tide – an example of *moon-phase spawning*.

Where eggs are internally fertilized, as in the coelacanth, the young usually develop inside the female, hatching at or soon before expulsion. Internal fertilization is normal in cartilaginous fishes, the males of which have the pelvic fins adapted as *claspers*, to help maintain contact during copulation and to assist in funnelling in sperm. The common dogfish and skates produce their eggs in hard black capsules with corner tendrils, sometimes called 'mermaids' purses'.

Adult fish generally desert their eggs, but there are examples of guarding and nursing behaviour. The Nile mouthbrooder

carries its newly hatched young inside its mouth, while the discus of South America carries its young on its sides, where they feed on the mucus covering its scales. Male Siamese fighting fish make a nest of bubbles for the young, while the European stickleback uses plant material, and the male guards the eggs until they hatch.

Most hatched young are miniatures of their parents, but there are exceptions. The North American and European eel undergoes an extraordinary multistage development (see p. 170). The young of flatfishes – such as flounders and plaice – are round-bodied, but as they mature, the body twists to the left or right (depending on the species), so that both eyes end up on one side, with the mouth at the edge. Males and females of most fishes differ in appearance, if only in size and sometimes in brightness of colour.

Distribution and habitats

Fishes are *ectotherms* – their metabolic system is generally adapted to the temperature of their habitat, so they are effectively cold-blooded. Fast swimmers such as tuna maintain their body temperatures 3–12 °C (5–22 °F) higher than the surrounding water by eating almost constantly. Antarctic cod survive water temperatures of −2 °C (28 °F) using a protein-based blood antifreeze.

In the twilight zone at depths of 200–1000 m (660–3300 ft), the commonest fish in the oceans, the luminous cyclothone, is found in great shoals. In this region, *luminescence* becomes commoner as location of mates, prey or predators by sight is impossible: up to 80% of fish species carry 'lights' of some kind, often as lures to trap prey.

In the deepest parts of the oceans, below 2000 m (7000 ft), fishes have evolved bizarre adaptations to their habitat (see photo). Many anglerfishes have a luminous 'fishing rod', formed from a ray of the dorsal fin, which extends above the mouth and attracts prey with its fleshy 'bait'. Others, such as the gulper eels, trawl for food with their huge mouths gaping open.

Perhaps the richest habitats for colourful fishes are the tropical coral reefs. Many of these fishes have beaks as well as teeth, which they use to graze on coral and seaweed. The clownfish lives in a symbiotic relationship with stinging sea anemones, thereby gaining protection from predators (see photo, p. 175).   ML-E

A female anglerfish with two parasitic males. In the deepest parts of the oceans the most bizarre fishes of all are found. They are often black or transparent, with light-producing organs and huge eyes to see their food. In several families of anglerfishes, the diminutive males become parasitic on the larger females. They attach themselves by biting into the skin, after which the skin becomes fused and the blood supplies linked.

An Australian grey nurse shark. All sharks are carnivorous, and most are voracious predators, feeding on a very wide range of aquatic animals. Several of the larger sharks have been known to attack humans and small boats, notably the huge 9 m (30 ft) white (or man-eating) shark. However, around 90% of all shark species present no real threat to humans, because they are too small, their teeth are inadequate, or they live at too great a depth.

Amphibians

Amphibians, the majority of which are frogs and toads, have never achieved a total separation from water, and usually spend at least one stage of their life in water. Sharing a common ancestry with lungfishes (see p. 128), they often possess gills as well as lungs, and most have a moist skin, to allow air to pass through it. Their eggs are generally covered in gel, and lack shells and complicated membranes.

The class Amphibia contains over 4000 species and is subdivided into three orders: Anura (frogs and toads); Urodela (newts and salamanders); and Apoda (caecilians). Strictly speaking, the term 'toad' is applied to the members of the family Bufonidae, while 'frog' is used of the family Ranidae. In common usage, however, the two words are used more or less indiscriminately, an anuran with a smooth moist skin being termed a frog, one with a drier, warty skin being referred to as a toad.

Anatomy

The structure of amphibian skin allows oxygen dissolved in water to pass through it and to be absorbed directly into the bloodstream. On land the skin is kept moist by glands that secrete mucus and other protectants, thus allowing some oxygen from the air to dissolve and pass through it. Most frogs and salamanders are highly efficient at 'skin-breathing', but toads are much more reliant on their lungs, and will die if unable to get out of water.

Frogs and toads have well-developed fore-legs and fingers, adapted for digging or holding, while the hind limbs are elongated for leaping or running. Tree frogs have adhesive discs on their toes, making landing more secure. All frogs and toads have large eyes and eyelids, which they blink when they swallow. Many also have a functional *nictitating membrane* – the third eyelid, which lubricates and cleans their eyes – and colour vision with a special sensitivity for blue light, which helps them to find water quickly.

Amphibians – like fish, reptiles and birds – have a single passage, the *cloaca*, for release of eggs and sperm, and expulsion of body wastes. A special feature of many frogs and toads is a highly extendable tongue, which is flicked out, tipped with sticky saliva, to trap unwary prey.

The skeleton of frogs and toads is highly modified, with a single neck vertebra, a short trunk and very short fused ribs. The lower spine and pelvis are fused to form the *urostyle* – the double-arched, saddle-shaped structure that gives adults their squat, humped shape and acts as a shock absorber for leaping. The tail is absent, hence the name 'Anura' (from the Greek word meaning 'tailless').

By contrast, newts and salamanders have well-developed necks and tails, up to 100 vertebrae, and lack the urostyle found in frogs and toads. In general, they spend more of their lives in water than frogs and toads, keep internal gills into adulthood, and can 'breathe' through their skins. Fully aquatic species are often *neotenous* – they retain juvenile features even when sexually mature (see box).

The eyes and limbs of caecilians are small or vestigial, their main sense organs being tentacles on their cheeks. They have up to 250 vertebrae and lack tails. Unlike other amphibians, they often have scales buried in their skin, which is ringed like an earthworm's. These are all adaptations to a burrowing life.

Amphibians' teeth are often poorly developed or absent, and they rely on adhesive tongues or gripping jaws to capture and subdue their prey. Large amphibians can eat nestling birds, snakes, mice, other amphibians, and even bats, while smaller amphibians rely for their diet on insects, fish, tadpoles, slugs and snails.

Amphibian life cycles

The gel-covered eggs of frogs and toads are externally fertilized, like those of most fish. The smell of water and algae attracts both sexes to ponds, streams and damp places. Closeness of male and female is vital and is ensured by a clasping reflex (the *amplexus*). Females may carry males on their backs for weeks before laying eggs, at which point sperm is immediately shed by the male through the cloaca.

Successful fertilization results in the familiar masses of eggs or *spawn*, frogs laying in clumps that float at the surface and toads in strings in deeper water. Once the eggs have been laid, the adults generally take no further interest in them, leaving them to develop on their own (see illustration).

In most other amphibians, fertilization is internal and takes place underwater in the case of newts and salamanders, or underground in the case of most caecilians. Male newts and salamanders have glands on their cheeks or in the cloaca that release chemical signals called *pheromones* (see p. 166), which attract females and make them relax during mating. This allows the transfer of a gel-covered sperm package, the *spermatophore*, which is released by the male and sinks to the bottom, and is then picked up by the female using her cloaca. Male caecilians have a copulatory organ for internal fertilization.

In most cases the eggs are kept inside the female until hatching. The European salamander and some caecilians go one

A European green tree frog. Male frogs and toads attract females by producing croaks distinctive to their species. This is achieved by trapping air in the sac beneath the chin and pumping it backwards and forwards across the vocal cords.

THE LIFE CYCLE OF THE COMMON FROG

1. The fertilized eggs, or **spawn**, remain in their protective gel for about a week. They then hatch into larvae called **tadpoles**, which bear no resemblance to the adult form.

2. During its early weeks, the tadpole feeds mainly on algae. It breathes by means of feathery external gills, which wither away within the first month and are replaced by internal gills.

3. By the time the tadpole is about ten weeks old, the hind limbs and toes have appeared. The tadpole has developed teeth, and can eat small insects, worms and other tadpoles. Meanwhile the front limbs develop within the internal gill chambers, ready to push through. Within a week or so, lungs will have taken over from the gills, allowing the tadpole to breathe air.

4. After four months the limbs are developed, the tail has all but disappeared, and the vertebral column has taken on its final form – the tadpole is now essentially a young frog.

5. The frog is sexually mature by about its third year, and returns to its native pond to breed.

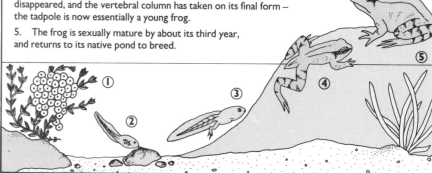

European marbled newts. Adult newts of many species spend much of the year on land, but have to return to water – ponds or stretches of still water – in order to breed.

stage further – the young develop inside the mother's body, and are nurtured by internal secretions. The immature forms of newts and salamanders resemble adults more closely than do frog tadpoles, except that they have external gills and tail fins.

Breeding variations

Some frogs and toads are *ovoviviparous* – they keep their eggs in the oviduct within their bodies, only releasing metamorphosed young from the cloaca as the eggs hatch. The male may carry the eggs, wrapped round the hind legs in the case of the European midwife toad, in the vocal sac in the case of Darwin's frog from South America. The female Surinam toad implants fertilized eggs in her back, where the young develop before finally erupting through the skin. Amazon tree frogs use the water-filled 'vases' at the centre of certain tropical plants, laying their eggs on leaves and carrying the tadpoles on their backs to the water.

Distribution and habitats

Amphibians are *ectotherms*, i.e. cold-blooded. They rely on external heat to maintain normal activity, and this fact is reflected in their habitats and behaviour.

Frogs and toads are found in all continents except Antarctica, with a greater concentration of species in warmer parts. They have exploited water, land and trees equally well. The Javan flying frog glides between trees, using highly developed footwebs. Some have adapted to dry conditions, such as the Arizona spadefoot toad, which spends the dry months in undergound burrows, only emerging after

the seasonal rains – an example of aestivation (see p. 171).

The majority of newts and salamanders are found in the northern hemisphere and are well represented in more temperate regions. Their ability to breathe through the skin as well as the lungs allows some salamanders to live in mud and swamps, such as the mud puppy of the Great Lakes region of North America and the mud eel of southeastern USA. The olm lives in the underground cave pools of Croatia, and has lost both its sight and its pigmentation. Salamanders can also withstand the cold – some species are even found in the Himalaya and Siberian Arctic.

Caecilians are the most specialized amphibians, living in water and earth burrows exclusively in the Equatorial belt.

Life in the deepfreeze

Only recently has it been discovered that some North American frogs – the grey tree frog, the spring peeper, the wood frog and the chorus frog – can survive periods of freezing between 0 and −8 °C (32 and 18 °F). When freezing starts, there is an extremely rapid accumulation in their blood of glucose – or glycerol in the case of the grey tree frog – which acts as a kind of antifreeze. The vital internal organs are insulated from further cooling by the frog's frozen exterior and its glucose- or glycerol-rich cell fluids.

Defence behaviour

Most amphibians are relatively defenceless. Frogs scream or squeak, and toads puff themselves up with air and stand on their tiptoes, appearing to grow to three or four times their normal size. Toads, some salamanders and the great crested newt have another line of defence. Salivary glands in the head and glands in the

● MIGRATION p. 170
● HOW ANIMALS MOVE p. 172
● ECOSYSTEMS: AQUATIC p. 178

NEOTENY

A Mexican axolotl

Typical features of the larval stage of amphibians are the *gills* – loops of tiny blood vessels, clearly seen as feathery clumps on each side of the head. The internal gills are similar, hidden inside pouches in the neck region. Adult newts and salamanders do not lose their internal gills, and some species also keep the external pair. This persistence of juvenile features into sexual maturity is called *neoteny*, and is most clearly seen in the axolotl of Mexico.

An orgy of common toads. Group sex maximizes the chances of at least some tadpoles surviving the stresses of heat and weather to achieve metamorphosis. The tight grip of the male toad on the right – the so-called *amplexus* reflex – ensures that the release of sperm and egg occurs as closely together as possible.

body skin secrete poisons – *bufotoxins* – that affect blood pressure, nerves and muscles in predators. These poisons are extremely potent, hence the use of frog poison by Amazonian Indians to tip their arrows.

Pregnancy diagnosis

African clawed toads are the most aquatic of all toads and frogs, and are highly active breeders, laying more than 100 000 eggs each year. To support this activity they even eat some of their own tadpoles. The first reliable early-pregnancy test for humans was carried out by injecting test urine into mature female clawed toads, which are highly sensitive to pregnancy hormones, and which responded within a few days by profuse egg laying.   ML-E

SEE ALSO

Dinosaurs

The dinosaurs, the most advanced reptiles of all time, dominated the Earth for 140 million years – compared with the 2 million that man has been on the planet. Unlike living reptiles – which either crawl, or walk with their limbs extended out to the sides – dinosaurs walked with their limbs directly under their bodies, just like modern mammals and birds. However, like modern reptiles, most of the dinosaurs were probably cold-blooded.

Many dinosaurs were of gigantic size, some weighing up to 100 tonnes (tons). Nearly 1000 species have been identified, and although the word 'dinosaur' is from the Greek for 'terrible lizard', there were herbivores as well as carnivores.

Beginnings

The ancestors of the dinosaurs are found among the early *thecodonts* ('socket teeth') that lived in the early Triassic period 235 million years ago. Primitive thecodonts were somewhat like modern crocodiles (which also evolved from them). They developed thick, flattened muscular tails for swimming, and longer and more powerful hind limbs to provide the initial thrust for lurching at their prey.

When they emerged onto dry land, the difference in the length of the fore and hind limbs meant that the hind limbs had the potential to move at a greater speed than the fore. This problem was overcome by the first dinosaurs lifting their fore-limbs and running on their hind limbs as bipeds, with the heavy muscular tail acting as a counterbalance. Another crucial factor that enabled dinosaurs to colonize terrestrial habitats was the development of the reptilian egg with its protective shell (see p. 134).

The Triassic period

The first true dinosaurs appeared in the late Triassic period, about 205 million years ago – actually a little later than the first mammals (see p. 140). From the very beginning, two different orders of dinosaur can be distinguished, the Saurischia and the Ornithischia. The *saurischian* ('lizard-hipped') dinosaurs had a pelvic girdle structured like that of modern lizards, whereas the pelvic girdle of *ornithischian* ('bird-hipped') dinosaurs was like that of birds.

The first ornithischians were *ornithopods* ('bird-footed'), and were small bipedal herbivores, about 1 m (40 in) long. Like some modern crocodiles, they seem to have spent the hot summers dormant in their burrows (a process known as *aestivation*; see p. 171).

The first saurischians were the *theropods* ('beast-footed'), a group of bipedal carnivores about 2 m (6½ ft) in length. There were two contrasting kinds: a heavily built, large-headed carnosaur, and a lightly built, long-necked, small-headed coelurosaur. From one group of coelurosaurs eventually evolved a group of giant herbivores, the *sauropods* ('lizard feet').

The sauropods included several massive quadrupedal types such as the brontosaur and the diplodocus, but the largest was the brachiosaur, 25 m (80 ft) long and weighing 100 tonnes (tons). These giants spent much time browsing in lakes and rivers. The water helped to support their weight, and the fact that they could also swim is shown by fossil trackways of the prints of the forelimbs alone.

The Jurassic period

During the Jurassic period, 205–135 million years ago, the giant sauropods were the dominant herbivores. At the same time the carnosaurs developed into huge, ponderous 12 m (40 ft) scavengers. In dramatic contrast, the lightly built coelurosaurs remained small, active hunters – one group was only 60 cm (2 ft) long.

During this period, some reptiles (not strictly dinosaurs) began to return to the sea. Notable examples, both with paddle-like limbs and growing up to 12 m (40 ft) long, were the dolphin-shaped ichthyosaur, which had dorsal and tail fins, and the long-necked plesiosaur. The pterosaurs, another group of reptiles including the pterodactyl, took to the skies, flying on membranous wings with spans of up to 11–12 m (36–39 ft).

SEE ALSO

● GEOLOGICAL TIME CHART p. 85
● EVOLUTIONARY TABLE p. 109
● THE BEGINNINGS OF LIFE p. 110
● EVOLUTION p. 112
● REPTILES p. 134
● EARLY MAMMALS p. 140

TRIASSIC PERIOD (250–205 million years ago)   **JURASSIC PER**

THECODONT
(Protosuchus)

THECODONT
(Shansisuchus)

PTERODACTYL

ORNITHOPOD
(Lesothosaur)

COELUROSAU
(Compsognathus)

The small herbivorous ornithopods continued with little change to the very end of the age of the dinosaurs, apart from a remarkable development that took place in all the ornithischians. This was the development of muscular cheeks, grinding teeth and the formation of a secondary palate separating the nasal passages from the main cavity of the mouth, which allowed them to breathe and chew food at the same time.

Another change that occurred during this period was the appearance of large ornithopods, such as the herbivorous iguanodon. From the evidence of footprints the large ornithopods lived in herds of up to 30 individuals, and such numbers must have afforded protection against predators. An alternative method of defence was illustrated by the stegosaur, which had two pairs of sharp spikes at the end of its tail. The stegosaur also had a double row of vertical bony plates (in some cases spines) running down its back and tail, but it is thought that these were primarily for display.

The Cretaceous period

A more solidly armoured type developed in the Cretaceous period (135–65 million years ago). This was the ankylosaur ('fused lizard'), so called because the thick bony plates covering its back and tail were often fused into a solid sheet over the pelvic region.

From the small bipedal herbivorous ornithopods there eventually evolved such giants as the three-horned triceratops with its huge bony frill extending over the vulnerable neck region. Although the horns were obvious defensive structures, it is now believed that they were mainly used for trials of strength among one another. Other descendants of the small ornithopods included the bone-head dinosaurs, the tops of whose skulls were up to 30 cm (12 in) thick. The bone-heads were perfectly adapted to head butting in the manner of sheep and goats, and they probably lived in herds with a dominant male presiding.

The most successful of the herbivorous dinosaurs were the duckbilled dinosaurs, which evolved from the large ornithopods. They also lived in herds, and maintained communal 'dinosaur nurseries', with the adults caring for the young in much the same way as crocodiles do today.

As the herbivores became more advanced, so too did the carnivores, such as the fearsome-looking tyrannosaur, a bipedal scavenger 6.5 m (21 ft) tall. But by far the most formidable carnivores, although only 3 m (10 ft) long, were the clawed dinosaurs. Hunting in packs, and capable of leaping onto their prey, these bipedal predators bore a large sickle-like claw on the hind foot for ripping open their victims. They also had binocular vision, and well-developed brains – not all dinosaurs had the walnut-sized brain of the stegosaur.

Extinction

One of the greatest unsolved problems relating to the dinosaurs is why they suddenly vanished 65 million years ago. Numerous theories have been put forward, from changes in plant life that made the dinosaurs constipated, to small mammals eating up their eggs.

One of the most popular theories is that the Earth was struck by a large meteorite, 15 km (9 mi) in diameter. This idea is based on the discovery of a thin layer of clay with a high concentration of iridium, a rare metal normally only found in such concentrations in meteorites. If such an object had struck the Earth, it would have thrown up a cloud of dust that could have obscured the Sun for several years. This would explain the disappearance of large land dwellers and the survival of smaller animals.

The problem with this theory is that the dinosaurs had begun to decline 5 million years before their final extinction. In addition, around this time other forms of life became extinct – but these extinctions were separated by tens of thousands of years. Furthermore, they were highly selective, some groups of plants and animals apparently being unaffected.

For a theory of extinction to carry conviction, it must take into account the exact timing of extinctions and their curious selectivity. To date no theory has been able to do this, and the disappearance of the dinosaurs remains a mystery.　　BH

The first bird, the archaeopteryx, appeared about 175 million years ago. In many respects it was indistinguishable from small carnivorous dinosaurs, but the fact that it was covered in feathers indicates that it was warm-blooded – and that it could fly. Many scientists think that at least some of the dinosaurs did not become extinct, but survive in the form of birds.

◀35 million years ago)　　**CRETACEOUS PERIOD** (135–65 million years ago)

TYRANNOSAUR

CLAWED DINOSAUR
(Deinonychus)

DIPLODOCUS

...SAUR

ANKYLOSAUR

TRICERATOPS

Reptiles

Reptiles have succeeded in making a complete break from water by developing two features lacking in living amphibians – scaled waterproof skins and shelled yolk-bearing eggs. It is particularly due to these developments that reptiles have succeeded in adapting to a far wider range of habitats than amphibians.

Nile crocodiles hatching (right). In response to the high-pitched squeaks of her young, the female has opened the nest, exposing the eggs and allowing the young to hatch without suffocating. When they have all hatched, they will join their mother in a nursery area.

The class Reptilia is divided into four orders: Archosauria (the crocodilians – crocodiles, alligators and the gavial, or gharial); Chelonia (the chelonians – turtles and tortoises); Squamata (lizards, snakes and amphisbaenids); and Rhynchocephalia (the tuatara). Of the 6250 or so species of reptile, over 95% are lizards or snakes.

Anatomy

Reptilian scales are developments of skin keratin (a protein also found in hair, nails, hooves, etc.). Scales are small and granular in many lizards, smooth and iridescent in snakes, and large, thick and shield-like in tortoises and alligators. Scales may be periodically shed in flakes, or – in the case of snakes – cast off in a slough of the whole skin.

A green turtle. Turtles may travel thousands of kilometres a year, but they do so at such a leisurely pace that barnacle larvae are able to settle on their shells and grow.

The vertebral column of reptiles is well developed, with snakes having up to 450 vertebrae, each with a pair of ribs. Like fish, birds and amphibians, reptiles have a single passage (the *cloaca*) through which eggs and sperm are released, and body wastes expelled. Almost all reptiles have tails.

Most lizards and all crocodilians have four well-developed limbs, with up to five toes on each. Chelonians have powerful limbs, often heavily clawed for digging, or beautifully adapted as paddles for life in the ocean. The limbs of snakes, burrowing lizards and amphisbaenids are absent or vestigial (reduced in size and function).

The distinguishing feature of turtles and tortoises is their box-like shell, which protects the soft inner organs. It is composed of an upper section, the *carapace*, and a lower plate, the *plastron*. In many species the head, tail and limbs can be withdrawn into the shell for safety.

An obvious feature of snakes and some lizards is the forked tongue. This is flicked rapidly in and out of the mouth, carrying odour molecules to a special sense gland in the roof of the mouth.

The 100 or so species of amphisbaenid, or worm lizard, have their scales arranged in rings, lack limbs and are blind. They burrow in forest floors or sandy, dry or desert areas.

The tuatara of New Zealand is the most archaic reptile, with little change in structure since it first appeared in the Triassic period, over 200 million years ago. Lizard-like in appearance, tuataras have a third eye underneath the skin in their forehead. They also have a much lower metabolic rate than other reptiles: they have been known to live for over 75 years, and their eggs take 15 months to hatch.

The life cycle of reptiles

Fertilization in reptiles is internal, and follows a courtship ritual in which female chemical signals called *pheromones* (see p. 166) and tactile stimulation are important. The annual mass-mating of American garter snakes is a striking example of this. Clutches of eggs are laid, usually in holes in the earth or in mud.

Reptilian eggs are well protected by chalky or leathery shells. Within the shell, the embryo is surrounded by the *amnion*, a membrane that assists gas exchange. Wastes are collected in another membranous sac, the *allantois*. These membranes are characteristic of the *amniote vertebrates*, which also include birds and mammals. Unlike amphibians, reptiles do not pass through an aquatic larval stage (see p. 130), and the hatchlings are miniatures of the parents.

Many species of lizard and snake are *ovoviviparous* – they retain their eggs in the oviduct during the development of the young, which hatch as the eggs are laid. A few species of skink (burrowing lizards) are *viviparous* – they have placenta-like arrangements in the oviduct, similar to those of mammals, supplying nutrition to the developing young. Most species of sea snake hatch their young within the body, so they do not have to leave the water to breed.

Most reptiles abandon their eggs. There are exceptions, however. All crocodiles provide nests for their eggs and protect them until they are ready to hatch. A female may also respond to the call of her young at hatching time, and help them to emerge from the eggs. Some species of crocodile also provide parental care after hatching (see photo). Cobras and the Indian python coil themselves around their eggs and warm them by rapid muscle tremors.

Distribution and habitat

Reptiles are *ectotherms* – they are dependent on their surroundings to maintain their normal body temperature, and are therefore generally cold-blooded. They actively seek warmth when they are cold and avoid it if there is a danger of overheating. If the body temperature of a reptile falls below the optimum (between 25–30 °C/75–85 °F for most reptiles), metabolic functions are reduced and the animal becomes sluggish. Reptilian kid-

heys are highly efficient at water conservation, however, so reptiles have been able to exploit colder, hotter and drier conditions than amphibians.

Many reptiles, including certain turtles, tortoises, snakes and lizards, hibernate during the colder months, slowing their metabolism dramatically. River turtles even have blood-rich patches of membrane in the mouth and cloaca, which help them to absorb oxygen while they are buried in mud.

Diet

Most reptiles are carnivorous, eating invertebrate and vertebrate prey, their particular diet being related both to size and to habitat. Some are herbivores, including many land tortoises and the marine iguana of the Galápagos Islands. Snakes can open their mouths very wide, owing to elastic ligaments between the lower jaw and the skull, which enables them to swallow large prey whole. Anacondas and pythons can even swallow prey the size of young deer and goats.

Pit vipers and boas locate their prey at night using a pair of sense organs in pits in their snouts, and are able to detect temperature differences of as little as .2 °C (0.36 °F). They can pinpoint the position of prey at distances of around half a metre (20 in) by comparing signals from left and right pits.

Saltwater reptiles such as sea snakes, marine turtles and the marine iguana need to have some means of excreting the salt they take in. Snakes and lizards achieve this through a nasal gland (similar to that of birds; see p. 136), and turtles by weeping highly salt tears.

Movement

Snakes move on the ground or in trees or water by using their ribs, side muscles and body scales in various combinations (see p. 172). The sidewinder of southern USA and Mexico minimizes contact with hot sand by sideways wriggling and throwing its body forwards. Some snakes, such as the black mamba of Africa, can exceed 16 km/h (10 mph) for short bursts by lifting the front of their bodies off the ground and 'running' on their ribs. Sea snakes have bodies flattened from side to side and wriggle through the water.

Lizards are generally agile when warmed up. The South American basilisk can even run on its hind legs on water – hence its local name, the Jesu Cristo lizard. With their streamlined shape, marine turtles make graceful and powerful swimmers. Using their strong forelimbs as synchronized paddles, they travel many thousands of kilometres a year.

Escape and defence

Although many lizards have sharp teeth, most rely on their agility to escape predators. A varied repertoire of other defence strategies is also found, however. Some chameleons resemble dead leaves, while others alter their skin colour in response to changes in their surroundings (see box). The frilled lizard of Australia stands on its hind legs, opens its brightly coloured mouth, and expands its neck ruff

The red diamondback, a venomous front-fanged rattlesnake. The pit visible at the front of the snout houses one of two heat-sensitive organs used to detect prey at night. The distinctive rattle is used to warn intruders of the snake's presence.

to scare away predators or rivals. The hooded scaly-foot, another Australian species, resembles a snake, and closely mimics the threat display of a certain poisonous cobra. Only two species of lizard – the Gila monster and beaded lizard of the drylands of the southern USA and Mexico – have poisonous bites, with venom glands located in the lower jaw.

A defensive mechanism known as *autotomy* allows some lizards to cast off a length of tail, which breaks off at a fracture plane running through the tail vertebrae. The discarded tail continues to wriggle as the lizard makes its escape. The soft part of the tail regrows, although never to the original length, but the vertebrae are not replaced.

Snake poisons

The salivary glands of many snakes produce *venom*. The chemical composition of snake venom varies from species to species. The usual effects of snakebite are paralysis of muscles and breathing, and damage to blood and body tissues. However, although thousands of people die each year as a result of snakebite, most snakes are in fact more likely to flee humans than to attack them.

In front-fanged snakes, two very large teeth swing down like the blades of a penknife as the mouth opens wide, and the snake stabs its prey and injects venom in a single movement. The front-fanged cobras are particularly feared because – in addition to biting – they can spit their venom accurately over distances of more than a metre (over 3 feet). Rear-fanged snakes inject venom through grooved teeth closer to the throat, and are less dangerous to humans.   ML-E

SEE ALSO

● DINOSAURS p. 132
● MIGRATION p. 170
● HOW ANIMALS MOVE p. 172

CHAMELEONS

Mainly found in East Africa and Madagascar, chameleons are bizarre-looking creatures that have adapted superbly to life both in trees and on the forest floor. Equipped with excellent natural camouflage, arboreal species grip branches by means of their pincer-like toes and prehensile tails. Special cells in the skin may be contracted or relaxed under nervous control, so producing a range of colours to match the animal's surroundings.

Capable of remaining immobile for hours on end, chameleons vigilantly watch for prey or predator. Their eyes stand well out from their sockets, protected by bulging fused eyelids with a central round hole. The eyes can move in completely different directions from one another, or can be rotated forward to gauge the distance to an insect or small bird with binocular precision. Suddenly, the chameleon's hollow tongue, usually kept collapsed on the floor of the mouth, is shot out, mucus-laden, and retrieves the prey, returning to the mouth like a piece of elastic.

Birds
1. Birds of the Sea and Air

Birds are four-legged vertebrates, with the forelimbs adapted as wings. They share a common ancestry with reptiles – the first bird, the archaeopteryx (see p. 133), had many characteristics in common with certain dinosaurs – and, in common with reptiles, birds have the characteristic of laying eggs in which the developing embryo is protected by a fluid-filled bag (see p. 134). Unlike reptiles, however, birds are warm-blooded, generating their body heat from the breakdown of their food – a feature they share with mammals.

A black-chested harrier eagle (right). Birds of prey, such as vultures, condors and eagles, have broad, splay-feathered wings, perfectly suited to soaring and floating on thermals over land. Eagles typically soar until they sight prey on the ground, whereupon they swoop down to stun and kill it.

Of the 28 orders and 8600 species that make up the class Aves, to which all birds belong, 6 orders and nearly 15% of species are birds of the sea and air. Four of these orders, with nearly 500 species, are made up primarily of sea birds: Sphenisciformes (penguins; 18 species); Procellariiformes (albatrosses, petrels, shearwaters, fulmars; 100 species); Pelecaniformes (pelicans, gannets, frigate birds, boobies, cormorants, shags; 60 species); and Charadriiformes (shore and island birds such as waders, gulls, terns and auks; over 300 species). The birds of the air – including many of the most accomplished flyers, some of which spend the greater part of their lives airborne – are classified in two orders: Falconiformes (falcons, hawks, eagles, condors, vultures; 300 species) and Apodiformes (swifts and hummingbirds; almost 400 species).

SEE ALSO
- BIRDS 2 p. 138
- TERRITORY, MATING, SOCIAL ORGANIZATION p. 168
- MIGRATION p. 170
- HOW ANIMALS MOVE p. 172
- ECOSYSTEMS pp. 178–87

Aerodynamics

The wings of flying birds create lift in exactly the same way as the wings of an aircraft – by causing air to move faster over the convex upper surface than the concave lower surface. Forward thrust is provided as the wings are flapped down and back (see p. 173).

Emperor penguins, the largest of the penguins, are agile and rapid swimmers even under ice, where they hunt fish and squid. They leave the water only to breed and to raise their chicks on the surface of the permanent Antarctic icepacks.

The wings are attached to the body by mobile shoulder joints, by the wishbone (or *furcula*), which increases the spring of the wing beat, and by massive pectoral muscles, attached to a deep breastbone. Greatly lengthened and fused digits form the outer third of the wing, supporting the main flight feathers. Manoeuvrability is assisted by rotation of the wings at the shoulders, angulation of the tail, and alteration of the position of the tail and flight feathers.

The wings of birds of the sea and air are shaped to make the most of their habitats. Albatrosses, terns and swifts – airborne for much or most of their lives – have long thin wings for gliding on the trade winds of the oceans. Vultures, condors, buzzards and eagles (see photo) have broad splay-feathered wings for soaring and floating on thermals over land. The effortless soaring of the wandering albatross – with a massive wingspan of over 3 m (9¾ ft) – contrasts sharply with the extraordinary aerobatics of the tiny hummingbirds, some of which can even fly backwards.

Birds adapted to swimming and diving in the sea are often stubby and bullet-shaped, with blade-like wings and streamlined bodies. Auks, guillemots, puffins and penguins (see photo) are typical, with webbed feet far back on the body, giving them an upright posture on land and excellent steering abilities in water.

Anatomy

The most characteristic feature of birds is their feathers. *Feathers* are made of keratin, the same protein as in mammalian hair and nails. Each feather has a central shaft (the *quill*) and its own blood and nerve supply. Many soft hair-like projections called *barbs* are set out in two rows, one on each side of the quill; the barbs interlock to provide insulation and minimal air resistance. Closer to the skin is a layer of soft short feathers (*down*), which give added insulation. Feathers (like hair) can be erected in order to regulate temperature.

The flight feathers on the wings and the tail feathers have the strongest quills, in order to withstand the tremendous stresses of flight and steering. In addition, the feathers on the wings are embedded in the armbones. To maximize insulation and water-repellence, the feathers of penguins are particularly soft and filamentous, and are closely packed on the skin.

Next to a bird's tail is the *preen* (or *uropygeal*) *gland*, which secretes skin oil. This oil is particularly important in sea and water birds, because it waterproofs the surface feathers as a bird preens itself. The secretions from this gland may also give birds their characteristic smell, such as the muskiness of storm petrels. Several ocean-going birds such as gannets and albatrosses excrete excess salt (from sea water taken in with food) not through the kidneys, but through modified tear glands, ejecting the salt-rich fluid from their nostrils or mouth.

Vision

Sea and air birds have large eyes and good vision. Those that sight their prey while flying are able to detect movement and detail at much greater distances than humans. Hawks have a double *fovea* (part of the retina) in which there are only *cones* – nerve cells sensitive to fine detail in bright light – and this allows them to pinpoint their prey. Vultures have a higher magnification in the centre of their field of view, enabling them to recognize prey even if it is not moving. Penguins, on the other hand, have flat corneas (the transparent part at the front of the eye) ideal for underwater vision but making them very short-sighted on land.

Many sea birds are attracted to red, possibly because oil droplets in their retinal cones absorb green and blue light. Nestlings peck at red spots on the beaks of adult birds, stimulating regurgitation of food. Penguins, which make nests out of pebbles, habitually steal the 'best' ones from their neighbours' nests, and a pile of red pebbles put at one edge of a penguin rookery will rapidly migrate towards the other side.

Diet

Modern birds lack teeth. Instead, they have *beaks* or *bills* – horny coverings to their jaws – the shape of which often reflects their diet (see illustration).

Most ocean birds are fish-eaters, and their bills are sharp and strong, with serrated edges and often hooked tips to hold slipery fish. Pelicans dive into the sea and catch fish with their long bills, storing them in a pouch under the bill. Storm petrels of the southern hemisphere skip at the surface of the sea, collecting small fish, plankton and crustaceans. Groups of gannets dive from heights of up to 30 m (100 ft) to take shoaling fish. Ocean birds follow their food wherever it is most abundant, often to the extremes of Arctic and Antarctic seas.

Coastal birds such as fulmars and auks live on rocky cliffs. Others, including terns, waders and some gulls, prefer flatter ground, while puffins live in burrows. All either catch fish by diving and swimming or gather invertebrates from the intertidal zones. The Atlantic puffin has a stout bill striped yellow and red with which it catches several fish at a time, diving underwater and swimming strongly with its wings. Waders such as the oystercatcher, redshank and avocet, all birds of Atlantic beaches, probe for crustaceans, shellfish and insects on mud flats and shores with their long beaks.

Some birds are scavengers, such as the snowy sheathbill of the South Atlantic and Antarctica, which eats seaweed, carrion and young seals. Although feeding on fish at other times, its counterpart in the North Atlantic, the great skua, harries nesting and feeding birds during its own nesting season to steal their eggs, chicks and food. The frigate bird of the Galápagos Islands has a long hooked beak with which it scoops up fish, squid and jellyfish. It also terrorizes other birds into regurgitating their food, which it then steals. Many gulls have adapted to feeding on human refuse, and are steadily moving inland in some areas.

Birds of prey are almost all carnivores, taking birds, reptiles, mammals, and sometimes fish. They have strong hooked beaks, and their toes, arranged three forward and one back, are armed with long sharp curving claws (talons).

Old and New World vultures are carrion-eaters. They have featherless heads and necks, and sharp beaks to cope with dead animals. They belong to different families, however, their similarities being an example of convergent evolution. The small Egyptian vulture also eats animal droppings, preferring lion faeces, which are high in undigested protein.

The osprey is widely distributed throughout the world and eats fish, diving at them feet-first and gripping them with its claws and spiked soles. The American bald eagle is also a fish-eater, and often follows salmon on their spawning runs to catch exhausted fish. Most hawks and eagles perch or soar until they sight prey on the ground, then drop from a height to stun and kill it. Others, such as the peregrine falcon, hobby and goshawk of the northern hemisphere, are aggressive and acrobatic hunters, chasing and catching birds on the wing.

Hummingbirds are nectar-sippers (see illustration), some long-tubed flowers even using them as pollinators (see p. 121). They also eat insects, catching them in flight or on flowers. Except when nesting, swifts spend all their life in the air, and feed entirely on insects, which they catch in flight.

Breeding habits

Many sea and coast birds such as auks, gannets, penguins and boobies nest in huge colonies (see photo). The passage from egg to independence may take as little as six weeks, as in the North Atlantic razorbill, while albatrosses may take as long as 12 months to lay and incubate their eggs, and to rear the chicks until they can fly. The young albatross then sets off to ride the trade winds round the globe for years before it reaches sexual maturity and begins to seek a nesting site. Emperor penguins do not make nests: the single egg is transferred to a pouch between the male bird's belly and feet as soon as it is laid and then several thousand males huddle together, so that the eggs are protected from the cold of the Antarctic ice.

Swifts glue their nests together with saliva. Those of cave swiftlets – used to make Chinese bird's-nest soup – are entirely made up of hardened saliva. Most birds of prey make their untidy nests in or on trees, or on rocky ledges. Sparrowhawks and peregrines have even been known to nest on the window ledges of high city buildings.   ML-E

Cape gannets on Bird Island, South Africa. Many sea birds nest in huge noisy colonies, each pair establishing a tiny territory and mates recognizing one another by voice and by pair-bonding displays. The vast colonies formed by penguins are similarly spectacular (see photo, p. 169).

Toco toucan. Toucans have huge beaks, almost as long as their bodies. The beak is used to pluck fruit from branch tips, and may be important in display.

Caribbean flamingo. Towering on their long thin legs, flamingos hold their beaks upside down to sieve water fleas and small fish from shallow lakes and ponds.

Rufous hummingbird. Hummingbirds use their bills to reach to the bottom of tubular flowers, from which they suck nectar through their tube-shaped tongues.

Gold-and-blue macaw. Parrots have powerful beaks, enabling them to lever themselves up trees and to break open the hardest nuts; however, they can also be used with great delicacy in grooming and courtship.

Goshawk. Birds of prey have sharp beaks ideally suited to slashing and dismembering their prey. Their nostrils are protected from clogging with blood by tufts of feather.

Black skimmer. Skimmers feed on the wing, with the lower jaw cutting the surface water and the upper jaw ready to snap down on any aquatic life that is channelled in.

Birds
2. Birds of the Land and Water

Of the 8600 species of bird, about 7500 – over 85% of all species – live in close association with land or fresh water. In land and water birds, there are often clear differences between the sexes, in size, colour and feather patterns. The diversity of their habitats and diets in comparison to sea birds has led to a greater range of territorial and mating behaviour, as well as great variations in size, shape and aerodynamics. Most of the land birds belong to a single order (the perching birds), and it is with these that the clearest distinction between land and sea birds – birdsong – has reached its greatest development.

The order Passeriformes (perching birds) contains between 4500 and 5000 species – more than half of all bird species. Three orders of birds are particularly important to man as sources of food and domesticated birds: Columbiformes (pigeons, doves; over 300 species), Galliformes (pheasants, turkeys, fowl, game birds; 270 species) and Anseriformes (ducks, geese, screamers, swans; 170 species). The members of the orders Caprimulgiformes (nightjars, frogmouths; about 90 species) and Strigiformes (owls; over 145 species) share nocturnal habits and fascinating adaptations associated with their life style. Amongst the most colourful of birds are those in the orders Psittaciformes (parrots, cockatoos, macaws; 315 species), Piciformes (woodpeckers, barbets, tou-cans; almost 400 species) and Trogoniformes (quetzals, trogons; 35 species).

Ground and perching birds

While the forelimbs of birds are modified into wings (see p. 136), the hind, or pelvic, limbs – the legs – are usually covered in scales and armed with curving nails, the *claws*. Ground birds use their claws to dig and gather food, while perching birds use them to grip branches. Three digits face forwards for propulsion, one faces backwards as a support, but is sometimes vestigial (reduced in size and function).

Owls and tree-living birds such as woodpeckers and trogons are *zygodactylous* – the third toe also faces backwards, increasing the strength of their grip. In owls, all toes are equally well developed, with very sharp talons for grappling with prey. Parrots use their beaks for climbing, using the upper part to lever themselves up. Young hoatzin, primitive South American galliforms, have clawed thumbs on their wings, which they use for scrambling through trees.

Flightless birds

The 10 species of flightless birds (or ratites) are the most primitive birds, and are the remnants of a group once found worldwide. They have flat breastbones, often large legbones and wings that are reduced in size. It is now thought that such birds were probably never capable of flying.

Apart from the kiwi of New Zealand, 50 cm (20 in) tall, flightless birds range in size from 1.5 m (5 ft) to the largest living bird – the ostrich of Africa (see photo, p. 113), towering above humans at up to 2.75 m (9 ft). The group also includes the cassowaries of Australia and New Guinea, the rheas of South America (see photo, p. 113) and the emu of Australia. Their feathers are hair- or plume-like. Several females often lay in the same nest, and the eggs are then incubated by the male. The egg of an ostrich is equal in volume to 25–40 chicken eggs, while the huge extinct ele-phant birds of Madagascar laid eggs that weighed around 10 kg (22 lb).

Some species of flying bird, such as the New Zealand rails and the kakapo, a nocturnal parrot, have become flightless, usually in island habitats in the absence of predators. Such birds are now under severe pressure both from humans and from introduced predators.

Swimmers and divers

Unlike sea birds such as penguins, which use their wings as flippers, propulsion in water birds is generally achieved by kicking with powerful legs. Ducks, swans and loons (divers) have webbed feet, while grebes and finfoots have fringed paddle-like toes. Most water birds dabble and dive for plants, insects, molluscs and crustaceans. Some, such as the mergansers and red-throated divers of North Atlantic and Pacific waters, dive for fish. The dipper, a passerine that hunts crustaceans and larvae in fast mountain streams in the northern hemisphere, lacks strong legs, and swims using its wings instead.

Dippers and divers have flexible lenses in their eyes, allowing them to see as well under water as in the air. Like sea birds, water birds have well-developed preen glands (see p. 136) to waterproof their feathers.

Feather colours

The colours of birds' feathers are produced by a combination of structural effects and actual pigments in the feather keratin. Light may be absorbed or dispersed by feathers, resulting in unshiny dark or light areas, or may be diffracted by the feather filaments, producing the marvellous iridescence and metallic sheens seen, for example, on starling and peacock feathers.

Most reds and oranges result from the presence of carotenoid pigments related to vitamin A, and the light-sensitive reti-

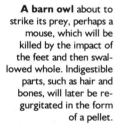

A barn owl about to strike its prey, perhaps a mouse, which will be killed by the impact of the feet and then swallowed whole. Indigestible parts, such as hair and bones, will later be regurgitated in the form of a pellet.

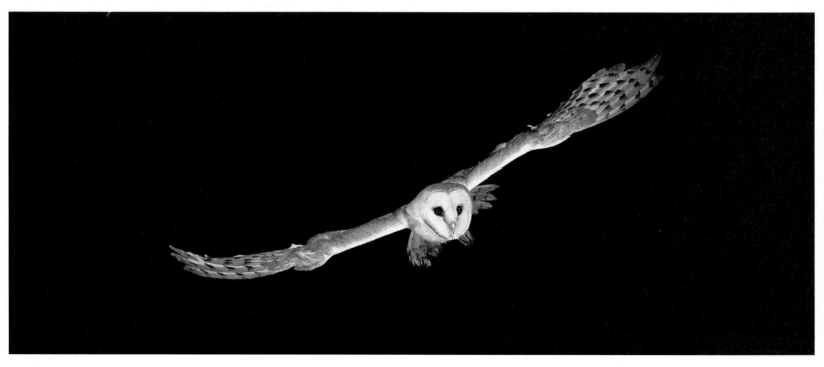

nal pigment rhodopsin, which comes from foodstuffs. Melanin, the dark pigment associated with keratin in mammalian hair and dark skin, is responsible for yellows, browns, greens and blues. Turacos, African birds related to cuckoos, have brilliant red and green colours different from those of all other birds. These colours are based on copper-containing pigments related to haemoglobin, the oxygen-carrying protein in red blood cells.

Bird senses

For most birds, vision is the most important sense. Nocturnal birds, such as owls, frogmouths and nightjars, have large eyes with a high proportion of *rods* – retinal cells sensitive to movement in dim light. The barn owl's sight is up to 100 times better than a human's (see photo).

Acute hearing can, also be important. Owls have left and right earflaps in slightly different positions on their heads, allowing them to fix the position of noises more accurately. They also have large eardrums to amplify tiny sounds. Their feathers are very soft, resulting in almost soundless flight – an adaptation that fishing owls lack, not needing silence to catch their prey. Oilbirds, relatives of the nightjar, also rely on their hearing, although not in order to detect prey – they eat seeds and fruits. They live in dark caves where they navigate by listening to the echoes of their vocal clicks.

Smell is generally poorly developed in birds, but a notable exception is the kiwi. It has very small eyes and detects earthworms and grubs by smell, having nostrils at the very tip of its long flexible beak. The part of the kiwi's brain associated with smell is far better developed than in all other birds. Parrots use their tongues a great deal, rolling nuts and seeds round in their beaks to test their shape and find a good place to start chewing.

Birdsong

Song is part of a bird's territorial and mating behaviour. In songbirds, which make up over 40 of the 60 or so families in the order Passeriformes, the *syrinx*, an organ at the base of the windpipe, with its own muscles and nerve supply, is especially well developed. As air vibrates the syrinx membranes, the muscles alter their tension, allowing tones of different pitch and timbre to be produced. The chick's basic noise patterns are inherited, but more complex patterns are learned from older birds. Canaries are well known for their varied repertoire. At the end of each breeding season, brain cells die and songs are lost; at the beginning of the next season new cells grow and new songs enter the repertoire.

Some birds are less selective about the sounds they copy. Starlings will even imitate the ringing of telephones, and the mynas of Asia are accomplished mimics. Members of the parrot and crow families – reckoned to be the most intelligent groups of birds – will learn and repeat phrases of human language. African grey parrots are particularly skilled and may have vocabularies of around 1000 words. However, this ability is pure mimicry, and does not indicate an understanding of human speech.

Dances and displays

Dances and displays are also part of territorial and mating behaviour. The need for male birds to impress and attract females has led to the evolution of spectacular feather coloration and bizarre mating rituals, as in the birds of paradise and the bowerbirds (see photos, and p. 168).

Many relatives of the chicken also have spectacular displays. Male argus pheasants of Southeast Asia and Indian peacocks attract females by spreading and vibrating their fan-shaped tails and elongated wing feathers. Males of the grouse family, such as the European blackcock and the prairie chicken of the central USA, have display grounds called *leks* (see p. 168), where all the males dance, jump and court the females. The prairie chicken stamps its feet and has a loud booming call, accentuated by orange-skinned neck pouches, which are inflated as resonators. All members of the crane family make displays – not only in the breeding season – that involve huge leaps, wing-flapping, bowing and dancing on tiptoe.

Breeding behaviour

Apart from species such as swans and grebes, where pair-bonding is the norm and may be renewed from year to year (see photo), most birds exhibit patterns of behaviour or body characteristics that attract females to males that are superior in some way (see pp. 168–9). Fighting for females is not always involved: European pheasant females, for instance, prefer to mate with males that have longer legspurs, a feature that appears to be genetically associated with greater fertility. In the case of the European swallow, it is the length of the male's outer tail feathers that determines attractiveness.

Fertilization in all birds is internal, by cloacal contact – although anseriforms (such as ducks and geese) and the flightless ratites have a protrusible cloaca that serves as a penis. As the fertilized ovum passes down the female's oviduct to the exterior, it is gradually coated in various layers. First it is provided with a food supply (the *yolk*), and then robed in *albumen* (the egg white), which acts as a cushion and supplies water. The albumen is then coated in membranes (to offer protection against bacteria), and finally covered in several shell layers. Shells are protective and waterproof, but have pores and allow gas transfer. The eggs are incubated in a nest, mostly by the female, who may strip feathers off her breast to improve transfer of heat from her skin. Many species of cuckoo are parasitic – they lay their eggs in the nest of a bird of another species, leaving the young to

The greater bird of paradise. Mainly found in New Guinea, birds of paradise make spectacular courtship displays. The males of many species dance on branches or hang upside down and swing to and fro while shimmering their brilliant feathers.

Male bowerbirds (above) of Australasia construct elaborate display grounds called bowers, which they adorn with all manner of objects. Females are attracted to the bower for mating, and subsequently care for the eggs and young unaided.

SEE ALSO

● BIRDS I p. 136
● ANIMAL COMMUNICATION p. 166
● TERRITORY, MATING, SOCIAL ORGANIZATION p. 168
● MIGRATION p. 170
● HOW ANIMALS MOVE p. 172
● ECOSYSTEMS p. 178–87
● LIVESTOCK FARMING p. 190

be reared by the foster parent (see photo, p. 174).

An unusual method of incubation is found in the mallee fowl and scrub fowl, both members of a strange family restricted to Australasia and Indonesia. They build huge mounds of vegetation or earth (depending on habitat) in which females lay their eggs. The male then guards his mound and tests the temperature with special heat-sensors on his back: too hot, and he scrapes off material; too cool, and he builds up the mound. The mallee fowl chick can fly within a day of hatching. In most other bird species, however, chicks are helpless and are fed by one or other parent until their flight feathers emerge and they are ready to leave the nest. ML-E

Great crested grebes. Pair-bonding is essential in grebes because both parents are involved in nest building and rearing of young. The bond is formed and then reinforced by elaborate and highly ritualized courtship displays, which include head shaking, preening, diving and weed carrying.

Early Mammals

The word *mammal* is derived from the Latin *mamma* ('the breast') and refers to the fundamental feature of the group: the production of milk from the mother. In virtually all mammals the foetus develops inside the *uterus* (womb) of the mother. The exceptions are the *monotremes*, which – like their reptilian ancestors and the birds – lay eggs (see p. 142).

In the *marsupial mammals* (see p. 142) the foetus is surrounded by a thin membrane within the uterus, and is kept in a pouch when born. In the *placental mammals*, which comprise the vast majority of modern species – including man – nutrients and oxygen are passed to the foetus via an organ within the uterus called the *placenta* (see pp. 202–3).

In order that the young can suckle and breathe at the same time, the food and air passages of mammals are separated by a bony secondary palate. This also allows food to be processed in the mouth, and mammals have developed different types of teeth for accomplishing different tasks: *incisors* for biting, *canines* for stabbing and *cusped teeth* (*premolars* and *molars*) for chewing and grinding.

Mammals are warm-blooded, maintaining a constant internal temperature (*homoiothermy*) by means of a high metabolic rate in conjunction with an insulating covering of hair or fur. The final characteristic of the mammals is their intelligence: the neocortex (that part of the brain responsible for intelligence) is more highly developed in mammals than in any other kind of vertebrate.

The ancestors of the mammals

The first reptiles that conquered the land about 295 million years ago were the mammal-like reptiles or *paramammals*. From the detailed structure of paramammal skulls it is presumed that the mammals originated from them. All early paramammals were carnivores, the smallest ones feeding on insects and worms, the larger ones on the smaller reptiles. However, by about 250 million years ago one major group, the *dicynodonts* ('two dog tooths'), had become herbivores. By the Triassic period, 235 million years ago, the paramammals – such as the mainly carnivorous *cynodonts* ('dog tooths') – were much more mammalian in their appearance: in the structure of their skeletons, their stance and gait, their feeding and chewing, and in the inferred development of warm-bloodedness, fur, and possibly milk production.

In one of the most striking faunal turnabouts in the history of life on Earth, the paramammals began to go into a serious decline. By the Jurassic period, 185 million years ago, only a few herbivores had managed to survive. In place of the paramammals had come the dinosaurs, which emerged about 205 million years ago and which were to dominate life on land for the next 140 million years (see p. 132).

The first mammals

It was during the later Triassic, about 220 million years ago, that the first true mammals appeared. Throughout the age of the dinosaurs, the mammals remained small, and were shrew-like or rat-like in appearance and life style. Because of their fur and warm-bloodedness, they could adapt to nocturnal activity, unlike the cold-blooded dinosaurs. By the end of the Cretaceous, 65 million years ago, the first primate, *Purgatorius*, had made its appearance. This bore a striking resemblance to a present-day group of mammals, the *tree shrews* (see illustration).

When the dinosaurs became extinct at this time, and the ecological niches they had occupied became vacant, the mammals began to extend their range and to adapt themselves to a wide range of habitats. They were by no means dominant at first: for a time giant flightless flesh-eating birds – about 2 m (6½ ft) tall and with skulls as large as horses' heads – were the dominant carnivores. In spite of this the mammals were able to establish themselves.

The age of the mammals begins

When the dinosaurs had begun to spread over the planet, all the continents were united in the single land mass of Pangea: in contrast, when the age of mammals began 65 million years ago, the continents were separate (see pp. 78–9). Similar-looking mammals evolved independently on the different continents to fill the same kinds of niches. Although not directly related, these animals would have shared a common ancestor. Hence, for example, on the grasslands of South America there were animals resembling modern camels, horses, rhinoceroses and elephants, and even a large marsupial cat. There were also unique creatures, such as the giant ground sloths and armoured glyptodonts, which survived into historic times.

A major event in the history of the mammals occurred during the Miocene epoch, 23 million years ago, when Africa collided with Eurasia at either end of what is now the Mediterranean. This new land connection allowed the mammals of Europe and Asia to invade Africa, and by the same token the unique African mammals, the elephants and apes, migrated north to conquer Eurasia.

The grasslands

Fundamental changes in mammalian life came about with the gradual replacement of forests and woodlands by grasslands

GLYPTODONT
(*Daedicurus*)

SOUTH AMERICAN MAMMALS
65–23 million years ago

GIANT GROUND SLOTH
(*Megatherium*)

LITOPTERN
(*Theosodon*)

MARSUPIAL CAT
(*Thylacasmilus*)

A green tree shrew, one of the 16 species of tree shrew that make up the unique order Scandentia. Tree shrews range from 10 to 22 cm (4 to 8 ½ in) in length, excluding tail. Although similar to shrews and other insectivores in appearance, their closest resemblance is to the very first primates, which first appeared 65 million years ago.

SEE ALSO

● EVOLUTION p. 112
● DINOSAURS p. 132
● MAMMALS pp. 142–65
● PHYSICAL EVOLUTION (HUMAN) p. 200
● ANATOMY AND PHYSIOLOGY pp. 202–23
● HUMAN PREHISTORY p. 362
● PREHISTORIC ART p. 504

not adapted, and so it was the generalists rather than the specialists that dominated life in the Pleistocene.

Cattle (in the form of bison in North America), sheep and pigs were the key herbivores everywhere, and the most adaptable of the carnivores – the cats and dogs – held their own by virtue of their superior intelligence. But it was the rats and mice that became the most numerous and successful of all the mammals. One other highly adaptable mammal, with an ability to use tools and harness fire, also began to emerge: man.

When the ice caps spread from the polar regions into central Europe, the permafrost and tundra reached as far south as the Alps and Himalaya. The great plains of Eurasia and North America were inhabited by woolly mammoths and woolly rhinoceroses, which grazed on the tundra – the tundra at this period supported a much richer plant-life than it does today. These large mammals were preyed upon by carnivores such as the sabre-toothed cat, with its long stabbing canine teeth. Caves became important as shelters for many animals, including humans and the large cave bears that they hunted. Indeed, much of our detailed knowledge of the appearance of ice-age mammals comes from the figurines of Cro-Magnon man of 30 000 years ago, and from later cave paintings (see p. 504).

Why are many of these great mammals of the Pleistocene no longer around? One theory suggests that they were victims of man's improving technology and were simply hunted to extinction: these extinctions seem to correlate with the advent of the hand-axe culture of early man and his use of fire. With the end of the last Ice Age 10 000 years ago, the plant-rich tundra disappeared, and this may also have contributed to the extinction of so many species. BH

during the late Oligocene and early Miocene epochs (28–18 million years ago). Horses, which had been browsers of leaves, became long-legged, fast-running grazers. The same basic changes occurred among the cattle and antelopes. As well as being able to run fast, they were able to observe the approach of predators over large distances on the open grasslands. This had startling consequences for the main groups of carnivores, which in fact became extinct.

In this new environment there was a premium on intelligence, and it was on the grasslands that modern cats and dogs evolved in the Miocene epoch (23–5.3 million years ago). Neither cats nor dogs can catch their prey by simply chasing it – they do not have the speed capability. Instead they use complex stratagems:

dogs hunt in packs, and cats, although solitary, use cunning and stealth to pounce on their victims.

Another consequence of the great reduction of forests was that the tree-dwelling primates found themselves on open grasslands. But because of their intelligence and ability to work together in teams, the savannah-living apes of the Miocene epoch in Africa and Eurasia were able not only to survive but to spread over vast areas.

The present-day game reserves of East Africa – with their great variety of specialized mammals – represent the type of ecosystem that first arose in the Miocene grasslands. This diversity came to an end in most parts of the world with the ice ages of the Pleistocene epoch, 1.6 million to 10 000 years ago (see p. 90).

The epoch of the ice ages

During the wide range of conditions and types of plant life that follow one another with dramatic climatic change, it is hardly possible for any animal to specialize on one type of food or indeed to specialize at all on anything. The key to survival and success is to be adaptable,

ICE AGE MAMMALS
1.6 million–10 000 years ago

WOOLLY MAMMOTH
(Mammuthus primigenius)

SABRE-TOOTHED CAT
(Machairodus latidens)

WOOLLY RHINO
(Coelodonta tichorhinus)

Monotremes and Marsupials

The monotremes and marsupials are the most primitive living mammals, and are distinguished from all other mammals by their methods of reproduction. Whereas the majority of mammals – the *placental mammals* – typically retain their young within the uterus (womb) until fairly well developed, this is not the case with either monotremes or marsupials. Monotremes are unique among mammals in that they lay eggs, and – although females have mammary glands – they do not have nipples. Marsupials, on the other hand, give birth to minute, near-embryonic young. These then clamber up the mother's hair to her nipples, which are usually situated within a pouch (the *marsupium*) on the abdomen, where the young complete their development.

Two families make up the order of monotremes (Monotremata), with a total of just three living species, all confined to Australasia: the single species of the platypus family, and the two species of echidna, or spiny anteater. There are some 250 species of marsupial mammal (order Marsupialia), divided into 15 families, the majority of which are found only in Australasia.

The duck-billed platypus and the two species of echidna are the only mammals to lay eggs. The young are no more than about 1.5 cm (³/₅ in) long at the time of hatching, and – because female platypuses lack teats – are nourished by lapping milk from the fur on their mother's abdomen.

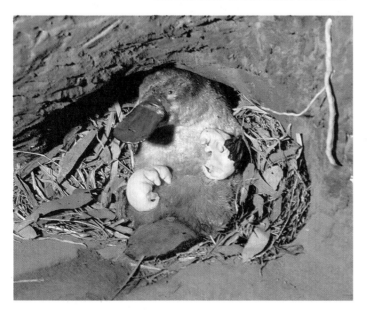

Monotremes

Despite laying eggs and sharing certain anatomical similarities with reptiles, the monotremes exhibit two essential mammalian features – body hair and mammary glands. Male monotremes have a spur on each ankle, which – in the platypus – is connected to a poison gland.

The duck-billed platypus of eastern Australia and Tasmania is of such extraordinary appearance that when the first specimen was brought to Europe in 1798, it was thought to be a fake. The platypus's distinctive characteristics – leathery duck-like bill, flattened tail and webbed feet (see photo) – are admirably suited to its semi-aquatic life style. It is a strong swimmer and eats freshwater shrimps and insect larvae. The feet are clawed and used for burrowing in riverbanks, where the platypus makes its home.

The echidnas, or spiny anteaters, of Australia and New Guinea are burrowers. They are superficially like hedgehogs in appearance, and – like hedgehogs – may roll into a ball when threatened. They have powerful claws for digging, and long snouts and sticky tongues with which to trap their insect prey.

Marsupials

Australia separated from other land masses (see p. 78) before placental mammals were able to establish themselves, so it is chiefly in Australia that marsupials have been able to realize their full potential. In the absence of competition from other mammals, marsupials have filled most of the ecological niches occupied by 'true' mammals elsewhere, and range from tiny shrew-like insectivorous species to wolf-like carnivores. Thus, for instance, there is a marsupial mole, remarkably similar in appearance and life style to placental moles – although it has rodent-like grinding teeth. Another marsupial – the wombat – shares the burrowing life of the badger, and resembles the badger in shape and size.

Tree kangaroos are remarkably agile, despite showing few adaptations to their specialized habitat. The hind feet are notably unsuited to tree climbing, and the tail – while offering considerable stability – is not prehensile.

Marsupials are found in other parts of Australasia, particularly in New Guinea, and are represented in the Americas by the opossums. They do not occur in such great diversity outside Australia, however, perhaps because these other areas were colonized early on by placental mammals.

Kangaroos

The members of the kangaroo family (Macropodidae) include the largest living marsupials. There are over 50 species of kangaroo, the biggest of them – the red kangaroo of the arid plains of central Australia – growing to a height of 1.5 m (5 ft) or more. They are mainly grazers, filling the niche occupied by sheep or antelope in other parts of the world. The smaller kangaroos known as wallabies fill some of the niches occupied elsewhere by rabbits and hares. A few, such as the tiny musk rat-kangaroos, are largely insectivorous.

Kangaroos are the only mammals – with the exception of man – to move mainly or solely on two legs. The forelimbs are small and generally held clear of the ground, while the enlarged, well-muscled hind limbs provide the propulsive force for their bounding movement (see p. 173). The larger kangaroos attain considerable speeds as they move forward in huge leaps of 6 m (20 ft) or more. The kangaroo's long powerful tail acts as a counterweight, providing stability on landing. The tail also serves as a balance for the handful of species – the tree kangaroos – that live in the tropical forests of New Guinea and Queensland (see photo).

Dasyurid marsupials

The main group of carnivorous and insectivorous marsupials, the dasyurids (family Dasyuridae), contains nearly 50 species, most of which are nocturnal. They range in size from tiny marsupial 'mice' (dunnarts) around

THE THYLACINE

Until its extinction, the largest carnivorous marsupial was the thylacine, or Tasmanian wolf. It often grew to a length of over 1.5 m (5 ft) from nose to tail, and was the only native carnivore capable of bringing down the larger kangaroos. It once occurred on the Australian mainland as well as Tasmania, but was probably exterminated by competition with dingoes (see p. 154), brought to Australia by the Aboriginal settlers. By the time of the arrival of European colonists in 1788, thylacines were already confined to Tasmania. Here they were persecuted and exterminated by sheep farmers, the last probably dying in the 1930s.

9.5 cm (3¾ in) long to native 'cats' (in fact more similar to genets), such as the quoll, nearly 1 m (39 in) long. The smaller species, such as the shrew-like planigale and the antechinus, are voracious predators, often killing prey – insects, reptiles and small mammals – almost as big as themselves. Some species of dunnart, especially those living in arid habitats where food supplies can be erratic, are capable of accumulating fat reserves in the tail. They can also become torpid, sleeping with their energy consumption very much reduced (see p. 171).

The powerful and heavily built Tasmanian devil (see photo) was formerly found over much of Australia, but is now confined to Tasmania. Its squat body supports a massive head with powerful hyena-like jaws that enable it to smash through the bones of carrion.

The koala

The koala of eastern Australia superficially resembles a small thick-set bear (see photo). It is a highly specialized tree-climbing species, lacks a tail, and feeds almost exclusively on eucalyptus trees, eating as much as 1.5 kg (3¼ lb) of leaves a day. The koala's single offspring remains in the mother's pouch for as long as six months, and then rides around on her back until it is about a year old.

New World marsupials

Three families of marsupial, containing around 83 species, are found in the Americas – the only marsupials found outside Australasia. About 70 of these species belong to the opossum family (Didelphidae), and most of the others resemble opossums. The majority of opossums are rat-like in appearance, even having similar scaly hairless tails, but some are more reminiscent of shrews. Most are forest-dwellers, but one – the water opossum, or yapok – has adapted to an aquatic life.

The Virginia opossum – the largest species of opossum, and the only one found north of Mexico – has adapted well to life with man, following the spread of agriculture and often scavenging in urban refuse. It is a prodigious breeder, with up to three litters a year. The young are smaller than honeybees at birth, and litters of 18 have been recorded, but since there are only 13 teats in the mother's pouch, fewer survive. The expression 'playing possum' comes from the animal's habit of feigning death when cornered by a predator.

JAB

A koala. Until recently koalas were threatened with extinction through a combination of hunting for the fur trade, loss of habitat and epidemic disease. Now under strict protection, the few thousand that survived have rebuilt, and the koala is now once again fairly abundant.

SEE ALSO

● EARLY MAMMALS p. 140
● ANIMAL BEHAVIOUR pp. 166–75
● ECOSYSTEMS pp. 178–87

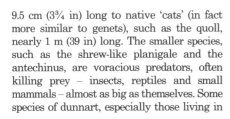

The Tasmanian devil (left), despite its fearsome name and its reputation as a sheep-killer, is chiefly a scavenger. Although capable of bringing down prey larger than itself, it formerly relied mainly on carcasses discarded by the now extinct thylacine.

Edentates, Pangolins and the Aardvark

Although not closely related, pangolins, the aardvark and the group of animals known as edentates – armadillos, anteaters and sloths – have a superficial similarity in that they lack some or all of their teeth. This reduction or loss of teeth is associated with the specialized diet of these animals: with the exception of sloths, which depend on plant matter, all of them feed mainly or solely on insects, especially ants and termites.

The giant anteater is ground-dwelling, and walks on its knuckles to keep its claws sharp. It can eat around 30 000 ants or termites in a single day, gathering them in with its extraordinarily long tongue, which can be extended over 60 cm (24in).

Three families of edentates with a total of just 30 species make up the order Edentata (which literally means 'toothless'): the armadillo family (Dasypodidae) with 21 species; the anteater family (Myrmecophagidae) with 4 species; and the sloth family (Bradypodidae) with 5 species. The 7 species of pangolin form a single family (Manidae) in a single order (Pholidota). The aardvark was once classified as an edentate, but the similarities are due to convergent evolution rather than close relationship. It is now considered the sole species of a family (Orycteropidae) that is the single family in its order (Tubulidentata).

Armadillos

The 21 species of armadillo are found in Central and South America, with one species – the nine-banded armadillo – also occurring in the southern USA. They range in size from the endangered giant armadillo at around 1.5 m (5 ft) long to the tiny pichiciegos, or fairy armadillos, some 15 cm (6 in) long.

The Spanish name 'armadillo' refers to the animal's armour-like plates, which are made of bone and covered in horny scales. They are set in bands and cover most or all of the exposed upper part of the body, including the head and tail. The plates are interspersed with flexible skin, and most armadillos can roll up into a ball for protection.

Armadillos have powerful claws and are efficient burrowers, loosening the soil with their forefeet and kicking it clear with the hind feet. The tiny pichiciegos brace themselves against their stiff tails when digging. Armadillos feed mostly on insects, worms and other invertebrates. Some species also eat plant matter, and can cause significant damage to sprouting maize and other crops.

The nine-banded armadillo is an adaptable animal, readily colonizing arable land. It has spread steadily over the southern parts of the USA, where it is a frequent casualty on the roads. Its normal litter consists of four young, which all come from a single fertilized egg – and hence are genetically identical quadruplets. As a consequence, these animals have become important in laboratory research, especially into multiple births.

Anteaters

The four species of anteater occur in tropical forests and savannah from southern Mexico as far south as northern Argentina. All species are toothless, and have long tapering snouts and sticky tongues to trap ants or termites. The forelimbs are armed with powerful claws for ripping open insect nests, the claw on the middle digit being especially long and sharp. The largest species is the giant anteater, which is ground-dwelling and grows to over 2 m (7 ft) long (see illustration).

The two species of lesser anteater, or tamandua, and the silky (or pygmy) anteater are tree-dwelling, and have prehensile tails. The latter, growing to a body length of just 15 cm (6 in), has hind feet with jointed soles, allowing it to grasp branches both with its tail and with its claws.

Sloths

There are two groups of living sloths: three species of three-toed sloth and two species of two-toed sloth (the distinction is based on the forelimbs – all sloths have three toes on each hind limb). All five species are found in the tropical forests of Central and South America. They are slow-moving, tree-dwelling vegetarians that spend almost their entire life upside down (see photo). Their hands and feet have hook-like claws with which they hang from branches: they eat, sleep, mate and give birth upside down.

Because sloths are so slow-moving, their fur often has a growth of algae, which gives a greenish tinge and acts as camouflage. Although almost all other mammals – even giraffes – have seven neck vertebrae, the three-toed sloths have eight or nine. The extra length allows great flexibility – an advantage in an animal otherwise so restricted in movement.

When man first colonized the Americas, there were several species of ground-dwelling sloth in the Caribbean, as well as a spectacular giant ground sloth, growing to some 6 m (20 ft), in southern South America (see illustration, pp. 140–1). Since their remains have been found with pottery and other human relics, it is highly probable that they were exterminated by man.

Pangolins

Like the aardvark, the pangolins, or scaly anteaters, were once classified as edentates. They do indeed bear a striking superficial resemblance to armadillos, except that their armour is in the form of scales rather than bands of bony plates (see photo). Four species of pangolin are found in Africa and three in Asia, and all are active at night, when they go in search of their insect prey – chiefly ants and termites. On finding a nest, they tear it open with their five strong claws on each front foot.

Pangolins typically have a tapering body, a small pointed head, and a broad tail, sometimes nearly as long as the rest of the animal's body. All species are covered with large overlapping horny scales, and can roll into a ball if alarmed and squirt a foul-smelling liquid from glands in the anus. The largest, the giant pangolin of western Africa, grows to a total length of over 1.5 m (5 ft).

Pangolins do not have any teeth at all, but their stomachs have muscular walls with a horny lining embedded with tiny stones,

enabling them to crush and grind ants and other insects. Perhaps the pangolin's most remarkable feature is its tongue. The roots of the tongue muscles are anchored to the pelvis, and the tongue itself can be extended for nearly half the length of the animal's body, in order to extract termites and other insects from their nests. When attacked by ants, pangolins can close the openings to their ears and nostrils, and their eyes are protected by thick eyelids.

The aardvark

The aardvark (meaning 'earth-pig' in Afrikaans) grows to a length of 1.4 m (4½ ft), and is found throughout Africa south of the Sahara (see photo). It spends the day sheltered in excavated burrows, coming out at night in search of its insect prey – ants and termites. Once it has sniffed out an ant or termite nest, the aardvark rips open the nest with its large powerful claws and extracts the insects with its long sticky tongue – up to 30 cm (12 in) long.   JAB

The aardvark (above left) has huge ears that are folded back to exclude dirt when burrowing, and its muzzle is protected by thick bristles. It uses its powerful claws to rip open ant or termite nests.

A three-toed sloth (above). Sloths spend most of their lives hanging upside down. As an adaptation to this unusual life style, their hair grows from belly to back – unlike all other mammals – so that it hangs downwards in their normal inverted posture.

Temminck's ground pangolin (below) of Africa. Pangolins are the only mammals to have scales – large, overlapping plates made of a horny material. Although entirely lacking teeth, pangolins have extremely long tongues, which they use to sweep up their insect prey.

SEE ALSO

● EARLY MAMMALS p. 140
● ANIMAL BEHAVIOUR pp. 166–75
● ECOSYSTEMS pp. 178–87

Bats

Although certain other mammals are capable of gliding – sometimes for considerable distances – bats are the only mammals capable of true flight. The flying membrane of bats consists of skin stretched between the four extremely elongated fingers of each hand; only the thumb remains free, and is used for grooming. The elastic membrane is attached to the bat's ankles, and in many species it is also connected to the tail. While many species of bat have light fluttery flight, others are powerful fliers capable of covering great distances. Migratory species, such as the European mouse-eared bat, regularly fly 400 km (250 mi) or more.

Bats occur all over the world except the colder regions, above the tree line, and on some remote oceanic islands. They are extremely numerous and diverse, second only to rodents in number of species: well over 900 species have been described, and new ones are regularly discovered, particularly in the tropical forests.

The order Chiroptera, to which all bats belong, is divided into two unequal groups: the Megachiroptera consists of a single family (Pteropodidae) of about 170 species of fruit bat, or flying fox; the Microchiroptera includes all other species of bat – around 800 species in 18 distinct families.

Because all bats fly at night, they are mostly rather drab-coloured – usually various shades of brown. A few are more striking, however, such as the white bat of Central America and the Rodriguez fruit

The greater horseshoe bat. The grotesque folds of skin on the nose and face are used to project and focus the high-pitched squeaks used in *echolocation* – the sophisticated sonar system that enables most bats to fly in complete darkness. Accuracy in determining the direction of incoming signals is enhanced by the large ears.

bat of Rodriguez Island (near Mauritius in the Indian Ocean), which has golden fur. Bats vary in size from one of the smallest known mammals, Kitti's hog-nosed bat of Thailand, which is about the size of a bumblebee and weighs around 2 g (¹⁄₁₄ oz), to the fruit bats, which may weigh over 1.5 kg (3⅓ lb) and have wingspans in excess of 1.5 m (5 ft).

Fruit bats

The fruit bats, or flying foxes, are found in the tropical and subtropical regions of Australia and the Old World (see photo, p. 173). As their name suggests, fruit bats mostly eat fruit, but some feed on nectar as well. Their alternative name is also apt, as most fruit bats have dog-like faces, and many have the rusty coloration of the red fox. Most fruit bats have large eyes and rely principally on their sight, and are therefore usually active at dusk or dawn, flying up to 70 km (44 mi) in search of fruit. A few are nocturnal, however, using echolocation for navigation (see below).

Fruit bats often live in the tops of trees in communal roosts. They frequently occur in huge numbers – a single colony sometimes numbering over a million members. Some of the smaller fruit bats roost in the roofs of caves, in colonies of up to nine million members. They often move in flocks of a thousand or more to suitable feeding sites, as figs or other fruit ripen on a particular tree. These feeding movements play an important part in the dispersal of the seeds of trees in tropical forests. Fruit bats sometimes feed in citrus and other plantations, but since they normally eat fruit that is ripe or over-ripe, and most commercial harvesting is of under-ripe fruit, they actually cause little damage. Despite this, they have been extensively persecuted by fruit farmers.

Echolocation

With the exception of most species of fruit bat, the majority of bats are dependent for navigation on *echolocation* – an extremely sophisticated form of sonar. Echolocation involves emitting high-pitched squeaks (mostly above the range of human hearing) and measuring how long it takes for the noise to bounce back from intervening objects. By this means bats are able to fly in total darkness.

Many species, such as the horseshoe and

Hunting on the wing. Most bats rely principally on insects for their food, but some – including this American leaf-nosed bat – feed on larger prey. As well as frogs, carnivorous bats may feed on shrews, small rodents, birds, lizards and even other species of bat.

GLIDING MAMMALS

Although bats are the only mammals that have achieved true flight, some others can glide, often for long distances and with a great deal of control. The sifaka, a large lemur from Madagascar, has small membranes between its limbs that probably do little more than assist stability in its enormous leaps of up to 10 m (33 ft). The two species of colugo, or flying lemur, of Southeast Asia – unrelated to the Madagascan lemurs – can easily glide 100 m (330 ft) or more. They have the most extensive membranes of any gliding mammal, the skin-fold (*patagium*) extending from the neck to the wrists, between the front and back limbs, and back to the tail.

Other species of gliding mammal include a marsupial – the tiny pygmy gliding possum of Australia, weighing around 12 g (less than ¹/₂ oz) – and the similar-sized flying squirrels of North America and Eurasia. A number of species of squirrel and possum have gliding membranes stretching along their sides between their limbs, on which they can glide from tree to tree, and several have cartilaginous rods extending from the wrist or elbow that stiffen the membrane when in flight.

A North American flying squirrel coming in to land.

leaf-nosed bats, have elaborate folds of skin on the nose and face that are used in echolocation (see photo). Because certain insects, particularly night-flying moths, have learnt to take evasive action when they hear bats approaching, some bats have huge ears and use very low-volume squeaks for navigation.

Feeding techniques

Bats have evolved a wide variety of feeding techniques. Most are insectivorous, often consuming huge numbers of tiny insects such as midges and mosquitoes in the course of a single night. In the tropics many species feed on nectar and pollen, and are often extremely important pollinators for night-flowering trees, cacti and other plants. Flower-feeding bats tend to have long extensible tongues or pointed snouts in order to reach into flowers.

The three species of vampire bat, confined to the New World, are the most specialized of all bats, feeding entirely on the blood of warm-blooded vertebrates. Their front teeth are modified into two triangular razors, which they use to make a small incision, rarely felt by the victim. They then lap up the blood. The bat's saliva contains anticoagulants to prevent the blood from clotting, and the victim may continue to bleed after the bat has finished feeding. Although vampires are a problem in some parts of the New World,

particularly in cattle-rearing areas and where rabies is common, the dangers are often greatly exaggerated.

A few species of bat are carnivorous (see photo), the largest being the Australian giant false vampire, which feeds on mice, small marsupials, birds and even other bats. Other species of false vampire occurring in Central and South America feed on opossums, lizards and other bats. There are also a few species that regularly catch fish.

Bat roosts

Many species of bat roost in caves or crevices, and some of the larger roosts are among the biggest known concentrations of any one mammal (see photo). A single colony of free-tailed bats in Eagle Creek, Arizona, once contained some 50 million members. This number subsequently fell to about 600 000, probably as a result of the widespread and often indiscriminate use of insecticides in North America in the 1960s.

While roosting, most bats hang upside down by their feet, and may even give birth in this posture. The dung, or *guano*, of cave-dwelling bats has been mined in many parts of the world as a rich source of agricultural fertilizer.

In certain tropical caves, such as those in Borneo, several million bats of a number

of different species live together. Complete ecosystems have evolved that are dependent on these bats. A wide range of invertebrates feed on the bats' dung and food remains, while snakes, insectivores and other vertebrates prey on the invertebrates and the bats themselves.

Hibernation

Most species of bat living in temperate regions either migrate in winter to areas where food is available or hibernate (see p. 171). During hibernation bats use about a tenth of the oxygen needed when active, and can rely on energy stored as fat. Most bats allow their body temperature to drop and their metabolism to slow down both when sleeping and when hibernating.

Declining populations

In parts of the world where there is intensive farming, especially in Europe and North America, bat populations have undergone catastrophic declines in the past few decades. Damage to habitat has been a significant factor, but the widespread use of persistent pesticides in agriculture and of highly toxic insecticides for treating building timbers has also played a major part. Although most bats produce only one offspring a year, this low rate of reproduction is normally balanced by the fact that they are long-lived animals, with even small bats known to live 20 years or more in the wild. As a result, declines in numbers can take a long time to be noticed – and even longer to be reversed.   JAB

SEE ALSO

● MIGRATION p. 170
● HOW ANIMALS MOVE p. 172

Female Mexican free-tailed bats form vast summer nursery roosts in 13 caves in Texas, USA. Previously totalling around 100 million individuals, their numbers crashed catastrophically in the 1960s to perhaps 2 to 3 million, probably because of the indiscriminate use of the insecticide DDT. Now banned in the USA, DDT is still used in Mexico, where the bats spend the winter.

Insectivores

The seven families of insectivores, which include the shrews, the moles and the hedgehogs, contain around 375 species of mammal, together making up the order Insectivora. They are thought to bear a close relationship with the primates, and some of the simpler forms appear to be very similar to primitive, unspecialized ancestral mammals (see p. 140).

Insectivores are generally small, have long narrow snouts, and simple peg-like teeth. They have five clawed digits on each limb, and usually have minute eyes and flat feet. Most species live on or under the ground, and generally eat insects, as their name implies, although some are carnivorous.

Shrews

The most numerous family of insectivores is the shrews (Soricidae), with around 265 species found in all parts of the world except the colder regions, Australia and New Zealand, some islands, and most of South America. They are generally small mouse-like animals, with dense fur and pointed snouts. Although mostly ground-dwelling, a few species have adapted to an aquatic life, and several species of water shrew have fringes of stiff hairs on their feet to aid swimming.

The pygmy white-toothed shrew has the distinction of being one of the world's smallest mammals, weighing about 2 g ($^1/_{14}$ oz). The hero (or armoured) shrew of central Africa, on the other hand, is one of the most resilient: it has a reinforced vertebral column of such extraordinary strength that it can sustain the weight of an adult human, apparently without suffering damage.

A number of shrews (as well as some other insectivores) have poisons in their saliva, which – although only mildly toxic to larger animals – can incapacitate invertebrates such as earthworms. In the case of some shrews, predators are also deterred from attacking by acrid-smelling secretions from glands in the animal's flanks.

Shrews are very active, feeding in short bursts, then resting. In order to meet its energy requirements, the common shrew may eat well over its own weight in food in a period of 24 hours. Shrews never hibernate, even those species living in colder regions – it would be impossible for them to build up sufficient reserves of food. When alarmed their heart rate may rise to 1200 beats a minute.

The 16 species of tree shrew – despite their name and shrew-like appearance – have certain peculiar features that have led them to be classified separately from the insectivores. They are now usually placed in an order of their own (see photo, p. 141).

The star-nosed mole's snout is fringed with 22 highly sensitive fleshy tentacles. These are constantly moving as the animal grubs about for worms and other food.

Moles

All of the 27 or so species of mole (family Talpidae) are confined to the northern hemisphere. They are adapted to life underground and to digging, and so are generally restricted to habitats with soft soil. Their shovel-like forepaws are permanently turned outwards, and they have short thick arms with powerful muscles. The fur is short and velvety, and can brush in any direction, thus allowing the mole to move backwards and forwards through its tunnels with equal ease. They have very small eyes and are virtually blind, but have long sensitive snouts.

The diet of Old World moles is principally made up of earthworms, which are trapped as they inadvertently fall into the mole's system of burrows. Any surplus worms are stored away, having first been immobilized by having their front segments bitten off. One species, the star-nosed mole of North America, has highly sensitive tentacles on its snout with which it searches for food (see photo).

Desmans are a type of aquatic mole, and have webbed hind feet to aid swimming. The Russian desman is the largest of the moles, growing to around 40 cm (16 in). It is one of the few insectivores to have been hunted commercially for its fur, although moleskins were traditionally used in Britain for countrymen's waistcoats. The only other species, the Pyrenean desman, is rather smaller.

Golden moles

The 18 species of golden mole (family Chrysochloridae) are confined to Africa, where they are found from Cameroon and Uganda to the Cape. Although similar in structure to the true moles, they are only distantly related. Their thick woolly fur has a lustre often giving them a golden or bronze appearance. Some species – despite being blind – hunt on the surface, but usually only after rain, or at night. Most species feed on invertebrates, but

A bicoloured white-toothed shrew with young. When the young are older but not yet independent, their mother will lead them around in a 'caravan': each young shrew holds the base of the tail of another in its jaws, with the leader hanging on to the mother.

some also eat legless lizards up to 20 cm (8 in) long – over twice their own length.

Tenrecs

All but 3 of the 34 species of tenrec (family Tenrecidae) are confined to Madagascar and the nearby Comoro Islands. In the absence of other insectivores, they have adopted the life styles of insectivores elsewhere. In most cases the Madagascan tenrecs have been little studied, and several species are rare. The common (or tailless) tenrec has rather spiny fur (see photo), while the hedgehog tenrecs are so spiny as to be superficially very similar to the true hedgehogs.

The three other species of tenrec – the otter shrews – are found in western Africa, and are indeed rather otter-like in appearance. The largest, the giant otter shrew, found in the rain forests of central Africa, grows to around 75 cm (2½ ft) and has a flattened muzzle covered with stiff whiskers. Its nostrils can be closed with flaps of skin when swimming, and it has a powerful flattened tail.

Hedgehogs

The hedgehog family (Erinacidae) consists of two main groups, the moon rats (or gymnures) of Southeast Asia, and the true hedgehogs. The moon rats lack spines, but have long blunt-nosed snouts like true hedgehogs, and are among the largest insectivores, weighing up to 2 kg (4½ lb).

The true hedgehogs are native to Africa and Eurasia. They are covered in spines, and when alarmed can curl into a defensive ball (see photo). Hedgehogs feed on a wide range of small invertebrates, such as slugs, snails, insects and their larvae, as well as young mice, birds' eggs and other small animals when they find them. They have adapted well to suburban gardens – but their spines are no protection against road traffic. They are mostly ground-dwelling, but can swim and climb – if they fall they use their spines to absorb the impact.

In the northern part of its range the European hedgehog and its close relative, the Romanian hedgehog, hibernate. The more southerly species, such as the desert hedgehog, do not normally hibernate, although they may aestivate (become torpid in the summer heat; see p. 171).

Solenodons

The two living species of solenodon (family Solenodontidae) are confined to the islands of Cuba and Hispaniola in the Caribbean. They resemble large robust shrews, and can weigh up to 1 kg (2.2 lb). Although they mostly eat insects and fruit, they also feed on reptiles and poultry. Both species are legally protected, but are in imminent danger of extinction, particularly as a result of deforestation and predation by introduced cats and dogs. Soon after the arrival of the Spaniards in the Caribbean in the 16th century, another family of shrew-like animals (Nesophontidae), which was found on Hispaniola, Cuba, Puerto Rico and other islands, became extinct.

Elephant shrews

The 15 species of elephant shrew (family Macroscelididae) are such bizarre creatures that they are sometimes classified in an order of their own. They are usually grouped with the insectivores, however, on account of their dentition.

All the species of elephant shrew are found only in Africa. They take their name from their long flexible snout, which, while not prehensile, can be moved round as the animal searches for food. The largest – growing to around 50 cm (20 in), of which just under half is tail – is the chequered elephant shrew of central Africa, which feeds mainly on ants, termites and beetle larvae. Some species carry a type of malaria that is not transmitted to humans, and have consequently been used in medical research.

JAB

SEE ALSO

● EARLY MAMMALS p. 140
● HIBERNATION p. 171

A European hedgehog (above) raises its spines at the warning hiss of an adder. A band of muscles running along the border of the prickly coat are contracted to draw the hedgehog into its protective ball.

A young tenrec. The common, or tailless, tenrec is one of the most prolific mammals known. There is a recorded case of a litter of 31 – all but one of which survived – although the normal litter is only about half this size.

Rodents, Lagomorphs and Hyraxes

Rodents are easily the most numerous mammals in the world, with many species having populations running into millions. Because species such as rats and mice live alongside man, they also have the widest distribution of any wild mammals. The lagomorphs – rabbits, hares and pikas – have certain structural features that distinguish them from rodents, but recent studies of animal body proteins indicate that they are closely related to rodents. The same studies show that hyraxes – despite their small size and rodent-like appearance – have no close relatives but the elephants.

The pacas of South and Central America are among the larger rodents, growing to around 70 cm (28 in) in length. Timid and usually solitary, they lie up during the day in riverside burrows, emerging after dark to forage for roots, grasses and other plant matter. They are good swimmers, readily taking to water to escape predators.

The order Rodentia is by far the largest order of mammals, containing around 1650 species in 28 families. Rodents account for about 40% of all known mammal species, and occur on all continents except Antarctica. The exact relationship between the various rodent families is much disputed. One possible classification divides them into three suborders, the distinction being based primarily on the structure of the skull: Sciuromorpha – squirrels and squirrel-like rodents; Myomorpha – rats, mice and related species; and Hystricomorpha – porcupines, cavies and their relatives (see table).

Rodents: common features

Despite the large number of species, rodents are remarkably uniform in structure. All have a similar arrangement of the teeth, with two pairs of incisors, one above and one below, then a gap before the cheek teeth – the canines and the anterior premolars are missing.

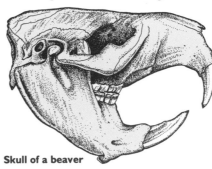

Skull of a beaver

In all species the characteristic incisors grow continuously throughout the animal's life. They are coated with enamel on the outside surface only, and therefore wear down faster on the inside; and because the upper pair grow over the lower pair and constantly work against them, the incisors are self-sharpening. Many species of rodent have cheek pouches, used for carrying food.

Rodents are primarily vegetarian, feeding on seeds, leaves, roots and other plant matter. Although some species are extremely specialized, rodents in general eat a remarkable variety of foods. Many desert-dwelling species – the Australian native mice, for example – can live their entire lives without ever drinking. They manage to derive all the water they need from the seeds and grains upon which they feed.

Most rodents are relatively small. The largest – the capybara – grows to 50 kg (110 lb) or more, but the majority are less than 1 kg (2.2 lb) and there are many species weighing less than 10 g (⅓ oz).

Squirrels and squirrel-like rodents

Squirrels are found in most parts of the world except Australia, but are particularly diverse in Asia, where the majority are tree-dwelling and often very agile. Squirrels are generally keen-sighted, and most species are active by day and often extremely brightly coloured. Some species – the flying squirrels – are capable of gliding on a membrane stretched between the front and hind feet (see p. 147).

Ground squirrels are particularly widespread in North America, and some spe-

RODENT FAMILIES

Family	Number of species	Representative species	Africa	N. America	S. America	Asia	Australasia	Europe
SCIUROMORPHA ('squirrel-like')								
Aplodontidae	1	Mountain beaver		▪				
Sciuridae	251	Squirrels, marmots, chipmunks	▪	▪	▪	▪		▪
Geomyidae	25	Pocket gophers		▪	▪			
Heteromyidae	63	Pocket mice, kangaroo rats and mice		▪	▪			
Castoridae	2	Beavers		▪		▪		▪
Anomaluridae	7	Scaly-tailed squirrels	▪					
Pedetidae	1	Springhare (or springhaas)	▪					
MYOMORPHA ('mouse-like')								
Muridae	1063	Rats, mice, hamsters, lemmings, etc.	▪	▪	▪	▪	▪	▪
Gliridae	16	Dormice	▪			▪		▪
Seleviniidae	1	Desert dormouse				▪		
Zapodidae	11	Jumping mice		▪		▪		▪
Dipodidae	29	Jerboas	▪			▪		▪
HYSTRICOMORPHA ('porcupine-like')								
Hystricidae	11	Old World porcupines	▪			▪		▪
Erethizontidae	10	New World porcupines		▪	▪			
Caviidae	16	Cavies (or guinea pigs)			▪			
Hydrochoeridae	1	Capybara			▪			
Dinomyidae	1	Pacarana			▪			
Dasyproctidae	15	Agoutis, pacas		▪	▪			
Chinchillidae	6	Chinchillas, viscachas			▪			
Capromyidae	13	Hutias, coypu (or nutria)			▪			
Octodontidae	8	Octodonts			▪			
Ctenomyidae	38	Tuco-tucos			▪			
Abrocomidae	2	Chinchilla rats			▪			
Echimyidae	58	Spiny rats		▪	▪			
Thryonomyidae	2	Cane rats	▪					
Petromyidae	1	Dassie rat	▪					
Bathyergidae	8	African mole rats	▪					
Ctenodactylidae	2	Gundis	▪					

cies – the prairie dogs – are often highly gregarious. Prairie dogs live in huge colonies known as 'towns', which sometimes have populations running into millions and in which a complex system of social organization operates. At the turn of the 20th century a single town in Texas was estimated to cover 64 000 km² (25 000 sq mi) and to contain 400 million individuals.

The largest of the squirrels are the marmots, which can grow to 7.5 kg (16 lb). They are found over much of the northern hemisphere, particularly in mountainous areas. Unlike the majority of rodents, marmots hibernate (see p. 171), and several species make hay in summer and store it underground for use in winter during spells of mild weather.

The two species of beaver are among the larger rodents. They are well adapted to their semi-aquatic life style: the ears and nostrils can be closed when the animal is submerged, while the webbed hind feet and paddle-shaped tail provide excellent propulsion and control when swimming. Beavers are capable of modifying their environment in ways that few animals other than man can rival: they fell trees

RODENTS AND ECONOMICS

The impact of rodents on mankind has chiefly been negative. The brown rat, black rat and house mouse in particular cause billions of dollars' worth of damage to crops, stored foodstuffs and property. In the USA alone the damage caused by the brown rat has been put at a billion dollars a year.

Rats also spread disease. Fleas carried by rats in turn carried the bacterium responsible for bubonic plague, the disease that killed a third of the population of Europe in the 14th century (see p. 402) and 11 million people in India between 1892 and 1918. Other diseases passed to humans by rats include Rocky Mountain spotted fever and leptospirosis (sewerman's disease).

Rodents have proved useful in other ways, however. Several rodents, such as the cane rat in West Africa and the cavy (or guinea pig) in South America, are important food animals. Others are important fur-bearers, the chinchilla being the most valuable. The domesticated brown rat is one of the most important laboratory animals, used extensively for research and in testing products such as medicines, cosmetics and poisons.

and build dams to create the swampy conditions they favour. The American beaver was in the past of considerable economic importance – its fur was once the mainstay of the Canadian economy. The Eurasian species is very similar in appearance and habits to its American relative.

Rats, mice and their relatives

Rats and mice are found in almost all parts of the world, and have been introduced into regions where they do not occur naturally. Characterized by their long snouts and naked scaly tails, they are among the most successful and adaptable of all mammals. Their impact on humans has chiefly been negative: as well as carrying diseases, they cause considerable damage to crops and property (see box).

Perhaps the most bizarre rodents are those belonging to the African mole rat family. Living entirely in underground burrows and feeding on plant roots and bulbs, they are virtually blind, but are superb diggers and can even gnaw their way through soil. They work together in teams, and exhibit an extraordinary system of social organization (see p. 169).

Because of their large numbers, species of rodent such as voles and lemmings are important prey for owls, foxes and many other predators. In northern areas rodent populations are often cyclical, building up over periods of three to four years into plague proportions, before crashing when they overexploit their food supply. This population crash is often followed by that of their predators.

Porcupines, cavies and their relatives

Most species of porcupine are active by night, and feed on a variety of plant matter. They are characterized by the long spines (formed from modified hair) that grow thickly on the back and sides. The African and Asian species have particularly long spines, which can grow to 35 cm (14 in) in length. The New World porcupines are broadly similar in appearance to the Old World species, but – unlike the latter – most of them are tree-dwelling (see photo).

The cavies, or guinea pigs, are ground-dwelling rodents found only in South America. Most species are social, and have the rather thick-set body form of the domestic guinea pig. Although in a separate family, the capybara of South America – the largest of the rodents – has the appearance of a giant guinea pig. It is semi-aquatic and has partially webbed feet. It too is a social animal, always living in family groups.

Rabbits, hares and pikas

The order Lagomorpha is made up of just two families: around 40 species of rabbit and hare (Leporidae) and 14 species of pika (Ochotonidae). Unlike rodents, the lagomorphs have two pairs of incisors in

the upper jaw, although only one is functional, the other being tiny and undeveloped. All lagomorphs are herbivorous, and have the curious habit of eating their own fecal pellets, thus gaining extra nutritional value from their food. They live in a wide variety of habitats, including woodlands and swamps, but generally favour open grassy habitats.

Rabbits and hares are highly successful and adaptable mammals. The hind limbs are strong and disproportionately large, giving these animals their swift bounding movement. Although the names are often used loosely, 'rabbit' is usually used to describe those species that live in burrows and give birth to small undeveloped young. Hares, on the other hand, live in shallow surface depressions known as forms, and their young are well developed at birth, with eyes already open and a full coat of hair. As well as enhancing hearing, the large ears typical of rabbits and hares help species that live in dry, hot areas to disperse excess heat.

One species, the European rabbit, has been domesticated. It has been introduced into areas of the world where it is not native and has become a serious pest, causing widespread damage to grasslands and crops. Attempts to control it have included the introduction of the myxomatosis virus, a disease originally found in a South American species of rabbit.

Pikas, or conies, have short rounded ears, a rounded body, and a stubby tale. All species live on rocky slopes, mostly in the mountainous parts of north and central Asia, with two species occurring in western North America. They collect green plants in summer, which they dry and store away for use in the colder months, but they do not hibernate. The Tibetan pika occupies one of the highest habitats of any mammal – up to 6000 m (20 000 ft) in the Himalaya.

Hyraxes

The seven species of hyrax (also called dassies), although superficially rodent-like, are quite unrelated, and are placed in an order of their own (Hyracoidea). All species are herbivorous, and are found in Africa and parts of the Middle East. Most species are sociable, living and grazing in small colonies. Hyraxes have curious hoof-like feet, used effectively by some species for climbing in trees.   JAB

A North American porcupine (left). Whereas the Old World porcupines are mainly ground-dwelling and rather cumbersome, the New World species are generally more agile, and most have adapted to life in trees: they have strong broad feet, well suited to climbing, and some have prehensile tails, which they use to grasp branches.

SEE ALSO

● GLIDING MAMMALS p. 147
● ANIMAL COMMUNICATION
   p. 166
● TERRITORY, MATING, SOCIAL
   ORGANIZATION p. 168
● MIGRATION p. 170

Mad as a March hare: at the beginning of the breeding season, male hares – such as these common (or European brown) hares – indulge in wild antics. Striving for the attention of females, rivals box, kick and bite, only stopping when one of the combatants turns tail and runs. Females not yet ready to mate may also join in the fray, to ward off over-eager suitors.

Carnivores
1. Cats, Civets, Hyenas

Although the name 'carnivore' is applied generally to any carnivorous, or flesh-eating, animal, the term is used specifically to describe the group of mammals belonging to the order Carnivora. Most members of this order are indeed carnivorous – they are flesh-eating predators, feeding on other vertebrates. Some are active hunters, while others are mainly scavengers. However, many carnivores eat plant matter and insects as well as flesh, and a few are even vegetarian.

The order Carnivora contains around 245 species in seven families. There are believed to have been two distinct lines of evolutionary development within the order, allowing these families to be divided into two groups. The suborder Aeluroidea contains three families: cats (Felidae); civets and their relatives (Viverridae); and hyenas (Hyaenidae). The other suborder, Arctoidea, contains four families: dogs and their relatives (Canidae); bears (Ursidae); raccoons and their relatives (Procyonidae); and weasels and their relatives (Mustelidae).

The natural range of living carnivores is very broad, encompassing virtually all parts of the world except Australasia, Antarctica and many oceanic islands. Carnivores are highly diverse in form, but – despite great differences in appearance – are most readily distinguished as a group by the structure of their teeth. The small, sharp incisors at the front of the jaw are suitable for nipping off flesh, while the canines are usually enlarged and dagger-like, well adapted for stabbing and tearing.

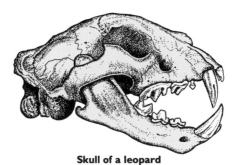

Skull of a leopard

Highly carnivorous species, such as cats, weasels and hyenas, have well-developed cheek teeth (*carnassials*) that interlock in a scissor-like action to cut through tough flesh and sinew. This adaptation is generally absent or little developed in more omnivorous species such as bears and raccoons.

Cats

Despite differences in size and colouring, the 37 living species of cat (family Felidae) are remarkably uniform in shape and structure, all of them essentially resembling the familiar domestic cat.

All cats are predatory and their characteristic adaptations are perfectly suited to the life of a hunter. As well as specialized teeth, all species (except the cheetah) have claws that can be withdrawn into sheaths, thus keeping the claws razor-sharp and allowing the animal to stalk noiselessly on its pads. All senses, especially sight, scent and hearing, are well developed. Most cats climb trees, and feed on prey ranging from monkeys and birds to mice and insects – almost anything, in fact, that they are capable of catching.

The tiger is the biggest of the cats, with a head-and-body length sometimes in excess of 2.5 m (8 ft). Formerly ranging widely over most of southern Asia, it is now almost entirely restricted to parks and reserves, with fewer than 5000 left in the wild. Although coloration is variable, all subspecies of tiger are striped, offering excellent camouflage in their forest habitat. Nocturnal and usually solitary, tigers tend to take large prey, and can eat about 23 kg (50 lb) of meat in a single meal (see photo).

Like the tiger, the lion has been exterminated from much of its former range. Within historic times, lions were found in southern Europe, across the Middle East as far east as India, and over most of Africa. They are now almost entirely confined to subsaharan Africa. Generally only slightly smaller than the tiger, male lions are larger than females and are further distinguished by the heavy mane around the neck and shoulders. Unlike most other cats, lions live together in groups called prides, which usually contain about nine individuals. They inhabit open savannah and are typically active by day. Lionesses do most of the hunting, preying mainly on mammals such as zebra, wildebeest and other antelope (see photo).

The leopard has proved more adaptable than the other big cats, and is still relatively common throughout its extensive range, covering southern Asia and much of Africa. It typically grows to around 1.5 m (5 ft) excluding the tail. Most leopards are marked with characteristic rosette-shaped spots, but they can be entirely black (in which case they are known as panthers). Like most other cats,

SEE ALSO

- TERRITORY, MATING AND SOCIAL ORGANIZATION p. 168
- HOW ANIMALS MOVE p. 172
- ECOSYSTEMS: GRASSLANDS p. 184

The lionesses within a group (or 'pride') of lions are responsible for most of the hunting. Here they are seen digging a warthog from its hole.

the leopard is solitary and generally nocturnal, but in Sri Lanka – where lions and tigers are absent – it is active by day.

Several other cats are superficially similar to the leopard. The jaguar – the largest of the New World cats – resembles the leopard in proportions and coloration, but is of slightly heavier build and is not quite so agile. The snow leopard also has spotted markings, but its fur is thicker and softer, and it has a longer tail – almost as long as its body. It is smaller than a leopard and one of the rarest of the larger cats, being restricted to the Himalaya and the Altai Mountains of Mongolia. It is a particularly agile jumper – only matched by the New World puma (also called the cougar, or mountain lion).

The cheetah, or hunting leopard, formerly of widespread distribution, is now confined to isolated populations in Asia, and to eastern and southern Africa. It is the fastest land animal, and is superbly adapted for speed, with long legs and a slender, supple body. The cheetah hunts in open plains, and relies on bursts of speed that may exceed 80 km/h (50 mph) to run down its prey, mostly gazelles.

Among the smaller cats, the wildcat is one of the most widely distributed. It occurs in a wide range of habitats, from forest to semi-desert, in many parts of the Old World. Like an oversized domestic cat in appearance, the wildcat is largely solitary and nocturnal. Although an agile climber, it mainly stalks small mammals and birds on the ground. The name 'wildcat' is sometimes applied to other medium-sized cats, including the Old World caracal, the North American bobcat, and the lynx, which is widespread throughout the northern hemisphere.

Civets and their relatives

The viverrids – civets, genets, mongooses and linsangs – belong to some 75 species that together make up the civet family (Viverridae). They have a wide distribution from southern Europe across southern Asia, down through Africa and into Madagascar. Viverrids are variable in habit and appearance, but tend to have long lithe bodies, short legs, pointed snouts, and very long tails – in a few cases, even longer than the rest of the animal's body. Many civets, genets and linsangs are boldly spotted or stripped, with banded tails. Nearly all viverrids have scent glands in the anus, the secretion from which is used both in perfumery and medicine.

Viverrids have adapted to a wide range of habitats, from tropical forest to savannah. Some, such as the otter civet of Southeast

Asia and the Congo water civet, have adapted to spending much of their life in water. Most species are strong climbers, and the binturong of Southeast Asia is one of only two species of carnivore to have a prehensile tail (the other being the kinkajou; see p. 155). Most viverrids are solitary in behaviour, but some species are notably gregarious (see photo).

Mongooses are famous for their ability to prey on venomous snakes. Despite popular belief, they are not immune to snake venom, but rely on their agility and coarse fur as protection against cobras and other snakes. Because they are effective and voracious predators of small mammals such as rats and mice, mongooses have been introduced onto islands where these rodents have become pests. Unfortunately, in most cases the mongooses have in turn become serious pests, by preying on native birds, reptiles and other wildlife.

Hyenas

Despite their superficial resemblance to dogs, the four species in the hyena family (Hyaenidae) are in fact more closely related to the cat and civet families. The aardwolf, found in the drier habitats of subsaharan Africa, is of lighter build than the other hyenas, and has weak jaws and minute teeth. It is also the most specialized, feeding almost exclusively on termites and other insects.

The other three species – the spotted, brown and striped hyenas – are very dog-like in appearance. Their distinctive sloping gait is due to their hind legs being shorter than their forelegs. All have massive heads and powerful jaws capable of crushing bones. Whereas the brown hyena is confined to southern Africa, the spotted hyena (the largest member of the family) is found throughout subsaharan Africa, and the striped hyena occurs in dry habitats across northern Africa and into Asia as far as eastern India. The spotted hyena is particularly noted for its laughing cry – the other species are less vocal.

Although noted as scavengers, the hyenas – especially the spotted hyena – are also effective predators (see photo). On the plains of the Serengeti, a quarter of all carcasses on which lions feed are animals killed by hyenas. When available, they also eat considerable quantities of fruit such as melons. JAB

A spotted hyena. Hyenas have a reputation for scavenging, but they are also effective predators. They hunt in packs of up to 30, and in some areas kill about 80% of their food, including wildebeest and zebra.

Meerkats, or suricates (above), live in groups of 10 to 15 and exhibit a highly complex social structure. Some act as nursemaids for the young, some as hunters and foragers, while others keep watch for predators. Such gregarious behaviour is unusual in the civet family, most members of which are solitary.

A tiger (left) with a sambar (a species of deer). The larger cats, including lions, leopards, tigers and jaguars, often take large prey, such as sheep, deer and monkeys. The causes of man-eating, particularly in tigers, have been much discussed, but the likely reason is simply that man falls within the natural range of their prey and may on occasion be preyed on.

Carnivores
2. Dogs, Bears, Raccoons, Weasels

The 37 species of *dogs and their relatives* (family Canidae) occur in almost all habitats and – even excluding the domestic dog – in virtually all parts of the world. The dingoes of Australia are descended from domesticated dogs introduced by the Aboriginal settlers more than 10 000 years ago, while huskies are still used as sled dogs in the Arctic.

Canids are typically long-legged, with a muscular torso and bushy tail. The muzzle is usually elongated, and the teeth exhibit the normal carnivorous adaptations: the canines are long and sharp, and the carnassials are well developed (see p. 152). Canid senses – particularly smell and hearing – are acute. Unlike cats, canids have blunt claws that cannot be retracted. Most canids are strictly terrestrial and are excellent runners, although one species – the grey fox of the New World – often climbs trees.

Canids are principally meat-eaters. Species such as the African hunting dog and the dhole (or Asiatic wild dog) are quite strictly carnivorous, while others, including the foxes, are generally more omnivorous, feeding on both animal and vegetable matter as available. Several canids, including the jackal of Asia and Africa, obtain much of their food by scavenging; the jackal is also an effective hunter, however, and in Africa is the chief predator of Thomson's gazelle.

The ancestor of the domestic dog is the wolf. The grey wolf was once widespread and abundant throughout most of the northern hemisphere, and had the greatest natural range of any terrestrial mammal other than man. However, the wolf has been ruthlessly persecuted ever since man first started herding animals. Although still found in thousands in parts of Canada, Russia and China, it is now extinct over much of its range. Wolves are gregarious animals, living and hunting in family groups, or packs (see photo, p. 181). he pack a strict social hierarchy is reinforced by ritual gestures and posturing.

The North American coyote resembles a small wolf, and has been far more successful at surviving human persecution. It has moved into the prairies, where it has forced out wolves, and has even managed to colonize city suburbs. The maned wolf of South America – despite its name – is in fact more fox-like in appearance. It lives mainly in savannah, where its exceptionally long legs enable it to see above tall grass.

As well as the wolf, several other species of canid, such as the dingo, the African hunting dog and the dhole, are notable for their social behaviour. Cooperative hunting is particularly important for the more carnivorous species, especially those relying on larger prey, since success may depend on organized attack.

Several fox species, on the other hand, including the red fox, are more opportunistic in their feeding and therefore have less need of cooperative activity. The red fox is usually solitary, and although it may take poultry and sick lambs, it mostly feeds on small animals such as voles or even insects. It has proved as adaptable as the coyote, with a wide distribution throughout the northern hemisphere, and has even taken to scavenging in urban refuse.

The Arctic fox, by contrast, is confined to the Arctic regions of North America and Eurasia. This species exists in two colour forms: the white form, which turns brown in summer, and the less widespread blue form, which is the same bluey-grey throughout the year. Although living in large dens, Arctic foxes hunt alone, with lemmings as their chief prey. They are extremely hardy animals: they can survive temperatures as low as −80 °C (−112 °F), and make some of the longest dispersal movements known for any terrestrial mammal, covering distances of around 1500 km (940 mi). At the other extreme, the fennec fox – the smallest of the foxes – has adapted to the harsh arid conditions of deserts. Its huge ears both enhance hearing and help it to lose heat.

The raccoon dog of eastern Asia is similar in appearance to the New World raccoons (see below), with squat body, short legs and a black facial mask. It feeds mainly on fish, amphibians and other small mammals. Unlike all other dogs, it enters a state of semi-hibernation for over four months of the year. It does not become completely torpid, however, and emerges at intervals to feed.

Bears

Within historic times, the eight living species of the bear family (Ursidae) oc-
curred throughout almost the entire northern hemisphere, extending as far south as North Africa, Malaysia and the Andes of South America. Bears are now distributed patchily over their range. Despite some variation, bears are characteristically large and heavily built. They have stocky bodies, flat feet with long curved claws, and the tail is short or absent. The large head is dog-like, pointing to the common ancestry of bears and dogs.

Among the bears are the largest living carnivores – the brown bears and the polar bear of the Arctic regions. An adult male polar bear weighs on average about 400 kg (880 lb), and grows to a length of 2.5 m (over 8 ft), but much heavier specimens have been reported. There are several subspecies of brown bear, including the giant North American grizzlies and the Old World brown bears, still found in remote parts of Europe. The largest members of the species are those found on Kodiak Island in Alaska, which – although usually not much exceeding the polar bear in length – may be more than 100 kg (220 lb) heavier.

Most bears are omnivorous and opportunistic in their feeding, eating a wide range of food including roots, leaves, berries, nuts, insects and small mammals (see photo). The only exception is the polar bear, which is largely carnivorous, feeding mostly on seals.

The sun bear (or honey bear) of Southeast Asia – although the smallest of the bears, growing to a length of about 1 m (39 in) – is nevertheless powerfully built and a good tree-climber. It spends most of the day sleeping or sunbathing in trees, only becoming active in the cool of the night. It mainly eats plants, but may also strip off bark with its sharp claws in search of honey or insects.

The sloth bear of the Indian peninsula and Sri Lanka lacks upper incisors, and has lips and tongue modified for its specialized diet of ants and termites. After it has dug open an ant or termite nest with its claws, it purses its mobile lips, closes its nostrils and sucks up insects like a vacuum cleaner.

The giant panda shows so many specialized anatomical modifications that it has often been classified quite separately from the bears. However, recent studies of animal body proteins indicate that bears and the panda

Bears are typically omnivorous – they eat a wide variety of plant material and meat, depending on availability. The Alaskan brown bear shown here feeds on fish during the summer salmon migration, but at other times relies principally on plants.

All mustelids have well-developed anal scent glands, which are generally used for marking the boundaries of their territory. In some species – most notably the polecats, such as the African zorilla and the ratel, and the skunks of North and Central America – the scent glands are also used as a very effective deterrent to would-be intruders. A foul-smelling liquid is ejected – with remarkable accuracy – in the form of an aerosol vapour from two glands located just inside the anus. The skunks and other mustelids that use this defensive strategy often have conspicuous coloration, usually black and white, which is intended to warn potential attackers to steer clear.

Badgers are found throughout Eurasia and North America. Most species are broadly similar in size and appearance, generally being stockily built and having distinctive black-and-white facial markings. All badgers are efficient burrowers and are typically active by night, when they emerge from their burrows to feed on a wide diet of animal and plant material. The American badger is mostly solitary, whereas the Eurasian badger is social, living in family groups in extensive underground burrows known as setts. The oriental stink badgers and ferret badgers both use defensive strategies similar to that of the skunks.

All otter species show adaptations for life in water, typically having streamlined bodies and webbed feet, as well as broad tails to give propulsion when swimming. Most specialized of all are the sea otters – the smallest of all marine mammals – which are capable of living their entire life without ever coming on shore (see photo). Unlike most aquatic mammals, such as whales and seals, otters lack a thick layer of blubber, and are insulated from the cold water by a layer of air trapped in the fibres of their dense fur. Sea otters can close their nostrils when diving, and can dive for several minutes without surfacing.

JAB

The sea otter (left) is one of the very few mammals to make use of tools: while floating on its back, it cracks open clams and other shellfish by pounding them against a stone balanced on its chest.

SEE ALSO

● ANIMAL COMMUNICATION p. 166
● TERRITORY, MATING AND SOCIAL ORGANIZATION p. 168
● HIBERNATION p. 170
● HOW ANIMALS MOVE p. 172

The red panda is more closely related to the raccoons than to the giant panda. However, it shares with its more famous namesake a feature known as the 'sixth finger' – an extra pad on the forepaw that helps it to grasp plant stems.

---

are indeed closely related. Formerly more widespread, the panda is now confined to three small areas of mountainous bamboo forest in western China, where it feeds almost exclusively on bamboo shoots. The front paw has a special pad – the so-called sixth finger – that enables pandas to hold bamboo stems. This adaptation is also found in the red panda (see below), but the two species are not thought to be closely related. The nutritional value of their bamboo diet is relatively poor, so pandas need to spend 10 to 12 hours a day eating. Being such specialized feeders, the panda populations suffer when a natural disaster affects bamboo. About a hundred pandas starved to death following such a disaster in the 1970s.

Raccoons and their relatives

The raccoon family (Procyonidae) is made up of 19 species of small to medium-sized mammals. With the exception of the red panda, all the procyonids are confined to the Americas.

There are six species of raccoon proper, all growing to a body length of around 50 cm (20 in). The most widespread and one of the commonest mammals in North America is the common raccoon. Like other procyonids, the raccoon is an active and inquisitive animal, and a good climber. It can also use its forepaws with extraordinary dexterity, and is very adept at fishing, flicking crayfish, small salmon and other fish from the water. It has proved highly adaptable to urban and suburban life, and it is often seen – conspicuous by its black face mask and ringed tail – rummaging among garbage cans.

The kinkajou of the tropical forests of Central and northern South America spends almost its entire life in trees, where it is active at night and feeds mainly on fruit. It is also fond of honey, and – like the sun bear – is sometimes called the honey bear. It is similar in body size to the raccoon, but is not so stockily built and has a longer tail. Its tail is prehensile, adding to its great agility in climbing from branch to branch.

The olingo is similar in appearance and distribution to the kinkajou, and is also an adept climber. However, its tail is bushier and banded like the raccoon's, and is not prehensile. The South American coatis are notable for their long banded tails, and their pointed, flexible snouts, with which they probe for insects and other invertebrates. Unlike most other procyonids, which tend to be solitary, female coatis live in groups of a dozen or more members, although males are solitary outside the breeding season.

The red, or lesser, panda is found from the Himalaya to southern China (see photo). It is like the raccoon in size and build, with a bushy banded tail, but its coat is a lustrous rusty red. It is also known as the cat bear, from its habit of sleeping during the day, curled up on a branch with its tail over its head. It generally feeds on the ground at night, eating mainly bamboo shoots and other plant matter.

Weasels and their relatives

The weasel family (Mustelidae) contains nearly 70 species, and includes weasels, skunks, badgers and otters. Mustelids occur on nearly all land masses except Australasia, and have adapted to a wide variety of habitats. Mustelids tend to have long supple bodies, often arched near the hindquarters. At the front, the body typically tapers into a long neck supporting a relatively small pointed head. The tail is usually long, and sometimes bushy.

Mustelids are generally highly carnivorous, with well-developed carnassials (see p. 152). Most species are skilled hunters. The wolverine of the subarctic regions of America and Eurasia, although only around 1 m (39 in) from nose to tail, is a fearsome predator. It often preys on animals larger than itself, and has been known to drive bears and pumas off their kills. Its alternative name – the glutton – is indicative of its voracious appetite. The ratel, a polecat of subsaharan Africa and southern Asia, is another tenacious predator. Its favourite food, however, is honey – hence its other name, the honey badger.

The least weasel, found in most temperate parts of the northern hemisphere, is the smallest living carnivore, growing to a total length (including tail) of about 20 cm (8 in). In the northern parts of its range, its fur turns white in winter. A similar colour change is undergone by the slightly larger but closely related stoat, whose white winter coat provides the ermine used for trimming robes and regalia. Another close relative, the mink, is now farmed for its luxuriant fur, while the martens (which include the sable) are also prized for their dense, soft pelts.

Elephants and Perissodactyls:

Horses, Rhinos, Tapirs

Over 200 species of mammal – collectively known as *ungulates* – are distinguished from all others by their possession of hooves. Ungulates walk on their toes, with the heel raised off the ground, and these toes have evolved into hooves, formed by the broadening of the bone at the tip of the toe. A structure equivalent to claws and nails in other mammals has become modified to surround this bone, while a soft pad in the centre of the underpart absorbs shock as the foot strikes the ground. With the exception of pigs and peccaries, almost all ungulates are strictly herbivorous, whether as grazers (feeding on grasses) or as browsers (feeding on foliage).

Ungulates are divided into two orders, distinguished by the number of toes possessed by their member species. Much the larger order (Artiodactyla) – with nearly 200 species in nine familes – is made up of the even-toed ungulates, or *artiodactyls*, and includes deer, cattle, pigs and others (see pp. 158–61). The smaller order (Perissodactyla), with just 17 species, is made up of three families of odd-toed ungulates, or *perissodactyls* – horses, rhinoceroses and tapirs.

Elephants (see opposite) are not hoofed – their feet are essentially large flattened pads – and are therefore not classified as ungulates.

Common zebras fighting. Zebra stallions are often aggressive, both to predators and to other stallions. Fighting frequently arises when a stallion in possession of a harem of females strives to ward off an intruding male.

A black rhinoceros with young. Rhino calves (like other perissodactyls) are well developed at birth, and will accompany their mother until the next offspring is born. Except for female white rhinos and mothers of other species with young, adult rhinos are solitary.

Horses and their relatives

The eight species of horse, ass (donkey) and zebra – the equids – are all closely related, and grouped together in a single family (Equidae). All species are superbly adapted as fast and elegant runners. Equids are naturally gregarious, living together in herds. They feed almost exclusively on grasses, and the characteristic elongated jaw houses teeth adapted for their diet – the incisors for cropping grass and large cheek teeth for grinding.

The wild horse – the ancestor of the domestic horse – is now extinct in the wild, although until well into historic times it ranged from Eastern Europe as far east as Mongolia. Other equids have also suffered drastic reductions in their range. The Asian wild ass, formerly abundant in the more open, arid habitats of southern Asia, is now limited to isolated populations. The African wild ass – the ancestor of the donkey – was once widespread over much of northern Africa, but is now on the brink of extinction in the wild. However, descendants of the wild horse and wild ass have been widely domesticated (see p. 191).

South of the Sahara, four species of zebra were once widespread. The southernmost – the quagga – is now extinct, and the mountain zebra has been reduced to a few isolated populations in southwestern Africa. The common zebra (Burchell's zebra; see photo) is still relatively widespread in eastern and southern Africa. Grevy's zebra – distinguished from the common zebra by its slightly larger size and its narrower, more numerous stripes – is still found in northern Kenya and Ethiopia.

Rhinoceroses

There are five living species of rhinoceros, or rhino – two in Africa and three in Asia. They are all massively built, with short stocky legs terminating in three hoofed toes, and a large head that has one or two horns on the top of the snout. The horns are composed of compressed hair (keratin) and are fibrous. All species are herbivorous, whether as browsers or as grazers. Rhinos are generally promiscuous, rarely forming even semi-permanent pairings.

The largest species is the white rhinoceros (the animal is in fact generally greyish in colour – 'white' is a corruption of an Afrikaans word referring to the rhino's wide lip; see photo, p. 168). It is the largest living land mammal after the elephants, standing up to 2 m (6½ ft) at the shoulder and weighing over 3.5 tonnes (tons). In common with the black rhino (the other African species) and the Sumatran rhino, the white rhino has two horns. It is primarily a grazer, with distinctive square lips for cropping grass, and is less solitary than the other rhinos.

The black rhino is also misleadingly named – it too is usually grey (see photo), albeit a shade darker than the white rhino. It is principally a browser, and – like all the Asian species – has a hooked upper lip tapering into a finger-like point, which is used to cull leaves and twigs from trees. Both African species were formerly widespread in open grasslands and woodlands south of the Sahara. Indiscriminate hunting, however, has reduced both species to scattered populations, mostly confined to national parks and reserves.

The Sumatran rhinoceros is the smallest of the rhinos, growing to a shoulder height of up to 1.5 m (5 ft). It is also known as the hairy rhinoceros, because of its scattering of bristly hairs over its thick skin. It feeds by browsing, usually in pairs. Its original range was from eastern India in the northwest to Sumatra and Borneo in the southeast, but it is now reduced to scattered and isolated populations.

The largest of the Asian species is the Indian rhinoceros. Although much the same height as the white rhino, it is far less massively built, weighing around 2 tonnes (tons). It has a single horn, and its thick skin is heavily folded at the joints, giving the appearance of armour-plating. Although still an endangered species, the Indian rhino is slowly increasing in numbers, at least in some of the reserves and parks where it is protected.

The Javan rhinoceros is like a small version of the Indian rhino in appearance, with similar folded skin and a single horn. This animal has the dubious distinction of being one of the world's most endangered mammals. It was once found in many parts of Southeast Asia from Vietnam southwards, but is now reduced to a single population in a reserve in Java, and a handful of isolated individuals in mainland Asia. There are fewer than 50 left in total, and given the animal's low birth rate, it is unlikely that the species can survive.

One of the main reasons for the decline in rhinoceros numbers is the high value placed on their horns in Asia. Among other reputed medicinal values, the horns are mistakenly thought to have aphrodisiac qualities. With the decline in the Asian species, widespread publicity by conservationists of the high prices that horn commands may ironically have led to the rapid expansion of poaching in Africa in order to supply the illicit export market.

Tapirs

One species of tapir is found in Southeast Asia, the other three in Central America and northern South America. They are shy browsing animals, never found far from water. Despite their wide geographical separation, all species are structurally very similar, with four toes on the front feet and three on the hind feet. The head tapers into a flexible proboscis, or trunk, which overhangs the upper lip; it is used to scoop leaves and other vegetable matter into the mouth. As adults, the different species of tapir vary greatly in coloration, but the young of all species are very similar, with distinctive stripes and blotches (see illustration).

The Malaysian tapir is larger than the other species, growing to a head-and-body length of up to 2.5 m (8¼ ft). Solitary and nocturnal, it occurs mainly in swampy forests from Thailand and Burma south to Sumatra. Its striking black-and-white coloration provides perfect camouflage in the moonlit forests. The Brazilian tapir is uniformly brown and further distinguished by a short erect mane on the back of the neck. The mountain tapir is the most thickly furred, the other species having short bristly fur.

Elephants

Within the geologically recent past, giant

Brazilian tapir

Malaysian tapir

mastodons and mammoths – close relatives of the elephants – occurred in the New World and across northern Eurasia (see p. 141). Today, the order Proboscidea is represented by just two species – the Asian elephant of India and Southeast Asia and the African elephant of subsaharan Africa. Two races or subspecies of the latter are recognized – the bush elephant and the smaller forest elephant.

Both African and Asian species are gregarious, living in herds in habitats from forest to savannah (see photo). Elephants are entirely vegetarian, and – despite their massive bulk – are surprisingly graceful and swift on their feet. The gestation period of elephants is very long – between 20 and 22 months, after which usually a single calf is born.

The African elephant is the largest living land animal: a large male may stand over 3.5 m (11½ ft) at the shoulder, and weigh around 7 tonnes (tons). The Asian elephant is smaller, with a shoulder height of 3 m (10 ft) and weighing up to 6 tonnes. As well as by size, the African elephant is

distinguished by its larger ears, sparser hair and less domed head. The female Asian elephant usually lacks tusks, and the male's tusks are generally much smaller than those of the African species. This size difference may be the result of evolution – the Asian elephant has been hunted for ivory for several thousand years (and hence only small-tusked strains have survived), whereas the African species has only been hunted with any intensity for just over two centuries.

The most obvious feature of all elephants is the long, flexible, muscular trunk. The trunk is formed by an enormous elongation of the nose and upper lip. The nostrils are at the tip, and the sensitive grasping lip can be used to pluck foliage or to pick up objects as small as a nut. As well as providing an efficient means of gathering food, the trunk is also used for drinking and smelling, and for producing the loud trumpeting sounds used in communication and courtship.

An elephant's tusks are in fact highly modified teeth – continuously growing upper incisors. The largest tusks measure around 3.5 m (11½ ft) and pairs can weigh over 110 kg (240 lb) – with record pairs weighing nearly twice this. However, because of relentless hunting, huge 'tuskers' are now rare, and it is unusual to see an elephant with tusks weighing much more than 30 kg (66 lb). Elephants' cheek teeth are also unusual in that they do not succeed one another vertically like those of most other mammals, but move successively from the rear, pushing out the foremost tooth as it becomes worn and useless.

Asian elephants have been tamed (although not strictly domesticated, since they are not normally captive-bred but captured and then tamed). They are used in forestry for moving timber, and also as ceremonial beasts, when they are often elaborately decorated. The African elephant can also be tamed – as the Carthaginian general Hannibal proved over 2000 years ago (see pp. 376–7). JAB

SEE ALSO

● EARLY MAMMALS p. 140
● TERRITORY, MATING, SOCIAL ORGANIZATION p. 168
● MIGRATION p. 170
● HOW ANIMALS MOVE p. 172
● LIVESTOCK FARMING p. 190

A herd of African elephants roaming in search of food. Both Asian and African elephants are highly social, living in family groups led by an old cow. An injured member of the herd will be shielded by its comrades and assisted in moving to a place of safety, while an orphaned calf will be fostered by another cow.

Artiodactyls
1. Pigs, Peccaries, Hippos, Camels

The artiodactyls, or even-toed ungulates, comprise the nine families of pigs, peccaries, hippos, camels, deer, chevrotains, giraffes, bovids and the pronghorn. It is the larger and more diverse of the two orders of ungulates, or hoofed mammals (see p. 156). There are nearly 200 species, and they are native to all the larger land masses except Australasia and most oceanic islands. The foot of most artiodactyls has four toes, but only the middle two are normally hoofed and bear the weight of the animal. The other two (the dew claws) are small, and do not touch the ground. Many species are of considerable economic importance, either as game animals or domestic livestock.

Wart hogs are more active in the daytime than most pigs, and are generally found in more open habitats. At night they shelter in burrows – from which they are often dug out by lions (see photo, p. 152).

Pigs and peccaries are omnivorous, but all other species of artiodactyl are herbivorous, and have teeth specialized for cutting and grinding plant material. With the exception of pigs, peccaries and hippos, all artiodactyls are ruminants (see box, p. 161).

Pigs

The eight species of pig form a single family (Suidae) that has a widespread distribution throughout the Old World. Pigs characteristically have short legs and heavy bodies, and the long pointed head terminates in a large flexible snout. The body of most wild pigs is covered in coarse bristly hair, which in males (boars) sometimes forms a crest along the spine.

The snout is sensitive but resilient. It is strengthened at the end with a cartilaginous disk, and is further reinforced by a bone not found in most other mammals. The upper incisors and canines often form sharp tusks, the edges being sharpened by contact with the teeth in the lower jaw. In males the tusks grow continuously throughout the animal's life and are often large, and can be extremely dangerous weapons.

All pigs are primarily forest and woodland species, and are largely nocturnal. They eat much vegetable matter, but will feed on anything edible, including carrion. In addition to grazing and browsing, they grub in forest litter using their snouts and tusks in search of insect larvae, worms and other invertebrates.

Most pigs live in small family groups, or 'sounders', of 4 to 6 members, although some species, such as the wart hog and the wild boar, are often found in much larger sounders. Pigs are notable breeders. Males produce large amounts of semen, and a female may have two or more litters a year. After a gestation of 3 to 5 months, they generally have litters of up to 6 or 8. The domestic pig and the feral boar normally have larger litters – up to 12 is common.

Although the range of several pig species has contracted, the wild boar of Eurasia – in the guise of its descendant, the domestic pig – has been spread by human agency to many parts of America, Australasia and elsewhere. Because of centuries of careful selective breeding, the domestic pig has changed strikingly from its wild ancestor, the latter being generally smaller and lighter, with a straight tail, a longer snout and a coat of thick bristles. On the continent of Europe, the wild boar is still widespread and even manages to survive in countries as densely populated as the Netherlands. It was originally found in Britain too, but became extinct in the 17th century.

The boar also occurs in North Africa, but south of the Sahara it is replaced by three other species. The African bush pig, or red river hog, occurs both on the African mainland and on Madagascar and the Comoros, where it was possibly introduced. The wart hog – so called because of the wart-like outgrowths on its face – is still abundant in many areas, and is a familiar sight in East Africa's national parks (see photo). Despite being the largest of the African pigs, the giant forest hog was one of the last really large mammals to become known to science – it was not described until 1904.

The smallest pig is the pygmy hog from the foothills of the Himalaya, which is only around 50 cm (20 in) long. Despite attempts to breed it in captivity, the species is one of the most endangered mammals in the world. Another threatened species – although not to the extent of the pygmy hog – is the babirusa of Sulawesi (Celebes) in Indonesia. The upper tusks of the babirusa grow upwards through the top of the muzzle before curving down, while the lower ones project upwards out of the mouth. These tusks cannot be used as weapons, and their precise function is unclear.

Peccaries

The three species of peccary (Tayassuidae family) are found in Central and South America. They are essentially modified pigs, and are broadly similar to pigs both in appearance and in habits. They are slightly smaller than pigs, however, and are further distinguished by the tusks, which curve downwards rather than upwards, and by a prominent scent gland on the back. Their sounders tend to be large, sometimes numbering up to a hundred. All the members of a sounder turn collectively on any predator – the animal's main method of defence.

The collared and white-lipped peccaries are the only artiodactyls to have three toes on the hind feet and four on the front feet. The Chacoan peccary was only known from fossil remains until the early 1970s, when specimens were found alive in the Gran Chaco of Bolivia, Paraguay and northern Argentina.

Hippopotamuses

The two species of the hippopotamus family (Hippopotamidae) are found only in Africa. The common hippopotamus, or hippo, originally occurred throughout most of Africa, including the delta of the River Nile, but within historic times its range has contracted considerably, through a combination of changes in habitat and overhunting. Despite this overall decline, hippos can still be found

the wild. It is found only in the remote deserts of Mongolia and China.

Both camel species are superbly adapted to life in desert conditions. Their feet (like those of other camelids) have two toes joined by a web of skin that can be splayed, so preventing the animal from sinking into soft sand. The eyes are protected from sand by heavy lashes, while the nostrils can be closed to exclude sand. The fatty humps act as food stores in case of shortage.

The camel's well-known ability to go for long periods without drinking – for over a week while travelling long distances – is due to a number of adaptations designed to conserve water. The number of sweat glands is heavily reduced, and camels do not start to sweat until the temperature reaches 40 °C (104 °F); heat accumulated in the body during the day is dissipated in the cool of the night. Camels can survive a water loss of about 40% of their body weight without suffering damage, and the water content of the urine is minimized by the kidneys. Following a prolonged period without water, camels have been known to drink over 100 litres (22 imperial gallons / 26 US gallons) in a matter of minutes.

Four species of camelid are found in South America: the vicuna, the guanaco, and the guanaco's two domesticated relatives, the llama and the alpaca. All four species are similar in size, growing to a body length of around 1.5 m (5 ft). They are slender-legged animals, with a long neck supporting a head that resembles that of the Old World camels, except that the ears are larger. Grasses form the basis of their diet, and in all species the hair is soft and woolly.

Guanacos are territorial and live in small herds (or troops) of up to 10 females and a single male. They are found in arid plains and mountains, where they move with speed and agility over the rugged terrain. The vicuna is also gregarious, but is confined to mountainous terrain. The alpaca is bred primarily for its wool, while the llama is used as a beast of burden. Llamas are famous for their spitting – a protective device performed by blowing out saliva and nasal mucus through the mouth. Since alpacas and llamas have been domesticated for around 4500 years, their precise relationship with the guanaco is uncertain.   JAB

in dense concentrations – densities of nearly 20 per km² (50 per sq mi) have been recorded along a stretch of the Nile in Uganda.

The common hippopotamus is one of the largest terrestrial mammals – only surpassed in weight by the elephants. Hippos can weigh up to 4.5 tonnes (tons), and stand 1.5 m (5 ft) at the shoulder. They are amphibious, spending most of the day sleeping and resting in water (see photo). They emerge at night to graze, mostly on grasses, which they crop with the front teeth and lips. Although strictly herbivorous, hippos are not ruminants. When lying in water, hippos can submerge almost the entire body, with only their nostrils, eyes and ears – all of which are set on top of the huge bulbous head – appearing above the surface. The belief that hippos 'sweat blood' derives from the fact that they have glands in the skin that exude droplets of an oily fluid that appear red. This secretion in fact gives protection to the hippo's virtually hairless skin.

The pygmy hippopotamus is confined to the forests of West Africa. Although similar in appearance, it is much smaller than its giant relative, standing about 85 cm (2¾ ft) at the shoulder and weighing around 225 kg (500 lb). It is less aquatic than the common hippo, not gregarious, and has probably always been rare.

Camels

Formerly more widespread, the camel family (Camelidae) is today represented by just six species – two species of camel in the Old World, and four related species confined to South America. All camelids ruminate, but are peculiar among ruminants in that the digestive glands are located in sacs in the

The dromedaries, or one-humped camels, of the Middle East and North Africa have been domesticated and used as beasts of burden for several thousand years, and no longer survive in the wild. They have been introduced into several countries, including Australia, where a large feral population exists.

lining of the rumen (see p. 161). All species show adaptations for life in arid or semi-arid plains, grasslands and deserts.

The Old World camels are among the largest of the artiodactyls. The two-humped Bactrian camel grows to over 2 m (7 ft) at the shoulder, while the one-humped dromedary is usually slightly taller, at 2.4 m (8 ft). The dromedary is native to North Africa and the Middle East, and only survives in its domesticated form (see photo). The Bactrian camel has also been domesticated and is now endangered in

Hippopotamuses are excellent swimmers. They can close their ears and nostrils, and stay submerged for up to half an hour. They often swim out to sea and return up another river, and can even walk on the bottom of rivers and lakes.

Artiodactyls 2. Deer, Giraffes, Bovids, etc.

The thirty-eight species of the *deer family* (Cervidae) are widespread throughout the northern hemisphere and in South America. They have adapted to a broad range of habitat, from tropical forest to arctic tundra. Typically, deer are delicately built, with long legs terminating in cloven (split) hooves, and all are swift and elegant runners. Their senses are also acute – vital in species otherwise so vulnerable to predators. Most species are fairly uniform in size, growing to a body length of 1 to 1.5 m (40 to 60 in) – although the largest species, the elk (known as the moose in North America), can exceed 2.5 m (8¼ ft) in length.

All species of deer are ruminants (see box). They are mainly browsers – feeding on leaves – but red deer also graze, and deer have generally adapted to grazing on grass and other vegetable matter in areas where forests have been cleared.

The characteristic feature of deer – branching antlers – are not found in any other family of animals. In most species, antlers are carried by males alone – only in the case of the reindeer (caribou) of the Arctic do both sexes possess them. The musk deer of Asia and the Chinese water deer are the only species lacking antlers, although the males of both species have short tusks formed from elongated upper canines. Antlers consist of bone and grow yearly from knobs on the skull. While growing, they are covered in soft velvety fur, but once fully grown, the blood supply is cut off, and the fur peels off, leaving only the hard bony core. Each successive set of antlers is larger and more branched than the one before, until a deer reaches maturity, after which the antlers may decline.

Although the sexes typically live in separate herds for the rest of the year, during the breeding season, or *rut*, the males of many deer species become territorial and defend harems of females (see photo). Once the rut is over, the antlers are shed, to be grown anew the following year. Most deer have only one or two young, which are well developed and

The okapi, restricted to the dense tropical forests of Zaïre, is the giraffe's only living relative. More solitary than its gregarious relative, the okapi is likewise a browser, using its long tongue to gather foliage. The tongue is indeed so long that it can be used to clean the animal's eyes. Such is the okapi's unobtrusive life style that – despite being the size of a large zebra – it remained unknown to science until 1901.

Reindeer stags and males of most other deer species establish a territory during the breeding season (or rut), and use their antlers to ward off rival males. Occasionally the antlers may get locked together – in which case the animals concerned will starve to death.

often able to follow their mother within hours of birth. Unlike adults, which tend to be drab brown, the young are frequently heavily spotted.

Chevrotains

The four species of chevrotain, or mouse deer – although placed in a separate family (Tragulidae) – are fairly closely related to deer. They are like tiny deer in appearance, growing to between 20 and 35 cm (8 and 14 in) at the shoulder. Generally found near water in the tropical forests and swamps of Africa and Asia, chevrotains graze and browse at night on the forest undergrowth. They lack horns or antlers, but in males the upper canines have developed into tusks.

The giraffe family

The giraffe family (Giraffidae) consists of only two living species – the elusive okapi of the tropical forests of Zaïre (see illustration) and the giraffe. Male okapis and giraffes of both sexes have two or three distinctive skin-covered horns, which are formed from bony outgrowths and are never shed. Both species are ruminants. Formerly found in open habitats throughout Africa, the giraffe is now restricted to subsaharan Africa, but is still relatively abundant in eastern and southern Africa. The giraffe's characteristic pattern of brown blotches is highly variable, and a number of distinct geographical races are recognized.

With its long slender legs and enormously elongated neck, the giraffe is by far the tallest land animal. Male giraffes grow to a height of about 5.5 m (18 ft) – about a metre more than females. Although the giraffe's neck has only seven vertebrae – the same as most other mammals – the bones are greatly elongated and the joints

are of the ball-and-socket kind (see p. 206), giving extra flexibility. In order to allow blood to ascend to the head and to prevent a sudden surge of blood when the animal bends down to drink, there is a series of valves within the neck to regulate the blood supply. When giraffes walk or run, the neck moves rhythmically backwards and forwards, thus shifting the centre of gravity and maintaining balance. Giraffes have long tongues – nearly 45 cm (18 in) in length – enabling them to browse on the tops of bushes and trees. They usually remain standing even when sleeping.

Bovids

The bovid family (Bovidae) is a highly diverse group containing 128 species of antelope, cattle, sheep and various related species. The family includes some of man's most important domestic animals (see p. 191). Bovids are most numerous and diverse in Africa, but they are well represented in most parts of Eurasia and North America, and also occur on some Arctic and Southeast Asian islands. Although bovids have adapted to a wide range of other habitats, the majority of species favour open grassland, scrub or desert. Diversity in habitat is matched by great diversity in size and form: at one extreme is the tiny royal (or pygmy) antelope of West Africa, standing a mere 25 cm (10 in) at the shoulder; at the other, the massively built bisons of North America and Europe, growing to a shoulder height of 2.2 m (7¼ ft).

Despite differences in size and appearance, bovids are united by the possession of certain common features. All species are ruminants and almost exclusively herbivorous. Typically their teeth are highly modified for browsing and grazing: grass or foliage is cropped with the upper lip and lower incisors (the upper incisors are missing), and then ground down by the large check teeth.

Skull of a bison

As well as having the cloven hoof common to other artiodactyls, the males of all bovid species and the females of most carry horns. Bovid horns have bony cores covered in a sheath of horny material that is constantly renewed from within; they are unbranched and never shed. They vary in shape from the long corkscrew spirals of the greater kudu of Africa to the ramshorn spirals of the American bighorn. The horns of a large Indian buffalo may measure around 4 m (13 ft) from tip to tip along the outer curve, while the various gazelles have horns with a wide variety of elegant curves.

The lines of development within the bovid family are not clearly understood, but five groups or subfamilies may be distinguished. The subfamily Bovinae comprises most of the larger bovids, including the African bongo and nilgai, elands, bison and cattle, all of which (unlike most other bovids) are non-territorial. The spiral-horned elands of Africa range from the giant eland – the largest of all antelopes, sometimes weighing over 900 kg (1985 lb) – to the tiny bushbuck, about a tenth of the weight of its massive relative. The ancestors of the various species of domestic cattle – banteng, gaur (or Indian bison), yak and water buffalo – are generally rare and endangered in the wild, while the aurochs (the ancestor of the domestic cattle of Europe) is extinct.

The term 'antelope' does not designate a precise zoological grouping – the name is used somewhat loosely to describe a number of bovids that have followed different lines of development. Antelopes are typically long-legged, fast-running species, often with long horns that may be laid along the back when the animal is in full flight. The majority of antelopes belong to two subfamilies: Hippotraginae, which includes the oryxes and the addax, wildebeest (or gnus), roan antelopes and kobs; and Antilopinae, which generally contains slighter and more graceful animals such as gazelles, the impala and the springbok.

Antelopes are mainly grassland species, but many have adapted to flooded grasslands: pukus, waterbucks and lechwes are

all good swimmers, usually feeding belly-deep in water, while the sitatunga has long splayed hooves that enable it to move freely over swampy ground. Some species of antelope, such as the addax and the oryxes (see photo), can survive for very long periods without drinking.

The subfamily Caprinae includes sheep and goats, together with various relatives such as gorals, serows, takins and tahrs. Most are woolly or have long hair. Several species, such as wild goats, chamois and ibex, are agile cliff- and mountain-dwellers. Tolerance of extreme conditions is particularly marked in this group: barbary and bighorn sheep have adapted to arid deserts, while Rocky Mountain sheep survive high up in mountains and musk ox in arctic tundra.

The duikers of Africa (subfamily Cephalophinae) are generally small and solitary, often living in thick forest. Although mainly feeding on grass and leaves, some duikers – unlike most other bovids – are

believed to eat insects and carrion, and even to kill small animals.

The pronghorn

The pronghorn of North America is the sole survivor of a New World family of herbivorous ruminants (Antilocapridae), similar in habits and appearance to the Old World antelopes. Males and most females carry horns that consist of a bony core covered with a horny sheath, rather like branched cattle horns, but – unlike the horns of cattle – the sheath is shed after each breeding season. Although greatly reduced in numbers since the advent of European settlers and the subsequent enclosure of grasslands, the pronghorn is still found in considerable numbers throughout North America from Washington State to Mexico. When alarmed by the approach of wolves or other predators, hairs on the pronghorn's rump stand erect, so emphasizing the animal's white rump-patch. At this signal, the whole herd gallops off at speeds of over 64 km/h (40 mph).   JAB

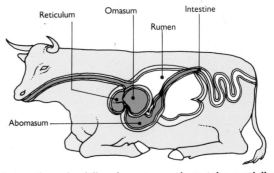

Gemsbok and other species of oryx have adapted well to arid conditions. They can survive for very long periods without drinking, relying on dew and moisture from roots and bulbs. Like most other antelopes, oryxes are gregarious, and may gather in large herds, particularly after the rains.

SEE ALSO
● UNGULATE CLASSIFICATION p. 156
● ARTIODACTYLS I p. 158
● ANIMAL COMMUNICATION p. 166
● TERRITORY, MATING, SOCIAL ORGANIZATION p. 168
● MIGRATION p. 170
● ECOSYSTEMS pp. 180–7
● LIVESTOCK FARMING p. 190

RUMINATION

GRAZING

RUMINATING

Reticulum   Omasum   Intestine
Rumen
Abomasum

Apart from pigs, peccaries and hippopotamuses, all artiodactyls are *ruminants*: they ruminate, or 'chew the cud', as an important part of their digestive process. For this purpose, camels have a three-chambered stomach and show certain exceptional features (see p. 159), but other ruminants have a specialized stomach with four chambers.

While grazing, ruminants crop plant matter as fast as possible, masticating it with their large and mobile tongue. When swallowed, the food passes into the *rumen* (the large storage chamber) and the *reticulum*, where the cellulose of plant cell walls (which cannot be digested by gastric juices) is broken down by symbiotic micro-organisms (see p. 175).

Later, the animal lies down to ruminate: the partially digested plant material, known as 'cud', is regurgitated, chewed further, and reswallowed. The food now passes into the *omasum*, where most of the water is absorbed, and then into the *abomasum* – the 'true' stomach, corresponding to the stomach of other mammals – where it is acted on by ordinary digestive juices.

Rumination allows animals to exploit coarse grasses and other plant matter that would otherwise be unusable. It also reduces the time taken to amass food – important for animals that often graze in places where they are vulnerable to predators.

Marine Mammals

In the course of evolution, some mammals returned to the sea, where millions of years previously their fish ancestors had lived. Some, such as seals, have to return to land to breed, but whales, manatees and others are entirely aquatic: they eat, sleep and give birth in water. Although united by their dependence on water, the various groups of marine mammals have separate origins. The carnivorous pinnipeds (seals and the walrus) are related to the land carnivores (see pp. 152–5), while the sirenians (manatees and the dugong) share a common ancestry with elephants and – like elephants – are herbivorous. The cetaceans (whales and dolphins) form a completely separate group, related neither to the seals nor to the sirenians.

Internally the bones and organs of marine mammals all closely resemble those of land mammals, and – although superficially fish-like – their paddles are in fact modified limbs. Like all other mammals, marine mammals breathe by taking in oxygen from the air, and so have to return to the surface at intervals to breathe. In some species, the respiratory system is similar to that of land mammals, but in the whales, the nose – or blowhole – is set high up on the head, and the nostrils can be closed by valves to prevent water from entering the lungs during dives.

An American manatee. The sirenians or sea cows – manatees and the dugong – are the only herbivorous marine mammals. Among other adaptations to life as shallow-water grazers, they lack air spaces in their bones, allowing them to sink effortlessly and remain submerged.

Manatees and the dugong

The order Sirenia contains just four species – the single surviving species of dugong (family Dugongidae), and three species of manatee (family Trichechidae). The sirenians are also known as sea cows, as they are the only herbivorous marine mammals, feeding mainly on seaweed and other marine plants.

Manatees are found in the tropical and subtropical coastal waters of the Atlantic and adjacent river systems (see photo), while the dugong is found at similar latitudes in the Indian Ocean, the Red Sea and the western Pacific. Another species of sirenian – and the largest, growing to about 7.5 m (24½ ft) in length and weighing around 4 tonnes (tons) – was Steller's sea cow, which was confined to the Bering Sea and was the only species adapted to cold water. It had been hunted to extinction within three decades of its discovery in 1741.

The surviving species of sirenian grow to about 4 m (13 ft) in length. All have heavy but streamlined bodies, tapering to the rear. The forelimbs are modified into paddles, and the hind limbs are absent. The tail is horizontally flattened – the dugong's into a crescent-shaped fluke, the manatees' into an oval fluke. Although the body is virtually hairless, the muzzle is covered in thick stiff whiskers. The dugong has a flexible overhanging upper lip, which it uses to uproot clumps of seaweed and other plants, and males have tusks formed from the incisor teeth. Manatees have a deeply split upper lip, allowing each half to be moved independently. The dugong is mainly solitary, while manatees are more gregarious, sometimes gathering in large herds.

Seals and the walrus

The order Pinnipedia includes three families: the eared seal family (Otariidae) – distinguished by the possession of external ears – which includes 13 species of fur seal and sea lion; 18 species of earless (or 'true') seals (family Phocidae); and the single species of the walrus family (Odobenidae). The pinnipeds are closely related to the order Carnivora, and are indeed sometimes included in that order.

Walruses are social animals, forming vast herds in the breeding season, up to 3000 strong. Males set up and defend territories, in which they gather together and mate with a number of females. Usually a single pup is born, which (unlike most pinnipeds) remains with its mother for about two years.

All species are predatory, feeding mainly on fish and squid.

The hands and feet of pinnipeds are flattened into flippers, and the body is streamlined. All species have thick layers of insulating blubber, and most species have a covering of coarse hair to protect the skin when on shore. Although pinnipeds are more at home in water, all species are capable of moving on land – and have to return to the shore to breed and to moult. Walruses and the eared seals are able to bring their hind limbs forward to facilitate movement on land – an ability lacking in the true seals.

Most pinnipeds are highly gregarious. During the breeding season, they gather in large numbers at traditional breeding grounds called rookeries. Males (much larger than females in most species) typically become highly territorial, with dominant males seeking to defend harems of females (see photo, p. 168). All sea lions and many other seal species give birth to young conceived during the previous breeding season, so allowing birth and mating to be synchronized in the short period when adults are together on land.

Although less mobile than other pinnipeds on land, earless seals are superb swimmers and divers. The Weddell seal of the Antarctic, for instance, regularly dives to depths of over 300 m (985 ft), and one was recorded at 600 m (1970 ft), where it remained for 43 minutes. To facilitate prolonged dives, seals are able to shut off the blood supply to all the organs except the brain (the muscles operate on their

SEE ALSO

● ANIMAL BEHAVIOUR
  pp. 166–73
● ECOSYSTEMS: AQUATIC
  p. 178
● FISHING p. 194

own stored oxygen), and the blood itself has a higher oxygen-storage capacity than that of other mammals.

Walruses are usually found in the shallow coastal waters of the Arctic (see photo). Male walruses can grow to around 3.5 m (11½ ft) and weigh around 1.5 tonnes (tons). Tusks formed from the upper canine teeth are present in both sexes, but are larger in males. They grow continually for up to 30 years, reaching lengths of over 1 m (39 in). The walrus uses its tusks to heave itself onto ice floes and to keep open breathing holes in the ice. They are also used to plough up the sea bed in search of molluscs and for sparring with rival males in the breeding season.

Several species of seal have been brought to the brink of extinction by hunting for meat, oils and hides. However, under protection, most seals show remarkable powers of recovery. The huge northern elephant seal, for instance, once found from Alaska to California, was reduced to fewer than 100 individuals by 1900. Now protected, its numbers have grown to over 60 000.

Whales, dolphins and porpoises

The order Cetacea is divided into two groups: one of toothed whales (dolphins, porpoises and most of the smaller whales); the other of baleen whales, which contains most of the giants of the sea, including the blue whale, the largest animal ever known to have existed.

Unlike all other marine mammals, the cetaceans spend their entire life in water. They occur in all oceans, as well as a few of the larger river systems and lakes connected to them. Their adaptations to marine life are similar to those of seals: the body is streamlined, there is an insulating layer of blubber, and the limbs are modified into paddles. In cetaceans, however – like sirenians – the hind limbs are absent, and instead there is a horizontally flattened tail fluke, which provides the principal means of propulsion (see photo, p. 172). To varying degrees, all whales are gregarious, forming groups known as *schools*.

The five families of **toothed whales** (the larger of the two cetacean groups) include the dolphin and porpoise family (Delphinidae, 40 species); the river dolphin family (Platanistidae, 6 species); and three families of whales – sperm whales (Physeteridae, 3 species), white whales (Monodontidae, 2 species), and beaked whales (Ziphiidae, 18 species).

All species have teeth, ranging from a single pair in some of the beaked whales to as many as 260 in some dolphin species – a record for any mammal. Toothed whales feed mainly on fish, octopus and squid. In order to detect prey, most species use a form of ultrasonic sonar, similar to the echolocation used by bats (see p. 146), emitting rapid high-pitched squeaks and clicks in order to gauge the position of surrounding objects.

Most dolphins are characterized by their streamlined form and beaked snouts. They are extremely gregarious, forming schools sometimes of over a hundred individuals (not necessarily of a single species), in which a well-developed social hierarchy is established. Dolphins generally grow to between 2.5 and 4 m (8¼ and 13 ft) and the largest of them – the killer whale (see photo) – can grow to over 9 m (30 ft). Dolphins produce a single offspring, which – like all marine mammals – is well developed at birth. The calf is usually born tail-first, and is helped to the surface by its mother to take its first breath of air.

River dolphins are found in the major river systems of India, South America and China. They have long slender beaks and domed foreheads. Because their native rivers are muddy and murky, they are heavily dependent on echolocation to avoid obstacles and detect prey, and some species, such as the Ganges dolphin, are blind.

The porpoises are the smallest of the whales. They are very similar to dolphins, but are shorter and stockier, and do not have a beaked snout. They are generally found in coastal waters, often venturing up rivers for several kilometres.

The largest of the toothed whales is the sperm whale. Males formerly grew to about 24 m (79 ft) – roughly twice the size of females – but two centuries of intensive hunting have led to a considerable decrease in size. The most striking feature of the sperm whale is its huge squarish head, which contains the largest brain of any animal – weighing around 9.2 kg (over 20 lb). The majority of the head, however, is filled with spermaceti wax – nearly 2000 litres of it – which gives the whale its name. The precise function of this wax is not known, but it may be involved in sound transmission, or help to regulate buoyancy during dives. Sperm whales can dive to around 1000 m (3280 ft) and remain submerged for up to 75 minutes. They feed mainly on deepwater squid.

The two species of white whale are restricted to Arctic coastal waters. One of them, the narwhal, has an extraordinary spiral tusk, which may grow to over 2.5 m (8¼ ft) – sometimes as long as the whale's body. It is in fact a hugely elongated upper incisor, but its precise function is unclear.

There are three families of **baleen whales**: the single species of the grey whale family (Eschrichtidae) of the coastal waters of the northern Pacific; three species of right whale (Balaenidae); and six species of rorqual whale (Balaenopteridae). Despite their great size, all baleen species feed by filtering food from sea water. In the southern oceans, krill (tiny planktonic crustaceans) form the principal part of their diet, but other planktonic animal life and even small fish may also be eaten. In order to accommodate this specialized diet, the teeth are replaced by hundreds of sheets of horny brush-like material known as *baleen* (or *whalebone*), which hang from the upper jaw. The inner edges of these sheets are fringed with long fibres, which mat together to form a sieve. In order to feed, a baleen whale takes a huge mouthful of water, half shuts the mouth, and then presses the tongue forward: the water is forced out, while the krill (or other food) remains behind and is swallowed.

Rorquals are distinguished from other baleen whales by the many grooves – up to 94 in the case of the blue whale – running along the throat. The vast blue whale grows to around 30 m (100 ft) and can weigh over 150 tonnes (tons). It feeds only during the summer months, but during this time may consume over 2 tonnes of krill per day.

The humpback whale – another rorqual – is more gregarious than the blue whale, and is usually seen in family groups of three or four members. As is the case with other rorquals, these whales are great migrants. They move from their summer feeding grounds off Alaska to spend the winter in the tropical waters off Hawaii, where they produce the calves conceived during the previous breeding season, mate, and indulge in their famous singing. Their complex songs usually last for about 10 minutes, and may be repeated for hours on end. Their purpose is not clear, but they seem to be mainly confined to the breeding season and are specific to different populations. They may aid identification and help to coordinate movement during migration.

Right whales are so called because they were regarded by whalers as the 'right' whales to kill: they are stockier and less streamlined than other baleen whales, and so more easily overtaken. They lack throat furrows and have enormous heads, which accommodate 700 baleen plates. Right whales have been hunted commercially in such numbers that today they are rare. Their fate is typical of other large whales, almost all of which have been hunted to the point of extinction (see p. 195).   JAB

The killer whale is the world's largest predator of warm-blooded prey, moving in packs to hunt for seals, penguins and even other species of whale. Although closely related to dolphins, the killer whale is not only much bigger, but is further distinguished by its unbeaked snout and exceptionally tall dorsal fin – growing to nearly 2 m (6 ½ ft) in adult males.

Primates

Although the similarity between man and the apes has long been recognized, the likeness was regarded by many as purely coincidental and no particular significance was placed on the fact. Indeed, when Linnaeus (see p. 108) classified man as a primate in 1758, it was generally regarded as a great blow to human dignity, and subsequent classifications persisted in placing man in a separate order. Only after Darwin (see p. 112) was it generally accepted that man does indeed belong with the primates.

The order Primates consists of around 180 species, ranging in size from the tiny mouse lemur to the powerful gorilla. Apart from man, they are largely confined to the tropical regions of the world. Within the order, two suborders are recognized: the *prosimians*, or primitive primates, which include lemurs, the aye-aye, lorises and tarsiers; and the *anthropoids*, or higher primates, which include marmosets, monkeys, apes and man. Tree shrews (see p. 141) have traditionally been classified as primates on the basis of structural similarities, but recent analysis of molecular data has placed them in an order of their own, far removed from the primates.

Primate characteristics

Although highly varied in form, primates are distinguished as a group by certain common characteristics, including a flexibility of behaviour that is linked to their relatively large brains. Many of their distinguishing characteristics are related to their essentially arboreal (tree-dwelling) nature. While smell is the most important sense for most ground-living mammals, the primates – particularly the anthropoids – have a well-developed visual system, with forward-facing eyes and binocular (i.e. stereoscopic) vision, and a highly refined sense of touch, with sensitive tactile pads on fingers and toes and flat nails rather than claws. It is possible that it was this development of

The aye-aye, found in the dense forests of Madagascar, is the only species in its family (Danbentoniidae). It has large, naked ears, rodent-like incisors, and long, slender fingers, particularly the third one. It taps on a tree trunk to locate insect larvae, listens for movement, then uses its long finger to extract its prey. Sometimes it first tears open the wood with its powerful teeth. The young are produced only every 2–3 years, and are suckled for a full year.

sight and touch that has allowed primates – particularly man – to become so highly versatile in their behaviour. The large brains of primates, notable for the complexity and elaboration of the cerebral cortex, resulted in the development of intelligence, particularly in the higher primates such as man.

Another characteristic primate feature is their prehensile (grasping) hands and feet, vital for moving around safely in trees, and the opposable thumb and big toe, which are capable of being moved freely and rotated. Although less well developed in the prosimians, this ability gives primates both power and precision in their grip.

Most primates usually have single births or twins, and all have a long life-cycle and gestation period relative to their size. But the most notable feature of primates is not in the gestation period itself but in the length of time the young remain psychologically dependent on their parents – 2½ years in lemurs, 3½–4 years in monkeys, 3–5 years in apes, and 12–14 years or more in man. These periods of dependence seem to be correlated with brain size and complexity of social system.

Lemurs

Most species of lemur are confined to the forests of Madagascar, although some are found in the nearby Comoro Islands, where they may have been introduced by man. Lemurs are primarily arboreal but may come down to the ground to look for food. Their diet includes insects, small vertebrates, fruit buds, shoots, leaves and bark. Many species are nocturnal. All except the indri have long tails – often longer than the head and body combined. The young are usually produced annually and suckled for 6 months. Both sexes have special scent glands to mark their territorial boundaries.

The smallest are the 7 species of mouse lemur (family Cheirogaleidae), with a head-and-body length of 12.5–15 cm (5–6 in), while the true lemurs (Lemuridae; 16 species) grow to around 45 cm (18 in). The ring-tailed lemur has a conspicuous bushy tail banded in black and white; it is active by day and spends much time on the ground. The indri (family Indriidae) is the largest lemur, up to 90 cm (3 ft) long and almost tailless. The closely related sifakas are around half their size, and can leap considerable distances from tree to tree – up to 10 m (33 ft) – aided by gliding membranes (see p. 147).

Lorises, pottos and galagos

Eleven species of the family Lorisidae – the lorises, pottos and galagos (or bushbabies) – are found in Africa and southern Asia. They are largely nocturnal and arboreal, with large, round eyes. The lorises and pottos are small (less than 40 cm / 16 in long), and have no tails. Although slow-moving and not known to leap or jump, they are skilled climbers. Feeding largely on insects, they approach their prey stealthily and then seize it with their hands. The galagos, by contrast, are agile leapers and have long furry tails. The largest species, the greater galago, grows to 37 cm (14½ in) plus a tail of 47 cm

The Marimonda spider monkey, with its long limbs and prehensile (grasping) tail, is among the most agile and acrobatic of all New World monkeys. Spider monkeys use their tails as a fifth limb to grasp branches or gather food.

(18½ in) and the smallest, Demidoff's galago, to around 10 cm (4 in) with a tail of 15 cm (6 in). Galagos eat a wide variety of insects and other small animals, as well as gums and nectar.

Tarsiers

The three closely related species of tarsier (family Tarsiidae) are found in the forests and other thickly vegetated habitats of the Philippines and Indonesia. They are at the most 16 cm (6½ in) long, with a naked tail up to 27 cm (11 in). Their most obvious features are their huge eyes, which are 16 mm (⅔ in) in diameter. They have short arms and long legs, and the fingers and toes are all tipped with soft round pads enabling them to grip almost any surface. They are proficient jumpers: on the ground they can leap distances of 1.7 m (5½ ft) and to a height of 0.6 m (2 ft), and can make even greater leaps from tree to tree.

Marmosets and tamarins

The marmosets and tamarins (family Callitrichidae) are the smallest of the an-

Male mandrills are distinguished by their bright facial and posterior markings. Along with the olive baboon, the heavily built mandrill is the largest of the Old World monkeys, weighing up to 19.5 kg (43 lb) and with a body length up to 1 m (3¼ ft).

thropoids, with a body length of 13–37 cm (5¼–15 in) and long tails. Many have tufts or ruffs of fur round their heads, and all have claws on hands and feet, with a flat nail only on the big toe. These and the monkeys of the Cebidae family (see below) are the only non-human primates found in the New World. Both families have flat noses with widely spaced nostrils, in contrast to the Old World monkeys (see below). The marmosets and tamarins live mostly in tropical forest, particularly around the Amazon basin. Like all the anthropoids except the night monkey, they are active by day. They are mainly arboreal, bounding swiftly through the trees rather like squirrels. They have a varied diet including nuts, insects, bark and sap, and are sociable animals living in small family groups.

The New World monkeys

The 31 species of New World monkey belong to the family Cebidae, and include capuchins, howlers, spider monkeys and woolly monkeys. They are mostly confined to the tropical forests of South America and are largely arboreal. Apart from the uakari, they all have long, often strongly prehensile tails, which serve as a fifth limb when swinging through the forest. They range in size from the squirrel monkeys, which are around the size of marmosets, to the massive howler monkeys, with a body length of 80–90 cm (32–36 in). Howlers are noted for their powerful voices, which can be heard up to 3 km (1.9 mi) away. The male howler calls loudly for periods of up to half an hour to signal possession of a territory. All New World monkeys are gregarious, living in family-based groups with much visual and vocal communication. Their diet is largely vegetarian.

The Old World monkeys

The 85 species of Old World monkey (family Cercopithecidae) include the macaques, mandrills, mangabeys and others. They are found in Africa, Asia and Indonesia, in a much greater range of habitats than the South American monkeys. All walk on all fours and have thin noses with forward-pointing nostrils, and none have prehensile tails. Some species, such as baboons (see photo p. 167), are found in open, often rocky, arid areas, and spend most of their time on the ground – although they generally sleep in trees. The Japanese macaque is the only primate other than man that lives in latitudes where winter temperatures drop below freezing.

The Old World monkeys are generally larger than the South American primates, and often have heavy manes and bare buttock pads, sometimes brightly coloured. The male proboscis monkey of Borneo has a huge pendulous nose that straightens out when it makes its loud honking call. The females are generally smaller – sometimes only half the size – and less brightly coloured, with lighter manes or none at all. Old World monkeys are primarily vegetarian, but some may supplement their diet with insects and small animals.

The gibbons

All members of the ape family (Pongidae) have protruding jaws and lack tails, but the slender, agile gibbons are otherwise very different from the sturdy, powerful great apes. The nine species of gibbon are all found in the forests of Southeast Asia and Indonesia. They are perhaps the best adapted of all mammals for moving swiftly through the forest canopy, using their extremely long arms and hooked hands to swing from branch to branch. The largest is the siamang, with a body length of 90 cm (3 ft) and a spread of 1.5 m (nearly 5 ft) from hand to hand. Most male gibbons have an inflatable throat sac used to amplify their voice. The loud calls are important both for communicating within the family group and for defining their territory. Gibbons are primarily fruit eaters, and live in family groups of two to six.

The great apes

The four species of great ape are man's closest living relatives. The arboreal orang-utan, confined to the rainforests of Borneo and Sumatra, is the second largest primate, weighing up to 90 kg (almost 200 lb). Males are much larger and heavier than females, and as they grow old they develop distinctive cheek flaps. Orang-utans live alone or in small family groups. Fruit is their staple diet.

The chimpanzee is found in Africa, having a relatively wide range in woodland and forest south of the Sahara and north and east of the Zaïre River, while the pygmy chimpanzee is found only in Zaïre. Like gorillas and man, chimpanzees are largely terrestrial, and

both chimpanzees and gorillas walk on the knuckles of their hands. Chimpanzees are intelligent and social animals, using a wide range of gestures and sound for communication. They live in groups of varying composition, sometimes having as many as 50 members. When standing, the male can measure up to 1.7 m (5 ft 8 in) and is strongly built with long powerful arms. They eat a wide range of food, basically vegetarian, but also including insects, birds' eggs, and small birds and mammals. They use sticks as tools to winkle termites or ants from their mounds, hurl stones at intruders, and use leaves as sponges to soak up water. They build nests to sleep in, constructing a fresh one each night. The young live with their mothers for about 3 years.

The largest of the primates is the gorilla, found in the forests of the Zaïre basin, with isolated populations of mountain gorillas on the slopes of the mountains between Rwanda and Zaïre. When standing they are not much taller than large chimpanzees, but they are much more heavily and powerfully built. A male gorilla may measure up to 175 cm (70 in) around the chest and weigh up to 275 kg (605 lb). Although females and young gorillas climb trees, males rarely do so because of their size. Gorillas live in family groups of 12 to 14 with a 'silverback' (a mature male) at the head. Gorillas are almost exclusively vegetarian in their diet; like chimpanzees, they build a nest each night to sleep in.   JAB

SEE ALSO

● THE CLASSIFICATION OF LIFE p. 108
● EVOLUTION p. 112
● EARLY MAMMALS p. 140
● ANIMAL COMMUNICATION p. 166
● TERRITORY, MATING AND SOCIAL ORGANIZATION p. 168
● PHYSICAL EVOLUTION (HUMAN) p. 200
● HUMAN ANATOMY, PHYSIOLOGY AND PSYCHOLOGY pp. 202–33

Gorillas – despite their reputation for ferocity – are gentle, intelligent and social animals, living in close-knit family groups. Encounters with neighbouring groups are avoided by drumming on the ground from a distance. Old males threaten younger rivals by standing erect and beating the chest, roaring and sometimes tearing up and throwing plants.

Animal Communication

The roar of a stag and the faint whiff of a scent, the flash of a brightly coloured wing and the complex speech of humans – these are all means of communication. They are signals produced by one individual, the *signaller*, and they carry information about the state of the signaller to another individual, the *recipient*.

The signal is intended to broadcast information about the signaller's present state. The meaning of the signal to a recipient depends on the recipient's status. To a neighbouring male the territorial song of a bird reveals the presence of a rival, possibly to be challenged. To an unmated female the same song indicates a potential mate, while a mated female ignores it.

Functions of communication

A major function of communication is to bring the sexes together for reproduction. It is the means by which the species, sex, reproductive state and sometimes even the particular individuals concerned are identified. Courtship often involves complex displays in which one or both partners posture and perhaps call to each other. Such displays enable partners to learn to recognize each other and to assess each other's suitability as mates.

Communication is also important in spacing out animals, in marking territorial boundaries, and in establishing a position in a hierarchy through aggression and submission. Size or pitch of voice may indicate competitive status, as may the possession of weapons such as antlers (see photo, p. 160). Submission is often signalled by particular postures (see photo).

Defence against attack by rivals or predators often involves intense or sudden signals. Mammals often let out loud low-pitched roars or screams when threatened. Rabbits and deer use tail flashes to warn others of impending danger, while birds use various kinds of alarm call. Vervet monkeys use different alarm calls to indicate different predators, such as snakes, eagles and leopards. Unpleasant-tasting or poisonous animals such as wasps and snakes often indicate their unpalatability by adopting bright warning coloration, typically black, with bands of red or yellow (see box).

Information on food sources may be communicated through transmission of the odour or taste of the food from a successful forager to other members of the group. This method is used by both bees and rats. Bees also transmit information about food sources through complex dances (see box).

Communication signals

The form of communication signal differs

Chemical signals released by animals to affect the behaviour of members of their own species are commonly known as *pheromones*. Among many uses, they serve to mark trails, to indicate territorial boundaries, to signal alarm and to attract sexual partners. Such signals can be perceived with extraordinary sensitivity: some male moths, for example, use their antennae to detect the pheromone released by females over distances of several kilometres.

depending on the information to be conveyed, the distance over which it has to travel, and the habitat of the animals concerned.

Chemical signals depend on the sense of smell and sometimes the sense of taste. Such signals can travel over long distances if carried on wind currents, but can only be perceived downwind. They may be used for long-term signalling, as when mammals such as hyena and deer mark their territory, while the food trails left by ants are a form of short-term signalling. Specific chemicals that have particular effects are called *pheromones*. In honeybee colonies, for instance, the queen produces a pheromone, 'queen substance', that prevents the ovaries of the worker bees developing (see p. 127). Pheromones serve a wide variety of other purposes, and are particularly important as sex attractants (see photo).

Acoustic signals can change very rapidly in pitch and intensity, and so can be used to convey a wide range of information. They also travel very fast and in all directions from the signaller, and are easy for the recipient to locate. The intensity of the signal – and hence the distance it travels – is enhanced by some ingenious devices. Mole crickets construct a horn-shaped burrow that increases the sound produced by the cricket some twenty times. Howler monkeys, and some birds, frogs and toads have large vocal sacs that amplify the sound made by the animal (see photo, p. 130).

Because low sound frequencies travel further than higher ones, large animals such as whales and elephants use very low frequencies – below the human hearing range – to communicate over long distances. Sound travels especially well in water, and the songs of baleen whales can travel over hundreds of kilometres. Some whales and dolphins emit a wide variety of whistles and squeaks. Humpback whales produce songs that generally

Submission to a dominant individual within a social hierarchy may be signalled by particular postures. Within a wolf pack, submission is indicated by a crouching posture, with ears held back and tail between the legs.

DO ANIMALS HAVE LANGUAGE?

To qualify as language, a communication system must be symbolic and must be able to denote abstract ideas, as well as things and events that are distant in time and place. It used to be thought that language was an exclusively human attribute, but some animal communication systems show features in common with language.

The 'dance language' of bees is a well-known example. When a worker bee has found a good source of food a hundred metres or so from the hive, she returns to the hive and performs on the vertical comb a dance in the form of a flattened figure of eight. The worker waggles her abdomen to and fro as she marks out the figure, and each waggle is accompanied by a burst of sound. The further away the food is from the hive, the slower the rate at which the bee dances; the more intense the waggle and the sound, the greater the food supply. The angle at which the straight part of the dance is performed indicates the direction of the food source. The top of the comb is equivalent to the position of the Sun outside, and the dance is performed at the same angle to this vertical position as the food source is to the Sun. The dance is therefore symbolic, and codes for the direction, the distance and the abundance of the food source.

Another example of possible language in animals is the controversial attempts to teach chimpanzees and gorillas to communicate with humans using speech or symbols. All attempts to teach chimps to talk have failed because they do not have the necessary vocal apparatus to produce sounds as we do, but attempts to teach them to use sign language have been more successful. A young female chimp called Washoe was taught well over a hundred symbols of the American Sign Language used by deaf people. She learned to use the symbols in the appropriate contexts and to string them together to indicate, for example, 'gimme sweet' or 'come open'. Another chimp, Sarah, was taught to use coloured plastic symbols to represent words, and could answer questions with the appropriate symbols. These tests show that chimps can certainly learn to use abstract symbols to indicate objects and actions, but how far this – or the dance language of bees – can be equated with human language is an area of continuing debate.

Tactile signals are particularly important among primates, as indications of friendship and appeasement. Grooming of one individual by another, as seen in these Guinea baboons, serves to strengthen bonds between family members and partners – as well as helping to remove unwanted parasites.

and brightly coloured, and is waved in a characteristic way to attract females. The bright colours and patterns of butterfly wings and of many male birds attract mates over short distances, while bowerbirds build special mating areas to attract females (see p. 139).

As they fly at night, male lampyrid beetles produce flashes of light in characteristic patterns to which the females on the ground respond with their own flashes. Females of a different species mimic these responding flashes, and then eat the unsuspecting males as they fly down to mate with them.

Tactile signals can only be used close at hand (see photo), while *vibration signals* are operative only over short distances. Male orb-web spiders indicate their presence to females by vibrating their webs in a characteristic way, thus dissuading females from treating them as prey (see p. 125). Male water striders make ripples on the water surface that are detected by the antennae of recipients – rival males and potential mates. Mole rats bang their heads against the roofs of their underground tunnels to communicate with both rivals and mates – a method also employed by tunnelling insects, such as deathwatch beetles.

Electrical signals are used by some fish that live in muddy rivers in South America and Africa. These signals can pass through solid objects and are used aggressively and in courtship, as well as for purposes of navigation (see p. 129). GS

SEE ALSO

- ● ANIMAL GROUPS pp. 122–65
- ● TERRITORY, MATING, SOCIAL ORGANIZATION p. 168
- ● TOUCH, TASTE, SMELL p. 216
- ● SEEING AND HEARING p. 218
- ● THE POWER OF SPEECH p. 226
- ● BODY LANGUAGE (HUMAN) p. 228
- ● HOW LANGUAGE WORKS p. 608
- ● THE LANGUAGE OF SIGNS p. 610

last 10 minutes, although songs up to 30 minutes long have been recorded. The songs probably help to keep groups of whales together and to aid cooperation between them (see pp. 162–3).

Visual signals are used by many different animals. They can be turned on and off very rapidly, but can generally only be used in daytime and are easily blocked by objects such as trees. Visual signals are often bright or consist of jerky movements to make them conspicuous. One of the claws of the male fiddler crab is enlarged

---

CRYPSIS, DECEIT AND MIMICRY

To avoid being eaten, some animals attempt to deceive potential predators. In order to remain inconspicuous, certain animals are *cryptic*, blending in with their background by using various types of camouflage. For example, stick insects and praying mantises (see photo, p. 126) show extraordinary likenesses to leaves and twigs. Some toads adopt the colour and patterning of stones, and the larva of the swallowtail butterfly looks like bird droppings.

Other animals startle predators by sudden displays. Many moths open their wings to reveal owl-like 'eyes', while the snake caterpillar extends its front end to mimic the head of a snake. A fulgorid beetle has false eyes and antennae on the rear of its body, and so appears to run backwards when attacked.

The bright warning colours of distasteful species such as wasps are sometimes mimicked by species such as hover flies, which are themselves harmless. This is known as *Batesian mimicry*. There must never be too many mimics, however, or the predator would not readily learn to

avoid the brightly coloured, but generally distasteful, animals. Sometimes distasteful species come to mimic each other, so that if the predator takes one species, it then avoids all the others. This is called *Müllerian mimicry* and occurs in some butterflies.

A stonefish. As if its camouflage were not sufficient, the stonefish has a second line of defence: it has highly poisonous spines in its dorsal fin, which are erected if the fish is disturbed.

Territory, Mating, Social Organization

Animals interact with other members of their own species in a wide variety of ways. Some animals, such as hamsters, are largely solitary in their behaviour, only coming together to mate. Other animals form groups of varying size and structure: shoals of fish are essentially loose aggregations of individuals, while in primate groups, for instance, roles of social dominance and subordination can be recognized and there is often division of labour.

Whatever the social organization, it may be necessary – in order to obtain sufficient food or shelter – for one or more animals to keep a particular area for their sole use and to keep out other members of the same species. An area in which vital resources are defended in this way is known as a *territory*.

Territory

Territories may be held by any number of animals: hamsters and mice, for instance, hold their territories singly, gulls in pairs, hyenas, lions and prairie dogs (see p. 150) in larger groups. While many animals, such as robins and badgers, hold large multipurpose territories for feeding, mating and rearing of young, other territories are used for one purpose only. Male sage grouse and Uganda kob, for example, gather in traditional mating grounds called *leks*, where each male defends a small mating territory (see p. 139). Females are attracted to the leks and prefer to mate with males holding particular territories, often those in the centre of the lekking area. Colonial nesting gulls feed at sea and so defend an area around the nest solely for the purpose of bringing up their young. Many animals patrol the boundaries of their territories regularly

and attack any intruder, using various signals to indicate their possession of a territory (see photo).

A territory is only worth defending if the benefits – in terms of food obtained or young successfully reared – outweigh the cost in time, energy and potential injury. The golden-winged sunbird, for instance, defends a territory containing its food source, nectar from *Leonotis* flowers. The energy it obtains from the flowers just exceeds that used in feeding and in defending the territory, so the bird makes a small net gain in energy.

Mating

It takes more time and energy for a female to produce eggs than for a male to produce sperm. Mating with a poor or sterile partner is consequently more costly for a female than for a male. Females therefore tend to be choosy about potential mates, with the result that males have to compete among themselves for the attentions of females. This is believed to have led to the evolution in males of weapons such as horns and antlers, and of conspicuous ways of attracting females, such as the brilliant colouring and complex songs of many male birds (see p. 139).

SEE ALSO

● ANIMAL GROUPS pp. 122–65
● ANIMAL COMMUNICATION p. 166
● MIGRATION p. 170
● HUMAN SOCIAL ORGANI-ZATION pp. 254–67

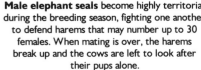

Male elephant seals become highly territorial during the breeding season, fighting one another to defend harems that may number up to 30 females. When mating is over, the harems break up and the cows are left to look after their pups alone.

Courtship is the means by which males advertise themselves and their intentions and by which females assess potential mates. Males are judged either on their ability to provide resources and help for the young, or on their prowess in competing successfully against other males.

Whether a male mates with one or more females, or vice versa, often depends on the type of parental care the male provides. *Polygyny* is the mating system in which a male mates with more than one female. The males often show no parental care. In many mammals, such as red deer and elephant seals (see photo), and in lekking birds, the males mate with many females, which are then left to care for the young alone. Some males – red grouse and yellow-bellied marmots, for instance – mate with a few females and defend territories in which the females raise the young. In some cases, where eggs are fertilized externally, for example in sticklebacks and the midwife toad, the male may mate with several females and then care for the eggs himself.

Where the male is needed to help feed the young, as is the case with many birds, the common mating system is *monogamy*, where one male mates with a single female (see photo). The pairing may be for life as in swans, geese and eagles, or for a single season as in many garden birds. Monogamy also occurs in mammals such as wolves, because a lactating female cannot hunt and the male is thus required to bring back food for the female. Another example of monogamy in mammals is the marmoset. In this case the male helps to carry the twin young, so that the small female can preserve her energy for feeding.

A few birds have a mating system called *polyandry*, in which a female mates with more than one male, with each male

A white rhino marking its territory. Possession of a territory is indicated by various signals. Rhinos and many other mammals, including hyenas, badgers and deer, use dung, urine or scent to mark the boundaries of their territory. Other methods include birdsong and the boundary displays performed by male sticklebacks.

then being left to look after his own offspring. This may occur in birds such as the jaçana because the risk of predation is high. Alternatively, it may take place where abundance of food allows the female to lay several clutches of eggs in a single season, as is the case with the spotted sandpiper, which can lay as many as five clutches in 40 days.

Competition between males for access to females may continue after mating. Male damselflies have a special appendage to remove the sperm of a previous mating from the female before he deposits his own. Some insects and rodents produce a copulatory plug that reduces the chance of other males mating effectively, while in fruit flies and some butterflies the male places an anti-aphrodisiac substance on the females that inhibits mating by other males.

Social organization

Living in social groups has many advantages. Important among these is that some degree of cooperation is possible – in finding and collecting food, in looking out for danger, and in defence against predators.

One of the simplest types of social group is the *family*, where both parents remain with the young for a given period of time. Examples of this kind of family are the groups formed by jackals, swans and many songbirds. Some birds – mallard ducks, for instance – and many mammals, such as bears and rodents, form one-parent families where the females show parental care. In the case of some fish and amphibians, it is the male that guards the young.

Extended families are formed when the offspring remain and help rear succeeding generations. Ants, termites, and some bees and wasps are called *eusocial* ('truly social') insects, because they live in large groups and show extreme division of labour, with only one individual, the queen, reproducing. In the case of bees, all other females remain sterile because of a pheromone produced by the queen (see p. 166), while males are required only to fertilize new queens (see p. 127).

In a termite colony, different tasks are performed by different castes – the queen, who lays the eggs, and sterile wingless workers and soldiers. Periodically winged males and females are produced, which are capable of reproduction and which leave the nest to start new colonies (see photos, above right and p. 127).

The naked mole rat – a species of rodent that lives in large groups in underground burrows – exhibits a similar type of social organization. Only one pair breeds. Small non-breeding animals of either sex dig the tunnels, while larger ones stay near the breeding female, feeding her and brooding the young.

Harems are composed of a single breeding male and a group of females, each with her own young. Permanent harems are formed by animals such as zebra and patas monkeys, whereas red deer and sea lions, for instance, form temporary harems that only stay together for the duration of the breeding season. For the rest of the year the females and their young generally form female groups. The males either live in *bachelor herds* – as is the case with red deer – or they may live alone.

Multi-male groups are formed by several animals, including common baboons, hyenas and lions. A number of males and females breed, although there may be a hierarchy in both sexes to determine which animals breed most often and when they will do so. At adolescence male baboons frequently leave their home groups and join another group. A male lion may abandon its own group to take over another group of females by force.

The social organization of a species is not rigidly fixed. As with red deer and elephant seals, it often changes with the season. Many garden birds live in monogamous pairs only during the summer; in winter, species such as chaffinches and starlings live in large flocks, while robins, for instance, live alone. Female robins are indeed seldom seen during the winter – their whereabouts is a mystery. GS

Termites are an extreme example of an extended family, living together in large numbers and performing different functions depending on their caste. Here the queen – enormously bloated with eggs – is seen surrounded by massive-jawed soldiers, whose task is to defend the colony, and by the smaller workers, who look after the queen and her eggs.

Monogamous pairing (below) is particularly common in birds, where males are needed to help rear the young. In spite of the vast size of their nesting colonies, penguins usually return to their mate of the previous year, each parent taking it in turns to incubate the eggs. After their initial rearing, the chicks join groups of their contemporaries in communal crèches, usually presided over by a few adults.

Migration

Pacific sockeye salmon battling up a waterfall to reach their spawning grounds. Salmon breed in fresh water, but the young migrate to the sea to feed and grow. After several years the mature adults return to breed, often to their native rivers. All Pacific salmon die soon after spawning, but some Atlantic salmon make it back to the sea and survive to spawn again.

Many different animals make *migrations* – periodic movements from one habitat to another. Some migrants such as birds move annually between summer breeding grounds and overwintering sites, often returning to the same areas each year, while salmon and eels take several years to complete their migrations. Locust migrations occur irregularly, and no individual returns to its birth place. The mass movements of lemmings and voles that occur every few years are often referred to as *emigrations* or *invasions*.

Blue wildebeest making a river crossing – a perilous undertaking that may result in many being drowned or swept away. At the beginning of the wet season, wildebeest migrate in large numbers across the open plains of East Africa in search of water and fresh grass. They are able to sense rain up 100 km (60 mi) away.

All migrations involve some active movement by the individuals concerned, often for many days. Smaller migrants such as plankton, aphids and locusts also use water or wind currents, while birds use trade winds and thermal upcurrents.

Migration serves many different purposes. Some animals migrate to escape harsh winters or hot summers, others to find suitable breeding grounds. The need to avoid predators may also be a motivating factor: caribou (reindeer) move from the arctic tundra in autumn to spend the winter in the great coniferous forests further south, where they gain shelter both from the harsh winter and from wolves. Migrating locusts and lemmings move away from dense populations to new areas and new food supplies.

Migration in invertebrates

Plankton gather in the surface waters at night to feed, but during the day move down to deeper, cooler waters, sometimes reaching depths of 1200 m (4000 ft). Here they save energy, as metabolism is reduced at lower temperatures, and they also avoid the fish that hunt by day. By moving between different currents they may also find new food sources.

The small crustaceans called sand hoppers live in wet sand just above the high-tide mark but feed on rotting seaweed higher up the shore. On moist nights they move many metres inland to feed, returning before day to their sandy refuges. Land crabs may travel up to 240 km (150 mi) to lay their eggs in salt water.

The migratory habits of locusts are of great importance to man. The normal form of locust is solitary in its behaviour. However, when food is scarce or breeding grounds are restricted, individuals crowd together and the migratory form develops. This form is gregarious and gathers in vast swarms, which are carried downwind towards areas of rain and so of fresh vegetation. The swarms invade large areas of Africa and the Near East, devastating valuable crops.

Fish, amphibians and reptiles

Fish such as herring, plaice and cod undertake regular annual migrations. In the North Sea, for example, each population follows a seasonal anticlockwise migration cycle, feeding in one area and breeding in another. Salmon, on the other hand, make less frequent journeys (see photo).

The adults of the North American and European eel live in rivers, but migrate to breed deep in the Sargasso Sea, an area of warm water in the Atlantic southeast of Bermuda. The very young eels, called leptocephali larvae, remain in the sea for 30 months, then metamorphose into small eels called *elvers*. These migrate in vast numbers up rivers, sometimes wriggling overland for short distances to reach their feeding grounds. Here they may remain for as long as 19 years before returning to the Sargasso Sea to breed and die.

Many newts, salamanders, frogs and toads migrate annually over distances of a few kilometres from their hibernation sites to the ponds or streams where they breed. Some reptiles such as turtles make much longer migrations. Green turtles live and feed off the coast of Brazil but migrate thousands of kilometres to lay their eggs above the high-water mark on the beaches of Ascension Island. After hatching, the young turtles go straight down the beach to the sea and then disappear for about a year before appearing at the adult feeding sites.

Birds

The most spectacular migrations are performed by birds. The arctic tern migrates between the Arctic and the Antarctic and back each year – a round trip of 40 000 km (25 000 mi). Great shearwaters breed in the South Atlantic and then follow the prevailing winds in a clockwise direction, first to Newfoundland, then on to Greenland, and finally south again in the autumn. European summer visitors, such as swallows, warblers and white storks, overwinter in central or southern Africa. Rather than fly directly across the Mediterranean many birds cross at the Strait of Gibraltar or take a route around the eastern coast of the Mediterranean.

Many migrants show great feats of speed and endurance. The tiny ruby-throated hummingbird migrates 1000 km (620 mi) across the Gulf of Mexico. There is no chance to stop and rest, and many birds complete the journey in 20 hours. One sandpiper flew 3680 km (2300 mi) from Massachusetts to the Panama Canal in 19 days – an average speed of 164 km (125 mi) per day.

Mammals

Large herbivores such as caribou, wildebeest and zebra are the most significant mammal migrants. On the plains of East Africa, wildebeest, zebra, antelope and elephants gather in huge numbers round water holes in the dry season, spreading out into smaller herds in the wet season.

Other mammalian migrants include bats, whales and seals. Seals return each year to the same beaches to breed. Grey whales living in the eastern Pacific feed in the Bering Sea and move south to breed off California, where the water is warmer for the calves but less rich in food.

The timing of migrations

Migrations are often correlated with regular natural events such as the seasons or the phases of the Moon. Before migrating, birds put on weight and show restless behaviour – even caged birds attempt to fly in the migratory direction. These changes are probably controlled by the pituitary gland (see p. 214), which affects weight gain and reproduction, and by the pineal organ, which appears to measure day length and to control annual rhythms of reproduction.

The exact timing of departure tends to depend on environmental conditions such as changes in temperature or decline in

food supplies. Some animals appear to have an internal clock (probably associated with the pineal gland) that triggers migration at the appropriate time. In European garden warblers the internal clock apparently determines when the birds leave on their migration, when they change route, and when they stop flying.

Orientation and navigation

How animals find their way during migration is still something of a mystery. Close to the home site familiar landmarks undoubtedly play a part, and geographical features such as coastlines and mountain ranges may be followed for part of the way. Birds may also listen for infrasonic sounds – very low-frequency sounds produced by natural features such as waterfalls, waves and the wind over woodland and hills. Smell may also be important. Salmon can tell the particular river in which they hatched by its smell, and mammals may follow scent trails.

Many animals – insects and fish as well as birds – use the Sun as a compass for orientation, thus maintaining a particular direction. Such animals use their internal clock to compensate for the movements of the Sun during the day. Birds can also use the stars for orientation, and both birds and bees use the Earth's magnetic field, which may be sensed by magnetic material in their bodies.

Most migrations can be accomplished by orientation alone, but many birds show evidence of navigation – the ability to reach a distant goal even if displaced from their original route. This means that the animals know the position of their home site, rather than just its general direction. They must therefore have some form of internal 'map' of their route, the nature of which is still unknown. It may involve the Earth's magnetic field and, near to home, familiar landmarks, as well as guideposts offered by smell and sound.

Monarch butterflies cluster in vast numbers on tree trunks in Mexico, where they spend the winter. In spring, successive broods of monarchs migrate thousands of kilometres to breed on the milkweeds of North America, reaching as far north as Canada.

GS

HIBERNATION AND AESTIVATION

While some animals avoid harsh conditions by migrating, others stay at home and hide away in burrows, caves or other safe refuges. This method of enduring winter conditions is called *hibernation* and occurs in some amphibians, reptiles and mammals.

Hibernating animals build special nests or find shelter beneath tree stumps or under leaves. Bats use crevices or may migrate to suitable caves. Hibernators become *torpid* – they enter a sleep-like state in which both heart rate and respiration are slowed, and in mammals the body temperature drops, often to within a few degrees of the environmental temperature. When the temperature of the pocket mouse's immediate surroundings approach freezing point, its body temperature drops to 2–3 °C (35.5–37.5 °F). The hedgehog may stop breathing for periods of up to an hour, separated by only a few minutes of respiration.

Many hibernators remain inactive for several months. They use very little energy, and can survive on the fat stores built up before hibernation. Some animals, such as dormice, become active at intervals, and feed on the caches of nuts and seeds they stored away in the autumn. Brown and black bears also spend most of the winter months hibernating, but do not undergo the extreme metabolic and respiratory changes found in smaller mammals.

Aestivation is the avoidance of harsh summer conditions. Earthworms hollow out chambers deep in the soil where they can remain moist. South American and

A garden dormouse hibernating

African lungfish dig chambers deep in the mud when their home rivers dry up, and can survive for up to six months using air for respiration. The Californian ground squirrel remains underground from August to March, and so protects itself from summer temperatures that may reach 43 °C (110 °F).

SEE ALSO

● ANIMAL GROUPS
pp. 122–65
● TERRITORY, MATING AND
SOCIAL ORGANIZATION
p. 168
● HOW ANIMALS MOVE p. 172
● ECOSYSTEMS pp. 178–87

How Animals Move

All animals need to move at some stage in their lives – to find food, to invade new habitats, to reproduce. Many move actively, using muscles and skeletons or fine hair-like projections. Some creep along the ground or swim through water. Others fly or glide through the air, or burrow through earth, wood or even flesh.

Certain animals are carried passively by wind or water currents. Such animals often have projections such as fine hairs, or are flattened to increase their surface area. Jellyfish can move themselves through the water by pulsations of the bell (see photo, p. 123), but they can also be carried passively in the surface waters over great distances. Some very young spiders move by 'ballooning'. Climbing to the top of a twig or branch, they produce a fine silk thread that is caught by the wind, so carrying the tiny spiders away.

Movement in very small animals

Single-celled organisms such as amoebas (see p. 111) move by flowing. The outer jelly-like layer of the cell is converted at the rear end to a fluid, which flows forward and is converted back to jelly at the front. Other protists have either a whip-like structure called the *flagellum*, which undulates, or rows of hundreds of tiny hair-like projections called *cilia*, which beat one after another, so that waves of movement sweep across the organism's body. Tiny flatworms crawl over surfaces by beating rows of cilia in a fine film of mucus that they secrete.

Muscles and skeletons

Most animals move by using muscles that can contract and so are able – when anchored to a rigid skeleton – to move parts of the body attached to them. As muscles are capable only of contraction, not extension, they are generally arranged in *antagonistic pairs*, where the contraction of one muscle extends another (see pp. 206–7).

In vertebrates, skeletons are internal and made of cartilage or bone. Invertebrates such as insects and crustaceans have hard external skeletons (see p. 124), while others – worms, coelenterates and molluscs, for instance – have internal fluid-filled (or *hydrostatic*) skeletons.

Crawling

Animals without tails, fins or legs move by alternately shortening and lengthening either the whole or parts of their body. Leeches extend the body by contracting circular muscles running around the body while attached to a surface by a sucker at the rear end. The front sucker then attaches, and the body is drawn forward by contraction of longitudinal muscles running the length of the body.

In earthworms the body is divided into segments, each with its own set of circular and longitudinal muscles and hydrostatic skeleton. When the longitudinal muscles are contracted, the segment is short and fat and pushes against the ground, being anchored by means of mucus and tiny bristles called *chaetae* (or *setae*). When the circular muscles contract, the segment is thin and elongated. During crawling waves of contraction, first of one set of muscles then of another, pass down the worm's body. When burrowing, the chaetae at the rear end anchor the body in the burrow while the front part pushes forward between the soil particles.

Slugs and snails have a single large flat foot. Waves of muscular contraction pass over the foot, lifting small areas off the ground and moving them forwards. In many snakes the body is thrown into waves that travel from head to tail (see p. 135). At the crests of the waves the body pushes back against the ground, so moving the snake forward. In sidewinders, first the head and then successive sections of the body are moved sideways.

Movement in water

Long aquatic animals such as lampreys, eels and water snakes swim by throwing their body into lateral undulations that push back against the water – the method of movement probably used by early vertebrates. In most fish, however, the tail is the main propulsive force. This pushes sideways and backwards against the water on each stroke, driving the fish forwards. The fins keep the fish stable and are used for fine adjustment of position. Marine mammals such as whales and dolphins use a similar method of propulsion (see photo), while walruses and seals

Jumping is both a rapid means of moving from one place to another and an efficient one, in terms of energy consumption. As well as frogs (such as the edible frog shown here), kangaroos, grasshoppers and fleas all hop or jump by rapidly straightening their long powerful hind legs.

The fluked tail of a blue whale. Propulsion in water is most commonly achieved by powerful strokes of the tail, pushing back against the water. Tail movement in fish is from side to side, while the tails of marine mammals such as dolphins and whales are set horizontally and are moved up and down.

flap their hind feet from side to side. Rays and flatfish move all or parts of their body up and down when swimming. In rays these undulations run down the side of the broad lateral fins, but in flatfish the whole body is flapped up and down.

Some animals row themselves through the water – sea lions use the front flippers like oars, while water boatmen (a kind of insect) use a pair of legs covered with fine hairs. Penguins flap their flippers up and down when swimming, and almost seem to fly through the water (see photo, p. 136). Squids and their relatives move by jet propulsion. Water is drawn into a large muscular-walled cavity, and then forced out in a particular direction through a narrow flexible funnel.

Walking, running and jumping

Movement on land often involves the use of legs. When walking, two-legged or *bipedal* animals – humans and birds – always keep at least one foot on the ground at any one time, but in running there are times when both feet leave the ground. Dinosaurs were also bipedal and presumably moved in a similar way (see p. 132).

Animals with four legs often show various gaits, which differ in the order in which the legs are moved and in their speed. Elephants, for instance, have two gaits – a walk and an amble (a fast walk); horses have four gaits – a walk, a trot, a canter and a gallop. In most mammals walking involves moving one leg at a time – first a front leg, then the opposite hind leg, then the other front leg, and finally the other hind leg. In all other mammalian gaits, such as trotting, cantering, galloping and bounding, two, three and even all four legs can be off the ground at the same time. Long legs and large strides, separately or in combination, lead to increased speed in fast runners such as dogs and cheetahs (see photo, and p. 153).

Many reptiles and amphibians have long bodies and hold their limbs out to the side. They bend their body as they walk in a similar manner to the lateral undulations of fish, and move their legs in diagonally opposite pairs. Similar patterns of movement are seen in the fins of fish such as the coelacanth and the lungfishes (see pp. 128–9), which are thought to be closely related to four-legged vertebrates.

Insects, with six legs, move the legs in sets of three, the first and third on one side and the second on the other. The other three legs form a triangle or rotating tripod on which the animal balances. Millipedes and centipedes, which may have a hundred legs or more, move the legs on each side of the body in order, one after another (see photo, p. 125). Depending on the species, waves of leg movement travel backwards or forwards along the body, and opposite legs move either simultaneously or alternately.

Frogs, kangaroos, grasshoppers and fleas all hop or jump by pushing off the ground with long back legs (see photo). Kangaroos have elastic tendons in the legs that are stretched on landing and store energy to push the animal off as the tendons recoil (see p. 142). Fleas and grass-

True flight is found today only in insects, birds and bats (such as the flying fox, or fruit bat, shown here). The modifications necessary to achieve flight are very great, particularly in heavier animals. However, the advantages conferred by flight can readily be judged by the success of those animal groups that have achieved it.

hoppers store energy in an elastic protein in the legs by slow muscular contraction. A release mechanism triggers the recoil of the protein, catapulting the animal into the air. Fleas are the most accomplished leapers in the animal kingdom, being able to jump more than a hundred times their own height.

Gliding and flight

The use of extended flaps of skin for gliding or parachuting is seen in several groups of animals. Flying fish have enlarged lateral fins, flying amphibians use long webbed toes as parachutes, flying dragons (flying lizards) support a web of skin on elongated ribs, flying snakes flatten the body, and flying squirrels, possums and lemurs have a flap of skin between the fore and hind limbs (see p. 147). In these animals 'flight' is more or less uncontrolled and somewhat erratic.

True flight occurred in pterosaurs (including the pterodactyl, see p. 132), and is seen today only in insects, birds and bats. These have wings that can move up and down and be held at different angles. When the wing is held at an angle to the air flowing over it, the air has to move further over the upper surface. This creates a lower pressure above the wing and higher pressure below it, thus producing a lifting force. This lift operates in gliding and flapping flight. When the wings are also moved downwards, both lift and a forward thrust are produced. On the

upward stroke the wing is twisted to reduce reverse thrust.

Birds and bats have powerful chest muscles, attached to large projections on the breastbones, to produce strong downward wing movements on the power stroke. In birds the wings are formed from extended forearms covered with feathers (see p. 136). In bats, the hands are enlarged and the wing surface is a double flap of skin (see photo, and p. 146).

Insect wings project between the top and the sides of the thorax (see p. 127). In fast-flying insects the flight muscles are not attached directly to the wing. One set of muscles, running from the roof to the floor of the thorax, contracts in such a way that the muscles pull the roof downwards and so raise the wing through a lever system at the base of the wing. The upstroke occurs when longitudinal muscles attached to each end of the thorax contract, so buckling the roof upwards. Once set in motion the muscles extend each other and then contract at a very high rate, giving flight speeds of up to 40 km/h (25 mph) in some moths.   GS

Fast runners such as cheetahs arch the spine upwards as they run to bring the hind feet as far forward as possible, thus increasing stride length and so speed. At the highest speeds, the hind legs land in front of the previous position of the forelegs.

SEE ALSO

● ANIMAL GROUPS pp. 122–65
● MIGRATION p. 170
● HOW PEOPLE MOVE p. 206

Parasitism and Symbiosis

There is no such thing as a truly independent organism. In all ecosystems, animals, plants and microorganisms interact and interfere with one another in a wide variety of ways. Some of these interactions are casual, short-term and unspecialized in nature. Others are the very special inter-relationships that occur between members of the same species in family or social groups. In addition to these types of association, however, almost all groups of living things involve themselves in highly intimate associations that form between *different* species and that typically result in clear-cut patterns of harm and benefit for the organisms concerned.

Associations of this kind are generally long-term interactions, often involving close physical contact between the species concerned, together with many adaptations for life together. Two such associations – parasitism and symbiosis – require similar degrees of adaptation for the organisms concerned, but may be differentiated on the basis of their distinct ecological implications.

Types of association

In *parasitism*, one species, the *parasite*, lives in or on another species, the *host*. Internal parasites are called *endoparasites*, whereas those living on the outer surface of their hosts are known as *ectoparasites*. The host is harmed by the parasite. The harm can take a number of unpleasant forms, but the net result of infection by a parasite is that the host survives less well and/or produces fewer offspring. The parasite, on the other hand, benefits from the relationship, usually gaining food or other resources from the host's body. The partnership is therefore an unequal one – the parasite gains, the host loses.

Symbiosis, in contrast, is a more balanced partnership. In a typical symbiotic association, the species participating, called *symbionts* (or *symbiotes*), derive mutual benefit from it. It is usual for both species to survive and reproduce more suc-

A common cuckoo being fed by a tree pipit. Many species of cuckoo are *brood parasites* – they lay a single egg in the nests of a number of host species, which are then left to rear the young cuckoos themselves. To minimize the chances of rejection, the coloration of the cuckoo's egg may mimic that of a particular host's egg. Soon after hatching, the young cuckoo 'evicts' the host's own eggs or nestlings, so that it does not have to compete for the limited food provided by its small foster parents.

cessfully when living symbiotically than when living apart.

A third kind of association, known as *commensalism*, occurs when an organism of one species (the *commensal*) derives benefit from associating with an organism of a different species (the *host*), which itself receives neither benefit nor harm from the relationship. Barnacles, for instance, attach themselves to whales, thereby obtaining anchorage and transportation, while the whales remain unaffected.

Types of parasite

All types of organism can lead parasitic ways of life. *Microparasites* – microscopic organisms such as parasitic viruses, bacteria, fungi and protists – typically multiply directly on a host. *Macroparasites* – larger organisms such as worms, insects, ticks, vertebrates and plants – usually produce offspring on a host that then leave it to establish new infections.

Parasites show adaptations for locating their preferred host species and for establishing themselves on or in them. Usually included among these adaptations are methods for feeding from host tissues and for maintaining transmission from host to host. The latter traits become tied together into often complex life cycles, sometimes – in the case of *multi-host* life cycles – involving several hosts of different species. In a typical multi-host cycle, a parasite infects different hosts at different stages of its development, making specific adaptations as it passes from one host to another.

Human parasites

We think of ourselves, as a species, as

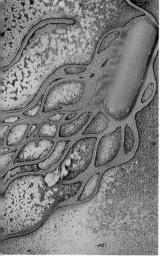

A salmonella bacterium (above), magnified in a false-colour image. All members of the genus *Salmonella* are intestinal microparasites, found in man and other animals. A wide range of diseases are caused by salmonella bacteria, including typhoid, paratyphoid and food poisoning.

Many species of lamprey are parasitic on other fishes, attaching themselves to the host species by means of their sucker-like mouths. Their saliva contains an anticoagulant, to prevent the host's blood from clotting. They feed on the victim's blood and body tissue until it is virtually 'sucked dry' – by which time it is often too weak to survive.

being in control of our own ecological destiny, but we can in fact be infected by diseases caused by almost every kind of parasitic organism.

Among the microparasites, we can suffer viral infections ranging from the mild common cold to the fatal and incurable AIDS virus. We are prone to hundreds of different bacterial illnesses, from acne to bubonic plague. We also get skin diseases caused by fungi – athlete's foot, for example, and ringworm – as well as some very serious protist diseases, such as malaria and sleeping sickness.

Malaria and sleeping sickness are examples of parasites with multi-host life cycles. In each disease the infection is spread to new humans when an already infected mosquito (in the case of malaria) or tsetse fly (in the case of sleeping sickness) bites a person in order to feed on their blood. These insect hosts are called *secondary hosts*. Similarly, the insects themselves become infected when they remove blood from a person already suffering from the disease.

Human macroparasites cause several of the most serious tropical parasitic diseases. One such disease, filariasis, is caused by nematode roundworms (see p. 122), which are spread from person to person by mosquitoes. The presence of these worms causes inflammation and eventual blockage of the lymph vessels, which can result (in severe cases) in the dreadful disfigurement known as elephantiasis.

A typical parasitic life cycle

Another serious tropical disease, schistosomiasis (formerly known as bilharzia), is the result of infection by a flatworm blood fluke of the genus *Schistosoma*. The life cycle of this fluke, which infects more than 250 million people in the world today, illustrates well the types of adaptation that take place in the world of parasites.

The human disease is caused by pairs of worms, a male and female locked together in permanent copulation, which live in the blood vessels of either the intestine or the bladder. The female worms in these pairs produce thousands of spined eggs, some of which escape from damaged blood vessels into the faeces or urine of an infected person. This is the parasite's subtle escape route for continuation of the life cycle.

Each egg contains a larva called a *miracidium*, which is stimulated to hatch when it reaches fresh water. It then swims to infect a freshwater snail. Within this secondary host, parasite numbers are dramatically increased by a form of cloning – thousands of new larvae called *cercariae*, genetically identical to the single invading miracidium, are produced in the snail's tissues.

The cercariae then emerge from the snail and swim in water for about 48 hours, until their finite food reserves are exhausted. If they come into contact with human skin during this period, the cercariae bore into the skin to establish a new human infection. Because of the

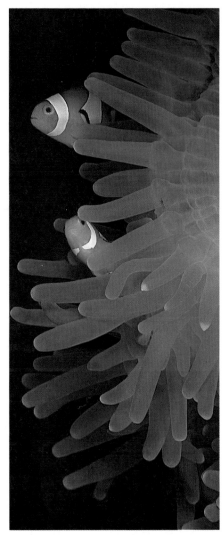

organization of this life cycle, the disease is commonest in developing countries in the tropics, where sanitation is poor and where there is much human contact with infected fresh water – as in paddy fields and irrigation ditches.

Symbiosis

The mutually beneficial partnerships of symbiosis are used by a remarkably diverse range of organism pairings.

Fungi and cells of algae collaborate in a delicately balanced metabolic interaction to produce a whole new life form – the lichens (see photo, p. 118). These plant-like growths have a body based on fungal threads, but derive photosynthetic benefit from the algae embedded in the fungal base.

In the intestines of many animals (including humans) there are populations of symbiotic microorganisms – the so-called *gut flora* – some of which aid digestion. Cows and termites, for instance, are only able to digest their cellulose-rich diet because their guts are populated by a mixture of symbiotic bacteria and protists (see box, p. 161). These microorganism species can only survive in the oxygen-free conditions of termite and ruminant guts. Termites even have nitrogen-fixing bacteria in their gut flora. With these

Clownfishes locked in a symbiotic pairing with a sea anemone. Immune to the anemone's stinging cells, these little fishes live among its tentacles, so gaining protection from predators. In return, the clownfishes ward off other predators, and it is even thought that they may lure larger fishes into the anemone's tentacles, so providing their protector with food.

they can obtain organic foods containing nitrogen derived from the gaseous nitrogen in the atmosphere.

The same metabolic trick is used by one family of flowering plants – the legumes (see also p. 116). This very successful group of plants, with over 20 000 species, includes the peas, beans and acacias. These plants are able to grow well even in nitrate-poor soils because their roots possess nodules populated with nitrogen-fixing bacteria that initially invade the roots from the soil. The bacteria gain nutrients from the plant tissues, while the plant gets fixed nitrogen from the microorganisms – the type of two-way help typical of symbiosis.

Symbiosis occurs everywhere in the natural world. Many insects and even some bats and birds (such as hummingbirds) are linked to plants by the bond of pollination symbiosis (see p. 121). Certain ant colonies symbiotically protect the spiny acacias in which they build their nests. Sea anemones are locked in symbiotic pairings with clownfishes and hermit crabs (see photos).

There is even a suggestion that around 1500 million years ago the complex cells typical of the higher organisms evolved from simpler bacteria-like cells by a symbiotic route (see p. 111). If this theory is correct, we exist today because of a series of symbioses that first happened many millions of years ago.   PWh

SEE ALSO

● THE BEGINNINGS OF LIFE p. 110
● PLANT PHYSIOLOGY p. 116
● PRIMITIVE ANIMALS p. 122
● RUMINATION p. 161
● THE BIOSPHERE p. 176
● THE IMMUNE SYSTEM p. 212
● INFECTIOUS DISEASES p. 238
● PREVENTING DISEASE p. 244

Hermit crabs are often involved in complex associations with other animals. The empty mollusc shell inhabited by this hermit crab carries two sea anemones, which symbiotically protect the crab in return for scraps of discarded food. The anemones may be carefully transferred when the crab moves into more spacious lodgings. The adopted shell may also carry commensal hydroids, which gain anchorage and food but apparently give nothing in return.

The Biosphere

The biosphere is the layer around our planet in which all living organisms exist. It contains all the different ecosystems, and all the water, minerals, oxygen, nitrogen, phosphorus and other nutrients that living things need in order to survive. The biosphere has been called the 'skin of life' – it extends only a few kilometres above and below sea level, and only a few metres into the soil. It surrounds the Earth like a cellular blanket, regulating the temperature by allowing the Sun's rays to enter and by letting waste heat back into space.

Everything in the biosphere is interrelated. The atmosphere (see p. 77) helps to purify water by recycling it in the hydrological cycle (see pp. 94–5), and also provides carbon dioxide for plant photosynthesis (see p. 117) and oxygen for respiration in both plants and animals. Plants provide food for animals as well as releasing oxygen (the waste product of photosynthesis) for them to breathe. The soil provides nutrients and water for plants (see pp. 116–17), and when the plants die they release the nutrients back into the soil. Both animals and plants convert food into energy by the process of respiration (see pp. 116–17 and 210–11). The waste product of respiration is carbon dioxide, which is absorbed by plants in photosynthesis.

Ecological niches

All the millions of different species of plants and animals exist within the biosphere in an orderly and precise fashion. This has not happened by chance, but by the process of evolution (see p. 112). Each species is thought to have evolved to take advantage of a particular habitat and a particular position in the food chain, and this is called its *ecological niche*. By remaining in its ecological niche a species maximizes its chance of survival, for within its niche it will find all requirements necessary for life. In theory, each species will occupy a separate niche, and so competition with other species is minimized. In practice, however, different niche spaces may overlap, and where this occurs then competition for resources takes place and aggressive behaviour may sometimes be seen.

Communities

Each part of the biosphere contains particular combinations of climate and soil. These areas provide life-support conditions for groups of species that have adapted to those environments, and so may be said to have broadly similar ecological niches. Such groups of species are called *communities*. There are many thousands of different communities, but they can all be divided into a simple classification:

Aquatic	Terrestrial
Freshwater	Forest
Marine	Grassland
	Desert

These communities are looked at in more detail on the following pages.

Components of ecosystems

An *ecosystem* is a self-regulating natural community of living organisms (the *biotic* components) interacting both with one another and with the non-living (*abiotic* or *physical*) environment that surrounds them. Ecosystems are 'models' devised by ecologists in order to simplify the complexity of the real world, but by studying ecosystems we can sometimes gain a better idea of how, for example, forests, lakes and grasslands actually function as complex groups of interrelated species. In the earliest stages of the history of our planet some 4000–5000 million years ago only the physical components existed. An erratically changing climate and geology resulted in environments that were unstable. Gradually, a stability developed in which simple living organisms evolved (see p. 110). These biotic components were totally dependent for their existence upon the abiotic components.

As the complexity of plants and animals increased then so they bound together all the physical, chemical and biological components. The links that join together the different parts of an ecosystem can be thought of as pipe-lines along which food, energy and waste products continually pass (see diagram).

The power source for life

Energy is the driving force behind all life in the biosphere. The Sun provides 99.99% of all the radiant energy required for life on Earth; the remaining 0.01% comes from heat contained within the planet (see p. 76). Because the Sun's energy has existed for at least 4600 million years and

ECOLOGICAL NICHES AND COMPETITION

NICHE 1
Maximum competition
Moderate competition
Minimal competition
Moderate competition
NICHE 2
Minimal competition
Minimal competition
NICHE 3
Minimal competition

Wherever possible, species appear to avoid competition by spacing out their niche areas. This example shows how three closely related species of North American birds that feed on the same conifer tree have different feeding zones.

Cape May Warbler   Bay-breasted Warbler   Myrtle Warbler

AN ECOSYSTEM MODEL

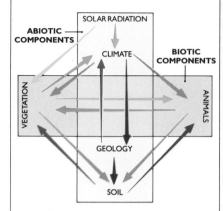

SOLAR RADIATION
ABIOTIC COMPONENTS
CLIMATE
BIOTIC COMPONENTS
VEGETATION
ANIMALS
GEOLOGY
SOIL

Sun provides energy for plant photosynthesis.

Amount of solar radiation varies with latitude and hence affects climate. Solar radiation also powers weather systems.

Volcanic activity, mountain ranges, etc., can also affect climate.

Climate interacts with geology in soil formation, and provides water for soil. Climate (in the form of ice, water and wind erosion) also weathers rocks.

Soil provides water and nutrients for plants, together with a physical base in which plants can root themselves.

Plants provide food for animals.

Animals alter vegetation by browsing and grazing. Humans have significantly altered vegetation patterns through modifications for agriculture.

Vegetation gives off water vapour, which helps to stabilize the climate of the planet.

Climate restricts the types of plants and animals that can survive in a particular ecosystem. Water and temperature are the two main climatic controls.

Dead plants and animals decompose and return nutrients to the soil. Nutrients are also returned to the soil through animal excrement.

Soil provides a habitat (including water and air) for many invertebrates. In addition many animals have evolved specialisms to cope with different soils, for example, the feet of camels.

THE NITROGEN CYCLE

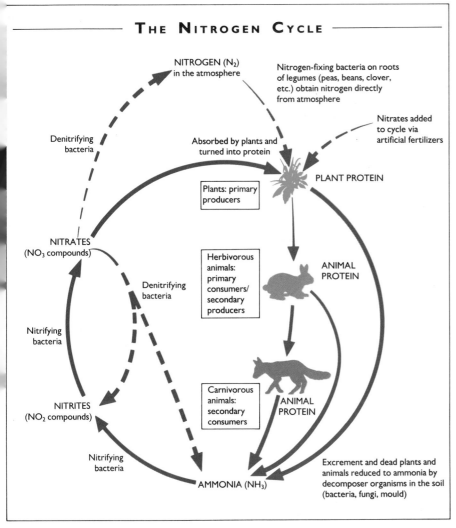

NITROGEN (N₂) in the atmosphere

Nitrogen-fixing bacteria on roots of legumes (peas, beans, clover, etc.) obtain nitrogen directly from atmosphere

Nitrates added to cycle via artificial fertilizers

Denitrifying bacteria

Absorbed by plants and turned into protein

PLANT PROTEIN

Plants: primary producers

NITRATES (NO₃ compounds)

Denitrifying bacteria

Herbivorous animals: primary consumers/ secondary producers

ANIMAL PROTEIN

Nitrifying bacteria

Carnivorous animals: secondary consumers

ANIMAL PROTEIN

NITRITES (NO₂ compounds)

Nitrifying bacteria

AMMONIA (NH₃)

Excrement and dead plants and animals reduced to ammonia by decomposer organisms in the soil (bacteria, fungi, mould)

These are the so-called *macroelements*. About 97% of human bodies are made from these elements. The remainder is made up of *microelements*, which may include between 14 and 24 different elements, depending on the organism. The exact chemical composition of organisms varies and can depend upon the abundance of microelements, the age of the organism, the season of the year and the location in which the individual organism has lived.

When a plant or animal dies, the chemical compounds locked in its body are gradually released back to the soil and the oceans via the decomposer organisms. Apart from the nitrogen compounds (see diagram), most of the compounds become incorporated into vast, slow-moving *biogeochemical cycles*. In these cycles the compounds become locked into the formation of new rocks and thus become unavailable for reuse until the rock is weathered into new soil and the compounds are taken up once again by plants, so starting a new cycle (see also the rock cycle, pp. 84–5, and the hydrological cycle, pp. 94–5).

The entire cycle of nutrient movement takes many tens of millions of years to complete. It is a sobering thought to realize that the chemical elements in our bodies may have previously formed part of some ancient organism such as a dinosaur living at least 65 million years before the present, and may already by then have been recycled several times in the history of life on Earth.   GJ

SEE ALSO

● THE EARTH'S STRUCTURE AND ATMOSPHERE p. 76
● CLIMATIC AND VEGETATION REGIONS p. 104
● THE CLASSIFICATION OF LIFE p. 108
● THE BEGINNINGS OF LIFE p. 110
● EVOLUTION p. 112
● ECOSYSTEMS pp. 178–87
● THREATS TO THE ENVIRONMENT p. 300

---

will probably continue as far again into the future it is described as an *infinite resource*. The Sun's radiant energy arrives at the outer edge of the atmosphere as very high-energy short-wave radiation. As this radiation travels through the atmosphere about half of its energy is absorbed, scattered and reflected by water vapour. At the outer edge of the atmosphere the ozone layer (see p. 77) plays a crucial role in trapping the biologically harmful ultraviolet radiation emitted by the Sun. This layer is currently under threat from man-made chemicals (see pp. 300–1). Of the energy that reaches the surface of the Earth, 95–99% is absorbed by the oceans, leaving, at most, 5% available to green plants for photosynthesis.

Primary and secondary producers

Living organisms have two remarkable properties: firstly, they can replicate themselves (that is they can *reproduce*), and secondly, the green plants and blue-green algae can manufacture their own food supply from inorganic materials by the process of photosynthesis. The products of photosynthesis – the plants themselves – are then consumed by animals, thus forming the beginning of a *food chain*.

As the photosynthesizing organisms and certain bacteria (see p. 110) make their food from inorganic materials, they are called *autotrophs* (self-feeders), and

form the group called *primary producers*. All other organisms (in particular, the animals) are known as *heterotrophs* or *consumer organisms*, as they consume other living organisms.

The heterotrophs can be divided into several subgroups. Those animals that eat plants are the *herbivores* or *primary consumers*. In turn, they are preyed upon by *carnivorous* animals, the *secondary consumers*.

Eventually, when plants and animals die, they are broken down by the *decomposer organisms* (mostly bacteria, moulds and fungi) and their nutrients are released into the soil, whereupon the nutrients can be reused by new living organisms. This process is called *nutrient recycling*.

Nutrient sources for life

Nutrient recycling is necessary because, unlike solar energy, the nutrients held within the soil are scarce commodities existing in fixed quantities. Hence they are called *finite resources*. Nutrients are scarce because the biosphere only includes the topmost 2 or 3 m (6 to 10 ft) of the Earth's surface. Plant roots and soil microorganisms cannot penetrate much beyond this depth, and thus the bulk of the nutrients held within the Earth's crust are inaccessible.

The bodies of plants and animals consist mainly of the elements carbon, oxygen, hydrogen, nitrogen, phosphorus and sulphur, in various chemical compounds.

PRIMARY PRODUCTION IN THE BIOSPHERE

The term *primary production* usually means the amount of material trapped by autotrophs via the process of photosynthesis, and *productivity* is the amount of material stored by autotrophs per unit of time.

It is useful to measure the *net primary productivity* (NPP) of different ecosystems in order to compare their efficiency. The NPP is the total amount of material assimilated by autotrophs, minus the material lost in respiration.

Measurement of NPP is not easy, and a number of different and complex techniques have been devised. In spite of many variations, research has shown that forests, swamps and estuaries are the most productive ecosystems within our biosphere, and that a strong productivity gradient exists from the tropics (high) to the poles (low). Research also indicates that our agricultural systems are, for the most part, relatively unproductive in terms of primary production.

The main factors that control primary production are the length of the growing season and the length of daylight, both of which are partly related to latitude. Because of the distribution of the land masses, some 80% of land on the Earth's surface falls within the less productive regions.

VEGETATION TYPE

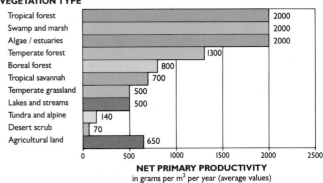

Vegetation type	NPP
Tropical forest	2000
Swamp and marsh	2000
Algae / estuaries	2000
Temperate forest	1300
Boreal forest	800
Tropical savannah	700
Temperate grassland	500
Lakes and streams	500
Tundra and alpine	140
Desert scrub	70
Agricultural land	650

NET PRIMARY PRODUCTIVITY
in grams per m² per year (average values)

Ecosystems: Aquatic

Water covers 71% of the surface of the Earth. This fact, combined with the great depth of many of the oceans (average depth 3700 m / 12 140 ft), provides a living space estimated to be 200 times larger than all the land ecosystems. Aquatic ecosystems can be divided into marine systems (salt water) and freshwater systems (rivers and lakes).

Aquatic ecosystems are better able to support life than the terrestrial ecosystems. However, because of the constancy of the water environment when compared to the land environment, the diversity of life in the vast aquatic ecosystems is relatively small.

The aquatic environment

A watery environment was almost certainly the original source of all life on this planet (see p. 110). Water provides a protective shield around plants and animals, preventing the drying out of cells, providing buoyancy, transporting food to the organism, and carrying waste products away. Water also makes fertilization much easier than on land, preventing the developing young from becoming dry, maintaining an even temperature, filtering out harmful ultraviolet light from the Sun, and dispersing the young after birth.

One of the most remarkable properties of water is its dissolving power. Chemical compounds can be dissolved, transported, and precipitated out with virtually no chemical alteration due to the neutrality of rainwater (pH about 6.5, i.e. just slightly acid). In some places, however, acid rain (see pp. 300–1) has increased the acidity of water, with harmful consequences for the organisms living in it.

Plants and animals that live in water can dispense with a rigid structure (woody tissue in plants, bones in animals). One major group of fish has developed a supple cartilaginous framework that provides attachment for the muscle system. The contrast in the supportive capability of air and water is shown below.

Medium	Density Value (grams per cc at 4 °C and at mean sea level)
Air	0.0013
Sea water	1.028
Fresh water	1.001
Protoplasm	1.028

Notice that the density of protoplasm (the jelly-like substance within all living cells) is identical to that of sea water. That is why we float in sea water more easily than in fresh water. Some biologists believe that as the density of protoplasm is identical to that of sea water it is possible that all animals had an earlier ancestral form that lived in the oceans.

Controlling factors

Various factors control the nature of different aquatic ecosystems. The most important is *salinity* (the saltiness of water), which depends principally upon the amount of sodium chloride dissolved in it, along with small amounts of bromides, carbonates and sulphates of the elements sodium, potassium, calcium and magnesium. Salinity is lowest – typically 30 parts per thousand (ppt) – near the estuaries of large rivers where the addition of fresh water dilutes the concentration of salts. High salinity (70 ppt) is recorded where rainfall is low and evaporation rate is high – in the Red Sea, for example. The amount of salinity divides aquatic ecosystems into two main groups.

The first group, the *freshwater ecosystems*, includes standing water such as reservoirs, lakes, ponds, marshes and wetlands, and the flowing water of rivers and streams. These ecosystems are normally of very low salinity, usually between 15 and 30 ppt.

By contrast, the waters of the second group, the *marine* or *saltwater ecosystems* (which include oceans, estuaries, mangrove swamps and coral reefs), contain considerably more salts, typically between 35 and 70 ppt. The saltiness of the

A mangrove swamp on the northeast coast of Brazil. Mangrove trees and shrubs belong to a variety of families, but all send out 'prop' roots from their trunks, among which sediment is trapped. Mangroves, which are restricted to the tropics and subtropics, grow in dense thickets in salt marshes and along tidal estuaries and muddy coasts. Mangroves form unique ecosystems, and support a variety of aquatic animals such as the guaiamu crab seen here.

oceans is ultimately derived from minerals and salts eroded and washed away from rocks and soils, and eventually transported to the sea by rivers.

The temperature of the water in aquatic ecosystems is also critically important for life forms. Of the ultraviolet light that reaches the surface of the planet, about 95% is absorbed as heat by the oceans. The effect of this is to make the seas behave like giant radiators that warm the northern hemisphere in winter and cool it in summer (and vice versa in the southern hemisphere). On average, the annual variation in surface-water temperature of the oceans is about 10 °C (18 °F), but at a depth of 20 m (66 ft) the annual variation may be as little as 1 or 2 °C (2 to 4 °F). Because of the evenness of temperatures, most aquatic life forms have little or no need for temperature-control mechanisms such as those found in land-based life forms.

The third controlling factor is oxygen, a vital component of all aquatic ecosystems. Most oxygen is found at the surface of water bodies, especially in turbulent streams or when waves break. The amount of dissolved oxygen in water can be severely altered due to human activity. In particular, the dumping of untreated sewage and industrial wastes directly into seas and rivers has caused a huge increase in the demand for oxygen by the organisms that feed on the effluents (see pp. 300–1). Organic debris, phosphates from soap powders and ammonia from agricultural sources and sewage all provide a rich food supply for bacteria and scavenger organisms. They feed rapidly on these effluents, growing and reproducing much more quickly than in unpolluted waters. The increase in numbers consumes most, or even all, of the dissolved oxygen, and this in turn asphyxiates other aquatic life forms.

A fourth factor is the speed at which sunlight disappears in water. This depends upon the quantity of suspended materials and floating organisms in the water. Usually some 50% of red, orange and yellow light is absorbed in the top 2 m (6½ ft) of water, and by 20 m (65 ft) only small amounts of blue-green light remain to give water its typical 'colour'. The rapid removal of sunlight makes all aquatic ecosystems that are more than several metres deep into dark, relatively cold environments. Even at the equator, the temperature of deeper water does not exceed 4 °C (39 °F).

Marine ecosystems

Marine ecosystems provide ecological niches for about 250 000 different plant and animal species. Many of these are very simple, single-celled phytoplankton (plant-like) or zooplankton (animals), which provide the food sources for other larger species, notably fish.

Ocean ecosystems can be divided into two main types: the *coastal* or *neritic zone*, and the *ocean deeps*. Coastal ecosystems extend from low water to the edge of the continental shelf (see p. 101) and they do not exceed 200 m (660 ft) in depth. This zone represents less than 10% of the ocean area yet contains 98% of marine life forms. It is the location of most commer-

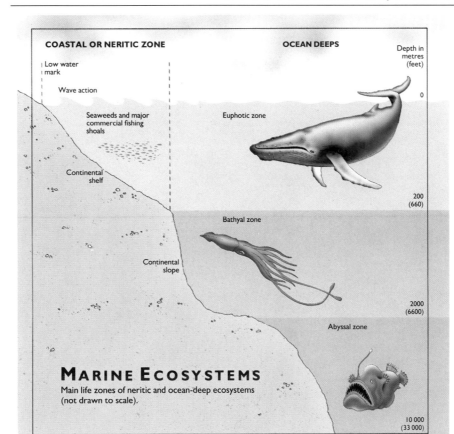

COASTAL OR NERITIC ZONE
Low water mark
Wave action
Seaweeds and major commercial fishing shoals
Continental shelf

OCEAN DEEPS
Euphotic zone
Depth in metres (feet)
0
200 (660)
Bathyal zone
Continental slope
2000 (6600)
Abyssal zone
10 000 (33 000)

MARINE ECOSYSTEMS
Main life zones of neritic and ocean-deep ecosystems (not drawn to scale).

SEE ALSO

- RIVERS AND LAKES p. 94
- THE OCEANS p. 100
- THE BEGINNINGS OF LIFE p. 110
- PRIMITIVE ANIMALS p. 122
- ARTHROPODS: CRUSTACEANS p. 124
- FISHES p. 128
- AMPHIBIANS p. 130
- REPTILES p. 134
- BIRDS pp. 136–9
- MARINE MAMMALS p. 162
- THE BIOSPHERE p. 176
- FISHERY p. 194

cial fishing, and increasingly for off-shore oil platforms. Unfortunately, it is also the most heavily polluted part of our oceans.

The ocean deeps usually occur far away from land masses, and so are mostly relatively unpolluted. Three distinct zones can be found: a surface or *euphotic zone* to 200 m (660 ft), which contains most life forms, a middle *bathyal zone* (200–2000 m / 660–6600 ft), and a cold, dark, bottom layer or *abyssal zone* (below 2000 m / 6600 ft). Surprisingly, about 98% of the species in the ocean deeps are in the deepest zone, but most are bacteria involved in decomposition.

Freshwater ecosystems

Freshwater ecosystems are highly variable and their characteristics depend upon the surrounding geology, land use,

and pollution levels.

Most freshwater ecosystems are *eutrophic*, i.e. there is an accumulation of nutrients and organic matter. This accumulation takes place over time and can be thought of as an 'ageing' process, particularly in lakes. Unfortunately, extreme eutrophication can also occur when raw sewage or agricultural wastes are allowed to enter fresh water, with a resulting depletion in oxygen (see above).

In contrast, fresh water that flows off ancient acid rocks or that drains from peaty areas often has a very low nutrient content. Such freshwater ecosystems are described as *oligotrophic*. They have clear water (apart from brown staining from peat) and usually have very few life forms.   GJ

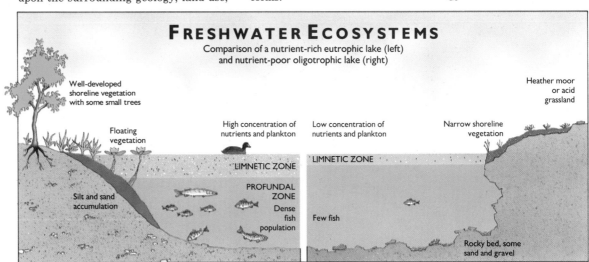

FRESHWATER ECOSYSTEMS
Comparison of a nutrient-rich eutrophic lake (left) and nutrient-poor oligotrophic lake (right)

Well-developed shoreline vegetation with some small trees
Floating vegetation
High concentration of nutrients and plankton
Low concentration of nutrients and plankton
Narrow shoreline vegetation
Heather moor or acid grassland
LIMNETIC ZONE
LIMNETIC ZONE
Silt and sand accumulation
PROFUNDAL ZONE
Dense fish population
Few fish
Rocky bed, some sand and gravel

Ecosystems: Coniferous and Temperate Forests

The extensive northern latitudes between 35° and 70° are the locations of the main *extra-tropical* forests. Many different extra-tropical forest types existed in the past. Some have been totally cleared, while others have been simplified by selective felling. Two contrasting tree types are found in these forests. North of latitude 55° N, the softwood conifer tree predominates, while to the south, the broadleaf hardwood tree is dominant. In the southern hemisphere, apart from New Zealand, parts of eastern Australia and in Tasmania, the temperate broadleaf forest is present only in small amounts, while the conifer (or *Boreal*) forest is virtually absent.

Although broadleaf hardwoods and some conifers can be found in both hemispheres, the species composition is usually totally different. This suggests that at some time in the past a common ancestor for conifers and another for broadleaf hardwoods existed, probably within the equatorial forest. Migration of tree species, combined with significant movement of the Earth's plates, carried species north and south and in the process distinct lines of evolution took place, thus separating the species of the two hemispheres.

The evolution of the mid-latitude forests

The ancestors of present-day forest species were already in existence during the Tertiary period, some 20 million years ago. About 1 million years ago there was a major cooling of the atmosphere, resulting in the ice ages. The mid-latitudes of both hemispheres were largely covered by snow and ice, destroying many forested areas.

From about 20 000 years ago, the climate gradually improved and the plants and animals that had migrated towards the equator to avoid the ice ages reinvaded the mid-latitudes. Animals could fly or walk to the ice-free land, but plants relied on the wind, rivers or animals to transport the seeds. Small, light seeds – such as those of birch and pine trees – were carried faster and farther than the heavy seeds, such as those of oak and beech.

Such a reinvasion (as far as plants are concerned) is an example of a *vegetation succession*. In a vegetation succession many different plant types take part, but these eventually come to be dominated by 'closed' forest communities – that is, forests in which all the living space is used by trees.

The last ice age finally ended about 10 000 years ago, and a succession of flowering plants quickly developed and reached its peak about 3000 BC, when the average world temperature was about 2 °C (3.6 °F) warmer than at present. This high point is called the *climatic optimum* and was characterized by the most luxuriant development of forest that the planet had seen for about 20 million years. During this time only the highest mountains and exposed coastal lands of the mid-latitudes remained unforested.

After 3000 BC two events occurred which changed the distribution of world forests. First, the climate became slightly cooler and moister. Peat began to form in the wetter areas and prevented the regrowth of trees. More significantly, humans began to emerge as an increasingly successful animal. At first, human impact on the forests was slight: people gathered berries and nuts, cut timber for shelters and made clearings in which to keep the first domesticated animals.

By the end of the 19th century many mid-latitude forests had been felled to make way for agriculture, towns and industry. On average, only 33% of the mid-latitudes remained forested, and in Britain, for example, only 2% of the country was covered by mature forest by 1918.

Most mid-latitude countries now recognize forests as a vital resource, of great economic and scientific wealth. As such, the remaining areas of forest (on average about 20% of the land area) are carefully managed, either as commercial forests, or in the form of protected areas such as national parks.

Coniferous or Boreal forest

A vast area of forest extends from about 45° to 65° N or even 70° N in Siberia (see map, p. 105). This is called the *Boreal* forest. A short growing season of 3 months is too restricting for the broadleaf hardwood trees. Instead, coniferous, softwood gymnosperms (see p. 119) predominate, the most common types being spruce, pine, fir and larch. Apart from the latter species, the conifers are evergreen, a condition thought to increase their ability to use any short, favourable growing season.

In the river valleys some deciduous hardwood species, such as willow and birch, occur as alternatives to the vast areas covered by conifers. On the forest floor is a thick layer of poorly decomposed acidic needles. These in turn are covered by mosses and sedges. Tree growth in the harsh conditions of these latitudes is slow, with trees taking 150–200 years to reach maturity. Although large areas of Boreal forest have been cut over and replanted, there still remain extensive areas of coniferous forest barely touched by man, particularly in the vast remoteness of Siberia.

Broadleaf hardwood forest

In the northern hemisphere an extensive belt of forest occurs between latitudes 35°

Temperate rain forest (left) in Tasmania. Temperate rain forests are found in particularly wet areas in the mid-latitudes, including Tasmania, southern Chile, and the northwest coast of North America. Such forests may be predominantly coniferous or broadleaved, but all are characterized by an abundance of ferns and mosses.

and 50° N (see map, p. 105), although vast areas of this belt have been felled, especially in Europe. These forests have more variety of species than their coniferous counterparts to the north. Oak, ash, beech, maple, elm, alder and hickory can form the dominant species depending upon site conditions. Beneath these large trees further layers of smaller trees, shrubs and herbs can be found. Each layer supports its own population of birds, small mammals and insects.

In spring and summer, these forests teem with life and provide a wide variety of shape, form and colour. In winter, at the northern extremity of these forests, average monthly temperatures fall to less than 5 °C (41 °F) and the growing season comes to an end. The response of the trees is to shed their leaves, that is they become *dormant*, a condition that persists until the next spring when the temperature once again rises above 5 °C. Although in these northern areas the broadleaf species tend to be deciduous, evergreen species of oak and chestnut, for example, may be found in areas such as southern Europe.

Very few undisturbed areas of temperate forest now remain. Only in the protected areas of the Appalachian Mountains of the USA and the Polish and Czechoslovak national parks can a semblance of the former luxuriance be found.

Many other forest types exist. In the southern hemisphere a very distinctive drought-resistant *Eucalyptus* forest can be found in southeastern Australia, while in New Zealand and the southern tip of South America, large natural forests of southern beech clothe the mountains.

Animal life

Throughout the coniferous and temperate forests animals have evolved alongside the developing vegetation. Together, animals and plants form an integrated community, reliant upon each other. The animals feed on the plants, while in return the plants benefit from the animals through pollination by insects, and through the constant clearing of vegetation by the grazing animals, thus making space for new plant growth.

In the Boreal forest the cold, dark winters

inhibit animal life. Animals survive either by hibernating or by migrating to warmer areas (see p. 170). In summer, however, the forest teems with life. The waterlogged forest floor provides an ideal breeding ground for flies, mosquitoes, leeches and snails. The verdant mosses and lichens are greedily searched out by large herbivores such as moose, elk, reindeer and caribou (all closely related species). Their diets are supplemented by the nutritious young shoots of birch and willow trees. The herbivores are migratory, seldom remaining in one area long enough to overgraze it.

More problematic are the myriads of insects. They defoliate the trees, feed on bark and roots, extract sap, form galls and bore into the living wood. Species such as the larch sawfly, pine sawfly and spruce budworm reach epidemic proportions and can devastate vast areas of forest before their life cycle is brought to an abrupt close by the onset of winter. Other insects feed on the animals (including humans), biting, taking blood and spreading diseases. The timber wolf, lynx, arctic hare, bear and wolverine are all preyed on by parasitic creatures, as are large birds such as the spruce grouse and the capercaillie.

The mosaic of forest habitats produces a similar diversity of animal life. Logging or fire damage opens out the forest, allowing voles, deer and ground-feeding birds to colonize. In the closed forest, squirrels and crossbill finches feed on the seeds contained in the cones. In turn these species are preyed upon by owls, hawks and pine martens.

The temperate forest, with its milder winters and more fertile soils, supports a far greater diversity of animals. Three main habitats exist – the foliage of the canopy, the decaying leaf litter of the forest floor, and the dying and dead wood of the forest. The foliage-feeders – mainly small herbivorous invertebrates but also including a wide range of caterpillars – can totally defoliate a tree in a matter of days. Epidemics of the poplar hawk moth can destroy its host tree, the poplars. Bark and sap are also consumed.

The large number of insects provide a great attraction for the insectivorous birds. The tit family of Europe and the chikadees of North America eat a wide variety of insects. The different birds feed in specific parts of the forest, thus reducing competition.

On the forest floor, the abundant grassy herb layer provides grazing for deer. Formerly, the European bison and its North American counterpart could be found grazing the forest glades. Rodents such as voles, mice, squirrels and chipmunks consume vast amounts of herbage. The droppings of all of these animals help to fertilize the soil and recycle the nutrients (see pp. 176–7).   GJ

The Boreal forest (left) of northern Eurasia and America is the home of the wolf. Hunting in packs, wolves can bring down prey larger than themselves, such as caribou, which they follow north to the tundra in the brief arctic summer.

The broadleaf forests (below left) of more temperate latitudes – such as those in New England seen here – are largely composed of deciduous trees. These provide glorious autumn colours as they prepare to shed their leaves prior to entering their period of winter dormancy.

SEE ALSO

● CLIMATIC AND VEGETATION REGIONS p. 104
● NON-FLOWERING PLANTS p. 118
● FLOWERING PLANTS p. 120
● MIGRATION p. 170
● THE BIOSPHERE p. 176
● FORESTRY p. 192

Ecosystems: Tropical Forests

Tropical forests contain some of the richest ranges of wild-life and vegetation to be found anywhere in the world. Some 30–40 million km² (12–15 million sq mi) – between around one fifth and one quarter of the Earth's total land area – is covered with tropical forests. There are four main types of tropical forest: evergreen forest, moist forest, deciduous forest and dry woodland. Strictly speaking, any forest between the tropics of Cancer and Capricorn can be called 'tropical forest', but the term is usually applied to forests within 10° north and south of the equator (see map, p. 105).

Our understanding of ecological relationships in tropical forests is steadily increasing. For example, it has been discovered that many trees have evolved chemical defences against leaf eaters (especially insects, which tend to cause the most damage). Another important discovery is the way in which certain fruit have evolved in shape and timing to be available to animals that disperse the seed (by excreting undigested seeds), but not to those that destroy the seed as they eat it. However, with the vast amounts of species that occur in the forests, and the practical difficulty of studying them, there are doubtless many fascinating discoveries still to be made.

Tropical evergreen forest

Tropical evergreen forest – also called *tropical rain forest* – is located in the *equatorial belt*, within 4° north and south of the equator. Although predominantly evergreen, such forests do contain many deciduous species. Tropical evergreen forest receives at least 4000 mm (156 in) of rainfall each year (with no dry season), and average monthly temperatures are between 21 and 27 °C (70 and 80 °F). In these hot, humid conditions vegetation attains its most luxuriant development. The leaves and branches of the trees form a *closed canopy*, through which very little light can penetrate downwards. Where a gap is left by a fallen tree, young trees compete to reach the light, and hence forest trees typically have tall, thin, branchless trunks, only putting out branches and leaves at the top where the light is. This competition encourages a very rapid rate of growth – as much as 10 m (33 ft) in 5 years. The top layer of vegetation consists of scattered trees (up to 60 m / 200 ft in height) that tower above a closed-canopy layer. These are the so-called *emergent trees*. Below these the

vegetation is sometimes classified into various layers, although this is more a convenience for description and analysis than a reality, as layers often overlap and merge.

Despite serious deforestation, tropical evergreen rain forest remains the single most extensive vegetation type at about 10–12 million km² (4–5 million sq mi). Although the amount of carbon dioxide absorbed by vegetation (see p. 117) is small compared to that absorbed by the oceans, the sheer amount of vegetation in tropical forests does contribute something to the reduction of the 'greenhouse effect' (see pp. 300–1), and so helps to regulate the heat balance of the planet. More importantly, however, the vast amounts of carbon dioxide given off when tropical forests are cleared and burnt are a significant factor in the build-up of the greenhouse effect.

It is estimated that at least 2 million different species of plants and animals exist in tropical evergreen forest, only one in six of which has been identified and named. Variety of shape and form is infinite. In the Malay peninsula alone there are 2500 different tree species.

Tropical moist forest

Seasonal rainfall variation soon becomes apparent around 4° from the equator. Total annual rainfall is reduced to 2000–3000 mm (78–117 in) and up to three months each year there may be as little as 100 mm (4 in) rainfall per month. In response, the forest becomes less luxuriant. Trees are less closely spaced, fewer layers of vegetation occur, and the number of different plant and animal species becomes fewer. Normally the trees are evergreen, but in the occasional long (14-day) dry spell, they actually shed a variable proportion of their leaves.

Tropical deciduous forest

Moving yet further from the equator, (5°–15° north and south), the seasonality of rainfall becomes greater and the dry season lasts for four to six months. Annual rainfall may be as low as 1500 mm (58 in). The trees becomes shorter, leaves become smaller and a deciduous phase becomes the only way to survive the dry period. Frequent fires ravage the forest and many species show fire-resistant features, such as thick bark, seeds that only germinate after exposure to heat, and branches that leave the trunk high above the ground.

Tropical open dry woodland

By 15–20° north and south of the equator extreme seasonal aridity occurs and rainfall of less than 1000 mm (39 in) per year is typical. Here, the forest is replaced by small, gnarled trees around 5 m (16½ ft) high, many of which are covered by green thorns up to 5 cm (2 in) long. Burning and the constant foraging of grazing animals (such as antelope, zebra, giraffe and elephant) keep the forest in check. This kind of woodland only occurs on the high African plateau but, following at least 2 million years of human use of the landscape, trees today are secondary to the grasses. These areas form the great tropical grasslands or *savannahs* (see p. 184).

Fertility

In the past it was assumed that the luxuri-

ant tropical forests must inevitably overlie a rich and fertile soil. Scientists conveniently overlooked the evidence from the *slash-and-burn* economies of the native peoples in which areas of forest were felled, then burnt to provide ash in which crops were grown. After two or three years the fertility of the site was lost and a new area was opened up. How had the fertility been lost?

The answer, when it was discovered, was a surprise. Because decomposition is so rapid, and because clay particles go into solution owing to the constantly high temperatures, it is not possible for a *clay-humus complex* to form. In all other latitudes the clay-humus complex is the method whereby soil fertility is retained. Without a clay-humus complex, tropical eco-systems have devised their own unique method of retaining fertility. The nutrients are held in the living portion of the forest, i.e. above ground. When a leaf falls to the forest floor it quickly decomposes (36–72 hours) and the nutrients are re-absorbed by the roots. If the forest is cut away there is then no mechanism for holding on to nutrients – and hence massive and rapid *leaching* (washing away) of nutrients takes place. In many areas the soils are also inherently infertile, as they have been leached by heavy rain storms over such a long period.

Human influence

There are two main pressures on tropical forests, both of which have led to massive deforestation: unmanaged commercial forestry (see p. 193), and farming. In the past commercial agricultural interests were attracted by the apparent luxuriance of the forests, but found that the fertility of the soil quickly disappeared once the forest was cleared (see above). In recent decades it has been desperation resulting from population expansion that has increasingly forced poor peasant farmers to encroach on the tropical forests, often with a similar lack of success – which forces them in two or three years to clear yet another area of forest.

Each year 120 000 km² (46 300 sq mi) of tropical evergreen forest are cleared – an area of land almost equal to the size of England. A further 100 000 km² (38 600 sq mi) of evergreen forest is being affected by partial destruction. Most authorities agree that if the current rate of forest depletion continues then all tropical forest will have disappeared by about the year 2050.

It is as a renewable resource that the forest can make its greatest yield. Instead of clear felling, continuous harvesting of products can generate a constant income. For example, Brazil earns $22 million each year from the export of essential oils extracted from forest species and destined for the pharmaceutical industry.

Within the forest are immense natural riches that could supply untold wealth for the developing countries. The tropical forest helps to balance the world's climate, while its vast collection of species holds the 'blueprints' of evolution, both that which has already occurred and that which remains to take place in the future. By destroying the forest and its inhabitants we would inflict irreparable damage on the biosphere and possibly even hasten our own demise.   GJ

SEE ALSO

- CLIMATIC AND VEGETATION REGIONS p. 104
- PLANT PHYSIOLOGY p. 116
- FLOWERING PLANTS p. 120
- THE BIOSPHERE p. 176
- FORESTRY p. 192

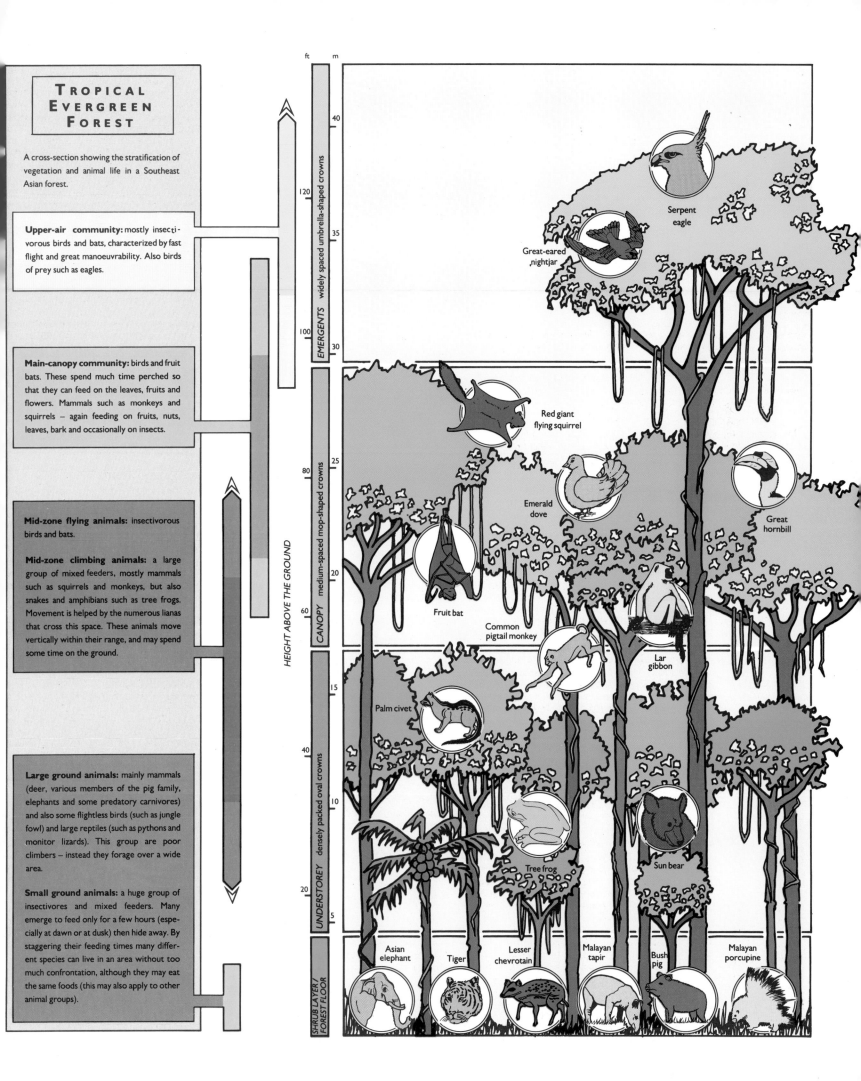

TROPICAL EVERGREEN FOREST

A cross-section showing the stratification of vegetation and animal life in a Southeast Asian forest.

Upper-air community: mostly insectivorous birds and bats, characterized by fast flight and great manoeuvrability. Also birds of prey such as eagles.

Main-canopy community: birds and fruit bats. These spend much time perched so that they can feed on the leaves, fruits and flowers. Mammals such as monkeys and squirrels — again feeding on fruits, nuts, leaves, bark and occasionally on insects.

Mid-zone flying animals: insectivorous birds and bats.

Mid-zone climbing animals: a large group of mixed feeders, mostly mammals such as squirrels and monkeys, but also snakes and amphibians such as tree frogs. Movement is helped by the numerous lianas that cross this space. These animals move vertically within their range, and may spend some time on the ground.

Large ground animals: mainly mammals (deer, various members of the pig family, elephants and some predatory carnivores) and also some flightless birds (such as jungle fowl) and large reptiles (such as pythons and monitor lizards). This group are poor climbers — instead they forage over a wide area.

Small ground animals: a huge group of insectivores and mixed feeders. Many emerge to feed only for a few hours (especially at dawn or at dusk) then hide away. By staggering their feeding times many different species can live in an area without too much confrontation, although they may eat the same foods (this may also apply to other animal groups).

ft   m

40

120

35

100

30

HEIGHT ABOVE THE GROUND

EMERGENTS   widely spaced umbrella-shaped crowns

25

80

CANOPY   medium-spaced mop-shaped crowns

20

60

15

UNDERSTOREY   densely packed oval crowns

40

10

20

5

SHRUB LAYER / FOREST FLOOR

Serpent eagle

Great-eared nightjar

Red giant flying squirrel

Emerald dove

Great hornbill

Fruit bat

Common pigtail monkey

Lar gibbon

Palm civet

Tree frog

Sun bear

Asian elephant

Tiger

Lesser chevrotain

Malayan tapir

Bush pig

Malayan porcupine

Ecosystems: Grasslands

In undisturbed forest ecosystems, grasses form a small proportion of the ground-layer vegetation, occurring mainly as small, isolated clumps. Once the forest is removed, and the grasses are exposed to direct sunlight, however, they grow rapidly to produce a continuous carpet of grass called a *sward*.

Leopards (right), whose range extends from Africa across southern Asia, are creatures both of the forest and of more open bush, where the grasslands are interspersed with trees. Leopards are agile climbers, both sleeping and storing their kills in trees.

Almost 30% of the Earth's land surface is covered by grassland. Most grassland has appeared within the last 2000 years, as pastoral agriculture (the rearing of sheep, cattle, etc.) has spread at the expense of forests. Apart from these young agricultural grasslands there are also some very old 'natural' grasslands – although there is some doubt over just how natural they are. The North American prairie, the Russian steppe, the South America pampas and the African savannah are all examples of very ancient grassland. They were 'discovered' by European settlers from about 1650 onwards and were immediately recognized as the perfect location for cattle and sheep farming.

It was once thought that the areas occupied by old grasslands marked the occurrence of special types of climate that were in some way unsuitable for the growth of trees. Certainly, they all suffer cold (or very cold) average winter temperatures (typically –10 °C / 4 °F) and summers are invariably hot (28 °C / 82 °F). The biggest climatic limitation against trees is the low rainfall – as low as 500 mm (20 in) per annum and rarely more than 1000 m (40 in) – and the high evaporation rate in summer. Even this climate, however, would not prevent the growth of dry, thorn forest.

It is now known that the critical factor in the creation and maintenance of grasslands has been fire. The dry climate would have allowed natural fires caused by lightning strikes to have burnt areas of forest. Repeated and frequent burning (every 5–10 years) would have been sufficient to prevent the recolonization of the area by trees. Once established, natural grasslands became the centres of development for huge numbers of mammals, which consumed vast amounts of grass and trampled and nibbled any young trees that attempted to grow.

The biology of grasses

Grasses belong to the gramineae family and include a wide diversity of species. Grasses can grow in every imaginable habitat, from the very dry to the very wet, from salty sea-level sites to windswept mountain summits. Unlike other plants, grasses generally grow faster if they are grazed by animals. They are also able to survive both burning and flooding. The grass family has a vigorous genetic structure, and this has been utilized by generations of farmers for the breeding of grain crops (wheat, barley, oats, sorghum, rice, etc.).

Grasses increase their numbers in two ways. If their flowers are cross-pollinated (see p. 121), seeds are produced from which new plants grow, so encouraging vigour in the stock. Grasses also rely on *vegetative reproduction*. In this process, side shoots quickly develop their own leaves and roots.

Unlike most other plants, grasses can make new growth from two quite separate points. They possess the customary apical growing points located at the tip of each stem (see p. 116). In addition, they have many intermediate growing points at intervals along the stems. If the top of the stem is eaten by a grazing animal then the intermediate growing points become activated and develop side shoots. Provided grazing is not continuous, grassland can support a large animal population.

Major natural grasslands

Within the tropics are found the *savannah* grasslands. They are most extensive in Africa. Sustained by the summer rains, the savannah grasses grow to at least 2 m (6½ ft) and sometimes 3 m (10 ft) tall. They support a huge population of seed-eating birds and large herbivorous mammals (antelope, wildebeest, zebra), and nowadays increasing herds of domestic cattle and goats. The large wild herbivores in

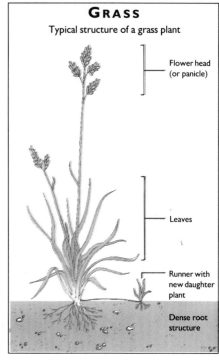

GRASS
Typical structure of a grass plant

- Flower head (or panicle)
- Leaves
- Runner with new daughter plant
- Dense root structure

turn support large carnivores (lion, leopard, cheetah, hyena, jackal).

Beyond the tropics, extensive areas of old grassland can be found in North America and in Russia. Both areas experience generally similar climates – very cold, snowy winters (with several months below 0 °C / 32 °F) and hot summers (average temperatures above 21 °C / 70 °F).

In North America, the European settlers cut their way through the eastern deciduous forests suddenly to be confronted by a 'sea of grass', the *prairies*. Grassland existed in a huge tract from the Appalachian Mountains westwards to the foothills of the Rocky Mountains. Vast herds of bison migrated across the prairie, following the seasonal distribution of rainfall and the associated new growth of the grasses.

Wherever the bison was to be found so too was the prairie dog. These small ground-living squirrels (not dogs) dig extensive burrows up to 3 m (10 ft) into the prairie soils. It has been estimated that in an area of 110 500 km² (42 640 sq mi) there once lived some 40 million prairie dogs. Their burrows caused buildings to collapse, roads to subside and farm animals to break their legs as they fell into the burrows. As a result the prairie dog has been hunted almost to extinction in some parts of North America.

Evidence from North American Indian cultures suggests that bison and grasslands have existed for about 10 000 years. It was assumed that the prairie was a natural vegetation unit that had developed in response to soil or climatic factors. It is now thought that the prairies are the result either of frequent natural fires or of fires started by the indigenous Indian population, who burnt the vegetation every few years in order to eliminate trees and encourage the grasses. These in turn supported the all-important bison. With the coming of European settlers and firearms, the bison were hunted to the verge of extinction.

The *steppes*, located almost entirely in the USSR, have a remarkably similar botanical structure to the prairies. In the summer, grasses grow to just over 1 m (3¼ ft) high and die quickly in the first frosts of autumn. They remain covered by the winter snows until the following spring, when they quickly decompose to form a thick humus material.

Soils beneath the grasslands are typically very dark brown or black. The colour is due to the large quantities of humus, which constitutes up to 15% of the soil. In North America these soils are called 'prairie earth', while in Russia the famous 'chernozem' soils occur.

Southern-hemisphere grasslands

At one time there were vast areas of grassland south of the Tropic of Capricorn, though as in the northern hemisphere, the original vegetation has been much changed due to agriculture.

In Uruguay and northern Argentina a type of grass known as *pampas* once occurred. It grew up to 2 m (6½ ft) high and consisted of 'bunch' grasses with bare soil between the tussocks. A similar tussock grassland, known as *veld*, once covered a large area of the high plateau of southern Africa. The extent of the original veld has grown considerably since the 1960s into a barren, overgrazed and eroded area. This has partly been caused by the ravaging droughts that have hit southern Africa, and partly by unsuitable farming practices.

In the South Island of New Zealand an area called the *Canterbury Plains* has been an extensive grassland for at least 250 years, and possibly for several thousands of years. It is now thought probable that the earliest Polynesian settlers burnt the original forest to encourage grasses for huge flightless grazing birds (the moas, extinct from about 1750), upon which the Maori population were once totally dependent.

The fate of the grasslands

Few areas of natural grassland either in the tropics or in the mid-latitudes now remain. The temperate grasslands have been largely converted to agricultural use, being particularly suited for the production of cereals – they are sometimes called the 'bread baskets' of the world. The North American prairies alone will be producing almost 200 million tonnes (tons) of grain for export by the year 2000.

Tropical grasslands are also being converted to agriculture, although with mixed success. Tropical diseases and the variability of the annual rains have made food production an erratic process. The famines that occurred in many north African countries in the mid-1980s was due in part to the unsuccessful conversion of the savannahs.   GJ

SEE ALSO

● CLIMATIC AND VEGETATION
  REGIONS p. 104
● PLANT PHYSIOLOGY p. 116
● FLOWERING PLANTS p. 120
● BIRDS p. 136–9
● MAMMALS p. 140–65
● THE BIOSPHERE p. 176
● ARABLE FARMING p. 188
● LIVESTOCK FARMING p. 190

The open savannah of East Africa is home to vast herds of large herbivores, such as these wildebeest in the Serengeti National Park of Tanzania. The herbivores are in turn preyed upon by hunters and scavengers – big cats, hyenas, jackals and vultures.

Ecosystems: Extreme

Most habitats found on the planet have at least one factor in their environmental make-up which acts as a limiting factor on plants and animals. These limits make their greatest impact in the deserts, alpine regions and polar areas. But even in such extreme environments it is remarkable how many plants and animals have adapted successfully to the harsh conditions.

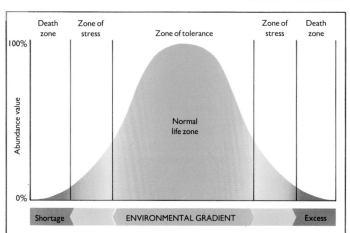

The environmental gradient, showing the zone of tolerance in which most plants and animals flourish. However, some specially adapted species actually thrive better in the zone of stress, as there is less competition with other species.

All species are said to possess an environmental *tolerance range* within which they must live. The diagram of the *environmental gradient* shows that at the extreme points the population size becomes restricted because either a severe shortage or an excess of a commodity creates conditions of stress and causes death. Only when the life-giving necessities are available in *optimum* amounts do plants and animals reach the maximum numbers as in the centre of the diagram.

Most species will migrate to those regions in which they find their own unique blend of environmental requirements. Some plants and animals seem especially able to survive in areas that at first sight appear hostile to the very existence of life. However, with few species able to colonize the edges of the zone of tolerance and fewer still in the stress zone, competition between species is actually reduced. For some hardy plants and animals, life in these marginal areas can actually be easier than fighting for survival in the over-populated zone of optimum conditions.

Desert ecosystems

Deserts receive small and erratic amounts of precipitation, usually less than 250 mm (10 in) per annum. Of greater importance than the amount of rainfall is the effectiveness of the moisture. If a desert receives 100 mm (4 in) of rainfall per annum in only two heavy storms then the effectiveness of the moisture is less than if the rain falls on 20 occasions as fine drizzle of 5 mm (0.2 in). Temperature is also important. When it exceeds 20 °C (68 °F), evaporation rates become very high.

Deserts cover more than one third of the Earth's land surface, but only quite a small proportion of desert area is sandy – the rest is bare rock or covered with scree-like debris. As well as hot deserts

such as the Sahara and Kalahari Deserts there are also temperate and cold deserts such as the Gobi. Many such deserts owe their origin to being many thousands of kilometres from the oceans, and hence the rain-bearing winds never reach them (see also p. 92).

The vegetation in all deserts shows extreme adaptation to suit the droughty conditions. Smallness of size, leaves reduced to spines, long, deep roots and the ability to grow very quickly at the onset of rains are some of the most useful adaptations. The seeds of many desert plants can remain dormant for up to five years awaiting the occurrence of damp conditions suitable for germination. Other species have adapted to the long dry spells by storing water in enlarged, fleshy stems. These are the so-called *succulent plants* of which the New World cacti are the best-known examples. The most spectacular cactus is the barrel cactus, which was traditionally used as a water reserve by the American Indians. In the Old World the *Euphorbia* group of plants predominate in deserts. The stems of these plants are filled with sticky latex, which resists evaporation.

Animal life is surprisingly varied. Most desert animals are active primarily at night or during the brief periods of early morning and late afternoon when the heat is not as intense. During the day they remain in cooler underground burrows, or in the shade of overhanging rocks. Rodents, snakes, lizards, a few birds, spiders and insects are the main animal types (although there are also a few larger herbivores and carnivores). Many desert animals – including the dromedary (see p. 159) – show strange adaptations for life in these extreme conditions.

Neither the Saharan jerboa (a tiny rodent) nor the North American kangaroo rat, for example, appear to drink any water, but instead obtain their moisture directly from their food. They do this by oxidizing food substances containing hydrogen, and this provides sufficient quantities of water. Many desert animals have unusually efficient excretion systems in which the waste products of salts, urea and solids contain virtually no water. An absence of sweat glands, large skin flaps (particularly large ears) from which an excess of heat can be lost and an ability to lose a large proportion of body weight in the dry season are common characteristics of desert animals.

Each year some 120 000 km² (46 300 sq mi) of new desert is formed by a process called *desertification*. This is due to over-cultivation, deforestation, over-grazing and poor irrigation. Desertification in the southern fringes of the Sahara contributed to the famines in that region in the 1970s and 80s.

Alpine ecosystems

Strong winds, low temperatures and short (three-month) summers characterize the alpine ecosystem. Spring and autumn are

A lone cactus in the Nazca Desert on the Pacific side of the Andes. Cacti survive long periods of drought by their ability to store water in enlarged, fleshy stems. Their leaves are reduced to spines to minimize evaporation.

ften completely missing: the winter snows melt quickly as the air temperature rises above 0 °C (32 °F), while at the end of summer, active life for all plants and animals is brought to an abrupt end at the onset of the first snows.

There is no precise elevation at which alpine conditions can be said to begin (see diagram). At or near the equator alpine conditions begin within the range 4000–5300 m (13 100–17 400 ft). That figure falls gradually until by latitude 60° north – in Norway for example – alpine conditions begin about 300 m (1000 ft).

The alpine environment is one of extreme contrast. A plant may find its leaves in bright sunlight and at a temperature of more than 10 °C (50 °F) while its roots may be embedded in ice crystals at 0 °C (32 °F). Many alpine plants show *xeromorphic features* (modifications to ensure water conservation). At the highest elevations more than 5000 m / 16 400 ft), a far greater amount of intense ultraviolet light is received due to the thinner atmosphere. This light can stimulate intense growth rates. It also causes genetic mutations and probably explains why alpine plants are able to hybridize with an ease not seen in other ecosystems.

Alpine vegetation is usually very low growing, seeking the protection of any rock or furrow in order to escape the almost persistent strong winds. They often grow as 'cushions', which help build up heat within the plant. In early summer, alpine plants become a blaze of colour to attract the plentiful insects. Individual plants may survive for many years.

Animal life is confined to small mammals, such as marmots and voles, which live in burrows. However, larger herbivores such as chamois, ibex, bighorns and yaks also survive at high altitudes, as do carnivores such as foxes, bears and snow leopards. Many birds visit these areas in summer, laying their eggs in shallow nests shaped more from stones than from twigs and grasses.

Tropical alpine areas show many unique features, in particular a tendency for plants which occur lower down the mountain to grow to a giant size. Thus on Kilimanjaro giant lobelias and groundsel reach 2 m (7 ft) high, and in the tropical Andes giant members of the daisy family occur.

Polar or high-latitude ecosystems

Beyond the Arctic and Antarctic Circles the main limiting factors are those of the long winter darkness and the perennially low temperatures. For up to six months of the year darkness prevails, temperatures remain below 0 °C (32 °F), snow covers the surface, and permafrost cracks open the ground. Life in these circumstances is severely restricted – but is still possible.

Summers are short (in some cases only 8 weeks) but long days allow temperatures to reach 10 °C (50 °F). The ground thaws to a sticky mass, insects abound and plant life becomes active. Inconspicuous mosses and lichens cover the ground along with sedges, grasses and flowering plants. In some areas tiny trees (willow

Alpine plants – such as these *Ranunculus glacialis* (members of the buttercup family) – are often characterized by low height and a habit of forming cushions to preserve heat.

and aspen) grow horizontally to escape the cold winds. This is the area of the *tundra*.

Few animals remain in the tundra during the long winter. Those that do must develop thick insulating coats of fur or feathers. The musk ox of North America and Greenland has a double layer of hair, as does the arctic fox, while resident birds such as the ptarmigan have a special layer of insulating feathers. Thus equipped, these animals can survive temperatures as low as –50 °C (–58 °F). In some animals the colour of the coat also changes from a summer brown to a protective winter white.

Hibernation (see p. 170) is not common amongst the animal inhabitants – the conditions are probably too severe to make such an adaptation a reliable form of survival. Small rodents such as lemmings, shrews and voles burrow under the snow and remain active all winter. Tunnels and nests insulated with grass and warmed by the animals' bodies often provide temperatures of 10 °C (50 °F) when external conditions are below freezing. Food is obtained from eating plant roots and stems.

By far the greatest means of survival is for animals to migrate to less hostile areas (see p. 170), returning in the spring or early summer. Mobility and navigation skills are thus essential features. Birds such as ducks, geese and swans are particularly successful migrants. To save essential time, pairing occurs before they arrive at the summer breeding grounds and old nest sites are reused. Food is abundant in the short but favourable summer, although the animals must be prepared to change their food supply to coincide with whatever is available –

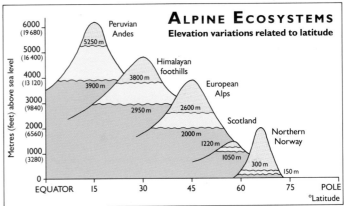

ALPINE ECOSYSTEMS
Elevation variations related to latitude

insects, molluscs, worms, and young plant shoots.

Because life is so marginal in the extreme ecosystems, they are highly vulnerable to changes wrought by humans. Hunters, mineral prospectors and tourists all take their toll. The extreme ecosystems will never provide us with much food, but they are often rich in minerals and are exploited by the developed nations. These remote areas represent the last remaining under-utilized land on this planet – they are the last true wildernesses.   GJ

SEE ALSO

- MOUNTAINS p. 86
- ICE p. 90
- DESERTS p. 92
- CLIMATIC AND VEGETATION REGIONS p. 104
- NON-FLOWERING PLANTS p. 118
- FLOWERING PLANTS p. 120
- THE BIOSPHERE p. 176

Polar bears on the winter tundra of northern Canada. The polar bear's adaptations to its environment include thick fur, camouflage coloration, and hairy soles to help its paws grip on the ice.

Arable Farming

Arable farming is the practice of cultivating land to produce crops for human or animal consumption. Horticulture, the growing of fruit and vegetables, is regarded as a specialized branch of arable agriculture. Some crops are grown for purposes other than food: for example, cotton and jute are turned into fabrics, cooking oil is extracted from maize and sunflowers, esparto grass is used in the manufacture of paper and rope, and tobacco is used for smoking materials. Although there are about 80 000 edible plants, just four plants (rice, wheat, maize and potatoes) make up more of the world's total food production than all the others combined.

Land used for arable farming is usually cultivated by ploughing (or often by digging in the Third World). Seed or small plants are then planted in the prepared soil. In the developed world, the crop is usually fertilized and sprayed with a variety of chemicals in order to ensure rapid and healthy growth. In Third World countries less reliance is placed on these additives and more attention is given by the farmer and his family to weeding, hoeing and selective spraying to control pests *after* they have appeared.

The geographical limits

The geographic boundaries of arable farming are controlled by soil, relief and climate. Soils must be fertile, stone free and well drained. Generally, slope should not exceed about 15° from the horizontal in order to minimize soil erosion and prevent the overturning of tractors. However, the building of terraces can enable steeper slopes to be cultivated.

At temperate latitudes only land near sea level is suitable for arable farming. Above about 200 m (660 ft) the growing season becomes too short and night-time frosts can damage crops. However, in lower latitudes, arable agriculture is successfully practised on high plateaux up to 2000 m (6600 ft) above sea level, while in the tropical Andes potatoes are cultivated at 4300 m (14 100 ft). Apart from temperature, availability of moisture is of critical importance. Rainfall should be evenly distributed through the growing season, although nowadays any deficiency can often be offset by irrigation.

The development of arable farming

Arable agriculture first emerged in the Middle East in the period 9000–7000 BC, immediately following a world-wide improvement in climate after the last Ice Age. The crops grown were primitive forms of einkorn (a variety of wheat) and barley. Evidence of agricultural development in many of the fertile river valleys of the Far East, India and the Nile Valley, and from Central and South America, have also been discovered, all dating from between 6000 and 4000 BC. When the crops grown at these sites are listed they appear remarkably similar to our present crops (rice, oats, beans, peas, maize, casava, etc.).

Gradually, a *subsistence* arable agriculture was developed in which at least enough crops for survival were produced, using human labour perhaps supplemented by draft animals. At best there would be some crops left over to barter, or to put aside for hard times.

Two types of subsistence farming could be found, both of which are still practised in the Third World. The first was labour intensive, in which one crop was continually produced (*monoculture*) – for example, rice in the Far East. The second was land intensive, in which a number of crops were produced (*polyculture*) from a small area of land until soil fertility became exhausted and a new area of land was developed. A typical example of this is the *slash-and-burn* agriculture found within the tropics (see pp. 182–3).

In the mid-latitudes neither of these farming types was possible. Instead, during the Middle Ages, small strips of land were cultivated to the point of soil exhaustion. The need to rotate crops and to add manure was poorly understood.

Gradually, during the course of the 18th century, the first Agricultural Revolution (see p. 420) occurred in Europe. Land was periodically rested (left *fallow*) and crops rotated between two, and later three and four fields. A four-field system would typically have involved a grain crop (oats, barley or wheat), followed by a root crop (turnip or potato), followed by a different grain crop, followed by a fallow year of grass or clover (the latter helping to restore nitrogen to the soil – see p. 116.) The alternation of crops helps to maintain the fertility of the soil, and to prevent the build-up of pests and diseases specific to a particular crop.

The increased productivity that resulted from rotation, and from improvements in techniques such as ploughing and sowing, enabled many farmers to grow a large proportion of their produce as *cash crops*, i.e. crops that can be sold at a profit. These surpluses were used to feed the increasing urban populations.

PROPORTIONAL LAND USE

At present, 11% of the world's total land area is devoted to arable farming. A further 13% of the total is potential arable land.

NORTH and CENTRAL AMERICA	SOUTH AMERICA	EUROPE	AFRICA	SOUTH ASIA	NORTH and CENTRAL ASIA	SOUTHEAST ASIA	AUSTRALIA and NEW ZEALAND

KEY | ARABLE and CROPLAND | GRAZING LAND | FOREST | OTHER LAND

MAIN FOOD CROPS OF THE WORLD

WHEAT
Distribution: non-tropical regions throughout the world, extending to about latitude 60°N and 50°S.
Uses: flour for bread-making and baking.
Annual production: 596 million tonnes (tons). Wheat can hybridize with ease, not only between different cultivated varieties but also with grasses. This gives it its great potential as an agricultural species, and has resulted in a great many varieties. There are two main groups of modern wheat. *Spring wheat* is sown in March and harvested in September (in the northern hemisphere), and is usually found in higher-latitude locations such as Canada and Russia. It produces a hard grain well suited to bread making. *Winter wheat* is slower growing and less tolerant of winter cold. It is planted in September and harvested the following July (in the northern hemisphere). It is a softer grain more useful for general baking. Modern cultivation methods rely on hybrid seed and inorganic fertilizers to boost the yield.

RICE
Distribution: any region where growing-season temperatures exceed 21°C (70°F) and irrigation is possible.
Uses: boiled as a staple food, and milled to rice flour.
Annual production: 521 million tonnes (tons). More than half the world's population depends on rice for sustenance, mainly in Asia and in Central and South America. Only 2% of annual rice production enters the international commodities market.

Most rice in Asia is of the 'paddy' variety, that is, grown in standing water until the time of harvest. Elsewhere, 'upland rice' is grown, which relies on abundant rainfall. Paddy rice gives the highest yields, and up to three crops per year can be obtained. Traditionally, rice has demanded intensive labour, although mechanization of some of the cultivation stages has now become possible. Genetic improvements since 1962 have resulted in a 700% improvement in yield.

MAIZE (CORN)
Distribution: originally from the Americas but introduced to Europe in 1492 and now extensively grown in all tropical, sub-tropical and warm temperate regions.
Uses: consumed by humans in the form of maize flour and breakfast cereals, and as a vegetable ('sweet corn'). Milled for animal feed, and used as a source of oils, vitamins and industrial starch. Also fermented for maize beer.
Annual production: 469 million tonnes (tons). Maize is unique in that it produces distinctive 'cobs' each made up of several hundred grains. Under optimum growth conditions maize is three times as productive as wheat. Maize flour is ideal for cake making, pancakes and unleavened bread. When fed to pigs and cattle it can result in spectacular increases in meat tissue. Experiments have shown it to be ideally suited for the production of industrial alcohol, and the plant residue can be decomposed to produce methane gas (biofuel).

BARLEY
Distribution: northern hemisphere mid-latitudes.
Uses: animal feedstock. In its 'malted' (germinated) form it is used in the manufacture of beer and whisky.
Annual production: 181 million tonnes (tons). Barley is the fourth most important cereal in terms of world production. Its use as a food stuff is almost completely confined to animal feed.

PULSES (PEAS AND BEANS)
Distribution: worldwide.
Uses: oils for human and industrial use and increasingly as alternative sources of high-quality protein in meat-free diets. Extracts from pulses are used in putty, paint, waterproofing materials and leather dressings.
Annual production: 110 million tonnes (tons). The most important pulse today is the soyabean, and now 40% of world soyabean output comes from the USA. The bean produces valuable oil, and the residue is fed to animals.

POTATOES
Distribution: temperate and high latitudes throughout the world.
Uses: as a vegetable for humans.
Annual production: 268 million tonnes (tons). The potato originated in the mountains of the northern Andes of South America. It was brought to Europe at the end of the 16th century, doing particularly well in the cool, damp conditions of Western Europe. The potato is particularly rich in carbohydrate and also supplies protein, iron, vitamins B and C, as well as 50% of phosphorus and 10% of calcium requirements. The potato is vulnerable to diseases such as the dreaded potato blight, which decimated the Irish potato crop in the 1840s. The potential of the potato has hardly been realized. Their natural variety makes them ideal subjects for genetic engineering, and new varieties have already been developed for tropical latitudes – potentially revolutionizing the diets of many Third World populations.

SWEET POTATOES
Distribution: in the tropics, and increasingly in temperate latitudes.
Uses: as a staple food and also as a flavoursome vegetable.
Annual production: 133 million tonnes (tons). Originally confined to the tropics of South America, the sweet potato accompanied the Portuguese and Spanish voyagers of the 16th century. The swollen root is rich in starch, sugar, iron, calcium and a Vitamin A substitute. It is unusual amongst crops in that it is always grown from cuttings (rarely if ever from seed).

CASSAVA
Distribution: originally the tropics of the New World, but now more extensive in Africa.
Uses: fried, roasted, boiled, sun-dried or fermented for human consumption.
Annual production: 148 million tonnes (tons). Cassava is a versatile crop, and will tolerate drought conditions. Some species contain the poisonous substance hydrogen cyanide, and this must be carefully removed before eating. It contains virtually no protein (at best 1%) and people who eat mainly cassava develop kwashior-kor, a protein-deficiency disease characterized by swollen stomachs.

OATS AND RYE
Distribution: cool, damp climates of the higher latitudes.
Uses: mainly as cattle and horse feed, but oats are used for porridge and rye as a specialist bread flour.
Annual production: 80 million tonnes (tons). These two cereals are of lesser importance than formerly, and now account for only about 5% of the world's cereal production. The advantages of both are that they can grow in poor soils in poor climates. They are also extremely nutritious, with a higher fat content than most cereals and an excellent grade of dietary fibre.

Modern arable farming

In the early 1900s the mechanization of farming began to speed up, first in America, later in Europe. Petrol-driven tractors hauled bigger ploughs, and this allowed larger areas to be cultivated. From 1918 the number of people employed in agriculture began to fall. In the 1930s the first large-scale use of chemical products began. These included artificial fertilizers rich in nitrogen, phosphate and potash, together with fungicides, insecticides and herbicides to control moulds, insect pests and weeds respectively. There were dramatic increases in productivity levels, although wider environmental problems have sometimes resulted (see pp. 300–1). Environmental problems have also arisen from the destruction of hedges, felling of trees and drainage of boggy areas, all of which leaves a landscape open to the ravages of wind and water erosion.

By the 1960s plant geneticists were able to breed crops for specific environments, heralding the so-called 'Green Revolution'. By the 1970s biochemists were able to recombine the genetic structure of plants to produce new hybrid crop varieties with greater yields and increased disease resistance. In the 1980s the cloning of plants allowed the mass production of young plants that all had identical properties: characteristics such as height, fruit size, leaf size and rate of maturing can all be made very similar within a crop produced from cloned stock. As a result, harvesting costs have been reduced and yield increased.

Other changes have also occurred in arable agriculture. High capital investment is necessary to buy fertilizers, pesticides and machinery, with the result that large-scale specialization has been a feature of agriculture in the developed world, with many family farms being brought into corporate ownership. Agriculture has become big business – agribusiness.   GJ

Hydroponics is a technique for growing fruit and vegetables in gravel or polythene, through which water containing dissolved inorganic salts is pumped. This gives the plants all the nutrients they need. In this purpose-built hydroponics building in the far north-west of Scotland, such plants as strawberries, sweetcorn, vines and bananas can be grown.

SEE ALSO
- PLANT PHYSIOLOGY p. 116
- FLOWERING PLANTS p. 120
- LIVESTOCK FARMING p. 190
- THE FOOD-PROCESSING INDUSTRY p. 196
- FOOD, DIET AND DIGESTION p. 208
- POPULATION AND HUNGER p. 296
- THREATS TO THE ENVIRONMENT p. 300

Livestock Farming

Livestock farming is concerned with the rearing of animals for their meat, meat products, dairy products, hides, skins, wool, glue and gelatin. The term *pastoralism* is also used for this branch of agriculture, although technically it does not include the intensive indoor rearing of animals such as pigs and chickens.

Meat and meat products are used for both human and animal consumption. Dairy products are based on milk – usually from cows, but also from goats and sheep – and include butter, cream, cheese and yoghurt. Hides and skins are mostly used for clothing and footwear, usually in the form of leather. Leather is made by the process of *tanning*, by which the skin or hide is made smooth and flexible by removing the hair and treating it with various natural or man-made chemicals. Wool – sheared from the animal annually – is spun into yarn and then woven or knitted into garments: sheep are the main producers, but goats, camels, vicuna, alpaca and others are also important. Glue and gela-

tin are made by boiling bones, skin and horns, fertilizers from ground hoof and horn.

Livestock farming around the world

Although dogs were domesticated as early as 10 000–8000 BC in North America, Europe and the Middle East, the first agricultural animal to be domesticated was the sheep: this occurred in the Middle East around 9000 BC. Goats, cattle and pigs soon followed, and livestock farming started to spread to Europe in around 6000 BC. The domestication of draught animals (such as horse, ox, camel) allowed the mechanization of agriculture to begin.

Today, all forms of livestock farming can still be found around the world, from the nomadic Bakhtiari pastoralists of Iran to the extensive commercial ranching of sheep and cattle in Australia and North America, and the intensive techniques of Western Europe. Nine types of domesticated animals predominate (see box) and in all these require 30 000 000 km² (11 580 000 sq mi) of grazing land (compared to the total area of arable land of 15 000 000 km² / 5 790 000 sq mi). The proportions of grazing land compared to other land uses in different continents are shown on pp. 188-9.

Modern pastoralism

Meat and meat products are too expensive for most of the world's people to consume, because large herbivores are too inefficient at converting plant material (their main source of food) into meat for human consumption. For example, rangeland cattle are less than 4% efficient in terms

of their ability to convert grass into meat. The other 96% is lost in keeping warm, moving, breathing and digesting the vast quantities of leafy food. However, as the wealth of a population increases then so more of its disposable income is spent on meat. This reaches its maximum development in the USA, where more than half of all the grain produced is fed to cattle for eventual consumption as steaks and burgers.

In an attempt to make livestock farming a more productive method of producing food, many forms of specialization have developed. Intensive farming in Western Europe has been based on centuries of carefully controlled breeding to produce an animal well suited for market requirements. Grazing lands have been ploughed and reseeded with the most productive mixtures of grasses, clovers and vetches.

In many animals, breeding has been made more efficient in the 20th century by the use of *artificial insemination*, by which semen from a single male exhibiting the desired characteristics can be stored at low temperatures for months and be used to fertilize a large number of females. Totally new varieties have been made possible by the genetic engineering of specific animal types to suit particular locations. Thus the strength of the yak has been combined with the meat and milk quality of the cow to improve the main livestock type used in the foothills of the Himalaya.

Factory farming

The most recent trend in intensive animal rearing has been towards *factory farming,*

Wodaabe nomads travelling with their herds of cattle in Niger, to the south of the Sahara Desert. For such nomadic peoples, their cattle provide virtually all their physical needs, and ownership of cattle often lends social status.

The geep, born at Cambridge in 1982. The result of genetic engineering, the geep grew from a mixture of cells from the embryos of a sheep and a goat.

Factory farming has been considered by some people to be morally offensive in that animals are no longer free to range. More recently, factory farming has been criticized for the practice of feeding growth hormones and chemical additives to animals in an effort to boost the quantity and quality of the product. Some authorities believe these substances are cumulative in the human food chain and can cause health problems.

in which animals are housed in heated buildings. This is done to minimize energy losses through movement and heat loss. All food is brought to the animal and all waste products removed. Pig farms, battery houses for hens, stall-fed cattle and the animal feedlot found around large American cities are all examples of this trend.

It should be stressed, however, that if we continue to demand large quantities of red meat (itself now under suspicion as a cause of human illness such as heart disease) and dairy products then we shall be forced to rely upon factory-farming methods. Extensive free-range pastoralism is too inefficient to provide sufficient food.   GJ

Factory farming of hens in California.

SEE ALSO

● ARABLE FARMING p. 188
● THE FOOD-PROCESSING INDUSTRY p. 196
● FOOD, DIET AND DIGESTION p. 208
● POPULATION AND HUNGER p. 296

THE MAIN TYPES OF DOMESTICATED ANIMAL

CATTLE
Worldwide numbers: 1283 million.
Distribution: worldwide.
Uses: meat, meat products, milk, dairy products, leather, draught animals (oxen).

Many different varieties exist, some bred principally for beef, others for milk production; in addition different varieties have been bred for different climatic conditions. Cows can be bred at any time of the year. Following the birth of the calf, the mother remains in milk for up to 10 months. Good cows can be kept in an almost continuous cycle of calf production and milk yield from about 18 months of age to 10 years. Most male calves are castrated and reared for beef, being ready for slaughter at 18 months. In contrast, animals destined for veal production are fed only on milk, and slaughtered at about 14 weeks.

PIGS
Worldwide numbers: 861 million.
Distribution: worldwide.
Uses: every part of the pig can be used, and products include meat, meat products, leather, hair for brushes, fat for industrial use.

Traditionally, pigs have been allowed to roam through woodlands rooting for worms, slugs, roots and young shoots. Nowadays, economic pressures have forced pig farmers to keep their animals in purpose-built buildings. Maize (corn) is fed direct to the pigs to ensure rapid, high-quality meat production. Pigs intended for pork are slaughtered at 40–50 kg (88–110 lb) body weight, while for bacon, a weight of 80–100 kg (176–220 lb) is acceptable.

SHEEP
Worldwide numbers: 1194 million.
Distribution: mainly Old World, Australia and New Zealand.
Uses: wool; meat, skins; locally milk for cheese making.

An amazing variety of domestic types have been bred, showing all extremes of size, with or without horns and with or without a fleece. Two major categories can be identified, the *hairy sheep* kept for milk and meat (especially in Africa), and the *woolly sheep* with fluffier hair and found mainly in the higher latitudes. Sheep can generally survive on poorer pasture than cattle. Male lambs are usually castrated and reared for slaughter. On average, a sheep yields about 3.5 kg (7½ lb) of wool per year.

HORSES
Worldwide number: 60 million.
Distribution: worldwide.
Uses: transportation, sport.

The domesticated horse shows a great variety of types, but is often divided into two main groups. The *Arabian stock* produces a fine-boned, smooth-skinned animal, well suited for running and pulling light carriages but with a nervous disposition. The so-called *cold-blooded stock* is characterized by a heavy frame, a shaggy coat, and a quiet temperament, making such animals suitable for farm work.

ASSES AND MULES
Worldwide numbers: 58 million.
Distribution: mainly Africa, Asia and South America.
Uses: human transport, agricultural work and to power machines (especially water wheels and grinding apparatus). Also for meat in China and the Middle East.

No other domesticated animal will perform so much work for so little food and attention as the ass (or donkey). They are very resistant to disease and can have a working life of 40 years. Mules are crosses between horses and asses, and are more versatile and less flighty than horses. Mules are sterile, and therefore each generation has to be bred afresh from horse and ass parents.

GOATS
Worldwide numbers: 556 million.
Distribution: Africa, Middle and Far East.
Uses: milk, wool, skins, fine leather, meat, horns.

Unfortunately, goats are destructive foragers and will overgraze an area if their population is too high. The goat has been called the 'poor man's cow' due to its association with the poorest of agricultural economies, although the Cashmere and Angora varieties are valued for their high-quality wool.

CAMELS
Worldwide numbers: 19 million.
Distribution: North Africa, Middle East, Central Asia.
Uses: transportation (carries a load, can be ridden and pulls wagons), hides, dung for fuel, meat in emergencies.

The camel is the ideal animal for use in dry environments. A good camel can walk 80 km (50 mi) in a day, though the average would be only 20 km (12½ mi). Camel caravans travel at 4 km/h (2½ mph) and take frequent rests. A female lactates for 11–15 months and yields between 1–7 litres of milk per day.

WATER BUFFALO
Worldwide numbers: 126 million.
Distribution: mostly in India, Pakistan, and East and Southeast Asia.
Uses: draft animal, meat (eaten by some Indian castes), skins and horns used commercially.

The water buffalo has been the most important tropical domestic animal. Its numbers are now declining slowly because it interbreeds freely with cattle, but by so doing becomes highly susceptible to bovine diseases. Increasing agricultural mechanization is also leading to its demise. Water buffalo are still widely used to work the rice fields, where they pull ploughs and carts, and can even be ridden. There are many local varieties, all of which, however, are characterized by massive size (1000 kg/2200 lb). If the strain can be kept pure, the water buffalo exceeds all other cattle in terms of strength, resistance to disease, and intelligence. It can work for 12–15 hours each day but requires frequent access to water.

POULTRY
Worldwide numbers: 9600 million.
Distribution: worldwide.
Uses: meat, eggs, feathers.
Types: chickens, turkeys, ducks, geese.

Poultry are mostly low-grade grazers and foragers that can survive on the leftovers around farmyards or kitchen wastes. In developed countries, poultry rearing has been revolutionized by the breeding of smaller birds that can be kept in small cages (battery farming).

Forestry

Trees present the largest and most highly developed form of plant life on this planet. Trees grow together in continuous and extensive tracts of woodland, or forests. Forests are the most extensive, complex and biologically productive of all the ecosystems on this planet. They have been used by mankind since the earliest times, but in recent years their overuse has led to a serious deforestation problem.

Two thousand years ago, forests probably extended over some 60 million km (23 million sq mi), but continuous felling has reduced this amount to an estimated 28 million km² (11 million sq mi), two fifths of the world's land surface, with a further fifth – 13 million km² (5 million sq mi) – of open, scrub-like forest. The proportions of forest compared to other land uses in different continents are shown on pp. 188–9.

The two main types of forest

Trees can be divided into two main types: the *softwoods*, all of which are coniferous gymnosperms (see p. 119), and the *hardwoods*, all of which are broadleafed angiosperms (see p. 120).

Softwoods are mainly found in the colder, high latitudes, while the hardwoods occupy the mid and low latitudes (see map, p. 105). However, this natural distribution is changing as mankind cuts down the natural forest and replants with species of high commercial value.

The usefulness of trees

We only eat 4% of the material contained in forests (mainly seeds and fruits), the remaining woody tissue being inedible. But it is this hard tissue that is of particular use to humanity. Along with chipped flints, wood was the first implement used by early man. Until the 18th century – when brick making became widespread – wood was the prime material for building dwelling places. Wood was also extensively used for charcoal making and as fuel, and is still used widely as

such, especially in Third World countries. The Industrial Revolution (see p. 420) increased the demand for timber, which was used for such things as pit props and railway sleepers. Deforestation became widespread throughout Europe, with the previous 80% forest cover reduced to little more than 30%.

Today, softwood timber is used for floorboards, roof trusses, packing cases and cheap furniture, and increasingly for conversion into cellulose pulp and paper. Hardwoods, being more expensive and capable of being worked, are used mainly for furniture making.

Unmanaged forestry

By the end of World War I, the advent of cheap world shipping allowed timber to be transported easily from both the tropics and from the great softwood forests of Siberia, Canada and Scandinavia. Forests were seen as inexhaustible reserves of timber, and provided the rate at which the trees were cut down did not exceed the natural rate of growth then forests were indeed renewable resources.

By 1950, most European countries were deficient in some or all home supplies of timber, and more of the virgin forests of the world were brought into extensive production. This was particularly so of the tropical forests. In the search for species such as mahogany, teak, deal, rosewood and sandalwood, vast areas have been destroyed for the sake of a small number of valuable trees. The proportion of commercially useful to useless tree species is often in the order of one to a hundred. Attempts to restock these felled areas have varied. In the worst cases they are allowed to regenerate as best they can, but with the commercially significant trees removed there are no seed sources to allow a complete sequence of species to begin the forest succession anew (see p. 180). Soils – particularly tropical soils – have been severely eroded by deforestation.

It is in the tropics that the absence of a coordinated forestry policy has had the greatest consequence, with 120 000 km² (46 300 sq mi) cleared annually. Commercial logging has often been followed by burning the forest waste to encourage the growth of grasses in place of trees so that cattle ranching can be introduced, as in Brazil. Where tropical forests have been cleared, the soil is usually too thin to support arable agriculture for long, and even grass for grazing can only be supported for about three years.

Managed forestry

Forest management plans exist for only a small proportion of the world's forests. The UN Food and Agriculture Organization (FAO) has estimated that plans exist for only 23% of forests. Management plans are necessary to coordinate replanting, thinning, spraying against disease,

Logs in Lake Kamloops, British Columbia. The vast river and lake systems of North America provide a cheap means of transporting timber from forest to sawmill or paper mill.

A MANAGED CONIFEROUS FOREST

Typical life cycle in a developed country

Week 0 Cells taken from an ideal parent tree for cloning. The 'daughter cells' are cultured in a laboratory then transferred to a 'growth chamber' to achieve rapid growth.

Week 24 Seedlings transferred to nursery area for 'hardening off'.

18 months Planting out by hand begins in the forest. Site has been ploughed and young trees are planted into the overturned turfs. A planting density of 250 000 trees per km² (650 000 trees per sq mi) is commonplace.

2–5 years Periodic clearing of competing vegetation until trees are tall enough (2 m / 6½ ft) to shade out their competitors.

10–20 years Gradual thinning of weaker trees to give a typical density of 150 000 trees per km² (390 000 trees per sq mi). Periodic aerial spraying with pesticides to control disease. On infertile soils, aerial spraying of fertilizers may be carried out.

30 years onwards The first saleable timber destined for the pulp mill is produced. Minimum sawmill size is about 80 mm (3 in) diameter and 1 m (3¼ ft) in length. Pesticides are applied as and when required. Thinnings continue as the forest matures until by about 60 years only 30 000 trees per km² (78 000 trees per sq mi) remain. Only the straight trunk wood is sold; everything else is allowed to decompose on the forest floor.

60 years onwards The forest may be 'clear felled', that is, all remaining trees are removed and the land reploughed ready for the next crop of trees. Alternatively, the mature trees can be underplanted with shade-tolerant trees to produce a forest of more natural appearance.

---

fertilizing and ultimately harvesting and marketing the timber crop.

Because trees take up to 100 years to reach sawmill size, private investment in forestry must usually be encouraged through provision of government grants to cover the establishment costs of the forest. Tax relief on the profits gained from the sale of timber are also sometimes given. Alternatively, the government of a country can establish its own department of forestry that effectively becomes responsible for the management of the forest resource. In some countries, notably the USA, forest management is interpreted in a much wider sense and embraces wildlife management, watershed management, prevention of soil ero-

---

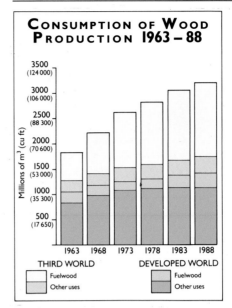

CONSUMPTION OF WOOD PRODUCTION 1963 – 88

THIRD WORLD — Fuelwood / Other uses
DEVELOPED WORLD — Fuelwood / Other uses

SEE ALSO

- NON-FLOWERING PLANTS p. 118
- FLOWERING PLANTS p. 120
- ECOSYSTEMS: CONIFEROUS AND TEMPERATE FORESTS p. 180
- ECOSYSTEMS: TROPICAL FORESTS p. 182

sion, and provision of recreation and leisure facilities.

Managed forests differ in almost every respect from natural forests. One or two species are extensively planted in blocks forming even-aged forests that can be more easily managed than the highly variable natural forest. In temperate latitudes, species such as spruce, pine, fir and eucalypts now predominate, with species selected for rate and quantity of wood production. The trees are planted close together to ensure straight growth. This is necessary for the mechanized handling and processing of the timber.

The species planted in an area are often *exotic* conifers, that is they are not native species. The exotic species are used because they often have faster growth rates than native species. They produce softwood timber much in demand for conversion into paper pulp. However, because they are non-native, such plantations cannot support the native birds, insects and mammals that were adapted to the vegetation of the area prior to forestation. Thus even managed forestry can destroy delicate ecosystems – for example in the wetlands of the Flow Country in northeast Scotland.   GJ

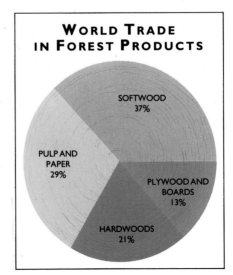

WORLD TRADE IN FOREST PRODUCTS

SOFTWOOD 37%
PULP AND PAPER 29%
PLYWOOD AND BOARDS 13%
HARDWOODS 21%

Fishing

Fishing is the harvesting of fish and other marine animals from the oceans and inland waters to provide food for humans. Fish can be processed to make fishmeal (an important animal food), and to make oils, glues, fertilizers and drugs. From the earliest times, fishing has been one of humanity's most important means of feeding itself. Spears, lines and nets were used to catch fish, at first by fishermen standing at the edges of the water. Gradually, the use of boats allowed fishing to move into deeper waters, a trend that has continued up to the present day.

The present annual marine catch totals about 76 million tonnes (tons). More than 75% of this total is caught in the northern hemisphere – despite the fact that 90% of the surface of the southern hemisphere is covered with water. Traditionally, fishing has been concentrated on the continental shelves, where the shallow waters receive sufficient sunlight and nutrients washed in by rivers to support large amounts of plankton, the tiny plants and animals that provide the main source of food for fish. The principal fishing nations today are Japan (accounting for 13% of the world catch), Russia (12%) and China (8%).

Because of the perishable nature of fish, the fishing industry was traditionally based on many small ports each serving its own immediate area. The advent of railways and, later, of refrigerated lorries has meant that fish can now be transported longer distances, and commercial fishing has generally become concentrated on a small number of ports, each with its own processing and freezing factories.

In 1950 the total annual catch was 21 million tonnes (tons), most of which came from *inshore* fishing, that is from fishing grounds within about 100 km (60 mi) of a port. Small boats netted the *pelagic* species (those fish that live in the surface waters), such as herring, mackerel and

The danger and discomfort of fishing in the North Atlantic is vividly captured in this photograph taken on board a Breton trawler.

anchovy. Further out to sea, beyond the continental shelves, the deep-sea or *demersal* fish (cod, hake, plaice, skate) were caught by larger vessels that remained at sea for up to a week before discharging their catch.

Between 1950 and 1970 the commercial fishing industry was revolutionized by technological advances. Larger boats with on-board refrigeration plants enabled vessels to remain at sea for up to a month. Underwater sonar (see p. 332) allowed shoals of fish to be detected with comparative ease, and powerful hydraulic winches made possible the use of larger nets.

Overfishing and ocean management

In the 20 years up to 1970 the annual world catch increased by 7% per annum, but in 1971/72 a serious slump occurred. This was due mainly to the collapse of the Peruvian anchovy industry following uncontrolled overfishing. Elsewhere, the 'vacuum cleaning' of the oceans by large factory fishing fleets had so depleted the world fish reserves that in the North Sea, for example, the estimated stock of herring fell by 75%, from 4 million to 1 million fish. The Californian sardine industry had collapsed through overfishing in the 1950s. A similar fate befell the South African pilchard industry in the 1970s, followed by haddock in the northwest Atlantic (the catch in 1974 was only 8% of what it had been in 1965) and the Alaskan pollack in 1975/76 (though this species had recovered by the 1980s).

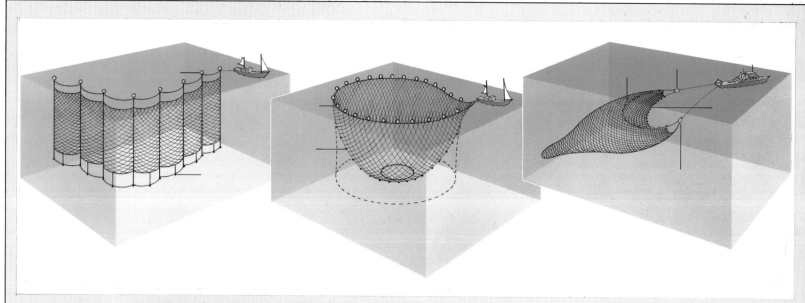

There are two main techniques of commercial fishing. The first is *drift* fishing, in which the surface-living species are caught by means of special nets. The second is *trawl* fishing, in which different kinds of nets are used to catch species that live in deep water or inhabit the ocean floor. There are many variations in these techniques.

Drift fishing techniques can be used to catch the shoaling species of surface fish (such as herring and anchovy) that live no deeper than 15 m (50 ft) below the surface. Nets can be strung out in a line to form *drag seines* or *drift seines*. A line of corks or buoyancy chambers along the top edge and a series

of weights along the bottom position the net vertically and at the required depth in the water. These nets are slowly dragged through the surface waters pulled by a small boat called a *drifter*. The mesh size of the net is set so that small, immature fish can pass through while the larger fish are trapped.

A variation of this method is the *purse seine*, a large net that is either fired out over a shoal, or pulled round the shoal by two boats. Weights around its edge allow the bottom of the net to fall slowly down to make an enclosure round the fish. The bottom of the net is then closed underneath the fish by pulling tight a line – like drawing shut the neck of an

old-fashioned purse. All seine nets are very efficient means of gathering fish.

Trawl fishing techniques are used to catch fish (such as cod and flatfish) at depths greater than about 15 m (50 ft). All trawl nets resemble a huge funnel shape. Small trawl nets can be towed along by one boat (a *trawler* – generally larger than a drifter), while large trawl nets need two boats, one at each side, to pull them through the water. The most common type of trawl net is the so-called *otter trawl*, a conically shaped bag with two large 'otter boards' designed to force open the mouth of the net.

In theory, the oceans represent vast, sustainable sources of food for human consumption. Some experts believe that a sustainable annual harvest of 90–100 million tonnes (tons) could be achieved if a carefully managed and internationally coordinated fishing policy were developed. The persistent overfishing and removal of undersized, juvenile fish has led most countries to establish fishing limits around their shores. Within these limits, set variously between 19 km (12 mi) and 320 km (200 mi) offshore, foreign vessels are strictly licensed and the domestic fleet is restricted as to the type and amount of fish which may be caught. Annual limits are set following careful research into the general size and state of health of the breeding population of fish species. Fish quotas and fishing exclusion zones have led to international disagreements – notably between Iceland and Britain in the 1950s and 1970s (the 'Cod Wars'), and between Argentina and Britain over the area round the Falkland Islands in the 1980s.

In an attempt to introduce a management policy for the use of the sea and its resources the United Nations has established a Convention on the Law of the Sea (1982). Some 160 countries have signed the document. The concept of a 364 km (200 mi) Exclusive Economic Zone (EEZ) off the coast of each country – both for fishing and for the extraction of mineral resources such as oil – is central to the UN initiative.

Fish farming

Deep-sea fishing is expensive in terms of the fixed costs of boats, equipment, fuel and manpower. It is also a hard and dangerous means of providing human food. As a result, the deliberate rearing of fish in tanks or netted enclosures in lakes and coastal waters has now become commercially important. The products of fish farms attract a ready market, providing a guaranteed quality and size of product that is difficult to match from traditional fishing sources.

Fish farming (*aquaculture*) has its origins in China, perhaps as long ago as 2000 BC. Modern fish farming now supplies 100 000 tonnes (tons) per year – 13% of the world catch – and this figure is set to rise. Not all 'wild' fish can be reared in fish farms. Traditionally, the freshwater carp has been the main species, particularly in Third World countries. Since the 1970s, developed countries have invested vast sums in research, and trout, salmon, shrimps, crabs and lobsters are all now successfully produced in large amounts. Very rapid growth is achieved by the direct feeding of grain or grain by-products supplemented with high-quality protein.

There is great concern over the potential for transmission of disease and genetic damage to native fish species through interbreeding with the escaped fish-farm stock. In Norway alone, an estimated 500 000 salmon escaped from fish farms in 1988, and farmed fish now form 15% of the entire catch of sea salmon. The threat to wild fish is not to entire species, but to

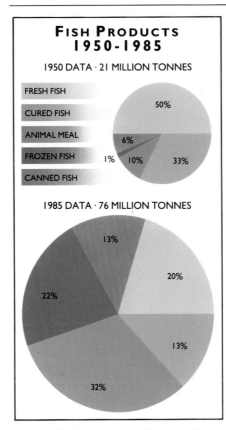

FISH PRODUCTS 1950-1985

1950 DATA · 21 MILLION TONNES

- FRESH FISH
- CURED FISH
- ANIMAL MEAL
- FROZEN FISH
- CANNED FISH

50% | 33% | 10% | 1% | 6%

1985 DATA · 76 MILLION TONNES

13% | 20% | 13% | 32% | 22%

genetically distinct varieties that live in specific rivers.

Fish as a food source

Fish and other marine animals (particularly crustaceans such as lobsters, crabs, shrimps, prawns and krill, and cephalopods such as squid and octopus) supply humans on average with about 15% of their protein, rising to a maximum of 60% in Japan. Some 25% of all animal feedstock is derived from fish, representing about one third of the total fish catch. One tonne (ton) of fish meal can produce half a tonne (ton) of pork or poultry meat, a notably inefficient use of protein resources. It is ironic that the protein-deficient Third World countries sell much of their fish catch to the industrialized northern hemisphere nations for eventual use as animal feed.

International trade in fish and fish products now exceeds $15 billion per year. The price of fish has risen more rapidly than that of other foods – largely because of the increase in processing and packaging costs.

A major potential source of food is krill, a shrimp-like creature 4–6 cm (1½–2½) long, which lives in vast shoals in the cold waters of the Atlantic and Pacific. Krill form a major source of food for whales, but with the decline in whale numbers the amount of unharvested krill has increased. Already 450 000 tonnes (tons) of krill are caught each year, mainly by the Russian and Japanese fleets. The potential annual catch is estimated at 50 million tonnes (tons), which would provide a major source of nutritious food for humans as well as a foodstock for animals. GJ

Stilt fishing in Sri Lanka. Such techniques are a far cry from the intensive 'vacuum-cleaning' of the seas by the fishing fleets of the developed nations.

WHALING

The hunting of whales for their meat and valuable oils has always been carried out by peoples such as the Inuit (Eskimos) of Arctic North America. Commercial whaling only began in the 18th century. Initially it was a highly risky business, with the actual catching being done by a hand-thrown harpoon from a small rowing boat. Once killed, the whale was towed back to the land for processing. With the coming of steam power and guns that fired harpoons with explosive heads into the whale the balance became disastrously weighted against the whale.

In 1900 an estimated 4.4 million whales of all types existed. Hunting, combined with the effects of pollution, has reduced this number to 1 million, of which the bulk comprise the sperm whale and the minke whale, the latter species being rescued from extinction by the newly awakened concern for whales in the 1970s. One by one the commercially important species have been hunted to the verge of extinction – first the humpback (early 1900s), then the blue whale (1930s), finwhale (1940s), sei whale (1965) and the smaller species such as the minke whale by 1970.

The International Whaling Commission called for a complete ban on whaling from 1985/86 and now only Japan continues to catch whales, ostensibly for 'research' purposes. A report on whale numbers published in 1989 suggested that fewer than half the number of whales may actually exist than was previously thought likely.

SEE ALSO

- THE OCEANS p. 100
- FISHES p. 128
- MARINE MAMMALS p. 162
- ECOSYSTEMS: AQUATIC p. 178

Food Processing

For thousands of years people have processed natural food-stuffs to improve their keeping qualities, nutritional value or flavour. Natural processes have been harnessed to create entirely new foods and drinks, or to change the characteristics of a raw material completely. Biotechnology and advanced engineering are now used to enhance what can be done with the world's harvest, and will undoubtedly shape some of the foods and drinks of the future.

The oldest processing techniques improve the digestibility and enhance the keeping qualities of foodstuffs. Examples include grain-milling, the cooking of meat, and the fermentation of grapes to make wine.

Fermentation and enzymes

The most widely used biological technique is *fermentation* – the changing of food components such as carbohydrates into natural preservatives, or more easily digestible nutrients, by the action of yeasts, fungi or bacteria. Bread-making, the brewing of beers, and the manufacture of yoghurts and cheeses are typical examples. Fermentation is also used for the preservation of proteins, as for example in meats such as pastrami and salamis. In Japan, fermentation has been used for centuries both for food conservation and in order to produce new flavours, such as rice sake, soya bean sauce, and whole fermented soya beans (natto).

Enzymes – proteins that are produced by living organisms – are used as catalysts in biochemical reactions in a number of food-processing techniques. For example, *rennet*, derived from rennin (an enzyme found in the stomachs of cud-chewing animals such as cows), is used to curdle milk in the manufacture of cheese.

Dairy foods

Milk, butter, cheese and yoghurt are *staples* – basic components of many diets all over the world. Milk is mainly water, with some protein, fat, lactose (milk sugar) and salts. It sours easily, and can also be a vehicle for human diseases. Louis Pasteur (1822–95), the great French microbiologist, devised a method of heating liquids to temperatures that destroy harmful microorganisms. His work in the 1860s concentrated on wines and beers, where spoilage caused great economic losses. He found that heating to temperatures as low as 57 °C (135 °F) for a few minutes extended the safe shelf-life without spoiling the taste. *Pasteurization* of milk is undoubtedly one of the most significant advances in public health of the last hundred years.

In 1907, Ilya Mechnikov (1845–1916) of the Pasteur Institute in Paris published the results of his research into the long life-spans of Bulgarian farming families. He was convinced that their diet of natural yoghurt was the cause. Since then yoghurts have shown a greater worldwide market growth than any other dairy product. In the manufacture of yoghurt, certain bacteria are responsible for turning the lactose in milk into lactic acid, so enhancing the milk's nutritional value and preventing other organisms from causing rancid sourness.

Bread and alcohol

Grains are another staple of the human diet. Modern milling of cereals such as wheat and maize separates fibrous, floury and proteinaceous components. The fibre is known as *bran* and the protein as *germ*, which often has a high oil content. The flour is either used for baking or processed further, by means of biochemical enzymes, into fructose or glucose syrups. These are then used in all kinds of snacks, processed foods, cakes and confectionery. The germ and bran are often sold separately as health foods. Bakeries are now often recombining the separate ingredients in 'multi-grain', bran-enriched and 'natural' breads, to take advantage of a consumer trend for foods with a healthier image. Enzyme-based whole-grain processes are now being developed to retain protein and fibre in the end-product and avoid separation techniques.

Other types of grain are used to make drinks. Barley is *malted* – the grains are sprouted in warm, wet conditions that encourage natural enzymes to turn the starchy component into maltose, another sugar. After drying, the malted barley is

Monosodium glutamate is a white crystalline powder, seen here in a false-colour scanning electron micrograph. It is prepared from wheat gluten and other proteins.

used as one of the sugar ingredients in making beer and lager; special yeasts act on these sugars to turn them into carbon dioxide and alcohol.

Other sugary or starchy materials – such as cactus juice, potatoes, wild fruits, rye and sugar cane – can be fermented. The resulting juice (*must*) is then heated to drive off the alcohol, which is condensed by cooling and collected as a high-alcohol liquor. Each of the resulting liquors has its own distinctive character – the materials mentioned above producing (respectively) tequila, vodka, eaux de vie, bourbon and rum.

Drying and cooking

The simplest and among the most ancient processing methods are drying and cooking. Drying is still used for preserving foods for long journeys or for eating out of season. The aim is to reduce the level of water to below that at which microorganisms can grow. Examples include meats, such as North American *pemmican* from deer and buffalo; fishes such as Bombay duck (or bummalo) of India; and fruits, including apricots, grapes (currants) and plums (prunes). Tea leaves, coffee berries and the pulp around the cocoa bean are dried and allowed to undergo natural fermentation before final preparation. Drying over slow-burning wood gives foods such as fish, sausages and cheese an attractive smoked flavour. Coffee – the most common substance preserved by *freeze-drying* – is frozen rapidly and then dried in a vacuum.

Cooking is a necessary preparation of many foods. Cooking also helps preserve food for short periods, but the continued presence of water allows the eventual growth of organisms and the development of rancid and other 'off' flavours. Baking, boiling, roasting and frying all sterilize foods through the direct or prolonged effects of heat. In cooking, the protein structure is altered, which tends to improve the palatability of meats and vegetables. For some foods, such as dried cereals and pulses, boiling is essential to rehydrate them, to soften fibre and to inactivate lectins, naturally occurring anti-insect poisons that are found in, for

A Calvados brewery in Normandy. Calvados is an apple brandy that is distilled from cider.

FOOD ADDITIVES

There is a long tradition of using additives to improve both the appearance and the taste of food products. Orange-coloured plant dyes are used to make cheeses look richly flavoured, berry juice to darken thin wines, and chalk to whiten coarse-floured bread. Salt, spices, and natural sources of monosodium glutamate are used to give foods a meaty or savoury flavour.

Vinegar, salt and sugar all act as preservatives. In foods such as pickles, cured meats and jams, they remove free water and inhibit the growth of spoilage yeasts and various bacteria associated with food poisoning.

During the 19th century, as the techniques of chemical synthesis developed, the creation of new flavours and colours became a focus for many researchers. Sometimes their aim was to replace scarce or old-fashioned ingredients such as cochineal, a red dye made from squashed cactus-bugs; sometimes entirely new compounds were made, such as saccharin, synthesized in the USA in 1879 as a nonfattening replacement for sugar. This rapid proliferation of products often led to the use of materials that were untested for safety.

Many additives have since been banned as possible health hazards. Acceptable and established additives are now classified as 'Generally Regarded as Safe' (GRAS); new ones must undergo years of testing to ensure freedom from harmful effects. In the USA, the Food and Drug Administration has stringently regulated food additives since 1960. The European Community also assesses additives and grants permitted ones *E numbers*, which must appear on food labels. Many of these 'E-number' additives are natural (or identical to natural) substances, such as Vitamin C (ascorbic acid, an anti-oxidant and acidulant). Others are artificial, such as tartrazine, a yellow-orange dye currently implicated in food allergies.

Modern additives perform a wide range of functions. They include agents to control mould, anti-oxidants to preserve fats and oils from rancidity, gelling agents to give products a pleasant texture, and emulsifiers to stabilize mixtures of ingredients.

example, peas and beans. Baking breaks down storage carbohydrates and thus increases the nutrient value of such staples as plantain bananas, yams, Jerusalem artichokes and potatoes.

Canning

As the demand for perishable foods grew, methods were sought to allow safe long-distance transportation and preservation. Commercial 'canning' – originally in sealed glass pots – dates from the time of the Napoleonic Wars in the early 19th century. The spread of canning technology went hand in hand with the advance of the railways, the 1860s and 1870s being the time when American corned beef spread throughout the world. Since then, canning has been revolutionized by advances in controlled heating, the use of additives to improve flavour and appearance, and the design and manufacture of the cans themselves – plastic coatings, shaped aluminium and sophisticated sealing.

Freezing

Although freezing was being used as a food preservation technique by the end of the 19th century, the freezing itself took a day or more and food tended to be damaged in the process. The modern frozen-food industry, using quick-freezing methods that take only a few minutes or a few hours, started in the 1930s. Today, with the deep-freeze a common item of household equipment in developed countries, frozen foods are an extremely popular convenience food. Additives are rarely needed, most of the nutritional value of food is maintained, and a wide variety of precooked frozen foods is available.

Food presentation

Many of the older food-processing techniques alter the flavour, appearance or texture of foodstuffs. Even freezing – despite its advantages – can alter texture and taste on thawing, because of the disruptive effect of ice crystals.

The 20th century has seen an increasing emphasis on freshness, visual appeal and freedom from additives. The retailer's aim is to make food items look and taste as if they have just been harvested or freshly prepared. Chilling, vacuum-packing, controlled-atmosphere packing and irradiation are all possible ways of achieving this aim. Of these, *irradiation* – the controlled use of gamma or beta rays – is the most effective anti-microbial technique and preserver of quality, but it is not widely used in Europe and America because of fears about its safety. *Chilling* is particularly useful for foods that are sold and eaten within a few days of preparation. Chilling approximates to household-refrigerator conditions, and slows down spoilage considerably. However, the bacterium *Listeria*, which can cause food poisoning, can persist at chill-temperature. *Controlled-atmosphere packing* involves the use of unreactive gases such as nitrogen, which slow down the rate of spoilage.

Biotechnology in food processing

The possibility of altering the genes of a food source to change the characteristics of a food product is now real. Raw materials may be manipulated to give new effects, or effects currently achieved only by using additives. Currently under research are animals with a better lean-to-fat ratio, and soya-bean proteins with better 'foaming' properties to help make certain desserts more attractive to eat. New sweeteners such as aspartame and thaumatin are produced using genetic-engineering techniques or mass-culture of plant cells. Tomatoes have been created that contain genes preventing the softening of skin associated with ripening, thus prolonging shelf life. Diagnostic tests, based on monoclonal antibodies and gene-probes, have been developed to detect food-poisoning bacteria in raw and processed foods, and toxins in fish that come from the algae they eat.

Other technologies

Spectacular growth has been made in extruded food, where ground materials such as cereal flours, grains, potatoes, flavours and spices are mixed with water or other fluids, and forced out of nozzles under pressure and cooked. This is the technique used for centuries by the Chinese and then the Italians for noodles and pasta. The snack – food and sweet – biscuit industries are now using many innovations in extrusion.

The need to detect foreign bodies such as fish bones and fruit stones has led to the use of sophisticated lasers or computerized density-sensors in food-processing lines. An electronic 'potato' developed in England accompanies real potatoes down the processing line to detect where bruising and damage occur.   ML-E

SEE ALSO

● THE BEGINNINGS OF LIFE p. 110
● ARABLE FARMING p. 188
● LIVESTOCK FARMING p. 190
● FISHING p. 194
● FOOD, DIET AND DIGESTION p. 208
● POPULATION AND HUNGER p. 296

Irradiation of foodstuffs. A technician manoeuvres a cylindrical casket of fruit above an accelerator pool, submerged in which is a 2 000 000 electron-volt accelerator, a source of the X-rays that are used to preserve foodstuffs. The irradiation operation is carried out under water to protect the technician from exposure to radiation.

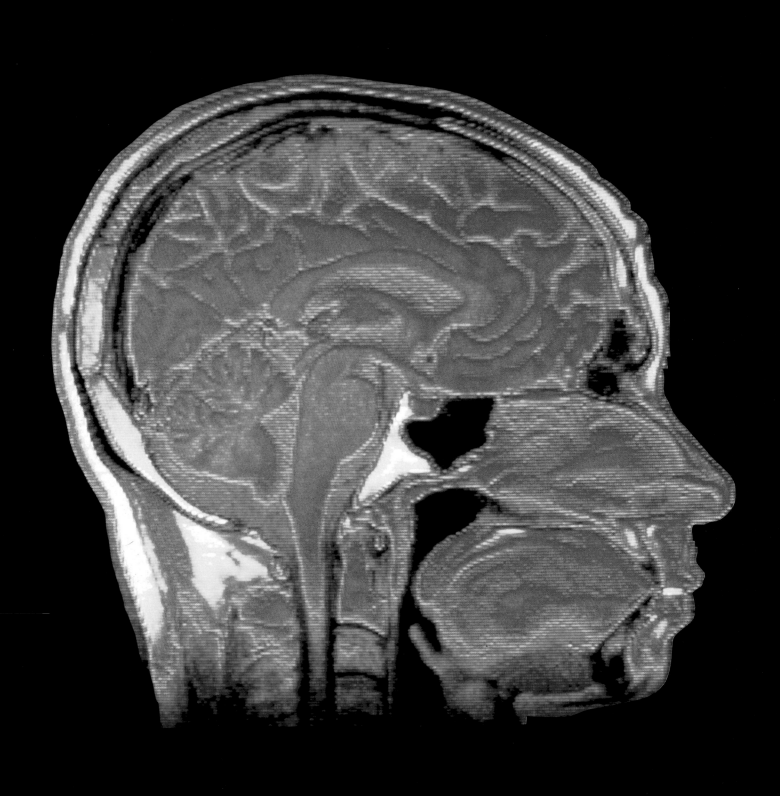

THE HUMAN ORGANISM

*'What a piece of work
is a man!'*

William Shakespeare

Physical Evolution

Human beings are unusual in being the only living species representing an entire biological family, the Hominidae or hominids. The human species is exceptionally widespread, having colonized most land masses of the world. Although closely related to the great apes, such as the gorilla and chimpanzee (see p. 165), humans are distinct from them and all other mammals in many important features. These include bipedal locomotion (walking on two legs) and the large size of the brain in relation to the body. Humans are marked out even more by behaviour, in particular the great dependence on learning passed on from generation to generation. This is transmitted largely by language, or by means of other symbols.

Skulls of Neanderthal man (left) and Cro-Magnon man.

Palaeoanthropology is the branch of learning that is concerned with investigating the origins and evolution of the hominids, which in the past have been represented by at least several species. This includes the study of early apes, but much of the interest is centred on the period since our ancestors diverged from the apes. This separation is now generally believed to have occurred 6–8 million years ago. Detailed pictures have been built up of ape species living in East Africa 18–14 million years ago. Species in the genus *Proconsul* may be typical of the common ancestors of the African apes and the hominids. Other work in Pakistan in sediments about 8 million years old has shown the presence of apes in southern Asia related to the orang-utan.

Early hominids

There is very little fossil evidence of the apes from the last 8 million years, but two lines of evidence strongly indicate that hominids diverged early on during this period. The first is provided by the fossil remains of early hominids from the period 3 to 4 million years ago that have been recovered in East Africa since the mid-1970s. The other is biochemical evidence, which demonstrates a very close genetic relationship between human beings and the living African apes. The relationship is apparent from the form of the chromosomes, sequences of DNA, and resemblances in proteins (see pp. 114–15). Evidently our ancestors and those of the gorilla and chimpanzee had a common line for several million years after they separated from the orang-utan ancestors.

Early hominids have been found in Laetoli in Tanzania and Hadar in Ethiopia. Those found at Hadar are just over 3 million years old and include the famous 'Lucy', whose skeleton is over 40%

complete. The remains give us a picture of small, slender but very strong hominids, whose pelvis and lower limb bones were already adapted for upright walking. Although the body had already assumed a near-human form, their brains were no larger than those of apes, and the teeth still retain signs of ape ancestry. The finds from Laetoli, close to the Olduvai Gorge, are 3.5–3.8 million years old. The fossils resemble those from Hadar, but even more spectacular is the preservation of hominid footprints (see box).

The australopithecines

All earlier hominids known so far are normally grouped in the genus *Australopithecus* ('southern ape'). They were given this name because the first discovery of the remains of such a hominid was made at Taung in South Africa in 1924. The finds are restricted to eastern and southern Africa.

There is little direct evidence about the behaviour of the australopithecines, but these creatures show that the human bodily adaptation was successful before the great development of the brain that has shaped the modern human head. It is likely that the hominids lived in more open country than the great apes, but returned to the trees to avoid danger.

Early Homo

In the late Pliocene epoch, about 2 million years ago, one line of the australopithecines began to develop a larger brain. Fossils of these hominids are sufficiently human-like that they are classed in our own genus, *Homo* ('man'). The best known specimens of this line are the *Homo habilis* ('handy man') found at the Olduvai Gorge in Tanzania.

In the same general period stone tools began to appear, giving us the first direct archaeological evidence of behaviour. It cannot be proved that the stone tools are all linked with *Homo*. Species of hominids such as *Australopithecus robustus* and *Australopithecus boisei* survived until about 1 million years ago. They may also have made tools, but as the archaeological record continues without a break after their extinction, the importance of *Homo* as a tool-maker has to be acknowledged.

Stone tools clearly imparted a major advantage to the hominids leading a hard life on the savannah. They provided sharp edges, allowing the hominids to cut hides, meat and roots and probably to shape wood. It is not clear to what extent animals were hunted rather than scavenged.

Homo erectus

By 1.7 million years ago a variety of *Homo* rapidly achieved stature similar to that of modern human beings. Brain size increased to about 800–1000 cc (cubic centimetres), compared with the modern average of about 1500 cc. *Homo erectus* ('upright man'), first known from sites in Java and China, is the principal species of this age. Most of the Asian specimens are little more than 500 000 years old, but similar, far older, fossils have been found in Africa, especially from the area of Lake Turkana in Kenya.

Homo erectus is found in Africa, Asia and Europe, indicating a spread of human occupation out of the tropics. How human *Homo erectus* was in behaviour is still debated, but it is clear that they had the ability to adapt to the seasonal climate of the temperate zone.

Early Homo sapiens

Through the Pleistocene epoch (1.6 million to 10 000 years ago) the trend towards

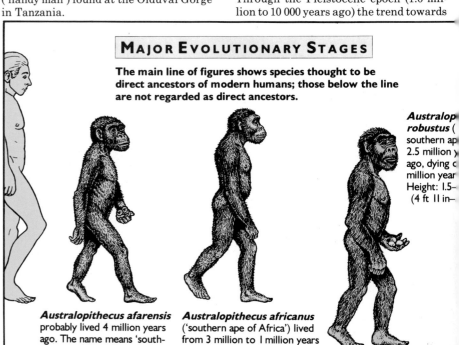

MAJOR EVOLUTIONARY STAGES

The main line of figures shows species thought to be direct ancestors of modern humans; those below the line are not regarded as direct ancestors.

Australopithecus afarensis probably lived 4 million years ago. The name means 'southern ape of Afar', from finds made in Ethiopia's Afar Triangle. Height: 1–1.3 m (3–4 ft).

Australopithecus africanus ('southern ape of Africa') lived from 3 million to 1 million years ago and probably evolved from *Australopithecus afarensis*. Height: 1–1.3 m (3–4 ft).

Australop robustus (southern ap 2.5 million y ago, dying o million year Height: 1.5– (4 ft 11 in–

large brains continued. *Homo sapiens* ('wise man') appeared about 300 000 years ago as the successor of *Homo erectus*. Early specimens are known from Europe and Africa, but Asia remains a blank except for rare traces in India and China.

In this period there is no sudden change in stone tools to mark the transition to *Homo sapiens*, but by about 250 000 years ago techniques of manufacture had reached a new sophistication (see p. 362).

Wood now appears in the archaeological record, usually surviving only on water-logged sites. A possible club from Kalambo Falls in Africa and a spear from Essex in England are among the most suggestive evidence that hunting was now practised, although plant foods undoubtedly remained important.

The 'Eve hypothesis'
Select studies of DNA in human populations suggest that there is more variety in Africa than in other populations. The DNA in the mitochondria – specialized structures within cells – is a special case, inherited from the mother only. The increased variety in Africa can be taken to suggest that modern populations originated in this continent. It has been suggested that all living human beings have mitochondrial DNA originating from a single woman who lived in Africa about 200 000 years ago. This dramatic view does not conflict with the evidence of fossils, but even if this 'Eve' existed, we would have derived only a minimal fraction of our genetic heritage from her.

The Neanderthals
Neanderthal man (named after a valley in Germany) is the best known variety of early *Homo sapiens*. Widespread in Europe and parts of Asia, they flourished between about 100 000 and 30 000 years

ago, but appear to have evolved gradually from about 200 000 years ago.

The Neanderthals are easily recognizable by their combination of long low skull, large face and robust bodily skeleton. Generally they are regarded as a subspecies of *Homo sapiens* (*H. sapiens neanderthalensis*). For many years there has been controversy concerning their status – were they ancestors of modern human beings, or an evolutionary sideshoot?

Dates obtained from Skhul and Qafzeh in Israel now show that 'early moderns' much more like ourselves than the Neanderthals already existed about 100 000 years ago. These dates rule out the possibility that modern human beings evolved from Neanderthals. Although the Neanderthals disappeared by about 30 000 years ago it remains likely that modern *Homo sapiens* obtained some genes from them through interbreeding.

Modern man
The most plentiful evidence for early specimens of anatomically modern human beings (*Homo sapiens sapiens*) comes from Ice Age Europe. It is in Europe that the remains of Cro-Magnon man are found, dating from about 30 000 years ago. The Cro-Magnons are named after a cave in France, but other specimens are distributed across Europe. It is evident that anatomically modern humans had evolved at an earlier date outside Europe.

Even before modern industrial technology, human populations had colonized all the continents except Antarctica, and also many islands. The spread outside the Old World probably happened within the last 100 000 years and can be linked with the relatively advanced skills and technologies associated with *Homo sapiens sapiens*.   JGo

SEE ALSO
- EVOLUTION p. 112
- GENETICS AND INHERITANCE p. 114
- PRIMATES p. 164
- DISCOVERING THE PAST p. 360
- HUMAN PREHISTORY p. 362

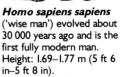

Australopithecus boisei was named after the Englishman Charles Boise, who funded excavations in the 1950s. It lived in East Africa 2.5 million to 1 million years ago.. Height: 1.6 m–1.78 m (5 ft 3 in–5 ft 10 in).

Homo habilis ('handy man') was the first known species of the genus *Homo* and lived 2–1.5 million years ago. Height: 1.2–1.5 m (4–5 ft).

Homo erectus ('upright man') lived 1.6 million – 500 000 years ago, probably evolving in Africa and spreading to Europe, East Asia and Southeast Asia. Height: 1.5–1.8 m (5–6 ft).

Homo sapiens neanderthalensis ('wise Neanderthal man') takes its name from finds in the Neander Valley in West Germany. The subspecies evolved about 200 000 years ago. Height: 1.7 m (5.7 ft).

Homo sapiens sapiens ('wise man') evolved about 30 000 years ago and is the first fully modern man. Height: 1.69–1.77 m (5 ft 6 in–5 ft 8 in).

Reproduction

Every human being begins life as a single cell no bigger than the dot above the letter i and grows to be an individual composed of 6 million million cells. In that first cell and every subsequent one is DNA – the material that lays down the blueprint of what an individual will be like, from the colour of eyes to the size of feet.

SEE ALSO
● PHYSICAL DEVELOPMENT
   p. 204
● GLANDS AND HORMONES
   p. 214

A baby develops from the union of one of its mother's eggs and one sperm cell from its father. Each of these cells carries 23 *chromosomes* – threadlike structures that

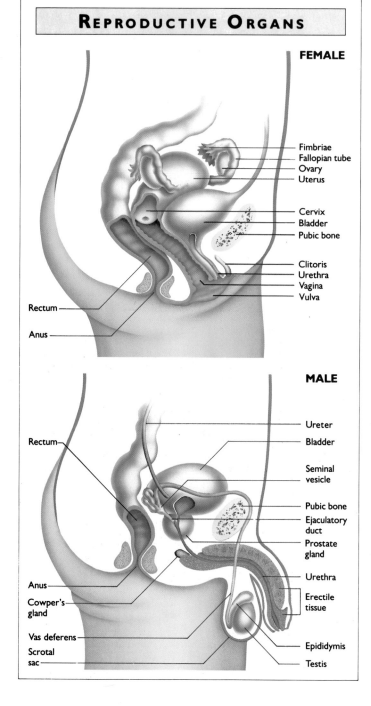

REPRODUCTIVE ORGANS

FEMALE

Fimbriae
Fallopian tube
Ovary
Uterus

Cervix
Bladder
Pubic bone

Clitoris
Urethra
Vagina
Vulva

Rectum

Anus

MALE

Rectum

Ureter

Bladder

Seminal vesicle

Pubic bone

Ejaculatory duct

Prostate gland

Urethra

Erectile tissue

Anus

Cowper's gland

Vas deferens

Scrotal sac

Epididymis

Testis

bear *genes* containing DNA (see p. 114). Every cell that grows from the fused egg and sperm will contain 46 chromosomes.

Sperm and ova

Even before birth a female baby possesses her full quota of *ova* or eggs which develop in the *ovarian follicles* (see pp. 204–5). These are stored in the *ovaries* – two glands that in adults are about the size of pigeons' eggs. Only a few ova will ever ripen and have the potential to be fertilized by sperm.

The human male, too, is born with cells that will produce sperm in adult life. Sperm are manufactured in *seminiferous tubules* in the testes at the rate of 1000 per second, and stored in the *epididymis*.

Each sperm starts with 46 chromosomes but sheds half of these as it matures (a process that takes 74 days). If it loses its Y chromosome and goes on to fertilize an egg, the resulting baby will be a girl; if the X chromosome has been shed the child will be a boy (see also p. 114). A mature sperm is still less than 0.05 mm ($^1/_{500}$ in) long.

Ovulation and menstruation

Each month one ovum ripens, breaks free from its protective follicle and is swept up by the fringe-like endings (*fimbriae*) of one of the *fallopian tubes*. Its journey down the fallopian tube to the *uterus* or womb lasts four days. For a few hours only it is in a state of readiness to be fertilized by a sperm. Unfertilized, it will pass on and out of the woman's body. The enriched blood supply lining the uterus in preparation for receiving a fertilized ovum is shed soon after. This loss of blood is *menstruation*, more commonly referred to as a 'period'.

Coitus and fertilization

During sexual intercourse or *coitus*, the erect penis is inserted into the vagina and rhythmical movements lead to orgasm and the ejaculation of *semen* – sperm in a nutrient fluid. A sperm swims by using rapid movements of its long, threadlike tail, and the head of the sperm contains stores of glucose to provide energy for its long swim to the ovum. If it is the first of the 2–3 million sperms released during an ejaculation to reach the ovum, its genetic material will mix with the ovum's chromosomes.

Cell division and implantation

Within hours of conception a fertilized ovum, called a *zygote*, begins to divide. To do this it needs to be surrounded by the hormone *progesterone*, which is supplied by cells that develop in the egg's discarded follicle – the *corpus luteum*. Progesterone also prevents any further ovulations. Three days after fertilization, the zygote has divided three times producing eight cells. Four days later, containing 16 cells, the zygote reaches the uterus.

Three days after that, the zygote implants itself into the uterine wall. Now called a *blastocyst* and 0.1 mm ($^1/_{250}$ in) in size, its cells change into two types – *embryoblast* cells that will eventually become the baby, and *trophoblast* cells that will form the

placenta and nourish the growing foetus. The embryo cells themselves soon change into an inner and an outer layer.

The developing embryo

By the start of the third week the inner layer has organized into a pear shape and the outer covering develops a split, allowing a third layer to develop between the other two. Each layer will eventually form specific parts of the body structure.

As the third week ends, two tiny tubes covered by muscle cells merge into one, forming the heart. By week 4 it is already pumping blood through tiny arteries and veins to reach inner cells that are beginning to form internal organs.

In the first month, the embryo has grown to a length of 4 mm ($^1/_6$ in) with one end bigger than the other. Groups of cells have clustered in readiness to become specific organs or limbs. The middle layer has begun to lay down what will be the spine and the nervous system, heart and blood vessels.

By the fifth week, the eyes, ears, nose and the nerve cells that interpret sight, smell, sound, taste and touch have started to appear. Arms and legs are beginning to emerge with translucent flipper-like plates showing the forerunners of fingers and toes.

One week later the 10 mm ($^2/_5$ in) embryo is already bending its elbows and moving its hands, which have clearly defined fingers. The face is forming recognizable eyes, mouth and ears. The brain has divided into its various parts responsible for thinking, memory, reflexes and emotions. Throughout the embryo cartilage begins to turn to bone.

By the fourteenth week the foetus is completely formed, and from this time on – until week 40 when it is ready to be born – it grows in size rather than complexity.

Birth

When the foetus reaches maturity or outgrows its food supply from the placenta it

Thousands of sperm will attach themselves to the ovum but only one will succeed in penetrating it. Once penetrated, it discharges enzymes to create an impenetrable barrier to other sperms. The magnification is 1000 times in this false-colour electron micrograph.

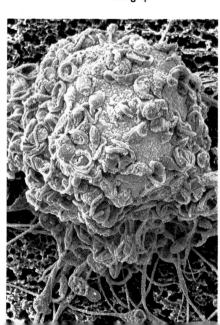

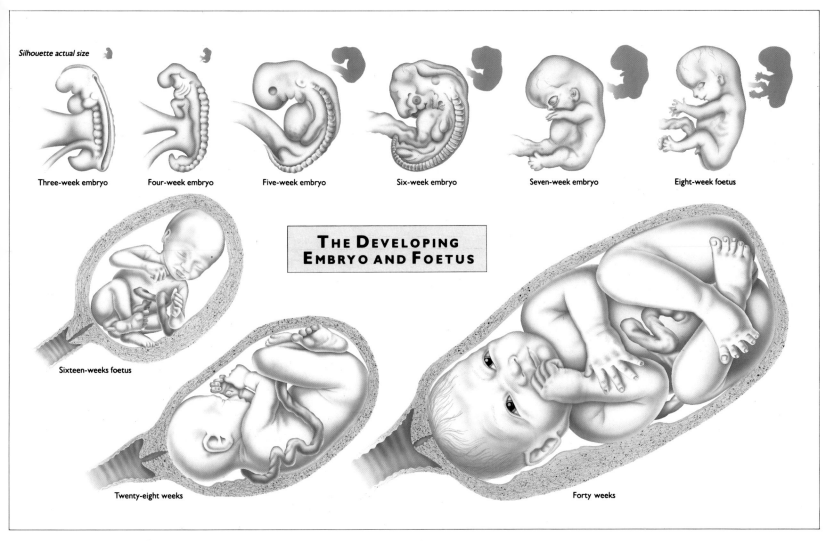

Silhouette actual size

Three-week embryo Four-week embryo Five-week embryo Six-week embryo Seven-week embryo Eight-week foetus

THE DEVELOPING EMBRYO AND FOETUS

Sixteen-weeks foetus

Twenty-eight weeks

Forty weeks

triggers off the start of labour. The hormone *oxytocin* begins to circulate in the mother's blood, softening the *cervix* (the neck of the womb) so that it will be able to stretch and accommodate the baby's head. There are three clearly defined stages of labour. In the *first stage*, the muscular wall of the uterus gradually builds up the force and frequency of its contractions as it draws up the edges of the now thinned and softened cervix until it is fully dilated (i.e. widened). The first stage of labour is the longest, taking an average of 8 – 10 hours for a first baby. At the end of the first stage the membranes rupture, releasing the *amniotic fluid*, which surrounds the foetus in the uterus – this is known as the breaking of the waters.

The *second stage* is shorter (½ – 2 hours) but harder. This is the stage where the baby is moved down the birth canal (the

cervix and vagina) and is born. The uterus contracts swiftly and forcefully and the mother experiences an overwhelming desire to 'bear down' or push with her

abdominal muscles to help the baby to be born.

The *third stage* is the delivery of the placenta or 'afterbirth'.   OGO

The human foetus at 12 weeks, showing the head, upper limbs and umbilical cord, which connects the foetus to the placenta.

CONTRACEPTION

There are five main methods of contraception practised at present: hormonal, intra-uterine device, barrier, sterilization and rhythm.

Hormonal
The Pill is the best-known hormonal contraceptive. Millions of women have used it since it became widely available in the 1960s and have enjoyed a freedom from unwanted pregnancies undreamt of by previous generations. The Pill is highly effective and may protect woman against some gynaecological cancers, such as ovarian cancer. Older versions of the Pill that contained higher doses of oestrogen and progesterone than today's Pills carried a slightly increased risk of circulatory disease and breast cancer.

Sterilization
In women sterilization involves blocking the fallopian tubes by either cutting or tying them. Male sterilization involves cutting the *vas deferens*, the channel that transports sperm. The operation, called a *vasectomy*, can be performed as an out-patient procedure.

Barrier
Barrier methods of contraception consist of the condom (sheath) worn over the man's penis, and the diaphragm, which covers the woman's cervix. They are less reliable than the Pill in preventing pregnancies, but have no effects on other body systems. The spread of AIDS has made the condom a popular

choice since it forms a complete barrier, the diaphragm may also give some protection against cancer of the cervix. The spermicide normally used with the diaphragm and used to coat some brands of condom has been shown to immobilize the AIDS virus under laboratory conditions.

IUDs
The *intra-uterine device* (IUD or 'coil') is a small object made from plastic and metal wire, often copper, inserted into the uterus. It probably works by preventing a fertilized egg from implanting into the uterine wall. IUDs have lost popularity since they have been associated with infections and infertility in some women and heavy, painful periods in others. Their advantage is that women can forget about contraception for years at a time.

Rhythm
This is one of the oldest methods of contraception and relies on restricting intercourse to the days in a woman's menstrual cycle when she is unlikely to become pregnant. It is the least reliable way to prevent unwanted pregnancies. More recently, other signs of fertility such as an increase in clear mucus or body temperature have been used by couples to either increase or reduce their chances of conceiving.

Other methods
Many other methods of contraception are currently being researched, including a male pill, a female condom, hormonal implants, an IUD that will prevent sexually transmitted diseases, and pregnancy vaccines.

Physical Development

Growth begins at conception and proceeds at an increasing rate during the first six months of pregnancy. From this time onwards there is a slowly decelerating growth through infancy and childhood, with a brief increase in rate during puberty. Growth in height stops towards the end of the second decade. Most early growth takes place through cell division, but growth in cell size becomes increasingly important once the full complement of cells has been established. This is why damage to the developing foetus has particularly severe long-term consequences on growth.

Growth that takes place in the *uterus* or womb and in the first year of life depends almost entirely upon nutrition. Babies grow more quickly if they are given more food – children who are underfed lose out on this phase of infantile growth, which contributes approximately one half of the total growth of the human.

Growth in childhood

Towards the end of the first year of postnatal life, the control of the growth process switches from dependence on nutrition to dependence on growth hormone secretion (see p. 214). Growth hormone is released from the pituitary gland and the rate at which children grow depends on the amount of growth hormone secreted – tall children become tall adults by growing consistently at a faster rate than their shorter peers.

Growth in childhood continues at a slowly decelerating pace until the deceleration is interrupted by the onset of puberty. The increase in height in childhood is roughly the same as that during the first year, but it is the amount and timing of the pubertal component of growth that determines the adult height of men and women.

Puberty

During the 12th year of life secondary sexual characteristics will have become apparent in 50% of girls and boys. These include development of breasts in girls, enlargement of the testes and, later, deepening of the voice in boys, and growth of axillary (underarm) and pubic hair in both sexes. Such developments occur before the age of 9 years in 3% of children, and 97% show some secondary sexual characteristics by the age of 14 years.

As soon as the ovary begins to secrete sufficient oestrogen to promote breast enlargement (the earliest change in female puberty), the growth rate increases as a result of an increase in the secretion of growth hormone. Until this age, the heights achieved by boys and girls are virtually the same so that a girl starts her pubertal growth from an average height of about 140 cm (4 ft 7 in). Female pubertal growth adds approximately 20 cm (8 in) to this height. As puberty progresses, girls grow increasingly quickly for about 18 months and then the growth rate begins to fall. By this time the cyclical waxing and waning of oestrogen has induced sufficient thickening of the lining of the uterus for the falling oestrogen level to induce shedding of the lining, with some blood loss (menstruation or a 'period'; see p. 202). The timing of the first period has relatively little biological importance but has occurred in 97% of girls by the age of 15. After the onset of the first period, most bleeding occurs at irregular intervals because ovulation does not become reliably established for at least 18 months.

Secondary sexual characteristics in boys appear at more or less the same time as breast development in girls. Boys continue growing along the childhood (decelerating) curve during the first two years of their pubertal development, and reach an average height of about 150 cm (4 ft

---

MAIN STAGES OF PHYSICAL DEVELOPMENT

A child's height at 1 year is roughly equal to the height gain in the rest of childhood, and the height at 2 years is roughly half the final adult height. The growth rate slows down after the age of 1, but accelerates again at puberty. Although the majority of both sexes begin puberty (the development of secondary sexual characteristics) in their 12th or 13th years, the adolescent growth spurt starts two years earlier in girls than in boys. On average, girls will reach their final adult height by the age of 15, and boys by the age of 16.

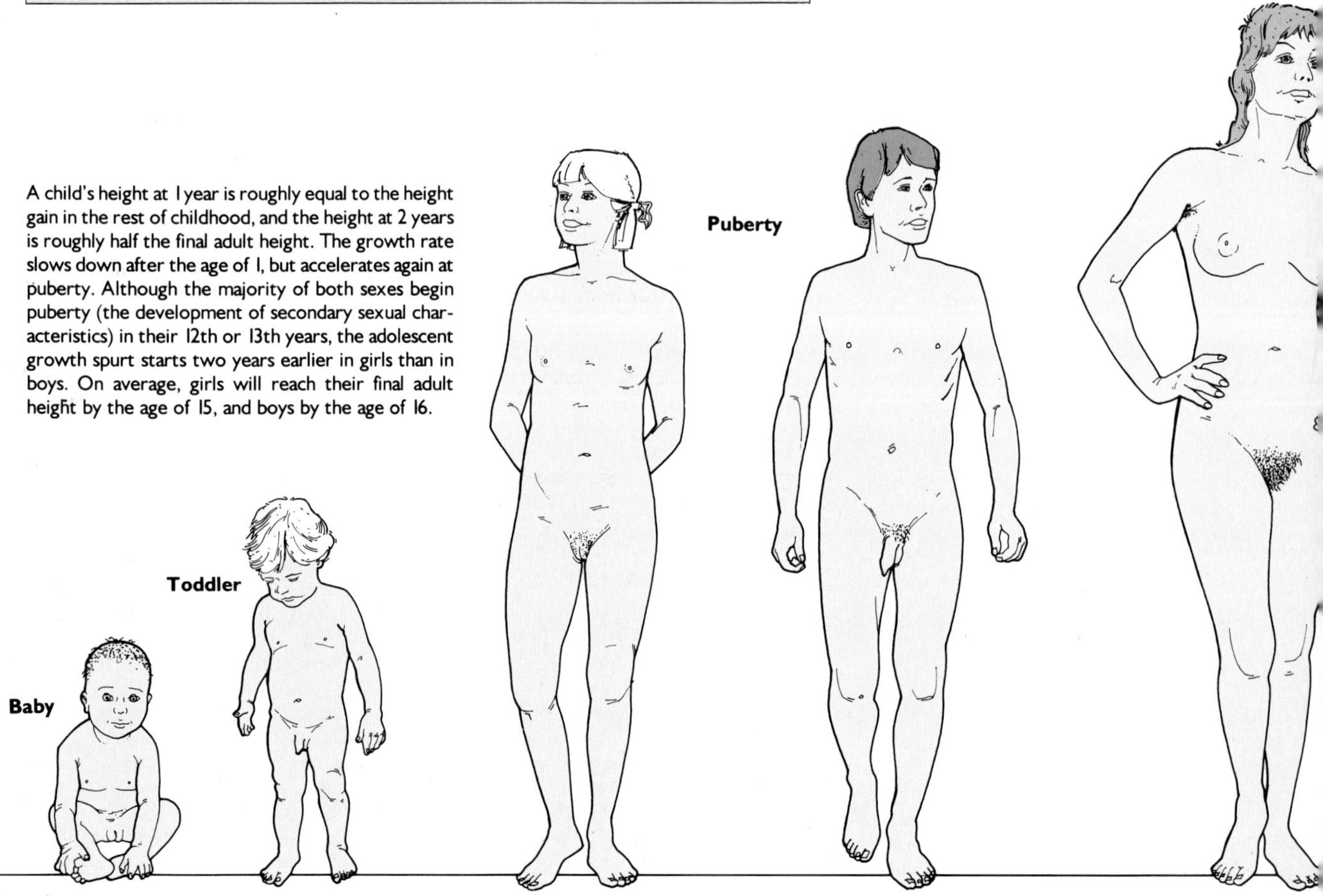

Baby

Toddler

Puberty

11 in) before the pubertal growth spurt starts. As testosterone produced by the testes is a better stimulator of growth than oestrogen, the peak of a boy's growth rate is greater than that of a girl, but it passes more quickly. Whereas boys start to grow during puberty two years later than girls, they stop growing only about one year later – at about 16 rather than 15 years of age on average.

The male growth spurt adds approximately 25 cm (10 in) in height and the final height of adult men is consequently an average 12.6 cm (5 in) greater than that of adult women. This is mainly due to the prolongation of childhood growth in men and not to the contribution of the puberty growth spurt, which is only slightly greater in boys than in girls. As soon as testosterone secretion occurs in the testes, *spermatogenesis* (the production of sperm) begins in the seminiferous tubules (see diagram, p. 202). Testosterone also promotes muscle development and the growth of body hair, for instance on the chest.

The menopause

The developing female is equipped at birth with all the ovarian follicles – in which the ova or eggs develop – she will require for life (see p. 202). The follicles disappear at a rate proportional to the number of follicles remaining – quickly at first, then increasingly slowly. The newborn infant has approximately 1 000 000 follicles, but this has already reduced to 100 000 by the time menstruation begins.

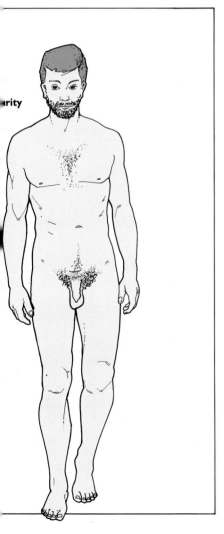

GIANTISM AND DWARFISM

A disturbance of the pattern of growth hormone secretion is usually the reason why children who otherwise look normal become excessively large (*giantism*) or small (*dwarfism*). However, there are also a number of congenital and/or hereditary causes of grossly abnormal stature. In the most extreme cases of excessive or restricted growth, there is a limited amount that the physician can do to alleviate the problem. Mental retardation is *not* a characteristic feature of dwarfism or giantism.

The tendency to excessive or restricted growth is usually present at birth and becomes apparent in the early months of life. Some children with giantism may be born large and show an accelerated growth rate from birth. In others the growth rate may speed up abnormally just before puberty and continue up to maturity – most often such growth patterns are due to over-secretion of growth hormone by the pituitary gland (see p. 214) because of a pituitary tumour, but the interaction with changes occurring at puberty is relevant to the determination of final height. In this case the problem can be alleviated by surgery.

Dwarfism in children may be hereditary or due to under-secretion of growth hormone by the pituitary. In the latter case it most commonly becomes apparent if the onset of puberty is delayed, and therapies are available in cases where final height may be severely restricted.

Robert Wadlow (1918–40), the tallest recorded giant in medical history, grew to a height of 2 m 72 cm (8 ft 11 in).

An 8-year-old dwarf (left) with normal-sized children of the same age.

Since approximately 20 ovarian follicles are required for each menstrual cycle (from which only one is selected to ovulate) the average woman requires about 250 follicles for each year of reproductive life.

The average age of the menopause is 51 years, so there is an enormous surplus of follicles present in the infantile ovary. The menopause in women is not determined by the use of follicles in the menstrual cycle but by the process of their disappearance. This process is to some extent influenced by environmental circumstances – for example, the age at menopause is lower in women who smoke than in those who do not.

The sudden decline in oestrogen secretion in women at the menopause has been blamed for many symptoms, but the only symptoms clearly associated with oestrogen deficiency are hot flushes, vaginal dryness and skin changes, *osteoporosis* (loss of bone density, making them more liable to fracture), and an increase in the rate of development of *atherosclerosis* (hardening of the arteries). These changes can cause severe psychological and physical symptoms, which is why the question of hormone replacement therapy for post-menopausal women is so important. Now that life expectancy has increased so greatly, a woman can expect three or more decades of post-menopausal life in which the consequences of diminishing oestrogen can develop. Men are less severely affected by hormonal changes, since the decline in male sex hormone concentrations occurs over a much longer period.

Old age

The physical changes associated with old age have been much less intensively studied than those of childhood. It is obvious that old people become thinner, more wrinkled through loss both of skin elasticity and of subcutaneous (under-skin) fat, shorter through vertebral compression, and more vulnerable to disease. However, there are no standards comparable to those established in childhood with which to assess individual subjects. As longevity increases, the need for such standards becomes increasingly important.   CB

SEE ALSO

● REPRODUCTION p. 202
● GLANDS AND HORMONES p. 214

How People Move

Bones, joints, muscles and nerves are the essential requirements for human movement, whether for top athletes or just ordinary people going about their daily lives. Normally, people are born with the same set of anatomical equipment – bones, joints and voluntary muscles supplied with an almost identical network of nerves and blood vessels. Bones account for one sixth of body weight, and muscles make up two fifths.

The speed and control with which individuals move and the suppleness of their bodies depend partly on luck in inheriting the right genes from parents. The length and thickness of bones and the laxity of joint ligaments are determined to a great extent before birth, but regular exercise can strengthen muscles and improve skill in movement.

Bones

Without the rigid support provided by bones we would all be shapeless bags of organs. But the skeleton performs a number of important functions besides giving the body shape and form.

Bones such as the skull, ribs and vertebrae encase vital organs such as the brains, lungs, heart and spinal cord, protecting them from injury.

Other bones such as the femur, tibia and fibula – the long bones of the legs – and the humerus, radius and ulna in the arms serve primarily as levers providing attachments for muscles that propel the body forward or allow it to reach and retrieve objects.

Some bones, including the ribs, pelvis and sternum (the breast bone), contain bone marrow. This is the substance responsible for manufacturing the millions of red blood cells essential to life (see p. 210). Bones also act as reservoirs for calcium and other minerals needed to maintain health.

At birth bones are made up of two thirds fibrous material and one third mineral, while in old age they are two thirds mineral and one third fibrous. Broken bones in children are called *greenstick fractures* – they are more flexible and do not break completely. In old people bones contain less calcium and break more easily.

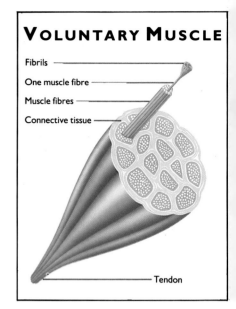

VOLUNTARY MUSCLE

Fibrils

One muscle fibre

Muscle fibres

Connective tissue

Tendon

Joints

Bones meet one another to form joints, of which there are six main types (see below). The degree of movement possible at a joint is determined by the surface of the bone ends and the joint space and fluid between them.

The hip joint is an example of a *ball-and-socket joint*, where both bone ends have a large area of smooth surface covered in cartilage and lubricated by *synovial fluid*. Movement is possible in all directions.

SEE ALSO

● FOOD, DIET AND DIGESTION p. 208
● RESPIRATION AND CIRCULATION p. 210
● THE NERVOUS SYSTEM p. 220

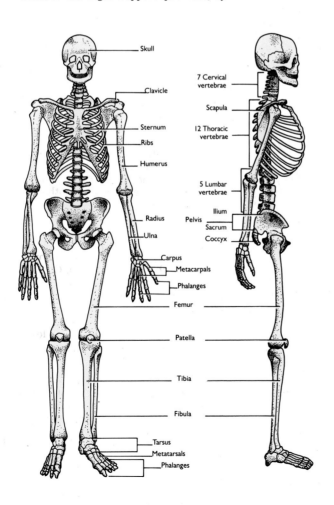

Skull
Clavicle
Sternum
Ribs
Humerus
Radius
Ulna
Carpus
Metacarpals
Phalanges
Femur
Patella
Tibia
Fibula
Tarsus
Metatarsals
Phalanges

7 Cervical vertebrae
Scapula
12 Thoracic vertebrae
5 Lumbar vertebrae
Pelvis
Ilium
Sacrum
Coccyx

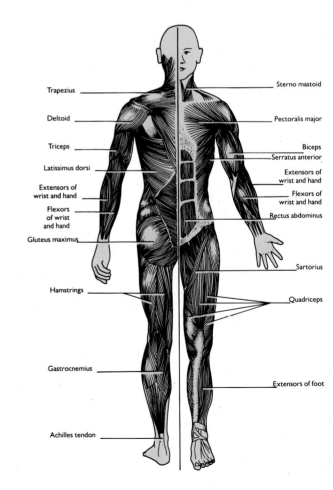

Trapezius
Deltoid
Triceps
Latissimus dorsi
Extensors of wrist and hand
Flexors of wrist and hand
Gluteus maximus
Hamstrings
Gastrocnemius
Achilles tendon

Sterno mastoid
Pectoralis major
Biceps
Serratus anterior
Extensors of wrist and hand
Flexors of wrist and hand
Rectus abdominus
Sartorius
Quadriceps
Extensors of foot

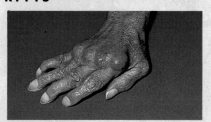

Biceps
contracts

Triceps
relaxes

Biceps
relaxes

Triceps
con-
tracts

Muscles usually function in pairs. When one – known as the agonist – contracts, the other – the antagonist – relaxes, producing a smooth movement.

The knee and elbow are *hinge joints*, with movement mostly in one plane. The joint between the thumb and hand is a *saddle joint* permitting movement in a number of directions, while the joint between the base of the spine and the pelvis – the sacro-iliac joint – is a *plane joint* where very little movement is possible except during pregnancy, when the pelvis expands to accommodate the growing foetus.

Where the first vertebra – the *atlas*, so named because it holds the weight of the head – joins the next vertebra, the *axis*, a *pivotal joint* is formed. Movement occurs between the ring of the atlas and the toothlike peg of the axis, allowing rotation or turning of the head to look over the shoulder.

Condyloid joints are those between the

bones of the hand and the fingers and the foot and toes.

Muscle types

Muscle is basically of two types: the sort we can control, known as *voluntary*, *striped*, or *skeletal muscle*, and the sort we cannot control, otherwise known as *smooth*, *autonomic* or *involuntary muscle*. Although the heart muscle is not under our direct control it is usually classed separately as *cardiac muscle*.

Voluntary muscle

Voluntary muscle is composed of long thin cells or fibres enclosed in an outer coat. Under the miscroscope the fibres show alternate light and dark bands, which is why they are sometimes referred to as striped. The dark bands contain the protein *myosin* while the light ones contain *actin*. In the middle of the dark bands is a lighter area called the H band. In the middle of the light bands is a slim dark band called the Z area and the space between two Z areas is known as a contractile unit or *sarcomere*.

When a message to move is sent by the brain to a muscle via the nerves (see pp. 220–221) or if an electrical stimulus is applied to a muscle fibre, it will contract – the light bands shorten and the actin and myosin filaments slide past each other. When a muscle contracts it can shorten and become thicker – an *isotonic* contraction – or it can remain the same length but increase in tension – an *isometric* contraction. If a weight is picked up and the elbow bent, the biceps contract isotomically. If we try to bend the elbow while applying pressure with the other hand to prevent it actually bending, the biceps contracts isometrically.

Although we can directly cause voluntary muscles to contract, we rarely do so. The usual course is to direct a movement like walking upstairs. Such a command initiates action in whole groups of muscles that act in harmony to perform a coordinated manoeuvre. Some of the muscles perform the move obvious actions like bending the hip and knee, while others come into play to stabilize the trunk and increase strength in the opposite leg, which temporarily bears the entire body weight.

Habitual movements patterns are so well established that the way we move is largely performed unconsciously. Only the dedicated few – for example, tennis players wanting to improve their backhand stroke – study precisely which muscles are working and develop the conscious ability to make fine adjustments to the way they perform.

Involuntary muscle

Involuntary or smooth muscle is found in the walls of the digestive tract, in the respiratory system and in the urinary and reproductive tracts. It is the main tissue in the middle coat of the smaller arteries and determines the diameter of these vessels. By regulating the resistance of the vessels it controls the distribution of blood to the various tissues and organs and helps control the blood pressure.

In the eye, involuntary muscle controls the amount of light entering by adjusting the size of the pupil (see pp. 218–19) and in the skin it causes the hair to stand erect when we are cold or frightened.

Involuntary muscle is the simplest type of muscle in construction, consisting of spindle-shaped fibres each with a single nucleus. But it is capable of very strong contractions. During birth the smooth muscle of the uterus contracts powerfully to expel the foetus, and the act of defecating or vomiting brings smooth muscle in the digestive tract into play with considerable force.

Cardiac muscle

The heart muscle is unique in construction, consisting of long cylindrical fibres arranged in sheets and bundles. Certain special fibres in the heart muscle make up the conducting system by which electrical impulses spread to the other fibres and bring about the rhythmical sequence of contraction and relaxation that allows the heart to empty itself of blood and then refill (see pp. 210–11).

All types of muscle are influenced by psychological factors. Most people have experienced how feeling nervous can make the hands and legs tremble and the heart beat faster. There may also be a need to rush to the lavatory as the urinary and digestive tracts empty faster than they would under more relaxed circumstances. Some people learn to control unwanted muscle actions using meditation and relaxation techniques. OGO

ARTHRITIS

One of the commonest causes of difficulties in moving is arthritis. The term itself means inflammation of a joint, but there are several different reasons why joints can become inflamed, swollen and stiff.

Most people with arthritis suffer from *osteoarthritis*. This used to be considered to result from general wear and tear because it affects so many old people and people who have suffered an injury affecting joint surfaces. Now it is thought some other unidentified factor is also involved. In osteoarthritis the cartilage covering joint surfaces becomes thinner and bony outgrowths called *osteophytes* proliferate around the edges of the bone ends. Usually only one joint is affected, such as a hip or knee.

***Rheumatoid arthritis* is a more crippling disease, believed to be an autoimmune condition (see p. 212). It affects people earlier in life than osteoarthritis, and usually several joints are involved at any one time. The disease begins in the *synovial membrane*, which lines the joint capsule and provides lubrication. This membrane becomes eaten away by an inflammatory substance that spreads**

Arthritis affecting the joints of a hand.

over the bone ends destroying cartilage, bone and even affecting surrounding muscles. This arthritis is extremely painful and causes sufferers a general illness during times when the condition flares up. Damage to the joints can lead to deformity, particularly noticeable in the hands, since the knuckles are often the first joints to be affected.

Less common forms of arthritis can result from infections, including sexually transmitted diseases.

Arthritis is usually treated with anti-inflammatory drugs and pain killers, and antibiotics if an infection is present. Rest is important during attacks but otherwise exercise and physiotherapy is advised to keep the joints from stiffening.

TYPES OF JOINT

BALL AND SOCKET

SADDLE

HINGE

CONDYLOID

PIVOTAL

PLANE

Food, Diet and Digestion

Unlike plants, which can synthesize everything they require using energy from the Sun, animals, including humans, must obtain their nutrients and energy from food. Digestion is the process in which the energy and nutrients contained in food are broken down into a suitable form to be absorbed by the body and utilized as a source of energy, or to synthesize substances such as proteins, enzymes and hormones that are required for the normal functioning of the body.

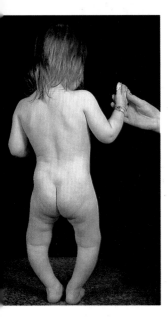

A child suffering from rickets: a disease caused by deficiency of vitamin D in which the bones of growing children are malformed and fail to harden.

A BALANCED DIET

When a baby is born, its mother's milk provides all the nutrients it requires. Once an infant has been weaned, and for the rest of its life, it is necessary to select a diet from a wide range of food sources. An individual's personal requirements depend on many factors such as age, sex and size. It is impossible to know how much of a particular nutrient an individual requires without doing complicated biochemical tests. It is possible, however, to estimate the amount of each nutrient needed by virtually everybody in the population. These 'Recommended Daily Amounts' are defined for different ages and different states – for example, requirements are greater in pregnancy.

A person's energy requirements also depend on their level of activity. Any excess energy taken in is stored in the form of fat. It is therefore important to ensure that the energy taken in is not greater than the amount expended.

The proportion of energy derived from fat, carbohydrate and protein is important, and current dietary guidelines suggest that no more than 35% of energy should come from fat, 10% from protein and 55% from carbohydrates. A diet high in fat, particularly 'saturated fat' (as found in, for example, red meat and dairy products), has been linked to the development of coronary heart disease. Most people would benefit from reducing their total fat intake, particularly if it contains a lot of saturated fatty acids.

To ensure the right balance of nutrients in a diet it is important to base one's eating on a wide range of foods. This should also ensure that adequate amounts of vitamins and minerals are consumed.

The nutrients required by the body are proteins, carbohydrates, fats and vitamins. Water is not a nutrient but an adequate intake is essential to replace the water that is lost each day through the skin and lungs and in urine and faeces.

Proteins

Proteins are made up of large numbers of *amino acids*. There are about 20 amino acids and they can be arranged in any order to produce a larger number of different proteins. Eight amino acids must be provided by the diet – these are called the *essential amino acids*. The others can be synthesized from one of the other amino acids.

Proteins provide cell structure, help fight infections, transport substances around the body and form enzymes and hormones. They can also provide energy. Meat, eggs, milk and pulses are all rich in proteins.

Carbohydrates

Carbohydrates contain carbon, hydrogen and oxygen and provide energy. The simple carbohydrates are the *monosaccharides* (glucose, fructose and galactose) and the *disaccharides* (sucrose, lactose and maltose). A disaccharide consists of two molecules of a monosaccharide. Sucrose (table sugar) contains a molecule of glucose joined to a molecule of fructose. Good sources of simple carbohydrates are fruits; honey, milk and table sugar.

Complex carbohydrates (*polysaccharides*) contain many hundreds of monosaccharides. Starch is a polysaccharide of glucose. Good sources of complex carbohydrates are bread, rice and potatoes. Dietary fibre consists mainly of complex carbohydrates that cannot be digested. It provides bulk and aids bowel function. Sources includes unrefined cereals, fruit and vegetables.

Fats

Fats are made up of *triglycerides*. A triglyceride has a backbone of *glycerol* with three *fatty acids* attached to it. Fatty acids can either be *saturated* or *unsaturated* (see box). Fats provide twice the amount of energy as carbohydrates and proteins.

Minerals

Mineral salts are essential for many of the body's chemical reactions. *Sodium* in the fluid surrounding the cells regulates the cells' external environment, while *potassium* plays the same role inside the cell. Haemoglobin, which transports oxygen, contains *iron*; many enzymes contain *zinc*; the transmission of nerve impulses requires sodium and potassium, and the mineral salts *calcium* and *phosphorus* are found in bone.

Vitamins

Vitamins are complex chemical compounds that are essential in small

VITAMINS

VITAMIN A (Retinol)
Functions: Essential for growth; vision in poor light; health of cornea and resistance to infection. Deficiency causes stunted growth, night blindness and susceptibility to infection.
Sources: Dairy products, fish-liver oils, egg yolks. Carotene, found in carrots and green vegetables, can be converted by the body into retinol.

VITAMIN B1 (Thiamin)
Functions: Essential for carbohydrate metabolism and nervous system functioning. Deficiency causes beriberi, with symptoms either of fluid retention or of extreme weight loss.
Sources: Yeast, egg yolks, liver, wheatgerm, peas and beans.

VITAMIN B2 (Riboflavin)
Functions: Essential for tissue respiration. Deficiency causes inflammation of tongue and lips.
Sources: Yeast, yeast and meat extracts, milk, liver, kidneys, cheese, eggs, green vegetables.

FOLIC ACID
Functions: B vitamin essential for maturing of red blood cells in bone marrow.
Sources: Spinach, liver, broccoli, peanuts.

NICOTINIC ACID (Niacin)
Functions: B vitamin essential for metabolism of carbohydrates; functioning of digestive tract and nervous system. Deficiency causes pellagra, characterized by scaly skin, diarrhoea and depression.
Sources: Yeast, yeast and meat extracts, fish, meat, cereals, peas and beans.

VITAMIN B6 (Pyridoxine)
Functions: Essential for metabolism of fat and protein.
Sources: Liver, egg yolks, meat, peas and beans.

VITAMIN B12 (Cyanocobalamin)
Functions: Essential for maturing of red blood cells in bone marrow.
Sources: Liver, fish, eggs, meat.

BIOTIN
Functions: B vitamin essential for metabolism of fat.
Sources: Egg yolks, liver, tomatoes, raspberries, artichokes.

VITAMIN C (Ascorbic acid)
Functions: Essential for formation of red blood cells, antibodies and connective tissue; formation and maintenance of bones; maintenance of strength of blood capillaries. Deficiency causes scurvy, with symptoms of swollen bleeding gums, weakness and dizziness.
Sources: Blackcurrants, citrus fruits, green vegetables, potatoes.

VITAMIN D
Functions: Essential for absorption of calcium and phosphorus. Deficiency causes rickets.
Sources: Fish-liver oils, eggs, butter, cheese. Humans can synthesize vitamin D from sunlight.

VITAMIN E
Functions: Has antioxidant properties, thought to prevent oxidation of unsaturated fatty acids in cells.
Sources: Vegetable oils, cereals, green vegetables, eggs, butter.

VITAMIN K
Functions: Associated with clotting mechanism of blood.
Sources: Green vegetables, liver; can be synthesized in the human gut.

quantities for many chemical reactions. If a vitamin is lacking in the diet a deficiency disease arises – for example, lack of vitamin C leads to scurvy (see p. 244). An excess of certain vitamins can also be dangerous.

Digestion and absorption

The gastrointestinal tract is a long tube about 9 m long, which passes through the body from the mouth to the anus. Here the complex structures present in food are mixed with *enzymes* (proteins that act as catalysts in certain biochemical reactions) and broken down into their simple constituents. These are small enough to be absorbed through the wall of the intestine into the bloodstream.

Food is chewed in the mouth and mixed with saliva. It passes through the *oesophagus* into the *stomach*. The stomach acts as a temporary store and mixes the food until it is in a semi-fluid state called *chyme*. This is then released slowly into the *duodenum*.

Most digestion takes place in the duodenum. Enzymes, secreted by the pancreas into the duodenum, split proteins into amino acids, fats into fatty acids and glycerol and polysaccharides into glucose and fructose. These are then absorbed through the walls of the *ileum* (part of the small intestine). Glucose, fructose and amino acids are absorbed into the bloodstream and carried to the liver (see below). Fatty acids and glycerol are absorbed into the lymphatic system (see p. 212), and enter the bloodstream later.

Substances that cannot be digested pass into the *colon* (the large intestine). Some compounds are fermented by the bacteria there and others are excreted as waste products in the faeces via the *rectum*.

Storage and use of nutrients

The blood carries the absorbed nutrients from the intestine to the liver. After a meal the liver prevents the levels of glucose and amino acids in the blood from rising too much by removing them from the blood. Glucose is stored as *glycogen* and can be converted back into glucose when the blood levels of glucose begin to fall. Any excess glucose is converted into *triglyceride* and is stored in *adipose tissue* – connective tissue packed with fat cells.

Amino acids are stored as proteins, which can be broken down to release the amino acids when they are required. Excess amino acids are converted to carbohydrate by the removal of the 'amino' group, and used as an energy source. The 'amino' group is converted to *urea*, a waste substance that is excreted in the urine.

Fatty acids are also an energy source. When the supply of glucose begins to fall, triglycerides are broken down in the liver and adipose tissue, and fatty acids are released into the blood to be taken up by other cells.

Energy is produced by the oxidation of either glucose or fatty acids and is stored

in the high-energy molecule ATP *(adenosine triphosphate)*. ATP can later release this energy to drive other chemical reactions in the cell. The oxidation of fatty acids produces more than twice as many molecules of ATP as the oxidation of glucose. Carbohydrates and proteins provide 4 kilocalories (17 kilojoules) of energy per gram, and fat 9 kilocalories (39 kilojoules) per gram.

Excretion

Many of the chemical reactions that take place in the body produce compounds that would be toxic if allowed to accumulate. Blood must therefore be purified and the toxic waste products excreted. This takes place in the *kidney nephron*. There are many hundreds of nephrons in each kidney (see diagram bottom right). BNF

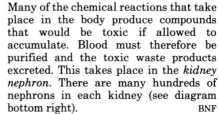

Kwashiorkor is a form of malnutrition due to a diet deficient in protein. The abdomen becomes distended as a result of water retention.

SEE ALSO

● ARABLE FARMING p. 188
● LIVESTOCK FARMING p. 190
● THE FOOD-PROCESSING INDUSTRY p. 196
● RESPIRATION AND CIRCULATION p. 210
● TOUCH, TASTE AND SMELL p. 216
● NON-INFECTIOUS DISEASES p. 236
● PREVENTING DISEASE p. 244

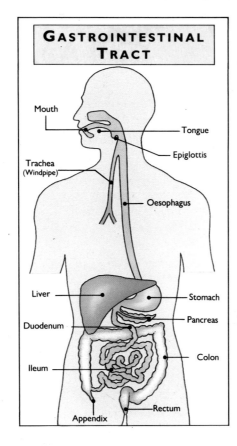

GASTROINTESTINAL TRACT

Mouth
Tongue
Epiglottis
Trachea (Windpipe)
Oesophagus
Liver
Stomach
Pancreas
Duodenum
Colon
Ileum
Rectum
Appendix

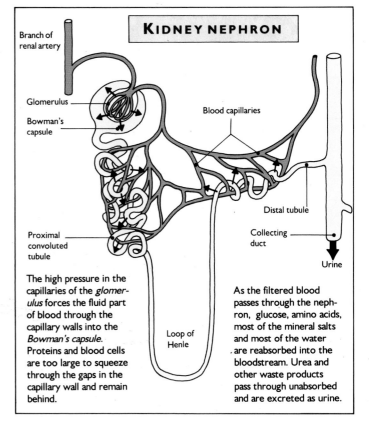

KIDNEY NEPHRON

Branch of renal artery
Glomerulus
Bowman's capsule
Blood capillaries
Distal tubule
Collecting duct
Proximal convoluted tubule
Loop of Henle
Urine

The high pressure in the capillaries of the *glomerulus* forces the fluid part of blood through the capillary walls into the *Bowman's capsule*. Proteins and blood cells are too large to squeeze through the gaps in the capillary wall and remain behind.

As the filtered blood passes through the nephron, glucose, amino acids, most of the mineral salts and most of the water are reabsorbed into the bloodstream. Urea and other waste products pass through unabsorbed and are excreted as urine.

Respiration and Circulation

Every cell of the body requires a constant supply of oxygen and nutrients. The immediate source of these is the interstitial fluid, which surrounds the cell and is continuously replenished by the blood supply. Carbon dioxide and other waste produced by the cells are then carried away by the blood.

SEE ALSO

● HOW PEOPLE MOVE p. 206
● FOOD, DIET AND DIGESTION p. 208
● GLANDS AND HORMONES p. 214
● NON-INFECTIOUS DISEASES p. 235

Carrying gases is one of the many functions of blood, which consists of three types of cell. Suspended in a liquid called *plasma* are red corpuscles, white corpuscles and platelets. The main function of white corpuscles is to fight infection (see p. 212) and the platelets initiate the clotting mechanism, which ensures that when a blood vessel is damaged the wound is sealed before much of the 5 litres (8 pints) of blood that the average person possesses is lost.

Each litre of blood contains about 5×10^{12} red blood corpuscles containing *haemoglobin* – a substance which combines with oxygen in the lungs and carries it to the tissues, where the oxygen is exchanged for carbon dioxide. This carbon dioxide is then carried to the lungs, where it is exchanged for more oxygen. If a person has a reduced number of red corpuscles or if the corpuscles have a reduced amount of haemoglobin, they are said to be suffering from *anaemia* and not enough oxygen is carried to the tissues. This results in tiredness and breathlessness, particularly on exertion.

Respiration

The oxygenation of blood in the lungs, the use of oxygen and production of carbon dioxide by the tissues and the removal of carbon dioxide from the blood in the lungs is called respiration.

Air enters the respiratory system through the nose or mouth and passes down the *trachea*, which branches in the lungs into smaller and smaller tubes or *bronchioles* and finally into *alveoli*, where blood and gas are in close contact and gases can exchange freely. This occurs as a result of muscle contraction. Breathing in (*inspiration*) occurs when two sets of muscle contract – the *diaphragm*, which separates the chest from the abdomen, and the *intercostals*, which lie between each rib. Contraction of these muscles increases

the volume within the *thoracic cavity* (chest). This causes the lungs to expand and air to rush in. When the muscles stop contracting, they relax passively and the lungs deflate again, forcing the air out (*expiration*).

Circulation

William Harvey (see pp. 248–49) proved that the heart and blood vessels formed a closed system, with the blood continuously circulating around it. The centre point of this system is the heart – the pump which forces the blood through the blood vessels to every part of the body. The heart is in fact a double pump – a right and a left pump, each consisting of two chambers, an *atrium* and a *ventricle*. The right atrium receives blood from all parts of the body and passes it on to the right ventricle, which then pumps it to the lungs (*pulmonary circulation*). The oxygenated blood then returns to the left atrium and into the left ventricle, which pumps it to all parts of the body (*systemic circulation*). The heart is a very powerful muscle, contracting between 60 and 200 times a minute depending on the level of activity. To ensure that the blood moves in only one direction through the heart, the openings between the atria and ventricles and between the ventricles and blood vessels are guarded by valves.

The blood vessels leaving the heart are called arteries, with the *pulmonary artery* going to the lungs, and the *aorta* to all the organs and tissues of the body. As they get further from the heart, they branch into smaller and smaller arteries. Arteries appear circular in cross section, with thick muscular walls. The smaller arteries eventually become *capillaries* – thin-walled vessels through which the transfer of oxygen and other substances between the blood and interstitial fluid occurs. At the same time, carbon dioxide and other waste products leave the interstitial fluid and enter the blood. The capillaries then converge, forming larger and larger vessels known as *veins*, which are thin-walled and of indefinite shape. Veins contain valves, which aid the movement of blood from the lower parts of the body against gravity. Eventually they merge into two large veins, the *superior vena cava* and *inferior vena cava*, which return blood to the right atrium.

The effects of exercise

As the body changes from a state of rest to one of activity, its requirements alter. At rest the body uses about 0.25 litres of oxygen each minute, and this can rise to three litres a minute in heavy exercise. To make this possible, both the heart and the respiratory system must increase their level of activity. At rest the heart pumps about five litres of blood per minute to the lungs and the same amount around the rest of the body. In heavy exercise, this volume is increased to about 30 litres per minute – the heart rate increases from about 60 to 200 beats per minute and the amount of blood pumped out with each beat is doubled. Because the amount of blood passing through the lungs increases

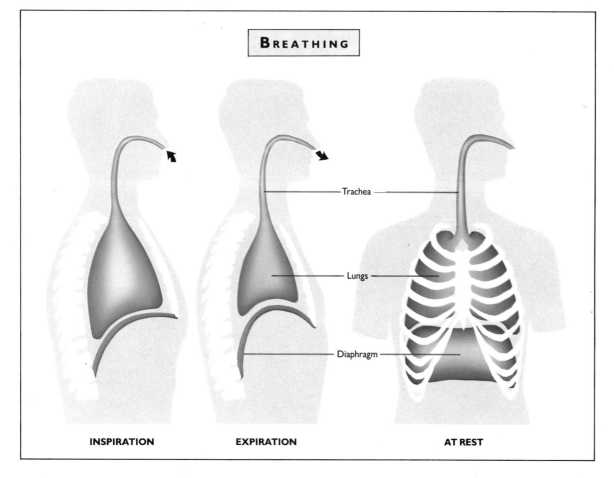

BREATHING

Trachea

Lungs

Diaphragm

INSPIRATION   **EXPIRATION**   **AT REST**

BLOOD CIRCULATION

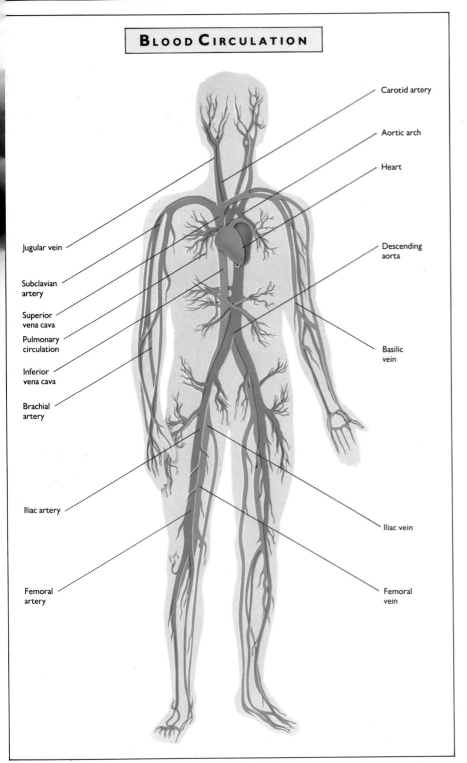

Carotid artery

Aortic arch

Heart

Descending aorta

Basilic vein

Iliac vein

Femoral vein

Jugular vein

Subclavian artery

Superior vena cava

Pulmonary circulation

Inferior vena cava

Brachial artery

Iliac artery

Femoral artery

BLOOD FLOW THROUGH THE HEART

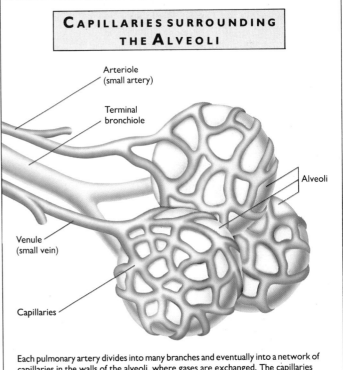

Right pulmonary artery

Superior vena cava

Right atrium

Right ventricle

Inferior vena cava

Aorta

Left pulmonary artery

Left pulmonary veins

Left atrium

Left ventricle

The right side of the heart deals with deoxygenated blood, while the left side deals with oxygenated blood.

CAPILLARIES SURROUNDING THE ALVEOLI

Arteriole (small artery)

Terminal bronchiole

Alveoli

Venule (small vein)

Capillaries

Each pulmonary artery divides into many branches and eventually into a network of capillaries in the walls of the alveoli, where gases are exchanged. The capillaries rejoin and become two pulmonary veins, conveying oxygenated blood back to the heart.

about six times, more air must be brought into the lungs to provide the necessary oxygen, and this is achieved by breathing more frequently and more deeply. The circulatory and respiratory systems can be finely controlled in this way to meet the prevailing requirements of the body.

Other functions

Nutrients, eaten and digested (see p. 208) are absorbed into the bloodstream and transported to the liver and tissues which need them. Water, which accounts for about 60% of the body, is constantly moving around the body and this is brought about by movement into and out of the bloodstream. Hormones are secreted into the bloodstream by the endocrine glands and transported to their target tissues (see p. 214). Waste products are carried to the kidneys for excretion in the urine (see p. 209). Drugs taken by mouth or injected enter the bloodstream and are carried to the organs on which they are expected to act.

Injury or infection causes inflammation – local blood vessels dilate and the increased flow of blood brings microphages, macrophages and antibodies to the area (see p. 212). Blood also plays a part in regulating body temperature: in hot weather vessels in the skin dilate allowing heat to escape and in cold weather they contract, conserving body heat. BND

The Immune System

Everyday of our lives there is a constant battle between our bodies and a multitude of microbes. To bacteria, viruses and fungi, many of which cause disease, the human body represents a warm haven where food is plentiful. Before a microorganism can install itself, however, it has to breach the body's first line of defence.

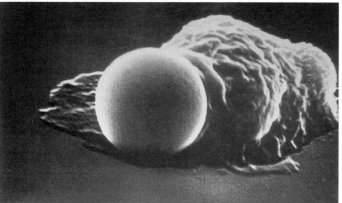

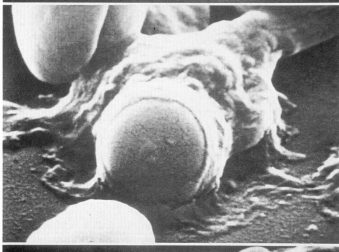

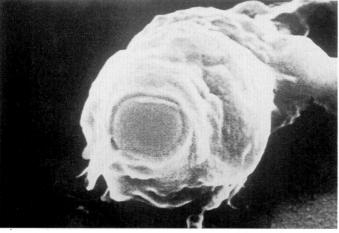

A macrophage (a type of white blood cell) approaching, engulfing and consuming a red blood cell that has reached the end of its life.

The most obvious of these is the skin, which forms a waterproof layer over most of the body. The sebum secreted by the sebaceous glands in the skin contains a substance called *lysozyme* – also present in tears and nasal mucus – which kills bacteria and viruses.

Those parts of the body open to the exterior have their own specialized defences. Any bacteria or viruses inhaled may become entangled in mucus produced by the cells lining the tubes leading to the lungs. Tiny hair-like *cilia* in these tubes constantly beat the mucus upwards towards the throat, where it is either coughed up or swallowed. If it is swallowed, the acid in the stomach juices will usually kill any microorganisms present.

Microorganisms can also enter the body via the urinary opening or, in women, the vagina. In both men and women, the flushing action of urine tends to wash any invading bacteria out of the body. In women, harmless bacteria in the vagina help to prevent those that cause disease from establishing themselves. Harmless bacteria in the gut play a similar role.

Bacteria, viruses, fungi and other microorganisms that cause diseases sometimes manage to evade these defences and begin to multiply in the body. One of the main functions of the immune system – that of protecting the human body against invading microbes – then comes into play. The immune system can also recognize and reject foreign material, such as transplanted organs, and identify and destroy cancer cells.

The components of the immune system

White blood cells known as *lymphocytes* form one of the most important components of the immune system. The cells destined to become lymphocytes originate in the bone marrow. Some of them travel in the blood to the *thymus gland* in the neck, where they mature into *T-lymphocytes*. The thymus gland seems to have a role in ensuring that only those T cells that recognize foreign proteins (as opposed to the body's own proteins) are released into the circulation. Some of the immature cells remain in the bone marrow for the rest of their development, however, and they become *B-lymphocytes*. Once mature, the T and B cells migrate in the blood to the *spleen*, the *lymph nodes* and other components of the *lymphoid tissue*, such as the tonsils. The spleen is an organ found on the left side of the body, just below the diaphragm. One of its functions is to filter circulating microorganisms from the blood. Lymphocytes present in the spleen are ready to respond to any foreign microbe that appears.

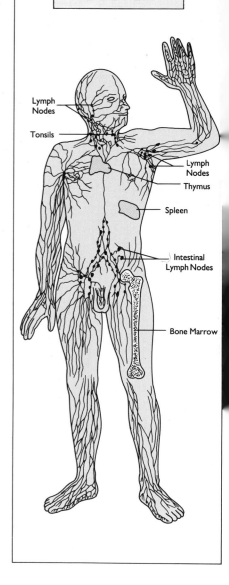

THE IMMUNE SYSTEM

Lymph Nodes
Tonsils
Lymph Nodes
Thymus
Spleen
Intestinal Lymph Nodes
Bone Marrow

The lymph nodes, present throughout the body, filter the *lymph* – a clear fluid that drains from the body tissues. The lymph collects in the vessels of the *lymphatic system*, and eventually returns to the blood. It first passes through the lymph nodes and any microorganisms or cancer cells are filtered out. If an infection is present, lymphocytes respond by multiplying, which accounts for the swelling of the nodes – for example, in the armpits and under the lower jaw – that sometimes occurs. Vast numbers of other types of white blood cell, e.g. *microphages* (neutrophils) and *macrophages*, can engulf and destroy microorganisms. They also destroy red blood cells that have reached the end of their 120-day life span. These so-called *phagocytic* cells are found in the tissues, lymph nodes and spleen.

Antigens and antibodies

An *antigen* is any foreign substance – for instance, the protein on the coat of a bacterium – that can stimulate an immune

AIDS AND THE IMMUNE SYSTEM

The *human immunodeficiency virus* (HIV), which causes AIDS (acquired immune deficiency syndrome), strikes at the heart of the body's defences. The virus destroys the immune system, including the very cells that should be capable of eliminating it. In infected people the virus is found in the blood, semen and – to a lesser extent – vaginal secretions. It can be transmitted if any of these fluids gains access to another person's blood stream. This can occur through sexual contact involving exposure to semen, as the virus could enter even the most minute cut or abrasion in the vagina or the more delicate rectum. It can also be spread among drug users via shared hypodermic needles.

People infected with HIV may remain apparently well for many years. After a variable incubation period, which may average as long as 9 or 10 years, many affected people – although no one knows exactly what proportion – will go on to develop AIDS. The disease develops when the individual's level of T-helper cells falls drastically.

Without the T-helper cells, which orchestrate many of the components of the immune system, it becomes impossible for

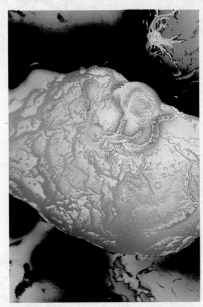

An AIDS virus (orange) budding from the plasma membrane (blue) of an infected T-lymphocyte, viewed through a false-colour electron microscope.

the body to fight off infectious agents. The person falls prey to a variety of *opportunistic infections*, so called because they have taken advantage of the failing immune system. Certain cancers, including the skin cancer known as *Kaposi's sarcoma*, may also develop in AIDS.

Medical scientists studying AIDS have been puzzled by the observation that HIV seems to infect only a very small proportion of T-helper cells circulating in the blood. Even if these infected cells died, the body would produce T cells at such a rate that they would easily be replaced.

One theory to explain the loss is that some effects of the virus on uninfected cells may be to blame. For example, viral proteins circulating in the blood may attach themselves to the cells that HIV attacks. Cytotoxic T cells may then see these cells as infected (even though they are not) and kill them.

HIV infects not only T-helper cells, but also macrophages. Sometimes the virus can multiply within the macrophages to the point where the cells are bursting with viruses. Possibly, the primary defect in AIDS may lie with the macrophages.

SEE ALSO

- REPRODUCTION p. 202
- RESPIRATION AND CIRCULATION p. 210
- GLANDS AND HORMONES p. 214
- NON-INFECTIOUS DISEASES p. 236
- INFECTIOUS DISEASES p. 238
- PREVENTING DISEASE p. 244

response. When T cells meet antigens they respond by multiplying and dividing, releasing molecules that stimulate other cells of the immune system (including other T cells) to grow.

There are many different kinds of T cells. *Cytotoxic T cells* can recognize and kill cells infected with viruses. *T-helper cells* can help macrophages to kill microorganisms. T-helper cells also have an important role in stimulating B cells.

Once stimulated, a B cell multiplies. Its offspring mature into *plasma cells*, which secrete *antibodies*. These are specialized molecules that can latch on to antigens and help the rest of the immune system eliminate the foreign particle. There is potentially an infinite variety of antibodies, one for every conceivable antigen. Once a B cell is stimulated, the result is a *clone* of plasma cells, all dedicated to manufacturing the antibody that recognizes the antigen in question.

Immunity and memory

A few of the cells that result when a B cell divides in response to an antigen are so-called *memory cells*. These remain in the body for life: when the individual meets the same antigen again, they are ready to respond, faster and with more force than before. This explains why people who have one attack of rubella (German measles), for example, are immune to subsequent infections by this virus.

Immunization (see pp. 244–45) works on this principle. Vaccines aim to prime the

immune system to recognize disease-causing organisms, so that it will spring into action when it encounters the microorganisms concerned. Several vaccines consist of bacteria or viruses that have been killed or weakened; they provoke a protective immune response, but no longer have the capacity to cause the disease.

Autoimmune diseases

Many common diseases – for example rheumatoid arthritis (see pp. 206–7) and some types of diabetes mellitus and thyroid disease (see pp. 214–15) are thought to be caused by an *autoimmune response*, in which the body's tissues are attacked by its own antibodies. SK

Severe combined immune deficiency is a rare condition in which the immune system is seriously defective. Even a mild infection can prove fatal to affected children, who can only survive in the sterile environment of a biological isolation unit. This child lived until the age of 8 in a unit at Texas Children's Hospital, USA.

Glands and Hormones

As multicellular organisms evolved, it became necessary to establish ways in which cells could communicate with one another. Two basic mechanisms perform this task: the nervous system (see p. 220) and the *endocrine system*. The latter consists of the endocrine glands, scattered throughout the body. The endocrine glands produce chemicals (*hormones*) that are transported in the blood to distant tissues (*targets*) whose activity they modify. Hormones exert their effects in four broadly defined biological areas: reproduction, growth and development, control of the internal environment and regulation of energy production.

A eunuch of the Turkish Sultan's harem (c. 1800). Castration before puberty results in a lack of the male sex hormone testosterone. Without testosterone, secondary sexual characteristics – body and facial hair, deepening of the voice – fail to develop. Because of their sexual impotence, eunuchs were often employed as servants in harems.

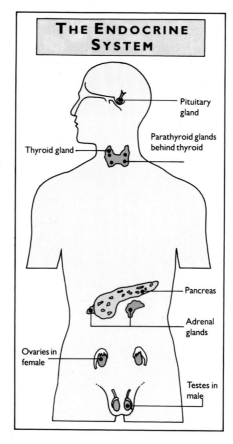

THE ENDOCRINE SYSTEM

Pituitary gland

Parathyroid glands behind thyroid

Thyroid gland

Pancreas

Adrenal glands

Ovaries in female

Testes in male

The first demonstration of hormonal activity came in 1849 when it was noticed that castration caused the loss of secondary sexual characteristics in the cockerel (as a result of the loss of testicular hormones). Since then, a host of different hormones have been identified and a number of disorders resulting from the impairment of endocrine function have been described.

The anterior pituitary

The *pituitary* gland consists of two lobes, anterior and posterior. It sits in a cavity of the skull, underneath the brain, and despite its small size – less than 1 cm in diameter and 0.5 g in weight ($\frac{1}{50}$ oz) – it performs a crucial function within the endocrine system. In particular, by their actions on other glands throughout the body, the hormones of the anterior pituitary play a fundamental role in the control of both reproduction and metabolism. The anterior pituitary is itself controlled by the *hypothalamus*, an area of the brain that receives information about the internal environment of the body and adjusts pituitary output accordingly.

Reproduction

Reproductive function in both sexes is controlled by the anterior pituitary *gona-*

DIABETES MELLITUS

Diabetes is an extremely common and – as yet – incurable metabolic disease. In Western societies 1–2% of the population are affected, while the incidence can reach 15% in certain subpopulations, e.g. Australian Aboriginals and North American Indians.

In many cases the disease is genetically determined but it can also be precipitated by certain viral infections, toxins, chronic disease or pregnancy. In all cases, the primary defect is an absolute or relative deficiency of *pancreatic insulin*. Insulin plays a pivotal role in the control of the metabolism. It allows glucose, which is derived from food, to enter the cells. There it is broken down in order to generate energy for the work of cells; it promotes the synthesis of new protein and suppresses the breakdown of fat.

Insulin deficiency results in profound metabolic derangements, the most consistent of which is *hyperglycaemia* (blood glucose levels above the normal range of 50–120 mg per 100 millilitres). As blood sugar rises, glucose appears in the urine, carrying water with it and giving rise to the increased urine output and thirst that characterize the disorder – *diabetes* is the Greek word for 'syphon'. Fat metabolism may also be enhanced, leading to the accumulation of acidic by-products (keto-acids) which, if unchecked, can result in coma or death.

Many diabetic patients are treated by dietary restrictions and the use of drugs but some are dependent upon daily administration of insulin to control their symptoms. Until recently animal insulins were used, but today, using modern techniques of molecular biology, bacteria can be made to synthesize the human hormone. Administration is either by injection, usually before meals, or continuously using a specially-designed mini-infusion pump.

Although the major clinical manifestations of diabetes can usually be controlled, it is difficult to maintain blood glucose levels within the normal range. Consequently, diabetic patients become susceptible to degenerative complications involving the nerves, eyes, kidneys and blood vessels, and it is these secondary problems that make diabetes such a devastating disease.

dotrophins (FSH and LH) and the *steroid hormones* from ovary or testis. In women, fluctuations of these hormones govern each menstrual cycle, stimulating ovulation and preparing the uterus (womb) for pregnancy (see p. 202). After delivery, *prolactin* and *oxytocin* control milk production and expression. In men, pituitary gonadotrophins are responsible for sperm production and fertility.

The sex steroids also bring about the development of secondary sexual characteristics – beard growth, deep voice and muscle increase in males, and breast development in females. The male steroids are anabolic and are among the banned substances occasionally used by athletes to encourage muscle development and enhance performance.

Growth

Many hormones participate in the coordination of growth, both of individual organs and of the whole body. *Growth hormone* (GH) is particularly important for growth of the skeleton during childhood, while *thyroid hormone* (TH) is crucial for the maturing of the central nervous system. In the absence of thyroid function during early infancy, physical and mental development fail, giving rise to *cretinism* – restricted height and mental retardation. An excess of GH in adult life leads to *acromegaly*, characterized by abnormal thickening of bones and soft tissues.

The internal environment

For the body to function efficiently its internal environment – for example, the volume and composition of the blood – must be carefully controlled. A multitude of hormones participate in such regulation. *Antidiuretic hormone* from the posterior pituitary and *aldosterone* from the cortex of the adrenal gland regulate the excretion of water and salt by the kidney; *parathyroid hormone*, together with vitamin D, controls the level of the minerals calcium and phosphorus in the blood, while the functions of liver, muscle and fat are influenced by GH, insulin, glucagon, adrenaline, sex steroids and cortisol.

Metabolism

The body must convert food into usable energy while storing part of that energy for use in times of fasting. The pancreatic hormones *insulin* and *glucagon* have key roles to play here. In addition, *thyroxine* stimulates metabolism, helping to generate large amounts of energy in the form of heat. People with thyroid insufficiency suffer a variety of metabolic disorders – including extreme cold sensitivity and mental slowing – while in Graves disease (overactive thyroid) metabolic rate is elevated and the patient loses weight and feels hot, hyperactive and anxious.

Hormone secretion

The output of a hormone is usually regulated so as to allow a response to a biological need without a prolonged high

level of secretion. Hormones or the effects they produce often inhibit their own output by negative feedback – their secretion is self-limiting. Many hormones are released in response to stress, while some show a daily (*circadian*) pattern. ACTH and the adrenal cortical hormones show such a 24-hour rhythm, with a peak occurring in the early morning, probably to prepare the body for the stress of getting up. The symptoms of jet lag (see p. 232) may be due to the desynchronization of daily activity with hormonal rhythms.

Measurement of hormones

Hormones are present in tiny amounts in body fluids but modern techniques allow many of them to be measured accurately. Pregnancy, for example, is confirmed by the presence of *human chorionic gonadotrophin* (HGC) in urine, while the success of *in vitro* (test tube) fertilization relies on the accurate detection of pituitary gonadotrophins and ovarian hormones. The presence of certain tumours can be detected from abnormal levels of hormones in the blood. GP

MAJOR GLANDS AND THEIR HORMONES

Gland	Hormone	Chief Target Tissue
Brain (hypothalamus)	Releasing hormones responsible for controlling output of anterior pituitary hormones, e.g. thyrotropin releasing hormone (TRH), which stimulates secretion of TSH.	Anterior pituitary
Anterior pituitary	Gonadotrophins (luteinizing hormone, LH; follicle-stimulating hormone, FSH)	Gonads (ovaries and testes)
	Prolactin	Breast
	Adrenocorticotrophic hormone (ACTH)	Adrenal cortex
	Thyroid stimulating hormone (TSH)	Thyroid gland
	Growth hormone (GH)	Most cells
Posterior pituitary	Antidiuretic hormone (ADH)	Kidney
	Oxytocin	Breast
Thyroid gland	Thryoxine	Most cells
Adrenal cortex	Steroids: cortisol	Most cells
	aldosterone	Kidney
Ovaries and testes	Sex steroids: oestrogens progesterone testosterone	Reproductive system
Placenta	Sex steroids, human chorionic gonadotrophins (HCG)	Uterus, breast
Pancreas	Insulin and glucagon	Most cells
Parathyroid glands	Parathyroid hormone (PTH)	Bone, kidney
Adrenal medulla	Adrenaline, noradrenaline	Heart, blood vessels

SEE ALSO

● REPRODUCTION p. 202
● PHYSICAL DEVELOPMENT p. 204
● FOOD, DIET AND DIGESTION p. 208
● RESPIRATION AND CIRCULATION p. 210
● NON-INFECTIOUS DISEASES p. 236

Crystals of progesterone – (left) a female sex hormone – seen through a polarized light microscope.

Touch, Taste and Smell

The skin covers the body completely, forming a waterproof, protective coat that constitutes the first barrier to invading organisms (see p. 212). It also has sensory and excretory functions, and plays an important part in regulating body temperature. The skin continues in a modified form in the mucous membrane, which lines the nose, mouth and digestive tract. Like the skin, the senses of smell and taste have a protective function and can alert us to the presence of, for example, food that has gone bad.

The skin is composed of two layers – the epidermis and the dermis – with a layer of fatty tissue underneath. The *epidermis*, or outer layer, itself consists of several layers. Replacement cells are required as the surface cells are shed or rubbed off continuously. The lowest layer or *stratum basale* contains constantly dividing cells, providing new cells that rise through the layers, gradually becoming flattened and finally reaching the *stratum corneum* – the outermost layer, in which the cells are flat, thin and filled with the fibrous protein *keratin*. The epidermis derives oxygen and nutrients from the interstitial fluid (see p. 210).

The *dermis* is the layer of living tissue, and consists of connective tissue with blood capillaries, lymph vessels, sensory nerve endings, sweat glands and pores, hair follicles and sebaceous glands.

Touch

The sense of touch is primarily exploratory. Buried within the skin and other exposed surfaces, such as the eyeball and the mouth, are the *sensory nerve endings*, which have lost their protective myelin sheath (see p. 220) and branch out into fine filaments. These are responsible for telling the brain what is in contact with the body and alerting the brain to specific sensations – pressure, warmth, cold and pain. An electrical response is produced in the stimulated nerve ending, and this travels up the sensory fibres of a nerve to the *cortex* or outer layer of the brain (see p. 222). Certain areas – such as the lips, palms of the hands, soles of the feet and the genitalia – have a far greater concentration of nerve endings than, for example, the skin on the back and are thus more sensitive than other areas.

Specific areas of the brain are responsible for the sense of touch or pain in certain areas of skin. If, at any point in its journey, the nerve is damaged, then the electrical impulse will not be able to travel and the area from which the impulse came will feel numb.

The sensation of touch is not dependent solely on nerve impulses travelling up to the brain. The brain can be selective in what it does with this information, and in some cases can decide to ignore it (see box). It can, for instance, decide to get 'used' to the more repetitive stimuli, such as the weight of clothes on the body, and will cease to register them unless its attention is focused on them specifically.

Hair

The skin also contains hairs, whose roots (*hair follicles*) are embedded in the dermis and expand at their base to form bulbs, which contain dividing cells. Newly formed cells push older cells upwards; these are converted to keratin and form the root and shaft of the hair. Nerves attached to the follicles are activated every time the hair moves, telling the brain that it has just been touched. The *sebaceous glands* are associated with the hair follicle and produce *sebum* or oil, which lubricates the hair and skin.

Temperature regulation

The skin is able to regulate body temperature by means of the sweat glands and pores. The *eccrine* sweat glands, present throughout the skin but more numerous in the palms of the hands, soles of the feet, armpits and groin, produce sweat, which is released through the sweat pores. The evaporation of sweat from the skin cools the body (see latent heat, p. 25). It also has an excretory function, in that it carries away wastes such as urea and lactic acid. The amount of sweat produced is controlled by the hypothalamus (see p. 214). The *apocrine* sweat glands, situated in the armpits and genital areas, produce a thicker secretion and do not become active until puberty. The action of bacteria on apocrine sweat is capable of causing a strong odour.

Smell

In humans, the sense of smell is relatively under-developed when compared to that of the dog or the pig, for example, which depend on it to a far greater extent.

The sense of smell is derived from tiny nerve endings that pass through the *cribriform plate* from the *olfactory nerve* at the base of the brain into the damp lining of the nose, known as the *nasal mucosa*. This mucous membrane contains thousands of tiny glands whose job it is to produce the wet, sticky substance known as *mucus*. Microscopic hairs – *cilia* – direct the mucus back towards the throat, where it is swallowed. Infection by the common cold virus irritates the lining of the nose, which then produces an excess of mucus.

Substances that have an odour give off molecules, which are present in the air and are breathed in. They dissolve in the

A sweat pore from the palm of a man's hand, viewed through a false-colour electron microscope (magnification 180). The skin on human hands is arranged in ridges, with sweat pores appearing as miniature depressions tunnelling into the ridges.

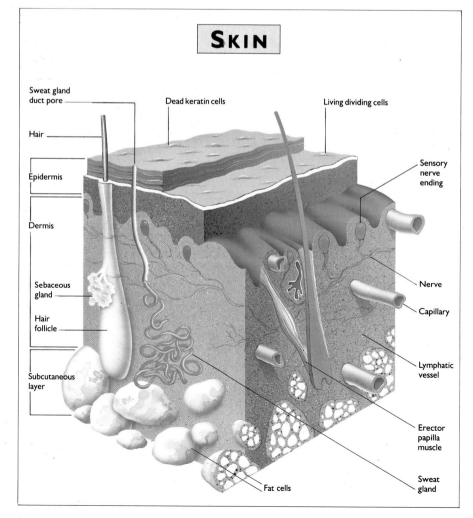

SKIN

Sweat gland duct pore

Dead keratin cells

Living dividing cells

Hair

Epidermis

Sensory nerve ending

Dermis

Sebaceous gland

Nerve

Hair follicle

Capillary

Subcutaneous layer

Lymphatic vessel

Erector papilla muscle

Sweat gland

Fat cells

PAIN

Pain results from the stimulation of nerve fibres in the skin or internally. The sensation of pain can vary from a mild ache to an overpowering agony. Itching is considered to be a very mild form of painful stimulus.

Research has shown that pain stimuli travel at different speeds within these nerves, hence the sensation of 'double pain'. If a finger is put in scalding water there will be sudden, sharp, 'first pain' followed a few moments later by a duller 'second pain'. The first pain is carried quickly in one sort of nerve fibre (A fibres), the second more slowly in another (C fibres).

Pain receptors in the brain are called *nociceptors*. They respond very quickly to the chemicals that are released from damaged cells. This sensitivity to chemicals allows pain to be treated using pain-killing chemical drugs (*analgesics*) such as aspirin.

The brain plays an immensely important role in the perception of pain. Indian 'fakirs' for instance sleep on beds of nails or apparently walk over smouldering coals in their bare feet without apparently feeling anything. How can this be?

The concept of pain 'tolerance' is important here. A person can put up with almost any degree of pain depending on their state of mind.

An interesting experiment along these lines was carried out in the 1960s by an American professor. He allowed his students to lower a slowly turning drill onto the backs of their hand. He then assessed how much pressure and pain they could withstand. Many appeared to be able to withstand a good deal.

He then allowed the students to rest and to think about what had gone on, then invited them to repeat the experiment. Armed with the knowledge of what it had felt like at the last attempt, all the students found they could now stand only a fraction of the pain that they had happily stood before. Their pain tolerance was much lower than before.

At its most extreme, this tolerance of pain allows the body to deal with major injuries that occur in war or in severe accidents. Many victims claims they feel nothing immediately following the injury, and only later begin to experience the pain.

Pain may sometimes be felt in an area of the body some distance away from the part actually damaged or diseased – for instance, a pain resulting from heart disease is often felt across the chest and down the left arm. This phenomenon is known as *referred pain*, and results from the fact that sensory nerves from different parts of the body share the same pathways in the spinal cord. *Phantom limb pain* is often felt by people who have lost limbs: an itch or pain is felt in a part that is no longer there. These phantom sensations are caused by the cut sensory nerves continuing to send messages to the brain.

Pain tolerance: a woman walking across burning coals.

SMELL

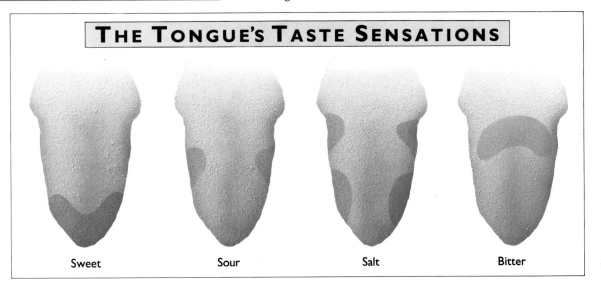

Frontal sinus

Olfactory nerves passing through the cribriform plate of the ethmoid bone to the olfactory bulb of cranial nerve

Specialized nasal mucosa for detecting smell

Palate

Tongue

Sensory nerves from the taste buds reach the central nervous system through branches of the facial, glossopharyngeal and vagus nerves (cranial nerves VII, IX and X).

SEE ALSO

● ANIMAL COMMUNICATION p. 166
● SEEING AND HEARING p. 218
● THE NERVOUS SYSTEM p. 220

when suffering from a cold. This condition is known as *anosmia* and, while it may not hinder the ability to operate effectively, it is potentially dangerous since smell is relied on to detect such things as gas leaks, fire or food that has gone off.

Taste

Taste is a complex sensation. The tongue can distinguish between only four basic tastes: sweet, sour, salt and bitter – and nothing else. The surface of the tongue is covered with small projections called *papillae*, which contain the nerve endings concerned with the sense of taste. These specialized sensory receptors – the *taste buds* – are stimulated by particles of food dissolving in the saliva. Nerve impulses are sent to the brain via the facial nerve and the glossopharyngeal nerve. The range of tastes normally associated with food depends, in fact, more on the sense of smell than on that of taste – people who lose their sense of smell notice that their food suddenly tastes bland and uninteresting.   MG

nasal mucus, thereby stimulating the olfactory nerve. This information is then passed back to the olfactory lobes in the brain and also to a primitive part of the brain called the limbic system or *rhinencephalon*.

In lower animals the olfactory lobes are very large, sometimes making up over half the brain mass. Undoubtedly these animals produce smell 'pictures' by which they feed and find a mate (see also pp. 166–7). Hence the importance dogs, for instance, place on 'marking' their territory (see also pp. 168–9). Most animals, including humans, produce certain fatty acids called *pheromones*, which attract members of the opposite sex.

Some people lose their sense of smell completely – permanently, for instance as the result of an accident, or temporarily,

THE TONGUE'S TASTE SENSATIONS

Sweet

Sour

Salt

Bitter

Seeing and Hearing

**Sight and hearing are the key senses, giving vital inform-
ation about what is going on in the world around us and
allowing our bodies to react appropriately. The eye is the
dominant sense organ, situated in the orbital cavity and
supplied by the optic nerve. The eyeballs, measuring about
2.5 cm (1 in) in diameter, function as a pair – each sees a
slightly different version of the object being looked at. This
3-D or stereoscopic vision is particularly important in order
to judge distances, and hence to judge at what speed things
are travelling.**

The *sclera*, or white of the eye, is a firm
membrane that forms the outer layer of
the eyeball. At the front of the eye it
continues as the *cornea*, a transparent
convex membrane that refracts the light
rays to focus on the *retina* (see below). The
lacrimal glands, situated in recesses just
above each eye, secrete tears composed of
water, salts and the bacteria-killing
enzyme *lysozyme*. The eyelids form a pair
of protective shutters, closing instantly if
injury is feared; the eyelids also spread
tears over the cornea, keeping it moist
and free from infection. The *choroid*,
which is rich in blood vessels, lines the
inner surface of the sclera.

The *ciliary body*, which continues from
the choroid, consists of muscle fibres and
is connected to the *suspensory ligament*,
which is attached at its other end to a
capsule containing the *lens* (see below).
The *iris* – the part of the eye that regulates
the amount of light that enters – lies
behind the cornea in front of the lens. It
forms a pigmented muscular body with a
central aperture, the *pupil*, which varies
in size depending on the intensity of light.
In bright light the circular muscle fibres
of the iris contract, causing the pupil to
constrict; in dim light a set of radiating
muscle fibres contract and the pupil
dilates. The *lens*, a transparent crystalline structure, is enclosed in a thin clear
capsule and situated behind the pupil. It
bends light rays reflected by objects in
front of the eye. It is highly elastic,
changing focus by increasing or decreasing its thickness – this is brought about by
contraction of the *ciliary muscle*. The
nearer the object, the thicker the lens
needs to be in order to bring it into focus.
The chamber behind the cornea and in
front of the lens is filled with a watery
fluid known as *aqueous humour*, while the
chamber behind the lens contains a jelly-
like substance, the *vitreous humour*.

The *retina* is the light-sensitive layer
lining the eye. It contains nerve fibres and
specialized cells – *rods* and *cones*. The
rods, numbering about 125 million, are
essential for seeing in dim light. They
contain a pigment known as *visual purple*,
which is broken down in the light and
regenerated in the dark. The 6–7 million
cones function in bright light and are
necessary for sharp vision; they are most

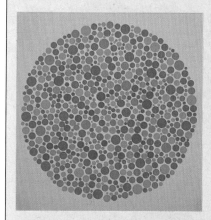
concentrated in the *fovea* – a small
depression in the retina.

To allow vision in different directions
without turning the head, the eye can be
swivelled around in its socket by a
complex set of *ocular muscles*.

The brain and vision

The human eye is similar in structure to a
camera (see p. 324) and the principles of
vision lie within the basic physical theories of optics (see p. 32). The light image
focused by the lens onto the retina is
converted into electrical impulses, which
are then transmitted to the brain via the
optic nerve. These electrical messages
from the nasal half of each retina actually
cross to opposite sides of the head en route
for the brain (see p. 230). Because visual
images are split in this way, it can mean
that, if a person has an injury to one side
of the head, rather than losing all the
sight from the right or the left eye, half the
sight is lost from each. Those who suffer
migraine may sometimes experience this.

Once inside the brain, the electrical
image of what the eyes are looking at must
be interpreted according to the brain's
past experience, so that the image can be
'recognized' (see also p. 224). If the eye is
shown a table, for instance, the brain will
receive electrical messages telling it that
something with a horizontal surface and
four vertical legs is present. The brain
sorts through all the other images it has

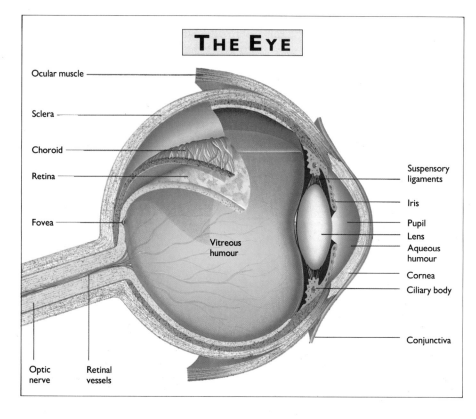

THE EYE

Ocular muscle

Sclera

Choroid

Retina

Fovea

Vitreous
humour

Suspensory
ligaments

Iris

Pupil

Lens

Aqueous
humour

Cornea

Ciliary body

Conjunctiva

Optic
nerve

Retinal
vessels

SEE ALSO
- ACOUSTICS p. 30
- OPTICS p. 32
- PERCEPTION p. 224
- THE POWER OF SPEECH p. 226
- LEARNING, CREATIVITY AND INTELLIGENCE p. 230

seen that resemble this – four-legged animals, beds, etc. – eventually matching it up with a table seen in the past and giving it a label. Although complicated, the process takes only a fraction of a second. Even today, the most advanced computers can do nothing so complex so quickly.

Visual impairment

The most common reasons for not being able to see properly are *myopia* (short sight) and *hypermetropia* (long sight). Short-sighted people find that objects get progressively more blurred the further away they are because parallel light rays are brought to a focus in front of the retina. The condition can be corrected by spectacles with concave lenses. In the case of long sight, parallel light rays are brought to a focus behind the retina, so that close objects appear blurred. Wearing spectacles with convex lenses can restore normal sight. *Presbyopia*, a condition common in later life, is caused by a gradual loss of elasticity in the lens – it becomes less able to increase its curvature in order to focus on near objects.

Cataract is also a common cause of poor sight. The lens begins to become opaque, and the condition may eventually prevent any light coming through at all. Cataract is particularly common in later life – it

THE EAR

Semicircular canals

Auditory nerve (Cranial nerve VIII)

Auditory ossicles in middle ear (malleus, incus and stapes).

Cochlea

Eustachian tube leading to nasopharynx

Eardrum

External auditory canal

The auditory ossicles, seen here through a false-colour electron microscope, are the bones responsible for the conduction of sound waves in the middle ear. At the top left is the *malleus* (hammer), which strikes the *incus* (anvil), seen to the right of the malleus. The incus is joined to the *stapes* (stirrup), which conducts sound towards the inner ear. The stapes is the smallest bone in the body, measuring 2.6–3.4 mm (0.10–0.17 in). Sound waves entering the ear cause the eardrum to vibrate and the bones transmit the vibrations to the structures of the inner ear – the footplate of the stapes presses into the fluid-filled *scala vestibuli* of the cochlea, which converts vibrations into nerve impulses.

may be congenital, or may be due to a metabolic disease such as diabetes. It can be treated by surgical removal of the lens.

Glaucoma, or tunnel vision, is an inherited condition in which the pressure of fluid within the eye builds up, thus destroying the nerve cells in the retina. Eventually only a small patch of nerve cells in the centre of the retina remains, giving the sufferer the sensation of constantly looking down a tube.

Hearing

The ability to hear has two elements – a mechanical element and an element involving electrical nerve impulses. Sound enters through the *external ear* or *auricle* – that part of the ear that is visible. Its scalloped shape ensures that as much sound as possible is reflected into the inside of the ear. In some mammals the ear can actually be swivelled round to face the point from which the maximum amount of noise is coming.

Inside the ear, sound travels down a short tube, the *external acoustic meatus*, until it hits a very thin sheet of skin called the *eardrum* or *tympanic membrane*. The mechanical force of the sound waves (see p. 30) sets the eardrum vibrating. This vibration is then transmitted across the cavity, or *middle ear*, on the other side of the eardrum by a series of tiny bones (*auditory ossicles*), which form a series of movable joints with each other. The *stapes* is a stirrup-shaped bone; the *incus*, an anvil-shaped bone, is situated in the middle, and the *malleus*, a hammer-shaped bone, is in contact with the tympanic membrane.

Beyond the middle ear is the *inner ear* or *cochlea*. This helix-shaped structure is basically a fluid-filled tube lined with nerve endings. Like many musical instruments, it is wider at one end in order to pick up low-pitched sounds and narrower at the other in order to pick up high-pitched ones.

The *semicircular canals*, three tubes that open into the inner ear, are not connected with hearing but are concerned with balance. Each canal registers movement in a different plane and sends nerve impulses to the brain. The semicircular canals are thus essential in establishing our sense of physical position.

If the vibrations passing through the ear are at any stage impeded – perhaps by a burst eardrum, by damage to the ossicles of the middle ear or by degeneration of the nerves taking the sound messages to the brain, then the individual will become partially or completely deaf in that ear. Children are particularly susceptible to middle-ear infections, and these can frequently lead to eardrum damage. The drum will eventually heal and hearing will be restored, but if the child experiences too many such infections the drum will become scarred and unable to vibrate properly, causing permanent partial deafness.

Elderly people often become slightly deaf because of degeneration of the auditory nerve cells. Hearing aids can be used to boost the sound impulse, thus helping the nerve cells that remain to pick up more of the sound vibration.   MG

The Nervous System

The nervous system is a vast, complex network that regulates every aspect of human life and endeavour, from breathing to running a marathon. The system weaves throughout the body, picking up, interpreting and acting upon data both from outside and from within.

Governing the network is the *central nervous system* (CNS), consisting of the brain (see p. 222) and spinal cord. The role of the CNS is largely to do with sensations and voluntary movement. Messages passing to and from the CNS are carried by way of the branching fibres of the *peripheral nervous system*, which reaches all the way to the body extremities.

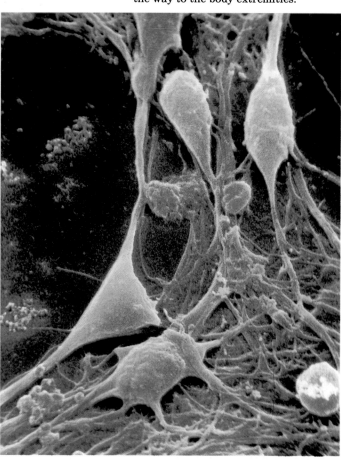

Neurones (nerve cells) from the cerebral cortex, seen through a false-colour electron microscope. Neurones exist in different sizes and shapes throughout the nervous system, but all have a similar basic structure. From the cell body, which contains the nucleus, extend several *processes*: the nerve fibre or *axon* carries impulses away from the cell body, while the *dendrites* (which vary in number) receive impulses from other neurones.

The nerve cell

The basic functional unit of the nervous system is the nerve cell or *neurone*. From the cell body containing the nucleus, branching outgrowths called *processes* trail in all directions. The cell's longest process – its 'main cable' – is the *axon*, which carries outgoing signals. An axon may extend all the way from the CNS to a finger or toe to connect with the muscle on which it acts. Processes known as *dendrites*, which vary in number, pick up messages from other cells.

Axons are like telephone cables, in that they have a central electrical conductor surrounded by an insulating layer. The high electrical resistance of the core, and the thinness of the membrane, would cause simple electrical signals to die out over very short distances. This difficulty is overcome by actively regenerating the signals into discrete, all-or-nothing, on-or-off electrical impulses (as in a digital computer) that are continuously renewed and kept up to strength throughout their transmission.

COMMUNICATING CELLS

The functional unit of nervous tissue is the nerve cell or *neurone*. There are billions of these in the central nervous system (CNS). They vary greatly in shape and size, but all communicate electrochemically with their neighbours, forming an intricate network that far outstrips in complexity the circuitry of the most advanced electronic computer.

Neurones can be classified into three types: *interneurones* lie entirely within the CNS, while sensory or *afferent* and motor or *efferent* neurones have segments outside the CNS. In response to physical or chemical stimuli, receptors at the far ends of the afferent neurones send impulses to the CNS. Efferent neurones conduct signals outwards from the CNS to target tissues, such as muscles. The interneurones, which are by far the most numerous nerve cells in the CNS, form highly complex connections between the terminations of sensory nerves in the CNS and the origins of motor nerves. Higher activities – such as language – involve millions of interneuronal pathways.

The neurone consists of a cell body, with its nucleus, and projecting filaments – the *dendrites* and the *axon*. These may show extensive branching, and sometimes carry information over long distances in the body. Information is coded as discrete electrical impulses in the neurones. The nature of the information transmitted depends on which particular set of anatomical pathways is being activated, and the intensity or magnitude of the signal depends on the frequency of impulses and the number of pathways carrying the message. The axon terminates at the *synapse* – the junction where it makes contact with the dendrites or cell bodies of other neurones, or with secretory cells or muscle cells. At the synapse, the electrical signal in the axon causes the release of a small amount of a chemical transmitter – such as *acetylcholine* or *noradrenaline* – which carries the message to the next cell.

There is a profusion of known neurotransmitters, which enable nerve cells to communicate with each other. Acetylcholine and noradrenaline are the best known, but there is a whole range of substances, including quite complex

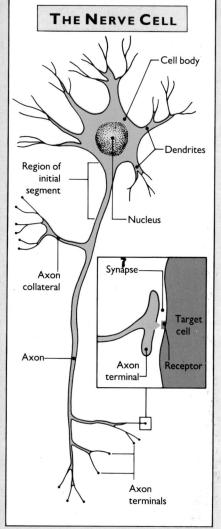

THE NERVE CELL

- Cell body
- Dendrites
- Nucleus
- Region of initial segment
- Axon collateral
- Axon
- Synapse
- Target cell
- Axon terminal
- Receptor
- Axon terminals

molecules such as peptides, that may be released from nerve-cell terminals in the CNS. Transmitters generally stimulate the adjacent cell, but sometimes they inhibit some on-going activity. Some chemical substances produce much more diffuse effects, acting beyond the immediate vicinity of the cells from which they were released, changing the levels of excitability in whole groups of neurones. They are not neurotransmitters in the true sense of the word, since their action is not confined to the synapse where they were released; they are therefore described as neuromodulators.

SEE ALSO

● TOUCH, TASTE AND SMELL
  p. 216
● SEEING AND HEARING p. 218
● THE BRAIN p. 222

THE NERVOUS SYSTEM: ANATOMY

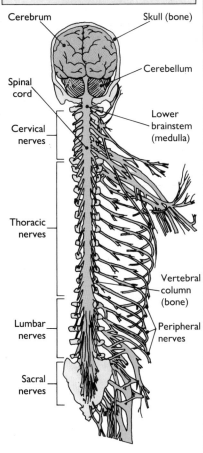

The human nervous system (shown from behind) comprises two major divisions: the *central nervous system* (CNS), which consists of the brain and spinal cord, and the *peripheral nervous system*, which consists of cranial nerves (12 pairs) and spinal nerves (31 pairs) arising from the CNS. Shown here are the spinal nerves; not shown are the cranial nerves, which derive from the brain.

Smaller axons conduct impulses smoothly and slowly – about 1 m (3¼ ft) per second – but larger fibres have specially increased layers of insulation, made up of the fatty substance known as *myelin*. In these myelinated fibres conduction is much faster – up to 100 m (328 ft) per second. Loss of the myelin sheath, in a disease such as multiple sclerosis, blocks or greatly slows down conduction.

The peripheral nervous system

The central nervous system communicates with the peripheral nervous system through 12 pairs of cranial nerves and 31 pairs of spinal nerves, which leave the brain and spinal cord. It is these fibres that eventually make their way to the body extremities.

Individual fibres in a nerve may arise from either afferent or efferent neurones. *Afferent neurones* are those carrying signals towards the CNS, while outgoing signals are conducted by *efferent neurones*. Groups of afferent fibres enter the spinal cord at the rear, where they form the dorsal roots; efferent fibres leave the spinal cord at the front, by way of the ventral roots.

The efferent fibres of the peripheral nervous system are divided into the *somatic* (bodily) *nervous system* and the *autonomic* (self-regulating) *nervous system*. Somatic fibres activate skeletal (voluntary) muscle control, whereas autonomic fibres act on smooth or involuntary muscle (such as that found in the gut), as well as cardiac muscle and the various internal organs and glands (see pp. 206 and 214).

Because the activity of the neurones in the somatic nervous system leads to contraction of muscles, they are often called *motor neurones*. Damage to the cell bodies of motor neurones, which are present in clusters in the brain and spinal cord, results in impaired movement.

The autonomic system

The autonomic nervous system, concerned with involuntary function, breaks down further into the *sympathetic* and *parasympathetic nervous systems*. These two components, often present in the same gland or organ, keep each other in check. Broadly, the sympathetic division takes over when rapid action is needed. It enables the appropriate circulatory, metabolic and other adjustments to be made in order to engage in 'fight, flight or fright'.

The autonomic system has been called the 'involuntary nervous system' because of its role in controlling physiological events in which normally there is no conscious input. These include routine matters of body maintenance, such as breathing, heart rate, blood flow, temperature control, digestion, glandular secretion and excretion.   PP

The Russian physiologist *Ivan Petrovitch Pavlov* (1849–1936), who developed the concept of the *conditioned reflex*. The autonomic nervous system is involved in reflexes that depend on sensory input to the brain or spinal cord; these reflexes are coordinated in the brain without conscious control. In the case of a conditioned reflex, a response occurs not to the stimulus that usually causes it but to another stimulus that has been learned to be associated with it. Pavlov experimented with dogs and showed that nerves stimulated by the presence of food carried a message to the brain which, via other nerves, stimulated the secretion of saliva. He then demonstrated that, if a bell is rung every time a dog is shown food, it will eventually salivate every time the bell rings, even when no food is present.

The Brain

The brain is a highly developed, dense mass of nerve cells that forms the upper end of the central nervous system. An adult brain weighs on average 1400g (49 oz), constituting about 2% of the total body weight. Nerve cells without myelin sheaths (see p. 220) form the 'grey matter' of the brain, while those with myelin form the 'white matter'.

Nervous tissue is composed of two types of cells: the *neurones*, which are the basic functional units of the nervous system (see p. 220), and, sustaining and supporting them, the non-communicating *glial cells* (or *neuroglia*). Both the brain and the spinal cord are encased in bone and further protected by three encircling membranes, the *meninges*. The *cerebrospinal fluid* (CSF), derived from the choroid plexuses and circulating in the cerebral ventricles, helps to cushion delicate nerve tissue.

Divisions of the brain

The brain has three major divisions. The *brainstem* and *cerebellum* are basic structures concerned with life-support, posture and coordination of movement. The *forebrain* (see below) is relatively more developed in humans than in other species. The brainstem – the oldest structure in evolutionary terms – forms the stalk of the brain, where vital functions such as breathing and circulation are integrated.

The cerebellum, like the cerebrum (see below), consists of two hemispheres, one on either side. Also like the cerebrum, it has a grey outer covering (*cortex*) with a core of white matter. The cerebellum is chiefly involved with the coordination of movement. It ensures coherent muscle function and tone and helps to maintain posture.

The forebrain

Overlying these structures is the forebrain, consisting of a central core (the *diencephalon*) and the *cortex*. Key landmarks in the diencephalon include the *thalamus*, a relay station and integrating centre for sensory messages on their way to the cerebral cortex (see below). Below it lies the *hypothalamus*, which is responsible for regulating the body's internal environment (see p. 215).

In human beings the great mass of the brain is formed by the *cerebrum*, separated by a deep cleft into two *cerebral hemispheres*, which are linked at the bottom by a communicating bridge, the *corpus callosum*. Each cerebral hemisphere has specialized functions (see box, and p. 230).

The cerebrum is the most recently evolved part of the brain, responsible for intelligence, intellectual and creative skills and memory. The *cerebral cortex* (or 'grey matter'), the fissured outer layer of the cerebrum, processes information that reaches it from the thalamus and other lower centres.

The higher centres

The cerebral cortex, then, is the most sophisticated part of the brain, where incoming information of all kinds is processed. The cortex sifts, sorts and generally makes sense of the vast mass of stimuli flooding in from the periphery. It organizes these data into the intelligible sights, sounds, impressions and thoughts that are needed to cope with daily living. The cortex therefore perceives and comprehends. It also initiates, for it is here that decisions are taken and instructions are issued for their implementation.

Anatomists divide the cerebral cortex into four lobes – the frontal, parietal, temporal and occipital lobes, all named after the skull plates beneath which they lie. The *frontal lobe*, extending back behind the forehead and temples, is the largest of the four, as well as the newest in evolutionary terms. Not surprisingly, therefore, it bears the greatest responsibilities and is regarded as the seat of the most advanced mental processes. The frontal lobe governs all voluntary actions, from the simplest physical movements to the intricate matters of thought, language and speech.

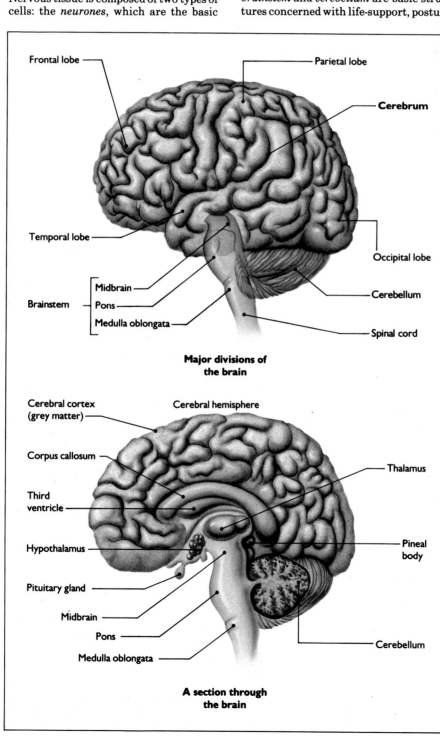

Major divisions of the brain

A section through the brain

SEE ALSO

● THE NERVOUS SYSTEM
  p. 220
● PERCEPTION p. 224
● THE POWER OF SPEECH
  p. 226
● LEARNING, CREATIVITY AND
  INTELLIGENCE p. 230
● SLEEP AND DREAMS p. 232
● MENTAL DISORDERS p. 234
● ARTIFICIAL INTELLIGENCE
  AND CYBERNETICS p. 336

THE INJURED BRAIN

The 4th-century Greek philosopher Aristotle (see p. 487) took a dim view of the brain. He believed that the sole purpose of the brain was to cool the blood; the heart, he said, was the seat of the soul. In this he was out of step with many early physicians, who recognized the pre-eminence of the brain. They came to this realization not least through observing that disorders of mental functioning can result from physical injury to the head and brain. Blows to the head, the growth of brain tumours, or impairment of the brain's blood supply (as in a stroke) can all have serious effects upon our ability to speak and understand, to recognize objects and people, to perform skilled actions or remember past events.

Disorders of language after brain damage (*aphasia*) come in many forms (see also pp. 226–7). The brain-injured person may, for example, no longer be able to formulate coherent sentences. Asked to detail the history of his early life, one man said simply: 'School, marbles, farm, errands, engineer, Glasgow, Philadelphia'. Perhaps we are to gather from this that he enjoyed playing marbles at school, he grew up on a farm and ran errands, trained as an engineer in Glasgow and emigrated to Philadelphia.

Problems with perception and recognition (*agnosia*) are common after brain damage, even in people with intact vision. Such a person, for instance, might be able to copy a drawing accurately, but be quite unable to recognize what object they had drawn.

Some neurological patients can recognize common objects, but have specific problems identifying faces. They may not recognize the faces of family members or even their own reflections in a mirror. In this condition (*prosopagnosia*) the person knows a face is a face, but has no idea which one, and is forced to identify individuals by voice or by particular articles of clothing.

A more common consequence of brain damage is *visual neglect*. Despite having free movement of the head and eyes, the brain-injured person ignores information from one half of the visual field. In extreme cases, he or she may only eat the food on one side of the plate, or shave or apply make-up to just one side of the face.

Sometimes the capacity to sequence actions correctly, or to direct them appropriately in three-dimensional space, is impaired. Asked to demonstrate how to brush the teeth, the patient may make an accurate brushing movement, but do so nearer the forehead than the mouth. Or, asked to make a cup of tea, he or she may tip the sugar into the milk jug, stir the water in the kettle with a spoon, and pour the milk into the kettle.

Although none of us have perfect memories, we can remember what we had for breakfast or where we went on holiday. Some forms of brain damage impair these autobiographical memories (*retrograde amnesia*). In severe cases, a doctor can talk to a patient for half an hour, leave for 10 minutes, and return to find that the patient has no recollection of ever having seen them before.

Alcoholism is a common cause of brain damage, in that it destroys areas responsible for the acquisition, storage and retrieval of experienced events. There is often a 'temporal gradient' to retrograde loss of memory, so that events from the distant past may be remembered better than more recent ones. Not all forms of learning are impaired in *anterograde amnesia*. A patient who solves the same jigsaw day after day may become progressively faster at it, without possessing any memory of having seen it before.

These very specific types of cognitive impairment can be seen in people whose knowledge, skill and ability in other areas is intact. In fact it was from observations of brain-damaged patients that doctors first began mapping the brain, assigning particular functions to its various areas. For instance, the brain appears to be a paired organ: two apparently identical hemispheres connected by a large fibre-tract, the corpus callosum. So we might expect the two half-brains to be equivalent in terms of what they do. Yet the 19th-century French physician *Paul Broca* (1824–80) noted that language disorder typically follows damage to the left (and not the right) hemisphere.

At about the same time, the English neurologist *John Hughlings Jackson* (1835–1911) observed that many disorders of visio-spatial perception were associated with right-hemisphere damage. In our own time this notion of 'hemispheric specialization' has been confirmed in patients who have had the corpus callosum surgically severed (for the relief of intractable epilepsy). In these patients, two brains – and perhaps two minds with different capacities, thoughts and feelings – coexist in one body.

There is further specialization of function within a hemisphere of the brain. In the right hemisphere, visual neglect of the left half of space is associated with damage at the rear, while frontal regions (of both hemispheres) are involved in more general functions involved in the planning and regulation of behaviour. In the left hemisphere, different areas are concerned with the expression and the comprehension of language, and yet other areas with the organization of skilled movements. Some capacities, including autobiographical memory, are represented equally in both hemispheres.   JMa

The size of each body part in this distorted photograph indicates the size of the area of the brain given over to controlling that part. (Colorific/Grodsinsky/Life Magazine)

contain the centres for auditory perception, with both ears represented on each side of the brain. If one of the temporal lobes is damaged, hearing is not lost, as vision is if one of the *occipital lobes* comes to harm. The smallest of the four, at the rear of the cortex, the occipital lobes receive and process visual images.

Since the information from one sense alone does not always give us a complete picture, all incoming signals are supplemented by, and integrated with, other data being processed simultaneously. This integration process, fulfilled by what are known as *association areas* in the cortex, gives us total awareness of our surroundings.

Instinctive behaviour and emotions

The *limbic system* is the oldest part of the forebrain and consists of a rim of cerebral cortex around the stalk of each central hemisphere, together with a group of deeper structures concerned with instinctive behaviour and the emotional and physical changes that accompany them. These include sexual drive, thirst, hunger, fear and anger.   PP

Behind the frontal lobes are the *parietal lobes*, straddling each hemisphere towards the rear. Within the parietal lobes are the primary reception areas for the sensation of touch, as well as zones associated with spatial perception (recognition of body position). Damage in these areas would plunge us into a topsy-turvy world.

Running along the base of the parietal lobes, the *temporal lobes* lie approximately on a level with the ears. They

Perception

How the brain experiences the world of objects through information from the senses – sight, hearing, taste, smell and touch – forms the study of *perception*. Perception has evolved from the reflexes of the most primitive animals, and is also present to some degree in plants, many of which sense gravity to grow upright and grow towards sunlight (see p. 117); some even have touch-sensitive tendrils.

The study of human perception is important for medicine, because perception can go wrong. For example, schizophrenia (see pp. 234–5) is associated with visual and auditory hallucinations: knowing why this is so may help the understanding of schizophrenia and its causes. It is important for art, for problems such as dyslexia, for skills such as flying and driving, wine tasting and music, for designing instruments such as telescopes and microscopes (see p. 33) to match the optics of the eye and predilections of the brain, and for philosophers concerned with how we know and understand (see pp. 488–91). Although hardly, if at all, a subject in schools, perception is central both to all human discovery and knowledge, and to our everyday experience.

SEE ALSO

- ACOUSTICS p. 30
- OPTICS p. 32
- TOUCH, TASTE AND SMELL p. 216
- SEEING AND HEARING p. 218
- THE NERVOUS SYSTEM p. 220
- THE BRAIN p. 222
- LEARNING, CREATIVITY AND INTELLIGENCE p. 230
- ARTIFICIAL INTELLIGENCE p. 336
- KNOWLEDGE AND REALITY p. 488
- MIND AND BODY p. 490

Visual perception

There are two essentially different ways of explaining or describing how we see. Classically, vision was supposed to be direct knowledge, picked up by the eye rather in the same way as the sense of touch operates, with the fingers having direct contact with objects. But a lot of guessing is needed to identify objects by touch, and even more for visual perception. It has been known since the early 17th century that vision works from optical images (upside down and right-left reversed) cast on the retina at the back of the eyes. The retina has 120 000 000 light-sensitive 'rod' cells signalling light and dark, and 7 000 000 'cone' cells, of three kinds, signalling colour (see p. 218). These cells convert light intensities and frequencies into small pulses of electricity, transmitted to the brain through the bundle of 1 000 000 fibres of the optic nerves. Specialized regions at the back of the brain (see p. 222) respond to and analyse particular visual characteristics – movement, orientation, colour and so on. Somehow these separate representations are combined to create perceptions that are (usually) consistent.

We now know that the classical account is incorrect: vision is indirectly and tenuously linked to the world of objects by complicated physiological processes, some of which are now understood in considerable detail. These processes convert received stimuli into neural signals that are analysed and 'read' in terms of our knowledge of objects. Perceiving is affected by experience and learning while sensing is not. Sensations produced by a specific stimulus remain essentially unchanged from one time to another, but our perception of these sensations may be different, depending on what we have learned in the meantime (see also box, p. 217). We may say that 'bottom up' signals from the senses are read by the brain with 'top down' knowledge of the world, derived from past experience, some of which is inherited.

Space and distance

Space is perceived in three dimensions – height, width and depth. The eyes, positioned at different points in the skull, receive two slightly different images of the environment, projected upside-down onto each retina. These two retinal images are then combined in the brain into one three-dimensional image, perceived the right way up. The degree of difference between the two images – known as the *binocular parallax* – depends on the difference between the angles at which an object is fixed by each eye. The greater the difference, the nearer the object is perceived to be. (See also the parallax method, p. 5.)

Space perception does not, however, depend solely on vision. Balance (see p. 219) is also an important factor in orienting ourselves in the environment. Hearing, and to some extent smell, are, like sight, 'distance' senses: they are capable of obtaining information from distant points. Other senses – touch and taste – provide information about objects in direct contact with the body.

What are perceptions? They are far richer than this mass of data from the senses. They are internal descriptions of the world out there, and of ourselves. They go beyond available data – for example, assuming that partly hidden objects are really complete – and they are predictive into the immediate future. So although there is a reaction-time delay in physiological signalling of about a twentieth of a second, we can hit a cricket ball, play fast table tennis or drive a car, generally anticipating what is about to happen before it happens. It may therefore be said that perceptions are *predictive hypotheses of reality*.

Illusions

Perceptions can be wrong, leading to the experience of *illusions* (see box). Some illusions are due to *physiological* abnormalities (which may be permanent, but are usually temporary, such as the after-images that result from seeing a bright light that fatigues or adapts retinal receptor cells). Alternatively, an illusion may

Paradoxes: the Dutch artist M. C. Escher (1898–1971) made use of realistic detail and ambiguous perspectives to achieve his 'impossible' representations. (Archiv für Kunst/© 1990 M.C. Escher/ Cordon Art–Baarn–Netherlands)

ILLUSIONS

Optical illusions can be divided into four types – ambiguities, distortions, paradoxes and fictions. Many of these phenomena of perception are not simply physiological in origin; it is far more likely that many are due to cognitive misreading of the available sensory data.

Ambiguities are spontaneous perceptual changes, the result of searching for the best bet when there are two (or more) equally likely kinds of objects out there. *Distortions* can be caused by errors of physiological signalling, but most are due to misreading size and distance. Errors are made in judging size, distance, shape or curvature. Objects indicated by perspective, or other cues, as being distant are perceptually expanded in pictures. *Paradoxes* are figures or objects that appear impossible. They are also related to depth perception, as when near and far features happen to line up and touch. *Fictions* – edges and surfaces that are not actually there but are clearly seen – lead to the assumption of the presence of an object or a surface. The ghostly surface,

though seen, is not really there. Indeed, this going beyond the sensory data to see what 'ought' to be there could be the cause of many reported apparitions.

Auditory illusions are also frequently experienced. For example, the *Doppler effect* (see p. 31) is the term used to describe the impression that a horn sounded by an approaching car changes its pitch as it passes by – it sounds higher as it approaches, and drops again as the car retreats into the distance.

Tactile illusions may occur, as, for instance, in the case of the sensations of heat and cold. The skin has different receptors that respond to one or other of these sensations, but not to both; a heat stimulus to a specific small area may therefore produce a sensation of cold. Abrupt changes in temperature may also result in confusion. If one hand is put in hot water and the other in cold, they will after a time adjust to these temperatures; if they are then placed in lukewarm water, the hot hand will feel cold and the cold one will feel warm.

be due to the coded signals from the senses being '*cognitively*' misread, due to the fact that sensory signals are ambiguous. For example, a given retinal image may be of a small near object or a more distant, larger object, and the same image may be given by an object that could have any of an infinite range of possible shapes – although some options are usually far more likely than others. For perception from sensory data, our very lives depend on guessing, or betting, on what objects are out there.

The philosophers of classical Greece, and the British Empiricists of the 18th and 19th centuries – and indeed most philosophers – have sought essential certainty from perception on which to base beliefs on the nature of things (see pp. 488 and 490). But the data from instruments and the experimental techniques of science have revealed a very different world; appearances from the senses and from the accounts of science can be very different, and even conflicting. Thus the Moon looks the size of an orange, and appears to be quite near; yet we know it to be far larger than anything on Earth and 384 400 km (238 700 mi) away. Knowledge and sensory experience are different perceptions, which we somehow have to reconcile – to link and harmonize how things appear with what we believe them to be. This is a conflict that stimulates art, but it makes science hard to explain to non-scientists.

This appearance/reality conflict makes the study of illusions of vision and the other senses significant for science. The philosophy of knowledge (*epistemology*) and the phenomena of illusions are important for revealing processes of normal perception, as well as being tools for the artist. Cognitive errors (see above) can

occur when normally useful rules, or assumptions of various kinds, do not quite apply, or are not adequate for choosing between possibilities. If we think of perceptions as internal descriptions, hypotheses of the external world and of our own bodies, it is interesting to note that the phenomena of visual illusions can be neatly classified into the same kinds of error we find in written or spoken descriptions with words.

A great challenge for computer technology (see pp. 334 and 336) is to design and build machines that can not only recognize patterns (such as printed or written letters, or spoken words) but to perceive in the full sense – to recognize objects from new view-points, and handle unfamiliar or even entirely unknown objects appropriately. We should expect seeing robots to have cognitive illusions similar to ours, but different physiological ones.   RLG

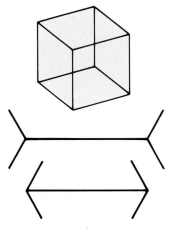

Ambiguities: a meaningful picture will probably be perceived when the drawing above is first seen, but it may then be abruptly replaced by another image. It is not known why the image of a vase first appears to some people and that of two faces to other people, nor is the reason for the sudden change clear. Similarly, the cube below appears to change orientation when looked at continuously.

Distortion: in the diagram above, two lines of equal length are made to appear unequal by the addition of the lines at each end, which lead the eye either inward or outward. The tops of the circles below seem to form a curved line, but in fact are aligned in a straight line. The brain is misled because of the strong curve formed by the bottoms of the circles.

Fictions: the edges of the white triangle overlapping the circles are not physically present, but are clearly perceived.

If looked at for a sufficient length of time the patterns of squares in this picture will be perceived as a recognizable image of Abraham Lincoln: presented with very little visual information, the brain 'fills in' the missing details.

The Power of Speech

Speech is the formation of sounds in a meaningful sequence. It depends on the ability of the speaker to reproduce *phonemes* – vocal 'units' (see p. 608) – and to use acquired language. Correct *phonation* – the articulation of speech – in turn involves the coordination of complex neurological, anatomical and physiological apparatuses.

Language distinguishes speech from mere utterance. A one-year-old baby may babble using a wide repertoire of sounds, and may show good comprehension of spoken language. Babies only become *lingual*, however, when they pronounce, for the first time, a word that has the same meaning for them as for the listener. This single spoken word raises a baby's use of language to the level of communication.

The ability to give form to ideas, to share emotions and to express one's personality imparts to speech a dimension far beyond the mere vocalization of language. The two-way aural/oral process (hearing and producing sound) begins shortly after birth, when a newborn baby already exchanges sounds with its mother and connections begin to develop in the infant brain, linking auditory stimulus and spoken response.

This experience is lacking in babies who are born deaf. If the speech reception centre in the brain is not stimulated from early on, devices such as the cochlear implant (which restores hearing; see p. 240) can never be used, because their brain cannot make sense of sound.

The production of speech

Newborn babies display a willingness to communicate. But, even apart from their neurological immaturity, their bodies are not ready to speak: the shapes of the skull and of the oral cavity make phonation impossible.

Vocal production makes use of three 'systems': the *phonatory system*, including the larynx (voice-box) and its accompanying structures; the *respiratory system*, including the airways, muscles and nerves that support breathing; and the *resonatory system*, which is made up of the structures of the skull and the oral and nasal cavities and affects the acoustics of speech.

Voice is produced when air passes through the larynx, a cartilagenous structure positioned in the trachea (see pp. 210–11). Two ligaments – the *vocal cords* – are attached front and back to bridge the airway. During normal breathing these remain wide apart. If necessary they can be brought together to close off the airway and protect the lungs from an inhaled foreign object. This movement has been adapted for speech. As the cords are brought together, air passing between them under pressure causes them to vibrate.

The larynx is served by a rich nerve supply and 17 sets of muscles. All of these control vocal-cord and laryngeal movement to allow the wide repertoire of sounds possessed by the human voice. Each person's voice has a natural frequency (see p. 29), but changes in cord length, tension and mass can alter pitch, volume, intonation and intensity of sound.

The respiratory system – lungs, diaphragm and muscles attached to the ribs – draws air in and expels it from the lungs. Prolonged phonation uses a continuous column of air coming from the lungs under steady pressure. Breathing for speech requires fine control of exhalation. Without this control, the speaker would only be able to sigh or utter a few sounds before running out of breath. Too much pressure results in distorted sound, and can damage the delicate vocal cords.

The resonatory system, or vocal tract, is made up of all the other structures that modulate the quality of the voice – its richness, depth and pronunciation of vowels and consonants. The vocal tract comprises the throat, the nose and mouth, the soft palate and the sinuses (hollow spaces in the skull). All the sounds used in speech are created by changing the position of the tongue, lips, soft palate and lower jaw. Changes in the shape and size of the throat and mouth affect the acoustic properties of the voice. Without these features, the most impassioned speech would be reduced to a monotonous drone.

Neurological input

The verbal expression of language brings into play sophisticated neurological pathways. In adults, the language centre is usually situated in the left hemisphere of the brain (see pp. 222–3 and 230). It comprises areas that perceive language (written and spoken), comprehend it, formulate expression and translate it into coherent speech.

The idea or structure of a phrase arises in one of these areas, *Wernicke's area*, and reaches another area, *Broca's area*, via association fibres. From here a 'program' of instructions for vocalization passes to the motor cortex. The phonatory system is served by four cranial nerves, while the resonatory system is served by five.

Speech development

The human infant is, in the most literal sense, a pre-lingual creature: *infans* in Latin means unable to speak. Speech begins when the necessary neurological pathways are established and the necessary skeletal changes take place. Early articulation of sounds encompasses a much wider range than will be needed for the mother tongue – for example, babies go through a phase of experimenting with blowing raspberries. Gradually, phonetic contraction reduces the phonemes that a baby can distinguish or make. A Japanese baby soon loses the ability to tell the difference between 'l' and 'r' sounds (see p. 608). At the same time, variations in pitch, tone of voice and emphasis develop so that the babbling sounds remarkably like speech.

Despite limitations in their ability to articulate, babies can certainly discrim-

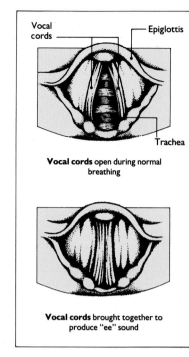

Vocal cords open during normal breathing

Vocal cords brought together to produce "ee" sound

A cross-section of the head and neck, showing the parts involved in the production of speech

- Nasal cavity
- Oral cavity
- Pharynx
- Soft palate
- Tongue
- Epiglottis
- Larynx
- Vocal cords
- Trachea
- Oesophagus

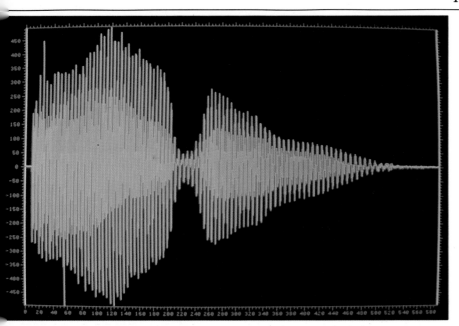

A computer graphics image of the amplitude waveform of the word 'baby', produced on a speech synthesizer.

permanent loss of the natural voice. As something must be able to vibrate in order to create sound, an alternative to the vocal cords is needed. This can be provided by an artificial larynx, or the patient can learn oesophageal speech (see below). Whichever means of vocalization is used, patients must relearn how to articulate individual sounds.

Post-operatively, about 60% of people who have their larynxes removed eventually learn oesophageal speech. This is achieved by filling the oesophagus with air, then releasing it under controlled pressure to produce vibrations at the pharyngo-oesophageal segment, the place where the gullet leads off from the throat. Fluent oesophageal speech depends on the continuous intake and expulsion of air. While the voice is fairly low in pitch and husky, it is possible to speak at a rate of more than 100 words a minute.   ESa

SEE ALSO

● ACOUSTICS p. 30
● THE RESPIRATORY SYSTEM p. 210
● TOUCH, TASTE AND SMELL p. 216
● SEEING AND HEARING p. 218
● THE BRAIN p. 222
● BODY LANGUAGE p. 228
● LEARNING, CREATIVITY AND INTELLIGENCE p. 230
● HOW LANGUAGE WORKS p. 608

nate between sounds. This was pointed out by a researcher at Harvard, who echoed a young child's pronunciation of 'fis' – and was corrected repeatedly by the child until the researcher finally said, 'fish', the word the child knew she was saying.

Children who are brought up in a multilingual home retain the phonemes found in each of the native languages they have heard from birth. Similarly, those who learn a second language at an early age very easily learn to reproduce the different sounds.

Aphasia

When the inability to use speech arises in the brain the condition is known as *aphasia*. Even slight damage to the language centres has grave consequences. Damage in Wernicke's area leaves sufferers with the ability to articulate sounds fluently, but deprived of language comprehension. They can neither make sense of the words of others nor give meaning to their own words.

When a stroke or haemorrhage damages Broca's area, language comprehension is unaffected. Instead, the victim is left with *expressive aphasia*, and is unable to transform language into speech or writing, because the program that instructs the three vocal systems is no longer sent to the motor cortex. It is very difficult to assess the language competence of someone with expressive aphasia because communication is, in effect, cut off.

Global aphasia is the term used for the destruction of the entire language centre. It leaves its victim bereft of comprehension and expression.

Damage to the pathway between Broca's area and the motor cortex, or to the motor cortex itself, prevents the necessary stimuli from reaching the vocal apparatus.

Speech malfunction occurs, likewise, whenever any of the nerves forming the connections between the brain and the organs of speech are injured or severed.

Vocal therapy

The absence, or loss, of coherent speech is extremely distressing. The sufferer is deprived of the principal means of communication. The deficit can occur at any level, from the brain to the speech apparatuses. The cause may be congenital – as in the case of cleft palate – or acquired as a consequence of disease (for instance, in multiple sclerosis or Parkinson's disease). The vocal cords may be damaged by infection or through over-use. Articulation and resonation also deteriorate in the person who becomes deaf.

Speech therapists are professionals who are trained to diagnose and assess a person's voice. They evaluate all the systems involved in sound production, and decide on appropriate treatment. In many cases, a programme of exercises will improve the voice. Treatment may also require medical or surgical intervention. The child with cleft palate will have the defect closed; polyps on the vocal cords may be removed; drugs are given to relieve tremor in Parkinson's disease.

Although the deaf cannot hear their own voice, they can see it with the aid of monitors, which translate sound into visual signals. By using this feedback technique and appropriate exercises, they can retain good speech.

Surgical removal of the larynx means

A 'Token and Reporter' test is used to evaluate a subject's receptive and expressive language. The test can be used to screen for *aphasia*, a disorder of language affecting the generation of speech and its understanding, rather than a disorder of articulation. Aphasia is caused by organic brain disease in the dominant left brain hemisphere in a right-handed person, and of the dominant right brain hemisphere in a left-handed person.

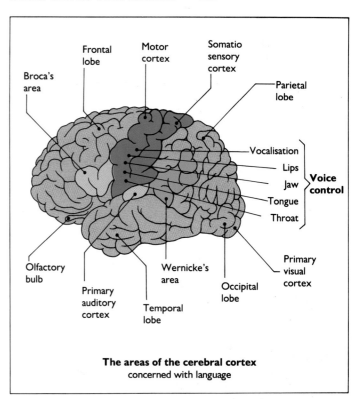

The areas of the cerebral cortex concerned with language

Body Language

Even in the most casual of conversations, extra messages are communicated by various parts of the body. It is often these signals, rather than the words themselves, that are the more influential – they convey what the speaker truly feels. 'Body language' is the popular term for non-verbal communication – it refers to all those signals that are not transmitted through the verbal channel.

Deliberate gestures – for example, a shrug of the shoulders, a raised eyebrow or a movement of the hand – can often transmit a message more clearly, and with greater economy, than a lengthy spoken phrase. Unconscious messages are also constantly being transmitted, for instance in the way a person sits or stands, or the position of their hands or feet.

Facial expressions

Facial expressions are, perhaps, the most obvious of all non-verbal channels of communication. It is possible that some expressions are innate – they are reactions we possess from birth, rather than something we have to learn. Facial expressions of emotions such as happiness, sadness, fear or anger are basically the same all over the world. Even people who are born blind, and never have the chance to see other people's expressions, grow up using the same emotional signals as people with sight.

Cultural differences

Other elements of body language are learned through imitating others, and may vary from culture to culture. For instance, in the West nodding the head up and down indicates an affirmative answer and shaking the head from side to side means a negative one; in some countries, such as India, the meanings of these gestures are reversed.

The eyes

It has often been claimed that the eyes are a kind of window on the soul – they reveal our innermost feelings. Eye signals, while communicating basic feelings and emotions, are also very important in ordinary, everyday conversation. In a conversation between two people, one speaker will gaze at the other when starting to speak, then look away, then look back at the other person to check the response to what has been said. Similar signals are used during a conversation between a group of people. By holding the gaze of the person who is speaking, we can indicate that we want to speak ourselves. When we want to give

SEE ALSO

● ANIMAL COMMUNICATION
  p. 166
● THE POWER OF SPEECH
  p. 226
● WRITING SYSTEMS p. 604
● HOW LANGUAGE WORKS
  p. 608
● THE LANGUAGE OF SIGNS
  p. 610

BARRIER GESTURES

Hiding behind a barrier is symbolized by crossing one or both arms across the chest.

The standard arm cross signifies a negative or defensive state of mind – it is commonly seen in situations where people feel insecure. It can also indicate that a listener disagrees with what is being said.

If the arms are crossed and fists are clenched, the attitude is more strongly defensive and negative.

A partial barrier can be formed by folding one arm over the body to grasp the other arm – this often signifies a lack of self-confidence.

someone else the chance to speak, we look up, meet their eyes and in doing so invite them to take over – avoiding lengthy, often embarrassing silences and ensuring that not everybody tries to talk at once.

During friendly encounters, eye contact is held slightly longer than it is in neutral ones. People sexually attracted to each other may gaze at each other for long periods – in this situation the pupils will be dilated. People who dislike one another may also engage in prolonged mutual staring, but in this case the pupils will be constricted. The length of time one person can comfortably gaze at another during conversation also varies from culture to

culture – the Japanese keep eye contact to a minimum, while in southern European countries a much longer gaze is permissible.

Posture

Close friends adopt open postures with the arms away from the body and the general direction of movement towards the other person. They will usually assume very similar positions, perhaps crossing their legs in the same way or leaning forward at the same angle. When one moves, the other may echo the movement.

People who have their arms tightly folded

across their chests and their feet and legs pointing away from the other person are clearly not getting on very well. One posture to avoid is the 'oblique' posture. This occurs when one person's body is slanted away from the other person's by about 45 degrees so that they talk to them across their shoulder – this gives a very aloof and unfriendly impression.

Personal space

Humans are territorial – they need to have a territory that is 'theirs'. Similarly, people tend to carry with them their own 'personal space' – an invisible area around them into which other people do not intrude. If others enter this space uninvited, we feel threatened. In a crowd, personal space inevitably shrinks and we allow people to move closer to us than we otherwise would. In a very crowded situation, as on a train in the rush hour, personal space cannot exist at all and bodily contact is inescapable. People usually cope with this by ignoring others completely and avoiding eye contact.

The distance between two people is a good indicator of the relationship between them – in general, people who like each other sit and stand closer together than those who dislike each other. However, different cultures have different concepts of personal space. In southern European or Arab countries, for example, a fairly close distance between two people is acceptable, whereas in northern Europe people tend to stand further apart. This can result in tension during a conversation between two people of different cultures – one person may feel threatened if their personal space is invaded, or the other may feel rejected if their companion stands too great a distance away.

Touch

Touch is a very basic form of body language and varies from country to country. In Mediterranean countries, for example, people touch each other, even in casual conversations, much more frequently than British people do. Even in northern France, teenagers greet each other with kisses on the cheek and touches on the arms and shoulders. Touching, if done appropriately, can be a way of establishing friendly relations with people of both the same and opposite sex, which is why the formal handshake is used as a basic method of greeting strangers. Perhaps surprisingly, psychological research shows that it is girls and women who respond most positively to social touching, so long as it is not seen as an unwelcome sexual advance or a patronizing 'put-down'.

These different types of body language do not, of course, occur in isolation. Gestures, facial expressions, eye movements and changes in posture all occur at the same time and combine to increase the

— PUPIL SIGNALS —

The pupil alters its size according to the amount of light available (see p. 218). However, it also changes according to our moods,* and can thus transmit strong emotional messages. When we are looking at something pleasing, particularly a person of the opposite sex, the pupil will often expand considerably. An angry, negative mood will cause the pupil to contract. Dilated pupils therefore have the effect of making the face more attractive. Shown two pictures of a face – one with dilated pupils and one with constricted pupils, but identical in every other way – and asked to choose which they prefer, people will choose the face with dilated pupils without being aware of the reason for their choice.

power of the messages that they convey. Basic social skills – the ability to get on with other people and to establish relationships – develop as people begin to 'translate' the body language of others and learn to present themselves in a way which is seen as friendly, open and inviting. *PeM*

BATON SIGNALS

Some gestures are like words – they have specific meanings, and most of them are fairly rude. There is, however, another kind of gesture called a 'baton signal', which has a different function. Baton signals are those typical movements of the hands and arms that accompany speech. People 'beat time' as they speak. Being able to use these movements appropriately is important because they do two things – they put emphasis on certain things that are being said, and they maintain the rhythm of the conversation. Experienced politicians speaking on television or addressing meetings are adept at using these gestures, keeping the attention of the audience, stressing the important issues and highlighting the promises they want us to believe.

Holding the hand with the thumb and forefinger lightly touching shows that the speaker is striving to express him or herself with great precision.

Making a grasping motion in the air indicates that the speaker is attempting to gain control of the situation.

Chopping downwards, with the hand straight and rigid, is typical of an aggressive speaker feeling the need to cut through a problem.

Jabbing the fingers towards the listener is an aggressive gesture with the aggression directed at the listener.

The raised forefinger is an authoritative gesture and can also appear threatening – the finger is a symbolic weapon ready to deliver a blow.

Holding out both hands with the palms up is reminiscent of a beggar's gesture: the speaker is begging the listener to agree.

Extending the hands with the palms downwards is a restraining gesture, used when the speaker wants to calm down the listener.

Holding the hands up with palms facing outwards makes the speaker appear to push away the listener or something another speaker has said.

Learning, Creativity and Intelligence

Learning, creativity and intelligence are all concerned with the acquisition and use of knowledge. Philosophers have argued about the nature of knowledge, and how we come by it, for thousands of years. Some have claimed that knowledge is acquired through experience and others that we have inborn ideas about the world. Psychologists have now begun to answer more modest – but solvable – questions. Why is it that some people seem to learn faster than others? Are differences between people due to genetic or environmental influences? What factors make someone creative?

If the kinds of thinking involved in different subjects or *knowledge domains* – for example, how we solve problems in mathematics or how we remember events in history – are analysed we find that they are found to be specific to that domain. A child's understanding of the world seems to be very different from that of an adult: for example, a child might think that the wind is made by trees moving. Such observations led to the idea that intelligence is simply a random collection of independent pieces of knowledge and thinking skills. Yet there are striking regularities in the data that suggest that intelligence and knowledge are not the same thing.

Intelligence

Our ability to think and reason improves as we become older, and this improvement follows the same pattern for all abilities. The major improvements take place in early childhood and end by the late teens.

Everyone has differences between their abilities – some, for instance, do better at science than art, others do better at history than geography. However, when individuals of the same age are compared, someone who is relatively good at one kind of thinking will also tend to be good at others. In other words intelligence is general.

Despite the obvious and large changes in our knowledge over the years, IQ (intelligence quotient; see box) is relatively stable throughout life. So what is it that gives rise to these regularities?

One explanation is that although different subjects require different kinds of thinking and reasoning skills, all thought processes are influenced by the biological properties of the brain.

MEASURING HEMISPHERIC DIFFERENCES

When the eyes focus on a spot (*fixation point*) in the middle of the field of view, everything to the right of that spot (*right visual field*) will be projected on to the left cerebral hemisphere and everything to the left (*left visual field*) will be projected to the right cerebral hemisphere. Since both eyes receive information from both visual fields this means that half of the fibres from each eye must cross over on their way to the projection centres of the brain. They do this at the *optic chiasma*.

Scientists can take advantage of this anatomical feature of the visual system to test the specialization of the cerebral hemispheres by varying the kind of information that is presented in each visual field. Although the cerebral hemispheres communicate with each other by sending messages through the *cerebral commissures* (the bundle of nerve fibres that connects the two halves of the brain), we know that information in one visual field will be received first in the opposite cerebral hemisphere. Presenting the information in each visual field for a shorter time than it takes to change fixation (about one fifth of a second) ensures that it is only being projected onto the one hemisphere. Any systematic differences in the kinds of information that are processed in each hemisphere can be seen.

If people are asked to make decisions about pictures or about words (for example, are they the same or different?) we find that performance is faster and more accurate for pictures if they are presented in the left visual field (right hemisphere) and for words if they are presented in the right visual field (left hemisphere). This has led scientists to suppose that the right hemisphere is more specialized for visual imagery and the left for verbal processing. Some believe that the difference is more general than this, with the right hemisphere dealing with more intuitive forms of reasoning and the left with more analytical and sequential thinking.

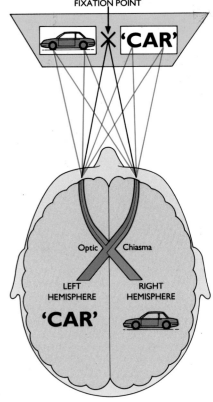

The above diagram illustrates an experiment in which people are shown on a screen a series of pictures, of which half are cars and half are other objects, and a series of words, of which half are 'car' and the remainder other words. They are asked to focus on a fixation point in the middle of their field of view. The images are flashed onto the screen at random, in either the right or left field of vision, very briefly so that there is no time to change fixation.

They are asked to press a red button if they see a picture of a car or the word car, and an orange button if they see other words or objects. It is found that when a *picture* is presented to the left field of vision the response is faster than when it is presented to the right; when a *word* is presented to the right field of vision the response is faster than when it is presented to the left.

Alternatively, it could be that general intelligence is a result of our environment rather than a property of our brains. In other words, it may be that the environmental circumstances of some individuals provide better learning opportunities.

Nature versus nurture

The study of twins has been the most common method for estimating the relevance of genetic factors to intelligence. *Monozygotic* (identical) twins have the same genetic constitution (*genotype*), whereas *dizygotic* (non-identical) twins have only 50% of their genotype in common (i.e. no more than any two offspring of the same biological parents). The extent to which identical twins are similar in intelligence compared to the extent of similarity in non-identical twins

gives us an estimate of the degree to which intelligence is inherited. If identical twins were no more similar than non-identical twins then we could conclude that there is no genetic contribution to intelligence. Because twins have more than their genotype in common – they often have similar environments for example – studies concentrate on twins reared apart.

Identical twins reared apart are more similar in intelligence than non-identical twins reared apart, and so there is little doubt that there is some genetic contribution to intelligence. The best estimate is that at least 50% of the total variance in intelligence in our population is due to inherited differences. Of course, this leaves at least 50% that could be environmental in origin. Heritability estimates apply to populations and tell us that on average genes contribute half of the variation in intelligence. However, we cannot say that half of any particular individual's intelligence is due to genes and half to environment. Either the environmental circumstances or the genetic history of an individual, if extreme enough, could totally determine the level of intelligence.

Learnability

It is also interesting that some things that have proved impossible for computers to learn seem remarkably simple for all human beings, irrespective of the level of general thinking ability. For example, there is no computer that has fully mastered the ability to understand human language (as opposed to specially designed computer languages), and yet almost all human beings can do so. Similarly, the process of constructing our perception of the visual world from a retinal image – the image projected onto the light receptors in our eyes – is beyond the capability of any computer but is within the mastery of the human infant. This suggests that evolution has furnished us with specialized brain structures that are unrelated to our ability to think. Occasionally such structures may go wrong, producing people with anomalous abilities (see below).

Specific learning disorders

Undoubtedly some individuals perform less well than we would expect from their level of general intelligence. For example, dyslexic children usually have great difficulty with reading, writing and spelling and yet are of normal intelligence – a complex brain process usually involved in the analysis of words may not be working. There are also cases in which a brain structure is spared the consequences of general brain damage and a spectacular anomalous ability occurs, where some individuals of very low measured intelligence display a single isolated – sometimes remarkable – ability. These abilities

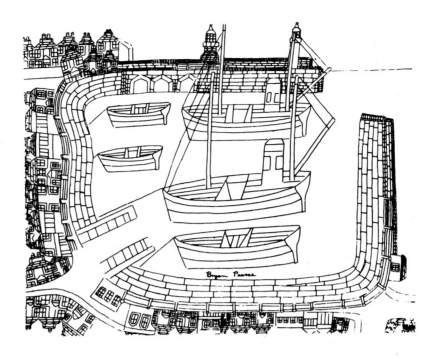

range from knowledge of numbers and number systems (for example, being able to say almost immediately what day of the week it was or will be on any given date) to musical and artistic abilities. Some of these individuals appear so talented that they have been used as evidence that creativity is independent of intelligence.

What is creativity?

Creativity is usually thought of as depending on some special talent that some people are born with. It has been suggested that creativity depends on properties of the right, as opposed to the left, cerebral hemisphere.

While it is true that the two hemispheres seem to be specialized for different kinds of thinking (see box), there is no evidence to suggest that one or the other is specialized for any creative abilities. If we

A drawing by an *idiot savant*
– a person who, although possessing very low intelligence and limited communicative ability, has one outstanding talent.

analyse the life history of creative individuals there are few, if any, that would be regarded as generally unintelligent.

It is also clear that many factors such as personality, motivation, parental involvement and practice contribute to an individual's creativity. In addition, because much of creativity, particularly in art, may be in the eye of the beholder, many social factors determine whether someone will be called creative or not. Perhaps here, more than in any area related to human intelligence, we see the limitations of analysing the brain independently of the environment in which it develops.   MA

SEE ALSO

● GENETICS AND INHERITANCE p. 114
● THE BRAIN p. 222
● PERCEPTION p. 224
● THE POWER OF SPEECH p. 226
● EDUCATION p. 260
● HOW LANGUAGE WORKS p. 608

INTELLIGENCE TESTS

Intelligence tests – which were first invented in 1904 by the French psychologist Alfred Binet (1857–1911) – come in many forms. Some test factual knowledge or vocabulary. Other tests include arranging blocks into shapes, quickly substituting geometric symbols for digits, performing calculations and keeping as many numbers as possible in the memory.

Constructing an intelligence test is highly technical. Items are arranged in order of difficulty (an item should not be so easy that everybody gets it right or so hard that everybody gets it wrong) and are given to a representative cross-section of the population. This cross-section provides the sample on which the test's *norms* are calculated. On the basis of these norms – for example the average score for 12-year-olds

– such statistics as *mental age* or *IQ* (intelligence quotient) can be calculated from an individual's test score. Mental age is the age for which that test score would be average. Thus a child has a mental age of 7 if its score is typical of a 7-year-old.

IQ is an indication of how the test score compares with that of other children of the same age. An IQ of 100 would mean that the test score was the average score for the child's age group. An IQ greater than 100 indicates that a child has performed better than average for its age. In any age group, 66% will have an IQ between 85 and 115. An IQ less than 70 usually indicates that a child has learning difficulties.

An intelligence test is a sophisticated instrument, and like any instrument the measure-

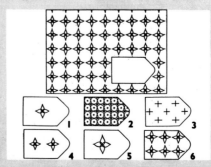

ments are meaningless if they are not used in the proper way. So, for example, while it is true that someone can improve their score on any intelligence test by practising at the test, it does not mean that they become more intelligent.

A non-verbal reasoning test: choose which of the six boxes completes the pattern. This is a simple example, reduced in size, taken from a series of tests designed for older children and adults; the tests become progressively harder.

Test A5 from *Raven Standard Progressive Matrices*, copyright J.C. Raven Limited. Answer: 6

Sleep and Dreams

Sleep and wakefulness come and go as a biological rhythm, wakefulness being a time for achievement and sleep for renewal. Sleep is necessary and without it alertness and effort become impaired. Dreams can occur at any time in sleep but the phase known as REM (rapid eye movement) sleep is richest in dreaming. Sleep is less refreshing when there are worries and responsibilities, and it becomes more broken in middle and later life.

Sleep is a time when the brain imposes rest upon itself and the body. Throughout the animal kingdom wakefulness and sleep alternate: the Earth rotates every 24 hours and humans, like all creatures, have through evolution incorporated a 24-hour activity-rest cycle into their genetic material.

This daily rhythm will more forcefully be brought to our attention if, for example, we fly to Tokyo. We then suffer jet lag, which means that for the first few days we are sleepy and inefficient when local people are awake, but lie awake in bed while they sleep.

Why do we fall asleep?

Chiefly we fall asleep when the powerful sleep-wakefulness rhythm forces us to be sleepy, though we also fall asleep more easily if we are short of recent hours of sleep, immobile, warm or bored. Wakefulness and attention are maintained by change; a constant environment makes us drowsy.

If the body is deprived of sleep, then more and deeper sleep is taken later as compensation. Body tissues are at all times being broken down and renewed, but there is relatively greater breakdown when we are awake, and greater renewal during sleep. If people have been kept unnaturally awake, they can by special effort briefly perform what may be required of them, but they progressively lose the ability to sustain that effort, make more and more mistakes, and finally drop off to sleep regardless of surroundings. After sleep, the brain's powers are restored.

What happens in sleep?

As we fall asleep the body becomes inert and the flow of saliva decreases so we do not drown. Heart rate, oxygen consumption, breathing and temperature all diminish, and the electrical brain waves (measured by a machine called an electroencephalogram) take on changed appearances. Whereas in wakefulness the levels of the stimulant hormone *adrenaline* in the blood are high and help achievement regardless of cost, in sleep those levels are low and the body-building hormone, *somatotrophin*, reaches a sustained peak.

In the brain, memory traces of the day are strengthened, but durable new traces are not laid down: dreams are quickly forgotten, and you cannot learn a new language from tape recordings played through the night.

Dreaming

In dreams we are not passive observers of pictures. People blind from birth do not

---

FREUD, JUNG AND THE UNCONSCIOUS

Many bodily functions are controlled by a part of the nervous system over which we have very limited conscious control (see p. 220). Similarly, much of our mental life is directed by unconscious processes within the central nervous system; a thought suddenly comes into our heads and we have no idea where it came from. The concept of the unconscious was central to the theories of the Austrian neurologist Sigmund Freud (1856–1939) and to those of the Swiss psychiatrist Carl Gustav Jung (1875–1961).

According to Freud and Jung, dreams are the most obvious manifestation of the unconscious, which they conceived of as a vast repository of hidden instincts, memories, ideas and emotions that exists in all of us. They believed that one key to the knowledge of our conscious behaviour lay in the unconscious. Freud thought that unpleasant experiences or guilt-provoking desires were *repressed*, or banished from the conscious mind, but gave rise to such symptoms as anxiety, depression, phobias and 'hysterical' paralysis. Both Freud and Jung hoped to prove that many psychiatric illnesses could be treated successfully by *psychoanalysis*. Psychoanalysis aims to enable the analyst and the patient to gain access to the unconscious mind through discussion, free association – in which the patient says whatever comes into his or her mind – and dream analysis. Through this method the patient remembers the experience and the emotions associated with it, and is cured.

Freud grew to believe that the experiences, wishes or emotions that were repressed were often sexual and could be traced back to early childhood. He believed that these repressed impulses affected our thoughts and actions, and that dreams are disguised fulfilments of repressed, usually sexual,

Sigmund Freud

wishes, with disturbing ideas represented by symbols. Patients could be cured of their symptoms by a successful interpretation of their dreams, their slips of the tongue and of their neurotic behaviour itself.

Freud identified five stages in sexual development. The *oral* stage lasts for the first year of life when the child's pleasure is focused on feeding. The *anal* stage lasts from the ages of 1 to 3 when the child is learning to control its bowels. The *phallic* stage, with the penis or clitoris as the centre of attention, follows at the age of 3 or 4. There is then a *latency* period during which sexual impulses are 'sublimated' into other pursuits – social, intellectual, athletic. Finally, the mature *genital* stage is entered at puberty.

In addition to these stages Freud put forward the concept of the *Oedipus complex*, a perfectly normal phase through which all male children passed at the age of 4 or 5. During this phase the boy becomes sexually attracted to his mother and wants her totally for himself, so developing aggressive feelings towards his father. These feelings lead to the fear that his father will retaliate by castrating him. The theory takes its name from the Greek myth of Oedipus who, abandoned at birth by his parents, later marries his mother and kills his father.

Freud thought that the mind was divided into three parts – the *id*, concerned with basic, inherited instincts, the *ego*, concerned with the tasks of reality and the sense of self within the world, and the *superego*, a kind of conscience that represents ideals and values derived from parents and society, and that controls the impulses of the id and ego.

According to Jung, dreams are communications from the unconscious but are not necessarily concerned with wishes. Jung divided the unconscious life into two parts – the personal and the collective. The *personal unconscious* consists of contents that have been forgotten or repressed, while the *collective unconscious* is an inherited pattern of memories, instincts and experiences common to everyone. He formed his theory of the collective unconscious when he noticed that delusions and hallucinations in different patients seemed to contain similar themes, and often could not be explained as products of the patients' own experiences.

Jung also developed the idea of dividing people into *extroverts*, or outward-looking personalities, and *introverts*, or inward-looking personalities – although he recognized that most people combine aspects of both types.

Few of the theories of Freud and Jung are now seen as being capable of scientific testing. However, they had a profound effect on the way we look at the human mind and opened the way for modern psychiatry and psychotherapy. SM

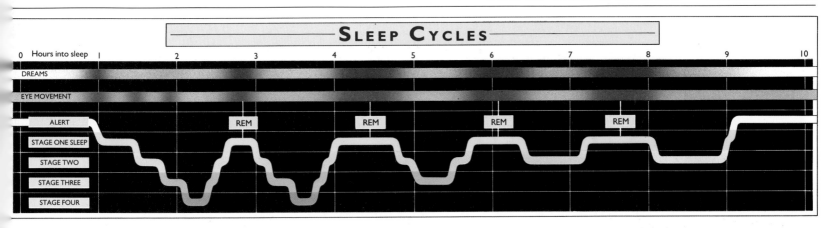

SLEEP CYCLES

| 0 | Hours into sleep | 1 | 2 | 3 | 4 | 5 | 6 | 7 | 8 | 9 | 10 |

DREAMS

EYE MOVEMENT

ALERT — REM — REM — REM — REM

STAGE ONE SLEEP

STAGE TWO

STAGE THREE

STAGE FOUR

see in dreams, but like all of us they live in a fantasy world whilst asleep.

Throughout history it has been believed that dreams foretell the future and that they contain symbols. In the early 20th century there was a flowering of interest in dreams through the writings of Sigmund Freud and Carl Gustav Jung, who hoped that by understanding symbols in dreams it would be possible to help people with psychological difficulties (see box). Their writings greatly influenced the imagery of creative artists such as the Surrealists (see p. 550), but their hopes have not been realized, and modern psychiatrists usually rely upon the reality of people's waking feelings, relationships and behaviour to achieve understanding.

In the 1950s interest in dreaming revived, thanks to research into sleep. Everybody experiences two states of sleep, which alternate four or five times a night. Rapid eye movement (REM) sleep occupies about 20% of the time, and if sleepers are deliberately awakened from REM sleep they are especially likely to describe a dream.

In REM sleep, periods of which last 5–30 minutes, there are intermittent flurries of jerky eye movements accompanied by finger, toe and facial twitchings, erection of the penis or increased vaginal blood flow, and general bodily paralysis. We need both REM and non-REM sleep, and catch up on either if selectively deprived. Although awakenings from REM sleep yield the richest harvest of dreams, mental life goes on all night: dreams are very common when we are merely drowsy at the start of the night, and the most vivid of all dreams, night terrors, occur in non-REM sleep. REM sleep itself is in fact most prominent in infancy (and before birth) when memories and knowledge for the creation of dreams are not available.

When people are awakened from their sleep and their dream reports tape-recorded, most dreams are found to be quite dull and to do with everyday events. Just occasionally there are bizarre or erotic developments that tend to be remembered in the morning. Outside noises may get woven into the dream: for example, in one experiment the name 'Robert' repeatedly spoken to the sleeper led to a dream of 'a rabbit and it looked distorted', while 'Gillian' (the name of an ex-girlfriend) produced a dream of 'an old woman who came from Chile' (a Chilean).

Sleep troubles

The amount of sleep needed varies greatly from individual to individual. Most babies sleep 14–16 hours per 24, most adults 7 or 8. Young adults usually sleep heavily but, as the years pass, sleep becomes more broken and is increasingly felt to be lighter, so that by their fifties about 25% of all women and 15% of men feel dissatisfied with the quality of their sleep. Their rest is also more easily disturbed by noises or caffeine-containing drinks.

At any age, worry or depression will impair sleep. Since long before Shakespeare's 'drowsy syrups', drugs, including alcohol, have been taken to try to improve sleep. Today's sleeping drugs are safer, give satisfying sleep if used for a short time, and are used mainly by older people. However, over-dependency is a danger and it is wise to use them only occasionally.

SEE ALSO
● THE NERVOUS SYSTEM p. 220
● THE BRAIN p. 222
● DRUG ABUSE p. 246

The Nightmare (left) by Henry Fuseli (1741–1825).

10

Mental Disorders

Throughout history people have explained mental disorders in ways that have suited their particular culture and society. In some societies people with mental disorders were regarded as being possessed by devils and were tortured to drive them out, while in others, such people were thought to be divinely inspired. In the case of some artistic geniuses – such as Vincent van Gogh – there appears to have been a link between mental illness and creativity.

In general, however, the mentally ill were badly treated – even King George III of Britain was tied up and beaten. In the 19th century large asylums were built for the mentally ill as places of safety, although these too have been the sites of some appalling treatment. Not until recently, with the introduction of powerful drugs

and new pyschological theories, has medicine had the means of effectively treating mental illness.

Classification

Mental distress is often treated in the first instance by the general practitioner, who may decide to refer the patient to a psychiatrist for an expert opinion. Mental disorders can be broadly divided into psychosis, neurosis, organic and other disorders.

Psychosis is perhaps what most people think of when they talk of madness. It means being out of touch with reality, and is characterized by frequently bizarre behaviour in a seemingly normal setting. The mental symptoms are of a severe disturbance of beliefs and perceptions – the psychotic person may have delusions (false beliefs) and hallucinations (seeing things that are not there, or hearing imaginary voices). Psychotic people are often not aware – at least during severe episodes – that they are ill. The two psychotic disorders are *schizophrenia* and *affective illness*.

Schizophrenia can affect every aspect of a

person's mind and personality. One of the most distressing symptoms is the belief that one's thoughts are not one's own, and even that one's physical actions are initiated by someone else. The term schizophrenia ('split mind') was first used in 1911 to describe this splitting of mental functions.

Affective or mood disorder can take two forms: *mania* and *depression*. Mania is characterized by excessive cheerfulness, overactive behaviour and impaired judgement. Depression is classified as psychotic when beliefs and perceptions are distorted.

A *neurosis* is a psychological illness that causes distress but is understandable in terms of more normal mental processes. In *anxiety neurosis* anxiety is the predominant emotion to the extent that it becomes impossible to live a normal life. An *obsessive-compulsive disorder* can involve long complicated rituals, frequently related to the fear of contamination – repeatedly washing the hands, for example. The ritual is omitted only at the cost of unbearable anxiety. In the case of *phobias*, anxiety is focused on particular objects or situations. Usually these are objects that we have an instinctive capacity to fear, such as snakes or confined spaces. *Depressive neurosis* involves depression as the principal emotion, and is different from psychotic depression in that perceptions are not

Bethlehem Royal Hospital in London was infamous for its cruel treatment of mentally ill patients. In the 18th century a tour round the hospital – known as Bedlam – was a popular entertainment.

As well as individual psychotherapy sessions, people can be seen in groups or with their families. Group therapy is especially beneficial for a number of people with the same problem. Family therapy is a particularly useful tool as it acknowledges that individuals are affected by their families and vice versa. It is widely used by therapists working with children and adolescents.   CBe

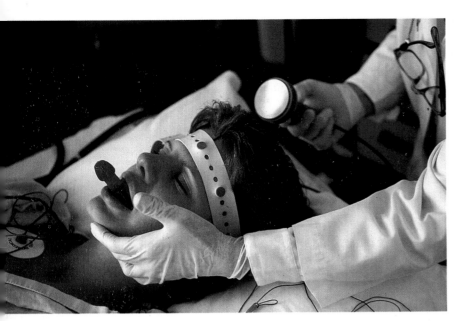

In electroconvulsive therapy the patient is anaesthetized and a modified alternating current is passed through the head between two electrodes placed on the temples, producing a seizure.

distorted. *Hysteria* is a complicated problem that can take many forms. It involves symptoms with no physical cause that enable the sufferer to escape from an intolerable situation – these can be connected with memory, as in amnesia, or with the body as in hysterical paralysis or blindness. Occasionally more complicated forms, such as multiple personality, may occur.

In *organic disorders*, mental illness is caused by physical disease. *Delirium* is an acute, short-term clouding of consciousness, as with a high fever or in delirium tremens (DTs or alcohol withdrawal, see p. 246). *Dementia* is a chronic or long-term brain dysfunction, which is most commonly seen in old age. It can also be a result of tertiary syphilis (general paralysis of the insane) or of brain damage caused by illness or drugs. There are other mental disorders that may be the province of the psychiatrist, but that are not necessarily termed mental illness. These include personality disorders and problems such as drug abuse and sexual dysfunction.

Causes

Many factors are involved in the origins of mental disorder, including heredity. Exactly what form the inheritance takes is only poorly understood, but some disorders have been shown to be more prevalent in family members of afflicted individuals. Such disorders include schizophrenia, manic-depressive psychosis and alcoholism.

Upbringing too plays its part. It was once thought that mothers were the cause of severe mental illness (such as schizophrenia), but this theory is no longer accepted. The odd ways in which families with a mentally ill member behave are now seen as understandable, given the stress these families live with. Cruelty or neglect, however, do have serious implications for mental health, and family patterns of behaviour may contribute to the development of neuroses (see also p. 257).

Precipitating factors are easier to identify than original causes. Perhaps the best way to view the development of a mental breakdown is to see people as being more or less vulnerable because of their genes, early life and personality. Stress in their environment, such as leaving home or starting a new job, can be the final straw. In particularly vulnerable people the actual stress may be very minor indeed.

Treatment

Drug therapy came of age in psychiatry in the early 1950s with the introduction of antipsychotic drugs called *phenothiazines*. Until then the old asylums were overcrowded with psychotic patients for whom little could be done, but with the introduction of phenothiazines vast numbers of people have been helped to lead normal lives.

Anti-depressant drugs have also proved effective in many cases. Tranquillizers – *benzodiazepines* – have a place in short-term treatment, but they are only rarely useful in the longer term, and can be addictive (see p. 246).

Most of the old physical treatments have now fallen into disrepute. One, however – *electroconvulsive therapy* (ECT) – is still useful. For a specific, selected group of patients ECT can bring about a recovery more rapidly than any other treatment, although it is not known how it works. These people may be severely depressed, unable to eat or sleep, hearing accusatory voices, and genuinely believing that they are totally worthless – perhaps even thinking that they are dead. It is clear then that a recovery as soon as possible is important.

Psychotherapy is a form of treatment that is aimed at helping patients to understand themselves. It is a broad term that covers therapies from classic psychoanalysis (see p. 232) to counselling, drama therapy, music therapy and art therapy. These treatments can be used to help people with almost all forms of mental disorder. They can be combined with drug therapy, as drugs and counselling can be aimed at different facets of the same problem.

JOAN OF ARC
A CASE STUDY

One of the most fundamental parts of the Joan of Arc story (see p. 401) is that she heard voices. Yet this feature is one which is usually associated with mental illness. So the question arises: was Joan of Arc mentally ill?

To answer this it is necessary to look more closely at the nature of psychosis and at her experiences.

Joan of Arc heard voices talking to her, telling her that she was special and that she had a mission. Her mood at the time is not known, but perhaps it involved an element of elation. Later in her life she remained convinced that the voices were from God. She did as the voices told her and was both single-minded and effective, succeeding in defeating the English army in battle.

How do these features fit in with mental illness? Schizophrenia is characterized by the disintegration of the personality; voices usually speak about the affected person and are persecutory. The sufferer may hold beliefs about being special or chosen, but motivation is frequently affected adversely. In the longer term, the afflicted person may recover and see their experiences as hallucinations, or the disease may progress to a state of severe handicap. Only rarely will a delusion persist in an intact personality, and even in such an instance stress would be likely to provoke a more severe relapse.

Manic depressive psychosis is primarily a disorder of mood. We can rule out depression, but could Joan have been manic? Here the mood disorder is elation or irritability with voices frequently being heard talking to, rather than about, the afflicted person. There is an inability to concentrate, a rapid, mid-sentence switch of ideas, and eventual exhaustion. Depression, often longer lasting, is a common outcome.

On balance, then, it would appear to be extremely unlikely that Joan suffered from a mental disorder as we understand it. Was she swept up in the religiosity of her time? A farm girl with a yearning for something more? Perhaps most compelling is the fact that the people of her time did not think of her as mad, but admired and followed her.

SEE ALSO

- THE BRAIN p. 222
- SLEEP AND DREAMS (BOX) p. 232
- DRUG ABUSE p. 246
- DEVIANCE, CRIME AND LAW ENFORCEMENT p. 262

Non-Infectious Diseases

Diseases that are not transmitted have now replaced infections as the primary health problem – at least in developed countries. Infectious diseases such as smallpox, tuberculosis and diphtheria have been ousted from their positions as major killers by cancer, heart disease and strokes.

A Down's syndrome child (right). The condition is caused by a chromosome defect – there are three number 21 chromosomes instead of the usual two, resulting in the characteristic slanting eyes, short stature, a varying degree of mental retardation and, sometimes, structural abnormalities of the heart and kidneys.

A patient undergoing radiotherapy to treat Hodgkin's disease – a cancer of the lymphatic system. The illuminated discs over the patient's chest indicate the areas that are to receive radiation.

While factors such as an inappropriate diet, lack of exercise, excessive intake of alcohol and tobacco smoking have to take the blame for many of the diseases that afflict people today, they are not the only culprits. The genes that each of us inherits from our parents may also put us at risk of developing heart disease, schizophrenia, rheumatoid arthritis or certain types of cancer, for example. Often several genes will contribute to an individual's risk of developing such a disease.

The role of heredity

There are many different types of inherited disease. Some are apparent from birth, while others may take decades to reveal themselves. Abnormalities of the chromosomes (see p. 114) may be to blame. In *Down's syndrome*, for example, the affected child has an extra copy of chromosome number 21.

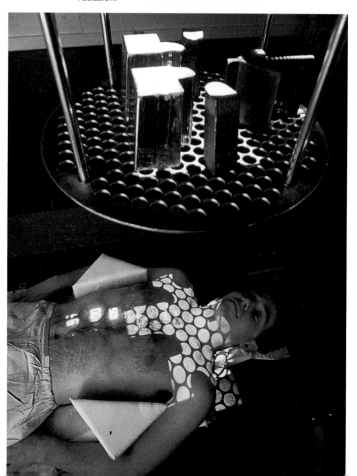

More than 4000 genetic diseases result from the inheritance of a mutant gene. They include achondroplasia (dwarfism; see p. 204), cystic fibrosis, Huntington's chorea and the blood disorders sickle-cell disease and thalassaemia. Affected couples may seek genetic counselling in order to assess their risk of passing on the disease to their children.

In *cystic fibrosis*, the mutation results in abnormally thick mucous secretions in the lungs and intestine. Treatment for digestive problems and lung infections can help to prolong the lives of people with cystic fibrosis, many of whom now survive into their mid-twenties. Hopes are high that, now that the exact mutation responsible for this disease has been identified, it may be possible to devise more effective treatments.

Huntington's chorea, which affects about one in 20 000 people, is a particularly distressing disease. Dementia (a disorder of the mental processes) and uncontrolled movements occur, but the symptoms fail to become apparent until the affected person has reached middle age. By this time, he or she has often already had children who risk suffering the same fate.

Sickle-cell disease is a hereditary blood disease that affects mainly people from Africa and their descendants. An abnormal type of haemoglobin (see p. 210) is produced in the red blood cells. When carrying oxygen it functions normally, but after passing oxygen to the tissues the haemoglobin molecules change shape and pack together, distorting the blood cells and causing them to become sickle-shaped. Anaemia occurs as these cells are destroyed prematurely by the body. *Sickling crises* may also be brought about when the oxygen level is reduced, for example after strenuous exercise. In such circumstances, large numbers of red blood cells become sickle-shaped and can cause obstructions in the blood vessels, with possible damage to organs such as the kidneys and the brain. No satisfactory

treatment has yet been developed.

Thalassaemia, common in Mediterranean countries, Asia and Africa, is also caused by a haemoglobin abnormality. Affected red blood cells cannot function normally, resulting in anaemia, enlargement of the spleen and bone-marrow disorders. The disease can be treated by repeated blood transfusions.

The influence of genes

Many common diseases such as heart disease, diabetes and some types of cancer may result from the inheritance of a blend of 'predisposing' genes, particularly when combined with environmental factors such as diet.

Diabetes (see p. 214) may 'run in families'. The brother or sister of a diabetic person is more likely to develop diabetes than a member of the general population. Obesity may also play a role in encouraging the onset of the disease.

Physical and chemical causes of disease

Environmental hazards such as radiation and pollutants account for some types of disease. People normally encounter only small doses of radiation, from diagnostic X-rays or perhaps as a treatment for cancer. In addition, everyone is exposed to low background levels of natural radiation from the Sun and from some types of rock. However, excessive doses of radiation may follow accidents at nuclear reactors or the detonation of nuclear weapons.

People who experience such high exposures develop radiation sickness, with loss of cells from their bone marrow and the lining of their intestine. The person loses appetite and suffers diarrhoea, sickness, chills, fever and extreme tiredness. Death may follow because of the damage to the bowel and bone marrow resulting in loss of resistance to infection and severe anaemia. Long-term survivors are at increased risk of developing cancers,

SEE ALSO

- GENETICS AND INHERITANCE p. 114
- PHYSICAL DEVELOPMENT p. 204
- HOW PEOPLE MOVE (ARTHRITIS) p. 207
- FOOD, DIET AND DIGESTION p. 208
- THE IMMUNE SYSTEM p. 212
- PREVENTING DISEASE p. 244
- DRUG ABUSE p. 246

CANCER

Cancer occurs when cells grow out of control. A single cell can accumulate changes in its genes that allow it to replicate in an uncontrolled way. Such a cell can give rise to a *tumour*, which may manifest itself as a palpable lump or a mass. Once cells become cancerous they lose the function that they once had: they simply reproduce themselves indefinitely.

A tumour is considered to be *benign* if it remains localized in the place where it originated. Nevertheless, benign tumours can be life-threatening if they jeopardize normal structures. Benign tumours of the brain, for example, can be fatal.

Malignant tumours have the capacity to spread around the body. Individual cells, or groups of cells, can detach themselves from the *primary tumour*, migrate via the blood or the lymph around the body and become deposited in other organs such as the brain, the bones or the lungs. There they form *secondary tumours*. This process is called *metastasis*, and the secondary tumours are known as *metastases*.

In many cases the cause of cancer is unknown, and will vary according to the type of cancer. Studies of women who have had breast cancer have provided some indication of the factors at work in the development of this disease. Breast cancer is more common in women who have a close relative, such as a mother or sister, who has also had the disease. This suggests that – in some cases at least – genetic influences are at work.

Cancer of the breast is also more common in women who begin their periods early, who have their first child later in life and who have a late menopause. These observations indicate that hormonal influences on the breast are important. The same appears to be true of cancer of the ovary:

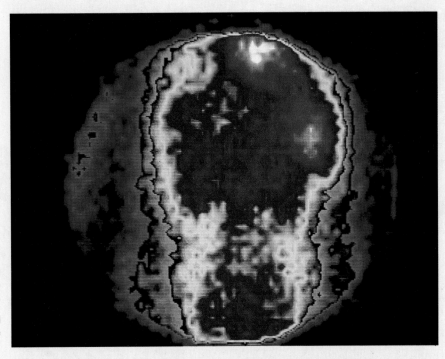

this is less common in women who have taken oral contraceptives for several years, thus suppressing the normal monthly cycle of activity in the ovaries.

Environmental factors undoubtedly play a part in the development of some cancers. Excessive exposure to ultraviolet light in sunlight seems to be responsible for *melanoma*, or cancer of the skin. Almost a third of all deaths from cancer could be avoided if people abandoned smoking tobacco.

Treatment for cancer varies according to the type of tumour, the site of the primary tumour and the extent of the spread of cancerous cells. *Chemotherapy* (drug therapy) can produce long remissions in some forms of the disease but side effects occur as

Secondary cancer *(metastases)* (above) of the spleen, arising from a primary ovarian cancer. The image was taken by gamma camera scanning (see caption, p. 332) and the cancerous cells are indicated by the bright red, pink and white regions.

normal cells are also damaged and the white blood cells become depleted. *Radiation therapy* uses ionizing radiation – including X-rays and gamma-rays – to destroy cancer cells. Chemicals can be used to sensitize malignant cells to radiation, leaving healthy cells undamaged. Surgery is used to remove malignant growths but is only completely effective if cancer cells have not migrated into other parts of the body.

---

including cancers of the blood, and cataracts (see p. 218).

Chemical hazards are probably more often encountered at work than at home. The list of industrial diseases is a long one and includes poisoning by lead, mercury and other heavy metals. Many industrial diseases result from inhaling some harmful substance. *Asbestosis*, for example, results from inhaling fibres of asbestos. The lungs become fibrous and the affected person not only experiences increasing breathlessness, with failure of the heart and lungs, but also has an increased risk of developing cancer of the lung.

Autoimmune disease

Some diseases result from the immune system (see p. 212) attacking the body's own tissues or other components. In *thyrotoxicosis*, antibodies produced by the immune system bind to cells of the thyroid, stimulating them to produce excessive amounts of thyroid hormone. In *rheumatoid arthritis* (see box, p. 207), there is

evidence that the damage to the lining of the joint results from a faulty immune response within the joint.

Diet

The Western diet has been criticized for being too low in fibre and too high in sugar and other refined carbohydrates and in fat. Heart disease, diabetes, cancer of the colon and of the large bowel, constipation, haemorrhoids and obesity are among the many diseases that may result.

A diet too high in saturated fat may result in an elevated level of blood cholesterol leading to *atheroma* – degeneration of artery walls due to the formation of fatty deposits. People with this disease are prone to *angina* (severe pain in the chest on exertion) and heart attacks, which may be fatal.

Obesity can also encourage unwanted health problems. People who are overweight are more likely to suffer from heart disease, diabetes and strokes.

Alcohol

Apart from the social cost of alcohol-related diseases, excessive intake of alcohol exerts a huge toll on physical health. The long-term effects of alcohol taken to excess include cirrhosis of the liver (in which liver cells are replaced by scar tissue), alcoholic hepatitis (inflammation of the liver) and liver cancer. Alcohol can damage the heart, brain and nerves. Cancers of the larynx, oesophagus and pancreas are also associated with consumption of alcohol.

Smoking

Cancer of the lung is 10 to 15 times more common in regular tobacco smokers than in people who have never smoked, and up to 40 times commoner in very heavy smokers. Smoking also increases the risk of cancer of the pancreas, oesophagus and larynx. Smokers are more likely than non-smokers to suffer heart attacks, chronic bronchitis and *emphysema*, a condition in which the sufferer commonly experiences increasing breathlessness.   SK

Infectious Diseases

An infectious disease is one in which one living organism inhabits and multiplies on or within another, harming it in the process, either by the production of toxic substances or by damaging, digesting or destroying part or all of its cellular structure. Such harmful organisms are mostly microscopic – viruses, bacteria and protozoans – but also include various larger organisms such as various kinds of fungi, worms and arthropods.

SEE ALSO

- THE BEGINNINGS OF LIFE p. 110
- PARASITISM AND SYMBIOSIS p. 174
- THE IMMUNE SYSTEM p. 212
- PREVENTING DISEASE p. 244
- THE HISTORY OF MEDICINE p. 248

The parasitic flatworm Schistosoma, which causes schistosomiasis.

Leprosy is a chronic inflammatory disease that affects the skin, mucous membranes and nerves.

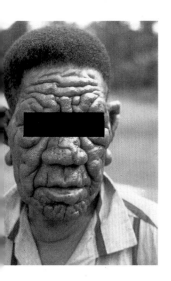

Human beings may be efficient at killing each other, but these other organisms are even more efficient: more people died in the outbreak of Spanish influenza following World War I than died in the war itself. From conception onwards, human beings are under attack from infectious organisms ranging from the rubella virus, which damages embryos, to pneumonia, which quietly ends the lives of many old people.

The existence of bacteria was first demonstrated in the 17th century by Anton van Leeuwenhoek (see p. 250) who detected them through a microscope in scrapings of the white film on his teeth. With later microscopes (see pp. 32–3) scientists were able to find many more of his 'animalcules', now calling them microorganisms. Some – the viruses – are so small that they can only be seen with an electron microscope (see pp. 332–3). The vast majority of microorganisms are harmless; some live with human beings in harmony, each helping the other in a *symbiotic* relationship (see also pp. 174–5). For example, certain bacteria manufacture some of the vitamins of the B complex in the intestines, at the same time absorbing a tiny amount of our food. However, many organisms are harmful, and such organisms are called *pathogens*. Pathogens are divided into four main groups: viruses, bacteria, fungi and parasites.

Viruses

Viruses (see p. 110) are by far the smallest of the pathogens. They need to live inside the body cells of other organisms to survive, and in reproducing themselves they destroy the host cell.

Our only natural defence against viruses is the formation of antibodies from B cells manufactured in the bone marrow (see pp. 212–13). One other natural substance that is effective against viruses is interferon, but this has proved so difficult to produce commercially that it is not used in the routine treatment of viral disease. Only two or three drugs are of any use, and these only against a limited number of viruses. Treatment at the moment has to be by prevention in the form of immunization, which produces the antibodies in our system before the virus itself attacks (see pp. 212–3). Considerable research has recently been going on into *oncogenic* (cancer-causing) viruses, which appear to stimulate cells to become malignant, and the near future may well see significant advances in this field.

Bacteria

Bacteria (see p. 110) are much bigger structures, and unlike viruses are visible under the ordinary light microscope. They have four main shapes: round (*cocci*), straight rods (*bacilli*), curved rods (*vibrios*), and coils (*spirochaetes*).

Two groups of drugs are used to treat bacterial infection. The first group, the *bacteriostats*, prevent the multiplication of bacteria. The second group, the *antibiotics*, either disrupt the cell membranes or metabolic pathways of bacteria, or act as direct poisons. Matching the infecting bacteria to the appropriate antibacterial drug involves growing the bacteria on a culture dish, and then placing discs impregnated with antibiotics in the dish. With an effective antibiotic the disc will show a clear space around it where the organism does not grow. It is then said to be 'sensitive' to the antibiotic.

Fungi

Fungi (see pp. 118–19) are probably the most widespread of organisms, inhabiting virtually every animal and plant species and their habitats. Thus there is essentially no difference between fairy rings on a lawn and ringworm on the skin – the characteristic spreading ring indicates fungi growing in both media.

The Plague by the Swiss painter Arnold Böcklin (1827–1901).

Very few fungi infect human beings, and those that do mostly colonize the surface (skin, nails and hair). However, there are geographical differences: in North America, for example, there are many deeply invasive fungi, causing such diseases as pneumonia. These fungi are not found in the UK or Europe.

Spores of fungi, carried in the air, may be responsible for asthma and many allergies in human beings, but are not infections in the strictest sense (see p. 236).

Parasites

Parasites are divided into three groups – protozoans, worms and arthropods.

Protozoans, although still microscopic, are generally larger than bacteria and possess a more evolved cell structure (see pp. 110–11). They include the amoeba that causes amoebic dysentery. Protozoans are not damaged by antibiotics in the concentrations that would be lethal to bacteria. Some, such as the malaria parasite, go through complicated life cycles.

Parasitic *worms* affect human intestines in various ways, and in some cases migrate to various other organs of the body, sometimes causing large cysts or swelling of limbs as in elephantiasis. They include threadworms, roundworms, hookworms, flatworms, flukes and tapeworms.

Arthropods (see pp. 124–7) such as lice, fleas and mites not only infest or infect humans, but some also act as carriers (*vectors*) of microorganisms, such as those that cause typhus and plague. LH

TRANSMISSION OF INFECTIONS

Airborne: Transmitted through infected droplets in the air from the nose, throat/lungs or saliva, or from dust particles from fallen skin.

Contamination: Contamination of food or water supplies usually by infected faeces or urine.

Direct contact (contagion): Disease is caught from close contact with an infected person.

Sexual transmission: Transmitted by vaginal or anal intercourse or oral sex. Use of condoms can reduce risk of transmission.

Blood borne: Transmitted by injection of contaminated blood or blood products or by improperly sterilized instruments. Common among haemophiliacs and intravenous drug users; occasionally from tattooing or acupuncture.

Animal carrier (vector): Injection of contaminated saliva as in malaria; flea bites as in bubonic plague.

SOME INFECTIOUS DISEASES

AIDS
Cause: HIV virus.
Transmission: Sexual; transfusion; contact with infected blood.
Characteristics: Destruction of immune system. Always fatal.
Prevention: Avoidance of unprotected sex and infected blood.
Treatment: Antiviral drugs (of limited use).

CHOLERA
Cause: Bacterium.
Transmission: Faecally contaminated water. Largely restricted to tropics.
Characteristics: Vomiting and diarrhoea leading to dehydration. Often fatal.
Prevention: Clean water supply. Vaccination effective 6–9 months.
Treatment: Antibiotics.

COMMON COLD
Cause: Viruses.
Transmission: Airborne; direct contact.
Characteristics: Inflammation of nose and upper respiratory tract causing sneezing, coughing, sore throat.
Prevention: Avoidance of direct contact.
Treatment: Rest. Proprietary medicines may relieve some symptoms but are of limited use.

DIPHTHERIA
Cause: Bacterium.
Transmission: Airborne.
Characteristics: Infection of pharynx; breathing obstructed; Heart inflammation. Often fatal. Now rare in developed countries.
Prevention: Immunization.
Treatment: Antibiotics.

DYSENTERY
Cause: Amoeba or bacteria. Amoebic dysentery confined to tropics.
Transmission: Contaminated food or water.
Characteristics: Diarrhoea, weight loss, dehydration. With amoebic dysentery, liver abscesses.
Prevention: Hygiene, clean water supply.
Treatment: Antibiotics, emetine, rehydration.

FOOD POISONING
Cause: Bacteria, including *Salmonella*, *Listeria* or more rarely *Clostridium botulinum*, which causes botulism. Viruses.
Transmission: Contaminated food or water.
Characteristics: Vomiting and diarrhoea. Botulism affects central nervous system and is often fatal.
Prevention: Food hygiene, clean water supply.
Treatment: Antibiotics, rehydration.

GLANDULAR FEVER
Cause: Virus.
Transmission: Direct contact.
Characteristics: Swollen lymph nodes, fever, sore throat, fatigue.
Prevention: Avoidance of direct contact.
Treatment: Rest.

GONORRHOEA
Cause: Bacterium.
Transmission: Sexual.
Characteristics: Discharge, pain on urinating; if not checked can cause sterility and inflammation of heart valves.
Prevention: Avoidance of unprotected sex.
Treatment: Antibiotics.

HEPATITIS A
Cause: Virus.
Transmission: Contaminated food or water.
Characteristics: Inflammation of liver causing fever, sickness and jaundice.
Prevention: Immunization.
Treatment: No effective antiviral drug.

HEPATITIS B
Cause: Virus.
Transmission: Sexual or blood borne.
Characteristics: see above.
Prevention: Immunization; avoidance of unprotected sex and infected blood.
Treatment: No effective antiviral drug.

HERPES SIMPLEX
Cause: Virus.
Transmission: Direct contact.
Characteristics: Small blisters on mouth or genitals. Virus lies dormant and symptoms may recur.
Prevention: Avoidance of close contact.
Treatment: Acyclovir.

HERPES ZOSTER (SHINGLES)
Cause: Reactivation of virus that causes varicella (chickenpox).
Characteristics: Virus affects a nerve of the face, abdomen or chest causing severe pain and blisters in surrounding skin.
Treatment: Acyclovir.

INFLUENZA
Cause: Virus.
Transmission: Airborne.
Characteristics: Fever, loss of appetite, weakness. In elderly people can be fatal.
Prevention: Immunization against certain viruses.
Treatment: Rest.

LEPROSY
Cause: Bacterium.
Transmission: Prolonged or close contact.
Characteristics: Thickening of skin and nerves, numbness, deformity and disfigurement.
Prevention: Avoidance of direct contact.
Treatment: Control with sulphone drugs.

LEGIONNAIRES' DISEASE
Cause: Bacterium.
Transmission: Airborne: carried in water droplets from contaminated supplies, often through air-conditioning systems or showers.
Characteristics: Fever, cough, chest pain, breathlessness. Can be fatal.
Prevention: Attention to cooling towers and hot water.
Treatment: Antibiotics.

MALARIA
Cause: Parasite.
Transmission: Mosquito bites.
Characteristics: Destruction of red blood cells causing fever and anaemia. Can be fatal.,
Prevention: See box, p. 244.
Treatment: See box, p. 244.

MEASLES
Cause: Virus.
Transmission: Airborne.
Characteristics: Fever, rash, possible middle-ear infection or bronchopneumonia.
Prevention: Immunization.
Treatment: Antibiotics if infections present.

MENINGITIS
Cause: Virus or bacteria.
Transmission: Airborne or direct contact.
Characteristics: Inflammation of membranes surrounding brain causes headache, fever, convulsions. Can be fatal.
Prevention: Avoidance of direct contact.
Treatment: Bacterial meningitis: antibiotics. Viral meningitis: rest.

MUMPS
Cause: Virus.
Transmission: Airborne.
Characteristics: Fever, swelling of parotid salivary glands. In adults, testicular and ovarian inflammation.
Prevention: Immunization (immunity short-lived).
Treatment: Rest.

PLAGUE
Cause: Bacterium.
Transmission: Airborne or via flea bites.
Characteristics: Fever, weakness, delirium, painful buboes (swelling of lymph nodes). Often fatal.
Prevention: Immunization (partial protection).
Treatment: Antibiotics.

PNEUMONIA
Cause: Bacteria or viruses.
Transmission: Airborne; direct contact.
Characteristics: Inflammation of lung causing pain and breathing difficulty. Can be fatal.
Prevention:
Treatment: Antibiotics if caused by bacteria.

POLIOMYELITIS
Cause: Virus.
Transmission: Direct contact.
Characteristics: Infection of central nervous system causing fever, headache, stiffness of neck. Possible paralysis in minority of cases.
Prevention: Immunization.
Treatment: Use of respirator if respiratory paralysis occurs. Physiotherapy if muscles remain affected.

RUBELLA (GERMAN MEASLES)
Cause: Virus.
Transmission: Direct contact.
Characteristics: Headache, sore throat, fever, swelling of neck, pink rash. Can damage developing foetus if caught by pregnant woman.
Prevention: Immunization.
Treatment: Rest.

SCHISTOSOMIASIS (BILHARZIA)
Cause: Parasitic flatworm *Schistosoma*.
Transmission: Eggs excreted in faeces or urine of infected people undergo part of larval development in freshwater snails. Larvae released by snails penetrate skin of person bathing in infected water and colonize blood vessels of intestine.
Characteristics: Diarrhoea, enlarged spleen and liver, cirrhosis of the liver. Can be fatal.
Prevention: Clean water supply.
Treatment: Various drugs.

SCARLET FEVER
Cause: Bacterium.
Transmission: Airborne.
Characteristics: Fever, sore throat, scarlet rash, possible ear and kidney infections.
Prevention: Avoidance of contacts.
Treatment: Antibiotics.

SYPHILIS
Cause: Bacterium.
Transmission: Sexual; can also be passed to foetus via placenta.
Characteristics: Hard ulcer on genitals followed by fever, malaise, rash on chest. Eventual heart and brain damage, blindness, general paralysis of the insane.
Prevention: Avoidance of unprotected sex.
Treatment: Antibiotics.

TAPEWORMS
Transmission: Through infested meat.
Characteristics: Weakness, hunger, weight loss caused by parasite absorbing nutrients.
Prevention: Avoiding undercooked meat.
Treatment: Antithelmintics.

TETANUS (LOCKJAW)
Cause: Bacterium.
Transmission: Bacterium entering wounds.
Characteristics: Muscle stiffness, spasm and rigidity, high fever, convulsions, extreme pain. Can be fatal.
Prevention: Immunization.
Treatment: Penicillin and antitoxins.

THREADWORMS
Transmission: Direct contact.
Characteristics: Anal itching caused by female worm emerging at night to lay eggs.
Prevention: Hygiene.
Treatment: Piperazine.

THRUSH
Cause: Fungus *Candida albicans*.
Transmission: Fungus (*Candida albicans*) lives in alimentary tract and vagina; thrush arises when growth of fungus increases, in some cases following course of broad-spectrum antibiotics. Can be passed to baby at birth.
Characteristics: White patches in mouth or irritation of vagina.
Prevention: Avoidance of broad-spectrum antibiotics.
Treatment: Antifungals.

TUBERCULOSIS
Cause: Bacterium.
Transmission: Airborne; unpasteurized milk.
Characteristics: Bacteria inhaled into lungs cause a *tubercle* or lesion leading to fever, weight loss, coughing up blood. Bacteria from infected milk affect abdominal lymph nodes. Formerly often fatal.
Prevention: Immunization, pasteurizing milk.
Treatment: Antibiotics.

TYPHOID
Cause: Bacterium.
Transmission: Faecally contaminated food or water.
Characteristics: Infection of digestive system causing high fever, red rash, possible inflammation of spleen and bones. Formerly often fatal.
Prevention: Immunization.
Treatment: Antibiotics.

TYPHUS
Cause: Parasite *Rickettsia*, spread by lice, fleas or ticks.
Characteristics: Severe headaches, rash, high fever, delirium.
Prevention: Hygiene.
Treatment: Antibiotics.

VARICELLA (CHICKENPOX)
Cause: Virus.
Transmission: Airborne.
Characteristics: Mild fever, itchy blistering rash.
Prevention: Immunization.
Treatment: Rest.

WHOOPING COUGH
Cause: Bacterium.
Transmission: Airborne; direct contact.
Characteristics: Infection of trachea and bronchi producing coughs followed by involuntary intakes of breath.
Prevention: Immunization.
Treatment: Rest.

Surgery

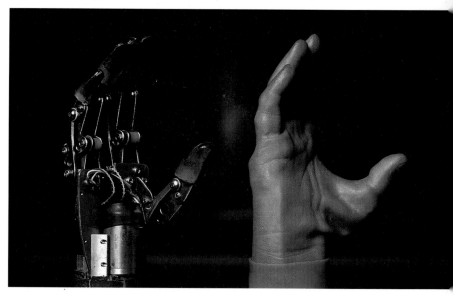

The practice of surgery is very old indeed. From the remains of skulls we know that the technique of trepanning – removing a disc of bone from the skull – was carried out about 10 000 years ago. This operation released the build-up of fluid in the skull, and may have been originally based on the belief that it let out an evil spirit. But it was only in the last century and a half that certain key events laid the foundations for safe, effective surgery as we know it today.

The _prosthesis_ (right) (an artificial replacement for a missing or malfunctioning part of the body) is a major part of medical technology. The picture shows an 'intelligent' prosthetic hand. Electrodes built into prosthetic hands can be activated by the patient's muscle contractions, and the electrical current generated by the contractions is amplified by electrical components and batteries to control movement.

Landmark developments included the introduction of anaesthesia; the acceptance of the germ theory of disease, which inspired measures to limit post-operative infection; the discovery of blood groups, paving the way for safe transfusions; and the development of techniques for surgical _anastomosis_ – joining the severed ends of tubular structures such as blood vessels or the intestine.

Necessity or choice

At the beginning of the 20th century, two kinds of surgery began to emerge: elective and non-elective. Non-elective (often emergency) surgery is for the most part life-saving. Few people would question the need for the removal of an acutely inflamed appendix, amputation of a gangrenous limb or repair of a ruptured aorta. But with elective procedures there is often the element of choice: when to have the operation; which of several different techniques to choose; or whether to forgo surgery in favour of some other treatment.

The most notably successful elective procedure is hip replacement, which involves removing the diseased joint and inserting an artificial replacement or _prosthesis_. Degeneration of the hip joint due to age and arthritis (see p. 207) can be overcome by this operation, freeing the patient from pain and restoring mobility.

The range of prostheses available includes the artificial pacemaker. This is an electronic device supplied to patients with a condition known as heart block, in which the conduction of the electrical impulses generated by the heart's natural pacemaker is impaired, slowing down the heart beat. The pacemaker stimulates the heart to beat at the desired rate.

A more recent innovation is the cochlear implant, also an electronic assembly, which restores hearing in some cases of deafness attributable to damage in the inner ear (see p. 219).

Spare-parts surgery also includes grafting of organic tissues – for instance, the _corneal graft_, in which diseased parts of the cornea (see p. 218) are replaced by corneal tissue from a donor.

Obsolete procedures

Some early operations, such as _thoracoplasty_ (causing partial collapse of a lung) for pulmonary tuberculosis, have been replaced by more effective medical treatments. _Psycho-surgery_ – surgical attempts to rectify mental disorders – has also become largely obsolete. For instance, _leucotomy_ – an operation to sever connections to the frontal lobes of the brain – was pioneered in the 1930s for the relief of severe mental illness. It reduced severe anxiety, but often at the expense of personality and intellect. It came to be seen as inhumane, and was rendered superfluous by the advent in the

---

ORGAN TRANSPLANTS

The first human organ to be successfully transplanted – in the 1950s – was a kidney. The fact that the donor and recipient were identical twins meant that there were no problems with rejection – normally a problem with such transplants because the body's immune system (see p. 212) identifies the transplant as a foreign object and so sets about destroying it. It was another two decades, however, before organ transplants – kidney grafts in particular – began to be routinely employed to replace organs that had completely failed. Since then, the biggest single contribution to survival has been the discovery in 1978 of the drug _cyclosporin_, which suppresses the immune system and so prevents rejection.

Four major transplant procedures have moved from the experimental category to become treatments of choice: kidney, liver, heart and heart-lung. Kidney grafting is most in demand.

There is no mechanical support for the failing liver, and liver transplant – one of the most challenging of all operations – is increasingly sought. Children tolerate it slightly better than adults. However, because of the difficulty of finding suitably-sized organs, some younger children now receive segmental grafts fashioned from adult livers.

The fact that none of the first recipients of transplanted hearts (pioneered by Christiaan Barnard (1922–) in South Africa in 1967) survived for long meant that this operation lost its appeal for some years. It came back into its own in the late 1970s, and now enjoys a one-year survival rate of 80%. Candidates for heart transplants include newborn babies with hitherto inoperable heart disease.

Heart-lung transplantations – technically more feasible than grafting the lungs alone – was developed for patients with severe lung disease, such as cystic fibrosis (see p. 236). Single lung transplants are rarely performed.

Donor kidneys are preserved prior to transplantation in this 'Max-100' machine at the University of Minneapolis Hospital, USA.

SEE ALSO

- OPTICS p. 32
- MEDICAL TECHNOLOGY p. 242
- HISTORY OF MEDICINE p. 248

1950s of effective drug therapy (see p. 235). More recently, the need for exploratory surgery has been lessened by the introduction of non-invasive imaging techniques, such as ultrasound, CT-scan and magnetic resonance imaging (see pp. 242–3 and 332–3). Laparotomy – laying open the abdomen – was and still is the commonest exploratory procedure, but is now performed less frequently.

Keyhole surgery

Endoscopy – examination of the interior of the body by direct viewing – also provides a minimally invasive aid to diagnosis. *Endoscopes* are flexible viewing tubes fitted with a built-in fibre-optic light source (see fibre optics, p. 33) and adapted for specific parts of the body. A *bronchoscope*, for instance, is used for viewing the bronchial passage (see p. 210), while the *gastroscope* allows the interior of the stomach to be seen. *Tissue biopsy* (the removal of a small piece of tissue for examination) and small, localized treatments can be performed by means of fine instruments introduced through the endoscope. This approach is known as *keyhole surgery*.

Open-heart surgery

A major new development in the last quarter of a century has been open-heart surgery. This requires the heart to be stopped and the blood to be pumped by way of an *extra-corporeal circulation* (ECC), and had to await the advent of the heart-lung machine in the late 1950s.

In the 1970s, a significant addition to the heart surgeon's repertoire was *coronary artery bypass grafting* (CABG). This is an operation to replace sections of coronary arteries that have become severely narrowed by an accumulation of fatty deposits (*plaque*). Furred vessels are replaced by lengths of vein, usually taken from the patient's leg. The operation relieves the crippling pain of angina and restores an adequate blood supply to the heart muscle.

For some patients an alternative technique is available for dealing with blocked arteries – *balloon angioplasty*, developed in Switzerland in 1977. This involves passing a balloon-tipped catheter into a large artery in the groin and advancing it until the tip comes to rest in the narrowed coronary vessel. Here the balloon is inflated, compressing the plaque against the artery wall so as to re-establish an adequate channel for blood-flow to the heart. If balloon angioplasty fails, or – as often happens – the plaque recurs, the procedure can be repeated.

Balloon angioplasty is not without risk, but it is performed under local anaesthesia and is quicker than the open-heart procedure. Another consideration is that it is a much cheaper option, entailing a hospital stay of only two to three days instead of the ten days or so required for CABG. However, the newer procedure may itself be improved (or even superseded) if current experimental work with

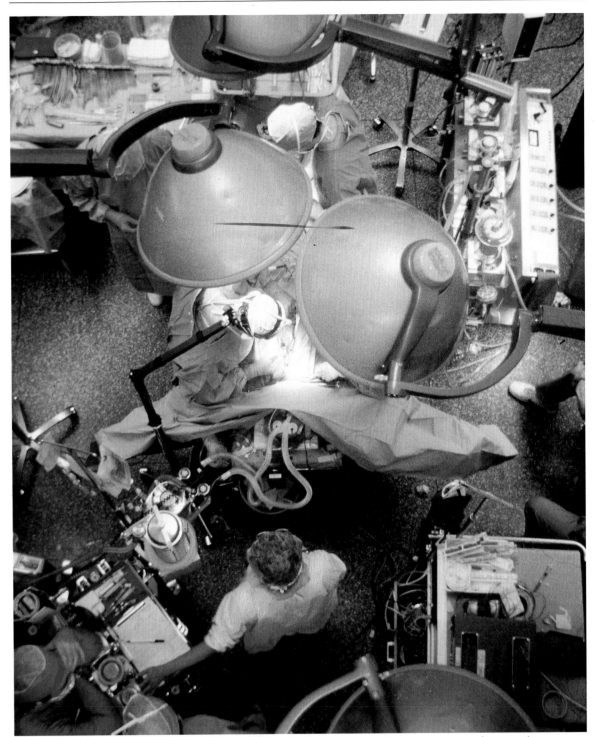

lasers (see below) is seen to be more effective.

Bloodless surgery

Two areas where use of the medical laser has proved revolutionary are the treatment of cervical cancer (cancer of the neck of the womb) and eye problems such as glaucoma and diabetic eye disease. With fine precision, lasers can be made to cut, coagulate or vaporize body tissue. Tumours lying close to vital nerve fibres, bleeding gastric ulcers, some cancers, and even unsightly birthmarks can all be treated quickly and relatively painlessly. However, the full potential of 'bloodless surgery' has yet to be realized.

(For an account of the principles behind the laser, see p. 33.)

Safe anaesthesia

It is often not realized to what extent successful surgery relies on competent anaesthesia. Dramatic advances in anaesthetic techniques over the last few decades have contributed to the development of high-profile surgery (such as transplants, etc.), as well as to cheaper, safer options for routine treatments, In particular, the versatility of anaesthetic techniques underlies the growth of same-day surgery, which is increasingly popular with patients.　　　　PP

An operation in progress in a modern operating theatre. Since the 19th century, operations have been carried out in aseptic (i.e. germ-free) environments. Prior to carrying out operations, surgical staff wash thoroughly and change into sterilized clothing. The operating theatre and all its instruments are also sterilized. Before the advent of asepsis and antiseptics, most patients died from infected wounds following surgery (see pp. 248–9).

Medical Technology

The practice of medicine is based on diagnosis and treatment. Diagnosis – identifying a disease or condition – depends on recognizing and assessing changes from normal function. With this information the doctor decides on the appropriate course of action. Increasingly sophisticated medical technology underlies both diagnosis and treatment.

The physician of a century ago could call upon few instruments to aid diagnosis. He relied on a stethoscope and percussion of the chest, a few urine and blood tests and, from the turn of the century, the *sphygmomanometer* to measure blood pressure, as well as the skilful observation of physical signs. The internal effects of the disease process could only be learned after death, by dissecting and studying the body (*autopsy*). And, while diagnosis became increasingly accurate, little could be done to influence the outcome of a disease.

Over the century, X-rays and penicillin perhaps represent medicine's most radical advances. Röntgen's mysterious rays (see p. 332) first brought to light the secrets of the living body. Penicillin was the first of several drugs – the *antibiotics* (see p. 249) – that have proved successful in treating an enormous range of bacterial infections (see pp. 238–9). These early discoveries have since been joined by an array of technologies that have not only given clearer insights into the living body, but also provided increasingly diverse means of support for the sick.

Medical imaging

Medical imaging has progressed far beyond the early days of still X-rays, although these are still an important diagnostic tool. Routine procedures now reveal organs and bones, joints in motion, blood flow through the heart and vessels, and cell activity at the molecular level.

Digital subtraction angiography (DSA) builds up multiple X-ray images by computer into a coherent digital picture. For instance, a *radiograph* (X-ray photograph) can be taken of a major blood vessel and radio-opaque dye (a dye that does not allow X-rays to pass through) then injected into a vein. A second radiograph is taken and the computer 'subtracts' the first image from the second, leaving only the differences between the two – in this case a clear outline of the blood supply to the brain, kidney or one of the limbs.

Ultrasound (see p. 332) is best known for its role in providing images of the foetus in pregnancy, since it would be damaged by X-rays. *Echocardiography*, now an essential diagnostic tool for cardiologists (heart specialists), also uses ultrasound to study the heart in motion. *Doppler ultrasonography* translates blood flow into an image, using the Doppler effect (see p. 31). As blood passes through a narrowed vessel or damaged heart valve the changing sound of the flow is reflected to pinpoint the damage. This is proving of great value in the diagnosis of heart conditions in young children and babies.

Computerized Axial Tomography (CAT scanning) measures the attenuation of X-rays entering the body from different angles. The computer reconstructs thin sections or 'slices' of the interior of the body. The technique is valuable in that it allows images of soft tissues, such as the liver and kidneys, to be differentiated.

Magnetic resonance imaging (MRI) is a wholly new technique. Brief radio impulses, emitted within a very powerful magnetic field surrounding the body, cause the nuclei of atoms first to spin and then to emit signals as they realign themselves to the magnet. Each tissue gives off characteristic signals, which are converted by computer to produce startlingly clear images. For the first time it has become possible to observe degenerative conditions of the central nervous system, such as multiple sclerosis.

Medical monitoring

The importance of physiological monitoring has been appreciated for many centuries. Recognizing that disease affects the way the body functions, early physicians felt pulses and tasted urine (for sugar in diabetes). Present technologies reflect the same principle: that every condition produces typical changes that can be observed and measured. These findings are the key to diagnosing disease and to determining its treatment.

Electrocardiography (ECG) is a safe, non-invasive means of studying heart function. Electrical impulses generated by the heart are transmitted to an oscilloscope by means of electrodes placed on the skin. Abnormal rhythms and damage caused by a heart attack produce characteristic patterns that can be 'read' on the ECG tracing. A miniature ECG worn for 24 hours records heart activity throughout a routine day, while cardiac monitors used in hospital intensive care units provide a continuous picture of heart function in the critically ill.

A recent, non-invasive monitoring device, the *pulse oximeter*, measures oxygen concentrations in arterial blood. The probe, which simply clips on to a fingertip or ear lobe, detects pulsions of blood in the capillaries lying near the skin surface. It has two light-emitting diodes on one side – which flash up to 500 times a minute – and a photodetector on the other. The reading – based on the differing amounts of light absorbed by oxygen-carrying haemoglobin and haemoglobin without oxygen – gives a good indication of the blood supply to vital organs. A dangerous drop in oxygen can be detected – and treated – before damage occurs.

Physiological support

Before the invention of artificial respiration in the 18th century, the cessation of breathing meant the end of life. It is not surprising that the first resuscitation technique provoked a degree of hysteria: if the dead could be restored to life, who could say when a person was dead? Societies and ingenious devices sprang up everywhere to forestall the horrors of premature burial. The implications are no less problematic today. With the technology to support failing organ systems, how do we choose when to support and when to withdraw support?

Ventilators are used to maintain oxygen levels in the blood when unassisted breathing is inadequate. These machines – popularly known as 'life-support

INTENSIVE CARE

The intensive care unit is at the forefront of high-technology medicine. Here, a multitude of equipment and techniques are brought together to monitor, support and treat patients who are in imminent danger of death. Many of these devices have a vital preventive function, alerting staff to potentially fatal conditions before they become irreversible.

And yet the human element still prevails. Doctors must choose appropriate treatment and appreciate the consequences of each intervention. And it is nursing care and experience, not technology, on which the patient's life ultimately depends. Technology is a useful tool, but only in the right hands.

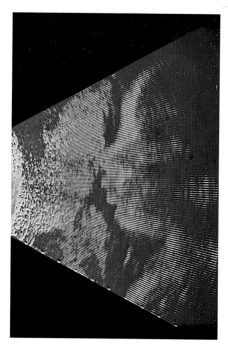

A false-colour ultrasound image of a human foetus in the womb after 7 months' development, showing the face and shoulders in profile.

machines' – deliver humidified gases to the lungs through a tube inserted into the trachea, either through the mouth or through a surgical incision in the throat. Modern ventilators control the proportion of oxygen, the pressure used to inflate the lungs and the rate of respirations. Some types initiate every respiration; others support the patient's own breathing.

Dialysis replaces kidney function in renal failure by removing toxic wastes from the blood. By means of diffusion across a semipermeable membrane, waste products and excess water are transferred to a *dialysate* fluid. For *haemodialysis*, the blood passes through a dialyser with membrane and dialysate, and is returned to the circulation.

Continuous ambulatory peritoneal dialysis (CAPD) uses the peritoneum (the membrane lining the abdominal cavity), which is about 2 m² (21½ sq ft) in area. Two litres of warmed dialysate are introduced into the abdomen through a catheter, left for several hours while waste products accumulate, and are then drained out. CAPD is carried out round the clock so that the patient is able to continue leading a normal life.

One of the foremost life-saving techniques is *defibrillation*. Each beat of the heart begins with electrical stimuli arising in the heart's own conductive tissue. In the condition known as fibrillation, the stimuli, and therefore the heart beat, become chaotic. Defibrillation uses a direct current shock to convert the twitching movement to normal rhythm. Two paddles, one negative and the other positive, are applied to the patient's chest, and the counter-shock delivered to the heart causes the myocardial cells to resume their proper electrical function.

This technique is being taken into the community to save the lives of people with heart disease. Defibrillators installed in ambulances either have a built-in computer or can be linked by telephone to the hospital. If a patient develops chest pains, the two paddles – which also take ECGs – are placed in position. If the machine has its own computer, this analyses the ECG and advises whether to defibrillate. Alternatively, the ECG can be relayed by telephone to a consultant, who can activate the defibrillator if necessary. Automatic battery-powered defibrillators that can be implanted in the patient's body are also available.

Drug therapy

Drugs – the term includes any substance that acts on living cells – may treat or prevent a disease or condition, or may support a stressed or failing organ. The earliest effective drugs to be used – still of great value – include quinine, to treat malaria, and digitalis, to strengthen the weakened heart. Since the beginning of the 19th century, and particularly since World War II, drugs have been discovered and developed to treat every body system

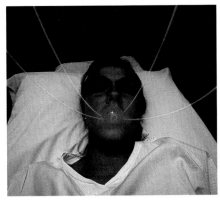

A low-power red argon laser, directed through 4 fibre-optics waveguides to treat a cancerous tumour in the patient's throat. The low-power beams activate a drug previously injected into the patient – the drug does not affect normal cells, but is absorbed by cancerous ones. The products of the photochemical reaction initiated by the laser are toxic to cancerous cells.

and many diverse features within each system. Mentioned here are just some of the latest major developments.

Peptic ulcers occur when part of the lining of the digestive tract is digested by acid and the digestive enzyme *pepsin*. H_2*-receptor antagonists* such as cimetidine and ranitidine, which reduce gastric acid secretion, have revolutionized treatment of this potentially lethal condition. Management of ulcers was once limited to diet and major surgery; now most cases respond to a course of medication over 3–4 weeks. However, the ulcers may recur.

Thrombolytics are improving both short- and long-term survival after a heart attack. When a blood clot (*thrombus*) lodges in one of the coronary arteries, the heart muscle is deprived of blood and begins to die. Injected intravenously, preferably within the first few hours of the attack, both streptokinase and tissue plasminogen activator (t-PA) dissolve the thrombi effectively, preventing irreversible damage to the heart muscle.

Controversial though it may be, there has long been interest in an abortion pill to spare women the trauma of surgical termination. Developed in France, RU 486 is proving an effective abortion pill – 95% successful in terminating pregnancies of up to nine weeks. The embryo is implanted in the lining of the uterus, which is rich in blood vessels and maintained by the hormone progesterone. When progesterone is replaced by the synthetic hormone mifepristone (RU 486), the uterine lining and embryo are usually shed within 48 hours. Side-effects include moderate to severe pain and possible heavy bleeding.　　ESa

SEE ALSO

● ACOUSTICS p. 30
● OPTICS p. 32
● SURGERY p. 240
● HISTORY OF MEDICINE p. 248
● SEEING THE INVISIBLE p. 332

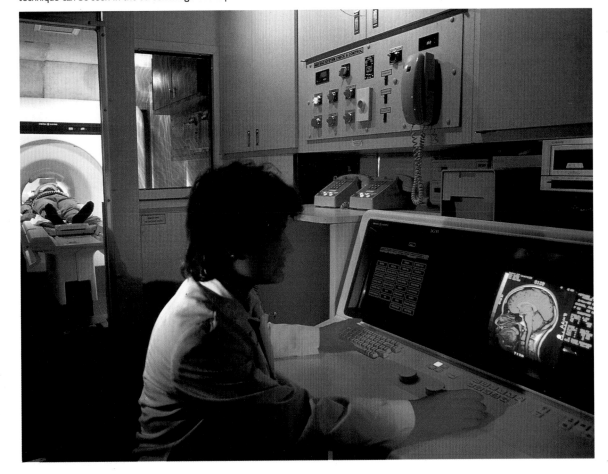

A mobile magnetic resonance unit. The remarkable clarity of the information obtained with this technique can be seen in the screen image of the patient's head.

Preventing Disease

Methods of disease prevention range from simple precautions taken in the home – washing the hands, for example – to expensive international campaigns to eradicate illnesses. Until the 19th century there was little understanding of how disease was spread – earlier people often thought that diseases such as plague were a punishment from angry gods. We now know that plague is a possibly fatal infection passed to man from rat fleas (see p. 402).

Throughout history, sailors on long voyages suffered from *scurvy*, a disease characterized by bleeding gums and stiff limbs. The discovery in the mid-18th century that eating citrus fruits could cure these symptoms demonstrated the importance of diet in preventing disease, and ships began to carry supplies of limes. In the 20th century it was discovered that citrus fruits are particularly rich in ascorbic acid (vitamin C), and that it is a lack of this substance that causes scurvy (see p. 208). As our understanding increases, so we are better equipped to prevent disease.

Public health measures

Adequate housing is a basic human need and plays an important part in preventing disease. Overcrowded living conditions lead to the rapid spread of disease – for example, evidence of millions of disease-carrying parasites and worms have been found in human remains discovered by archaeologists in primitive settlements. Without toilets and drainage systems, such infestations are passed easily from one person to another. Two thousand years ago, Romans realized the importance of fresh water supplies and sewage systems, and the ruins of Pompeii include fountains, toilet areas and drains. Systems to cope with human waste are essential, since it is a common source of infection if not properly disposed of. Typhoid, for example, can be easily spread by a faulty sewer pipe leaking into the supply of drinking water. In London a cholera outbreak in 1854 was traced to a public well, the Broad Street Pump, which was being contaminated in this way.

Industrialization has brought new problems of pollution and waste disposal (see also p. 300). Industrial accidents may also have major environmental effects, notably accidents at chemical factories or nuclear power stations, and governments impose rigorous safety regulations to prevent these – although the disasters at the chemical factory in Bhopal in India in 1984 and at the nuclear power station at Chernobyl in Ukraine in 1986 show that such regulations are not always fool-proof. The effects of radioactivity are particularly long-lasting, and may produce cancers years after the exposure to radiation. People working with dangerous substances such as radiation – for example taking X-rays in hospital – have to take precautions to protect themselves and others.

International disease control

The World Health Organization in 1980 declared that smallpox, an often fatal disease, was officially extinct. This was the result of a successful worldwide vaccination programme. It was hoped that the same success would be achieved with malaria, but unexpected difficulties have prevented the success of this programme (see box).

An older method of preventing disease from spreading from country to country – dating from 15th-century Venice – is quarantine. Quarantine (from the Italian *quarantina,* 40 days) is a period of isolation in which animals (and formerly humans) are detained before being allowed to enter a country – so allowing time for symptoms of a disease to develop before it can be transmitted. In this way, some countries have been successful in preventing *rabies* entering their territory. This serious illness is spread by animals, often foxes and rodents, but potentially also by domestic animals. In the United Kingdom strict quarantine arrangements for all animals entering the country have prevented the disease from becoming established.

Immunization programmes

Much protection from disease is given to children through immunization in the

Overcrowded housing in the past contributed to the rapid spread of diseases such as tuberculosis, while poor sanitation was often a major factor in outbreaks of cholera and typhoid.

MALARIA

Every year in the tropics, more than 1 million people still die of malaria and 2 million new cases appear, despite worldwide effects to control the disease. The current situation is now more complex and difficult to solve than ever before.

All efforts at controlling the disease focus on the mosquito that is the carrier of the malaria parasite. A person catches malaria when bitten by a female mosquito. The parasite may then stay dormant in the human liver for months or even years before causing symptoms. There are different types of malaria, some more likely than others to be fatal.

Control of the mosquito population helps to control the disease. This is done by destroying breeding sites – still water such as ponds – through land drainage, treating water with chemicals to destroy mosquito larvae, and the use of insecticides to kill mosquitoes.

Drugs can be used to treat infected humans, and measures – such as the use of nets, repellents and suitable clothing – can be taken to prevent the mosquito biting.

Throughout the 1950s and 1960s the World Health Organization had enormous success in malaria eradication, particularly in the USA and Europe. The programme also led to a 500-fold decrease in malaria in India. Unfortunately resistance of mosquitoes to the insecticide DDT then developed and in many areas in the 1970s the eradication began to falter. Some countries still have widespread malaria.

Travellers to areas where malaria is prevalent must take anti-malarial tablets before setting out, during their stay, and for at least four weeks after their return. The wide variety of drugs needed to prevent malaria reflects the emergence of the malaria parasite's resistance to certain drugs. This has further hampered control of the disease. Travellers must be careful to match their drug to the exact area they are travelling to in order to ensure its effectiveness.

first year of life (see p. 212). This has greatly decreased the incidence of previously common illnesses. In the USA certain immunizations – against measles, for instance – are required before a child can be admitted to school.

Rubella (German measles) is a mild illness, but if caught by a woman in the first three months of pregnancy it can affect the developing foetus, resulting in permanent damage such as blindness and deafness. National programmes exist in all developed countries to prevent this risk. Before the development of a vaccine many people died or were crippled due to *poliomyelitis* infection, but two drops of vaccine on the tongue can now provide effective protection for up to 10 years. Immunization is also standard in many

countries against diseases such as tuberculosis, diphtheria and tetanus.

In addition to childhood immunization programmes, immunization is available to the international traveller to prevent the risk of being affected by a wide range of illnesses.

Health education

Although much health education is undertaken by doctors, nurses, and health visitors, many people obtain health information from other sources. Magazines, newspapers and television carry increasing amounts of information on illnesses and their prevention. National campaigns to increase public awareness have been particularly successful.

In the UK, for example, widespread use of sophisticated advertising concerning the AIDS virus (see p. 212) led to significant changes in public attitude. It is also thought to have contributed to a reduction in the spread of the disease. In Australia there is a high incidence of *malignant melanoma* – a skin cancer common in those exposed to strong sunlight. A media campaign has helped to save lives by providing information on early detection and on precautions that prevent melanoma from developing. In the USA the fictional character *Superman* has been enlisted in a television campaign to encourage people to check their blood cholesterol level. A high level may increase the risk of heart disease; cutting down on fats and eating unsaturated instead of saturated fats (see p. 208) can help to reduce it.

Alcohol and tobacco

Cigarettes are known to cause cancer, lung disease and heart disease. Many governments impose restrictions on their advertising and sale, and increasingly on where they are smoked, since it is now recognized that it is possible to develop cancer from inhaling other peoples' cigarette smoke. Alcohol causes brain and liver damage and some types of cancer, as well as numerous accidents. Recent health campaigns have focused on the amount people can drink without risking these effects (see p. 246).

Health checks

In France the government links social security benefits to pregnant women to their attendance at antenatal clinics. This encourages attendance, which can lead to the early detection and prevention of diseases in the mother and the child.

Health-screening checks are used to detect various diseases, resulting in early treatment and fewer deaths. Finland and Scotland have succeeded, through regular screening, in reducing the number of deaths in women from cancer of the

cervix. X-ray techniques that can detect breast cancer are now widely available. Blood pressure can be tested to make sure that it is not dangerously high, and diabetes can be detected by the presence of sugar in the urine (see p. 214). Blood tests can reveal the existence of many conditions, from anaemia to the presence of the AIDS virus.

Although expensive to implement, health-screening checks – like other preventive measures – save money in the longer term on expensive treatments once diseases develop. They also save lives. RM

Smallpox has now been completely eradicated as a result of worldwide immunization programmes.

SEE ALSO

- FOOD, DIET AND DIGESTION p. 208
- THE IMMUNE SYSTEM p. 212
- NON-INFECTIOUS DISEASES p. 236
- INFECTIOUS DISEASES p. 238
- DRUG ABUSE p. 246
- POPULATION AND HUNGER p. 296
- THREATS TO THE ENVIRONMENT p. 300
- INDUSTRIAL SOCIETY (SOCIAL REFORMS) p. 434

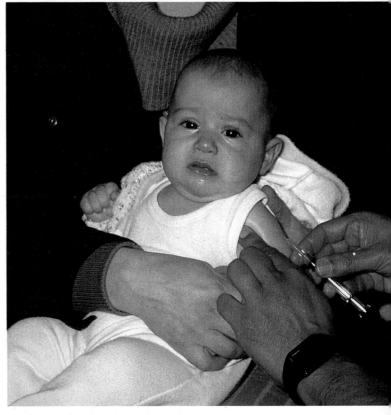

Children are vaccinated against a variety of diseases, including polio, tuberculosis, diphtheria, tetanus, whooping cough and measles.

Drug Abuse

People have been taking drugs for medicinal, spiritual or pleasurable purposes since the dawn of recorded history. Drug abuse is to be found among all known societies and cultures. Drug use is a subjective term implying dangerous use, usually of an illegal substance, and often reveals more about what is socially acceptable than what is truly harmful. In some societies heavy drinking and tobacco smoking are not generally considered to be drug abuse.

More precise terms have recently come into use: taking drugs for pleasure is referred to as *recreational*, as opposed to medical, use. Drug use which causes harm to the user is *problem* use, and can result from both medical and recreational use.

Physical and psychological dependence

Drug use can sometimes result in dependence, a craving to use again and again. This dependence may be physical, with unpleasant or dangerous symptoms when use of the drug is terminated, or psychological. Psychological dependence is often a greater problem than physical dependence and can occur with activities unrelated to drugs – gambling, for instance.

Such repeated activities can become harmful compulsions, especially if the person concerned faces problems such as lack of housing or employment, is susceptible to peer-group pressures, or is having difficulties with relationships.

Psychological factors can even influence the experience of physical dependence. The more a user fears withdrawing from a drug, the worse the physical withdrawal symptoms are likely to be. The dosage to which they have become accustomed is largely irrelevant. Regular sustained drug use can become an emotional crutch, with the routine of buying and taking the drug assuming a more important role than the physical effects.

Drugs and society

Different cultures use different drugs in different ways. For Sadhus – Hindu ascetics in India – cannabis is a sacred substance believed to assist the path to true understanding. The Christian world generally punishes cannabis use, but uses alcohol in religious services. Most Islamic societies ban both.

The social context in which drugs are taken influences how they are used. Alcohol is a physically addictive drug, dangerous by any standards, which causes immense harm when used excessively. Were it not for the fact that the majority of people drink without problems, most of the Western world would be facing widespread alcoholism and imminent social collapse. People have developed 'safe' drinking habits, reinforced by social pressures, such as not drinking alone, not drinking in the morning, or not drinking and driving. Other cultures control other drug use in similar ways.

Advertising, price structures, availability and the law all play a role in influencing who uses what drug, and how they use it.

Legal and illegal drugs

Despite international statutes that prohibit or restrict production and sale of certain drugs, differing cultural attitudes to drugs remain partially reflected in different laws. Cannabis is still legally available in certain Indian states, and may be used in limited quantities in some European countries and American states. Public tobacco smoking is becoming increasingly restricted.

There is an important distinction between laws prohibiting drugs and statutes regulating their production, sale and public consumption such as the UK alcohol licensing laws. Prohibition forces production and consumption underground, creating rich illegal cartels as in the USA in the 1920s. The wealth and power of many organized criminal syndicates in the USA, now dealing in heroin and cocaine, grew from this era. Estimating the present size of world illicit markets is difficult, since these businesses tend not to publish their accounts. In Bolivia and Colombia the value of the illicit drug trade, largely cocaine, probably exceeds the combined value of all legal trade. In Europe, particularly the UK and Scandinavian countries, amphetamines are one of the most commonly used drugs and widespread domestic production generates huge sums.

Sniffing cocaine can cause ulceration of the mucous membranes in the nose; death from respiratory arrest is possible after high doses.

There are no documented examples of prohibition eradicating the sale and use of an illegal drug. There are also many abused substances – such as lighter fuels, aerosols, cleaning fluids or the solvents in glue – which for practical reasons cannot be banned, although in some countries such as the UK and Eire retailers may not knowingly sell these for inhalation.

People are unlikely suddenly to stop using drugs, legal and illegal, and one proposed solution has been legal, strictly regulated supply and consumption of currently illegal drugs. However, it may be many years before legal consumption and supply curbs the power of illicit suppliers.

Nor is unrestricted legal supply a sensible solution. Restrictions controlling advertising, taxes to control relative price structures, and prescribing regulations making drugs such as heroin and amphetamines available to dependents are increasingly recognized as valid tools for minimizing problem drug use.

Prohibition: (right) the illegal manufacture and sale of alcohol was widespread in the USA during the 1920s. The picture shows the destruction of 18 000 bottles of confiscated beer.

New Drugs

The quest for safe, non-addictive substitutes for commonly abused substances has been a long one. Heroin was advertised as a miracle cure for many diseases and as a non-addictive substitute for morphine and opium when it was first introduced in the late 19th century. Barbiturates were tried as a safe substitute for heroin, until they were found to be far more physically addictive, more liable to cause death through overdose and even capable – unlike heroin – of causing death during withdrawal. The benzodiazepines were in turn seen as a safe substitute for barbiturates until it was discovered, too late for many medical users, that they also induced both physical and psychological dependence.

Illicit chemists have been working for years on drugs similar in effect to banned substances, yet chemically distinct and therefore legal – until the law is changed.

MDMA, known as XTC, ecstasy or adam, was one such drug, 'designed' as a substitute for LSD. It is now illegal in the UK.

Treatment

There is no single cure for problem drug use. Different treatments suit different people. It is generally accepted that withdrawing from physical addiction presents less of a problem than coping with psychological dependence. Successful treatment often has little to do with the drug itself, and may focus on personal counselling or practical assistance in finding work or a home. In recent years the concept of helping users learn safe drug use has become more acceptable as an option where total abstinence is unrealistic. Distributing clean syringes to combat HIV infection (see p. 212), prescribing opioids to maintain dependents on stable doses, and teaching sensible drinking habits are all examples of this approach.   TM; approved by ISDD

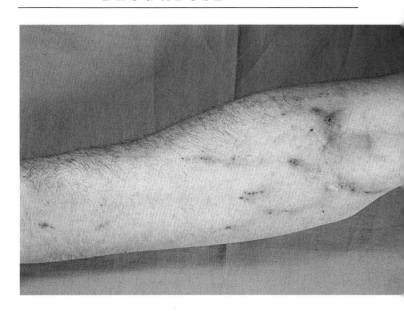

The injection-scarred arm of an intravenous drug user.

TYPES OF DRUG

ALCOHOL
Short-term effects: Intoxication lasting several hours.
Long-term effects: Increased risk of liver disease, high blood pressure, diseases of the nervous system, strong physical and psychological dependence. Withdrawal after very heavy use can lead to delirium, which can be fatal. Regular heavy drinking during pregnancy can cause permanent damage to the baby.

BARBITURATES
Medical use: As hypnotics (sleep inducers).
Short-term effects: Drunkenness if sleep does not occur. Overdose deaths possible after less than 10 times usual dose. Extremely dangerous with alcohol. Effects last 3–6 hours.
Long-term effects: Chronic inebriation, respiratory problems. Risk of overdose death even when tolerance has built up. Strong psychological and physical dependence. Withdrawal can cause seizures and delirium, and can be fatal.

BENZODIAZEPINES
Medical use: As tranquillizers and hypnotics; include Valium, Librium, Ativan, Mogadon, etc.
Short-term effects: Relief from anxiety. Overdose death only possible with massive doses.
Long-term effects: Lethargy, physical and psychological dependence. Withdrawal causes anxiety, restlessness and tremors.

SOLVENTS AND GASES
Short-term effects: Immediate intoxication lasting 15–45 minutes. Deaths due to accidents, suffocation and heart failure possible.
Long-term effects: Impairment of mental and physical functions – clears up when sniffing stopped. Prolonged use can cause brain damage. Aerosols and cleaning fluids especially harmful.

OPIATES AND OPIOIDS
Opiates – natural derivatives of the opium poppy – include heroin and morphine. **Opioids** – synthetic drugs similar to opiates – include methadone and pethidine.

Medical use: Pain reduction
Short-term effects: Feeling of warmth and contentment lasting 3–6 hours.
Long-term effects: Psychological and physical dependence, respiratory problems, constipation, lack of sexual drive, instability of mood. Overdose death possible.

AMPHETAMINES
Medical use: Stimulation of nervous system.
Short-term effects: Increased alertness, mood elevation, diminished fatigue lasting 3–4 hours. After repeated doses and consequent sleep loss over several days, temporary psychotic state possible.
Long-term effects: Paranoid thinking and psychotic states, which clear up when use is stopped. Poor health due to lack of sleep and appetite. Withdrawal effects can be severe.

COCAINE
Short-term effects: Similar to amphetamines but lasting for shorter periods. Repeated use over several hours may lead to extreme agitation and paranoid states. Death from respiratory arrest possible after large doses. Cocaine freebase, which includes 'crack', gives more immediate and intense effects of shorter duration.
Long-term use: Short-lived 'high' is followed by extreme mood swings and eating disorders. Paranoid thinking and psychotic behaviour possible. If sniffed, possible nose damage; if smoked, possible respiratory problems. Withdrawal effects less intense than with amphetamines but can be severe.

CAFFEINE
Short-term effects: Mild stimulant. After drinking, effects evident within an hour, lasting 3–4 hours. Overdose death possible after huge doses, but rare.
Long-term effects: Stomach irritation. Irregular heartbeat in susceptible people after high doses.

NICOTINE
Short-term effects: Mild stimulant, also felt to be relaxing by regular users. Inhaled in tobacco smoke. Almost immediate but rapidly declining effects.
Long-term effects: Other components of tobacco smoke can cause respiratory diseases, including lung cancer, and heart and circulatory disorders; at least 100 000 tobacco-related deaths in the UK alone each year. Smoking during pregnancy can cause premature birth and smaller babies. Strong psychological dependence.

LSD
Short-term effects: Major perceptual distortions, usually known to be unreal, which peak after 2–6 hours and fade after 12 hours. Hallucinations and usually temporary psychotic episode possible. **Long-term effects:** Flashbacks (re-experiencing a small part of the episode later) possible. Prolonged psychotic episodes rare but may occur. No physical dependence. Further doses ineffective after several days' continuous use.

HALLUCINOGENIC MUSHROOMS
Short-term effects: Similar to mild LSD experience, but shorter (4–9 hours). Danger of mistakenly picking poisonous mushrooms.
Long-term effects: No physical or psychological dependence. Repeated doses ineffective after several days' continuous use.

CANNABIS
Short-term effects: Relaxed feeling, talkativeness, heightened perceptions. Perceptual distortions possible after high doses.
Long-term effects: Possible psychological dependence. Respiratory problems, including lung cancer if smoked.

PHENCYCLIDINE (PCP)
Medical use: As veterinary anaesthetic.
Short-term effects: Unpredictable – stimulation or depression, hallucinations, distortion of time and space, paranoia. Higher doses can cause coma and death.
Long-term effects: Disorientation and severe depression, psychosis, possible physical and psychological dependence.

The information in this table is based on data provided by the Institute for the Study of Drug Dependence and reproduced with their permission.

SEE ALSO

- RESPIRATION AND CIRCULATION p. 210
- THE NERVOUS SYSTEM p. 220
- MENTAL DISORDERS p. 234
- DEVIANCE, CRIME AND LAW ENFORCEMENT p. 262
- YOUTH MOVEMENTS p. 294

The History of Medicine

Disease is as old as life itself. Medicine, on the other hand, is of quite recent origin. In most early civilizations medicine was closely linked to religion. Diseases were believed to be caused by gods who might also effect cures, and treatment involved rituals and incantations. In ancient Egypt physicians were priests trained in special temple schools, and one famous physician, *Imhotep* (c. 2900 BC), was made a god of healing.

Papyrus fragments such as the Ebers Papyrus show that Egyptian medicine was sophisticated in observation and diagnosis, if not in treatment. In ancient Babylon the Code of Hammurabi, the world's first legal code, contained laws regulating a large and well-organized medical profession.

The concepts of early Indian medicine are set out in sacred texts called the Vedas, which may date back to the 2nd millennium BC. Numerous herbal remedies are described.

Greek medicine

At its peak Greek medicine was rational, scientific and clearly separated from religion. The Greek philosopher *Hippocrates of Cos* (c. 460–370 BC) is regarded as the 'father of modern medicine'. His teachings were written down by his fol-

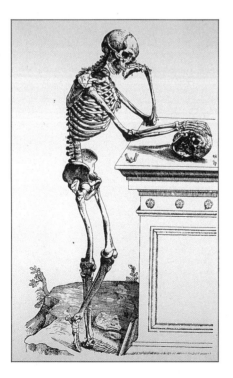

An engraving from the first edition of *De Humani Corporis Fabrica* by Vesalius, published in 1543.

lowers in a collection known as the Hippocratic Corpus. Hippocrates believed that moderation in all things is the key to health. He also set out a code of ethics for physicians, and the *Hippocratic Oath*, taken by doctors, is based on this code.

The Greek theory of the four *elements* and the four *humours* – which originated with the philosophers *Empedocles* (c. 490–430 BC) and *Aristotle* (384–322 BC) – influenced the shape of medicine for many centuries (see box). At the time of the Roman Empire the Greek physician *Galen of Pergamum* (Latin name Claudius Galenus, AD 130–201) carried out dissections on animals but none on human specimens, and this led to many errors in his anatomical descriptions. Galen combined the theory of the humours with his own studies in anatomy and physiology to produce an erroneous system of medicine, which nevertheless lasted more than 1000 years.

Medieval medicine

As the Roman Empire declined and fell, civilization moved eastward. Greek learning was preserved and developed by Arab scholars such as *Razes* (Arabic name al-Rhazi, AD 860–932) and *Avicenna* (Arabic name Ibn Sinna, AD 980–1036), and from about AD 1000 ancient knowledge began to return to the West via centres such as the medical school at Salerno. Later, medicine was taught in new universities (see p. 406) such as Montpellier in France and Bologna in Italy – two places where, in the 14th century, anatomy lessons included the public dissection of corpses. Because in this period a physician was expected to have had an academic schooling, he became known as 'doctor' – an academic title. However, the Church prohibited clerks from shedding blood and this meant that medieval universities did not teach surgery. In this field students had to be trained by a practising surgeon. In general, medieval medicine was a mixture of ancient physiology, empirical knowledge of the effects of some drugs and superstitious incantation. By the

14th century thousands of hospitals had been founded in Europe.

The 16th century

Before this time individual doctors had frequently doubted Galen's authority on specific points, but it was only after the invention of printing (see p. 322) that such doubts could become widely known. For example, in his book *De Humani Corporis Fabrica* ('On the Fabric of the Human Body') the Flemish anatomist *Andreas Vesalius* (1514–64) showed the inadequacies of Galen. It is the first accurate anatomy book, based on the dissection of human corpses, and laid the foundations of modern anatomy. Surgery was advanced at the same time by the Frenchman *Ambroise Paré* (1517–90), who opposed the use of *cauterization* (the application of red-hot irons or boiling oil) to treat wounds.

The Italian *Girolamo Fracastoro* (Latin name Fracastorius, 1484–1553) speculated that epidemic diseases might be caused by minute germs, invisible to the naked eye. He argued that germs are *specific*, i.e. that each kind causes a particular disease, but his theory was not proved until the 19th century. The idea that specific diseases required specific treatments was pioneered by a Swiss physician and alchemist, *Philippus Aureolus Paracelsus* (real name Theophrastus Bombastus von Hohenheim, 1493–1541). He also introduced the use of chemicals into medicine, pioneering the use of mercury and laudanum (an opiate; see p. 247)).

The 17th and 18th centuries

The main medical event of the 17th century was the discovery by *William Harvey* (1578–1677), an English physician, of the true nature of the heartbeat and the circulation of the blood. His book *De Motu Cordis* ('On the Movement of the Heart') laid the foundation of all modern physiology – although Harvey did not realize *why* the blood circulates.

A further aid to the study of physiology – and to medical science generally – was

---

ELEMENTS AND HUMOURS

The ancient Greeks believed that everything was made out of combinations of air, water, earth and fire – and that these corresponded to four *qualities* – cold, wet, dry and hot. They thought that in the body the elements blend to form four *humours*: blood (hot and wet), yellow bile (hot and dry), black bile (dry and cold) and phlegm (cold and wet). Good mental and physical health was supposed to depend on the correct balance of the humours. This view of human physiology remained current until the 17th century, and is still preserved in words indicating a dominance of one humour, such as 'phlegmatic' (not easily excited), 'sanguine' (cheerful and confident, from the Latin *sanguis*, 'blood') and 'bilious' (irritable – yellow bile was supposed to cause anger, and black bile melancholy. In the 2nd century AD Galen refined the physiology of the Greeks with his early theory of circulation. The theory stated that nutriments from the stomach moved to the liver, where they were made into blood. Blood moved into the right side of the heart, and passed through the wall of the heart to the left side where it mixed with *vital spirits* from the lungs. Some now travelled to the organs and limbs, and the remainder went to the brain where *animal spirits* were formed.

It was this false physiology that Harvey replaced in the 17th century when he found that blood is pumped by the heart into the arteries and returned to the heart by the veins.

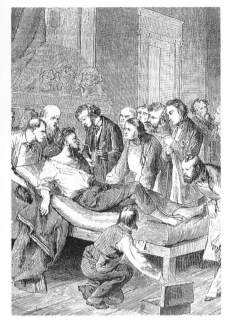

The first operation using anaesthetic, carried out in 1846 at the Massachusetts General Hospital, USA. The operation – a tooth extraction – was performed by William Morton. The engraving shows sulphuric acid ether being administered to the patient through the mouth.

provided by the invention of microscopes (see p. 33). The Dutchman **Anton van Leeuwenhoek** (1632–1723) showed the value of these fundamental research tools by using them to investigate blood cells, spermatozoa and even microbes.

During the 18th century a number of great medical schools, including Vienna and Edinburgh, were founded. Surgery was established on firm scientific principles by the Scot **John Hunter** (1728–93), who also proved the value of experimental surgery. The science of neurology was pioneered by the Swiss physiologist **Albrecht von Haller** (1708–77), with his theory that nerve fibres acted on 'irritable' muscle to produce movement.

Giovanni Battista Morgagni (1682–1771), an Italian anatomist, argued that disease is *localized* in parts of the body rather than spread throughout, while the invention of the stethoscope by the French physician **René Théophile Hyacinthe Laennec** (1781–1826) was to prove a major aid in the diagnosis of disease.

Although the practice of medicine up to this point often did more harm than good to patients, one of the first scientific steps in preventing disease was the introduction of vaccination by the English physician **Edward Jenner** (1749–1823), when he discovered in 1796 that inoculation with the cowpox virus gives immunity to smallpox. Immunization against various other diseases (see pp. 244–5) was to be introduced over the next two centuries, and smallpox itself was finally eradicated from the world in the 1970s.

The 19th century

The 19th century was the century of progress in medicine. One of the most important discoveries was the demonstration by the Frenchman **Louis Pasteur** (1822–95) and the German **Robert Koch** (1843–1910) that diseases such as rabies and tuberculosis are caused by microorganisms called *bacteria* (see pp. 110 and 238). They showed precisely which bacteria cause which disease, and between 1875 and 1906 over twenty fatal diseases were understood and made preventable through immunization.

Although by the 19th century many kinds of surgical operation had been successfully carried out, patients died in large numbers from infections entering their bodies during operations or childbirth, or through wounds. They also had to endure the agony of being fully conscious during operations. Pain control by *anaesthesia* (loss of feeling induced by drugs) was pioneered by the Americans **Horace Wells** (1815–48), using nitrous oxide, and **William Thomas Green Morton** (1819–68), using ether. In Britain general anaesthesia – rendering the patient unconscious – by means of chloroform was introduced by the Scottish surgeon **Sir James Young Simpson** (1811–70). In the 1840s the Hungarian **Ignaz P. Semmelweiss** (1818–65) showed the crucial importance of *asepsis* (a germ-free environment) in childbirth wards, and in 1865, following Pasteur's theory of bacterial infection, the Scottish surgeon **Joseph Lister** (later Lord Lister) (1827–1912) introduced *antisepsis* (the destruction of bacteria), spraying the area being operated on with carbolic acid.

The century also saw many measures introduced to improve public health. Chief among these were improved sewage and sanitary conditions (see p. 244), and such preventive measures improved the life expectancies of millions.

Finally, the century saw the emergence of modern nursing, largely due to the efforts of the Englishwoman, **Florence Nightingale** (1820–1910), who showed that good nursing had a dramatic effect on reducing death rates in hospitals.

The 20th century

The 20th century has been an era of technological innovation in medicine, particularly in diagnosis. In 1895 the German physicist **Wilhelm Konrad Röntgen** (1845–1923) discovered X-rays (see p. 332), the medical applications of which had been realized by the turn of the century. Other inventions of the early part of the century included the *electrocardiograph* (for measuring heart activity) and the *electroencephalograph* (for measuring brain activity). The introduction of ultrasound scanning (see pp. 242 and 332) in the 1970s allowed even more accurate pictures than X-rays, which cannot safely be used for long exposures or on pregnant women.

Work on the chemistry of nutrition by the German **Emil Fischer** (1852–1919) gave rise to *biochemistry* (the study of the chemistry of living organisms), and the chemical study of disease is now a basic medical approach. Out of Fischer's work came the discovery by the British biochemist **Sir Frederick Gowland Hopkins** (1861–1947) that certain substances – later called *vitamins* (see p. 208) – are essential to the diet in minute amounts, and that disease occurs if these are absent.

Chemotherapy, treatment by chemicals that attack disease agents with minimum harm to the body, was pioneered by the German scientist **Paul Ehrlich** (1854–1915), who discovered that synthetic dyestuffs could kill bacteria. The *sulphonamides*, derived from dyestuffs and introduced in 1932, greatly reduced the number of post-operative infections. Ehrlich also initiated the study of the body's immune system (see p. 212). A large number of bacterial infections – many of which were previously fatal – were rendered curable by a new range of drugs, the *antibiotics*. These drugs were developed from the accidental discovery by the British microbiologist **Sir Alexander Fleming** (1881–1955) that a growth of penicillin mould had destroyed a bacterial culture he was working on.

Surgery has also been aided by technology (see p. 240), and now lasers are sometimes used for very precise work. The greater understanding of the immune system has led to the possibility of transplants of organs from one body to another. Kidney transplantation, first attempted in 1902, is now a well-established operation. Heart transplantation was first performed by the South African surgeon **Christiaan Barnard** (1922–) in 1967 ▷▷

SEE ALSO

- HISTORY OF SCIENCE p. 60
- NON-INFECTIOUS DISEASES p. 236
- INFECTIOUS DISEASES p. 238
- SURGERY p. 240
- MEDICAL TECHNOLOGY p. 242
- PREVENTING DISEASE p. 244

Louis Pasteur (1822–95) in his laboratory. Pasteur's demonstration that many diseases are caused by specific microorganisms was a major breakthrough in medical science. Pasteur also did important work on the microbiology of fermentation (see p. 196).

Alternative Medicine

Alternative medicine encompasses all the forms of healing that lie outside the sort of medicine people normally receive from a GP or hospital. It includes a wide variety of different therapies used by millions of people worldwide to treat every ill imaginable. That they appear to work in some cases is beyond doubt. How they work, however, is still to a large extent a mystery.

SEE ALSO

● HOW PEOPLE MOVE p. 206
● THE NERVOUS SYSTEM p. 220
● THE BRAIN p. 222
● NON-INFECTIOUS DISEASES p. 236
● INFECTIOUS DISEASES p. 238
● MEDICAL TECHNOLOGY p. 242

Medical science has made great advances and has long seemed to promise a 'pill for every ill'. Virtually every drug, however, has been shown to have some side effects and many patients have become dissatisfied with the inability of orthodox treatments to cure certain conditions – particularly chronic diseases such as arthritis. The common feature that seems to run through every one of the alternative treatments is the importance placed on the whole person, not just on specific symptoms – this is known as the *holistic* approach.

Herbalism

Herbalism is an ancient form of medicine. From the dawn of humanity, people have been using plants to cure their illnesses. From the Middle Ages, herbals – manuals listing the names of plants and what they could be used for – were widely used. In the 17th century **Nicholas Culpeper** (1616–54) combined herbalism with astrology in his *Herbal*. Herbalists today use the roots, leaves, stems, flowers and seeds of plants to produce medicines. A large number of orthodox modern medicines are also derived from plants – the heart drug *digoxin* is produced from the foxglove, and the group of painkillers known as *opiates* are derived from the opium poppy (see p. 246).

Once a diagnosis has been made, the herbalist will dilute a concentrated extract of a certain herb in water or mix it into a paste to form a cream or ointment.

Conditions such as arthritis, colds and coughs, skin problems, digestive disorders and minor injuries are regarded as the most likely to benefit from herbalism.

Homoeopathy

Homoeopathy was invented by a German doctor, **Samuel Hahnemann** (1755–1843). He reasoned that since many of the symptoms people suffer during illness – fever or pain, for example – are actually visible signs of the body's own defences working against the disease, it would make sense to try to boost these defences. He based his therapy on the principle that 'like cures like', giving patients tiny quantities of substances known to produce exactly these symptoms in healthy people. One homoeopathic remedy for fever, for instance, is sulphur, which produces a feeling of heat and promotes sweating if taken by mouth in larger doses.

Homoeopathy offers remedies for virtually every medical complaint, but it is less frequently used in acute or life-threatening illness. Homoeopathic remedies are prescribed by some GPs as well as by homoeopaths.

Aromatherapy

Aromatherapy is principally a massage technique in which essential oils derived from herbs, flowers and spices are rubbed into the skin and eventually inhaled. The natural fragrances these oils produce are said to be particularly effective for psychological complaints such as anxiety or depression, but are used to treat a range of conditions including skin disorders and burns.

Acupuncture

Acupuncture originated in China over 5000 years ago. The technique uses fine needles inserted at specific points on the body in order to restore the balance of an inner 'life force' known as *chi* energy and believed to

Acupuncture: 17th-century Chinese study figure. Meridians and points are mapped out across the body surface.

An acupuncturist (far right) treating a patient for persistent headaches.

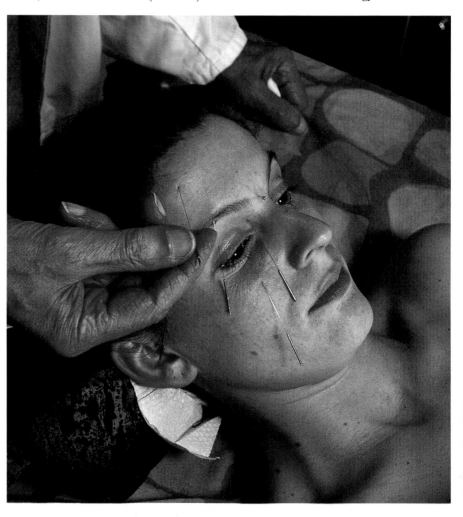

sions on surrounding muscles, tendons and ligaments.

Osteopaths tend to concentrate their work on the spine since this contains the spinal cord and all the nerves that control the body. Back pain is the disorder most commonly treated by an osteopath.

Chiropractic

The central philosophy of chiropractic is that malalignments of the bones in the spine cause disturbances of the nervous and vascular systems leading to disease not only in the bones and muscles themselves, but in any organ of the body.

Chiropractitioners work with the help of X-rays to discover where the malalignments are and to identify 'intersegmental dysrelationships'. They then manipulate the bones using short, but very forceful thrusts to the joint, thus relieving the root cause of the problem. However, chiropractic should not be used in any case of bone malignancy (cancer) or where the spinal cord is compressed. The rapid, forceful thrusts can lead to fracture and paralysis in these cases.

The Alexander Technique

The Alexander Technique is a method of producing postural changes, which are claimed to relieve a number of physical disorders. The technique was developed in the 19th century by an Australian actor, *Matthias Alexander* (1869–1955). He realized that the position of his head and neck were the cause of his frequent loss of voice during performances, and found that by altering his posture he could cure himself.

During a series of lessons – 12 or more – the person 'relearns' how to use the body, breaking harmful postural habits. The technique is claimed to be beneficial for everyone, but in particular for those who have suffered long spells of general ill health – lethargy or poor sleeping, for example.

Biofeedback

Biofeedback is a technique used to help people learn to control physical phenomena governed by the autonomic nervous system, such as blood pressure, heartbeat and temperature. Electrodes placed on the body pick up electrical impulses produced by physical changes. The impulses are transformed by the biofeedback machine into an electronic sound, or shown by the rise and fall of a needle on a dial. The person concentrates on changing the tone of the sound or on causing the needle to move and in doing so learns, for instance, to lower the blood pressure or slow down the heartbeat.   MG

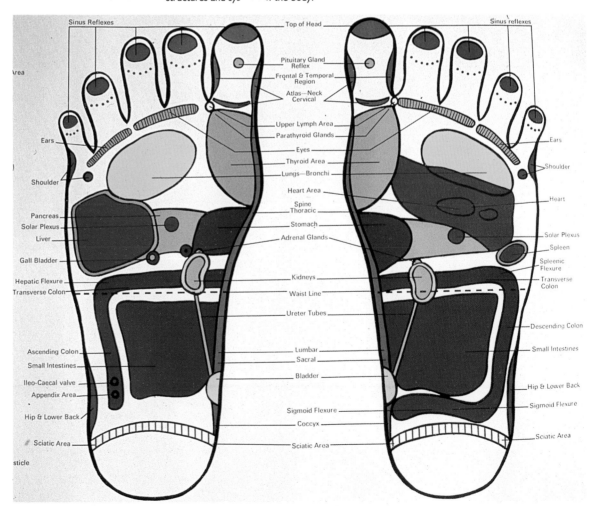

A reflexology chart showing the areas of the feet that correspond to various organs, structures and systems of the body.

flow along a number of *meridians* or channels in the body. Each of the 12 main meridians is believed to have its own pulse – six in each wrist – and the acupuncturist checks these carefully in order to decide which points to stimulate.

The technique has been shown to be remarkably successful at stopping pain, and in China major operations have been carried out using only acupuncture for pain relief. Scientists have discovered that the needles appear to make the body produce its own natural painkillers, *endorphins*. Acupuncture is also claimed to be effective in treating a wide range of diseases, including respiratory, digestive, bone and muscle disorders.

Reflexology

Like acupuncture, reflexology is based on the idea that the body contains channels of 'life force'. Reflexologists believe that this force exists in 10 'zones' of energy that each begin in the toes and end in the fingers.

By touching and feeling the toes and feet, reflexologists claim to be able to feel blocks in these channels of energy (they say these feel like crystals below the skin surface), and by manipulating and massaging the foot in a specific way they try to move the blockage, thus curing the illness. Like acupuncture, reflexology is used to treat most conditions.

Osteopathy

Osteopathy is a manipulative technique founded by the American doctor *Andrew Taylor Still* (1828–1917). Joints are pushed and occasionally pulled so as to restore them to their normal positions, thus relieving ten-

THE WORLD TODAY

'We have it in our power to begin
the world over again.'

Thomas Paine

Age Roles and Rites of Passage

Age is an important marker of social differences in all societies. Everywhere some people are treated differently from others according to their age, and are expected to behave in a socially approved way. These expectations define the roles that people play and thus are known as *age roles*. Although age roles are universal, the expectations that define them are cultural; that is, they are the product of a people's shared history and experience and therefore they vary from society to society and over time.

A Greek Orthodox wedding. Marriage ceremonies often include visible signs of the new social status of the bride and groom, such as wedding rings, distinctive headdress and garments, and ornaments.

Rites of passage are rituals or ceremonies that mark the movement of individuals or groups from one social status to another (such as birth, puberty, marriage, and death). Since many changes of social status are associated with age – becoming an adult, for example – there is often a close connection between rites of passage and changing age roles.

Significance of age roles and rites of passage

Societies differ in the importance they attach to age roles and changes in social status. Until recently, traditional tribal societies in Africa and elsewhere attached great significance to age as a determinant of social position. The Masai of East Africa, in common with many other pastoral, nomadic societies, organize their social, political and economic life around age groupings. These age groupings, which anthropologists call *age sets, age grades*, or *age cohorts*, typically span 10–15 years.

Both males and females are divided into age groupings among the Masai. Male age sets are the most significant in the public sphere. Masai distinguish between boys, warriors and elders, and rites of passage mark the transitions between them. Boys have no independent role in Masai society: they learn from men and are close to their mothers, sisters and other females. Boys become warriors in an initiation ceremony that marks them physically and removes them socially from the sphere of women. All Masai boys are circumcised, although individual groups of Masai follow different practices relating to facial scarification and the removal of teeth.

Warriors have the responsibility of herding the cattle – the mainstay of Masai life. The search for water and pasture for the cattle may take them away from the home camps for many months of the year. They live a communal and egalitarian life. After 10–15 years' service the warriors become elders. It is the role of the elders to stay at home and run public affairs. They are the decision-makers of Masai society. Men are allowed to marry only when they become elders.

Age roles in traditional and modern societies

The spread of new ideas and technologies from the developed world produces new ways of living in traditional Third World societies. Most significantly, men and women become less dependent on traditional structures for their opportunities in life. Age roles and rites of passage cease to be dominant features of social life in a modernized society.

Although modern societies stress individualism and personal achievement, social relations are still frequently recognized by age. Age is formally and legally signifi-cant in many areas of life in modern societies. It determines when people go to school, when they may leave school, when they may marry, when they may enter full-time employment, when they have to leave employment and so on. Age is often used as the basis for assigning rights and duties to people in society. Ideas of physical and psychological growth and change often support the divisions based on age.

In recent times the term *ageism* has been used to describe the assessment of people solely in terms of age. As with the pejorative terms *sexism* and *racism*, the term implies criticism of the use of unchangeable (*ascribed*) characteristics (see p. 254) as a criterion of assessment by a society that purports to judge people according to what they have achieved.

Anthropologists have noted that in both traditional and modern societies the relationships between *adjacent generations* (parents and children) tend to be difficult. In contrast the relationships between *alternate generations* (grandparents and grandchildren) tend to be less problematic. It has been suggested that the social maturing of children signals to parents their own social decline. Grandparents and grandchildren are not in competition for power and control and so enjoy relatively harmonious relations.

Analysis of rites of passage

The French anthropologist and folklorist Arnold van Gennep (1873–1957) demonstrated that all rites of passage have a common form. He identified three phases in every ritual ceremony: the phase of *separation*, the phase of *transition* and the phase of *incorporation*. As individuals change status they are separated from their old associations and relationships. They move into limbo, a state of betwixt and between, in which they have left the old but not yet assumed the new. In the final phase they take on their new status and join others of like status.

Van Gennep pointed out that different rites of passage stress different phases, though all are present within each ritual or ceremony. In funeral ceremonies the emphasis is on the separation of the deceased and the bereaved. In Christian baptism (see p. 474) and in the Jewish *brit milah* (circumcision; see illustration and p. 472) the emphasis is on incorporation – the joining of a religious community.

The Scottish New Year celebration of *Hogmanay* illustrates Van Gennep's three phases. A stranger (one who is separate) crosses the threshold (transition between inside and outside) just after midnight (transition in time from one day to another) and is welcomed (incorporated) into the household as the bringer of the New Year (having left the old year behind). Hogmanay is a rite of passage in the sense that it marks the symbolic death and rebirth of the year.

There is no generally accepted scheme for classifying different types of rites of passage, and there tends to be much overlap between the categories sometimes used to describe related types of rite. *Life-cycle ceremonies* are connected with the bioogical changes of life and include rituals surrounding childbirth, puberty, marriage and death. *Ceremonies of social transformation* include all such life-cycle ceremonies, but many rites of social transformation, such as initiation into clubs or common-interest societies, have no immediate connection with biological changes. *Ceremonies of religious transformation* signal changes in religious status, and can involve lay people (as in the Jewish *bar mitzvah*; see below and p. 472) or priests (as in Christian ordination).

Puberty rites

Coming of age' parties in Western societies celebrate the transition in time from child to adult. In tribal societies the rituals that mark the movement into adult status are sometimes called *puberty rites*, and mark a movement into a sexual world from a non-sexual one. Sometimes this transition is marked physically by ritual scarring or body mutilation.

Puberty rites amongst Australian Aborigines are highly complex and involve a symbolic re-enactment of death in order to achieve new life as an adult. Among the Dinka people of the southern Sudan, the passage from boyhood to manhood is marked by a ceremony in which boys of similar age undergo hardship together, including ritual feeding in 'fattening camps'. The abandonment of the activity of milking cows – which had marked their status as children and servers of men – symbolizes the boys' entry into manhood.

The Jewish ritual of *bar mitzvah* can be seen both as a puberty ritual and as a ceremony of religious transformation. Bar mitzvah transforms a boy into a full member of the Jewish male religious community. Similarly, Christian baptism and confirmation (see p. 474) confer membership of a religious community.

Weddings and childbirth

Wedding ceremonies display separation, transition and incorporation. In Christian wedding ceremonies in Britain the relatives and friends of the bride and groom are physically separated; the bride is 'given away' by her father or senior male relative to the groom (separated from her family to be incorporated into a new family); the bride and groom leave the ceremony together (separate from both sets of relatives and friends as they form a new union); after the ceremony relatives and friends of the couple mingle together, symbolizing the restructuring of their relationships brought about by the marriage.

Pregnancy and childbirth are traditionally seen as dangerous and polluting, especially to men. Pregnant women are in a transitional phase between being one person and being two or more. Transitional phases are confusing because the people who inhabit them do not belong to the ordered categories of society – they are between them. Until quite recently it was common in Western societies for women who had given birth to be *churched* – ritually cleansed and received back into the community of the Christian Church.

Funeral rites

In most societies death is marked by elaborate ritual, generally of a religious nature. In traditional China, the dying were specially prepared for death, having their heads shaved and their bodies washed and placed in a sitting position to allow the soul to leave the body easily. In Catholic Christianity, the dying make a last confession of their sins to a priest, and receive absolution.

The actual disposal of the body displays varying degrees of complexity and religious significance in different societies. In ancient Egypt, the dead underwent a particularly intricate process of ritual embalming (mummification) to prepare them for a proper afterlife (see p. 460). In most societies, burial or cremation are the favoured methods of disposing of the dead. However, the Parsis of India (see p. 467) expose their corpses on 'towers of silence' to be devoured by crows, kites and vultures. This is to avoid polluting by burial or cremation the sacred divine creations of earth and fire.

In Western countries, despite a tendency for funerals to become less elaborate (simple cremation is increasingly preferred to burial), religious rites and customs surrounding death continue to be observed even though the beliefs that inspired them have been discarded or forgotten. In all societies funeral ceremonies mark the movement from life to death and help the bereaved adjust to the loss of a member of the community.

Other rites

The action of joining is stressed in other ceremonies including the many secular rites of passage. For instance, after the

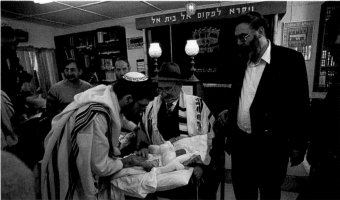

A Jewish circumcision ceremony in Israel. In Judaism male children undergo circumcision – performed by a specially qualified *mohel* – on the eighth day after birth. The ritual also involves the blessing and naming of the child, who becomes a member of the Jewish religious community and is henceforth bound to obey the Law of Moses.

SEE ALSO

● THE FAMILY p. 256
● SOCIAL STRATIFICATION AND DIVISIONS p. 258
● RELIGIONS pp. 462–79

successful completion of their studies undergraduates become graduands (i.e. people who are about to graduate) and then graduates at degree-awarding ceremonies. The graduates are members of an academic community. Other significant social changes which do not involve initiation into organized social groups are attended by ritual. These include festivities marking retirement from work and various other award ceremonies.

Whatever their form and content, age roles and rites of passage are ways in which human beings try to structure and organize their relationships with one another. Rites of passage provide an ordered framework for individuals in which their rights and obligations are made clear to them in a public context.   EB

The Mexican day of the dead. In all societies the passage from life to death is marked by ritual. In many societies the dead continue to be honoured in elaborate ceremonies such as the annual day of the dead in Mexico, when relations mount a night-long vigil around the graves of their loved ones, offering up chants and prayers to appease the souls of the deceased.

The Family

A family is a group of people who are related to each other by blood (for instance a brother and sister), or by marriage (for instance a husband and his wife's sister). A wider group of related families is referred to as a *kinship system*. Family relationships are universal in the sense that everyone has blood relatives. However, the patterns of family, marriage and kinship relationships vary both geographically and historically.

Marriage is the bond that makes families possible. Typically it involves a legal agreement between a man and a woman to enter into a long-term socio-sexual relationship for the purposes of establishing a home, satisfying sexual needs and raising children. Marriage also creates rights and responsibilities, such as the economic support of spouse and offspring.

Marital relationships are usually formalized and solemnized by an elaborate ritual, known as a wedding ceremony, often with relatives of the couple in attendance. This can take place in a building officially recognized for holding such events, such as a church, temple or registry office. In Western societies, marriage is the final stage in a social process that involves dating, courtship and engagement. In many non-Western societies, for example in rural China, marital partners are selected by parents or other matchmakers rather than the couple themselves.

The expectations of what marriage should be and the laws governing who a person can marry and how many people a person can marry vary considerably from one society to another.

Although all known societies prohibit marriage and/or sexual relations between certain categories of relatives (*incest*), the categories themselves differ according to the culture in question. Exceptionally, in ancient Egypt brother-sister marriages were permitted within the family of the pharaoh in order to preserve the blood purity of the ruling dynasty. This is in marked contrast to the traditional family

The nuclear family, spanning two generations, is the characteristic family unit of developed industrial societies. Although the nuclear family is generally believed to allow greater mobility and individual freedom, it has also been blamed for increases in stress and tension, rising divorce rates and increases in delinquency.

system of China, which prohibits marriage among a wide range of relatives, including distant cousins. The universally strong feelings that incest arouses have led to it becoming a taboo subject and practice.

Similarly, rules concerning the number of husbands or wives a person is allowed at one time vary between societies. Basically, there are two types of marriage: *monogamy*, where the individual has only one spouse at a time; and *polygamy*, where two or more spouses are recognized socially. Polygamy can involve husbands having two or more wives (*polygyny*) or wives having two or more husbands (*polyandry*). Polygyny is much more common than polyandry, and is particularly widespread in Islamic areas of Africa, where Muslim men are allowed to have up to four wives.

Polygamy is the most frequently found form of marriage, but monogamy, which is characteristic of Western societies, is spreading under the influence of Western culture. However, due to the increasingly high incidence of divorce and remarriage in Western societies, the practice of having many spouses consecutively (*serial monogamy*) is becoming more common.

Divorce rates vary considerably in different societies. For example, in countries where a marriage is essentially regarded as a civil contract, such as Britain, the USA and Russia, the divorce rate tends to be high. However, in countries dominated by the Catholic Church (which officially forbids divorce), such as Ireland, Spain, Italy and Mexico, the divorce rate is either not calculated or is very low. There are also many other ways of ending a marriage, including desertion, separation and annulment (legal cancellation). Consequently, divorce rates are an imperfect measure of marital breakdown.

An extended family group at the seaside in Britain in 1900. Extended families, in which three or more generations live together under one roof, have become far less common in Western societies, but are still found in some non-Western cultures.

Family and kinship

A person who marries leaves the *family of origin* to set up his or her own *family of procreation*. In the process he or she simultaneously becomes a member of a kinship system consisting of three families: the family of origin, the spouse's family of origin and the new family of procreation. A family comprising two generations only, namely parents and children, is known as a *nuclear family*. A family comprising three or more generations living together, namely parents, children and grandparents, is known as an *extended family*.

Typically, especially in Western societies, all the members of a nuclear family live in one household. In pre-industrial Western societies it was common for extended families consisting of parents, married and unmarried children and their spouses and offspring to live together under one roof. In the present day, extended family households are mainly found in non-Western cultures, for instance in Islamic societies. For most people the need for social and geographical mobility makes it impractical to share a household with a large number of relatives throughout their lives. Consequently, the typical family form in contemporary Western societies is not the isolated nuclear or extended type, but the *modified extended family*. This type of family is characterized by a nuclear family household that maintains social, economic and emotional ties with wider kin. Moreover, it is a family form that seems to be spreading with industrialization and urbanization.

Family functions

Notwithstanding the historical and regional variation in family types, the family performs the same range of functions to a greater or lesser extent in all societies: regulating sexual activity; ensuring economic survival; preparing young people for adulthood; and providing emotional security.

As societies have developed economically and have grown in size and complexity, the family has lost its monopoly regarding these social functions. For example, although no society allows total sexual freedom, in Western societies there has been a tendency during the 20th century to relax the norms and rules governing sexual behaviour. As a result, sex outside marriage is more common and more widely accepted now than in the immediate past. In the case of its economic and socialization functions, the family no longer operates alone in training young people to produce or supply goods and services. It does so indirectly in conjunction with schools, colleges, factories and offices. However, in Western societies, people still consume goods and services in a family context (for instance watching television and eating meals) and the majority of children are born within marriage, even if many are conceived outside it.

The historical decline of the social and economic functions of the family has tended to enhance the emotional function. In addition, this function has been heightened by the increasing importance attached to romantic love and marital satisfaction in Western societies. Hence, increasingly it is only within the family that an individual experiences close and enduring emotional ties. Outside the family – at school, work and at leisure – impersonal relationships have become the norm. It is in this important sense that the modern Western family home is often described as a haven.

Family disharmony and alternative families

The model of family life in which parents and children live together is generally considered to be the ideal, and has become the predominant pattern in Western societies. But even in this context there are problems and exceptions. The increasing emotional weight that the modern family has to bear, along with other factors such as inequalities within the family and the pressure to be economically successful, have caused certain family problems.

For example, a high rate of marital breakdown and a corresponding increase in *single-parent families* is apparent in many industrial societies. Also, the social and economic limitations of two-generation households, often revealed by the problem of caring for very young or very old family members, has been largely responsible for the persistence of extended family households.

Some people choose to reject conventional domestic arrangements and set up alternative household groups. Multi-family households such as communes or kibbutzes, frequently inspired by political or religious ideas, continue to exist in Western societies as a minority pattern.

The emotional intensity of family relationships, combined with other pressures on the modern family, is also thought to be responsible for the increasing prevalence of family conflict and violence. This includes child and wife abuse, and family murder. Some sociologists have attributed cases of mental illness and even suicide to the stresses of living in an excessively private family, especially in times of economic insecurity. According to this view, the modern family is not always an emotional haven – it can be a prison.   SE

SEE ALSO
- AGE ROLES AND RITES OF PASSAGE p. 254
- SOCIAL STRATIFICATION AND DIVISIONS p. 258

Men of the Hewa people of Papua New Guinea. In some traditional societies all the men of a community live together – rather than with their wives and children – in order to be able to cooperate more easily in activities such as hunting and defending the village.

Social Stratification and Divisions

The hierarchical classification of social differences in terms of one or more dimensions of social inequality – such as wealth, power or prestige – is known as _social stratification_. The particular pattern that predominates in any one society tends to vary over time. There is some controversy as to whether social stratification is a universal feature of human societies. In preliterate or 'primitive' societies, membership of a _clan_ (a group tracing its descent from a common male ancestor) or _tribe_ (a distinctive ethnic and cultural group) is the main determinant of social inequality.

In addition to the hierarchical classification of social differences that divides societies into horizontal layers, it is also possible to divide societies vertically into blocks or pillars. Physical and cultural divisions based on factors such as sex/gender, race, ethnic identity, language and religion tend to cut across hierarchically ranked social groups, thereby fragmenting a society even further.

The caste system of social stratification

Caste is found in its most developed form in the Hindu-based system of social stratification in India. Its exact origins are obscure, although it is known to have existed for at least 2000 years. Social groups known as _castes_ are separated from each other by religious rules of ritual purity and are ranked hierarchically on a scale that ranges from pure to impure. Thus each caste is 'purer' than the one below it. Contact between castes is prohibited on the grounds that lower castes could 'pollute' higher ones by coming too close.

Membership of caste is inherited and regarded by Hindus as divinely ordained. Caste members are required to marry within their caste. Traditionally, castes are associated with particular kinds of work, and this reinforces social segregation. Because caste membership is permanent and unchangeable, social mobility – the ability to move up (or down) the social ladder via marriage or individual effort – is impossible within a rigid caste system.

The main castes and their associated occupations are:

1. Brahmin (priests)
2. Kshatriya (warriors and landlords)
3. Vaishya (farmers and traders)
4. Sudra (rural and urban labourers)

Subsequently, another caste was added to the bottom of the classification: _Harijans_ or _'untouchables'_, who undertake the most menial of tasks such as cleaning streets and toilets. In addition to the main castes, several thousand subcastes known as _jatis_ have been identified at the local village level. As in the wider caste system, jati membership is inherited and is therefore permanent and unchangeable.

Legal discrimination based on caste has been abolished in modern India and industrialization has created many new occupational groups. This has led to an increase in both individual and collective social mobility which in turn has loosened some of the rigidities of the caste system.

The estate system

Social groups known as _estates_ existed in Europe from the time of the Roman Empire to as late as 1789 in France. The estate system reached its zenith during the feudal era in Europe (see p. 404) and there was also a similar system in Japan (see p. 386). Estates were created by laws that provided for a clear structure of rights and duties, privileges and obligations. Estates were also related to the prevailing economic division of labour. 'The nobility were ordained to defend all, the clergy to pray for all, and the commons to provide food for all.' An estate system was not an entirely closed system of social stratification. Social mobility was possible but not very widespread.

The main estates were:

1. The nobility
2. The clergy
3. The commons (also known as serfs and peasantry)

The decline of the estate system in Europe coincided with the rise in the economic and political power of the urban _bourgeoisie_ (merchants, manufacturers, financiers, etc.), a distinctive social group that developed within the estate system. According to some theories, this group played a major part in transforming and overthrowing the estate system of social stratification.

Class systems

Class systems of social stratification are characteristic of industrial capitalist societies. _Classes_ are defined in economic rather than religious terms (as in caste systems), or political-legal terms (as in estate systems). There are no formal barriers to economic achievement in modern democratic societies, hence class systems tend to be less characterized by inherited factors and are correspondingly more open than other types of social stratification. In a class system, social mobility is the norm rather than the exception. Following the pioneering sociological theories of the Germans Karl Marx (see p. 268) and Max Weber (1864–1920), there are two main models of class.

The Marxian model of class

In Marxist theory, a class is a group of people who have the same relationship to capital (property, such as land, factories or money,

Two boys from Harrow, one of Britain's most prestigious private schools, outside Lord's Cricket Ground in 1937 during the annual match between Harrow and their great private-school rivals, Eton. The existence of both private and state education systems is seen by some as perpetuating class divisions.

sed for profit). Thus his classification is strictly economic. In this theory there are two main and two minor classes:

1. Bourgeoisie (large-scale owners of capital / employers)
2. Workers (non-owners of capital / employees)
1a Petty bourgeoisie (small-scale owners of capital / employers)
2b New middle class (managers and professional employees)

The relationship between workers and employers, together with the conflict that it inevitably gives rise to, is the key point of Marx's theory of class. With industrialization, Marx expected the petty bourgeoisie to decline and the new middle class to expand, which has in fact happened. He also expected conflict between the two main classes to increase, resulting in the revolutionary overthrow of the dominant class, the owners, by the much larger subordinate class, the workers. This has not occurred in the most economically developed Western societies, but it has in several other societies, such as the former USSR, China and Cuba.

Weber's theory of class

In addition to those differences based on the individual's relationship to capital, Weber suggested that class is also determined by a person's relationship to the market (see p. 274). People have qualifications or skills for which there is a large or small demand depending on the situation. There is, for example, a higher demand for aircraft pilots than for neon-sign designers during a war. Weber's theory of class tends to have more class categories than the Marxian one because it includes the ownership/non-ownership of knowledge as well as that of capital.

The occupational status system

Weber also emphasized the concept of *status*, which he defined as social prestige. Social status is not unique to modern societies and can be influenced by many factors, including birth, education, occupation and lifestyle. As a result of the increased economic and social significance of work in modern societies, *occupational status* (also sometimes called *occupational class*), is often used as an alternative to class models of social stratification. The rank order of occupations can vary between societies and change over time. For example, since the 19th century, nursing has increased in skill and has therefore moved up the ranking, whereas clerical work has been deskilled and has consequently declined in status.

The main occupational status groups are:

1. Higher managerial and professional (e.g. doctor, lawyer)
2. Lower managerial and professional (e.g. teacher, nurse)
3. Skilled non-manual (e.g. insurance agent, secretary)
4. Skilled manual (e.g. carpenter, hairdresser)
5. Semi-skilled manual (e.g. bus driver, cashier)
6. Unskilled manual (e.g. cleaner, labourer)

Market research companies in Britain, the USA and many other industrial capitalist societies use a comparable *social grading of occupation*:

A Upper middle class (higher managerial and professional)
B Middle class (lower managerial and professional)
C1 Lower middle class (routine white-collar)
C2 Skilled working class (manual)
D Semi-skilled and unskilled working class (manual)
E Residual (including those dependent upon the state)

The terms *middle class* and *working class* are widely used by sociologists and market researchers to refer to non-manual and manual occupational groups respectively in the above classifications.

Other social divisions

Such social distinctions as gender, race, ethnic identity, language and religion have been widely used as the basis for discrimination, both official and unofficial, in many societies. In the 19th century, for example, in many countries women were not allowed to own property or to enter certain professional occupations (see p. 292). Under the apartheid system in 20th-century South Africa, political, economic and social discrimination was officially practised by the dominant White race in relation to the non-White races. When discrimination is legally abolished, it often persists informally. Consequently, disadvantage in the competition for wealth, education, work, power and prestige continues to be experienced by certain groups, notably women and Blacks.

The term *plural society* refers to one that is divided into different racial, ethnic, linguistic, and/or religious groups. The degree of segmentation varies between societies and depends on several factors, such as the extent to which different groups have their own social institutions. Modern Dutch society is a particularly good example of advanced pluralism. In the Netherlands there are Catholic, Calvinist and non-religious

political parties, trade unions, education organizations and broadcasting institutions. Many other societies are similarly divided, sometimes to such a degree that conflict between the major social groups occurs. Such tensions exist between Catholics and Protestants in Northern Ireland, Hindus and Sikhs in India, Greeks and Turks in Cyprus, and Muslims and Christians in Lebanon. The USA is highly pluralistic – as was the former USSR – in that it is made up of many large ethnic groupings, some of which coexist harmoniously, others less so.

Extreme tensions between groups with different cultural traditions can lead to political movements for *separatism*. Groups such as the Basques in Spain, and the French-speaking nationalists in Quebec in Canada have at times campaigned for their own separate state. Protestants in what is now Northern Ireland chose to stay outside the newly independent Irish Free State in 1922, agitating for the six counties where their communities are concentrated to remain a part of the United Kingdom. In India, extreme violence between Muslims and Hindus led to the partitioning of the country on independence in 1947 into two separate states – predominantly Hindu India, and predominantly Muslim Pakistan. SE

A group of 'untouchables' in India. Legislation to emancipate untouchables from the religious, occupational and social restrictions to which they are traditionally subjected has begun to break down the divisions between caste groups in India.

SEE ALSO

- AGE ROLES AND RITES OF PASSAGE p. 254
- THE FAMILY p. 256
- GOVERNMENT AND THE PEOPLE p. 266
- POLITICAL THEORIES OF THE LEFT p. 268
- POLITICAL THEORIES OF THE RIGHT p. 270
- CIVIL AND HUMAN RIGHTS p. 290

Violence on the streets of Northern Ireland. The tensions that have dogged Northern Ireland since its creation in 1922 have their roots in a centuries-old religious and cultural division between Catholic Irish and Protestants proclaiming allegiance to the UK. Although the Protestant community tends to be economically dominant, the division cuts across the normal class structure.

Education

Education is the process that allows each new generation to learn and sometimes challenge the knowledge, skills, values and behaviour that have been developed by previous generations. It may be acquired formally, in schools, colleges, universities and workplaces, or informally, in the home, on the streets, or in places of leisure. Although some people educate themselves, most learn from others, either from teachers who are paid to teach them, or from parents, relatives, friends and workmates.

Without education even advanced societies would sink back into a primitive state within a few years. We rely on education to ensure a supply of doctors, engineers, scientists and teachers, as well as to provide all citizens with a good foundation of basic knowledge and skills. In order to achieve this most countries have established a formal system of schooling. Children usually start attending school on a regular basis at the age of 5 or 6, although nursery and other forms of pre-school education may begin earlier.

The history of education

Accounts of many early civilizations contain descriptions of teaching. In ancient societies it was crucial to be able to hunt, cook, make weapons and utensils, and to know important rituals such as tribal dances and songs. Such skills and knowledge were passed on to children by their elders.

The main quadrangle of Christ Church, Oxford University's largest college, is dominated by Sir Christopher Wren's magnificent 'Tom Tower'. Founded in the 12th century, Oxford – along with Paris and Bologna – was one of Europe's first universities. Established as centres of advanced learning, there were more than 70 universities in Europe by the start of the 16th century.

A ragged school in London in the 1850s. The ragged schools were charitable institutions that provided elementary schooling, industrial training and religious instruction for nearly 300 000 destitute children. The schools died out after the introduction of compulsory education in Britain in 1870.

When societies became more advanced they needed teachers. Teachers were sometimes paid by the community out of taxes, or by parents. Some became well known. In the 5th century BC Kongfuzi (Confucius; see p. 470) wandered round China with his disciples, who in turn became teachers, and wrote down his philosophy of teaching in the *Analects*. One of his sayings was 'If out of the four corners of a subject I have dealt thoroughly with one corner and the pupils cannot find out the other three for themselves, then I do not explain any more.'

In ancient India knowledge of the sacred texts was regarded as very important for teachers. They would live with and follow their own teachers or *gurus* until they had acquired enough wisdom to be teachers themselves. This was also the pattern adopted by Jesus and his disciples.

In Classical Greece and Rome, mastery of *rhetoric* (the skill of persuasion and communication in debate and public speaking) was highly valued. Athenian parents were willing to pay well-known teachers, such as Protagoras, as much as 10 000 drachmas to turn their sons into successful orators and men of affairs within three or four years. In Rome Cicero and Quintilian (see p. 615) analysed teaching methodology in considerable detail, and taught their pupils how to deliver a talk on a subject, or how to write in the style of different authors.

From about AD 1200 education gradually began to be made available to the ordinary people, not just the children of the wealthy (see p. 406). The Church played a big part in this: in many European countries the first schools for the poor were run by the local church, with the priest doubling up as teacher. As countries became industrialized there was political pressure to have a better educated workforce, and in the 19th century the first forms of official public education for all began to emerge (see pp. 434-5).

During the 20th century the formal education of children in schools has spread throughout the world. In cities like New York the schools are huge and cater for thousands of pupils. In contrast, rural primary schools may only have a teaching staff of one and just a handful of children. Some schools simply teach their country's national curriculum (if it has one), while others may be founded on less conventional principles and adopt radically different teaching styles. Summerhill, founded in England in 1921 by the Scottish educationalist A.S. Neill (1883–1973), stresses freedom of choice for children, with optional attendance at lessons and a 'parliament' of teachers and pupils. Gordonstoun, founded in Scotland in 1935 by the German Kurt Hahn (1886–1974), emphasizes the benefits of a spartan outdoor regime and the achievement of ambitious intellectual and physical objectives. Hahn had established a similar school in Germany, but was forced to flee by the Nazis.

Aims and methods

Most official documents on education would claim that the aim of schooling is to develop children's talents to the full. In reality, however, there is some variety in what different schools try to achieve.

The primary or elementary phase of education usually covers the period from the start of compulsory schooling up to the age of 11 or 12. This is a time when pupils receive a general education and a basic grounding in foundation subjects – especially in their own language and mathematics – often, though not always, from a single teacher. Many primary schools have been influenced by the philosophy of European thinkers on education, such as the German Friedrich Froebel (1782–1852) and the Italian Maria Montessori (1870–1952), who both stressed

EDUCATION AROUND THE WORLD

The organization of education varies considerably from one country to another. In some countries, such as France, there is a national system and curriculum controlled by the central government. Other countries favour local control, as in Germany, where the regional government in each *Land* (state) decides how schools are run. In the USA there is even more decentralization, with hundreds of school districts, some quite small, organizing local education.

The United Kingdom has a number of different systems. England and Wales have a mixture of local and national control, the curriculum, since 1988, being prescribed by the government but most day-to-day decisions about teachers, methods, books and buildings being decided at school level. In Scotland the Scottish Education Department exercises central control of the curriculum and examinations.

In many countries the state or the Church exerts a powerful influence on schooling. Before 1989–91, in Eastern Bloc countries such as the USSR and Bulgaria, the state determined that education was provided according to the principles laid down by Marx and Lenin. In some Islamic countries such as Saudi Arabia and Pakistan, education is dedicated to promoting the principles of the Muslim religion, and much time in schools is devoted to the teachings of the Qur'an (Koran). In Ireland the Roman Catholic Church controls the administration of the vast majority of the country's schools.

Though the predominant form of schooling in most countries is that provided by the state, many countries have a private sector. Most private schools charge fees, although some are free, and the number varies from none at all in countries where independent schools are not permitted, to parts of the USA where there may be more private than public provision.

'mixed ability' classes? All these questions are commonly asked.

In addition, the speed of technological change is such that education is having to change rapidly. The development of radio, television, the microcomputer and the interactive videodisc have already influenced the way people learn and will continue to do so. With a source of electrical power and a telephone link, even the remotest areas can have access to the greatest stores of information in the world.

Furthermore, the many rapid changes in society and the realization that human beings are capable of learning throughout their lives – even into old age – have combined to produce a demand for permanent educational opportunities. In the 21st century people will need to be able to learn and retrain throughout their lives, not just during the brief years of compulsory schooling.   ECW

An English lesson in a progressive school in London in the 1960s. Progressive education developed at the end of the 19th century in opposition to formal school structures and teaching methods. The movement favours child-centred teaching, a playing down of the importance of academic examinations, and – as the picture suggests – relaxed discipline.

the importance of creative play, self-motivation and practical activity.

Certain countries, especially the less wealthy, do not provide any education beyond the primary level. Even in Britain it was not until the Education Act of 1944 that secondary education was made available to all children. In some countries, such as Germany, children undergo a selection procedure to determine which type of secondary school they should attend. In others, like the United States and most of the United Kingdom, all pupils in an area attend the same secondary or high school.

During the secondary phase pupils usually study a variety of subjects taught by specialist teachers. The curriculum in some countries consists entirely of traditional academic subjects such as mathematics, history, science and both their native and a foreign language. In other countries there may be a more vocational bias. Pupils in the USA, for example, may be able to have classes in such fields as journalism.

Further and higher education

Once the compulsory years of education are over, those who wish to continue learning can choose either to teach themselves, learn in their workplace, or attend an institution of further or higher education. Colleges of further education usually provide a wide range of courses for people wanting to study either part or full time. Most of these courses are below degree level, often leading to a professional or technical qualification, but such colleges may offer courses of general education or 'second chances' to those who were not able to obtain academic qualifications earlier in their careers.

Institutions of higher education include universities and polytechnics, which offer courses at first-degree level or beyond. Students either attend for their general education, or they may pursue a course related to a future career in, for example, medicine, engineering or law. Numbers

attending degree-level courses may vary from a tiny percentage of the population in less wealthy countries, to one in three in Japan and parts of the USA.

Issues in education

There are few parts of the world where education is not a contentious issue. In countries with high unemployment it may be a passport to one of the few good jobs available, so parents will be anxious to secure the best opportunities for their children. Particular controversy attaches to the question of equal opportunities for all. Do children of all backgrounds get a fair deal? Do boys have a better education than girls? Are children from different religious, ethnic and social groups given the same opportunities as others? Should children attend selective schools according to their ability, or should all attend a common high school or comprehensive school? And within the school should they be grouped according to their ability – in streamed classes – or be taught in

A school classroom in Communist Cuba (left). The map on the classroom wall shows Cuba's revolutionary leader Fidel Castro looking towards Lenin, the leader of the Russian revolution. Cuba's state-run education system links schooling to manual labour, stresses ideological teaching, and encourages continued study by working people.

SEE ALSO

- PERCEPTION p. 224
- THE POWER OF SPEECH p. 226
- LEARNING, CREATIVITY AND INTELLIGENCE p. 231
- MEDIEVAL AND RENAISSANCE CULTURE p. 406
- INDUSTRIAL SOCIETY p. 434
- HOW LANGUAGE WORKS p. 608

Deviance, Crime and Law Enforcement

Deviants are people who do not conform with the social, moral or legal rules of a society, although the term is most often used to refer to those who actually break the criminal law (see p. 265). As societies evolve and become more complex, views on what constitutes deviance and crime may change.

The Fleet prison in London – described in several of Charles Dickens's novels – served mainly as a debtors' prison until it was demolished in 1848. The imprisonment of people until they could pay their debts was widespread until the second half of the 19th century.

Although the central core of criminal wrongdoing – offences such as murder, theft and assault – has remained more or less unchanged over the centuries and from country to country, other behaviour may be regarded as criminal at one time or place but not at another. In Britain, for instance, suicide was a crime until 1961 and eavesdropping until 1967, and homosexual behaviour was legalized in some situations in the same year.

On the other hand, many new crimes have been created. Insider dealing – the unfair use of information about stocks and shares to make a personal profit – was made a crime in several countries in the 1980s, and many countries are considering making computer 'hacking' a crime. In South Africa, the apartheid system, which segregates people according to their skin colour, is enforced by criminal law. In countries with a strict system of Islamic law, it is a criminal offence to commit adultery, or to drink alcohol.

Generally crimes can be classified in four broad groups: firstly there are *crimes against the person*, such as murder, manslaughter, assault and sexual offences; secondly *crimes against property*, such as theft, burglary and criminal damage; thirdly *crimes against public order*, such as riot, affray and incitement to racial hatred; and fourthly *crimes against the state*, such as treason and sedition. Some laws are designed to protect health, such as quarantine laws and laws against the possession and use of dangerous drugs, or to protect people's feelings and beliefs, such as the laws of libel and blasphemy.

Crimes and the state

The notion that the criminal law always enforces morality is a mistaken one. While the criminal law can be used to enforce the Ten Commandments, for example, it can also be used to bolster the most repressive political regimes, such as Nazi Germany (see p. 442). For the society that has made the law, crimes are wrongs committed not just against an individual victim, but also against society as a whole (see pp. 264–5). Thus prosecutions are almost always brought by the state and only rarely by individual citizens. In most countries the prosecution must prove an accused person's guilt beyond reasonable doubt.

For all serious crimes, the prosecution must prove that the accused committed the wrongful act, such as killing the victim, and that this was done with a guilty mind – that is to say on purpose rather than by accident. Even if the prosecution can prove these elements of the crime, the accused person may be able to rely on a defence – such as insanity or duress – to show the court that in the circumstances he or she should not be found guilty after all. However, if pleading insanity the accused may be detained in a mental institution.

Crime rates

Many people think that crime is on the increase, but it is difficult to be certain of this. Official crime statistics generally record only those offences that are reported to the police and recorded by them. An increase from one year to another in, say, the number of thefts recorded in the statistics might not reflect a real increase in that crime, but only an increase in the number of thefts reported, or be caused by changes in police recording practices.

There is also the problem of the extent of unrecorded crime, which does not appear in these figures at all. The only way to measure the 'dark figure' of unrecorded crime is to conduct surveys, asking people for details of cases where they have been crime victims but have not reported the matter to the police. A survey like this has been carried out regularly in Britain by the Home Office since 1983. It shows that there are twice as many burglaries, 5 times as many serious assaults and 13 times as much criminal damage as the official statistics show.

The police

The police have the job of investigating and detecting crime. In England and Wales their powers to arrest and question suspects and search for evidence are set out in various Acts of Parliament, notably the Police and Criminal Evidence Act of 1984. One of the first organized police forces was created in Dublin in 1786, though the office of constable – unpaid, locally appointed and answerable to justices of the peace – had existed for hundreds of years before that.

The Metropolitan Police force was established in London in 1829 and local forces were set up elsewhere in Britain during the 1830s. These early policemen were known as 'Bow Street Runners' and later as 'Peelers', after Sir Robert Peel, the statesman who set up the force.

The British police are unusual in the world today in maintaining the tradition of not routinely carrying firearms. Some European police forces, such as those in France and Italy, are highly centralized and paramilitary in nature. In the USA, federal, state and local police forces operate independently. Police forces in most countries have developed special squads of officers to deal with riots, and specially trained officers to detect complex crimes, such as fraud.

Punishment

After a person is convicted of an offence by a criminal court (see p. 264), the court proceeds to sentence him or her. Judges often have a

Masked gunmen hijacked an American airliner at Beirut Airport in 1985, demanding the release of Shiite and Palestinian prisoners by Israel. The perpetrators of politically motivated terrorist acts are regarded as violent criminals by many in the international community, but are seen by their supporters as freedom fighters in a just cause.

...wide discretion over which sentence to impose. Under many legal systems their decision is subject to an appeal by the offender, if he or she thinks the sentence is too severe, and conversely by the prosecution if they think the sentence is too lenient.

Capital punishment (the death penalty) was once widely used in Britain, for offences as diverse as defacing the coinage and sheep stealing. It was effectively abolished in 1965, although theoretically it can still be imposed for a crime of treason. The death penalty still exists in other countries, such as China, the USA and South Africa. A death sentence is often not carried out immediately, and prisoners on 'Death Row' may face months or years of uncertainty until they know whether an appeal against their sentence will be successful, or whether the government will commute their sentence to one of imprisonment.

Imprisonment was not originally designed as a punishment. Prisons were places used to hold people securely until they paid their debts, were executed, or transported overseas. In many countries imprisonment is now the most severe sentence a court can impose. It may be for a fixed term stated by the judge, or for life. In either case the actual period served may be reduced, sometimes quite considerably, by the prisoner's good behaviour and a decision by the authorities to release a prisoner early, under supervision. Prison sentences, and the equivalent sentence of detention in a youth-offender institution for those under 21, are used in about half the cases sentenced in the British Crown Courts.

Courts can opt for *non-custodial* sentences as alternatives to prison. Prison sentences can be suspended, which means that the offender will only serve the sentence if he or she commits a further offence within a specified time. In Britain fines are the most frequently imposed non-custodial sentence, though in the USA they are seldom used. In Germany and Sweden a system exists where-by offenders are fined a percentage of their income, rather than being fined a fixed amount for the crime committed.

Community service – introduced first in Britain in 1972 – and in many countries since – requires the offender to do up to 240 hours of unpaid work in the community to repay his or her debt to society. This may be hard physical labour, such as clearing derelict

THE FORENSIC LABORATORY

The methods by which crimes are investigated have become increasingly sophisticated during the 20th century. The modern forensic laboratory is equipped with a formidable array of scientific instruments and facilities, and employs a number of chemical, photographic and other techniques to analyse and identify physical evidence.

Modern methods of *fingerprinting* are based on techniques established in the late 19th century and officially introduced by the London Metropolitan Police in 1901. Fingerprinting is particularly useful as a means of identifying suspects since no two people have the same pattern of ridges on their fingers and thumbs. Dusting techniques have made the revelation and identification of 'invisible' fingerprints a commonplace, and chemical tests have been devised that can detect the presence of fingerprints that are several years old.

The use of chemical tests is crucial in the examination of blood, semen, urine and other body fluids. Once blood has been detected, categorization according to blood group is possible, as well as an estimate of the age of the bloodstains. A recent advance in forensic investigation is the technique of *genetic fingerprinting* (see p. 114), which allows exact identification of a suspect by an examination of DNA molecules in body fluids and tissues.

Chemical tests also enable scientists to identify specific drugs or poisons. *Toxicological analysis* by a forensic laboratory may be necessary to establish whether a death was accidental, murder or suicide.

Sophisticated photographic techniques, particularly infrared and ultraviolet photography, allow the detection of invisible writing, alterations to documents, and stains in clothing and fabric.

Photomicrography (photographing objects through a microscope) is of particular use to *ballistics* (firearms) experts. Minute imperfections on the inside of a gun barrel leave tiny scratches on a bullet fired from it – every gun leaves a different pattern of scratches. Photomicrography can be used to compare such markings on a test bullet fired from a suspect firearm with those on a bullet found at the scene of a crime, and positive identification can then be made.

The distance from which a weapon was fired can be determined from the shape and size of a bullet hole or wound and the extent of the burnt area around it. Tests also exist to detect traces of chemicals left by cartridge primers on the hands and clothing and thereby establish whether a suspect has recently fired a gun.

land, or social work alongside professional carers and volunteers with the disadvantaged or handicapped. A *probation* order places the offender under the supervision of a probation officer for a period of up to three years. In the USA some offenders on probation are required to wear an electronic anklet or tag, so that the probation officer can check their whereabouts by radio monitoring.

In many cases where the offender can afford to pay, he or she will be required by the criminal court to pay money in compensation to the victim of the crime. Alternatively, a victim who has suffered physical injury may be able to claim some compensation from the state. The first scheme of this type started in New Zealand in 1960 and most countries now have one.   MW

SEE ALSO

● THE LAW: CIVIL AND CRIMINAL p. 264
● GOVERNMENT AND THE PEOPLE p. 266
● CIVIL AND HUMAN RIGHTS p. 290

Los Angeles police use a battering ram to break into a house during a drugs raid. The best way of policing increasingly violent inner-city areas is a matter of considerable debate: some favour community policing, where there is frequent liaison between police and local residents, while others favour a hard-hitting approach to stamp out crime, even when this might alienate sections of the local community.

The Law: Civil and Criminal

At the root of all systems of law is the notion of justice. *Justice*, associated with the principles of fairness and impartiality, is often personified as a blindfolded fligure holding a pair of scales, to symbolize the impartiality of the law. It is said that justice must be done and be seen to be done.

A medieval trial by combat fought before judges. Trial by ordeal – which included trial by fire and immersion in water as well as trial by combat – was based on the belief that God woulc intervene to protect an innocent person. Most forms of trial by ordeal died out in the 13th century, although in some parts of Europe trial by combat persisted until the 15th century.

What happens in court is reported by the press, and courts often have a public gallery where anyone can sit and watch the law in action. In the USA it is quite common for important cases to be televized, but this is not permitted in Britain. Judges should be neutral and have no personal interest in the outcome of the case. No person should act as both prosecutor and judge. With a few exceptions, anyone can be called as a witness, and be required to give evidence.

Nazi leaders in the dock during the war crimes trials held in Nuremburg in 1945 and 1946. Nazi atrocities, such as mass extermination and transportation, were defined not only as war crimes, but as crimes against humanity. Twelve Nazi leaders were sentenced to hang in the trials, which established the precedent that war crimes are the responsibility of the individual, as well as of the state.

Ancient legal systems, particularly those of Greece and Rome, still influence the modern law. Around the world, there are now four distinct 'schools' of law. The first is based on *Roman law* and is the chief influence on the legal systems of many Western European countries. A characteristic of Roman law systems is the writing down of laws in the form of general codes. Perhaps the most famous of these is the French Napoleonic code (see p. 427). The second type is based on *common law*, and is found in Britain and in those countries – such as the USA and Commonwealth countries – whose legal systems are modelled on British law. The third type is *socialist law*, strongly influenced by Marxism-Leninism (see pp. 268–9), and found in Eastern Europe (where it is under review) and some Asian countries. Fourthly, *Muslim law* is based on the Qur'an (Koran; see pp. 478–9).

The sources of the law

The first and most important source of the law is *statute law*. In Britain a statute is an Act of Parliament passed by both Houses of Parliament; similarly, in other countries, laws are passed by a majority in the representative assembly (*legislature*; see p. 266). European Community laws are having an important effect in standardizing the laws of all countries that are members of the EC (see p. 286). In the USA statutes may apply at either state or federal level, but the most important statute is the US Constitution itself (see p. 423). Sometimes the wording of a statute or code may be unclear, in which case a judge must give a ruling on the meaning of the new law. This process is called *statutory interpretation*. In Roman-law systems, the main task of the judge is to apply the codes.

The second source of the law is previous court decisions. The doctrine of *precedent*, which is found in all legal systems, says that the judge must generally follow an earlier decision of any higher court on the same point of law that he is considering. A *litigant* who wants to challenge that law must take his or her case on appeal to a court high enough to overturn the earlier decision (see diagram). The system of precedent means that a legal system must have detailed accounts of previous cases, known as *law reports*.

Common-law systems are *adversarial*, which means that lawyers on each side put opposing arguments to the judge, who then decides which argument wins. The role of the judge is rather like an umpire – he or she ensures fair play and then announces the result. In some kinds of cases, the jury has the role of deciding the result (see criminal law, below).

A quite different system, the *inquisitorial* one, operates in Roman-law, socialist and Islamic systems. Here, the judge or magistrate actively investigates the case and questions the witnesses in court before reaching his or her decision.

Civil law

Civil law governs rights and duties between citizens. The law of *contract* deals with important business matters such as trade, credit and insurance, but also

overns more commonplace agreements (for example a bus ticket is a contract between the passenger and the bus company).

The law of *tort*, or *delict*, governs liability following breach of a duty of care between citizens, such as a case in which a person is injured by another's negligent driving, or has property damaged by animals that have escaped from a neighbour's farm, or where a person's reputation is damaged by defamatory statements in a published work.

A famous tort case in Britain is *Donoghue versus Stevenson* in 1932, in which a woman obtained compensation from the manufacturers of a bottle of ginger beer. She had fallen ill after drinking the ginger beer, which, because of the manufacturer's negligence, contained the decomposed remains of a snail.

In civil cases the person injured (known in England and Wales as the *plaintiff*) will use the law to bring an action against the *defendant* in a civil court (see diagram), probably seeking the remedy of *damages*, which is a payment of compensation. Another civil remedy is an *injunction*. This might be used where one neighbour sues another to stop them having noisy parties or making unpleasant smells on their land. In such cases the plaintiff does not want compensation; the court is being asked to order the offending behaviour to be stopped.

Civil law covers other important areas of life, such as the purchase of a house, the disposal of property where a marriage ends in divorce, and the care and custody of the children of that marriage.

Criminal law

Criminal law deals with the situation where the *accused* person is said to have broken a law that has caused an injury not just to another individual, but also to the state (see p. 262). This law covers offences that range from murder, manslaughter, assault and sexual offences, to offences against property such as theft, burglary and criminal damage. The purpose of the criminal law is quite different from that of the civil law. The state prosecutes accused persons in a criminal court (see diagram) not in order to obtain compensation, but to punish them for what they have done.

In common-law systems, serious criminal law cases are dealt with by a judge and *jury*, but most cases can be decided by *magistrates*, or *justices of the peace*, who are not lawyers and are unpaid. With the exception of some libel cases, a jury is never used in a civil case in Britain, and juries are hardly ever used in Roman-law, socialist or Islamic legal systems. In England and Wales a jury is composed of 12 impartial people, aged between 18 and 70. At the end of the case they decide if the accused is guilty or not guilty. In most countries that have a jury system a unanimous verdict is needed, but in England and Wales a majority verdict, with up to two dissenters, is allowed. If the jury cannot agree, there may be a retrial. In Scotland, juries consist of 15 people, and a bare majority verdict of 8:7 is acceptable.

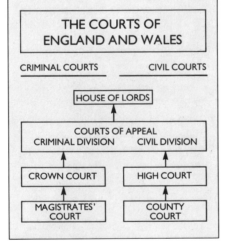

THE COURTS OF ENGLAND AND WALES

The arrows indicate where a right of appeal lies from one court to another. The more serious criminal cases start off in the Crown Court and more complicated civil cases in the High Court.

Three judges sit in the Court of Appeal. They are known as Lords Justices of Appeal. Five judges sit in the House of Lords. They are known as Lords of Appeal in Ordinary, or the Law Lords.

The head of the Civil Division of the Court of Appeal is the Master of the Rolls. This title derives from his historical custodianship of the court record, or rolls. The head of the Criminal Division of the Court of Appeal is the Lord Chief Justice. The head of the House of Lords is the Lord Chancellor. The Lord Chancellor is the only judge who is also a member of the Government.

THE COURTS OF ENGLAND AND WALES

CRIMINAL COURTS | CIVIL COURTS

HOUSE OF LORDS

COURTS OF APPEAL
CRIMINAL DIVISION | CIVIL DIVISION

CROWN COURT | HIGH COURT

MAGISTRATES' COURT | COUNTY COURT

The accused's guilt in a criminal case must be proved by the prosecution beyond reasonable doubt. The rules governing what evidence can be heard in court are complex and vary between different legal systems. In Britain the accused's previous convictions cannot be discussed, nor can *hearsay* evidence, where one person testifies as to what another person told him. Opinion evidence is not allowed, unless it is the opinion of an expert, such as a forensic scientist or handwriting expert (see p. 263).

Lawyers

In Britain the legal profession is divided into two groups. *Solicitors* have a general knowledge of most of the law, and it is a solicitor to whom a client would go with a legal problem. In many cases the solicitor is able to deal with the matter alone. If, however, the problem involves a complex issue in a specialized area of law, or there is likely to be a case in a higher court, the solicitor briefs a barrister.

Barristers (called *advocates* in Scotland) specialize in a particular area of the law. In France there is a similar distinction, between the *avoué* (solicitor) and the *avocat* (barrister). In most countries, one lawyer does both jobs. In the former USSR lawyers were regarded as the servants of the state, and were appointed to cases by a governing body, the *Prokuratura*, rather than being chosen by the person in need of a lawyer. In many countries with common-law or Roman-law systems, lawyers are paid a fee whether the case is won or lost. In damages cases in the USA a system of *contingency fees* is sometimes applied, whereby all parties agree that the lawyer will only be paid if the case is won.

In Britain judges are almost always appointed from the ranks of senior barristers, though it is also possible for solicitors to become judges. In due course a judge may be promoted to sit in the appeal courts: these are the Court of Appeal, which is split into Civil and Criminal Divisions, and the House of Lords (see diagram). Judges, once appointed, hold office until their retirement, unless they resign or are removed from office by a complex procedure involving resolution by both Houses of Parliament.

In many other European countries judges are not appointed from the ranks of barristers. In Switzerland and France, for instance, judges have a special legal training, and are appointed for life. US Federal judges, including those in the Supreme Court, are appointed by the President, subject to confirmation by the Senate. State judges are, however, elected to their jobs.

In the former Soviet Union and in some of its former satellites in Eastern Europe, in theory, any citizen could be elected a judge – legal training was not a requirement. In Argentina, Brazil and Chile, Supreme Court judges are appointed for life. Elsewhere all judges are appointed for fixed terms varying from 3 to 10 years.

It can be very expensive to bring a legal case, especially one that reaches the higher courts. Many civil cases can, however, be resolved between the lawyers of the two parties without going to court. For those people who cannot afford to pay, there are systems of legal advice and legal aid available in most countries to help with some, or all, of a person's legal expenses.　　　　MW

SEE ALSO
● DEVIANCE, CRIME AND LAW ENFORCEMENT p. 262
● GOVERNMENT AND THE PEOPLE p. 266
● CIVIL AND HUMAN RIGHTS p. 290

The appeal court in Paris. The 35 appeal courts in France are empowered to pass judgement on decisions pronounced by magistrate's courts and high courts, as well as specialized courts such as industrial tribunals and commercial courts. Most judicial systems have a hierarchy of courts allowing for a decision in a lower court to be reversed on appeal to a higher court.

Government
and the
People

The word 'government' comes from the Latin word *gubernator*, meaning helmsman. Well before Roman times, people living in early societies started to develop special institutions to look after their common well-being. Government is needed to make decisions on matters affecting the people of a state as a whole. Effective government means the ability to arrive at a balance between conflicting pressures, and to steer the state towards shared community goals.

The frontispiece of *Leviathan* (1651) (right) by Thomas Hobbes. The crowned giant – representing the absolute power of the sovereign – wields a sword and bishop's crozier, symbols of civil and ecclesiastical supremacy. The tiny figures within the giant's body represent the state, which is made up of all the individuals within it. Hobbes believed that individuals came together to create the state by surrendering power to an absolute monarch, whose duty it is to preserve their peace and safety.

The original purposes of government were to protect a people from attack from external aggressors, and to provide them with a body of laws to bring order to their everyday lives. Since the 19th century, the tasks of government have grown to cover education, health and pensions (the 'welfare state', see pp. 268-9). Some people think that modern governments take on too wide a range of tasks.

The ancient Athenian city-state (see pp. 370–1) is often viewed as the basic model of democracy. It was certainly more democratic than anything that had come before it; but, by modern standards, Athenian democracy was limited by the inferior status of women, the reliance on slavery, and an unequal sharing of power among male citizens. The Roman republican system (see pp. 376–7) saw a further development of popular control of government, in particular in the acceptance of the idea that sovereignty rests in the people as a whole rather than in one small group.

In the medieval period, the task of government was effectively divided between the state and the Church, with each claiming their own set of rights. The

A new session of the French National Assembly opens. The Assembly is the lower house of the French parliament under the 1958 constitution, and is made up of 577 deputies (members of parliament). Deputies in the Assembly are elected for terms of five years by a simple majority vote in single-member constituencies. But in a two-stage electoral system, only the leading candidates in the first ballot survive to the second round.

medieval view was that the authority of one person to rule over another came from God – the so-called 'divine right of kings'. The Italian political theorist Niccolò Machiavelli (1469–1527) broke away from accepted ideas towards a secular view of the state. He favoured a popular form of government that he saw as having existed in the Roman Republic.

The social contract

The emergence of the idea of the *social contract* in the 16th century reintroduced the notion that government rests on the consent of the people. The English political philosopher Thomas Hobbes (1588–1679) described the chaos in which he believed people lived when they did not have a proper government. He claims in his most important treatise, *Leviathan* (1651), that the life of man in his natural, ungoverned state is 'solitary, poor, nasty, brutish and short'. Hobbes's doctrine is that men can only live together in peace if they agree to obey an absolute sovereign, and this agreement Hobbes called 'the social contract'. Hobbes's concern about what happened when government broke down, as in the English Civil War (see p. 412) during his lifetime, led him to suggest that considerable power should be placed in the hands of the sovereign.

In his two *Treatises of Government* (1690), the English philosopher John Locke (1632–1704; see also p. 418) also makes use of the idea of a social contract. However, Locke opposed absolutism, and saw the free consent of the governed as the basis of legitimate government. Obedience depends on governments ruling for the good of the governed, who have the right to rebel if they are oppressed. This idea would appear quite acceptable today, but was seen as radical at the time – being adopted, for example, by the American Revolutionaries of 1776 (see p. 422).

The French philosopher Jean-Jacques

Rousseau (1712–1778; see also pp. 419 and 630-1) faced the question that had troubled all social-contract theorists since the decline of the idea of a God-given authority. If laws are made by citizens, why should other citizens obey them? Rousseau made it clear that citizens must exist within a system of law, but citizens can only be bound by those laws if they take part in making them. In his *Social Contract* (1762), Rousseau offers an account of the ideal democracy based on popular sovereignty. The exercise of power, Rousseau argues, should accord with the 'general will' and have the consent of all the people.

Types and tasks of government

By developing the idea of *separation of powers*, the French enlightenment philosopher Montesquieu (1689–1755; see also p. 418) pointed the way to the modern view of the three branches of government. The *legislature* is responsible for the making and amending of laws; the *executive* is responsible for carrying out laws and the *judiciary* is responsible for the administering of justice. This division of governmental powers provides a basis for popular control. For example, a supreme court (the highest court of the judiciary) can rule whether the government (executive) has broken the law. In the United States, the constitution is based on a system of 'checks and balances' between the different branches of government.

Liberal or western democracies take a number of forms, but have in common the regular election of governments by free choice between competing parties. Countries such as France and the USA have *presidential* systems in which executive power is vested in an elected president. A president's power is usually limited to some extent by the legislative assembly, which is responsible for the day-to-day running of the government.

In a *parliamentary* system, a *Prime Minister* – usually the leader of the majority party in the legislative assembly – heads the executive branch of government. In a *constitutional monarchy*, such as Britain, the prime minister serves under a sovereign who has only cere-monial powers (see feature).

Communist states, such as the Soviet Union until 1990–91, depended on one-party rule by the Communist Party. In 1989–91, the power of the Communist Party was eroded in the countries of Eastern Europe, which moved towards democratic political systems. Many countries, particularly in the Third World, are governed by the military. However, since the 1970s, there has been a trend for military regimes to be replaced by democracies, first in southern Europe, later in Latin America and most recently in Africa .

A *federal* system, as in Germany, divides power between central government and a number of regional governments. A *unitary* system concentrates executive authority in the hands of central government.

Political participation

Modern democracy has developed as a system in which the people are able to take part in government decision making. The most basic form of political participation is voting to elect public officials. This may be direct or indirect. In the system of indirect election in the United States, the people choose a body of electors – an *electoral college* – which then elects a president. Some countries have a first-past-the-post electoral system in which the candi-date with the most votes in a constituency (i.e. a particular area) is elected (see feature). France uses a two-stage system, while many other European countries use a variety of systems of *proportional representation* in-tended to ensure that parties are represented in parliament in relation to the number of votes they receive from the electorate as a whole. In Australia and Belgium it is illegal not to vote in a general election.

Some countries, such as Switzerland, make extensive use of referenda to allow the electorate to decide directly on current issues. Referenda have been used in Britain on the issues of membership of the European Com-munity and devolution for Scotland and Wales.

Citizens may become more directly involved in politics. They may join a political party, or form or join a pressure group campaigning on a single issue. They may decide to stand for public office themselves. Even in the freest society, political participation is dependent to a certain extent on social and economic factors that give some individuals and groups more power and influence than others.

The administration

The German sociologist Max Weber (see p. 258) saw bureaucracy as a more efficient form of administration than, for example, the ear-lier system based on the members of a mon-arch's court. However, the very efficiency of bureaucracy, and the permanent status of most civil servants, raises serious questions about the accountability of bureaucrats to the people.

The civil service, particularly its senior mem-bers, is important both in terms of offering advice on policy, and putting policies into operation. The central position of bureau-cracy in modern government has created a need for new ways of dealing with complaints from citizens about unfair treatment. In Britain, the *ombudsman* is an official who investigates claims of maladministration against national and local government.

Reforms such as this can help to deal with complaints from individual citizens, but they do not solve the more general problem of the accountability of bureaucrats. The power of the bureaucracy is something that Montes-quieu did not anticipate when writing about the separation of powers, and poses the most serious problem for popular control.   WG

Unarmed 'people power' in the Phi-lippines ended the repressive 20-year rule of President Ferdinand Marcos in 1986. The uprising that brought Mrs Corazon Aquino to power, after Marcos's refusal to acknowledge electoral defeat, was a rare example of the bloodless overthrow of illegitimate government by popular pressure.

GOVERNMENT AND PEOPLE IN BRITAIN

The United Kingdom uses a 'first-past-the-post' system for electing Members of Parlia-ment. Each constituency elects one MP, the person gaining the most votes being elected. In a contest between four parties, it would be possible for an MP to be elected with less than a third of the total vote. At national level, it is possible for the party that obtains the largest number of votes not to win the election, as happened in 1951 when the Labour Government lost office to the Conservatives.

The first-past-the-post system favours parties that appeal to a particular social class (such as the Conservative and Labour parties) or to a region (such as the Nation-alist parties in Wales and Scotland). Parties that have an appeal across the electorate gain fewer seats.

The British system tends to produce major-ity governments that do not have to rely on coalition partners to govern. Systems of proportional representation, such as those of Germany and Italy, can give a lot of influence to very small parties whose sup-port is needed by larger parties to enable them to form a government .

The monarch is head of the United Kingdom, although the *crown* is seen as a symbol above and beyond the monarch. Legislative power is vested in parliament, with the *royal assent* needed for a bill to become law. The Commons is elected for a term of not more than five years. Parlia-ment is *dissolved* by the monarch on the advice of the prime minister. After a gen-eral election, the monarch appoints the head of the winning party as the new prime minister, although if no one party had a working majority, the monarch would have to seek advice on who to ask first to try and form a government.

Britain operates a system of *cabinet government* in which ministers in charge of departments are drawn from the two Houses of Parliament, largely from the *Commons* (lower house) rather than the *Lords* (upper house). If the government loses a vote of confidence in the House of Commons, even by only one vote, as hap-pened to the Labour Party in 1979, it has to resign.

Because modern governments have so much to do, the Cabinet increasingly works through a system of committees. Some are permanent committees dealing with tasks such as managing the economy, while others are formed to deal with particular problems. The Cabinet as a whole remains crucial in shaping the general policy of the Government, although the Prime Minister is clearly its most important single member.

Much of the work of governing Britain is done by local government. Local authorities (county councils and district councils in England and Wales, regional and district councils in Scotland) are responsible for services such as education, social services, local authority housing, and the fire brigade. There has been some loss of tasks by local government in the 1980s, with some metropolitan authorities (notably the Greater London Council) being abolished and schools being allowed to opt for direct funding by central government.

SEE ALSO

● SOCIAL STRATIFICATION AND DIVISIONS p. 258
● POLITICAL THEORIES OF THE LEFT p. 268
● POLITICAL THEORIES OF THE RIGHT p. 270
● THE ENLIGHTENMENT p. 418

Political Theories of the Left

In politics the Left is the polar opposite of the Right. The metaphor of left, right and centre originated in the French Revolution of 1789 (see pp. 424–5). In the French Estates General the aristocracy sat on the King's right, whereas the commoners (or 'third estate') sat on his left. Subsequently, in French and other European assemblies, radical democrats, radical liberals and socialists sat on the left of the President's or Speaker's chair. The French revolutionary commitment to 'liberty, equality and fraternity' remains the simplest way to understand the numerous political theories of the Left, as these core values lie at the centre of the Left's arguments.

The tensions between liberty, equality and fraternity help explain much of the internal debate and fragmentation within the Left. However, all these values and tensions are subsumed within a broad philosophical commitment to 'political rationalism'.

Liberty

The Left, especially its liberal and democratic components such as the socialist, labour and social democratic parties of Western Europe, are distinguished by their fundamental commitment to democracy, understood as government based on popular consent and popular participation in the formation and exercise of political authority. The Left hold that human freedom requires political freedom – freedom to choose the government and to dissent from it – and civil rights of assembly, expression and participation (see pp. 290–1) which make the realization of such freedom effective.

The Left have always been divided, however, over how and to what extent to increase democracy. The liberal and social democratic Left embrace the institutions of representative government (the periodic election of parliaments and/or presidents under universal suffrage) and the rule of law (the regulation of all social activity by constitutional and other legislation). They have sought more rarely to extend democracy to non-governmental organizations. In contrast, socialists and Communists have emphasized the merits of 'workers' control', 'industrial democracy' (the control of an organization by those who work in it), 'economic democracy' or, more generally, 'participatory democracy'. They have believed in the

Chartist riots (right) in 1839. Chartism was the first significant mass working-class protest movement against the injustices of 19th-century industrial capitalism in Britain. Chartists campaigned for universal suffrage for men, annually elected parliaments, equal electoral districts, payment of Members of Parliament, voting by ballot, and the waiving of ownership of property as a qualification for Members of Parliament.

merits of politicizing such formally neutral institutions as state bureaucracies, the police and the judiciary (see p. 266). The ultra-Left, who resemble anarchists (advocates of the abolition of formal government) in their political beliefs, would entrust ultimate authority to mass meetings of active people rather than to laws or constitutions which give power to small groups.

In part these differences reflect conflict within the Left over the relative importance of liberty and equality. The more extreme Left believe that greater equality requires the extending of democracy to all institutions, whereas others believe that too much 'democratization' threatens other values of the Left, such as liberty, and may not necessarily produce democratic institutions.

The Left have also been divided over how to achieve their commitment to liberty. *Reformists*, i.e. liberals, social democrats and democratic socialists, believe that the Left should work within the institutions of liberal democracy to extend support for their values. They usually organize themselves in mass socialist, social democratic or labour parties for these purposes. By contrast *revolutionaries*, especially those committed to the political theories of Communism or Marxist-Leninism (see box), believe that liberal democracy is a sham: a facade for 'bourgeois' or 'capitalist' democracy. They believe that 'true democracy', i.e. proletarian or working-class democracy, can be achieved only through insurrectionary means. They have usually organized themselves in elite parties to achieve these purposes, using the Russian Bolsheviks (see p. 438) as their model. However, the Marxist-Leninist or Communist commitment to democracy has been fundamentally compromised since the Russian Revolution of 1917. It has been historically associated with the 'dictatorship of the proletariat', which in practice has meant the dictatorship of the Communist Party. Such parties have monopolized state power in the Soviet Union and Eastern Europe (until 1989), China, Indochina and Cuba.

All components of the Left also believe in 'positive' as opposed to 'negative' freedom, i.e. the importance of people being free *to* achieve their objectives and realize their talents. Mere freedom *from* government, or 'negative' liberty, is considered insufficient to build a good society. The Left believe that such positive freedom can be built only in societies committed to egalitarian and fraternal values.

Equality

The Left are perhaps best known for their commitment to 'equality'. First, they are opposed to hereditary privilege – especially aristocratic patronage but also any form of nepotism – on the grounds that such privilege has nothing to do with merit. This principle is considered indispensable to the creation of a 'classless society'. Second, the Left believe that 'equality of opportunity' requires governmental regulation of private property and family rights to ensure that equality is realized in meaningful, practical terms. Thus a redistributive *welfare state*, based upon progressive taxation of income and wealth, which ensures equality of access to such basic social goods as education, health care and insurance, is considered vital to enable people to have a fair chance of benefiting from equality of opportunity. Third, the Left believe that inequalities between people in income, wealth or resources have to be justified by the benefits such inequalities generate for the rest of society. This requirement sets limits to differences in income and wealth which can be accepted within the principles of social justice. Here the Left differ from those who believe that equality of opportunity means merely equality of opportunity to achieve unequal rewards.

Fourth, the Left have progressively extended the principle that all adults should be treated as meriting equal respect and possessing equal rights before the law, because of their equal humanity. Thus they have been hostile to *imperialism* – the conquest and coercive domination of some ethnic groups by others; to *racism* – the belief that some races are generally superior to others; and to *sexism* – the belief that men are generally superior to women. Moreover, they are prepared to rectify discrimination against ill-treated groups, whether defined by their race, ethnic identity, religion, sex, sexual preference or physical traits, by advocating 'affirmative action' to ensure that members of such groups are fully integrated into modern society as equal citizens.

Finally, and most controversially, the Left have been associated with an egalitarian philosophy which opposes the free market (see pp. 271 and 274–5) and private property rights. Thus many early socialists and Marxist-Leninists favoured the replacement of the free market by a planned economy, and state or social ownership as opposed to private ownership of the means of production, distribution and exchange. They argued that such policies were necessary to control the anarchy and inequalities of capitalist markets, to abolish class privileges, and to create the genuine solidarity which

SEE ALSO

● GOVERNMENT AND THE
  PEOPLE p. 266
● POLITICAL THEORIES OF THE
  RIGHT p. 270
● ECONOMICS pp. 272–9
● CIVIL AND HUMAN RIGHTS
  p. 290
● YOUTH MOVEMENTS p. 294

MARXISM

The economic and political doctrine known as Marxism was outlined by the German theorists Karl Marx (1818–83) and Friedrich Engels (1820–95). Their most famous joint work was *The Communist Party Manifesto* (1848), and Engels helped finish Marx's major work *Das Kapital* (1867–94).

According to Marx and Engels' theory of *historical materialism*, human history – a process of gradual technological advance – has seen the existence of a number of progressive modes of production. Each mode of production, except the Communist modes, is characterized by fundamental class division and exploitation. The ruling class own the means of production (land or capital or people) and extract 'surplus labour' from subordinate classes.

Marx believed that the ruling class of each mode of production, who controlled the state, would be challenged and replaced by a new ruling class when their rule ceased to advance the progress of production. Thus the feudal nobility, who were dominant because they owned the land, were replaced – with the growth in trade and industrialization – by the capitalist middle class (the 'bourgeoisie'), who gained ascendancy because of their control of capital; while the bourgeoisie in their turn were doomed to be replaced by the indus-

trial working class (the 'proletariat').

Changes in modes of production occurred through *class struggle* and polarization and were always signalled by revolution. Marx and Engels believed that the socialist revolution would be characterized by a temporary 'dictatorship of the proletariat' – in which the means of production would be owned by the state – which would build the conditions for a classless communist society, with the means of production collectively owned by all members of society, and goods and services distributed justly according to people's needs.

Through its profound influence on revolutionary Communists such as Lenin (1870–1924; see pp. 438–9) and Mao Zedong (1893–1976; see pp. 446–7), as well as its lesser influence on evolutionary socialists and social democrats, Marxism has had a dramatic impact on the history of the 20th century. Lenin deviated from Marx not in preaching the necessity for violent proletarian revolution, but by advocating the creation of an elite party of professional revolutionaries to hasten this end, and by arguing for the dictatorship of this party rather than the working class as a whole. Lenin's revolutionary philosophy – Marxist-Leninism – became the guiding doctrine of the Soviet Union and spread

Karl Marx, the founder of modern Communism.

throughout the world. Mao Zedong's interpretation of Marxist-Leninism was based on the revolutionary potential of the rural peasantry, and on guerrilla warfare, and adapted Marx and Lenin's ideas to Chinese conditions.

they believed should characterize a socialist society. This 'state socialist' tradition has been the dominant one amongst the Left, especially the Marxist Left, and was applied in the Soviet Union from the late 1920s, and after 1945 in places as diverse as Eastern Europe, China, Indochina and Cuba.

However, the 'state socialist' tradition has never been universal on the Left. Western democratic socialists have argued that markets can be regulated to achieve socialist ends (i.e. liberal, egalitarian and fraternal outcomes) without supplanting them by state planning. They have agreed with the Right (see p. 270) that monopolistic state ownership and planning endanger liberty and reduce efficiency without necessarily producing either greater equality or solidarity. In the 1980s the 'state socialist' tradition became totally discredited as President Gorbachov's programme of *perestroika* (restructuring) in the Soviet Union revealed the fundamental failures of the planned economies of the Communist bloc. This discrediting has permitted the democratic socialist Left in Western Europe, such as the Swedish and German Social Democrats, the British Labour Party, and the French Socialists, to clarify their commitment to economic pluralism, i.e. a mixed economy (see pp. 276–7) in which markets are regulated by governments to maximize liberty, equality and community.

Fraternity

The Left have been historically associated with the value of 'fraternity' or, in more explicitly sexist language, with sup-

porting 'the brotherhood of man'. Fraternity is the least precise of the Left's core values and has been interpreted in various ways. It has been understood first as a commitment to 'internationalism' – the rejection of the idea that political activity should be bound within the confines of one nation or territory, and support for global political organization and principles. It has also, and to the contrary, been understood as a commitment to nationalism, the emotional solidarity of all citizens of the self-governing nation. Finally, it has been understood as a generalized commitment to collectivism or 'communitarianism' which is opposed to the egoistic individualism espoused by some of the Right. The understanding of fraternity as collectivism, very prevalent on the Left, is linked to egalitarianism. Historically the Left's commitment to fraternal solidarity was associated with an exclusive commitment to the interests and aspirations of the (manual and male) working class, especially those organized in trade unions. But today the democratic Left extend their conception of community to the people as a whole. More recently a 'Green' Left have emerged, who argue that the commitment to solidarity and equality with other humans must be extended to nature itself if human existence is to be preserved in a tolerable form (see p. 301).

Rationalism

The Left's values of equality, liberty and community are usually expressed in rationalist political argument. The Left believe that the world can be understood through, and only through, the powers of

human reason – although this belief is challenged by some socialist feminists. The Left also think that all political institutions must be justified by reason, rather than by appeals to traditions, emotions, religions, intimations or instincts. Unlike conservatives (see p. 271) the Left do not regard human beings as unimprovable or inherently evil. They believe that most, if not all, political problems and conflicts are soluble through the application of reason. Such rationalism, which entails optimistic conceptions of human nature and the human condition, distinguishes the political theorists and supporters of the Left, whatever their many internal differences over the relative importance of liberty, equality and fraternity, and over the ways in which these values can be implemented.   BO'L

A rally of the ruling Worker's Party, from 1984 to 1991 the sole legal party in Ethiopia. States under Communist control have been characterized by centralized economies and vast administrative bureaucracies. In their suppression of free speech and competing political parties, and in their regulation of every aspect of human life, totalitarian dictatorships of the Left are virtually indistinguishable from those of the far Right.

Political Theories of the Right

The Right are defined as the opponents of the Left (see pp. 268–9). Like the Left, the Right encompasses a wide range of beliefs. However, four core values lie at the heart of right-wing political thought: authority, hierarchy, property, and community. Though there is much disagreement amongst right-wing political theorists over their interpretation and justification, these four values are generally subsumed under a 'common-sense' political philosophy that rejects the idea that human beings can be made perfect.

Edmund Burke (above right), the conservative political theorist, defended the merits of tradition and advocated gradual evolutionary progress. Shown here is a detail from a 1771 portrait by the studio of Sir Joshua Reynolds. (National Portrait Gallery)

Varying degrees of commitment among those on the Right to each of these core values is reflected in the existence of different parties of the Right, and in the co-existence of opposed emphases within individual right-wing parties. The British Conservative Party, and the German Christian Democratic Party, for instance, include traditional conservatives whose notions of paternalistic Christian duty lead them to accept essentially socialist concepts such as the welfare state and some state intervention in the economy (see p. 268). On the other hand, they also include many 'economic liberals', who believe the market should be allowed to function free from government interference – hence they dislike, for example, controls on the labour market (see p. 275) and reject government ownership of industry or services such as transport, power or health care (see p. 276). Such 'economic liberals' should not be confused with 'political liberals' – non-socialist upholders of tolerance, freedom of expression and individual liberty who occupy the centre ground of politics between Left and Right, and are found in such parties as the British Social and Liberal Democratic Party and the German Free Democratic Party.

Authority

Right-wing political thought in Europe began as a defence of authority. The French Revolution (see pp. 424–5) prompted the 'reactionary' Right to defend the old European order. Its French exponents, notably Joseph de Maistre (1754–1821), defended traditional religious authority against radical scepticism and liberal secularism. They also supported the established, legitimate monarchies against the enthusiasts for liberal republicanism, and rejected any querying of patriarchal authority in the family. Authority was defended above all because it preserved order. Questioning authority threatens social chaos, de Maistre claimed, so obedience to traditional and religiously sanctified rulers is imperative. The law must enforce Christian morality: for there is no distinction between law and morality in such authoritarian thinking. De Maistre asserted that Europe required the restoration of the authority of 'the pope and the executioner'. Present-day religious fundamentalists of the Christian and Islamic faiths embrace a similar authoritarianism.

While the European reactionary Right believed in Catholic authority and absolute monarchy, such positions were not possible for the conservative Right in Britain and America. They defended a Protestant faith, and either a constitutional monarchy (see p. 413) or, in the case of the USA, a republic (see p. 422). The Irishman Edmund Burke (1729–97) provided the most coherent expression of this philosophy in his *Reflections on the French Revolution* (1790). There he predicted that the French Revolution would degenerate into dictatorship, and that the revolutionary destruction of hallowed customs would fragment rather than improve the world, encouraging the unbridled abuse of freedom. Since authority preserves traditions containing the accumulated wisdom and experience of past generations, we should be wary of tampering with it. Authority, Burke argued, permits human beings to evolve while preserving the inheritance of the past. Legitimate authority, based on centuries of evolution, is preferable to a system of naked power manufactured by rationalist revolutionaries; the authoritarian preservation of established morality is superior to the excessive and dangerous freedom of permissive libertarianism.

The tension between the absolutism of de Maistre's reactionary conservatism and Burke's evolutionism illustrates a characteristic division on the Right. Reactionaries seek to restore a vanished and frequently wholly imagined authoritarian past, offering the politics and religion of a better yesterday; evolutionists argue against radical change, but not against all change. This tension explains the existence of separate political parties on the Right, but it is also found within every conservative political movement.

North American and European liberals who reject the reactionary Right's assumptions about the unquestionable merits of ancient authority and religious tradition have nonetheless often found common cause with conservatives in defence of authority. Economic liberals believe that order, stability and traditional family values are essential for the rule of law and the development of a free but disciplined market economy; thus they can sometimes come to pragmatic agreements with conservatives. However there exists a fundamental and enduring political division between reactionary conservatives and political liberals. The former have no qualms about government's prerogative to exercise unlimited power, as seen for example in the doctrine of 'Parliamentary sovereignty' (the supreme and unrestricted power of Parliament) in Britain. Liberals, by contrast, embrace a political philosophy that seeks to limit and fragment governmental authority – through such devices as the separation of powers (see p. 266) and bills of rights (see pp. 290–1). Others on the Right have emphasized the virtues of free markets as a protection against an over-mighty state.

Hierarchy

Reactionaries and conservatives such as de Maistre and Burke unite in defending the merits of traditional hierarchies. The hereditary principle – whether understood as a title to property or status – is considered sacrosanct. Reactionaries and conservatives therefore support monarchy and aristocracy as well as private-property rights. By contrast, both economic and political liberals oppose the universal application of the hereditary principle: they believe in inherited property rights but not in hereditary political rights or titles.

In much right-wing thought, hierarchy is considered the natural form of human existence. Equality by contrast is regarded as the artificial condition. Hierarchy is defended because it provides continuity and encourages diversity. Right-wing political thinkers tend to agree with the ideas of 19th-century Social Darwinism (developed by analogy with Darwin's theory of evolution; see pp. 112–13) – in which existence is seen as a struggle for survival of the fittest, and hierarchy as the natural outcome of this struggle. Today they are inclined to believe certain sociobiologists who argue that there are fundamental and immutable intellectual and emotional differences between the races and sexes. Such ideas may easily slip into racism or sexism, and these inclinations lead some on the far Right to defend racial domination and segregation (as practised under the system of apartheid from 1948 in South Africa; see p. 291) or from 1933 to 1945 by the Nazis in Germany; see pp. 442–3), and to demand the return of women to their traditional roles of child-rearing and domestic labour (see pp. 202–3).

Hierarchicalism also explains why in the past the Right have sometimes been suspicious of democracy, because of its egalitarian tendencies and its rejection of principles of privilege in favour of the belief in the political equality of all adult citizens. The Right today often regard egalitarianism as inevitably taking everybody down to the lowest common denomnator – 'levelling down' rather than 'levelling up'; however, they do in general agree on the need for equality of opportunity. Traditional conservatives gradually accepted democratic institutions, such as universal suffrage (see p. 435), when they became persuaded that they would not automatically lead to the removal of privilege. However, most contemporary right-wing thinkers support representative democracy because they see it as the best system of government for a free-market society (see p. 275): they defend representative democracy as a means rather than as an end. Nonetheless, many on the far Right are prepared to sacrifice democratic principles in pursuit of other values – especially when they believe that democratic institutions favour socialist practices or the dilution of racial purity.

Property

Conservatives share with all liberals a firm commitment to individuals' rights to private property – in contrast with socialists and Communists (see pp. 268–9). They cite two arguments for the justice of strong private-property rights. The first, deriving from the English philosopher John Locke (see pp. 266 and 487), suggests that individuals have a natural right to property on which they have worked, and that this right is transferable. The second, best developed in the work of the German philosopher G.W.F. Hegel (see p. 487), suggests that private property rights are essential if individuals are to be free, and able to exercise their freedom. The Austrian philosopher Friedrich Hayek (1899–1992) argues that without strong private-property rights there are no real individuals – only members of tribes or the 'serfs' of collectivist states such as the Soviet Union under Stalinism.

Traditional conservatives differ from economic liberals, however, in recognizing that the claims of authority or community must sometimes have precedence over the rights of individuals. This difference explains why conservatives on the Right, especially in the European Christian Democratic tradition, sometimes accept the principles of the welfare state (see p. 268) – including progressive taxation and state provision of education and health care – which economic liberals consider to be restrictive intrusions on property rights. Economic liberalism – based on the doctrine of the 18th-century Scottish economist Adam Smith (see p. 275) – has been on the ascendant amongst the Right in the last two decades. Political exponents of this philosophy, known as the 'New Right', have been especially active in the English-speaking democracies. Supporters of Margaret Thatcher in Britain and former President Reagan in the USA have vigorously pursued tax-cutting, privatization (selling public enterprises into private ownership; see p. 277) and the freeing of business from governmental restrictions, arguing that leaving people free to exploit their property is the best means to advance general prosperity.

Community

Conservatives and economic liberals on the Right also differ on the question of commitment to 'community'. Reactionaries and traditionalists, as well as 20th-century Fascists (see pp. 442–3), advocate the building of strong national communities, united by bonds of affection, blood, ethnic identity, language and culture. They argue that economic liberals are merely concerned to establish social relationships on the basis of their practical usefulness, and are self-interested individuals who conduct all their social relations on a contractual basis. 'Romantic' conservatives, like socialists, argue that industrialized economies ordered according to free-market principles produce rootless individuals belonging to no community and consequently lacking a sense of shared cultural traditions. In the past such feelings were expressed in loyalties to the king, the lord, or the village communities of feudal times. Subsequently the traditional Right replaced such loyalties with loyalty towards the nation. To paraphrase Burke, the idea of the nation cuts across class distinctions to unite all in community with the dead, the living and as yet unborn. Present-day 'New-Right' governments, adhering to economic liberal beliefs, do not believe in a community other than that of the nation-state, and regard society as composed of individuals striving for economic benefits for themselves and their families.

The traditional Right, unlike those economic liberals who believe that national governments should not intervene in the market, are rarely internationalists. Traditional right-wing thinkers support capitalism because they see it as a means of preserving order, hierarchy and property rights, but insist it must be regulated in the national interest. Where capitalism threatens the core values of the traditional Right, then intervention by the government is considered justified. This fact explains why the traditional Right, unlike economic liberals, sometimes justify protectionism as opposed to free trade (see p. 278). It also explains why conservative political thinkers see no inconsistency in rejecting free choice in matters of sexual preference, literature and the dramatic arts: censorship and moral regulation are considered essential to preserve a stable national community. However, the New Right include many libertarians who would like to extend individual freedom, for example by legalizing banned drugs.

Anti-rationalism

The defence by the traditional Right of aristocracy, religion and patriarchy was rarely based on an explicit philosophy. Traditionalists, from the 18th to the 20th century, argue that liberals and socialists produce abstract, unfeeling, ideological and rationalist doctrines, which should be rejected by right-thinking people. Rationalists are accused of seeking to judge all social activity by the yardstick of reason alone, and of remorselessly eroding the complex web of habits and customs that preserve social order and social well-being. Right-wing traditionalists see socialist theorists as ideologues who believe it is possible to plan and change society as if it were a machine, and accuse them of embracing benevolent and simple-minded conceptions of the goodness and rationality of human nature, so ignoring the spontaneous drives and emotions that can be tempered only by the discipline of traditional civilization. This distrust of human capacities and lack of belief in the prospects for human progress is distinctive to the traditional conservative temperament. However, economic liberals – following the ideas of Adam Smith – although agreeing that humanity itself is innately unimprovable, believe that the driving force of economic progress is 'enlightened self-interest', whereby the self-seeking efforts of the wealth creators will eventually lead to greater prosperity for all.

Right-wing political thought has shown a remarkable capacity to absorb opposed ideas. Thus many contemporary right-wing thinkers are influenced by the arguments of liberals and socialists. Their defence of capitalism and private property typically borrows from liberals, and their defence of community often borrows from socialists. The fusion of traditionalism with other ideas can produce a dangerous irrationalism on the Right. For instance, a curious mixture of right-wing doctrine and some socialist ideas lies behind Fascism, which exalts the organic unity of the nation, rejects 'bourgeois' democracy in favour of one-party rule, uses anti-capitalist rhetoric, and singles out racial and other minorities as causes of social stress.   BO'L

SEE ALSO

- GOVERNMENT AND THE PEOPLE p. 266
- POLITICAL THEORIES OF THE LEFT p. 268
- ECONOMICS pp. 272–79
- CIVIL AND HUMAN RIGHTS p. 290
- NATIONALISM IN EUROPE p. 428
- THE GROWTH OF TOTALITARIANISM p. 442

Neo-Nazi demonstrators in Dresden, Germany, in 1992. Since the demise of the Communist governments of the former Soviet bloc (1989–91), various Fascist and extreme nationalist movements have appeared in Germany, Russia and the Balkans. The rise in the number of refugees seeking asylum in the West has also fostered Fascist and nationalist groups in Western Europe.

Economic Systems

Economics is concerned with the problem of using the available resources of a country as efficiently as possible to achieve the maximum fulfilment of society's unlimited demands for goods and services. The ultimate purpose of economic endeavour is to satisfy human wants for products. The problem is that although wants are virtually without limit, the resources – natural resources, labour and capital – available to produce goods and services are limited in supply.

Since resources are scarce – relative to the demands they are called upon to satisfy – mechanisms are required in order to allocate resources between individual end uses (*microeconomics*; see p. 274) and to ensure that all the available resources are fully employed (*macroeconomics*; see p. 276). An economy can be organized in a number of ways. These are usually described as market, command and mixed economies.

Market economies

In a *market* or *private enterprise* economy the means of production are privately held by individuals and businesses. Economic decision-making is highly decentralized, and resources are allocated through a large number of individual markets for goods and services. The *market* brings together buyers and producers. By establishing prices for products and suitable profit rewards for suppliers, the market will determine how much of a product will be produced and sold.

Proponents of enterprise systems highlight the inefficiencies and rigidities usually associated with state bureaucracies (command economies), and suggest that competition, far from being wasteful, acts as an important spur to efficiency and encourages enterprise, leading to lower prices and better goods and services.

Command economies

In a *command*, *centrally planned* or *state* economy, economic decision-making is centralized in the hands of the state. The means of production – except labour – are under collective ownership. The state bureaucracy decides which products – and how many of each – are to be produced in accordance with some centralized national plan. Resources are allocated between producing units by quotas.

Advocates of this system emphasize the benefits of synchronizing and coordinating the allocation of resources as a unified

FINANCIAL INSTITUTIONS AND MARKETS

Financial institutions can be classified into two broad groupings – *deposit-taking institutions* and *longer-term savings institutions.*

Deposit-taking institutions comprise the commercial banks, savings banks, merchant banks, building societies (called savings and loan societies in the USA) and finance houses. Such institutions rely mainly on deposits from individuals and businesses for their funds. They pay interest on deposits and make a profit on their operations by lending out money or buying securities at higher rates of interest.

The *commercial banks* provide a money-transmission service for their depositors (for instance redeeming cheques and paying standing orders) and are involved in all three categories of short-term finance, as well as mortgage finance (see box on Capital). The other deposit-taking institutions operate in narrower areas. *Building societies* specialize in mortgage finance (loans for buying houses); *finance houses* specialize in instalment loans (i.e. hire purchase) and leasing (buying business assets such as machinery and cars, which are then hired out to companies); *savings banks* invest most of their funds in loan and share capital and government stocks; *merchant banks* specialize in business loans and 'underwrite' new share issues on the stock market (i.e. agree to buy up shares that are not sold on the open market).

Longer-term savings institutions include: *pension funds* (institutions that collect personal savings from contributors to provide them with pension payments in their retirement), *insurance companies* (com-panies that collect funds from individuals and businesses on a long-term basis, providing insurance to cover loss of life and injury, or to cover personal and business property against loss or damage), *unit trusts* and *investment trust companies* (institutions that issue, respectively, 'units' and shares, principally for purchase by small investors).

The financial markets comprise two main channels for bringing together borrowers and lenders, and savers and investors. These are the *money market*, which deals primarily in short-term financial securities (such as bills of exchange and Treasury bills) and inter-bank loans; and the *stock market*, which deals mainly in company stocks and shares and government stocks. The stock market performs two important functions: it provides a 'new-issue' market where companies and the government can raise capital by the sale of new stocks and shares, and it provides a secondary market for the day-to-day buying and selling of existing stocks and shares.

Shares provide a permanent source of finance for as long as the company continues to exist. The shareholders of a company are its legal owners and are entitled to a share in its profits. During the 1980s, the growth of multinational companies and financial institutions led to an opening-up of stock markets around the world and a greater interdependency between them. Shares in companies can now be traded simultaneously across stock markets based in New York, London and Tokyo, using new satellite and computerized communication systems for transmitting deals.

The stock exchange in Frankfurt, Germany. Other major international exchanges are found in London, Tokyo, Paris, Hong Kong and New York (Wall Street). Computerization has revolutionized international dealings in stock and shares.

whole, avoiding the 'wastes' of duplication inherent in competition. However, the fundamental failure of the planned economies of the Communist bloc in the late 1980s has totally discredited the theories behind command economies.

Mixed economies

In a mixed economy the state provides some goods and services (for example, postal services, medical care, education, etc), while others are provided by private enterprise. The precise 'mix' of private enterprise and state activities to be found in particular countries varies substantially and is influenced by the political philosophies of the government concerned (see pp. 268–71).

The creation of the European Community (see p. 286), programmes of privatization in Britain, France, and many other countries, and the collapse of the command economies of the countries of the former Soviet bloc, bear testimony to the current ascendancy of the 'free market' economy and the mixed economy.   CP

LABOUR

Labour represents people's contribution to productive activity; it includes both manual tasks such as laying a pipeline, and mental and organizational skills such as managing a business. The labour force of a country consists of employers, employees and the self-employed, together with those registered as unemployed. An economy is working near to its maximum productive capabilities when there is full employment; *unemployment* represents 'wasted' labour resources and thus 'lost' output potential.

Notable trends in the labour forces of the major Western industrialized countries over the past two decades include an increase in the proportion of women in the labour force, a decline in the average number of hours worked per week and an increase in the number of part-time employees, especially women. A significant trend in the distribution of labour has been the fall in the proportion of the labour force employed in manufacturing industry and a continuing expansion of the service industries. Generally, this is consistent with a change in the pattern of demand and the composition of output in favour of services, but in some countries, notably Britain, employment in the manufacturing sector has been adversely affected by foreign competition.

People who take on a particular job are required to accept the terms and conditions specified by their employers in an employment contract. Failure to meet the requirements of that contract, either through non-compliance or incompetence, may result in dismissal. Individually, workers tend to be in a relatively weak position in relation to their employers, especially in large companies. For this reason, workers have found it expedient to

Jobless Berliners queueing outside an employment exchange in the early 1930s.

SEE ALSO

● POLITICAL IDEOLOGIES p. 268–71
● MICROECONOMICS p. 274
● MACROECONOMICS p. 276
● TRADE p. 278

organize themselves into *trade unions* to increase their bargaining power.

Trade unions are organizations of workers whose primary objective is to protect and advance the economic interests of their members by negotiating pay deals with employers (*collective bargaining*), and coming to agreements on hours and conditions of work (including paid holidays, and redundancy and dismissal procedures). Trade union membership has declined in

many countries in recent years, owing to a lack of interest in and dissatisfaction with trade union policies, and most importantly the structural shifts in the labour force away from the manufacturing industries, the traditional strongholds of union power, towards the less unionized service sector. However, unions continue to play a significant role in the functioning of national economies, in particular by influencing the level of wage rates and, through this, supply costs and prices.

CAPITAL

Capital refers to investment in such things as factories, training and research; *money capital* constitutes the means of financing such investment. The three main types of capital investment are capital stock, human capital and research and development.

Capital stock is investment in business and social assets. This comprises investment by private businesses and public corporations in factories, offices, machinery and equipment, etc., and investment by the government in the provision of *social capital* – roads, railways, schools, hospitals, etc. *Capital formation* (the process of adding to capital stock) expands the productive capacity of an economy, enabling a greater quantity of goods and services to be supplied. This, together with similar investments in the provision of social capital, contributes significantly to improving a country's general standard of living.

Human capital refers to investment by governments in general education and by government and businesses in vocational training. A better educated and skilled workforce not only helps to increase productivity (output per employee) in the economy, but also assists in the more rapid

development and introduction of new, superior technologies and products.

Research and development (R & D) is investment in the invention and introduction of new technologies and products. Technological advance frequently involves the removal of existing capital and its replacement by superior production processes and equipment (which help to reduce supply costs), while the introduction of new, more sophisticated and reliable products benefits the consumer.

Investment has to be financed, and this requires savings and borrowing facilities. In some cases a business, individual or government may be able to finance investment out of their own resources: a business might use its retained profits (*corporate savings*) to buy a new machine. In a large number of cases, however, businesses, individuals and governments have to use other people's money, raising the finance they need by borrowing or issuing *financial securities* such as *stocks and shares* (see box on Financial Institutions and Markets). It is in this latter capacity that a country's *financial system* plays an important role, by channelling savings and other funds into

investment uses, as well as financing spending on personal consumption (such as loans to purchase a new car).

The three main types of short-term finance are: a *loan* (a specified sum of money advanced to a borrower by a lender to cover, for example, personal consumption and the day-to-day financial requirements of a business), an *overdraft* (a credit facility offered by banks that allows an individual or business to 'overdraw' their bank account up to an agreed limit), and *commercial bills of exchange* and *Treasury bills* (fixed-interest securities issued respectively by businesses and the government, and purchased by discount houses and banks).

There are four main types of long-term finance: a *mortgage* (a specified sum of money advanced to a borrower, to be used to purchase a house, factory, land, etc.), *loan capital* (fixed-interest securities such as *loan stock* and *debentures* issued by a company as a means of borrowing money for a specified period of time, usually upwards of 10 years), *share capital* (money subscribed to a company by shareholders), and *government bonds* or *stocks* (fixed-interest stocks issued by the government).

Microeconomics

Microeconomics is concerned with how resources that are scarce are allocated to produce a multitude of goods and services to meet the demands of consumers for these products. In capitalist economies the allocation of resources is dealt with through exchange mechanisms known as _markets_. Markets provide opportunities for buyers and sellers to communicate with one another and exchange their goods and resources. Markets also send out signals that help consumers decide which products and how much of them to buy, and help producers decide which products and how much of them to make.

At the heart of a market system are the forces of _demand_ and _supply_. The interplay of these forces determines the prices of products, how much of a product will be produced and sold, the prices of resources, and how each product will be made.

Consumers' demand for goods and services depends on several factors. The most important of these are the number of potential customers, their tastes or preferences for products, how much of their income is available to spend on products (_disposable income_), the price of the product, and the prices of other products that consumers could buy.

The amount of a product that producers are prepared to supply (i.e. sell at a given price) depends on the prices that they pay for the materials, labour and capital (see p. 272) needed for making the product. Producers need to cover these production costs if it is to be worthwhile for them to make the product. They will also bear in mind alternative products that they could make with their resources, and will only continue to supply a particular product if its price covers supply costs, including a 'fair' profit on the capital investment made and the risks taken.

The following simple example explains how the interplay of demand and supply works.

The price system

Let us assume two products, chicken and beef, and that initially prices are such as to equate supply and demand for these products in their respective markets. If there is a change in consumer demand away from beef and towards chicken, the increased demand for chicken – coupled with an unchanged supply of chicken in the short-run – results in an _excess demand_ for chicken at the prevailing price. This extra demand causes the price of chicken to rise. By the same token, the fall in demand for beef – coupled with an unchanged beef supply in the short-run – results initially in an _excess supply_ of beef at the prevailing price and a fall in the price of beef as suppliers seek to clear unsold stocks.

These changes in prices will affect the profits of chicken and beef suppliers. The rising price of chicken will increase the profitability of supplying poultry and the falling price of beef will decrease the profitability of supplying beef. In the long term, existing poultry farmers will expand production and new producers will enter the market, causing the price of chicken to fall until a new _equilibrium price_ – at which supply will again equal demand – is reached. Similarly, the falling price of beef will drive less efficient suppliers out of the market, while other suppliers will cut their output. The resulting decline in beef supply will continue until beef supply adjusts to the lower level of demand and prices stabilize, restoring the equality of supply and demand.

The diagram shows how farmers and firms would respond to changes in demand for chicken and beef and the resulting changes in the prices of these products, the profitability of their producers and the prices of resources used in these two markets. Such forces can affect the regio-

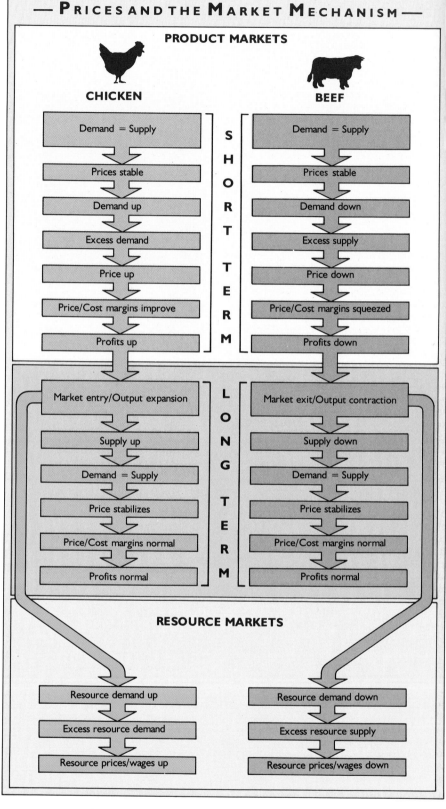

— PRICES AND THE MARKET MECHANISM —

PRODUCT MARKETS

CHICKEN   **BEEF**

SHORT TERM	CHICKEN	BEEF
	Demand = Supply	Demand = Supply
	Prices stable	Prices stable
	Demand up	Demand down
	Excess demand	Excess supply
	Price up	Price down
	Price/Cost margins improve	Price/Cost margins squeezed
	Profits up	Profits down

LONG TERM	CHICKEN	BEEF
	Market entry/Output expansion	Market exit/Output contraction
	Supply up	Supply down
	Demand = Supply	Demand = Supply
	Price stabilizes	Price stabilizes
	Price/Cost margins normal	Price/Cost margins normal
	Profits normal	Profits normal

RESOURCE MARKETS

CHICKEN	BEEF
Resource demand up	Resource demand down
Excess resource demand	Excess resource supply
Resource prices/wages up	Resource prices/wages down

ADAM SMITH

The workings of the market mechanism (see main text) were first outlined by the Scottish economist and philosopher Adam Smith (1723–90) in his influential book *An Inquiry into the Nature and Causes of the Wealth of Nations* (1776). Smith emphasized the benefits of specialization and exchange. His contention was that if producers were free to seek profits by providing goods and services, then the 'invisible hand' of market forces will ensure that the right goods and services are produced. Provided that markets remain free of government regulation, competition will ensure that production is dictated by what buyers want.

The theory of *economic liberalism* (see p. 270) – based upon the doctrine of Adam Smith – rose to prominence on the political Right during the 1980s. Political exponents of this philosophy, known as the 'New Right', have been especially active in English-speaking democracies. The adoption of the market by most of the former Communist states has added to current interest in the theories of Adam Smith.

MICROECONOMIC POLICY

Because of the problems involved in responding to market mechanisms (see main text), governments often attempt to improve the allocation of resources by using a variety of industrial, competition, regional and labour policies. *Industrial policy*, for example, can be used to reorganize industries beset by excess capacity, by compensating firms for leaving the industry or encouraging firms to merge and close down redundant plant. Industrial policy can be used to foster innovation by providing grants and tax benefits to firms investing in research and development and to provide retraining facilities to improve occupational mobility.

Competition policy can be used to prevent dominant firms from profiteering at the expense of consumers and to outlaw price-fixing agreements between firms. Similarly, competition policy can be used to prevent mergers and takeovers likely to have anti-competitive consequences.

Regional policies can be used alongside macroeconomic policies (see p. 276) to stimulate employment opportunities by encouraging new firms and industries to invest in areas of high unemployment to replace declining industries. It is also possible for a government to improve the functioning of resource markets through *labour policies* – for example, attacking restrictive labour practices and reducing the monopoly power of trade unions.

Inner city renewal schemes have been undertaken by many governments to promote the revival of old urban industrial areas. Here in London Docklands, a government-funded development corporation has encouraged new office, industrial and commercial schemes to create employment opportunities. Public finance has also been made available to help establish the necessary infrastructure, for example, the light railway.

al distribution of industries and employment within a country. If beef production was concentrated in the north of a country and chicken production in the south, the effects on unemployment of the mechanism traced in the diagram would be considerable.

The market mechanism

In the diagram, market changes were initiated by changes in consumer demand for products, which in turn led to changes in the demand for, and price of, resources. But changes in the relative scarcity and price of resources can also affect markets. For example, if beef is produced through labour-intensive grazing, while chickens are reared in mechanized battery units needing little labour, then overall increases in wage rates caused by labour shortages would affect beef and chicken production differentially. Chicken producers would find their production costs hardly affected and so would need to raise their prices very little; while beef producers would have a strong incentive to mechanize production and substitute capital for comparatively expensive labour to keep production costs down, or would be forced to raise beef prices substantially to cover increased costs and lost sales as demand declined.

The response to supply within the price system to changes in consumer demand may be very slow and painful, because less efficient producers are not eliminated quickly but linger on making low profits or losses. In addition, resources cannot always be easily switched from one activity to another. For example, in the case of labour, a significant amount of retraining may be required or workers may be required to move from one area of the country to another. Thus, occupational and geographical immobilities may inhibit effective resource redeployment.

Monopolies

The market forces depicted in the diagram will only operate properly where markets are competitively structured. Without numerous sellers to provide competition, suppliers have no incentive to keep prices down to levels that just cover costs and offer a normal profit or return on the capital employed. Furthermore, in market situations with only a single supplier (*monopoly*) or only a few large suppliers (*oligopoly*), there exists a number of barriers to market entry of new suppliers. Such factors as heavy advertising (causing strong consumer preferences for existing brands), and the control of raw materials and market outlets by estab-

lished firms, may prevent new firms from moving into the markets. Increased consumer demand in such markets may simply lead to higher prices and profits for the monopolist or oligopolists, without any increase in the resources deployed there.

To counter potential exploitation of consumers by monopolies, most governments have regulatory bodies such as the Office of Fair Trading (OFT) and the Monopolies and Mergers Commission (MMC) in Britain, and the Anti-Trust Division of the Supreme Court in the USA. Such bodies monitor the behaviour of monopolists and investigate mergers between suppliers.   CP

SEE ALSO

- POLITICAL THEORIES p. 268–71
- ECONOMIC SYSTEMS p. 272
- MACROECONOMICS p. 276
- FROM RAW MATERIAL TO THE CONSUMER p. 280
- BUSINESS ORGANIZATION AND ACCOUNTING p. 282

Macroeconomics

Macroeconomics is concerned with how the economy as a whole 'works'. It seeks to identify the factors that determine the levels of national income, output and spending, employment and prices, and the balance of payments.

The premise of macroeconomics – and the rationale for governments 'managing the economy' – is that there are certain 'forces' at work in the economy that transcend individual markets (see p. 172). The level of spending in the economy affects all markets to a greater or lesser degree as well as affecting the overall levels of employment and prices in the economy. Thus, if total spending (i.e. *aggregate demand*) is too low relative to the output potential of the economy (i.e. *aggregate supply*) the result is likely to be rising unemployment. If total spending is too high, causing the economy to 'overheat', the result may be inflation (see box) and/or rising levels of imports, leading to balance of payments problems.

Income and expenditure

'Households' purchase goods and services from 'businesses', using incomes received from supplying economic 'resources' (their labour and/or capital) to businesses. Businesses produce goods and services using resources supplied to them by households. This basic model can be developed to incorporate a number of 'injections' to and 'withdrawals' from the flow of national income (see box on Gross National Product).

Businesses not only produce *consumer goods*, they also produce *investment* or *capital goods* (factories, machines, etc). Investment injects funds back into the income flow. Part of the income received by households is taxed by the government and serves to reduce the amount of income that consumers have available to spend. *Taxation* is a withdrawal from the income flow. However, when governments spend their taxation receipts by providing public goods (schools, roads, etc.) and benefits such as old-age pensions and unemployment benefit, they inject income back into the flow.

Households spend part of their income on goods and services produced abroad. Imports are a withdrawal from the income flow. On the other hand, some output is sold to overseas customers. Exports represent spending by foreigners on domestically produced goods and services and so constitute an injection into the income flow (see p. 176).

Macroeconomic policy

Governments attempt to manage or control income and spending flows in the economy in order to ensure that they are consistent with their overall economic objectives. Typically, governments are concerned to secure four main macroeconomic objectives:

Full employment – unemployment is to be avoided not only because of its social consequences but also because it results in 'lost' output to the country;

Price stability – inflation is to be avoided because it produces harmful effects, for example people on fixed incomes – such as pensioners – suffer a fall in their standard of living;

Economic growth – growth enables the economy to produce more goods and services over time, serving to increase living standards;

Balance of payments equilibrium – a persistent excess of imports over exports is to be avoided since this is likely to lower domestic income and lead to job losses.

Governments use four main methods to control the level and distribution of spending in the economy – fiscal policy, monetary policy, prices and incomes policies and management of the exchange rate.

Fiscal policy

Fiscal policy involves the use of various taxation measures to control spending. If spending needs to be reduced, the authori-

---

EXCHANGE RATES

German children playing with virtually worthless banknotes in November 1923. During the early 1920s Germany experienced rampant inflation, with the value of the mark falling to 4 200 000 000 to the US dollar. The causes of, and cures for, inflation are the subjects of economic and political debate, but contributory factors include an increase in the money supply, excess spending and unsatisfied demand.

Exchange rates are *fixed* when countries use specific measures of a metal, for example gold, or some other agreed standard to define how much the currency is worth. When supply and demand (see p. 172) or speculation determines the value of a currency, it is said to be *floating*. Most currencies – including the Russian rouble since 1992 – are allowed to float but do so within limits managed by individual governments.

The *ERM* (Exchange Rate Mechanism) is an agreement between most of the members of the European Community (EC; see p. 178) to limit movement in the value of their currencies. ERM members agree a set of exchange rates against each other's currencies and a margin on either side of these *central rates* to allow for daily movement in the markets. Within such a system, a currency may become overvalued, leading to pressure upon the government concerned to *devalue* the currency.

When the currency of a country is devalued it becomes worth less in terms of other currencies. The goods and services offered by that country therefore become cheaper on the international market and the *terms of trade* are said to be in its favour, at least in the short term. However, imports, including raw materials from abroad, will be more expensive and the cost advantage enjoyed by exports may not last long. If a currency is *revalued* – becoming worth more in terms of other currencies – its exports become more expensive, but its imports become cheaper.

SEE ALSO

● POLITICAL THEORIES p. 268
● MICROECONOMICS p. 274
● TRADE p. 278

...ies can, for example, increase *direct taxes* on individuals (raising *income tax* rates) and companies (raising *corporation tax* rates). Spending can also be reduced by increasing *indirect taxes* – an increase in the *value-added tax* (VAT) on products in general, or an increase in *excise duties* on particular products such as oil or beer will, by increasing their prices, lead to a reduction in purchasing power. Alternatively, the government can use changes in its own expenditure to affect spending levels; a cut in current purchases of products or capital investment by the government, for example, will reduce total spending in the economy.

Taxation and government expenditure are linked together in terms of the government's overall fiscal or budget position. A *budget surplus* (with government taxation and other receipts exceeding expenditure) serves to decrease total spending, while a *budget deficit* (where expenditure is greater than taxation receipts) serves to increase total spending in the economy.

Monetary policy

Monetary policy involves the regulation of the *money supply* (notes and coins, bank deposits, etc.), and of credit and interest rates in the economy. If, for example, the authorities wish to reduce the level of spending they can seek to reduce the money supply by an *open market operation* such as selling government securities to the general public. Buyers pay for these securities by running down their bank deposits – an important component of the money supply. This forces the banks in turn to reduce the amount of bank loans to personal and business customers.

The authorities can also seek to reduce spending by making borrowing more expensive, i.e. by increasing interest rates on loans used to buy cars, televisions, houses, etc. This is done by direct government intervention in the money markets to reduce the availability of monetary assets relative to the demand for them, and so forcing up base lending rates. The authorities may use more direct methods to limit credit by, for example,

'instructing' the banks to limit or reduce the amount of loans they make available.

Prices and incomes policies

Prices and incomes policies are statutory controls on costs and prices of goods, raw materials, wages and salaries. In Britain, Germany and the USA policies to restrain increases in prices and in incomes have been implemented through voluntary agreements with trade unions and business. In Scandinavian countries, wage increases have been arrived at through centralized collective bargaining. Communist governments, for example, in the former USSR, controlled the prices of staple items of food, heating costs and rent.   CP

Exchange rates

The management of the exchange rate – the price of the currency of one country against the price of the currency of another country – influences a country's external trade and payments position (see box).

Homeless unemployed people sleeping rough on the streets of London. Full employment is a major macroeconomic objective. During a recession, labour is laid off as demand for goods and services falls. Homelessness increased sharply in Britain and the USA in the early 1990s when the loss of employment meant that some people were no longer able to keep up their mortgage payments.

GROSS NATIONAL PRODUCT

Gross National Product (GNP) is generally considered the best way of measuring the economic power of a country. GNP comprises the GDP (see below) plus income received from abroad, less payments made abroad.

Gross Domestic Product (GDP) is the sum of all output produced domestically. It is usually stated to be equal to total domestic expenditure plus the value of exports, less the value of imports. There are, however, three ways of estimating GDP in use by different countries: the *expenditure basis* estimates GDP on the basis of how much money has been spent in a country; the *output basis* or *net material product* (NMP) estimates GDP on the basis of the value of goods that have been sold in a country; the *income basis* estimates GDP on the basis of how much income has been earned in a country.

National income is the sum of all income received in an economy during one particular period of time, usually one financial year. It is equal to GNP less depreciation.

The GNPs of the major industrial powers in 1990–91 were as follows:

Country	GNP in US dollars
USA	5 670 000 000 000
Japan	4 000 000 000 000
Germany	1 950 000 000 000
France	1 360 000 000 000
Italy	1 170 000 000 000
United Kingdom	1 000 000 000 000
Canada	588 000 000 000
Spain	540 000 000 000
China	475 900 000 000
Brazil	393 000 000 000
Mexico	382 000 000 000
South Korea	354 000 000 000

ECONOMIC DOCTRINES

For most of the period since 1945, monetary policy has been widely used as a short-term measure but has largely taken second place to fiscal policy – the regulation of taxation and government spending as a means of controlling the level and composition of spending in the economy (see main text). This reflects the dominance of the ideas of the British economist John Maynard Keynes (1883–1946). However, in a number of countries, the recent influence of *monetarist* ideas has led to long-term control of the money supply taking centre stage in government economic policy. The depression of the early 1930s led Keynes to argue that unemployment can only be avoided by government spending on public-works programmes. His advocacy of government intervention in the economy caused several nations to adopt spending programmes in the 1930s, for example, Roosevelt's 'New Deal' in the USA. Despite the current popularity of monetarist policies, *Keynesian economics* continues to influence many governments today.

Monetarism as an economic doctrine emphasizes the role of money – in particular the money supply (see main text) – in the functioning of the economy. Unlike Keynesian economists, monetarists believe that with the exception of managing the money supply, governments should not intervene in the economy. The historical roots of modern monetarism – associated with the work of the American economist Milton Friedman (1912–) – lie in the *quantity theory of money*, which indicates that excessive increases in the money supply will lead to inflation. In policy terms, this means that the amount of money in the economy used to finance purchases of goods and services (*aggregate demand*) has to be 'balanced' with the economy's ability to produce goods and services (*aggregate supply*). If the money supply is increased at a faster rate than the supply capacity of the economy, then the excess demand created will result in inflation. Monetarist policies were adopted by the governments of a number of countries in the 1970s and 1980s, including Britain, the USA and Argentina.

Trade

All countries to a greater or lesser degree are dependent on international trade. Trade is a two-way process involving imports and exports. Countries receive payment from trading partners for domestic goods and services exported; they make payments to trading partners for goods and services imported.

International trade can be divided into two main groups of products: trade in goods, consisting of agricultural produce, minerals and manufactured goods; and trade in services, consisting of earnings from shipping and air freight, banking, insurance and management services, as well as receipts and payments from foreign investments and government transactions.

In 1990 Western Europe accounted for about 45% of total world trade, followed by Asia (20%) and North America (17%). The 'top ten' exporters of goods are Germany, the USA, Japan, France, the UK, Italy, Russia, Canada, the Netherlands and Belgium (with Luxembourg). The 'top ten' exporters of services are the USA, the UK, France, Germany, Japan, Belgium (with Luxembourg), Italy, the Netherlands, Switzerland and Spain. Both sectors are dominated by the older developed countries, although in the goods trade a number of 'newly industrializing' countries (Taiwan, Hong Kong and South Korea) are also becoming significant exporters.

In recent years, international trade flows have become increasingly complex, with the continued rapid growth of *multinational companies*. Ford Motors, for example, make car engines in Britain and gearboxes in Germany. These – along with other parts – are then shipped to Spain and assembled into complete vehicles for export to other European markets.

SEE ALSO

- ECONOMIC SYSTEMS p. 272
- MICROECONOMIC SYSTEMS p. 274
- MACROECONOMICS p. 276
- FROM RAW MATERIALS TO THE CONSUMER p. 280
- INTERNATIONAL ORGANIZATIONS 2 p. 286

TRADE, THE EXCHANGE RATE AND THE BALANCE OF PAYMENTS

The graph shows the rate, or price, at which British pounds (£s) might exchange for US dollars ($s). The downward demand curve for £s (DD) reflects the fact that if £s become less expensive, British goods and services will become cheaper to Americans. This results in Americans demanding greater quantities of British products and therefore larger amounts of £s with which to purchase those products. The upward supply curve for £s (SS) reflects the fact that as the $ price of £s increases, American goods become cheaper to the British. This results in the British demanding greater quantities of American goods – hence the greater supply of £s offered in exchange for $s with which to purchase these products.

The intersection of the demand and supply curves for £s will determine the 'equilibrium' $ price of £s. In this case British-American trade and the balance of payments are in equilibrium: British exports to America create a demand

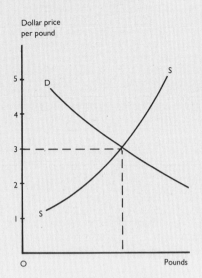

The dollar/pound exchange rate

for £s equal to the quantity made available from the imports of American products.

International trade grew at an annual rate of around 8% from the late 1950s until 1973. During this period trade was stimulated by high rates of economic growth and the pursuit of 'free trade' policies (see below). Although the major oil price increases of 1973 and 1979 reduced economic growth rates and created balance of payments and debt problems for many countries (see box), international trade has continued to expand at an annual average rate of around 4% since 1973.

The benefits of international trade

Countries trade with one another for the same reasons that individuals, firms and regions within a country engage in the exchange of goods and services – to obtain the benefits of specialization. By exporting its own products in exchange for imports of products from other nations, a country can enjoy a wider range of goods and services (many of which, such as scarce raw materials or high technology products, may be unobtainable from domestic sources), and obtain them more cheaply than would otherwise be the case. An international division of labour in which each country specializes in the production of only some of the goods that it is capable of producing enables total world output to be increased. It can also help to raise countries' standards of living.

A country's choice of which products to specialize in will be determined to a large extent by the *comparative advantages* it possesses over others in the production of particular products. Such advantages

A meeting of OPEC (The Organization of Petroleum Exporting Countries; see p. 287). OPEC's decision to raise oil prices sharply in 1973 and again in 1979 caused balance of payments deficits, inflation and protracted recession in the major oil-importing nations. The price of oil has a greater effect on international trade than any other product.

LEADING EXPORTERS OF GOODS AND SERVICES, 1989

	Goods % of World Total		Services[1] % of World Total
1. USA	11.8	USA	19.1
2. Germany[2]	11.0	UK	14.4
3. Japan	8.9	Japan	10.1
4. France	5.8	France	8.4
5. UK	4.9	Germany[2]	6.8
6. Italy	4.6	Belgium & Luxembourg	5.3
7. Canada	3.9	Italy	4.3
8. USSR	3.5	Netherlands	3.7
9. Netherlands	3.5	Switzerland	3.4
10. Belgium & Luxembourg	3.2	Spain	2.6
Total of above	61.1		78.1

[1] includes investment income; [2] West Germany only

occur largely as a result of differences between countries in their *factor endowments* (the availability and cost of raw materials, labour and capital) and their level of economic sophistication and skills.

Free trade and protectionism

The achievement of the potential benefits of international trade is best secured by conditions of *free trade*, that is, the absence of any form of restriction on the free movement of goods and services from one country to another. Countries have attempted to promote free trade both by the General Agreement on Tariffs and Trade (GATT; see p. 284) and the formation of various regional free trade blocs. GATT has achieved significant tariff cuts on many products, and on the some items the complete elimination of tariff and quota restrictions. Free trade blocs are more limited in scope. While

A consignment of Italian grapes destroyed by French farmers protesting about reduced state support for farming under the EC Common Agricultural Policy. French opposition to free trade in agricultural products was a major factor in delaying the conclusion of a new GATT accord in the early 1990s (see main text).

they promote free trade between member countries, they also involve trade restrictions against non-members. There are three main types of trade bloc:

A *free trade area* (such as EFTA; see p. 286), where members eliminate trade barriers between themselves but each separately continues to operate its own particular barriers against non-members.

A *customs union*, where members eliminate trade barriers between themselves but establish uniform barriers against non-members.

A *common market* (such as the EC; see p. 286), a customs union that also establishes common rules, standards and practices so that members' economies are harmonized into a 'single market'. It also allows the free movement of labour and capital across the national boundaries.

In practice the benefits of international trade are often unequally divided between countries and this tends to produce situations where national self-interest is put first. *Protectionism* occurs when governments take measures to protect their domestic industries from foreign competition or seek to reverse a balance of payments deficit. The most direct forms of protectionism are:

Tariffs, the imposition of taxes or duties on imported products. This raises their prices in the domestic market, thereby encouraging buyers to switch to domestically produced substitutes;

Quotas, the use of physical controls to limit imports of a product to a specified number of units;

Exchange controls, the limitation by the monetary authorities (central banks) of the amount of foreign currency made available for the purchase of imported products.

COMPARATIVE ADVANTAGE

In its most simplified form – a world economy consisting of two countries (Orania and Techland), and two products (corn and cars) – the theory of comparative advantage generates the following relationship of international production and trade.

Assuming Orania has an abundance of cheap labour but little capital, while Techland has an abundance of cheap capital but a small labour force, and that corn production is labour-intensive and car production is capital-intensive, then Orania has a comparative advantage over Techland in the production of corn, while Techland has a comparative advantage over Orania in the production of cars.

It follows that both countries gain from specialization and trade. Orania produces corn and exports some of it in exchange for imports of cars. Techland produces cars and trades some of them for imports of corn.

TRADE AND THE BALANCE OF PAYMENTS

A country's balance of payments represents the *net* results over a particular time period (usually one year) of its trade and financial transactions with the rest of the world. The table shows Britain's balance of payments for 1990. The *current account* shows the country's profit and loss in day-to-day dealings.

The *visible trade balance* indicates the difference between the value of Britain's exports and imports of goods (raw materials, fuel, foodstuffs and manufactures). The *invisible trade balance* includes earnings from and payments for such services as shipping, banking, insurance and tourism; interest, profits and dividends on investments and loans; and government receipts and spending on defence, overseas administration, etc.

The *investment and other capital transactions account* covers the purchase of physical assets (such as new factories) and financial assets (such as stocks and shares) by British and overseas individuals, companies and governments, and a variety of interbank dealings in sterling and foreign currencies. Also included in the capital transactions account are movements in Britain's stock of international reserves of gold and foreign currencies. An overall balance of payments deficit is financed by a fall in the reserves (and/or increased borrowing), while a surplus leads to an addition to the reserve position.

BRITAIN'S BALANCE OF PAYMENTS, 1990

Current Account

	£ million	
Visible balance[1]		
Food, beverages and tobacco	−4620	
Basic materials	−3280	
Oil, lubricants	387	
Manufactures	−11440	
Other items	278	
		−18675
Invisible balance[2]		
Services balance	5201	
Interest, profit and dividends balance	4029	
Transfers balance (mainly government European Community payments)	−4935	
		4295
Current balance		−14380
Transactions in UK assets and liabilities (investment and other capital transactions)		
UK external assets (increase)	−72300	
UK external liabilities (increase)	84381	
Net transactions		12081

[1] Visible trade – flows of goods which are recorded by the customs and excise authorities as they enter or leave the country.
[2] Invisible trade – transactions that are recorded by the Bank of England from company and bank foreign currency receipts and payments data.

Indirect forms of protectionism include complex import documentation requirements and customs procedures, local market standards requiring imported products to be modified, and government subsidies to domestic firms to lower their costs and compete more effectively with imports. CP

From Raw Material to the Consumer

A country's economy is made up of a complex and varied amalgam of industries. Some of these produce goods and services such as motorcars, soap powder and banking services for the *final consumer*, while others are engaged in the provision of *intermediate* products. These include raw materials such as farm products (wheat, livestock, cotton, etc.), natural products (crude oil, timber, iron ore, etc.) and component parts (steel, textiles, small motors, etc.). The passage of goods from raw materials to the final consumer requires a business *infrastructure* consisting of factories, offices, road and rail networks and a range of facilitating services, most importantly finance, distribution, insurance and marketing.

SEE ALSO

- FOOD PROCESSING p. 196
- CAPITAL AND LABOUR p. 272
- THE MARKET p. 274
- GOVERNMENT AND THE NATIONAL ECONOMY p. 276
- THE INTERNATIONAL ECONOMY p. 278
- BUSINESS ORGANIZATION AND ACCOUNTING p. 282
- OIL AND GAS p. 310
- MINING, MINERALS AND METALS p. 312
- IRON AND STEEL p. 314
- RUBBER AND PLASTICS p. 316
- TEXTILES p. 318
- CHEMICALS AND BIOTECHNOLOGY p. 320

In fact, the manufacture and distribution of a typical consumer product involve a long chain of related activities. These start with the extraction and processing of raw materials, then move through various component and manufacturing stages and via a number of distribution channels before reaching the final consumer.

From raw materials to finished product

The diagram illustrates the various end products that can be produced in the chemical and petrochemical industries from the basic raw materials of oil and natural gas (see also pp. 310–11, 316–17 and 320–1).

The chain begins with the extraction of crude oil from land- and sea-based oil wells; this is then transported by pipeline or shipped to an oil refinery located either close to the oil wells or in a major industrial centre. At the refinery crude oil is broken down into various 'primary' base materials such as ethylene, butadiene and propylene. These primary derivatives are then processed and combined with chemicals and other materials to form 'secondary' materials, such as polyethylene and phenol, to produce a diverse range of products, including pharmaceuticals, cosmetics, paint, detergents, tyres and clothing.

To take the example of a plastic bread bin, a firm engaged in plastic fabrication might use ethylene as a basic raw material in the processing of various chemicals to produce secondary materials such as polyethylene, polystyrene, polypropylene and polyvinylchloride (PVC). These materials in turn would be processed further, combined with other materials and subjected to various treatments and assembly operations before finally emerging as finished products.

Each of these activities may be undertaken by firms specializing at a particular level, or combined and performed as part of a vertically integrated operation. For example, oil companies such as BP and Shell are involved in oil exploration and extraction, and in refining and manufacturing. (They are also involved in the distribution of some products, for instance the retailing of petrol through company-owned filling stations.) In other cases chemical companies, such as ICI and Hoechst, combine the production of base chemicals and the manufacture of finished products.

From manufacturer to buyer

Products reach markets through distribution channels. These incorporate a sequence of value-adding activities that assist the passage of goods from raw materials to the final consumer. Manufacturers typically produce large quantities of a limited variety of goods, while consumers normally want a limited quantity of a broad range of goods. Consequently, a number of distribution tasks must be undertaken to ensure that goods of appropriate quality and form are provided to customers in the right quantities, at the right time and at convenient locations. Market information must be gathered, storage must be provided for goods, and large quantities (such as pallets) must be broken down into smaller lots (such as individual packs). Also, retail outlets need to be set up close to consumers, and credit and service facilities established.

The performance of these tasks is essential for the effective provision of goods. Firms may choose to integrate these operations and carry them out themselves or, alternatively, they may use intermediaries, i.e. independent firms employed for their specialist skills and efficiency in making contacts between producers and consumers (see box). In advanced economies the use of intermediaries is common, and a typical distribution channel consists of three basic types of closely related operation: manufacturing, wholesaling and retailing.

Wholesalers

Wholesalers buy products in large quantities from manufacturers. They store them in warehouses and earn profits by selling them in smaller quantities and at higher prices to *retailers*. Wholesalers thus act as 'middlemen' between producers and retailers of products, removing the need for suppliers themselves to stock and distribute their goods to retailers, and for retailers to run their own warehouses. Wholesalers provide market coverage, offer product assortments, aid in processing orders, handle inventories and gather market information. Traditionally they provided their retail customers with services such as credit facilities, technical assistance and delivery, i.e. they were *full-function wholesalers*. In recent years, however, *limited-function wholesalers* such as 'cash-and-carry' operations have become a prominent feature of distribution systems. As its name implies, 'cash and carry' involves retailers themselves collecting goods from the wholesaler's warehouse and making an immediate

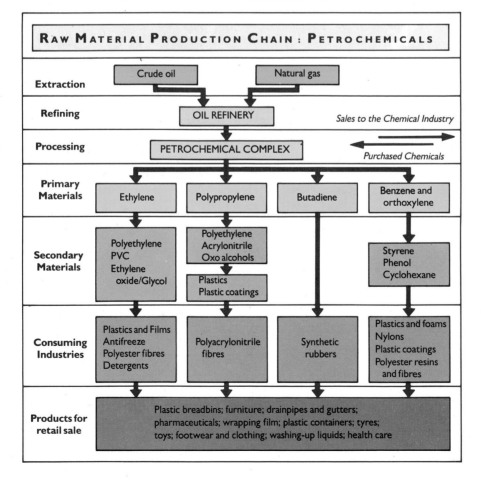

RAW MATERIAL PRODUCTION CHAIN : PETROCHEMICALS

Extraction	Crude oil / Natural gas	
Refining	OIL REFINERY	Sales to the Chemical Industry
Processing	PETROCHEMICAL COMPLEX	Purchased Chemicals
Primary Materials	Ethylene / Polypropylene / Butadiene / Benzene and orthoxylene	
Secondary Materials	Polyethylene, PVC, Ethylene oxide/Glycol / Polyethylene, Acrylonitrile, Oxo alcohols / Plastics, Plastic coatings / Styrene, Phenol, Cyclohexane	
Consuming Industries	Plastics and Films, Antifreeze, Polyester fibres, Detergents / Polyacrylonitrile fibres / Synthetic rubbers / Plastics and foams, Nylons, Plastic coatings, Polyester resins and fibres	
Products for retail sale	Plastic breadbins; furniture; drainpipes and gutters; pharmaceuticals; wrapping film; plastic containers; tyres; toys; footwear and clothing; washing-up liquids; health care	

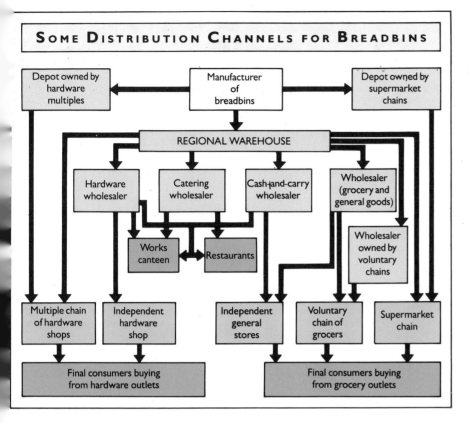

SOME DISTRIBUTION CHANNELS FOR BREADBINS

visit a shop, there also exist various 'home shopping' systems. These can take a variety of forms, with customers filling in and returning coupons in newspapers for advertised goods, or ordering goods from a mail order catalogue for delivery direct to their homes.

For many products distributive arrangements are multi-dimensional, with a number of different channels being used by a manufacturer to maximize sales potential. The diagram illustrates a number of ways in which a bread bin might reach the final buyer.

Distribution systems similar to those described above are to be found in most advanced industrial countries, although in some – most notably Japan – there exist many more 'layers' of distribution intermediaries. This can make it more difficult for foreign products to break into such markets.   CP/CE

Tea-picking in Burundi. Natural products such as tea, coffee, cotton and rubber are bought and sold by brokers on behalf of clients in commodity markets in major cities such as London and New York. India and Sri Lanka – two of the world's largest tea-producers – operate their own commodity markets for tea.

cash payment for them. Generally, though, independent wholesalers have declined in importance: distribution tasks previously within their province have increasingly been taken over by large chain-store retailing groups (see below).

Retailers

Retailing is the provision of a 'point of sale', such as a shop or store, vending machine or kiosk, which a prospective buyer of a product can visit to make a purchase. Retailers create product assortments that anticipate and/or fulfil consumer needs and wants. They offer products in appropriate quantities for family consumption and provide the facility for the 'final exchange of value' – i.e. payment for the good. Retailers earn profits by selling goods at prices above those they pay to either wholesalers or manufacturers.

Although some retailers are involved in the preparation and packaging of products before their final sale (for example, butchers and fruit and flower retailers), most are engaged in selling a range of pre-packed complete items. Retailers in Britain used to play a relatively passive role in the distribution channel, merely providing a convenient point of sale for manufacturers' products. The controlling influence of suppliers was evident in, for example, 'resale price maintenance', a practice that sets the retail price of the products. However, with the emergence of large multi-shop retailing chains, such as supermarkets and do-it-yourself (DIY) groups, the balance of power has shifted towards retailers. Retailing groups have increasingly combined the wholesaling and retailing functions and, by dealing directly with manufacturers, they have been able to exploit their bulk-buying power to obtain substantial price dis-

counts. Through the development of the 'self-service' concept and the introduction of electronic storage and check-out systems, a few large groups have been able to increase their market share by offering customers highly competitive prices. Moreover, the scale of their operations has made it advantageous for retailers to develop an extensive range of 'own-label goods' (i.e. products bearing the retailer's own brand name), which they sell in direct competition with manufacturers' brands. Similarly, small retailers have banded together in 'voluntary groups' such as SPAR and MACE to obtain bulk-buying price concessions from manufacturers.

Retail outlets include:

Specialist shops: outlets concentrating either totally on a particular type of product or on a narrow range of related products, for example a shoe shop or a chemist's shop.

Discount stores: outlets specializing in a limited range of products that they sell at highly 'discounted' prices (i.e. at prices substantially below manufacturers' listed prices).

Department stores: outlets selling a very wide range of products, being divided up into a number of 'departments', each offering its own distinctive product range.

Supermarkets or *hypermarkets*: outlets selling a comprehensive range of products at competitive prices. Supermarkets initially appeared mainly in the grocery sector, but they now often provide non-food lines, such as hardware, decorating materials, footwear and clothing, radio and television.

In addition to the traditional form of retailing in which prospective buyers

CHANNELS OF DISTRIBUTION

As the diagram below illustrates, there are a number of possible distribution channels for moving goods to the final consumer. The channel used will reflect the relative costs and marketing effectiveness of the various systems, and will also depend upon 'tradition' in the trade, the nature of the product and the characteristics of the markets being served.

Line 1 shows a conventional channel structure with the products being moved through independent intermediaries at each separate stage. Line 2 shows a distribution channel favoured by retailers such as supermarket chains, who buy in bulk direct from manufacturers and undertake the wholesaling function themselves as part of an integrated wholesaling–retailing operation. Line 3 shows a combined manufacturing–wholesaling–retailing operation, with a manufacturer combining all three operations and selling directly to the final consumer by – for example – mail order.

The most fundamental trend in distribution in recent years has been the move towards Vertical Marketing Systems (VMS), in which firms integrate the various elements of the supply chain (vertical integration) or attempt to establish effective control over distribution processes by tight contractual agreements. *Franchising*, for example, involves one firm assigning to another the right to supply its product or products.

One simple truth underpins the total 'cost of distribution': no matter who undertakes the various distribution tasks, the costs incurred will be included in the selling price paid by the final consumer.

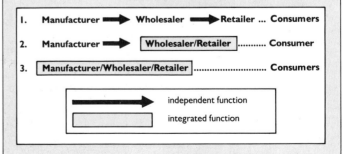

Business Organization and Accounting

Businesses are set up by people who believe they can provide goods or services that other people want. A business has to satisfy the needs of its customers and make a profit in order to meet its running costs and provide opportunities for future growth. People who start and then develop a new business have to contend with legal requirements and the challenge of organization and management.

Businesses involved in the provision of goods or services are all ultimately concerned with transforming *factor inputs* (materials, labour, etc.) into higher-value products. Such businesses vary greatly in size and in the way they are legally constituted. They range from small one-man businesses such as local corner shops, window cleaners or painters and decorators, to giant multinational companies such as Unilever or Shell.

Types of business organization

Most small businesses start up as *sole proprietorships* in which the firm is owned and controlled by a single person or family. The proprietor provides the capital necessary to finance the business from his or her savings and borrowings, makes all the business decisions, and reaps all the rewards in the form of profits. On the other hand a sole proprietor bears all the business risks: the sole proprietor has *unlimited liability* and may have to sell his or her home and other personal possessions to pay off the business's debts if it

fails and has to be wound up. Many businesses in retailing and other services, such as hairdressing or plumbing, are organized as sole proprietorships.

Some businesses are organized as *partnerships*, with two or more people jointly owning and controlling the business. This provides a larger pool of managers and workers for the business. Partners provide the capital for the business and share profits and losses according to a legal partnership agreement. They are all jointly responsible for any business debts and have unlimited liability for these debts. Providers of professional services such as general medical practitioners, solicitors and accountants are often organized as partnerships.

As businesses grow they generally need to attract extra capital to invest in additional factories and machinery. However, investors are reluctant to invest in a business if the failure of that business could lead to the loss of all their possessions. To facilitate the raising of capital, businesses are often formed as *joint-stock companies*, whereby the liability of any investor or shareholder is limited to the amount of capital that they invest. By placing a limit on the amount of potential losses, many more investors can be encouraged to subscribe capital. To warn potential creditors or lenders that their claims against such a joint-stock company will be limited in total to the amount of the company's share capital, British companies have the term 'Limited' (Ltd) or 'Public Limited Company' (PLC) after their names. Public limited companies (PLCs) can have their shares traded on the stock exchange, while shareholders in a private limited company (Ltd) can only sell their shares with the permission of existing shareholders.

Joint-stock companies raise finance by issuing shares in the company to investors. Shareholders own the company in proportion to the number of shares they own and they elect a *board of directors* to manage the company, headed by the *chairman* of the board. They may also appoint one director as *managing director* responsible for the day-to-day management of the company. In the UK and USA companies have a single board of directors, but several European countries, notably Germany, have two-tier boards with a supervisory board composed of shareholder and employee representatives (see p. 273), which in turn appoints an executive board – the latter having a management function.

Every year the directors of a company call an *annual general meeting* of shareholders, when they present to the shareholders their annual report on the company's performance and the company's financial statements (see box). At this meeting shareholders elect directors

for the forthcoming year. (Such elections are generally a formality, with the retiring directors being re-elected.) Shareholders are entitled to a cash *dividend* from the company's profits after all other outlays (production costs, overheads, tax payments, etc.) have been met. The rate of dividend per share is decided upon at the annual general meeting.

Legal requirements

To form a new joint-stock company, the company founders must first draw up a legal document called a *memorandum of association*, which governs the external relationship between the company and other people. The memorandum lists the name of the company, its objects (i.e. what it is in business for), the country in which the company is situated, the amount and division of share capital, and the names of the company founders. Next, the company must set out its legal constitution or *articles of association*, which deal with the rights and duties of shareholders and directors, and with dividends and voting rights. The company can then apply to a government official (in Britain the *Company Registrar*) for a *certificate of incorporation*, which sets up the company. At this point the company usually issues a *prospectus*, inviting investors to subscribe money in return for shares in the company. The shareholders provide the company's capital, and in the event of the company being wound up by voluntary liquidation or bankruptcy, they are entitled to any remaining company assets after all company debts have been discharged.

Once shareholders have subscribed for shares in a company, the capital they have thus invested becomes permanent finance for the company as long as the company remains in existence – so shareholders cannot get their money back from the company. However, shareholders in a public limited company can usually convert their investment into cash by selling their shares to someone else through an established *stock exchange* (see p. 272). Most large public limited companies have their shares listed on the major world stock exchanges in London, New York and Tokyo and smaller exchanges such as the French *Bourse* and the Italian *Borsa*. The daily buying and selling of these shares on the stock exchanges establishes market prices for them (see pp. 274–5). These share prices are published each day in specialist financial newspapers such as the *Financial Times* in London and the *Wall Street Journal* in New York.

In Britain, public limited companies are obliged by law to maintain an up-to-date *register* of the names of shareholders and the number of shares each shareholder owns, the register being amended as shares are sold. By contrast, in the USA companies issue numbered *bearer stocks and shares*, which are not registered under the names of particular holders. In Britain and the USA the majority of shares in large companies are held by institutional investors such as pension funds and insurance companies, with the

A meeting of business executives. The success of an executive is typically judged on his or her contribution to maximizing the company's earnings, through increasing sales or productivity, or by achieving reductions in costs or expenditure.

PROFIT-AND-LOSS ACCOUNT

The profit-and-loss account matches the *sales revenue* for a particular period with the *costs* involved in generating that sales revenue. After all appropriate deductions have been made from sales, the residual sum of *net profit* for the year can be determined.

Firstly, sales revenue is compared with the cost of goods sold to determine *gross margin. Cost of goods sold* is not usually the same as the cost of finished goods made because firms can sell more units than they make by running down stocks of finished goods and vice versa. Consequently an adjustment has to be made for changes in the stock of finished goods, as shown in the table.

Once the gross margin on trading has been determined, indirect operating expenses such as manufacturing, selling and administration costs are deducted to arrive at *Trading profit*. Financing costs can then be deducted to arrive at *Net profit*.

BALANCE SHEET

The balance sheet shows what the business owns (*assets*) and what it owes (financial obligations) at the end of the trading period. The assets show how funds are used in the business, and the financial obligations show the sources of these funds.

Assets fall into two major groups:

1. *Fixed assets*, such as buildings and machinery, are those bought for use in the business rather than for re-sale. Generally they are retained in the business for long periods. Each year a proportion of the original cost of fixed assets will be *written off* against (deducted from) profits. This *depreciation* (reduction in value) of the assets reflects their diminishing usefulness over time. (Consequently, fixed assets are usually shown at cost less depreciation charged to date.)

2. *Current assets*, such as stocks of goods not yet sold and debtors (i.e. those who have not yet paid the company for goods supplied), are those that will be converted into cash in the normal course of business. They tend to turn over relatively quickly as raw materials are made up, sold and eventually paid for. Stock has to be valued accurately; its value must not be overstated as this directly affects profit. Stocks are usually valued at cost (i.e. what it cost to make them) or market value (i.e. what price could be expected for them), whichever is the lower.

Financial obligations fall into three major groups:

1. *Current liabilities* are obligations to pay out cash at a date in the near future. They include amounts owed by the business to trade creditors and banks.

2. *Shareholders' capital employed* consists of the share capital invested by the owners plus any profits ploughed back into the business as reserves.

3. *Long-term liabilities* are those that do not have to be repaid in cash for 12 months or more. They include long-term loans, mortgages, etc.

Working capital (net current assets) is the difference between current assets and current liabilities. It shows the money tied up in financing company production and selling operations. Increases in the volume of company trading will lead to increases in stocks and debtors, and so to an increase in working capital required to finance the business. Reductions in delays between paying for material and wages and getting cash in from customers – i.e. increasing the *cash flow* – will tend to reduce the working capital needed.

XYZ LTD
PROFIT-AND-LOSS ACCOUNT
YEAR ENDED 31.12.19—

Revenue from sales of finished goods		120000
less cost of finished goods sold:		
Opening stock	6000	
Cost of goods made (materials & labour)	87000	
Closing stock	(9000)	84000
Gross margin		36000
less indirect costs or overheads:		
Manufacturing:		
Depreciation of equipment		7000
Selling and distribution expenses:		
Salesmen's salaries	4000	
Transport costs	5000	9000
Administration expenses:		
Office salaries, heating, lighting, office equipment, etc.	4500	20500
Trading profit		15500
Other expenses:		
Loan interest (interest on money borrowed from bank)		500
Net profit		15000

XYZ LTD
BALANCE SHEET FOR
YEAR ENDED 31.12.19—

Fixed Assets	Cost	Depreciation	
Freehold land and buildings	45000	5000	40000
Plant and machinery	23000	13000	10000
Motor vehicles	12000	7000	5000
			55000
Current assets:			
Stocks			
– raw materials	11000		
– work in progress	4000		
– finished goods	9000	24000	
Debtors		11000	
Cash and bank balances		3000	38000
less current liabilities:			
Creditors (money owed by the company)		15000	
Taxation owed		6000	21000
Net current assets (working capital)			17000
Total net assets			72000
Shareholders' capital employed:			
Share capital		50000	
Retained profits		12000	62000
Long-term liabilities (loans)			10000
			72000

---

minority of shares being owned by small individual shareholders (see p. 272).

Company financial statements

All businesses are obliged by law to keep accounting records. These records serve two main purposes within a business:

1. They record a company's day-to-day financial transactions, keeping managers informed of the state of play at any time. For example, records show the value of raw materials purchased by the company and any amounts owing to suppliers for these. They also show the value of goods sold and any amounts owed by customers for these goods.

2. These records can be summarized at the end of a particular period to show how the business has fared financially. The two principal summaries are the *profit-and-loss account*, which measures the income earned by the business over a period, and the *balance sheet*, which summarizes the assets and liabilities of the business at the end of the period to show its financial position (see box).

Accounting

In order to ensure that the financial statements presented to shareholders are accurate and meaningful, limited-liability companies are required by law to appoint independent professional accountants as *auditors* to scrutinize the accounts prepared by the company's own accountants and directors.

The measurement principles used in preparing company financial statements can differ from one country to another, depending upon the legal codes and taxation rules operating in different countries. In response to the development of international capital markets there has been a movement towards international and regional harmonization of accounting principles, to improve comparability of financial statements. For example, the Fourth Company Law Directive of the European Community (see p. 286) stipulates the form and content of the annual accounts of limited-liability companies throughout Europe, while the Eighth Company Law Directive lays down minimum educational and experience requirements for auditors.   BL

SEE ALSO

● CAPITAL AND LABOUR p. 272
● THE MARKET p. 274
● GOVERNMENT AND THE NATIONAL ECONOMY p. 276
● THE INTERNATIONAL ECONOMY p. 278
● FROM RAW MATERIAL TO THE CONSUMER p. 280

International Organizations 1:
The United Nations

The world today consists of over 190 states. Each state has a defined territory, a people or peoples and a sovereign government, with the result that humanity is represented politically by numerous individual state governments. Thus humanity lacks a world government, but it does have an international organization where virtually all states can meet around the conference table. That organization is the United Nations.

Afghan refugees (above right) wait for UN food aid. The UN High Commissioner for Refugees aims to provide humanitarian and economic assistance to refugees and to aid their repatriation or permanent resettlement.

UN troops at a checkpoint in southern Lebanon. A UN peacekeeping force was deployed in southern Lebanon from 1978 in an attempt to limit hostilities between warring factions in the area.

The United Nations was planned at two conferences held by the Allied powers towards the end of World War II. Earlier in the war, the Allies had agreed to create a new international organization to replace the ill-fated League of Nations (see pp. 441 and 443), and at the Dumbarton Oaks (August-October 1944) and San Francisco (April-June 1945) conferences the Allies worked out what form this new body should take. The institution they created formally came into existence on 24 October 1945. It was called the United Nations Organization (UNO) or simply the United Nations (UN) – a name that had been devised by American president Franklin D. Roosevelt and had been adopted on 1 January 1942 by the anti-Axis (see p. 444) nations.

Purposes and principles of the United Nations

The founding fathers of the UN gave their creation three basic purposes, each of which was seen as a counter to the aggressive policy of the Axis powers that had culminated in World War II. The founders determined that the first and principal purpose of the UN should be to maintain international peace and security. Secondly, they decreed that their creation should, 'develop friendly relations among nations based on respect for the principle of equal rights and self-determination of peoples...'. Thirdly, they declared that the UN should 'achieve international co-operation in solving international problems of an economic, social, cultural, or humanitarian character' and promote and encourage 'respect for human rights and for fundamental freedoms for all without distinction as to race, sex, language, or religion...'. In effect, the founding fathers inserted into the UN Charter (the organization's 'constitution') the liberal-democratic ideals enunciated by the Allied powers – especially the USA – during the war.

The founding fathers gave the UN the authority to discuss disputes, to make recommendations for the settlement of such disputes, and, if necessary, to order collective measures to enforce the peace. This authority was vested primarily in two of the Organization's principal organs, the *General Assembly* and the *Security Council* (see box). The Assembly was empowered to discuss disputes and make recommendations on matters of international peace and security. The Security Council could go further, being entitled not only to make recommendations for the peaceful settlement of disputes but also, if these efforts proved ineffective, to direct member-states to impose diplomatic or economic sanctions, or even take military action, against a target government or regime.

The Assembly was also entitled to discuss and make recommendations on virtually any matter falling within the scope of the Charter. It was to be aided in the pursuance of the UN's second purpose by the now effectively defunct *Trusteeship Council* and of the third by the *Economic and Social Council* (see box).

All UN activities (with the exception of enforcement) were subject to the proviso that the organization should not 'intervene in matters which are essentially within the domestic jurisdiction' of any state. This measure was designed to safeguard the principle of state sovereignty, and has in practice been subject to differing interpretations by member-states.

The record of the United Nations

The UN's efforts to give effect to its main purpose of keeping the peace have been undermined by deep political divisions, especially those associated with the Cold War (see p. 450), and the General Assembly's meetings have as often reflected disunity as harmony among nations. The Security Council has similarly been hampered by a lack of unanimity among the great powers, and has rarely exercised its enforcement powers. The only exceptions are its decision to give military assistance to South Korea in June 1950 (see p. 450) – the Soviet delegation was absent from the Council at the time – and its decisions to impose diplomatic and economic sanctions against Southern Rhodesia in 1966 and against Iraq in 1990, and an arms embargo against South Africa in 1977.

However, the UN's contribution to the maintenance of international peace and security extends beyond enforcement. The Security Council has mounted several 'peacekeeping' operations, in which forces drawn from member-states have acted as buffers between warring states or

SEE ALSO

- INTERNATIONAL ORGANIZATIONS 2 p. 286
- NUCLEAR ARMAMENT AND DISARMAMENT p. 288
- CIVIL AND HUMAN RIGHTS p. 290
- THE THIRD WORLD AND THE DEVELOPED WORLD p. 298
- DECOLONIZATION p. 448
- THE COLD WAR p. 450
- THE MIDDLE EAST p. 454

...ctions, at the request of the government(s) concerned, so as to make a ...sumption of hostilities less likely. UN ...eacekeeping forces have been deployed ... various combat zones, including ...yprus, the Golan Heights, the Lebanon, ...ambodia and the former Yugoslavia.

...he General Assembly's debates, though ...ten degenerating into exchanges of pro-...aganda, have at least provided a forum ...here states can 'let off steam'. Succes-...ve Secretary Generals (see feature) have ...ayed a significant part in arbitrating ...ternational disputes, and the *International Court of Justice* has contributed, ...oviding an opportunity for states to ...ke their disputes to legal settlement.

...he UN's importance in facilitating the ...nd of armed conflicts and military in-...olvements was most clearly illustrated ...1988 and 1989, when the UN played a ...ignificant role in dealing with three ...ng-standing and difficult problems. It ...elped establish and monitor a ceasefire ...the Iran-Iraq war (see p. 455); it assisted ...e process of Soviet military withdrawal ...om Afghanistan (see p. 451); and it ...ayed a key role in securing and obser-...ing the settlement of Namibia. Many of ...ese events were made possible by the ...ncreasing degree of cooperation among ...e five permanent members of the Secur-...ty Council in the late 1980s. In 1990–91, ...his cooperation led to the Security ...ouncil authorizing armed action by a ...US-led coalition to liberate Kuwait from ...raqi occupation. However, in 1992–93 the ...UN had less success dealing with the civil ...var in the former Yugoslavia. UN arms ...nd trade sanctions against Serbia were ...outed, UN resolutions ignored and UN ...elief convoys attacked. The inability of ...he UN and other international bodies to ...alt the conflict was but one of numerous ...lements of actual and potential disorder ...o threaten the emerging 'new world ...rder' of the early 1990s.

...he UN can boast of some successes in the ...ursuance of its other basic purposes. It ...as helped to accelerate the progress ...owards self-government of the peoples of ...ormer colonies and has done much to ...nake the private cruelties of states a ...natter for the whole international com-...nunity. It has also endeavoured to ...lleviate economic, social, educational, ...ealth and related shortcomings in the ...Third World, particularly through spe-...cialized agencies such as the WHO and ...UNICEF (see box). However, the UN has ...often been criticized for denouncing ...violations of human rights in some states ...while condoning such violations in ...others, and for allowing the specialized ...agencies to waste large proportions of ...their budgets on unnecessary bureau-...cracy, to the detriment of the intended ...recipients.

...he UN's overall record, therefore, has ...been uneven. The organization has not ...lived up to the ideals of the founding ...fathers, but it has not failed entirely, and ...has proved its usefulness in many con-...flicts. The UN is a free association of ...states based upon the principle of state ...sovereignty. In other words the UN can ...only do as much – or as little – as its ...member-states allow it to do.

THE UN SYSTEM

The UN has five principal organs. These are listed below, together with an outline of their size and role. All are based in New York, with the exception of the International Court of Justice, which is based in The Hague.

THE GENERAL ASSEMBLY
This is composed of all member-states and can discuss anything within the scope of the Charter. It takes decisions by a qualified majority (two thirds) of those present on 'important' questions, and by a simple majority on other issues, each member having one vote.

THE SECURITY COUNCIL
This is the main organ for maintaining international peace and security. It has 5 permanent members – China, France, Russia, the UK and the USA, states that constituted the 'great powers' at the end of World War II – and 10 other seats taken by other member-states in turn. Decisions are reached through 9 out of 15 members voting for a measure. However, any one of the permanent members can invalidate a decision by exercising its right of veto. This system therefore institutionalizes the world authority of the great powers.

THE ECONOMIC AND SOCIAL COUNCIL
This has 54 members. It has acted as a coordinating body for the numerous specialized agencies created by the UN with the aim of achieving international cooperation in the economic, social and related fields.

THE INTERNATIONAL COURT OF JUSTICE
This is the UN's principal judicial organ, available to offer legal rulings on any cases that are brought before it.

THE SECRETARIAT
This acts as a sort of international civil service. Its head is the **Secretary General**, who combines the task of being the organization's chief administrative officer with that of being an international mediator. The post has had five incumbents so far:

Trygve Lie (Norway) 1946–53
Dag Hammarskjöld (Sweden) 1953–61
U Thant (Burma) 1961–72
Kurt Waldheim (Austria) 1972–81
Javier Perez de Cuellar (Peru) 1982–92
Boutros Boutros Ghali (Egypt) 1992–

THE SPECIALIZED AGENCIES
These are intergovernmental agencies related to the UN and attached to it:
International Labour Organization (ILO)
Food and Agriculture Organization (FAO)
United Nations Educational, Scientific and Cultural Organization (UNESCO)
World Health Organization (WHO)
International Bank for Reconstruction and Development (IBRD, or World Bank)
International Development Association (IDA)
International Finance Corporation (IFC)
International Monetary Fund (IMF)
International Civil Aviation Organization (ICAO)
Universal Postal Union (UPU)
International Telecommunications Union (ITU)
World Meteorological Organization (WMO)
International Maritime Organization (IMO)
World Intellectual Property Organization (WIPO)
International Fund for Agricultural Development (IFAD)
Industrial Development Organization (UNIDO)

In addition to these agencies, which report to the Economic and Social Council, there are two other agencies:
International Atomic Energy Agency (IAEA). This reports to the General Assembly and, as appropriate, to the Security Council.
General Agreement on Tariffs and Trade (GATT). This lays downs rules for international trade (see pp. 278–9).

Among the subsidiary organs set up by the UN are the following:
United Nations High Commissioner for Refugees (UNHCR)
United Nations International Children's Emergency Fund (UNICEF)
United Nations Relief and Works Agency (UNRWA)

Membership

According to its Charter, applicants for membership of the UN have to satisfy the Security Council and a two-thirds majority of the General Assembly that they are peace-loving states, accept the obligations of the UN Charter, and are able and willing to carry out these obligations. In practice, the UN has granted applicants membership almost as of right, with the result that the organization has grown from an initial complement of 51 member-states to 100 by the end of 1960 and 181 since 1992. Most of these new members are former colonial or dependent territories.

The Charter also allows for the suspension or expulsion of any member-state that has persistently violated the principles of the organization. The UN has not yet taken such action.

In 1971 the UN decided to replace the Republic of China (Taiwan) with the People's Republic of China as the representative of the Chinese people. Since then, other than Taiwan, the only states without UN membership are Switzerland, which maintains its strict interpretation of neutrality, and a number of states in the Pacific and Europe.   FT

A meeting of the UN Security Council.

International Organizations 2

The growth in the number and functions of all types of international organizations since 1945 has been very marked – so much so that they have sometimes been seen as super-seding the state, or indeed as changing the whole character of international relations. The numerous bodies that form parts of the United Nations system (see pp. 284–5) have a global membership and role, but these are by no means the only significant international organizations.

There are many other international organizations, some very important, that are not strictly speaking parts of the UN system. Most of them have a more limited membership, bringing together groups of states with a common interest – whether

in matters of economics, security, shared language and culture, political orientation, or protection of the environment.

European and transatlantic organizations

Some Western European governments began to press for a united Europe almost immediately after the end of World War II. Representatives of many European states attended the Congress of Europe in 1948, which resulted in the creation of the *Council of Europe* in May 1949. The Council of Europe aims to foster greater unity between member-states, and their economic and social progress. One of the Council's major achievements was the establishment in 1950 of the *European Convention for the Protection of Human Rights* (see pp. 290–1). The majority of West and Central European states are members and it is the largest organization of the European democracies, although it has not taken on supra-national powers.

By contrast, the establishment of the *European Coal and Steel Community* (ECSC) by the Treaty of Paris of March 1951 paved the way for a measure of economic and political integration in Europe. Belgium, France, Italy, Luxembourg, the Netherlands and West Germany – the founder members of the ECSC – went on to create the *European Economic Community* (EEC or Common Market) and the *European Atomic Energy Authority* (EAEA or EURATOM). The EEC aimed to abolish import and export duties on goods in general, and EURATOM to promote a common effort in the development of nuclear energy for peaceful purposes. Both bodies were authorized by the treaties signed in Rome in March 1957. The 'Six' were joined in these organizations by Denmark, Ireland and the UK in 1973, by Greece in 1981, and by Spain and Portugal in 1986. These 12 states form what is now known as the *European Community* (EC; see box), whose 345 million people provide a market larger than the USA, Russia or Japan. The enlarged Community – in accordance with the stated intention of the Rome treaties of an 'ever closer union' – moved towards economic integration ('the single market') in 1993, allowing free movement of capital, labour, goods and services within the Community. The EC looks set to expand again in the mid-1990s with applications for membership from Austria, Sweden, Norway, Finland, Malta, Cyprus and Turkey.

Three of the more recent members of the EC – Denmark, Portugal and Britain – had formerly been members of an economic association called the *European Free Trade Association* (EFTA). Formed in 1959 by Austria, Denmark, Norway, Portugal, Sweden, Switzerland and Britain, EFTA's underlying aim was to achieve free trade (see p. 278) in industrial products between member-states. Although the 'Seven' were to lose Denmark, Portugal and Britain, they gained Iceland (1970), Finland (1986) and Liechtenstein (1991). The EC and EFTA are creating a single European trading area for goods, services, capital and labour – the

EUROPE: MAIN ECONOMIC GROUPINGS

ICELAND
NORWAY
SWEDEN
FINLAND
RUSSIA
ESTONIA
LATVIA
DENMARK
RUSSIA
LITHUANIA
IRELAND
THE NETHERLANDS
UK
POLAND
BELARUS
GERMANY
BELGIUM
LUXEMBOURG
CZECH R
UKRAINE
FRANCE
SLOVAKIA
MOLDOVA
AUSTRIA
SWITZER-LAND
HUNGARY
ROMANIA
ITALY
SLOVENIA
CROATIA
YUGOSLAVIA
BULGARIA
PORTUGAL
SPAIN
BOSNIA-HERZEGOVINA
ALBANIA
GREECE
TURKEY

EUROPEAN COMMUNITY (EC)	EUROPEAN FREE TRADE AREA (EFTA)
ORGANIZATION for ECONOMIC COOPERATION and DEVELOPMENT (OECD)	

OECD also includes Australia, Canada, Japan, New Zealand and the USA.

(see pp. 284–5)

European Economic Area (EEA) – which would not, however, replace either of the two existing trading groups.

All the member-states of the EC and EFTA are also members of a wider economic grouping called the *Organization for Economic Cooperation and Development* (OECD). The organization began life as the *Organization for European Economic Cooperation* (OEEC), a body set up in 1948 by the governments of 16 European states to further European economic recovery after World War II using aid supplied from the USA by the Marshall Plan (see p. 450). It became the OECD in September 1961, when Canada and the USA became full members and economic development was added to its original purpose of economic coordination. Since 1961, Australia, Canada, Finland, Japan, New Zealand and Turkey have also joined the OECD. Yugoslavia's special status as an associate member was suspended in 1992. In effect, the OECD is the Western world's vehicle for harmonizing economic and development policies.

CONSTITUENT BODIES OF THE EUROPEAN COMMUNITY

The EC's equivalent of an executive body is the *Council of Ministers*. Meetings of the Council are attended by government ministers with responsibility for the issue under consideration. These ministers represent national interests, but are supposed to arrive at unanimous decisions. In addition, heads of government meet regularly to discuss EC policy matters and foreign affairs.

The Council acts mainly on legislative proposals provided by the *European Commission*, whose members are duty bound to act in the interests of the Community as a whole rather than those of individual countries. The Commission is based in Brussels and has 17 members, two appointed by France, Italy, Spain, the UK and Germany, and one by the other member-states. They are appointed by the member governments for a 4-year renewable term.

The Commission is answerable to the *European Parliament*, which can vote the former out of office. Based in Strasbourg, the Parliament has 567 members elected to serve for five-year periods. These members have been directly elected by universal adult suffrage since 1979. The allocation of seats per state varies according to population ratios. Germany has 99 members, France, Italy and the UK 87, Spain 64, Netherlands 31, Belgium, Greece and Portugal 25, Denmark 16, Ireland 15 and Luxembourg 6. The Parliament is split along party lines similar to those in the national parliaments of member-states.

The *European Court of Justice* – based in Luxembourg – consists of 13 independent judges, whose task is to settle disputes arising out of the application of Community Law.

1992 the newly-democratic countries Poland, the Czech Republic, Slovakia and Hungary signed the *Central European Free Trade Agreement* (CEFTA) under which they agreed to set up a free trade area between them by 2001.

The West's main military alliance is the *North Atlantic Treaty Organization* (NATO). In March 1948 five West European states – Belgium, France, Luxembourg, the Netherlands and Britain – had agreed to help each other in the event of an armed attack. These five signatories to the Brussels Treaty were joined in April 1949 by a further seven states – the USA, Canada, Denmark, Norway, Iceland, Italy and Portugal – as signatories to the North Atlantic Treaty, which established NATO. These 12 states agreed that an attack against any of them would be regarded as an attack against all, and that if such an attack occurred they would take appropriate measures, including armed force if necessary, to assist the party attacked. The original 12 were joined by Greece and Turkey (1952), West Germany (1955) and Spain (1982). French forces were withdrawn from NATO's integrated military structure by President de Gaulle (1966). The former East Germany became part of NATO and the EC in 1990. NATO was principally set up to defend the West against the perceived military threat of the Eastern Bloc countries, embodied in the Warsaw Pact. The latter's dissolution in 1991 has obliged NATO to re-examine its role.

The aims of the *Conference on Security and Cooperation in Europe* (CSCE) – established in 1975 by a security conference held in Helsinki, Finland – were formulated by the Charter of Paris (1990), which has been described as the formal end of the Cold War (see p. 451). Members affirm an adherence to democracy and human rights, and a commitment to settle disputes by peaceful means. Its members comprise over 50 North American, European and former Soviet states.

Other regional organizations

In 1945 the *League of Arab States* or *Arab League* was formed to promote economic and cultural links, and to minimize conflict between Arab states. The League now includes all Arab states as well as the Palestine Liberation Organization (PLO; see p. 454), which the League regards as the representative of a legitimate state.

Soon afterwards came the formation of the *Organization of American States* (OAS), set up in 1948 to promote solidarity among the states of the Americas. Its 35 members include the USA and Canada as well as Latin American and Caribbean countries.

In 1963, 32 African states established the *Organization of African Unity* (OAU), chief amongst whose objectives were the eradication of colonialism (see p. 448) and the promotion of economic and political cooperation between member-states. Since its founding, the OAU has grown to include all the African states except South Africa. In 1985, Morocco, a founder member, withdrew.

Other regional bodies created by Third World states include the *Association of South East Asian Nations* (ASEAN), established by Indonesia, Malaysia, the Philippines, Singapore and Thailand in 1967 to promote their mutual economic development, and the *Caribbean Community* (CARICOM), a West Indian common market that came into existence in 1973. The *Economic Community of West African States* (ECOWAS) was founded in 1975 to promote trade and cooperation between member states. In 1990 an ECOWAS force intervened in an attempt to stop the civil war in Liberia.

The Latin America Free Trade Area was replaced by the *Asociación Latinoamericana de Integración* (ALADI) in 1980. Like its predecessor it aims to encourage trade and remove tariffs between member states which include Argentina, Brazil and Chile. A similar free-trade area – with a common external tariff – was established in northern and eastern South America with the establishment of the *Andean Pact* in 1992. It was signed by Bolivia, Colombia, Ecuador, Peru and Venezuela. Canada, Mexico and the USA signed the *North American Free Trade Agreement* (NAFTA) in 1992 under which they agreed to eliminate tariffs, quotas and import licences between member states.

Following the dissolution of the USSR in December 1991, 11 of the former Soviet republics – Armenia, Belarus, Kazakhstan, Kyrgyzstan, Moldova, Russia, Tajikistan, Ukraine and Uzbekistan – formed the *Commonwealth of Independent States* (CIS). Azerbaijan withdrew in 1992. The CIS maintains some elements of the economic, military and political coordination that existed within the former USSR.

Producer cartels

Producers of particular commodities, such as copper, coffee, oil, etc., have formed bodies to protect their mutual economic and commercial interests. The best-known of such organizations is OPEC – the *Organization of Petroleum Exporting Countries* – set up to safeguard the collective interests of Third World petroleum-exporting states. This oil cartel sprang into world prominence during the October 1973 Arab-Israeli War, when members restricted the supply and quadrupled the price of their oil exports, causing serious economic problems for the consumer nations of the West. OPEC's 12 members are Algeria, Gabon, Indonesia, Iran, Iraq, Kuwait, Libya, Nigeria, Qatar, Saudi Arabia, the United Arab Emirates and Venezuela. Ecuador withdrew in 1992.

Non-regional organizations

Many organizations and associations draw on states from all over the world – often on the basis of mutual interests, shared history or language.

The countries of the Third World are not short of organizations or associations through which they advance their collective interests. The broadest of these is the *Non-aligned Movement*, the brainchild of Nehru (the first prime minister of independent India), Nasser (prime minister then President of Egypt, 1954–70) and Tito (president of Yugoslavia, 1945–80). Their stated aim was to create a new force in international politics, outside the two major power blocs (see pp. 450–1) and dedicated to the principles of non-alignment, peaceful co-existence and national self-determination. The principle of non-alignment was proclaimed at the organization's founding conference in Belgrade in 1961. Membership of the movement varies from one conference to another. Yugoslavia and India have been the most influential members of the movement, which now has over 90 members, most of them African or Asian.

Many Third World countries could also claim that the formerly British *Commonwealth* has become 'their' association too. The Commonwealth is an association of sovereign states that are, or have been at some time, ruled by the UK. However, from being a 'club' of Western states, the Commonwealth has been transformed by an influx of newly independent former British colonies in Africa, Asia and the Caribbean into a predominantly Third World association.   FT

SEE ALSO

● TRADE p. 278
● THE UNITED NATIONS p. 284
● NUCLEAR ARMAMENT AND DISARMAMENT p. 288
● CIVIL AND HUMAN RIGHTS p. 290
● THE THIRD WORLD AND THE DEVELOPED WORLD p. 298
● DECOLONIZATION p. 448
● THE COLD WAR p. 450
● THE MIDDLE EAST p. 454
● COUNTRIES OF THE WORLD p. 660 on

Non-aligned leaders listen to PLO leader Yasser Arafat at a meeting in Harare in 1986. A grouping of over 100 Third World countries and liberation movements, the Non-Aligned Movement rejects the system of world power blocs, promotes world peace and aims to bring about the more even distribution of the world's wealth.

Nuclear Armament and Disarmament

On 16 July 1945 scientists in the USA, working on the Manhattan Project, successfully tested the world's first atomic device, at Alamogordo in the New Mexico desert. The fruits of more than three years of intensive research, it was an awesome spectacle, producing an explosion equivalent to thousands of tons (kilotons) of conventional TNT. President Harry Truman had no hesitation in using the new weapon against the Japanese. On 6 August a B-29 Superfortress bomber dropped an atomic bomb on Hiroshima, killing some 80 000 people instantaneously; three days later Nagasaki was hit, killing a further 35 000. These attacks hastened the Japanese surrender and the end of World War II (see p. 445). The atomic age had dawned.

These early atom bombs were based on the theory, first propounded by the German chemist Otto Hahn (1879–1968) in 1938, that if the atoms of a heavy element such as uranium were bombarded with neutrons, they would split and create a chain reaction – *nuclear fission* – releasing an enormous burst of energy. The Hiroshima bomb achieved this by firing one piece of fissile material (uranium-235) into another; the Nagasaki bomb 'imploded' an outer casing of TNT onto the fissile material. The results were the same: heat, blast and a searing flash of light capable of achieving widespread devastation.

The spread of nuclear weapons

Other countries sought to equal the US achievement. In 1949 the USSR test-exploded a device, followed in 1952 by the UK. France joined the 'atomic club' in 1960 and China in 1964. By then nuclear capability had been taken further with the advent of the thermonuclear (hydrogen) bomb, first tested by the USA in 1952. In the thermonuclear bomb the hydrogen nuclei of deuterium and tritium are fused together – *nuclear fusion* – under the pressure of a fission explosion to release the equivalent of millions of tons (megatons) of TNT. Such an explosion, even if confined to one megaton, would blind people up to 160 km (100 mi) away and devastate anything within 6 km (3.75 mi).

No one has used a thermonuclear device in anger, for possession of such weapons forced a change of attitude towards war. Traditionally force had been used to gain a political objective, often after all other methods of persuasion had failed, but now the results of such a policy would be so damaging as to be self-defeating, especially if the opponent could also deliver nuclear weapons. Instead, the nuclear powers began to use their weapons to deter war, threatening nuclear attack to force an opponent to reconsider a particular course of action. In the early years of the atomic age this was a one-way process, as the USA had a monopoly of capability and delivery means, but as the USSR caught up in the 1960s a rough parity between the superpowers emerged.

MAD and its weaknesses

This led to the development of the theory of MAD (mutual assured destruction), in which each side had the ability to absorb a first-strike surprise attack whi[le] retaining sufficient weapons to hit ba[ck] in a retaliatory second strike of devasta[t]ing potential. Thus, if the Soviets attac[k]ed first, aiming to destroy US landbas[ed] ICBMs (intercontinental ballistic m[is]siles), the USA would probably still ha[ve] sufficient ICBMs – as well as mann[ed] bombers and SLBMs (submarine-launc[h]ed ballistic missiles) – to hit back.

MAD depended on the maintenance of [a] balance of capability, for if one side ha[d] gained the means to carry out a devasta[t]ing first strike that deprived the other [of] its retaliatory capability, or develope[d] defensive systems that left it substantial[ly] protected against attack, deterren[ce] would have failed. Both superpowe[rs] strove to improve the accuracy of the[ir] warheads, making them capable of see[k]ing out and destroying more and mo[re] targets in a nuclear strike. By the la[te] 1960s the Americans were experimentin[g] with MRVs (multiple re-entry vehicles[)] which enabled each missile to carry up t[o] five separate warheads. These were soo[n] developed into MIRVs (multiple indepen[?] dently targeted re-entry vehicles), eac[h] capable of spinning off to find a separat[e] target. The Soviets followed suit. If eac[h] target was, say, an ICBM launch silo, [it] was now possible to swamp the oppositio[n] with so many warheads that its ICB[M] force would be wiped out, seriously redu[c] ing its ability to launch a second strik[e.]

As experiments have taken place in Ame[r] ica with MARV (manoeuvrable re-entr[y] vehicles), each capable of gaugin[g] whether or not a particular target ha[s] been hit already and, if it has, of spinnin[g] off to a secondary target, the sophist[i] cation is awesome. This would not affec[t] the SLBMs, still the mainstay of secon[d] strike capability. But if either side coul[d] successfully track the missile-carryin[g] SSBN (sub-surface ballistic nuclear) sub[?] marines as they cruised in deep-ocean

The aftermath of the nuclear attack on Hiroshima in August 1945. The blast destroyed most of the city and is estimated to have killed some 80 000 people. Many more have died from the effects of radiation in the years since. Hiroshima has now become a major centre of the peace movement.

SEE ALSO

- ATOMS AND SUBATOMIC PARTICLES p. 38
- WORLD WAR II p. 444
- THE COLD WAR p. 450

CHEMICAL AND BIOLOGICAL WEAPONS

Chlorine gas was used by the Germans against the Russians in January 1915 and against British and French forces in Flanders three months later. Despite the development of protective gas masks, both sides made widespread use of gas during World War I (see p. 436). The Germans replaced chlorine with the more lethal phosgene, and (in 1917) with mustard gas, a blistering agent that was much used by both sides. Disgust at the use of gas led to the international prohibition of chemical weapons (poison and nerve gases) in 1925, but this did not stop the Iraqis using them against Kurdish rebels at Halabja in March 1988.

During the 1991 Gulf War, it was feared that the Iraqis would use chemical and biological weapons (virus gases) against US-led coalition forces or the populations of Saudi Arabia and Israel (see p. 455). In the event, the threat did not materialize, but international concern about the spread and possible use of chemical and biological weapons remains. These weapons – often described as the 'poor man's atomic bomb' – are now available to a wide range of states.

Poison gases come in two forms: choking gases such as phosgene, which attack the lungs and restrict breathing; and blistering gases such as mustard gas, which cause horrific burns. Nerve gases – such as tabun and sarin – impair muscle control, making breathing impossible, while biological weapons carry the spores of deadly diseases such as plague or anthrax. Constituent parts of these weapons are relatively easy to manufacture and store in secret; delivery is effected by missiles or bombs.

Attempts have been made to control chemical and biological weapons. In 1972 an international convention banned biological devices, but chemical weapons have proved more difficult to define or identify. It is almost impossible to distinguish between factories involved in the manufacture of chemical or biological weapons and those engaged in more peaceful pursuits.

The combination of chemical and biological substances with the advanced technology of missiles is capable of inflicting precise and devastating damage on an enemy without the need for expensive mobilization of armies. These benefits have encouraged the spread of such weaponry. In recent years both the USA and the former USSR agreed to reduce their stockpiles, but a wider international agreement to stop the manufacture, storage and use of all chemical weapons has yet to emerge.

ventional Forces in Europe) talks. Both sides began to update and increase their intermediate-range nuclear systems (missiles stationed in and targeted against points in Europe), but under Mikhail Gorbachov the Soviet government became more flexible. Both superpowers agreed in December 1987 to abolish land-based INF (intermediate nuclear forces), namely the Soviet SS-20 and American Pershing II and GLCM (ground-launched cruise missile). The USA and USSR, anxious to cut defence spending, continued with START, but little headway was made until 1991 when a treaty was finally signed to cut strategic arsenals to 6000 weapons on each side by 1998. This heralded a new era in superpower relations, but the break-up of the USSR left the USA sufficiently worried to retain the option of Star Wars.

In 1991, Presidents Bush and Gorbachov announced that all land-based tactical missiles and nuclear artillery shells were to be eliminated, and NATO decided to scrap up to 50% of its nuclear bombs unilaterally. However, the problem of proliferation – the spread of nuclear weapons to states without them – is growing: there is, for example, evidence that Iraq and North Korea are pursuing nuclear capability. The dissolution of the USSR (1991) left strategic nuclear weapons stationed not only in Russia but also in Belarus, Ukraine and Kazakhstan, which agreed to the eventual transfer of the weapons to Russia for destruction. JP

A demonstration against nuclear weapons by the Campaign for Nuclear Disarmament (CND) in London. Along with anti-nuclear groups in other Western countries, CND was founded in the 1950s to mobilize public opinion in favour of the unilateral abandonment of nuclear weapons. The revival of the Cold War in the early 1980s led to a resurgence of anti-nuclear activity in Britain and elsewhere.

areas of the world, they could be targeted in a first strike and destroyed.

Star Wars

Of far more concern was that if either side developed a substantial defence against incoming missiles or warheads, the balance of MAD would disappear. In the 1960s both superpowers experimented with ABMs (anti-ballistic missiles) – rockets that could intercept and destroy incoming weapons – but this proved both costly and potentially destabilizing. Then, in March 1983, President Ronald Reagan announced his decision to fund a space-based defensive system for the USA, known officially as SDI (the Strategic Defense Initiative) but more popularly as 'Star Wars'. In its most ambitious form – centred upon an elaborate system of laser and charged-particle-beam weapons in space, ready to destroy an incoming Soviet nuclear strike – SDI was likely to be ruinously expensive, and much less than 100% effective. Reagan's view was that, if deployed, it would render nuclear weapons as useless as offensive instruments. More feasible was a less ambitious system to protect ICBM sites.

Arms control and disarmament

There was, of course, an alternative approach – to negotiate mutual disarmament. Since the 1950s there has been pressure from disarmament groups – such as CND (the Campaign for Nuclear Disarmament) in Britain – for unilateral nuclear disarmament, in which one side gives up its nuclear weapons in the hope that the other will follow. But the chances of this happening in a distrustful world affected by the Cold War (see p. 450) were poor. Instead, the superpowers approached the problem through arms control, designed to create and maintain the central balance so essential to MAD. In the late 1960s, as ABM technology threatened the balance, the Americans and Soviets met to discuss control and in 1972, after three years of negotiation, an ABM Treaty, limiting deployment to two systems only in each superpower homeland, was signed as part of the SALT I (Strategic Arms Limitation Talks) package. This was refined at Vladivostok in 1974 to impose 'ceilings' on the number of nuclear delivery vehicles (bombers, ICBMs and submarines) deployed by each side. The process was taken a stage further by SALT II in 1979, when the ceilings were reduced, but the Soviet invasion of Afghanistan in December 1979 prevented ratification by the US Senate.

Further attempts at arms control or disarmament failed as the superpowers entered the 'New Cold War' of the early 1980s. The follow-up to SALT, known as START (Strategic Arms Reduction Talks), made slow progress. Similar attempts to extend the principle of control to conventional (non-nuclear) weapons in Europe – MBFR (Mutual and Balanced Force Reduction) – fared worse, and after 15 years of negotiations were stopped and replaced by a new forum, the CFE (Con-

Civil and Human Rights

The concepts of civil and human rights are closely linked with ideas of justice – both as ideals towards which laws should strive, and as limits on what such laws can require of individuals. Human rights are often thought of as being divine or supernatural in origin. While much writing on human rights is based on Western European traditions, other traditions such as those of Confucianism, Buddhism, Hinduism, and Islam have strong doctrines of what law should be.

The Declaration of the Rights of Man and of the Citizen was drafted in 1789 and incorporated as the preface to the French constitution in 1791. Influenced by the American Declaration of Independence of 1776, the ideas of the Enlightenment, and the English Bill of Rights of 1689, the Declaration asserted the equality of all men before the law, and their right to freedom of speech and ownership of property.

Although the terms 'human rights', 'civil rights' and 'civil liberties' are often used interchangeably, there are differences in emphasis. 'Human rights' is used mostly in international law to mean the rights to which all human beings are entitled. These are often divided into 'civil and political rights' (such as the right to free speech and to vote) which governments should not restrict, and 'economic, social and cultural rights' (such as the right to health care and education) which governments should strive to provide. 'Civil rights' and 'civil liberties' are expressions used more often to describe freedoms protected by the laws of a particular country.

Historical origins

In the West, the development of the concept of human rights can be traced to the writings of Plato (see p. 488) and other Greek and Roman philosophers, but they also have a religious foundation in the Judaeo-Christian traditions. Thomas Aquinas (see p. 488) developed a religious theory of 'natural law' based on Christian principles against which secular law – the actual law of the state – was to be measured. In the 17th and 18th centuries the philosophers of the Enlightenment (see p. 418) attempted to develop theories of natural law that could be discovered by the exercise of reason rather than by divine revelation. Writers such as Locke, Rousseau and Paine (see pp. 226 and 425) put forward theories of government based on the rights of individuals that were subordinated only in degrees to the governmental power to be exercised for the general welfare.

The idea that government derived its authority from the consent of the governed rather than from divine authority carried with it the possibility that such consent could be withdrawn. It was a revolutionary idea and was used to justify the American and French revolutions at the end of the 18th century (see pp. 266 and 422–5). The English revolution of a century before (see p. 412) had been influenced by such ideas, but not to the same degree. Three important milestones in the establishing of basic rights in Britain were the *Magna Carta* of 1215, a charter defining certain limitations on royal power; the *Habeas Corpus Act* of 1679, a law requiring that a prisoner be brought before a court to determine whether his detention is lawful; and the Bill of Rights of 1689 (see p. 413). But none of these has the same fundamental status as the Declaration of the Rights of Man in France (see p. 424) or the Bill of Rights in the USA (see p. 423).

Although doctrines of human rights served as the bases for revolutions in France and America, the notion that human rights should be enshrined as articles of international law developed only gradually during the 19th century. The anti-slavery movement was one example of a growing conviction that human beings have basic rights according to a higher law to which all nations are subject (see pp. 416 and 430–1).

From around the middle of the 19th century many states began to agree that prisoners of war and non-combatants had rights that other states were bound to respect. The *Geneva Conventions*, a series of treaties signed by many countries between 1864 and 1949, provided for humane treatment of civilians in wartime, the protection of sick and wounded soldiers, and the fair treatment of prisoners of war. The emblem adopted by the Geneva Convention of 1864 lent its name to the first international body formed to observe and encourage respect for such rights. Founded in 1863, the *Red Cross* (known as the *Red Crescent* in Islamic countries) now has over 100 national societies and its work has expanded to include aid to refugees and disaster relief.

Human rights in the 20th century

The systematic atrocities of World War II inspired the United Nations to adopt the *Universal Declaration of Human Rights* in 1948 (see p. 284). The rights set out in the declaration are repeated with variations and extensions in other international human-rights documents such as the *European Convention on Human Rights* (see p. 286), *The Inter-American Convention on Human Rights* and the *African Charter on Human and People's Rights*. They include rights of personal security against arbitrary state treatment; rights of conscience; rights of fair trial; rights to privacy and a family; political rights; economic rights; and rights of equality.

Since the Universal Declaration, emphasis has been laid on the difference between civil and political rights on the one hand, and economic, social and cultural rights on the other. Civil and political rights, such as freedom of expression and the right to travel, are essentially limits on what the state can do to individuals. In this sense, the right to life is the right not to be killed by the state. Economic, social and cultural rights, such as the right to education, housing or health care, are more likely to require action on the part of the state. But the differences between them are not clear-cut: the right to life, for example, can also mean the right to be protected from ill-health by the state through access to food and health care. This distinction is expressed in the two United Nations documents adopted to give force to the Universal Declaration: the *International Covenant on Civil and Political Rights* and the *International Covenant on Economic, Social and Cultural Rights*. It is also reflected in regional documents such as the *European Social Charter*.

The implementation of the rights declared can be achieved through governmental and non-governmental methods. Governments working together have established international bodies, such as the *Human Rights Commission* and the *Human Rights Committee* of the United Nations. Such bodies consider reports from countries about their development and promotion of human rights, and investigate reports of human rights violations by particular states.

Traditional international law did not recognize individuals, and was principally concerned with disputes between nations. Complaints by one state about another's violations of human rights could be used for political ends, or not publicized at all if the states had a common interest in concealing such violations. The European Convention on Human Rights was the first to allow individuals to complain directly to an international body about human rights

TWO 20TH-CENTURY CIVIL RIGHTS MOVEMENTS

Despite the guarantee of full citizenship rights for Blacks contained in the 13th and 14th amendments to the US Constitution, laws passed in the Southern states of the USA in the 1890s reduced Blacks in these states to second-class citizens and established racially segregated public facilities.

In December 1955 a campaign to desegregate the bus service in Montgomery, Alabama, was organized by a charismatic young Black Baptist minister, Martin Luther King (1929–68). Its success gave impetus to a mass protest movement to end segregation and inequality in the Southern states with King at its head. Using non-violent methods such as sit-ins, boycotts and protest marches, the movement spread across the Southern states, forcing desegregation of public transport, shops, cinemas and libraries, and eventually gaining the support of the administration of President John F. Kennedy. The campaign culminated in the passing by Congress of the 1964 Civil Rights Act and the 1965 Voting Act, outlawing discrimination in public housing, schools, employment and voting on grounds of race, colour or religion.

After King's assassination in 1968, the movement fragmented somewhat, and more militant organizations briefly came to the fore. These organizations included the Black Panthers, who advocated violent protest and armed self-protection by Blacks.

In Northern Ireland, a predominantly Roman Catholic Civil Rights Association was launched in 1968 to end discrimination by the majority Protestant community in housing, employment and voting rights in local elections. The ambushing by militant Protestants of peaceful protest marches led to bloody sectarian confrontation between Catholics and Protestants in Belfast and Londonderry. In 1969 British troops were sent to Northern Ireland to attempt to contain the strife. The civil-rights campaign was to win some reforms from the British government, which had assumed direct rule of the province in 1972. But the protests of the minority community were only part of a deeper political and cultural divide between Catholics and Protestants. This divide remains a source of violence and terror in Northern Ireland to this day.

violations perpetrated by particular countries. Other systems have begun to provide for similar complaints.

Non-governmental organizations have been important in the promotion of human rights in the 20th century. Although organizations such as the Red Cross and *Amnesty International* (which works for the freeing of political prisoners and other prisoners of conscience) may be consulted by international governmental bodies, they owe much of their influence to their independence of governments. They have no legal authority, however, and their influence is based almost entirely on careful documentation and publicizing of human-rights abuses.

Human and civil rights

Human rights in particular countries are often called civil rights or civil liberties. In the USA and many other countries they are enshrined as doctrines in written constitutions (see p. 423) and have a higher status than ordinary legislation. Measuring laws against such fundamental principles may be achieved in several ways: by advice to the legislature while it is making law, or by cases brought to challenge laws that have been enacted (including many of the cases brought before the US Supreme Court). The interpretation of such rights in particular countries may be influenced by interpretations in other countries or by international bodies.

Britain has no written constitution or bill of rights – the 1689 Bill was largely concerned with restricting royal powers. Many basic rights, such as freedom of speech, are not protected by statute, but are rights in common law (see p. 264), whose continued existence is dependent on the will of Parliament. In recent years, however, legislation has been passed to protect the rights of certain minorities, notably the *Race Relations Act* (1968), which prohibits discrimination on grounds of race, and the *Sex Discrimination Act* (1975).

There are still many countries whose citizens are denied basic human rights. In South Africa, under the apartheid system,

The Ku Klux Klan. The 19th-century Klan – an anti-Black terrorist organization – was founded after the US Civil War to restore White supremacy in the Southern states. The 20th-century Klan, founded in 1915, added bias against Jews and Catholics to its hostility towards Blacks. The civil-rights activism of the 1950s and 1960s prompted a resurgence of Klan violence against Blacks and civil-rights workers. The picture shows a night gathering of hooded Klansmen initiating new members into the group in 1915.

SEE ALSO

- THE LAW: CRIMINAL AND CIVIL p. 264
- GOVERNMENT AND THE PEOPLE p. 266
- POLITICAL THEORIES pp. 268–71
- INTERNATIONAL ORGANIZATIONS pp. 284–7

the dominant White minority denied the majority Black population many rights. Communist countries such as the former Soviet Union and China traditionally stressed the importance of social rights, such as the right to work, but often at the expense of human rights, such as freedom of speech.

The implementation of human rights in national and international law has been one of the most important developments in law and government in the 20th century. Although largely divorced from particular religions, it still represents a form of law that is higher than ordinary law. Human rights are both limits on government, in specifying what may not be done, and goals towards which laws should be directed.   JM

Human rights protesters in Argentina. In the early 1980s the mothers of missing political activists – the so-called 'Disappeared' – gathered once a week in the centre of Buenos Aires to demonstrate against the human-rights violations of the military juntas that ruled Argentina from 1976 to 1982.

The Women's Movement

Although feminist ideas have been voiced in many ages and cultures, the women's movement in its organized form is a comparatively modern development. Over 150 years, organized feminism has flourished in many countries around the world and has been responsible for obtaining significant improvements in the lives of women. Behind a general belief in equality between the sexes lies a history of campaigning for specific political, legal and social rights.

In 1792 the Englishwoman Mary Wollstonecraft (1759–97) wrote one of the great classics of feminist literature, *A Vindication of the Rights of Women*. Her vision of an education for girls that would enable them to fulfil their human potential was to provide inspiration for many future reformers. The emancipation of women was very much part of the liberal and progressive reform movements of the 19th and 20th centuries. In its significance, the emergence of the women's movement can be compared with the abolition of slavery, the rise of nationalism in colonial empires, and the political organization of the working classes.

The first wave of feminism

In the first half of the 19th century in the newly industrialized societies of the USA and Britain, the lives of middle-class women were circumscribed by social constraints. Great emphasis was placed on their domestic duties and on voluntary religious and charitable work, but paid employment, particularly outside the home, was discouraged. Working-class women were barred from many of the better paid and traditionally male jobs, and more frequently worked in unskilled sectors of the labour market or in sweatshops (workshops where employees worked long hours in poor conditions for very low wages). All women were denied access to higher education, apprenticeships and professional training, and were legally prevented from the right to suffrage (i.e. the right to vote).

At the Seneca Falls Convention in New York State in 1848 – the first women's rights meeting – the delegates declared that 'all men and women are created equal'. This principle underscored the work of Susan B. Anthony (1820–1906) and Elizabeth Cady Stanton (1815–1902), two of the most prominent campaigners in the powerful American suffrage and equal rights movement. They founded the National Woman Suffrage Association in 1869.

THE SPREAD OF WOMEN'S SUFFRAGE			
New Zealand	1893	Ceylon	1932
Australia	1902	(now Sri Lanka)	
Finland	1906	Philippines	1937
Norway[1]	1913	Jamaica	1944
Denmark	1915	France	1945
Soviet Union	1917	Italy	1945
Britain[2]	1918	Japan	1945
Germany	1918	China	1949
Poland	1918	India	1949
Netherlands	1919	Mexico	1952
Canada	1920	Egypt	1956
USA	1920	Kenya	1964
Ireland	1922	Switzerland	1971
Brazil	1934	Jordan	1982

[1] Women in Norway gained partial suffrage in 1907.

[2] Women aged 30 and over were granted the vote in 1918; in 1928 this was extended to women aged 21 and over.

In Britain, feminists started to organize in the 1850s and 1860s, initially concerning themselves with opening up employment opportunities, improving girls' education, and reforming the property laws. Dr Elizabeth Garrett Anderson (1836–1917) qualified as the first woman medical practitioner in 1865, in spite of strong opposition from the medical profession. In 1878 London University became the first such institution to admit women to all its examinations and degrees. A significant legal reform occurred in 1882 when married women obtained the right to own property.

The suffrage movement in Britain began in 1866 when the radical MP and philosopher John Stuart Mill (1806–1873) presented the first female suffrage petition to parliament. By 1900 the National Union of Women's Suffrage Societies, led by Millicent Garrett Fawcett (1847–1929), had become the largest suffrage organization in the country. Its members, called 'suffragists', campaigned for the vote using constitutional and peaceful means. In 1903 a new association of 'suffragettes' was formed – the Women's Social and Political Union – led by Emmeline Pankhurst (1858–1928) and her daughter Christabel (1880–1958). Their more militant methods – such as chaining themselves to railings, breaking windows and hunger strikes – were controversial and sometimes outside the law.

By the early 20th century women were also campaigning for social reforms such as birth control information and baby clinics. Women workers tried to improve their economic position through trade unions such as the National Union of Women Workers, formed in 1906.

In other European countries and in Australia and New Zealand, a strong women's movement also emerged in the mid to late 19th century. French feminists, for example, founded the journal *Le Droit des Femmes* in 1869 and successfully campaigned for entry into the legal profession in 1900 and the right of married women to control their own earnings in 1907. A small but highly effective move-

Suffragette leader Emmeline Pankhurst is arrested outside Buckingham Palace in 1914. In Britain the more militant members of the women's suffrage movement attacked property, staged demonstrations, refused to pay taxes, and were repeatedly sent to prison, where many underwent forcible feeding after going on hunger strike. The notorious 'Cat-and-Mouse Act' allowed the release of sick suffragettes, but made them liable to re-arrest once they had recovered their health.

ment in New Zealand won the vote for women in 1893 – New Zealand thus becoming the first country to grant national women's suffrage.

Contemporary feminism

Although the first wave of feminism had reached its peak by 1930, the middle decades of the 20th century saw continued efforts to improve the position of women, but on a much reduced scale. The widespread use of female labour during World War II, often in the traditionally male-dominated sectors of agriculture and industry, was to be short-lived. At the end of the war many women gave up the new skills they had learned and returned to the home. In the subsequent 'baby boom' years of the 1950s, traditional ideas about women's role in society regained a strong foothold, particularly in the Western world, and the achievements of the first feminists were largely hidden from history. When Simone de Beauvoir (1908–1986) published her analysis of woman's condition in *The Second Sex* in 1949, her views were regarded by many as being outrageous and even offensive.

The women's movement re-emerged in the late 1960s and early 1970s and was much influenced by radical student politics in North America and Western Europe (see p. 295). At that time it was frequently referred to as the 'Women's Liberation Movement'. In 1963 the American Betty Friedan (1921–) wrote her classic *The Feminine Mystique*, which together with *The Female Eunuch* (1970) by Australian-born Germaine Greer (1939–) presented a feminist critique of women's subordinate position in society. Women were still conditioned to accept their feminine, domestic and maternal role as paramount. They found it difficult to be active in the men's world of public and political affairs and to enter male-dominated sectors of the economy such as business, industry and banking.

In terms of organization, the women's movement has never been a unified whole, but rather a network of separate campaigns and interest groups. Methods have varied from political lobbying to mass demonstrations and there has been much emphasis on the need for women to work together in separate, women-only groups – for example, the consciousness-raising groups of the 1970s.

Somewhat different in style and aims from the first wave of feminism, the contemporary women's movement has emphasized issues of childcare, sexuality, male violence and the role of men and women in the home. It has raised questions as to how and why men and women are different in the 'nature versus nurture' debate – in other words, apart from physical differences, are women different from men because of their genetic make-up or because of their upbringing? As not all feminists agree on priorities and objectives, division has surfaced since the early 1970s between those who are most concerned with gaining equal rights, those who adopt a 'radical' stance and argue for women's separation from men in political and sexual ways (often adopting lesbianism as a political statement), and those who link feminist aims with other objectives such as socialism (see p. 268).

The international dimension

The women's movement is very much a global phenomenon with organized activity on all continents. Its objectives are often determined by existing conditions and laws in individual countries and cultures.

In the early 20th century nationalist movements sometimes provided women with a liberal framework within which to organize. An Indian Women's Association was founded in 1917 to campaign for suffrage, education and Hindu law reform. In Egypt the Egyptian Feminist Movement, formed in 1923, campaigned for an end to purdah (see p. 478) and the compulsory custom of wearing the veil, as well as for suffrage, better working conditions, and educational opportunities. The movement's leader, Huda Shaarawi (1879–1947), became first president of the

pan-Arab Feminist Union at its foundation in 1944.

More recently, in Eastern Europe and the Soviet Union, a small but autonomous women's movement has appeared, quite separate from the official women's organizations that have been run by the state. Although the Communist states have provided women with free nurseries and abortion facilities, and have encouraged women to work outside the home – often in traditionally male spheres – dissatisfaction remains. Feminists criticize the double burden of housework and employment and a family structure in which the roles of men and women are still traditional.

Conclusion

Although much has been achieved by the Women's Movement, much remains to be done. In Britain, in spite of campaigns for equal pay since World War I and the Equal Pay Act of 1970, a woman's 'rate for the job' is still less than a man's in many occupations, and women's average earnings on a national scale are approximately only three quarters the average earnings of men. With the exception of the Scandinavian countries, women active in government, in the higher levels of bureaucracy and in the trade unions are in a very small minority. Women are still living in a society largely governed by men.   LW

Present-day feminists demonstrating in Rome. Feminists of differing political convictions continue to campaign on issues as diverse as childcare provision, women's health, access to abortion, nuclear disarmament, and lesbian and gay rights.

Women working in an aircraft factory in Britain during World War II. The widespread use of female labour in traditionally male jobs during both World Wars was to prove a short-lived phenomenon. Once war had ended women were encouraged to give up the skills they had learned and to return to their more traditional roles in the home.

SEE ALSO

● POLITICAL THEORIES OF THE LEFT p. 268
● CIVIL AND HUMAN RIGHTS p. 290
● INDUSTRIAL SOCIETY p. 434

Youth Movements

Young people are not merely passive recipients of adult authority, but active participants in their own history. Past generations of radical students have played a part in fomenting protests and revolutions against the existing order of society. The revolutionary uprisings of 1848 (see p. 428) saw students fighting alongside workers on the barricades in capital cities across Europe. A youth movement, in this sense, must have an explicit ideological or political framework and considerable youth involvement in both leadership and organization.

Hell's Angels (above right) in Hyde Park, London, for the Rolling Stones' open-air concert in July 1969. Hell's Angels, organized into rival 'chapters', based their life style around powerful motorbikes, heavy-metal rock music, and often violently antisocial behaviour.

Two boy scouts scramble over rope bridges during a bridge- and raft-building competition in England in 1926. Outdoor pursuits intended to enhance boys' physical and moral development figure largely in adult-led youth organizations.

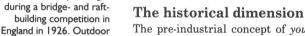

Ordinary young people are more likely to have belonged to a youth movement through membership of an adult-led, voluntary youth organization, such as the Scouts or Guides. Such youth movements offer the limited aim of propagating a code of living, studiously avoiding overt politics or youth activism. Fashion-led 'youth cultures', identified by modes of dress, music and language, represent movements created by and for youth, then rapidly absorbed into the commercial mainstream. The term 'youth movement' is so all-embracing that it can refer to Woodstock Nation and Punk Rockers as well as Woodcraft Folk and the Young Conservatives.

The historical dimension

The pre-industrial concept of *youth*, extending from the age of 15 to 25, was much broader than the generally accepted meaning of *adolescence* today. The concept of adolescence, covering the teenage years and implying those that are neither children nor adults, was 'discovered' and institutionalized by the 19th-century middle class. Examples of this institutionalization include the reform of the English public-school system and the creation of reformatories for working-class delinquents – who would previously have been sent to an adult jail.

In 1904 the American child psychologist G. Stanley Hall (1844–1924) published his formidable two-volume *Adolescence*, which gave scientific respectability to the concept. In addition, the abolition of child labour, the introduction of compulsory education (see pp. 434–5), the progressive raising of the school leaving age, rising rates of juvenile crime, and the advent of a teenage consumer market for leisure, are all seen as ushering in the concept of adolescence over the last hundred years.

Adult-led youth movements

The world's first voluntary, uniformed youth organization was the Church-based Boys' Brigade, founded in Glasgow, Scotland, in 1883 by William Alexander Smith (1854–1914), and dedicated to the 'advancement of Christ's Kingdom among Boys, and the promotion of the habits of Obedience, Reverence, Discipline, Self-Respect, and all that tends towards a true Christian manliness'.

In the 1900s, middle-class students in the German *Wandervögel* (ramblers) movement, inspired by Karl Fischer, rejected stuffy conventions and took up open-air tramping. Richard Schirrmann, a German school teacher, opened the first youth hostel in a small castle, Burg Altena, in 1909. Youth hostels – providing cheap accommodation mainly, though not exclusively, for young people – are now found in most areas of the world.

In England, Major-General Robert Baden-Powell (1857–1941), hero of the siege of Mafeking in the Boer War, founded a uniformed woodcraft movement – the Boy Scouts – in 1908. Like the Boys' Brigade the Scout movement has spread around the world. A sister organization to the Scouts, the Girl Guide Association, founded in 1910, also has a large membership worldwide.

Mass political movements – youth sections

In 1927 the Italian Boy Scouts were suppressed by Mussolini's Fascists (see p. 442) in favour of their youth section, the *Balilla*. Uniformed youth have contributed to the militancy of mass political movements of both left and right, particularly in the 1930s. Catholic, Protestant and other youth movements in Germany were swallowed up by the Nazi Hitler Youth after 1933, membership of which later became compulsory.

In Britain, some disaffected youth joined the Blackshirts of the British Union of Fascists. The Austrian Red Falcons were an active 1930s socialist youth movement. Soviet Russia had Young Communist groups: *Komsomol* (age 14–28), *Pioneer*

9–14) and *Octobrist* (7–9). Totalitarian regimes invariably recognize the importance of organizing youth, as in present-day North Korea, where the young must subscribe to Communist leader Kim Il-Sung's personality cult.

Postwar youth cultures

The heightened visibility of youth since World War II has led the media to sensationalize the activities of deviant or violent youth cults, rather than report the dull conformism of most young people. British prototypes, much influenced in the 1950s by American cultural icons such as James Dean, Marlon Brando and Elvis Presley, have been eagerly followed elsewhere in Europe, appealing to a wide cross-section of youth experiencing the contradictions of adolescence.

The *Teddy Boys* of the 1950s, with their long, draped jackets, velvet collars, drainpipe trousers and crêpe-soled shoes, were the first of the rebellious working-class youth cults. In the early 1960s came new groups such as the *Mods*, dressed in Italian-style clothes, and their leather-clad rivals, the *Rockers*, associated with motorcycles and rock-and-roll music. The *Hippies* of the late 1960s and after were more middle-class, direct descendants of the novelist Jack Kerouac (1922–69) and the American 'Beat Generation' of the 1950s (the *Beatniks*). They experimented with drugs, lived in communes, grew their hair long, and were attracted to radical politics.

Skinheads, combining elements of both Mods and Rockers and associated with the racism of the far right, arrived on the football terraces from the late 1960s onwards. *Punk Rockers* achieved notoriety through the attentions of the media in the late 1970s, with their unique hairstyles, cast-off clothes and aggressive music. Outside these white and largely male-dominated subcultures, *Rudies* and *Rastas* represent West Indian youth culture. Several of these youth cultures were recycled in the 1980s.   JSp

French riot police in action against student demonstrators, Paris, May 1968.

1968: STUDENTS IN REVOLT

In 1968 middle-class student activists challenged the established order from Prague to Paris, London to Tokyo, San Francisco to Turin, threatening capitalist and socialist regimes alike. Che Guevara and Ho Chi Minh (see pp. 451–3) were idolized as fighters against imperialism. Each student demonstration had its own localized grievances, often taking the form of 'sit-ins' – occupations of university buildings in an attempt to gain a greater say in the way universities were run. However, protest against America's war in Vietnam (see p. 452) was common to many, as was a far-left (often Trotskyist) ideology. The exaggerated revolutionary optimism of the late 1960s soon faded away, but the capacity of Western parliamentary democracies for social transformation without violence was severely tested.

THE USA
In 1967–68 police used tear gas on students protesting against the draft (compulsory conscription into the army) and the war in Vietnam. The confrontational stance of *Students for a Democratic Society* (SDS) gained widespread support, as did the provocative 'happenings' of the *Youth International Party* (Yippies), contrived by Jerry Rubin and Abbie Hoffman. On 28 August 1968, the American Democratic Party's National Convention in Chicago was disrupted by a brutal police attack on anti-war demonstrators, and in 1970 four student protesters were shot dead by National Guardsmen at Kent State University. Domestic protests against the war contributed to the US withdrawal of its troops from Vietnam in 1973.

BRITAIN
On 17 March 1968 anti-war students in London, led by the activist Tariq Ali and the Vietnam Solidarity Campaign, marched to Grosvenor Square and attempted to storm the American Embassy. There were also sit-ins in many universities. People's Democracy students from Queen's University, Belfast, among them Bernadette Devlin, later a Nationalist MP, demonstrated for the civil rights of the minority Catholic population in a divided Northern Ireland (see p. 291).

FRANCE
In May 1968 students took to the barricades in the Latin Quarter of Paris, in Nantes, Bordeaux, Lyon and several other cities, provoking a violent reaction from the police. Media prominence was given to Nanterre University student leader Daniel Cohn-Bendit. The students were mainly protesting against the government's high defence spending at the expense of education and social services, and their demands were reinforced by a wave of industrial strikes. At one point the stability of President de Gaulle's Fifth Republic seemed to be seriously threatened, but the government survived by granting concessions to the workers and placating the students with educational reforms.

WEST GERMANY
Students demonstrating against the authoritarian Emergency Powers Act, and demanding a greater voice in their education, were radicalized by the attempted assassination of influential student leader Rudi Dutschke at the hands of a right-wing fanatic. Militants in the German Socialist Students League (SDS) occupied universities, proclaiming the imminence of social revolution.

CZECHOSLOVAKIA
Soviet tanks entered Czechoslovakia on 20 August 1968 to end reforms initiated by the liberalizing regime of Alexander Dubček during the 'Prague Spring' of that year. They encountered some student resistance, including 'sit-in' protests throughout Bohemia and Moravia. On 16 January 1969 the student Jan Palach burnt himself to death in Wenceslas Square, Prague, as a protest against the Soviet occupation. A vast display of patriotic solidarity was shown at his funeral.

JAPAN
On 4 September 1968, riot police cleared out radicals who had been occupying the private Nihon University for three months. Groups of helmeted students ran in phalanx formation across the campus while their leaders blew whistles. At Tokyo University, on 19 November, Communist and radical students massed into rival armies, each some 6000 strong, both factions insisting on separate negotiations with the administration. Fifty were injured when the two groups clashed.

CHINA
The Cultural Revolution of 1966–69 (see p. 447) began with demonstrations by students and high-school children, out of which emerged the infamous *Red Guards*. Fanatical upholders of Chairman Mao's thought, they were instruments of one radical faction competing for domination of the state, rather than student revolutionaries. (Almost forty years after the Communist take-over of China, on 4 June 1989, students campaigning for basic democratic rights were massacred by the People's Army in or near Tiananmen Square, Beijing.)

The disappointment of the more radical ideals of the generation of 1968 led some, notably the *Baader-Meinhof* group in West Germany and the *Red Army* faction in Japan, to adopt terrorist strategies in the 1970s.

SEE ALSO
- POLITICAL THEORIES OF THE LEFT p. 268
- POLITICAL THEORIES OF THE RIGHT p. 270
- THE INDUSTRIAL SOCIETY p. 434
- THE GROWTH OF TOTALITARIANISM p. 442
- CHINA IN THE 20TH CENTURY p. 446
- WARS IN VIETNAM p. 452

A group of punks in Paris sport 'Mohican' hairstyles and vivid eye make-up. Punk rock, typified by the anarchic, anti-establishment songs of the Sex Pistols, began to appear in Britain from the mid-1970s, and has spread all over Europe and North America. Both the music and the appearance of punks deliberately went against what was thought of as conventionally attractive.

Population and Hunger

Somewhere between 24 June and 11 July 1987, the human population of the planet Earth reached 5 billion. Yet, two hundred years before that, when the world's population was barely more than one billion, political economists such as Thomas Malthus and David Ricardo were already predicting that the human species would breed itself into starvation. Nevertheless, despite their predictions the human population keeps increasing – but so too does the food supply. Were the prognoses of Malthus and Ricardo wrong? Or, with the inexorable rise in population growth, is it just a matter of time before mass hunger and starvation prove them right? What is the relationship between population and hunger?

Famine victims at a camp in Ethiopia. The Ethiopian famine of 1984 is estimated to have killed at least 800 000 people. The chronic problems of the country's under-developed economy were exacerbated throughout the 1980s by failed harvests and continuing civil war. Further famine threatened as the decade drew to a close.

A direct relationship between population and hunger was indicated 1800 years ago by Tertullian, an early Christian writer from North Africa, when he said 'We weigh upon the world; its resources hardly suffice to support us. As our needs grow larger, so do our protests that already nature does not sustain us.' Over the past 200 years this concern has intensified. With more effective means of communication and more accurate record keeping, knowledge about the disparities in living conditions of peoples all over the world has become more accessible. The Chinese famine of 1876–79 claimed approximately 13 million lives, the 1943 Bengal famine 3 million and the Ethiopian famine of 1984 at least 800 000.

Two contending views have emerged concerning the extent to which burgeoning populations affect food supply. The first is that population must be controlled if persistent malnutrition and starvation are not to become the inevitable lot for a substantial portion of the globe. The second is that, even with a projected global population of 10 billion by the year 2070, there is sufficient food to feed everyone.

These views reflect differing assumptions. Those who link hunger directly with overpopulation adhere to the Malthusian principle that in a world of relatively finite resources, increases in human numbers lower the demand for labour. This in turn lowers the wages of labour, leaving large portions of the population without the means to purchase food. Unless human beings seek to restrict their own reproduction through voluntary celibacy, late marriages, abortion and contraception, so, the neo-Malthusians argue, only the natural forces of war, epidemics and starvation will control the balance between population and food availability.

Such assumptions have been challenged by Karl Marx (see p. 269), who believed that the ways society was structured and its resources allocated were more important than population and finite resources. Others consider the prevalence of hunger as an issue more related to the way that people are deprived of access to food rather than one of its insufficiency.

Although the debate continues, increasing evidence would seem to support the structural view. Over the past 25 years, increases in food production have outstripped unprecedented global population growth by about 16%. Based upon this figure, it can be deduced that there is sufficient food in the world today to supply every individual with a daily intake of 3600 calories, although 900 million people live on the precipice of malnutrition (2100 calories per day for adult maintenance) or acute hunger (1750 calories per day for short-term adult survival).

Population and poverty

The greatest increases in population continue to occur in countries that are the poorest in terms of their Gross Domestic Product (see p. 276). The populations of many Third World countries depend upon subsistence agriculture (see p. 188) as their principal economic activity. These countries have limited social services and lack most forms of advanced agricultural technology. Under such conditions, rural families tend to have large families, ensuring a degree of labour as well as support for members of the family in their old age. Hence, large families – as was formerly the case in the developed world (see p. 256) – continue to be an essential norm for the poor, who represent the majority in most Third World societies.

Ironically, the emphasis placed upon eliminating disease amongst the young – for example through mass immunization programmes – has lowered levels of infant mortality. This has increased the population in many Third World countries, often leaving members of families without prospects for work. Thus towns and cities are seen as havens for alternative employment, although urban centres in underdeveloped countries offer limited job opportunities, and migration to towns and cities has done little to break the poverty cycle.

Hunger and poverty

There is a general belief that the forces of nature are principally to blame for the hunger that threatens much of humanity. Yet the effects of nature cannot be divorced from the issue of man-made poverty. In the USA in 1987, an extensive area in the southeast of the country was stricken by drought. No one died, no lives were threatened. During the same period, drought-affected Ethiopia needed over 1.3 million tonnes (tons) of emergency food to save the lives of over 4 million affected people. The differences between the two situations underscore the relationship between poverty and hunger. In the USA, available resources had been invested in extensive irrigation and water schemes. Food was available, if required, from a well-developed food-reserve system, and farmers were ultimately protected by insurance and loan schemes provided by the federal and state governments. Alternative employment was generally available to those whose assets were not otherwise protected.

In Ethiopia, as in many other Third World countries, the resources required to develop such support systems are generally not available. Without them, people become more and more vulnerable to the forces of nature, and their poverty intensifies. Ecological degradation demonstrates this well. With few resources, farmers in the Third World must till their

fields continuously, leaving no respite for their recovery. Fertilizers are expensive, and therefore not readily available. The topsoil of these lands may have been held in place by trees that have now been felled to be used as fuel for which the poor have no real alternatives. The trees become the victims of poverty as does the land. Rain washes away valuable topsoil and the farmer gets less and less for his efforts. His situation, faced with an inevitably declining income, deteriorates. Subsistence agriculture teeters ever more frequently on the brink of disaster.

Poverty, population and development

If the world produces sufficient food to feed itself but the impoverished are increasingly exposed to threats of malnutrition and starvation, the issue seems to be how best to give the poor access to the food that is clearly available rather than one of population reduction. Greater access can be achieved through effective development. Such development must either help rural families to farm more effectively for profit – so enabling them to purchase a wider variety of foods – or allow them to find alternative means of generating income.

But there are three barriers to effective development that need to be overcome. On the international level, the majority of Third World countries are saddled with international debts (see p. 299) that prevent them from funding the extensive development programmes that they require. Foreign exchange to pay these debts and to seek new loans is often hindered by the trading restrictions of the developed nations, or by the fluctuations in international market prices for the few goods that poor nations may have to sell. And even when development assistance comes from outside donors, all too often it is aid that is tied to the sorts of projects that may benefit the donor and the recipient government, but not necessarily citizens at the grass-roots level.

At the national level, many of the poorest countries are faced with contending demands that cannot be met with their limited resources. The fact that domestic and regional instability is also often prevalent means that a high proportion of national wealth is spent on armaments rather than development. Third World governments also have to expand resources on providing subsidized food for potentially volatile populations in towns and cities – which is often purchased by governments at prices that leave no incentives for farmers. Governments of developing countries, frequently prompted by developed countries, may also view development itself as a 'top-down' process: in other words, more visible large-scale projects such as road and dam construction are pursued, instead of projects that contribute directly to improving the lives of the poor.

It is at local levels that the cumulative effects of instability and lack of effective development take their hardest toll. These effects are often compounded by a strict adherence to traditions, sometimes reinforced by religions that rationalize but do not necessarily ease the plight of the poor. Lack of education and appropriate technology means that traditional working methods are rarely abandoned, and consequently the poverty of the poor is intensified.

Although with increases in family incomes the size of families decrease, this fact does not diminish the more general point that poverty rather than population size lies at the heart of hunger. Whether a population is large or small, there is little evidence that size in itself influences the way societies are structured or the way resources are allocated. In short, population is related to hunger but it is far from being its necessary cause.

The role of the international community

Since the World Food Conference of 1974, the international community has sought to play a greater role in relieving the crises of hunger found in many parts of the world. International organizations such as the United Nations World Food Programme, the Food and Agriculture Organization, the United Nations Children's Fund and the United Nations Development Programme (see p. 284) have all attempted to assist countries where threats of famine and severe malnutrition are rife. These international organizations are supported by the efforts of donor governments (which either give assistance through international organizations or directly to affected countries) or through voluntary non-governmental organizations that are working in affected countries (see p. 299).

These organizations work on two levels. In times of severe food shortages they provide food and medicines for the hungry; frequently

A Chinese government poster urging couples to have one child only; in China it is now illegal to have more than one. Since World War II many governments have instituted campaigns to restrict population growth, but these have generally been more effective in the developed world than in the Third World.

SEE ALSO

● INTERNATIONAL ORGANI-
ZATIONS p. 284–7
● THE THIRD WORLD AND
THE DEVELOPED WORLD
p. 298

they also fund development programmes to stimulate economic growth. Although in the past these development efforts have not always addressed the real causes of hunger, increasingly both Third World governments and members of the international community recognize the need to focus their assistance directly upon the poor.   RK

POPULATION FACTS

Growth of world population by billion and year

World population	Year	Elapsed years
1 billion	1805	indefinite
2 billion	1926	121
3 billion	1960	34
4 billion	1974	14
5 billion	1987	13
6 billion	1998	11
7 billion	2010	12
8 billion	2023	13
9 billion	2040	17
10 billion	2070	30

The projected slowing down of world population growth to a peak of 10 billion in 2070 is based on the following assumptions: increased use of contraception in developing countries, and an ageing of the global population (with fertile adults making up a smaller percentage of the whole).

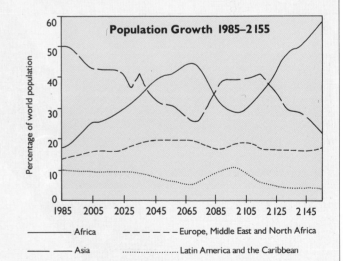

Population Growth 1985–2155

- Africa
- Asia
- Europe, Middle East and North Africa
- Latin America and the Caribbean

Population growth by geographic region, 1985-2025

Region	Population (millions)		Growth rate (%)		Birth rate (per 1000)		Death rate (per 1000)	
	1985	2025	1985-90	2020-25	1985-90	2020-25	1985-90	2020-25
WORLD	4,840	8,188	1.71	0.94	26.9	17.6	9.8	8.2
Africa	560	1,495	3.05	1.74	45.0	24.1	14.5	6.7
Asia	2,819	4,758	1.80	0.89	27.4	17.0	9.2	8.1
America	666	1,035	1.58	0.72	23.4	15.3	7.9	8.2
Europe	770	863	0.45	0.15	14.7	13.0	10.3	11.5
Oceania	25	36	1.37	0.59	19.6	15.0	8.2	9.1

The Third World and the Developed World

The international system that emerged after World War II was designed and dominated by the developed nations. Apart from the Latin American countries, most Third World countries were still under colonial rule. Although there was a genuine feeling among European governments that decolonization was just and proper, there were other reasons for changes in this area after 1945.

Economically, France and Britain could no longer sustain major commitments abroad. Moreover, they believed they could retain the advantages of colonialism while granting independence to their colonies. The newly independent countries had no choice but to participate in an existing international system and economic order that reflected the needs of the developed world. Thus Britain and France found it was possible to respond positively to demands for independence without sacrificing trade and economic links that were important to them. The

A slum colony in Delhi. Unlike most developing countries, India has a sophisticated industrial base, and an advanced administrative and political structure. However, it remains dogged by the fundamental economic problem of how to feed, clothe and house its ever-growing population, the majority of whom have incomes well below the subsistence level.

USA developed similar ties with Latin America.

Change was not automatic, however, and nationalist movements often had to organize mass protests or even armed struggle against colonial rule (see pp. 448–9). With the immense costs incurred by Britain and France in fighting World War II, followed by the independence of India in 1947, it seemed inevitable that the tide of decolonization could not be reversed.

The legacy of colonization

The common feature of the newly independent countries is that, alongside Latin America, they are poorer than the developed world. They are very often in debt to the developed world or its banking institutions; and, in a significant number of cases, they are poverty-stricken. Moreover, there appears to be no way in which they can escape poverty and debt except by dependence upon the developed world. Most developing countries are in the southern hemisphere, hence the relationship is also a North-South issue. Following the end of the Cold War (see p. 451), the North-South relationship has replaced East-West rivalry as a cause of concern.

The transfer of resources from North to South is of immediate importance: firstly, to help the Southern states face the future with confidence; secondly, to correct the imbalance in the transfer of resources that took place during the period of colonization; and thirdly, because effective demand from the South would stimulate Northern economies, create employment and increase global political stability. But to achieve such goals, the countries of the South must also undertake reforms so that they can attain their full economic potential.

Because of their weak economies, development has been difficult, and national unity has often been impossible to sustain in Third World countries. Many Third World countries gained their indepen-

An irrigation scheme in Ethiopia, financed by UNICEF. The drought and resultant famine of 1983–85 exacerbated the existing problems of underdevelopment in Ethiopia's agricultural economy. The devastating legacy of the drought – continuing serious shortages of food, grain, farm implements and livestock – will only be reversed by a long-term programme of outside aid.

dence with the same boundaries that had been established by the colonial powers. In many cases, these boundaries differed from those reflecting traditional tribal, economic and cultural links. The attempts of modern states to create a national unity over and above traditional patterns of interaction have not always been successful and are not helped by underdevelopment and poverty. Particularly in Africa, very few local inhabitants had been properly trained by the colonial powers to become the skilled administrators and technicians of the new, independent states. Viewed in this light, the achievements of many Third World countries since independence – the establishment of transport, education and health networks, and the extension of public administration – are impressive.

Zones of conflict

With the emergence of the USA and the USSR as the two opposing superpowers after World War II, both countries looked for allies in the Third World. The numerous regional conflicts of the Cold War often saw one superpower engaged in hostilities with the allies of the other (see pp. 450–1).

The protagonists in the wars between Israel and its Arab neighbours were armed and supported by the USA and the Soviet Union respectively (see pp. 454–5). In southern Africa, the USA was for some time supportive of South Africa's military incursions into neighbouring independent Angola, because the Soviet Union and Cuba, in turn, supported the Marxist government of Angola. In such cases, it was the Third World countries involved who suffered most. War added to the problems of underdevelopment.

The USA and the Soviet Union did not confine their competition in the Third World to visible military clashes. Both attempted to secure allies through large-scale aid programmes. Under Khrushchev's leadership (1953–64), the USSR sought to use aid to win over recently independent African countries, and spent most money on those they thought might develop along socialist lines.

Later Soviet leaders tended to confine significant aid to countries of strategic value, such as Ethiopia, which is of importance because of its position near the Red Sea and the Suez Canal, through which a great deal of the world's shipping continues to pass. The USA has developed a very large aid budget, but the largest portions of this aid go firstly to Israel and secondly to Egypt, precisely to maintain influence in the Middle Eastern and Red Sea areas. Aid (much of which is directly military) has often been given, therefore, not for the sake of development within a Third World country, but for the sake of political advantage in the competitive world of international relations.

Current economic domination

Aid by itself usually forms only a small part of the finance a country needs to operate properly. When it comes to large-scale economic transactions, the West rather than the East has dominated the Third World. The economic domination of the Third World by developed industrial nations is sometimes referred to as *neo-imperialism*. The 24 richest Western states together account for 60% of world industrial production, 73% of world trade, and 80% of all aid to developing countries. More importantly, all of the great commercial banks are found in the West, as are the world's two great financial institutions, the International Monetary Fund (IMF) and the World Bank (see p. 285). Originally, the IMF and World Bank helped Europe to redevelop after World War II but, as Third World countries became independent, they also turned to these organizations. These, together with the commercial banks, loaned money for development, to the Third World and (since 1989–91) to Eastern Europe.

Difficult international economic conditions in the 1970s and 1980s involved rising oil costs and deteriorating terms of trade for many other raw materials: developing nations had to pay more for oil but received less for their own exports. They therefore had to borrow from the commercial banks who at that time, because they were handling oil revenues, had much to lend. As economic recession hit the West, however, interest rates rose and Third World countries were obliged to pay more interest on their loans than they had expected. Meanwhile, income from exports continued to decline. Particularly after 1982, commercial banks grew reluctant to make further large new loans to the Third World countries, which increasingly turned to the IMF.

The IMF, however, made finance available only if a country organized its financial planning and management with the IMF's approval. But local development was often thereby compromised and living conditions for Third World citizens became harsher. Indeed for many such countries, *debt servicing* (payment of interest on loans) can absorb the largest portion of income earned from exports, leaving very little for development or even for maintaining current facilities and infrastructure (schools, hospitals, transport systems, etc.). In the late 1980s, several African countries exported more money in the form of loan and interest payments than anything else.

THE BRANDT COMMISSION

The most comprehensive plan for confronting both the problems of debt and slow development was that put forward in 1979 in the *Brandt Report*. This was prepared by the Independent Commission on International Development Issues under the chairmanship of former West German Chancellor Willy Brandt (1913–92).

The Report made four major sets of recommendations: firstly, a global food programme to stimulate food production in the fight against hunger and famine; secondly, a global energy programme; thirdly, greater participation for Third World countries in organizations such as the IMF and World Bank; fourthly, and most importantly in the immediate term, increased financial aid to Third World countries, both in the form of grants and low-interest loans, and in the reduction or cancellation of many existing debts, to allow Third World countries to rescue themselves from the current debt trap and recommence the process of development. The Report also stressed that vast expenditure on arms by the rich nations of the West takes potential resources away from the impoverished countries of the Third World.

Although the Brandt Report argued that its proposed plan was in Western self-interest, Western governments paid little attention to it. However, it enabled the Western public to become aware of what could and should be done in the mutual interest.

The world's largest debtor nations are found in Latin America. So great is the debt of Mexico, Brazil and Argentina together that it is thought that any refusal or inability to repay it would cause chaos within the Western banking system. Thus the lending banks may become vulnerable to their borrowers.

Current aid

Despite the refusal of Western governments to implement the proposals of the Brandt report (see box) there has been Western action to help meet emergency conditions. Famine in Ethiopia and Mozambique brought disaster relief from both governments and the public. In many countries voluntary charities are deeply involved in raising money for the starving in the Third World. Bob Geldof's Band Aid was one example of work by private citizens to raise money for the hungry.

The problem with emergency aid is that often it does not address fundamental problems. Ethiopia, for example, was a zone of conflict subject to East-West competition. In Mozambique, the war between the government and rebels supported by South Africa has prevented any chance of national development.

Brandt was correct in saying that North-South relations are as important as East-West relations. The tragedy of the 20th century is that, while one part of the world has developed, the larger part has suffered the loss of its chance for development in this century. It is a loss that in the long run could also imperil the well-being of the developed world. SC

SEE ALSO

- THE INTERNATIONAL ECONOMY p. 278
- THE UNITED NATIONS p. 284
- REGIONAL, ECONOMIC AND MILITARY ALLIANCES p. 286
- POPULATION AND HUNGER p. 296
- DECOLONIZATION p. 448
- THE COLD WAR p. 450

Soviet troops withdraw from Afghanistan in 1989. Third World countries have been the battleground for many of the confrontations of the Cold War. Throughout the Soviet Union's ten-year military involvement in Afghanistan, their Muslim fundamentalist adversaries received military backing from the West. Like the USA in Vietnam, the Soviets were to discover that the economic and human cost of such military commitments is impossible to sustain.

Threats to the Environment

Perhaps the most disturbing surprise of the late 20th century has been the discovery of the frailty of the world's environment. The last wildernesses have almost gone, and it is possible that our children will see the large mammals only in zoos or on film. The tropical rain forests of South America, Africa and Southeast Asia, which provide much of the oxygen we breathe, are disappearing at an alarming rate; the ozone layer, which protects us from harmful radiation, is being eaten away. As the threat of a nuclear war recedes with the easing of tensions between the superpowers, the new battle is to protect the Earth's biological and natural systems from human exploitation.

Trees damaged by acid rain in the Black Forest, Germany.

At the time of the last great extinction on Earth – the disappearance of the dinosaurs 65 million years ago (see p. 132) – only a handful of species every thousand years were becoming extinct. Now we are losing perhaps a hundred species a day. This is the time of the greatest mass extinction of life forms in the history of life on Earth.

The rise of industry in the northern hemisphere has brought with it material wealth at the expense of the local environment. Opencast mining in Europe and elsewhere has scarred the countryside. Cities and factories have spread, and the smoke from their chimneys has released harmful chemicals into the air. Cars to transport burgeoning populations are multiplying, adding their own pollutants to the atmosphere.

The source of the environmental problems of today lies in the lifestyle of the industrialized nations. The widespread use of disposable convenience goods that are 'energy inefficient' is wasteful of scarce resources; the batteries that power personal stereos, for example, take 50 times more energy to manufacture than they produce. A developed Third World that follows the environmentally damaging practices of the developed nations could propel the Earth into an ecological holocaust within decades.

Air pollution

The internal combustion engine that powers the motor car produces carbon monoxide, an odourless gas that is highly poisonous and possibly a cause of cancer. Car engines also emit hydrocarbons and nitrogen oxides, which, under the influence of sunlight, form *low-atmosphere ozone*, a major irritant and air pollutant. It is the main ingredient in the photochemical smog that afflicts the cities of Los Angeles, Tokyo and Athens.

The other major threat in car exhausts is lead, which is added to petrol to improve performance. Excess lead levels in the atmosphere can lead to damage to the brain and nervous system, especially in children. Lead-free petrol is becoming more popular, but the switch to unleaded fuel has brought its own problems. In America, the aromatic hydrocarbon content of petrol – benzine, toluene and xylene – has been doubled to help performance. These compounds are known carcinogens (causes of cancer).

But the major form of air pollution comes from another source. Coal-fired power stations and other industrial processes emit sulphur dioxide and nitrogen oxides, which, when combined with atmospheric moisture, create *acid rain* (dilute sulphuric or nitric acid). Acid rain (or snow) is the main atmospheric fallout of industrial pollutants, although these may also occur as dry deposits (such as ash). Acid rain damages forests, plants and agriculture (see illustration), raises the acid level in lakes and ground water, killing fish and other water-bound life, and contaminating drinking water.

Temperate forests have been seriously damaged by acid rain. The Black Forest in Germany has been steadily losing its trees through *Waldsterben* (tree death). But Britain has the highest percentage of damaged trees in Europe – 67%. In southern Norway 80% of the lakes are devoid of fish life, and Sweden has 20 000 acidified lakes.

Acid rain upsets the fine chemical balance in lakes that are home to numerous species of fish. Salmon, roach and trout are highly sensitive to pH (i.e. acid) levels in their habitat. Even a slight dip in pH levels causes heavy metals such as aluminium, mercury, lead, zinc and cadmium to become more concentrated, decreasing the amount of oxygen the fish can absorb and eventually causing their death. The absence of large fish destabilizes the ecosystem and the effects are felt throughout the food chain. The ecosystem is seriously depleted, and only some smaller creatures, such as water beetles, seem able to survive.

Acid rain also causes damage to the soil. High levels of acid rain in the soil cause lead and other heavy metals to become concentrated and interrupt the life-cycles of microorganisms. The bacteria and fungi that help break down organic matter into nutrients are disturbed (see the nitrogen cycle, p. 177), and soils can lose their ability to support forests or agriculture.

There are various methods of reducing the amount of pollutants reaching the atmosphere, such as lead-free petrol, catalytic converters attached to car exhausts (which destroy some of the harmful gases), and filter systems that reduce dangerous emissions from power stations and industry.

Water pollution

Rivers and seas are also used as dumping grounds for waste products. Excessive amounts of domestic sewage, fertilizers and other toxic chemicals thus disposed of can destroy the life forms that live in water. (Oil spills at sea such as the *Exxon Valdez* disaster off Alaska in 1989 can cause the deaths of thousands of sea birds and fish.) Water itself is also used to cool industrial factories, but when returned to rivers and lakes can cause an increase in the temperature, so destabilizing the natural habitat. Industrial waste products can also contaminate drinking water.

Some of the most toxic materials used by man are *polychlorinated biphenyls* (PCBs). PCBs are widely used in light fittings, kiss-proof lipstick and in commercial cooling systems and transformers. PCBs are water-soluble but find their way into the food chain through their propensity to dissolve in fats. The chemicals lie in sediments after being released into the environment and pass into the fat of smaller animals, eventually reaching the higher mammals at the top of the food chain.

Pesticides

Increasingly high levels of pesticides are also present in the bodies of most creatures. More than 2 300 000 tonnes (tons) of pesticides were produced in the world in 1986, and their use is increasing worldwide at a rate of nearly 13% per year. Like PCBs they become concentrated in the bodies of animals at the top of the food chain, animals such as seals and humans.

While producers claim that without pesticides the world population would starve, there is little evidence to support this. Pests tend to become immune to pesticides, while their predators are contaminated by them and consequently decline

THE OZONE LAYER

Ozone is a gas made up of three oxygen atoms (O₃). It is inherently unstable, and is formed partly by the action of sunlight on normal oxygen, which is made up of pairs of oxygen atoms (O₂). Ozone is a minor constituent of the atmosphere, found in varying concentrations between sea level and a height of 60 km (37 mi). Most ozone is in the layer of the atmosphere called the stratosphere (see p. 77), which extends from around 10–12 km (6–7.5 mi) to about 45–50 km (28–31 mi) above the Earth's surface.

The ozone layer filters out harmful ultra-violet radiation from the Sun. Ultraviolet radiation can cause skin cancer and eye cataracts, and can damage crops. During every southern-hemisphere spring since the 1970s, holes have developed in the ozone layer above Antarctica (see illustration). There the effects are minimal, but there are signs that similar holes are appearing over the heavily populated northern latitudes, which include Europe,

North America and Russia.

The culprits are chlorofluorocarbons (CFCs) – man-made gases used in air conditioning, fridges, many aerosols and some foam-blown cartons. The gases released from these products collect in the upper atmosphere and there decay into chloride gas, which destroys the ozone.

The development of safe substitutes for aerosols, plastic-foam materials and for refrigeration and air-conditioning systems is lagging behind the need for a rapid phasing-out of CFCs. Even if all production of CFCs was banned immediately, the chemicals would take centuries to fall to the levels of the mid-1970s, and until 2050 even to drop to the level of 1985.

A hole in the ozone layer, as shown on a satellite map on October 15, 1987. The hole is visible here as the deep blue, purple, black and pink area covering Antarctica (outlined in white) and beyond. The colours represent Dobson units, a measure of atmospheric ozone.

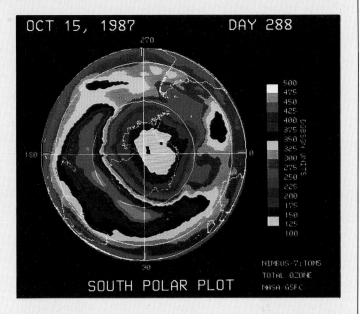

OCT 15, 1987   DAY 288

SOUTH POLAR PLOT

---

n population. The resulting imbalance creates more pests rather than fewer because their natural enemies have been poisoned.

Global warming

Pollution can have subtler but potentially more devastating effects on the environment than just poisoning. Carbon-dioxide emissions now threaten the world's climate, by causing a gradual warming of the planet – the so-called *greenhouse effect*.

Average temperatures on Earth have increased by 0.5 °C (0.9 °F) in the last century. 'Greenhouse' gases (particularly carbon dioxide) – produced by burning fossil fuels – are accumulating in the atmosphere and trapping heat that would normally escape into space, rather like the glass in a greenhouse. Not only will the weather become hotter as a result, but the polar ice caps will release more water into the oceans, raising sea levels across the globe. It has been estimated that the temperature will rise by 1.5–4.5 °C (2.7–8.1 °F) by the year 2050. Estimates of the resulting rise in sea level vary from 0.3–0.7 m (1–2 ft) to 0.8–1.8 m (2½–6 ft). The larger projected rise could result in the disappearance of small, low-lying islands such as the Maldives in the Indian Ocean. A rise of 1.8 m (6 ft) would seriously threaten cities such as London, New York and Venice.

Nuclear power

While the nuclear industry has always maintained that its reactors are safe and clean, accidents at Three Mile Island in the USA in 1979 and at Chernobyl in Ukraine in 1986 (see illustration), have cast doubt on these claims. The National Radiological Protection Board in Britain estimates that 2000 people will develop cancer in Europe over the next 50 years because of the accident at Chernobyl.

But other agencies put the figure closer to 40 000.

The Chernobyl accident was the result of an experiment involving the deliberate switching-off of the safety systems. Power rose to 480 times the normal levels before the reactor exploded, contaminating vast tracts of Eastern Europe and Scandinavia. Even four years after the explosion some parts of Scandinavia remained contaminated by radioactive fallout.

Quite apart from the horror of accidents such as Chernobyl, the nuclear industry poses the problem of how to dispose of the waste that it produces. Much of its waste will remain highly toxic and radioactive for tens of thousands of years. In the USA, high-level waste is stored in stainless steel tanks, which are cooled and buried. But in Britain high-level waste is stored in a process called vitrification. This involves solidifying the radioactive material in glass to make it easier to handle.

Lower-level waste is usually buried in shallow sites, or in abandoned mines. The problem of nuclear waste disposal has merely been delayed. Most methods involve moving the waste to safer places ready for the future. It has even been suggested that waste be 'injected' out into space. The *Challenger* space shuttle disaster (see p. 19), however, has killed such ideas.

Environmental awareness

There are signs that the world is waking up to the environmental threats facing it. However, most governments have not faced up to the unpalatable economic policies necessary to rectify the situation. Governments have failed to agree on reductions in carbon-dioxide emissions because they say this would hamper economic growth. However, the Montreal Convention of March 1989 commits the international community to a 100% reduction of CFCs by the year 2000. Western concern to preserve the biodiversity of many areas – particularly in developing countries – was high-lighted at the 1992 Rio Conference on the Environment. However, many developing countries would prefer to exploit their land and resources in order to develop economically. As yet the richer Western countries have not provided sufficient funds to help developing countries implement painful environmental policies.

Public opinion will determine whether economic growth continues to be put before the health of the environment as 'Green' politics have become a major force in society. But the phenomenon of green consumerism is the most powerful force for change. Consumers are increasingly opting for goods that are environmentally less damaging. When industry finds that it is not economically viable to be environmentally irresponsible then the tide will have turned.   AS

SEE ALSO

- SMALL MOLECULES p. 48
- WEATHER AND CLIMATE pp. 102–5
- PHOTOSYNTHESIS p. 117
- THE BIOSPHERE p. 176
- ECOSYSTEMS pp. 178–87
- AGRICULTURE AND FOOD pp. 188–97
- ENERGY pp. 304–7
- MINING, MINERALS AND METALS p. 312
- RUBBER AND PLASTICS p. 316

Nuclear decontamination at Chernobyl (left) in northern Ukraine. The explosion of the nuclear reactor at Chernobyl in 1986 necessitated the immediate evacuation of 130 000 people from the disaster zone. But the effects of radioactive fallout from the blast were felt all over Eastern and Northern Europe.

TECHNOLOGY AND INDUSTRY

*'The machine does not isolate man
from the great problems of nature
but plunges him more deeply into them'*

Antoine de Saint Exupéry

Energy
1. Coal, Oil and Nuclear

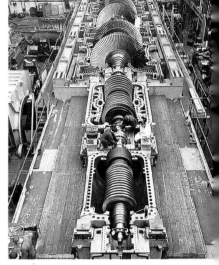

In the industrialized world, the vast amount of power that we demand is most often provided by means of electricity – the most convenient and flexible medium in which to transfer power from its source to where it is needed. However, in deciding how best to generate electricity in ever-increasing quantities, we are confronted with an unenviable choice. On the one hand, there is the gradual but inevitable damage to the environment caused by burning coal and oil; on the other, the unlikely but potentially catastrophic risks associated with nuclear power.

A 660-MW steam turbine (right) at the Drax coal-fired power station in England.

The principle of electromagnetic induction – on which the electrical generator depends – was demonstrated by Michael Faraday as early as 1831 (see p. 34). However, it was not until the mid-1870s that electricity was first used to light streets and public buildings. The first experiments in providing a combined public and domestic electricity supply were made in 1881, when a limited service was made available to the people of Godalming in Surrey, England.

Today, almost all the energy used to generate electricity in the developed world comes from burning coal or oil, or from nuclear fission. In each case the heat produced by the fuel is used to raise steam, which turns the blades of a steam turbine (see photo and p. 308). The turbine rotor is connected to the shaft of an electrical generator (see p. 36). In most developed countries and increasingly in the Third World, the power output is fed into a national grid system (see box).

Most developed countries have extensive and complex supply networks. Power stations are interlinked and centrally controlled, allowing power to be channelled to where it is required and extra stations to be started up to meet peaks in demand.

Pollution and efficiency

The burning of fossil fuels in power stations leads to the emission of several by-products that are potentially damaging to the environment. *Fly ash*, which results from burning pulverized coal, is effectively removed by passing the flue (or waste) gases from the furnace through an *electrostatic precipitator* – a series of electrically charged plates that hold back the tiny particles of ash.

However, other by-products pass straight out of the chimney and into the atmosphere, including sulphur dioxide and nitrogen oxides, major causes of acid rain, and carbon dioxide, which contributes to the greenhouse effect (see pp. 300–1). Some of the biggest power stations are already being fitted with burners to minimize the production of nitrogen oxides, and major coal-fired stations are likely to include desulphurization equipment.

At present, less than 40% of the energy released by the burning of fuel is finally transmitted as electrical energy. The remainder is dissipated as waste heat. The efficiency of small stations near cities can rise to nearer 80% if the energy that would otherwise pass uselessly into the environment is used to heat water, which is then piped into a district heating scheme, serving radiators in blocks of flats and offices. Such schemes are already in operation, notably in Iceland and Russia.

Nuclear power

In terms of electricity generation, the only difference between nuclear power stations and conventional stations is the means of raising steam to drive the turbines: the coal- or oil-burning furnace is simply replaced by a nuclear reactor. However, this entails a whole industry of its own.

Uranium-235 (U-235) is the form (or isotope) of the element uranium used as the fuel in most nuclear reactors. However, it is only present in tiny quantities – less than 1% – in mined uranium. The rest is made up of uranium-238. For many reactors, the proportion of U-235 has to be increased by a complex and very costly process known as *enrichment*. The fuel – enriched or natural uranium as required – is packed into fuel rods, which are placed in the core of a nuclear reactor.

The nuclei of U-235 atoms sometimes break apart when struck by neutrons, in a process known as nuclear fission (see

SEE ALSO

● ELECTRICITY IN ACTION p. 36
● ATOMS AND SUBATOMIC PARTICLES p. 38
● THREATS TO THE ENVIRONMENT p. 300
● ENERGY 2 p. 306
● OIL AND GAS p. 310
● MINING, MINERALS AND METALS p. 312

ELECTRICITY GENERATION AND TRANSMISSION

Steam from boiler/reactor

Water to boiler/reactor

Steam turbine   Generator   25 000 volts   Transformer   400 000 volts   Pylon   Substation   125 000 volts   Pylon   Substation   Heavy industry 33 000 volts   25 000 volts   33 000 volts   Substation   14 000 volts   Light industry 415 volts   120/240 volts

Condenser

Heat is produced by burning oil or coal in the furnace of a conventional power station, or by nuclear fission in a nuclear reactor. In the case of a coal-fired power station, the fuel is first pulverized to a fine powder, which is then pumped in a stream of air through jets into the furnace. The heat is used to boil water circulating through tubes in the boiler/reactor, so creating steam. The steam is then superheated until it reaches temperatures of up to 600 °C (1112 °F).

The superheated steam is channelled to a steam turbine, where it is used to drive the turbine shaft at high speed. The steam is then passed through a condenser, where it is turned back into water, thus creating a partial vacuum and so improving the flow of steam through the turbine. The condensed water is pumped back to the boiler/reactor under pressure.

The turbine shaft is linked to a generator, where – in the case of the largest modern generators – electricity is generated at around 25 000 volts of alternating current. For efficient transmission, the voltage is stepped up by transformers to very high voltages, typically as high as 400 000 volts — otherwise, significant amounts of energy would be lost through resistance in the transmission cables.

In many countries, the output is fed into a national grid system, by means of overhead cables suspended from pylons. A single row of pylons is able to carry the entire output from an average power station. At substations at various points on the grid, the supply is stepped down to suitable levels for distribution to consumers, typically at around the voltages shown in the diagram.

. 38). As the nucleus splits, two or three more neutrons are released. These go on to bombard other nuclei and may cause them to split, thus setting off a chain reaction. The reaction is essentially a controlled version of what happens when an atomic bomb explodes. To increase their chance of fissioning U-235 (rather than being captured without fission by U-238), the neutrons are slowed down using a *moderator* such as graphite. So much energy is released as the fuel is fissioned that a single tonne (ton) of uranium is equivalent to 25 000 tonnes of coal.

The vessel in which the fuel rods are placed is filled with a *coolant*. As nuclei split, energetic fragments fly off and are brought to rest in the surrounding coolant, so causing its temperature to rise. The coolant is constantly circulated through the core, so preventing the core from overheating and at the same time acting as the medium by which heat is channelled away from the core to raise steam. The nuclear reaction can be slowed down or stopped altogether if control rods containing a material that absorbs neutrons, such as boron, are lowered into the reactor core.

Types of nuclear reactor

The first commercial nuclear power station, opened in 1956 at Calder Hall in Cumbria, England, was a *magnox reactor*. Magnox reactors are so called because their fuel – natural (unenriched) uranium – is clad in an alloy of magnesium and aluminium called magnox. They are cooled by carbon dioxide gas. In the 1970s a new generation of much bigger gas-cooled reactors was developed in Britain – the *advanced gas-cooled reactors* or AGRs (see diagram). Meanwhile, the Canadians have developed reactors that use 'heavy water' (deuterium oxide). Because heavy water (unlike ordinary water) absorbs few neutrons itself, reactors using it as moderator and coolant can operate with unenriched (and thus cheaper) fuel. The economy in fuel costs is offset, however, by the additional expenditure involved in producing heavy water.

Today, the most widespread nuclear power plants are *light-water reactors*. The coolant and moderator – ordinary ('light') water – is readily available and cheap, but the uranium fuel has to be highly enriched. In the case of *boiling-water reactors* (BWRs), the water is allowed to boil to make steam, which is less efficient at cooling and moderating the reactor, and so must be prevented from building up in the reactor core. In *pressurized-water reactors* or PWRs (see diagram), the water must remain at even higher pressure than is required in a BWR, so that it can reach useful temperatures without boiling.

The world's reserves of uranium will not last for ever, but one sort of reactor could make them go a lot further – the *fast breeder reactor* or FBR (see diagram). The drawback of fast reactors is that they require the reprocessing of spent nuclear fuel both to extract plutonium (its main fuel) in the first place and to recover it from the uranium blanket. Reprocessing is a highly complex and expensive opera-

tion – as well as being unpopular with environmentalists. Nevertheless – and in spite of funds for FBR programmes generally being cut back – prototypes exist, including one at Dounreay in northern Scotland, a large one on the River Rhône in France and one in India.

Nuclear safety

In April 1986 a nuclear power plant at Chernobyl in Ukraine suffered the world's worst nuclear accident. The reactor – a design of BWR peculiar to the former USSR – was operated in such a way that water was allowed to boil to steam inside the reactor. This led to a reduction in cooling and a build-up of pressure. Finally steam reacted with the graphite moderator in the reactor core, producing hydrogen, which exploded. Thirty-three people died of radiation sickness as a direct consequence, but many more throughout northern Europe may ultimately suffer cancer as a result of exposure to the radioactive cloud that escaped.

As a result of Chernobyl and another costly, though less serious, accident at a PWR on Three Mile Island in the USA, many countries have slowed or halted their nuclear programmes. Italy stopped building nuclear reactors just as the first one was being completed, and Sweden has decided to abandon its extensive nuclear programme. France and Russia, however, continue to build new nuclear plants, and Britain has decided to go ahead with a PWR at Sizewell in Suffolk. More are planned, but all arouse intense public debate.

Nuclear fusion

The ultimate dream of the nuclear industry is not to split big nuclei as at present, but to combine small ones – to exploit nuclear fusion (see p. 38) rather than nuclear fission. In principle nuclear fusion sounds the perfect answer. The fuel required – deuterium and tritium, isotopes of hydrogen – can be produced relatively simply and in almost unlimited quantities. Although parts of the reactor will be made radioactive by energetic neutrons, there is no radioactive waste from the fuel itself.

There is a problem, however: to produce a continuous fusion reaction would effectively involve mimicking conditions in the core of the Sun or in a hydrogen bomb explosion (see p. 288). The hydrogen isotopes must be heated to extremely high temperatures – to such an extent that electrons are stripped off their nuclei, and the nuclei collide at such high energy levels that they fuse to form helium, releasing energy in the process. Temperatures of hundreds of millions of degrees will probably be required, so that the materials involved will have to be contained by laser beams or strong magnetic fields. Technologies have been stretched to the limits to make experimental reactors at centres around the world. It is unlikely, however, that power from nuclear fusion will become a commercial reality until the middle of the 21st century.

MRe

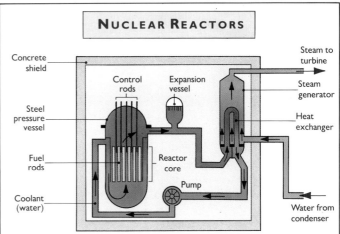

NUCLEAR REACTORS

The pressurized-water reactor (PWR). A PWR is essentially a closed loop in which the combined coolant and moderator – ordinary ('light') water – is pressurized to about 150 atmospheres, and pumped through the reactor core. The core, made up of fuel rods containing pellets of enriched uranium dioxide, heats the coolant to around 325 °C (617 °F), which then passes through a heat exchanger, where it transfers heat to a separate reservoir of water. This water is vaporized to steam, which is piped off to drive the turbine.

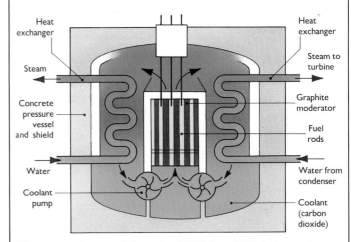

The advanced gas-cooled reactor (AGR). In an AGR, the heat exchangers are located within the pressure vessel itself. The carbon-dioxide coolant is pressurized and heated up to 600 °C (1112 °F) or more as it is pumped through the core, which is made up of fuel rods filled with enriched uranium dioxide.

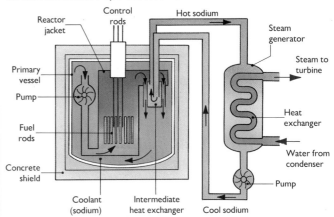

The fast breeder reactor (FBR). In an FBR, the neutrons released from the highly enriched fuel (uranium-235 and plutonium) convert a surrounding blanket of uranium-238 into more plutonium – the reactor 'breeds' plutonium. The reactor is 'fast' because no moderator is used to slow down the neutrons in the core. The coolant is liquid sodium, which is efficient at conducting heat away from the compact core and capable of dealing with the high temperatures involved. The coolant flow is isolated from the steam generator by a second, entirely independent sodium flow.

Energy
2. Other Sources

Even the biggest man-made power stations are dwarfed by the Earth's principal source of energy – the Sun. Directly or indirectly, it provides nearly all the energy we need, for the Sun warms the planet and ultimately drives the wind and waves. Even the chemical energy of the world's reserves of coal, oil and gas came originally from plants and algae, which themselves derived their energy from sunlight.

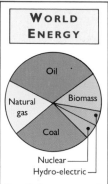

WORLD ENERGY

Oil

Natural gas

Biomass

Coal

Nuclear

Hydro-electric

By their nature, all renewable sources of energy are virtually impossible to quantify. However, the above diagram gives a fair indication of how the world derived its energy in 1988 – as well as showing the continuing dominance of traditional fossil fuels.

SEE ALSO

● THE SUN AND THE SOLAR SYSTEM p. 10
● ELECTRICITY IN ACTION p. 36
● THE FORMATION OF ROCKS p. 84
● THE OCEANS p. 100
● FORESTRY p. 192
● ENERGY 1 p. 304

'Solar One' in California, USA, is the largest solar power plant in the world, with a peak output of 10 MW. Over 1800 mirrors are individually programmed to track the movement of the Sun and to reflect its heat to the collector at the centre of the complex.

The Earth intercepts hundreds of billions of megawatts of power from the Sun. Although most of this is radiated back into space and is not available for use, the amount of solar energy that is absorbed by the Earth in a single year is still far greater than the energy that could be derived from the world's entire recoverable reserves of fossil fuels. If we made full use of just a tiny fraction of this solar energy, we would satisfy our present needs. The Sun will continue to shine for billions of years, so the energy forms derived from it on a daily basis are called *renewable sources*.

Biomass

On a global scale, *biomass* – vegetable matter used as a source of energy – meets a significant proportion of our energy needs. In Ethiopia, Tanzania and Nepal, for instance, it accounts for over 90%. In most other developing countries, wood, crop residues and animal dung provide over 40% of the fuel burnt. Such fuel is the only source of energy for cooking and heating for some 2000 million people.

In many developing countries, the wood used as fuel comes mainly from unmanaged forestry (see p. 193), in which trees are felled but not replanted. There are developments under way, however, that will make both the production and the combustion of biomass more efficient. Crop residues, such as straw, which were once left to rot or burnt on the fields, can now form the fuel for compact boilers used to heat farms or factories, to generate power, or to fuel industrial processes. Farmers, particularly in the Third World, are beginning to plant fast-growing tree species in forests or between rows of crops to provide a regular supply of firewood.

Many tractors in Africa are being converted to run on sunflower oil instead of diesel. Crops rich in starch and sugar can be fermented to produce alcohol, which is added to petrol in many countries, notably Brazil, to form what is known as 'gasohol'.

Rubbish

Domestic and commercial waste is expensive to dispose of in dumps, yet it could form a valuable fuel. A dry weight of 100 million tonnes (tons) of rubbish – perhaps a tenth of the total collected in the USA each year – could replace about 15 million tonnes of coal. In Sweden, there is already a scheme in operation known as 'district heating'. Twenty-three refuse incinerators burn roughly half the country's domestic refuse, and the energy produced – rather than being used to generate electricity – is used to heat nearby homes and offices.

Where waste is dumped into the ground, it can still yield useful energy. As rub-

bish decomposes, it produces methane (the principal component of natural gas). More than 30 large sites in the USA already extract gas from buried refuse dumps, and the technology is being introduced elsewhere.

Even sewage can be used as a source of energy. Millions of rural homes in the developing world have *biogas plants*. At their simplest, these consist of cement-lined tanks buried in the ground, which receive human waste or animal manure. Bacterial action produces methane, or 'biogas'. An estimated 20 million people in China use it for cooking and heating.

Sunshine

Direct solar energy is one of the simplest sources of power. Building designs, old and new, take advantage of it for heating and lighting. Today, more active designs are becoming widespread. Each square metre (11¾ sq ft) of a solar collector in northern Europe receives roughly 1000 kilowatt-hours of solar energy in the course of a year, and can use about half of this energy to heat water. A similar collector in California receives twice as much energy as this (see photo).

Solar (or 'photovoltaic') cells, which use the Sun's radiation to generate electrical energy, are also becoming cheaper and more efficient. Earlier cells, made from large slices of crystalline silicon, were very expensive, but new materials, such as amorphous silicon and gallium arsenide, are bringing the price down towards the goal of about one dollar per watt. The latest experimental solar cells are able to convert about a third of the energy in sunlight into electricity. Solar cells are already proving the best option for producing electricity reliably in remote locations.

Wind

The traditional windmill has tapped the energy of the winds for centuries. Its modern counterpart is far more sophisticated. The biggest ones have blades resembling giant aircraft propellers up to 60 m (200 ft) across, and can generate 3 MW of electricity. Two such machines provide much of the electricity for the Orkney Islands, and several large 'wind farms' have been built at coastal sites both in Europe and in the USA (see photo). Another approach, pioneered in Britain, is a wind turbine with blades like a giant letter H, which rotate around a vertical axis. The mechanism tilts the blade tips inwards in high winds, thus regulating the supply.

Water power

The average power in waves washing the North Atlantic coast of Europe is 50 kW per metre of wave front. Many ingenious techniques have been devised to harness this power, ranging from systems of rafts or floats known as 'ducks', rings of air bags known as 'clams', or columns in which water is forced up and down. Much effort has gone into the development of such techniques, but it has proved difficult to design structures capable of withstanding the force of the waves with-

A wind farm at Palm Springs, California, USA. The traditional use of windmills to grind corn has been extended in recent years to the generation of electricity. Several large wind farms have been built in Europe and the USA, principally at windy coastal sites. Modern designs have chiefly been of two types: horizontal-axis turbines, which resemble gigantic aircraft propellers; and vertical-axis turbines, which have the advantage that they do not need to be orientated towards the wind.

out excessive maintenance. It has become clear that wave power will not easily produce the hoped-for quantities of cheap energy.

The power of running water has long been exploited by water mills – one of the most ancient means of harnessing the power of the elements. In some countries, *hydro-electric power*, or 'hydropower' (see box), is the most important source of energy. Hydropower provides 8% of Western Europe's energy, and worldwide it provides roughly as much energy as nuclear power. Major projects can be controversial as they may involve flooding environmentally sensitive areas. However, the latest design of low-head water turbines has reduced the necessary height difference (the 'head') between the turbine and the surface of the reservoir, so making it possible to build smaller barrages or even to place turbines directly into river beds.

Tidal movements – ultimately derived from the Earth's rotation (see p. 100) – are potentially a vast source of energy. Where tidal currents are funnelled into river estuaries, there is an opportunity to harness this energy. There are currently six tidal power stations in the world, the biggest of them at the Rance Estuary in Brittany, France (see box). Proposed tidal power schemes across the Severn

Estuary in Britain and the Bay of Fundy in Canada would be much bigger.

Geothermal power

Just 30 km (19 mi) beneath our feet, the rock has a temperature of around 900 °C (1650 °F). This heat comes primarily from the gradual radioactive decay of elements within the Earth. Strictly speaking, this source of power is not renewable, but it is immense. There is enough heat in the top 10 km (6 mi) of the Earth's crust, at depths accessible with current drilling techniques, to supply all our energy needs for hundreds of years.

In some parts of the world, including Iceland, the amount of geothermal heat reaching the surface is distinctly greater than elsewhere, and can be used directly as a means of domestic heating. In other countries, blocks of flats are heated by hot water from wells 2 to 3 km (1 to 2 mi) deep.

The biggest reserves of geothermal heat, however, are to be found deeper still, at 6 km (4 mi) or so. As the rocks at this depth are dry, it is harder and more costly to get the heat out, because it is necessary to pump down water in order to bring the heat up. In an experimental project in Cornwall, England, three boreholes drilled to a depth of 2 km (1¼ mi) have been interconnected with a· system of cracks, allowing water to be pumped from one borehole to another. There are plans to drill holes to three times this depth, but even at current depths the water returns to the surface hot enough to produce steam to drive turbines. Some estimates suggest that in Cornwall and other areas where the rocks are hotter at shallower depths, schemes of this kind could ultimately yield energy for Britain equivalent to 10 billion tonnes (tons) of coal.

Energy in the future

No single form of renewable energy is likely to be as dominant in the future as oil and coal have been in the past. Taken together, however, such sources could answer most of the world's needs, replacing fossil fuels as they run out or become environmentally unacceptable. If fuel-saving measures such as improved insulation and waste-heat recovery are also widely implemented, it may be that our energy needs will fall even as our prosperity grows.   MRe

HYDROELECTRIC POWER

In a typical hydroelectric power plant, a river is dammed to create a reservoir that can provide a steady and controllable supply of running water. Water from the reservoir is channelled downstream to the power plant, where it causes a turbine to rotate, which in turn drives an electric generator. The electricity generated is then stepped up by transformers at a substation to the high voltages suitable for transmission.

In areas where there are considerable fluctuations in electricity demand, pumped-storage plants may be installed. The surplus power available at off-peak periods is used to pump water to a separate reservoir. At peak times, the stored water is released to generate extra electrical power.

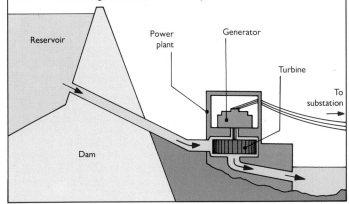

TIDAL POWER

The tidal power station at La Rance in Brittany, France, opened in 1966, consists of a barrage blocking the 750 m (2460 ft) wide estuary of the River Rance. The tidal waters are channelled through 24 tunnels in the barrage (seen in cross-section below). Each tunnel houses a reversible turbine generator that can operate efficiently both on the flood tide (when the water flow is from sea to basin) and on the ebb tide (from basin to sea). At high tide, the sluices are closed, trapping the water in the tidal basin. The water can then be released to turn the turbines when the tide is low but when demand for power is high. Each of the 24 turbines can generate up to 10 MW – the total output of the plant being sufficient to satisfy the needs of around a million consumers.

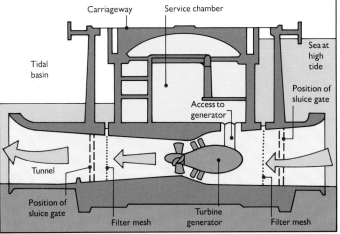

Engines

The tempo of human life, the jobs we do, and the structure of society itself were all transformed by the invention of *heat engines* – engines that use energy provided by heat to do work (see p. 24). The steam engine, invented in the 18th century, greatly extended mass production in factories, as well as providing power for railways and ships. The internal-combustion engine, invented at the end of the 19th century, greatly increased personal mobility through the motorcar. And the jet engine, the 20th century's contribution, has made travel to the ends of the Earth an everyday occurrence.

SEE ALSO

● SPACE EXPLORATION p. 18
● THERMODYNAMICS p. 24
● TRANSPORTATION pp. 342–55
● THE INDUSTRIAL REVOLUTION p. 420

Before the invention of heat engines, man depended on animals to draw the plough and provide transport, and on water-wheels and windmills to supply power for industry. But even the biggest mills generated no more than 10 horsepower – about 7 kilowatts.

The power of steam

The first engines to use steam were pumps used to lift water from mines, developed in

Charles Parsons's *Turbinia*. Parsons's triumphant demonstration of the steam turbine 1897 revolutionized marine propulsion. The turbine rapidly supplanted the reciprocating steam engine in naval craft and other ships.

THE DOUBLE-ACTING STEAM ENGINE

Diagram labels: Feedwater reservoir; Beam; Flywheel; Piston rod; Valve; Feedwater valve; Cylinder; Safety valve; Boiler; Steam; Water; Furnace; Cooling water in; Condenser; Cooling water out; Condensed water out

The principal components of a typical Watt double-acting steam engine, as built c. 1790. Steam from a boiler was introduced alternately on either side of the piston, so that the engine was 'double-acting' – both the upstroke and the downstroke were powered by steam. After passing through the cylinder, the steam was condensed to water, which was extracted by means of an air pump. As the steam condensed, a partial vacuum was created in the part of the cylinder into which the piston was moving. Thus – although the steam pressure in Watt's engines did not exceed 1½ atmospheres – the relative pressure difference within the cylinder increased the effective power of the engine.

England in 1698 by a military engineer, Captain Thomas Savery (c. 1650–1715), and improved in 1712 by a Devon black-smith, Thomas Newcomen (1663–1729). In Newcomen's atmospheric engines, steam from a boiler was admitted to the lower part of a cylinder, so driving a tightly fitting piston upwards. The steam was then condensed (turned back into water) by cooling the cylinder itself, thus creating a partial vacuum and allowing atmospheric pressure to force the piston down in the power stroke. The piston was attached to a beam pivoted in the centre, the other end of which was connected to the pumping rod.

The most significant improvements to the design of steam engines were made in the second half of the 18th century by the Scottish inventor James Watt (1736–1819). Watt's first and most important step was taken in 1769, with the introduction into Newcomen's basic design of a condenser separate from the cylinder. This meant that the cylinder did not need to be alternately heated and cooled; the result was a dramatic reduction in fuel consumption and thus in operating costs.

In 1781 Watt's invention of the so-called 'sun-and-planet' gear allowed the reciprocating (up-and-down) motion of the cross-beam to be used to drive a wheel. In the following year, Watt improved the design of his engine still further by making it double-acting (see diagram).

Steam engines were applied first in industry – mining, manufacturing and textiles – and then in transport. By the early 19th century, the first commercially successful steamboats, the *Charlotte Dundas* and the larger *Clermont*, were operating in Scotland and New York State respectively. By this time Richard Trevithick (1771–1833), a Cornish engineer, had built steam engines operating at much higher pressures than Watt's. He installed one of his engines in a locomotive that could pull a load of 10 tonnes (tons) on a cast-iron tramway between Penydarran Ironworks and the Glamorganshire Canal in Wales,

at a speed of 8 km/h (5 mph). The irresisible rise of steam had begun.

Today the only important form of stea power is the *steam turbine*. Instead driving a piston (in a reciprocatin motion) the steam in a turbine expand past a series of sets of blades mounted on single axle, generating power withou vibration. It was developed by Charl Parsons (1854–1931), an engineer fro Newcastle, whose triumph came at th Naval Review at Spithead in 1897. H little yacht *Turbinia* wove its way in an out of the ponderous warships at th unprecedented speed of 34 knots or km/h (39 mph).

Steam turbines found their ideal functio in generating electricity. Fed by stea from coal, oil or nuclear boilers, an attached directly to alternators, hug steam turbines produce almost all th electricity we use (see p. 304).

Petrol and gas engines

In steam engines the fuel is burnt outsid the engine – they are external-combustio engines. But *internal-combustion engin* – in which the fuel is burnt inside th cylinder, expanding to drive the piston have proved even more versatile. The combination of lightness and power mad possible the motorcar, the aeroplane, th tractor and the tank.

The first practical internal-combustio engine was built in 1860 by a Belgia inventor, Étienne Lenoir (1822–1900). ran on coal gas, had a single cylinder, an consumed a lot of fuel. A much bett engine was built in 1876 by the Germa engineer Nikolaus August Otto (1832–9 who re-invented the four-stroke princip (or Otto cycle) first put forward in 18 but subsequently forgotten. The *fou stroke engine* has had a greater impa han any other type of engine, and is used o drive most of the cars on the road today see box).

The *two-stroke engine* is a simpler version f the four-stroke. It dispenses with valves nd uses the rotation of the crankshaft nside a pressurized crankcase to force he fuel into the cylinder. It has essenially the same ignition system as the our-stroke, however, and it too is fuelled y petrol and air (although it requires a roportion of oil in the fuel). Such engines till find uses, for instance in some motorikes and in chainsaws.

Some engines dispense with spark plugs ltogether, relying on the increase in emperature caused by the compression troke to ignite the mixture. They are alled compression-ignition engines, or *diesel engines*, after their inventor Rudolf Diesel (1858–1913), a German engineer. Air is fed into the cylinder, and comressed so that it reaches a temperature higher than the ignition temperature of the fuel. The fuel is then injected by a pump, and ignites. More economical than petrol engines, they are used in ships, trucks, taxis and increasingly in private cars.

Like the steam engine, the internalcombustion engine also has a turbine equivalent – the *gas-turbine* (or *jet*) *engine*

THE FOUR-STROKE ENGINE

In the four-stroke (or Otto) cycle, the piston makes four movements in each power cycle. Most cars have at least four cylinders linked to the same crankshaft, both cylinders and crankshaft being set within a heavy cast-iron cylinder block. The crankshaft also drives a camshaft, which opens and closes the valves at the top of each cylinder in the correct sequence. The four cylinders fire in turn, usually in the order 1–3–4–2, so that there is a power stroke for every half-revolution of the crankshaft.

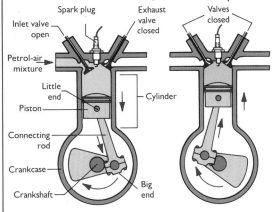
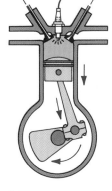
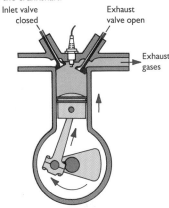

I. The induction stroke. The piston moves down as the crankshaft is turned (by the starter motor, in a car), causing a reduction in pressure inside the cylinder. The partial vacuum thus created draws petrol and air (mixed in the carburettor or by a fuel-injection system) through the open inlet valve into the cylinder.

2. The compression stroke. The fuel-air mixture is compressed as the piston ascends with both valves closed.

3. The power stroke. The mixture is ignited by the spark plug, timed to produce a brief spark at the top of the compression stroke. The piston is driven down as the burning fuel expands.

4. The exhaust stroke. The exhaust valve opens and the piston rises, expelling the burnt mixture from the cylinder to make room for fresh fuel on the next induction stroke.

REFRIGERATION

The operation of a domestic refrigerator is based on the fact that the working fluid – the *refrigerant* – becomes cooler as it expands and changes from liquid to vapour while circulating through pipes within the cold box. As it does so, it takes in heat from the warmer air within the fridge, so cooling the interior.

The refrigerant – now vapour – is withdrawn by a pump. The pump then compresses the refrigerant, so raising its temperature above that of the room and allowing it to transfer heat through a heat exchanger into the air outside the fridge. Becoming liquid again as it cools, the refrigerant is then ready to pass into the cold box to repeat the cycle.

This system – the *vapour-compression cycle* – is the basis of most domestic and industrial refrigeration. A commonly used refrigerant is the chlorofluorocarbon (CFC) Freon-12. Otherwise inert and ideally suited for refrigeration and other uses, this and other CFCs react with ozone and are responsible for depleting the ozone layer (see p. 300).

(see box). Very high speeds and temperatures are reached in the operation of such engines, making great demands on the materials used.

The first efficient gas turbines were installed at an oil refinery in the USA in 1936 by the Swiss firm Brown Boveri. In Britain Frank Whittle (1907–) realized that the gas turbine could be used to power aircraft if the exhaust gases were forced through a nozzle to produce a powerful jet. The first aircraft powered by jet engines were flying by the end of World War II, and the jet has gone on to transform air travel (see pp. 348–9).

Rocket engines

There is an easier way to produce a jet – by burning fuel in a container with a single nozzle through which the exhaust is driven. This is the principle of the rocket engine, first demonstrated as long ago as the year 1200 by Chinese and Mongolian soldiers. The first long-range rocket, the V-2, was developed by a team led by Wernher von Braun (1912–77) and used by the Germans to bombard London and Antwerp during 1944 and 1945.

Rocket fuels may be either solids that burn steadily rather than exploding, or liquids (such as liquid hydrogen and oxygen) that react with each other. Unlike jet engines, rockets need no external source of oxygen, so they can work in space.   NHa

---

THE JET ENGINE

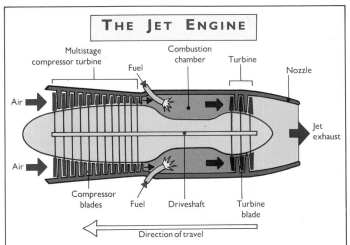

The *turbojet* (above) is the simplest form of gas-turbine (or jet) engine. Forward thrust is created by the rapid expulsion of high-pressure exhaust gases through the nozzle at the rear of the unit. The compressor turbine, initially set in motion by an electric motor, acts like a series of fans to compress air drawn in at the front of the engine. The hot compressed air passes into the combustion chambers, where it is mixed with fuel (kerosene) and ignited. Once ignited, the temperature within the engine – typically in excess of 450 °C (840 °F) – is sufficient to keep the fuel-air mixture burning. Before exiting through the tail nozzle, the exhaust gases pass through a second turbine, which itself drives the compressor turbine via the driveshaft.

The basic turbojet has been modified in several ways. In a *turboprop* engine, the driveshaft is used to rotate a conventional propeller mounted in front of the compressor. The *turbofan* engine, used to power the biggest aircraft, has a large fan in the air intake at the front of the engine. This fan takes in extra air, most of which is channelled around the combustion chambers and out through the tail nozzle, so increasing efficiency and reducing noise.

Oil and Gas

For hundreds of millions of years before man first trod the Earth, plants and simple single-celled organisms had flourished. After they had died and decayed, they gradually formed deposits of coal, oil and natural gas – the fossil fuels upon which modern society largely relies. We live, quite literally, upon the reconstituted rubbish of the past.

Oil and natural gas are hydrocarbons – organic compounds built from just two elements, hydrogen and carbon (see p. 52). Hydrocarbons range from light gases like methane (CH_4) to heavy solids like asphalt. Crude oil is a mixture of hydrocarbons – some light, some heavy – and is often found in conjunction with natural gas. Three types of rock are needed to form an oil reserve: the sedimentary rocks in which the hydrocarbons form; porous rocks that can store the oil and gas like a sponge; and an impervious layer of rock over the top, ideally in the form of a dome, to form a trap.

Finding oil

Three surveying techniques are used to pinpoint areas where oil and gas are likely to have formed. In *gravimetric* and *magnetic surveys*, small variations in the force of gravity or in the Earth's magnetic field give clues to the type of rock in an area. *Seismic surveys* use shock waves, usually created by detonating small explosions (see p. 332). These waves are reflected from the various layers of rock beneath the ground and measured at the surface. Computer analysis of the reflected waves enables a cross-section of the subterranean rocks to be drawn.

Drilling for oil

When a likely area has been identified, exploratory drilling begins. The first oil well was drilled in 1859 in the USA, at Titusville, western Pennsylvania, by Colonel Edwin Drake. He was attracted to the spot by a stream whose water was often contaminated by oil seeping to the surface. He found oil 21 m (69 ft) down, using a drill that pounded away at the ground in an up-and-down motion. Today's drilling rigs work by rotary action and must drill much deeper to strike oil, often to depths of several kilometres (see diagram).

If economic amounts of oil are found, production wells are drilled. From a single derrick, many holes can be drilled, fanning outwards to reach all corners of the reserve. This is done with a tool called the *whipstock*, which forces the flexible drillstring to bend slightly. A large field may be drilled from several different platforms. Each hole is lined with steel casing embedded in concrete, and explosives are used to punch holes through the casing, to allow the oil to get into the hollow casing from the surrounding rock.

Once the well has been drilled, an arrangement of pipework and valves – called a 'christmas tree' because of its shape – is installed at the surface to control the flow. The pressure of the oil may be enough to drive it to the surface, but pumps can also be used. As pressure falls, it may be artificially increased by pumping water down other holes. Even with such techniques no more than 30 to 40% of the oil in place can be recovered.

Production and transportation

Oil is seldom found exactly where it is needed. In most cases, the biggest oil-producing countries – principally in the Middle East, Africa and Latin America –

ROTARY DRILLING RIG

Modern drills work by rotary action. The rock is cut by the *drill bit*, which is attached to a *drillstring* made up of 9 m (30 ft) sections of steel piping. The top piece of the string – the *kelly* – is usually square-shaped, and fits into the *rotary table*, which is powered by a motor and causes the whole drillstring to rotate. In order to concentrate weight on the bit, an extra-heavy section of piping called the *drill collar* is fitted immediately above the bit. As the well gets deeper, fresh sections of pipe are added to the top of the drillstring.

The chips of fragmented rock are carried to the surface by pumping 'mud' (actually a mixture of water, clay and added minerals) through the hollow drillstring. The mud is forced out through the bit and returns to the surface, where it is filtered before being recycled. The mud helps to keep the bit cool, and its weight prevents blowouts and gushers – uncontrollable escapes of oil and gas – if the drill should encounter a region of oil and gas under high pressure.

Drilling speeds vary with the type of rock, from 60 m (200 ft) an hour in soft shales to only 6 m (20 ft) a day in the hardest rocks. When the bit is blunt, the whole drillstring must be removed section by section, and a new bit fitted. The process of removal and reassembly can take as long as 10 hours if the well is deep.

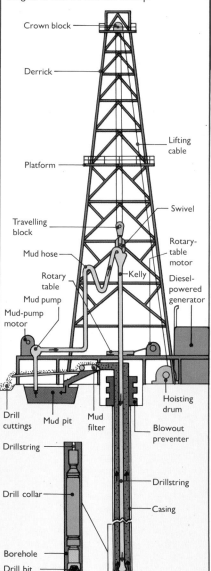

OIL AND WORLD POLITICS

During the 19th century coal was the dominant fuel, but in the 20th century coal has been eclipsed by oil. Although renewable sources of energy are becoming increasingly significant, the dominance of fossil fuels in the global picture is still largely undiminished (see pie chart, p. 306). Oil and natural gas meet about half the world's energy needs, while coal still accounts for more than a quarter. By contrast, nuclear power provides just 5% of global requirements. In addition, oil is the principal raw material from which plastics and polymers are produced (see pp. 316–17). Without it, modern society could not long continue to flourish.

During the 1970s the producer nations, particularly in the Middle East, realized that their mineral wealth was being used up by the developed economies of the USA, Europe and Japan, and that the price these countries were paying did not reflect the true value of the product. The oil-producing nations therefore got together to form OPEC (Organization of Petroleum Exporting Countries; see p. 287) – a cartel, or 'producers' club', intended to gain a greater share of the wealth derived from oil for those who were fortunate enough to have territory containing it.

In 1973 and again in 1979, OPEC was strong enough to enforce huge increases in the price of oil, placing a big burden on the world economy and sparking off world-wide inflation (see also p. 278). The extra burden imposed by higher oil prices led to a slump in industrial output and world trade, and although the oil producers became rich, the fall in the value of the dollars they had earned eliminated much of the gain. Today the growth of oil production outside OPEC has reduced the organization's hold over the market, and oil prices have fallen back to values lower in real terms than they were before the second 'oil shock' of 1979.

recovered. The processing of gas involves separating it from any liquids and 'sweetening' it by removing gases such as hydrogen sulphide and carbon dioxide. The end product consists mostly of methane (more than 80%) combined with smaller amounts of ethane, propane and butane (see p. 52).

A diminishing resource

How long will oil last? Although very large, supplies cannot be inexhaustible. The difficulty is that we cannot simply divide the world's known reserves by its annual production to work out how many years' supply is left. If we do that, the figure comes to no more than 20 years or so. In reality, however, as stocks diminish and prices rise, many new sources of oil are discovered, always keeping reserves ahead of production. While geologists accept that there must be a limit eventually, it remains a long way off. So far we have used no more than a quarter, and perhaps as little as a tenth, of all the oil that can be extracted.   NHa

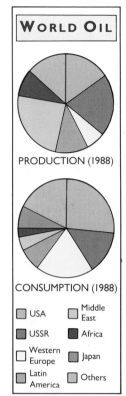

WORLD OIL

PRODUCTION (1988)

CONSUMPTION (1988)

- USA
- USSR
- Western Europe
- Latin America
- Middle East
- Africa
- Japan
- Others

---

are not themselves major consumers, and are therefore able to export much or most of the oil they produce (see pie charts). Russia and the USA also possess large oil reserves, but both are major consumers as well, the latter being by far the greatest single consumer. At the other extreme, Japan – another big consumer – has virtually no reserves of its own. This geographical imbalance between production and consumption has meant that the transportation of oil has become a vast business in itself.

The easiest way to transport oil overland is through pipes. Pipelines are made up of welded steel sections, and may be up to 1.2m (4 ft) in diameter. Pumping stations are installed at regular intervals to maintain pressure. For sea transport, huge tankers are used (see p. 344). Natural gas can also be carried in ships, if it is first liquefied by refrigeration.

Oil refining

To turn crude oil into useful products it must be refined. Two basic processes are used. *Fractional distillation* allows lighter fractions to be separated from heavier ones (see diagram). *Catalytic cracking* uses heat, pressure, and certain catalysts to convert or 'split' some of the heavier fractions obtained by distillation into lighter, more useful ones. Today the most valuable product is petrol (gasoline used to drive the world's cars, so a growing proportion of each barrel is converted into that.

Gas

Natural gas is often found together with oil, because it is formed in the same way and collects in the same kind of geological formations. The development of long-distance pipelines and ships that carry liquefied natural gas has greatly increased the market for gas, which is both an excellent fuel and a useful raw material for the chemical industry (see p. 320). Gas flows more readily than crude oil, so as much as 80% of the gas in place may be

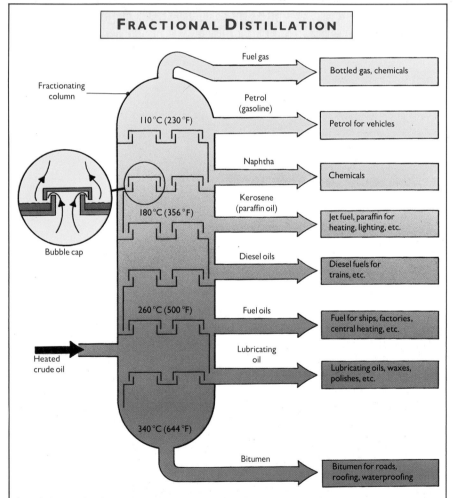

FRACTIONAL DISTILLATION

Fractionating column

Bubble cap

Heated crude oil

110 °C (230 °F)

180 °C (356 °F)

260 °C (500 °F)

340 °C (644 °F)

Fuel gas → Bottled gas, chemicals

Petrol (gasoline) → Petrol for vehicles

Naphtha → Chemicals

Kerosene (paraffin oil) → Jet fuel, paraffin for heating, lighting, etc.

Diesel oils → Diesel fuels for trains, etc.

Fuel oils → Fuel for ships, factories, central heating, etc.

Lubricating oil → Lubricating oils, waxes, polishes, etc.

Bitumen → Bitumen for roads, roofing, waterproofing

In order to yield useful products, the various liquids and dissolved solids of which crude oil is composed must be separated. The principal method by which this is achieved is fractional distillation. Crude oil is heated in a furnace to around 350 °C (660 °F), and the oil vapours passed into the lower part of a *fractionating column*, a cylindrical tower about 50 m (165 ft) high, in which 30 or so perforated trays are placed at regular intervals.

As the vapours rise up the column, the temperature falls. Constituents (or *fractions*) of the oil with high boiling points, such as lubricating oils, condense lower down the column, while fractions that boil at lower temperatures, such as petrol, continue to rise until they reach a level cool enough for them to condense.

Modern distillation units generally have a capacity well in excess of 100 000 barrels a day. The *barrel* is the unit most commonly used in the oil industry and is equivalent to 160 litres (42 US gallons, or 35 imperial gallons).

SEE ALSO

- ENERGY pp. 304-7
- CHEMICALS AND BIOTECHNOLOGY p. 320
- SEEING THE INVISIBLE p. 332
- SHIPS 2 p. 344

Mining, Minerals and Metals

The Earth's crust, a thin layer that accounts for only about 0.6% of the planet's total volume (see p. 76), provides the fuels, metals and minerals upon which developed societies depend. The quantities of most metals in the crust are small – only iron, aluminium and magnesium are really plentiful. We are able to extract them only because they are not evenly distributed but occur in local concentrations where mining is economically possible. There are far greater concentrations of some metals, such as iron and nickel, in the Earth's mantle and core, but for the moment they are beyond our reach.

Longwall mining (right) is more expensive than opencast methods but is more suitable for deeper deposits, such as those commonly found in Europe. Huge cutting machines pass along the face of the seam, shearing off a thickness of up to 1 m (3 ¼ ft) of material at a time.

The first metals to be used by man were those that occurred in their natural state and appeared in outcrops on the surface – gold, silver, iron (in the form of fallen meteorites) and copper. However, supplies of elemental iron and copper soon ran out, and during the Bronze and Iron Ages it was discovered how to extract metals from their ores, in which they are chemically combined with other elements, most often oxygen or sulphur. A variety of techniques have been developed for finding and then recovering ores and other minerals.

Mining methods

There are basically two kinds of mine – underground mines and opencast (or surface) mines (see diagram). In an underground mine, horizontal tunnels several kilometres long are cut to get at a seam containing the desired mineral. Various techniques are then used to remove the mined material from the seam. In *room-and-pillar mining*, a common technique in coal mines in the USA, the coal is broken up by means of explosives and drills, and then removed to form large underground caverns, with the roof supported by pillars of unmined material. *Longwall mining* is more suitable for deeper deposits, such as those generally found in Europe. A working face of 100 m (320 ft) or more is cut by huge machines, and the coal is transported back along roadways by automatic conveyors. Powered roof supports are used to prevent falls of rock at the working face. Some deep mines are very deep indeed: gold is mined in South Africa at depths of more than 3500 m (11 500 ft), where the temperature of the rock may reach 49 °C (120 °F).

In opencast mining, the desired material is first exposed by removing any overlying material (the *overburden*) by means of scrapers, excavators, or draglines (huge buckets pulled along by steel cables). Relatively soft materials, such as coal, may then be removed by draglines, while for harder minerals the rock must first be broken up by blasting. In deep surface mines, such as the copper mines of Chile and Bingham Canyon in the USA, the ore is dug out in a series of terraces, or 'benches', that gradually expand and

COAL

Coal is a carbon-based mineral that formed over many millions of years as a result of the gradual compacting of partially decomposed plant matter. Three basic types of coal are found: lignite, bituminous coal and anthracite. Lignite (brown coal) has the lowest heat value, since it was formed more recently and contains less carbon and more water than the other varieties. About half the coal mined is used for generating electricity (see p. 304), with another quarter going to the steel industry as coking coal. The remainder is used in other industries or for home heating. In the past, coal was the chief raw material for the plastics industry, but in this function it has been largely superseded by crude oil.

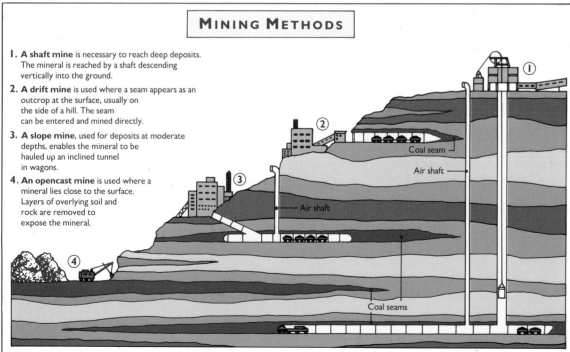

MINING METHODS

1. **A shaft mine** is necessary to reach deep deposits. The mineral is reached by a shaft descending vertically into the ground.

2. **A drift mine** is used where a seam appears as an outcrop at the surface, usually on the side of a hill. The seam can be entered and mined directly.

3. **A slope mine**, used for deposits at moderate depths, enables the mineral to be hauled up an inclined tunnel in wagons.

4. **An opencast mine** is used where a mineral lies close to the surface. Layers of overlying soil and rock are removed to expose the mineral.

Coal seam

Air shaft

Air shaft

Air shaft

Coal seams

The mining method chosen to extract coal or other minerals depends principally on the depth of the seam or deposit. **Opencast mines** (also called **open-pit** or **strip mines**) are appropriate for deposits close to the surface. Various types of **underground mine** – **drift**, **slope** or **shaft mines** – are suitable for deeper deposits.

parts per million of the Earth's crust, and lead only 20 parts per million (see table). But the availability of metals does not depend so much on their abundance as on how easy it is to find and exploit their ores.

Sometimes bodies of ore advertise their presence by appearing at the surface, perhaps where erosion has scoured the rocks on a cliff face. Hidden reserves can be found by *magnetic* or *gravimetric* surveys – a mountain rich in iron ore will affect the Earth's magnetic field and the force of gravity in the immediate vicinity. Seismic and satellite surveying and knowledge of the local geology may also indicate the likelihood of a particular ore occurring (see pp. 332–3).

The mere presence of an ore – even a valuable one – is no guarantee that it can be exploited economically. If such a deposit is too far from its final market, it may not be able to compete with poorer ores that are more favourably placed. In Brazil there are huge iron-ore reserves, amounting to some 50 000 million tonnes (tons), but because of their remoteness they have only begun to be used since the early 1970s.

Will minerals run out?

As the poorer nations of the world strive to catch up with the rest, the consumption of all metals and minerals is rising fast. Will there be enough to go round? A number of studies carried out since the early 1960s have cast doubt on this. While iron and aluminium are abundant, there are many important metals – lead, zinc, tin, silver, platinum and mercury – the supplies of which seem less certain. In many cases, as one metal becomes scarcer, it can be replaced with another, or with a plastic or composite material, but this is not always possible. For instance, there is as yet no substitute for silver in photographic emulsions or for platinum as an industrial catalyst.

At the same time it is important to remember that in mining we have only begun – quite literally – to scratch the surface. While many of the richest sources of metals have already been exhausted, higher prices and better technology make it feasible to extract metals economically from poorer ores and to tap less accessible deposits. Few mining engineers or geologists believe that there is any real danger of running out of important minerals in the immediate future.   NHa

Opencast mining (left) is now used to obtain the bulk of most minerals – although the environmental damage is severe. At Bingham Canyon near Salt Lake City in the USA (seen here), the scale of the operation is vast: 38 electric shovels, 62 locomotives, 1268 wagons and 28 tonnes (tons) of explosives are used to remove 96 000 tonnes of ore (containing only 1% copper) and 225 000 tonnes of waste every day.

SEE ALSO

● ELEMENTS p. 42
● THE EARTH'S STRUCTURE p. 76
● THE FORMATION OF ROCKS p. 84
● ENERGY 1 p. 304
● OIL AND GAS p. 310
● THE INDUSTRIAL REVOLUTION p. 420

METALS

Element (mineral)	Abundance in crust (parts per million)	Major uses
Aluminium (bauxite)	81000	Conductors, aircraft, ships, cars, foil
Chromium (chromite)	under 700	Chromium-plating, stainless steel
Copper (many)	100	Conductors, alloys (brass, bronze), coinage, plumbing
Gold (naturally occurring)	under 0.005	Source of value, jewellery, some electronic uses
Iron (see p. 314)	50 000	Structures, machines
Lead (galena)	20	Batteries, roofing, radiological protection
Magnesium (magnesite, etc.)	25 000	Low-density alloys for aircraft, machinery, etc.
Mercury (cinnabar)	under 1	Explosives, scientific instruments, dentistry
Nickel (garnierite, pentlandite)	under 80	Nickel-plating, steel alloys, gas-turbine engines, coinage
Platinum (naturally occurring, sperrylite)	under 0.005	Catalyst in chemical processes and in car exhausts
Silver (many)	under 1	Jewellery, silverware, photographic emulsions
Tin (cassiterite)	1.5	Tin-plating, alloys (bronze and pewter)
Tungsten (wolframite, scheelite)	1.5	Lamp filaments, electronics, steel alloys, cutting tools
Uranium (pitchblende)	under 7	Nuclear power stations
Zinc (sphalerite)	under 80	Alloys (brass), galvanizing steel

enlarge the pit. Roadways spiralling to the surface are provided for trucks to carry away the ore (see photo).

Alluvial mining, often used to recover tin and gold, makes use of the erosion of ores by water. Carried down by the flow of water, the ores (or native metal in the case of gold) can be recovered from the bottom of lakes and rivers by dredging or suction. The most primitive version of this is the panning technique used by gold prospectors. In Malaysia, huge dredges are used to pick up the tin-bearing gravels from the bottom of lakes.

An unusual method is used for mining sulphur, an element vital to the chemical industry (see p. 320). Developed by the American engineer Herman Frasch (1851–1914) at the end of the 19th century, the system uses three tubes of different diameters, one inside another, that are drilled down into reserves of naturally occurring sulphur. Water under pressure and at a temperature of 160 °C (320 °F) is pumped down the outer pipe, melting the sulphur. Compressed air is then pumped down the centre tube, driving the molten sulphur up through the middle tube. Sulphur obtained in this way is 99% pure. Today a considerable proportion of the world's sulphur is produced as a by-product of the purification of natural gas.

Common salt (sodium chloride) is found as salt deposits and in sea water. The salt deposits can be mined, while salt is recovered from sea water by evaporation in shallow pools. Magnesium chloride is also found in sea water in small but consistent amounts, and is extracted by reacting the sea water with lime, causing the magnesium to be deposited as a precipitate.

Discovering minerals

Fortunately for mankind, metals and minerals occur unevenly. Copper, tin, nickel, zinc, lead, mercury, silver and gold – all vital to our industrial society – are in fact extremely rare. Copper makes up only 100

GEMS

Hundreds of stones are mined as gems. The most important is diamond (a form of carbon) because its great hardness makes it important for tools in industry. The major source of diamonds is South Africa, where they are recovered from rock by deep mining. Where gemstones have been eroded from rocks by water, they may be found in gravel deposits. Sapphires and rubies, for instance, occur in such deposits in Sri Lanka.

Rough and polished diamonds

Iron and Steel

The Iron Age began in the Near East in the 2nd millennium BC, and we still live in it today. Iron and steel account for almost 95% of the total tonnage of all metal production. Ships and trains, cars and trucks, bridges and buildings – all these and thousands of things besides depend on the strength, flexibility and toughness of steel.

Iron is extracted industrially from naturally occurring ores. The two most important of these are iron oxides – hematite (Fe_2O_3) and magnetite (Fe_3O_4). Mixed with carbon and heated to 1500 °C (2730 °F), iron oxides are reduced to metallic iron, the carbon combining with the oxygen to form carbon dioxide. This process is called *smelting*. In the Middle Ages charcoal was used to provide the carbon, but in 1709 Abraham Darby (1677–1717) of Coalbrookdale in Shropshire, England, succeeded in smelting iron with coke, which could readily be produced from coal. This made possible a huge increase in iron production during the Industrial Revolution (see p. 420).

The first link in the production of iron is the *blast furnace*, in which iron ore is reduced to iron (see diagram). The biggest modern blast furnaces are huge constructions up to 30 m (100 ft) tall, with walls more than 3 m (10 ft) thick, and capable of making more than 10 000 tonnes (tons) of iron a day. The iron produced in the blast furnace is still contaminated with some residual impurities. Depending on the ore, it usually contains some 3 to 5% carbon, 1% manganese and 3% silicon.

From iron to steel

The iron tapped from a blast furnace i[s] a raw material, not a finished product. T[o] be useful, it must be converted either int[o] cast iron or into steel. *Cast iron* is pro[-] duced by remelting pig iron (iron that ha[s] been cast into moulds and allowed to coo[l]) and carefully adjusting the proportion[s] of carbon, silicon and other alloyin[g] elements (see table below). Strong an[d] resistant to wear, cast iron can b[e] machined and is easily cast into quit[e] complex shapes. The moulds into which i[t] is cast are made of sand contained i[n] moulding boxes. The shape to be cast i[s] impressed into the sand, and the molte[n] iron poured into it. When solid, the cast[-] ing is removed and the sand re-used t[o] make a fresh mould.

The great bulk of the iron produced in [a] blast furnace is converted into steel, b[y] greatly reducing the carbon content. A[?] way of removing carbon economicall[y] from pig iron was discovered in 1857 by[?]

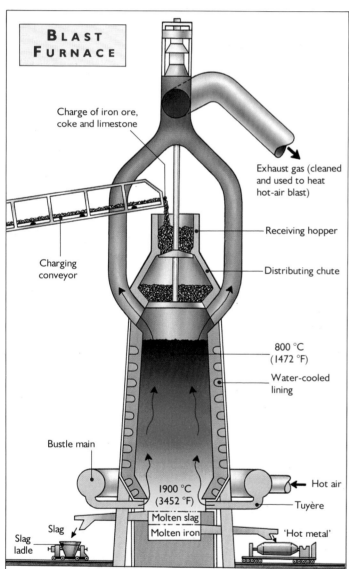

BLAST FURNACE

- Charge of iron ore, coke and limestone
- Charging conveyor
- Exhaust gas (cleaned and used to heat hot-air blast)
- Receiving hopper
- Distributing chute
- 800 °C (1472 °F)
- Water-cooled lining
- Bustle main
- 1900 °C (3452 °F)
- Hot air
- Tuyère
- Molten slag
- Molten iron
- Slag
- Slag ladle
- 'Hot metal'

A mixture of fused ore and coke (known as *sinter*) and limestone is poured into the top of the furnace, while a blast of hot dry air is blown through the mixture from below. The coke burns at a high temperature and reacts with the oxygen in the air to produce carbon monoxide. This reduces the ore to liquid iron, which flows down to the bottom of the furnace. The limestone reacts with impurities in the ore – principally silicon from sand, clay and stones – and prevents them from contaminating the iron. Instead the silica and limestone form a *slag*, which is lighter than molten iron and floats on the surface.

From time to time liquid iron (known as 'hot metal') is tapped off from a hole at the bottom, gushing out as a white-hot stream. The slag is drained off at regular intervals from another hole higher up. The iron-making process is continuous and may carry on without a break for 10 years or more, until the furnace's heat-resistant lining begins to deteriorate and has to be replaced.

Electric-arc furnaces (below) take a charge consisting entirely of cold scrap – hot metal is not used. Because very precise control of the composition of the final product is possible, such furnaces are generally used to make the more expensive steels, including alloy and stainless steels. Modern arc furnaces produce up to 150 tonnes (tons) of steel in less than 1½ hours.

hardened by heating it to red heat – around 850 °C (1560 °F) – and then quenching it in water, but such a steel is also brittle. The hardness can largely be retained and the brittleness reduced by a second heating to a lower temperature – to around 250 °C (480 °F). The steel is then allowed to cool in air. Such steel is said to be *tempered*.

Alloying steel with other elements in addition to carbon is also important. A steel containing 3% nickel, for example, is immensely tough, and is used for gears and shafts that have to take a lot of strain. Steels containing up to 13% manganese have very hard edges, and are used for items such as rock-breaking machinery. The metal molybdenum is added to alloy steels to reduce brittleness. *Stainless steels*, containing around 14% chromium and sometimes nickel as well, do not rust because of the formation of an impermeable oxide layer on their surface. Such steels are now widely used for cutlery, kitchen sinks and the cladding of buildings.
NHa

Molten steel (left) is formed into standard basic shapes, such as billets (bars) or slabs, before being rolled or formed into products for sale. In the past, all molten metal passed through an intermediate ingot stage before being reheated and rolled, but the development of continuous casting has allowed the molten metal to be poured directly into a casting machine to produce billets or slabs.

SEE ALSO

- METALS p. 50
- MINING, MINERALS AND METALS p. 312
- THE INDUSTRIAL REVOLUTION p. 420

the English engineer Henry Bessemer (1813–98). In the *Bessemer process*, air blown through the molten iron combined with some of the carbon, carrying it away as carbon monoxide and carbon dioxide. It also oxidized some of the iron, which then combined with the silicon and manganese to form a slag. After just 15 minutes, several hundred tonnes (tons) of iron had been converted into steel. The entire converter rotated on an axle like a cement mixer to pour out the molten steel.

A much slower and more controllable process was invented in the 1860s by a number of engineers – the *open-hearth process*. In this process gas from low-grade coal was used to heat pig iron in a shallow furnace. The chemical changes were the same as in the Bessemer converter, but the process had the advantage that scrap steel could be added to the mixture. The process took up to 12 hours to produce steel, allowing very careful control of the final composition.

Today both the Bessemer and the open-hearth processes have been superseded in most countries by a process that combines the merits of both. In the *L-D process* (short for Linz-Donawitz), a jet of almost pure oxygen is blown through a lance onto the surface of molten iron. The process is quick and can absorb up to 20% scrap, while producing steel of very high quality. The addition of lime to the oxygen enables iron of higher phosphorus content to be converted, and in this form the process is known as the *basic oxygen furnace*.

For the more expensive steels, including alloy and stainless steels, *electric-arc furnaces* are used (see photo). Heat is provided by three carbon electrodes, which are lowered into a mixture of scrap and alloying additions. Silicon, manganese and phosphorus are removed as slag, and

carbon is removed by adding some iron ore, which reacts just as in the blast furnace. The fact that an electric-arc furnace can melt a charge consisting entirely of scrap is a big advantage in developed countries where recycled steel makes up a large proportion of total production (see box).

Types of steel

Steel is sold in the form of cast slabs, or rolled into plates, strips, rods (for nails, screws and wire) or beams (for buildings, bridges and other constructional uses). To make it suitable for a particular use, the characteristics of a steel can be altered by a number of processes, including heat treatment and alloying.

Type of steel	Carbon content (%)	Typical uses
Mild steel	0.08	Car bodies, tin cans
	0.2	Buildings, bridges, ships
Medium-carbon	0.25–0.45	Gun barrels, railway wheels
High-carbon	0.45–1.5	Tools, scissors, cutlery
Cast iron	2.5–4.5	Machine tools, engine blocks, ironmongery

The most important factor in any steel is the carbon content. High-carbon steels are harder and stronger, but they are also more brittle and cannot be welded. For adequate weldability, carbon contents below 0.2% are needed. The precise characteristics of any steel also depend on heat treatment, which determines the microstructure of the steel. Steel can be

SCRAP

The availability of recyclable scrap steel is an important factor in determining the most suitable kind of steel-making process. In a typical developed economy, there is so much scrap available that as much as half of any newly manufactured steel object may consist of recycled scrap: new cars have old cars driving around inside them. In developing economies, where there is less old steel around, a much lower proportion of scrap is used.

Not all scrap, however, comes from products that have reached the end of their life. A lot of scrap is produced in the steelworks itself, from material that is not up to the required standard, while offcuts from industry are returned to steel mills for reprocessing.

Rubber and Plastics

The natural product of a tropical tree and the man-made creations of a chemical factory could hardly have more different origins. But rubber and plastics play similar and equally important roles in modern life.

Rubber was known to the Mayas and Aztecs in Pre-Columbian America. They heated the latex – a whitish milky fluid – that flowed from the bark of the rubber tree until it coagulated. From it they made balls with which they played games. The Spanish, who conquered most of South America, used rubber to waterproof soldiers' cloaks, but it was a Frenchman, Charles de la Condamine (1701–74), who first brought it back to Europe.

SEE ALSO

● CHEMISTRY pp. 52–7
● TEXTILES p. 318
● CHEMICALS AND BIOTECHNOLOGY p. 320

Vulcanization of rubber

Beyond its curiosity value, raw rubber

Rubber-tapping. Although millions of tonnes of natural rubber are produced annually, the substance from which it is made – latex – is still tapped from rubber trees in the traditional way. A diagonal cut is made into the bark of the tree a metre or so from the ground. A spout is then driven into the lower end of the cut, and a cup is attached to catch the latex as it flows out.

had relatively few uses. It was given its name by the chemist Joseph Priestley (chiefly known as the discoverer of oxygen), who observed in 1770 how useful it was for rubbing out pencil marks. In 1823 the Scottish chemist Charles Macintosh (1766–1843) made his name immortal (though universally misspelt) by inventing the 'mackintosh' – a waterproof raincoat made from a fabric produced by sandwiching a layer of sheet rubber between two pieces of cloth.

It was a Philadelphia hardware merchant, Charles Goodyear (1800–60), who transformed the future of rubber. Looking for a way of preventing it going sticky when hot and hard when cold, he mixed it with sulphur and heated it. The result was a far more stable and useful product – tougher and more consistent in its properties, yet retaining all the resilience of untreated rubber. The name *vulcanization* was given to this process. Vulcanized rubber could be used for a whole new range of applications – conveyor belts, hoses, valves, insulation of electrical cables, and, on the horizon – the biggest use of all – pneumatic tyres for road vehicles. By the end of the 19th century Michelin in France, Dunlop in England and Goodrich in the USA were all producing tyres for the motorcar.

Rubber production

Although other plants have sometimes been used, most of the world's rubber originates in cultivated plantations of *Hevea brasiliensis*, a tree native to Brazil. Seeds from this tree were brought to England in 1876 and exported to parts of the British Empire where the climate was suitably tropical and humid. Today more than 4 million tonnes (tons) of rubber is produced annually, 90% of it from Southeast Asia, principally from Malaysia.

Latex is still tapped from rubber trees in the traditional manner (see photo). At the factory the latex is first caused to coagulate (usually by the addition of chemicals) and then masticated – kneaded and worked between steel rollers rotating in opposite directions – to break it down and make it flexible. Next, the rubber is mixed with various compounding agents to improve its performance. Carbon black may be added to reinforce the rubber, while antioxidants are incorporated to prolong its life. The colour of the rubber may be altered by adding various pigments. The sulphur for vulcanizing is also added at this stage. The rubber is then shaped on a variety of machines into its final form, and only then is it vulcanized,

usually by heating it in a metal mould. For tyres, the final shaping and vulcanization are carried out at the same time by applying heat and pressure in metal moulds.

Rubber is used in a vast array of different products, from delicate surgical devices at one extreme to huge conveyor belts at the other. Artificial substitutes for rubber have been made, but for all but a few specialist purposes they are not as good as natural rubber.

The first plastics

Chemically, rubber is a polymer – a compound containing large molecules that are formed by the bonding of many smaller, simpler units, repeated over and over again. The same bonding principle – *polymerization* – underlies the creation of a huge range of plastics by the chemical industry.

The first plastic was developed as a result of a competition in the USA. In the 1860s $10 000 was offered to anybody who could replace ivory – supplies of which were declining – with something equally good as a material for making billiard balls. The prize was won by John Wesley Hyatt with a material called celluloid. *Celluloid* was made by dissolving cellulose, a carbohydrate obtained from plants, in a solution of camphor dissolved in ethanol. This new material rapidly found uses in the manufacture of products such as knife handles, detachable collars and cuffs, spectacle frames and photographic film. Without celluloid, the film industry could never have got off the ground at the end of the 19th century.

Celluloid can be repeatedly softened and reshaped by heat, and is known as a *thermoplastic*. In 1907 Leo Baekeland (1863–1944), a Belgian chemist working in the USA, invented a different kind of plastic, by causing phenol and formaldehyde to react together. Baekeland called it *Bakelite*, and it was the first of the *thermosets* – plastics that can be cast and moulded while hot but cannot be softened by heat and reshaped once they have set. Bakelite was a good insulator, and was resistant to water, acids, and moderate heat. With these properties it was soon being used in the manufacture of switches, household items such as knife handles, and electrical components for cars.

Plastics proliferate

Chemists soon began looking for other small molecules that could be strung together to make polymers. In the 1930s British chemists discovered that the gas ethylene would polymerize under heat and pressure to form a thermoplastic they called *polythene* (see photo and p. 321). *Polypropylene* followed in the 1950s. Both are used to make bottles, pipes and plastic bags. A small change in the starting material – replacing a hydrogen atom in ethylene with a chlorine atom – produced *PVC* (polyvinyl chloride), a hard, fireproof plastic suitable for drains and gutters. By adding certain chemicals, a oft form of PVC can be produced, suitable as a substitute for rubber in items such as waterproof clothing. A closely related plastic is *Teflon* or *PTFE* (polytetrafluoroethylene). It has a very low coefficient of friction, making it ideal for bearings, rollers, and non-stick frying pans.

Polystyrene, developed during the 1930s in Germany, is a clear glass-like material, used in food containers, domestic appliances and toys. Expanded polystyrene – a white rigid foam – is widely used in packaging and insulation (see photo). *Polyurethanes*, also developed in Germany, found uses as adhesives, coatings, and – in the form of rigid foams – as insulation materials. All these plastics are produced from chemicals derived from crude oil, which contains exactly the same elements – carbon and hydrogen – as many plastics.

Man-made fibres

In the 1930s the first of the man-made fibres was created – *nylon*. Its inventor was a chemist called Wallace Carothers (1896–1937), who worked for the Du Pont company in the USA. He found that under the right conditions two chemicals – hexamethylenediamine and adipic acid – would form a polymer that could be pumped out through holes and then stretched to form long glossy threads that could be woven like silk. Its first use was to make parachutes for the US armed forces in World War II. In the postwar

Low-density polythene (or polyethylene) (below) being formed into film by *extrusion* – ejection under pressure through a suitably shaped nozzle. This form of polythene is widely used for the manufacture of plastic bags and other kinds of packaging. High-density polythene, produced at lower pressures using special catalysts, is a more rigid product, and can be injection- or blow-moulded into items such as plastic kitchenware, milk crates and large drums.

years it completely replaced silk in the manufacture of stockings.

Many other synthetic fibres joined nylon, including Orlon, Acrilan, and Terylene. Today most garments are made of a blend of natural fibres, such as cotton and wool, and man-made fibres that make fabrics easier to look after (see pp. 318–19).

Plastic waste

The great strength of plastic – its indestructibility – is also something of a drawback. Beaches all over the world, even on the remotest islands, are littered with plastic bottles that nothing can destroy. Nor is it very easy to recycle plastics, as different types of plastic are often used in the same items and call for different treatments.

Plastics can be made biodegradable by incorporating into their structure a material such as starch, which is attacked by bacteria and causes the plastic to fall apart. Other materials can be incorporated that gradually decay in sunlight – although bottles made of such materials have to be stored in the dark, to ensure they do not disintegrate before they have been used.   NHa

Large blocks of expanded polystyrene being used instead of normal infill in the construction of a trunk road. The adaptability of plastics has meant that they have been able to replace traditional materials in many areas: as well as offering economies in cost and time, plastic substitutes are often more suitable for a given purpose.

Textiles

Mankind has always needed clothes, so the history of textiles is a long one. More than 3000 years before the birth of Christ, Egyptian mummies were laid in their tombs wrapped in linen, a fabric woven from flax. The Chinese were weaving delicate patterns in silk by about 1000 BC.

Raw cotton – one of the many natural fibres used in the production of textiles. Natural fibres, whether derived from plants or animals, are relatively short, and must first be spun into long strands (yarn) before being woven or knitted into fabric.

The creation of textiles requires two processes: the spinning of yarn, and the weaving of cloth. The basic principles of these two crafts have not changed since the earliest times, although the materials used have been supplemented in the 20th century by man-made fibres.

Natural fibres

Natural fibres come from a variety of sources: wool from sheep, cotton from the seed pod of the cotton plant, flax from the stem of the flax plant, silk from the delicate webs spun by silkworms fattened on the leaves of the mulberry tree. Among the more specialized fibres, the Angora goat produces mohair, while cashmere comes from the Kashmir goat. Camel hair and the fleece of the vicuña, a relative of the llama, are used in rugs and overcoats. Jute, a plant fibre, is used for making sacks and carpet backings, while hemp, another plant fibre, is used in sailcloth and canvas.

In their natural state, none of these fibres is very long. Wool fibres may be up to 20 cm (8 in) long, and flax a metre or more, but cotton fibres are rarely more than a few centimetres and are often as short as 3 mm (⅛ in). In order to make a continuous strand or *yarn*, the fibres have to be laid out in parallel lines and twisted together in the process called *spinning*.

Spinning

Having first been cleaned, the fibres are carded (laid parallel) by rolling them

Textile printing provides an alternative to weaving as a means of producing patterns on fabric. Here a sheet of cloth is seen running through a colour press, with large vats of dye standing in the foreground.

between two surfaces faced with points. Then they are combed to remove short fibres, and rolled in machines that pull out the yarn and give it a twist, which helps to hold the fibres together. Stronger yarns are created by twisting two or more yarns together, and mixtures are made by combining fibres from different sources, such as wool and polyester. Finally the finished yarn is dyed and wound on bobbins (spools) for dispatch.

Spinning was originally done on a simple *spindle* – basically a hanging stick, weighted to make it spin round. A measure of mechanization was achieved by the spinning wheel, but it was not until the late 18th century that the process was industrialized. The spinning jenny, invented around 1764 by the Englishman James Hargreaves (c. 1719–78), allowed several strands to be spun simultaneously. Within a few years Richard Arkwright (1732–92) had brought mechanical power to spinning in the form of the water frame. Another British inventor, Samuel Crompton (1753–1827), combined the advantages of both earlier machines in his spinning mule of 1779, which increased the speed and improved the quality of yarn production. Continuous improvement in mechanization since the 18th century has led to modern machines that are capable of producing thousands of metres of yarn an hour.

Unlike natural fibres, man-made fibres like nylon are continuous (see p. 317). In principle, therefore, they can be used without spinning to make items such as net curtains, nylon stockings or tights. For more substantial garments, however, several filaments are wound together to make a thicker yarn. Synthetic fibres may also be cut into shorter lengths, and then blended with natural fibres and spun into a combination yarn.

In knitting, fabric is produced by knotting continuous yarns into a series of interlocking loops. Knitted fabrics are generally more stretchable than woven ones, and the range of patterns that can be produced is more limited. Here a worker is seen checking for a rough beam flange on a high-speed nylon knitting machine.

Weaving

Two techniques are available for turning yarn into fabric: weaving and knitting. Traditionally knitting has been used for hosiery (including nylon stockings), for sweaters, and for women's dresses. Weaving is used to create bolts (rolls) of cloth, both for clothing and for furnishing fabrics (see diagram).

Hand looms have been in use since ancient times, but it was not until 1785 that the British industrialist Edmund Cartwright (1743–1823) invented a power loom, in which the shuttle was moved across the warp mechanically. In 1801 the Frenchman Joseph-Marie Jacquard (1752–1834) mechanized the weaving of complex fabrics by controlling the loom with a series of punched cards that allowed warp threads to be lifted and lowered in the correct sequence. The punched cards were linked together as a sequence, and it took many thousands of them for the most elaborate fabrics.

The pattern of the weave can be altered to produce different effects. *Satin* gets its glossy appearance because the warp threads are interwoven not with every weft thread, but with every fourth or fifth. In *damask*, the same technique is used, but places where the warp lies on top are alternated with places where the weft does, producing subtle variations of shading. *Twill weaves* are used to produce gaberdine, serge and whipcord, and *pile weaves* for corduroy, plush, velour and velvet. The pile in such fabrics is created by cutting some of the threads after weaving, so that they stand out vertically from the surface of the fabric.

Printed patterns

Not all fabric patterns are produced by weaving. Colour printing, using as many as 16 different colours, can also be used (see photo). This method originated in India, and the Hindi word 'tchint', meaning 'mottled', is believed to be the origin of *chintz*, the bright printed fabric widely used in furnishing.

Printing is done on a series of rollers, one for each colour that is to be applied. Each roller, engraved with a part of the pattern, picks up dye from a trough as it rotates. The pattern is transferred to the fabric as it passes between the rollers, care being taken to ensure that the fabric cannot slip – otherwise the pattern would get out of register. After coming off the final roller at speeds of up to 180 m (590 ft) a minute, the fabric is dried in an oven.

Knitting

In knitting, the yarns are not interwoven with one another but knotted (see photo). The range of patterns is more limited, but with modern knitting machines far more ambitious designs can be achieved than had previously been possible. The use of modern combination fabrics in which wool is mixed with man-made fibres has also allowed garments to be knitted that are easier to look after and that keep their shape better.   NHa

SEE ALSO

- RUBBER AND PLASTICS p. 316
- THE INDUSTRIAL REVOLUTION p. 420

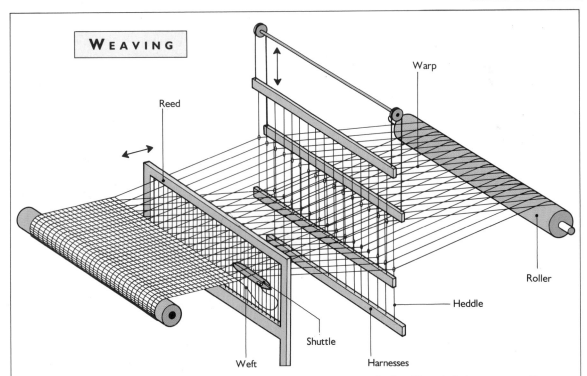

WEAVING

Reed · Warp · Roller · Heddle · Shuttle · Weft · Harnesses

Although modern looms are fully automated and electrically driven, the basic weaving operations performed are the same in principle as in earlier looms.

Two separate yarns are used, the warp and the weft. The *warp* runs along the length of the cloth, while the *weft* runs crosswise, alternately under and over the warp threads. The warp is mounted on a roller as wide as the bolt (roll) of cloth will be, and each warp thread passes through an eyelet at the midpoint of a fine wire called a *heddle*, all the heddles being supported in frames called *harnesses*. As the harnesses are raised and lowered, they separate the warp threads, allowing the weft to pass through the gap created. The weft is carried by a hollow boat-shaped object called the *shuttle*. After each pass, the weft is beaten down by a hinged, comb-like device called the *reed*, so that the most recent weft thread is pressed close to the previously woven cloth.

The weaving process can be elaborated almost infinitely, by varying the colours of the threads or by altering the pattern in which the yarns are interwoven.

Chemicals and Biotechnology

The chemical industry turns readily available raw materials into thousands of useful products. Principally from coal, oil, natural gas, air, water, limestone, salt and sulphur, the industry manufactures drugs, fertilizers and pesticides, soap and detergents, cosmetics, plastics, acids and alkalis, dyes, solvents, paints, explosives and gases.

SEE ALSO

- CHEMISTRY pp. 40–57
- MEDICAL TECHNOLOGY p. 242
- THREATS TO THE ENVIRONMENT p. 300
- OIL AND GAS p. 310
- RUBBER AND PLASTICS p. 316
- TEXTILES p. 318

Biotechnology also produces useful products, but by biological rather than chemical methods. Living organisms – or substances produced from them – are used to make drugs, to improve crops, to brew alcohols, and even to extract minerals. Some of its methods, such as fermentation, are ancient, while others are so new that they are barely out of the research laboratory.

The birth of the chemical industry

The first chemical to be produced on a large scale was *soda* (sodium carbonate), which was needed primarily in glass and soap manufacture. In 1787 the French chemist Nicolas Leblanc (?1742–1806) devised a method of mixing common salt (sodium chloride) with sulphuric acid to produce sodium sulphate, which was then mixed with coal and limestone and roasted. The resultant 'black ash' was

dissolved in water and then evaporated to extract the soda. Subsequently the Leblanc process was replaced by a process using salt, carbon dioxide and ammonia. Soda is typical of most products manufactured by the chemical industry in that it requires further processing to make useful products.

Other important landmarks in the growth of the chemical industry were the production of bleaching powder (a bleaching agent and disinfectant) in 1799, and the invention of synthetic dyes, beginning with Perkin's mauve in 1856. The production of artificial fertilizers, which supply plants with nitrogen, potassium and phosphorus, was also significant. The first of these was *superphosphate*, manufactured from 1834 onwards by mixing phosphates with sulphuric acid. The use of electrolysis to extract valuable chemicals by passing electrical currents through salt solutions began in 1894 with the Castner–Kellner process for making pure caustic soda.

The chemical industry today

The modern chemical industry can be divided for convenience into three categories: the heavy inorganic sector, which includes fertilizers and other chemicals produced in large amounts; the fine chemicals sector, which includes drugs and dyes; and the heavy organic sector, which includes plastics, man-made fibres and paints. The term 'organic' was originally used to designate any chemical found in living organisms, but today the term refers to any chemical containing carbon. Because of the facility with which carbon atoms link to form molecules, the variety of such compounds is enormous – literally

A BP acetic acid plant in Hull, England. As well as dilute acetic acid produced as vinegar by biochemical means (fermentation), huge quantities of acetic acid are prepared by chemical synthesis – one of the many products of the heavy organic sector of the chemical industry. Industrially, acetic acid is processed further into various types of acetate, which are used (among other things) as solvents for paints, in textiles and in plastics.

millions of carbon compounds can be synthesized (see p. 52).

In the heavy inorganic sector, *sulphuric acid* is by far the largest single product. Nearly half is used to produce superphosphate, with the rest going to a variety of chemical processes, including the production of explosives and artificial fibres. In 1908 the German chemist Fritz Haber (1868–1934) developed a catalytic method for combining the nitrogen in air with hydrogen to form *ammonia*, which is chiefly used in the manufacture of explosives and nitrate fertilizers (see also p. 48).

In the fine chemicals sector, chemical substances are produced in much smaller quantities than is the case with (say) fertilizers, but higher prices are charged. Dyes are produced in a huge range of colours, originally from coal but now mostly from crude oil. Many drugs are also synthesized using the methods of organic chemistry, and some are produced biochemically (see below).

In the heavy organic sector, materials are produced in large quantities, usually as raw materials for further processing into plastics, fibres, films or paints. Typical examples are benzene, phenol, toluene, vinyl chloride and ethylene (see diagram). The raw material generally used is crude oil, which contains a range of hydrocarbons – chemicals made up of carbon and hydrogen. From crude oil individual hydrocarbons can be extracted by distillation or catalytic cracking (see p. 311). The hydrocarbons obtained in this way are then used to build more complex molecules by polymerization (see p. 316).

Biotechnology

The technique of *fermentation*, in which microorganisms such as yeast convert

The pharmaceutical industry, producing drugs, forms a major part of the fine chemicals sector of the chemical industry. Here, a scientist is seen in strictly controlled clean-room conditions, working on the production of pharmaceutical compounds based on precious metals such as platinum. Such compounds include recently developed anti-cancer drugs.

raw materials into useful products, has been known since earliest times. By the middle of the 19th century, industrial alcohol was being produced by fermentation in much the same way as beer or wine. After the price of crude oil went up in the 1970s, alcohol produced in this way has been able to compete under some circumstances with petrol, and large fermentation plants have been built in the USA and Brazil to convert plant material such as maize into fuel (see p. 306).

A number of acids can also be produced by fermentation – vinegar (dilute acetic acid) being an important example. Citric acid, widely used in food and drinks, was originally produced from citrus fruits, but a fermentation process developed by the US Pfizer company in the 1920s soon dominated the market. Pfizer still produces half the 250 000 tonnes (tons) of citric acid used every year. Other chemicals that can be produced by fermentation include glycerol, acetone and propylene glycol.

Fermentation has proved equally useful in the drug industry. Following the discovery of the antibiotic penicillin in 1928 (see p. 249), large-scale fermentation methods were developed in the 1940s to produce the drug commercially. Today a large number of drugs are produced in this way, as well as other biochemicals such as enzymes (biochemical catalysts), alkaloids, peptides and proteins.

The technique of *genetic engineering* (see p. 115) has greatly increased the range of possible products. By altering the genetic blueprint of a microorganism, it can be made to produce a protein quite unlike anything it would produce naturally. For example, if the short length of the genetic material DNA responsible for producing growth hormones in humans is inserted into cells of a certain bacterium, the bacterium will produce the human hormone as it grows. It can then be extracted and used to treat children who would otherwise not grow properly. The same methods can be used to produce insulin for diabetics, while sheep have been genetically engineered so that they produce a human blood-clotting agent in their milk.

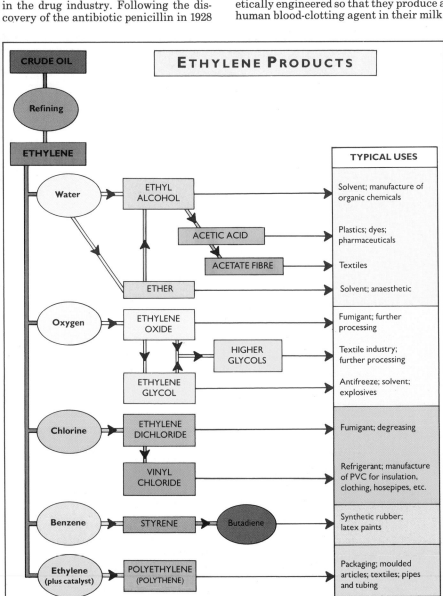

ETHYLENE PRODUCTS

	TYPICAL USES
CRUDE OIL	
Refining	
ETHYLENE	
ETHYL ALCOHOL	Solvent; manufacture of organic chemicals
ACETIC ACID	Plastics; dyes; pharmaceuticals
ACETATE FIBRE	Textiles
ETHER	Solvent; anaesthetic
ETHYLENE OXIDE	Fumigant; further processing
HIGHER GLYCOLS	Textile industry; further processing
ETHYLENE GLYCOL	Antifreeze; solvent; explosives
ETHYLENE DICHLORIDE	Fumigant; degreasing
VINYL CHLORIDE	Refrigerant; manufacture of PVC for insulation, clothing, hosepipes, etc.
STYRENE / Butadiene	Synthetic rubber; latex paints
POLYETHYLENE (POLYTHENE)	Packaging; moulded articles; textiles; pipes and tubing

(Reactant labels: Water, Oxygen, Chlorine, Benzene, Ethylene (plus catalyst))

Unlike other manufacturing industries, where several raw materials are typically required to make a single product, the chemical industry derives thousands of useful products from a smaller number of raw materials.

For example, ethylene – a product of the refinement of crude oil – is used to form a few major chemicals, which in turn spawn hundreds of derivative products.

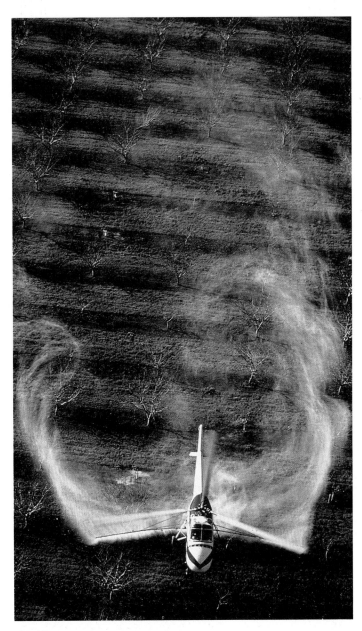

Environmental hazards

The damage done to the environment by the growth of the chemical industry is an issue of widespread concern (see p. 300). The first attempts at controlling pollution by legislation were made in the 19th century, and today the chemical industry throughout the world is heavily circumscribed by legislation. Such legislation is not always successful, however, since poisonous discharges into streams still continue, and there is little control of the dumping of toxic wastes.

A longer-term hazard is posed by the use of fertilizers. Although nitrates have contributed enormously to the production of food, they can pollute lakes and streams, and by percolating through the soil can reach groundwater. Controls on the use of such agricultural chemicals may soon be needed. There is also anxiety about the use of genetic engineering techniques. It is possible, for example, that an accident could produce super-resistant species of germs or pests.   NHa

A vast range of pesticides is produced by the chemical industry. They are a crucial element in the battle against insects and other pests that cause economic damage to crops or that produce disease in humans and domestic animals.

Printing

Books spread knowledge and ideas, make universal education possible, and provide access to techniques invented by others. When the first printed books appeared in Europe in the 15th century, the progress of learning began to gather pace. The information revolution that still dominates our lives was under way.

By the end of the 2nd century AD the Chinese had invented paper, ink and a block with a picture or letters cut into it – the basic requirements for printing. The blocks were made of wood, and text was engraved on them by cutting around the characters so that they stood out in relief. By the 14th century, individual blocks had been carved for each of the 80 000 Chinese characters. They could be arranged in any order to make up a page – the principle of *movable type*.

Typesetting

The really decisive advances, however, were made in Europe in around 1450, by Johannes Gutenberg (c. 1398–1468) and Johann Fust (c. 1400–66). Both goldsmiths by trade, they used metal type – far longer lasting than wooden blocks – and a vice-like press to transfer the ink from the blocks to the paper. Each letter was separately cast, using a low melting-point alloy of lead, tin and antimony. The letters were then arranged side by side along a strip of wood called a *stick* to form

words, and the lines were *justified* (made to fit a fixed width or *measure*) by inserting small pieces of lead between the words. By 1448 they had printed the Bible in Latin, each page taking a printer a day to set in type. A similar process to Gutenberg's was adopted by the Englishman William Caxton (c. 1422–91). He printed his first book – the first book printed in English – in 1475.

Printing using hot metal lasted more than 500 years. Its speed was improved by inventions such as the *Linotype machine* – produced in 1884 by Ottmar Mergenthaler (1854–99) in the USA – which could cast a whole line at once from individual letters typed by the operator on a keyboard. It was used mainly for newspapers. Its principal rival was the *Monotype machine*, invented in 1887 by Tolbert Lanston (1844–1913), also in the USA. The Monotype operator keyed in the text, which was coded into a punched tape, together with information about the spaces between words needed to justify the line. This information came at the end of each line, but the tape was fed to the typecaster backwards, so that the correct spacing was known before the line was cast. The Monotype machine produced high-quality results and was used for a wide range of printing jobs.

Today typesetting – as well as other stages in the production of printed material – has been almost entirely taken over by computers (see box).

Printing methods

Three methods of printing are of particular significance (see diagram). In *letterpress printing*, the method used by

SEE ALSO
● PHOTOGRAPHY AND FILM p. 324
● COMPUTERS p. 334
● MEDIEVAL AND RENAISSANCE CULTURE p. 406
● ART TECHNIQUES 2 p. 502

THE COMPUTER REVOLUTION

Computer technology has revolutionized every stage in the production of printed matter. In a fully computerized system, it is entirely feasible that the material to be printed will never have been set down on paper before it finally passes through the printer's press.

Text may be keyed directly into the computer typesetting system, or an author's word-processed disks may be made compatible with a particular system. The text is displayed on screen, where it may be edited or corrected; typesetting commands – specifying the desired typeface, type size and so on – are also added at this stage. A designer may then assemble the page on screen, juggling pictures and text into the final layout.

The layout of the page being designed on screen.

Next the text is set in type by a laser guided by the computer. The laser scans to and fro across a sheet of film or photographic paper ('bromide'), tracing the shapes of all the characters according to the instructions prepared at the page-layout terminal. After development, the result is a positive or negative film, or a bromide; in the latter, the characters traced by the laser appear black against a white background. The film or bromide can then be used to prepare printing plates.

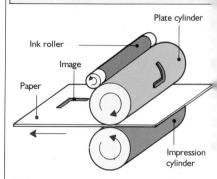

In letterpress printing, the image is transferred to paper by means of type that stands out in relief from the printing plate.

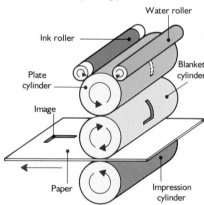

In lithography, the image is localized on a flat printing plate by means of chemicals that attract ink, while blank areas are covered by a film of water.

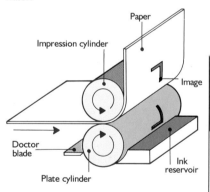

In photogravure, the image is etched into depressions on the printing plate. The plate is then inked, and the ink removed from blank (i.e. non-recessed) areas by means of a blade.

Gutenberg, the raised surfaces of the typeset page are covered in ink by rollers, and paper is pressed against it in a press to transfer the image.

The principle of *lithography* (or 'litho'), which has now almost entirely taken over from letterpress, was invented in 1796 by a Bavarian, Aloys Senefelder (1771–1834). The technique depends on the fact that water and grease do not mix. The images to be printed are transferred to flexible metal plates photographically, in such a way that the areas to be printed consist of chemicals that attract ink and repel water, while the blank areas attract water and repel ink. First water and then ink is applied to the plate; all the ink congreates in the areas of the image, and can be transferred to paper in a rotary press (see below). A better image is achieved if the cylinder carrying the plate first transfers the image to a rubber-coated cylinder, which in turn transfers it to paper. This rubber 'offset' cylinder gives the method its name – *offset litho*.

A third technique is widely used for printing colour supplements and magazines. In *gravure* (short for 'rotogravure' or 'photogravure') the image is etched on the plate photographically, forming cells whose depth depends on the intensity of the colour. As the plate rotates, it picks up ink, which is wiped off blank areas by a blade. When the paper passes between the cylinders of the press, the deeper cells produce denser images, while the shallower ones produce lighter ones. In a related process, known as *copperplate gravure* or *line intaglio*, the image consists of discrete lines that vary in depth and width. It is the preferred method for printing stamps and banknotes.

Printing presses

Several designs of printing press have been developed over the centuries. Historically, the various kinds of press were all designed chiefly for the purposes of letterpress printing. The methods that have largely superseded letterpress – gravure and litho – are carried out almost exclusively on some variant of rotary press (see below).

In *platen presses*, the type is carried in a flat bed and pressure is applied by the platen – a second flat surface, which is fed by sheets of paper. In *flat-bed* or *cylinder presses*, the type is carried in a mobile flat bed that moves back and forth beneath an impression cylinder, around which a sheet of paper is wrapped.

Greater printing speed, particularly important for newspaper production, was achieved by *rotary presses*, which operate cylinder to cylinder. Letterpress type was formed into a curve by a process known as *stereotyping*, invented in 1727. An impression was taken of the typeset page using papier-mâché, which was then curved into a half circle and used as a mould to cast copies of the typeset page. The curved page was fitted together with another page around a cylinder and locked in place. Rotary presses may be sheet-fed or web-fed; in the latter case a continuous roll (or *web*) of paper passes between the cylinders. Rotary printing allows much more rapid production than flat-bed methods.

Screening. In lithography and letterpress printing, it is impossible to produce gradations of tone by varying the thickness of ink deposited at different points of the printed image. Areas of different tone in an illustration are therefore reproduced by a process known as *screening* (also known as the *halftone process*). The image is photographed through a fine screen, so dividing the image into a series of evenly spaced dots; the size of the dots determines the density of the ink at a given point – the larger the dot, the darker the tone.

Inks

Water-based inks are unsuitable for printing, since they tend to collect in droplets on metal type and smudge when pressed on paper. The solution, quickly discovered, was to use inks made of pigments dissolved in oil. Vegetable or mineral oils may be used, depending on the type of printing. The black pigment used is generally carbon black.

Paper

The earliest documents were written on clay tablets, and then on parchment, made from the skin of sheep or goat, or vellum, made from calfskin. A writing material prepared from the stem of the papyrus plant was also known to the Ancients. These materials, however, were quite inadequate for the huge volume of printed matter that was made possible by Gutenberg's inventions.

The answer was paper, invented by the Chinese nearly 2000 years ago, but not widely known in Europe until the 12th century. Paper can be made from virtually any fibrous material. The commonest in use today is wood pulp, but recycled material such as rags or waste paper are also used. After felling, trees are turned into chips and then digested into pulp using sodium sulphate. The pulp is bleached and then flows through a narrow slit onto a moving screen that allows the water to drain away. The paper is then pressed to remove more water and dried by steam-heated cylinders. Finally the paper is treated with pigments such as clay to give it a smoother finish, or given a glossy surface with chalk or titanium dioxide.   NHa

Photography and Film

At least as early as the 4th century BC, the ancient Greeks were familiar with the principle of the *camera obscura* – a darkened chamber in which an inverted image of the world outside is projected through a small opening onto a flat surface within. However, it was not until the first half of the 19th century that a process was developed by which an image could be made permanent.

A *camera* is essentially a box that is lightproof except where the optical component, the *lens* (see p. 32), projects an image onto a sheet of material inside the camera. This material, usually film, is coated with an emulsion whose chemical properties are changed by exposure to light, and which – after appropriate processing – can reproduce the image.

The *emulsion* is made of silver halide grains (often silver bromide or iodide), suspended in gelatin. After exposure to light and chemical processing (*development*), the grains become black metallic silver. When the unexposed silver halide in the parts wholly or partially untouched by light is dissolved away, the picture becomes permanent, or *fixed*. It is, however, a reversed, or *negative*, image, with the original light areas reproduced as dark areas, and vice versa. The conversion of the negative to a true, or *positive*, picture was at first a problem, until a negative/positive technique was evolved (see below), which brought the bonus that an unlimited number of positive prints could be produced from a single negative.

The early pioneers

In 1826 the Frenchman Nicéphore Niepce

SEE ALSO

- OPTICS p. 32
- RADIO, TELEVISION AND VIDEO p. 326
- SEEING THE INVISIBLE p. 332
- PHOTOGRAPHY AS ART p. 556
- CINEMA pp. 558–65

The world's first photograph, 1826: view of a barnyard from Nicéphore Niepce's country estate in Chalon-sur-Saône, France. This image was recorded on a pewter plate after an exposure of eight hours.

THE SINGLE-LENS REFLEX CAMERA

In a single-lens reflex (SLR) camera, a single lens is used both for viewing and for taking the picture. A hinged mirror set at 45° directs the image projected through the lens onto a ground-glass focusing screen above the mirror. The laterally reversed image on the screen is then reflected off the sides of a pentaprism (five-sided prism), so that the image – upright and the right way round – is seen through the viewfinder. The image is then focused on the screen, and the iris diaphragm is set to contract automatically to the correct aperture as the picture is taken. As the shutter-release button is pressed, the mirror swings up and the shutter opens, thus allowing the image to strike the film.

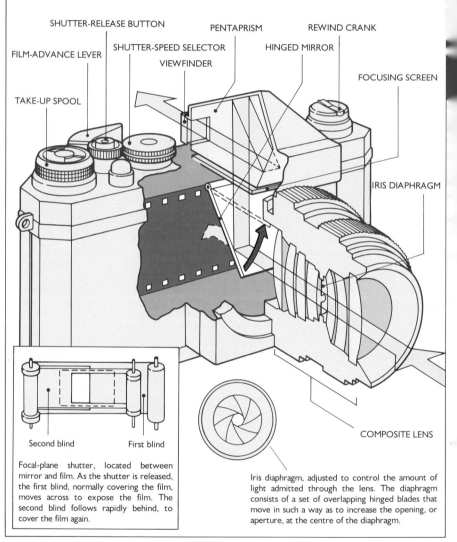

SHUTTER-RELEASE BUTTON
PENTAPRISM
REWIND CRANK
FILM-ADVANCE LEVER
SHUTTER-SPEED SELECTOR
HINGED MIRROR
VIEWFINDER
FOCUSING SCREEN
TAKE-UP SPOOL
IRIS DIAPHRAGM
COMPOSITE LENS

Focal-plane shutter, located between mirror and film. As the shutter is released, the first blind, normally covering the film, moves across to expose the film. The second blind follows rapidly behind, to cover the film again.

Second blind   First blind

Iris diaphragm, adjusted to control the amount of light admitted through the lens. The diaphragm consists of a set of overlapping hinged blades that move in such a way as to increase the opening, or aperture, at the centre of the diaphragm.

(1765–1833) produced the world's first photographic image (see photo). In 1839 Niepce's partner Louis Daguerre (1789–1851) marketed his *daguerreotype*, which used a copper plate coated with light-sensitive silver chloride, and required a half-hour exposure. There was no development in the modern sense, but by using mercury vapour to whiten the exposed silver and common salt to fix it, Daguerre produced a positive picture.

In 1841 the Englishman William Fox Talbot (1800–77) patented his negative/positive process (the *calotype* process). The paper negative was placed face-to-face against another, unexposed, piece of sensitized paper, and then light was passed through the back of the negative. The sensitive paper, when developed, became a positive print.

Later developments

The growth of photography as a profession was greatly assisted by the introduction of a *wet-plate* process in 1851. A jelly-like solution called collodion was poured onto a glass plate, which was then dipped in silver nitrate solution. The plate was then exposed in the camera and developed before it dried. Portrait and landscape pictures could now be made to order, and intrepid photographers set off on expeditions laden with darkroom tent, glass plates, and chemicals.

The invention of a *dry-plate* process in the 1870s led to the commercial manufacture of glass plates in which dry gelatin replaced wet collodion. The emulsion was also very much more sensitive. Using a spring-operated shutter, exposure times could therefore be reduced to 1/25 second, thus making a tripod unnecessary.

In 1888 the American George Eastman (1854–1932) produced his first Kodak camera with the slogan 'You press the button, we do the rest.' It was in the well-tried form of a box, but instead of plates used a roll of sensitive paper (later nitrocellulose, or 'film'), which could be wound on between exposures. It took 100 shots, after which the camera was sent back to the manufacturer for development and replacement of the film.

In the 1920s the Leica camera was introduced – the first commercially successful 'miniature' camera able to use 35 mm cinema film. This and subsequent miniature cameras became extremely popular with professionals as well as amateurs. Even smaller cameras were later introduced for the mass market, but were not favoured by professionals.

In the mid-20th century the Polaroid camera was invented by the American Edwin Land (1909–91), making 'instant' pictures by processing the film inside the camera itself. This was achieved by incorporating developing agents in the film, activated by bursting a pod containing alkaline solution as the exposed film was pressed between rollers.

Modern cameras

Unlike more traditional 35 mm cameras, which have a simple see-through viewfinder, the 35 mm single-lens reflex camera allows the user to see the exact picture being taken (see box). Larger cameras may also use the reflex viewfinder. In the case of the twin-lens reflex, the mirror is fixed and has its own lens, of the same characteristics as the taking lens. Although the 35 mm film size is the most popular, larger formats, using sheet film or roll film, are still used where convenience of use is less important than final picture quality.

More sophisticated 35 mm cameras have their own *exposure meters*, which measure the amount of light falling on the subject and adjust the shutter speed and lens aperture accordingly. They may also incorporate electronic controls and automatic focusing: the user is required only to frame the picture and press the trigger.

Film and colour photography

Emulsions have improved continuously. An early step was the introduction of *panchromatic* film, which was sensitive to red and therefore gave a better tonal rendering. Subsequent films of still greater sensitivity enabled pictures to be taken in poor light, but tended to be less sharp because the silver grains were larger – although this problem was itself solved by the later introduction of sensitive fine-grain films.

Cumbersome ways of making colour pictures were evolved in the late 19th century, but it was the appearance of Kodachrome and Agfacolor in the 1930s that introduced modern colour films. These were multi-layer films in which three separate emulsions recorded the blue, green and red parts of the image. They were then processed by dyeing each layer with the corresponding complementary colour (yellow, magenta and cyan), thus producing three positive images one above the other, which together reproduced the original colours of the image (see p. 323). The final picture was a transparency, to be looked through or projected, but a negative/positive system was soon introduced to produce colour prints.

Applied photography

Photomicrography produces enlarged pictures of tiny objects, and is achieved either by using a short-focus lens on a long-bodied camera, or by taking photographs through a microscope. It has applications in biology and criminology, among other fields.

High-speed photography shows successive phases of movement too fast to be observed by the human eye. Apart from the use of high-speed shutters (see photo), a technique known as *stroboscopy* may be used, in which cameras with open shutters register successive images of a moving object illuminated by intermittent flashes. Such techniques can be used for studying phenomena as disparate as a dancer's movements, explosions, or fracturing metal.

Photography has numerous other specialized applications that have widened the possibilities of many activities and revolutionized others. Using lens filters and special film, for instance, it is possible to select parts of the electromagnetic spectrum (see p. 34) other than visible light as the illuminant. X-ray and infrared photography are among the important applications of this technique (see pp. 332–3). JW

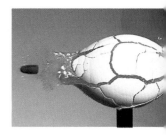

Faster than the human eye: a bullet travelling at 450 m (1476 ft) per second is captured as it passes through an egg. High-speed photography generally uses shutter speeds of less than 1/1000 second, and has many applications in science and technology.

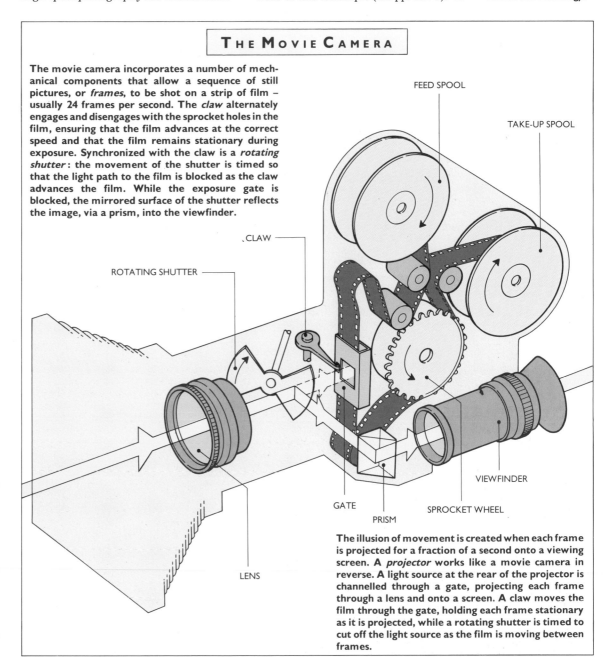

THE MOVIE CAMERA

The movie camera incorporates a number of mechanical components that allow a sequence of still pictures, or *frames*, to be shot on a strip of film – usually 24 frames per second. The *claw* alternately engages and disengages with the sprocket holes in the film, ensuring that the film advances at the correct speed and that the film remains stationary during exposure. Synchronized with the claw is a *rotating shutter* : the movement of the shutter is timed so that the light path to the film is blocked as the claw advances the film. While the exposure gate is blocked, the mirrored surface of the shutter reflects the image, via a prism, into the viewfinder.

FEED SPOOL

TAKE-UP SPOOL

CLAW

ROTATING SHUTTER

GATE

PRISM

SPROCKET WHEEL

VIEWFINDER

LENS

The illusion of movement is created when each frame is projected for a fraction of a second onto a viewing screen. A *projector* works like a movie camera in reverse. A light source at the rear of the projector is channelled through a gate, projecting each frame through a lens and onto a screen. A claw moves the film through the gate, holding each frame stationary as it is projected, while a rotating shutter is timed to cut off the light source as the film is moving between frames.

Radio, Television and Video

The use of electromagnetic waves to carry sound and pictures has revolutionized communications in the 20th century. News, entertainment, sport and education have all been transformed by radio and television. Television has become the single most significant leisure-time activity in developed countries.

The media used to carry information are *radio waves*, which lie at the low-frequency end of the electromagnetic spectrum (see p. 35). Radio waves occur naturally in space, emitted by stars and galaxies, but for broadcasting purposes, they are generated by accelerating electrons inside an *aerial* (or *antenna*) – a device used both to emit and receive radio waves. Like all electromagnetic waves, radio waves travel at the speed of light – 300 000 km (186 000 mi) per second in a vacuum.

Long, medium and *short* radio waves, with wavelengths between 2 km and 10 m (1¼ mi and 33 ft), can diffract or 'bend' around obstacles such as hills and are therefore suitable for local radio broadcasting. They are reflected both by the Earth and by the ionosphere (a layer in the atmosphere, see p. 77), and thus can 'bounce' between the two and be transmitted over very long distances. Short waves are reflected best, and are generally used for international broadcasting. *VHS* (very high frequency) and *UHF* (ultra-high frequency) waves have shorter wavelengths. They can only travel in a straight-line path, and pass through the ionosphere. They are chiefly used for television and local radio.

Radio

The simplest form of radio transmission is to use a radio *transmitter* (or, strictly speaking, an emitter) to create a radio wave of a fixed frequency, and a receiver tuned to that frequency to pick it up. By turning the wave on and off, a series of dots and dashes can be transmitted, sending a message in Morse code (see p. 330). In 1894 the Italian Guglielmo Marconi (1874–1919) put together the discoveries of others to create radio. In the attic of his parents' house near Bologna he made a bell ring by sending a radio message across the room. By 1901 he had transmitted the letter S in Morse code across the Atlantic from Cornwall in England to Newfoundland in Canada.

A more sophisticated system is needed to transmit voices and music. A *carrier wave*, instead of being turned on and off like a tap, must have a second signal imposed on it. This is the process known as modulation. One possibility is *amplitude modulation* (AM), where the amplitude of the wave is varied; a second is *frequency modulation* (FM), where the frequency of the wave is varied (see pp. 28–9). A microphone produces a small electrical current representing the sounds made into it. The wave profile corresponding to this current is then superimposed on the carrier wave, broadcast, and finally separated out again at the other end by the radio *receiver*. An amplifier increases the power of the signal, so that it can operate a loudspeaker, recreating the original sounds made into the microphone. (For the basic operation of amplifier, loudspeaker and microphone, see pp. 328–9.)

Television

The idea of using radio waves to carry visual information dates back to the early days of radio, but became practical only in 1926. The basic principle is to break up the image into a series of dots, which are then transmitted and displayed on a screen so rapidly that the human eye perceives them as a complete picture (see box).

In 1926 the Scottish inventor John Logie Baird (1888–1946) demonstrated television based on a mechanical method of scanning an image into lines of dots of light. Baird's system had little future, however, and was rapidly superseded by an all-electronic system. This was developed by Vladimir Zworykin (1889–1982), a Russian-born engineer working in the USA. His first practical camera, made in 1931, focused the picture onto a mosaic of photoelectric cells (see pp. 36–7). The voltage induced in each cell was a measure of the light intensity at that point, and could be transmitted as a signal. A modern TV camera operates in essentially the same way, measuring the light intensity at each point of the image. This information is then encoded on the radio wave and transmitted.

At the receiving end, the signal has to be decoded. A TV set is basically a *cathode-ray tube*, in which a 'gun' fires a beam of electrons at a luminescent screen. As they strike it, the screen lights up. To make up the whole picture the beam is scanned to and fro in a series of lines (625 in modern sets), covering the entire screen in ¹/₂₅ second.

Satellite and cable TV

Because the VHF and UHF wavebands on which television signals are transmitted are not significantly reflected by the ionosphere, many transmitters are needed for complete coverage of all but the smallest countries. For intercontinental TV, some other way of bouncing the signal back from space is needed. This is achieved by satellites above the Earth that pick up the signals and broadcast them back to Earth. The satellite signals are not powerful enough to be picked up by ordinary TV aerials, so they are re-broadcast by ground transmitters. Special dish-shaped aerials can pick up satellite signals, however, making possible continent-wide direct broadcasting by satellite (DBS). Such satellite channels already operate in the USA and Europe.

John Logie Baird transmitted televised objects in outline in 1924, recognizable human faces in 1925 and moving objects in 1926. In 1928 he demonstrated a rudimentary form of colour television.

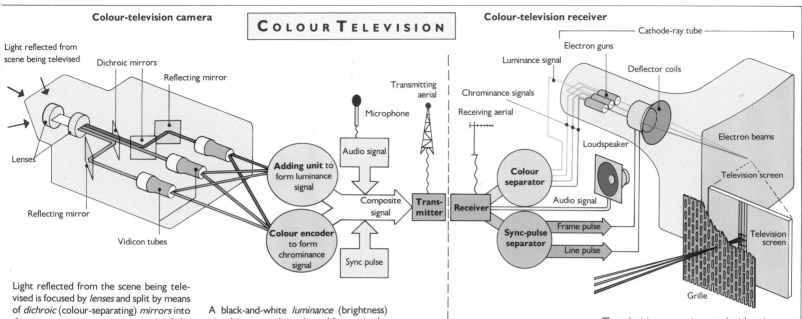

Colour-television camera

Light reflected from scene being televised
Dichroic mirrors
Reflecting mirror
Lenses
Reflecting mirror
Vidicon tubes
Adding unit to form luminance signal
Colour encoder to form chrominance signal
Microphone
Audio signal
Transmitting aerial
Composite signal
Sync pulse
Trans-mitter

COLOUR TELEVISION

Colour-television receiver

Receiving aerial
Receiver
Colour separator
Sync-pulse separator
Audio signal
Frame pulse
Line pulse
Cathode-ray tube
Electron guns
Luminance signal
Chrominance signals
Deflector coils
Loudspeaker
Electron beams
Television screen
Television screen
Grille

Light reflected from the scene being tele-vised is focused by *lenses* and split by means of *dichroic* (colour-separating) *mirrors* into three separate images, one in each of the three primary colours – blue, green and red. Each beam of coloured light is then directed into one of three identical *vidicon tubes*. The pattern of light falling on a photoconductive layer within each tube causes a varying pattern of electrical resist-ance; as an electron beam scans the photo-conductive area from behind, a varying electric current is induced in a circuit connected to the conductive layer. The pattern of dark and light in each primary-colour image is thus converted into one of three varying electrical signals.

A black-and-white *luminance* (brightness) *signal* is created in the adding unit, by combining information from each of the three colour signals. At the same time, the colour encoder produces a single *chromi-nance signal*, which defines the hue and saturation of each primary colour. The luminance and chrominance signals are combined into a composite *video signal*. Prior to transmission, the *audio signal* is incorporated, together with a *synchroniz-ing pulse* ('sync pulse'), which ensures that the electron scanning in the receiving system matches that of the transmitting system.

The composite signal picked up by the receiving aerial is decoded, separating out the various constituent signals. The lumi-nance signal controls the overall output of three electron guns in the cathode-ray tube of the receiving set, so determining the balance of light and shade in the final picture. The chrominance signal – now split into the three primary-colour signals – regulates the relative strength of each electron beam. The sync pulse, divided into line and frame components, controls the deflection of the beams across and down the screen.

The television screen is coated with stripes of different phosphors, which glow red, blue or green when struck by electrons. Immedi-ately behind the screen is a *grille*, or *shadow mask*, which contains many perforations. Travelling at slightly different angles as they pass through the perforations, the electron beams are caused to diverge before striking the screen, in such a way that the electrons from each gun can only reach phosphor stripes of the appropriate colour. Each image on the screen thus consists of stripes of varying brightness and colour that merge together to form the complete picture.

TV signals can also be fed down cables, making possible networks in which films, news, sport and other programmes are available exclusively to those willing to pay a subscription.

Videotext

TV sets can also be used to display written information, in the form of videotext. The written information is transmitted as part of the signal, and decoded by the TV receiver. Each page of information takes about one quarter of a second to transmit. The system runs through a magazine of about 150 pages, taking 30 seconds to complete the cycle before starting again. The user can stop the cycle at any page by keying the number of that page on a keypad. A limit is effectively put on the size of such systems – of which British Ceefax and Oracle are examples – by the fact that if more than 150 pages were transmitted, delays in displaying would be unacceptably long. There is no such limit on the amount of material that can be provided on interactive systems, in which the signal is not broadcast but carried on telephone lines. In these sys-tems, the TV screen is used to display information held in a central computer and accessed by dialling into it over an ordinary telephone line (see p. 331).

Video recorders

TV programmes can also be recorded on

magnetic tape. The principle is the same as that of an audio tape recorder (see pp. 328–9), but the technology is more complex. The signals are recorded as mag-netic patterns on the tape, but because a video signal contains much more informa-tion than an audio one, it is necessary to pack it more efficiently onto the tape. Early experimental video tape recorders

(VTRs) used fixed recording heads and fast running tape, but needed 32 km (20 mi) of tape to record one hour's TV. The answer was to use a recording head that rotated as the tape ran past it, so that the information was effectively laid out di-agonally across the tape, reducing the length of tape needed. This is the principle used by all today's VTRs. NHa

SEE ALSO

- WAVE THEORY p. 28
- ELECTROMAGNETISM p. 34
- ELECTRICITY IN ACTION p. 36
- PHOTOGRAPHY AND FILM p. 324
- HIFI p. 328
- TELECOMMUNICATIONS p. 330
- CINEMA pp. 558–65
- JOURNALISM p. 654

A high-definition tele-vision system being demonstrated by a scientist. The Electronic Group is developing this advanced TV, which dis-plays an image composed of 2000 lines. This gives a resolution 32 times better than that of the usual 'studio quality' systems.

Hi-fi

The enjoyment of recorded music depends on a series of mechanical, electronic and optical inventions. Although sound has been recorded and reproduced for more than 100 years, techniques have been revolutionized in the 1980s, producing much greater fidelity, convenience and reliability.

SEE ALSO

● ACOUSTICS p. 30
● OPTICS (LASERS) p. 33
● ELECTROMAGNETISM p. 34
● ELECTRICITY IN ACTION p. 36
● RADIO, TELEVISION AND VIDEO p. 326
● TELECOMMUNICATIONS p. 330
● COMPUTERS p. 334
● MUSIC pp. 568–91

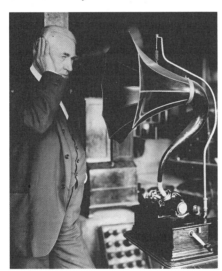

Thomas Edison with his wax-cylinder phonograph. Edison's inventive genius is witnessed by more than 1000 patents in fields as diverse as telephony, the generation of electricity, storage batteries, photography and cinematography.

Three forms of recorded sound now exist: records in which a fine stylus travels along grooves; tapes in which sounds are recorded as magnetic patterns; and digital ('compact') discs in which beams of laser light read patterns of binary digits.

Mechanical recording

The first decisive step in the recording of sound was taken by the American inventor Thomas Edison (1847–1931) in 1877. Edison's *phonograph* worked by converting sound vibrations into grooves on the surface of a cylinder covered in tinfoil.

The grooves were cut by a sharp steel needle (*stylus*) mounted on a diaphragm at the narrow end of a large horn. Sound channelled through the horn made the diaphragm vibrate, causing the steel point to go in and out and to cut a line of varying depth. The sound could be reproduced by putting the needle back to the start position and rotating the cylinder at the same speed as it had travelled during the recording. Better results were obtained when wax cylinders replaced tinfoil in 1888.

A major drawback of cylinders was that they could not be easily mass-produced. The German-born American Emile Berliner (1851–1929) resolved this difficulty in 1888 with the invention of flat discs. In his *gramophone records*, the groove ran in a spiral from the edge of the disc towards the centre, and the vibrations were recorded and played by side-to-side movements of the needle, rather than up-and-down movements as in Edison's phonograph. Once a master disc had been cut, it could be turned into a metal die, which could then be used to produce as many copies as required. The earliest records were made from vulcanized rubber, but a more suitable material proved to be *shellac* (a resinous substance derived from insects), which was in use from 1895.

In the 1920s the quality of recordings was greatly improved by the change from acoustic to electrical recording methods. Instead of relying on a vibrating diaphragm, *microphones* converted sounds into electrical currents, which could then be used to drive cutting machines to create the grooves. In playback, the vibrations picked up by the stylus were used to generate an electrical current, which could be amplified by electronic circuits and played through loudspeakers that converted the electrical signals back into sound.

Record decks

Today's record decks use fundamentally the same principles as the original gramophone. Long-playing records (LPs), made of vinyl plastic instead of breakable shellac and rotating at 33 rpm (revolutions per minute) instead of 78 rpm, were first produced in 1946. They required much lighter stylus pressures to avoid grinding away the soft plastic; and because the grooves were narrower, the styluses needed finer points, usually provided by the use of diamond or sapphire.

Instead of a maximum of about 4 minutes playing time per side, LPs offered more than 20 minutes. For the first time, really accurate reproduction of sound quality became possible: the age of high fidelity or hi-fi – had arrived.

Magnetic recording

In 1898 the Danish inventor Valdemar Poulsen (1869–1942) devised the *telegraphone* – a forerunner of the modern tape recorder – which recorded sound by the alternating magnetization of a steel wire. In the 1930s, steel tapes were used successfully by radio stations. However, the invention that made tape recording widely available was the introduction of strong plastic tape covered with iron oxide powder, developed in 1935 by two German companies, AEG Telefunken and IG Farben. Domestic tape recorders using such tape first appeared in the 1950s. Sounds are recorded by passing the tape in front of a recording head that consists of an electromagnet fed by electrical signals from a microphone. A magnetic pattern corresponding to the sounds is created on the tape as the fragments of iron oxide align themselves with the magnetic field. In playback, the tape passes in front of a second head, inducing in it an electrical current that is proportional to the magnetization of the tape. The current is then passed through an amplifier to loudspeakers, as in a stylus-playback system.

Today, the commonest format for tapes is the *compact cassette*, introduced by Philips in 1963, which is much more convenient and easily handled than open-reel tapes. The latter are still used, however, in situations where very high quality is

Disc cutting. The electrical signals produced by microphones are used to drive cutting machines to create grooves on a master disc. In order to make copies of a master disc, negative metal replicas have to be made by electroforming – a wet silvering process makes the surface of the master electrically conductive so that it may be plated (usually with nickel) to create a negative mould from which a metal master is cast. A limited number of plastic copies may be obtained from the metal master, but in order to produce commercial quantities numerous pressing masters – known as stampers – are produced from moulds made by electroforming the metal masters. Synthetic resin – thermoplastic – is melted between two stampers in a heated press to make individual records.

A diamond stylus travelling through the grooves of a long-playing stereo record. The frequency at which the stylus moves from side to side in the groove dictates the pitch of the music, and the amount of the displacement dictates the loudness, thus the wavy groove seen here indicates a loud piece of music. The inner wall of the groove carries the signal from the left-hand microphone; the outer wall carries the right-hand signal. The stylus illustrated in this false-colour scanning electron micrograph is encrusted with dirt, even though it has been thoroughly cleaned.

equired, as, for example, in multi-track studio recording. The effectiveness of apes as a hi-fi medium has been enormously increased by the noise-reduction system developed by the American engineer Ray Dolby (1933–). The *Dolby system* uses electronic processing to reduce the steady background hiss that is otherwise audible.

Stereo

The principles of stereophonic sound were first demonstrated by the British company EMI in 1933, but stereo recordings did not become widely available until 1958. In cutting a stereo disc, two microphones are set up at a distance from one another, and each of them records its own set of sound signals. The aim is to simulate the way in which we hear sounds: having two ears, we simultaneously hear two sounds, which are slightly different and come from slightly different directions. The two channels are recorded on the record in a V-shaped groove with a 90° angle. The inner wall of the groove carries the signal from the left-hand microphone, while the outer wall carries the right-hand signal. In playback, the stylus moves from side to side, sending the signals to two loudspeakers. The effect to a listener placed in the right position is to create an illusion of the left-to-right spread of the music. The same effect is achieved on a tape by recording the two signals as separate strips along the tape, then playing them back through two speakers.

Amplifiers and loudspeakers

At the heart of any hi-fi system is the *amplifier*. An amplifier is essentially a set of electronic circuits that boost the signal from the stylus or the tape deck, which is about one thousandth of a watt, to the 10 watts or more needed to operate the loudspeakers. The circuits are now made from transistors (see p. 37) rather than valves, and much effort has gone into designing amplifiers that produce the minimum distortion of the signal.

Loudspeakers convert the electrical signal from the amplifier back into sound again, usually operating on the moving-coil principle. The current from the amplifier flows around a coil of wire that is placed inside the field of a permanent magnet. The interaction between the field produced by the current flowing through the coil and that of the permanent magnet makes the coil vibrate. The coil is attached to a cone of stiff lightweight material that vibrates with it and creates the sounds. No loudspeaker works without distortion over the whole frequency range, so it is common to have several different speakers within the same cabinet. Each speaker serves only that part of the range for which it is designed: low frequencies (i.e. low pitches) are produced by a 'woofer', high ones by a 'tweeter', while more sophisticated loudspeakers may also include a mid-range 'squawker' and a very low-range 'sub-woofer'.

Compact-disc players

Conventional record players are *analogue systems*, in which the shape of the grooves is a direct and continual physical representation of the sounds of music or speech. An alternative system of recording, made possible by modern electronics, records the sounds digitally, as a series of binary digits, or *bits* (see pp. 65 and 334). In a *digital system*, the sound is 'sampled' 40 000 times a second, and its amplitude and frequency (volume and pitch) are recorded as a binary number. Recordings made in this way can be turned into ordinary analogue discs, but the advantages of low distortion and a good signal-to-noise ratio are better preserved in the form of digital ('compact') discs.

Compact discs – which were launched commercially in 1982 – record the bits as a series of pits or blank spaces in the surface of the disc, each pit measuring less than one hundredth of a millimetre across. The discs are made of clear PVC, coated with shiny aluminium and finished with a clear coating of plastic laminate. The pits are 'read' by a laser device (see p. 33), the light from which is either reflected or scattered, depending upon whether it strikes a pit or a blank space. As it scans the record, therefore, it picks up a series of signals, either 1s or 0s, which are the original binary digits of the recording. These signals are then converted to analogue currents that can be amplified and fed to loudspeakers.

The advantages of compact discs are high fidelity and robustness – dust and finger marks have no effect – and they have already superseded LPs in sales. In the early 1990s the *Digital compact cassette* (DCC) and *Mini Disc* were developed. DCC is a digital recording and playback system based on tape. A mini disc is a miniature version of the compact disc that records.   NHa

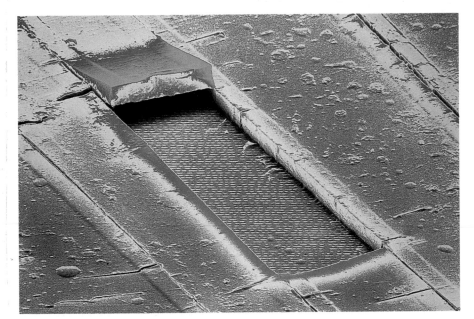

The surface of a compact disc. In this false-colour scanning electron micrograph the plastic covering on the surface of the CD has been cracked to show the pits and blank spaces that are 'read' by a laser device. To reflect the laser light, the pitted surface is covered with a layer of transparent plastic. Further layers of plastic protect the surface from dust and scratches that could affect the sound quality.

Telecommunications

The transfer of information by wire or by radio waves is the basis of telecommunications, which is now one of world's biggest and fastest-growing industries. Currently, the most important systems are the telephone, the telegraph, telex, facsimile, and information systems based on the telephone or television.

SEE ALSO

- AMPLITUDE AND FREQUENCY MODULATION p. 29
- FIBRE OPTICS p. 33
- ELECTROMAGNETISM p. 34
- RADIO, TELEVISION AND VIDEO p. 326
- COMPUTERS p. 334

Today it is possible to send information in different forms – telephone conversations, data and images of documents – around the world in seconds.

Post

Letters have long been the principal form of communication over a distance. By the 17th century in Britain letters and official dispatches were carried by stagecoaches. The recipient paid for the cost of the letter until the introduction of postage stamps in 1840, the first of which was the British 'Penny Black'. For a penny, paid by the sender and registered by fixing a stamp on the envelope, the Royal Mail undertook to deliver a letter weighing not more than half an ounce (about 14 grams) anywhere in the country. Before the penny post, 82 million letters a year were sent, but within 30 years the number had risen to 917 million. Other countries soon followed suit with their own postage stamps.

Telegraphy

Efficient as the 19th century postal system was, a quicker method of communication was needed, particularly to co-ordinate the movements of the rapidly growing railways. The answer was the *electric telegraph*. This resulted from the work of a number of pioneers, following the publication by the Danish physicist Hans Christiaan Oersted (1777–1851) of his discovery that a magnetized needle could be deflected by an electric current flowing in a wire (see pp. 34–5).

The electric telegraph was put into a practical form by two Englishmen, Sir Charles Wheatstone (1802–75) and William Cooke (1806–79), who were granted a British patent in 1837. The following year the American inventor Samuel Morse (1791–1872) – in partnership with Alfred Vail (1807–59) – devised the *Morse code*, in which individual letters of the alphabet and digits are represented by different sequences of dots and dashes. This enabled messages to be sent using a single circuit at a rate of 10 words a minute. The operator tapped a key to send the message as a series of electrical impulses. At the other end it was printed out as pen marks on paper tape and decoded. However, the pen was soon replaced by a *sounder* when it was found that operators could decode messages faster by hearing the sounds of the pen making dots and dashes than by reading the marks on paper.

In 1851 the first telegraph cable was laid across the English Channel, and the first transatlantic cable was laid in August 1858, although it soon failed. In 1866 a more successful cable was laid, and by 1872 the majority of the world's great cities were in contact with one another by telegraph. Telegraphy remained the principal form of telecommunication until just before World War I, when the telephone began to take over.

Telephones

Transmitting the sound of the human voice required further inventions – the *microphone* and the *receiver*. A microphone controls the current in a circuit operating a receiver, which generates a sound similar to that received by the microphone. The first successful telephone was made by the Scottish inventor Alexander Graham Bell (1847–1922) in 1876 (see photo).

The introduction of automatic exchanges early in the 20th century made possible a huge growth in the telephone system (see box). However, a number of technical problems remained. Because even high-quality metal conductors show electrical resistance, it is difficult to send a signal over a long distance. For this reason, amplifiers – known as *repeaters* – had to be installed at regular intervals to compensate for the loss of power. The cost of providing and maintaining repeaters was considerable, and long distance telephony only became effective once long-lived repeaters had been developed.

Alexander Graham Bell. Bell's interest in transmitting the sound of the human voice grew out of his research into speech mechanics while training teachers for the deaf.

Early telephone subscribers had to rely on human operators to connect their calls by means of a plug-and-socket arrangement. The first practical automatic switching device was invented in 1889 by a Kansas City undertaker, Almon B. Strowger. Fearing that his local operator – the wife of a business rival – was diverting his calls, he devised an automatic exchange – a 'girl-less, wait-less' telephone.

The Strowger system proved so successful that it formed the basis of subsequent mechanical exchanges. A series of electrical pulses, produced by means of a dial, caused a contact arm to rise and rotate through a corresponding number of steps, so making the desired connection. It was not until the 1960s, with the emergence of electronic exchanges, that the dominance of the Strowger system began to be challenged, and some Strowger exchanges are still in use today.

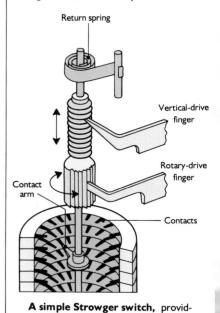

A simple Strowger switch, providing a connection to number 34.

During the 1960s *electronic exchanges* began to be introduced. Dialled numbers are stored electronically and routed to their destination automatically and at great speed. Such exchanges have few moving parts, less noisy lines because there are no mechanical switches, and can operate quickly enough for push-button rather than dial phones to be used.

Multiplexing

In the early days of telephony, each subscriber telephone was connected to the exchange by an individual circuit, and every link between exchanges was achieved by cables transmitting single calls. The result was not only chaotic and unsightly, but also expensive as telephone wires are costly to install and maintain. From 1910, this problem was resolved by the introduction of *multiplexing*, which allowed more than one call to be sent down the same set of wires at the same time. At its simplest, this is achieved by allocating carrier waves of different frequencies (see p. 29) to different calls. These waves are then sepa-ted out at the receiving exchange by a ning arrangement rather like that used a radio sets.

In modern telephony, multiplexing is achieved by *pulse-code modulation*. The continuous waveform of the human voice is converted into a digital signal by means of sampling at fixed intervals – normally 000 times a second. These samples are transformed by an *encoder* into a code that is transmitted in a series of regular pulses and pauses. At the other end, the pulses are separated again into individual conversations, and converted back into a form that is analogous to the human voice so that they can be heard on the telephone. In this method, numerous calls can be transmitted on the same line by using the gaps between the samples.

Optical cables

An even better way of transmitting more calls along the same line is to replace electrical currents with microwaves (see p. 35) or with light. The amount of information that can be carried is higher for high-frequency carrier waves, but very-high-frequency carrier signals are quickly weakened by ordinary wires. Both microwaves and light produced by lasers offer much higher frequencies, with the capacity to handle thousands of calls along a single link. Cables made of optical fibre, which can transmit laser light over long distances without loss (see p. 33), are now replacing the old copper cables. Optical cables are cheaper to make, tough, flexible, and immune to electrical interference. Each glass fibre in the cable can handle thousands of telephone calls at once, each one at a different frequency.

Microwaves and satellites

Radio waves at very high frequencies – *microwaves* – may be focused into beams and used for the transmission of telephone messages over middle-range distances. Unlike other radio waves with longer frequencies, microwaves are not reflected by the ionosphere (see pp. 77 and 326) and so cannot be used for long-distance telecommunications unless they are transmitted via satellites. The first effective telecommunications satellite was *Telstar*, launched in 1962. Orbiting the Earth in 150 minutes, the satellite was used to transmit a single television link or a limited number of telephone calls for 20 minutes in each orbit.

Telecommunications satellites now orbit the globe high above the Equator in 24 hours. By this means the satellites are always in the same location relative to stations on Earth and can therefore be used constantly. Satellite telecommunications are largely regulated by half a dozen international organizations, the most prominent of which is the consortium Intelsat, with nearly 120 member states and some 180 stations. Each of its satellites – numbering 13 in 1989 – can link over 30 000 telephone calls and 60 television channels.

Radio waves are used in mobile telephones in cars; these are commonly called *cordless telephones*, but more accurately referred to as *cellular radio*. Because the number of users is greatly in excess of the number of radio channels available for this service, the area over which cellular radio operates is divided into cells in each of which there is a low-power radio transmitter whose operations are confined to the users in its area. By this means the number of calls on the system can be multiplied by the number of cells. Calls between cells are transmitted via a central control.

Data transmission

Telephones are not restricted to communication by voice. Increasingly they are being used to send data from computer to computer, and images of documents by facsimile transmission (fax). In many Western countries telephones are widely used to send information for display on a TV set. These services are known generically as *viewdata*. They offer a great range of information, which is stored centrally on a computer database and covers topics as varied as stock-market prices, sports and general news, holiday information, job advertisements, weather forecasts and entertainment guides.

For transmission of computer data, a *modem* – modulator-demodulator – is needed at each end of the line. A modem converts the digital signals from the computer into a form that can be transmitted by telephone and reconverts them at the other end. Provided the telephone lines are good enough, portable computers can now be connected up to the telephone system anywhere in the world, and used to send information elsewhere. Where lines are poor, *telex systems* – the descendants of the telegraph – survive. These send images of documents along the line, letter by letter, to be printed out at the far end.

Facsimile transmission – fax – is one of the fastest growing of the new telephone services. It has been available for many years – particularly in Japan, where the language, with its many symbols, makes telex too complex. Fax has only really begun to grow rapidly, however, with the availability of much cheaper machines. Fax works by scanning a sheet of typed or handwritten material, and turning the result into a digital signal that can be sent over the telephone network to a designated fax machine somewhere else. It is by far the quickest way to transmit images of drawings or typed documents.

The telephone network can also be used to send electronic mail from terminal to terminal, and to replace the use of cash for purchasing goods. *Electronic funds transfer* (EFT) is a system for automatically debiting a customer's bank account and transferring money to that of the store, without handling cash, cheques or credit cards. EFT is still in its infancy, but offers great economies over the existing paper-laden systems and is likely to grow. NHa

A spray of polymer optical fibres. Optical fibres have a core of perspex and a thin outer covering of polymer. The fibres illustrated are used for lighting, but those used in optical cables to transmit telephone calls are similar.

Satellite dishes at Raisting in Germany: a ground-based receiving station for radio signals retransmitted by communications satellites.

Seeing the Invisible

The light by which we see is only one of many means at our disposal for detecting, measuring and observing things. We can also use sound, beams of electrons, and radiation in various parts of the electromagnetic spectrum, such as infrared radiation, gamma rays, X-rays and radio waves. By these means we can penetrate the depths of outer space and gain access to a hidden world inside our own bodies, deep in the oceans and under the Earth's crust.

These forms of radiation – like light – exhibit wave-like properties and travel in straight lines (see p. 28). In certain circumstances, therefore, they can be used to provide sharp shadows or clear images of objects that would otherwise be invisible.

X-rays

When Wilhelm Röntgen (1845–1923) discovered X-rays in 1895, the effect was sensational. By directing X-rays through the body of a living person, the bones within the flesh – which absorb X-rays – could be seen as shadows cast on photo-

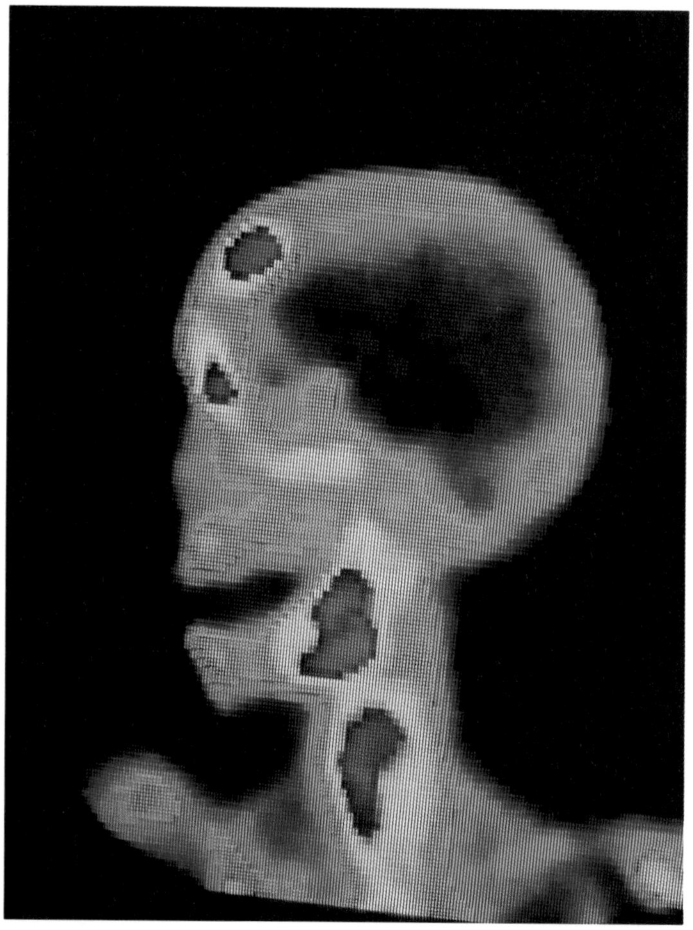

A gamma-camera scan of the skull of a patient suffering from secondary bone cancer. This colour-coded image shows the position and intensity of gamma rays emitted from a radioactive isotope injected into a blood vessel supplying the skull region. The technique depends on the fact that the radioisotope forms greater concentrations in tumours and cancerous bone (shown here in red) than in unaffected areas.

graphic emulsions or fluorescent screens. Within months X-rays were in use for diagnosing bone fractures. It was quickly found that the digestive tract could also be seen, if the patient were 'fed' with a chemical such as barium sulphate that absorbs X-rays and therefore shows up when scanned.

X-rays were so called because Röntgen did not know what they were and gave them the name mathematicians give to an unknown quantity. They are in fact a form of short-wave electromagnetic radiation emitted by cathode-ray tubes (see p. 326). More than a momentary exposure to X-rays damages tissue, which has given them a second use in radiotherapy, where they are used to destroy cancers in the body.

The use of X-rays in diagnosis was revolutionized by the development in 1973 of *computerized axial tomography*, applied first to the skull and later to the whole body. Earlier tomography techniques had provided cross-sectional images, but with nothing like the clarity of this new method. The patient is placed inside a machine in which the body is scanned by a rotating source of X-rays. Variations in the density of the tissues are detected, and assembled by a computer into a cross-section of the brain or body.

In addition to their medical applications, X-rays may also be used to examine inanimate objects, such as baggage at airport check-ins or to detect subsurface defects in materials. Gamma rays are sometimes used for similar purposes, while historical documents (for instance) are studied in very much the same way using beta rays.

Sound

Animals such as bats, whales and dolphins have long been known to use high-pitched sounds to locate objects in the dark (see pp. 146 and 163). In the 1920s *sonar* or *ultrasound devices* – closely mimicking the ultrasonic technique used by animals – were developed, primarily for naval use in detecting enemy submarines. A series of pulses of sound in the ultrasonic region – above the range of human hearing – are sent out and their reflections detected. From the time taken for the pulses to return, the position of intervening objects can be determined. Whereas bats use ultrasonic emissions (with very short wavelengths) because they need to locate tiny objects such as insects, sonar uses ultrasonics to avoid the excessive spreading of the beam in water. Such techniques are also commonly used to measure the depth of water,

and can be used by fishing boats to gauge the position of shoals of fish, or by geologists to study the sea bed.

Ultrasound has applications in medicine, where it has distinct advantages over X-rays. Whereas X-rays cannot be used on pregnant women for fear of injuring the foetus, *ultrasound scanning* has no damaging effects. The images obtained are so precise that they can even be used to guide operations on the unborn child to relieve a number of dangerous conditions.

Yet another application of sound is in *seismic surveying* in the search for oil and minerals (see pp. 310 and 313). A loud impact on the ground, created by an explosive charge or by dropping a heavy weight, creates sound waves that travel down into the Earth and are reflected back from underground rock layers. The sound waves are detected by an array of instruments at the surface, and the data can be processed and displayed by computer. From the arrangement of the rock layers, geologists can estimate the chances of finding particular minerals or a reservoir of trapped oil or gas.

Radar

Radio waves – like sound waves – are reflected off solid objects. This fact led to the development of *radar* (short for 'radio detection and ranging'), following studies by a number of scientists in the 1930s. In order to give suitably narrow beams, of adequate intensity and able to offer accurate location of objects, the shortest wavelengths then attainable were used. Initially this meant wavelengths of several metres, but this was gradually reduced, microwaves coming into use in the early 1940s. Radar sets were installed in Britain in time to provide early detection of the oncoming squadrons of German fighters and bombers in the Battle of Britain in 1940.

Microwaves are transmitted in the form of pulses, with the gaps between pulses chosen so that there is time for the reflected pulse to return and be detected before the next is sent out. From the time taken for the pulse to bounce back, the distance to the object can be calculated. If the object under surveillance is moving, the frequency of the echo will change, and from this variation in frequency – known as the Doppler shift (see p. 31) – it is possible to determine both the object's speed and its direction of movement.

Radar today has many uses, both military and civilian. The biggest radar sets are used to give advance warning of a nuclear attack by detecting missiles soon after launch. Both the navigation of ships in crowded sea lanes and air-traffic control would be impossible without radar. It can also be used in weather forecasting and for mapping. *Radar altimeters* in aircraft work by sending signals to the ground and measuring the time it takes them to return. The data is then used to calculate the aircraft's altitude.

Radio astronomy

In 1931 it was discovered that there are radio waves emanating from sources in

space. They were first detected by an American engineer, Karl Jansky (1905–1950), who was studying static, the noisy crackling sound that interferes with radio reception. He discovered a source of radio waves far outside the solar system, in the constellation of Sagittarius.

After World War II a number of *radio telescopes* were built to investigate these sources. Some extraordinary and unexpected features of the universe were revealed, including *pulsars*, tiny col-

A scanning electron micrograph of a dust mite among household dust, shown in false colour and magnified 500 times. Scanning electron microscopes are capable of magnifying objects up to a million times their real size, and have been responsible for some of the most dramatic pictures ever taken.

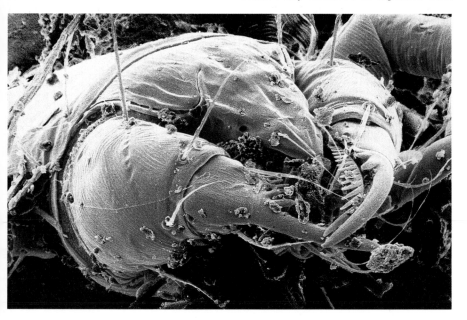

lapsed stars rotating at up to 30 times a second and emitting intense beams of radio waves. Radio astronomy was also responsible for discovering the most distant objects ever detected – *quasars*, quasi-stellar objects that are thousands of millions of light years away and emit as much radio energy as a whole galaxy. *X-ray telescopes* carried by satellites have also been used for astronomical observation.

Electron microscopy

However powerful an optical microscope, there is a limit to its resolving power, set by the wavelength of visible light (typically about 5×10^{-7} m). Although particles much smaller than this wavelength can be detected, it is not possible to resolve any detail or to separate close objects. The answer is to use a beam of electrons. Such beams typically have wavelengths 10 000 times shorter than that of visible light, and much shorter wavelengths are possible; they can be focused (by means of electric or magnetic fields) to form images.

The first *electron microscopes* were built in the 1930s. A thin slice is taken from the material to be examined. A beam of electrons is then passed through the slice, and the electrons strike a screen to produce an image. An alternative is the *scanning electron microscope*, in which the beam scans across the surface of the object, producing a detailed three-dimensional image (see photo). Its one limitation is that it cannot study living specimens, because the object must be kept in a vacuum to prevent air molecules interfering with the beam.

Image intensifiers

Image intensifiers can be used to amplify electronically the image or shadow produced by detection techniques using various types of radiation. Particularly in military contexts, image intensifiers have been adapted for use at night, to boost the tiny quantities of moon- or starlight reflected from targets or other objects. Essentially they work like TV cameras, turning the image into a signal that can be amplified and displayed on a screen.

Devices sensitive to emissions of *infrared radiation* (see p. 34) can be used for a variety of detection and imaging purposes. In military contexts, infrared sensors are used to detect heat given out by engines or even individual soldiers. Because infrared devices can operate in complete darkness, photographic emulsions sensitive to infrared light can be used at night or in conditions of poor visibility.　　　　　　　　NHa

SEE ALSO

- WAVE THEORY p. 28
- ACOUSTICS p. 30
- OPTICS p. 32
- ELECTROMAGNETISM p. 34
- ATOMS AND SUBATOMIC PARTICLES p. 38
- MEDICAL TECHNOLOGY p. 242
- FINDING OIL p. 310
- DISCOVERING MINERALS p. 313
- APPLIED PHOTOGRAPHY p. 325

Computers

A computer is a machine that manipulates data according to a predetermined sequence of commands to produce a desired result. Initially computers were seen solely as devices for performing mathematical calculations, but they have far exceeded the expectations of their original designers. Almost any kind of information can be represented in a form that can be handled by a computer – letters of the alphabet, dots that form pictures, telecommunication signals and graphs, to name but a few.

In order to manipulate information, computers are fed instructions known as *programs* (see below). There are many different types of computer program (collectively known as *software*), all of which tell the *hardware* (the machinery of the computer) precisely what to do at some point in the process of communication or data handling. The machine does exactly what it is instructed to do by the software, only much quicker than a human – hence the illusion of intelligence.

Any computer has four essential elements:

(1) a *storage device* to record data;
(2) a *processor* to manipulate data;
(3) an *input/ouput device* to get data into and out of the machine;
(4) a *program* to control the process.

Types of storage device

All data is stored and manipulated in a computer in *binary* – a number system that uses just 1s and 0s (see p. 65). Each of the binary digits, or *bits*, is represented by an electronic circuit, or other device, that can have only one of two positions, either 'on' or 'off'.

Bits are grouped into *bytes* – the fundamental unit used to determine the *address*, or location, of an item of data in the memory of a computer. Most com-

EDSAC (1946), containing 3500 valves, was the first stored-program computer in operation. It is seen here with its designers, Maurice Wilkes (left) and W. Renwick.

puters use 8-bit bytes. Modern computers often have large amounts of data and programs that are loaded when the computer is built. This data – which cannot be changed by the user – is called *ROM* (Read-Only Memory).

A ROM is one type of *integrated circuit* or *chip* that is used to make a computer (see photo). Each of these chips is a single piece of silicon that has millions of transistors (see p. 37) within it, all interconnected to form an array of circuits, in which each tiny memory circuit stores a single bit of information. Complex chips of this nature are constructed using *VLSI* – Very Large-Scale Integration.

Computer memory that can be changed is called *RAM* or *DRAM* – Dynamic Random Access Memory. DRAMs hold the data as a static electric charge that must be refreshed regularly before the charge leaks away.

Information that is to be kept on a long-term basis, or even removed from the computer, is stored on magnetic disks or tapes. These store a signal in exactly the same way as a domestic tape recorder (see pp. 326–7). Computers can also use a modified form of compact-disc player (see p. 327) called a *CD-ROM* to hold large quantities of read-only data. CD-ROMs can store 600 times as much information as can be held inside the computer or on a removable magnetic disk, for about the same cost as an audio CD. They are used to store directories and other reference material. A further development is *CDI* (CD-interactive), which allows interaction between program and user.

The processor and microprocessor

Many powerful computers use large numbers of integrated circuits mounted on printed circuitboards to make the processor. *Microcomputers* use a processor that is all on a single chip – a *microprocessor*. Microprocessors were originally designed to be used in, for example, digital wrist watches, desk calculators and control · circuitry for washing machines and video players.

Each instruction that the processor executes manipulates the data through operations such as the addition and subtraction of values by setting and clearing individual bits. It then selects which instruction to execute next by testing the results of these operations.

Computers are now classified into the following categories:

(1) *microcomputer* – this has a single-chip processor;
(2) *minicomputer* – a computer (often used for small office networks) that is intermediate in capacity between a microcomputer and a mainframe;
(3) *mainframe* – the most powerful general-purpose computer;
(4) *supercomputer* – a computer designed specifically for speed (see pp. 336–7).

Software

The *program* is a series of coded instructions held as numbers, each of which

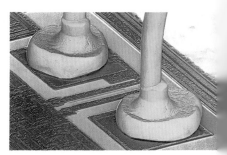

Part of an integrated circuit, or silicon chip, colour-enhanced and magnified 110 times, showing two connecting wires bonded to terminal pads on the edge of the device. The small squares at the end of the two tracks running between the pads are transistors, which act as switches to control the input and output to the connecting wires.

makes the computer perform a simple movement or manipulation of an item of data.

Machine-code programming is the most detailed way of programming a computer. It involves coding the instructions in numbers that can be directly obeyed by the computer. Programmers write the instructions in groups of three or four bits, and since each group can have 8 or 16 values, these systems are called *octal* and *hexadecimal*.

Gradually a method of writing down programs was developed using mnemonics (a device to assist the memory) instead of numbers. A special program, called an *assembler*, takes the original text, written in mnemonics, and translates it into binary values for the machine-code instructions.

However, programming in this way still relies on an intimate knowledge of the internal workings of the computer. FORTRAN and COBOL were the first *high-level computer languages* to be used that did not require a programmer to be familiar with the details of how the computer worked.

Most programs contain errors or *bugs*. Discovering and removing bugs is both difficult and time-consuming. Some computer languages – such as BASIC (Beginners' All-purpose Symbolic Instruction Code), which was developed as a language suitable for beginners – speed up debugging by interpreting each line of the program just before it is executed. This avoids the need to recompile the program after each bug is traced and eliminated.

As computers became more sophisticated, the need arose for the manufacturers to provide an *operating system* to control access and to assist the use of the machine. A typical operating system includes utility programs for common operations and a method of storing and filing information on a disk.

There is now such great demand for software that programs must be written using still higher levels of abstraction. *Fourth-generation languages* (4GL) have been developed to enable a programmer to describe the problem and the data, and to leave the computer to write the actual programs. Although this may produce programs that are less efficient, it makes

LANDMARKS IN COMPUTING

1790 Joseph-MarieJacquard(1752-1834)used punched cards to control a weaving loom (see p. 319).

1842 Charles Babbage (1791–1871) designed the Difference engine – a semi-automatic mechanical calculator.

1890 Herman Hollerith (1860–1929) successfully used punched cards to record the American census.

1941 Konrad Zuse(1910–)made a mechanical computer complete with mechanical memories and arithmetic units made from relays.

1945 COLOSSUS I was developed to decode secret messages during World War II.

1945 ENIAC, the first general-purpose machine was designed by J. P. Eckert and J. W. Maunchly. It was used to calculate the trajectories of bombs and shells. ENIAC had 18 000 valves, weighed 30 tonnes, consumed 140kW, and occupied 85 cubic metres.

1946 EDSAC (Electronic Delay Storage Automatic Calculator), the first stored-program computer in operation (see photo, far left). This machine was similar to the EDVAC, designed in the USA by a team led by John von Neumann (1903–57).

1947 Transistor demonstrated.

1952 First use of germanium semiconductor diodes in a machine called Gamma 3.

1957–59 Programming languages such as FORTRAN (FORmula TRANslator), ALGOL (ALGOrithmic Language), and COBOL (COmmercial Business Orientated Language) were introduced.

1958 First computers to use transistors, e.g. Elliott 802.

1964 First integrated circuits, e.g. IBM System 360.

1965 BASIC (Beginners All-purpose Symbolic Instruction Code) – the most common interpreted language – developed by Kemeny and Kurtz.

1965 Digital Equipment made the PDP-8, the first mass-produced computer.

1974 First microprocessor-based computer systems developed by Intel using an 8-bit microprocessor.

1978 First 32-bit minicomputer, the VAX-11/780.

1979 The IBM Personal Computer launched.

1989 Optical computer demonstrated.

SEE ALSO

- FIRBRE OPTICS p. 33
- ELECTRICITY IN ACTION p. 36
- NUMBER SYSTEMS p. 64
- SETS AND LOGIC p. 67
- HI-FI p. 328
- TELECOMMUNICATIONS p. 330
- ARTIFICIAL INTELLIGENCE p. 336

mance increased about one million times. The speed of the basic circuitry improved only about 10 000 times; the remainder of the improvement came from changes in the internal organization of computers.

The amount of work done in a processor as a result of a single instruction is determined by *word length* – the number of bits that are processed at a time. The earliest microprocessors handled only four bits at a time, although the first general-purpose microcomputers had eight-bit words. Common computers now use 16-, 32- and even 64-bit words, and are correspondingly more powerful.

Most computers can be made to operate faster by making things happen in parallel. A well-designed computer has all the parts working at the same instant of time; however, many low-cost computers have very fast memories and processors, but relatively slow disks. Various techniques, called *cacheing* and *memory-resident disks*, have been developed to try to restore the balance.

Supercomputers have been designed to operate at very high speed (see pp. 336–7). Many computers that are used for military purposes are specifically designed for their task and have very high performance. They perform tasks such as tracking aircraft on radar. In practice, the maximum power of a computer is limited by the heat that it generates internally, and by the time taken for a signal to travel within it. Research is currently being conducted into replacing electronic signals within computers by laser light (see p. 33). If successful, this promises to produce even more powerful computers.   SD

the best use of the most valuable resource – the human programmer.

'Off the shelf' programs are called *applications*. The most common type on larger computers is the database, but small computers are predominantly used for word processing. A *database* allows information to be collected, stored, classified and looked up at random. These types of actions require a large mass of information to be stored in an organized way. Modern database programs use some form of standard 'structured query language' (SQL) to express what information is required from a database. Other popular types of programs include the *spreadsheet*, which produces the results of elaborate calculations on rows and columns of numbers on several sheets, computer-aided design (see p. 337), and *multimedia* educational programs that combine sound, words and visual displays.

Increasing performance

Between 1950 and 1990 computer perfor-

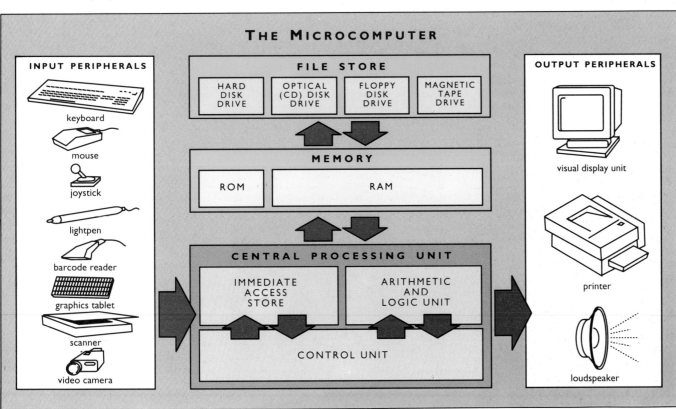

THE MICROCOMPUTER

INPUT PERIPHERALS
- keyboard
- mouse
- joystick
- lightpen
- barcode reader
- graphics tablet
- scanner
- video camera

FILE STORE
- HARD DISK DRIVE
- OPTICAL (CD) DISK DRIVE
- FLOPPY DISK DRIVE
- MAGNETIC TAPE DRIVE

MEMORY
- ROM
- RAM

CENTRAL PROCESSING UNIT
- IMMEDIATE ACCESS STORE
- ARITHMETIC AND LOGIC UNIT
- CONTROL UNIT

OUTPUT PERIPHERALS
- visual display unit
- printer
- loudspeaker

Artificial Intelligence

Computer scientists have long dreamt of building machines that can think. So far they have failed, but in the process they have taught us much about the way that humans think. The problem for the field of artificial intelligence (AI) has been in defining intelligence and demonstrating that machines are capable of it.

The British mathematician Alan Turing (1912–54) designed an experiment to test whether a machine shows intelligence. In Turing's experiment a human conducts a dialogue – by means of a computer terminal – with both a machine and another human, hidden behind a screen. Both respondents must answer every question put to them. Turing argued that if the questioner could not decide which of the two respondents was the machine, then the machine would have demonstrated intelligence.

AI researchers have adopted two very different approaches to building intelligent machines. Some have tried to build machines that use the same principles as biological intelligence, while others have chosen examples of intelligent behaviour (such as chess playing or language) and tried to build machines that copy it.

Since its origins in the mid 1950s, AI research has attacked a wide range of problems. These include problem solving, natural language and vision.

Problem solving

The first attempts to tackle problem solving (often used as a measure of intelligence) produced the Logic Theorem program in the 1950s. As its name suggests, it was capable of proving theorems. Later came a more advanced program called the General Problem Solver, which was able to tackle more complex mathematical problems.

Since then computer scientists have made great strides in improving the problem-solving abilities of computers, but these are still confined to those problems that lie within the realms of logic (see p. 394).

Language

A major goal of AI research is to enable humans to interact with computers using natural language – language that is written and spoken by humans, as distinct from computer-program languages (see p. 334).

To understand and interpret such language, much more knowledge is needed than was once thought. Computers have to be able to work out the context in which a word is uttered in order to interpret what is being said. To this end AI researchers have made use of the ideas of the linguist Noam Chomsky (see p. 608), who suggested that language obeys a set of rules that can be expressed in mathematical terms.

Running parallel with this work on natural language, research has been undertaken into speech recognition. Speech-recognition systems use information about the structure and components of speech and are typically 'trained' in on one person's voice. The challenge is to develop a machine that can recognize what any one of a variety of speakers is saying – even if their voice is affected by, for instance, a cold – and distinguish speech from background noise.

Storing knowledge

Computers are able to store a vast amount of information, but this cannot be stored in an orderless mass – the computer has to be able to get at the relevant bits of information to solve a given problem (see box).

To decide how computers should store information most efficiently for the purposes of AI, scientists have explored how humans store and access the knowledge in their brains. As a result much has been discovered about how humans learn.

Expert systems

The most tangible and practical result of

Speech recognition systems: an engineer tests a talk-writer computer, which allows the machine to interpret and act upon human voice patterns. The interpretation of voice patterns is a criterion for the development of fifth-generation computer systems, in which extreme user-friendliness – the ability to communicate in natural language – would be a major feature. Fifth-generation computers will be radically different from existing machines and will be based on expert systems, very high-level programming languages, decentralized processing and Very Large Scale Integration (VLSI) microchips.

AI research has been expert systems. These are designed to help humans make decisions, typically in solving problems where it would otherwise be necessary to call in an expert in a particular area.

Many early expert systems tackled medical diagnosis, but industry and commerce have now begun to take them seriously. Finance companies use them to advise on whether a customer should be given a loan, or what type of insurance would best suit their needs. Expert systems have also been used in mineral prospecting and chemical analysis, and to build computers. They are particularly valuable where decisions have to be made in a hostile environment, such as nuclear power plants.

An expert system has three components:

(1) a database or *knowledge base*, in which the knowledge and experience of an expert are summarized in the form of rules;
(2) an *inference engine*, which is a program that searches the knowledge base for the best possible answer to a question;
(3) a *user interface*, which allows the user to 'talk' to the system.

The software needed to build an expert system – a so-called *shell* – is already widely available. Although a shell lacks only the knowledge base, building the knowledge base proves in practice to be difficult and time-consuming. Experts often find it difficult to explain to a computer engineer exactly how they reach their decisions, and translating the mechanics of these decisions – which may rely heavily on experience and intuition – into the exact mathematical logic required by a computer is a complex task.

Robotic arms working on the assembly line of a Citroën car production plant.

building the knowledge base has spawned the new field of knowledge engineering – the process of getting the knowledge out of the human expert and translating it into a database of rules.

Expert systems are of no use where intuition or common sense is necessary – they can only be used where the decision-making process follows a simple, well-defined logic path. But such systems are very valuable where experts are scarce, or as a means of preserving knowledge and transferring it to others as individuals retire or change jobs.

Neural computing

As neurophysiologists have begun to unravel the structure of the brain, computer scientists have seized upon their findings as a potential basis for a computer architecture.

The brain is essentially a complex network of interlinking neurones (nerve cells; see pp. 220 and 222) and it is this interlinking that is the key to solving problems quickly. The idea of building a neural network has been around since the 1940s, but only since the early 1980s has interest been rekindled. In this time computer technology has advanced rapidly, making the prospect of building neural computers more realistic.

Neural networks offer big advantages over conventional (von Neumann) computers (see p. 334) in searching large databases for close matches, or storing and accessing data. They consist of a large number of processors (nodes) – the points at which the information is processed – linked by communication channels. Neural computers learn by example; they are not programmed like conventional computers, which means that they are not simply given a series of instructions to carry out. They use the concept of feedback – where part of the output of a node is returned as input for another process, for self-correction – and hence they can interact with their environment.

They also differ from conventional computers in that changing the interconnections between nodes alters the behaviour of the network, making it suitable for a particular kind of problem solving.

Neural networks are now finding their way into the commercial world; early applications are in financial advice, recognizing intruders, and detecting explosives.

Robotics

Another major branch of AI is robotics. The technology is still in its infancy, however – the idea of an intelligent robot replacing the fallible human is still a long way off.

While robots are used on the production lines of most car manufacturing plants – for assembly and simple spot welding – they are very primitive. They inhabit a 'perfect' world, and have no ability to sense and react to their environment.

One important field of AI research – three-dimensional vision – is crucial to developing practical systems. A wide range of techniques is being developed for extracting the salient features of an image; this would allow a robot to recognize and pick up an object from the production line, for example, even if the object were not in its correct position.

Thinking machines?

The road to the thinking machine is proving longer and more difficult than the AI pioneers of the 1940s and 1950s believed. There is still much debate in the AI community about whether computers will ever be able to think, or to display the traits normally considered essential for intelligence.

But the pursuit of the thinking machine has brought us robots, machine translation, computer systems capable of obeying verbal instructions and recognizing faces, and a chess-playing program capable of beating some of the world's top players. While the debate continues, research into AI is bringing a better understanding of brain function and our own intelligence, and an insight into such things as speech disorders and learning problems.   AM

SEE ALSO
- THE BRAIN p. 222
- THE POWER OF SPEECH p. 226
- LEARNING, CREATIVITY AND INTELLIGENCE p. 230
- COMPUTERS p. 334
- LOGIC AND ARGUMENT p. 494
- HOW LANGUAGE WORKS p. 608

STORING INFORMATION

There are many ways of storing information. Some commonly used approaches include:

Trees: here the relationship between chunks of knowledge is expressed as rules (or branches).

Frames: similar to a series of boxes, where related facts can be stored or pigeon-holed.

Semantic nets: these show the relationships between different chunks of knowledge.

Shown here are different ways of organizing the knowledge that birds and mammals are animals; sparrows and penguins are birds; sparrows can fly but penguins cannot; whales and cats are mammals; whales can swim.

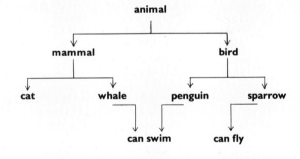

TREE STRUCTURE

animal
- mammal
  - cat
  - whale → can swim
- bird
  - penguin → can swim
  - sparrow → can fly

FRAME

Animal

bird
instance – penguin
can fly – no
can swim – yes

mammal
instance – whale
can fly – no
can swim – yes

SEMANTIC NET

animal
- is a → bird
  - is a ← sparrow → can fly
  - is a ← penguin → cannot fly / can swim
- is a → mammal
  - is a ← whale → can swim
  - is a ← cat → cannot swim

COMPUTER-AIDED DESIGN

Complex tasks such as meteorological forecasting, or determining airflow over car or aircraft bodies, require many related computations. Supercomputers are able to perform such calculations at very high speed. Shown here is a computer-graphics image of the airflow over an F-16 jet fighter aircraft, produced by a Cray supercomputer.

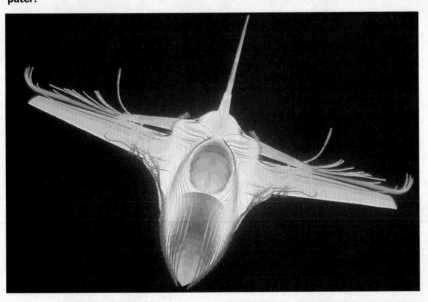

Building Construction

The essential task of building construction is to satisfy that most basic of human needs – a roof over one's head. Buildings have many purposes and construction is not confined to providing dwellings: it embraces the provision of shelter for most human activities.

The purpose of a roof is to cover a floor, and floor area is the prime feature of a building's specification. In modern times, building design has aimed to minimize the cost per square metre of floor, while observing local or national building and planning regulations. *Building regulations* specify approved techniques and materials, chiefly with the aim of enhancing safety, but because they generally favour well-tried methods, they tend to delay innovation. *Planning regulations* are concerned rather with the appearance of a building and its suitability to a particular location. In cities, where land is expensive, high-rise buildings may be cheaper per square metre, despite the greater construction costs.

Parts of a building

The part of a building above ground level is called the *superstructure*; the part falling below ground level is referred to as the *substructure*. The stability of a building depends on its load-bearing components. There are three kinds of load:

1. *Dead* – resulting from the weight of the building itself;
2. *Live* – the result of furnishing, equipment and bodies;
3. *Lateral* – the result of sideways pressure, typically due to wind.

In a typical house, the load is borne principally by load-bearing walls. Internal dividing walls or partitions may or may not carry loads. Larger buildings may also use columns, arches and domes to support loads. The load-bearing substructure is known as the *foundations*, or *footings*, and for a house this is usually concrete supports for the load-bearing walls. Where the ground is soft, *raft foundations* may be used, which distribute the load evenly over the area occupied by the building. For larger buildings, *piles* may be driven through the ground to connect the substructure with ground of sufficient strength to support the building.

An alternative to load-bearing walls is *skeleton construction*, in which a structu-ral frame carries the load, and the walls (*curtain walls*) are used simply to enclose space. In most conditions, load-bearing walls are not suitable for structures of more than four floors.

The development of building construction

The *post-and-lintel technique*, in which vertical posts support horizontal lintels, has a long history; it is exemplified in its basic form by the ancient stone circle at Stonehenge in England. The method has been used from antiquity for supporting roofs, the posts often taking the form of pillars, as in Egyptian and Greek temples. It is suitable for timber as well as masonry construction.

A way of spanning larger openings is provided by the *arch* (developed by the Romans), but this is not required in smaller, domestic buildings. The *pointed arch*, a feature of Gothic architecture (see p. 522), foreshadowed modern skeleton building in that loads were not transferred from the arch to the walls, but to load-bearing ribs, buttresses, shafts and piers. This enabled walls to be pierced for large openings.

In most countries timber was the favoured material for dwellings. Where wood was plentiful, planks or split trunks could form walls, but elsewhere the spaces between the wooden frame were filled with wattle (intertwined sticks and twigs) covered in clay and, later, with brick or tile. By about 1600 – when good wood was already becoming scarce – most town houses in Europe were *half-timbered*, having a load-bearing oak frame filled in with various materials. The box-like frame was often designed to allow the upper storey to overhang, thereby casting rainwater at a safe distance from the lower storey. Foundations were usually of stone.

The large floor area needed by the factories of the 18th and 19th centuries was provided by the use of timber or cast-iron pillars to support beams and floors. The construction of the Crystal Palace in London for the Great Exhibition of 1851 encouraged the design of buildings with cast-iron frames, and it was experience with cast-iron structures such as these that eventually led to steel-framed multi-storey buildings and finally to the sky-scraper. The latter became possible with the introduction of steel-skeleton construction, first used in the Home Insurance Building in Chicago in 1880, while the use of lifts (elevators) from 1860 onwards was a practical necessity.

Modern structural design

After World War II, skeleton-frame buildings became increasingly popular, especially for offices. Walls could be thin and light, thereby allowing the frames to support a greater weight of floor. The outer face of the building could take many decorative or practical forms, including aluminium or stainless-steel sheeting, enamelled steel, glass and bronze. Sometimes these faces had a fire-resistant backing consisting of a concrete layer, insulation, seal and internal finish, forming a *prefabricated sandwich*.

Domestic dwellings saw fewer changes in the postwar years. Skeleton-frame construction, however, was used in the form of timber-framed housing, in which the timber members carried the loads and were covered by curtain walls on the outside, and by plasterboard or other finishing materials on the inside. In many countries, especially where skilled labour was scarce, *prefabricated* or *industrialized building systems* were introduced, in which the main components were made in factories for easy assembly on site. *Panel systems*, in which the walls were load-bearing, became popular, as did *box systems*, in which prefabricated boxes consisting of wall, roof and floor were designed to be assembled in various configurations.

Materials

Over the long history of building construction, there has been a steady substitution of man-made materials for natural ones. Brick, concrete and steel have largely replaced natural stone, such as granite and sandstone, as the latter require expensive skilled labour both in preparation and in assembly. In the same way, thatch and slate have given way to tile for roofing and cladding.

Although wood is still widely used for construction purposes, it too is increasingly being replaced by cheaper composite materials such as plywood (glued layers of wood) and particle board (wood and resin). Concrete and steel are now used for many building purposes, while synthetic materials such as PVC are becoming ever more common in non-structural applications.

New technology

In recent years building innovation has centred around the use of new materials and the potential for saving energy by means of refined insulation and ventilation techniques. The *dome* has also been resurrected as a means of covering the greatest area at the least cost. The stressed-skin dome, in which thin aluminium is stretched over a ribbed framework to form a combined curtain wall and roof, has been successful in specialized uses. In a refined version known as the geodesic dome, the somewhat heavy ribs are replaced by metal tubing in the form of linked hexagons and triangles.

Another trend is towards the development of *tensile structures*, in which the roof is supported by means of cables stretched from pylons. This frees the space beneath the roof from any supporting structure, thereby increasing the usable area. The most notable application is in new sports stadiums, such as the Munich Olympic Stadium.   JW

SEE ALSO

● CIVIL ENGINEERING p. 340
● VISUAL ARTS pp. 504–53

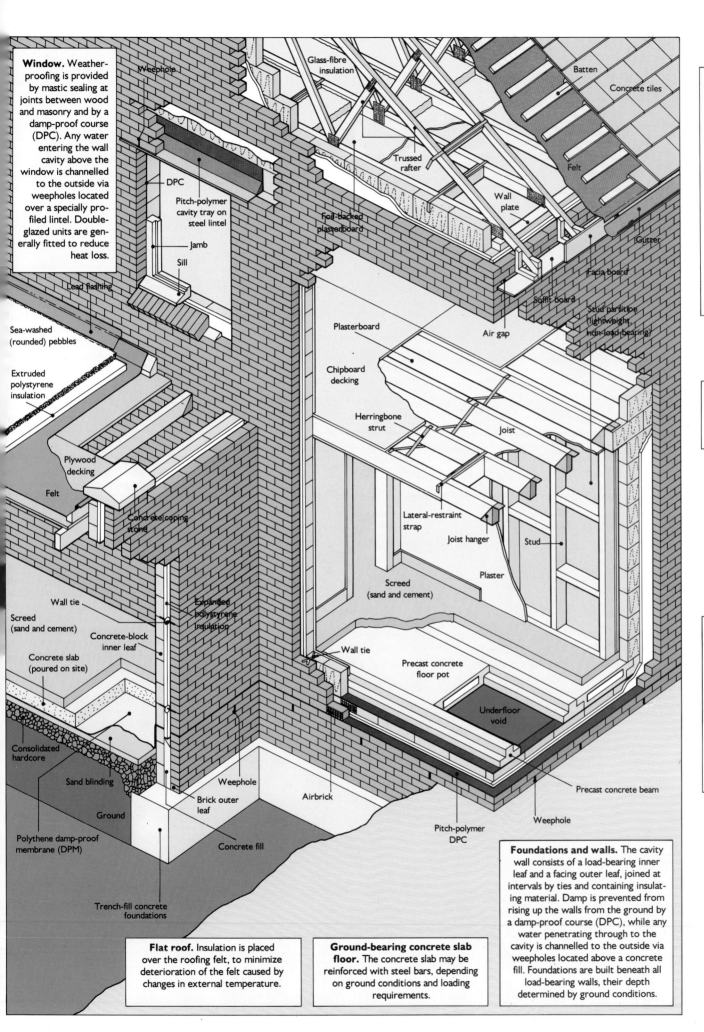

Window. Weather-proofing is provided by mastic sealing at joints between wood and masonry and by a damp-proof course (DPC). Any water entering the wall cavity above the window is channelled to the outside via weepholes located over a specially pro-filed lintel. Double-glazed units are gen-erally fitted to reduce heat loss.

Weephole

Glass-fibre insulation

Batten

Concrete tiles

Trussed rafter

DPC

Pitch-polymer cavity tray on steel lintel

Jamb

Sill

Foil-backed plasterboard

Wall plate

Felt

Gutter

Facia board

Soffit board

Lead flashing

Sea-washed (rounded) pebbles

Extruded polystyrene insulation

Plasterboard

Air gap

Stud partition (lightweight, non-load-bearing)

Chipboard decking

Plywood decking

Felt

Herringbone strut

Joist

Concrete coping stone

Lateral-restraint strap

Joist hanger

Stud

Wall tie

Screed (sand and cement)

Expanded polystyrene insulation

Plaster

Screed (sand and cement)

Concrete-block inner leaf

Wall tie

Concrete slab (poured on site)

Precast concrete floor pot

Underfloor void

Consolidated hardcore

Sand blinding

Ground

Polythene damp-proof membrane (DPM)

Brick outer leaf

Weephole

Airbrick

Precast concrete beam

Concrete fill

Weephole

Pitch-polymer DPC

Trench-fill concrete foundations

Roof. Prefabricated trussed rafters, offering economies in timber and construc-tion time, are increas-ingly replacing traditional cut-timber roofs. Condensation in the roof void is minimized by ade-quate ventilation (typically provided by a continuous air gap running under the eaves) and by a vapour barrier (foil-backed plasterboard), which prevents mois-ture rising from the living area below.

Suspended timber floor. Rigidity is pro-vided by herringbone strutting and lateral-restraint straps.

Suspended concrete pot-and-beam floor. Sus-pended concrete floors can offer better insulation and allow speedier and drier construction than ground-bearing floors, but loading limits are more restricted. The underfloor void is typically ventilated by means of airbricks.

Flat roof. Insulation is placed over the roofing felt, to minimize deterioration of the felt caused by changes in external temperature.

Ground-bearing concrete slab floor. The concrete slab may be reinforced with steel bars, depending on ground conditions and loading requirements.

Foundations and walls. The cavity wall consists of a load-bearing inner leaf and a facing outer leaf, joined at intervals by ties and containing insulat-ing material. Damp is prevented from rising up the walls from the ground by a damp-proof course (DPC), while any water penetrating through to the cavity is channelled to the outside via weepholes located above a concrete fill. Foundations are built beneath all load-bearing walls, their depth determined by ground conditions.

Civil Engineering

In its aims, civil engineering is one of the most ancient of human activities: it is concerned with altering the natural environment for the greater convenience of mankind. It embraces the design and building of major structures and systems, usually concerned with transport: roads and railways, bridges, canals and tunnels, harbours and airports. The first person to call himself a civil engineer – as distinct from a military engineer – is thought to have been John Smeaton (1724–92), designer of the Eddystone Lighthouse (1759) in England.

Although there were highway links in Mesopotamia from as early as 3500 BC, the Romans were probably the first road-builders with fixed engineering standards. At the peak of the Roman Empire in the 1st century AD, Rome had road connections totalling about 85 000 km (53 000 mi).

Roads

Roman roads were constructed with a deep stone surface for stability and load-bearing (see diagram). They had straight alignments and therefore were often hilly. The Roman roads remained the main arteries of European transport for many centuries, and even today many roads follow the Roman routes. New roads were generally of inferior quality, and the achievements of Roman builders were largely unsurpassed until the resurgence of road-building in the 18th century.

The 18th-century engineers, with horse-drawn coaches in mind, preferred to curve their roads to avoid hills. The road surface was regarded as merely a face to absorb wear, the load-bearing strength being obtained from a properly prepared and well-drained foundation. The Scottish engineer John McAdam (1756–1836) typically used a surface layer of only 5 cm (2 in), composed of crushed stone compacted with a mixture of stone dust and water, and then rolled. McAdam's later roads were surfaced with a layer of *tarmacadam* (or *tarmac*) – hot tar on which a layer of stone chips were laid. Roads of this kind were known as *flexible pavements* (see diagram).

By the early 19th century – the start of the railway age – men such as John McAdam and Thomas Telford (see box) had created a British road network totalling some 200 000 km (125 000 mi), of which about one sixth was turnpikes (privately owned toll roads). In the first half of the 19th century many roads in the USA were built to the new standards, of which the National Pike from West Virginia to Illinois was perhaps the most notable.

In the 20th century the ever-increasing use of motor vehicles threatened to break up roads built to 19th-century standards, so new techniques had to be developed. On routes with heavy traffic, flexible pavements were replaced by *rigid pavements*, in which the top layer was concrete, 15 to 30 cm (6 to 12 in) thick, laid on a prepared bed. Nowadays steel bars are laid within the concrete. This not only restrains shrinkage during setting but also reduces expansion in warm weather. As a result it is possible to lay long slabs without danger of cracking.

The demands of heavy traffic led to the concept of high-speed, long-distance roads, with access or slip lanes spaced

The Brenner Highway, completed in the early 1970s, provides a vital trade link between Austria and Italy over the Brenner Pass (1372 m / 4501 ft). The Highway is a spectacular example of a combined civil-engineering project, relying on both bridging and road-building techniques. On the Austrian side alone, there are 10 km (6 mi) of viaducts and 44 bridges.

TYPES OF ROAD

Roman road (materials varied according to locality)

Curb — Paving stones set in mortar — Stones in concrete

Flat stones — Broken stone and mortar

Flexible pavement

Bituminous surface (bitumen with sand or gravel)

Subgrade

Base course (sand, gravel or crushed stone, often mixed with cement or bitumen) — Sub-base course

Concrete road

Granular shoulder — Concrete with steel bars inset

Sub-base

THOMAS TELFORD

The Scotsman Thomas Telford (1757–1834) trained as a stonemason but went on to become one of the most celebrated civil engineers. The peak of his career was reached in the early 19th century, when he built roads, bridges, canals and harbours. His roads were noted for their level alignments. The lower course was made up of hand-placed stone, to a depth of 18 cm (7 in). The upper course was the same depth, but constructed of broken hardstone. His roads were finished with a 25 mm (1 in) layer of gravel, and would typically measure 5.5 m (18 ft) in width. The London-to-Holyhead road, including the famous suspension bridge over the Menai Strait (1825), was regarded as his masterpiece.

SEE ALSO

● POWER 2 p. 306
● BUILDING CONSTRUCTION p. 338
● RAILWAYS p. 346

widely apart. The US Bronx River Parkway of 1925 was followed by several variants – Mussolini's autostradas, Hitler's autobahns, and the Pan American Highway. Such roads – especially the intercity autobahns with their separate multilane carriageways for each direction – were the predecessors of today's motorways.

Bridges

The development of the *arched bridge* in Roman times marked the beginning of scientific bridge-building; hitherto, bridges had generally been crossings in the form of felled trees or flat stone blocks. Absorbing the load by compression, arched bridges and viaducts are very strong. They were usually built of stone, but brick and timber were also used. A fine early example is at Alcantara in Spain, built of granite by the Romans in AD 105 to span the River Tagus. In modern times, metal and concrete arched bridges have been constructed. The first significant metal bridge, built of cast iron in 1779, still stands at Ironbridge in England.

Steel, with its superior strength-to-weight ratio, soon replaced iron in metal bridgework. In the railway age the *truss* (or *girder*) *bridge* became popular. Built of wood or metal, the truss beam consists of upper and lower horizontal booms joined by vertical or inclined members. The truss thus formed is designed to resist the three forces of tension, compression and shear.

The *suspension bridge* has a deck supported by suspenders that drop from one or more overhead cables. It requires strong anchorage at each end to resist the inward tension of the cables, and the deck is strengthened to control distortion by moving loads or high winds. Such bridges are nevertheless lightweight, and therefore the most suitable for very long spans. The Clifton Suspension Bridge, designed by the English engineer Isambard Kingdom Brunel (1806–59) to span the Avon Gorge in England, is famous both for its beautiful setting and for its elegant design. The 1980 Humber Estuary Bridge in England has the longest span of any suspension bridge at 1410 m (4626 ft).

Cantilever bridges, such as the 1889 Forth rail bridge in Scotland, exploit the potential of steel construction to produce a wide clearwater space. The spans have a central supporting pier and meet in midstream. The downward thrust where the spans meet is countered by firm anchorage of the spans at their other ends. Although the suspension bridge can span a wider gap, the cantilever offers better stability, which was important for 19th-century railway-builders. The world's longest cantilever span – 549 m (1800 ft) – is that of the Quebec rail bridge in Canada, constructed in 1918.

In the 20th century, new forms of construction have been facilitated by the use of *prestressed concrete* – concrete surrounding tensioned steel cables that counter the stresses that occur under load. The *box girder* – a massive hollow box-shaped girder, which is both strong and light – has become a key component of concrete bridges.

Navigational engineering

The Pharos lighthouse, built at Alexandria in Egypt in about 280 BC and still standing until the 14th century, testifies to the antiquity of navigational engineering. Canals also have a long history, although it was not until the invention of the mitre gate in the 16th century that extensive canal-building was undertaken. The *mitre gate*, formed by two leaves meeting at an angle and pointing upstream, greatly simplified the construction of locks, which are used where canals pass over rising ground. In the 19th century, inland waterways suffered from railway competition, but canals for ocean-going ships remained practicable, and the Suez Canal of 1869 and the Panama Canal of 1914 shortened key shipping routes.

Tunnels

Tunnel-building was developed in the 18th century to enable canals to penetrate hills, and the same techniques were exploited by the 19th-century railway-builders. Tunnels through hard rock could be unlined, but in soft or moist ground millions of bricks were used as lining. The world's largest tunnel is the Seikan railway tunnel in Japan (1985), which is 54 km (33 mi) long. This is about 4 km longer than the projected length of the Anglo-French Channel Tunnel (also an underwater rail link), work on which began in 1987.

Dams

Dams, initially used for flood control and water storage, are of great antiquity. The crescent (horizontally arched) dam, which first appeared in the Byzantine Empire in the 6th century AD, enabled a much greater weight of water to be held than was possible with earlier constructions. Correct judgement of underlying rock strata is as important as good design, and a number of catastrophic dam failures have occurred because the foundations proved inadequate in the long term. Concrete is now the preferred material for dam-construction, but earth, rock, stone and brick have been used in the past. JW

The Thames Barrier at Woolwich, London, is the world's largest tidal barrier. Opened in 1984 to protect the city from flooding, the barrier consists of nine massive concrete piers running in line from bank to bank. The wider central gaps in the barrier, each spanning 61 m (200 ft), are closed by specially designed 'rising-sector' gates. When open, these gates sit in curved concrete sills on the river bed; when required to block the tide, they are rocked into a vertical position.

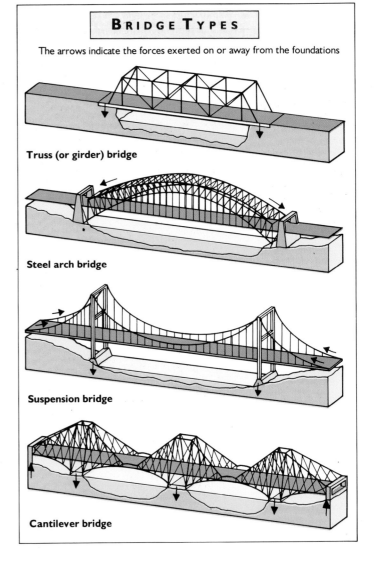

BRIDGE TYPES

The arrows indicate the forces exerted on or away from the foundations

Truss (or girder) bridge

Steel arch bridge

Suspension bridge

Cantilever bridge

Ships
1. Development

The basic design of ships has changed little over the past 3500 years. The Egyptians, Phoenicians and Greeks in the Mediterranean, and the Chinese in the East, built large fleets for trade, exploration and war; and from these emerged the ancestors of the Arab dhow, the Chinese junk and other types of craft.

SEE ALSO

- ENGINES p. 308
- MODERN SHIPPING p. 344
- ARCHAIC AND CLASSICAL GREECE p. 370
- THE INVASIONS (VIKINGS) p. 396
- THE VOYAGES OF DISCOVERY p. 405
- EUROPEAN EMPIRES IN THE 17TH AND 18TH CENTURIES p. 416
- THE INDUSTRIAL AND AGRICULTURAL REVOLUTIONS p. 420
- THE REVOLUTIONARY AND NAPOLEONIC WARS p. 426
- WORLD WAR I p. 436
- WORLD WAR II p. 444

The differing needs of commerce and warfare soon created two distinct types of ship. Warships were designed with speed and manoeuvrability in mind, and thus tended to have long, narrow hulls and to be oar-powered. The oared fighting ship, or *galley*, with its lateen-rigged (i.e. triangular) sail was supreme in Mediterranean sea warfare from the time of the Phoenicians. Some had a single bank of oars but others two or three (these were known as *biremes* and *triemes* respectively). The Phoenicians generally used two banks, but the Greeks, and later the Romans, favoured three. Medieval galleys had single banks of long oars with wide outriggers. For trading vessels, on the other hand, carrying capacity was the major consideration, so they were generally shorter and broader than warships, and relied mainly on sails.

The longship and the cog

Sometime in the 7th or 8th centuries AD a new form of construction appeared in Northern Europe – the Viking *longship* (see photo, p. 396). The bow and stern were formed nearly at right angles to the keel, and the hull planking tapered to form distinct stem- and sternpieces. Although relying upon oars for fighting, the longship had a much larger and efficient sail than the galley, the longer keel and pointed ends providing a more stable and efficient sailing form. The longship was an awesome raiding craft, faster and more seaworthy than the Mediterranean galley, and enabled the Vikings to sail as far as North America. Longships based on the Viking design were used in the Norman invasion of England in 1066 (see p. 397).

The rise of the Hanseatic League (an association of northern German trading towns) in the 14th century led to the development of the *Hansa cog*. This broad, sturdy vessel, typically about 30 m (100 ft) long, had a good cargo-carrying capacity. It had a square sail on a single mast and built-up 'castles' at the stem and stern.

The evolution of the sailing ship

Early ships were manoeuvred by means of a steering oar or paddle on the quarter (i.e. the side near the stern). Between 1200 and 1500 the gradual replacement of the steering oar by the wooden rudder brought about an enormous improvement in ship-handling. As ships grew larger the single mast gave way to two, three or even four masts. These features were incorporated in the Mediterranean *carrack*, which became the standard large ship in the 15th and 16th centuries.

A smaller version of the carrack, the *caravel*, was used along with the carrack by the Spanish and Portuguese to make their epic voyages of discovery (see p. 405). The caravel was easy to handle and large enough for ocean voyages, yet small enough to be rowed if there was no wind.

During the 15th century the warship also grew much bigger. Ships with a displacement of 250 tonnes (tons) at the beginning of the century had been replaced by ships of 1000 tonnes or more by 1500. Guns were used at sea in English men o' war from about 1340 and many of the Spanish galleys at the Battle of Lepanto in 1571 carried heavy armaments (see illustration, p. 411). Gunports were provided in French and Spanish ships before 1500.

The huge expansion of the known world in the 16th century had a lasting effect on the ships of the trading nations. In Northern Europe the cog was expanded, while Spain and Portugal continued to develop the carrack. By the time England faced the Spanish Armada in 1588, *galleons* were the new model of fighting ship on both sides. But English shipwrights favoured low-charged (low-sided) ships, while the Spanish clung to the high-charged carrack hull (see illustration, p. 412).

During the 17th and 18th centuries the warship developed into a vessel of considerable strength, with massive double-planked sides (see illustration, p. 416). Under the rating system that evolved, only 1st to 3rd rates, mounting at least 64 heavy cannon, were designated as 'ships of the line'. Their purpose was to fight in the great sea battles. Smaller ships, the 4th, 5th and 6th rates, were for 'cruising' or independent operations; 5th and 6th rates were known as *frigates* and *sloops* respectively.

Merchantmen were built on broadly similar lines, but devoted internal space to cargo rather than weapons. Speed was not crucial, but small vessels adopted improvements to rigging to save manpower. Only the *clipper* used a finer form, sacrificing cargo space to speed in order to dominate trade in perishable commodities such as tea. Their 19th-century heyday was brief, however, as their huge spread of canvas required large crews.

The age of steam

With the end of the long military struggle between Britain and France in 1815 designers turned their attention to ways of improving propulsion and hulls. Mechanical means of driving ships had been talked about for centuries, but it was the invention of an efficient steam engine towards the end of the 18th century (see p. 308) that made major improvements possible.

A small paddle steamer briefly sailed on the River Saône in France in 1783, and another on the Delaware River in the USA in 1786. The first practical and commercially successful steamer, however, was the *Charlotte Dundas*, which ran on the Forth and Clyde Canal in Scotland in 1802. Other inventors pressed on with designs, and by 1816 there was a service running across the English Channel. In 1821 the Royal Navy ordered its first class of paddle steamers for auxiliary missions, such as towing ships of the line. Not being dependent on the strength and direction of the wind, steam tugs made movement in restricted areas easier and safer. Steam also meant that time schedules could be maintained, which was important on long voyages. In 1838 the *Sirius* and the *Great Western* (the latter designed by Brunel; see p. 341) crossed the Atlantic, proving that steam power on its own was also suitable for long voyages.

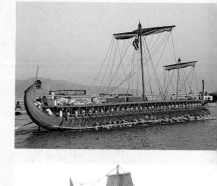

The ancient Greek trireme (top) marked the ultimate development of the Mediterranean galley, its three tiers of rowers giving it unsurpassed speed. This photograph is of a modern reconstruction.

A carrack (bottom) of the 15th century, similar to Columbus's ship the *Santa Maria*. Columbus also sailed with the caravels *Pinta* and *Niña*. Caravels are even smaller ships with lateen rigs (i.e. triangular sails).

Iron hulls and the screw propeller

The introduction of steam put excessive weight into wooden hulls that were already reaching their maximum size, with warships approaching 7000 tonnes (tons). An early precaution was to stiffen hulls with iron bracing, and it was not long before all-iron hulls were proposed. The first iron steamer operated successfully from 1820, and several small warships followed.

Navies were reluctant, however, to build large warships with iron hulls and paddle engines. The iron hull was found to affect the compass on long voyages, and tests in the 1840s showed that solid shot would fracture on impact with wrought iron, causing lethal splinters.

As well as being inefficient, the paddle wheel – in naval contexts – restricted armament and was vulnerable to enemy shot. These drawbacks were overcome by the invention in 1836 of the screw propeller, credit for which is shared by the Swedish-American John Ericcson and by the Englishman Francis Pettit-Smith. After a series of experiments this new method of propulsion gained widespread approval, with the Royal Navy ordering its first screw steamer (HMS *Rattler*) in 1840, and Brunel redesigning the SS *Great Britain* for screw propulsion later that same year. The Royal Navy initiated a major programme to convert sailing ships

of the line to steam, cutting ships in two to provide volume for coal bunkers, boilers and engines. But iron for large warships did not find favour until the Crimean War (1853–56), when the threat from explosive shells forced the British and French to build armour-plated 'floating batteries'. This led to a desire to apply armour to a line-of-battle ship. The French built the *Gloire*, which was a wooden ship covered in armour. The British then built the much superior HMS *Warrior*, which had an iron hull with armour added.

In the ensuing arms race, heavily armoured ships, known as *ironclads*, became the focus of ship technology. Such ironclads saw action in the US Civil War. Until the end of the 19th century, the use of heavier and heavier armour-plating was matched by the ever-increasing power of naval guns, some in turret mountings. HMS *Inflexible*, completed in 1881, had four 80-tonne guns in twin turrets, and was also equipped with torpedo tubes and even electric lighting. Great Britain, with ample supplies of iron and coal, came to dominate world shipbuilding in a way that had not been possible when wood was the standard material. From being a large-scale operator of merchant ships, Britain became shipbuilder to the world.

As steam engines became more reliable, auxiliary sailing rig became redundant, and by 1900 sail-and-steam ships were a

thing of the past. Cheap steel was now available and had replaced wrought iron.

20th-century developments

Brunel's *Great Eastern* (1858) – which was over 200 m (nearly 700 ft) long – was ahead of its time, but it proved that there was no practical limit to the size of iron ships. By the early years of the 20th century, liners were plying a regular transatlantic trade. When it sank after hitting an iceberg on its maiden voyage in 1912, the *Titanic* was setting new standards for luxury and comfort.

By the turn of the century the demand for higher speeds, both in passenger liners and warships, forced engineers to look for an alternative to the reciprocating steam engine. The Parsons steam turbine (see p. 308) offered reduced vibration at maximum power, and after experiments in destroyers, the Royal Navy adopted steam turbines for the revolutionary battleship *Dreadnought* (1905). Shortly afterwards the Cunard Line made a similar decision for its new liners.

Between 1900 and World War II the picture was one of steady development to meet changing needs and to take advantage of changing technology. Amongst merchant ships there was the growth of transatlantic liners with ever-increasing size, speed and standards of comfort culminating in the *Queen Mary* and *Queen Elizabeth*. Oil tankers grew in size and number as the demands of industry and transport for oil increased. The diesel engine (see p. 309) was widely adopted as a cheap propulsion unit for merchant ships and minor naval craft. Larger warships and the large liners retained their steam turbines, but with engineering advances providing increased power in less space.

In the military field the early years were dominated by the introduction of HMS *Dreadnought* (see above), the first all-large-gun fast battleship. It gave its name to a type of battleship, and prior to World War I the major naval powers embarked upon building numbers of them to maintain the credibility of their fleets. Advances in technology brought the submarine from a virtual toy to become a major factor in both World Wars (see pp. 437 and 444). Armed with torpedoes it became a lethal weapon system and its covert operations were aided in World War II by the 'snort mast' which enabled it to run its diesels at periscope depth. Destroyers, frigates and corvettes were developed to combat the submarine, using sonar (see p. 332) to detect it and weapons such as the depth charge to attack it.

The other major change came about with the introduction of aircraft. Special ships were designed to carry and operate them and new weapons developed to combat them. The aircraft carrier started as a primitive auxiliary vessel in World War I, but with the destruction of the US Pacific fleet at Pearl Harbor in 1941 by Japanese carrier-borne aircraft, the aircraft carrier came to displace the battleship. AP

Ship of the line (top) of the late 18th and 19th centuries evolved from the galleons of the century, but had heavier timbers to allow and more numerous guns to be carried. This shows HMS *Redoubtable* in action at Trafalgar (1805).

French ironclad warships (bottom) of the 1860s, together with (in the left-centre foreground) an early submarine, *Le Plongeur*. The ship is *Le Magenta*. At this period auxiliary rig was still carried on steam ships, but by the late 19th century, as steam engines became reliable, sails were finally dispensed with.

The battleship HMS *Dreadnought* (top) was the first large ship to use the Parsons steam turbine. The *Dreadnought* gave its name to a class of battleships carrying ten 12-inch guns, and which were faster than any other large warship. The race among the European powers to build such ships reached a climax in World War I.

Transatlantic liners (bottom) such as the Cunarder *Mauretania* ran a fast and dependable service in the first half of the 20th century, giving passengers the illusion of living in a luxury hotel. Such liners are now largely used for cruises, the transatlantic route having been taken over by jet airliners.

Ships 2. Modern Shipping

Over the last 50 years the design of commercial and naval ships has undergone radical changes both as a result of advances in technology and as a response to changing economic pressures and military threats. In all types of ship automation has helped to reduce crew size and the cost of construction and operation.

The LNG carrier *Khannar*. LNG (liquefied natural gas) carriers have special insulated tanks in which the gas is carried under pressure and at low temperature (−100 °C / −148 °F).

with complex electronic and computer systems.

Advances in technology have both posed threats and provided opportunities to commercial shipping. Since World War II the main influences have been the growth in air travel, the tremendous increase in demands for energy, the need to transport large volumes of cargo around the world, and the increase in leisure time among the affluent societies of the West.

Passenger shipping

The growth of relatively cheap air travel has meant that virtually all long-distance passenger transport is now by air. After World War II a few large liners such as the *Queen Elizabeth II* were built, but as the greater speed and convenience of air travel became apparent, liners were either scrapped or converted to cruise ships or floating hotels. However, on shorter sea crossings, car and passenger ferries have expanded their activities to cope with the growth of demand for holidays abroad. Partly for economic reasons and partly in order to win customers, ferries have grown in size and speed, with particular attention being paid to on-board amenities and provision for fast boarding and unloading. The roll-on/roll-off design is now common. On some routes, the greater speed of the hovercraft has made it attractive to travellers.

With increasing leisure time, a demand has grown for sea cruises. Initially converted liners were used, but now most ships are specifically designed for the cruising trade. Visits are made to a number of ports where passengers can disembark for excursions to places of interest. Often the ship travels from port to port over night, so the passenger has the advantages of a travelling hotel without the need to pack and unpack. Larger cruise liners can carry some 3000 people in relative luxury and with all facilities – such as swimming pools and dance halls – on board.

Cargo shipping

The rapid growth in demand for energy has meant that large volumes of oil need to be shipped around the world. To keep the price per tonne (ton) of oil as low as possible, the size of tankers has grown

Container ships have revolutionized cargo shipping. The containers are built to an international standard size, and can be loaded direct onto lorries and railway rolling stock without having to unpack and repack the freight.

In spite of competition from the air, ships still carry the great majority of cargoes; and although the great transatlantic liners have disappeared, cruise ships and ferries flourish. In the military field, the need to cope with high-speed missiles – both in attack and defence – has meant that modern warships are now equipped

SPECIAL SHIP TYPES

A number of special ship types have evolved either to meet a new demand or to utilize some advance in technology. *Twin hulls* provide a large deck area together with great stability. This is useful for helicopter operation, for towing a variety of hydrographic equipment, or as a base for operating small submersibles or diving bells. When a large part of the hull is kept well below the sea surface, the ship is known as a *semi-submersible*. Such vessels are much less affected by waves than conventional hulls and are therefore suitable for oil exploration. A variant of this, which is of interest in military and hydrographic fields, is the *small waterplane area twin hull* (SWATH) ship. The small waterplane means a much reduced response to surface waves and hence small ship motion.

The *hydrofoil* has been in existence for many years. It uses fins to create sufficient hydrodynamic lift to raise the hull clear of the water. Hydrofoils are suitable for small high-speed ferries, as they provide a comfortable ride in moderate sea conditions. The *hovercraft* is also used for ferries.

A hovercraft landing. Large hovercraft such as this are used to ferry passengers and cars over relatively short distances, such as across the English Channel.

The hull is carried on an air cushion, and in some variants there are no elements of the ship in the water. Such craft can run over flat areas of land such as mudbanks and beaches as easily as they can over water. In other variants the craft has sidewalls that remain partly submerged and an underwater propulsor. These are not amphibious.

dramatically. Whereas before 1956 there were no tankers larger than 50 000 tonnes, ships of 100 000 tonnes were built in the 1960s. There are now Very Large Crude Carriers (VLCC) of between 200 000 to 400 000 tonnes and Ultra Large Crude Carriers (ULCC) of more than 400 000 tonnes. To transport natural gas to where it is needed has led to the development of the Liquefied Natural Gas (LNG) carrier (see photo).

Whilst the extraction of gas and oil from shallow-water off-shore sites had long been carried out, the need for more oil caused oil companies to look further afield to deeper, more exposed areas, such as the North Sea (see also p. 310). In order to remain stationary while drilling,

The USS _Carl Vinson_. This nuclear-powered American carrier is here seen with F-14 Tomcats and an E-2 Hawkeye (to starboard) parked on the stern. The angled flight deck, arresting gear and four steam catapults facilitate the operation of high-performance aircraft with full supporting facilities on board.

drilling ships with dynamic position control systems were required, as were saturated diving systems, production rigs and supply vessels of specialized design.

Bulk carriage of grain and metal ores was influenced by the need to keep transport as cheap as possible, with minimum manpower and minimum time in port. Bulk carriers therefore grew in the same way as tankers, and like them had machinery and accommodation aft with holds or tanks forward. Some large ships are designed to be able to take different cargoes (say oil or ore) on different occasions. Load distribution is then important to ensure that the strength limits of the hull are not exceeded.

Other cargoes carried in bulk bring their own problems. For instance, the bulk movement of cars has been facilitated by the use of roll-on/roll-off ships, a concept that has also found favour in large car ferries. For general cargoes, there is the same need to reduce time of loading and off-loading in order to maximize the use of the ships. This need led to the development of container ships, which carry a large number of 'standard' containers stacked in special holds. As with bulk carriers, the machinery and accommodation is grouped aft, with the hold forward. Special facilities are needed at the docks to load and unload, this being more economical than providing such facilities on each ship. The ship in this case is only one element in an integrated transport system. Containers can be loaded at the factory or source point and then carried by road and/or rail to the docks. Large ships, typically around 60 000 tonnes, carry the containers between major ports, where they are transferred to road, rail or to smaller vessels for transfer to smaller ports or to their final destination.

Warship defences

The design of warships is dictated both by the need to carry out certain types of operation and by the need to counter the threat posed by an enemy. During World War II the pace of change accelerated and

has continued to do so since. With developments in materials, electronics and computers, the growing complexity of the threats posed has been matched by the sophisticated means used to combat them.

One example is the threat posed by mines, which can be laid covertly, often before hostilities begin, to be activated at a later date. World War II saw the appearance of _influence mines_, which are triggered by the magnetic, acoustic and/or pressure 'signature' of the target. The result of the development of mines and homing weapons (such as missiles and torpedoes, which use similar sensor devices) is that great emphasis has been placed on reducing ship signatures and thus their susceptibility to attack. The radar reflection of modern warships is reduced in a variety of ways: special materials are used, and much attention is paid to shaping and to minimizing the above-water profile. The magnetic signature of a ship can be significantly reduced by _degaussing_, a process in which special equipment is used to produce an opposing magnetic field (see p. 34). The acoustic signature can be reduced by specially designed propulsion units and by isolating noise sources within the ship. Finally, the susceptibility to infrared detection can be decreased by reducing hot spots within the ship.

Special vessels have also been developed to hunt out mines that cannot be swept. The mines are then destroyed by charges placed close to them by small remotely operated vehicles. To ensure that the magnetic signature of mine-countermeasures vessels is minimized, their hulls are now made of glass-reinforced plastic.

As well as reducing signatures, other defences include the use of jamming to confuse enemy detection or homing systems, the use of decoys to seduce homing weapons away from their target, and 'hard-kill' weapons to destroy the enemy weapon before impact.

It is not always possible to prevent weapon hits, and ships must be robust enough to withstand some damage and still remain effective fighting units. Various means of reducing vulnerability include protective plating against splinters, duplication of important systems, subdivision of the ship, and limiting the area of the ship over which a hit can put any particular system out of action.

Modern battle fleets

A modern battle fleet is provided with a 'layered' defence. Aircraft carriers can deploy early-warning aircraft and intercept enemy aircraft at a distance with their fighters. The introduction of take-off ramps, angled flight decks, steam catapults and deck landing aids have all helped the carrier to operate high-performance aircraft. Carriers, destroyers and frigates can also deploy helicopters to combat submarines at a distance. In effect, aircraft extend the eyes, ears and weapon radius of the fleet. The next layer of defence is provided by long-range missile systems that can defend a given area of sea. The inner ring is a self-defence capability provided by close-range weapons.

Modern fleets also need to be able to combine with land forces in amphibious operations. A variety of specialized ships have been developed for such operations. Small craft are used to land men, tanks and equipment on exposed beaches. Often the small craft are carried to the vicinity of the beach by mother ships, sometimes in the form of mobile floating docks. The need to support large fleets at great distances from base led to the 'fleet train', comprising tankers, supply ships and repair ships. Systems have been developed to enable solids and liquids to be transferred while the ships are moving.

Thus a modern navy is likely to comprise carriers, guided-missile ships of various sizes, mine-countermeasure ships, anti-submarine vessels, amphibious forces and support ships. All are provided with increasingly complex electronics, rely heavily on computer-based systems and require highly trained crews to operate them.

It is important that these very expensive ships are available for duty for as much of the time as possible. Special paint systems reduce the need to dock, while major items of equipment are replaced rather than repaired in situ. Thus the gas turbines in many modern warships are readily replaced through the associated ducting, while diesel engines, air-conditioning plants and pumps are provided with special removal routes.   ECT

SEE ALSO

● ENGINES p. 308
● OIL AND GAS p. 310
● SEEING THE INVISIBLE p. 332
● SHIPS I: DEVELOPMENT p. 342
● WEAPONRY p. 356

SUBMARINES

The advent of space satellites means that an enemy is likely to know the disposition of all major surface units. This has increased the value of the submarine, which is much more difficult to detect. Nuclear power has enabled submarines to remain submerged for long periods, and, because of their low vulnerability, such vessels provide effective launch vehicles for nuclear missiles (see also p. 288).

L'Indomptable, a French nuclear submarine, carries 16 ballistic missiles in a hull about 128 m (420 ft) long with submerged displacement of almost 9000 tonnes (tons). Propulsion power is provided by a pressurized water reactor (PWR), giving a reported submerged speed of 25 knots.

Railways

The ancient Babylonians and Greeks laid short lines of grooved stones, while in medieval Europe horse-drawn wagons running on wooden planks were occasionally used in mining. But railways as we know them resulted from the combination of two elements – mechanical traction, provided by the steam engine (see p. 308), and the flanged metal wheel running on metal rails.

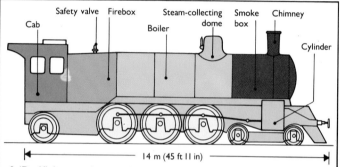

A 'Pacific' steam locomotive, one of the most popular wheel arrangements for fast passenger service. Under the Whyte system of classification, this is a 4–6–2 arrangement: four small carrying wheels at the front, six driving wheels, and a pair of wheels supporting the firebox.

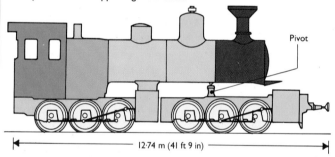

A Mallet locomotive. For steam locomotives, pulling power depended on the number of driving wheels, but too many such wheels meant a long rigid wheelbase that would grind against curved track. This problem was solved by the introduction of articulated locomotives, which had flexible chassis. In a Mallet locomotive, articulation was achieved by allowing the front set of driving wheels to pivot.

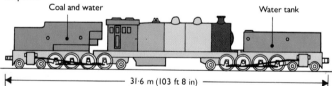

A Garratt locomotive. Another means of articulation was provided by the Garratt locomotive, in which two separate locomotive chassis support each end of the boiler. The one shown here, with a 4–8–2 + 2–8–4 wheel arrangement, was the largest locomotive ever built in Britain.

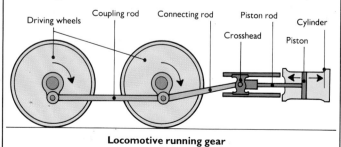

Locomotive running gear

The Stockton & Darlington Railway, designed by George Stephenson and opened in 1825, was the first public railway to use steam locomotives and the first to carry both freight and passengers. Initially steam traction was used for goods trains only, but from 1833 the use of locomotives was extended to passenger service, which had previously been provided by carriages drawn along the tracks by horses.

Being both a stimulus and a result of the Industrial Revolution, railways have had an enormous social and economic impact over the last 175 years. Although railways have provided a public service for most of their history, it was in fact from old horse-drawn industrial lines used in the British coalfields that the modern railway developed.

The first steam railways

In 1812 steam locomotives began regular service in England on the industrial Middleton Railway near Leeds, and in 1814 the English engineer George Stephenson introduced his first steam locomotive at the Killingworth Colliery, near Newcastle-upon-Tyne (see historical box). Stephenson went on to complete the Stockton & Darlington Railway, the first public steam line, in 1825 (see photo). In 1830 the first intercity railway, the Liverpool & Manchester, was opened, and in the same year the initial length of the first US public steam line, the Baltimore & Ohio Railroad, was completed.

Many continental European countries built their first railways in the 1830s, often using Stephenson locomotives. Canada built a line in the same decade, but more distant parts of the British Empire waited longer, with Australia's first line opening in 1854, South Africa's in 1860, and New Zealand's in 1863.

In Europe and North America the great period of railway building was the second half of the 19th century. The peak British mileage of 32 908 km (20 449 mi) was reached in 1931, but 90% of that had been built before 1900. The US peak mileage was reached in 1916, at 408 762 km (254 000 mi). In developed countries competition from road transport has since caused many lines to close, but elsewhere in the world new railways are still being built.

Nationwide systems

Creating national railway networks requires substantial engineering works to overcome water or mountain barriers. In Britain the Severn Tunnel (1886) and Forth Bridge (1890) were two outstanding achievements. British engineers gave high priority to the avoidance of steep gradients, and therefore made great use of tunnels and viaducts. They often worked at the very limit of their technical knowledge – sometimes with catastrophic consequences, as when the Tay Bridge collapsed in a gale in 1879 while a train was crossing: all 73 passengers and the crew of 5 were drowned.

In North America the Rockies presented a difficult obstacle to several lines, including the first US transcontinental, the Union Pacific–Central Pacific line (1869) from Nebraska to California. The Canadian Pacific, Canada's first transcontinental (1887), running from Montreal to Vancouver, used a series of spiralling tunnels to cross the Rockies. Russia's Trans-Siberian (1904) from the Urals to the Pacific had to make an expensive detour to pass Lake Baikal, while the Trans-Australian Railway (1917) faced a problem of a different kind in the arid Nullarbor Plain, over which a dead straight line was driven for 478 km (297 mi).

Outside North America, most private railways were eventually taken into state ownership. In 1948 British Railways (later British Rail) took over the four big companies that had owned the British system since 1923.

Technical progress

Nineteenth-century innovations included

LANDMARKS IN LOCOMOTIVE DEVELOPMENT

1804 Richard Trevithick (1771–1833) successfully operates his steam locomotive in South Wales.

1812 Matthew Murray (1765–1826) puts his steam cog locomotives into service at Middleton Colliery, Yorkshire.

1813 William Hedley (1779–1843) and Timothy Hackworth (1786–1850) build a smooth-wheeled steam locomotive for Wylam Colliery, Northumberland.

1814 George Stephenson (1781–1848) builds the *Blücher*, his first locomotive.

1827 Hackworth's *Royal George* is the first locomotive with six coupled wheels (to increase wheel-to-rail adhesion), and the first with cylinders driving direct to the wheels.

1829 At the Rainhill locomotive trials the *Rocket*, designed by Robert Stephenson (1803–59) and his father George, impresses the Liverpool & Manchester Railway management.

1897 The German Wilhelm Schmidt (1858–1924) introduces the first successful superheater, enhancing steam locomotive performance.

1900 Electrification of the Paris–Orléans line begins.

1913 A diesel railcar begins running successfully in Sweden.

1923 The American Locomotive Company introduces successful diesel-electric locomotives.

1932 The record-breaking diesel train *Flying Hamburger* begins running between Berlin and Hamburg.

1934 The *Burlington Zephyr*, the first diesel-electric streamliner, covers the 1626 km (1010 mi) from Denver to Chicago at an average speed of 125 km/h (77.6 mph).

1938 The British streamlined locomotive *Mallard* wins the all-time steam speed record by reaching 203 km/h (126 mph).

1958 A French electric locomotive reaches 331 km/h (206 mph).

1960 Regular mainline steam traction ends in the USA.

1968 Regular mainline steam traction ends in Britain.

1981 The French TGV reaches 380 km/h (236 mph) in trials.

automatic train brakes controlled from the locomotive and, in passenger service, corridor trains with toilet and dining facilities, steam heating, and electric lighting. Luxury trains, including sleeping cars with a high degree of personal service, have been successfully operated, mainly by the Pullman company in the USA and Wagons-Lits in Europe.

In the 20th century the steam locomotive was gradually replaced by electric and diesel traction. Electrification enabled trains to run more cheaply, more cleanly, and in practice more often, while the greater power of electric locomotives allowed heavier trains and higher speeds. Diesel traction was particularly advantageous on lines where traffic was not heavy enough to justify the cost of electrification.

To keep up with the image created by aircraft and racing cars, railways introduced streamlined trains – or 'streamliners' – in the 1930s, with trains such as the *Silver Jubilee* in England averaging 112 km/h (70 mph) or more. In the USA many of the streamliners were diesel-powered.

In some countries, including Britain but not the USA, freight traffic has diminished since the 1920s. Freight trains tended to become faster and more specialized. 'Piggyback' (road trailers carried on flatcars) and removable containers were widely used from the 1950s to combine the long-haul advantage of the train with the door-to-door advantage of the motor vehicle.

In 1964 high-speed trains, running on special track, appeared in Japan. The French TGV service between Paris and Lyon began in 1981 (see photo), and has running speeds of up to 270 km/h (168 mph). In Britain the 200 km/h (125 mph) High-Speed Train (HST) differs from the Japanese and French examples in that it is diesel, not electric, and runs on existing track. Maglev (magnetic levitation) trains, which dispense with the steel rail and flanged wheel, became technically feasible in the 1970s, but seem unlikely (at least in the short term) to prove economic except for specialized short-haul transit (see box).

Gauge

The *gauge* of a railway track – the distance between the two rails – is partly a matter of convention but can also be varied to suit particular purposes. The gauge used by Stephenson – 1435 mm (4 ft 8½ in) – became known as *standard gauge*, and has been used for more than half of the railway track ever laid. The advantage of narrow gauge is that it is cheaper to build, especially in hilly terrain, and allows the use of smaller and lighter rolling stock, which is cheaper to operate. Broad gauge, on the other hand, is suitable for larger rolling stock and generally allows higher running speeds, because of greater lateral stability.

The inconvenience of different gauges is exemplified by Australia, where Victoria and South Australia chose 1600 mm (5 ft 3 in), Western Australia and Queensland 1067 mm (3 ft 6 in), and New South Wales standard gauge. These gauges are still in use, but the mainland state capitals now have standard-gauge connections. Sometimes, to accommodate trains of different gauges, a third rail is laid to create *mixed gauge*.

The impact of railways

Railways revolutionized economic and social life. They enabled industries to be located far from their fuel sources and to enjoy nationwide markets for their products. People could choose from a wider range of commodities and easily travel

The French TGV ('Train à Grande Vitesse') is electrically powered by overhead cables and aerodynamically designed to minimize energy consumption; it is the fastest commercial train ever to operate, reaching peak running speeds of up to 270 km/h (168 mph). Entering regular passenger service between Paris and Lyon in 1981, the TGV had cut the scheduled time for the 425 km (264 mi) journey to exactly 2 hours by 1983.

SEE ALSO

● ENGINES p. 308
● THE INDUSTRIAL REVOLUTION p. 420

outside their own district for business and pleasure. The cheap mass movement of people and commodities that was now possible caught the popular imagination and encouraged new enterprise, thus changing static agrarian communities and nations into dynamic industrialized societies. JW

FLOATING TRAINS

The friction between flanged metal wheels and steel track imposes an upper limit on the speeds that can be obtained by conventional trains. To overcome this barrier, experiments have been conducted with vehicles that are suspended over a guideway on a 'cushion' of air, but perhaps the most promising progress has been made with maglev (magnetic levitation) trains.

Maglev designs have been of two main types. The German Transrapid programme has used an 'attractive' system, in which electromagnets in the wings of the train lie beneath the guideway and are drawn up towards the steel rail as the power is turned on. Meanwhile the Japanese have developed a 'repulsive' maglev, in which superconducting magnets (see p. 54) in the guideway create a magnetic field of the same polarity as magnets set in the train itself; the train is thus levitated as the two fields repel one another.

Prototype of the German Transrapid 07.

Aircraft
1. Development

Until the invention of the powered aeroplane, the only method of sustained ascending flight was by lighter-than-air aircraft – balloons and dirigibles. Balloons enabled pioneering aeronauts to undertake voyages across land and sea as early as 1784/5. By the middle of the next century, the dirigible (or airship) had arrived, bringing with it both a system of propulsion and a method of steering.

The heyday of the airship came in the first three decades of the 20th century. During this time the airship was widely used in both commercial and military contexts. Its success was short-lived, however: hastened on by a series of horrific accidents, the eclipse of the airship by the aeroplane was complete by the late 1930s.

Balloons and dirigibles

Although the principle of the hot-air balloon had been successfully demonstrated at the beginning of the 18th century, the experiments of the French pioneers Joseph (1740–1810) and Jacques-Étienne (1745–99) Montgolfier are better remembered, as they finally led to the first manned flight. Following successful experiments with unmanned hot-air balloons earlier in the same year (see illustration), on 19 September 1783 the Montgolfier brothers launched a balloon that safely carried the first airborne passengers – a cock, a duck and a sheep. Less than a month later, on 15 October, François Pilâtre de Rozier became the first person to ascend in a balloon, using a tethered Montgolfier hot-air balloon.

On 21 November, with the Marquis d'Arlandes, de Rozier also made the first free balloon flight, remaining airborne over Paris for about 25 minutes. Only a few days were to pass, however, before Jacques Charles and one of the Robert brothers flew a distance of about 43 km (27 mi) in a hydrogen balloon.

The unpredictable nature of ballooning soon led to attempts to design dirigibles. Dirigibles are airships (powered lighter-than-air aircraft) that can be guided or steered. Before long, dirigibles moved away from the spherical envelope typical of balloons, and some were of rigid structure. The first manned and powered dirigible was demonstrated by the Frenchman Henri Giffard (1825–82) in 1852. Starting from Paris on 24 September, Giffard flew about 27 km (17 mi), his craft being driven forward at an average speed of just 8 km/h (5 mph).

A name closely associated with dirigibles is the German Count Ferdinand von Zeppelin (1838–1917), whose first craft,

the *LZ 1*, made its maiden ascent on 2 July 1900. Zeppelins built for the German army and navy were used with considerable effect in World War I, with Zeppelin raids over Great Britain beginning in January 1915. Before the outbreak of war Zeppelins had also been used for the world's first commercial passenger service.

The early years of the aeroplane

The American pioneers Wilbur (1867–1912) and Orville (1871–1948) Wright were the first to conduct a sustained flight with a man-carrying, powered and controllable heavier-than-air aircraft. On 17 December 1903 Orville made the first historic flight in their aeroplane *Flyer* (see photo) – although the flight lasted only 12 seconds and covered just 36 m (120 ft). Two other flights were made that day, the longer of the two lasting 59 seconds and covering 260 m (852 ft).

From about 1906 the Wright brothers gradually began to lose their almost total dominance over all other pioneer aviators. Successful trials were conducted in Europe at this time, and on 25 July 1909 the Frenchman Louis Blériot (1872–1936) became the first man to fly an aeroplane across the English Channel. In the same

year the British Short brothers set up th[e] first aeroplane production line, construc[t]ing six Wright Model As before going o[n] to their own designs.

Military developments

World War I witnessed massive aircra[ft] construction programmes. Although ai[r] frame design improved during these year[s] the most significant advances were i[n] speed, lifting capability, and rel[i] ability, due to greatly improved engine[s] Well into the 1930s, open-cockpit biplane[s] with wire-and-strut bracing remained th[e] most common aeroplane design. The 1930[s] saw aircraft with cantilever monoplan[e] wings begin to take over, often wit[h] enclosed cockpits, retractable under[carriages, all-metal construction an[d] heavier armament. Speeds also increase[d] dramatically.

In 1944 Britain and Germany pioneere[d] the introduction of gas-turbine engine[s] (turbojets; see p. 309) to warplanes, wit[h] the Gloster Meteor and Messerschmitt M[e] 262 jet fighters respectively. Althoug[h] only slightly faster than piston-engine[d] fighter planes at higher altitudes, the ne[w] jets were about 160 km/h (100 mph) faste[r] at sea level. During the 1950s piston engined warplanes were almost com[pletely replaced by those powered b[y] turbojets.

The Montgolfier brothers' first public demonstration. Launched from the market place at Annonay in France on 4 June 1783, this hot-air balloon rose to an altitude of 1830 m (6000 ft), and travelled more than 1.6 km (1 mi) before landing. This successful experiment paved the way for the historic manned flights later in the same year.

The first powered and controlled flight by an aeroplane (top): Wilbur Wright looks on as Orville pilots *Flyer* at Kitty Hawk, North Carolina, on 17 December 1903. **Charles Lindbergh** (bottom), the first man to make a non-stop solo crossing of the Atlantic, alongside *Spirit of St Louis*. His historic flight lasted 33 hours 39 minutes from take-off on 20 May 1927.

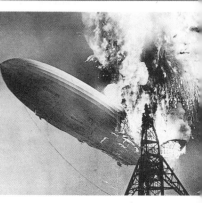

The Boeing Model 247 (top), first flown i[n] heralded the age of the modern airliner. The [247,] the first all-metal monoplane airliner with ca[ntilever] low-mounted wings and retractable underc[arriage.] **The German airship** *Hindenburg* (b[ottom)] engulfed in flames as it approaches its moo[rings at] Lakehurst, New Jersey, on 6 May 1937: the [age of] large passenger-carrying airships was over.

On 14 October 1947 the American Bell X-1 research aircraft flown by Captain Charles ('Chuck') Yeager became the first aircraft to fly faster than the speed of sound. The North American F-100 Super Sabre fighter introduced sustained supersonic capability in level flight to production aircraft during the 1950s. On 18 January 1957 three US Air Force eight-engined Boeing B-52 Stratofortress bombers completed the first ever non-stop round-the-world flight, giving a vivid demonstration that any target in the world was now within the range of nuclear or conventional weapons. The greatest advances since the 1970s have been in the field of aircraft electronics (avionics) and in the use of light composite materials for airframes.

Commercial flying

Passenger, mail and freight services by airlines began in earnest immediately after World War I, often using ex-military pilots and aircraft. At the same time, many hazardous long flights were undertaken to prove routes and sometimes to win prizes. The first non-stop flight across the Atlantic was made on 14–15 June 1919, by the Englishmen Captain John Alcock (1892–1919) and Lieutenant Arthur Whitten Brown (1886–1948) in a Vickers Vimy bomber. It was not until 1927, however, that the first solo crossing was made (see

photo). During the 1920s and 1930s large multi-engined flying boats were widely used for long-distance over-water services, but they rapidly declined with the development of long-range landplanes just before and during World War II.

The first scheduled passenger flight by an airliner with a turboprop engine (see p. 309) – the British Vickers Viscount – was made in 1950. Turbojet power came to commercial aviation two years later, with another British airliner, the de Havilland Comet. The first American turbojet-powered airliner was the larger and commercially more successful Boeing 707, which began airline operation in 1958 on the route between New York and Paris. The Anglo-French Concorde was the world's first supersonic airliner, starting scheduled passenger flights in 1976.

Vertical flight

In 1907 the French Breguet-Richet *Gyroplane 1* became the first helicopter to lift a man from the ground. It was not until the 1930s, however, that fully successful helicopters appeared. The most important of these were the French Breguet-Dorand *Gyroplane Laboratoire*, the German Focke-Wulf Fw 61, and the American Vought-Sikorsky VS-300. All three could fly well but had very limited lifting capacity. However, both the German and American types led to the development of

better machines, which saw limited service during World War II. Widescale military use of helicopters was first seen in the early 1950s, during the Korean War.

Many forms of vertical take-off aeroplane have been designed and tested over the decades of aviation history. The world's first operational V/STOL (vertical/short take-off and landing) aeroplane was the Harrier, first built by Hawker Siddeley (now part of British Aerospace), which entered service with the Royal Air Force in 1969. This uses the thrust-vectoring technique, in which the direction of the engine's thrust can be altered to provide power for vertical and horizontal flight.

The Bell-Boeing V-22 Osprey combines the advantages of aeroplane and helicopter. First flown as a prototype in March 1989, it uses the *tilt-rotor* concept: engines driving large rotors are mounted at the tips of the wings to swivel upwards (vertical) in helicopter flight mode and swivel forward (horizontal) in aeroplane mode. Although less efficient than a simple aeroplane in cruising flight, the Osprey is vastly superior to a helicopter, being able to fly – for the same payload and fuel consumption – about three times as far in the same time.   MT

SEE ALSO
● ENGINES p. 308
● HOW AIRCRAFT WORK p. 350

Hughes H4 Hercules (top), the largest flying [boat] ever built, with a wingspan of 97.54 m (320 ft). [By the] time of its first and only flight in November [1947] the age of the flying boat was virtually over. [The] Vought-Sikorsky VS-300 (bottom), seen [pi]loted by designer Igor Sikorsky, was the first [succes]sful American helicopter. It made its maiden [flight] on 13 May 1940.

The Messerschmitt Me 262A-2a jet fighter-bomber (top). The German Me 262 and the British Gloster Meteor ushered in the age of the turbojet in July 1944. Prototype de Havilland Comet (bottom). The Comet introduced turbojet power to commercial aviation in 1952.

British Aerospace Harrier GR.Mk 3 (top): the Harrier, entering service in 1969, was the first operational aeroplane with the capacity to take off and land vertically. The Bell-Boeing Osprey prototype (bottom), first flown in March 1989, demonstrating the tilt-rotor concept.

Aircraft
2. How Aircraft Work

The term 'aircraft' includes every man-made device that flies in the atmosphere. The most important group of aircraft, called *aerodynes*, are not naturally buoyant – they are heavier than air. Aerodynes obtain their lift in a variety of ways: by jet thrust; by means of rotating blades; or by means of fixed wings, with a separate propulsion system to make the wings move through the air.

SEE ALSO

● ENGINES p. 308
● AIRCRAFT I p. 348

A smaller group is the *aerostats*, which are naturally buoyant – they are lighter than air. Those without power are called balloons (gas-filled or hot-air), while those with propulsion and some means of steering are called airships or dirigibles (see p. 348).

The principle of flight

When the *weight* of an aircraft (due to the force of gravity) is exceeded by the *lift* (the upward force created by the wings or by hot air or lighter-than-air gases), the aircraft will rise in the air. In the case of aeroplanes and gliders, lift is produced as a result of the characteristic profile – the *aerofoil section* – of the wing. The wing is rounded and thicker at the front (the *leading edge*), and tapers away to a sharp edge at the back (the *trailing edge*).

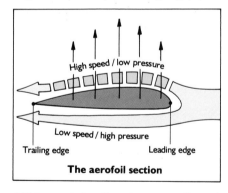

High speed / low pressure

Low speed / high pressure

Trailing edge   Leading edge

The aerofoil section

Lift is created as the wings move through the air at speed and relies on the fact that air pressure drops as air speed increases. As air passes over the wing, it has to move further, and thus faster, over the more curved upper surface than the lower surface. This causes a considerable reduction in pressure above the wing, especially at the front, where the wing is thickest and the upper surface most sharply curved. Lift can be increased both by increasing the speed of airflow over the wing and by increasing the curvature of the upper wing surface.

Any aircraft with propulsion also experiences *thrust* – the resultant force pulling or pushing it through the air; and *drag* – the equal and opposite force caused by the resistance of the air to the frontal surfaces of the aircraft. Drag is effectively wasted energy, so the aim of aircraft designers is to reduce drag without sacrificing lift.

Gliders, lacking an independent source of propulsion, have to fly downhill from the moment they are cast off after takeoff. The pilot thus seeks columns of rising warmer air, called *thermals*. Modern gliders are so efficient that they have climbed to nearly 15 000 m (49 200 ft) and flown 1460 km (907 mi).

Aircraft stability

In the absence of other forces, an aircraft's centre of gravity would have to be at the same point as its centre of lift for the craft to remain in equilibrium. In practice, however, because of thrust and drag, nearly all aeroplanes are designed to be naturally stable in the longitudinal plane, but with the centre of gravity ahead of the centre of lift. This causes a downward movement of the nose, which is counteracted by a constant download on the horizontal tail. Any disturbance tending to tilt the aircraft nose-up or nose-down is countered automatically by the change in the angle of the wings and of the horizontal tail.

Today, thanks to extremely fast computers, fighter planes can be deliberately made naturally unstable (see photo). This has two advantages: instead of a download the tailplane imparts an upload, thus helping the wing instead of fighting it; and as the fighter is always trying to depart from straight flight (restrained by computers that apply restoring forces 40 or more times per second), the aircraft can be made exceptionally agile.

Aircraft controls

Aeroplanes and gliders are controlled in the longitudinal (*pitch*) axis by *elevator* on the tailplane (see diagram), or by having a fully powered pivoted tailplane. A few modern designs have a foreplane instead of a tailplane, and a very few have both. Directional control is provided by a vertical *rudder*, which is usually located on the tailplane as well. The rudder is also an important control surface if a multi-engined aircraft should suffer failure of an engine mounted far out on a wing.

Lateral (*roll*) control was formerly provided only by *ailerons* – pivoted portions of the trailing edge near the tips of the wings – but today roll control can be effected by asymmetric use of the tail planes or by asymmetric deflection of *spoilers*. The spoilers are door-like surfaces hinged along the top of the wing. Differentially they control roll, and symmetrically they serve as airbrakes by increasing drag. Spoilers can also be used in *direct lift control* to enable the aircraft trajectory to be varied up or down without changing the attitude of the fuselage. On landing, spoilers act as 'lift dumpers', instantly killing wing lift and thus increasing the weight on the wheels and the effectiveness of the brakes.

All early aircraft used cables in tension or push/pull pivoted rods to convey pilot commands to the control surfaces. From about 1950 powered controls were widely introduced, in which the surfaces were moved by hydraulic actuators, the pilot's controls being provided with some form of artificial 'feel' so that he could sense what was happening. By 1970 *fly by wire* was

British Aerospace's active-control demonstrator (foreground) seen flying with a stable RAF Tornado. The demonstrator is a modified SEPECAT Jaguar, deliberately destabilized by 10% by fitting wing leading-edge strakes and aft ballast.

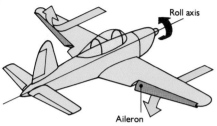

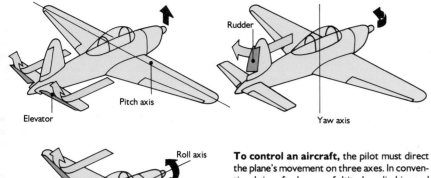

Pitch axis

Elevator

Rudder

Yaw axis

Roll axis

Aileron

To control an aircraft, the pilot must direct the plane's movement on three axes. In conventional aircraft, changes of altitude – climbing and descent – are achieved by moving the nose up or down (on the *pitch axis*) by means of *elevators*. Directional control (on the *yaw axis*) is provided by the *rudder*, while lateral control (on the *roll axis*) is effected by trailing-edge flaps called *ailerons*.

rapidly becoming common, in which the pilot's controls send out small electrical signals, which are carried through multiple wires to the surface power units. Today *fly by light* is being introduced: pilot signals are conveyed as variable light output along optical fibres (see p. 33), thus offering colossal bandwidth and data-handling capacity.

The high-lift system

An aircraft has to work hardest during take-off and landing, when airspeed is at its lowest and yet maximum lift is required. To facilitate these manoeuvres, most aircraft have a *high-lift system*, brought into action for the approach and landing, and usually also for take-off.

Along the leading edge of the wing there may be *slats*, slender portions of the wing moved out and away on parallel arms, or alternatively *Krüger flaps*, which swing down and around from underneath the leading edge. These full-span devices greatly increase the available lift, especially from a thin wing suitable for fast jets.

Along the trailing edge are fitted *flaps*. These again come in many forms, but all swing back and down from the wing. When selected to a take-off setting, such as 15°, they increase lift and slightly increase drag; when fully down, at the landing setting of perhaps 40°, they increase lift even more but also greatly increase drag.

Aircraft propulsion

Until 1939 virtually all aeroplanes were powered by piston engines driving a *propeller*, which provides thrust by accelerating air through aerodynamic rotating blades. Almost all modern propellers are of the variable-pitch type – the angle at which the blades attack the air can be altered. The blades are set to fine pitch for take-off to match high engine speed with low aircraft speed, and then automat-

ically adjusted to coarse pitch for cruising flight, to match economical low engine speed to high forward speed. After landing, some propellers can be set to reverse pitch to help brake the aircraft.

During World War II, engines grew rapidly in power. The Spitfire Mk I, for example, had a two-blade propeller, while the Mk XIV had five blades, in order to absorb the increased power within the limited available propeller diameter. Today some turboprop airliners (see p. 309) have six-blade propellers, turning at relatively low speed for minimum noise.

During and after World War II, the propeller gave way to the turbojet for most purposes. The turbojet itself was largely eclipsed by the turbofan, which offers better fuel economy and reduced noise levels (see p. 309).

Helicopters and autogyros

A helicopter is lifted by a *rotor* (sometimes two rotors), which is constructed of between two and eight slender blades, which effectively act as rotating wings. Lift is created as the rotor is driven round under power, forcing the air obliquely downwards. Because the rotor can create lift even when the aircraft itself is stationary, a helicopter is able to hover, and to take off and land vertically. In forward flight, the airflow through the rotor is complex. In order that the greater lift produced by the advancing blade does not destabilize the aircraft, the blades are hinged at the rotorhead, so that they flap up and down once every revolution.

An autogyro has no mechanical drive to the rotor (except sometimes to pre-spin it), but uses a separate propulsion system, usually driving a propeller. This propels the machine forward, the airflow through the rotor causing it to spin of its own accord. The air flows obliquely up through the rotor disc.   MT

Pilot's-eye view (above) of a modern fighter cockpit (F-16C). Several advanced systems are used to reduce the pilot's workload, including a wide-angle holographic display and keyboard, to project data onto the see-through screen above the instrument console. The control stick is on the pilot's right-hand side; the backward-tilted seat and raised heel line enable him to tolerate high g-forces.

The Stealth Fighter. The shape and materials used to make the Stealth Fighter have made it almost undetectable to hostile radars and other sensors. The low, flat shape was designed to reflect radar energy in directions other than back to the radar.

The Motorcar
1. Development

A motorcar can be defined as a passenger-carrying road vehicle powered by an internal-combustion engine. As such, its history extends for little over a century. However, such vehicles owe much both to the steam-powered vehicles that preceded them and to the horse-and-carriage. Features essential to the success of the motorcar, including wheels, axles, spokes and suspension systems, had all been developed and improved in earlier types of road vehicle. It was only when these features were linked to the recently developed four-stroke engine (see p. 309) that a motorcar similar in essentials to its modern counterpart could emerge.

SEE ALSO

● ENGINES p. 308
● OIL AND GAS p. 310
● THE MOTORCAR 2 p. 354

In late 1885 the German inventor Karl Benz (1844–1929) announced his Motorwagen, a single-cylinder, petrol-engined tricycle (see photo). Although the immediate impact of this invention was not great, its significance cannot be overestimated. Within 10 years, dozens of manufacturers had appeared; the first motor race – the 1895 Paris–Bordeaux–Paris race – had been run; and the rich were buying cars both as status symbols and as a means of transportation.

The early years of the car
At the turn of the 20th century, the development of the car began to gather pace. Within 10 years, the 'horseless carriage' had replaced the horse as the preferred form of transport – at least for those who could afford it. The awkward tiller steering with which the first cars were equipped was abandoned in favour of the steering wheel, which was much easier to operate. Engines grew in size and the speed of the fastest cars was now well in excess of what any team of horses could muster. Even the cynics who had dismissed the car as a passing craze were beginning to realize that the day of horse-drawn vehicles was nearing its end.

A major landmark in the history of the car came in 1906, when Rolls-Royce produced the 'Silver Ghost' (see photo). A seven-litre, six-cylinder luxury tourer, it was capable of travelling practically unlimited distances with complete reliability, often at speeds of over 100 km/h (62.5 mph). At the same time it offered unrivalled comfort, looks and quietness.

Mass production
Up until 1908, the car had been very much the toy of the rich, far beyond the reach of the less affluent. In October 1908, this situation was dramatically changed by the American industrialist Henry Ford (1863–1947), with the introduction of mass-production. Instead of individually hand-crafting each car, he designed a car – the famous Model T Ford (see photo) – that could be made on a production line with standardized parts. Available only in a single colour (black), each car came off the line in around 90 minutes. More than 15 million Model Ts were made in its 19-year career, many being sold for as little as $250. By the start of the 1920s, every major manufacturing country had started to produce cars for general transport, rather than for the use of a privileged minority.

The age of innovation
Many of the features that make modern cars comfortable and safe were developed in the years between the launch of the Model T and the start of World War II.

Independent front suspension, which no modern family car would be without, was first introduced in a practical form on the 1922 Lancia Lambda, although it was not common practice to fit such systems until after 1945. Supercharging (see box) was pioneered in the 1920s by Mercedes, who also put the first diesel-engined production car on the road in 1936, in the form of the Mercedes-Benz 260D. The French company Citroën produced the first successful front-wheel-drive car in 1934, when it launched the Traction Avant (see photo); today, over half the cars in the world use their front wheels to transmit power to the ground.

The evolution of the car progresse[d] rapidly up until 1939, but during Worl[d] War II the pace of innovation slowe[d] dramatically. The only real advance [at] this time was the further development [of] four-wheel drive in the form of the Jee[p] (see photo), which – thanks to its powe[r] being driven through all four wheels [–] could traverse terrain that would b[e] unpassable in a normal car. After the wa[r] manufacturers found themselves turnin[g] out 10-year-old designs; it was only as th[e] 1950s approached that innovation bega[n] to return.

Modern cars
In August 1959, Austin Morris launche[d] the Mini Minor (see photo), which ha[s] profoundly influenced all subsequen[t] small-car design. By mounting the engin[e] *across* the chassis, its Greek-born d[e]signer, Sir Alexander Issigonis (1906–88[)] created a small car with more interi[or] space than many large saloons of the da[y]. The Mini also used the then relative[ly] unusual technology of front-wheel driv[e] which obviated the need for a bulky tran[s]mission tunnel in the car. Today virtual[ly] all small cars use this layout.

Cars have now evolved to the extent tha[t] most can reach speeds in excess of 16[0] km/h (100 mph) and achieve over 50 k[m] (31 mi) per gallon. At the same tim[e] standards of reliability have improve[d] dramatically, so that cars generally gi[ve] thousands of kilometres of trouble-fr[ee] motoring – and all for a fraction of t[he] money it would have cost (in real terms) [to] buy an equivalent car in the 1920s. At th[e]

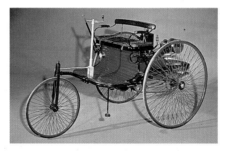

The Benz Motorwagen (1885; above), the first practical petrol-driven car. It developed less than one brake horsepower and could achieve no more than 16 km/h (10 mph).

The Rolls-Royce Silver Ghost (1906; above right). In 1907 the original model completed 23 127 km (14 371 mi) without an involuntary stop, so setting a new world reliability record. The engine and chassis cost £985, the body being built separately by leading coachbuilders. Rolls-Royce sold all their cars in this way until 1949.

Model T Fords (right) at Ford's first moving assembly line, located at Highland Park, Michigan. This photograph, taken in around 1913–14, shows the use of the exterior of the building for lowering the body onto the chassis.

The *performance* of a car is normally assessed on the basis of its top speed and its acceleration – how fast it can go and how long it takes to reach a given speed. The *power* of a car's engine may be expressed in several ways. The power (as a physical quantity – the rate at which mechanical work is done; see p. 24) may be expressed in brake horsepower or kilowatts (1 bhp being equivalent to 0.746 kW).

The power and the performance of a car are sometimes confused, but one is not always a reliable guide to the other. Even with a seemingly advantageous power-to-mass ratio, the performance of a vehicle is largely dependent on how effectively its power is developed and then delivered to the wheels.

Basically, the efficiency of an engine depends on the mass of fuel–oxygen mixture that can be pumped through it and effectively combusted in a given period of time. This factor is known as the *volumetric efficiency*.

To this end a number of systems have been developed to increase the power output of engines without increasing their size. For example, *supercharging* and *turbocharging* both force the fuel–air mixture into the combustion chamber at high pressure. Multi-valve cylinder heads have also been developed to improve the volumetric efficiency or 'breathing' of an engine.

The Porsche 959 (1986): the 2850 cc engine develops 450 bhp and delivers drive to all four wheels.

upper end of the market, many cars are turbocharged (see box), fuel-injected (see p. 354), have four-wheel drive and are capable of around 240 km/h (150 mph).

In recent years Japanese cars have made the greatest technical progress, and the Far East is now the world-leader in engine-design. US manufacturers have had trouble shedding their reputation for producing 'gas-guzzlers', but are now designing economy-conscious cars with greater international appeal. Europe, the traditional breeding ground of car innovation and design, will have to change direction as the car evolves further.

The move is now towards cars that give out less toxic waste and do less damage to the environment. This has led in many countries to legislation enforcing the use on cars of *catalytic converters*, which detoxify many of the harmful substances in the exhaust gases. However, concern about the burning of fossil fuels and the consequent environmental damage is sure to continue, and it seems clear that the car will have to change radically in the coming decades if it is to survive. AF

The Citroën Traction Avant (1934; above) the first successful front-wheel-drive car. It also the first car to be fitted with radial-ply tyres (in 1948). In all, when production ended in 1957, over 700 000 had been built.

The Jeep (from GP, 'general purpose'; above centre), introduced in 1940, was the first vehicle to realize the potential of four-wheel drive. Here, paratroopers remove the harness from a Jeep that has been dropped with them during an airborne operation in the Korean War.

The Mini (above). Following the Suez Crisis of 1956, petrol rationing led to a demand for smaller cars, and BMC's chairman asked Alec Issigonis to design the smallest possible car that could still carry four adults and luggage. The result was the Mini, launched as the Morris Mini Minor / Austin 7 in 1959 and still in production today. It established the engine and transmission layout used by almost all subsequent small cars.

The Audi Quattro (left), when it was first introduced in 1980, became the first mass-production saloon car with permanent four-wheel drive. This capability, combined with its 5-cylinder 2144 cc turbocharged engine, made it a highly successful rally car.

The Motorcar
2. How Cars Work

The engine is the power unit of a car, providing the motion that is ultimately transmitted to the driven wheels. However, a series of interconnected mechanisms, including the clutch, the gearbox and the differential, is required to transmit the power of the engine to the wheels in a usable form. At the same time, a number of subsidiary systems, including steering and brakes, are necessary in order to give adequate control over the movement of the car.

Most cars today are fitted with an overhead-valve, four-stroke, petrol engine, with four or six cylinders (see opposite and p. 309). Although the primary function of the engine is to spin the flywheel – the first link in the chain by which the engine's power is transmitted to the wheels – the rotary motion of the crankshaft is also used to turn the *alternator*, which generates the current needed by the car's electrical systems. At the same time, the rotation of the camshaft – again dependent on the crankshaft – drives both the oil pump and the distributor.

The ignition system

The purpose of the ignition system is to produce a spark of sufficient strength to ignite the petrol–air mixture at the exact moment when each piston in turn is nearly at the top of the compression stroke (see p. 309). The spark is produced as an electric current jumps (arcs) between the two electrodes of a spark plug; however, the voltage supplied by the battery is insufficient for this purpose. The voltage from the battery is first boosted by the *coil* to around 15 000 volts before passing to the *distributor*, in which a spinning rotor (driven by the camshaft) directs the current to each spark plug in turn.

The fuel system

For efficient and economical combustion within the engine, the precise proportions of petrol and air in the fuel mixture entering the cylinders must be carefully regulated. This is generally achieved by a *carburettor*. Although different types of carburettor exist, nearly all are in the form of a tube into which air is drawn by the downward movement of the pistons on their successive induction strokes (see p. 309). As the air accelerates through the narrowed middle section of the carburettor, its pressure falls, so causing a jet of fuel to be drawn through a nozzle from a reservoir, which is itself fed by a pump from the petrol tank. Within the carburettor, on the engine-side of the fuel jet, a circular flap (known as a butterfly valve) is actuated by the accelerator pedal in such a way as to control the volume of

air–fuel mixture drawn into the engine, thus regulating engine speed. In most designs, a similar valve (the *choke*) on the air-intake side of the fuel jet regulates the amount of air entering the carburettor and thus the richness of the fuel mix.

Increasingly, direct *fuel-injection* is being used in place of the carburettor. This is more efficient and economical than the carburettor, since accurately metered and appropriate amounts of fuel can be delivered to each cylinder's combustion chamber. There are several systems – both mechanical and electrical – but the basic principle is that fuel is injected at high pressure into the combustion chamber from a point behind the inlet valve.

Transmission

The term 'transmission' embraces all the components that are responsible for transferring the engine's power from the flywheel to the driven wheels. The spinning motion of the flywheel is transmitted to the *gearbox* via the *clutch* (see diagram). When the clutch pedal is depressed, the spinning flywheel is disconnected from the shaft transmitting power to the gearbox, so allowing the car to move off gently and smooth gear-changes to be made.

A gearbox is necessary because – unlike (say) an electric motor – most internal-combustion engines develop their full power and torque (turning effort) within a relatively narrow band of engine speeds (usually between 3000 and 5000 revolutions per minute). By means of the gearbox (and partly by the differential; see below), the engine speed is kept within these limits while allowing the car to operate at widely varying speeds and in a wide range of driving conditions.

For example, a steep hill requires a low gear, because it is only at high engine speeds that the engine is able to deliver enough torque to keep the wheels turning. On the other hand, where little torque is required, as when travelling at speed on a level road, a high gear may be used, thus matching high road speed with (relatively) low engine speed. In this way engine life is prolonged, passenger comfort enhanced and fuel consumption kept to a minimum.

After passing through the gearbox-and-clutch assembly, the drive is transferred to the *differential*. In front-wheel-drive cars, transmission from gearbox to differential is direct; in rear-wheel-drive cars, if the engine is mounted at the front of the car, the differential is driven by a crown wheel and pinion at the end of a propeller shaft.

The rotation rate of the shaft from the gearbox is further stepped down by the differential (normally to about a quarter of the gearbox speed). However, the differential's distinctive function is to allow power to be divided between the driven wheels in whatever proportion is required. Such a mechanism is necessary when cornering, because the outside driven wheel needs to be turned more rapidly than the inside wheel. **AF**

Engine. Four pistons fit tightly in four cylinde[rs] bored into the cylinder block. Each pisto[n is] driven downwards in a fixed sequence on t[he] power stroke of the four-stroke cycle (s[ee] p. 309). A *connecting rod* from each cylinder [is] attached to a cranked (dog-legged) shaft (t[he] *crankshaft*), which is turned a half-revolution [with] each successive power stroke. To one end [of] the crankshaft is bolted a heavy disc called t[he] *flywheel*, which provides the drive to the gea[r-] box via the clutch; at the other end, a belt-an[d-] pulley system causes the *camshaft* to rotate [at] half the speed of the crankshaft. Pear-shap[ed] lobes (*cams*) along the length of the camsh[aft] act on a series of rocker mechanisms that cau[se] the inlet and exhaust valves on each cylinder [to] open and close in exact timing with the fo[ur] strokes of the pisto[n]

Suspension. The *MacPherson strut* is a very common suspension arrangement, consisting of a spring mounted on an arm that runs from the wheel to a secure place on the bodyframe. The arm moves up and down with road irregularities, so compressing the spring and absorbing bumps.

To counteract the compressed spring's tendency to rebound, a *shock absorber* is fitted (within the spring, in the case of the MacPherson strut). This is essentially a fluid-filled piston-and-cylinder assembly. The piston moves in and out to the same extent as the spring, so forcing the thick fluid back and forth through channels in the piston and thus deadening the bounce of the spring.

MacPherson strut

Coil spring

S[ ] lower a[ ]

Clutch-and-gearbox assembly. The clutc[h] consists of the flywheel (driven round by th[e] crankshaft), a clutch (or friction) plate and [a] pressure plate. When the clutch is engaged (i.e[.] with the pedal released), powerful springs forc[e] the clutch plate against the flywheel, thereb[y] linking the flywheel to the shaft transmittin[g] power to the gearbox. When the clutch i[s] disengaged, levers work against the springs t[o] separate the clutch plate from the flywheel, s[o] disconnecting the transmission. The frictio[n] linings on the clutch plate allow the plate to sli[p] before becoming fully engaged, so preventing [a] shuddering jerk on starting[.]

The gearbox allows optimum (i.e. high) engin[e] speed to be matched to a wide variety o[f] driving conditions. By means of selector fork[s] actuated by the gearstick, different-sized gear[s] linked to the input shaft can be engaged wit[h] different-sized gears on the shaft transmittin[g] power to the differential. A (relatively) smal[l] gear on the input shaft engaged with a larg[e] gear on the transmission shaft produces lo[w] speed but high power; high speed and lo[w] power are achieved by reversing the gear ratio[s] on the input and output shafts. In top gear, n[o] gears are engaged and transmission passe[s] directly through the gearbox to the differential.

SEE ALSO
● ENGINES p. 308
● OIL AND GAS p. 310
● THE MOTORCAR I p. 352

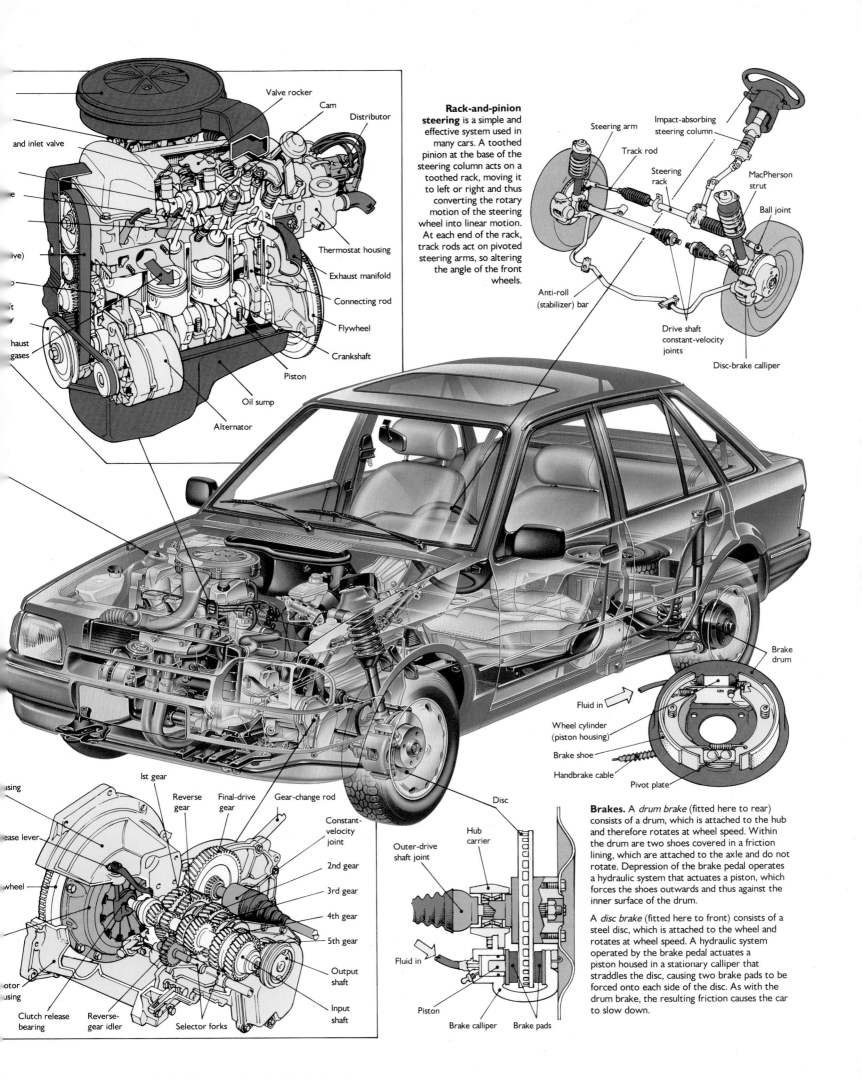

Valve rocker

Cam

Distributor

and inlet valve

Thermostat housing

Exhaust manifold

Connecting rod

haust gases

Flywheel

Crankshaft

Piston

Oil sump

Alternator

Rack-and-pinion steering is a simple and effective system used in many cars. A toothed pinion at the base of the steering column acts on a toothed rack, moving it to left or right and thus converting the rotary motion of the steering wheel into linear motion. At each end of the rack, track rods act on pivoted steering arms, so altering the angle of the front wheels.

Steering arm

Impact-absorbing steering column

Track rod

Steering rack

MacPherson strut

Ball joint

Anti-roll (stabilizer) bar

Drive shaft constant-velocity joints

Disc-brake calliper

Brake drum

Fluid in

Wheel cylinder (piston housing)

Brake shoe

Handbrake cable

Pivot plate

1st gear

Reverse gear

Final-drive gear

Gear-change rod

Disc

Hub carrier

using

ease lever

wheel

Constant-velocity joint

2nd gear

3rd gear

4th gear

5th gear

Output shaft

Input shaft

otor using

Clutch release bearing

Reverse-gear idler

Selector forks

Outer-drive shaft joint

Fluid in

Piston

Brake calliper

Brake pads

Brakes. A *drum brake* (fitted here to rear) consists of a drum, which is attached to the hub and therefore rotates at wheel speed. Within the drum are two shoes covered in a friction lining, which are attached to the axle and do not rotate. Depression of the brake pedal operates a hydraulic system that actuates a piston, which forces the shoes outwards and thus against the inner surface of the drum.

A *disc brake* (fitted here to front) consists of a steel disc, which is attached to the wheel and rotates at wheel speed. A hydraulic system operated by the brake pedal actuates a piston housed in a stationary calliper that straddles the disc, causing two brake pads to be forced onto each side of the disc. As with the drum brake, the resulting friction causes the car to slow down.

Weaponry

Throughout recorded history, man has searched for ways to gain advantage over his opponents on the field of battle. As new weapons have been developed, countermeasures have been sought, so invariably initiating further change. The result is a pendulum, swinging between opponents in terms of advantage and accelerating as technological expertise has grown.

A French crossbow of the early 16th century.

Until the 14th century, technology played a limited role in warfare. Before then, weapons were little more than hunting tools – spears, axes, sling-shots and swords – put to a different use. Technology was confined to weapons that depended on tension to project missiles over distance. An early example was the Roman *ballista*, a catapult that used ropes to pull back a wooden pivot, the release of which threw large rocks against enemy defences. The same principle was used by the *longbow* and the more mechanical *crossbow* (see photo), both dependent on human muscle to tauten a string, which projected an arrow when released.

Early firearms

The real breakthrough came with the use of gunpowder to provide projectile power. Invented by the Chinese, *gunpowder* is a mixture of saltpetre (potassium nitrate), sulphur and charcoal, which – when ignited in an enclosed space – explodes. A weapon was produced when this explosion took place in a tube closed at one end, with a projectile, such as a ball or a bullet, introduced at the other end. The result was the gun, examples of which were in use in European armies by the 1320s.

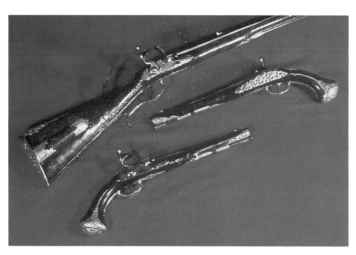

A set of imperial flintlock pistols (1732)

Although early guns were not very accurate, improvements came steadily, and by the late 17th century the *flintlock* had appeared. A soldier armed with a flintlock musket would bite the end off a paper cartridge, empty a small amount of powder into the pan above the trigger, tip the remainder down the barrel, add a ball and the cartridge case as wadding, ram it tight and cock the weapon. When he pulled the trigger, a piece of flint struck a 'steel' that covered the pan to produce sparks, which ignited the main charge and sent the ball out of the barrel at speed. Cannon worked on the same principle, except that a match needed to be applied to the touch-hole to produce the explosion.

Breech-loaded weapons

Major changes occurred in the 19th century. In the 1830s the flintlock began to be replaced by *percussion firing*, whereby a hammer struck a detonator to produce the necessary spark. This allowed the development of self-contained cartridges, comprising detonator, gunpowder and projectile. This in turn dispensed with the need for muzzle-loading and led to the introduction of *breech-loaded weapons*, in which the cartridge was fed directly into the breech, or firing chamber.

By the 1880s breech-loading had been refined to incorporate the use of magazines, each containing a number of cartridges, fed into the breech as the soldier worked a bolt (see box). Artillery also benefited from these developments, using self-contained breech-loaded shells that could be fired rapidly one after another. The invention of smokeless powder, such as cordite, also allowed firing to take place from concealed positions.

Automatic weapons

In terms of infantry weapons, the logical next step was to eliminate the working of the bolt by hand, by harnessing the explosive action of the gun to do the job automatically. Early machine guns such as the Maxim did this by using the recoil of the weapon to open the breech, eject the used cartridge and feed the next one in.

In other designs, automatic loading was achieved by diverting gases produced by the explosion back into the weapon.

A British World War I tank

THE BOLT-ACTION MAGAZINE RIFLE

In the second half of the 19th century, muzzle-loaded rifles were replaced by weapons in which a cartridge fed from a magazine was loaded into the breech by working a bolt. Such bolt-action rifles remained standard infantry issue until generally displaced by automatic weapons after World War II.

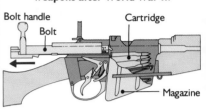

As the bolt is withdrawn, a cartridge is fed by the spring-loaded magazine into line with the bolt.

As it is pushed forward, the bolt engages with the cartridge and moves it into the breech.

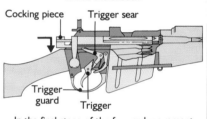

In the final stage of the forward movement of the bolt, a protruding piece of the bolt assembly catches the trigger sear, so cocking the weapon. The bolt is rotated to lock the cartridge in the breech. The weapon can now be fired by pressure on the trigger.

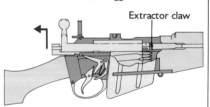

When the bolt is released and drawn backwards, a claw on the bolt engages with the rim of the spent cartridge, so removing it from the breech. Once clear, the cartridge is ejected.

Experiments during World War I enabled the same system to be incorporated into much lighter weapons, producing the submachine gun and, eventually, the automatic rifle (see box). Modern assault rifles such as the British SA-80 and the Soviet AK-47 work on this principle (known as 'blow-back') and give the ordinary soldier unprecedented firepower.

Tank warfare

On the ground, the face of battle was changed by the introduction of the tank

nd its antidotes. The tank was invented
y the British in 1915 as an armoured
aterpillar-tracked machine designed to
ross the mud and trenches of a World
War I battlefield.

he tank was later developed into a war-
winning weapon by the Germans, who
ecognized its potential to break through
nemy lines and produce rear-area para-
ysis. *Blitzkrieg* ('lightning war'), depen-
ent on a mixture of mobility and air
upport, was effective in the early years of
World War II, but was slowly countered
y new technology. Tanks proved vul-
erable to other tanks, especially those
rmed with bigger guns and special anti-
ank shells. Infantry soldiers were also
quipped to deal with the threat, using
pring-loaded weapons such as the British
PIAT ('projectile, infantry, anti-tank') or
he German Panzerfaust.

Long-range warfare

During the two World Wars the ability to
hit distant targets improved dramatically,
ulminating in the development of pilot-
ess bombs and surface-to-surface missiles
- the German V1 and V2 weapons.

The V1 was a pulse-jet powered machine,
ired from a special ramp towards its
arget, which it hit when it ran out of fuel.
The US-produced *Cruise missile* of the
1970s owed its origins to V1, but was far
more sophisticated. It incorporated
an on-board 'terrain contour-matching
(TERCOM) guidance system', which
'read' the ground over which the missile
was flying, compared it to a pre-set computer memory, and corrected the flight
path to ensure pin-point accuracy.

The V2 had a liquid-fuelled rocket engine
that burned for about 70 seconds, during
which the missile shot vertically to an
altitude of 96 km (60 mi). It then fell
back to Earth in a predetermined arc,
hitting its target at a speed of 3840 km/h
(2386 mph). It was the forerunner of the
nuclear-armed ballistic missiles of the
modern era (see p. 288).

Since 1945 missiles have been preferred
both for anti-tank and for anti-aircraft
roles. By the early 1970s, wire-guided
anti-tank missiles such as the Soviet AT-3
Sagger and British Swingfire had been
developed, being fired towards the target
and guided onto it by electronic signals
transmitted down a command wire trailing behind. Since then, the wire has been
discarded and the missile fired down a
pre-set laser beam: the missile has a
sensor in its nose, which – when locked
onto the beam – carries it unerringly to its
destination.

Current developments take this further,
with the on-board sensor homing in on
infrared or heat emissions from the
target. As such missiles will seek out their
own targets, they are known as 'fire-and-
forget' weapons. Similar developments
have affected surface-to-air missiles
(SAMs), which are designed to home in on
the heat and light emitted by the jet exhausts of modern aircraft (see photo). JP

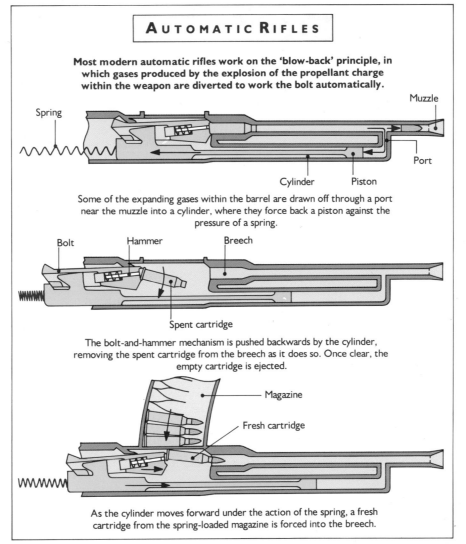

AUTOMATIC RIFLES

Most modern automatic rifles work on the 'blow-back' principle, in
which gases produced by the explosion of the propellant charge
within the weapon are diverted to work the bolt automatically.

Spring · Muzzle · Port · Cylinder · Piston

Some of the expanding gases within the barrel are drawn off through a port
near the muzzle into a cylinder, where they force back a piston against the
pressure of a spring.

Bolt · Hammer · Breech · Spent cartridge

The bolt-and-hammer mechanism is pushed backwards by the cylinder,
removing the spent cartridge from the breech as it does so. Once clear, the
empty cartridge is ejected.

Magazine · Fresh cartridge

As the cylinder moves forward under the action of the spring, a fresh
cartridge from the spring-loaded magazine is forced into the breech.

SEE ALSO

- NUCLEAR ARMAMENT AND DISARMAMENT p. 288
- SHIPS pp. 342–5
- AIRCRAFT pp. 348–51
- HELLENISTIC ARMIES p. 373
- THE ROMAN ARMY p. 378
- MEDIEVAL ARMOUR p. 401
- MEDIEVAL AND RENAIS-SANCE WAR AND FORTIFI-CATION p. 407
- NAPOLEON'S MILITARY REVOLUTION p. 427
- WORLD WAR I p. 436
- WORLD WAR II p. 444

The US Stinger is a
portable surface-to-air
missile (SAM), vital in
situations where troop
mobility is required.
The Stinger is a 'fire-
and-forget' missile,
automatically homing in
on the heat emissions of
aircraft exhausts. This
advantageous mode of
operation is partially
offset by the missile's
susceptibility to heat flares
ejected as decoys from
target aircraft.

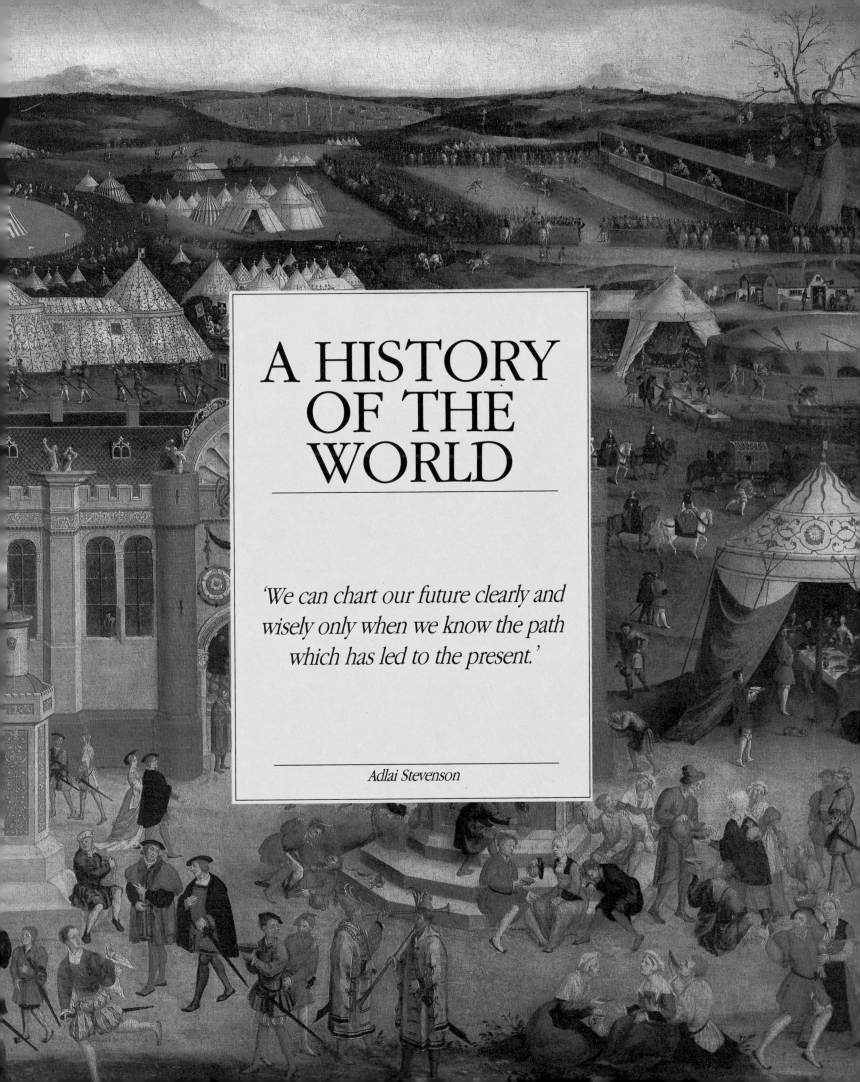

A HISTORY
OF THE
WORLD

'We can chart our future clearly and
wisely only when we know the path
which has led to the present.'

Adlai Stevenson

Discovering the Past

History in its widest sense is the study of humanity's past. In a narrower sense, history is often contrasted with archaeology, the former studying written and oral records, and the latter examining physical remains such as buildings and artefacts. While history in this sense has been written since the time of the ancient Greeks, true archaeological investigation only began in the 18th century.

The basic aims of history are to record and explain. This was recognized already by the 'Father of History', Herodotus (c. 485–c. 420 BC), who wrote his account of the war between Persia and the Greeks 'in order to preserve the memory of past events, and the fame of the great and wonderful achievements of both Greeks and Persians, and in addition to show how the two peoples came to make war on one another'.

Other historians have combined these basic aims with their own philosophies. The Chronicles of Raphael Holinshed (d. ?1580), for example, are Tudor propaganda, doing down the English kings (such as Richard III) whom the Tudors replaced. The 19th-century Whig historians in Britain, such as Lord Macaulay (1800–59), saw history in terms of progress towards the present, while Marxists interpret it as an illustration of the class struggle (see p. 268).

Most historians today try to adopt as impartial a view as possible, but history can never be a wholly objective study – even the selection of facts is an act of interpretation reflecting the culture and ideology of the historian, and the period in which he or she is writing.

As much as possible, however, historians try to avoid applying the values and beliefs of the present to their interpretation of the past. It is not valid, for example, to denounce 19th-century European imperialism *simply* as an exploitation of the colonized countries, when many of the imperialists themselves felt they were bringing a 'higher civilization' to those countries. We may argue that they were mistaken, but to understand their motives it is important to try to put ourselves in their shoes – an exercise of historical imagination known as *empathy*.

Historical evidence

Before the historian can begin to impose a pattern on the facts, those facts must first of all be established. The raw material of history is found in *primary sources* – records written by the people involved in the events being studied. Such records may be government and legal papers, wills, maps, leases, letters or diaries. In addition, statistical evidence may be extracted from census returns or birth and marriage registers. *Secondary sources* are studies of primary sources made at a later date, and may include anything from newspaper reports to the writings of previous historians.

All sources may include (sometimes unknowingly) an interpretation of events. In these cases the critical reader must ask 'What is the attitude of the writer to the events he or she is describing? How close to the events was he or she?' This is also true of oral evidence – the recollections of living people – since memories distort and fade.

Archaeological evidence

In addition to written or oral evidence, the historian may also draw on archaeological evidence – not only for periods for which no written records exist, but also for later periods where the written records are scarce or fragmentary.

Artefacts such as pottery, glass and most metals survive well (though usually in fragments), while objects made of organic substances (wood, leather and textiles) often only survive in waterlogged sites such as ports or rivers or in exceptionally arid conditions, as in Egypt. When objects are found in their original (*primary*) position in buildings, as opposed to being

Rescue archaeologists uncovering the Roman basilica in the City of London. Each layer or piece of masonry is recorded at a scale of 1:20 with the aid of aluminium frames of various sizes. Each context (layers, ditches, walls, etc.) must be drawn before the evidence is removed.

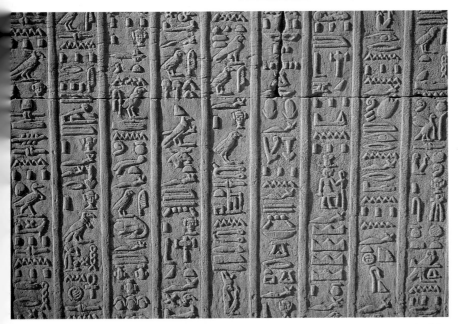

Egyptian hieroglyphs. Such written records are the raw materials of history.

thrown away somewhere else (*secondary*), we can reconstruct the functions of rooms or spaces – how they were used for industrial, ceremonial, or domestic purposes.

Human bones provide details of the age- and sex-structure of the population, congenital disorders, famine, weather conditions, blood types and diseases of the skeleton. Animal bones, shells and dried excrement furnish information on diet and farming techniques. Environmental factors such as climate or pollution can be studied by looking at seeds, pollen counts, insects and the remains of microscopic organisms.

Excavation

Some archaeological research is designed to answer specific questions, but much of it nowadays is *rescue archaeology*, which attempts to preserve a record of what was there before a site is destroyed by building work, deep ploughing, quarrying or new roads.

The first question every archaeologist is asked is 'How did you know where to dig?' There are two kinds of helpful evidence: previous written records (including maps) of what stood on the site and what it was used for, and prospecting methods such as aerial photography (which, with the use of specialist techniques, can also identify monuments beneath the ground) or remote sensing on the ground.

The main task of archaeological recording is to note even the smallest evidence of past human activity – a layer, a ditch, a wall. These are called *contexts*, and they are given numbers so that information about them, and the artefacts from them, can be stored separately (see box). The context will be surveyed and probably photographed before it is removed to uncover the one below; it may also be sampled for environmental or industrial residues.

The contexts are ordered to show the

succession of layers representing the history of the site – construction, occupation, destruction, decay – and natural actions such as river flooding or erosion. The *stratigraphy* of a site is the record of its various layers, which can be shown in a scale drawing and in diagrammatic form as a *matrix* (see box). The stratigraphy is the basis of all future research. Once the dates are established, these are then added to the matrix.

Methods of dating

Dates may be established by examining historical records, or by comparing the finds with similar finds of known date – a method known as *typology*.

Various scientific techniques are also used. *Radiocarbon dating* is based on the fact that all living material (such as wood) absorbs small amounts of radioactive carbon-14, which reduces by a known amount over time once the material is dead. In general this method is useful only for prehistoric periods, because of its margin of error.

Dendrochronology (tree-dating) is far more precise, being based on the annual growth rings in trees, and is especially useful for the Roman and later historic periods. Variations in the width between rings correspond with climatic changes, and so timber used in a building can be compared with other timber of known age.

The range of history and archaeology

Archaeologists, particularly those working on the prehistoric period, have looked at very wide factors over large regions, giving rise to conflicting theories as to whether cultures spread by invasion – the *invasion hypothesis* – or by autonomous development – the *continuity hypothesis* (see p. 375 for an example). Today, in addition, the archaeologist is interested in identifying small groups within com-

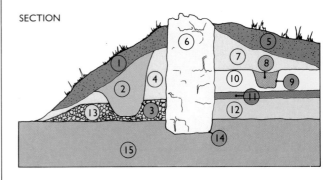

ANALYSIS OF AN ARCHAEOLOGICAL DIG

SECTION

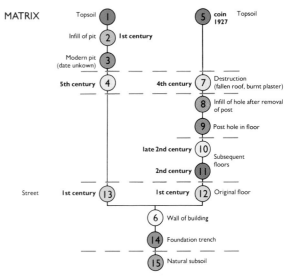

This diagram shows how the archaeologist analyses strata in the ground, as shown by a *section* (vertical cut) through the wall of a building. The layers or *contexts* are numbered as they are excavated, and their stratigraphic links shown in the *matrix*. The sequence of construction, use and destruction of the building can be reconstructed using the matrix. The latest dates from each layer – from artefacts or dating mechanisms such as carbon-14 – will be added to the matrix, to find out the overall dates for the phases shown. Note that some layers have no finds.

The above example shows a Roman street and building laid out in the 1st century AD, with internal floors renewed in the 2nd century. The street and building were destroyed in the 5th century: note how layer 4 has later material than layer 7, and therefore the destruction is dated by the later material. Note also the misleading finds in layer 2, filling the pit 3; this pit was dug after the 5th century, but contains *residual* 1st-century finds (probably from layer 13).

munities – village, town or city – and working out how these groups rose and fell, interacted with each other, and disappeared from view.

Similarly, while some historians are concerned with large-scale patterns underlying the changes in societies and civilizations, others restrict themselves to particular aspects or specific locations. History is not just about the actions of monarchs and statesmen, but may also concern itself with such things as the ebb and flow of population, variations in standards of living, fashions, and the spread of technology. All human activity belongs to history, and we ourselves cannot stand apart from it. History starts yesterday.   JS

SEE ALSO

- HUMAN PREHISTORY p. 362
- THE ANCIENT NEAR EAST p. 364
- ANCIENT EGYPT p. 366
- MINOANS AND MYCENAEANS p. 368
- THE CELTS p. 374

Human Prehistory

Prehistory is the period of time before written documents, the normal means by which historic events are recorded and dated. Before the development of scientific dating methods after World War II (see p. 361), dating methods were largely *relative* **– in other words, definite dates were not assigned, but instead it was simply indicated whether a period came before or after certain important technological developments of unknown date.**

A Neolithic house (right) at Skara Brae, in the Orkney Islands, dating from c. 3000 BC. There are several such semi-underground houses at the site, interlinked by covered passages. Because there were no local trees, furniture was made out of stone. Buried by sand for centuries, the site was exposed by a great storm in 1850.

The division of human prehistory into the *Stone Age*, *Bronze Age* and *Iron Age*, based on the materials used for tools, was introduced in the early 19th century. This 'Three Age System' was further developed in the late 19th century by subdividing the Stone Age into the *Palaeolithic* ('Old Stone'), *Mesolithic* ('Middle Stone'), and *Neolithic* ('New Stone') Ages. These technologically based divisions remain useful for European prehistory, but they are not always valid in other parts of the world.

The Palaeolithic

Most of the Palaeolithic developments in Europe, and in Asia outside the tropics, occurred against a background of a much colder climate, associated with the growth of vast ice sheets in northern latitudes, and extensive glacier development in more southerly latitudes, including the Alps and the Balkans. This was the last Ice Age (see p. 91).

STONE AGE TOOLS

As Palaeolithic flintworking progressed, the numbers of stages and flaking-blows involved in tool manufacture increased.

Early Homo erectus hand axe, dating from the earliest part of the Lower Palaeolithic. This was rough-hewn from a single piece of flint in a single stage involving about 25 blows.

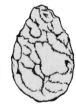

Later Homo erectus hand axe, dating from the later part of the Lower Palaeolithic. This was made in the same way as the earlier axe, but involved two stages and around 65 blows.

Neanderthal knife, dating from the Middle Palaeolithic. This was made in three stages, involving chipping a flake from a flint core and then working on the flake. Over 100 blows would have been needed.

Cro-Magnon knife, dating from the Upper Palaeolithic. This incredibly sharp knife represents the most advanced Palaeolithic stone-working technology. A total of nine stages and 250 blows were required.

The causes, and exact number, of the cold periods, which were separated by warmer phases, are not clearly understood; nor is their age well established, since scientific methods have as yet not been very successful in dating this geological time span. However, the last cold phase ended about 10 000 years ago and the different warm and cold phases can be recognized archaeologically because of the preservation of the bones of characteristic animals and even the pollen of particular trees, which indicate warmer or colder periods. They thus provide a useful *relative chronology* in which to place human developments. Archaeologists also use developments in stone-tool types to subdivide the Palaeolithic into *Lower* (i.e. earliest), *Middle*, and *Upper* phases.

The Lower Palaeolithic

No certain finds of human fossils at the australopithecine stage of evolution, dated between 2 and 5 million years ago (see p. 200), have appeared outside Africa. The earliest human fossils in Europe and Africa belong to the *Homo erectus* evolutionary stage, dated between 1.5 million and 200 000 years ago, although in Europe and Asia outside the tropics there is no good evidence for human occupation before 1 million years ago. *Homo erectus* fossils have been discovered in France, Germany, China and Java.

The *industries* (i.e. tool types) used by *Homo erectus* belong to the Lower Palaeolithic. The most characteristic tool is the hand axe, a general-purpose implement made by striking off pieces of stone (*flakes*) from a lump of stone until the correct shape and cutting edge were produced. Simple tools made of flakes removed from a lump of stone (a *core*) were

also used, sometimes improved by further flaking of the edges. Tools in materials other than stone very rarely survive, but a Lower Palaeolithic wooden spear point has been found in Essex, England. Even at this early stage humans used fire, as exemplified by the fire hardening of the spear.

While Lower Palaeolithic tools continued until about 100 000 years ago, it seems that between 300/200 000 and 100 000 years ago *Homo erectus* evolved into a more developed stage, at least in Europe. However, there is little evidence of this stage.

The Middle Palaeolithic

The Middle Palaeolithic stage, from 100 000 to as late as 30 000 years ago, is associated with the remains of Neanderthal man (*Homo sapiens neanderthalensis*, named after the Neandertal, a valley in Germany where remains were first found). While *Homo erectus* only occupied Eurasia during relatively warm periods, Neanderthals could exploit the arctic environments of the full glacial phases, living in caves and in skin tents held down by mammoth bones.

Middle Palaeolithic stone tools, made mainly from flakes, were more specialized than earlier tools, and included spear heads, knives and scraping tools for wood and hides. Neanderthals were the first humans to bury their dead, and they also had a sense of beauty: scientific analysis shows that at Shanidar cave in Iraq a Neanderthal was buried on a bed of spring flowers.

The Upper Palaeolithic

There is still much scientific debate about the date of the first appearance of anatomically modern humans (*Homo sapiens*

THE THREE AGES OF NEAR-EASTERN AND EUROPEAN PREHISTORY

AGE	STONE AGE						BRONZE AGE	IRON AGE
	PALAEOLITHIC			MESOLITHIC	NEOLITHIC			
	LOWER	MIDDLE	UPPER					
PERIOD BEGAN (approximately)	1 million years ago	100 000 years ago	30 000 BC	10 000 BC	9000-4000 BC (spreading from Near East to W Europe)		3000-2000 BC (both periods earliest in Near East and SE Europe, spreading to W and N Europe)	1200-500 BC
DOMINANT HOMINID	Homo erectus	Neanderthal man (H. saplens neanderthalensis)	Modern man (Homo sapiens sapiens)					
TECHNOLOGY	Simple stone tools, e.g. hand axes Use of fire	More specialized stone tools, e.g. spear heads, knives	Development of stone blades and bone tools Beginnings of art	Use of bow and arrow	Beginnings of agriculture First towns in Near East		Bronze artefacts First cities	Iron artefacts

The standing stones at **Carnac** in France, erected around 2000 BC. This megalithic ('giant stone') monument consists of nearly 3000 standing stones (or *menhirs*) arranged in several long, parallel rows – some over 1 km (0.6 mi) in length. The amount of manpower and effort involved in constructing such megaliths as Carnac and Stonehenge indicates the strong social and cultural cohesion of local Neolithic societies.

sapiens, also called Cro-Magnon man, after a cave in the Dordogne, France). However, it seems likely that in Europe and northern Asia they appeared relatively late – perhaps as late as 30 000 BC in Western Europe – although in some other parts of the world they had appeared before 40 000 BC.

In Eurasia, Upper Palaeolithic tools, associated with modern humans, have a number of characteristic features: stone tools were now based on *blades* (long, thin flakes), which were made into an even wider variety of specialized tools than previously. Bone tools also appear regularly for the first time. Another Upper Palaeolithic cultural achievement is the Ice Age art found, for example, in the prehistoric cave sites of France and Spain (see p. 504).

The achievements of these early modern humans include the peopling of the previously unoccupied continents of Australasia and the Americas (see pp. 388–90). A less positive achievement is the extinction of a number of large mammal species (see p. 140) towards the end of the last Ice Age (about 8000 BC), at least partially as a result of the efficient hunting methods of Upper Palaeolithic peoples.

The Mesolithic

The end of the Ice Age saw significantly increased temperatures and rainfall in Europe and parts of Asia. A largely treeless environment was replaced by forest, especially in Europe north of the Alps, and mammal species adapted to tundra and steppe environments were replaced by forest species. Humans adapted to these changes by living in smaller groups and exploiting the increased numbers of wildfowl and fish. In Eurasia use of the bow and arrow became important in this period.

The Neolithic

The earliest Neolithic cultures, defined by the appearance of agriculture as a way of life, are found in the Near East, in an area between Turkey and Israel in the west and Iran in the east. In this area the wild ancestors of wheat and barley, and of sheep, goats, pigs and cattle all occurred. The earliest Neolithic sites date to the period 9000–7000 BC, contemporary with the Mesolithic period in Europe. But in the Near East the climatic changes associated with the end of the Ice Age were far less marked than in Europe, and population pressure is a more likely explanation for the beginnings of agriculture than climatic change. By 6000 BC some substantial towns existed in the Near East.

The spread of agriculture was relatively rapid: Neolithic sites in Greece start before 6000 BC and appear in Britain by 4000 BC. During the 2000–3000-year lifespan of the Neolithic, considerable social distinctions emerged along with increasingly centralized political power. These developments are associated with the building of large burial and ceremonial monuments in earth and stone that began in many parts of Europe at this time (see p. 504). Specialized production of, and widespread trade in, a variety of objects and materials also developed.

The Bronze Age

Copper and gold were the main metals used during the Bronze Age (bronze is an alloy: a mixture of copper with a little tin). The production of metal objects is a complex process, but the discovery of metallurgy probably occurred independently in several places, including the Near East, southeast Europe and southwest Asia. In parts of Europe and the Near East, small numbers of simple copper objects were in use many centuries before the beginning of the Bronze Age: this transitional period is called the *Chalcolithic* ('copper-stone') Age.

Social distinctions increased as more powerful individuals displayed their status via bronze weapons and gold jewellery. The status and power of certain individuals was particularly marked in the Later Bronze Age, as shown by various imposing grave monuments and offerings, such as the Mycenaean shaft graves (see p. 369), and bronze weapons and armour in a number of central European graves.

The Iron Age

The development of iron working in the Near East and its spread, starting at about 1000 BC, had little immediate effect on late Bronze Age cultures. The recognizably Celtic societies of Iron Age temperate Europe (see p. 374) developed directly out of later Bronze Age cultures. European Iron Age societies had increasing contacts with Greece and Rome, first through trade, but later through the invasion of much of Celtic Europe by the Romans. This put an end to prehistory in those areas. However, the peripheries of Europe (Ireland, Scotland, Scandinavia, northern Germany) were never colonized by the Romans. The emergence of these areas from prehistory only occurred gradually, within the last 1500 years, after their conversion to Christianity.   HF

SEE ALSO

- PHYSICAL EVOLUTION p. 200
- DISCOVERING THE PAST p. 360
- THE ANCIENT NEAR EAST p. 364
- MINOANS AND MYCENAEANS p. 368
- THE CELTS p. 374
- FOR PREHISTORY OUTSIDE EUROPE AND THE NEAR EAST pp. 382–91
- PREHISTORIC ART p. 504

The Ancient Near East

The Ancient Near East has been called the cradle of Western Civilization. To its people we owe the invention of agriculture, the wheel, writing and the alphabet. The region known as the Near East comprises the countries on the eastern shores of the Mediterranean, together with modern Turkey, Iran (ancient Persia), Egypt (see p. 336), and Iraq (ancient Mesopotamia, consisting of Babylonia and Assyria). This agriculturally rich area is sometimes called the 'Fertile Crescent'.

The world's first cities arose between 4000 and 3000 BC in Mesopotamia, which in Greek means 'the land of the two rivers'. These rivers, the Tigris and Euphrates, flooded their banks during the spring and made the surrounding plain extremely fertile.

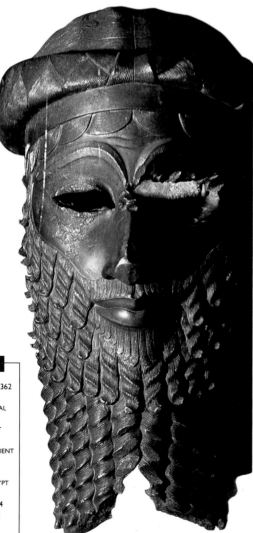

SEE ALSO

- HUMAN PREHISTORY p. 362
- ANCIENT EGYPT p. 366
- ARCHAIC AND CLASSICAL GREECE p. 370
- ALEXANDER THE GREAT p. 372
- RELIGIONS OF THE ANCIENT NEAR EAST p. 460
- ART OF THE ANCIENT MIDDLE EAST AND EGYPT p. 506
- WRITING SYSTEMS p. 604
- THE MAKING OF MYTHS p. 612

The Mesopotamian farmers had to build a complex system of canals, dykes and reservoirs to control the annual floods. This required a great deal of organization and cooperation. Variations in the fertility of the soil led to differences in individual wealth – and hence to the emergence of social classes. Food surpluses allowed some people to give up farming and become craftsmen, labourers, merchants and administrators. These developments created a need for centralized decision making, regulation and control: the beginnings of urban civilization.

The Sumerians

In southern Babylonia, between 3500 and 3000 BC, buildings became progressively larger and more elaborate. The best example is the White Temple at Uruk, built on a high platform. The wheel was invented at around the same period. The earliest writing – simple pictures drawn on clay – developed probably because of the need for record keeping in an ever more complex society (see also p. 604).

We call these people Sumerians, from the ancient name for southern Babylonia, 'Sumer'. Each Sumerian city had a king, whose power was believed to come from the gods. Throughout the so-called Early Dynastic period (c. 2900–2370 BC) the Sumerian rulers fought each other for supremacy over their land.

The Akkadians and the Sumerian renaissance

About 2370 BC, Sargon of Akkad conquered Babylonia. He and his successors spoke a Semitic language we call Akkadian. Akkadian was written in the cuneiform script (see p. 604) borrowed from Sumerian, and it replaced Sumerian as the official language. The Akkadian empire expanded rapidly, but was faced with constant rebellions. It was overrun about 2200 BC by the mountain people of Gutium.

After 100 years of anarchy, the Third Dynasty of Ur (c. 2113–2006 BC) was founded by Ur-Nammu. He and his successors were great warriors, but this was also a century of prosperity. The kings created an efficient, centralized administrative system, rebuilt temples, and encouraged a renaissance in Sumerian art and literature.

Hammurabi of Babylon

The end of Sumerian rule was marked by the sack of Ur in c. 2006 BC by the Elamites (a people of ancient Iran). The small kingdoms of Mesopotamia fought for sovereignty for 200 years. Many were ruled

Sargon of Akkad, who in around 2370 BC conquered Babylonia and founded a short-lived empire extending across much of the Near East. Legend has it that a gardener found him as a baby floating in a basket on the river, and brought him up to follow in his footsteps.

by Amorites, originally nomads from the Syrian desert.

Eventually one of these Amorite kings, Hammurabi of Babylon (c. 1792–1750 BC) defeated his rival states of Ashur and Mari and conquered the whole of Mesopotamia. He is best known for his law code, whose harsh punishments were tempered by its clarification of individual rights. After Hammurabi's death, the empire was weakened, and Babylon was plundered by the Hittites (see below) in c. 1595 BC.

Empire and diplomacy

The period from c. 1600 to 1200 BC in the Near East is one of powerful empires struggling for control through military and diplomatic means. There was a balance of forces between the Kassites in Babylonia, the Mitannians in Palestine and eastern Syria, the Egyptian empire in Palestine and southern Syria, and later the Assyrians in northern Mesopotamia and the Hittites in Anatolia (modern Turkey) and northern Syria.

With its capital at Hattusas (modern Boghazkoy), the Hittite empire was founded in about 1650 BC. The empire reached its peak under Suppiluliumas I (c. 1380–1350 BC), who extended its frontiers and clashed with the Egyptian empire in Syria. Hostilities between the two powers continued until c. 1283 BC when the Hittite king, Hattusilis III, signed a treaty with Ramses II of Egypt.

Cuneiform was still the international script, although the first alphabet was invented in Syria or Palestine in the 16th century BC (see p. 604). A 14th-century BC archive of cuneiform letters from Amarna in Egypt reveals correspondence between the 'Great Kings'. They frequently sent envoys and presents, and even married each other's daughters.

About 1200 BC many of the Near Eastern kingdoms collapsed. A major cause were the 'Sea Peoples', marauders from the eastern Mediterranean, who were eventually defeated by the Egyptian pharaohs Merenptah and Ramses III.

Iron Age kingdoms

After c. 1200 BC there was a new look to the Near East. The Philistines, on the coast of southern Palestine, were originally one group of the Sea Peoples. Their battles against the Israelites are recorded in the Old Testament.

The Phoenicians, on the Lebanese and Syrian coast, became great seafaring traders, sailing as far as Britain to purchase Cornish tin. They also founded colonies such as Carthage in North Africa. Carthage in turn grew to dominate the western Mediterranean, until finally defeated by the Romans in the 3rd century BC (see p. 376).

The Aramaeans occupied Syria and frequently fought the Assyrians and Israelites. Aramaic became the international language and script of the Near East, and was the original language of some of the later books of the Old Testament.

The survivors of the Hittite empire, whom

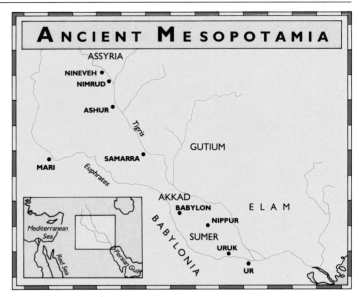

Assyrians fighting Arabs – the latter mounted on camels. This typically warlike Assyrian relief comes from the palace of Ashurbanipal (c. 650 BC) in Nineveh. Ashurbanipal's palace also housed an immense library of clay tablets, dealing with such subjects as mathematics, chemistry and botany.

we call Neo-Hittites, ruled seven city-states in northern Syria. They fought successfully against the Aramaeans, but were conquered by the Assyrians in the 8th century BC.

The Israelite exodus and conquest

The Old Testament records the exodus of the Jews from Egypt under Moses, and their conquest of Canaan (Palestine) under Joshua. The Israelites destroyed many Canaanite towns, notably Jericho and Ai. The conventional date for the conquest is c. 1230 BC.

However, archaeological evidence does not appear to confirm the biblical version. It is likely that in reality the process was more complex, with different tribes coming into possession of the land at different times and in different ways.

About 1000 BC a united kingdom of Israel arose, with Saul and David as its first kings. Following the death of David's son and successor, Solomon, the kingdom divided into two – Israel in the north and Judah in the south.

The Assyrian empire

The kingdom of Assyria, with its traditional capital at Ashur, was located in northern Mesopotamia. From the 9th century BC on, its kings campaigned to the west against the Aramaeans. Eventually they reached the Mediterranean Sea and even briefly invaded Egypt. Tiglathpileser III (744–727 BC) proclaimed himself king of Babylon, and for the next hundred

years Babylonia struggled for independence from Assyria.

Conquered areas paid tribute in food and animals to supply Assyrian troops. A common Assyrian practice was to deport the populations of whole cities or areas as punishment for rebellion, and resettle them elsewhere in the empire.

Assyria was always vulnerable on its eastern and northern frontiers to peoples like the Medes and Scythians. Towards the end of the 7th century BC Assyrian cities fell one by one. Nineveh was destroyed in 612 BC by an alliance of Medes and the Chaldaean kings of Babylonia.

The Neo-Babylonian empire

The Babylonian success was short-lived. Nebuchadnezzar defeated the Egyptians at Carchemish in 605 BC and campaigned extensively in Syria and Palestine. He captured Jerusalem in 587 BC and deported thousands of Jews to Babylonia.

However, his successors were weak; the last king, Nabonidus, spent several years of his reign at Teima in Arabia. In 539 BC Babylon fell without resistance to the Persian ruler Cyrus, of the Achaemenid dynasty.

The Persian empire

The empire of the Persian Achaemenids became the largest yet known in the Near East. From their homeland in what is now Iran, the successors of Cyrus conquered Egypt, northern India and Asia Minor (modern Turkey), and frequently came into conflict with the Greeks (see pp. 370–1).

Darius I (521–486 BC) reorganized the provinces (satrapies) and the army, introduced coinage, legal and postal systems, and dug a canal linking the Nile with the Red Sea. His successor, Xerxes (486–465 BC), crushed rebellions ruthlessly and is

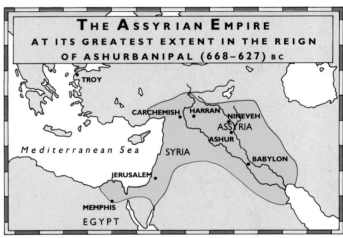

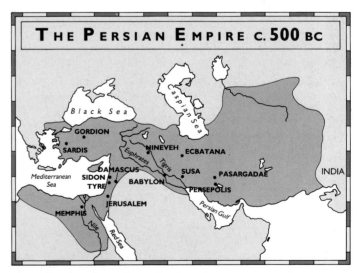

generally thought to have instigated a new policy of suppressing foreign religions. This was a reversal of the religious tolerance of Cyrus, who had freed Babylonia's Jews and given them permission to build their temple in Jerusalem.

Economic decline, revolts, murder and harem conspiracies weakened the Persian throne. The capital Persepolis fell to Alexander the Great in April 330 BC (see p. 372), and the last Achaemenid, Darius III, was murdered in the same year.   PB

Ancient Egypt

'Concerning Egypt itself, I shall extend my remarks to a great length, because there is no country that possesses so many wonders.' So wrote the Greek writer Herodotus in the 5th century BC. Egypt's ancient civilization has continued to interest and fascinate. Geographically isolated by deserts and sea, it developed a unique and self-contained culture that lasted three thousand years. Its dry climate has contributed to the preservation of a wealth of monuments: ancient cities, pyramids, temples and sumptuous artefacts that are a source of wonder today, as they were in antiquity.

With the decipherment of hieroglyphic script in 1822 by the French scholar Jean-François Champollion, it became possible to read and understand the written documents of the ancient Egyptians: religious and historical texts, literary compositions, and the many documents that illustrate aspects of their daily lives.

Geography and resources

Ancient Egypt consisted of the Nile Valley – a long and narrow strip of land extending some 600 miles from Aswan to the area south of modern Cairo, where the river opened up into the Delta. On either side of the valley stretched vast expanses of desert. The Nile was not only the unifying feature of the country, it was also its main source of life. In Egypt rainfall is negligible, but in antiquity the regular annual inundation of the Nile between July and October covered most of the land in the valley and in the Delta, laying down a rich layer of fertilizing silt. Agriculture involved careful management of the waters of the river through the creation of irrigation basins and channels. The main crops were cereals, but pulses, vegetables and fruit were also grown. Flax was used for clothing, sails and ropes, and the pith of the papyrus plant to produce a type of paper. The

SEE ALSO

- THE ANCIENT NEAR EAST p. 364
- ALEXANDER THE GREAT p. 372
- THE RISE OF ROME p. 376
- RELIGIONS OF THE ANCIENT NEAR EAST p. 460
- ART OF THE ANCIENT NEAR EAST p. 506
- WRITING SYSTEMS p. 604
- THE MAKING OF MYTHS p. 612

The Step Pyramid complex of Pharaoh Djoser at Saqqara, the first monument in Ancient Egypt to be built completely out of stone. It was designed by the architect Imhotep around 2700 BC. Uniquely, this pyramid is surrounded by a re-creation (part of which can be seen in the foreground) of the royal capital of Memphis, so that after his death the pharaoh would continue to rule his kingdom.

Egyptians also kept cattle, pigs, goats and sheep, and hunting and fishing provided some additional variety to their diet.

Ancient Egypt was rich in mineral resources – gold, copper and turquoise – and building and semi-precious stones were also quarried. Trading expeditions brought to Egypt the resources that the country lacked: wood from the Lebanon; oil, wine and silver from western Asia; lapis lazuli from Afghanistan; and incense, ebony, ivory, precious stones and exotic animals from the semi-mythical land of Punt, situated somewhere in the area of modern Eritrea or Somalia.

The Early Dynastic Period and the Old Kingdom

It is customary to divide the history of ancient Egypt into thirty dynasties of pharaohs (as the kings of ancient Egypt were known; see table). The history of Pharaonic Egypt begins around 3100 BC with the unification of Upper and Lower Egypt under a king known to history as Menes. Though it is impossible to trace the events leading to the unification of the country, evidence suggests that the Delta area was conquered by rulers from the south.

During the Early Dynastic (or Archaic) Period, a considerable administrative organization of the state took place. A new capital, Memphis, was founded at the junction of Upper and Lower Egypt. There was a dramatic development in the science of writing, no doubt to keep pace with the requirements of a centralized bureaucratic government. Burial customs became more complex, and the first pyramid was built – the Step Pyramid at Saqqara.

This formative period led to the tremendous achievements of the Old Kingdom, the great pyramid age of Egypt. Written records indicate that all aspects of government and administration were controlled by the pharaoh from the royal residence at Memphis. The monumental size of the Great Pyramids at Giza – in which the pharaohs were buried – clearly shows that the pharaoh was the dominant figure of the state, acting as an intermediary between the gods and mankind. The construction of these enormous monuments is also evidence of the degree of state organization that the Egyptians had achieved. At the same time the horizons of the Egyptians expanded, with trading expeditions to Nubia, Sinai, Libya and the Levant all recorded.

The Middle Kingdom

A relaxation of the strong personal authority of the pharaohs towards the end of the 5th and during the 6th dynasty resulted in a complete breakdown of royal power during what has been called the First Intermediate Period. For about a hundred years, a number of rival princes claimed the kingship of Upper and Lower Egypt. Civil wars broke out and there is evidence of famine.

Pharaoh Mentuhotep II of the 11th dynasty finally succeeded in taking control of the whole country. The period that followed this reunification of Egypt is known as the Middle Kingdom, and it was regarded in later tradition as the 'classical' period of Pharaonic civilization. Under the strong kings of the 12th dynasty, Egypt once again became a highly centralized and well-administered state, and a new capital, Itj-towy, was founded south of Memphis. The practice of co-regency was instituted at the very beginning of the dynasty, whereby the ruling pharaoh nominated his successor

THE PERIODS AND DYNASTIES OF ANCIENT EGYPT

Dates (BC)	Period	Dynasties	Main events
3100–2725	Early Dynastic Period	1–3	Unification of Upper and Lower Egypt under Menes. Foundation of Memphis. Building of Step Pyramid.
2575–2134	Old Kingdom	4–8	Centralized administration. Building of Great Pyramids at Giza.
2134–2040	First Intermediate Period	9–11	Egypt divided. Political fragmentation. Control by local monarchs.
2040–1640	Middle Kingdom	11–13	Reunification under Mentuhotep II. Foundation of Itj-towy. Administrative reforms. Co-regencies. Conquest of Nubia.
1640–1552	Second Intermediate Period	14–17	Hyksos rule. Theban dynasty liberates Egypt.
1552–1070	New Kingdom	18–20	Imperial Egypt: empire extends from Syria to southern Sudan. Capital at Thebes. Great building programme.
1070–712	Third Intermediate Period	21–24	Egypt divided: priesthood of Amun rule in Thebes, while pharaohs rule in Tanis.
712–332	Late Period	25–30	Reunification of Egypt under 26th Dynasty. Persian invasion. Conquest by Alexander the Great: end of the line of native pharaohs.

Ploughing the fields and sowing following the annual flood of the Nile. This scene comes from the tomb of Sennedjem and his wife. Sennedjem was a master craftsman who lived around 1300 BC. Such scenes are one of a series of standard scenes found in the tombs of the ancient Egyptians, depicting aspects of daily life that they hoped to recreate in the afterlife.

as co-regent and reigned with him for the last years of his rule.

Administrative reforms removed from the provincial nobility much of the power they had acquired during the First Intermediate Period. In foreign affairs, contacts with the Levant were re-established and in Nubia a series of fortresses was constructed along the Nile, to secure the southern boundaries and to regulate all trade into Egypt.

A series of short-lived reigns during the 13th dynasty was followed by the Second Intermediate Period, during which the political control of the land was once again fragmented. Of the four dynasties assigned to this period, two are native Egyptian (the 14th and 17th dynasties), while two are allotted to foreign Asiatic rulers, the Hyksos kings (the 15th and 16th dynasties). The Hyksos rulers were remembered later as hated foreign usurpers, and were eventually expelled by a new Theban dynasty.

The New Kingdom

The memory of the Hyksos domination of Egypt was largely responsible for shaping the policies of the New Kingdom rulers. The pharaohs of the 18th and 19th dynasties were true war leaders: at the head of their armies, they extended their territories from Syria to southern Sudan. Egypt became the largest empire of the ancient Near East. Diplomatic contacts were established with other great powers of the period – the Hittites, Babylonians and Assyrians (see p. 364) – and peace treaties were concluded between them, often cemented by dynastic marriages between the pharaohs and foreign princesses.

Enormous wealth poured into Egypt from the various regions of the empire. From the ancient capital of Memphis and their new religious centre of Thebes, the New Kingdom pharaohs undertook a large number of building projects. The grandiose temple complex of Karnak was built not only as the main cult temple for the state god Amun-Ra, but also as the treasury of the state. The royal tombs were situated, for security reasons, in the 'Valley of the Kings', a remote canyon on the west bank of the Nile at Thebes. Vast mortuary temples, palaces and shrines were erected, and during the reign of Ramses II, a new capital city was founded at Per-Ramesses in the Delta. The artistic output of this period is unsurpassed, both in quantity and in craftsmanship.

The Late Period

However, around the late 19th and 20th dynasties, Egypt once again went into decline. Invaders from Libya and the 'Sea Peoples' from the eastern Mediterranean were among those Ramses III claimed to have repulsed. Egypt's control over her empire disintegrated, and a series of weak kings resulted in much of royal power being usurped by the high priest of Amun.

The final collapse of the New Kingdom saw once more the division of the country into two halves, with Upper Egypt ruled by the priesthood of Amun in Thebes, while the pharaohs governed from their new capital at Tanis in the Delta. This period is usually referred to as the Third Intermediate Period.

During the 25th dynasty, Egypt was taken over by Nubian pharaohs. It was not until the 26th dynasty that the country was reunited under the rule of the strong and able Saite kings, who restored order and recreated some of the splendour of the past. But in 525 BC the Persians under Cambyses invaded Egypt. The conquest by the Achaemenid Persians meant the end of Egypt's independence. In 332 BC Alexander the Great defeated the Persians and was crowned pharaoh of Egypt (see p. 372). At his death, his general Ptolemy took control of the country, founding a line of kings who were to rule for some three hundred years until Egypt was annexed as a province of the Roman Empire.   ND

Akhenaton (below), in the form of a sphinx. Under the rule of Akhenaton and his wife Nefertiti (c. 1350 BC) a cultural revolution took place. The traditional gods were replaced by the cult of a single god, represented by the sun disc, the *Aten* (also depicted here). After his death Akhenaton was vilified as a heretic, and all traces of his rule were obliterated, including his new capital Tell-el-Amarna.

Minoans and Mycenaeans

Long before the classical era two great civilizations flourished in the area of the Aegean Sea. The existence of the Minoans and the Mycenaeans was unknown until late in the 19th century. The Minoans were named after the legendary King Minos, and the Mycenaeans take their name from one of the major centres of their culture, the city of Mycenae, home of Agamemnon, the mythological king who led the Greeks against Troy.

The palace at Knossos, the greatest of the Minoan palaces on Crete. The palace was excavated and partially restored between 1899 and 1935 by the British archaeologist, Sir Arthur Evans, the first man to discover the remains of Minoan civilization. The complex floor-plan of the palace may have given rise to the later Greek myth of the labyrinth, in which the Minotaur – a man with a bull's head – lurked in wait for Theseus.

Minoan civilization, based on the island of Crete, reached its peak in the Middle and Late Bronze Age between 2200 and 1450 BC. The height of the Mycenaean culture of mainland Greece is slightly later – about 1500 to 1150 BC.

The rise of Minoan civilization

Early in the Middle Bronze Age, about 2200 BC, the first palaces began to be built on Crete, most notably at the sites of later palaces at Knossos and Phaistos. At this time writing also appeared in the Aegean region. The script, called Linear A, was mostly impressed on unbaked clay tablets, but signs painted or scratched on vases are also common. The language is as yet undeciphered, and practically all that can be determined is that the Minoans were not Greek-speakers. Some writing appears in religious contexts, although mostly it seems to have been used for administrative purposes.

It is not clear whether there was one great Minoan 'king' or several smaller leaders ruling on Crete. There are several important palace sites – for example, Phaistos, Aghia Triadha and Mallia – but the palace at Knossos is by far the largest, so perhaps the most important king resided there. Another indication of centralized power is the fact that there is little local variation in Minoan, especially late Minoan, pottery, which may suggest it was controlled by (if not made in) a single centre.

The Minoans were great seafarers, and there is evidence of some Minoan presence on the Aegean islands. There are many representations of ships and other marine motifs on pottery and wall paintings, and the palaces are full of beautiful things brought back from abroad. Crete is also mentioned in ancient Egyptian documents as 'Kheftiu'.

The palace at Knossos

The palace, along with the luxurious houses that surrounded it, reveals much about the life of the Minoan elite. The palace alone covers about 1.3 ha (3 acres). There is a large central courtyard, and the floor-plan is very complicated, with hundreds of rooms.

Little is known about the upper storeys of the palace – there was at least one – but the ground floor and the basement rooms, which are probably not the grandest, are better preserved. Most striking are the large numbers of storage rooms, some filled with enormous storage jars, probably to hold wine and olive oil. Other rooms probably contained metals, textiles and dry foodstuffs like grain. Such remains show that the rulers who lived here had the power to collect tribute and to redistribute it to their allies and friends.

In many rooms of the palace at Knossos the walls are beautifully painted with scenes from Minoan life. Most are of people – beautiful young men in kilts and women in elegant, topless dresses. There are also scenes vividly depicting plant and animal life.

The palace suffered several phases of destruction, but it is not known for

The Lion Gate at Mycenae, set into the huge irregular blocks ('Cyclopean walls') typical of Mycenaean construction. It is probable that this massive gateway was only a side entrance to the citadel.

ertain what caused any of these events, and the chronology is shaky. It has been suggested that the damage around 1500 BC might be related to earthquakes occurring between 1550 and 1500, when the great eruption of Thera occurred (see p. 52), but this is only a remote possibility. Since palace records after a destruction around 1450 BC are in Mycenaean Linear B script (see below), it has been suggested that Mycenaean invaders might have been responsible.

Minoan religion

Some wall paintings from Knossos and elsewhere seem to depict religious scenes, such as those of young men and women performing acrobatics over charging bulls. It has been suggested that the arena for these extraordinary games might have been the courtyard of the palace itself. Some of the women may be goddesses and some religious symbols are present, like the sign of the double axe or the bulls' horns.

The true complexity of Minoan religion is still beyond the reach of archaeologists. There are no Minoan 'temples' as such, but there are a few shrines, one of which is in the basement of the palace at Knossos. Perhaps, given its underground location, it was dedicated to an earth deity. Some sites, like that of Aghia Triadha, seem to have had special religious significance.

The Mycenaeans

The Mycenaeans, who replaced the Minoans as the dominant power in the Aegean from about 1450 BC, were based in citadel cities with great palaces throughout mainland Greece. The most important sites include Mycenae, Tiryns, Pylos, Thebes, Gla and Athens. It is unlikely that any one king controlled the whole of Greece in this period, although

Linear B script on a clay tablet from Pylos. For many years the script of the Mycenaeans remained undeciphered, but in 1952 Michael Ventris and John Chadwick successfully decoded it, identifying the language as an early form of Greek.

THE TROJAN WAR: FACT OR MYTH?

It has long been asked if the later Greek tradition of the Trojan War preserves memories of the glorious Mycenaean past and the destruction of Mycenaean civilization. It is certainly true that some elements of the *Iliad* and the *Odyssey* belong in the Bronze Age, although the poems – traditionally attributed to Homer – were probably written down in their final form around 750–700 BC (see p. 614).

It is difficult to relate these epics to the archaeological remains of Mycenaean civilization with any certainty. Clearly, there were Mycenaean contacts with Troy (probably the mound at modern Hissarlik in northwest Turkey). There is more Mycenaean pottery from this site than from any other site in Anatolia, but Mycenaean pottery still represents only a minute proportion of the total pottery found there. Perhaps the Homeric traditions contain genuine memories from the troubled times at the end of the Bronze Age. But if they do, it is impossible for historians to dissect the poetry to find the truth.

some palaces are clearly much richer than others.

The earliest evidence of a powerful Mycenaean nobility comes from the shaft graves of Mycenae, which are arranged in two circles outside the city walls and which date from c. 1600 BC. The large amounts of gold and other metals deposited in them provide an awesome reminder of the wealth and strength of the city's rulers.

Mycenaean cities and palaces

The cities themselves were massively fortified, the walls made of huge, irregular blocks. The actual palaces were much simpler than in Crete, the most important feature being the *megaron*, a hall with a central hearth flanked by two columns.

From the records at Pylos, Mycenae, Thebes and other sites, we know that Mycenaean palaces, like those of the Minoans, were centres of political and economic control. These records were written on unbaked clay tablets in a script called Linear B, which is similar to Minoan Linear A, but the language is a form of Greek (see illustration).

It is clear from these records that the Mycenaean kings had control of vast

A gold funeral mask from the shaft graves at Mycenae. 'I have looked upon the face of Agamemnon', declared the German archaeologist, Heinrich Schliemann, when he discovered this mask in 1876. However, subsequent research has shown that the mask dates from about 1600 BC, around 400 years too early for the 'historical' Agamemnon.

amounts of land, full of flocks and crops, and worked on by great numbers of slaves. The palaces seem to have supervised the manufacture and trade of many crucial commodities, such as metals.

Like the Minoan palaces, Mycenaean palaces were full of treasures and works of art commissioned by the nobility. Walls were painted, but not usually so elaborately as in Crete. Many luxury items were imported from abroad, and Mycenaean pottery is found in Syria, Palestine, Egypt and elsewhere.

Mycenaean religion

The Linear B tablets reveal that the Mycenaeans worshipped many of the gods and goddesses familiar from later Greek religion (see p. 462). There were priests and priestesses who received offerings for the deities at their shrines. The remains of several Mycenaean shrines, with religious statues, have been found.

The end of the Greek Bronze Age

Around 1200–1100 BC several of the palaces seem to have been destroyed, and it is still a mystery why such rich and powerful civilizations suddenly declined at this period. Many suggestions have been made, including internal dissent and revolution, climatic change, and foreign invaders – the Dorians – from the north. It is probable that the true reasons for their decline are complex, and possible that all the suggestions made are partially right in some way. It has been securely established now that at least some Mycenaeans settled on Cyprus at this time. Whatever the cause of Mycenaean decline, Greece at this time entered a 'dark age' from which it did not emerge until the beginning of the Archaic period, in about 800 BC (see p. 370).   LF

SEE ALSO

● HUMAN PREHISTORY p. 362
● ARCHAIC AND CLASSICAL GREECE p. 370
● PRIMAL RELIGIONS: ANCIENT TIMES p. 462
● CLASSICAL LITERATURE p. 614

Archaic and Classical Greece

The typical unit of political and social organization in ancient Greece was the *polis* or independent city-state. City-states arose in many parts of the Greek-speaking world during the 8th century BC at the beginning of the so-called Archaic period (c. 800-500 BC). This development marked the end of a long period of poverty that had followed the collapse of Mycenaean civilization (see p. 369). The Archaic period was followed by the Classical period (c. 500-338 BC), during which the Greeks made radical experiments with political, artistic and philosophical ideas, all of which have had a lasting impact on Western civilization.

The geography of Greece, with many small plains and valleys surrounded by high mountains, encouraged the formation of many small states. A city-state usually consisted of an agricultural territory (in which the vast majority of its citizens worked), and a walled town centre. The individual identity of each city-state was reinforced by religious ties and a shared involvement in the making of political and legal decisions.

The Archaic city-state

Initially each city-state was dominated by a few noble families, although decisions might be put to assemblies of all citizens. However, from about 750 BC on this aristocratic dominance was progressively undermined. Firstly, the reintroduction of literacy into Greece (c. 750 BC) led to the public display of the laws, enabling citizens to question what had previously been under the strict control of the aristocrats. Secondly, from c. 750–600 BC, many new Greek city-states were established around the Aegean, Adriatic and Black Seas. The setting up of new cities, with new laws and a fresh distribution of land, also encouraged questioning of the distribution of power and wealth at home. Thirdly, the introduction of *hoplite* armour and tactics (see illustration) gave the ordinary people a greater potential power.

A consequence was that new laws began to restrict the power of the nobles. In a number of cities government by hereditary nobles was replaced by the rule of a *tyrant*, a usurper who seized power with the support of the hoplites. As a result of such upheavals, in many city-states power was held by a small group (an *oligarchy*), defined by wealth rather than by birth, although important issues might still be put to the citizens.

Archaic Sparta

During the Archaic period, two city-states, Sparta and Athens, became particularly important. They developed in very different ways. In the 8th century the Spartans gained control of most of the southern Peloponnese (the large peninsula in southern Greece), and the majority of the defeated peoples became 'state serfs' (*helots*).

In the mid-7th century BC a major helot revolt occurred, and at about the same time Spartan citizens, now organized in a hoplite army, successfully agitated for reforms. The citizens won more political rights and more equal shares of land, but socially Sparta was transformed into a tightly regimented and authoritarian state. Its citizens were subjected to a rigorous training programme from the age of 7 onwards.

During the 6th century BC the reformed and strengthened Sparta, through military and diplomatic means, created the 'Peloponnesian League', a network of alliances throughout the Peloponnese, and became the most powerful state in Greece.

Archaic Athens

The first steps towards democracy in Athens were made by Solon (?638–?559 BC), who was appointed in 594 to create new laws after a period of serious unrest between rich and poor. Solon did much to establish the peasants in ownership of their lands, and encouraged all citizens to participate in the assembly and in legal processes. He introduced a division of all citizens based on wealth, but restricted the various offices to the better-off classes.

Political discontent continued, and the leader of the poorer peasants, Peisisratos, established himself as tyrant. He and his sons ruled Athens from about 545 to 510 BC. Like Solon, they helped to secure the peasants on their lands, but the regime became unpopular and cruel in its later years.

In 507 BC new reforms proposed by Cleisthenes (d. 508 BC) created more democratic means of decision-making at local and at city level, including the new 'Council of Five Hundred', selected from representatives of local areas. The Council prepared business for the assembly and performed an increasing number of administrative activities. In order to prevent tyranny and to resolve disputes Cleisthenes introduced the institution of *ostracism*, whereby Athenians could vote for a politician to be banished from the city for 10 years. Helped by these reforms Athens also became a more effective military power.

The Persian Wars

The growing power of the Persian Empire had led by c. 500 BC to its dominance over the Greek cities of Asia Minor (modern Turkey). Athenian support for an unsuccessful revolt against Persian rule by these cities (500–494 BC) led in 490 BC to the first invasion by the Persians of the Greek mainland. This was repulsed by the Athenians in the land battle at Marathon.

A much more serious invasion followed in 480 BC, under the new Persian king, Xerxes (ruled 485–465). An anti-Persian alliance was formed under the leadership of Sparta, which provided the most powerful infantry, while the largest fleet belonged to Athens. After the initial

The Acropolis, Athens. Under Pericles, Athens used the profits of its empire on a spectacular public building programme that saw the Acropolis decorated with buildings and sculptures, such as the Parthenon (centre), the Propylaea (left) and the great statues of Athena.

Hoplite warriors following a chariot, c. 490 BC. The introduction of heavier body-armour and weapons, and the development of infantry formations in which the disciplined cohesion of a large force of men counted for more than the leadership and gallantry of a few, meant that the security of the city-state was seen to depend on large numbers of ordinary farmers, not just on the traditional nobles.

heroic defeat at Thermopylae, the combined Greek forces defeated the Persians at sea at Salamis (480), and on land the next year at Plataea. These victories confirmed Sparta and Athens as the two major Greek powers. One Athenian, Themistocles (c. 528–462 BC), seems to have been the main driving force behind the development of the Athenian navy and the strategy adopted in 480–479 BC.

Athenian empire and Athenian democracy

The Greek fleet pursued the Persians across the Aegean and 'liberated' the Greek cities from Persian rule. In 478 BC Athens assumed leadership of a new alliance, the Delian League, and by c. 450 BC active fighting ceased.

Meanwhile the League was increasingly dominated by Athens, to whom the members were forced to pay tribute. Athenian interference in the politics and economies of its allies grew, to Athens' own advantage and also that of the poorer allied citizens. By the 440s the League could more appropriately be described as an Athenian empire.

During this period Athens completed the development of its democracy. The popular juries heard all law suits except homicide, and the scrutiny of all office-holders and their conduct was shared between the Council of Five Hundred, the assembly, and the juries.

From 462 BC until his death the statesman and orator Pericles (c. 495–429 BC) took an increasingly major part in developing Athenian policies, and at this time Athens was at its most prosperous, successful and powerful. But its use of power did not lead to the unity of Greece: many in its empire resented Athenian control, and the rival Peloponnesian League remained fearful of its growing power.

The Peloponnesian War

The immediate origins of the Peloponnesian War (431–404 BC) lay in areas such as Corinth where the interests of Athens and the Peloponnesians overlapped. In 431 BC the complaints of the Athenian allies and the refusal of Athens to compromise, led the Spartans to declare war. The fundamental reason, perhaps, was Spartan fear of losing control over its own allies in the Peloponnese.

Sparta was strong on land and Athens strong at sea, and for long each avoided a decisive battle. Since one side tended to support democracies and the other oligarchies, and each tried to win over the other's allies, the war greatly intensified the political and economic struggles inside many Greek cities. In Athens itself after the death of Pericles, a more populist set of politicians appeared, and as each vied for power, political and social tensions increased.

A temporary peace was made in 421 BC, but in 415 Athens made the serious mistake of attempting to conquer Sicily, which appealed for Spartan help. Athens' most inspired leader, Alcibiades (c. 450–404 BC), was implicated in religious scandals and fled to Sparta, giving the Spartans useful strategic advice. In 414 Sparta came to the help of the Sicilians, and the Athenian fleet was destroyed in 413.

What was decisive in the long run was that the Persians increasingly contributed to the expenses of the Spartan fleet. Inside Athens, the democracy took much of the blame for the defeat in Sicily, and in 411 there was a brief period of non-democratic rule. Despite all these difficulties – and further mistakes – Athens fought on until its final defeat at sea in 404 BC. Thus the great war ended in complete victory for Sparta. However, most of the Greek cities, although liberated from Athenian 'tyranny', found themselves either ruled once more by the Persians, or by narrow, Spartan-backed oligarchies.

In Athens defeat was followed by the brief and savage rule of an oligarchy, the 'Thirty Tyrants' (404–403 BC). When this was overthrown, the restored democracy won credit by declaring an amnesty for all except the chief oligarchs. But the execution of the philosopher Socrates (see p. 488) on charges of corrupting the young and of impiety did lasting damage to Athens' reputation. He was used as a scapegoat, and blamed for his association with young men such as Alcibiades.

The emergence of Macedon

The Athenian defeat did not bring peace. The harsh policies of Sparta, and the reversal of its former policies by attacking Persian rule in Asia Minor, led to a coalition against it. This consisted of its former allies, Corinth and Thebes, and its old enemies Athens and Argos, supported by Persian gold. A succession of wars continued until the middle of the century, with Thebes, as the leader of the Boeotian Confederacy, achieving major military successes over Sparta. Sparta failed to recover, largely owing to the gradual breakdown of its economic and social system. Athens did recover some of its former power, and from 378/7 created a new Aegean Confederacy. However, this was only a shadow of its former empire.

The main Greek states thus became weaker, a weakness often exacerbated by civil war. Into this power vacuum came Macedon, a previously backward kingdom in northeast Greece. In 359 BC Philip II became king of Macedon, and immediately undertook a total reorganization of the army and the kingdom. He went on by a combination of diplomacy and force to achieve a position of dominance in mainland Greece, achieving final victory at the battle of Chaironea (338). Philip was assassinated in 336, leaving his son Alexander to carry out his plan to invade Persia (see p. 372). Although the Greek city-states were to maintain a degree of self-government for centuries, from now on power in Greece was to depend ultimately on outsiders. NF

SEE ALSO

- MINOANS AND MYCENAEANS p. 368
- ALEXANDER THE GREAT p. 372
- THE EVOLUTION OF PHILOSOPHY p. 488
- GREEK AND ROMAN ART p. 508
- CLASSICAL LITERATURE p. 614

Greek vase painting of a symposium. Male social life in Greek cities was dominated by the institutions of the athletic training grounds, the gymnasia and the *symposia* – drinking parties, to which 'respectable' women were not permitted, but where other women – dancing girls or prostitutes – were available, and where the relatively open homosexual relationships between young men and adolescents also flourished.

Alexander the Great
and the Hellenistic Age

The conquests of Alexander the Great brought the whole of the former Persian Empire under the control of Greek-speaking rulers. The monarchies that were established after his death enabled Greek culture to penetrate through Syria, Mesopotamia and Iran to India. The *Hellenistic Age* (from the Greek *Hellenistes*, 'an imitator of the Greeks') is the period from Alexander's death (323 BC) until the gradual extinction of these kingdoms, most of which were absorbed by the Roman or Parthian Empires in the 2nd and 1st centuries BC.

Alexander was born in the summer of 356 BC, eldest son of Philip II, king of Macedon (359–336 BC). Alexander was educated by – among others – the philosopher Aristotle, and acquired all the skills needed by a future ruler. When Philip won complete control over the Greek city-states at the battle of Chaironeia in 338 BC, Alexander commanded the Macedonian army's victorious left wing. On the assassination of Philip in 336 BC he was immediately proclaimed king. Some of the states subject to Macedon tried to take advantage of the new king, but he crushed the uprisings. A series of swift and brutal campaigns in Thrace and Greece culminated in the defeat of the Thebans and the destruction of their city in 335 BC.

Alexander the Great on his horse Bucephalus. According to the popular story, no one could ride the fiery horse until the 12-year-old Alexander managed to tame it. Bucephalus became Alexander's favourite horse for twenty years, and when it died Alexander named a city after it.

The conquest of the Persian Empire

Having secured his position in Europe, Alexander was able to continue the Greek offensive against the Persian Empire. This had been initiated by his father and was explicitly portrayed as revenge for the desecrations of Xerxes (see p. 370) and liberation for the Greeks of Asia Minor (modern Turkey). In practice this meant replacing Persian rule with Macedonian rule by right of conquest.

Alexander crossed into Asia Minor in 334 BC with an army of 32 000 infantry and 5000 cavalry. He engaged the massed forces of the western Persian provinces at the River Granikos and defeated them. He proceeded through Asia Minor, entering some cities as a welcome deliverer and others as a resisted conqueror. When he came to the edge of Asia proper he was faced by a larger Persian army commanded by Darius III himself, the Achaemenid king of Persia (336–330 BC). At the Battle of Issos in 333 BC Alexander won a brilliant victory, personally leading his cavalry into the heart of the battle. Darius fled, leaving his family to be captured, while Alexander entered Egypt and was accepted as its new ruler by the Egyptian priests.

A final stand by Darius ended in total defeat at Gaugamela in 332 BC. The fleeing king was eventually murdered by his own nobles, only hours before Alexander caught up with him. Alexander became his successor, although it took a great deal more campaigning before Alexander had subdued all of the Persian Empire. He led his army across Asia to the edge of the Himalaya and the northern provinces of India. As he progressed further away from Greece he began to use Persian soldiers and appoint Persian nobles to positions of authority, much to the dismay of the Macedonians. After a mutiny by his tired army in 324 BC he turned back towards the west, only getting as far as Babylon, where he fell ill and died in 323 BC.

In ten years Alexander had created the largest empire that the world had ever known, stretching from the Greek mainland to the River Indus, incorporating all or part of 17 modern states. His outstandingly successful career made him the ideal king, against whom all others were judged and whose deeds all tried to emulate. Just before his death he may have planned further campaigns against the powerful states of the western Mediterranean – after his conquest of the Persian Empire anything was possible.

The successors of Alexander

There was no clear rule of succession for Macedonian kings. Alexander's wife Roxane was pregnant when he died and a regent was appointed. Both the child and his mother were murdered in the disputes that followed. The leading Macedonian generals immediately fought amongst themselves over who should govern the various parts of the empire and several

The Battle of Issos, Alexander's brilliant victory over the Persian king, Darius. Alexander is shown leading his cavalry (left), while Darius is shown in his chariot (centre-right). This Roman mosaic from Pompeii is a copy of a Greek painting from the time of Alexander.

tried to set themselves up as kings. Three main dynasties were eventually established – by Ptolemy (Egypt), Seleucos (Asia) and Antigonos (Macedon and Greece). Smaller vassal kingdoms and city-states existed within their territories, especially in parts where their authority was weakest. In time some of these became more powerful and achieved independence from the main dynasties.

In Macedon the kingship was to a limited degree elective – the king was approved by his subjects, especially the army, and he ruled by consent. The Antigonids retained this idea, so that their monarchy closely resembled that of Philip II and Alexander, before the conquest of Persia. In Egypt and Asia, however, native concepts of absolute monarchy and the divine nature of the king's authority produced monarchies more like those of the pharaohs and the Achaemenids. The Seleucids and the Ptolemies were worshipped as gods, supposedly descended from Apollo and Dionysos or their local equivalents. Divine nature was also attributed to their families. All over the Hellenistic world Alexander was honoured as a god, from whom all kings claimed descent.

Kingdoms and cities

The nature of the Hellenistic kingdoms varied greatly. The Antigonids ruled Macedon securely, but their control over central and southern Greece was not always so firm. Two federations of city-states, Aitolia and Achaia, were dominant from c. 240 BC onwards. The Ptolemaic kingdom was limited to Egypt and some coastal areas of the eastern Mediterranean. It had the most effective navy and the least rebellious population. The Seleucid kingdom included many peoples spread over a huge area. Much of their original territory fragmented into ethnic kingdoms, such as Bactria, Armenia, Bithynia and Pontus. Those areas that they did retain were controlled like the Achaemenid Empire by local governors (*satraps*).

The basic social and political unit of the Hellenistic world was the city, made up of an urban centre and surrounding countryside. Alexander founded many cities bearing his name as part of the process of spreading Greek culture and ideas throughout his empire. He even named one city after his horse, Bucephalus. Some of these cities, like Alexandria in Egypt, have endured to the present day. His successors copied this idea (e.g. Antiochia, Seleucia). Cities were centres of wealth and power, to be controlled and exploited. Many were free to administer their own affairs and to behave almost as independent states, although this could lead to rebellion.

Eumenes, the governor of Pergamon, transformed the city from a Seleucid fortress and treasury into an independent state. In 238 BC his son Attalos I became a king. The territory of Pergamon was

small, but favourable circumstances and location enabled it to develop into one of the most prosperous and beautiful of all the Hellenistic cities.

The competitive spirit

The Hellenistic Age was marked by a highly competitive spirit affecting individuals at all levels of society. Kings were rivals on a grand scale in war and politics. They fought each other for the control of people and places, sometimes with force, sometimes diplomacy. Vassals and cities competed for a monarch's favour and protection.

Citizens tried to amass larger fortunes than their fellows through agriculture and trade. They showed off their riches by financing splendid buildings or festivals for their cities, and were rewarded with extravagant honours and titles. Most public works were paid for by private wealth, and official posts were occupied by men, and occasionally women, who could afford to be generous. Wealth determined how easy or hard life was. If a person was captured by the ubiquitous pirates, for example, whether they were sold into slavery or ransomed depended on how rich they or their patrons were.

The decline of the Hellenistic world

Competition was not always beneficial. The Hellenistic monarchies weakened each other through constant wars, and fell victim to outsiders. Macedon was conquered by the Romans in 167 BC, and Greece became a Roman province in 146 BC. Attalos III of Pergamon bequeathed his kingdom to Rome in 133 BC to avoid further internal strife. The Seleucid

HELLENISTIC ARMIES

All the Hellenistic kings were generals first and rulers second. It was possible to be a king without a kingdom, but not without an army. Wars were fought for booty and prestige as much as for territory. The basic infantry unity of Hellenistic armies was the *phalanx*, 1000 or more men standing close together in lines 16 deep. They were armed with a sword, a shield and a spear, the *sarissa*, about 4 m (13 ft) long. The spear points of the first five rows made an impenetrable barrier ahead and the others held their spears overhead to ward off missiles. Cavalrymen in squadrons of 200 protected the wings. Both Philip II and Alexander used the strong but unwieldy *phalanx* to engage the enemy and break up his line. The cavalry would then charge on the flanks and win the battle. Later monarchs employed elephants for a shock effect. The early *phalanx* was composed of Macedonian peasant soldiers. In the second and first centuries BC mercenaries from all over the Hellenistic world served together in the armies of the various monarchs.

family quarrelled over an ever-shrinking kingdom as the provinces rebelled under local leaders, overthrowing Greek rule in favour of native rulers. Egypt was the longest lived of the Hellenistic kingdoms, thanks largely to the speed with which Macedonian rule was assimilated into the traditional pattern of Egyptian monarchy. It was at the Battle of Actium in 31 BC that the Hellenistic Age came to a close, with the defeat of Cleopatra VII, last of the Hellenistic monarchs (see p. 377).   PDS

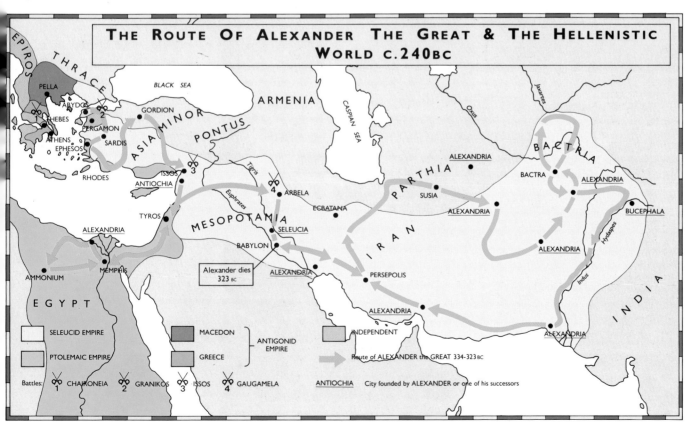

THE ROUTE OF ALEXANDER THE GREAT & THE HELLENISTIC WORLD C.240BC

Alexander dies 323 BC

SELEUCID EMPIRE

PTOLEMAIC EMPIRE

MACEDON

GREECE

ANTIGONID EMPIRE

INDEPENDENT

Route of ALEXANDER the GREAT 334-323 BC

Battles: CHAIRONEIA 1 GRANIKOS 2 ISSOS 3 GAUGAMELA 4

ANTIOCHIA City founded by ALEXANDER or one of his successors

SEE ALSO

● THE ANCIENT NEAR EAST p. 364
● ARCHAIC AND CLASSICAL GREECE p.370
● THE RISE OF ROME p.376
● GREEK AND ROMAN ART p. 508
● CLASSICAL LITERATURE p. 614

The Celts

Prehistoric Europe was populated by a large number of different groups. Most of them are quite obscure to us now, but the way of life of those societies, located on the fringe of literate Mediterranean cultures, may be reconstructed in some detail. Best known of all are the late Iron Age inhabitants of present-day France and Britain and their neighbours.

Archaeologists have no way of knowing either the languages spoken by most of these peoples or even their own names for themselves. Greek explorers and Roman conquerors referred to them all as *Gauls* or *Celts*, and more recently the term *Celtic* has been applied to a group of languages. But it is a modern (and mistaken) idea that the Celts were a single people with a common language and a common culture, who shared a history extending from prehistory to the present day.

Europe in the first millennium BC

Temperate Europe is a land of rolling hills and wide plains and plateaux. Most of this landscape was covered in woodland until a few thousand years ago, when groups of settled farmers began to clear large areas for cultivation. With the discovery of iron technology (see p. 363), the rate of clearance accelerated. Marshes were drained, hillsides were deforested and the fertile river valleys supported dense populations long before the Roman invasions.

Iron Age agricultural systems were fairly sophisticated. Most areas depended on a variety of grains – emmer, spelt, barley and millet being the most important. Stock breeding was also used to develop valued traits in cattle, pigs and sheep. Regional specialities developed – cattle in the Low Countries for example – but most communities were probably self-sufficient in basic foodstuffs.

Most of the population lived in villages. The traces of scattered farmsteads are found in some regions, and at some periods massive fortifications were constructed – the hillforts that still dominate the landscape of many parts of the countryside. But we cannot be sure that all these fortifications were permanently inhabited, and, except in mountainous areas like northern Scotland or the Alps, hillforts were only built and used for brief periods of prehistory.

Iron Age society was village based. Most people were peasant farmers who lived with their relatives near to the land they farmed. Villages may have had headmen, but kinship was probably equally important in organizing daily life.

By the time the Romans invaded, many areas were also organized into larger political units. Hereditary nobles owned much of the land, and dominated society with their bands of followers. Noble society was violent – young men won praise and wealth by raids, duels and in war. Iron Age groups were probably no more warlike than any other ancient society, but they have acquired a reputation for ferocity both from the accounts of Roman generals who fought them and from the splendid weaponry of the nobility.

Material culture and art

Archaeology allows us to reconstruct a detailed picture of everyday life in late prehistoric Europe. Houses were built of wood and wickerwork and coated in mud to weatherproof them. Food was stored, cooked and served in pottery vessels, most of them coarse by modern standards but some brightly painted or covered in a shimmering coat of graphite. Bone was used to make needles, and clothes were woven on looms from flax and wool.

But it is the metalwork of prehistoric Europe that has most excited the admiration of recent generations. Weapons, ornaments and drinking equipment show a high degree of metallurgical proficiency. A great quantity of iron was produced: the largest hillfort ramparts used hundreds of tons merely for nails to hold together wooden timbers. The quality of ironworking was also very high; some late Iron Age swords will still spring back when bent.

Gold and silver were used to make necklaces (*torques*) and brooches decorated with stylized artwork. Animals and religious motifs combine with graceful curves and elaborate decoration to form wonderfully balanced overall designs. The interests of the nobility are graphically illustrated by the beautiful weapons and drinking equipment with which they were buried or which they threw into rivers as offerings to the gods.

Art historians have identified two widely used styles, now known after the sites at which they were first observed. *Hallstatt* art (named after an Austrian village), which flourished between 900 and 500 BC, originated in central Europe and spread

Detail from the Gundestrup Cauldron (right), showing a Celtic god with antlers. This masterpiece of Iron Age metalwork dates from around 100 BC.

Maiden Castle, an Iron Age fort in Dorset, England. The site was settled from Neolithic times, and later earthworks subsequently added. A stronghold of the Britons, it was captured by the Romans in AD 43.

widely on the continent. *La Tène* art (named after a part of Lake Neuchâtel, Switzerland) developed around 450 BC under the influence of civilizations of the south and east. The style first appears in the Rhineland, but spread even further than Hallstatt art, reaching Ireland and Spain in the west and Hungary in the east.

The invasion hypothesis

Archaeologists used to imagine that particular styles of material culture (tools, weapons, pots, etc.) corresponded to particular peoples, with distinctive beliefs, languages, customs and identities. They believed that movements of peoples could be traced through the archaeological records by looking for key artefacts. This theory is known as the *invasion hypothesis.*

So the spread of Hallstatt and La Tène styles and artefacts used to be interpreted as migrations of Hallstatt people or La Tène warrior bands. One or both groups were thought to be the ancestors of 'the Celts'. The case seemed to be proved by Greek and Latin accounts of 'barbarian invasions'.

Modern archaeology and anthropology have shown that the relationship between material culture and particular peoples is more complex. Firstly, the same kind of material culture is often used by individuals who think of themselves as belonging to quite different groups. Secondly, the whole idea of fixed 'peoples' is now seen to derive from those ideas of race developed during the 1930s and long discredited in most parts of the world.

Most anthropologists prefer to talk of *ethnicity,* the sense of identity created for itself by a group in a particular time and place. Ethnicity, unlike race, is culturally defined and changes over time, just as

individuals can change their ethnicity by becoming part of another group.

No doubt there were population movements in prehistoric Europe (although they may be invisible to archaeologists) but ethnicities must have been continually forming and breaking up and reforming just as they do today.

What happened to the Celts?

Who are today's Celts? After the Roman conquest of much of Europe, Iron Age cultures fed into the Romanized culture of the empire. Local traditions remained but the overwhelming influence was Mediterranean.

Celts appear again on the fringes of the Roman world after the fall of the empire. Modern scholars use the term to refer to the early medieval groups who inhabited present-day Scotland, Ireland, Wales, Cornwall and Brittany. Many contemporary inhabitants of these areas now think of themselves as 'Celtic' – that is they have adopted a Celtic 'ethnicity'.

The creation of the modern Celts has to be seen in the context of the rise of nationalism in the 19th century (see p. 428). All over Europe, disadvantaged minorities adopted new ethnicities, often based on linguistic divisions. In fact, no Classical writers ever speak of Celts in Ireland. But the myth of the Celts has become a powerful symbol in the struggle of many groups for autonomy and independence from the larger political units in which they are embedded.   GW

SEE ALSO

- HUMAN PREHISTORY p. 362
- THE INVASIONS p. 396
- THE PRIMAL RELIGIONS: ANCIENT TIMES p. 462
- THE WORLD'S LANGUAGES p. 602

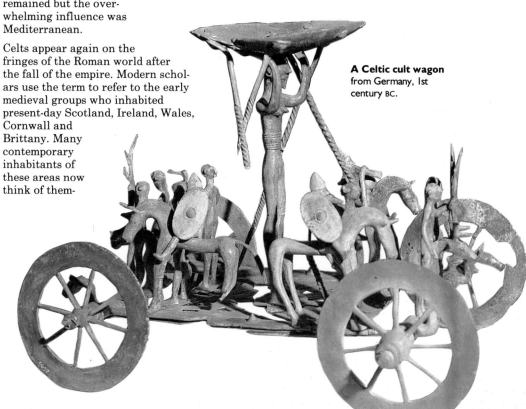

A Celtic cult wagon from Germany, 1st century BC.

The Rise of Rome

The beginnings of Rome are lost in legend. According to the story, the city took its name from Romulus, a shepherd king who founded a settlement on the banks of the Tiber after killing his twin brother Remus, traditionally in 753 BC. Romulus was the first of seven kings of Rome, the last of whom, Tarquin the Proud, was expelled in 509 BC when a republic was set up.

It is difficult to know how much truth there is in the legends of early Rome. Archaeologists have established that one or more villages existed on the site from the end of the Bronze Age (c. 1000 BC),

THE ETRUSCANS

The Etruscans, whose civilization flourished from the 8th century BC, lived in the region of central Italy between the Tiber and the Arno. Scholars are uncertain whether they were an indigenous people or immigrants, but are agreed that the Etruscan civilization took shape in Italy – albeit under strong external influences, particularly from the Greeks. In the 6th century BC Etruria was divided into fiercely independent city-states. To begin with these rivalled Rome, but in the 4th and 3rd centuries they were gradually conquered and subsequently 'Romanized'.

The Etruscan cities are known to us mainly from their material remains, particularly their cemeteries. Tombs decorated with wall paintings and sculptures tell us much about Etruscan religion, society and daily life. Archaeology remains the chief source of information because the Etruscan language, though surviving in thousands of mainly short inscriptions, is still poorly understood.

An Etruscan couple on a sarcophagus from the 7th century BC.

and that by 600 BC the settlement had developed into a substantial city.

At the time of the overthrow of Tarquin, Rome possessed an extensive territory, a strong army and a wide network of commercial and diplomatic contacts, not only with other Latin-speaking towns, which it dominated, but with the powerful Etruscan states to the north (see box), the Greek colonies in the south, and even with distant Carthage, a Phoenician trading city on the North African coast.

The early Republic

Under the Republic, established in 509 BC, power was exercised by two annually elected *consuls*, who ruled the city and commanded the army. They were advised by a council of elders (the *Senate*), and in the course of time were assisted by more junior officials, who were also elected annually. Only in emergencies was a single *dictator* appointed, for a maximum of six months.

At first these posts were held almost exclusively by the *patricians*, a hereditary elite of obscure origin. But in the 4th century BC other wealthy citizens, representing the rest of the population (the *plebeians*), also obtained access to high office. The plebeians had formed their own assembly and elected their own officials, called *tribunes*, to represent them. In 287 BC the plebeians obtained the right to pass laws in their assemblies, and at this point the struggle between the patricians and plebeians was finally ended.

The growth of the Empire

In the 4th century BC, after a temporary setback in 390 when the city was sacked by Gallic raiders from northern Italy, the Romans gradually expanded their power. The neighbouring peoples whom they conquered were obliged to become allies and to fight alongside them in subsequent wars. Part of the land they conquered was colonized by the poor (allies as well as Romans), while the rest was left to its original owners, who were enrolled as allies and invited to share in future conquests. By 272 BC the conquest of peninsular Italy was complete.

Shortly afterwards the Romans became involved in a major overseas war, when in 264 BC they challenged the Carthaginians for the control of Sicily. In spite of immense losses the Romans eventually emerged as victors in 241 BC in what is known as the First Punic War (from *Punicus*, 'Carthaginian'), and Sicily became the first Roman province. The Second Punic War began in 218 when the Carthaginian general Hannibal (247– c. 183 BC) sought revenge by crossing the Alps and invading Italy with an army of 26 000 men and several war elephants. In

spite of spectacular victories at Trasimene and Cannae, Hannibal failed to win over Rome's Italian allies and was gradually worn down by the tactics of Quintus Fabius Maximus (d. 203 BC). Hannibal withdrew from Italy in 204 BC and was finally defeated in 202 at Zama in Africa by Scipio Africanus (236–183 BC).

As a result the Romans obtained further provinces from the former Carthaginian possessions in Spain, and in the following decades the Romans decisively defeated the major Hellenistic kingdoms in Greece and Asia Minor (see p. 373), and by 167 BC Rome dominated the whole Mediterranean. After the Third Punic War (149–146 BC) Carthage was destroyed and 'Africa' (i.e. roughly modern Tunisia) became a Roman province. Greece was made a province at the same time; Asia (i.e. western Turkey) followed in 133, and then Southern Gaul (Provence) in 121, Cilicia (southern Turkey) in 101, and Cyrenaica (eastern Libya) in 96.

The consequences of Roman imperialism

These overseas successes vastly increased the power and wealth of the upper classes, who hastened to invest their gains in large landed estates, worked by war captives imported as slaves. Slave labour replaced the small peasant proprietors, who formed the backbone of the Roman army but found that prolonged military service in distant lands made it increasingly difficult to maintain their farms. Many peasants were thus driven off their land to a life of penury and unemployment. One result of this was a problem in military recruitment, since the law laid down a property qualification for service in the army. Social tensions thus began to build up, and the earlier concensus came under increasing strain.

Meanwhile the rich began to adopt luxurious and increasingly sophisticated habits. The influence of Greek culture became pervasive, as Romans began to imitate the leisured style of the great centres of the Hellenistic world (see pp. 373 and 508).

The breakdown of the Republic

The widening gulf between rich and poor eventually gave rise to social conflict and political breakdown. In 133 BC a tribune, Tiberius Gracchus (163–133), introduced a land reform that proposed to redistribute among the poor the state-owned land that had been annexed by the rich. There was immense opposition, and Gracchus was murdered in a furious outbreak of political violence. Ten years later, his brother, Gaius (153–121), attempted to bring in a series of popular reforms, and suffered the same fate.

In the following generation Rome faced hostile military threats in every part of the Empire, including a serious revolt by the Italian allies (91–88). The ruling oligarchy showed itself corrupt and incompetent in attempting to respond to

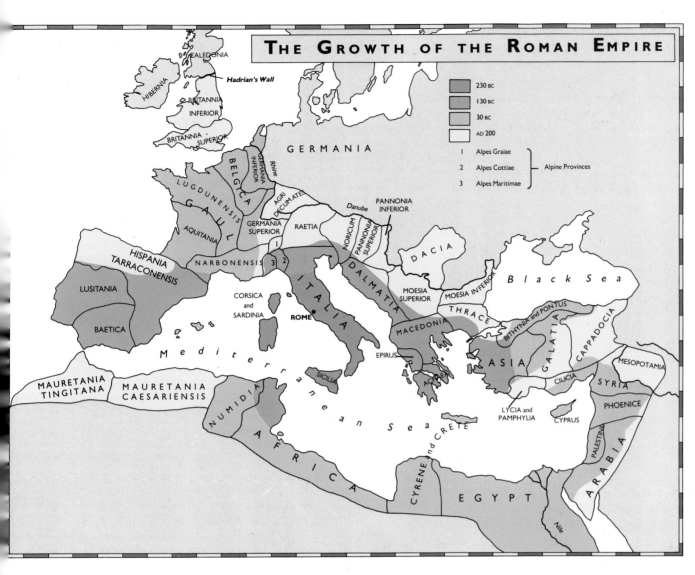

THE GROWTH OF THE ROMAN EMPIRE

�	230 BC
▪	130 BC
▪	30 BC
□	AD 200

1 Alpes Graiae
2 Alpes Cottiae — Alpine Provinces
3 Alpes Maritimae

SEE ALSO
- ALEXANDER AND THE HELLENISTIC WORLD p. 372
- THE ROMAN EMPIRE p. 378
- THE DECLINE OF ROME p. 380
- PRIMAL RELIGIONS: ANCIENT TIMES p. 462
- GREEK AND ROMAN ART p. 508
- CLASSICAL LITERATURE p. 614

these crises, which were only overcome by allowing able and ambitious individuals to take control of the government, and by creating a professional army from the proletariat.

These measures solved the military problems, but had fatal political consequences, because they provided the poor with a means to redress their grievances, and ambitious nobles with the chance to gain personal power by means of armed force. The first civil war was between the successful generals Gaius Marius (c. 157–86) and Lucius Sulla (c. 138–78). Both men marched against the city and massacred their political opponents, and in 81 Sulla set himself up as dictator. His attempts to reform the political system were ineffectual, however, and the same lethal trends continued.

A fresh series of military crises in the 70s enabled the popular general Pompey (Gnaeus Pompeius, 106–48) to gain a position of pre-eminence in the state. But he was unable to prevent other leaders from doing the same thing, and in 60 he joined Marcus Crassus (c. 115–53) and Julius Caesar (100–44) in the First Triumvirate. Following his conquest of Gaul (modern France) Caesar invaded Italy and once again plunged the Empire into civil war.

After defeating Pompey at Pharsalus in 48 Caesar became consul and dictator for life.

Caesar's monarchical tendencies went against republican tradition and offended the nobles. On 15 March (the 'Ides of March') 44 BC, he was stabbed to death by a group of senators led by Marcus Junius Brutus (?85–42) and Gaius Cassius Longinus (d. 42). The conspirators were unable to restore the Republic, however, because Caesar's chief aides, Mark Antony (Marcus Antonius, 83–31) and Marcus Lepidus (c. 89–12), had the support of his armies. In 43 Mark Antony and Lepidus joined together with Caesar's heir, the 19-year-old Caesar Octavian (the future Augustus, 63 BC–AD 14), to form the Second Triumvirate, and in the following year Brutus and Cassius were defeated at Philippi in Macedonia, and committed suicide.

Lepidus was soon squeezed out of the Triumvirate, and the Empire was uneasily divided between Octavian and Antony until 31 BC, when the issue was decided in Octavian's favour at the Battle of Actium, off the west coast of Greece. Mark Antony and his mistress, the Egyptian queen Cleopatra, committed suicide, leaving Octavian in complete control of the Roman Empire. TC

A war elephant on a Carthaginian coin from the 3rd century BC. The Carthaginians succeeded in training African elephants and Hannibal took 50 across the Alps. Although many died, those that survived provided a useful shock tactic against the Romans. The Romans later learnt to cope with the charging elephants by simply opening ranks to let them pass through.

The Roman Empire

After his victory at Actium (see p. 377) Octavian was faced with the problem of retaining the loyalty of the army while at the same time establishing a position of permanent power that would be acceptable to traditional opinion. Octavian's great achievement was to find a lasting solution to this problem. The name Augustus (meaning 'revered') was an honorary title conferred on him in 27 BC, when his position was formalized by the grant of special powers by the Senate and people. He later took on other powers, but made sure that they were voted to him, so as not to offend republican sentiment.

The Senate effectively became a branch of the administration and lost all political independence. The resentment caused by this loss of power was never entirely eliminated, and was the source of much political conflict during the century that followed.

Augustus (63 BC–AD 14), the first Roman Emperor, whose strong rule ended a long period of civil wars. Statues of Augustus were set up all over the Empire, in many parts of which he came to be worshipped as a god.

The work of Augustus

In general, however, the new regime was welcomed by the upper classes, since it brought peace, stability and a chance to prosper. In the provinces, which had suffered dreadfully from civil war, Augustus was hailed as a saviour and universal benefactor. Throughout the Empire formal cults of the emperor were established and became a focus for the loyalty of his subjects.

Augustus received the enthusiastic support of the people of Rome with free rations of grain, cash hand-outs, games and shows ('bread and circuses'). He also secured the loyalty of the army by settling veterans in colonies in the provinces and establishing a permanent standing force, with fixed terms of service and regular wages. This reform had the effect of taking the army out of politics, and guaranteeing its loyalty to the state.

Under Augustus the army was kept busy in wars of conquest. Northwest Spain, the Alpine regions and the Balkans were overrun by Augustus' generals, although the plan to extend Roman rule in Germany east of the Rhine had to be abandoned after the annihilation of three legions under Varus in the Teutoburger forest in AD 9.

Victories abroad and peace at home were the hallmarks of Augustus' long reign. Agriculture and trade benefited, city life prospered, and literature and the arts flourished in what came to be regarded as Rome's 'Golden Age'. On the negative side, political debate was suppressed and freedom of thought was discouraged. This trend intensified under Augustus' successors, with sinister results.

The imperial succession

Augustus was succeeded by his stepson Tiberius, whose long and peaceful reign (AD 14–37) was marred by conflicts with the Senate, treason trials, and palace conspiracies. These tendencies became more pronounced under the later rulers of the Julio–Claudian dynasty: the insane Caligula (37–41), the feeble and pedantic Claudius (41–54), and the colourful but vicious Nero (54–68).

Nero's suicide left the throne with no legitimate heir, and opened the way to civil war as the various provincial armies backed the claims of their generals. The chaos was finally ended by Vespasian, the commander of the eastern legions, who fought his way to power in late 69 and

Roman officers with their legion's standard. (Louvre, Paris)

established the Flavian dynasty. This too became a reign of terror under Domitian (81–96), who was eventually murdered.

The Senate replaced him with the weak and ineffectual Nerva (96–98), who only averted the possibility of renewed civil war by adopting a popular general, Trajan, as his successor. Trajan (98–117) was a successful military ruler who also won over the Senate, which regarded him as an ideal emperor. The atmosphere of stability and concord continued under Hadrian (117–138), Antoninus Pius (138–161) and Marcus Aurelius (161–180). Each of these beneficent rulers was adopted by

is predecessor in the absence of a natural
eir; the sequence broken by Marcus' son
commodus (180–192), who turned out to
e a maniac, thus confirming the Senate's
orst suspicions of dynastic succession.

he assassination of Commodus ushered
a period of turmoil which resembled the
vents of 68–69, and from which Septimius
everus emerged as the final victor.
everus' reign (193–211) was a naked
ilitary despotism, and the army became
olitically dominant under his succes-
ors. When Alexander Severus was mur-
ered by his soldiers in 235, the Severan
ynasty came to an end and the Empire
apsed into anarchy (see p. 380).

tate and subject

he Roman Empire embraced the terri-
ory of some 25 modern countries, and had
population of over 50 million people.
evertheless its administrative organi-

The villa of the Emperor Hadrian at
Tivoli, near Rome, gives some idea of the luxury
and elegance of life for wealthy Romans. Built in
the early 2nd century AD, the villa complex
and its gardens cover some 18 km² (7 sq mi).
As well as the villa itself, there were
theatres, pavilions, baths and libraries.

zation was rudimentary. The *Pax Romana*
('Roman Peace') was maintained in spite
of – or perhaps rather because of – the
inertia of the central government. The
state made only a minimal impact on the
daily lives of its subjects. The emperor,
who worked with a tiny secretarial staff of
domestic slaves and freedmen, delegated
his authority to the provincial governors
and lesser administrators called *procura-
tors*, none of whom had any significant
clerical staff to assist them. There was no

ECONOMY, SOCIETY AND CULTURE

A model of Rome as it was at its peak in the 2nd century AD. The Colosseum – the site of
gladiatorial combats – can be seen top right, while the Circus Maximus – where chariot races
were held – is at centre left. In between the two is the Palatine hill, with the imperial palace
complex. At this period the population of Rome may have reached over one million – many of
whom were unemployed, lived in overcrowded slums, and depended on state handouts.

Although trade and manufacture reached significant levels in the Roman Empire, growth was
hindered by backward technology, low investment and poor demand. Agriculture was always
the most important sector of the economy, and
engaged most of the population. Land was the
chief focus of investment, and the most respectable form of wealth. There was no significant class
of businessmen or entrepreneurs.

Society was sharply divided between the rich
landowners and the mass of rural peasants and
urban poor, who were heavily dependent on the
patronage of the well-to-do. Finally, there were
the slaves.

In the cities slaves were used largely as domestic
staff in the houses of the rich; but slave labour was
also used in quarries and mines, where conditions
of work were inhuman, and sometimes in the
fields, although the large-scale use of agricultural
slavery was probably not common outside Italy.
The Romans regularly freed their slaves, who
thereby obtained Roman citizenship, a consider-

able privilege. Many of them prospered, and
well-off freedmen became an important social
group.

A notable feature of Roman society was its
uniformity and ease of movement. People could
travel without a passport from York to Alexandria, or from Ankara to Tangier, get by with just
Latin and Greek, and always find themselves in
familiar surroundings. The large cities were
especially cosmopolitan and open to outside
influences.

In these circumstances new ideas spread rapidly.
Especially important were new religious beliefs,
including the so-called oriental mystery cults,
which offered converts a chance of personal
salvation through direct communion with divine
powers. The most important cults were the
worship of the Phrygian goddess Cybele, the
Egyptian Isis, the Persian Mithras (see pp. 460–3),
and above all the Palestinian-Jewish cult of
Christianity, which ultimately triumphed over all
its competitors (see p. 380).

bureaucracy or civil service.

The Empire functioned thanks to the
active cooperation of its subjects, who
largely governed themselves. The provinces formed a patchwork of self-governing cities, each with its surrounding
territory, whose local elite was responsible for day-to-day administration and
collection of taxes. Each city was a miniature version of Rome, with its own senate
and annual office holders, elected from
the wealthiest citizens. These men
attained status and prestige by spending
lavishly from their own fortunes on public
amenities, charities, and festivals. The
civic spirit shown by this local munif-
icence is a key feature of Roman civilization.   TC

SEE ALSO

- THE RISE OF ROME p. 376
- THE DECLINE OF ROME
  p. 380
- PRIMAL RELIGIONS: ANCIENT
  TIMES p. 462
- GREEK AND ROMAN ART
  p. 508
- CLASSICAL LITERATURE
  p. 614

The Decline of Rome

In the middle years of the 3rd century AD the Roman Empire was plagued by civil war, foreign invasion and economic breakdown. The political system collapsed, as emperors succumbed one after another to assassination or military revolt. In the fifty years to the accession of Diocletian (284) there were at least twenty emperors who could claim some sort of legitimacy, as well as countless usurpers who were proclaimed by the armies in different parts of the Empire.

The increased political significance of the army arose from the fact that the Empire now depended on it for survival. Pressure from German tribes beyond the Rhine and Danube became intense as Gaul and Germany were ravaged by the incursions of two newly formed tribal groups, the Franks and the Alemanni. Meanwhile the Goths on the lower Danube pressed hard on the Balkan provinces and made seaborne raids on Greece and Asia Minor (northern Turkey). In the east a new and aggressive power arose in the shape of the Persians, who made frequent attacks on eastern provinces. They overran Syria in 260 and captured the emperor, Valerian.

Military difficulties made increasing demands on the Empire's finances, which the taxpayers were unable to meet. The government responded by depreciating the currency, which resulted in galloping inflation. By the 250s the coinage was worthless and the monetary system of the Empire had collapsed. Taxes and payments to soldiers and officials began to be paid in kind, and the requisitioning of supplies became a form of organized looting by the armies.

In these circumstances trade and agriculture suffered, land became deserted, and banditry flourished. Famines and epidemics reduced the population, and cultural activity virtually ceased. Public buildings in the towns fell into disrepair, and the only new constructions were fortifications and city walls. Rome itself was surrounded by defensive walls under Aurelian (271–275), a clear sign of the weakness of the Empire – in earlier times an attack on the city would have been unthinkable.

Recovery under Diocletian and Constantine

The first signs of recovery occurred in the 270s with a series of significant military successes and a perceptible upturn in the economy. Political stability returned with Diocletian, who took office in 284 and managed to stay in power for 20 years. Recognizing that he could not rule the whole Empire on his own, Diocletian chose a colleague, Maximian, to whom he entrusted the management of the western provinces, while he took charge of the east. Shortly afterwards the two emperors (*Augusti*) each took on an assistant (*Caesar*).

This *tetrarchy* (rule of four) was intended to be a permanent institution, but when Diocletian retired in 305 civil war erupted between the various heirs. Constantine, son of Maximian's Caesar, was victorious in the west in 312, and in 324 defeated the eastern emperor. He thus reunited the Empire under his sole rule, which lasted until his death in 337.

Under Diocletian and Constantine the Empire was completely reorganized. The army was enlarged and divided between frontier guards and a mobile field army concentrated in fortified cities and ready to strike back against invaders. Commanders were professional soldiers appointed from the ranks.

The provinces were subdivided into areas of more manageable size, and their governors relieved of military command. The currency was reformed and attempt made to combat inflation. Diocletian also reformed the tax system, and it was he who invented the idea of an annual budget.

These measures reimposed order, but at a price. The central government became more oppressive, and a vast bureaucracy was established. This was self-serving, inefficient and corrupt – an intolerable burden on the taxpayer. Peasants and other workers found it increasingly difficult to make a living and to meet the demands of the state, which in turn attempted to prevent desertion and declining output by compelling workers and their descendants to remain in their jobs. Society thus became more rigid, and the peasants were gradually reduced to serfdom.

The rise of Christianity

From its beginnings in Palestine in the early 1st century AD Christianity spread rapidly. By the 2nd century the new faith had won adherents in all parts of the Empire. At this early stage most people were hostile to Christianity, which was seen as a bizarre and irrational cult, focused as it was on a man who had been executed as a common criminal in the

Defensive walls were constructed around Rome towards the end of the 3rd century AD. For the first time in centuries the heart of the Roman Empire felt itself threatened.

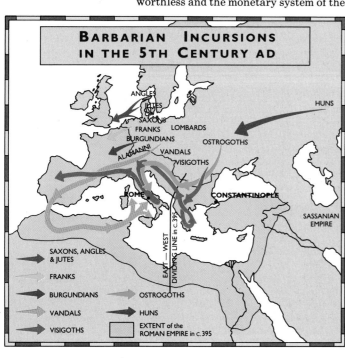

BARBARIAN INCURSIONS IN THE 5TH CENTURY AD

ANGLES
JUTES
SAXONS
FRANKS LOMBARDS
BURGUNDIANS
ALAMANNI OSTROGOTHS
VANDALS
VISIGOTHS
HUNS
ROME
CONSTANTINOPLE
SASSANIAN EMPIRE
EAST – WEST DIVIDING LINE in c.395

SAXONS, ANGLES & JUTES
FRANKS
BURGUNDIANS
VANDALS
VISIGOTHS
OSTROGOTHS
HUNS
EXTENT of the ROMAN EMPIRE in c.395

SEE ALSO

● THE ROMAN EMPIRE p. 378
● THE SUCCESSORS OF ROME
  p. 394
● THE INVASIONS p. 396
● THE PRIMAL RELIGIONS:
  ANCIENT TIMES p. 462
● GREEK AND ROMAN ART
  p. 508
● CLASSICAL LITERATURE
  p. 614

relatively recent past, rather than on a 'normal' god. The Christians were also considered antisocial atheists since they refused to believe in pagan gods or to take part in their festivals. The government was largely indifferent, however, and made no attempt to stamp out the cult – the earliest persecutions were spontaneous outbreaks of popular hatred.

The 3rd-century troubles swelled the membership of the Church but at the same time fuelled popular hostility. Official persecutions began at this time, and were intensified under Diocletian in 303. These persecutions were ruthless and bloody, but the courage of the martyrs served only to increase the prestige and strength of the Church. The point was not lost on Constantine, who issued an edict of toleration in 313.

Constantine's own personal attitude is uncertain, since he continued to endorse pagan cults and was only baptized on his deathbed. However, he honoured the Church and its leaders, and used his authority to settle theological disputes, which from now on become matters of political importance. All subsequent emperors were nominally Christians – with the exception of Julian the Apostate (360–363), who staged an abortive pagan revival – and Christianity became the officially established religion of the Empire.

The Eastern and Western Empires

In 330 Constantine inaugurated a new

Fragments of a giant statue to the Emperor Constantine, who is often credited with making Christianity the official religion of the Roman Empire – although he himself was only baptized on his deathbed.

capital at Constantinople (modern Istanbul). This move symbolized the declining importance of Rome and the growing separation of the eastern and western halves of the Empire. From the later 4th century they had separate emperors and their histories diverged. The West was menaced by foreign invaders, and at the start of the 5th century German barbarians overran Gaul, Spain, Africa and Italy. In 410 Rome itself was sacked by the Visigoths under Alaric. After these disasters things were patched up, and the Western Empire limped on until 476 when the last Roman emperor, Romulus Augustulus, was deposed and replaced in Italy by the Gothic king, Odoacer.

The East survived, however, partly because it faced fewer military problems. Thrace (a region of the eastern Balkans) was continually attacked by Goths and Huns in the 5th century, and by Avars and Bulgars in the 6th, but these threats were dealt with relatively easily, and diplomacy secured peace with the Persians in the east. The Byzantine Empire, as the Eastern Empire became known, although steadily reduced by Arab and then Turkish conquests, was to survive until the 15th century (see p. 395). TC

WHY DID ROME FALL?

Historians have long puzzled over the causes of the decline and fall of the Western Empire, and have offered a bewildering variety of explanations. Excessive taxation, military weakness and population decline were all relevant factors, but were themselves symptoms of the condition that needs to be explained, and cannot be considered causes in their own right. The same is true of such explanations as moral corruption, while supposed environmental factors such as climate change or poisoning from lead water pipes seem contrived and unconvincing.

Much depends on the subjective view of the historian. For instance, Edward Gibbon (1737–94) in his monumental *Decline and Fall of the Roman Empire* deeply lamented the disappearance of an enlightened and rational culture, swept away on a tide of barbarism and superstition. Christians have not unnaturally challenged this view of the triumph of their faith. Modern academic historians are more neutral. They tend to emphasize the prosaic fact of the German invasions, which arose from external causes. Barbarian pressure on the frontiers had not existed under the early Empire, but built up in the 3rd century and became irresistible in the 5th. The conclusion of this view is that the Roman Empire did not fall – it was pushed.

China to the Colonial Age

Since the fall of the Roman Empire, China has been the largest state in the world, and until the European Renaissance, technologically the most advanced. The Chinese continue to call their country the Middle Kingdom, and for long they thought of it as the centre of the world. Beyond the limits of its power were only outer darkness and barbarity.

The historic core of China was the area around the middle reaches of the Yellow River (Hwang He), what is now the northern part of Henan. There, on the fertile, easily worked soil that colours the river, the domestication of millet resulted in well-established Neolithic farming by 4000 BC. From this heartland, farming spread out in all directions, reaching

The terracotta warriors from the grave of the 'First Emperor', Shi Huangdi (259–210 BC). The massed ranks of more than 6000 life-sized soldiers were found when excavation of the tomb began in 1974 – an army for the dead emperor in the afterlife.

the other great river basin, that of the Yangtze (Chang Jiang), by 2500 BC. As agriculture reached the warmer south, it adopted a more suitable local staple crop, rice. By 1500 BC, fully developed rice farming had spread south into Indochina and, by 500 BC, northeast into Korea.

Early civilization in the Chinese heartland

In the Yellow River heartland, the scale and organization of the farming communities increased and their technology improved. By 2000 BC, they had developed bronzeworking and ceremonial centres of some size, even a shadowy dynasty, the Xia. Around 1500 BC the first historical rulers emerged, the kings of the Shang dynasty. The remains of Shang cities and tombs reveal a civilization clearly ancestral to classic Chinese culture. Its script was of the ideographic type still used by the Chinese today, and its capital cities were laid out on a grid system oriented to the points of the compass, as all subsequent Chinese capitals have been. In addition, its bronze, pottery, jade and silk artefacts conformed to a style that the Chinese have held to ever since.

Civilization gradually spread outwards from the core area ruled by the Shang. To the west, the rulers of the Zhou acquired their essentials efficiently enough to displace the Shang as overlords of the Chinese heartland around 1000 BC. The Zhou expanded their power north as far as Manchuria and south over the Yangtze

CENTRAL ASIA & THE SILK ROUTE

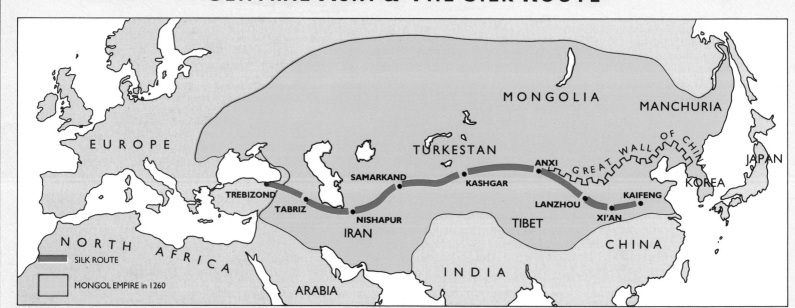

Central Asia lay between the two main areas of World civilization: China in the east, and the Middle East and Mediterranean in the west. It gave these civilizations a common enemy – the nomads who roamed Central Asia and periodically burst out over the settled lands around them – and also a tenuous trade link along the Silk Route.

The Silk Route first flourished at the beginning of the Christian era, when it linked the Han and Roman Empires at the height of their prosperity. Silk, and later porcelain, travelled from east to west; in exchange came gold, silver, gems, ivory and natural rarities unobtainable in China.

The passage of technological ideas along the same route mainly benefited the

West. The Chinese developed paper, printing, gunpowder and the magnetic compass well before the West. It is likely that the Silk Route carried these ideas westwards, where much more advantage was eventually taken of them. In the 16th century the arrival in the East of Western ships steered with compasses and defended by guns marked the end of the usefulness of the Silk Route.

The map shows the Silk Route in the 13th century. The broad line of the route remained much the same through the centuries, but its terminuses varied with changes in the politics and economics of China and the Middle East. The map also shows the boundary of direct Mongol rule in 1260, the year in which their empire was split between the descendants of Genghis Khan, bringing to an end the only period when a single nomad power ruled the whole of Central Asia.

basin. Within those boundaries, advances in agriculture (irrigation) and technology (ironworking) made it possible to support powerful local rulers, their courts and warriors. As the centuries passed, power devolved to these smaller states which eventually – from the mid-5th century BC – became the 'Warring States'.

When they were not making war, the rulers of the fiefs of Zhou China found time to consider the nature of power and government. At their courts, the essentials of Chinese views on the good society were developed. The most prominent administrator-philosopher was Kongfuzi (Confucius; 551–479 BC) who, around 500 BC, set out the basis of an ethic of civilized life that was to influence Chinese society down to the 20th century (see p. 470).

The beginnings of empire

The westernmost of the Warring States, Qin – which was the most remote from the origins of Chinese culture – emerged the final victor. In 221 BC, its ruler became Shi Huangdi (259–210) – 'the First Emperor' – and in the 11 years of his reign established the framework of the greatest state the world had so far seen. His empire spread out to touch the South China Sea and Central Asia. In the north, its boundary with the nomads was defined by the largest single human artefact ever made: the Great Wall. Within these borders, the inhabitants were conscripted to build a massive road system as well as the Wall. The laws, administration, script, currency, weights and measures of the empire were all reorganized and standardized.

Qin rule did not long outlast Shi Huangdi, but the foundations of empire had been firmly laid. Under the succeeding Han dynasty, the Chinese empire defined its traditional bounds. At the end of the 2nd century BC, it spread west into Central Asia, south into Vietnam, and east into Korea. However, these lands were too far away to be held for long, and though they always remained under strong Chinese influence they subsequently went their own way politically.

One result of the expansion of the Han Empire and its contacts with other societies was the arrival of Buddhism (see p. 468). Buddhism spread from India along the Central Asian trade routes that

flourished in this period. Although it never displaced native philosophies such as Confucianism, Buddhist beliefs became and remained a major component of popular religion and culture in China.

The Han empire also set the pattern of Chinese government. At the centre was the emperor and his court. He ruled through a highly educated bureaucracy selected by rigorous examination. The emperor also had a religious role: the welfare of the empire and its people was bound up with his well-being and correct performance of ritual duties. The carefully planned imperial city was the focus of ritual, bureaucracy, wealth and culture. The Chinese capitals – with populations of up to half a million – were easily the largest and most magnificent cities in the world between the fall of Rome and the rise of London.

The history of the Han empire and of the later dynasties followed a similar pattern. Each dynasty started with a period of just and efficient government and imperial expansion. Then, slowly and inevitably, decline and disintegration set in. In the provinces, generals and governors built up separate local centres of power. Peasants rebelled as the burdens of tax and conscription weighed more heavily. Nomads pressed on the northern frontiers and sometimes broke through.

A pattern of dynasties

The next longstanding dynasty, the Tang, saw the empire rise to a classic perfection in the 7th, 8th and 9th centuries AD, ruled with rigid efficiency from Changan, the most crushingly magnificent of the imperial capitals. Song China, between the 10th and 12th centuries, had a more complex structure. It was larger, too, containing over 100 million subjects at its peak. Among its most prosperous parts were the great new commercial cities along the Yangtze and the southern and eastern coasts, with trading links well beyond the traditional bounds of empire. These cities marked a drift of the centre of gravity of imperial China away from the Yellow River and towards the south.

The south proved sufficient to sustain a reduced 'southern Song' empire when the Yellow River basin fell under the rule of the Jin nomads from Manchuria in 1126. The northern Jin empire in turn succumbed to more powerful nomads, the Mongols under Genghis Khan (c. 1162–1227), who swept over northern China in a devastating campaign between 1211 and 1215. In the mid-13th century the Mongol attack was renewed and, by 1280, after more destruction, all China was under the rule of the Mongol Kublai Khan (1215–94).

The Yuan dynasty of the Mongols lasted a century. Although it adopted many of the trappings of traditional empire, it was overthrown in 1368 by a nationalist revolt. The first emperor of the new dynasty, the Ming, was Hongwu (Hung-Wu; 1328–98), who had started life as a peasant. The Ming re-established the empire in its old form, and this empire flourished for over two centuries, then collapsed in the face of a peasant revolt in

the mid-17th century. Order was restored by another nomad dynasty, the Qing, originating in Manchuria.

The last empire

The Qing (Manchu) dynasty, which ruled for two and a half centuries from 1659, formed an alien veneer on an empire that remained in its essential workings the traditional Chinese state. Under the Qing the empire reached new heights of power, expanding to include Tibet, Turkestan and Mongolia. The population within its borders eventually rose past the 400 million mark. Its capital, Beijing (Peking), with a population approaching a million, remained the largest city in the world until the end of the 18th century.

The decay and collapse of Qing authority in the 19th century was in part a repetition of the old cycle. Population pressure, official corruption and increased taxation made peasant life a misery and revolt an attractive alternative. Thus far the old patterns held – but the barbarians pressing on the empire were different: this time they were Europeans.

The Europeans did not want to rule; they wanted to trade at a profit. The Chinese empire was unwilling to expand its trade with the West, partly from a desire to remain self-sufficient, and partly out of incomprehension. However, trade was forced on the empire, in particular the import of opium from British India. Following the two Opium Wars (1839–42 and 1856–58), the conditions of trade were imposed by the European powers (see pp. 432–3).

In exchange, the Western powers helped to put down the most formidable peasant rebellion of the 19th century, in which several million people died. The Taiping ('heavenly peace') movement controlled much of the south of China during the 1850s in the name of a peasant egalitarianism influenced by elements of Christianty borrowed from Western missionaries. However, European arms and generalship helped to bring it to a blood-soaked end in 1864. The Boxer Rebellion that broke out at the end of the century, which was turned against the Europeans by the Qing court, was equally effectively suppressed by Western forces in 1901. The court was punished for its complicity by being obliged to make further trading and other concessions. With China divided into Western (and Japanese) spheres of influence, the stage was set for the final act (see p. 446). RJ

The Great Wall of China, the largest single construction ever made. Begun in the 3rd century BC to keep out nomadic invaders from the north, it was largely rebuilt in the 15th and 16th centuries AD. On average some 9 m (30 ft) high, it stretches 2400 km (1490 mi) across northern China.

SEE ALSO

- JAPAN TO THE 20TH CENTURY p. 386
- THE PEAK OF EMPIRE p. 432
- CHINA IN THE 20TH CENTURY p. 446
- RELIGIONS OF CHINA AND JAPAN p. 470
- CHINESE AND JAPANESE ART p. 514
- THE LITERATURE OF ASIA p. 616

IMPERIAL DYNASTIES OF CHINA

Shang	1480 BC–1050 BC
Zhou	1122 BC–256 BC
(Warring States	481 BC–221 BC)
Qin (Ch'in)	221 BC–206 BC
Han	202 BC–AD 220
Jin (Tsin)	265–316
Sui	589–618
Tang	618–907
Song (Sung)	960–1127
(in south only	1127–1279)
Yuan (Mongol)	1271–1368
Ming	1368–1644
Qing (Manchu)	1644–1911

India and Southeast Asia to the Colonial Age

The history of civilization in the Indian subcontinent begins in the northwest (now mainly Pakistan). This region formed an extension of the Middle-East/Iranian cultural zone and it was from that direction that it acquired Neolithic farming techniques by 5000 BC. The techniques spread on, first to central India and then to the far south by 2000 BC.

Up in the northwest, Mesopotamian patterns were repeated (see p. 364). Settlements became larger, bronze working was introduced, and ruling elites – probably priestly – emerged. A climax was reached in the Harappan civilization, which flourished in the Indus Valley between 2300 and 1700 BC, focused on the two cities of Harappa and Mohenjo-Daro. In these cities the full repertoire of Bronze Age urban society was displayed: a literate elite, carefully organized and controlled water and food supplies, and densely packed artisan quarters – a society of rank and order that was reflected in the detail of its urban planning. The urban civilization of the Indus Valley flourished for 600 years and then collapsed for reasons that remain unclear, although life in the villages went on much as before.

The northeast of the subcontinent took a different line. It too, formed part of a wider zone, that of tropical Southeast Asia. As in other tropical areas, the development of settled farming took varied forms, rather more horticultural than agricultural, eventually adopting rice as its staple crop. By 1500 BC this part of India, the Ganges basin, had evolved a Bronze Age culture of its own and succeeded the Indus Valley as the core area of Indian civilization.

The shift from the Indus to the Ganges is associated with the entry into the subcontinent of the Aryans – Indo-European pastoralists from the Iranian steppe. The Aryans imposed themselves on the native Dravidians, and the resulting amalgam became the Hindu society that has been the majority community of India ever since. This amalgam contained elements from both cultures: the gods and the language were Aryan but many of the customs, including the all-important caste system (see p. 466), were Dravidian.

Kingdoms and empires

The Hindu kingdoms of the Ganges valley entered the Iron Age in around 800 BC. Some

Mohenjo Daro, one of the main cities of the Harappa civilization. This civilization – one of the world's earliest – flourished in the Indus Valley between 2300 and 1700 BC.

ANGKOR AND ANURADHAPURA

Angkor, the ancient temple-city of Cambodia. The city was founded in the 9th century AD as the Khmer capital, abandoned in the 15th century, and rediscovered, covered in jungle, in 1860.

Hindu kingship left its most haunting relics in the deserted temple-cities of southern Asia, above all, Angkor in Cambodia and Anuradhapura in Sri Lanka. The kings of these Hindu (and later Buddhist) kingdoms took on divine characteristics at their accession to power. In their lifetime, their palaces intermingled with the temples of their fellow gods; after death, their shrines were added to those of the other deities. Because they were the residences of gods, the cities symbolized the universe in microcosm, with temple-topped mounds and artificial lakes recreating the mountains and seas of the real world.

The god-king was responsible for the spiritual and material well-being of his people. If he failed in that responsibility, he and his city had failed to please the other gods. The solution to a national disaster was therefore to start again with a new and auspicious capital. We can understand what happened in earlier centuries from what we know of the movement of

capitals in 18th- and 19th-century Burma. When the capital was moved from Ava to Amarapura in 1783 or from Amarapura to Mandalay in 1857, the rejected city was deserted almost overnight. Wooden palaces and houses were moved from the discarded city to the new site and most of the inhabitants went with them.

Anuradhapura failed to protect the Sinhalese against Tamil invaders from southern India and was discarded in favour of Polonnaruwa in the 8th century AD (itself abandoned in the 13th century). The divine protection embodied in Angkor failed to protect the Khmer against Thai invaders in the 15th century and the city was abandoned to be replaced by Phnom Penh.

For all their splendour, the temple-cities we see today were – in the end – magnificent failures.

00 years later the region produced one of history's great religious teachers, Prince Gautama, the Buddha ('enlightened one'; see p. 468). The dominant kingdom then and for several centuries subsequently was Magadha: its pre-eminence increased with the advent first of the Nanda dynasty (362–321 BC), then of the Mauryans. Chandragupta Maurya (321–297 BC) conquered most of northern and central India, and his grandson Ashoka (272–232 BC) placed inscriptions even further afield, in Afghanistan and the southern Deccan.

An Indian empire of this extent was exceptional. Mostly the Indus valley belonged to empires that lay to the west – to Persia between the late 6th and 4th centuries BC and to Alexander the Great at the end of the 4th century BC. After Ashoka, the Greeks returned to the upper Indus basin and a rich Indo-Greek society developed in the area; they in their turn were supplanted by nomad rulers from Central Asia, notably the Kushans (1st to 5th centuries AD).

The expansion of Hindu culture

The decline of the Mauryan dynasty after Ashoka saw the north and centre of the subcontinent revert to a glittering mosaic of regional kingdoms. They were only briefly brought under the sway of later empire builders – the Guptas in the 4th century AD and Harsha in the first half of the 7th century.

Hindu expansionism was mercantile and cultural rather than imperial, although Ceylon (Sri Lanka) was brought within its influence by invasion from the north of India around 500 BC. First the relatively backward tribal areas of southern India were brought into contact with the centre and north, and then overseas trading links were developed to the east. Trade planted the seeds of Indian culture far and wide. By the 3rd century AD, Hindu kingdoms were beginning to spring up all over previously tribal Southeast Asia – in Burma, Thailand, Cambodia, Java and Sumatra.

Buddhism followed Hinduism into Southeast Asia at a time when its influence at home in India was declining, and established itself as the dominant faith in Burma, Thailand and Cambodia. The splendour of Indian culture in Southeast Asia was to reach its climax between the 9th and 13th centuries in the great Buddhist Khmer empire of Cambodia and the wide Hindu maritime kingdom of Shrivijaya, centred on Sumatra.

Back in the subcontinent during this period there were no great empires but only regional kingdoms. For the first time, the south produced an important kingdom – Vijayanaga (c. 1350–1550).

Islam in India

The first Muslim invasion of India occurred in the 8th century, when an Arab army marched in from Iran and made Sind (southern Pakistan) a province of the Caliphate. The next moves came much later, in the 11th and 12th centuries, with Muslim princes in Afghanistan launching a whole series of campaigns that eventually brought down the Hindu kingdoms of the Ganges

valley and replaced them with an Islamic state, the Sultanate of Delhi (1206). Temporarily, under Muhammed bin Tughluq (1325–1351), then more permanently under Akbar (1556–1605) and Aurangzeb (1658–1707) of the Mogul dynasty, the sultanate expanded until it embraced almost the entire subcontinent. The Moguls – the word is a variant of 'Mongol' – came from Central Asia and their artists from Iran, but this alien court created a culture which, in buildings such as the Taj Mahal, stamped its image on India forever.

After Aurangzeb, Mogul power declined and provincial governors, some of them Hindus,

began asserting their independence. There were also new players in the game by this time – the European trading companies. The Portuguese had been visiting India since the 16th century, and the Dutch, French and British arrived in the course of the 17th. At first the companies stuck to trading, then they became involved in local politics, and in wars between themselves and against native rulers. By the 1760s the British East India Company had emerged as the dominant power on the subcontinent (see p. 416). It was the beginning of a new phase of empire building that ultimately brought all India under British rule (see p. 432). RJ

Akbar's troops besieging a castle in 1568. Akbar, the greatest of the Mogul Emperors of India, successfully pursued a policy of imperial expansion. He also made many administrative reforms, and showed toleration and respect towards non-Muslims. (Victoria and Albert Museum, London)

SEE ALSO

● THE RISE OF ISLAM p. 392
● THE VOYAGES OF DISCOVERY p. 405
● EUROPEAN EMPIRES IN THE 17TH AND 18TH CENTURIES p. 416
● THE PEAK OF EMPIRE p. 432
● THE RELIGIONS OF INDIA p. 466
● BUDDHISM p. 468
● ISLAMIC ART p. 510
● ASIAN ART p. 512

Japan
to the 20th Century

Japan was first peopled from Asia in one of those periods in the last Ice Age when lowered sea levels joined offshore islands to the mainland. Over tens of thousands of years, hunting and gathering communities thrived on the Japanese islands. They were among the earliest societies in the world to develop pottery, probably around 10 000 BC, and, for much of the next ten thousand years, the pottery of the Jomon culture showed what could be achieved in material terms by a society living on the proceeds of hunting, gathering and perhaps some horticulture.

The techniques of fully developed rice farming reached the southern island of Kyushu from Korea, the nearest point on the Asian mainland, around 400 BC and spread up the island chain to reach the east coast of the central island of Honshu by AD 100. Progress further north was much slower: the northern island of Hokkaido was not brought into the farming zone until the 19th century, and the hunting-gathering culture of the Ainu survived there until recently.

Links with the Asian mainland were maintained and strengthened by the early farming communities of Japan. It is possible that considerable numbers of immigrants arrived, and certainly technical skills and cultural ideas were borrowed, including the Chinese script, Confucianism and the then popular Chinese form of Buddhism. These were added to Shinto, the traditional Japanese ancestor worship, to form a trio of often interrelated systems of belief (see pp. 468–471).

The castle at Kumamotu, central Kyushu. The castle was built in the l7th century, at a time when the Tokugawa shogunate was reasserting central control in Japan.

Imperial Japan

By the 7th century AD, Chinese concepts of government were being borrowed in the southern Yamato Plain of Honshu, whose rulers dominated much of central and western Japan by this time. A Chinese-style emperor was established at Nara (710–84) in a Chinese-style imperial city and the main features of the Chinese system of government were imitated. The court was moved to Heian (modern Kyoto) in 794, and the 9th century saw an elaboration of the imperial system there.

Having borrowed from China, the Japanese absorbed and transformed their borrowings. At the same time, contacts with China diminished. The imperial system, too, was transformed. The emperor became a religious figurehead, power being held by members of an aristocratic court family, the Fujiwara. Then power in turn slipped away from the Fujiwara and the court and into the hands of provincial governors and landowners.

Feudal Japan

By the 12th century, much of the real power in Japan was exercised by the provincial barons (*daimyos*) through bands of warriors (*samurai* – see box). In the mid-12th century, the head of one baronial family, Taira Kiyomori, seized power as a military dictator. His successor, Yoritomo, leader of the Minamoto family, took the logic of the separation of real power and imperial dignity to its conclusion. He ruled Japan after 1185 from Kamakura (near Tokyo), eventually under the title of *shogun*, in the name of a powerless emperor who remained in courtly isolation at Kyoto.

The Kamakura shogunate lasted a century and a half. For much of that time, the shogun himself was a figurehead, the real power being exercised by regents from the Hojo family. In the 14th century, the Ashikaga family instituted a new shogunate based at Kyoto. This fell apart into warring provincial baronies. An emperor and a shogun still nominally ruled in Kyoto, but real power was contested by the provincial daimyos and their military forces.

This was the Japan that came into contact with European (mainly Portuguese) traders and missionaries from the 1540s. During the 16th century, Western ideas, particularly Christianity, made a significant impact on Japan, but the impact that really mattered was that of European firearms. Three military leaders in turn – Oda Nobunaga (1578–82), Toyotomi Hideyoshi (1582–98) and Tokugawa Ieyasu (1600–16) – used muskets to fight their way out of the impasse of feudal anarchy and into control of a united Japan.

Tokugawa Japan

Under Ieyasu, the shogunate was established at Edo (Tokyo) in the control of the Tokugawa family. The emperor, with some dignity restored, remained at Kyoto.

THE SAMURAI

Samurai in traditional armour. By the time this photograph was taken in 1907, the rank of samurai had been abolished for some thirty years.

For much of the time between the 12th and the 19th centuries, Japan was ruled by a military government, the *bakufu* ('camp government'), under a *shogun* ('great general'). Beneath the shogun were the ranks of the military barons (*daimyos*), and beneath them their warriors – the *samurai*. Lower down the social scale were the civilian ranks of peasants, artisans and merchants.

The ties that bound this military society together were the ties of personal loyalty. Japanese society in this period is called feudal because it was held together in similar ways to feudal Western Europe during the Middle Ages (see p. 404). Power and protection flowed down from person to person through the ranks of society; loyalty, service and dues in cash and kind passed upwards in return. A samurai – the equivalent of the European knight – gave absolute loyalty to his daimyo and exercised the power of the sword on his behalf.

The samurai, like all expensive, heavily armed warriors on horseback, were a privileged elite. They were trained to a code of loyalty, honour, bravery, self-discipline and the stoical acceptance of death – self-inflicted if that were the only way to retain honour. The iron discipline of this warrior life was softened by an emphasis on culture and the arts: a samurai was an expert with the pen as well as the sword.

From the mid-17th century, the stability of Tokugawa Japan limited opportunities for actual fighting. Military duties became largely ceremonial and many samurai made good bureaucrats. As a final irony, many also fell into debt with the merchants who ranked at the bottom of the feudal society. Only a few samurai felt the loss of honour sufficiently to raise their swords in revolt when the Meiji reformers abolished their rank in the 1870s. Their days of glory were already long past.

The Tokugawa shogunate was built on feudal concepts but governed as a military bureaucracy. In particular, the daimyos were subject to close supervision from Edo and their local power diminished by long periods of compulsory residence at the court of the shogun. Their families remained at court the whole time as potential hostages.

Loyalty to the shogunate was further encouraged by excluding foreign influences. Christianity was suppressed, and the only foreign traders permitted were the Dutch, who were restricted to Nagasaki harbour. Firearms, having done

their work, were limited to the use of the government.

Hermetically sealed from outside influences, Japan went its own way between the mid-17th and the mid-19th centuries. Tokugawa Japan was a stable and, in many ways, a prosperous pre-industrial society, able to sustain great cities and a complex bureaucracy – and also eventually able to face the challenges of the 19th century.

Japan transforms

The industrial West arrived with Commodore Perry and an American fleet in 1853.

Japan was forced into the global trading system. The loss of face and the impact of the outside world destabilized an already weakening Tokugawa regime. In 1867–68, power was seized at Kyoto by a group representing daimyos from western Japan together with reforming imperial courtiers.

The prestige of the emperor was restored, the last Tokugawa shogun was overthrown and, in 1869, Emperor Mutsuhito was installed with executive power at Edo, renamed Tokyo ('the eastern capital'). The emperor adopted 'Meiji' ('enlightened government') as his throne name, and the term is also applied to the period of his reign (1867-1912).

The group of privy councillors who exercised power on behalf of the emperor then proceeded to transform Japan. Within ten years virtually all vestiges of feudalism had been removed. The daimyos and samurai were pensioned off and the peasants given ownership of the land they worked (and then heavily taxed). Western systems of law, administration and taxation were introduced in 1889, followed by a constitution and parliament along Western lines.

The Meiji reformers saw that survival in the modern world demanded not just Western institutions but also a Western-style economy. This was a little more difficult to achieve, but industrialization, sponsored by the state, was well underway by the beginning of the 20th century.

By then Japan was sufficiently well-established in world prestige to be accepted as an equal by the Western powers, who relinquished their unequal treaty rights. Japan even began to fight and win Western-type wars, against China in 1894-95 and Russia in 1904-5, coming away with the beginnings of a colonial empire in Taiwan, Korea and the south of Manchuria. The career of Japan as a major world power had begun (see p. 443). RJ

SEE ALSO
- CHINA TO THE COLONIAL AGE p. 382
- THE GROWTH OF TOTALITARIANISM p. 442
- WORLD WAR II p. 444
- BUDDHISM p. 468
- RELIGIONS OF CHINA AND JAPAN p. 470
- CHINESE AND JAPANESE ART p. 514
- THE LITERATURE OF ASIA p. 616

A Japanese view of Westerners: American, Dutch and Russian troops parade in Japan in 1860. Japan was forced to open up to US trade following two visits by Commodore Perry's fleet in 1853 and 1854, and soon other Western powers followed suit. Japan's 200-year period of isolation was over, and its development into a major industrial power was about to begin.

Africa, Australasia and Oceania

to the Colonial Age

Africa south of the Sahara is the cradle of the human race: the first man-like creatures evolved there, as did the first men (see p. 200). As the millennia passed, early man (*Homo erectus*) evolved into modern man (*Homo sapiens*), who in turn developed different varieties to suit different environments. Sub-Saharan Africa produced four: the Negroes in the West African bush, the Pygmies in the equatorial rain forest, the Nilo-Saharans of the middle Nile, and the Bushmen of the open lands in the east and south.

The relatively small area of Africa north of the Sahara belonged, then as now, to a different world; its peoples, sometimes referred to as Hamites, are relatives of the Semites of the Middle East. They can be divided into three main groups: the Berbers of the Maghreb (Morocco, Algeria and Tunisia), the Egyptians, and the Cushites of the Red Sea coast. The

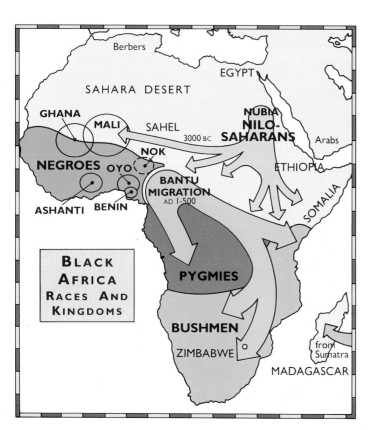

history of these peoples belongs largely to that of the Mediterranean and the Middle East (see pp. 366, 372, 376 and 392).

Australasia's history is short compared to Africa's. The first men only arrived in New Guinea and Australia around 50 000 BC, when the last Ice Age lowered the sea level sufficiently to make island-hopping along the Indonesian archipelago relatively easy. And, for a long time, that was as far as they got. Even relatively close Oceanic island groups like the New Hebrides and New Caledonia were not colonized before 2000 BC, and Hawaii and New Zealand were still undiscovered and uninhabited when the Christian era began.

Africa: the earliest farmers

The Nilo-Saharans of the Nile Valley had the closest contact with the Mediterranean and Middle Eastern world to the north. The practice of farming spread from the Middle East through Egypt to the middle Nile valley sometime before 3000 BC. When it spread beyond the Nile valley, it encountered an environment that was more suited to specialized pastoral farming. Soon, Nilo-Saharans and Cushites and their herds were moving west along the Sahel, the area of open savannah to the south of the Sahara, and into West Africa.

In West Africa the land was more suited to settled farming. In the course of the final millennium BC, village communities began to appear in this zone and the Negro peoples who lived in them subsequently developed other skills too, notably the ability to smelt iron. The first of these West African Iron Age communities recognized by the archaeologists is known as the Nok culture; it has been dated to the last few centuries BC.

The combination of agriculture and iron created a potent force in prehistoric society. Around the beginning of the

The massive walls of Zimbabwe embody the power and skill of this former African kingdom, which flourished from the 13th to the 15th centuries. Zimbabwe exported its gold via the coastal Arabs in return for a wide range of goods including Chinese pottery, fragments of which have been found at the site.

Christian era, Negro farmers – mainly Bantu – began to spread east and south out of West Africa, settling areas previously roamed by hunter-gatherers. By AD 500 they had reached as far as the east coast of southern Africa, leaving only the deep rain forest to the Pygmies and the Kalahari Desert to the Bushmen.

Africa and the wider world

Settled, agricultural Black Africa of the Iron Age had several major links with the wider world. That world – to the north and east – offered trade in exchange for Africa's gold, ivory and slaves and was eventually to offer monotheistic religion as well. Egypt had always been in touch with Nilo-Saharan Nubia (northern Sudan, known to the Ancient Egyptians as 'Cush'). Egypt had even been briefly ruled by a Nubian dynasty, the 25th, in the century around 700 BC. Later, Christianity found its way up the Nile to Nubia and to Ethiopia, to the kingdom of Axum (later Abyssinia), as early as the 4th century AD.

The eastern coast of Africa, too, had its contacts: longstanding ones with the Arabian peninsula, and occasional ones with lands further to the east. It was, however, probably an accident which brought the Malagasy people from Indonesia to settle Madagascar around AD 500. Arab expansion (see p. 392) brought Islam to the northeast coast, as far south as Somalia, by the 12th century, and the establishment of trading settlements along the coast down to Mozambique between the 9th and 13th centuries. In West Africa, trade began to reach across

he Sahara from Muslim North Africa
n the 8th century and Islam followed into
he Sahel in the 11th century.

African kingdoms

African contact with the Arab world
reveals for the first time something of the
political history of Black Africa and of the
rise and fall of its kingdoms. The profit
from that contact – particularly from the
gold trade – enabled some African kingdoms to establish themselves on a much
more lavish scale than before. In West
Africa, the kingdoms of Ghana (8th–12th
centuries) and Mali (13th–14th centuries)
dominated the routes between the goldfields and the desert trails to North
Africa. Similarly, the eastern kingdom of
Zimbabwe (13th–15th centuries) controlled that region's goldfields and its
trade with the coastal Arabs.

The pattern of African history was fixed
on this basis until the 19th century. From
the later 15th century, the Portuguese
took over much of the east-coast Arab
trade and went on to establish a similar
trade on the west coast (see p. 410), where
they were largely replaced by the Dutch
in the 17th century, who in turn were
replaced by the British and French in the
18th (see p. 416). Inland African kingdoms
– such as Benin (17th century), Oyo (18th
century) and Ashanti (18th and 19th centuries) in West Africa – lived in symbiosis
with the coastal traders, supplying them
with gold and slaves to work the plantations of the Americas in exchange for
textiles, iron goods and guns (see p. 416).

Only in the far south was there a different
type of development: Dutch colonists, the
Boers, began to settle that area in the
second half of the 17th century. By the end
of the 18th century Boer expansion had
led to clashes with the southernmost
of the Bantu kingdoms and begun a
pattern of war and colonization which
was to bring about the fall of all black

A Samoan war canoe,
photographed at the end
of the 19th century. In
such flimsy vessels as this
the Polynesians colonized
vast tracts of the Pacific.

African kingdoms except Abyssinia by
the end of 19th century (see p. 432).

Australasia

After the last Ice Age, the waters finally
rose to divide New Guinea and Australia
sometime around 5000 BC, and the two
great islands went their separate ways.
Both developed advanced Stone Age cultures. That of New Guinea – which was in
the course of acquiring Neolithic food
production methods from Southeast Asia
at the time – was based on horticulture,
and that of Australia on hunting and
gathering.

The Aboriginal culture of Australia was
largely isolated from this time. It was not
unchanging in its isolation, but neither
internal pressures nor sporadic contacts
with the rest of the world led to the
development of agriculture. Instead,
roving hunter-gatherers reacted in sophisticated ways to a wide variety of
environments. The rich cultural life sustained by this successful adaptation to
time and place has all but disappeared
under the destructive impact of European
settlement, leaving little more behind it
than myths of the 'Dream Time' and a
fading legacy of rock paintings.

Oceania

With their particular brand of food production fully developed in New Guinea,
Melanesian horticulturalists began to
settle the islands to the east, reaching the
New Hebrides and New Caledonia by
2000 BC. At the same time, other peoples –
originally of east Asian stock – were
moving east from the Philippines and
surrounding islands to settle Micronesia
and the northern and eastern fringes of
Melanesia.

These newcomers to the area brought
with them a different language and culture from those previously developed
in Melanesia. But they also brought
a similar Neolithic horticulture which,
combined with fishing, was well suited to
the smaller islands of the Pacific. Settlers
from such a background had reached Fiji
by 1500 BC, spreading from there to Tonga
and Samoa. It was in this area over the
next millennium that the language and
culture of the Pacific islanders developed
the traits we recognize as Polynesian.

An outstanding aspect of Polynesian culture was a magnificent tradition of seafaring. Time and again, Polynesians set
out into the unknown on outrigger
canoes loaded with the essentials of their
life – coconut, taro, yam, banana,
breadfruit, pig and chicken, none of
which was native to the area – and used
their skill and luck to colonize islands all
over the vastness of the Pacific.

The canoes reached as far as Easter
Island, where Polynesian culture produced one of its strangest manifestations,
the great stone heads with diminutive
bodies which have puzzled outsiders
since the first European contacts of the
18th century (see p. 513).

In the south, the main islands of New
Zealand were much larger than the other
Polynesian islands and lay in the temperate zone. In this different environment, Maori culture developed its own
variations. At first, the peculiar fauna of
New Zealand, particularly the flightless
moa, made hunting an important part of
life. When there were no more moas, the
Maori turned to an agriculture founded
on sweet potatoes and fern rhizomes, and
developed a warrior culture based on
fortified villages. They were to become
the only Pacific people to offer major
armed resistance to European advances
in the 19th century, and peace between
the Maoris and the British colonists was
only finally achieved in 1871.   RJ

SEE ALSO

● ANCIENT EGYPT p. 366
● THE RISE OF ISLAM p. 392
● THE PEAK OF EMPIRE p. 432
● DECOLONIZATION p. 448
● THE PRIMAL RELIGIONS:
 MODERN TIMES p. 464
● ASIAN, AUSTRALASIAN AND
 OCEANIC ART p. 512
● NATIVE AMERICAN AND
 AFRICAN ART p. 516

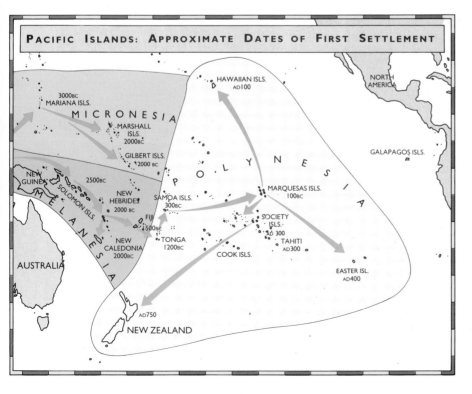

PACIFIC ISLANDS: APPROXIMATE DATES OF FIRST SETTLEMENT

HAWAIIAN ISLS.
AD 100

NORTH
AMERICA

3000BC
MARIANA ISLS.

MICRONESIA

MARSHALL
ISLS.
2000BC

GILBERT ISLS.
2000 BC

GALAPAGOS ISLS.

NEW
GUINEA

2500BC

POLYNESIA

NEW
HEBRIDES
2000 BC

SAMOA ISLS.
300BC

MARQUESAS ISLS.
100BC

FIJI
1500BC

SOCIETY
ISLS.
AD 300

TONGA
1200BC

TAHITI
AD300

NEW
CALEDONIA
2000BC

COOK ISLS.

MELANESIA

SOLOMON ISLS.

AUSTRALIA

EASTER ISL.
AD400

AD750
NEW ZEALAND

Pre-Columbian
America

America was the last of the habitable continents to be colonized by man, an event that occurred during the last Ice Age. Two opposing geographical changes made it possible. First the sea level fell because of the amount of water locked up in the icecaps: this led to the appearance of a land bridge connecting Asia and Alaska. Then the melting of the North American icecap removed the barrier to movement between Alaska and the rest of North America. There was just enough time for a few families of Siberian mammoth hunters to make the journey before the rising sea level obliterated the land bridge.

This happened in around 10 000 BC, and within 1000 years the descendants of these few families had spread over North and South America. Nearly all the American Indians derive from this stock: the only exceptions are the Athapascan tribes of Canada and western North America, and the Inuit (Eskimo) of the far north; these two peoples arrived by boat five or six thousand years later.

As the climate improved and the mammoths disappeared from the American scene, the early Americans found it difficult to support themselves by big-game hunting alone; many of them turned to smaller game, and to the gathering of edible seeds and fruit. In the end, around 2500 BC, this led to the appearance of agricultural communities in Meso-America (Mexico and Central America) and the central Andean region of South America (Equador, Peru and Bolivia).

The early agriculturalists

In Meso-America the staple crop was maize. In the Andes, and on their western side, a number of crops were domesticated, including the potato, and, after 1500 BC, maize. By 1000 BC a third area of farming – relying largely on manioc – had developed in the tropical area now covered by Colombia and Venezuela.

Later in the first millennium BC maize farming reached what is now the southwest USA and spread from there into the Mississippi basin around AD 500. By that time, the whole western part of the continent between Mexico and northern Chile was occupied by maize farmers, while tropical farmers were settled on river banks along the whole length of the Amazon river system and had reached the Caribbean islands as well. Tropical farming continued to spread after this, reaching south to the Paraná basin by AD

A Mayan wall painting from Bonampak, south of the Yucatán peninsula. Between 300 and 900 AD the Mayans emerged as one of the greatest civilizations of the western hemisphere.

1000 and then moving north up the Brazilian coast.

Not all Americans turned to agriculture, however. Along the coastline, on the open plains of both North and South America and in the deep tropical jungle of the Amazon basin, specialist fishers, hunters and gatherers maintained rich and varied ways of life up to the 19th or 20th centuries.

The development of civilization

As in the Old World, the acquisition of agriculture was only the beginning of a sequence of developments which culminated in civilization. Settled farmers can support settled places of worship. After a while, by coming together in sufficient numbers, they can build temples of some size and maintain the priestly elites to go with them. This development had taken place separately by 1500 BC in both of the core areas of temperate agriculture, Meso-America and the central Andes, and spread as far as the Mississippi basin by the 8th century AD (the Temple Mound culture).

The steps in the organization of society beyond tribal farming and local religious centres were taken only in Meso-America and the central Andes. The initial focus of the development of civilization in these two areas was religious, centring on the building of increasingly grandiose temples and then temple-cities. This phase

Machu Picchu, (left), a city of the Incas perched high in the Andes of Peru. The site occupies an area of 13 km² (5 sq mi), and includes a temple, a fortress, and terraced gardens. The city escaped destruction at the hands of the Spanish Conquistadores, and was only rediscovered in 1911.

THE NORTH AMERICAN INDIANS

It is difficult to get back beyond five centuries of disruption (and destruction) to obtain a clear picture of the life of the native Americans north of the Rio Grande before 1492. It is even difficult to separate the Indian brave from his horse – a European import which the Plains Indians took over with great enthusiasm in the 18th century.

The million or so inhabitants of North America in 1492 were scattered across the whole continent and gained their living in a wide variety of ways. In and around the Mississippi basin and over to the east coast were well-established farmers living in villages of solid wooden houses. They relied largely – but not exclusively – on agriculture for their subsistence. In the southwest were other farmers, living in a more hostile and arid environment, but occupying even more solid, stone-built pueblos. Along the northwest coastline were prosperous villagers who relied on the ample resources of the sea and rivers for their main food supply.

Elsewhere, life was more mobile: following game on the Plains or gathering plants in the deserts and hills west of the Rockies. There were hunters in the forests beyond the Great Lakes and then up towards the Arctic were the Inuit (Eskimo) fishers and hunters.

The villagers and some of the more organized bands of hunter-gatherers were grouped into tribes. Tribes shared a local language and culture and often claimed a common descent. They were governed by meetings of tribal elders and came together from time to time to worship and socialize. Tribes further distinguished themselves from other tribes by a readiness to fight them.

Plains Indians. An engraving by George Catlin, who made extensive studies of North American Indians in the mid-19th century.

War called for individual leadership. Among the villagers of the east and the northwest, this had led to the grouping of some of the tribes into more permanent confederations under the rule of chiefs. Chiefs could claim more extensive rights of government and a greater share of resources for themselves and their warriors than was possible among the individual tribes – and they took them. However, with the coming of the Europeans, the Indians were forced further and further west, until by the end of the 19th century all their lands had been lost (see p. 430).

MAJOR TRIBES OF NORTH AMERICA AD 1500

reached its peak in the Maya cities of lowland Meso-America, at Teotihuacán in the Mexico valley, and at Tiahuanaco high up in the Andes, all at the height of their splendour in the first millennium AD. At the heart of these ceremonial cities were great artificial temple mounds ('pyramids') set within rigid geometric layouts that had astronomical significance. In Meso-America, an obsession with the calendar led to complex mathematical calculations and the development of hieroglyphic means of record. Another obsession of Meso-American religion was human sacrifice, presumably intended to appease the gods and maintain the pattern of the seasons.

In the 7th century Teotihuacán was abandoned and the same fate gradually overtook all the other pyramid cities of Mexico and Yucatán. No one knows why – perhaps the rituals had simply become too onerous to sustain. The setback was not permanent, however, and by 900 new cities were under construction, notably

Tula, the capital of the Toltecs, just to the north of present-day Mexico City.

Toltecs, Aztecs and Incas

These temple-cities were not primarily the capitals of political states. They were the religious and social centres of agricultural peoples – organized into tribes and chiefdoms – who periodically came up to their temples to worship and celebrate. States grew out of the dominance that the warriors of certain tribes established over their neighbours during this period.

In Meso-America, the earliest warrior state of major importance was probably Teotihuacán, which in the 6th century AD was sending armed embassies far afield. The next was that built up by the Toltecs, who dominated a large part of central Mexico and the Yucatán between the 10th and 12th centuries AD from their base at Tula and Chichen Itza.

The following period was one of warring local states, none of which established

more than a brief regional dominance. Then from the mid-14th century the Aztecs, based on their great island city of Tenochtitlan in Lake Texcoco (the site of Mexico City), spread out to bring a large part of Meso-America under their rule. Theirs was the most impressive empire Meso-America had seen – and the last native one, falling to Spanish invaders under Cortez in 1519–21 (see p. 410–411).

In South America, the first military hegemony of some size was that established from Huari between the 9th and 12th centuries AD. It was succeeded, after a period in which regional states reasserted themselves, by the coastal power of Chimu from the late 14th to mid-15th centuries, and then by the highland rule of the Incas of Cuzco.

By the end of the 15th century, Inca power spread over virtually the whole of the area from modern Ecuador to northern Chile. The Inca empire was another first and last empire, scarcely established before it was overthrown by Spanish forces under Pizarro in 1532–33 (see p. 410).

The Aztec and Inca empires fell in unequal struggles. They were at a cultural level roughly equivalent to the Old World Bronze Age (see p. 363). They had built their first proper cities and had begun to organize themselves to collect tribute efficiently from the tribes and chiefdoms they dominated. The Incas had also built a system of roads and forts to control their domains more effectively. None of these could protect them against such instruments of advanced Old World civilization as the iron sword, the firearm and the horse-borne warrior. RJ

SEE ALSO

● THE SPANISH AND PORTUGUESE EMPIRES p. 410
● THE BIRTH OF THE USA p. 422
● THE EXPANSION OF THE USA p. 430
● NATIVE AMERICAN ART p. 516

The Rise of Islam

In the early 7th century of the Christian era something extraordinary happened in the Arabian peninsula. A charismatic figure united its tribes, who then embarked on a century-long campaign of conquest. The man was Muhammad, called the Prophet, and his religion was Islam – meaning 'submission to the will of God' (see p. 478). Islam spread rapidly eastwards to Persia and westwards into North Africa and Spain. After these initial successes Muslim conquests peaked around 750. Then in the 13th century it won new adherents in Central Asia – the Mongols (see p. 382). The 13th century also saw Islam spread to India (see p. 385). During the 14th and 15th centuries Islam continued to spread – to large areas of Africa, and even Southeast Asia. Today it is one of the world's major religions.

Islam's initial success was due to a number of factors. Before he died in 632, Muhammad urged a *jihad* ('holy war') against unbelievers, although the causes of Arab expansion were more complex than a simple crusade. The first targets of this expansion were areas adjacent to Arabia belonging to the Byzantine and Sassanid (Persian) Empires. These two great powers had exhausted themselves after decades of continuous warfare. In addition the Christians of the region belonged to sects that had no love for the Byzantine Empire. In a decade Arab armies conquered Syria (636–638), Egypt (640–642) and Mesopotamia (639–646). Persia collapsed within the same timescale. Muslim tolerance of Christians and Jews meant that many welcomed their rule.

The early caliphates

The Umayyad dynasty (651–749), reigning in Syria, created a strong, flexible state, under its *caliphs* (successors of the Prophet). However, Islam was split when a combination of dynastic and theological issues produced the breakaway Shiite (or Shia) sect. This consisted of followers of the Prophet's son-in-law Ali, who had been murdered in 661.

In 749 regional separatism and Shiite opposition produced a revolution and the establishment of the Abbasid dynasty. The new caliphs removed their power base to a new capital – Baghdad. The Umayyads held on only in their most recent conquest, Spain. Eventually, in 929, the Umayyad ruler of Córdoba took the title of caliph for himself.

The political unity of the Muslim world – *Dar-al-Islam* – was further fractured in the 9th and 10th centuries. The Fatimids (claiming descent from the Prophet's daughter, Fatima) established another caliphate in Tunisia. In 969 they conquered Egypt. Once again Shiite forces from the periphery had conquered a centre of Muslim power. Meanwhile within the Baghdad caliphate real power had fallen into the hands of Turkish army commanders. Although the Abbasid dynasty was to survive until 1258, the power of the caliphs was considerably diminished.

Dealing with the 'barbarians'

Between the 11th and 13th centuries the Islamic world suffered a series of shocks at the hands of peoples it regarded as barbarians: Seljuk Turks, Western Europeans, and Mongols. However, whereas both Seljuks and Mongols were in time converted to Islam, the advancing Europeans – the Crusaders – remained Christian, and indeed saw themselves as fighting a kind of holy war of their own (see p. 398).

By the early 13th century the Muslims had lost nearly all of Spain to the Christians (see p. 399), and this loss was to be permanent. In Syria, Christian conquests – the Crusader states – were more short-lived. They were too close to the twin heartlands of Islamic power – Egypt and Iraq – ever to have much chance of survival. In 1187 Saladin, sultan of Egypt and Syria, recaptured Jerusalem and in the late 13th century his work was completed by the Mamluk sultans of Egypt (see p. 398). The Mamluk sultans, moreover, had managed to keep their independence when much of the Muslim world collapsed before the Mongol advance in the mid-13th century. Once converted, however, the Mongols took Islam even further afield, into India and China.

Ottoman expansion

From small beginnings around 1300, the

THE ARAB EMPIRE AT ITS GREATEST EXTENT AD 700–850

- ARAB EMPIRE
- BYZANTINE EMPIRE

In many areas of intellectual and material culture, the Islamic world dwarfed Christian Europe. Although defined by the Qur'an (Koran), Hadith and Sharia (see p. 478), Islam proved itself very receptive to cultural influences. The older civilizations of Egypt, Greece, Persia and India all contributed to produce a fusion that was distinctive to each region, fusions that are most obvious in the visual arts (see p. 510).

In the sciences – mathematics, chemistry and medicine – and also in philosophy, Muslim intellectuals made great strides. The greatest scholar of the conquest period was Abd Allah ibn Abbas, renowned for his interpretation of the Qur'an. Under the early Umayyads, al-Zuhri developed the art of jurisprudence and wrote a biography of Muhammad. Both these developments helped to create a Muslim self-identity.

In the early Abbasid period, al-Kindi became the first important Islamic philosopher. He had a good knowledge of ancient Greek works and ideas, and these were to have a profound effect on Islamic thinking. Towards the end of the 9th century, al-Yaqubi's history provided both a chronological framework and a study of Greek science. He is also regarded as the founder of geography in the Islamic world.

From Hindu mathematics the Arab mathematician al-Khwarizmi took what we now call 'Arabic' numerals, including the symbol for zero. He also introduced the writing down of calculations in place of using an abacus (the term 'algorithm' derives from his name), and extended algebra (the word derives from Arabic *al-jabr*, 'transposition'). It was through the Arabs that algebra reached Europe.

The study of medicine was central to Islamic science, with no less than 70 scholars producing works on the subject. The great caliph Harun al-Rashid founded a hospital in Baghdad in AD 800, and individual physicians were in demand all over the medieval world. The names of the greatest scholars became well-known in the West: Razes (ar-Rhazi), the medical encyclopedist, Haly Abbas (al-Majri), and Avicenna (Ibn Sinna), the 11th-century physician and philosopher.

Such men contributed enormously to the rediscovery of classical knowledge in Christian Europe. It was Avicenna, under the influence of his mentor al-Farabi, who brought Aristotle's *Metaphysics* to the attention of Christian scholars. This single work was to dominate the development of philosophy in Europe. Interestingly, the Aristotelian commentaries of ibn-Rushd, known as Averroës (1126–98), had more influence on Christians than on Muslims.

By 1200, on the threshold of an intellectual renaissance in Europe (see p. 406), Islam had begun to follow the strictures of the 11th-century thinker al-Ghazali: the study of 'foreign sciences' had to conform to Islamic doctrine. It was this reassertion of theological control in the Islamic world that was at the root of the growing scientific and technological dominance of Europe, a dominance that was to become apparent by the end of the Middle Ages.

The Turkish siege of Vienna in 1683 marked Islam's deepest penetration into Europe. Following an appeal from the pope, an army drawn from Germany, Lorraine and Poland came to the city's aid. After a 15-hour battle the Christian forces under Jan Sobieski defeated the Turks, and the siege was lifted. However, the Turks were to remain dominant in southeast Europe for another two centuries.

SEE ALSO

● THE SUCCESSORS OF ROME p. 394
● CHRISTIANITY RESURGENT p. 398
● NATIONALISM IN EUROPE p. 428
● THE MIDDLE EAST p. 454
● ISLAM p. 478
● ISLAMIC ART p. 510
● THE LITERATURE OF ASIA p. 616

Ottoman Turks emerged as the foremost Muslim power. They made Anatolia (Asian Turkey) the centre of attacks on the Byzantine capital, Constantinople – the great fortress city that had withstood Arab sieges in the 670s and in 717–718 (see p. 395). By the end of the 14th century, devastating Ottoman raids into the remaining Byzantine territory had reduced the Byzantine Empire to the walls of Constantinople. The city was saved, not by the misbegotten crusade of 1396, which the Turks easily crushed, but by invaders from Central Asia under their fearsome leader, Tamerlane. Tamerlane (or Timur; c. 1336–1405) – who claimed descent from the Mongol Genghis Khan – had led his armies from his capital in Samarkand in an orgy of conquest and destruction across Mongolia, India, Russia and the Middle East, and in 1402 he defeated and captured the Ottoman sultan. This was merely a stay of execution for Constantinople, however, since Sultan Mehmed II's artillery and huge forces overwhelmed resistance in 1453.

From their new capital, now named Istanbul, the Ottoman sultans embarked on campaigns of expansion. In 1517 Selim I conquered Egypt, and under his successor, Suleiman the Magnificent (1520–66), the Ottoman Empire reached its peak.

Certainly the Ottomans did much to encourage the spread of Islam. The northern boundary of their conquests in Europe was marked by the failed sieges of Vienna in 1529 and 1683, but the Ottomans were to hold on to most of southeast Europe until the 19th century (see p. 429). The naval defeat at Lepanto in 1571 (see p. 411) meant that Mediterranean expansion was effectively over by 1600, although the Ottomans were able to conquer Crete in 1669. Christian Spain expelled its Muslim population – the Moriscoes – in the mid-17th century.

Despite this check in Europe, overall the picture was still one of expansion. Just as the Christian Spanish and Portuguese spread their religion along the trade routes (see p. 410), so Ottoman venturers carried Islam to Africa and Southeast Asia. During the 14th and 15th centuries Malaya and Indonesia were converted to Islam, and its status as a worldwide religion was assured. MB

An Arab ship from a 12th-century manuscript. The Arabs were great seafarers, not only dominating the Mediterranean for centuries, but also trading down the east coast of Africa and as far as Southeast Asia.

The Successors of Rome

The Roman Empire has had many imitators. After AD 400 the western part of the Empire (though not yet the east) began to disintegrate into various kingdoms ruled by Germanic peoples (see p. 381). Around 800, Charlemagne reunited many of them to create a Frankish empire in Rome's image. This later became known as the Holy Roman Empire. With the failure of Charlemagne's Carolingian dynasty in the 10th century, the Eastern Franks took over the Empire, whose base moved to Germany and Italy. The Empire was ruled by successive European dynasties until the Habsburgs monopolized the succession from the 15th century onwards. This Empire lasted, latterly in the guise of the Austro-Hungarian Empire, until 1918 (see p. 440).

SEE ALSO

- THE DECLINE OF ROME p. 380
- THE RISE OF ISLAM p. 392
- CHRISTIANITY RESURGENT p. 398
- THE SPANISH AND PORTU-GUESE EMPIRES p. 410

The eastern Roman Empire was based on Constantinople (modern Istanbul) and ruled separately from 380 onwards (see p. 381). Here decline was slower. This empire became known as the Byzantine Empire, after Byzantium, the Greek name for Constantinople. The Byzantine Empire survived the Arab invasions and numerous attacks from both east and west for centuries, alternately expanding and contracting. It was only finally extinguished by the Ottoman Turks in 1453. Even then many of its traditions continued in the Ottoman Empire, which itself did not dissolve until after World War I (see p. 440).

The Sack of Rome

Although the image of the Goths sacking Rome in 410 (see p. 381) is a powerful one, the act was more symbolic than significant. Germanic peoples had been pressing on Roman borders for centuries and had already broken through once, in the 3rd century. However, the conquest of the 5th century was to prove permanent. By around 500, successor states were established by the Visigoths in Spain, the Vandals in North Africa, the Ostrogoths in Italy, and the Franks in Gaul (France). It was the Franks who were to survive and attempt to recreate Rome's empire. The others fell either to Justinian's 'reconquest' in the mid-6th century (see below) or to Islam (see p. 392).

The Carolingian Empire

The Carolingian dynasty was based in northern France. It was named after Charlemagne ('Charles the Great'), king of the Franks from 768 to 814. Charle-magne's father, Pepin the Short (751–768), had ousted the old Merovingian dynasty that had ruled the Franks from c. 500 to 751. The Carolingian rise to power was due to military success. Charlemagne's grandfather, Charles Martel, had checked the Muslim advance at Poitiers in 732, and Charlemagne himself went on to conquer Italy, Hungary and Germany. He created the largest state in the West for 400 years. More than that he consciously declared it Roman and Christian.

Charlemagne had himself crowned emperor of the West by the pope in Rome on Christmas Day 800. His court at Aix-la-Chapelle (Aachen) became the centre of a cultural renaissance without which much classical learning would have been lost. Charlemagne also did much to strengthen the administration of the Empire.

But a combination of the Frankish system of partible inheritance (division amongst heirs) and external attack worked against the Empire's survival. Charlemagne's son Louis the Pious (814–840) divided the Empire between his three sons. In the late 9th century, the imperial leadership proved itself ineffective against Muslim, Viking and Magyar (Hungarian) raids. The result was that power slipped into the hands of regional aristocracies.

The German Empire

The East Frankish (German) aristocracy became particularly prominent. In the early 10th century, its leaders – the dukes of Saxony – replaced the Carolingians as kings east of the Rhine. By first checking and then defeating the Magyars (Battle of the Lech, 955) and by keeping the Vikings at bay, Henry I (919–936) and his son Otto I 'the Great' (936–973) established claims to empire. Otto entered Italy with his army in 951 and was crowned emperor at Rome in 962.

The ending of the custom of partible inheritance meant that this empire lasted until the end of the Middle Ages and beyond. When the Saxon (Ottonian) dynasty died out (1024), first the Salians took over (until 1125), then the Hohenstaufen dynasty (until 1254).

The efforts that these rulers made to keep control over Italy led to a series of quarrels both with cities such as Milan – which were increasingly wealthy and independent – and with popes intent on asserting the 'liberty of the Church' against secular interference (see p. 398). The quarrels with popes led to the emperors insisting on the God-given dignity of their own position; thus in the 13th century the term 'Holy Roman Empire' came into vogue.

The Holy Roman Empire

In theory the Empire had become an elective (rather than a hereditary) monarchy in the 12th century, and in 1356 the procedure by which a college of seven electors chose the emperor-to-be was laid

Byzantine warriors on a 10th-century ivory box. At this period the Byzantine Empire underwent a military revival. After one victory over the Bulgars, the Byzantine emperor Basil II – 'the Bulgar Slayer' – is said to have blinded virtually all his prisoners, letting them find their way home by leaving one eye for every hundred men.

down in detail. Yet – apart from a period from the mid-13th to the mid-14th century – in practice the electors were content to elect the dynastic heir. Thus Charles IV (1346–78) was succeeded by his heirs until they died out in 1437. From then on until the end of the Empire in 1918 the Austrian Habsburgs remained firmly on the throne.

By far the most prominent of the Habsburg emperors was Charles V. Holy Roman Emperor from 1519 until his abdication in 1556, and combining the Habsburg, Burgundian and Spanish inheritances in a single pair of hands, he ruled over the largest European empire since Charlemagne (see p. 410). Ironically, however, it was the troops of this most Christian emperor that sacked Rome in 1536.

The Eastern Empire under Justinian

Secure within the walls of Constantinople the Eastern Empire weathered the storm of the 5th century. During the reign of Justinian (527–565) it underwent an intellectual, administrative, architectural and military revival. A new law code, the great church of Hagia Sophia and an attempt to enforce religious uniformity set the tone for the rest of Byzantine history.

Justinian's most ambitious project was to reconquer the Empire's lost western provinces, and so turn the Mediterranean once again into a 'Roman lake'. In the 530s his great general Belisarius achieved some stunning triumphs: the reconquest of Africa, Sicily and most of Ostrogothic Italy. But in 542 bubonic plague struck. This and subsequent epidemics may have reduced the Empire's population by as much as one third. While Justinian wrestled with the devastating economic and financial consequences, the Ostrogoths took the opportunity to fight back. Yet by the early 560s Justinian's armies had once again gained control of Italy and reconquered southern Spain from the Visigoths. At the time of the emperor's death his greatly extended empire was still intact.

Charlemagne as depicted in a stained-glass window (c. 1200) in Strasbourg Cathedral.

Crisis, survival and recovery

In 568 new invaders, the Lombards, entered Italy. Conceivably they might have been thrown out, but Justinian's over-confident successors chose this moment to break with Rome's ancient enemy, Persia. There followed a long and destructive series of wars, and in 626 the Persians, in alliance with the Avars, laid siege to Constantinople itself. The soldier-emperor Heraclius (610–641) chose this moment to launch a counter-attack on the Persian heartlands, and while Constantinople's walls held firm, the Persian Empire crumbled.

But the emperor's conjuring trick was in vain. In the 630s and 640s his exhausted empire was unable to prevent the loss of its richest provinces – Syria, Egypt, Mesopotamia and then Africa – to the Arabs (see p. 392). The tax revenues of Egypt alone were about one third of those of the whole Empire. This was a blow from which the Empire never entirely recovered.

The 7th century also saw the Lombards make further advances in Italy, while the Danube frontier collapsed as Slavs moved in and settled the Balkans in increasing numbers. This was a century that left its mark on the map: from now on the Middle East was to remain a Muslim preserve, and the Balkans a largely Slav one.

For Constantinople itself worse was still to come – not only the great Arab sieges of the city in the 670s and 717–718, but also the incessant pressure of Arab raids into Asia Minor (modern Turkey) in these and subsequent decades. Fortress towns took the place of the old 'open' cities of antiquity. The feeling that God had forsaken them led to a radical questioning of religious practices, notably the veneration of icons (images of Christ and the saints). The result was an *iconoclast* ('icon-breaker') movement, which disturbed Byzantine society from the 720s until the final restoration of the icons in 843. Yet several of the 'iconoclast' emperors were able soldiers and, within its reduced borders, the Empire survived.

In the 10th century there was something of a revival. Talented military emperors pressed east into Armenia and even campaigned in Syria again. In the 960s Crete and Cyprus were recovered – although in the West the Arabs completed their conquest of Sicily. The main achievement of this period was the combination of Byzantine military power and Greek cultural influence, which led to the acceptance of Orthodox Christianity by the Bulgars and Russians.

The legacy of Byzantium

The mid-11th century, however, found the Empire once again on the retreat. Normans occupied southern Italy (see p. 397) and, more seriously, Seljuk Turks overran the interior of Asia Minor. In the 12th century the Bulgars regained their independence. Disaster followed in 1204 when the Fourth Crusade, diverted from its original goal by Venetian policy, ended by sacking Constantinople, the greatest city of the Christian world. Although the Latin Empire set up by the Crusaders in Constantinople lasted only until 1261, the re-established Byzantine Empire was to be but a shadow of its former self.

The last two centuries of Byzantine history are a record of decline in the face of pressure from the Ottoman Turks. The final fall of Constantinople to the Ottomans in 1453 was a case of an elephant crushing a flea.

Yet Byzantium had always meant more than merely its territories. It created Orthodox Christianity and it preserved Greek culture. For centuries this preservation of Greek culture was to be a source of inspiration to the West, either directly or indirectly through the Arabs (see p. 393). In the end its Turkish conquerors were themselves captured by the image of Byzantium. They chose to rule, in Byzantine manner, from the place they called simply 'Stamboul' – the city.   MB

The Turkish siege of Constantinople. The fall of Constantinople to the Ottoman Turks in 1453 was the culmination of centuries of decline. (Bibliothèque Nationale, Paris)

The Invasions

Following the great barbarian invasions that had eaten into, and finally destroyed, the western part of the Roman Empire, further movements of people continued in Europe, especially in the northwest. Between the 5th and 11th centuries AD, Britain in particular was the target of a series of invasions that fundamentally changed its culture, language, institutions and history. The sea, which subsequently proved Britain's main defence, was used as a highway by many invaders – Celtic and Germanic peoples, Vikings, and finally the Normans.

For 400 years the Romans had colonized Britain south of the Solway. The native Britons, who were Celts (see p. 374), had been largely Romanized, and Christianity had been established. But in AD 407, pressure from barbarians on other parts of the Empire led to the final withdrawal of Roman forces from Britain, leaving a power vacuum that other peoples were eager to exploit.

Picts and Scots

Already in the 4th century the Picts – who occupied what is now Scotland – were raiding Britain south of Hadrian's Wall, but they made no settlements. Then the Picts themselves became the target of the Scots, who originated in Ireland. In the 5th and 6th centuries Scots from Antrim took over Argyll, Bute and Arran, establishing the kingdom of Dal Riada. In 603 southward expansion by the Scots was halted by the Northumbrian English, but cultural and dynastic penetration of the Pictish heartland of northeastern Scotland continued until the 9th century, when the last of the Picts were absorbed into the kingdom of Scotland under Kenneth MacAlpine (846–58).

The Anglo-Saxon invasions

The chief threat to southern Britain came from pagan Germanic invaders – principally Angles, Saxons and Jutes, but also Frisians and Franks (see map). Collectively, these peoples are known as Anglo-Saxons, and it is from their language that modern English derives (see p. 606).

An account by the British priest Gildas, written a century later, indicates that in c. 450 British leaders hired Saxon mercenaries to help repel the Picts. However, the Saxons sent for reinforcements and turned on their former employers. Gildas goes on to describe how the British fought back, winning a great victory at 'Mount Badon' (whose date and location are not known).

Although later Welsh legends associate King Arthur with this phase of British resistance, there is no secure evidence that he existed at all (see also p. 618).

The Anglo-Saxon advance resumed in the later 6th century. In the first half of the 7th century Anglo-Saxon control reached the Firth of Forth in the north and the borders of Wales in the west. However, in the southwest (Cornwall) and northwest (Strathclyde) the British retained their independence.

The Anglo-Saxon kingdoms

Throughout the 7th and 8th centuries there was a fluctuating number of Anglo-Saxon kingdoms, sometimes as many as a dozen. Gradually, however, a 'big three' emerged: Northumbria, Mercia and Wessex – the three kingdoms that were the cutting edge of expansion northwards and westwards.

Yet it is clear that relations between native British and Anglo-Saxon invaders were not exclusively hostile. In Wessex and Mercia some kings bore British names, and in their western parts many British place names survive. It is possible that Wessex, Mercia and Northumbria were mixed British and Anglo-Saxon societies in which Anglo-Saxon (English) culture came to be dominant – except in one respect. Christianity – the religion of the Britons – had been reintroduced. In 597 St Augustine had been sent from Rome to convert the English and to bring the British Churches under Roman authority.

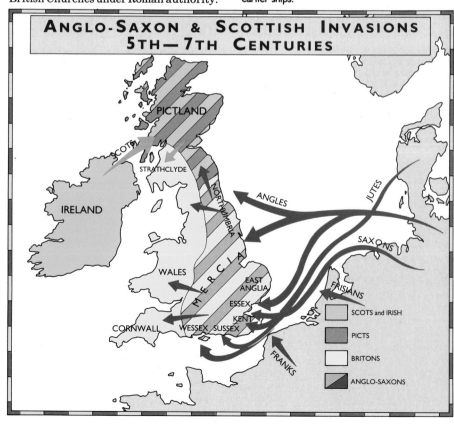

Reconstruction of a Viking long-boat, from Norway. In boats such as this the Vikings not only attacked great areas of northern Europe, but also sailed the Atlantic as far as North America. The longship, which carried a single sail, was revolutionary in its design: its longer keel and tapered ends made it both faster and more seaworthy than earlier ships.

ANGLO-SAXON & SCOTTISH INVASIONS 5TH – 7TH CENTURIES

PICTLAND

SCOTS

STRATHCLYDE

NORTHUMBRIA

ANGLES

JUTES

IRELAND

WALES

MERCIA

SAXONS

EAST ANGLIA

ESSEX

FRISIANS

CORNWALL

WESSEX SUSSEX

KENT

FRANKS

SCOTS and IRISH

PICTS

BRITONS

ANGLO-SAXONS

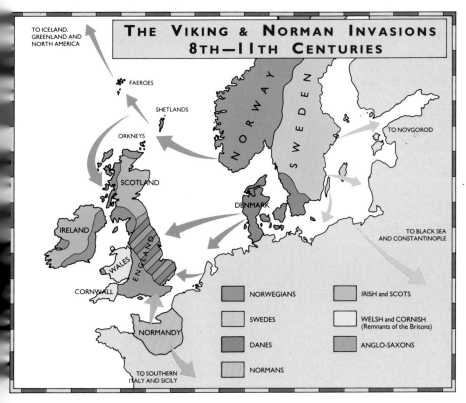

THE VIKING & NORMAN INVASIONS 8TH–11TH CENTURIES

TO ICELAND, GREENLAND AND NORTH AMERICA

FAEROES

SHETLANDS

NORWAY

SWEDEN

ORKNEYS

TO NOVGOROD

SCOTLAND

DENMARK

IRELAND

TO BLACK SEA AND CONSTANTINOPLE

WALES

ENGLAND

CORNWALL

NORMANDY

TO SOUTHERN ITALY AND SICILY

NORWEGIANS

SWEDES

DANES

NORMANS

IRISH and SCOTS

WELSH and CORNISH (Remnants of the Britons)

ANGLO-SAXONS

Augustine founded the church at Canterbury, but further north the main work of conversion was carried out by Scottish monks.

During the 7th and 8th centuries Anglo-Saxon kings were more concerned with a struggle for supremacy over each other than further expansion at the expense of the Welsh. This internal struggle was interrupted by raids carried out by fierce seafarers from across the North Sea – the Vikings.

The Vikings

The Vikings (or 'Norsemen') in fact came from three distinct parts of Scandinavia – Norway, Sweden and Denmark. They were brilliant seamen, their longships taking them from the Black Sea in the east to America in the west. Viking armies were small, usually to be numbered in hundreds, and were not militantly anti-Christian – by the end of the 11th century they had all been converted to Christianity. The Vikings shared many values with the rulers of the societies they attacked in western Europe and found it easy to stay as settlers.

The Norwegians were active on both shores of the Irish Sea, ultimately settling in eastern Ireland, western Scotland, the Isle of Man and northwest England, as well as the Orkney, Shetland and Faeroe Islands. They also sailed the Atlantic to colonize Iceland. It was from Iceland that Eric the Red sailed west in c. 986 to discover Greenland, where a settlement survived into the 15th century. In around 1000 the Norwegians, under Leif Eriksson, also briefly settled in northeast North America, which they called *Vinland* (possibly Newfoundland).

The Swedes went east into Russia where they formed the first organized states. Sailing down the great river systems to the Black Sea, they also traded with – and even

assaulted – the Byzantine capital, Constantinople.

The Danes directed most of their energies against the Anglo-Saxon and Frankish kingdoms (the latter in what is now France and north Germany). By the end of the century the kingdoms of Northumbria, East Anglia and Mercia had been taken over. These Viking kingdoms in the area known as the *Danelaw* were shortlived, but they were to have an important impact on the culture and language of England. Only Wessex (England south of the Thames) survived the onslaught, under a remarkable king, Alfred the Great (871–899). By 960 his successors had conquered the rest of England, forming one kingdom for the first time. Ironically the elimination by the Vikings of Wessex's Anglo-Saxon rivals had paved the way for the unification of England.

Viking attacks were renewed during Ethelred II's reign (978–1016). After prolonged resistance the English kingdom finally capitulated to the Danish king, Cnut, in 1016. However, this conquest did not involve a major new settlement of Scandinavians in England, and in 1042 Ethelred's son, Edward the Confessor, recovered his throne.

The Normans

In 911 a Viking leader named Rollo was granted control of the lower Seine valley by the West Frankish king. In the following decades Rollo's descendants and their followers extended their grip on the Channel coast. Thus they created the duchy of Normandy, 'the land of the Northmen', but in the process lost their Viking character and merged into the aristocracy of northern France.

In the 11th century the Normans were one of the most successful peoples in Europe.

Early in the century Norman mercenaries began to carve out territories for themselves in southern Italy, ultimately seizing the whole area from its Greek and Lombard rulers, and then taking Sicily from the Arabs.

The Norman conquests in southern Italy were acts of private enterprise. The conquest of England, on the other hand, was organized by the duke of Normandy himself, with all the resources of his duchy behind him. In 1051 Duke William (later known as 'the Conqueror') had been made heir to his cousin, the childless Edward the Confessor. But in England the most powerful man after the king was Harold Godwinson, and when Edward died (January 1066), the English acclaimed Harold king.

Harold's defence of his crown was complicated by the necessity to repel a Norwegian invasion under Harold Hardrada, which he crushed in a great battle at Stamford Bridge near York. Meanwhile William landed on the southeast coast. In a daring campaign (September–December 1066) he demonstrated his superior military skill, defeating and killing Harold at the Battle of Hastings. He was then crowned king on Christmas Day 1066.

William had seized control of a richer and more powerful kingdom by a bold and well-organized coup. Until 1071 the Norman grip on England was severely tested by revolts and Danish invasions, but this opposition hastened the destruction of the English ruling class and its replacement by a new Norman-French nobility. For more than 300 years the language of the rulers of England was to be a form of French, which left a lasting impact on the English language (see p. 606). Yet initially only some 10 000 newcomers were involved, and there were many things they could not, indeed did not, wish to change. The more sophisticated administrative structures of Anglo-Saxon England were taken over virtually unchanged, and these formed the framework of English government not just in the Middle Ages, but down to the present day. NH

SEE ALSO

● THE DECLINE OF ROME p. 380
● THE SUCCESSORS OF ROME p. 394
● THE HUNDRED YEARS WAR p. 400
● EARLY MEDIEVAL ART p. 518
● THE STORY OF ENGLISH p. 606
● EPICS AND ROMANCES p. 618

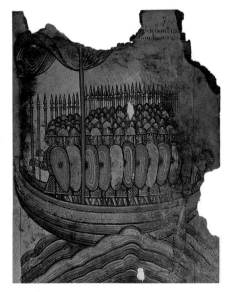

Norman soldiers crossing the English Channel in 1066, as depicted in a medieval manuscript illumination. During the period 1066–1204, when the kings of England were also the dukes of Normandy, ships like this would have carried troops, courtiers, officials, horses and supplies between England and Normandy as regularly as cross-Channel ferries do today.

Christianity Resurgent

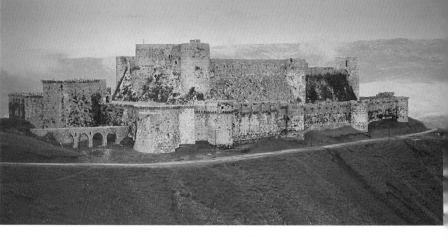

The era of the Crusades saw Christian Europe once more on the offensive. Inspired by a reformed and revitalized papacy, knights flocked to rescue Jerusalem from Islam. Even though in the long run the Crusader states that they set up in the Holy Land were to prove vulnerable to the Muslim 'counter-crusade', elsewhere the crusading spirit was to achieve more permanent results. In Eastern Europe missionaries and warrior monks extended Christendom into previously pagan areas. In a process known as the *Reconquista*, Spain was recovered from the Islamic Moors after four centuries of conflict. And in the motives of men like Prince Henry the Navigator, organizer of the Portuguese exploration of Africa, the crusading outlook moved out into a wider world (see pp. 405 and 410).

In the mid-11th century, for the first time in European history, a series of popes placed themselves at the head of a radical reform movement – sometimes known as the Gregorian Reform, after the most controversial of these popes, Gregory VII (1073–85). The aim of the reformers was to abolish both the family life of the clergy and secular control of the Church. Not surprisingly they ran into fierce opposition from clergy who wanted to keep their wives and from secular rulers who wished to retain their traditional powers, notably the right to appoint and invest (i.e. ceremonially install bishops and abbots.

The siege of Antioch during the First Crusade. In June 1098 the city eventually fell to the Crusaders, who proceeded to massacre the Muslim population. This illustration is from the Chronicles of William of Tyre (late 12th century).

In time the reformers' struggle for what they called the 'freedom of the Church' – a struggle known as the *Investiture Contest* – was to produce some strange martyrs, above all St Thomas Becket, murdered in Canterbury Cathedral in 1170. But its immediate effect was to put the papacy at the storm centre of European politics and to create a new style of militant Christianity. Those warriors who took up their swords on the pope's behalf were promised the rewards of heaven.

The Crusades

No sermon has ever had greater impact than that delivered by Pope Urban II at Clermont in 1095. It set in motion the whole crusading movement. All that had been intended was to send some military assistance to the Byzantine Emperor, Alexius I, who was battling against Turkish nomads in Asia Minor. In the west, however, men believed that these Turks were making life intolerably difficult for pilgrims on their way to Jerusalem – the Holy City – and in consequence the response to Urban's preaching was on a totally unexpected scale. In 1096 several huge armies set out on the long march to Jerusalem. Their

Krak des Chevaliers, a Crusader castle in what is now Syria. The castle was built in the early 12th century to guard the eastern border of the County of Tripoli, one of the Christian states established by the Crusaders in the Near East.

intention was to free the Christian churches in the East and recapture the Holy City, which had been in Muslim hands since the 7th century.

Despite great difficulties the knights of the First Crusade took Jerusalem and established a handful of small states. These were vulnerable to Muslim counterattack and Saladin (?1137–93, sultan of Egypt and Syria) recaptured the Holy City in 1187. All military attempts to recover the city proved futile (see table) – even Richard the Lionheart failed. Only the diplomacy of Emperor Frederick II brought about its temporary recovery (1228–44).

For much of the 13th century the Crusaders held on to the coast of Syria and Palestine, but this too gradually fell into the hands of the powerful Mamluk sultans of Egypt. When the port of Acre fell in 1291 the Crusaders lost their last base in the Holy Land. In the 14th century, crusades were little more than raids. The last one, in 1396 – which took a French and Burgundian army as far as Nicopolis (on the Danube) – was ignominiously defeated by the Ottoman sultan.

Although the primary motive of most Crusaders was religious fervour, there was also a good deal of self-interested adventurism involved. At times quarrels broke out between the various European contingents. The Fourth Crusade never even reached the Holy Land. Instead, at the instigation of Venice, the Crusaders captured Christian Constantinople, the capital of the Byzantine Empire, Venice's rival in the eastern Mediterranean.

In the 13th century, crusades were mounted within Christendom, both against heretics (such as the Cathars in southern France; see p. 403) and against the papacy's political enemies, such as Emperor Frederick II. In the 15th century crusading became limited to Eastern Europe, against the Turks or the

PRINCIPAL CRUSADES AGAINST ISLAM

Crusade	Dates	Region	Principal leaders	Results
First	1096–99	Holy Land	Counts and dukes of France, Germany and southern Italy	Capture of Jerusalem and establishment of Crusader states
Second	1146–49	Holy Land	Louis VII, king of France (1137–80) Conrad III, German emperor (1138–52)	Failed siege of Damascus
Third	1189–92	Holy Land	Emperor Frederick I 'Barbarossa' (1152–90; died en route) Richard I 'the Lionheart', king of England (1189–99)	Capture of Acre, defeat of Saladin at Arsuf (1191), failure to take Jerusalem
Fourth	1200–4	Intended for Holy Land	Conrad, marquis of Montferrat Baldwin, count of Flanders Dandolo, doge of Venice	Capture of Constantinople and establishment of Latin empire of Constantinople (until 1260)
Fifth	1216–21	Egypt	Papal legate	Failed attack on Cairo
Sixth	1228	Holy Land	Emperor Frederick II (1215–50)	Recovery of Jerusalem by treaty (until 1244)
Seventh	1248–52	Egypt	Louis IX (St Louis), King of France (1226–70)	Failed attack on Cairo; all Crusade leaders captured

Hussite heretics of Bohemia – generally without success.

The Reconquista

In the Iberian Peninsula it was a different story. In the mid-11th century the small Christian kingdoms of northern Spain, principally Castile and Aragon, began to expand at the expense of the Muslim states that had long dominated their peninsula (see p. 392). In 1139 the kingdom of Portugal was founded but initially the progress of reconquest was by no means irreversible. On two occasions, in 1085 and 1145, Islam was reinforced by waves of Berber tribesmen from North Africa. They defeated Christian armies and briefly united the Muslims.

Towards the end of the 12th century, however, the tide was turning inexorably in favour of the Reconquista. The Castilian victory at Las Navas de Tolosa in 1212 set the seal on this process, and swift advances followed. By the mid-13th century Muslim rule was confined to the Emirate of Granada. This state survived until 1492, when it was finally snuffed out by the dual monarchy of Ferdinand of Aragon and Isabella of Castile (see p. 410).

The papal-imperial conflict

Although from 962 onwards the medieval emperors were German, they drew the bulk of their revenues from Italy. This led to tension with the papacy since for centuries the popes had been trying to establish a state of their own in central Italy. When the Hohenstaufen emperor, Henry VI (1190–97), conquered Sicily in 1194 it looked as though the encircled papal state was doomed. But Henry died in 1197 and the civil war that followed enabled Pope Innocent III (1198–1216) to rebuild the papal states. Yet Henry's descendants, notably Frederick II (1215–50), remained as dangerous neighbours until in 1268 the pope employed a French prince, Charles of Anjou, to defeat and kill the last Hohenstaufen.

Exile, schism and reform

Central Italy, however, was rarely at peace and early 14th-century popes decided to stay in the relative security of Avignon in France, even though this led to them being regarded as puppets of the French monarchy. It also upset many devout Christians who believed that the pope's place was in Rome. Ironically the papacy's return to Rome in 1377 was followed immediately by what the faithful regarded as an even greater scandal: the outbreak of what became known as the *Great Schism*. From 1378 until 1417 there were always either two or three men simultaneously claiming to be the rightful pope. At the same time reformist movements – Lollards in England and Hussites in Bohemia (see p. 403) – believing that the Church was corrupt, turned against a papal establishment that no longer had the will to reform. These currents of opinion were early signals of the Protestant Reformation that was to break out a century later (see p. 408).   MB

SEE ALSO

- THE RISE OF ISLAM p. 392
- THE SUCCESSORS OF ROME p. 394
- CRISIS IN EUROPE p. 402
- THE REFORMATION p. 408
- THE SPANISH AND PORTUGUESE EMPIRES p. 410

The momument to El Cid, at his burial place near Burgos, Spain. 'El Cid' ('the lord') was the name given to Rodrigo Díaz de Vivar (c.1043-99), whose role in fighting the Moors in Spain made him into a national hero. In fact, El Cid was also involved in fighting rival Spanish Christians, and at one point was even in the service of the Muslim ruler of Saragossa.

THE MILITARY ORDERS

The reformed papacy's call for knights to serve Christ and the pope led to the creation of a new type of warrior: the soldier monk. In 1128, St Bernard of Clairvaux (?1090–1153) devised a 'Rule' by which men might live as trained knights devoted to fighting a holy war, while simultaneously sharing the monastic obligations of poverty, chastity and obedience.

The first order to be created was the Knights Templar, named after the Temple of Solomon, their base in Jerusalem. Soon afterwards the Knights of St John, or Hospitallers, were converted from a purely medical to a military role. Both orders were predominantly French in composition. In imitation and competition German knights formed the Teutonic order, and Spain provided several other groups, such as the knights of Calatrava.

The military orders were the cutting edge of the Crusader states and on all the borders of Christendom. Donations of land in Europe gave them great wealth,

enabling them to carry out their military role. The Templars also became great bankers. But after the fall of Acre they were rich men without a cause. This proved too much of a temptation for Philip IV of France (see p. 400): in 1306 he had the Order of the Temple dissolved and profited from its riches.

The other orders survived and adapted to changed circumstances. The Teutonic Order returned to its homeland and headed the drive to the east into Slav lands, creating a Baltic empire in what later became Prussia. After playing a large part in the warfare and politics of Eastern Europe, they were defeated by the Poles at Tannenberg in 1410.

The Hospitallers established themselves on Rhodes. From there they harried Muslim coasts and shipping for two centuries. Chased off the island by the Turks in 1520, they defended Malta against the same enemy in 1565. There they survived, although with declining military significance, until overrun by Napoleon's forces on their way to Egypt in 1798.

The Hundred Years War

In the 14th and 15th centuries, rivalry between the kingdoms of France and England became the dominant political feature of northwestern Europe. From 1337 until 1453 the two states fought out an irregular succession of wars. At issue was the English king's claim to the French crown, as well as control of lands the English kings held in France. This conflict is known as the Hundred Years War.

During the course of the 13th century a series of powerful rulers belonging to the Capetian dynasty, Philip Augustus (1180–1223), Louis IX (St Louis, 1226–70), and Philip IV ('the Fair', 1285–1314), had made France the outstanding kingdom in Europe. They could raise taxes and muster armies on a grander scale than any other European ruler. Even so their success depended on the cooperation of the great and independent-minded nobles of France. These nobles owed allegiance to the king, shared in the profits of taxation and enjoyed wide-ranging rights of justice over their extensive lands. One of these nobles held the title 'duke of Aquitaine'. He was also the king of England.

The origins of the conflict

Ever since 1066, when the duke of Normandy took the English throne as William I (see p. 397), the Norman kings and their Plantagenet successors had continued to enjoy possession of huge territories in France. This straddling of the English Channel reached its height in the 12th century with Henry II, whose marriage to Eleanor of Aquitaine established a Plantagenet empire that incorporated most of western France. However, King John's incompetence meant that in a few years between 1203 and 1206 most of these territories were lost to Philip Augustus, and by the 1330s only Gascony (the southwest of Aquitaine) was still retained by the English king. Yet even these much-reduced dominions continued to provide ample cause for conflict.

As duke of Aquitaine the king of England owed formal allegiance to the French crown. Moreover his Gascon subjects were only too willing, whenever it suited their own private interests, to appeal from the duke's court to the court of the king of France.

Tension in the 1330s

What added spice to the long-standing wrangling between the two monarchies was that when the Capetian dynasty died out in the direct male line in 1328, then the Plantagenet Edward III (1327–77), as maternal grandson of Philip the Fair, had an excellent claim to the French throne. In fact, however, the crown passed to a nephew, Philip of Valois, who became Philip VI (1328–50). Soon the two kings were fighting a kind of border war, the initial phases of the struggle being confined to Scotland and Flanders.

From the 1290s, when Edward I of England had attempted to conquer Scotland, the Scots had found common cause with France in the 'Auld Alliance' against England. More significantly, the merchants and workers in the thriving Flemish cloth towns – Bruges, Ghent and Ypres – found themselves drawn by economic self-interest to the English side – for it was from England that they imported the raw material, wool, indispensable to their industrial prosperity. Yet the county of Flanders 'belonged' to France, and so they owed allegiance to Philip VI. It would therefore ease their consciences if Edward III proclaimed himself the true French king. At Ghent in January 1340 Edward duly assumed the title 'king of England and France', which was to be borne by his successors for nearly five centuries, until 1801.

The first phase: 1337–1360

Initially Edward's claim to the French crown may have been a bargaining counter by which he hoped to obtain French recognition of English sovereignty over Gascony. He built up an alliance with the towns and nobles of the

A battle between the Scots and English during the Hundred Years War. Scotland's 'Auld Alliance' with France against England began in the early 14th century, and was to continue until the mid-16th century. By and large the Alliance tended to work against the interests of the Scots, who found themselves encouraged into several disastrous military campaigns against their more powerful southern neighbours.

Low Countries (including Flanders), and took an army there in 1338–39. In 1340 an English naval victory at Sluys, off the Flemish coast, put an end to a threatened French invasion of England.

France was a much richer country than England, however, and at this stage the war was proving an immense strain on Edward's resources. Not until some Breton and Norman nobles deserted the Valois cause did the fortunes of the war on land begin to go Edward's way. In 1346 the main French army was routed by the firepower of English archers at Crécy. In 1347 Edward captured Calais, which was to remain an English possession until 1558. At the Battle of Poitiers, ten years after Crécy, the English archers, this time under the command of Edward, Prince of Wales (the 'Black Prince'), repeated their slaughter of the over-confident French knights. At Poitiers the French king, John II (1350–64), was taken prisoner, and after four years of ransom negotiations the French agreed at Brétigny to hand over no less than a third of the land of France in full sovereignty. In return Edward was to renounce his claim to the throne.

French recovery

But the Treaty of Brétigny was never quite ratified in full. Both sides preferred to leave loopholes that might be exploited later if opportunity arose. Meanwhile Edward rapidly occupied his new territories and created his eldest son 'prince of Aquitaine'. But the Black Prince's stern rule aggravated a number of the leading Gascon nobles and they appealed for help to the new king of France, Charles V (1364–80). In 1369 Edward formally resumed his French title and war broke out anew. Under the shrewd leadership of Charles V and of captains such as Bertrand du Guesclin, the French avoided pitched battles. Instead they settled down to use their greater resources in the piecemeal reconquest of territory. Generally the English found themselves outmanoeuvred and in 1396 the English king, Richard II (1377–99), was happy to agree to a 28-year truce.

Henry V and the Burgundian alliance

Charles VI of France (1380–1422) suffered recurrent bouts of mental illness. This unleashed a ferocious struggle for control between the dukes of Burgundy and Orléans, both of them representatives of junior branches of the royal house. Here was a situation which the English warrior-king, Henry V (1413–22), was ideally equipped to exploit. This marked the opening of the third phase of hostilities, and after his stunning victory at Agincourt in 1415 Henry launched a full-scale war of conquest.

On the French side things became even more chaotic when in 1419 the heir to the throne (the *dauphin*, later Charles VII) became implicated in the murder of Duke John 'the Fearless' of Burgundy on the bridge at Montereau. As a result John's son, Duke Philip 'the Good', determined to throw all his weight behind the English cause. Within a year of the murder at

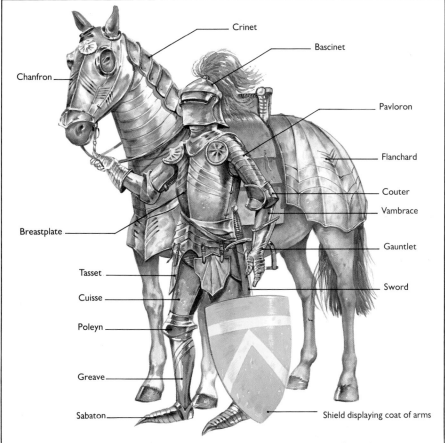

A 15th-century knight The main weapon used during charges would have been a lance. When riding into battle, a shield would probably not have been carried as the development of such effective plate armour had by this time made it superfluous.

Crinet
Bascinet
Chanfron
Pavloron
Flanchard
Couter
Vambrace
Breastplate
Gauntlet
Tasset
Sword
Cuisse
Poleyn
Greave
Sabaton
Shield displaying coat of arms

SEE ALSO
● THE INVASIONS p 396
● MEDIEVAL AND RENAISSANCE CULTURE p 406
● THE RISE OF BRITAIN p 412

Joan of Arc (below), the national heroine of France. Born the daughter of a peasant in around 1412, she claimed to have heard the voices of Saints Michael, Catherine and Margaret urging her to rid France of the English invaders. She led a French army that defeated the English at Orléans in 1429, enabling the French *dauphin* to be crowned as Charles VII. Captured by the English, Joan was burnt as a heretic in 1431. She was made a saint in 1920.

Montereau, Charles VI had agreed to name Henry V as his successor (the Treaty of Troyes). The Anglo-Burgundian regime took control of Paris and much of northern France. As it turned out, however, Henry V died two months before Charles VI.

Victory for France

In the early years of his reign Charles VII (1422–61) was confined to the lands south of the Loire (the kingdom of Bourges), but in 1429 a French revival, in part inspired by Joan of Arc, recaptured the initiative. By 1435 Duke Philip had swung back to the French royal side. For more than a decade the English held on stubbornly. Then suddenly, between 1450 and 1453, both Normandy and Gascony were lost forever.

From now on the monarchies of France and England, bound together in a troubled relationship since 1066, went their separate ways. In England the shock of the unexpected defeat led to civil war, with the Wars of the Roses (1455–85) between the houses of Lancaster and York. In France the monarchy garnered the rewards of victory, and of the reorganization of government that victory had entailed. Following the break-up of the Burgundian state after the death of Duke Charles 'the Bold' (1467–77), the French kings once again enjoyed unrivalled power in France.   MR/JG

Crisis in Europe

In the 14th century Europe was dealt a series of blows that made it the most calamitous century before our own. Early in the century appalling weather resulted in harvest failures and famine (1315–17). Then, in mid-century, bubonic plague – the Black Death – wiped out a significant proportion of the population; consequently demand for basic foodstuffs contracted sharply. For many landowners, accustomed to seeing their products eagerly sought after, this was a rude awakening.

In some regions the miseries of war added to the sense of confusion. Criticism of the Church, the appearance of new heresies and a series of popular uprisings all added to the fundamental challenges faced by medieval society.

The Black Death

Bubonic plague originated in the Far East, and was brought to Europe in 1346–47 by Italian merchant ships from the ports of the Crimea on the Black Sea. As well as Ukrainian grain they carried the rats whose fleas spread the disease. The plague spread rapidly from the Mediterranean ports, reaching southern England in 1348 (see map). Victims developed fever and hard black *buboes* (swollen lymph nodes in the groin and

Death strikes down all impartially in this symbolic representation of the Black Death from a 14th-century French church.

armpits). More than half of those infected died. The pneumonic strain affected the lungs and was spread by coughing, making it more virulent in winter when the bubonic form was less active. This strain, and the septicaemic variety – which attacked the bloodstream and brought death before symptoms could develop – were almost always fatal. Contemporary medicine knew no treatment for the terrifying affliction.

Death rates are difficult to calculate. In some pockets mortality was light, while small parts of southwest France, Flanders and northern Italy, and most of Silesia and Poland escaped the Black Death altogether. Elsewhere it is accepted that one third of the population perished in the 1348–49 epidemic. Recovery from even this severe blow might have been quick had it not been for recurrent epidemics in the 1360s and 70s. These attacked children in particular and so the future breeding stock was reduced. An age of population decline set in and plague became a fact of European life for more than three centuries.

Economic and psychological effects

The first onslaught of the Black Death was followed by labour shortages and disruption of production. Wages and prices both rose sharply. In England the government panicked and passed laws, such as the Statute of Labourers (1351), designed to freeze wages. However, there was a rapid recovery in the next few years.

While unproductive marginal fields were abandoned there was no shortage of takers for vacant tenancies, an indication of overpopulation on the eve of the pestilence. Long-term effects were more marked. Consumption and production of basic foodstuffs declined as the population did. Within a few decades acute labour shortages meant that serfdom (see p. 404) had to be abandoned and that real wages for rural labourers reached levels unmatched for centuries to come. For the surviving peasantry the plague was thus a blessing, inaugurating a golden age of improved conditions and relative plenty.

The immediate psychological effect of the Black Death was to encourage survivors to live for the day. When it became clear that this was not the end of the world there were varied reactions. Some blamed the Jews, while others took to self-flagellation to mollify the anger of God. The ever-present threat of pestilence may be responsible for a mood of pessimism in the literature and art of the period. The plague was no respecter of rank. The Church suffered heavily, a consequence of its duties to the sick. The rich derived some protection from their better living conditions, but princes and great lords died of the plague as well as the poor.

War and taxation

Warfare in the 14th and 15th centuries was more widespread and intensive than

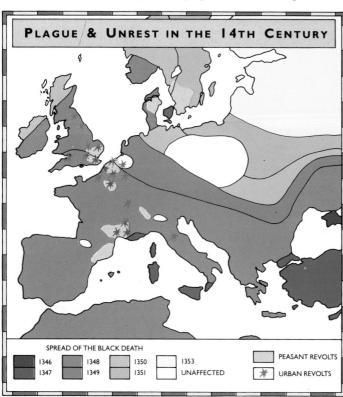

PLAGUE & UNREST IN THE 14TH CENTURY

SPREAD OF THE BLACK DEATH

1346	1348	1350	1353
1347	1349	1351	UNAFFECTED

PEASANT REVOLTS

URBAN REVOLTS

n the previous two centuries. The Hun-red Years War (see p. 400) involved cotland and Spain as well as France and England. In the 15th century Turkish advances turned southeast Europe into a one of near permanent war (see pp. 393 nd 395).

he brunt of medieval warfare was born y civilians. Medieval armies obtained heir supplies by plundering, and the assage of such an army through a istrict often meant famine. Where war-are became static, as along the borders of English-held Normandy and Gascony rom the 1420s until the 1450s, uncul-ivated deserts were created. In times of eace unemployed soldiers continued to perate by plundering, now on their own ccounts.

The costs of wages, armour, artillery and ortifications made war increasingly bur-densome to the tax-paying population. Even successful kings like Charles V of France could overstretch the willingness of their subjects to pay for their wars. Aggressive wars fought on foreign soil could be profitable as well as prestigious – as Edward III and Henry V of England showed – but failure in war always brought political instability in its train.

Popular revolts

Economic change and the burdens of warfare inspired widespread challenges o authority. In Flemish and Italian towns clothworkers had economic grievances against their masters and wanted a greater say in government. The popular French revolt of 1358 followed the humili-ating defeat of the French aristocracy at the Battle of Poitiers (see p. 401). This revolt was known as the Jacquerie, after the contemptuous name 'Jacques Bon-homme' given to French peasants. The Peasants' Revolt in England (1381) was sparked off by the weight of taxation at a time when the Hundred Years War was going badly for the English. Its deep-rooted cause, however, was anger at the government's attempts to keep wages at pre-plague levels and to prevent men moving to lords offering better terms. Although these and similar revolts else-where in Europe were suppressed, in the long run the authorities found the pressure of changed economic circum-stances harder to resist.

Anticlericalism and heresy

The wealth and worldliness of the Church attracted criticism from those who believed in a simpler and more devout way of life. Many ecclesiastics and laymen satisfied their desires for a purer life within the limits of the Church. Criticism was not incompatible with orthodoxy. English legislation in the mid-14th century to limit papal interference was based more on a notion that 'the pope has become a Frenchman' – the popes at this time were resident in Avignon (see p. 399). Demands that the Church be stripped of its land were often inspired by a feeling that it did not pay its share of taxation. The authority and repute of the Church was further undermined by the Great

Schism of 1378–1417, which saw first two, then three concurrent popes (see p. 399).

Some critics transgressed into heresy. The alternative Cathar (or Albigensian) Church in southern France had been broken in the 13th century by crusades and persecution. During the Great Schism two new heresies surfaced. In England the Oxford theologian John Wyclif (?1330–84) based his criticism on a fundamentalist study of Scripture, re-jecting the authority of the papacy and the doctrine of transubstantiation in the Eucharist (see p. 474). His ideas were condemned but found favour with a few knights of Richard II's court, and they protected Wyclif's followers, who were insultingly known as 'Lollards'. Only in 1401 were severe penalties prescribed for these English heretics. The reaction became hysterical when in 1414 Sir John Oldcastle organized an abortive plot to murder Henry V. The Lollards were only a tiny minority and Oldcastle's treason robbed them of their remaining support among the ruling classes. Despite perse-cution, however, they survived until the next century and the Reformation (see p. 408).

The Czech scholar Jan Hus (?1372–1415) shared some of Wyclif's ideas – indeed Hussites and Lollards corresponded – and rejected the authority of the Church. He

was condemned and burned in 1415, but his ideas became far more of a threat than Wyclif's owing to their connection with Bohemian nationalism. Under the able command of John Zizka the Hussites defeated crusaders from Germany, Aus-tria and Hungary. Their resistance ended only in 1436 after a compact that recog-nized both their distinctive beliefs and the fact that many nobles had used the troubles to get their hands on Church estates.

A century of calamities?

It is important not to exaggerate the effect of the 14th-century crisis. It has already been said that life may have been better for the survivors of the shocks of the 14th century. They almost certainly enjoyed a more varied diet; this was because farmers, faced by a declining demand for grain as the numbers of mouths fell, grew vegetables instead, or turned to livestock. In the wake of natural and man-made calamities European society was to show great powers of recovery in the 15th century – the century of the printing press and of overseas exploration and expansion (see p. 404).

NH

The burning of Jan Hus. Hus was lured to appear before a Church council at Constance under the promise of safe conduct. However, he was put on trial for heresy and convicted. Eyewitnesses recalled how he prayed loudly at the stake until the smoke choked him.

SEE ALSO

● CHRISTIANITY RESURGENT p. 398
● THE HUNDRED YEARS WAR p. 400
● MEDIEVAL AND RENAIS-SANCE ECONOMY AND SOCIETY p. 404
● MEDIEVAL AND RENAIS-SANCE CULTURE p. 406
● THE REFORMATION p. 408

Medieval and Renaissance Economy and Society

The medieval world was essentially a rural one. It depended on a hard-working peasantry, fair weather and good harvests. At first, in the centuries after the fall of Rome, both people and money were in short supply. There then followed a long period of economic, commercial and population growth. This growth was slow at first – in the 9th and 10th centuries – but then accelerated through the 12th and 13th centuries. The catastrophe of the Black Death brought a century of uncertainty before expansion was resumed in the later 15th century.

Even though the population of Europe in 1600 may have been no greater than in 1300, the basic fact remains that for most of the Middle Ages the population of Europe was a growing one. This meant pressure to bring more land into cultivation and to improve the processing and distribution of basic necessities: food, fuel and clothing. Water mills proliferated, and in the 12th century a new invention, the windmill, provided a supplementary source of power. Bulk-carrying ships were developed and, on land, improved harness design enabled the much faster horse cart to replace the ox cart.

Slaves, serfs and freemen

Throughout these centuries the greater part of the work was done by small tenant farmers (i.e. peasants) and their servants – though initially, as in the ancient world, slave labour was employed on many estates. By 1200, however, slavery and the slave trade had both died out in Europe north of the Alps. Some tenants were obliged by the terms of their tenure to work their lord's land as well as their own; those whose obligations were particularly burdensome tended to be called *serfs* or *villeins*, and after the demise of slavery it was these men who were regarded as 'unfree'. Then the long period of labour shortage following the Black Death in the 14th century (see p. 402) led to the end of serfdom. From then on virtually all tenants either owed a share of their harvest or a money rent; as the volume of coinage in circulation increased, the latter became more common. Thus in northwestern Europe the Middle Ages witnessed the end of both slavery and serfdom – two important moments in the history of liberty.

The 'feudal system'

Most of Europe was dominated by landlords throughout these centuries. Small local landlords owed rent or service or both to greater landlords, and so on all the way up the social hierarchy to the ruler. At each level tenants owed the kind of service – financial, administrative or military – appropriate to their status. Thus tenants of knightly status might be expected to perform 'knight service' in return for *fiefs*, estates granted them by their lords. Historians have often called this kind of society 'feudal' – from the latin *feudum* meaning a fief – though neither the word nor the concept 'feudal' existed in the Middle Ages.

Moreover the 'feudal system' was not a static one. From the 12th and 13th centuries onwards lords increasingly secured men's service by paying them in cash. At the same time the demand for administrators rose sharply – for men who were both literate and numerate. To meet this demand schools were founded all over Europe (see p. 406). For men who gave their lords good service there were plenty of opportunities to rise in the world.

Town life

From the 11th century onwards a rising population led to a massive growth in the number and size of towns throughout Europe, most of them functioning principally as local markets. Most towns were small by today's standards – though by 1300 London may have had a population of 100 000 and Paris twice as many.

Townspeople struggled to win certain freedoms, notably the right to supervise their own markets and to elect their own magistrates. Successful towns obtained charters from the king – in England and Scotland such towns became known as *boroughs*. A characteristic feature of towns everywhere was the existence within them of a number of associations and clubs, known variously to contemporaries as *guilds*, *fraternities*, *companies* or *crafts*. Some of them were based on particular trades or crafts and were responsible for regulating their members' economic activities, but they also performed a wide range of social, religious and charitable functions.

In the more urbanized parts of Europe many towns – such as Milan, Florence, Cologne and Bruges – were able to become *communes*, self-governing municipalities capable of independent political action. This was particularly so in northern Italy where a fiercely competitive society of rival city-states, not unlike the society of Classical Greece (see p. 370), had emerged by the 13th century. This was the seedbed of the Italian Renaissance.

The commercial revolution

By the 13th century Italian businessmen had developed a sophisticated system of credit finance and were acting as international bankers. These facilities helped to make Italy the hub of international trade. Venice, Pisa and Genoa fought each other for control of the highly lucrative commerce of the Mediterranean. Italian merchants like Marco Polo's father travelled overland to China, but it was to be the increasing volume of seaborne trade between the Mediterranean and Northern Europe that led to the crucial improvements in ship design (see p. 342) that made possible the voyages of discovery (see opposite).   JG

An agricultural scene in the early 16th century. This painting depicting July is one of a series of the 12 months attributed to the school of Master Bering of Bruges.

SEE ALSO

● CRISIS IN EUROPE p. 402
● MEDIEVAL AND RENAIS-
  SANCE CULTURE p. 406
● THE SPANISH AND PORTU-
  GUESE EMPIRES p. 410

Marco Polo (c. 1254–1324)
Trade between Europe and China along the Silk Route (see p. 383) had long been established, and in 1260–69 Marco Polo's father and uncle made a trading expedition there. Marco Polo accompanied them on their second expedition, reaching China in 1275. There he entered the service of the emperor, Kublai Khan, and remained in China until 1292.

Prince Henry the Navigator (1394–1460)
Son of John I of Portugal, Henry was the leading patron of Portuguese exploration in the early 15th century. By his death his ships had discovered the Cape Verde Islands, and advanced down the west coast of Africa as far as Sierra Leone.

Zheng He (or Cheng Ho; died c. 1433)
In the early 15th century China was also expanding its horizons and Admiral Zheng He led several expeditions to India, Arabia and the coast of East Africa. At this point, however, the Chinese government decided against further exploration.

Bartolomeu Dias (?1450–1500)
In 1488 the Portuguese navigator Bartolomeu Dias rounded the Cape of Good Hope and could report that a sea route to the spices and other wealth of the East now lay open.

Vasco da Gama (1469–1524)
Setting out from Portugal in 1497, da Gama followed a slightly different course to that of Dias and reached Calicut on the southwest coast of India, returning home in 1499. The route from Portugal to the East was now confirmed.

Christopher Columbus (1451–1506)
Because the Italian navigator Christopher Columbus believed that the world was much smaller than it is, he was confident that he could reach the East by sailing west. It had been known for centuries that the world is round, but for a long time Columbus' schemes were rejected by experts who had a much more accurate idea of the actual size of the globe. Not until 1492 was he given the backing of the Spanish Crown. His flotilla of three ships led by the *Santa Maria* reached the Bahamas in 33 days. On subsequent voyages Columbus reached the American mainland. He died still convinced, however, that he had reached the East, or the Indies, hence the name 'West Indies'.

John Cabot (c. 1450–?98)
An Italian navigator in the service of Henry VII of England, Cabot discovered Cape Breton Island in 1497, and is sometimes credited with the discovery of North America – though the Vikings had reached there, via Iceland and Greenland, five hundred years earlier.

Ferdinand Magellan (c. 1480–1521)
A Portuguese navigator sponsored by Spain, in 1519 Magellan set off with five ships to seek a western route to the East Indies. He negotiated the strait named after him between Tierra del Fuego and the South American mainland. The expedition crossed the Pacific and reached the East Indies in 1521, where Magellan was killed. Only one ship returned to Spain in 1522, so completing the first circumnavigation of the world.

The first landing of Columbus in the New World. On 12 October 1492 he landed on San Salvador Island in the Bahamas, and is so credited with the discovery of America. So convinced was Columbus that he would reach Asia that he took along a man who spoke some Arabic, in case they met the 'grand Khan'. Even when he reached the West Indies, Columbus continued to sail in search of Japan – which he thought he had found when he discovered Cuba.

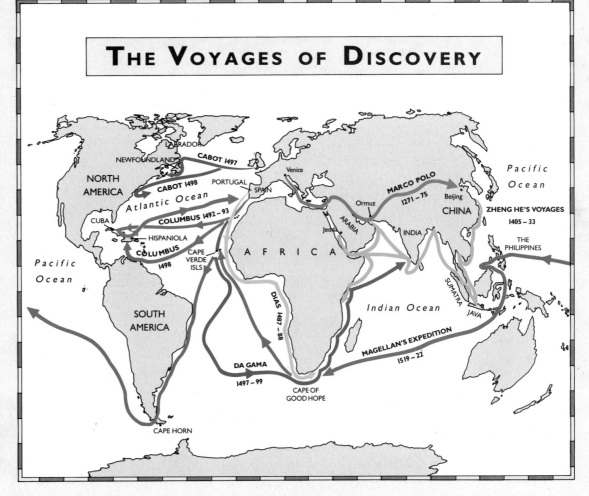

THE VOYAGES OF DISCOVERY

Medieval and Renaissance Culture

After the fall of the western Roman Empire, people in Western Europe gradually lost touch with the centres of culture in the eastern Mediterranean. Much of the learning of the ancient world was lost. What survived the 'Dark Ages' – the 7th to 10th centuries – did so because it was preserved in monasteries. For centuries formal education was not much more than a by-product of religion.

The medieval nobleman was expected to be able to play chess as well as he could fight, hunt, dance and play music. This scene shows Otto IV of Brandenburg (1266-1309) with a lady.

In the 12th and 13th centuries all that changed. Through a variety of channels, classical learning (in philosophy, law and the sciences) was recovered. Schools and universities, medical schools and hospitals (see p. 248) were founded. At the same time there was a new architecture – Gothic (see p. 522) – and a remarkable flowering of vernacular literature (see pp. 618–21). In the most urbanized region in Europe – northern Italy – a rather different style took root, and by the 16th century Renaissance Italy was setting the fashion for the rest of Europe, a development assisted by a powerful new invention: the printing press.

The monastic centuries

Christianity was adopted as the official religion of the Roman Empire in the 4th century AD, and Christians found that they had become part of the imperial establishment – an experience which was not to the liking of all of them. Many preferred to turn their backs on the material comforts and pleasures that society now offered. In Egypt and Syria – the most urbanized and prosperous parts of the Roman world – so many followed this course that hundreds of new communities dedicated to religious self-denial were established, often in the desert. These were the first monasteries. During the 5th and 6th centuries this style of religious life caught on in the West, and while the Roman cultural world collapsed, monasteries survived, islands of stability, quiet, and traditional learning.

For four or five hundred years there were few men (except in Italy, where there always seem to have been town schools) who learned to read and write anywhere but in a monastery school. Moreover, the accumulation of pious gifts over the centuries meant that many monasteries became great landowning corporations, and could afford to employ the finest builders, sculptors and artists. In these circumstances it was probably inevitable that early medieval culture should come to have a distinctly ecclesiastical tinge.

Schools and universities

By the 12th century Western Europe was a more populous and more complex society (see p. 404). All over Europe, teachers began to set up new schools, including some in quite small towns and villages. The 'lost' learning of the ancient world was translated out of Arabic into Latin and so made generally available to European scholars (see p. 393).

It was in this receptive and expansionist educational environment that the earliest universities – Paris, Bologna and Oxford – were established (by around 1200), and they set a trend that was to last for centuries. By 1500 more than 70 more universities had been founded, among them Cambridge, Prague, Heidelberg and St Andrews. Most students were *clerks* – in other words, they were nominally churchmen. Relatively few, however, chose to become theologians or parish priests. Most studied for the 'arts' degree; of those who went on to take a higher degree most chose one of what were known as the 'lucrative sciences' – law or medicine. Their ambitions were professional and worldly.

Chivalry and secular culture

Outside the Church there had always of course been another culture – even in the 'Dark Ages'. The Church might have been a rich patron, but the nobles were even richer. However, in the early Middle Ages the culture of the European aristocracy was essentially an illiterate one. Except in Anglo-Saxon England, its ideas and values were rarely fixed in writing and in consequence we know little about them.

But the vernacular literature of the 12th and 13th centuries throws a whole new flood of light on the upper levels of secular society. It shows us the world of chivalry – a society that valued knightly prowess, courage, loyalty, generosity and courtesy (particularly when in the company of ladies). It was a very courtly world. The ideal nobleman was expected not only to be a warrior and huntsman, but also a fine musician, a graceful dancer, an eloquent and shrewd speaker in several languages, and to possess polished manners. The idea of the all-round 'Renaissance man', embodied in *The Book of the Courtier* by Baldassare Castiglione (1478-1529), had in fact been around long before the Renaissance, and one of the reasons for the book's success across Europe was that it was preaching – and with rare eloquence – to an audience that had been converted for centuries.

In the 12th and 13th centuries it became normal for members of the upper classes – gentry as well as business people, women as well as men – to be able to read. Many of them employed clerks to do their writing for them, just as businessmen today employ secretaries. By the 15th century a reading public existed that was large enough to absorb the enormous increase in books produced by the new printing presses (see below).

Humanism and the Renaissance

In the 14th century, the Italian poet Petrarch (1304–74) inspired a new kind of enthusiasm for the writings of ancient Greece and Rome – an enthusiasm for their style as well as for their content. Following this lead, a diverse group of scholars, known as the *humanists*, came to regard classical texts as models for public speaking, writing and conduct. Initially based in northern Italy, by 1500 humanist ideas began to spread to northern Europe, where Erasmus (see below) was the most important scholar.

Because the humanists laid weight on being able to speak and write like the Roman orator and writer Cicero, this tended to make them contemptuous of all those who had not even tried to do so. Thus they popularized the idea of the 'Dark Ages', a period of supposed barbarism stretching between the ancient world and their own time.

Undoubtedly their enthusiasm for antiquity led them to discover previously unknown classical texts, notably some works by the Greek philosopher Plato. By translating such texts into Latin – for knowledge of Greek remained rare throughout the Renaissance – they made them more widely available. Whether their enthusiasm for classical models led them to a new or 'modern' view of the world and of man's place within it, is a question that historians still debate. In 15th-century Florence, humanist language was used to encourage active citizenship and loyalty to the state – but these were qualities of which rulers everywhere approved. Although humanism did not involve a rejection of Christian doctrine, it did undoubtedly focus on man's – as opposed to God's – role in the world, but so also did the 'old-fashioned' secular ideals of chivalry and good lordship.

The importance of printing

In 1450 the first printing press was set up at Mainz in Germany by Johannes Gutenberg (?1398–1468; see p. 322). The new technique spread rapidly, particularly in the urbanized regions: 90% of European book production before 1500 was concentrated in Italy and the Rhineland. In 1475 William Caxton (c. 1422–91) introduced the technique into England. Printing – pictures as well as words – meant that writers could reach a much larger international audience than ever before.

When the Florentine, Niccolò Machiavelli (1469-1527), argued in his book *The Prince* that the need to ensure the survival of the state justified acts that otherwise might be regarded as immoral, he was not doing much more than laying bare the way governments had always acted – but in the new world of the printed book this was enough to make his name synonymous with duplicity. More importantly, when the Dutch scholar Desiderius Erasmus (1466–1536) edited the Greek New Testament, and when in letters and tracts such as *In Praise of Folly* he called for Church reform, his words, now in print, reached minds and hearts that earlier writers had failed to reach. This anticipated the way in which printing was to play a crucial role in the spread of the Reformation (see p. 408). JG

A 15th-century joust in an Italian town. By this time the joust had largely superseded the *mêlée* – a mock battle involving many horsemen. Up until the end of the 13th century, the contestants often used unblunted swords and lances, and death or serious injury was not unusual. (National Gallery, London)

WAR AND FORTIFICATION

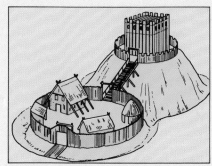

11th century: motte and bailey

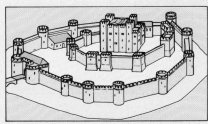

12th–13th centuries: stone castle

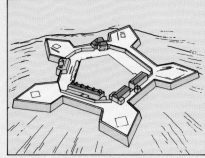

14th century onwards: bastion

SEE ALSO

● THE HISTORY OF SCIENCE
  p. 60
● THE HISTORY OF MEDICINE
  p. 248
● PRINTING p. 322
● MEDIEVAL AND RENAIS
  SANCE ECONOMY AND
  SOCIETY p. 404
● THE REFORMATION p. 408
● MEDIEVAL AND RENAIS
  SANCE ART AND ARCHITEC
  TURE pp. 518-29
● PLAINSONG AND POLY
  PHONY p. 570
● DANCE pp. 592-5
● MEDIEVAL AND RENAIS
  SANCE LITERATURE
  pp. 620-5

Chivalry was a code of conduct that laid down how men were expected to behave when at court or when jousting. However, when at war the leaders of the cult of chivalry were as professional and ruthless as soldiers anywhere. They had no 'chivalrous' objections to the use of new weapons, such as the 12th-century crossbow and 14th-century gun.

Throughout this period battles were rare and war largely revolved around control of strongpoints, castles or towns. Thus an important aspect of the great rebuilding

that took place in the 12th and 13th centuries was the replacement of basic earthwork and timber fortifications (including the motte-and-bailey castle) by vastly more expensive stone walls. High stone walls and towers were designed to counter the high-trajectory siege catapults of the period.

But from the 1370s onwards the advent of effective siege guns – capable of delivering a massive horizontal blow – presented military architects with a new problem. Their solution was the bastion. It was low,

and was built of rubble and brick so that it absorbed cannon shot, instead of fracturing on impact as stone did. Above all it was itself a gun platform, enabling the defenders to hit back at any attacker.

Everywhere in Europe – though rarely in Britain – the old town defences were pulled down and a new wide ring of bastions built. Every European city from the Baltic to North Africa took on a new appearance, and wherever Europeans settled overseas, from Havana to Goa, they built towns on this new plan.

The Reformation

The Reformation was the outcome of dissatisfaction with abuses within the Roman Catholic Church, and also with the role of the clergy and with the direction of the Church. The close link which often developed between Protestant reformers and secular rulers resulted in the development of national churches and the appropriation of Church property. The publication of the Bible in various national languages was also a very important effect of the Reformation.

The success of the reformers transformed the Catholic Church. From the late 16th century a revitalized Catholic Church was making great efforts to recover lost ground. However, the success of the Counter-Reformation depended ultimately on the power of Catholic rulers. They made a determined effort to turn the clock back in the early 17th century, but with only partial success. Protestantism for its part had lost much of its dynamism by 1650 – but had survived.

The background

The desire for reform was not new. The weakness of the papacy in the late 14th and early 15th centuries had stimulated the progress of Lollardy in England and Hussitism in Bohemia, both of which anticipated the Protestant Reformation (see p. 403). However, their success was limited and the late 15th century saw a revival of papal authority.

The popes had St Peter's rebuilt (see p. 528) so that Rome should be a fitting capital, and they paid for this and other projects by exploiting their headship of the Church to raise money throughout Europe. They sold indulgences (remissions of the penance imposed on confessed sinners), dispensations and cardinalships, and at the same time resisted calls for reform in an increasingly corrupt and secular Church. In Germany this provoked a strong anti-Italian feeling based on the belief that the papacy was extorting great sums from the Germans.

The humanists' new scholarly work on the texts of the Bible (see p. 407) drew attention to the great gulf between the early and contemporary Church, and gave added strength to the growing hostility to the clergy and the papacy. The invention of printing played a crucial role in the spread of the ideas both of the humanists and of the new reformers (see p. 407).

Martin Luther and Protestantism

In 1517 Martin Luther (1483–1547), a German monk and theologian, published his opposition to indulgences and other abuses in the Church. Attempts to silence him only clarified his ideas. Luther believed that the foundation of all faith must be the Bible, and that all people should have access to it, not just those who understood Latin. Those religious doctrines and practices not founded in Scripture, such as monastic orders and the cult of Mary and the saints, he regarded as abuses; only faith in God brought salvation. Luther also denied the special status of the clergy administering the sacraments: to him the priesthood comprised all true believers, and each believer stood alone and equal before God. Following his excommunication in 1520 Luther rejected papal authority.

Luther's protest, spread by the new printing presses and by preachers, was popular in Germany. The poor thought it meant freedom from some of their burdens. However, Luther urged the brutal suppression of the Peasants' Revolt (1525) by the German princes, whom he needed to defend the Reformation against the hostility of Charles V, the Holy Roman Emperor. Yet Charles's commitments elsewhere prevented him from having time or strength enough to root out Protestantism in Germany. In 1555 he had to agree to the Peace of Augsburg, which allowed each prince, Lutheran or Catholic, to decide the religion of his subjects.

By that time Lutheran Churches had been established in a number of states in Germany, and in Sweden and Denmark, while the new state Church emerging in England (see p. 412) was influenced by Lutheran doctrines. A number of rulers ordered Reformation in their states because they profited from the seizure of Church property, and increased their

The St Bartholomew's Day Massacre of French Protestants, 1572. The massacre was ordered by the French queen mother, Catherine de' Medici. Some 3000 Protestants were killed in Paris, and many more in the provinces. This event was just one of the many atrocities carried out by both Protestants and Catholics in the turbulent century following the Reformation.

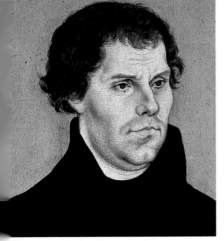

Martin Luther, painted by Lucas Cranach (see p. 527) in 1526. Luther made public his criticisms of the Roman Catholic Church in 1517, when he nailed his 'Ninety-five Theses' to the church door at Wittenberg. The main statement of belief of the Lutheran Churches, the 1530 Augsburg Confession, was in fact drawn up by Philip Melanchthon (1497–1560), who took over the leadership of the German Reformation from Luther.

authority by creating a clergy subject to them and not to Rome.

Calvin and Calvinism

Reform was also effected in Zürich by Ulrich Zwingli (1484–1531). But the most influential of the other reformers was John Calvin (1509–56), a French lawyer. Calvin, like Luther, based his ideas firmly on Scripture, but went beyond Luther in believing that salvation was predestined or determined by God. He also went further than Luther in rejecting religious ceremonial and imagery.

Calvin reformed both the Church and the government of Geneva, ensuring a closer link between the two and a greater supervision of the religious and moral life of its citizens. Geneva provided a model for Calvinists, who in the late 16th century took the lead in the reform movement. However, their different beliefs often meant conflict with Lutherans as well as with Catholics.

In Scotland, a successful revolt against the Catholic Mary Queen of Scots was followed by reform of the Church on Calvinist lines by John Knox (?1514–72). In France the Huguenots (as French Calvinists were known) became involved in the rivalries of the noble factions in the French Wars of Religion (1559–98). The strength of the Huguenots fell considerably after the St Bartholomew's Day Massacre of their leaders (1572). Yet they were strong enough to obtain toleration in 1598 under the Edict of Nantes.

Calvinist resistance contributed to the success of the Dutch revolt against Philip II (see p. 411), a Calvinist Church being set up in the Dutch Republic. Calvinist Churches were also established in Bohemia, Hungary, Poland, and parts of Germany (where Calvinism was not included in the settlement of 1555). Not surprisingly, Calvinism was associated with rebellion.

The Counter-Reformation

The success of the Reformation increased the pressure for a council to reform the Roman Catholic Church from within. Such a council was indeed established, and met at Trent between 1541 and 1563.

Yet the Council of Trent made few concessions to Protestant criticisms. Instead it restated traditional doctrine regarding the sacraments, the Bible and papal supremacy. It also declared that Catholics should be better instructed in their faith, and provided for a trained clergy to do this.

The Council was followed by a great missionary effort to recover the areas lost to Protestantism. A leading part in this was played by the Jesuits (the Society of Jesus), founded by a Spaniard, Ignatius Loyola (1491–1556). The Jesuits were distinguished both as missionaries in Europe, America and Asia, and as teachers in their European colleges. As royal confessors they urged Catholic rulers to ignore Protestant rights as a limitation on their power.

This reflected the dependence of the Counter-Reformation on the support of monarchs such as Mary of England (1553–58), who tried to recatholicize her kingdom (see p. 412), and Philip II of Spain (see p. 411).

In Spain, as elsewhere in Catholic Europe, the Inquisition investigated suspected heretics, passing serious offenders to the secular authorities for punishment. It also enforced the 'Index' of books whose content was regarded as heretical and not to be read by Catholics. The Index was constantly revised, and was not abandoned until 1966.

The Thirty Years War

The religious tensions that had built up over the previous 60 years or more finally erupted in a complex series of struggles known as the Thirty Years War.

The war began with a revolt in 1618 in Bohemia against the anti-Protestant and centralizing policies of the Austrian Habsburg emperor, Ferdinand II. By 1620 this revolt had been crushed, but the struggle quickly became entangled with wider European conflicts.

Spain, the ally of the Austrian Habsburgs, resumed its war with the Dutch in 1621. During the course of the war the Spanish occupied the Palatinate – in western Germany – whose ruler had led the Bohemian revolt. By 1629 Habsburg power seemed dominant in Germany, and in that year Ferdinand II attempted to reimpose the religious settlement of 1555, thus ending the unofficial toleration of Calvinism. Fear of Habsburg and Catholic power led Gustavus Adolphus, king of Sweden (1611–32), to invade Germany in 1630. After some brilliant successes he was killed at the battle of Lützen in 1632.

The war was now becoming an essentially political struggle, especially with the entry of France, the greatest anti-Habsburg power, in 1635. The growing difficulties of both the Spanish and Austrian Habsburgs led in 1648 to the Peace of Westphalia, which confirmed the

THE EUROPEAN WITCH CRAZE

The fierce religious struggles of the Reformation stimulated even further the growing obsession with witchcraft. Witchcraft – defined as making a pact with the devil to obtain magic powers – was first declared a heresy in 1484 by Pope Innocent VIII, who appointed two inquisitors to stamp it out in Germany.

Between about 1580 and 1650 the number of witch trials rocketed throughout western Europe. Both Roman Catholic and Protestant theologians identified witchcraft with active heresy. Indeed witchhunts were used by Calvinists in Scotland in the 1590s and Catholics in Poland from the 1650s to purge their opponents. In Catholic countries where there was no real Protestant threat the Inquisition's witchcraft cases were often no more than efforts to stamp out superstitions such as the use of love potions.

The witch craze died down in western Europe from about 1650 as fierce religious warfare ended and Protestant and Counter-Reformation teaching eradicated pre-Christian beliefs. However, persecution of suspected witches was by no means over: 19 people were executed in Massachusetts in 1692 following the infamous Salem witchcraft trials.

Three German witches being burnt alive in 1555.

1555 Augsburg settlement, and now included the Calvinists.

In parts of Germany up to a third – and in a few areas up to two thirds – of the population may have died during the war, mainly through disease and famine brought about by economic disruption. The struggle between France and Spain went on until 1659, but the age of religious, or partly religious, wars was over. The religious divisions of Europe (see map) were now fixed essentially as they are today.　　　　　　　　　CS

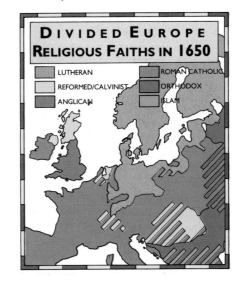

DIVIDED EUROPE
RELIGIOUS FAITHS IN 1650

◼ LUTHERAN   ◼ ROMAN CATHOLIC
◻ REFORMED/CALVINIST   ◼ ORTHODOX
◼ ANGLICAN   ◻ ISLAM

SEE ALSO

● CHRISTIANITY RESURGENT p. 396
● CRISIS IN EUROPE p. 402
● MEDIEVAL AND RENAISSANCE CULTURE p. 406
● THE SPANISH AND PORTUGUESE EMPIRES p. 410
● THE RISE OF BRITAIN p. 412
● WORLD CHRISTIANITY p. 476

The Spanish and Portuguese Empires

The 16th century saw the creation of the first large colonial empires by European powers. The empires of Spain and Portugal resulted from their sponsorship of the great voyages of discovery (see p. 405). In the case of Spain its empire would not have been created without the achievement of political unity at home. This came about in 1469, when Isabella of Castile married Ferdinand of Aragon. With his support she restored order and royal authority in Castile. In 1492 they completed the conquest of the Moorish kingdom of Granada, bringing to a conclusion the Reconquista, the reconquest of Islamic Spain (see p. 399).

The achievement of Ferdinand and Isabella rested on the cooperation of their two realms. Aragon feared being swallowed up by the far richer Castile and made little contribution to Spain's subsequent greatness. Yet the union was held together, first by Ferdinand and Isabella, and then from 1516 by the Habsburgs, initially in the person of Charles V. Charles inherited both realms and was also elected Holy Roman Emperor in 1519. Spain's incorporation into the Habsburg Empire offered it the opportunity to use its own resources and those of its American empire on a wider stage. Spain assumed the role of leading power in Europe until well into the 17th century.

Spain and Portugal divide the world

Following Columbus's successful voyage of 1492, Isabella needed to establish her right to colonize the Americas. After arbitration by the pope, Spain and Portugal came to an agreement at the Treaty of Tordesillas in 1493. All lands west of an imaginary north-to-south line drawn 370 leagues west of the Azores and Cape Verde Islands were to go to Spain, and all those east of it to Portugal. The result of this was that Portugal got Brazil, and Spain virtually all of the rest of South and Central America, and even parts of North America.

The Spanish impact on native life

Before settlement of the Americas could begin, the existing native empires (see p. 390) had to be subdued. This was the achievement of the conquistadores. In a short time and against vastly greater numbers – but aided by an overwhelming technological superiority – Cortez overthrew the Aztec empire in Mexico (1519–21), Alvardo conquered the Mayas in Yucatán (1524), and Pizarro subdued the Inca empire in Peru (1531–33).

Spanish colonization accelerated, and the native Indians were subjected to a colonial administration headed by two viceroys – in Mexico and Peru – responsible to the king in Spain. The Indians were obliged to work on the Spaniards' lands and in the gold and silver mines. The Spanish missionaries destroyed the Indians' temples and idols, established mission churches, and began a process of wholesale, sometimes forcible, conversion. The Roman Catholic Church

A map of Brazil, 1519, based on a Portuguese atlas of the period. North is towards the bottom of the picture. The initial attraction of Brazil to the Portuguese was the valuable red dye that could be extracted from a native tree – seen here being purchased from the Indians. Colonization began in 1530, and soon great parcels of land were being turned into sugar plantations.

thereby acquired massive numbers of believers in the Americas. The disruption of the Indians' way of life, together with the introduction of diseases to which they were not immune, contributed to a massive decline in their numbers – from perhaps 25 million in Mexico alone in 1519 to just over 1 million in 1600.

Trade, gold and silver

Gold had been the original attraction of the Americas for the conquistadores, and tales of El Dorado, a fabled city rich in gold, continued to fuel exploration. However, silver soon made up 90% of the precious metals sent back to Spain. These metals went as taxes and to pay for the goods the colonists received from Spain. Spain tried to prevent foreigners trading with their colonies, but this proved difficult. The silver stimulated the Spanish economy, and then that of the whole of Europe, contributing to the general inflation in the 16th century. However, in the 17th century, colonial self-sufficiency and economic recession, combined with a fall in silver exports, all contributed to a depression in the European economy.

Portugal's empire in Africa and Asia

Portugal's empire was much more dispersed than that of Spain. Limited to a few coastal settlements in Brazil, the Portuguese also had a handful of forts and 'trading' factories in West Africa and along the Mozambique coast, and a scattering of settlements between India and the Pacific.

This pattern reflected the importance of trade with the East. Portugal drew from the East an impressive range of spices, which then attracted high prices in Europe. The Portuguese also obtained gold from China and silver from Japan. Some of these goods were traded locally, but many were carried back to Lisbon, and on to Antwerp for European distribution. Since the only way to Portugal from the East was round the Cape of Good Hope, the forts and factories along the African coast protected this trade. Africa also provided gold – particularly from the Gold Coast (now Ghana) – and slaves. The latter were especially valued as labour on the developing sugar plantations of Brazil.

The number of White settlers in both the Portuguese and Spanish Empires was always far inferior to the number of non-Whites, but many Whites, including missionaries, were attracted to the colonies. The Portuguese, like the Spanish, condoned conversion of the native populations by force, so it is not clear how genuine the conversions were.

Spanish power in Europe

In 1556 Charles V abdicated. His brother had long ruled the Habsburg lands in Austria, and now kept them. Everything else went to Charles's son, Philip II (who ruled 1556–98). Spain now dominated

The Battle of Lepanto, 7 October 1571. It was off Lepanto (the western Greek port of Návpaktos) that a combined Spanish and Venetian fleet defeated the Ottoman Turks, so preventing Turkish expansion into the western Mediterranean. The Christian fleet was commanded by Don John of Austria, the half-brother of Philip II of Spain. Among the combatants was Miguel de Cervantes – the creator of Don Quixote (see p. 628) – who lost an arm during the fighting. The battle was the last great naval engagement involving oar-powered galleys. This painting by Andrea Micheli hangs in the Doge's Palace, Venice.

much of Italy and therefore the whole of the western Mediterranean. It also surrounded France – and threatened England – through its possession of the Netherlands. Spain also led the Christian fight against the Turks at sea: it was a largely Spanish fleet that defeated the Turks at Lepanto in 1571, although this did not end Turkish power in the Mediterranean (see p. 393).

Following the death of the king of Portugal in battle in Morocco in 1578, Philip added the Portuguese Empire to that of Spain. Apart from making Spain a major power in the East, this made Philip much stronger in Europe. The Spanish Empire in 1600 was the biggest the world had ever seen.

Portuguese women in Goa, as depicted by a 16th-century Indian painter. Goa, one of the first European settlements in India (1510), remained a Portuguese territory until it was forcefully taken over by India in 1961.

Spain's great military strength was used in a long struggle to suppress the revolt of the Protestant Netherlands from 1567. However, Philip was unable to devote himself wholly to ending the revolt, and his enemies aided the rebels in order to weaken Spain.

The failure of Philip's Armada against England in 1588 (see p. 412) meant that these distractions continued. Warfare on this scale was too expensive even with the silver of the Americas, and Spain was unable to beat the Dutch rebels.

The decline of Spain

The recovery of France from the weakness inflicted by the Wars of Religion (see p. 408) proved disastrous for Spain. Spanish troops proved very successful in the first half of the Thirty Years War (see p. 409), but their victories ended after France's entry into the war in 1635. At the same time Castile was less able to carry the cost of empire alone, largely owing to decline

in its population, agriculture and industry, and to the American recession. Yet the non-Castilian realms refused to shoulder more of the costs. Catalonia revolted in 1640 when Castile attempted to pass on some of the burden, as did Portugal, whose empire Spain had proved incapable of defending.

Spain recovered Catalonia but was obliged to recognize Dutch (1648) and Portuguese (1668) independence. Portugal then rebuilt its colonial empire around Brazil.

Although Spain continued to decline, the support of other states, now concerned to resist France rather than Spain, meant that the Spanish Empire was still vast enough to be worth fighting over when the last Habsburg king of Spain died (the War of the Spanish Succession; see pp. 414–5).   CS

SEE ALSO

● PRE-COLUMBIAN AMERICA p. 390
● CHRISTIANITY RESURGENT p. 398
● THE VOYAGES OF DISCOVERY p. 405
● THE REFORMATION p. 408
● THE RISE OF BRITAIN p. 412
● LOUIS XIV p. 414
● EUROPEAN EMPIRES IN THE 17TH AND 18TH CENTURIES p. 416

THE CONQUEST OF MEXICO

Hernán Cortez (1485–1547), like many other conquistadores, was a younger son of an impoverished noble family and was inspired by a variety of motives: he wanted to spread the faith but he also wanted to make his fortune.

In 1519 he led a private expedition to explore the interior of Mexico, accompanied by only 600 volunteers. He burnt his boats before marching inland towards the Aztec capital, Tenochtitlan, taking the ships' guns with him. Cortez was aided by Indian tribes who resented paying tribute to the Aztecs, particularly their demand for human sacrifices.

The Aztec leader, Montezuma, discouraged Cortez from entering Tenochtitlan, which was built on a lake and entered across a causeway. But the Spaniards insisted, attracted by the presents of gold they had received. Reluctantly, Montezuma allowed them in. The Aztecs revolted, murdering Montezuma and attacking Cortez, who was forced to fight his way out, losing a third of his men.

The Spaniards then besieged Tenochtitlan. Cortez cut off all supplies and built boats on which he mounted his guns. The guns bombarded the town and protected the Spanish troops as they crossed the causeway. The Aztecs – already weakened by the smallpox brought by the Spaniards from Cuba – surrendered. Within two years of the Spaniards coming, a civilization had collapsed.

The Rise of Britain

Between the end of the 15th and the middle of the 18th centuries England became Great Britain. By 1763 Britain had emerged as a leading power in Europe and the world, with a vast colonial empire. This position was achieved by the development of political stability after the upheavals of the 16th and 17th centuries. Stability was associated with the establishment of a Protestant, parliamentary monarchy from 1688. The achievement of effective control over the previously independent realms of Scotland and Ireland (Wales had been subjugated in the 13th century) contributed to the success of that new system.

The defeat of the Spanish Armada, 1588 (right). Among the commanders of the English fleet were Sir John Hawkins and Sir Francis Drake, under the Lord High Admiral, Howard of Effingham. After their defeat at Gravelines, the Spanish fleet tried to escape round Scotland and Ireland, suffering further losses by storm and shipwreck. Of the 130 Spanish ships that originally set out, only 86 returned. (Painting attributed to Nicholas Hilliard, Society of Apothecaries, London)

England's future success was not obvious when Henry Tudor defeated Richard III at Bosworth in 1485, so becoming Henry VII (1485–1509). It remained to be seen whether Henry could end the cycle of civil war known as the Wars of the Roses, which had started in 1455. These wars did little real damage to the wealth of England, but reduced the prestige and authority of the Crown, which had often proved incapable of enforcing obedience from the great nobles. The Crown had become the plaything of factions, being claimed by the Houses of York (the white rose) and Lancaster (the red rose). Scotland remained an independent kingdom inclined to ally with France against England (see also p. 400).

The early Tudor achievement

Henry married Elizabeth, daughter of Edward IV, ensuring that their children were heirs of both Lancaster and York. He defeated Yorkist attempts to seize his throne, and gained foreign support by a policy of marriage alliances and peace. Henry had no police or army and could restore royal authority only by channelling patronage (grants of land and offices) to those who obeyed him.

Henry VII's success was such that Henry VIII (1509–47) succeeded without question to a rich and powerful Crown, financially independent thanks to Henry VII's careful exploitation of the Crown's extensive landed estates. Henry VIII revived the traditions of the Hundred Years War (see p. 400), invading France in 1513. In his absence the Scots invaded England, but were defeated at Flodden. The man who organized the French expedition, Cardinal Thomas Wolsey (1473–1530), became Henry's chief minister.

The English Reformation

Henry VIII's wife, Catherine of Aragon, had five children, but only Princess Mary survived. The security of the Tudor dynasty required that Henry be followed by a son. The pope, not wishing to offend Catherine's uncle, Emperor Charles V, refused Henry a divorce. Henry therefore declared himself Supreme Head of the Church in England, which then granted him a divorce. Henry and his new chief minister, Thomas Cromwell (1485–1540), then dissolved the monasteries – thereby increasing the landed revenue available to the Crown – and reformed the Church.

Opposition to Henry's policies was brutally suppressed. In the interests of security, Wales was incorporated into the English Crown (1536, 1543), Henry was declared king of Ireland (1541), and efforts were made in the 1540s to subject the Scots.

Under Edward VI (1547–53), Henry VIII's son by his third wife, Jane Seymour, the Reformation continued. However, Edward was succeeded by his half-sister, Mary (1553–58), who hoped to restore Catholicism and papal authority in England, burning nearly 300 Protestants in the process. Mary might have been successful, but died in 1558 leaving no children to carry on the work. She was succeeded by Elizabeth I (1558–1603), Henry's daughter by his second wife, Anne Boleyn.

Elizabeth re-established the Church of England (also known as the Anglican Church) on the basis of the Thirty-Nine Articles (1559), disappointing those 'Puritans' who wished for a purer Protestant Church. Fear of Spanish power led her to support the Dutch rebels against Philip II (see p. 411). Following the discovery of plots against Elizabeth's life by Philip and Mary Queen of Scots (held prisoner by Elizabeth since 1570), Mary was executed in 1586. In 1588 Philip attempted the conquest of England by means of the Armada. It failed, but Philip continued to threaten Elizabeth, aiding the Catholic Irish chiefs who rebelled against Elizabeth in 1599. Ireland was not reconquered until 1603, the year of Elizabeth's death. Elizabeth never married and so left no heir. Instead she left the Crown to her Stuart relative, James VI of Scotland, who became James I of England (1603–25).

Parliament, the Stuarts, and the English Civil War

Elizabeth's wars, and the great inflation of the 16th century, eroded the financial achievement of the early Tudors. The

The Battle of Culloden, 1746 – the last pitched battle on British soil. The final defeat of Bonnie Prince Charlie's Highlanders marked the end of the Jacobite cause, and the end of the traditional Highland way of life. (By gracious permission of Her Majesty the Queen)

Crown sought Parliamentary help since Parliament's consent was necessary for full-scale taxation. This gave MPs the opportunity to criticize the Crown, and to attempt to influence its policy. The ending of the war with Spain by James I did not end these problems, but the situation was far worse under James's son Charles I (1625–49).

Charles expected to be obeyed, and after fierce arguments over his efforts to pay for an expensive foreign policy, he ruled without Parliament from 1629, raising money on his own authority. This, and the religious policies of Archbishop Laud – which seemed to threaten the return of Catholicism – were unpopular. However, Charles succeeded until Presbyterian Scotland rebelled against his efforts to impose an English-style Church there. The Scots invaded England, and Charles's need for money obliged him to call Parliament. Parliament's distrust of Charles and its efforts to obtain a share of government led him to begin the Civil War in 1642. The creation of the successful New Model Army helped Parliament to victory by 1649.

The Parliamentarians felt that Charles could not be trusted. He was therefore beheaded, and England was declared a republic (1649). The Parliamentary commander, Oliver Cromwell (1599–1658), then asserted the authority of the Parliamentary regime in Ireland and Scotland by force. English foreign policy in the 1650s was more aggressive and successful than under the Stuarts. However, the problem of a permanent replacement for the monarchy proved insoluble. Cromwell ruled as 'Lord Protector' (1653–58), but on his death the only solution seemed to be the restoration of the Stuart monarchy, stripped of the powers that had proved so offensive under Charles I.

The Glorious Revolution and parliamentary monarchy

Exploiting the widespread fear of another civil war, Charles II (1660–85) advanced towards an absolute monarchy, supported by a small standing army. He also used this fear to defeat attempts to exclude his Catholic brother James from the succession. However, the efforts of James II (1685–88) to recatholicize England led supporters of the Anglican Church to invite William of Orange, husband of James's daughter Mary, to come to save them. William and his army landed in England in November 1688, and James fled to France. No blood was spilt, and the 'Glorious Revolution' had been achieved.

In the Bill of Rights of 1689 Parliament declared some of the royal powers used by James illegal, and offered the Crown jointly to William (1689–1702) and Mary (1689–94), obliging them to call Parliament regularly. Aided by Louis XIV, James led a revolt in Ireland, but was defeated by William at the Battle of the Boyne (1690). This laid the foundations of effective British control of Ireland. Scotland also rejected James's political and religious policies in 1688–89, offering the Scottish Crown to William and Mary, but retaining its own parliament. Under William and Mary, and then Anne (1702–14),

THE GROWTH OF LONDON

London lay at the heart of Britain's growing power. The city's population trebled between 1500 and 1600 to 220 000 – about 5% of the population of England. Despite the loss of 10 000 people in the last of the great plagues to hit London (1665), its population had more than doubled to 550 000 by 1700 – 10% of the population of England. By 1800, 1 million people lived in London – about 11 or 12% of the population of England. By contrast, only about 2% of the population of France lived in Paris at the outbreak of the Revolution in 1789.

London was the centre of the country's political life. The expanding administration surrounded the monarchs in their palaces in the London area: Whitehall, Hampton Court, Kensington Palace and Buckingham Palace. Parliament met at Westminster, while the Inns of Court became busier as more people used legal means, rather than violence, to settle disputes.

London was already the country's leading commercial centre. In the 16th century, England's most valuable export, wool, was shipped from London to the Netherlands. From the later 17th century fortunes were made in the booming colonial trades. These trades, and the needs of government, stimulated the development of banking and insurance services, and a market in stocks and shares, while foreign money was attracted to the City of London. London's growth stimulated the economy of the rest of England, which provided most of London's food, fuel and other needs.

The development in London of a fashionable consumer society, frequenting the coffee houses and theatres, created employment and helped to attract immigrants from the countryside. The City had been partially rebuilt after the loss of 13 000 homes in the Great Fire of 1666. Soon, however, new suburbs had to be developed beyond the City gates, which

were demolished in the 1760s. As London grew so did the problem of maintaining order. The London mob was one of the few remaining unstable elements in the political life of Britain by the middle of the 18th century.

A view of London around 1600, showing the old St Paul's Cathedral that was destroyed in the Great Fire of 1666.

England's growing army and navy played a major part in defeating Louis XIV (see p. 415), obliging him to recognize the Revolution settlement.

These wars required enormous loans – often raised by the Bank of England, founded in 1694 – which in turn contributed to the growth of the national debt. These loans were secured by regular grants from Parliament, to which governments became more accountable for their policies. Ministers controlled Parliament by the use of patronage (basically a form of bribery), a system perfected by Sir Robert Walpole, the first 'Prime Minister' (1721–42).

Anne, the last Stuart monarch, left no surviving heir, so the Elector George of Hanover, in virtue of his descent from a daughter of James I, became king as George I. The most obvious threat to the new Hanoverian dynasty came from the Jacobites, supporters of the son (Prince James Francis Edward Stuart, the 'Old

Pretender') and grandson (Prince Charles Edward Stuart, the 'Young Pretender') of the exiled James II. In Scotland – which had lost its separate parliament by the 1707 Act of Union – Jacobite sympathies remained strong, particularly in the Highlands. These sympathies broke out in two major revolts, in 1715 and 1745–46, which were, however, defeated. The final defeat of the Jacobites was followed by the collapse of the old Gaelic-speaking society and culture of the Scottish Highlands.

Secure at home, Great Britain had triumphed abroad by 1763 with its victories in the Seven Years War and acquisition of vast new colonial territories (see p. 417). This stability, combined with its growing empire, enabled Britain to embark on a process of industrialization that was to make it the world's most powerful country in the 19th century (see pp. 420 and 432).   CS

SEE ALSO
- THE INVASIONS p. 392
- THE HUNDRED YEARS WAR p. 400
- THE REFORMATION p. 408
- EUROPEAN EMPIRES IN THE 17TH AND 18TH CENTURIES p. 416
- THE INDUSTRIAL AND AGRICULTURAL REVOLUTIONS p. 420
- THE REVOLUTIONARY AND NAPOLEONIC WARS p. 426
- THE PEAK OF EMPIRE p. 432

Louis XIV

Between the end of the Thirty Years War and the French Revolution the most characteristic form of government in Europe was absolute monarchy. In this style of government not only were kings unhindered by the need to refer to representative assemblies, but they also developed ways of controlling their states more firmly. The archetype of the absolute monarch was Louis XIV, king of France (1643–1715), whom many other rulers took as their model. Despite practical limitations on his absolutism, Louis was able to threaten Western Europe with French domination.

The sciences flourished under Louis' patronage. Here the king visits the Académie des Sciences.

For much of the first half of the 17th century, France had been ruled by two chief ministers. Louis XIII (1610–43) had given great power to Cardinal Richelieu (1585–1642), and when Louis died his widow acted as regent for his son Louis XIV – then a child – though much power was in the hands of another chief minister, Cardinal Mazarin (1602–61). Resentment of Mazarin's influence contributed to the outbreak of civil war in France (the so-called 'Frondes') in 1648–53.

Louis' personal rule in France

When Mazarin died in 1661, the 22-year-old Louis declared that henceforth he would rule personally. He did so until his death in 1715. His persistence owed a great deal to his belief (commonly held at that time) that kings ruled by divine right, receiving their power from God, and so must rule justly and in person. This belief is summed up in the famous words attributed to Louis, *'L'état c'est moi'* ('I am the state').

Louis had a number of very capable ministers, notably Jean Baptiste Colbert (1619–83) and the Marquis de Louvois (1641–91), but made it clear that they were his servants and dependent on his favour. He also adopted the Sun as his personal emblem and commissioned artists and writers to glorify him as the Sun King (*le roi soleil*).

Louis XIV, painted by Hyacinthe Rigaud in 1701. Even in old age Louis was determined to project an image of great majesty. (Louvre, Paris)

Royal academies were set up to promote and direct the arts and sciences. Colbert set up state trading companies and state-subsidized factories in order to stimulate the economy. This growing cultural and economic regulation, together with Colbert's efforts to increase tax revenue, greatly stimulated the development of a centrally controlled bureaucracy.

Efforts were also made to end disorder. The nobles, who had been so unruly during the Frondes, were encouraged to attend Louis' court at Versailles (see box). Far away from their power bases in the provinces, and under the watchful eye of the king, they were less likely to cause mischief.

At the same time the king's power to

SEE ALSO

● THE SPANISH AND PORTU-
  GUESE EMPIRES p. 410
● THE RISE OF BRITAIN p. 412
● EUROPEAN EMPIRES IN THE
  17TH AND 18TH CENTURIES
  p. 416
● THE ENLIGHTENMENT p. 418
● THE FRENCH REVOLUTION
  p. 424

WARS OF LOUIS XIV

Dates	Main Opponents
1667–68	Spain
1672–78	Netherlands, Spain, Holy Roman Empire
1689–97	Netherlands, Spain, Holy Roman Empire, Britain
1701–13	Netherlands, Holy Roman Empire, Britain

suppress dissent was increased once Louvois had completed the creation of a large standing army. Religious division was strongly disapproved, and in 1685 Louis revoked the Edict of Nantes (see p. 409), which had declared toleration for Protestantism in France. Louis also asserted his authority over the Church in France against the pope, but subsequently allied with him to suppress the Jansenists, a radical and anti-papal school of thought within the French Church.

Louis and Europe

Louis' identification of himself with the state was most evident in his foreign policy. He was always jealous of his personal reputation, or *gloire* ('glory'), which he considered to be inseparable from that of France. Louis' main concern, however, was France's vulnerability, and for this reason he had great fortresses built along the eastern and northeastern borders. Louis also believed in dynastic right, and asserted his claim to the Spanish Empire that ringed France (see p. 410). Skilled French diplomacy was backed by the army, and by a large navy built by Colbert.

Between 1667 and 1713 Louis fought a series of increasingly large-scale and expensive wars (see table) in an effort to strengthen France's frontiers and assert his own prestige and dynastic rights. As time went on the fear he aroused led to the formation of large coalitions against him; and the fact that after the Glorious Revolution of 1688 (see p. 412) England finally joined his enemies was a serious setback.

The peace of 1697 saw Louis forced for the first time to return some of his previous gains, while the War of the Spanish Succession (1701–13) brought France close to collapse. When Louis died in 1715, he left France territorially strengthened, but at a heavy economic and social cost.

Yet French influence remained great. Other rulers in Europe envied Louis' authority in France and his success abroad. Those who had not already introduced absolutist measures copied his bureaucracy, his tax system, his standing army, his academies, and his style of personal rule. In imitation of Versailles, many set up court in great new palaces away from their capitals, and French fashions and manners were widely imitated.

The limits of absolutism

Yet despite greater central control, a large number of individuals, groups and provinces enjoyed privileges restricting Louis' authority. Since Louis had neither the resources nor the inclination to end these privileges, the administration of France was by no means completely centralized or uniform. Much of it remained in the hands of independent officials. Louis therefore depended on the co-operation of the privileged groups, and their desire for order. His government also depended increasingly on huge loans from private financiers.

These limits were made clear in the 1690s and 1700s, when Louis' wars demanded more money. More offices were sold, and the tax burden and government debt vastly increased. The growing burden on the mass of the population became even heavier when accompanied, as in 1693–94 and in 1709, by harvest failure and famine.

Nevertheless absolute monarchy was still intact in 1715. It declined under Louis XIV's successors because neither Louis XV nor Louis XVI had the same capacity to run the machine. Even so, its survival until the Revolution in 1789 (see p. 424) contributed to the long-term centralization of French government.   CS

VERSAILLES

The palace of Versailles remains the most enduring monument to Louis XIV's absolute rule. Louis had a great passion for building, and he also had unpleasant memories of Paris during the civil wars of his childhood. He therefore built the greatest of his palaces at Versailles outside Paris.

Originally a hunting lodge, it was transformed between 1670 and 1700 by the addition of two wings designed by J.H. Mansart (see p. 531), and the laying out of extensive formal gardens by André Le Nôtre. The interior was redesigned by Charles Le Brun, with much gilt and glass, and many tapestries. These were often supplied by the subsidized factories, such as the famous Gobelins tapestry factory. Paintings celebrated Louis' military successes in the Dutch Wars and his achievements within France. The image of the Sun – Louis' personal emblem – was everywhere.

Louis personally directed much of the works, which employed 36 000 men in the 1680s and cost 70 million livres. They were still unfinished when he and his court took up residence from the 1670s. Eventually 15 000 people lived there and in the adjacent town.

Versailles remained the residence of the absolute monarchy until 1789. Here Louis saw his ministers, gave his orders, and received foreign princes and ambassadors. Spectacular entertainments stressed the king's magnificence, many of these being contrived by the playwright Molière (see pp. 626-7) and the composer Lully (see pp. 572-3). Life at Versailles revolved around Louis' daily routine: it was claimed that the time could be told simply by knowing what Louis was doing.

The nobles were expected to attend the court as a sign of loyalty, and there they competed with each other to perform menial tasks around Louis – since that was the means to royal favour. Banishment from Versailles and the king's presence became a severe punishment. In this way Louis reduced the independence of the nobility and reinforced his own power.

The Palace of Versailles with Paris in the distance. As well as being Louis XIV's greatest memorial, Versailles was also to become the scene of Britain's recognition of American independence (1783), the crowning of Wilhelm I as the first emperor of Germany (1871), and the signing of the main peace treaty after World War I (1919).

European Empires

in the 17th and 18th Centuries

European expansion overseas in the 16th century had been limited to Spain and Portugal (see p. 410), and the Spanish colonial empire remained the largest in the world in the 17th and 18th centuries. However, in the 17th century new colonial empires were created by the maritime states of northwest Europe – Britain, France and the Dutch Republic. Much of this was at the expense of Spain and Portugal, but Europeans were also making their presence felt in new areas. These new empires provided Europe with a wide range of colonial products and stimulated the demand for and production of European manufactured goods.

The wealth of their new trading empires increased the importance of Britain and the Dutch Republic in European politics. These states were therefore eager to defend and add to their colonies, and this led to wars that were fought all over the world. The decline of a number of European states in the 18th century also allowed the emergence of a number of new powers, particularly in Eastern Europe, which did not rely on overseas trade and colonization.

Colonial trade, mercantilism and settlement

Europe's overseas trade boomed in the 17th and 18th centuries owing to growing demand for a wider range of goods: timber and other naval stores, furs, tobacco, rice and fish (all from North America), tea, cotton and silk (from the East), coffee (from Java, the Americas and the East), but above all sugar (from Brazil and the West Indies). The sugar, tobacco, and coffee plantations depended on regular supplies of African slaves. A trade 'triangle' developed. Traders from Europe would buy slaves in West Africa, carrying them to the Americas. There they traded them for colonial products with which they returned to Europe. In Europe processing industries refined those products for re-export to other parts of Europe.

The attitude of the governments of the period towards their colonies was influenced by the theories of *mercantilism*. These theories assumed the amount of wealth in the world to be fixed, and therefore that individual states had to ensure that their subjects achieved the largest share possible of world trade. Since success depended on a favourable trade balance, governments felt that their policies should encourage manufactured exports, and discourage their import. It was thought that a country's trade should be monopolized by its own subjects, and that colonies existed only to benefit the mother country.

Although mercantilists thought colonial settlement encouraged demand for home exports, colonies were regarded more as sources of profit rather than as outlets for

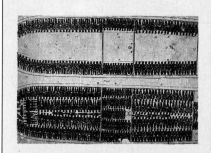

The layout of a slave ship. Europeans entered the slave trade in a major way in the 16th century, capturing or buying slaves from West Africa for transportation to the plantations of the Americas. Conditions on the ships were appalling, and on average one fifth of the slaves died before reaching their destination.

In 1807 the reformer William Wilberforce (1759–1833) persuaded the British Parliament to make the slave trade illegal, and in 1834 slavery itself was abolished in all British territories. France followed suit in 1848. Although the USA also abolished the slave trade in 1807, the continuance of slavery in the southern states was one of the major causes of the US Civil War (see p. 430).

The surrender of the *Royal Prince* to the Dutch in 1666, by the great marine painter Willem van de Velde. Although the English emerged from the three Anglo-Dutch Wars as the victors, the second war saw a succession of Dutch naval victories, culminating in the burning of the English fleet at its base in Chatham, Kent.

xcess population. Settlement, which was eaviest in the Americas, was often dependent of government sponsorship ee p. 422).

he Anglo-Dutch Wars

rofits from the Dutch domination of the aritime trade between the Baltic and outhern Europe provided capital for olonial projects. In the first half of the 7th century the Dutch seized most of ortugal's scattered East Indian empire, long with its valuable spice trade. They lso captured many of its African forts, nd temporarily held part of Brazil. uring the English Civil War, the Dutch lso gained a hold on England's trade ith her North American colonies.

he Dutch were therefore the target for he mercantilist policies of their rivals. rom 1651 the Navigation Acts reserved he produce of England's colonies for ngland, and their carriage to English hipping. The Acts led to a series of nglo-Dutch Wars (1652–54, 1665–67, 672–74) fought out – mostly at sea – in nany parts of the world. England ousted he Dutch from North America and West frica (and so from the slave trade) and gradually excluded them from its foreign nd colonial trade. Expensive land wars gainst France overstrained Dutch re-sources, and by 1713, when the wars of ouis XIV ended (see p. 415), the Dutch vere being overtaken by both Britain and rance.

The Anglo-French colonial struggle

Britain and France now increasingly felt that each was the other's natural trading and colonial rival. French colonization had begun in a number of West Indian islands and Canada early in the 17th century, and in Louisiana (which then comprised much of the Mississippi basin) at the end of the 17th century. In 1713 Britain took advantage of victory in Europe to secure her position in North America, gaining Nova Scotia, New-foundland and Hudson's Bay. The two countries were on opposing sides during the War of the Austrian Succession (1740–48), when for the first time the

An official of the British East India Company enjoying a water pipe. Many of the Company's officials made personal fortunes, and one such official, Warren Hastings (1732–1826), became the first governor of India in 1774. Although a brilliant administrator, on his return to England in 1785 Hastings was impeached for corruption. He was eventually acquitted in 1795.

British and French East India Companies fought each other in India. Neither country gained a decisive advantage in this war, and the struggle continued.

Fighting in North America contributed to the outbreak of the Seven Years War (1756–63). While Prussia distracted France in Germany, the British navy achieved dominance over the French at sea. Most of France's main colonies were captured, including Canada, thanks to the victory of General James Wolfe (1727–59) at Quebec. In India, under the generalship of Robert Clive (1725–74), victories over Indians and French made the British East India Company a large private colonial power, which dominated the subcontinent. France renewed the struggle during the American War of

Independence (1776–83; see p. 422). Yet, despite Britain's loss of its American colonies, the war did not reverse Britain's long-term victory in the colonial struggle.

The non-colonial empires of Europe

While the maritime states sought wealth and power overseas, new great powers emerged in 18th-century Europe without the aid of colonial wealth. The Baltic empire that Sweden had built up during the 17th century collapsed during the Great Northern War (1700–21). That war saw the first appearance of Russia as a European power. Russia had been emerging in the later 17th century, a process greatly accelerated by Peter the Great (1682–1725). He created a large Russian army and navy and gave Russia a Baltic outlet. Russia continued to expand into Siberia in the 18th century, and in the reign of Catherine the Great (1762–96) exploited Turkish decline to expand southwards – a process continued in the 19th century (see p. 429).

Austria had reconquered Hungary from the Turks by 1700 and had been revi-talized after losing Silesia to Prussia in the 1740s. Prussia had been a small and scattered kingdom in 1740. However, a superb administration and a large and effective army enabled Frederick the Great (1740–86) to seize Silesia in 1740, and to resist Austrian efforts (supported for most of the Seven Years War by Russia) to recover it. In 1772 Prussia, Russia and Austria agreed to the first partition of Poland, which for most of the 18th century had been a Russian satellite. Subsequent partitions, in 1793 and 1795, saw the disappearance of independent Poland and the further enlargement of Austria, Prussia and Russia.   CS

THE OPENING UP OF THE PACIFIC

Spanish, Portuguese and Dutch explorers began to explore the Pacific in the 17th century. At first they believed that Australia (then known as New Holland) was part of a larger southern continent. In 1642 the Dutchman Abel Tasman (1603–59) discovered Tasmania and the south island of New Zealand, and by sailing round Australia proved it to be an island. However, the Pacific remained largely unknown, too distant and too poor to attract European trading inter-est.

France's expulsion from America and India, and the belief that the East offered great wealth, turned European attention to the Pacific in the 1760s. In 1767 the British reached Tahiti, to be followed in 1768 by a French expedition under Louis Antoine de Bougainville (1729–1811).

Captain James Cook (1728–79) visited Tahiti on the first (1768–71) of three Pacific voyages. He charted the New Zealand coasts and landed on the east coast of Australia at Botany Bay. On his second voyage (1772–75) Cook dis-covered Easter Island, the Society and Friendly Islands, the New Hebrides, New Caledonia, Norfolk Island and the Sand-wich Islands (Hawaii). On his last voyage, to discover the Northwest Passage from the Pacific to the Atlantic via the Arctic (1775–79), Cook was killed in Hawaii.

However, the new lands were still too poor to be settled without government intervention. American independence obliged the British government to trans-port convicts elsewhere. They were sent to Botany Bay, where the first batch arrived in 1788.

SEE ALSO

- THE SPANISH AND PORTU-GUESE EMPIRES p. 410
- THE RISE OF BRITAIN p. 412
- THE ENLIGHTENMENT p. 418
- THE BIRTH OF THE USA p. 422
- NATIONALISM IN EUROPE p. 428
- THE PEAK OF EMPIRE p. 432

The Enlightenment

In the late 17th century English thinkers provided the foundation for a body of ideas that were developed in France in the 18th century and then spread through Europe. For their adherents these ideas represented an attempt to bring humanity into the light of reason out of the darkness of tradition and prejudice – hence the term *the Enlightenment*. This 'enlightenment' was to be achieved by the application of critical and rational thought to assumptions hitherto taken for granted.

At its peak in the 1750s it seemed that this bold, liberating movement had captured the minds of monarchs – the so-called *enlightened despots* – and that this explained the major reforms being attempted in many states in the later 18th century. Yet the practical influence of the Enlightenment was never great, and its intellectual impetus declined in the later 18th century. Tradition and the Church, the great enemies of the Enlightenment, survived the attack.

The development of the Enlightenment

The scientific discoveries of the first half of the 17th century undermined traditional explanations of the universe. A new explanation was devised by the French philosopher, René Descartes (1596–1650). Descartes was sceptical about all knowledge derived from the senses, and saw the universe as a mechanical system ordained by God, a system explicable by abstract mathematical laws. By 1700 *Cartesianism* – as Descartes' philosophy became known – was the general intellectual orthodoxy in much of Europe. However, the continued progress of experimental science, and Newton's discoveries in physics and optics (see pp. 20 and 32), showed that Descartes' system had no basis in reality.

That system was therefore discredited in favour of an explanation of reality based on experiment (an approach known as *empiricism*). The English philosopher John Locke (1632–1704) provided an intellectual basis for this empiricism. He argued that ideas were the product of sensation and experience and that people were not born with ideas (not even of God, contrary to what the Church and Descartes himself believed). According to Locke, human behaviour was based on two desires – to avoid pain, and to seek pleasure.

Newton and Locke provided the basis of a sustained critical movement, popularized by a group of French writers known as the *Philosophes*. The greatest of these was Voltaire (1694–1778), who introduced the ideas of Newton and Locke to France in his *Philosophical Letters* (1734). Encyclopedias and dictionaries were a favourite way of spreading the new ideas. The Philosophe Denis Diderot (1713–84) was largely responsible for the 28-volume *Encyclopédie* (1751–72), which incorporated the latest knowledge and progressive ideas, and which helped to spread the ideas of the Enlightenment in France and in other parts of Europe.

The Enlightenment consensus

There was no single 'Enlightenment' attitude. However, there was a consensus of enlightened opinion in the 1750s, symbolized by the *Encyclopédie*. This consensus was founded on the belief that the combination of reason and personal experience could discover the rules underlying the workings of nature. Such ideas led to a practical humanitarianism. The Italian legal theorist Cesare Beccaria (1738–94) urged the abolition of torture and the reform of penal codes. Some Philosophes were also critical of the way governments inflicted the horrors of war on their peoples.

Morality came to be seen as the product of circumstance, rather than an absolute truth – a view known as *relativism*. In his *Spirit of the Laws* (1748) the French philosopher Montesquieu (1689–1755) analysed how different circumstances in different societies produced different laws. The discovery of non-Christian societies by overseas exploration encouraged such relativism. Since there was no monopoly of truth or right, Enlightenment thinkers – notably Voltaire – called for toleration and attacked the Church as a powerful and repressive authority.

In place of established religion many of the Philosophes proposed the 'natural religion' of *Deism*, which required that religion conform to the workings of the universe as discovered by reason. Miracles and religion dependent on divine revelation were rejected as mere superstition. The Deists proposed a God who was simply a benevolent force. He had endowed individuals with reason and control of their fate, but otherwise played little part in human affairs.

Enlightened despotism

Apart from Montesquieu, Enlightenment writers said little about political theory or organization. Although the Philosophes were generally liberal in outlook, some looked to autocratic rulers to carry out their ideas. Catherine the Great (1762–96) drew on Enlightenment ideas when initiating reform in Russia. The transformation of Prussia by Frederick the Great (see p. 417), who corresponded with Voltaire, seemed a triumph of enlightened despotism. Both Frederick and Emperor Joseph II of Austria (1765–90) saw authority as a trust, to be used to promote the welfare of their subjects.

Yet Joseph's major reform of the Habsburg monarchy was largely a continuation of the reforms begun by his very conservative mother, Maria Theresa. Both wished to make Austria powerful again – the object of reform in most big states. Joseph wished to abolish serfdom mainly so that peasants could pay higher taxes. For the same reason, the humanitarian aspect of the Enlightenment was largely ignored in Prussia. Genuinely enlightened reform was often easier in the smaller states of Germany and Italy. Elsewhere tradition and privilege remained powerful. Most of Joseph II's reforms were withdrawn in the face of the hostility of various privileged groups.

Design for a cenotaph for Newton, by Étienne-Louis Boullée (1784). This unrealized design sums up Enlightenment rationalism, and the debt it owed to the great English scientist. 'O Newton,' wrote Boullée, 'as by the extent of your wisdom and the sublimity of your genius you determined the shape of the Earth, I have conceived the idea of enveloping you in your own discovery.'

SEE ALSO

- THE SCIENTIFIC METHOD p. 58
- THE HISTORY OF SCIENCE p. 60
- GOVERNMENT AND THE PEOPLE p. 266
- THE BIRTH OF THE USA p. 422
- THE FRENCH REVOLUTION p. 424
- THE EVOLUTION OF PHILOSOPHY p. 488

THE SCOTTISH
ENLIGHTENMENT

Scotland played an important role in
the Enlightenment and in 18th-
century intellectual life in general.
There were several reasons for this.
Though still much poorer than
England, Scotland was enjoying substantial economic growth, helped by
the Union of 1707 with England (see p.
413). Glasgow grew rich on trade with
America, and there was considerable
industrial and agricultural development in the Lowlands (although the
Highlands remained much poorer and
more backward). The Lowlands also
had one of the best school systems in
Europe, provided by the dominant
Presbyterian Church, while the two
main universities, Glasgow and
Edinburgh, were intellectually active
in an age when universities generally
were stagnant and unproductive.

Scottish intellectual achievement in
this age was many-sided. David Hume
(1711–76) produced, in his *Treatise on
Human Nature* (1739), an extremely
radical criticism of accepted philosophical assumptions. His attack on
the validity of inductive reasoning in
particular is a landmark in the history
of philosophy (see p. 58).

In 1776 Adam Smith (1723–90)
published his *Wealth of Nations*.
Although less original than Hume's
work – it owed a good deal to the
writings of Smith's French contemporaries – it had more practical influence. Its stress on a more natural
economic system and on free enterprise and free trade was found widely
attractive and the book was translated into many European languages.

Adam Ferguson (1723–1816) and John
Millar (1735–1801) were among the
forerunners of modern sociology,
while Joseph Black (1728–99), a professor at Glasgow, did fundamental
work on the science of heat. This
helped James Watt (1736–1819) to
develop a more efficient steam engine
(see p. 308), an invention essential to
the future development of industry
throughout the world. It is perhaps
significant of Scottish intellectual
vitality in this period that the first
edition of the *Encyclopaedia Bri-
tannica* was published in Edinburgh
(1768–71).

Voltaire in his study
(left). Best known today
for his novel *Candide*
(1759), Voltaire was also
a playwright, philosopher,
scientist and moralist. He
infused all of his work
with a concern for
humanity and truth, and
constantly pleaded for
toleration. 'I may disagree
with what you say,' said
Voltaire, 'but I will defend
to the death your right to
say it.' (Musée Carnavalet,
Paris).

Reform was often forced on governments.
The suppression of the Jesuits in 1773
was not the result of Enlightenment influence, but nevertheless obliged governments to establish new educational
institutions to replace those previously
run by the Jesuits (see p. 409).

The impact of the Enlightenment

The Enlightenment provided some of the
ideas and language of the American and
French Revolutions (see pp. 422 and 424),
but did not cause them. Since the vast

Some pages from the *Encyclopédie* (right),
the multi-volume monument to Enlightenment
thinking. Masterminded by Diderot, the *Encyclopédie* include Voltaire and Rousseau among its
contributors.

majority of Europeans remained uneducated, the number of those directly influenced by the Enlightenment was very
small.

In the second half of the 18th century the
Enlightenment faced growing competition from irrational movements. The
reaction against reason was expressed
most forcefully by Jean Jacques Rousseau
(see p. 630). Formerly a Philosophe, Rousseau now rejected the values of the
Enlightenment, arguing that natural
instinct was the best guide. Individual
feeling, not universal reason, was what
mattered. This attitude was the core of
Romanticism, the movement that was to
sweep across Europe at the end of the 18th
century (see pp. 536, 576 and 630).   CS

The Agricultural and Industrial Revolutions

A rapid and unprecedented rise in population occurred in Britain during the second half of the 18th century, and later in most other European nations. New and more efficient farming methods had to be found to feed the increased numbers, as traditional farming, based on subsistence methods, could not cope with the rise.

SEE ALSO

- ARABLE FARMING p. 188
- LIVESTOCK FARMING p. 190
- CAPITAL AND LABOUR p. 272
- ENGINES p. 308
- MINING, MINERALS AND METALS p. 312
- IRON AND STEEL p. 314
- TEXTILES p. 318
- CIVIL ENGINEERING p. 340
- THE DEVELOPMENT OF THE SHIP p. 342
- RAILWAYS p. 346
- INDUSTRIAL SOCIETY p. 434

The Industrial Revolution, which also began in Britain during the 18th century, spread to much of the northern hemisphere throughout the 19th and early part of the 20th centuries. The advent of mechanized mass production heralded the transformation of the countries of Europe and North America into predominantly industrial rather than agricultural nations, with their populations increasingly concentrated in the cities.

The Agricultural Revolution

In Britain almost all traces of the ancient 'open-field' system of arable farming disappeared, and between 1760 and 1820 over 20 000 km² (7700 sq mi) of open field and common land were enclosed. Similar processes took place elsewhere. The process of enclosure involved wealthier farmers and landowners taking over land previously farmed by peasants who could not demonstrate legal ownership.

Once fields began to be enclosed, it was possible to keep animals away from others that might be diseased or underweight, and landowners began to experiment with

A steam-driven threshing machine in action in 1872. The mechanization of farming accelerated after the introduction of steam power, with a consequent requirement for fewer and fewer people to work the land.

carefully planned selective livestock breeding. Animals could be kept alive during the winter months, as extra fodder crops, such as turnips, were now grown. The introduction of four-field crop rotation (see pp. 188–9) made it possible to use all fields to the full every year.

New types of agricultural machinery such as the seed drill invented by Jethro Tull (1674–1741) in 1730 also led eventually to a great improvement in crop production. But new machines required fewer men to operate them. In some areas, farm workers forced farmers to destroy them, or did so themselves. Enclosures often led to great hardship, and to the eviction of many peasant farmers, which in some places led to riots and revolts, and in Ireland and the Scottish Highlands, for example, to mass emigration.

Throughout Europe the enormous agricultural changes made it possible for a reduced number of people working on the land to produce more food for the growing numbers of people who left the countryside to live in the industrial towns and cities. This process was helped by the increased use of artificial fertilizers and the cultivation of 'new' staple crops: potatoes in northern Europe and maize in the south. More and more potential farmland was put to use, but despite this, by the early 20th century imported North American grain was essential to feed Europe's growing population.

The beginnings of the Industrial Revolution

Why did the Industrial Revolution begin in Britain? Britain had the advantage of being a united country with a relatively stable internal political situation, free from internal customs duties and with well-established banking and insurance facilities. In the 18th century Britain became the dominant international trading power (see p. 416), and many British merchants had accumulated large sums of capital. In addition, the Agricultural Revolution produced huge profits for some farmers. This made it possible for ambitious new schemes to be financed at very low rates of interest.

Britain's secure position as an island, combined with its proximity to the principal sea routes between northern Europe and the rest of the world, gave it great natural advantages. In addition, Britain's large numbers of natural harbours and navigable rivers – many linked by new canals in the 18th century – meant that internal and overseas trade were easily linked. Acquisition of a colonial empire became vitally important for Britain and later for other powers, so as to provide markets and raw materials (see pp. 416 and 432).

Rapid industrial development was also precipitated by a need to tackle Britain's fuel crisis. By the mid-18th century it was apparent that the forests were seriously

depleted; opencast and shallow underground coal mines (see p. 312) were nearing exhaustion and existing technologies for draining deeper mine shafts were inadequate. The invention of steam pumps as a far more efficient way to drain mines and the discovery of a process for smelting iron using coke made possible a more intense exploitation of Britain's mineral resources. The geology of Britain – with sources of coal and iron ore close to each other – also played its part.

Textiles

Woollen cloth had long been one of Britain's most important products, but as the 18th century progressed, it became difficult to fulfil the greatly increased demand. Inventions such as the spinning jenny (see p. 318) produced larger quantities of thread more quickly, especially cotton. Cotton was imported in increasing quantities from the USA, and became vital to the British textile industry. Further mechanical spinning devices such as the water frame and the spinning mule (see p. 318) appeared in the 1770s, and in 1785 the introduction of Cartwright's power loom (see p. 318), capable of being operated by relatively unskilled labour, marked the end of handloom weaving. The initial development of mechanized textile industries in the USA and much of continental Europe was dependent on many of these British inventions.

Only those with capital could invest in the new machinery, and those without it could not produce thread or cloth as cheaply. Thus mechanization of the textile industry gave rise to the factory system. Instead of being self-employed and working at home, women and children (who had always been expected to work for their living) – and later men as well – went 'out to work' for wages in the factories, where steam engines set the pace. Attempts to destroy the new machinery by disgruntled weavers ('Luddites') were severely repressed.

Iron, steel, steam and coal

The breakthroughs in iron smelting and production in the 18th century (see p. 314) were vital for early industrialization. Iron was used for machinery, ships, and railways. Although high-quality cast steel was produced from the 1740s, it was not until 1857 that a cheap method of mass producing mild steel was discovered (the Bessemer process; see p. 314). This process was developed and improved by others, and large-scale production of steel using these techniques was an important factor in the rapid industrial growth of Germany and the USA.

Experimental attempts to drain water from mines led to the early steam engines of Savery (1698) and Newcomen (1712). However, it was not until James Watt redesigned Newcomen's device (patented in 1769) that a cheaper and more efficient steam pump became available (see p. 308). With the addition of rotary motion achieved by Watt in 1781, steam engines quickly became ubiquitous. As well as pumps, steam engines powered all kinds of factory machinery, railway locomotives, and ships. Without steam many of the later developments of the Industrial Revolution would have been impossible.

Coal production was dramatically increased as a direct result of the availability of practical steam pumps and other innovations. However, deeper, more mechanized mining proved more dangerous to the mineworkers, who included children of 4 years old and upwards. Coal was the basic fuel for steam engines, and throughout Europe and the northeast USA heavy industry grew up in areas close to rich coal seams. Such areas included the Scottish lowlands, South Wales, the Ruhr and Silesia.

By the 1880s, the development of electrical energy as a power source, pioneered by Michael Faraday (1791–1867), heralded the introduction of a rival that was eventually to supersede steam. British industries, unlike those in Germany and the USA, were slow to abandon steam engines until well into the 20th century.

Other industries, such as the potteries of Josiah Wedgwood (1730–1795), were transformed during the 18th century by the invention of new chemical processes. Development of accurate and standardized machine tools was also a very important aspect of the Industrial Revolution.

Transport

The need for reliable and cheap access to raw materials and markets made improvements in transport an essential part of the Industrial Revolution.

Road building enjoyed a long overdue revival in the 18th century, pioneered in Britain by such men as McAdam and Telford (see p. 340). Initially more important, however, were canals, which provided the cheapest way of transporting goods and materials in bulk. A massive canal-building programme got under way in the 18th century, and by 1830 there were over 6400 km (4000 mi) of canals in Britain alone, linking all the main industrial areas. However, with the advent of the railways, the canals fell rapidly into disuse.

Following the opening of the first public steam line in 1825 (Stephenson's Stockton & Darlington; see p. 346), private railway companies in Britain proliferated rapidly, with the result that a national network evolved with little attempt at planning. In continental Europe the railways were subject to a greater degree of state regulation and control. This was especially true of Belgium and Germany.

By providing a rapid means of transporting in bulk both raw materials and manufactured goods, the growth of railway networks greatly assisted the process of industrialization. The railways also provided an impetus for other developments, such as the electric telegraph (see p. 330), and in the USA they played a key role in opening up the interior after the Civil War (see p. 430). The railways also played a social and cultural role: by providing a means of cheap and swift long-distance passenger transport they opened up a wider world to millions of people.

Industrialization outside Britain

Although Britain initiated the Industrial Revolution, other European nations, notably Belgium, were close behind. In France, industrialization proceeded more slowly, but was still impressive. The 'second phase' of the Industrial Revolution (from the 1880s onwards) was dominated by electricity and by the internal combustion engine. Superior expertise in these technologies resulted in Germany overtaking Britain as Europe's leading industrial power. Government encouragement of a systematic programme of scientific and technical education also contributed to Germany's success.

The USA enjoyed vast supplies of raw materials and a rapidly increasing population – supplemented by large-scale immigration. The difficulties of developing an adequate transport system to cover vast distances held industrialization in check for a while. However, by the start of the 20th century the USA had become the world's leading industrial power.

For Russia and Japan, industrialization during the later part of the 19th century was a result of deliberate government policy. In the 1850s, both powers were largely agricultural societies dominated by ancient feudal systems, but by the start of the 20th century Japan had emerged as a serious industrial, military and economic rival to the world's industrial giants (see p. 387).

Russia's industrialization was hampered by the country's vast size and poor communications, and even more so by the backwardness of a society still run as a feudal system, and by the inertia of the autocratic rule of the Tsars. A succession of foreign loans and internal reforms gradually made it possible to increase production and build up a railway network, and in the early years of the 20th century state aid was used to encourage growth. However, the strain of war, in

1904–5 (against Japan) and again in 1914–17 (World War I), caused the government's final collapse. Industrialization continued following the Bolshevik Revolution, but under circumstances of extreme difficulty (see p. 438).   PO

Steel making (above) using the Bessemer process in a German foundry. Large-scale production of steel in the later 19th century contributed to the emergence of Germany and the USA as major industrial powers.

A train of second-class carriages (below) pulled by Robert Stephenson's *Jupiter*, built in 1831 for the Liverpool and Manchester Railway. As a cheap and rapid method of long-distance transport – carrying workers and materials to where they were needed – railways provided a great impetus to the process of industrialization in virtually every country in the world.

The Birth of the USA

Continuous European settlement of North America dates from the beginning of the 17th century. The first British plantation, Virginia, was established in 1607, with its centre at Jamestown. In November 1620 Protestant separatists (Puritans) reached Cape Cod after sailing from Plymouth in the *Mayflower* two months earlier. Their Massachusetts Bay colony became a refuge for Puritans fleeing religious strife in England. Other British settlements followed, notably New York (formerly Dutch New Netherland) and Quaker Pennsylvania. In the South the tobacco plantations were worked by imported African slaves. By 1700 most of the colonies possessed governors appointed by the Crown and had been integrated into Britain's Atlantic empire.

An English customs officer is tarred and feathered by American patriots angry at the British tax on tea. The Americans resented having to pay taxes levied by a London parliament.

In 1756–63 Britain won mastery of the continent by defeating the French in the Seven Years War (see p. 417). France surrendered Louisiana (then comprising much of the Mississippi basin) to Spain (regaining it in 1800) and Spain in turn gave up Florida to Britain but retained its own settlements in the southwest. The British victory was a costly one, for the national debt almost doubled during these years. It was time, the British Parliament concluded, that the colonists made a greater contribution to their own defence.

Origins of the Revolution

During the first half of the 18th century Americans became used to a good deal of self-government. Wealthy planters, lawyers and merchants played leading roles in colonial society. Although they regarded themselves as British, they resented their lack of representation in Parliament and their economic subordination within the Empire (particularly restrictions on their ability to trade). In 1765 Parliament's imposition of a stamp duty on legal documents and merchandise unleashed the cry of 'no taxation without representation'.

Although widespread opposition to these measures forced the British government to back down – both on this occasion and again in 1767 – Parliament continued to insist that it had full power to make laws for the colonies and left a tax on tea as proof of its authority. In 1773 it allowed the struggling East India Company to dump its tea on the American market, still retaining the controversial duty. When the first consignment reached Boston, Massachusetts, a group of patriots – as the American radicals now called themselves – disguised themselves as Indians. They proceeded to throw the tea chests into the harbour, in what became known as the 'Boston Tea Party'. America was now ripe for revolution.

First blows

Britain instituted repressive measures against Massachusetts, and Americans reacted by sending delegates to the First Continental Congress in September 1774. This banned the import of goods from Britain, while colonial pamphleteers insisted that traditional freedoms were being threatened by a corrupt and tyrannical enemy. In April 1775, when British troops moved to seize a store of arms outside Boston, they were confronted at Lexington by armed Massachusetts farmers, and retreated without achieving their objective.

The Declaration of Independence

King George III and his government in Britain now regarded the Americans as traitors who must be suppressed. To this end large numbers of British troops and German mercenaries were sent across the Atlantic. The Americans themselves were divided as to how they should react. Most of those at the head of the patriot movement, however, believed Britain's policy of coercion had severed the ties of empire. In mid-1776 a Virginia planter, Thomas Jefferson (1743–1826), drafted a formal Declaration of Independence. This also announced a potentially revolutionary new doctrine: 'that all men are created equal, that they are endowed by their Creator with certain unalienable rights, that among these are life, liberty and the pursuit of happiness'. Congress approved the document on 4 July.

The War of Independence

In the eight-year-long struggle for independence the Americans had a number of crucial advantages. They were fighting in conditions familiar to them but to which the British had to adapt; and the considerable number of Americans who remained loyal to the British Crown proved a relatively ineffective force. Even more important, the Americans had interior lines of communication, whereas the enemy was dependent on a 5000 km (3000 mi) long supply route from Europe. Moreover the rebels owed much to the leadership of George Washington (1732–99), a cautious but inspiring commander.

Finally, France's decision to support the American cause after the patriot victory at Saratoga in 1777 diverted much of Britain's resources and threatened the Royal Navy's mastery of the seas. When a British army under Cornwallis found itself besieged by Washington at Yorktown in 1781 a French fleet in Chesapeake Bay cut off the only avenue of escape. Cornwallis surrendered on 19 October, and Yorktown turned out to be the decisive engagement of the war. Two years later, in 1783, Britain recognized American independence. The United States of America had entered the community of nations.

The Constitution

Until 1788 the only legal basis for the USA was the Articles of Confederation, which delegated very restricted powers to Congress. However, by the mid-1780s Congress's inability to respond effectively to economic pressure from European powers revealed clearly the shortcomings of the Articles. Moreover many conservatives feared serious social unrest in the aftermath of the war. The Articles, it seemed, would have to be replaced.

Fifty-five delegates from 12 of the states gathered in Philadelphia in May 1787 to draft a new constitution. Although Washington was president of the Convention and was to become the first president of the new republic in 1789, it was his fellow Virginian, James Madison (1751–1836), who had most influence on the proceedings. His 'Virginia Plan' proposed to create a stronger national government that should operate directly on individuals rather than states.

After much debate the Plan was modified, and as it finally emerged the Constitution was a compromise between the various regional interests in the Convention (see box). In spite of serious flaws it was a remarkably democratic document for its time. Critics who disliked its strengthening of central government were placated in 1791 by the passage of a Bill of Rights (see box), which formed the first ten amendments to the Constitution.   RC

THE US CONSTITUTION AND BILL OF RIGHTS

The main provisions of the **US Constitution** (ratified in 1788) were:

1. A stronger central government divided into three branches – a president chosen by an Electoral College; a Federal judiciary; and a popularly elected House of Representatives and a Senate chosen by the state legislatures.

2. While representation in the House was based on population, each state sent two delegates to the Senate.

3. Congress was given full power to levy import duties and taxes.

4. For representation and tax purposes a Black slave was to be enumerated as three fifths of a White person.

5. The African slave trade was not to be abolished before 1808.

The **Bill of Rights** (ratified in 1791) formed the first 10 amendments to the Constitution. These ruled against:

1. Abridgement of freedom of religion, speech, the press, petition, and peaceful assembly.

2. Infringement of the right to bear arms.

3. The illegal quartering of troops.

4. Unreasonable searches and seizures.

5. The capital trial of any person for the same offence; deprivation of life, liberty or property 'without due process of law'; self-incrimination; uncompensated seizure of property.

6. Infringement of an accused person's right to a speedy and public trial before an impartial jury.

7. Depriving persons of the right to trial by jury in common-law suits where the value in question exceeded $20.

8. Excessive bail and punishments.

Amendments **9** and **10** declared that the listing in the Constitution of certain rights should not be taken to deny others retained by the people, and reserved to the states all powers not delegated to the Federal government by the Constitution.

Jefferson described these rights as 'what the people are entitled to against every government on earth', and several of them have been enshrined in the constitutions of other democratic countries.

George Washington (above) at the Constitutional Convention in Philadelphia, 1787. (Virginia Museum of Fine Arts)

The Battle of Bunker Hill, 17 June 1775, the first major engagement of the War of Independence. Although the Americans were defeated by the British, their heroic defence and low casualties helped raise American morale. (Painting by John Trumbull, Yale University Art Gallery)

SEE ALSO

● GOVERNMENT AND THE PEOPLE p. 266
● EUROPEAN EMPIRES IN THE 17TH AND 18TH CENTURIES p. 416
● THE ENLIGHTENMENT p. 418
● THE EXPANSION OF THE USA p. 430

The French Revolution

Between 1789 and 1791 the political and social institutions that had characterized France for the previous century and more were overthrown. In 1792 France became a republic, and between 1793 and 1794 experienced a revolutionary dictatorship (the 'Reign of Terror'). Thereafter a reaction set in, culminating in the establishment of a military dictatorship under Napoleon Bonaparte (1769–1821). With the overthrow of the republic, many of the institutions and practices of pre-Revolutionary France were reintroduced. In 1815, following Napoleon's final defeat (see p. 427), the Bourbon dynasty was restored.

The Tennis Court Oath (above right), 20 June 1789. When the commoners (the Third Estate) of the States-General declared themselves a National Assembly on 17 June, they were shut out of their usual meeting place at Versailles. They met instead in one of the royal tennis courts, where they vowed to stay until Louis XVI agreed to a written constitution. This copy of a painting by Jacques-Louis David hangs in the Musée Carnavalet, Paris.

Yet the French revolution remains an event of major importance. It was the first 'modern' revolution, in that it attempted to transform the whole social and political system. It put into circulation modern notions of democracy, nationalism, and even socialism. In these respects, and in its resort to violent dictatorship to effect this programme, the French Revolution was very different from the earlier revolutions in England (see p. 412) and America (see p. 422).

The background to the Revolution

The France of the *ancien régime* – the term given to the political and social system prior to the Revolution – was a centralized, absolute monarchy ruled by Louis XVI (1774–92) from Versailles (see p. 414). Yet it remained a patchwork of privilege with the great mass of taxation being paid by the unprivileged urban poor and by the peasantry, who had the additional burden of feudal dues. The wealthiest non-nobles (the *bourgeois*), although by no means unprivileged, had less legal and social rights than the aristocracy.

Some nobles and bourgeois (particularly those influenced by Enlightenment ideas, see p. 418) agreed that merit should be the true basis of social status. They were also critical of royal absolutism and the corruption of the court. The monarchy was further undermined by the weak character of Louis XVI, and by the unpopularity of his Austrian queen, Marie Antoinette.

The immediate background to the revolution was the government's bankruptcy following French intervention in the American War of Independence (see p. 422), and a trade recession coinciding with harvest failure. At a time of growing discontent among the poor, Louis XVI was obliged to call the States-General (a national assembly that had not met since 1614) to consider reform of the tax system, including a reduction in privileges.

The events of 1789

The Third Estate (the commoners) of the States-General declared itself a National Assembly, intending to introduce reform. Louis ordered troops to Paris and Versailles. On 14 July, fearing an attack on Paris and the Assembly, the Paris mob seized the Bastille (a royal fortress and prison) in order to obtain arms. An independent municipal government (*commune*) and National Guard were established in Paris, and other towns followed suit. Since the army was divided and unreliable, royal authority collapsed. The National Assembly survived.

Following a wave of peasant revolts, the Assembly abolished feudal and other privileges in August 1789. This abolition was confirmed in the Declaration of the Rights of Man. This stated that the natural rights of man and the citizen (liberty, property, security, and the right to resist oppression) could never be given up. All men were free and equal, and equally liable to taxation, and the king derived his authority solely from the will of the people.

France becomes a republic 1791–93

The Assembly prepared a 'modern' constitutional government. Henceforth legislative power lay with a new elected assembly, and local government and the legal system were completely reorganized. Religious toleration for Protestants and Jews ended the privileged position of the Catholic Church, and the confiscation and sale of Church lands

The storming of the Bastille. The medieval fortress of the Bastille in Paris had long been used to hold political prisoners, but only seven remained when the Paris mob stormed the building on 14 July 1789. The Bastille was seen as a symbol of the oppression of the *ancien régime*, and its fall a symbol of the Revolution. Ever since 1880, Bastille Day has been a French national holiday.

SEE ALSO

● LOUIS XIV p. 414
● THE ENLIGHTENMENT p. 418
● THE REVOLUTIONARY AND NAPOLEONIC WARS p. 426
● NATIONALISM IN EUROPE p. 428

THE REVOLUTIONARY CALENDAR

One of the more radical measures associated with the Revolution was the new calendar introduced in September 1793. Because of its associations with the Church, the Gregorian calendar (see p. 7) was replaced by one in which the year was divided into 12 new months, whose names evoked the season; for example, Thermidor (heat) lasted from 19 July to 17 August, and Brumaire (mist) from 22 October to 20 November.

Each month consisted of three 'decades' of 10 days. Originally each day was to consist of 10 equal parts. The 5 days left at the end of the year became the *sans culottides*, feast days in honour of the *sans culottes*. The sixth day of a leap year was the *françiade*, on which Frenchmen came from all parts to Paris to celebrate the Revolution and its slogan of 'Liberty, Equality and Fraternity'.

The calendar was dated from the declaration of the Republic in France, so Year One ran from September 1792 to September 1793. In 1806 Napoleon restored the Gregorian calendar.

solved the problem of the national debt while a fairer tax system was being devised.

In October 1789 Louis XVI and the Assembly had been forced to leave Versailles for Paris. There the mob, organized by members of political clubs (notably the left-wing Jacobins), could influence events. After a failed attempt to flee the country in 1791, Louis XVI was obliged to approve the new constitution. By the end of 1791 the Revolution had – relatively peacefully – put an end to absolute monarchy and transformed French society.

Yet the Revolution was by no means over. In 1792 foreign powers, anxious to nip the Revolution in the bud before it spread to their own countries, invaded France (see p. 426). This stimulated suspicions of plots to betray the Revolution. A thousand suspected counter-revolutionaries were massacred in the prisons of Paris (September 1792), and France was declared a republic (November). In the following year Louis XVI and Marie Antoinette were tried for treason and guillotined.

The Reign of Terror 1793–94

Not all Frenchmen supported the Revolution. Many left France (the so-called *émigrés*), but many more remained. In 1793 revolt broke out in the Vendée in the west, and also in Normandy and the south. Against the background of civil and foreign war some people – for example the influential journalist Jean-Paul Marat (1743–93) – called for a revolutionary dictatorship.

This was brought about by the Jacobins in the summer of 1793, following the expulsion from the Convention of the moderate Girondin deputies. The Girondins were so

called because they were from the Gironde area of southwest France, and their expulsion was effected by the revolutionary mob known as the *sans culottes* ('without breeches' – working men wore trousers). Marat himself was murdered by Charlotte Corday, a Girondin sympathizer.

Virtually dictatorial powers were assumed by the Committee of Public Safety, of which Maximilien Robespierre (1758–94) was the most prominent member. The Committee unleashed what became known as the 'Reign of Terror' against suspected counter-revolutionaries. All over France at least 300 000 people were arrested, and of these about 17 000 were executed.

In the spring of 1794 the Terror intensified. The Committee eliminated its political opponents, including those on the left responsible for a policy of dechristianization. Robespierre – believing that religion was necessary to social stability – introduced a 'Cult of the Supreme Being'. Other victims included the moderate Georges Danton (1759–94), himself a former head of the Committee. Suspects' rights were reduced and no mercy shown to those convicted. Fearing for their own lives, and that Robespierre's power was too great, his enemies had him arrested on 27 July 1794 (the coup of 9 Thermidor; see box) and executed. A new regime, a group of five known as the Directory, was established.

The end of the Revolution

The Terror was brought to an end, the Jacobin club closed, and the Paris commune abolished. The more democratic constitution of 1793 was replaced. The Paris mob resented these moves but was powerless against the army, whose support proved crucial to the continuance of the Directory. Frequent military interventions in politics culminated in 1799 in

the coup of 18 Brumaire (8 November; see box) on behalf of General Napoleon Bonaparte. In 1800 Bonaparte became first Consul, and in 1804 Emperor Napoleon I, so ending the First Republic. His military dictatorship saw the restoration of central control of local government, the end of representative assemblies, and the creation of a new aristocracy.

The debate on the Revolution

The Revolution divided informed opinion throughout Europe. The views of its opponents were expressed by the Anglo-Irish Edmund Burke (1729–97) in *Reflections on the Revolution in France* (1790). Burke denied that there was any virtue in destroying established social institutions, and refused to see any evils in pre-Revolutionary France. He predicted that the Revolution would consume itself in violence. He was answered by the Anglo-American radical, Thomas Paine (1737–1809), whose *Rights of Man* (1792) defended the right of the nation to reform what was corrupt. The British government, afraid of revolution, persecuted Paine and other radicals. Governments elsewhere repressed reform movements, putting an end to the progress of the Enlightenment.   CS

REGIMES AND ASSEMBLIES

Louis XVI	1774–92
States-General	May–June 1789
National Assembly	June–July 1789
Constituent Assembly	1789–91
Legislative Assembly	1791–92
Convention	1792–95
Directory	1795–99
Consulate	1799–1804
First Empire	1804–14/15

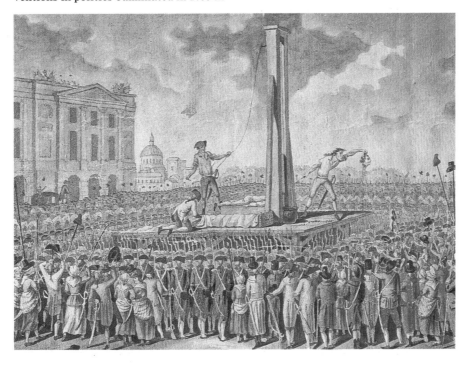

The execution of Louis XVI, 21 January 1793. A weak and reactionary king, Louis failed to come to terms with the fact of the Revolution and continued to plot with both French and foreign counter-revolutionaries. Evidence of his intrigues led to his conviction and execution for treason.

The Revolutionary and Napoleonic Wars

The French Revolution transformed Europe and the relations of its states with France. From 1792 the French were obliged to defend their Revolution against a series of foreign enemies, who feared the spread of revolutionary ideas to their own countries. For their own part, the French appealed to peoples everywhere to rise up against their rulers. The war became an ideological crusade on both sides. Obliged to wage 'total war' at home and abroad, France was soon on the offensive, and its expansion meant the end of some old-established states.

Napoleon strengthened the imperialist trend in French policy and his empire became the largest in Europe since that of Rome. French domination inspired 'national' resistance, which contributed to the collapse of Napoleon and his empire in 1815. However, Napoleon's downfall was mainly the work of the 'Great Powers' – Russia, Prussia, Austria, and particularly Britain.

The First Coalition 1793–97

Those Frenchmen who fled France after 1789 urged foreign monarchs to suppress the Revolution. Eventually in 1792 the Austrians and Prussians invaded France, but were repulsed, and France went onto the offensive. French success, particularly the conquest of the Austrian Netherlands, alarmed Britain, which declared war in 1793. By offering cash subsidies Britain built up the First Coalition against France. The Coalition included most of Europe and all of France's neighbours, but it lacked an effective strategy. The French introduced conscription, which gave France the largest army in Europe (750 000 men in 1794), and in 1794–95 French armies carried all before them. French leaders put forward the idea of 'natural frontiers' to justify their first annexations of territory. One by one the allies settled with France. The brilliant French campaign in Italy in 1796–97 – led by a young general, Napoleon Bonaparte – forced Austria to surrender Belgium in exchange for the previously independent state of Venice. The French, cooperating with local enthusiasts, established 'sister republics' in the United Provinces, Italy and Switzerland. Napoleon, having secured the Revolution against foreign enemies, set off to conquer Egypt in 1798.

The Second Coalition 1798–1802

Britain's naval power had enabled it to survive, even to score a number of victories against France. However, if it were to defeat France it needed continental allies. Again using subsidies, Britain built up the Second Coalition, consisting of Russia, the Ottoman (Turkish) Empire, Austria, Portugal and Naples. After some initial successes, the allies were weakened by the mutual jealousies of Austria and Russia. Despite the defeat of the French fleet at the Nile (1798) by the British under Admiral (later Lord) Horatio Nelson (1758–1805), Napoleon returned to Europe, and seized political power in France (see p. 425).

Having defeated the Austrians at Marengo (1800) in Italy, Napoleon forced them to recognize French domination of Italy. Britain's other allies were soon forced to settle with France. Nelson's destruction of the Danish fleet at Copenhagen (1801) destroyed the threat posed

NAPOLEON'S MILITARY REVOLUTION

In the 18th century, armies had been relatively small, professional and expensive. Warfare had largely been a matter of siege and manoeuvre, because troops were too expensive to lose in battle. With their massive conscript armies, the French developed – and Napoleon perfected – new formations and tactics.

Napoleon always sought decisive victory, concentrating his troops against his enemy's weakest point. He divided his armies into corps of 25–30 000 men. These could be deployed over a wide front (keeping the enemy guessing as to where the attack would come) and then be reunited before the decisive battle. Napoleon was a master of rapid manoeuvre, and developed an appropriately flexible logistic system, including living off the land as his troops marched on. In a poor country such as Russia, however, this system left his troops highly vulnerable.

The success of Napoleon's approach was founded on good communications and supply, a vast reservoir of new conscripts, and on his popularity with his troops. This popularity was helped by a system of promotion through the ranks, and many of Napoleon's generals – such as the great Marshal Ney (1769–1815) – had risen in this way.

by a league of neutrals resentful of British efforts to end their trade with France. But Britain found it too expensive to carry on alone, and settled with France (the Peace of Amiens, 1802).

The Third Coalition 1805–07

Peace did not end the antagonisms between Britain and France, or put an end to French expansion. In 1803 Britain declared war again. Napoleon declared himself Emperor in 1804 and proceeded to assemble an army to invade England, but his plans were frustrated by Nelson's defeat of the Franco-Spanish fleet at Trafalgar (1805). Yet Britain again depended on European allies. Napoleon's proclamation of himself as king of Italy led Austria, Russia and Naples to join the Third Coalition. Britain again provided subsidies. However, Prussia remained neutral (as it had since 1795), and a number of smaller German states joined Napoleon.

In a lightning campaign, Napoleon's troops left the Channel ports for Germany, marching 800 km (500 mi) in five weeks. Defeating the Austrians at Ulm (October 1805), he occupied Vienna, before defeating an Austro-Russian army at Austerlitz (December). Austria was forced to recognize French supremacy in Italy and Germany.

The Battle of Aboukir Bay, 1799 (opposite). Following the French invasion of Egypt, Napoleon's army of 7000 defeated 18 000 Ottoman Turks. This victory was the more remarkable, given the fact that the French fleet in the Eastern Mediterranean had been annihilated the previous year by Nelson at the Battle of the Nile, cutting off Napoleon's supply line from France.

Prussia decided to restrain Napoleon, but suffered a disastrous defeat at Jena (1806). Prussia lost much territory as Napoleon reorganized Germany: the Holy Roman Empire was abolished and a French satellite organization, the Confederation of the Rhine, was established. In 1807 Russia too was beaten, settling with Napoleon and declaring war on Britain. Austria, having been defeated again in 1809, decided to join France. Napoleon, having divorced Josephine (his first wife), married an Austrian princess.

The Continental System

Napoleon was at the peak of his power in 1807, and determined to destroy Britain by ruining its export trade – the basis of its wealth and so of its continued opposition to France. Napoleon banned the import of British goods into all parts of Europe under French control. This blockade (the *Continental System*) created serious difficulties for Britain, including an inconclusive war in 1812–14 with the USA over the trading rights of neutrals. However, the System was not effective. Its unpopularity contributed to growing disillusionment with and resentment of French occupation in many parts of Europe.

The collapse of the Napoleonic Empire 1807–15

In 1808 Napoleon imposed his brother as king of Spain, sparking off a popular revolt. Henceforth large numbers of French troops were tied down in Spain, fighting a savage guerrilla war. Britain sent an expeditionary force to the Iberian peninsula, and many years of fighting (the Peninsular War) followed. After their victory at Vitoria (1813) under the command of Arthur Wellesley (1769–1852) – later the Duke of Wellington – British troops entered France in 1814.

By that time, French prestige had suffered disastrously in Russia. Relations between the two countries had deteriorated to the point that in 1812 Napoleon invaded Russia. Despite defeating the Russians at Borodino and reaching Moscow, Napoleon could not force the Russians to terms, and was himself obliged to retreat. The bitter winter combined with Russian attacks and the inadequacies of the French logistic system took a terrible toll: only 40 000 of the original French army of 450 000 men returned.

The Russian fiasco stimulated the formation of a Fourth Coalition. This included Prussia and Austria, and was again financed by British subsidies. In France itself the constant drainage of manpower led to growing resistance to conscription, and to Napoleon's rule in general. Fighting on two fronts, Spain and Germany, Napoleon was defeated at Leipzig (1813). In 1814, following the capture of Paris by the allies, he abdicated and was exiled to Elba. However, in March 1815 Napoleon exploited the unpopularity of the new Bourbon king, Louis XVIII, to return to France, seize power and renew the war. His 'Hundred Days' ended with his defeat at Waterloo (June 1815) by allied forces under Wel-

lington and the Prussian general, von Blücher. Napoleon was sent to St Helena in the South Atlantic, and Louis XVIII was restored.

The peace settlement

The peace settlement was worked out at Paris and the Congress of Vienna in 1814–15. It was a compromise between restoring pre-Revolutionary Europe, rewarding the victors, and preventing France from again dominating Europe. A ring of strong states was established around France, including a new kingdom of the Netherlands and a Prussian presence in the Rhineland. The Confederation of the Rhine was abolished, but security needs meant that not all the small states were restored. Austria kept Venice, and Russia was rewarded by the acquisition of most of Poland. In order to prevent future threats to their peace settlement, the victorious allies planned to hold regular meetings. The settlement effectively suppressed much radical and nationalist sentiment in Europe, which was to come to the boil in 1848 (see p. 428).   CS

SEE ALSO

● THE FRENCH REVOLUTION p. 424
● NATIONALISM IN EUROPE p. 428

THE NAPOLEONIC CODE

One of the most permanent achievements of the Revolution was the Napoleonic Code. Codification of the mass of legislation enacted in France since 1789 had begun in 1792. It was completed in 1804, and renamed the *Code Napoléon* in 1807. The Code restated in legal terms the egalitarian principles of 1789, including religious toleration, and confirmed the abolition of feudal rights. However, it put greater emphasis on the rights of property, reflecting the conservatism of French political life after the Terror. It also stressed the rights of husbands and fathers, reducing the status of women. This reflected Napoleon's personal views.

The Code, one small volume containing 2251 articles, spread the basic principles of the Revolution across Europe. Many states had little choice, since the Code was often imposed by Napoleon on those states incorporated into his empire. It was also adopted by his satellites and allies. In many states the Code survived the fall of Napoleon, and continued to play a vital part in national life. It contributed to the unification of states that before the wars had been divided by different sorts of law. In this way it ensured the permanent impact of the Revolution.

Nationalism in Europe

Nationalism is based on a feeling of common identity shared by a large group of people with the same language, culture, ethnic origins and history. Nationalism manifests itself politically in a sense of loyalty to a 'mother country', particularly where that country has not yet become a sovereign state in its own right. During the 19th century, nationalist sentiment sprung up throughout Europe, and provided the ideological cement for the construction of two new powers in Europe: Germany and Italy. Conversely, the effect of nationalism among peoples such as the Hungarians, Serbs, Poles and Greeks was to encourage rebellion against the larger and more powerful empires that controlled them.

Liberalism and Romanticism (see p. 630) were often closely associated with nationalism. Some, although by no means all, 19th-century nationalist movements combined their demands for national freedom or unity with the demands of the middle classes for a liberal form of government. Paradoxically, however, most successful movements for national unity resulted

Giuseppe Garibaldi, whose popular charisma led many to follow him in the cause of Italian unification. With his Redshirts – a band of irregular guerrilla fighters – he was responsible for many of the military successes of the Risorgimento, but his radical republicanism and independent ways often put him at odds with more conservative Italian leaders.

in the formation of states dominated by a strong monarchy.

The revolutions of 1848

Many of the European revolutions of 1848 were associated with nationalist demands. The uprising in Paris on 22 February 1848 led to the overthrow of the Orléans monarchy and the installation of a republican government, and was to inspire revolts right across Europe.

In Italy outbreaks of revolution occurred throughout the Italian peninsula, leading to wholesale expulsion of the Austrians occupying the north. However, disunity among the nationalists led to the Austrians (and the Spanish Bourbons in the south) regaining control.

In the vast, multilingual Austrian Empire, the revolutionaries of 1848 set their sights on overthrowing Austrian rule. The Hungarians, Croats and Czechs all managed to assert their independence from the Austrians and set up their own states for a brief period. However, the old rulers soon returned to power, partly by exploiting the divisions between the various national groupings.

Popular uprisings also occurred in many of the German states, and a liberal 'German National Assembly' met in Frankfurt in May, but by the end of 1849 the attempt to construct a constitutional unified German state had ended.

Italian unification

At the Congress of Vienna in 1815 (see p. 427), Napoleonic Italy was divided into 13 separate states, of which only 2, the Papal States and the kingdom of Sardinia (including Piedmont), were ruled by Italians. Austria dominated the peninsula. Nationalist secret societies such as the Carbonari ('charcoal burners') staged several risings and conspiracies during the 1820s and 30s, but none succeeded in dislodging Austrian rule. Other groups, including the Young Italy movement of Guiseppe Mazzini (1805–72), fared little better.

At the forefront of the Risorgimento ('resurrection') – as the movement for Italian unification came to be known – was Piedmont, which was by far the most industrialized and economically prosperous Italian state. Camillo di Cavour (1810–61), Piedmont's prime minister from 1852, seized every opportunity to advance the cause of Italian unification, and successfully solicited French help in driving the Austrians out of most of northern Italy in 1859.

In 1860 the nationalist guerrilla leader Guiseppe Garibaldi (1807–82) landed in Sicily with an army of 1000 volunteers and swiftly took control. He crossed to the mainland and swept aside minimal Bourbon resistance in southern Italy. Cavour moved troops to the Papal States in order to assert Piedmontese control of the newly united Italy.

In 1861 the 'Kingdom of Italy' comprised the entire peninsula, with the exception of Venetia (in the northeast) and Rome. Venetia was eventually acquired from Austria after Italian help had been given to Prussia in the 1866 'Seven Weeks War' (see below). Rome, with the exception of the Pope's own territory of the Vatican, was taken over when the French garrison left in 1870.

German unification

One man, Otto von Bismarck (1815–98), Prussian prime minister (1862–71) and then German chancellor (1871–90), is credited with masterminding the process of German unification. Germany at the close of the Napoleonic Wars existed only as a loosely grouped, weak confederation of 39 states. Economic unity preceded political unification, with the Prussian-led Zollverein ('customs union') being established in 1818. The 1848 revolutions rocked the rulers of states throughout Germany. However, by 1851, having crushed its own revolutionary unrest, Austria rather than Prussia had reverted to the position of dominant power within the reinstated German Confederation. Bismarck determined to change this through a policy of 'blood and iron' which unfolded in three main stages.

The first stage involved Prussia allying with Austria against Denmark over the thorny and complicated question of who should control the duchies of Schleswig and Holstein. In 1864 Prussia invaded and swiftly defeated Denmark, and then took control of Schleswig, while Austria took Holstein.

In the second stage Bismarck isolated Austria by means of skilful diplomacy and then provoked a war with Austria and various north German states in June 1866. This 'Seven Weeks War' culminated in a decisive Prussian victory over Austria at Sadowa. Austria was forced to accept that Prussia was now pre-eminent in north German affairs. The still independent south German states (Bavaria, Württemberg and Baden) were associated with the new, Prussian-dominated North German Confederation in an economic alliance.

In the final stage, the fears of the southern Germans of possible French aggression were exploited by Bismarck as a means of compelling them to draw closer to Prussia. Bismarck manoeuvred France into declaring war on Prussia in 1870 (the Franco-Prussian War). Following the swift and humiliating French defeat, the whole of the 'German' area of Europe was finally unified under Prussian control, and Prussia also gained Alsace and Lorraine from France (see also p. 440). The new German Empire was proclaimed on 18 January 1871, with the Prussian king declared Kaiser Wilhelm I of Germany.

peoples, and appalled by the cruelty with which the Turks put down Pan-Slavist rebellions, the governments of those two countries were more concerned by Russian territorial ambitions in the region. Russian interest in and encroachment on Afghanistan and Persia (present-day Iran) also caused tension with Britain, as it appeared to threaten the security of British India. Austria-Hungary, meanwhile, was alarmed at the prospect of Slav nationalism spreading to its own subject peoples, such as the Czechs and Slovaks.

British and French fears of Russian ambitions were confirmed when Russia occupied the eastern Balkan territories of Moldavia and Walachia in 1853. The following year the Russians sank a Turkish fleet, and Britain and France sent an expeditionary force to the Crimea, a Russian peninsula in the Black Sea. The Crimean War (1854-56) cost the lives of half a million men, largely owing to disease and military incompetence, and did not in the end forestall Russian ambitions.

Further Russian encroachments into Turkish territory in the Balkans were halted at the Congress of Berlin in 1878. In return, Turkey recognized Serbia, which became the largest independent Slav state in the region. However, Slav nationalists – encouraged by Russia and Serbia – greatly resented having to exchange Turkish for Austro-Hungarian control, as happened in Bosnia-Herzegovina. The Balkan Wars of 1912 and 1913 led to success for Slav nationalist aspirations: the territory of the Ottoman Empire was much reduced, and Serbia increased its size and strength. Austria was their next target. It was a Slav nationalist who assassinated the Austrian Archduke Franz Ferdinand in Sarajevo in 1914 – an event which precipitated the outbreak of World War I and the final break-up of the Austro-Hungarian Empire into independent nation-states following its defeat in the war (see pp. 436 and 440).   PO

SEE ALSO

- THE RISE OF ISLAM p. 392
- THE SPANISH AND PORTU-GUESE EMPIRES p. 410
- EUROPEAN EMPIRES IN THE 17TH AND 18TH CENTURIES p. 416
- THE FRENCH REVOLUTION p. 424
- THE REVOLUTIONARY AND NAPOLEONIC WARS p. 426
- THE PEAK OF EMPIRE p. 432
- WORLD WAR I p. 436

French troops in action during the Franco-Prussian War, 1870–71. Prussian victory led to German unification and the establishment of the Third Republic in France, whose government agreed to a humiliating peace treaty. Angered by this and by the conservatism of the new government, radical republicans and socialists set up the self-governing Paris Commune. This was bloodily suppressed by French troops in May 1871, and 20 000 communards were killed or executed. (Musée, Versailles)

'The Eastern Question'

In Eastern Europe, the nationalist aspirations of the various peoples under foreign domination became confused with the attempts by various of the great European powers to fill the power vacuum being created by the decline of the Ottoman (Turkish) Empire. This was particularly so in the Balkans, where the Turks had ruled a variety of mostly Slavic peoples for centuries, and which were seen by Russia, France and Britain as the key to dominance of the strategically important eastern Mediterranean.

The first crisis arose in Greece, where a popular uprising was put down by the Turks in 1821. The following year a National Greek Assembly declared Greece independent, and liberal and nationalist sympathizers from all over Europe pledged their support. The governments of the European powers remained officially uninvolved, until massacres perpetrated by the Turkish Sultan's troops goaded Russia into declaring its intention to intervene. In 1826, in order to forestall Russian domination in the area, Britain and France put pressure on the Sultan to grant a measure of autonomy to Greece, and when he refused, a joint British and French naval force sunk his fleet in Navarino Bay in 1827. Greek independence was eventually guaranteed by Britain, France and Russia in 1830.

In the previous year Russia had gained some territory and considerable rights and privileges in the Balkans from Turkey. The Russians also turned nationalist sentiments in the region to their advantage with the doctrine of 'Pan-Slavism', by which Russia took upon itself the right, as the largest Slav nation, to promote the desires of other Slav peoples for independence. Help to Balkan nationalists tended to coincide with Russian foreign-policy aims, particularly for power in the eastern Mediterranean, and control of the strategically vital entrance to the Black Sea. In other areas, where Russia's own interests were not likely to be furthered by the promotion of local nationalist aspirations, any such stirrings were quickly and firmly crushed – as happened in Russian-ruled Poland in 1830 and 1863.

Although liberal opinion in Britain and France was very much in sympathy with the national aspirations of the Balkan

The Crimean War (1854–56) was the first major conflict to be captured by the camera. The main aim of the Anglo-French expeditionary force was to capture the Russian port of Sevastopol. The first major battle was at Balaclava (October 1854), where a mistaken order led the Light Brigade to charge straight at some Russian artillery positioned at the end of a narrow valley. The battle was indecisive, although the following month the Russians were defeated at Inkerman. Sevastopol was eventually abandoned by the Russians in September 1855, and a generally inconclusive peace agreed in 1856.

The Expansion of the USA

The 19th century saw the transformation of the USA from an undeveloped, rural nation into an industrial giant. Population growth combined with economic and geographical expansion to produce by 1900 a dynamic, ethnically diverse republic stretching from the Atlantic Ocean to the Pacific.

This transformation was not accomplished smoothly. In addition to the inevitable problems that accompanied tremendous social dislocation, the USA was confronted at mid-century by a regional conflict over slavery and the rights of the individual states that threatened to destroy the Union. A bloody civil war was the result of this clash between North and South, a war from which the industrial North emerged the victor.

The early national period

Although a majority of Americans welcomed the creation of a stronger national government in 1787 (see p. 423), the initial unity produced by the Constitution was quickly undermined by a debate over the future of the country. On the one hand the Federalists, followers of Secretary of the Treasury Alexander Hamilton (1755–1804), demanded a sound system of public finance that would attract capital for commerce and manufacturing. On the other hand Democratic-Republicans, supporters of President Thomas Jefferson, hailed the virtues of an agrarian republic in which the states would check the excesses of federal power.

In 1812 aggressive British economic policy and American hopes of conquering Canada led to a second war between the two countries. The conflict dragged on until 1814, but resulted in military stalemate (see also pp. 426–7). New England Federalists flirted with treason during this period, thereby hastening the demise of their party. By the mid-1830s most Jeffersonians had become members of President Andrew Jackson's new pro-Southern Democratic Party, which endorsed the idea that the US had a 'Manifest Destiny' to expand over the whole of North America.

The westward movement

In spite of increasing industrial growth occasioned by canal and railroad construction after 1825, the USA remained a predominantly agricultural nation until after the Civil War. The aim of many Americans was to possess their own farm. To this end millions of people moved westward during the 19th century, lured from their homes by the prospect of settling on the fertile soils of the Mississippi basin and the Pacific coast. This process resulted in the displacement and settlement on separate, economically depressed reservations of most of the native Indian tribes.

Slavery and the territorial issue

In 1793 a New Englander, Eli Whitney (1765–1825), invented an improved cotton gin to separate seeds from the fibres of the cotton plant. Ten years later President Jefferson purchased the territory of Louisiana from Napoleon for $11.5 million. These events paved the way for the expansion of cotton growing into the southwest and reinforced the need for slaves to work the plantations (see p. 416).

Notwithstanding the development of a domestic abolition movement in the 1830s, most Northerners were unwilling to endanger the Union by agitating the slavery question. However, the US military defeat of Mexico in 1846–48 added a vast tract of land to the national domain (see map) and unleashed a bitter debate over whether slavery should be excluded from the new territories (notably California). In 1854 Congress passed the Kansas-Nebraska Act repealing a previous ban on slavery in the northwest. This appeared to open up all the new territories to slave labour, and Northern and Southern hotheads became embroiled in a vicious guerrilla war to make Kansas a state in their own image.

The crisis deepened as Northerners perceived the South's ruling planter class as a threat to their own freedoms and began voting for the new Republican Party. This organization, which represented Northern evangelical sentiment and economic interests, demanded Federal prohibition of slavery expansion. Southerners, on the other hand, believed their slave-based society to be under attack from abolitionists. When the Democratic Party split into Northern and Southern factions over the slavery issue, the Republican candidate, Abraham Lincoln (1809–65), won the 1860 presidential election. The seven Deep South states responded by seceding from the Union and forming an independent Confederacy.

When Confederates bombarded Federal troops at Fort Sumter, South Carolina, in April 1861, most Americans assumed the conflict would be brief. They were wrong. In spite of serious disadvantages, the South was able to prolong the issue for four bloody years. Six hundred thousand men – White and Black – perished in this, the first great modern war in history (see box).

Reconstruction

The North's triumph in the Civil War preserved the Union, ended slavery, and

A wagon train moves west. Throughout the 19th century, millions of people settled in the western USA, a process accelerated with the coming of the railways.

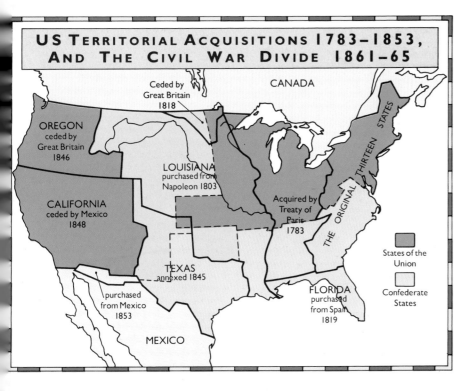

US TERRITORIAL ACQUISITIONS 1783–1853, AND THE CIVIL WAR DIVIDE 1861–65

THE CIVIL WAR

The Upper South's decision to join the Confederacy when war broke out bolstered the region's military effort. Virginia furnished the most talented strategist of the period, Robert E. Lee (1807–70). Indeed, until 1863 Southern generalship as a whole was markedly superior to the North's, particularly in the vital eastern theatre.

For most of 1861–63 the Northern cause looked bleak. Union armies suffered a string of serious reversals. Lincoln himself was attacked by fellow Republicans for his tentative approach to the war, and particularly for his reluctance to alienate the loyal slave states (Maryland, Delaware, Kentucky, and Missouri) by tackling the slavery question. However, on 1 January 1863 Lincoln signed the famous Emancipation Proclamation declaring that all slaves outside Union lines were free.

On 4 July 1863 the Union army of General Ulysses S. Grant (1822–85) finally broke through in the west by taking the Confederate stronghold of Vicksburg. The previous day Lee had been repulsed at Gettysburg, Pennsylvania. These two defeats sealed the fate of the Confederacy. Over the next two years the armies of Grant and William T. Sherman (1820–91) ground down the rebels in Virginia, Georgia, and the Carolinas. On 9 April 1865 Lee surrendered at Appomattox. The dream of an independent Southern nation was over.

Abraham Lincoln consults with his generals during the Civil War.

confirmed the dominance of the North's free-labour system. But it also created new problems. How should the South be reintegrated into the nation and what was to be done about 4 million ex-slaves (formally liberated by the 13th Amendment to the Constitution in 1865)?

Radical Republicans hoped that after Lincoln's assassination on 14 April 1865 his successor, Andrew Johnson, would join them in seeking to reconstruct Southern society before readmitting Southern delegates to Congress. In fact Johnson, a Tennessean, proved to be an ally of the defeated planter class. A fierce political struggle evolved during which moderate and Radical Republicans united to give Southern Blacks the vote.

During the 1870s Deep South states with large Black populations sent Black delegates to Congress for the first time in US history. However, after the onset of economic recession in 1873, the Northern electorate lost interest in Reconstruction, and the Republicans abandoned their Southern allies to the racist White majority. During the 1890s Southern Blacks were deprived of the vote by state laws, and they remained second-class citizens until the mid-20th century.

The industrial giant

Between 1880 and 1900 the USA emerged as a major industrial power. Large corporations such as Standard Oil and US Steel took advantage of new urban markets for manufactures and raw materials. Unprecedented numbers of immigrants, many of them from southern and eastern Europe, journeyed to the USA to take up jobs produced by postwar economic growth. By 1900 the nation's population totalled 76.1 million, more than double what it had been 30 years previously.

An originally insignificant, parochial republic was now on the threshold of claiming an imperial role. This had been hinted at as early as 1823 by the Monroe Doctrine (enunciated by President James Monroe), which had warned European nations not to seek further colonies in the New World. In 1867 the USA purchased Alaska from Russia, and in 1898 assumed control over Puerto Rico, Cuba, and the Philippines after winning a brief, jingoistic war against Spain. Not all Americans were pleased with their country's aggressive rise to great-power status, but neither they nor the rest of humanity could deny that the USA had at last arrived on the world stage. RC

SEE ALSO

- THE BIRTH OF THE USA p. 422
- THE PEAK OF EMPIRE p. 432
- WORLD WAR I p. 436
- THE POSTWAR SETTLEMENT AND THE DEPRESSION p. 440
- WORLD WAR II p. 444
- THE COLD WAR p. 450
- THE WARS IN VIETNAM p. 452

Emigrants embarking for the USA (left) from Hamburg in 1880. Escaping poverty and sometimes persecution at home, great waves of European immigrants arrived in the USA throughout the 19th and early 20th centuries. First came the Irish and Germans, and then the Italians and many nationalities from Central and Eastern Europe.

The Peak of Empire

The 19th century witnessed one of the most remarkable events in world history. In 1800 most people in the world were self-governing. By 1914 about one quarter of the globe had been taken over as colonies by half a dozen states. At the time many people argued that imperialism was needed to increase trade and find new materials for the economies of Europe. Others wanted to gain more territories to increase their strategic power in relation to other states. In the 19th century the various motives of the imperialists – economic, political and strategic – came together and encouraged the drive for Empire.

By the late 18th century various European empires had been established (see pp. 410 and 416) but these had either been in relatively under-populated areas, such as Canada and Australia, or had already shown signs of growing independence, as in the United States (1776; see p. 422) and South America in the early 19th century. The one serious exception was the rule of the British East India Company.

The British in India

By 1805 the East India Company was dominant in India. Wars against Nepal (1814–16), Sind (1843) and the Sikh kingdom of the Punjab (1849) extended the frontiers to the natural boundaries of the subcontinent in the north. To the east the British had annexed the Burmese empire by 1886.

Within India the traditional system of landholding was destroyed and the British introduced private ownership. Production of food did not keep pace with

The French flag is raised in Timbuktu, 1894. The 'scramble for Africa' in the 1880s and 1890s resulted in huge areas of the continent being carved up between the European powers. Possession was often a matter of whose army first arrived in an area.

the growth in population (some 190 million in 1871) and famine was a continuous threat. As a result the land quickly passed into the hands of relatively few large landowners, creating a large number of landless peasants.

The Indian Mutiny was the last effort of traditional India to oppose British rule. Princes, landlords and peasants were all united by the speed and tactlessness of the changes imposed by the British. The revolt began in 1857 as a mutiny of the Company's Indian soldiers. This spark ignited into rebellion all those who resented the growing British interference in Indian customs and believed that the introduction of Western education would destroy the indigenous culture of India. Economic tensions such as those arising out of the increased payment of land tax also played their part. Opposition to the British centred around the large number of rulers, including the Mogul emperor himself, who had been dispossessed by the Company. The British brutally ended the revolt in 1858 after 14 months of bitter struggle.

After the Indian Mutiny the British government took direct control of India, and embarked on a programme of modernization. By 1927 92 000 km (57 000 mi) of roads had been built; education in English was introduced; and, most importantly, a railway network was constructed. The railways made possible the exploitation of Indian raw materials and the introduction of cash crops, such as tea. On the other hand, the British refused or failed to modernize industry, destroying, for example, the Indian cotton industry so that it could not compete with the British.

Fears of a Russian threat to the Indian subcontinent led to ill-fated British expeditions to Afghanistan in 1839–42 and again in 1878–80. The fiercely independent Afghan tribesmen managed to oust the British, and their country remained as a buffer between the British and Russian Empires.

European imperialism

After 1870 there was a rush to acquire colonial possessions by the major European powers. Two major areas of the world were almost entirely divided up: Africa and the Pacific. There were a number of reasons for this striking change.

The development of commerce in the 19th century created a global economic system. Many formerly remote areas of the world were being settled and developed: Canada, the USA west of the Mississippi, Australia and New Zealand. Ancient civilizations – such as Persia (Iran), China (see p. 383) and Japan (see p. 387) – were being opened to European penetration. In Africa and Asia missionaries and traders were arguing the enormous potential value of colonies as a treasure house of souls and raw materials.

The second major factor was the development of new technologies that depended on raw materials found mostly in remote

places: for example, the motor car depended on oil and rubber, and copper from Africa and South America was needed for the new electrical industry. In addition the new mass consumption of sugar, tea, coffee, cocoa and fruit led to the development of tropical plantation economies. So the scramble for natural resources provided a fresh impetus for expansion.

In Europe there was increasing competition between the old imperial powers – Britain and France – and the emerging nations, especially Germany and Italy. Each feared being left behind by its rivals. Missionaries, traders, military and naval men and the public came together in the European capitals to press for imperial advances.

The scramble for empire

Before the 1880s the Africans, aided by the climate, had largely resisted European conquest, even forcing the Portuguese out in 1690. Even in the late 19th century the Ashanti, the Zulu and the Abyssinians were capable of strong resistance, but the balance of military technology was now decisively in favour of Europe. Large areas of the globe, particularly in Africa and Oceania, were carved up between the Western powers (see map).

The French gained most of north and west Africa as well as Madagascar and Indochina. Germany acquired an empire in the Cameroons, Togoland, South West Africa, Tanganyika, China, part of New Guinea and some Pacific islands (all lost to the Allies after World War I). Italy obtained Libya, Eritrea and part of Somaliland, but failed in 1896 to conquer Abyssinia (see also p. 443). The British made the greatest gains, including Egypt (although nominally still part of the Ottoman Empire), the Sudan, Uganda, Kenya, British Somaliland, Nigeria, Ghana, the Rhodesias and Nyasaland, as well as strategically important areas of the Pacific such as Singapore, Malaya and Fiji. The British also consolidated their rule of South Africa with their victory in the Boer War (1899–1902) over the Boers (or Afrikaners: settlers of Dutch descent).

The old empire of the Dutch remained in Indonesia, while the Portuguese reasserted control of Angola, Mozambique and Guinea, although their largest colony, Brazil, had become independent in 1822. What remained of the Spanish Empire after the successful wars of independence in its South American colonies (1810–29), however, was largely taken over by the USA after a brief war in 1898. The Americans acquired Puerto Rico, Guam and the Philippines from Spain, and also the Panama Canal, Hawaii and other Pacific bases.

The imposition of colonial rule varied. In the Congo the personal rule of King Leopold of Belgium led to horrific atrocities. In South West Africa the Germans massacred the Hereros to impose their rule. Many Africans revolted against colonial rule: for example, the Ndebele and Shona rose in rebellion in Rhodesia (1896–97) and the Zulus in South Africa (1906). These movements, while trying to maintain traditional independence, also prefigured future nationalist movements.

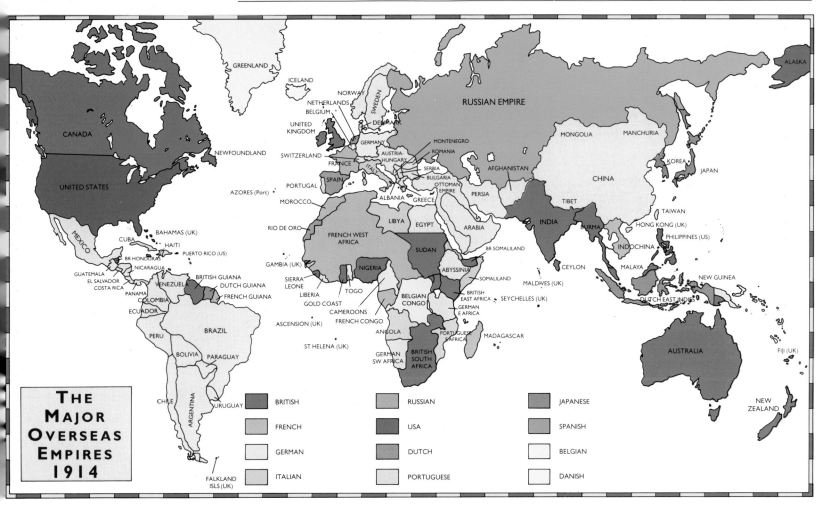

THE
MAJOR
OVERSEAS
EMPIRES
1914

BRITISH

FRENCH

GERMAN

ITALIAN

RUSSIAN

USA

DUTCH

PORTUGUESE

JAPANESE

SPANISH

BELGIAN

DANISH

Imperial acquisitions 1876-1914

During this period, nearly one fifth of the Earth's land surface was colonized. The shares taken by the various imperial powers are shown in this pie chart.

Total 30 million km² (10·8 million sq mi)

China

Once a great empire, by the 19th century China was politically weak and corrupt. It remained closed to outsiders until in the first Opium War of 1839–42 the British forced the Chinese to allow the traffic of drugs into China, and established five British-dominated treaty ports. British and French victory in the second Opium War (1856–60) forced the Chinese to open further ports. China seemed doomed to disappear under colonial rule. Russia

exercised influence in Manchuria, the Germans carved out bases in the north, Britain enlarged its Hong Kong colony, and the rising power of Japan annexed Taiwan in 1894–95 and Korea in 1910 after defeating the Russians in the Russo-Japanese War of 1905.

The Western powers were able to unite to put down the Boxer Rising and to occupy and loot Beijing (Peking) in 1900, but they were unable to agree how to divide the immense Chinese empire. As a result China remained independent, but the strains of foreign interference helped cause the final collapse of the world's most ancient civilization in 1911 (see p. 446).

Imperial rivalry and World War I

There is no simple connection between imperialism and the outbreak of World War I. Colonial disputes – such as the Fashoda Incident in 1898 between the French and British, and the crises over Morocco in 1906 and 1911, involving Germany – were successfully defused. Nevertheless, the drive for empire and control of the world economy created new antagonisms between the major powers. The rivalries between the powers, formerly confined to Europe, were now global and imperial.

The legacy of imperialism

Imperialism was both a massive movement and a very brief experience for those

involved. The entire experience of colonialism in many parts of the world can be fitted within a single life – decolonization started after World War II, accelerated in the 1960s and was virtually complete by the 1980s (see p. 448). For most people the cultural impact of imperialism was very limited, though a minority did have Western education and many of these later became the leaders of anti-imperialism.

Perhaps the most significant long-term impact of imperialism is continuing resentment against the imposition of Western ideas and against the economic dominance of the West over large areas of the Third World (see p. 298).   MP

SEE ALSO

● THE THIRD WORLD AND THE DEVELOPED WORLD p. 298
● THE SPANISH AND PORTU-GUESE EMPIRES p. 410
● EUROPEAN EMPIRES IN THE 17TH AND 18TH CENTURIES p. 416
● DECOLONIZATION p. 448

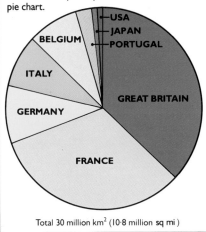

British troops in the Boer War (1899–1902). The guerrilla tactics of the Boers initially proved successful against superior British forces. To counter these tactics, the British devastated the country-side and rounded up Boer women and children into concentration camps, where at least 20 000 died of disease.

Industrial Society

Although the growth of industrial society created great wealth and caused nations to become rich, the cost in terms of human suffering was very great. The development of industry, especially in the textile factories and mines, brought long hours of work in harsh conditions. Child labour is often seen as one of the worst aspects of industrialization, although most children in pre-industrial society also had had to work exhausting hours. The principle of *laissez faire* (no state intervention in the regulation of industrial and economic affairs) was extremely influential, but campaigners such as Lord Shaftesbury in Britain secured legislation to limit the employment of young and female workers.

The Great Exhibition of 1851, held in the specially built Crystal Palace, was a showcase for British industrial, technological and imperial achievements. Other international exhibitions soon followed, in which each country vied to demonstrate its superiority.

During the second half of the 19th century improvements were also made in housing conditions and public health, and free education for children began to be introduced on a wider scale. Most of these reforms were introduced by the wealthy and powerful who controlled government. But many working people also agitated for improvements, and formed themselves into trade unions to achieve better pay and working conditions. There was also agitation for all adults to have a vote, which in many countries was restricted to men who owned property.

Working conditions

Campaigns for a 10-hour working day for all started up in many countries. In the USA, a 10-hour day became mandatory in New Hampshire in 1847, and in several other states soon after, but loopholes in the law made it ineffective. In Britain the 10-hour day was agreed in 1874, but in Japan, for example, it was not until 1916 that hours for women and children under 12 were eventually restricted to 11 per day. By the beginning of the 20th century, many children in the USA still spent 12 to 14 hours a day in the textile mills, and, by the time of World War I, despite being the world's largest and richest industrial state, the USA had far fewer laws than the industrialized nations of Europe for the protection of workers and the regulation of hours and conditions of employment.

Although various countries established work houses in the 19th century for those with no means of support, conditions in poor houses tended to be punitive. The first steps to what we now think of as the welfare state came with state insurance schemes, by which workers and employers paid regular premiums into a state-run scheme. Should a worker become sick or unemployed, payments were made to them out of the scheme. Old-age pensions were also often paid out of such schemes. The first such schemes were introduced in Germany in 1883–89, and in Britain and Russia, for example, in the years prior to World War I.

Social reforms

As industrial towns and cities developed, extensive areas of jerry-built housing appeared, which quickly turned into squalid slums.

In Britain the ravages of cholera in the 1830s and 40s at last prompted government action in the form of the first Public Health Act (1848). Later, demolition of slums and the rebuilding of better standard working-class housing became a function of local government. In 1882 the powers of local authorities were increased, leading to schemes for adequate sewage disposal, water supply and street lighting.

In the USA legislation was introduced in 1901 to improve conditions, but this was not particularly effective, and the corruption of some administrations allowed such conditions to continue unchecked. However, by 1920 many of the worst abuses had disappeared.

By the beginning of World War I, most major European cities had some experience of slum-clearance schemes, and of increased provision of public health and other municipal facilities. In France, the Second Empire (1852–70) saw the large-scale demolition of slum housing, and of rebuilding, especially in Paris. Even in Tsarist Russia a number of civic improvements were made. In Japan, although by 1907 both Tokyo and Osaka had waterworks and other public facilities, many cities still remained without amenities such as complete modern sewage schemes.

Education

As manufacturing processes became more complex, the need for an educated workforce led for the first time to state provision of more or less universal and compulsory systems of elementary education in most industrialized countries. The Church remained involved in educational provision, and serious conflicts sometimes arose between Church and state – particularly in France and Germany.

In Britain, cheap non-denominational elementary education became widely available from 1870. With further acts in 1902 and 1918, a free system for all was established with increased access to secondary education. Provision of free education in the USA predated its arrival in Europe. However, most Northern states were better off than the South. Many private schools were run by religious bodies in the USA, but there were no arguments between Church and state over control of education. In Japan, compulsory, state-run elementary schools were set up from 1872, with a curriculum laid down by the government.

Trade unions

Attempts by workers to organize themselves in defence of their own particular trade were made in all industralized countries. Trade unions often had another function, providing support for members in time of hardship or misfortune. Most governments saw the uncontrolled association of working people as a threat – particularly with the emergence of socialism as an ideology and political force (see p. 268).

In the USA, 'combinations' of workers had begun to appear during the last few

SEE ALSO

- EDUCATION p. 260
- GOVERNMENT AND THE PEOPLE p. 266
- POLITICAL THEORIES OF THE LEFT AND RIGHT pp. 268-71
- CAPITAL AND LABOUR p. 272
- THE WOMEN'S MOVEMENT p. 292
- THE INDUSTRIAL AND AGRICULTURAL REVOLUTIONS p. 420

SPREAD OF UNIVERSAL SUFFRAGE		
	Men	**Women**
Britain	1918	1918 (over 30) 1928 (over 21)
France	1871 (briefly in 1848)	1945
Germany	1870	1918
Russia	1917	1917
Japan	1925	1945

A slum in the East End of London, 1912, illustrates the gloomy and crowded conditions in which the urban working classes were obliged to live.

years of the 18th century, developing into unions in the 1820s and 30s. From the mid-19th century, American unions began to amalgamate in larger federations, including the National Labour Union (1866), the Knights of Labour (1869), the American Federation of Labour (1886) and the Industrial Workers of the World (1905) – the 'Wobblies'. With the exception of the AFL these organizations were socialist-inspired. Despite opposition in the courts and from many employers, and the bad publicity resulting from various anarchist-inspired acts of violence, trade unionism in the USA proved durable and effective, but only the AFL survived into the period following World War I. Socialism in the USA also reached its peak before 1914.

Britain was the first European country to allow 'combinations' of workmen (1824), although it took some time for trade unions to become both accepted and sustainable. The failure of the scheme of the utopian socialist factory owner, Robert Owen, for a 'Grand National Consolidated Trade Union' in the 1830s, and the case of the Tolpuddle Martyrs (1834), both bear witness to these difficulties. It was not until 1868 that the Trades Union Congress (TUC) first met.

In France, the first official acceptance of trade unions came in 1864, and in 1884 the Third Republic accorded full legal recognition. The Confédération Générale du Travail (CGT) was formed in 1895 as a united national body, and it resolutely refused to align itself with any political grouping. Separate Catholic trade unions were also set up. By 1913 there were 1 million trade-union members in France.

From 1886 onwards the size of the union movement throughout Europe was suddenly swelled by the recruitment of thousands of semi-skilled or unskilled members stirred into action by an economic slump. Previously these workers had not been sought or accepted by many of the older craft unions. In Britain, for example, membership of the TUC had increased to 4 million by 1913. In 1900 the forerunner of the British Labour Party was formed with the purpose of sending working-class representatives to Parliament. Germany's trade-union movement, legalized after Bismarck's departure from power in 1890, also grew rapidly. As in France, Catholic and other Christian workers had their own unions, and the original 'craft' unions also remained a distinct group. However, the socialist trade unions had by far the largest membership.

All such activity was suppressed as subversive in Russia throughout the 19th century, and those unions that did exist did so in secret. For a short period following the revolution of 1905 (see p. 438), unions of a limited kind were permitted, but repression quickly resumed. Metal workers and railway employees attempted to form unions in Japan in the late 1890s, but early efforts met with repression. The 'Yuaikai', a national labour organization, was set up in 1912. It began as a kind of self-help group, but in 1919, renamed as the Federation of Labour, it rapidly began to expand its membership.

The spread of suffrage

With the transition from an agricultural to an industrial economy, a major transfer of political power took place. The landowning classes were compelled to share their once exclusive access to government, first with the newly rich manufacturers and industrialists, and eventually with an increasingly broad section of the middle and working classes. This development led to the adoption of the principle of universal suffrage, in which every adult citizen had the right to vote.

The basis of the US system of government, the Declaration of Independence (1776), enshrined the ideas of equality and democratic rights for all (see p. 422) – although in practice most states imposed property qualifications for the right to vote and stand for office. All White men had voting rights by the end of the Civil War (1865), and the 14th amendement to the US Constitution sought to extend the vote to all Black citizens. However, this had little real effect (see p. 431). It was not until 1920 that all women throughout the USA gained the vote.

Ideas of democracy had been spread in Europe by the French Revolution of 1789 and the revolutions of 1848 (see pp. 424 and 428). By the end of the 19th century, the principles of democratic government had been accepted in most industrialized Western European countries: these principles included the right of public association, and some measure of freedom of speech and of the press. Until the 20th century, in many countries the right to vote and to be elected was restricted to men who owned property (see table). PO

Child workers (left) on a spinning machine in the USA, c. 1907/8. At this time many children in the USA were still working 12 or even 14 hours per day, although in other industrialized countries far tighter controls on the use of child labour had been instituted.

World War I

By 1914 Europe was divided into two armed camps based upon political, territorial and economic rivalries. In the centre of Europe was a recently unified Germany, allied to Austria-Hungary since 1879 and Italy since 1882, fearful of attack from France and Russia (allied since 1894), yet threatening expansion against either or both. Britain, traditionally aloof, viewed German industrial development, naval expansion and colonial ambitions (see p. 432) with distrust and since 1904 had been associated with Germany's rivals.

On 28 June 1914 the Archduke Franz Ferdinand, heir to the throne of Austria-Hungary, was assassinated in Sarajevo, capital of Bosnia, a region of the Balkans then part of the Austro-Hungarian Empire (see p. 429). The Austrians – supported by the Germans, who feared for the disintegration of their ally – blamed the newly independent neighbouring state of Serbia and threatened to attack. The Serbs in turn appealed for aid from their fellow Slavs in Russia, who began to mobilize their vast army.

Fearing attack, Germany put into action a strategy known as the *Schlieffen Plan*, and delcared war on both Russia and France. The Plan was designed to knock out France (Russia's ally) before the Russians completed mobilization, so avoid-ing a two-front war. As German troops crossed into neutral Belgium as a preli-minary to their attack on France, Britain (which had guaranteed Belgian indepen-dence) declared war on Germany.

The battle lines were drawn. On the one side were the *Allies* (Britain, France and Russia), and on the other the *Central Powers* (Germany and Austro-Hungary). Italy held back. By 4 August Europe had been plunged into a conflict that was to last for over four years, killing an esti-mated 20 million people.

Opening moves

Everyone expected a short war, but pre-vious military plans soon became irrele-vant. The French, intent on recovering the provinces of Alsace and Lorraine (lost to the Germans in 1870, see p. 428) mounted a major attack around Metz on 14 August, only to suffer enormous casualties. Meanwhile the Germans swept into Belgium towards northeastern France, aiming to take Paris in a huge outflanking movement. However, the Germans, with large distances to cover, lost momentum in the broiling heat of summer. This allowed the French to scrape together a new army to defend Paris, counterattacking across the River Marne in early September to force the Germans back. Both sides then tried to outflank the other to the north, but neither could gain advantage. The rival armies dug in and, by October, had created a line of trenches from the Chan-nel to the Swiss border.

By then the Germans had been forced to divert armies to the east. The Russians had initially made a ponderous advance into East Prussia in August, but were defeated in a series of battles around Tannenberg. Further south the Russians were more successful, pushing the Austrians back in Galicia, necessitating a

The sinking by U-boats of three British war-ships in 1914. Despite the effectiveness of the German U-boat campaign, by the end of the war the British navy had the upper hand at sea, starving Germany of essential supplies.

German reinforcement to prevent defeat. By Christmas 1914 a two-front war had become a reality for Germany.

The trench nightmare

Warfare on the Western Front was char-acterized by the trench system. This emerged to a large extent because of new weapons that gave the advantage to the defender. If one side wished to attack – as Britain and France did in order to liberate northeastern France and Belgium – their soldiers had to do so through mud, across barbed wire and into the teeth of machine guns and quick-fire artillery. In 1915, as casualties mounted alarmingly, the nature of the war changed, forcing all the major combatants to raise large armies and to mobilize their societies to produce new armaments. Anglo-French offensives failed to break the deadlock in the west, while on the Eastern Front the situation, although more fluid, similarly denied victory to either side.

Instead, the war expanded. In October 1914 the Turks declared war on the Allies, and in May 1915 Italy – in return for Allied promises of territorial gains from Austria-Hungary – declared war on the Central Powers, opening up new fronts that drained resources. In mid-1915 the Ger-mans forced the Russians back through Poland, taking pressure off Germany's eastern border, and in October Bulgaria joined the Central Powers. Only in Serbia was a decisive campaign fought: by December 1915 the country had been con-quered by the Central Powers.

The nightmare deepened in 1916. In Feb-ruary the Germans made an attack

The faces of British soldiers show something of the horror of the Western Front. Despite the deadlock of trench warfare, both sides continued to throw millions of men into attacks that might only gain a few hundred metres – at the cost of hundreds of thousands of casualties.

around Verdun on the River Meuse, designed to 'bleed France white'. The French obliged by pouring in reserves until, by December, the fighting had cost each side about 700 000 men. On 1 July the British tried to break through on the River Somme, losing 57 000 soldiers in the first few hours; by November this figure had risen to 460 000. On the Eastern Front it was even worse: a Russian offensive in June enjoyed initial success near the Carpathian Mountains, only to be turned back three months later at a cost of a million men. The Russian Army came perilously close to collapse.

Things were no better in 1917: after a failed French offensive in Champagne in April, elements of the French Army mutinied, while at Passchendaele in July the British entered a nightmare of mud that cost a further half million casualties. Only on the Austrian-Italian front was there a breakthrough of the stalemate, with the massive defeat of the Italians at Caporetto.

Alternatives to trench deadlock

In such circumstances alternatives to attritional deadlock were sought. Britain, for example, devoted part of her effort to attacks against the outer edge of the Central Powers, searching for weaknesses. As early as 1914 British forces had seized many of Germany's colonies in Africa, but a greater opportunity arose when Turkey came into the war.

Already regarded as the 'sick man' of Europe, a knock-out blow against Turkey would, it was argued, open up the southern flank of the Central Powers. In April 1915 a seaborne attack was made on the Gallipoli peninsula, on the Dardanelles Straits between the Aegean and Black Seas, with the main aim of taking Constantinople (now Istanbul). It failed, at a cost of 265 000 Allied troops, many of them Australian and New Zealand volunteers. A similar campaign in Mesopotamia (now Iraq) ended in disaster at Kut, on the road to Baghdad, in April 1916. Only later, in Mesopotamia and Palestine (the latter aided by an Arab revolt coordinated by T.E. Lawrence, 1888–1935) was success achieved, but the costs were high and resources diverted from the war in France.

Other alternatives were also tried, using the sea and air to reinforce the pressures of conflict on land. At sea, fleet actions were rare – the only major engagement between the British and Germans, at Jutland in May 1916, ended in stalemate – but from the start of the war both maritime powers attempted to impose blockades on their rivals. Britain was successful, but Germany was not.

The German U-boat (submarine) offensive caused heavy British losses, but in 1917, with a declaration of unrestricted warfare against any ships suspected of trading with Britain, it helped to trigger a declaration of war against the Central Powers by the USA. Using protected convoys and new anti-submarine weapons, the British gradually gained the initiative. By late 1918 the British blockade of

Germany had led to starvation and social unrest, but that year the Central Powers gained the Ukraine with its rich harvests. Germany mounted bombing raids on England by Zeppelin airships and aircraft, but they had little effect on the war effort. In the end, whoever won the land battles would prevail, and this meant looking to new weapons and tactics to break the trench deadlock.

New weapons and tactics

In 1915 the Germans used poison gas at Ypres, and the British soon reciprocated, but generally gas led to no major breakthroughs. On the Somme in 1916 Britain first deployed the tank as a means of crossing the mud and barbed wire of no-man's-land between the trenches and countering the effects of machine guns. However, it was not until Cambrai in November 1917 that the full offensive potential of massed tanks began to be seen. On this occasion the Germans counterattacked using select groups of 'stormtroops' to infiltrate rather than attack head on. By the end of 1917 the ingredients for tactical success were emerging.

Allied victory

By the end of 1917 the balance of power between the two sides had shifted. In late 1917 Russia dissolved into revolutionary chaos (see p. 438) and the Germans took the opportunity to attack with decisive results: by March 1918 a peace treaty between the two countries had been signed. This enabled the Germans to concentrate their forces in the west for a major assault on the British and French before American troops arrived in Europe in large numbers.

The German offensive enjoyed some success in March, using the new stormtrooper tactics tried out at Cambrai, but

by the middle of April Allied forces had rallied and stopped the advance. In August they moved onto the offensive, using tanks supported by ground-attack aircraft and, significantly, involving the first of the newly arrived American divisions. Elsewhere, the Central Powers began to crumble, first in the Middle East, where British troops took Jerusalem and Damascus and defeated the Turks, then in Italy, where the Austro-Hungarians were defeated at Vittorio Veneto and forced to seek terms. By November the Germans were isolated. With public confidence in the government evaporating, Communism spreading from the East and the Allies closing in, the German Kaiser fled to Holland and an armistice was arranged. At 11 AM on 11 November 1918 the fighting ceased.   JP

German propaganda print, depicting Scottish soldiers trampling on Greek virtue. Allied troops were sent to Salonika in 1915, in an attempt to open another front against the Central Powers. However, they failed to launch a successful attack on Bulgaria – Germany's ally – until 1918.

SEE ALSO
- NATIONALISM IN EUROPE p. 428
- THE PEAK OF EMPIRE p. 432
- THE RUSSIAN REVOLUTIONS p. 438
- THE POSTWAR SETTLEMENT AND THE DEPRESSION p. 440

The war in the east was generally more mobile than that in the west. Here German troops move through the burning streets of a Russian town.

The Russian Revolutions

At the turn of the 20th century Russia was a feudal state. Tsar Nicholas II ruled, as his ancestors had ruled before him, as an autocratic monarch. Nicholas had the backing of a large and inefficient bureaucracy, but remained supreme. His will was enforced by the state police and the army, and his officials controlled education and censored the press. Dissent was ruthlessly crushed. It was a situation ripe for revolution.

The vast majority of Russian subjects were poverty-stricken peasants, controlled through 'land captains' appointed by the government. Although serfdom (virtual ownership of the peasants by the land-owning classes) had been abolished in 1861, the peasants were closely bound to the land by a communal system of land holding.

Nevertheless, increasing numbers migrated to the cities, for Russia began to industrialize rapidly in the first decade of the 20th century with the aid of Western, particularly French, capital. Life for the 15 million or so members of the urban working class was harsh. Housing and conditions in the factories were poor, providing fertile ground for the growth of radical and revolutionary political parties. The two most important such parties were the Social Democrats and the Social Revolutionaries. The effective leader of the former was Vladimir Ilyich Ulyanov, better known as Lenin (1870–1924).

The roots of revolution

In 1904–5 Russia fought and lost a war with Japan. Even before this, unrest had been growing in both urban and rural areas. The defeat at the hands of the Japanese precipitated a revolution. On 'Bloody Sunday' (22 January 1905) troops opened fire on a peaceful demonstration near the Tsar's Winter Palace in the capital, St Petersburg (now Leningrad).

About 1000 protestors – including women and children – were killed. This was followed by a general strike, peasant uprisings in the countryside, rioting, assassinations and army mutinies. In October 1905 the Tsar agreed to elections to a *Duma*, or parliament. This rallied moderate political reformers to the side of the government, which was able to crush the revolt.

The first two Dumas proved to be too radical for the Tsar's taste, but in 1907 a conservative Duma was elected after electoral changes. Some reforms did take place under the chief minister, Petr Arkadievich Stolypin (1863–1911), who curbed the power of the land captains and helped to create a small class of peasants who owned their own land. However, Stolypin was unpopular with both Left and Right, and was assassinated.

World War I placed Russian society under tremendous strain. After three years of war the army had suffered 8 million casualties and over 1 million men had deserted. Inflation was rife and the peasants began to stop sending their produce to the cities, leading to food shortages. Respect for the Imperial government – which was seen to be dominated by the corrupt and debauched monk Grigori Efimovich Rasputin (c. 1872–1916) – had crumbled and revolutionary propaganda began to spread among the soldiers and workers.

On 8 March 1917 revolution broke out in Petrograd (as St Petersburg had been renamed in 1914). *Soviets* (councils) of soldiers, workers and peasants were set up all over Russia. On 15 March the Tsar abdicated and a moderate provisional government was set up. In the summer of 1917 Aleksandr Fyodorovich Kerenski (1881–1970) became the chief minister, but the powerful Petrograd soviet was controlled by Lenin's Bolsheviks. On 7–8 November (25–26 October in the old Russian calendar) Kerenski was ousted in a coup led by Lenin.

Lenin and the Bolsheviks

Lenin had studied the ideas of Karl Marx (see p. 268) and aimed to replace capitalism with a Communist workers' state. He decided that the Russian people needed to be led by a well-educated, dedicated revolutionary elite. His opponents in the Social Democratic Party, who wished to build a mass party, were dubbed *Mensheviks* (or the minority), although in fact it was the followers of Lenin, the *Bolsheviks* (or majority), who formed the smaller group.

When the March revolution began, Lenin was in exile in Switzerland, but in April 1917 he was allowed by the Germans to return to Russia in a sealed train. He immediately began to plot the downfall of the provisional government, which had misguidedly decided to continue the war with Germany and was slow in introducing land reform. Lenin's promise of 'bread, peace and land' won many to the Bolshevik cause. After he seized power in November 1917, Lenin moved against rival socialist groups, using the Cheka (secret police) as a weapon, and executed the deposed Tsar and his family.

The Bolsheviks were forced to accept a harsh peace with Germany at Brest-Litovsk in March 1918, but this allowed the Bolsheviks to turn their attention to the civil war that had begun in Russia. The 'Reds' were opposed by the 'Whites' – a loose coalition of

SEE ALSO

- POLITICAL THEORIES OF THE LEFT p. 268
- INDUSTRIAL SOCIETY p. 434
- WORLD WAR I p. 436
- THE GROWTH OF TOTALI-TARIANISM p. 442
- WORLD WAR II p. 444
- THE COLD WAR p. 450

Lenin, the leader of the Bolshevik revolution and founder of the USSR. This idealized portrait was painted in 1930.

Bolshevik revolutionaries in action in Petrograd (Leningrad) in November 1917. The coup itself was virtually bloodless, but was followed by several years of civil war.

democrats, socialists and reactionaries, united only by their opposition to Lenin – and by armies sent by Britain, France, Japan and the USA.

However, the various White factions were unable to coordinate their strategy, and they were defeated piecemeal by the Red Army created by Leon Trotsky (1879–1940), a former Menshevik. By mid-1920 it was clear that the Bolsheviks had triumphed. Russia was then attacked by Poland, which was intent on seizing territory in western Russia. The Red Army weathered the attack and then advanced as far as Warsaw before suffering a defeat on the Vistula. During the civil war the Red Army also reconquered the various non-Russian areas of the former Tsarist empire; these had formed their own republics in 1918. The Union of Soviet Socialist Republics was formally established in 1922.

Economic problems and the NEP

In November 1917 the new Bolshevik government faced many economic problems. They divided up the old estates, giving the land to peasants, which gained them considerable support. In June 1918 Lenin was forced to introduce 'War Communism', by which there was wholesale nationalization and state control of agriculture. This led to the collapse of industrial production and

serious food shortages. In March 1921, after a serious naval mutiny at Kronstadt, the New Economic Policy (NEP) was introduced. This returned small businesses to private hands and allowed farmers to sell their crops. Previously, surplus produce had simply been requisitioned by the state, but now a class of *kulaks* (affluent peasant farmers) emerged. The NEP improved both industrial and agricultural output.

The death of Lenin in 1924 initiated a power struggle among his successors. By 1929 Joseph Stalin had emerged victorious and he remained the unchallenged ruler until his death in 1953. His chief rival had been Trotsky, who had advocated spreading revolution across Europe. In the mid-1920s Trotsky was eased out of power and eventually went into exile in Mexico, where he was murdered in 1940 by a Spanish Communist, probably acting for Stalin.

Stalin's policy of building 'socialism in one country' was undoubtedly more realistic, given the weakness of the USSR. Stalin aimed to catch up with the Western capitalist powers by a crash programme of industrialization and agricultural collectivization. This policy was to cause untold suffering to the Soviet people.

In 1928 Stalin ordered that land be taken away from its peasant owners and used to create collective farms, which were supposed to be more efficient as well as egalitarian. In the process the kulak class was destroyed, with perhaps 10 million deaths in 10 years. The disruption caused by the collectivization programme led to famine.

THE GREAT PURGE

In 1934 a senior Communist official, Kirov, was murdered – probably on Stalin's orders. Stalin claimed the murder was part of a widespread plot against the Soviet leadership, and used it to initiate the 'Great Purge'. For four years a whole series of Stalin's potential rivals were brought before show trials, convicted and shot, including 1108 delegates to the 17th Party Congress.

The Purge also claimed the lives of intellectuals, army officers and indeed anyone who might be considered a threat to Stalin. The officer corps of the Red Army was ripped apart. About 20 000 officers were killed or imprisoned, and Marshal Tukhachevski, perhaps the greatest of all Soviet generals, was shot. Altogether tens of millions of people were executed, exiled, or put in prison. The damage the USSR suffered as a result of the Purge can never be properly assessed, but the Red Army was certainly to pay dearly for this bloodletting when the Germans invaded the USSR in 1941.

The first of the Five-Year Plans to improve Soviet heavy industry also began in 1928. Generally, the targets were too ambitious; nonetheless Soviet industry did begin to catch up with the West. As in pre-revolutionary days, such rapid industrial growth caused much hardship. Living standards plummeted as the industrial workforce swiftly doubled to 6 million, and Soviet officials were quick to punish underproduction by imprisonment in labour camps.

The USSR and Europe

Although European governments feared that the USSR was bent on spreading revolution to their countries, the Soviets played relatively little part in European affairs in this period. The 1922 Treaty of Rapallo brought the USSR together with Germany, but with the emergence of Hitler, the Soviets began a bitter war of propaganda against the Nazis.

From 1934 onwards Stalin moved towards Britain and France. However, disillusioned by the policies of appeasement and worried at the prospect of Soviet isolation, Stalin signed a non-aggression pact with Hitler in 1939, agreeing to partition Poland between their two countries. This gave the Soviets a breathing space, but it was only to last until June 1941, when Hitler invaded the USSR (see p. 444).

JP

A poster for the Third International, the association of national Communist parties established in 1919. The aim of the organization – which was also known as the Comintern – was to promote world revolution. Largely a tool for Soviet control over Communist parties in other countries, the Comintern was dissolved by Stalin during World War II in order to reassure his non-Communist allies.

LONG LIVE THE THIRD COMMUNIST INTERNATIONAL!   VIVE LA TROISIÈME INTERNATIONALE COMMUNISTE!
EVVIVA IL TERZA INTERNAZIONALE COMUNISTA!   ES LEBE DIE DRITTE KOMMUNISTISCHE INTERNATIONALE!

The Postwar Settlement

Two months after Germany was forced to ask the Allies for an armistice to end World War I (see p. 437), the Paris Peace Conference opened. Although 32 states (but neither Germany nor Russia) sent representatives, most of the major decisions were taken by the 'Big Three' – the British and French prime ministers (David Lloyd George and Georges Clemenceau) and the US president (Woodrow Wilson). What they decided was to lay the foundations for the future of the world.

France had lost 1.4 million men in the war and Clemenceau was determined to weaken Germany so that it could never again threaten French security. Among his demands was a demilitarized 'buffer zone' in the Rhineland. Lloyd George, despite having exploited anti-German hysteria to win the December 1918 election, attempted to moderate the more extreme of Clemenceau's demands. In January 1918 Wilson had announced his 'Fourteen Points', which were to form the basis of a moderate peace based on national self-determination. However, during the Conference the idealistic Wilson had to compromise with the demands of the French and British. The terms of the resulting Treaty of Versailles with Germany were severe (see below), including a clause in which Germany accepted responsibility for the war.

Redrawing the map of Europe

The break-up of the German, Russian, Turkish and Austro-Hungarian empires gave the Big Three the opportunity to redraw the map of Europe and build up buffer states around Germany and Russia – the latter because of fears of its Communist revolution (see p. 438) spreading to other countries.

Under the *Treaty of Versailles* (signed on 28 June 1919), the Polish state was created and awarded the 'Danzig Corridor' – a belt of former German land that gave the Poles access to the sea and separated East Prussia from the rest of Germany. Danzig (the modern Polish Gdansk) became a free city administered by the newly created League of Nations (see below). Germany also lost northern Schleswig to Denmark, and Eupen and Malmedy to Belgium. The provinces of Alsace and Lorraine (seized in 1870, see p. 428) were returned to France. The Saarland was to be governed by an international commission for 15 years, until a referendum to decide its future, and the coalmines of the area given to France. The Rhineland was occupied by Allied troops and a 50 km (31 mi) wide swathe of land east of the Rhine was demilitarized. Control of German colonies overseas passed to the Allies under the guise of mandates from the League of Nations. The size of the German army was limited to 100 000 men, conscription was forbidden, and Germany was banned from

The signing of the Treaty of Versailles, 28 June 1919, in the Hall of Mirrors, Versailles. The choice of venue had symbolic significance, as it was here that the unified German Empire had been declared after the defeat of France in 1871. In the centre can be seen (from left to right) President Wilson of the USA, Prime Minister Clemenceau of France, and Prime Minister Lloyd George of Britain. (Imperial War Museum, London)

THE FOURTEEN POINTS

President Wilson of the USA proposed his 'Fourteen Points' on 8 January 1918. They enunciated the USA's aims in World War I, and Wilson hoped they would provide the basis of a lasting peace. However, at the Paris Peace Conference, Wilson was forced by Britain and France to give way on many of them.

1. An open peace treaty, with no secret diplomacy.

2. Freedom of navigation in international waters.

3. The removal of international trade barriers.

4. Reduction in the armaments of all countries.

5. Impartial settlement of conflicting colonial claims, taking into account the interests of the colonial populations concerned.

6. The evacuation of foreign troops from Russian territory, and no further interference in Russia's own political self-determination (see p. 438).

7. The evacuation of German troops from Belgium, and a guarantee of Belgian Sovereignty.

8. The evacuation of German troops from France, and the restoration of Alsace and Lorraine.

9. The adjustment of Italian frontiers on the basis of nationality.

10. Self-determination for all nationalities within the Austro-Hungarian Empire.

11. Removal of occupying forces from Romania, Montenegro and Serbia, and access to the sea for Serbia.

12. Guarantee of sovereignty of the Turkish portion of the Ottoman Empire, and self-determination for other nationalities within the Empire, plus free passage for all nations through the Dardanelles (between the Mediterranean and the Black Sea).

13. An independent Poland with access to the sea. (Poland had been partitioned between Prussia, Austria and Russia in the 18th century; see p. 417).

14. The formation of a 'general association of nations' – which was to become the League of Nations (see main text).

possessing tanks, military aircraft and large naval vessels. In addition, heavy reparations were imposed (see below).

The victorious powers also signed treaties with Austria-Hungary. By the *Treaty of St Germain* (10 September 1919) Austria lost Bohemia (including the Sudetenland) and Moravia to the newly created state of Czechoslovakia; Galicia went to Poland; and Trieste, Istria and the South Tyrol to Italy. By the *Treaty of the Trianon* (4 June 1921) Hungary, the other half of the old Dual Monarchy, was stripped of two thirds of its territory to help form Czechoslovakia, the new state of Yugoslavia and Poland. Under the terms of the *Treaty of Neuilly* (26 November 1919) Bulgaria ceded land to Greece. Austria, Hungary and Bulgaria – like Germany – were all forbidden to build up their troops beyond a certain level.

The Allies were forced to sign two treaties with Turkey. The first, the *Treaty of Sèvres* in August 1920, gave substantial parts of the old Ottoman Empire as mandates to France (which received 'Greater Syria') and Britain (which gained Palestine, Iraq and Transjordan; see also p. 454). However, an attempt by Greece, Britain and Italy to occupy parts of the Turkish homeland provoked a nationalist revolt led by a distinguished Turkish general, Mustapha Kemal (Kemal Atatürk, 1881–1938). His military and diplomatic successes cleared much of what is now present-day Turkey of foreign troops, and in 1923 he signed the *Treaty of Lausanne*, which gave Turkey much improved terms.

The seeds of future conflict

The seeds of future conflict were sown by these treaties. The various peoples of Europe were too mixed up to be neatly separated into nation-states, and the territorial settlement caused resentment and strife. Versailles, for example, resulted in ethnic Germans being placed under Polish and Czech rule in the Polish Corridor and the Sudetenland respectively. Italy, which had suffered heavy losses, left the Peace Conference disgruntled at her treatment by the Big Three, having failed to gain all the territory it had been promised when it entered the war on the Allied side. Above all, Germany emerged from the postwar settlement weakened and embittered but still the strongest power in central Europe. With the USA withdrawing into isolationism, France faced the prospect of a resurgent Germany alone, except for the unenthusiastic support of Britain and the weak and vulnerable states of Eastern Europe. The grievances of both Italy and Germany were to help undermine the fragile democratic systems in those countries (see p. 442).

The Versailles settlement has often been criticized for being too harsh; it has also been argued – in retrospect – that it was too mild and that only occupation and partition could have prevented future German aggression. One of the most bitterly resented aspects of the Treaty of Versailles was the imposition of monetary reparations. Britain and France demanded the payment of reparations from Germany both to satisfy their desire for revenge and to pay off their enormous war debts to the USA: Britain owed $5 billion and France about $4 billion.

John Maynard Keynes, the British economist (see also pp. 276–7), warned that reparations would be damaging to the economies of the victorious powers as well as Germany, but he was ignored. In 1923, during a period of rampant inflation in Germany, the payment of reparations was unilaterally suspended. The French Army marched into the German industrial area of the Ruhr, which caused the German economy further damage. A promise that reparations would once again be paid induced the French to pull out in September 1923. Reparations were scrapped in 1932 without having been paid in full.

The League of Nations

Some of the events of the 1920s made the international scene appear somewhat brighter. For example, the League of Nations had been created at the Peace Conference in 1920 in an attempt to outlaw war. It was intended that aggressor states would be punished by economic sanctions, or in the last resort by military action by states that were members of the League. Unfortunately for the idea, the US Senate refused in 1920 to ratify the Treaty of Versailles, and the USA did not join the League. Thus the League was weakened from the outset, and was to prove unable to stand up to international aggression in the 1930s (see p. 443).

'How much can the German donkey carry?' A reflection from the German satirical magazine *Simplicissimus* on the enormous burdens placed on Germany after World War I.

However, the notion of 'collective security' survived and by the *Locarno Treaties* of 1925 Germany's western frontiers were guaranteed by Italy and Britain. At this time Germany joined the League. The *Kellogg-Briand Pact* (named after the US and French foreign ministers who proposed it in 1928) renounced war as a means of settling disputes, and was signed by 65 nations. However, like Locarno, it proved to be of little lasting value. Growing rivalry in the Pacific between Japan and the USA appeared to have been defused by the *Washington Naval Conference* of 1921–22. This established a ratio of tonnage of capital ships (i.e. battleships and heavy cruisers) of 5:5:3 between the fleets of the USA, Britain and Japan. JP

SEE ALSO

● WORLD WAR I p. 436
● THE GROWTH OF TOTALITARIANISM p. 442
● WORLD WAR II p. 444

THE DEPRESSION

The Wall Street Crash was to terminate the era of collective security. On 24 October 1929, after a period of apparent prosperity, confidence in the New York Stock Exchange collapsed, leading to panic selling of shares. The Wall Street Crash threw first the USA and then the world economy into recession. As world trade suffered, unemployment rose steeply, leading to poverty, homelessness and misery for millions.

The Depression, as it became known, placed enormous strains on democratic political systems. In 1931 an attempt to deal with Britain's economic problems by cutting public spending led to the resignation of the Labour government and a constitutional crisis. British democracy survived, while in the USA President Franklin D. Roosevelt's liberal 'New Deal' policies had some success in tackling the social problems of the Depression. In Germany, however, the Depression made possible Hitler's rise to power (see p. 442).

An American family in the Dust Bowl of the Midwest during the Depression. The Dust Bowl – a vast area where the topsoil was eroded by droughts and overfarming – added to the misery caused by economic recession.

The Growth of Totalitarianism

From an ancient Roman symbol of authority, the *fasces*, is derived the name of one of the most significant ideologies of the 20th century – *Fascism*. Fascism grew out of the unstable political conditions that followed World War I. Its mass appeal derived from its promises to replace weak democratic governments with strong leadership and to rectify the grievances of individuals and states arising out of the postwar settlement (see p. 440). In the 1920s Fascist dictators began to gain power in several countries. Once they did, tensions arose between themselves and the democratic states – tensions that would lead eventually to war.

A Nazi gathering. One of the features of totalitarian states is the highly regimented mass rally of party members. Those held annually by the Nazis at Nuremberg involved huge open-air gatherings in a specially built stadium. The Nazi leaders used these occasions to rouse their followers into a frenzy of devotion, and to deliver important policy statements.

Fascism was not a coherent doctrine like Marxism (see p. 268), but all Fascists believed in a strong, nationalist, authoritarian state, ruled by a charismatic dictator backed by a single paramilitary party. Fascists were fanatically opposed to democracy, socialism, Marxism and liberalism, and were often racist and antisemitic. Both in opposition and in power, Fascists made effective use of propaganda and terror to win support and to dispose of political rivals.

Mussolini gains power

Italy appeared to be threatened by Communist revolution after World War I. One of the many extremist right-wing groups that was formed in response was the Fasci di Combattimento (usually shortened to 'Fascists'), led by Benito Mussolini (1883–1945). By 1922, largely through Mussolini's brilliant oratory and shrewd political sense, the Fascists had gained enough support to attempt to seize power. In October, 25 000 Fascist 'Blackshirts' marched on Rome and King Victor Emmanuel III was forced to ask Mussolini to form a government.

In 1926 Mussolini made himself dictator, awarding himself the title 'Il Duce' ('the Leader'). His most notable achievement was the Lateran Treaty of 1929, which ended the hostility between the Catholic Church and the Italian State. Massive programmes of public works were undertaken, but this did not prevent Italy from suffering badly in the Depression (see p. 441).

The rise of the Nazis

In Germany the weak Weimar Republic (set up in the aftermath of World War I, and named after the town where its parliament first met) came under attack in 1919 from Communist 'Spartacist' revolutionaries, and in 1920 right-wing paramilitary units launched an abortive coup – the 'Kapp Putsch'. In 1923 Adolf Hitler (1889–1945), leader of the small National Socialist German Workers' (or Nazi) Party, tried to overthrow the Bavarian government. The 'Beer-Hall Putsch' was unsuccessful and Hitler, a former army corporal, was arrested, serving a short prison sentence. During his imprisonment he wrote *Mein Kampf* ('My Struggle'). In it he set out his

beliefs on race: that 'Aryan' Germanic peoples were superior to Slavs, Negroes and, above all, Jews, and that the German 'Master Race' must conquer territory in the east to achieve *lebensraum* ('living space').

The Depression rang the death knell of the Weimar Republic. In 1930 a political crisis developed over plans to cut government spending on welfare services and President von Hindenburg (1847–1934) began to rule by decree. The Nazis were well placed to exploit the crisis. Hitler was a masterly orator and one of his principal lieutenants, Josef Goebbels (1897–1945), had a genius for propaganda. Hitler denounced democratic politicians for stabbing the undefeated German Army in the back at the end of World War I by signing the Treaty of Versailles (see p. 440), and blamed the Depression on Jewish financiers. Nazi tactics were ruthless but effective: the brown-shirted 'Stormtroopers' of the SA (Sturmabteilung) intimidated and murdered opponents. The Nazis began to receive support from all classes who longed for firm government.

In the 1932 election the Nazis won 230 seats, becoming the largest party in the Reichstag (the German parliament), and on 30 January 1933 Hitler became chancellor (prime minister). The move to totalitarianism was swift. The Nazis used the burning of the Reichstag on 27 February 1933 – which was probably the work of the Nazis themselves – as an excuse to arrest opposition politicians. The Nazis also forced through a law giving Hitler dictatorial powers.

Hitler in power

After von Hindenburg's death in August 1934 Hitler became 'Führer' ('Leader') with the powers of chancellor and president. The Nazis outlawed all other political parties, banned trade unions, and tightened their grip on the state by the use of censorship and by establishing a hierarchy of Nazi officials down to the lowest levels. Hitler's will was enforced by the SS (Schutzstaffel, 'protection squad') and Gestapo (Geheime Staatspolizei, 'secret state police'), both under the authority of Heinrich Himmler (1900–1945). Ernst Roehm, the head of the SA and a potential rival to Hitler, was murdered along with 150 of his followers on the 'Night of the Long Knives' (30 June 1934).

In accordance with Hitler's hatred of the Jews, the 1935 Nuremberg Laws stripped German Jews of their remaining rights; eventually 6 million Jews were murdered in concentration camps (see p. 445). By reintroducing conscription and rearming in defiance of the Treaty of Versailles, Hitler not only reduced unemployment but also restored national pride – both of which made him genuinely popular in Germany in the 1930s.

Totalitarianism in Japan

Other European states – notably Hungary, Yugoslavia, Poland and Romania – were also ruled by right-wing dictators during the interwar years. However, the growth of totalitarianism was not con-

Axis meeting, Rome, 1938. From left to right: Mussolini, Hitler, Count Ciano (the Italian foreign minister), Goebbels, Himmler, Hess, and King Victor Emmanuel III of Italy.

fined to Europe. Japanese governments in the 1920s tended to be weak, and even before the Wall Street Crash (see p. 441) the country suffered from serious economic problems. Faced with the power of big business on the one hand and the development of left-wing movements on the other, Fascist-style ideas, combined with a revival of emperor-worship, began to influence army officers. Many sections of Japanese society supported the idea of strong military government and military expansion at the expense of Japan's neighbours – particularly the European colonial powers.

The army began to demonstrate increasing independence from the government. In 1931, following a clash with Chinese troops at Mukden, the army occupied Chinese Manchuria on its own initiative. Four years later it attempted to seize power in Tokyo. Although the coup failed, the army came to have a dominating influence on the government, with General Hideki Tojo (1884–1948) becoming prime minister in 1941. Domestic policies began to resemble those of European Fascist states.

The failure of the League of Nations

The League of Nations proved unable to prevent war. When in 1933 a League commission denounced the Japanese attack on Manchuria the Japanese simply left the League and began a war of conquest in China proper in 1937. Similarly, in 1935–36 Mussolini invaded and conquered Abyssinia (Ethiopia). All the League of Nations did was to impose – for a brief period – ineffective economic sanctions on Italy. Three years later, in March 1939, Mussolini struck again, attacking and occupying Albania.

Meanwhile Hitler began to threaten the peace of Europe. In 1934 Germany left the League and in 1935 Hitler announced his rearmament programme. The following year he marched into the demilitarized zone in the Rhineland. This was a gamble: German forces were still very weak and the French might have driven them back. However, Britain and France did nothing. Also in 1936 Mussolini and Hitler became allies in the Rome–Berlin Axis, and Japan joined Germany in the Anti-Comintern Pact, aimed against the USSR.

Appeasement and the road to war

British and French policy towards Hitler has been called 'appeasement' – that is, they gave way to what they believed to be Hitler's reasonable demands in the hope that he would be content and not go to war. In March 1938 German troops marched into Austria and the *Anschluss* (union of the two countries) was proclaimed. Hitler next began to threaten Czechoslovakia, using the alleged ill-treatment of German-speaking peoples in Czech Sudetenland as a pretext. Britain and France at first supported the Czechs, but at the Munich conference in October 1938 the British and French prime ministers agreed to Hitler's demands, and the Sudetenland was handed over to Germany. The British prime minister returned to Britain announcing that he had achieved 'peace in our time'.

This peace lasted for approximately 12 months. In March 1939 Hitler seized what was left of independent Czechoslovakia, in defiance of the Munich agreement. He then turned his attention to Poland, demanding the return of Danzig and access across the Polish Corridor to East Prussia (see p. 440). War once again seemed inevitable and the British and French began half-heartedly negotiating with the USSR. But on 24 August Germany signed a 'non-aggression pact' with the USSR. Hitler, convinced that the British and French would do nothing, attacked Poland on 1 September 1939. World War II had begun. **JP**

SEE ALSO

- POLITICAL THEORIES OF THE RIGHT p. 270
- THE RUSSIAN REVOLUTIONS p. 438
- THE POSTWAR SETTLEMENT p. 440
- WORLD WAR II p. 444
- CHINA IN THE 20TH CENTURY p. 446

THE SPANISH CIVIL WAR

In Spain in 1936, alarmed at the left-wing policies of the Republican government and the breakdown in civil order, General Francisco Franco (1892–1975) mounted an armed revolt. A bloody three-year civil war began. Franco's Nationalists received military and economic support from Italy and Germany, and the Republican forces were aided by the Soviet Union as well as 'International Brigades' of largely pro-Communist volunteers.

The fighting was bitter and many of the tactics of 'total war' were tried out, especially by the Nationalists. In April 1937 German aircraft razed the Basque town of Guernica in a foretaste of the city bombing of 1940–45 (see p. 444). In April 1939 the war ended in Nationalist victory and Franco became the leader of a neo-Fascist Falange government.

Republican snipers in Toledo, 1936, during the Spanish Civil War.

World War II

Between September 1939 and September 1945 the world experienced a 'total war', fought by countries that devoted their full human and material resources to the complete destruction of their enemies. In the process the fighting spread to almost every continent and ocean, and all the ingenuity of man was used to produce new weapons of mass destruction. By the end of it all, over 50 million people had died.

The conflict began in Europe when, on 1 September 1939, Germany invaded Poland in pursuance of its territorial demands (see p. 443). Britain and France declared war on Germany two days later but could do nothing to help the Poles. On 17 September, following the Nazi-Soviet Non-Aggression Pact, Soviet units advanced from the east to link up with Hitler's armies. Poland ceased to exist.

Europe and the Mediterranean

After a pause known as the 'Phoney War', Hitler turned towards the west. In early April 1940 German forces invaded Denmark and Norway, then on 10 May turned their blitzkrieg ('lightning war') tactics on the Netherlands, Belgium and France, spearheading their attacks with dive bombers and fast-moving tank units. Anglo-French forces moved into Belgium, but found that the Germans had advanced across their rear. Trapped on the coast the British rescued over 300 000 men from Dunkirk, leaving the French to fight on alone. France surrendered on 22 June, and a pro-German French government was set up in the town of Vichy.

By then Britain was besieged. Since September 1939 the Germans had been conducting a naval campaign against British merchant shipping, and the German U-boats (submarines) were beginning to have an effect. In the aftermath of Dunkirk this threat was reinforced by air attacks on Britain. Initially the Germans tried to destroy the RAF as a preliminary to invasion, but were defeated in the Battle of Britain in the summer of 1940. They then tried to undermine British resolve by bombing cities in the 'Blitz' (September 1940–May 1941).

Nor was the fighting confined to Europe. On 10 June 1940 Italy declared war on Britain and France, taking the opportunity of their weakness to seize Somaliland (Somalia) and invade Egypt. In the event both attacks were defeated, with British counterattacks to take Italian-held Abyssinia (Ethiopia) and eastern Libya. This triggered a German response to prevent Italian humiliation. In North Africa General Erwin Rommel (1891–1944) pushed the British back to the Egyptian border, while in the Mediterranean the key island of Malta came under air attack. In the Balkans, where an Italian invasion of Greece (October 1940) had come close to disaster, German forces swiftly overran Yugoslavia, Greece and Crete (April–May 1941). British fortunes were at a low ebb, boosted only by a growing friendship with the USA. This resulted in the provision of war materials to the UK under 'Lend-Lease'.

The war spreads

The war suddenly escalated on 22 June 1941, when Hitler's forces attacked the USSR. As German tanks thrust deep into western Russia, massive pockets of Soviet troops surrendered. But Hitler could not make up his mind about objectives, first of all shifting forces to the north, then to the south. It was not until October that a major drive on Moscow began. As German units approached the city the winter snows began, enabling the Russians to recover. In December they counterattacked, forcing the Germans into winter enclaves.

By then the war had spread to the Pacific. On 7 December 1941 Japanese aircraft struck Pearl Harbor in the Hawaiian islands, crippling the US Pacific Fleet. In the next few weeks Japanese forces attacked the Philippines, Malaya, Hong Kong and the Dutch East Indies. By May 1942 all these colonies, together with Burma and Singapore, had been lost, and even Australia was under attack.

These escalations were to spell long-term disaster for the Axis powers (Germany, Italy and Japan), for a Grand Alliance (including Britain, the USA and the USSR) now emerged. Cooperation between the three main Allies was not always smooth, but a series of meetings, initially between British prime minister Churchill and President Roosevelt of the USA, then including the Soviet leader Stalin, gradually developed a concerted strategy for the defeat of the Axis, based on a demand for unconditional surrender.

The tide turns in the west

The first priority was the defeat of Germany. The Americans favoured an immediate cross-Channel invasion, but Britain was not enthusiastic. By early 1942 North Africa had still to be cleared, and Allied shipping in the Atlantic was still under heavy attack by German U-boats. Churchill therefore persuaded

The Normandy Beachhead, July 1944. Operation Overlord, which commenced on D-Day (6 June 1944), was the greatest seaborne invasion in history. Within a month 1.1 million Allied troops and 200 000 vehicles had been landed on the beaches of north-west France.

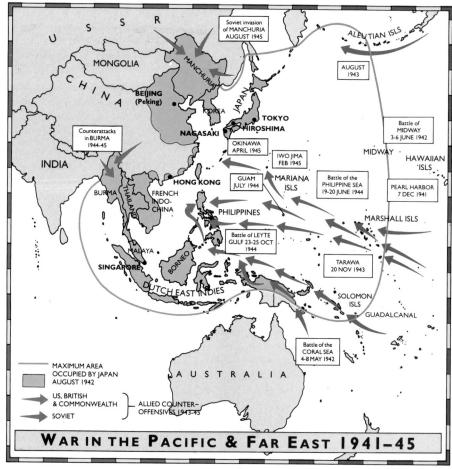

WAR IN THE PACIFIC & FAR EAST 1941-45

THE WAR IN EUROPE 1939-45

➤ US, BRITISH, COMMONWEALTH & OTHERS

➤ SOVIET

ALLIED COUNTERATTACKS 1942-45

■ MAXIMUM EXTENT OF AXIS EMPIRE, NOVEMBER 1942

■ UNOCCUPIED ALLIED POWERS

■ NEUTRAL

the Americans to concentrate on these two areas first, together with a combined bombing offensive against German cities.

By early 1943 new tactics and weapons had given victory to the Allies in the Atlantic. In North Africa, the tide was turned at Alamein in October 1942 by British forces under General (later Field Marshal) Bernard Montgomery (1887–1976). Simultaneously Anglo-US forces invaded French North Africa and, although the Axis forces fought stubbornly for Tunisia, victory was attained by May 1943.

The Americans called again for a cross-Channel assault, but the Mediterranean still took priority. In July 1943 Allied forces invaded Sicily then, in September, southern Italy. Mussolini was overthrown and the Italians surrendered, but German units rushed south to fill the breach. The Allied advance soon stalled in mountains to the south of Rome, centred on Monte Cassino. Despite an amphibious landing at Anzio (January 1944), Cassino was not taken until May. Rome was liberated on 4 June.

The defeat of Germany

The build-up of Allied forces in Britain was now complete. On 6 June 1944 (D-Day) they crossed the Channel under the overall command of General Dwight D. Eisenhower (1890–1969) to seize beachheads on the coast of Normandy. Bitter fighting ensued, but by early September Paris had been liberated, an invasion of southern France had taken place and Anglo-US forces were closing in on Germany. An attempt to use airborne forces

to 'jump' the lower Rhine at Arnhem in the Netherlands failed in September, and an autumn stalemate developed.

The Soviets meanwhile, under Marshal Georgi Zhukov (1896–1976), had advanced from the east. Their victory was hard-won, beginning in early 1943 when a German push towards the Caucasus had been stalled in the shattered streets of Stalingrad (now Volgograd). This enabled the Soviets to begin pushing westwards and by July 1943 their forces had re-entered the Crimea and advanced as far as Kursk, where a major German counterattack was decisively defeated. In 1944 a series of coordinated attacks all along the Eastern Front pushed the Germans out of the Ukraine in the south, to the gates of Warsaw in the centre (where an uprising by Polish resistance fighters was put down brutally by the Germans) and to the former Baltic provinces in the north. Leningrad, under German siege since 1941, was relieved in January 1944, having cost over one million Russian lives. Advances into the Balkans finally cleared the Germans from Soviet territory in late 1944.

The end came swiftly for Germany. Attacked from the air by massive fleets of Anglo-US bombers, its cities lay in ruins and, despite a desperate German counterattack through the Ardennes in December 1944, the Allies closed in. In the east the Russians drove from Warsaw to the gates of Berlin; in the west the Anglo-Americans crossed the Rhine and reached the River Elbe; in Italy the Germans were pushed over the Alps. Hitler committed suicide in late April 1945 and Berlin fell to

the Soviets in early May. On 8 May Germany surrendered unconditionally.

The defeat of Japan

This left the Japanese. Their initial wave of success had been halted at the Battle of Midway (June 1942) as well as in New Guinea and Guadalcanal (Solomon Islands). The Americans immediately went onto the offensive, conducting a two-pronged advance – under General Douglas MacArthur (1880–1964) in the southwest and under Admiral Chester Nimitz (1885–1966) in the central Pacific. Simultaneously British forces prepared to counterattack in Burma in conjunction with Chinese units. The Solomons/New Guinea campaign achieved success by late 1943, enabling MacArthur to prepare for the liberation of the Philippines; at the same time forces under Nimitz began an 'island-hopping' campaign, aiming for Taiwan.

By early 1944 it had been decided that both prongs should converge on the Philippines. As Nimitz closed in, taking the Marshall and Mariana Islands by June, he defeated a major Japanese naval force at the Battle of the Philippine Sea; as MacArthur invaded Luzon in October, he did the same at the Battle of Leyte Gulf. Both victories enabled the Americans to step up the pressure, fighting to liberate the myriad of islands in the Philippines while initiating a bombing campaign on Japan from the Marianas. In Burma a Japanese attack towards Imphal was defeated and the British went on to the offensive, liberating Rangoon by May 1945.

By then Iwo Jima had been captured and Okinawa invaded, although as US troops got closer to Japan the level of resistance grew more fanatical. Presented with the means to knock Japan out of the war and thereby save thousands of US soldiers, the new US president, Harry Truman, authorized the use of the newly developed atomic bomb on Hiroshima (6 August) and Nagasaki (9 August; see also p. 288). The latter coincided with a Soviet invasion of Manchuria and this finally broke Japanese resolve. The Pacific war ended on 15 August, although the surrender was not formally signed until 2 September. It was the end of six years of war.　JP

SEE ALSO

● NUCLEAR ARMAMENT AND DISARMAMENT p. 288
● THE POSTWAR SETTLEMENT p. 440
● THE GROWTH OF TOTALITARIANISM p. 442
● CHINA IN THE 20TH CENTURY p. 446
● THE COLD WAR p. 450

Buchenwald following its liberation in 1945. The implementation of the Nazis' 'Final Solution' – the extermination of those they considered sub-human – began in 1940. By 1945, at such camps as Buchenwald, Auschwitz, Treblinka, Dachau and Belsen, an estimated 20 million people had died, either in the gas chambers or from starvation and disease. Among the victims were some 6 million Jews – two thirds of Europe's Jewish population – together with Slavs, Gypsies, homosexuals, and political prisoners.

China in the 20th Century

At the beginning of the 20th century China was in turmoil. Despite a remarkable continuity of civilization dating back to at least 2000 BC, the authority of the emperor had been weakened in the 19th century by outside powers greedy for trade, and by huge rebellions which had left large areas of the country beyond the control of central government (see pp. 382 and 432-3). In 1911 a revolution, led by the *Guomindang* (*Kuomintang* or Nationalists) under Sun Zhong Shan (Sun Yat-sen; 1866–1925), overthrew the last of the Manchu emperors. Strong in the south (where Sun established a republic in 1916), the Nationalists faced problems in the north, which was ruled by independent warlords resentful of central interference.

Zi Xi or Tz'u-hsi, the imperial concubine who became empress on the birth of her son in 1856. She retained effective power during the reign of her son, and then during the reign of her nephew – whom she imprisoned and eventually had murdered shortly before her own death in 1908. Her reactionary policies inspired widespread discontent, culminating in the Nationalist revolution of 1911.

By the time of Sun's death in 1925 it was obvious that if the republic was to be extended to the whole of China, force would have to be used: indeed, Sun's successor, Jiang Jie Shi (Chiang Kai-shek; 1887–1975), gained his new position primarily because he commanded the Nationalist armies. Some inroads were made into the north, only to be undermined by the emergence of another, potentially powerful political force – the Communists.

Mao Zedong and the Communist revolution

The Chinese Communist Party (CCP) was formed in Beijing (Peking) in 1921, taking as its model the Bolshevik revolution in Russia four years earlier (see p. 438). But the Russian Communists had based their revolution on the discontented urban working class, and this the Chinese – an overwhelmingly peasant people – lacked. By 1928, after a series of disastrous urban uprisings, easily and brutally suppressed by Jiang, the CCP seemed doomed to extinction.

While this was going on, however, a relatively unknown member of the CCP, Mao Zedong (Mao Tse-tung; 1893–1976), had been experimenting with new ideas. Recognizing that any successful revolution needed popular support and that in the China of the time such support could only come from the peasants, he concentrated on the rural areas, setting up 'safe bases' among the people, which would act as a strong foundation for future action against the Nationalist government. Operating initially in his own home province of Hunan, in south-central China, then in the remote and inaccessible mountains of neighbouring Jiangxi, Mao proved so successful that by the early 1930s he was posing a direct challenge to Jiang's authority.

Jiang responded with military action, gradually reducing the Jiangxi base until, in October 1934, Mao was forced to withdraw. During the next 12 months he led his followers on a 9000 km (5600 mi) trek known as the 'Long March', moving from Jiangxi to the even more remote northwestern province of Shaanxi. Jiang, convinced that he could do no more damage, let him go.

The Sino-Japanese War

But by this time Jiang was facing a much more immediate threat – that of Japanese expansion. This had begun in 1931 with the Japanese seizure of Manchuria (one of the few centres of Chinese industry), and this was followed six years later by an all-out attack that led to the Japanese occupation of Beijing as well as of substantial parts of the Chinese coast (see also pp. 442-3).

Despite an alliance between Jiang and Mao, the Nationalists (who bore the brunt of the fighting) could do little to counter Japanese aggression. Only after the extension of the war to the Pacific and Southeast Asia in 1941–42 (see p. 444) could Jiang be guaranteed the outside support he needed, especially from the USA, but even then the record of the Nationalists was poor. They were still facing the Japanese occupation of large parts of China when Japan surrendered to the Allies in August 1945.

Part of the pressure exerted on Japan in the final days of the war was a Soviet invasion of Manchuria. In its aftermath the Soviets tried to ensure that Mao's Communists took over the area, hoping to accelerate the revolution. During the Sino-Japanese War Mao had extended his influence and gathered strength, waiting for an opportunity to attack the weakened Nationalists. In 1946 he marched into Manchuria.

Mao Zedong, the former teacher and son of a prosperous farmer. By bringing Communist rule to China, he transformed the lives of a quarter of the world's inhabitants.

The civil war and Communist victory

This began a civil war in China that was to last for three years. At first the Nationalists held on to Manchuria, but gradually lost their grip in the face of guerrilla attacks. By 1948 Manchuria was in Communist hands and, when this was followed by attacks on Beijing, Jiang's forces began to collapse. On 1 October 1949 Mao proclaimed a People's Republic in Beijing. Jiang fled to the offshore island of Taiwan, where a Nationalist government was set up. The Communists periodically exerted military and political pressure against the Nationalists, most notably in 1958 when Mao's forces tried to seize the Nationalist-controlled islands of Quemoy and Matsu. However, the Nationalist government in Taiwan still exists today.

Meanwhile, in 1949 Mao's first priority was to ensure Communist control over the whole of mainland China, sending the newly created People's Liberation Army (PLA) to root out 'class enemies' and the remnants of the Nationalist armies. This led in 1950 to the first of a series of moves beyond the borders of China, when PLA units entered Tibet, an independent state since 1916. Repressive Communist rule alienated the native Tibetans, loyal to their religious leader, the Dalai Lama, and in 1959 they rose in revolt, only to be ruthlessly suppressed. Tibet has remained under Chinese control ever since.

Border wars

Expansion such as this highlights one of the chief priorities of the Chinese Communists – to secure the borders of China against outside interference. From late October 1950 PLA 'volunteers' saw action in Korea, triggered by an advance by United Nations forces into Communist North Korea after the North Koreans had been pushed back from their invasion of the South (see p. 450). As the UN advance seemed to be approaching the Yalu River on the border with China, Mao felt justified in committing his troops, initiating a costly but (in Chinese eyes) ultimately successful campaign that lasted almost three years. At the end of the Korean War in 1953 all of the North had been restored to Communist control and the threat to China's border removed.

Similar intervention in the Himalayan border region against India in 1962 prevented what was seen as a threat from that direction, while in 1979 an incursion into northern Vietnam, albeit less successful militarily, continued the trend.

The Sino-Soviet split

The incursion into Vietnam had its origins in a Chinese fear of Soviet encirclement, for by then Vietnam was supported by the USSR. Such a fear had seemed justified ever since relations between China and the USSR deteriorated in the late 1950s, triggered by ideological clashes over the true nature of Communism and fuelled by border clashes in Manchuria. One of the results was an acceleration of Chinese research into atomic weapons – they test-exploded their first device in 1964 – but of far more significance was the effects of the split on Chinese domestic and foreign policy. In foreign-policy terms, Mao mended fences with the USA in the early 1970s, playing the West against the East in a new twist to the Cold War (see p. 451), while at home he tried to radicalize the revolution to ensure its ideological strength.

The Cultural Revolution and its aftermath

The process of radicalization had begun in the 1950s, when the PLA (always primarily a political rather than a military instrument) had been sent into the countryside to spearhead the 'Great Leap Forward', an ambitious programme of land collectivization and education. It had largely failed, suggesting to Mao that the PLA had lost its revolutionary zeal.

After appropriate reforms in the PLA, Mao tried again in the mid-1960s, determined to spread more radical revolutionary ideas to the people in the so-called Cultural Revolution. He stirred up a hornets' nest, with militant students forming groups of 'Red Guards' to attack the existing hierarchy, which they regarded as bourgeois, over-Westernized and technocratic. Thousands died, and thousands more bureaucrats and intellectuals were sent to work in the fields. Mao was lucky to survive, having to turn to the PLA for support against the Red Guards when they went out of control. The power struggle that ensued between the militants and the now influential PLA was still being played out when Mao died in 1976.

After Mao's death China – under the leadership of Deng Xiaoping (1904–) – followed a more careful course both at home and abroad. Border disputes were settled more peacefully, and relations with the USSR were cautiously re-established in 1989. Foreign affairs generally were characterized by more open friendship with previously hated enemies. The agreement to negotiate the future of Hong Kong, which is to cease to be a British colony and revert to Chinese control in 1997, is a case in point.

The reason for this opening up to foreign countries is that the Party leadership had recognized the need for industrialization and modernization if China was to compete in the world, and this would be impossible if foreign crises occurred. Western technology was needed, and for this to be available and effective in China, less extreme policies had to be introduced. Economic liberalization and the opening up to Western cultural influences has led to internal pressures for political change, culminating in the massive pro-democracy demonstrations by students and workers in early 1989. These were brutally repressed by an ageing leadership apparently unwilling to loosen its hold on political power. In the face of an international outcry, China seemed to be turning inwards again.

China is currently at a crossroads: if it succeeds in modernizing its industry it has great potential; if it reverts to repression and international distrust, the record of violence and war so characteristic of its history in the 20th century could continue. JP

A lone demonstrator confronts the army in Beijing, June 1989. In April and May of 1989 millions of students and workers participated in demonstrations for greater democracy in cities across China. After a period of indecision, China's ageing Communist rulers sent in the tanks. Thousands died, and many more were arrested in the subsequent repression.

SEE ALSO

- POLITICAL THEORIES OF THE LEFT p. 268
- CHINA TO THE COLONIAL AGE p. 382
- WORLD WAR II p. 444
- THE COLD WAR p. 450

Decolonization

The process of decolonization, or withdrawal from empire, is by no means a novelty peculiar to the second half of the 20th century. In classical times, for instance, the Persians, Greeks and Romans in turn abandoned their once-expansive empires; in the early 19th century Spain and Portugal proved unable to maintain their colonies in Latin America in the face of an outburst of nationalist feeling. More recently Germany lost its overseas holdings in Africa and the Pacific as a result of defeat in World War I (see p. 440), while both Italy and Japan lost theirs as a result of defeat in World War II. The theme of decolonization is therefore a well-established one and, like the process of setting up and maintaining an empire – imperialism – a recurrent one in world history.

For all that, however, the decolonization process that has taken place since 1945 can be distinguished from previous imperial retreats by the sheer magnitude of what has happened. Whereas the Roman Empire of antiquity was restricted to the Mediterranean basin, Western Europe and parts of the Middle East, the retreat from empire by Western European powers during the modern period has affected virtually the entire world.

It is instructive to contrast the political map of the world in 1945 with its equivalent 30 years later. In 1945 there were some 70 independent sovereign states in existence, and much of the globe – especially vast tracts of Africa, the Indian subcontinent, Southeast Asia and the Middle East – were controlled by European colonial powers, either as colonies or as protectorates or 'mandates' from the now defunct League of Nations (see p. 440, and also the map on p. 433). Thirty years later there were more than 170 independent states on the map, the increase being accounted for almost entirely by decolonization, and there were hardly any non-self-governing areas left. The age of European colonialism was over, the nationalist revolution having wrought a massive change in the international political system.

Pressures for change

That such a transformation came about has been explained by some historians in terms of a 'push-pull' concept – in other words, that the colonial powers abandoned their empires both because of the 'push' provided by the rise and spread of nationalism within their colonies, and because of the 'pull' provided by liberal opinion in the home countries. The two processes coincided with dramatic effect during the second and third quarters of the 20th century to produce the wholesale withdrawal from empire.

The 'push' – rising demand for self-government and independence – may be explained by a number of factors. One of

these, the basis for the growth of nationalist sentiment within colonial territories, was the tendency of the colonial powers to provide Western-style education to their colonial subjects, albeit a minority of those subjects only and usually no more than a small elite. Education was provided for reasons of self-interest as well as altruism – an educated elite was a valuable asset in terms of local administration and development. But the consequences were the same: the emergence of a group of people who understood Western ways and who were imbued with notions such as freedom, self-determination and equality, and determined to enjoy such advantages themselves.

Another equally significant factor was the development in many colonies of an economic infrastructure (roads, railways, schools, etc.) and even some commerce and industry. This helped to stimulate 'detribalization' (the breaking down of barriers between different groups of people within a colonial area) and, allied to the spread of education, this produced groups of colonial subjects susceptible to the nationalist message.

Finally, the clash of cultures brought about by imperialism created upheaval. The imperialists were alien in terms of race and religion in most cases, and local people – often for the first time – became aware of their own unique characteristics. In the Middle East, for example, the importance of the Islamic religion and the steady growth of an awareness of the Arab race as a distinct social and cultural grouping undoubtedly fuelled the rise of Arab nationalism – a force of some potential as early as the 1920s and 1930s.

The myth of White invincibility

If the effect of these factors could be seen from such an early stage, World War II gave a tremendous boost to the growth of nationalist feeling – especially in areas occupied by Axis forces or cut off from the imperial power.

In Southeast Asia, for example, French and British territories were exposed to revolutionary ideas following the Japanese conquests of 1941–42 (see p. 445). Having shattered the myth of White invincibility, the Japanese encouraged local anti-colonial movements. After the war, these movements were superseded or enlarged by anti-Japanese nationalists – many of them Communists. Winning considerable popular backing, these elements

SEE ALSO

- THE THIRD WORLD AND THE DEVELOPED WORLD p. 298
- THE PEAK OF EMPIRE p. 432
- WORLD WAR II p. 444
- THE WARS IN VIETNAM p. 452
- THE MIDDLE EAST p. 454
- COUNTRIES OF THE WORLD p. 660 on

Dutch troops in action (above left) against Indonesian nationalists in 1948–49. Following the occupation by the Japanese in World War II, Indonesia declared its independence in 1945, but this was only formally recognized by the Netherlands in 1949–50.

A Mau Mau irregular (below left). During the 1950s the Mau Mau waged a campaign of terror against White settlers in Kenya, but were disbanded in 1963 following independence.

White settlers (above) riot in Algiers in 1960 in protest at President de Gaulle's apparent intention to grant independence to Algeria. Independence was eventually granted in 1962.

Independence in the Belgian Congo (now Zaïre) in 1960 (below) was followed by a bloody civil war between tribal factions in which UN, Belgian and mercenary forces also became involved.

were able to persuade or coerce the returning imperialists into granting independence – in Burma with minimal violence but in the Dutch East Indies (Indonesia) and French Indochina (Vietnam, Laos and Cambodia) only after prolonged and bloody conflict in the late 1940s and early 1950s (see also p.452).

In Africa, too, nationalist sentiment developed rapidly as a result of World War II. Its rise was fuelled by a variety of factors: the humiliation of France and Britain in 1940 and of Italy by 1943; economic and commercial development during the war; and, of course, by inspiration offered by Asian countries such as India and Pakistan, which gained their independence (albeit to the accompaniment of widespread sectarian violence) in 1947. By then, the Philippines had gained

independence from the USA (in 1946), Britain had given notice of her intention to withdraw from the mandate of Palestine (in 1947; see p. 454), and Indonesia formally became independent of the Dutch in 1949.

World War II, or more accurately the effects of that war, also encouraged the growth of anti-imperialist feeling in the mother countries themselves. Many of these countries, notably Britain, France, Belgium and the Netherlands, had been devastated or virtually bankrupted by the war and were finding it difficult to provide the necessary resources to rebuild their shattered economies, provide greater living standards at home and, at the same time, continue to bear the 'White man's burden' of empire. Imperial glory began to feel like imperial strain.

Moreover, the colonial powers began to find themselves overstretched not only economically and militarily but also, in a sense, morally. West European leaders and public opinion in general became responsive to the idea that colonial peoples should be allowed, indeed encouraged, to achieve the same rights of self-determination that Europeans had claimed for themselves long before. In short, the colonial powers began to lose the will, as opposed to just the power, to hang on to their empires indefinitely. The 'push' and the 'pull' thus came together and the imperial powers withdrew from empire in the third quarter of the 20th century almost as systematically as they had rushed into it in the latter half of the 19th. The days of empire, for better or worse, were over.

The end of empire

Setting the pace of decolonization were the British, who had established the largest of the overseas empires. Britain had begun the process long before World War II, granting independence to the countries of White settlement – Canada, Australia, New Zealand and South Africa – and this was followed in 1947 by the concession of independence to the largest non-White territory, India (split along

religious lines into Hindu India and Muslim Pakistan).

Then, under successive governments, colonies in Asia, Africa, the West Indies and Oceania followed suit, the process being greatly accelerated by the Suez Crisis of 1956, when Britain, having invaded Egypt (in conjunction with the French and Israelis) in an effort to reverse President Nasser's decision to nationalize the Anglo-French Suez Canal Company, was forced to withdraw under intense diplomatic and economic pressure from the USA (see also p. 454). The implication was that, even if Britain wished to maintain an empire, it could no longer do so in a superpower-dominated world.

Decolonization gathered pace in the 1960s, presaged by Prime Minister Harold Macmillan's recognition of a 'wind of change' blowing through the colonies. Empire was replaced by the concept of a multiracial Commonwealth, formed for the most part from states that had gained independence without recourse to violence, although the British did have to fight in places such as Malaya (1948–60), Kenya (1952–60), Cyprus (1955–59), Borneo (1963–66) and Aden (1964–67) to ensure, or try to ensure, the emergence of friendly governments.

The French also withdrew from empire, though only after two protracted and bitter conflicts against nationalists in Indochina (1946–54; see p. 452) and Algeria (1954–62) had persuaded them to abandon the concept of an indivisible French Union. The Portuguese, too, tried to preserve an indivisible empire, but gave up in 1974–75 after prolonged insurgencies in their three African territories of Angola (1961–74), Mozambique (1964–74) and Guinea–Bissau (1963–74).

In contrast, the Dutch accepted more quickly that they could not reassert their authority in the East Indies (Indonesia), while the Belgians granted independence to their main overseas holding, the Congo (Zaïre) in 1960, although this was followed by a bitter civil war. Even Spain decided to abandon her African colonies, Guinea and the Spanish Sahara, in 1968 and 1976 respectively.

By the late 1970s the world had changed dramatically, producing new political, territorial and economic rivalries as well as new opportunities for alliances and trade. One significant political development was the establishment in 1961 of the non-aligned movement (mostly consisting of African and Asian states), which encourages foreign policies independent of Eastern and Western superpower blocs. However, despite the technical independence of Third World states, many of them continue to be influenced strongly – politically and economically – by either the superpowers or a former colonial power – a situation sometimes described as *neo-imperialism* or *economic imperialism* (see p. 298). JP

Some key figures in Third World nationalism (from the top): Gandhi (India), Nehru (India), Sukarno (Indonesia), Nasser (Egypt), Nkrumah (Ghana), Sékou Touré (Guinea), Kenyatta (Kenya), Machel (Mozambique).

The Cold War

The Allied victory in World War II was largely due to the massive military involvement of the USA and the USSR. With Europe in ruins, it was these two giants that emerged as the world's superpowers. Two new opposing military alliances emerged in Europe: NATO in the West, and the Warsaw Pact in the East (see p. 286). The *Cold War* is the name that has been given to the confrontation between the superpowers and their respective allies that continued with varying degrees of hostility for four decades after 1945.

The term 'Cold War' derives from the fact that the superpowers themselves were never in direct military conflict, partially for fear of nuclear war. Instead there was a conflict of ideologies – Western capitalism versus Eastern Communism – exacerbated by what each side believed was the other's desire for economic and political domination of the world.

The division of Europe

In February 1945 Roosevelt, Churchill and Stalin met at Yalta to decide on the fate of postwar Europe. It was implicitly agreed that the USSR should maintain its influence in the areas occupied by the Red Army in Eastern Europe. Germany itself was to be divided into four zones of military occupation, with the UK, USA and France in the West and the USSR in the East. Berlin, lying within the Soviet sector, was to be split along the same lines.

Contra rebel soldiers. Financed by the USA, right-wing Contra rebels fought against the Sandinista government of Nicaragua. The USA accused the Sandinistas of receiving aid from Cuba and the USSR and introducing Communism. The Reagan administration in particular campaigned for more financial aid for the Contras from the US Congress. A ceasefire between the Contras and Sandinistas was agreed in 1989.

By 1949 Soviet-dominated Communist governments ruled East Germany, Romania, Bulgaria, Poland, Czechoslovakia, Hungary and Albania. Yugoslavia too was Communist. All opposition was suppressed, and many freedoms curtailed. Europe was effectively divided from the Baltic to the Adriatic, and the so-called *Iron Curtain* had fallen.

Until 1989, only Yugoslavia, Albania and Romania had managed to break with the Moscow line. When other Eastern European countries tried to implement independent policies the USSR quickly reasserted its domination. For example, the reforming governments of Hungary (1956) and Czechoslovakia (1968) were overthrown by military invasion.

What the USSR effectively created in Eastern Europe was a series of buffer states between itself and the West. The fact that in World War II the USSR lost 27 million dead, many of them civilians, contributed to a kind of siege mentality, and in particular a determination to keep Germany divided. This fear of invasion was undoubtedly replenished by periods of virulent anti-Communism in the West. However, it should not be forgotten that Russia even in the 19th century had had extensive imperial ambitions in Eastern Europe and Asia, and that all Soviet leaders up to the mid-1980s espoused a doctrine of world revolution.

Early confrontations

Once Hitler had been defeated, the wartime friendship and cooperation between the Allies quickly crumbled, and the old ideological hostility re-emerged. In 1947 President Truman declared the intention of the USA to resist Communist expansion. This policy – the *Truman Doctrine* – has been pursued by all subsequent US governments. US military and economic aid was sent to the governments of Greece and Turkey, who were fighting Communist insurrections. In addition, European reliance on the USA was ensured by the *Marshall Plan*, which pumped $13 billion of aid into Western Europe.

When the Western Allies proposed currency reform throughout occupied Germany, the USSR vetoed the idea. The Western Allies unilaterally instituted the reforms in their own occupation zones. In retaliation, Soviet forces blocked off all land links to West Berlin (June 1948). However, the USA and the UK organized an enormous airlift of supplies, and the blockade was finally lifted in May 1949.

Anti-Communist feeling in the West was further intensified by the explosion of the first Soviet atom bomb, the Communist victory in China (both in 1949), and the outbreak of the Korean War in 1950. In the USA the 'Red Scare' came to a head with Senator Joseph McCarthy's witch hunt of suspected Communists (1950–54).

The Korean War

Korea, which had been a Japanese territory, was divided in 1945 into two occupation zones, with the Soviets to the north of the 38th parallel of latitude and the Americans to the south. The eventual reunification of Korea was planned, but in each zone the occupying forces set up governments that reflected their own ideologies.

The occupation ended in 1948, and in 1950 North Korea launched a massive invasion of the South. The UN Security Council, which was then being boycotted by the USSR, sent armed forces to intervene. The UN forces rapidly pushed the North Koreans back over the 38th parallel, and continued to advance northwards ignoring Chinese warnings. China attacked in response, and the UN forces retreated back into South Korea. Fighting continued for another two years along the border. In 1953, after the USA threatened to use nuclear weapons, an armistice was signed, restoring the status quo.

Latin America and the Caribbean

Since the formulation of the Monroe Doctrine (see p. 431) the USA has regarded the Americas as its sphere of influence. With the onset of the Cold War this policy was adapted to resist Communist penetration of the region. Sometimes this has led to covert American involvement in the overthrow of democratically elected governments that the USA considers dangerously left-wing, as in Chile in 1973. It has also led the USA to support authoritarian governments of the right.

A long-standing irritation to the USA has has been Cuba, where in 1959 Castro's left-wing government came to power. Castro's nationalization of American-owned property led the US government to back an unsuccessful invasion by Cuban exiles at the Bay of Pigs (1961). Castro retaliated by adopting full-blooded Communism, and allowed the USSR to build missile bases on the island in 1962. The USA saw this as a direct threat, and told the Soviets to withdraw the missiles or

SIGNIFICANT EVENTS & ALLIANCES OF THE COLD WAR

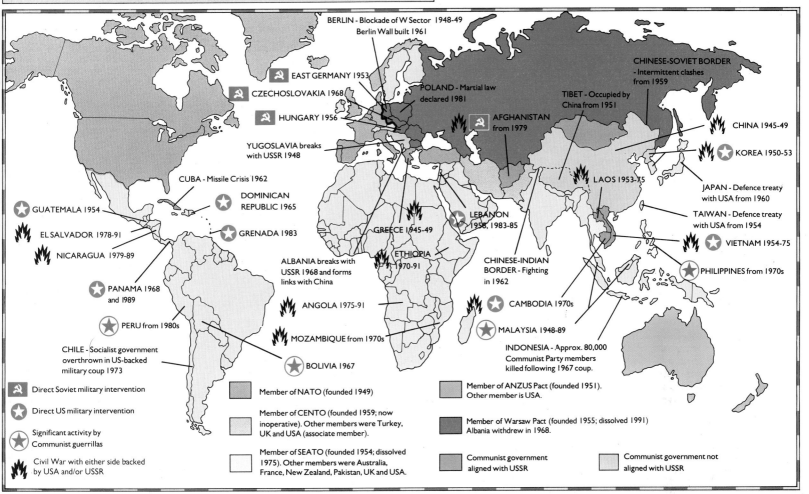

BERLIN - Blockade of W Sector 1948-49
Berlin Wall built 1961

EAST GERMANY 1953

CZECHOSLOVAKIA 1968

HUNGARY 1956

POLAND - Martial law declared 1981

AFGHANISTAN from 1979

CHINESE-SOVIET BORDER - Intermittent clashes from 1959

TIBET - Occupied by China from 1951

CHINA 1945-49

KOREA 1950-53

YUGOSLAVIA breaks with USSR 1948

CUBA - Missile Crisis 1962

DOMINICAN REPUBLIC 1965

GUATEMALA 1954

EL SALVADOR 1978-91

NICARAGUA 1979-89

GRENADA 1983

GREECE 1945-49

LEBANON 1958, 1983-85

ETHIOPIA 1970-91

JAPAN - Defence treaty with USA from 1960

TAIWAN - Defence treaty with USA from 1954

VIETNAM 1954-75

ALBANIA breaks with USSR 1968 and forms links with China

CHINESE-INDIAN BORDER - Fighting in 1962

PHILIPPINES from 1970s

PANAMA 1968 and 1989

ANGOLA 1975-91

CAMBODIA 1970s

PERU from 1980s

MOZAMBIQUE from 1970s

MALAYSIA 1948-89

CHILE - Socialist government overthrown in US-backed military coup 1973

BOLIVIA 1967

INDONESIA - Approx. 80,000 Communist Party members killed following 1967 coup.

Direct Soviet military intervention

Direct US military intervention

Significant activity by Communist guerrillas

Civil War with either side backed by USA and/or USSR

Member of NATO (founded 1949)

Member of CENTO (founded 1959; now inoperative). Other members were Turkey, UK and USA (associate member).

Member of SEATO (founded 1954; dissolved 1975). Other members were Australia, France, New Zealand, Pakistan, UK and USA.

Member of ANZUS Pact (founded 1951). Other member is USA.

Member of Warsaw Pact (founded 1955; dissolved 1991) Albania withdrew in 1968.

Communist government aligned with USSR

Communist government not aligned with USSR

face nuclear attack. The brinkmanship succeeded; the missiles were removed. Cuba attempted to export its revolution to various Third World countries. Notably active in this effort was Ernesto ('Che') Guevara. In the 1980s Cuba supported the left-wing Sandinista government of Nicaragua, while the USA supplied extensive aid to the right-wing 'Contra' rebels.

Towards détente

Following the Cuban Missile Crisis both the USA and the USSR realized how close they had come to mutual annihilation. Both sides sought thereafter to defuse tensions between them and to try to achieve a measure of 'peaceful coexistence'.

Although the most dangerous phase of the Cold War was over, both sides were to become embroiled in local conflicts, carefully avoiding direct confrontation with the other. Without doubt the worst of these conflicts was in Vietnam (see p. 452). The beginning of the Vietnam peace talks in 1968 coincided with a broader effort at *détente* – the term applied to a reduction in tensions between states. The USA, China and the USSR all began to adopt a more realistic, less ideologically motivated attitude to world affairs.

One of the first signs of this process was the re-establishment of friendly relations between the USA and Communist China, which by this time had established itself

as the third superpower. China had broken with the USSR in the 1950s (see p. 447), since when relations between the two had steadily deteriorated. With China making friends with the USA, the USSR saw the necessity of improving relations with the Americans. There was also the realization by both the USA and the USSR that it would be too risky to intervene militarily in the Arab-Israeli wars of 1967 and 1973 (see p. 454).

The results of détente included the SALT and ABM agreements in the 1970s at which the USA and USSR agreed to limitations in the nuclear arms race (see p. 289). There was also the Helsinki Conference of 1973–75, which was designed to reduce tension and increase cooperation within Europe.

A major setback to détente occurred in 1979 with the Soviet invasion of Afghanistan. The West immediately condemned the invasion and sent military aid to the anti-Soviet Afghani guerrillas in the subsequent civil war. For several years East-West relations were extremely frosty, with both sides accelerating the arms race. Regional conflicts broke out not only in Afghanistan but also in Central America and Africa.

The end of the Cold War

With the advent of Mikhail Gorbachov as the Soviet leader in 1985 the climate began to change. Gradually Gorbachov

initiated liberalizing reforms at home, and made a series of initiatives on arms reductions (for example agreeing the INF Treaty with the USA in 1987 – see p. 289). Like the Americans in Vietnam before them, the Soviets realized they could not win the war in Afghanistan without unacceptable losses, and in 1989 all Soviet forces were withdrawn.

Gorbachov also encouraged change in Eastern Europe, making it clear to the old-guard Communist leaderships that they should give way to reformers. This process was accelerated by massive popular demonstrations in many East European countries, and by the beginning of the 1990s all the former Soviet satellites were on the path to multi-party democracy. The Berlin Wall was opened in November 1989 and, in October 1990, West and East Germany were reunified. A month later, the Charter of Paris for a New Europe, signed by 34 countries representing the old East-West divide, marked the official end of the Cold War. The Charter included agreements on human rights, territorial boundaries and arms reduction. In September 1991, following the abortive coup by hardliners in the USSR, the Soviet Communist Party was suspended and major political reforms were implemented. However, with the USSR breaking up and Yugoslavia embroiled in civil war, Europe was clearly still subject to internal conflict. IDC

SEE ALSO

● POLITICAL THEORIES pp. 268–71
● INTERNATIONAL ORGANIZATIONS pp. 284–7
● NUCLEAR ARMAMENT DISARMAMENT p. 288
● THE THIRD WORLD AND THE DEVELOPED WORLD p. 298
● THE RUSSIAN REVOLUTIONS p. 438
● WORLD WAR II p. 444
● CHINA IN THE 20TH CENTURY p. 446
● THE WARS IN VIETNAM p. 452
● THE MIDDLE EAST p. 454

The Wars in Vietnam

Indochina, the area of Southeast Asia including Vietnam, Laos and Cambodia, has suffered almost continuous conflict since the early 1930s. In the process all three countries have come under Communist rule, and two Western powers – France and the USA – have experienced the humiliation of political and military defeat. Under the Communists conflict has continued, with fighting between differently aligned groups.

Communism in Indochina had its roots in nationalist opposition to French colonial rule. The Vietnamese Communist Party was founded in 1930 by Ho Chi Minh (1892–1969), dedicated to securing independence and political power. When French authority in the region was weakened by Japanese domination (and eventual occupation) during World War II, the Communists – known as the *Viet Minh* – set up 'safe bases' in remote areas and organized a strong political structure. In September 1945, after the Japanese surrender but before the French return, Ho Chi Minh declared independence for Viet-

nam – only to face French opposition. By 1947 he had withdrawn to the safe bases, determined to wear down his enemy using political subversion and guerrilla warfare.

The First Indochina War

The First Indochina War began in earnest in 1950 with Viet Minh attacks against isolated French outposts, forcing the colonial rulers back to defensive positions around Hanoi. In 1951 the Communists assaulted these positions head on, and were badly defeated. But Ho Chi Minh did not give up. Reverting to guerrilla tactics, he waited for his enemy to make a mistake. This came in November 1953 when, in response to a Viet Minh move into northern Laos, French airborne forces seized the isolated valley of Dien Bien Phu, close to the Laotian border. The Viet Minh surrounded the French base, and after a 55-day onslaught, forced the French to surrender in May 1954.

Their defeat was reflected in the Geneva Accords, signed in July 1954, which granted independence to Laos, Cambodia and Vietnam. Vietnam was split along the 17th parallel of latitude, with a Communist government in the North and a Western-style government in the South, on the understanding by the North that there would be nationwide elections in 1956. The South refused to cooperate in such elections, and by 1959 the South was facing renewed pressure from the North,

intent on reunification under Communist rule.

The start of the Second Indochina War

Communist guerrillas in the South, known as the *Viet Cong* (VC), began to mount attacks in rural areas. They were supported by the North via a network of jungle paths in Laos and Cambodia known as the *Ho Chi Minh Trail*. The Americans – viewing South Vietnam as a bulwark against the spread of Communism in Asia – committed advisers to train the South Vietnamese army (the Army of the Republic of Vietnam, or ARVN). It did little good: by 1963 nearly 60% of South Vietnam was affected by VC activity, and the ARVN was proving ineffectual. In November 1963 there was a military coup and South Vietnam entered a period of political chaos.

American commitment

The Americans were drawn in to fill the vacuum. In August 1964, President Lyndon Johnson claimed that North Vietnamese gunboats had attacked US warships in the Gulf of Tonkin, thereby gaining US Congressional approval for an expanded military commitment to South Vietnam and for retaliatory air strikes against the North. With VC attacks against military bases in the South increasing, and the North Vietnamese army (NVA) beginning to threaten the borders, US Marines were put ashore to guard Da Nang, just south of the Demilitarized Zone (DMZ) on the 17th parallel (March 1965). The Marines were soon

The Battle of Dien Bien Phu. This aerial shot was taken on 1 April 1954 during the siege of the French base by the Viet Minh. The French surrender here in May 1954 led to Vietnamese independence, but the wars in Vietnam still had more than twenty years to run.

US patrol craft in action in South Vietnam.

nducting major operations against VC
ses, and US Army units began to be sent
the South.

etween 1965 and 1968 the Americans
nsciously avoided full-scale commit-
ent of their forces, yet found themselves
awn ever deeper into the conflict. The
S strategy was to use their own 'main-
rce' units to guard the most vital
egions of South Vietnam against VC and
VA attack, and to deter the North from
ore active involvement by bombing
lected targets beyond the DMZ. The
RVN, with its US advisers and some
ain-force support, struggled to remain
fective. Australia, New Zealand, Phil-
ppine, South Korean and Thai forces also
ntered the war, but America's NATO
llies refused to assist.

lajor battles took place on the borders,
 which US firepower and technology
variably prevailed, but at heavy cost in
asualties and material. US forces were
creasingly diverted to the defence of
e populated areas, although they also
ounted multi-divisional 'search-and-
estroy' operations in which vast areas of
ountryside were cleared using firepower
nd mobile units – but this did nothing to
ain the support of the local people. The
C, adept at living underground in tunnel
omplexes, merely waited for the opera-
ons to end and then re-emerged to conti-
ue their activities.

et and US withdrawal

evertheless by early 1968 American
enerals were confidently stating that
ictory was in sight. So when in late
anuary the NVA and VC mounted a
eries of coordinated attacks throughout
e South (the *Tet Offensive*), the sense of
hock in the USA was profound. It
eepened as TV pictures of the fighting
ppeared in American homes, leading
any people to question the effectiveness
f Johnson's policies despite the ultimate
efeat of the Tet attackers. Under mount-
g pressure, Johnson refused to stand for
resident in the forthcoming elections,
alled for peace talks (which began that
ear in Paris) and, as a preliminary,
alted the bombing of the North. In
lovember 1968 Richard Nixon was
lected in his place, determined to end the
JS combat commitment. By then, the
mericans had over 550 000 troops in
ietnam.

lixon's strategy was 'Vietnamization' –
anding responsibility for the war to the
RVN so that US troops could be with-
rawn. The defeat of the Tet attackers
llowed the withdrawal to begin, but the
IVA was still active, leading to conti-
ued fighting and US casualties. Ameri-
an troop morale began to suffer and US
ublic opinion turned even more strongly
gainst the war. Nixon had no choice but
o continue withdrawals, buying time by
ermitting air attacks and limited ground
ncursions into Cambodia (1970) and
aos (1971), aimed at the Ho Chi Minh
rail, by now an elaborate supply route.
he pro-US Cambodian army mounted a
uccessful coup against Prince Sihanouk,
nd abandoned his policy of neutrality.

However, these incursions merely spread
the war, leaving both countries increasingly vulnerable to pressure from their
own indigenous Communist groups, the
Khmer Rouge in Cambodia and *Pathet Lao*
in Laos.

The North Vietnamese exploited the
diversion of US and ARVN attention by
mounting an all-out invasion of the South
in March 1972. They were halted partly by
ARVN resolve but more significantly by
US airpower, including renewed attacks
on the North. The damage was extensive
and the North Vietnamese agreed to a
ceasefire, signed in Paris in early 1973,
which left their forces in place in South
Vietnam. The Americans and other allies
completed their withdrawal. Over 47 000
US servicemen had been killed without
the satisfaction of a clear-cut victory.

Peace stood little chance. Nixon was
forced to resign over the Watergate scandal in 1974 and his successor, Gerald Ford,
lacked the political strength to maintain
support to the South. When the NVA
attacked again in early 1975 the ARVN
collapsed and by late April Saigon was in
Communist hands. In all, 1.3 million Vietnamese had died. Simultaneously the
Khmer Rouge took the Cambodian capital
Phnom Penh, and, a few months later,
Laos fell to the Pathet Lao. It was a major
defeat for US policy.

Continuing conflict

The violence did not end. In Cambodia the
Khmer Rouge leader Pol Pot (1925–)
initiated a bizarre experiment in 'social
re-education', forcibly moving city dwellers to rural areas to work the land. An
estimated 1.4 million people died, either of
famine or at the hands of the Khmer
Rouge. At the same time, Cambodian
forces exerted pressure on the border with
Vietnam, triggering a Vietnamese invasion in December 1978, which by 1979 had
pushed the Khmer Rouge back to the Thai
border. China tried to help Pol Pot by
launching a four-week punitive attack on
northern Vietnam (which was Moscow-
orientated), but the Chinese army did not
perform well (see p. 447). The Vietnamese
remained in Cambodia until 1988–89 when
the withdrawal of their forces created a
vacuum that Pol Pot attempted to fill.
However, in August 1991 Cambodia's
warring factions agreed on most aspects
of a UN-supervised peace plan.

Since 1975 there has been a mass exodus of
refugees from Vietnam to countries such
as Malaysia, the Philippines and Hong
Kong. The 'Boat People' stretch the resources of their reluctant host countries,
most of whom favour the forced repatriation of what they regard as economic,
rather than political, refugees. The
ripples caused by the violence of Indochina have not yet been calmed.   JP

The fall of Saigon to North Vietnamese forces in April 1975 marked the final victory of the Communists – although South Vietnamese resistance had by this stage collapsed. Saigon was renamed Ho Chi Minh City, and Vietnam reunited.

SEE ALSO

● DECOLONIZATION p. 448
● THE COLD WAR p. 450

The Middle East

From Libya in the west to Iran in the east, from Turkey in the north to Yemen and Oman in the south, the Middle East has long been a centre of tension and conflict. Lying astride some of the most important trade routes of the world – linking Africa, Asia and Europe – and containing valuable deposits of oil, it has attracted interference from a variety of outside powers. As a centre of three major religions – Judaism, Christianity and Islam – it has endured a high level of internal discord, fuelled in more recent times by nationalist and territorial disputes.

The Suez Crisis (right). A grief-stricken Arab woman in the streets of Port Said during the Anglo-French-Israeli invasion of Egypt, 1956.

Until the end of World War I in 1918, much of the region was under Ottoman (Turkish) rule, but Western colonial powers – Britain, France and Italy – had already established their influence there, particularly since the opening of the Suez Canal in 1869 had offered a much shorter route from Europe to the Far East. After World War I major parts of the Ottoman Empire were given as 'mandates' of the League of Nations (see p. 440) to Britain and France, with the intention of preparing them for eventual independence. France received 'Greater Syria' (part of which became the predominantly Christian state of Lebanon in 1920), while Britain received Iraq, Transjordan and Palestine.

The creation of Israel

From the time of the Roman Empire, the majority of Jews had been dispersed from Palestine. Since the late 19th century

The destruction of the Arab-Israeli conflict is summed up in this photograph taken in Sinai during the 1973 Yom Kippur War.

Palestine had been claimed by the Zionists, a group of Jews led by Theodor Herzl (1860–1904) who demanded a revived Jewish homeland on the basis of biblical rights. In November 1917, in an effort to ensure Jewish support for the war effort, the British foreign secretary, Arthur Balfour, had pledged his government to 'view with favour' the establishment of such a homeland once the Turks had been defeated. To the British in the 1920s and 1930s, the 'Balfour Declaration' meant no more than permitting restricted Jewish immigration to Palestine. But to the Arabs it was a first move in a Jewish seizure of their land and to the Zionists it was the first step in the creation of an independent Jewish state.

Britain faced growing Arab and Jewish unrest. Violence, particularly from extremist Jewish groups, grew in the aftermath of World War II, leading Britain in 1947 to hand the area over to the United Nations (UN) as successor to the League of Nations. Palestine was partitioned be-

ween Arabs and Jews, allowing the state
f Israel to emerge in 1948.

he response of neighbouring Arab coun-
ries – newly independent from Western
ule and imbued with a growing sense of
ationalism – was immediate. Five armies
– from Egypt, Jordan, Iraq, Syria and
ebanon – invaded the new state, but
vere defeated. By early 1949 Israel had
ecured its existence, but in order to
urvive with slender resources it evolved
emarkably capable armed forces.

uez

he prowess of the Israeli armed forces
vas shown in October 1956 when Israel, in
ollusion with Britain and France – angry
it Egypt's nationalization of the Suez
Canal Company (see p. 449) – invaded the
lesert region of Sinai. It was a short,
harp war, with the Israelis quickly occu-
ying Sinai, and French and British
orces attacking the area round the
Canal. There was an international out-
ry, and the USA in particular exerted
pressure that led to a withdrawal. A UN
peacekeeping force moved into Sinai to
keep the two sides apart.

The 1967 War

After 1956 Arab nationalism grew, particularly under the leadership of the Egyptian president, Gamal Abdel Nasser
(1918–70). His contacts with Syria and
Jordan alarmed Israel and when, in May
1967, he moved troops into Sinai and
demanded that the UN force withdraw, it
looked to Israel as if an attack was about
to take place. The Israelis responded with
a shattering strike against the Arab air
forces on 5 June, followed immediately by
a rapid campaign. In six days Israel
defeated the Egyptians in Sinai, the Jordanians on the West Bank (that part of
Jordan west of the River Jordan) and the
Syrians on the Golan Heights overlooking northern Galilee. This time, however, Israel had the backing of the USA –
which was concerned about Soviet friendship with Egypt and Syria – and refused
to withdraw. Israel's territorial gains
placed it behind more defendable borders
but ensured continued Arab enmity.

The 1973 War

Intent on recovering lost territory, Egypt
and Syria aimed to force Israel to the
conference table on the terms of UN
Resolution 242, which called for a return
to the borders of 1949. A war of attrition
was fought along the Suez Canal in
1969–70, and on 6 October 1973 Egypt and
Syria simultaneously mounted major
attacks, under cover of the Jewish religious holiday Yom Kippur.

Caught by war on two fronts, the Israelis
were hard pressed, but they devised tactics to counter new Soviet weapons and
defeated Egypt and Syria after 16 days of
hard fighting. During the war, a US
nuclear alert – triggered by apparent
Soviet moves to commit troops to the
support of Egypt and Syria – reminded the
world of the volatile nature of the Middle
East and helped to initiate a peace process
that culminated at Camp David in the
USA in 1979. In exchange for promises of
peace, Egypt regained Sinai.

The Palestinians and Lebanon

Since 1948 Palestinian Arabs had opposed
the loss of their homeland to the Israelis,
initially by looking for Arab support and
then, with the creation of the Palestine
Liberation Organization (PLO) in 1964,
by recourse to guerrilla warfare and
terrorism. By 1970 the PLO, organized as
a 'state in exile', was threatening the
internal stability of Jordan, forcing King
Hussein to commit his army against them.
In response many Palestinians fled to
Lebanon, taking advantage of the internal chaos of that country, which was split
between Christian and Muslim sects.

A civil war between these sects in 1975–76
caused the Syrians (who had never accepted the creation of a separate Lebanon) to intervene. The Israelis regarded
this as another threat to their security,
made worse by increasing attacks by the
PLO. In June 1982 Israeli forces invaded
southern Lebanon, intent on destroying
PLO forces based there. They also aimed
to create a buffer of Christian Lebanese
between Israel and the Syrian positions.

The Israelis advanced to Beirut in less
than six days, but the lack of an immediate UN-sponsored ceasefire condemned Israel to a war of attrition. A local ceasefire
in August allowed the PLO to withdraw
from Lebanon. However, a subsequent
Israeli move into Muslim-controlled West
Beirut (during which pro-Israeli Lebanese forces massacred Palestinian civilians at Sabra and Chatilla refugee
camps) revived the fighting. By June 1985
the Israelis, weakened by the seemingly
endless commitment to Lebanon, had withdrawn, leaving a buffer zone on their
border in the hands of the South Lebanese
Army. Lebanon disintegrated into ungovernable chaos, within which various extremist factions emerged. The situation
was made worse by splits in the Muslim
ranks, brought about by the rise of Islamic
fundamentalism in Iran (see box) and by
the return to Lebanon of elements of the
PLO. However, in 1991 Syrian forces defeated the Lebanese Christian militia and
the Lebanese government established control over the whole of Beirut, but parts of
the country remain beyond its control.

In 1988 the Palestinian Arabs in the occupied territories began widespread demonstrations against continued Israeli rule,
known as the *Intifada*. The often brutal
response of Israeli armed forces led to
condemnation abroad. Israel looked
increasingly isolated, especially after the
PLO Chairman, Yasser Arafat (1929–),
shifted the emphasis of his campaign, and
went as far as to recognize the state of
Israel. The large influx of Soviet Jews into
Israel since 1990 has given extra impetus
to the Intifada. After the Gulf War (1991)
there was renewed international pressure
to resolve the Arab–Israeli conflict. The
'peace process' began in October 1991
with deep mutual distrust and arguments
over Palestinian representation. No
agreements were reached, and the Israelis
rejected Arab demands for their complete
withdrawal from the occupied territories,
where Israelis had settled. JP

SEE ALSO

● DECOLONIZATION p. 448
● THE COLD WAR p. 450
● JUDAISM p. 472
● ISLAM p. 478

WARS IN THE GULF

In early 1979 the Shah of Iran was overthrown by Shiite Muslims under the Ayatollah Khomeini (1900–1989), intent on a
fundamentalist Islamic revival. This inevitably led to tensions with Arab countries in the Middle East ruled by more
secular Sunni Muslims. In its most dramatic form it led to the Iran-Iraq War.

Territorial disputes over the Shatt-al-
Arab waterway, coupled to religious and
ethnic differences, led to an Iraqi invasion
of Iran in September 1980. The fighting
was to continue for eight years, and it is
estimated that 1 million people died. As
each side tried to starve the other of
valuable oil revenues, the war spilt over
into the waters of the Gulf, both sides
mounting air and naval attacks on predominantly Western-owned oil tankers.

Eventually American, Russian, French and
British warships were deployed in the Gulf
to protect shipping, despite the possibility
of escalation to more general war. A
ceasefire in 1988 imposed a shaky peace,
but the world had been reminded yet
again of the potential dangers of the
Middle East. What had been intended by
Iraq as a quick victory resulted in the
virtual bankruptcy of the country.

In an attempt to restore Iraq's economic
fortunes, President Saddam Hussein ordered the invasion of neighbouring oil-rich
Kuwait (2 August 1990). The international
community was almost unanimous in its
condemnation of the invasion and UN
sanctions against Iraq were imposed. Iraq
annexed Kuwait, declaring the emirate to
be its 19th province, and refused to withdraw despite repeated UN demands. The
UN Security Council authorized armed
action by a US-led coalition to liberate
Kuwait from Iraqi occupation, and on 16
January 1991 the Gulf War began with a
massive coalition air campaign. The following month, coalition forces entered
Iraqi and Kuwaiti territory in a short
ground war that put an end to the occupation of Kuwait.

When the future of the Ba'athist Party
dictatorship of Saddam Hussein appeared
to be in danger, Iraq accepted all the UN
resolutions regarding Kuwait and agreed
to a ceasefire. During March and April –
with coalition forces occupying part of
southern Iraq – Saddam suppressed
revolts by Shiites in the south and Kurds in
the north. International efforts were
made to feed and protect over 1 million
Shiite and Kurdish refugees who fled to
Iran and Turkey. The Gulf War illustrated
an increasing degree of international
cooperation: the USA, Saudi Arabia,
Egypt, the UK, France and 23 other
nations contributed troops, aircraft or
warships to the coalition. Syria's participation in the coalition against its old rival
Iraq gained greater international acceptance for Syria, which had attracted
criticism for its sponsorship of terrorism.

RELIGION AND PHILOSOPHY

'Religion is a candle inside a multicoloured lantern. Everyone looks through a particular colour, but the candle is always there.'

Muhammad Naguib

What is Religion?

Religion is one of the most universal activities known to humankind, being practised across virtually all cultures, and from the very earliest times to the present day. Although various writers have attempted a wide and general definition, none of these definitions have been universally accepted.

Buddhist worshippers in Tibet. As in many Communist countries, religion in Tibet was long repressed, as it was seen to be in conflict with the materialism and atheism of Marxism-Leninism, the official state ideology. As in many religions, followers of Marxism-Leninism have at times adhered to its doctrines with unquestioning faith, persecuting those who believe differently.

Religion appears to have arisen from the human desire to find an ultimate meaning and purpose in life, and this is usually centred around belief in a supernatural being (or beings). In most religions the devotees attempt to honour and/or influence their god or gods – commonly through such practices as prayer, sacrifice or right behaviour.

Religion, magic and ideology

The question arises as to what can be included in what we call religion. Can we, for example, call Marxism-Leninism a religion, or humanism (the belief in humanity and reason rather than a god)? It is true that some people would be willing to include such beliefs in a modern definition of religion as 'anything to which we give ultimate allegiance'; however, such beliefs do not normally include any reference to a supernatural or ultimate being (or god). It is therefore better to describe them as ideologies, rather than religions, though they may share many of the characteristics of religion.

Among many peoples, for example in Africa and Latin America, there is a widespread belief in magic – the ability to change the physical world through ritual action (such as making someone sick by putting a curse on them). Can we call this religion? Again, though it shares some of the characteristics of religion, it differs in at least one major respect. In most religions there is a belief, in some form or other, in the sovereignty of a god or gods – that is, a belief that ultimately we cannot command the divine being or ultimate reality, but merely try to influence it in our favour. In magic, however, the world is understood in such a way that certain ritual actions automatically bring about the desired physical changes. This difference between the automatic result believed in by practitioners of magic on the one hand, and the provisional result as understood in

A Jain icon of the released spirit. A lack of attachment to material things and bodily pleasures is seen as essential to spirituality in many religions, and this has led to the emergence of monasticism in various different cultures. In the religions of the Indian tradition – particularly Buddhism, Jainism and Hinduism – this lack of attachment is essential if the spirit is to be released from the eternal cycle of death and rebirth.

most religions on the other, means that it is better not to regard magic as belonging to what we would normally call religion.

The constituent parts of religion

Religion is made up of both beliefs and practice. The academic discipline of theology (especially in the West, and in relation to the Christian religion) has tended to concentrate on belief. It is important to realize, however, that in some societies there is no word for religion. It is not a separate compartment of life – it is a way of understanding and living life itself.

Nevertheless, it is possible to distinguish several different aspects in most religions. One widely accepted classification identifies the following aspects: faith, cult, community, creed and code. *Faith* is the internal part of religion; what people believe, their feelings of awe and reverence, individual prayer, etc. *Cult* is all that is involved in worship – buildings, images, altars, rituals, holy songs, community gatherings and so on. *Community* is the social aspect of religion – the worshippers at a particular church or temple, the wider denomination or sect, monks and nuns, etc. *Creed* involves all the beliefs and ideas held by the religion as a whole. It includes scriptures, and ideas about God, angels, heaven, hell and salvation. *Code* has to do with the way people behave because of their religious beliefs, and includes ethics, taboos, and ideas of sin and holiness.

Families of religions

The religions of the world can be divided into two major groups. The first of these groups is often called the *primal reli-*

gions. These include the traditional religions of Africa, Australasia, Oceania, some parts of Asia and the original peoples of the Americas (see p. 464). They also include the pre-Christian religions of Europe (see p. 462) and the religions of other ancient peoples (see p. 460). These religions, though differing in detail, have several features in common. They all tend to be local – they are tailored to the particular tribe or people who practise them and their practitioners do not generally regard them as relevant to other peoples. Thus many of the myths and stories of such religions deal with the origin of one particular tribe. Secondly, modern primal religions tend to depend largely on oral traditions rather than on written scriptures. Finally, such religions are generally non-missionary, i.e. they do not seek converts.

The other main group is made up of what are often called the *universal religions.* This name implies that they see themselves not as local but as potentially universal – i.e. they have significance for the whole world. To varying degrees, therefore, they are missionary, i.e. they try to make converts. In addition, they have usually developed written scriptures that play a central part in the religion. Islam and Christianity are characteristic examples of this type of universal religion.

Within the universal group certain main families can be identified. The *Semitic family* includes Judaism, Christianity and Islam (see pp. 472–7), all of which share a common historical and geographical background. The *Indian family* is made up of Hinduism, early Buddhism, Jainism and Sikhism (see pp. 466–9). The *Far Eastern family* includes Confucianism, Daoism (Taoism) and Shinto (see p. 470). Though any given religion will normally claim to have been inspired by God, it is important to remember that all religions begin and develop in particular historical, geographical and cultural situations that influence and mould the particular form that religion takes.

Another way of classifying groups of religions is to distinguish those with a single god (*monotheistic* religions) and those with several gods (*polytheistic* religions). Monotheistic religions include Judaism, Christianity and Islam, while the polytheistic religions include Hinduism, the ancient Greek and Germanic religions, and many present-day primal religions.

Religion and secularism

In the present century, particularly in the West, some people have seen evidence of a decline in religion, and its replacement by *secularism* (a belief that the physical world is self-contained, and can be perfectly well understood by the insights of modern science, without reference to any supernatural explanations). While it is perfectly true that in some societies there seems to be a decline in organized religion, there is

SEE ALSO
● POLITICAL THEORIES pp. 268–71
● RELIGIONS OF THE WORLD pp. 460–79
● WORSHIP, PRAYER AND PILGRIMAGE p. 480
● SACRED SPACE, SACRED TIME p. 482
● GOOD AND EVIL p. 484
● PHILOSOPHY pp. 486–97

The Festival of the Supreme Being in Revolutionary France, 1794. At the outset of the French Revolution there was considerable anti-Christian feeling. However, within a few years the Revolutionary leadership had come to believe that religion was necessary for social stability, and introduced a Cult of the Supreme Being. This cult was based on Deism, the Enlightenment idea of a 'natural religion' based on human reason (see pp. 418 and 425).

little evidence of a decline in religiosity (religious feeling). Thus, while few people in Britain regularly attend church, most still claim to believe in God. This may indicate changing patterns of religiosity, rather than its decline.

One example of this is the widespread growth of new religious movements in many Western societies, offering alternative religious traditions not previously available. Thus movements such as Transcendental Meditation, the Unification Church (Moonies), the Hare Krishna movement and many others

attract followers because at a time of rapid change many people are disillusioned with traditional religions, yet retain a basic religiosity.

It must also be remembered that while organized religion may seem to be declining in the West, in most other parts of the world the major universal religions (especially Christianity and Islam) are increasing at a considerable rate. Thus religion – always living and changing – nevertheless remains the near universal phenomenon it has always been.   TJT

Religions of the Ancient Near East

The development of writing systems in the ancient Near East from around 3000 BC lays flesh on the archaeological bones of the region, revealing a considerable variety of religious beliefs and practices. Popular and private religion, while conforming to local norms, appears to have been fairly uniform, consisting of devotion to personal deities who were believed to answer prayers, often accompanied by sacrifices. Greater variation attended funerary practices and beliefs about human destiny beyond death.

SEE ALSO

● THE ANCIENT NEAR EAST p. 364
● ANCIENT EGYPT p. 366
● JUDAISM p. 472
● ART OF THE ANCIENT NEAR EAST p. 506
● THE MAKING OF MYTHS p. 612

Regional and national differences are most marked in community and national cults. There is evidence of this in extensive temple remains, ritual and mythological texts, official inscriptions, and monuments. All the national cults (see below) – apart from Zoroastrianism and Judaism (see p. 472) – were polytheistic, and gods and goddesses tended to be rationalized into hierarchical or family groupings. Superficially, these appear to have been 'nature religions', worshipping the natural forces of the world, but in fact they were more complex structures, symbolizing cultural and individual identity, and the realities of social hierarchies and power, as well as natural/environmental factors in communal life.

Egypt

The pharaohs of ancient Egypt (see p. 366) were regarded as divine, and were called 'Horus' and 'Son of Re'. The autocratic rule of the pharaohs was legitimized by the mythology of Re as the Sun god and the ruler of gods; as 'Son of Re' the pharaoh embodied the life-giving power of the Sun. Horus was the son of Isis, the Divine Mother, and of Osiris, the god of the inundation, vegetation and the dead. As Horus, the pharaoh embodied the periodic renewal of life and fertility borne

on the annual inundation of the land by the Nile. The temple cults reflected the pharaoh's divinity, and his rule of justice was further reinforced by the conflict myth – Horus as order conquering Seth, god of disorder. To augment their powers, local deities were often linked with national ones; the most significant was Amun, the god of invisibility, one of the characteristic elements of chaos out of which the Earth emerged. From c. 2000 BC he was combined with Re to become Amun-Re of Thebes, whose temple at Thebes was to become the most powerful and wealthiest in Egypt. The short-lived 'Amarna revolution' (c. 1350 BC) under Akhenaton promoted the cult of the Aten (whose creative power was manifest in the disc of the Sun), in opposition to Amun-Re (see illustration p. 367, and p. 507).

In the Old Kingdom, the pyramid became the means of royal burial and a symbol of the pharaoh's ultimate power as the son of Re (see p. 366). In the later pyramids, ritual texts known as pyramid texts first began to appear. These texts contain spells and accounts of the afterlife, and later appeared in democratized form as coffin texts in the tombs of the Middle Kingdom nobles (see pp. 366–7). They later developed into the Book of the Dead, a collection of spells and prayers designed to secure a safe and prosperous life for all people in the Land of the Dead, the Land of Osiris. The destiny of divine kings thus filtered down as a promise of future happiness to the common people.

The Egyptians could not imagine death to be different to life in the land of Egypt and so the preservation of the body was one of the prerequisites for survival in the afterlife. Detailed methods of preservation and mummification were developed and refined over the centuries. By the New Kingdom, elaborate burial rites, once the prerogative of the royal family and their entourage, were considered the norm for those who could afford them. The body was buried alongside servant statuettes, food, clothes, tools, jewellery and other luxuries, and the tomb walls were inscribed with hymns, incantations, spells and colourful illustrations of life in the next world. Even the poorest Egyptian could hope for a place in the Land of Osiris with the appropriate texts and the most basic tomb provisions and methods of embalming. It was believed that the body and contents of the tomb were brought to life by a priest during a ceremony known as the 'Opening of the Mouth'. The dead man or woman would then go forward to be judged by the gods of the underworld but, armed with the Negative Confession, a denial of 49 possible offences contained in the Book of the Dead, a future in the Land of Osiris was assured.

Canaan

The Western Semitic city-states of the Levant were never unified, but often under the control of the great powers. Relatively homogenous religious patterns prevailed, apart from the monotheistic religion of the Jews (see p. 472).

Baal, one of the most important of the Canaanite gods. This figurine, dating from the 13th century BC, comes from Ugarit (Ras Shamra in Syria).

Our chief source of information, Ugarit (Ras Shamra in northwest Syria), has yielded extensive texts discovered in a priest's house adjoining the temple of the god Baal. The Ras Shamra texts reveal a pantheon of gods under the control of El, the 'Creator of Created Things', and his counterpart, Asherah (the mother goddess). Texts narrate the conflict of Baal (the storm god) with Yam (the ruler of the sea) and with Mot (death and sterility). In his struggle against other gods and forces, Baal is aided by his sister and vindicator Anat, goddess of fertility and war. A third goddess associated with fertility is Astarte, the Canaanite version of the name Ishtar, the Semitic mother goddess. Astarte's functions were superseded by Anat, although there is a tendency for the distinctive features of Asherah, Anat and Astarte to fuse together. The myths associated with the Canaanite pantheon are commonly interpreted as an allegory of the seasons, but it is perhaps better to interpret them as a reflection of the fragile maintenance or order (cosmos) in opposition to disorder (chaos)

Cult in these religions seems largely to have consisted of animal and occasionally human sacrifices, the dramatization of myths, and enactments of the sacred marriage (which may, however, have been no more than public consummations of royal marriages). Kings were regarded as divine, and former kings were invoked as 'saviours'. The dead were thought to sleep in their tombs, and were nourished with offerings of food and drink.

Mesopotamia

Of unknown provenance, the Sumerians (see p. 364) had settled in southern Iraq before 3000 BC. They developed writing and thus left the first records of religion in the region. Developing cities each had their own pantheon of deities, though many were assimilated to dominant types (Nanna – Moon, Utu – Sun, An – sky, Ea – storm, Enki – Earth, Inanna – the mother goddess, equivalent to the Semitic Ishtar). Sacred marriage myths and rites were especially popular. Semitic migrations led to the rise of successive empires – Akkad, Babylon and Assyria, (see pp. 364–5). The resulting religions preserved many archaic Sumerian features, although

Anubis, the jackal-headed god, here seen in his role as patron of the embalmers and god of the necropolis. Anubis also played a role in the judgement of the dead, weighing the heart of the deceased against Maat, goddess of truth and justice, while Osiris as judge of the dead looks on.

adapted to the new cultures. Superficially nature deities, the gods of Mesopotamia were, as further west, complex beings who also symbolized moral and social values. They witnessed and guaranteed treaties, chose kings, led them to war, and overthrew cities, thus participating in history.

As elsewhere in the ancient Near East, temple cult consisted largely of sacrificial offerings to divine images. Temples tended over a period to develop into ziggurats (see illustration). It was on the ziggurats that the Akitu festival was celebrated: the creation myth was narrated, proclaiming the victory of Marduk (Babylon) or Asshur (Assyria) over Tiamat (the primordial deep). After ritual humiliation, the king was confirmed in his rule – as the earthly agent of Marduk's life-giving blessings – and then performed the sacred marriage.

These ancient religions of Egyptian, Sumerian and Semitic origins overlay older forms, and were in Asia further influenced by Indo-European peoples (see table, p. 603) appearing in the area.

Anatolia (modern Turkey)

The Hittite empire of the second millennium BC (see p. 364) has left little clear information on religious matters. Many mythological texts were translations of Hurrian (see below) or Semitic originals. The myth of the dragon Illuyankas and the storm god has Indian, Greek and Semitic equivalents. The Telepinu myth (of a disappearing god whose departure brings disaster) may relate to the Persephone tradition that also appears in Greek mythology. Cult appears to have conformed to patterns observed elsewhere.

Following the decline of the Hittites the kingdom of Phrygia emerged in the same area. Phrygia was the centre of the cult of Cybele, an Earth goddess whose priests were eunuchs. This cult later spread to Greece and Rome.

Mitanni

In the third millennium BC, people called Hurrians seem to have emerged from Armenia and appear in significant numbers in various Near Eastern cities. By the mid-second millennium, they were ubiquitous in Syria and northern Mesopotamia. At this time Indo-Aryan migrants (see table, p. 603), bringing horses and chariots to the region, formed an aristocracy among the Hurrians, and developed the great empire of Mitanni in northern Mesopotamia and eastern Syria.

As with the Hittites, their religion appears to have been eclectic, incorporating various features met with in the Vedas of India (see p. 466). These in turn influenced local cults, and there is evidence of 'Vedic' gods such as Indra and Mitra as far south as Palestine. The story of Mitra (meaning 'treaty') may lie behind the biblical motif of the covenant between God and his chosen people. It has even been proposed that the Hebrew divine name *Yahweh* derives from the Indo-European *Dyaus* (meaning 'Day' or 'Bright One', the name of an ancient sky god).

Persia and Zoroastrianism

Later waves of Indo-Europeans entering Persia (Iran) pushed the Indo-Aryans into India and the Near East. These later Indo-Europeans also practised a religion akin to that of the Vedas. Many ancient myths are related to Indian versions, and the same deities are found. In northeast Persia in the late second millennium (possibly c. 1200 BC) a religious reformer named Zarathustra (Zoroaster in Greek) preached a simplification of the old polytheistic cosmology. Life meant a choice between Ahura Mazda ('wise lord') and Angra Mainyu ('hostile spirit'), embodying good and evil respectively. Ahura Mazda was assisted in his divine purposes by angelic beings, the Amesha Spentas ('bountiful immortals'), who represented moral values. A person's destiny after death (i.e. whether they went to heaven or hell) was determined by his or her choice. Zoroastrianism appears to be the earliest 'salvation religion' in history.

After an obscure prehistory, Zoroastrianism appears, already in a much developed form, as the national cult of the Persian Achaemenid Empire (see p. 365). Zoroastrian dualism (i.e. seeing the universe in terms of a struggle between good and evil) may have influenced some strains of Greek and early Jewish thought, and Zoroastrian ideas on the end of the world may also have contributed to later Jewish ideas. Zoroastrianism survives in the religion of the Parsis of India (see p. 467). Persia was also the home of Mithraism (see p. 462), which became an important cult in the Roman Empire.   NW/JO'B

THE PRINCIPAL GODS OF ANCIENT EGYPT

AMUN	God of Thebes, sometimes represented as a man, sometimes with an erect penis.
ANUBIS	The jackal-headed god of the necropolis, patron of the embalmers.
ATEN	Creator god manifest in the Sun disc.
ATUM	The original Sun god of Heliopolis.
BASTET	Cat goddess.
BES	Domestic god, usually depicted as a dwarf.
EDJO	Cobra goddess who appears as the pharaoh's protector on the royal diadem.
HATHOR	Often represented as a cow, a cow-headed woman, or a woman with a cow's headdress. Recognized as the suckler of the pharaoh.
HORUS	Falcon god, identified with the pharaoh during his reign. The son of Osiris and Isis, Horus grew up to avenge his father's murder by Seth.
IMHOTEP	Architect of the Step Pyramid (see p. 366), chief minister of Djoser (c. 2700 BC). Later venerated as the god of learning and medicine.
ISIS	Wife of Osiris and mother of Horus.
KHEPRI	The scarab-beetle god, identified with the Sun god Re as creator god.
MAAT	Goddess of truth, justice and order, depicted as a woman with an ostrich feather on her head.
NEKHBET	Vulture goddess, who sometimes appears beside Edjo on the royal diadem.
NEPHTHYS	Sister of Isis.
OSIRIS	God of the dead. Identified with the dead king and depicted as a mummified king. Also god of the inundation of the Nile and of vegetation.
PTAH	Creator god of Memphis and patron of craftsmen. Represented as a mummified man.
PTAH-SOKER-OSIRIS	God combining the principal gods of creation, death and the afterlife. Represented as a mummified king.
RE or RA	The Sun god of Heliopolis and the supreme judge. Other gods aspiring to universal recognition would often link their name to his, e.g. Amun-Re.
RE-HARAKHTI	Falcon god, incorporating the characteristics of Re and Horus.
SEKHMET	Lion-headed goddess, wife of Ptah, venerated in the area of Memphis. Regarded as the bringer of sickness and destruction to the enemies of Re.
SETH	God of violence and storms. Brother and murderer of Osiris, represented as an animal of unidentified type.
SOBEK	Crocodile god.
THOUERIS	Hippopotamus goddess, the patron of women in childbirth.
THOTH	The ibis-headed god of Hermopolis, scribe to the gods and inventor of writing.

The ziggurats of ancient Mesopotamia were brick-built temple towers, generally consisting of a series of rectangular terraces of diminishing size. They were regarded as 'stairways to heaven', at the top of which gods and men communicated, and probably provided the basis of the biblical story of the Tower of Babel. This example was built in the 15th century BC.

The Primal Religions: Ancient Europe

The earliest evidence of what seems to be religious activity and belief in an afterlife dates from the Upper Palaeolithic period (30 000–10 000 BC). Cave paintings dating from 15 000–11 000 BC found in France appear to show rituals connected with hunting, and figurines as old as 25 000 BC suggest a mother goddess or fertility figure. But reconstructing the religion of preliterary times is a hazardous task – there is so much we can never know.

Some scholars believe the religions of all the Indo-European peoples (see table, p. 603) had common features; but Greek, Roman, Celtic and Germanic religion (not to mention old Iranian and Vedic religion, also belonging to Indo-European peoples) display important differences and have complex histories.

Ancient Greek religion

Written evidence about religion in Europe begins with the Linear B texts of Mycenaean civilization (see p. 369). These show the importance of Poseidon the sea god and of 'the Lady' of various locations (presumably a mother goddess). Some other divine names occur, including Zeus and Hera, which later appear in the epic poetry of Homer (see p. 612). Homer's gods lived ageless and immortal on Mount Olympus, but acted like humans – and not the best-behaved humans. They could change shape, intervene in human life, and might respond to gifts and prayers to change human destiny – but they did not change human nature.

The Olympian gods were taken for granted in the literature of Classical Greece (see p. 614). They were incorporated into the workings of secret societies (for example, the Eleusinian mysteries), and into healing and divination cults (for example, the oracle at Delphi). By the 6th century BC they were part of the official worship of the Greek city-states. But ancient Greek religion had little to do with morality, and the moral, metaphysical and scientific concerns of the Athenian philosophers of the 5th and 4th centuries (see pp. 486–7) led to very different ideas of God. These ideas challenged popular religion, and in 399 BC the philosopher Socrates was condemned for atheism and corrupting youth by undermining the gods of the state.

The conquests of Alexander the Great (see p. 372) spread Greek language and ideas through Asia Minor, Syria, Egypt and the Middle East. The resulting Hellenistic civilization fused Greek and Oriental cultures and outlooks. The names and worship of the Olympians spread everywhere, but other cults – of the Egyptian Isis and the Phrygian Cybele, for instance (see pp. 460–1) – spread too. The Greek philosophical use of reason was combined with Oriental mysticism and the quest for immortality, and Greek rulers realized the political usefulness of Eastern ideas of divine kingship (see p. 372).

Rome

Early Roman religion was probably shaped by the Bronze Age culture of the Etruscans (see p. 376) and was concerned with the

A domestic shrine from Herculaneum, one of the towns destroyed by the eruption of Vesuvius in AD 79. At such shrines, Roman families would worship their own household gods – the *lares* and *penates*.

agricultural cycle. Two forms of religious expression developed. Domestic piety recognized household gods (*lares* and *penates*), while the state cult – conducted by a high priest (the *pontifex maximus*) and other specified officials – ensured corporate wellbeing. As Rome encountered Greek culture, the state deities were identified with Olympian equivalents. As the Roman Empire expanded, its armies brought back foreign cults and religious ideas. The most important of these cults – until the official Roman adoption of Christianity in the 4th century AD – was Mithraism. This cult was based on the worship of Mithra or Mithras, the Persian god of light, truth and justice, whose killing of a cosmic bull was echoed by his devotees in ritual sacrifices. A male-only mystery cult, Mithraism reached Rome in the 1st century BC, and became particularly popular in the army.

Apollo, the Greek god of the arts, considered to be the archetype of male beauty. The Olympian gods were not regarded as models of morality – Apollo, for example, devised a variety of unpleasant fates for the women who refused his advances.

THE 'TWELVE GODS' OF MOUNT OLYMPUS

('By the Twelve!' was a form of oath)

ZEUS
(Roman **Jupiter**) — Sky deity, ruler of the immortals. 'Father of gods and men' (but not creator).

HERA
(Roman **Juno**) — Consort of Zeus, guardian of marriage and childbirth.

POSEIDON
(Roman **Neptune**) — 'The earthshaker', ruler of the sea.

DEMETER
(Roman **Ceres**) — Goddess of corn and crops.

APOLLO
(No direct Roman equivalent) — Averter of evil, source of prophecy and divination; sometimes associated with the Sun, music and poetry.

ARTEMIS
(Roman **Diana**) — Virgin goddess of hunting and wild animals; originally a mother goddess, and sometimes associated with the Moon.

ARES
(Roman **Mars**) — God of war.

APHRODITE
(Roman **Venus**) — Goddess of love and fertility.

HERMES
(Roman **Mercury**) — Messenger of the gods, guardian of the market place.

ATHENA
(Roman **Minerva**) — Goddess of wisdom and virgin protector of the household; patron of Athens.

HEPHAESTOS
(Roman **Vulcan**) — God of fire and volcanoes; patron of smiths.

HESTIA
(Roman **Vesta**) — Goddess of the hearth; patron of the city of Rome.

Divinities not among the Twelve but important in popular religion included: **DIONYSUS** (Roman **Bacchus**), associated with wine and crops, and worshipped with orgiastic rituals; and **ASKLEPIOS** (Roman **Aesculapius**), source of healing.

Generally speaking, however, Roman official religion resisted innovations, or admitted them only when of proven worth. Divine honours were accorded to Julius Caesar after his assassination, and to Augustus, most of his successors, and various members of the imperial family at death. In the Eastern provinces of the Roman Empire living emperors were saluted as divine. The Christian rejection of the Olympian gods and the Oriental cults was partly foreshadowed by the Greek philosophers; it was the conflict with state cult that eventually brought about the official persecution of Christianity.

Celtic religion

The Romans have left us descriptions of the religions of the Celtic and Germanic 'barbarians' on the fringes of their empire. The Romans recognized some divinities with similar functions to certain gods of Rome, and archaeology shows how Roman and Celtic religion could merge. But we have no 'insider's' account of pre-Christian Celtic religion and much remains uncertain. Some Irish stories hint at a Celtic High God, but the commonest Celtic religious image is a male figure with horns – evidently a fertility figure (see illustration p. 374). Sometimes the horned god has an 'earth mother' consort. Traces of places of worship occur close to fertility-giving water – at springs, wells and river sources. Human sacrifice seems to have been common, and the human head to have had special significance. Severed heads often occur in Celtic imagery, and the frame of a great sanctuary found in France has niches to hold heads.

Several observers mention 'druids' conducting sacrifices and divination ceremonies.

Germanic religion

The religions of the Germanic peoples survived into the Middle Ages: Denmark, Norway, Iceland and Orkney did not become Christian until the 10th and 11th centuries, and Sweden not till the 12th. We know most about the later forms, especially from Norse literature; but the Norse stories were themselves written down in Christian times and give no complete picture even of Viking belief and practice, still less that of the Anglo-Saxons and other North European peoples.

Germanic religion had many divinities. In early times, three in particular were worshipped: Wotan or Woden (Norse Odin), father of the gods and the slain; Tiw or Tiwaz (Norse Tyr), the giver of law; and Thor, the thunder deity. (These gods gave their names to Wednesday, Tuesday and Thursday respectively.) In the Norse literature, Tyr plays little part. Odin and Thor belong to the Aesir, the gods of Asgard, who defeated the Vanir, another race of gods. Aesir and Vanir became reconciled, and the Vanir Frey and his female counterpart Freya, closely associated with fertility, are major figures. There is no High God, only a chaos of divine energy. The worshipper chose the divinity thought most likely to serve him. Odin was the natural patron of warriors, and his Valkyries took dead heroes to his great hall, Valhalla. Thor seems to have been the most popular divinity,

PEOPLES AND PLACES IN NORSE RELIGION

AESIR	The race of gods including Odin and Thor. Defeated the Vanir.
ASGARD	Home of the gods.
BALDER	'The Beautiful', son of Odin, tragically slain by Loki.
FENRIR	'Great Wolf', son of Loki; bound up by Tyr, but will break free at Ragnarok.
FREY	Fertility god, one of the Vanir.
FREYA	Frey's sister, consort of Odin.
FRIGG	Odin's wife. Her name is preserved in 'Friday'.
HEL	Kingdom of the dead; also personified as Loki's daughter.
LOKI	The trickster god of Asgard. Imprisoned in a cave for the murder of Balder, he will break loose at Ragnarok.
MIDGARD	The world of men. It is held by a coiled serpent, who will show himself at Ragnarok.
NJORD	Father of Frey and Freya, associated with ships and sailing.
NORNS	Three maidens who rule the fates of men and daily water the world tree Yggdrasil.
ODIN (Old Germanic **Wotan**, Anglo-Saxon **Woden**)	Chief of the Aesir; god of battle, poetry and death.
RAGNAROK (German **Götterdämmerung**)	'The twilight of the gods', the coming day of destruction for Asgard and Midgard and their inhabitants in a battle with the forces of evil.
THOR	God of thunder.
TYR (Old Germanic **Tiwaz**)	A war god, has bound Fenrir.
VALHALLA	Odin's great hall for warriors.
VALKYRIES	Spirit maidens who guide in battle and conduct the chosen slain to Valhalla.
VANIR	The race of gods associated with fertility. Defeated by the Aesir.
YGGDRASIL	The self-renewing world tree, which forms the centre of the worlds of gods, giants and men. Odin hung for nine days in its branches to gain secrets from it.

and images of his hammer were used for protection. In the end, the gods themselves pass away in the great combat of Ragnarok; the Tree of Life, Yggdrasil, will renew itself and the world when they have gone. AW

Lid of a cremation urn from the pre-Viking Danish Bronze Age. The obvious fertility symbolism is reinforced by the corn motif behind the female figure.

SEE ALSO

- HUMAN PREHISTORY p. 362
- ANCIENT GREECE AND ROME pp. 368–81
- THE CELTS p. 374
- THE INVASIONS p. 396
- WHAT IS PHILOSOPHY? p. 486
- CLASSICAL LITERATURE p. 614
- EPICS AND ROMANCES p. 618

The Primal Religions: Modern Times

The primal religions that survive today are the religions of non-literate, usually tribal societies. Unlike the universal religions such as Christianity, Islam, Hinduism and Buddhism – which have a wealth of written records and scriptures – the primal religions have no written sources. This does not mean, however, that primal religions are without history or are in some way 'fossilized' remnants of a past age. Like the universal religions, they have long and complex histories.

SEE ALSO

- AGE ROLES AND RITES OF PASSAGE p. 254
- AFRICA, AUSTRALASIA AND OCEANIA TO THE COLONIAL AGE p. 388
- WHAT IS RELIGION? p. 458
- WORSHIP, PRAYER AND PILGRIMAGE p. 480
- SACRED SPACE, SACRED TIME p. 482
- THE MAKING OF MYTHS p. 612

The word 'primal' is used to convey the idea that these religions came first in human history, and underlie all the major religions of the world. By studying the religious beliefs and customs of primal peoples we can learn much about the religious heritage that we all share. It is wrong to think of these religions as primitive. They often contain beliefs and ideas about the world that achieve high levels of sophistication.

Where are primal religions found?

There are many thousands of primal societies scattered throughout the world – in North and South America, Siberia, the Arctic, Central Asia, Australia, Southeast Asia and the Pacific Islands. There are over 700 separate peoples in subsaharan Africa alone. Some societies number only a few hundred members, others a few million. They live in very different environments, ranging from the Arctic tundra to the tropical rainforests.

Every primal society has its own culture and its own unique religion – in fact there are as many primal religions as there are primal societies. However, these religions have enough in common in terms of beliefs and practices to make it possible to group them together as primal religions.

Components of the spirit world

In almost all primal religions there is a

A ceremonial headdress from Vanuatu, west Pacific Ocean. The lower head represents the ogress Neviubum Baau, while the figure on top is either her son or her husband. Among many primal societies, headdresses or masks are frequently worn during religious ceremonies, indicating that the participants are no longer ordinary humans but have been taken over by some spirit.

conception of a *supreme god*, sometimes prominent in religious life, sometimes remote and uninterested in human affairs. The Ashanti of central Ghana call their god Nyame and other West African peoples have similar names for their god – Nyonmo, Nyama, Ngewo. The supreme god of the Yoruba people of Nigeria is known as Olorun, 'Owner of the Sky'. He is the creator of all things, the giver of life and breath, and the final judge of all people. Belief in a supreme god is found throughout the African continent, but in many parts he is considered so great and remote that he is not worshipped. Divinities and ancestors, who act as intermediaries between people and the supreme god, are worshipped instead. Only in times of extreme distress is the god directly approached by people.

Divinities are powerful named spirits, each with their own specific characteristics. In West Africa, the Americas, Asia and Polynesia, people believe in a multitude of divinities other than the supreme god. Many West African peoples have large pantheons of gods who are involved in daily human life. They require many temples, shrines, priests, images, rituals and offerings. Among the Igbo of Nigeria, the earth deity Ala is the most important divinity, and every village has its shrine to Ala. This shrine is the most important in the village, and the priest who tends it is the head priest of the village. Offerings of wine and yams are made to Ala before planting the land, and at harvest.

Virtually all primal peoples believe in spirits or souls of *ancestors* that survive the body after death and are capable of interfering in the lives of the living for good or ill. They have the power to do harm, but at the same time they are respected and thought of with affection. Their power to intercede in the lives of the living is connected with their desire to maintain social harmony. They can send illness or other misfortune to those who misbehave towards their fellow kin. Ancestors are honoured by the living through ritual offerings and prayers.

As well as powerful divinities and ancestor spirits, most primal peoples believe in numerous *minor spirits*, who may be good, malevolent or capricious. They may be the souls of the forgotten dead, who haunt the living and play tricks on them. Spirits live in all sorts of places – in rocks, caves, mountain passes, river crossings, even in animals and insects. They are unpredictable and people are careful not to offend them. They must be treated with proper respect, and small offerings of food are left when people pass by their dwelling places. Among Arctic hunting peoples, spirits commonly take animal form. Inuit (Eskimo) hunters enter into a special relationship with animal spirits, who help them in their quest for game animals.

Mana is a spiritual power or life force that is believed to permeate the universe. Originally a Melanesian word, it is now applied by anthropologists to spiritual power in other primal religions. Mana is not a spirit, and it has no will or purpose – it is impersonal and flows from one thing to another, and can be manipulated to achieve certain ends. Charms, amulets and medicines contain this power for the benefit of the wearer or user. It can be used for good or evil purposes – it is thought to be present, for example, both in a sorcerer's poisons and in Western medicines.

Structures of religious life

The *sacrifice* of an animal or plant is a communication and communion with the spirit world. The animal or object sacrificed acts as an intermediary between people and a being of the spirit world. For the Nuer of Sudan, for example, sacrifice is the most typical and expressive act of their religion. Most Nuer sacrifices consist of an offering of an ox to Kwoth (their supreme god).

Initiation ceremonies take place in all primal religions to mark the transition of a person from one religious and social status to another – from bachelor to married man, for example, or from dead person to ancestor (see also rites of passage, pp. 254–5). Initiation can also mark the entry into a religious profession. Novice shamans (see box), for example, have to undergo special initiation ceremonies. At the heart of initiation is an encounter with the spirit world from which a person emerges spiritually transformed. The most common type of initiation marks the transition from childhood to adulthood. During these ceremonies adolescents learn behaviour patterns, myths and sacred traditions of their people, the names of the gods, and above all the relationship between people and the spirit world as it was established at the beginning of time.

There are a whole range of *religious specialists*, from the priests, prophets, diviners and sacred kings of Africa to the medicine men of North America and the shamans of Siberia and the Arctic (see box). Their role is to mediate between people and the spirit world. A priest's role is to serve a divinity or divinities, and to carry out specific ritual and ceremonial duties. A prophet is someone chosen by a spirit to deliver a special message. This message often involves changes to the social and religious order. Diviners, with the help of spirits or by using various techniques, diagnose disease or solve problems for people.

Myths are sacred narratives about the beings of the spirit world. All primal peoples have their own set of stories that express their understanding of the world and their place in it. Myths are often creation stories relating the origin of the world, and of human beings and animals (see also p. 612).

Primal religions today

Most primal peoples today have been profoundly influenced by contact with more 'sophisticated' and powerful societies and their religions. This has led to the development of new movements within primal religions, and in some cases to new religions. Most of these movements have developed out of interaction with Christianity. In Papua New Guinea and some other Pacific Islands, for instance, primal and Christian elements have combined in movements, often called 'cargo cults', to create a new society, and in North America renewed resistance by Native American ('American Indian') peoples to White domination is expressed in a revival of some elements of traditional Native American religion.   PBa

A tree-worship shrine in Nigeria. In all parts of the world, not only trees but also rocks, rivers and lakes have at some time been regarded as sacred – either because they are the home of particular spirits, or because they are associated with some god or goddess.

A Voodoo ritual in Haiti. Voodoo – which combines elements of West African religions with elements derived from Roman Catholicism – is practised by the descendants of Black African slaves in parts of the Caribbean and South America. In Voodoo rituals, dancers enter trances, and an animal (usually a chicken) is sacrificed.

The Religions of India

India is home to what is – alongside Judaism – the world's oldest surviving religion. Hinduism, generally referred to as *sanatana dharma* or 'eternal tradition' by Hindus themselves, has a history of some 4000 years. Its earliest roots lie in the Indus valley civilization in the period before the Aryan invasion of north India in around 1500 BC (see p. 384). It was the Aryans who developed much of what is now commonly associated with the Hindu tradition.

Although officially a secular state, India is still a highly religious state, with 80% of the population (550 million) being Hindu. There are also other important religious traditions: over 80 million Muslims (see p. 478), 27 million Christians and 14 million Sikhs, together with smaller numbers of Buddhists, Jains, Parsis, Jews and those following tribal religions.

Hinduism, Buddhism, Jainism and Sikhism, though differing, have some common themes. They all share the idea of a continuing cycle of birth, death and rebirth (*samsara*), and the belief that individuals suffer the consequences of their actions (*karma*). Both of these ideas are linked to the idea of *transmigration* – that the soul is continually reincarnated in different bodies (human or animal) after the last body dies, and that what form this body takes depends on actions in the previous incarnation.

Krishna (centre), one of the incarnations of the great Hindu god Vishnu, with Radha (left). Krishna spent his youth as an amorous cowherd, his flute playing inspiring the wives and daughters of the other cowherds (including his favourite, Radha) to dance ecstatically with him.

The Hindu tradition

All the religions speak of *dharma*, usually said to mean 'law', 'duty', 'way' or 'nature'. Both Hindus and Sikhs refer to their religious leaders and teachers as *gurus*, and all the religions except Sik-

hism hold up celibacy and asceticism (the renunciation of pleasure and luxury) as ideals.

The earliest scriptures, the *Vedas*, were compiled by the Aryans. In these texts sacrificial rituals and the role of the *brahman* priest are described. The authority of the *brahmans* in Indian religion has continued to be significant – despite the many movements that have challenged it, such as Buddhism (see p. 468) and Jainism (see below).

Between 500 BC and AD 500, in addition to the rise of Buddhism and Jainism, India saw the growth of the Hindu tradition, building on the Vedic past but developing in new ways. The great epics, the *Ramayana* and the *Mahabharata* (incorporating the *Bhagavadgita*) were compiled. They told the stories of Rama and Krishna, both of whom were seen as *avataras* or incarnations of the great god, Vishnu. These gods became increasingly popular along with Shiva (the destroyer god) and the goddess Devi, and later became the inspiration for devotional poets and religious sects.

All these gods and goddesses have innumerable manifestations, i.e. they appear in many different forms and with different names. There are also a large number of minor gods, spirits and demons. Reflecting this, within Hinduism there are a large number of different sects worshipping a particular god or goddess, or even a particular manifestation.

Hindu worship and pilgrimage

The social and religious aspects of life for all Hindus is inseparable. Closely bound up with Hindu belief and practice is the *caste* system, a hierarchical system of social and religious stratification (see p. 258). Everyone is born into a particular caste, and for Hindus, this and their stage of life – as student, householder, retired person, etc. – determines how they live.

Most homes have a corner set aside for worship at which family members offer food, flowers, incense and the light of a candle. It is often the women who lead these daily *puja* rituals, although everyone can take part.

Many different gods and goddesses are worshipped, some well known (such as Krishna, Shiva and Durga) and others (like the goddess of smallpox) renowned for particular activities. Some are known only to people in a particular area and may be worshipped to ensure local protection. Hindus believe that the divine can be manifested in any number of gods, objects or people, which then become worthy of worship.

The brahman priests are required to keep a high level of purity and a knowledge of the ancient Sanskrit language and of ritual practice. They lead the rites of passage at times of initiation, marriage and death. In a village there may be other specialists who are responsible for communicating with local spirits for such purposes as healing, blessings or exorcism.

| HINDU GODS AND GODDESSES | |

HINDU GODS AND GODDESSES

GODS OF THE VEDAS

Indra	Thunder god, god of battle
Varuna	Guardian of order; divine overseer
Agni	God of fire
Surya	God associated with the Sun

MAJOR GODS OF HINDUISM

Brahma	The creator; linked with goddess Saraswati
Vishnu	The preserver; with Shiva, one of Hinduism's great gods. Vishnu has ten incarnations or *avataras*, and is married to Lakshmi.
Shiva	A great god, associated with destruction. In Hindu mythology, Shiva is married to Parvati and is the father of Ganesh.
Ganesh	The elephant-headed god, worshipped as the remover of obstacles and god of good luck
Hanuman	The monkey warrior-god associated with the god Rama

VISHNU'S TEN AVATARAS

Matsya	The fish
Kurma	The tortoise
Varaha	The boar
Narasimha	The man-lion
Vamana	The dwarf
Parasurama	Rama bearing the axe
Ramachandra	Otherwise known as **Rama**, identified by his bow and quiver of arrows. The god of the *Ramayana* epic, married to Sita.
Krishna	The important god featured in the *Bhagavadgita*. He is worshipped particularly as a baby and as a flute-playing cowherd and lover of Radha.
The Buddha	The great teacher from the 6th–5th century BC and founder of Buddhism (see p. 468)
Kalki	'The one to come'; a future *avatara*

THE GODDESSES

The goddesses are manifestations of the great creative spirit or **Shakti**. The most popular are:

Parvati	Wife of Shiva; also known as **Uma**
Durga	All-powerful warrior goddess, also known as **Amba**, and linked with Shiva
Kali	Goddess associated with destruction
Lakshmi	Goddess of beauty, wealth and good fortune, wife of Vishnu
Saraswati	Goddess of learning, arts and music, and wife of Brahma

A sadhu, a Hindu holy man, practising yoga meditation. Sadhus submit themselves to various physical and spiritual disciplines, take vows of poverty and celibacy, and depend on charity. There are also Buddhist and Jain sadhus.

A Hindu temple (*mandir*) may be a huge, ornate building dedicated to the worship of a major deity – visited particularly during festivals and pilgrimages – or it may be a small shrine by the roadside at which offerings to a local spirit are made. The Hindu calendar celebrates the anniversaries of deities and saints, seasonal events, and the new year. At these times, many Hindus undertake pilgrimages to nearby sites or to major religious centres such as Varanasi (Benares) to immerse themselves in the sacred waters of the River Ganges. It is here that a Hindu may go to die with the hope of achieving final liberation (*moksha*) from the cycle of death and rebirth. After death, the body is cremated, a practice dating back to the time of the Vedas.

Jainism

Founded by the ascetic Mahavira in the 6th century BC at around the same time as Buddhism, Jainism shares with Buddhism a belief in no god. With the rise in popularity in India of the gods Vishnu and Shiva, Buddhism gradually declined. Jainism, however, has not died out and remains strong in the west of India.

Non-violence or *ahimsa* is central to Jain life and has influenced those of other religions too, like Mahatma Gandhi. Jains believe that all living creatures have souls and must not be harmed. They are therefore strict vegetarians. Many are nuns or monks, the ascetic life being encouraged as the true path to non-violent, personal liberation.

The Parsis

Parsiism is a monotheistic religion derived from Zoroastrianism (see p. 461), whose adherents fled Persia (modern Iran) in the 8th century AD to escape Arab persecution. Most Parsis are now found in western India, particularly Bombay.

Parsi worship is centred in fire temples where a sacred fire – the representative of God or Ahura Mazda – burns continuously. Rather than burying or cremating their dead, which they believe would contaminate earth, fire and water, Parsis expose the bodies in circular 'towers of silence', where they are eaten by vultures and other birds.

Parsis have maintained their communal identity by keeping the symbols of the sacred shirt (*sudre*) and cord (*kusti*), by encouraging marriage within the faith

and by supporting Parsi business and educational ventures, charitable concerns and housing colonies.

The Sikhs

The Sikhs, like the Jains, are comparatively small in number in India. Sikhism, however, is an important religion, particularly in the north, where there has been a call for a separate Sikh homeland, *Khalistan*, in the Punjab. In the 1980s, a minority of extremist Sikhs began a campaign of terrorism to achieve this aim (see Countries of the World: India).

Sikhs are proud of their history and still remember, in their prayers and festivals, many of the events in the lives of their ten gurus. Sikhism is a monotheistic religion, and was founded by the first of the ten gurus, Nanak (1469–1539). The Sikh gurus were critical of the ritual and social aspects of Hindu tradition, rejecting the caste system. They were political as well as religious leaders, evolving the idea of the warrior-saint and standing up against the rule of the Muslims who had dominated north India since the 13th century.

The foundations of Sikh life are the teachings of Nanak on how to lead a good life and seek final union with God. Also of fundamental importance was the formation by the last guru, Gobind Singh (1666–1708), of the Sikh community, with its shared symbols and the names 'Singh' and 'Kaur' for men and women respectively. The shared symbols are the so-called *five K's* worn by Sikh men (see photo).

Equality is an important Sikh ideal, and this is symbolized by the sharing of food in the *gurdwara*. This is the place of worship where Sikhs meet and where they are in the presence of their holy book, the *Guru Granth Sahib*. The most important Sikh temple is the Golden Temple at Amritsar, built in the late 16th century.

Many Sikhs begin and end the day with prayers from the holy book. Their aim is to sanctify ordinary life, keeping the mind and heart set on God. Of the four major religions of India, it is only Sikhism that has turned away from the ideals of asceticism and celibacy and focused instead on the householder.

Indian religions around the world

Half of the world's Sikhs, though Indian by origin, live in other countries, notably Britain, the USA and Canada. This is also true of India's other religious groups. In Nepal and parts of Southeast Asia, Hinduism is now an indigenous religion, originally exported from India many centuries ago. More recently, migrant Indians have taken Hinduism, Jainism and Parsiism with them all over the world, to Fiji and Mauritius, Trinidad and Guyana, Britain, the USA and Canada.

The impact of India's religions now extends far beyond India itself, and from the 1960s many people in the West began to be attracted to Indian religions – not only Buddhism, but also various Hindu sects, such as the Hare Krishna movement. Some such sects have in fact evolved particularly to appeal to Westerners.

KK

MAJOR FESTIVALS IN INDIA

April	Hindu / Sikh	New Year
	Jain	Mahavira's birthday
July	Hindu / Jain	Monsoon begins
August	Hindu	Krishna's birthday (*Janamashtami*)
September	Hindu	Remembering ancestors (*Shradh*)
October	Hindu	Celebration of goddesses (*Durga Puja*)
	Hindu	Rama's victory over Ravana (*Dashera*)
November	Hindu / Jain / Sikh	Festival of Lights (*Divali*)
	Sikh	Guru Nanak's birthday
December	Sikh	Guru Gobind Singh's birthday
January	Hindu	Pilgrim fairs (*Kumbha Mela*)
February	Hindu	Festival for Shiva (*Mahashivaratri*)
March	Hindu / Sikh	Spring harvest celebration (*Holi*)
	Parsi	New Year (*No Ruz*)

Two Sikhs. All Sikh men wear the symbols of their faith, the so-called 'five K's': *kesh* (uncut beard and hair, the latter worn in a turban); *kangha* (comb, to keep the hair clean); *kara* (metal bracelet); *kaccha* (knee-length undershorts); and *kirpan* (dagger).

SEE ALSO

- INDIA AND SOUTHEAST ASIA TO THE COLONIAL AGE p. 384
- BUDDHISM p. 468
- ISLAM p. 478
- WORSHIP, PRAYER AND PILGRIMAGE p. 480
- SACRED SPACE AND SACRED TIME p. 482
- GOOD AND EVIL p. 484
- ASIAN ART p. 512

Buddhism

Buddhism originated in India around 500 BC with the life and teaching of Gautama the Buddha ('enlightened one'). According to tradition, Prince Gautama (?563–483 BC) was born into luxury, but after seeing an old man, a sick man and a corpse he realized that he too would grow old, become decrepit, and die. A meeting with a wandering religious seeker inspired Gautama to leave home and seek liberation from the endless cycle of birth and death through *yoga* or meditation.

SEE ALSO

- ● THE RELIGIONS OF INDIA p. 466
- ● THE RELIGIONS OF CHINA AND JAPAN p. 470
- ● WORSHIP, PRAYER AND PILGRIMAGE p. 480
- ● SACRED SPACE AND SACRED TIME p. 482
- ● GOOD AND EVIL p. 484
- ● ASIAN ART p. 512

After unsuccessfully attempting to gain liberation by depriving the body of food and comfort, Gautama rejected asceticism and sought a *middle way* between luxury and self-mortification. He sat in meditation through the night, and attained awakening or *nirvana* (literally the 'blowing out' of the flames of passion and craving), overcoming the attachments that would have caused him to be reborn in the world.

The Buddha attracted disciples, and these formed the nucleus of the Buddhist community or *sangha*. Initially a wandering religious order, their resting places later developed into Buddhist monasteries.

Propagated throughout India as a creed of righteousness and non-violence by the great Mauryan king, Ashoka (272–232 BC), Buddhism spread through southern and eastern Asia. Two main branches developed, Theravada and Mahayana (see below). However, in India itself, Buddhism had virtually died out by the 13th century AD.

The nature of Buddhism

Buddhist teachings (called *dharma*) are distinctive because the Buddha taught that there is no permanent 'self'. Indeed, Buddhist teachings stress that nothing at all exists permanently – there is only perpetual change. Family, friends, possessions, even our own mind and body – all the things cherished as 'me' or 'mine' – are subject to perpetual change and decay. Yet people become mentally and emotionally attached to them as if they were permanent, so when any of them changes – for instance if someone dies – people suffer. Even moments of happiness are unsatisfactory, because they never last.

The Buddha taught that since impermanence is an unalterable fact of life, we can be truly happy only by becoming detached from the delusive notions of 'me' and 'mine'. Such detachment may be achieved through techniques of meditation.

Buddhism shares with Hinduism the concepts of *samsara*, an eternal cycle of death and rebirth, and *karma*, the idea that individuals suffer the effects of past actions (see p. 446).

Theravada Buddhism

Theravada ('Teaching of the Elders') is found mainly in Sri Lanka, Cambodia, Thailand, and other countries of Southeast Asia. Theravadins view Gautama as a human being who achieved nirvana after many lifetimes of moral and spiritual development (inspiring tales of the Buddha's previous human and animal lives are a favourite method of teaching about Buddhism). To imitate the Buddha by becoming a monk is the best way to attain enlightenment.

A Theravadin monk follows a strict discipline, eating only donated food, remaining celibate, and not harming living beings. The monastic routine helps monks forget worldly concerns, so enabling them to concentrate on Buddhist teachings and to control the mind through meditation.

Monasteries depend entirely on the goodwill of the wider community. People give generously to the monastery, believing that such acts of merit will help them gain a better rebirth, perhaps become a monk

An image of the Buddha from Anuradhapura, Sri Lanka. The Buddha is usually depicted in a meditative position.

MEDITATION

The following instructions are condensed from the *zazen* (sitting meditation) instructions of Zen master Dōgen (1200-53 AD). A session of *zazen* may last half an hour or longer.

Find a quiet room.

Take food and drink only in moderation.

Do not think about good and evil or right and wrong.

Set all thoughts aside – give up even the idea of becoming enlightened.

Put a mat on the floor and a round cushion on the mat.

Sit in either the full or half crosslegged position. The full position is right foot on left thigh, left foot on right thigh. The half position is left foot on right thigh.

Clothing should be loose but neat.

Rest the back of your right hand on your left foot, and your left hand palm-up in the right hand, the tips of the thumbs just touching.

Sit straight upright without leaning. Line up ears and shoulders, nose and navel.

Keep your lips and teeth closed and your tongue against the roof of your mouth. Keep your eyes always open, and breathe regularly through the nose.

When you have arranged yourself like this, take a deep breath, sway to right and left and then sit firmly like a rock.

As thoughts and feelings arise just accept them and let them pass naturally.

After meditating, get up calmly without sudden movements.

With practice, you will forget all attachments, and pure concentration will arise spontaneously. This is the basis of meditation, and meditation is the gateway of peace and bliss.

in a future life. In return, lay people receive spiritual guidance from the monks and emulate them by following some of the rules of the Buddhist life.

Lay Buddhists pray to local gods and spirits for mundane benefits such as a good harvest – for although gods, like people, are impermanent, they may still be able to help.

Theravada Buddhist festivals vary from country to country, but typically celebrate the Buddha's birth and enlightenment and important events in the history of Buddhism in that country.

Mahayana Buddhism

Mahayana ('Great Vehicle') is a strand of Buddhism originating in India which spread to China, Korea, Japan and Tibet. According to Mahayana scriptures, the Buddha is not Gautama but an eternal, formless, cosmic principle, constantly

A Buddhist mandala. Mandalas are intricate geometric pictures used by some Buddhists and Hindus as aids to meditation.

...cting to liberate us from suffering exist-ence. The eternal Buddha uses wise and compassionate 'skilful means' (such as appearing in human form as the Buddha Gautama) if this will help deluded beings out of the cycle of rebirth.

Mahayanists recognize several Buddhas and many *bodhisattvas* ('enlightenment-beings'), near-Buddhas who have delayed entering final nirvana to help all beings attain enlightenment.

Underlying Mahayana Buddhism are two important religious concepts. One is the idea of *emptiness* – that nothing at all has any permanent substance; even Buddhist doctrines are 'empty' and one should not become attached to them. The other is 'mind-only', meaning that the world we experience is a product of the mind, like a dream. The task of the Buddhist is to 'awaken' from the dream of existence.

Mahayana takes several forms. In *Pure Land,* by visualizing the Buddha Amida's beautiful form or chanting his name, a devotee is assured of rebirth in Amida's 'Land of bliss', where conditions are better for attaining final nirvana.

Zen ('meditation') Buddhism emphasizes the hard discipline of silent meditation, with unusual methods such as shouting and slapping used sometimes by Zen masters to shock the monk's mind into 'awakening'. Japanese Zen profoundly influenced the martial arts and the tea ceremony.

Esoteric, Tantric or *'Diamond'* Buddhism became popular in Tibet and Japan. It holds that enlightenment is fully present within the disciple and with the correct spiritual technique passed on privately by a master, enlightenment can be had here and now.

Nichiren Buddhism, named after a 13th-century Japanese monk, contains eso-teric elements such as a *mantra*, a re-peated phrase with special power (see p. 471).

Festivals in Mahayana countries vary according to the tradition and are often a blend of Buddhism and other religions. There are numerous Mahayana cults focusing on different Buddhas and bodhi-sattvas to whom people pray for help with problems. In Japan, Buddhist priests are mainly responsible for funeral and mem-orial services for the ancestors.

The contemporary relevance of Buddhism

Buddhism has now spread worldwide, with Buddhist centres in most Western countries, and Buddhists today are de-bating the future role and direction of Buddhism. Some hold that Buddhism necessarily involves withdrawing from the world and social involvement is con-trary to the 'middle way'. Others feel that the Buddha's teaching provides a blue-print for a better society, and Buddhists should therefore engage in social-reform movements.

The appeal of Buddhism in modern indus-trial society may lie in its emphasis on individual well-being, its non-exploit-ative approach to life, and its inner-directed philosophy. A Buddhist would say that people are drawn to Buddhism in this life because they performed acts of merit in a previous life.   BBO

Theravadin Buddhist monks in Bangkok, Thailand. Theravadin Buddhists believe that to imitate the Buddha by becoming a monk is the best way to attain enlightenment.

THE FOUR NOBLE TRUTHS

Buddhists believe that Gautama's teaching can be expressed succinctly in the Four Noble Truths:

1. To exist is to suffer.
2. Suffering is caused by attachment to impermanent things.
3. Suffering ceases once attachment ceases.
4. There is a 'Way' to end suffering.

This 'Way' varies with different kinds of Buddhism. Pure Land Buddhists rely on the power of Amida to help them (see main text). Zen Buddhists rely on meditation. Theravadin Buddhists have a formula that describes the Way – the ***Noble Eightfold Path***:

1. Perfect understanding or knowledge.
2. Perfect attitude or resolve.
3. Perfect speech.
4. Perfect action.
5. Perfect occupation or living.
6. Perfect effort.
7. Perfect mindfulness.
8. Perfect composure or meditation.

Some Buddhists believe that these 'perfections' can only be obtained by long meditation and by living a strictly moral life. Others believe that the Buddha helps those who turn to him for assistance, or that these perfections are complete and innate within all of us.

Religions of China and Japan

Chinese religion comprises a basic belief in the power of gods, fate, spirits and ancestors, and three great religions with separate origins: Confucianism and Daoism (Taoism), which originated in China between 500 and 300 BC, and Buddhism, which entered China about AD 100 (see p. 468). In practice these religions are thoroughly blended in the rites and festivals of Chinese religion.

Buddhism is also important in Japan, where it takes three main forms: Zen and Pure Land (see pp. 468–9), and Nichiren (see box). Japan's oldest religion, however, is Shinto, which has always been the religion of the emperors. Many new religions have also emerged in Japan in the last hundred years. Some offer totally new teachings, while others aim to revitalize the practices and values of older traditions.

Confucianism

Confucianism is an approach to life and way of thinking based on the teachings of Kongfuzi (Confucius; 551–479 BC). Kong-fuzi was a scholar-official who taught that man's duty and happiness lay in conforming to the 'Will of Heaven' – a supreme spiritual principle that is believed to regulate the course of events and relationships between people. When people live according to the Will of Heaven, society is stable and people are happy and prosperous. However, if people follow their selfish desires and contravene the Will of Heaven, conflicts and natural disasters occur, and the whole universe becomes disordered.

Kongfuzi himself is considered to represent the Confucian ideal of the 'noble man'. Gradually through diligent training and study ('self-cultivation'), he was able to remould his own character to conform to the Will of Heaven. Proper respect, family love, reciprocity among friends, benevolence to strangers and loyalty to the state are the five noble Confucian qualities to be cultivated.

Kongfuzi's teachings were developed by Mengzi (Mencius; 372–289 BC) and became the basis of Chinese ethics and behaviour, in which there is an emphasis on the preservation of the family and the state, and the performance of proper rites for the ancestors.

Daoism (Taoism)

Dao or *Tao* ('the Way') is a word of deep significance in Chinese thought. It refers to the mystical power behind all events, the flow of events themselves, and the religious path one should follow. The central text of Daoism is the *Dao de jing* (*Tao Te Ching*), dating from the 4th century BC but traditionally ascribed to Lao Zi (Lao-tzu), a semi-legendary philosopher of the 6th century BC. Also dating from the 4th century BC are the writings of Zhuang Zi (Chuang Tzu). In these texts the Dao is described as unfathomable and indescribable. It includes good and evil, darkness and light, stillness and motion (see Yin/Yang illustration). Another text normally regarded as a blend of Daoist and Confucian thought is the *Book of Changes (Yijing* or *I Ching)*, an oracular work that claims to predict the future from chance events, such as throwing sticks in a pattern.

Unlike Confucianism, Daoism advocates spontaneity and naturalness, abandoning oneself to the current of the Dao. Everything, good or bad, is the sublime operation of the Dao and should not be interfered with. Daoists naturally tended to solitude, meditation and simple living. Their techniques of quiet contemplation were similar to Buddhist meditation. Indeed, the Chinese word later used for Buddhist enlightenment was 'Dao'.

Oneness with the Dao was believed to confer immortality, and Daoist alchemy originated as an attempt to find an elixir that would transmute the perishable self into an Immortal. Though seemingly opposed to Confucianism in its advocacy of 'non-action', Daoists shared the Confucian aim of a harmonious existence, and most Chinese combine Daoism and Confucianism in their way of thinking.

Chinese religion in practice

Chinese festivals follow the cycle of the agricultural year and reflect concern for ancestors, health and prosperity. The Daoist rite of cosmic renewal (*jiao*) is carried out in early winter, and the Ch'ing Ming ('clear and bright') festival in the spring involves repairing ancestors' graves and offering food and paper 'spirit' money to the souls of the ancestors. Daoist and Buddhist priests as well as *shamans* (intermediaries between this world and the spirit world) assist in these festivals and in the rituals marking events in the life cycle, such as birth, marriage and death.

Rural people in mainland (Communist) China tend to be more religious than Chinese living in capitalist countries such as Hong Kong and Taiwan, but practising any religion has been difficult in China since Marxism became the official belief system in 1949 (see p. 447). A more liberal policy towards religion emerged in the late 1970s, but Chinese rulers throughout history have suppressed religions that do not support the government.

Shinto

Shinto ('the Sacred Way') is the native religion of Japan. Shinto existed in Japan long before the introduction of writing from China (5th century AD), but its earliest texts date from the 8th century. These texts include semi-mythological histories of Japan, tracing the line of emperors

SEE ALSO

● ALTERNATIVE MEDICINE p. 250
● CHINA TO THE COLONIAL AGE p. 382
● JAPAN TO THE 20TH CENTURY p. 386
● THE GROWTH OF TOTALI-TARIANISM p. 442
● CHINA IN THE 20TH CENTURY p. 446
● BUDDHISM p. 468
● CHINESE AND JAPANESE ART p. 514
● THE LITERATURE OF ASIA p. 616

The Hall of Annual Prayer, part of the Temple of Heaven, Beijing. The Temple of Heaven is a complex of several buildings, layed out in a geometrical pattern representing the belief that heaven is round and the Earth square.

MODERN JAPANESE BUDDHISM

Nichiren (AD 1222–82) was a Japanese monk who preached faith in the *Lotus Sutra*, a major scripture of Mahayana Buddhism. Unusually for a Buddhist, Nichiren violently criticized all other forms of Buddhism as heresy.

Civil war, famine and disease were threatening Japan in Nichiren's time. He believed these calamities were due to people's lack of faith in the *Lotus Sutra*, for the sutra warns those who scorn it that they will suffer.

Though Nichiren failed to convert all Japan to his cause, his form of Buddhism eventually became very popular in Japan. One group of followers was called *Nichiren Shōshū* (the 'True Nichiren Sect').

Nichiren Buddhists chant the Japanese title of the *Lotus Sutra*, 'Namu-myō-hō-renge-kyō'. Nichiren taught that this chanting has the power to make one enlightened, by awakening one's already-present Buddha-nature.

Sōka Gakkai ('The Society for the Creation of Value') was founded in the 1930s by Makiguchi Tsunesaburo, a schoolmaster who intended to combine Nichiren Buddhist practice with his own progressive educational theories. Although the movement was suppressed and Makiguchi died in prison during World War II, his successors Toda Josei and Ikeda Daisaku built up Sōka Gakkai membership in the 1960s to approximately 10 million members – the most successful lay religious movement in Japan.

Sōka Gakkai attracted converts by promising healing, business success and happiness, and in the 1970s the movement began to spread to other countries under the name *Nichiren Shōshū*. Many people – including pop stars and business and professional people – have been attracted to this accessible form of Buddhism. It teaches that chanting can bring anything one desires, from a new job to a Rolls Royce. People who chant for material goods, however, discover that having everything one desires is not the same as being happy. They begin to study the deeper meaning of Buddhism taught by Nichiren.

Despite its rapid growth since 1945, Sōka Gakkai points out that it is not a 'new' religion but a lay movement attached to the 'True Nichiren Sect', and that it regards Nichiren himself as the Buddha for the present age.

back to Amaterasu, the Sun goddess, so bestowing divine status on the imperial line.

Adherents of Shinto seek vitality, growth and prosperity through the worship of *kami* ('deity' or 'sacred energy'). The many Japanese gods are described as kami, and kami may also be found in sacred trees, rocks, waterfalls, mountains, and in the emperor and other outstanding individuals.

Shinto shrines throughout Japan house the kami of the locality. Shinto priests perform rituals of purification and renewal, and during festivals the kami is ceremonially carried through the streets in a *mikoshi* or portable shrine and entertained with a ceremony or a strenuous contest among the young men.

Shinto coexisted peacefully with other religions in Japan until the 1870s, when the modernizing government suppressed other religions and adapted Shinto teachings for government propaganda. Up to the Japanese defeat at the end of World War II, *State Shinto* taught that a citizen's religious duty was obedience to the divine emperor (see pp. 442–3). In 1946 Emperor Hirohito renounced all claims to divinity, and the new postwar constitution safeguards religious freedom and prohibits any association between religion and state.

Modern Japanese religions

With freedom of religion, many new religions appeared in postwar Japan, while others, suppressed before the war, expanded rapidly.

Some so-called 'new' religions actually began in the 19th century but had been restricted until 1945. The new religions are usually lay movements based on the personality and teaching of a founder, who may be a female shaman (see above). Founders may reveal new truths about the meaning of life, or may simply renew people's faith in more traditional teach-

Daoist sages admire a painting of the Yin/Yang symbol in this Chinese illustration from the 17th–18th century. Yin and Yang are complementary opposites, Yin being dark, feminine and negative, while Yang is light, masculine and positive. The interplay of Yin and Yang maintains the harmony of the universe and affects all things.

ings. Some new religions offer magical solutions to difficulties, while others encourage positive thinking as the solution to life's problems.

Several new religions teach that family problems are caused by selfishness and by neglect of the spirits of the family ancestors, who make their anger felt by disrupting life. Religious rites are prescribed to pacify the ancestors and thus solve the problem. These new Japanese religions are continuing ideas and practices dating back to the earliest known forms of Chinese religion.　BBo

The Seven Japanese Gods of Good Fortune in their treasure ship. This print is by the Japanese artist Hiroshige (1797–1858).

Judaism

The biblical account of the origin of the Jewish religion traces its history back to the revolt by Abraham against the idol-worship of his native Mesopotamia (now Iraq), when he smashed his father's idols and fled to Canaan (present-day Israel). His fundamental belief in one God is enshrined in God's covenant 'with you and your descendants, to be a God to you and your descendants after you' (Genesis 17:7).

SEE ALSO

- THE ANCIENT NEAR EAST p. 364
- THE GROWTH OF TOTALI-TARIANISM p. 442
- WORLD WAR II p. 444
- THE MIDDLE EAST p. 454
- RELIGIONS OF THE ANCIENT NEAR EAST p. 460
- CHRISTIANITY: BELIEF AND ACTION p. 474
- WORSHIP, PRAYER AND PIL-GRIMAGE p. 480
- SACRED SPACE, SACRED TIME p. 482
- GOOD AND EVIL p. 484
- THE MAKING OF MYTHS p. 612

When Canaan was struck by famine, Abraham's grandson Jacob (who was renamed Israel by an angel) was forced to take his twelve sons to find food in Egypt, where they were enslaved. God's promise to Abraham to make his descendants into a nation and to give them the land of Canaan in perpetuity was fulfilled when the twelve tribes of Israel, the descendants of Jacob's sons, were led out of Egypt by Moses (c. 1300 BC). During their 40-year journey to the Promised Land, the Ten Commandments were revealed to Moses by God on Mount Sinai, along with the foundations of the legal and moral system of the Jewish religion.

The Written Law and the Oral Law

Orthodox Judaism regards all religious authority as deriving from this revelation, as embodied in the *Torah*, the first five books of the Hebrew bible. The

A Hebrew Bible from 13th-century Spain. On the right is a representation of the *Menorah*, the seven-branched candlestick that once stood in the Temple in Jerusalem. On the left are other Temple implements.

Jewish bible (known to Christians as the Old Testament) also contains the historical books of the Prophets, and the 'Writings' which include such poetical and ethical books as Psalms and Proverbs.

The word 'Torah' literally means 'instruction' or 'law', and the term is also used to refer to the 613 commandments that tradition identifies in the Five Books of Moses, and to the whole body of social and religious law developed around them. Tradition holds that an *Oral Law* containing the key to the interpretation of the Written Law was revealed to Moses together with it. After the destruction of the Jewish state by the Romans in AD 70, this was codified as the *Mishna*, whose 63 'Tractates' are grouped into six 'Orders' dealing with agricultural law (in the land of Israel), sabbaths and festivals, family law, damages, temple ritual and dietary laws, and laws of purity.

During the following centuries debate amongst the Rabbis continued, and much of this is recorded in the *Gemara*. The *Talmud*, the great encyclopedia of Jewish teaching, consists of the interwoven texts of the *Mishna* and *Gemara*, usually printed with later commentaries around the page.

Beliefs

The Jewish religion is based on the belief in one God, Creator and Lord of the Universe, whose special relationship with the Jewish people consists in their undertaking to keep God's laws faithfully. Although Judaism expects non-Jews to observe certain basic ethical laws, it does not regard Jewish ritual as obligatory and does not seek converts. In fact, God promises the righteous of all people a place in the world to come, and the eventual re-establishment of the royal house of David; the *Messiah* (meaning 'anointed') will inaugurate an age of universal peace and security. (See also box on Thirteen Principles.)

Ritual and worship

Jewish law lays down a complex set of laws of *kashrut*, which distinguishes permitted (*kosher* or *kasher*) from prohibited (*treifa*) foods. Only mammals that have both cloven hoofs and chew the cud, such as cows and sheep, are permitted as food, and then they must be killed by a skilled *shochet* in a way that minimizes pain to the animal and drains as much blood as possible. Fish must have fins and scales (so that eels and sturgeon are forbidden), and shellfish and birds of prey are prohibited. In addition, milk and meat and their derivatives must be strictly separated and must not be cooked or prepared together, nor eaten at the same meal.

The Jewish day starts at sunset, and the week on Sunday, so that *Shabbat*, the day of rest ordained by the Torah, is observed from dusk on Friday to nightfall on Saturday. This day of rest derives from the account of the creation in the Bible,

where God rested on the seventh day. During Shabbat, productive work and kindling fire are prohibited; the prohibitions include carrying, writing, cooking and travelling (except a limited distance on foot).

Synagogues were first built to serve as temporary places of worship after the destruction of the Temple in Jerusalem by the Babylonians in 586 BC, but although the Jews did rebuild the Temple, the practice of local houses of prayer continued. However, the second Temple was also destroyed, this time by the Romans, and never rebuilt, and to this day the synagogue service is modelled upon, and refers to, the Temple service. The central role of the synagogue in Jewish religious life is attested by its Hebrew names, which translate as 'house of meeting' and 'house of study', as well as 'house of prayer'.

Although there are no requirements for a specially built building, and prayer can take place anywhere, many synagogues incorporate such ancient Jewish symbols as the Star of David, the *Menorah* (the seven-branched Temple candlestick), and the two tablets containing the Ten Commandments (Exodus 20) in their decoration. The congregation usually faces the Ark, a cupboard containing the Torah scrolls, which are handwritten on parchment by a specially trained scribe. Above the Ark, which is usually in the wall facing Jerusalem, a light is kept burning as a sign of God's eternal presence.

Services are held in the evening, morning, and afternoon. Each service has at its centre a silent prayer, which is recited standing and facing Jerusalem. Morning and evening prayers also contain the *Shema*, the central declaration of Jewish faith, beginning 'Hear, O Israel: the Lord is our God; the Lord is One' (Deuteronomy, 5), which is also the last rite of a Jew on his deathbed.

For a formal service to take place, a *minyan* or quorum of ten men is required; otherwise the Torah is not read and certain prayers cannot be said, including the *Kaddish*, a declaration of faith recited by mourners during the year after their bereavement. Any of the minyan may lead the prayers and read the Torah, not only the rabbi, whose main function is as teacher and interpreter of the Law.

Rites of passage

Birth. As a sign of the covenant between God and the Jews, the Torah lays down that every baby boy must be circumcised. The service is performed by a specially trained person, a *mohel*, on the eighth day after birth. Girls are named by their father in the synagogue.

Bar mitzvah. When a Jewish boy is 13 years old, he is regarded as being old enough to take responsibility for himself and for his observance of the Law. He is then 'bar mitzvah' (Hebrew for 'son of the commandment'), an adult in religious terms. He can then take an active part in services, and be counted in the minyan. One of the privileges of a Jewish man is to be called to read a passage of the Torah, in Hebrew, in a synagogue service, and in many communities the first occasion when he can do this is made the pretext of a party. In Orthodox Judaism, girls celebrate their coming of age at 12, and in some congregations this is marked by a *bat chayil* ceremony. In Progressive synagogues girls may have a *bat mitzvah* ('daughter of the commandment') ceremony at the age of 13.

Marriage. A Jewish marriage ceremony takes place under a canopy, the *chuppah*, and can be held anywhere, but is usually held in a synagogue or out of doors. After the bridegroom places a ring on the bride's forefinger, the ketubah or marriage contract is read out, and seven blessings are recited. At the end of the ceremony, the bridegroom breaks a glass underfoot, recalling the destruction of the Temple in Jerusalem. In Orthodox circles, the celebrations continue for a week, with the seven blessings repeated each night.

Death. Jewish law requires that a body must be buried in consecrated ground as soon as possible after death. It is first washed, anointed with spices, wrapped in a white sheet, and placed in a plain wooden coffin. Orthodox Jews regard cremation as a denial of belief in bodily resurrection. At the funeral, mourners tear their clothes, and for the next year they recite *Kaddish* (see above) during every synagogue service; *Kaddish* is also recited annually on the anniversary of death.

Jewish traditions and sects

For the Orthodox Jew, all authority derives from the divine will as expressed in the Torah and interpreted in the rabbinic tradition; the main role for human reason is in working out the precise details of that law. Ritual observance and the obligation to study are not thought of as different from ethical behaviour. Nonetheless, there are diverse traditions within Orthodox Judaism: the *Ashkenazi* tradition developed in the communities of Germany and Poland; while the *Sephardic* tradition is traced back to the Jews who lived in the lands of the Near East and Mediterranean (particularly Spain) under Muslim rule in and before the Middle Ages. When the Sephardic Jews of Spain and Portugal were expelled in 1492 they settled in various countries, but have preserved different traditions from the Jews of northern Europe. The *Hassidic* sects of eastern Europe and some of the Oriental and North African communities also evolved their own rites. These groups, however, recognize each other's legitimacy in so far as they subscribe to the traditional concept of divine authority.

In the 19th and early 20th centuries various trends in Europe and America moved away from traditional or Orthodox observance, giving rise to Reform, Liberal, Conservative, Reconstructionist and other forms of Judaism. They reject the divinity of the Torah and rabbinic authority, and believe, to varying degrees, that Jewish practice must adapt to changing circumstances. They have introduced changes such as holding services partly in the vernacular (rather than Hebrew).   EJB

A Passover meal in a Jewish home. When the youngest child of the family asks 'Why is this night different from other nights?', the father responds by recounting the story of the Jewish Exodus from slavery in Egypt. At the special meal or *seder*, foods with symbolic significance are eaten, and traditionally an extra place at table and a glass of wine is set aside for the Prophet Elijah.

MAJOR JEWISH FESTIVALS

The normal Jewish year consists of 12 lunar months of 29 or 30 days. An extra month is added to 7 years of every 19-year cycle to bring the calendar back in time with the solar year.

The Jewish months are as follows:

Nisan (March–April), Iyyar (April–May), Sivan (May–June), Tammuz (June–July), Av (July–August), Ellul (August–September), Tishri (September–October), Cheshvan (October–November), Kislev (November–December), Tevet (December–January), Shevat (January–February), Adar (February–March).

PESACH (Passover), 15–22 Nisan. Formal meal to commemorate Exodus from Egypt; also originally thanksgiving for barley harvest. No leaven eaten.

SHAVUOT (Pentecost), 6–7 Sivan. Commemorates giving of Torah; also originally thanksgiving for wheat harvest.

FAST OF AV, 9 Av. 24-hour fast to commemorate destruction of the Temple in Jerusalem by Nebuchadnezzar in 586 BC and by the Romans in AD 70.

ROSH HASHANA, 1–2 Tishri. New Year; commemorates 'Birthday of the World'. White worn for repentance, and ram's horn blown to commemorate Abraham's covenant with God.

YOM KIPPUR, 10 Tishri. Day of Atonement, marked by 24 hours of fasting and prayer for forgiveness of past sins.

SUKKOT (Tabernacles), 15–22 Tishri. The 40 years of wandering in the desert are commemorated by eating and sleeping in huts roofed with branches. Also originally thanksgiving for harvest.

SIMCHAT TORAH, 22–23 Tishri. Marks completion of annual cycle of Torah readings and commencement of new cycle.

CHANUKAH or **HANUKKAH** (Festival of Lights), 25 Kislev–3 Tevet. Candles are lit in a nine-branched *Menorah* or *Chanukiah* to commemorate rededication of the Temple in Jerusalem by Judas Maccabeus in 165 BC.

TU B'SHEVAT, 15 Shevat. Trees planted.

PURIM, 14 Adar. Readings of Book of Esther, giving of charity and sending of gifts all commemorate the deliverance of the Jews of Persia from destruction.

Two new dates are observed by many Jews: **YOM HA'ATZMA'UT** (5 Iyyar) celebrates the establishment of the State of Israel, and **YOM HASHOAH** (27 Nisan) is a memorial for the 6 million Jews who died in the Nazi Holocaust.

Christianity: Belief and Practice

The Western calendar, shaped and determined by Christianity, sees the birth of Jesus of Nazareth, known as the Christ, as the turning point of history. In dating the modern era from the supposed date of his birth (it seems likely Jesus was actually born c. 4 BC), Christianity was making a profound statement about the significance of Jesus Christ.

SEE ALSO

- THE DECLINE OF ROME p. 380
- THE SUCCESSORS OF ROME p. 394
- CHRISTIANITY RESURGENT p. 398
- MEDIEVAL AND RENAISSANCE CULTURE p. 406
- THE REFORMATION p. 408
- WHAT IS RELIGION? p. 458
- JUDAISM p. 472
- WORLD CHRISTIANITY p. 476
- WORSHIP, PRAYER AND PILGRIMAGE p. 480
- SACRED SPACE, SACRED TIME p. 482
- GOOD AND EVIL p. 484

For Christians, the Jewish child born in Bethlehem was no ordinary human. He was and is, both human and divine, the Son of God. While it is possible to say that a historical person named Jesus lived between c. 4 BC and AD 30, it is only faith that can claim that he was the Christ, the anointed one of God, the long awaited Messiah of the Jews.

The nature of God

Christians believe that God is the creator of the universe and all life. They believe that Jesus Christ is the only Son of God, who has existed with God the Father from before time began. Jesus was incarnated (given human form), when by the power of the Holy Spirit, his human mother, Mary, gave birth to him. The purpose of his incarnation was to reconcile humanity with God, as human sinfulness had broken the relationship with God. Through Jesus' death upon the cross God broke the power of sin and evil, and through the rising of Jesus from the dead on the third day God showed the triumph of life over death, of good over evil, and gave the promise of everlasting life to those who believe in Jesus.

After his death, Jesus appeared to his disciples a number of times, and then ascended to heaven. He promised to send the Holy Spirit to guide and enlighten the Church. Christians believe that Jesus will return at the end of time to judge the world.

The Nativity – the birth of Jesus – by the 15th-century Flemish painter Robert Campin. The Gospels recount how the Angel Gabriel announced to Mary that she was to conceive the Son of God by the Holy Spirit, and that, although married to Joseph, she remained a virgin. In both the Orthodox and Roman Catholic Churches, Mary is regarded as a mediator between God and man. (Musée des Beaux-Arts, Dijon/ Explorer)

The *Trinity* expresses the Christian belief that there are three persons who are of the same substance – God, namely the Father who created, the Son who revealed God's love and purpose to humanity and creation, and the Holy Spirit, through which God seeks to guide and instruct the world today.

The teachings of Jesus

What we know of Jesus' teachings and life is recorded in the Gospels and in several quotes and stories found in the other books of the New Testament. These were all written by Christians who believed Jesus to be in some way both human and divine. Our knowledge of Jesus therefore comes through the pens of believers. Jesus taught that God was like a father who cares for every person on Earth. He taught that through repentance and forgiveness, God calls all humanity to him in love and seeks for every individual to do his will on Earth. Jesus taught that through living as God wishes, the Kingdom of God – justice, love, mercy and peace – could come upon Earth, either in individual lives or possibly to the world as a whole. What we cannot be sure of is quite how Jesus understood his role. He certainly rejected the model of the *Messiah* that the Jews of his day had. They longed for a righteous warrior who would free them from Rome and give them their own country again. But whether Jesus understood himself to be divine is a hotly debated issue. He certainly talked of the kingdom to come – but not a political or military one, rather one established in people's hearts and minds.

The Church holds that through the twelve key disciples of Jesus, the apostles, authority on Earth was given to the Church, which is to be seen as the body of Christ on Earth. The Church is therefore held to be essential to salvation – to being freed from sin and to the possibility of everlasting life.

The Bible

The Jewish Bible is called the *Old Testament* by Christians, and the Gospels, Acts of the Apostles, Letters and Revelation are called the *New Testament*. In so doing, the Church shows that it considers itself to be the true heir of Israel, to whom the Old Testament or covenant was given (see p. 472). But Christians believe Israel failed to recognize Jesus as the fulfilment of the Old Testament, and so the special relationship with God enjoyed by Israel passed to the Church.

Some Christians believe the Bible is a factual, historical and scientific account of life on Earth, its purpose and meaning. Other Christians hold that it reveals, through story and myth, the nature of humanity's relationship with God and with one another. For both, the Bible plays a central role in helping to determine Christian responses to moral, social and spiritual issues.

The Bible the first Christians knew was the Jewish one, in which Christians see Jesus foretold. The Jewish Bible was known to the early Christians in two forms, the original Hebrew and the Greek translation known as the *Septuagint*. This was because Christianity started amongst Jews – Jesus appears to have had few non-Jewish (Gentile) followers during his life on Earth. Very soon, however, Christians were attracted from non-Jewish groups and they read the Jewish Bible in the common language of their time, Greek. The New Testament was entirely written in Greek, showing how the Gentile world

MAJOR CHRISTIAN FESTIVALS

Of the Christian festivals, the following are the most significant – although every day of the year has its saints, and there are many minor festivals.

ADVENT and CHRISTMAS

Advent runs for some four or five weeks prior to 25 December (Christmas Day) and is a time of preparation for the coming of Jesus in the past, in the present and in the future. Christmas Day celebrates the birth of Jesus and is traditionally followed by the twelve days of Christmas, ending with Epiphany, which celebrates the visit of the wise men to the child Jesus.

LENT and EASTER

This is the major festival of the Church. For 40 days before Holy Week and Easter – a period known as Lent – Christians fast or go without certain foods to remind themselves of Jesus' 40 days in the wilderness and of the sufferings he endured on the cross. Holy Week begins with Palm Sunday, which recalls Jesus' entry into Jerusalem when the people covered the road with palm leaves to celebrate his arrival. Good Friday – so called because it brought redemption to humanity – is the day Christians commemorate the death of Jesus upon the cross. Easter Sunday celebrates the rising from the tomb by Jesus and his first appearance to his disciples and friends.

ASCENSION DAY

Ascension Day comes 40 days after Easter and celebrates the ascension of Jesus into heaven – the last earthly appearance of Jesus.

PENTECOST

Whitsunday or Pentecost comes ten days later, and celebrates the gift of the Holy Spirit upon the disciples and the founding of the Church.

The **Ascension of Christ** as depicted in a 14th-century French manuscript. (Explorer)

became more important to the Church than the Jewish world. Jesus himself spoke Aramaic (a Semitic language), and a few words of this remain in the New Testament.

The earliest history of the Church is captured in the Acts of the Apostles, while the four Gospels portray the life of Jesus in different ways. The New Testament also contains letters from St Paul and others to the early churches, in which Christian theology and reflection on Jesus begins to develop. At the end of the New Testament is the Book of Revelation, which envisages the end of the world and the Second Coming of Jesus. The early Church seems to have expected Jesus to return very soon and to establish God's rule on Earth. When this did not happen, this Second Coming became an event in the distant future, when all would be judged for their behaviour and the just rule of God would come on Earth.

The Church and ritual

The life of the Church has been formed by both the Bible and by Christian teachings and doctrine. Through a dynamic interaction between Bible and tradition the Church has developed its teachings, beliefs and creeds as well as liturgies, sacraments and festivals. These impart to the believer the essence of the Christian faith and imbue the significant stages of life with Christian meaning and purpose. The following account draws primarily upon Roman Catholic and Anglican practices; there is in fact a wide divergence of belief and practice within the Christian faith.

There are two rites or *sacraments* that were instituted by Jesus himself, namely baptism and the eucharist. Other rites celebrated at times of grace or blessing include confirmation, marriage, ordination to the priesthood, confession, and extreme unction just before death.

The *eucharist* (or *holy communion*) – in which bread and wine is consecrated and offered to the congregation – is the central service of many Churches, because Jesus at the last Supper (just before the crucifixion) told his disciples to remember him when they broke bread and drank wine. There is a wide diversity of understanding of the role of the bread and the wine. In Roman Catholic theology it is believed that the bread and the wine become the body and blood of Christ – a process known as *transubstantiation*. In Protestant thought the term *consubstantiation* covers one understanding – that the body and blood of Christ are present in the bread and the wine. Protestant thought also has the idea that the bread and wine are simply a memorial to the blood and body of Christ.

Baptism (or *christening*) marks the acceptance of a new member into the Church, and involves sprinkling holy water on the head of the person concerned, or may, in some traditions, involve total immersion. The ritual recalls the baptism of Jesus by John the Baptist, and Jesus' own baptizing of his disciples.

Many Churches have professional clergy. These fall into two main types, priests and ministers. The role of the *priest* in, say, the Orthodox or Roman Catholic tradition is to act as an intermediary between God and the world. The priest has a formal, liturgical role that does not necessarily involve a pastoral dimension. In contrast, the *minister* in many Protestant Churches does not act as an intermediary, as each person is believed to be in direct communication with God, or capable of being so. The minister's role is to guide reflection on the Word of God and to help Christians in the daily conduct of their lives according to Christian principles. In such Churches there is a belief in the priesthood of all believers.

The term 'church' needs to be explored, for it has two distinct meanings. With a capital 'C', it is applied to the whole body of believers, as in the Church of England. It does not just mean the clergy, but all who profess Christ's name and belong to him through the Church. The second meaning, with a lower-case 'c', is the physical place of worship for the community of believers. Most churches have their sanctuary, where the altar is kept, and provide places for communal worship, reading of the Bible, preaching and administration of the eucharist and other sacraments such as baptism. In certain traditions the church faces towards Jerusalem.

Forms of Christianity

Christianity has three major forms: Roman Catholic with the pope as head of the Church; Orthodox, with the patriarch of Constantinople as the first amongst equals of the various patriarchs of the different Orthodox Churches such as the Russian Church; the Protestant movement, made up of main denominations such as the Lutherans, Methodists, Anglicans, Baptists, United Churches and so forth, as well as the many smaller splinter Churches. Worldwide, Christianity has over 1500 million adherents, of which the majority are now to be found in the Third World – Africa, Latin America and Asia. More details on these different traditions will be found on pp. 476–7. ICOREC

A baptism in Cuba (left). Baptism marks the acceptance of a new member into the Church, holy water symbolizing purification from sin. Although infant baptism is practised in most Churches, some traditions such as the Baptists believe that children are too young to understand the significance of the ritual, and usually only baptize adults.

World Christianity

In every form of Christianity the same scriptures are used, the God of Israel is worshipped, and Jesus Christ is seen as having ultimate significance. The differences in expression and forms of worship among Christians are immense, as Christianity has adapted to different cultures and historical circumstances. To understand this diversity it is necessary to consider how Christianity has spread.

The earliest Christians were all Jews, and the first Christian centre was Jerusalem. The belief that Jesus was Israel's Messiah led to a rethinking of Israel's history and scripture. Many Gentiles (non-Jews) were attracted already to the monotheism of Judaism and found in Christianity a way that brought Jewish and Greek thought together. Crucially, the Christians decided that non-Jewish followers of Jesus should not become converts to Judaism. This meant that the new Christians (who were soon the majority) had a quite different lifestyle from the first followers of Jesus.

Greco-Roman Christianity
Christianity spread in all directions from Palestine, but most rapidly in the Roman Empire, where it had to adapt to Greek philosophy and popular (and later official) hostility. Though local forms of Christianity developed, a process of consensus produced statements of teaching regarded as *catholic* (universal) and *orthodox* (right thinking). The methods of Greek philosophical debate were employed to define and state Christian teaching. After 313 the Roman state began to favour Christianity and eventually made it the official religion (see p. 380).

The Emperors generally wanted religious uniformity and so 'catholic' and 'orthodox' formulations came to have state sanction. In the Empire's eastern provinces, Christians were thinking about Christ not only in terms of Greek philosophy, but also in terms of Syrian and Egyptian thought; and Christians outside the Empire were not always involved in the consultative process at all. *Monophysitism* and *Nestorianism* are names given to teachings about Christ rejected at Empire-based councils in the 5th century. The issues are complex, but the basic conflict was probably between mainstream Greco-Roman and non-Greek ways of thinking. At any rate, most Syriac and Coptic Christians formed Monophysite or Nestorian Churches, and Churches of these types spread in the Middle East and northeast Africa, across Central Asia, and over to southern India (see Oriental Churches, below).

Christianity and Europe
By 400, Christianity was established in Roman-Greek culture. After the collapse of Rome (see p. 381) the Empire continued in the east at Constantinople until 1453 (see p. 395), but its eastern provinces were gradually conquered by Muslims (see p. 392). In Central Asia, too, the Muslim advance drastically reduced the Christian presence. But by 1000 the majority of tribal peoples from Ireland to Russia had become Christian, some under Roman, some under Greek influence. Roman or Greek culture was added to tribal heritages to form new, distinct Christian civilizations in Western Europe and Russia.

The linguistic and cultural differences meant that Eastern and Western Christians increasingly grew apart. Western Christians used Latin and looked to Rome; Eastern Christians used Greek or Slavonic languages and looked to Constantinople. Despite various attempts at reconciliation, the breach between Eastern and Western Christianity had hardened by the 11th century.

Christianity expands again
From the late 15th century, Western Europeans learned of new routes and hitherto unknown lands (see p. 405); and, from the 16th century, Russia explored its vast Asian hinterland. Both thought it a duty to bring Christianity to their new neighbours.

In Spanish America, Christianity was enforced by conquest (see pp. 410–11). In most other areas, conquest was out of the question. The result was missionary endeavour on the part of the Roman Catholic Church in Africa and Asia from the 16th century. Orthodox missions in Siberia and Protestant missions elsewhere developed in earnest in the 18th century. Though missions sometimes profited from imperial ventures (as in the Treaty ports in China), many preceded the major imperial expansions of the late 19th century (see p. 432).

Until the 20th century the success of the missions appeared modest. In 1900, about 83% of the world's professing Christians lived in Europe or North America. Today between 50% and 60% live in Africa, Asia, Latin America and Oceania, and the proportion is rising – in Africa alone there are now 224 million Christians, where there were only 10 million in 1900. In the West, especially in Europe, Christian belief has declined, making Christianity increasingly a religion of the southern continents.

The Eastern Churches
Most of the Churches called Orthodox derived from the ancient Greek Christianity of the Eastern Mediterranean. The direct link with Churches founded by apostles and the memory of a Christian Roman Empire (the Byzantine Empire) that lasted until 1453 heighten the importance of tradition as the guide of the Church. Tradition includes the scriptures, the early Church councils and the writings of the Church Fathers (the early medieval writers on Christian doctrine), the liturgy and the veneration of holy pictures (icons). The Ecumenical Patriarch of Constantinople is the senior figure, but each autonomous Church (the Russian being much the largest) has its

World Peace Day, 27 October 1986. At the invitation of Pope John Paul II, leaders of many Christian denominations and non-Christian faiths gathered in Assisi – the home of St Francis – to pray for an end to war, violence and intolerance.

own patriarch and is self-governing. Apart from Russia, Orthodox Christianity is particularly important in the Balkans, Greece, Cyprus, Romania, Bulgaria and parts of Yugoslavia.

The Oriental Churches

The Oriental Churches include the surviving parts of the ancient Monophysite and Nestorian Churches (see above). The Monophysite Churches include the Coptic Church of Egypt – one of the earliest Churches; the Ethiopian Church founded in the 4th century; the Syrian Church – again one of the earliest, and which includes the Thomarists of India; and the Armenians – who became the first nation to officially adopt Christianity, at the end of the 3rd century.

The Nestorian Church at one time covered most of Persia (modern Iran), and had reached into China by the 7th century. However, with the rise of Islam, the Nestorian Church was largely extinguished.

Except in Ethiopia and India, other Churches exist primarily within Muslim states, where they are tolerated, although evangelization is usually not permitted. The Ethiopian Church underwent a difficult period with the Marxist regime in Ethiopia (1976–91), but has held its place as the major humanitarian agency in the famine-struck country.

The ancient Church of South India has a complex history, with both Monophysite and Nestorian (as well as Catholic and Protestant) influences.

The Roman Catholic Church

Rome was the only Western Church founded by an apostle (St Peter). From Ireland to the Carpathians, Christians came to acknowledge the bishop of Rome as pope (from Vulgar Latin *papa*, 'father'), and used Latin for worship, scripture-reading and theology. In the 16th century most of northern Europe broke the link with Rome to form reformed Protestant Churches (see p. 408 and below). This division of Western Christianity led to the terms 'Protestant' for these northern Churches and 'Roman Catholic' (though to its members it was simply 'the Church') for Latin Christianity.

Supreme in southern Europe, Catholic Christianity was extended to the Americas and to parts of Asia and Africa. Missions in the 19th and 20th centuries extended it further, and the Roman Catholic Church today is found worldwide, forming the largest single Christian body. It has a strong central authority based on the idea of the Church as the possessor and interpreter of the tradition of Christ. Since the Second Vatican Council (1962–65) Latin has for most purposes given way to local languages. Some smaller non-Latin Churches, such as the Ukrainian Church and the Lebanese Maronites, accept the leadership of the pope. These are known as 'Uniate' Churches.

The Protestant Churches

In 16th-century Europe, movements to reform the Church accompanied fresh interpretations of the Bible and the use of everyday language in place of Latin. These movements rejected Roman authority and established reformed national forms of Christianity in the various states of northern Europe, such as Lutheranism in Sweden and parts of Germany, Calvinism in Geneva and Scotland, and Anglicanism in England. This process is known as the Reformation (see p. 408). The majority Protestant movement aimed to reform the Church within each state while keeping the idea that the Church embraced the whole community. The Radical (or Anabaptist) movement insisted that the Church consisted solely of those who

---

RELATED GROUPS

Various movements related to Christianity stand apart from the forms mentioned above. Wide variations in teaching include distinctive interpretations of the Bible. Some of these movements have supplementary literature, and most reject trinitarian belief and the divinity of Christ. Western examples include some forms of Unitarianism, the Watchtower Movement or Jehovah's Witnesses, and the Church of Latter-Day Saints of Jesus Christ or Mormons. The latter two are of 19th-century American origin.

---

made a commitment to Christ, and broke the link with the state. A minority in Europe, this movement produced the dominant Christian forms in North America.

The 18th century saw movements for spiritual renewal in Protestant countries – Pietism in Germany and the Evangelical Revival in Britain, North America and elsewhere. These brought the majority and radical Protestant streams closer together. European emigration brought all the Protestant traditions to America, including the Pietist and Evangelical movements. They took new life and new shapes in a huge community – largely Christian, but multi-ethnic and with no national Church. Some completely new forms of Christianity also arose – notably Pentecostalism, with its stress on gifts of tongues and healing. Today the American religious scene is characterized by a large number of denominations.

New expressions of Christianity

New expressions of Christianity are appearing in the southern continents as Christians there meet situations not encountered in the West. There are some signs that a tradition of Christianity is developing that may be as distinctively African as Catholicism and Protestantism have been Western, in that African Independent Churches reflect African ways of worship and address issues of African life. In India, united Churches of South India and North India have developed, and these replace the denominational Churches of Western origin. Latin America has produced new developments such as 'liberation theology' and 'basic Christian communities' (radical movements within the Roman Catholic Church that work for social justice), and a surge of Pentecostalist Christianity.

Christianity today

One characteristic of Christianity today is the increased understanding and cooperation both between Christians in different parts of the world and between Christians of different backgrounds and traditions. The word *ecumenical* is used to describe such spirit and action. Though sometimes used in a narrower sense to refer to the movement associated with the World Council of Churches (founded in 1948), the word simply means 'worldwide' (from the Greek *oikumene*, 'inhabited world'). It is a sign that Christianity is a world faith to a greater extent than ever before, and that in itself means diversity.

In the 1990s female ordination became a major issue in Anglican Churches, some of which – including those in the USA and New Zealand – already have women priests, but the decision of the Church of England to admit women to the priesthood (1992) threatened a secession of traditionalists to Roman Catholicism. AW

The Amish (left) are a radical and pacifist Protestant sect that originated in Switzerland in the 16th century. They began to emigrate to America in the 18th century, and are now mostly settled in close communities in Pennsylvania. Denying themselves all forms of modern technology, they largely support themselves by farming.

SEE ALSO

● THE DECLINE OF ROME p. 380
● THE SUCCESSORS OF ROME p. 394
● CHRISTIANITY RESURGENT p. 398
● CRISIS IN EUROPE p. 402
● MEDIEVAL AND RENAISSANCE CULTURE p. 406
● THE REFORMATION p. 408
● JUDAISM p. 472
● CHRISTIANITY: BELIEF AND ACTION p. 474
● PHILOSOPHY pp. 486–97

Islam

Islam is an Arabic word meaning 'submission'. Muslims are those who submit themselves to Allah – whom they regard as the one true God – by accepting the faith of Islam. The sacred book of Islam is the Qur'an (Koran), the word of God revealed to the Prophet Muhammad. Five basic beliefs are central in Islam. These are the Articles of Faith and consist of belief in the oneness of God; the holy books he has revealed for the guidance of humanity; the prophets; the angels; and the hereafter.

The founder of Islam was the Prophet Muhammad. Born around AD 570 at Mecca in western Arabia, Muhammad received his call to prophethood when he was about 40 years old. He claimed that he had been sent to bring good news and to warn his people against idolatry, so that they might turn to the true God. Those who believed and obeyed the laws in the Qur'an would be rewarded in paradise, whereas those who rejected the message would be punished in hell.

Gradually opposition built up against Muhammad, especially among the rich merchant class, and he and his followers migrated from Mecca to Medina, a city 450 km (280 mi) to the north of Mecca. This migration is known as the *Hijra* and it took place in July 622, marking the beginning of the Islamic calendar. At Medina, Muhammad became the head of a new religious community. He fought his Meccan opponents until his final conquest of Mecca in 630. He died in 632, having spread the message of Islam through much of Arabia.

God, revelation and the Qur'an

Muslims insist on God's oneness and believe that no one and nothing should be worshipped alongside him. God is seen as the creator, the giver and taker of life, present everywhere in the universe and quite unlike any other being. He is described by many 'beautiful names' such as All-Powerful, All-Seeing, All-Hearing, Merciful, Compassionate, Forgiving. From a Muslim viewpoint God can be known most reliably through his revelation of himself in the Qur'an.

According to Islamic doctrine, the Qur'an is the collection of God's revelations to the Prophet Muhammad through the medium of the angel Gabriel. Revealed in Arabic over 22 years from AD 610 to 632, it is seen not as an earthly-inspired book but as the exact words of God, taken from a heavenly tablet. It is regarded as a miracle and great care has been taken to preserve it without change.

Muslims maintain that in the Qur'an God speaks of his own nature, of his relationship with human beings, and of how they will be held accountable to him at the Last Judgement. Although the Qur'an refers directly to Muhammad and the early Islamic community, it offers moral guidance to people of all times and all races. In addition, earlier prophets – including Abraham, Moses and Jesus – are recognized.

Religious leaders

Prayers in the mosque are led by an *imam*. Any male Muslim can act as an imam, but there are usually professional imams attached to mosques and they may also preach, teach and conduct marriages and funerals. The word 'imam' can also be used to mean the leader of all the Muslims. After Muhammad's death, the Sunni Muslims used the word in this way, but no longer have such a leader. The Shiite sects have varying beliefs about the imam as head of the community, but stress the importance of his spiritual leadership.

Scholars of religion provide guidance for the community in matters of theology and the Holy Law. Among the Twelver Shiites the senior theologians, known in Iran as *ayatollahs*, exercise great authority in the absence of the Imam. The title of *mullah*, also used in Iran, is a general term for a Shiite religious scholar.

Sufism is the name given to the mystical movement in Islam. Sufi shaikhs provide leadership for their followers in the mystical brotherhoods, guiding the initiates on their spiritual journey. In some areas of the Islamic world, for example in parts of West Africa, they remain a powerful influence.

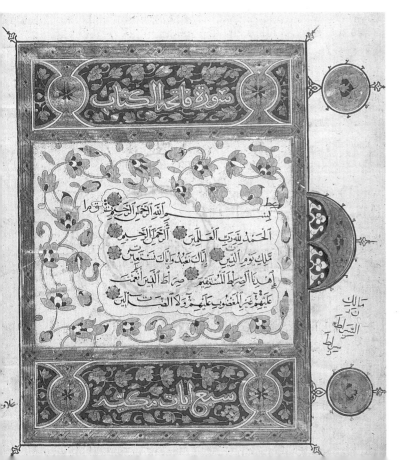

An ornately decorated Qur'an (Koran) from the 14th century. It is traditionally forbidden in Islam to portray living figures, so Muslim calligraphers developed highly ornamental styles based on geometric shapes and plant motifs.

The sects of Islam

The *Sunnis*, who form about 90% of Muslims, are known more fully as 'the People of the Sunna and Collectivity'. Their name derives from their claim to follow the *sunna* or 'trodden path' (the name given to the words and actions of Muhammad and his first four successors), and also from their claim to adhere to the ways of the 'collectivity' of Muslims.

The *Shiite* sects originated in a dispute as to who should head the Islamic community after the Prophet's death. Supporters of his cousin and son-in-law, Ali,

The Kaaba the shrine near the centre of the Great Mosque in Mecca. Pilgrims to Mecca circle the Kaaba seven times and kiss and touch the Black Stone built into the eastern wall. According to tradition, the Black Stone was given to Adam when he was expelled from paradise to enable him to obtain forgiveness for his sins. Originally white, it has become black by assimilating the sins of millions of pilgrims.

became known as the *Shiat Ali* or 'Party of Ali'. All Shiites recognize lines of Ali's descendants as imams. They are divided into three main subsects.

The first of the Shiite subsects consists of the *Zaidis*, who differ little from Sunni Muslims, but recognize a line of imams possessing no supernatural qualities. The Zaidi imams ruled Yemen until their overthrow in 1962.

The majority of Shiites are *Twelvers* or *Imamis*. This subsect forms most of the population of Iran, with considerable numbers in Iraq, Lebanon, Pakistan and India. They recognize twelve imams, the last of whom disappeared in AD 878 and is expected by them to return as the *Mahdi*, a Messiah-like figure who will usher in an age of justice before the end of the world. The Twelvers regard the imams as perfect and sinless, partaking of divine qualities through the emanation into them of the Divine Light. In modern times the title 'imam' has also been given to other major religious leaders of the Twelvers, such as Imam Khomeini of Iran.

The last main Shiite subsect is formed by the *Ismailis*, who recognize a continuing line of infallible imams descended from Ismail, the eldest son of the sixth Twelver imam. The doctrines of the Ismailis are strongly influenced by neoplatonic and Indian thought, introduced especially in their interpretation of the Qur'an, in which they saw inner truths different from the external meanings. The Fatimid caliphs of Egypt (see p. 392) were Ismailis. Modern branches are the Khojas, led by the Aga Khan (mainly in India and East Africa), and the Bohras of India and Yemen.

Life under the Holy Law

Islamic law is called the *Sharia*, the 'high-

way' along which God commands the Muslims to walk. The scope of the Sharia is wider than that of Western secular law and covers all aspects of life. Religious duties are specified in detailed regulations for performing prayer, pilgrimage, etc. Punishments are laid down for certain offences, for example, the amputation of a hand for theft, 80 lashes for drinking alcohol. Family organization is determined by laws dealing with marriage, divorce, custody of children and inheritance.

Women and Islam

The status of women in Muslim countries is changing rapidly. A man is allowed up to four wives, but this is rare nowadays and most men have only one. Traditionally, a man can divorce his wife by saying three times that he intends to divorce her, but she cannot divorce him. However, reform in the law in some countries now allows a woman to divorce her husband in some circumstances – for example, if he takes another wife after writing in their marriage contract that she would be his only wife.

Some women wear strict Islamic dress covering all parts of the body, including face, hands and hair. Others allow just their face and hands to show, and some wear modest Western dress, keeping Islamic dress for attendance at the mosque and prayers at home. These variations can even be seen within one family. Many younger married women work, and some run their own companies or have attained senior positions in government.   ES

SEE ALSO
● THE RISE OF ISLAM p. 392
● THE MIDDLE EAST p. 454
● WORSHIP, PRAYER AND PILGRIMAGE p. 480
● SACRED SPACE AND SACRED TIME p. 482
● ISLAMIC ART p. 510
● THE LITERATURE OF ASIA p. 616

A Muslim university in India run by the Bohras, a branch of the Ismaili sect. The Ismailis see esoteric hidden meanings in the Qur'an, and distinguish between ordinary Muslims and the initiated.

Worship, Prayer and Pilgrimage

In religion the word *worship* (originally *worth-ship*) means the acknowledgement of the worth and position of the supreme being and of lesser divinities (or occasionally ancestors), and the giving to them of such veneration as is appropriate. More specifically, the word is often applied to the particular rites and ceremonies through which this acknowledgement is given expression. Thus one might talk of Jewish or Muslim worship to indicate the way in which followers of these religions actually demonstrate their veneration of the supreme being.

Jain monks meditating in India. Meditation is a form of non-verbal prayer. Although Jains, like Buddhists, have no god, meditation is an important element in the lives of Jain monks and nuns.

In this second sense, much of what is thus called worship might more accurately be referred to as *ritual*. Ritual refers to conscious and voluntary actions regularly carried out (usually in a stylized and symbolic way) to establish contact with, and give honour to, whoever (or whatever) is being worshipped.

Varieties of ritual

Different purposes are apparent in different kinds of ritual. Some, for example, are designed to bring about health and healing – the laying on of hands in some religions would be an example of this, as would various forms of exorcism to drive out evil spirits. Other rituals may aim at influencing God (or nature spirits) to change or improve aspects of nature. Thus in time of drought, many religions have rituals aimed at helping to bring about rain. Yet other rituals emphasize changes in social or biological status (see also p. 254). Many religions have ceremonies around the time of puberty to mark the transition to adulthood: the Jewish bar mitzvah is one example of this, the rite of circumcision amongst many tribal peoples another.

Prayer

Although not always regarded as such, prayer is a form of ritual. Prayer may be defined broadly as a human attempt at communication with the divine, or with other spiritual beings. Across the religions, prayer takes many different forms. It can be personal or communal, spontaneous or formal, spoken or silent.

Where a religion stresses the *transcendence* (or separateness) of God, prayer is a means of bridging the gap between humanity and divinity; where the *immanence* (or 'presentness') of God is stressed prayer often serves to make the worshipper more aware of 'the God within'.

The purposes of verbal prayer include *adoration* (acknowledging the existence and attributes of the divine), *thanksgiving* (expressions of gratitude for divine favours), and *petition* (the making of particular requests to the divine).

In many religions there is a tradition of non-verbal prayer or *meditation*. In meditation – as, for example, in the Hindu and Buddhist tradition of yoga (see pp. 480–1) – the purpose of the exercise is union with the divine, sometimes called *enlightenment*, or, in the Christian mystical tradition, *the beatific vision*.

Across many religious traditions there are different aids to prayer. Rosaries (or prayer beads) are used in several religions to help remember a series of prayers; prayer wheels are used in Buddhism; and holy pictures of several sorts may aid

concentration. In Roman Catholicism these may be of Jesus Christ or the saints, and in the Eastern Orthodox tradition take the particular form of *icons*. In Hinduism and Buddhism they often take the form of intricate geometric pictures known as *mandalas* (see illustration, p. 469). By contrast, Islam traditionally prohibits the making of images of any living creature.

Sacrifice

Sacrifice is the making of an offering or gift to a supernatural being, which often (though not always) involves the destruction of the object being offered. Almost anything can be offered as a sacrifice, although, since one of the purposes of sacrifice is to honour the deity, the object offered should usually be of value to the donor.

In some religions, human sacrifices have been made, for example amongst the Aztecs; more often animal or vegetable sacrifices are offered. These were common in earlier Judaism, but died out after the destruction of the Temple in Jerusalem in AD 70. Partly for that reason, and partly because they saw the death of Christ as the ultimate sacrifice, the early Christians spiritualized sacrifice to mean the giving up for religious reasons of something otherwise desirable in life. In Islam, although the ritual slaughter of animals takes place as part of the pilgrimage to Mecca, it is not, technically speaking, sacrifice, which is seen more as the duty to give alms to the poor. Generally Buddhism has rejected physical sacrifice as a valid religious activity.

The purposes of sacrifice are diverse. Certainly it seems likely that the practice of sacrifice depends upon belief in a god and/or lesser divinities who can be influenced by human actions. In a sense sacrifice is a form of prayer, and several of its purposes mirror those of prayer (see above). Thus a sacrifice may be carried out to praise, thank or petition the recipient. Praise sacrifices are comparatively rare; thanksgiving offerings are much more common. One of the most frequent forms of the latter are first-fruit offerings when the crops ripen – remnants of this can be seen in Christian harvest festivals, which are still held today even in industrialized areas. An additional purpose of sacrifice is *expiation* (sometimes also called *atonement* or *propitiation*). Such sacrifices are carried out to pay for some moral lapse or to appease the anger of the divinity. Some Christians would see the death of Jesus in this way – as a sacrificial payment for the sins of humanity.

Pilgrimage

Most religions have a tradition of pilgrimage – journeying to some holy place as a religious duty, and in order to obtain some spiritual or physical benefit.

Several elements are central to the idea of pilgrimage across religious traditions. The first is the journey itself, usually undertaken in groups, and producing a feeling of fellowship and solidarity. The second is the place to which the journey is

SEE ALSO

- WHAT IS RELIGION? p. 458
- RELIGIONS OF THE WORLD pp. 460–79
- SACRED SPACE AND SACRED TIME p. 482
- GOOD AND EVIL p. 484

A **Bantu initiate** sacrifices a goat. In the religion of the Bantus of southern Africa, spirits of the ancestors are the only links between mortals and the supreme being, and only priestly *sangomas* (faith healers) can communicate with the spirit world. The initiation of a new sangoma centres on an animal sacrifice, with blood, tobacco and other foods being offered to the spirits to keep their favours.

made. This almost always has a special religious significance and is regarded as a place of power. It may be the birthplace or burial place of a founder or saint – for example, Christians make pilgrimages to Bethlehem and Jerusalem. It may be a place of special historical importance in the development of the religion, such as Mecca in Islam. Other pilgrimage destinations are places of particular spiritual power, such as the River Ganges in Hinduism, while others again may be sites associated with unusual manifestations, such as Lourdes in France, or, more recently, Medjugorje in Bosnia, where the Virgin Mary is said to have appeared.

A third element central to pilgrimage is the carrying out of some special religious duties or rituals at the place of pilgrimage itself. Thus at Mecca pilgrims process seven times around the Kaaba (see illustration, p. 479), and during the huge Hindu festival of Kumbha Mela (which in 1989 attracted 15 million participants) pilgrims wash ritually in the sacred waters of the Ganges.

Pilgrimages may be undertaken for several reasons: to obtain religious merit by personal hardship; to make amends for sins previously committed; or in obedience to specific religious demands – for example, all Muslims are expected to visit Mecca at least once in their lives. One of the most common purposes of pilgrimage is to seek healing at a place of spiritual power – as at Lourdes.

Far from pilgrimage declining in the modern world, improved methods of transport have meant that pilgrimages previously possible for only a very limited number – and taking a long time – have become much more accessible to large numbers of people.   TJT

Santiago de Compostela in Spain has been a site of Christian pilgrimage since the 9th century, when the supposed tomb of St James (one of the Twelve Disciples) was discovered there.

Sacred Space, Sacred Time

In many parts of the world, the only remaining vestiges of forests or of wildlife exist around sacred sites such as mountains, temples or holy rivers. For archaeologists and historians, holy sites often provide the best-preserved selection of historic buildings, from the great temples of the Incas or the shrines of the Buddhists to the parish church or local mosque. In most faiths, the setting aside of a place or building as sacred gives that site a special quality that often leaves it untouched or unaltered over long stretches of time. Sacred space and time are closely related.

Some places are sacred because of their importance in religious history; such places include the place of enlightenment of the Buddha at Bohdi Gaya, the empty tomb of Jesus in Jerusalem, and the Kaaba in Mecca. Other places may have their roots in a historical event, but their real significance is that they are places where the same power is believed to be present to this day.

In many indigenous traditions, sites are believed to be imbued with a continuous power or spirit that needs to be worshipped or attended if life itself is to continue. Australian Aborigines believe that in performing the rituals and telling the stories of the Dreamtime, they keep alive the creative forces of the world. In venerating the Ganges and in placing the ashes of the dead upon its waters, Hindus believe that the reincarnational flow of life through the Earth and the universe is both sustained and partaken of by the believers. To place ashes on the waters of the Ganges is to send them on a journey that is both physical and spiritual.

Spiritual geography

The central and determinative role of place and time is clearly seen in the way peoples centre the world. In traditional Christian cartography, Jerusalem was the centre of the world – the famous Mappa Mundi in Hereford Cathedral, drawn by an Englishman, shows this perfectly, with Britain placed on the extreme edge of the map and Jerusalem in the centre. Likewise, traditional Muslim cartography places Mecca at the centre of the world. Even today, many Christian churches face Jerusalem and Muslims pray in the direction of Mecca.

But it is not just religious traditions that manifest this need to find and express our understanding of where we are in time and space. World maps produced in Europe still usually put Europe in the centre. The Chinese have likewise seen themselves as the centre of the world: the Chinese name for China is 'the Middle Kingdom' and that is quite literally where the Chinese saw themselves, right in the middle.

Sacred places

In Eastern Orthodox Christianity, the two worlds of the physical and the spiritual literally meet on the altar of any Orthodox church, which is why only priests are allowed within the special enclosed area behind the *inconstasis* (scene of icons). This idea of special areas within places of worship is found in many faiths.

Association with specific sacred places often makes whole areas themselves sacred – with the result that such areas are often saved from destructive modern developments. The island of Patmos was declared a Holy Island by the Patriarch of Constantinople in 1988, because in a cave on the island St John had his 'revelation', which he described in writing and which became the last book of the Bible. Wat Phai Lom, a Thai Buddhist temple north

Jews praying at the Wailing Wall – also known as the Western Wall – in Jerusalem. As the last surviving part of the Temple of Herod, it is sacred to Jews as a focus for prayer and pilgrimage.

A holy site of the blacksmiths of the Dogon people in Mali, West Africa. The baobab trees were planted some 400–500 years ago in an elliptical ring, and on the artificial hill in the centre iron has been extracted from laterite. Today the site is still used for secret ceremonies.

of Bangkok, is the last remaining breeding place of the open-billed stork, which would be extinct in Thailand were it not for the protection afforded by this special site. In the jungles of the Amazon, the sacred nature of the rivers, lands and especially trees has made it possible for the indigenous peoples to evolve a workable lifestyle with their harsh but fragile environment. This environment is now being destroyed by outsiders, who, through a failure to understand the local cultures, are destroying the balance.

In certain cultures, the presence of a sacred object endows an area or building with special power and authority. For instance, any Sikh home that has a full copy of the Sikh scriptures, the Guru Granth Sahib, sets aside a special room that becomes a temple. In medieval Christianity, possession of a particularly significant relic would give any otherwise ordinary church, cathedral or monastery a far greater attraction to worshippers and pilgrims. In many faiths, if not all, the physical presence of the body or a part of the body of a saint, guru or wise person likewise makes the space especially holy. This illustrates the very close links between the idea of sacred space and time. The devotion to the body of a dead saint is devotion to a living spiritual force, and the presence of the relic brings sacredness to a site. The Buddha never visited Sri Lanka, but the presence of his tooth in the city of Kandy makes that place a sacred place of Buddhism.

In even the most universalistic of faiths, the need to have a special place and a special time to remember or be in direct relationship with the divine is still found. While there may appear to be a difference between the folk Daoist worshipping a tree and the Muslim praying in the mosque, both denote the same need for a focus to the spiritual life. Sacred places provide such focuses and it is no accident that they are often the centre or

SEE ALSO

● THE UNIVERSE AND COS-
   MOLOGY p. 4
● TIME p. 6
● WHAT IS RELIGION? p. 458
● RELIGIONS OF THE WORLD
   pp. 460–79
● WORSHIP, PRAYER AND PIL-
   GRIMAGE p. 480
● TEMPLE AND CHURCH
   ARCHITECTURE pp. 504–19,
   522–5, 528–31, 534, 538,
   552

focus of the community, both believing and non-believing, which lives around them. The traditional heart of the European village or town is the church. When developers in inner-city areas demolish old rows of houses, they usually leave two buildings intact – the church and the pub.

Sacred time

Within the major faiths of the world, there are two very distinct concepts of time, which fundamentally shape the outlook and doctrines of the faiths.

The first model of time is the *cyclical model*. This model views time as without a beginning and without an end. Its most famous expression and most graspable manifestation is in the belief in reincarnation. The notion that this life is not the only life, but one of tens of thousands of lives to be lived, forms the heart of Hindu, Buddhist and Sikh teaching. This is not just a concept applied to individual lives. In Hindu thought, for instance, even the gods die and are reborn. The very universe is but the most recent in an unending chain of universes that have come into being, matured, declined and finally become extinct. This cycle is reflected in the three main Hindu deities: Brahma creates the world and the universe, Vishnu sustains it, and Shiva destroys it. However, Shiva is also described as the re-creator, for from destruction comes the next world and/or universe, and so the cycle starts again.

The result of this is that history is not really very important. There are no unique events in time, but there is a constant reiteration of the eternal truths, time after time. Time itself becomes a trap and freedom comes from the escape from rebirth, from having to live in time. This stands in distinct contrast to the other model of time.

The *linear model* of time – as found in Judaism, Christianity and Islam – posits that there is a definite beginning to time and that there will be a definite end. Time progresses, never repeating, but moving inexorably from A to Z. This gives rise to such standard Christian/Western concepts as 'you only live

once'. The difference that this makes in contrast to the cyclical model is very clear. In the cyclical model, the individual does not have to succeed in this life – a long-term view can be taken. This can lead to a more passive understanding of the significance of the individual. In the linear model, the individual has to make maximum use of this one chance. Therefore the linear model develops concepts of judgement after death whereby the soul goes to heaven or hell, whereas the cyclical model has no such concept. You are simply reborn in an appropriate body – human, animal, or whatever.

Another major consequence of the linear model is that history becomes purposeful. The traditional understanding of the journey from A to Z is from start to completion. This means that linear-dominated belief sees history as moving towards an ultimate purpose, which, once it has been achieved, will mean the end of history. History thus becomes charged with salvationary powers and meaning, in complete contrast to the cyclical model.

All faiths use the cycle of the year to reflect or draw particular attention to core beliefs within the faith. Festivals tend either to follow an agricultural structure or to tell the story of the faith. In Judaism there is an essentially agricultural cycle with issues of wider significance grafted onto the original festivals (see p. 473). The succession of major Christian festivals tells the story of Jesus from birth to death, resurrection and the coming of the Holy Spirit (see p. 475). The construction of calendars also reflects the faith's interest in or use of time as a vehicle of meaning. The dating of the Muslim calendar from the time of Muhammad's journey to Medina makes a statement about the role of history as a means of emerging salvation.

The setting aside of a distinct day each week for worship is distinctive of faiths with linear time models, such as Judaism or Christianity. The link of the seven days of the traditional week with the seven days of Creation reinforces the links between the faith and the whole process of time as a salvationary

process to which the faith holds the key. In contrast, cyclical faiths have no such concept, but use the main periods of the year as a focus for worship and ritual.　　ICOREC

The Hindu god Shiva as king of the dancers. Shiva's dance symbolizes the Hindu concept of time as an eternal cycle of cosmic creation and destruction. Shiva's multiple arms represent pairs of complementary opposites – life and death, good and evil, asceticism and sensuality, and so on.

Good and Evil

Religions and moral philosophy share a common concern with the question, 'What is the good life for humanity?' – that is, with morality. However, the ways in which philosophy and the religions of the world answer this question differ. Whereas contemporary philosophers tend to discuss morality without reference to anything beyond the human, religions see good and evil within a wider cosmological framework.

This cosmological framework usually involves, over and above human activity, the activities of supernatural beings – God, gods, angels, ancestors, Satan, demons, etc. Religions also maintain that the full significance of good and evil can only be appreciated in terms of beliefs about the continuance of human life beyond the grave.

Primal religions

Primal religions see 'good' mainly as that which enhances and strengthens the health, wealth and harmony of the individual and the community, and 'evil' as that which weakens the community or the individual. Both good and evil may result from human activity, but they may also be the result of the activity of gods, ancestors or spirits, whose will must be discovered by religious specialists, and who need ritual offerings from time to time to ensure their continued goodwill and to ward off evil intent. In primal societies any unwelcome events – sickness, accidents, bad luck – are usually attributed to the activity of supernatural beings, although they may also be the result of the activity of humans, as in the practice of witchcraft and sorcery.

Notions of rewards or punishments in an afterlife – for good or evil done in this life – are rare in surviving primal religions, but not unknown. The greatest reward is to be 'born again' into the human community.

Religions in the Indian tradition

Hinduism, Jainism, Buddhism and Sikhism see human life in terms of *samsara* – an eternal cycle of birth and rebirth operating according to the moral law of *karma*. Under this law, observance of *dharma* (religious duty) is rewarded by a good rebirth, while non-observance is punished by a bad rebirth. While this cycle is not of itself evil, it is not desirable, and the aim of all the religions in the Indian tradition is to secure the release (*moksha*) of the individual from samsara. This is the individual's ultimate good.

At the level of popular understanding, elements of primal religion remain, and rituals are performed to ensure the goodwill of gods, goddesses and spirits, and to ward off evil. The great gods of the Hindus, such as Vishnu or Shiva, are often thought of as being the originators of both good and evil. In this respect, Hinduism differs from religions in the Semitic tradition.

Buddhism sees the world not as evil in itself, but as the source of evil, with the human condition characterized by suffering (*dukka*) caused by individuals clinging (*tanha*) to existence in the world. The therapy for this is for the individual to renounce tanha and to search for the good of *nirvana* (see also p. 468). Buddhism also has a conception of an evil spirit, *Mara*, who tries to tempt men and women from seeking release from the eternal round of birth and rebirth.

Sikhism, being monotheistic, sees humanity's good as responding in loving devotion (*bhakti*) to the voice of the divine guru – God. This is the way to obtain release from samsara. This is also the case in some Hindu sects, such as those devoted to the worship of Vishnu or Shiva.

Religions in the Semitic tradition

Judaism, Christianity and Islam – perhaps influenced by Zoroastrianism, which historically did much to sharpen the duality of good and evil (see p. 461) – see the world as the battleground of a cosmic struggle between the forces of good (led by God) and the forces of evil (led by the Devil or Satan). Men and women are caught up in this struggle. While, on the cosmic level, the ultimate outcome is never in doubt, individual destinies (heaven or hell) are decided by obedience to the will of God (as revealed in the scriptures of the three religions) and by rejecting the temptations of the Devil and his demons (known in Islam as *Jinn*). Angels and saints may aid human beings in their struggle to overcome evil and do good, and so to reap the reward of paradise and eternal life. The alternative is hell, a place of eternal punishment.

The attempt to reconcile belief in a God who is all-good and all-powerful with the fact of evil and suffering in the world constitutes the theological and philosophical problem known in these three religions as 'the problem of evil'.

While Judaism and Islam emphasize obedience to the revealed law of God as the way to obtain good things in this life and in the world to come, Christianity has tended to emphasize love of God and of fellow humans, and to believe that men and women are ultimately saved from the consequences of doing evil by appealing to the crucifixion of Jesus as constituting 'a full and perfect sacrifice' for their sins.

The mystical tradition in these religions has, however, tended to see human good and human fulfilment not in terms of rewards and punishments for obedience or disobedience to divine commands, but rather in terms of the uniting of the human soul with 'the divine ground of all being'. This brings the idea of the final good of men and women in this tradition nearer to that found in the Vedanta tradition in India.

The snake is a symbol of evil in many religions. For example, in Genesis, it is a serpent that tempts Eve. In this ancient Egyptian wall painting, the lynx goddess Tefnut kills the evil snake Apophis.

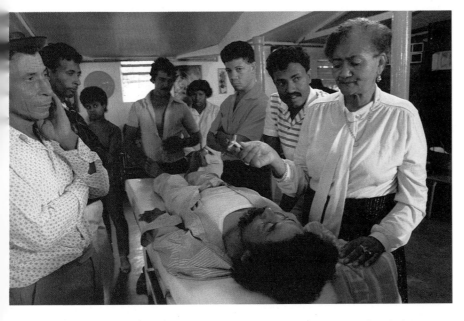

An exorcism ritual in the Indian Ocean island of Réunion. In many religions – including various Christian traditions – it is thought possible for people to become possessed by evil spirits. In such religions, there are usually set rituals, known as exorcism rituals, to purge the afflicted person of the possession.

China and Japan

In China, while the Confucian code of conduct has guided men and women in their relations with one another, and Daoism (Taoism) has sought to show how the harmony of men and women with the natural order of the world can be maintained for the benefit of all, it has been Buddhism or, more precisely, Buddha and the *bodhisattvas* – saint-like beings who have renounced nirvana so as to help others achieve it – who, in the popular imagination, determine the ultimate destiny of the soul. In Chinese Buddhism, however, this destiny is thought of not so much as release from the eternal round of *samsara*, but rather in terms of traditional Chinese cosmology, where the souls of the departed are first purified through punishment in the infernal regions before the hoped-for entry into heaven. Certain Buddhist ceremonies are thought to aid release from the infernal regions.

Although Buddhism is widespread in Japan, the traditional religion of Shinto preserves the primal outlook and seeks, through a variety of ceremonies, to reap material good for men and women, and to ward off evil by placating the *kami*, or spiritual forces, believed to operate in the natural world. In Shinto (as in Hinduism) evil is thought of primarily as ritual pollution – something that cuts men and women off from the *kami* and makes their prayers and offerings unacceptable. The Shinto code of conduct is designed to enable men and women to avoid this. Where pollution occurs, Shinto prescribes certain rituals for its eradication. In Shinto all good things ultimately derive from the Sun goddess Amaterasu, and all evil things from her brother Susano-o.

As in traditional Chinese cosmology, the dead go first to the regions below the Earth (*Yomi-no-kuni*), where evil spirits seek to detain them, before being transported to the land of the blessed (*Tokoyo-no-kuni*). As in China, Buddhist rituals are also thought to aid this process. *Yomi-no-kuni* is not, however, thought of as a place of punishment for evil deeds.

Morality and religion

Most religions maintain that much of the good and evil things that happen in the world occur, not as the result of what men and women do, but as the result of the activity of supernatural beings – although men and women can seek, by ritual means, to influence these beings. Men and women are, however, considered to be responsible for many of their actions and will be held accountable for them. In most religions the code of conduct by which men and women should behave is seen as something directly revealed to humanity by God or other divine beings.

In religions, therefore, morality only makes sense within the context of a total religious understanding of the world. In philosophy, however, attempts have been made, and are still being made, to establish morality on foundations that owe nothing to a religious outlook on the world.   JT

SEE ALSO

● WHAT IS RELIGION? p. 458
● RELIGIONS OF THE WORLD pp. 460–79
● WORSHIP, PRAYER AND PILGRIMAGE p. 480
● ETHICS p. 492

The torments of hell, as depicted by an unknown Portuguese painter from the early 16th century. The idea of hell as a place of eternal punishment for those who have sinned is common to all three religions of the Semitic tradition – Judaism, Christianity, and Islam. (Museum of Ancient Art, Lisbon/Explorer)

What is Philosophy?

Everyone puzzles over such questions as 'Is there a God?', 'Should we believe what scientists tell us?', 'Is there always a right answer to moral dilemmas?' and 'Does a person survive after death?' But academic philosophy takes these familiar questions much further, and in doing so has developed techniques and a vocabulary of its own.

SEE ALSO

● THE SCIENTIFIC METHOD
  p. 58
● THE HISTORY OF SCIENCE
  p. 60
● SETS AND PARADOXES p. 66
● THE ENLIGHTENMENT p. 418
● WHAT IS RELIGION? p. 458
● GOOD AND EVIL p. 484
● KNOWLEDGE AND REALITY
  p. 488
● ETHICS p. 490
● MIND AND BODY p. 492
● LOGIC AND ARGUMENT
  p. 494
● THE PHILOSOPHY OF
  LANGUAGE p. 496

The word 'philosophy' is derived from the Greek meaning 'love of wisdom'. Until the 19th century the term was used to include what we now distinguish as 'science' (from the Latin for 'knowledge'), and this terminology persists in the names of some university courses, such as 'natural philosophy' for physics and 'moral sciences' for what we now call philosophy. Current usage, however, is more specialized: we now think of science as involving experimental testing of theories about how specific parts of the natural world work (see p. 58), while the concerns of philosophy are more general.

Philosophy and philosophies

We often talk of someone's 'philosophy of life', by which we mean the general principles by which they live, their goals, their values, or their yet more general view of the world and their place in it. Similarly, when we speak about the philosophy behind some government proposal, we mean the principles or rationale in terms of which the proposal is justified. Some Eastern philosophies are generalizations of these kinds of questions, seeking a reason, in some sense, for life or the universe, or seeking to reinterpret human experience within some larger scheme of things.

That this is what one tends to find on the philosophy shelves of bookshops and libraries often irritates academic philosophers, who think that such discussions of ultimate purpose are more a matter for theology than philosophy. Western academic philosophy, by contrast, is generally concerned with clarification rather than explanation – except when it is the nature of explanation itself that it seeks to clarify – perhaps because for two thousand years explanation in the West has been thought of in terms of causes rather than reasons (see pp. 58–9).

There is, of course, a connection between this academic discipline and philosophy as rationale or world-view: philosophy at any level is concerned not with concrete but with abstract questions, and academic philosophy deals with these questions at their most general, posing questions not about whether a particular theory or explanation is true, but about, for example, whether it even makes sense or, even more generally, questions about what it is for something to be a theory or explanation at all.

Philosophy as a second-order activity

Explanation and justification depend on argument, and *logic* is the branch of philosophy that studies this. Clearly whether an argument is a good or a bad one does not depend upon what it is about, so logic is concerned with the *form* of an argument rather than its *content*. Similarly, questions about knowledge, or about the relation between mind and language, or about language and the world, are general and independent of what is known or thought or said.

Philosophy, then, is not a *first-order activity*, concerned to discover the truth about some specific subject, but a *second-order activity*, whose true subject is the first-order activity itself.

This is perhaps most obvious in the field of *ethics*, where the first-order activity – *moralizing* – seeks to establish the correctness of certain rules of conduct, while second-order theorizing – *moral philosophy* – is concerned with questions that arise whatever first-order theory we adopt. Not all philosophers, however, have observed this distinction, and many philosophers of the past have been concerned with how we should behave and what constitutes a good life. Indeed, there remain live philosophical disputes about whether certain second-order theories about the nature of morality force us to adopt particular first-order moral principles. In any event, conceptual clarity can only help us to reach reliable moral decisions, so there must remain a role for philosophy even in unambiguous moralizing (see p. 492). On the other hand, discussions of how moral language works, of whether there are moral absolutes, or of the logic of moral disagreement do not lead to conclusions about right conduct. On the contrary, these questions are not specific to ethics, but are more generally about truth and reality, about knowledge and justification, about logic and language.

Changing preoccupations in philosophy

These very general questions reflect the distinct preoccupations of three different eras in the history of philosophy. Ancient Greek philosophers and their followers through medieval times were mainly concerned with *metaphysics* – that is questions about the ultimate nature of reality. The existence of God, the nature of time, and the relation of mind and body (see p. 490) are metaphysical questions that are still discussed, albeit with different emphasis.

One major change was the stress placed since the 17th century on *epistemological* questions (see p. 488). For example, René Descartes sought to reconstruct all human knowledge systematically on the model of Euclid's geometry (see p. 63).

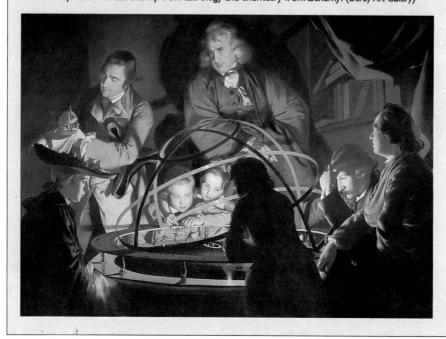

A Philosopher Lecturing on the Orrery (1766), by Joseph Wright of Derby. Science can be regarded as growing out of philosophy. Often issues first crop up in a purely speculative way, without any reference to experience or experiment, and only as a result of such philosophical speculation does agreement begin to emerge about what kind of experiment would settle the question. Only then does a science begin to emerge, and even then there remain philosophical questions about the methods of investigation, the concepts used and the validity of the inferences made. This pattern can be seen in the development of biology between Aristotle and Darwin and the separation of astronomy from astrology and chemistry from alchemy. (Derby Art Gallery)

Reacting to this *rationalist* search for mathematical certainty, the *empiricists* such as John Locke and David Hume questioned the origin of human knowledge, and regarded philosophy as clearing the ground for science. Their speculation about how the mind works (out of which grew the empirical science of psychology) led to the condemnation of metaphysics as beyond the limits of knowability.

More recently, philosophy in the English-speaking world has turned to consideration of the nature of language itself. In the light of the insights gained from this, many traditional philosophical problems have been reinterpreted as arising from mistaken presuppositions about the way language works. Philosophical problems are then seen as a matter of 'losing one's way' conceptually, and the task of philosophy is reduced to what Ludwig Wittgenstein called 'showing the fly the way out of the fly-bottle' (see p. 496).

Teaching philosophy through its history

It seems obvious that the history of philosophy is not itself philosophy. Yet – although it would be odd, for example, to teach chemistry by giving lectures on alchemy – philosophy is often taught by reviewing its past. This is because philosophical methods of reasoning do not break down, like arithmetic, into simple skills that can be easily taught and practised: if they can be taught at all, it is by example. So one reason for studying the great philosophers of the past is to learn from their example.

One does not, however, become a philosopher by learning what others have thought; we have to learn how to solve problems for ourselves. And this suggests another reason for studying the great philosophers of the past – namely as a source of arguments and opinions that the newcomer can subject to rigorous scrutiny.

There is no contradiction here between treating past philosophers both as examples to emulate and as perpetrators of fallacies that even a beginner can recognize: much philosophical discussion is about which past theories should be accepted and which rejected. It is this search for new arguments about old positions that distinguishes teaching philosophy through its history from teaching a history of ideas. While history involves the accumulation of facts, philosophy is concerned with the assessment of argument and the teaching of a skill – philosophizing. The gulf between philosophy and the history of ideas is thus that between knowing *how* to do something and knowing *that* some statement is true – a distinction that has itself been the subject of much philosophical debate in the 20th century.   EJB

MAJOR PHILOSOPHERS

Heraclitus (c. 540–c. 480 BC), Pre-Socratic philosopher (see p. 488) whose doctrine is often represented as 'everything is change'.

Parmenides (born c. 515 BC), Pre-Socratic metaphysician who believed that time, motion and change are all illusory (see p. 488).

Socrates (c. 470–399 BC), Greek philosopher, who, through his pupil Plato (see p. 492) is perhaps the crucial influence on the development of Western thought.

Plato (427–347 BC), Greek philosopher, whose works form the foundation of Western philosophy (see pp. 488, 492 and 496).

Aristotle (384–322 BC), Greek philosopher and scientist, whose works have influenced the whole of Western philosophy (see pp. 488 and 492 and also p. 60).

St Augustine (AD 354–430), North African convert to Christianity, who saw philosophy as auxiliary to faith and interpreted Christian doctrine in the light of Platonic philosophy.

St Anselm (1033–1109), Italian monk, who first propounded the ontological argument (see p. 488).

St Thomas Aquinas (1225–74), Italian philosopher and scholastic theologian (see pp. 290 and 488).

Thomas Hobbes (1588–1679), English empiricist philosopher, author of *Leviathan*, best known for his political philosophy (see p. 266).

René Descartes (1596–1650), French philosopher, scientist, and mathematician – generally regarded as the father of modern philosophy (see pp. 488 and 490, and also pp. 63, 70 and 418).

Baruch (Benedict) Spinoza (1632–77), Dutch rationalist philosopher, who was accused both of atheism and of pantheism (see p. 488).

John Locke (1632–1704), English empiricist philosopher and political theorist (see pp. 266, 290, 488 and 496).

Gottfried Wilhelm Leibniz (1645–1716), German rationalist philosopher and mathematician (see pp. 488 and 490, and also p. 70).

George Berkeley (1685–1753), Irish bishop and empiricist philosopher who produced a paradoxical response to scepticism and atheism (see p. 488).

David Hume (1711–76), Scottish empiricist philosopher and historian, a major influence on subsequent Western philosophy (see pp. 59, 488 and 494, and also p. 419).

Jean-Jacques Rousseau (1712–78), Swiss-born political philosopher (see pp. 266, 290, 419 and 631).

Immanuel Kant (1724–1804), influential German philosopher and scientist (see pp. 489 and 492).

Jeremy Bentham (1748–1832), English legal philosopher, who attempted to quantify utilitarianism by devising a 'hedonic calculus' (see p. 492).

Georg Wilhelm Friedrich Hegel (1770–1831), German philosopher, who applied logical concepts to historical processes, so that history becomes a *dialectic* in which one process, the *thesis*, is contradicted by another, the *antithesis*, and then both are subsumed in a *synthesis*.

Arthur Schopenhauer (1788–1860), German anti-Hegelian follower of Kant, who distinguished *noumenal* and *phenomenal* aspects of the Self, and emphasized the role of the (possibly unconscious) will, from which art is the only escape.

John Stuart Mill (1806–73), English philosopher, economist and social reformer (see p. 492).

Søren Kierkegaard (1813–55), Danish philosopher and theologian, whose rejection of objectivity as an illusion that leads us to accept rules of ethical conduct greatly influenced the later existentialists.

Karl Marx (1818–83), German revolutionary and social theorist, whose philosophical position was largely a materialist reinterpretation of Hegel (see p. 269).

Charles Sanders Peirce (1839–1914), American physicist, logician and philosopher (see p. 610) who proposed the *pragmatist* doctrine that concepts are to be understood in terms of their practical significance.

William James (1842–1910), American medical professor and pragmatist philosopher (see p. 496), brother of the novelist Henry James (see p. 639). He applied Peirce's pragmatism to the dissolution of metaphysics, saw truth in terms of productiveness and believed that emotions are caused by bodily events.

Friedrich Nietzsche (1844–1900), German-born philosopher, who argued that the will to power is the primary human drive, and that the goal of history is to produce a society of supermen. These ideas were later taken up by Nazi ideologists (see p. 442).

Gottlob Frege (1848–1925), German mathematics professor, who established the foundations of mathematics as a discipline (see pp. 67 and 496).

Edmund Husserl (1859–1938), German mathematician and philosopher, whose *phenomenology* was intended as an account of the content of the consciousness.

John Dewey (1859–1952), American pragmatist philosopher and psychologist who synthesized the ideas of Peirce and James and developed the notion that ideas, statements and theories are instruments of prediction, and are to be judged for their usefulness rather than their truth.

Bertrand Russell (1872–1970), English philosopher, logician and social reformer (see pp. 67, 494 and 496).

Ludwig Wittgenstein (1889–1951), Austrian-born philosopher, and the most influential figure in 20th-century philosophy (pp. 496–7).

Martin Heidegger (1889–1976), German philosopher, who followed Husserl in denying the distinction between consciousness and the external world, and saw the human predicament in terms of the necessity of constant choice, in which the rejected possibilities are condemned to 'nothingness'.

Jean-Paul Sartre (1905–80), French philosopher and intellectual, generally regarded as the chief exponent of existentialism (see pp. 490 and 648).

Willard van Orman Quine (1908–), American logician, who rejects as 'Two Dogmas of Empiricism' the distinction between analytic and synthetic (see p. 488), and the reductionist interpretation of observation language.

Sir Alfred (A.J.) Ayer (1910–89), English logical positivist philosopher (see pp. 488 and 492).

Knowledge and Reality

Philosophy has traditionally been seen as a search for the most general and well-founded knowledge, or knowledge of ultimate truth. Yet philosophy has also been concerned to evaluate, systematize or justify the claims to knowledge made by others. Both approaches raise questions about the nature and extent of possible knowledge – and indeed about whether true knowledge is ever possible at all. The philosophical study of the validity, methods and scope of knowledge is known as *epistemology*.

SEE ALSO

- THE SCIENTIFIC METHOD p. 58
- WHAT IS PHILOSOPHY? p. 486
- MIND AND BODY p. 490
- ETHICS p. 492
- LOGIC AND ARGUMENT p. 494
- THE PHILOSOPHY OF LANGUAGE p. 496

Change is paradoxical: on the one hand change – by definition – destroys identity; on the other, it is the same entity, albeit with different properties, that survives

— **PLATO'S CAVE** —

In the *Republic* Plato likens mankind to lifelong prisoners who sit in a darkened cave, chained so that they can only see what is directly in front of them. Their only experience is of the shadows of objects thrown by a fire behind them onto the wall opposite. According to Plato, our knowledge of reality is as incomplete as that of the prisoners. Only when a prisoner is unbound and shown the puppets and the fire, and is then dragged outside and shown the puppeteers and the Sun, will he attain true knowledge. Finally, in an apologia for the perennially misunderstood philosopher, the enlightened prisoner returns to the cave, where his floundering in the darkness makes others think that freedom has ruined his sight.

the change. This paradox was addressed by the earliest philosophers whose works have survived – the Greek Pre-Socratics of the 6th and 5th centuries BC. They offered two radically opposed solutions. On one side, Heraclitus believed that all things are related by an 'ever-living fire, ever flaring up and ever extinguished', so that identity is illusory and even truth is unstable. Others, such as Parmenides, held that it is time, motion and change that are illusory, while reality is indivisible and unchanging. It was against this background that the three greatest Greek philosophers – Socrates, Plato and Aristotle (see p. 494) – conducted the inquiries that have influenced the whole of Western thought.

The theory of Forms

One of the best known of all philosophical theories is the theory of Forms. According to Plato, although general terms such as 'justice', 'circle' or 'horse' can be applied to a number of different things, what they really refer to is an abstract object – a 'Form' or 'Idea', an archetype of justice or circularity or horsiness. A particular circle on a page is thus a circle because it somehow partakes of, or is a pale copy of, the archetypical circle. These Forms do not exist in the world of experience; they are independent of human understanding.

Change is therefore located in our everyday world, while reality belongs to the unchanging world of Forms. Since ordinary material objects are changeable, their properties cannot be known infallibly. The same thing may be an acorn one day, later a sapling, still later an oak, and in due course die, decay, and become nothing at all. But no such change affects the world of Forms: there an acorn is for all time a seed, an oak for all time a tree. Only there is true knowledge attainable. All we can hope for in the world of changing physical reality is mere opinion or belief, so neither observation nor science can yield true knowledge. Knowledge and belief are thus totally distinct: they are not even concerned with the same objects.

Knowledge, doubt and certainty

'Modern' philosophy is often taken to begin some 2000 years later with the work of the 17th-century French scientist and philosopher René Descartes, but he too was primarily concerned to set the highest possible standard for knowledge. He was greatly struck by both the certainty and the systematic nature of mathematics; his aim was to encompass all human knowledge within a single theory with the same certainty and generality as mathematics.

Descartes's best-known work, the *Meditations* (1641), addresses the issue of whether knowledge is ever possible. His 'method of doubt' seeks to weed out any beliefs about which we cannot be certain. Since the same table may sometimes look round and sometimes oval – if viewed from different angles – reason alone confirms

the unreliability of the senses. All sensory experience must therefore be cast aside; it is also possible that we might merely be dreaming that certain beliefs are true, and such beliefs must also be cast aside. Even arithmetic succumbs to a 'hyperbolic doubt' occasioned by the thought that there might be an 'evil demon' who forever deceives us.

In the midst of this extreme scepticism, however, Descartes identifies an inalienable certainty. This is his famous statement, 'I think; therefore I exist' (*Cogito ergo sum*): however deep my doubt, I must exist in order to doubt; thus from the very fact that I have the thought that I might not exist, I can know with complete certainty that I do. Subsequent philosophers have discussed the *Cogito* in great detail: some have argued that Descartes begs the question by starting from 'I think' rather than 'There is a thought', while others have questioned whether the *Cogito* can really be an argument at all, since the all-encompassing doubt is supposed to challenge even the reliability of logic.

Reason and rationalism

Descartes's influence lay not so much in the detail of his doctrine as in his approach. From his single certainty, he goes on to argue that God exists and would not have created me only in order to deceive me; so that my senses and memory can in general be relied upon, provided that I am cautious. From this it follows that science is in principle possible.

He thus argues that everything we know about the world can be deduced from a single basic truth that is discoverable by reason alone rather than experience. This is a controversial belief, and indeed, the major division in subsequent philosophy has been between *rationalists*, who uphold it, and *empiricists*, who repudiate it.

Among Descartes's immediate successors, the most influential were Spinoza and Leibniz (see p. 492). Both stressed the deducibility of all knowledge (see deduction, p. 59) and constructed metaphysical theories in which this was possible. Spinoza believed that since everything is deducible from a small number of self-evident axioms, everything happens necessarily as it does. Leibniz shared the fundamental rationalist conviction that everything is explicable by reason alone, believing that it is in principle possible to deduce a complete description of the world, including its future, from a description of any one of the infinitely many simple immaterial substances (*monads*) that exists. The only 'sufficient reason' for the existence of this world rather than another is that God, who can thus determine which is the best possible world, wills it: human experience is thus subordinated to an independent and divinely ordained reality.

Ideas and experience

The competing British empiricist school developed largely in response to Descartes; indeed, Thomas Hobbes when a refugee in France wrote a set of 'Objections' that were published in the same volume as the *Meditations*.

In his *Essay concerning Human Understanding* (1690) John Locke argued

you have no access to my ideas nor I to yours, we can never tell whether this transfer has been successful. Worse, if all we experience are ideas, we cannot even know that these ideas represent a world outside themselves. Faced with Locke's difficulty, Berkeley gave the paradoxical response that 'external' objects are just ideas; the reality and intelligibility of the perceived world then consists in its being observed by an 'all-wise Spirit', God, who is also the active agent in those regularities described by science.

Experience and the limits of thought

Perhaps the most influential of the empiricists was the Scotsman David Hume, who remarked that Berkeley's sceptical arguments 'admit of no answer but produce no conviction'. Instead he sought to secure the foundation of knowledge by avoiding all subjects beyond the scope of human reason; that is, by restricting intellectual consideration to ideas that can be shown to be directly or indirectly derived from experience. He uses this principle to cast doubt on the reality of the 'self' and of causal connection, but concludes that these ideas are indeed derived – albeit by a complex route – from experience.

Hume's other major principle, known as *Hume's Fork*, was the division of all statements between 'relations of ideas', which can be known by reason alone, and 'matters of fact', which can always be imagined to be otherwise and require experience to adjudicate. However, Hume argues, neither reason nor experience can justify how we learn from experience; his solution is strikingly modern, and insists that induction (see pp. 59 and 495) cannot in fact be justified, but is merely a 'habit or custom', a 'principle of human nature', part of what Wittgenstein calls our 'form of life' or 'the natural history of our species' (see p. 497).

These doctrines had a profound effect, not least upon Immanuel Kant. Although his

early work was in the rationalist tradition of Leibniz, reading Hume 'interrupted [his] dogmatic slumbers' and spurred him to develop a new synthesis, which he referred to as *transcendental idealism*. In the *Critique of Pure Reason* (1781) Kant agreed with Hume that metaphysical error arises from trying to apply concepts derived from experience beyond the scope of experience; he nonetheless believed that 'transcendental' argument about the conditions for intelligible experience could yield metaphysical truths.

In order to state clearly the issue between them, Kant replaced Hume's Fork with two distinctions. The first distinction is a matter of logic: if it is self-contradictory to deny some statement, that statement is *analytic*; otherwise it is *synthetic*. Kant claims, however, contrary to Hume, that the epistemological distinction between a statement that may be knowable without experience (*a priori*) and one that requires experience to determine its truth (*a posteriori*) does not coincide with the first distinction. For Kant, human understanding is not merely passive, but itself contributes *synthetic a priori* propositions such as that every event has a cause. These are not learnt from experience but form the conceptual framework by virtue of which we are able to make sense of experience at all.

The retreat from metaphysics

Hume's Fork and Kant's reworking of it have continued to define the terms of much 20th-century debate. Positivists such as A. J. Ayer and Karl Popper (see pp. 58–9), for example, have been forced to address the status of these putative synthetic a priori truths in order to reinstate their own versions of Hume's Fork. Thus Ayer's 'verification principle' and Popper's criterion of falsifiability are both intended to exclude metaphysical statements as meaningless.

Not all modern philosophers have been so opposed to metaphysics. The Oxford philosopher Peter Strawson (1919–), for example, finds a role for 'descriptive metaphysics [that is] content to describe the actual structure of our thought about the world'. However, this project is more akin to Wittgenstein's conception of philosophy as 'assembling reminders' about the use of language (see p. 497) than it is to traditional 'revisionary' metaphysics

ehemently
hat all ideas are
derived from experience, and that knowledge is the 'perception of the agreement or disagreement of two ideas'. Although conceptual truth could still be independent of any particular experience, the acquisition of the concepts themselves could not. For example, although whales would be mammals whether or not anyone had ever discovered the fact, I cannot understand this sentence unless I know what whales and mammals are, which requires a chain of definition ultimately terminating with direct experience.

Locke argued that if everything had a unique name, we would not only be unable to communicate with one another, but we would not even be able to record our own thoughts. Consequently we 'abstract' from the ideas of diverse things whatever they have in common, and we designate the idea of that common property by a general term. Thus, for example, the word 'red' does not refer to anything independent of red things and of human observers of those things; on the contrary, it refers to the thought of red that is common to all perceptions of red things.

The Irish philosopher George Berkeley objected that Locke's general ideas must have contradictory properties. The general idea of a triangle, he said, would have to be equilateral and scalene (i.e. having all sides of unequal length), and the general idea of a man would have to be tall and short, fat and thin, and so on. Berkeley therefore suggested that general words do not stand for general ideas, but for images of particular instances that somehow represent the whole class. This is no real improvement, however, as it simply shifts the problem of generality from the idea itself to its relation with its instances.

Language, according to Locke, is a process for communicating or transferring ideas from one mind to another. But since

Immanuel Kant, (left) 18th-century German philosopher and scientist. In the *Critique of Pure Reason* (1781) he suggested that human understanding contributes twelve *categories*, which are not learnt from experience but which form the conceptual framework by virtue of which we make sense of it. Similarly, the unity of science is not discovered by science but is what makes science possible. He believed, however, that by *transcendental* argument it is possible to infer the bare existence of a world beyond experience.

MEDIEVAL CHRISTIAN PHILOSOPHY

St Thomas Aquinas (1225–74), the philosopher and scholastic theologian, sought in his writings to reconcile Christian theology with Aristotelian philosophy. Aquinas believed that the existence of a first cause or Supreme Being (i.e. God) could be deduced from our observation of causation, motion and order in the universe. He nevertheless believed that faith and reason are distinct.

Another famous argument for the existence of God, the *ontological argument*, had been put forward by the Italian monk St Anselm two centuries earlier. Since God is by definition that than which nothing greater can be conceived, he must exist. Otherwise a being greater than God could exist – one with the same characteristics plus existence.

St Thomas Aquinas

Mind and Body

Many religions subscribe to the belief that human beings have an immaterial mind or soul as well as a body – a belief that gives rise to problems that have been discussed by philosophers since the time of Plato. The key questions centre on the evidence for the existence of the mind and – if it does exist – how its apparent interaction with the body occurs. Another common religious belief is that the soul survives the death of the body, and this gives rise to a second group of questions, about *personal identity* – that is, about the conditions under which someone remains the same person through a process of change. Both issues, however, must first address the question of what a person *is*.

What constitutes a person has always been a vexed philosophical conundrum. If one holds that the defining characteristic of a person is intelligent or voluntary behaviour, one faces the challenge of framing criteria that include the mentally handicapped and the incurably comatose,

René Descartes, 17th-century French philosopher, scientist and mathematician, often regarded as the father of modern philosophy. He believed that all knowledge could be derived from axioms self-evident to reason and independent of experience. His method of systematic doubt (see p. 488) had the effect of breaking the hold of theology over philosophy, while his dualistic theory of mind and body (see text) created a puzzle that has exercised philosophers ever since.

while excluding higher primates and fifth-generation computers. If one instead holds the dualist view (see below) that persons are distinguished from animals by their possession of an immaterial mind or soul, one faces the no less difficult challenge of spelling out the criteria by which to determine whether or not such a mind is present.

Dualism

People are often thought of as consisting of a physical body and an immaterial entity – the soul, mind or spirit. A physical body has a position in space from which it excludes other things, it can be moved around or dismembered, it has a chemical composition, and it is subject to all the laws of physics. A mind or soul, on the other hand, cannot be directly observed, cannot be analysed chemically or influenced by the laws of physics, and competes neither with other such entities nor with bodies for its position in space. It is the mind and soul with which we think, feel, desire, understand, regret, and so forth, and which is held to distinguish us from animals. This set of beliefs forms the core of metaphysical *dualism*.

Dualism certainly reflects the way ordinary language speaks about people, but it is a metaphysical rather than a linguistic theory, making a fundamental claim about the nature of reality. Regarded in this way, the theory is clearly incomplete: it may be that we are each an amalgam of two utterly distinct entities, but dualism says nothing whatever about the relationship between them. The traditional answer is that the bodily senses convey information about the world to the mind, which then exercises reason to decide upon a course of action; the mind then somehow conveys instructions to the body for it to carry out.

This is essentially the view formulated by the French philosopher Descartes in the 17th century. Unfortunately his theory, known as *interactionism*, raises more questions than it answers. The most obvious is that, since immaterial substance is by definition not affected by physical substance and the body is itself a physical object, his theory is actually committed to denying that such an interaction can take place. Descartes himself thought he could meet this difficulty by locating the interaction within the brain, but this does no more than localize the interaction – and the problem – and so misses the point.

In an attempt to bridge the gap, Descartes' younger contemporary Nicolas Malebranche (1638–1715) proposed instead that God constantly intervenes to bring about the apparent interaction (a version of the theory known as *occasionalism*), while Leibniz believed in a world of infinitely many distinct, simple substances (*monads*) that are incapable of interaction but are like two clocks that God has set to keep time with each other

without any direct causal interaction (a doctrine known as *parallelism*).

Neither of these theories, however, explains how the non-physical can interact with the physical, since both ascribe a crucial role to a God who is no more a part of the physical world than the mind.

Knowledge of other minds

Dualism gives rise to another problem: how do we know that minds other than our own do exist? Of course we see other human bodies around us, we hear seemingly articulate speech emanating from them, and we can apparently affect the behaviour of these bodies in a way that suggests they have heard and understood our words and acted accordingly. But, for the dualist at least, none of this is conclusive evidence that other people have minds.

The development of computers has given the *other-minds problem* a new lease of life. The languages of computing and human intellect have come to infect one another: we talk of a machine or a program deciding how to process a form, and of children being programmed by their early experiences. Although we know that computers merely apply rules in a determinate manner and do not really think, such expressions no longer sound metaphorical, and the development of computers that are able to learn from their mistakes by amending their own programs offers the vision of a machine whose behaviour is indistinguishable from that of a person (see p. 336).

Perhaps another case sheds some light on this: the fact that scientists have taught chimpanzees to communicate in sign language at about the level of a 5-year-old child does not make them persons, yet we clearly regard this achievement as more significant than teaching a dog to walk on its hind legs. Dogs are said to recognize their owner's voice, horses refuse to jump, cats want to be let out, but frogs do not refuse and worms do not want. This suggests that whether we are prepared to talk of something as a person or treat it as a member of the moral community is not a matter of the existence or otherwise of some kind of immaterial entity, but rather of how close an analogy there is between its behaviour and our own.

The same ranking emerges in morality: few people have qualms about killing flies, while experiments on dogs cause more upset than those on rats; even the Nazis had first to portray their victims as 'sub-human' before wholesale murder could be presented as morally permissible. Perhaps then the concept of a person is itself a moral one: persons are those with whom we interact in terms of duties and obligations.

Materialism and behaviourism

The other-minds problem arose as a consequence of dualism, but dualism is not the only possible view of mind and body. Many philosophers have held instead that there is only one kind of substance. *Materialism* is the theory that all that exists is

Chimpanzees have been taught to communicate in sign language at about the level of a 5-year-old child, while the development of a computer whose behaviour is indistinguishable from that of a human may not be so far away. Yet we are not inclined to refer to them as 'people'. On what basis do we – or should we – make the distinction?

material, physical substance, so that minds or souls as generally conceived do not exist. It is often suggested that neurology provides direct evidence for this, since mental impairment seems to be both the symptom and the consequence of brain damage (see p. 223). However, this is not conclusive against Descartes' view that the mind and body interact through the brain, for it could be that it is only the connections that are damaged and not the mind itself. Indeed, the common experience of stroke victims, who seem to know what they want to say and show frustration at their inability to express it, seems to be neurological evidence against materialism.

Another problem with materialism is that the very fact that we understand each other's talk of minds and mental events suggests that there must be something about which we are talking. One form of *behaviourism* denies that there are such things as minds, but avoids this objection by rejecting the naive referential view of how language works (see p. 496) from which it would follow that mentalistic language is meaningless. Instead it is suggested that what look grammatically like expressions that refer to mental objects and events are in reality abbreviations for complex descriptions of behaviour. This was the view of the English philosopher Gilbert Ryle (1900–76), who argued that we do not judge someone a good chess player by enquiring about their mental processes but by observing that they consistently make the right moves. He claimed that Descartes' theory portrayed the mind as no more than a 'ghost in the machine', just as someone who had never before seen a car might insist that there must be a horse in it somewhere, albeit invisible and intangible.

Personal identity

Suppose that, in a world just slightly more

EXISTENTIALISM

Existentialism is not a single philosophical system, but is typified by certain attitudes. Its name derives from the proposition that 'existence precedes essence' – that one becomes what one is by virtue of the decisions one makes, rather than being determined by nature, society or even reason. In *Being and Nothingness* (1943) Jean-Paul Sartre distinguishes the 'being in itself' of inert matter from the 'being for itself', which is capable of free choice by virtue of its awareness of 'not-being'. Human beings are therefore condemned to the anxiety (*angst*) of freedom, but can take refuge in 'bad faith' (*mauvaise foi*): thus they may blame society for their own decisions, for example, or 'objectify' themselves by playing the role society expects of them.

Jean-Paul Sartre

---

advanced than ours, you suffer a serious accident in which your entire body is crushed, but your skull and brain are intact. At about the same time I, quite literally, blow my brains out, and our mangled remains arrive simultaneously at the same hospital. Suppose, too, that there is no technical obstacle to implanting your uninjured brain in my body and that this procedure is carried out. Who then survives the operation – me (with a new brain), you (with a new body), or someone different from either of us?

This (in our imagined world) would not merely be an academic question. Many things would hang on which of us was deemed to be alive and which dead. Who is tried for your bank robbery, for instance, and who inherits which estate? If we say the survivor is you because he has your memories, will that cut much ice with your family and friends when you – a male – come home in my – female – body? If we say the survivor is me because he has my body, or that he is a new person altogether, how do we explain his memories, which seem linked to your past in (almost) the normal way?

Now let us make the story worse. The human brain consists of two more or less separate and autonomous hemispheres, each of which controls the opposite side of the body and is specialized in various ways; nonetheless people have survived the loss of one half of their brain, and have lived reasonably normal lives. Note that the fact that we talk of survival entails that we judge the person who emerges from the operating theatre to be the same person as the person who went in. Now suppose that my brother and I both blow our brains out, and half of your brain is transplanted into each of our heads. If you thought before that the survivor was you because he had your brain and so your memories, do you now think that both survivors are you? And does that mean that they are now one and the same person, occupying two bodies? nd what if my body receives a second half-brain from another donor? The patient now has two sets of memories, one from each hemisphere; is he then two people in the same body?

Personal identity survives some kinds of physical and mental change: I am the same person now as the child I remember being and as the old man for whose retirement I am planning. But what are the limits to such change? Is there some part of me – my brain, my mind (as Descartes argued), my memory (as Locke held) – which is the essential me?   EJB

SEE ALSO

● ANIMAL COMMUNICATION p. 166
● THE BRAIN p. 222
● LEARNING, CREATIVITY AND INTELLIGENCE p. 230
● SLEEP, DREAMS AND THE UNCONSCIOUS p. 232
● ARTIFICIAL INTELLIGENCE p. 336
● WHAT IS PHILOSOPHY? p. 486
● KNOWLEDGE AND REALITY p. 488
● ETHICS p. 492
● LOGIC AND ARGUMENT p. 494
● THE PHILOSOPHY OF LANGUAGE p. 496

Ethics

Frequently in our everyday lives we encounter ethical concepts, such as rights and duties, benefit and harm, right and wrong, good and bad. Such concepts are also the stuff of politics, as is clear from every letter to the editor about the legalization of drugs, every demonstration for or against abortion, every government debate on capital punishment. Moral philosophy studies these ethical concepts, seeking not a unique solution to all our ethical dilemmas but a better understanding of the concepts themselves.

Disagreement about matters of taste are equally familiar: if you think cabbage tastes disgusting and I disagree, we just agree to differ. Although we seem to contradict one another, in reality we do not, any more than if I say I feel warm and you say you do not. One statement is about you, the other about me: there is nothing to which we are ascribing incompatible properties.

Taste and morality

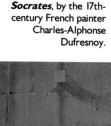

The Death of Socrates, by the 17th-century French painter Charles-Alphonse Dufresnoy.

It is sometimes suggested that people's moral outlooks can differ from one another in this way too. But, if this were so, a disagreement about whether eating people is wrong would be like a disagreement about whether cabbage tastes disgusting, rather than being analogous to a factual disagreement, such as whether cabbage contains vitamins. Most people, however, simply do not take this view of ethical disagreements: we cannot agree to differ while one of us practises cannibalism and the other refrains from it; on the contrary, if you stand by and watch without protest while another person kills and eats somebody else, your behaviour is equally reprehensible. In fact, it casts doubt on your claim to believe that cannibalism is wrong, because if you did you would not just refrain yourself but also try to prevent others. This is one sense in which moral judgements are said to be *universalizable*.

They are, however, like factual disagreements in being amenable to argument: if we disagree about whether cabbage contains vitamins, we can attempt to cite arguments to persuade one another, and might even conduct an experiment to settle the matter; but if we dispute whether it tastes good, there is nothing either of us can do or say to convince the other. Judgements of artistic merit seem to fall somewhere between the two extremes: argument may convince us of the *aesthetic* merit of a painting or a play, but we can still insist that we nonetheless just don't like it. In ethics, however, it does not seem possible, without irrationality, both to accept an argument and to demur from its conclusion. Of course in a moral dilemma there will be arguments on both sides, and even after reaching a decision you may still have doubts – but what you cannot rationally do is to bring the argument to a conclusion about where your duty lies and yet still insist on making the opposite judgement.

Values and facts

Both judgements of taste and moral judgements are *value judgements*. While all such judgements can have the form of grammatical statements, it is not always natural to talk of them as being true or false. 'That's not true' seems appropriate as a reply to the claim that cabbage contains vitamins but not to the statement that cabbage tastes nice.

Despite such considerations, it is clear that moral judgements are related in some way to facts – after all, it is about the facts that we make the judgements, and it is argument about the facts that makes us change our minds. The simplest theory is that there are moral facts and that moral judgements are true if they report those facts correctly, and false otherwise; this is

known as *descriptivism*. Descriptivist theories fall into two camps: on the one hand there are *naturalistic* theories that attempt to define ethical terms such as 'right' or 'good' in non-ethical language; on the other there are *non-naturalistic* theories that claim that, while there are moral properties and moral facts, these cannot be defined in non-ethical terms.

Defining moral terms

Naturalistic theories are manifold: *hedonistic* theories, for example, define 'good' in terms of human pleasure or happiness, while *egoistic* theories define moral obligation in terms of seeking one's own advantage; *theistic* theories define right action as that which is commanded by God. The best-known hedonistic theory is the *utilitarianism* of Bentham and Mill, which holds that in any moral conflict the right thing to do is that which results in the 'greatest happiness for the greatest number'.

Any such theory can, however, be criticized for committing what the Cambridge philosopher G.E. Moore (1873–1958) called the *naturalistic fallacy*. This can be illustrated by considering the theory that 'right' means 'promoting general happiness'. Obviously not everyone accepts the theory, so it must remain contentious whether it is right to promote general happiness. But because it is about the *meaning* of 'right', the theory has the absurd consequence that this supposedly contentious question means the same as the vacuously uncontentious one of whether it is right to act rightly. This argument suggests that there is a gulf between 'facts' and 'values' (or, as is sometimes said, between 'is' and 'ought') too wide to be bridged by any naturalistic definition.

Some moral philosophers, including G.E. Moore himself, have therefore concluded that ethical terms ascribe some indefinable non-natural moral property. But such a doctrine immediately raises the problem of how we could ever resolve moral disputes. Colour may be indefinable, but disputes can be settled by appealing to the consensus of people with normal vision. In the case of deep ethical disagreement, however, there will be no consensus about whose 'moral vision' is normal, nor any way of settling the matter independent of the original disagreement.

The force of moral judgements

One way out of these difficulties is to defend a naturalistic account of the correct use of ethical terms, but to insist that it does not exhaust their meaning. A more radical response is to reject the descriptivist presupposition common to both naturalism and non-naturalism.

Both these responses share an underlying belief that part of the explanation of the meaning of an expression must be an account of what *speech act* it performs and that the grammatical structure of an expression is at best only a superficial guide to how it is used. Where the two approaches differ is about whether fact-stating remains part of the force of moral

judgements; if it does, they retain a truth value, but if value judgements do not state facts at all, they can never strictly speaking be true or false.

Since moral judgements clearly do have a prescriptive force and often reflect an individual's attitudes, the commonest analogies for the force of moral judgements are commands and exclamations. Expressions of either kind can clearly be said to contradict one another, so that some of the logical properties of moral argument can be accounted for. The *prescriptivism* of the Oxford philosopher Richard Hare (1919–) holds that moral judgements have the force of universalized commands and that this accounts for their authority, while the *emotivism* of A.J. Ayer suggests that a moral judgement does not report but actually expresses an attitude.

While emotivism explains why sincerity may seem a more appropriate measure than truth, treating 'Eating people is wrong' as equivalent to 'Down with cannibalism' hardly conveys the seriousness of moral judgement: rational ethical debate is surely more than the chanting of competing slogans.

Good and duty

Neither emotivism nor prescriptivism lays down any logical restrictions on the content of a person's moral views. This may not be an objection, however: once we have restricted our attention to the question of how moral language works, we should not be surprised that the answer is as limited as the question. The objection should perhaps rather be to the suggestion that this is all there is to say about moral language. The fact that we can make sense of ascribing to a Nazi a moral outlook that is abhorrent to us shows that we do distinguish between those of a person's beliefs that count for that person as a morality and the question of whether we ourselves adjudge those views moral. Only beliefs that are moral in the first sense can be moral or immoral in the second sense; otherwise they are non-moral – simply not in the ethical arena at all.

Granting, then, that our moral beliefs are those to which we have certain attitudes and which we regard as binding and universal, what permits us to say that the Nazi's beliefs are morally abhorrent, even though they pass all such tests? The obvious answer is that they sanction cruelty, murder, and senseless war. Such a response implicitly appeals to a naturalistic criterion of morality, but this time there is no threat of fallacy, because a criterion is weaker than a definition. In fact many of those who believe that the meaning of ethical terms is best explained in terms of their force nonetheless regard the general good as a criterion of moral value.

Even this weaker claim, however, falls foul of the suggestion that duty must be done for its own sake, and not to achieve some further end such as human happiness. This is the view taken in the 18th century by Kant, who proposed a number of formulations of what he referred to as the *categorical imperative*. According to

this principle, you should only act in a manner that could be adopted by everyone, and you should always treat people as ends in themselves rather than means to an end. He argued that it is part of the very concept of duty that, even if you do what duty dictates, but you do it for some extraneous reason, your action is not praiseworthy. Morality is thus, for Kant, concerned with motive rather than outcome, and the only right action is that motivated by duty for its own sake.   EJB

John Stuart Mill, English philosopher, economist and social reformer, whose *On Liberty* (1859) is the classic statement of the principle of maximum individual liberty for all. He tempered Jeremy Bentham's utilitarian 'greatest happiness principle' with egalitarianism, and argued for female emancipation and universal suffrage.

SEE ALSO

● CIVIL AND HUMAN RIGHTS p. 290
● GOOD AND EVIL p. 484
● WHAT IS PHILOSOPHY? p. 486
● KNOWLEDGE AND REALITY p. 488
● MIND AND BODY p. 490
● LOGIC AND ARGUMENT p. 494
● THE PHILOSOPHY OF LANGUAGE p. 496

UTILITARIANISM AND JUSTICE

Utilitarianism (at least in a naive form) is an implausible criterion of right action: it might, for example, justify slavery on the grounds that depriving a few people of their liberty increases the average standard of living. One suggestion is that what is wrong here is that the position of the worst-off members of society is worsened by the pursuit of the *maximizing* principle of utilitarianism.

The American philosopher John Rawls (1921–) therefore suggests that when drawing up rules for society we should try to ensure *fairness* by laying down that the right action in any dilemma of moral choice is the one that would produce the situation in which the worst-off person is least badly off. This doctrine seems to be reflected in the taxation and social-welfare systems of modern democracies. Most people think it better that society as a whole should be slightly worse off on average than that unrestricted economic activity should result in even a very few people starving.

Logic and Argument

Logic is the study of good and bad argument. During the 20th century, a number of distinct branches have developed: formal or mathematical logic studies symbolic systems that are intended to model certain kinds of argument, while philosophical logic discusses the relationship between such systems and ordinary language, and between language and the world (see p. 496).

Logic is about *argument* – that is, about rational means of persuasion. The typical situation in which an argument may arise is when the person with whom you are discussing something does not believe something you say; you then offer reasons or grounds for your point of view. On the other hand – for example in mathematics – it may be you yourself who are actually or notionally unsure of something, and you construct a *proof*, the purpose of which is to convince yourself and anyone who may study it.

The force of argument

What makes such an argument or proof convincing? The first requirement is obviously that the argument starts from a position that is itself accepted. There is no point in trying to persuade an atheist of the existence of God using premises that implicity assume what you intend to prove; that is just begging the question. In a mathematical context, the starting point is likely to be a set of *axioms* – propositions that are stipulated to be true and about which there can be no argument, since they are what define the theory. In ordinary persuasive rhetoric, the premises need only meet the weaker condition that the other party accepts them; the point of the argument is then to show that he or she *must* as a consequence of the premises accept the intended conclusion.

What then is the force of this 'must'? It is precisely that acceptance of the premises commits you to the conclusion; that to accept the premises but persist in denying the conclusion would be *inconsistent*. If we believe that an inconsistent pair of statements, such as 'It is raining outside' and 'It is not raining outside', are both true, we can no longer use our belief in the truth of the first to rule out the truth of the second. We thereby rob ourselves of any distinction between truth and falsehood, and the whole point of argument – that it lets us choose which of two competing statements is true – is undermined. It is indeed possible to construct an argu-

David Hume, Scottish empiricist philosopher, whose avowed aim was to secure the foundation of knowledge by demonstrating that 'false and adulterate metaphysics' only arises when we address subjects beyond the scope of human reason. He used the principle that all legitimate ideas must be derived from experience to cast doubt on the reality of the self and of causal connection. He claimed that inductive reasoning (see text) cannot be justified; it is merely a 'habit or custom', a 'principle of human nature'.

ment that shows that from any pair of inconsistent statements anything at all can be deduced.

Correct arguments

Thus, for an argument to be *convincing* (or *sound*), it must not only have true (or accepted) premises, but these premises must make the conclusion inescapable. These questions can be considered independently: for example, a mathematician often shows a supposition to be false precisely by deducing an absurdity from it – but that requires him to recognize that the absurdity is logically inescapable given the supposition. Clearly we judge arguments without knowing whether their premises are true. What is at issue is whether the conclusion would have to be true if the premises were true. This property of arguments is called *correctness* or *validity*, and consists in it being inconsistent to accept the premises while denying the conclusion. For example,

(1) John is a bachelor, so he is unmarried

is a correct argument, since the conclusion follows from the definition of a 'bachelor'. On the other hand

(2) I have never seen a swan that was not white; so all swans are white

is not a correct argument, since it is perfectly possible for the premise to be true but the conclusion false; this is the case simply because I have limited experience of swans.

The use of counterexamples

The explanation of why (2) is incorrect suggests a way of demonstrating that any argument is not correct. A correct argument will never let us down, irrespective of the truth or falsehood of its premises; so to show that an argument is not correct, all we need to do is find a *counterexample* – a situation in which the argument *does* let us down, i.e. in which the premises are true but the conclusion false. The counterexample need not itself have true premises: it is sufficient that it is *possible* for the argument to let us down for us to have to reject it as invalid.

This is decisive because it shows that the argument is not *infallibly truth-preserving*: it cannot be relied upon never to lead from truth to falsehood. It would therefore always be an open question whether it had let us down on the very occasion we tried to use it.

This clearly reflects our ordinary conception of what constitutes a good argument. We recognize, for example, that

(3) Pigs have wings; if pigs have wings they can fly; so pigs can fly

a correct argument, even though the first premise and the conclusion are false. In fact, a correct argument can have false premises, and an incorrect argument can have true premises; the only combination that cannot occur is true premises, correct argument, but false conclusion.

Formal validity

There is clearly a difference between arguments like (1) above and those like (3). The correctness of the former depends on the meanings of the words, and it is impossible to generalize beyond the context of those words. On the other hand, we can recognize that (3) is in some sense the same argument as

(4) Today is Saturday; if today is Saturday I can stay in bed; so I can stay in bed.

The reason we recognize it as the same argument is that the 'shape' or *form* of the argument is the same. If we use letters to replace the component sentences of (3) and (4), we obtain the same form in each case:

(5) P; if P then Q; so Q.

In this case it is possible to generalize beyond the context of a particular argument, since it is obvious that the correctness of (3) and (4) does not depend on what they are about but on their common form. This special case of correctness is called *formal validity*; it is important because it is possible to develop tests of correctness that are independent of the particular argument and depend only on its form.

Symbolic systems that model certain kinds of argument and enable validity to be determined are known as *logics*. For example, (5) is derived from (4) by replacing component sentences with symbols. The elements whose pattern determines the validity of these arguments are sentences; the arguments are therefore said to be *sententially valid*, and (5) is known as a *sentential form*. On the other hand,

SEE ALSO

- THE SCIENTIFIC METHOD p. 58
- LOGIC, SETS AND PARADOXES p. 66
- WHAT IS PHILOSOPHY? p. 486
- KNOWLEDGE AND REALITY p. 488
- MIND AND BODY p. 490
- ETHICS p. 492
- THE PHILOSOPHY OF LANGUAGE p. 496

(6) All philosophers are bearded; some Glaswegians are philosophers; so some Glaswegians are bearded

is clearly formally valid rather than merely correct, but its validity does not depend on a sentential form. The structure that makes this argument work is at the level of subjects and predicates, and its form can be written

(7) All A are B; some C are A; so some C are B

where A, B and C represent the *terms* of the argument. Different logics are thus needed to test the validity of different kinds of argument: a system of sentential logic obviously cannot assess an argument like (7). One way to test the validity of arguments like this is to use Venn diagrams (see p. 66).

Induction and deduction

Not all argument falls into the kind of mould we have been discussing. As we saw, (2) is not even correct, far less formally valid, yet we build our lives around inferences of this kind, and they are a common tool by which science develops theories out of observations. Arguments like this, which go beyond their premises to a conclusion that is not necessitated by the premises, are known as *inductive* arguments, by contrast with *deductive* arguments, such as (3) and (6), in which the conclusion is strictly a consequence of the premises (see also pp. 58–9).

Since with inductive reasoning there is no guarantee that true premises will ever yield a true conclusion, philosophers have often discussed how it can be justified (see pp. 58–9). Expedients such as choosing a large sample from diverse sources do not address the fundamental concern that the conclusion might still turn out to be false. Nor can inductive reasoning be justified because it works, since that is itself an inductive argument of precisely the kind we are seeking to justify. It is, of course, always possible to turn an argument like (2) into a formally valid argument by adding as an additional premise that the observed sample is typical of the entire population, or that the future will resemble the past, and so forth. But that does not make the argument any more convincing, since the truth of the new premise is no less doubtful than the correctness of the original argument.

Discussion of the justification of inductive argument has proved inconclusive. Indeed, many philosophers in the tradition of Hume and Wittgenstein have argued that the demand for justification is itself at fault. We do not seek a justification of deduction, and if one is in fact offered, it must be inherently circular. Likewise, arguing inductively – learning from experience – is part of what we mean by behaving rationally and does not stand in need of any other justification. EJB

Bertrand Russell, English philosopher, logician and social reformer. In the 3-volume *Principia Mathematica* (1910–13), he and A.N. Whitehead worked out a reduction of mathematics to logic, thereby leaving a lasting impression on both subjects. In the philosophy of language his identification of meaning with reference (see p. 496) led him to explain all meaning in terms of 'logically proper names', which refer infallibly to the contents of immediate experience (sense data).

SLIPPERY SLOPES

Abortion is a vexed moral issue, but both parties in the debate agree that, except in certain extreme conditions, it is morally wrong to kill a living person; the disagreement is about whether the foetus is a living person. The opponent of abortion cites the foetus just prior to delivery: surely this is as much a living person as five minutes later when it is at its mother's breast. The advocate of the 'right to choose' abortion cites the foetus immediately after conception: surely this is no more a living person than the same cells were five minutes earlier before they combined.

As they stand, these positions are not in conflict; they seem to support what is the legal position in many countries – that abortion before a certain date is permissible and after that date is wrong. Such laws, then, are not simply a compromise: they follow from arguments about when the foetus should be ascribed the status of a living person.

In the absence of any metaphysical argument for one instant rather than another, both camps agree that from conception to delivery there is no relevant difference between one instant and the next, and so no instant at which the foetus changes from not being a living person to being one; this is why their positions are in conflict. For consider the three statements:

(1) The foetus immediately after conception is not a living person;

(2) The foetus immediately prior to delivery is a living person;

(3) There is no instant at which the foetus changes from not being a living person to being one.

Clearly these form an inconsistent set – they cannot all be true. But which of the three should be rejected? All we can conclude is that if any pair of them is true, then the third must be false. The outright opponent of abortion thus argues from (2) and (3) to deny (1); the advocate of an absolute 'right to choose' might argue from (1) and (3) to deny (2); and the law appears to deny (3) on the grounds of arguments for both (1) and (2).

Which of these arguments should we accept? For an argument to be convincing two things are required: that its premises are true and that its form is valid. All these arguments are equally valid, so we seem to be thrown back on assessing which of the three statements is false – which is the very question we were attempting to answer. Many people, presented with each of these statements separately, or presented with a trio of the same form but about a less emotive subject, actually assent to all three – even when their apparent contradiction is pointed out.

Modern philosophy does not seek to square this circle. Instead it uses examples like this to show that the logic of contradiction is not as clear-cut as it at first seems: perhaps statements can be other than true or false; perhaps there are shades of grey, at least when we are dealing with concepts that are themselves vague or a matter of degree. Perhaps we should stop thinking of the world as divided sharply between persons and non-persons; perhaps even this basic moral notion is a matter of degree. Wherever we place the blame, we have come a long way for a solution: we began with a real practical moral and political debate, and we have found in it reason for questioning the very basis of all reasoning – the logic of truth and falsehood itself.

The Philosophy of Language

The most unproblematic way of explaining the meaning of a word seems to be to point to what that word stands for (its *reference*), and indeed philosophers have traditionally identified the meaning of a word with its reference. But this theory appears to fall foul of the simple observation that we often talk of things that do not exist (for example fictional characters and ghosts) and such talk is not meaningless. But the referential model is so powerful that philosophers have generally preferred to postulate various kinds of abstract entities for the words to refer to, rather than admit that the theory is wrong.

John Locke, English empiricist philosopher and political theorist. He regarded philosophy as clearing the conceptual ground for science, and began his *Essay concerning Human Understanding* (1690) by rejecting the doctrine of innate ideas and postulating instead that all ideas are derived from experience (see p. 488 and text). Shown here is a contemporary copy of a portrait by Godfrey Kneller (1697).
(Archiv für Kunst)

SEE ALSO

● ARTIFICIAL INTELLIGENCE p. 336
● WHAT IS PHILOSOPHY? p. 486
● KNOWLEDGE AND REALITY p. 488
● MIND AND BODY p. 490
● ETHICS p. 492
● LOGIC AND ARGUMENT p. 494
● HOW LANGUAGE WORKS p. 608
● THE LANGUAGE OF SIGNS p. 610

Plato, for example, thought that general terms like 'justice' or 'circle' or 'horse' name Forms – abstract entities existing in some unchanging metaphysical realm that is accessible only to properly trained reason – while Locke believed that they name abstract ideas that enter the mind by a process of abstraction from experience (see p. 488). For all the differences of detail, Plato and Locke agree in their underlying theory of meaning: both held that the meaning of a word is simply the thing that it names; all they disagree about is what kind of thing this might be.

Meaning and reference

This *referential* theory looks quite plausible for one class of words. Names of people, places and things seem to do no more than label them; the meaning of the name 'Fido' is simply the dog Fido.

Names thus seem to contrast with descriptions like 'red' or 'round', whose function is to ascribe a property. Nonetheless, in the absence of any alternative to reference as an account of meaning, philosophers from Plato to Bertrand Russell were faced with the problem that if an expression lacked a reference it seemed to be just meaningless. It was thus to provide meanings for general terms that philosophers such as Plato and Locke advanced the theories they did.

Sense and reference

At the end of the 19th century, the German philosopher Gottlob Frege argued that there must be more to meaning than reference, even for names. After all, he said, if 'Cicero' and 'Tully' are two names used by the same Roman, 'Cicero was Cicero' and 'Cicero was Tully' are equally true, but there is obviously a difference between what these two sentences tell us. Frege proposed that in addition to a reference a word has a *sense*, which is how it determines its reference. The reason 'Cicero was Tully' is informative is that the two names have different senses which determine the same reference in different ways.

The divergence of sense and reference is quite clear in the way we use, for example, the personal and demonstrative pronouns in ordinary language. Obviously the reference of a word such as 'you' or 'here' depends upon where and when it is used. But we do not ordinarily want to say that these words are *ambiguous*: the reason their reference is so variable is that their meaning depends on the context of use. Frege's notion that sense determines reference is analogous to this obvious fact.

Names and descriptions

Bertrand Russell also recognized that ordinary names could not function purely referentially – not least because we meaningfully give names to things that do not exist at all. His solution looks similar to Frege's, since they both claimed that behind an ordinary name there is a description that really determines what is referred to, but in fact their solutions are radically different. This difference can be seen in practice in the way they treat a sentence such as 'Sherlock Holmes is bald', which seems to refer to someone who does not exist.

According to Frege, the sense of the name 'Sherlock Holmes' might be, say, 'the detective who lives at 221B Baker Street', and our sentence will be true if that detective is bald and false if he is not. But in this case, since there is no detective who lives at 221B Baker Street, nothing at all satisfies the description, so no one is picked out as having baldness ascribed to him; for Frege the given sentence is therefore neither true nor false.

For Russell, on the other hand, only meaningless sentences can lack a truth value, and it is clearly not meaningless to say that Sherlock Holmes is bald. Russell's *theory of descriptions* involves two steps of analysis: first, since he has no concept of sense, he regards the description as actually the meaning of the name (so the name just abbreviates the descripion); secondly, it is part of the meaning of names and definite descriptions that they denote exactly one individual, and this can only be explained in the context of the whole sentence. Thus, for example, 'Sherlock Holmes is bald' is analysed into three separate claims:

1) there is at least one detective who lives at 221B Baker Street;

2) there is at most one detective who lives at 221B Baker Street; and

3) any detective who lives at 221B Baker Street is bald.

Since (1) is clearly false, Russell judges that the given sentence is false.

More recently, the Oxford philosopher Peter Strawson (1919–) offered a resolution of this conflict: he pointed out that it is linguistic expressions that have meaning, while uses of them have reference or truth; for example, 'you' only has one meaning (say, 'the person being spoken to'), whereas its reference changes from conversation to conversation. Thus Frege is right that the sentence is meaningful but lacks a truth value, while Russell is right about how to determine its truth value when it has one.

Meaning and meanings

Even Frege postulated abstract entities ('concepts') to be the references of general terms. More recently, however, the presupposition that for a word to be intelligible it must refer to something has been challenged at a deeper level, principally by Ludwig Wittgenstein.

To be fair, the idiom of the English language is against us: we talk of words having a meaning and of ambiguous words having more than one meaning. It is then natural to ask what these meanings are, and how we establish whether or not the meanings as independently existing entities of two words are the same. However, language is often misleading and the fact that we distinguish expressions with meaning from those without is insufficient to show that there exist meanings as independently existing entities that the former possess and that the latter lack.

What is more, as Wittgenstein argued, both Platonic Forms and Lockean mental images would drop out of the kind of explanation we actually give of how we use language. Let us suppose either of these accounts correct, and consider how, for example, we would determine whether a child has yet learnt some concept. We have no way of directly examining either the ideas in its mind or its grasp of a Form; instead what we invariably do is to base our judgement upon whether or not the child *behaves as if* it has grasped the concept. We are thus doing no more or less than judging whether the child's use of the term accords sufficiently with our own; abstract or mental entities make as little difference to this judgement, says Wittgenstein, as would a paper crown on a chess piece to its moves in a game.

This kind of argument not only undermines the conception of a meaning as some kind of mystical entity, but it also opens our eyes to the fact that words do not all have sharply defined uses. On the contrary, once we have learnt the use of a word, we are bound to go beyond the limited range of cases in which our teachers corrected our errors; we are all familiar with arguments about whether turquoise is blue or green and about where its boundaries are. In fact, when we meet a new phenomenon, our usage is not determined by previous use, but we have to decide how to extend previous usage. We do not, of course, have complete freedom to call a fish a bicycle; we try to make our new usage conform to previous usage, but this is as much a new case of conforming as it is a potentially new kind of fish, and we are to that extent free to choose here too.

Thus language is indeed dynamic and open-ended in a way that earlier theories could not allow, and its relation with the world can be equally multi-faceted. As Wittgenstein remarked, there is no more to supposing that all language works like names do, by referring, than there is to supposing that deep down all tools are somehow hammers.   EJB

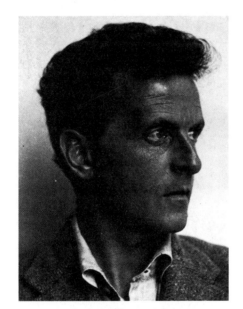

Ludwig Wittgenstein

LUDWIG WITTGENSTEIN

Despite publishing very little, Ludwig Wittgenstein (1889–1951) became the most influential philosopher of the 20th century. He developed two highly original but incompatible systems of philosophy, both dominated by a concern with the relations between language and the world.

The early doctrines of the *Tractatus Logico-Philosophicus* (1921) are based on a highly structured logico-metaphysical theory: 'the world is the totality of facts . . . not of things' and these can be analysed into 'atomic facts', which are literally 'pictured' by 'atomic propositions'. However, the philosophical propositions of the *Tractatus* itself, being about – not of – the world, can only be shown, not said, and 'whereof we cannot speak, thereof we must keep silent'. Believing that he had said all that could be said, Wittgenstein, true to his word, abandoned philosophy and became a teacher. However, his interest was reawakened by contact with the Vienna Circle of logical positivists, and he returned to Cambridge where his unpublished lectures influenced another generation of philosophers.

His later view, as expressed in the *Philosophical Investigations* (1953), is that language is a varied social phenomenon for which there is no single criterion of correctness nor a single explanatory metaphor. There can be no criterion to distinguish following a private rule from thinking one is doing so; so the rules of language in particular cannot depend upon any essentially private entities such as Lockean ideas. The later Wittgenstein consistently walks a narrow path between the two competing orthodoxies: he denies both that there is some external fact by virtue of which all red things are red, and that there is nothing whatever to determine our usage of the word. Likewise 'Pain is not a something, but it is not nothing either' – it is neither a private mental entity nor is it merely to be identified with behaviour. The other-minds problem (see p. 490) thus arises from typical philosophical misunderstanding of metaphorical language. Philosophy should not construct grandiose theories which tend to distort language, but merely 'assemble reminders' about its use.

DOING THINGS WITH WORDS

The variety of language use has been stressed by others as well as Wittgenstein. The Oxford philosopher J.L. Austin (1911–60) remarked that some sentences do not report facts but instead perform acts, and so cannot be true or false but only appropriate or inappropriate; 'I hereby appoint you my deputy' is such a *performative utterance*.

Another theory in the same tradition is that of the English philosopher H.P. Grice, who identified a number of 'maxims of conversational cooperativeness', such as 'always give as much information as you can' or 'stick to the subject'. He then suggested that we are entitled to infer whatever is necessary to explain an apparent breach of these maxims. For example, if I ask you where my coat is and you reply 'Either in the hall or in the wardrobe', I am entitled to believe that you yourself do not know which, since if you did you could have given a better answer. This theory of *conversational implicature* has been used to clarify a variety of traditional problems. For example, if – as is commonly said – knowledge is justified true belief, then 'John knows he is ill' must imply 'John believes he is ill', yet by saying the latter I seem to suggest he isn't really. If, however, we distinguish truth from appropriateness, then saying that 'John believes he is ill' is not false but inappropriate, because the presupposition that I am complying with the maxims requires me to give the stronger answer if I am in a position to do so.

This is a very fruitful theory, and has the merit of treating language as a species of deliberate behaviour. Thus, just as I can infer from your behaviour a rational explanation for your acting as you did, so I make similar inferences not just from what you say but also from how you say it.

THE VISUAL ARTS

'Art happens – no hovel is safe from it, no prince may depend upon it, the vastest intelligence cannot bring it about.'

James McNeill Whistler

Art Techniques 1: Painting and Drawing

The great variety of painting techniques reflects the range of surfaces that are painted on: for instance, tempera technique is used for painting on wood panels and fresco technique for painting on walls. Oil painting is done mainly on canvas, while acrylic, watercolour, gouache and pastels can all be used to paint on paper.

The earliest paintings known are some 15 000 years old, found in the caves of Altamira in Spain and Lascaux in France (see p. 504). The pigments used in these prehistoric sites include burnt wood, bone, chalk and earth colours.

Pigments

Pigments (colours) can be derived from earths, natural dyes and minerals or chemically synthesized. In addition to the pigments used by prehistoric man, *verdigris* (copper resinate; green), *ultramarine* (lapis lazuli; blue), *white lead*, *azurite* (copper carbonate; blue), *madder* (red), *lead-tin yellow* and *vermilion* (cinnabar; red) were in use in the 14th century and form the basis of the painter's palette even today. Not until *Prussian blue* was discovered in 1705 and *Naples yellow* in the 1750s were significant additions made. During the 19th century, however, the range of colours expanded to include new chemical colours such as purples and greens. The identification of pigments can often help in the dating of paintings, based on the knowledge of their discovery and availability to artists.

Drawing tools

The range of drawing tools used by artists begins with the *silverpoint*, a metal point used mainly in the 15th century on prepared paper, often coloured, to show the marks of the implement. The development of the graphite pencil in the 17th century avoided the need for a prepared ground and also enabled the artist to draw in a variety of styles.

From the 16th century *charcoal* (charred wood), *black chalk* (black stone) and *red chalk* (mineral) were extensively used in preparatory drawings. These allow a great freedom of handling, and passages of light and shade are achieved by hatching – drawing fine parallel or crossed lines – smudging and the use of white highlights. Pen and ink may be used for preparatory drawings, either alone or in combination with charcoal or chalk.

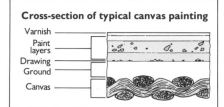

Cross-section of typical canvas painting

- Varnish
- Paint layers
- Drawing
- Ground
- Canvas

Tempera

Tempera is one of the oldest painting techniques. It is based on a mixture of a water-based liquid with an oily or waxy medium. Traditionally egg white and egg yolk are used together with an oil such as linseed oil, but egg (which acts as a binder) may also be used with water alone. Its quick-drying properties and luminosity of colour account for the attraction of tempera. The ground (base) for wood panel tempera paintings was traditionally *gesso* (calcium sulphate) in Italy, and chalk (calcium carbonate) in northern Europe, both mixed with *size* (animal glue). This is built up in a series of layers and finally polished to form a smooth surface. On this the painter would draw his design in silverpoint or charcoal or by transferring a design by *pouncing* – tapping charcoal through a pricked drawing onto the gesso. He would build up the composition with thin layers of paint and washes. Modelling and detail is done with *cross hatching* (crossed lines), *stippling* (light dabs and flecks of paint) and transparent glazes applied with fine brushes. Early medieval tempera paintings were modelled from a green earth ground, which formed the shadows, to the paler highlights, often against a gold leaf ground with punched decoration as in the painting of the *Madonna* by Duccio. Drapery was treated in a similar way.

Fresco

Fresco (Italian 'fresh') is a wall-painting technique in which powdered pigments are mixed in water and applied to a wet lime-plaster ground. The colours fuse with the plaster, forming a permanent waterproof surface. Best suited to a warm climate, it was widely used in Italian medieval and Renaissance painting, but it was also used during Classical Roman times, for instance at Pompeii. Most Italian fresco painters used the same technique: a charcoal design was drawn onto the fresh lime-plaster, the main outlines were cut into the surface and the lines of the design were strengthened with *sinopia* (red ochre). In the 16th century a *cartoon* (drawing) was used to transfer the design by pouncing onto the plaster. Next, the *intonaco* (a layer of fine plaster) was applied in small sections over the rough plaster and the design was pounced onto the wet plaster again. These sections are called *giornate* (from Italian *giorno*, day) since each represents the area of fresh (that is, wet) plaster that the painter can paint in one day; this can be seen in Giotto's (see p. 520) fresco of the mourning of Christ in Padua, where the divisions of each day's plaster are visible around the angels. Mainly natural pigments were used, and the modelling techniques are similar to those used in tempera painting. Finally, finishing touches might be made on the dry plaster in *secco* (dry), usually an egg tempera. Mistakes were corrected with difficulty, as this usually involved removing the area of plaster and reapplying a fresh layer. The painter needed to be assured and to work in broad strokes.

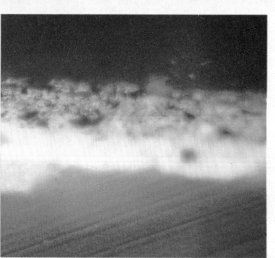

Lorenzo Monaco's *Coronation of the Virgin* (1430). The cross-section illustrates the modelling techniques used in medieval painting. The layers of white, cream and tan paint overlaid by a reddish-brown translucent glaze (with some black particles) form the brown shadow of the sleeve of the right-hand angel. Tempera technique is still in use today: the American painter Andrew Wyeth (1917–) and the British painter David Tindle (1932–) are major exponents. (Gambier-Parry Collection, Courtauld Institute Galleries, London)

Dürer's *Hands of an Apostle* (1508), a study for the Heller altarpiece, is a brush drawing on blue paper. (The Albertina Collection/Austrian Embassy, London)

This is evident in Michelangelo's (see p. 528) Sistine Chapel frescos, where subtle and complicated transitions of colour and tone are achieved with remarkably broad strokes of colour.

Oil

Oil painting techniques were first widely used in 15th-century Netherlandish painting, above all by Jan van Eyck (see p. 526), who developed an oil technique which produced a highly refined glass-like finish. Sixteenth-century Venetian painters explored this medium with great success and it has been the most widely used technique since then.

Oil paint is based on a mixture of dry pigment and vegetable oil, commonly linseed, poppy or walnut oil. It is slow-drying, so the artist is able to make revisions and build up layers of colour. Canvas primed with white lead and linseed oil is most commonly used to paint on, although Netherlandish painters often painted on wood panel and copper.

The composition is outlined with charcoal or transferred from a squared drawing onto the ground. An underpaint is painted over this: the red ground favoured by Titian (see p. 529), the black ground used by Tintoretto (see p. 529) and the grey and umber wash laid on by Rubens (see p. 530), for instance, would determine the overall tonality of the painting. The composition is built up in layers of thicker or thinner paint. Over opaque paint a final translucent glaze might be applied, lending a luminosity to highlights or intensifying colours.

Variety in brushwork can have significant visual effect. Paint can be thickly applied with a loaded brush or palette knife, as in Van Gogh's paintings (see p.

544), but brushstrokes are imperceptible if paint is thinned to a runny consistency. Surface textures are achieved by *scumbling* (applying thin layers of lighter colours over darker underpainting), *stippling* (applying paint in light dabs) and *frottage* (taking a rubbing from a rough surface such as wood and applying paint on the resulting textured surface). The final surface is a wax or resin varnish.

Acrylic

Acrylic paint is manufactured from pigment bound in a synthetic resin, normally acrylic or PVA. It is a 20th-century development, initially used in wall painting. Acrylic is an opaque, water-soluble, quick-drying paint. The colour, unlike that of oil paint, does not alter with time, and it can be diluted to translucency if required. It has been used to great effect in the paintings of David Hockney (see p. 554).

Watercolour and gouache

Watercolour is made with pigment bound in a gum arabic medium. It was used as a paint in Egyptian and Oriental painting, although it was most fully explored by 18th- and 19th-century British landscape artists.

Watercolour is distinguished by its translucent quality; it is also extremely versatile. Hand-made paper is preferable as a ground. Over a preparatory sketch in pencil, pen and ink or chalk, the light ground and texture is exploited by overlaying with transparent washes, and by using uncoloured areas for highlights. Some watercolours are *monochrome* – painted only in one colour, such as *bistre* (soot brown) or *sepia* (ink from cuttle fish), for example Claude Lorraine's landscape sketches (see p. 531).

Gouache is a related technique, although the binding medium is glue, and white pigment is added to give it some opacity. Used by French painters since the 18th century, it is widely used in commercial illustration today.

Pastel

Pastels are sticks of pigment made by mixing powdered pigment with gum or resin binder. Pastels can be easily blended with the finger, resulting in soft contours which retain their freshness of colour. Rosalba Carriera (see p. 535) pioneered its use in Venice and Degas experimented by mixing it with turpentine or steam to achieve different effects (see p. 542). AB

One of two frescos painted by Botticelli (1445–1510) at the Villa Lemmi in Florence. It shows Venus leading the Graces with an offering for the young woman on the right. (Louvre, Paris/R.M.N.)

SEE ALSO

● PHOTOGRAPHY AND FILM p. 324
● ART TECHNIQUES 2: SCULPTURE AND PRINT-MAKING p. 502

Art Techniques 2: Sculpture and Printmaking

Images were first printed from engraved wooden blocks onto parchment some 3000 to 4000 years ago. In the West, the development of printing coincided with the invention of movable type in the 15th century. Since then, a great variety of different printing techniques has evolved. The enormous popularity of the print is explained by its reproductive character, which makes artistic images accessible to a wide market at a cheap price.

SEE ALSO

- PRINTING p. 322
- PHOTOGRAPHY AND FILM p. 324
- ART TECHNIQUES I: PAINTING AND DRAWING p. 500

The two main sculpture techniques are *carving* and *modelling*. The carved image is created by cutting unwanted material away from a block of hard material, usually stone or wood. Modelling, by contrast, involves manipulating some soft and yielding material such as clay, wax or plaster until the desired image is reached. Carving is the most ancient sculpture technique, but both were known in prehistoric times. Because modelling materials are basically soft, models are generally turned into a more lasting form, either by heating, as with clay, or by *casting* them in bronze or some other metal. The Egyptians cast bronze models over 3500 years ago.

Relief techniques

Relief techniques of print-making include woodcuts, wood engravings and linocuts, and are characterized by an image printed from the raised surface of a block.

Woodcuts were used as early as the 14th century for making cheap pilgrims' images and playing cards. The technique was extensively used by Dürer (see p. 527) and revived by the German Expressionists in the 20th century (see p. 547). The design is drawn onto the wood and cut away along the grain with gouges and

A wood engraving from Thomas Bewick's *History of Quadrupeds*, published in 1800. (The Mansell Collection)

knives, leaving only the raised lines of the image ready to be inked. The block is printed by laying paper onto the inked block and rubbing this with a spoon or, later, by a mechanical press to record the image.

Wood engraving, thought to have been invented by Thomas Bewick (1753–1828), differs from woodcutting in that normally a hard, fine-grained wood like maple or boxwood is cut into across its end grain, using a lozenge-shaped tool (a *burin*) similar to the sort used for engraving. The resulting image is usually much finer than a woodcut. Commonly used for fine book illustrations during the 19th century, it was also popular with illustrators such as Eric Ravilious during the 1920s.

Linocuts are made using the floor covering material linoleum, a cheap and easily carved surface that can be worked with gouges and knives similar to those used for woodcutting and engraving. Although it does not allow great subtlety of detail, it was favoured by artists in the 1920s, including Picasso (see p. 548).

Intaglio techniques

Intaglio techniques differ from relief techniques since the image is printed from lines cut into a metal plate, either with metal engraving tools, or by acid biting into the exposed areas of the plate.

Engraving techniques stem originally from those used in gem carving and in the decoration of armour. The 15th-century Italian *niello* or line engraving technique was used by many Italian and German Renaissance artists for their prints. A zinc or copper plate is engraved with a sharp tool. The plate is then inked with a tacky ink and all the uncut surfaces wiped clean – leaving ink only in the recessed furrows. The print is then produced by passing the plate and a sheet of dampened paper through a press. The pressure forces the paper into the engraved lines, producing the raised lines characteristic of this technique.

Etching was used as a technique during the 17th and 18th centuries by artists such as Rembrandt (see p. 533), and revived in the late 19th century by Whistler (1834–1903). The design is etched onto a copper plate coated in a blackened acid-resistant material (the hard ground), using a steel needle, which exposes the metal. The plate is then immersed in a bath of acid, which bites into the exposed lines; these are characterized by blunt ends, rather than the tapered lines of engraving. To accentuate areas of light and shade or to add lines, parts of the plate are protected or 'stopped out' with a varnish and the plate is then re-immersed in the acid. Some lines might even be reinforced by engraving. The plate is then cleaned of all ground, inked, wiped clean and printed using the same method as for engraving.

Aquatint is commonly used to imitate the effect of watercolours and was probably developed by Jean-Baptiste le Prince (1734–84). A copper plate is coated with powdered resin. When it is immersed in an acid bath, small areas of copper between the particles of dust are exposed. The acid biting into the copper produces a rough

Picasso's etching on zinc, *The Frugal Repast* (1904), illustrates the fine detail that can be achieved with this technique. (Explorer)

granular surface, and it is this roughness that holds the ink. In successive immersions areas not protected by a varnish are bitten into further, producing the tonal effects. The design can be drawn or etched onto the plate before the ground is laid, or the stopping out can be done without any drawing for guidance.

Mezzotint was a very popular technique during the 18th and 19th centuries for reproductions after oil paintings. It was probably invented in 1642 by Ludwig von Siegen (1609–76), and developed by Prince Rupert of Bavaria. The ground is prepared by passing a serrated rocker over the metal, leaving a varying number of indentations in which ink will collect and produce the tonal values. The tone engraving is then achieved by scraping away for darker tones and burnishing for highlights.

Planographic methods

Planographic techniques are those characterized by surface-printing methods.

Lithography – the term literally means 'stone drawing' – depends upon the mutual incompatibility of water and grease. A limestone slab several centimetres thick (a grained alloy plate is now normally used) is either polished to a smooth surface, or given a texture or 'tooth'. The design is drawn or painted onto the stone with a greasy material such as crayon or lithographic ink. A solution of nitric acid and gum arabic is applied to the unmarked areas, which repels the lithographic ink wiped onto the surface of the dampened stone before printing. Paper is then laid onto the inked stone and passed through a press. The drawn areas attract the ink, while the moist surfaces repel it. The method was used by Honoré Daumier (see p. 541) for his satirical cartoons and by Toulouse-Lautrec (1864–1901) for posters. Since the mid-19th century, many technical developments have aided the expansion of lithographic methods for commercial use, particularly *photolithography* and *offset lithography* (see p. 322).

Screen printing was developed in the 20th century. A screen of silk or gauze is tautly stretched over a wooden or metal frame. The design is applied to the screen in the form of a stencil so that areas not to be coloured are blocked out. Ink is wiped across the screen with a wiper (or *squeegee*) and the ink is pushed through the mesh onto the paper. The development of photo-screen printing offered Pop artists such as Andy Warhol and Robert Rauschenberg a suitable modern technique for their images (see p. 554).

Sculpture carving techniques

Stone carving can be done from granite, limestone, sandstone, alabaster and a variety of marbles. The basic set of tools employed by the stone carver includes the mallet and point or punch, for knocking off chips to give a rough shape, and a square hammer (*boucharde*) to work the surfaces roughly; they are then refined with a series of flat, bull-nosed and tooth or claw chisels. For undercutting or defining hair and recessions a drill is used. Lastly, surfaces are finished by polishing with rasps and rifflers (files) and abrasives.

Wood carving frequently reflects the local availability of a certain species of wood: for instance, limewood, commonly used by Renaissance German sculptors, was cheap and abundant – while in England oak was more frequently carved. Sculpture and reliefs are carved from the heartwood of the tree and in the direction of the grain. The exception is in the use of extremely fine-grained fruit woods such as boxwood, where the sculptor can carve in any direction. The basic tools are similar to the stone carver's but lighter and sharper. In Europe wooden and stone sculpture would originally have been polychromed, providing a protective surface. In the 20th century a natural oiled or varnished surface is preferred, and enhances the grain and colour of the wood.

Other materials that are commonly carved for small-scale sculpture are ivory, amber, shells and semi-precious stones.

Modelling techniques

Materials such as clay, wax and plaster are employed both in the preparatory stages of sculpture in other media and as finished modelled sculpture.

Depending on the materials, normally a three-dimensional shape is built up around an *armature* (framework) in metal or wood, which provides an inner support and surface for working. In the case of a relief, this is provided by a board studded with nail heads that act as a key for the material. The material is modelled with the fingers, with knives used for cutting the mass and scrapers for smoothing the surfaces. Models in clay are fired, while wax or plaster models are left in their raw state. *Maquettes* (models) are often used by carvers (e.g. Henry Moore, 1898–1986) as a means of working out the design of a sculpture before carving. Often these are scaled up by a mechanical pointing machine for transfer to stone or wood.

Casting techniques

The two principal casting techniques – the lost-wax process and sand casting – have been employed by bronze casters for thousands of years. Bronze, a copper and tin alloy, is the main metal cast in these ways, although brass may also be used.

The lost-wax process involves building up a wax layer, to the thickness of the eventual bronze, around a solid core model made from plaster and *grog* (previously fired clay ground up and mixed with fresh clay). Wax rods, termed *risers* and *runners*, are fixed at angles to the model and when the wax has burnt away these act as channels for the escaping gases and for the molten bronze. The model is covered in plaster with the rods projecting and meeting in a funnel-shaped depression at the base. This is then placed, inverted, in an oven heated to around 650 °C (1200 °F). This causes the core to harden and the wax to burn away, forming a thin cavity into which the molten bronze is poured through the funnel. Once the bronze has cooled down, the plaster investment is broken off, and the plaster core chipped out. The surface of the metal is then *chased* (polished and chiselled) and a final *patina* (a chemical colouring) applied as a decorative enhancement of the metal, which is then sealed with lacquer.

Sand casting involves making a mould of a model using special casting sand, which will retain a detailed impression even when inverted. The dampened sand is placed in two rectangular metal frames. The mould is made by packing round each half of the mould in turn with the sand. Each frame then contains half a mould. These *piece-moulds* are then matched exactly and clamped together to form a *flask*. Channels are cut into the sand as vents and gates, with a wider channel for the pouring end. A cavity for the molten metal is created by suspending an inner sand core within the metal, held in place with metal rods. The whole is hardened in an oven. Molten metal is then poured in, and once cooled the mould is broken away and the core chipped out. The characteristic raised lines left by the piece mould were often used to decorative advantage (as in Chinese bronzes; see p. 514) but more often filed off when the metal surface was chased.

Modern sculpture techniques include welding and construction, which borrow methods from industrial metalworking methods.   AB

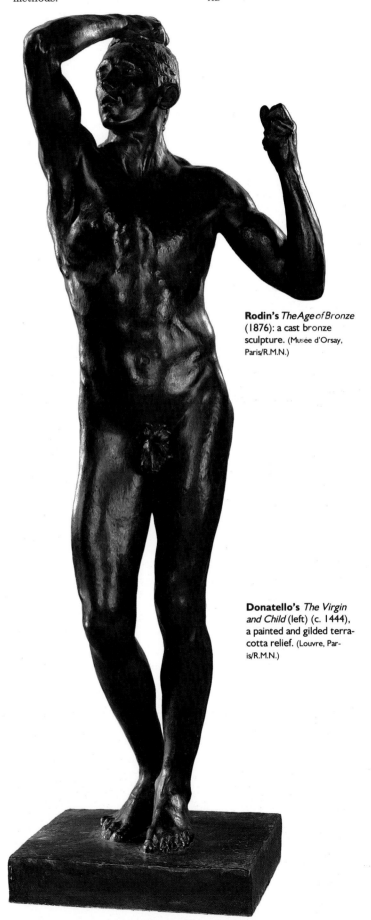

Rodin's *The Age of Bronze* (1876): a cast bronze sculpture. (Musée d'Orsay, Paris/R.M.N.)

Donatello's *The Virgin and Child* (left) (c. 1444), a painted and gilded terracotta relief. (Louvre, Paris/R.M.N.)

Prehistoric Art

The world's most ancient works of art date from 30 000 BC. This is vastly earlier than the first written records and means that the greater part of art history is, in fact, prehistoric. It was during the prehistoric period that virtually all the major artistic media evolved, including drawing, painting, sculpture, ceramics and, arguably, architecture.

The study of prehistoric art differs from traditional art history in two fundamental ways. Firstly, there is little opportunity to identify individual artists – instead, works of art are discussed with reference to archaeological evidence. Secondly, prehistoric art is usually the art of relatively simple, non-urban societies.

Humans 'invented' art independently in various regions around the world. There are examples of ancient rock art in Africa, particularly in the Sahara, and there is recent evidence that the tradition of rock art in Australia dates from at least 17 000 BC. Pottery was invented during the prehistory of the Near East in the 7th millennium BC. However, the Palaeolithic (Old Stone Age) art of Europe is the earliest and most splendid prehistoric art, while the traditions that succeeded it until the Roman conquests are the most intensively researched in the world.

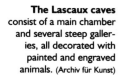

The Lascaux caves consist of a main chamber and several steep galleries, all decorated with painted and engraved animals. (Archiv für Kunst)

Palaeolithic sculpture

Body painting is probably the most ancient of visual arts, but sculpture is the first for which evidence has survived. From 30 000 BC hunters and gatherers shaped figurines out of clay, bone, stone, wood and ivory. These figurines, which have been found scattered over a wide area from Spain to Siberia, depict both animals – such as bears and horses – and humans. Some, typified by the famous 'Venus' of Willendorf in Austria, portray women with exaggerated breasts and buttocks, and have been linked to a supposed fertility cult. Others, such as the female head from Brassempouy, France, are more elegant and naturalistic. Tools, particularly spear-throwers, were also decorated by this sculpture-in-the-round technique. However, decorated tools are generally much later than the early figurines and are closely related to cave art.

Cave art

Painting, engraving and relief sculpture on the walls of caves began later than figurine sculpture, and flourished soon after 16 000 BC. Cave art is found mostly in southern France and northeastern Spain, sometimes deep within cave systems, and sometimes near cave entrances or in shallow rock shelters.

The hunters who created cave art were inspired by the animals around them, particularly by large mammals such as deer, horses, wild cattle, bison, woolly rhinoceroses and mammoths. They drew a few human and semi-human figures, but never trees or plants or any landscape.

One of the mysteries of cave art is that although 'panels' of rock often contain many images of animals, these are rarely arranged in compositions. Often the animals are drawn to different scales, or are even made to overlap one another. Despite this, many galleries are very impressive, including those at Lascaux, France, which show leaping and galloping wild cattle and horses.

Since cave art began to be accepted as Palaeolithic in the late 19th century, it has been interpreted in many ways. An early theory claimed that many of the animals were shown dead or wounded in order to bring luck in hunting. Other ideas were that the animals illustrated tribal mythologies or clan totems, or that they marked out sacred areas used for initiation or fertility rites. More recently it has been noticed that certain animals tend to occur together, such as horses with bison, or in specific parts of the caves. One controversial theory interprets all the images within each cave, together with the non-representational marks that sometimes accompany them, as part of an elaborate system of opposed symbols centred around the male/female relationship. A more widely accepted idea is that specially decorated caves helped to promote group identity among hunters who depended upon each other for survival.

Early pottery

In the Neolithic (New Stone Age) period, farming and settled village life spread across Europe (c. 6500–4000 BC). This

CYCLADIC SCULPTURE

Between 3000 and 2000 BC some of the most accomplished prehistoric European sculpture was created on the Cyclades islands of the Aegean. An early tradition of grinding the local translucent marble into simple schematic idols was refined to produce striking figurines up to 1.5 m (5 ft) long.

The most famous type of figurine is a naked, slender, usually female figure with her arms folded above her waist. The elegance and simplicity of such figures attract the modern eye; however, it should be remembered that the faces, now featureless except for a prominent nose, may originally have been painted.

The folded-arm figurines were relatively easy to manufacture as the limbs were often differentiated from the body only by simple incisions. There is a more elaborate group of figurines in which the limbs are fully rounded and the pose much more relaxed (some are even seated). The most remarkable of these portray musicians with harps and flutes, while a rare grouped example depicts two men whose linked arms support a smaller figure.

A Cycladic figurine: the face may originally have been painted. (National Museum, Athens/Scala)

A Celtic bronze helmet overlaid with decorative hoops. The top and bottom hoops are of open iron with enamel inlay and between them is a gilded bronze hoop. (Ancient Art and Architecture Collection)

was elaborated in the later temples, and the blocks of stone were carefully shaped to create impressive façades. Beautifully balanced spiral carvings still decorate some temples, and many of the walls were originally covered with painted plaster. At the complex temple of Tarxien there are animal friezes and the surviving half of a monumental sculpture depicting a hugely corpulent deity. This fat deity is also portrayed in smaller works, and these provide an interesting contrast to the elegant contemporary sculpture of the Cyclades (see box).

Bronze and Iron Age

During later European prehistory, despite advances in pottery and architecture, the most exciting artistic innovations arose from the development of metalwork. In the 2nd millennium BC in Eastern Europe, early cast bronze weapons and jewellery were delicately engraved with curvilinear (curved-line) designs. Similar decoration appears on Scandinavian metalwork: a remarkable ritual object found at Trundholm, Denmark, consists of a cast bronze horse pulling an engraved gold-covered sun symbol.

During the earlier 1st millennium BC many more bronze figures were cast, notably in Scandinavia, central Europe and Sardinia. Engraving remained common, but the beating or embossing of metalwork grew in importance. Embossed friezes on the bronze 'buckets' or *situlae* of northern Italy and Slovenia (c. 600–350 BC) illustrate religious processions and other lively scenes.

Situla art was partly inspired by the art of the Near East (see p. 506) and Greece (see p. 508). This is also true of the last great prehistoric tradition, that of the Celts (see p. 374). However, even the earliest Celtic art (c. 450 BC) subverted the influence of the civilizations to the east and attempted to integrate abstract patterns and representational images. The Celts decorated weapons, vessels and pieces of jewellery in such a fluid style that it is often impossible to separate the stylized Celtic heads and animals from the surrounding plant-like ornament. It is the use of these supple motifs within a wonderfully balanced overall design that characterizes the finest Celtic art.   RJa

encouraged both the use of pottery and the development of architecture.

Shaped and decorated vessels were produced almost everywhere, but the most prolific and inventive potters lived in Eastern Europe. The Vinca culture of Serbia produced thousands of fired-clay figurines, including some dramatically stylized heads found at Predionica, Serbia. Related cultures manufactured pots shaped like human figures, animals or even houses. Eastern Neolithic pottery was often painted: the designs of the Cucuteni culture of Romania employed both powerful swirls and intricate geometric patterns.

Houses, tombs and temples

Houses in Neolithic Europe varied in design from small mud-brick buildings in the southern Balkans to timber long houses in central and western Europe. The well-preserved village of Skara Brae (c. 3000 BC) in the Orkneys, Scotland, consists of drystone houses equipped with stone furniture (see illustration, p. 362). Stone was also used to erect massive walls and bastions around the town of Los Millares, Spain, which dates from the same period. However, the most impressive Neolithic buildings are the *megalithic* ('large-stone') monuments of the Atlantic seaboard (see illustration, p. 363).

The passage grave of Newgrange in Ireland (c. 3200 BC) is a particularly brilliant example of megalithic design. The passage leading to the tomb chamber was carefully constructed to allow sunrays to illuminate the chamber at midwinter. The

huge cairn covering the chamber is ringed by kerbstones carved with spirals and other patterns, similar to those found on many tombs in Ireland, Brittany and Spain.

Some of the hundreds of stone circles erected in Britain and Ireland also contain astronomical alignments, including the famous circle at Stonehenge. The design of Stonehenge was remarkably ambitious in its use of dressed stone and lintels balanced on uprights, but perhaps the most sophisticated Neolithic architecture developed on Malta.

The Maltese temples (c. 3600–2500 BC) were built of large blocks of stone to a ground plan that was originally shaped rather like a three-leaf clover. This design

A bronze situla (left) (c. 600–350 BC) with embossed friezes, found in Slovenia. (National Museum, Ljubljana/Scala)

SEE ALSO

- EARLY MAMMALS p. 140
- PHYSICAL EVOLUTION (HUMAN) p. 200
- HUMAN PREHISTORY p. 362
- THE CELTS p. 374

The Art of the Ancient Near East and Egypt

Early civilizations flourished along the great river valleys of the Nile in Egypt, and the Tigris and Euphrates from Anatolia (present-day Turkey), through Syria into Mesopotamia (present-day Iraq). The rivers linked these regions in an extensive trade network that also encompassed Persia (present-day Iran) to the east, but variations in climate, geography, natural resources and population resulted in corresponding variations in artistic traditions.

Persepolis: (right) the capital of the Achaemenid rulers of Persia (6th–4th centuries BC). (Keystone Press Agency)

Mesopotamia depended on imports for the raw materials it lacked, and exported manufactured goods that influenced the art of Persia, Syria-Palestine and Anatolia. Ancient Near Eastern art varied according to the degree of Mesopotamian cultural dominance, and much of it was politically motivated. In contrast the conventions of Egyptian art remained remarkably consistent throughout the dynastic period. Egyptian artists created sculptures in order to represent the things that they wanted to enjoy after death.

Mesopotamia

Monumental sculpture appeared in the Uruk period (c. 3500–3000 BC) and is typified by the life-size Warka head, which displays a classical serenity. The Mesopotamians preferred relief carving, however: lively hunting and battle scenes decorate Assyrian reliefs of the 9th–7th centuries BC. Thousands of miniature reliefs have survived on small cylinder-shaped seals of stone that were used from

A Phoenician ivory found at the Assyrian capital Nimrud (9th century BC). (Ancient Art and Architecture Collection)

c. 3500 for more than 3000 years. Particularly fine examples, many of lapis lazuli, were found in the Royal Graves at Ur (c. 2600 BC) along with metalwork, jewellery, and mosaic panels inlaid with shell and stone.

Mud-brick was the principal building material. In the Ubaid period (5th millennium BC) huge circular buildings occur alongside T-shaped units. In the Uruk period T-shaped temples 80 m (260 ft) long, with elaborately niched and buttressed façades, display a monumentality only paralleled by *ziggurats* (temple towers) constructed from the late 3rd millennium BC onwards, and by palaces built by the Assyrians and Babylonians around huge courtyards in the first half of the first millennium BC.

Ancient Persia

Susa in southwest Persia developed an urban civilization contemporary with that of Uruk, but the cultural diversity of other sites reflects their geographical location in isolated valleys. As a result many distinctive pottery styles flourished, some of them beautifully painted with stylized animal designs. Metalwork excelled at all periods and the life-size, cast-bronze statue of Queen Napirasu (13th century BC) is a technical masterpiece. The Luristan bronzes of the late 2nd and early 1st millennium BC display bizarre combinations of lions, birds and humans.

The Achaemenid rulers of the 6th–4th centuries BC sought to unite their empire culturally and created an imperial style that drew on the traditions and craftsmen of the whole ancient Near East and Egypt. This style is best seen at their capital, Persepolis, with its halls of tall columns and reliefs depicting tribute-bearers from all parts of the empire.

Syria-Palestine

Carved stone masks, plastered human skulls and votive figures of gypsum plaster over a framework of reeds have been found at many sites of the 8th millennium BC, notably at Jericho, where a huge, circular tower was built of stone. Objects and paintings from the palaces at Mari and Ebla, 3rd–2nd millennium, incorporate Mesopotamian and Anatolian features, but Egyptian and Aegean motifs adorn the jewellery and ceremonial weapons of the coastal cities of Byblos and Ugarit.

In the 1st millennium BC Phoenician bowls and ivory carving were widely traded and, according to the Bible, Hiram of Tyre was employed to cast metal objects for Solomon's Temple at Jerusalem.

Anatolia

Extraordinary scenes – with vultures, bull-dances, textile patterns, and what might be a landscape with a volcano erupting – decorated shrines from the 6th-millennium BC at Çatal Hüyük in central Anatolia. The site has also produced numerous stone and clay figurines of women, youths and leopards.

Combinations of metals characterize Anatolian metalwork, notably the figure of a stag with huge, stylized horns, made of bronze inlaid with electrum, from Alaca Hüyük (c. 2300 BC). The extraordinary inlaid furniture in the Tomb of Midas at Gordion reflects, in wood, the same taste for combining colours and textures.

The massive city walls of the Hittite capital at Bŏgazköy and the foundations of its temples survive, as does a rock-cut shrine with reliefs depicting processions of deities. The monumental quality of Hittite art continued into the 1st millennium BC at Carchemish and other sites along the Syrian frontier, where palaces with columned porticoes were decorated with lively reliefs. These and gateway figures of lions inspired the Assyrians.

Egypt

Egyptian artists were concerned more

Akhenaton and Nefertiti (c. 1360–1330 BC). Under the reign of Akhenaton artists were able to create more naturalistic, less stylized works. (Louvre, Paris/Explorer)

An Egyptian glazed hippopotamus (Middle Kingdom, c. 1900 BC). (Art History Museum, Vienna/Austrian Embassy, London)

with religious ritual than with decorative effect or aesthetic achievements. They created sculptures and paintings primarily in order to represent the things that they wanted to continue to enjoy after death. Because they wanted to reproduce things in their entirety rather than simply as they appeared from one viewpoint, they often depicted elements of objects that would not usually be visible. The conventions of Egyptian art remained remarkably consistent throughout the dynastic period. Only in the reign of Akhenaton – the Amarna period (c. 1360–1330 BC) – were artists permitted to depict scenes with any real freedom and innovation.

The Egyptians were skilled in many forms of painting, from illuminated papyri to sketches on chips of rock or pottery. Their greatest achievements, however, were in the decoration of the walls of tombs, such as those in the Valley of the Kings at Thebes. The rock or brick surface was prepared with a smooth layer of plaster, and the lines of the paintings were executed by a skilled 'outline scribe', employing a grid of red lines in order to maintain the convention of 18 fists for the height of each human figure. Teams of artists would then paint the designs with the appropriate colours.

Egyptian sculptures dating from around 3000 BC took the form of ceremonial palettes and maceheads. Throughout the dynastic period Egyptian sculpture was enormously varied, both in materials and subject matter, ranging from the series of delicately carved wooden panels decorating the tomb of Hesyre (c. 2620 BC) at Saqqara to the huge statues of Amenophis III (c. 1370 BC) at Western Thebes, known as the Colossi of Memnon.

The many masterpieces of life-size statuary include a magnificent diorite seated figure of the 4th-dynasty pharaoh Chephren (c. 2500 BC) and a standing wooden figure of the 5th-dynasty priest Ka-aper (known as the Sheikh el-Beled), both from the necropolis at Giza. The contents of the tomb of the Pharaoh Tutankhamun, discovered in 1922, give some idea of the wide range of types of statue that would have been placed in a royal tomb.

The first houses and shrines in Egypt were made of organic materials, often bonded together with mud. Out of the earliest Predynastic graves (shallow pits covered with sand) developed the *mastaba* tomb, the forerunner of the pyramid, which consisted of a pit or maze of corridors covered by a mud-brick superstructure. *Mastaba* tombs of members of the earliest Egyptian royal families have been excavated at Saqqara and Abydos.

In the time of Djoser (c. 2620 BC) the earliest pyramid – the Step Pyramid – was built at Saqqara by the first known architect, Imhotep. From the reign of Djoser until the end of the Middle Kingdom virtually every pharaoh was buried in a pyramid complex, usually of stone. The 4th-dynasty Great Pyramids at Giza are the largest and best preserved. During the pyramid age, the pharaoh's wealthier sub-

Ramses II: a stone figure from the 19th dynasty (1270 BC), found at Thebes.

jects continued to be buried in *mastaba* tombs and rock tombs.

In the 16th century BC, the pharaohs and their families began to be interred in secret burial chambers in Western Thebes (the Valley of the Kings), probably in an attempt to prevent plundering of their grave goods. These New Kingdom royal tombs consisted of long corridors with

SEE ALSO

- THE ANCIENT NEAR EAST (HISTORY) p. 364
- ANCIENT EGYPT (HISTORY) p. 366
- RELIGIONS OF THE ANCIENT NEAR EAST p. 460
- THE MAKING OF MYTHS p. 612

painted walls that showed mythological scenes.

Secular buildings throughout Egyptian history were built mainly of mud brick, while virtually all Egyptian temples were constructed of stone. The vast Temple of Amun at Karnak, the core of which dates to the New Kingdom, contains most of the basic elements of the Egyptian temple, including a *hypostyle* (columned) hall with a huge forest of columns covering an area of 6000 m² (7200 sq yd). By the Ptolemaic period (from 305 BC) temple reliefs had become formulaic and uninspired. DC/IS

A rare Egyptian sculpture in green stone of a lion falling on a calf (Late Period, c. 500 BC). (Art History Museum, Vienna/Austrian Embassy, London)

Greek and Roman Art

The arts of Greece and Rome are characterized by a sense of proportion, harmony and balance. Since the Renaissance, Classical decoration, whether ornate or simple, has frequently provided architects with a fruitful source of ideas, and Classical imagery has enriched the work of poets, painters and sculptors. In general, Classical form has exerted a largely civilizing influence over the past two and a half millennia.

SEE ALSO

- ARCHAIC AND CLASSICAL GREECE p. 370
- ALEXANDER THE GREAT AND THE HELLENISTIC AGE p. 372
- ROMAN HISTORY pp. 376–81
- PRIMAL RELIGIONS: ANCIENT EUROPE p. 462
- CLASSICAL LITERATURE p. 614

This influence has been achieved in part by the surviving architecture, sculpture and ceramics (which have been surveyed, collected and catalogued with mixed success since the 18th century), and in part by the writings of ancient Roman scholars. Among these scholars were Vitruvius (1st century BC), whose writings on architecture inspired Palladio (see pp. 528–9) in the 16th century; and Philostratus (?2nd/3rd century AD), to whom Mantegna and Rubens looked for their knowledge of the lost works of the Greek painters Apelles and Zeuxis.

The concentration on what has survived, and the elevation of some of it to the first rank of artistic excellence in modern eyes, have tended to obscure the fact that we now possess very little of what ancient Greeks and Romans might have considered to be artistically important. Although today even fragments of Greek pots, for example, are highly valued, the Greeks and Romans themselves were more materialistic, and tended rather to appreciate highly wrought works in gold and silver. Since articles of precious metal were the first to be seized or melted down in times of war or hardship, such works have virtually all vanished, but contemporary accounts of shrines and temples, as well as of the houses of rich individuals, speak of great amounts of sculpture and vases made of gold and silver, and it was in these media that eminent craftsmen preferred to work.

The Archaic period

What remains of Archaic Greek art (of the 6th and earlier 5th centuries BC) consists mostly of marble and pottery, with a little bronze. Luxury arts are represented by seals cut in semiprecious stones, jewellery, and coins. Apart from the silver ox at Delphi, perhaps the most impressive surviving object of the period is the huge (1.64 m / 5 ft 5 in high) Vix crater (a wine-mixing bowl). The figurine of a woman on the lid and the warriors on the frieze on the neck display the famous 'archaic smile' – Lucian's 'holy and forgetful' smile – that characterized much Archaic sculpture well into the 5th century. We are used to seeing it on the anonymous marble *kouroi* (youths) and *korai* (maidens) that have survived in considerable numbers, or on the painted decoration of archaic Greek pottery.

If, however, we consider the artefacts thought worthy of note by contemporaries, we get a rather different picture. One of the most sought-after artists in the 6th century was Theodore of Samos. He made a gold wine crater and a vine set with jewels for the bedroom of Darius, the king of Persia. He made the ring of the tyrant Polycrates, and a silver bowl that was among the gifts sent by Croesus, king of Lydia, to Delphi. Other gifts included a statue of a woman in gold, 1.8 m (6 ft) high. This object may have been of solid gold, but it was more usual for temple sculpture to be of wood or marble covered with gold sheathing. Thus a statue of Apollo at Sparta was considered to be unfinished until it was gilded. A statue stolen by a Persian from Delos in 490 is said to have been covered with gold, and the same is true of one of the earliest statues carved in Greek marble presented by an Egyptian pharaoh to a temple at Lindos in the mid-6th century BC. The practice seems to have had its origins in the Near East, and continues today in the modern Greek custom of covering icons with precious metal.

Reconstruction of the Athena Parthenos, the huge gold and ivory statue by Phidias (5th century BC) that once adorned the Parthenon.
(Royal Ontario Musem)

Greek libation bowl (detail) from c. 400 BC, found in a tomb at Thrace (modern Bulgaria). The bowl is made of silver, with gold-figure ornament showing a chariot race. This effect was evoked by the artisans who decorated Athenian pottery.
(Michael Vickers)

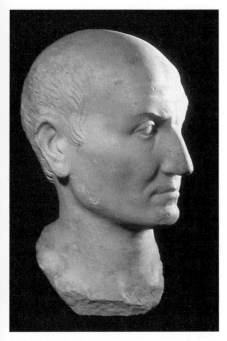

A **Roman portrait bust** from the 1st century BC. In contrast to the idealized portraits of the Greeks, the Romans preferred realistic depictions of individual personalities. (Vienna Classical Art Collection/Austrian Embassy, London)

THE CLASSICAL ORDERS OF ARCHITECTURE

Corinthian
(from the Portico of Hadrian, Athens)

Ionic
(from the Erechtheum on the Athenian Acropolis)

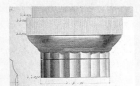

Doric
(from the Parthenon, Athens)

The differences between the 'Orders' of Classical architecture can most clearly be seen in the capitals at the tops of pillars. In buildings employing all three orders, Doric was used for the lowest level, Ionic for the middle, and Corinthian at the top. These illustrations are from Stuart and Revett's great 18th-century work on Classical architecture. (Ashmolean Museum, Oxford)

The Classical period

In the Classical period (5th and 4th centuries BC) there is again a marked discrepancy between what there is and what we know there was. The marble sculpture that once adorned the Parthenon in Athens (see illustration, p. 370) is rightly regarded as exemplifying the Classical ideal, but it is frequently forgotten that it only cost about 4% of the total cost of the building, and that 50% went on Phidias' gold and ivory cult-figure of Athena Parthenos. More than 10 m (33 ft) high, and incorporating gold worth some $20 million at today's prices, this and Phidias' other great masterpiece, the Zeus at Olympia, are what the Greeks would have considered to be the greatest works of their time. The Zeus was still being tended by Phidias' descendants in the 2nd century AD, but was stripped of its precious metal by the first Christian emperor, Constantine, and its remains taken to Constantinople, where they were destroyed by fire in the 5th century. However, the image of a majestic seated and bearded deity survived, and was adopted by Byzantine Greek artists as the model for Christ Pantocrator (Christ had hitherto been shown beardless), thus providing the basis for a potent image that has lasted until today.

Painted pottery appears prominently in today's picture of Classical Greece, but its role in antiquity is currently being reassessed. Most of it comes from the graves of rich Etruscans, who seem to have had the pots as substitutes for silver table vessels. Black and red pottery evokes the appearance of vases of patinated ('oxidized') silver decorated with gold-figure ornament. The imagery preserves something of the imagery on the few pieces of Classical plate that have escaped the melting pot. Of the major Classical paintings, nothing survives except awestruck contemporary accounts of the ability of the greatest painters to mimic nature. Classical paintings presented an idealized vision of the past, retold in the light of the Greeks' recent victories over the Persians. Allegory in art was another major Greek contribution.

The Hellenistic period

Alexander the Great's conquests (which included the capture of 4680 tons of gold and silver from the Persians) led to an emphasis on the aggrandizement of the ruler, rather than that of the city-state. There was even a plan to carve the Athos peninsula (some 32 km / 20 mi long) in the shape of a reclining Alexander. Alexandria in Egypt, Antioch in Syria, Pergamon in western Asia Minor (modern Turkey) were major artistic centres. The Great Altar of Zeus from Pergamon (now in Berlin) gives us some idea of Hellenistic splendour. The 'Tazza Farnese' (now in Naples) is one of the few pieces of court art of the period to have survived. The red mould-made pottery reflects the use of gold vessels on the tables of the rich.

Roman art and architecture

Rome was the successor to all of this. Republican simplicity gave way to the flamboyant luxury of the Caesars, but once more we only have the husks of a few great buildings, which would once have been covered with exotic marbles and rich mosaics. The frescoes and mosaics from Pompeii and

Herculaneum are but a pale reflection. Sculptors were commissioned to make portraits of the emperor that would be set up throughout the Empire, and to decorate public monuments such as Trajan's Column or the Arch of Constantine with idealized renditions of imperial triumphs and expressions of official propaganda. Occasional finds, such as the Hildesheim Treasure, give us an idea of the great artistry that went into the production of gold and silver plate. Glass has survived in some quantity, but it was rarely a luxury item, and pottery never was. Arretine pottery does, however, preserve something of the appearance of lost work in gold.

The ordinary inhabitants of the great cities of the Empire, such as Rome, Milan and Trier, might share in the imperial splendour in their great public buildings. Temples, market places, assembly halls (basilicas), amphitheatres and circuses were built on a large scale, frequently incorporating arches, vaults and domes in their construction. The applied use of the Classical architectural 'Orders', however, served to humanize them and to clothe them with dignity.   MV

Allegory of Africa, a mosaic from the Roman villa at Piazza Armerina, Sicily. (Scala)

The Treasury at Petra, an ancient city situated in a rocky defile in what is now Jordan. The capital of the Nabateans, an Arab people, Petra became part of the Roman Empire in AD 106. Its buildings and tombs – cut into solid rock – show strong Hellenistic and Roman influences. (Spectrum)

Islamic Art

Geographically Islamic art extends from Indonesia in the east to Morocco and Spain in the west. The word 'Islamic' reflects a culture and society united by Islam, but as artistic influences from Arabia (the birthplace of Islam) were minimal, Islam can in some ways also be seen as a catalyst for the development of existing Byzantine, Persian and later Indian styles that prevailed when the conquering Muslim armies arrived.

The Blue Mosque, Istanbul (right). (Explorer)

The faith and practice of Islam had a particular influence on architecture and calligraphy. Although by no means absolute, traditionally there is a ban on the representation of living figures in a religious context, which accounts for the often semi-abstract nature of Islamic ornament and for the virtual absence of sculpture. However, there is a fine tradition of miniature painting.

SEE ALSO

● THE RISE OF ISLAM p. 392
● INDIA TO THE COLONIAL AGE p. 384
● ISLAM (RELIGION) p. 478
● THE LITERATURE OF ASIA p. 616

The origins of the mosque

The early mosque was a simple building that was roughly based on the Prophet Muhammad's house at Medina, which had a *minbar* or pulpit added to it so that his voice could reach the increasingly big crowds that gathered around him. With the early Arab conquests (see p. 392) the congregational or Friday Mosque developed. This typically included a minaret, a tower from which the faithful are called to prayer. Reflecting its use as both a religious building and a popular debating hall and law court, the mosque took on a rectangular form like the Roman forum or the Greek agora.

The early mosques and the place of government of the Umayyad dynasty (661–750) – which ruled from Damascus – both reflected the increasing authority of the caliph ('deputy' of the Prophet) and of the state. The Umayyads drew on Byzantine and Persian tradition, recycling materials from churches and temples without inhibition, not only as a quarrying procedure but also to symbolize the triumph of Islam.

The Caliph al-Walid introduced the *mihrab* (recess indicating the direction of Mecca) when he had the Prophet's house at Medina rebuilt. At Basra its governor installed a screened enclosure (*maqsura*) between the mosque and his place of government so that he as imam (spiritual leader) would not have to pass among the people.

Some suggest that the most famous Umayyad building, the *Qubbat al-Sakhra* or Dome of the Rock in Jerusalem, was built to rival the Great Mosque at Mecca, and it has also been compared with earlier Christian shrines. Al-Walid's slightly later Great Mosque of Damascus already owes less to Christianity, despite the re-use of Byzantine materials.

Early Persian influence

Romano-Byzantine influences gradually gave way to Persian ones with the fall of the Umayyads and the establishment of the Abbasid capital at Baghdad in 762. Baghdad was to be the embodiment of the palace-city with the caliph's palace at the heart of a concentric circular design.

Further up the Tigris the palace complex of Samarra was built in 836. With its Persian and even Chinese and Indian influences, Samarra saw the coming of age of Islamic art. It was famed both for its wall decorations – employing geometric and vegetal (plant and flower) motifs capable of infinite repetition – as well as for its walled courtyards, rectangular pools and canals bordered with flowers.

The flowering of art in Spain

The Umayyad dynasty founded in Spain in 756 developed the complex decorative traditions of Andalusia with the help of Christian converts to Islam. The Great Mosque of Córdoba was enlarged by stages, developing to a point where pillars, arches and walls were almost entirely covered with carving. The marvels of the Great Mosque of Seville, begun in 1172, were to be tragically replaced by a 15th-century cathedral. The concentration of Muslim Spain's intricate stucco

CALLIGRAPHY AND MINIATURE PAINTING

Calligraphy is in one sense the most important of the Islamic arts, since Muslims believe that God revealed himself in an Arabic book, the Qur'an (Koran), whose words therefore have a sacred character. The traditional Islamic ban on the representation of living figures directed Muslim artists towards ornamental styles based on plants and flowers, geometrical shapes, and actual Arabic script. In architecture this was reflected in peculiarly Islamic styles such as the curvilinear *arabesque*. More important, however, was its influence on calligraphy, which became ornate and decorative, and by the 10th century, six classical scripts had emerged (see illustration, p. 478). Calligraphy in turn became closely associated with architecture, and – particularly in Spain and Persia – entire surfaces were often covered with verses from the Qur'an or with sayings of the Prophet.

An extension of calligraphy was book illustration. Initiated by the Mongol Il Khans in Persia, book illustration became the starting point of miniature painting. The miniature reached its peak under the Safavids in Persia and the Moguls in India.

An **Indian miniature** featuring a Mogul prince speaking to a dervish (an Islamic mystic). (Bodleian Library, Oxford/Archiv für Kunst).

tracery is best exemplified in the Alhambra palace at Granada.

The development of Cairo

Muslim urban planning evolved in the 10th century with the founding by the Fatimids of the city of Cairo, with its many gates and its new university mosque of Al-Azhar. Under the Fatimids originated the *muqarnas* or stalactite vault. Saladin, who succeeded the Fatimids, began construction of the citadel, one of Cairo's great medieval monuments. Persian influences were increasingly felt after the fall of Baghdad to the Mongols in 1258, when its artisans sought refuge in Egypt, and Egypt's most imposing mosques were built by the Mamluk dynasty in the 14th and 15th centuries.

A Persian golden age

Although in Persia the Arab-style mosque with pillar-supported roof was used to begin with, the Persian *kiosk* (an open-sided pavilion) based on the Zoroastrian fire temple (see p. 461) also appeared. The Great Mosque of Isfahan was initially of Arab-style baked bricks with cylindrical piers supporting a wooden roof. A *maqsura* and, later, a huge brick dome were also added. Further additions were continually made until the 15th century.

The Seljuk dynasty (1038–1194) excelled in the use of brick masonry and stucco. Sadly, many of the great Seljuk monuments in Iran were destroyed by the Mongols in the 13th century and by Tamerlane (Timur) in the 14th.

Under the early Safavids (1501–1732), painting, textiles, metalwork and ceramics flourished, but Safavid architecture only developed with the dynasty's move to Isfahan under Shah Abbas I (1588–1629). His Isfahan was one of the best examples of Islamic urban planning. He surrounded the *meidan* or square with covered bazaars, which were separated from a central market square by trees and water channels. The Shah's Mosque was built at

the south end of the *meidan*. The city's central boulevard, lined by gardens and pleasure pavilions, ended in a vast garden rising in a series of 12 terraces. Other notable buildings in Isfahan include the *Chehel Sutun* ('forty columns') – which was surrounded by formal gardens and four pavilions for the use of lovers – and the Mosque of Shaykh Lutfullah with its superb glazed tilework.

The evolution of an Ottoman style

Architecture in Turkey was at first almost wholly influenced by Persian and Arab styles. But after the Ottoman Turks conquered Constantinople in 1453, Turkish architects were faced by the challenge of converting the great Byzantine church, the Hagia Sophia (see p. 518), into a mosque. It was in this conversion that a distinctly Ottoman style evolved: the great central dome is visually reflected by a series of half domes, and slim minarets are placed at each corner; courtyards are integral to the whole plan and, unlike Persian styles, façades are only slightly decorated. This style was to be repeated throughout the Ottoman domains. The greatest of Ottoman architects and a near contemporary of Michelangelo was Koca Sinan (1490/1–1588).

The great buildings of India

The development of Islamic art and architecture in India began with the first Muslim invaders in the 12th century, but it only reached its peak with the monumental buildings of the Moguls, who ruled from 1526 (see p. 385). The Tomb of Humayun, the deserted city of Fatipur Sikri and the Taj Mahal and Pearl Mosque at Agra are but a few examples of a marvellous fusion of Central Asian, Ottoman and Safavid styles.

Modern Islamic art

While many Muslim countries have tried to preserve and even reconstruct traditional Islamic buildings, attempts have also been made to adapt modern styles to Islamic themes. Hasan Fathy's New Gourna village project in Upper Egypt in 1948 was an attempt at this, although the

buildings of his fellow Egyptian Abd al-Wahid Wakil are a better example of contemporary Islamic architecture. Saudi Arabia and other Gulf states tend increasingly to use Islamic themes to enhance the cultural identity of their modern mega-buildings.   TMo

---

CERAMICS, TEXTILES AND METALWORK

The minor arts of Islam reached maturity under the Abbasids. In pottery the emphasis was on decoration rather than shape. The best surviving metalwork is Iranian silver dishes and ewers, but the dearth of silver in the 11th century made bronze and brass popular. While Iranian metalwork focused on courtly scenes, the Mamluks preferred heraldic statements.

The most important textiles are silks and carpets, the former usually for ceremonial use. The earliest surviving carpets are 13th-century Anatolian. Later carpets are best represented by vivid Safavid scenes of the 16th century.

A Persian carpet (1539–40). (Victoria and Albert Museum/E.T. Archive)

The Great Mosque of Córdoba in Spain: the painted ceiling illustrates the geometric and plant motifs that lend themselves to infinite repetition.

(Ancient Art and Architecture Collection)

The Arts of Southern Asia, Australasia and Oceania

India's earliest civilization flourished in the Indus Valley between 2300–1700 BC and was centred on the cities of Harappa and Mohenjo-Daro. Its architecture is utilitarian, but some fine statues in sandstone and slate were produced. Little survives between the time of the Harappa civilization and that of the Mauryas (321–185 BC), during whose rule Persian and Greek influences are apparent, notably in architecture.

The Ellora caves, India (above right) – a series of temples excavated out of rock cliffs in the 5th–8th centuries AD. (INCAFO)

In the early centuries of the Christian era India's already ancient culture began to influence the culture of Southeast Asia. By the 2nd century AD two-way trade extended as far as Indonesia, and Buddhist monks brought Indian culture to the region.

In contrast, the arts of Australia and Oceania reflect their comparative isolation. Australia itself was divided from New Guinea in about 5000 BC and, although many of the peoples of Oceania had common origins, distinctive cultures evolved in the different island groups of the Pacific (see p. 389).

Architecture in Southern Asia

One of the most distinctive Buddhist architectural forms is the *stupa* or burial mound – originally earthen, but later built of unburnt brick covered with burnt brick and plaster. The Sanchi stupa (2nd century BC) is one of the finest, although the Abhayagiri Dagaba stupa (2nd century AD) in Sri Lanka is larger. Stupas became increasingly ornate, as seen in the elaborate Sarnath and Nalanda stupas, the former dating from the Guptas (AD 300–647). One of the greatest monuments of Buddhist architecture is at Borobudur in Java. It was probably built during the dynasty of the Indian King Sailendra, who created an empire in the Malay peninsula, Sumatra and Java during the mid-8th century AD.

Another distinctive Indian architectural form is the man-made cave, first carved out at the time of the Mauryas. Among the most famous caves are those at Ajanta, near Hyderabad (2nd century BC–7th century AD) and the nearby Ellora caves (5th–8th centuries AD). Many regard Ellora's Kailasanatha Temple as India's greatest single architectural work.

Temples

The earliest known free-standing temple in India is a small one with a Buddhist stupa at Bairat near Jaipur. Greek influ-

Borobudur, Java: several stupas can be seen behind the figure of Buddha. Built in the 8th century AD, Borobudur is one of the world's most magnificent Buddhist monuments, influenced by the Gupta art of India. The monument consists of a small hill surrounded by a succession of terraces, each terrace containing reliefs depicting a higher stage of enlightenment. (Ancient Art and Architecture Collection)

ence is apparent in the later Fire Temple at Jandial (50 BC–AD 65) near Taksasila. Under the Guptas small wooden temples proliferated, and the most famous of these is the temple of Deogahr (6th century AD) near Jhansi. Subsequently wood gave way to stone or brick in the building of temples. The northern Indian style tended to be a tower with rounded top and curvilinear outline, while the Southern Indians preferred a tower shaped as a rectangular, truncated pyramid.

Meanwhile, the Hindu tradition extended into Cambodia where the first of the great temple-cities (see p. 384) was built by Yasovarman (AD 889–910), although the famous city of Angkor, with its immense temple complex, was to be built in the 12th century. Burma's most famous temple, the temple of Ananda at Pagan, was first built by Indian Buddhist monks in the 11th–12th centuries and shows Bengali influence.

Sculpture in Southern Asia

After the decline of the Harappan civilization, it was not until that of the Mauryas that a revival of sculpture occurred. Under Ashoka, the great Mauryan king (272–232 BC), the capitals of columns were finely carved with figures such as tree spirits. Soon came the carvings on the railings and gateways of the great Buddhist sites at Bharhut, Gaya and Sanchi (all 1st–2nd centuries BC). The gateways of Sanchi are massively adorned with teeming human and animal life. Indian sculpture peaked with the temples of Khajurao (c. AD 1000), which are covered with graceful divinities and pairs of lovers.

The realistic Buddhas of the Gandhara school, which peaked in the 2nd century AD, owed much to increasing trade with the West, when Rome's prosperity was at its height. However, some of the finest bronze Buddhas in the style of the 2nd and 3rd centuries AD are found in Sri Lanka, and others as far away as Dong Duong in Vietnam. Stone carving was also important in Sri Lanka; in the 12th century AD the 15-metre (50-ft) long Parinirvana statue of the sleeping Buddha was chiselled. Until the 6th century AD the Buddhas of Thailand were heavily influenced by the art of the Indian Guptas. As in pre-Khmer Cambodia, Indian missionaries imported Hindu as well as Buddhist ritual art into Thailand.

Painting in Southern Asia

Surviving painting from pre-Mogul India is restricted to the murals of certain cave temples. Of these the Buddhist 'frescoes' in the Ajanta caves (see above) are among the most marvellous of any ancient civilization. Although painted for religious purposes, they are secular in style, and often erotic. A similar sensuality is found in the *apsaras* – figures of women – painted on Sri Lanka's great Sigiriya rock. With the spread of Islamic influence Indian painters turned to miniatures and book illustration in the Persian style (see box, p. 510).

Australia

When Europeans arrived in Australia its natives knew nothing of pottery or metalwork. However, in 1839 cave paintings representing men and women in a naturalistic way were discovered along the Glenelg River in southeast Australia. Similarly naturalistic paintings, the most famous of which depicts a man with a halo carrying a kangaroo, were found in northwest Australia.

Later, more abstract paintings were found in the Warramunga district of central Australia. These consisted of circles and straight lines in brown and white. Such symbols had their own meanings, the concentric rings indicating resting places and the connecting lines tracks, for example. Various materials were used, the Australian Aborigines often making thumb-nail drawings on smoke-blackened bark or painting with ochre or clay on the walls of caves.

Melanesia

Melanesia, northeast of Australia, boasts some of the region's richest works of art.

An Australian bark painting depicting a funeral ceremony. (Musée des Arts Africains et Océaniens, Paris/R.M.N.)

Here, influences from Malaya and New Guinea led to a flourishing of the decorative arts. In parts of Melanesia every household utensil and every tool was decorated. Soot drawings on bark represent wood demons and other magic creatures. Totemism – the belief in the kinship of groups, symbolized by a common totem such as a species of plant or animal – was strong in Melanesia, and many objects made by the Melanesians serve as such totems. Popular ancestral figures included the 'Uli' – statues with huge heads, small bodies and tiny legs. Indian sculpture, brought by Indian merchants, was later to influence this region. Some Chinese influences have also been noted.

Polynesia

Polynesia (the many islands) extends from Hawaii to New Zealand and Easter Island. Under the pressure of the Mongoloid races the Polynesians left Asia from 1000 BC onwards. Skilled sailors, they created networks of communication among the islands. Life was regulated by the positive force called *mana* and the negative force called *tapu* (taboo). The artisans belonged to the priest caste, were considered to possess *mana* and had the monopoly of canoe-building and religious carving. They were, indeed, among the greatest wood-carvers of all time. In the Austral Islands they carved with light incisions, while the Maoris made tattoo-like patterns. Each island had its own style. Wood and stone were the only materials used until the Europeans brought metal. However, the arts of bark painting, plaiting, weaving, tattooing and the making of articles of personal adornment reached a great degree of perfection, particularly in New Zealand and in Samoa.   TMo

A 5th-century rock-face fresco at Sigirya, Sri Lanka. (Ancient Art and Architecture Collection)

SEE ALSO

● INDIA AND SOUTHEAST ASIA TO THE COLONIAL AGE p. 384
● AUSTRALASIA AND OCEANIA TO THE COLONIAL AGE p. 464
● THE RELIGIONS OF INDIA p. 466
● BUDDHISM p. 468

THE EASTER ISLAND HEADS

The Easter Island heads are carved from a soft volcanic stone; some of the statues weigh over 50 tonnes (tons). (Keystone)

When the Dutch landed on Easter Island in 1722, they discovered over 500 gigantic stone carvings of men's heads, between 3 and 12 m (10 and 40 ft) high. However, when the Dutch enslaved the Polynesian people in 1862, they slaughtered its kings and priests and were consequently unable to decipher the inscriptions on wooden tablets that they discovered. Recent research has shown that the statues – thought to be cult objects (possibly deifications of dead people) – were erected between AD 1000 and 1600. The fact that there are many unfinished and toppled statues on the island indicates that the cult was ended suddenly by a brutal civil war. Some traditions record such a war, in which the 'Short Ears' overthrew their warlords, the 'Long Ears', together with their statues.

Chinese and Japanese Art

China is the longest surviving civilization in the world, with an art history stretching back at least 4000 years. Because it was the most advanced country in Eastern Asia, China influenced many of its neighbours and later the Islamic world and Western Europe. The distinctiveness of Chinese art has been complemented by very high technical skills, and for many centuries ceramics, bronzes, jade carvings, silk and lacquer were produced at standards surpassing all other cultures.

Japanese art has throughout its history borrowed inspiration and techniques from China, with the introduction of Buddhism in the 6th century exerting a considerable influence. However, different requirements and technical skills resulted in a creative originality distinct from that of China. Japanese colour prints and pottery, influenced by Western culture in the 19th century, have in turn been an important influence on 19th and 20th century Western art.

Pre-imperial culture

During China's Neolithic period, painted pottery was the principal artefact made. In the *Shang* and *Zhou* dynasties (1480 BC – 221 BC) very sophisticated bronze vessels, regarded as some of the finest ever produced, were manufactured. Ritual carvings reveal the Chinese reverence for jade, the other important medium in this early culture.

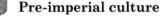

A Chinese Shang dynasty bronze cooking vessel from the latter half of the 2nd millennium BC. (British Museum/E.T. Archive)

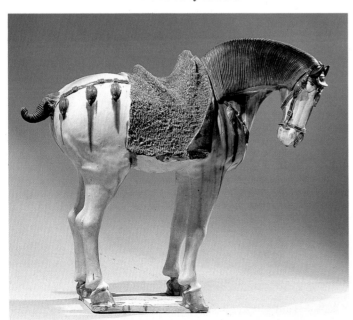

A Chinese scroll painting from the Yuan period: *Dwelling in the Fuchun Mountains* (1350) by Huang Gongwang. (National Palace Museum, Taiwan/E.T. Archive)

Early empire

In the Chinese *Qin* and *Han* dynasties (221 BC – AD 220) ceramic tomb sculptures featuring servant figures provided for the afterlife of the dead – in place of the earlier practice of human sacrifice. Mythical creatures of sculpted stone line the routes to the tombs. In Xian, the Qin capital, thousands of life-sized terracotta warriors and horses demonstrating great technical skill have been excavated (see illustration p. 382). Buildings were often decorated with murals, and lacquer became an important industry. Silk weaving developed and lead glazes were applied to pottery.

The introduction of Buddhism into China from India in the 1st century AD brought a demand for religious art. Temple architecture flourished and sculptured Buddhist images of stone, marble and gilt bronze were made. By the 6th century the style had evolved from Indian to characteristically Chinese.

Middle empire

The *Tang* dynasty (AD 618–907) was a golden age for Chinese art. Buddhist sculpture was made on a monumental scale. Jewellery and metalworking in gold show foreign influences. Tomb figures and other pottery are often decorated with a three-colour glaze. The invention of porcelain (about 1000 years before its discovery in Europe) meant that ceramics became highly prized abroad. To the Chinese, *calligraphy* – the art of handwriting – and painting have always been the most important of the arts. They share the same materials (brush, ink and paper) and format – often long handscrolls and

A glazed pottery model horse from the Chinese Tang dynasty (AD 618–907). (Idemitsu Museum of Arts, Tokyo/Werner Forman Archive)

tall hanging scrolls. Figure painting now reached a peak, and landscape painting emerged as an important genre.

In the *Song* dynasty (960–1279) calligraphy became more individualistic. Song landscape paintings portray angular mountains and gnarled trees, with mists enhancing the effect of distance. Human figures are reduced to a minute scale to indicate their relative unimportance. Chan Buddhist-inspired painting, with its wildly splashed, impressionistic ink effects, was particularly admired in Japan. Song ceramics reached a peak of perfection in technique and design.

In the Mongol *Yuan* dynasty (1271–1368) some painters reverted to archaic styles and the human figure became more important. In ceramics *underglaze* painting (pigments applied before the glaze) in red and blue and *overglaze* painting (applied after the glaze) in enamels were introduced. The art of carving red lacquer was developed. The Mongols also inspired much Buddhist sculpture.

The *Ming* dynasty (1368–1644) rebuilt Peking, now known as Beijing, and many of the city's monuments date from this period. Ceramics were concentrated in huge industrial complexes at Jingdezhen, where the famous blue and white and other wares were produced under imperial supervision. Reign marks were now first used and decoration using many different colours was developed. Lacquer work was inlaid with different coloured lacquers and mother-of-pearl. Cloisonné enamelling – in which a wire outline is filled in with coloured enamels – and miniature works in glass, jade and ivory were also produced.

End of empire

From the *Qing* dynasty (1644–1911) technical perfection began to take precedence over innovation. Some Qing artists painted in a traditional style reinterpreting Song and Yuan landscapes. Enamelled porcelain was popular and much exported to Europe. After 1949, the emphasis has seemed to be more on mass production than artistic inspiration. However, there is a revival of interest in painting, with artists inspired by their own past culture as well as being influenced by Western techniques of perspective. Many artists today are government supported.

Chinese architecture

Most Chinese public buildings were made of wood on a stone foundation and had tiled roofs with upturned edges. The roofs were supported by wooden columns connected to the ceiling beams by wooden brackets. Buildings were often designed around a central courtyard and their settings were considered important. Most buildings were one storey, but there were also many-storied towers called pagodas, a notable feature of Chinese architecture.

Early Japan

Amongst the earliest artistic finds in Japan are ceramics with intricate patterns of raised lines, tomb figures of clay and engraved bronze bells.

The introduction of Buddhism brought to Japan not only religion but the influence of Chinese civilization. It was an important impetus in Japanese art as it stimulated demand for temples, paintings and images. During the *Nara* period (710–784) the capital was built on a grand scale with wooden temples and fine bronze sculpture. Buddhist art, particularly sculpture in wood, began to take on a more Japanese character.

Imperial Japan

In the *Heian* period (794–1185) Buddhist sculptured figures possess an elegance and mysticism more characteristically Japanese than Chinese. A Japanese school of scroll painting combining decorative and narrative features now developed.

Feudal Japan

In the *Kamakura* period (1185–1392) the *Samurai* (knightly caste) dominated the arts, as it did politics. Wooden sculpture was more realistic, and Buddhist paintings more emotionally expressive. Horizontal scroll paintings depict historical tales and legends in an animated style with few Chinese precedents.

Despite incessant clan warfare in the *Muromachi* period (1333–1568) the arts flourished. *Zen* Buddhism with its emphasis on the natural and unadorned influenced all the arts including the landscaping of gardens, architecture and the austere pottery utensils of the tea ceremony. Zen paintings favoured the ink

Japanese ivory netsuke (left) (late 19th century) representing the Chinese general Gentoku. (Victoria and Albert Museum)

style using few brush strokes that had also been popular in China.

The *Momoyama* period (1568–1614) was a luxurious age when art became more secularized and new styles were introduced. The demands of the warlords and the rising middle classes resulted in lacquer ware, ceramics and textiles of this period being famous for the brilliance of their design and technical perfection. Use of gold and silver leaf reveals the love for sumptuousness that somehow coexisted with the restrained and understated style typical of the tea ceremony's pottery utensils.

Tokugawa Japan

The *Ukiyo-e* prints (pictures of the floating world) of the *Edo* period (1615–1868) were produced by artists such as *Hokusai* and *Utamaro*. They drew their subject matter from the entertainment life of Edo (modern Tokyo), depicting the courtesans and actors of the time. This popular art was mass-produced in coloured wood block prints, and print-making flourished throughout the 18th and 19th centuries. These prints were very influential on post-impressionist painters of the West (see p. 544). Sculptural art was now often directed towards miniatures such as *netsuke* carving – ornamental toggles used to fasten purses or tobacco pouches to garments – but lacquer ware, often decorated with gold dust, flourished as did ceramics. By the late 19th century European influence began to transform Japanese art and many of its native traditions had exhausted themselves.

Japanese architecture

Most Japanese buildings were of wood and therefore ancient buildings have not survived, though the more important monuments have been rebuilt several times. Many architectural monuments are Buddhist temples which have tiled roofs with upturned edges. Japanese architecture tends to emphasize the harmony between buildings and the natural beauty around them, and is closely linked to landscape gardening, which has long been a highly developed art in Japan. The interiors of houses have always been very simple and adaptable, with sliding screens for walls and doors.   CM

SEE ALSO

● CHINA TO THE COLONIAL AGE p. 382
● JAPAN TO THE 20TH CENTURY p. 386
● BUDDHISM p. 468
● RELIGIONS OF CHINA AND JAPAN p. 470
● THE LITERATURE OF ASIA p. 616

Hokusai's *Boats in the Waves*, an Ukiyo-e print from the Japanese Edo period. (Musée Guimet/ R.M.N.)

Native American and African Art

The greatest architecture and stone sculpture of the Americas is divided between the ancient civilizations of Mesoamerica and the Central Andes (see pp. 390–1). Before and after the arrival of Europeans, tribal North America excelled in wooden sculpture, textiles and pottery.

An Aztec crystal skull. (above right) (Museum of Mankind, London/E.T. Archive)

SEE ALSO

● AFRICA, AUSTRALASIA AND OCEANIA TO THE COLONIAL AGE p 388
● PRE-COLUMBIAN AMERICA p 390
● PRIMAL RELIGIONS: MODERN TIMES p 464

The Mayan pyramid of Kukulcan (10th–12th century) in Yucatán. Named 'El Castillo' by the Spanish, it is crowned by a temple dedicated to Quetzalcoatl. In the foreground is the corridor of 1000 columns bordering the Temple of the Warriors. (Werner Forman Archive)

African art, excluding the products of Egypt and the Muslim north (see pp. 506 and 510), is concentrated in the rain forests and savannah woodland of central western Africa. Far to the north and south lies the ancient rock art of the Sahara and southern Africa.

The early civilizations of the Americas

The Chavin culture, which spread over much of Peru between about 1000 and 200 BC, is named after a temple complex at Chavin de Huántar. Inside the complex the essentially graphic nature of Chavin sculpture can be seen in the outline of a semi-feline figure, sprouting snakes instead of hair, incised on a large block of granite. Chavin pottery similarly blends animal and human elements, and this cultural trait is paralleled in the man-jaguar and other motifs engraved on *stelae* (stone columns) and jade objects by the Mesoamerican Olmecs (1500–600 BC).

The Olmecs also sculpted dynamic and naturalistic three-dimensional figures, but their most famous works are colossal human heads (1.5–2.8 m / 5–9 ft high) with thick lips and flattened noses. Four of these occur at the site of La Venta, which is also strewn with carved stelae and altars. The platforms and courtyards of La Venta, dominated by a clay pyramid, form an early example of a planned ceremonial centre.

The 'Classic' art of Mesoamerica

The construction of religious complexes reached an early climax in the huge pyramids and regular avenues of imperial Teotihuacán, Central Mexico (c. AD 100–600). The Temple of Quetzalcoatl is an impressive combination of sculpture and architecture; out of the vertical facings of each platform juts a series of serpents' heads, alternating with a series of geometric faces with circular staring eyes.

This severe style, seen again in the schematic statue of a water deity found near the Pyramid of the Moon, is somewhat tempered in the florid wall-paintings. A mural in the palace of Tepantitla shows people playing and catching butterflies while a central figure weeps and the Rain God sprinkles the scene with water from above.

In the southeast of Mesoamerica lie the ceremonial centres of the Maya (c. AD 100–1000). These are loosely arranged collections of platformed single-storey 'palaces', plazas with carved stelae and altars, and tall, slender pyramids. On top of the pyramids are temples capped with 'roof-combs', and both these and the palaces are decorated with low reliefs of painted stucco and stone.

Mayan reliefs often combine lively, richly dressed human figures with complex hieroglyphic motifs. The elaborate, almost 'baroque' Mayan style is also apparent in the rare wall-paintings at Bonampak (c. AD 800). These illustrate a battle, prisoners-of-war having their fingernails torn out, and victory celebrations (see illustration, p. 390).

Mayan sculpture is not often three-dimensional, but striking pottery figurines were manufactured on the island of Jaina. A few of these depict spirits, but most seem to portray earthly figures such as dancers and priests wearing headdresses.

Mochica and Nazca art

The fundamentally naturalistic art of the Mochica people of the Andean region (c. 200 BC–AD 800) is perfectly expressed in their pottery vessels. Some of these are painted with vivid scenes of everyday life, religious rituals or warfare. Others consist of a moulded human face with a handle attached to the top of the head; many of the faces are so realistic and individual that they seem to be actual portraits.

In contrast, the pottery of the adjacent Nazca culture (c. 200 BC–AD 700) is characterized by stylized designs and bold colours. The pottery motifs are echoed in the exquisite Nazca textiles, and some, such as the owl and spider, appear again among the famous 'Nazca lines' in the Palpa Valley region. These were created by scraping the weathered desert surface to reveal lighter clay below, and thus outlining huge geometric patterns, birds and animals.

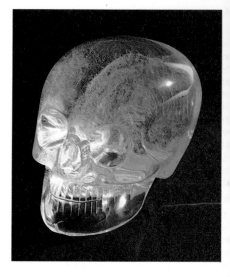

Aztec and Inca art

The great Mesoamerican tradition that began at Teotihuacán flowed through the succeeding Toltec and Mixtec civilizations and culminated in the art and religion of the Aztec Empire (c. 1420–1519). Perhaps the Aztec love of war and sacrifice accounts for the terrifying statue of Coatlicue, Goddess of Earth and Fertility, found at Tenochtitlan. The face of the goddess is replaced by two serpent heads, her chest is covered with amputated hands and hearts, and writhing snakes form a skirt beneath a staring death head. More delicate and naturalistic sculpture was also produced together with mosaics, jewellery and sophisticated featherwork, revealing the complexity of Aztec culture.

The expansion of the Inca Empire from 1440 in the Andean region paralleled the rise of the Aztecs. Inca pottery and metalwork is sophisticated but standardized; the most impressive products of the Incas are their palaces and fortresses built of huge stones.

The naturalistic style of the art of the African kingdom of Ife (AD 1100–1600) is exemplified by this terracotta head. (Werner Forman Archive)

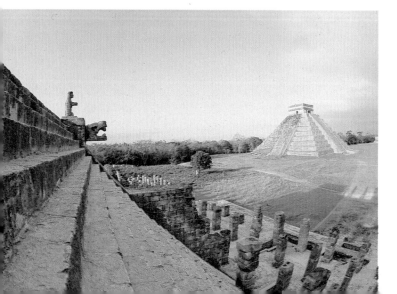

North America

The Inuit (Eskimos) of the extreme north fashion bone, driftwood and ivory into miniature figures of men, seals, polar bears and other Arctic animals. On a more massive scale, the Indians of the north-west coast traditionally carved totem poles depicting chiefs, spirits and animals. In the same region dancers still wear brightly painted masks and elaborate costumes during rituals. The southern Kwagiutl people create dramatic masks of cannibal birds with hooked beaks and shredded cedar bark hair.

All over the continent animals skins were intricately decorated; the Plains Indians painted buffalo hides with hunting scenes. To the west the Indians of Oregon and California embellished their fine basketry with geometric and animal motifs. Further south the colourful textiles of the Navajo also combine geometric and pictorial motifs (such as horses and birds). A similar tension between depiction and abstraction can be traced in the brilliantly coloured pottery of the Pueblo Indians.

This bronze plaque (16th century) shows the level of sophistication attained in metalwork by craftsmen in the kingdom of Benin. (British Museum, London/Werner Forman Archive)

African rock art

The earliest paintings and engravings in the Sahara may date from c. 6000 BC, and depict giant masked figures, hunters and animals now extinct in the area such as hippopotamuses and buffalo. Later, less naturalistic works chart the introduction of cattle and chariots pulled by horses. The smallest and most schematic paintings reveal present-day fauna such as camels.

The San (Bushman) rock art of South Africa and Namibia may be even more ancient. The tradition continued into the 19th century AD, and some paintings show San fighting Bantu and Europeans. Many works depict the graceful eland, a type of antelope central to San mythology; recent research among surviving San groups suggests that the numerous elaborate dancing scenes illustrate magical trance ceremonies.

The African kingdoms

The earliest known sculptural tradition of sub-Saharan Africa emerged c. 500 BC in northern Nigeria. Its products are grouped together as the 'Nok culture', and consist of naturalistic terracottas of animals and more stylized terracottas of human figures; the figures often have simplified bodies, disproportionately large heads and distinctive eyes.

Nok sculpture may have influenced the art of the Kingdom of Ife in southwest Nigeria (c. AD 1100–1600). The Ife terracottas and bronzes are in the form of realistic, if idealized, heads and figures, some of which may portray local rulers. The famous bronzes of the kingdom of Benin (1500–1700) similarly depict full figures and heads, but include plaques decorated in high and low relief with scenes of warriors, chiefs and Portuguese traders.

African architecture

The Benin bronze plaques also illustrate the local architecture, revealing major palace structures with tall central towers. These towers were surmounted by large cast-bronze birds, and long bronze pythons were draped down the tower roofs. West African architecture relies principally on wood and mud, often used in a strikingly sculptural manner. The smooth surfaces of major buildings, such as the pyramidal tower of the early 14th-century mosque at Timbuktu, are often spiked with wooden beams used for maintenance. Africa also possesses monumental stone architecture, notably at the site of Zimbabwe (c. 1400–1800). Here a massive, roughly circular wall 9 m (30 ft) high surrounds various other dry-stone structures, including a tall conical tower. Throughout much of Africa huts are made of interlaced sticks, mud and thatch. Many great buildings were also made of ephemeral materials, such as the barrel-vaulted halls (up to 30 m / 98 ft long) constructed out of wood, rafia stems and grass in the 19th-century Mangbetu kingdom, Zaïre.

Wooden sculpture and masks

Carved wooden masks and sculptures have come to typify African art. Although many of the most famous works were collected in the 19th and early 20th centuries, the tradition is very ancient and persists in certain regions even today.

Western artists such as Picasso (see pp. 548–9) were greatly influenced by African sculpture, believing it to be free of the constraints of naturalism or realism. This is only partly true, and even the most schematic styles possess strong conventions of their own.

Both masks and figures tend to face forward and to be symmetrically arranged around a vertical axis. Figures are usually carved from a single piece of wood, while masks are often embellished with beads, feathers, hair or fibre. The dance masks of the Bakuba of central Africa are particularly elaborate. Sometimes masks and figures are combined, as in the Yoruba *epa* mask which is crowned with a vividly painted sculptural superstructure up to 2 m (7 ft) high.

Both figures and masks were created for specific occasions, such as initiation and healing rites, or to communicate with spirits. Many figures, like those in the elegantly stylized tradition of the Dogon and Bambara of Mali, form part of an ancestor cult. RJa

A mask of painted wood from the Ivory Coast, surmounted by figures of a leopard devouring a sheep. (Musée des Arts Africains et Océaniens, Paris/R.M.N.)

Early Medieval and Byzantine Art

The period between the Classical Age and the Renaissance has sometimes been described dismissively as the 'Dark Ages'. This is both inaccurate and misleading. These centuries formed an essential artistic bridgehead, when new approaches to pictorial form were worked out and deeper spiritual values attached to works of art. The major pattern became the Christian Church, and most of the greatest monuments are related to churches and monasteries.

Before the break-up of the Roman Empire, Christianity had already established itself at the heart of civilized society in Europe. The art of the early Christians is, therefore, a branch of late Roman art. From a stylistic point of view, and in terms of some of its subject matter, this art at first very much resembled its pagan counterpart.

Because Christians were initially persecuted, the earliest Christian symbols in the catacomb paintings of Rome and on 3rd- and 4th-century sarcophagi are all conveniently neutral: the Good Shepherd, philosophers, and *orant* (praying) figures abound. Only in the 4th and 5th centuries did a specifically Christian *iconography* (a vocabulary of images) develop, and scenes from the Old and New Testaments of the Bible became widespread on the walls of churches and in illuminated manuscripts. The move away from Classical naturalism, already evident in late Roman art, was hastened as more emphasis was given to story-telling and simple iconic images.

Early Christian architecture

The first Christian buildings were simply houses that served as meeting places for the faithful. But soon larger churches were needed. The earliest grand churches in Rome took the form of the *basilica* – a single nave with a lower aisle on each side and an apse at the end. The largest of these required transepts (wings) for the increasing congregations and this form of church changed remarkably little until the Gothic period. Circular Christian buildings – *martyria* (martyr's churches) and *baptisteries* (places where baptisms took place) – were also derived from earlier pagan mausoleums and baths. The vast expanse of wall provided by the basilicas – above the nave arcade and in the apse – was the ideal space for pictorial decoration: all of these major early churches were painted or covered in mosaic pictures.

Early Byzantine art and architecture

With the demise of the Roman Empire in the West, the power base shifted to the East, to Constantinople (formerly Byzantium; see p. 394). From the 5th century the Byzantine emperors provided lavish patronage for artists and architects. As a result brilliant innovations took place, in architecture especially, as the Byzantines experimented with the circular church plan and developed the domed basilica. The outstanding example of the latter is Hagia Sophia at Constantinople (now Istanbul), built in the 6th century under the great emperor Justinian. Much of the

mosaic decoration in the church is now covered over, but some idea of its former richness is conveyed by the nearly contemporary mosaics in the church of San Vitale in Ravenna. The history of art in the Byzantine world is complicated, however, and there was often strong and concerted opposition to imagery; this

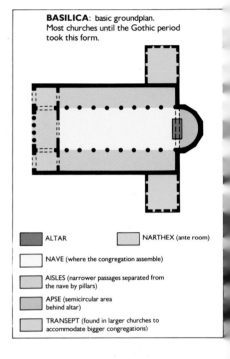

BASILICA: basic groundplan. Most churches until the Gothic period took this form.

ALTAR	NARTHEX (ante room)

NAVE (where the congregation assemble)

AISLES (narrower passages separated from the nave by pillars)

APSE (semicircular area behind altar)

TRANSEPT (found in larger churches to accommodate bigger congregations)

A 6th-century mosaic (right) from S Apollinare Nuovo in Ravenna typifies the stylized Byzantine approach to the depiction of the human figure.
(Explorer)

The interior of Hagia Sophia (below), the great Byzantine cathedral of Constantinople. With the fall of Constantinople to the Ottoman Turks in 1453, the cathedral became a mosque, and the name of the city was changed to Istanbul.
(Explorer)

culminated in a period of iconoclasm (726–843), when all representations of people in religious art were banned in the East.

The spread of Byzantine art

From the 9th century through to the fall of Constantinople to the Turks in 1453, Byzantine art and architecture is notable for its continuity. Right across the Empire – from southern Italy to Armenia – there was a remarkable similarity of style. Typically Byzantine domed church buildings with fresco cycles are still numerous in Greece and Yugoslavia. The Byzantine style of decoration spread outwards to neighbouring regions, so that similar schemes of mosaic decoration may be seen, for example, in Venice (St Mark's) and Sicily (Cefalu, Monreale and Palermo).

Anglo-Saxon art

In the West, the fall of the Roman Empire in the 5th century brought fragmentation and a power vacuum. The barbarian tribes overran Europe (see pp. 381 and 396), producing a cultural climate hardly conducive to ambitious church building. The products of these (largely nomadic) civilizations are mostly portable, and the jewellery produced by them clearly shows links with a Celtic past. The Anglo-Saxons excelled at abstract, highly patterned ornament (often involving interlace designs), and the masterpieces of their art – such as the Lindisfarne Gospels – stand comparison with the most sophisticated products of any civilization. The stone high crosses found in the British Isles are rare examples of large-scale sculpture before the Romanesque period.

Carolingian art

Charlemagne, crowned Holy Roman Emperor in the year 800, consciously evoked the grandeur and learning of Rome at his court at Aachen (see p. 394). For his Palace Chapel there he closely followed Late Antique prototypes, and even re-used Roman building materials. Sumptuous manuscripts were produced, many with beautifully carved book-covers of ivory and jewels. Largely through the efforts of the Carolingians and Byzantines the Classical heritage, both in literature and the visual arts, was preserved for later ages.

Romanesque

In the decades following the year 1000 (the year prophesied by many as the end of the world) a huge increase in church building took place. A contemporary chronicler described Europe at that time as 'clothing itself everywhere in a white robe of churches'. These new churches swept away the older, smaller structures, and over the years new building techniques developed, such as the barrel-and-rib vault, the latter seen for the first time at Durham Cathedral in northern England.

The term 'Romanesque' for the art of the 11th and 12th centuries was first used in the early 19th century because many of the greatest churches of the period have a grandeur unmatched since Roman times,

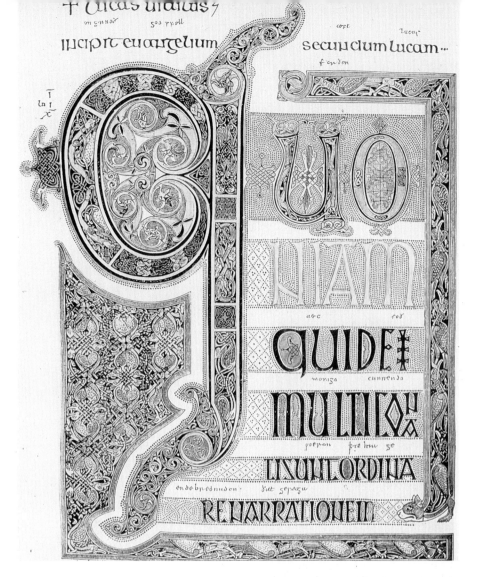

The Lindisfarne Gospels (left), dating from c. AD 690–700, are a masterpiece of Anglo-Saxon manuscript illumination. This page is the beginning of St Luke's Gospel. (Hulton-Deutsch)

SEE ALSO

- THE SUCCESSORS OF ROME p. 394
- THE INVASIONS p. 396
- GREEK AND ROMAN ART p. 508
- GOTHIC PAINTING AND SCULPTURE p. 520
- GOTHIC ARCHITECTURE p. 522

Durham Cathedral (below), started in 1093, is possibly the finest example of Romanesque architecture in England. The Romanesque style became popular following the Norman invasion of 1066, and hence is known in England as 'Norman'. (Spectrum)

and because one of the recurring features of the architecture is the rounded Classical arch. In England this style has often been referred to as 'Norman', as it first emerged at the time of the Norman Conquest (1066).

The Romanesque style was disseminated throughout Europe quickly because of the network of related monasteries ruled over by single great houses. The most influential of these was Cluny in Burgundy, under whose rule were 2000 monasteries served by 10 000 monks. The rise in popularity of pilgrimages to holy sites also meant that new innovations in the arts at any one centre were rapidly picked up and passed on. Although regional variations did occur, there is thus a certain uniformity of style that is instantly recognizable. An especially popular decorative device – found in sculpture, metalwork and manuscript illumination – is the *inhabited scroll*, where men and animals are found amongst foliage.

The art of large-scale sculpture was revived during the Romanesque period to decorate the inside and outside of the new churches. Special attention was paid to the embellishment of capitals surmounting columns and to doorways – the *tympanum* (the semicircular space between the door and the arch) was usually elaborately carved, often with a figure of Christ in Majesty. **PW**

Gothic Painting and Sculpture

Gothic painting and sculpture flourished alongside architecture. The Romanesque world of fantastic beasts is largely left behind and a new emphasis is placed on nature and humanity's place within its hierarchy. This is shown in a more human relationship between God and the individual and the expression of human emotions.

There are obvious stylistic variations in treatment over the period and in different regions, but Gothic art is often characterized by elegant, sometimes elongated figures, decorative surface treatment, and an attention to detail.

Architectural sculpture

Gothic figure sculpture became more naturalistic and less dependent on its architectural support as time progressed. The early French column figures, as at the Royal Portal of Chartres Cathedral (c. 1150), were contained within the shape of the column. The extreme elongation of the figures and narrow, parallel folds of drapery produce an unnatural elegance. By the mid-13th century, at Rheims Cathedral, the sculptures of the Visitation and Annunciation groups (c. 1224–45) are well

Giotto's *Saint Francis receiving stigmata.* Saint Francis was said to have been visited by an angel who caused the wounds of Christ to appear on his body. (Louvre/R.M.N.)

proportioned and the drapery is used to create a greater sense of form as the figures appear to move freely in front of the columns.

In Germany too, naturalism was accentuated by an expression of contemplation in the faces, as seen in two examples of secular figures in cathedrals, the Rider at Bamberg (mid-13th century) and Ekkehard and Uta at Naumberg (c. 1250–60). Most medieval sculptures were originally painted, making them even more realistic.

Italian Gothic

Towards the end of the 13th century the anatomical realism of classical sculpture was taken up by the Pisan sculptor **Nicola Pisano** (active 1258–84) who, with his assistant, the Florentine **Arnolto di Cambio** (active 1265–1300), began the move into the realm of the Gothic. However, it was in the hands of Nicola's son, **Giovanni Pisano** (active 1265–1314) that the style blossomed, especially on his pulpit in S Andrea, Pistoia (1301), where a wealth of human emotions are expressed. In the panel of the *Massacre of the Innocents* the anguish of the mothers is visible both on their faces and in their exaggerated postures.

Beneath the drapery the human form is clearly delineated. This sculptural approach was paralleled in the works of the painters, particularly the Florentine **Giotto di Bondone** (c. 1267–1337). The first attempts at this type of realism are apparent in the *Sta Trinità Madonna* (Florence, Uffizi, c. 1280), attributed to an earlier Florentine, **Cimabue** (active 1272–1302), although the artist still produces the iconic image of his Byzantine predecessors. It is dramatically developed by Giotto in the *Ognissanti Madonna* (Florence, Uffizi, c. 1310–15) with its solid figures, more convincingly set into space, but even Giotto retains the traditional gold background. In contrast, the early work of the Sienese painter **Duccio di Boninsegna** (active 1278–1319) concentrates on a two-dimensional decorative surface treatment which was to continue in Sienese art.

However, other concerns often governed an artist's approach – the need to produce a clear narrative, for example. In the frescoes of the Arena Chapel (Padua, 1304–13), Giotto's figures are mainly ranged along the front of the picture plane, and this, while unnaturalistic, assists in the story-telling. On the back of Duccio's majestic *Maestà* (Siena, Opera del Duomo, 1308–11), the artist uses a

Pisano's *Massacre of the Innocents* (1300–01; detail). The grief of the mothers is powerfully conveyed by this expressive sculpture. (S. Andrea, Pistoia/Scala)

SEE ALSO

● MEDIEVAL AND RENAIS-
SANCE CULTURE p. 406
● EARLY MEDIEVAL AND
BYZANTINE ART p. 518
● GOTHIC ARCHITECTURE
p. 522
● THE EARLY RENAISSANCE
p. 524
● EARLY NETHERLANDISH
AND GERMAN ART p. 526

inity of setting in many of the scenes treated here in a more convincing spacial arrangement), and individual characters are distinguished by different colours.

During this period the identity of artists became more publicly known and their status increased. Giovanni Pisano included a self-laudatory inscription on the Pistoia pulpit to ensure his name was known, and Giotto was mentioned by both Petrarch and Dante (see pp. 618–19).

The importance of the patrons and their requirements must also not be overlooked. Major decorative schemes were commissioned by the Church, the guilds, wealthy individuals and city governments. An especially important project was the decoration of the double church of S Francesco at Assisi where virtually all the painters of note, from Cimabue to the Lorenzetti (see below), were employed. Among them was the Sienese *Simone Martini* (active 1315–44), whose linear rhythms, sensitive use of colour and graceful figure style create a spirituality that obviously appealed to many different types of patron. These qualities were evident in his *Maestà* at Siena Town Hall (1315) and the S Martin Chapel frescoes at Assisi (1320–?30), but more particularly in his panel painting.

The Sienese painters *Ambrogio* and *Pietro Lorenzetti* (active c. 1319–48) produced works which marry Sienese tradition with sculptural, Giottesque form. Their expression of emotion clearly illustrates Gothic humanism and especially the close mother-and-child relationship in, for example, Ambrogio's *Madonna del Latte* (c. mid-1320s). The Lorenzetti both seem to have perished in the Black Death of 1348 (see p. 402), which set back artistic development in the second half of the century.

International Gothic

At the end of the 14th and the beginning of

MANUSCRIPT ILLUMINATION

Small-scale sculptures and manuscripts were produced in large numbers to satisfy both liturgical needs and the personal contemplation of individual worshippers. Manuscripts were often richly decorated, and examples include the *Belleville Breviary*, which is believed to have been illuminated by *Jean Pucelle* (active early 14th century) in Paris before 1343. Pucelle's delicate and sensitive figure style displays a knowledge of Sienese painting (see below). The beautifully painted plant and animal life in the margins (unrelated to the religious function of the manuscript) illustrate the detailed naturalism which later became a feature of International Gothic (see below).

At the beginning of the following century the *Limbourg Brothers* (Paul, Jean and Herman; d. c. 1416) began probably the most famous Gothic manuscript, the *Très Riches Heures* of the Duc de Berry. The calendar is illustrated with scenes from everyday life; the figures are simply set out, but the landscapes contain naturalistic and fantastic elements, both earthly and spiritual.

The miniature paintings of the *Très Riches Heures* by the Limbourg Brothers illustrate each month with a scene of peasants at work or noblemen at leisure; naturalistic detail is combined with an elegant style probably influenced by Italian art. (Musée Condé, Chantilly/Archiv für Kunst)

the 15th century a new development in art, aptly known as International Gothic, combined the French court style, Sienese tradition and Central European features. It is characterized by a preciousness and delicacy of handling, and attention to detail, particularly evident in the *Très Riches Heures* of the Limbourg Brothers (see above). It is also seen in the mon-

umental figures of the Flemish sculptor *Claus Sluter* (active c. 1380– d. 1405/6) at the Chartreuse de Champmol, Dijon (1390s–1403), in which the use of naturalistic facial expression and swaying drapery is typical of the style.

In Italy International Gothic existed alongside the growing development of Renaissance classicism. The bronze doors of the Baptistery in Florence, begun by Ghiberti in 1403 (see p. 524), retain a Gothicism in figure style and layout while demonstrating a greater awareness of the antique.

The influential *Adoration of the Magi* (Florence, Uffizi, 1423) by the Venetian painter *Gentile da Fabriano* (c. 1370–1427) displays a clear knowledge of Simone Martini's figure style. This painting appears to be have been used as a model by *Lorenzo Monaco* (c. 1370/2–1422/5) for his *Adoration* (Florence, Uffizi, c. 1424). The combination of linear contours and colourism in his elongated figures betrays his Sienese background.

A close relationship can also be seen between International Gothic painting and tapestries, which were produced mainly in Flanders and were highly prized. This is especially clear in the work of the Veronese *Antonio Pisanello* (c. 1395–1455/6), in paintings such as the *Vision of St Eustace* (London, National Gallery, 1435–38), where the subject is treated in a largely two-dimensional way, with detailed plant and animal life dotted about the surface. PE

Simone's *Annunciation* (left) (1333) was painted in collaboration with his brother-in-law Memmi. It was his last major work in Italy. (Uffizi, Florence/Archiv für Kunst)

Gothic Architecture

The Gothic style emerged in the 12th century and survived in some areas of Northern Europe until the 16th. In Italy it was largely superseded by the Renaissance at the beginning of the 15th century. The term 'Gothic' was first applied to architecture, and it was architectural forms that were to dominate the art of the period.

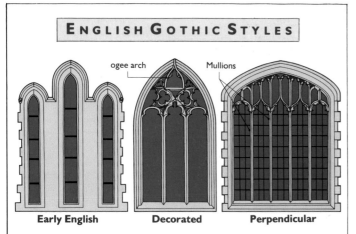

ENGLISH GOTHIC STYLES

ogee arch   Mullions

Early English   **Decorated**   **Perpendicular**

English Gothic is generally divided into three stylistic periods and, like the High Gothic in France, these are characterized by their window styles (see box on stained glass).

Early English lasted c. 1190–1250 and tall, lancet windows without tracery are typical. This was succeeded by **Decorated**, c. 1250– c. 1360, characterized by the **ogee arch** (appearing in doorways and windows) and decorated wall surfaces. During this period window tracery changed from geometric to flowing. Finally came **Perpendicular**, c. 1330–c. 1550, which, as its name implies, emphasized vertical features. The mullions continue through the tracery to the full height of the window.

In Gothic architecture a transcendental quality is evoked by pointed arches, vaulted ceilings, and an emphasis on light through large pointed windows, frequently decorated with stained glass. As the style developed, many of the functional elements were elaborated to create densely decorative forms.

The Gothic cathedral

The first features that can be recognized as Gothic appeared in France at St Denis (near Paris) as early as the 1140s. A sculptured triple *portal* (doorway) with twin square towers – only one of which was completed – was built under Abbot Suger, and a new choir and *ambulatory* (aisle running behind the altar) with radiating chapels were added to accommodate the vast number of pilgrims who visited the shrine of St Denis. The style was immediately developed in several northern French cathedrals, notably Chartres (c. 1140–50).

The development of the *ribbed vault* from its early beginnings at Durham (1093) had enabled stone vaults to be erected, thus increasing the height of the roof while reducing the risk of fire, which had proved a major problem with earlier wooden ceilings. More elaborate and decorative vaulting systems were to follow, such as *lierne vaults* (Salisbury, crossing tower, 15th century) and *fan vaults* (Gloucester, cloisters, late 14th century; and Henry VII chapel, Westminster, early 16th century). *Bosses* covered the joins of the ribs and were carved with foliage or figurative scenes.

The desire to create light interiors (see box on stained glass) led to dramatic developments in construction. Large areas of wall surface were replaced by windows, and the thick walls with passages typical of the Romanesque were replaced with thin walls. Although much lighter, the walls still required support and *flying buttresses* were sometimes added to the exterior of the building, as at Notre Dame, Paris (about 1180).

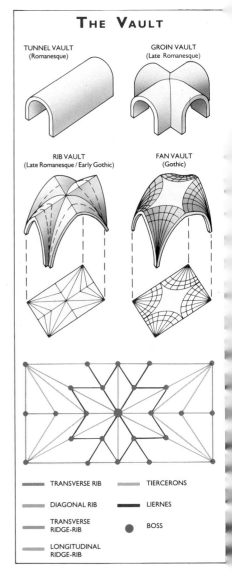

THE VAULT

TUNNEL VAULT (Romanesque)   GROIN VAULT (Late Romanesque)

RIB VAULT (Late Romanesque / Early Gothic)   FAN VAULT (Gothic)

TRANSVERSE RIB	TIERCERONS
DIAGONAL RIB	LIERNES
TRANSVERSE RIDGE-RIB	BOSS
LONGITUDINAL RIDGE-RIB	

With its tall pointed arcades, the interior of the Gothic church was elegant, light and uncluttered by heavy structural features. It was therefore possible to pursue a love of decoration at every opportunity. *Blind arcading* (walled-up windows) was added to wall surfaces, the

STAINED GLASS

The passing of light through glass was seen as symbolizing the spirit of God passing into the Virgin without violation of her purity. When the glass was stained and painted this symbolism was accentuated by the light taking on the colour of the glass and decorating the interior of the church or cathedral.

The design of the window was drawn onto a wooden panel and the glass cut to fit suitable contours of the figure or pattern. The outlines were then drawn in dark pigment and the glass painted before being fired in a kiln. The segments were joined together with strips of lead and each window was set into an iron frame. The dominant colours of 12th-century glass are red and blue, but technical developments

Rose window, Chartres Cathedral.

during the 13th and 14th centuries made other colours available, notably yellow. Glass painted in *grisaille* (or grey) is also common, particularly in lesser churches that could not afford expensive stained glass.

Most medieval glass has been destroyed over the centuries, particularly during the Reformation in England, but major schemes have survived at Chartres, Ste Chapelle (Paris) and Canterbury, where pilgrims would have been taught the biblical stories illustrated in the glass by guides, much as visitors are today. Splendid rose windows decorate the east, west or transept ends of most major Gothic cathedrals. The French *rayonnant* (c. 1230–c. 1350) and *flamboyant* (c. 1350–c. 1525) styles of Gothic architecture were named respectively after the radiating and flame-like nature of their window tracery.

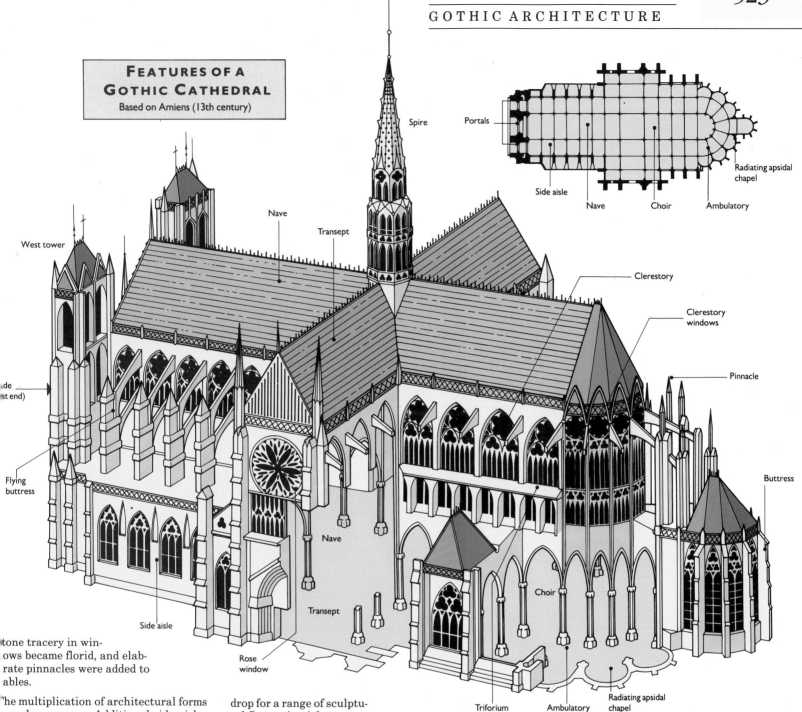

**FEATURES OF A
GOTHIC CATHEDRAL**
Based on Amiens (13th century)

Spire

Nave

Transept

West tower

Clerestory

Clerestory windows

Pinnacle

...de
(...st end)

Flying
buttress

Nave

Buttress

Side aisle

Nave

Transept

Triforium

Choir

Ambulatory

Rose
window

Portals

Side aisle

Radiating apsidal
chapel

Nave

Choir

Ambulatory

Radiating apsidal
chapel

tone tracery in win-
ows became florid, and elab-
rate pinnacles were added to
ables.

he multiplication of architectural forms
vas also common. Additional side aisles
vere added (Bourges, late 13th century;
nd Milan, late 14th century) and double
ransepts were built (Salisbury, early 13th
entury). The three-storey Romanesque
nd early Gothic elevation was occa-
ionally increased to four (Laon, late 12th
early 13th century). This illustrates the
rench preference for height, whereas in
ngland the emphasis is much more on
ength. Despite its elegant central tower,
alisbury Cathedral looks squat and long
n comparison to Amiens. This impression
s partly exaggerated by the screen façade
decorated interior partition), an English
eature that developed in the early 13th
entury, and which is also seen at Wells
nd Lincoln. Unlike the portal, which
eflects the nave and side aisles behind,
he screen façade partially disguises the
rchitectural layout and provides a back-

drop for a range of sculptural figures in niches.

Regional differences also became
apparent in Germany. The first Gothic
cathedrals in the mid-13th century, such
as Marburg, Trier and Cologne, closely
followed the French style. However, even
at Marburg the first signs of the German
innovation of the more open style of the
Hallenkirche ('Hall church') are visible,
where the aisles are almost the same
height as the nave and the interior is lit
from large aisle windows.

Secular architecture

The major examples of secular architecture to survive are castles, (see p. 407),
palaces and civic buildings. In England,
an important contribution was made to
military architecture by Edward I at the
end of the 13th century, when a major
building programme was undertaken,

exemplified by
Carnarfon Castle. In view of
the continuous unrest in medieval
Europe, the need for fortified buildings
often formed part of everyday life. In
Florence, for example, the Palazzo Vecchio (1299–1310) was built to house the
Priori (or council) but displays battle-
ments, small pointed windows and impressive rusticated stonework. On the
other hand, in Venice the palaces were
elegant and decorative. Both the Palazzo
Ducale (Doge's Palace, 1340–after 1425)
and the Ca'd'Oro (1422–c.1440) display a
use of colour and multiplicity of decorative architectural forms that were to survive well into the 15th century.   PE

SEE ALSO

● MEDIEVAL AND RENAIS-
SANCE CULTURE p. 406
● EARLY MEDIEVAL AND
BYZANTINE ART p. 518
● GOTHIC PAINTING AND
SCULPTURE p. 520
● THE EARLY RENAISSANCE
p. 524
● EARLY NETHERLANDISH
AND GERMAN ART p. 526

The Early Renaissance

The term *Renaissance* ('rebirth') was first coined in the 19th century to describe a period of intellectual and artistic renewal that lasted from about 1350 to about 1550. The dominant theme of this period is the revival of interest in classical literature and art by 14th- and 15th-century humanists (see p. 406) and the rediscovery by artists of their cultural past. Florence was the first centre of such rediscovery, with Padua, Venice and finally Rome rivalling Florence in the pursuit of antiquarian learning and artistic excellence. After 1500, the movement also spread to northern Europe (see p. 526).

A panel from Ghiberti's second set of doors (1426–52) for the Florence Baptistery, an important landmark in Renaissance art. In comparision with the Gothic detail of his first set of doors (1403–23), the second set – the so-called 'Gates of Paradise' – include highly sophisticated representations of space and form. (Scala)

This flowering was accompanied by a change in the status of artists – from craftsmen to honoured members of cultured society – and was aided by enlightened civic, private, royal and papal patronage. Civic spending on the arts helped to fund several important public projects, in which many individual artists and architects were involved. Although the demand for paintings and sculpture of religious subjects was as great as before, the choice widened to include mythological, historical and allegorical subjects.

Stylization and realism

The courtly decorativeness of International Gothic (see p. 521) was the immediate precursor of the Italian Renaissance. *Gentile da Fabriano* (c. 1370–1427) and *Antonio Pisanello* (c. 1395–1455) were the supreme exponents of this style in Italy. In the latter's paintings there begins to be a concern with perspectival views, although Gothic stylization still dominates.

The growing interest in perspective and in the use of Classical motifs is clearly revealed in the early work of both *Filippo Brunelleschi* (1377–1446) and *Lorenzo Ghiberti* (1378–1455), such as the bronze panels of the *Sacrifice of Isaac*, that each submitted to the Florence Baptistery doors competition in 1402. The success of Ghiberti's composition led to his commission for the first set of bronze doors (1403–23), followed by the gilded doors, the so-called 'Gates of Paradise' (1426–52) featuring Old Testament scenes.

An advance in the realistic depiction of the draped standing and seated figure can be seen in the sculpture of *Donatello* (c. 1386–1466), many of whose figures were also commissioned for Florentine civic projects. The realism of Donatello's sculpture probably influenced the figures of *Masaccio* (1401–c. 1428), such as those

The dome of Florence Cathedral, designed by Brunelleschi, was a magnificent technical feat. In his *Lives of the Most Eminent Painters, Sculptors and Architects* (1568), Giorgio Vasari described the dome as 'the finest of all the achievements of ancient and modern times'. (Spectrum)

in the frescoes for the Brancacci Chapel (see illustration). In his fresco of the *Trinity* (1426–27) the realism of the architectural setting for the figures owes much to Brunelleschi's architectural designs (see below).

As popular to contemporary tastes were the paintings of *Fra Angelico* (c. 1399–1455) and *Fra Filippo Lippi* (c. 1406–69), which retain many of the refined features of Gothic religious painting, yet show an awareness of the need for a realistic depiction of space and form. The gilded splendour of Fra Angelico's *Coronation of the Virgin* (c. 1430–40) contrasts with his simplified and spare scenes of monks in contemplation, while the crowded space of Lippi's Virgin-and-Child compositions are like painted depictions of high-relief sculpture.

Space in art and architecture

Paolo Uccello (c. 1397–1475) was one of the first of the Florentine painters to experiment in perspectival compositions, as in his fresco of the *Deluge* and the three panels depicting the *Rout of Romano*. These illustrate the way in which he employed this new method to produce works with dramatic foreshortening and distant vanishing points.

The application of mathematical rules in painting was pursued by *Piero della Francesca* (?1420–92). His compositions and figures, as seen in the frescoes illustrating the *Story of the True Cross* in Arezzo, have a monumentality and geometric purity unequalled by his contemporaries. This simplicity is also seen in Brunelleschi's Classically inspired architecture, where he applies pure geometry

One of Masaccio's *Scenes from the Life of St Peter*, a series of frescoes for the Brancacci Chapel of S Maria del Carmine, Florence (c. 1425). The strongly modelled forms and statuesque poses seem to be observed for the first time from life. (Archiv für Kunst)

SEE ALSO

● MEDIEVAL AND RENAIS-
SANCE CULTURE p. 406
● GOTHIC PAINTING AND
SCULPTURE p. 520
● EARLY NETHERLANDISH
AND GERMAN ART p. 526
● THE HIGH RENAISSANCE

in his designs for churches and secular buildings.

Brunelleschi's successor in this tradition was the humanist, architect and artist **Leon Battista Alberti** (1404–72), who conciously attempted to revive the architecture of the ancient Romans. Indeed, his own influential treatises on architecture, sculpture and painting are based upon Classical Roman prototypes. His church of S Andrea in Mantua was based on a Classical description of an Etruscan temple, and in his façade design for the Palazzo Rucellai in Florence the correct use of the Classical orders (see pp. 508–9) is employed for the first time.

The antiquarian pursuits and application of artificial perspective in the work of the North Italian **Andrea Mantegna** (c.1430–1506) led him to depict Classically clothed figures and sculpture in steeply foreshortened scenes in the Overtari Chapel (Padua, Eremitani Church, 1459). The scenes of the Gonzaga family and the illusionistic ceiling decoration in the Camera degli Sposi in Mantua (1474) prefigure 16th-century painted illusionism.

Narrative and mythological painting and sculpture

The Italian medieval tradition of religious narrative fresco decorations in churches continued in the 15th century. But now the desire to decorate private palaces with secular narratives of historical or mythological subjects gave painters new areas for exploration. The mythological paintings of **Sandro Botticelli** (c. 1445–1510), such as *Primavera* ('Spring', 1477–78), and the *Birth of Venus* (c. 1485–90), reflect contemporary interest in esoteric Neoplatonist philosophy. In these enchanted visions Botticelli explores his distinctively linear style to the full.

In the more robust religious narratives of **Domenico Ghirlandaio** (1449–94), such as the *Scenes from the lives of the Virgin and St John* (1486–90), the religious scenes are cast in contemporary settings and include portraits of the patron and his family, or are set against distant landscapes. Sculptural equivalents of such narratives are found, for example, in the altar reliefs of **Antonio Pollaiuolo** (c. 1432–98) and **Andrea Verrocchio** (c. 1435–88).

Venice

Through its geographical position and historical trade links, Venetian painting reflected the impact both of Byzantine decoration and of north European painting, particularly in the use of oil painting. The local demand for devotional works and portraits was well suited to the Venetian style, in which surface brilliance and sumptuous colour was more important than the inclusion of Classical forms.

Lay confraternities in Venice played a significant role in their patronage of painted narrative cycles for their headquarters. In the *Miracle of the Relic of the True Cross* (1494–95) of **Vittorio Carpaccio** (c. 1460–1523/6) the depiction of the miraculous event is relegated to a side position on a Venetian canal setting, barely observed by the throng of confraternity members represented. **Giovanni Bellini** (c. 1430–1516) probably learnt oil painting from the Sicilian, **Antonello da Messina** (c. 1430–79), who had probably learnt the technique in the Netherlands. Bellini's use of this medium profoundly affected the direction of Venetian art. His still, contemplative altarpieces and portraits, initially depicted with linear, sculptural form, later became increasingly saturated with colour and light, a quality he also brought to his landscape compositions.

Leonardo da Vinci

Leonardo da Vinci (1452–1519) represents the true Renaissance artist: not only was he proficient in all the arts, but he was also an engineer, inventor, scientist, mathematician and philosopher. His inventions include designs for a parachute and flying machines, and he made many studies of subjects as diverse as hydraulics and anatomy.

As a painter, he developed the use of aerial perspective (see box) and monochrome effects in such paintings as the *Adoration of the Kings* (1481) and the *Mona Lisa* (1503), and yet his technical experiment in *The Last Supper* (1495–98) resulted in the immediate decay of one of his great masterpieces. His reputation was enormous during his lifetime, and has continued to be so. One of his greatest legacies is a vast collection of compositional and technical drawings, many of them in his notebooks, in which he wrote in mirror writing.   AB

Leonardo's *The Annunciation* (c. 1472–77). Even this early work demonstrates a staggering mastery of composition and technique. On his death in 1519, a contemporary wrote 'It is not in the power of nature to reproduce another such man.' (Uffizi, Florence/Scala)

PERSPECTIVE

Piero della Francesca's *Flagellation of Christ*, a striking demonstration of perspective, in which the recession to a single 'vanishing point' is emphasized by the converging lines in the floor and ceiling. (Galleria Nazionale delle Marche, Urbino/Scala)

Perspective is a mathematical method of depicting three-dimensional space in two dimensions. In the 14th and 15th centuries the growing desire to represent naturalistic space in compositions led to the development of a system of perspective by Brunelleschi in the early 15th century.

This system involved the depiction of objects receding in proportional diminution to one or more *vanishing points*, the point or points at which all receding parallel lines appear to meet: this was determined by the position of the viewer's eye and distance from the *picture plane*, the imaginary plane on which the perspective of a painting meets the eye of the viewer.

Piero della Francesca and Alberti formalized the theoretical rules of perspective in their treatises. Uccello experimented with a less rigid perspective, and Leonardo explored *aerial perspective*, in which colours are paled and tones cooled toward blue with receding distance.

Early Netherlandish and German Art

The Netherlandish and German art of the period from around 1400 to 1570 is often described under the blanket term 'Northern Renaissance'. While this label recognizes the originality and vitality of the northern contemporaries of the Italian Renaissance masters, it obscures the very important divide between the 15th and 16th centuries. In the earlier century the rediscoveries of the Italians aroused little interest north of the Alps, but in the 16th century Netherlandish and German artists became increasingly fascinated by classical antiquity.

The Temptation of Saint Anthony (right) by Bosch (detail). Carl Gustav Jung described Bosch as 'this master of the monstrous . . . the discoverer of the Unconscious'. (National Museum of Ancient Art, Lisbon/Explorer)

Sometimes the term 'Late Gothic' is applied to the 15th-century northern art and 'Northern Renaissance' is restricted to that of the following century. This is unsatisfactory, as a taste for naturalism and a delight in experimentation were common to both. A fundamental problem

The Ghent Altarpiece by Jan and Hubert van Eyck (detail): this panel shows the Virgin Mary. (Cathedral of Saint-Baron, Ghent/Scala)

is that the roots of art-historical terminology are Italian-based and encourage a viewpoint not entirely suited to the understanding of northern art.

The new realism in the Netherlands

At the monastery of Champmol near Dijon the weighty figures of prophets carved by Claus Sluter (see p. 520) mark as dramatic a break with the still flourishing International Gothic. *Robert Campin* (1378/9–1444) of Tournai – also known as the *Master of Flémalle* – was impressed by Sluter's grim realism, as is apparent from the massive figures, robed in heavy folds, who inhabit his paintings.

However, it was his contemporary, the Flemish painter *Jan van Eyck* (active 1422–41), who is remembered as the 'father' of the early Netherlandish painting. A court painter and trusted follower of the Duke of Burgundy, he excelled both as a portraitist and as a painter of altarpieces. By contrast, almost nothing is known about his elder brother and co-painter of the Ghent Altarpiece, *Hubert van Eyck* (d. 1426). This altarpiece, completed in 1432, abounds in innovations including portraiture, nudes, meticulously accurate details and distant landscapes, spatial illusionism and the careful depiction of light and shadow. The brothers Van Eyck were the first to grasp fully the capacity of oil paint to render effects of light, colour and texture. This new realism invested the age-old motifs of Christian art with a powerful new impact, permitting ever more complex levels of meaning.

After Jan Van Eyck, the Flemish painter most praised by contemporaries was *Rogier van der Weyden* (c. 1399–1464), a student of Campin. Aided by a brilliant sense of abstract design, he explored the emotive possibilities of the new style in his masterpiece, the Madrid *Descent from the Cross*. Van Eyck's Flemish pupil *Petrus Christus* (active 1444–72/3) continued his teacher's more contemplative style and made the first Netherlandish experiments with the Italian technique of one-point perspective.

The spread of the new style

By the mid-century collectors as far afield as Italy and Spain were eagerly acquiring paintings by the Netherlandish pioneers. Inspired by their example, German masters from *Steven Lochner* (active 1442–51) in Cologne to *Konrad Witz* (c. 1400–46/7) in Basel formulated local variants of the new style. In Colmar in Alsace *Martin Schongauer* (active 1469–91) translated Rogier van der Weyden's figure style into the new technique of engraving, and so the style was widely disseminated through prints. In the low countries, *Dierick Bouts* (active 1448–75) and *Hans Memling* (active 1465–94) also took their starting point from Rogier, while *Hugo van der Goes* (active 1467–82) turned repeatedly to the monumental grandeur of Jan van Eyck.

The impact of Italy and the Reformation

During the early 16th century many northern artists developed an essentially traditional style to ever increasing levels of complexity. Among such artists, the Flemish painter *Hieronymus Bosch* (active 1480/1–1516) is particularly notable. Bosch specialized in large, panoramic compositions peopled with myriad tiny figures and creatures. Although his paintings frequently utilize the triptych (triple-panel) format usual in altarpieces, it is more likely that they were intended as moral allegories for the entertainment and edification of private collectors.

The German painter and hydraulic engineer *Grünewald* (Mathis Neithardt-Gothardt, active 1501–28) is the most expressionist of Renaissance artists, concentrating on religious themes. His masterpiece, the shutters of the Isenheim altarpiece (1515), vividly embodies the poetic mysticism of late medieval theology.

Other painters followed the lead of the German *Albrecht Dürer* (1471–1528). A visitor to Venice in 1494–95 and 1505–07, he studied perspective and the theory of human proportions with Italian artists and read the treatises of the classical authorities Vitruvius and Euclid. Displaying an immensely fertile imagination and brilliant technical skill, his paintings impressed the Venetian master Giovanni Bellini (see p. 524). The designer of over 400 woodcuts and engravings, Dürer elevated printmaking to the status of a major medium with such works as the humanist-inspired *Melancholia* of 1513.

The Germans *Albrecht Altdorfer* (c.

Dürer's *Melancholia*. In this complex allegory, Dürer achieved a range of tone not seen before in engraving. (Private collection/Explorer)

1480–1538), *Hans Baldung Grien* (1484/5–1545), and *Lucas Cranach* (1472–1553) consolidated Dürer's foundation of the greatest school of painting and printmaking in German history. Artists in Catholic regions continued the traditional subject matter of altarpieces, while others such as Cranach and the German *Hans Holbein the Younger* (1497/8–1543) played a major role in the spread of the Reformation through their Protestant paintings and book illustrations. Holbein was also the principal portraitist of his day and, as the court painter of the English king, Henry VIII, the founder of what became the British school.

Despite Dürer's visit to Antwerp in 1520–21, the growth of an Italianate style in the low countries was on the whole an independent development. *Quentin Massys* (1464/5–1530) had access to draw-

ings by Leonardo da Vinci, who moved to France in 1517, and *Jan Gossaert* (also known as *Mabuse*; active 1503–32) visited Rome in 1508–09. *Lucas van Leyden* (c. 1489–1533) studied Italian and German prints, and his own engravings were celebrated by Vasari as the equal of Dürer's own work.

In 1522 the Dutch painter *Jan van Scorel* (1495–1562) visited Rome, where the Dutch Pope Hadrian VI appointed him briefly as Raphael's successor in the post of curator of the Vatican collection of antiquities. His student *Maerten van Heemskerck* (1498–1574) also visited Italy and popularized classical form and subject matter in numerous paintings and engravings. Antwerp Mannerism was brought to its ultimate level of refined complexity by *Frans Floris* (flourished 1517–70). In contrast to such transplanted Italianism, *Joachim Patenir* (c. 1480–1524) – also active in Antwerp – developed the 15th-century fascination with landscape until it became an independent subject. The domestic scenes of the Dutch painter *Pieter Aertsen* (1508/9–75) conceal a religious message, but his delight in the details of everyday life foreshadows 17th-century Dutch *genre painting* (the term used for scenes of everyday life, particularly featuring peasants; see p. 532).

The pictures of *Pieter Bruegel the Elder* (c. 1525–69) were painted in the last years before the Revolt of the Netherlands destroyed the Netherlandish School. Although Bruegel mainly painted scenes of peasants and the countryside, his works often illustrate moral themes. Thus the famous *Peasant Dance* is best inter-

preted as a criticism of the lust and hypocrisy of the peasants who abuse a saint's day by regarding it as an excuse for a party. Some multi-figure landscapes such as his *Procession to Calvary* (1564) treat traditional religious themes. The breathtaking naturalism of Bruegel's paintings also marks the birth of a new, secular outlook, which was to flourish in the Golden Age of Dutch painting (see p. 532).

ME

Bruegel's *The Land of Cockaigne* depicts an imaginary land of luxury and idleness.
(Alte Pinakothek, Munich/Scala)

Cranach's *The Fee* (1532) – the theme of the ill-matched couple was a popular one in northern Europe at the time. (Statens Konstmuseer, Stockholm)

SEE ALSO

- MEDIEVAL AND RENAISSANCE CULTURE p. 406
- THE REFORMATION p. 408
- GOTHIC PAINTING AND SCULPTURE p. 520
- THE EARLY RENAISSANCE p. 524
- THE DUTCH SCHOOL p. 532

The High Renaissance and Mannerism

The focus of artistic activity in Italy shifted during the early 16th century from Florence to Rome, with the rise of papal patronage. Before the Sack of Rome by the Imperial forces in 1527 (see p. 380), one of the most concentrated groups of artistic genius ever known was gathered in the papal city. The role of the artist changed even more dramatically than in the previous century, and a number of academies were established, confirming the professional status of the artist.
At the same time, the artistic innovations of the Italian Renaissance began to spread to northern Europe (see p. 526).

Michelangelo's *David* (1501–4). (Accademia, Florence/Spectrum Colour Library.)

Raphael's *'La Belle Jardinière'* (Mary with Jesus and John the Baptist; 1507). (Louvre, Paris/Archiv für Kunst.)

Artistic innovation later led to the superficial elegance of Mannerism, a style which became popular all over Catholic Europe. However, the Counter-Reformation brought in restrictions on both subject matter and treatment of religious art, and by the end of the 16th century Mannerism had lost much of its vigour.

Rome and papal glory

The role of the pope in establishing Rome as a centre of artistic prominence had begun in the 15th century. This was continued at a greater pace in the 16th century, with a succession of popes employing the foremost artists and architects of the day in the decoration and rebuilding of Rome. The triumvirate dominating the scene were Michelangelo, Raphael and Bramante. These three established a style that was to be copied throughout Italy.

Michelangelo Buonarroti (1475–1564) started his artistic career in the humanist environment of Florence, where the Medici had been his patrons. On his first visit to Rome he carved his first great sculptures, such as the *Pietà* (1499), and on returning to Florence produced his giant marble *David* (1501–4). His second stay in Rome started in 1505, at the summons of Julius II. This was to work on the pope's tomb, a project on which he spent thirty years. Of the carved figures originally planned only the monumental *Moses* was finally placed on the much modified tomb. Even in their incomplete state, the languid and pent-up energy of the *Slaves*, also intended for the tomb, testify to Michelangelo's assertion that sculpture is locked into the block of stone, only waiting to be unleashed by the sculptor. His next major project, for the ceiling of the Sistine Chapel (1508–1512), was undertaken without assistance. In scenes from the Old Testament – in which figures of Prophets, Sybils and nudes are set into the architectural framework – Michelangelo demonstrated his powers as a draughtsman and innovative colourist, and as the creator of painted figures of almost sculptural presence and beauty. Michelangelo worked in Florence from 1516 to 1534, but on his return to Rome he painted the *Last Judgement* (1536–41) on the altar wall of the Sistine Chapel.

Raphael (1483–1520), who had been based in Florence in 1504–8, was also involved in extensive decorative schemes in Rome: in paintings for the *Stanze* and loggias of the Vatican Palace (1509–14), such as *The School of Athens*, and on the series of cartoons (drawings) for a set of tapestries for the Sistine Chapel (1517–18). These richly classical works, together with other works such as his portraits and Virgin-and-Child paintings, form the basis for High Renaissance art. Their wealth of invention and harmonious compositions were copied by artists for centuries.

Donato Bramante (1444–1514) arrived in Rome from Milan in 1499. In his designs for palace architecture, town planning and the series of courtyards connecting the Vatican Palace and the Villa Belvedere, he introduced the first truly classical architecture in Rome. Very little of his plan for St Peter's was completed, but his designs formed the basis for all subsequent work on the basilica, including the dome built by Michelangelo.

Patronage: the Medici

Apart from two periods of exile (1494–1512 and 1527–1530), the Medici family dominated artistic life in Florence in the 15th and 16th centuries. Under the patronage of Lorenzo the Magnificent, and the grand dukes Cosimo I, Francesco and Ferdinand I, Florence experienced a wealth of artistic activity.

During the absence of Michelangelo, Raphael and Leonardo (see p. 524) from Florence, the scene was dominated by *Fra Bartolommeo* (c. 1474–c. 1517) and *Andrea del Sarto* (1486–1530), whose altarpieces and frescoes represent the epitome of the harmonious and quietly classical Florentine style prior to the advent of Mannerism.

The middle years of the 16th century were dominated by a series of decorative schemes for the Palazzo Vecchio, the building of the Uffizi, the enlargement of the Pitti Palace and the Boboli Gardens. Directing many of these works was the painter and architect *Giorgio Vasari* (1511–74), who, as author of the *Lives of the Artists*, was responsible for attributing to contemporary Florentine artists, in particular Michelangelo, the supreme triumph of having surpassed both nature and the ancients in their art.

Mannerism

Mannerism is a style of exaggerated sophistication and virtuosity – sometimes combined with a heightened emotionalism and religiosity – that grew out of the example of High Renaissance art and was partly a reaction to it. In Florence, *Jacopo Pontormo* (1494–1556) and *Agnolo Bronzino* (1507–1572) perfected a style that featured figures posed in elegant tension, contrasts of colours, and dense, complicated compositions. In sculpture this tendency is represented by the brilliant goldsmith's work and bronzes of *Benvenuto Cellini* (1500–71) and in the work of *Giambologna* (1529–1608), such as the spiralling group of the *Rape of the Sabines* (1579–83).

p. 580). Most of his buildings are in and around Vicenza, including the Villa Malcontenta and the Villa Rotonda, although he also introduced a true classicism into his Venetian church designs. In his *Four Books of Architecture* (1570) Palladio devised a comprehensive architectural system, and Palladianism was to be a recurring theme in European architecture for the next two centuries.

The seven books of architecture compiled by the Italian **Sebastiano Serlio** (1475–1554) and his designs for buildings at Fontainebleau and the Château d'Ancy formed the basis for a new style in French architecture. The square court for the Louvre (1546–51) by **Pierre Lescot** (1500/15–78) represents the first example of classical French architecture.

At Granada in Spain, an Italianate influence is seen in Charles V's Palace in the Alhambra (1527–68). Later in the century the austerity of the Escorial palace near Madrid is more in keeping with the severe tastes of Philip II.

In England **Robert Smythson** (c. 1536–1614) combined influences from Serlio and Flemish architecture in a highly personal and romantic brand of Classicism, seen in such great houses as Longleat, Wollaton Hall and Hardwick Hall. However, it was not until the early 17th century that Inigo Jones introduced Palladianism to England (see p. 531).   AB

Titian's *Flora* shows the artist's rich, expressive colouring. (Uffizi, Florence/Archiv für Kunst.)

SEE ALSO

- MEDIEVAL RENAISSANCE CULTURE p. 406
- THE EARLY RENAISSANCE p. 524
- THE BAROQUE AND CLASSICISM p. 530

El Greco's *Adoration of the Shepherds*. The elongated figures, harsh colours and elaborate composition are typical of El Greco's distinctive Mannerist style. (Prado, Madrid/Scala.)

In Mantua, Raphael's assistant, **Giulio Romano** (1492–1546), combined architecture and painting in his witty application of Mannerist details in the designs for the Gonzaga family's Palazzo del Tè, begun in 1526. **Antonio Correggio** (c. 1495–1534) developed a rich painterly style in his altarpieces and frescoes, based on knowledge of Mantegna, Michelangelo and Raphael. In his illusionistic ceilings for the Cathedral dome and S Giovanni Evangelista in Parma he anticipated the illusionistic ceilings of the next century. Influenced by Correggio, **Parmigianino** (1503–40) evolved a style that delighted in elegant, if bizarre, distortion of the human figure, for instance in his *Madonna of the Long Neck* (c. 1535).

In 1532 the French king, Francis I, summoned **Primaticcio** (1504–70) and **Rosso Fiorentino** (1495–1540) to provide the painted and stucco decorations for his château at Fontainebleau. The elaborate decorations had a profound effect on French artists such as **Jean Goujon** (active 1540–62) and **Germaine Pilon** (c. 1535–90). However, the formal court portrait style of **François Clouet** (d. 1540/1) remained unaffected. In the Spanish Netherlands and at the Habsburg court of Rudolf II at Prague, the style was enthusiastically taken up in all the arts, but adapted to suit existing tastes. In Spain, **El Greco** (1541–1614) produced a highly personal Mannerist style characterized by acid colours, elongated figures and mystical visions, seen for instance in his *Burial of Count Orgaz* (1586).

Venetian colour

At the beginning of the 16th century Venetian art was dominated by Giovanni Bellini (see p. 524) and **Giorgione** (c. 1476/8–1510). Giorgione's works introduced a new category of paintings depicting esoteric subjects – such as *The Tempest* – intended for private collectors. Giorgione also pioneered dream-like pastorals, in which figures and landscape became harmoniously integrated.

This genre was also taken up by **Titian** (c. 1487/90–1576), considered to be the greatest of the Venetian painters. As Court Painter to Charles V he established an influential style of court portraiture, and his sensual allegorical works contain a lyrical richness that relies on colour and tone rather than on drawing and line.

Mannerism in Venetian painting is represented by the darkly dramatic, sharply foreshortened compositions of **Jacopo Tintoretto** (1518–94) in his series decorating the confraternity headquarters of the Scuola di San Rocco. In contrast to these dark visions are the large canvases of **Veronese** (1528–88) depicting religious, historical and allegorical events in sumptuous Venetian settings.

16th-century architecture

After Bramante the major architect in Rome was **Giacomo Vignola** (1507–73), who continued the work on St Peter's. He codified the classical orders (see p. 530), and applied these in buildings such as the influential single-nave church of Il Gesù in Rome (begun 1568) and the Palazzo Farnese at Caprarola.

In northern Italy **Andrea Palladio** (1508–80) transformed villa and palace architecture, basing his designs on ancient Roman public buildings, and in particular the theories of Vitruvius (see

The Baroque and Classicism

Classicism and the Baroque were the two dominant trends in the visual arts of the 17th century, particularly in Catholic countries and most importantly in Italy and France. Although frequently divergent and opposed, they both originated in the reaction in Italy at the end of the 16th century against the aridity of Late Mannerism. A return to the naturalism, harmonious equilibrium and compositional coherence of the High Renaissance was combined with a new physical realism, emotional immediacy and dynamic vigour.

The Baroque style combined the dramatic effects of energetic movement, vivid colour and decorative detail with expressive originality and freedom. Classicism deployed more restrained qualities of directness and precision to enliven traditional ideas of balance and decorum.

The Early Baroque in Italy

The most remarkable painter of the Early

Caravaggio's *The Young Bacchus* uses a sexually ambiguous low-life character to model the god of wine. (Uffizi, Florence/Explorer)

Rubens' *The Garden of Love* (below) displays the full flamboyance of the Baroque. (Prado, Madrid/ Archiv für Kunst)

Baroque was **Michelangelo Merisi da Caravaggio** (1573–1610). His earlier works were controversial, celebrating sexually ambiguous low-life characters and representing holy figures as ordinary people, aspects combined in the *Calling of St Matthew* (c. 1599). His religious imagery was powerful, expressed in gestures, shadowed backgrounds and dramatic use of light and shade (*chiaroscuro*). His turbulent career in Rome culminated in his flight from a murder charge in 1606. The altarpieces he subsequently painted in Naples, Malta and Sicily were among his finest creations, increasingly sombre, poignant and dramatic.

Ludovico Carracci (1555–1619) and his cousins **Agostino** (1557–1602) and **Annibale** (1560–1609) represented the ortho-

Las Meniñas (1656) by Velasquez. The appearance of the artist himself in the left of the picture, together with the mysterious figures in the doorway and mirror, are all components in this complex exploration of illusion and reality. (Prado, Madrid/Archiv für Kunst)

dox side of the Early Baroque revolution, founding the first true example of the modern artistic academy, in Bologna in the 1580s. Their works revived the dignity of the Renaissance, enhanced by richer contrasts and colours, weightier figures and complex compositional relationships.

Annibale's most talented pupils were **Guido Reni** (1575–1642) and **Domenichino** (1581–1641). Their very different approaches were already evident in their companion frescoes of *Scenes from the martyrdom of St Andrew* (1608–9), in which Reni's decorative elaboration contrasts with Domenichino's concentration on narrative. Reni's development, while occasionally encompassing some of the drama of Caravaggio, was towards idealized beauty, rhythmic grace and surface elegance. Domenichino, on the other hand, created an austerely original Classicism, with simplified and static compositions, grandiose figures and archaeologically accurate details.

Developments outside Italy

Peter Paul Rubens (1577–1640) studied in Italy, but subsequently transformed his Italian influences through a vigorous imagination and a brilliant technique. His paintings embody all the energy, colour and sensuality of the Baroque. But he was equally capable of tenderness and sensitivity, particularly in portraiture; and his landscapes, allegorical schemes

Rubens' enormous output required the help of a large studio of assistants, the most distinguished being *Jacob Jordaens* (1593–1678), who coarsened the master's style, and *Anthony Van Dyck* (1599–1641), who refined it. Van Dyck's superbly elegant portraits were popular in Genoa and later in England, where they immortalized the court of Charles I.

Portraiture also became the chief medium of expression for the Spanish painter *Diego Velasquez* (1599–1660). His early works were scenes of everyday life, probably influenced by Caravaggio, and his religious and mythological pictures are charged with a sober naturalism. In his portraits too his level gaze never faltered as he moved from the power-mongers of the Spanish government to the pathetic court dwarfs and frail royal children, described with ever subtler handling of paint.

The High Baroque in Rome

Perhaps the greatest figure of the Italian High Baroque was *Gianlorenzo Bernini* (1598–1680). The brilliant naturalistic forms of his sculpture expressed ideas of daring originality. He went on to combine sculpture with architecture and painting, as in the *Ecstasy of St Teresa* (1645–52). He transformed the square in front of the Baroque façade of St Peter's (of 1607–10) into an oval piazza enclosed by colonnades, to represent the embracing arms of the Church.

Although his compositions were complex, the architectural forms employed by Bernini were comparatively simple and firmly within the Classical tradition of the Renaissance. Quite different was the work of the architect *Francesco Borromini* (1599–1667), whose inventions were of an often bizarre power. An equal contrast is provided by the sensuous richness and formal harmony of the architecture and the painting of *Pietro da Cortona* (1596–1669). In Cortona's later works the development of architectural simplicity and pictorial lightness indicates an increasing awareness of the new Classicism.

The challenge of Classicism

Bernini's dominance of the Roman artistic scene can obscure the presence there of an important group of artists who were opposed to the emotional drama and formal licence of the Baroque. Instead they combined Baroque colour and solidity with a revival of antique forms. The dominant figure of the group was the Frenchman *Nicolas Poussin* (1593/4 –1665), who was strongly influenced by Domenichino. The graceful poetry of some of his earlier works found admirers in Rome, but the increasingly sober, abstract qualities of his later mythologies and religious pictures appealed to the more rigorous intellectual climate of Paris. As part of this development Poussin often turned to pure landscape as an expression of mathematical order and contemplative grandeur.

A new spirit was infused into landscape

painting by another Frenchman, *Claude Lorraine* (1600–82). His sensitivity to nature and magical light effects transformed the stylizations of northern European landscape artists into poetic evocations of the changing moods of the Italian countryside. The wild and rocky scenes of the Italian *Salvator Rosa* (1615–73) were seen in the 18th century as precursors of the Sublime (see p. 536).

Architecture and decoration in France

French architecture of the 17th century moved from the elaborate decorative licence of the previous period towards the rational refinements of Classicism. In buildings such as the Palais de Luxembourg, Paris (1615) an understanding of Classical rules was first wedded to the realization of three-dimensional mass. *François Mansart* (1598–1666) replaced the traditional steep pitch roof with the lower-angled form of the *mansard roof*, showing his devotion to Classical principles of unity.

The eclectic and decorative style of the architect *Louis Le Vau* (1612–70) found its most fruitful outlet in collaboration with the grandiose decorative schemes of the painter *Charles Lebrun* (1619–90) and the vast formal layouts of the gardener *André Le Nôtre* (1613–1700). This team was used by Louis XIV for the creation of Versailles (see p. 414); but it was the enormous new wings of the garden front, and the glittering interior of the *Galerie des Glaces*, both created by *Jules Hardouin Mansart* (1646–1708), that transformed the palace into such a potent symbol of glamour and authority.

Architecture in England

Fifty years earlier a precursor of Versailles had been designed by *Inigo Jones* (1573–1652) in an unexecuted project for a palace at Whitehall for Charles I. Jones's Classicism, strongly influenced by Palladio (see p. 528), was of a rigorous purity exemplified by his Queen's House at

Greenwich (1616–35). But it was also without immediate influence, presenting too extreme a contrast to the prevailing Jacobean mode. The eclecticism of English taste is indicated by the fact that Jones's ultra-Classical Banqueting House at Whitehall (1619–22) was soon decorated with Rubens' ultra-Baroque ceiling paintings. Some idea of the Italianate grandeur of Jones's lost larger works is given by the wing built by a pupil of his as the first part of Greenwich Hospital (1663–67).

By the Restoration in 1660 a more modest Classicism of Dutch and French inspiration had become the norm for grand domestic architecture. This used to be associated with *Christopher Wren* (1632–1723); but Wren was in fact the great ecclesiastical architect of the period, as is attested by his rebuilding of St Paul's (begun 1675) and the City churches destroyed by the Great Fire of London in 1666. His additions to Hampton Court (1690–96) and Greenwich Hospital (from 1694) show a monumental grandeur.

The power and gloom that permeates some of Wren's designs is probably due to his assistant, *Nicholas Hawksmoor* (1661–1716). Hawksmoor too showed his true genius in church architecture. However, he also worked as an assistant on the country houses of *John Vanbrugh* (1664–1726), whose vast Baroque inventions contrast strong movement with massively weighty masonry, as at Castle Howard (begun 1699) and Blenheim Palace (1705–24). NG-R

The Dutch School

In the 17th century a sudden flowering of the art of painting in the Netherlands coincided with the overthrow of Spanish rule and Dutch mercantile success throughout the world. The stubborn tenacity that enabled them to triumph over apparently superior forces at home and abroad was reflected in the solid sobriety with which the Dutch viewed their surroundings.

Brouwer's *Singing Farmers* – (right) a typical tavern scene in which the vulgarity of his subject contrasts with the delicacy of his style. (Kunsthaus, Zurich/Archiv für Kunst)

SEE ALSO

● EUROPEAN EMPIRES IN THE 17TH AND 18TH CENTURIES p. 416
● EARLY NETHERLANDISH AND GERMAN ART p. 526

Having saved their country and their possessions for themselves, they wanted to see them safely depicted, a calm reflection of their vision of reality. To achieve this their artists concentrated on the types of painting in which they had long specialized – still life, genre, landscape and portraiture.

Still life

Early 17th-century Dutch still lifes faithfully render domestic objects and flowers in brilliant colour and light, but almost haphazardly against dark backgrounds. Often a watch, skull or other reminder of the passage of time is included. More subtle compositions were gradually developed, using restricted colour harmonies and more atmospheric tones and settings.

Kalf's *Still Life with Fruit and China Vase.* The watch in the bottom left-hand corner is included as a reminder of the passage of time. (Archiv für Kunst)

In the second half of the century, lower viewpoints, combined with greater depth in the composition, produced a naturalistic effect. The works of **Willem Kalf** (1619–93) – daringly composed arrangements of sculpted silver, blue and white Delft ware and ripe fruit – are typical.

Genre

Genre painting is the depiction of scenes of everyday life, originally (as with still life) with an allegorical intention. Its translation in the Netherlands into pure narrative was partly due to the influence of Caravaggio, who had incorporated aspects of both still life and genre into his works (see p. 530). These aspects were taken up and popularized by his followers, who included Dutch artists in Rome such as **Hendrick Terbrugghen** (1588–1629) and **Gerard van Honthorst** (1590–1656). They founded the Utrecht School, which produced occasional religious pictures (Utrecht was a Catholic centre), but chiefly colourful groups of low-life characters in fancy dress, distinguished by Caravaggesque use of dramatic light and shade.

More realistic were the works of **Adriaen Brouwer** (1605/6–38), a Fleming who worked mainly in the Netherlands. In his tavern scenes, boorish men carousing or snoring are sympathetically depicted in delicate colour harmonies with subtle lighting. Also related to the Flemish tradition were Dutch pictures of butchers' shops and market stalls, which combined still life with picturesquely vulgar figures. Vulgarity, ostensibly with a moralizing message, was also the keynote of the boisterous, colourful and highly detailed scenes of **Jan Steen** (1626–79).

Quite different was the quiet atmosphere of the genteel interiors of **Gerard Terborch** (1617–81), which often feature precise renderings of silks and carpets. Equally quiet, but far subtler and more daring in the handling of light and perspective, were the interior and exterior views of **Pieter de Hooch** (1629–84). An air of mystery is often added to the realism of his homely rooms and courtyards by the interpolation of further, gently lit views into subsidiary background spaces.

Jan Vermeer (1632–75) of Delft is best known for his domestic interiors whose restricted colours, simplified forms, delicate rendering of light effects and skilful compositions built up from geometrical shapes transformed the humdrum into the poetic.

Landscapes and other views

The earliest Dutch landscapes combined the artificial compositions of Mannerism (see p. 528) with a minute description of realistic detail, but a more naturalistic style later developed. In the 1630s and 1640s, parallel with changes in still life painting, atmosphere and tonal subtleties created a new sense of light and space. After 1650 these achievements were gradually combined with a richer colour range, and a greater feeling for natural drama.

The most accomplished figure of this last period was **Jacob van Ruisdael** (1628/9 –82), whose works are as varied and as inventively composed as Claude's (see p. 530), though less idealized. Those of **Meindert Hobbema** (1638–1709), a former pupil of Ruisdael, concentrate on decorative, sunlit forest scenes, while his best known work, *The Avenue at Middelharnis,* (1689) derives its strong central focus from an avenue of tall trees receding into the distance. Contrastingly Italianate are the golden light and warm tonalities of **Aelbert Cuyp** (1620–91), which lend his simple groupings of trees, cows or ships a poetic monumentality.

Townscapes became popular later in the 17th century, under the influence of Italian examples, and in their turn contributed to the topographical aspect of 18th-century view painting. Specifically Dutch, however, were the church interiors of **Pieter Saenredam** (1597–1665), perhaps the nearest things to popular Dutch religious pictures. Their spatial complexity and monumental architectural values reflect the intellectuality as well as the tenacious realism of Protestantism.

Other artists were equally specialized. The ice scenes of **Hendrik Avercamp** (1585–1634) are decoratively joyous and detailed. **Willem van der Velde** (1633–1707) painted seascapes, often collaborating with his father of the same name on superbly atmospheric yet splendidly detailed arrangements of ships at sea. See p. 416 for an example of his work.

Ruisdael's *The Ray of Sunlight*.
Ruisdael's landscapes are often
dominated by a vast, cloudy sky.
(Louvre, Paris/Scala)

Portraits

In portraiture, the most popular branch of painting in the Netherlands, developments occurred at a rapid pace. This was due to the brilliant talent of *Franz Hals* (1580/85–1666), who soon dominated the field, his lively brushwork vividly capturing fleeting expressions. The immediacy of his group portraits gives life to potentially static compositions, while single sitters are portrayed directly, with apparently spontaneous handling of paint pro

viding visual excitement. His technique became even freer, and his colours more limited, during the 1640s and 1650s. His final works, painted when he was destitute, show a more sensitive approach that may indicate an awareness of the late Rembrandt (see box). NG-R

Vermeer's *The Geographer* (1669;
also known as *The Astronomer*).
(Städelsches Kunstinstitut, Frankfurt/Archiv für
Kunst)

REMBRANDT

Rembrandt van Rijn (1606–69) stands apart from the rest of the Dutch School not only through his imagination and depth of human sympathy, but also because of the variety and originality of his subject matter and his superlative technical skills. The last were evident from his earliest works, which include experiments in Caravaggio's dramatic chiaroscuro (contrast of light and shade) and Rubens' colourful vigour.

However, Rembrandt made his name through his success in portraiture. His first triumph in Amsterdam was *The Anatomy Lesson* (1632), and his single portraits were equally convincing and imaginative, often employing illusionistic tricks.

Subtler illusionistic effects and an even more ambitious compositional use of light appeared in another group portrait, the so-called *Night Watch* (1642); this extraordinary picture combines an almost abstract disposition of its naturalistic parts with a Baroque sense of dramatic movement.

This was the high point of Rembrandt's worldly success. His fortunes subsequently declined, largely because he had begun to live extravagantly, and refused to concentrate on the sort of work that would have made him rich. His interest in Old Testament subjects had begun early, as shown by the *Jeremiah* of 1630, opulently coloured and richly detailed, with only the dramatic fall of light illuminating the prophet's sorrow. Subsequent examples, such as *Bathsheba* (1654), are more direct in composition, more restrained in colour and comparably deeper in psychological insight.

More conventional religious feeling was expressed in Rembrandt's etchings, though with unconventional means – vast sweeps of light, tense groupings of figures and sudden detail create great emotional dramas, often in a tiny area. His technical mastery is equally evident in the range of his drawings.

Rembrandt's range and development can most clearly be seen in his series of self-portraits. These were painted over forty years and charted his personal journey from unconventional beginner to young master, disillusioned middle-aged bankrupt to weary sage, by which time he had achieved an extraordinary freedom and expressiveness in his handling of paint.

Rembrandt's engraving, the so-called *'Hundred Guilder Print'*, depicts scenes from St Matthew's Gospel, chapter 19. It is probably his most complex engraving in terms of composition and demonstrates his masterly use of light.
(The Albertina Collection/Austrian Embassy, London).

Rococo and Neoclassicism

The synthesis in later 17th-century Italy of Classicist idealization and Baroque vigour was taken up in France and spread throughout Europe as the accepted courtly 'Grand Manner'. It was soon diluted by the 18th-century desire for the informal and the undemanding, which found its artistic expression in the style known as Rococo. For perhaps the first time the primary function of art was perceived as decorative, rather than illustrative or didactic.

Neither the attitude nor the style were fully accepted in England, where Baroque licence had already been challenged early in the new century by the more 'rational' concept of Palladianism. By the 1750s a reaction to the still freer and more exotic forms of the Rococo appeared not only in England but in France, cradle of the style. Archaeological discoveries in Italy and Greece prompted a re-examination of the origins of European civilization. French intellectualism developed this into international Neoclassicism, and also into the cults of the primitive and of the individual. The latter aspects were forerunners of the Romanticism of the early 19th century (see p. 536).

The Rococo in France

The origins of Rococo can be seen in the later works commissioned by Louis XIV, such as the châteaux of Marly and La Ménagerie, where redecorations included curving forms, curved mirrors and cornices, and plain ceilings with central rosettes. During the reign of Louis XV, Rococo dominated interior design. Its trend was towards lightness and freedom, abstraction of decorative detail, and the

Watteau's *Le Gilles.* There is always a sadness beneath the gaiety in Watteau's dreamlike scenes of open-air festivities, and in this portrait of a clown, the melancholy is nearer the surface than usual. (Louvre, Paris/Explorer)

dominance of curves. Decoration was derived from foliage, sunbursts, grotesques and shellwork (or *rocaille*, giving rise to the later, contemptuous name 'Rococo'). The shapes of these forms were reflected in the rooms themselves, which were wholly or partly circular or elliptical. Colour-schemes typically featured ivory white, pale blue, and gold.

Decorative elegance also characterized contemporary French painting, although neither of its two greatest figures, **Antoine Watteau** (1684–1721) and **Jean-Baptiste-Siméon Chardin** (1699–1779), can be thought of properly in terms of Rococo. While Watteau refined the Flemish mythologies of Rubens and Van Dyck (see pp. 530–1) into scenes of melancholy charm, Chardin poeticized the prosaic Dutch gentleness of de Hooch and Ter Borch (see pp. 532–3). More in harmony with Rococo interiors were the paintings of **François Boucher** (1703–70), the favourite of Madame de Pompadour (Louis XV's mistress) and the even frothier confections of **Jean-Honoré Fragonard** (1732–1806).

Some of the most original creations of French Rococo were in the applied arts: curved furniture, richly inlaid and gilt-mounted; porcelain, notably the elaborate and vividly coloured products of the Sèvres factory founded by Pompadour and Louis XV; and silverware in often boldly asymmetrical shapes.

Rococo in Germany, Italy and Britain

Such elements of asymmetry and inventive fancy (relegated to minor details in French Rococo) were developed to imaginative heights as central features of German Rococo, which elaborated the basics of the style with fantasy and humour. In the exquisite Amalienburg pavilion (1734–39) – at the Schloss Nymphenburg near Munich – the smooth French elegance of the exterior is enlivened by whimsical details; the central salon reduces the grandeur of Versailles' Galerie des Glaces to a playful oval where the variously shaped mirrors reflect spiralling drifts of birds, flowers, foliage and graceful figures, all in silver on a pale blue ground.

Yet more original were the decorations of pilgrimage churches like the Wieskirche, Bavaria (1745–54; see photo), and Vierzehnheiligen, Franconia (1743–72). The architectural forms are those of Italian Baroque, but the plan of Vierzehnheiligen, by **Balthasar Neumann** (1687–1753), is an ingeniously interlocking series of oval and circular spaces, which creates a truly Rococo sense of fluidity. The exterior of Neumann's Würzburg Residenz (1719–44) is also Baroque, but the grandeur of the interior is lightened by sparkling Rococo details.

The lightness of the Kaisersaal and Treppenhaus at Würzburg is brilliantly enhanced by the illusionistic ceiling frescoes (painted 1750–52) of the Venetian **Giambattista Tiepolo** (1696–1770), perhaps the greatest genius of the Rococo. His dazzling effects, luminous colour and

The Wieskirche, Bavaria, epitomizes German Rococo style, its light-filled interior seemingly alive with flickering and surging ornament. (Spectrum)

seemingly endless invention ensured that he was in demand throughout Europe.

The other masters of Venetian Rococo were Tiepolo's brothers-in-law, **Gianantonio** (1699–1760) and **Francesco** (1712–93) **Guardi**. The real and imaginary views of Venice painted by Francesco after his brother's death evoke the changing hues of water and sky as freely as the landscapes of the Impressionists. But even the more precise scenes of **Antonio Canaletto** (1697–1768) were imbued with a poetry only partly due to the decorative fantasy of Venice itself. Indeed the contemporary architecture of the city was one of Classical revival. The true architectural expression of the Italian Rococo is seen in the grandiose scale and elegant curves of the Spanish Steps in Rome (1723–26).

In Britain Rococo elements also appeared in painting, in the graceful landscapes of **Thomas Gainsborough** (1727–88), whose portraits (see box) represent a rather different mode. Rococo elements can also be detected in the crisp line of **William Hogarth** (1697–1784), whose moralizing satires were otherwise quite contrary to the whimsicality of the Rococo. (For examples of Hogarth's works, see pp. 234 and 629.)

Apart from the minor arts of silverware and porcelain, the true spirit of Rococo was only fully expressed in England in chinoiserie (a Chinese-inspired decorative style) and Gothic decoration. But the Gothic Revival (see pp. 538–9), even in the mid-18th century, was rarely without intellectual and emotional resonances relating it to the ideas of the Sublime and Picturesque (see p. 536). The pioneering gardens of the poet **Alexander Pope** (1688–1744; see also p. 627) and **William Kent** (1685–1748), based in part on supposed Chinese ideas of asymmetry, had a very Rococo air with their sinuous lines and artfully composed surprises. The later, more open and apparently natural designs of **Lancelot 'Capability' Brown** (1716–83) were in fact controlled by defined concepts of Classical harmony and balance.

Neoclassicism in Britain

The 'natural' parks of Kent and Brown were considered ideal settings for the 'rational', and therefore equally 'natural', buildings of the Palladians. The Palladians were imitators of the restrained and beautifully proportioned designs of the Renaissance architect Antonio Palladio (see pp. 528–9). Leading architects in the movement included Kent himself and *Colen Campbell* (d. 1729), whose buildings include Stourhead (1720) and Houghton Hall (1722). Both Kent and Campbell were encouraged by *Richard Boyle, Earl of Burlington* (1694–1753), who also turned his own hand to architecture, designing his villa at Chiswick House (1725) in a typically concentrated yet pedantic version of Palladianism.

The Palladian revival, although attempting to re-create ancient Roman architecture for the new 'Augustan' age, was stylistically a revival of Renaissance forms. In the 1750s and 1760s new archaeological discoveries in Italy and Greece, and new ideas in France, led to the emergence of the Neoclassical movement, which encouraged a return to Antique prototypes. The most brilliant figure of this movement in Britain was *Robert Adam* (1728–92). His interiors, contrasting with the heavy forms and restricted colours of the Palladians, created an overall harmony of subtle pastel shades and low-relief patterns. More sober were the works of *William Chambers* (1723–96) and *Henry Holland* (1745–1806), who introduced elements of the elegant simplicity and refined details of French Neoclassicism.

Neoclassicism in Italy and France

The intellectual and philosophical basis of Neoclassicism originated and was developed in Rome and Paris. The ideas of various French theorists and the accurate recording of Greek and Roman antiquities provided food for thought as well as matter for stylistic change. The Louis XVI style of decoration (actually begun under Louis XV) replaced curves with straight lines, sculptural movement with low-relief restraint, and natural and abstract forms with stylized Antique detail. The architectural equivalent can be represented by the classic simplicity of the Petit Trianon (1762–68).

Neoclassicism in painting is best represented by the severely noble canvases of *Jacques-Louis David* (1748–1825). Lacking Antique examples of his art, David relied on the achievements of Nicolas Poussin (see p. 531); but his forms were more simplified and his details more archaeological. At his height he could achieve the poetic realism of the *Death of Marat* (1793) without losing his Classical poise. (For another example of David's work, see p. 626.) As David was the leading Neoclassical painter, so the Italian *Antonio Canova* (1757–1822) was the leading Neoclassical sculptor. However, where David was austere, Canova tended towards the sentimental, setting the style for much 19th-century sculpture. NG-R

David's *Leonides at Thermopylae* (1814) recalls the heroic event in which 300 Spartans took on the whole Persian army. David was virtually the official painter of the French Revolution, a position he maintained under Napoleon. As such, David found in Neoclassical style and subject matter a means of conveying the heroic and civic virtues regarded as desirable by the new order in France. (Louvre, Paris/Archiv für Kunst)

SEE ALSO

● THE BAROQUE AND CLASSICISM p. 530
● ROMANTICISM p. 536
● ARCHITECTURE AND THE APPLIED ARTS IN THE 19TH CENTURY p. 538

Romanticism

Romanticism was a movement in art that emerged in the late 18th century, and that flourished until the middle of the 19th. The movement was a reaction both against the aesthetic and ethical values of Classical and Neoclassical art, and against the ugliness and materialism of the Industrial Revolution. The influence of Romantic writers such as Rousseau, Schiller, Goethe, Scott and Byron was particularly important in providing both subject matter and a philosophy for the Romantic painters.

Liberty Leading the People (1830) by Eugène Delacroix (right). The painting celebrates the revolution of that year, and demonstrates a hatred of tyranny shared by many of the Romantics.

The values of the wider Romantic movement (see p. 630) are central to an understanding of the visual art of the period. Indeed it is the *content* of Romantic painting and the attitude of the artists themselves that give the movement coherence, as in terms of style and technique there are enormous variations.

The Romantic artist

The Romantic image of the artist is of the solitary hero, struggling to recreate his inner vision on the canvas: 'Genius is the fire of a volcano,' wrote Géricault, 'that must and will break forth.' There was a determination to paint the world as *they* saw it, and for many Romantic painters this meant the modern world with all its imperfections, rather than the statically balanced pictures of noble Greeks and Romans favoured by the Neoclassicists.

In Neoclassical art the struggle and feel-

Friedrich's *Abbey in the Oakwoods* (1810). Gothic ruins and brooding skies appealed to the contemporary taste for melancholy and mystery.

ings of the artist are deliberately concealed under a smooth surface in which the main masses are sharply defined. In contrast, the greatest Romantic painters – Constable, Turner, Goya, Delacroix and Géricault – shunned an over-emphasis on line, applying paint freely and boldly in a way that draws attention to the artistic process itself. However, modern subjects and painterly techniques were by no means universal among Romantic painters.

Precursors of Romanticism

For some Romantics the art of the Middle Ages represented their version of an ideal world, a world redolent of knights and chivalry and Christian purity. In architecture the Gothic Revival began in England in the first half of the 18th century, and continued right through the 19th century (see p. 538).

The 18th-century taste for the Gothic went hand in hand with a liking for ivy-clad ruins, evoking a melancholy sense of a lost and mysterious past. Such 'ruins' were often deliberately constructed in grounds laid out in a more 'natural' and unpredictable way than earlier formally patterned gardens.

Theoreticians of the 18th century held up such quaint and irregular landscapes (whether natural or man-made) as examples of the *Picturesque*. This notion had a great impact on landscape painting in the later 18th century, and was to be absorbed by both Constable and Turner. The Picturesque was contrasted with the order and regularity of the *Beautiful* (qualities central to the Classical conception of art), and with the awesome grandeur of the *Sublime*. The Sublime was exemplifed in mountain scenery and storms, which previously had been regarded as ugly and useless, but which from the mid-18th century began to be admired as thrilling manifestations of a power greater than man.

The Romantic landscape

The Sublime was central to the Romantic idea of landscape. For the Romantics, landscape contained a meaning beyond and above its mere visual appearance – an idea that frequently emerges in the works of such poets as Wordsworth and Shelley.

Many Romantic painters attempted to imbue their landscapes with this sense of transcendent meaning. The German painter **Caspar David Friedrich** (1774–1840) used an almost photographic technique to bring out every detail in his landscapes. Mountains, forests, oceans,

skies and ruins dominate tiny figures, evoking a melancholy sense of the infinite. Friedrich saturates his scenes with the light of storm or moon or dawn or sunset in such a way as to give a sense that a visionary experience is close yet unattainable.

The English painter **John Martin** (1789–1854) was also a maker of vast imaginary landscapes. But whereas Friedrich seems to be on the verge of genuine vision, Martin is merely a sensationalist. In his great apocalyptic extravaganzas, drawn largely from the Bible, the destructive forces of nature are exaggerated to a degree that is now difficult to take seriously, but which thrilled his contemporaries. Indeed the taste for 'dramatic' landscape in the manner of Friedrich and Martin continued through much of the 19th century.

A unique contribution to Romantic landscape was made by **Samuel Palmer** (1805–81), a follower of the visionary poet and artist William Blake (see p. 632). As a young man living at Shoreham in the North Downs of Kent, Palmer produced a series of intense visions of the fecundity of nature, painted in a totally personal linear style.

Painting nature – Constable and Turner

Although for many of the Romantics nature was a veil through which the Eternal might sometimes be glimpsed, for the two greatest Romantic landscape painters – both English – the portrayal of nature for its own sake was paramount.

The quiet East Anglian landscapes of **John Constable** (1776–1837) do not immediately strike one as typically Romantic. What is Romantic about them is Constable's honesty to his own experience of nature. Changing moods in the weather, the play of light on clouds and trees and water – all these Constable captured on canvas with unprecedented directness and skill. He had no desire to idealize or generalize the particular scene before him, and if it contained a broken-down old cart (as in *The Hay Wain*, 1821), in it would go. His influence on French painting was profound, particularly on the landscapists of the Barbizon school (see p. 540).

Like Constable, **Joseph Mallord William Turner** (1775–1851) was far more concerned with the business of painting nature as he saw it than with any Romantic philosophy. Initially inspired by the 'Picturesque' landscapes of Claude and the 17th-century Dutch masters, Turner gradually introduced more obviously Romantic subject matter into his work. His exploration of the visual effects of great elemental forces such as Alpine storms was accompanied by increasingly free brushwork. In later works such as *Rain, Steam and Speed* (1844) light and atmospheric effects dominate the picture to such an extent as to make it virtually abstract, looking forward to the Impressionists (see p. 542) and beyond.

Explorers of the irrational – Goya and Fuseli

Henry Fuseli, originally Johann Hein-

rich Füssli (1741–1825), was a Swiss painter who settled permanently in England in 1788, where he became a friend and admirer of Blake. In his most famous work, *The Nightmare* (1782; see p. 232), a grotesque demonic dwarf squats on the body of a sleeping woman, while through the curtains bursts the head of a fearsome horse. Although not an outstanding painter, his explorations of the darker side of human nature were highly influential within the Romantic movement.

A far greater painter was **Francisco de Goya y Lucientes** (1746–1848). As painter to the Spanish court he produced fine portraits painted with a free and masterly technique. However, his dislike for the reactionary establishment led him to such works as the *Caprices* (1799), a series of prints intended to mock the follies and superstitions of society. The result was a series of nightmare images, on which he commented 'The sleep of reason produces monsters.' In another series of prints, *The Disasters of War* (1810–20), and in his great painting *The Third of May* (1814), Goya gave graphic witness to the horrors that result when men abandon reason in war. In his last great works, such as *Saturn Devouring One of his Children* (c. 1820–23), hideous giant figures loom out of the frenzied paintwork, giving a more symbolic expression to the dark forces within humanity.

The French Romantics – Géricault and Delacroix

In 1812 **Théodore Géricault** (1791–1824) virtually overthrew the dominance of Neoclassicism in France with one picture, his *Charging Chasseur*. This gallant cavalry officer on his wild, rearing horse struck the contemporary imagination as a magnificent image of Napoleonic glory. For Géricault, horses represented the epitome of untamed Romantic power, and they feature in many of his finest paintings. Géricault also had a more morbid streak, which found its greatest expression in *The Raft of the Medusa* (1819). Based on a recent event, it depicts the dead and dying abandoned on a raft following a shipwreck. Transcending the sensationalism of the subject, Géricault transforms the terrible scene into one of timeless drama.

Like many of the Romantics, **Eugène Delacroix** (1798–1863) was sympathetic to liberal and nationalist aspirations. This is reflected in works such as *Liberty Leading the People* (1830), a celebration of the revolution in that year that overthrew the reactionary Bourbons from the French throne. What was striking about this picture was its lack of idealization: the revolutionaries at the barricade – and even Liberty herself – are far from genteel or classically heroic.

Delacroix was also attracted by more exotic subjects – often featuring sex and violence – which he painted in brilliant clashes of vibrant colour. For example, in *The Death of Sardanapalus* (1827) the dying Assyrian tyrant looks on indifferently as his naked concubines are butchered to join him in death. Delacroix often gave his compositions an apparently ran-

Goya's series of prints entitled *Caprices* (1799) contains many bizarre images, demonstrating a fascination with the irrational typical of many artists of the period.

SEE ALSO

- THE ENLIGHTENMENT p. 418
- ARCHITECTURE IN THE 19TH CENTURY p. 538
- ROMANTICISM IN EUROPE p. 630
- THE BRITISH ROMANTICS p. 632

dom structure, suggesting an extraordinary sense of movement and actuality.

Medievalism

The nostalgia for things medieval that first emerged in the Gothic Revival is also seen in such writers as Scott and Keats, and in two groups of Romantic painters in particular. The first of these, the **Nazarenes**, were a group of German artists working in Rome in the early 19th century, who drew their inspiration from late medieval German art.

In England the **Pre-Raphaelite Brotherhood** (founded 1848) tried to recreate what they saw as the innocent naturalism of 15th-century Italian painting. Leading members of this group were Dante Gabriel Rossetti (1828–82), John Everett Millais (1829–96) and William Holman Hunt (1827–1910), who in turn strongly influenced William Morris (1834–96) and Edward Burne-Jones (1833–98). Like that of the Nazarenes, the work of the PRB lacked the vigour of the original, and the subjects chosen often veered towards the pious or the sentimental.   IDC

Turner's *Norham Castle, Sunrise* (c. 1845). In late works such as this, Turner floods his canvas with light, whose effects he captures with an extraordinarily free handling of paint.

Architecture and the Applied Arts in the 19th Century

Neoclassicism (see p. 534) had seen architecture and design enriched both by archaeological discoveries of ancient buildings and by intellectual interest in primitive cultures. The latter, combined with an equally radical concentration on geometric forms, had contributed to the creation, in the last years of the 18th century, of what is known as Romantic Classicism – the architectural counterpart of Romanticism in the other arts (see p. 536) – in France, England and Germany. This was characterized, in a series of grandiose but mostly unrealized projects, by freedom from stylistic dependence on the past.

SEE ALSO

- BUILDING CONSTRUCTION p. 338
- CIVIL ENGINEERING p. 340
- ARCHITECTURE AND THE APPLIED ARTS IN THE 20th CENTURY p. 552

The most original of those projects that were executed was the remodelling of the Bank of England by *John Soane* (1753–1837) between 1788 and 1833; the interiors particularly demonstrated Soane's genius for the creation of dramatic shapes, as can still be seen on a small scale in his house in Lincoln's Inn Fields, London (1812–13).

Regency eclecticism

The converse of Soane's individualism was the lavish eclecticism of *John Nash* (1752–1835). His planned transformation of London's fashionable West End, with a triumphal commercial way linking the Prince Regent's residence with a newly developed Regent's Park, surrounded by terraces and dotted with villas, was a successful application of Picturesque ideas of variety and asymmetry to a city setting. Nash was equally inventive in other styles – most famously in Indian and Chinese, as in the Royal Pavilion, Brighton (1815–21).

The variety of Regency styles was reflected with less exuberance in architecture abroad. But in furniture, silverware, china and interior design they were adopted with abandon throughout Europe. A further style, Egyptian, was added to the list in celebration of the campaigns of Napoleon and Nelson. By contrast Classical designs, especially in furniture, showed an elegant simplicity.

Soon, however, Classical architecture was to appear in a richer guise. The precise neo-Greek of Neoclassicism was being replaced by such lavishly columned Graeco-Roman structures as the Madeleine in Paris (1806–42), the British Museum in London (1832–47) and many other, even grander, public buildings from St Petersburg to Naples. Smaller commissions, too, were being executed in elaborately detailed Italian Renaissance

The British Museum, London: a Neoclassical design by Sir Robert Smirke. It was begun in 1823, but the great columned entrance front was completed only in 1847.

styles. This trend was represented in England by the work of *Charles Barry* (1795–1860), who designed the Travellers' (1829–31) and Reform (1838–40) Clubs, London. His greatest work, the Houses of Parliament (1837–60) in London, though asymmetrical as a Classical palace, was decked inside and out with convincing Gothic detail by his collaborator *A.W.N. Pugin* (1812–52); it thus became a monument of the first great movement in 19th-century architecture, the Gothic revival.

The Gothic revival

In the 18th century Gothic architecture had been considered quaintly decorative. But as early as 1772 Goethe had seen Strasbourg Cathedral as a vivid expression of the German soul, and such attitudes later spread to France and England. To Pugin, however, Gothic was supremely the Christian style, which had found its expression in ecclesiastical structures through the spiritual worth of its architects and craftsmen. This religious and moral dimension, echoed in the influential writings of *John Ruskin* (1819–1900), inspired Pugin's followers to create a vast array of Gothic buildings of all kinds, at their best not imitations at all but possessing real originality.

In France similar enthusiasm was shown by *Eugene Viollet-le-Duc* (1814–79), who was certainly one of the most zealous 19th-century restorers of medieval buildings. In Germany Gothic was adopted equally enthusiastically, although it was an Englishman, *George Gilbert Scott* (1811–78), who designed the first true German Gothic Revival church, the Nikolaikirche, Hamburg (1845–63). Scott was the most successful architect of the Victorian age, producing two of its most typical creations, the Midland Hotel, St Pancras (1866–71), and the Albert Memorial (1863–72), both in London.

New technology

Scott's claim that the chief principle of architecture was to decorate construction expressed a feeling common among contemporary architects. His St Pancras Hotel is a façade screening the equally magnificent iron and glass vault of the train shed (1863–67).

Schloss Neuschwanstein, the fairy-tale castle built by Ludwig II of Bavaria (1848–86). The interiors were decorated with scenes from Wagner's romantic operas. (Images)

Cast-iron constructions had been used extensively since the erection of the Iron Bridge, Coalbrookdale (1777–79), both for engineering purposes and to strengthe conventional architecture – even the Albert Memorial was built around a cast-iron core. The most conspicuous example of exposed metal construction was the Eiffel Tower, built for the Paris International Exhibition of 1889.

The combination of iron and glass was also widely used, not just in the railway stations of cities throughout Europe, but in a great variety of other structures, from the Gothic Conservatory (1811–12) of the Prince Regent's Carlton House, London, to the vast shopping arcade of the Galleria Vittorio Emanuele, Milan (1865–77), where the consultant engineers were British. But the greatest example was undoubtedly London's Crystal Palace (1850–51; destroyed 1936), created by *Joseph Paxton* (1801–65) on the model of his conservatories at Chatsworth, Derbyshire, on the site of the Great Exhibition of 1851.

The battle of styles

The Great Exhibition had been conceived by Prince Albert as an opportunity for British artists and craftsmen to display their talents in the application of Fine Art to manufactured goods (the ultimate result of the endeavour was the Victoria and Albert Museum). Pugin, who happily applied his virtuous Gothic to interior fittings from wallpaper to door-handles, was well represented with carved furniture and stone fireplaces. But the public was more impressed by the lavish and massive 'Jacobethan' pieces, by sideboards writhing with naturalistic ornament and by the bulbously curved forms of neo-Rococo.

Such stylistic variety also characterized the International Exhibitions held in Europe and America during the following decades. French influence was particularly noticeable in interior design, where an often vulgarized version of 18th-century Rococo (see p. 534) – known confusingly in England as 'Louis Quatorze' – was popular throughout the century. Its architectural equivalent, the only mode of Continental origin to gain currency in Britain, featured steep mansard roofs and rich French Renaissance detail, and was used for buildings such as hotels and town halls. A Baroque elaboration of this style produced such splendid results as the Paris Opera (1861–74),

J.F. Bentley's design for Westminster Cathedral, London (1895–1903), was influenced by both Italian and Byzantine architecture. Built of red brick with bands of white stone, it has an asymmetrically placed campanile similar to that on Siena Cathedral, Italy.

and the wedding cake extravagance of the Victor Emmanuel Monument, Rome (1885–1911).

The Gothic style had opponents even in England, as Scott discovered when Lord Palmerston forced him to produce a Classical design for the Foreign Office, Whitehall (1860–75). New and more original alternatives were also found, such as 'Old English' and 'Queen Anne'. These hybrid creations combined medieval and Tudor styles, with much half-timbering, and 17th-century details executed in brick; soon, however, the styles became mixed. They were popularized by the work of *R. Norman Shaw* (1831–1912), who had worked in Gothic and who was to develop a more formal Classical range based on the architecture of Christopher Wren and his contemporaries, and a free handling of Baroque (see p. 530). The varied stylistic experiments of *Edwin Lutyens* (1869–1944) moved from Old English and 'Wrenaissance' to the still more formal Neo-Georgian, a popular British mode.

The Arts and Crafts and Aesthetic movements

The medieval vernacular origins of Shaw's and Lutyens' Old English manner gave its products a strong resemblance to those of Arts and Crafts architects. The Arts and Crafts movement was inspired by the vigorous social theories of *William Morris* (1834–96). Morris thought that the social and artistic levels of industrialism could be transformed by a return to the dignity of medieval craftsmanship and a rationalization of design. He set up a firm to manufacture his own wallpapers and textiles, which replaced elaborate pattern repeats with all-over patterns of flowing, semi-stylized forms more suited

to two-dimensional surfaces. His firm also reproduced the furniture of like-minded friends – some of them Pre-Raphaelites (see p. 536) – based on traditional rural models. Subdued 'natural' tones were preferred to garish colours and vivid contrasts.

During the 1870s the influence of Japanese artefacts, suddenly available in huge quantities in Europe, began to be felt. In France this chiefly affected painting (see p. 544); in Britain the slender shapes of furniture, the stylized and even abstract patterns of textiles and porcelain, and the delicate colours and simple forms of interior design were enthusiastically adopted by the Aesthetic middle classes. It was the heady combination of the Aesthetic and Arts and Crafts movements which led to the creation on the Continent of Art Nouveau (see p. 522).

Equally influential, in Europe and America, was the simple rationalism of Arts and Crafts architecture; here too, however, the simplicity of hand-crafted stone and timber cottages was soon modified by the urban elegance and 'art for art's sake' code of the Aesthetes. The architect who most successfully combined simplicity and elegance was *C.F.A. Voysey* (1857–1941); he quickly developed his characteristic combination of white plastered walls, stone-framed ribbon windows and huge, sweeping slate roofs. His smaller, symmetrically gabled examples provided straightforward, easily imitated models that were adapted to suburban semi-detached houses by British architects for the following 30 years. Some of his more original followers combined Voysey's external style with fluid interior arrangements based on American ideas, prefiguring the open planning revolution of the Modern Movement (see p. 522). NG-R

Realism

Realism was a movement that flourished between 1840 and 1880, originating in France, and soon spreading throughout Europe and to America. The Realists reacted against the subjectivity, individualism and historical obsessions of many of the Romantics, adopting instead a style of art based on truth to nature. The grand, heroic subject matter of the Romantic movement was replaced by simple views of everyday life, and Romantic emotionalism was abandoned in favour of detached, objective observation.

Corot's *The Gust of Wind* (right)(c. 1865–70). In such landscapes as this, Corot looked forward to the spontaneity of the Impressionists. (Museé Saint-Denis, Rheims/Archiv für Kunst)

The term 'realism' applies to both style and subject matter. Usually Realists avoided the vivid, dramatic brushstrokes favoured by artists such as Delacroix (see pp. 536–7), preferring to make their paintings distinct and precise, with straightforward subjects. Their motto was, 'It is necessary to be of your own time.'

The beginnings of Realism

In France the Revolution of 1848 brought in the Second Republic, overturning the old bourgeois order and replacing it with a more democractic government (see p. 428). The ideals and aims of democracy and socialism were discussed by a number of writers, artists and intellectuals in a Parisian café, the Andler Keller. *Gustav Courbet* (1819–77) attended these meetings and was inspired to represent the new ideas in his art.

Courbet was a largely self-taught artist who wanted to render the outside world as faithfully as possible. He hoped to translate his sense impressions directly onto the canvas, instead of relying on the standard practice of copying the style and subject of Old Masters. In 1850 he created a scandal in Paris with the exhibition of his paintings *The Peasants at Flagey Returning from the Fair*, *The Burial at Ornans* and *The Stonebreakers*.

In these works he showed humble villagers, peasants and labourers, rather than the gods, heroes and biblical figures that the Parisian public was accustomed to as subjects for paintings. *The Stonebreakers* represents a man too old to be working, and a boy too young to be working. Their clothes are ragged, their faces are obscured; yet through their monumental forms they symbolize the dignity of the working man. Courbet's painting represented his political beliefs and his desire to show the world as it is, rather than as it should be.

Realist landscape

Realism also had an impact on landscape. The French painter *Camille Corot* (1796–1875) was an important link between the idealized Romantic landscape and the landscape painted directly from nature. He made several trips to Italy, and his early works bring a new tonal style to the old traditions of ideal landscape as practised by Claude Lorraine and Nicolas Poussin in the 17th century (see p. 531).

Corot's silvery tonal landscapes were popular in his own time, but he was not satisfied with them. As his style developed, he began to exhibit sketches that he had made out of doors. This move was particularly controversial because landscape painters traditionally made sketches out of doors, but finished the painting in the studio.

Corot was especially influential on the *Barbizon School* – a group of artists who moved to Barbizon in the Forest of Fontainbleau, southeast of Paris. There they immersed themselves in the study of nature and painted *'en plein air'* (out of doors), in order to represent nature as faithfully as possible. *Théodore Rousseau* (1812–67), the leader of the group, favoured a rational, almost geological approach to nature. He was interested in the changing effects of weather and tried to capture them on canvas. *Charles-François Daubigny* (1817–78), an artist closely associated with the Barbizon School, had a studio on a boat, which allowed him to float up and down the Oise river making sketches from nature.

Millet and the noble peasant

Perhaps the most unusual member of the Barbizon group was *Jean-François Millet* (1814–75). Millet was from a peasant background, and had been raised on a farm. He studied painting in Paris, but his attempts exasperated his teachers and he soon settled into his own distinctive and unusual style. His subjects consisted mainly of peasants working in the fields, sowing, gleaning (gathering left-over corn) or mowing, endowed with grace and dignity by Millet's cool classical style.

In 1849 Millet settled in Barbizon and adopted the ideals of the Barbizon painters, living a life of poverty in a cottage with his wife and 14 children. His noble peasants and calm, peaceful landscapes later influenced Van Gogh (see p. 544).

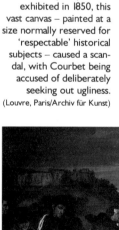

Courbet's *The Burial at Ornans* (1849). When exhibited in 1850, this vast canvas – painted at a size normally reserved for 'respectable' historical subjects – caused a scandal, with Courbet being accused of deliberately seeking out ugliness. (Louvre, Paris/Archiv für Kunst)

Painters of modern life

Realism was not confined to landscapes and views of peasant life. The Realists' desire to be modern, rather than historical, led to a series of paintings representing scenes of middle-class life. City life was the main subject in the work of *Gustave Caillebotte* (1848–94), who painted precise, almost photographic, views of busy Paris streets.

Eugène Boudin (1824–98) applied the *plein air* methods of Corot and the Barbizon painters to such scenes of fashionable life. Boudin painted a number of landscapes at the beach resorts of Trouville and Deauville and, in contrast to Courbet and Millet, depicted French middle-class, bourgeois society. His paintings influenced Claude Monet, whom he persuaded to become a landscape painter.

Apart from Monet, other Impressionists such as Degas and Renoir adopted Realist modern-life subject matter in their scenes of cafés, Paris streets, theatres and parks (see pp. 542–3). Standing somewhat apart from the Impressionists, Edouard Manet (see p. 542) took his role as 'the painter of modern life' very seriously.

Realism and caricature

The unique contribution of *Honoré Daumier* (1808–79) to Realism was a series of caricatures that combined fantasy with Realism. These often bitter satires attacked both political evils and social foibles. Daumier was arrested and imprisoned in 1832 for publishing a caricature of King Louis Philippe, after which his attacks became less specific, concentrating instead on universal types – doctors, lawyers, businessmen. One of Daumier's recurring character types was Ratapoil, an evil imperialist with a greasy moustache. (For an example of Daumier's work, see pp. 634–5.)

European Realism outside France

In 1855 the Exposition Universelle (Universal Exhibition) was held in Paris, and

Realist paintings were prominently on display. Artists from many countries saw the works, and soon the Realist movement became international. Britain, Russia, Italy, Germany and Scandinavia all produced examples of Realist art.

In England, *William Powell Frith* (1819–1909) adopted the fashionable beach scene for his painting of *Ramsgate Sands* (1854), which was bought by Queen

Victoria, and he extended the idea of a modern crowd in works such as *Derby Day* (1858) and the *Railway Station* (1862). (For an example of Frith's work, see p. 637.) A more serious form of Realism can be seen in the works of artists such as *Luke Fildes* (1843–1927) and *Hubert*

Herkomer (1849–1914). Fildes's *Applicants for Admission to a Casual Ward* shows a group of impoverished and ill patients waiting in the cold for a place in the hospital.

The social beliefs of *Ford Madox Brown* (1821–93) are embodied in his most famous painting, *Work* (1852–65). Stylistically

Madox Brown was an important influence on the Pre-Raphaelites (see p. 537), although they did not generally depict modern subjects; Holman Hunt's *The Awakening Conscience* (1853–54) is a notable exception.

In Germany, the first great Realist was *Adolph von Menzel* (1815–1905), whose style anticipated that of the Impressionists. Also notable are the scenes of village life by *Wilhelm Leibl* (1844–1900), such as *Three Women in Church* (1882).

Realism in America

In America, Realism was also known as *Naturalism*, and its main exponents were *Thomas Eakins* (1844–1916) and *Winslow Homer* (1836–1910). Homer began his career as an illustrator for the periodical *Harper's Weekly*, acting as a war artist during the American Civil War (see p. 431). His views of the front provided a detached impression of the more trivial details of war. In the 1860s and 1870s he painted scenes of rural America, which were influenced by *plein air* paintings he had seen in France. After a visit to England in 1881, he became fascinated by the sea and seafaring people. He moved to the Maine coast and spent the rest of his life as a recluse, painting views of the coast and coastal life.   SW

SEE ALSO

● ROMANTICISM p. 536
● IMPRESSIONISM p. 542
● REALISM AND NATURALISM (LITERATURE) p. 634
● THE NOVEL IN 19TH CENTURY BRITAIN p. 636

Winslow Homer's *Game of Croquet* (1866). In his scenes of modern life, Homer vividly captured the freshness of the open air. (Art Institute, Chicago/Scala)

Millet's *The Gleaners* (left)(1857). Millet devoted himself to the depiction of the harsh life of French peasants, and the stoical dignity with which they endured it. (Louvre, Paris/Archiv für Kunst)

Impressionism

Although often regarded as the first of the modern movements, Impressionism was neither a school nor a movement with a clearly defined programme. Instead it is better regarded as an ill-defined association of artists who joined together for the purpose of mounting independent group exhibitions, rather than compromise their art in order to be included in the Paris Salon, the official state-sponsored exhibition. While they had no stated aims or manifesto their work shared some techniques and certain subjects.

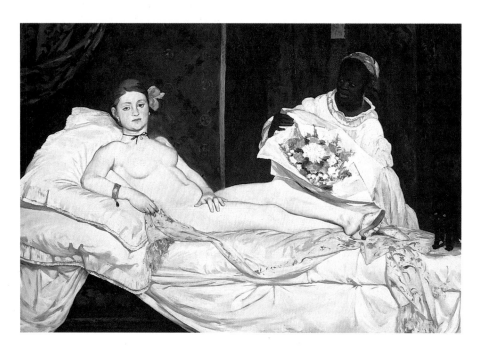

Manet's *Olympia* (1863) caused a major scandal because it dealt with a traditional subject in a shockingly contemporary mode – Manet used a prostitute to masquerade in the pose of a Classical Venus. (Jeu de Paume, Paris/ R.M.N.)

Player, the paintings Manet submitted to the Salon of 1863 were refused, along with thousands of others. Since artists depended largely on the Salon to attract potential customers at a time before the private dealer was a common phenomenon, there was a tremendous outcry at this apparent injustice. Eventually the Emperor Napoleon III decreed that a counter-exhibition should be hung – alongside the official Salon – in which the public could judge for themselves the merits of the refused works. This was the *Salon des Refusés* and the work which aroused the most hostile reaction at this exhibition was Manet's *Déjeuner sur l'herbe* ('Picnic on the grass', 1863).

Despite its apparently innocuous subject, the painting evoked strong feelings in its viewers because Manet had chosen to rework a classical theme – the nude in a landscape – and place it within a clearly identifiable modern setting. Because of the presence of the two men in modern dress and the direct gaze of the seated woman, the painting was seen to portray two prostitutes with their clients. A similar scandal was caused at the next official Salon (1865), where Manet exhibited his *Olympia* (1863).

While the Impressionist painters did not by and large share Manet's subject matter nor his techniques, they recognized that in the late 1860s and 1870s he was the leader of the artistic avant-garde in Paris, both because of his forceful painting style and also because of his uncompromising stance against hallowed art institutions.

Impressionist style

In the summer of 1869 the French painters **Claude Monet** (1840–1926) and **Pierre Auguste Renoir** (1841–1919) worked together at a popular bathing spot known as La Grenouillère on the River Seine just outside Paris. Painting in collaboration, they produced a series of canvases that are generally regarded as being the first examples of the fully developed Impressionist style.

Artists began to produce finished paintings, rather than mere sketches, in the open air ('*en plein air*'). This meant that their canvases had to be much smaller and more intimate than the large works Manet sent to the Salon. In order to represent the effect of sunlight on water they used the characteristic 'broken' brushstroke, in which dabs of pure pigment were laid side by side on the canvas rather than smoothly modelled as had previously been the case. Unlike Manet, they eliminated all the earth colours, and particularly black, from their palettes and concentrated instead on the three primaries (red, yellow and blue) and their immediate derivatives. They observed that the colours of objects were modified by their surroundings and introduced colour reflections into the shadows. Although the essential features of the Impressionist style were formed by 1869, it was another five years before the first group exhibition gave the group any kind of coherent identity.

SEE ALSO

● REALISM p. 540
● POST-IMPRESSIONISM p. 544
● SYMBOLISM p. 546

Neoimpressionism had little to do with Impressionism although its two chief exponents, Seurat and Signac, exhibited with the Impressionist group. It was much more clearly systematized than Impressionism and drew on current scientific research – such as the interest in colour theory – in a much more coherent way than that adopted by painters in the Impressionist circle.

Manet and the Salon des Refusés

The French artist **Edouard Manet** (1832–83) is frequently linked with the Impressionist group although he declined ever to exhibit with these artists and shared few of their artistic aspirations. He continued to strive for success and recognition at the all-important Salon, producing large-scale canvases painted entirely in the studio using heavy earth colours and rich, velvety blacks, all of which were to be abandoned by the members of the Impressionist group.

After an early success at the Salon of 1861 with his painting *The Spanish Guitar*

Monet's *Gare Saint-Lazare* (right) (1877). Although well-known for his rural landscapes, Monet was also a painter of modern life. (Jeu de Paume, Paris/Scala)

Further exhibitions

In all there were eight exhibitions of the Impressionist group, held from 1874 to 1886. Of the original group, only Pissarro exhibited at all eight, and by the time of the last their character had changed fundamentally with the inclusion of artists such as Gauguin, Seurat and Signac, whose contributions were not always admired by some of the older artists.

Impressionist subject matter

Monet, Sisley and Pissarro favoured landscapes; Pissarro's *The Harvest at Montfoucault* (1876), shown at the third exhibition, is a depiction of timeless rural activity, while Monet's *Arrival of the Normandy Train at Gare Saint-Lazare* (1877) takes its inspiration from the rapidly industrializing French capital. This canvas was also shown at the 1877 exhibition and represented the glass roof of the station filled with smoke from the approaching train.

Renoir produced a number of figure studies and Degas in particular shunned the notion of working in the open, preferring instead to work in the traditional manner, finishing canvases in his studio from rough sketches done on the spot. He produced a number of oil paintings that took horse racing as their theme, and specialized in ballet scenes.   LS

Renoir's *Lunch on the Riverbank* (left), a typically joyous celebration of the good things of life. (Art Institute, Chicago/Scala)

Degas' *Ballet School* (below left). Degas' composition, with its oddly cut-off figures, shows the influence of photography on his work. (Archiv für Kunst)

The first exhibition

Although the idea of a group exhibition had been considered for some time, it was not until 1874 that the first Impressionist exhibition was held at the studio of the photographer Nadar. They were motivated partly by disillusionment at their persistent rejections at the Salon and partly out of a desire for sales. The 39 artists exhibiting included not only Monet and Renoir but also Paul Cézanne (see p. 544), **Edgar Degas** (1834–1917), **Berthe Morisot** (1841–95), **Camille Pissarro** (1831–1903) and **Alfred Sisley** (1839–99). At later exhibitions they were joined by the American **Mary Cassatt** (1844–1926), Paul Gauguin (see p. 544), **Georges Seurat** (1859–91) and **Paul Signac** (1863–1935).

At the exhibition of 1874 they called themselves the 'société anonyme des artistes peintres, sculpteurs, graveurs' – that is they formed a limited company. It was not until later that they adopted the name 'Impressionists' for themselves. However, the name 'Impressionist' had been coined at the 1874 show by the critic Louis Leroy in response to a work by Monet entitled *Impression: Sunrise*. This depicted boats in a port seen through a mist, which led to a dissolution of form and complete lack of detail or description. Leroy was so incensed at the apparent sloppiness of the work that he failed to see that the painting's real subject was a faithful rendition of an atmosphere. Taking the name 'Impressionist' from the offending work he extended it to the group as a whole.

NEOIMPRESSIONISM

At the final Impressionist exhibition, Seurat, Signac and Pissarro all showed canvases using the latest *divisionist* (or *pointillist*) techniques. This involved the use of pure colours applied in such small patches (often dots) that they appeared to fuse to form an intermediary tone when viewed from an appropriate distance. Hence grass might be composed of touches of blue alongside areas of yellow. These ideas were not new, but had been used in a much less systematic way by the Impressionist painters. However, the static quality of works such as Seurat's *Bathers at Asnières* (1884) and its large format marked a departure from the aims of orthodox Impressionism.

Seurat's *The Circus.* (Jeu de Paume, Paris/Scala)

Post-Impressionism and Fauvism

Just as the Impressionists reacted against the established art of their day, a succession of artists later reacted against Impressionism itself. The Post-Impressionists, as they became known, were active mainly in France between about 1880 and 1905. They included artists who painted in a wide variety of styles but who shared a desire to go beyond pure naturalism and to give more emphasis to colour, emotions and imagination. From these individuals the major art movements of the 20th century emerged.

The term Post-Impressionism was first used by the British critic and artist Roger Fry when he arranged an exhibition entitled 'Manet and the Post-Impressionists' in London in 1910. The principal artists in this exhibition were Cézanne, Gauguin and van Gogh; according to Fry these were the three great artists who had moved beyond Impressionism in the search for a new art. Also included were paintings by the Neoimpressionists Seurat and Signac (see p. 543), Redon (see p. 546), Picasso (see p. 548), Matisse, Derain, Vlaminck, Rouault, and Marquet. In 1912 Fry arranged a second Post-Impressionist exhibition and the term later grew to include the Fauves (see

SEE ALSO

● IMPRESSIONISM AND NEO-
   IMPRESSIONISM p. 542
● SYMBOLISM, SECESSION AND
   EXPRESSIONISM p. 546
● CUBISM AND ABSTRACTION
   p. 548

below) and the Neoimpressionists as well as artists from other countries who had not been included in Fry's exhibitions.

Post-Impressionism in France

As a young man, **Paul Cézanne** (1839–1906) painted dark romantic pictures, often using a palette knife to depict scenes of violence and eroticism. In the early 1870s, encouraged by the Impressionist Camille Pissarro, he began to work out of doors and gradually lightened his palette. Cézanne soon developed away from the Impressionists and their depictions of a fleeting moment in time, which he felt resulted in a lack of structure. Like the Impressionists he wanted to paint directly from nature, but also to recapture the grandeur and order of the masters of Classicism such as Poussin (see p. 531). Part of his greatness lies in his struggle to combine these two aims and to achieve a monumental, timeless fusion of forms. Cézanne spent most of his life in the south of France, where he mainly painted still lifes and landscapes – often depicting Mont Sainte-Victoire, a mountain near his native town of Aix.

Like those of Cézanne, the early works of **Vincent van Gogh** (1853–90) were dark in colour. These works – the most famous of which is *The Potato Eaters* (1885) – reflect the plight of poor peasants at work in his native Netherlands. After moving to Paris in 1886 he adopted the brighter colours of the Impressionists. Van Gogh's most powerful works were painted after 1888, when he moved to Arles in Provence. In numerous self-portraits and landscapes his emotions are conveyed through brilliant colours, thick paint and strong rhythmic brushstrokes. He was subject to periodic fits of depression and eventually committed suicide.

Paul Gauguin (1848–1903) gave up his life as a prosperous Parisian businessman to become a painter. He lived in Brittany,

Gauguin's *Ea Haere Ia Oe* (Where are you going? 1892). In his Tahitian period, Gauguin often combined mysterious subjects with vivid experiments in colour and line. (Staatsgalerie, Stuttgart)

Martinique, Tahiti and finally the Marquesas Islands, attracted by the apparently simple life of these communities. In monumental compositions such as *Nevermore* (1897), forms are portrayed as broad flat areas of rich colour surrounded by sinuous lines. Like van Gogh, Gauguin used colour for emotional rather than naturalistic effect, although Gauguin was closer to the Symbolists (see p. 546).

The turn of the 19th century was a period of great developments in art. Cézanne, van Gogh and Gauguin all influenced subsequent art movements, including Symbolism and Expressionism (see p. 546), Fauvism (see below) and Cubism (where Cézanne's influence was central; see p. 548). However, individualism also flourished and many artists appeared who cannot easily be grouped into schools. **Henri Rousseau** (1844–1910), known as 'Le Douanier' because of his job in the Paris Customs service, was self-taught and was the first untrained, 'naive' painter to win recognition as a major artist. He painted pictures of great clarity and brightness, which, despite his knowledge of perspective, are full of subtlety and charm. **Henri de Toulouse-Lautrec** (1864–1901) was influenced by Degas (see p. 542) and took his subjects from Parisian music halls and brothels. His style was at its most effective in the simplified lines of such poster designs as *Moulin Rouge* (1891).

Post-Impressionism in Britain

Despite initial public hostility to the London exhibitions, British artists were soon influenced by the new European art. **Walter Sickert** (1860–1942) and the Camden Town Group applied the new approach to their paintings of lower-class London life, while the Bloomsbury artists also looked to the continent for inspiration.

The Intimists

The French painters **Pierre Bonnard**

Cézanne painted Mont Sainte-Victoire countless times. His works – embodying his aim to 'treat nature in terms of the cylinder, the sphere, the cone' – were a crucial influence on the Cubists. (Metropolitan Museum of Art, New York/Archiv für Kunst)

Van Gogh's *Wheatfields*, executed in the typically turbulent brushstrokes and expressive colours of his late works. (Van Gogh Museum, Amsterdam/Explorer)

1864–1947) and ***Edouard Vuillard*** 1868–1940) were both retiring in character and concentrated chiefly on depicting their immediate environments. Intimate interior scenes of bourgeois life, informal portraits and nudes were their chief subjects. Many of Vuillard's paintings show his mother, while Bonnard frequently used his wife as a model.

Matisse and the Fauves

Another Frenchman, ***Henri Matisse*** (1869–1954), was one of the most important and influential artists of the early 20th century. He was a master of colour and line as well as a major sculptor and illustrator. In his paintings of female nudes, still lifes and interiors, Matisse combined a sensitivity of line with decorative pattern and rich flat colour. In 1908 Matisse wrote, 'What I dream of is an art of balance, of purity and serenity devoid of troubling or distressing subject matter'. In his later years, unable to paint, Matisse made large compositions from brilliantly coloured paper cut-outs.

With ***André Derain*** (1880–1954), Matisse was the founder of ***Fauvism***, the first modern movement of the 20th century.

Matisse's colours became brighter after he painted with the Neoimpressionist painter Signac (see p. 543) at Saint Tropez in 1904. The following year he worked in the south of France with Derain (who had been influenced by van Gogh), and their paintings were transformed into explosions of bold brushstrokes and brilliant colours.

When their works were exhibited at the Salon D'Automne in Paris in 1905 the name *fauves* ('wild beasts') was given to them by the critic Louis Vauxcelles. He was not referring to the artists' characters, but to their bold shocking colours. The only Fauve who could be described as wild in character was ***Maurice de Vlaminck*** (1876–1958), a professional cyclist whose love of speed was reflected in the immediacy of his paintings – he frequently used thick pigment squeezed directly from the tube on to the canvas.

One of the artists connected with the Fauves for a short period was ***Raoul Dufy*** (1877–1953). He soon abandoned Fauvism, but retained bright colours throughout

Derain's *Port of London* exemplifies the bright, primary colours and simplified forms of the Fauves. (Tate Gallery, London/Archiv für Kunst)

his life in his cheerful scenes of race courses and the seaside. Under Matisse's influence ***Albert Marquet*** (1875–1947) used bright Fauve colours in his paintings of flag-lined streets and seaside billboards, but soon turned to carefully composed atmospheric scenes in muted tones that seem to look back to the Impressionists. The Dutch artist ***Kees van Dongen*** (1877–1968) painted scenes of Parisian night life in bold Fauve colours. ***George Rouault*** (1871–1958) exhibited with the Fauves but did not belong to the movement; his paintings of human corruption and religious images, with their deep glowing colours, place him closer to Expressionism (see p. 546). AJ

Matisse's *Decorative Figure* (1927). Matisse was fascinated by the patterns of furnishings, and his figures are often absorbed into the background to make a deliberately two-dimensional composition. (Succession H. Matisse/DACS/Archiv für Kunst)

Symbolism, Secession and Expressionism

The Symbolist movement emerged in the 1880s as a reaction against the naturalist movement (the idea that art was an imitation of nature) and against modern industrialism and materialist values. The Symbolists sought to escape into the past or into the world of fantasy, including dreams. They believed that art existed alongside, not in direct relation to, the real world, and that it had its own rules.

Moreau's *The Apparition* (1876) portrays Sâlomé – the ultimate *femme fatale* – witnessing a vision of the head of John the Baptist. (Musée Gustave Moreau, Paris/R.M.N.)

The anti-naturalism of the Symbolists was also shared by many of the artists of the German and Austrian Secessions of the 1890s, and by a diverse group of later artists known as the Expressionists, who wished to emphasize – often through unnaturalistic distortion – the importance of emotion and the artist's inner vision. Expressionism was also an impor-

Munch's *The Scream* (1893) expresses the anguish of human existence. (Nasjonalgalleriet, Oslo/Archiv für Kunst)

tant movement in cinema (see pp. 558–9) and drama (see pp. 642–3)

Symbolism in France

Symbolism in art was linked to a legacy of Romanticism in art and literature. In 1857 the poet Charles Baudelaire published *Les Fleurs du Mal* (see p. 640). Among the subjects that he treated was Sâlomé, the temptress and ultimate *femme fatale*. The subject of Sâlomé was depicted many times by **Gustave Moreau** (1826–98) in pictures such as *The Apparition*, which he submitted to the Paris Salon of 1876. Its jewel-like colours and extravagant, ornamental details, together with its atmosphere of mystery and menace, were characteristic of his anti-naturalistic approach. The *femme fatale* – seductive, exotic and evil – was to become a recurrent theme in Symbolist art of the so-called 'decadent' kind.

The work of **Odilon Redon** (1840–1916) dealt with fantastic subject matter, dream or nightmare imagery and strange, hallucinatory beings in a mixture of the emotional and the irrational. He worked almost exclusively in black and white until around 1890, when he began making pastels and oil paintings in radiant colours. Moreau and Redon pioneered the way to Symbolism in art in France and were especially influential in suggesting the existence of a mysterious reality beyond appearances.

Another particularly influential figure was **Paul Gauguin** (see also p. 544), who

turned away from Impressionism in the late 1880s and started to work from memory and imagination, using bold, rhythmical outlines and arbitrary colours. His figure compositions from then on have an air of ambiguity and mystery.

Symbolism in England

In England, the Pre-Raphaelite paintings produced by Dante Gabriel Rossetti (see p. 537) were an important source. Rossetti's works, filled with poetic feelings of suppressed sexuality and depicting visions of the Middle Ages in a highly decorative manner, were a major influence on **Sir Edward Burne-Jones** (1833–98) and **Aubrey Beardsley** (1872–98), among others. Beardsley produced fluid yet economical black-and-white drawings as illustrations for literary works such as *Sâlomé* by Oscar Wilde and *Le Morte d'Arthur* by Sir Thomas Malory (both 1894). His drawings were often sexually explicit.

The Secessions

In Austria and Germany in the 1890s the growing revolt against the academicism of conventional painting led to the formation of *Secessions* – breakaway groups of artists. The first was formed in Munich in 1892 in protest against the overcrowding and lack of selectiveness of the official salons. That of Berlin – led by

Max Liebermann (1847–1935) and *Lovis Corinth* (1858–1925), who were pioneering the German version of Impressionism – was sparked off by the hostility of academic painters towards new art.

It was the Vienna Secession (1897), led by Gustav Klimt (see below), that was the most radical. It was successful in its aim of promoting and encouraging Austrian painters, architects and craftsmen. The major styles of the artists of the Vienna Secession were Symbolism and *Jugendstil*, the German and Austrian form of Art Nouveau (see p. 552). The independent nature of the Secessions paved the way for later artists' groups such as Die Brücke and Der Blaue Reiter (see below).

Precursors of Expressionism

Expressionism as a movement reached a peak around 1910. There were, however, earlier artists whose work showed an approach that attempted not just to depict the visual, but to express the emotional. Expressionist styles varied, although there was a general tendency towards distorted forms and unnaturalistic colours. Van Gogh (see p. 544) was an important influence.

The Norwegian *Edvard Munch* (1863–1944) produced paintings and prints whose subject matter and its treatment could be described as hysterical, neurotic and intense. In works such as *The Scream* (1893) he portrayed anxiety, fear and despair, not only in the shrieking figure, but also in the tortured sky. In Munch's work, the turbulence of the paint often enhances the powerful subjects of love, sickness and death. *James Ensor* (1860–1949), a Belgian artist, included grotesque elements such as skeletons and carnival masks in his works, giving them a latent black humour. Executed in thick paint and sometimes close to caricature, they are often seen as Expressionistic.

In Austria the development from Symbolism to Expressionism via Jugendstil can be seen in the work of three artists. *Gustav Klimt* (1863–1918), produced highly decorative paintings in which erotic female images are combined with areas of luxuriant, mosaic-like Jugendstil patterning.

Although badly received by the public,

Klimt's *The Kiss* (1908) makes use of flat decorative pattern and gold leaf. (Österreichische Galerie, Vienna/Austrian Embassy, London)

Klimt's work was an important influence on *Egon Schiele* (1890–1918) and *Oskar Kokoschka* (1886–1980). Despite his brief career, Schiele became one of the major Austrian Expressionists. He is famous for his contorted and often sexually explicit nudes, which frequently convey a psychological tension. Kokoschka's many portraits and figure compositions, such as *The Tempest* (*Bride of the Wind*) (1914), are treated with a nervous linearity through which he tried to reveal the subject's intimate feelings and neuroses.

German Expressionism

The artists' group known as *Die Brücke* ('The Bridge') was formed in Dresden in 1905, and lasted until 1913. Its members included *Ernst Ludwig Kirchner* (1880–1938), *Erich Heckel* (1883–1970), *Karl Schmidt-Rotluff* (1884–1976), *Max Pechstein* (1881–1955) and, for a short time, *Emil Nolde* (1867–1956). The group was united by a desire to create a revolutionary new art, and their name signified their hope that this new art would serve as a bridge to the future. The bridge motif often appeared in paintings and prints by the group's members.

The artists of Die Brücke were influenced by Gauguin and the Fauves (see pp. 545–6), and also by African sculpture and German medieval woodcuts (a medium they revived). Though to some extent the German equivalent of Fauvism, their work was deliberately rougher and cruder, with broken, unnaturalistic colours and heavily expressive, stylized forms.

Another independent group that gave German Expressionism further impetus was *Der Blaue Reiter* ('The Blue Rider'), formed in Munich in 1911. The members included the Russian *Wassily Kandinsky* (1866–1944), *August Macke* (1887–1914) and *Franz Marc* (1880–1916), and the name of the group derives from the cover of their periodical – designed by Kandinsky and Marc – which depicted a horse and rider in blue and black. Der Blaue Reiter was a more varied group than Die Brücke and, rather than promoting one particular tendency, its aim was for each artist to achieve an individual style. They did, however, share a use of bold colours and a tendency to develop towards abstraction. The death of Marc and Macke during World War I led to the group's dissolution. Although the Russian *Alexej Jawlensky* (1864–1941) never joined Der Blaue Reiter, his work was in a similar vein. Works such as *Head of a Young Girl* show a use of bold outlines and deep rich colours.

For many artists the trauma of World War I had a powerful effect on their work. The pre-war works of the German *Max Beckmann* (1884–1950) had already shown Expressionist tendencies, but it was works such as *The Night* (1918–19) that had the greatest impact, depicting the horror of torture in a Germany undergoing radical changes and uprisings. The stylized figures crowded together in a shallow space resemble German late Gothic wood carvings. *George Grosz* (1893–1959), a painter and draughtsman who had been a member of the Berlin Dada group (see p. 550), similarly tackled

Kokoschka's *The Tempest* (*The Bride of the Wind*) (1914) is symbolic of the stormy relationship between the artist and his mistress, Alma Mahler. (Kunstmuseum, Basle/Colorphoto Hinz)

contemporary issues and subjects such as the decadent capitalism of the Weimar Republic (see p. 442). His satirical caricatures were especially savage. The rise of Nazism in Germany, and later in Austria, led to the work of many leading artists being attacked as 'degenerate'. They were banned from exhibiting, and a number of them fled abroad. SR

Erich Heckel's *Scene from Dostoevski* (1912). This woodcut, with its angularity and strong contrasts, is typical of the Expressionism of Die Brücke.

SEE ALSO

- ARCHITECTURE AND THE APPLIED ARTS IN THE 19TH CENTURY p. 538
- IMPRESSIONISM AND NEO-IMPRESSIONISM p. 542
- POST-IMPRESSIONISM p. 544
- CUBISM AND ABSTRACTION p. 546
- ARCHITECTURE AND THE APPLIED ARTS IN THE 20TH CENTURY p. 552
- SILENT FILMS p. 558
- SYMBOLISM (IN LITERATURE) p. 640
- EXPERIMENTAL THEATRE p. 642

Cubism and Abstraction

In the first half of the 20th century a revolution occurred in the practice of art. The Cubists led this revolution by breaking with the convention that art should provide a faithful representation of the world. From 1910 artists in different countries began to produce abstract or non-figurative art, sometimes abstracting from a landscape or still life until the subject disappeared.

At other times they produced an art that had no obvious reference to the real world. In this so-called non-objective art, all connection with objective reality has been severed and the work of art becomes the expression of the artist's personal perception.

Braque's *Clarinet and Bottle of Rum on a Mantelpiece* (1913). The inclusion of stencilled letters was a Cubist innovation. (© DACS 1990/Tate Gallery, London/Bridgeman Art Library)

Early Cubism

Cubism, one of the most important movements in 20th-century art, was originated in France by the Spanish artist **Pablo Picasso** (1881–1973) and the

Frenchman **Georges Braque** (1882–1963). The movement lasted from about 1907 into the 1920s and, as with Impressionism and Fauvism (see pp. 542 and 545), the term 'Cubism' was coined by a critic and intended to be derogatory. Following the example of Cézanne (see p. 542), the Cubists sought new answers to the age-old question of how to depict the three-dimensional real world on a flat two-dimensional canvas. They began to analyse objects, breaking them down into their geometrical shapes and restructuring them in order to show each form's many facets in a single image. They were therefore representing what is known about an object rather than what is actually seen. These early *Analytical Cubist* works, as they became known, generally depict either single figures or still lifes and were painted in a restricted range of greys and browns.

The Cubists were also influenced by the recently discovered African Negro art and this is first exemplified in the right-hand side of Picasso's *Les Demoiselles d'Avignon* (1907), where two faces have been broken down into simple, mask-like forms.

Later Cubism

From 1909 to 1913 Picasso and Braque worked in close association and their works during this period were so similar that it is often difficult to differentiate between them. By 1910–11 their paintings had developed to a point where they were almost abstract meshes of colour and line – the subject was identifiable only by a few clues, such as a pipe, a moustache or the indication of a chair back. To combat

Boccioni's *Unique Forms of Continuity in Space* (1913) is a representation of bodily movement. (Private collection/ Scala)

this move towards abstraction the artists began to add references to the real world, firstly by adding lettering or by simulating actual textures such as wood or fabric. Eventually even sand and newspaper cuttings were glued to the canvas to make a *collage* (from the French *coller*, to glue). Brighter colours were used in this phase, which was known as *Synthetic Cubism*.

Several important artists worked in these styles early on in their careers. **Fernand Léger** (1881–1955) took the modern mechanical world as his subject for his Cubist works. The Spanish artist **Juan Gris** (1887–1927) is regarded by some as the originator of Synthetic Cubism; and the paintings of **Robert Delaunay** (1885–1941) are Cubist in origin but composed in the pure colours of the spectrum.

Developments outside France

Futurism was founded in Italy by the poet Filippo Marinetti (see p. 640), who proclaimed the Futurists' revolutionary aims in their first manifesto of 1909. He urged artists to turn their backs on the art of the past and to seek inspiration from industrial society and the dynamism of modern life. He wrote, 'We declare that the splendour of the world has been enriched with a new form of beauty, the beauty of speed . . . a race-automobile which seems to rush over exploding powder is more beautiful than the *Victory of Samothrace*' (this last being a much-admired Classical statue).

The Futurists wanted to apply these aims to all aspects of life, and the movement included poets and designers as well as painters and architects. In order to realize their aim of depicting objects in motion, the Futurists made use first of Divisionist (see p. 543) and later of Cubist techniques. By painting successive movements simultaneously, artists such as **Giacomo Balla** (1871–1958) and **Carlo Carra** (1881–1966) were able to suggest dynamic movement. **Umberto Boccioni** (1882–1916) sought to depict feelings or states of mind through broken strokes of colour, as in *The Laugh* (1911). Later, many of the Futurists were to become associated with the emergent Italian Fascist party (see p. 442).

The **Rayonist** movement in Russia owed a considerable debt to the Futurists. During the years 1912 to 1914 artists such as **Natalia Goncharova** (1881–1962) combined the influences of Cubism and Futurism in their works, which are characterized by almost abstract diagonal rays of colour.

The **Vorticists** shared some of the revolutionary aims of the Futurists, and the crisp geometrical forms and jagged lines of their works reflect the aggressive nature of this British group. The term 'Vorticism' was coined by the American poet Ezra Pound and the movement's aims were expressed in the periodical *Blast* (see p. 641). **Wyndham Lewis** (1882–1957) was the leader of the movement and his *Work-*

Picasso's *Guernica*
(1937). (© DACS
1990/Museum of Modern Art,
New York/Archiv für Kunst)

SEE ALSO

● POST-IMPRESSIONISM p. 544
● SYMBOLISM, SECESSION AND
  EXPRESSIONISM p. 546
● DADA AND SURREALISM
  p. 550

shop (c. 1914–15) comes close to abstraction. *David Bomberg* (1890–1957) was not a member of the Vorticist group but his *Mud Bath* (1914) has an agitated rhythm that is typically Vorticist, as is the half-man, half-machine sculpture *Rock Drill* (1913–14) by *Jacob Epstein* (1880–1959). Vorticism did not survive World War I and its leading sculptor *Henri Gaudier-Brzeska* (1891–1915) was killed in action.

Abstraction before World War II

By about 1910, a greater emphasis on colour and form rather than subject matter had led many artists from different countries to move towards abstraction. Some, such as the Russian *Wassily Kandinsky* (1866–1944), approached abstraction through Expressionism (see p. 547). Others, like the Dutchman *Piet Mon-* *drian* (1872–1944), developed through Cubism, abstracting from a tree or a windmill until the original subject almost completely disappeared. Mondrian gradually restricted his colours and used only vertical and horizontal lines in his compositions. The other members of the Dutch *De Stijl* movement, to which Mondrian belonged, also worked in geometrical abstract shapes, as did the artists of the Russian *Suprematist* movement, which was founded by *Kasimir Malevich* (1878–1935) in 1915.

It was another Russian artist, *Naum Gabo* (1890–1977), who, with his brother *Antoine Pevsner* (1886–1962), co-founded the abstract movement *Constructivism*. Gabo used plastic and other new man-made materials to construct completely abstract sculptures that have something of the character of mathematical models. Far less rigorous in his abstraction was

the Swiss painter *Paul Klee* (1879–1940), whose playful, witty works are rarely entirely abstract.

Romanian by birth, but working for most of his life in France, *Constantin Brancusi* (1876–1957) usually took a shape, such as a head or a bird, as a starting point and gradually simplified it until he had eliminated all inessential details, arriving at an almost abstract form of great purity. *Amedeo Modigliani* (1884–1920) worked with Brancusi and, although he was not an abstract artist, his stylized, elongated heads echo the same shapes.

During the 1930s, the painter *Ben Nicholson* (1894–1982) and the sculptors *Henry Moore* (1898–1986) and *Barbara Hepworth* (1903–75) tried to bring Britain into line with its continental neighbours. All had visited France and were aware of the current developments towards abstraction.   AJ

Mondrian's *Composition with Red, Yellow and Blue* (left) (1939–42). Striving for purity and clarity, Mondrian restricted his artistic vocabulary to horizontal and vertical lines and his palette to black, white, grey and primary colours. (© DACS 1990/Tate Gallery, London/Archiv für Kunst)

Dada and Surrealism

The aftermath of World War I brought a crisis of faith in a society whose intellectual and moral values were held responsible for the appalling destruction of the war. There already existed a growing revolt against traditional values, derived from the writings of Darwin, Marx and Freud. Two art movements that grew out of this climate were Dada and Surrealism. Although they were essentially different in purpose and character, some common ground existed, and a number of Dada artists later joined the Surrealist movement.

Arp's *Concrete Union.* In his sculptures Arp created a type of abstract art based on smooth, rounded forms of a semi-organic character. (Musée de l'Art Moderne, Paris/Scala)

Höch's *Cut with the Kitchen Knife* (1919): the technique of photo-montage was ideal for the overtly political work of Berlin Dada.
© 1990/Staatliche Museen Preussischer Kulturbesitz, Nationalgalerie, Berlin)

Dada was international and was a 'state of mind' rather than a coherent artistic movement. It rejected existing social values and art as products of the existing order. Instead Dada was anarchistic, outrageous and deliberately provocative, aiming to shock people out of a state of complacency. Dada sought to create an art freed from the values and ideas that had preceded it, and so was simultaneously art and anti-art.

Zurich Dada

Dada was born in neutral Switzerland in 1916 where a group of young writers, poets and artists had converged in Zurich. Founded by the playwright and actor **Hugo Ball** (1880–1927), it was officially launched at the *Cabaret Voltaire*, a nightclub and venue for Dada activities. The name Dada is thought to have been chosen at random from a French–German dictionary by the writer **Richard Huelsenbeck** (1892–1973) and means child's rocking horse.

Dada was a heterogeneous movement embracing literature, the visual arts and performance. Ball believed that conventional language in poetry, like the human figure in painting, was an outmoded form of expression, and introduced abstract poetry consisting of made-up words that relied for their effect entirely on their sound and rhythm.

Tristan Tzara (1886–1963), a Romanian poet, was the main spokesman for the group. His experiments included using words cut out from newspapers and then arranged at random in order to create poems.

There is a visual equivalent of this use of chance in the work of the Dada artist **Jean (Hans) Arp** (1887–1966), an Alsatian who arrived in Zurich in 1915. Between 1916 and 1917 he experimented with torn pieces of coloured paper scattered randomly on a paper background. He stated that 'These works like nature were ordered according to the laws of chance. . .'.

New York Dada

The French artist **Marcel Duchamp** (1887–1968) embarked in 1911 on a version of Cubism that became more and more eccentric, with mechanical and intestinal forms. Together with the Frenchman **Francis Picabia** (1879–1953) he began to depict imaginary machines that often had an erotic character. In 1915 both Duchamp and Picabia moved temporarily to New York, where they became the focus of a proto-Dada movement that was joined by the American **Man Ray** (1890–1976). Duchamp had largely given up painting by this time, apart from work on his masterpiece *The Bride Stripped Bare by her Bachelors, Even* (1915–23), which is partly a fantastic and ironic mechanical diagram of sexual intercourse. He also carried on the practice he had started in Paris in 1913 of designating selected everyday objects – such as a hat rack or a urinal – as works of art, terming them 'ready-mades'.

German Dada

In 1917 Richard Huelsenbeck returned to Berlin, where he found an atmosphere of disillusionment. He was joined by the painters **Raoul Hausmann** (1886–1971), **George Grosz** (1893–1959) and **Hannah Höch** (1889–1978), and a *Club Dada* was formed. More political in nature than Dada groups in the other centres, it quickly took on a Communist direction.

The influence of Cubist collage is evident in the Dadaists' development of photomontage, a collage technique using photographs and words. It was used by Hausmann, Grosz and **John Heartfield** (Helmut Herzfelde, 1891–1968), a German artist who had anglicized his name to show his sympathy with America.

In Hanover, **Kurt Schwitters** (1887–1948) developed a variant of Dada which he called *Merz*. The name was taken from the word 'Commerzbank' found on a torn piece of paper. Schwitters collected rubbish – such as cigarette wrappers, tickets, and newspapers – to incorporate into his collages, known as *Merzbilden*.

Max Ernst (1891–1976) was the major exponent of Dada in Cologne. His work was rooted in Late Gothic fantasy drawn from Grünewald and Bosch (see p. 526) and included series of collages such as *Here Everything is Still Floating* (1920), in which images from such sources as 19th-century steel engravings were pasted together to create dreamlike scenes. He later made paintings that had a similar character.

Paris Dada

In 1919 Tzara arrived in Paris, Duchamp returned from New York and Dadaists from other European cities descended on the French capital. In 1920 a Paris Dada group was launched with a manifesto by Picabia. The French writer **André Breton** (1896–1966) had been contributing to Dada publications since 1918 and Tzara had begun to write for Breton's periodical *Littérature*. The Dada spectacles and noisy demonstrations that took place drew large crowds and were even more extravagant than before. After 1920 Breton, increasingly frustrated by Dada's anarchic activities, broke away and established a group of writers – including many former Dadaists – which later became the Surrealist group. By 1920 the Dada group had almost totally disbanded.

Surrealism

Surrealism was founded in Paris in 1924 in reaction to the rationalism and materialism of Western society. Breton's theories were derived from his reading of Freud's psychoanalytical experiments (see p. 232). The potential of the subconscious mind as a source of fantastic and dreamlike images was central to the Surrealists' interests. Breton defined Surrealism in the first *Surrealist Manifesto* (1924) as 'Pure psychic automatism, by which it is intended to express, verbally, in writing, or by other means, the real process of thought. Thought dictated in the absence of all control exercised by reason, outside any aesthetic or moral preoccupation.' Art and literature were viewed as a means of expressing the fusion of the seemingly contradictory states of dream and reality into a 'sort of absolute reality, a surreality'.

The movement was revolutionary in spirit and from 1925 gravitated towards the Communist party. Subsequently the Communists disassociated themselves from

Miró's *Dutch Interior* (1928). Miró's sense of childish humour differs from the black humour of the other Surrealists. (© ADAGP, Paris/DACS 1990/ Museum of Modern Art, New York/Scala)

the Surrealists because of an ever-widening and unbridgeable gap in their respective aims.

In the visual arts Surrealism took two directions. The first adapted the automatic writing techniques of the Surrealist poets in order to liberate the mind from conscious control and produce a flow of ideas from the subconscious. The works produced in this way could be either abstract or figurative. The other stream was based on elaborate, meticulously detailed reconstructions of a dream world in which objects were often placed in unexpected juxtaposition. Both reflected the Surrealists' interest in the use of chance. They greatly admired the Comte de Lautréamont (1846–80), a 19th-century poet, and his simile 'Beautiful as the chance encounter of a sewing machine and an umbrella on an operating table' became their touchstone. The pioneer of this approach in painting was the Italian **Giorgio de Chirico** (1888–1978), whose early work of about 1912–17 was highly influential. De Chirico painted dreamlike visions of Italian piazzas, in which he introduced enigmatic imagery – classical statues, tailor's dummies, trains, gloves.

The automatic painters

In 1925, Ernst invented the new technique of *frottage*. Rubbings were taken from textured surfaces such as wooden floorboards, leaves or ropes and used to suggest fantastic images as in *Forest and Dove* (1927). Many of his paintings employ a method known as *decalomania*. This involved placing paint on a surface such as glass, metal or shiny paper and then pressing this onto a canvas or paper support. The shapes and forms in the resulting impression could then be developed imaginatively.

In 1924 the Spanish painter **Joan Miró** (1893–1983) joined the Surrealists. In *The Harlequin's Carnival* (1924–5), he crossed the boundary between, on the one hand, observation of the 'external model' and, on the other, freely invented signs flowing

from the subconscious. Though based on drawings made in a state of hallucination induced by hunger, its composition is highly organized through the intervention of conscious control.

André Masson (1896–1987) was the first surrealist artist to surrender himself to trance-like states as part of his working method, as seen in the drawings he began to make from around 1924. The images he created suggest brutal forces in nature as in *Battle of the Fishes* (1927). Technically this work is important, not only in the automatic drawing which is then consciously reworked, but in the way paint is poured onto the surface, a method which later influenced the Abstract Expressionists (see p. 554).

The oneiric (dream) painters

René Magritte (1898–1967) rejected as unauthentic the supposed spontaneity of automatism because it appeared to be contrived and mechanical. Instead he began to work with images that often appeared stiffly conventional at first sight, but which were given a bizarre, dreamlike character by wildly impossible juxtapositions or changes of scale.

In 1929 **Salvador Dali** (1904–89) became an official member of the Surrealist group and gave it a new impetus with his method of *paranoiac-critical activity*, which combined the delusions associated with paranoia with a certain degree of objective detachment and control. Dali was particularly interested in abnormal mental conditions and, in particular, hallucinations. His strange dream imagery was depicted in sharp focus and as realistically as possible in a mode of painting that resembled colour photography.

Dali's contribution to Surrealism also included the development of the surrealist object and experimentation in the medium of film. He collaborated with the film maker **Luis Buñuel** (1900–83) on *Un Chien Andalou* (1929) and *L'Age d'Or* (1930).

The painter **Marc Chagall** (1887–1985), though not a member of the Surrealist group, also developed a dreamlike style featuring irrational juxtapositions that often involved imagery derived from his Russian Jewish childhood. **RH**

SEE ALSO
- CUBISM AND ABSTRACTION p. 548
- MOVEMENTS IN ART SINCE 1945 p. 554
- PHOTOGRAPHY AS ART p. 556
- SYMBOLISM, AESTHETICISM AND THE BIRTH OF MODERNISM (LITERATURE) p. 640

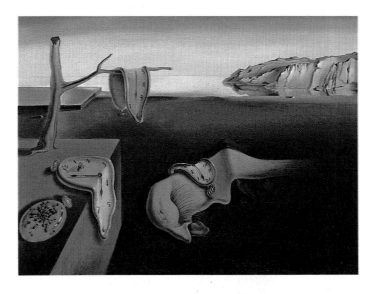

Dali's *The Persistence of Memory* (1931) represented dreamlike images with an almost photographic accuracy. (© Demart Pro Arte BV/ DACS 1990/Museum of Modern Art, New York/Archiv für Kunst)

Architecture and the Applied Arts in the 20th Century

The 20th century has made more difference than any other to the way people live. The forms and scale of modern architecture have transformed existing towns and cities and created new ones. While local traditions of building and design did not entirely die out, and throughout the century revivals of earlier styles continued, modernism became the first truly international style, with broadly similar products originating in the United States, Europe, Africa and Asia.

SEE ALSO

- BUILDING CONSTRUCTION p. 338
- CIVIL ENGINEERING p. 340
- ARCHITECTURE AND THE APPLIED ARTS IN THE 19th CENTURY p. 538

Gaudi's Casa Battló, Barcelona. In its shapes and surfaces, the building was intended to echo the landscape of Catalonia. (Explorer)

In the closing years of the 19th century, however, architects and designers were increasingly willing to mix many styles – Classical, Gothic, Oriental or Celtic – within a single building or piece of furniture. The continuing influence of the Arts and Crafts movements (see p. 538) meant that design could vary more from country to country, even when stylistic sources were apparently the same.

Art Nouveau

As the name suggests, *Art Nouveau* (New Art) was seen as an entirely new style in both architecture and the decorative arts. Although it owed some inspiration to Celtic art and to the Gothic Revival return to naturalism, its whiplash curves and motifs of entwining plant-forms, flowers and women's hair were entirely original. The style first appeared in painting (for example in the late works of Seurat; see p. 542) and it emerged fully formed in Brussels in 1892 with the flowing forms of the ironwork and mosaics of the Tassel house, designed by **Victor Horta** (1861–1947). It achieved its fullest expression in Paris following the *Exposition Universelle* of 1900, in particular in the Metro stations and entrances by **Hector Guimard** (1867–1942), and in the bizarre architecture of **Antonio Gaudi** (1852–1926) in Barcelona, such as his Parc Güell (1900–14).

Different expressions of the Art Nouveau spirit were taking place in Austria (see p. 546) and Scotland. **Charles Rennie Mackintosh** (1868–1928) designed furniture, buildings, metalwork and posters which, in their exuberant floral motifs, show an affinity with continental Art Nouveau. However, his designs have a sparseness and economy that is quite different. His Glasgow School of Art buildings (1897–1909) are revolutionary in their use of simple shapes and lack of decoration.

In 1905 the Austrian architect and

Le Corbusier's Chapel of Notre Dame du Haut (1950–55), Ronchamps, France. The walls of the chapel were built to a double thickness for visual effect, and the sloping roof rests on a series of supports. (Spectrum)

designer **Josef Hoffmann** (1870–1956) designed the Palais Stoclet, a large house in Brussels. This has an overall simplicity of form, like the Glasgow School of Art. The intentions of Mackintosh and Viennese designers such as Hoffmann were quite different from those of the French and Belgian exponents of Art Nouveau, and in many ways can be seen as precursors of Modernism (see below).

Modernism – the 'International Style'

The central ideal of Modernism was that the beauty of designed objects – buildings, furniture or anything else – depended on the extent to which they functioned well. Thus it was both a moral and an aesthetic imperative that, for instance, the form of a building should reflect its function and express its construction.

Advances in technology made possible the realization of modernist aspirations. Reinforced concrete and steel-framing, where the stresses in a building are carried not by the walls but by a steel frame arranged in a series of boxes, meant that buildings could be built much more cheaply and simply. It also allowed the construction of skyscrapers, pioneered by the American **Louis Sullivan** (1856–1924) in such works as the Wainwright building, St Louis, Missouri (1890).

The skyscraper was just one of the many modes of building used by **Frank Lloyd Wright** (1867–1959). Until the 1930s he made a speciality of medium-sized, often suburban, houses. The culmination of his flexible planning, where the interiors and exteriors flow into one another via terraces and cantilevered roofs, is Falling Water, Bear Run, Pennsylvania (1936–37), a series of rectangular concrete boxes built up over a waterfall.

In Austria and Germany Modernism grew out of a widespread desire for simplicity in design. The Fagus Works factory (1911–12) at Alfeld-an-der-Leine, designed by *Walter Gropius* (1883–1969), is a startlingly novel construction, with a complete façade in glass revealing the apparently unsupported concrete staircase within.

Gropius was a founder in 1919 of the *Bauhaus* art and design school in Weimar (later in Dessau), which he saw as continuing the Arts and Crafts traditions of architects, designers and craftsmen working in close collaboration. The main difference was that at the Bauhaus mass production, standardization and new materials were fully accepted and celebrated, so that their buildings were economical to build and their designs could be cheaply produced in large quantities.

The Swiss architect *Le Corbusier* (1887–1965) expounded similar ideas, but went further by claiming that architecture should be based on geometric figures – cubes, cones, etc. – with these spaces within a building connected by simple means such as ramps. In the same spirit all fittings and furnishings should be standardized, as, he claimed, houses were 'machines for living in'. All these ideas are realized in his Villa Savoie, Poissy (1929–31).

Le Corbusier believed that just as individual buildings should be based on these purist, geometrical and rational principles, so should towns. His projects for a 'Contemporary City' (1922–5) and 'Radiating Town' (1935) are complex grids of intersecting squares and rectangles with areas for business institutions (contained in 60-storey skyscrapers), cultural institutions, industry and blocks of housing, with separate vehicular and pedestrian traffic.

Art Deco

The uncompromising austerity of modernism was countered almost as soon as it began. *Art Deco*, which applies to both architecture and design, took its name from the 1925 Paris *Exposition Internationale des Arts Décoratifs et Industriels Modernes*. Early Art Deco was characterized by stylized flowers but from the early 1920s these gave way to more geometric forms such as sunbursts and ziggurats, reflecting the discoveries of Aztec temples in Mexico and Tutankhamun's tomb in Egypt.

These zigzag motifs also served to signify speed, for Art Deco celebrated the modern age in as lighthearted a way as the modernists were serious. The English ceramicist *Clarice Cliff* (1899–1970) designed 'Bizarre' pottery in the 1930s in simple shapes with triangular-handled straight-sided cups and bold, stylized decoration in primary colours.

The postwar scene

The destruction wrought in Europe by six

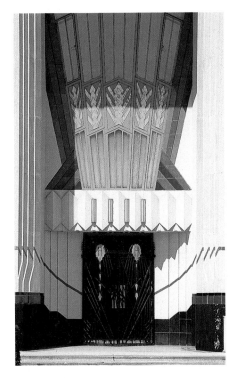

years of war saw the implementation in the 1950s and 1960s of many of Le Corbusier's and the other Modernists' ideas about city planning. In developing countries this went a stage further, as in Brazil where a capital city, Brasilia, has been designed from scratch and largely built by the Brazilians themselves. In the applied arts there was a more lighthearted spirit, perhaps as a reaction to postwar gloom. Typical were the textile designs of *Lucienne Day*, whose 'Calyx' fabric (1951) featured abstract shapes, inspired by Mirós paintings, in primary colours joined by spidery lines.

Hi-tech

In the 1970s a distinct development in architecture took place, partly as a result of the 1960s drawing-board experiments by such groups as Archigram. The Georges Pompidou Centre in Paris (1970–77), designed by *Richard Rogers* (1933–) and *Renzo Piano* (1937–), has water pipes and electrical conduits coated in brightly coloured plastic and located, along with the escalators, prominently on the exterior of the building. The purpose of this is to stress the building's various technological functions and not just its structure.

Post-Modernism

Post-Modernism emerged in the 1970s as a reaction against the austerity and public criticism of such products of Modernism as high-rise blocks of flats. The term literally applies to any style which has developed since Modernism, but is particularly associated with a style pioneered in the USA by *Michael Graves* (1934–). Graves adorned his Portland Public Building, Portland, Oregon (1982), with colourful, non-structural pediments, keystones and ribbon garlands.

Graves has designed furniture in a similar style, using brightly coloured plastic lam-

inates and imitation marbles for Memphis of Milan (founded 1981), an international group of architects and designers led by the designer *Ettore Sottsass* (1917–). Sottsass himself uses these materials and also shapes derived from Classicism, Art Deco and 1950s design.

Post-Modernism as practised by Graves and Sottsass is self-consciously 'fun' and, unlike Modernism, not based on polemical or didactic theories. It is perhaps too soon to judge whether it is a viable alternative to Modernism, but its influence can already be seen in shops, hotels, offices and restaurants across Europe and America.   AR

Art Deco: the main entrance of the Hoover Factory (1932), Perivale, UK, features the characteristic stylized sunburst motif. (Spectrum)

The hi-tech design (below) of Richard Rogers' Lloyd's of London building (1981–86) with Leadenhall Market, built exactly 100 years earlier, in the foreground. (Zefa)

Movements in Art since 1945

The postwar period is characterized by extremely varied approaches to the problems of art. Although much of the best work has been abstract, some artists have continued to work in more traditional styles. The Swiss sculptor *Alberto Giacometti* (1901–66) and the English painter *Francis Bacon* (1909–92) developed highly original treatments of the human figure, expressing feelings of anguish and isolation.

Pollock's *Full Fathom Five.* (© DACS 1990/Museum of Modern Art, New York/Bridgeman Art Library)

Abstract Expressionism

The first new movement to emerge after the war was Abstract Expressionism, which was also the first major art movement to originate in the United States. Stimulated by the presence in New York during the war of most of the leading Surrealist artists as refugees, a group of American painters began to make abstract pictures in much freer, more improvisatory styles influenced by the Surrealists' notion of automatism. This new way of painting was pioneered by *Jackson Pollock* (1912–56), who went on to paint pictures on canvases laid flat on the floor. He moved around them, dripping rhythmical interweaving trails of paint from a brush or stick, so that the images grew unpredictably in the course of painting. But although expressive brushwork is characteristic of certain types of Abstract Expressionist painting, such as the work of *Willem de Kooning* (1904–) and *Franz Kline* (1910–62), there are also other types in which the paint is applied more evenly to create all-over fields of intense, saturated colour, as in the work of *Mark Rothko* (1903–70) and *Barnett Newman* (1905–70). Many Abstract Expressionist paintings are very large, and have an air of grandeur and drama.

Art Informel

Art Informel is the name given to most abstract painting produced in Paris in the immediate postwar years, on account of its loose, improvisatory character, with free brushwork and sometimes a heavily textured surface. It is also sometimes known as *Tachism* after the French word *'tache'*, meaning 'spot' or 'stain'. Though similar in some respects to American Abstract Expressionism, it developed independently and tended to be less daring, and smaller in scale. Typical artists were *Nicolas de Staël* (1914–55), *Pierre Soulages* (1919–) and *Hans Hartung* (1904–).

Cobra

Cobra was a movement created by artists from Denmark, Belgium and the Netherlands (Co = Copenhagen, Br = Brussels, A = Amsterdam). It was founded in Paris in 1948 and only lasted officially until 1951, though some of the artists, such as *Asger Jorn* (1914–73) and *Karel Appel* (1921–) continued painting in Cobra styles for many years afterwards. In their search for spontaneity and irrational 'uncivilized' forms of expression, the artists turned for inspiration to primitive art, children's art and graffiti. In many of their paintings fantastic heads or animals seem to be emerging from a turbulent paint surface.

Performance art

Performance art began in the late 1950s, though its origins can be traced back to the Dada movement (see p. 550). The earliest events, such as those created by the American *Jim Dine* (1935–), were known at the time as *Happenings*. Per-

Lichtenstein's *Whaam!* When seen at full size, Lichtenstein's enlargements of comic-strip images take on an almost abstract quality. (© DACS 1990/Tate Gallery, London/Archiv für Kunst)

formance works are the creation of artists trained as painters or sculptors; they tend to be extremely unconventional, have a strong visual character and are presented not in theatres but in art galleries or other such venues. Performance can take many forms, ranging, for example, from the strange rituals of the German *Joseph Beuys* (1921–87), using such props as a stuffed hare, felt and butter, to the 'Singing Sculpture' of the British team *Gilbert and George* (1943– and 1942–), in which the artists mimed, robot-like, to a piece of music.

Pop

The late 1950s saw a reaction against Abstract Expressionism, which had become well established in both America and Europe. Younger artists felt that it had become introspective, decorative and unrelated to the reality of contemporary life, which was changing rapidly thanks to the growing prosperity of the postwar years.

A fascination with the power of advertising formed the central focus of the work of American artists such as *Andy Warhol* (1928–87). Warhol's *Coca-Cola Bottles* and *Marilyn* series (1962), amongst others, expressed the essence of the American dream where both products and celebrities were the icons of contemporary life. *Roy Lichtenstein* (1923–) painted pictures based on comic strips, enormously enlarged.

Pop art was closely linked to a revival of interest in Dada, and artists such as *Jasper Johns* (1930–) and *Robert Rauschenberg* (1925–) were described as Neo-Dadaists at the time. Rauschenberg's *Combine* paintings brought together images from the media and everyday 'found objects' with areas of Abstract Expressionist-type brushwork.

In Britain, where the notion of pop culture had developed in the mid-1950s, *David Hockney* (1937–) produced a contemporary version of Hogarth's *A Rake's Progress* following his travels in the USA, while the more conceptually oriented *Richard Hamilton* (1922–) took a critical view of the liberated sixties in works such as *Swinging London*, which dealt with the arrest of Mick Jagger and the London gallery owner Robert Fraser on drugs charges.

Nouveau Réalisme

The French Nouveau Réaliste (New Realist)

group was founded in 1960. The artists sought to revitalize the School of Paris through the use of commercial images and consumer goods drawn from the contemporary environment. They incorporated actual machine-made objects in their works, either by a process of assemblage or by using them as scrap material which could be radically reshaped. For instance, **Arman** (Armand Fernandez, 1928–) produced accumulations of objects such as paint tubes or shaving brushes, which he encased in solid blocks of transparent plastic; **Christo** (Christo Javacheff, 1935–) wrapped up cars, chairs and so on; and **César** (César Baldaccini, 1921–) compressed car bodies in industrial machines made for this purpose.

Op

The term Op art (short for 'optical art') is applied to a type of abstract art, usually of a geometrical kind, that explores optical phenomena such as the interaction of colours, after-images, and effects of dazzle and vibration, often in a systematic manner. Its pioneers included the German **Joseph Albers** (1888–1976), who used a standardized composition of squares within a square to

Vasarély's Supernovae *exploits the optical effects of pattern.* (© DACS 1990/Tate Gallery, /Bridgeman Art Library)

explore effects of advancing and receding colours, expanding and contracting space; and the Hungarian **Victor Vasarély** (1908–), with grid-like compositions in dazzling juxtapositions of black and white. It reached its peak in the 1960s.

Kinetic art

Whereas some Op works create an illusion of movement, Kinetic works actually move, either by means of an electric motor or through the intervention of some outside force such as air currents. Leading Kinetic artists include the American **Alexander Calder** (1898–1976), with his *Mobiles* consisting of painted cut-out metal shapes freely suspended from metal rods; and the Swiss **Jean Tinguely** (1925–91), whose Kinetic metal sculptures, often incorporating junk materials, have an anarchic, fantastic character.

Minimalism

From the mid-1960s, various artists, mainly sculptors, developed an awareness of the 'literalness' of objects and materials. The Americans **Donald Judd** (1928–) and **Sol LeWitt** (1928–) pioneered the use of industrial manufacturing techniques and materials in the creation of art, placing strong emphasis on their specific physical qualities. Much Minimal art was made by industrial craftsmen from artists' designs and is characterized by anonymous handling and the use of simple, repeated geometric forms such as cubes.

Conceptual art

Conceptual art grew partly out of Minimal art (the importance of the idea behind the work) and partly as a reaction against the sheer bulk of minimal work. This led to what has been called 'the dematerialization of the art object'. Artists started to make works of a temporary character utilizing different types of process and system, inscribing imaginary geometric patterns on the landscape, and working with photographs and texts.

Photo-Realism

Photo-Realism, a mainly American movement, began in the late 1960s and reached its peak in the 1970s. It developed as a return to realism, but instead of working directly from nature, the painters worked from photographs. Most, like **Richard Estes** (1936–), painted street scenes with buildings and shop fronts depicted with great clarity and as if frozen in a moment of time.

Neo-Expressionism

Neo-Expressionism is primarily a West German movement, although a number of other European and American artists have been associated with it. Executed with great vigour in styles sometimes reminiscent of German Expressionism (see page 546), it has marked a return to myths, religion and mysterious symbolism as subject matter for painting. The monumental paintings of **Anselm Kiefer** (1945–) touch on subjects related to Germany's past – in particular the rise of the Nazis – but also on wider-ranging subjects such as ancient literature, and deal with the problems of contemporary history painting.
JR/RA

Christo's Surrounded Islands (1983): Christo used pink plastic to surround 11 islands in Biscayne Bay, Florida, USA. His art reflects the emphasis placed on packaging by modern consumer society.

SEE ALSO

● CUBISM AND ABSTRACTION p. 548
● DADA AND SURREALISM p. 550
● ARCHITECTURE AND THE APPLIED ARTS IN THE 20TH CENTURY p. 552
● PHOTOGRAPHY AS ART p. 556

Kiefer's Margarethe (1981): a combination of oil paint and straw on canvas. (Saatchi Collection, London)

Photography as Art

'From today painting is dead!' declared the French painter Paul Delaroche in 1839, the year Louis Daguerre announced his discovery of a process for making photographic images or daguerreotypes. Delaroche voiced the expectations of many: that the camera's ability to capture in an instant every detail of the real world would spell the end of painting and drawing, and that photography was the art form of the future. An equally vocal opposing camp claimed that photography was a science, not an art – a purely mechanical process that could never rival in feeling or expression the sensitive hand of the painter or draughtsman.

Julia Margaret Cameron's *The Angel at the Sepulchre* (right) shows the influence of Pre-Raphaelite painting. (E.T. Archive)

Since 1839, photography has assumed a vast range of forms and uses – in science and medicine, geographic exploration, anthropology, journalism and advertising – but its close relationship with art has continued throughout.

The 19th century

A French daguerreotype (1855). The composition is influenced by academic painting of the time. (Musée d'Orsay, Paris/R.M.N.)

One of photography's first uses was as an aid to artists: painters accustomed to painting from life found photographs an invaluable source of reference for detail and composition. High-speed photographs taken by Eadweard Muybridge (1830–1904) in the 1880s showed artists (and scientists) for the first time the

frozen image of a galloping horse or a leaping man in motion. Many painters, most notably the French Impressionist Edgar Degas (see p. 542), explored the unusual 'snapshot' views captured by the camera, and its ability to still a moment in time.

By contrast, many early photographers attempted to gain status and approval by self-consciously adopting the high moral themes – and even copying the forms – of 19th-century painting; others, of the 'pictorialist' movement, favoured the deep tones and soft focus that suggested the delicate sweep of brushstrokes for their portraits and picturesque landscapes – 'painting with light' as they saw it. Despite this, and with gradual improvements in photographic technology over the decades, photographers came to respect the photograph for its unique immediacy, its ability to capture a real sense of life. The best of them, such as the great Victorian portraitist *Julia Margaret Cameron* (1815–79), were able to infuse their work with a strong vitality, and to convey in their portraits a sense of genuine psychological insight.

Modernism

Photography began to gain new status as

an independent medium in the early 20th century. The famous American photographer *Alfred Stieglitz* (1864–1946) – through his work and writings, his Gallery 291 in New York, and his magazine *Camera Work* – advocated a 'pure' photography with aesthetic value beyond its descriptive or utilitarian function. This modernist view influenced a generation of photographers including the Americans *Edward Weston* (1886–1958) and *Paul Strand* (1890–1976), who believed in the honest, 'straight photograph', and whose sharp, objective images found significant form and beauty in simple objects, figures and elements in the landscape. An inheritor of this purist tradition was *Ansel Adams* (1902–84), renowned for his fine printing and perfect images of the vast untamed American landscape.

While many Americans sought inspiration in solitary nature, in Europe close ties were being forged between photographers and avant-garde artists such as the Italian Futurists (see p. 548), who looked to photography to celebrate the rhythm and speed of modern society, the dynamism of the machine age. For the Dadaists in Germany (see p. 550), and especially *John Heartfield* (1891–1968), *photomontage* (influenced by cubist collage techniques) brought different images of reality into collision and became a tool for biting social and political satire. After Dada, the Surrealists (see p. 550) also found photography a shortcut to the unusual and bizarre, and exploited its ability to cast the ordinary in a strange light, to mystify, confuse and outrage. Foremost among them was the American *Man Ray* (1890–1976), whose innovative techniques and provocative wit initiated a still-continuing trend of 'surreal' photography.

An alternative way of seeing the world was proposed by the 'new objectivity' photographers led by *László Moholy Nagy* (1895–1946), the Hungarian-born artist who was closely involved with the Utopian design school, the Bauhaus, in Germany (see p. 552). They found the unexpected in the commonplace not by imposing on it any surreal distortions, but by looking at it directly, from unusual angles, and with almost scientific detachment. Thus a plant seen close up looks machine-made, and a street scene from above becomes an almost abstract pattern of texture: ordinary things transformed by a point of view.

Documentary photography

Many photographers now regarded as great masters would never have thought of themselves as artists at all. Three photographers who inspired the Surrealists, or detected surreal qualities in everyday life, were *Eugene Atget* (1857–1927), *André Kertesz* (1894–1985) and *Brassaï* (1899–1984). All three documented the life they saw around them, and so fit into a broad documentary approach that encompasses a vast span of attitudes and subject matter. In America *Walker Evans* (1903–1975) recorded the lives of the rural poor, the sharecroppers and tenant farmers. He created stark, powerful and dignified images that bear witness to social inequality and the harsh everyday struggle for existence. The pictures of the Frenchman *Jacques-Henri Lartigue* (1894–1986) brilliantly chronicled the amusing events and small happenings of French bourgeois society around him and took the apparently casual snapshot approach to new heights. In England, *Bill Brandt* (1904–83) produced memorable, haunting and poetic images scrutinizing life in the 1930s right across the social spectrum.

Their work prefigured that of the 'concerned' photographers of the postwar years who roamed the world intent on changing it for the better through their pictures of human suffering and hope. This approach is best seen in the influential work of *Henri Cartier-Bresson* (1908), whose brilliantly judged images sought that elusive 'decisive moment' that resulted in perfect composition and a lucid message.

Photography since 1945

Since World War II photographers have continued to innovate and find new ground. In America in the 1950s and 60s, a new, seemingly informal approach to urban or 'street' photography evolved

through the work of those such as *Lee Friedlander* (1934), *Robert Frank* (1924) and *Diane Arbus* (1923–71). Mirroring the Cold War loss of faith and post-Holocaust sensibility, these photographers portrayed a less optimistic world view in which they often cast themselves as the alienated outsider, adrift in a concrete jungle.

At the same time, photography and art have become more closely aligned. Pop artists like *Andy Warhol* (1928–87) and *Robert Rauschenberg* (1925) both used photographic images and concepts in their work and realigned 'High Art' in the direction of popular culture. Photography has also been employed to record

minimalist, conceptual and performance art (see p. 554), helping to break down the idea of the unique, hand-made physical art object.

As photography has become ubiquitous in recent years, so its audience is now increasingly sophisticated in its reception of photographic images, and less inclined to accept simple notions of photographic objectivity or 'truth'. In recent years, many photographers have turned their attention from the world 'out there' to express themselves by staging their own events, and literally constructing their own images for the camera – a retreat into the private world of their own imagination.   MC-S

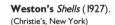

Cartier-Bresson: an untitled photograph (c. 1930). Cartier-Bresson saw the camera as 'an extension of the eye', capturing fleeting moments in time. (Christie's, New York)

Weston's *Shells* (1927). (Christie's, New York)

SEE ALSO

● PHOTOGRAPHY AND FILM p. 324
● CINEMA pp. 558–65

The Silent Cinema

Long before the invention of the Kinematograph – or cinema as we usually call it today – the *camera obscura* and the magic lantern had been used to project images upon a screen. Although lantern slides sometimes had mechanical parts that made the image move, 'films' make use of the phenomenon known as 'persistence of vision' to give an optical simulation of movement, and their development only became possible with the invention of photographic film.

A Praxinoscope consists of a revolving drum with mirrors in the centre. On the inside of the drum is a sequence of drawn figures, each in a slightly different phase of movement. Spinning the drum creates the illusion of movement that is essential to 'motion pictures', which consist of a series of still photographs or *frames* shown one after another.

There are several claims to the invention of cinema. The American **Thomas Edison** (1847–1931; see also p. 328) – already inventor of the phonograph and the incandescent electric light – was first to market a successful film machine, but it was in Europe that the potential of cinema was first recognized. Then came World War I and the American film industry, uninterrupted by the conflict that held back development in Europe, began its long dominance.

The inventors

The first photographer to record actual movement was English-born Eadweard Muybridge (see p. 556). He photographed animals and people in motion and invented a *Zoopraxiscope* to project these images (1880).

More practical than Muybridge's line of cameras was a photographic 'gun' – invented in 1882 by Frenchman **Etienne Marey** (1830–1904) – that took a sequence of pictures on a revolving photographic plate. But it was the invention of flexible film by George Eastman (see p. 324) that enabled Edison to invent a really practical method of photographing movement.

Edison wanted to provide a moving image to accompany his phonograph. His first attempt was a sequence of images on the phonograph cylinder, viewed through a magnifier. Then, using Eastman's film cut in half to 35 mm (1.38 in) and with sprocket holes along the sides, Edison's assistant **W.K.L. Dickson** (1860–1935) developed both a camera (the *Kinetograph*, patented 1891) and a viewer (the *Kinetoscope*). The film moved horizontally and in the viewer was a continuous 1.5 m (5 ft) loop of film, a shutter disc interrupting the light source. This was launched commercially in 1894 as a slot machine for solo viewing. Edison thought that projected films could be seen by too many people at once to make money.

Should Edison have the credit for inventing motion pictures? British inventor **William Friese-Greene** (1855–1921) had written to him outlining his own ideas for a camera and projector, and there were well over 100 different machines developed in the early 1890s by French, Czech, German and other inventors. The most successful projection system was developed by two French brothers, **August** (1862–1954) and **Louis** (1864–1948) **Lumière**, after seeing a demonstration of the Kinetoscope. Their *Cinematographe* was a camera and projector in one. It combined most of the earlier ideas and added a claw system to move the film. The Lumières gave their first public show in Paris on 28 December 1895. Three months later Edison demonstrated a projector, the *Vitascope*, invented by **Thomas Armat** (1866–1948), in New York.

The first films

Edison's first film, *Fred Ott's Sneeze*, showed a laboratory assistant sneezing, and was less than a minute long. Edison's other films featured snippets of vaudeville acts, markswoman Annie Oakley, strongman Eugene Sandow and even *The Execu-*

Intolerance (1916), Griffith's second film, intercut 4 stories of intolerance through the ages, linked by the image of a mother holding her baby. Costing $2 million, it was at the time the most expensive film ever made, with huge, spectacular sets, particularly for the Babylon sequences (shown above).

SEE ALSO

- PHOTOGRAPHY AND FILM p. 324
- RADIO, TELEVISION AND VIDEO p. 326
- HOLLYWOOD p. 560
- WORLD CINEMA p. 562
- HOW A FILM IS MADE p. 564

tion of Mary Queen of Scots, with the axe falling and her head rolling in the dust. They made no attempt to tell a story and were filmed in a studio with unwieldy equipment. The Lumières had a portable camera and filmed real life, making a great impact with a film of a train arriving at a station.

Illusionist **Georges Méliès** (1861–1938) was very excited by the Lumières' shows. He turned his theatre into a cinema, and made films like theirs. On one occasion his camera stopped working for a while, so that the developed film showed a hearse suddenly replacing the cart in the previous frame. The magician realized the potential in this kind of *stop action* photography and in other tricks like *double exposure*, exploiting them in fantasy films such as *Voyage to the Moon* (1902).

Méliès' films were very theatrical, but films like **Edwin Porter's** (1869–1941) 12-minute *The Great Train Robbery* (USA, 1903) and **Cecil Hepworth's** (1874–1956) *Rescued by Rover* (UK, 1905) were shot on outside locations. At one point in Porter's film the camera pans sideways to follow some horsemen; the film ends with a sudden close-up of a gunman firing straight at the audience. However, Porter did not develop these innovations further.

Famous players

The early US cinemas, known as 'nickelodeons', attracted only the lower classes, who paid 5 cents to see a 20-minute programme of short films. A little later, French films of successful plays running an hour or more, featuring stage actors, brought in patrons who would pay $1 a ticket. Gaumont's *Queen Elizabeth* (1912), with the celebrated Sarah Bernhardt, made so much money for **Adolph Zukor** (1873–1976) that he founded his own company – Famous Players – with Porter directing films such as *The Count of Monte Cristo* and *The Prisoner of Zenda*.

For a time Italy took the lead in filmmaking with a series of spectacular productions of historical subjects including *The Last Days of Pompeii, Quo Vadis!* (1913) and the two-hour long *Cabiria* (1914), about the Punic Wars.

D.W. Griffith

It was D.W. Griffith (1875–1948), a director for the US company Biograph, who began to make more adventurous use of the camera. He experimented with lighting, long-shots and close-ups, takes of different lengths, different camera setups and angles within a scene, realizing that all these affect audience reaction. He also omitted unnecessary scene-setting and

took his scenes straight into the important action.

Realizing that close-up acting demands skills different from the flamboyant style of many stage actors, he built up a team of cinema actors – including **Mary Pickford** (1893–1979), **Dorothy** (1898–1968) and **Lillian** (1899–93) **Gish** and **Lionel Barrymore** (1878–1954). He was probably the first American director to make a film lasting more than one reel (12 minutes) and, in 1910, one of the earliest to take his crew to California.

Griffith's epic *The Birth of a Nation* (1915), about the American Civil War and its aftermath, amazed the world with what films could do. Made from a Southern viewpoint, the inbuilt racism of the film caused concern but did not obscure its cinematic achievement.

The silent comics

Mack Sennet (1884–1960) was a younger director who learned rapidly from Griffith. He developed a comedy troupe at Biograph, then went off to join the newly founded Keystone company in California. His most famous films featured the cleverly edited, speeded-up antics of the Keystone Cops, and were made to a regular formula of chases and slapstick, using stop and reverse action filming combined with carefully planned stunts. Keystone films also featured such famous names as **Roscoe 'Fatty' Arbuckle** (1881–1932), **Charlie Chaplin** (1889–1977) and **Buster Keaton** (1895–1966).

European silent classics

In the years after World War I the European cinema could not compete with Hollywood commercially but led in terms of experiment. **Robert Weine's** (1881–1938) *Cabinet of Dr Caligari* (1919), using expressionist settings, and **F.W. Murnau's** (1888–1931) *Nosferatu* (1921, an early Dracula) drew attention to German cinema, which went on to produce many films notable for their distinctive style and social awareness, such as **Georg Pabst's** (1887–1967) *Pandora's Box* (1928) and the Austrian **Fritz Lang's** (1890–1976) *Metropolis* (1927).

In France intellectuals experimented with the film as a serious art form: examples include **Jean Cocteau's** (1889–1963) *Blood of a Poet* (1930) and **Luis Buñuel's** (1900–83) *Un Chien Andalou* (1928), made in collaboration with Salvador Dali. **René Clair's** (1898–1981) farce *An Italian Straw Hat* (1927), **Abel Gance's** (1899–1981) *Napoleon* (1927) – which used a wide screen with three overlapping images – and **Renée Falconetti's** (1901–46) *The Passion of Joan of Arc* are among those recognized as silent classics.

The Soviet leader Lenin saw Griffith's *Intolerance* and recognized the power of cinema, declaring it 'the foremost cultural weapon of the proletariat'. Some brilliant Russian directors emerged. The greatest of these, **Sergei Eisenstein** (1898–1948), used symbols to reinforce ideas and edited shots to make a 'collision' of images, emphasizing conflict in the subject. The cutting rhythms in his *Battleship Potemkin* (1925) are a virtuoso demonstration of these skills.

The introduction of colour

Early feature films were often tinted with a colour appropriate to the scene, or even with several colours applied by stencil for parts of a major film. *Kinemacolor*, invented in Britain in 1906, used two colour filters in the camera and projector and two reels of film exposed alternately, and was the first of several 'natural colour' systems. *Technicolor*, developed in America in about 1915, at first used a prism to split colour to two film reels. The company replaced it with several different processes before, in 1941, they introduced a three-colour system on a single film. *Eastman Color* superseded Technicolor in 1952 – a negative three-colour movie from which Technicolor or Eastman Color prints can be made.

The coming of sound

In silent films, dialogue or any information that could not be presented as part of the action had to be conveyed by text inserted between the pictures. Additional atmosphere was supplied by live music, ranging from a honkytonk piano to a full symphony orchestra.

Separate sound recordings were used with film in Berlin as early as 1896, and a sound-on-movie process was patented by **Eugene Lauste** (1856–1935) in 1906, though it was not at first effective for speech. In 1926 Warner Brothers presented a synchronized music track on disc to accompany their *Don Juan*. This was followed by *The Jazz Singer* (1927), which included songs and a snatch of dialogue and is generally accepted as the first 'talkie'. Sound-on-movie, the sound being recorded as a varying strip of light, came into use the following year, mainly using systems based on that developed by the German TOBIS company.

Audiences demanded 'talkies'. To provide them, directors abandoned all their cinematographic skills. The problems of sound recording brought back the static shorts of very early cinema, for the camera had to be encased in a cumbersome soundproof box. With new equipment, including the invention of the *boom*, a movable pole from which the microphone is suspended, it became possible for cameras to move again. Skills in editing sound began to match those of image editing, and sound too began to be used creatively. HL

Charlie Chaplin's screen persona as a pathetic, endearing little tramp was developed through a series of films and made him one of the first Hollywood stars.

Hollywood

Hollywood is not so much a place as a whole style of films and film-making. Within a year of the Nestor Studio opening in this suburb of Los Angeles, California, in 1911 there were 15 other studios close by, and Hollywood rapidly became the centre of both the industry and the film community. For 40 years the 'majors', the handful of big production companies, dominated world cinema. 'Tinseltown' and 'dream factory' are appropriate epithets, for the ethos of Hollywood has been one of surface glamour. But Hollywood was also an efficient production machine. Top directors such as John Ford (1895–1973), King Vidor (1894–1982) or Cecil B. De Mille (1881–1959) were capable of turning out as many as six productions in a year.

In the early years of cinema, films were made all over the United States, but three factors led to the development of Hollywood as a film centre. The first was the weather – the Los Angeles Chamber of Commerce guaranteed sunshine 350 days a year. The second was the great variety of location scenery. The third was the Motion Picture Patents Company – set up in 1909 by the equipment patentees – which tried to restrict US film-making to its nine member companies. It fixed the length of films at one reel (8-12 minutes) and insisted on the anonymity of actors. Independent companies fled to the West Coast to escape its detectives and thugs; the Patents Company's hirelings followed, but its power was broken by 1913.

Studios and the star system

The growth of the big studios, with expensive equipment and a permanent staff of technicians, scene builders and painters, meant that films were scheduled to strict shooting programmes. Talent was contracted for a period or a number of films at a time, and writers, directors and actors found their professional lives out of their own control.

In 1910 the ban on naming players was broken, pleasing both the public and the actors, who were eager for recognition. In addition, as individual popularity with audiences became established, actors could demand more money. They were not just local celebrities, as most stage actors had been, but might be known all over the world. Soon 'star' salaries became a major part of a film's budget. However, actors who signed a contract with a studio had to do what they were told. Carefully promoted by the studio, they were the company's greatest assets. Details of their real or imaginary private lives were fed to gossip writers, and if they were caught doing anything which might spoil their public image their contract could be cancelled. Only a handful, such as **Mary Pickford** (1893–1979), **Douglas Fairbanks** (1883–1939) and **Charlie Chaplin** (1889–1977), who formed their own company, United Artists, were able to preserve their independence. Old-style stars were not necessarily very good-looking or great actors – often they were mere creations of the studio publicity machine. Today's stars tend to be better actors and more able to retain control of their own careers.

The Hollywood film

The production line of the studio system produced technically proficient, professionally made films. These were usually straightforward narratives, realistically presented – there was no time for risk-taking and experiment. If a particular film was successful with the public then it was likely that others like it would follow.

Historical romances and adaptations of novels and stage successes were among the earliest feature films, but soon films began to be produced that were recognizable as belonging to particularly cinematic genres.

The Magnificent Ambersons (Orson Welles, 1942) was adapted from Booth Tarkington's novel by Welles himself and tells the story of the decline of a wealthy, proud mid-Western family.

Westerns

The western, with its emphasis on action, was ideal for the silent cinema and a number of stars specialized in cowboy roles. The roles of 'goodie' and 'baddie' were usually clear-cut, whether the conflict involved outlaws or Indians. Chases, stunts and often comedy were regular elements and in the 1930s, after the coming of sound, there was a vogue for singing cowboys. After World War II distinctions between good and bad become more blurred, and the traditional folk hero was replaced by more complex characters. Gunfight violence became more realistic and a more balanced view of 'wild west' life was presented. Films with quite different settings, such as the science fiction *Star Wars* (1977), are sometimes seen as a reworking of the original western formula.

Gangster films

A few silent films, such as **Josef von Sternberg's** (1894–1969) *Underworld* (1927), dealt with organized crime, but it was after the advent of sound and the American experience of prohibition that gangster films became a popular genre, often based on identifiable real-life criminals. **Edward G. Robinson** (1893–1972) – especially as Al Capone in *Little Caesar* (1930) – **James Cagney** (1899–1986) and **Humphrey Bogart** (1899–1957) all built their reputations in gangster roles. Later films often showed social problems as a reason for turning to crime. In 1959 **Billy Wilder** (1906–) parodied the form in the hilarious *Some Like it Hot* (1959), while *Bonny and Clyde* (1967) and *The Godfather* (1971) were sophisticated treatments of the gangster film.

Musicals

With the talkies came the musical. **Al Jolson's** (1886–1950) *The Jazz Singer* (1927) had only interpolated songs, but in his *The Singing Fool* (1928) they became part of the action. *The Broadway Melody* (1929), the first 'all-talking, all-singing, all-dancing' film, was so successful that over 70 musicals appeared within a year. It used a backstage story as an excuse for revue-style numbers, a formula often repeated in subsequent films. Others were based on, or echoed, the styles of operetta and stage musical comedies. *42nd Street* (1933), another backstage story, introduced the spectacular dance sequences of

Stagecoach (1939), directed by John Ford, represents the classic mature western, featuring a group of characters on board a stagecoach that is in danger from Indians. John Wayne (1907–79) became a major star following his role in the film.

HOLLYWOOD REBELS

The Hollywood studios occasionally appeared to give talent its freedom, but usually tried to crush anyone going against the system.

Erich von Stroheim (1885–1957), an actor who played 'the man you love to hate' in silent films, was also a fine director who achieved his effects through detail in extended shots. After directing a number of successful films for Universal he was suddenly fired.

His next, and most ambitious, project was *Greed* (1913) for Goldwyn. He shot a film for 42 reels, which he then shortened by half, for showing in two parts. But it was cut first to 4 ½ hours then to 'commercial length' by a cutter who had read neither the script nor the original book. Having spent $4 470 000 on the film, MGM (of which Goldwyn was now part) now failed to publicize it, preferring to write it off against tax.

A further eight of Stroheim's films were mutilated before distribution, and his only film with sound was given to another director to remake in a form more acceptable to the studio. After a few years in menial jobs he went to France to act in Jean Renoir's (1894–1979) *La Grande Illusion* (1936) and years later had a successful role in *Sunset Boulevard* (1950).

Orson Welles (1915–85), after a great success in New York theatre and radio, was offered total freedom to make *Citizen Kane* (1941), in which his abandonment of a chronological narrative and innovative low-angle and deep-focus camerawork (by Gregg Toland) all broke new ground.

Though acclaimed as a masterpiece, in some places it flopped. RKO refused to allow him to complete the editing of his next film, *The Magnificent Ambersons* (Orson Welles, 1942). They cut 40 minutes and shot a new ending without his permission; he completed neither of his next films and was then fired. Welles spent most of his life acting, sometimes in inferior films, to raise money for the films he wanted to make.

The Wizard of Oz (1939): the Tin Man, Dorothy and the Scarecrow follow the Yellow Brick Road to the Emerald City. MGM wanted child star Shirley Temple (1928–) to play Dorothy, but Twentieth Century Fox, to whom she was contracted, refused permission. The part of 9-year-old Dorothy went to Judy Garland (1922–69), then aged 17.

Other genres

There have been many other Hollywood genres: thrillers – of which the British director *Alfred Hitchcock* (1889–1980) was such a master – horror, detection, disaster subjects, war and action films as well as the whole range of romance, historical drama, social problem stories and comedy, ranging from the zany *Marx Brothers* to the sophistication of *Frank Capra* (1897–1991) or the introspection of *Woody Allen* (1935–) – but the musical and the western are the ones particularly associated with Hollywood.

Hollywood's social conscience

The coming of sound gave greater power to the writer and, with the heightened political awareness generated by the Depression, a number of films began to tackle social issues, culminating in *John Ford's* (1895–1973) version of Steinbeck's *The Grapes of Wrath* (1940). After World War II this continued with films like *William Wyler's* (1902–81) *The Best Years of our Lives* (1946) about GIs readjusting to civilian life, *Edward Dmytryk's* (1908–) *Crossfire* (1947) about anti-semitism, and *Otto Preminger's* (1906–86) *The Man with the Golden Arm* (1955) about drug addiction. In the early 1950s, however, the anti-Communist witch-hunt, led by Senator

McCarthy (see p. 450), drove many progressive talents out of Hollywood and threw some into jail. One director who testified before the Un-American Activities Committee and could therefore continue to work was *Elia Kazan* (1909–). One of the founders of the Actors' Studio, he introduced Method acting (see p. 642) to the cinema and helped launch *Marlon Brando* (1924–) and *James Dean* (1931–55) as stars.

Competing with television

The popularity of television in the 1940s and 50s dramatically reduced cinema attendance. Hollywood retaliated with spectacular epics and innovations such as ultra-wide Cinerama, 3-D and stereophonic sound.

For a time Hollywood transferred production to British, Italian or Spanish studios to cut costs. Exotic locations have been seen as a way of attracting audiences, and recently there has been an emphasis on elaborate special effects and on films aimed at the American teenage market.

In 1949 the Hollywood 'majors' were forced to shed their distribution arms. Later, economic pressures led to the selling off of 'back-lots' (where old sets were kept standing for re-use), auctioning of costumes and properties, and disposal of film rights. Independent companies are now responsible for a larger proportion of film releases although finance may still come from the big studios, which are now part of multinational companies such as Coca-Cola. Much production in Hollywood is now designed for television.

Anti-Hollywood

Since the success of *John Casavettes'* (1929–89) *Shadows* (1960) there has been a strong underground film movement in the USA catering for art and campus cinemas, ranging from the experiments of *Andy Warhol* (see p. 554) and Paul Morrissey (1939–) to social documentaries.   HL

Busby Berkeley (1895–1976). For 30 years he produced dazzling dance routines designed for the camera, often featuring kaleidoscope-like effects. Singers and dancers such as *Fred Astaire* (1899–1987), *Judy Garland* (1922–69) and *Gene Kelly* (1912–) soon became some of Hollywood's most valuable properties. From *The Wizard of Oz* (1939) to *Singing in the Rain* (1953), Metro-Goldwyn-Mayer (MGM) in particular made a series of musicals of great quality, but the cost of making this kind of film had soared and in the years that followed most musicals were film versions of big box office stage shows. A notable exception was *Bob Fosse's* (1925–88) ambitiously experimental *All That Jazz* (1979).

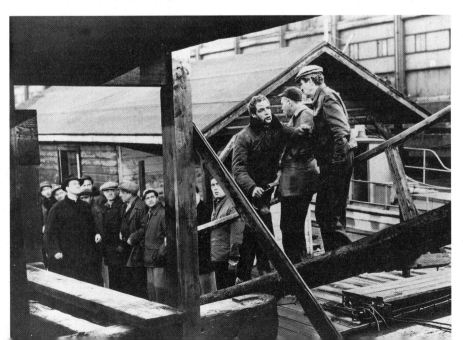

On the Waterfront (Elia Kazan, 1954) was one of Marlon Brando's earliest films. He stars as the young stevedore who takes on the waterfront gang boss.

World Cinema

Despite Hollywood's long dominance in world cinema, the country producing the highest number of films per year has long been India, apart from a period in the 1950s when there was a boom in production in Japan. Hong Kong also produces large numbers of films and even France often exceeds America in the number made each year. Indigenous film production is important everywhere to preserve national identity and offset foreign cultural dominance, and many countries have some kind of state support for national film industries.

Freedom from some of the pressures of Hollywood has enabled film makers to be more personal and often more thoughtful in their films, able to reflect the societies in which they work. It has allowed them to risk experiment and to explore subjects unacceptable to the US film industry's Production Code.

In the early days of cinema, France, Italy and Britain were as important as the USA, and the first 60-minute feature, *The Story of the Ned Kelly Gang* (1906), was made in Australia. From the 1970s Australia again began to make a mark in world cinema with sensitive films such as *Picnic at Hanging Rock* (Peter Weir, 1975) and commercial properties like *Mad Max* (1979), *Crocodile Dundee* (1986) and their sequels.

The coming of sound made foreign films inaccessible to many film-goers. Although some art-house cinemas existed, few non-Hollywood films gained wide distribution in countries where a different language was spoken. Even now only a comparatively small number are seen outside the art-house and ciné-club circuits, though

Saturday Night and Sunday Morning (Karel Reisz, 1960) displayed a new attitude towards illicit sex and was extremely influential. Albert Finney (1936–), in his first starring role, played the Nottingham factory worker who gets into trouble through an affair with a married woman.

television enables more to be seen in some countries.

British cinema

Initially, British feature films made little impact on world markets, apart from **Alfred Hitchcock's** (1899–1980) suspense thrillers, beginning with *Blackmail* (1929). From 1932, however, Hungarian-born **Alexander Korda** (1893–1956) set up London Film Productions to challenge Hollywood, producing such successes as *The Private Life of Henry VIII* (1933) and *Things to Come* (1936). In the 1930s, Britain pioneered the creation of a documentary tradition, led by **John Grierson** (1898–1972).

Towards the end of World War II Britain started to produce a string of high-quality films, including **Laurence Olivier's** (1907–89) *Henry V* (1944), **David Lean's** (1908–91) *Oliver Twist* (1948), **Carol Reed's** (1906–76) *The Third Man* (1949) and the work of **Michael Powell** (1905–) and **Emeric Pressburger** (1902–88), especially *The Red Shoes* (1948). At the same time Ealing Studios began a string of delightful comedies from *Kind Hearts and Coronets* (1949) to *Lady-killers* (1955), many exploiting the talents of Alec Guinness (1914–).

From the late 1950s, influenced by a parallel movement in literature and theatre, a series of British films focused on provincial working-class life: examples include **Karel Reisz's** (1926–) *Saturday Night and Sunday Morning* (1960) and **Lindsay Anderson's** (1923–) *This Sporting Life* (1963), a tradition continued by **Ken Loach's** (1936–) *Kes* (1970). Hammer Films meanwhile established a reputation in the horror genre and **Ken Russell** (1927–) displayed a maverick talent ranging from the carefully created *Women in Love* (1969) to the extravaganza of *Tommy* (1975). Also in Britain, fleeing McCarthy's witch-hunt, was US director **Joseph Losey** (1909–84), noted for psychological studies such as *The Servant* (1963) and *Accident* (1967).

More recent British successes, especially those like the Oscar-winning *Chariots of Fire* (Hugh Hudson, 1981), *Gandhi* (Richard Attenborough, 1982) and *The Killing Fields* (Roland Joffe, 1984) have been typical international productions, although a more indigenous cinema continues with films such as **Bill Forsyth's** (1947–) *Gregory's Girl* (1980) and *Local Hero* (1983).

French cinema

In the 1930s **Jean Renoir** (1894–1979) reflected the mood of anti-militarism in *La Grande Illusion* (1937), while in *La Règle du Jeu* (1939) he offered a bleak social satire. **Jean Gabin** (1904–76) became a popular actor playing a series of doomed heroes in such films as **Marcel Carné's** (1909–) *Le Jour se Lève* (1939).

Carné's *Les Enfants du Paradis* (1945), **Jean Cocteau's** (1889–1963) *Beauty and the Beast* (1946) and Orpheus films, together with the austere films of **Robert Bresson** (1907–) were among the very personal statements characteristic of intellectual French cinema. A series of comedies made by and featuring Jacques

Tati (1908–82), beginning with *Monsieur Hulot's Holiday* (1951), also found international audiences.

Influential in the late 1950s was a group of critics turned directors, led by **François Truffaut** (1932–84), **Jean-Luc Godard** (1930–), **Claud Chabrol** (1930–) and **Alain Resnais** (1922–). Collectively dubbed the *Nouvelle Vague* (New Wave), they emphasized personal style rather than conventionally 'well-made' films in successes such as *Les Quatre-cent Coups* (Truffaut, 1959), *Hiroshima Mon Amour* (Resnais, 1959) and *A Bout de Souffle* (Godard, 1960). France continues to produce many stylish and thoughtful films from established directors like **Eric Rohmer** (1920–), **Agnès Varda** (1928–) and **Louis Malle** (1932–) and from newcomers like **Claude Berri** (1954–), whose *Jean de Florette* (1986) and *Manon des Sources* (1986) were international successes.

Eastern European cinema

The relaxation of controls after the death of Stalin saw a flowering of creative cinema in Eastern Europe. With films such as *Ashes and Diamonds* (1958) the Polish **Andrzej Wajda** (1926–) displayed a major talent, while **Roman Polanski** (1933–), known mostly for his films made in the West, is another ex-student of the highly regarded Polish Film School.

In Czechoslovakia, **Milos Forman** (1932–) attracted attention with films such as *The Fireman's Ball* (1967), as did **Jiři Menzel** (1938–) with *Closely Observed Trains* (1966) before the extinction of the 'Prague Spring'.

In Russia, **Sergei Eisenstein** (1898–1948) began work on his great *Ivan the Terrible* trilogy in 1943 – but the second part was not released until 1958, five years after Stalin's death, and little of the third part was shot. Liberalization under Khrushchev allowed more individual expression in films such as **Grigori Chukrai's** (1921–) *The Forty-First* (1956) and **Mikhail Kalatzov's** (1903–73) *Cranes are Flying*. Later films of note included fine versions of *Hamlet* (1964) by **Grigori Kozintsev** (1905–73) and of *War and Peace* by **Sergei Bondarchuk** (1920–). **Andrei Tarkovsky** (1932–88) was widely acclaimed abroad for films which ranged from *Andrei Rublev* (1966), a subjective study of a medieval painter, to the science fiction *Solaris* (1971). Tarkovsky's increasingly obscure films met with official disapproval and he ended his life working abroad.

The Balkan countries have made little contribution to world cinema, but **Michael Cacoyannis'** (1922–) early films *Stella* (1955) and *Electra* (1961) attracted attention to Greek cinema, as did blacklisted US director **Jules Dassin's** (1911–) *Never on Sunday* (1959). **Theodor Angelopoulos'** (1935–) *Travelling Players* (1975) also gained wide acclaim.

Northern European cinema

The work of Danish director **Carl Dreyer** (1889–1968) and occasional films such as the Swedish *Witchcraft through the Ages* (Benjamin Christensen, 1922) and *The*

Atonement of Gosta Berling (Mauritz Stiller, 1924) attracted attention in other countries – but **Greta Garbo** (1905–90), launched in the latter film, was Scandinavian silent cinema's best-known export. In the 1940s **Alf Sjöberg** (1903–80) had some overseas success, especially with *Frenzy* (1944), but it was his scriptwriter **Ingmar Bergman** (1918–) who came to dominate modern Swedish cinema. After his allegorical *The Seventh Seal* (1957) he increasingly turned to obsessional studies of relationships.

In Germany, **Georg Pabst's** (1887–1967) *Threepenny Opera* (1931) and *Kameradschaft* (1931) were notable early talkies and **Fritz Lang** (1890–1976) made *M* (1931) before moving to Hollywood. The rise of Hitler put cinema in a straitjacket, though the propagandist *Triumph of the Will* (1934) and *Olympia* (1938) showed **Leni Riefenstahl** (1902–) to be an accomplished film-maker.

From the 1960s a group of new young directors began to attract international attention to German cinema. **Werner Herzog** (1942–) is best known for *Aguirre, Wrath of God* (1973) and *Fitzcarraldo* (1982), and **Wim Wenders** (1945–) for *The American Friend* (1981) and *Wings of Desire* (1987). The films of **Rainer Werner Fassbinder** (1946–82) vary in quality but delve deeply into the plight of their characters.

Italian and Spanish cinema

Censorship under Mussolini's fascist regime stifled all except elegantly glamorous films, but with *Obsessione* (1942) **Luchino Visconti** (1906–76) broke the romantic conventions, attracting the description 'neorealist' for films showing real life in real surroundings. With the liberation of Italy, **Roberto Rossellini** (1906–77) launched the new style, using a mainly non-professional cast in *Rome, Open City* (1945), a resistance story planned while the Germans still held Rome but shot after the entry of the Allies. Impressive films dealing with social problems followed, including **Vittorio de Sica's** (1901–74) *Bicycle Thieves* (1948) and *La Terra Trema* (Visconti, 1948).

Neorealism influenced cinema widely from India to Brazil. In Spain, still under fascist dictatorship, young directors such as **Juan Badem** (1922–) and **Luis Garcia Berlanga** (1921–) were particularly affected. Badem was responsible for **Luis Buñuel's** (1900–83) return to Spain to direct *Viridiana* (1961), where it was immediately banned. At last, with **Victor Erice's** (1940–) *Spirit of the Beehive* (1973), Spanish cinema was able to look back honestly at Spain's recent history.

In Italy meanwhile, **Federico Fellini** (1920–) moved from neorealism to an exploration of his own guilts and fantasies in films such as *La Dolce Vita* (1959) and *8½* (1963), while **Michelangelo Antonioni** (1912–) attracted attention with the enigmatic and slow-moving *L'Avventura* (1960). **Pier Paolo Pasolini's** (1922–75) 1967 film was a dazzling treatment of *Oedipus Rex* while his *Gospel According to St Matthew* (1964) was the best ever life of Christ. **Franco Rossi**

(1919–) and **Bernardo Bertolucci** (1940–) have continued the radical critique of Italian society begun by the neorealists although working with much more elaborate resources. Bertolucci has since become famous for productions such as *The Last Emperor* (1988).

Latin-American cinema

Influenced by neorealism and the ideas of Brazilian director **Glauber Rocha** (1938–), there have been a number of attempts by South American film-makers to develop a polemical cinema, such as the Brazilian *Cinema Nuovo*, which would reflect their own cultures and counter the

In *Kagemusha* (Kurosawa, 1980), set in 16th-century Japan, the double or *kagemusha* of a clan chief actually takes his place when he dies. One of Kurosawa's most impressive works, it features spectacular battle scenes with horses and men dying in slow motion.

commercialism of most Latin American films. The many comedies starring Mexican comedian *Cantinflas* (1911–) made him a star comparable to Chaplin in the Spanish-speaking world, but few films achieve international showing. From *Los Olivados* (1950) to *The Exterminating Angel* (1962), Luis Buñuel worked in Mexico, while Argentinian **Leopoldo Torre-Nilson** (1924–78) is well known abroad for *The Hand in the Trap* (1961) and other Bergman-like films. Isolated films such as **Lima Barreto's** (1905–82) *The Bandit* (Brazil, 1953), **Tomás Gutiérrez Alea's** (1928–) *Memories of Underdevelopment* (Cuba, 1968) and **Hector Babenco's** *Kiss of the Spiderwoman* (Brazil/US, 1985) have also achieved wide success.

Asian and African cinema

The Indian cinema produces three times more films annually than the USA. Its output is largely sentimental melodrama built around song and dance sequences and dominated by Hollywood-style stars. Both Hindi and Bengali cinema also have a lesser tradition of socially aware films, but the only films widely known elsewhere are those of **Satyajit Ray** (1921–92), whose work has had an international following since *Pather Panchali* (1955).

Japan at one time exceeded even India's output, though few films have made the international circuits, apart from the battle-centred historical dramas of **Akira Kurosawa** (1910–) such as *Seven Samurai* (1954) and *Ran* (1986). **Nagisa Oshima** (1932–) and **Yasujiro Ozu**

(1903–63) are now becoming known outside Japan for their fine studies of family and social life, while the trilogy *The Human Condition* (1959–61) by **Masaki Kobayashi** (1916–) deserves a place alongside the great European anti-militarist films.

China has a thriving film industry, although its output is little known to non-Chinese, but Hong Kong producers, serving the international Chinese communities, for a time gained wide distribution for martial arts films, such as *Enter the Dragon* (1973) and other films starring American-born **Bruce Lee** (1940–73).

The most important film-maker to emerge from the Middle East is Turkey's **Yilmaz Güney** (1937–84) who, despite imprisonment by the authorities, made powerful films such as *The Wall* (1982) and *Yol* (1981).

Although Egypt has been producing films for local audiences since 1918, little African cinema has found an audience elsewhere. Nevertheless indigenous films from black Africa are now achieving considerable quality, as in the work of **Souleymane Cissé** (1940–) from Senegal, whose *Yeelan* (1988) gained international screenings.   HL

Les Quatre-Cent Coups (Truffaut, 1959). Jean-Pierre Léaud (1944–) played the neglected 12-year-old Antoine Doinel, who takes to petty crime and is placed in a reform school. Léaud went on to play Doinel in four further Truffaut films, following the character through adolescence, marriage, fatherhood and divorce.

SEE ALSO

● PHOTOGRAPHY AND FILM p. 324
● RADIO, TELEVISION AND VIDEO p. 326
● SILENT FILMS p. 558
● HOLLYWOOD p. 560
● HOW A FILM IS MADE p. 564

How a Film is Made

The technology of cinema has developed considerably during its first century. Improvements in film stock, lenses, lighting, sound reproduction and colour have all contributed, but the basic methods of film production have changed little since the coming of sound and are the same whatever kind of film is being made. Prop makers and scene builders now make use of new materials such as plastics, but the major recent change has been in the use of computers, not so much to create images as to control the positions and precise movements of subjects and cameras for complex special effects.

D.W. Griffith (see p. 558) improvised many of his early films from a few notes on the back of an envelope, but feature films usually involve a great many people and much detailed planning. The making of a film can be divided into three broad areas: preproduction, production and postproduction.

Preproduction

A film begins either with a *screenwriter* or a *director* developing an idea and interesting a producer, or with a *producer* having an original idea or deciding that an existing book or play would make a good film.

The producer, whether on the staff of a big film company or an independent developing his or her own films, is responsible for the business side of the project. The producer raises the finance, which may come from corporations, individual investors, distributors (who will later profit from renting the film out to cinemas) or television and video companies

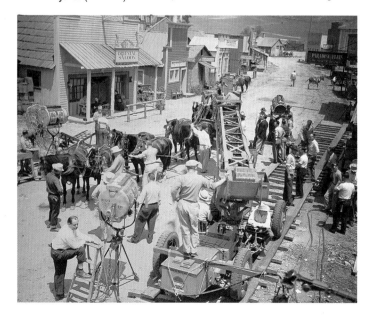

A film crew at work on the Hollywood western *Duel in the Sun* (King Vidor, 1946), famous for its final gory shoot-out between Gregory Peck (1916–) and Jennifer Jones (1919–).

(who want to acquire the right to show or rent it). A budget and filming schedule will be drawn up. The producer will also engage all the personnel required, although the director – and possibly the leading actors, when contracted – may have a say in who is taken on.

The producer, sometimes with the involvement of the director, will have a script developed. First comes a *treatment* – a synopsis of the action – which is often essential for raising finance. This is then developed into a *shooting script*, which contains dialogue and scene descriptions and can go through many versions before a final form is agreed.

Studio space must be booked, suitable locations found and transportation problems solved. Everyone involved must be fed and found somewhere to stay. Finally, the cooperation of local people and the police needs to be obtained for any public filming before such scenes can be filmed.

Production

Some directors like to rehearse actors away from the film set, while others simply run through a scene immediately before filming it. Even when actors are encouraged to improvise, the camerawork is usually carefully planned in advance. Often a *storyboard* – a sequence of drawings showing the contents of the picture for each change of image or viewpoint – is prepared beforehand.

Some *shots* (uninterrupted sequences of filming) – such as a building being demolished or a car crashing over a cliff – may be difficult to restage and have to be got right first time. However, a shot often has to be taken again and again because of something unwanted appearing within the picture or on the soundtrack, quite apart from any mistake the actors make. Each *take* is identified by filming a *clapperboard*, with scene and take numbers chalked on it, at the beginning of each shot. The *clapperboy* brings down a wooden bar on the edge of the board to make a clap to guide synchronization of sound and image when the film is edited. Sometimes film is shot without sound (especially in Italy) and dialogue is dubbed over afterwards. This avoids some

Make-up artist Christopher Tucker took 7 hours to transform John Hurt (1940–) for his role in *The Elephant Man* (1980), using previously made-up models to help him. The film is based on the true story of a grotesquely deformed man rescued from a fairground freak show by a doctor.

problems in filming, but adds complications later.

Filming is often out of continuity as far as the story is concerned – for instance, when all scenes on one set, or involving one actor, are filmed together. In *Serpico* (Sidney Lumet, 1973) **Al Pacino** (1939–), as an undercover detective, had to grow a disguise of hippy beard and hair. The unit could not wait for his hair to grow between shots so he grew it first and scenes were filmed in reverse order, with the beard and hair gradually cut off so that the cleanshaven look was filmed last.

The time taken in preparing each shot and in retakes makes film-making a slow and expensive business. Often it takes a whole day to film only a few minutes of final action, and the budget of an average feature film is in the region of $10 million.

Postproduction

Postproduction is when a film is put together. The *editor* assembles satisfactory takes, or parts of takes (of which continuity will have kept a record), in a sequence to tell the story and make the cumulative or contrasting effects the director requires. This *rough cut* is without a soundtrack.

Now special effects and optical links – *mixes* (or *dissolves*), *fade-ins, fade-outs* and *wipes* (when the picture is replaced by another moving across it) – and sound are added, including sound effects that may not be on the original soundtrack. The editing will be tightened up to perfect each transition and to regulate the overall pace of the film, and titles and credits will be added. Actors now *dub* scenes recorded mute or badly, watching the projected film and synchronizing speech with their lip movements on the screen. Finally, music is composed and recorded to fit the *final cut*, which is made from the master negative, earlier editing having been done on replaceable working prints.

Distribution

The film now passes to the *distributors*, who buy from the producers the right to rent out the film to cinemas. Sometimes they may insist on changes being made to the content or length of the film to suit their ideas of what will be successful. Finally, the film may be seen by a censorship body, which can insist on deletions of sequences they consider offensive or limit viewing to audiences over certain ages. Television channels that show films will also make their own cuts to fit time schedules or to make the film more suitable for their viewers. Sometimes the producers will make special television versions that may, for example, exclude swearing or explicit sex scenes that are considered acceptable in the cinema but not on television.   HL

SEE ALSO

● PHOTOGRAPHY AND FILM p. 324
● RADIO, TELEVISION AND VIDEO p. 326
● SILENT FILMS p. 558
● HOLLYWOOD p. 560
● WORLD CINEMA p. 562

SPECIAL EFFECTS

Filming has many tricks to show things that are not really there. *Double exposure* and *stop action* were used by Georges Méliès (see p. 558), and in the silent days techniques had already been developed to avoid the need for building huge sets or to add elements to location shooting. The area of the scene in which the actors do not appear is painted on glass, or made as a model, then carefully lined up on camera so that the image fits precisely with the full-scale set or location. However, this works only if the camera is stationary. An alternative method is to block off the unwanted area with a mask or *matte* while filming or in optical printing, instead of combining the image in the camera. When the image is copied frame by frame, the replacement image can then be photographed on another film and the two combined. A similar masking technique can be used for filming the same actor as twins, or for other double exposures.

Sequences combining several different matte shots and involving complicated camera movements are now possible with the help of computers that control the camera and any movable elements in models with an accuracy that produces a perfect match.

Models are frequently used to produce scenes – such as floods and devastated cities – that would be impossible to stage full-scale. Shots of the model are then intercut with full-scale action shots. For creations like *King Kong* (1933) a whole series of sizes may be used, from a scaled figure climbing a model skyscraper to a huge mechanized hand in which an actress can be held for close-ups.

The shark in *Jaws* (1975) was played by life-sized models – each 7.5 m (25 ft) long. Two had complex hydraulic, pneumatic and electronic equipment to enable them to leap and dive but could only be shot from the opposite side to the controls; the third, simpler version was used for overhead shots. Each cost $250 000 to build and $1 million to operate during filming.

ANIMATED FILMS

Animated films, whether using drawn cartoons or models, depend on stop-action photography. The film is exposed one frame at a time and the picture changed, or the model moved, a fraction between each exposure. A few animators actually repaint the picture between each shot and others draw directly on the film, but in most cartoons backgrounds are created and characters and other moving elements are painted on acetate overlays called *cels* (originally celluloid was used). Only the moving elements are redrawn, although sometimes as many as eight layers of cels may be used in a single frame. Since five seconds of animation may require up to 60 different drawings, the cel technique saves a lot of work compared with redrawing the whole picture. In recent years computers have been used to help create the graphics for cartoons.

Bob Hoskins (1942–) has trouble with Roger Rabbit in *Who Framed Roger Rabbit?* (1989), which combines cartoon and real-life characters. The action shot (top) in which an extension to the tap produces the stream of water that will come out of Roger Rabbit's mouth, and the cartoon drawing (centre) are combined to make the complete shot (bottom).

THE CREW

Director: has overall artistic control of the film; second unit or assistant directors may handle scenes shot on distant locations or help to handle large-scale filming.

Art director: designs sets and chooses locations; controls set dressers and costume designers.

Director of photography (cinematographer): a specialist in the film image, responsible for lighting, camerawork and manipulation; controls camera operators (who run cameras) and assistants (who load film, focus cameras and move them about).

Sound mixer: a specialist in capturing and using sound images; supported by recordists and microphone operators.

Continuity ('script girl'): keeps records of shots made and details of action, with responsibility for ensuring consistency, e.g. same clothes worn, props in same positions and every detail matching other shots of the same scene – even to how far a cigarette has been burned down – especially when taken at different times.

Gaffer: places and rigs lights; controls an assistant known as 'best boy' in Hollywood.

Key grip: the head prop person (props are all the movable things on a set from furniture to food).

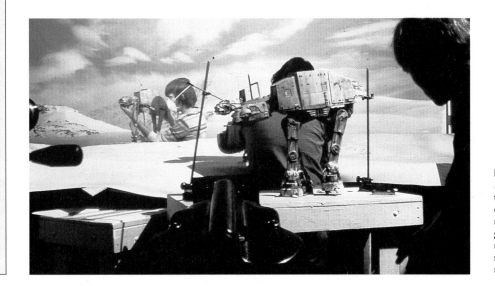

Making *The Empire Strikes Back* (1980). In the Star Wars films, computers were used to merge model backgrounds, explosions, moving sky patterns and spaceship interiors into a single image.

MUSIC
AND DANCE

*'Music is an invisible dance,
as dancing is silent music.'*

Jean Paul

What is Music?

Music, more than ever before, forms part of our lives – in shops, restaurants, bars, hotels, buses, aircraft, cars, it has become almost inescapable. With the help of a portable-cassette or compact-disc player, it can accompany you wherever you go. If you play these instruments too loudly through earphones, you may (as the manufacturers warn) grow deaf. Most people, however, seem already deaf to background music, so ever-present has it become.

Yet if asked to define music, most of us would find it hard to answer. Surprisingly, the multi-volume *New Grove Dictionary of Music and Musicians* takes the subject so completely for granted that it does not attempt a definition. The *Collins English Dictionary* calls it 'an art form consisting of sequences of sounds in time, especially tones of definite pitch organized melodically, harmonically, rhythmically and according to tone colour'.

But not all music aspires to being an art form, and not all music is melodic, harmonic, or rhythmic. John Cage's piano piece, *4' 33" for Henry Flint,* requires the performer to sit at the keyboard for a specified amount of time, without touching the instrument. What the audience 'hears' is the silence, or absence of silence, for Cage's 'music' inevitably incorporates every sound or rustle that occurs within earshot during the piece's duration. Electronic music, which modern composers have developed into a heavy industry, likewise defies preconceptions. Many listeners still refuse to accept it as legitimate music, yet, as a distinguished critic once pointed out, if that's not music, so much the worse for music.

Music, then, is an art that is difficult to tie down. Its components may include melody, rhythm, harmony, pitch and timbre (tone colour), not necessarily all at the same time.

The origins of music

In its most primitive form, music may evoke the sound of the elements – earth, air, fire, water. Since humans have always been imitative animals, it seems natural that nature itself should have provided the scope for the earliest music and the materials for the earliest musical instruments. Where these materials – sticks, stones, bones, bells, reed pipes or whatever – were not available, the human voice was a more than adequate substitute, relieving loneliness, making contact with other people, reflecting the rhythms of manual labour or simply of walking, celebrating victories, or paying tribute to primitive deities – often in combination with dancing (see p. 592).

The sophisticated evolution of music – even the notes of a simple scale or chord – took place over a period of centuries. There was certainly a rich musical tradition in the years before Christ – for example in India, China, Egypt and Greece, much of it tantalizing because it was passed on orally, not written down. Even today, in Asia particularly, this tradition persists, because music is regarded as improvisatory and contemplative, ceaselessly changing, rather than something perfected and fixed on paper.

In Europe, much of what we today call music emerged through the spread of Christianity and of Judaism, particularly through medieval *plainsong* chants, which were single lines of notated vocal melody in free rhythm (i.e. not divided into bar lengths) sung in churches, and through *Gregorian chant*, named after Pope Gregory I, in whose time (around AD 600) it was systematized. This still forms part of Roman Catholic musical ritual. However, its *modes* (or 'scales') gradually gave way to the modern scale.

The components of music

A musical *note*, therefore, is more than just a 'noise'. It is a single sound of definite pitch and duration, which can be identified in writing. The *pitch* of a note is its height or depth in relation to other notes, or in relation to an absolute pitch. This absolute pitch has internationally been set at A = 440 Hz (hertz); that is, the A above middle C has a frequency of 440 cycles or vibrations per second (see also Wave Theory, pp. 28–9, and Acoustics, pp. 30–1).

A *scale* is a progression of notes in ascending or descending order, while a *melody* (or tune) assembles a series of notes into a recognizable musical shape. However, to suggest, as some people do, that modern music lacks 'melody' may merely mean that the listener has failed to identify, or come to terms with, the melodies it contains – even Beethoven and Verdi, to some ears, once seemed unmelodic.

A melody usually, though not necessarily, possesses *rhythm*, which listeners often assume to mean *beat*. In fact, the beat of a piece of music is simply its regular pulse,

determined by the *bar lines* by which music is metrically divided (two beats in the bar and so forth). Rhythm can be an infinitely more complex arrangement of notes into a mixture of short and long durations (or time values; see box) within a single bar or across a series of bars. The *time* in which a piece of music (or section of a piece) is written is identified by a *time signature* at the beginning of the piece or section. Thus 3/4 time (three-four time), which is waltz time, represents three crotchets to the bar. This means that the main beat comes every three crotchets: 1 2 3, 1 2 3, etc.; 4/4 time, which is march time, has four crotchets: 1 2 3 4, 1 2 3 4, etc.; 3/8 and 6/8 represent three and six quavers, respectively. There are also many more complex time signatures.

A melody may have *harmony*. This means that it is accompanied by *chords*, which are combinations of notes, simultaneously sounded. It may also have *counterpoint*, whereby another melody, or succession of notes with musical shape, is simultaneously combined with it. 'Rules' of harmony and counterpoint, stating which notes could be acceptably combined and which could not, have been matters of concern to scholars, teachers and pupils in the course of musical history. But as with any other grammar, progressive composers have known when to break or bend the rules to the benefit of their own music.

Tonality

The old modes, or scales, employed in the Middle Ages gradually gave way in the 17th century to a modern *tonality* – scales laid out in 12 major and minor *keys*, each consisting of a sequence of seven notes, divided into tones and semitones. Each of the 12 major and minor scales starts on one of the 12 semitones into which an octave is divided (see illustration). Melodies in a specific key use the notes of that scale, and the order in which the notes are used determines the nature of the melody. On a piano the scale of C major consists entirely of white notes, starting on C.

The notes from C to the next C, either above or below, form an *octave*. A note and another note an octave above sound 'the same' because the higher note has double the frequency (see above). For example, the A above middle C is 440 cycles per second, and the A above that is 880 cycles.

From C to D (the first 'white' note above) represents an interval of a tone, from C to C sharp (the first 'black' note) an interval of a semitone, so called because it represents half a tone. But from E to F, and from B to C, also forms a semitone (on a piano there is no black note between them). A scale therefore consists of a mixture of tone and semitone intervals. A *chromatic scale*, on the other hand, employs nothing but semitones, and thus requires all 12 of the white and black notes to be used. The *whole-tone scale* – used, for example, by Debussy – moves entirely in tones. Starting on C, it would consist of the notes C–D–E–F sharp–G sharp–A sharp.

In musical terminology, a sharp (♯) indicates a semitone rise in pitch, and a flat (♭)

SEE ALSO

- WAVE THEORY p. 28
- ACOUSTICS p. 30
- HIFI p. 328
- WESTERN MUSIC pp. 570–81
- THE SYMPHONY ORCHESTRA AND ITS INSTRUMENTS p. 582
- MUSIC FROM AROUND THE WORLD p. 590
- THE WORLD OF DANCE p. 592

TIME VALUES OF NOTES

Each note has half the duration or time value of the note above. The symbol for each note is followed by the symbol for the equivalent rest. The breve is rarely used. A dot after a note increases its value by half.

Note symbol	Rest symbol	British name	US name
		Semibreve	Whole note
		Minim	Half note
	Ɣ or Ɂ	Crotchet	Quarter note
	7	Quaver	Eighth note
		Semiquaver	Sixteenth note
		Demisemiquaver	Thirty-second note
		Hemidemisemiquaver	Sixty-fourth note

a semitone fall. A natural (♮) is a note that is neither sharp nor flat, though the indication sign needs only to be used in special circumstances.

The first note of a scale is known as the *tonic*, or 'keynote'. The tonic of the scale of C is therefore the note C. All other scales require one or more black notes to be played in order to produce the same sequence of intervals. The sequence of intervals between the notes in a major scale is therefore as follows (using C major as an example):

C [tone] D [tone] E [semitone] F [tone] G [tone] A [tone] B [semitone] C.

Minor scales employ a different sequence of notes from major, and incorporate, in particular, a flattened third (in the scale of C minor the note E, a 'third' higher than the note C, is 'flattened' to the black note immediately below, i.e. E flat). It is this that gives minor keys what listeners traditionally identify as their element of 'sadness' compared with major ones. There are two commonly used forms of the minor scale, and the sequence of intervals are as follows (using A minor as an example):

Harmonic Minor: A [tone] B [semitone] C [tone] D [tone] E [semitone] F [1½ tones] G sharp [semitone] A.

Melodic Minor: A [tone] B [semitone] C [tone] D [tone] E [tone] F sharp [tone] G sharp [semitone] A.

There is a different descending sequence in melodic scales:

A [tone] G [tone] F [semitone] E [tone] D [tone] C [semitone] B [tone] A.

It is important to remember that these scales are conventions – conventions to which our ears are attuned through familiarity. The modes of ancient Greece and medieval Europe employed different sequences of tones and semitones, and the scales used in Indian music and some modern jazz, for example, may use quarter tones.

The development of tonality was cele- brated by Johann Sebastian Bach (1685– 1750) in 24 keyboard preludes and fugues, one in each key, known as the *Well-tempered Clavier*. These displayed the advantages of the (at the time) novel system of *equal temperament*, whereby all of the notes of a keyboard instrument were 'tempered' to be precisely a semitone apart. The notes C sharp and D flat thus became identical, which was not (and still is not) the case with other instruments. On a string instrument, where the notes are not pre-set, C sharp and D flat are slightly different from each other – imper- ceptibly so to the ears of most listeners, though there is a passage in Wagner's *Siegfried Idyll* where the violins do aud- ibly move from a sustained A sharp to a sustained B flat, an effect impossible on a piano.

In the course of a piece of music, a composer may often *modulate*, or change key, in order to avoid monotony. In Bach's time, and beyond, an established and logical change was to the key based on the fifth note of the scale, known as the *dominant* (the note G in the key of C). Harmonically this is closely related to the tonic note, so the transition could be made from one key to the other, and back to the home key, without difficulty. But modulations to harmonically more 'dis- tant' keys, though at one time frowned on for pedantic reasons, were soon found to be a source of dramatic effects, as also was the sudden contrast between a minor key and a major, exploited by composers such as Beethoven with increasing freedom. By the time Wagner composed *Tristan and Isolde* (1865), modulation had become so fluid that it was only a step away from *atonality*, or the composition of music in no fixed key at all. Atonality was syste- matized by Schoenberg (see p. 578) in what he described as *dodecaphonic* or 'twelve- note' music. In this method of composi- tion, one of the major influences on 20th- century music, the twelve notes within an octave were employed in such a way that there was no home key and no reliance on modulation in the old sense, though key relationships did often remain implied, even if not specifically stated.   CW

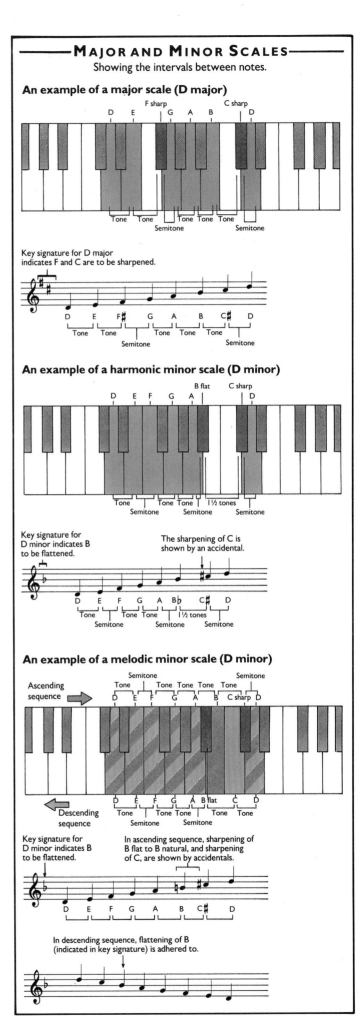

MAJOR AND MINOR SCALES
Showing the intervals between notes.

An example of a major scale (D major)

Key signature for D major indicates F and C are to be sharpened.

An example of a harmonic minor scale (D minor)

Key signature for D minor indicates B to be flattened.

The sharpening of C is shown by an accidental.

An example of a melodic minor scale (D minor)

Ascending sequence

Descending sequence

Key signature for D minor indicates B to be flattened.

In ascending sequence, sharpening of B flat to B natural, and sharpening of C, are shown by accidentals.

In descending sequence, flattening of B (indicated in key signature) is adhered to.

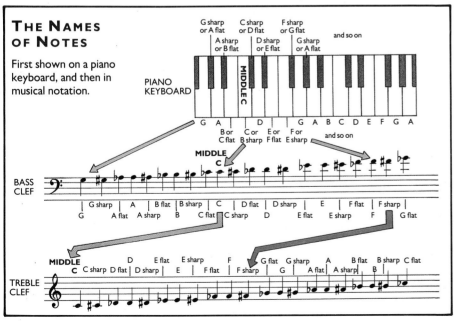

THE NAMES OF NOTES

First shown on a piano keyboard, and then in musical notation.

PIANO KEYBOARD

MIDDLE C

BASS CLEF

TREBLE CLEF

MIDDLE C

Plainsong and Polyphony

The beginnings of Western music lie in the cultures of the ancient Near East, where music is believed to have been used as an accompaniment to religious worship, dance, and work. The musical culture of the Eastern Mediterranean was transplanted to the Western Mediterranean by the Romans, and after the decline of the Roman Empire, it was the Christian Church that perpetuated and extended the musical heritage of antiquity.

An ensemble of medieval instruments, including flutes and rebecs (a type of early bowed instrument). Watching the players in this 13th-century manuscript illustration is the lyric poet and musician Heinrich Frauenlob, who is dressed in the costume of the 'king of the minstrels'.
(Heidelberg Library/Explorer)

Two of the crucial developments in the early history of Western music were *plainsong* and *polyphony*, both of which came about through the spread of the Christian religion, and whose musical foundations lay partly in Jewish chant, partly in Greece and Rome, and almost anywhere else where Christianity had taken root.

Plainsong

Plainsong, consisting of a single line of vocal melody in 'free' rhythm (i.e. not divided into metred bar lengths), gained ground during the early years of Christianity and reached its peak in Gregorian chant (see p. 568), still used in the Roman Catholic Church today. Other parts of Europe produced their own ritual music of similar type. Byzantine music largely consisted of the liturgical chant of the Eastern Orthodox Churches; Spanish church music showed Moorish influences; the French had their Gallic Rite; and through Ambrosian Chant, named after the 4th-century St Ambrose of Milan, there spread the practice of *antiphons*, whereby two separate bodies of singers performed plainsong chants in response to one another.

Monophony and polyphony

Plainsong, being confined to a single line of unaccompanied melody, falls into the category of *monophonic* music – Greek for 'single sound', implying absence of harmonic support or other melodies performed simultaneously with the original. *Polyphony*, conversely, means 'many sounds', and indicates the simultaneous sounding of two or more independent melodic lines to produce a coherent musical texture. The melodies in polyphony are described as being in *counterpoint* to each other, and the resulting music as *contrapuntal*. The art of polyphony began to emerge in Europe in the 12th and 13th centuries.

Ars Antiqua and Ars Nova

The most influential centre of musical activity in the 12th and 13th centuries was the church of Notre Dame in Paris, where the choirmasters **Léonin** (active 12th century) and **Pérotin** (c.1160–1240) developed a musical style based on plainsong and *organum*, an early form of polyphony involving the addition of parts to a plainsong melody. Such music was described by writers of the early 14th century as 'Ars Antiqua' (Latin for 'old art') to distinguish it from its successor 'Ars Nova' (Latin for 'new art'). Ars Nova, which flourished in France and Italy in the 14th century, incorporated significant innovations in the areas of rhythm and harmony.

France's proclaimed flower of Ars Nova was **Guillaume de Machaut** (c. 1300–77), a composer of brilliant ingenuity and a champion of *isorhythms*, whereby rhythm and melody followed strictly repeated patterns that were not in synchronization with each other. In addition to his important innovations in the mass and the motet (see box), Machaut was also a pioneer of the polyphonic setting of poetry in fixed song forms, such as the *ballade*, the *rondeau* and the *virelai*. Collectively these song forms are known as *chansons*.

Secular song

Secular compositions such as these were greatly influenced – especially in their metric system – by the flourishing medieval tradition of monophonic secular song that preceded them. In France the *troubadours* – itinerant poet-musicians, often of aristocratic birth – were active in Provence in the 11th and 12th centuries. Their German equivalents were the *Minnesinger* (German 'love singers'; see also p. 618), whose successors, the guilds of *Meistersinger* ('Mastersingers'), established themselves in some German cities in the 15th and 16th centuries.

The Renaissance

Generally, the beginning of the Renais-sance in music is reckoned to be found in the increasing secularization of music that took place at the court of Burgundy in the early years of the 15th century. Among the leading musicians of Western Europe attracted to the courts of Philip the Good and Charles the Bold (see p. 401) were the Franco-Flemish composers **Guillaume Dufay** (c. 1400–74) and **Gilles Binchois** (c. 1400–60). Also active in France at this time was the influential English composer **John Dunstable** (c. 1385–1453).

During this period significant developments occurred both in religious and secular musical forms. In the domain of religious music, composers concentrated their efforts on the forms of the mass and the motet (see box). Plainsong melodies had formed the basis of earlier polyphonic settings for the mass, but Dufay began the practice of borrowing secular songs for the same purpose.

Musicians from the Low Countries continued to dominate the European musical stage in the second half of the 15th century. **Johannes Ockeghem** (c. 1425–c. 1495) spent his career in the service of kings of France, while his pupil **Josquin Desprès** (1440–1521) worked in both France and Italy before returning to his native Flanders. In their sacred polyphony, Ockeghem, Josquin and their contemporaries added further parts, so increasing the breadth of sound. While the mass, the motet and the *chanson* continued to be the chief forms of composition, new forms were also emerging, notably, in northern Italy, the *frottola* – a simple chordal precursor of the madrigal (see below).

The polyphonic style established by Ockeghem and Josquin persisted to the beginning of the 16th century, but gradually different national styles and forms began to emerge. An important harmonic development was the use of chromaticism (the use of notes outside the mode of the composition), which foreshadowed the passing of the medieval modal system (see p. 568). Different types of mass setting developed, especially where the Reformation had established Protestant worship. In Germany the Lutheran chorale (later to exercise a deep influence on the music of J.S. Bach; see p. 572) took root, while in England the anthem (the Protestant equivalent of the Latin motet) took its place in the liturgy of the Church of England. But as the 16th century progressed, it was Italy that emerged as the crucially important musical centre.

The polyphonic mass reached its apogee in the work of three great composers: the Italian **Giovanni Palestrina** (c. 1525–84), the Spaniard **Luis de Victoria** (c. 1548–1611), and the Flemish **Roland de Lassus** (1532–94). The harmonic vividness and smooth, flowing lines of Palestrina's polyphony are displayed in over 100 masses and 250 motets embracing many different styles and numbers of voices. The masses of Victoria are characterized by subtle expressive polyphony and intense dramatic feeling. Roland de Lassus represents the high-water mark of Flemish polyphony. In a prolific and cosmopolitan career, he produced nearly 2000 works including masses, motets, psalm settings, chansons, madrigals and canzonas (see below).

In Venice, a more flamboyant polychoral (multi-choir) style was developed by the Venetians *Andrea Gabrieli* (c. 1510–86) and his nephew and pupil *Giovanni Gabrieli* (1557–1612). Giovanni's motets featured a rich instrumental accompaniment, and made use of the antiphonal effects that it was possible to obtain in St Mark's Church in Venice, where the congregation was framed by two balconies.

The European polyphonic tradition was introduced into England by *Thomas Tallis* (c. 1505–85). Tallis's works include masses, two settings of the Magnificat, and the extraordinary 40-part motet, *Spem in alium*. He was one of the first composers to provide settings of the Anglican liturgy.

Although based in Protestant England, *William Byrd* (1543–1623) – a Catholic – composed his greatest music for the Roman liturgy. Byrd produced three masses and numerous motets for the Roman Catholic Church, as well as anthems and psalm settings for the Anglican Church in a style which, while showing him to be versed in the work of Palestrina and the continental masters, is marked by genuine individuality as well as technical mastery.

Byrd was active in other genres. In his music for virginal (an early keyboard instrument similar to the harpsichord) he developed the variation form and prepared the ground for the achievements of other English keyboard composers such as *John Bull* (c. 1562–1628), *Orlando Gibbons* (1583–1625) and *Thomas Tomkins* (1572–1656). Byrd's fantasias for viol consort established a style of composition that was to influence a whole generation of Jacobean composers. His secular songs, composed for solo voice accompanied by viol consort, draw on a native English tradition and, unlike the madrigals of his contemporaries, show little Italian influence.

The madrigal

The art of the madrigal – a secular polyphonic composition for several voices, usually based on poems of some literary merit – had its roots in Italy, where early forms of the madrigal first appeared in the 14th century. The type of madrigal that emerged in the 16th century was the result of the marriage of the *frottola* with the more sophisticated musical techniques of the Flemish and those trained by them. Early madrigal composers were Flemish composers resident in Italy, and their madrigals were written for three or four voices. A larger number of voices and a more consistently polyphonic style became the norm as the century progressed. In the hands of composers such as *Luca Marenzio* (c. 1553–99), *Carlo Gesualdo* (c. 1560–1613) and, above all, Claudio Monteverdi (see below), the madrigal became a highly sophisticated and dramatic genre, incorporating many colourful effects and vivid word-painting.

Italian madrigals began to appear in England in the late 16th century. A native English tradition of madrigal composition incorporating features of the secular song as exemplified by Byrd and Gibbons was quickly established by composers such as *Thomas Morley* (1557–c. 1602), *Thomas Weelkes* (c. 1576–1623) and *John Wilbye* (1574–1638).

Another vocal genre popular in England was the *ayre*, a less contrapuntal form than the madrigal, usually performed to lute or consort accompaniment. Preeminent among England's school of lutenist song composers was *John Dowland* (1563–1626), the melancholy beauty of whose music made him famous throughout Europe.

Instrumental music

In the Middle Ages instruments were principally used to double voices in vocal polyphony or to provide music for dancing. The real burgeoning of instrumental music took place in the 16th century. Dance forms such as the stately *pavan* and vigorous *galliard* emerged, and were often composed in pairs, prefiguring the instrumental dance suites of the 17th century. Non-dance forms included the *canzona*, the *ricercare* and the *fantasia*. The canzona – an intricate fugal form – began life as a vocal composition, and developed as an instrumental form for keyboard, lute or instrumental ensemble. Similar to the canzona in its use of melodic imitation was the *fantasia*, a composition for consorts of string or wind instruments, which enjoyed a particular vogue in England in the 16th and 17th centuries. The *ricercare* – another elaborate fugal form – first appeared as a form of lute composition in the early 16th century, but later examples of the form were written for organ and consorts of viols.

Instrumental music in the 16th century was performed principally on the lute, the organ, the virginal and other stringed keyboard instruments and by instrumental ensembles. The lute in particular enjoyed immense popularity as a domestic instrument for solo playing and song accompaniment. Instrumental ensembles of the Renaissance period never became standardized, but consorts of viols, and groups of wind instruments such as cornetts and sackbuts were common.

Towards the Baroque

Claudio Monteverdi (1567–1643) is chiefly celebrated today as the composer of three innovative operas (see p. 584) and the *Vespro della Beata Vergine* ('Vespers of the Blessed Virgin'; 1610), which runs the entire gamut of contemporary types of sacred music. Monteverdi's church music displays two contrasting trends: one following the traditional polyphonic style, the other tending towards the newer Baroque style of brilliant and expressive writing for solo voices and chorus.

The greatest German composer of the 17th century was *Heinrich Schütz* (1585–1672), who encountered the new Italian style while a pupil of Giovanni Gabrieli in Venice. In his compositions for the

Claudio Monteverdi, the Italian composer of operas, madrigals and sacred music, painted by Bernardo Strozzi in 1640. Only three of the 12 operas Monteverdi is known to have written have survived, but their blend of rich orchestral texture, dramatically effective recitative, songs and choral writing ensure their status as landmarks in the history of musical drama. (Museum Ferdinandeum, Innsbruck/Archiv für Kunst)

Lutheran Church, Schütz adopted the Venetian polychoral style of the Gabrielis, the operatic style of Monteverdi, and the emerging *concertante* style of his Italian contemporaries – and then married these with the native German polyphonic tradition. Schütz's choral style was to prove an influence on German composers up until the time of Bach and Handel (see pp. 572–3). CW

SEE ALSO

● WHAT IS MUSIC? p. 568
● MUSIC OF THE BAROQUE p. 572
● CLASSICAL MUSIC p. 574
● THE SYMPHONY ORCHESTRA AND ITS INSTRUMENTS p. 582
● OPERA p. 584

MASSES AND MOTETS

The Mass is the principal service of the Roman Catholic Church, which composers set to music as part of their duty to God and to their employers. From the 11th to the 13th centuries composers used original plainsong melodies as the basis for polyphonic settings of selected parts of the Mass. The first known integrated setting of the 'Ordinary' of the Mass (*Kyrie*, *Gloria*, *Credo*, *Sanctus* with *Benedictus*, and *Agnus Dei*) was the 14th-century composer Guillaume de Machaut's *Messe de Notre Dame*. It was only in the first half of the 15th century that settings of the whole Ordinary of the Mass became the norm.

Though early masses had no written instrumental parts, performances between the 15th and 17th centuries often alternated sung passages with passages played on the organ: these were known as *organ masses*. By the 18th century, masses with instrumental accompaniment had established themselves, as Bach's great B minor Mass, with its sonorous high trumpet parts, confirms.

A *missa brevis* was a concise version of the Mass, while a *missa parodia* was not a 'parody' in the modern sense of the word – the name merely referred to a type of mass, prevalent in the 15th and 16th centuries, in which composers drew elements from other works.

Requiem masses for the dead consisted of a somewhat different sequence of movements, including an opening *Requiem aeternam* ('Grant them eternal rest') and a *Dies irae*. Palestrina, Lassus and Victoria all produced requiems and, via Mozart, Berlioz and Verdi, the practice has continued to our own day, as Benjamin Britten's *War Requiem* (1962) testifies.

A motet is a short choral work, often unaccompanied, whose origins go back to the 13th century. The early motet was a polyphonic composition for three voices, two accompanying voices being added in counterpoint to a plainsong or other melody sung by a tenor. The Renaissance motet – also polyphonic, and setting sacred Latin texts for four to six voices – reached its summit in the compositions of Victoria, Palestrina, Byrd and Tallis.

Music of the Baroque

Baroque, Classical and *Romantic* are the categories to which most music performed in the concert hall or opera house are assigned. But the boundaries of each are hazy, and the word Baroque is particularly difficult to define. A word of obscure origin, by the 17th and 18th centuries Baroque had become a term for the ornate, particularly ecclesiastical, architecture of the period (see pp. 530–1). Other than defining a particular period between 1650 and 1750, Baroque has little meaning in application to music, though in its suggestion of ornateness of style it is obviously descriptive of certain types of 17th- and 18th-century composition. A distinction is generally made between composers of the 'early Baroque' (such as Monteverdi and Schütz; see p.571), and those of the 'late Baroque' (most notably Bach and Handel).

The vocabulary and techniques of instrumental and vocal composition underwent a massive expansion in the 17th century. Revolutionary change took place also in the formal organization of music: the medieval modes that had been the basis of polyphonic composition in the 16th century giving way during the 17th century to a system involving the exclusive use of modern scales (see p. 568). In addition, innovations such as the *concertato* style – in which specific instrumental or vocal parts were accompanied by a *basso continuo*, or 'thorough bass' (involving a low-pitched instrument such as a cello or bass viol combined with a harpsichord, organ or lute) – distinguish the Baroque from the Renaissance that preceded it.

Italy

As well as providing the emerging vocal genres of opera (see p. 584), cantata and

The Harpsichord Lesson by the Dutch painter Jan Steen (1626–79). From the Middle Ages through to the early 20th century, the ability to play an instrument or to sing was regarded as an essential accomplishment in polite society – particularly for women. (The Wallace Collection, London/Archiv für Kunst)

oratorio (see box), Italy was the principal source of instrumental ensemble music throughout the 17th century. The development of the two major new instrumental genres of the Baroque – the sonata and the concerto (see box) – was largely the work of Italian composers. The violinist *Arcangelo Corelli* (1653–1713) was perhaps the most gifted and influential of the pioneer composers of concertos and sonatas. His 12 *Concerti Grossi* (1714) established the form of the concerto grosso (see box) and were imitated all over Europe. While Corelli's output was relatively small and limited to instrumental compositions, his later compatriots, the composer-priest *Antonio Vivaldi* (1678–1741) and *Tommaso Albinoni* (1671–1750) wrote prodigious amounts of instrumental and vocal music. But Vivaldi is chiefly known for his development of the solo concerto: his set of violin concertos known as *The Four Seasons* – representing but four concertos out of an output of more than 460 – has become perhaps the best known of all Baroque compositions. The publication of many of Vivaldi's concertos in his own lifetime enabled their influence to spread throughout Europe, and their three-movement structure became a model for many composers of concertos, including Johann Sebastian Bach.

In contrast with his sonatas and concertos, Vivaldi's many operas have never been successfully revived. A similar fate has befallen the 115 extant operas of the prolific Neapolitan *Alessandro Scarlatti* (1660–1725; see also p. 584). One of Scarlatti's important innovations was the three-movement form of the Italian opera overture or *sinfonia*, regarded by many as being the earliest forerunner of the Classical symphony (see p. 574). The new freedom of expression Scarlatti imported to opera was given to harpsichord music by his son *Domenico Scarlatti* (1685–1757). The younger Scarlatti's 550 single-movement sonatas for harpsichord considerably extended the technical and musical possibilities of keyboard writing.

France

In France, as in England and Germany, composers were strongly influenced by Italian models of instrumental music. However, the greatest achievements of the French Baroque were in the domain of harpsichord music and opera.

The Italian-born Frenchman *Jean-Baptiste Lully* (1632–87) established the form of the French opera (see also pp. 584 and 596), which was to reach its peak in the operas of Jean-Philippe Rameau. The overtures and dance movements from Lully's operas enjoyed a flourishing life outside the operatic context. So-called French overtures on the Lullian model were used by Handel in some of his operas and oratorios, and became an integral part of the Baroque orchestral suite (see box). Stylized dance movements such as the minuet and the allemande, as well as being central to the suite, were also sometimes incorporated in concertos.

Louis Couperin (c. 1626–61) – the first significant member of a famous musical dynasty – has left a tantalizingly small body of works for harpsichord and organ, distinguished by passion, invention and

Jean-Philippe Rameau by Jacques-André-Joseph Aved. Rameau began his musical career as a provincial organist, but the publication of his influential treatises on harmony brought him wider fame and recognition. His move to Paris in 1732 heralded an active and successful second career as a fashionable harpsichord teacher and the composer of the greatest operas of the French Baroque. (Fine Arts Museum, Dijon/Explorer)

harmonic daring. *François Couperin* ('*Le Grand*'; 1668–1733) composed in a wider range of genres than his uncle, but is best known for his elegant harpsichord pieces, many of which bear fanciful titles and characterize people or objects.

The early career of *Jean-Philippe Rameau* (1683–1764) was dominated by harpsichord composition and the writing of influential treatises on harmony, but he was to enjoy a second and highly successful career as a composer of opera (see p. 584 and illustration).

Germany

The German composer *Johann Sebastian Bach* (1685–1750) is held by many to be the greatest of all Baroque composers, though it was not until after his death that his stature was recognized. In his concertos, sonatas, cantatas and keyboard music, Bach took to a summit of achievement the forms that had developed in Italy during the 17th century. Johann Sebastian was the most distinguished of a vast family of musical Bachs, but in his lifetime he was a provincial composer whose highest aspiration was to become organist and choirmaster of St Thomas's Church in Leipzig. He never journeyed outside his homeland, but was nevertheless aware of musical trends elsewhere, as his *French Suites* and *Italian Concerto* for harpsichord testify. Lutheran hymn tunes were a further influence on his style, whose components included (particularly in his instrumental music) an exhilarating use of rhythmic syncopation, along with an unrivalled grasp of counterpoint that was later to prove an inspiration to such composers as Mozart, Beethoven and Mendelssohn. To suggest that Bach's music is 'dry' or 'intellectual' is to misunderstand its remarkable range

MUSICAL FORMS OF THE BAROQUE

CONCERTO

A work for one or more solo instruments and orchestra, usually in three movements following a quick-slow-quick pattern also employed by later composers. Bach's concertos, mostly for harpsichord or violin (though the so-called *Brandenburg Concertos* of 1721 used a more intricate array of instruments) were among the greatest of the Baroque period.

CONCERTO GROSSO

Grosso in Italian means 'great' or 'big'. A concerto grosso incorporates an interplay between a large body of instruments and a smaller one, each group usually consisting of strings, though sometimes with wind players also. Corelli and Handel were two of the greatest exponents of the form.

CANTATA

From the Italian word *cantare*, 'to sing', this is a vocal work with solo voices or chorus (or sometimes a combination of both), accompanied by a solo instrument or orchestra. Bach's numerous cantatas were mostly written for church services, while Alessandro Scarlatti and Handel were both prolific exponents of the secular cantata.

FUGUE

A contrapuntal composition – instrumental, orchestral or choral – written in two or more 'parts' or voices, at the start of which the voices enter successively in imitation of each other and are subsequently combined with varying degrees of intricacy (the word is from the Italian 'fuga', meaning 'running away' or 'flight'). *Canons* and *rounds* are simpler, earlier forms of the fugue.

SONATA

From the Italian *suonare*, 'to sound or play an instrument', the sonata developed from its 16th-century origins into a major musical form, employing one or more solo instruments and structured usually in three or more movements. Bach's most famous sonatas are those for violin, either unaccompanied or with *basso continuo*. A *trio sonata* was so called because the composer wrote the music in three parts (two solo instruments – usually violins – and basso continuo), although four players usually participated in the performance if the bass notes were to be underlined by a cello.

SUITE

A work consisting of a group of dance movements, usually in the same key. The Baroque suite was refined from earlier models by harpsichord composers such as the Frenchman *Jacques Champion de Chambonnières* (c. 1602–72 and the German *Johann Jacob Froberger* (1616–67). Bach's *French Suites* for harpsichord (c. 1722) are typical examples of the genre, expanding the traditional sequence of allemande–courante–sarabande–gigue with 'galant' French movements such as minuets and gavottes. French composers such as Rameau and François Couperin often gave the movements of their suites (or 'ordres' in Couperin's case) fanciful or evocative titles. Orchestral suites were written by Bach, Handel and Telemann, amongst others. Handel's *Water Music* (composed c. 1715 for a royal boat trip on the Thames) is one of the best-known examples.

ORATORIO

An unstaged dramatic composition, usually on a biblical theme, for soloists, chorus and orchestra, which was developed in Italy by composers such as *Giacomo Carissimi* (1605–74). Important composers of oratorio were: in Germany, *Heinrich Schütz* (1585–1672; see p. 571) and Bach; in France, *Marc-Antoine Charpentier* (1634–1704); and in England, Handel, whose works in the genre were characterized by extensive and flexible use of the chorus.

---

rary, Bach. He left his native Saxony, travelling first to Hamburg (to become a violinist in the opera orchestra), then to Italy (where he met Corelli and Alessandro Scarlatti and became deeply imbued with Italian styles of vocal and instrumental writing), and finally to London, where he settled and took British nationality.

Handel's music combines the Italian solo and instrumental style, German counterpoint and the English choral tradition he encountered in Purcell. Out of these, in his operas, oratorios, concertos and suites, he created a brilliant, highly individual style of writing, which, while in essence a stylistic hybrid, is completely and triumphantly his own.

As befitted a man who spent the bulk of his career as a composer of Italian operas (now rarely performed; see p. 584), Handel was at heart a dramatic composer. Deep humanity and a gift for perceptive and sympathetic characterization permeates all his vocal writing – be it solo cantata, opera or oratorio. But the opera-composer's aptitude for beguiling and expressive melody reveals itself also in his concertos, sonatas and suites. When the Italian opera went into a decline in London, Handel turned his attention to a genre – the English oratorio – which he had first experimented with 20 years earlier, and which he now brought to its first, and greatest, flowering. Of his numerous oratorios, *Messiah* (1741) has always held pride of place, at the expense, sadly, of his other masterpieces in the form, notably *Saul* (1739), *Solomon* (1748) and *Jephtha* (1751).   CW

SEE ALSO

- WHAT IS MUSIC? p. 568
- PLAINSONG AND POLY-PHONY p. 570
- CLASSICAL MUSIC p. 574
- THE SYMPHONY ORCHESTRA AND ITS INSTRUMENTS p. 582
- OPERA p. 584
- CLASSICAL BALLET p. 596

George Frideric Handel, indefatigable composer of Italian opera, and inventor of the English oratorio, painted by Thomas Hudson in 1749. Handel is here shown clutching the score of *Messiah*, his most famous and popular oratorio, the first version of which he composed in the space of three weeks in the summer of 1741. (University Library, Hamburg/ Archiv für Kunst)

---

of emotions – the latter being particularly evident in his great choral works inspired by Christ's Passion and in his Mass in B minor for soloists, chorus and orchestra (see p. 571).

A number of Bach's many sons were also distinguished composers. The symphonies and concertos of *Carl Phillip Emanuel Bach* (1714–88) show a reaction against his father's polyphony and counterpoint, while in his sonatas can be detected the growth of the thematic treatment of different keys, which was to develop into Classical sonata form (see p. 575). The London-based *Johann Christian Bach* (1735–82), a composer of operas and symphonies in a 'galant', pre-Classical style, was an influence on the young Mozart (see p. 574).

Posterity has accorded *Georg Phillipp Telemann* (1681–1767) a lowlier status than his friends Bach and Handel. But Telemann's exalted reputation during his own lifetime is attested by the fact that he, rather than Bach, was first choice for the post of choirmaster in Leipzig eventually offered to Bach. Telemann absorbed all of the principal compositional styles of the period and wrote with astonishing fecundity in all of the principal genres of the Baroque. While he only rarely achieved the sublimity of Bach or Handel, Tele-mann wrote with a keen sense of the possibilities of individual instruments, and his music – especially his concertos and orchestral suites – is distinguished by engaging melody and buoyant rhythms.

England

Like Mozart, *Henry Purcell* (1659–95) was a composer of genius whose early death has deprived us of a potentially even greater body of masterpieces. In his odes, theatre music, church music, string fantasias and sonatas Purcell's style combines a sublime gift for melody, harmonic invention and a mastery of counterpoint. His best-known work – and for some his greatest achievement – is the miniature opera *Dido and Aeneas* (see p. 584), though his incidental music for a hack version of Shakespeare's *A Midsummer Night's Dream* – entitled *The Fairy Queen* (1692) – similarly achieves passionate musical expression that transcends the doggerel of the words.

The greatest composer working in England during the late Baroque was the German-born *George Frideric Handel* (1685–1759). Impresario, musical director, virtuoso keyboard player and sought-after teacher, as well as composer, Handel was a more cosmopolitan and worldly figure than his great German contempo-

The Classical Period

If the music of J.S. Bach represents the summit of the Baroque era, that of his sons, particularly Carl Philip Emanuel and Johann Christian (see also p. 572), provides a link with the period loosely known as Classical. It was a time of new developments in the art of the symphony and concerto, of the birth of the string quartet and piano sonata, and of the humanizing of opera.

Vienna, the capital of the Austrian Habsburg Empire, now became the centre of musical progress, with *Franz Joseph Haydn* (1732–1809), *Wolfgang Amadeus Mozart* (1756–91) and, before long, *Ludwig van Beethoven* (1770–1827) as its principal representatives. In the next generation *Franz Schubert* (1797–1828) was to sustain Vienna's musical preeminence. Both Beethoven and Schubert were to extend the Classical forms and infuse them with a Romantic sensibility (see also p. 576). All four composers collectively became known as the First Viennese School (for the Second Viennese School, see p. 578).

By 1790 Haydn and Mozart were both resident in Vienna. The Salzburg-born Mozart had settled there in 1781 after a quarrel with his employer, the Archbishop of Salzburg, while Haydn had only just arrived after his retirement at the age of 58 from the post of resident composer

with the Esterházy family. At the palace of Esterháza, Haydn had had the privacy to work in peace ('There was nobody near to confuse me, so I was forced to become original', he once declared) – yet he was famed throughout Europe. Beethoven, born in Bonn in Germany, did not make Vienna his home until two years later, by which time Mozart was dead at the age of 35. However, Haydn was to become (briefly and none too happily) his teacher.

Classicism in music

Classicism, in musical terms, has been defined as a style accepting certain basic conventions of form and structure (see box), and using these as a natural framework for the expression of ideas. Unlike Romantic music (see p. 576), which developed out of Classicism, it saw no need to break the set boundaries, although in a discreet way its greatest practitioners did so more often than not.

Only in pedantic hands did Classicism lead to rigidity of structure. Its strength derived from the ability of composers to concentrate the intensity of their inspir-

Mozart at the age of 6 at the court of the Empress Maria Theresa and her son, the future Emperor Joseph II. Although Mozart had a huge success as a child prodigy, as an adult he had continual financial difficulties, and was finally buried in an unmarked pauper's grave.

ation within a formal framework, and to express themselves with clarity through the use of moderate resources. The Classical period also saw the development of the symphony – and thereby the symphony orchestra – as a vehicle for well-argued musical discourse.

The symphony

The word *symphony* derives from the Greek word for 'consonance' (i.e. pleasing harmony). In the Baroque period the symphony tended to be no more than a prelude or interlude (such as the 'Pastoral Symphony' in Handel's *Messiah*). But out of the three-section form of many operatic overtures (or *sinfonias*) came the basic structure of what was subsequently to establish itself as the self-sufficient symphony, intended for concert performance.

The three short, usually interconnected movements grew in scale and became more clearly separated from each other; in due course a fourth movement was added. The Classical symphony orchestra was somewhat larger than Bach's orchestra, although less expansive than those of the later Romantics. It drew extra colour from the woodwind family (usually pairs of flutes, oboes, bassoons and the then novel clarinets), from horns, and from the 'pompous' combination of trumpets and kettledrums. Most of these instruments had already been employed by Bach and Handel, but not normally together.

Haydn, with his own orchestra and a benevolent patron at Esterháza, was ideally placed to perfect symphonic form the way he wished. In the end he produced more than a hundred symphonies remarkable for their resourcefulness, terseness of structure (whole movements often growing out of a single theme), and harmonic and rhythmic verve enchanced by warmth of expression.

SEE ALSO

● ROCOCO AND NEOCLASSI-
  CISM (VISUAL ARTS) p. 534
● WHAT IS MUSIC? p. 568
● MUSIC OF THE BAROQUE
  p. 572
● MUSIC OF THE ROMANTICS
  p. 576
● THE SYMPHONY ORCHESTRA
  AND ITS INSTRUMENTS
  p. 582
● OPERA p. 584
● CLASSICISM IN LITERATURE
  p. 626

Rehearsing a cantata in around 1775.

But elsewhere, too, the symphony was spreading like wildfire. At Mannheim, the presence of an outstanding orchestra had resulted in the founding of the 'Mannheim School' of composers – including *Johann Stamitz* (1717–57) and his son *Karl* (1745–1801). These composers established brilliant scale passages ('Mannheim rockets') as a symphonic feature, along with startling contrasts between soft and loud, and pioneered the disciplined orchestral *crescendo* and *decrescendo* (increases and decreases in volume).

The young Mozart, on a visit to Mannheim, benefited from what he heard there. Mozart also reacted in his own way to the 'Paris style', with its fashionable *premier coup d'archet* (the arresting bowstroke signalling the start of a symphony), which he encountered during his visit to France in 1778 and commemorated in his *Paris symphony* (no. 31 in D).

More important than symphonic gestures such as the *coup d'archet*, however, was the actual structure of the symphony (see box). Although this structure seems rigid, the Classical symphony nevertheless gave composers considerable scope for self-expression, as a comparison between the sombre passion of Mozart's 40th symphony and the Olympian purity of the 41st (the *Jupiter*) makes plain. The last 6 of Mozart's 41 symphonies, and the last 12 of Haydn's 104, represent the summit of the Classical style. Beethoven, in his 9 symphonies, built on the work of his predecessors, but was to extend the form considerably in scale and take it into the beginnings of the Romantic era (see p. 576), as was Schubert in the last 2 (the *Unfinished* and the *Great* C major) of his 9 symphonies.

Other forms

But what was achieved symphonically at this time was also reflected in the progress of the concerto, the string quartet (with its offshoots, the string trio and quintet), the piano trio and the piano sonata. Mozart, on leaving the security of Salzburg, found himself living by his wits in Vienna as the world's first major 'freelance' composer. Up to that point composers generally worked full time either for a wealthy patron or the Church. As a freelance, Mozart attempted to earn money by giving public subscription concerts, the first of their kind, incorporating new piano concertos written for himself (or star pupils) to play. But if the initiative was commercial, the works themselves (particularly the last dozen) were epoch-making, achieving a perfection that was only to be equalled by Beethoven.

What Mozart achieved on behalf of the concerto, Haydn (and, under his influence, Mozart also) did for the string quartet, entrusting a group of four players (two violinists, a viola player and a cellist) with his most intimate musical thoughts. Haydn wrote sets of quartets all his life, and these sublime instrumental conversation-pieces now form the basis of the quartet repertoire, along with those of Mozart, Beethoven (see p. 576) and Schubert. Haydn's piano trios, too, set a standard other composers could emulate but never surpass, and his keyboard sonatas, along with Mozart's, paved the way for Beethoven's 32 unparalleled masterpieces in the form.

Church music was also an important part of a Classical composer's workload, just as it was in Bach's and Handel's time. To their Masses and other choral works, Haydn and Mozart brought a distinctively Austrian flavour that was at times almost operatic, quite different from those of Bach. But then – thanks to Mozart – opera itself had changed personality (see p. 584).   CW

Beethoven in middle age, a copy of Stieler's somewhat idealized 1819 portrait. Unlike Mozart, who would compose all the details of complete movements in his head before writing them down, composition for Beethoven was always a struggle, involving frequent revisions of his original sketches.

Music of the Romantics

Romanticism in music was not necessarily born in 1800. But the first year of the 19th century, when Beethoven had just produced the first of his nine symphonies, is as good a time as any by which to commemorate the establishment of composers as individual artists – rather than as servants of rich patrons, which had been the case throughout the Baroque and Classical periods.

An 1846 caricature of Berlioz conducting his own music. One aspect of 19th-century Romanticism was the growth in the number and range of instruments in the symphony orchestra. Although Berlioz was lampooned for the overwhelming volume of his orchestral effects, some of the finest moments in his music are achieved with quiet subtlety.

Mozart had pointed the way by provoking the Archbishop of Salzburg into dismissing him, and later by composing (purely for himself) his 40th symphony, a work of dark and passionate Romanticism, albeit within a Classical format. His opera, *Don Giovanni*, with its swashbuckling but doomed hero, provided another pointer. Significantly it was this more than any other 18th-century masterpiece that fired the Romantic 19th-century imagination by demonstrating how it was possible to break the bounds of 18th-century formality.

Beethoven and the beginnings of Romanticism

So when in 1800 **Ludwig van Beethoven** (1770–1827; see also pp. 574–5) produced not only his first symphony (which in size and appearance seemed quite Mozartian but had the explosiveness of a time bomb) but also his C minor piano concerto (which had a startling assertiveness absent from his two previous works in the form), it was clear that winds of change were sweeping through music in Vienna. This was confirmed in 1803 by the unleashing of the *Eroica* symphony, originally intended by Beethoven to be a homage to Napoleon. This in itself was a Romantic act – Napoleon for a time being regarded as the champion of republican liberty – just as was the composer's subsequent decision to delete Napoleon's name when the French general declared himself emperor. But the special achievement of the *Eroica*, Beethoven's third symphony, was that it finally shattered the bounds of Classicism. It was not only the biggest symphony ever written until that time (though Beethoven himself was to surpass it in his ninth), it was also recognized to be a personal testament in music, the first of its kind, symbolizing Beethoven's battle with the growing deafness that was to destroy his career as a public performer, but which intensified his inspiration as a composer.

Beethoven has been called the 'poet of heroism', a title to which his fifth symphony and his solitary opera, *Fidelio*, as well as the *Eroica* bear tribute. The idea of a symphony beginning ominously in C minor and ending triumphantly in C major was a symbol of Romanticism in music, emulated 70 years later by Brahms (see below) in his first symphony. The crucial role played by Beethoven in the progress of symphonic form, and of the art of the string quartet and piano sonata, was something no later composer could ignore. In his last quartets in particular, Beethoven explored the most profound emotional and spiritual tensions with a musical daring not seen again for another century. In Italy, Verdi (see p. 585) slept with Beethoven's quartets by his bedside. In France, **Hector Berlioz** (1803–69) stated Beethoven to be a primary influence on his style. In Germany, the symphonic structure employed by **Richard Wagner** (1813–83; see also pp. 584–5 and below) in his music dramas had Beethoven's ninth symphony as source.

Literary influence

But apart from inspiring autobiographical symphonies (such as Berlioz's *Symphonie fantastique*; see below), and heroic concertos such as Beethoven's so-called *Emperor* (1809), in which soloist and orchestra were often deemed to be opponents rather than partners, the age of Romanticism also increased the influence of literature on music.

Beethoven's *An die ferne Geliebte* ('To the Distant Beloved', 1816) was the first song cycle of importance, paving the way for *Die schöne Müllerin* ('The Beautiful Maid of the Mill', 1823) and *Winterreise* ('Winter Journey', 1827) by **Franz Schubert** (1797–1828; see also pp. 574–5), the most gifted and one of the most prolific of all song writers. The art of the song cycle, which required songs to be grouped in a particular order and to possess some specific literary theme, was nourished in Germany after Schubert's early death by **Robert Schumann** (1810–56) in his *Dichterliebe* ('Poet's Love') and *Frauenliebe und -Leben* ('Woman's Love and Life'), both written in 1840, and by Berlioz in his exquisite *Nuits d'été*, ('Summer Nights', 1841).

Though composers of the period were often attracted to high-quality texts – Berlioz, a highly literary composer, chose Théophile Gautier's poetry for his *Nuits d'été*, Schumann chose Heinrich Heine for *Dichterliebe* – great songs were not necessarily dependent on great poetry for their inspiration. Schubert, through his music, raised minor verse to the level of Goethe. Wagner wrote his own operatic texts, employing alliteration to bring flow and cohesion to such works as *Tristan and Isolde* and *The Ring*.

Programme music

Inevitably, the 'composer as artist' was also attracted to representational or *'programme music'* – music that evokes pictorial scenes or finds some way to tell a story in purely musical terms.

As early as 1808, Beethoven wrote his *Pastoral* symphony, describing its often quite precise imagery rather cautiously as 'the expression of feelings rather than painting'. His E flat piano sonata (opus 81a) of the following year was also an

expression of feelings; its three movements were entitled 'Farewell', 'Absence' and 'Return', the sonata being dedicated to the Archduke Rudolph on his departure from Vienna during the siege by Napoleon's troops. But that Beethoven's piano music often seemed to evoke pictures, in a way that Haydn's or Mozart's did not, cannot be denied – hence, for example, the nickname *Moonlight* given by a critic to Beethoven's C sharp minor piano sonata.

In Germany, *Felix Mendelssohn* (1809–47), in such works as *The Hebrides* (1830–32) and his *Scottish* and *Italian* symphonies, evoked landscapes within conventional forms, while Schumann – a great champion of the new Romantic style – evoked scenes of sentiment, chivalry and humour in his piano music.

More significant in terms of breaking traditional formal boundaries was the piano music of *Frédéric Chopin* (1810–49), a Pole who settled in France. Chopin's nocturnes, ballades, mazurkas, polonaises, preludes, studies, waltzes and scherzos, inspired all sorts of poetic responses in their listeners, although Chopin himself, it is true, seldom supplied these pieces with 'programmes', and indeed, as his sonatas disclose, he was a far more rigorous composer than he has been given credit for. Bach, rather than raindrops, was the source of his 24 preludes, Op 28, though the undeniable 'poetry' of his music and of his performance of it in fashionable French salons – along with the fact that he was tubercular – was bound to enhance his reputation in Romantic terms.

Berlioz's *Symphonie fantastique* (1830) contained a far more deliberate 'programme', each movement depicting a scene from a tragic imaginary love affair, inspired by Berlioz's own unhappy love affair with the actress Harriet Smithson. However, it was *Ferencz* or *Franz Liszt* (1811–86) who developed the art of programme music into a heavy industry. Born in Hungary, Liszt subsequently toured all over Europe as a hugely popular piano virtuoso. Liszt coined the term *symphonic poem* for his series of 13 descriptive orchestral works, each written in a single 'symphonic' movement, and also wrote numerous piano pieces inspired by poems, paintings and places (his collections of *Années des pèlerinage*, or 'Years of Pilgrimage', being specially notable). Like Wagner, whose music he conducted and did much to publicize, Liszt was a believer in what he called 'the music of the future'. Through his symphonic poems, and above all through his single-movement piano sonata in B minor (1852–53), he developed the idea of musical *metamorphosis*, whereby the transformations of a single theme, through changes of tempo, rhythm, contour and harmony, could form the argument of an entire piece. Some of Liszt's later piano pieces, such as *Nuages gris* ('Grey Clouds', 1881), proved far-reaching in their harmonic innovation, and possessed an austerity of utterance far different from the flamboyance of his early and middle years.

Nationalism in music

The rise of nationalist feeling all over Europe in the 19th century (see p. 428) inspired many Romantic artists, including composers. Although Liszt's Hungarian Rhapsodies lacked Hungarian authenticity (in that Liszt mistook gypsy music for Hungarian folk music), nationalism in music was becoming a major force.

Folk rhythms, folk dances, folk songs, folk legends and folk harmonies (see p. 586) served as important sources of inspiration to such composers as *Bedřich Smetana* (1824–84) and *Antonín Dvořák* (1841–1904) in what is now Czechoslovakia, *Edvard Grieg* (1843–1907) in Norway, and *Mily Balakirev* (1837–1910), *Modest Musorgsky* (1839–81) and *Pyotr Ilyich Tchaikovsky* (1840–93) in Russia. These composers often employed nationalist subjects for their operas (Smetana's *Dalibor* and Musorgsky's *Boris Godunov* being examples), while their symphonic works, particularly Tchaikovsky's first four, gained an intensity and identity of their own by combining recognizably nationalistic colouring with the established structural procedures of the German mainstream.

Wagner, Brahms and after

But that mainstream itself was undergoing change. On the one hand Wagner was abandoning all constraints of scale and conventional musical structure in his vast music dramas (see pp. 584–5). In these complex tapestries of interwoven themes he built on Liszt's ideas of metamorphosis, and cultivated tonal chromaticism – the frequent introduction of notes foreign to the key of the music. On the other hand, composers such as Berlioz in France and *Johannes Brahms* (1833–97) in Germany were exploring the tensions arising from containing Romantic emotions within strict Classical structures. It was inevitable that Brahms and Wagner in their time were considered to represent opposite musical poles, and that listeners (encouraged by the critic Eduard Hanslick, who favoured Brahms) tended to take sides.

In the long term, however, it was Wagner

who proved the major influence. The nine symphonies of the Austrian *Anton Bruckner* (1824–96) employ Wagnerian harmony yet have roots in Schubert's *Great* C major symphony (1825), an Austrian masterpiece written on a similarly spacious scale. Wagner and Schubert also provided the foundations of the ten symphonies (the last unfinished) of Bruckner's fellow-Austrian *Gustav Mahler* (1860–1911), who exploited elements of anguish and ecstasy beyond anything previously attempted in symphonic music, and in his later works there are strong premonitions of the chaos and uncertainty that the new century was to bring. In Germany, *Richard Strauss* (1864–1949) absorbed aspects of both Liszt and Wagner into his operas and symphonic poems, though some of his works, particularly his opera, *Der Rosenkavalier* (1911), reveal a degree of Mozartian nostalgia. At heart Strauss remained a lifelong Romantic: a year before he died in 1949, he wrote his *Four Last Songs* for soprano and orchestra, an almost unbearably poignant farewell. However, it was Wagner's tendency towards atonality rather than his high Romanticism that was at the root of mainstream musical development in the 20th century.   CW

Richard Wagner (centre) with his wife Cosima and her father Franz Liszt. While still married to the conductor Hans von Bülow, Cosima had a child by Wagner, and subsequently eloped with him. The unconventionality of Wagner's private life was matched by the unconventionality of his music, and both attracted moral censure.

SEE ALSO
- ROMANTICISM (IN PAINTING) p. 536
- THE CLASSICAL PERIOD p. 574
- MODERNISTS AND OTHERS p. 578
- THE SYMPHONY ORCHESTRA AND ITS INSTRUMENTS p. 582
- OPERA p. 584
- FOLK MUSIC p. 586
- CLASSICAL BALLET p. 596
- ROMANTICISM (IN LITERATURE) pp. 630–3

Brahms at the piano. Encouraged as a young man by Schumann, Brahms was deeply upset by Schumann's madness and death. His distress was increased by his awareness that he was in love with Schumann's wife Clara. However, he suppressed his love, and later cultivated the image of a gruff old bachelor.

Modernists and others

If the decades surrounding 1800 were an important period in the development of Romanticism in music, those around 1900 marked the beginnings of Modernism. Wagner's *Tristan and Isolde* (1865) was the German fountainhead, with Debussy's *Pelléas and Mélisande* (1902) as its French counterpart. From these two operas, the major trends in 20th-century music all flowed.

SEE ALSO

● MODERN ART pp. 544–55
● MUSIC OF THE ROMANTICS p. 576
● THE NEW MUSIC p. 580
● OPERA p. 584
● CLASSICAL BALLET p. 596
● MODERN DANCE p. 598
● SYMBOLISM, AESTHETICISM AND MODERNISM (LITERATURE) p. 640

Modernism in music – as in the visual arts and literature – involved a radical break with existing conventions. It also involved what often appears as a greater distancing between the artist and audience – certainly audiences in all the arts have tended to find Modernist works 'difficult'. However, although Modernism has been at the intellectual forefront of music in the 20th century, many composers have followed more accessible paths.

The Second Viennese School

Wagner's chromaticism (see p. 577) had a powerful influence on the young Austrian composer **Arnold Schoenberg** (1874–1951). In early works such as *Verklärte Nacht* ('Transfigured Night') for string sextet (1899), the ties of conventional tonality begin to be loosened, a process continued by Schoenberg and his disciples **Alban Berg** (1885–1935) and **Anton Webern** (1883–1945), and these three formed what has become known as the Second Viennese School (for the First Viennese School, see p. 574).

The music of Schoenberg and his German and Austrian contemporaries is sometimes described as 'Expressionist'. This

term (also used in painting – see p. 546) is particularly applicable to works such as Schoenberg's *Erwartung* ('Waiting', 1909) for soprano and vast orchestra, which displays the nightmarish despair of a woman awaiting an absent lover who may or may not be dead. Schoenberg's *Pierrot Lunaire* (1912) and Berg's operas *Wozzeck* (1922) and *Lulu* (1935; see also p. 585) are also archetypically Expressionist, and the expressive force of *Pierrot Lunaire* and *Wozzeck* is devastatingly reinforced by the use of *Sprechgesang* ('speech song'), in which notes are half-sung, half-spoken.

However, Schoenberg himself was to move away from Expressionism towards a more sparingly written, abstract music, and by the 1920s he had formulated *dodecaphony*, or *twelve-note music*, a method of composition whereby all 12 notes within the octave (the 7 white and 5 black keys on a piano keyboard) are treated as equals, with no chords or groups of notes dominating as in conventional harmony. Dodecaphony was to be employed by many later composers in the 20th century, although Schoenberg himself used it far less rigorously after the 1920s.

Similarly sparingly written and epigrammatic was the music of Webern, who also adopted dodecaphic techniques. Webern's influence, through his extraordinarily compressed chamber symphony (1924), Chamber Concerto (1934) and sets of tiny yet intense, at times even fierce, orchestral pieces, Op 6 and 10 (1910 and 1913), has been profound.

Debussy and the French

Claude Debussy (1862–1918), although admiring Wagner's achievement, regarded him as a dead end – he once referred to him as 'that old poisoner'. Compared to Schoenberg's *Erwartung*, the fastidiously pared down music of Debussy's *Pelléas and Mélisande* transforms a similarly dreamlike subject almost into an anti-opera from which anything as vulgar as a melody has been ruthlessly excluded. The action – in essence a triangular drama about two half-brothers involved with the same woman – may take place on the stage, where Debussy's setting of Maurice Maeterlinck's Symbolist play does nothing to demystify the ambiguities of the story; but what gives this masterpiece its cool yet extraordinary intensity is what goes on in the orchestra pit.

Debussy's sense of instrumental colour, whether pure or misty, was what earned him his 'impressionist' label – much to his annoyance, critics characterized him as a musical equivalent of Claude Monet (see p. 542). Many of Debussy's works, such as his three orchestral *Nocturnes* (1901) and his piano preludes, had visual associations, but poetry – particularly that of Symbolists such as Mallarmé (see p. 640) – also influenced Debussy and his fellow French composers, **Gabriel Fauré** (1845–1924) and **Maurice Ravel** (1875–1937). Although Fauré is best known today for his Requiem (1887), he was to develop more modern idioms, and both he and Ravel wrote exquisite songs as well as

Claude Debussy, one of the key figures in the birth of musical Modernism. In 1913 he declared, 'A century of aeroplanes deserves its own music. As there are no precedents, I must create anew.'

sharing Debussy's delight in instrumental colour. This was particularly so of Ravel in works such as *Rapsodie espagnole* (1907), *La Valse* (1920) and *Boléro* (1928), although later works such as his two piano concertos (1931) show a sparer, more ironic approach. The strain of ironic playfulness detectable in some of the music of these French composers is also apparent in smaller-scale works, such as the piano miniatures of **Erik Satie** (1866–1925) and the output of his six disciples – nicknamed **Les Six**, and including **Francis Poulenc** (1899–1963) and **Darius Milhaud** (1892–1974). The work of Les Six was produced during the aftermath of, and in reaction to, World War I.

Satie, whose choice of titles (e.g. 'Three Pear-shaped Pieces') caused him to be dismissed as an eccentric, has proved more durable than was initially expected. His *Vexations* (1893), an early example of what came to be known as 'minimalism' (see pp. 580–1), required a few bars of music to be repeated 840 times over a period of a whole day. Dadaism, the movement that had invaded French visual arts with its irrationality and irreverence (see p. 550), found in Satie its musical champion; yet the third of his three *Gymnopédies* (1888) is adored by listeners everywhere not because it is irrational but simply because it is an exquisite, haunting melody, unpredictably harmonized.

Stravinsky and Bartók

Debussy's rhythmic intricacy and progressive ideas on harmony, as well as his extraordinary sense of timbre (tone colour), proved immensely influential, not only on French composers but on others also. The Russian-born **Igor Stravinsky** (1882–1971) and the Hungarian **Béla Bartók** (1881–1945) were major figures of 20th-century music who came under his spell. The opening notes of Stravinsky's sensational ballet, *The Rite of Spring* (1913), have their roots in Debussy's *Prélude à l'après-midi d'un*

The Schoenberg family portrayed in appropriately Expressionist style by the Austrian painter Richard Gerstl. Gerstl killed himself in 1908 after running off with Schoenberg's wife. (Museum der 20 Jahrhunderts, Vienna/Austrian Embassy, London)

faune (1894), even if the bludgeoning rhythms of the rest of the work do not. Likewise it is possible to hear in Bartók's *Music for Strings, Percussion and Celesta* (1936) the shimmering timbres that had so fascinated Debussy when he encountered an Indonesian gamelan orchestra at the Paris Universal Exhibition in 1889.

Although Stravinsky's changes of style seemed as frequent as his changes of residence (educated in Leningrad, Stravinsky spent a vital part of his career in Paris and ended up, like Schoenberg, in Los Angeles), he can now be seen to have straddled, like nobody else, the 20th century. Stravinsky was acutely aware of, and responsive to, all the modern trends, and capable of transforming them into pure Stravinsky. His changes of direction can all be seen as revelations of different aspects of one and the same formidable mind. First came the blockbuster early ballets for Diaghilev's Ballets Russes (see p. 597) – their rich orchestration influenced as much by his fellow-Russian *Nikolay Rimsky-Korsakov* (1844–1908) as by Debussy. Then came Stravinsky's more ascetic 'neoclassical' period represented in the 1920s by *Apollon-Musagète* and *Pulcinella*, and these in turn led to his even more pared-down later works such as *Movements* for piano and orchestra (1959) and the 'pocket' requiem which he entitled *Requiem Canticles* (1966).

Unlike Stravinsky, Bartók was to remain in his native Hungary until 1940, when he was forced into unhappy exile in the USA. Bartók's study of Hungarian folk music (see p. 586) liberated him from the influence of the German Romantics, and he went on to develop a very individual approach to composition – with sometimes forbiddingly dissonant but always compelling results. His works ranged from exciting orchestral scores to the severe abstractions of piano music such as *Mikrokosmos*, and his six string quartets were the first to extend the possibilities of the form since Beethoven.

Britain

From all these continental trends, Britain as an island found itself largely – and willingly – shut off. The musical voice of *Edward Elgar* (1857–1934) was that of his native Worcestershire (of which his *Introduction and Allegro* for strings, of 1905, is redolent). However, the influence of Schumann and Wagner was strong, and there were times when he seemed to carry the whole weight, the pain and the glory, of Victorian England on his shoulders, as in his two symphonies and concertos, and the touching *Enigma Variations*.

In the music of *William Walton* (1902–83) a vein of satire flickered sporadically in such works as the Sitwell-inspired *Façade* (1921), but Walton never lived up to his early promise, and even the dramatic cantata *Belshazzar's Feast* (1931) – which at the time seemed excitingly modern – now merely sounds noisily provincial. *Benjamin Britten* (1913–76) was actively prevented as a young man from studying under Alban Berg in Vienna, because it was feared this would do him harm – although he was the one British composer of his period who might have benefited

from such exposure. Despite this, Berg's operas, with their psychological concerns, were to prove a major influence on those of Britten, especially *Peter Grimes* (1945), *The Turning of the Screw* (1953) and *Death in Venice* (1973).

Ralph Vaughan Williams (1872–1958), after a brief period in Paris when he flirted with the music of Ravel, returned home to produce the intensely English, often folk-song inspired, music for which he was revered (see also p. 587). Each of these composers, like *Frederick Delius* (1862–1934; see also p. 587) and *Gustav Holst* (1874–1934), succeeded in discovering his own individually English voice, but it was Britten above all who found an idiom, at once English and international, which enabled his music to cross boundaries more freely than that of the others.

Scandinavia

Also set apart from European mainstream was the Finnish composer *Jean Sibelius* (1865–1957), whose tone poems and seven symphonies possess their own lonely grandeur and integrity. The Dane *Carl Nielsen* (1865–1931) was another very individual symphonist. His first symphony (1892) was novel in its introduction of 'progressive tonality' (in other words it began in one key and ended in another), while in his fourth (*The Inextinguishable*) and fifth symphonies a side drum does battle with the orchestra, attempting, unsuccessfully, to drown it out.

America

'Beauty in music is too often confused with something that lets the ears lie back in an easy chair', wrote *Charles Ives* (1874–1954). Largely ignorant of developments in Europe, in the first two decades of the 20th century Ives was experimenting with note clusters (produced by pressing a piece of wood across the keys of the piano), chance elements and improvisation, and even evolved a form of dodecaphony before rejecting it as 'wallpaper design music'. However, he is perhaps best known for his use of multiple orchestras to re-create the sound of his hometown on holidays, when two different bands would be playing different tunes simultaneously.

Although Ives's music was largely ignored by the public during his lifetime, there were other experimenters at work in America in the earlier part of the 20th century, notably Ives's great champion *Carl Ruggles* (1876–1971), *Henry Cowell* (1897–1965), and the French-born *Edgard Varèse* (1865–1965). More conventional was the music of *Aaron Copland* (1900–90), much of it based on American folk idioms; these can be heard particularly in works such as *Billy the Kid* (1938) and *Appalachian Spring* (1944). The music of his contemporary, *Virgil Thomson* (1896–), was more international in outlook; during his stay in Paris (1925–32) Thomson absorbed influences from Stravinsky and the new French school.

Russia

Before the Revolution, the mystical and voluptuous music of *Alexander Skryabin* (1872–1915) – who expressed the desire to 'suffocate in ecstasy' – soon proved a dead end. *Sergey Rakhmaninov* (1873–1943), who spent several years abroad before his final departure from Russia in 1917, was content to exploit his own greatly rewarding vein of Romantic nostalgia.

Far more modernist in spirit was *Sergey Prokofiev* (1891–1953), who also left Russia during the Revolution and lived in Paris from 1922 until his return to the Soviet Union in 1934. It was left to Prokofiev and *Dmitri Shostakovich* (1906–75) to compose progressive and individual music conforming with political pressures to produce easily accessible works for the masses. Shostakovich's increasingly bleak and inward-turning music (including 15 symphonies and the same number of string quartets) was a poignant testimony to how compromise could actually be made to work, because, in Shostakovich's case, enforced jollity could never hide the skull beneath the skin. CW

Igor Stravinsky rehearsing for a concert at the age of 83. Like the painter Pablo Picasso, Stravinsky's long career was marked by numerous changes of style and a continual delight in innovation.

The New Music

Music since 1945 has evolved in many different ways. For many composers – especially in the 1950s – the once revolutionary twelve-note techniques of Schoenberg (see p. 578) became the new orthodoxy, while the avant-garde in the 1960s and 1970s enthusiastically embraced the novel sound possibilities offered by the development of electronic instruments. For a while it seemed as though conventional tonality had been banished from any music aspiring to be 'serious'; indeed tonality still tends to be the exception rather than the rule.

However, the advent of Minimalism in the late 1960s – a movement that came to maturity in the 1980s – saw the restoration of tonality (and even of melody) to respectability, at the same time finding a wider audience for serious music, verging as it does on the fringes of certain developments in jazz and rock. There has also, in recent years, been a decline in interest in electronic music, as the sounds offered by the new medium have become commonplace, rather than strange and exciting. With the reversion to conventional instruments (and voices) there has often come an opening up to influences from further back in the Western musical tradition, and also to influences from non-Western traditions.

To an extent standing aloof from these changes in fashion, certain composers stand out as having identifiably individual voices and styles – even though they themselves are often fathers of movements of one kind or another.

Italy

The Communist *Luigi Nono* (1924–90) maintained an austere position as Italy's leading guru, with an output uncompromising in its severity, from his opera *Intolleranza 1960* onwards. However, it is in the music of *Luciano Berio* (1925–) that listeners have recognized a more appealing Italian theatricality, lyricism and sharpness of observation, rooted in Italian musical history from Monteverdi onwards. Berio's works include his Mahler-inspired *Sinfonia* (1969), his 'recital' entitled *Recital* (1972) and his sequence of *Sequenze* for various soloists.

Britain

Standing centre-stage in postwar Britain is the music – especially the operas – of Benjamin Britten (see p. 579). More idiosyncratic is the music of *Michael Tippett* (1905–), whose musical personality derives from a heady mixture of Elizabethan madrigals, Beethoven, Carl Jung and T.S. Eliot, shot through with elements of jazz and pop songs. The result is about as inimitable as Berlioz. In addition to orchestral and chamber works, Tippett has written several operas, including *The Midsummer Marriage* (1955) and *The Knot Garden* (1970), and his most recent opera, *New Year* (1989), has a story (written as always by the composer himself) set in 'Terror Town', where the heroine is a child psychologist, the Belfast Troubles are touched on, the action incorporates a time-travelling spaceship, and the music includes references to reggae.

Tippett's younger compatriot **Peter Maxwell Davies** (1934–) has proved similarly open-minded, using parody (of anything from plainsong to foxtrots) as an inspirational device in such audacious pieces of music theatre as *Vesalii Icones* (1969), a darkly sardonic tour of the Stations of the Cross, and *Eight Songs for a Mad King* (1969), a ferocious portrait of King George III. In recent years, through the influence of the Orkney landscapes and seascapes amid which he now works, Davies's music has grown more romantic and picturesque.

America

Set somewhat apart from the mainstream is the music of *Elliott Carter* (1908–), whose music combines romance and high intellectuality. Carter has concentrated on intricately wrought and beautifully fashioned orchestral and chamber music, not invariably abstract (his Symphony of Three Orchestras, written in 1977, was inspired by Hart Crane's poem *The Bridge*), but demanding the utmost concentration on the part of its performers and listeners. His third string quartet (1971) consists of two elaborate duos, geared to be performed simultaneously, yet independently and at different speeds.

In comparison, *John Cage* (1912–92) was a maverick whose musical anarchy had its roots in America's iconoclastic and exhilarating pioneer, Charles Ives (see p. 579).

Cage, a pupil of Schoenberg and Henry Cowell (see pp. 578–9), established the *prepared piano*, whereby foreign bodies were introduced to the instrument's interior in order to produce new sonorities. Like Ives in his vanguard orchestral piece, *The Unanswered Question* (1906), Cage was a champion of what was later to be called *aleatory music*, the performance

Stockhausen at work in the electronic studios of West German Radio at Cologne in the 1950s. In some of Stockhausen's later pieces the performers are presented not with printed notes but with instructions such as the following:
Think NOTHING
Wait until it is absolutely still within you
When you have attained this
Begin to play . . .

of which involves a deliberate degree of indeterminacy, or elements of chance, with the result that no two performances are ever the same. Thus *Music of Changes* (1951), a seminal work, was created by Cage with the help of the *I Ching* (see p. 470) and the tossing of coins. (Mozart and Haydn once made similar experiments, but only in a peripheral way, whereas in Cage's case they grew from a long study of oriental philosophy.)

Cage's use of chance elements extended to his interest in electronics, his *Imaginary Landscape No 4* (1951) requiring 12 radios to be manipulated by 24 players – each performance depending on what could be heard on local radio stations. But though his *HPSCHD* (1969) called for seven harpsichordists and 51 or more tape recorders, Cage had by then been succeeded by Stockhausen as the high priest of electronic music.

Germany

Working from West German Radio's studios in Cologne, *Karlheinz Stockhausen* (1928–) brought to his art the same sort of single-minded devotion Wagner brought to *The Ring*. No task, whether involving electronics, conventional instruments or a combination of both, seemed too great for him. He formed his own ensemble, directing its sounds through synthesizers and amplifiers that he controlled himself; he studied phonetics and acoustics, evolving a theory of parameters, or dimensions in sound, and applied his researches to a series of monster compositions dominated by his seven-part opera cycle entitled *Licht* (one part for each day of the week), on which he has been at work since 1984. Though people have dismissed Stockhausen as a theorist whose output has been all hot air,

MINIMALISM

Minimalism in music was first evolved by the American composer *Terry Riley* (1935–) in the late 1960s. Minimalist music involves the extensive repetition of the simplest of melodies or rhythms over slowly changing harmonies, and the overall effect, for those with the patience to listen, can be compellingly hypnotic. The style continues to be vigorously exploited by such American composers as *Steve Reich* (1936–) and *Philip Glass* (1937–). The latter has worked with Ravi Shankar (see p. 590), and classical Indian music has been an important influence on his work. Glass has also brought Minimalism to the opera house, with pieces such as *Einstein on the Beach* (1976) and *Akhnaten* (1984). However, it has taken the 'post-Minimalist' political opera *Nixon in China* (1987) by *John Adams* (1947–) to prove to some listeners that there is more to Minimalism than at first meets the ears.

he has demonstrated in such works as *Gruppen* for three orchestras (1957), *Hymnen* (1967), *Prozession* (1967), *Stimmung* (1968), *Jubilaeum* (1977) and a cycle of scores inspired by his son and other members of his closely integrated family that he remains one of the most-formidable figures of modern music, who tirelessly promotes his cause around the world.

Hans Werner Henze (1926–), on the other hand, has been content to employ traditional musical forms, producing an imposing series of operas, six symphonies, and a massive, neo-romantic piano concerto. In Henze's music, his respect for German musical convention is shot through with an Italian lyricism – he prefers Italian life to that in his homeland. Henze's involvement with Communism has yielded such works as his oratorio *The Raft of the Medusa* (1968), whose Hamburg premiere was brutally broken up by the West German police, and his war opera (to a text by the English playwright Edward Bond) *We Come to the River* (1976).

France

One of the most original and impressive composers to have emerged since World War II is *Olivier Messiaen* (1908–92). Messiaen has combined an indebtedness to the French tradition of Berlioz, Franck and Debussy – the latter notably in the piano work *Catalogue d'oiseaux* ('Bird Catalogue', 1958) – with influences as diverse as bird song, plainsong and oriental music. A devout Catholic, Messiaen wrote many of his works on religious themes, and produced the most powerful organ music since Bach.

The earlier works of Messiaen's pupil *Pierre Boulez* (1925–), such as *Le Marteau sans maître* ('The Hammer without a Master') for voice and chamber orchestra (1953–55) and *Pli selon pli* ('Fold upon Fold') for soprano and chamber orchestra

(1957–62), employ twelve-note techniques, and Boulez has also experimented widely with electronic sounds. Although he has composed less in recent years, as a conductor Boulez has remained a tireless champion of new music.

Another pupil of Messiaen, mainly active in France, is the Romanian-born Greek *Iannis Xenakis* (1922–), who is not only one of the most important composers of the 20th century, but also a mathematician, logician, poet and architect; in this last capacity he at one time worked with Le Corbusier (see pp. 552–3). Mathematics (particularly probability theory) has played an important role in his music, which, although mostly scored for conventional instruments, he has often written with the aid of a computer.

The Soviet Union

The pressures put upon Shostakovich (see p. 579) to produce 'people's music', and which resulted in some masterpieces quite extraordinary in their inner tension, were gradually relaxed after his death. Subsequent Soviet and post-Soviet composers have had access to all the latest trends, and have had brilliant ensembles to perform the fruits of this new musical freedom. From this more temperate climate two composers in particular, *Edison Denisov* (1929–) and *Alfred Shnitke* (1934–), appear to have benefited. Both have produced imaginative and original music, Shnitke's possessing sometimes a blackly humorous element of send-up, as in his violin concerto incorporating a 'silent' cadenza that the soloist has to go through the motions of playing, with Paganini-like frenzy.

Eastern Europe

In Poland this state of musical freedom was achieved somewhat sooner, thanks

partly to the Warsaw Festival, an annual autumn ferment of new ideas. Thus *Witold Lutoslawski* (1913–) was able to apply all the modern techniques at his disposal to works (such as his string quartet of 1964 and cello concerto of 1970) that were at the same time products of an exceptionally lucid and, for the listener, by no means daunting mind.

His younger compatriot, *Krzysztof Penderecki* (1933–), was prone to employ more sensational effects, such as dense note-clusters and huge orchestral and choral *glissandi*, yet in his *Threnody for the Victims of Hiroshima* for 52 solo strings (1960), his *St Luke Passion* (1966) and his opera *The Devils of Loudun* (1969) he composed music that, for all its apparent complexity, proved shattering in its impact.

To write with this sort of boldness, the Hungarian composer *Gyorgy Ligeti* (1923–) had to move to the West before unleashing his requiem (1965) and his opera *Le Grand Macabre* (1978). Ligeti's music, like that of all the above composers, has travelled widely. *Le Grand Macabre*, an operatic equivalent of the Theatre of the Absurd (see pp. 642–3) with Bosch, Bruegel, Kafka and Lewis Carroll among its influences, had its premiere in Stockholm but was soon seen in Britain, Germany, France, Spain and America. His *San Francisco Polyphony* (1974), a brilliant orchestral spider's web of sound, beat America's West Coast Minimalist composers (see box) at their own game, and showed how tiny repeated wisps of tune could be spun into a work of beauty, intricacy and substance.   CW

A scene from *Akhnaten*, Glass's opera about the unconventional Egyptian pharaoh (see p. 367).

The Symphony Orchestra and its Instruments

The rise of the symphony orchestra, consisting of 80 or more instrumentalists performing for a conductor in a concert hall, was one of the great musical developments of the 19th century. Its roots lay in the much smaller groups of players that formed the opera orchestras of the 17th and 18th centuries, and in the ensembles that took part in performances in cathedrals and churches. In the Baroque period, these tended to be based on a small body of strings, supported by keyboard continuo (either harpsichord or organ), and sometimes with woodwind players in addition.

The arrival of the classical symphony, via Haydn and Mozart, brought larger forces into play: more strings and woodwind (with the clarinet gradually added to the flute, oboe and bassoon), a pair of horns, plus ceremonial trumpets and kettle-drums. Throughout the 19th century these forces continued to be augmented: Beethoven's fifth symphony (1808) incorporated trombones, a piccolo and a double bassoon (all new to the concert hall), and Berlioz's *Symphonie Fantastique* (1830) added cornets, tubas and extra percussion.

By the start of the 20th century, the range of instruments at a composer's disposal had grown still larger. Stravinsky's *Rite of Spring* (1913) required eight horns and quintuple woodwind (i.e. five instruments in each woodwind section). Strauss's *Alpine Symphony* (1915) included wind and thunder machines, and Respighi's *The Pines of Rome* (1924) the recorded sound of a nightingale.

Platform placing

In general, the 19th-century structure of the orchestra has been maintained, though seating positions have been altered since Haydn's and Beethoven's day. The first and second violins, formerly placed to the left and right of the conductor, are now massed together on the left. Though this achieves greater brilliance of sound, it is at the expense of spatial interplay between the two sets of instruments, an effect (often witty) that was deliberately built into Classical scores.

Furthermore, the modern practice of placing the cellos and double basses at the right of the platform, instead of more centrally, has destroyed the original sense of balance and the solid foundation of tone that the basses provided when they stretched round the back of the platform, facing straight into the audience. Though some 20th-century conductors (Otto Klemperer and Sir Adrian Boult were two) adhered, as far as they could, to the old layout, most of today's star conductors prefer the modern arrangement, and orchestras have become accustomed to it.

For some idea of how Classical symphonies were meant to sound, however, one can turn to the increasing number of specialist ensembles that have been revolutionizing the concert platform and grabbing for themselves an increasingly large slice of the symphonic repertoire. But no matter whether an orchestra uses modern or 'original' placings and instruments (or at any rate ones designed to correspond as closely as possible to their 18th- or 19th-century predecessors) these instruments continue to fall into four families: strings, woodwind, brass and percussion.

Strings

Of the string instruments, the *violins* produce the highest sound, with the violas, cellos and double basses following in descending order (the larger the instrument the deeper the sound). Their forerunners, employed until about 1700, were the *viols* and were likewise of various

A Ruckers harpsichord dating from the early 17th century. The Ruckers family of Antwerp were famed for the quality of their instruments, many of which were still in use in the late 18th century.

KEYBOARD INSTRUMENTS

The *organ* is the oldest of the keyboard instruments, being known to the ancient Greeks and Romans. Probably sometime in the 13th century, levers began to replace the clumsy sliders previously used to admit air into the pipes of the organ. These levers provided the basis of the modern keyboard. The organ grew in size over the years, the medieval portative (i.e. transportable) and the gentle Baroque organ being very much smaller than the more familiar multi-keyboard 19th-century organs. But whatever the size, the operation – involving bellows blowing air through pipes to sound the notes – is the same. At one time the bellows were worked by hand, until electric motors made the process easier. With the help of 'stops' (which mechanically control the tone), extra keyboards (including the 'pedal-board' for the feet), and a swell-box to increase or reduce the volume of sound, the organist gradually gained a formidable armoury of sonic effects. The modern electronic organ has done away with the need for pipes, but (though cheaper to buy and easier to maintain) is regarded as a feeble substitute for the real thing.

The *harpsichord*, roughly akin to a grand piano in shape, originated in the 15th century – or even earlier – but acquired its most developed form in the Baroque period (see pp. 572–3). The harpsichord may have one, two, or (exceptionally) three keyboards. Its strings, unlike those of the piano, are plucked mechanically rather than struck. The smaller, softer-toned *clavichord*, dating from the same period, was essentially a domestic instrument, its strings being hit by a small blade or brass known as a 'tangent'.

From these instruments there derived the *pianoforte* (so named, in Italian, because it could play both softly and loudly). At first it was sometimes called the *fortepiano*, and the name is nowadays abbreviated to 'piano'. In essence, the names fortepiano and pianoforte mean the same, the terms now being used principally to differentiate the light, clear, silvery-toned 18th-century instrument (the correct vehicle for Mozart's piano concertos) from the larger, weightier, more brilliant concert grand, built from the 19th century by such firms as Steinway, Bechstein, Bösendorfer and Blüthner.

Other keyboard instruments, such as the ethereal-toned *celesta*, invented in France in 1886, and the wailing electronic *ondes martenot*, also of French origin, are also sometimes employed in an orchestral context. The latter instrument was really an early form of *synthesizer*; this modern instrument, as well as imitating many acoustic instruments, can make sounds of its own – both music and sheer noise.

sizes. (In fact the modern double bass, with its characteristic sloping shoulders, is modelled on the old double-bass viol.) Today, many specialist groups have revived the art of viol playing, and the cello-like bass viol (often called the viola da gamba) has in particular regained its place in the concert hall.

The *viola* is a larger, lower-pitched relative of the violin, and is likewise placed beneath the player's chin. Its mellow, often gravely eloquent tone blends into the string ensemble and in solo passages achieves high expressiveness (as in Mozart's series of string quintets). The *cello* (whose full name is *violoncello*) has a still darker tone, though its lighter upper register can be exploited to magical effect. All these are four-stringed instruments (the strings originally being of gut, later replaced by wire or wire-wound gut); so, too, is the *double bass*, though five-string basses, giving the instrument an even deeper register, are also found.

Woodwind

The woodwind are so called because they were all originally made of wood – although most flutes today are actually made of metal. The woodwind are of two types: those that are blown directly (the various kinds of flute and recorder) and those that are blown by means of a single or double reed.

The highest, most piercing flute is the *piccolo*. Pitched an octave lower is the standard *flute* (often, like the other woodwind instruments, employed in pairs in the orchestra), with a compass from middle C upwards for three octaves. Lower still, and considerably longer, is the *alto flute*, whose special tone quality proved popular with various 20th-century composers, particularly Ravel and Stravinsky. Unlike the rest of the woodwind, the flute is played sideways, the sound being produced by blowing across an aperture cut into the top of the tube at one end.

The oboe and its lower-toned relative, the cor anglais, are both blown through a double reed, as also (in descending order of pitch) are the bassoon and double bassoon. The *oboe*, 'reedier' in sound than the pure-toned flute, has a range from the B flat below middle C upwards for more than 2½ octaves, though some modern virtuosi have stretched this compass farther. The *cor anglais* ('English horn'), is neither English nor a horn but a large oboe, recognizable by its bulb-shaped bell and darker tone quality. It is pitched a fifth lower than an oboe. The *bassoon*, which is the bass member of the woodwind family, consists of a long tube doubled back on itself (in Italy it is called the *fagotto* or bundle of sticks). Though sometimes employed to comic effect, its nasal tone is capable of eloquence and, at the top and bottom of its compass, which stretches from the B flat below the bass stave upwards for 3½ octaves, it can also sound sinister. The even more unwieldy *double bassoon* is pitched an octave lower. The *clarinet*, which looks like an oboe, differs by being blown through a single reed. Its creamy tone was much loved by Mozart, who was the first composer to realize its full potential, both as a member of the woodwind and as a solo instrument. The clarinet family is a large one, the instruments originally being made in several sizes to facilitate playing in different keys. But by the time the symphony orchestra was fully established, only two sizes – the B flat (with a compass stretching three octaves from the D below middle C) and the A (with a compass a semitone lower than the B flat) – were in regular use. These, however, were merely the 'standard' clarinets, and to them were added the high E flat clarinet, whose piercing tone quality was exploited by Berlioz in his *Symphonie Fantastique*; the *basset horn*, a low-toned clarinet adored by Mozart but not much used by other composers; and the *bass clarinet*, pitched an octave lower than the B flat clarinet and shaped like a saxophone.

The *saxophone* itself, though of more recent vintage (it was invented by Adolphe Sax in 1840), is also a species of clarinet, using a single reed, but producing a more vibrant, wailing oily tone. It too comes in several sizes and plays a vital role in jazz, though Classical composers have also made use of it.

Brass

Brass instruments are made of metal and their sound is produced by vibration of the lips against a cup-shaped mouthpiece. The horn, trumpet, trombone and tuba are the brass instruments most commonly used in the symphony orchestra, though the *cornet* (resembling a trumpet but with a wider bore and an expressiveness all its own) also appears and has been particularly popular with French composers from Berlioz onwards.

The *horn*, distinguished by its coiled shape, was at one time capable of producing only a limited number of notes. But in its modern form, through the addition of valves, it is more versatile and provides a complete chromatic compass from B below the bass stave upwards for 3½ octaves. Of the brass instruments it is the most mellow, though it can also be assertive and agile. In Britain, the horn is often referred to as the 'French horn', because it was in France that the instrument was perfected.

The modern *trumpet*, like the horn, has valves and considerable versatility. Originally, however, it was a straight tube with a limited number of notes at its disposal, and its use was primarily ceremonial. The more familiar type of folded trumpet first appeared in the 15th century, and the addition of 'crooks' – detachable sections of tubing that altered its pitch – gave it greater scope. The modern trumpet uses valves to open up different sections of tubing, and in the case of the B flat trumpet has a compass from E below middle C upwards for about three octaves (jazz trumpeters often push it still higher). There are also smaller, higher modern trumpets.

Trombones, which come in tenor and bass versions (as well as others less frequently used), operate with the help of valves and U-shaped slides that move along the length of the instrument and provide a compass from E below the bass stave upwards for about three octaves in the case of the tenor trombone, and from the lower D flat in the case of the bass – though even lower notes can be produced. The solemnity of trombone tone was effectively used by Mozart in *The Magic Flute*, and grandly exploited by Wagner in his music dramas. The *tuba*, an instrument of more recent invention, underpins the trombones and comes in tenor, bass and other versions (though the bass is the one most regularly employed in the symphony orchestra). Its great girth, and its upward facing bell, make it instantly recognizable. Its compass, founded on the F an octave below the bass stave, stretches upwards as high as three octaves. The so-called 'Wagner tuba', designed for use in Wagner's *Ring*, is really a large, modified horn, and comes in two sizes.

Percussion

Percussion instruments are either struck or shaken, and may be either pitched or non-pitched. The copper-bottomed *timpani*, or *kettledrums*, are the most important and versatile of all the instruments in this section. Of Arab origin, they were first used orchestrally in the 17th century, when they were played in pairs and were capable of only two notes, one tuned to the tonic and the other to the dominant of whatever key was being performed, the pitch being adjusted by screws on the rim of the drums. From Beethoven's time onwards, however, the instruments gained other tunings – in the 20th century with the help of foot pedals, which add *glissandi*, to their range of effects – and they began to be used, whether loudly or softly, to increasingly attractive purpose.

Side drum, tenor drum, bass drum, cymbals, triangle and *castanets* are the instruments of indefinite pitch most frequently seen in the symphony orchestra, though today the variety of such instruments is endless. Keyed percussion instruments, such as the *xylophone, glockenspiel, vibraphone* and *marimba*, are tuned to a definite pitch, and have proved increasingly popular with modern composers. The *piano* and the *celesta* are also, technically, percussion instruments (in that they are struck) and even the *harp* is sometimes listed as a member of the percussion family, even though its strings, encompassing seven octaves, are plucked. CW

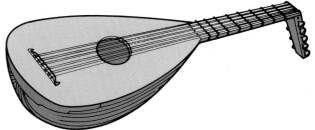

A lute. The lute and guitar families are not normally used in an orchestral context, tending to be used as solo instruments or to accompany a singer. The lute has been traced back to around 2000 BC in ancient Mesopotamia, and reached the peak of its popularity in the 16th and 17th centuries. The guitar was introduced into Spain by the Moors in the Middle Ages.

SEE ALSO

● WAVE THEORY p. 28
● ACOUSTICS p. 30
● WHAT IS MUSIC? p. 568
● WESTERN MUSIC pp. 570–81
● FOLK MUSIC p. 586
● MUSIC FROM AROUND THE
   WORLD p. 590

From left to right: **Oboe, cor anglais and clarinet**

Opera

Opera is the Italian word for 'work'. But, as an abbreviation of *opera in musica* (a 'musical work'), it began to be used in 17th-century Italy for music dramas in which singers in costume enacted a story with instrumental accompaniment. The narrative element was what differentiated these pieces from earlier entertainments known as *intermedii*, or 'interludes', which were written to celebrate weddings, birthdays and similar events at the Italian courts, and incorporated lavish balletic and vocal sections.

Papageno, the bird-catcher from Mozart's mystical opera on masonic themes, *The Magic Flute*. The opera is named after the flute given to the prince Tamino to safeguard him against evil as he attempts to free Pamina, daughter of the Queen of the Night, from Sarastro, High Priest of Isis and Osiris. In fact, on reaching Sarastro's temple Tamino finds that Sarastro is wise and good, and the Queen of the Night evil. Next to Papageno in this 1819 engraving is the chime of magic bells given to him as protection as he accompanies Tamino in his quest.

Jacopo Peri's *Euridice*, first performed at the Pitti Palace, Florence, in October 1600, may not have been the first opera ever written, but it was the first to survive, along with Emilio de Cavalieri's sacred drama, *The Representation of Soul and Body*, composed in the same year for performance in Rome.

Early opera

The first true masterpieces in the form, however, were by the Venetian composer, **Claudio Monteverdi** (1567–1643; see also p. 571). Monteverdi's *Orfeo* of 1607, followed by *The Return of Ulysses* (1640) and *The Coronation of Poppea* (1642), gradually took opera out of the court and into the public domain with music of great beauty and sophistication. Each work dictated its own form, with the music providing the dramatic weight. Brief arias (solo songs), madrigals (part songs), declaimed recitatives (sung speeches), duets and ensembles were the materials Monteverdi worked with, and he used them with a freedom that his successors might have envied.

Many of the most prominent opera composers of the late 17th and early 18th centuries came from Naples, giving rise to the term the *Neapolitan School*, even though their operas tended to be first performed in Rome or Venice. One such composer was **Alessandro Scarlatti** (1660–1725; see p. 582) in whose work the conventions of *opera seria* (see below), including the *da capo* aria, were established.

In France a native form of opera was developed by **Jean-Baptiste Lully** (1632–87), who reduced the extended Italian aria to shorter 'airs' and introduced a declamatory style of recitative, and assigned a major role to ballet interludes and choruses (see pp. 582 and 596). The operatic style established by Lully reached the high point of its development in the operas of **Jean-Philippe Rameau** (1683–1764) – especially *Hippolyte et Aricie* (1733) and *Castor et Pollux* (1737) – with their complex and brilliant orchestration, rich and sometimes dissonant harmony, and pervasive atmosphere of sensuous and languid melancholy.

Just as in France the acceptance of opera was hampered by the strength of the tradition of the court ballet, so in England its development was delayed by the popularity of the masque (see p. 623). But England did produce one operatic masterpiece in *Dido and Aeneas* (1689) – the one 'true' opera of **Henry Purcell** (1659–95; also see p. 583) – which, despite its brevity, offers an astonishing range of dramatic expression, vivid characterization and depth of human understanding.

The 18th century

The greatest operas of the first half of the the 18th century were written in England – but their composer was German-born, and the language of their texts (because of the rage for *opera seria*) was Italian. By the time **George Frideric Handel** (1685–1759; see also p. 573) arrived in London from Italy in 1710, opera had become more formalized. The *da capo* aria (so called because its introductory section was repeated *da capo*, or 'from the beginning', after a contrasting middle section) reigned supreme. For all the melodic beauty Handel was able to bring to such arias in his 39 operas, the unhurried progress of the music, together with the seemingly stilted nature of many of the plots, demands a degree of patience on the part of a modern audience. Nevertheless

the rewards provided by a sympathetic performance of operas such as *Rodelinda* (1725), *Orlando* (1733) or *Alcina* (1735) speak for themselves.

Opera seria ('serious opera') was the apt title later given to the form favoured by Handel and his contemporaries, and Italian remained the favoured language, even when (as in Handel's case) the works were written for a London audience. But because operas were performed with the house lights up (not until Wagner's time was the auditorium plunged into darkness) people were able to follow the action with a copy of the text.

The term *opera seria* was strictly applied to operas whose subjects were taken from Classical and medieval history, but it is more loosely used to include operas on mythological themes. The principal roles in *opera seria* were usually taken by *castrati* (male sopranos or contraltos). Today, the idea of a 'castrated' Nero or Julius Caesar makes the art of *opera seria* seem dramatically implausible, as also does the insistence on happy or semi-happy endings, even for potentially tragic stories.

Even though the brilliant, florid-voiced *castrati* were the stars of their day, they ultimately provoked composers such as the German **Christoph Willibald von Gluck** (1714–87) to rebel against what seemed the increasingly rigid conventions of *opera seria,* and to demand a complete reform of the art.

Orpheus and Eurydice (1762) and *Alceste* (1767) were the first fruits of Gluck's determination to make opera more genuinely dramatic, and to 'restrict music to its true office by means of expression and by following the situations of the story'. Working in Paris (where opera, in the form of *opéra ballet*, suffered from other rigid traditions) as well as in Vienna, Gluck fell victim to the French capital's rival operatic factions, which had already (in 1752) prompted the so-called *Guerre des Bouffons*, or 'war of the comedians' between supporters of Italian comic opera and the stately French tradition of Lully and Rameau.

But if, in the end, he was a disillusioned man, Gluck's operatic beliefs were soon to find inspired expression in the great masterpieces of **Wolfgang Amadeus Mozart** (1756–91; see also pp. 574–5). Mozart's operas straddled the worlds of comedy and *opera seria*, and of Italian and German opera, in a way nobody else achieved. Whether in *Idomeneo* (1781), the most human *opera seria* ever written, or in his penetrating human comedies – *The Marriage of Figaro* (1786), *Così fan tutte* (1790), *Don Giovanni* (1787) and *The Magic Flute* (1791) – Mozart was the supreme operatic genius of his age. He accepted the convention of the 'number' opera (in which the music is divided into arias, duets, ensembles and so forth,

Atys (1676) by Jean-Baptiste Lully. In recent years many productions have attempted to create authentic stagings of 17th- and 18th-century operas. The career of Lully, a powerful and scheming member of Louis XIV's court, was cut short by his death from blood poisoning – the result of striking his foot with the wooden staff he was using to beat time while conducting a *Te Deum*.

Tristan and Isolde, by Richard Wagner, was unsuccessful when first produced in 1865, but is now recognized as occupying a crucial place in opera history. *Tristan* is one of a group of works in which Wagner sought to create a totally new art form, which he called music-drama rather than opera. Shown here is a scene from the Paris Opera's 1985 production.

known as 'numbers') but provided a new continuity that found its high watermarks in the finale of Act Two of *The Marriage of Figaro* and the climax of *Don Giovanni*

The 19th century

With Mozart as an example, operatic structure became increasingly continuous. In *Fidelio* (1814), **Ludwig van Beethoven** (1770–1827; see also pp. 574–5) used the methods of a traditional German *Singspiel* ('song-play', employing speech and song in alternation) to create a sublime music drama on the subject of love and liberty. *Der Freischütz* (1821) by **Carl Maria von Weber** (1786–1826), along with the same composer's *Oberon* (1826), bridged the gap between Mozart and Wagner.

With its Romanticism and its open-air scenario, *Der Freischütz* was a milestone on the road to Wagner's *Ring*, completed half a century later. By then, with characteristic single-mindedness, the German **Richard Wagner** (1813–83; see also pp. 576–7) had expanded and transformed the art of opera into what he himself preferred to describe as 'music drama'. Laid out in four parts, intended to be spread over four nights, *Der Ring des Nibelungen* ('The Nibelung's Ring') is the longest opera ever written. *The Ring* was the outcome of some 20 years of its composer's life, culminating in its first complete performance in 1876. By the time he completed it, having already produced *The Flying Dutchman* (1843), *Lohengrin* (1850), *Tristan and Isolde* (1865) and *Die Meistersinger* (1868), Wagner had made each act of his operas wholly continuous. He had also expanded his responsibilities as a composer by writing the words as well as the music of each of his works. He also acted as his own producer and designer, and built his own revolutionary theatre at Bayreuth in Bavaria, complete with a covered orchestra pit.

Simultaneously in Italy, **Giuseppe Verdi** (1813–1901) was following a parallel, if more cautious, course. Verdi inherited the tradition of the 'number opera' from his Italian predecessors. Notable among these were **Gioacchino Rossini** (1792–1868), whose operas include *The Barber of Seville* (1816) and *William Tell* (1829);

Vincenzo Bellini (1801–25), best known today for *Norma* (1831); and the prolific **Gaetano Donizetti** (1797–1848), whose most famous works, *Maria Stuarda* (1834) and *Lucia di Lammermoor* (1835), are based on works by the Romantic writers Schiller and Scott (see pp. 630–3) respectively. Verdi gradually rebelled against this tradition, while retaining a lyrical Italian feeling for the art of *bel canto* ('beautiful singing'). *Il Trovatore* (1853) marked the turning point. Though today, in some respects, it may sound like just another number opera, it nevertheless represents a conscious effort on Verdi's part to escape from what he regarded as dead traditions. *La Traviata* (1853) – a more intimate opera – took him farther along the road to structural freedom, as indeed did each of his subsequent operas, right through to the two sublime masterpieces of his old age, *Otello* (1887) and *Falstaff* (1893). These two operas – both based on Shakespeare – demonstrated that Verdi had reached Wagner's goals by his own route, without sacrificing his abiding gift for melody. When told that *Falstaff* lacked 'tunes', Verdi could with justice reply that it was all melody – the only difference between it and its predecessors being that the tunes were no longer within inverted commas.

A significant trend in opera in the second half of the 19th century was the increasing use by composers of realistic subjects. *Carmen* (1875), by the French composer **Georges Bizet** (1838–75), is the savage tale of the fickle affections of a girl who works in a cigarette factory. In Italy a move towards down-to-earth representation of contemporary life (*verismo*) is registered in *Cavalleria rusticana* (1890) – a one-act opera by **Pietro Mascagni** (1863–1945). *Pagliacci* (1892) – a brief *verismo* opera by **Ruggero Leoncavallo** (1858–1919) is often performed with Mascagni's opera as a double bill, the two works together being popularly known as 'Cav' and 'Pag'. *Verismo* influence is also seen in some of the operas of Puccini (see below).

The 20th century

From Verdi to **Giacomo Puccini** (1858–1924) in Italy – as from Wagner to **Richard Strauss** (1864–1949) in Germany –

was inevitably a downhill progress. But the theatricality of Puccini's *La Bohème* (1896), *Madama Butterfly* (1900) and *Tosca* (1904), along with their sure-fire sense of melody and brilliance of orchestration has kept them in the repertoire, just as have the bloodcurdling ferocity of Strauss's *Salome* (1905) and *Elektra* (1909), and the bitter-sweetness of *Der Rosenkavalier* (1911), with its application of a vast Wagnerian scale to a Viennese chocolate-box story.

Opera's real genius of this period, however, emerged from Czechoslovakia, as audiences have only recently come to realize. In *Jenufa* (1904), *Katya Kabanova* (1921), *The Cunning Little Vixen* (1924), *The Makropoulos Case* (1926), and *From the House of the Dead* (1930), **Leoš Janáček** (1854–1928) showed himself to possess a deep compassion for his characters.

To state, as some authorities have done, that the history of opera ended with Puccini's unfinished *Turandot* in 1926 suggests that he manipulated his admirers all too well. Yet as early as 1902, **Claude Debussy** (1862–1918; see p. 578), had shown in the dreamlike shadowy world of *Pelléas and Mélisande* (his answer to the symbolism of Wagner's *Tristan* and *Parsifal*) that opera was capable of taking new directions. The same was proved by the searing, yet compassionate Expressionist dramas, *Wozzeck* (1925) and *Lulu* (1937), by the Austrian **Alban Berg** (1885–1935; see also p. 578).

More recently, Benjamin Britten (1913–76), Michael Tippett (1905–), Harrison Birtwistle (1934–) and Peter Maxwell Davies (1934–) in Britain, Hans Werner Henze, (1926–), Aribert Reimann (1936–) and Karlheinz Stockhausen (1928– ; see also pp. 580–1), Bern-Alois Zimmermann (1918–70) in Germany, Luciano Berio (1925–) and Luigi Nono (1924–90) in Italy, Olivier Messiaen (1908–92) in France and John Adams (1947–) in America are among those who have demonstrated opera to be alive and kicking, even if few composers today aspire to the prodigious output of a Handel or Donizetti. (For more details on some of these composers, see pp. 581–3.)   CW

SEE ALSO

- MUSIC OF THE BAROQUE p. 572
- CLASSICAL MUSIC p. 574
- MUSIC OF THE ROMANTICS p. 576
- MODERNISTS AND OTHERS p. 578
- THE NEW MUSIC p. 580
- CLASSICAL BALLET p. 516
- CLASSICISM IN LITERATURE p. 626
- ROMANTICISM IN LITERATURE pp. 630–1

Folk Music

All the world's peoples have their different styles of community music, generally of anonymous authorship, which has been handed down, usually orally, from one generation to the next. In the West this music is called 'folk music', in order to distinguish it from the great Western 'classical' tradition. The original term was 'folk song', which was simply a translation of *Volkslied*, the German term for 'popular song'.

In music outside the Western tradition – now often referred to as 'world music' (see p. 590) – there may also sometimes be distinctions between popular music and self-conscious 'art' music; this is particularly so in India and the Far East. However, all such distinctions tend to be blurred – as are the distinctions between the status of Western folk music and the community music of non-Western peoples. As Big Bill Broonzy once said, 'I guess all songs is folk songs. I never heard no horse sing 'em.'

Though traditionally the product of musically uneducated rural and urban communities, folk music has proved, time and again, to be capable of immense subtlety, fascinating and memorable in itself, and capable also of inspiring formally trained composers to make use of it in their works, either by quotation or by imitation.

Folk music, although usually geographically specific in its origin, often evolves as it spreads – which is why, for example, some 'American' folk songs may sound Scottish. It is also the reason why there are often many variations in words and tune of the same basic song. Since those who created and performed such music usually had no academic training, the survival of folk songs and dances was dependent on the strength of the oral tradition. In this way, a variety of memorable, often strongly rhythmic melodies gained currency. Their moods might express happiness or sadness, conviviality or loneliness, and their range of subjects was wide. Love songs, lullabies, work songs, narrative songs, patriotic songs and drinking songs featured strongly, as one would expect.

Preservation

Naturally, once musical notation was devised, there was the possibility that surviving folk music could be preserved in writing for posterity, either by those who performed it or by listeners educated enough to write it down. This was largely haphazard until the 20th century, when various composers – notably Béla Bartók (see p. 579) and Zoltán Kodály in Hungary – methodically set about tracking down and preserving as authentically as possible the folk music of their homelands. In this process of scrupulous rediscovery it became clear that what, in the 19th century, has passed for folk music (in such works as Liszt's *Hungarian Rhapsodies* for solo piano) was often a soft-edged distortion of the real thing. At the end of the 19th century, the French composer Debussy (see p. 578) wryly commented on this distorting process: 'From east to west the tiniest villages have been ransacked, and simple tunes, plucked from the mouths of hoary peasants, find themselves, to their consternation, trimmed with harmonic frills.'

In contrast, Bartók's keyboard folk dances, including many valuable teaching pieces, were an instant revelation when they began to establish themselves

The champion Irish fiddler, Tommy Flyn. The fiddle has become one of the main folk instruments in Ireland and Scotland, alongside older instruments such as the pipes and the harp. In the Scottish Highlands the fiddle was taken up when the bagpipes, alongside the wearing of the kilt, were banned after the Jacobite Rebellion of 1745–46. Folk fiddling traditions are also strong in America and Norway. The Norwegian Hardanger fiddle has additional strings that vibrate sympathetically without being touched.

early in the 20th century: the music was notably harder-edged, rhythmically more complex, harmonically more abrasive, melodically more irregular than the previous century's 'Germanization' of Eastern European folk song, and it exerted an exhilarating influence on Bartók's own compositional style.

Nationalism

What was true for Hungary proved equally true elsewhere. Though folk song had on occasion been introduced into European classical music, it was with the rise of musical 'nationalism' in the mid-19th century that it became a frequent feature. Edvard Grieg (see also p. 577) championed the folk music of his native Norway in numerous piano pieces and songs, employing dissonance in so individual a way that it had to be recognized as peculiarly Norwegian.

To that extent Grieg quoted genuine folk songs in his music, and to what extent he composed music in the style of folk songs, has never been fully clear. The same can be said for Antonín Dvořák (see also p. 577), whose symphonies contain melodies so reminiscent of folk songs that it comes as a surprise to learn that Dvořák composed most of them himself. But then, in many Western countries, the bulk of folk melodies are themselves relatively recent. What passes as German folk music, for instance, dates largely from the 19th century, which is partly why Brahms' (see p. 577) folk song collection, with piano accompaniment, sounds so Brahmsian. Many Italian folk songs, especially the 'Neapolitan' ones purveyed by world-famous tenors from Beniamino Gigli to Luciano Pavarotti, are even younger than their German equivalents, and are indeed indistinguishable from such popular touristic ditties as 'Santa Lucia' and 'O sole mio', which are not genuine folk songs at all.

British folk music

In Britain, folk music has a longer and richer history, many songs being traced to at least the 16th century, while the modal

May Day celebrations in a German village in the early 19th century. The May tree is visible in the background. While much folk music is intended for dancing, many songs, particularly ballads, are a form of story-telling. Most folk traditions include both types of music, and there is often considerable overlap.

nature of some melodies indicates an imitation of medieval plainsong chant (see p. 568).

In Britain the founding of the Folk Music Society in 1898, and the work of Cecil Sharp (1859–1924) on behalf of both British folk songs and of those of the Appalachian Mountains in America (where many originally British folk songs had survived in an isolated community of immigrants), were steps on the road towards the expanding academic study of the music of communities all over the world, a field now given the title of *ethnomusicology*. However, Sharp's patronizing intent, to replace 'coarse music-hall songs' with folk tunes, and so 'do incalculable good in civilizing the

Spanish pipers at an Easter parade. Although today the Scottish, Irish and Breton bagpipes are the best-known forms of the instrument, the bagpipes probably originated in Asia. They were introduced to Europe by the Romans, and subsequently spread all over the Continent. When the bag is squeezed under the arm, a steady supply of air is forced through the chanter, a reed instrument (akin to the oboe or clarinet) on which the tune is played. Most kinds of bagpipes have one or more drone pipes, each of which plays a single accompanying bass note. The bag itself is filled either from the lungs or by bellows squeezed between the thighs.

masses', is not an attitude that would be shared by many modern ethnomusicologists.

While Sharp was helping to lay the foundations of what came to be known as the English folk song and folk dance revival, Majory Kennedy-Fraser (1857–1930) was doing the same for Scotland in her collections of Hebridean songs. But Scottish folk music, for all its richness and variety, was not enhanced by Kennedy-Fraser type 'arrangements' with their emasculated harmonies – though many people still assume this to be real Scottish music, in all its purity. Not until singers and song collectors such as Ewan McColl established themselves in the mid-20th century could Scottish folk music be heard in all its rawness and pungency. The *Kelvin* collection of Scottish folk songs, compiled in the 1960s by some of Scotland's leading composers, proved a similar corrective to the more sugary versions of traditional tunes. The melody of 'The Bonnie Earl o' Moray' was thereby stripped of its false sentimentality, and the result was a revelation.

A similar freshness of sound was brought by Benjamin Britten (see p. 579) to the various folk-song arrangements he prepared for the singer Peter Pears, and for himself as piano accompanist. Though some listeners deemed them too 'mannered', they at least cast a more accurate light upon music that had had much of its cutting edge removed. The same, more recently, has been done on behalf of old Christmas carols, many of which had become enfeebled by vulgarized arrangements.

Roots

But a return to roots, rather than the unquestioning acceptance of distortions, is the welcome trend in the folk-music movement, which in recent years has developed into an increasingly heavy industry in many parts of the world. At worst, this has resulted in the commercialization of folk music, but even at that level it has helped to open people's ears to the sound of ethnic instruments such as the Appalachian dulcimer, a species of zither employed in the Appalachian Mountains since the 18th century and popularized in modern times by performers such as John Jacob Niles and Jean Ritchie.

Hearing folk music performed on the right instruments by gifted exponents has been a major factor in the continuing rise of interest (not only among specialists) in the subject as a whole. Fiddle music can be Scottish or it can be Cajun. Indeed, how French folk music reached Louisiana from Nova Scotia in the 18th century, and became 'Cajun' through merging with the music of local Blacks and adding the sound of the accordion to that of the fiddle, is a good example of the complex processes by which folk music evolves and is enriched. CW

SEE ALSO

● MUSIC OF THE ROMANTICS (NATIONALISM) p. 577
● POPULAR MUSIC IN THE 20TH CENTURY p. 588
● MUSIC FROM AROUND THE WORLD p. 590
● FOLK AND SOCIAL DANCING p. 594

Popular Music in the 20th Century

Popular music shares some features in common with folk music. Both types of music have a wider appeal than classical music, and have in many cases been disseminated by oral means. Unlike folk music, however, popular music is produced by professional musicians and predominantly from an urban milieu. The 20th century has witnessed an increasing uniformity of styles of popular music, largely because of the powerful cultural influence of the USA.

Not until Wagner set down his musical principles did composers recognize a distinct division between 'serious' and 'popular' music. From the mid-19th century onwards the serious and the popular increasingly flowed down separate channels. Operetta (i.e. 'light opera') and dance music were purveyed, to perfection, by **Johann Strauss** (1825–99) in Vienna, by **Jacques Offenbach** (1819–80) in Paris, and by the so-called Savoy Operas (really operettas) of **W.S. Gilbert** (1836–1911) and **Arthur Sullivan** (1842–1900) in Victorian London. Musical comedy and the Broadway musical were the 20th-century offspring of operetta, and of the old German *Singspiel* (see p. 584).

Whatever species they belong to, these works had as their common factor the alternation between spoken words and sung ones. In their simplicity they were all, in a sense, light operas, but they were capable of considerable subtlety and

Charlie Parker and Miles Davis. Parker was one of the leaders of the bebop movement in jazz, which revolted against the dominance of swing in the 1940s. Davis, a devotee of Parker's harmonic and rhythmic innovations, later made attempts to fuse jazz with rock elements.

melodic distinction. The wit, both musical and verbal, of *The Mikado* (1885) by Gilbert and Sullivan has proved indestructible. Musical comedy, in comparison, tended to be more lyrical, especially in the works of the Irish-born American **Victor Herbert** (1859–1924) and **Jerome Kern** (1885–1945), whose *Show Boat* (1927) contained some of the best American songs of the period. Songs such as 'Ol' Man River' were popularized by Paul Robeson (1898–1976), the first Black bass to achieve international fame. Robeson also championed the Negro spiritual, i.e. the religious songs of Black America, enduring examples of which include 'Go down Moses' and 'Deep River'.

Broadway

The Broadway musical preserved the lyricism of musical comedy in such successes as *Oklahoma!* (1943) by Rodgers and Hammerstein, and *My Fair Lady* (1958) by Loewe and Lerner, but also proved capable of bringing new edge and vitalilty to the form. With **Lorenz Hart** (1895–1943) as his sardonic literary partner, **Richard Rodgers** (1902–80) proved an infinitely sharper composer in *Pal Joey* (1940) than with the more sentimental **Oscar Hammerstein II** (1895–1960) in *The Sound of Music* (1959). But for sheer punch and incisiveness, *West Side Story* (1958) – a New York updating of Shakespeare's *Romeo and Juliet* with music by **Leonard Bernstein** (1918–90) and lyrics by **Stephen Sondheim** (1930–) – remains unsurpassed.

All these works have survived on the strength of their melodic resourcefulness and (particularly in Bernstein's case) rhythmic vitality. The popular song, whether written in isolation or for a stage production, has always been an American speciality. Notable exponents of the genre include **Irving Berlin** (1888–1989), composer of 'White Christmas' and 'Alexander's Ragtime Band'; **Cole Porter** (1893–1964), whose dapper songs, often with witty inner rhymes, include 'Let's do it', 'You're the top', and 'I get a kick out of you'; and above all **George Gershwin** (1898–1937), whose melodic perfection, reaching its high water-mark in 'The man I love' and in the music of his most ambitious work, the opera *Porgy and Bess* (1935), has caused him to be hailed by some as an American Schubert.

Blues and jazz

At its best, whether in Gershwin or in the often despairing music of the 12-bar blues, which follows a precisely set sequence of chords, the American popular song achieved the status of an art form, with the Black singers, **Bessie Smith** (1898–1937) and **Billie Holiday** (1915–59), as its greatest exponents. The blues has been Black America's most eloquent gift to the world of music – a major influence on jazz and, since the 1950s, on rock. The blues is also the probable source of the term 'blue note', referring to certain notes of the scale (in particular the third and seventh) that are slightly flattened, or 'leaned upon', in the performance of jazz and blues, and add their own special colouring to the music.

Though jazz is usually said to have been born in the early years of the 20th century,

Bill Haley and the Comets set America and the rest of the world alight in the 1950s with the heavy dance beat of 'Rock Around the Clock'.

its roots lie in the music that began to develop in the Black communities of the Southern States of the USA towards the end of the 19th century. Particularly in New Orleans, the fusion of Black and European cultures enabled jazz to formulate and gain its own identity, at first in saloon bars and brothels but also in the street parades that were part of New Orleans life. Street bands playing slow marches for funeral processions, and fast ones for celebrating the memory of the deceased as the mourners returned home, were thus one of the original elements of jazz.

Ragtime – an early form of jazz and one that was sometimes composed rather than improvised – was characterized by witty syncopation of simple tunes. Ragtime was particularly associated with solo piano performance, the most famous exponent of the 'rag' being the Black pianist and composer, **Scott Joplin** (1868–1917).

In the early days the form and harmony of jazz were simple; the complexity came from the way the performers improvised collectively upon the simple melodies, and from their command of syncopation. Jazz music inevitably soon swept northwards to Chicago and other cities, before spreading abroad. **Louis Armstrong** (1900–71) was one of the first to carry the message beyond New Orleans, where he was born. As a solo cornet player and singer, by the 1920s Armstrong had created his own instantly recognizable style, basing his improvisations on the harmonic sequence of tunes rather than the melodies themselves. This was a development of immense importance and, by the 1940s, had led to jazz performances in which the original melody was sometimes never stated at all, but merely implied by its underlying harmonies. Armstrong was a practitioner of the style known as *Dixieland*, which married elements from both ragtime and blues with its own distinctive improvisations.

Though jazz in Armstrong's early days was predominantly the music of Black Americans, White musicians – such as **Bix Beiderbecke** (1903–31), another brilliant cornet player – proved that it was not exclusively a Black preserve. As the popularity of jazz began to spread, so the bands, which had tended to comprise five, six or seven players, began to grow larger. During what became known as the 'swing' era, which dominated jazz just before World War II, bands such as that of **Benny Goodman** (1909–86), consisting of brass and reed sections blowing against each other over a solid beat, grew fashionable. Goodman's Carnegie Hall concerts in New York were deemed by some to have made jazz 'respectable'.

Swing to bebop

Crucial to the success of the bands were their virtuoso instrumentalists, including Goodman (an outstanding clarinettist), the trombonist **Glenn Miller** (1904–44), and the tenor saxophonist **Lester Young** (1909–59). Miller formed his own band, developed the saxophone-dominated 'Miller Sound' and achieved a phenomenal success during World War II with such hits as 'Moonlight Serenade' and 'In the Mood'. Young – a member of **Count Basie's** (1904–84) band – was to prove influential on the development after World War II of what became known as 'modern' jazz. By that time the saxophone (whether soprano or alto, tenor or bass) had established itself as the equal of any brass instrument in the performance of jazz. However 'primitive' jazz may once have been, it soon produced brilliant performers who both sustained the art of improvisation after classical music had lost it and were soloists of stunning virtuosity. The blind Black pianist **Art Tatum** (1910–56) was positively Lisztian in his technique.

The major jazz watershed occurred, significantly, in 1945, at the end of World War II, when 'traditional' jazz, with its simple harmonies, gave way to the complexity, tension, abrasiveness and virtuosity of 'modern' jazz, whose key figures have included the saxophonists **Charlie 'Bird' Parker** (1920–55) and **Ornette Coleman** (1930–), and the trumpeters **Dizzy Gillespie** (1917–93) and **Miles Davis** (1926–91). Whether identified as 'cool' jazz, or as 'bop', 'bebop' or 'rebop' – an onomatopoeic description of one of its characteristic sounds – modern jazz gains much of its intensity of expression from the contrast between a steady beat and a convoluted, often apparently agonized, solo line. Though traditionalists tend to say that jazz came to an end in 1945, and continue to perform or listen to traditional jazz as if modern jazz had never been invented, at least one of the greatest jazzmen, the pianist and band leader **Duke Ellington** (1899–1974), succeeded in straddling both camps and broke new ground with his *Such Sweet Thunder* suite, inspired by Shakespeare.

Rock

Although some people claim that jazz no longer forms part of popular music at all, because it has become much too specialized, it has nevertheless exerted a powerful influence on more obviously popular music. 'Rhythm and blues', an offshoot of the blues, featured an ensemble rather than a solo voice, and produced its own Negro-spiritual-inspired offshoot known as 'soul music'. 'Reggae', an Afro-Jamaican hybrid, originated in the 1960s and employs topical lyrics. 'Country and western' is America's modern equivalent of the European country dances of pre-

vious centuries. But above all jazz has inspired rock, a hybrid of American popular forms, both Black and White: blues, rhythm and blues, gospel, and country-and-western music. Since the advent of 'rock 'n' roll' in the 1950s, rock music – usually performed by groups using electronically amplified instruments – has established itself as the major force of present-day popular music.

In the 1950s Black artists such as the guitarist **Chuck Berry** (1926–) vied for popularity with Whites such as **Buddy Holly** (1936–1959) and, most notably, **Elvis Presley** (1935–77), whose blend of physicality and tremulous baritone delivery in such numbers as 'Heartbreak Hotel' inspired an almost religious devotion in his millions of fans.

The most significant developments in rock music in the 1960s took place in Britain, where the **Beatles** introduced a more sophisticated lyricism to the genre, and the **Rolling Stones** brought an overt sexuality to their vigorous and pungent dance numbers. The 'Mersey Sound', associated with the Beatles in the 1960s, was not only a skilful brew of British and American trends of the period, but also combined genuine melodic flair with words (the best of them by **John Lennon**, 1940–80) of real literary merit. Nor did the talents of the Beatles suffer from the short-windedness of some pop music. Their LP album, *Sergeant Pepper's Lonely Hearts Club Band* (1967), was the pop equivalent of an integrated classical song cycle, a milestone in the progress of popu-

lar music. A similar literary distinction has stamped the songs of the American **Bob Dylan** (1941–), who achieved a synthesis of elements of rock and roll and folk in his songs of protest.

Other 1960s rock trends were the drug-influenced *acid rock* of such performers as the American guitarist **Jimi Hendrix** (1942–70), and the highly amplified, rhythmic style of rock and roll, known as *hard rock*, practised by such bands as the **The Who**. A significant development in the late 1960s was the use of rock music in stage works or 'rock operas' such as *Hair*, *Jesus Christ Superstar* and The Who's *Tommy*.

In the early 1970s the *progressive rock* of British bands such as **Pink Floyd** and **Genesis** involved longer tracks, more advanced harmonies, and more complicated instrumental solo passages. It was partly in response to what some perceived as the artistic pretensions and pompous self-indulgence of such music that *punk rock* exploded onto the scene in Britain in the mid-1970s. In common with certain songs of the Rolling Stones, notably 'Street Fighting Man', punk rock gave vivid and sometimes anarchic expression to working-class discontent, most notably in the abrasive and nihilistic anthems of its most notorious practitioners, the **Sex Pistols**.

The 1980s saw an increasing divergence of styles and a growing use of electronic equipment. An increasingly influential role was played by production teams in the creation of rock music. CW

SEE ALSO
● OPERA p. 584
● FOLK MUSIC p. 586
● MUSIC FROM AROUND THE WORLD p. 590
● FOLK AND SOCIAL DANCING p. 594

The Beatles in 1968. The immense success of the Beatles was due in large part to the song-writing talents of John Lennon and Paul McCartney. The Beatles' use of different moods, themes and musical styles has not been matched by any other rock group.

Music from around the World

In the West, when we speak of music, we think in terms of the Western 'classical' tradition; but there are many other musical traditions in the world that are highly developed. Distinct classical traditions, as opposed to folk or popular traditions, also exist in countries such as Arabia, India, Indonesia, China, Japan and Korea. Traditional music is generally associated with the activities of everyday life. Because it is not normally written down, this music is passed from one generation to another by word of mouth and imitation; traditional repertoires are constantly changing to meet the needs, either political or social, of a particular society.

A Moroccan musician and dancer at a festival in the Atlas Mountains.

Modes, scales and rhythms vary from country to country, but the interval of an octave is a universal concept (see p. 568). The octave is generally divided into three (*tritonic*), five (*pentatonic*), six (*hexatonic*) or seven (*heptatonic*). These intervals are not necessarily of equal size.

Africa

Song in Africa is a communal activity; song celebrates, comments on or spreads news of all aspects of African life. The main instruments are drums, rattles, xylophones, harps, lyres, single-string fiddles, flutes and side-blown trumpets. Instruments can be played solo, in groups or to accompany singing, and as some instruments are believed to possess supernatural powers, they act as mediators between people and gods. Drums can be played so that they imitate the rhythms and pitches of African tonal languages, and they are often used to transmit verbal messages. The ownership of trumpets and drums represents power, prestige and authority. The social organization of a tribe is often reflected by the instruments they play: for example, pygmies have few instruments, usually small in size so that they can be easily carried, while the music of nomadic tribes is mainly vocal and is often accompanied by clapping, slapping the body or a leather apron, and stamping.

The texts of African songs are often freely improvised, the singer acquiring inspiration from his surroundings – for example, at wedding celebrations advice is often given to the bride and bridegroom on how they should conduct their married life together. The music usually consists of only two phrases that are constantly repeated, the first being sung by the soloist and the second by everyone present. The music is nearly always accompanied by steady rhythmic clapping.

The rhythms of African music are often *additive* (of unequal sections). In a time span of twelve beats in Western music the beat would be divided into 4 + 4 + 4 or 3 + 3 + 3 + 3, but in African music the beat could be divided into 5 + 7 or 3 + 4 + 5 units of time. Each drummer has his own basic rhythm to play; in a group only one player at a time may improvise.

Arabia

The most important instruments in Arabic music are the *ūd* (short-necked lute), the *qānūn* (psaltery), the *rabāb* (fiddle), the *nāy* (vertical flute), the *kamānja* (violin), the *darbukka* (drum) and the *duff* (tambourine). Often orchestras of many different instruments play in unison.

The text for many Arabic songs is derived from ancient literary traditions; heroic tales, love songs and death laments are popular and are generally for solo voice or choir with instrumental accompaniment.

The song is divided into three sections, in which the melodies are developed by contrasting improvised and fixed melodic passages, and is accompanied by a group of instrumentalists. Arabic music is particularly remarkable for its rhythm. The time cycle (called a 'chain') may be ex-

tremely long, yet the players can always mark the strong and weak beats precisely on each recurrence of the chain. The scale used in Arabic music consists of small intervals, and a tone can be divided into three or four microtones, while folk music favours the three-quarter tone for its melodies. Within the folk tradition melodies are harsh and dissonant, in contrast to the more delicate classical styles. Texts are often imaginative and express the personal feelings of the singer on loneliness or rejection by a lover.

China

From earliest times music has played an important role in Chinese society – at feasts and festivals, and in theatre, dance-pantomimes, and puppet shows. Today it is used for political, social and educational purposes.

Traditionally instruments are classified according to the material from which they are made – metal, stone, clay, skin, silk, wood, gourd and bamboo. The oldest known traditional instruments are the *qin* (zither) and *piba* (lute); today other instruments are popular, such as the *zheng* (16-stringed zither), *dizi* (bamboo flute), *erhu* (2-stringed fiddle), *yang-qin* (dulcimer) and *sona* (oboe). There are large bells, and magnificent tuned gongs that can be played singly or in groups of ten or thirteen.

Each Chinese scale is selected from twelve basic pitches called *lü*; each *lü* is roughly equivalent to a semitone, but they are unequal. The commonest scale chosen from these notes is the pentatonic scale, followed by the heptatonic.

There are four categories of Chinese opera. The *Kunqu,* which is today staged mainly by amateurs, is characterized by a very sophisticated singing style and prominent use of dance. It is mainly accompanied by flute melodies. Both the *Kunqu* and the *Pi-huang* (Beijing or Peking opera) use the same fragments of melodies for different songs throughout the opera. The character of the melodies is changed by contrasting the tempo and rhythm. The main melody instrument is the *jinghu* (high-pitched two-stringed fiddle). The *Gaoqiang* opera takes local folk song as its musical basis while the *Clapper* opera, true to its name, is accompanied by a wooden clapper.

India

In India there are two main traditions of classical music: the north Indian or Hindustani, and the south Indian or Carnatic tradition. In northern India, music is divided into distinct styles, and most performers specialize in one particular genre. Great emphasis is placed on improvisation and the creation of new ideas within the strict rules of the classical tradition. In southern India more emphasis is placed on the performance of set pieces.

Within the classical tradition there is a predominance of string instruments and drums. The main instruments are the *vīnā* (stick zither), *sitār* (long-necked lute with moveable frets), *tambūrā* (long-necked lute with wire strings), and *sarāngī* (fiddle

Ravi Shankar, perhaps the most famous exponent of the sitār, has spread appreciation of Indian music around the world with his rāga recitals.

played with a short bow). The most important drum in north India is the *tablā* – which is in fact a set of two drums, one smaller than the other, that produce an astonishing variety of sounds. In folk music, flutes, horns and bagpipes are common, as well as bells, cymbals, gongs, clappers and rattles of many shapes and sizes.

As in Chinese music the octave is divided into twelve semitones from which a variety of scales are formed, called *thāt* in north India, and *melakarta* in southern India. From each scale a set of fixed note-patterns is chosen, called a *rāga*, and this forms the basis of an improvisation. Each improvisation is accompanied by a drone, a combination of the basic note and the fifth note of the scale. The *rāga* creates an atmosphere, and some are believed to have magic powers – for example, creating rain or healing diseases. The basic song is short, but the skill of the performer is shown as he improvises, developing the ideas of his chosen *rāga*.

Indonesia

In Indonesia music has been important in religious and state ceremonies, puppetry and dance drama since the 8th century. Once a preserve of royal courts, it is today heard in cities, towns and villages. The main instrumental unit in the classical tradition is called the *gamelan*. This is a term for an orchestra of instruments, chiefly gongs of various sizes; there are also metallophones (instruments like chime-bars), zithers, two-stringed fiddles and various drums.

There are two styles of playing. The first is soft, creating a feeling of mysticism and timelessness; it is performed by singers, and is associated with refined dances and puppet plays. The second is a strong style;

its powerful sounds are suited to 'heroic' dances. There are two tuning systems. The *sléndro* has five fixed, almost equal pitches to the octave, and the *pélog* has seven unequal pitches. As there is no standard *sléndro* or *pélog* scale, each gamelan has its own tonal characteristics and sound colour.

Folk music is a little more free in style, and groups of gongs, violins and bamboo rattles are common.

Japan

There are two distinct traditions in Japanese music: folk music and art music. Japanese folksong is normally associated with work, dance, ceremony or feasts; it is sung with or without the accompaniment of hand-clapping or instruments. Instrumental pieces are usually played for dancing or at local ceremonies, and the instruments include the *fue* (bamboo flute), *taiko* (drum), *bin-zasara* (bamboo clappers) and *suzu* (bell). Art music is associated with the court, and with the religious ceremonies of Shintoism. It is performed by a male choir with instru-

mental accompaniment. The instruments played in art music are many; they include the *koto* (13-stringed zither), *wagon* (6-stringed zither), *biwa* (short-necked lute), *shamisen* (three-stringed lute), *fue* (bamboo flute) and *shō* (mouth-organ, used exclusively in court music). Percussion instruments include bells, drums, rattles and gongs.

In Japan the octave is divided into twelve fixed pitches, and scales normally contain five or seven notes.

The musical Noh drama (see also p. 617) is one of the most admired theatrical forms. The dances in Noh drama are of four types: ritual and comic dances, and those connected with prayer and warriors. These are accompanied by a flautist and three drummers playing stick-drum, shoulder-drum and hip-drum. The drummers play very intricate rhythmic patterns while the flute plays the melody.

There is also a long tradition of narrative song based on classical poetry, accompanied by *koto*, flute and drums.   CTG

SEE ALSO

● ISLAMIC ART p. 510
● ASIAN ART p. 512
● CHINESE AND JAPANESE ART p. 514
● WHAT IS MUSIC? p. 568
● FOLK MUSIC p. 586
● THE WORLD OF DANCE p. 592
● THE LITERATURE OF ASIA p. 616

A modern Japanese drum performance. In many countries traditional music may only survive by adapting to the changing tastes of audiences. At worst this may result in a debased commercialization, but at best may result in exciting new musical syntheses.

The World of Dance

Forms of dance vary from those that employ the whole body in free and open movement to those in which movement is restricted to certain parts – just to the eyes in the case of one Samoan courtship dance. Dance is usually rhythmic, often with an element of repetition, and forms a pattern in both time and space. Dance can be a simple expression of pleasure in the movement of the body or an art form of complex patterns and significant gestures.

Thai dancers. Eastern dance tends to place more emphasis on subtle use of the hands and fingers than is the case in Western dance, where the emphasis is more on patterns made by the whole body moving through space.

Children dance almost as soon as they can stand, and since spontaneous dancing requires no spoken language, tools or taught skills, it is likely to have been one of the first forms of human artistic expression. Dance may generate its own rhythms and patterns but usually has some kind of musical accompaniment, which helps to maintain unison among groups of dancers. This may be vocal or instrumental – or just the sound of hands clapping or feet stamping in the dance itself. Music may simply reinforce the rhythm of a dance, but dance may also seek to interpret a piece of music, giving physical expression to its structure and content. Sometimes, as in some Indian forms, dancer and musician improvise variations, each challenging the other's skills.

Ritual and magic

Cave paintings dating from thousands of years ago show prehistoric people who from their postures can only be dancing. We do not know their steps, but from the evidence of later cultures and of anthropological studies we can deduce that these dances were probably ritualistic. Dancers sometimes wore masks and animal skins imitating the movements of the prey, while others enacted the hunt. Such hunting dances were partly a magical way to bring success and partly an offering to the hunted animal. In the same way war dances were a kind of spell to bring success in battle, and such dances also induced courage and a sense of invincibility in the participants.

Repetitive movement, especially when accompanied by chants or clapping, can induce a trance-like state. In such trances voodoo dancers in Haiti are able to step over hot coals, and the whirling dervishes of Turkey and the Barong dancers of Bali can slash themselves with knives or pierce themselves with weapons without coming to lasting harm. In Arizona the Hopi Indians grip live rattlesnakes between their teeth in a dance to invoke rain – the Hopi believe that when the snakes are released they carry the message to the gods.

In cultures throughout the world, dances have been performed to ensure fertility and to celebrate the rites of passage – birth, initiation into adulthood, and death. In many dance rituals a performer wears a mask and may sometimes be considered to become the god, ancestor or animal that the dance evokes. Sometimes the steps are very precise and must be exactly followed for their magic to work. For certain dances in the Pacific islands of the New Hebrides archers stood by

An energetic dance from Burundi. In tribal societies, dance is often deeply rooted in ritual.

SEE ALSO

- OPERA p. 584
- MUSIC FROM ROUND THE WORLD p. 590
- FOLK AND SOCIAL DANCING p. 594
- CLASSICAL BALLET p. 596
- MODERN DANCE p. 598

ready to shoot any dancer who made a mistake.

Dance forms

Complicated dances demanded training and specialist performers, such as a shaman or priest or a group of temple dancers. From them developed theatrical dance. For some traditional Indian, Chinese and Japanese performances the stage is still ritually consecrated. Western theatre also had its roots in dances at Greek religious festivals (see p. 614). Although dances might be conceived as an offering to the gods, spectators would still appreciate the skill of the performers and enjoy the art of the dance, and in time such dances came to be performed in secular situations. For example, when Muslim rulers took power in India some forms of Hindu dance began to be given at court. Similarly, erotic dances originally offered in the worship of Shiva or the fertility cults of the Middle East became an accomplishment of courtesans and slave girls.

The rites that the whole community performed became the basis of folk dance the whole world over, and dances to select a mate have developed into modern paired social dances (see p. 594). Many dances provide an opportunity for solo display and introduce a competitive element, such as the back-bending limbo dancer trying to dance beneath the lowest pole – a Caribbean dance that has its roots in West Africa. Many folk traditions include this element and it periodically reappears in social dance – as in contemporary jazz and break dancing.

East and West

Every culture has evolved its own dances, but some broad differences seem to exist between Eastern and Western forms. Dances of European origin usually cover space, the pattern of the dance being a floor design or the interaction of bodies. Far Eastern dances are often performed from a fixed position with the pattern being contained within the reach of the body. Eastern dance makes complex and subtle use of the hands and fingers, whereas in the West the hands are often held passively. However, this was not true in Classical times, as we can see from Seneca's description of Roman performers: 'We admire the dancers because their hands can describe all things and all sentiments, and because their expressive gestures are as quick as words. Every change of the position of the hands and of the individual fingers expresses a different meaning.'

The Christian Church in general came to disapprove of dancing, partly because of its association with pagan faiths and partly because of its sensuality. There were a few isolated cases of ritual retaining dance, but it is only in relatively recent years that, along with other kinds of performance, it has been welcomed back in some Churches. There are still extreme groups who consider any dancing sinful – although the Bible describes King David dancing 'before the Lord with all his might', and the Psalms call for dance in praise of God. There are also sects such as the Shakers and the Holy Rollers for whom dance is an integral part of their devotions.

Medieval and Renaissance dance

Although dancing was turned out of the

Kathakali dancers in India are all male. In several societies (including Europe up to the end of the 17th century) female dancers were associated with prostitution, and so professional dance became restricted to male performers.

Church, people enjoyed it too much for it to be totally suppressed. Many folk dances continued as festive dances, although their symbolism might not be openly acknowledged. In the castles and palaces of medieval Europe the nobility turned the peasant dances into stately parades and developed more formal steps (see European court dances, p. 594). By the 15th century dancing teachers were common and rules for dances were set down. Teachers took a newly fashionable dance from one court to another, and in addition the development of printing made it easier to disseminate new music, so helping to spread the dances that went with it.

Court dancing tended to be very ordered – in Italy in particular – with suites of different dances performed in sequence. These suites became a formal spectacle and for special occasions might be linked with verse and songs on a particular theme (often from Classical mythology) to form an elaborate entertainment with sumptuous costumes and ornate settings. Dance episodes were also incorporated in the pageants to welcome important visitors and even inserted in revivals of Classical drama.

The Florentine princess, Catherine de' Medici (1519–89), was a particularly notable dance enthusiast. Following her marriage to the French king she promoted many such entertainments, in which the whole court took part. Later, as queen mother, then regent, she even used such *masques* or *ballets* – as they came to be known – as a political tool. In one, *La Defense du Paradis* (1572), her son Charles IX defended the earthly paradise against attack by the Protestant Henri of Navarre. A few days later, thousands of Protestants were killed in the St Bartholomew's Day Massacre (see p. 408) – an atrocity for which she is largely held responsible. However, court ballets usually ended with a scene of concord and harmony

and were followed by a ball in which performers were joined by spectators, symbolically bringing them into accord with the ideas expressed.

In Italy spectacles placed a growing importance upon singing, leading to the development of opera as the fashionable form (see p. 584) with dance only a subsidiary component. At the French court, however, dance remained most important. In the 17th century, when Louis XIV (see p. 414) made many triumphant appearances as a dancer, it was France that provided the most sought-after dancing masters and it was in France that the strict forms of classical ballet were developed (see p. 596). HL

Louis XIV of France as the Sun in a court ballet of 1651 called *The Night*. It was Louis' interest in dance that led to the establishment of classical ballet.

Folk and Social Dancing

Folk dances, the traditional dances of particular areas, are dances that have evolved rather than been invented. They often retain features that once had magical and ritual significance. Emphasis is usually on the group, although pairs or individuals may be featured or encouraged to give bravura displays. Social dances developed from courtship dances and, although some may involve unison dancing by the group, the emphasis is usually placed on couples.

The traditional dances of Africa, Asia and the Pacific are usually more closely related to early rituals than are European folk dances. They might best be described as ethnic dances, although they are now often performed as tourist or theatrical attractions.

European folk dance

European dances may have become divorced from magic and ritual but their origins are often still clear to see. The *horn dance* performed annually at Abbot's Bromley, England, by a band of men wearing deer's antlers, is a direct link with Stone Age animal worship. The *hora* of eastern Europe, the *sardanas* of Catalonia and many similar dances use a closed magic circle with hands held or linked by handkerchiefs. There are winding chain dances – of which the *conga* is a modern equivalent – whose serpentine forms may have some link with snake worship. *Maypole dances* are reminders both of tree worship and fertility ritual. There are numerous 'battle' dances – such as the *morris dance* (see box) – which perhaps originally represented the fight against the darkness of winter, but which have subsequently become linked with historic battles.

In most folk dances women have gentle gliding movements and small steps, while leaping and kicking is reserved for men. Male dancing often allows for a competitive display of athleticism. In the Tyrolean courtship dance, the *Schuhlplattler*, the man circles his partner with much stamping and slapping of knees, thighs and heels, and sometimes even turns somersaults and cartwheels and jumps right over the woman. The Cossack kicks out from a full knees bend, and in *flamenco* dancing the Spanish Gypsy stamps out the staccato rhythms of the *zapateado* – although in this case the women are almost as exhibitionist and flamenco has always been a performance rather than a communal dance.

Folk dances often incorporate imitative gestures. They may copy the movements of an animal or mimic work activities. Farmers' dances use the movements of sowing, reaping and haymaking, while sailors haul on ropes and fishermen on nets – one Danish dance even uses the actions of women washing clothes.

European court dances

The social dances of the nobility at first differed little from formal peasant dances. The basic medieval dance – the *basse danse*, or low dance – used small gliding steps with only a lift onto the toes, the feet scarcely losing contact with the floor. There were also *haute*, or high, leaping dances, but such steps were probably mainly for men, rather than for women with their long trains and high headdresses.

The circling glide of the 13th-century *carole* was danced to grave religious music, but with the new brighter secular music of the 15th and 16th centuries came faster livelier paces, made easier when heels were added to shoes, and skirts became shorter. The *pavane* and the *allemande* were still stately processional dances, but the *sarabande* involved advances and retreats and couples passing between rows of dancers, while the *courante* included the elegant bending of the knees. Then there was the sprightly jigging *galliard* and the twirling *volta*, in which the woman was lifted from the floor and bounced upon the man's knees.

Another lively dance was the *gavotte*, developed from a Provençal folk dance. It gave each couple a chance to dance on their own and reached its greatest popularity in 17th-century France at the court of Louis XIV. Another favourite at the French court was the delicate *minuet*, which often followed the boisterous gavotte as a contrast. Based on a figure-of-eight folk dance from Poitou, the minuet was to become fashionable throughout Europe in the 18th century.

Village dancers from medieval Europe. It was from such dances as this that most European court dances derived.

'Country dancing'

In Britain in the 17th century, lively longways (facing rows) and circle dances became very popular. They involved simple walks, runs, and skipping and hopping steps, often with couples changing position within a set. In 1650 John Playford (1623–86) published *The English Dancing Master*, which describes a great many different forms. They were taken up in France and Italy and taken across the Atlantic by American colonists where, with promptings from a caller, they became the popular American *square dance*.

The waltz

In Austria the *Ländler*, a traditional dance in which the partners turned in each other's arms with a hop and a step, was taken up at court. Simplified to make it easier in fashionable clothes and on smooth ballroom floors it emerged in the early 19th century as the *waltz*. It spread slowly because the physical contact involved scandalized so many people. In 1818 the London *Times* called it 'that indecent foreign dance' and felt it a duty 'to warn every parent against exposing his daughter to so fatal a contagion' – and that was with considerable space between the partners. It took nearly a century before the bodies actually made contact in the close embrace that dancers use today. Nevertheless, its popularity grew and it became the leading ballroom dance of the 19th century.

The waltz and the bouncing *polka*, which appeared in the middle of the century, both allowed improvisation by the dancers. Although some new group dances were developed – such as the *Paul Jones* and the *lancers* in the 19th century, and the serpentine *conga* and the jokey *hokey-cokey* in the 20th century – the emphasis now shifted to couples dancing together.

New rhythms

Most of the new dances of the 20th century originated in America, and had their roots in the offbeat syncopated rhythms originally brought by Black slaves from Africa. Other influences included the jigs and clog dances of Irish immigrants and the mixing of African, Spanish and Portuguese styles in Latin America. Often dances have been invented for particular shows or films, or to promote sheet music and record sales.

At the beginning of the 20th century the most important innovators were the American husband-and-wife team, Irene and Vernon Castle. They introduced new steps in public exhibitions of ballroom dancing and popularized the *one step*, the *foxtrot*, the *tango* (already introduced from Argentina by Joseph Smith), and many other dances, usually accompanied by syncopated and jazzy music. Later dancing couples, like Fred and Adele Astaire, gained equal fame as exhibition dancers, but were not dance makers.

The 20th century has seen rapid changes of fashion in music and dance. The Jazz Age of the 1920s saw a succession of zany dances, including the kicking and flexing

knees of the *charleston*. The *samba*, *rumba* and *cha-cha* all have Latin rhythms and have become established ballroom dances. The *lindy hop*, in which the male partner broke away to improvise, developed into the *jitterbug* or *jive*, which in the 1950s was danced to rock-and-roll music. With rock-and-roll there also came the *twist* in the early 1960s, and with the punk rock of the later 1970s came the *pogo*, which simply involves jumping up and down as energetically as possible. In contrast, only the hips and arms move to the Jamaican reggae beat, while the feet stay more or less rooted on the spot.

Freestyle

The foxtrot, jitterbug, twist and many modern dances consist of basic steps on which to improvise rather than formal dance patterns. Now dancers often invent their steps and body movements. They do not necessarily mirror a partner, and in discos lone dancers may often be seen giving a display of individual virtuosity.

The 1980s saw the introduction of *robotics*, based on angular, jerky mechanical-looking movements, and *break dance*, which features acrobatics and ground spins pivoted on the head and shoulders. Both might as often be seen on the street or subway as in dance hall or disco and they are not really social dances but performances.   HL

SEE ALSO
- FOLK MUSIC p. 586
- POPULAR MUSIC IN THE 20TH CENTURY p. 588
- THE WORLD OF DANCE p. 592
- CLASSICAL BALLET p. 596
- MODERN DANCE p. 598

London's Vauxhall Gardens, opened to the public in 1660, became a favourite venue for dancing and music. The pleasures to be found there eventually became notorious, and the Gardens were closed in 1859.

Originally known as the lindy hop (below), this exuberant dance developed into the jitterbug or jive, much loved by rock-and-rollers in the 1950s.

Classical Ballet

Ballet is a theatrical dance form based upon a set of positions, steps and expressive gestures that demand considerable skill and training. Ballet may tell a story or offer abstract patterns of movement. Though generally aiming at an appearance of effortless grace, it can also be highly dramatic. Balletic entertainments were first developed in the French court in the 16th century (see p. 593), but ballet companies in many countries have created their own distinctive national styles.

There are several ways in which ballet differs from other forms of dance. Most obvious is the 90° 'turned-out' position of the feet, which permits a remarkable degree of balance in all positions. Ballet also requires a tension and arching of the foot and Achilles tendon to provide a powerful jump and to cushion landing. Dancers begin training at a very early age to achieve the positions required, and must continue to exercise every day.

The beginnings of ballet

In 1661 the French king, Louis XIV, established a group of dancing instructors, the Académie Royale de Danse, to codify court dances. Its director, **Charles Louis Beauchamp** (1636–1705), is credited with inventing the 'five positions', though he may just have followed existing practice. As greater skills were demanded of performers, trained professionals began to replace the aristocratic amateurs who had previously participated in courtly entertainments.

Louis XIV danced his last role in 1670, and this made it less fashionable for amateurs to perform. After the founding of the Académie Royale de Musique et de Danse under the composer Lully (see p. 572) in 1672 there was a permanent demand for professional dancers. In 1713 the Paris Opéra – as the theatre of the Académie became known – established a permanent company of dancers and a school to train them.

Dancers in the ballets that featured prominently at the Opéra wore heavy court costume and hid their faces behind masks. This was supposedly because they thought that ancient Greek performers wore them, but it may have had as much to do with the fact that court ladies had preferred to disguise their faces, and also that at the Opéra female roles were danced by men. It was not until 1681 that a woman professional danced at the Opéra.

Ballet redefined

The early ballets had consisted of a succession of dances with music and poetry, but from 1661 the actor-dramatist Molière (see p. 626) began to use dance as part of the action in his plays. At the Opéra, ballet was still accompanied by vocal music providing a text, but interest grew in making ballet a dramatic form in which the dance itself carried the story and emotion.

The greatest instigator of change was **Jean Georges Noverre** (1727–1810). Noverre created dances in London for David Garrick's Drury Lane Theatre, and also in Stuttgart and Vienna – both of which he helped to make important ballet centres – before becoming ballet master at the Opéra in his native Paris in 1776. Noverre's aims were to get rid of heavy wigs, masks and big padded skirts, and also to introduce more natural gestures into dance along with a greater emphasis on dramatic action.

Although the male star **Gaetano Vestris** (1729–1808) had abandoned his mask when dancing at the Opéra in 1770 there was considerable resistance to Noverre's reforms in France. They were adopted most fully in Denmark in the work of **August Bournonville** (1805–1879), son of one of Noverre's pupils. A free, more lyrical technique with realistic characterization is still typical of Danish ballet.

However, long before Noverre's arrival some changes had been initiated. **La Camargo** (Marie Anne de Cupis de Camargo, 1710–70) was acclaimed for her jumps, especially the *entrechat*, in which the feet beat together in the air. She danced in heel-less slippers to aid her footwork, which she displayed to better effect by shortening her skirts to mid-calf. While La Camargo made her name as a technician, her contemporary and rival **Marie Sallé** (1707–56) placed more emphasis on plot and interpretation.

Romantic ballet

Sometime after 1800 women began to dance 'on point' (on the tips of the toes), stiffening the ends of their slippers to give more support. Pointwork became a key

Frederick Ashton's *Ondine*, with Anthony Dowell and Maria Almeida of the Royal Ballet. The ballet, with music specially composed by Hans Werner Henze, was created in 1958, and tells the story of a water sprite and her human lover. The great British prima ballerina Margot Fonteyn (1919–91) took the title role in the first production.

feature of choreography for women. It requires strengthening of the muscles in foot and leg and can cause injury if attempted prematurely.

As in the other arts, the fashion now was for Romanticism (see pp. 536, 576, 630), which in ballet took the form of stories of princes in love with nymphs and of unrequited love. The Romantic style was exemplifed by *Giselle*, first danced in 1841, in which the spirit of an abandoned country girl appears to her untrue princely lover.

Milan became important for ballet in the Romantic period because the ballet master at La Scala, **Carlo Blasis** (1797–1878), was a famous teacher. The practice exercises which he developed – with deep knee bends and stretching of the feet and thighs – still form the basis of the dancer's daily class.

Although there were still some virtuosi male dancers, in Romantic ballets men tended to be mere partners, literally supporting the women. Even ostensibly male roles were often danced by women dressed up as men. A famous example is the role of Franz in *Coppelia* (created 1870), although this ballet has a more lively plot and structure than earlier Romantic ballets.

Russian ballet

A French dancer and choreographer, **Maurice Petipa** (1822–1910), and a Danish teacher, **Christian Johansson** (1817–1903), were responsible for a particular flowering of ballet in Russia in the second half of the 19th century. Ballets like the still popular *Sleeping Beauty* and *Swan Lake* (both to Tchaikovsky's music) filled the whole evening. Dancers achieved a distinctive national style, making ballet the equal of opera in artistic status.

In 1919 the impresario **Serge Diaghilev** (1872–1929) mounted a season of Russian ballet in Paris, calling his company the Ballets Russes (see box). His dazzling dancers and stunning stagings attracted wild enthusiasm. For the next 20 years Diaghilev toured his company in Europe and the Americas, creating a new enthusiasm for ballet and launching the careers of many international stars.

Several of today's great ballet companies have their origins in Diaghilev's company. **George Balanchine** (1904–83), founder-choreographer of the New York City Ballet, **Ninette de Valois** (1898–), founder of Sadlers Wells (now the Royal) Ballet, and **Marie Rambert** (1888–1982), who shares with de Valois the credit for the creation of British ballet, are only a few of the key figures who were at one time members of his company.

Modern ballet

Russia has continued to produce superb dancers such as **Galina Ulanova** (1910–) and **Maya Plisetskaya** (1929–) and several who have made their names in the West: **Rudolph Nureyev** (1939–93), **Mikhail Baryshnikov** (1948–) and **Natalia Makarova** (1940–). Innovation and experiment, however, have shifted elsewhere. Many countries, from Canada to

Japan, Cuba to Australia, now have major national companies. Choreographers like **Jerome Robbins** (1918–) in the USA, **Frederick Ashton** (1904–88) and **Kenneth Macmillan** (1929–92) in Britain, the Dane **Harold Lander** (1905–), **Roland Petit** (1924– , French), **John Cranko** (1927–73, South African but working mainly in Britain and Germany), and **Jiri Kylian** (1947– , Czech, working in Holland) have extended the vocabulary of dance while remaining within the classical world.

HL

SEE ALSO

● OPERA p. 584
● THE WORLD OF DANCE p. 592
● MODERN DANCE p. 598

DIAGHILEV'S BALLETS RUSSES

No impresario has ever brought together such a dazzling display of great artists from every field. A few of them are listed here.

Choreographers and dancers included: Michel Fokine (1880–1942), Anna Pavlova (1881–1931), Vaslav Nijinsky (1889–1950), Tamara Karsavina (1885–1978), Leonide Massine (1895–1979), Serge Lifar (1905–86), Bronislava Nijinsky (1891–1977), George Balanchine, Anton Dolin (1904–83), Alicia Markova (1910–).

Designers included: Alexandre Benois (1870–1960), Leon Bakst (1866–1924), Pablo Picasso (1881–1973), Henri Matisse (1869–1954), André Derain (1885–1954), Marie Laurencin (1885–1956).

Composers included: Claude Debussy (1862–1918), Igor Stravinsky (1882–1971), Sergei Prokofiev (1891–1953), François Poulenc (1899–1963), Eric Satie (1866–1925).

Ballets included: *Les Sylphides* (originally created for Marykinsky Theatre, 1906), *Scheherazade* (1910), *Firebird* (1910), *Le Spectre de la Rose* (1911), *Petrushka* (1911), *L'Aprés-midi d'une faune* (1912), *The Rite of Spring* (1913), *Parade* (1917), *The Three-Cornered Hat* (1919), *Les Noces* (1923), *Apollon Musagète* (1928), *The Prodigal Son* (1929).

Costume design for *Sheherazade* by Leon Bakst. The ballet – with choreography by Fokine and music by Rimsky–Korsakov – was first performed in 1910 by Diaghilev's Ballets Russes.

The ethereal Marie Taglioni (1804–84), the epitome of the 19th-century ballerina. Contemporaries said that on point and in soaring jumps she seemed to float above the ground before landing apparently noiselessly.

THE FIVE POSITIONS

In strict classical ballet, all movements start and end with the feet in one of these positions. The hand positions match the foot positions to give a graceful line.

First position

Second position

Third position

Fourth position

Fifth position

feet: open
arms: *en avant*

feet: crossed
arms: *en haut*

arms: *en haut*
(with *en avant*
and *en bas* marked
by dotted lines)

Modern Dance

Reaction against the formal rules of classical ballet (see p. 596) saw the development of freer styles during the 20th century, and these styles are collectively known as *modern dance*. Like all the arts, dance has been affected by contemporary ideas in other areas. Modern dance may reflect the minimalist ideas found in late 20th-century music and painting, use as its materials a combination of natural movements, or follow idiosyncratic individual inspiration.

Dancing as a component of more popular stage entertainment – sometimes described as *show dancing* – has its roots in earlier troupes of fair and street performers, which usually included dancers and acrobats. Dancing girls were also a feature of private entertainment in many cultures, and stage dance sometimes exploited the exoticism and erotic elements of non-European styles, as well as the acrobatic skills of performers. Stage dancing often also reflected existing folk and social dances (see p. 594), but was sometimes a result of the dancers'

Isadora Duncan, one of the founders of modern dance. Her colourful life ended when her scarf caught in the wheel of a sports car in which she was travelling.

own invention. Today, the gap between modern and show dance has narrowed, as each draws on the influence of the other.

Show dancing

One of the most famous show dances is the high-kicking, leg-twirling *cancan*, which emerged in Paris in the 1840s, and which was widely copied in musical comedy and burlesque theatres. However, the biggest influences on show dancing, in the 20th century were tap and jazz dancing, which were exclusively American developments.

The minstrel shows of 19th-century America offered a mixture of Irish jigs, clog dances and African stamping, and this mixture evolved into a new style from which two main dance forms developed: an active, fast dance done in wooden-soled shoes that became known as *buck and wing*, and the smooth, relaxed *soft-shoe shuffle*.

By the mid-1920s, when steel tips were introduced so that shoes would make more noise, *tap dancing* was combining both forms. It was mainly a male style, with dancers such as **Bill 'Bojangles' Robinson** (1878–1949) and **Fred Astaire** (1899–1987) developing more and more complex footwork. But women were very much involved in group precision dancing featuring both tap and high kicks. Such chorus lines became a feature of a number of spectacular revues, and groups such as the Rockettes at New York's Radio City, the Bluebell Girls in Paris and the Tiller Girls in London put on remarkable displays of technical skill.

Free forms

At the forefront of a reaction against the formal constraints of classical ballet were three Americans, all influenced by the ideas of **François Delsarte** (1811–71), a Frenchman who had analysed gesture and movement.

Isadora Duncan (1878–1927) sought to express emotion through dance based on the grace of natural movement, and to this end she danced barefoot and in a costume modelled on ancient Greek dress. She found success in Europe, where she may have influenced Fokine's early work for Diaghilev (see p. 597). In 1920 she was invited to start a school in post-revolutionary Russia, but neither this nor her schools in Germany and the USA survived, although her influence persisted.

Like Duncan, **Ruth St Denis** (1879–1968) first attracted attention with recitals for fashionable New York parties. St Denis and her husband **Ted Shawn** (1891–1972) also sought a free dance form, but they explored folk and national dance for their inspiration, especially that of the Orient. They opened the Denishawn School in Los Angeles, and subsequently Shawn's all-male company helped to break down prejudice against male dancers.

Graham and Cunningham

A dancer with St Denis's company for some years, **Martha Graham** (1894–1991) eventually tired of its mixture of styles and its exotic decors. From about 1927 she developed a new style, apparently angu-

lar and abstract but rooted in the expression of emotion. Like St Denis's style it emphasized contact with the ground, as in oriental dancing, rather than the constant attempt to escape gravity typical of classical ballet. Instead of trying to hide the effort of the dancer, Graham's approach celebrates the energy of muscular action. To equip dancers for the demands of her style she evolved a highly developed training system.

Graham's pupils and members of her company – such as **Robert Cohan** (1925–), director of the London Contemporary Dance Theatre – continue her influence. Another of Graham's protegés, **Merce Cunningham** (1919–), rejected her strong links to story and meaning to create a more abstract dance, sometimes involving elements of chance. In one piece he even breaks off a virtuoso dance sequence for some unrelated activity like riding a bike. **Paul Taylor** (1930–), a dancer with both Graham's and Cunningham's companies, has incorporated everyday movement into his lyrical ballets.

Laban and his followers

The Hungarian-born movement analyst and choreographer **Rudolph Laban** (1879–1958) was the theorist behind an important European modern dance movement. He founded a Dance Institute in Munich and later devised his 'Laba-notation', a system of symbols to record all the body's movements, which is now the most widely used way of writing down dance. He paid much attention to the relationship between the individual and the surrounding space, also a feature of the choreography of his pupil **Mary Wigman** (1866–1973). Another pupil was **Kurt Jooss** (1901–79), whose expressionist anti-war ballet *The Green Table* (1932) became the most famous of modern works between the two world wars.

Contemporary dance

Recent years have seen the creation of many modern dance companies drawing on existing styles and experimenting with new ideas. Not only have choreographers invented new figures within the classical discipline, but techniques from various styles have been combined.

Classical purists have criticized choreographers such as the Frenchman **Maurice Béjart** (1927–) for breaking all the rules of formal classicism in his spectacular theatrical ballets, but these have found particular favour with young audiences. **Michael Clark** (1962–), the iconoclastic ex-Royal Ballet dancer, is gaining a new young audience by attempting to shock his elders. One of the best-known of the many innovative American choreographers is **Twyla Tharp** (1942–), who has created works both for Baryshnikov and for the skater John Curry. She has choreographed work for the wide spaces of New York's Central Park, and experimented with texts and songs that parallel the dance.

All over the world there are many other talented choreographers extending the parameters of modern dance. Performers with a background in rock music, paint-

Soldat (above), a recent dance work by the choreographer Ashley Page, here performed by the Rambert Dance Company.

SEE ALSO

● FOLK AND SOCIAL DANCING
  p. 594
● CLASSICAL BALLET p. 596
● EXPERIMENTAL THEATRE
  p. 642

ing and sculpture, without formal dance training, have turned to using their bodies to create original movement works. With the increasing integration of styles, virtuoso disco and break dancers may also be called upon to display their skills within dance works.

New directions

Linked both to the idea of living sculpture and to Zen concentration on detail is a recent Japanese dance style known as *butoh* – in full *ankoku butoh* ('dance of utter darkness') – first developed by **Kazuo Ohno** (1906–), his son **Yoshito**, and **Tatsumi Hijikata** (d. 1986). It features a slowly evolving transition from one shape to another – shapes that may be animals or even inanimate objects as well as human. But it can also encompass improvisation, as when a single dancer performs with a live peacock, mirroring and complementing the free movement of the bird.

Another recent movement is the German *Tanztheatre*, best known abroad through the Wuppertal company of **Pina Bausch** (1940–), which demands a similar concentration of its audience to observe action that is frequently slow moving and repetitive. But Bausch's work, drawing its actions from ordinary daily life, is definitely about people, and her performers often speak. Sometimes beautiful images emerge, but Bausch seems more concerned with human bitterness, brutality and failure to communicate. For those with patience to develop empathy with the performers, Bausch's work can achieve a hypnotic power.   HL

A break dancer (below) in action. Modern dance has increasingly seen an integration of all kinds of dance, including virtuoso disco and break dancers.

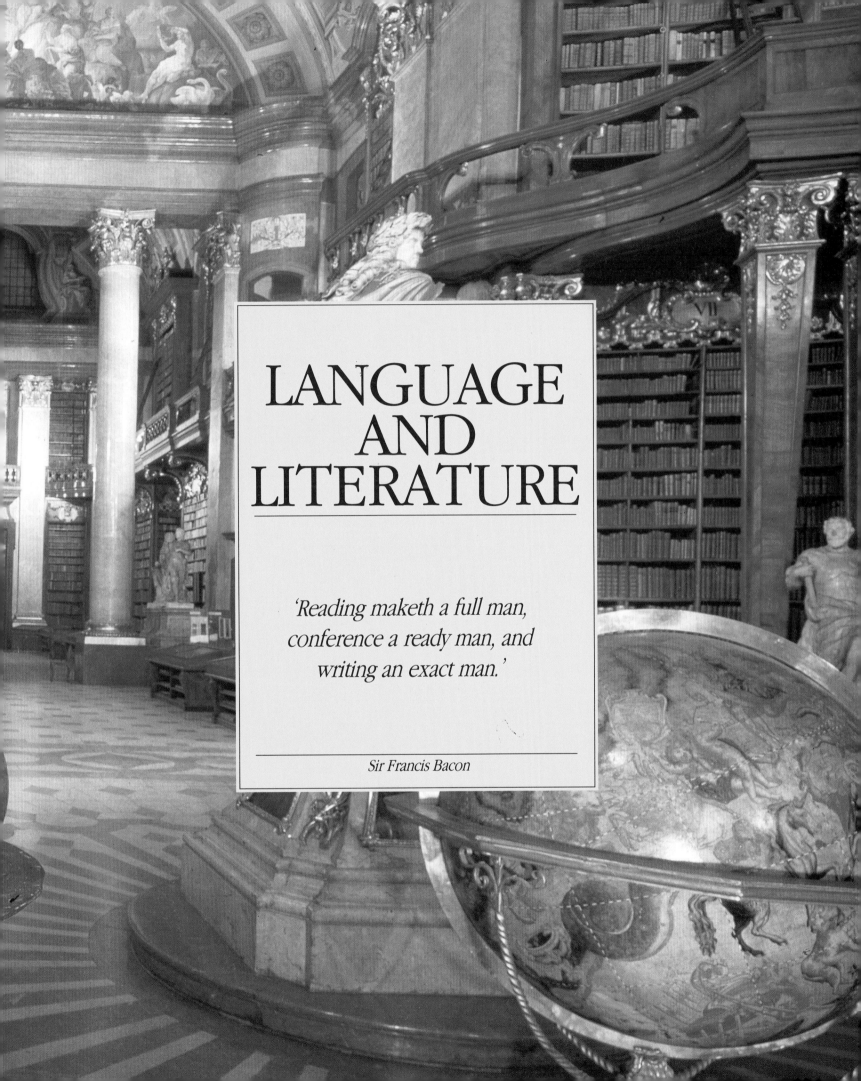

LANGUAGE AND LITERATURE

'Reading maketh a full man,
conference a ready man, and
writing an exact man.'

Sir Francis Bacon

The World's Languages

No one is certain how many living languages there are in the world, but it is likely that the number exceeds 5000. Nor has any scholar been able to account for the fact that languages outnumber races by at least one thousand to one. Each world language is unique in that each has its own system of sounds, words and structures, and yet each is related either closely or distantly to other languages found in the same part of the world. Thus English, French, Igbo and Yoruba are all distinct languages, but English and French share many linguistic features with each other and with other languages in Europe, whereas Igbo and Yoruba have more in common with each other and with other African tongues.

Wilhelm von Humboldt, the German educationist and language scholar. Humboldt's ideas, notably on the relationship between language, thought and culture, prefigure modern linguistic study. His work includes studies of the Basque language and the languages of Java.

The world's languages are as unique as individual people, but like people they can also be classified in terms of families. Tree diagrams such as that illustrated here are often used in descriptions of languages to show the relationships that are thought to exist within language families. The 'tree' shows the main branches of the *Indo-European* family of languages.

Language families

Language trees were used by 19th-century *philologists* (historical linguists). They all derive, to some extent, from the work of scholars such as the Englishman Sir William Jones (1746–94), who in 1786 described the relationship that exists – especially in the area of vocabulary – between Latin and Greek, the Germanic languages, Hindi and Persian:

Dutch	English	German	Greek
broeder	brother	Bruder	phrätër
vader	father	Vater	patër
moeder	mother	Mutter	matër

Irish	Latin	Sanskrit
brathair	frater	bhrätar-
athair	pater	pitar-
mathair	mater	mätä

In the 19th century, two further developments occurred: phonological and syntactic evidence (see pp. 608–9) was used to reinforce relationships already clear from similarities of vocabulary between languages, and other language families were established. The German philologist and folklorist Jacob Grimm (1785–1863) – also famous for his and his brother Wilhelm Carl's collection of folk tales – formulated a law which, with certain modifications proposed by the Danish linguist Karl Verner (1846–96), gave a systematic account of the sound differences in the related Indo-European languages. An initial 'p' in proto-Indo-European – assumed to be the mother language of the Indo-European family – was retained as 'p' in Latin and Greek, changed to 'f' in the Germanic languages and often disappeared in Irish Gaelic:

Latin	English	Irish
piscis	fish	iasc
pater	father	athair
periculum	fear	eagla

Similar correspondences could be found for other consonants:

Latin	English	Irish
canis	hound	cú
centum	hundred	céad
cor	heart	croidhe
caballus	horse	capall

and for vowels, with 'a' in one language often corresponding to 'o' or 'e' in another:

Latin	English	French
frater	brother	frère
mater	mother	mère

The second development in historical language study was the recognition of additional groupings of languages. Today, as well as the Indo-European family, other large families have been recognized. These include:

Altaic – e.g. Mongolian and Turkish.
Amerindian – North American Indian languages such as Chinook and Nootka.
Austronesian – languages of the southwest Pacific such as Fijian and Kuanua.
Bantu – Sub-Saharan African languages such as Herero (a language of Namibia) and Zulu.
Dravidian – languages of central and southern India and Sri Lanka such as Tamil and Telugu.
Finno-Ugrian – e.g. Finnish, Lappish and Magyar (spoken in Hungary).
Indo-Chinese – e.g. Chinese and Tibetan.
Japanese – apparently unrelated to other languages.
Papuan – languages of Papua New Guinea such as Chimbu and Huli.
Semitic-Hamitic – languages spoken in North Africa and southwest Asia such as Arabic and Hebrew.

Whether these families are related to one another is a question that cannot be answered because the necessary evidence is not available.

Language types

Other approaches to the relationship between languages have also been pursued. The German philologist Wilhelm von Humboldt (1767–1835), followed by August Schleicher (1821–1868), helped to establish a branch of language study that has sometimes been called *typological linguistics* and has proved useful in classifying languages according to their structural type. According to this approach the three main groups of languages are agglutinative, fusional (or inflectional) and isolating. Von Humboldt's approach dealt mainly with *morphology*, that is, the structure and forms of words (see p. 608).

Agglutinative languages, like Turkish, typically form structures by means of a string of *morphemes* (see p. 608), each with a specific meaning or function. Thus in Turkish 'to love' is *sevmek* ('love' + infinitive), 'to be loved' *sevilmek* ('love' + passive + infinitive) and 'not to love' *sevmemek* ('love' + negative + infinitive).

Fusional or *inflectional languages*, like Latin, have words where there is not a one-to-one correspondence between a morpheme and a meaning. The Latin word equus, for example, fuses the features nominative case + masculine + singular as well as the meaning ('horse'). Cases change in fusional languages; for example, the nominative case *equus* would be used where the word is the subject of a sentence, and the accusative case *equum* where the word is the object of a sentence.

In *isolating languages*, each word consists of just one morpheme – and words don't change their form at all – so the distinction between word and morpheme is not very useful. There are very few pure isolating languages in the world, but Vietnamese is the best example. Some *pidginized* languages (languages based on one language but containing elements of another) are, to a large extent, isolating. In Kamtok, the pidginized English of the Cameroon, one morpheme can function without change as a noun (singular or plural), as a verb, as an adjective and as an adverb. Thus *bad* can be the equivalent of 'sin/sins' in *i bin du bad* ('he did bad things'), 'be bad' in *i bad* ('he is bad'), 'bad' in the sense of 'naughty' in *di bad pikin* ('the naughty child') and of 'very' in *di pikin fain bad* ('the child is very good-looking').

In contrast to isolating languages, there are *polysynthetic* languages, ones in which few, if any, words contain just one morpheme. Polysynthetic languages, including many American Indian languages, are characterized by long, complex words that express the meanings of whole phrases and even clauses.

These ways of grouping languages all reveal useful information about the characteristics of languages, but no language belongs solely to one type. English, for example, has characteristics of all four types. A word such as 'unworkmanlike' is agglutinative in that one can distinguish four morphemes each with a recognizable meaning. 'Took' is fusional in that it incorporates the meaning of past tense + the meaning of 'take'. The fact that 'fish' can be a singular or a plural noun as well as a verb shows that parts of English resemble isolating languages. A word such as 'disestablishmentarianism' has the complex structure of a word from a polysynthetic language.

Contemporary linguists consider other factors in identifying language groups, including phonological patterns, such as

THE INDO-EUROPEAN LANGUAGES: A simplified family tree

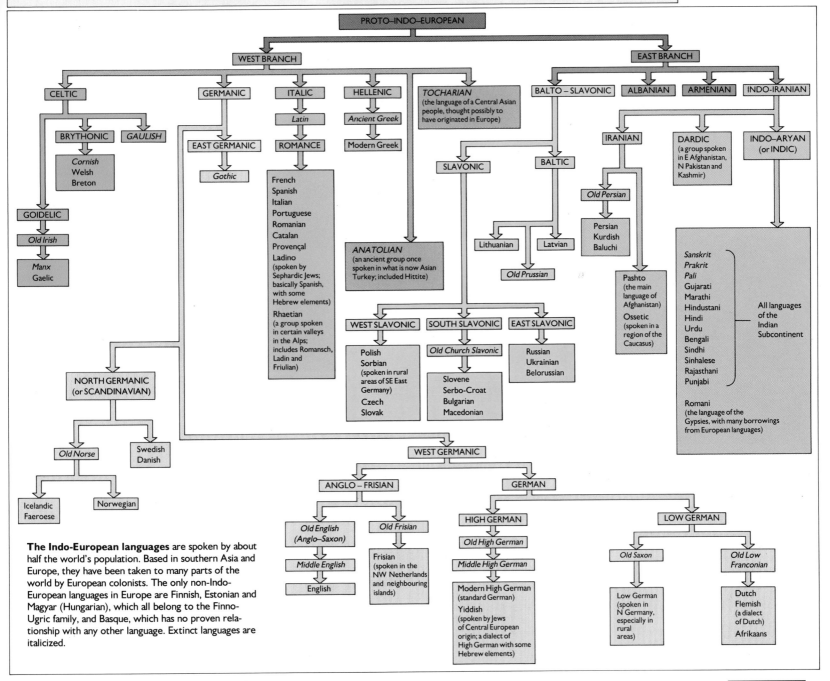

The Indo-European languages are spoken by about half the world's population. Based in southern Asia and Europe, they have been taken to many parts of the world by European colonists. The only non-Indo-European languages in Europe are Finnish, Estonian and Magyar (Hungarian), which all belong to the Finno-Ugric family, and Basque, which has no proven relationship with any other language. Extinct languages are italicized.

the use of tone to distinguish meaning. Chinese, for example, is a tone language. An important way of classifying language types is by word order. Typically, English has the basic order subject-verb-object ('I – ate – the apple'); it is an SVO language, as are Greek and Swahili. But Hindi, Japanese and Turkish, for example, are basically SOV ('I – the apple – ate', as it were). And Hebrew, Maori and Welsh are examples of VSO languages ('Ate – I – the apple'). Languages in each group (and these are not the only ones possible) generally have other syntactic features in common.

General features of languages

From the evidence currently available to linguists the following generalizations can be made about world languages.

1. All languages change through time because of internal pressures. These include the desire to regularize ('dived' rather than 'dove' is now used in British English as the past tense of the verb 'dive'); and changes of meaning (the word 'silly' in English used to mean 'holy'). External pressures often result in vocabulary borrowed from other languages – in this respect English has been one of the greatest borrowers. English has also changed from a highly inflected to a relatively uninflected language (see p. 606).

2. Language change may be slow or very rapid. Icelandic has changed less in the last 1000 years than English did in 20 as it was pidginized on the sugar plantations of Queensland in the 19th century.

3. All languages are equal to the needs of their users. There are no inferior languages.

4. All language users use different styles of their language in different contexts, e.g. formal and ritual occasions, story-telling and literature (either written or oral), within families, within peer groups.

5. Any human language can be translated into any other, although there may be losses in nuance and cultural reference in the process.

6. Any normal child will learn the language or languages of his or her environment irrespective of the family the language may belong to. In other words, an English child exposed to Hindi or Swahili will learn it as easily and as naturally as he or she learns English.

LT

SEE ALSO

● WRITING SYSTEMS p. 604
● THE STORY OF ENGLISH p. 606
● HOW LANGUAGE WORKS p. 608

Writing Systems

Human beings are believed to have kept records since the last Ice Age, about 20 000 years ago. Bones and antlers have been found with regular groups of incisions thought by some archaeologists to be calendars. Such objects may have been used to keep track of the migrating animals on which hunters of the Palaeolithic period (see p. 362) depended. However, true writing was not invented until much later.

SEE ALSO

- THE ANCIENT NEAR EAST p. 364
- ANCIENT EGYPT p. 366
- MINOANS AND MYCENAEANS p. 368
- THE WORLD'S LANGUAGES p. 602
- THE STORY OF ENGLISH p. 606
- HOW LANGUAGE WORKS p. 608

The distinguishing feature of a proper writing system is that the written symbols transmit the actual words and sounds of a particular language, and not simply ideas. Thus a picture of a horse does not constitute writing since it could be 'read' in any language, for example as *cheval, hippos, equus, sisu* or *horse*. In contrast, all of the words listed express the same idea – horse – but the writing reproduces the sounds of several different languages: French, Greek, Latin, Akkadian (ancient Babylonian) and English.

Writing systems are not the same as languages. One writing system, such as the modern Roman alphabet in which English is written, can be used to write a number of European languages. Similarly, the Arabic alphabet has been used to write Turkish and Persian as well as the Arabic language.

The earliest writing

Writing developed independently in several areas, including the Near East, China, the Indus Valley (in what is now Pakistan) and Central America. The writing systems that evolved in each of these areas are different and not influenced by the others. The earliest known true writing system was the cuneiform (wedge-shaped) script of Mesopotamia (modern Iraq), which dates back to at least 3100 BC.

Why did people invent writing? The answer can perhaps be guessed at from the first things they wrote. In most places where writing was independently invented, the oldest surviving written documents are labels (often on storage jars) and lists, or the names of rulers. Generally, the societies that produced these documents were ones in which some people were much richer than others, power being concentrated in the hands of small groups. It is usually assumed that writing was invented because the members of such groups needed to monitor the movements of commodities and people in order to maintain their control over them. However, where writing is scarce, written words are also powerful symbols of authority. The monumental writing of a ruler's name – for example on gigantic stone slabs in Central America, or on oracle bones in China during the Shang period (1480–1050 BC) – served to indicate the ruler's special status, and thus enhanced his power and control.

In many (though not all) societies, writing soon came to be used for other purposes as well. For example, in early Mesopotamia (see p. 364), contracts and other business documents, letters, laws, religious rituals and even literature were written down. By contrast, in Central America (see p. 390) writing was for a long time restricted to inscriptions on royal monuments. In societies where writing was intended for the use of a small ruling group, very few people actually knew how to read and write. Often special scribes were the only ones with the ability to read and write, and not even kings themselves were literate. This is not altogether surprising since many scripts were very difficult to learn. In Mesopotamia, for example, temples ran special schools that trained boys (but only rarely girls) to be scribes.

Chinese and Japanese Writing

Chinese script – reckoned to be more than 4000 years old – is the oldest script still in use today; it consists of *logograms* (signs for words) and syllabic signs. Types of Chinese script sign include picture signs (as in 1 below), symbolic pictures (as in 2), and symbolic compounds (as in 3).

	Sign	Meaning	Explanation
1.	木	tree	branches above and roots beneath
2.	言	to speak, word	mouth with breath coming out
3.	炎	very hot	two fires

The Chinese writing system appeared in Japan in the 5th century AD, Chinese word-signs being taken over by the Japanese and read with Japanese rather than Chinese values. Some Chinese word-signs were given phonetic values and used as syllabic signs to express the grammatical determinatives of the Japanese language. Despite the development of a stable system of syllabic signs, the Japanese continue to make extensive use of Chinese logograms in their writing and printing today.

Logographic scripts

According to the way they work, writing systems can be classified as *logographic, syllabic* or *alphabetic*. Sometimes, particular writing systems use more than one of these principles simultaneously. Ancient Egyptian, for instance, used all three at once.

In *logographic* writing systems each symbol stands for a whole word. In many such systems *grammatical determinatives* (special symbols indicating changes in meaning or grammar such as compound or plural forms of words) are added to the basic signs. Below are the additions that would be made to the basic sign for 'man' in Sumerian – the oldest known script – used in southern Mesopotamia from about 3100 BC.

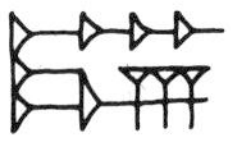 LU =man

 LU.MESH =men (with special sign for the plural form)

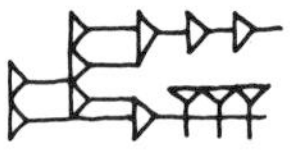 LUGAL =king (literally, 'great man')

While logographic writing systems were principally used by ancient civilizations, some logographic systems are still used by modern languages, most notably Chinese.

The most obvious difficulty with logographic writing systems is that an enormous number of symbols is necessary to express every word in a language. The Chinese script consists of about 50 000 characters, though not all are in regular use. It is hardly surprising that in imperial China few people were literate. Even in the modern period, it took several decades to develop a Chinese typewriter.

Syllabic scripts

Syllabic writing systems use symbols to express syllables. Many early writing systems were syllabic: Babylonian and Assyrian cuneiform in the ancient Near East, two scripts of pre-Classical Greece (known as Linear A and B), Japanese, and the ancient Mayan script of Central America.

Babylonian cuneiform is a good example of the use and diffusion of a syllabic script. It was originally derived from logographic Sumerian writing. Both scripts were written by pressing wedge-shaped marks onto wet clay tablets. Words were composed by stringing syllabic signs together. Shown below is the composition of the words for 'father' and 'brother' in Akkadian, the language of ancient Babylonia.

 a-bu (abu) = father

 a-hu (ahu) = brother

The syllabic cuneiform script had a long life in the ancient Near East, being in use between c. 3100 BC and c. 100 BC. As well as Akkadian, it was also used to write other, unrelated languages such as Hittite (spoken in central Turkey; see p. 603) and Elamite (spoken in southeastern Iran). Similarly, while Japanese is largely a syllabic writing system, the symbols it uses are derived from Chinese logographic characters (see box).

Although syllabic writing systems are less cumbersome than logographic ones, they remain difficult and were generally used only by professional scribes. Babylonian cuneiform has about 600 symbols, but many of these are used for several different syllabic values. For example, the symbol that usually represented the syllable 'pa' could sometimes also stand for the syllables 'ba', 'had', 'hat', 'sak', 'shag' or 'hats', depending on the context.

Alphabetic scripts

Most modern languages use *alphabetic* writing systems, in which each symbol stands for a basic sound. English and most modern European languages are written in Roman-derived alphabets. The great advantage of alphabetic systems is that many fewer symbols need to be learned than in logographic or syllabic writing systems, since most alphabets have fewer than 30 characters.

Ironically, the invention of the first alphabet may have been inspired by ancient Egyptian script, one of the most complicated writing systems ever devised. Egyptian *hieroglyphics* used logographic, syllabic and alphabetic symbols in combination. By the middle of the second millennium BC communities dwelling in the Sinai peninsula realized that all the sounds of their West Semitic tongue (related to Hebrew) could be expressed by a small number of alphabetic symbols. (They were perhaps derived from the alphabetic signs in Egyptian hieroglyphics; see box.) To this day, rough rock-cut inscriptions in the Sinai Desert bear witness to their innovation, which was to lead to the creation of the familiar alphabetic writing systems of the present.

By 1150 BC alphabetic writing systems derived from the original Sinai script must have been widespread in the Levant (modern Israel, Jordan, Lebanon and Syria). However, because alphabetic writing was largely done on perishable materials, such as parchment (dried and processed sheepskins) or papyrus (an early form of paper used in and imported from Egypt), very little original material survives. Although papyrus has been preserved in Egypt because of the dry, bacteria-free conditions in the desert, it has rotted away in the wetter conditions of the Levant.

Early examples of alphabetic writing dating from between 1450 and 1150 BC have been found on the site of the ancient Canaanite city of Ugarit (modern Ras Shamra in Syria). In order to write in Ugaritic (a West Semitic language related to Hebrew) a writing system was developed here consisting of 30 cuneiform symbols. Documents in Ugaritic script were written on clay tablets, which last almost forever once baked. The development of this script suggests that the inhabitants of Ugarit, a cosmopolitan port town, were also more familiar with the more common tradition of Semitic alphabetic writing on perishable materials.

A much later and very rare example of the survival of original Semitic parchments is the *Dead Sea Scrolls*. This collection of enigmatic religious texts in Aramaic and Hebrew dating from between 100 BC and 68 AD was found in jars in a desert cave in Israel between 1947 and 1956. After 1200 BC the development of alphabets of the Levant used for Semitic languages such as Phoenician, Hebrew and Aramaic becomes slightly easier to trace since there are a few inscriptions carved in stone.

The Semitic use of alphabetic scripts (including Hebrew, Arabic, Phoenician and Aramaic) differs from the modern European use of alphabetic writing in two notable ways. Firstly, the normal direction of writing in Semitic scripts was right to left (as is still the case in Hebrew and Arabic), rather than left to right. Secondly, the vowel sounds and diphthongs of the languages that use Semitic scripts (a, e, i, o, u, ou, ai, oo, etc.) are not written, and only the consonants (b, k, d, f, g, etc.) are recorded.

The writing of vowel sounds seems to have been an accident, rather than a brilliant invention. Greeks became acquainted with alphabets of the Levant when they came into regular contact with the Phoenicians and other Levantine peoples, probably some time between 950 and 800 BC, when both Greeks and Phoenicians established trading posts all over the Mediterranean. Some letters that represent consonants in Semitic were heard in Greek as vowels. For example, the Semitic glottal stop consonant (which is similar to the gulp heard in the colloquial English pronunciation of the word 'bottle' as 'bo'ul'), was heard by Greeks as the vowel sound 'a'. The Greeks also seem to have been responsible for changing the direction of writing. The earliest Greek inscriptions run both right to left and left to right (sometimes both in the same text), but after about 150 years, left to right became standard.

The Greeks also brought their alphabet to Italy, where it was adapted to writing Etruscan, Latin and other languages. The Roman Empire (see pp. 376–81) helped spread the alphabet over much of Western Europe, though the Greek alphabet continued to be used in the eastern Empire. By the time the Western Roman Empire fell in the 5th century AD it was a Christian Empire. Writing (in Latin) had by this time become essential to the administration of the Church. Both the Roman writing system and Christianity outlasted the Empire within which they had developed. During the early medieval period the Latin alphabet was adapted for writing local spoken languages such as Gothic, Old Irish, Frankish and Anglo-Saxon (see p. 603). Meanwhile, in the east, Greek Orthodox Christianity spread north to the Balkans and Russia and with it went the Greek alphabet. It is reputed that two Orthodox clerics, St Cyril and St Methodius, adapted the Greek alphabet to write Slavonic languages. Hence the alphabet used today in Russia, Bulgaria and some other parts of Eastern Europe is called *Cyrillic*, after St Cyril. Thus the Semitic, Greek, and Roman alphabets were the basis of most of the alphabets now used in modern Europe, the Middle East and the Indian subcontinent. LF

THE DEVELOPMENT OF THE ROMAN ALPHABET

The modern Roman alphabet, as well as the other major alphabets in use today – Greek, Cyrillic, Hebrew and Arabic – developed from a script (North Semitic) that evolved on the Eastern shores of the Mediterranean during the second millennium BC. The table below traces the development of six modern Roman characters from their earliest hieroglyphic form.

It is generally believed that North Semitic script took over elements from ancient Egyptian hieroglyphic script in order to reproduce the consonant sounds of the North Semitic language. According to one theory, the name of the object indicated by the hieroglyphs was translated into the North Semitic language, and the Semitic word then provided the new alphabetic value of the sign. Thus the hieroglyph for house was translated into Semitic as *bet* and used as the letter for *b*.

Egyptian hieroglyphic	Proto-Sinaitic Script	North Semitic (Phoenician)	Hebrew	Greek (with local variations)	Cyrillic	Latin
(ox)		('alep)		(alpha)	A	A
(building, house)		(bet)		(beta)	Б	B
(head)		(resh)		(rho)	Р	R
		(shin [tooth])		(sigma)	C	S
(eye)		('ayin)		(omikron)	O	O
(fence)		(he)		(epsilon)	E	E

The Story of English

The English language is a rich mixture, both in its origins and in the variety of ways in which it is spoken in the world today. The origins of English lie in the *Germanic* group of languages – from which other modern languages such as German and Dutch are also descended – but its vocabulary includes a very large proportion of *Romance* words, which are derived from Latin and are related to modern languages such as French and Italian.

Britain's colonial past has ensured the extraordinary expansion in the use of English from being spoken only in a small island to becoming the most widely-used language in the world. As such, it is used worldwide for air-traffic control, and it is the most common language used in technical publications. It is also taught as the principal foreign language in many countries.

Old English

Before the 5th century AD, various *Celtic* languages were spoken in Britain. But the real ancestors of English began to develop in the 5th century, when the Celtic languages were displaced by successive invasions from the eastern coasts of the North Sea (see p. 396). These invaders spoke *Germanic* languages (Frisian, Saxon, Jutish). It is from these languages that *Old English* (the language of the Anglo-Saxons) developed. Although Old English is as different from Modern English as a foreign language, it provided the basis of modern English both in the way sentences are formed and in most of the short, non-abstract words that are used in ordi-

Sir James Murray, surrounded by quotation slips for the monumental *Oxford English Dictionary,* of which he was the original editor. After the first volume appeared in 1884, Murray estimated that the book would take a further 12 years to complete. It was eventually finished in 1928, some 50 years after Murray began work on it, and 13 years after his death. The dictionary contains 414 825 headwords and 1 827 306 illustrative quotations.

nary speech. The Celtic languages did survive in the west and north, however, developing into Welsh and Gaelic. In England, Celtic languages only survive in a few place names (especially rivers), such as Avon.

The most obvious difference between Old English (OE) and any later form of the language is that the function of words in a sentence was indicated not by the order in which they appeared, but by *inflections* – endings that change the form of words (see p. 608). Thus 'a dog bites the man' could take any of the forms: *hund thone guman biteth, thone guman biteth hund, hund biteth thone guman.* 'A man bites the dog', on the other hand, might be *thone hund guma biteth.* Furthermore, as in many modern languages, all nouns had *grammatical gender* – masculine, feminine or neuter – and adjectives changed their form to agree with the gender of nouns. OE 'wif-mann' ('woman'), for example, was in fact a masculine noun. OE (like Modern German) was thus a richly inflected language and the history of English is in part the history of the gradual loss of this inflectional system. Some of it remains, however, most notably in our present-day pronouns (e.g. *he, him, his*).

The 7th-century Christian missions to Britain brought learning and literacy. At first this was entirely Latin (the words 'bishop', 'monk' and 'church' derive from Latin borrowings into OE), but an OE written literature did emerge, at first in the northeast and later, and most notably, in the West Saxon kingdom of Alfred the Great, who reigned AD 871–899. From the late 8th to the 10th century, the vocabulary was influenced by further invaders from Scandinavia – the Vikings (see p. 397) – whose *Norse* tongue gave us several words, including 'happy', 'husband', 'wrong' and the pronoun 'they'. Norse also left its mark in place-names, for example *beck* ('stream') in 'Troutbeck' and *fell* ('hill') in 'Scafell'.

Middle English

The Norman Conquest in 1066 (see p. 397) not only changed the government of England – it also changed the way in which the English language developed.

English now became the language of a conquered people and ceased to be the 'national language'; a Romance language – Norman French – was the language of the court, and a Normanized Latin the language of government, learning and the Church. The social division between French and English speakers can be seen in the contrast between the words *pig, sheep, cow* (English words for beasts of the fields), and *pork, mutton, beef* (French words for meat on the table).

Nevertheless, literature was still written in English, with dialect forms in different parts of the country. For three hundred years after the Conquest, English and French slowly merged as the separation between Norman and Saxon became less rigid. By the end of the 14th century,

BIBLE TRANSLATIONS

The following translations of Matthew Chapter 6 verses 25–6 illustrate the development of English.

Old English (10th century)
Fortham ic secge eow, thæt ge ne sin ymbhydige eowre sawle, hwæt ge eton; ne eowrum lichaman, mid hwam ge syn ymbscrydde. Hu nys seo sawl selre thonne mete, and eower lichama betera thonne thæt reaf? Behealda heofonan fuglas, fortham the hig ne sawa ne hig ne ripath, ne hig ne gadriath on berne; and eower heofonlica fæder hig fet. Hu ne synt ge selran thonne hig?

John Wycliffe, or one of his circle (c. 1390)
Therfore Y say to you, that ye ben nat besie to youre lijf, what ye shulen ete; othir to youre body, with what ye shuln be clothid. Where youre lijf is nat more than mete, and the body more than clothe? Beholde ye the fleeyinge foulis of the eir, for thei sowen nat, ne repyn, neither gadren in to bernys; and youre fadir of heuen fedith hem. Wher ye be nat more worthi than thei?

William Tyndale (1525)
Therefore I saye vnto you, be not carefull for youre lyfe, what ye shall eate, or what ye shall dryncke, nor yet for youre boddy, what rayment ye shall weare. Ys not the lyfe more worth then meate? and the boddy more off value then rayment? Beholde the foules of the aier: for they sowe not, neder reepe, nor yet cary into the barnes, and yett youre hevenly father feedeth them. Are ye not better then they?

Authorized or King James Version (1611)
Therefore I say vnto you, Take no thought for your life, what yee shall eate, or what ye shall drinke, nor yet for your body, what ye shall put on: Is not the life more then meate? and the body then raiment? Behold the foules of the aire: for they sow not, neither do they reape, nor gather into barnes, yet your heauenly father feedeth them. Are yee not much better then they?

New English Bible (1961)
Therefore I bid you put away anxious thoughts about food and drink to keep you alive, and clothes to cover your body. Surely life is more than food, the body more than clothes. Look at the birds of the air; they do not sow and reap and store in barns, yet your heavenly Father feeds them. You are worth more than the birds!

English was being used for official purposes; pleadings in law courts were first made in English in 1362. By 1400 a language had developed that, despite its many dialect variations, was recognizably the beginnings of the English we know today. The greatest writer in Middle English was the poet Geoffrey Chaucer (?1345–1400), whose *Canterbury Tales* show the range and power of expression of the emergent language (see p. 620).

This language was different in two ways from Old English. Its vocabulary no longer came from a single source but showed an inextricable mixture of Germanic and Romance words. Often the more basic word today is Germanic and the derived word Romance; we take our *teeth* (Germanic) to a *dentist* (Romance) and things connected with the *moon* (Germanic) are *lunar* (Romance). The other important difference relates to the simplification of the inflectional system. Grammatical gender was entirely lost in Middle English (and so adjectives ceased to 'agree' with nouns) and the inflectional endings of OE were already disappearing, with word order being used to signal meaning as in present-day English.

The Renaissance

By 1500 English was not very far removed from the language we use today. With the revival of classical learning known as the Renaissance (see p. 406), it was a common view, which endured well into the 17th century, that Latin was the only suitable language for serious writing. English, however, was itself influenced, both in its vocabulary and in the sentence structure of scholarly style, by the classical models of Latin and Greek. This, combined with the establishment of a strong central government, led to English being accepted once again as the national language for all public purposes. Besides, as the poetry and plays of the Tudor period (notably the works of Shakespeare) had clearly shown, the language was well established as capable of literary as well as popular use (see pp. 622–3).

Shakespeare's works show the language in transition. The form 'thou' and the inflection '–est' as in 'thou knowest' ('you know') were still used in speaking to one person regarded as an intimate or an inferior, though the usage was not consistent. As regards the formation of questions: in *Macbeth*, Lennox asks 'Goes the king today?' where we would use the verb 'do' as in 'Does the king go today?', though both forms were available, as shown by Polonius's question in *Hamlet* 'What do you read, my lord?' Notice also that we would say 'What are you reading?' The present-day distinction between 'I read' (simple present tense) and 'I am reading' was only just emerging at this stage.

The introduction of printing into England by William Caxton in the 15th century (see p. 322) brought more books in English, and printers began to regularize spelling and punctuation. Although regional dialects continued to be spoken, the idea of a standard form of written English was now accepted. The establishment of this standard and the status of English, as against Latin, was strengthened by the writings of the Reformation (see p. 408), notably the *Book of Common Prayer* (1549 and 1552; see illustration) and the *Authorized* or *King James* translation of the Bible (1611).

Modern English

From the late 17th century, English usage became more regular and consistent. The idea of an Academy similar to the one in France (see p. 626) was unpopular, but individual scholars and writers tried to preserve what they regarded as the 'purity' of their native language. Standards of spelling and meaning were supported by dictionaries, the most famous being that of Samuel Johnson in 1755 (see p. 631). Grammarians made recommendations for correct English usage, based on

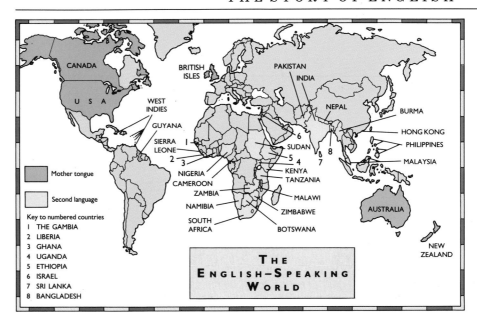

THE
ENGLISH-SPEAKING
WORLD

Mother tongue

Second language

Key to numbered countries
1 THE GAMBIA
2 LIBERIA
3 GHANA
4 UGANDA
5 ETHIOPIA
6 ISRAEL
7 SRI LANKA
8 BANGLADESH

Latin and regarded as a prescriptive set of rules for all to follow.

The grammar of English did not greatly change after the middle of the 17th century. The third-person singular of the present tense of the verb ended in *-s* instead of *-eth*, and the singular pronoun *thou* disappeared with the universal use of *you*. The main development over the last three centuries has been the growth of vocabulary. Some words have become obsolete or changed their meanings (for example 'nice' had a range of meanings it no longer has, and 'quick' meant alive), but many more have been introduced.

In the late 19th century new discoveries, inventions and ideas brought further expansion of vocabulary. This coincided with another great literary period marked by the acceptance of the novel as a serious literary medium (see pp. 623–3 and 636–7), as well as poetry, memoirs, biographies and political writing. Academic study of language principles brought better understanding of the history and nature of English. A notable contribution was the *Oxford English Dictionary*, begun by James Murray (1837–1915; see illustration) in 1879.

The 20th century has witnessed continuing growth. Technical advances have brought still more new words as well as adapting old ones. A word like *computer* is introduced and the word *screen* takes on a special meaning in connection with it. There have been few changes in grammar, but a tendency to drop some forms; the inflected form *whom* is seldom heard in speech today. A more significant change is the use of *they* and *them* in connection with singular common-gender words like *person* and *student* instead of the masculine form.

English in the world

The language of Shakespeare was the language of some 5 million people, the population of Britain in the late 16th century. Since that time English has spread throughout the world, beginning with the colonies in North America (see p. 422). The speech of the early settlers developed into American English, with some differences in vocabulary, grammar and spelling. As the British Empire expanded during the 18th and 19th centuries (see pp. 416 and 432), English became the language of countries such as Canada and Australia, occupied mainly by people of British origin. It was also the official language in India, many parts of Africa and elsewhere. When these countries gained independence, they usually kept English for use in international communication and between speakers with different first languages. These speakers, like those in the USA, have adapted English for their own purposes, thereby creating new varieties of the language that are legitimate in their own right.

The variety of English known as 'British English' is in fact now spoken by a minority among the English-speaking peoples of the world. It has been estimated that there are over 300 million people for whom English is their native language, perhaps 1000 million for whom it is a second national language, and an unknown number who have learned it as a foreign language. The teaching of English as a second or foreign language, both in Britain and abroad, has greatly expanded and is now academically and commercially important. The emergence of the predominantly English-speaking USA as a superpower undoubtedly played a role in the international importance of English.

British English was itself affected by world use. It has readily absorbed new words ever since the Norman Conquest and today has words from many languages: examples include *bungalow* from Hindi, *pyjamas* from Urdu, *gong* from Malay and *boomerang* from Australian aboriginal. The English that emerged about the end of the 14th century as a mixed and developing language has now a very extensive vocabulary. RCh

SEE ALSO

● THE WORLD'S LANGUAGES p. 602
● HOW LANGUAGE WORKS p. 606
● RENAISSANCE THEATRE p. 622
● THE NOVEL IN 19TH-CENTURY BRITAIN p. 636
● MODERN POETRY IN ENGLISH p. 646

How Language Works

Language is the most important and widespread of sign systems; all human technology, civilization and culture depend upon it. Its use demands the coordination of immensely complex physical and mental activities. Since these activities are normally subconscious, language is usually taken for granted and treated as a transparent medium through which we entertain ideas and acquire information about the world.

Ferdinand de Saussure, the Swiss linguist, in 1909. Saussure's idea of language as a system of signs, whose component parts can only be defined in relation to one another, not only provided the inspiration for modern 'structural' linguistics, but also exerted a significant influence on the social sciences and on literary criticism.

Language usually manifests itself in the form of writing (see pp. 604–5) or speech, though not necessarily so. The sign languages used by the deaf are as complex as spoken languages. Speech develops before writing, both in societies and in individuals.

There are an estimated five thousand living languages (see p. 602). Making this calculation is hindered by the difficulty in distinguishing languages from dialects (see below); distinctions are often drawn for political reasons rather than linguistic ones.

Linguistics: the study of language

The academic study of language is known as *linguistics*. Its aim is to understand how language in general works. Following the ideas of the Swiss linguist **Ferdinand de Saussure** (1857–1913), often thought of as the father of the subject, it focuses on the linguistic system ('*la langue*') underlying people's linguistic behaviour ('*la parole*'). It aims to describe the system underlying the way people actually speak their own language – rather than telling them how they ought to speak it, or teaching them foreign languages. In other words, linguistics is *descriptive*, rather than *prescriptive*. Saussure was the first to suggest that *synchronic* linguistics, which is the study of languages as they are at a given point in time, could be independent of *diachronic* (historical) linguistics, which is the study of how languages have developed through the centuries (see p. 602).

At the centre of linguistics lies the study of *grammar*, which can be divided into phonetics, phonology, morphology, syntax, and semantics.

Sounds in language

Speech is a continuous stream of sound that the speaker's mind divides into units. The physical study of such sounds, and how they are produced in the vocal tract, is called *phonetics*. Linguists use a special *phonetic script* to represent speech sounds because there is seldom a one-to-one correspondence between speech sounds and the symbols of ordinary spelling *(graphemes)*. Think, for example, how 'ough' is pronounced in 'bought', 'bough', 'enough', 'through' and 'hiccough'.

By contrast with phonetics, which deals with the physical aspects of sound, *phonology* is concerned with the linguistic significance of sounds in a given language. Not all phonetic (physical) differences in sound are linguistically significant in a given language. In English the physical difference between [l] and [r] is significant and functional: it serves to distinguish words from one another (e.g. 'lip' and 'rip', 'light' and 'right'). 'l' and 'r' are thus different *phonemes* in English, and the difference between them is described as a *phonemic* difference. But in the Ewe language (spoken in Ghana), the distinction is not phonemic. In Ewe, no two words are distinguished from each other simply by that difference in sound: indeed speakers of Ewe find it difficult to hear the difference. Similarly, English speakers tend not to notice any difference in the 'p' sounds in 'pot' and 'spot' or the 't' sound in 'team' and 'steam'. There is a difference, represented phonetically as [pʰ] and [tʰ] versus [p] and [t], but it is not phonemic in English, though it is phonemic in Thai, where the word pronounced [pʰa] means 'aunt' and the word pronounced [pa] means 'cliff'.

Noam Chomsky, the influential American linguist and political activist. In his writings he argued that the ease with which children master the grammar of their native language suggests an innate predisposition to acquire language. Chomsky, who sees his ideas about language as related to those of the rationalist philosophers of the 18th century, has sought to make linguistics an integral part of modern psychology and philosophy.

Words and sentences

Some sequences of phonemes or graphemes represent *morphemes*, which are the smallest units of meaning in the structure of words. (The study of word structure is called *morphology*.) For example, the sequence of graphemes *d + o + g* represents the English morpheme 'dog', while the sequence *o + l + s* represents no English morpheme. Morphemes may stand as words in their own right or combine with other morphemes to form complex words. For example, the word 'dogs' consists of two morphemes: 'dog' (a kind of animal) + '-s' (plural); and 'uninvited' divides into 'un-' and 'invited' which in turn divides into 'invite' and '-ed'. In some languages there is a tendency for morphemes to correspond to words; in others, words tend to contain more than one morpheme (see p. 602).

We are more conscious of using the words (the vocabulary) of our language than we are of using any other kind of linguistic unit. But words by themselves don't make a language. Languages include rules for combining words into larger grammatical units – for combining words into *phrases*, phrases into *clauses*, and clauses into full *sentences* (see below). These rules constitute the *syntax* of the language. The most influential present-day linguist, the American **Noam Chomsky** (1928–), emphasizes that it is these rules that allow speakers to create an infinity of new sentences from a finite stock of morphemes.

For example, 'away' can combine with 'ran' to form the phrase 'ran away'; 'poor' can combine with 'John' to form the phrase 'poor John'. In turn, those two phrases can combine to form the clause 'poor John ran away' (see diagram). A clause can act as a complete sentence as it stands or as a unit within the structure of another sentence as in 'She said poor John ran away'. Words are assigned to *word classes* according to the ways in which they can combine with other words and phrases: *noun, verb, adjective* and so on. These classes are sometimes called the *parts of speech*.

In English (as in French and Italian) the structure and meaning of sentences are indicated by the order of words (see p. 603). In other languages, such as Russian, Arabic, and Latin, the order of words is fairly free because structure and meaning are indicated by special morphemes at the end of words. These are called *inflections*. For example, the English sentence 'Brutus killed Caesar' translates into Latin as either 'Brutus Caesarem tuit' or 'Caesarem Brutus tuit', while 'Caesar killed Brutus' translates as either 'Caesar Brutum tuit' or 'Brutum Caesar tuit'.

Meaning

For many people the most obvious point about language is that it carries meaning. The study of literal linguistic meaning is known as *semantics*. The meaning of a sentence depends not only on the meanings of its words or morphemes; it depends also on how these are combined in the structure of sentences. Although the two English sentences 'the reluctant farmer followed the noisy cow' and 'the noisy reluctant cow followed the farmer' contain exactly the same words, they have different meanings, and 'farmer cow the noisy the followed reluctant' means nothing, even though each word is meaningful. Sentence meaning thus depends on how sentences are structured by the rules of language.

By contrast, and as Saussure pointed out, what meaning a morpheme has does not depend on rules, but is a matter of arbitrary convention within each language. The connection between the English morpheme 'tree' and any actual tree is no more natural or inevitable than the connection between the French morpheme 'arbre' and any actual tree.

Meaning depends on much more than morphemes and grammar, however. Speakers convey or communicate much more than the literal meanings of the sentences they utter. What is communicated depends on who the speaker is, who the hearer is, and on the context in which the sentence is used. The meaning of 'I am the victor of Waterloo' depends on whether it is said by Wellington (in which case it is true) or Napoleon (false). Compare also 'That was fun!' said of a day at the fair, as against a day spent in solitary confinement. 'It's cold in here!' will communicate that the hearer should do something about it if it is said by Lord X to his butler, but not if the butler says it to Lord X.

The study of these contextual aspects of meaning is called *pragmatics*. Since pragmatics is about meaning in context it is also concerned with how sentences are structured into coherent discourse (this aspect of pragmatics is sometimes called *discourse analysis*). Pragmatics also covers the contribution to communication made by how something is said: by stress and intonation (variations in pitch), voice quality, body movement and facial expression. In short, pragmatics is the study of the relationship between the linguistic system itself and people's use of that system in their linguistic behaviour.

Language acquisition

Every human being acquires proficiency in at least one language during infancy, without conscious effort or teaching. This is their *native language*. The extreme ease and speed of language acquisition led Chomsky to suggest that human beings are unique in that they are genetically programmed to develop a native language, and that certain very general principles governing all human languages are built into the human mind regardless of nationality or intelligence. The study of these principles is known as *universal grammar*. It is possible to switch languages or acquire new ones until roughly the age of puberty, but thereafter it is more difficult and requires conscious effort. In addition to the native language used at home, many people have to use a different language in the society in which they work. This is called their *second language* to distinguish it from any other *foreign language*. For example, English is used as a second language in Malaysia, as is French in Morocco.

Language variation

Speakers of a given language speak it in different ways. For example, English is a language, but it is spoken differently in Australia, California, Jamaica, Scotland, southern England and Northern Ireland. The most noticeable difference is that of accent, but there are also differences in syntax and vocabulary (see illustration). A variety of a language associated with geographical location (especially where there is variation in vocabulary) is called a *dialect* of that language. In fact, most linguists do not consider that there is a 'proper' form of a language, together with a cluster of 'non-standard' dialects, but rather that *all* forms of a language are in fact dialects. However, it may be that one dialect may be appropriate for use in a domestic or social situation, and another, more formal, dialect may be appropriate in a work situation or in writing. The whole subject of variation in language in general, its causes and effects, is called *sociolinguistics*.

Linguistics and cognitive science

The capacity of human beings to store and to structure information, to reason and solve problems, to engage in rational interaction with others and perceive the world in a purposeful way, is heavily dependent on their language capacity. Linguistics thus relates to psychology on the one hand and to the computer study of *artificial intelligence* (see p. 336) and *synthetic speech* on the other. The connections between these fields are the concern of *cognitive science*. Indeed, linguistics is coming now to be seen as a branch of this relatively new science.   NB-R

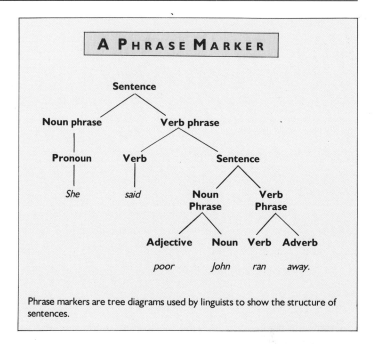

A PHRASE MARKER

Phrase markers are tree diagrams used by linguists to show the structure of sentences.

SEE ALSO

● THE WORLD'S LANGUAGES p. 602
● WRITING SYSTEMS p. 604
● THE STORY OF ENGLISH p. 606
● THE LANGUAGE OF SIGNS p. 610
● LITERARY THEORY AND LITERARY CRITICISM p. 650

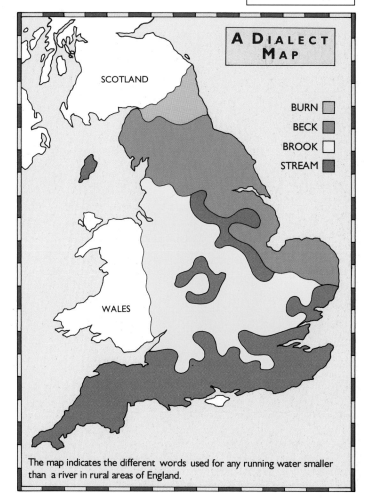

A DIALECT MAP

BURN
BECK
BROOK
STREAM

SCOTLAND

WALES

The map indicates the different words used for any running water smaller than a river in rural areas of England.

The Language of Signs

A sign is something that communicates a meaning. The English word 'cat' is a sign because it has meaning. But, although words are the most obvious signs, they are by no means the only things that communicate meanings. In the various senses of the word 'mean', a smile means friendship, a top hat means formality, and smoke means fire. Languages are made up of signs in the form of words. But if we allow that a language is any way of communicating meaning, then there are other kinds of 'language', with other kinds of signs. A beefburger and a beefsteak are more or less the same object (although they are prepared differently). But they 'say' very different things; they have different associations for us.

Linguistic signs are the most obvious because they have no function in life except as signs. The things that serve as signs in the 'language' of clothes or food have other functions, however. The language of clothing contains signs like 'blue jeans', 'bowler hat', and 'pink socks'; someone wearing one of these items is – consciously or not – sending signals telling us something about themselves. And just as words combine into sentences, so items of clothing combine into outfits. An outfit such as 't-shirt, jeans, sneakers' is a sort of sentence in the language of clothing. Just as particular combinations of words mean particular things, so particular combinations of clothes mean particular things: wearing pink socks with a bowler hat is a 'fashion statement' – a sentence in the language of clothes with a particular meaning. What meaning it is depends on context: a bowler hat sends one signal in the financial world and another at a student party; braces with a city suit mean something different from braces with jeans and 'Dr. Martens' boots. Wearing swimwear at work would send signals different from those it would send on the beach.

The Swiss linguist Ferdinand de Saussure (see pp. 608–9 and 650–1) showed that linguistics looks at a particular kind of sign – the word, and its combinations. He correctly predicted that linguistics would influence the more general science of *semiotics* or *semiology*, which studies all signs and every kind of meaning.

Kinds of meaning

While it is correct to say that a sign means something, it must be remembered that there are different relations between signs and their meanings. Smoke means fire, but not in the same way that the word 'fire' means fire. The American philosopher **C.S. Peirce** (1839–1914) suggested that there were three different kinds of sign:

1. Smoke means a fire because it is caused by, and thereby indicates, fire; Peirce called smoke an *index* of the fire.
2. A photograph or painting of a fire means the fire because it imitates, or represents it; Peirce called the picture an *icon* of the fire.
3. The word 'fire' means fire for no other reason than because this is the convention people use when they use the English language (see p. 608). Speakers of the Fon language follow the different convention that the word 'zò' means fire. Peirce called the word a *symbol* of the fire.

Signs are interesting because they are invented by a culture as tools for communication between people within that culture. Examining them tells us a lot about the workings of the culture, and what people in it consider to be valuable and important. For example, decisions about the shape and materials of a building are in part decisions about signs. A state-owned block of flats might express the value 'equality and uniformity among the masses'; a skyscraper might express the value 'corporate aspiration and achievement'; marble columns and floors might express the value 'long-established and respected authority'. Symbols are particularly interesting because they are connected to what they mean only by convention. This connection can be quite loose, with the result that symbols can have vague or wide-ranging or complicated meanings.

The world of codes

Because the word 'language' has so many meanings, semiologists use the more specific word '*code*' instead. A code is a system of signs, each one with a meaning. The three colours of traffic lights (red for stop, amber for caution, green for go) are an example of a well-known and very fixed code; but there is also a code of clothing, less fixed in its meanings, but still meaningful. Just as you can learn the English language, so you can learn any code. Semiologists argue that we learn many codes without realizing it, and that we are constantly being spoken to – by the things we see as well as the things we hear – in the many codes that surround us.

This idea is part of the basis of structuralism (see p. 651). Structuralism is a theory that was originally developed in anthropology by **Claude Levi-Strauss** (1908–), who was influenced by the linguistics of Saussure. It was taken further by the French structuralist critic **Roland Barthes** (1915–80; see pp. 650–1), who developed a theory of the structures (including codes) that hold a culture together, involving signs from fields as varied as wrestling, toys, and Hollywood cinema. Barthes was responsible for identifying clothing as a code and carried

SEE ALSO

● HOW LANGUAGE WORKS
  p. 608
● LITERARY THEORY AND
  LITERARY CRITICISM p. 650

Contrasting meanings are communicated by a 1950s Oldsmobile and a Citroën 2 CV. The fins and chromium-plated gleam of the American car suggest that the vehicle is as fast as a spaceship. The unspectacular, primitive shape of the French car – largely unchanged since it first appeared in 1949 – bespeaks frugality and lack of pretension, qualities that have endeared it to the mainly young, anti-nuclear, anti-macho, environmentally concerned middle-class professionals who drive it today.

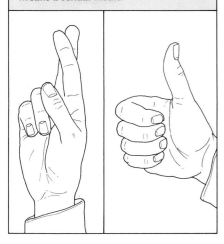

out a semiological analysis of fashion. Structuralists have tried to show that the same codes exist in different cultures. Levi-Strauss tried to show that raw food, cooked food, and rotten food are three signs that are found, sometimes concealed, in many different cultures, and that provide a pattern for the way people think about food (and even about other things in the culture). For example, different makes of car send different signals and project different images (see illustration). As advertisers recognize, people tend not to choose a make of car on the basis of how efficiently it will transport them, but on the basis of what image of themselves they want to project to the world.

Semiology – the radical science

Semiology has been at the centre of many controversies. Semiologists themselves do not always agree about basic issues. Other controversies come from the challenge made by semiology to the assumptions of other disciplines. Semiology looks at works of literature, music and art, for example, as systems of meaning to be examined and experimented with rather than as works of creative genius to be valued. When Barthes used the same science to study both fashion and the plays of the 17th-century dramatist Jean Racine (see p. 626), it was interpreted as an attack on the literary establishment. In this way semiology led to lasting disagreements about the nature of literature and the arts.

Semiology is radical in another way. Semiologists translate the messages that are constantly being transmitted in a culture; they are like detectives following up clues and catching up with the signs that speak to us without our realizing it. Some people feel that the very act of examining the sub-conscious messages that surround us is subversive or inappropriate. But understanding signs is important as a skill – for example, for advertisers, who use semiology to create their messages, as well as for the public, who must learn how to resist (if they choose) the advertiser's hidden meanings.

What are signs for?

Food gives us nourishment. But food can also be pleasant to eat – it gives us pleasure. In the same way, a sign gives us information but it can also be 'pleasant to think'. This is because the sign is not exactly the same as its meaning. A sign has its own independent existence as well. In the code of music, a particular rhythm might be a sign meaning 'rock 'n' roll'. But at the same time it might have a pleasure in itself, simply as a rhythm. Because a sign is not the same as its meaning, it can develop new meanings in addition to the original one. These further meanings might combine. Because signs 'pick up' extra meaning in this way, people find that individual signs become associated for them with particular memories, and particular pleasures. As a species we seek out meaning and constantly consume information. Signs carry meaning and information in complex ways; this is why we need them. This is the basis of personal symbolism as well as personal style – a person's symbolic shaping of themselves for the 'readers' in the world outside; a hat might have a general meaning for their society, but might have personal associations just for its owner as well.

Semiology and the arts

Semiologists see the world as a gigantic crossword puzzle, a collection of signs and clues to be interpreted and made sense of. Individual human beings are born into this complex network of communicative possibilities and grow up using it. What people can say is partly shaped but also restricted by the cultural codes of the society that they are part of.

In an extension of this idea some semiologists proclaimed 'the death of the author'. They meant by this that the author of a book is like a machine that plugs into the codes of a culture and arranges and displays them in the form of a book. The meaning of the book comes from the codes rather than from the author, regardless of the latter's intentions.

Semiology has become a part of Western culture. Although it started as a way of viewing language and then as a way of reading texts, it now more generally invites us to 'read the world' as if it were a text. Inevitably, it has influenced how other arts are now received (or 'read'), including films (witness the book *How to Read a Film*, by James Monaco), photographs, paintings, and music. In fact, it has influenced writing itself. The most famous recent example of this is the novel *The Name of the Rose* (1981; see illustration), by the Italian semiologist **Umberto Eco** (1932–). This is about a medieval monk who tries to understand the signs around him in order to solve a multiple murder mystery in a monastery. The novel encourages us to think of the monk as a medieval semiologist; furthermore, it invites the reader himself or herself to be a semiologist of the novel itself, to investigate the novel in imitation of its hero's investigations. Eco is drawing our attention to the fact that all detective fiction can be seen as exercises in semiology on the part of both detective and reader.

Films have been particularly influenced by the ideas of semiology, notably Jean-Luc Godard's *Alphaville* (1965), Peter Greenaway's *The Draughtsman's Contract* (1982) and George Lucas's *Star Wars* (1977).   NFa

The Name of the Rose. Umberto Eco's best-selling novel – a medieval whodunnit and intellectual tour de force – has for its hero a monk who uses semiological methods to investigate a series of grisly and baffling murders in a monastery. Illustrated here is a scene from the 1986 film version.

The Making of Myths

Myths are one of the means by which human societies have attempted to interpret creative forces, natural phenomena and events beyond their control. They attempt to explain, for instance, how evil and death were brought into the world, or how time relates to eternity; they also describe events such as the beginning or the end of the world, or the exploits of cultural heroes. Myths offer insight into the human condition and are a source of inspiration or comfort when human beings are confronted with the apparently irreconcilable.

While scientific discovery may appear to have invalidated the literal truth of many myths, they still remain powerful emotional and spiritual models. For the historian and archaeologist myths also provide an illuminating record of religion, history, politics, racial migration and fusion.

In all of the main mythological traditions certain types of myth have a particular importance, principally those relating to the creation of man, and the creation of the universe (the latter being known as *cosmogonies*).

An Egyptian creation myth as depicted on a papyrus dating from 1000 BC. Nut, the sky goddess, arches herself over Geb, the Earth god, while Re, the Sun god, travels between them in his solar barge.

Gilgamesh, the legendary Sumerian king, fighting two lions. This impression is taken from a cylindrical seal found in the ancient city of Ur and dates from between 2500 and 2400 BC.

Mesopotamian myth

The myths of the ancient civilizations of Mesopotamia (see pp. 364–5), which date back to at least the 3rd millennium BC, are evidence of humanity's struggle to understand its relationship to the natural environment and to assert control over its unpredictable forces. In a land dominated by the capricious floods of the Tigris and Euphrates rivers, it is inevitable that the triumph of order over watery chaos should be a central theme. The myths were first recorded by the Sumerians and later appropriated by the Semitic peoples in southern Mesopotamia in the Old Akkadian period or the later Amorite period. They were to some extent taken over by the Assyrians in northern Mesopotamia from 1200 BC until the fall of their empire in 612 BC (see p. 365).

Mesopotamian mythology includes interpretations of the cosmic forces that shaped creation and legends of heroic human journeys and epic conflicts such as the *Epic of Gilgamesh* (see below). There are also myths of city gods that reflect the political intrigues of the automonous city-states of the region.

Each year ritual and myth were re-enacted at the Babylonian New Year festival when order was threatened by the spring floods. The myth from the liturgy of this festival was used on the fourth day of the eleven days of celebration. The opening verses of the myth describe the forces at work during creation. Long before the Earth or heaven had a name, Apsu, the sweet water, and Tiamat, the bitter water, joined forces to produce the tumultuous waves from which all life came. Their first creations were the gods Lakhmu and Lakhamu, but before they were fully grown they produced even stronger gods, Anshar and Kishar, the representatives of the celestial and terrestrial worlds. The inert forces of Apsu and Tiamat became increasingly resentful as the creation of energetic and effective gods continued from their original waters. The myth develops with an account of their conflict and culminates in the triumph of Marduk, champion of the heavenly court, who upholds order against the menace of primeval chaos. The battle for the maintenance of order over chaos is also reflected in Canaanite myths, most notably the *Baal Epic*, recorded on tablets found at the ancient city of Ugarit in Syria (see p. 460).

The version of the Akkadian *Epic of Gilgamesh* that has come down to us dates from the 1st millennium BC. It tells of how Gilgamesh, ruler of the southern Mesopotamian city of Uruk, defeats and then befriends the wild man Enkidu and rejects the advances of the love goddess Ishtar. After the death of Enkidu, Gilgamesh sets out to learn the secret of eternal life from his aged ancestor, Utnapishtim, who is, however, unable to help him. Gilgamesh hears of and finds a plant alleged to restore youth and vigour, only to see it eaten by a snake on his return journey.

The Old Testament

The creation story of the Jewish people – and the account subsequently adapted in the Christian Church – is found in the Book of Genesis, the first book of the Old Testament. Genesis uses images borrowed from Babylonian mythology, but moulds them to put across its own view of the relationship of God and man. Out of darkness and the void, God creates heaven and Earth, resting on the seventh day after six days of labour. God creates man (Adam) out of dust and breathes the breath of life into him. A woman (Eve) is created for Adam out of one of his ribs, and man and woman are placed in the garden of paradise (Eden). But Eve is persuaded by a guileful serpent to eat the forbidden fruit of the tree of knowledge, some of which she also gives to Adam to eat. God punishes Adam and Eve for their disobedience by driving them out of the idyllic garden into the world of pain and death. With the banishment from the garden, human history – the history of imperfect mankind – begins. The tale of Adam's son, Cain, who in killing his brother Abel commits the first murder, again emphasizes human imperfection and man's estrangement from God.

Myths of ancient Egypt

During the Old Kingdom (2575 BC–2134 BC) the powerful priesthoods in the three main theological centres of Egypt – Heliopolis, Memphis and Hermopolis – attempted to rationalize and centralize the many cults that existed during predynastic and early dynastic times (see p. 366). Each priesthood worked to assert the supremacy of its creator god and his control over the lesser gods and humans. Many myths came to be associated with the cosmic force of the Sun and its relation to the Earth and sky – the powerful natural phenomena that framed Egyptian life. During this period of religious rivalry the Heliopolitan cosmogony proved to be the most influential. It tells how Atum, who came to be completely identified with the Sun god Re, emerged from Nun, the primeval ocean. Re-Atum then generated Shu, the god of the air, and Tefnut, goddess of moisture. Together they produced Geb, the Earth god, and Nut, the sky goddess. Geb's children were the noncosmic deities, Osiris, Isis, Nepthys and Seth (see p. 461).

Besides the cosmogonies, other myths were born of local cults, special religious sites or of animals imbued with human or spiritual qualities. One of the most important mythological themes, however, was death and resurrection. The god Osiris came to be recognized as both the god of vegetation – the bringer of new life after the Nile floods had receded – and as the god of the dead, who welcomed the deceased to a new life in the Land of the Dead (see p. 460).

Osiris was believed to have been murdered and dismembered by his jealous brother, Seth. His body was then scattered across the land of Egypt, but the pieces were retrieved by his devoted wife, Isis. She restored Osiris by magic and conceived a child, Horus, by him. Horus eventually fought Seth to avenge his father's death. Their dispute was settled by a tribunal of gods who declared in favour of Horus. Osiris was then brought back to life and reinstated as king and judge of the dead (see p. 460).

Hindu myths of India

The various Hindu accounts of the creation differ substantially, but no two are mutually exclusive. The earliest account of creation is given in the *Rig Veda*, one of the ancient sacred texts of the Hindus. Hymns relate how Indra, the storm god, measured out the heavens and the Earth, while in others Varuna, guardian of the cosmic law, is said to have performed this task. Another hymn tells how the gods sacrificed a giant and as a result the Moon sprang from his mind, the Sun from his eye, Indra and Agni (the god of fire) from his mouth, the wind from his breath, the air from his navel, the sky from his body, and the Earth from his feet. The four castes (see p. 258) also rose from his mouth, arms, thighs and feet. They became respectively the teachers, soldiers, merchants, and workers.

Most Hindu creation myths acknowledge a primal male deity who formed creation from chaos, although one account contained in the ancient Sanskrit texts known as the *Upanishads* describes how the Universal Soul took the shape of a man who, realizing his sole existence,

declared 'This I am', thus producing the name 'I'. Feeling desire for another he divided himself in two to form male and female, but felt disunited and thus joined the two parts together as husband and wife. Together they produced mankind and then, assuming the form of pairs of animals, they produced all other creatures.

The two great Hindu epics, the *Ramayana* and the *Mahabharata* (see also p. 466), have traditionally been the most accessible and popular Hindu myths. They are regarded by many Hindus as a reflection of the moral and spiritual dilemmas and responsibilities of human existence. Both myths are peopled with characters who display neither perfect good nor absolute evil, and although they culminate in epic battles that result in the triumph of good

The Tower of Babel painted by Peter Bruegel the Elder in 1569. The story of the Tower of Babel, told in the Old Testament Book of Genesis, attempts to account for the existence of the diversity of different languages in the world. Noah's descendants in Babylon (all of whom spoke one language) tried to build a tower reaching to heaven. But God, to punish their presumption, disrupted the work by causing them to speak in different languages (thus losing the ability to speak intelligibly to one another). The tower of the myth was probably inspired by the terraced temple towers (*ziggurats*) of ancient Mesopotamia (see p. 463).

over evil, no being, whether god or man, can represent absolute good. The notion of good and evil arises out of the inability of the mortal mind to realize the oneness of the Supreme Being, the ultimate reality.   JO'B

GREEK MYTH

Greek accounts of creation tell how Uranus, the sky god, is born of Gaia, the Earth goddess. Uranus marries Gaia, who bears him giants, including the Titans, as children. At Gaia's instigation, Cronus, the last-born Titan, castrates Uranus for imprisoning her children within her body (an action which perhaps represents the separation of Heaven and Earth). Cronus now rules over his brothers and sisters, and fathers other gods by Rhea, his wife and sister. Cronus eats these gods as soon as they are born, with the exception of Zeus, who later overthrows his father and forces him to restore the children he has swallowed. Later, war breaks out between the younger gods – led by Zeus – and the older Titans, from which the younger faction emerges victorious. Zeus is elected king by the other gods, and reigns on the craggy heights of Mount

Olympus, accompanied by his wife Hera, whose cult was originally that of a mother goddess. Authority over the sky, sea and underworld was divided between Zeus, Poseidon and Hades, the sons of Cronus. The family of gods is further extended through marriages and birth, and many myths revolve around the responsibilities, jealousies, sorrows and deeds of this divine family.

Some of the most celebrated Greek myths centre on the exploits of Herakles (known to the Romans as Hercules), a son of Zeus by the mortal Alcmene. At birth Herakles strangles two snakes sent by the jealous Hera to kill him, and goes on to perform feats of superhuman strength and courage. His most famous feats are the Twelve Labours, which included the cleaning of the Augean Stables and the Descent to the

Underworld. Herakles later became revered as a god – particularly by the Romans.

Herakles' heroism is emulated by his friend Theseus, an Athenian hero noted for his slaying of the Cretan Minotaur and subsequent escape from the labyrinth with the help of Ariadne's thread, and the conquest (with Herakles) of the Amazons, a tribe of female warriors.

Greek mythology extends beyond the Olympian gods through a catalogue of other characters – notably Perseus and Jason – involved in heroic deeds and emotional struggles. Cults developed out of the myths of individual gods such as Dionysus, the god of wine, who was celebrated in orgiastic rites, and Orpheus, a poet and lyre-player.

SEE ALSO

- THE ANCIENT NEAR EAST p. 364
- ANCIENT EGYPT p. 366
- RELIGIONS OF THE ANCIENT NEAR EAST p. 460
- CLASSICAL LITERATURE p. 614

Classical Literature

Western literature begins with the literature of Greece and Rome, and the literatures of Europe have constantly imitated, adapted, reacted against and returned to this inescapable Classical inheritance. The 1500 years from Homer to the early Middle Ages saw the birth of almost all the major forms of prose and poetry, and the very concept of literature itself as a separate activity first made its appearance.

From this varied inheritance, the Renaissance (see pp. 622–5) fashioned an image of Classicism as a static entity whose values were order, unity and stability. But on closer inspection the literatures of Greece and Rome present a more varied and discordant scene.

Early Greek literature

The earliest extant documents in Greek are Mycenaean clay tablets of the second millennium BC written in the 'Linear B' script (see p. 605), but literature begins with two epics: the *Iliad* and the *Odyssey* of **Homer** (?8th century BC). These may not in fact be the work of one man; certainly a long tradition of oral poetry lay behind them. The *Iliad* describes the war waged against Troy by the Greeks to recover Helen, wife of Menelaus – Helen having been abducted by Paris, son of Priam, the king of Troy (see illustration). The *Iliad* focuses especially on the wrath of Achilles, the foremost Greek warrior, and its tragic consequences. The *Odyssey* tells of the wanderings of Odysseus (known to the Romans as Ulysses) as he returns from Troy to claim his wife and

Sappho, the Greek poetess of the 7th century BC, was the pioneer of the brief subjective love poem. Sappho's passionate lyrics were apparently written for a circle of admiring women and girls on the island of Lesbos, where she lived. This wall-painting from the Roman city of Pompeii dates from the 1st century AD.
(National Museum, Naples/Archiv für Kunst)

throne. Together these two poems established the form and themes of the epic genre for the West.

Homer's near-contemporary **Hesiod** (?8th–7th centuries BC) wrote the first didactic poetry in his *Works and Days* (an account of a farmer's life) and *Theogony* (an account of creation and the gods). More significant, however, is the first appearance of personal poetry in the works of the rumbustious soldier-poets **Archilochus** (mid-7th century BC) and **Alcaeus** (7th–6th centuries BC), and above all in the passionate love-songs of **Sappho** (born mid-7th century BC; see illustration), the first Western poetess.

The golden age of Athens

Philosophical and historical writing in the 6th century BC marks the beginning of Greek literary prose. Meanwhile **Pindar** (c. 520–445) and **Bacchylides** (6th–5th centuries BC), with their choral songs for victorious athletes, continued the themes of the lyric age. But in the 5th century BC an unparalleled explosion of literary innovation occurred, particularly in Athens, the centre of a newly created empire (see p. 371).

Tragedy is believed to have its beginnings in primitive rituals. However, it was in the plays of **Aeschylus** (c. 525–456 BC), most notably in his great trilogy the *Oresteia* (458 BC), that tragedy acquired the intense interest in human suffering and responsibility that has marked it ever

The Trojan Horse, depicted on the neck of a terracotta amphora of the 7th century BC. The story of the Trojan Horse is referred to in Homer's *Odyssey*. After the death of Achilles, the Greeks pretended to depart, but left behind them a wooden horse, which the Trojans, in spite of the warnings of their prophets, took into the city. While Troy slept, Greek warriors concealed inside the horse opened the gates to the Greek army, which proceeded to sack Troy. (Mykonos Museum/Archiv für Kunst)

since. The same issues are to be found in the plays of **Sophocles** (c. 497–405 BC) notably *Oedipus Rex* (c. 430 BC) and *Antigone* (441 BC), whose passionately intense heroes are brought into uncomfortable proximity with the everyday world of the audience. With **Euripides** (c. 485–406 BC) the genre took an intellectual turn, exploring the ambiguous power of language. But passion was not abandoned: there is no greater representation of the extremes of emotion than Euripides' *Medea* (431 BC), in which the heroine kills her own children.

Presented at the same time as the tragedies were the comedies of **Aristophanes** (c. 445–385 BC), riotously obscene yet politically engaged fantasies in which men ride to heaven on a dung-beetle (*Peace*; 421 BC) or women take over the city (*Lysistrata*; 411 BC). The story of the wars with Persia at the beginnings of the 5th century (see p. 370) was told by the 'father of history', **Herodotus** (c. 490–c. 425 BC), in a work that showed a sympathetic interest in the civilizations of the Middle East and Egypt. His younger contemporary **Thucydides** (c. 455–c. 399 BC) related the history of the later disastrous Peloponnesian War (see p. 371) in an intensely personal style that stretched and tortured the Greek language to express the tragic fall of Athenian imperial power.

The Hellenistic age

The 4th century BC was an age of prose. The greatest writers worked in genres often now excluded from the category of literature: **Plato** (c. 427–347 BC) and later **Aristotle** (384–322 BC) in philosophy (see p. 487); **Isocrates** (436–338 BC) and **Demosthenes** (384–322 BC) in oratory. But to the Greeks themselves the prose of Plato and Demosthenes ranked among their finest literary achievements, while it is to Aristotle in his *Poetics* that we owe many of the central concepts of literary theory (see p. 650).

The rise of Macedon and the end of traditional Greek freedom (see p. 371) caused yet another shift in literary fashion. The continuing vigour of literary activity in Athens is evident in the 'New Comedy' of dramatists such as **Menander** (342–c. 292 BC), whose witty but stylized humour of situation and intrigue lacks the satirical edge of Aristophanes. But the centre of balance moved to the kingdoms of the dynasts who succeeded Alexander the Great, above all to the court of the Ptolemies in the new city of Alexandria (see pp. 372–3).

The greatest figure of this 'Alexandrian' or 'Hellenistic' age was the scholar-poet **Callimachus** (c. 310–240 BC). For him, artistry in literature was all, and he railed against 'big books' and empty archaism. Also notable are the beginnings of pastoral poetry in the *Idylls* of **Theocritus** (3rd century BC), where for the first time in the Western tradition the figure of the herdsman came to symbolize the tensions between city and country, art and life.

Greece under the Romans

The 2nd century BC saw the growing power of Rome (see pp. 376–7) impinge

more and more on Greece, but this by no means ended the story of Greek literature. In the work of figures such as *Plutarch* (c. AD 46–120) – best known for his *Parallel Lives* of eminent Greeks and Romans (much used by Shakespeare) – it displayed an assured confidence in the continuity of Greek culture. Christianity was as easily assimilated, and the flowering of the new Eastern capital of Byzantium (Constantinople; see p. 381) has left us more works than survive from the rest of Greek history put together. Byzantine literature ended only with the sack of the city by the Turks in 1453 (see p. 395) – and by then the great works of Greek literature had once more begun to make their way to the West.

Early Roman literature

From its beginning Latin literature was heavily influenced by Greek. The first work of real independence was the *Annals* of *Ennius* (239–169 BC), a historical epic of which only fragments survive. Better preserved are the adaptations of Greek New Comedy by *Plautus* (c. 250–184 BC) and the North African *Terence* (c. 185–159 BC), in which the native Latin traditions of wit rejuvenate the bland Greek originals.

The golden age of Rome

It was in the middle years of the 1st century BC that Latin really began to rival Greek as a vehicle for literary creativity. Both *Lucretius* (98–c. 55 BC) with his didactic poem *On the Nature of Things* and *Catullus* (c. 84–c. 54 BC) with his short poems of love and hate showed that the pressures of following Greek tradition could be a positive rather than a negative force. The backdrop to their poems was the death of the Roman Republic in war and civil strife, a demise that Rome's greatest orator *Cicero* (106–43 BC) tried to

stop. When he failed, he returned to philosophy – although this did not stop Mark Antony demanding his head after Julius Caesar's murder in 44 BC.

The greatest period of Roman literature began, however, under the new emperor Augustus (see p. 378). Under the patronage of Augustus' minister Maecenas, *Virgil* (70–19 BC) wrote the exquisite *Eclogues* and *Georgics* and his national epic the *Aeneid* (29–19 BC), while the lyric poet *Horace* (65–8 BC) vied with Sappho and Alcaeus in his *Odes* and created new genres of colloquial poetry in his *Satires* and *Epistles*. At the same time two writers of elegiac love poetry – *Tibullus* (c. 55–19 BC) and *Propertius* (c. 50–after 16 BC) – celebrated their own erotic enslavement, rather than the new regime, in learned yet passionate poems.

Glory and decadence

Though writing under Augustus, Virgil and Horace in many ways represented the end of Republican poetry. The prolific *Ovid* (43 BC–AD 17) was the first real Imperial poet, and his clever burlesques of love elegy such as the *Art of Love* (c. 1 BC) show that the influence of Roman literature itself was now beginning to be felt as a burden and challenge. His great *Metamorphoses* (which recounts both Greek and Roman myths and legends) is both epic and anti-epic, a reply to Virgil but also the only way possible to continue the tradition.

As the empire became established, the past became more important. Already the Republican historian *Sallust* (86–35 BC) and the Augustan *Livy* (59 BC–AD 17) had used the history of Rome's past to make points about the present, but it was the cynical and sardonic *Tacitus* (c. AD 56–117) who brought this mode to perfection. Yet his style was a contemporary

one, characterized by a pointed 'silver' Latin (in contrast to the Latin of the 'golden age'). 'Silver' Latin had been developed a generation earlier by writers such as the philosopher and dramatist *Seneca* (AD 4–65), whose plays of violent rhetoric exerted a potent influence on Shakespeare (see pp. 622–3).

This creative tension between tradition and innovation was the main dynamic of the literature of the Empire. It revealed itself in a low-life comic novel, the *Satyricon* of *Petronius* (d. AD 65), in *The Golden Ass*, a romance by *Apuleius* (active AD 155), in the biting and often obscene miniatures of the epigrammatist *Martial* (c. AD 40–104), and in the hard-hitting verse satire of *Juvenal* (?AD 60–?140). More straightforward imitation, especially of Virgil, was not lacking; but the greatest writers were able to infuse a new spirit. An example of this is to be found in the civil war epic of *Lucan* (AD 39–65); in this bitter work the traditional gods are replaced with blind Fortune and relentless Fate.

Latin Literature lasted even longer than Greek: late antiquity could provide in *Claudian* (4th–5th centuries AD) and *Boethius* (c. AD 476–524) poets to equal Ovid and at times even Virgil, and the vast Latin literature of the Middle Ages and the Renaissance cannot even be touched upon here. When Greek was rediscovered, the enthusiasm for the new wonders that discovery revealed led at first to an underestimation of Latin on grounds that it was derivative. But the same charge can be levelled at the whole of Western culture. The distinctive contribution of Latin was precisely to articulate that sense of 'coming after', and to suggest strategies for dealing with it – strategies that even today we cannot avoid as we try to come to terms with the Classical inheritance. **DF**

A Greek theatre. The well-preserved amphitheatre at Epidaurus was built by Polycleitus in the 4th century BC. All large Greek theatres were open to the sky, the drama being acted out on a level circular space (the *orchestra*) while spectators looked on from the vast terraced auditorium.

SEE ALSO

● THE MAKING OF MYTHS p. 612
● THE LITERATURE OF ASIA p. 616
● RENAISSANCE LITERATURE pp. 622–5
● CLASSICISM IN LITERATURE p. 626
● LITERARY THEORY AND LITERARY CRITICISM p. 650

The Literature of Asia

The diverse cultures of the Middle East, China and Japan have produced bodies of writing which, while relatively unknown in the wider world, nonetheless offer a richness and scope equal to that of any of the world's great literary traditions. Literature written in Arabic owes much of its inspiration to the emergence of Islam in the 7th century AD. Persia – conquered by the Arabs shortly afterwards – possessed a literature more varied in its forms and content than that written in classical Arabic, and was to enrich the Arabic literary tradition with new genres such as the epic poem.

The Assemblies of al-Hariri, a collection of tales by the 11th-century Arab scholar Abu Muhammad al-Kasim al-Hariri, is one of the most popular works in Arabic. It relates – in a witty and refined style – the deceptions of a learned and eloquent confidence trickster. Shown here is a 13th-century illustration of one of the tales.

China's literary heritage dates back 3000 years, and is particularly distinguished by its poetry, which was generally sung to musical accompaniment. Chinese literature exerted a major influence on that of Japan, which, despite its briefer history, boasts high achievement in poetry, drama and the novel.

Arabic literature

Prior to the life of the Prophet Muhammad the literary tradition of Arabia was oral and mainly poetic. The three principal forms of poetry were the *qasida* (ode), eulogy, and *hija* (satire). At this time the spoken word carried such weight that even a more powerful army might flee before the *hija* of the enemy poet.

The first Arabic book was the Qur'an (Koran), considered by Muslims to be the word of God (see p. 478). Dating from the 7th century AD, it has remained until today the standard of correct Arabic style. Under the early caliphs the Muslim armies carried the Qur'an and with it the Arabic language into regions previously ruled by the Byzantine and Persian Empires (see p. 392).

The most common early secular prose was *adab* or 'polite literature' – courtesy books that took their inspiration from the Near East and India. Although at first applying to a professional code of polite behaviour, the term *adab* was soon used to describe literature in general.

In the early years of the Abbasid dynasty (AD 750–1258), poets turned away from the Bedouin traditions of the Arabs towards more classically Persian themes, often involving the praise of women and wine. One of the greatest of these poets was *Abu Nuwas* (c. AD 762–c. 813), whose verses broke new ground by sometimes concentrating entirely on the praise of wine. Later Abbasid poetry, however, was increasingly influenced by mysticism.

Some of the greatest Arabic writing is in the fields of history, biography and travel, but in terms of imaginative writing the 12th century onwards saw the emergence of popular prose epics extolling tribal and Islamic heroes, as well as Islamicized folk tales. The best known among the latter are found in the collection of stories entitled *The Thousand and One Nights*, which evolved in its present form under the Mamluk rulers (1250–1517) of Egypt. The narrative framework for the stories is provided by Scheherazade, who – married to a king in the habit of killing his wives the morning after their wedding night – cleverly saves her life by recounting a succession of diverting tales including 'Sindbad the Sailor' and 'Ali Baba and the Forty Thieves'.

In modern Arabic literature the novel and drama, both heavily influenced from the West, became the new medium of expression at the expense of poetry. Particularly notable is the work of the Egyptian novelist *Najib Mahfuz* (1911–), who won the Nobel prize for literature in 1988. The Swedish Academy ranked his descriptions of Cairo alongside Dickens's London and Zola's Paris (see pp. 635 and 636).

Persian literature

The Arab conquest of Persia (modern Iran) between AD 635 and 652 led to the conversion of most of its people to Islam. Arabic, the language of the Qur'an, quickly became the language both of government and religious instruction, and also the main language of literature, although Arabic poets of Persian origin, such as Abu Nuwas (see above), used Arabic to revive Persian tradition.

Much surviving medieval Persian literature was written far from the centres of Arabic culture, under the patronage of rulers such as the Samanids (AD 819–1005). The Samanid era is considered an age of decorum and good taste. After the Samanids there evolved the Persian *qasida* and the *masnavi* (verse epic in rhyming couplets), of which the *Shah-Name* ('Book of Kings') of *Firdausi* (933–1031) is the great example. The *Shah-Name*, a 50 000-verse narration of the legendary history of Persia from the creation to the end of the Samanid era, is a national epic that has above all served to keep the Persian identity distinct from that of other Muslim peoples.

The period from the beginning of the Seljuks in 1038 until the Mongol invasion of 1220 was the most creative and productive phase in the history of Persian literature. It saw both the spread of Persian culture into India and Anatolia (modern Turkey) and the rise of the Sufi fraternities (see p. 478). One of the most famous of the Sufi poets is *Omar Khayyám* (?1048–?1122), whose *Rubaiyat* eulogized in four-line verses (*ruba'is*) women and wine as apparent symbols of mystical union with God. The *Rubaiyat* has become well known in the West through its translation by the Victorian poet Edward Fitzgerald (1809–83).

Some of the most famous classical poets, such as *Rumi* (d. 1273), *Sa'di* (d. 1294) and *Hafiz* (1319–89), wrote during the period following the ferocious Mongol invasion, although their ouput is considered as the fulfilment of the flourishing literary tradition born under the Seljuks. In the *Gulistan* and the *Bustan*, Sa'di used many stories to expound Sufi wisdom, while the *Diwan* of Hafiz contains erotic poems with mystical interpretations.

Western influence began to be felt in the 19th century, since when many writers have been concerned with social and political issues. Since the Islamic revolution of 1979 in Iran, literature concerned with martyrdom and pan-Islamic themes has become dominant.

Chinese literature

China's earliest writings are ritualistic inscriptions dating from the Shang dynasty (1480–1050 BC). The first of the five early Confucian classics was the *Yijing (I Ching)* or *Book of Changes*, a book of divination whose first part dates from early Zhou times (1122 BC–256 BC). The other four classics are the *Book of Documents* (c. 600 BC), the *Book of Odes* (also referred to as the *Book of Songs*), the *Ritual Canons*, and the *Spring and Autumn Annals*. Zhou tradition maintains that Kongfuzi (Confucius; see p. 470) himself edited the Annals. Commentaries on the Confucian classical texts were produced continuously from Han times, and by the Song dynasty the Confucian classics numbered 13, including several philosophical texts.

Early poetry, contained in the *Book of Songs* or *Shijing*, is anonymous and dates from 850 to 600 BC. The first identifiable poet was *Qu Yuan* (4th–3rd century BC), whose poetry – allegorical in form and influenced by shamanism (see p. 464) – was collected in an anthology of local poets called *Chuci* or *Songs of the South*. The *Shijing* and the *Chuci* together established the two principal strains of poetic tradition for the following centuries. During the Han period (202 BC–AD 220) a poetic form (*gushi* or 'ancient verse') evolved which, along with the *lüshi* of the Tang period (see below), became one of the main verse styles of traditional Chinese literature. Contemporary with *gushi* verse were the ballads collected by the Han music bureau (the *Yuefu*). In the 3rd century AD poetry became more philosophical and intellectual, influenced by Daoism (Taoism; see p. 470).

The Tang dynasty (AD 618–907) was the golden age of Chinese poetry, producing two of China's greatest poets: **Du Fu** (Tu Fu; 712–770) and **Li Bai** (Li Po; 701–762). Much of Du Fu's verse looks back wistfully at the short period he spent at the imperial court and treats themes of social injustice and suffering caused by civil strife. The poetry of Li Bai, a Daoist, wine-lover and bohemian, reveals an exciting, mercurial personality. Tang poetry is remarkable for the emergence of new forms of *lüshi* ('regulated verse'), which laid down strict rules regarding tone and numbers of lines and syllables. A skill in this form of poetry became an indispensable social and bureaucratic prerequisite for aspiring gentlemen.

The poetry of the Song dynasty (960–1279) was dominated by the *ci* genre – a form with strict tonal patterns and rhyme schemes written in fixed numbers of lines and words – which had originally emerged in the Tang period. The Yuan dynasty (1271–1368) saw the emergence of the *sanqu* ('non-dramatic songs') – a new poetic melody with tonal patterns modelled on tunes drawn from folk music – which remained popular throughout the Ming (1368–1644) and Qing (1644–1911) dynasties as well.

While a vast array of popular theatrical forms had existed from Song times onwards, it was the Yuan period that saw the full flowering of Chinese dramatic literature. A new type of play developed – typified by the love story *The Western Chamber* by **Wang Shifu** (c. 1250–?1337) – usually consisting of four acts and consisting of songs and dialogues in language approximating to that spoken at the time. Poetic dramas containing up to 40 scene changes and a number of different plots – the *chuanqi* ('tales of mystery') – became popular during the Ming period. It was not until the end of the 18th century that the popular Peking opera emerged as a distinctive theatrical form.

From the 12th century AD storytelling – a profession initially organized into guilds – became extremely popular. In time oral literature sometimes won more respect than written texts. Popular anecdotal literature, short stories and religious ballads developed after the Han period. The novel emerged in the 14th century with episodic accounts of heroic adventures such as *The Water Margin*, attributed to

Luo Guan-zhong (active 14th century). During the 18th century the novel became more refined: *The Dream of the Red Chamber* by **Cao Xueqin** (1715–63), for example, is a novel of manners charting the downfall of a great Chinese family.

Traditional themes and styles were not challenged until the early decades of the 20th century, and at first the strongest influence on fiction was from pre-revolutionary Russian writers (see p. 634) and Ibsen. After the People's Republic of China was founded in 1949, all the arts fell under centralized Communist control (see p. 446) and Soviet-style *socialist realism* (see p. 635) became the dominant approach in all forms of literature.

Japanese literature

Japanese literature has its origins in the Nara period (AD 710–94), when the first attempts were made to write Japanese with Chinese characters in the chronicles called the *Kojiki* ('Records of Ancient Matters') which appeared in 712, and the slightly later *Nihongi* ('Chronicles of Japan'; 720). The greatest literary accomplishment of the Nara period was the *Manyoshu*, a collection of 4496 poems of which 4173 are examples of the *tanka* – a short poem of 5 lines and 31 syllables giving a complete picture of an event or mood.

The best-known work of the Heian period (794–1185) was *'The Tale of Genji'*, written about 1000 by the woman writer **Murasaki Shikibu** (973–1014). *'The Tale of Genji'* has had immense influence on later Japanese literature and is recognized as the greatest masterpiece of Japanese prose narrative and, possibly, the earliest true novel in world literature. Its language and style brought together the early traditions of tales and romances and provided the model for subsequent courtly novels until the 15th century. The middle Heian period saw a flowering of prose writing by women, notably the miscellany of stylish commentary and gossip on court life, *The Pillow Book* of **Sei Shonagon** (966/7–1013).

The Kamakura period (1185–1335) produced the third great anthology of the Japanese poetry. The *Shinkokinshu*, compiled by six editors between 1201 and 1205, is considered by many to represent the apex of tanka composition.

The finest literary works of the 15th century are the *No* plays. Written in elaborate poetry, many reflected the Zen Buddhist goal of detachment. The ideals of the No plays are mystery and depth, and they invoke an invisible world through highly stylized speech and movement, using dance, mime, masks and minimal scenery. Most of the No plays still performed today date from the Muromachi period (1338–1513). The 16th and 17th centuries saw the development of *bunraku* (puppet plays) and *kabuki* (popular theatre). Kabuki, which is usually based on heroic legends from Japanese history

A performance of No theatre in modern Japan. A stylized drama involving music, dancing and elaborate costumes, and taking its themes from religious stories and myth, No developed in the 15th century and remains highly popular today.

and has a more concentrated plot form than No drama, remains extremely popular today.

Throughout most of the Tokugawa period (1603–1867) Japan was closed to the outside world, encouraging an inward-looking literature. During this period the *haiku* developed as an important genre and began to replace the older classical form of the tanka. The haiku is a tiny poem of only 17 syllables arranged into three lines, which had first emerged in the early 16th century as a fragment of a longer poetic form called *waka*. **Matsuo Basho** (1644–94), whose verse reflects the quietness and loneliness he found in nature, was responsible for making the haiku into a literary form in its own right. Basho is also known for his popular travel book, *The Narrow Road to the Deep North*.

The 17th century also saw the appearance of many fine novels, notably *The Life of an Amorous Man* (1682) by **Ihara Saikaku** (1642–93), an erotic account of one man's sexual adventures from childhood to old age. Saikaku's novels, which depict very realistically the times in which he lived, reflect the increasing interest of writers of the shogunate period (see pp. 386–7) in the bourgeoisie.

The opening up of Japan to the West in the mid-19th century, and Japan's subsequent modernization, provoked conflict between the traditional writers and the modernists. Japan's first modern novel was *The Drifting Cloud* (1887–89) by **Futabatei Shimei** (1864–1909). It was influenced by Russian literature (see p. 634) and written in colloquial Japanese.

Japan's best-known modern writer is the right-wing **Mishima Yukio** (1925–70). His novels, including *The Temple of the Golden Pavilion* (1956), and the tetralogy *The Sea of Fertility* (1965–70), demonstrate a preoccupation with homosexuality and death. Mishima called for a return to traditional military values before committing harakiri (ritual suicide) in 1970.   TMo

SEE ALSO

● CHINA TO THE COLONIAL AGE p. 382
● JAPAN TO THE 20TH CENTURY p. 386
● THE RISE OF ISLAM p. 392
● CLASSICAL LITERATURE p. 614
● MEDIEVAL TALES p. 620

Medieval Epic and Romance

Epic and Romance are loose terms used to describe the narrative literature of medieval Western Europe, most of which was in the form of long poems about men who became mythical heroes in the culture of their races. In epic and romance, modern European literature first flowered in the national languages which replaced the old universal literary language, Latin. This literature retains its vividness and immediacy and continues to spawn new creations – either based on it or influenced by it – in all of the arts. All of the major medieval epics and romances can be read in modern English translation.

SEE ALSO

● MEDIEVAL TALES p. 620
● RENAISSANCE POETRY p. 624

Generally speaking, the heroes of epics, such as the English Beowulf and the French Roland, are historical characters whose courage and honour, and almost superhuman deeds in the service of their overlords, provided a national ideal. Such epics – as in the ancient world – were dramatically chanted to harp accompaniment before audiences such as noble courts, tribal gatherings and groups of travellers. Accordingly, the epic is regarded as the loftiest kind of poetry. The heroes of romances, though presented as historical, are largely fictional characters such as King Arthur (see p. 396) and the knights of his Round Table, whose warrior qualities are especially revealed in the service of love. Their stories often proceed by 'romantic' event, involving not only women, but also the supernatural and the magical. Epic tends to be rooted in a real society – the family, the tribe, the nation; while romance expresses a fanciful aristocratic way of life. Though both kinds of narrative may include material from primitive folklore – monsters, ghosts and so on – medieval feudal and Christian values permeate all but the earliest works.

Epics of the Teutonic North

The cultural life of pre-Christian Scandinavia and Germany is reflected in a collection of Icelandic poems known as the *Elder* (or *Poetic*) *Edda* (before AD 1000). Mostly in *alliterative* verse, in which three or four stressed syllables in a line begin with the same sound, they tell stories of Germanic heroes and mythological characters, and relate a history of the Norse gods from creation to apocalypse (see also pp. 462–3). They also contain an early form of the *Nibelungenlied* (Song of the Nibelungs; c. 1200), a German poem celebrating the warrior Siegfried, his treacherous murder and the revenge of his widow, Kriemhild.

The *Sagas* ('stories') of Iceland and Norway are powerful semi-historical fictions of feudal life, mostly about manslaughter and revenge, but also about love and magic. The best are the sagas of *Njál* and *Grettir*.

The Anglo-Saxons were also a Germanic people, and the old English (i.e. Anglo-Saxon) alliterative poem *Beowulf* (c. AD 800) is the epic masterpiece of the age. In honourable defence of his people, its hero first kills the monster Grendel, who comes to devour his sleeping warriors, and then the monster's mother, who comes the next night to avenge her son. When old, Beowulf also kills a fire-breathing dragon while in his own death-throes. The Christian values found in *Beowulf* are strongly developed in Old English literature generally. *Biblical epics*, such as the poetic versions of the Books of *Genesis* and *Exodus*, also survive from this period.

Epics of France and Spain

The best-known heroes of early France and Spain were both real knights whose deeds were celebrated in magnificent epic poems. Roland was killed leading a rearguard action – the Battle of Roncevaux – in the Pyrenees in AD 778, and El Cid (see pp. 399 and 626) died in 1099. *La Chanson de Roland* ('The Song of Roland') is one of some eighty French epics about the knights of Charlemagne (AD 742–814; see p. 394) and other kings. They are known as *chansons de geste* ('songs of deeds'), the values of which are Christian and chivalric. It is a well-known tradition that William the Conqueror's minstrel, Taillefer, sang an early version of the Song of Roland at the Battle of Hastings in 1066. The version we have may have been composed in England.

The *Poema del Cid* emphasizes the hero's honour as he successfully strives to prove his loyalty to his king and to obtain justice for the dishonour done to his daughters. Like the Song of Roland, the poem generates its fervour and its sense of honour from the hero's exploits against Muslim invaders from the south. The poetic form of the two poems is similar, with verses made up of irregular numbers of lines rhyming by vowel sound only (*assonance*).

The world of Romance

The French word *roman*, which now means 'novel' (see p. 628), in the Middle Ages described verse and prose tales about three main kinds of subject; *Arthurian*, *Carolingian* (that is, about Charlemagne and his court) and *Classical* (mostly concerning the Fall of Troy and Alexander the Great).

Romances expressed the spirit of *Courtly Love*, a semi-religious philosophy of love between man and woman in which the woman is placed on an exalted pedestal, and the man ennobles himself by adoring and serving her. It developed first among Provençal lyric poets, the *troubadours*, in the 11th century, and spread to France, Germany and, less strongly, to England. It dominated the lyric in Italy and Spain as

The Sleep of King Arthur in Avalon. The subject of numerous medieval romances, the legendary figure of King Arthur has continued to be a source of inspiration to a wide range of creative artists, including the 19th-century poet Tennyson and the Pre-Raphaelite painter Sir Edward Burne-Jones, whose depiction (1894) of Arthur's final resting-place is illustrated here.
(Fine Art Photographic Library)

well as France, and the **Minnesingers** ('love singers') of Germany – some of whom were also epic poets – enriched their already fine love poetry with it. In *La Vita Nuova* ('the new life'), a collection of 31 love poems, Dante (see below) saw his beloved Beatrice as saving his soul.

The 13th-century *Roman de la Rose* ('The Romance of the Rose') is a dream allegory (see p. 621) of courtly love in two parts. The first 4058 lines by **Guillaume de Lorris** (d. 1237) describe the Lover's attempt to make the Lady respond, and he gets as far as kissing her despite his opponents, who represent aspects of her character such as Shame, Danger and Fear. The remaining 17 722 lines, composed by **Jean de Meun** (?1250–?1305) forty years later, extend the discussion of love into debates, supporting stories and satire, until at last the Lover wins the Lady. The work profoundly influenced the poetry of Europe for the next two hundred years. Among the romances affected by it is Geoffrey Chaucer's (see p. 620) *Troilus and Criseyde*, one of several long medieval works set in the period of the Trojan War, the subject of Homer's *Iliad* (see p. 614). Chaucer tells of the love affair, the role of Pandarus – Criseyde's uncle and guardian – in bringing the couple to bed, Criseyde's infidelity and Troilus's death in despair. Pandarus (from whose name we derive our word 'pander') is a debased example of the character of the Friend, who in the *Roman de la Rose* pleads the cause of the Lover.

Arthurian Romance

In real life Arthur may have been a Romano-British chieftain of the 5th century. His first appearance in literature was in early Welsh poetry and Latin histories of Britain written by Welsh monks. In 1155 the account of Arthur by **Geoffrey of Monmouth** (d. 1155) was expanded by the Jersey poet **Wace** (c. 1100–?1171), whose Norman-French poem was dedicated to Henry II's queen, Eleanor of Aquitaine (1122–1204), the famous patron of the arts and of courtly literature in particular. Wace's account was absorbed and enormously developed by the Frenchman **Chrétien de Troyes** (active 1170–90), whose five long poems in octosyllabic couplets represent the greatest achievement in Arthurian literature. Lancelot's adultery with Arthur's queen, Guinevere, and the resultant catastrophe in the treachery of Arthur's nephew Mordred and the end of the Round Table fellowship, figure in the slightly later French prose romances.

Chrétien's romances very soon inspired German versions, of which *Tristan and Isolde* (another adulterous love story; ?1210) by **Gottfried von Strassburg** (active 1210) and *Parzival* (?1212) by **Wolfram von Eschenbach** (?1170–?1220) are the most distinguished. *Tristan and Isolde* deals in a heightened tragic way with the consequences of the administering of a magic love potion, and *Parzival* with the search by Arthur's knights for the Holy Grail, the miraculous bowl – used, according to legend, by Jesus at the Last Supper – which will bring them spiritual happiness as well as earthly triumph.

GVI COELVM GENIT MEDIVMQVE IMVMQVE TRIBVNAL · LVSTRAVIT QVE ANIMO CVNCTA POETA SVO · DOCTVS ADEST DANTES SVA QVEM FLORENTIA SAEPE · SENSIT CONSILIIS AC PIETATE PATREM · NIL POTVIT TANTO MORS SAEVA NOCERE POETAE · QVEM VIVVM VIRTVS CARMEN IMAGO FACIT

In Britain and throughout Europe – from Sicily to Scandinavia – many minor Arthurian romances were written, some in ballad form. The major achievement in Britain was *Sir Gawain and the Green Knight* (c. 1390), whose hero defends the honour of the Round Table by entering into a fearful compact with a green giant. He chops off the giant's head, only to see its mouth remind him that he has agreed to stand a return blow in a year's time. He survives because he resists the Green Knight's wife's attempt to seduce him, so preserving the honour of Arthur's court. The manuscript of *Sir Gawain and the Green Knight* also contains the biblical epics *Patience*, on Jonah and the Whale, and *Cleanness*, on the Flood, Sodom and Gomorrah, and Belshazzar's Feast. All three poems are believed by many to be the work of the same author.

Like *Sir Gawain and the Green Knight*, the 14th-century *Morte Arthure* is an alliterative poem which in spirit looks back to heroic Norse times. It is a tragic epic, a battle poem of the same ferocity as the Song of Roland. It details Arthur's European conquests; when he is about to humble the Pope, news reaches him of Mordred's treachery and seduction of Guinevere. He returns to fight his last battle, in which he dies from a wound he receives in killing Mordred.

After the end of the period, the best-known English Arthurian romance was written in prose. This was the *Morte D'Arthur* ('The Death of Arthur') of **Sir Thomas Malory** (d. 1471), which collects and binds into unity all the major Arthurian legends. Its title refers strictly to the content of the last of its 21 books.

Italy and Dante

The spirit of courtly love was strong in medieval Italy. In his sonnets, **Petrarch** (1304–74) idealizes his beloved but unobtainable Laura. Both the spiritual substance and the form of the Petrarchan sonnet influenced French and English poets of the following two centuries (see pp. 624–5). Among writers of longer poems, Giovanni Boccaccio (see p. 620) wrote the *Filostrato* ('he who is struck by love') and the *Teseida*, on both of which Chaucer based romances (see p. 620).

But the towering figure of medieval Italy is **Dante Alighieri** (1265–1321; see illustration), whose *Divine Comedy* is one of the greatest poems of Western civilization. It is written in *terza rima* – lines of 11 syllables arranged in rhyming groups of three – and consists of three parts: the *Inferno*, the *Purgatorio* and the *Paradiso*. *The Divine Comedy* is a Christian epic in which the poet journeys through Hell and Purgatory with the Latin poet Virgil (see p. 614), and reaches Paradise guided by his beloved Beatrice, who in her death has become the handmaiden of God. It is a poem of both present and future life – seen by the poet as it were through the eyes of God – and is full of Dante's passion and prodigious learning in philosophy, astronomy, natural science and history. It ends on a pinnacle of bliss, in which the poet's soul achieves salvation through his idealized love for Beatrice. BS

Dante Alighieri, by Domenico di Michelino (1465). Dante's native Florence appears on the right, with the rest of the painting dominated by Hell, Purgatory and Heaven, through which Dante journeys in his great poem, *The Divine Comedy*. To the left of the poet is Hell, conceived by Dante as a descending spiral whose 'circles' accommodate the different categories of sinners. The mountain behind Dante represents Purgatory, with groups of repentant sinners on its circular ledges, and the Earthly Paradise at its summit. Above this are the spheres of Paradise itself through which Dante ascends with his beloved Beatrice until God is eventually revealed to him. (Florence Cathedral/Scala)

Medieval Tales

The chief glory of medieval European literature lies in its stories, which were composed in poetry or prose for reciting, or in the form of plays for acting. They covered the known world, both its past (see pp. 618–19) and its present. All human life, from peasant hardship to aristocratic privilege, and the rising world of modern commerce in between, was the province of story. In subject and technique, stories ranged from comic bawdiness to scholarly wit, from pure romance to pungent satire, from folk superstition to elevated Christian doctrine. Stories were the main source of popular and aristocratic entertainment and education. Since few people outside the Church and the nobility could read and write, the stories that have survived were written down and preserved within religious or noble communities.

The three most famous medieval collections of stories are the *Thousand and One Nights* (see p. 616), Boccaccio's *Decameron* and Chaucer's *Canterbury Tales*. The *Thousand and One Nights* – a collection of Indian, Persian and Arabic stories first made in the 10th century – became known in Europe only in the 17th century. But many of its stories circulated long before that, and the Italian writer *Giovanni Boccaccio* (1313–75) incorporated several in his *Decameron* ('The Ten Days' Work'). This comprises a hundred tales supposedly told over a ten-day period by a group of young Florentine aristocrats who take a villa in the country to escape an outbreak of the plague in the city in 1348. While the *Thousand and One Nights* deals, in an oriental setting, with the fabulous and the romantic as well as with intrigue and sexual adventures, Boccaccio's stories are nearly all realistically set in his own Italian world, with sex and intrigue predominating.

The Canterbury Tales

Geoffrey Chaucer (?1343–1400) drew on the *Decameron* for certain of his *Canterbury Tales* – an unfinished collection of 24 stories extending to 17 000 lines of verse and prose. In the *Canterbury Tales*, 30 pilgrims – representing the most diverse trades and social classes – gather at an inn in Southwark and agree to engage in a storytelling contest as they ride to the shrine of St Thomas Beckett in Canterbury. The tales they tell are preceded by a prologue presenting vivid and humorous character sketches of the pilgrims, and are linked together by vigorous exchanges between them. Prologue, tales and 'links' combine to present a unified whole – a profound and satisfying portrayal of medieval England – from which Chaucer's genius for characterization and understanding of social rela-

Geoffrey Chaucer (right), author of the *Canterbury Tales*, as portrayed in the Ellesmere manuscript. Chaucer includes himself amongst the group of pilgrims who tell stories to shorten the journey to Canterbury, and recounts two of the 24 tales.
(Victoria and Albert Museum, London/E.T. Archive)

tionships shines forth. The *Canterbury Tales* presents a highly varied collection of different types of story: courtly romance (in the classical *Knight's Tale*, a shortened version of Boccaccio's epic, the *Teseida*), allegorical tale, devotional tale, beast fable (see p. 621) and racy fabliau.

The *fabliau*, a short verse tale usually in couplets with lines of eight syllables, originated in France in the 12th century. In England fabliaux written by Chaucer and others used material drawn from France, or from Boccaccio and his eastern and Mediterranean sources. They dealt with farcical situations of everyday life in which knockabout sex and satire of Church people were prominent. In Chaucer's *Miller's Tale*, for example, a dull-witted carpenter is cuckolded by his student lodger, who – in a riotous finale – is then branded on the bare behind. The *Reeve's Tale* that follows is an equally bawdy riposte to the Miller for recounting a tale of the duping of a carpenter, the Reeve's profession. Sex and marital fidelity are explored in a more sophisticated style in the *Merchant's Tale*, an account of an ageing husband's relationship with a young wife.

Perhaps the most memorable example of Chaucer's delineation of character is contained in the 856-line prologue to the *Wife of Bath's Tale*. This account of how the teller gained the upper hand over each of her five husbands is so colourful and vital as to cause the courtly tale that follows to fall rather flat.

A number of the *Canterbury Tales* have religious themes, recounting miracles and the lives of saints, and three are actually sermons. The *Pardoner's Tale* contains an *exemplum* – a story illuminating the message of a sermon – warning against covetousness. Three young 'rioters', who have decided to seek out and kill Death, are told by an old man that they will find him at the foot of a tree. In attempting to cheat one another for possession of the gold they find there, they kill each other.

VILLON

The greatest poet of late medieval France was *François Villon* (b. 1431), who, from the scant details known of him, appears to have led a life of criminal excess. Villon was arrested in 1463 for his part in a brawl and condemned to be hanged, but the sentence was commuted to a ten-year banishment from Paris. After this nothing further is known of him.

Villon's major surviving works are *Le Lais* and *Le Testament*, long poems written mainly in stanzas of eight octosyllabic lines, but also containing ballads and rondeaux. The ballads mingle reflection on the happiness and transience of earthly pleasures with a horror of sickness, old age and death. Probably the most famous single poem of *Le Testament* is the 'Ballad of the ladies of yesteryear', with its oft-quoted refrain 'Where are the snows of yesteryear?' Villon's poetry speaks with directness of love and death, and is permeated by a compassion for suffering humanity and regret for a wasted past.

Besides the *Pardoner's Tale*, the *Canterbury Tales* include two exquisite tales of religious meaning. The *Man of Law's Tale* concerns Constance, daughter of a Christian emperor of Rome, and focuses on the heroine's trust in God, which endures through several attempts made to murder or rape her. The *Clerk's Tale* tells of the extreme conjugal obedience of 'patient Griselda', who is set a number of cruel tests by her husband.

Chaucer's interest in building a series of individual stories into a larger whole was shared, but less successfully realized, by his contemporary *John Gower* (?1330–1408). In Gower's *Confessio Amantis* ('The Lover's Confession') the poet encounters a priest of Venus, goddess of love, who recounts a series of exampla illustrating the seven deadly sins.

Alliterative religious poetry

Modern preference for Chaucer's secular tales and fabliaux tends to obscure the fact that religion was the chief subject of medieval literature. Even a hundred years later, of all the works printed by William Caxton (see p. 322), *The Golden Legend* – a manual of ecclesiastical lore containing stories of the lives of saints, sermons and other religious material – was the most popular.

The greatest medieval religious poetry was *alliterative* (see p. 619). Besides the two Bible epics attributed to the author of *Sir Gawain and the Green Knight* (see p. 619), *Piers Plowman* (c. 1360–80) by *William Langland* (c. 1330–c. 1386) is particularly noteworthy. Langland, who seems to have been a lay priest, worked on the poem for 20 years. In structure it is a dream vision of a type suggested originally by the Book of Revelation, the last book of the Bible. But Langland's allegorical vision is of the whole range of life in England, viewed by an observant religious man whose aim is to discover how a good Christian can save his soul. He satirizes vice, and shows the good way forward. The hero of the poem, Piers, is at first an ordinary English farmer, but gradually becomes a kind of Christ-figure.

In *Pearl*, a dream vision also thought to be the work of the 'Gawain poet', the poet is advised by the spirit of his young daughter not to feel immoderate grief at her death. The girl describes to her father her blissful state in paradise, and he wakes from his dream with his faith in God reaffirmed and strengthened. *Pearl* is brilliantly ornate, being both heavily rhymed and alliterative.

Mystery plays

At religious festivals throughout medieval Europe, *mystery plays* were performed based on the Christian story from the Creation to the Last Judgement, and on the lives of saints. They were scripted by churchmen and performed by townspeople with staging as magnificent as that of noble tournaments and pageants. They were acted in or outside churches, often on stages built for the purpose, or on huge pageant carts that moved about the town to designated audience positions. In England, four cycles of plays survive, from York (48 plays), Chester (25), Wakefield (32) and 'N-Town' (so called because it is not known where they were performed). Except at 'N-Town', the plays were put on by craft guilds (see p. 404). (It is believed by some that the name 'mystery' derives from the French word *métier*, meaning job or trade, though the word has always had the meaning 'religious truth'.) Thus at York the Crucifixion play was staged by the Pinners (nailmakers) and Painters, and at Chester the Noah play was staged by the Waterleaders and Drawers of Dee. Many mystery plays not belonging to the main cycles were also staged, particularly at York. Though the subject matter of mystery plays is serious, the treatment is often down-to-earth and amusing. In many versions of the Nativity story, for example, Herod appears as a splendid pantomime villain.

Morality plays

In the 15th century, dramatized sermons called *moralities* developed. Broadly, they show man's fight against sin, and the process by which he saves his soul. The best-known are *The Castle of Perseverance* (late 15th century) and *Everyman* (c. 1510). Later moralities were more political: both *Ane Pleasant Satyre of the Thrie Estaitis* by the Scottish poet **Sir David Lindsay** (c. 1486–1555) and *Magnyfycence* by **John Skelton** (?1460–1529; better known for his earthy colloquial verse) castigate vices in public life and offer good advice to rulers.

Allegories

Morality plays were *allegories* – metaphorical narratives in which the characters represented abstract qualities, such as the Seven Deadly Sins and their virtuous opposites. The medieval tradition of allegory developed from *The Romance of the Rose* (see p. 618), and was to continue through later centuries in

such works as *The Faerie Queene* by Edmund Spenser (c. 1552–99; see pp. 624–5) – a grand political and religious compliment to Elizabeth I – and the prose allegory *The Pilgrim's Progress* (1684) by the non-conformist **John Bunyan** (1628–88), a dream vision charting the pilgrim's path to the Celestial City.

Fables

In literature the term *fable* describes a short verse or prose tale with a moral, which approaches its subject through extraordinary or mythical events. Thus, some of the religious stories mentioned above could be called fables. The Middle Ages were particularly rich in *beast fables*, following a tradition established by **Aesop**, a probably legendary Greek of the 6th century BC. Chaucer's *Nun's Priest's Tale* retells the familiar fable of the Cock and the Fox in mock-heroic style: the vain and self-important Cock is persuaded by the Fox to display his

prowess at crowing, and is thus caught off guard when the Fox seizes him, but nevertheless succeeds in getting away by flattering the Fox in turn. Chaucer presents the tale as a comic allegory on human behaviour and the Church, though his insistence on the 'morality' of his tale is perhaps to be taken with a pinch of salt.

Reynard the Fox is the favourite hero – or villain – of medieval beast fable. Other fables include the 13th-century *Owl and the Nightingale*, a religious debate on marriage between the Owl, who represents the orthodox view of the Church, and the Nightingale, who represents the philosophy of courtly love (see p. 618).

The tradition of the fable continues through European literature until well after the Middle Ages; well-known examples include the *Fables* of the Frenchman **Jean de La Fontaine** (1621–95), the *Fables* of the English poet **John Gay** (1685–1732), and the modern political fable *Animal Farm* (1945), by **George Orwell** (1903–50; see p. 649), in which Napoleon, the chief pig, represents the Soviet dictator Stalin (see p. 442), while Boxer, the plodding carthorse, embodies the decent common man.

The heritage of medieval tales

Medieval tales have had a lasting and enriching influence on the world's literature and drama. They confirm the universal and eternal thirst for good stories, whether for reading or performance. In the drama, mystery and morality plays provided the basis for the *interludes* (short episodic plays like dramatic fables) of the 15th and 16th centuries, which rapidly expanded into the extraordinary dramatic achievements of Shakespeare and his contemporaries (see pp. 622–3). The major mysteries and moralities are often revived today, and new works inspired by them have been composed, such as the opera *Noye's Fludde*, by Benjamin Britten (1913–76; see p. 579).　BS

RABELAIS

The Frenchman *François Rabelais* (c. 1494–c. 1553), a distinguished humanist and physician, wrote a voluminous comic prose satire – *Gargantua and Pantagruel*. The fantastic progress of the giant Gargantua and his son Pantagruel, and Pantagruel's education at the University of Paris, military exploits and employment of the rascally Panurge, are recounted in a parade of satirical attacks on human folly and the worlds of learning and politics. Encyclopedic, wildly funny, often startlingly obscene, *Gargantua and Pantagruel* is permeated by the values of Renaissance humanism (see p. 407). Rabelais proposes a responsible life of freedom and self-expression for which there is no medieval precedent, except perhaps implicitly in some of Chaucer's poems.

The Decameron, by Giovanni Boccaccio, is a collection of 100 tales told by a group of young aristocrats in the garden of a country villa. This illustration of one of the tales features Saladin, the great Muslim warrior who retook Jerusalem from the Crusaders in 1187. (Bargello, Florence/ Scala).

The Dog and the Wolf depicted in a 14th-century French manuscript of Aesop's fables. (Bibliothèque Nationale, Paris/ E.T. Archive)

SEE ALSO

● THE LITERATURE OF ASIA p. 616
● EPICS AND ROMANCES p. 618
● RENAISSANCE LITERATURE pp. 622–25

Renaissance Theatre

The drama of the Renaissance is intelligible to us in ways that medieval literature never can be, because it springs from a historical moment when humanity finally elbows God aside to occupy the stage of its own consciousness. The drama of the Middle Ages is religious drama, reflecting Christian ritual (see p. 621); the drama of the 16th century is a secular theatre of human activity. The stage no longer represents Heaven and Hell, but the world of history and the material present; the essence of the drama is no longer the salvation of the individual soul, but the fate of kingdoms, countries, families and races. The Renaissance historicized the drama as it secularized culture; drama, like history in Karl Marx's formulation, became 'nothing more nor less than the spectacle of man pursuing his aims'.

The Globe Theatre in Southwark, in which many of Shakespeare's plays were first performed. Playhouses such as the Swan, the Rose and the Globe were the focus of the professional theatre that flourished in the Elizabethan period. Built in 1599, the Globe was burnt down in 1613, re-built in 1614 and finally demolished in 1644 (the professional theatres having been closed by Act of Parliament in 1642).

In Britain this break with the past is clear and sharply defined. Henry VIII's Reformation crushed the old religious drama, since it was recognized as the ritual of the Catholic Church. The new-style monarchy of the Tudors disarmed the old feudal aristocracy, realigned itself against Catholic Europe, and set about building a modern apparatus of government (see p. 412). The culture of this new nation-state, shaped by a newly-powerful ruling class, was royalist, imperialist and secular. As the economic revolution freed new social forces for entrepreneurial action, the profession of acting was transformed from a feudal service to an independent business concern. Formerly the clients of aristocratic patrons, actors in the later 16th century became small independent producers, selling their wares directly to an eager and growing market.

The new theatres

Most importantly, from the 1570s onwards actors had their own purpose-built theatres, the first to be constructed in Britain since Roman times. These open-air amphitheatres, such as the Rose, the Swan and the Globe (see illustration), provided a large, bare, thrust stage around which the audience stood or sat in galleries lining the inner walls of the theatre. The stages used no scenery or artificial lighting, and operated entirely without theatrical illusion. The buildings could hold audiences of several thousands, and the price of admission could be as low as a penny; they were popular theatres. The focus of attention in such a theatre was on the actors – their bodies, faces, costumes and voices: English Renaissance drama is a drama of language and gesture rather than one of pictorial effect.

Spanish drama

This cultural pattern was not confined to Britain alone, however. Generally in Europe, theatre remained split between refined courtly shows and popular entertainment. In Spain, however, a parallel historical development, occurring somewhat later than in England, produced a flowering of the professional theatre that has been termed 'the golden age' of Spanish drama.

Lope de Vega (1562–1635) wrote prolifically for popular audiences in urban theatres. His prodigious output – he claimed to have written 1500 plays, of which only 500 survive – includes dramas of intrigue and chivalry, dramas on biblical subjects, and dramas with involved plots taken from Spanish history. Lope's dramas made flexible use of the unities (see p. 630), and were to exercise a pro-found influence on 17th-century French drama (see p. 630).

The versatile genius of the Spanish theatre was *(Pedro) Calderon (de la Barca)* (1600–81), who wrote popular plays, religious dramas and court spectacle. A master of allegory, Calderon built on the dramatic form and conventions established by Lope de Vega. His secular tragedy *The Mayor of Zalamea* (c. 1643) contrasts the nobility and the people and rejects the traditional assumptions of the aristocratic code of honour, showing honour to be the prerogative of all who display moral integrity, regardless of their social class.

The new drama

In England, the plays of **Christopher Marlowe** (1564–93) offered radical dramatic reworkings of traditional materials. Marlowe's *The Tragical History of Dr Faustus* (c. 1589) took up the theme of the battle between good and evil for the fate of the Christian soul (see pp. 620–1): but instead of a simple warning against transgression, the play becomes an affirmation of the need for knowledge and freedom. In *Tamburlaine the Great* (1587–8) Marlowe expressed all the unappeased hunger of his age for experience and power. In *Edward II* (1592) Marlowe helped to establish the genre of the Elizabethan history play.

In contrast with Marlowe, whose dramas are relatively intellectual in character, other dramatists were producing plays in popular genres such as the *revenge tragedy*. **Thomas Kyd** (1558–94) in *The Spanish Tragedy* (1592) created out of the popular raw materials of violence and blood-revenge a complex plot suggestive of Shakespeare's later tragedy *Hamlet*.

Shakespeare

The remarkable dramatic achievement of the dramatist and poet **William Shakespeare** (1564–1616) should be assessed in the context of a flourishing and progressive cultural industry: in this sense it was not the work of one man alone.

Certainly no other dramatist had such success in so many different genres. In comedies such as *Twelfth Night* and *As You Like It* (both c. 1600), Shakespeare excelled in a particular type of romantic, festive drama, often with a Utopian setting, depicting the maturing of a romantic hero with the help of an assertive and powerful woman. No other dramatist attempted to construct a huge cycle of historical plays covering the whole of English history from 1399 to 1485, from the deposing of Richard II to the death of Richard III at the Battle of Bosworth. In tragedy Shakespeare began with the materials of crude Senecan melodrama (see p. 615), and later, in plays such as *Hamlet* (c. 1600), *King Lear* (c. 1605), and *Macbeth* (c. 1606), wrote dramas which seem to chronicle the universal catastrophe of an age as well as the agonizing death of a hero. After these great tragedies, as theatrical fashion veered towards romantic tragi-comedy, Shakespeare wrote some extraordinary and complex plays, notably *The Tempest* and *The Winter's Tale* (both 1611), which re-examine, within a framework of romance, the conventions of comedy, history and tragedy.

Although the plays of Shakespeare were written by a dramatist of genius, it must not be forgotten that they were the product of a collective form of cultural production – theatre – which involved actors, businessmen and audience as well as writers; and of a vigorous theatrical culture in a dynamically developing new society.

Citizen comedy

Only one of Shakespeare's plays (*The Merry Wives of Windsor*; c. 1602) deals principally with bourgeois characters in a contemporary English setting. The plays of his friend **Ben Jonson** (1572–1637) are, by contrast, teeming with the middle- and working-class life of the London streets and are addressed directly to the follies and vices of contemporary society.

With a new mercantile class flourishing in early Jacobean England, Jonson directs a satirical offensive against those greedy for money and power. The style of Jonson's drama is derived from Classical comedy (see pp. 614–15), but its subject matter is recognizably derived from contemporary London. *Volpone* (1605) is a comedy of deception set in a corrupt Venetian society where only the most ruthless and quick-witted survive. In satirical plays such as *The Alchemist* (1610) and the exuberant *Bartholemew Fair* (1614) Jonson presented and explored a wide range of contemporary manners. Jonson produced masques for the court (see below) from 1605 onwards.

Bartholemew Fair is an example of a type of drama known as 'Citizen Comedy'. Dealing with middle-class life in a bustling urban setting, Citizen Comedy was the staple of the various indoor 'Boy's Companies' (acting troupes consisting of the children of choir schools at St Paul's and the Chapel Royal), which, in the early years of the 17th century, briefly equalled in popularity the outdoor adult companies.

Jacobean tragedy

By the time James I succeeded Elizabeth I in 1603, the world of the Renaissance stage was beginning to narrow. The focal points of significant dramatic activity were no longer in the popular public theatres, but in the exclusive and expensive indoor ('private') venues such as the Blackfriars Theatre, and in the royal court itself. In the Jacobean private theatre there developed a new kind of tragedy which, in plots of sensational

intrigue and artistically refined violence, portrayed the world – or at least the court – as hopelessly corrupt. **Thomas Middleton** (1580–1627) – in such plays as *The Revenger's Tragedy* (c. 1605), *Women Beware Women* (1621), and *The Changeling* (1622; with William Rowley) – presented the Renaissance court as a scene of cruel sexual exploitation and violent blood-revenge. In *The White Devil* (1612; see illustration) and *The Duchess of Malfi* (1613–14), his contemporary **John Webster** (c. 1578 – c. 1632) elevated melodrama to tragedy by pitting a sinister and depraved world against female heroines, who display some measure of corrupt nobility.

Court theatre

Meanwhile, the court of James I began to stage hugely expensive *masques* and shows, written by dramatists such as Ben Jonson and with ornate staging by artists such as Inigo Jones (see p. 531). The masque was a spectacular court entertainment involving music and dancing, in which masked performers enacted allegorical plots. Ben Jonson's *Oberon* (1601) provides an interesting contrast with Shakespeare's comedy *A Midsummer Night's Dream* (c. 1595): although both works use similar materials, the play is a celebration of imagination and popular energy, while the masque – which featured James's heir Prince Henry as a star performer – praises and celebrates royalty.

The theatre companies, which had always been persecuted by the Puritan citizens who dominated London social and economic life, gradually crept closer to the monarchy for protection. Shakespeare's company was known during the Elizabethan period as the 'Lord Chamberlain's Men', but after Elizabeth's death became the 'King's Men', personal servants to James I himself. When Shakespeare retired from the theatre in 1613, he left a space to be filled by lesser dramatists and courtly amateurs. His successors as principal writers for the King's Men were **Francis Beaumont** (1584–1616) and his collaborator **John Fletcher** (1579–1625), whose characteristic emphasis on romantic tragedy and tragicomedy influenced the drama until the Civil War and beyond. Another versatile dramatist of this period was **John Ford** (1586–?1639), who explored the taboos surrounding the incestuous love between a brother and sister in his tragedy *'Tis Pity She's a Whore* (1632). The Renaissance drama in England comes to a close in the reign of Charles I, with a stage dominated by Royalist writers such as **James Shirley** (1596–1666) and **Sir William Davenant** (1606–68), whose work foreshadows the satire and social comedy of the Reformation (see p. 627).

It was inevitable that the outbreak of the Civil War (see p. 413) between king and Parliament would result in the actors, and to some extent drama itself, being identified with the court. The closure of the theatres in 1642 marks the end of Renaissance drama in England.　　GHo

William Shakespeare (left) as he appeared in an engraving by Martin Droeshout on the title-page of the First Folio. Although some works were published individually, Shakespeare's plays were not collected together for publication during the playwright's lifetime. Thanks to the efforts of Shakespeare's fellow-actors John Heminges and Henry Condell, the majority of the plays appeared in collected form as the First Folio in 1623.

● MEDIEVAL TALES p. 620
● RENAISSANCE POETRY p. 624
● CLASSICISM IN LITERATURE p. 626

The White Devil by John Webster. The play's sensationalized Italian setting, together with its ingredients of lust, insanity and bloody revenge, are typical of Jacobean tragedy. *The White Devil* and Webster's later *Duchess of Malfi* have been revived more frequently in the modern theatre than any plays of the period apart from Shakespeare's. Illustrated here is a scene from the 1969 National Theatre production.

Renaissance Poetry

Renaissance poetry, while less often celebrated than Renaissance painting, sculpture and architecture (see pp. 524–9), or the drama (see pp. 622–3), is equally characteristic of this rich and vital period. An earlier literary flowering in Italy, including Boccaccio, Dante, and Petrarch (see pp. 619 and 620), prepared the ground, and Renaissance poetry flourished from the late 15th to the mid-17th century throughout Western Europe.

Sir Philip Sidney by an unknown artist. Poet, courtier, artistic patron, diplomat and soldier, Sir Philip Sidney is traditionally regarded as the complete Renaissance gentleman. He died of his wounds while fighting the Spanish in the Netherlands in 1586, allegedly giving his water-bottle to a dying soldier as he himself was carried mortally wounded from the field.
(National Portrait Gallery, London)

The Renaissance – which saw itself as an age of rebirth, awakening to the light after centuries of darkness – was fully alive in its poets. Its interest in Classical learning, its reaction against the alleged barbarism of the Middle Ages, and atmosphere of optimism and confidence in the discovery of the world and man, are all infused into its poetry, although anxieties are also recorded.

Renaissance poets showed a deep and imaginative interest in antiquity, its civilizations and especially its literature, and sought to imitate the ancients (see pp. 614–15). They combined a Classical-pagan and Judaeo-Christian culture and world-

Jerusalem Delivered by the Italian poet Torquato Tasso is an epic of the First Crusade describing the capture of the Holy City by Geoffrey of Bouillon, the leader of the Christian armies besieging Jerusalem. A blend of historical, romantic and fabulous elements, *Jerusalem Delivered* is one of the greatest and most influential poems of the 16th century. Illustrated here is the frontispiece of the first edition (1581).

view. They believed strongly in poetry's capacity to elevate the mind and had a corresponding sense of high vocation. The major poets of the Renaissance demonstrated enormous ambition, revealed in attempts to write on an epic scale, while many, both major and minor, delighted in exhibiting their learning and expressed a patriotic pride in their native tongue. They treated perennial themes: love, war, death, time, nature, beauty – but in ways that reflected their new confidence and ambition, while retaining much of medieval thinking.

Change and continuity

While reaction against the medieval world is evident in Renaissance poetry, so too is deep continuity with it. Renaissance poets did not replace medieval with modern. Some of their work can seem obscure to the modern reader, embodying as it does a world-view vastly different from our own; therefore an appreciation of the historical and ideological contexts in which the poetry of this period was written is important for understanding.

Despite the advent of the 'new philosophy', the gradual and partial replacement of a Ptolemaic by a Copernican universe (see p. 16) and the beginnings of modern science (see p. 60), the Renaissance conception of the world remained based on ancient and medieval ideas that were essentially poetic. Poetry and science were interfused and not distinct and opposed, as they are for us.

Poets often wrote on what we would now consider purely scientific subjects. The English poet *Edmund Spenser* (1552–99) in his 'Mutabilitie Cantos' (1609), the Englishman *John Davies* (1569–1626) in his delightful poem *Orchestra* (1596), and the French Protestant *Guillaume Du Bartas* (1544–90) in his *La Sepmaine* (1578) – a long poem extolling the creation – were three poets among many basing their work on medieval 'science', yet essentially Renaissance in expression and outlook.

Classical and Christian

Renaissance poetry was deeply Christian, notwithstanding its veneration of pagan antiquity – which it nevertheless sought to Christianize. Religious conflict, following the Reformation (see p. 408), was endemic and frequently if obliquely reflected in the poetry of the age. While poets were rarely concerned with explicit religious doctrine – John Milton (see box) being a notable exception – their religious beliefs were important. The poetry of Spenser, Du Bartas and the Englishman *Sir Philip Sidney* (1554–86) is informed by their Protestantism, while the hostility of the French Protestant Huguenots (see p. 409) to *Pierre de Ronsard* (1524–85) and the *Pleiade* – the group of poets associated with him – indicates Ronsard's role as spokesman for Catholic France.

Poets were eager nonetheless to combine Christian faith and Classical learning and, though not new, this ambition was implemented with unprecedented vigour and exuberance. *Neoplatonism*, a philosophical and religious system that sought to reconcile pagan and Platonic ideas (see p. 487) with Christian faith, influenced many poets, including Spenser and Sidney in England, Ronsard and *Joachim Du Bellay* (1525–60) in France, and *Pietro Bembo* (1470–1547) and *Torquato Tasso* (1544–95) in Italy. Tensions in the combination of Classical and Christian ideas appear in these poets and others – most profoundly in Milton. Yet the 'antique world' also offered escape from the pressures of Christendom – with the inevitability of salvation or damnation at the Last Judgement – to a Golden Age of happy paganism.

Delight and instruction

Notwithstanding a wealth of lighter verse in the period, the conviction that poetry should instruct while pleasing its reader was paramount. Belief in the power and duty of poetry to edify was drawn from Classical sources, notably Plato, Aristotle and Horace (see pp. 487 and 615). It emerged in the claim of Spenser's *Faerie Queene* (1590–96) to present twelve Aristotelian 'moral virtues'; in Tasso's defence of heroic poetry; and superlatively in Milton's proposal to 'justify the way of God to men' in *Paradise Lost* (see box).

Roles: courtier and lover

These high aspirations were accompanied, however, by practical considerations: the poet had to live. Renaissance poets usually had a small audience – generally an aristocratic one. The poet was often a courtier – especially in the

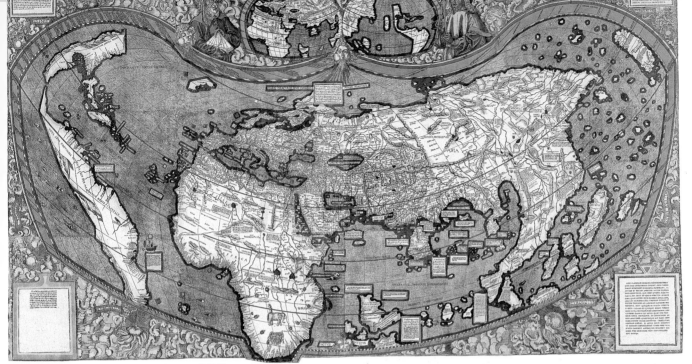

A world map of 1507. The Renaissance saw a vast expansion of man's knowledge of the globe through the pioneering voyages of navigators such as Columbus and Magellan. This spirit of discovery permeates Luis de Camoëns's great epic of Portuguese exploration, *The Lusiads* (1572). An account of the voyage of Vasco de Gama from Portugal to India around the Cape of Good Hope, it combines realistic description, mythological fantasy and Portuguese history.

SEE ALSO

- MEDIEVAL EPIC AND ROMANCE p. 618
- MEDIEVAL TALES p. 620
- RENAISSANCE DRAMA p. 622
- CLASSICISM IN LITERATURE p. 626

PARADISE LOST

The great Christian epic *Paradise Lost* (1667) was the work of a formidably erudite poet – *John Milton* (1608–74). In the poem – the story of Satan's rebellion against God and the casting out of Adam and Eve from the Garden of Eden – Milton draws on a wealth of earlier poetry, both Classical and Renaissance. The medieval world-view persists in *Paradise Lost*, but it is counterpoised by Renaissance values; Classical learning suffuses the poem, in tension with a Protestant faith steeped in Scripture; the moral aims of Spenser and Tasso (both absorbed by Milton) are raised to a yet higher power. Yet this power is exhaustive: *Paradise Lost* is the last successful epic, the supreme example of the scope and confidence of Renaissance poetry. There is also in Milton much of the luxuriance and energy of the Baroque (see p. 530), which promises new growth after the sterility of late Renaissance Mannerism. Milton is the last great Renaissance poet but also an important influence on the poetry, especially the English poetry, of the post-Renaissance world.

earlier Renaissance – eager to please, if not flatter, his patron. Spenser idealized Elizabeth I as Gloriana; Sidney was the model courtier and ideal Renaissance man: lover, scholar, soldier (see illustration); *Lodovico Ariosto* (1474–1533) served the Italian ducal house of Este, as did Tasso, less happily, later; Ronsard was laureate to two kings of France during the wars of religion (see p. 409).

The role of lover, real or affected, was almost indispensable for the poet, and the topic of love was almost universal. Love might be erotic (following the Classical models of Ovid and Catullus; see p. 615), romantic (with medieval chivalry often the setting; see p. 618), or Platonic (in the sense of being free from sexual desire) – and frequently involved an intermingling of all these elements. The medieval courtly love tradition (see p. 618) per-

sisted in modified form, sometimes associated with the spiritualized love of Neoplatonism. The sonnet sequence (see below) was a favoured mode of treating love's diversity and vicissitudes: in Ronsard's *Amours* (1553), Spenser's *Amoretti* (1595), Sidney's *Astrophel and Stella* (1591), Shakespeare's and *Michelangelo Buonarotti's* (see p. 528) *Sonnets*, and quantities of Elizabethan verse. Love was treated wittily and profoundly, if often cynically, by the Metaphysical poets (see box). Ariosto's romantic epic *Orlando Furioso* (1532) recounts humorously and vividly the passion of the medieval knight Roland (see p. 618) for Angelica.

Forms: lyric, sonnet, epic

Renaissance poetry is richly diverse in form and style and includes romantic epic (see p. 618), narrative verse, and varieties of lyric – some extremely complex, some unaffectedly simple. Many lyrics were set to music, and traditions of song were elaborated in England by poet-musicians such as *John Dowland* (1563–1626) and *Thomas Campion* (1567–1670) or, very differently, by the guilds of professional poets or *Meistersingers* in Germany. The most famous composer of Meisterlieder was *Hans Sachs* of Nuremburg (1494–1576).

The poets relished difficult lyric forms, such as the *sestina* (a poem of six six-line stanzas) and *canzone*, and the multiple meanings of allegory. Rhetorical language was characteristic, especially in the earlier Renaissance: 'ornament' was generally approved, though there are preferences for plain style, often associated with Puritan sympathies.

The Renaissance was also an age of literary theorizing, interested in poetic categories modelled on Classical examples, which the poet sought to emulate. The genres of satire, epigram, elegy, ode, eclogue, comedy, tragedy, and epic, and the work of Greek and (chiefly) Roman poets (Ovid, Virgil, Horace pre-eminently) were widely imitated and translated. The models were often creatively transformed rather than merely copied, as in Spenser's *Shepheardes Calender* (a

series of 12 eclogues; 1579) or Milton's *Lycidas* (an elegy; 1638). Also Classical is the idea of decorum – the poet's duty to employ a style and language suited to his subject.

The most celebrated lyric form was the *sonnet*, which enjoyed a Europe-wide vogue in the later 16th century. The model for writers of sonnets was Petrarch (see p. 619), whose influence was enormous. His *Rime* – a series of love poems – supplied the model of the 14-line poem (modified slightly in French and English) and the persona of the unrequited poet-lover.

The epic or 'heroical poem' (see p. 618) is the most ambitious of the genres, demanding a lofty subject as well as great gifts and dedication from the poet. Tasso spent years composing and revising *Jerusalem Delivered* (1580–81), his highly romantic but deeply serious epic of the Crusades (see illustration). Spenser died with *The Faerie Queene* only half written.

Epic also gave appropriate expression to the burgeoning patriotic pride of the Renaissance, as in *The Lusiads* (1572), the Portuguese national epic, by *Luis de Camoëns* (1524–80), based on Vasco da Gama's voyage of discovery (see p. 405). The choice of epic form for a vernacular poem, consciously evoking Classical precedent (da Gama is Camoëns's Aeneas), is in itself a patriotic statement.   JL

THE METAPHYSICAL POETS

The term *Metaphysical*, coined by Dr Johnson in the 18th century (see p. 627), is used to describe a number of early 17th-century English poets whose verse – witty and intellectual – makes use of abstract ideas and paradoxes to express feelings.

John Donne (1572–1631) was the foremost Metaphysical poet: his love poetry is characterized by a dazzling and often cynical wit, while his religious poems explore vividly the paradoxes of Christian belief.

George Herbert (1593–1633) was a religious poet. Like Donne, he was an Anglican searching out issues and problems of faith, though in a less dramatic, and more reflective mode. Other Metaphysical poets of note include *Henry Vaughan* (1621–95), *Andrew Marvell* (1621–78), *Richard Crashaw* (1612/13–49) and the young Milton.

Classicism in Literature

Knowledge of and interest in the works of ancient Greek and Roman authors was a key aspect of the Renaissance (see p. 624). After that explosive fusion of old and new ideas came a period when *Neoclassical* writers tried to imitate in modern languages what they thought was the spirit and style of the classics. *Neoclassicism* was especially strong in the French theatre during the 17th century and in England from the Restoration of 1660 to the end of the 18th century.

The virtues seen in ancient Classical writers were an appeal to reason rather than emotion; a concern with ideas and experiences of a universal validity; and a style characterized by clarity, control and dignity. Alexander Pope's translation of Horace's (see p. 614) dictum 'What oft was thought but ne'er so well expressed', conveys in its balanced phrasing the harmony of style and subject matter cherished by the Neoclassicists.

The French Classical theatre

In his *Poetics* Aristotle (see p. 614) discussed the unified organization of a tragedy. Later writers – notably the influential Italian Renaissance critic *Lodovico Castelvetro* (1505–71) – developed Aristotle's ideas into a set of rules, known as the *unities*. The unity of *action* restricted the action to a single plot. The unity of *time* restricted the span of events on stage to 24 hours and the

SEE ALSO

● CLASSICAL LITERATURE
  p. 614
● RENAISSANCE LITERATURE
  pp. 622–5
● THE BEGINNINGS OF THE
  NOVEL p. 628
● ROMANTICISM pp. 630–3

unity of *place* limited the action to a single spot. The unities of time and place were intended to help the audience 'believe' what they saw. When they are skilfully handled, as in the best plays of Corneille and Racine, these constraints can produce drama of great power and concentration; less adroitly applied, they can engender much clumsy contrivance in order to squeeze characters into one location and action into one day.

Pierre Corneille (1606–84) began by writing comedy, but then attempted a classical tragedy. *Le Cid* (1637) is based on the life of the 11th-century Spanish hero (see p. 399) and explores the moral clash of passion and duty. The play was immensely successful, but broke the unity of action, thereby displeasing the newly formed Académie française, a literary academy founded in 1634 and devoted to maintaining the standards of the French language. This controversy led to final acceptance of the unities and the exclusion of sub-plots from French Classical drama thereafter. Corneille went on to write three great plays – *Horace* (1640), *Cinna* (1641) and *Polyeucte* (1643) – which conform strictly to these rules, and deal with conflicts between family affection and public duty and the rival claims of justice and mercy.

In all these plays the central characters are put under severe mental pressure. Their moments of emotional stress are presented in long, rhetorical speeches in a style that is elevated rather than natural. In accordance with the Neoclassical virtue of restraint, there is little action on stage. The plays are written in six-beat rhyming couplets (*Alexandrines*) that were held to give the speech true Classical dignity.

Corneille lived to see his place as France's greatest tragic dramatist usurped by *Jean Racine* (1639–99), who drew upon Greek,

Roman and Biblical sources for most of his plays. The tragedies *Andromaque* (1667), *Britannicus* (1669), *Bérénice* (1670) and *Bajazet* (1672) respectively explore themes of emotional rejection, tyranny, the conflict of love and duty, and revenge. But it is in *Phèdre* (1677) that Racine's central theme of the destructive power of passion is most memorably dramatized. Phèdre – one of a succession of agonized heroines in his drama – is torn between her love for a young man and her guilt because he is her stepson. Racine uses the formal and stylistic conventions of Neoclassicism to write tragedies of power and psychological depth unrivalled in French literature. His plays adhere rigidly to the unities; his plots are stark and simple; all is focused on a poetic language of masterly flexibility and concentration.

The greatest writer of Classical French comedy was the playwright, actor and producer *Molière* (the pen name of Jean-Baptiste Poquelin, 1622–73). The ancient Greeks saw comedy as a way of ridiculing the absurdities of men, and this Molière did supremely well. But as well as exposing the foibles and falsity of a whole gallery of misfits, obsessives and hypocrites in such plays as *The School for Wives* (1662), *Don Juan* (1665), and *The Miser* (1668), he also celebrates tolerance and generosity of spirit.

Molière's plots, which often involve a romantic element and clever, contriving servants, are influenced by Terence and Plautus (see pp. 614–15) in their use of certain stock characters, and by the improvised farce of the Italian *Commedia dell'arte*. But Molière's characters take on an individuality and a vitality of their own. In *Tartuffe* (1664) he derided religious hypocrisy so effectively that he outraged all shades of religious opinion. Molière's greatest play, *The Misanthrope* (1666), stops only just short of tragedy in its perceptive depiction of an uncompromising and self-righteous critic of the sins of society.

Subtle analysis of feeling and sentiment characterizes the plays of *Pierre Marivaux* (1688–1763). Despite their verbal preciosity, *The Game of Love and Chance* (1730) and *The False Confidences* (1737) show an increase in realism, establishing precise social settings and giving the servant characters real feelings.

The chief theorist of Neoclassical French literature was the poet and critic *Nicolas Boileau* (1636–1711), who wrote epistles and satires on Horatian models. His *Poetic Art* (1674) defined principles of literary judgement that were put into practice in England by Dryden and Pope.

The influence of French Neoclassicism throughout Europe was deep but not always beneficial. In Germany the critic *Johann Christoph Gottsched* (1700–66) determined to improve German literary style using French models and wrote vigorously in support of this aim. But the dramatist and critic *Gotthold Ephraim Lessing* (1728–81) – who used English literature as his model in his comedy *Minna von Barnhelm* (1767) and his domestic tragedy *Miss Sara Sampson* (1755) – helped free German literature from slavish imitation of French Neoclassicism.

The Oath of the Horatii by the French painter Jacques Louis David. Ancient Roman legend tells of an uncompromisingly patriotic soldier (one of three brothers – the Horatii), who kills his sister when she weeps at the death of her lover – an enemy of Rome whom he has slain in single combat. This tale of martial virtue provided the basis for Pierre Corneille's Neoclassical drama *Horace* (1640), an austere tragedy of the conflict between family affection and public duty.

Lessing's drama exemplified a new trend in drama to select subjects from everyday life, rather than the doings of the great.

The wave of egalitarianism that swept through European literature in the late 18th century is seen in two plays by **Pierre-Augustin Caron de Beaumarchais** (1732–99), which take the character of the clever servant to its highest expression. *The Barber of Seville* (1775) and *The Marriage of Figaro* (1784) explore the master-servant relationship in the household to attack despotic government and hereditary privilege. The plays inspired operas by Rossini and Mozart (see p. 584).

English Restoration drama

Exiled in France during the years of Cromwell's Protectorate (see p. 412), Charles II and many of his court brought back a taste for French theatre to England in 1660. This included the use of actresses to play women's parts, an innovation that introduced new possibilities for the exploration of sexual relationships into drama.

Essentially Restoration comedy is a mocking view of the manners of London society. Smart rakes and fops, sexually voracious wives and tedious, jealous husbands are the chief players in a drama of sexual intrigue, often with money as the motive. The plots are complicated, the style fast, witty, and at times very bawdy.

The Country Wife (1675) by **William Wycherley** (1641–1715) makes hilarious use of ribald innuendo, and is fiercely satirical in its presentation of a society so dedicated to pleasure that it has lost touch with real human values. His last play, *The Plain Dealer* (1676), is based on, but radically reworked from, Molière's *The Misanthrope*.

A more restrained and elegant approach to social satire is found in the plays of **William Congreve** (1670–1729). His comedy of deception, *The Way of The World* (1700), is distinguished by brilliant dialogue and makes serious points about the social pressures on love and marriage. Other notable writers of comedies include **Sir John Vanbrugh** (1664–1726) and **George Farquhar** (1678–1707).

This tradition of social comedy continued in milder form into the 18th century with **Richard Sheridan** (1751–1816) – with plays such as *The Rivals* (1775) – into the 19th century with Oscar Wilde and into the 20th century with Noel Coward (see p. 644).

Elevated heroic tragedies also played in the Restoration theatre. Influenced by French tragedies, these plays involved heroes caught in stock situations of conflicting loyalties. The rhetoric and strict form of classical tragedy never became popular in England, although the poet and dramatist **John Dryden** (1631–1700) did manage a successful adaptation of Shakespeare in the blank-verse play *All for Love* (1678), where he squeezed the story of Antony and Cleopatra within the limits of the unities with some success.

The Augustan Age

Dryden was altogether more successful as

a poet, mastering the ode and, in the allegorical poem *Absalom and Achitophel* (1681), writing some of the keenest satire in the English language. (Hugely inventive prose satire is also found in the works of Jonathan Swift, see p. 629.)

The fifty or so years following Dryden's death are named after the Roman Emperor Augustus, under whom poets such as Virgil and Horace flourished (see p. 614). The natural successor to Dryden was **Alexander Pope** (1688–1744). Dryden had translated some of Juvenal's satire (see p. 614) using the heroic couplet to stinging effect. Pope began by writing pastoral verse and later translated Homer into formal English. But like Dryden he was most effective as a satirist, writing in mock-heroic vein in *The Rape of the Lock* (1712–14), and achieving a wicked elegance in his great attack on literary mediocrity, the *Dunciad* (1728–43). In his *Essay on Criticism* (1711) he laid down the rules for writing in the neoclassical manner with an emphasis on a high degree of polish and a harmony of style and sense.

Another aspect of 18th-century poetry,

and one visible in early Pope, is a taste for natural description, meditation and melancholy introspection. **Oliver Goldsmith's** (?1730–74) *The Deserted Village* (1770) laments a lost golden age of English village life, despoiled by the effects of the enclosures (see p. 420). This introspective tendency becomes more noticeable in the poetry of **Thomas Gray** (1716–71), who produced little but wrote with great care, perfecting the *Elegy Written in a Country Churchyard* (1751) over ten years. Of one part of it Dr Johnson said that while he had seen the ideas nowhere else, 'he that reads them here persuades himself that he has always felt them'. Although the poem is of the 18th century in its language, its mood of wistfulness and gloom looks forward to the early Romantics (see p. 632).

Many Neoclassical writers described landscape either in idealized, *pastoral* terms, or in terms of the *picturesque* (see p. 536). But by the end of the 18th century poets such as **George Crabbe** (1754–1832) were focusing on the harsh realities of the lives of the poor and contrasting these with the artificiality of pastoral verse. JC

DR JOHNSON

In Samuel Johnson (1709–84) can be seen the best, the worst and perhaps the end of the Augustan Age. He wrote English as though it were Latin, using many ponderous words of Classical origin. He was interested in general ideas, not particular feelings, and deeply distrusted emotion. Yet in his great edition of Shakespeare, Johnson dismisses the notion of the unities of time and place – which Shakespeare totally ignored – with brisk common sense.

Johnson was enormously versatile, writing plays, a novel, works of criticism and biography, and his famous *Dictionary of the English Language* (1755). But his reputation rests to a considerable extent on his friend James Boswell's (1740–95) portrait of him – learned, opinionated and a brilliant conversationalist – in his *Life of Samuel Johnson* (1791).

Samuel Johnson – literary critic, scholar, lexicographer and celebrated conversationalist – takes tea.

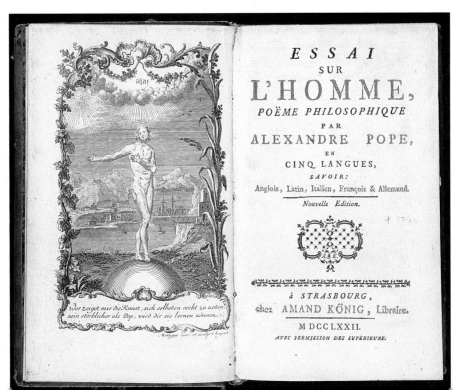

Alexander Pope's *Essay on Man* (1732–34) is a philosophical poem that sets out to demonstrate the perfection of God's scheme for the universe. Illustrated here are the frontispiece and title-page of a five-language edition of the poem published in Strasbourg in 1772. Pope was the first English poet to enjoy international fame during his own lifetime. His European reputation is reflected in the flattering couplet in German at the foot of the frontispiece.

The Beginnings of the Novel

One of the most dramatic shifts in literary fashion occurred in the early 18th century, when a relatively new form, the *novel* – an extended prose narrative treating in a realistic manner the story of fictional individuals within a recognizable social context – achieved popularity with a wide audience and came to be seen as a vehicle for serious literary expression.

Up to the 16th century the dominant literary mode had been verse, often of an elevated character and dealing with high-born heroes and heroines. There had also been, however, examples of prose fiction treating less exalted themes – works such as the *Satyricon* of Petronius and *The Golden Ass* of Apuleius (see pp. 614–15). The Italian *novella* – a type of short tale of a humorous nature found in Boccaccio's *Decameron* (see p. 620) and elsewhere – lent its name to the more extended prose fictions of Defoe, Richardson and Fielding.

A number of important strands can be discerned in the early novel. Some novels show a strong emphasis on *realism* – the representation of life as it is. The use of

SEE ALSO

● MEDIEVAL TALES p. 620
● CLASSICISM IN LITERATURE p. 626
● ROMANTICISM pp. 630–3
● REALISM AND NATURALISM p. 634
● THE NOVEL IN 19TH-CENTURY BRITAIN p. 636

Don Quixote on his horse Rosinante, painted by the 19th-century French artist Honoré Daumier. Cervantes's tale of the often absurd adventures of Don Quixote – a poor gentleman of La Mancha whose brain is addled by excessive reading of tales of chivalry – and his more earthy and pragmatic servant Sancho Panza, presents a vivid picture of all levels of Spanish society.

first-person narrative creates an impression that authentic experience is being described, underpinning the illusion of reality. *Epistolary novels* – written in the form of letters – were intended to enhance this illusion, by allowing the intimate recounting of recently lived experience. But the most important early influence on the development of the novel was the tradition of the picaresque.

The picaresque novel

The term *picaresque* derives from the Spanish word *picaro*, meaning a wily rogue. Picaresque tales appeared in Spain in the 16th century and typically relate the adventures of rascally servants who defraud their social superiors before repenting their ways. The term picaresque has subsequently been applied to any novel that is structured in episodes (often a series of adventures) linked only by one or more characters – as opposed to a novel with a more tightly integrated plot.

Simplicissimus (1669), by the German **J.J.C. von Grimmelshausen** (c.1621–76) was closely modelled on the Spanish picaresque novel and presents a vivid social picture of a fearful and chaotic Germany torn apart by the Thirty Years War (see p. 408). Satirical, ribald, and abounding in realistic and even grotesque detail, the novel charts the progression of its 'strange vagabond' hero through the roles of simpleton and debauched cynic to world-weary hermit (see illustration). *Simplicissimus* is one of the first – and greatest – novels in German; it addresses the principal themes of its age with philosophical depth and religious insight.

An interesting variation on the picaresque theme is found in *Don Quixote* (1615) by the Spanish writer **Miguel de Cervantes** (1547–1616). In what is widely regarded as the first true novel, the impossible idealism of the chivalric knight Don Quixote is contrasted with the earthy pragmatism of his servant Sancho Panza. By parodying the ballads and romances of chivalric literature – as in the scene where Quixote tilts at windmills in the mistaken belief that they are giants – Cervantes helped establish the humorous prose narrative as a serious literary genre.

The rise of the English novel

The works of the English writer **Daniel Defoe** (1660–1731) were influenced by the picaresque tradition and show a similar concern with low-life characters. His novel *Moll Flanders* (1722) purports to be an autobiographical account of a woman who is at times wife, prostitute, pickpocket and finally mistress of a plantation in Virginia. The first-person narrative emphasizes her strong personality but also dwells on the social injustices that determine her colourful story. Based on a true story, Defoe's most famous novel, *Robinson Crusoe* (1719), has an exotic desert-island setting, but its shipwrecked hero proves to be a

resolute defender of bourgeois values, re-creating in the wilderness the ordered world of 18th-century mercantile society.

The Irish clergyman **Jonathan Swift** (1667–1745) took the convention of the tale of the shipwrecked mariner into the realms of satirical fantasy in his classic *Gulliver's Travels* (1726). Lemuel Gulliver's adventures takes him to such fantastical locations as the island of Lilliput (inhabited by midgets), Brobdingnag (peopled by giants), and the flying island of Laputa. In the petty squabbles of their various inhabitants, Swift satirizes the intellectual pretentions and vanity of the philosophers, scientists and political and literary factions of the time. In the last section of the book, he extends this into a strident denunciation of the degradation of human life.

Defoe's immediacy of expression and close recording of realistic detail is heightened in the novels of **Samuel Richardson** (1689–1761). Richardson employed the epistolary technique, allowing his characters to speak in their own private voices through letters that detail not just events but also the varied emotional and psychological responses of the characters to those events.

Richardson's *Pamela* (1740–1) records the experiences of a young woman in domestic service who resists the lecherous advances of her unscrupulous employer. Her patience is rewarded when her virtue eventually ensures her suitor's rehabilitation and leads to a model marriage. The apparently simple-minded morality of Pamela was parodied in a spoof novel – *Shamela* (1741) by Fielding (see below).

In Richardson's later masterpiece *Clarissa* (1747–8) he again resorted to the epistolary technique, but this time to register the psychological collapse of a young woman who is drugged and raped by the appropriately named rake, Lovelace. Although a remorseful Lovelace is eventually killed in a duel, and Clarissa regains her sanity to die in Christian dignity, the emphasis throughout is on Clarissa's suffering rather than the easy rewards of virtue.

Novels such as Richardson's, in which extreme sensitivity is allied to true virtue, are sometimes known as *novels of sentiment*. But the highly emotional way in which Richardson's characters respond to life reflects a wider cult of feeling, or *sensibility*, that arose in Europe in the mid-18th century. The cult, which drew on philosophical beliefs in the innate goodness of man and prefigures Romanticism in its exalting of emotion (see p. 632), is also evident in the novels of Marivaux (see below), in Fielding and Sterne, in the characters of Rousseau's novels and in Goethe's *Sorrows of Young Werther* (see p. 630).

The apparently easy moral distinctions of Richardson cannot be made in the case of the novels of **Henry Fielding** (1707–54). *Tom Jones* (1749) tells the adventures of a generous-hearted foundling who is almost cheated of his rightful inheritance by mean-spirited relations. By the end of the novel he regains his legitimate fortune and captures the heart of the virtuous heroine – but not before indulging in a variety of sexual escapades along the way. The style of the novel is graphic, ironic and often bawdy, and the account of Tom Jones's journeyings allows a wide-ranging view of English society of the period.

Tobias Smollett (1721–71) employed a similar technique to Fielding, although the incidents he relates are often sordid and violent, and his tone lacks Fielding's tolerance and humanity. In his masterpiece, *The Expedition of Humphry Clinker* (1741), he achieves a comic fusion of the methods of Fielding and Richardson, the novel recording the varied adventures of a travelling group through a series of vividly expressed letters.

Standing somewhat apart from the main realistic tradition of 18th-century fiction is a highly original novel, *The Life and Opinions of Tristram Shandy* (1759–68), by the clergyman **Laurence Sterne** (1713–68). The surname of the novel's first-person narrator implies crankiness and absurdity, and the work abounds in idiosyncrasies that mock the conventional form of the novels of Sterne's contemporaries. The novel opens at the moment of the hero's conception and his birth is not described until well into the book, even then being interrupted by the overdue insertion of a Preface. Sterne constantly reminds readers of the unreality and illusion of fiction, indulging in abrupt time shifts and obscure philosophical speculation, leaving blank pages, making typographical allusions to events being described, and at times abandoning any sense of coherent plot. Nothing comparable to *Tristram Shandy* appears in literature until the novels of James Joyce in the 20th century.

The novel in France

Heroic romances with pastoral or antique settings and highly implausible plots enjoyed a vogue in France throughout the 17th century. The psychological realism and acute analysis of character that were to become the hallmark of the 18th-century French novel are seen for the first time in a novel by **Madame de la Fayette** (1634–93). *The Princess of Cleves* (1678) forsakes the idealized pastoral settings of its predecessors to present a tragic tale of married life and the temptations of romantic love in the realistic setting of a French court. As in the Neoclassical dramas of Corneille (see p. 626), the protagonists conquer their passion through the exercise of will-power.

Character and emotion receive yet closer analysis in the novels of **Antoine-François (l'Abbé) Prévost** (1697–1763), an admirer and translator of Richardson. *Manon Lescaut* (1731) is a first-person account of the mutually destructive passion of a refined but weak-willed nobleman and an alluring but amoral young woman. The novel celebrates passion with extraordinary intensity, most notably in the heroine's protracted death in the arms of her lover in the

The frontispiece and title-page of Grimmelshausen's picaresque novel *Simplicissimus* (1669). The grotesque monster was designed by the author himself and represents the vanity and inconstancy of earthly existence – an important theme of the novel. The long sub-title on the title-page contains the novelist's pen name 'German Schleifheim von Sulfsort' – an anagram of Grimmelshausen's full name. Grimmelshausen's authorship of *Simplicissimus* was not established until the 19th century.

Louisiana desert. But there is down-to-earth realism too, in the hero's precise noting of financial costs. *Manon Lescaut* inspired several operas, including one by Puccini.

The influence of the picaresque tradition is evident in two novels by **Pierre Marivaux** (1688–1763; see p. 626). *The Life of Marianne* (1731–41) and *The Fortunate Peasant* (1735) are first-person narratives whose heroes recount their upward progress in society. While both novels have elements of social realism strongly reminiscent of Defoe, their keynote is psychological analysis of motive and feeling. In the importance that they attach to emotion and intuition, and their rejection of authority and tradition in favour of simple morality and naturalness, Marivaux's novels, like Richardson's, look forward to the Romantic period. The cult of nature and simplicity is promoted most vigorously in the novels of Rousseau (see p. 631).

In contrast to Rousseau's unrealistic idealism is the practical philosophy of the Enlightenment thinker **Voltaire** (see p. 418). In his most famous work, *Candide* (1759), the hero sees and suffers so much that he comes to reject the philosophical dogma of his optimistic tutor, Dr. Pangloss, that this is 'the best of all possible worlds' (a doctrine derived from the German philosopher Leibniz; see p. 487). He decides instead that the secret of happiness is to 'cultivate one's garden' – an intensely practical philosophy that rejects excessive idealism and convoluted metaphysics.

Denis Diderot (see p. 418) shared with Voltaire an enthusiasm for English culture. His novel *Jacques the Fatalist* (1773) – which marries the tradition of the picaresque novel to the philosophical tale – shows the influence of Sterne in its awareness of the artificiality of the novel form.

Acute analysis is applied to the domain of sexual psychology with consummate skill in *Dangerous Liaisons* (1782), a finely crafted epistolary novel by **Choderlos de Laclos** (1741–1803). The novel takes the form of an exchange of letters between two cynical aristocrats who use innocent youth as a pawn in their sexual and emotional power struggle. Whether it is seen as a satire on the emptiness and corruption of aristocratic society prior to the French Revolution (see p. 424) or as an account of erotic psychology, *Dangerous Liaisons* is unquestionably a masterpiece.

In stark contrast is the idealized natural paradise depicted by **Bernardin de Saint-Pierre** (1737–1814) in *Paul et Virginie* (1787). The love of the two innocent children of the title flourishes on the idyllic island of Mauritius, until the intrusion of civilization leads to tragedy. The influence of dawning Romanticism – and particularly the notion that goodness and innocence reside only in the state of nature – can be discerned in this rich evocation of an exotic wilderness.   GH

Hogarth's frontispiece for *Tristram Shandy*. The conventions of the still youthful novel form were comprehensively satirized in Laurence Sterne's idiosyncratic work, in which the highly tenuous plot is constantly interrupted by lengthy and sometimes ribald digression. The book's typographical oddities include blank pages, rows of dashes and asterisks, and a variety of different typefaces.

Romanticism in Europe

'Romantic' used to mean simply the kind of thing found in a tale of romance (see pp. 618–19). The word was first used in a more profound sense around 1800 by the brothers *Schlegel, August Wilhelm* (1767–1845) and *Friedrich* (1772–1829). These German intellectuals idealized the era of classical antiquity, especially the culture of ancient Greece, and then contrasted it with the literature of the Christian era from the Middle Ages up to their own time. This second era they called modern – as distinct from ancient – and defined as Romantic.

Idealization of Antiquity (see pp. 614–15) had long been commonplace (Classical models had influenced European art, literature, and especially architecture since the Renaissance). The Schlegels believed the human spirit had found in Classical Greece a state of perfect harmony with its earthly surroundings. The modern spirit, by contrast, they thought to be restlessly pursuing goals which are never fulfilled on earth; it is inevitably self-conscious and ironic, and its characteristic passion is yearning. Naturally these writers regarded themselves as belonging to the modern, Romantic tradition, and they soon became known as Romantics.

'Sturm und Drang'

Germany was at that time enjoying a great cultural renaissance in literature, philosophy, and music. The country was still far from being a single nation state (see p. 428), and there was a widespread desire to discover and affirm a national identity. The literary renaissance had begun when the critic and cultural historian *Johann Gottfried Herder* (1744–1803) and the greatest German poet, *Johann Wolfgang von Goethe* (1749–1832), had proclaimed the need to stop imitating French culture (see pp. 626–7). This had been for two centuries Neoclassical in character – based on Greco-Roman models – and therefore itself an imitation rather than truly modern; it was also associated with the kind of monarchic and repressive rule which had long prevailed not just in France but throughout Europe.

Goethe, Herder, and Schiller (see below) were the principal figures in a movement of young writers known as *Sturm und Drang* ('Storm and Stress'). Strongly influenced by Rousseau (see p. 631), they rebelled against convention in both art and life, and exalted the free, the natural, and the spontaneous. Naturalness of emotion and a feeling for nature were the keynotes of Goethe's youthful poetry, while his plays dramatized the struggle for freedom. His novel, *The Sorrows of Young Werther* (1774), with its story of an artist's unrequited passion and suicide, made the new sensibility famous throughout Europe.

Young Germans felt immediate sympathy for the French Revolution, which seemed to promise escape from the old everywhere, now that the *ancien régime* had been overthrown in its homeland (see pp. 424–5 and 632). Instead came the Terror and a new French Empire established by

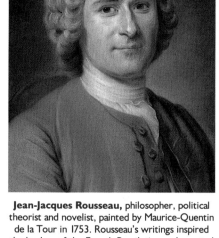

Jean-Jacques Rousseau, philosopher, political theorist and novelist, painted by Maurice-Quentin de la Tour in 1753. Rousseau's writings inspired the leaders of the French Revolution and exerted a massive influence on the Romantic movement throughout Europe.

Napoleon, which left monarchies and Neoclassical taste still in place. Thinkers and writers grew uncertain of their early liberalism, and many started to look backward, often to the Middle Ages, for a better social ideal.

The Schlegels' ideas helped to make most German Romantics idealize medieval culture. Goethe, by contrast, developed a Neoclassical style of his own. He lived in the court circles of Weimar, and he came to regard Romanticism as a sickness. He did not simply suppress his former inspiration, but disciplined it to a wiser perfection. His novel, *Wilhelm Meister* (1795–6), educates its Werther-like hero to accept his place in society. *Faust*, a dramatic poem Goethe worked on all his life, finally saves the hero's restlessly striving soul. The best achievements of Goethe's 'Classical' maturity are the verse dramas of reconciliation and renunciation – *Iphigenia* (1787) and *Torquato Tasso* (1790).

The dramatist and poet *Friedrich Schiller* (1759–1805) similarly turned away from the rhetoric of rebellion towards the measured verse of a purely spiritual freedom. The moral idealism of his mature dramas, *Wallenstein* (1798–9) and *Maria Stuart* (1800) is more profound psychologically and dramatically than that of *The Robbers* (1781), a wild *Sturm und Drang* production. Schiller's philosophical essays on art and morality, and especially his concept of a beautiful soul, have been widely influential.

The German Romantics

Apart from much speculative writing about culture and the creative personality, Romantic scholars developed German philology, collected the nation's folk-songs and tales, and translated Shakespeare and other kindred spirits of the Romantic age. A host of minor talents wrote poems and even fairy stories in a folkloric manner, some of which have been immortalized by being

Goethe in the Roman Campagna, painted by J.H.W. Tischbein in 1787. After a youth of restless Romantic aspirations, Goethe learnt to accept life's necessary forms. His encounter with Classical art during his stay in Italy from 1786 to 1788 provided creative renewal for his astonishingly diverse genius.

composed into Romantic *Lieder* (see p. 576).

The best poet of such song-like lyrics was *Heinrich Heine* (1797–1856), whose ironic intelligence, personal sufferings, and political principles lent this simple style some depth of interest. The danger facing all Romantics was escapism into self-indulgent emotions and fancies. Where this tendency was not corrected by a maturer sense of reality (as it was with Goethe), it required some unusual intensity of inwardness to raise fantasy above private make-believe.

Such intensity is present in the poetic meditations of *Novalis* (the pen name of Friedrich Leopold von Hardenberg; 1772–1801) on art and death, in the elegiac laments of *Friedrich Hölderlin* (1770–1843) for the loss of the ancient gods, and in the tragic stories and plays which *Heinrich von Kleist* (1777–1811) wove out of his sense that men are enclosed in illusion. Novalis willed himself to die for love, Hölderlin went mad, and Kleist committed suicide.

The philosophical background to Romanticism

None of these developments, from Schlegel's definition of Romantic to Kleist's tragic view of the human condition, would have taken place without the all-pervading presence throughout Germany of a new kind of philosophy. Known as idealist thinking, it originates with Kant (see p. 486), and it analyses how much the world is shaped through human understanding of it. What appears to be reality is, in truth, a projection of the human mind. The specifically Romantic philosophers, *F.W.J. von Schelling* (1775–1854) and *J.G. Fichte* (1762–1814), showed how nature therefore corresponds with the mind, being in a sense identical with it. *G.W.F. Hegel* (1770–1831) saw in human history and culture a direct manifestation of absolute spirit (or God). Coleridge learnt this view of nature from Schelling and taught it to Wordsworth (see p. 632); Marx learnt his philosophical method, though not his political message from Hegel (see p. 486). Few aspects of modern European culture remain untouched by the influence of this period in philosophy.

The French Romantics

In 1810, the French writer *Mme de Stael* (1766–1817) wrote a journalistic report, based on personal contacts, praising this renaissance of German culture. Her influential book *On Germany* was suppressed in France, on Napoleon's orders, for belittling French culture. And in truth, the change in outlook that was now becoming known as Romanticism owed as much to the French writer *Jean-Jacques Rousseau* (1712–78), as to any German.

As early as 1750, in his *Discourse on the arts and sciences*, Rousseau had begun to resist the rationalism and artificiality of the Enlightenment (see p. 418), and to plead for naturalness of feeling, freedom from constraint, and a better social order.

Rousseau argued that man's inherently perfect nature is corrupted by society. His novel *Emile* (1762) proposed a new type of 'natural' education, in which the child is shielded, like the 'noble savage', from the harmful influence of civilization. From Rousseau's novel *La Nouvelle Héloïse* (1761), which shows sentiment, virtue, and introspection flourishing in an idyllic setting, all Europe learned a new sensibility and appreciation of nature (see p. 536). From his political treatise, *The Social Contract* (see p. 266), a new revolutionary generation learned their most radical ideas of freedom. Rousseau's influence on both the Romantic movement and the French Revolution (see pp. 424–5) can hardly be exaggerated.

By the time a generation of avowed Romantics appeared in France, still further influences were at work. There was a mood of religious revival, encouraged by Napoleon, and captured by *François René de Chateaubriand* (1768–1848) in *Le Génie du Christianisme* (1802). This apologia for the cultural and psychological significance of religion – 'the genius of Christianity – includes his famous autobiographical tale of Romantic melancholy, *René*.

Besides this, there was admiration for the work of Byron and Scott (see pp. 632–3). Many historical novels were written by authors not considered Romantic, like Balzac (see p. 634) and Alexandre Dumas. The finest was produced in Italy by *Alessandro Manzoni* (1785–1873) – *The Betrothed* (1827).

A more or less 'Byronic' poetry of lonely intellectual genius, isolated in an alien world, bewailing its fate and addressing nature, was variously practised by such well-born writers as *Alphonse de Lamartine* (1790–1869), *Alfred de Vigny* (1797–1863), and *Alfred de Musset* (1810–57). The greatest was *Victor Hugo* (1802–85), whose high-minded idealism lent his later poetry a prophetic and visionary quality, drove him into political exile, and made him at last a national hero.

For these writers, Romanticism also meant an opportunity to break with the regularities and restrictions of Neoclassical forms, both in verse and in drama. Hugo's preface to his play *Cromwell* (1827) rejected conventions observed in France since Boileau (see p. 626), and pointed to Shakespeare to justify, for instance, mixing comedy and tragedy in the same play. *Cromwell* failed, but its preface became a Romantic manifesto, and another play, *Hernani*, triumphed in 1830, causing a near riot. The preface to Hugo's volume of poems, *Les Orientales* (1829), similarly proclaimed complete freedom of inspiration for poetry. However, the medium in which Hugo's wonderfully vivid and dramatic imagination expressed itself most freely was fiction, notably *The Hunchback of Notre Dame* (1831) and *Les Misérables* (1862).

A shift from Romanticism towards Aes-

theticism and Symbolism is evident in the work of Théophile Gautier (see p. 640) and the poet and prose-writer *Gérard de Nerval* (the pen name of Gérard Labrunie; 1808–55). Nerval translated Goethe's *Faust* as a young man, but his greatest achievement is his sonnet sequence *Les Chimères* (1854). These densely symbolic and allusive poems prefigure the poetry of Baudelaire and Mallarmé (see p. 640).

'National' poets

The great 'national' poets of other countries were also active at this time: *Adam Mickiewicz* in Poland (1798–1855), *Giacomo Leopardi* in Italy (1798–1837), and *Alexander Pushkin* in Russia (1799–1837). Their work goes far beyond the typical concerns of Romanticism, although these are present too in, for instance, the folkloric material and ironic self-awareness of Mickiewicz; in the solitariness, self-consciousness, and melancholy of Leopardi; and in the nature scenes and yearning passions of Pushkin.

Mikhail Lermontov (1814–1841) who shared Pushkin's rebelliousness against Russia's backward regime and society, is more obviously a Romantic, both in his lyric poems and in his novel, *A Hero of Our Time* (1840), which portrays a cynical Byronic outsider. Like the hero of his masterpiece and like Pushkin whom he admired, Lermontov was killed in a duel. Russians found in the landscape and people of the Caucasus their image of the simple and natural, which generations of Romantics – under Rousseau's influence – longed for. The most interesting Romantic literature grew from the realization that this ideal was unattainable. AT

SEE ALSO
- CLASSICISM IN LITERATURE p. 626
- THE BEGINNINGS OF THE NOVEL p. 628
- THE BRITISH ROMANTICS p. 632
- REALISM AND NATURALISM p. 634
- SYMBOLISM, AESTHETICISM AND THE BIRTH OF MODERNISM p. 640

Victor Hugo dominates the literary institutions of France in a contemporary caricature. The leader of the Romantic movement in the 1830s, Hugo was elected to the Académie française in 1841, became a peer in 1845, and was the object of public veneration in his later years.

The British Romantics

During the period of Germany's great cultural revival (see p. 630), Romanticism in British literature emerged, in the 1780s, in parallel with the revolutionary struggles of the French people against the Ancien Regime (see pp. 424–5). The initial passionate enthusiasm of the early British Romantics for the republican ideals of the French Revolution is reflected in Wordsworth's exhilarating affirmation 'Bliss was it in that dawn to be alive, but to be young was very heaven.'

The French Revolution itself was a contradictory historical movement. It intended to establish the reign of Reason on Earth but habitually used the tools of political violence and terror. It aspired to secure universal freedom, but released the great personality cult of Napoleon. It aimed to sweep away oppression by destroying the aristocracy, but ended by establishing new forms of domination for a new ruling class – the bourgeoisie.

In the same way British Romanticism contains many contradictory aspects and impulses. To one degree or another the Romantic poets all espoused radical or liberal sympathies with the progressive forces of the time. Yet they were also responsible for developing a new self-consciousness, a new emphasis on the individual, which distanced them from the masses. They wanted to liberate literature from the possession of the old ruling class of aristocratic patrons, to find a new popular audience and to write of the experience of the poor and oppressed. Yet at the same time they saw their art as a specialized activity set apart from common life. They tried to emphasize the positive powers of the human spirit and imagination, singing of joy and delight, energy and affirmation. Yet their songs of celebration were continually shadowed by an undertone of melancholy and hopelessness, a constant return to disillusionment and failure of the will.

Certain features, however, can be regarded as the common characteristics of the English Romantics. They rejected the rules and conventions of Neoclassical civilization (see pp. 626–7), and embraced artistic freedom, experimenting with many and varied poetic forms. They were out of sympathy with industrialization and the growth of the city, choosing to concentrate on rural or pastoral settings. They respected the irrational, and were not averse to writing of dreams, or of the supernatural, or experimenting with hallucinogenic drugs. They were for imagination, and against reason; for energy and against control; for revolution and against the old empires.

Romantic prose

Whereas in Europe Romanticism tended to seek a home in the novel and the drama (see pp. 630–1), in Britain the movement was largely a poetic one; but it also manifested itself in certain types of prose. Among these were *Gothic* novels, tales of the macabre and the fantastic set in wild landscapes of rugged mountains, haunted castles and ruins. These novels are the ancestors of the modern horror story (see p. 650). At one level they operated as an indulgence in the casual shudder, but at another level they began to explore unresearched depths of the human psyche. *The Castle of Otranto* (1765) by **Horace Walpole** (1717–97) is a pioneer of the genre; but the most popular and successful Gothic novels were those of **Mrs Ann Radcliffe** (1764–1823), of which the most celebrated is *The Mysteries of Udolpho* (1794).

The Romantic poets were to draw on this Gothic inheritance. Indeed it was Shelley's wife, **Mary Wollstonecraft Shelley** (1797–1851), who constructed one of the most enduring myths of science-fiction terror in *Frankenstein* (1818). Later 19th-century novelists could also tap into this cultural reservoir for serious purposes: Emily Brontë's *Wuthering Heights* (see p. 636) is a tale of love, death and the supernatural with a strong Gothic flav-our; yet it is recognized as one of the most extraordinary fictional experiments of the period. On the other hand the irrationality of the Gothic could be mocked by the solid common-sense approach of Realist fiction, as in Jane Austen's *Northanger Abbey* (see p. 636).

Scotland

The Scottish writer **Sir Walter Scott** (1771–1832) was in some ways the most European of British Romantics. He was well read in early French and Italian poetry, studied the German Romantics, and translated Goethe (see p. 630). As a poet he established a taste for the medieval, and gave currency to the ballad form in his collection of ballads *Minstrelsy of the Scottish Border* (1802–3).

As a novelist Scott virtually invented the historical novel, writing vivid pageants of medieval life such as *Ivanhoe* (1819), and more genuinely historical treatments of recent Scottish history, such as *The Heart of Midlothian* (1818).

Robert Burns (1759–96) was the first major poet to write in Scottish dialect. With his background as a ploughman and labourer on his father's poor farms, he was initially celebrated by the aristocratic society of Edinburgh as a 'peasant poet', and he went on to collect, edit and write over 700 dialect songs (including such well-known lyrics as 'Auld Lang Syne'). But he also wrote with facility in 18th-century English, and such verse has affinities with Neoclassical poetry. Burns deals equally with tales derived from Scottish folklore, as in his narrative poem *Tom o'Shanter* (1791).

Blake: poetry and revolution

The poet, painter and engraver **William Blake** (1757–1827) was the most consciously revolutionary and the most politically involved of the English Romantics, writing poems celebrating the American War of Independence and the French Revolution. His most successful works were the *Songs of Innocence* (1789) and *Songs of Experience* (1794), which juxtapose the linked opposites of existence, and capture perfectly the tense and conflictory nature of the age: childlike hope confronts adult disillusion, passion encounters moral oppression, the submissive gentleness of 'The Lamb' sits at irreconcilable odds with the violent energy of 'The Tyger'.

The 'Lake Poets'

The 'Lake Poets' was the collective name given to Wordsworth, Coleridge and their lesser associate Robert Southey (1774–1843), all of whom lived in the English Lake District for long periods after 1800. **William Wordsworth** (1770–1850) developed the use of imagination and feeling to explore a deeper understanding of human relationships and social existence. The natural landscape and peasant inhabitants of the Lake District, where he was brought up, provided the substance for much of his poetry. In 1795 Wordsworth had met Coleridge (see below) and, as neighbours in Dorset, the two poets worked closely together, publishing the

The Marriage of Heaven and Hell (1790–93), William Blake's main prose work, consists of a series of paradoxical aphorisms. The frontispiece shown here was etched and printed – as were all Blake's works – by the writer himself.

Lyrical Ballads (1798), a collection of poems dealing with common life, and written in popular ballad and lyrical forms. Despite his desire to reach out towards the common people, and his image of the poet as 'a man speaking to men', Wordsworth was the great poet of the self. In his huge psychological epic *The Prelude* (1798–1805), he attempted to link the development of his own experience with the revolutionary changes of his age.

The poetic gifts of **Samuel Taylor Coleridge** (1772–1834) were in some ways the opposite of Wordsworth's. His imagination dwelt on the strange and fantastic and on dream and hallucination. His contribution to the *Lyrical Ballads*, 'The Rime of the Ancient Mariner' – the tale of a nightmare sea-voyage and an enduring myth of psychological extremity and isolation – is regarded as one of the great poems of Romanticism. His 'Kubla Khan', supposedly half-remembered from an opium dream, creates an exotic Romantic landscape of the mind. With their use of the narrative and figurative devices of the popular ballad, both poems imprint themselves indelibly on the imagination, and are deservedly two of the best-known poems in the English language.

At the same time Coleridge was the great intellectual among the British Romantics: together with his poetry, he experimented with the characteristic forms of European Romanticism, philosophical discourse, cultural theory and the drama. He often failed to complete such projects, as if in him the visionary poet and the Romantic intellectual were at odds.

The second generation

Lord Byron (George Gordon Byron, 1788–1824) epitomized the more flamboyant aspects of Romanticism, and lived out the fantasies of his own verse. In the triumphantly successful *Childe Harold's Pilgrimage* (1812) Byron established as a typical Romantic figure the type of the melancholy, isolated 'Byronic' hero, exiled from his native land for some nameless and mysterious crime. Having scandalized public opinion by a rumoured

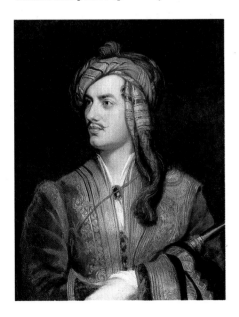

Lord Byron in Greek national costume, by the painter Thomas Phillips. Undeterred by the handicap of a club foot, Byron led a fiercely energetic, flamboyant and sometimes debauched life. Living in exile in Europe from 1816, he went to Greece in 1824 to aid the nationalists in their struggle against the Turks, and died of marsh fever at Missolonghi in 1824. (National Portrait Gallery)

liaison with his half-sister (who probably bore his child), Byron left England in 1816 and lived the rest of his life in continental Europe (see illustration), where his verse remains popular today. His most substantial achievement was in a vein of Romantic satire, combining wit and sentiment, passion and humour, that remained relatively undeveloped in England. Its most effective expression was his epic satire *Don Juan* (1819–24).

Percy Bysshe Shelley (1792–1822) and **John Keats** (1795–1821) are often linked together like Wordsworth and Coleridge, but the respective imaginative impulses of their poetry are almost opposite. In his elegy on the death of Keats, *Adonais* (1821), Shelley compared life to 'a dome of many-coloured glass' that 'stains the white radiance of Eternity'. Shelley's poetic search was always a quest for that white radiance, the unblemished purity of the eternal. In politics he was an extreme radical and a utopian idealist: his vision of progress was realized in great utopian poems like *Prometheus Unbound* (1820), or channelled into harsh satirical anger against existing political conditions, as in *The Mask of Anarchy* (1832).

Keats on the other hand was fascinated by the colours, the appearances and the sensations of physical existence itself. His characteristic achievement, in poems like the great *Odes* (*To a Nightingale, On a Grecian Urn, To Autumn*; 1820), was a poetry which simultaneously achieves through a rich and sensuous language a firm grasp of physical reality, while acknowledging the elusive transitoriness of all things. Shelley was a transcen-

dental, Keats a materialist poet. Yet each repesents something fundamental to Romanticism.

Dream and disenchantment

Romantic poets either died young, with their dreams and aspirations intact, or they lived on, like Wordsworth, into old age and disillusionment. The dreams and passions of Romanticism were as hard to grasp and retain as the utopian aspirations of the French Revolution. The final note of Romanticism always seems to be one of melancholy disappointment, a feeling that (in Wordsworth's line), 'there hath passed away a glory from the earth'. Later poets who revived and extended the Romantic inheritance also inherited these contradictions. The poetry of the great Victorian **Alfred, Lord Tennyson** (1809–92) continually poses a set of irreconcilable conflicts between desire and duty, dream and reality, pleasure and public life. His poem *The Lotos-eaters* (1833) strikes a fine balance between criticism and admiration for the lives of those who give themselves up to Romantic dreams. In *Ulysses* (1842) he contrasts responsibility to the world against Romantic longing for a better.   GHo

A landscape by the British painter Richard Wilson (1713–82). While 18th-century writers such as Dr Johnson preferred to admire nature from the safety of a stagecoach, the Romantic poets sought a closer relationship with it. They found inspiration in the power of wild landscapes such as the English Lake District, the European Alps and the bays of Italy.

SEE ALSO

- ROMANTICISM (PAINTING) p. 536
- CLASSICISM IN LITERATURE p. 626
- THE BEGINNINGS OF THE NOVEL p. 628
- ROMANTICISM IN EUROPE p. 630
- THE NOVEL IN 19TH-CENTURY BRITAIN p. 636

THE BROWNINGS

With Tennyson, Robert Browning (1812–89) was one of the great poets of the early Victorian period that followed the Romantic age. In 1846 he secretly married Elizabeth Barrett Browning (1806–61), herself a lyric poet of some distinction. They were to enjoy 15 intensely happy years together.

Browning concentrated initially on verse drama, but found his preferred mode of expression in dramatic monologues, in which he applied a penetrating psychological realism to a variety of historical and fictional characters. His masterpiece in this form is *The Ring and the Book* (1868–69) – the account of a murder case in late 17th-century Italy. Told by a succession of speakers presenting subjective points of view relating to the murder, and pervaded by prodigious learning, a love of the grotesque and a feeling for the period, *The Ring and the Book* is one of the great long poems in English.

Realism and Naturalism

The term Realism is commonly used to describe works of art that appear to represent the world as it is, not as it might or should be. It can be applied to literature (and painting) from almost any period, but is especially associated with those 19th-century novelists and playwrights who claimed to be giving detailed, accurate and objective descriptions of life, in sharp contrast to what they saw as the idealizing and even sentimentalizing of their 18th-century predecessors (see pp. 626–7 and 630–3).

Fyodor Dostoevski
by the Russian painter Vassily Grigorievich Perov in 1872. Much of Dostoevski's life was beset by crippling problems, including imprisonment for radical political activity in his youth, gambling debts, and family bereavement. In his last years alleviation of his financial difficulties came with public recognition both in Russia and throughout Europe.

To some extent this charge was unjust. Realism as a self-conscious literary movement had already appeared in early 18th-century English drama, and gathered strength in the novels of Defoe, Richardson, Fielding and Austen (see pp. 628–9 and 636). These writers prided themselves on truthfulness to life, strength of feeling, moral seriousness and common sense – all features which have remained the dominant conventions of Realism. The term Realism, however, first appeared in France in the 1830s when it was used to characterize the work of Balzac and Stendhal.

French fiction

The enormously prolific *Honoré de Balzac* (1799–1850) embarked on the long series of novels collected as *La Comédie humaine* ('The Human Comedy') in 1829. His aim was to paint a comprehensive portrait of French society in the early 19th century. He does this by creating hundreds of characters and settings, some of whom recur, giving the sense of a complete world – a practice followed by many later writers. Among the masterpieces of 'The Human Comedy' are *Old Goriot* (1835), and *Lost Illusions* (1837–43), both of which chart the frustrated ambitions and disillusionment of young heroes in a callous and self-seeking society. Balzac is famous for his attention to physical detail, but his main interest is in psychology; and while he delights in describing everyday life, he is also fascinated by the melodramatic and the macabre: misers, murderers, poets and madmen.

To this extent he is not only a Realist but also a Romantic, like his great contemporary *Stendhal* (the pen name of Marie-Henri Beyle; 1783–1842). But where Balzac is sensational, Stendhal is ironic; where Balzac presents the world objectively, Stendhal shows it to us through the minds of his protagonists – especially in *Le Rouge et le noir* ('Scarlet and Black'; 1830) and *The Charterhouse of Parma* (1839).

Honoré de Balzac
(below) in a daguerreotype by the French photographer Nadar. A tireless worker, Balzac was sustained in the task of writing his vast novel sequence 'The Human Comedy' – and very probably poisoned – by large quantities of strong black coffee.

Stendhal's subtler and more disturbing notion of reality – as something conditioned by the way we perceive it – was developed by *Gustave Flaubert* (1821–80). Flaubert was an aesthete: that is to say he saw the reality of human life as a squalid business redeemed only by the beauty and perfection of art. For him and for his disciples, including the short-story writer *Guy de Maupassant* (1850–93) and the novelist Marcel Proust (see pp. 640–1), Realism is not so much a matter of copying reality as of reconstructing it in language. In Flaubert's *Madame Bovary* (1857), the story of a provincial housewife who drifts into debt and casual affairs is worked into a highly finished masterpiece in which the contrast between the novelist's everyday material and his exquisite workmanship is powerfully ironic. *Sentimental Education* (1869), described by Flaubert as 'the moral history of the men of my generation', shows artistic, emotional and social ideals destroyed by contact with reality.

The Russians

Irony – the perception that things are not what they seem – is perhaps the main link between the French and the Russian Realists. In other respects Russia, which had almost no literary traditions to speak of before Pushkin (see p. 631), is very different. On the one hand 19th-century Russian writers were profoundly and directly involved with the great social and political debates of their day. On the other, they often display a freedom and scope lacking in their Western counterparts – tending to the fantastic in Gogol and Dostoevski and to the poetic and epic in Turgenev and Tolstoy.

Ivan Turgenev (1818–83), who admired Flaubert, is perhaps closest in spirit to the French novel. His exquisitely polished tales of aristocratic life in the country reveal the seething moral and political torments which lie just under the surface, ranging from young love to revolutionary fervour. In *Fathers and Sons* (1862) he reveals the intrinsically tragic irony of life through an analysis of the political and social situation in contemporary Russia.

This situation was the principal theme of Russian fiction in the 19th century. For example, it is central to the works of *Nikolai Gogol* (1809–52), such as his comic masterpiece *Dead Souls* (1842), his short stories (especially 'The Overcoat'; 1842) and his play *The Government Inspector* (1836). But these works also show how the conventions of Realism (objectivity and accuracy) can be stretched to reveal the incredible lurking within the ordinary. In Gogol, Realism begins to turn into Surrealism (see p. 641) – this is not simple transcription of reality but a hallucinatory vision of it.

Gogol's fiction hovers between tragedy and farce in a way strongly reminiscent of Dickens (see p. 636). Both writers influenced *Fyodor Dostoevski* (1821–81) – one of the greatest of all novelists – who adapted their blend of satire, fantasy, comedy, pathos and stark realism to his own lofty purposes.

Dostoevski's first novel, *Poor Folk* (1846), was immediately hailed as a realistic masterpiece. But like Gogol – and unlike his French and English contemporaries – Dostoevski was a profoundly religious writer and he soon moved on from straightforward Realism. Where French and English writers tend to focus on personal, moral and social predicaments, he has no hesitation in tackling the largest political and religious issues, most famously in *Crime and Punishment* (1866) and *The Brothers Karamazov* (1880). Both are nominally murder stories, but the sensational plots, though brilliantly narrated, provide a framework within which he can discuss questions of profound existential importance.

These ultimate questions are also the concern of Dostoevski's great contemporary, *Leo Tolstoy* (1828–1910). But Tolstoy presents them in a very different way. In the vast *War and Peace* (1869) and in *Anna Karenina* (1877) there is none of the stylistic and narrative exuberance of Gogol and Dostoevski. These are apparently stories of ordinary people leading ordinary lives, told in a plain, lucid style, in some ways akin to that of the English novelist George Eliot (see p. 637). Tolstoy's type of Realism is not far distant from Classicism. It assumes the existence of a common human nature, and this allows the author to write about his characters as universal types, while at the same time focusing on individuals.

The German Realists

In German-speaking Europe, the writings of the Austrian prose-writer Adalbert Stifter (1805–68), the Swiss novelist Gottfried Keller (1819–90) and the German story-writer Theodor Storm (1817–88) display a Realism that is regional and sometimes pastoral in its inspiration. Their attention is focused on social reality, but not – as was the case with the Naturalism of Zola (see below) – on its ugly and sordid aspects. Sometimes referred to as *Poetic Realists*, they aimed to portray life in a way that reflected positive and enduring values, avoiding excessive idealism on the one hand and excessive realistic detail on the other.

A subtle brand of Realism characterizes the social novels of *Theodor Fontane* (1819–98), many of which are set in their author's native Berlin and are marked by gently ironic humour, psychological understanding and a deep awareness of changing social conditions. *Irrungen*

Wirrungen (1887) explores the themes of class pressure and social duty in a sensitive account of the liaison of a working-class seamstress and an aristocratic army officer. In his greatest novel, the tragedy *Effi Briest* (1895), Fontane's humane, non-moralizing treatment of the theme of adultery rivals Flaubert and Tolstoy.

Naturalism

The typical Realist novel concentrates on the moral predicament of a hero or heroine. But towards the end of the 19th century prose fiction assumed a new focus with the appearance of *Naturalism*, a specialized form of Realism based on the philosophical doctrines of materialism and determinism (see p. 486). For the novelist these amount to a belief that everything in the world – including human behaviour – has observable physical causes; and that the individual is therefore shaped by society.

These views are expounded in Zola's essay 'The Experimental Novel' (1880). *Émile Zola* (1840–1902) dismisses the minute pyschological and moral description typical of the traditional Realist novel in favour of sociological analysis. He was a political radical who believed that the writer's task is not merely to describe society but to reform it. *Germinal* (1885), set in a grim mining village, is less about individual characters than the appalling sufferings of a whole working-class community in an unjust social system. *Germinal* is but one in a 20-volume cycle – the *Rougon Macquart* novels – in which Zola set out to present 'the social and natural history of a family under the Second Empire'.

A similar approach is seen in the work of the Russian *Maxim Gorki* (1868–1936), the American *Theodore Dreiser* (1871–1945), the German *Gerhart Hauptmann* (1862–1946) and the Italian *Giovanni Verga* (1840–1922). These writers all began as Romantic sentimentalists, turning to Naturalism in revulsion against what they saw as the trivializing, self-indulgent influence of Symbolism (see p. 640) and Romanticism. Little read today, they had considerable influence – especially Gorki. An important figure in the Russian Revolution, Gorki ironically ended up veering back towards his earlier mode of writing. Dreary sentimentality and predictable proletarian heroics became the hallmark of the style Gorki enshrined as 'Socialist Realism' – which for decades was to be the only approach to literature allowed in many Communist countries.

The theatre

While Socialist Realism was turning the ideals of literary Realism and Naturalism on their heads, the immediacy of cinema (and later television) threatened to render them obsolete. The theatrical revival in Europe at the end of the 19th century can be seen as the final flowering of Realism.

The late 19th-century Realist drama has an important forerunner in the work of the German radical *Georg Büchner* (1813–37). *Danton's Death* (1835) is a complex and pessimistic drama of the French Revolution. The dramatic fragment, *Woyzeck* (1837), with its themes of poverty and mental derangement, and use of short abrupt scenes, is both in content and form far ahead of its time.

The Russian *Anton Chekhov* (1860–1904) wrote both stories and plays, including *The Seagull* (1896), *Uncle Vanya* (1900), *The Three Sisters* (1901) and *The Cherry Orchard* (1904). His eye for the comedy of human foibles and pretensions only underlines the pervasive melancholy of his work, which is both sympathetic yet detached.

The Norwegian *Henrik Ibsen* (1828–1906) is a more complex figure whose plays range from drawing-room comedy to poetic tragedy. His middle-period plays (*A Doll's House*, 1879; *Ghosts*, 1881; *An Enemy of the People*, 1882) deal explicitly with social and political problems in the claustrophobic world of the provincial bourgeoisie. His later plays, such as *Hedda Gabler* (1890) and *The Master Builder* (1892), are more symbolic and show greater concern with the subconscious. Ibsen is often seen as the first great dramatist to write tragedies about ordinary people. His addressing of issues such as the position of women within marriage, and the conflict of authority and individual freedom ensures him a continuing relevance to the modern age.

Finally there is the Swede *August Strindberg* (1849–1912), whose earlier work, such as *Miss Julie* (1888), resembles Ibsen, but in whose later plays – notably *The Ghost Sonata* (1907) – one observes the dissolution of classic Realism into Expressionism (see p. 642). PWa

SEE ALSO
- ROMANTICISM pp. 630–3
- THE NOVEL IN 19TH-CENTURY BRITAIN p. 636
- SYMBOLISM, AESTHETICISM AND THE BIRTH OF MODERNISM p. 640
- EXPERIMENTAL THEATRE p. 642
- THE MODERN NOVEL p. 648

The stark realism of Zola and the Naturalist school is also reflected in the visual arts of the period. Honoré Daumier's earthy lithograph depicts (albeit with rather more humour than Zola) bathers in a public bath house. (Archiv für Kunst)

The Novel in 19th-century Britain

With improved printing processes and the vogue for seriali-
zation in magazines, the novel became the dominant literary
form in 19th-century Britain. At its best it is both popular
and literary, as with the works of *Charles Dickens*, which
were often read aloud in the family circle. The world that
most 19th-century British novelists were writing about was
one characterized by increasing urbanization and industrialization – a world dominated by the owners of capital.

Sam Weller, shoeblack at
the White Hart and later
to become Mr Pickwick's
devoted servant, in an illustration by 'Phiz' (Hablot K.
Browne) for Charles Dick-
ens's *Pickwick Papers*.
Originally published in 20
monthly parts from April
1836 to November 1837,
the novel made Dickens
famous.

At the same time the novel was increasingly accepted as a serious art form. Its
major advances are seen in a deepening
realism, both of a pyschological and
social nature, and in the development of
regional writing. The 19th-century novel
at times reflects the optimistic energy of
the age, but is also concerned with corruption, injustice, and the uncaring
nature of capitalist industrial society. Its
hallmarks are a radical questioning and
probing, and a strongly moral emphasis

on personal relationships. Some writers
use the device of an ironic commentary
that establishes a close relationship between narrator and reader.

Romantics and post-Romantics

Jane Austen (1775–1817) is the mistress
of the ironic manner, though she is
writing about a very different society
from that of the Victorians, and for a
narrower readership. She was born in a
Hampshire rectory, and led a reflective
and retired life, with Bath and London as
the boundaries of her travel. Country
village life was her domain, defined as 'the
little bit (two inches wide) of ivory on
which I work'.

Her novels *Sense and Sensibility* (1811),
Pride and Prejudice (1813), *Mansfield
Park* (1814), *Emma* (1815) and *Persuasion*
(1818) are astutely observed comedies of
middle-class manners. They are unpas-
sionate romances with an emphasis on
morality – balanced and witty, concisely
ironic, employing natural dialogue that
reveals a refined and incisive mind. Her
early novel *Northanger Abbey* (1798)
mocks the sensational 'Gothic' novels of
the time (see p. 632).

The novels of *Charlotte* (1816–55) and
Emily (1818–48) *Brontë* both contain
Gothic elements. With their sister *Anne*
(1820–49), they were raised in the pars-
onage at Haworth, Yorkshire, and
adopted male pen names to get their work
published. Charlotte's *Jane Eyre* (1847) is
the story of an independent woman who
refuses to become the mistress of the man
she loves. After *Shirley* (1849) she wrote
Villette (1853), forsaking the regional
location and using her teaching experiences in Brussels. *Wuthering Heights*
(1847), the only novel of Emily Brontë, is
a complex and original masterpiece. It is
beyond moral and literary convention,
and concerns the consuming and self-
destructive love of Catherine and Heath-
cliff. The novel combines violence, poetry,
supernatural and Gothic devices, and the
story is filtered through a variety of
narrators.

The social novel

Benjamin Disraeli (1804–81), who later
became prime minister (1868 and 1874–80),
was concerned with what he saw as the
adverse effects of capitalism on the social
fabric of the nation. In the early part of his
career he outlined his social manifestos in
his trilogy of novels, *Coningsby* (1844),
Sybil (1845) and *Tancred* (1847).

A message of social reconciliation
emerges in the work of *Elizabeth Gaskell* (1810–65). The novels *Cranford*
(1851–3) and *Wives and Daughters* (1866)
are kindly and tolerant portraits of provincial life drawn with deft and delicate
humour. But in *Mary Barton* (1848) and
North and South (1855) she records her
social awareness of industrial problems,
while in *Ruth* (1853) she bravely tackles
the problem of illegitimacy.

Charlotte Brontë, the oldest of the three
novel-writing sisters, in a chalk drawing by
George Richmond in 1850. The failure of a collection of their poetry, *Poems by Currer, Ellis and
Acton Bell* (the pen names of Charlotte, Emily
and Anne), did not deter the sisters from seeking
publishers for their novels. (*National Portrait Gallery*)

Social concern is always present in the
work of the greatest mass communicator
of the 19th century, *Charles Dickens*
(1812–70). London, especially in its commercial and social aspects, permeates his
work. In *Oliver Twist* (1837–8) he attacked
Poor Law administration as well as exposing criminal low life; in *Nicholas Nickleby*
(1838–9) corrupt schools; in *Bleak House*
(1852–3) the law and social deprivation;
and in *Little Dorrit* (1855–7) debtors' prisons and financial swindling. His highly
developed social conscience derived in
part from his own experience of childhood
poverty and deprivation, in particular his
period of forced labour in a black-
ing warehouse. His two first-person narratives (see p. 628), *David Copperfield*
(1848–50) and *Great Expectations* (1861),
retain a strongly autobiographical flavour.

Dickens's social concern is combined
with a richly imaginative and intensely
humane presentation of character and
scene. He stands for human values
against hypocrisy, crime and snobbery.
His creations are vivid and often larger
than life; his humour is immediate, being
both verbal and pictorial in effect. The
numerous 20th-century film adaptations
of his work testify to his enduring popularity.

William Makepeace Thackeray
(1811–63) takes as his subject matter the
exploration of social and personal morality. He was both artist and writer, illustrating many of his own books. He
established himself as a major novelist
with *Vanity Fair* (1846–8), which is set in
the period of the Battle of Waterloo (1815),
and castigates the corruptions of society.
His other main works are *Pendennis*
(1848–50), *Henry Esmond* (1852) and *The
Newcomes* (1853–5), each embodying his
ironic view of life, his feeling of history
and period, his humour and command of
pathos.

George Eliot, the pen name of Mary Ann Evans (1819–80), was fervently religious as a young woman, but rejected her faith in 1842, and later scandalized conventional social prejudice by living openly with her lover and mentor, G.H. Lewes. But she retained throughout her life a high-minded sense of duty, moral responsibility and altruistic endeavour. Her chief works – *Adam Bede* (1859), *The Mill on the Floss* (1860), *Silas Marner* (1861) and her masterpiece *Middlemarch* (1871–2) – are all set in the Midland region where she grew up. They are realistic portrayals of provincial life, with ironic humour and incisive observation of human behaviour. In these novels, and in *Daniel Deronda* (1874–76), George Eliot penetrates the surface of social convention and lays bare the motives of human action.

The prolific **Anthony Trollope** (1815–82) was a friend of Thackeray's and wrote an admiring study of his work. He developed Thackeray's social concerns into perceptive studies in two important novel sequences, *The Barsetshire Novels* (1857–67), in which he created an imaginary county, and the political *Palliser Novels* (1864–80). Trollope is fascinated by the world of political machination and in particular with the pressures created by political responsibility. His late masterpiece *The Way We Live Now* (1875) attacks the financial corruption of his own society in a manner influenced by Thackeray's *Vanity Fair*.

Social institutions such as the family and the Church were minutely and scathingly analysed by **Samuel Butler** (1835–1902) in *The Way of All Flesh* (1903), which traced the fortunes of four generations of a middle-class family.

Both Butler and the novelist, poet, artist and printer **William Morris** (1834–96) explored social issues in the context of imaginary societies. In his novel *Erewhon* (1872), Butler depicts a remote district where moral virtue is equated with physical health in a crude version of Darwinism (see pp. 112–13). In *News from Nowhere* (1891), Morris wrote of a Utopian socialist future state where technology has been harnessed to serve man's needs rather than enslave him.

The regional novel

The greatest regional novelist is **Thomas Hardy** (1840–1928). His setting is Wessex, the name he gives to Dorset and the surrounding counties. Hardy's reputation was made by *Far from the Madding Crowd* (1874), but his characteristic view of man as subject to a malign fate is seen from *The Return of the Native* (1878) onwards. This was followed by the great tragedies *The Mayor of Casterbridge* (1886), *The Woodlanders* (1887) and *Tess of the D'Urbervilles* (1891). Despite being widely admired in literary circles, contemporary reviewers in the popular press castigated his so-called immorality and pessimism. Disgusted by the adverse reception of *Jude the Obscure* (1895), Hardy turned from fiction to concentrate on poetry and short stories and produced a verse drama, *The Dynasts* (1904–8), in his last years (see p. 646).

Poverty and Wealth. A poor child and his mother gaze enviously at their affluent middle-class counterparts in William Powell Frith's painting. A concern with social issues – notably the sufferings of the poor and unemployed, the excesses of capitalist industrialism, and administrative, legal and financial corruption – characterizes the novels of Disraeli, Dickens, Mrs Gaskell and Trollope.

Another regional novelist of some importance is the later writer **Arnold Bennett** (1867–1931), who produced stories and novels of ordinary small-town lives in the Midlands.

Towards the modern novel

The majority of the 19th-century novelists worked within the Realist tradition, but the strains inherent in late 19th-century society became apparent in the work of novelists writing at the end of the century, who often use techniques to be developed by the Modernists (see pp. 641 and 648–9).

Some of the most perceptive writing of this later period comes from novelists springing from American and European traditions, such as Henry James (see p. 639) and the Polish-born **Joseph Conrad** (1857–1924). Conrad's early sea stories, notably *Lord Jim* (1902), are in the Realist manner, but with *Heart of Darkness* (1902), he experimented with Modernist techniques to analyse the corruptions at the heart of imperialism and the human psyche. The journey of his narrator, Marlowe, up a West African river exposes the brutality of colonial rule in the Belgian Congo and relates this to a wider 'darkness' of the human soul.

Conrad's concern with instability and corruptibility is further developed in *The Secret Agent* (1907) and *Under Western Eyes* (1911). These novels, in which traditional linear narrative is disrupted by breaks in the time-sequence, depict the anarchic face of the modern industrial city and the underworld of international terrorism. In his masterpiece, *Nostromo* (1904), the façade of Western economic progress is exposed by an exploration of its adverse effects on the imaginary South American country of Costaguana. Conrad is now seen as one of the most important Modernist writers.   GH

KIPLING

The poet, novelist and short-story writer Rudyard Kipling (1865–1936) is often thought of as the chauvinistic glorifier of British imperialism, though his attitude towards it was probably more complex than that. Judgements of Kipling's vast and varied output were diverse: he was admired by the popular reader, but accused of vulgar jingoism by liberal intellectuals.

Plain Tales from the Hills (1888) are tales of British soldiers in India and Burma, whose cynical realism recalls Maupassant (see p. 634). His school stories, *Stalky & Co.* (1899), draw on memories of his own schooldays and recount the escapades, teasings, bullyings and beatings of English boarding-school life. His novel *Kim* (1902) presents a vivid portrayal of India through the experiences of an abandoned orphan who becomes a British agent. But Kipling's most durable and popular achievements are his tales for children: the *Jungle Book* (1894), and the whimsical *Just So Stories* (1902).

SEE ALSO

- THE BEGINNINGS OF THE NOVEL p. 628
- THE BRITISH ROMANTICS p. 632
- REALISM AND NATURALISM p. 634
- SYMBOLISM, AESTHETICISM AND THE BIRTH OF MODERNISM p. 640
- THE MODERN NOVEL p. 648

American Literature of the 19th Century

In the 19th century American literature took on a specifically national character in its treatment of certain themes and ideas. Uncontaminated by history or tradition, the New World presented exciting possibilities for the creative writer. The successful War of Independence (1775–83) gave the USA the right to set its own constitution and create its own society (see pp. 422–3). The writing of a native literature was a key factor in this process. From 1861 to 1865 the country was torn apart by the Civil War (see p. 431) and afterwards there was an even deeper need for literature to unite the nation and re-establish a national consciousness.

SEE ALSO

● ROMANTICISM pp. 630–3
● REALISM AND NATURALISM p. 634
● THE NOVEL IN 19TH-CENTURY BRITAIN p. 636
● SYMBOLISM, AESTHETICISM AND THE BIRTH OF MODERNISM p. 640
● THE MODERN NOVEL p. 648

In Fenimore Cooper's evocation of frontier life, Whitman's celebration of American democracy, Hawthorne's analysis of New England Puritanism and Thoreau's and Emerson's American brand of Romanticism can be seen conscious efforts to create a national identity.

Frontier literature

Washington Irving (1783–1859) was the first American author to achieve an international readership. His early writings included satirical essays and poems, but it was his collection *The Sketch Book of Geoffrey Crayon* (1819–20) that made him a celebrity both in America and Britain. The collection consists of essays, sketches of English life and American adaptations of German folk tales, including most notably 'Rip Van Winkle' and 'The Legend of Sleepy Hollow'. In later life he travelled extensively in the American West and wrote three books about his experiences, including *A Tour of the Prairies* (1835).

James Fenimore Cooper (1789–1851) was responsible for establishing the historical novel in the United States. His first success was *The Spy* (1821), an exciting tale of the American Revolution. *The Pioneers* (1823), the first of his *Leatherstocking Tales*, introduced the character of Natty Bumppo or Hawkeye, the archetypal American pioneer or wilderness man. This, and later novels in the sequence, notably *The Last of the Mohicans* (1826) and *The Pathfinder* (1840), describe in detail the frontier experience of the White settlers but also present a vivid picture of the traditions and customs of the American Indians. The novelty of Cooper's subject gained him popularity in both America and Europe. Its prime importance, however, was in its expression of themes of great and enduring significance in American fiction, such as the tension between innocence and experience, and wilderness and civilization.

The Transcendentalists

Ralph Waldo Emerson (1803–1882) and **Henry David Thoreau** (1817–1862) lived and worked in the same New England town, Concord in Massachusetts, and were the most important members of an intellectual movement known as *Transcendentalism*, which insisted on the oneness of all forms of life. The interests of the transcendentalists were as broad as those of the European Romantics who so influenced them (see pp. 630–3). In their periodical *The Dial*, questions of philosophy, religion, politics and economics were debated.

Emerson developed the idea of an 'Over-Soul', which included God, humanity and nature, and many of his writings, including the essay *Nature* (1836), are centrally concerned with this relationship. In his verse and prose there is a Wordsworthian reverence for nature.

Thoreau was a political radical who protested against slavery and the war with Mexico. His radicalism is expressed in his essay *Civil Disobedience* (1840), which advocated techniques of peaceful protest

An atmospheric illustration for Edgar Allan Poe's short story 'The Tell-Tale Heart' (1843). A nightmarish account of a man who is tormented by the imagined sound of the heartbeat of an old man he has murdered, the tale typifies Poe's interest in the pathological and the macabre.

taken up by Gandhi in the 20th century. His antimaterialist philosophy led him to embark on an experiment in self-sufficiency in the woods near Concord. *Walden, or Life in the Woods* (1854) describes his daily physical and spiritual existence in the cabin he built himself beside Walden Pond.

Nathaniel Hawthorne (1804–1864) lived in the experimental Transcendentalist community at Brook Farm for a brief period and used his experiences there in a novel, *The Blithedale Romance* (1852). A long stay in Italy provided the inspiration for *The Marble Faun* (1860). Hawthorne was at times a critic of what he saw as the excesses of Transcendentalist philosophy. He moves away from the concerns of this group in his great novel *The Scarlet Letter* (1850). Set among the original Puritan settlers in New England, the novel tells the story of a woman who is ostracized for bearing an illegitimate child, and explores the themes of sin, guilt and hypocrisy.

Psychological frontiers

The poet, critic and short-story writer **Edgar Allan Poe** (1809–1849) worked for much of his brief and difficult life as a magazine editor, an advantageous position from which to publish his work but not a lucrative one. Poe concentrated initially on verse, publishing three volumes of poetry before he was 25. His collection of stories *Tales of the Grotesque and Arabesque* (1840) established the tone of writing with which his name was to become synonymous – that of terror, mystery and the macabre. The collection includes Poe's best-known story 'The Fall of the House of Usher'. His later tale 'The Murders in the Rue Morgue' has been described as the first modern detective story (see p. 652) and introduced the character of the detective C. Auguste Dupin, who was to appear in several other tales. Poe's exploration of the darker side of human experience endeared him to the French Symbolists, and in particular to Baudelaire (see p. 640), who translated many of his works.

Herman Melville (1819–1891) went to sea at the age of 19 and was to bring many of his sea-going adventures into his fiction. His first book, *Typee* (1846), draws on his experience of being marooned on a South Sea Island among a tribe of cannibals. His experience on board a whaling ship is reflected in his most ambitious novel, *Moby-Dick* (1851). Here, like Hawthorne in *The Scarlet Letter*, Melville portrays a community set apart from the world, united in a common purpose but separated by individual motivations, and uses it to explore the complexities of the human condition.

On a simple narrative level, the novel is a powerful and dramatic account of Captain Ahab's obsessive and ultimately fatal quest for the giant white whale that has bitten off his leg. But behind the bare facts of the doomed voyage of the *Pequod* lies a rich pattern of symbols that have been interpreted in many different ways: the ship's multiracial crew as a microcosm of the USA and of wider humanity; the whale as nature, God and the universe. Largely unappreciated in Melville's lifetime, *Moby-Dick* is now recognized as a masterpiece. Its multifaceted and experimental narrative techniques, including the insertion of a dissertation on whales and whaling, prefigure the modern novel.

Melville also wrote many outstanding short stories, including 'Bartleby the Scrivener' (1856), and completed a novella, *Billy Budd, Foretopman*, shortly before his death.

National voices

When **Walt Whitman** (1819–1892) published his first collection, *Leaves of Grass*, in 1855, a distinctive American poetry was born. Whitman wrote: 'I celebrate myself, and sing myself', but believed that self to represent all humankind. His views were influenced by the work of Emerson and his work celebrates the simple fact of life, in all its forms – human, animal and the landscape of his country. Whitman was intensely patriotic and sought to encompass within his verse both the broadest of *Democratic Vistas* (1871) and the smallest of personal experiences. Democracy in America was Whitman's passion and his poetry expresses his ardour.

Mark Twain (the pen name of Samuel Langhorne Clemens; 1835–1910) helped define a national identity through the use of 'Yankee' humour. He made his name with a tall tale called 'The Celebrated Jumping Frog of Calaveras County' (1867), which was reprinted in newspapers all across the USA. He earned his living giving lectures to packed houses and writing fiction and travel letters for publication. Memories of his own childhood beside the Mississippi River colour *The Adventures of Tom Sawyer* (1876), *Life on the Mississippi* (1883) and his masterpiece *The Adventures of Huckleberry Finn* (1884). Twain used comedy and the misunderstandings arising from the naïvety of his characters as a way to attack the injustices of society, particularly the horror and cruelty of slavery.

Moral consciousness

Emily Dickinson (1830–86), although a prolific and brilliant poet, published only seven poems during her lifetime. She lived with her father in Amherst, Massachusetts, and rarely left her home, preferring to communicate with the outside world by letter. She often defies convention in her poems, using unusual metre and punctuation and – to great effect – unexpected language. Based on a deliberately limited world in which the largest of truths can be expressed, Dickinson's poems evoke in minute detail the vividness of lived experience, and sensitively explore the spiritual relations between the individual and her maker.

Unlike Emily Dickinson, *Henry James* (1843–1916) travelled widely and eventually chose to make his home in England

Whale and whalers (above) do battle in the South Seas. Personal experience of life on board a whaling ship is reflected in Herman Melville's novel *Moby-Dick* (1851). Despite its rich symbolism and powerful narrative, the novel was a relative failure when first published and was not recognized as a masterpiece until the 20th century.

(see p. 637). His early novels explore the impact of Europe on Americans. *The Portrait of a Lady* (1881) describes the European 'education' of a young American, Isabel Archer. Later novels such as *The Spoils of Poynton* (1897) analyse in far greater depth what James saw as the peculiarly English character. But in his last three completed novels, *The Wings of the Dove* (1902), *The Ambassadors* (1903), and *The Golden Bowl* (1904), he returned to his abiding interest in the contrast of the European and American character. These are truly psychological novels in that their chief events are the thoughts and realizations that 'happen' in the minds of the protagonists. While James was an inheritor of the main 19th-century Realist tradition (he was an admirer of Balzac and saw himself working in the tradition of Charles Dickens and George Eliot; see pp. 634–7), he anticipated the modern novel (see pp. 648–9) in his intellectual, psychological and linguistic concerns.   JaG

Walt Whitman caricatured by Max Beerbohm. Whitman expressed his passionate idealism in his free-verse collection *Leaves of Grass* (1855). A fervent advocate of American democracy, he is depicted here encouraging the American eagle – the 'bird of freedom' – to fly.

Symbolism, Aestheticism and Modernism

These closely related movements in 19th- and early 20th-century European literature have their roots in French poetry. They shared a belief in the absolute value of art, reinforced by various forms of contempt for the everyday world, and especially for people who served its interests. There resulted a rift between writers and the public at large, who were seen as 'bourgeois' in a disparaging sense – i.e. they were thought of as small-minded and materialistic. Artists lived for their art alone, sometimes flaunting their difference from the rest of society by affected or deliberately shocking behaviour.

This cult of art differed from the idealization of art by the Romantics (some still alive, such as Hugo, see p. 630), because it was no longer concerned with the good of society or humanity. Art's long-standing association with moral and religious values was rejected as these were felt to have degenerated into cheap notions of respectability and progress. 'Art for art's sake' was the cry of such poets as **Théo-phile Gautier** (1811–72), whose early extravagant Romanticism was to be replaced by a preoccupation with poetic form. Music became the most admired of all the arts because it was pure – that is, it did not reflect banal reality, but transcended it altogether.

The beauty of evil

One of the first Symbolists and Aesthetes was **Charles Baudelaire** (1821–67). He is seen by some as the father of Modernism, though no label really describes him adequately. He is amongst the greatest of all French poets. Rebel son of a respectable family, his lifestyle included drugs, drink, a coloured mistress, prosecution by the state for immorality in his poetry, and affliction with syphilis which eventually killed him. Yet Baudelaire found his inspiration in this misery; he transformed it into a profound and potent symbol of the wretchedness inherent in the human condition, which most people hypocritically close their eyes to. Hypocrisy and 'ennui' (a heightened form of boredom, in which he saw a revelation of man's desperate state) are two of his major themes, and so also, in poignant contrast to them, are the hopes and longings inspired by love and beauty. Out of the conflict between human degradation and human aspiration, death and dreams, Baudelaire composed poems of tragic intensity. They are, as he tells us in the title of his only volume of verse poems (he also wrote 'poems in prose'), 'the flowers of evil' (*Les Fleurs du mal*; 1857).

Pure poetry

Stéphane Mallarmé (1842–98) marks a further step in the development of Modernism, beyond personal tragedies and scandals, indeed beyond ordinary experience altogether, towards pure intellectual preoccupation with words – and also towards the kind of obscurity and difficulty that characterizes much modern art. He sought an ideal that he called '*the pure idea*' – an essence of things that can only be grasped when the reader is prevented from reading words as descriptions of real things and situations; thus it is hard to relate the language of his poems to any personal perspective or familiar way of thinking.

This elimination of the lyrical 'I', and more generally of the author's presence as a guide for the reader, has since become a further characteristic of modern styles of writing. It creates the possibility of experimenting with radically different ways of organizing a text. The poems and poetic prose of **Arthur Rimbaud** (1854–91) are an example of what can be done with words and images when personal control is abandoned. Violently antipathetic to any form of authority, Rimbaud latterly adopted a vagabond lifestyle that took him to Abyssinia and a brief career in gun-running. His demonic influence almost awakened a modern genius in his lover **Paul Verlaine** (1844–96), who reverted, however, to conventional and sometimes maudlin moods of personal sentiment.

Paris

With the dawn of the new century, Symbolism (and artistic experimentation generally) flourished in many countries. To mention only a few names, there was in Russia the poet **Alexander Blok** (1880–1921); in Italy the poet **Filippo Marinetti** (1876–1944; see p. 548); and in Germany the poet **Stefan George** (1868–1933). However, the true capital of the arts in Europe at this time was Paris.

Painters, musicians and writers from all over Europe and America were attracted there by the intellectual excitement and freedom from convention. New groups, styles and ideas flourished, and to be avant garde was everything. Whether in painting, sculpture, music or any of the genres of literature, there was a great eagerness amongst this generation to break out of conventional ways of using the medium itself. A shared sense of being revolutionary and experimental drew together artists from different fields – notably, the French playwright Jean Cocteau (1889–1963), the ballet impresario Diaghilev (see p. 597), and the composer Stravinsky (see p. 578). After knowing Picasso (see p. 548), the French poet **Guillaume Apollinaire** (1880–1918) experimented with Cubist principles and produced early examples of concrete poetry (see p. 647). Movements such as Dada and Surrealism (see p. 550), which explored distorted, irrational, nonsensical effects, expressed themselves equally in writing, theatrical performance and painting (as did the politically more progressive Futurist movements in Italy and Russia; see p. 548).

A number of philosophical influences, including psychoanalysis (see p. 233), Marxism (see p. 268), and Nietzsche (see p.

A gathering of Symbolist writers, including Verlaine and Rimbaud (seated on far left), as painted by Henri Fantin-Latour.

James Joyce painted by J.E. Blanche. Joyce's Modernist masterpiece *Ulysses* was first published in Paris in 1922, but remained banned in Britain until 1936. (National Gallery of Ireland)

486), contributed to the suspicion that society's conventional view of the world, – indeed civilization itself – was a mere façade, resting on misconception and illusion. The role of art, it was thought, should not be to reproduce and support such falsehood, but rather to expose it. This suspicion was intensified by the carnage of World War I and the virtual collapse of the old social order in Europe (see pp. 436–7).

Dissimilar styles of Modernism

To understand the connection between the diverse literary talents of this period, it is necessary to consider this background of cultural and social crisis. For instance, *Jules Laforgue* (1860–87), an influential poet in the history of Modernism, is notable for his use of free verse (unrhymed verse without any regular rhythm), free association of ideas, glimpses of urban landscapes, snatches of popular songs, everyday speech, and philosophic and technical terms. *Paul Valéry* (1871–1945), on the other hand, a no less important poet, wrote poems that are classically controlled in their form, thought and imagery. What Valéry wanted to explore in this more formal style were the workings of consciousness in sharp contrast with the physical vitality of existence. It was a comparable sense of contrast between what the mind thinks and the actual reality of existence that prompted Laforgue to keep shifting focus and tone of voice.

This contrast became, in fact, a central theme of Modernist literature, and there turned out to be many ways of responding to it. When *Ezra Pound* (1885–1972) advised his fellow American poet *T.S. Eliot* (1888–1965) to introduce still more fragmentation and shifts of tone and reference into *The Waste Land* (1922), they were following Laforgue's style of Modernism. This Modernist masterpiece evokes the sterility of modern civilization by means of a kaleidoscopic use of echoes and allusions – to myths and religions, to other poetry (including Shakespeare, Wagner, popular songs and nursery

rhymes), and to symbolic landscapes and characters. Eliot developed this technique further – and better, many believe – in *Four Quartets* (1943), a series of religious meditations on time and eternity. Here the shifts in tone, rhythm, theme and reference are less harsh and more profound. By contrast, the great Irish poet W.B. Yeats (see p. 646) rather resembles Valéry in the formal metres, stanzas, syntax and figures of speech of his poems, in which he depicts the interaction of intellect and body, soul and self, in love and art and history.

The Modernist novel

There were no English-born Symbolists, Aesthetes, or Modernists of genius before Virginia Woolf (see below). *Algernon Charles Swinburne* (1837–1909) – an admirer of Baudelaire – posed as one, but his lush fantasies of beautiful living lacked any contact (let alone contrast) with reality. *Walter Pater* (1839–94) and other members of the Aesthetic Movement in England theorized academically about art; even *Oscar Wilde* (1854–1900; see p. 644), whose understanding of the psychological dangers in Aestheticism can be seen in his only novel, *The Picture of Dorian Gray* (1891), tended to escape into sheer wit. The hero of this quite conventionally written novel is modelled on the character of Des Esseintes in *Joris-Karl Huysmans's* (1848–1907) *Against Nature* (1884) – a much more memorable prototype of the decadent Aesthete, who reads Mallarmé.

Modernism in English-language fiction begins in fact with the work of the Irishman *James Joyce* (1882–1941). He refined a gift for realism in his early short stories, *Dubliners* (1914), condensing descriptions and events into scenes of poetic and symbolic power. He also explored interior point of view in the autobiographical *Portrait of the Artist as a Young Man* (1914–15). The first great Modernist novel is Joyce's *Ulysses* (1922), which – like Modernist poetry – contains many different shifts in style; polished realism, literary and journalistic pastiches, interior 'stream of consciousness', surrealist fantasy as well as a complex pattern of allusion to (amongst other things) Homer's story of Odysseus. Joyce's later work, especially *Finnegan's Wake* (1939), experiments still further with the extent to which language can be played with 'for its own sake', and dissolve the ordinary world. Only Samuel Beckett (see p. 643) – also an Irishman – has maintained Modernist fiction at the limit where it is no longer about anything real at all, but becomes (as in *The Unnameable*; 1960) a form of pure writing.

Virginia Woolf (1882–1941) first wrote conventionally realistic novels, then reacted against realism based on the overseeing viewpoint of the author. Her novels *Mrs Dalloway* (1925) and *To the Lighthouse* (1927) use the narrative method known as 'stream of consciousness', which shows 'reality' as it flows through the minds of her characters – steeped in currents of memory, anticipation, feeling and thought.

The greatest novel of this kind, however, remains *Remembrance of Things Past* (1913–27) by *Marcel Proust* (1871–1922).

This immense work in seven parts explores a whole life from childhood to middle age, not as a chronological narrative, objectively reported, but as a process of ever-shifting realization, a reality continuously reborn through memory and transformed into thought.

Beyond personal vision

Almost all the poetry, fiction and drama written in the 20th century bears the stamp of Symbolism and Modernism (see pp. 642–9). The extraordinarily innovative work of two authors writing in German deserves particular mention here: that of the Austrian poet *Rainer Maria Rilke* (1875–1926) and of the Czech novelist *Franz Kafka* (1883–1924). Both evoke a sense of spiritual crisis caused by the failure of conventional values. Rilke gradually taught himself to write a poetry not of personal feeling but of suprapersonal vision – opening himself to the reality of things (he said) not as a man but as an angel might see them. Kafka similarly evokes a world in which personal viewpoints fail, though in his case the vision seems less angelic than demonic. He asked for his unpublished work to be destroyed, but the incomplete text of two novels appeared as *The Trial* (1925) and *The Castle* (1926). Both have a terrifying hallucinatory quality, and the word 'Kafkaesque' has been coined to describe a nightmarish sense of isolation and alienation in a dehumanized world. Rilke and Kafka believed in art alone as a source of salvation, though Kafka – with Jewish humour – wondered whether his intense preoccupation with writing were not also responsible for his intense sense of crisis. AT

SEE ALSO

● SYMBOLISM, SECESSION AND EXPRESSIONISM p. 546
● CUBISM AND ABSTRACTION p. 548
● DADA AND SURREALISM p. 550
● ROMANTICISM pp. 630–3
● REALISM AND NATURALISM p. 634
● EXPERIMENTAL THEATRE pp. 642–3
● MODERN DRAMA IN BRITAIN AND THE USA p. 644
● MODERN POETRY p. 646
● THE MODERN NOVEL p. 648

Blast, an iconoclastic Modernist magazine edited by the painter and novelist Wyndham Lewis and the poet Ezra Pound. The magazine attacked what it saw as the complacency and insularity of British culture. Illustrated here is the first page of the first number (1914); the second and last number appeared in 1915 and contained the first poems of T.S. Eliot to be published in England.

1

BLAST First (from politeness) **ENGLAND**

CURSE ITS CLIMATE FOR ITS SINS AND INFECTIONS

DISMAL SYMBOL, SET round our bodies,
of effeminate lout within.

VICTORIAN VAMPIRE, the **LONDON** cloud sucks
the **TOWN'S** heart.

A 1000 MILE LONG, 2 KILOMETER Deep

BODY OF WATER even, is pushed against us
from the Floridas, **TO MAKE US MILD.**

OFFICIOUS MOUNTAINS keep back **DRASTIC WINDS**

SO MUCH VAST MACHINERY TO PRODUCE

THE CURATE of "Eltham"
BRITANNIC ÆSTHETE
WILD NATURE CRANK
DOMESTICATED
          POLICEMAN
LONDON COLISEUM
   SOCIALIST-PLAYWRIGHT
DALY'S MUSICAL COMEDY
GAIETY CHORUS GIRL
TONKS

11

Experimental Theatre

The 20th century has witnessed an enormous expansion in experiment and innovation in European theatre. Radical developments have pushed back the frontiers of theatrical taste and fundamentally challenged the basic relationship between performers and spectators established in the 19th century. German Expressionism, Epic Theatre, the Theatre of Cruelty and the Theatre of the Absurd all began as experiments designed to break away from the dominant theatrical convention of Naturalism (see p. 635). Many dramatists, directors, designers and performers forcibly challenged naturalistic writing and realistic performance conventions in search of an alternative and more dynamic theatrical experience.

SEE ALSO

● REALISM AND NATURALISM
p. 634
● SYMBOLISM, AESTHETICISM
AND MODERNISM p. 640
● MODERN DRAMA IN BRITAIN
AND THE USA p. 644

Naturalism became established first as a literary convention through the work of the French novelist Émile Zola, but its influence can also be seen in many of the plays of European dramatists of the late 19th century, such as Ibsen, Strindberg, and Chekhov (see p. 635). By creating the *illusion* of reality on the stage and by focusing on closely observed portraits of individuals, often in a domestic or family context, Naturalistic writers sought to demonstrate the vital importance of the environment in determining human behaviour.

In Russia the director Constantin Stanislavsky (1863–1938) made a major contribution to the development of what is now generally referred to as naturalistic acting. In books such as *An Actor Prepares* he outlined his theories of acting and thus influenced the way in which the craft was taught, especially in America, where a Stanislavski-based approach became known as *Method acting*.

German Expressionism

German Expressionism, a deliberate movement away from Naturalism, began around 1910. It employed radically different performance conventions which, instead of attempting to imitate life, drew attention to themselves as art. It included exaggerated shapes, unusual and highly contrasting colour combinations, and robotic movement (see p. 547). Expressionists concentrated on *expressing* the hidden but deeply significant world of individual emotions rather than realistically depicting what they regarded as the superficial exterior of reality. Expressionists sought to discover spiritual truths rather than seeking to confront the social and political issues cherished by many Naturalistic dramatists.

Following World War I German Expressionism became more concerned with universal as opposed to purely individualistic concerns. In particular, it expressed fears of a general and imminent world catastrophe. Between 1919 and 1924 the movement exercised considerable influence not only in Germany, but also in the rest of Europe. Two dramatists in particular are associated with it: the Germans *Georg Kaiser* (1878–1945) and *Ernst Toller* (1893–1939).

Epic theatre

The rise of the Nazi party in Germany in the 1920s almost compelled artists to become concerned with collective as opposed to simply individual issues. Expressionism declined and another militant anti-naturalistic approach gained ground. Its leading light was the radical socialist theatre director *Erwin Piscator* (1893–1966). He attempted to create performances of plays specifically aimed at a working-class audience and designed to increase their political awareness. Piscator's objective was to use the theatre to teach people about social issues. Using stylized acting, filmed sequences and cartoons, his productions attempted to assist the audience in connecting the dramatic situations on the stage with those of real life.

Piscator's most famous disciple was the German dramatist and lyric poet *Bertolt Brecht* (1898–1956), whose concept of 'epic' theatre has exerted an enormous influence on the drama of the 20th century. Brecht's early work, notably *Baal* (1922) and *Drums in the Night* (1922), was influenced by the Expressionists. He collaborated with the composer Kurt Weill (1900–1950) on *The Threepenny Opera* (1928) and *Mahagonny* (1930). These highly original and successful works, with their cabaret-like style and pointed satire, marked a new approach to musical theatre. But in the 1920s Brecht had also begun to write plays and to devise a theory of performance designed to help audiences to look critically at social issues. He wanted to create in them not simply an emotional response to characters, but a passion for rational argument and debate. In order to achieve this Brecht wanted to distance audiences emotionally from the action and characters on the stage in order that they might more clearly see and understand the social and political contexts in which the characters acted.

Brecht later described the effect he sought to create as the *Verfremdungseffekt* ('alienation effect'). But Brecht certainly did not want to put people off theatre. Above all else he believed that theatre-going should be entertaining. He wanted audiences to see the known and familiar as if for the first time, and to question what they had previously taken for granted.

A communist since the late 1920s, Brecht was forced into exile by the Nazis; first in Europe and subsequently in the USA. From exile he wrote the dramas that best illustrate his dramatic techniques: *Mother Courage* (1937), *Galileo*, (1938–9; see illustration), *The Good Person of Setzuan* (1938–40), *The Resistible Rise of Arturo Ui* (1940), and *The Caucasian Chalk Circle* (1944–5). In these works stylized acting and use of songs are intended to draw the audience's attention to the fact that they are watching a play.

1612 - FLORENCE - 1612

The Life of Galileo, by Bertolt Brecht. In his 'epic' theatre Brecht sought to create what he called the 'alienation effect' – a critical detachment conducive to rational understanding of the social and political contexts in which his characters act. In the 1980 National Theatre production illustrated here, this effect is fostered by a backdrop setting the action in its geographical and historical context.

Monsieur Ubu in a woodcut by Alfred Jarry for the first production of *Ubu Roi* in 1896. The play, which blends ribald farce, violence and stylized stage conventions, describes how the grotesque, puppet-like figure of Ubu becomes King of Poland and is driven to commit savage atrocities by his uncontrollable lust for power. *Ubu Roi* is regarded as a milestone in the history of experimental theatre.

After World War II Brecht returned to communist East Germany and founded a theatre company: the Berlin Ensemble. The company toured widely in Europe and its revolutionary style was to have a profound impact on directors and audiences.

Theatre of cruelty

Between the wars in Europe a radically different form of theatrical experiment was evolving in France. The work of **Antonin Artaud** (1896–1948), and especially his book *The Theatre and its Double* (1938), was to exert an enormous influence on the subsequent development of the theatre.

Artaud entirely rejected the conventions of Naturalistic and Realistic theatre. He believed that it was too preoccupied with social and psychological issues and so failed to harness what he saw as the true potential of theatre: to make audiences feel totally involved in a powerful and even magical event. The theatre, Artaud believed, could exorcize man's destructive urges by purging the emotions, and appealing not to the rational mind, but communicating directly with the senses. He termed his ideal theatre a 'theatre of cruelty', because he felt that within it an audience would be continually confronted with their real selves, and such a confrontation would inevitably lead to deep feelings akin to physical pain and discomfort.

Artaud wanted to move performances away from traditional venues in purpose-built theatres and the associations they carried with them. He wanted to perform in factories and in the street, and to locate the action in unexpected places.

Elsewhere in Europe dramatists were also conducting theatrical experiments. In Italy **Luigi Pirandello** (1867–1936) was writing an extraordinary series of plays of which the best known remains *Six Characters in Search of an Author* (1921), in which he explored ideas of illusion and reality, the role of performers and spectators, and the very nature of the theatrical experience itself.

In Britain the work of the director **Peter Brook** (1925–) was influenced by Artaud. He, too, expressed the belief that 'the theatre has one precise social function – to disturb the spectator'. In experimental-theatre workshops, inspired by Artaud's ideas, Brook explored non-verbal communication and radical assaults on the sensibility of the audience. Perhaps Brook's greatest impact on British theatre came through his staging of Shakespeare. His famous production in 1970 of *A Midsummer Night's Dream*, which set the action in a gymnasium, with characters swinging acrobatically from trapezes, caused critics and audiences to re-evaluate not only the play itself, but also the conventional approaches to staging it.

Theatre of the absurd

The notion of the 'absurd', defining human existence as incomprehensible, bewildering and purposeless, was given currency by the philosophical writings of the French novelist Albert Camus (see p. 648) in the 1940s. The term 'theatre of the absurd' was coined by the critic Martin Esslin in 1961. It describes the work of a number of dramatists he regards as preoccupied with the 'absurdity' of the human condition, and which present a vision of mankind adrift in a world devoid of ultimate meaning.

While absurd drama is normally associated with dramatists writing after World War II, elements of the absurd can be found in the work of earlier writers, including the plays written by **Jean Cocteau** (1889–1963; see also p. 640) in the 1920s, and, most notably, a wild and grotesque production by the Frenchman **Alfred Jarry** (1873–1907). *Ubu Roi* (1896; see illustration) – an extravagant farce that savagely attacks conventional moral and aesthetic values – is considered by many to be the first work in the absurd tradition.

Of the postwar practitioners of absurd drama, the best known are the Romanian-born Frenchman **Eugene Ionesco** (1912–) and the Irishman **Samuel Beckett** (1906–89; see also p. 641). In common with the other experiments described above, absurd drama abandoned Naturalism. There were no familiar domestic settings, no comfortable structure containing a beginning, middle and end. Events were not linked together with any clear causality.

The scope for comedy afforded by an absurd view of existence is evident in Ionesco's anarchic early play *The Bald Prima Donna* (1948). However, sombre themes of isolation and the difficulty of communication are present in a scene in which two strangers, engaged in a trivial discussion of homes and families, are staggered to find that they are in fact man and wife. Ionesco's later plays – notably *The Killer* (1960) and *Exit the King* (1962) – show an increasing obsession with the horror of death.

Beckett's *Waiting for Godot* (1952) – one of the most influential plays of the 20th century – addresses nothing less than the human condition itself. It shows men trying hard to pass the time meaningfully as they await the only certainty: death. Here, and in Beckett's other plays (notably *Endgame*, 1958; and *Happy Days*, 1961; see illustration), language – manipulated in a variety of styles and with a poetic concentration of meaning – is virtually the only action. This, and Beckett's hard-edged comedy, relate him closely to his friend and countryman James Joyce (see p. 641). PR

Happy Days, by Samuel Beckett. Beckett's dramas typically strip reality down to its barest essentials in order to address fundamental aspects of the human condition. In *Happy Days* – a fable of human self-delusion in the face of the inevitability of death – Winnie, although sinking ever deeper into the ground, still chatters about mundane matters and shows great concern with the contents of her handbag. Shown here is Peggy Ashcroft as Winnie in the 1975 National Theatre production.

Modern Drama in Britain and the USA

Modern drama in Britain and America is distinctive for its concern with issues. These may, amongst other things, relate to politics, morality, racism, and/or religion. Equally, the main concerns of modern theatre may be to do with theatre itself – how it works; what it means; the nature of its conventions, and the kind of language it uses. Finally, the ideas explored in modern drama may be those specifically associated with Modernism (see p. 641). Foremost among these are the workings of time and memory; the problems surrounding communication, and a sense that life is meaningless.

SEE ALSO

● REALISM AND NATURALISM p. 634
● SYMBOLISM, AESTHETICISM AND MODERNISM p. 640
● EXPERIMENTAL THEATRE p. 642

Most theatrical epochs have also been concerned with the nature of theatre and its relationship to society. Modern British drama, however, follows the theatrically lean period of the 19th century, when the best creative writers chose the medium of the novel or poetry rather than the stage. Plays were written primarily as vehicles to display the per-

George Bernard Shaw in the garden of his home at Ayot St Lawrence in 1946. As well as writing over 50 plays Shaw was an accomplished journalist, a tireless public speaker, and an active socialist, serving on the executive committee of the Fabian Society, supporting women's rights, and advocating the abolition of private property.

sonalities of leading actors, and as the foundation on which to build elaborate spectacle.

Such was the situation in both Britain and America for most of the 19th century. The modern drama of issues and ideas emerged first in Britain, and can conveniently be broken into three distinct phases.

Britain before World War I

By the beginning of the 20th century two Anglo-Irish dramatists, **George Bernard Shaw** (1856–1950) and **Oscar Wilde** (1854–1900), had established their plays on the London stage as a rich alternative to the mediocrity of much late-Victorian drama. Both men combined a wonderful facility with words with a shrewd and often caustic wit, which they focused on the behaviour of high society. Wilde's plays, especially *The Importance of Being Earnest* (1895), were enormously successful, whilst those of Shaw continued to edify and entertain audiences for over half a century.

In contrast with many of his theatrical peers, Shaw was concerned with more than filling stages with spectacle and illusion. Like Henrik Ibsen, the Norwegian dramatist he so admired (see p. 635), he wanted to feed the intelligence of audiences with a diet of new ideas about society, such as socialism. 'I write plays with the deliberate object of converting the nation to my opinions', he once said, only half tongue-in-cheek.

Shaw's concern with ideas does not make his a weighty or dull drama. His work fizzes with wit and verbal dexterity. His powers were probably at their height in the years leading up to World War I, when he produced plays such as *Arms and the Man* (1894), *Man and Superman* (1905), *Major Barbara* (1905), and *Heartbreak House* (1920).

Britain between the wars

The inter-war period in Britain, although punctuated by the appearance of one or two remarkable plays, produced no significant school of dramatic writing, and genuine theatrical innovation is hard to find. A few notable plays from this period do continue to be revived. Foremost among these are **R.C. Sherriff's** (1896–1975) dramatization of the hellish life of soldiers on the front line in World War I, *Journey's End* (1928); several plays concerned with various aspects of time, notably *Time and the Conways* (1937), by **J.B. Priestley** (1894–1984); and the poet **T.S. Eliot's** (see p. 641) verse dramas such as *Murder in the Cathedral* (1935).

The London stage regularly enjoyed revivals and new plays by Shaw, and additionally it was now elegantly adorned

by the 'talent to amuse' of the young **Noel Coward** (1899–1973). Coward enjoyed a phenomenal success and made a reputation and a considerable fortune from the theatre.

Britain after 1945

The aftermath of World War II was a time when people wished to put the horrors of war behind them and look with optimism to the future rebuilding of society. However, a decade later many young people felt that the ideals of that postwar period had not been fulfilled and, by 1956, the year of the Suez debacle, optimism began to be replaced by anger. In London that year the innovative Royal Court Theatre put on a new play by a then young and unknown dramatist, **John Osborne** (1929–). This play, *Look Back In Anger*, seemed to many to express their own pent-up feelings of anger and frustration. The play, with its hero, Jimmy Porter – tagged the 'angry young man' – has subsequently been seen as a turning-point in the history of the modern British theatre.

The success of *Look Back in Anger* prompted a new generation of writers to use the theatre to make statements about themselves and their society. The Royal Court Theatre was instrumental in furthering the development of new writing in the aftermath of Osborne's success. Plays by **Arnold Wesker** (1923–) and others produced fresh images of predominantly working-class life for predominantly middle-class audiences. Their plays, often centred around domestic life, were sometimes referred to as 'Kitchen Sink' drama.

The Royal Court continued to sponsor and encourage new writing, notably that of **John Arden** (1930–), whose brilliant and original play *Serjeant Musgrave's Dance* was first performed there in 1959. Of the new but equally talented group of writers who emerged in the 1960s it was perhaps **Edward Bond** (1934–) who made the greatest immediate impact. His second play, *Saved* (1965), caused an uproar by depicting scenes of savage urban deprivation and representing the stoning of a baby on stage. The furore caused by the play was a major factor in hastening the abolition of stage censorship in 1968. Bond's subsequent plays explore complex social and political issues with the ultimate objective – one which he shares with Brecht (see p. 642) – of provoking social action.

Some dramatists, unlike Brecht and Bond, avoid creating plays which seem to have a clear social message. The work of **Harold Pinter** (1930–) steadfastly refuses to fit any particular classification, although some critics have linked his early plays *The Birthday Party* (1958) and *The Caretaker* (1960; see illustration) – with their use of banal repetition, pauses and colloquial speech – to the Theatre of the Absurd (see p. 643). Pinter's plays were successful in the commercial as well as the subsidized theatre, as were the black and anarchic dramas of his short-lived but equally popular contemporary **Joe Orton** (1933–67), such as *Loot* (1965) and *What the Butler Saw* (1969).

Powerful and original dramatists who have emerged in recent years include **Caryl Churchill** (1938–), **Howard Brenton** (1942–) and **David Hare** (1947–). However, in terms of popular appeal, two British playwrights – **Tom Stoppard** (1937–) and **Alan Ayckbourn** (1939–) – stand out from the rest. Stoppard's inventive early comedies

The Caretaker. Harold Pinter's second full-length play established his reputation. A typically enigmatic drama, *The Caretaker* is about a former mental patient who rescues a tramp from a brawl and brings him to the house he shares with his brother. Pinter's themes include family hatred, obsession and the difficulties of communication. Illustrated here is a scene from the 1980 National Theatre production.

Rosencrantz and Guildenstern are Dead (1966) and *The Real Inspector Hound* (1968) respectively use characters from Shakespeare's *Hamlet* and parody the conventions of the stage thriller. In *Jumpers* (1972) and *Travesties* (1974) Stoppard explores philosophical ideas with considerable wit and verbal skill. Although termed comedies, Ayckbourn's plays of middle-class suburban life – notably *Relatively Speaking* (1967) and *The Norman Conquests* (1974) – are often almost painful in the sharpness of their observation. An increasingly sombre note, with undercurrents of violence, can be detected in his later work.

The USA

It was not until after the end of World War I that a distinctive voice was heard in American theatre. It was then that the young **Eugene O'Neill** (1888–1953) began to make his mark. The characters in O'Neill's plays are always seemingly motivated by their struggle to find some significance in life, and O'Neill himself was never afraid to experiment with new and diverse dramatic techniques. *The Hairy Ape* (1922) used Expressionist techniques (see p. 642), while other plays were influenced by Symbolism, Realist conventions and the stream-of-consciousness technique (see p. 635 and 640–1). *Mourning becomes Electra* (1931) was the first play in a trilogy based on the *Oresteia* of Aeschylus (see p. 614). Two late works, *The Iceman Cometh* (1946) and the posthumously-produced *A Long Day's Journey Into Night* (1956), established O'Neill's international reputation.

After the end of World War II American theatre welcomed two young and highly talented dramatists whose work was to dominate the American stage for the next three decades: **Tennessee Williams** (1911–83) and **Arthur Miller** (1915–).

Williams's first play, *The Glass Menagerie* (1944; see illustration) – a painful family drama – was an enormous success. Later successes include *A Street Car Named Desire* (1947), which explored themes of sexual obsession and violence, and *Cat On A Hot Tin Roof* (1955) a study of a family in disintegration, with Freudian undertones. That Williams had his finger on the pulse of popular interests and preoccupations is demonstrated by the fact that all three plays were subsequently made into successful films.

Critical acclaim for the work of Arthur Miller has by and large been reserved for his early work, notably *Death of a Salesman* (1949), and *A View from the Bridge* (1955). The strength of these plays lies in their closely observed depiction of the lives of ordinary Americans, whose desire for material reward is in conflict with a need for spiritual renewal and personal happiness. *The Crucible* (1952) – a dramatic account of the Salem witch trials of 1692 – is a parable of the anti-communist witch-hunts in America in the 1950s (see p. 450).

Apart from the not inconsiderable output of Williams and Miller, little original dramatic writing has emerged from the United States since the end of World War II. The first full-length play by **Edward Albee** (1928–), *Who's Afraid of Virginia Woolf?* (1962) – the bitter and often savage story of a marriage in crisis – raised high hopes that a new and rich talent had been unleashed. However, with the exception of the work of **Sam Shepard** (1943–) and **David Mamet** (1947–), American dramatic writing remains largely in the doldrums.   PR

The Glass Menagerie. Tennessee Williams achieved his first major success in 1944 with this portrayal of a Southern family living in reduced circumstances. The drama centres round the efforts of a frustrated and domineering mother to persuade her rebellious son to find a 'gentleman caller' for her crippled daughter. Illustrated here is a scene from the 1950 film version.

Modern Poetry in English

Modern poetry includes both 'difficult' poetry and poetry that is more directly accessible to the reader. The difficult poetry is obscure and highly allusive in the Modernist manner exemplified by T.S. Eliot's *The Waste Land* and Ezra Pound's *Cantos* (see p. 641). The more accessible poetry – though not necessarily easy to understand – belongs to a tradition which does not break so abruptly with previous poetry.

The subject matter of this more accessible poetry may be just as much concerned with modern urban experience, and its language may also be colloquial and casual rather than self-consciously 'poetic', but it retains the traditionally rational structure of argument and does not relate to the same extent as Modernist poetry to a wide range of cultural reference. Modernity, in other words, is not exclusively a possession of the Modernists – though for a time, especially in the 1920s, it seemed rather like that.

Yeats and modern Irish poetry

W.B. Yeats (1865–1939) is regarded by many as the greatest of modern poets writing in English. His early poetry has a wistful, dream-like quality, tinged with

---

HOPKINS

Although written during the Victorian period, the strikingly original poetry of the Jesuit priest Gerard Manley Hopkins (1844–89) was not published until 1918. Hopkins's verse was principally religious in character: his nature poems display an extraordinary lyrical intensity and joyous – almost mystical – awareness of God through nature; while his so-called 'terrible sonnets' describe the poet's anguished fear of abandonment by his Creator.

Hopkins's originality and (some would say) modernity lie in his use of language and rhythm. He took liberties with word order and parts of speech, coined new words and created unexpected word combinations – all in the interests of expressive vividness. His rhythms (in particular his use of what he called 'sprung rhythm') were unusual in being based mainly on stress.

Too idiosyncratic to fit conveniently into categories such as 'Victorian' or 'modern', Hopkins's poetry was to exercise some influence on the poets of the 1930s, and is now regarded as the work of a major and innovative poet.

SEE ALSO

● SYMBOLISM, AESTHETICISM AND THE BIRTH OF MODERNISM p. 640
● THE MODERN NOVEL p. 648

---

nostalgia for a mythical Ireland. However, his involvement with the early phase of the Irish Nationalist movement and, in particular, with the founding of a national theatre (see p. 645), caused Yeats to become disenchanted with this atmosphere of 'Celtic Twilight'. He discarded his elaborate early vein and opted for a plainer and more muscular style. The spare yet tragically powerful 'Easter 1916', a poem which meditates on the abortive Nationalist uprising in Dublin, is an example of the new style. Yeats's later poems, including such masterpieces as 'Sailing to Byzantium', 'Among School Children' and 'Lapis Lazuli', brood on the problems of growing old and the difficulty of reconciling art and life.

After Yeats there has been a remarkable renaissance of Irish poetry, including such names as **Patrick Kavanagh** (1905–67) and **Seamus Heaney** (1939–). Heaney, while far from being an imitator of Yeats, shows the same capacity to deal realistically with the facts of a turbulent Ireland while seeing them in the perspective of history.

Auden and the poetry of the thirties

W.H. Auden (1907–73) is a political poet of the 1930s who became a Christian liberal in his postwar work. In his earlier phase, with fellow Oxford poets **Louis MacNeice** (1907–63) and **Stephen Spender** (1909–), he wrote prophetic verse from a left-wing standpoint (often in updated ballad forms) intended to shake suburban readers out of their supposed indifference to the threat of Fascism, as well as intellectually more exacting poems on fashionable themes such as Marxism and Freudian psychology. Later he adopted a more relaxed manner and expressed more orthodox views. Prolific, and technically one of the most inventive and skilful of modern poets, Auden is at his best in poems that use the Modernist's colloquial ease to express acceptance of humanity's imperfect nature.

Hardy and Lawrence

Poetry in English has ceased to be exclusively 'English' and London-based. Two outstanding poets (perhaps better known as novelists) – **Thomas Hardy** (see p. 637) and **D.H. Lawrence** (see p. 648) – are regional rather than metropolitan. Hardy's position is that of a man divided between the emotional values associated with his birthplace and the national culture of the city. Out of this dual experience he develops an individual blend of understanding and detachment. His recurrent themes are loss of faith and stoic acceptance of mortality, but he is also a humanely ironic and satiric poet.

In Lawrence's poems, the regional influence is to be heard in his down-to-earth tone of voice. This is an effective means of deflating pretentiousness, while allowing sympathy for forms of experience that are repressed by modern materialism to

---

POETRY OF WORLD WAR I

Rupert Brooke (1887–1915) gave conventional expression to the patriotic sentiments that inspired many recruits at the beginning of the 1914–18 war, notably in his sonnet 'The Soldier', which contains the well-known lines: 'If I should die, think only this of me: / That there's some corner of a foreign field / That is for ever England.' *Edward Thomas* (1878–1917) expressed his feelings indirectly. In 'As the Team's Head-Brass', he set the war against the background of the old, seemingly permanent rhythms of the countryside.

However, poets like Wilfred Owen, Siegfried Sassoon (1886–1967) and Isaac Rosenberg wrote more directly of the horrific realities of trench warfare. *Wilfred Owen* (1893–1918) showed his disgust with the falsely heroic image of war fostered by stay-at-homes. His graphic description of a gas attack in 'Dulce Et Decorum Est' is a form of shock tactics. In 'Anthem for Doomed Youth' and 'Strange Meeting' he expresses a more profound feeling for 'the pity of war'.

Isaac Rosenberg (1890–1918), a war poet from a working-class background, who, like Owen, was killed in the last days of the war, combined an apocalyptic imagination with gruesome detail in 'Dead Man's Dump'.

---

come through. In 'Snake', for example, he conducts a dialogue between two aspects of his self: 'the voices of my accursed human education', which tell him to kill the snake, and his deeper feelings which warm to the dark vitality of the snake, compelling him to recognize it as 'one of the lords / Of life'.

Postwar British poetry

If there is an 'English' tradition as such, it may be said to stem from these two writers, continuing through Edward Thomas, Wilfred Owen (see box) and Robert Graves to Philip Larkin, Ted Hughes and Geoffrey Hill. **Philip Larkin** (1922–85) is the chief inheritor from Hardy, and **Ted Hughes** (1930–) – the British Poet Laureate from 1984 – from Lawrence.

W.B. Yeats, the great Irish poet, painted by his father John Butler Yeats in 1900.

We are Making a New World (1918), by the official British war artist Paul Nash, presents an image of the devastation wrought by trench warfare as stark as that provided by Wilfred Owen in his poetry.

Larkin combines the provincial and the national in his faithful representations of ordinary life in the 1960s. Like Hardy, Larkin is often regarded as a pessimist, but he is essentially a realist. 'Aubade', for example, is a poem that looks unblinkingly at the inevitability of death.

The realism of Hughes is of a different kind. He emphasizes the brute instinct of the animal world, but sees it as untameable energy in, for example, 'Hawk Roosting' and 'The Jaguar'. The later *Crow* sequences (1970–72) create a harsh, caricatural mythology, but the purpose is still to explore powers lying outside the safety limits that human beings try to build round themselves.

The poetry of *Geoffrey Hill* (1932–) is more problematic; his *Mercian Hymns* (1971) echo the allusive Modernism of Eliot. This is also true of the leading modern Scottish poet, *Hugh MacDiarmid* (the pen name of C.M. Grieve; 1892–1978). MacDiarmid sought to reinstate Scots as a medium for serious national poetry. His masterpiece, *A Drunk Man Looks at the Thistle* (1926), is a hotchpotch of lyricism, philosophizing and outspoken commentary on sex, politics and Scottish society. It is nationalist in vein, but also internationalist – as signalled by the inclusion of extracts from the Russian Symbolist poet A.A. Blok (see p. 640). Other modern Scottish poets use Scots less aggressively, or not at all. For example, *Edwin Muir* (1887–1959) wrote in the received standard form of English,

taking local experience as material for universal themes.

The best-known Welsh poet is *Dylan Thomas* (1914–53), whose work is exclusively in English. His is a concentrated, cryptic, highly metaphorical poetry, full of surprising twists given to familiar phrases – for example, 'once below a time' and 'happy as the heart was long' (from 'Fern Hill'). Puzzling, yet stimulating, it is modern poetry at its most bardic, and sometimes extravagantly rhetorical. *R.S. Thomas* (1913–), on the other hand, is an English-Welsh poet of a more restrained kind. Religious, yet almost too disillusioned for faith, he writes grimly austere poetry on the decay of Welsh culture.

American poetry

T.S. Eliot affirmed the need for Americans to be conscious of their English and European ancestry, and for poetry to be impersonal rather than a private confession. This position is adopted and reinforced, both in theory and in their own practice, by poets such as *Allen Tate* (1899–1979), *John Crowe Ransom* (1888–1974; see also p. 653) and *Wallace Stevens* (1879–1955). Stevens, in particular, makes the art of poetry a major subject of his own work. In 'Anecdote of the Jar', the placing of a jar on a hill 'in Tennessee' becomes an analogy for the way that an artist's imagination endows formless nature with form, and so makes it interesting and comprehensible to the mind. Stevens's poetry is elegantly constructed – a product of self-conscious artistry.

William Carlos Williams (1883–1963), on the other hand, finds a specifically American quality in the democratically free existence of things in and for

themselves. His 'poetry', which has been dismissed by some as lacking rhyme or metre, interferes as little as possible with the subject-matter, selecting and arranging only enough to awaken the reader's dormant attention. At its extreme Williams's position becomes 'no ideas but in things' (*Paterson*, 1946–58), and his poems become a series of 'shots', like a film or television sequence.

Robert Frost (1874–1963) also exploits the distinctive rhythms of American speech. A popular poet (more widely read than other modern poets, and more accessible in style), Frost can also be deceptively easy. His best poems question and undermine the obvious in the interests of a more tentative, cautious wisdom.

In the work of *John Berryman* (1914–72) and *Robert Lowell* (1917–77) this underground, disturbing quality is brought more forcefully out into the open. They themselves led tormented, turbulent lives – Lowell suffered spells of mental illness, and Berryman committed suicide. Private and public material is combined in their poetry. Berryman writes in an idiosyncratic, abrupt, oscillating style that gives little quarter to the reader. *The Dream Songs* (1964) are 18-line poems, divided into three 6-line stanzas, in which he creates the ravaged figure of a middle-aged American called 'Henry'.

Lowell's 'The Quaker Graveyard in Nantucket' (1946) is a Catholic elegy on a Protestant subject, with echoes of the Bible, Melville's *Moby-Dick*, and T.S. Eliot. One of Lowell's most celebrated poems, 'Skunk Hour', has for its setting a vividly realized Maine sea-port where a car radio 'bleats' a mawkish love-song. The poet's own psychological condition intrudes on the scene ('My mind's not right'), and the disturbing climax comes with moonlit skunks marching up 'Main Street'.

Among more recent American poets the one who most strikingly continues this 'confessional' line is *Sylvia Plath* (1932–63), who, like Berryman, committed suicide. She also represents an important trend in women's writing. Plath's images can be bizarre and her situations morbidly histrionic. In the frequently anthologized 'Daddy', the Nazi concentration camps of Dachau, Auschwitz and Belsen are used to express her own sense of victimization by domineering males.
RD

Robert Lowell, the American poet, in 1971. Vehemently opposed to US involvement in Vietnam, plagued by bouts of depression and heavy drinking, and lionized as the greatest American poet of his day, Lowell achieved near-legendary status in his lifetime.

A concrete poem. Modern poetry has seen attempts to extend imaginative expression beyond the normal verse range to include verbal shapes on the printed page. Known as 'concrete poetry' this form is arresting, but limited. It sacrifices the possibility of developing an argument or elaborating subtle distinctions, but offers instead images that have a poster-like effect, or entertain the reader (viewer?) with witty arrangements of language. Shown here is *Target Practice, Dedicated to both sides in Vietnam* (1968) by Ronald Draper.

The Modern Novel

Towards the end of the 19th century and in the early years of the 20th, the great Realist consensus (see pp. 634–7) began to exhibit signs of strain, and finally broke up altogether. This development did not, of course, happen overnight, though there are signs of its origin in the later writings of Hardy, Conrad, James, Dostoevski, and even in those of the Realist novelist *par excellence*, Tolstoy himself.

There was, however, no instantaneous recognition of the Modernist revolution in fiction. In the period leading up to the end of World War I, those novelists now regarded as the great mainstream of modern prose fiction were struggling, neglected, or even persecuted by cultural and political authorities.

The Modernist revolution

It is in the work of a generation of novelists who sprang to prominence in the 1920s that the irrevocable collapse of Realism can be traced. In the novels of James Joyce (see p. 641), and in those of the English writer **D.H. Lawrence** (1885–1930; see illustration), especially *Sons and Lovers* (1913), *Women in Love* (1920) and *The Plumed Serpent* (1926), we can observe the main features of this fictional revolution. There is a fundamental change in the notion of 'character'. The stream-of-consciousness technique used by Joyce and Virginia Woolf (see p. 641) causes the experience of an individual to become more intensely realized and sharply focused. The work of both Joyce and Lawrence also challenged traditional assumptions about literature in more direct and provocative ways. Both, for example, wrote about sexual experience – which even the boldest Realists tended to fill in by suggestion – more directly, more overtly, and in more specific physical detail. Both Joyce and Lawrence had their books censored and banned by the authorities. Lawrence's *Lady Chatterley's Lover* (1928) was printed privately in Italy by the author, but in Britain not published in complete form until the 1960s. Even those novels now regarded as the central achievements of these authors, *Ulysses* (1922) and *Women in Love*, were initially both published abroad, in France and America respectively (see p. 641).

Corresponding to this new focus on the individual is a changed relationship with the 'real world'. The solid, reassuring earth of the Realist novel becomes a more uncertain, nebulous and even nightmare landscape, shaped by the visionary con-sciousness of the individual. Modernist novels manifest a breakdown in the conventional moral scheme that formed the basis of much Realist fiction. In Joyce the values of 'art' are more important than those of morality, and Lawrence, though a passionate moralist, re-evaluated all conventional ethical taboos against sex, cruelty and violence. Revolutionary narrative techniques also contributed to the production of novels that are Modernist in style as well as content. Their linguistic texture is denser and more difficult than that of the Realist novel. It directs the reader's gaze inwards towards the artistic medium rather than outwards towards a graspable world of reality.

The alienated individual absorbed in an intense inner consciousness, and more or less lost in an increasingly surreal, nightmare world, became an archetype of modern fiction. The classic expression of this pattern is to be found in the writings of Franz Kafka (see p. 641). Later in the century, this sense of bewildered isolation formed the basis for the fiction of the absurd (see also p. 643), in novels such as *The Outsider* (1942) by **Albert Camus** (1913–60), or *Nausea* (1938) by the French existentialist philosopher **Jean-Paul Sartre** (1905–80; see p. 487).

Elsewhere novelists tried to grasp the nature of this period, of World War I and the 1920s, with a more specifically sociological analysis, though this was often viewed from a pessimistic perspective. Three prominent American writers produced bleak, melancholy visions of a tragic age. In *Fiesta (The Sun Also Rises*; 1926) and *A Farewell to Arms* (1929) **Ernest Hemingway** (1899–1961) wrote of the mood of disillusionment of a so-called 'lost generation' of American expatriate writers. **F. Scott Fitzgerald** (1896–1940) in *The Beautiful and the Damned* (1922) and *The Great Gatsby* (1925) traced the tragic decline of the 'Jazz Age'. **William Faulkner** (1897–1962) chronicled the declining civilization of the American South in novels such as *The Sound and the Fury* (1929) .

Continuities

In contrast with the formal experimentation of the Modernists, a substantial number of writers continued to work within more traditional artistic frameworks: either as a reaction to the radically experimental and culturally élitist stance of the Modernists, or simply out of a conservative preference for more conventional forms and styles. This technical conservatism does not necessarily imply a conservative approach to their subjects, and many of these traditionalist writers used their fictions to develop, as the 19th-century novelists had done, some incisive moral and social criticism of the world they lived in.

In France **André Gide** (1869–1951), and in Germany **Thomas Mann** (1875–1955; see illustration) explored issues such as the social alienation of the artist, the decline of European civilization and the oppressive burdens of the past. Both wrote some remarkable shorter novels, such as Gide's *The Immoralist* (1930) and Mann's *Death in Venice* (1912), as well as working in the traditional full-length novel form. Gide's *The Counterfeiters* (1927) and Mann's *The Magic Mountain* (1924) both combined a critical perspective on contemporary Europe with a relatively conservative approach to fictional technique.

In Britain, **E.M. Forster** (1879–1970) displayed a concern for the imaginative life of humanity and emphasized the need for sincerity and sensitivity in human relationships (see p. 632). *Howard's End* (1910) shows English society in a state of change and expresses Forster's idealized wish for a union of the imaginative aspects of human nature with more practical values. In the highly symbolic novel *A Passage to India* (1924), Forster's concern for spontaneity and friendship is played out against a background of racial difference in British-ruled India.

The English novelist **Evelyn Waugh** (1903–66) began writing in the late 1920s. In *Decline and Fall* (1928) and *A Handful of Dust* (1934) he incorporated the comedy of manners and social satire into the novel form, depicting with great humour the frivolous futility of the post-World War I generation. Later works such as *Brideshead Revisited* (1945), with its parable of the decline of a Catholic aristocracy, introduced deeper notes of elegy and pessimism. The novels of **Graham Greene** (1904–91) express a similarly difficult relationship with Catholicism: but where Waugh's more conservative sympathies lay with the English past and with the landed aristocracy, Greene was drawn towards Communism and to the political landscape of the modern world. His major novels, compelling explorations of failure and betrayal, are usually set in colonial or Third World locations: *The Power and the Glory* (1940) in Mexico and *The Heart of the Matter* (1948) in Africa. Greene also experimented with popular fictional forms such as the political thriller (*The Honorary Consul*; 1973) or the spy novel (*The Human Factor*; 1978). These genres are also brilliantly parodied in lighter

D.H. Lawrence (right) in 1920. Lawrence's frank treatment of sexual relations in his work was to keep him in constant trouble with the law. His last – and most sexually explicit – novel, *Lady Chatterley's Lover*, was not published in full in Britain until 1960, when it was the subject of a famous obscenity trial. (National Portrait Gallery)

Thomas Mann, the German novelist, painted by Wolf Kitz in 1955. In his novels and short stories Mann relates the inner problems of the creative artist to the changing cultural values of Europe. (© Wolf Ritz 1955/Schiller Nationalmuseum/ Archiv für Kunst)

novels that Greene termed 'entertainments', including the ironically comic *Our Man in Havana* (1958).

Other British writers continued to extend prose fiction along these more traditional lines. *Anthony Powell* (1905–) observed the upper middle-class social landscape in a sequence of twelve novels, *A Dance to the Music of Time* (1951–75). *William Golding* (1911–), in novels such as *Lord of the Flies* (1954) and *The Spire* (1964), pared down the novel to a modern form of the fable (see p. 621). *Iris Murdoch* (1919–) combined fiction and philosophy in novels such as *The Bell* (1958) and *The Sea, The Sea* (1978), which explore complicated sexual relationships within melodramatic and highly symbolic plots.

In America, *Saul Bellow* (1915–) also combined technical conservatism with deep and painful fictional exploration of the self and civilization, notably in *Herzog* (1964). In Australia *Patrick White* (1912–90) achieved an almost Dostoevskian intensity in novels such as *Voss* (1957) – an epic celebration of a heroic Australian past – and *Riders in the Chariot* (1961).

The strength of the great Realist tradition in Russia, and the post-revolutionary concern with social realism (see p. 635), ensured the continuity of traditional fictional forms in writers such as *Boris Pasternak* (1890–1960), whose critical view of Soviet Russia, *Dr Zhivago*, was published in Italy in 1957, and *Alexander Solzhenitsyn* (1918–), whose short story *One Day in the Life of Ivan Denisovitch* (1962) exposed the world of Stalin's labour camps. *Mikhail Sholokhov* (1905–84), a writer broadly in sympathy with the Soviet Communist system, achieved in his four-volume epic novel *And Quiet Flows the Don* (1928–40) an artistically remarkable representation of post-revolutionary Russia.

Post-Modernist innovation

Modernist writers produced a type of fiction in which the world of reality is shaped and coloured by the activity of the individual character. 'Post-Modernist' writers have extended the Modernist search into the potentialities of human consciousness and the distinction between the individual and the objective world by means of a deliberate subversion of fictional conventions. This has made possible a whole range of new fictional techniques, opening up serious fiction to fantasy, surrealist allegory and 'Magic Realism'.

Vladimir Nabokov (1899–1977), an expatriate Russian, can be regarded as a major and typical practitioner of the 'Post-Modernist' novel. He is best known for his parable of sexual destruction, *Lolita* (1958), but his flexible uses of narrative and playful linguistic fertility can be seen at their most inventive in *Pale Fire* (1962). The sophisticated technical experiments of the French *Nouveau Roman* ('New Novel') also testify to the positive effects of modern fiction's liberation from Realism. This term refers to the work of a group of French writers, the best known being *Marguerite Duras* (1914–) and *Alain Robbe-Grillet* (1922–), who share a belief that the traditional novel, with its realistic narrative and omniscient narrator, creates an illusion of order and significance that is no longer (if it ever was) a true depiction of reality. The typical *Nouveau Roman*, such as Robbe-Grillet's *Jealousy* (1957), destabilizes narrative and avoids imposing on its subject matter any fixed or final interpretation. The impact of these developments on the British novel can best be seen in the work of *John Fowles* (1926–). *The French Lieutenant's Woman* (1969) is a semi-historical novel that contrasts the conventions of the Victorian novel (see pp. 636–7) with a more modern view of fiction. The novel's modernity lies in its acknowledgement that fiction essentially involves deception and manipulation, Fowles replacing the Victorian conventions with a sceptical and uncertain narrator – a 20th-century anthropologist who interrupts the action with his comments – and an open-ended narrative, including three alternative endings.

These writers tended to concentrate their innovations on formal devices and techniques, while their narratives still occupied the traditional territory of the novel, continuing to portray the lives of people in contemporary society. Elsewhere Post-Modernist fiction has moved further away from the landscape of social realism and entered realms of dream, myth and fantasy. The Argentinian writer *Jorge Luis Borges* (1899–1986) developed the Post-Modernist preoccupation with the complex relations of fiction, truth and reality, and in collections of short stories such as *A Universal History of Infamy* (1935) and *Fictions* (1945) he established the form of *Magic Realism*, based on the premise that

myth, fantasy and dream are no less 'real' than the familiar territory of social realism traditionally occupied by the novel. The Colombian writer *Gabriel Garcia Marquez* (1928–) has also mixed the ordinary and the fantastic, the real and the supernatural, in a manner typical of Magic Realism. His best-known novel, *One Hundred Years of Solitude* (1967), combines the unexpected and the everyday, the normal and the inexplicable in the fragmented and dispersed narrative style characteristic of Post-Modernist fiction. Affinities with Magic Realism can also be detected in the novels of the reclusive American *Thomas Pynchon* (1937–). *Gravity's Rainbow* (1973) employs a blend of fantasy, black humour, grotesque sexuality and esoteric language to portray human alienation and the chaos of contemporary society.

In Germany *Günter Grass* (1927–), in comic and experimental novels such as *The Tin Drum* (1959) and *Dog Years* (1965), similarly questioned the status of truth and reality in the modern world, but with strong political preoccupations. Although most Post-Modernist fiction is based on a sceptical view of reality. Grass – a committed and outspoken socialist – represents the possibility of reconciling Post-Modernist art with a positive social engagement. And there could be no better illustration of the power of Post-Modernist fiction to challenge and outrage authority than the career of the Anglo-Indian novelist *Salman Rushdie* (1947–). An exponent of Magic Realism, in *Midnight's Children* (1981) he offered to Western culture a new and original perspective on the East that was readily and rapidly embraced. But when Rushdie applied his blend of myth and reality, philosophy and fantasy to an examination of Islam from the viewpoint of a non-believer in *The Satanic Verses* (1988), he caused great offence to many Muslims. The late Ayatollah Khomeini, the fundamentalist spiritual leader of Iran, sentenced Rushdie to death for blasphemy, forcing the writer into hiding.   GHo

SEE ALSO

- THE LANGUAGE OF SIGNS p. 610
- REALISM AND NATURALISM p. 634
- THE NOVEL IN 19TH-CENTURY BRITAIN p. 636
- AMERICAN LITERATURE OF THE 19TH CENTURY p. 638
- SYMBOLISM, AESTHETICISM AND MODERNISM p. 640
- MODERN POETRY IN ENGLISH p. 646
- LITERARY THEORY AND LITERARY CRITICISM p. 650

Nineteen Eighty-four. George Orwell's nightmarish fable of a totalitarian future has had a deep and lasting impact on the 20th century, not least in the passing of many of its words and phrases – notably 'Freedom is Slavery' and 'Doublespeak' – into the English language. Illustrated here is a scene from the 1984 film version. Winston Smith is dominated by the face of 'Big Brother' – the all-powerful head of the ruling party.

Popular Literature

In literature, there is no necessary contradiction between popularity and moral seriousness. Dickens, for example, wrote many of his novels as magazine serials to reach a wide audience, but they have retained their popular appeal precisely because they probe moral issues seen as having broad relevance. Traditionally, however, popular literature (PL) has been understood to designate works of fiction that appeal to mass readerships but are considered unworthy of academic study by literary critics. Recently the attitude of some academics has changed. PL texts may now be studied at degree level, not for their literary merit, but for what they reveal about the society that produces and consumes them.

PL covers a wide range of genres (categories). While each of these genres is distinctive, they share several basic characteristics. The most fundamental of these is that all are read by a vast and wide-ranging audience.

The second general characteristic of PL is that it tends to be written to certain formulas. This is true even of most detective stories and thrillers, whose plots, though they depend on concealment, generally share a well-established structure.

Readers of most kinds of PL like to be able to anticipate what is going to happen. They do not wish to be surprised (apart from by twists in a plot), but to repeat the experience they have enjoyed of reading similar novels. In romances and best-sellers, for example, heroes and heroines may change names, countries, cars, and jobs, but basically are interchangeable. The predictability of the plots of romances and bestsellers reveals a desire to reject the ambiguity, chaos, and failure typical of real life. These types of PL offer a temporary escape from reality, even if set in what passes for the real world.

A shared feature of PL is a concentration on action and dialogue rather than internal speculations or relationships. PL also tends to use everyday language and to avoid extended descriptions. Each of these characteristics tends to accelerate the pace of the narrative and to distinguish it from the kind of writing traditionally valued by literary critics. Certain elements that one would expect to find in the serious novel – complex psychology and clashes of ideas, for example – are absent from most of the genres of PL.

Whatever its literary value may be, the scale on which PL operates means that it is a powerful source of information about the society that produces it. Potentially PL has the power either to maintain or to challenge prevailing beliefs. It is often believed that PL works in favour of established institutions and the current organization of society. In fact, the different genres of PL have different objectives, and need to be considered separately.

Detective stories and thrillers

The 19th-century *novel of sensation*, a type of fiction abounding in astonishing happenings and guilty secrets, was a key forerunner of the present-day detective novel. The most accomplished practitioner of the genre was the Englishman *Wilkie Collins* (1824–89), whose novels of mystery and suspense were distinguished by ingenious plotting and meticulous descriptive detail. In *The Moonstone* (1868) Collins wrote what many consider to be the first full-length detective novel in English.

The American writer Edgar Allan Poe (1809–49; see p. 658) had provided the model 25 years earlier in stories such as 'The Murders in the Rue Morgue' (1841), which featured the detective Dupin. But it was Collins and later British writers such as *Sir Arthur Conan Doyle* (1859–1930), creator of Sherlock Holmes, and *G. K. Chesterton* (1874–1936), author of 'Father Brown' stories, who established the popularity of the detective genre.

The 1920s and 1930s are sometimes described as the 'golden age' of the detective novel. During this period the 'classic' English detective story was developed and refined by writers such as *Dorothy L. Sayers* (1893–1957), creator of the aristocratic sleuth Lord Peter Wimsey, and *Agatha Christie* (1890–1976), perhaps the most famous of all writers of crime fiction, whose two main detectives are the highly cerebral Belgian, Hercule Poirot, and the engaging old spinster, Miss Marple. This period also saw the establishing of the

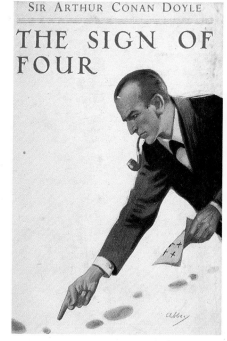

Sherlock Holmes, the brilliant and eccentric 'consulting detective', was the creation of Sir Arthur Conan Doyle. The occupants of 221B Baker Street – the hawk-eyed Holmes and his stolid friend and helper Dr Watson – are two of the most famous characters in all fiction.

rules of the genre: foremost among these was that the author must 'play fair' – no information vital to answering the question 'Whodunnit?' may be withheld from the reader.

In America a vogue for 'hard-boiled' crime fiction, characterized by a tough hero and a seedy urban setting, was established by *Dashiel Hammett* (1914–61) in such novels as *The Maltese Falcon* (1930). This vogue gathered pace after World War II in the detective novels and thrillers of *Raymond Chandler* (1888–1959) and *James M. Cain* (1892–1977). A number of Chandler's novels, notably *The Big Sleep* (1939) and *The Long Goodbye* (1953), featuring the lonely tough-guy hero Philip Marlowe, were made into successful films.

In recent years there have been signs that the spy story is superseding the traditional detective story. The forerunners of the modern spy thriller are the adventure novels of the Scots writer *John Buchan* (1875–1940). *The Thirty-Nine Steps* (1915) and *Greenmantle* (1916) are marked by simple characterization and much hectic action. In stark contrast to the stiff English heroism of Buchan's protagonist Richard Hannay is the suave toughness of James Bond – spy hero of the thrillers of *Ian Fleming* (1908–64). The exotic settings, technical marvels and stylized blend of sex and violence of such novels as *Casino Royale* (1953) and *Diamonds are Forever* (1956) have been made familiar to millions in highly popular film versions.

In recent years the spy novels of *John Le Carré* (the pen name of John Cornwell; 1931–), which blend austere realism with elaborate plots, have found favour with public and critics alike. The mild-mannered secret agent George Smiley appears in many of Le Carré's novels, notably *The Spy Who Came in from the*

The Jabberwock – an imaginary monster – is the subject of a poem in Lewis Carroll's popular fantasy *Through the Looking-Glass* (1872), in which Alice (heroine of the earlier *Alice's Adventures in Wonderland*, 1865) meets live chessmen, the fat schoolboys Tweedledum and Tweedledee, and Humpty-Dumpty. Shown here is Sir John Tenniel's picture of the Jabberwock – originally intended as a frontispiece, but banished by Carroll to the text of the book on grounds that it was too frightening.

Cold (1963) and *Tinker, Tailor, Soldier, Spy* (1974).

Horror and ghost stories

Tales of the supernatural abound in folk literature, but it was only with the emergence of the Gothic novel (see p. 632) in the second half of the 18th century that the creation of fear and curiosity for its own sake received literary expression. Gothic novels, with their atmospheric landscapes peopled by terrified heroines and sinister monks, are the precursors of the present-day horror story and ghost story. In the Romantic period the Gothic genre was further developed and its literary credibility heightened by Edgar Allan Poe in the USA and by *E.T.A. Hoffmann* (1776–1822) in Germany. In Britain its influence persisted throughout the 19th century and beyond in ghost stories and novels by *J.S. Le Fanu* (1814–73), Wilkie Collins, *Robert Louis Stevenson* (1850–94), *M.R. James* (1862–1936) and others.

Tales of vampires – corpses that rise nightly from their graves to drink the blood of the living – are widespread in Eastern European folklore. The present-day popularity of the vampire is largely due to the huge success of *Dracula* (1897), a Gothic-influenced novel by the Irish writer *Bram Stoker* (1847–1912). The figure of Count Dracula, the 'undead' Transylvanian with deathly pallor, sharp fangs and black cloak, became the model for countless imitators and inspired numerous film versions of the vampire legend (see illustration).

Vampire stories, as well as tales of devil worship and the occult, figure largely in the output of recent practitioners of popular horror fiction, notably *Dennis Wheatley* (1897–1977) in Britain and *Stephen King* (1946–) in the USA.

Science fiction

Science fiction (SF), a type of fiction presenting an imagined technological or scientific advance or a hypothetical and spectacular change in the human environment, has a celebrated 19th-century precursor in Mary Shelley's *Frankenstein*, a Gothic-influenced tale of scientific experimentation (see p. 632). But it was towards the end of the 19th century that the genre of SF as we recognize it today began to emerge in the scientific romances of the Frenchman *Jules Verne* (1828–1905) and the novels of the Englishman *H. G. Wells* (1866–1946). Wells's novels in particular introduced themes that were to dominate SF writing for years to come: time travel in *The Time Machine* (1895), invasion from outer space in *The War of the Worlds* (1898), and surgical experimentation in *The Island of Doctor Moreau* (1898).

Rapid developments in such fields as rocketry and computers after World War II gave further impetus to fictional explorations of the possible consequences of scientific progress. *Arthur C. Clarke* (1917–) in Britain and *Isaac Asimov* (1920–92) in the USA used their considerable astronomical and technical knowledge in novels whose themes include robots and interplanetary travel. The 1950s saw the appearance of the 'logical

fantasies' of the Englishman *John Wyndham* (1903–69), notably *The Day of the Triffids* (1951), in which domestic normality is shattered by a catastrophic invasion of mobile killer plants.

In recent years, 'New Wave' SF writers in Britain, such as *Brian Aldiss* (1925–), *J. G. Ballard* (1930–) and *Michael Moorcock* (1939–), have invested the SF genre with considerable literary merit. Their fantasies of technological breakdown and catastrophe contrast with the emphasis of earlier writers of SF on the benign possibilities of technical advance.

The concern of SF writers with the possibility of negative human advance is shared by a number of writers of more obviously 'serious' fiction. *Aldous Huxley* (1894–1963) in *Brave New World* (1932) and *George Orwell* in *Nineteen Eighty-four* (1949; see p. 649) offered nightmare visions of the future, in which certain political, social and scientific tendencies of the 20th century are presented in an extreme and unpleasant form.

Fantasy

Fantasy overlaps with SF in dealing with an alternative world in which unexpected, improbable or supernatural events take place. Fantasy writing, however, was first directed at juvenile audiences, though many 19th-century critics and educationalists, believing that children should be taught how to deal with the real world, rejected it as escapist.

Two of the earliest examples of children's fantasy writing were *Alice's Adventures in Wonderland* (1865) by *Lewis Carroll* (the pen name of Charles Lutwidge Dodgson; 1832–98) and *Pinnochio* (1883) by the Italian *Carlo Collodi* (1826–90). Much English fantasy was written between the two World Wars, the most influential example from this period being *The Hobbit* (1937) by *J.R.R. Tolkien* (1892–1973). *The Hobbit* creates a rich mythological fantasy world subsequently developed and expanded in *The Lord of the Rings* (1954–5), whose blend of 'sword and sorcery' was to be much imitated.

America became the source of most fantasy writing in the 1960s. Writers such as *Ursula Le Guin* (1929–) and *Madeline L'Engle* (1918–) continued the tradition established by Tolkien and his Oxford colleague *C.S. Lewis* (1898–1963) of creating fantasy worlds in which the battle between good and evil was clearly enacted.

Romance

Romantic fiction is read almost exclusively by women. Its plots centre around the fulfilment achieved through true love. Invariably this love is thwarted as part of the plot; but having proved herself worthy, the heroine generally wins her man.

Perhaps more than any other branch of PL, romance relies on formulaic plots and characters, and also uses many stock descriptions and phrases. These features

mean that experienced writers of romance employed by specialist romance publishers such as Mills and Boon may write their novels very rapidly indeed.

Romances are frequently given historical settings. Writers such as *Catherine Cookson* (1906–), *Georgette Heyer* (1902–74), and *Victoria Holt* (1906–) all use the past to provide the picturesque backgrounds, elegant lifestyles and virile men which they suggest are no longer readily available.

Despite romantic fiction's stereotyped depiction of women as passive and self-sacrificing, its popularity suggests that it addresses real problems in many women's lives. The fictional 'solutions' that romantic fiction offers may indicate ways in which women have accommodated themselves to the problems of being female in male-dominated societies. However, the fictional satisfactions provided by romance fiction are seen as problematic by many feminists because they seem to prevent women from working for real solutions.

Bestsellers

In that they are read by a vast and wide-ranging audience, all of the novels discussed under the categories above have attained the status of 'bestsellers'. But the term 'bestseller' is used in a narrower sense to denote a particular type of highly planned commercial novel aiming principally at short-term profit. Such novels are generally set in a glamorous, fast-paced world of big business and revolve around such subjects as the mafia, financial corruption and emotional power struggles, which are spiced with the key ingredients of sex, violence and marital infidelity. In other media, these themes have formed the subject of television 'soap operas' such as *Dallas*. The novels of the American *Harold Robbins* (1912–) – sales of which currently exceed 200 million – typify the bestseller genre.

KR

SEE ALSO

● THE HOLLYWOOD STYLE p. 560
● INTERNATIONAL CINEMA p. 562
● THE MODERN NOVEL p. 648

Nosferatu, the vampire. Werner Herzog's 1979 remake of the original *Nosferatu* (1922) is but one of numerous screen adaptations of Bram Stoker's famous tale of vampirism, *Dracula* (1897). In contrast to the elegantly threatening Transylvanian aristocrat of so many Hammer horror films, Herzog's vampire is hypnotically compelling despite a physically horrifying appearance.

Literary Theory and Literary Criticism

Interest in literature has produced theories about it since Aristotle first analysed tragedy around 340 BC. Until recent times, literature was generally assumed to be, like other forms of art, an imitation of life. Detailed discussion focused on the best means of making this imitation effective: on the appropriate form for a particular subject, on the right structure for a poem or play, and on correct stylistic usage.

Aristotle, the Greek philosopher. In his *Poetics*, one of the most influential works of aesthetic theory ever written, Aristotle analysed tragedy and praised poetry for its ability to tell universal truths, like philosophy, rather than particular facts, like history. The *Poetics* introduced concepts relating to the theory of tragedy that are still widely discussed today. (Vienna Classical Art Collection/ Austrian Embassy, London)

With the rediscovery of Greco-Roman literature during the Renaissance, the 'classics' provided models of good writing, and even rules for tragedy, which French Neoclassical dramatists followed (see p. 626). The best statement of Neoclassical principles was given by Nicolas Boileau (1636–1711), and echoed by Alexander Pope and Samuel Johnson, the first great critic in England (see pp. 626–7).

Assumptions changed with the coming of Romanticism (see pp. 630–33). Genius was held to be superior to any rules, and literature was thought to do something more profound and mysterious than merely imitate. Especially in Germany,

philosophers paid great attention to the essentially creative character of the mind, to the central role of the imagination, and to the special kind of significance embodied in art. These philosophical ideas were introduced into Britain by Samuel Taylor Coleridge (see p. 633), who argued that poetry does not simply state commonly accepted truths in ornate fashion, but creates a new form of truth, using essentially symbolic images to combine diverse aspects of reality into a unique whole. With this insight modern literary criticism was born. Its task was no longer to judge correctness or even excellence by an agreed standard, but to show the rich diversity of meaning within a literary work, and how it coheres.

French biographical and historical criticism

France again led the way in criticism during the 19th century, but in an anti-Romantic direction. *Charles Augustin Sainte-Beuve* (1804–69) developed his own explanation of the unity and meaning of literary works by relating them to the life and personality of their author. *Hippolyte Taine* (1828–93) investigated the determining influence of environment and race. *Ferdinand Brunetière* (1849–1906) worked out the evolution of literary genres.

By the early 20th century, France possessed a huge body of such scholarly criticism. French literature, systematized into periods, schools, styles, and backgrounds, was more rigorously studied than any other in Europe. (The first professor of English at Cambridge University, Arthur Quiller-Couch, was not appointed until 1912.) Before the development of a 'new criticism' in France in the 1960s, only a few creative writers, such as Proust (see p. 641), dared suggest that such academic scholarship was irrelevant to an understanding of the creative process.

A more philosophical style of criticism persisted in Germany, dominated by the idea of a 'spirit of the age' (*Zeitgeist*), that can be seen in similarities in the style and outlook of literary works produced in the same period. Literature was treated as prime evidence in the spiritual history of Europe.

Modern textual criticism

Matthew Arnold (1822–88) deplored the lack of informed knowledge of literature in Britain, by contrast with France and Germany. He preached the need for literary culture to replace declining religion and save society from anarchy. A similar concern with the civilizing function of poetry is shown by the Cambridge critic *I.A. Richards* (1893–1979), whose influential method of 'practical criticism' stressed the importance of close textual study, and trained and tested readers' responses. With *F.R. Leavis* (1895–1978) – also a Cambridge don – this approach became a crusade to defend the moral, social, and life-enhancing lessons of literature against mere academic know-

F.R. Leavis in a pen-and-ink drawing by Jeffrey Morgan. Leavis, whose critical method was characterized by close and detailed reading of literary texts, saw the study of literature as a civilizing activity in an age of cultural decline. He was one of the first to champion the poetry of T.S. Eliot and the novels of D.H. Lawrence.

ledge and theory, and also against the threat posed by the media and advertising. His periodical, *Scrutiny*, was contributed and subscribed to by those anxious to maintain standards of literary sensibility in mass industrial society. The poet and critic *William Empson* (1906–84), brought to the Cambridge method of textual analysis an insight into the multiple meanings of words (ambiguity) and the symbolic language of poetry, which recalls Coleridge.

This group of critics was influenced by the criticism of T.S Eliot (see p. 641), the first to go beyond Coleridge in defining how poetic symbols unify diverse thoughts and feelings. Eliot argued that thought and feeling had become 'dissociated' when the tradition which preserved such unifying symbolism broke down in the face of 17th-century science. The task of modern writers was to restore it; a tradition of poetic language and forms was the necessary complement of individual talent.

Eliot's ideas, together with the method of closely scrutinizing the texts to discover their pattern of unity and layers of meaning, were developed by a brilliant generation of so-called *New Critics* in the USA. Critics such as *John Crowe Ransom* (1888–1974) and *Cleanth Brooks* (1906–) rejected consideration of the writer's intentions and motives – 'the intentional fallacy' – in favour of analysis of the text in its own terms. Their insistence that a work of literary art achieves a unique significance, setting it apart from other kinds of thought, truth, or utterance, resulted in accusations of elitist aestheticism, and of cultivating personal sensitivity at the expense of social responsibility.

This charge was raised most fiercely by Marxist critics, for whom the significance of literature lies always in its reflection of historical and social reality. The most distinguished Marxist critic of this period was the Hungarian *Georg Lukács* (1885–1971), who generally condemned Modernist literature by comparison with the Realist tradition of the 19th-century novelists (see pp. 634–35).

From linguistics to structuralism

The growth of Modernism in literature (see pp. 640–41) was partly responsible for the tendency amongst modern critics to regard a literary text as a complex structure of words, rather than as a representation of the real world. This tendency was reinforced by other influences, most notably that of modern linguistics, which began with the work of Ferdinand de Saussure (see p. 610). The implications of linguistics for all types of writing were discovered by a post-World War II generation of French intellectuals, who were further influenced by the ideas of the pyschoanalyst Sigmund Freud (1856–1939; see p. 232) and the anthropologist, Claude Lévi-Strauss (1908–); both men pointed to the presence of deep symbolic systems of meaning within the mind, below the level of rational awareness.

In addition, the ideas were revived of a group of Russian critics interested in linguistics and known as *Formalists*

(notably Viktor Shklovski; 1893–). They had analysed the techniques writers use to give words a special artistic meaning different from the realistic one intended in practical speech. Banned in Russia, this work had continued in Prague, and became widely known through **Roman Jakobson** (1896–1982). He established the basic ways in which words can be linked together, for example by analogy (as in poetic metaphors) or by association (as in narrative description). The difference in meaning that results is due not to natural differences in the word, but to different kinds of linguistic structure.

The method of criticism known as *structuralism* has its roots in the linguistics of Saussure and Jakobson. It regards the literary text as a system of signs, and seeks out the underlying conventions or rules that cause these signs to generate meaning. Such criticism offers no traditional commentary on literary works in a social, psychological, moral or historical sense; it analyses their imaginative grammar – the interrelationship of their constituent parts.

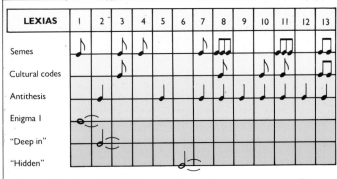

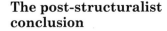

Roland Barthes (1915–1980) was one of the most original structuralist critics. In his analysis of a story by Balzac (see p. 634), he illustrates by means of musical notation the presence of a six-level structure of meanings in the text. He divides the text up into a numbered sequence of sense units (groups of phrases and sentences that he calls *lexias*), and likens them to bars in music. The six levels of meaning are like sounds from different instruments playing together when the story is read. Barthes analyses exactly what meanings are being sounded, from the most obvious story line (in the 'semes') down to deep suggestions of enigma, at every moment of Balzac's narrative.

The post-structuralist conclusion

Structuralism soon went beyond the neutral description of linguistic and literary structures. Critics began to consider the implications of the idea that meaning is only a matter of convention. Having learnt to dismiss the intentions of the author, and any reference to external reality, was a reader not free to find all manner of meanings in a literary work – or none? If writing is a form of play with words, should criticism itself not play with it, rather than try to fix it in a final analysis? And if a text pretends to achieve truth or realism, is it not criticism's job to expose this deception by 'deconstructing' its false façade?

Such *deconstruction* became the catchphrase of criticism designed to reveal the essential incoherence and inconsistency of any text that does not confess its own arbitrary play with meaning. The philosophical and cultural implications have been explored by **Michel Foucault** (1926–84) and **Jacques Derrida** (1930–) in France, while more or less 'deconstructive' criticism has also been practised in the USA. Deconstruction is often hard to understand, partly because it seems to ignore or demolish a text's conventionally obvious meaning, which it regards as some sort of political or psychological fabrication.

Many other and older types of literary criticism have continued to flourish. None is satisfied by merely personal impressions or judgements (as are often found in book reviews in newspapers). Conflicting moral, political, and philosophical assumptions have turned criticism into a battleground of values, concerning questions of spiritual openness or narrowness, social constraint or freedom, and sexual difference and prejudice (where specifically feminist criticism has had much to say).   AT

Matthew Arnold caricatured in 1871. A poet of some distinction, Arnold wrote little verse after the age of 40, turning to essays on literary, cultural and educational themes, and establishing himself as the leading English critic of his age. In works such as *Culture and Anarchy* (1869), Arnold called for greater emphasis on literary and cultural values to counterbalance what he saw as the philistinism and materialism of British life and culture.

SEE ALSO

● HOW LANGUAGE WORKS p. 608
● THE LANGUAGE OF SIGNS p. 610
● CLASSICAL LITERATURE p. 614
● SYMBOLISM, AESTHETICISM AND THE BIRTH OF MODERNISM p. 640

Journalism

Journalism is the gathering and redistribution of news either to a specific category of people or to as many people as possible, internationally, nationally or locally. The term journalism was originally applied to recording news by means of the printed word, usually in newspapers but also in magazines. Journalism now includes transmitting news electronically as, for example, by radio or television.

The power of the image. Photographs and television reports from Vietnam had a strong influence as pressure mounted to end the war. This well-known photograph, taken by Associated Press photographer Eddie Adams in Saigon in 1968, had considerable impact on American public opinion. It shows Brigadier General Loan, head of South Vietnam's national police, summarily executing a Viet Cong officer.

Before information could be written, or electronically passed through airwaves, poets and bards would memorize, embroider and sing or speak the news to the rich or powerful, who could afford or command their services. Access to information increased as more people became able to read and write. Journalism is often said to have begun with *Acta Diurna*, a daily news-sheet recording social and political news, published in ancient Rome from 59 BC. News-sheets circulated in German cities in the 15th century, but regularly published newspapers did not appear until the 17th century. *Nieuwe Tydingen*, published in Antwerp from 1605, was one of the earliest, although the oldest existing newspaper is the Swedish official journal *Post och Inrikes Tidningar*, founded in 1645.

Magazines developed from the learned journals that first appeared in the 17th century. Early examples contained comment and opinions on current events, but by the early 19th century mass-circulation illustrated magazines had appeared, including periodicals for specific interest groups.

The Fourth Estate

The power of the press to inform and to shape opinions was soon recognized. Thomas Carlyle (1795–1881), the Scottish essayist and historian, described the press as 'the Fourth Estate, more important than the three traditional powerful estates of the Monarch, the Lords and the Commons'. At the end of the 19th century the scope of journalism was enlarged as the new popular press added entertainment to the more traditional functions of information and interpretation. Lord Northcliffe (1865–1922), who did much to develop the modern popular press in Britain, identified a new reading public who wanted to read brief, rather than in-depth, news reports in papers that also offered them stories and amusing features. Differences between the style and presentation of the easily accessible 'popular press – aimed at a mass circulation – and the more informative 'quality press' date from the beginning of the 20th century when Northcliffe owned *The Times*, launched the *Daily Mail* and bought a stake in the *Daily Mirror*.

The right to know

From the 15th century, when printing (see pp. 322–3) increased the number of people who could obtain and read information and opinions, censors of the printed word became active. Throughout Europe there were strict controls on printers. In Britain, no book, pamphlet or news-sheet could be printed without a Royal licence until after the Civil War in the middle of the 17th century. Censorship in modern Western countries depends upon varying degrees of taste, restraint and self-censorship as well as upon how strict a state's laws of libel are. For example, the laws affecting the privacy of the individual are relatively strong in France. For this reason, 'revelations' regarding the private lives of French public figures are not possible in the popular press in France, but this is not generally thought of as a restriction on the freedom of information. In Western countries proprietors occasionally censor their journals or apply pressure for the inclusion of opinions and information sympathetic to their business or personal concerns. Advertisers can also exert influence. No newspaper would wish to upset advertisers and lose valuable revenue.

Governments exercise differing, often confusing, controls to protect official secrets. Sometimes official secrecy may be used to conceal mistakes or to suppress potentially embarrassing details. In the USA, the freedom of the press is guaranteed by the First Amendment of the Constitution (1787). In Britain the Official Secrets Act (1911, amended 1989) may be used to prevent the publication of information regarded as likely to endanger national security.

In dictatorships and Communist countries, the party in power is the censor. Opinions contrary to the official line are not usually printed and 'inconvenient' facts are suppressed. In the late 1980s, under the policy of *glasnost* (greater openness) in the USSR, articles criticizing officials and public bodies, but not the Communist system, began to be published. This editorial change was accompanied by a dramatic decline in the circulation of the staid daily newspapers, and a corresponding increase in readership of the innovative weekly paper *Argumenty I Fakty*.

The independence of TV and radio journalists depends on how the system is funded. In some countries, radio and TV may be wholly or partly financed by the state, with varying degrees of control. In Britain, the state-funded British Broadcasting Corporation (BBC) enjoys much freedom and runs regional radio stations and two TV networks, mainly financed by licence fees paid by the viewing public. It competes with commercial TV and radio networks funded by advertising revenue.

The scope of journalism

The Pulitzer prizes – awarded annually for achievement in American journalism – illustrate the scope of newspaper journalism. Awards are made for the best reporting of national news and of international

news, the most distinguished editorial, and the best local reporting (both with and without a deadline). There is also a Pulitzer award for the best news photograph, a reminder that news may be presented by the power of the image as opposed to the word. A single arresting photograph may say more than hundreds of words. Radio journalists employ different skills and styles to newspaper journalists, since their words are destined to be heard rather than seen. Television journalism marries the spoken word with images.

TV, radio, newspaper and magazine journalists employ certain common techniques. The story has to be written – or spoken – clearly, simply and in a logical order. Unless the journalist is working on a feature, which may be prepared long in advance, there is rarely a chance to rewrite or reassemble the components of the story, or *copy*, as it is more properly called. The kernel of the story comes first. Then come the 'W questions' – Who?, When?, Where?, Why? and so on. Until those essentials are in the copy, journalists cannot add the extra information that is relevant to the needs or interests of their readership.

Different media have different audiences. Thus, when a major storm wipes out the tea harvest in India, the popular press will blazon the number killed, a provincial newspaper may relate the experiences of a local resident who happened to visiting the disaster area at the time, while a specialist financial newspaper will highlight the effect on tea prices and commodity markets. The papers serve different markets. Readers, viewers and listeners will patronize the media that addresses their interests. In Britain, newspapers are not owned by political parties, but some offer editorial support to particular persuasions.

Reporters purvey facts, or *hard news*. In editorials those facts are summarized and interpreted through opinions. Feature writers provide background to the news through research and opinion. This may take the form of investigative journalism in which writers may have to research for weeks, even months, before being able to tell the story. The Watergate scandal (1972–75), which involved the revelation of illegal activities by the administration of former US President Richard Nixon, was, in part, uncovered because of investigative journalists working for the *Washington Post*. Interpretative material, particularly in magazines, is usually written by journalists specializing in fields such as finance, sport, cookery, gardening, crime, fashion and entertainment, and writing in various styles appropriate to their readership.

A journalistic style is also found in book form and is sometimes referred to as *new journalism*. This genre relates actual events, interpreting and embellishing them by the use of subjective imagery. The style is typified by *The Armies of the Night* (1968) – an account of the 1967 Vietnam peace demonstrations in Washington by Norman Mailer (1923–) – and *In Cold Blood* (1966) – a novel by Truman Capote (1924–84) based on multiple murders in Kansas.

Gathering news

Many stories are obtained by the media from news agencies. There are over 120 national agencies but five large international agencies dominate – Agence France-Presse, the American-based Associated Press and United Press International agencies, the Soviet agency Tass, and London-based Reuters. Agence France-Presse, for example, maintains news bureaux in over 150 countries, employs nearly 1100 journalists and permanent correspondents and over 1700 freelance journalists. The principal newspapers maintain their own permanent correspondents in major world cities and post others to various locations as important news stories develop. Among the latter are war correspondents who accompany armed forces and describe the conflict. The World War II despatches from the Pacific of the American war correspondent Ernie Pyle (1900–45) are distinguished examples.

Journalists have been described as people who do not know much but do know how to find out everything. At international, national and even local level, journalists rely upon a trusted network of contacts. Journalists need to know the leading figures in their own particular specialism or area to contact them for either attributable or non-attributable news and comments. At the same time journalists develop an innate mistrust of their contacts. Governments and companies planning takeovers or unpopular developments are among those who try to manipulate the media, and people tend to distort suffering or pleasure in the drama of interview. The best journalists learn to recognize and then simply relate the basic truth.

SPB

SEE ALSO

● PRINTING p. 322
● RADIO, TELEVISION AND VIDEO p. 326

NATIONAL PRESS

In Britain, national newspapers predominate as they rarely can in bigger countries in which distribution over a large geographical area can be problematic. However, developments in printing technology now allow simultaneous printing of editions in several centres. For example, the British newspaper *The Independent* is printed in Portsmouth, Bradford and Northampton. The UK has high circulation figures for daily newspapers, particularly for the popular press. In 1991 *The Sun* had an average circulation of nearly 3 700 000 copies and the *Daily Mirror* nearly 3 000 000 copies. Of the 'quality' British newspapers, only *The Daily Telegraph* had a circulation of over 1 000 000 copies, while *The Guardian*, *The Times*, *The Independent* and *Financial Times* all averaged sales of below half a million copies each.

In the USA there are more than 210 morning newpapers with an average circulation of over 50 000 copies. American daily papers place great emphasis on local news because of the strong interest in state, as opposed to national, affairs. The size of the country militates against the existence of a national press, although the *Wall Street Journal* and the *New York Times* (both of which are printed at several locations) and influential newspapers such as the *Washington Post*, the *Los Angeles Times* and the (Boston) *Christian Science Monitor* enjoy national readerships.

For historical reasons, some West European countries, in which regional identities have strongly developed, have few national papers. Major daily newpapers in Germany are edited and printed in over 60 provincial centres, and only *Bild Zeitung* – with average sales of over 4 700 000 copies – achieves a circulation similar to that of the popular press in Britain. No other newspaper in Germany sells more than half a million copies. Although nearly a dozen daily newspapers published in Paris have a national circulation, the provincial press has a major role in France. *Ouest-France* – published in Rennes – has a higher circulation than the most widely read Parisian daily newspaper, *Le Figaro*.

Japanese daily papers enjoy very high average circulations. In 1989 *Yomiuri Shimbun* attained a circulation of nearly 15 000 000 copies and was read in almost one quarter of Japan's households. There are over 100 other principal daily newspapers in Japan, where 569 copies of newspapers are printed for each 1000 people. A high population does not, however, guarantee the popularity or the power of the press. Brazil, with a slightly larger population than Japan, has neither a national press nor a tradition of newspaper readership. Only one paper – *O Globo* – has a circulation over a quarter of a million. Newspapers are relatively expensive and the majority of Brazilians rely upon television journalism rather than the printed word for information.

The lack of a single national language – for example in Canada, Belgium, India and Switzerland – also prevents the development of a national press. In the former USSR nearly 640 daily newspapers were printed in 55 different languages, and there was a also well-developed national press in the Russian language. Lenin recognized the power of the press, saying it was 'the most strong and powerful weapon of the Party'. The purpose of the press in the USSR was traditionally to disseminate Marxist-Leninism and to provide information on Soviet life. Newspapers were published by public organizations – *Izvestia* ('News') by the Supreme Soviet, *Pravda* ('Truth') by the Communist Party and *Trud* ('Labour') by the Central Council of Trade Unions. The very high circulation figures of these newspapers have shrunk since Russia gained a free press.

News may be coloured by views. The British popular daily newspaper *The Sun* left its readers in no doubt about its editorial opinion concerning the sinking of the Argentinian cruiser *General Belgrano* during the 1982 Falklands War.

THE COUNTRIES OF THE WORLD

---

*'The world is a great volume,
and man the index of that book.'*

John Donne

Sovereign States

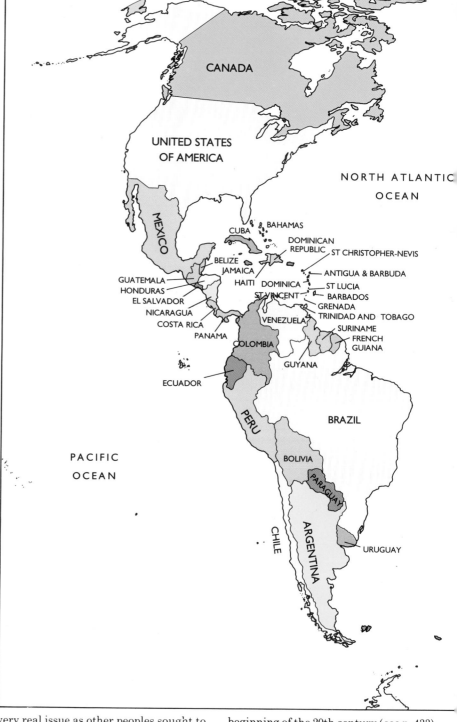

A country may be variously described as an area that is distinguished by its people, its geography or its culture, or as a land that enjoys political autonomy, more usually referred to as 'sovereignty'. This chapter describes the sovereign states of the world, that is the independent states that, in theory, exercise unrestricted power over their own destinies.

However, in some ways the concept of sovereignty is of limited value in the closing years of the 20th century. It could be argued that there is no such thing as a truly independent state. The overwhelming majority of sovereign states are members of one or more of the various economic and military alliances and groupings, such as NATO, the EC, the OAU and so on (see pp. 284–7). Most states have to recognize that the demands of security and trade bring agreed limits upon the freedom of action of individual countries. Countries rely upon their neighbours, and other states, at least economically, and are therefore restricted in their independence.

If a country is an area that may be recognized by its distinctive people, geography or culture, then many sovereign states may be said to contain other countries within their boundaries. For example, the UK comprises four distinct countries – England, Northern Ireland, Scotland and Wales – none of which has political autonomy. Conversely the states of Australia and the USA possess considerable political autonomy but have none of the characteristics of a country. Tibet (an autonomous region of China) is just one example of an area often thought of as a country, even though it is not an independent state. Poland disappeared from the map of Europe from 1795 until 1918 but it did not cease to be a country.

The number of sovereign countries is not a constant. After the Napoleonic Wars, the Congress of Vienna (1814–5) redrew the map of Europe delineating, for example, nearly 40 German-speaking states – almost the same as the total number of countries in Europe today. However, many of the ancient European countries have disappeared – the result of German and Italian unification and of two World Wars.

In the early 1990s the two German states created as a result of partition after World War II – the Federal Republic of Germany and the German Democratic Republic – achieved reunification, while in some East European states separatism was a

very real issue as other peoples sought to re-establish their autonomous political identity. The Yugoslav federation was destroyed by civil war. Following the failed coup by Communist hardliners in Moscow (1991), Estonia, Latvia and Lithuania achieved international recognition of their renewed independence, and in December 1991 the USSR was dissolved and the remaining 12 republics were recognized as sovereign states. Thus, even in a continent generally thought of as 'stable', countries can merge and emerge to renewed sovereignty.

In Africa, Asia, Oceania and the Caribbean over 80 countries have emerged from colonial rule since 1918, and more than one half of the countries shown on the world map on this page did not exist at the

beginning of the 20th century (see p. 433). Over 50 dependent territories remain, most of them small and not possessing that distinctive but intangible characteristic by which we may recognize a country.

Individual entries in this chapter detail:

Official name: Each sovereign state's official name in its own principal language(s).

Member of: Its membership of major international organizations (see pp. 284–7).

Area: Its area in square kilometres (and in square miles). In the case of some countries, more than one figure may be found for the area of the state. This is because that country's frontiers may be

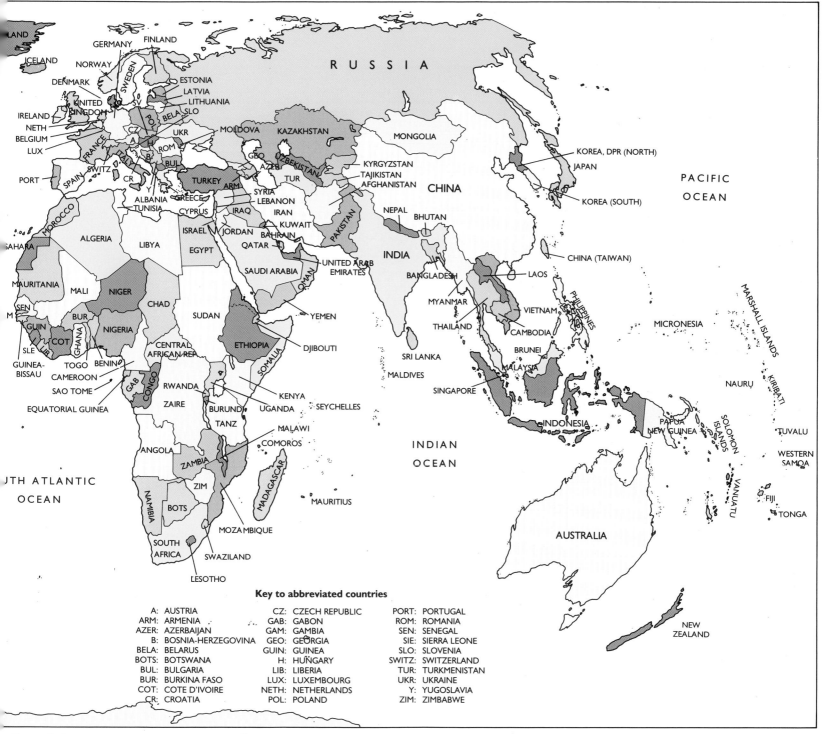

Key to abbreviated countries

A:	AUSTRIA	CZ:	CZECH REPUBLIC	PORT:	PORTUGAL
ARM:	ARMENIA	GAB:	GABON	ROM:	ROMANIA
AZER:	AZERBAIJAN	GAM:	GAMBIA	SEN:	SENEGAL
B:	BOSNIA-HERZEGOVINA	GEO:	GEORGIA	SIE:	SIERRA LEONE
BELA:	BELARUS	GUIN:	GUINEA	SLO:	SLOVENIA
BOTS:	BOTSWANA	H:	HUNGARY	SWITZ:	SWITZERLAND
BUL:	BULGARIA	LIB:	LIBERIA	TUR:	TURKMENISTAN
BUR:	BURKINA FASO	LUX:	LUXEMBOURG	UKR:	UKRAINE
COT:	COTE D'IVOIRE	NETH:	NETHERLANDS	Y:	YUGOSLAVIA
CR:	CROATIA	POL:	POLAND	ZIM:	ZIMBABWE

disputed (for example Israel), not defined (in the case of Oman) or because the country may lay claim to part of a neighbouring territory (for example Argentina).

Population: Its population according to figures given in the latest available census or official estimate. Where there is no reliable official estimate, an estimate of the national population from UN sources is given.

Capital and major cities: In many cases the names of cities in their local languages are given in brackets. Except where noted, the population figure given for a city relates to the agglomeration or urban area; that is the city, its suburbs and surrounding built-up area rather than for local government districts.

Languages: The principal languages only are indicated.

Religions: The principal religions only are indicated. As many censuses do not question respondents concerning their religious affiliation, the percentages given are approximations.

Dependent territories: The dependent territories of states are listed as appropriate. These include colonies, associated states – which enjoy varying degrees of autonomy (Puerto Rico, Belau and the Cook Islands, for example, enjoy complete internal self-government) – and overseas territories administered in a similar manner to local government units in the country to which they belong (for example the French overseas départements). Territorial claims in Antarctica

and other disputed areas – for example, the Western Sahara – are also included.

GOVERNMENT
The constitutional provisions of each state are summarized.

GEOGRAPHY
The main geographical features are described, including the principal rivers and a summary of the climate.

ECONOMY
The most important economic activities, resources and trends are summarized.

HISTORY
Summaries of the principal events and periods of history of each country with appropriate cross-references to pages in Chapter 7, A History of the World (see pp. 358–455).

SEE ALSO

● INTERNATIONAL ORGANIZATIONS pp. 284–7
● A HISTORY OF THE WORLD pp. 358–455

AFGHANISTAN

Official name: Jamhuria Afghanistan (Republic of Afghanistan)

Member of: UN

Area: 652 225 km² (251 773 sq mi)

Population: 16 121 000 (1990 est). There are almost 3 500 000 Afghan refugees (1990 est) in Pakistan and Iran

Capital and major cities: Kabul 1 425 000 (including suburbs), Kandahar (Qandahar) 226 000, Herat 177 000, Mazar-i-Sharif 131 000 (1988 est)

Languages: Pushto (52%), Dari (Persian; 30%) – both official

Religions: Sunni Islam (74%), Shia Islam (25%)

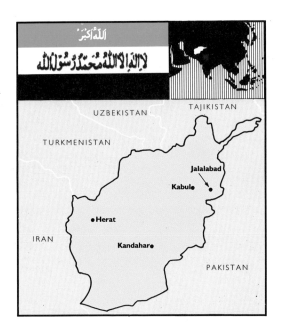

GOVERNMENT

The constitution provides for a two chamber National Assembly to be elected for four years by universal adult suffrage. The Loya Jirgha (the supreme state body) consists of the National Assembly and the Cabinet, and provincial, legal and tribal representatives. The Loya Jirgha elects the President, who appoints a Prime Minister, who, in turn, appoints the Council of Ministers. A provisional government was formed in 1992.

GEOGRAPHY

The central highlands, dominated by the Hindu Kush, cover over three quarters of the country and contain several peaks over 6400 m (21 000 ft). N of the highlands are plains, an important agricultural region, while the SW of the country is desert and semidesert.

Climate: The central highlands have very cold winters and short cool summers, while the desert regions have cold winters and hot summers. Except in parts of the highlands, it is dry.

ECONOMY

Most of the usable land is pasture, mainly for sheep, but cereal crops, particularly wheat and maize, are also important. Principal exports include fresh and dried fruit, wool and cotton. Natural gas, found in the northern plains, is also exported. Economic development has been retarded by civil war.

HISTORY

Afghanistan was ruled by the Persians until the 4th century BC when Alexander the Great invaded, but Greek control was short lived as Afghanistan fell to barbarians from the N. In the 7th century AD Arabs reached the borders, bringing Islam. Various Muslim empires followed until 1222 when the country fell under the harsh control of the Mongol Genghis Khan. The rule of Tamerlane (Timur) in the 14th century was equally devastating. In the 18th century, the Persians united the country. In the 19th century, rivalry between Russia and Britain, who regarded Afghanistan as the key to India, led to instability. Britain attempted to assert control in two disastrous wars (1839–42 and 1878–81). Independence was only achieved in 1921 after a third war with the British. A period of unrest followed until a more stable monarchy was established in 1933. A coup in 1973 overthrew the monarchy. A close relationship with the USSR resulted from the 1978 Saur Revolution, but the Soviet invasion (1979) led to civil war. In 1989 the Soviets withdrew, leaving the cities in the hands of the government and Muslim fundamentalist guerrillas controlling the countryside. In 1992 fundamentalists took Kabul and formed a provisional government, but factional – largely ethnic – fighting continues.

ALBANIA

Official name: Republika Shqipërisë (Republic of Albania)

Member of: UN, CSCE

Area: 28 748 km² (11 100 sq mi)

Population: 3 303 000 (1991 est)

Capital and major cities: Tirana (Tiranë) 238 000, Durrës 83 000, Elbasan 81 000 (1989 est)

Languages: Albanian (Gheg and Tosk dialects) – Tosk is the official language.

Religions: Sunni Islam (20%) – the practice of religion was banned from 1967 to 1990

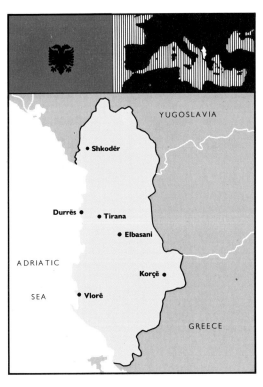

GOVERNMENT

A President and a 140-member People's Assembly are elected under a system of proportional representation by universal adult suffrage for four years. The Assembly elects a Prime Minister and a Council of Ministers.

GEOGRAPHY

Coastal lowlands support most of the country's agriculture. Mountain ranges cover the greater part of Albania, and reach 2751 m / 9025 ft at Mount Korab.

Climate: Hot, dry summers with mild, wet winters along the coast; equally hot summers but with very cold winters in the mountains.

ECONOMY

Albania is poor by European standards. The economy, which is still largely state-owned, relies on agriculture and the export of chromium. In 1990 Albania ended its self-imposed economic isolation and sought foreign financial and technical and humanitarian assistance. Nevertheless, the country has experienced famine and the collapse of much of its industrial infra-structure.

HISTORY

The revolt (1444–68) by Skenderbeg (?1403–68) against the Ottoman Turks – who invaded in the 14th century – is celebrated by Albanians as their national epic. Because most Albanians converted to Islam, they were able to secure autonomy and gain access to high positions in Ottoman service. By 1900, Ottoman enfeeblement encouraged Albanian nationalism, and in 1912, independence was declared. The country was occupied in both the Balkan Wars and World War I, and the formation of a stable government within recognized frontiers did not occur until the 1920s. Interwar Albania was dominated by Ahmed Zogu (1895–1961), who made himself king (as Zog I) in 1928. He fled when Mussolini invaded in 1939. Communist-led partisans took power when the Germans withdrew (1944). Under Enver Hoxha (1908–85), the regime pursued rapid modernization on Stalinist lines, allied, in turn, to Yugoslavia, the USSR and China, before opting (in 1978) for self-sufficiency and isolation. The liberal wing of the Communist Party won a power struggle (1990), instituted social and economic reforms, and held multi-party elections (1991). After the Socialists (former Communists) were defeated in 1992, a new government faced severe economic problems. Large numbers of Albanians have left the country in an attempt to find employment abroad.

ALGERIA

Official name: El Djemhouria El Djazaïria Demokratia Echaabia (the Democratic and Popular Republic of Algeria)

Member of: UN, OAU, Arab League, OPEC

Area: 2 381 741 km² (919 595 sq mi)

Population: 25 888 000 (1991 est)

Capital and major cities: Algiers (El Djazaïr or Alger) 1 722 000, Oran (Ouahran) 664 000, Constantine (Qacentina) 449 000 (1989; including suburbs)

Languages: Arabic (official), French, Berber

Religion: Sunni Islam (official)

GOVERNMENT

The constitution provides for the election of a President, who is head of state and of government, and a 296-member National People's Assembly by universal adult suffrage every five years. In 1992 the constitution was suspended and a military council was appointed.

GEOGRAPHY

Over 85% of Algeria is covered by the Sahara Desert. To the N lie the Atlas Mountains which enclose a dry plateau. In the SE are the Hoggar mountains, with Algeria's highest point, Mount Tahat (2918 m / 9573 ft). Along the Mediterranean coast are plains and lower mountain ranges.

Climate: The Mediterranean climate along the coastline is characterized by hot summers, mild winters and adequate rainfall. In the Sahara, it is hot and arid.

ECONOMY

Petroleum and natural gas are the main exports and important industries are based on oil and gas. Light industry is being encouraged but the country faces severe economic problems including high unemployment. One quarter of the adult population is involved in agriculture, but lack of rain and suitable land mean that Algeria has to import two thirds of its food. The small amount of arable land mainly produces wheat, barley, fruit and vegetables, while arid pasturelands support sheep, goats and cattle.

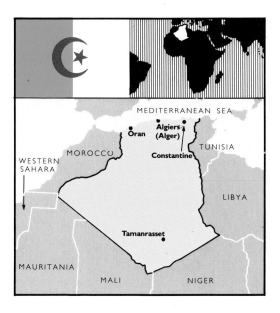

HISTORY

After the fall of Carthage in 146 BC, coastal Algeria became Roman. In the 7th century the Arabs brought Islam despite initial Berber resistance. Several Berber empires flourished in the Middle Ages. In the 16th century, Turkish corsairs defended Algiers against the Spanish, and placed the region under Ottoman control. During the 18th century, Algeria became a centre for piracy and in 1830 the French invaded on the pretext of protecting trade. Colonization followed, and coastal Algeria was attached to metropolitan France. By 1860 much of the best land was in French hands.

Nationalist riots in Sétif were ruthlessly suppressed in 1945, and in 1954 the Front de Libération Nationale (FLN) initiated a revolt that became a bitter war. A rising by French settlers, in favour of the integration of Algeria with France, led to the crisis that returned de Gaulle to power in France (1958). Despite two further risings by the settlers (see p. 449), and the activities of the colonists' terrorist organization, the OAS, Algeria gained independence in 1962. The first president, Ahmed Ben Bella (1916–), was overthrown in 1965 by Colonel Houari Boumédienne (1932–78), who established a one-party socialist state under the FLN. After his successor, Colonel Chadli Benjedid (1929–) introduced multi-party democracy (1990), Islamic fundamentalism became a political force. In 1992 the second round of multi-party elections was cancelled when fundamentalists gained a large lead in the first round. The military took power and suspended political activity.

ANDORRA

Official name: Les Valls d'Andorrà (The Valleys of Andorra)

Area: 467 km² (180 sq mi)

Population: 55 400 (1991 est)

Capital: Andorra la Vella 33 400 (town 20 400; 1990 est)

Languages: Catalan (30%; official), Spanish (59%), French (6%)

Religion: Roman Catholic

GOVERNMENT

Andorra has joint heads of state (co-princes) – the president of France and the Spanish bishop of Urgel – who delegate their powers to permanent representa-

tives. The 28-member General Council is elected for four years by universal adult suffrage, and (since 1981) choses an Executive Council (government). Major constitutional changes are in progress.

GEOGRAPHY

In the E Pyrenees, Andorra is surrounded by mountains up to 3000 m (9840 ft) high.

Climate: Mild in spring and summer, but cold for six months, with snow in the winter.

ECONOMY

The economy used to be based mainly on sheep and timber. Tourism has been encouraged by the development of ski resorts and by the duty-free status of consumer goods.

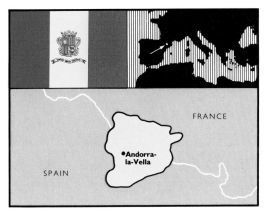

HISTORY

Andorra's joint allegiance to Spanish and French 'co-princes' dates directly from an agreement made in 1278 between the Spanish bishop of Urgel and the count of Foix, an ancestor of the Bourbon kings of France. Because of its peculiar constitution, Andorra found difficulties in obtaining international recognition. In 1993, however, a new constitution was proposed and independent diplomatic relations were instituted.

ANGOLA

Official name: A República de Angola (The Republic of Angola)

Member of: UN, OAU

Area: 1 246 700 km² (481 354 sq mi)

Population: 10 284 000 (1991 est)

Capital and major cities: Luanda 1 200 000 (1988 est), Huambo 203 000, Benguela 155 000 (1983 est)

Languages: Portuguese (official), Umbundu (38%), Kimbundu (27%), Lunda (13%), Kikongo (12%)

Religions: Roman Catholic (over 60%), animist (20%)

GOVERNMENT

A 318-member National Assembly and a President (who appoints a Premier and a Council of Ministers) are elected for a five-year term by universal adult suffrage.

GEOGRAPHY

Plateaux, over 1000 m (3300 ft), cover 90% of Angola. The highest point – Serra Mòco – reaches 2610 m (8563 ft). In the W is a narrow coastal plain and in the SW is desert.

Climate: Angola is tropical, with slightly lower temperatures in the uplands. October to May is the rainy season, but the SW is dry all year.

ECONOMY

The development of Angola has been hampered by war. The country is, however, rich in minerals, particularly diamonds, iron ore and petroleum. Although less than 5% of the land is arable, over half the adult population is engaged in agriculture. The main export crop is coffee.

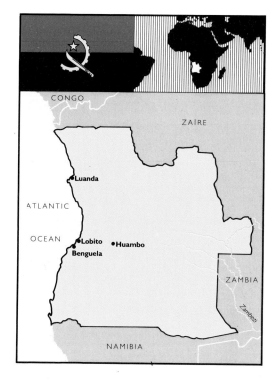

HISTORY

The Kongo and Ndongo kingdoms ruled much of the area when the Portuguese arrived in the late 15th century and developed a major slave trade. In the 20th century, forced labour, heavy taxation and discrimination from white settlers helped to stimulate nationalism. Portugal's repression of all political protest led to the outbreak of guerrilla wars in 1961. When independence was finally conceded (1975), three rival guerrilla movements fought for control of Angola. With Soviet and Cuban support, the (Marxist-Leninist) MPLA, under Dr Agostinho Neto (1922–79), gained the upper hand and repulsed an invasion from South Africa. In the 1980s, Cuban troops continued to support the MPLA government against the South African-aided UNITA movement in the S. Foreign involvement in the civil war ended in 1990. Following a ceasefire (1991), multi-party elections were held in 1992. However, UNITA forces resumed the conflict after rejecting the election results.

ANTIGUA AND BARBUDA

Member of: UN, CARICOM, Commonwealth, OAS

Area: 442 km² (170.5 sq mi)

Population: 81 600 (1991 est)

Capital: St John's 36 000 (1986 est)

Language: English

Religion: Anglican (44%), Moravian

GOVERNMENT

The 17-member House of Representatives is elected by universal adult suffrage for five years. The 17-member Senate is appointed. A Prime Minister and Cabinet of Ministers, commanding a majority in the lower house, are appointed by the Governor General, the representative of the British Queen as sovereign of Antigua.

GEOGRAPHY

Antigua is a low limestone island, rising in the W to Boggy Peak (402 m / 1319 ft). Barbuda – 45 km / 25 mi to the N – is a flat wooded coral island. Redonda is a rocky outcrop.

Climate: The tropical climate is moderated by sea

breezes. Rainfall is low for the West Indies, and Antigua island suffers from drought.

ECONOMY

Tourism is the mainstay of the country. In an attempt to diversify the economy, the government has encouraged agriculture, but the lack of water on Antigua island is a problem.

HISTORY

Antigua was discovered by Columbus in 1493, and colonized by English settlers in 1632. Black slaves were imported to work the sugar plantations. Barbuda was colonized from Antigua (1661) and run as a private estate by the Codrington family until it was annexed to Antigua in 1860. Britain granted Antigua complete internal self-government in 1967 and independence in 1981.

ARGENTINA

Official name: República Argentina (the Argentine Republic)

Member of: UN, OAS, ALADI, Mercosur

Area: 2 766 889 km² (1 068 302 sq mi), excluding territories claimed by Argentina: the Falkland Islands (Islas Malvinas), South Georgia, South Sandwich Islands, and parts of the Antarctic

Population: 32 880 000 (1990 est)

Capital and major cities: Buenos Aires 11 382 000, Córdoba 1 167 000, Rosario 1 096 000, Mendoza 729 000, La Plata 644 000 (all including suburbs; 1990 est)

Languages: Spanish (95%; official), Guarani (3%)

Religion: Roman Catholic (nearly 93%)

GOVERNMENT

The President and Vice-President are elected for a six-year term of office by an electoral college of 600 members who are chosen by universal adult suffrage. The lower house of Congress (the Chamber of Deputies) has 254 members elected by universal suffrage for four years, with one half of its members retiring every two years. The 46 members of the upper house (the Senate) are chosen by provincial legislatures to serve for nine years, with 18 members retiring every three years.

GEOGRAPHY

The Andes, whose highest point in Argentina is Cerro Aconcagua (6960 m / 22 834 ft), extend as a rugged barrier along the border with Chile. S of the Colorado River is Patagonia, an important pastureland – although much of it is semidesert. Nearly 80% of the population lives in the pampas, whose prairies form one of the world's most productive agricultural regions. The subtropical plains of NE Argentina contain part of the Gran Chaco prairie and rain forests.

Principal rivers: Paraná (4880 km / 3032 mi), Colorado (850 km / 530 mi)

Climate: Most of Argentina has a mild temperate climate, although the S is cooler and the NE is subtropical. The higher parts of the Andes have a subpolar climate. Rainfall is heavy in the Andes and the far NE, but generally decreases towards the S and SW which are dry.

ECONOMY

Argentina is one of the world's leading producers of beef, wool, mutton, wheat and wine. The pampas produce cereals, while fruit and vines are important in the NW. Pasturelands cover over 50% of Argentina – for beef cattle in the pampas and for sheep in Patagonia. However, manufacturing (including chemicals, steel, cement, paper, pulp and textiles) now makes the greatest contribution to the economy. The country is rich in natural resources including petroleum, natural gas, iron ore and precious metals, and has great potential for hydroelectric power. Argentina's status as an economic power declined between the 1930s and 1980s, but financial reforms greatly improved prospects in the 1990s.

HISTORY

NW Argentina was part of the Inca Empire (see pp. 390–91), while Patagonia and the pampas were home to nomadic Indians. The Spanish arrived in the La Plata estuary in 1516 but early colonization of the region was slow. During the Napoleonic Wars, nationalism grew. San Martín helped lead the revolution that ended Spanish rule. Independence was declared in 1816, but the war of liberation continued until 1820, and the first national government was only formed in 1826. Although it was reunited under the dictator de Rosas (1835–52), Argentina was wracked by disunity, and the powers of the provincial governments were not curbed until the 1850s. From 1880, large-scale European immigration and British investment helped Argentina to develop a flourishing economy. Prosperity was ended by the Depression (see p. 441), and, in 1930, constitutional rule was interrupted by a military coup.

In 1946, a populist leader, Juan Perón (1895–1974), came to power with the support of the unions. His wife Eva was a powerful and popular figure, and after her death (1952), Perón was deposed (1955) because of his unsuccessful economic policies. Succeeding civilian governments were unable to conquer rampant inflation, and the military took power again (1966–73). An unstable period of civilian rule (1973–76) included Perón's brief second presidency. In the early 1970s, urban terrorism grew and the economic crisis deepened, prompting another coup. The military junta that seized control in 1976 received international condemnation when thousands of opponents of the regime were arrested or disappeared. In April 1982, President Galtieri ordered tne invasion of the Falkland Islands and its dependencies, which had long been claimed by Argentina. A British task force recaptured the islands in June 1982, and Galtieri resigned. Constitutional rule was restored in 1983. Argentina's economic prospects have greatly improved since 1989 under President Carlos Menem.

ARMENIA

Official name: Haikakan (Armenia)

Member of: UN, CIS, CSCE

Area: 29 800 km² (11 500 sq mi)

Population: 3 376 000 (1989 census)

Capital and major cities: Yerevan 1 215 000, Kumayri (formerly Leninakan) 228 000, Karaklis 169 000 (1989 census)

Languages: Armenian (official; 93%), Azeri (5%)

Religion: Armenian Apostolic (Orthodox) majority

GOVERNMENT

A 259-member Assembly and an executive President are elected by universal adult suffrage for four years. A new constitution is to be drafted.

GEOGRAPHY

All of Armenia is mountainous – only 10% of the country is under 1000 m (3300 ft). The highest peak is Mt Aragats at 4090 m (13 418 ft).

Climate: Armenia has a dry continental climate with considerable local variations owing to altitude and aspect.

ECONOMY

The diverse industrial sector includes chemicals, metallurgy, textiles, precision goods and food processing. Major projects have provided hydroelectric power as well as irrigation water for agriculture. Steps have been taken to introduce a market economy but an effective blockade by Azerbaijan has devastated the economy.

HISTORY

Ancient Armenia was incorporated, in turn, into the Persian Empire (see p. 365), the empire of Alexander the Great (see p. 372) and the Seleucid Empire (see p. 373). Independent Armenian states appeared in the 2nd century BC and a united Armenian kingdom was established c. 55 BC. Christianity was adopted c. AD 300. In the 4th and 5th centuries Armenia was divided between the Byzantine Empire (see p. 394) and Persia. An independent kingdom (Greater Armenia) emerged in the 9th century, but was constantly threatened by invasion from the Arabs, Byzantines, Persians and Seljuks. When Greater Armenia fell to the Mongols (1236–42), many Armenians fled to Cilicia (modern SE Turkey) where a second Armenian kingdom (Little Armenia) flourished until the 14th century, when it was overrun by Mamluk armies from Egypt. In the 16th century Armenia was fought over by Persia and the Ottoman Turks. After 1620 W and central Armenia was ruled by the Turks and E Armenia (the present state) was annexed by Persia.

Russia took Persian Armenia between 1813 and 1828. The Armenians under Ottoman rule suffered persecution and, in 1896 and again in 1915, large-scale massacres. During World War I Turkey deported nearly 2 000 000 Armenians (suspected of pro-Russian sympathies) to Syria and Mesopotamia. The survivors contributed to an Armenian diaspora in Europe and the USA. Following the collapse of Tsarist Russia, an independent Armenian state emerged briefly (1918–22), but faced territorial wars with all its neighbours. Armenia became part of the Transcaucasian Soviet Republic in 1922 and a separate Union Republic within the USSR in 1936. After the abortive coup by Communist hardliners in Moscow (September 1991), Armenia declared independence and received international recognition when the USSR was dissolved (December 1991). Since 1990 Azeri and Armenian forces have been involved in a violent dispute concerning the status of Nagorno Karabakh, an enclave of Orthodox Christian Armenians surrounded by the Shiite Muslim Azeris – although Armenia maintains that it has no territorial claims on Azerbaijan.

AUSTRALIA

Official name: The Commonwealth of Australia

Member of: UN, Commonwealth, ANZUS, OECD.

Area: 7 682 300 km² (2 966 150 sq mi).

Population: 17 211 000 (1991 est).

Capital and major cities: Canberra 310 000, Sydney 3 657 000, Melbourne 3 081 000, Brisbane 1 302 000, Perth 1 193 000, Adelaide 1 050 000, Newcastle 429 000, Gold Coast 266 000, Wollongong 238 000, Hobart 184 000, Geelong 151 000, Townsville 114 000, Launceston 89 000 (including suburbs; 1990 est).

Language: English.

Religions: Anglican (26%), Roman Catholic (26%), Uniting Church in Australia (8%), Orthodox.

States and Territories (with areas, populations and capitals):

New South Wales – 801 600 km² (309 500 sq mi), 5 862 000 (1991 est), Sydney.

Queensland – 1 727 200 km² (666 875 sq mi), 2 939 000 (1991 est), Brisbane.

South Australia – 984 000 km² (379 925 sq mi), 1 448 000 (1991 est), Adelaide.

Tasmania – 67 800 km² (26 175 sq mi), 459 000 (1991 est), Hobart.

Victoria – 227 600 km² (87 875 sq mi), 4 407 000 (1991 est), Melbourne.

Western Australia – 2 525 500 km² (975 100 sq mi), 1 650 000 (1991 est), Perth.

Australian Capital Territory – 2400 km² (925 sq mi), 289 000 (1991 est), Canberra.

Northern Territory – 1 346 200 km² (519 750 sq mi), 158 000 (1991 est), Darwin.

External Territories (with areas, populations and capitals):

Ashmore and Cartier Islands – 5 km² (2 sq mi), uninhabited.

Australian Antarctic Territory – 6 120 000 km² (2 320 000 sq mi), no permanent population.

Christmas Island – 135 km² (52 sq mi), 1770 (1991 est), Flying Fish Cove.

Cocos (Keeling) Islands – 14 km² (5.5 sq mi), 600 (1990 census), Bantam Village on Home Island.

Coral Sea Islands Territory – 8 km² (5 sq mi), no permanent population.

Heard and MacDonald Islands – 292 km² (113 sq mi), no permanent population.

Norfolk Island – 34.5 km² (13.3 sq mi), 1980 (1986 census), Kingston.

GOVERNMENT

The Federal Parliament consists of two chambers elected by compulsory universal adult suffrage. The Senate has 76 members elected by proportional representation – 12 senators elected from each state for six years, 2 from both territories elected for three years. The House of Representatives has 148 members elected for three years. A Prime Minister, who commands a majority in the House of Representatives, is appointed by the Governor General, who is the representative of the British Queen as sovereign of Australia. The Prime Minister chairs the Federal Executive Council (or Cabinet), which is responsible to Parliament. Each state has its own government.

GEOGRAPHY

Vast areas of desert cover most of central and western Australia, a region of plateaux between 400 and 600 m (1300–2000 ft) with occasional higher regions, such as the Kimberley Plateau. In contrast to this scarcely populated area – which covers more than 50% of the country – are the narrow coastal plains of the fertile, well-watered E coast where the majority of Australians live. Behind the plains – which range from temperate forest in the S, through subtropical woodland to tropical rain forest in the N – rise the Eastern Uplands, or Great Dividing Range, a line of ridges and plateaux, stretching from Cape York Peninsula in the N to the island of Tasmania. The Australian Alps rise to Mt Kosciusko (2230 m / 7316 ft). The Great Artesian Basin extends from the Gulf of Carpentaria to the Murray River and Eyre Basins. Landforms in the basin include rolling plains, plateaux, salt lakes and river valleys, while the natural vegetation ranges from savannah and mixed forest to arid steppe and desert. Between the Murray River and Eyre Basins are the Flinders and Mount Lofty Ranges. Many of Australia's rivers flow intermittently.

Principal rivers: Murray 2589 km (1609 mi) with Darling 2700 km (1700 mi), Lachlan 2388 km (1484 mi), Flinders 837 km (520 mi)

Climate: The N is tropical with wet summers (January to March) and dry winters. The Timor Sea coast is subject to summer monsoons. The Queensland coast experiences tropical cyclones and has the heaviest rainfall, over 2500 mm (100 in) near Cairns. The interior is extremely hot and dry – over 30% of Australia has less than 255 mm (10 in) of rain a year. The coastal fringes in the S are either temperate or subtropical, with winter rainfall, hot or warm summers and mild winters. Winter snowfall occurs in the SE and Tasmanian highlands.

ECONOMY

Since World War II, Australia's economy has been dominated by mining. Minerals now account for over 30% of the country's exports. Australia has major reserves of coal, petroleum and natural gas, uranium, iron ore, copper, nickel, bauxite, gold and diamonds. Manufacturing and processing based upon these resources include iron and steel, construction, oil refining and petrochemicals, vehicle manufacturing and engineering. Food-processing and textile industries are also prominent. Australia's reliance on agriculture has fallen considerably, although the country is still the world's leading producer of wool. Major interests include sheep, cattle, cereals (in particular wheat), sugar (in Queensland) and fruit. A strong commercial sector, with banks and finance houses, adds to the diversity of the economy.

HISTORY

The Aborigines came to Australia around 50 000 years ago (see p. 389). They lived mainly along the N and E coasts and in the Murray Basin until British settlers drove them into the inhospitable interior. The Dutch are

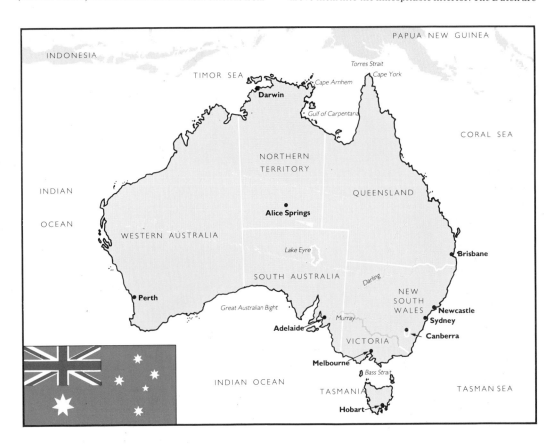

credited with the discovery of Australia. Willem de Janesz sighted Cape York Peninsula (1606), Hartog made the first landing in 1616 (in Western Australia), and Tasman explored the coasts (1642–44). However, the hospitable regions most suitable for colonization were not known to Europeans until Captain Cook landed at Botany Bay (1770), and claimed New South Wales for Britain.

In 1788, the first settlement was made at Port Jackson (Sydney), with over 700 British convicts and 250 free settlers. Penal settlements at Hobart and Launceston in Tasmania, and Newcastle (NSW) followed (1803–4). Moreton Bay (Brisbane) was established in 1824, Port Phillip (Melbourne) in 1826, and Albany (Western Australia) in 1827. Adelaide (South Australia), a settlement without convicts, was founded in 1837. Free migration was encouraged. The spread of sheep farming, and the discovery of copper (1840s) and gold (1851), attracted large numbers of migrants. The colonists campaigned to end transportation – the last convicts arrived in 1867 – and agitated for participation in government. In 1854, gold miners at Eureka Stockade (Ballarat) rebelled over the lack of representative government. This celebrated incident hastened reform. Between 1855 and 1870, all six colonies gained self-government. By 1900, 3 700 000 people, almost entirely of British and Irish ancestry, were living in Australia. Fear of invasion from Asia or German New Guinea, and the desire to achieve free trade between the colonies, encouraged federation. In 1901, the Commonwealth of Australia was founded.

Australia made an important contribution in World War I – one fifth of its servicemen were killed in action. The heroic landing at Gallipoli in the Dardenelles (see p. 437) is a national day of remembrance in Australia. The Depression hit the country badly (see p. 441), but the interwar years did see international recognition of Australia's independence. World War II, during which the N was threatened by Japan, strengthened links with America. Australian troops fought in Vietnam and important trading partnerships have been formed with Asian countries. Since 1945, migrants from all over Europe and many parts of Asia have gained assisted passage to Australia, further diluting the British connection and encouraging the growth of republicanism.

AUSTRIA

Official name: Republik Österreich (Republic of Austria)

Member of: UN, EFTA, CSCE, OECD

Area: 83 855 km² (32 367 sq mi)

Population: 7 812 000 (1991 census)

Capital and major cities: Vienna (Wien) 2 045 000 (city 1 533 800), Linz 434 000 (city 203 000), Graz 395 000 (city 232 000), Salzburg 267 000 (city 144 000), Innsbruck 235 000 (city 115 000) (1991 census)

Language: German (official; 96%)

Religion: Roman Catholic (84%)

GOVERNMENT
Executive power is shared by the Federal President – who is elected by universal adult suffrage for a six-year term – and the Council of Ministers (Cabinet), led by the Federal Chancellor. The President appoints a Chancellor who commands a majority in the Federal Assembly's lower chamber, the Nationalrat, whose 183 members are elected by universal adult suffrage according to proportional representation for a term of four years. The 63 members of the upper chamber – the Bundesrat – are elected by the assemblies of the nine provinces of the Federal Republic.

GEOGRAPHY
The Alps – much of which are covered by pastures and forests – occupy nearly two thirds of Austria. The highest point is the Grossglockner (3798 m / 12 462 ft). Lowland Austria – in the E – consists of low hills, the Vienna Basin and a flat marshy area beside the Neusiedler See on the Hungarian border. Along the Czech border is a forested massif rising to 1200 m (4000 ft).

Principal river: Danube (Donau) 2850 km (1770 mi)

Climate: There are many local variations in climate owing to altitude and aspect. The E is drier than the W, and is, in general, colder than the Alpine region in the winter and hotter, but more humid, in the summer. Areas over 3000 m (10 000 ft) are snow-covered all year.

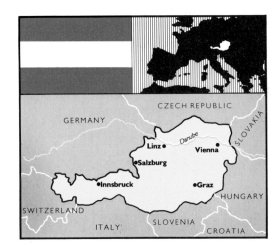

ECONOMY
Austria produces about 90% of its own food requirements, but farming employs only 8% of the labour force. The arable land in the E has fertile soils producing good yields of cereals and grapes for wine. Dairy produce is an important export from the pasturelands in the E and in the Alps. The mainstay of the economy is manufacturing industry, including machinery and transport equipment, iron and steel products, refined petroleum products, cement and paper. Natural resources include hydroelectric power potential and extensive forests. The Alps attract winter and summer visitors, making tourism a major foreign-currency earner. Austria retains economic links with Central European states that were once part of the Habsburg empire.

HISTORY
The Babenberg family ruled what became Austria from the late 10th century until 1250. Their successor as duke was defeated by Rudolf of Habsburg, the Holy Roman Emperor, in 1276, and from that date Austria became the heartland of the Empire. With one exception, every Holy Roman Emperor from 1438 to 1806 was a member of the Habsburg family (see pp. 344–5). In 1529, and in 1683, Austria repelled the Turks from the walls of Vienna and halted their advance across Europe. By the middle of the 16th century, the extent of the Habsburgs' territory had become unmanageable, and Charles V divided his inheritance, separating Spain from the Empire in central Europe (see pp. 410–11). In the 18th century, Maria Theresa and her son Joseph II reformed Austria and strengthened the multilingual Habsburg state. This was based on Austria, Hungary and Czech-speaking Bohemia, but it also included Polish, Croat, Slovak, Slovene and Italian areas (see pp. 417 and 418–9).

Napoleon I abolished the anachronistic Holy Roman Empire, but Francis II, foreseeing its dissolution, took the title Emperor of Austria. Metternich shaped the fortunes of Austria in the early 19th century and attempted to maintain the boundaries drawn by the Vienna Settlement (1814–15), but the Empire was bedevilled by national and ethnic divisions (see p. 428). Austria's partnership with the Hungarians – in the Dual Monarchy established in 1867 – did not ease these tensions. Defeat in the Austro-Prussian War (1866) excluded Austrian influence from Germany, and the Habsburgs were left to dominate unstable south-central Europe (see p. 429). In 1914, a Serb assassinated the heir to the Austro-Hungarian throne – an event which precipitated World War I (see pp. 429 and 436). In 1918–19, the Habsburg empire was dismembered (see p. 440). A separate Austrian republic was established despite considerable support for union with Germany. Unstable throughout the 1920s and 1930s, Austria was annexed by Germany in 1938 (the Anschluss, see p. 442). Austria was liberated in 1945, but Allied occupation forces remained until 1955 when the independence of a neutral republic was recognized. The collapse of Communism in Eastern Europe (1989–91) allowed Austria to renew traditional links with Hungary and the Czechs. Austria is a candidate for membership of the EC.

AZERBAIJAN

Official name: Azarbaijchan (Azerbaijan)

Member of: UN, CSCE

Area: 86 600 km² (33 400 sq mi)

Population: 7 137 000 (1989 census)

Capital and major cities: Baku 1 757 000, Gyanzha (formerly Kirovabad) 270 000 (1989 census)

Languages: Azeri (83%), Russian (6%), Armenian (2%)

Religion: Shia Islam majority

GOVERNMENT
An executive President and a 350-member Assembly are elected by universal adult suffrage for four years. A new constitution is to be drafted.

GEOGRAPHY
Azerbaijan comprises lowlands beside the Caspian Sea, part of the Caucasus Mountains in the N and the Little Caucasus in the SW. The republic includes the Nakhichevan enclave to the W of Armenia.

Climate: A wide climatic range includes dry and humid subtropical conditions beside the Caspian Sea and continental conditions in the mountains.

ECONOMY
Important reserves of oil and natural gas are the mainstay of the economy and the basis of heavy industries. Although industry dominates the economy, agriculture contributes a variety of exports including cotton and tobacco. Sturgeon are caught in the Caspian Sea for the important caviar industry. Initial steps have been taken to introduce a market economy, and trade agreements have been concluded with Turkey.

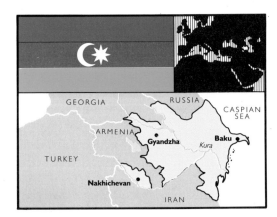

HISTORY
The Azeris were conquered by the Arabs in 632, but, although the region remained under Arab rule until the 11th century, Turkic rather than Arabic language and culture prevailed after the 9th century. The Mongols controlled Azerbaijan from 1236 to 1498, when the Azeris came under Persian rule. In the 18th century Tsarist Russia gradually expanded into the Caucasus. Russia took northern Azerbaijan in 1813, and Nakhichevan and the rest of the present state in 1828. However, the greater

part of the land of the Azeris remained under Persian rule. During World War I, a nationalist Azeri movement became allied with the Turks. An independent Azeri state was founded with Turkish assistance (1918), but was invaded by the Soviet Red Army in 1920. Azerbaijan was part of the Transcaucasian Soviet Republic from 1922 until 1936 when it became a separate Union Republic within the USSR. Independence was declared following the abortive coup in Moscow by Communist hardliners (September 1991) and was internationally recognized when the USSR was dissolved (December 1991). Since 1990 Azeri and Armenian forces have been involved in a violent dispute concerning the status of Nagorno Karabakh, an enclave of Orthodox Christian Armenians surrounded by the Shiite Muslim Azeris. Azerbaijan withdrew from the CIS in 1992.

BAHAMAS

Official name: The Commonwealth of the Bahamas
Member of: UN, Commonwealth, OAS, CARICOM
Area: 13 939 km² (5382 sq mi)
Population: 255 000 (1990 census)
Capital: Nassau 169 000 (1990 census)
Language: English
Religions: Baptist (29%), Roman Catholic (26%).

GOVERNMENT
The Senate (the upper house of Parliament) has 16 appointed members. The House of Assembly (the lower house) has 49 members elected by universal adult suffrage for five years. A Prime Minister, who commands a majority in the House, is appointed by the Governor General, who is the representative of the British Queen as sovereign of the Bahamas. The Prime Minister chairs the Cabinet, which is responsible to the House.

GEOGRAPHY
The Bahamas comprises some 700 long, flat, narrow islands, and over 2000 barren rocky islets.
Climate: The climate is mild and subtropical, with no great seasonal variation in temperature. Rainfall averages just over 1000 mm (39 in). The islands are liable to hurricanes.

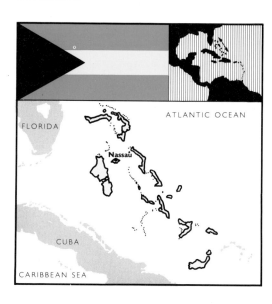

ECONOMY
Tourism – mainly from the USA – is the major source of income, and, with related industries, it employs the majority of the labour force. The islands have become a tax haven and financial centre.

HISTORY
Columbus landed in the Bahamas when he reached the

New World (1492). In the 17th century, English colonists attempted to settle, but development was slow. After the American Revolution, an influx of Loyalists and their slaves established cotton plantations, but the abolition of slavery (1834) ended this activity. Although the first representative assembly met in 1729, internal self-government was not achieved until 1964. Independence was granted in 1973.

BAHRAIN

Official name: Daulat al-Bahrain (The State of Bahrain)
Member of: UN, Arab League, OPEC, GCC
Area: 691 km² (267 sq mi)
Population: 516 000 (1991 est)
Capital and major cities: Manama 152 000, al-Muharraq 78 000 (1988 est)
Language: Arabic
Religions: Sunni Islam (33%), Shia Islam (60%)

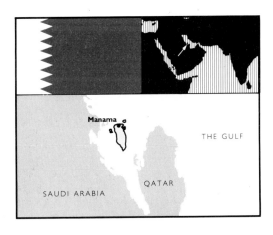

GOVERNMENT
Bahrain is ruled directly by an Amir (a hereditary monarch), who appoints a Council of Ministers.

GEOGRAPHY
Bahrain comprises an archipelago of the 35 small islands. Bahrain Island, the largest, consists mainly of sandy plains and salt marshes, and is linked to Saudi Arabia by causeway.
Climate: The climate is very hot. The annual average rainfall is 75 mm (3 in).

ECONOMY
The wealth of Bahrain is due to its petroleum and natural gas resources, and the oil-refining industry. As reserves began to wane in the 1970s, the government encouraged diversification. As a result, Bahrain is now one of the Gulf's major banking and communication centres.

HISTORY
Bahrain – part of the Arab Islamic world since the 7th century – was Persian from 1602 until 1783, when rule by the Sunni al-Khalifa family began. In the 19th century, Bahrain signed a series of treaties under which it became a British protectorate. Bahrain was the first Gulf state to develop its petroleum industry (from 1932). Since independence in 1971, there has been tension between the Sunni and Shiite communities. Bahrain joined the coalition forces against Iraq after the invasion of Kuwait (1990–91).

BANGLADESH

Official name: Gana Praja Tantri Bangla Desh (People's Republic of Bangladesh)

Member of: UN, Commonwealth
Area: 143 998 km² (55 598 sq mi)
Population: 107 992 000 (1991 census)
Capital and major cities: Dhaka 5 731 000, Chittagong 2 133 000, Khulna 1 029 000 (1991 census)
Languages: Bengali (97%), tribal dialects
Religion: Sunni Islam (over 85%; official), Hindu (12%)

GOVERNMENT
The Parliament (Jatiya Sangsad), comprises 300 members elected for five years by universal suffrage and 30 women chosen by the elected members. Parliament elects a President – who serves for five years – and a Prime Minister who appoints a Council of Ministers.

GEOGRAPHY
Most of Bangladesh is alluvial plains in the deltas of the rivers Ganges and Brahmaputra which combine as the Padma. The swampy plains – generally less than 9 m (30 ft) above sea level – are dissected by rivers dividing into numerous distributaries with raised banks. The S and SE coastal regions contain mangrove forests (the Sundarbans). The only uplands are the Sylhet Hills in the NE and the Chittagong hill country in the E – rising to 1230 m (4034 ft) at the Keokradong.
Principal rivers: Ganges 2506 km (1557 mi), Brahmaputra (Jumuna) 2900 km (1800 mi).
Climate: The climate is tropical with the highest temperatures between April and September. Most of the country's rainfall comes during the annual monsoon (June to October) when intense storms accompanied by high winds bring serious flooding. Rainfall totals range from 1000 mm (40 in) in the W to 5000 mm (200 in) in the Sylhet Hills.

ECONOMY
With a rapidly increasing population, Bangladesh is among the world's poorest countries and is heavily dependent on foreign aid. Over 70% of the labour force is involved in agriculture. Rice is produced on over 75% of the cultivated land, but although the land is fertile, crops are subject to floods and cyclones. A major Flood Action Plan, started in 1992, will alter the course of rivers and raise embankments. The main cash crops are jute – Bangladesh yields 90% of the world's production – and tea. Industries include those processing agricultural products – jute, cotton and sugar. There are reserves of natural gas.

HISTORY
A part of the Mogul empire from the 16th century, the area came under British rule within India after 1757. On partition in 1947, as the majority of its inhabitants were

Muslim, the area became the eastern province of Pakistan. Separated by 1600 km (1000 mi) from the Urdu-speaking, politically dominant western province, East Pakistan saw itself as a victim of economic and ethnic injustice. Resentment led to civil war in 1971 when Indian aid to Bengali irregulars gave birth to an independent People's Republic of Bangladesh ('Free Bengal') under Sheik Mujib-ur-Rahman. Mujib's assassination in 1975 led eventually to a takeover by General Zia-ur-Rahman, who amended the constitution to create an 'Islamic state'. Zia in turn was assassinated in 1981 and General Ershad took power in 1982. After Ershad was deposed (1990), a parliamentary system was reintroduced.

BARBADOS

Member of: UN, Commonwealth, OAS, CARICOM

Area: 430 km² (166 sq mi)

Population: 257 000 (1990 census)

Capital: Bridgetown 102 000 (city 7500; 1990 census)

Language: English

Religions: Anglican (40%), Pentacostalist, Methodist

GOVERNMENT
The 21 members of the Senate are appointed; the 27 members of the House of Assembly are elected by universal adult suffrage for five years. The Governor General, the representative of the British Queen as sovereign of Barbados, appoints a Prime Minister who commands a majority in the House. The PM appoints a Cabinet responsible to the House.

GEOGRAPHY
Barbados is generally flat and low, except in the N where it rises to Mount Hillaby (340 m / 1115 ft).

Climate: Barbados has a tropical climate. Rainfall is heavy, with totals everywhere above 1000 mm (40 in). The island is subject to hurricanes.

ECONOMY
Tourism – the main source of income – employs about one third of the labour force. The government has encouraged growth in banking and insurance. Sugar – once the mainstay of Barbados – remains the main crop.

HISTORY
Barbados was claimed and settled by the English in the 1620s. Black slaves were imported to work the sugar cane plantations, which, in the 18th century, made the island one of the most profitable parts of the British Empire. Slavery was abolished in 1834, but economic and political power remained with a small white minority. In the 1930s, economic and social conditions for black Barbadians were miserable. Riots in 1937 led to reforms and also greatly increased black political consciousness. As a result, Barbadians, such as Grantley Adams and Errol Barrow, became prominent in Caribbean politics. Barbados became independent in 1966.

BELARUS (BYELORUSSIA)

Official name: Respublika Belarus (Republic of Belarus). Formerly known as Byelorussia.

Member of: UN, CIS, CSCE

Area: 207 600 km² (80 200 sq mi)

Population: 10 260 000 (1989 census)

Capital and major cities: Minsk (Mensk) 1 589 000, Gomel (Homel) 500 000, Mogilev (Mahilyou) 359 000, Vitebsk 347 000 (1989 census)

Languages: Belarussian (also known as Belorussian) (79%), Russian (13%), Polish (4%)

Religions: Russian Orthodox majority

Government
A 300-member legislature and a President – who appoints a Council of Ministers – are elected by universal adult suffrage for four years.

GEOGRAPHY
Belarus comprises lowlands covered with glacial debris in the N, fertile well-drained tablelands and ridges in the centre, and the low-lying Pripet Marshes in the S and E. Much of the country is flat and the highest point, Dzyarzhynskaya Mountain, only reaches 346 m (1135 ft).

Climate: The continental climate is moderated by the proximity of the Baltic Sea. Belarussian winters are considerably milder than those experienced in European Russia to the E.

ECONOMY
Although Belarus has few natural resources, its economy is overwhelmingly industrial. Major heavy engineering, chemical, fertilizer, oil refining and synthetic fibre industries were established as part of the centrally-planned Soviet economy. Belarus is dependent upon trade with other former Soviet republics from which it imports the raw materials for its industries and upon which it relies as a market for its industrial goods. Little progress towards establishing a market economy has been made and the country faces severe economic problems. Agriculture is dominated by raising fodder crops for beef cattle, pigs and poultry. Flax is grown for export and the local linen industry. Extensive forests supply important woodworking and paper industries.

HISTORY
The Belarussian Slavs arrived in the region between the 6th and 8th centuries AD. A number of small Belarussian states flourished after c. 700 but were soon conquered by Kievan Rus'. When the Tatars overran Kievan Rus' (1240), the Belarussian lands came under Lithuanian rule. After 1569, when Lithuania and Poland became one state, the area was dominated by a Polish Roman Catholic aristocracy. In 1648–54, the Orthodox Belarussians, who had been reduced to serfdom, rose in revolt against a resented Polish elite that controlled the land, administration and trade. The Belarussians came

under Russian rule as a result of the three partitions of Poland (1772, 1793 and 1795).

The region suffered some of the fiercest fighting between Russia and Germany during World War I. Following the Russian Revolution (see p. 438), a Byelorussian Soviet republic was proclaimed (1919). The republic was invaded by the Poles in the same year and divided between Poland and the Soviet Union in 1921. Byelorussia was devastated during World War II. In 1945 the Belarussians were reunited in a single Soviet republic. A perceived lack of Soviet concern for the republic at the time of the accident at the Chernobyl nuclear power station (just over the Ukrainian border) strengthened a reawakening Belarussian national identity. Contamination from Chernobyl affected about 20% of the republic, causing some areas to be sealed off and necessitating the eventual resettlement of up to 2 000 000 people. Byelorussia declared independence following the abortive coup by Communist hardliners in Moscow (September 1991) and – as Belarus – received international recognition when the USSR was dissolved (December 1991).

BELGIUM

Official name: Royaume de Belgique or Koninkrijk België (Kingdom of Belgium)

Member of: UN, NATO, EC, CSCE, WEU, OECD

Area: 30 519 km² (11 783 sq mi)

Population: 9 849 000 (1991 census)

Capital and major cities: Brussels (Bruxelles or Brussel) 960 000, Antwerp (Antwerpen or Anvers) 920 000 (city 468 000), Liège (Luik) 590 000 (city 185 000), Ghent (Gent or Gand) 485 000 (city 230 000), Charleroi 429 000 (city 207 000), Malines (Mechelen) 293 000 (city 75 000), Courtrai (Kortrijk) 275 000 (city 76 000), Namur (Namen) 264 000 (city 104 000), Bruges (Brugge) 260 000, (city 117 000) (1990 est)

Languages: Flemish (58%), French (42%)

Religion: Roman Catholic (86%)

GOVERNMENT
Belgium is a constitutional monarchy. The Chamber of Deputies (the lower house of Parliament) comprises 212 members elected by universal adult suffrage for four years under a system of proportional representation. The Senate (the upper house) has 184 members: 106 directly elected, 51 chosen by provincial councils, 26 co-opted, plus the heir to the throne. The King appoints a Prime Minister, who commands a majority in the Chamber, and, upon the PM's advice, other members of

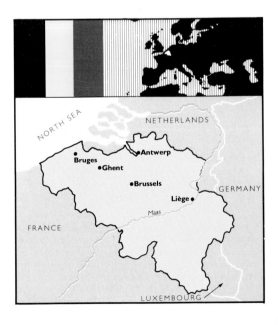

the Cabinet. The directly-elected regional councils of Flanders, Wallonia and Brussels have very considerable powers.

GEOGRAPHY
The forested Ardennes plateau – rising to Mount Botrange (694 m / 2272 ft) – occupies the SE. The plains of central Belgium, an important agricultural region, are covered in fertile loess. The flat, low-lying N contains the sandy Kempenland plateau in the E and the plain of Flanders in the W. Enclosed by dykes behind coastal sand dunes are polders, former marshes reclaimed from the sea.

Principal rivers: Scheldt (Schelde or Escaut) 435 km (270 mi), Meuse (Maes) 950 km (590 mi).

Climate: Belgium experiences relatively cool summers and mild winters, with ample rainfall throughout the year. Summers are hotter and winters colder inland.

ECONOMY
Belgium is a small, densely populated industrial country with few natural resources. In the centre and the N, soils are generally fertile and the climate encourages high yields of wheat, sugar beet, grass and fodder crops. Metalworking – originally based on small mineral deposits in the Ardennes – is the most important industry. Textiles, chemicals, ceramics, glass and rubber are also important, but, apart from coal, most raw materials required by industry now have to be imported. Economic problems since the 1970s have mirrored Belgium's linguistic divide, with high unemployment largely confined to the French-speaking (Walloon) S, while industry in the Flemish N has prospered. Banking, commerce and administration employ increasing numbers, and Brussels has benefited from its role as the unofficial 'capital' of the EC.

HISTORY
Belgium has been fought over by neighbouring powers for centuries. In the early Middle Ages, the area was divided into counties and duchies subject to the Holy Roman Emperor (see pp. 394–5). In the 12th–14th centuries, Bruges, Ghent and other Flemish textile centres were among the most prosperous cities in Europe. From 1384, most of modern Belgium was controlled by the rulers of Burgundy, whose territories were inherited by the Spanish Habsburgs in 1504. After the Protestant Dutch United Provinces rebelled and gained independence in the late 16th century, the Catholic south of the Low Countries ('Belgium') remained under Spanish rule.

By the Treaty of Utrecht (1713), the Spanish Netherlands passed to Austria. In the confusion of the French Revolutionary Wars, the Belgians expelled the Austrians (1791), but Belgium was annexed by France in 1793. After the Napoleonic Wars, which ended at Waterloo in Belgium (see p. 427), the Low Countries were reunited as the Kingdom of the Netherlands (1815). In 1830 the Belgians rebelled against Dutch rule and proclaimed their independence. Belgian neutrality was recognized by the Congress of London (1831) and the crown was offered to Leopold of Saxe-Coburg Gotha, Queen Victoria's uncle.

Belgium's neutrality was broken by the German invasion in 1914 (which led to Britain's declaration of war under the 1831 treaty). The brave resistance of King Albert in 1914–18 earned international admiration; the capitulation of Leopold III when Belgium was again occupied by Germany (1940–45) was severely criticized. The Belgian Congo (Zaïre), acquired as a personal possession by Leopold II (1879), was relinquished amidst scenes of chaos in 1960. Belgium is now the main centre of administration of the EC and of NATO, but it is troubled by acute rivalry between its Flemish and French speakers and has adopted a federal system based upon linguistic regions.

BELIZE

Member of: UN, Commonwealth, CARICOM, OAS

Area: 22 965 km² (8867 sq mi)

Population: 191 000 (1991 est)

Capital and major cities: Belmopan 4000, Belize City 50 000, Orange Walk 10 500 (1989 est)

Languages: English (official), Creole, Spanish (32%)

Religion: Roman Catholic (62%)

GOVERNMENT
The eight members of the Senate are appointed by the Governor General, the representative of the British Queen as sovereign of Belize. The 28 members of the House of Representatives are elected by universal adult suffrage for five years. The Governor General appoints a Prime Minister, who commands a majority in the House, and – on the PM's advice – a Cabinet, which is responsible to the House.

GEOGRAPHY
Tropical jungle covers much of Belize. The S contains the Maya Mountains – rising to 1122 m (3681 ft). The N is mainly swampy lowlands.

Climate: The subtropical climate is tempered by trade winds. Rainfall is heavy, but there is a dry season between February and May.

ECONOMY
The production of sugar, bananas and citrus fruit for export dominates the economy.

HISTORY
Mayan settlements flourished in Belize (see pp. 390–1) until 600 years before the arrival of the Spanish. Although Spain claimed the area, there were no Europeans living in Belize until English pirates and loggers settled in the 17th century. Black slaves were imported to cut timber. In 1862 the area formally became the colony of British Honduras. The colony gained independence – as Belize – in 1981, but Guatemala continued to claim it as part of her territory until 1991.

BENIN

Official name: La République du Bénin (Republic of Benin)

Member of: UN, OAU, ECOWAS

Area: 112 622 km² (43 484 sq mi)

Population: 4 776 000 (1991 est)

Capital and major cities: Porto-Novo 208 000, Cotonou 487 000 (1983 est)

Languages: French (official), Fon (47%), Adja (12%)

Religions: Animist (61%), Sunni Islam (16%)

GOVERNMENT
A President and an 80-member National Assembly are elected by universal adult suffrage for four years.

GEOGRAPHY
In the NW, the Atacora Massif reaches 635 m (2083 ft); in the NE, plains slope down to the Niger Valley. The plateaux of central Benin fall in the S to a low fertile region. A narrow coastal plain is backed by lagoons.

Climate: The N is tropical; the S is equatorial.

ECONOMY
The economy is based on agriculture, which occupies the majority of the labour force. The main food crops are cassava (manioc), yams and maize; the principal cash crop is palm oil. In the late 1980s, central planning was abandoned in favour of a market economy.

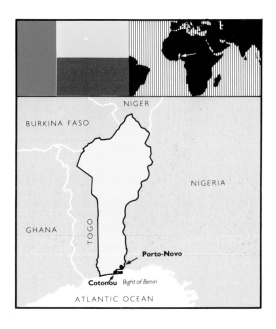

HISTORY
Benin was called Dahomey until 1975. From the 17th to the 19th centuries the kingdom of Dahomey was one of the principal slave trading states of W Africa. In the 1890s, Dahomey was conquered by the French. Political turmoil followed independence in 1960, and five coups took place between 1963 and 1972 when a Marxist-Leninist government came to power. A multi-party system was restored in 1991.

BHUTAN

Official name: Druk-yul (Realm of the Dragon)

Member of: UN

Area: 46 500 km² (17 954 sq mi)

Population: 1 442 000 (1990 UN est; 1992 Bhutanese government estimates give a population of over 700 000)

Capital: Thimphu 60 000 (1987 est)

Language: Dzongkha (Tibetan; official; 70%); Nepali (30%)

Religion: Buddhist (70%), Hindu (30%)

GOVERNMENT
Bhutan is a hereditary monarchy in which the King shares power with a Council of Ministers, the Buddhist Head Abbot and a 150-member National Assembly, comprising 100 members directly elected by universal adult suffrage for three years and 50 appointed members. There are no political parties.

GEOGRAPHY
The Himalaya – which in Bhutan rise to 7554 m (24 784 ft) at Khula Kangri – cover most of Bhutan. The valleys of central Bhutan are wide and fertile. The Duars Plain – a subtropical jungle – lies along the Indian border.

Climate: Hot and very wet in the Duars Plain, temperatures get progressively lower with altitude resulting in permanent snow cover in the N. Precipitation is heavy.

ECONOMY
Bhutan is one of the poorest and least developed countries in the world. Over 90% of the labour force is involved in producing food crops.

HISTORY
Tibetan influence over Bhutan from the 16th century was followed by Chinese overlordship (1720). Contact with British-dominated India (from 1774) led to border friction and partial annexation in 1865. In 1949 India returned this territory but assumed influence over Bhutan's external affairs. In 1907 the governor of Tongsa became Bhutan's first king. In the 1990s there has been discrimination against the Nepali minority.

BOLIVIA

Official name: République de Bolivia (Republic of Bolivia)

Member of: UN, OAS, ALADI, Andean Pact

Area: 1 098 581 km² (424 164 sq mi)

Population: 7 530 000 (1991 est)

Capital and major cities: La Paz (administrative capital) 1 050 000, Sucre (legal capital) 96 000, Santa Cruz 615 000, Cochabamba 377 000 (1988 est)

Languages: Spanish (official; 55%), Aymara (22%), Quéchua (5%)

Religion: Roman Catholic (official; 95%)

GOVERNMENT
The President (who appoints a Cabinet), the 27-member Senate and the 130-member Chamber of Deputies are elected for four-year terms by universal adult suffrage.

GEOGRAPHY
The Andes – whose highest point in Bolivia is Sajama (6542 m / 21 463 ft) – divide into two parallel chains between which is an extensive undulating depression (the Altiplano), containing Lake Titicaca, the highest navigable lake in the world. The lowlands in the E and NE include tropical rain forests (the Llanos), subtropical plains and semiarid grasslands (the Chaco).
Climate: Rainfall is negligible in the SW, and heavy in the NE. Temperature varies with altitude from the cold Andean summits and cool, windy Altiplano to the tropical NE.

ECONOMY
Bolivia is relatively poor, despite being rich in natural resources such as petroleum and tin. Lack of investment, political instability and high mining costs have retarded development. Agriculture is labour intensive, producing domestic foodstuffs (potatoes and maize), and export crops (sugar cane and cotton). The illegal cultivation of coca (for cocaine) is causing concern.

HISTORY
Until conquered by Spain in 1535 (see p. 410), Bolivia was part of the Inca Empire (see p. 391). As Upper Peru, Bolivia was ruled from Lima until 1776, when it became part of a viceroyalty based on Buenos Aires. A revolt against Spanish rule (1809) led to a power struggle between loyalists and nationalists, ending in independence in 1825. The remainder of the 19th century was characterized by political instability. In three devastating wars – the War of the Pacific (1879–83), alongside Peru against Chile, and the Chaco Wars (1928–30 and 1933–35) against Paraguay – Bolivia sustained great human and territorial losses. After 1935, political instability continued with a succession of military and civilian governments. Since 1982, however, Bolivia has had democratically elected governments.

BOSNIA-HERZEGOVINA

Official name: Bosna i Hercegovina (Bosnia-Herzegovina)

Member of: UN, CSCE

Area: 51 129 km² (19 741 sq mi)

Population: 4 365 000 (1991 census); 2 000 000 (late 1992 est; some 2 000 000 refugees left Bosnia in 1992 and over 200 000 were killed in the war).

Capital and major cities: Sarajevo 526 000 (including suburbs; by late 1992 the population of Sarajevo was c. 200 000), Banja Luka 143 000 (1991 census)

Languages: Serbo-Croat – a single language with two written forms

Religions: (pre-1992) Sunni Islam (44%), Serbian Orthodox (33%), Roman Catholic (17%)

GOVERNMENT
In early 1993 government authority was restricted to about 10% of central Bosnia.

GEOGRAPHY
Ridges of the Dinaric Mountains, rising to over 1800 m (6000 ft), occupy the greater part of the country and in places form arid karst limestone plateaux. The N comprises restricted lowlands in the valley of the River Sava. The combined length of two tiny coastlines on the Adriatic is less than 20 km (13 mi).
Climate: Bosnia (the N) has cold winters and warm summers; Herzegovina (the S) enjoys milder winters and warmer summers.

ECONOMY
The economy was devastated by war in 1992. Central and E Bosnia is forested. Agriculture is a major employer

and sheep, maize, olives, grapes and citrous fruit are important. Bosnia has little industry.

HISTORY
From the middle of the 12th century Bosnia came under Hungarian rule. In the 13th century, members of the Kotromanić family conquered Herzegovina and established an independent Bosnian kingdom. Bosnia declined in the 1390s and became a Turkish province in 1436. Under Ottoman rule – during which many Bosnians became Muslims – the region entered a long period of economic stagnation. During the 19th century, several revolts against Turkish rule were put down with ferocity. A major revolt (1875–6) attracted international concern, but the great powers overrode Bosnia's pan-Slavic aspirations at the Congress of Berlin (1877–8; see p. 429) and assigned Bosnia-Herzegovina to Habsburg Austro-Hungarian rule. In Sarajevo in 1914, Gavrilo Princip, a Bosnian student (ethnically a Serb), assassinated Archduke Franz Ferdinand, the heir to the Austro-Hungarian Empire – an event that helped precipitate World War I (see p. 436).

In 1918, Bosnia became part of the new Kingdom of Serbs, Croats and Slovenes, which was renamed Yugoslavia in 1929. Following the German invasion (1941), Bosnia was included in the Axis-controlled puppet state of Croatia. In 1945, when Yugoslavia was reorganized by Marshal Tito on Soviet lines, Bosnia-Herzegovina became a republic within the Communist federation. After the secession of Slovenia and Croatia and the beginning of the Yugoslav civil war (1991), tension grew between Serbs and Croats in Bosnia. The Muslim Bosnians reasserted their separate identity. In 1992, a referendum – which was boycotted by the Serbs – gave a majority in favour of Bosnian independence. International recognition of Bosnia-Herzegovina was gained in April 1992 but Bosnian Serbs, encouraged by Serbia, seized 70% of the country, killing or expelling Muslims and Croats in a campaign of 'ethnic cleansing'. Those areas of Herzegovina inhabited by ethnic Croats were effectively brought within the orbit of Croatia. International peace and humanitarian efforts were attempted.

BOTSWANA

Official name: The Republic of Botswana

Member of: UN, OAU, Commonwealth

Area: 582 000 km² (224 711 sq mi)

Population: 1 320 000 (1991 est)

Capital: Gaborone 130 000 (1991 est)

Languages: English (official), Setswana (national)

Religions: Animist (50%), Protestant Churches (50%)

GOVERNMENT
Thirty-four of the 40 members of the National Assembly

are elected by universal adult suffrage for five years. Of the remainder, four are nominated by the President; the Speaker and Attorney General are non-voting members. The President, who chairs and appoints a Cabinet, is elected for five years by the Assembly.

GEOGRAPHY

A central plateau divides a flat near-desert in the E of Botswana from the Kalahari Desert and Okavango Swamps in the W.

Climate: The climate is subtropical with extremes of heat and occasionally temperatures below freezing. Much of Botswana suffers drought.

ECONOMY

Nomadic cattle herding and the cultivation of subsistence crops occupies the majority of the labour force. The mainstay of the economy is mining for diamonds, copper-nickel and coal.

HISTORY

British missionaries had been active since 1813 in the area, which became the British protectorate of Bechuanaland in 1885. Development was slow, and many Africans had to seek work in South Africa. Nationalism was late to develop, and independence – as Botswana – was granted without a struggle in 1966. Under the first president, Sir Seretse Khama, and his successor, Botswana has succeeded in remaining a democracy.

BRAZIL

Official name: A República Federativa do Brasil (the Federative Republic of Brazil)

Member of: UN, OAS, ALADI, Mercosur

Area: 8 511 965 km² (3 286 488 sq mi)

Population: 153 322 000 (1991 est)

Capital and major cities: Brasília 1 864 000 (city 1 841 000), São Paulo 16 832 000 (city 9 700 000), Rio de Janeiro 11 141 000 (city 5 487 000), Belo Horizonte 3 446 000 (city 2 103 000), Recife 2 924 000 (city 1 336 000), Pôrto Alegre 2 924 000 (city 1 255 000), Salvador 2 362 000 (city 2 075 000), Fortaleza 2 169 000 (city 1 709 000), Curitiba 1 926 000 (city 1 248 000) (1991 est)

Language: Portuguese (official)

Religion: Roman Catholic (89%), Protestant Churches

GOVERNMENT

The President – who appoints a Cabinet – is elected for a five-year term by universal adult suffrage. The lower house of the National Congress (the Chamber of Deputies) has 503 members elected for four years by compulsory universal adult suffrage. The 91 members of the upper house (the Federal Senate) are elected directly for an eight-year term – one third and two thirds of the senators retiring alternately every four years. Each of the 26 states has its own legislature.

GEOGRAPHY

Nearly one half of Brazil is drained by the world's largest river system, the Amazon, whose low-lying basin is still largely covered by tropical rain forest, although pressure on land has encouraged deforestation. N of the Amazon Basin, the Guiana Highlands contain Brazil's highest peak – Pico da Neblina (3014 m / 9888 ft). A central plateau of savannah grasslands lies S of the Basin. In the E and S, a densely populated coastal plain adjoins the Brazilian Highlands – a vast plateau divided by fertile valleys and mountain ranges.

Principal rivers: Amazon 6448 km (4007 mi), Paraná 4880 km (3032 mi)

Climate: The Amazon Basin and the SE coast are tropical with heavy rainfall. The rest of Brazil is either subtropical or temperate (in the savannah). Only the NE has inadequate rainfall.

ECONOMY

Agriculture employs about one quarter of the labour force. The principal agricultural exports include coffee, sugar cane, soyabeans, oranges, beef cattle and cocoa. Timber was important, but environmental concern is restricting its trade. Rapid industrialization since 1945 has made Brazil a major manufacturing country. While textiles, clothing and food processing are still the biggest industries, the iron and steel, chemical, petroleum-refining, cement, electrical, motor-vehicle and fertilizer industries have all attained international stature. Brazil has enormous – and, in part, unexploited – natural resources, including iron ore, phosphates, uranium, copper, manganese, bauxite, coal and vast hydroelectric power potential. In the last two decades, rampant inflation has hindered development.

HISTORY

In 1500, Pedro Cabral claimed Brazil for Portugal (see pp. 410–1). Sugar was introduced in 1532. The plantations were dependent upon slaves, at first using native Indians, but gradually replacing them with Africans. In the 17th and 18th centuries, expansion S and W in search of gold and diamonds brought the Portuguese into conflict with Spain over borders. Threatened by a French invasion, the Portuguese royal family fled to Brazil (1808). The regent Dom João instituted reforms, making Brazil an equal partner with Portugal. In 1821, he returned to Portugal as king, leaving his son Dom Pedro as regent. When Portugal attempted to return Brazil to colonial rule, Pedro proclaimed Brazilian independence with himself as emperor (1822). After losing a war with Argentina (1828), Pedro abdicated (1831) in favour of his son, Pedro II, whose long reign brought stability and economic growth. Opposition from landowners (angered by the abolition of slavery in 1888) and the military (who were excluded from political power) led to a coup and the end of the monarchy in 1889.

The republic was initially stable, but social unrest mounted and, in 1930, Getúlio Vargas seized power. Vargas attempted to model Brazil on Mussolini's Italy, but was overthrown by the military in 1945. Vargas was elected president again (1950), but he committed suicide to avoid impeachment (1954). Short-lived civilian governments preceded a further period of military rule (1964–85), during which the economy expanded rapidly, but political and social rights were restricted. Civilian rule was restored in 1985 and in 1990 Brazilians were able for vote for a president for the first time in 29 years.

BRUNEI

Official name: Negara Brunei Darussalam (Sultanate of Brunei)

Member of: UN, Commonwealth, ASEAN

Area: 5765 km² (2226 sq mi)

Population: 264 000 (1991 est)

Capital: Bandar Seri Begawan 52 000 (1988 est)

Languages: Malay (official; over 50%), Chinese (26%), English

Religion: Sunni Islam (official; 66%), Buddhist (12%)

GOVERNMENT

The Sultan, a hereditary monarch, rules by decree, assisted by a Council of Ministers and a 21-member advisory council, both of which he appoints. There are no political parties.

GEOGRAPHY

Brunei consists of two coastal enclaves. The (larger) western part is hilly; the eastern enclave is more mountainous and forested.

Climate: Brunei has a tropical monsoon climate with rainfall totals in excess of 2500 mm (100 in).

ECONOMY

Exploitation of substantial deposits of petroleum and natural gas has given Brunei one of the world's highest per capita incomes. Most of the country's food has to be imported.

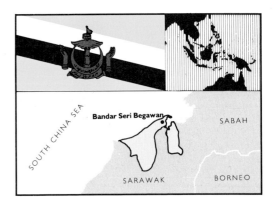

HISTORY

In the 16th century the sultans of Brunei ruled all of Borneo; by the 19th century they held a vastly reduced territory that had become a pirates' paradise. The British restored order and established a protectorate from 1888 to 1971. Oil was discovered in 1929. Independence was restored in 1984 under the absolute rule of Sultan Hassanal Bolkiah, allegedly the world's richest man.

BULGARIA

Official name: Republika Bulgariya (Republic of Bulgaria)

Member of: UN, CSCE

Area: 110 912 km² (42 823 sq mi)

Population: 9 005 000 (1991 est)

Capital and major cities: Sofia (Sofiya) 1 221 000, Plovdiv 379 000, Varna 315 000, Burgas 205 000, Ruse 192 000, Stara Zagora 165 000, Pleven 138 000 (1990 est)

Languages: Bulgarian (official; 89%), Turkish (11%)

Religions: Orthodox (80%), Sunni Islam (8%)

GOVERNMENT
The 240-member National Assembly is elected under a system of proportional representation every five years by universal adult suffrage. The President – who is directly elected for five years – appoints a Prime Minister who commands a majority in the Assembly. The PM, in turn, chooses a Council of Ministers.

GEOGRAPHY
The Balkan Mountains run from E to W across central Bulgaria. To the N, low-lying hills slope down to the River Danube. To the S, a belt of lowland separates the Balkan Mountains from a high, rugged massif, which includes Musala (2925 m / 9596 ft), Bulgaria's highest peak.

Principal river: Danube 2850 km (1770 mi)

Climate: The continental N has warm summers and cold winters, while the SE has a more Mediterranean climate.

ECONOMY
With fertile soils, and few other natural resources, Bulgaria's economy has a strong agricultural base specializing in cereals (wheat, maize, barley), fruit (grapes) and, increasingly, tobacco. Production is centred on large-scale, mechanized cooperatives. Agricultural products are the basis of the food processing, wine and tobacco industries. Other major industries include engineering, fertilizers and chemicals. Bulgaria's trade patterns and economy were disrupted by the collapse of the CMEA East European trading bloc. Industrial production has declined, but progress has been made towards the privatization of industry and agriculture.

HISTORY
The First Bulgarian Empire (681–1018) grew to dominate the Balkans and, under Simeon I (893–927), threatened Constantinople, but was defeated in 1014 by the Byzantine Empire (see p. 395). The Second Bulgarian Empire (1185–1393) succumbed gradually to the Ottoman advance (1362–1393). Five centuries of Turkish rule reduced Bulgarians to illiterate peasantry, but folk memories of past glories remained. Most Bulgarians remained Christian, and a 19th-century national revival sought to restore an independent Church as the first step towards the restoration of nationhood. Russian intervention produced both a Bulgarian Church (1870) and state (1878). The latter was an autonomous principality until 1908, and an independent kingdom until 1946. However, the boundaries, established at the Congress of Berlin (1878), failed to satisfy the Bulgarians, who waged five wars to win the lands they had been promised in the earlier Treaty of San Stefano (1877). Victorious in the first two wars (1885 and 1912), Bulgaria was on the losing side in the final Balkan War (1913) and in World Wars I and II (1915–1918 and 1941–1944), and forfeited territory. After the Red Army invaded (1944), a Communist regime, tied closely to the USSR, was established and the king was exiled (1946). Following popular demonstrations in 1989, the hardline leader Todor Zhivkov (1911–) was replaced by reformers who renounced the Communist Party's leading role. Free elections were held in 1990, since when short-lived coalitions have attempted to tackle Bulgaria's severe economic problems.

BURKINA FASO

Official name: Burkina Faso or République de Burkina (previously Upper Volta)

Member of: UN, OAS, ECOWAS

Area: 274 200 km² (105 869 sq mi)

Population: 9 261 000 (1991 est)

Capital and major cities: Ouagadougou 442 000, Bobo-Dioulasso 229 000, Koudougou 52 000 (1985 est)

Languages: French (official), Mossi (48%), Fulani

Religions: Animist (49%), Sunni Islam (40%)

GOVERNMENT
The constitution provides for elections by universal adult suffrage for a President every seven years, and a 77-member National Assembly every four years.

GEOGRAPHY
The country consists of plateaux about 500 m (1640 ft) high, rising to 747 m (2450 ft).

Principal rivers: Black Volta 1160 km (720 mi), White Volta 640 km (400 mi)

Climate: The country is hot and dry, with adequate rainfall – 1000 mm (40 in) – only in the savannah of the S. The N is semidesert.

ECONOMY
Burkina Faso, one of the world's poorest states, has been severely stricken by drought in the last two decades. Nomadic herdsmen and subsistence farmers – producing mainly sorghum, sugar cane and millet – form the bulk of the population. Cotton, manganese and zinc are exported.

HISTORY
Mossi kingdoms dominated the area for centuries before French rule began in the 1890s. In the colonial era, the country was a labour reservoir for more developed colonies to the S. Since independence in 1960, the country – which kept the name Upper Volta until 1984 – has had a turbulent political history, with a succession of military coups. Multi-party rule was restored in 1992.

BURMA see MYANMAR

BURUNDI

Official name: La République du Burundi/Republika y'Uburundi (The Republic of Burundi)

Member of: UN, OAU

Area: 27 834 km² (10 747 sq mi)

Population: 5 611 000 (1991 est)

Capital: Bujumbura 227 000 (1990 est)

Languages: Kirundi (majority) and French – both official, Kiswahili

Religion: Roman Catholic (65%)

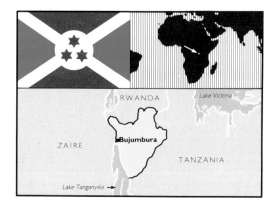

GOVERNMENT
Power is held by a 31-member military committee, whose Chairman is President. The Committee has appointed a civilian Council of Ministers.

GEOGRAPHY
Burundi is a high plateau, rising from Lake Tanganyika in the W to 2685 m / 8809 ft.

Climate: The lowlands are hot and humid. Temperatures are cooler in the mountains.

ECONOMIC ACTIVITY
Over 92% of the labour force is involved in agriculture, producing both subsistence crops and crops for export, such as coffee.

HISTORY
Burundi was kingdom in which the minority Tutsi people dominated the Hutu majority. Colonized by Germany in 1890, it was taken over by Belgium after World War I. Independence came in 1962, after much ethnic conflict. Following a military coup in 1966, a republic was established. The killing of the deposed king in 1972 led to a massacre of the Hutu. There have since been further coups and ethnic unrest.

CAMBODIA

Official name: Roat Kampuchea (Cambodia) – previously known as Kampuchea.

Member of: UN

Area: 181 035 km² (69 898 sq mi)

Population: 8 780 000 (1991 est)

Capital and major cities: Phnom-Penh 900 000 (1991 est), Battambang 45 000 (1987 est)

Languages: Khmer (official), French

Religion: Buddhist (official; majority)

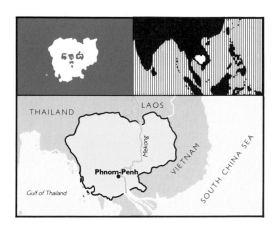

GOVERNMENT
Internationally supervised multi-party elections are scheduled for 1993 for a 123-member National Assembly, which will draft a new constitution. Government is exercised by the existing administration, assisted by the UN, although sovereignty is vested in the hands of a 12-member Supreme National Council, comprising 6 members of the government and two each from the three guerrilla factions that fought in the civil war.

GEOGRAPHY
Central Cambodia consists of fertile plains in the Mekong River valley and surrounding the Tonle Sap (Great Lake). To the N and E are plateaux covered by forests and savannah. The mountains in the S rise to the country's highest point, Phnum Aoral (1813 m / 5947 ft).

Principal river: Mekong 4350 km (2702 mi)

Climate: Cambodia is tropical and humid. The monsoon season (June–November) brings heavy rain to the whole country, with annual totals as high as 5000 mm (200 in) in the mountains.

ECONOMY
Invasion, civil wars, massacres of the civilian population (1976–79) and the (temporary) abolition of currency (in 1978) all but destroyed the economy. Aided by the Vietnamese since 1979, agriculture and – to a lesser extent – industry have been slowly rebuilt, but Cambodia remains one of the world's poorest nations. Rice yields – formerly exported – still fall short of Cambodia's own basic needs.

HISTORY
In the early 9th century, the Khmer king Jayavarman II established the Angkorian dynasty, with a new state religion. By the 12th century, Cambodia dominated mainland SE Asia, but, by the 15th century, Thai and Vietnamese expansion had constricted Cambodia to the Phnom-Penh area. A French protectorate was established in 1863 and continued, apart from Japanese occupation during World War II, until independence in 1953. Throughout this period, the monarchy remained in nominal control. In 1955, King (now Prince) Norodom Sihanouk abdicated to lead a broad coalition government, but he could not prevent Cambodia's involvement in the Vietnam War or allay US fears of his sympathies for the Communists (see pp. 452–53). In 1970 he was overthrown in by a pro-USA military junta, which, in turn, was attacked by Communist Khmer Rouge guerrillas, who sought to create a self-sufficient workers' utopia. The Khmer Rouge were finally victorious in 1975. Under Pol Pot, they forcibly evacuated the towns and massacred up to 2 000 000 of their compatriots. In 1978 Vietnam – Cambodia's traditional foe – invaded, overthrowing the Khmer Rouge. The hostility between the two countries was sharpened by the Sino-Soviet split (see p. 447) in which they took different sides. After Vietnamese troops withdrew in 1989, forces of the exiled government coalition invaded. In 1991 the country's warring factions agreed a peace plan that included free elections and UN supervision, and reduction of all Cambodian forces. A large UN peacekeeping force was deployed (1992) and UN participation in the administration of Cambodia was agreed. However, the Khmer Rouge subsequently withdrew from the peace plan.

CAMEROON

Official name: La République unie du Cameroun (The United Republic of Cameroon)

Member of: UN, OAU

Area: 475 442 km² (183 569 sq mi)

Population: 12 239 000 (1991 est)

Capital and major cities: Yaoundé 712 000, Douala 1 117 000, Nkongsamba 112 000 (1987 est)

Languages: French, English (both official)

Religions: Animist (40%), Sunni Islam (20%), Roman Catholic (20%)

GOVERNMENT
The 180 members of the National Assembly are elected for a five-year term by universal adult suffrage. The President – who is also directly elected for a five-year term – appoints a Council of Ministers.

GEOGRAPHY
In the W, a chain of highlands rises to the volcanic Mount Cameroon at 4069 m (13 353 ft). In the N, savannah plains dip towards Lake Chad. The coastal plains and plateaux in the S and the centre are covered with tropical forest.

Climate: Cameroon is tropical, with hot, rainy conditions on the coast, but drier inland.

ECONOMY
Cameroon is a major producer of cocoa, and other export crops include bananas, coffee, cotton, rubber and palm oil. The petroleum industry is a major foreign-currency earner. The diversity of the economy has given Cameroon one of the highest living standards in tropical Africa.

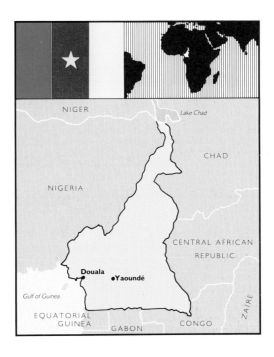

HISTORY
The area fell victim to Portuguese slave traders in the late 15th century. Germany declared a protectorate over Kamerun in 1884. After World War I, Cameroon was divided between the UK and France. The French Cameroons became independent in 1960. Following a plebiscite (1961), the N of the British Cameroons merged with Nigeria; the S federated with the former French territory. A single-party state was established in 1966 and a unitary system replaced the federation in 1972. Political pluralism returned in 1992, when multi-party elections were held.

CANADA

Member of: UN, Commonwealth, OAS, NATO, NAFTA, CSCE, G7

Area: 9 970 610 km² (3 849 674 sq mi)

Population: 26 991 000 (1991 est)

Capital and major cities: Ottawa 864 000 (city 301 000), Toronto 3 752 000 (city 612 000), Montréal 3 068 000 (city 1 015 000), Vancouver 1 547 000 (city 431 000), Edmonton 824 000 (city 574 000), Calgary 723 000 (city 636 000), Winnipeg 647 000 (city 595 000), Québec 622 000 (city 165 000) (1990 est; city populations 1986 census)

Languages: English (62% as a first language; official), French (25% as a first language; official); bilingual 16%

Religions: Roman Catholic (45%), United Church of Canada (15%), Anglican (10%)

Canadian provinces and territories: (with areas, populations and capitals)

Alberta – 661 199 km² (255 285 sq mi), 2 473 000 (1990 est), Edmonton.

British Columbia – 948 596 km² (366 255 sq mi), 3 139 000 (1990 est), Victoria.

Manitoba – 650 087 km² (250 947 sq mi), 1 091 000 (1990 est), Winnipeg.

New Brunswick – 73 437 km² (28 354 sq mi), 724 000 (1990 est), Fredericton.

Newfoundland and Labrador – 404 517 km² (156 185 sq mi), 573 000 (1990 est), St John's.

Nova Scotia – 55 490 km² (21 425 sq mi), 892 000 (1990 est), Halifax.

Ontario – 1 068 582 km² (412 582 sq mi), 9 748 000 (1990 est), Toronto.

Prince Edward Island – 5657 km² (2184 sq mi), 130 000 (1990 est), Charlottetown.

Québec – 1 540 680 km² (594 860 sq mi), 6 771 000 (1990 est), Québec.

Saskatchewan – 652 330 (251 866 sq mi), 1 000 000 (1990 est), Regina.

Northwest Territories – 3 379 285 km² (1 304 903 sq mi), 54 000 (1990 est), Yellowknife.

Yukon Territory – 482 515 km² (186 299 sq mi), 26 000 (1990 est), Whitehorse.

GOVERNMENT
The Canadian Federal Parliament has two houses – a Senate of 118 members appointed by the Governor General to represent the provinces, and the House of Commons, whose 295 members are elected for five years by universal adult suffrage. A Prime Minister, commanding a majority in the House of Commons, is appointed by the Governor General, who is the representative of the British Queen as sovereign of Canada. The PM, in turn, appoints a Cabinet of Ministers which is responsible to the House. Each province has its own government and legislature.

GEOGRAPHY
Nearly one half of Canada is covered by the Laurentian (or Canadian) Shield, a relatively flat region of hard rocks stretching round Hudson's Bay. Inland, the Shield ends in a scarp that is pronounced in the E, beside the lowlands around the St Lawrence River and the Great Lakes. To the W, a line of major lakes (including Lake Winnipeg) marks the boundary with the interior plains, the Prairies. A broad belt of mountains – over 800 km (500 mi) wide – lies W of the plains. This western

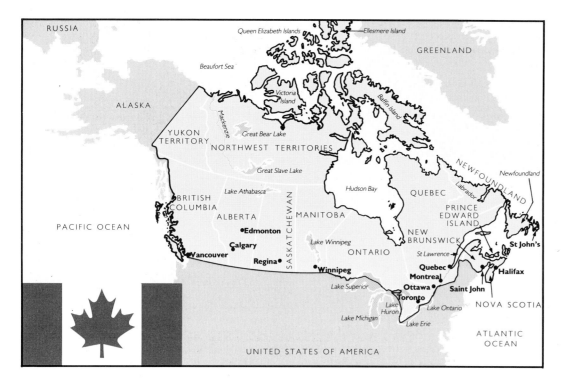

Area: 4033 km² (1557 sq mi)

Population: 341 000 (1991 est)

Capital and major cities: Praia 62 000, Mindelo 47 000 (1990 est)

Languages: Portuguese (official), Crioulu (majority)

Religion Roman Catholic (over 92%)

GOVERNMENT
The 83-member National Assembly is elected for five years by universal adult suffrage. The Assembly elects a President – also for five years – who appoints a Prime Minister and a Council of Ministers.

GEOGRAPHY
Cape Verde consists of ten volcanic, semiarid islands. Fogo Island, with its active volcano, reaches 2829 m (9281 ft).

Climate: Cooled by NE winds, temperatures seldom exceed 27 °C (80 °F). Rainfall is low.

ECONOMY
Lack of surface water hinders agriculture, and over 90% of Cape Verde's food has to be imported. Money sent back by over 700 000 Cape Verdeans living abroad is vital to the economy.

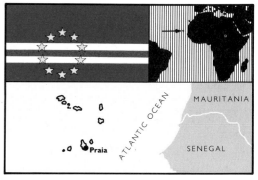

HISTORY
Settled by the Portuguese in the mid-15th century, the islands became a centre of the slave trade. A very mixed and impoverished population resulted. Independence was achieved in 1975 under a Marxist-Leninist regime. A free-market economy and a multi-party system were introduced in 1990.

CENTRAL AFRICAN REPUBLIC

cordillera comprises the Rocky, Mackenzie, Coast and St Elias Mountains, which include Canada's highest point, Mount Logan at 5951 m (19 524 ft). A lower, discontinuous, chain of highlands borders the E of Canada, running from Baffin Island to Nova Scotia.

Principal rivers: Mackenzie-Slave and Peace Rivers 4241 km (2635 mi), St Lawrence 3130 km (1945 mi), Yukon-Nisutlin 3185 km (1979 mi).

Climate: Much of Canada experiences extreme temperatures, with mild summers and long, cold winters. The climate in the far N is polar. Average winter temperatures only remain above freezing point on the Pacific coast. Precipitation is heavy in the W. In the rest of the country, rainfall totals are moderate or light. Most of Canada experiences heavy winter snow falls.

ECONOMY
Canada enjoys one of the highest standards of living in the world, due, in part, to great mineral resources. There are substantial deposits of zinc, nickel, gold, silver, iron ore, uranium, copper, cobalt and lead, as well as major reserves of petroleum and natural gas, and enormous hydroelectric-power potential. These resources are the basis of such industries as petroleum refining, motor vehicles, metal refining, chemicals and iron and steel. Canada is one of the world's leading exporters of cereals – in particular, wheat from the Prairie provinces. Other agricultural interests include fruit (mainly apples), beef cattle and potatoes. Vast coniferous forests have given rise to large lumber, wood-pulp and paper industries. Rich Atlantic and Pacific fishing grounds have made Canada the world's leading exporter of fish and seafood. The country has an important banking and insurance sector, and the economy is closely linked with that of the USA – tariff agreements exist between them.

HISTORY
The ancestors of the Indians came from Asia before 20 000 BC, while those of the Eskimos (Inuit) arrived in around the 6th millennium BC (see p. 390). In the 9th century, Icelanders fished Canadian waters, and after about 1000 short-lived Norse settlements were established in Newfoundland. In 1497, Cabot (see p. 405) explored the Atlantic coast for England, but Canada was claimed for France in 1534 by Cartier. In 1605, the first French colonists settled on the E coast. French settlement increased after the Company of New France was established (1627) to develop Canada. France and England were, however, in competition in Canada.

England claimed Newfoundland in 1583, and, in 1670, the Hudson's Bay Company was founded to assert English control of the vast area draining into Hudson's Bay. During European wars (1701–63), the French and English fought in Canada. France lost Acadia (1713) and – after Wolfe took Québec in the Battle of the Plains of Abraham (1759) – surrendered the rest of French Canada (1763; see p. 417). Britain granted toleration for the religion, institutions and language of the French Canadians.

Many of the loyalists who left the infant United States (see p. 422) settled in Upper Canada (Ontario), which was separated from French-speaking Lower Canada (Québec) in 1791. Severe economic problems, and a lack of political rights, led to rebellion in 1837. After the revolt, Ontario and Québec were united and granted self-government. Settlement spread rapidly W, but there was no national authority to develop the area between Ontario and British Columbia. Britain, anxious to be rid of responsibility for Canada, encouraged confederation, and in 1867 Ontario, Québec, New Brunswick and Nova Scotia formed the Dominion of Canada. Other provinces joined (1870–1905), but Newfoundland did not become part of Canada until 1949. The late 19th century saw important mineral finds, such as the Klondike gold rush, and the western provinces developed rapidly.

In World War I, Canadian forces distinguished themselves at Vimy Ridge, and Canada won itself a place as a separate nation at the peace conferences after the war. The Statute of Westminster (1931) recognized Canadian independence. The Depression of the 1930s (see p. 441) had a severe impact on Canada – Newfoundland, for example, went bankrupt. Canada played an important role in World War II and the Korean War, and was a founder member of NATO. Throughout the 1970s and 1980s, there was friction over the use and status of the French language. Since constitutional amendments recognizing Québec's special status were rejected in 1990, separatist pressure has increased in the province.

CAPE VERDE

Official name: A República de Cabo Verde (The Republic of Cape Verde)

Member of: UN, OAU, ECOWAS

Official name: La République centrafricaine (The Central African Republic)

Member of: UN, OAU

Area: 622 984 km² (240 535 sq mi)

Population: 2 937 000 (1991 est)

Capital and major cities: Bangui 598 000 (1988 est), Bambari 52 000 (1987 est)

Languages: French (official), Sangho (national)

Religions: Various Protestant Churches (48%), Roman Catholic (32%), animist (under 20%)

GOVERNMENT
The President – who appoints a Council of Ministers – is elected for a six-year term by universal adult suffrage. The Congress consists of a 52-member National Assembly (elected directly for a five-year term) and an Economic and Regional Council (half of whose members are elected by the Assembly; the remainder are appointed by the President).

GEOGRAPHY
The country is a low plateau, rising along the border with Sudan to the Bongos Mountains and in the W to the Monts Karre.

Climate: The N is savannah, with little rain between November and March. The S is equatorial with high temperatures and heavy rainfall.

ECONOMY
Subsistence farming dominates, although cotton and coffee are grown for export. Diamonds contribute over 30% of the state's foreign earnings. The country is one of the poorest in the world, largely owing to mismanagement under Bokassa.

HISTORY
French influence began in 1889, and the region became the French colony of Oubangi-Chari in 1903. It suffered greatly from the activities of companies that were granted exclusive rights to large areas of the colony. Independence – as the Central African Republic – was gained in 1960. Jean-Bédel Bokassa took power in a coup in 1965. In 1976 he declared himself emperor and was crowned in an extravagantly expensive ceremony. Revolts by students and schoolchildren helped to end his murderous regime in 1979. A multi-party system has been permitted since 1991.

CHAD

Official name: La République du Tchad (The Republic of Chad)

Member of: UN, OAU

Area: 1 284 000 km² (495 750 sq mi)

Population: 5 823 000 (1991 est)

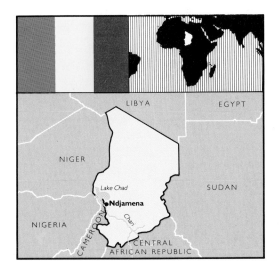

Capital and major cities: N'Djamena 594 000, Sarh 113 000, Moundou 102 000 (1986 est)

Languages: French and Arabic (both official)

Religions: Sunni Islam (50%), animist (25%)

GOVERNMENT
The constitution has provision for a 123-member National Assembly and a President to be elected for five years. Following a military coup in 1991, these provisions have been suspended.

GEOGRAPHY
Deserts in the N include the Tibesti Mountains, where the highest point – Emi Koussi – reaches 3415 m (11 204 ft). Savannah and semidesert in the centre slope down to Lake Chad. The Oubangui Plateau in the S is covered by tropical rain forest.

Climate: Chad is hot and dry in the N, and tropical in the S.

ECONOMY
Chad – one of the poorest countries in the world – has been wracked by civil war and drought. With few natural resources, it relies on subsistence farming, exports of cotton and on foreign aid.

HISTORY
Part of the medieval African empire of Kanem-Bornu, the area around Lake Chad became French in the late 19th century. The French conquest of the N was not completed until 1916. Since independence in 1960, Chad has been torn apart by a bitter civil war between the Muslim Arab N and the Christian and animist Black African S. Libya and France intervened forcefully on several occasions, but neither was able to achieve its aims. In 1987, an uneasy ceasefire was declared, but, following another civil war, military regimes took power in 1990 and 1991 and unrest continues.

CHILE

Official name: República de Chile (The Republic of Chile)

Member of: UN, OAS, ALADI

Area: 756 945 km² (292 258 sq mi)

Population: 13 385 000 (1991 est)

Capital and major cities: Santiago 5 343 000, Valparaiso (legislative capital) 277 000, Concepción 307 000, Viña del Mar 281 000, Talcahuano 247 000 (1991 est)

Language: Spanish (95%), Araucanian (5%)

Religion: Roman Catholic (79%), Protestant Churches

External territory: Chile claims sovereignty over part of Antarctica.

GOVERNMENT
Executive power is held by the President, who appoints a Cabinet of Ministers. The President is elected by universal adult suffrage for a single eight-year term. The National Congress has an upper chamber – of 38 senators directly elected for eight years and 10 senators appointed by the President – and a lower chamber of 120 deputies elected for four years by universal adult suffrage.

GEOGRAPHY
For almost 4000 km (2500 mi), the Andes form the eastern boundary of Chile. They rise to 6895 m (22 588 ft) at Ojos del Solado. Parallel to the Andes is a depression, in which lies the Atacama Desert in the N and fertile plains in the centre. A mountain chain runs between the depression and the coast, and, in the S, forms a string of islands.

Climate: The temperate climate is influenced by the cool Humboldt Current. Rainfall ranges from being negligible in the Atacama Desert in the N to heavy – over 2300 mm (90 in) – in the S.

ECONOMY
Agriculture employs nearly one fifth of the labour force. The central plains – the main agricultural region – grow

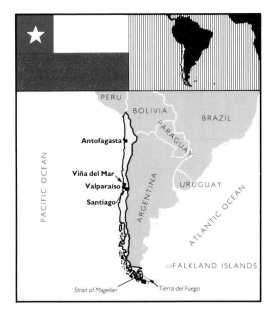

cereals (mainly wheat and maize) and fruit (notably grapes). Major fishing grounds yield a large catch of fish. There are considerable mineral resources and great hydroelectric-power potential. Chile is the world's largest exporter of copper, and has major reserves of iron ore, coal, petroleum and natural gas. Industry includes food processing, timber industries and textiles.

HISTORY
During the 15th century the Incas (see p. 391) moved into Chile, but were halted by the fierce Araucanian Indians. The Spanish approached Chile from Peru in 1537, and Pedro de Valdivia founded Santiago in 1541. Continuing S, Valdivia was killed by the Araucanians (1554), who were not finally defeated until the late 19th century. In 1810, a revolt – led by Bernardo O'Higgins (?1778–1842) – broke out against Spain. In 1817, troops led by José de San Martín crossed from Argentina to aid O'Higgins, who led Chile to independence in 1818. O'Higgins offended the powerful landowners and was exiled in 1823. For the next century – during which Chile gained territory in two wars against Peru and Bolivia – conservative landowners held power.

Between the late 1920s and the 1940s, Chile was governed by liberal and radical regimes, but social and economic change was slow. The election of the Christian Democrats (1964) brought some reforms, but not until Salvador Allende's Marxist government was elected in 1970 were major changes – including land reform – realized. Chile was polarized between right and left, and political chaos resulted in a US-backed military coup led by General Augusto Pinochet in 1973. Tens of thousands of leftists were killed, imprisoned or exiled by the junta. Pinochet reversed Allende's reforms, restructuring the economy in favour of landowners and exporters. Pressure on the dictatorship from within Chile and abroad brought the return of democratic rule in 1990.

CHINA

Official name: Zhonghua Renmin Gongheguo (The People's Republic of China)

Member of: UN

Area: 9 571 300 km² (3 695 500 sq mi)

Population: 1 150 000 000 (1991 est), Han (Chinese; 92%), with Mongol, Tibetan, Uighur, Manchu and other minorities

Capital and major cities: Beijing (Peking) 10 819 000, Shanghai 13 342 000, Tientsin 8 785 000, Shenyang 4 500 000, Wuhan 3 710 000, Guangzhou (Canton) 3 540 000, Chongquin 2 960 000, Harbin 2 800 000,

Chengdu 2 780 000, Xian 2 710 000, Nanjing (Nanking) 2 470 000, Zibo 2 430 000, Dalian (Darien) 2 370 000, Jinan 2 290 000, Changchun 2 070 000, Qingdao 2 040 000, Shenzhen 2 000 000, with 24 other urban municipalities with over 1 million inhabitants (1990 census)

Languages: Chinese (Guoyo or 'Mandarin' dialect in the majority, with local dialects in S and SE, e.g. Cantonese), small Mongol, Tibetan and other minorites

Religions: Officially atheist but those religions and philosophies practised include Confucianism and Daoism (over 20% together), Buddhism (c. 15%)

m / 29 078 ft). In the far S, the Yunnan Plateau rises to nearly 3700 m (12 000 ft), while in the far NE, ranges of hills and mountains almost enclose the NE Plain, formerly known as Manchuria. The Nan Ling Range of hills and mountains crosses central China and separates the basins of the Yellow (Huang He) and Yangtze (Chang Jiang). In E and central China, three great lowlands support intensive agriculture and dense populations – the plains of central China, the Sichuan Basin and the North China Plain. A vast loess plateau, deeply dissected by ravines, lies between the Mongolian

large-scale production is on collective farms, but traditional and inefficient practices remain. Almost half the arable land is irrigated, and China is the world's largest producer of rice. Other major crops include wheat, maize, sweet potatoes, sugar cane and soyabeans. Livestock, fruit, vegetables and fishing are also important, but China is unable to supply all its own food. Mineral and fuel resources are considerable and, for the most part, underdeveloped. They include coal, petroleum, natural gas, iron ore, bauxite, tin and antimony in major reserves, as well as huge hydroelectric power potential. The economy is centrally planned, with all industrial plant owned by the state. Petrochemical products account for nearly one quarter of China's exports. Other major industries include iron and steel, cement, vehicles, fertilizers, food processing, clothing and textiles. Recent reforms have promoted an 'open-door' policy under which joint ventures with other countries and foreign loans have been encouraged, together with a degree of small-scale private enterprise. Special Economic Zones and 'open cities' were designated in the S and central coastal areas to encourage industrial links with the W. Although foreign investment temporarily diminished after the 1989 pro-democracy movement was suppressed, sustained economic progress has been achieved in the Shanghai area and in southern China, in particular Guangdong where the new city of Shenzhen (near Hong Kong) is the centre of major industrial development. Very high growth rates have been achieved during the past decade.

HISTORY
The history of China is covered on pp. 382–3 and 446–7.

CHINA, REPUBLIC OF (TAIWAN)

Official name: Chung-hua Min Kuo (The Republic of China)

Area: 35 981 km² (13 893 sq mi)

Population: 20 489 000 (1991 est)

Capital and major cities: Taipei 2 720 000, Kaohsiung 1 393 000, Taichung 762 000 (1990 est)

Language: Chinese (northern or Amoy dialect)

Religions: Buddhist (24%), Daoist (14%), Roman Catholic (14%)

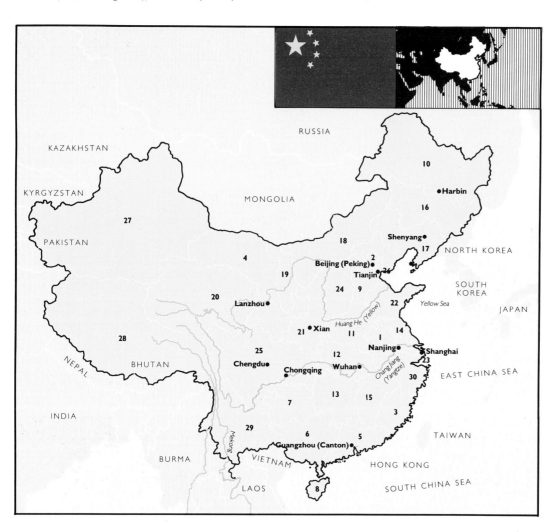

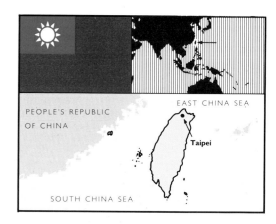

GOVERNMENT
The 2978 deputies of the National People's Congress are elected for a five-year term by the People's Congresses of the 22 provinces, five autonomous provinces and three municipal provinces, and by the army. The Congress elects a Standing Committee, a President (for a five-year term), a Prime Minister and a State Council (or Cabinet) – all of whom are responsible to the Congress. The only legal party is the Chinese Communist Party, which holds a Congress every five years. The Party Congress elects a Central Committee, which in turn elects a Politburo, and it is these two bodies that hold effective power.

GEOGRAPHY
China is the third largest country in the world in area and the largest in population. Almost half of China comprises mountain chains, mainly in the W, including the Altaï and Tien Shan Mountains in Xinjiang Uygur, and the Kun Lun Mountains to the N of Tibet. The Tibetan Plateau – at an altitude of 3000 m (10 000 ft) – is arid. In the S of Tibet is the Himalaya, containing 40 peaks over 7000 m (23 000 ft), including Mt Everest (8863

Plateau – which contains the Gobi Desert – and the deserts of the Tarim and Dzungarian Basins in the NW.

Principal rivers: Yangtze (Chang Jiang) 6300 km (3915 mi), Huang He (Yellow River) 5464 km (3395 mi), Xijiang (Sikiang) 2197 km (1323 mi)

Climate: In general, temperatures increase from N to S, and rainfall increases from NW to SE. NE China has a continental climate with warm and humid summers, long cold winters, and rainfall under 750 mm (30 in). The central lowlands contain the hottest areas of China, and have 750 to 1100 mm (30 to 40 in) of rainfall. The S is wetter, while the extreme subtropical S experiences the monsoon. The continental loess plateau is cold in the winter, warm in summer and has under 500 mm (20 in) of rain. The NW is arid, continental and experiences cold winters. The W – Tibet, Xinjiang Uygur, Gansu and Nei Monggol – experiences an extreme climate owing to its altitude and distance from the sea; rainfall is low and most of Tibet has ten months of frost.

ECONOMY
Agriculture occupies 60% of the labour force. All

GOVERNMENT
Under the terms of a new constitution (1991), the National Assembly comprises 325 members elected by universal adult suffrage for six years. The Assembly elects a President for a six-year term. The President appoints a Prime Minister and a Council of Ministers.

GEOGRAPHY
Taiwan is an island 160 km (100 mi) off the SE coast of

China. Its mountainous interior rises in the S to Yu Shan at 3997 m (13 113 ft). Most of the inhabitants live on the coastal plain in the W.

Climate: Taiwan – which is subtropical in the N, and tropical in the S – has rainy summers and mild winters. Tropical cyclones (typhoons) may occur between July and September.

ECONOMY
Despite Taiwan's diplomatic isolation, the island is a major international trading nation, exporting machinery, electronics, and textiles. Mineral resources include coal, marble, gold, petroleum and natural gas. Despite the fertility of the soil, agriculture has declined in relative importance.

HISTORY
Taiwan was originally inhabited by Malays and Polynesians. The first settlers from China came in the 7th century. Named Formosa ('beautiful') by the Portuguese in 1590, the island was the object of Spanish-Portuguese rivalry and then briefly (1662–83) independent under the Chinese general Koxinga. A period of Chinese rule and renewed migration lasted until a Japanese takeover (1895) began the modernization of agriculture, transport and education. In 1949, the Nationalist forces of Jiang Jie Shi (Chiang Kai-shek) were driven onto Taiwan by the Communist victory on the mainland (see pp. 446–47). Under US protection, the resulting authoritarian regime on Taiwan declared itself the Republic of China, and claimed to be the legitimate government of all China. America's rapprochement with the mainland People's Republic of China (see p. 447) lost Taiwan its UN seat in 1971 and US recognition in 1978. In 1991 Taiwan effectively recognized Communist China, but the island's international status remains problematic. By the late 1980s Taiwan was moving cautiously towards democracy, and in 1988 a native Taiwanese was elected President. A new constitution in 1991 marked the transition to a more Taiwanese, less Chinese, identity.

COLOMBIA

Official name: La República de Colombia (The Republic of Colombia)

Member of: UN, OAS, ALADI, Andean Pact

Area: 1 141 748 km² (440 831 sq mi)

Population: 33 613 000 (1991 est)

Capital and major cities: (Santa Fé de) Bogotá 4 820 000, Medellín 2 121 000, Cali 1 637 000, Barranquilla 1 029 000, Cartagena 564 000 (all including suburbs; 1990 est)

Languages: Spanish, over 150 Indian languages

Religions: Roman Catholic (official; over 95%)

GOVERNMENT
A President (who appoints a Cabinet of 13 members), a Senate of 102 members and a House of Representatives of 161 members are elected for a four-year term by universal adult suffrage.

GEOGRAPHY
The Andes run N to S through Colombia, reaching their highest point in the country at Pico Cristóbal Colón (5775 m / 18 947 ft). The greater part of Colombia lies E of the Andes in the mainly treeless grassland plains of the Llanos and the tropical Amazonian rain forest. A coastal plain lies to the W of the mountains.

Climate: The lower Andes are temperate; the mountains over 4000 m (13 100 ft) experience perpetual snow. The rest of the country is tropical. The coasts and the Amazonian Basin are hot and humid, with heavy rainfall. The Llanos have a savannah climate.

ECONOMY
Colombian coffee is the backbone of the country's exports; other cash crops include bananas, sugar cane, flowers and tobacco. However, profits from the illegal cultivation and export of marijuana and cocaine produce much revenue. Mineral resources include iron ore,

silver, coal, petroleum and natural gas. The main industries are food processing, petroleum refining, fertilizers, cement, textiles, clothing, and iron and steel.

HISTORY
The Spanish reached Colombia's N coast in 1500, and founded their first settlement in 1525. Meeting little resistance from the Indians, the conquistadores advanced inland reaching Bogotá in 1538. In 1718 the Viceroyalty of Nueva Granada was established at Bogotá. The struggle for independence from Spain (1809–1819) was fierce and bloody. Almost from that time, the centralizing pro-clerical Conservatives and the federalizing anti-clerical Liberals have struggled for control leading to civil wars (1899–1902 and 1948–1957) in which 400 000 people died. From 1957 to 1974 there were agreements between the Liberals and Conservatives to protect a fragile democracy threatened by left-wing guerrillas and right-wing death squads. In the early 1990s, a combination of security measures and amnesties curbed the activities of powerful drug-trafficking cartels, and left-wing guerrillas abandoned their armed struggle in favour of legitimate political activity.

COMOROS

Official name: La République fédérale islamique des Comores (The Federal Islamic Republic of the Comoros)

Member of: UN, OAU

Area: 1862 km² (719 sq mi) (excluding Mayotte, which is administered by France)

Population: 479 000 (1991 est; excluding Mayotte)

Capital: Moroni 60 000 (city 22 000; 1987 est)

Languages: French and Arabic – both official, Comoran (a blend of Swahili and Arabic)

Religion: Sunni Islam (official; 99%)

GOVERNMENT
The President – who is elected for a six-year term by universal adult suffrage – appoints a Council of Ministers. The 42 members of the Federal Assembly are directly elected for five years.

GEOGRAPHY
Ngazidja (Grande Comore) – the largest island – is dry and rocky, rising to an active volcano, Mount Kartala (2361 m / 7746 ft). Ndzouani (Anjouan) is a heavily-

eroded volcanic massif. Moili (Mohéli) is a forested plateau with fertile valleys.

Climate: The tropical climate of the Comoros is dry from May to October, but with heavy rain for the rest of the year.

ECONOMY
Poor and eroded soils, overpopulation and few resources combine to make these underdeveloped islands one of the world's poorest countries. Subsistence farming occupies the majority of the population, although vanilla, cloves and ylang-ylang are produced for export.

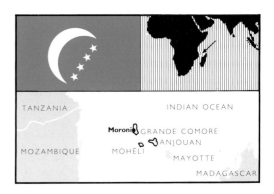

HISTORY
The four Comoran islands became a French colony in 1912. In a referendum in 1974, three islands voted to become independent, which they declared themselves without French agreement. The fourth island, Mayotte, voted against independence, and remains under French rule. From 1978 to 1990, when free elections were held, the republic was an Islamic single-party state.

CONGO

Official name: La République du Congo (The Republic of the Congo)

Member of: UN, OAU

Area: 342 000 km² (132 047 sq mi)

Population: 2 411 000 (1991 est)

Capital and major cities: Brazzaville 760 000, Pointe-Noire 388 000 (1990 est)

Languages: French (official), Lingala patois (50%), Monokutuba patois (40%), Kongo (45%), Teke (20%)

Religion: Roman Catholic (53%), animist (25%)

GOVERNMENT

The 153-member Assembly and the President – who appoints a Premier and a Council of Ministers – are elected for a five-year term by universal adult suffrage.

GEOGRAPHY

Behind a narrow coastal plain, the plateaux of the interior are covered by tropical rain forests and rise to over 700 m (2300 ft).

Principal river: Zaïre (Congo) 4700 km (2920 mi)

Climate: The Congo's tropical climate is hot and humid. Rainfall exceeds 1200 mm (47 in) a year.

ECONOMY

Petroleum and timber are the mainstays of the economy, which was centrally-planned until 1991. Congo is crippled by external debt. Subsistence agriculture – chiefly for cassava – occupies over 30% of the labour force.

HISTORY

Portuguese slave traders were active in the region from the 15th century. In the 1880s, the explorer Brazza placed the kingdom of the Teke people under French protection, and in 1905 the region became the colony of Moyen-Congo. Independence was gained in 1960. A Marxist-Leninist state was established in 1963, but a multi-party system was restored in 1991.

COSTA RICA

Official name: República de Costa Rica (The Republic of Costa Rica)

Member of: UN, OAS, CACM

Area: 51 100 km² (19 730 sq mi)

Population: 3 088 000 (1991 est)

Capital and major cities: San José 1 040 000 (city 294 000), Alajuela 158 000, Cartago 109 000 (1990 est)

Language: Spanish (official)

Religions: Roman Catholic (official)

GOVERNMENT Executive power is vested in the President, who appoints a Cabinet of Ministers. The President and the 57-member Legislative Assembly are elected for four-year terms by compulsory universal adult suffrage.

GEOGRAPHY

Between a narrow plain on the Pacific coast and a wider plain along the Caribbean coast rise a central plateau and mountain ranges whose highest point is Chirripó Grande at 3820 m (12 533 ft).

Climate: Rainfall is heavy along the Caribbean coast, but the Pacific coast is drier. Temperatures are warm in the lowlands, cooler in the highlands.

ECONOMY

Coffee is Costa Rica's major export. Bananas, sugar cane, beef cattle, cocoa and timber are also important.

HISTORY

Columbus reached Costa Rica during his final voyage in 1502. The area was under Spanish rule – as part of Guatemala – until 1821. Although it was part of the Central American Federation (1823–38), Costa Rica developed largely in isolation from its neighbours. Dominated by small farms, Costa Rica prospered, attracted European immigrants and developed a stable democracy. Following a brief civil war in 1948, the army was disbanded. Costa Rica has since adopted the role of peacemaker in Central America.

COTE D'IVOIRE

Official name: La République de la Côte d'Ivoire (The Republic of the Ivory Coast). Since 1986 Côte d'Ivoire has been the only official name.

Member of: UN, OAU, ECOWAS

Area: 322 462 km² (124 503 sq mi)

Population: 12 464 000 (1991 est)

Capital and major cities: Yamoussoukro (capital *de jure* and administrative capital) 120 000, Abidjan (legislative capital) 1 850 000, Bouaké 220 000 (1987 est)

Languages: French (official), Bete (20%), Senufo (14%)

Religions: Animist (60%), Christian (mainly Roman Catholic; 20%), Sunni Islam (20%)

GOVERNMENT

The President – who is elected for a five-year term by universal adult suffrage – appoints a Prime Minister and a Council of Ministers. The 175-member National Assembly is also directly elected for five years.

GEOGRAPHY

The N is a savannah-covered plateau rising to 1752 m (5748 ft) at Mont Nimba. In the S, tropical rain forest – increasingly cleared for plantations – ends at the narrow coastal plain.

Climate: The S is equatorial with high temperatures and heavy rainfall; the N has similar temperatures but is drier.

ECONOMY

The country depends on exports of cocoa, coffee and timber, and suffered in the 1980s when prices for these commodities fell. Natural resources include petroleum, natural gas and iron ore. Political stability has helped economic growth.

HISTORY

In the 16th century, Europeans established posts in the area for trading in ivory and slaves. Colonized by France in the 19th century, the Ivory Coast became a relatively prosperous part of French West Africa. Independence was achieved in 1960 under the presidency of Félix Houphouët-Boigny (1905–), who has kept close links with France in return for aid and military assistance, and is Africa's longest serving president. After over a decade of single-party rule, multi-party elections were held in 1990, but the opposition claimed electoral fraud.

CROATIA

Official name: Republika Hrvatska (The Republic of Croatia)

Member of: UN, CSCE

Area: 56 538 km² (21 829 sq mi), including the area (about one third) that is controlled by Serb forces

Population: 4 760 000 (1991 census). Since 1992 Croatia has received over 400 000 refugees from Bosnia

Capital and major cities: Zagreb 1 176 000 (city 704 000), Split 236 000 (city 189 000), Rijeka 193 000 (city 168 000) (1991 census)

Languages: Croat (75%) – the form of Serbo-Croat written in the Latin alphabet; Serbian (24%)

Religions: Roman Catholic majority, Orthodox minority

GOVERNMENT

The 356-member Parliament and an executive President are directly elected. A Prime Minister and Cabinet are appointed by the President.

GEOGRAPHY

Croatia comprises plains in the E (Slavonia), hills around Zagreb, and barren limestone ranges running parallel to the Dalmatian coast. Dubrovnik is detached from the rest of Croatia.

Climate: The interior is colder and drier than the Mediterranean coast.

ECONOMY

Manufacturing (aluminium, textiles and chemicals), mining (bauxite) and oil dominate the economy. Slavonia grows cereals, potatoes and sugar beet. In 1991–2 the economy was damaged by the Yugoslav civil war, and the lucrative Dalmatian tourist industry collapsed.

HISTORY

By the 10th century the Croat kingdom occupied most of modern Croatia. In 1102 Croatia passed to the Hungarian crown. After Slavonia was conquered by the Ottoman Turks (1526), the rump of Croatia came under the rule of the (Austrian) Habsburgs, who established a Serb military frontier zone (Krajina) against further

Ottoman expansion. Dalmatia came under Venetian rule in the 15th century, was annexed by Napoleon I in 1808, and was ceded to Austria in 1815. Ragusa (Dubrovnik) was an independent city-state from the 9th century to 1808. The Croats strove to preserve their identity within Habsburg Hungary and attempted secession during the 1848–9 Hungarian revolt. By 1900 a Croat national revival looked increasingly to independent Serbia to create a South ('Yugo') Slav state.

After World War I when the Habsburg Empire was dissolved (1918), the Croats joined the Serbs, Slovenes and Montenegrins in the state that was to become Yugoslavia in 1929. However, the Croats soon resented the highly centralized Serb-dominated kingdom. Following the German invasion (1941), the occupying Axis powers set up an 'independent' Croat puppet state that adopted anti-Serb policies. In 1945 Croatia was reintegrated into a federal Communist Yugoslav state by Marshal Tito, but after Tito's death (1980), the Yugoslav experiment faltered in economic and nationalist crises. Separatists came to power in Croatia in free elections (1990) and declared independence (June 1991). Serb insurgents, backed by the Yugoslav federal army, occupied 30% of Croatia including those areas with an ethnic Serb majority – Krajina and parts of Slavonia. The fierce Serbo-Croat war came to an uneasy halt in 1992 after Croatian independence had gained widespread diplomatic recognition and a UN peace-keeping force was agreed. Fighting in Krajina recommenced in 1993.

CUBA

Official name: La República de Cuba (The Republic of Cuba)

Member of: UN, OAS (suspended)

Area: 110 860 km² (42 803 sq mi)

Population: 10 700 000 (1991 est)

Capital and major cities: Havana (La Habana) 2 096 000, Santiago de Cuba 405 000, Camagüey 283 000, Holguín 228 000, Guantánamo 200 000 (1990 est)

Language: Spanish

Religion: Roman Catholic (39%)

GOVERNMENT
The Communist Party is the only legal political party. The 499-member National Assembly is directly elected for two and a half years by citizens aged 16 and over. The Assembly elects 31 of its members to form the Council of State, whose President – as head of state and government – appoints a Council of Ministers.

GEOGRAPHY
Three ranges of hills and mountains run E to W across Cuba, rising to 1971 m (6467 ft) at Pico Turquino.

Climate: The climate is semitropical. Temperatures

average 26 °C (78 °F), and rainfall is heavy. The island is subject to hurricanes.

ECONOMY
Sugar (the leading export), tobacco and coffee are the main crops. State-controlled farms occupy most of the land but are unable to meet Cuba's food needs. Rationing is in force. Nickel is Cuba's second most important export. The end of the Communist CMEA trade bloc and of Soviet subsidies have brought the Cuban economy to the verge of collapse.

HISTORY
Indian tribes inhabited Cuba when Columbus claimed the island for Spain (1492). Development was slow until the 18th century, when black slaves were imported to work the sugar plantations. The first war for independence (1868–78) was unsuccessful. The USA intervened in a second uprising (1895–98), forcing Spain to relinquish the island, but independence was not confirmed until after two periods of American administration (1899–1901 and 1906–9).

Under a succession of corrupt governments, the majority of Cubans suffered abject poverty. In 1959, the dictatorship of Fulgencio Batista was overthrown by the guerrilla leader Fidel Castro (1926–), whose revolutionary movement merged with the Communist Party to remodel Cuba on Soviet lines. In 1961, US-backed Cuban exiles attempted to invade at the Bay of Pigs, and relations with America deteriorated further in 1962 when the installation of Soviet missiles on Cuba almost led to world war. Castro encouraged revolutionary movements throughout Latin America, and his troops bolstered Marxist governments in Africa. The upheavals in the USSR and Eastern Europe (1989–91) left Cuba increasingly isolated as a hardline Marxist state.

CYPRUS

Official name: Kypriaki Dimokratia (in Greek) or Kibris Cumhuriyeti (in Turkish) (The Republic of Cyprus)

Member of: UN, Commonwealth, CSCE

Area: 9251 km² (3572 sq mi)

Population: 748 000 (1991 est)

Capital and major cities: Nicosia 338 000 (including the Turkish Cypriot zone Lefkosa), Limassol 135 000, Larnaca 63 000 (1990 est)

Languages: Greek (80%), Turkish (19%)

Religions: Orthodox (80%), Sunni Islam (19%)

GOVERNMENT A 56-member House of Representatives is elected by universal adult suffrage in the Greek Cypriot community for five years – an additional 24 seats for the Turkish Cypriot community remain unfilled. The President – who appoints a Council of Ministers – is elected from the Greek Cypriot community by universal adult suffrage for a five-year term. There is provision in the constitution for a Vice President to be similarly elected from the Turkish Cypriot community. In 1975, the administration of the Turkish Cypriot community unilaterally established the 'Turkish Republic of Northern Cyprus', which is unrecognized internationally except by Turkey.

GEOGRAPHY
The S of the island is covered by the Troodos Mountains, which rise to Mount Olympus 1951 m (6399 ft). Running E to W across the centre of Cyprus is a fertile plain, N of which are the Kyrenian Mountains and the Karpas Peninsula.

Climate: Cyprus has a Mediterranean climate with hot dry summers and mild, variable winters.

ECONOMIC ACTIVITY
Potatoes, fruit, wine, clothing and textiles are exported from the Greek Cypriot area, in which ports, resorts and an international airport have been constructed to replace facilities lost since partition. The Turkish Cypriot area – which exports fruit, potatoes and tobacco

– relies heavily on aid from Turkey. Tourism is important in both zones.

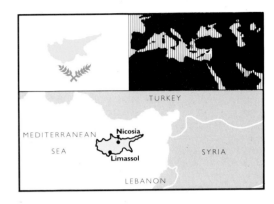

HISTORY
Greek settlements were established on Cyprus in the middle of the second millenium BC. The island was ruled by the Egyptians (from 323 BC) and was part of the Roman and Byzantine Empires. Captured by Crusaders (1191), Cyprus was an independent kingdom until 1489, when Venice acquired the island. In 1571, the Ottoman Turks took Cyprus. British administration was established in 1878. During the 1950s, Greek Cypriots, led by Archbishop (later President) Makarios III (1913–77), campaigned for Enosis (union with Greece). The Turkish Cypriots advocated partition, but following a terrorist campaign by the Greek Cypriot EOKA movement, a compromise was agreed. In 1960, Cyprus became an independent republic. Power was shared by the two communities, but the agreement broke down in 1963. UN forces intervened to stop intercommunal fighting. The Turkish Cypriots set up their own administration. When pro-Enosis officers staged a coup (1974), Turkey invaded the N. Cyprus was effectively partitioned. Over 200 000 Greek Cypriots were displaced from the N, into which settlers arrived from Turkey. Since then, UN forces have manned the 'Attila Line' between the Greek S and Turkish N. Attempts have been made to reunite Cyprus as a federal state.

CZECH REPUBLIC

Official name: Ceská Republika (Czech Republic)

Member of: UN, CSCE

Area: 78 880 km² (30 456 sq mi)

Population: 10 299 000 (1991 census)

Capital and major cities: Prague (Praha) 1 212 000, Brno 388 000, Ostrava 328 000 (1991 census)

Language: Czech

Religions: Roman Catholic (39%), Hussite (8%)

GOVERNMENT
The 200-member Assembly is elected by universal adult suffrage for five years. The Assembly elects a President, who appoints a Prime Minister and Government responsible to the Assembly.

GEOGRAPHY
In the W (Bohemia), the Elbe basin is ringed on three sides by uplands. The Moravian plain lies to the E of Bohemia. The highest point is Snezka at 1603 m (5259 ft).

Climate: The climate is continental with cold winters and warm summers.

ECONOMY
Apart from coal, there are few mineral resources, but the country is heavily industrialized and some areas have suffered heavy pollution. Manufactures include industrial machinery, motor vehicles and consumer goods. The country is switching from a state-controlled to a free-market economy, and has increasingly attracted foreign investment (80% German) and its economy is

increasingly linked to that of Germany. The timber industry is important. The main crops include wheat, maize, potatoes, barley and sugar beet.

HISTORY
Slavs first populated the region from the 5th century AD. A Moravian empire flourished in the 9th century, and, after its decline in the 11th century, the kingdom of Bohemia rose. In the 14th century, the greatest of the Czech kings, Charles IV, became Holy Roman Emperor. His support of Church reform eventually led to the Bohemian revolt against Rome known as the Hussite movement (see also p. 403). In 1526 Bohemia fell under Habsburg rule (see p. 410). The determination of the Catholic Habsburgs to control the mainly Protestant Czech nobility led to the Thirty Years' War (see p. 409). In 1620, the Czechs were defeated and remained under Austrian rule until 1918.

Nationalism grew in the 19th century, and on the collapse of the Austro-Hungarian Empire, the Czechs and Slovaks united in an independent state (1918) – largely due to the efforts of Thomas Masaryk, who became Czechoslovakia's first president. In 1938, Hitler demanded that Germany be granted the Sudetenland, where Germans predominated. Lacking allies, Czechoslovakia was dismembered (see p. 443). The Nazi occupation included the massacre of the inhabitants of Lidice (1942). Following liberation (1945), a coalition government was formed, but the Communists staged a takeover in 1948. In 1968, moves by Party Secretary Alexander Dubček to introduce political reforms met with Soviet disapproval, and invasion by Czechoslovakia's Warsaw Pact allies. In 1989, student demonstrations developed into a peaceful revolution led by the Civic Forum movement. Faced by overwhelming public opposition, the Communist Party renounced its leading role and hardline leaders were replaced by reformers. A coalition government was appointed and Civic Forum's leader – the playwright Vaclav Havel – was elected president. Free multi-party elections were held (1990), Soviet forces withdrawn (1991) and Czechoslovakia strengthened ties with Western Europe. Increased Slovak nationalism led to the division of the country in 1993, when the secession of poorer, more rural, Slovakia left the more developed Czech Republic as a likely eventual member of the EC.

DENMARK

Official name: Kongeriget Danmark (Kingdom of Denmark)

Member of: UN, EC, NATO, CSCE, OECD

Area: 43 092 km² (16 638 sq mi) – 'metropolitan' Denmark, excluding dependencies

Population: 5 194 000 (including Faeroes; 1991 census)

Capital and major cities: Copenhagen (København) 1 337 000 (city 465 000), Aarhus (Århus) 264 000, Odense 178 000, Aalborg (Ålborg) 156 000, Esbjerg 82 000 (all including suburbs; 1991 census)

Language: Danish

Religion: Lutheran (91%)

Danish autonomous dependencies: (with areas, populations and capitals):
Faeroe Islands – 1399 km² (540 sq mi), 48 400 (1990 est), Tórshavn.
Greenland – 2 175 600 km² (840 000 sq mi), 55 500 (1991 est), Nuuk (formerly known as Godthab).

GOVERNMENT
Denmark is a constitutional monarchy. The 179-member Parliament (Folketing) are elected by universal adult suffrage under a system of proportional representation for a four-year term. Two members are elected from both of the autonomous dependencies. The Monarch appoints a Prime Minister, who commands a majority in the Folketing. The PM appoints a State Council (Cabinet), which is responsible to the Folketing.

GEOGRAPHY
Denmark is a lowland of glacial moraine – only Bornholm, in the Baltic, has ancient hard surface rocks. The highest point, Yding Skovhøj – at 173 m (568 ft) – is on the Jutland Peninsula. The islands to the E of Jutland make up nearly one third of the country.

Climate: The climate is temperate and moist, with mild summers and cold winters. Bornholm – to the E – is more extreme.

ECONOMY
Denmark has a high standard of living, but few natural resources. Agriculture is organized on a cooperative basis, and produces cheese and other dairy products, bacon and beef – all mainly for export. About 20% of the labour force is involved in manufacturing, with iron and metal working, food processing, brewing, engineering and chemicals as the major industries. Petroleum and natural gas from the North Sea have reduced the costly burden of fuel imports.

HISTORY
Denmark became a distinct state in the 10th century. The Danes participated in the Viking invasions, which saw settlers and raiders penetrate much of W Europe, and, under Cnut, a short-lived Anglo-Danish empire was established (see p. 397). Medieval Denmark was beset by territorial wars and dynastic difficulties – the monarchy

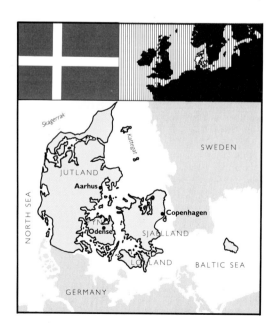

remained elective until 1660. Norway was acquired in 1380, and under the Kalmar Agreement (1397), Queen Margrethe I united all three Scandinavian kingdoms, but Sweden reasserted its independence in 1583. The Roman Catholic faction was defeated in a civil war (1534–36), and Lutheranism became the state religion. In the 17th century, Denmark was overshadowed by Sweden, its rival for control of the entrance to the Baltic. The Danes were defeated by Imperial forces in the Thirty Years' War (1626; see p. 409), but a decline in Swedish power after 1660 allowed Denmark to reassert itself.

Colonial ventures in the 18th century brought prosperity. An alliance with Napoleonic France proved disastrous, and in 1815 Denmark lost Norway to Sweden. The duchies of Schleswig and Holstein became the subject of a complicated dispute with Prussia (see p. 428). After a short war with Prussia and Austria (1864), Denmark surrendered the duchies, but N Schleswig was returned to Denmark in 1920. In the 20th century, Denmark's last colonial possessions were either sold (Virgin Islands) or given independence (Iceland) or autonomy (Greenland). The country was occupied by Nazi Germany (1940–45), and has since been a member of the Western Alliance. From the 1960s, Denmark's economic and political ties have increasingly been with Germany and the UK, rather than the traditional links with Norway and Sweden. Thus, in 1973, Denmark joined the EC, but the political consequence of joining the Common Market has been a further fragmentation of the country's political parties.

DJIBOUTI

Official name: Jumhuriya Jibuti (The Republic of Djibouti)

Member of: UN, OAU, Arab League

Area: 23 200 km² (8950 sq mi)

Population: 541 000 (1991 est)

Capital: Djibouti 290 000 (1988 est)

Languages: Arabic and French (both official); Somali (Issa; 37%)

Religion: Sunni Islam

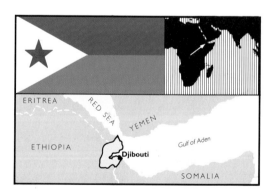

GOVERNMENT
The 65-member Chamber of Deputies and a President are by universal adult suffrage – respectively for five and six years. The President appoints a Prime Minister and Council of Ministers who are responsible to him.

GEOGRAPHY
Djibouti is a low-lying desert – below sea level in two basins but rising to 2062 m (6768 ft) in the N.

Climate: Djibouti is extremely hot and dry, with rainfall under 125 mm (5 in) on the coast.

ECONOMY
Lack of water largely restricts agriculture to grazing sheep and goats. The economy depends on the expanding seaport and railway, which both serve Ethiopia.

HISTORY
Islam came to the area in the 9th century. France acquired a port in 1862 and established the colony of French Somaliland in 1888. In the 1950s and 1970s, the Afar tribe and Europeans voted to remain French, while the Issas (Somalis) opted for independence. In 1977, the territory became the Republic of Djibouti, but the new state has suffered ethnic unrest and drought. From 1981 to 1992 Djibouti was a one-party state.

DOMINICA
Official name: Commonwealth of Dominica
Member of: UN, Commonwealth, OAS, CARICOM
Area: 751 km² (290 sq mi)
Population: 83 400 (1991 est)
Capital: Roseau 22 000 (city 8300; 1991 est)
Languages: English (official), French patois
Religion: Roman Catholic (80%)

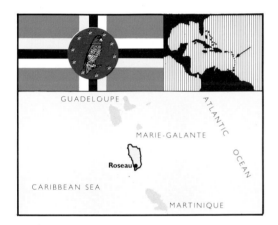

GOVERNMENT
Every five years, 21 members of the House of Assembly are elected by universal adult suffrage and 10 are appointed by the President, who is elected for a five-year term by the House. The President appoints a Prime Minister and Cabinet.

GEOGRAPHY
Dominica is surrounded by steep cliffs. Its forested mountainous interior rises to Morne Diablotin (1447 m / 4747 ft).
Climate: Dominica has a tropical climate with little seasonal variation and very heavy rainfall.

ECONOMY
Dominica is a poor island. It produces bananas, timber and coconuts, and exports water to drier neighbours. Tourism is increasing in importance.

HISTORY
Discovered by Columbus (1493), Dominica was occupied by Carib Indians who strongly resisted European settlement. Dominica was disputed by England and France, changing hands several times (1632–1783). Black slaves were imported to work plantations. Dominica was a member of the West Indies Federation (1958–62), gained autonomy in 1967 and independence in 1978.

DOMINICAN REPUBLIC
Official name: República Dominicana (The Dominican Republic)
Member of: UN, OAS, CARICOM
Area: 48 422 km² (18 696 sq mi)

Population: 7 320 000 (1991 est)
Capital and major cities: Santo Domingo 1 600 000, Santiago 308 000 (including suburbs; 1986 est)
Language: Spanish
Religions: Roman Catholic (official; over 90%)

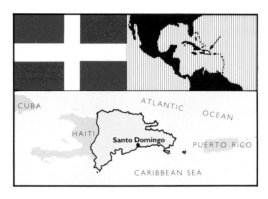

GOVERNMENT
The President and the National Congress – a 30-member Senate and a 120-member Chamber of Deputies – are elected for four years by universal adult suffrage. The President appoints a Cabinet.

GEOGRAPHY
The republic is the eastern two thirds of the island of Hispaniola. The fertile Cibao Valley in the N is an important agricultural region. Most of the rest of the country is mountainous, rising to Pico Duarte – at 3175 m (10 417 ft).
Climate: The climate is largely subtropical, but it is cooler in the mountains. Rainfall is heavy, but the W and SW are arid. Hurricanes are a hazard.

ECONOMY
Sugar is the traditional mainstay of the economy, but nickel and iron ore have become the principal exports. Tourism is now the greatest foreign-currency earner.

HISTORY
The island of Hispaniola was discovered in 1492 by Columbus. In 1697 Spain ceded the W of the island (Haiti) to France, and from 1795 the whole island was French. Returned to Spanish rule in 1809, the E declared independence as the Dominican Republic in 1821, but was annexed by Haiti (1822–44). The 19th century witnessed a succession of tyrants, and by 1900 the republic was bankrupt and in chaos. The USA intervened (1916–24). Rafael Trujillo (1891–1961) became president in 1930 and ruthlessly suppressed opposition. He was assassinated in 1961. Civil war in 1965 ended after intervention by US and Latin American troops. Since then, an infant democracy has faced grave economic problems.

ECUADOR
Official name: República del Ecuador (The Republic of Ecuador)
Member of: UN, OAS, ALADI, Andean Pact
Area: 270 670 km² (104 506 sq mi)
Population: 10 782 000 (1990 census)
Capital and major cities: Quito 1 388 000 (city 1 101 000), Guayaquil 1 764 000 (city 1 531 000), Cuenca 272 000 (city 195 000) (1990 census)
Language: Spanish (official; 93%), Quéchua
Religion: Roman Catholic (92%)

GOVERNMENT
The President is elected by compulsory universal adult suffrage for a single term of 4 years. The 72-member Chamber of Representatives is also directly elected – 60

members for two years, 12 members for four years. The President appoints a Cabinet of Ministers.

GEOGRAPHY
The Andes – rising to 6267 m (20 561 ft) at Chimborazo – divide the Pacific coastal plain in the W from the Amazonian rain forest in the E.
Climate: The Amazonian Basin has a wet tropical climate. The tropical coastal plain is humid in the N, arid in the S. The highland valleys are mild, but the highest peaks have permanent snow.

ECONOMY
Agriculture is the biggest single employer, and major exports include cocoa, coffee and, in particular, bananas. Petroleum is the major foreign-currency earner. High inflation and foreign debt are problems.

HISTORY
By the mid-15th century the Ecuadorian highlands had been incorporated into the Inca Empire (see p. 391). After being conquered by Spain (1532–33), the area was ruled as part of Peru. In 1822 Ecuador was liberated by the armies of Antonio José de Sucre (1795–1830) and Simón Bolivar (1783–1830). Initially federated with Colombia and Venezuela, Ecuador became completely independent in 1830. Throughout the 19th century there were struggles between liberals and conservatives. Since 1895 there have been long periods of military rule,

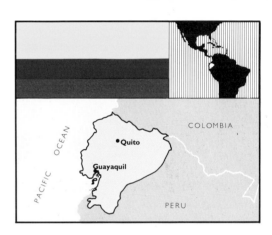

but democratically elected governments have been in power since 1978. Relations with neighbouring Peru have long been tense – war broke out in 1941, when Ecuador lost most of its Amazonian region and there were border skirmishes in 1981.

EGYPT
Official name: Jumhuriyat Misr al-'Arabiya (Arab Republic of Egypt)
Member of: UN, OAU, Arab League
Area: 997 739 km² (385 229 sq mi)
Population: 54 609 000 (1991 est)
Capital and major cities: Cairo (El-Qahira) 12 287 000 (with suburbs), Alexandria (El-Iskandariyah) 3 170 000, El-Giza 2 156 000 and Shubrâ El-Kheima 811 000 are both part of the Cairo agglomeration (1990 est).
Language: Arabic
Religion: Sunni Islam (90%), Christian (Coptic; 7%)

GOVERNMENT
Every five years, 444 members are elected by universal adult suffrage to the Majlis ash-Sha'ab (People's Assembly); the remaining 10 members are appointed by the President, who is nominated by the Assembly and confirmed by referendum for a six-year term. The President appoints a Prime Minister, Ministers and Vice-President(s).

GEOGRAPHY

Desert covers more than 90% of Egypt. The Western Desert – which stretches into Libya and Sudan – is low-lying. The Eastern Desert is divided by wadis and ends in the SE in mountains beside the Red Sea. The vast majority of the population lives in the Nile River valley and delta, intensively cultivated lands that rely on irrigation by the annual flood of the Nile. E of the Suez Canal, the Sinai Peninsula rises to Mt Catherine (Jabal Katrina) at 2642 m (8668 ft).

Principal river: Nile 6670 km (4145 mi)

Climate: Egyptian winters are mild and summers are hot and arid. Alexandria has the highest rainfall total – 200 mm (8 in) – while the area beside the Red Sea receives virtually no rain.

ECONOMY

Over 40% of the labour force is involved in agriculture, producing maize, wheat, rice and vegetables for the domestic market, and cotton and dates mainly for export. Petroleum reserves (small by Middle East standards), canal tolls and tourism are major foreign currency earners. The economy is held back by rapid population growth and the demands of a large public sector and food subsidies.

HISTORY

From 3100 to 332 BC, Egypt was ruled by 30 dynasties of pharaohs (see pp. 366–7). The country then formed part of the Ptolemaic kingdom (see pp. 372–3), the Roman Empire (see p. 377) and the Byzantine Empire (see p. 395). The Arabs invaded (639–42), and gradually transformed Egypt into an Arabic Islamic society, a province of the Abbasid caliphate. A rival caliphate was set up by the Fatamid dynasty in Cairo (973–1171). Mamluk armies – originally Turkish slaves – founded an independent sultanate (1250). In 1517 Egypt became part of the Ottoman (Turkish) Empire. After a French invasion (1798–1801), the Ottoman viceroy Mehemet Ali (1769–1849) made Egypt strong and established a dynasty that lasted until 1953. His successors gained territory and

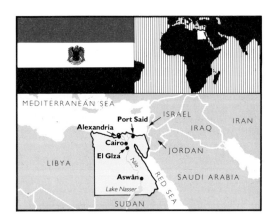

encouraged the construction of the Suez Canal, but they bankrupted Egypt. The UK – a major creditor – occupied Egypt (1882) and established a protectorate (1914–22).

The corrupt regime of King Farouk was toppled in a military coup (1952) and a republic was established (1953). The radical Gamal Abdel Nasser (1918–70) became president in 1954. He nationalized the Suez Canal (see pp. 449 and 454) and made Egypt the leader of Arab nationalism. Nasser was twice defeated by Israel in Middle East wars (see pp. 454–55), but his successor, President Anwar Sadat, made peace with Israel and was ostracized by the Arab world. Since Sadat's assassination (1981), Egypt has regained its place in the Arab fold. The prominent role played by Egypt in the coalition against Saddam Husain's Iraq (1991) confirmed Egypt as one of the leaders of the Arab world. The country faces severe economic problems, and there is a growth in Islamic fundamentalism.

EL SALVADOR

Official name: La República de El Salvador (The Republic of El Salvador)

Member of: UN, OAS, CACM

Area: 21 393 km² (8260 sq mi)

Population: 5 392 000 (1991 est)

Capital and major cities: San Salvador 1 151 000 (city 477 000), Santa Ana 224 000 (city 145 000) (1987 est)

Language: Spanish (official)

Religion: Roman Catholic (over 90%)

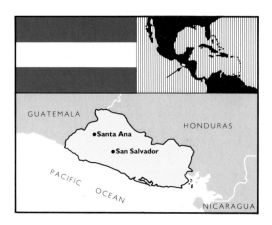

GOVERNMENT

The President – who appoints a Cabinet of Ministers – is elected by universal adult suffrage for a single five-year term. Every three years, direct elections are also held for the 60-member National Assembly.

GEOGRAPHY

The country is mountainous, with ranges along the border with Honduras and a higher volcanic chain in the S, rising to 2381 m (7812 ft).

Climate: The tropical coast is hot and humid, while the interior is temperate.

ECONOMY

Coffee and sugar cane are the country's main exports. The economy has declined since the 1970s owing to the state of near civil war.

HISTORY

Spain conquered the area in 1524 and governed it as part of Guatemala. El Salvador was liberated in 1821, but remained in the Central American Federation until 1838. The country has suffered frequent coups and political violence. In 1932 a peasant uprising was harshly suppressed. El Salvador's overpopulation has been partially relieved by migration to neighbouring states. After a soccer match between El Salvador and Honduras in 1969, war broke out because of illegal immigration by Salvadoreans into Honduras. Political and economic power is concentrated into the hands of a few families, and this has led to social tension. A state of virtual civil war existed from the late 1970s to 1992 with the US-backed military, assisted by extreme right-wing death squads, combating left-wing guerrillas. The government and guerrillas signed a peace agreement, which came into effect in 1992.

EQUATORIAL GUINEA

Official name: La República de Guinea Ecuatorial (The Republic of Equatorial Guinea)

Member of: UN, OAU

Area: 28 051 km² (10 831 sq mi)

Population: 358 000 (1991 est)

Capital: Malabo 37 000 (1988 est)

Languages: Spanish (official), Fang, Bubi

Religions: Roman Catholic majority

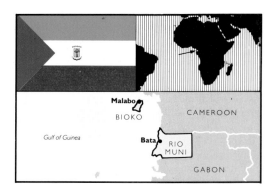

GOVERNMENT

The constitution provides for the election of a President for a seven-year term and a 41-member House of Representatives for five years. However, effective power is in the hands of the Supreme Military Council, whose President is head of state and of government.

GEOGRAPHY

The republic consists of the fertile island of Bioko (formerly Fernando Póo), the much smaller islands of Pagalu (formerly Annobón) and Corisco Group, and the district of Mbini (formerly Río Muni) on the African mainland.

Climate: The tropical climate is hot and humid with heavy rainfall.

ECONOMY

Mbini exports coffee and timber; Bioko exports cocoa. The economy relies heavily on foreign aid.

HISTORY

Fernando Póo was acquired by Spain in 1778. Río Muni was added in 1856 to create Spanish Guinea. The harsh plantation system practised during the colonial era attracted much international criticism. Independence in 1968 began under the dictatorship of Francisco Nguema, who was overthrown by a military coup in 1979. Severe economic decline was experienced throughout the 1970s.

ESTONIA

Official name: Eesti Vabariik (Republic of Estonia)

Member of: UN, CSCE

Area: 45 100 km² (17 413 sq mi)

Population: 1 589 000 (1991 est)

Capital and major cities: Tallinn 505 000, Tartu 115 000, Narva 82 000 (1991 est)

Languages: Estonian (over 62%), Russian (30%)

Religions: Lutheran (30%), Orthodox (10%)

GOVERNMENT

A 105-member Assembly and a President are elected by universal adult suffrage for four years. The President appoints a Prime Minister and a Council of Ministers who are responsible to the Assembly.

GEOGRAPHY

Estonia comprises a low-lying mainland – rising in the SE to 318 m (1042 ft) – and two main islands.

Climate: The moist temperate climate is characterized by mild summers and cold winters.

ECONOMY

Major industries include engineering and food processing. Gas for heating and industry is extracted from bituminous shale. The important agricultural sector is dominated by dairying. Since 1991 severe economic difficulties have resulted from Estonia's heavy dependency upon trade with Russia. The economy is still largely state-run, but some progress towards privatization has been made.

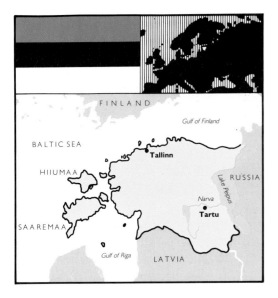

HISTORY
Estonia was ruled by Denmark (1227–1346), the (German) Teutonic Knights (1346–1558) and by Sweden (1558–1712) before becoming part of Russia. Estonian national consciousness increased throughout the 19th century. When the Communists took power in Russia (1917), Estonia seceded, but a German occupation and two Russian invasions delayed independence until 1919. Estonia's fragile democracy was replaced by a dictatorship in 1934. The Non-Aggression Pact (1939) between Hitler and Stalin assigned Estonia to the USSR, which invaded and annexed the republic (1940). Estonia was occupied by Nazi Germany (1941–44). When Soviet rule was reimposed (1945), large-scale Russian settlement replaced over 120 000 Estonians who had been killed or deported to Siberia. In 1988, reforms in the USSR allowed Estonian nationalists to operate openly. Nationalists won a majority in the republic's parliament, gradually assumed greater autonomy and seceded following the failed coup by Communist hardliners in Moscow (August 1991). The USSR recognized Estonia's independence in September 1991. The introduction of strict Estonian citizenship laws (1992) that denied full rights to most Russian-speakers increased tension with Russia.

ETHIOPIA

Official name: Ityopia (Ethiopia). Previously known as Abyssinia.

Member of: UN, OAU

Area: 1 223 600 km² (472 435 sq mi) – including Eritrea

Population: 51 617 000 (1991 est – including Eritrea)

Capital and major cities: Addis Ababa 1 739 000, Asmara 344 000, Dire Dawa 122 000 (1991 est)

Languages: Amharic (official), Arabic, Oromo (40%)

Religions: Sunni Islam (45%), Ethiopian Orthodox (40%)

GOVERNMENT
The constitution provides for the election by universal adult suffrage every five years of a 835-member National Assembly (Shengo), which elects a President and appoints a Cabinet. A federal system is to be instituted. The region of Eritrea has *de facto* been an independent state since 1991.

GEOGRAPHY
The Western Highlands – including Eritrea, the Tigré

Plateau and the Semien Mountains (rising to over 4000 m / 13 000 ft) – are separated from the lower Eastern Highlands by a wide rift valley.

Climate: Very hot and dry in the N and E, with a temperate climate in the highlands.

ECONOMY
Secessionist wars have damaged an impoverished, underdeveloped economy. Most Ethiopians are involved in subsistence farming. Coffee is the main foreign-currency earner. The economy is in serious difficulties owing to the end of aid of from former Communist states.

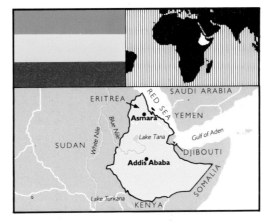

HISTORY
The kingdom of Aksum flourished in the first millennium AD, accepting Christianity in the 4th century. Later, Islam also entered the country. Under Menelik II, Ethiopia survived the European scramble for empire and defeated an Italian invasion (1896). However, the Italians occupied Ethiopia from 1936 to 1941. Emperor Haile Selassie (1892–1975) played a prominent part in African affairs, but – failing to modernize Ethiopia or overcome its extreme poverty – he was overthrown in 1974. Allied to the USSR, a left-wing military regime instituted revolutionary change, but, even with Cuban help, it was unable to overcome secessionist guerrilla movements in Eritrea and Tigray. Drought, soil erosion and civil war brought severe famine in the 1980s and 1990s. The Marxist-Leninist regime was toppled by Tigrayan forces in 1991. The interim authorities recognized the right of Eritrea to secede and a referendum on independence is scheduled for the province.

ERITREA
Area: 117 400 km² (45 300 sq mi). *Population:* 3 323 000 (1991 est). *Capital:* Asmara (Asmera) 344 000 (1991 est).

FIJI

Official name: Matanitu Ko Viti (Republic of Fiji)

Member of: UN

Area: 18 376 km² (7095 sq mi)

Population: 738 000 (1991 est)

Capital: Suva 141 000 (city 70 000; 1986 census)

Languages: English, Fijian (48%), Hindi (46%)

Religions: Methodist (45%), Hindu (over 40%)

GOVERNMENT
The 70-seat House of Representatives is elected by universal adult suffrage for five years to represent four ethnic voting lists – 37 members are elected by Fijians, 27 by Indians, 1 by Rotumans and 5 by others. The traditional Fijian Council of Chiefs elects the President and 24 of the 34 members of the appointed Senate. The President appoints a Prime Minister.

GEOGRAPHY
The mountainous larger islands are volcanic in origin. The smaller islands are mainly coral reefs.

Climate: Fiji experiences high temperatures and heavy rainfall with local variations.

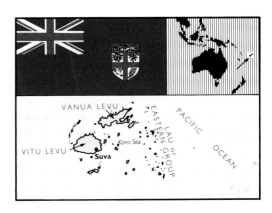

ECONOMY
Fiji's economy depends on agriculture, with sugar cane as the main cash crop. Copra, ginger, fish and timber are also exported. Tourism is becoming important.

HISTORY
Fiji was settled by Melanesians and Polynesians in around 1500 BC (see p. 389). Tasman reached Fiji in 1643, but Europeans did not settle until the early 1800s. During a period of great unrest, Chief Cakobau, who controlled the W, requested British assistance and ceded Fiji to Britain (1874). Indian labourers arrived to work on sugar plantations, reducing the Fijians, who retained ownership of most of the land, to a minority. Since independence (1970), racial tension and land disputes have brought instability. A military takeover in 1987 overthrew an Indian-led government and established a Fijian-dominated republic outside the Commonwealth.

FINLAND

Official name: Suomen Tasavalta (Republic of Finland)

Member of: UN, EFTA, CSCE, OECD

Area: 338 145 km² (130 557 sq mi)

Population: 4 999 000 (1990 census)

Capital and major cities: Helsinki (Helsingfors) 990 000 (city 492 000), Turku (Åbo) 265 000 (city 159 000), Tampere (Tammerfors) 261 000 (city 173 000), Espoo 173 000 and Vantaa 155 000 are part of the Helsinki agglomeration, Oulu (Uleaborg) 101 000 (1990 census)

Languages: Finnish (94%), Swedish (6%)

Religion: Lutheran (88%)

GOVERNMENT
The 200-member Parliament (Eduskunta) is elected for four years under a system of proportional representation by universal adult suffrage. Executive power is vested in a President elected for six years by direct popular vote. The President appoints a Council of State (Cabinet) – headed by a Prime Minister – responsible to the Parliament.

GEOGRAPHY
Nearly one third of Finland lies N of the Arctic Circle and one tenth of the country is covered by lakes, some 50 000 in all. Saimaa – the largest lake – has an area of over 4400 km² (1700 sq mi). During the winter months the Gulfs of Bothnia (to the W) and of Finland (to the S) freeze. The land is glaciated, and except for mountains in the NW – rising to 1342 m (4344 ft) – most of the country is lowland.

Climate: Warm summers with long, extremely cold, winters particularly in the N.

ECONOMY
Forests cover about two thirds of the country and wood products provide 30% of Finland's foreign earnings.

Metalworking and engineering (in particular shipbuilding) are among the main Finnish industries, which have a reputation for quality and good design. Apart from forests, copper and rivers suitable for hydroelectric power, there are few natural resources. However, Finland enjoys a high standard of living, but the collapse of trade with Russia – traditionally a major trading partner – brought severe economic difficulties to Finland in 1991–92. The fishing industry is large and the agricultural sector produces enough dairy products for export.

HISTORY

The Swedish conquest of Finland began in the 12th century and was complete by 1634. At the Reformation most Finns became Lutheran. Russia conquered much of the area in the early 18th century and gained complete control in 1809. Throughout the 19th century Finland was a grand duchy ruled by the Russian emperor. Tension grew as Russia sought to strengthen its political and cultural leverage. In 1906 Finland was allowed to call its own Duma (Parliament), but repression followed again in 1910. After the Russian Revolution of 1917, civil war broke out in Finland. The pro-Russian party was defeated and an independent republican constitution (still in force today) was established (1919). Finland's territorial integrity lasted until the Soviet invasion in 1939, after which land was ceded to the USSR. The failure of a brief alliance with Germany led to further cession of territory to the Soviet Union in 1944. Finland has, since 1945, retained its neutrality and independence. Finland has achieved some influence through the careful exercise of its neutrality, for example hosting the first sessions of CSCE, (the 'Helsinki accords'). Following the collapse of the USSR (1991), Finland renegotiated its close relationship with Russia and applied for membership of the EC.

FRANCE

Official name: La République française (The French Republic)

Member of: UN, EC, NATO, CSCE, G7, OECD

Area: 543 965 km² (210 026 sq mi) – 'metropolitan' France, excluding overseas départements and collectivités territoriales (whose status is between that of an overseas département and an overseas territory)

Population: 56 614 000 (1990 census) – 'metropolitan' France

Capital and major cities: Paris 9 063 000 (city 2 175 000), Lyon 1 262 000 (city 422 000), Marseille 1 087 000 (city 808 000), Lille 950 000 (city 178 000), Bordeaux 686 000 (city 213 000), Toulouse 608 000 (city 366 000), Nantes 492 000 (city 252 000), Nice 476 000 (city 346 000), Toulon 438 000 (city 170 000), Grenoble 400 000 (city 154 000), Strasbourg 388 000 (city 256 000), Rouen

380 000 (city 105 000), Valenciennes 336 000 (town 39 000), Cannes 336 000 (city 69 000), Lens 323 000 (town 35 000), Saint-Etienne 313 000 (city 202 0000), Nancy 311 000 (city 102 000), Tours 272 000 (city 133 000), Béthune 260 000 (town 26 000), Clermont-Ferrand 254 000 (city 140 000), Le Havre 254 000 (city 197 000) (1990 census)

Languages: French, with Breton and Basque minorities

Religions: Roman Catholic (74%), Sunni Islam (4%)

Overseas départements – integral parts of the French Republic (with areas, populations and capitals):
Guadeloupe – 1780 km² (687 sq mi) 387 000 (1991 census), Basse-Terre;
Guyane (French Guiana) – 90 000 km (34 750 sq mi), 115 000 (1990 census), Cayenne.
Martinique – 1100 km² (425 sq mi), 360 000 (1990 census), Fort-de-France.
Réunion – 2512 km² (970 sq mi), 597 000 (1990 census), Saint-Denis.

Collectivités territoriales – integral parts of the French Republic (with areas, population and capitals):
Mayotte – 376 km² (145 sq mi), 94 400 (1990 census), Dzaoudzi.
Saint-Pierre-et-Miquelon – 242 km² (93 sq mi), 6400 (1989 census), Saint-Pierre.

Overseas territories (with areas, populations and capitals):
French Polynesia – 4200 km² (1622 sq mi), 199 000 (1991 est), Papeete.
New Caledonia – 19 103 km² (7376 sq mi), 168 000 (1990 est), Nouméa.
Southern and Antarctic Territories – 451 600 km² (174 400 sq mi), no permanent population.

Wallis and Futuna Islands – 274 km² (106 sq mi), 13 700 (1990 est), Mata-Utu.

GOVERNMENT

Executive power is vested in the President, who is elected for a 7-year term by universal adult suffrage. The President appoints a Prime Minister and a Council of Ministers – both responsible to Parliament – but it is the President, rather than the PM, who presides over the Council of Ministers. The Senate (the upper house) comprises 321 members – 311 of whom represent individual départements, including overseas départements and territories – elected by members of municipal, local and regional councils. The remaining 10 senators are elected by French citizens resident abroad. Senators serve for nine years, with one third of the Senate retiring every three years. The National Assembly (the lower house) comprises 577 deputies elected for a five-year term by universal adult suffrage from single-member constituencies, with a second ballot for the leading candidates if no candidate obtains an absolute majority in the first round.

GEOGRAPHY

The Massif Central – a plateau of old hard rocks, rising to almost 2000 m (6500 ft) – occupies the middle of France. The Massif is surrounded by four major lowlands, which together make up over 60% of the total area of France. The Paris Basin – the largest of these lowlands – is divided by low ridges and fertile plains and plateaux, but is united by the river system of the Seine and its tributaries. To the E of the Massif Central is the narrow Rhône-Saône Valley, while to the W the Loire Valley stretches to the Atlantic. SW of the Massif Central lies the Aquitaine Basin, a large fertile region drained by the River Garonne and its tributaries. A

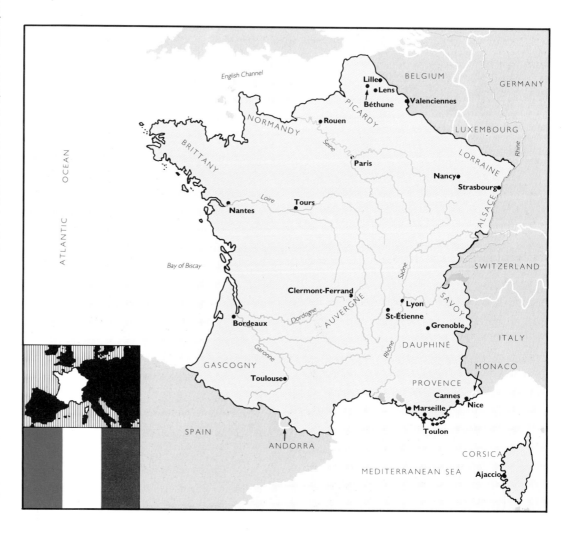

discontinuous ring of uplands surrounds France. In the NW the Armorican Massif (Brittany) rises to 411 m (1350 ft). In the SW the Pyrenees form a high natural boundary with Spain. The Alps in the SE divide France from Italy and contain Europe's highest peak, Mont Blanc (4807 m / 15 771 ft). The lower Jura – in the E – lie on the Swiss border, while the Vosges Mountains separate the Paris Basin from the Rhine Valley. In the NE the Ardennes extend into Belgium. The Mediterranean island of Corsica is an ancient massif rising to 2710 m (8891 ft).

Principal rivers: Rhine (Rhin) 1320 km (820 mi), Loire 1020 km (634 mi), Rhône 812 km (505 mi)

Climate: The Mediterranean S has warm summers and mild winters. The rest of France has a temperate climate, although the more continental E experiences warmer summers and colder winters. Rainfall is moderate, with highest falls in the mountains and lowest falls around Paris.

ECONOMY

Nearly two thirds of France is farmed. The principal products include cereals (wheat, maize, barley), meat and dairy products, sugar beet and grapes for wine. France is remarkably self-sufficient in agriculture, with tropical fruit and animal feeds being the only major imports. However, the small size of land holdings remains a problem despite consolidation and the efforts of cooperatives. Reafforestation is helping to safeguard the future of the important timber industry. Natural resources include coal, iron ore, copper, bauxite and tungsten, as well as petroleum and natural gas, and plentiful sites for hydroelectric power plants. Major French industries include textiles, chemicals, steel, food processing, motor vehicles, aircraft, and mechanical and electrical engineering. Traditionally French firms have been small, but mergers have resulted in larger corporations able to compete internationally. France is the world's fourth industrial power after the USA, Japan and Germany. During the later 1980s many state-owned corporations were privatized. Over 50% of the labour force is involved in service industries, in particular administration, banking, finance, and tourism.

HISTORY

The Gauls gradually spread over France from the E about 1500 BC. The ancient Greeks established settlements on the Mediterranean coast from the 7th century BC, and the Romans conquered Gaul from 123 BC. After the Romans departed in the 5th century AD, Germanic tribes invaded, among whom the Franks became dominant. The Frankish Carolingians built an empire under Charlemagne (reigned 768–814), and when his realm was divided in the 9th century, the W part became the ancestor of modern France (see also p. 394).

The French nation state was slow to emerge, however. In medieval times, a series of dynasties sought to extend their power over the area that is now France the Carolingians (768–987), the Capetians (987–1328), and the Valois (1328–1589). Territorial gains were repeatedly countered by invasion, while the strengthening of the monarchy did not occur without frequent dynastic crises. At the beginning of the Valois period (1328), Aquitaine, Brittany, Burgundy and Flanders were still outside the French royal domain, but by the 16th century they had all been included in the French state. For much of the medieval period, the French kings struggled to wrest control of northern and western France from the English, particularly in the Hundred Years War (see pp. 400–1). By 1453, however, only Calais remained in English hands. The question of frontiers – especially in the E – continued up to the Revolution and beyond. Between the 16th and 18th centuries conflict with Britain and France's other neighbours continued, particularly over colonial possessions and over control of the Low Countries and the Rhineland (see pp. 415–7).

Religious conflicts worked against the consolidation of France. The 16th century was scarred by civil wars between Catholics and Protestant Huguenots (see pp. 408–9). The Protestant Bourbon Henry of Navarre (1553–1610) succeeded the extinct Valois dynasty as Henry IV. Converting to Catholicism, he granted toleration to the

Huguenots, but the 17th century saw the gradual and often brutal suppression of these liberties, and the status of Protestants remained a sensitive issue until the Revolution. Provincial independence also hindered national unity, despite the efforts of the Bourbon monarchs – in particular Louis XIV (1638–1715) and his ministers (see pp. 414–15) – to weaken them.

By the 18th century France had achieved a high degree of centralization, and its glorification of the monarchy – typified by the palace of Versailles – was impressive. However, the Bourbon state was overextended. The national assembly – the Estates General – was unsummoned from 1614 to 1789, antagonizing the men of the Enlightenment (see p. 418). The Revolution of 1789 (see pp. 424–5) sprang from a detestation of heavy and unfair taxes and from a hatred of the economic privileges of the nobility and the Church. However, the Revolutionary regimes that followed the downfall of the monarchy took centralization further, attempting far more than they could achieve – for example, the suppression of the Church and the implementation of dramatic cultural reforms. The Revolutionary regimes also attempted to spread their ideas throughout Europe, especially under Napoleon (1769–1821; see pp. 426–7), whose centralized empire briefly outshone the monarchy of Louis XIV.

After Napoleon's defeat at Waterloo (1815), the less powerful monarchies of the first half of the 19th century – the restored Bourbons (1815–30) and the Orléanist monarchy (1830–48) – were toppled by revolt fed by popular memories of the liberties enjoyed under the Republic (see p. 428). The coup of Louis-Napoleon (a nephew of Napoleon I) turned the Second Republic into the Second Empire, with himself as Napoleon III. However, his reign (1852–70) was brought to an end by defeat in the Franco-Prussian war (1870–1; see p. 429). After this defeat, the Third Republic (1871–1940) was established, and immediately faced the revolt of the Paris Commune (see p. 429). Controversy over the role of religion in the state – particularly the question of religious-based or secular education – did not end until Church and state were finally separated in 1905.

In the 1890s the French colonial empire reached its greatest extent, in particular in Africa, SE Asia and the Pacific (see pp. 432–3). The Third Republic also saw continuing conflict over France's own boundaries Alsace-Lorraine was lost in 1870 but recovered in 1918 at the end of World War I, during which trench warfare in northern France claimed countless lives (see pp. 436–7). In World War II (see pp. 444–5), Germany rapidly defeated the French in 1940 and completely occupied the country in 1942. Marshal Philippe Pétain (1856–1951) led a collaborationist regime in the city of Vichy, while General Charles de Gaulle (1890–1970) headed the Free French in exile in London from 1940. After the war, the Fourth Republic (1946–58) was marked by instability, the Suez Crisis of 1956 (see p. 454), and nationalist revolts in some of the colonies, notably Vietnam (see p. 452) and Algeria (see p. 451). The troubles in Algeria – including the revolt of the French colonists and the campaign of their terrorist organization, the OAS – led to the end of the Fourth Republic and to the accession to power of General de Gaulle in 1959.

As first president of the Fifth Republic, de Gaulle granted Algeria independence (1962). While the French colonial empire – with a few minor exceptions – was being disbanded, France's position within Western Europe was being strengthened, especially by vigorous participation in the European Community. At the same time, de Gaulle pursued a foreign policy independent of the USA, building up France's non-nuclear armaments and withdrawing French forces from NATO's integrated command structure. Although restoring political and economic stability to France, domestic dissatisfaction – including the student revolt of May 1968 (see p. 295) – led de Gaulle to resign in 1969. De Gaulle's policies were broadly pursued by his successors as president, Georges Pompidou (in office 1969–74) and Valéry Giscard d'Estaing (1974–81). The modernization of France continued apace under the country's first Socialist president, François Mitterand (1981–).

GABON

Official name: La République gabonaise (The Gabonese Republic)

Member of: UN, OAU, OPEC

Area: 267 667 km² (103 347 sq mi)

Population: 1 133 000 (1990 est)

Capital and major cities: Libreville 352 000, Port-Gentil 164 000 (1987 est)

Languages: French (official), Fang (40%)

Religions: Roman Catholic (71%), animist (28%)

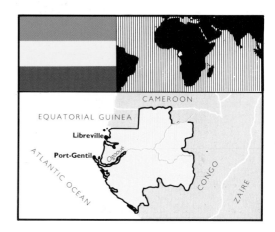

GOVERNMENT

The President – who is elected by universal adult suffrage for seven years – appoints a Council of Ministers (over which he presides) and a Prime Minister. The National Assembly has 120 members directly elected for five years.

GEOGRAPHY

Apart from the narrow coastal plain, low plateaus make up most of the country. The central Massif du Chaillu rises to 980 m (3215 ft).

Climate: The equatorial climate is hot and humid with little seasonal variation.

ECONOMY

Petroleum, natural gas, manganese, uranium and iron ore – and a relatively small population – make Gabon the richest Black African country, although most Gabonese are subsistence farmers.

HISTORY

The slave trade developed after the Portuguese arrived in the late 15th century. The French colonized Gabon in the late 19th century. Pro-French Léon M'Ba (1902–67) led the country to independence in 1960. Deposed in a coup (1964), he was restored to power by French troops. Under his successor, Albert-Bernard Bongo, Gabon has continued its pro-Western policies. From 1968 to 1990 Gabon was a single-party state.

GAMBIA

Official name: The Republic of the Gambia

Member of: UN, OAU, Commonwealth, ECOWAS

Area: 11 295 km² (4 361 sq mi)

Population: 883 000 (1991 est)

Capital: Banjul 147 000 (city 44 000; 1986 est)

Language: English (official)

Religions: Sunni Islam (90%), Protestant Churches (mainly Anglican; 9%)

GOVERNMENT

The President and 36 of the 50 members of the House of Representatives are elected by universal adult suffrage every five years; the remaining members are appointed. The President appoints a Vice-President – to lead the government in the House – and a Cabinet of Ministers.

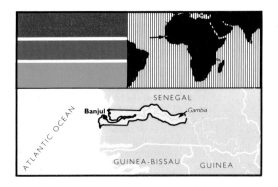

GEOGRAPHY
The Gambia is a narrow low-lying country on either bank of the River Gambia.

Climate: The climate is tropical, with a dry season from November to May.

ECONOMY
The economy is largely based on the cultivation of groundnuts. Tourism is increasing in importance.

HISTORY
Once part of the Mali empire, the area became involved in the slave trade following the arrival of the Portuguese in the mid-15th century. British traders later supplanted the Portuguese, and a British colony was established in 1843. The Gambia achieved independence in 1965 under Sir Dawda K. Jawara. In 1981 an attempted coup against his rule encouraged efforts to merge with the neighbouring French-speaking country of Senegal, but the confederation was dissolved in 1989.

GEORGIA

Official name: Sakartvelo (Georgia)

Member of: UN, CSCE

Area: 69 700 km² (26 900 sq mi)

Population: 5 464 000 (1991 est)

Capital and major cities: Tbilisi 1 264 000, Kutaisi 235 000, Rustavi 159 000 (1991 est)

Languages: Georgian (70%), Armenian (8%), Russian (6%), Azeri (3%), Ossetian (2%)

Religion: Georgian Orthodox majority

GOVERNMENT
The constitution provides for the election by universal adult suffrage of a 250-member Assembly and a President – who appoints a Council of Ministers – for four years.

GEOGRAPHY
The spine of the Caucasus Mountains forms the N border of Georgia. The highest peak, Elbrus, reaches 5642 m (18 510 ft). A lower range, the Little Caucasus, occupies S Georgia. Central Georgia comprises the Kolkhida lowlands.

Climate: Coastal and central Georgia has a moist Mediterranean climate. The rest of Georgia is drier. Climate varies considerably with altitude and aspect.

ECONOMY
Despite a shortage of cultivable land, Georgia has a diversified agricultural sector including tea, citrus fruit, tobacco, cereals, vines, livestock and vegetables. Natural resources include coal, manganese and plentiful hydroelectric power. Machine building, food processing and chemicals are major industries. The private sector is probably more highly developed than in any other former Soviet republic, but the economy was damaged by civil war (1991–92).

HISTORY
Georgia is the home of an ancient civilization established in the 3rd millennium BC. Georgian states, including Colchis and Iberia, flourished in the 1st millennium BC. Colchis fell to the Greeks before being ruled by Pontus and then Rome (65 BC). Christianity was adopted c. AD 330. From the 4th to the 7th centuries Georgia was fought over by the Byzantine Empire, the Persians and, later, the Arabs. In the 8th century the Bagratid family established several Georgian kingdoms. Bagrat III (975–1014) reunited Georgia. His descendant Queen Tamara (1184–1213) established an empire that included most of the Caucasian region, but national unity was destroyed by Mongol invasions, and dynastic quarrels.

From the 16th to the 18th centuries Georgia was disputed by the Ottoman Turks and the Persians. An independent Georgia was reunited in 1762 and sought Russian protection against Turkey and Persia. Russia deposed the Bagratids (1801) and annexed Georgia by degrees (1801–78). Following the Russian Revolution (1918), a Georgian republic, allied to Germany, was proclaimed. A British occupation (1918–20) in favour of the White Russians failed to win local support, and Georgia was invaded by the Soviet Red Army (1921). Georgia became part of the Transcaucasian Soviet Republic in 1921 and a separate Union Republic of the

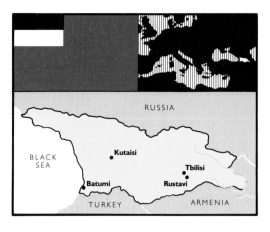

USSR in 1936. Following the abortive coup by Communist hardliners in Moscow (September 1991), Georgia declared independence. Locked into a fierce civil war, Georgia remained outside the CIS (the defence and economic community founded when the USSR was dissolved in December 1991). A temporary state council – led by Eduard Shevardnadze, the former Soviet Foreign Minister – replaced a military council in March 1992. The Abkhazian Muslims attempted secession (1992–93).

GERMANY

Official name: Bundesrepublik Deutschland (The Federal Republic of Germany)

Member of: UN, EC, NATO, G7, OECD, CSCE

Area: 357 050 km² (137 857 sq mi)

Population: 79 096 000 (1991 est)

Capital and major cities: Berlin (capital in name only) 3 410 000, Bonn (administrative capital) 284 000, Essen 4 700 000 (Essen-Ruhr; city 621 000), Hamburg 1 626 000, Munich (München) 1 218 000, Cologne (Köln) 940 000, Frankfurt 629 000, Dortmund (part of the Essen-Ruhr agglomeration) 589 000, Düsseldorf 570 000, Stuttgart 566 000, Bremen 546 000, Leipzig 539 000, Duisburg (part of the Essen-Ruhr agglomeration) 532 000, Dresden 516 000, Hannover 502 000, Nuremberg (Nürnberg) 482 000, Bochum (part of the Essen-Ruhr agglomeration) 390 000, Wuppertal 372 000, Bielefeld 313 000, Chemnitz 310 000, Mannheim 303 000 (1990 est)

Language: German

Religions: Various Protestant Churches (mainly Lutheran; 34%), Roman Catholic (35%)

GOVERNMENT
Each of the 16 states (Länder; singular Länd) is represented in the 79-member upper house of Parliament – the Federal Council (Bundesrat) – by three, four or six members of the state government (depending on population) appointed for a limited period. The lower house – the Federal Assembly (Bundestag) – has 662 members elected for four years by universal adult suffrage under a mixed system of single-member constituencies and proportional representation. Executive power rests with the Federal Government, led by a Federal Chancellor – who is elected by the Bundestag. The President is elected for a five-year term by the Bundesrat and an equal number of representatives of the states. Each state has its own Parliament and Government.

GEOGRAPHY
The North German Plain – a region of fertile farmlands and sandy heaths – is drained by the Rivers Elbe, Weser and Oder. In the W, the plain merges with the North Rhine lowlands which contain the Ruhr coalfield and over 20% of the country's population. A belt of plateaux, formed of old hard rocks, crosses the country from E to W and includes the Hunsrück and Eifel highlands in the Rhineland and the Taunus and Westerwald uplands in Hesse, and extends into the Harz and Erz Mountains in Thuringia. The Rhine cuts through these central plateaux in a deep gorge. In southern Germany, the Black Forest (Schwarzwald) separates the Rhine valley from the fertile valleys and scarplands of Swabia. The forested edge of the Bohemian uplands marks the Czech border, while the Bavarian Alps – rising to the Zugspitze (2963 m / 9721 ft) – form the frontier with Austria.

Principal rivers: Rhine (Rhein) 1320 km (820 mi), Elbe 1165 km (724 mi), Danube (Donau) 2850 km (1770 mi)

Climate: The climate is temperate, but with considerable variations between the generally mild N coastal plain and the Bavarian Alps in the S, which have cool summers and cold winters. The eastern part of the country has warm summers and cold winters.

ECONOMY
Germany is the world's third industrial power after the USA and Japan. The country's recovery after World War II has been called the 'German economic miracle'. The principal industries include mechanical and electrical engineering, chemicals, textiles, food processing and vehicles, with heavy industry and engineering concentrated in the Ruhr, chemicals in cities on the Rhine and motor vehicles in large provincial centres such as Stuttgart. From the 1980s, there has been a spectacular growth in high-technology industries. Apart from coal and brown coal, Germany has relatively few natural resources, and the country relies heavily upon imports. Labour has also been in short supply, and large numbers of 'guest workers' (Gastarbeiter) – particularly from Turkey and the former Yugoslavia – have been recruited. Since reunification in 1990 the labour shortage in the western part of the country has also been met by migration from the former GDR. Service industries employ almost twice as many people as manufacturing industry. Banking and finance are major foreign-currency earners and Frankfurt is one of the world's leading financial and business centres. Reunification has presented major problems. The GDR's economy had previously been the most successful in the Communist bloc, but, since 1990, many East German firms have been unable to compete with their Western counterparts. A trust (the Treuhandanstalt) was set up to oversee the privatization of the 8000 state-run firms in the E, but many have gone bankrupt and unemployment in the former GDR is high. The main German agricultural products include hops (for beer), grapes (for wine), sugar beet, wheat, barley, and dairy products. The collectivized farms of the former GDR were privatized in 1991. Forests cover almost 30% of Germany and support a flourishing timber industry.

HISTORY
Germany has only been unified between 1871 and 1945,

and since 1990. However, although for most of their history the German people were divided between a considerable number of states, they played a key role in Europe. Germanic peoples – who displaced Celts in what was to become Germany – helped to destroy the western Roman Empire. Most of the German lands were united under the Frankish Empire, but after the death of Charlemagne (768–814) the inheritance was divided (see p. 394). The Saxon kings – in particular Otto I – unsuccessfully attempted to reunite the Germans, although most of Germany was nominally within the Holy Roman Empire (see p. 394).

In the 12th and 13th centuries, the Hohenstaufen Holy Roman Emperors tried to make their mark in Italy as well as N of the Alps. This diversion allowed dozens of German princes, dukes, bishops and counts to assert their independence. Their small states formed an astonishing jigsaw on the map of Europe until the 19th century. In 1648 there were no fewer than 343 German states. The Habsburgs – Emperors for almost the entire period from 1437 to 1806 – were often so concerned with the fortunes of their territories in Austria, Hungary and Bohemia, that they were unable to control the subordinate electorates, principalities and bishoprics. The independence of local rulers was reinforced in the 16th century when a number of princes followed the lead of the Protestant reformer Martin Luther (1483–1547; see pp. 408–9). The Peace of Augsburg (1555) established the principle that a state's religion followed that of its prince. This was soon challenged by both Lutherans and Catholics, and became one of many factors contributing to the Thirty Years War (1618–48; see p. 409).

During the 18th century, some small German states – notably Saxe-Weimar under Duke Charles Augustus – became centres of enlightened government and of culture (see pp. 418–9). Other small territories became involved in the power politics of the major states. For example, after the accession of the elector of Hanover to the British throne in 1714 as George I, the British sovereign continued to be ruler of Hanover until 1837. The contribution of the small states was, however, overshadowed by the rise of Brandenburg-Prussia,

under the uncompromising leadership of the Hohenzollern family of electors (after 1701 kings). Frederick William, the Great Elector (ruled 1640–88) laid the foundations of Prussia's power. King Frederick William I (ruled 1713–40) expanded the army and did much to give Prussia its military nature, while Frederick II, the Great, (ruled 1740–86) greatly enlarged his kingdom at the expense of Austria and Poland (see p. 417). By the 18th century, Prussia was vying for supremacy in Germany with the Austrian-based Empire.

During the Napoleonic Wars (see pp. 426–7), France redrew the map of Germany, merging and annexing many territories, establishing new client states, and founding the Confederation of the Rhine. The Napoleonic period saw the upsurge of romantically inspired German nationalist sentiment. After the Napoleonic Wars, a German Confederation, initially composed of 39 states, was established. Although the Confederation contained important ancient states such as Bavaria, Hanover, Saxony, Württemberg, Hesse, Oldenburg, Baden and Mecklenburg, none could match Prussia or Austria in size or influence. The Confederation did not satisfy the longings of the German people for unity. In 1830, and again in 1848, liberal nationalist movements swept Germany, extracting short-lived liberal constitutions from autocratic princes (see p. 428).

Otto von Bismarck (1815–98) – prime minister of Prussia (1862–71), then German Chancellor (1871–90) – masterminded Prussia's ascendancy over Austria and the other German states (see also pp. 428–9). Military victories over the Danes (1864), Austria and her German allies (1866) and France (1871) earned Prussia extra territories and complete domination within Germany. In 1871, a German Empire – of four kingdoms, six grand duchies, five duchies and seven principalities – was proclaimed with the King of Prussia as Emperor of Germany (Kaiser). From 1871 to 1918, an expansionist unified Germany attempted to extend its influence throughout Europe, engaged in naval and commercial rivalry with Britain, and built a colonial empire. Under the mercurial Emperor William II (reigned 1888–1918), Germany was a destabilizing force in world politics.

Defeat in World War I (1914–18; see pp. 436–7) led to the loss of much territory in Europe and the colonies overseas, the end of the German monarchies, the imposition of a substantial reparations and the occupation of the Rhineland by Allied forces until 1930 (see pp. 440–1). The liberal Weimar republic (1919–33) could not bring economic or political stability. In the early 1930s the Nazi Party gained popularity (see pp. 442–3), urging the establishment of a strong centralized government, an aggressive foreign policy, 'Germanic character' and the overturn of the postwar settlement. In 1933, Adolf Hitler (1889–1945) became Chancellor and in 1934 President. His Third Reich (empire) annexed Austria (1938), dismembered Czechoslovakia (1939) and embarked on the extermination of the Jews and others that the Nazis regarded as 'inferior'. Invading Poland (1939), he launched Germany into war, defeat, occupation and division (see pp. 444–5).

In 1945, Germany lost substantial territories to Poland and was divided into four zones of occupation by the Allies – Britain, France, the USA and the USSR. Their intention was a united, disarmed Germany, but cooperation between the Allies rapidly broke down, and in 1948–49 the USSR blockaded West Berlin (see p. 450). The western zones of Germany were merged economically in 1948. After the merger of the western zones to form the Federal Republic of Germany, the German Democratic Republic was proclaimed in the Soviet zone (October 1949). The GDR's economic progress suffered by comparison with that of the Federal Republic. Food shortages and repressive Communist rule led to an abortive uprising in the GDR in 1953. West Germany gained sovereignty – as a member of the Western Alliance – in 1955. The division of Germany was only grudgingly accepted in West Germany. Chancellor Konrad Adenauer (1876–1967) refused to recognize East Germany as a separate state and relations with the Soviet Union remained uncertain. Major problems with

the Eastern bloc included the undefined status of the areas taken over by Poland in 1945 and the difficult position of West Berlin – a part of the Federal Republic isolated within Communist East Germany.

Relations between East and West Germany were soured as large numbers of East Germans fled to the West, and this outflow was stemmed only when Walter Ulbricht (East German Communist Party leader 1950–71) ordered the building of the Berlin Wall. Adenauer strove to gain the acceptance of West Germany back into Western Europe through reconciliation with France and participation in the European Community. The economic revival of Germany begun by Adenauer continued under his Christian Democrat (conservative) successors as Chancellor – Ludwig Erhard (1963–66) and Georg Kiesinger (1966–69). Under Social Democrat Chancellors – Willy Brandt (1969–74) and Helmut Schmidt (1974–82) – treaties were signed with the USSR (1970) and Poland (recognizing the Oder-Neisse line as Poland's western frontier), and relations with the GDR were normalized (1972). Under Helmut Kohl (Christian Democrat Chancellor from 1982) West Germany continued its impressive economic growth and enthusiastic membership of the EC, and acted as an economic and cultural magnet for much of Eastern Europe.

The root causes of the GDR's problems resurfaced in the late 1980s. The ageing Communist leadership led by Erich Honecker proved unresponsive to the mood of greater freedom emanating from Gorbachov's USSR. In 1989 fresh floods of East Germans left the GDR for the West by way of Czechoslovakia and Hungary. Massive public demonstrations in favour of reform resulted in a change of leadership and the opening of the Berlin Wall (November 1989), allowing free movement between East and West. Demonstrations in favour of more radical change continued, and a coalition government was appointed in the GDR. When the GDR's economy collapsed, West Germany proposed monetary union and the call for German reunification became unstoppable. Despite the initial opposition of the USSR, the reunification of Germany as a full member of the EC and NATO took place in October 1990. Soviet troops are scheduled to withdraw from the former GDR by 1994.

GHANA

Official name: The Republic of Ghana

Member of: UN, OAU, Commonwealth, ECOWAS

Area: 238 537 km² (92 099 sq mi)

Population: 15 509 000 (1991 est)

Capital and major cities: Accra 1 580 000, Kumasi 490 000, Tema (part of the Accra agglomeration) 190 000, Sekondi-Takoradi 175 000, Tamale 170 000 (1988 est)

Languages: English (official), Asante, Ewe, Ga

Religions: Various Protestant Churches (30%), Sunni Islam (20%), Roman Catholic (over 25%), animist (17%)

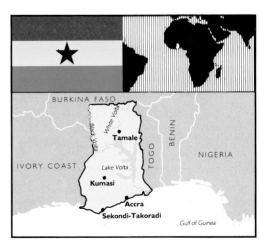

GOVERNMENT
A 140-member Assembly and a President are elected for four years by universal adult suffrage.

GEOGRAPHY
Most of the country is low-lying plains and plateaux. The central Volta Basin – which ends in steep escarpments – contains the large Lake Volta reservoir.

Principal river: Volta 1600 km (1000 mi)

Climate: The climate is tropical with 2000 mm (80 in) of rainfall on the coast, decreasing markedly inland. The N is subject to the hot, dry Harmattan wind from the Sahara.

ECONOMY
Political instability and mismanagement have damaged the economy. Nearly 50% of the labour force is involved in farming. Cocoa is the main cash crop. Timber and mining for bauxite, gold and diamonds are important.

HISTORY
Trade for gold, ivory and slaves led to the establishment of European coastal stations from around 1600. Britain ousted the Danes (1850) and the Dutch (1872) to establish the Gold Coast colony in 1874. The great inland kingdom of Ashanti was not finally conquered until 1898. After World War II, the prosperity of the cocoa industry, increasing literacy and the dynamism of Dr Kwame Nkrumah (1909–72), helped the Gold Coast set the pace for decolonization in Black Africa. After independence in 1957 – as Ghana – Nkrumah's grandiose policies and increasingly dictatorial rule led to his overthrow in a military coup in 1966. Ghana has since struggled to overcome its economic and political problems. There were six coups in 20 years, including two by Flight Lieutenant Jerry Rawlings (1979 and 1982). A multi-party system was restored in 1992.

GREECE

Official name: Ellenikí Dimokrátia (Hellenic Republic) or Ellás (Greece)

Member of: UN, EC, NATO, CSCE, OECD

Area: 131 957 km² (50 949 sq mi)

Population: 10 269 000 (1990 census)

Capital and major cities: Athens (Athínai) 3 097 000, Thessaloníki (formerly Salonika) 706 000, Piraeus (Piraiévs) 196 000 (part of the Athens agglomeration), Patras (Pátrai) 155 000, Lárisa 102 000, Heraklion (Iráklion, formerly Candia) 102 000 (1990 census)

Language: Greek (official)

Religion: Orthodox (98%; official)

GOVERNMENT
The 300-member Parliament is elected for four years by universal adult suffrage under a system of proportional representation. The President – who is elected for a five-year term by Parliament – appoints a Prime Minister (who commands a majority in Parliament) and other Ministers.

GEOGRAPHY
Over 80% of Greece is mountainous. The mainland is dominated by the Pindus Mountains, which extend from Albania S into the Peloponnese Peninsula and at Mount Olympus reach 2911 m (9550 ft). The Rhodope Mountains lie along the Bulgarian border. Greece has some 2000 islands, of which only 154 are inhabited.

Climate: Greece has a Mediterranean climate with hot dry summers and mild wet winters. The N and the mountains are colder.

ECONOMY
Agriculture involves 25% of the labour force. Much of the land is marginal – in particular the extensive sheep pastures. Greece is largely self-sufficient in wheat, barley, maize, sugar beet, fruit, vegetables, and cheese, and produces enough wine, olives (and olive oil) and tobacco for export. The industrial sector is expanding rapidly and includes processing local petroleum and

natural gas, lignite, and bauxite. Tourism, a large merchant fleet, and money sent back by Greeks working abroad are major foreign-currency earners. Greece receives special economic aid from the EC.

HISTORY
The Bronze Age Minoan civilization (c. 2200–1450 BC) was based in Crete (see pp. 368–9), while the slightly later Mycenaean civilization (c. 1500–1150 BC) flourished on the Greek mainland (see p. 369). Following a 'dark age', city-states began to emerge in the 8th century BC at the beginning of the Archaic period (see p. 370). The influence of the culture and political thinking of the Classical Greek period (c. 500–338 BC; see pp. 370–1) has since been felt throughout the world. The city-states declined and were conquered by the Macedonians who, under Alexander the Great, spread Hellenistic culture throughout the Middle East (see pp. 372–3). From 146 BC Greece formed part of the Roman Empire (see pp. 376–7). On the division of the Roman Empire, Greece formed part of the Eastern (Byzantine) Empire based in Constantinople (see pp. 394–5).

Most of Greece remained under Byzantine rule until 1204, when the Crusaders took Constantinople. From 1204 to the 15th century Greece was divided into four states – the Greek kingdoms of Salonika and Epirus in the N, and the Frankish monarchies of Athens and Archaia in the S. Venice gained the majority of the Greek islands. From the early 15th century, the Ottoman Turks gradually asserted control over the region. However, the continuing vitality of the Orthodox Church helped maintain a strong Greek national identity. As early as 1480 there was some resistance to Ottoman rule by klephts (rural bandits).

In the 18th century, various European powers, especially Russia, sought to use the Greeks in their quarrels with the Turks. The outbreak of revolution against Ottoman rule in 1821 attracted support throughout Europe (see p. 429). The leaders of the Greek state established in 1830 brought Western European constitutional institutions to Greece, but the monarchy established under a Bavarian prince in 1832 was swept away by revolution in 1862. Under a Danish prince – who became King George I in 1863 – Greece gained extra territory in 1863, 1881 and 1913, as Turkish power declined.

The 20th century has been marked by great instability. Eleuthérios Venizélos (1864–1936) dominated Greek politics from 1910 to 1935, a period of rivalry between

republicans and royalists. An attempt by his rival King Constantine I to seize Anatolia from Turkey (1921–22) ended in military defeat and the establishment of a republic in 1924. The monarchy was restored in 1935, but it depended upon a military leader, General Ioannis Metaxas (1871–1941) who, claiming the threat from Communism as justification, ruled as virtual dictator. The nation was deeply divided. The German invasion of 1941 (see p. 444) was met by rival resistance groups of Communists and monarchists, and the subsequent civil war between these factions lasted from 1945 to 1949, when, with British and US aid, the monarchists emerged victorious. Continued instability in the 1960s led to a military coup in 1967. King Constantine II, who had not initially opposed the coup, unsuccessfully appealed for the overthrow of the junta and went into exile. The dictatorship of the colonels ended in 1974 when their encouragement of a Greek Cypriot coup brought Greece to the verge of war with Turkey. Civilian government was restored, and a new republican constitution was adopted in 1975. Greece has forged closer links with Western Europe, in particular through membership of the EC (1981). Greek opposition prevented international recognition of the former Yugoslav republic of Macedonia in 1992.

GRENADA

Official name: The State of Grenada

Member of: UN, OAS, Commonwealth, CARICOM

Area: 344 km² (133 sq mi)

Population: 96 000 (1991 est)

Capital: St George's 36 000 (city 7500; 1989 est)

Language: English

Religions: Roman Catholic (over 60%), Anglican

GOVERNMENT
The 13-member Senate is appointed. The 15-member House of Representatives is elected for five years by universal adult suffrage. The Governor General – the representative of the British Queen as sovereign of Grenada – appoints a Prime Minister (who commands a majority in the House) and a Cabinet.

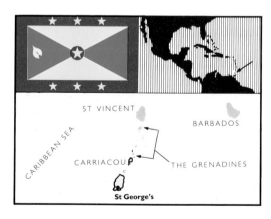

GEOGRAPHY
A forested mountain ridge – rising to 840 m (2706 ft) – covers much of this well-watered island. The island of Carriacou forms part of Grenada.

Climate: Grenada has a tropical maritime climate with a dry season from January to May.

ECONOMY
The production of spices, in particular nutmeg, is the mainstay of a largely agricultural economy. Tourism is increasing in importance.

HISTORY
Grenada was discovered by Columbus in 1498, colonized by France in 1650 and ceded to Britain in 1783. Independence was gained in 1974. The left-wing New Jewel

Movement seized power in a coup in 1979. In 1983 the PM Maurice Bishop was killed in a further coup in which more extreme members of the government seized power. Acting upon a request from East Caribbean islands to intervene, US and Caribbean forces landed in Grenada. After several days' fighting, the coup leaders were detained. Constitutional rule was restored in 1984.

GUATEMALA

Official name: República de Guatemala (Republic of Guatemala)

Member of: UN, OAS, CACM

Area: 108 889 km² (42 042 sq mi)

Population: 9 454 000 (1991 est)

Capital and major cities: Guatemala City 2 000 000, Puerto Barrios 338 000 (including suburbs; 1989 est)

Language: Spanish (official), Mayan languages (45%)

Religions: Roman Catholic (official; 70%), various Protestant evangelical Churches (30%)

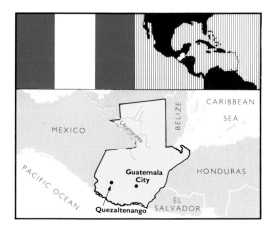

GOVERNMENT
A President – who appoints a Cabinet – and a 100-member National Congress are elected for a five-year term by universal adult suffrage.

GEOGRAPHY
A mountain chain – containing over 30 volcanoes including Tajumulco (4220 m/13 881 ft) – separates Pacific and Atlantic coastal lowlands.

Climate: The coastal plains have a tropical climate; the mountains are more temperate.

ECONOMY
More than one half of the labour force is involved in agriculture. Coffee is the major export, while the other main crops include sugar cane and bananas.

HISTORY
The area was the centre of the Mayan civilization between the 4th and 9th centuries (see pp. 390–91). After 1524, Guatemala was the administrative centre of Spanish Central America. Independence was proclaimed in 1821, but the country was part of the Central American Federation until 1839. Guatemala has a history of being ruled by dictators allied to landowners. However, in the 1950s President Jacobo Arbenz expropriated large estates, dividing them among the peasantry. Accused of being a Communist, he was deposed by the army with US military aid (1954). For over 30 years, the left was suppressed, leading to the emergence of guerrilla armies. Thousands of dissidents were killed or disappeared. Civilian government was restored in 1986, but unrest continues, and there have been serious abuses of human rights by the military.

GUINEA

Official name: La République de Guinée (The Republic of Guinea)

Member of: UN, OAU, ECOWAS

Area: 245 857 km² (94 926 sq mi)

Population: 7 052 000 (1991 est)

Capital: Conakry 705 000 (1983)

Languages: French (official), Fulani (40%), Soussou

Religion: Sunni Islam (85%)

GOVERNMENT
Power is exercised by the Military Committee for National Recovery, whose President is head of state and of government. There are no political parties.

GEOGRAPHY
Tropical rain forests cover the coastal plain. The interior highlands and plains are covered by grass and scrubland. The SW mountains rise to Mount Nimba 1752 m (5748 ft).

Climate: The climate is tropical with heavy rainfall. Temperatures are cooler in the highlands.

ECONOMY
Bauxite accounts for 80% of Guinea's exports. However, over 75% of the labour force is involved in agriculture, producing bananas, oil palm and citrus fruits for export, and maize, rice and cassava as subsistence crops. Despite mineral wealth, Guinea is one of the world's poorest states and relies heavily on aid.

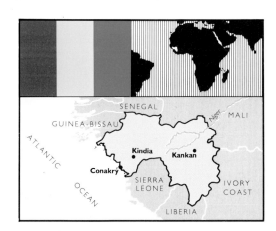

HISTORY
Portuguese slave traders visited the coast from the 15th century. In the 18th and 19th centuries the area was part of the Fulani tribe's Islamic kingdom. Increasing French influence in the 19th century led to the establishment of the colony of French Guinea (1890). Unlike the rest of French Africa, Guinea voted for a complete separation from France in 1958, suffering severe French reprisals as a result. The authoritarian radical leader Sékou Touré (1922–84) isolated Guinea, but he became reconciled with France in 1978. The leaders of a military coup (1984) have achieved some economic reforms.

GUINEA-BISSAU

Official name: Republica da Guiné-Bissau (Republic of Guinea-Bissau)

Member of: UN, OAU, ECOWAS

Area: 36 125 km² (13 948 sq mi)

Population: 994 000 (1991 est)

Capital: Bissau 125 000 (1988 est)

Languages: Portuguese (official), Crioulo

Religions: Animist (55%), Sunni Islam (40%)

GOVERNMENT
The 150-member Assembly – which is elected by univer-

sal adult suffrage – elects a President, who appoints a Prime Minister and a Cabinet of Ministers.

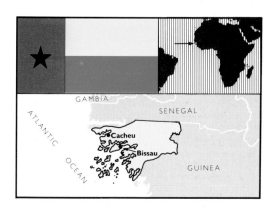

GEOGRAPHY
Most of the country is low-lying, with swampy coastal lowlands and a flat forested interior plain. The NE is mountainous.

Climate: The climate is tropical with a dry season from December to May.

ECONOMY
The country has one of the lowest standards of living in the world. Its subsistence economy is based mainly on rice. Palm kernels and timber are exported.

HISTORY
The area was much involved in the slave trade after the arrival of the Portuguese (1441). The colony of Portuguese Guinea was created in 1879. Failing to secure reform by peaceful means, the PAIGC movement mounted a liberation war (1961–74). Independence was proclaimed in 1973 and recognized by Portugal in 1974. Multi-party politics were introduced in 1991.

GUYANA

Official name: The Cooperative Republic of Guyana

Member of: UN, Commonwealth, OAS, CARICOM

Area: 214 969 km² (83 000 sq mi)

Population: 760 000 (1991 est)

Capital: Georgetown 187 000 (1986 est)

Languages: English (official), Hindu, Urdu

Religions: Hinduism (34%), with Anglican, Sunni Islam and Roman Catholic minorities

GOVERNMENT
The 65-member National Assembly is elected for five years under a system of proportional representation by

universal adult suffrage. The President – the leader of the majority in the Assembly – appoints a Prime Minister and Cabinet.

GEOGRAPHY
A coastal plain is protected from the sea by dykes. Tropical rain forest covers much of the interior. The Pakaraima range rises to 2772 m (9094 ft).

Climate: The interior is tropical, while the coastal plain is more moderate.

ECONOMY
Guyana depends on mining bauxite and growing sugar cane and rice. Nationalization and emigration have caused economic problems.

HISTORY
Dutch colonies on the Guyanese coast – established since the 1620s – were captured by the British in 1796 and merged to form British Guiana in 1831. From the 1840s large numbers of Indian and Chinese labourers were imported from Asia to work on sugar plantations. Racial tension between their descendants – now the majority – and the Black community (descended from imported African slaves) led to violence in 1964 and 1978. Guyana has been independent since 1966.

HAITI

Official name: La République d'Haïti (Republic of Haiti)

Member of: UN, OAS, CARICOM

Area: 27 750 km² (10 714 sq mi)

Population: 6 486 000 (1990 est)

Capital and major cities: Port-au-Prince 1 144 000, Jacmel 217 000 (all including suburbs; 1988 est)

Languages: Creole (90%), French – both official

Religions: Voodoo (majority), Roman Catholic (official)

GOVERNMENT
The constitution provides for a President, 27-member Senate and 77-member Chamber of Deputies elected for five years.

GEOGRAPHY
Haiti is the western part of the island of Hispaniola. Mountain ranges – up to 2800 m (8800 ft) – run from E to W, separated by densely populated valleys and plains.

Climate: Haiti's tropical climate is moderated by altitude and by the sea.

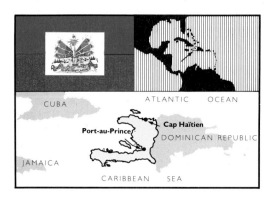

ECONOMY
Two thirds of the labour force is involved in agriculture, mainly growing crops for local consumption. Coffee is the main cash crop. With few resources, overpopulated Haiti is the poorest country in the western hemisphere.

HISTORY
Columbus discovered Hispaniola in 1492, and in the 17th century the French settled Haiti, which formally became a colony in 1697. Black slaves – who were imported to work plantations – revolted in 1791 and were freed in 1794. Toussaint l'Ouverture – a former slave – became

governor general (1801), but was unable to defeat a French force sent to restore the old order. Independence was proclaimed in 1804 during a revolt led by Jean-Jacques Dessalines and Henri Christophe, both of whom reigned as monarchs of Haiti. A united republic was achieved in 1820. Coups, instability and tension between Blacks and mulattos wracked Haiti until the US intervened (1915–35). President François Duvalier – 'Papa Doc' – (in office 1956–71) and his son Jean-Claude (1971–86) cowed the country into submission by means of their infamous private militia, the Tontons Macoutes. Several coups have followed the violent end to the Duvalier era. A free multi-party election – the first in Haiti's history – took place in 1991, but constitutional government was suspended following a military coup nine months later.

HONDURAS

Official name: La República de Honduras (Republic of Honduras)

Member of: UN, OAS, CACM

Area: 112 088 km² (43 277 sq mi)

Population: 4 708 000 (1991 est)

Capital and major cities: Tegucigalpa 648 000, San Pedro Sula 301 000, La Ceiba 72 000 (all including suburbs; 1988 census)

Language: Spanish (official)

Religion: Roman Catholic (85%)

GOVERNMENT
The President and the 134-member National Assembly are elected by universal adult suffrage for four years.

GEOGRAPHY
Over three quarters of Honduras is mountainous, with the highest point at Cerio las Minas 2849 m (9347 ft). There are small coastal plains.

Climate: The tropical lowlands experience high rainfall (1500–2000 mm / 60–80 in). The more temperate highlands are drier.

ECONOMY
Over 40% of Hondurans work in agriculture, but despite agrarian reform, living standards remain low. Bananas and coffee are the leading exports. There are few natural resources.

HISTORY
In 1502 Columbus reached Honduras and in 1523 the first Spanish settlement was established. Honduras gained freedom from Spain in 1821, but was part of the Central American Federation until 1839. Between independence and the early 20th century, Honduras experienced constant political upheaval and wars with neighbouring countries. US influence was immense, largely owing to the substantial investments of the powerfu United Fruit Company in banana production. After a short civil war in 1925, a succession of military dictators governed

Honduras until 1980. Since then the country has had democratically elected pro-US centre-right civilian governments.

HUNGARY

Official name: Magyarország (The Hungarian Republic) or Magyarország (Hungary)

Member of: UN, CSCE

Area: 93 036 km² (35 921 sq mi)

Population: 10 375 000 (1990 census)

Capital and major cities: Budapest 2 018 000, Debrecen 214 000, Miskolc 194 000, Szeged 176 000 (1990 census)

Language: Magyar (Hungarian; 97%)

Religions: Roman Catholic (56%), Calvinist

GOVERNMENT
The 386-member National Assembly is elected by universal adult suffrage, with 58 members elected from a national list, 152 elected on a county basis and 176 elected from single-member constituencies. The President – who is elected by the Assembly – appoints a Prime Minister and Cabinet from the majority in the Assembly.

GEOGRAPHY
Hungary W of the River Danube is an undulating lowland. The thickly wooded highlands of the NE contain the highest point, Kékes (1015 m / 3330 ft). The SE is a great expanse of flat plain.

Principal rivers: Danube (Duna) 2850 km (1770 mi), Tisza 996 km (619 mi)

Climate: The climate is continental with long, hot and dry summers, and cold winters.

ECONOMY
Nearly one fifth of the labour force is involved in agriculture. Major crops include cereals (maize, wheat and barley), sugar beet, fruit, and grapes for wine. Despite large reserves of coal, Hungary imports over 50% of its energy needs. The steel, chemical fertilizer, pharmaceutical, machinery and vehicle industries are important. Since the early 1980s, private enterprise and foreign investment have been encouraged, and most large state enterprises have been privatized.

HISTORY
The Magyars colonized the area from the E in the 9th century. The first Magyar king, Stephen (reigned 1001–38), encouraged Christianity and West European culture. Matthias Corvinus (reigned 1458–90) made Hungary a major power and did much to introduce the ideas of the Renaissance to central Europe. In the 16th century Hungary was dismembered by the Austrian Habsburgs and the Turkish Ottoman Empire. The

Habsburgs liberated Buda, the capital, from the Turks in 1686, and by the 18th century all the Hungarian lands were within the Habsburg Empire. Lajos Kossuth

(1802–94) led a nationalist revolt against Austrian rule (1848–49), but fled when Austria regained control with Russian aid. Austria granted Hungary considerable autonomy in the Dual Monarchy (1867) – the Austro-Hungarian Empire.

Defeat in World War I led to a brief period of Communist rule under Béla Kun (1919), then occupation by Romania. In the postwar settlement (see p. 441), Hungary lost two thirds of its territory. The Regent Admiral Miklás Horthy (1868–1957) cooperated with Hitler during World War II in an attempt to regain territory, but defeat in 1945 resulted in occupation by the Red Army, and a Communist People's Republic was established in 1949. The Hungarian Uprising in 1956 was a heroic attempt to overthrow Communist rule, but was quickly suppressed by Soviet forces, and its leader, Imre Nagy, was executed. János Kadar – Party Secretary 1956–88 – tried to win support with economic progress. However, in the late 1980s reformers in the Communist Party gained the upper hand, and established a fully democratic, multi-party state. Soviet troops left Hungary in 1990. The country has taken rapid steps to establish a free-market economy. The status of 3 000 000 Hungarians in neighbouring states has become an issue.

ICELAND

Official name: Lýdveldid Island (The Republic of Iceland)

Member of: UN, NATO, EFTA, CSCE

Area: 103 001 km² (39 769 sq mi)

Population: 258 000 (1991 est)

Capital and major cities: Reykjavik 146 000 (city 98 000), Akureyri 14 000 (1990 est)

Language: Icelandic

Religion: Evangelical Lutheran (93%)

GOVERNMENT
The 63-member Althing (Parliament) is elected under a system of proportional representation by universal adult suffrage for a four-year term and meets as an Upper House of 20 members and a Lower House of 43 members. The President – who is also directly elected for four years – appoints a Prime Minister and a Cabinet who are responsible to the Althing.

GEOGRAPHY
The greater part of Iceland has a volcanic landscape with hot springs, geysers and some 200 volcanoes – some of them active. Much of the country is tundra. The S and centre are covered by glacial icefields, the largest of which contains Hvannadalshnúkur at 2119 m (6952 ft) the country's highest peak.

Climate: The cool temperate climate is warmed by the Gulf Stream, which keeps Iceland milder than most places at the same latitude.

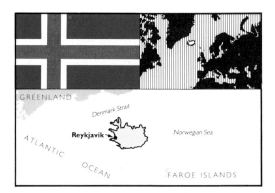

ECONOMY
The fishing industry provides the majority of Iceland's exports. Hydroelectric power is used to smelt aluminium; geo-thermal power warms extensive greenhouses.

Ample grazing land makes Iceland self-sufficient in meat and dairy products.

HISTORY
Norwegians settled in Iceland in the 9th century. From 930 Iceland was an independent republic, but Norwegian sovereignty was accepted in 1264 to end a civil war. When Denmark and Norway were united (1381), Iceland became Danish. Nationalism grew in the 19th century, and in 1918 Iceland gained independence, linked to Denmark only by their shared monarchy. In World War II the Danish link was severed and a republic was declared (1944). Disputes over fishing rights in Icelandic territorial waters led to clashes with British naval vessels in the 1950s and 1970s.

INDIA

Official name: Bharat (Republic of India)

Member of: UN, Commonwealth

Area: 3 287 263 km² (1 269 212 sq mi) – including the Indian-held part of Jammu and Kashmir

Population: 844 324 000 (1991 census)

Capital and major cities: Delhi 8 375 000 (city 7 175 000), Bombay 12 572 000 (city 9 910 000), Calcutta 10 916 000 (city 4 388 000), Madras 5 361 000 (city 3 795 000), Hyderabad 4 280 000 (city 3 005 000), Bangalore 4 087 000 (city 2 651 000), Ahmedabad 3 298 000 (city 2 873 000), Poona (Pune) 2 485 000 (city 1 560 000), Kanpur 2 111 000 (city 1 958 000), Nagpur 1 661 000 (city 1 622 000), Lucknow 1 642 000 (city 1 592 000), Surat 1 517 000 (1 497 000), Jaipur 1 514 000 (city 1 455 000); 11 other cities with over 1 million inhabitants (1991 census)

Languages: Hindi (30%; official), English (official), Bengali (8%), Telugu (8%), Marathi (8%), Tamil (7%), Urdu (5%), Gujarati (5%); over 1600 other languages

Religions: Hindu (83%), Sunni Islam (11%), Christian (mainly Roman Catholic) (nearly 3%)

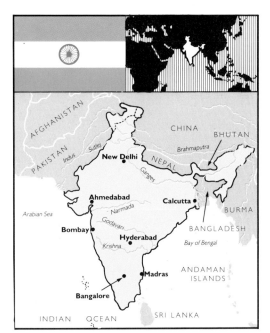

GOVERNMENT
The upper house of the federal parliament – the 250-member Council of States (Rajya Sabha) – consists of 12 members nominated by the President and 238 members elected by state assemblies. One third of the Council retires every two years. The lower house – the House of the People (Lok Sabha) – consists of 542 members elected for a five-year term by universal adult suffrage, plus two nominated members. The President – who serves for five

years – is elected by the federal parliament and the state assemblies. The President appoints a Prime Minister – who has a majority in the House – and a Council of Ministers, who are responsible to the House. Each of the 25 states has its own legislature.

GEOGRAPHY
The Himalaya cut the Indian subcontinent off from the rest of Asia. Several Himalayan peaks in India rise to over 7000 m (23 000 ft), including Kangchenjunga on the Nepal-Sikkim border – at 8598 m (28 208 ft) India's highest mountain. S of the Himalaya, the basins of the Rivers Ganges and Brahmaputra and their tributaries are intensively farmed and densely populated. The Thar Desert stretches along the border with Pakistan. In S India, the Deccan – a large plateau of hard rocks – is bordered in the E and W by the Ghats, discontinuous ranges of hills descending to coastal plains. Natural vegetation ranges from tropical rain forest on the W coast and monsoon forest in the NE and far S, through dry tropical scrub and thorn forest in the Deccan to Alpine and temperate vegetation in the Himalaya.

Principal rivers: Ganges (Ganga) 2510 km (1560 mi), Brahmaputra 2900 km (1800 mi), Sutlej 1450 km (900 mi)

Climate: India has three distinct seasons: a hot season from March to June, a wet season (when the SW monsoon brings heavy rain) from June to October, and a cooler drier season from November to March. Temperatures range from the cool of the Himalaya to the tropical heat in the S.

ECONOMY
Two thirds of the labour force are involved in subsistence farming, with rice and wheat as the principal crops. Cash crops tend to come from large plantations and include tea, cotton, jute and sugar cane – all grown for export. The monsoon rains and irrigation make cultivation possible in many areas, but drought and floods are common. India is a major industrial power. Major coal reserves provide the power base for industry. Other mineral deposits include diamonds, bauxite, and titanium, copper and iron ore, as well as substantial reserves of natural gas and petroleum. The textile, vehicle, iron and steel, pharmaceutical and electrical industries make important contributions to the economy, but India has balance-of-payment difficulties and relies upon foreign aid for development. Over one third of the population is below the official poverty line. Privatization of some state enterprises began in the early 1990s.

HISTORY
The history of the kingdoms and empires of India to the colonial age – and the expansion of Hindu culture and Islam in India – is covered on pp. 384–85. By the middle of the 18th century the British East India Company had established itself as the dominant power in India (see pp. 417 and 432). After the Indian Mutiny (1857–58; see p. 432) was put down, the Company ceded its rights in India to the British Crown. In 1877 the Indian Empire was proclaimed with Queen Victoria as Empress. The Empire included present-day Pakistan and Bangladesh, and comprised the Crown Territories of British India and over 620 Indian protected states. The latter covered about 40% of India, and enjoyed varying degrees of autonomy under their traditional princes.

From the middle of the 19th century the British cautiously encouraged Indian participation in the administration of British India. British institutions, the railways and the English language – all imposed upon India by a modernizing imperial power – fostered the growth of an Indian sense of identity beyond the divisions of caste (see p. 258) and language. However, ultimately the divisions of religion proved stronger. The Indian National Congress – the forerunner of the Congress Party – was first convened in 1885, and the Muslim League first met in 1906. Nationalist demands grew after British troops fired without warning on a nationalist protest meeting – the Amritsar Massacre (1919). The India Acts (1919 and 1935) granted limited autonomy and created an Indian federation, but the pace of reform did not satisfy Indian expectations. In 1920

Congress – led by Mohandas (Mahatma) Gandhi (1869–1948) – began a campaign of non-violence and non-cooperation with the British authorities. However relations between Hindus and Muslims steadily deteriorated. By 1940 the Muslim League was demanding a separate sovereign state.

By 1945, war-weary Britain had accepted the inevitability of Indian independence. However, religious discord forced the partition of the subcontinent in 1947 into predominantly Hindu India – under Jawaharlal (Pandit) Nehru (1889–1964) of the Congress Party – and Muslim Pakistan (including what is now Bangladesh) – under Mohammad Ali Jinnah (1876–1948) of the Muslim League. Over 70 million Hindus and Muslims became refugees and crossed the new boundaries, and thousands were killed in communal violence. The frontiers remained disputed. India and Pakistan fought border wars in 1947–49, 1965 (over Kashmir) and again in 1971 – when Bangladesh gained independence from Pakistan with Indian assistance. Kashmir is still divided along a cease-fire line. There were also border clashes with China in 1962.

Under Nehru – PM 1947–64 – India became one of the leaders of the nonaligned movement of Third World states. Under the premiership (1966–77 and 1980–84) of his daughter Indira Gandhi (1917–84) India continued to assert itself as the dominant regional power. Although India remained the world's largest democracy – despite Mrs Gandhi's brief imposition of emergency rule – local separatism and communal unrest have threatened unity. The Sikhs have conducted an often violent campaign for an independent homeland – Khalistan – in the Punjab. In 1984 Mrs Gandhi ordered the storming of the Golden Temple of Amritsar, a Sikh holy place that extremists had turned into an arsenal. In the same year Mrs Gandhi was assassinated by her Sikh bodyguard. Her son Rajiv Gandhi (PM 1984–89) was assassinated in the 1991 election campaign. Tension and violence between Hindus and Muslims has increased since a campaign (1990–) to build a Hindu temple on the site of a mosque in the holy city of Ayodhya.

INDONESIA

Official name: Republik Indonesia (Republic of Indonesia)

Member of: UN, ASEAN, OPEC

Area: 1 919 443 km² (741 101 sq mi) – including East Timor which has an area of 14 874 km² (5743 sq mi)

Population: 179 322 000 (1990 census) – including East Timor which had a population of 748 000.

Capital and major cities: Jakarta 7 829 000, Surabaya 2 345 000, Medan 2 110 000, Bandung 1 613 000 (all including suburbs; 1985 est)

Languages: Bahasa Indonesia (official), Javanese (34%), Sundanese (14%); about 26 other main languages

Religions: Sunni Islam (80%), Roman Catholic (3%), other Christians (7%), Hindu (2%)

GOVERNMENT

Every five years elections are held by universal adult suffrage for 400 members of the House of Representatives; 100 additional members are chosen by the President. The People's Consultative Assembly – which comprises the House plus 500 representatives of provincial governments, occupational and special interests – meets every five years to oversee principles of state policy and to elect the President, who appoints a Cabinet.

GEOGRAPHY

Indonesia consists of nearly 3700 islands of which about 3000 are inhabited. The southern chain of mountainous, volcanic islands comprises Sumatra, Java with Madura, Bali and the Lesser Sunda Islands. Java and its smaller neighbour Madura are fertile and densely populated, containing nearly 65% of Indonesians. The northern chain comprises Kalimantan (the Indonesian sector of Borneo), the irregular mountainous island of Sulawesi

(Celebes), the Moluccas group and Irian Jaya (western New Guinea), that contains the highest peak Ngga Pulu (or Carstenz Pyramid) at 5030 m (16 503 ft). Over two thirds of the country is covered by tropical rain forests.

Climate: The climate is tropical with heavy rainfall throughout the year.

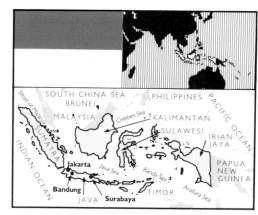

ECONOMY

Indonesia has great mineral wealth – petroleum, natural gas, tin, nickel and bauxite – but is relatively poor because of its great population. Over 50% of the labour force are subsistence farmers with rice being the major crop, but both estate and peasant farmers produce important quantities of rubber, tea, coffee and spices for export. Industry – largely concerned with processing mineral and agricultural products – is expanding and Indonesia achieved high economic growth rates in the 1980s and early 1990s.

HISTORY

Indian traders brought Hinduism to the East Indies (as Indonesia was formerly known) and by the 3rd century AD, Hindu kingdoms had been established in Java and Sumatra. Monks brought Buddhism from India, and both Hindu and Buddhist states flourished in the islands. The powerful Buddhist kingdom of Sri Vijaya on Sumatra (7th–13th centuries) was eclipsed by the Javan Hindu kingdom of Majapahit (13th–15th centuries). Arab traders brought Islam, which took the place of both established religions by the 16th century, while at the same time European incursions began. The struggle between the Portuguese, Dutch, Spanish and British for the rich spice trade ended in Dutch ascendancy in the 1620s. The East Indies became the major and most profitable part of the Dutch Empire.

Except for a brief period of British occupation (1811–14) and occasional local risings, the Netherlands retained control until 1942 when the Japanese invaded and were welcomed by most Indonesians as liberators from colonial rule. Upon Japan's surrender in 1945, Achmed Sukarno (1901–70) – the founder of the nationalist party in 1927 – declared the Dutch East Indies to be the independent republic of Indonesia. Under international pressure, the Dutch accepted Indonesian independence (1949) after four years of intermittent but brutal fighting. Sukarno's rule became increasingly authoritarian and the country sank into economic chaos. In 1962 he seized Netherlands New Guinea, which was formally annexed as Irian Jaya in 1969, although a separatist movement persists. Between 1963 and 1966 Sukarno tried to destabilize the newly-created Federation of Malaysia by armed incursions into N Borneo. General T.N.I. Suharto's suppression of a Communist uprising in 1965–66 enabled him to reverse Sukarno's anti-Americanism and eventually to displace him with the support of both the students and the army. Around 80 000 members of the Communist Party were killed in this period. The annexation of Portuguese East Timor by Indonesia in 1976 is unrecognized by the international community, and guerrilla action by local nationalists continues. International protests followed the killing of unarmed Timorese demonstrators by Indonesian troops

in 1991. An ambitious programme of resettlement has been attempted to relieve overcrowded Java, but the Javanese settlers have been resented in the outlying, underdeveloped islands.

IRAN

Official name: Jomhori-e-Islami-e-Irân (Islamic Republic of Iran). Known as Persia until 1935.

Member of: UN, OPEC

Area: 1 648 000 km² (636 296 sq mi)

Population: 57 050 000 (1991 est)

Capital and major cities: Tehran 6 022 000, Mashad 1 464 000, Isfahan 987 000, Tabriz 971 000 (all including suburbs; 1986 census)

Languages: Farsi or Persian (official; 45%), Azeri (26%); Kurdish, Luri and Baluchi minorities

Religion: Shia Islam (official; 98%)

GOVERNMENT

A Council of Experts – 83 Shiite clerics – is elected by universal adult suffrage to appoint the Wali Faqih (religious leader), who exercises supreme authority over the executive, legislature, judiciary and military. The 270-member Islamic Consultative Assembly (Majlis) and the President are directly elected for four years. The President appoints a Prime Minister and Cabinet who are responsible to the Majlis.

GEOGRAPHY

Apart from restricted lowlands along the Gulf, the Caspian Sea and the Iraqi border, Iran is a high plateau, surrounded by mountains. The Elburz Mountains in the N include the country's highest peak, Demavend at 5604 m (18 386 ft); the Zagros Mountains form a barrier running parallel to the Gulf. In the E, lower areas of the plateau are covered by salt deserts.

Climate: Iran has an extreme climate ranging from very hot on the Gulf to sub-zero temperatures in winter in the NW. The Caspian Sea coast has a subtropical climate with adequate rainfall. Most of Iran, however, is arid.

ECONOMY

Petroleum is Iran's main source of foreign currency. The principal industries are petrochemicals, carpetweaving, textiles, vehicles and cement, but the war with Iraq and the country's international isolation have severely interrupted trade. Over a quarter of the labour force is involved in agriculture, mainly producing cereals (wheat, maize and barley) and keeping livestock, but lack of water, land ownership problems and manpower shortages have restricted yields.

HISTORY

The Persian Achaemenid Empire grew under Cyrus from 539 BC (see p. 365). Under Darius I and Xerxes the Persians ruled from the Danube to the Indus, although their attempts to conquer Greece were eventually unsuccessful (see p. 370). Alexander the Great finally defeated the Achaemenids, taking the capital Persopolis in 330 BC (see pp. 372–3). Persia was part of the Hellenic Seleucid Empire until 247 BC, then ruled by the Parthians until 226 AD, when the Sassanians – an Iranian people – established an empire that lasted until the coming of the Arabs and Islam in the 7th century. The first Muslim dynasty, the Umayyads, were based on Damascus, but their successors the Abbasids moved the capital to Baghdad where Persian traditions predominated. Once Persia had recovered from the ruthless Mongol invasion of the 13th century, a golden age arose under the Safavid dynasty. The Safavids were great patrons of the arts, and established Shia – rather than Sunni – Islam as the state religion. The 18th century saw the rise of the Qajar dynasty, who moved the capital from Isfahan to Tehran. In the 19th century, Russia and Britain became rivals for influence in the region.

In 1921 an Iranian Cossack officer, Reza Khan Pahlavi (1877–1944), took power. Deposing the Qajars in 1925, he became Shah (emperor) himself as Reza I and modernized and secularized Iran. However, because of his pro-German sentiments, he was forced to abdicate by Britain and the USSR (1941) and was replaced by his son Mohammed Reza (1919–80). The radical nationalist PM Muhammad Mussadiq briefly toppled the monarchy (1953). Regaining his throne, the Shah tightened his grip through oppression and sought popularity through land reform and rapid development with US backing. However, Westernization offended the clergy, and an alliance of students, the bourgeoisie and religious leaders eventually combined against him, overthrowing the monarchy in 1979 and replacing it with a fundamentalist Islamic Republic inspired by the Ayatollah Ruhollah Khomeini (1900–89). The Western-educated classes fled Iran as the clergy tightened control. Radical anti-Western students seized the US embassy and held 66 American hostages (1979–81). In 1980 Iraq invaded Iran, beginning the bitter First Gulf War, which lasted until 1988 (see p. 455). Following the death of Khomeini in 1989, economic necessity brought a less militant phase of the Islamic revolution. The new president, Rafsanjani, emphasized pragmatic rather than radical policies and attempted to heal the diplomatic rift with Western powers. President Saddam Hussein of Iraq returned occupied Iranian territory following the invasion of Kuwait (1990). After the collapse of the USSR (1991), Iran began to look for closer ties with the Islamic former Soviet republics of Central Asia.

IRAQ

Official name: Al-Jumhuriya al-'Iraqiya (The Republic of Iraq)

Member of: UN, Arab League, OPEC

Area: 441 839 km² (170 595 sq mi)

Population: 17 754 000 (1990 est)

Capital and major cities: Baghdad 5 348 000 (including suburbs; 1988 est), Basrah 617 000, Mosul 571 000, Irbil 334 000 (1985 est)

Languages: Arabic (official; 80%), Kurdish (19%)

Religions: Sunni Islam (41%), Shia Islam (51%)

GOVERNMENT

The 250-member National Assembly is elected for four years by universal adult suffrage. The non-elected Revolutionary Command Council appoints the President, who appoints a Council of Ministers. The Arab Ba'ath Socialist Party is the only effective legal party.

GEOGRAPHY

The basins of the Rivers Tigris and Euphrates contain most of the arable land and most of the population. Desert in the SW occupies nearly one half of Iraq. In the NE, the highlands of Kurdistan rise to 3658 m (12 001 ft).

Principal rivers: Tigris (Dijlah) 1900 km (1180 mi), Euphrates (al Furat) 2800 km (1740 mi)

Climate: Summers are hot and dry with temperatures over 40 °C (104 °F). Most of the rainfall – ranging from 100 mm (4 in) in the desert to 1000 mm (40 in) in the mountains – comes in winter.

ECONOMY

Irrigated land in the Tigris and Euphrates basins produces cereals, fruit and vegetables for domestic consumption, and dates for export. Iraq depends upon its substantial reserves of petroleum but exports have been halted by international sanctions and the Second Gulf War (1991), during which the economy was devastated.

HISTORY

Iraq – ancient Mesopotamia – was the cradle of the Babylonian, Sumerian, Akkadian and Assyrian civilizations (see pp. 364–5). In the 7th century BC Iraq became part of Persia's Achaemenid empire (see p. 365). Conquered by Alexander the Great (see pp. 372–3), Iraq was then fought over by Parthia and Rome until it was absorbed by the Persian Sassanian Empire. In 637 AD Muslim armies from Arabia defeated the Persians. In 750 the Abbasid dynasty based its caliphate in Baghdad, which became the administrative and cultural capital of the Arab world. Abbasid power was ended by the Mongols in the 13th and 14th centuries, and Iraq was absorbed by the Turkish Ottoman Empire in 1534.

In World War I the British occupied the area, but Iraqi nationalists were disappointed when Iraq became a monarchy under a British Mandate (1920). In 1932 Iraq became fully independent. Following a military coup that brought pro-German officers to power in 1941, the British occupied Iraq until 1945. The royal family and the premier were murdered in the 'Free Officers' coup in 1958. A reign of terror against the left followed a further coup in 1963. In 1968 Ba'athist (pan-Arab nationalist) officers carried out another coup. Embittered by the Arabs' humiliation in the 1967 war and by US support for the Israelis (see p. 454), the regime turned to the Soviets.

In 1980 President Saddam Hussein attacked a weakened Iran, responding to Iran's threat to export Islamic revolution. What had been intended as a quick victory became the costly First Gulf War (1980–88) with many casualties (see p. 455). In an attempt to restore Iraq's economic fortunes Saddam invaded and annexed oil-rich Kuwait (1990). Following Iraq's failure to respond to repeated UN demands to withdraw, the UN authorized armed action by a US-led coalition. Kuwait was liberated in the short Second Gulf War (1991). After the war, Saddam suppressed revolts by Shiites in the S and Kurds in the N. International efforts established refugee camps for Kurds in a 'safe zone'. Despite being forced to accept UN inspection of Iraq's chemical and biological weapons and nuclear capacity, Saddam continued to defy UN demands concerning Iraqi disarmament.

IRELAND

Official name: Poblacht na h'Éireann (Republic of Ireland)

Member of: UN, EC, CSCE, OECD

Area: 70 282 km² (27 136 sq mi)

Population: 3 523 000 (1991 census)

Capital and major cities: Dublin 921 000 (city 478 000), Cork 174 000 (city 127 000), Limerick 77 000 (city 52 000), Dún Laoghaire 55 000 (part of the Dublin agglomeration), Galway 51 000, Waterford 41 000 (1991 census)

Languages: Irish (official), English

Religion: Roman Catholic (95%)

GOVERNMENT

The Seanad (Senate) comprises 60 members – 11 nominated by the Taoiseach (Prime Minister), the rest indirectly elected for a five-year term to represent vocational and special interests. The Dáil (House) comprises 166 members elected for five years by universal adult suffrage under a system of proportional representation. The President is directly elected for a seven-year term. The Taoiseach and a Cabinet of Ministers are appointed by the President upon the nomination of the Dáil, to whom they are responsible.

GEOGRAPHY

Central Ireland is a lowland crossed by slight ridges and broad valleys, bogs and large lakes, including Loughs Derg and Ree. Except on the E coast N of Dublin, the lowland is surrounded by coastal hills and mountains including the Wicklow Mountains, the Ox Mountains and the hills of Connemara and Donegal in the W. The highest uplands are the Macgillicuddy's Reeks in the SW, rising to Carrauntuohill (1041 m / 3414 ft). The rugged Atlantic Coast is highly indented.

Principal river: Shannon 370 km (595 mi)

Climate: Ireland has a mild temperate climate. Rainfall is high, ranging from over 2500 mm (100 in) in the W and SW to 750 mm (30 in) in the E.

ECONOMY

Manufactured goods – in particular machinery, metals and engineering, electronics and chemical products – now account for over 80% of Ireland's exports. Agriculture – the traditional mainstay of the economy – concentrates upon the production of livestock, meat and dairy products. Food processing and brewing are major industries. Natural resources include lead-zinc, offshore petroleum and natural gas, and HEP sites. Ireland suffers high rates of unemployment and emigration.

HISTORY

Christianity – traditionally brought by St Patrick in the 5th century – gave a cultural unity to the kingdoms of Celtic Ireland – Connacht, Leinster, Meath, Munster and Ulster. At the end of the 8th century, the Vikings invaded, settling in eastern Ireland, but were eventually defeated in 1014 by Brian Boru, who became effective king of all Ireland. However, throughout the early medieval period, the 'high kings' of Ireland seldom controlled the whole island. In 1171 the English king, Henry II, invaded Ireland and claimed sovereignty over the whole island. The disunited Irish kingdoms quickly succumbed, but the Anglo-Norman settlers and their descendants soon lost their identity and became absorbed by the Irish. For the greater part of the Middle Ages, only the area around Dublin (the Pale) remained loyal to English culture and administration. In the 16th and 17th centuries the English unsuccessfully attempted to convert the Irish to Protestantism. Following three major rebellions against Elizabeth I, new waves of Protestant settlers from England and later (under James I) from Scotland underlined English determination to control Ireland. Many Catholic landholders were deprived of their property following a series of English military actions, of which Oliver Cromwell's campaign (1649–50) is the most notorious.

The Catholic James II, having fled England in 1688, attempted to conquer Ireland. His defeat at the Battle of the Boyne (1690) at the hands of William of Orange (King William III of England) confirmed Protestant domination. The Protestant ascendancy was, however, split – Anglicans formed the Anglo-Irish ruling classes, while the Presbyterian descendants of Scottish settlers in Ulster were mainly working class. In the 18th century, both Presbyterians and Roman Catholics pressed for the civil rights that they were largely denied. In 1798 the failure of a nationalist revolt led by Wolfe Tone (1763–98) was followed by the amalgamation of the British and Irish parliaments and the establishment of the United Kingdom of Great Britain and Ireland (1801).

In the 1840s thousands died in the Irish potato famine.

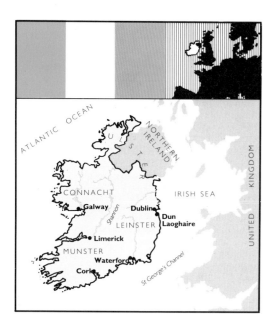

Many more were evicted by Anglo-Irish landowners and joined a mass emigration, especially to the USA – between 1845 and 1851 Ireland's population declined by almost 3 000 000. Daniel O'Connell (1775–1847) led a movement seeking to repeal the Union, and to gain land and civil rights for the Roman Catholic majority. His campaign helped lead to Catholic Emancipation (1829), after which Irish Catholics were able to become MPs in the British Parliament. However, relations between the Protestant and Catholic communities deteriorated, in part owing to increasingly violent actions by nationalist Fenians whose goal was Irish independence. English policy on Ireland vacillated between conciliation and coercion. Gladstone, recognizing the need for reform, disestablished the (Anglican) Church of Ireland and granted greater security of tenure to peasant farmers. In the 1880s Charles Stewart Parnell (1846–91) led a sizeable bloc of Irish MPs in a campaign to secure Irish Home Rule (i.e. self-government). Home Rule Bills were introduced in 1883 and 1893, but after their rejection by Parliament, more revolutionary nationalist groups gained support in Ireland.

Fearing Catholic domination, Protestant Unionists in Ulster opposed the Third Home Rule Bill in 1912. Nationalists declared an independent Irish state in the Dublin Easter Rising of 1916, which was put down by the British. After World War I, Irish nationalist MPs formed a provisional government in Dublin led by Eamon de Valera (later PM and President; 1882–1975). Except in the NE, British administration in Ireland crumbled and most of the Irish police resigned to be replaced by English officers – the 'Black and Tans'. Fighting broke

out between nationalists and British troops and police, and by 1919 Ireland had collapsed into violence. The British response in 1920 was to offer Ireland two Parliaments – one in Protestant Ulster, another in the Catholic S. Partition was initially rejected by the S, but by the Anglo-Irish Treaty (1921) dominion status was granted, although six (mainly Protestant) counties in Ulster – Northern Ireland – opted to remain British. The Irish Free State was proclaimed in 1922 but de Valera and the Republicans refused to accept it. Civil war broke out between the provisional government – led by Arthur Griffith and Michael Collins – and the Republicans. The fighting ended in 1923, but de Valera's campaign for a republic continued and in 1937 the Free State became the Republic of Eire. The country remained neutral in World War II and left the Commonwealth – as the Republic of Ireland – in 1949. Relations between S and N – and between the Republic and the UK – have often been tense during the 'troubles' in Northern Ireland (1968–   ). However, the Anglo-Irish Agreement (1985) provided for the participation of the Republic in political, legal and security matters in Northern Ireland.

ISRAEL

Official name: Medinat Israel (The State of Israel)

Member of: UN

Area: 21 946 km² (8473 sq mi), including East Jerusalem

Population: 4 821 000 (1991 est) – including East Jerusalem

Capital and major cities: Jerusalem (not recognized internationally as capital) 525 000, Tel-Aviv 1 157 000 (city 339 000), Haifa 395 000 (city 249 000) (1990 est)

Languages: Hebrew (official; 85%), Arabic (15%)

Religions: Judaism (official; 85%), Sunni Islam (13%), various Christian denominations

Occupied territories: (with areas and populations): Gaza – 378 km² (146 sq mi), 642 000 (1990 est); Golan – 1176 km² (454 sq mi), 26 000 (1990 est); West Bank (Judaea and Samaria) – 5879 km² (2270 sq mi), 955 000 (1990 est)

GOVERNMENT
The 120-member Assembly (Knesset) is elected by proportional representation for four years by universal adult suffrage. A Prime Minister and Cabinet take office after receiving a vote of confidence from the Knesset. The President is elected for a five-year term by the Knesset.

GEOGRAPHY
Israel – within the boundaries established by the 1949 cease-fire line – consists of a fertile thin coastal plain beside the Mediterranean, parts of the arid mountains of Judaea in the centre, the Negev Desert in the S and part of the Jordan Valley in the NE.

Climate: Israel's climate is Mediterranean with hot, dry summers and mild, wetter winters. The greater part of Israel receives less than 200 mm (8 in) of rain a year.

ECONOMY
Severe economic problems stem, in part, from Israel's large defence budget and political circumstances, which prevent trade with neighbouring countries. Israel is a major producer and exporter of citrus fruit. Much land is irrigated and over 75% of Israel's arable land is farmed by collectives (kibbutzim) and cooperatives. Mineral resources are few, but processing imported diamonds is a major source of foreign currency. Tourism – to biblical sites – is important.

HISTORY
Israel (Palestine) was occupied by the Hebrews around the 14th century BC. The kingdom of Israel was established about 1021 BC. King David made Jerusalem his capital, and under his successor, Solomon, the Temple was built and Israel prospered. In the 10th century, the kingdom was divided into Israel in the N and Judah in the S, both of which were eventually overrun by the Assyrians. In 587 BC Jerusalem was destroyed and many

of its people taken into captivity by the Babylonians. The Persians allowed the Jews to return 50 years later. Palestine was then ruled, in turn, by Alexander the Great, the Ptolomies of Egypt and the Seleucid Empire. Judas Maccabeus revolted against the Seleucids in 141 BC and established a Jewish state that lasted until the Roman conquest in 65 BC. After a revolt against the Romans in AD 135, the Jewish population of Palestine was dispersed – the Diaspora – and the Jews were scattered in small communities across the Middle East, North Africa and Europe.

Palestine was part of the Byzantine Empire, but in the 7th century an Arab invasion brought the area into the Islamic world (see p. 392). In the 12th and 13th centuries the Crusaders unsuccessfully attempted to retake the Holy Land (see pp. 398–9). The Turkish Ottoman Empire ruled the area from the early 16th century until 1917–18, when Palestine was captured by British forces. The Zionists (see p. 454) had hoped to establish a Jewish state, and this hope was intensified following the Balfour Declaration in favour of a homeland (1917). However, Palestine came under British administration and it was not until 1948–9 – after the murder of some 6 000 000 Jews in concentration camps by the Nazis (see p. 445) – that an explicitly Jewish state emerged. The establishment of a Jewish state met with hostility from Israel's neighbours, leading to a series of Arab-Israeli wars (see pp. 454–5). Israeli politics in the 1980s and 1990s have been characterized by political instability owing to the system of proportional representation and the large number of very small parties. The large-scale influx of Soviet Jews into Israel since 1990 has given extra impetus to the intifada (Palestinian uprising) against continued Israeli rule in Gaza and the West Bank. Israel has come under increased international pressure to achieve a Middle East settlement.

ITALY

Official name: Repubblica Italiana (Republic of Italy)

Member of: UN, EC, NATO, G7, OECD, CSCE

Area: 301 277 km² (116 324 sq mi)

Population: 57 590 000 (1991 census)

Capital and major cities: Rome (Roma) 3 000 000 (city 2 804 000), Milan (Milano) 3 700 000 (city 1 449 000),

Naples (Napoli) 2 900 000 (city 1 204 000), Turin (Torino) 1 003 000, Palermo 731 000, Genoa (Genova) 707 000, Bologna 417 000, Florence (Firenze) 413 000, Catania 366 000, Bari 355 000, Venice (Venezia) 321 000, Messina 275 000, Verona 259 000 (1991 census)

Languages: Italian (official), small German-, French- and Albanian-speaking minorities

Religion: Roman Catholic (over 90%)

GOVERNMENT

The two houses of Parliament are elected for a five-year term under a system of proportional representation. The Senate has 315 members elected by citizens aged 25 and over to represent the regions, plus former Presidents and five life senators, chosen by the President. The Chamber of Deputies has 630 members elected by citizens aged 18 and over. The President is elected for a seven-year term by Parliament and 65 regional representatives. The President appoints a Prime Minister – who commands a majority in Parliament – and a Council of Ministers (Cabinet) who are responsible to Parliament. The 20 regions have their own governments.

GEOGRAPHY

The Alps form a natural boundary between Italy and its western and northern neighbours. The highest point in Italy is at 4760 m (15 616 ft) just below the summit of Mt Blanc (Monte Bianco). A string of lakes – where the mountains meet the foothills – include Lakes Maggiore, Lugano and Como. The fertile Po Valley – the great lowland of N Italy – lies between the Alpine foothills in the N, the Apennine Mountains in the S, the Alps in the W and the Adriatic Sea in the E. The narrow ridge of the Ligurian Alps joins the Maritime Alps to the Apennines, which form a backbone down the entire length of the Italian peninsula. Coastal lowlands are few and relatively restricted but include the Arno Basin in Tuscany, the Tiber Basin around Rome, the Campania lowlands around Naples, and plains beside the Gulf of Taranto and in Puglia. The islands of Sardinia and Sicily are both largely mountainous. Much of Italy is liable to earthquakes. Italy has four active volcanoes, including Etna on Sicily and Vesuvius near Naples (see p. 82).

Principal rivers: Po 652 km (405 mi), Tiber (Tevere) 405 km (252 mi)

Climate: Italy enjoys a Mediterranean climate with warm, dry summers and mild winters. Sicily and Sardinia tend to be warmer and drier than the mainland. The Alps and the Po Valley have colder, wetter winters.

ECONOMY

N Italy, with its easy access to the rest of Europe, is the main centre of Italian industry. The S, in contrast, remains mainly agricultural, producing grapes, sugar beet, wheat, maize and tomatoes. Most farms are small – and many farmers in the S are resistant to change – thus average incomes in southern Italy (the 'Mezzogiorno') are much lower than in the N. Agriculture in the N is more mechanized and major crops include wheat, maize, rice, grapes (for the important wine industry), fruit and fodder crops for dairy herds. Industrialization in the S is being actively promoted. The industries of the N are well-developed and include electrical and electronic goods, motor vehicles and bicycles, textiles, clothing, leather goods, cement, glass and china. The N is also an important financial and banking area, and Milan is the commercial capital of Italy. Apart from marble and Alpine rivers that have been harnessed for HEP, Italy has few natural resources. Tourism and money sent back by Italians living abroad are important sources of foreign currency. A crippling public deficit has added to Italy's growing economic problems.

HISTORY

Italy has been united twice – in modern times, since 1861, and in ancient times under the Romans. The Roman Republic was established in 509 BC (see pp. 376–7), and by 272 BC all of peninsular Italy had been united under the rule of Rome. By 200 BC the foundations of the empire had been laid in the territories conquered from Carthage in N Africa and Spain (see p. 377). For the next five centuries Italy was the centre of the expanding Roman

Empire (see pp. 378–9). However by the middle of the 3rd century AD the Roman Empire began to decline, plagued by civil war, economic problems and foreign invasions (see pp. 380–1). Rome was sacked by the Visigoths under Alaric (410), but the beleaguered Western Roman Empire lasted until 476 when Odoacer established a Gothic kingdom based in Rome (see p. 381). Several centuries of chaotic conditions in Italy followed, during which the papacy brought the only stability. The early Middle Ages saw successive waves of invaders – the Byzantines, Lombards, Franks, Arabs, Germans, and, in the 11th century, the Normans (in the S). The papacy attempted to strengthen its position in Rome. The supremacy of the Bishop of Rome in the Western Church had been established in 443, but throughout the next thousand years the papacy had to struggle to maintain its position within the Catholic Church and its position as a temporal power in central Italy. Outside the Papal States, Italy was fragmented into smaller territories.

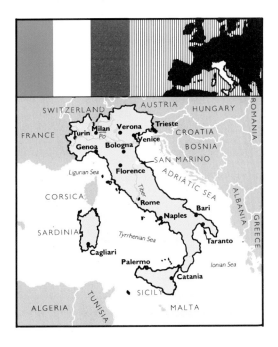

In 800, Charlemagne conquered Italy and had himself crowned Holy Roman Emperor by the pope in Rome (see p. 394). Successive emperors strove to maintain control of Italy, but this brought them into continued conflict with increasingly powerful and independent Italian cities – such as Milan – and also with the popes who were determined to assert the liberty of the Church (see pp. 394 and 398). Papal disputes with the Holy Roman Empire were common between the 10th and 13th centuries, and these conflicts had repercussions throughout Italy. By the end of the 13th century, Spanish rulers had established themselves in Sicily and Naples. At the same time, a number of important city-states – including Milan, Florence, Genoa and Venice – developed in the N. These city-states combined proud republican governments with commercial success and artistic splendour, although they were also afflicted by factional and class divisions, and frequent wars with their neighbours. The republics of Venice and Genoa became great sea powers and established Mediterranean empires in Greece, Cyprus and the Adriatic.

In the later Middle Ages, many of the city-states fell prey to powerful local families who established themselves as hereditary rulers – for example, the Visconti in Milan, the Gonzaga in Mantua and the Este in Ferrara and Modena. Perhaps the most famous were the Medicis, who took over Florence and eventually became Grand Dukes of Tuscany. The Italian ducal families were great patrons of the arts. The rivalry of their courts as cultural centres benefited sculptors, writers, artists and architects and Renaissance Italy became the artistic heart of

Western Europe (see pp. 524 and 528). Republican Venice stood out against the trend of establishing ducal dynasties in the city-states, but the city's role as a major Mediterranean trading power gradually declined. In the late 15th century N Italy was invaded by the French. After a bitter struggle for supremacy between the French Valois kings and the Habsburgs (see p. 410), the Habsburg Emperor Charles V gained control of much of Italy. On the division of his empire between the Austrian and Spanish Habsburgs, much of Italy passed to the Austrian branch. French withdrawal from the N was matched by the rise to power of the rulers of Piedmont-Savoy, who – after 1720 – also became kings of Sardinia. While some states, felt the effect of the Enlightenment or of more efficient government during the 18th century (see pp. 418–19), most Italian states hardly progressed in the 17th and 18th centuries. The kingdom of Naples (ruled by Spanish Bourbons) and the Papal States suffered reactionary and inefficient government.

During the Revolutionary and Napoleonic Wars (see pp. 426–7), Napoleon annexed part of the peninsula and redrew ancient boundaries. The 'old order' was essentially restored by the Congress of Vienna (1815) – with the kingdom of Sardinia(-Piedmont) and the Austrian provinces of Lombardy-Venetia in the N, the kingdom of the Two Sicilies (Naples) in the S, and the Papal States and minor duchies in the centre. Napoleon had, however, created a kingdom of Italy (based in Milan) and memories of this short-lived state – and of Napoleonic efficiency and modernization – remained. Revolts against the traditional rulers erupted in 1830 and again in 1848. Austrian control in Lombardy-Venetia and the duchies ensured that there would be no reform in the N, while Bourbon rule kept the S under a heavy yoke. Political activity was often confined to secret societies and was frequently expressed in violence. Reform and unity eventually came under the king of Sardinia (Piedmont) – Victor Emmanuel II (reigned 1849–78) – and his premier Count Camillo di Cavour (1810–61), who seized opportunities to advance unification with French assistance (see p. 428). The nationalist guerrilla leader Giuseppe Garibaldi (1807–82) liberated Naples and Sicily (the Two Sicilies) from the Bourbons, adding the S to the new kingdom of Italy – uniting most of the peninsula – that was proclaimed in 1861. Venetia (1866) and Rome (1870) were subsequently included (see p. 428).

Political development after unification was unsteady. Overseas ventures – such as the attempt to annex parts of Ethiopia (1895–96) – were often frustrated. Parliament was held in low esteem and the end of the 19th century saw a series of assassinations, including King Umberto I in 1900. Italy entered World War I on the Allied side in the expectation of territorial gains from Austria (see p. 436). However, Italy won far less territory than anticipated in the peace treaties after the war (see p. 441), when fear of Communist revolution led to an upsurge of Fascism (see p. 442). Benito Mussolini (1883–1945) became Prime Minister in 1922 with a programme of extensive domestic modernization and an aggressive foreign policy (see p. 443). In 1936 Italy allied with Germany in the Rome-Berlin Axis (see p. 443), and in 1940 war was declared on Britain and France. When Italy was invaded by Allied troops in 1943, Mussolini was dismissed by the king and Italy joined the Allies.

In 1946 a republic was proclaimed. Communist influence increased, both at local and national level. However, the dominance of the (conservative) Christian Democrats kept the Communists out of the succeeding coalitions that have ruled Italy and since 1989–90 the Communists have declined as a political force. Particularly in the 1970s, terrorist movements – of both the left and the right – have been active, kidnapping and assassinating senior political and industrial figures. Attempts have been made to effect a true unification of the country by encouraging the economic development of the S. However, the political structure of Italy remains unstable, with a succession of short-lived coalitions and in the 1990s public disillusion with state institutions grew. Italy was weakened by corruption, the activities of the Mafia and the growth of regional separatism in the N.

IVORY COAST see COTE D'IVOIRE

JAMAICA

Member of: UN, Commonwealth, OAS, CARICOM

Area: 10 991 km² (4244 sq mi)

Population: 2 420 000 (1991 est)

Capital and major cities: Kingston 662 000 (1990 est), Spanish Town 89 000 (1985 est)

Language: English

Religions: Church of God (17%), Anglican (10%)

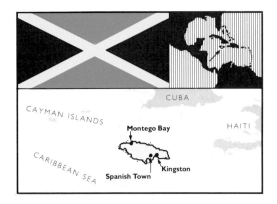

GOVERNMENT
The 60-member House of Representatives is elected for five years by universal suffrage. The 21-member Senate is appointed on the advice of the PM and the Leader of the Opposition. The Governor General – the representative of the British Queen as sovereign of Jamaica – appoints a Prime Minister who commands a majority in the House. The PM appoints a Cabinet of Ministers.

GEOGRAPHY
Coastal lowlands surround the interior limestone plateaux (the 'Cockpit Country') and mountains. The latter include the Blue Mountains, which rise to Blue Mountain Peak at 2256 m (7402 ft).

Climate: The lowlands are tropical and rainy; the highlands are cooler and wetter.

ECONOMY
Agriculture is the mainstay of the economy, with sugar cane and bananas as the main crops. Jamaica is a leading exporter of bauxite. Tourism is a major foreign currency earner.

HISTORY
Jamaica – which was originally inhabited by Arawak Indians – was sighted by Columbus (1494) and claimed for Spain. It became British in 1655. Black slaves were brought from Africa to work the sugar plantations. The abolition of slavery in the 1830s destroyed the plantation system. By the 1930s, severe social and economic problems led to rioting and the birth of political awareness. Since independence in 1962, power has alternated between the radical People's National Party – led until 1992 by Michael Manley – and the more conservative Jamaican Labour Party.

JAPAN

Official name: Nippon or Nihon ('The Land of the Rising Sun')

Member of: UN, G7, OECD

Area: 377 815 km² (145 874 sq mi)

Population: 123 612 000 (1990 census)

Capital and major cities: Tokyo 18 200 000 (city 11 855 000), Osaka 8 500 000 (city 2 624 000), Yokohama (part of the Tokyo agglomeration) 3 220 000, Nagoya 2 155 000, Sapporo 1 672 000, Kobe (part of the Osaka agglomeration) 1 477 000, Kyoto 1 461 000, Fukuoka 1 237 000, Kawasaki (part of the Tokyo agglomeration) 1 174 000, Hiroshima 1 086 000, Kitakyushu 1 026 000 (1990 census).

Language: Japanese

Religions: Shintoism (86%) overlaps with Buddhism (74%), Christian denominations (1%)

GOVERNMENT
The Emperor is head of state but has no executive power. The 252-member House of Councillors – the upper house of the Diet – is elected for six years by universal adult suffrage. One half of the councillors retire every three years. A system of proportional representation is used to elect 50 of the councillors. The 512-member House of Representatives is directly elected for 4 years. The Diet chooses a Prime Minister who commands a majority in the lower house. The PM in turn appoints a Cabinet of Ministers who are responsible to the Diet.

GEOGRAPHY
Japan consists of over 3900 islands, of which Hokkaido in the N occupies 22% of the total land area, and Shikoku and Kyushu in the S respectively occupy 5% and 11% of the area. The central island of Honshu occupies 61% of the area and contains 80% of the population. To the S of these main islands, the Ryukyu Islands – including Okinawa – stretch almost to Taiwan. Nearly 75% of Japan is mountainous. The population is concentrated into small coastal plains. The principal lowlands are Kanto (around Tokyo), Nobi (around Nagoya) and the Sendai Plain in the N of Honshu. The highest peak is Fujiyama at 3776 m (12 388 ft), an extinct volcano. There are also over 60 active volcanoes, and the country is prone to severe earthquakes.

Climate: Japan experiences great variations in climate. Although the whole country is temperate, the N has long cold snowy winters, while the S has hot summers and mild winters. Rainfall totals are high, with heavy rain and typhoons being common in the summer months.

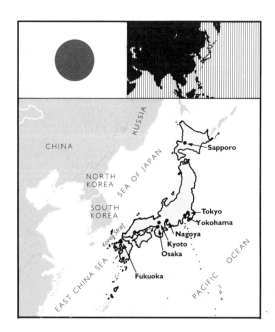

ECONOMY
Despite the generally crowded living conditions in the cities, the Japanese enjoy a high standard of living. The country has the second largest industrial economy in the world, despite having very few natural resources. Japanese industry is heavily dependent on imported raw materials – about 90% of Japan's energy requirements are imported and petroleum is the single largest import. Japan's economic success is based on manufacturing industry, which – with construction – employs 30% of the labour force. Japan is the world's leading manufacturer of motor vehicles, and one of the major producers of ships, steel, synthetic fibres, chemicals, cement, electrical goods and electronic equipment. Rapid advances in Japanese research and technology have helped the expanding export-led economy. The banking and financial sectors have prospered, and Tokyo is one of the world's main stock exchanges and commercial centres. Agriculture is labour intensive. Although Japan is self-sufficient in rice, agriculture is not a priority and a high percentage of its food requirements – particularly cereals and fodder crops – have to be imported. The traditional Japanese diet is sea-based and the fishing industry is a large one.

HISTORY
Japanese myth dates the first emperor, Jimmu, to 660 BC. However, the first known emperors reigned in Nara in the 8th century AD. The rise of imperial power, the feudal system and the shogunate in Japan are covered on pp. 386–7. At the end of the 19th century, the Meiji Emperor overthrew the last shogun and restored power to the throne. He encouraged Western institutions and a Western-style economy, so that by the beginning of the 20th century Japan was rapidly industrializing and on the brink of becoming a world power (see p. 387).

By the end of the Meiji era (1912), Japan had established an empire. Japan had defeated China (1894–95) – taking Port Arthur and Taiwan – and startled Europe by beating Russia (1904–5) by land and at sea. Korea was annexed in 1910. Allied with Britain from 1902, Japan entered World War I against Germany in 1914, in part to gain acceptance as an imperial world power. However, Japan gained little except some of the German island territories in the Pacific and became disillusioned that the country did not seem to be treated as an equal by the Great Powers. The rise of militarism and collapse of world trade led to the rise of totalitarianism and a phase of aggressive Japanese expansion (see pp. 442–3). Japan became allied to Nazi Germany and in 1941 Japanese aircraft struck Pearl Harbor in Hawaii, bringing the USA into World War II (see p. 444–5). An initial rapid Japanese military expansion across SE Asia and the Pacific was halted, and the war ended for Japan in disastrous defeat and the horrors of atomic warfare.

Emperor Hirohito (reigned 1926–89) surrendered in 1945. Shintoism – which had come to be identified with aggressive nationalism – ceased to be the state religion, and in 1946 the emperor renounced his divinity. The Allied occupation (1945–52) both democratized politics and began an astonishing economic recovery based on an aggressive export policy. The economy was jolted by major rises in petroleum prices in 1973 and 1979, but Japan maintained its advance to become a technological front-runner and, after the USA, the world's second largest economy. However, Japan's protectionism has led to accusations of unfair trading practices. By 1988 Japan surpassed the USA as the world's largest aid-donor. The Japanese political world is dominated by the Liberal Democrats, who have held office since 1955.

JORDAN

Official name: Al-Mamlaka al-Urduniya al-Hashemiyah (The Hashemite Kingdom of Jordan)

Member of: UN, Arab League

Area: 89 206 km² (34 443 sq mi) – East Bank only

Population: 3 285 000 (1991 est) – East Bank only

Capital and major cities: Amman 1 160 000, Zarqa 318 000, Irbid 168 000, Salt 134 000 (1986 est)

Language: Arabic (official)

Religion: Sunni Islam (over 80%)

GOVERNMENT
Jordan is a constitutional monarchy. The King appoints the 30 members of the Senate for eight years. The

80-member House of Representatives is elected for four years by universal adult suffrage.

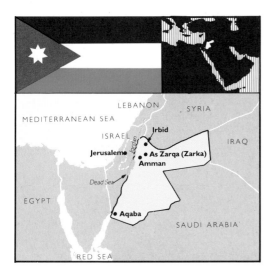

GEOGRAPHY
The steep escarpment of the East Bank Uplands – which rise to 1754 m (5755 ft) at Jabal Ramm – borders the Jordan Valley and the Dead Sea. Deserts cover over 80% of the country.

Principal rivers: Jordan (Urdun) 321 km (200 mi)

Climate: The summers are hot and dry; the winters are cooler and wetter, although much of Jordan experiences very low rainfall.

ECONOMY
Apart from potash – the main export – Jordan has few resources. Arable land accounts for only 5% of the total area. Foreign aid and money sent back by Jordanians working abroad are major sources of foreign currency.

HISTORY
After being incorporated into the biblical kingdoms of Solomon and David, the region was ruled, in turn, by the Assyrian, Babylonian, Persian and Seleucid empires (see pp. 364–5 and 372–3). The Nabateans – based at Petra – controlled Jordan from the 4th century BC until 64 BC when the area came under Roman rule. Jordan was part of the Byzantine Empire (see p. 394) from 394 until 636 when Muslim Arab forces were victorious in the Battle of Yarmouk. At first, Jordan prospered under Muslim rule but declined when the Abbasid caliphs moved their capital to Baghdad (see p. 392). In the 11th and 12th centuries, Crusader states flourished briefly in Jordan (see pp. 398–9). The area was conquered by the (Turkish) Ottoman Empire in the 16th century. In World War I the British aided an Arab revolt against Ottoman rule. The League of Nations awarded the area east of the River Jordan – Transjordan – to Britain as part of Palestine (1920), but in 1923 Transjordan became a separate emirate. In 1946 the country gained complete independence as the Kingdom of Jordan with Amir Abdullah (1880–1951) as its sovereign.

The Jordanian army fought with distinction in the 1948 Arab-Israeli War (see p. 455), and occupied the West Bank territories, which were formally incorporated into Jordan in 1950. In 1951 Abdullah was assassinated. His grandson King Hussein (reigned 1952–) was initially threatened by radicals encouraged by Egypt's President Nasser. In the 1967 Arab-Israeli War (see p. 455), Jordan lost the West Bank, including Arab Jerusalem, to the Israelis. In the 1970s the power of the Palestinian guerrillas in Jordan challenged the very existence of the Jordanian state. After a short bloody civil war in September 1979 the Palestinian leadership fled abroad. King Hussein renounced all responsibility for the West Bank in 1988. A ban on party politics ended in 1991. There has since been a major growth in support for Islamic fundamentalism.

KAZAKHSTAN

Official name: Kazakhstan

Member of: UN, CIS, CSCE

Area: 2 717 300 km² (1 049 200 sq mi)

Population: 16 793 000 (1991 est)

Capital and major cities: Alma-Ata (Almaty) 1 151 000, Karaganda (Qaraghandy) 615 000, Chimkent (Shymkent) 389 000 (1989 census)

Languages: Kazakh (40%), Russian (38%)

Religions: Sunni Islam majority, Russian Orthodox

GOVERNMENT
A 510-member legislature and a President are elected for four years by universal adult suffrage.

GEOGRAPHY
Kazakhstan comprises a vast expanse of low tablelands (steppes) in Central Asia. In the W, plains descend below sea level beside the Caspian Sea. Uplands include ranges of hills in the N and mountain chains, including the Tien Shan, in the S and E, where Khan Tengri, at 6398 m (20 991 ft), is the highest point. Kazakhstan has several salt lakes, including the Aral Sea, which is shrinking because of excessive extraction of irrigation water from its tributaries. Deserts include the Kyzylkum in the S, the Kara Kum in the centre, and the Barsuki in the N.

Principal river: Syrdarya 3019 km (1876 mi).

Climate: The Kazkah climate is characterized by bitterly cold winters and hot summers. Rainfall is low, ranging between 200 mm (8 in) in the N to 500 mm (20 in) or more in the SE, and negligible in the deserts.

ECONOMY
Kazakhstan is a major supplier of food and raw materials for industry to other former Soviet republics, particularly Russia. The transition to a market economy has hardly begun. Agriculture employs almost 50% of the labour force. Large collective farms on the steppes in the N contributed one third of the cereal crop of the former USSR. Other major farming interests include sheep, fodder crops, fruit, vegetables and rice. Kazakhstan is rich in natural resources including coal, tin, copper, lead, zinc, gold, chromite and oil. Industry is represented by iron and steel (in the Karaganda coalfield), pharmaceuticals, food processing and cement.

HISTORY
The Kazakhs first appear in written history in the late 15th century when they established a nomadic empire in the W and centre of the present republic. Between 1488 and 1518 Kazakh khans controlled virtually all the Central Asian steppes, but before 1600 the Kazakh khanate split into three separate hordes. In the 17th century the Kazakhs were constantly raided by the Oryats from Djungaria (Xinjiang in China). In the 18th century the Russians began to penetrate the Kazakh steppes and were initially welcomed as overlords in

exchange for protection from the Oryats. Revolts against Russian rule were suppressed (1792–4) and what little autonomy the khans still enjoyed was abolished between 1822 and 1848. During the Tsarist period there was large-scale Russian peasant settlement on the steppes, but Russian rule was resented and there was a major Kazakh revolt during World War I.

After the Russian revolution (see p. 438), Kazakh nationalists formed a local government and demanded autonomy (1917). The Soviet Red Army invaded in 1920 and established an Autonomous Soviet Republic. Kazakhstan did not become a full Union Republic within the USSR until 1936. Widespread immigration from other parts of the USSR became a flood in 1954–6 when the 'Virgin Lands' of N Kazakhstan were opened up for farming. By the time Kazakhstan declared independence – following the abortive coup by Communist hardliners in Moscow (September 1991) – the Kazakhs formed a minority within their own republic. When the USSR was dissolved (December 1991), Kazakhstan was internationally recognized as an independent republic. The vast new Kazakh state – in theory, a nuclear power because of former Soviet nuclear weapons on its territory – occupies a pivotal position within Central Asia.

KENYA

Official name: Jamhuri ya Kenya (Republic of Kenya)

Member of: UN, OAU, Commonwealth

Area: 580 367 km² (224 081 sq mi)

Population: 25 905 000 (1991 est)

Capital and major cities: Nairobi 1 505 000 (including suburbs; 1990 est), Mombasa 426 000, Kisumu 167 000, Nakuru 102 000 (1985 est)

Languages: Swahili (official), English, Kikuyu (21%), Luhya (14%), Luo (11%), with over 200 tribal languages

Religions: Roman Catholic (27%), Independent African Churches (27%), Protestant Churches (19%), animist

GOVERNMENT
The President and 188 members of the 202–member National Assembly are elected by universal adult suffrage every five years. The remaining 14 Assembly members, the Vice President and the Cabinet of Ministers are appointed by the President.

GEOGRAPHY
The steep sided Rift Valley divides the highlands that run from N to S through central Kenya and rise at Mount Kenya to 5199 m (17 058 ft). Plateaux extend in the W to Lake Victoria and in the E to coastal lowlands.

Climate: The coastal areas have a hot and humid equatorial climate. The highlands – which are cooler – experience high rainfall. The N is very hot and arid.

ECONOMY
Over 75% of the labour force is involved in agriculture. Major crops include wheat and maize for domestic consumption, and coffee, tea, sisal and sugar cane for export. Large numbers of beef cattle are reared, and Kenya is one of the few states in black Africa to have a major dairy industry. Tourism is an important source of foreign currency.

HISTORY
Arabs established coastal settlements from the 7th century, and the Portuguese were active on the Kenyan coast from 1498 until the 17th century, when they were evicted by the Arabs. The varied black African peoples of the area were brought forcibly under British rule in 1895 in the East African Protectorate, which became the colony of Kenya in 1920. White settlement in the highlands was bitterly resented by the Africans – particularly the Kikuyu – whose land was taken. Racial discrimination and attacks on African customs also created discontent. Black protest movements emerged in the 1920s and, after 1945, developed into nationalism, led by Jomo Kenyatta (c. 1893–1978), who in 1947 became the first president of the Kenya African Union. When the violent Mau Mau rising – which involved mainly

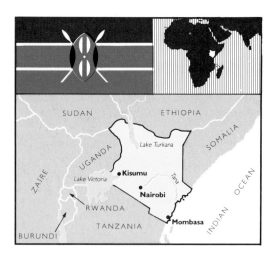

ECONOMY
Most islanders are involved in subsistence farming and fishing. Copra is almost the only export.

HISTORY
Kiribati has been inhabited by Micronesians for almost 4000 years (see p. 389). In the 18th century, the atolls were discovered by British sea captains, including Thomas Gilbert. The Gilbert Islands – which became British in 1892 – were occupied by Japan (1942–43). British nuclear weapons were tested on Christmas Island (1957–64). In 1979 the islands gained independence as Kiribati (pronounced Kiri-bass).

KOREA DPR (Democratic People's Republic of Korea)

Official name: Chosun Minchu-chui Inmin Konghwa-guk (Democratic People's Republic of Korea). Popularly known as North Korea.

Member of: UN

Area: 120 538 km² (46 540 sq mi)

Population: 21 815 000 (1991 est)

Capital and major cities: Pyongyang 2 640 000, Ham-hung 775 000, Chongjin 755 000 (1986 est)

Language: Korean

Religions: Daoism and Confucianism (14%), Chondism

GOVERNMENT
The Party Congress of the (Communist) Korean

Kikuyu people – broke out (1952–56), Kenyatta was held responsible and was imprisoned on doubtful evidence (1953–61). After the British had crushed the Mau Mau revolt in a bloody campaign, they negotiated with Kenyatta and the other nationalists. Independence, under Kenyatta's KANU party, followed in 1963. His moderate leadership and pro-capitalist policies were continued by his successor, Daniel arap Moi. Considerable restrictions on political activity followed an attempted military coup (1982). From 1969 to 1991, KANU was the only legal political party, but multi-party elections were held in 1993.

KIRIBATI

Official name: Republic of Kiribati

Member of: Commonwealth

Area: 717 km² (277 sq mi)

Population: 73 000 (1991 est)

Capital: Bairiki (on Tarawa) 25 000 (1990 census)

Languages: English (official), I-Kiribati

Religions: Roman Catholic (over 50%), Kiribati Protestant (Congregational; over 40%)

GOVERNMENT
The President and 39 members of the Assembly are elected by universal adult suffrage every four years. A member for Banaba, and an additional member, are appointed to the Assembly. The President appoints a Cabinet, which is responsible to the Assembly.

GEOGRAPHY
With the exception of the island of Banaba – which is composed of phosphate rock – Kiribati comprises three groups of small coral atolls.

Worker's Party elects a Central Committee, which in turn elects a Politburo, the seat of effective power. Unopposed elections are held every four years for the 687-member Supreme People's Assembly. The Assembly elects the President, Prime Minister and Central People's Committee, which nominates Ministers.

GEOGRAPHY
Over three quarters of the country consists of mountains, which rise in the NE to the volcanic peak Mount Paek-tu at 2744 m (9003 ft).

Climate: The country has long cold dry winters and hot wet summers.

ECONOMY
Over 30% of the labour force work on cooperative farms, mainly growing rice. Natural resources include coal, zinc, magnetite and iron ore. Great emphasis has been placed on industrial development, notably metallurgy and machine-building. The end of barter deals with the USSR (1990–91) brought a sharp economic decline.

HISTORY
Korea – a Japanese possession from 1910 to 1945 – was divided into zones of occupation in 1945. The USSR established a Communist republic in their zone N of the 38th parallel (1948). North Korea launched a surprise attack on the South in June 1950, hoping to achieve reunification by force. The Korean War (1950–53; see p. 450) devastated the peninsula. At the ceasefire in 1953 the frontier was re-established close to the 38th parallel. North Korea has the world's first Communist dynasty, whose personality cult has surpassed even that of Stalin. President Kim Il-Sung (1912–) and his son – and anticipated successor – Kim Jong-Il have rejected any reform of the country's Communist system. Since the collapse of Communism in the former USSR and Eastern Europe, North Korea has become increasingly isolated. The country's nuclear ambitions have caused international concern.

KOREA, REPUBLIC OF

Official name: Daehan-Minkuk (Republic of Korea). Popularly known as South Korea.

Member of: UN

Area: 99 143 km² (38 279 km²)

Population: 43 520 000 (1990 census)

Capital and major cities: Seoul (Soul) 10 726 000, Pusan 3 825 000, Taegu 2 248 000, Inchon 1 682 000, Kwangju 1 206 000 (1990 census)

Language: Korean (official)

Religions: Buddhist (24%), various Protestant Churches (16%), Roman Catholic (5%)

GOVERNMENT
The 299-member National Assembly is elected by universal adult suffrage every four years – 237 members are directly elected to represent constituencies; the remaining 62 members are chosen under a system of proportional representation. The President – who appoints a State Council (Cabinet) and a Prime Minister – is directly elected for a single five-year term.

GEOGRAPHY
Apart from restricted coastal lowlands and the densely-populated Han and Naktong basins, most of the country is mountainous. The highest point is Halla-san (1950 m / 6398 ft), an extinct volcano on Cheju island.

Climate: Korea experiences cold dry winters and hot summers during which the monsoon brings heavy rainfall.

ECONOMY
One fifth of the labour force is involved in farming. The principal crops are rice and barley. Industry is dominated by a small number of large family conglomerates. The important textile industry was the original manufacturing base. South Korea is now the world's leading

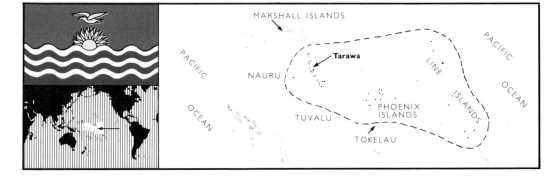

Climate: Kiribati has a maritime equatorial climate with high rainfall.

producer of ships and footwear and a major producer of electronic equipment, electrical goods, steel, petrochemicals and motor vehicles. Banking and finance are expanding. The country experienced high economic growth rates in the 1980s and early 1990s.

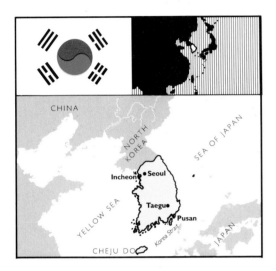

HISTORY

Even before the kingdom of Silla united the rest of Korea into a single state (668), the Korean peninsula acted as a bridge between China and Japan, adapting Chinese culture as it transmitted it to Japan. The Mongols overran the country in 1259 and ruled for a century, but Korea maintained its distinctive identity. The Yi dynasty (1392–1910) gave Korea a long period of cultural continuity. China helped the Koreans to repulse a Japanese invasion in 1592, exacting recognition of Chinese overlordship in return. From the 17th century, Korea became the 'Hermit Kingdom', cutting itself off from the outside world. In 1910 Korea fell victim to a harsh Japanese colonial rule. After World War II, the peninsula was divided into Soviet and US zones of occupation. In 1948 the Republic of Korea was established in the American (southern) zone. The surprise invasion of the South by the Communist North precipitated the Korean War (1950–53; see p. 450). The war cost a million lives and ended in stalemate with the division of Korea confirmed. Closely allied to the US, an astonishing economic transformation took place in South Korea. However, the country has experienced long periods of authoritarian rule including the presidencies of Syngman Rhee and Park Chung-Hee, but the election of ex-General Roh Tae Woo (1987) introduced a more open regime. Much prestige was gained through the successful Seoul Olympic Games, and trading and diplomatic contacts have been established with former Soviet republics and former Communist countries of Eastern Europe.

KUWAIT

Official name: Daulat al-Kuwait (State of Kuwait)

Member of: UN, Arab League, OPEC, GCC

Area: 17 818 km² (6880 sq mi)

Population: 1 100 000 (1992 est)

Capital: Kuwait City 750 000 (including agglomeration; 1992 unofficial est)

Language: Arabic (official)

Religions: Sunni Islam (official; 70%), Shia Islam (30%)

GOVERNMENT

Kuwait is a monarchy ruled by an Amir, who appoints a Prime Minister and a Cabinet. A 50-member National Assembly is elected for four years by literate male Kuwaiti nationals whose families fulfil stringent residence qualifications.

GEOGRAPHY

Most of Kuwait is desert, relatively flat and low lying.

Climate: Kuwait experiences extremes of heat in summer. Almost all the annual rainfall of 100 mm (4 in) comes during the cooler winter.

ECONOMY

The economy was devastated by the Iraqi invasion and Second Gulf War (1991), but reconstruction followed rapidly. Large reserves of petroleum and natural gas are the mainstay of the economy. Owing to lack of water, little agriculture is possible.

HISTORY

Islam came to Kuwait during the Prophet Muhammad's lifetime. In 1760 the Sabah family created the emirate that has lasted to today, although from 1899 to 1961 Kuwait was a British-protected state. Oil was discovered in 1938 and was produced commercially from 1946. In August 1990 Iraq invaded and annexed Kuwait. When Iraq failed to respond to repeated UN demands to withdraw, the UN authorized armed action. Kuwait was liberated by a US-led coalition early in 1991 in the short Second Gulf War, since when pressure for constitutional change has grown. Before 1990, Kuwait had a large

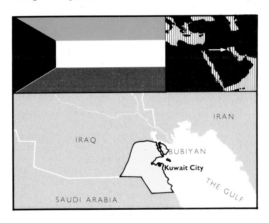

population of foreign workers, mainly Palestinians, who were perceived to have favoured the Iraqi occupation forces. Since 1991, most of the non-Kuwaiti Arab workers have fled or been deported, to be replaced by migrants from the Indian subcontinent on short-term contracts. As a result the population has decreased.

KYRGYZSTAN

Official name: Kyrgyzstan. Formerly known as Kirghizia

Member of: UN, CIS, CSCE

Area: 198 500 km² (76 600 sq mi)

Population: 4 422 000 (1991 est)

Capital and major cities: Bishkek (formerly Frunze) 626 000, Osh 213 000 (1989 census)

Languages: Kyryz (53%), Russian (21%), Uzbek (13%)

Religion: Sunni Islam majority

GOVERNMENT

A 250-member legislature and a President are elected for four years by universal adult suffrage.

GEOGRAPHY

Most of Kyrgyzstan lies within the Tien Shan mountains, rising at Pik Pobedy to 7439 m (24 406 ft). Restricted lowlands – including the Chu valley and part of the Fergana valley – contain most of the population.

Climate: The country's altitude and position deep within the interior of Asia combine to produce an extreme continental climate with low precipitation.

ECONOMY

Agriculture is dominated by large collectivized farms that specialize in growing fodder crops for sheep and

goats, and cotton under irrigation. Natural resources include coal, lead, zinc and considerable HEP potential. Food processing and light industry are expanding but the economy remains centrally planned.

HISTORY

The Kyrgyz – a Turkic people – are thought to have migrated to the region in the 12th century. Although nominally subject to Uzbek khans, the nomadic Kirghiz retained their independence until after 1850 when the area was annexed by Russia. Opposition to the Russians (who were given most of the best land) was expressed in a major revolt in 1916 and continuing guerrilla activity after the Russian Revolution. A Kirghiz Soviet Republic was founded in 1926 and became a full Union Republic within the USSR in 1936. After the abortive coup by Communist hardliners (September 1991), Kirghizia declared independence and – under its new name, Kyrgyzstan – received international recognition when the Soviet Union was dissolved (December 1991).

LAOS

Official name: Saathiaranagroat Prachhathippatay Prachhachhon Lao (The Lao People's Democratic Republic)

Member of: UN

Area: 236 800 km² (91 400 sq mi)

Population: 4 290 000 (1991 est)

Capital: Vientiane (Viengchane) 377 000 (1985 est)

Language: Lao (official)

Religion: Buddhism (57%), traditional local religions

GOVERNMENT

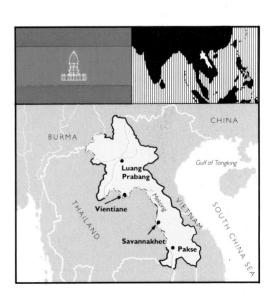

The President, Prime Minister and Council of Ministers are effectively responsible to the Central Committee of the (Communist) Lao People's Revolutionary Party. A new constitution is to be drafted.

GEOGRAPHY
Except for the Plain of Jars in the N and the Mekong Valley and low plateaux in the S, Laos is mountainous. Phou Bia (2820 m / 9252 ft) is the highest peak.

Principal river: Mekong 4350 km (2702 mi)

Climate: Laos has a tropical climate with heavy monsoon rains between May and October.

ECONOMY
Laos is one of the poorest countries in the world. Most Laotians work on collective farms, mainly growing rice. Western inverstment has been encouraged since 1990.

HISTORY
The powerful Laotian Buddhist kingdom of Lan Xang was established in the 14th century and divided into three in 1707. A French protectorate was established in 1893. Japanese occupation in World War II led to a declaration of independence which the French finally accepted in 1954 (see p. 452). However, the kingdom was wracked by civil war, with royalist forces fighting Communist Pathet Lao. The Viet Cong used Laos as a supply route in the Vietnam War (see p. 452), and US withdrawal from Vietnam allowed the Pathet Lao to take over Laos (1975). Since 1990 the government has begun to introduce reforms, but there is no suggestion that a multi-party system will be tolerated.

LATVIA

Official name: Latvija (Latvia)

Member of: UN, CSCE

Area: 64 589 km² (24 938 sq mi)

Population: 2 686 000 (1991 est)

Capital and major cities: Riga 917 000, Dagauvpils 128 000, Liepaja 115 000 (1990 est)

Languages: Lettish (over 52%), Russian (33%)

Religions: Lutheran (22%), Roman Catholic (7%)

GOVERNMENT
A President – who appoints a Prime Minister and a Cabinet – and a 100-member Assembly are elected by universal adult suffrage for three years.

GEOGRAPHY
Latvia comprises an undulating plain, lower in the W (Courland) than in the E (Livonia), which rises to 311 m (1020 ft).

Climate: Latvia has a moist, temperate climate with mild summers and cold winters.

ECONOMY
Engineering dominates a heavily industrialized economy. Latvia has relied on Russian trade and faces severe difficulties as it introduces a free market. Agriculture specializes in dairying and meat production.

HISTORY
Latvia was ruled by the (German) Teutonic Knights from 1237 until 1561. The E (Livonia) was Polish until 1629, then Swedish until 1710–21 when it was taken by Russia. The W (Courland) was an autonomous duchy until annexed by Russia in 1795. Latvian national consciousness grew throughout the 19th century. Following the Communist takeover in Russia (1917), Latvian nationalists declared independence (1918). A democratic system lasted until 1936 when General Ulmanis established a dictatorship. The Non-Aggression Pact (1939) between Hitler and Stalin assigned Latvia to the USSR, which invaded and annexed the republic (1940). After occupation by Nazi Germany (1941–44), Soviet rule was reimposed. Large-scale Russian settlement replaced over 200 000 Latvians who were killed or deported to Siberia. In 1988, reforms in the USSR allowed Latvian nationalists to operate openly. Nationalists won a majority in Latvia's parliament and seceded following the failed coup by Communist hardliners in Moscow (1991). The USSR recognized Latvia's independence in September 1991. Tension remains over the large Russian minority in Latvia.

LEBANON

Official name: Al-Lubnan (The Lebanon)

Member of: UN, Arab League

Area: 10 452 km² (4036 sq mi)

Population: 2 745 000 (1991 est)

Capital and major cities: Beirut 1 100 000, Tripoli (Tarabulus) 240 000 (including suburbs; 1990 est)

Language: Arabic (official)

Religions: Islam – Shia (31%) and Sunni (27%), Druze minority; Maronite Christian (22%), other Christian Churches (16%; Armenian, Greek Orthodox, Syrian)

GOVERNMENT
A 108-member National Assembly – comprising 54 deputies elected by Muslims, 54 by Christians – is elected by universal adult suffrage for four years. The Assembly elects a (Maronite) President, who appoints a (Sunni Muslim) Prime Minister, who, in turn, appoints a Council of Ministers (six Christians and five Muslims).

GEOGRAPHY
Beside a narrow coastal plain, the mountains of Lebanon rise to 3088 m (10 131 ft). Beyond the fertile Beka'a Valley, to the E, are the Anti-Lebanese range and Hermon Mountains.

Climate: The lowlands have a Mediterranean climate. The cooler highlands receive heavy winter snowfall.

ECONOMY
Reconstruction of an economy devastated by civil war began in 1991. The principal agricultural crops are citrus fruit (grown mainly for export), wheat, barley and olives. The illegal cultivation of opium poppies is economically significant. The textile and chemical industries and the financial sector are important.

HISTORY
Lebanon – the home of the ancient Phoenicians (see p. 364) – came, in turn, under Egyptian, Assyrian, Persian, Seleucid, Roman and Byzantine rule. The early Islamic conquests bypassed the Lebanese mountains, leaving important Maronite Christian enclaves. From the 10th century, Shia Islam (see p. 392) came to Lebanon, and in the 11th century the Druzes (a breakaway sect from the Shiites) became a significant force in the region. In the 12th and 13th centuries, the Crusader state of Tripoli (see pp. 398–9) flourished in Lebanon; in the 14th century the area was ruled by Mamluks from Egypt. In 1516 the Ottoman (Turkish) Empire took Lebanon, adminis-

tering it as part of Syria, although Druze princes enjoyed considerable autonomy. Intercommunal friction was never far from the surface. A massacre of thousands of Maronites by the Druzes (1860) brought French intervention. After World War I, France received Syria as a League of Nations mandate, and created a separate Lebanese territory to protect Christian interests. The constitution under which Lebanon became independent in 1943 enshrined power-sharing between Christians and Muslims.

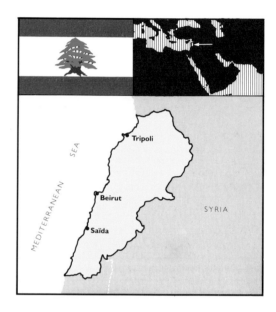

The relative toleration between the various religious groups in Lebanon began to break down in the late 1950s when Muslim numerical superiority failed to be matched by corresponding constitutional changes. Radical Muslim supporters of the union of Syria and Egypt in 1958 clashed with the pro-Western party of Camille Chamoun (President 1952–58). Civil war ensued, and US marines landed in Beirut to restore order. The 1967 Arab-Israeli war (see p. 455) and the exile of the Palestinian leadership to Beirut (1970–71) destabilized Lebanon. Civil war broke out in 1975, with subsequent Syrian and Israeli interventions (see p. 455). The war plunged the country into ungovernable chaos. In 1990 the defeat of Christian militia by Syrian troops allowed the Lebanese government to reassert its authority over the whole of Beirut. Most Lebanese sectarian militias were disarmed in 1991 when the civil war seemed to be over. However, Israeli-sponsored forces continue to occupy the S and the (Islamic fundamentalist) Hizbollah forces control the Beka'a Valley.

LESOTHO

Official name: The Kingdom of Lesotho

Member of: UN, Commonwealth, OAU

Area: 30 355 km² (11 720 sq mi)

Population: 1 806 000 (1991 est)

Capital: Maseru 110 000 (1988 est)

Languages: Sesotho and English – both official

Religions: Roman Catholic (44%), various Protestant Churches (49%)

GOVERNMENT
The kingdom of Lesotho is ruled by a Military Council, but a new constitution is to be drafted and the reintroduction of multi-party politics is scheduled.

GEOGRAPHY
Most of Lesotho is mountainous. Thabana Ntlenyana in the Drakensberg Mountains rises to (3482 m / 11 425 ft).

Climate: Lesotho has a mild subtropical climate with lower temperatures in the highlands.

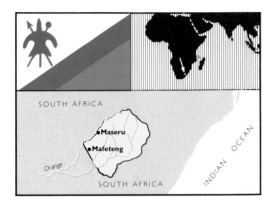

ECONOMY
Livestock – cattle, sheep and goats (for mohair) – are the mainstay of the economy. Natural resources include diamonds. Abundant water is exported to South Africa.

HISTORY
Lesotho was founded in the 1820s by the Sotho leader, Moshoeshoe I (c. 1790–1870). The kingdom escaped incorporation in South Africa by becoming a British protectorate (known as Basutoland) in 1868. Since independence (1966), land-locked Lesotho remains dependent on South Africa. Chief Jonathan (PM 1966–86) attempted to limit South African influence but was deposed in a coup. The Military Council removed the king's powers and (in 1990) placed his son on the throne.

LIBERIA

Official name: The Republic of Liberia
Member of: UN, OAU, ECOWAS
Area: 111 369 km² (43 000 sq mi)
Population: 2 607 000 (1990 est)
Capital: Monrovia 465 000 (1987 est)
Language: English (official)
Religions: Animist (50%), Sunni Islam (26%), Christian Churches (24%)

GOVERNMENT
The constitution provides for a President, 26-member Senate and 64-member House of Representatives to be elected for six years by universal adult suffrage. The President appoints a Cabinet of Ministers.

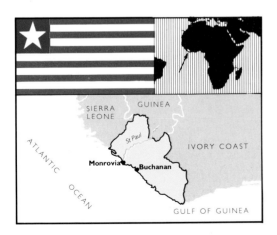

GEOGRAPHY
A low swampy coastal belt borders a higher zone of tropical forest. Further inland, plateaux rise to Mount Nimba at 1380 m (4540 ft).

Climate: Liberia has a tropical climate with a wet season in the summer and a dry season in winter.

ECONOMY
Over 70% of the labour force is involved in agriculture, producing cassava and rice as subsistence crops and rubber, coffee and cocoa for export. Liberia is a major exporter of iron ore. The economy has been disrupted by a civil war since 1990.

HISTORY
Founded by the American Colonization Society in 1821–22 as a settlement for freed slaves, Liberia was declared a republic in 1847. Black American settlers dominated the local Africans and extended their control inland. From 1878 to 1980 power was held by presidents from the True Whig Party, including William Tubman (President 1944–71). Samuel Doe, the first Liberian of local ancestry to rule, took power in a military coup (1980), but was overthrown in a civil war (1990). Despite the presence of an ECOWAS peace-keeping force civil war continues.

LIBYA

Official name: Daulat Libiya al-'Arabiya al-Ishtrakiya al-Jumhuriya (The Great Socialist People's Libyan Arab Jamahiriya)
Member of: UN, Arab League, OPEC
Area: 1 759 540 km² (679 363 sq mi)
Population: 4 325 000 (1991 est)
Capital and major cities: Tripoli (Tarabulus) 991 000, Benghazi (Banghazi) 485 000, Misurata (Misratah) 178 000 (1989 est). In 1988 government functions were decentralized to Sirte (Surt) and Al Jofrah as well as Tripoli and Benghazi.
Language: Arabic (official)
Religion: Sunni Islam (over 97%)

GOVERNMENT
Over 1110 delegates from directly elected local Basic People's Congresses, trade unions, 'popular committees' and professional organizations meet as the Great People's Congress, which chooses a Revolutionary Leader – head of state – and the General People's Committee (which is equivalent to a Council of Ministers). The appointed General Secretariat assists the Congress. There are no political parties.

GEOGRAPHY
The Sahara Desert covers most of Libya. In the NW (Tripolitania) coastal oases and a low plain support farming. In the NE (Cyrenaica) a coastal plain and mountains support Mediterranean vegetation. The Tibesti Mountains rise to Pico Bette (2286 m / 7500 ft).

Climate: Libya is hot and dry, with lower temperatures and higher rainfall near the coast.

ECONOMY
Libya is one of the world's largest producers of petroleum. Liquefied gas is also exported. Coastal oases produce wheat, barley, nuts, dates and grapes.

HISTORY
In the 7th century BC Phoenicians settled Tripolitania – which became part of the Carthaginian Empire (see p. 376) – and the Greeks founded cities in Cyrenaica. From the 1st century BC coastal Libya came under Roman rule. By the 5th century AD Libya – then part of the Byzantine Empire – was largely Christian. Arab armies brought Islam to Libya in the 7th century. Tripolitania came under Berber rule, and Cyrenaica became Egyptian, while the S – Fezzan – remained independent. In the 16th century, the whole of Libya was united under Ottoman (Turkish) rule, although autonomous local dynasties flourished.

In 1911 the Italians took Libya. The British Eighth Army defeated the Italians at El Alamein in the Libyan Desert (1942), and after World War II the country was divided between British and French administrations. Libya became independence in 1951 under King Idris, formerly Amir of Cyrenaica. Although oil revenues made Libya prosperous, the pro-Western monarchy became increasingly unpopular. In 1969 junior army officers led by Moamar al Gaddafi (1942–) took power. Gaddafi nationalized the oil industry, but his various attempts to federate with other Arab countries proved abortive. In the 1970s he began a cultural revolution, dismantled formal government, collectivized economic activity, limited personal wealth and suppressed opposition. Libya's alleged support of terrorism provoked US air raids on Tripoli and Benghazi in 1986, and UN sanctions in 1992.

LIECHTENSTEIN

Official name: Fürstentum Liechtenstein (The Principality of Liechtenstein)
Member of: UN, EFTA, CSCE
Area: 160 km² (62 sq mi)
Population: 29 000 (1991 est)
Capital and major towns: Vaduz 4800, Schaan 4900 (1990 est)
Language: German (official)
Religion: Roman Catholic (87%), Lutheran (8%)

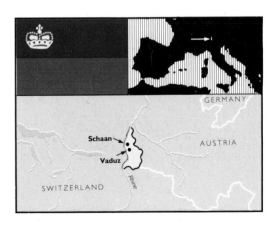

GOVERNMENT
The country is a monarchy ruled by a Prince. The 25-member Landstag is elected under a system of proportional representation by universal adult suffrage for four years. The Landstag elects a 5-member Cabinet including a Prime Minister.

GEOGRAPHY
The Alps in the E of the principality rise to the

Grauspitze at 2599 m (8326 ft). The W comprises the floodplain of the River Rhine.

Climate: The country has a mild Alpine climate.

ECONOMY
Liechtenstein has one of the highest standards of living in the world. Tourism, banking and manufacturing (precision goods) are all important.

HISTORY
In 1719 the counties of Schellenberg and Vaduz were united to form a principality for the Austrian Princes of Liechtenstein. Separated from Germany by Austrian territory, Liechtenstein was the only German principality not to join the German Empire in 1871. Since 1924 the country has enjoyed a customs and monetary union with Switzerland, although since 1989 the principality has taken a more active role internationally, for instance joining the UN and EFTA.

LITHUANIA

Official name: Lietuva (Lithuania)

Member of: UN, CSCE

Area: 65 200 km² (25 174 sq mi)

Population: 3 739 000 (1991)

Capital and major cities: Vilnius 593 000, Kaunas 430 000, Klaipeda 206 000 (1989 est)

Languages: Lithuanian (80%), Russian (9%)

Religions: Roman Catholic (80%), Lutheran minority

GOVERNMENT
The 141-member Parliament and a President are elected by universal adult suffrage for five years. The President, chooses the Prime Minister, who, in turn, appoints a Cabinet of Ministers.

GEOGRAPHY
Lithuania comprises a low-lying plain dotted with lakes and crossed by ridges of glacial moraine that rise to 294 m (964 ft) in the SE.

Climate: Lithuania has a transitional climate between the milder temperate areas to the W and the more extreme continental areas to the E.

ECONOMY
One fifth of the labour force is engaged in farming, mainly cattle rearing and dairying. Much of Lithuania is heavily forested. The engineering, timber, cement and food-processing industries are important, but Lithuania faces an uncertain future as it dismantles state control and breaks away from the former Soviet trade system.

HISTORY
The Lithuanians were first united c. 1250. Their 'grand princes' greatly enlarged the country, annexing Byelorussia and most of the Ukraine. The marriage of grand prince Jogaila to the queen of Poland (1386) united the crowns of the two countries, although Lithuania retained autonomy until 1569. Lithuania was annexed by Russia in 1795. Lithuanian national consciousness increased throughout the 19th century and Lithuanians rose with the Poles against Russian rule in 1830–31 and 1863. German forces invaded in 1915 and encouraged the establishment of a Lithuanian state. After World War I, the new republic faced invasions by the Red Army from the E and the Polish army from the W (1919–20). Internationally recognized boundaries were not established until 1923. The dictatorship of Augustinas Voldemaras (1926–29) was followed by that of Antonas Smetona (1929–40).

The Non-Aggression Pact (1939) between Hitler and Stalin assigned Lithuania to the USSR, which invaded and annexed the republic (1940). Lithuania was occupied by Nazi Germany (1941–44). When Soviet rule was reimposed (1945), large-scale Russian settlement replaced over 250 000 Lithuanians who had been killed or deported to Siberia. In 1988, reforms in the USSR allowed Lithuanian nationalists to operate openly. Nationalists won a majority in the republic's parliament, but their declaration of independence (1990) brought a crackdown by Soviet forces in Lithuania. Following the failed coup by Communist hardliners in Moscow (August 1991), the USSR recognized Lithuania's independence.

LUXEMBOURG

Official name: Grand-Duché de Luxembourg (Grand Duchy of Luxembourg)

Member of: UN, EC, NATO, CSCE, OECD

Area: 2586 km² (999 sq mi)

Population: 385 000 (1991 census)

Capital and major cities: Luxembourg 117 000 (city 78 000), Esch-sur-Alzette 24 000, Differdage 16 000 (1991 census)

Languages: Letzeburgish (national), French and German – both official

Religion: Roman Catholic (94%)

GOVERNMENT
Luxembourg is a monarchy with a Grand Duke as sovereign. The 64-member Chamber of Deputies is elected under a system of proportional representation by universal adult suffrage for five years. A Council of Ministers and a Premier – commanding a majority in the Chamber – are appointed by the sovereign.

GEOGRAPHY

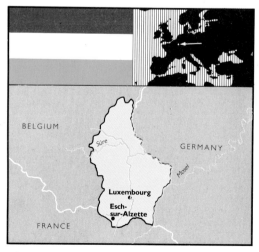

The Oesling is a wooded plateau rising to 550 m (1833 ft) in the N. The Gutland in the S is a lowland region of valleys and ridges.

Climate: Luxembourg has cool summers and mild winters.

ECONOMY
The iron and steel industry – originally based on local ore – is important. Luxembourg has become a major banking centre. The N grows potatoes and fodder crops; the S produces wheat and fruit, including grapes.

HISTORY
Luxembourg has changed hands many times through inheritance and invasion. In 1443, Luxembourg passed to the dukes of Burgundy, and was inherited by the Spanish Habsburgs in 1555–56. In 1713 the country came under Austrian rule, but was annexed by France during the Napoleonic Wars. In 1815 Luxembourg became a Grand Duchy with the Dutch king as sovereign, but in 1890 it was inherited by a junior branch of the House of Orange. Occupied by the Germans during both World Wars, Luxembourg concluded an economic union with Belgium in 1922 and has enthusiastically supported European unity.

MADAGASCAR

Official name: Repoblika Demokratika n'i Madagaskar (The Democratic Republic of Madagascar)

Member of: UN, OAU

Area: 587 041 km² (226 658 sq mi)

Population: 11 197 000 (1990 est)

Capital and major cities: Antananarivo (Tananarive) 802 000, Toamasina 145 000 (1990 est)

Languages: Malagasy and French (official)

Religions: Animist (47%), Roman Catholic (26%), Protestant Church of Jesus Christ in Madagascar (22%)

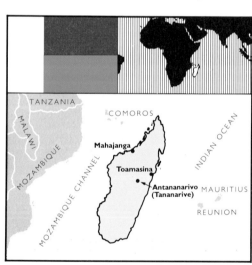

GOVERNMENT
A President – who appoints a Prime Minister and a Cabinet – is elected by universal adult suffrage for seven years. A 137-member National Assembly is directly elected for five years.

GEOGRAPHY
Massifs form a spine running from N to S through the island, rising to Tsaratanana peak at 2885 m (9465 ft). To the E is a narrow coastal plain; to the W are fertile plains.

Climate: The climate is tropical, although the highlands are cooler. The N receives monsoon rains, but the S is dry.

ECONOMY
Over three quarters of the labour force are involved in

agriculture. The main crops are coffee and vanilla for export, and rice and cassava for domestic consumption. The island is an important producer of chromite.

HISTORY
The first inhabitants were Polynesians from Indonesia in the early centuries AD, and were later joined by mainland Africans and by Arabs. In the early 19th century, the island was united by the Merina kingdom. Merina sovereigns attempted to modernize Madagascar but the island was annexed by France in 1896, although resistance continued until 1904. Strong nationalist feeling found expression in a major rising (1947–48) that was suppressed with heavy loss of life. Independence was finally achieved in 1960. Since a military coup in 1972, Madagascar has had left-wing governments, but political and economic reforms began in 1990.

MALAWI

Official name: The Republic of Malawi

Member of: UN, Commonwealth, OAU

Area: 118 484 km² (45 747 sq mi)

Population: 9 152 000 (1991 est)

Capital and major cities: Lilongwe 220 000, Blantyre 403 000, Mzuzu 115 000 (1987 census)

Languages: English and Chichewa (80%) – both official

Religions: Animist (67%), Roman Catholic (17%), Presbyterian (6%)

GOVERNMENT
Under the constitution the President is directly elected, but in 1971 Dr Hastings Kamuzu Banda was declared President for life. Elections are held by universal adult suffrage every five years for 112 members of the National Assembly. The President appoints additional members as well as a Cabinet of Ministers. The Malawi Congress Party is the only legal party.

GEOGRAPHY
Plateaux cover the N and centre. The Rift Valley contains Lake Malawi and the Shire Valley. The Shire Highlands on the Mozambique border rise to Mount Sapitawa at 3002 m (9849 ft).

Climate: Malawi has an equatorial climate with heavy rainfall from November to April.

ECONOMY
Agriculture is the mainstay of the economy, providing most of Malawi's exports. Tobacco, tea and sugar cane are the main crops.

HISTORY
David Livingstone and other British missionaries

became active in the area from the 1860s. A British protectorate, later called Nyasaland, was declared in 1891. In 1915 the Rev. John Chilembwe led a violent rising in the fertile S where Africans had lost much land to white settlers. Federation with the white-dominated Central African Federation (1953–63) was resented. The nationalist leader – later President – Dr Hastings Kamuzu Banda (c. 1902–   ) helped to break the Federation. Since independence as Malawi in 1964, Banda has provided strong rule and – despite criticism – maintained close relations with South Africa. In 1992–93 pressure to end the one-party state grew.

MALAYSIA

Official name: Persekutuan Tanah Melaysiu (The Federation of Malaysia)

Member of: UN, Commonwealth, ASEAN

Area: 329 758 km² (127 320 sq mi)

Population: 17 556 000 (1990 census)

Capital and major cities: Kuala Lumpur 1 233 000 (including suburbs; 1990 census), Ipoh 390 000, George Town 325 000, Johor Baharu 32? 000 (1990 est)

Languages: Bahasa Malaysia (Malay; official; 58%), English, Chinese (32%), Tamil

Religions: Sunni Islam (official; over 55%), Buddhist, Daoist and various Christian minorities

GOVERNMENT
The Yang di-Pertuan Agong (the King of Malaysia) holds office for five years. He is elected – from their own number – by the hereditary sultans who reign in 9 of the 13 states. The 70-member Senate (upper house) comprises 40 members appointed by the King and two members elected by each of the state and territorial assemblies for a three-year term. The 180-member House of Representatives is elected by universal adult suffrage for five years. The King appoints a Prime Minister and a Cabinet commanding a majority in the House. The states have their own governments.

GEOGRAPHY
Western (Peninsular) Malaysia consists of mountain ranges – including the Trengganu and Cameron Highlands – running N to S and bordered by densely populated coastal lowlands. Tropical rainforest covers the hills and mountains of Eastern Malaysia (Sabah and Sarawak, the northern part of the island of Borneo). The highest point is Kinabalu in Sabah (4101 m / 13 455 ft).

Climate: Malaysia has a tropical climate with heavy rainfall (up to 2500 mm / 100 in in the W). There is more seasonal variation in precipitation than temperature, with the NE monsoon (from October to February) and the SW monsoon (from May to September) bringing increased rainfall, particularly to Peninsular Malaysia.

ECONOMY
Rubber, petroleum and tin are the traditional mainstays of the Malaysian economy, but all three suffered drops in price on the world market in the 1980s. Pepper (mainly from Sarawak), cocoa and timber are also important. One third of the labour force is involved in agriculture. Large numbers of Malays grow rice as a subsistence crop. Manufacturing industry is now the largest exporter; major industries include rubber, tin, timber, textiles, machinery and cement. The government has greatly encouraged industrialization, investment and a more active role for the ethnic Malay population in industry, which – with commerce and finance – has been largely the preserve of Chinese Malaysians. Malaysia has experienced high economic growth rates since the early 1980s. The tourist industry is being promoted.

HISTORY
Malaysia's ethnic diversity reflects its complex history and the lure of its natural wealth and prime trading position. Most of the area was part of the Buddhist Sumatran kingdom of Sri Vayaja from the 9th century to the 14th century, when it fell to the Hindu Javanese. From the 15th century, Islam came to the region and the

spice trade attracted Europeans. The trading post of Malacca was taken by the Portuguese in 1511 and then by the Dutch in 1641. The British established themselves on the island of Penang (1786), founded Singapore (1819), and in 1867 established an administration for the Straits Settlements – Malacca, Penang and Singapore. Ignoring Thai claims to overlordship in the peninsula, the British took over the small sultanates as protected states. The British suppressed piracy, developed tin mining with Chinese labour and rubber plantations with Indian workers. Sarawak became a separate state under Sir James Brooke – the 'White Raja' – and his family from 1841, and was ceded to the British Crown in 1946. Sabah became British – as British North Borneo – from 1881.

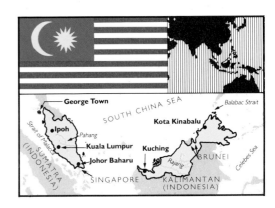

The Japanese occupied the whole of Malaysia during World War II. A Federation of Malaya – the peninsula – was established in 1948, but was threatened by Communist insurgency until 1960. Malaya became independent in 1957 with a constitution protecting the interests of the Malays who were fearful of the energy and acumen of the Chinese. Sabah, Sarawak and Singapore joined the Federation – renamed Malaysia – in 1963. Singapore left in 1965 but the unity of the Federation was maintained, with British armed support, in the face of an Indonesian 'confrontation' in Borneo (1965–66). Tension between Chinese and Malays led to riots and the suspension of parliamentary government (1969–71), but scarcely hindered the rapid development of a resource-rich economy. During the 1980s, the growth of Islamic fundamentalism led to a defensive re-assertion of Islamic values and practices among the Muslim Malay ruling elite.

THE MALDIVES

Official name: Dhivehi Jumhuriya (Republic of Maldives)

Member of: UN, Commonwealth

Area: 298 km² (115 sq mi)

Population: 213 000 (1990 census)

Capital: Malé 55 000 (1990 census)

Language: Dhivehi (Maldivian; official)

Religion: Sunni Islam (official)

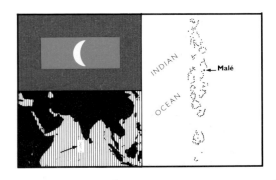

GOVERNMENT

The Majilis (Assembly) consists of 8 members appointed by the President, and 40 elected by universal adult suffrage for five years. The President – who is directly elected for five years – appoints a Cabinet. There are no political parties.

GEOGRAPHY

The country is a chain of over 1190 small low-lying coral islands, of which 203 are inhabited.

Climate: The tropical climate brings heavy rainfall brought by the monsoon between May and August.

ECONOMY

The tourist industry has displaced fishing as the mainstay of the economy. However, 35% of Maldivians subsist on fish and coconuts.

HISTORY

Settled from the S Asian mainland, the Maldives accepted Islam in the 12th century. Western contacts began with the Portuguese in the 16th century. From 1887 until independence in 1965 the Maldives were a British protectorate, but the ad-Din sultanate, established in the 14th century, was only abolished in 1968.

MALI

Official name: La République du Mali (The Republic of Mali)

Member of: UN, OAU, ECOWAS

Area: 1 240 192 km² (478 841 sq mi)

Population: 8 299 000 (1991 est)

Capital and major cities: Bamako 650 000, Ségou 89 000 (1987 census)

Languages: French (official), Bambara (60%)

Religions: Sunni Islam (80%), animist (9%)

GOVERNMENT

A President is elected by universal adult suffrage for six years and the 128-member National Assembly is directly elected for three years. (Thirteen of the deputies are elected by Malians living abroad.) The President appoints a Premier and a Cabinet.

GEOGRAPHY

The low-lying plains of Mali rise to 1155 m (3789 ft) in the Adrar des Iforas range in the NE. The S is savannah; the Sahara Desert is in the N.

Principal river: Niger 4200 km (2600 mi)

Climate: Mali is hot and largely dry, although the S has a wet season from June to October.

ECONOMY

Drought in the 1970s and 1980s devastated Mali's livestock herds. Only one fifth of Mali can be cultivated, producing mainly rice, millet and sorghum for domestic use, and cotton for export.

HISTORY

Mali is named after an empire in the area (12th–14th centuries). Conquered by France (1880–95), it became the French Sudan. Mali became independent in 1960. After an army coup in 1968, military governments ruled Mali until multi-party politics were restored in 1992.

MALTA

Official name: Repubblika Ta'Malta (Republic of Malta)

Member of: UN, Commonwealth, CSCE

Area: 316 km² (122 sq mi)

Population: 357 000 (1991 est)

Capital: Valletta 204 000 (city 9200; 1991 est)

Languages: Maltese and English – both official

Religion: Roman Catholic (official; 98%)

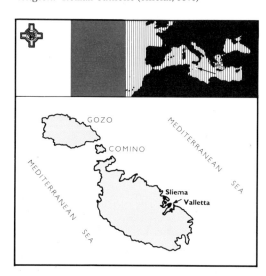

GOVERNMENT

The 65-member House of Representatives is elected by universal adult suffrage under a system of proportional representation for five years. The President – who is elected for five years by the House – appoints a Premier and a Cabinet who command a majority in the House.

GEOGRAPHY

The islands of Malta, Gozo and Comino consist of low limestone plateaux with little surface water.

Climate: The climate is Mediterranean with hot dry summers, and cooler wetter winters.

ECONOMY

The main industries are footwear and clothing, food processing and ship repairing. Tourism is the main foreign-currency earner. Malta is virtually self-sufficient in agricultural products.

HISTORY

Malta was ruled, in turn, by Rome (218 BC–394 AD), the Byzantine Empire (until 870), the Arabs (until 1091) and Sicily (until 1530). From 1530 to 1798, Malta was in the hands of the Knights of St John (see p. 399), who repelled a Turkish siege in 1565. The French held Malta from 1798 to 1800, provoking the Maltese to request British protection (1802). As a British colony (from 1814), Malta became a vital naval base, and the island received the George Cross for its valour in World War II. Malta gained independence in 1964. Maltese political life has polarized between the National Party and the Maltese Labour Party.

MARSHALL ISLANDS

Official name: The Republic of the Marshall Islands

Member of: UN

Area: 180 km² (70 sq mi)

Population: 49 000 (1991 est)

Capital: Dalap-Uliga-Darrit on Majuro 20 000 (1990 est)

Languages: Marshallese and English (official)

Religions: Protestant Churches (over 50%), Roman Catholic

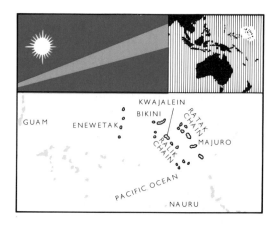

GOVERNMENT

The 33-member Nitijela (Parliament) and the President are elected by universal adult suffrage for four years.

GEOGRAPHY

The Marshall Islands comprise over 1150 small coral atolls and islands below 6 m (20 ft) high.

Climate: The tropical climate has heavy rainfall.

ECONOMY

With practically no resources, the islands depend on subsistence farming, tourism and US grants.

HISTORY

The earliest Micronesian settlements in the Marshall Islands date from c. 2000 BC. The Spanish navigator Saavedra was the first European visitor in 1529. The islands were under Spanish (1875–85), German (1885–1914), and Japanese (1914–45) administration before becoming part of the US Pacific Islands Trust Territory. In 1986, US administration was terminated, but the USA retains responsibility for the islands' defence. The islands' independence was recognized when the UN terminated the trusteeship in 1990.

MAURITANIA

Official name: Jumhuriyat Muritaniya al-Islamiya (Islamic Republic of Mauritania)

Member of: UN, OAU, Arab League

Area: 1 030 700 km² (397 950 sq mi)

Population: 2 053 000 (1991 est)

Capital: Nouakchott 600 000 (city 393 000; 1988 census)

Languages: Arabic (official; 81%); French

Religion: Sunni Islam (official; 99%)

GOVERNMENT

A President and a 77-member National Assembly are elected by universal adult suffrage for six years. A Senate (upper house) is indirectly elected. The President appoints a Prime Minister and a Council of Ministers.

GEOGRAPHY

Isolated peaks – including Kediet Ijill (915 m / 3050 ft) – rise above the plateaux of the Sahara Desert that cover most of Mauritania.

Principal river: Sénégal 1641 km (1020 mi)

Climate: The climate is hot and dry, with adequate rainfall only in the S.

ECONOMY
Persistant drought has devastated the nomads' herds of cattle and sheep. Fish from the Atlantic and iron ore are virtually the only exports.

HISTORY The French arrived on the coast in the 17th century, but did not annex the Arab emirates inland until 1903. Mauritania became independent in 1960. When Spain withdrew from the Western Sahara (1976), Morocco and Mauritania divided the territory between them, but Mauritania could not defeat the Polisario guerrillas fighting for Sahrawi independence and gave up its claim (1979). Tension between the dominant Arab N and Black African S led to violence in 1989. Military rulers held power from 1979. In 1992 free elections were held, but the opposition boycotted the poll.

MAURITIUS

Official name: The Republic of Mauritius

Member of: UN, OAU, Commonwealth

Area: 2040 km² (788 sq mi)

Population: 1 087 000 (1991 est)

Capital: Port Louis 142 000 (1990 est)

Languages: English (official), Creole (nearly 30%), Hindi (over 20%), Bhojpuri

Religions: Hindu (51%), Roman Catholic (25%), Sunni Islam (17%), with Protestant minorities

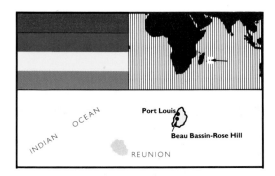

GOVERNMENT
Elections are held by universal adult suffrage every five years for 62 members of the Assembly; up to 8 additional members may be appointed. The President – who is appointed by the Assembly – appoints a Prime Minister who commands a majority in the Assembly. The PM, in turn, appoints a Cabinet responsible to the Assembly.

GEOGRAPHY
The central plateau of Mauritius is surrounded by mountains, including Piton de la Riviere Noire (826 m / 2711 ft). Other islands in the group include Rodrigues and the Agalega Islands.

Climate: The climate is subtropical, although it can be very hot from December to April. Rainfall is high in the uplands.

ECONOMY
Tourism and the export of sugar cane dominate the economy. Diversification is being encouraged, and the clothing industry is of increasing importance.

HISTORY
Known to the Arabs and the Portuguese, the island was settled by the Dutch in 1638. Mauritius was French from 1715 until 1814, when it became British. Black slaves were imported, followed in the 19th century by Indian labourers whose descendants are the majority community. Independence was gained in 1968 and a republic was declared in 1992.

MEXICO

Official name: Estados Unidos Mexicanos (United Mexican States)

Member of: UN, OAS, NAFTA, ALADI

Area: 1 958 201 km² (756 066 sq mi)

Population: 83 151 000 (1991 est)

Capital and major cities: Mexico City 19 480 000 (city 8 237 000), Guadalajara 3 187 000 (city 2 847 000), Monterrey 2 859 000 (city 2 522 000), Puebla 1 707 000 (city 1 055 000), Netzahualcóyotl 1 260 000 (part of the Mexico City agglomeration), León 1 081 000 (city 872 000) (all including suburbs; 1990 census)

Languages: Spanish (92%; official), various Indian languages

Religion: Roman Catholic (91%)

GOVERNMENT
The 64-member Senate and the President – who may serve only once – are elected by universal adult suffrage for six years. The 500-member Chamber of Deputies are directly elected for three years – 200 of the members are elected under a system of proportional representation; the remaining 300 represent single-member constituencies. The President appoints a Cabinet. Each of the 31 states has its own Chamber of Deputies.

GEOGRAPHY
Between the Sierra Madre Oriental mountains in the E and the Sierra Madre Occidental in the W is a large high central plateau. Volcanoes include Volcán Citlaltepetl (Pico de Orizaba) at 5610 m (18 405 ft), the country's highest point. The coastal plains are generally narrow in the W, but wider in the E. The Yucatán Peninsula in the SE is a broad limestone lowland; Baja California in the NW is a long narrow mountainous peninsula.

Principal river: Rio Bravo de Norte (Rio Grande) 3033 km (1885 mi)

Climate: There is considerable climatic variation, in part reflecting the complexity of the relief. In general, the S and the coastal lowlands are tropical; the central plateau and the mountains are cooler and drier.

ECONOMY
Over 20% of the labour force is involved in agriculture and many Mexicans are still subsistence farmers growing maize, wheat, kidney beans and rice. Coffee, cotton, fruit and vegetables are major export crops. Mexico is the world's leading producer of silver. The exploitation of large reserves of natural gas and petroleum enabled Mexico's spectacular economic development since the 1970s. An expanding industrial base includes important petrochemical, textile, motor-vehicle and food-processing industries. In the early 1990s low labour costs and the new NAFTA trade agreement encouraged major US companies to set up plant in Mexico. However, economic problems remain, and high unemployment has stimulated immigration – often illegal – to the US.

HISTORY
When the Spanish arrived in Mexico in 1519, the Maya civilization was in decline but Aztec power, centred on Tenochtitlan (Mexico City), was flourishing (see pp. 390–91). In 1519–21, the mighty Aztec empire was overthrown by a small band of Spanish invaders under Cortez (see pp. 410–11). For the next 300 years Mexico was under Spanish rule, its economy largely based on silver and gold mining and the produce of large estates owned by Spanish grandees (see p. 410). The first revolt against Spanish rule broke out in 1810, but Mexican independence was not gained until 1821 after a guerrilla war led by Vicente Guerrero. Initially an empire, Mexico became a republic in 1823, but conflict between federalists and centralists erupted, developing into civil war.

In 1836 Texas rebelled against Mexico, declaring independence. When the USA annexed Texas in 1845, war broke out, resulting in the loss of half Mexico's territory – Texas, New Mexico and California. A period of reform began in 1857, with a new liberal constitution. A civil war (1858–61) between reformists and conservatives was won by the reformists under Benito Juárez (1806–72), but the economy was shattered. After Mexico failed to repay debts, Spain, Britain and France invaded in 1863. Although Spain and Britain soon withdrew, France remained, appointing Archduke Maximilian of Austria (1832–67) as Emperor (1864). Under US pressure and Mexican resistance, the French withdrew in 1867. Maximilian remained in Mexico City and was captured and executed. Juárez re-established the republic.

The authoritarian rule of General Porfirio Díaz (President 1876–80 and 1888–1910) brought peace, but wealth was concentrated into a few hands. Revolution against the power of the landowners erupted in 1910. The reformist policies of President Francisco Madero (1873–1913) were supported by the outlaw Pancho Villa (1877–1923), but revolutionary violence continued, and in 1916–17 a US expeditionary force was sent against Villa. From 1924 the revolution became anticlerical and the Church was persecuted. Order was restored when the Institutional Revolutionary Party came to power in 1929. In the 1930s the large estates were divided and much of the economy was nationalized. Political opposition has been tolerated, although the ruling party is virtually guaranteed perpetual power.

MICRONESIA

Official name: The Federated States of Micronesia

Member of: UN

Area: 702 km² (271 sq mi)

Population: 111 000 (1991 est)

Capital: Palikir (on Pohnpei) 2000, Wenn (formerly Moen) 10 400, Kolonia (the former capital) 6300 (1990 est)

Languages: English, Trukese, Ponapean, Yapese, Kosraean

Religions: Roman Catholic, Assembly of God

GOVERNMENT
The President (who serves for four years) and the 14-member National Congress are elected by universal adult suffrage. Congress comprises one senator elected from each of the four states for four years, and ten senators elected by constituencies for two years.

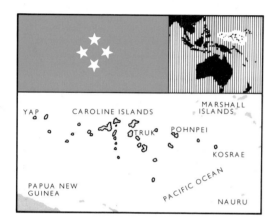

GEOGRAPHY
The Micronesian islands comprise over 600 islands in two main groups. The majority of the islands are low coral atolls, but Kosrae and Pohnpei are mountainous.

Climate: The climate is tropical with heavy rainfall.

ECONOMY
Apart from phosphate, the islands have practically no resources and depend upon subsistence agriculture, fishing and US grants.

HISTORY
The islands were first settled c. 3000 BC. The first European visitors were Spanish navigators who named the islands the Carolines. The islands were under Spanish (1874–99), German (1899–1914), and Japanese (1914–45) administration before becoming part of the US Pacific Trust Territory. In 1986, US administration was terminated, although the USA retains responsibility for the islands' defence. The Federated States' independence was recognized when the UN terminated the trusteeship in 1990.

MOLDOVA

Official name: Republica Moldoveneasca (Republic of Moldova). Formerly known as Moldavia

Member of: UN, CIS, CSCE

Area: 33 700 km² (13 000 sq mi)

Population: 4 367 000 (1991 est)

Capital and major cities: Chisinau (formerly Kishinev) 720 000, Tiraspol 182 000 (1989 census)

Languages: Romanian (64%), Ukrainian (14%), Russian (13%), Gagauz (4%)

Religions: Romanian Orthodox majority

GOVERNMENT
A 380-member legislature and a President – who appoints a Premier and a Cabinet – are elected for four years by universal adult suffrage.

GEOGRAPHY
Moldova comprises a hilly plain between the River Prut and the Dnestr valley.

Climate: The country experiences a mild, slightly continental climate.

ECONOMY
Collective farms grow fruit (particularly grapes for wine), vegetables, wheat, maize and tobacco. Little progress has been made to privatize agriculture or industry, which includes food processing and engineering.

HISTORY
Known as Bessarabia, the area was ruled by Kievan Rus' (10th–12th centuries) and the Tatars (13th–14th centuries) before becoming part of the Romanian principality of Moldavia – within the (Turkish) Ottoman Empire – in the 15th century. Bessarabia was intermittently occupied by Russia in the 18th century before being ceded to the Russians in 1812. Briefly restored to Moldavia (1856–78), Bessarabia remained Russian until World War I. An autonomous Bessarabian republic was proclaimed in 1917, but was suppressed by a Russian Bolshevik invasion (1918). The Russians were removed by Romanian forces and Bessarabia became part of the kingdom of Romania (1918). When Romania entered World War II as a German ally, the USSR reoccupied Bessarabia, which was reorganized as the Moldavian Soviet Republic in 1944. Following the abortive coup by Communist hardliners in Moscow (September 1991), Moldavia declared independence. As Moldova, the republic received international recognition when the Soviet Union was dissolved (December 1991). Civil war broke out in 1992 when Russian and Ukrainian minorities – fearing an eventual reunion of Moldova with Romania – attempted to secede. The intervention of CIS forces brought an uneasy peace.

MONACO

Official name: Principauté de Monaco (Principality of Monaco)

Member of: CSCE

Area: 2.21 km² (0.85 sq mi)

Population: 29 900 (1990 est)

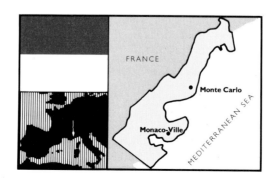

Capital and major cities: Monaco 1200, Monte-Carlo 13 200 (1990 est)

Languages: French (official), Monegasque

Religion: Roman Catholic (90%)

GOVERNMENT
Monaco is a constitutional monarchy. Legislative power is jointly held by the Prince and the 18-member National Council, which is elected by universal adult suffrage for five years. Executive power is held by the Prince, who appoints a four-member Council of Government and a French civil servant to head it.

GEOGRAPHY
Monaco comprises a rocky peninsula and a narrow stretch of coast. Since 1958 Monaco's area has increased by 20% through reclamation of land from the sea.

Climate: Monaco has a Mediterranean climate.

ECONOMY
Monaco depends upon real estate, banking, insurance, light industry and tourism.

HISTORY
The Grimaldi family has ruled Monaco since 1297. Monaco was annexed by France in 1793 but restored in 1814, under the protection of the king of Sardinia. The greater part of the principality was lost – and eventually annexed by France – in 1848. Since 1861 Monaco has been under French protection. Prince Rainier III granted a liberal constitution in 1962.

MONGOLIA

Official name: Bugd Nairamdakh Mongol Ard Uls (Mongolian People's Republic)

Member of: UN

Area: 1 565 000 km² (604 250 sq mi)

Population: 2 156 000 (1992 est)

Capital and major cities: Ulan Bator (Ulaan Baatar) 575 000, Darhan 90 000 (1991 est)

Languages: Khalkh Mongolian (official; 78%), Kazakh

Religion: Religion was suppressed from 1924 to 1990. Buddhism – the traditional religion – is now being encouraged.

GOVERNMENT
The 76-member Great Hural and a President are elected by universal adult suffrage for four years. The President appoints a Prime Minister and a Council of Ministers.

GEOGRAPHY
Mongolia comprises mountains in the N, a series of basins in the centre, and the Gobi Desert and Altai Mountains – rising to Mönh Hayrhan Uul (4362 m / 14 311 ft) – in the S.

Climate: Mongolia has a dry climate with generally mild summers and severely cold winters.

ECONOMY

Mongolia depends on collectivized animal herding (cattle, sheep, goats and camels). Cereals (including fodder crops) are grown on a large scale on state farms. The industrial sector is dominated by food processing, hides and wool. Copper is a major export. The former USSR was Mongolia's principal trading partner, but trade has been disrupted since 1991, leading to severe economic difficulties.

HISTORY

Mongolia was the home of the Huns – who ravaged both the Chinese and Roman empires (1st–5th centuries AD) – and of the strong Uigur state in the 8th and 9th centuries. In the 13th century the Mongol dynasty of Genghis Khan ('Perfect Warrior') created an immense but short-lived Asian empire. In the 17th century, Mongolia was annexed by China, but 'Outer' Mongolia – the N – retained autonomy as a Buddhist monarchy. In 1921, Outer Mongolia broke away from China with Soviet assistance and in 1924 the Mongolian People's Republic was established. Pro-democracy demonstrations led to a liberalization of the regime in 1990. The Communists won the first multi-party elections.

MOROCCO

Official name: Al-Mamlaka al-Maghribiya (The Kingdom of Morocco)

Member of: UN, Arab League

Area: 458 730 km² (177 115 sq mi), excluding disputed Western Sahara which has an area of 710 850 km² (274 461 sq mi).

Population: 25 208 000 (1990 est), excluding Western Sahara which had 185 000 inhabitants in 1987.

Capital and major cities: Rabat 1 472 000 (includes Salé), Casablanca (Dar el Beida) 3 210 000, Marrakech 1 517 000, Fez (Fès) 1 012 000 (with suburbs; 1990 est)

Languages: Arabic (official; 75%), Berber, French

Religion: Sunni Islam (official; 98%)

GOVERNMENT

Morocco is a constitutional monarchy. The 306-member Chamber of Representatives consists of 206 members elected by universal adult suffrage for six years and 100 members chosen by an electoral college representing municipal authorities and professional bodies. The King appoints a Prime Minister and Cabinet.

GEOGRAPHY

Over one third of Morocco is mountainous. The principal uplands are the Grand, Middle and Anti Atlas Mountains in the W and N – rising to Jebel Toubkal (4165 m / 13 665 ft) – and a plateau in the E. Much of Morocco – and all of the Western Sahara – is desert.

Climate: The N has a Mediterranean climate with hot dry summers and warm wetter winters. The S and much of the interior have semiarid and tropical desert climates.

ECONOMY

Over 40% of the labour force is involved in farming, producing mainly citrus fruits, grapes (for wine) and vegetables for export, and wheat and barley for local consumption. Morocco is the world's leading exporter of phosphates. Other resources include iron ore, lead and zinc. Many important industries and services are in state ownership. Tourism is growing.

HISTORY

The region became a Roman province in 46 AD. In the 7th century Morocco became Islamic. In the 11th and 12th centuries the Almoravid (Berber) empire – which included Muslim Spain – was based in Marrakech. Morocco was ruled by the Almohad dynasty who ruled a N African empire from 1147 until 1269. The Sharifian dynasty – descended from the Prophet Muhammad – rose to power in the 16th and 17th centuries, and still retains

the throne. In the 19th century Spain confirmed control of several long-claimed coastal settlements. In the 'Moroccan Crises' (1905–6 and 1911), French interests in Morocco were disputed by Germany. Under the Treaty of Fez in 1912 France established a protectorate over Morocco, although the Spanish enclaves remained. The 1925 Rif rebellion stirred nationalist feelings, but independence was not gained until 1956. King Hassan II (reigned 1961–) has survived left-wing challenges through strong rule and vigorous nationalism – as in his 1975 'Green March' of unarmed peasants into the then-Spanish (Western) Sahara. Morocco still holds Western Sahara despite international pressure and the activities of the Algerian-backed Polisario guerrillas fighting for the territory's independence. A ceasefire was agreed in 1991 but a scheduled UN-sponsored referendum on Western Sahara has yet to be held.

MOZAMBIQUE

Official name: A República de Moçambique (Republic of Mozambique)

Member of: UN, OAU

Area: 799 380 km² (308 641 sq mi)

Population: 15 656 000 (1990 est)

Capital and major cities: Maputo 1 070 000, Beira 292 000, Nampula 197 000 (1989 est)

Languages: Portuguese (official), Makua-Lomwe (52%)

Religions: Animist majority, with Roman Catholic and Sunni Islam minorities

GOVERNMENT

There is constitutional provision for elections by universal adult suffrage for a 250-member Assembly. The President – elected by the Assembly – appoints a Council of Ministers.

GEOGRAPHY

The Zambezi River separates high plateaux in northern Mozambique from lowlands in the S. Mount Bingo rises to 2436 m / 7992 ft.

Principal rivers: Limpopo 1770 km (1100 mi), Zambezi (Zambèze) 3540 km (2200 mi)

Climate: Mozambique has a tropical climate, with maximum rainfall and temperatures from November to March.

ECONOMY

Over 80% of the labour force is involved in farming, mainly growing cassava and maize. Fishing is a major employer – prawns and shrimps make up nearly 50% of Mozambique's exports. The economy has been devastated by civil war and drought, and famine is widespread. Mozambique is usually stated to be the poorest country in the world (in terms of GDP per head).

HISTORY

The Mozambique coast attracted Arab settlements from the 9th century AD. The Portuguese founded coastal trading posts from 1531, but only gained control of the interior at the end of the 19th century. Forced labour and minimal development fuelled nationalist feelings, and in 1964 the Frelimo movement launched a guerrilla war against Portuguese rule. Independence was gained in 1975, and a Marxist-Leninist state was established.

The pressures of poverty and the destabilization of the country by South Africa – through support for the Renamo guerrilla movement – led to renewed ties with the West. Marxism was abandoned by Frelimo in 1989. Political pluralism has been permitted since 1990. A ceasefire – and a UN presence in Mozambique – were agreed in 1992.

MYANMAR (BURMA)

Official name: Myanma Naingngandaw (The Union of Myanmar). The name Burma was officially dropped in 1989.

Member of: UN

Area: 676 552 km² (261 218 sq mi)

Population: 42 561 000 (1991 est)

Capital and major cities: Rangoon (Yangon) 2 513 000, Mandalay 533 000, Moulmein 230 000 (1983 census)

Languages: Burmese (official; 80%), Karen, Mon, Shan, Kachin

Religion: Buddhist (68%)

GOVERNMENT

Power is held by a 19-member State Law-and-Order Restoration Council. There is constitutional provision for a 489-member Assembly elected by universal adult suffrage, a Council of Ministers and a Council of State, whose Chairman is head of state.

GEOGRAPHY

The N and W of Burma are mountainous, rising to Hkakado Razi (5881 m / 19 296 ft). In the E, is the Shan Plateau along the Thai border. Central and S Burma consists of tropical lowlands.

Principal river: Irrawaddy 2090 km (1300 mi)

Climate: Burma is tropical, experiencing monsoon rains – up to 5000 mm (200 in) in the S – from May to October.

ECONOMY

Burma is rich in agriculture, timber, and minerals, but

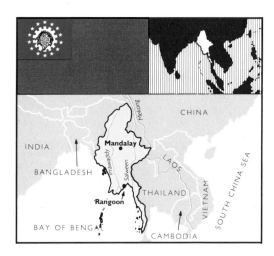

HISTORY

HISTORY
A German protectorate of South West Africa – excluding
Walvis Bay, which had been British since 1878 – was
declared in 1884. Seeking land for white settlement, the
Germans established their rule after great bloodshed –
over three quarters of the Herero people were killed in
1903–4. South Africa conquered the territory during
World War I, and (after 1919) administered it under a
League of Nations mandate. In 1966, the UN cancelled
the mandate, but South Africa – which had refused to
grant the territory independence – ignored the ruling.

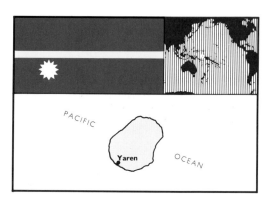

HISTORY
Germany annexed Nauru in 1888 after a request from
German settlers on Nauru for protection during unrest
between rival clans. Australia captured Nauru in 1914
and administered it – except for a period of Japanese
occupation (1942–45) – until independence in 1968.

NEPAL

Official name: Nepal Adhirajya (Kingdom of Nepal)

Member of: UN

Area: 147 181 km² (56 827 sq mi)

Population: 19 379 000 (1991 est)

Capital: Kathmandu 420 000 (city 235 000; 1987 est)

Languages: Nepali (official; 53%), Bihari (19%)

Religions: Hindu (official; 90%), Buddhist (5%)

GOVERNMENT
Nepal is a constitutional monarchy. The 205-member
House of Representatives (lower house) is elected for
five years by universal adult suffrage. The House elects
a Prime Minister and other Ministers. The National
Council (upper house) consists of 60 appointed and
indirectly elected members chosen for a six-year term.

GEOGRAPHY
In the S are densely populated subtropical lowlands. A
hilly central belt is divided by fertile valleys. The
Himalaya dominate the N, and include Mount Everest –
8863 m / 29 078 ft – on the Chinese border.

Climate: The climate varies between the subtropical S
and the glacial Himalayan peaks. All of Nepal experiences the monsoon.

---

because of poor communications, lack of development
and rebellions by a number of ethnic minorities, the
country has been unable to realize its potential. Subsistence farming involves about 80% of the labour force.

HISTORY
Burman supremacy over the Irrawaddy valley was first
claimed in 1044 by King Anawratha, who adopted
Buddhism from the rival Mon people. Chinese conquest
(1287) allowed a reassertion of Mon power until the 16th
century. After 1758 the Konbaung dynasty expanded
Burman territory until British counter-expansion led to
total annexation (1826–85). Separated from British India
in 1937, Burma became a battleground for British and
Japanese forces in World War II (see p. 445). In 1948,
Burma left the Commonwealth as an independent republic, keeping outside contacts to a minimum, particularly
following the coup of General Ne Win in 1962. Continuing armed attempts to gain autonomy by non-Burman
minorities have strengthened the role of the army,
which retained power following multi-party elections in
1990 and detained leaders of the winning party (including Aung San Suu Kyi, who was awarded the 1991 Nobel
Peace Prize). The government has come under strong
international pressure to introduce reforms but it has
continued to exert military pressure on minorities
including the Karen and Muslims.

NAMIBIA

Area: 823 168 km² (317 827 sq mi) – excluding the South
African enclave of Walvis Bay

Member of: UN, OAU, Commonwealth

Population: 1 334 000 (1991 est)

Capital: Windhoek 115 000 (1988 est)

Languages: Afrikaans and English (official)

Religions: Lutheran (30%), Roman Catholic (20%)

GOVERNMENT
A 72-member Assembly is elected by universal adult
suffrage. The President, who is elected by the Assembly,
appoints a Cabinet of Ministers.

GEOGRAPHY
The coastal Namib Desert stretches up to 160 km (100 mi)
inland and contains the highest point, the Brandberg, at
2579 m (8461 ft). Beyond the Central Plateau, the
Kalahari Desert occupies the eastern part of the
country.

Climate: Namibia has a hot dry tropical climate.
Average coastal rainfall is under 100 mm (4 in).

ECONOMY
Over 30% of the labour force is involved in farming,
mainly raising cattle and sheep, but Namibia is prone to
drought. The economy depends upon exports of diamonds and uranium, and is closely tied to South Africa.

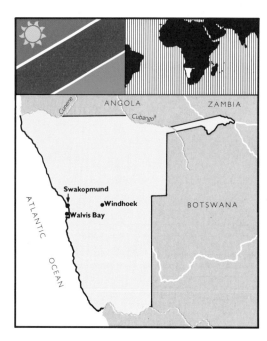

The main nationalist movement SWAPO began guerrilla warfare to free Namibia, the name adopted by the
UN for the state. South Africa unsuccessfully attempted
to exclude SWAPO's influence. After a cease-fire
agreement in 1989, UN-supervised elections were held in
November 1989 for a constituent assembly. Independence, under the presidency of SWAPO leader Sam
Nujoma, was achieved in 1990.

NAURU

Official name: The Republic of Nauru

Member of: Commonwealth (special member)

Area: 21 km² (8 sq mi)

Population: 9400 (1990 est)

Capital: No official capital; Yaren (no population
figure available) is capital *de facto*

Languages: Nauruan (official), English

Religions: Nauruan Protestant Church, Roman Catholic

GOVERNMENT
The 18-member Parliament – which is elected by universal adult suffrage for three years – elects a President,
who appoints a Cabinet of Ministers.

GEOGRAPHY
Nauru is a low-lying coral atoll.

Climate: Nauru has a tropical climate with heavy
rainfall, particularly between November and February.

ECONOMY
Nauru depends almost entirely upon the export of
phosphate rock, stocks of which are expected to run out
after 1995. Shipping and air services and 'tax haven'
facilities are planned to provide revenue when the
phosphate is exhausted.

ECONOMY
Nepal is one of the least developed countries in the
world. Most of the labour force is involved in subsistence farming, mainly growing rice, barley and maize.

Forestry is important, but increased farming has led to deforestation.

HISTORY

The Kathmandu Valley supported a Hindu-Buddhist culture by the 4th century AD. In 1768 the ruler of the principality of Gurkha in the W conquered the Valley, and began a phase of expansion that ended in defeat by the Chinese in Tibet (1792) and the British in India (1816). From 1846 to 1950 the Rana family held sway as hereditary chief ministers of a powerless monarchy. Their isolationist policy preserved Nepal's independence at the expense of its development. A brief experiment with democracy was followed by a re-assertion of royal autocracy (1960). Violent pro-democracy demonstrations (1990) forced the king to concede a democratic constitution. Multi-party elections were held in 1991.

THE NETHERLANDS

Official name: Koninkrijk der Nederlanden (The Kingdom of the Netherlands)

Member of: UN, EC, NATO, OECD, CSCE

Area: 41 785 km² (16 140 sq mi), or 33 937 km² (13 103 sq mi) excluding freshwater

Population: 15 065 000 (1991)

Capital and major cities: Amsterdam – capital in name only – 1 062 000 (city 702 000), The Hague ('s Gravenhage) – the seat of government and administration – 690 000 (city 444 000), Rotterdam 1 051 000 (city 582 000), Utrecht 535 000 (city 231 000), Eindhoven 386 000 (city 193 0000), Arnhem 303 000 (city 132 000), Heerlen-Kerkrade 268 000 (Heerlen city 94 000), Enschede 252 000 (city 146 000) (1991 est)

Language: Dutch (official)

Religions: Roman Catholic (under 30%), Netherlands Reformed Church (17%), Reformed Churches (Calvinistic) (8%)

Dependencies of the Netherlands (with areas, populations and capitals):
Aruba – 193 km² (75 sq mi), 66 000 (1991 est), Oranjestad.
Netherlands Antilles (The Antilles of the Five) – 800 km² (309 sq mi), 191 000 (1990 est), Willemstad

GOVERNMENT

The Netherlands is a constitutional monarchy. The 75-member First Chamber of the States-General is elected for six years term by the 12 provincial councils – with one half of the members retiring every three years. The 150-member Second Chamber is elected for four years by universal adult suffrage under a system of proportional representation. The monarch appoints a Prime Minister who commands a majority in the Second Chamber. The PM, in turn, appoints a Council of Ministers who are responsible to the Chamber.

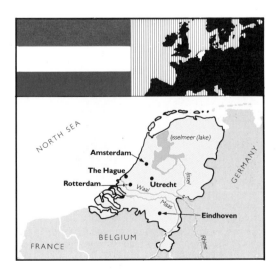

GEOGRAPHY

Over one quarter of the Netherlands – one of the world's most densely populated countries – lies below sea level. A network of canals and canalized rivers cross the W of the country where sand dunes and man-made dykes protect low-lying areas and polders (land reclaimed from the sea). The coast has been straightened by sea walls protecting Zeeland in the SW and enclosing a freshwater lake, the IJsselmeer, in the N. The E comprises low sandy plains, rising only to 321 m (1053 ft) at Vaalserberg, the highest point.

Principal rivers: Rhine (Rijn) – dividing into branches including Lek, Waal and Oude Rijn – 1320 km (820 mi)

Climate: The country has a maritime temperate climate, with cool summers and mild winters.

ECONOMY

Despite having few natural resources – except natural gas – the Netherlands has a high standard of living. Agriculture and horticulture are highly mechanized and concentrate on dairying and glasshouse crops, particularly flowers. Food processing is a major industry, and the country is a leading exporter of cheese. Manufacturing includes chemical, machinery, petroleum refining, metallurgical and electrical engineering industries. Raw materials are imported through Rotterdam – the largest port in the world – which serves much of Western Europe. Banking and finance are well developed.

HISTORY

In medieval times a patchwork of duchies, bishoprics and cities ruled the Netherlands. In the 15th century most of the area was governed by the dukes of Burgundy (see p. 401) and in the 16th century control of the Netherlands – the present kingdom, plus Belgium and Luxembourg – passed to the Spanish Habsburgs (see p. 411). The Spanish attempted to suppress Dutch Protestantism, and this provoked a revolt – initially led by Prince William ('The Silent') of Orange (1533–84) – that became a long struggle for independence. In 1579 – under the Union of Utrecht – the provinces of the Netherlands formed the United Provinces, which in 1581 broke away from Spanish rule, but did not gain international recognition as an independent state until 1648. Princes of the Orange family were stadholders ('governors') of the nation. In the 17th century, the Dutch began to acquire colonies, and became the greatest commercial power in Europe. This brought the Dutch into conflict with England (1652–74; see pp. 416–17), but when William of Orange became king of England in 1689, the fortunes of England and the Netherlands united in war against the expansionist policies of Louis XIV of France (see p. 414–15). Dutch power declined in the 18th century.

In 1795 the French invaded and ruled the country as the Batavian Republic (1795–1806) and the Kingdom of Holland (1806–10, under Louis Bonaparte). The Dutch lost important colonies to the British in the Napoleonic Wars, but kept an empire in Indonesia and the West Indies. The Congress of Vienna (1815) united all three Low Countries in the Kingdom of the Netherlands under the House of Orange, but Belgium broke away in 1830 and Luxembourg in 1890. The Dutch were neutral in World War I, but suffered occupation by the Germans from 1940–45. Following a bitter colonial war, the Dutch accepted that they could not reassert control over Indonesia after World War II. The Dutch have shown enthusiasm for European unity, and, with the other Low Countries, founded Benelux, the core of the EC. Dutch politics is characterized by a large number of small parties, some of a confessional nature, and a system of proportional representation has prevented any of these parties attaining a parliamentary majority. The formation of a new government after each general election has been difficult and time-consuming.

NEW ZEALAND

Official name: Dominion of New Zealand

Member of: UN, Commonwealth, ANZUS, OECD

Area: 269 057 km² (103 883 sq mi)

Population: 3 435 000 (1991 census)

Capital and major cities: Wellington 325 000 (city 150 000), Auckland 885 000 (city 316 000), Christchurch 307 000 (city 293 000), Manukau 227 000 and North Shore 151 000 are part of the Auckland agglomeration, Hamilton 149 000 (city 101 000), Napier with Hastings 110 000 (Napier city 52 000), Dunedin 109 000 (1991 census)

Languages: English (official), Maori

Religions: Anglican (24%), Presbyterian (18%), Roman Catholic (15%), Methodist (5%)

New Zealand Dependent Territories (with areas, populations and capitals):
Ross Dependency – 450 000 km² (175 000 sq mi), no permanent population.
Tokelau – 13 km² (5 sq mi), 1700 (1986 census), there is no capital as settlement is dispersed.

New Zealand Associated Territories (with areas, populations and capitals):
Cook Islands – 234 km² (90 sq mi), 19 000 (1991 est), Avarua.
Niue – 259 km² (100 sq mi), 2300 (1989 census), Alofi.

GOVERNMENT

The 97-member House of Representatives is elected by universal adult suffrage for three years to represent single-member constituencies, four of which have a Maori electorate. The Governor General – the representative of the British Queen as sovereign of New Zealand – appoints a Prime Minister who commands a majority in the House. The PM, in turn, appoints a Cabinet, which is responsible to the House.

GEOGRAPHY

On South Island, the Southern Alps rise at Mount Cook to 3754 m (12 315 ft). The mountains run from N to S through South Island, reaching the sea in the deeply indented coast of Fjordland. The Canterbury Plains lie to the E of the mountains. North Island is mainly hilly with isolated mountains, including volcanoes – two of which are active. Lowlands on North Island are largely restricted to coastal areas and the Waikato Valley.

Principal river: Waikato 435 km (270 mi)

Climate: The climate is temperate, although the N is warmer. Rainfall is abundant almost everywhere, but totals vary considerably with altitude and aspect, rising to over 6350 mm (250 in) on the W coast of South Island.

ECONOMY

The majority of New Zealand's export earnings come from agriculture, in particular meat, wool and dairy products. Forestry is expanding and supports an impor-

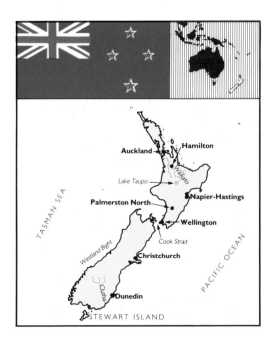

tant pulp and paper industry. Apart from coal, lignite, natural gas and gold, the country has few natural resources, although its considerable hydroelectric-power potential has been exploited to produce plentiful cheap electricity – an important basis of New Zealand's manufacturing industry. Natural gas – from North Island and off the Taranaki coast – is converted to liquid fuel. Despite its small domestic market and being remote from the world's major industrial powers, New Zealand has a high standard of living.

HISTORY

The Maoris migrated from Polynesia to New Zealand during the 8th century (see p. 389). Although the Dutch explorer Abel Tasman discovered the Westland coast in 1642, European settlement in New Zealand dates only from the late 18th century, partly because of the hostility shown by the Maoris towards the intruders. James Cook circumnavigated both main islands (1769–70), and his descriptions of the country encouraged colonization. By the beginning of the 19th century, a number of whaling stations had been established in New Zealand by Australian interests. As colonization increased, Britain determined to annex New Zealand. North Island was ceded to the British Crown by Maori chiefs under the Treaty of Waitangi (1840), while South Island was claimed by right of discovery. New Zealand was governed as a part of New South Wales until a separate colonial government was established in 1841.

The 1840s were marked by fierce armed resistance to British settlement by the Maoris, the majority of whom live in North Island. Relations between the Maoris and the white settlers deteriorated further during the 1850s as the colonists sought more land and Maori chiefs increasingly refused to sell it. When troops were used to evict Maoris from disputed lands in Waitara, war broke out (1860). Fighting continued for most of the decade in North Island, and guerrilla action in the King Country – the centre of North Island – was not suppressed until 1870. The Maori Wars retarded the European settlement of North Island, while – in the last quarter of the 19th century – the discovery of gold and the introduction of refrigerated ships to export meat and dairy products greatly stimulated the colonization and economy of South Island. However, by 1900, North Island was dominant again, and by 1911 migrants from Britain had boosted the country's population to one million. Subsequent immigration has remained overwhelmingly British, although there are sizeable communities of Samoans and Cook Islanders. Liberal governments (1891–1912) pioneered many reforms and social measures, including votes for women (1893) and the world's first old-age pensions (1898). Dominion status was granted in 1907, although New Zealand did not formally acknowledge its independent status until 1947.

In World War I, New Zealand fought as a British ally in Europe, achieving distinction in the disastrous Allied expedition to the Gallipoli peninsula during the campaign against Turkey (1915; see p. 387). When Japan entered World War II in 1941, New Zealand's more immediate security was threatened. The major role played by the USA in the Pacific War led to New Zealand's postwar alliance with Australia and America in the ANZUS pact, and the country sent troops to support the Americans in Vietnam. The entry of Britain into the EC in 1973 restricted the access of New Zealand's agricultural products to what had been their principal market. Since then New Zealand has been forced to seek new markets, particularly in the Far and Middle East. Under Labour governments (1972–75 and 1984–90), the country adopted an independent foreign and defence policy. A ban on vessels powered by nuclear energy or carrying nuclear weapons in New Zealand's waters placed a question mark over the country's role as a full ANZUS member.

NICARAGUA

Official name: República de Nicaragua (Republic of Nicaragua)

Member of: UN, OAS, CACM
Area: 120 254 km² (46 430 sq mi)
Population: 4 000 000 (1991 est)
Capital: Managua 979 000 (city 682 000; 1988 est)
Languages: Spanish (official), Miskito
Religion: Roman Catholic (90%)

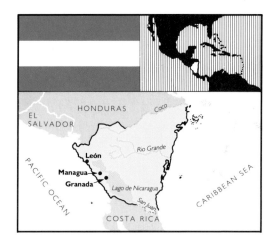

GOVERNMENT

The 92-member National Assembly is elected by proportional representation for six years by universal adult suffrage. The President – who appoints a Cabinet – is also directly elected for a six-year term.

GEOGRAPHY

Most Nicaraguans live on a fertile plain on the Pacific coast. Mountain ranges in the centre rise to Pico Mogotón at 2107 m (6913 ft). Tropical jungle covers the Atlantic coastal plain.

Climate: The climate is tropical and humid with a rainy season from May to October.

ECONOMY

The largely agricultural economy was damaged in the 1980s by guerrilla warfare, a US trade embargo and hurricanes. Privatization and strict austerity programmes have begun. Coffee, cotton and sugar cane are the main export crops.

HISTORY

In 1502 Columbus landed in Nicaragua, which remained a Spanish possession until independence was gained in 1821. Independent Nicaragua witnessed strife between conservatives and liberals. Early in the 20th century, the political situation deteriorated, provoking American intervention – US marines were based in Nicaragua from 1912 to 1925, and again from 1927 until 1933. General Anastasio Somoza became president in 1937. Employing dictatorial methods, members of the Somoza family, or their supporters, remained in power until overthrown by a popular uprising led by the Sandinista guerrilla army in 1979. Accusing the Sandinistas of introducing Communism, the USA imposed a trade embargo on Nicaragua, making it increasingly dependent on Cuba and the USSR. Right-wing Contra guerrillas, financed by the USA, fought the Sandinistas from bases in Honduras. A ceasefire between the Contras and Sandinistas was agreed in 1989. In free presidential elections in February 1990, the Sandinista incumbent Daniel Ortega was defeated by Violeta Chamorro.

NIGER

Official name La République du Niger (The Republic of Niger)
Member of: UN, OAU, ECOWAS
Area: 1 267 000 km² (489 191 sq mi)

Population: 8 024 000 (1991 est)
Capital: Niamey 398 000 (1988 census)
Languages: French (official), Hausa (85%)
Religion: Sunni Islam (85%)

GOVERNMENT

There is constitutional provision for a 93-member National Assembly to be elected by universal adult suffrage. The President – who appoints a Prime Minister – is elected for seven years.

GEOGRAPHY

Most of Niger lies in the Sahara Desert; the S and the Niger Valley are savannah. The central Aïr Mountains rise to just over 2000 m (6562 ft).

Principal river: Niger 4200 km (2600 mi)
Climate: Niger is dry and hot. The S has a rainy season from June to October.

ECONOMY

Livestock herds and harvests of subsistence crops – millet, sorghum, cassava and rice – have been reduced by desertification. Uranium is mined.

HISTORY

From the 15th century, the area was dominated in turn by the sultanate of Agadès, Hausa kingdoms and the Nigerian empire of Sokoto. The French territory of Niger was proclaimed in 1901, but much of the country was not pacified until 1920. Independence was gained in 1960. After the economy was wracked by a prolonged drought, the military took power in a coup (1974). Multi-party politics were restored in 1992 and free elections are scheduled for 1993.

NIGERIA

Official name: The Federal Republic of Nigeria
Member of: UN, OAU, OPEC, ECOWAS, Commonwealth

Area: 923 768 km² (356 669 sq mi)

Population: 88 514 000 (1991 census) – previous World Bank and UN estimates of Nigeria's population are 20 000 000 higher than this figure

Capital and major cities: Abuja (new federal capital) 379 000, Lagos 5 686 000 (city 1 340 000), Ibadan 1 263 000, Ogbomosho 644 000, Kano 595 000, Ilorin 420 000, Oshogbo 400 000 (1991 census)

Languages: English (official), with over 150 local languages including Hausa, Yoruba and Ibo

Religions: Sunni Islam (48%), various Protestant Churches (17%), Roman Catholic (17%)

GOVERNMENT
Since 1983 Nigeria has been ruled by the Armed Forces Ruling Council whose President is head of state and of government. Two political parties were legalized in 1989. Elections by universal adult suffrage are scheduled to be held for a 450-member Federal Assembly and a President to serve a six-year term. The 30 states each have their own state government.

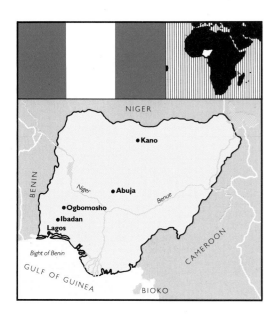

GEOGRAPHY
Inland from the swampy forest and tropical jungles of the coastal plains, Nigeria comprises a series of plateaux covered – for the most part – by open woodland or savannah. The far N is semi-desert. Isolated ranges of hills rise above the plateaux, the highest of which are the central Jos Plateau and the Biu Plateau in the NE. Vogel Peak (Dimlang) – near the Cameroon border – rises to 2042 m (6700 ft).

Principal rivers: Niger 4200 km (2600 mi), Benue 1083 km (673 mi)

Climate: The coastal areas are very humid and hot, with an average temperature of 32 °C (90 °F). Rainfall is heavy on the coast but decreases gradually inland – although there is a rainy season from April to October. The dry far N experiences the Harmattan, a hot wind blowing out of the Sahara.

ECONOMY
Nigeria is the major economic power in West Africa. The country depends upon revenue from petroleum exports, but a combination of falling petroleum prices and OPEC quotas has resulted in major economic problems, although it has encouraged diversification. Natural gas is to be exported in liquid form to Europe. Major industries include petrochemicals, textiles and food processing. Over 50% of the labour force is involved in agriculture, mainly producing maize, sorghum, cassava, yams and rice as subsistence crops. Cocoa is an important export.

HISTORY
The Kanem empire flourished in N Nigeria from the 11th to the 14th centuries, during which time Islam was introduced. Various Hausa kingdoms rose in the NW, which from the early 19th century contained the Fulani empire. Yoruba kingdoms and Benin occupied the SW, and Ibo kingdoms the SE. European intervention in the coastal region began with Portuguese explorers in the 15th century. From 1713 the slave trade in Nigeria came to be dominated by Britain. After British slave trading ended in 1807, British traders and explorers penetrated the interior. In 1861, Lagos was acquired, and in 1885 a British protectorate was established on the coast. In the scramble for empire, the commercial Royal Niger Company colonized the interior from 1886, and in 1900 its

territories were surrendered to the British Crown as the protectorate of Northern Nigeria. In 1914 the coast and the interior were united to form Britain's largest African colony. An unwieldy federal structure introduced in 1954 was unable to contain regional rivalries after independence (1960). In 1966, the first PM, Sir Abubakar Tafawa Balewa (1912–66), and other prominent politicians were assassinated in a military coup. After a counter-coup brought General Yakubu Gowon to power, a bitter civil war took place (1967–70) when the Eastern Region – the homeland of the Ibo – attempted to secede as Biafra. Although the East was quickly re-integrated once Biafra was defeated, Nigeria remained politically unstable. The number of states has been gradually increased from 3 to 30 in an attempt to prevent any one state becoming dominant. A military coup overthrew Gowon in 1975, and an attempt at civilian rule (1979–83) also ended in a coup. Another coup brought General Ibrahim Babangida to power in 1985. Free elections were held for the 30 state governments in 1992 and it is planned to reintroduce civilian rule at national level.

NORWAY

Official name: Kongeriket Norge (Kingdom of Norway)

Member of: UN, EFTA, NATO, CSCE, OECD

Area: 323 878 km² (125 050 sq mi), or 386 958 km² (149 469 sq mi) including the Arctic island territories of Svalbard (formerly known as Spitsbergen) and Jan Mayen

Population: 4 259 000 (1991 est)

Capital and major cities: Oslo 462 000, Bergen 213 000, Trondheim 138 000, Stavanger 98 000, Kristiansand 66 000, Drammen 52 000 (1991)

Languages: Two official forms of Norwegian – Bokmaal (80%), Nynorsk (or Landsmaal; 20%); Lappish

Religion: Lutheran (official; nearly 90%)

Norwegian Antarctic Territories (with areas):
Bouvet Island – 50 km² (19 sq mi), no permanent population.
Peter I Island – 180 km², no permanent population.
Queen Maud Land – as no inland limit has been made to the Norwegian claim, no estimate of the area of the territory can be made; no permanent population.

GOVERNMENT
Norway is a constitutional monarchy. The 165-member Parliament (Storting) is elected under a system of proportional representation by universal adult suffrage for a four-year term. In order to legislate, the Storting divides itself into two houses – the Lagting (containing one quarter of the members) and the Odelsting (containing the remaining three quarters of the members). The King appoints a Prime Minister who commands a majority in the Storting. The PM, in turn, appoints a Council of Ministers who are responsible to the Storting.

GEOGRAPHY
Norway's coastline is characterized by fjords, a series of long narrow inlets formed by glacial action. The greater part of Norway comprises highlands of hard rock. Galdhopiggen – the highest peak – reaches 2469 m (8098 ft). The principal lowlands are along the Skagerrak coast and around Oslofjord and Trondheimsfjord. Svalbard is a bleak archipelago in the Arctic.

Climate: Norway's temperate climate is the result of the warming Gulf Stream. Summers are remarkably mild for the latitude, while winters are long and very cold. Precipitation is heavy – over 2000 mm (80 in) in the W, with marked rain shadows inland.

ECONOMY
Norway enjoys a high standard of living. Agriculture is heavily subsidized and only a small proportion of the land can be cultivated – chiefly for fodder crops for dairy cattle. Timber is a major export for Norway, over 50% of which is forested. Fishing is an important foreign-currency earner, and fish farming – which has been encouraged by government development schemes – is

taking the place of whaling and deep-sea fishing. Manufacturing – which has traditionally been concerned with processing fish, timber and iron ore – is now dominated by petrochemicals and allied industries, based upon large reserves of petroleum and natural gas in Norway's sector of the North Sea. Petroleum and natural gas supply over one third of the country's export earnings. The development of industries such as electrical engineering has been helped by cheap hydroelectric power.

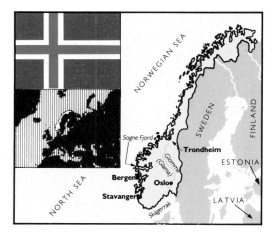

HISTORY
The period from the 9th to the 11th centuries was marked by the vigorous expansion of the Vikings from their Scandinavian homelands (see p. 397). Vikings from Norway plundered N Europe, settled in the British Isles, Iceland and Greenland and explored the Atlantic coast of North America. Norway itself was divided into a number of warring small kingdoms and was not united until 1015–30 under Olaf II Haraldsson, who converted many Norwegians to Christianity and later became the country's patron saint. However, the instability and civil wars that had preceded his rule returned in the 12th century, and unity under a strong monarch was not experienced again until the reign of Haakon IV (reigned 1217–63). The marriage of Haakon VI (reigned 1355–1380) to the future Queen Margrethe I of Denmark united the destinies of Norway and Denmark. Danish kings – who ruled Norway as a part of their own realm until 1814 – ensured the early adoption of the Lutheran religion by Norwegians. At the end of the Napoleonic Wars, Norway attempted to regain autonomy, but the country came under the rule of the kings of Sweden, although a separate Norwegian Parliament was allowed a considerable degree of independence.

Growing nationalism in Norway placed great strains upon the union with Sweden, and in 1905 – following a vote by the Norwegians to repeal the union – King Oscar II of Sweden gave up his claims to the Norwegian crown to allow a peaceful separation of the two countries. After a Swedish prince declined the Norwegian throne, Prince Carl of Denmark was confirmed as King of Norway – as Haakon VII – by a plebiscite. Norway was neutral in World War I, and declared neutrality in World War II, but was occupied by German forces (1940) who set up a puppet government under Vidkun Quisling. After the war, Norway joined NATO and agreed in 1972 to enter the EC, but a national referendum rejected membership. In 1992, a Norwegian reapplication for EC membership became a serious option.

OMAN

Official name: Sultanat 'Uman (Sultanate of Oman)

Member of: UN, Arab League, GCC

Area: 300 000 km² (120 000 sq mi)

Population: 1 502 000 (1990 est)

Capital: Muscat 380 000 (city 85 000; 1990 est)

Languages: Arabic (official), Baluchi

Religions: Ibadi Islam (75%), Sunni Islam (25%)

GOVERNMENT

Oman is an absolute monarchy. The Sultan rules by decree and appoints a Cabinet and a 52-member Consultative Council. There are no political parties.

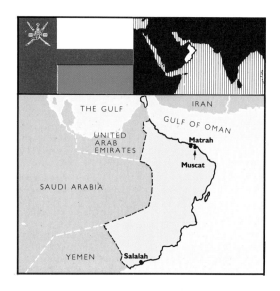

GEOGRAPHY

A barren range of hills rises sharply behind a narrow coastal plain and reaches 3170 m (10 400 ft) at Jabal ash Sham. Desert extends inland into the Rub' al Khali ('The Empty Quarter'). A small detached portion of Oman lies N of the United Arab Emirates.

Climate: Oman is very hot in the summer, but milder in winter and the mountains. The country is extremely arid with an average annual rainfall of 50 to 100 mm (2–4 in).

ECONOMY

Oman depends almost entirely upon exports of petroleum and natural gas. Owing to aridity, less than 1% of Oman is cultivated.

HISTORY

Persia ruled Oman from the 4th century AD until Muslim armies invaded bringing Islam in the 7th century. The area's flourishing trade with the E attracted the Portuguese (1507), who founded Muscat and occupied the coast until 1650. Ahmad ibn Sa'id, who became Imam in 1749, founded the present dynasty. His successors built an empire including the Kenyan coast and Zanzibar, but in 1861 Zanzibar and Oman separated. A British presence was established in the 19th century and Oman did not regain complete independence until 1951. Sultan Qaboos – who came to power in a palace coup in 1970 – has modernized and developed Oman. In the 1970s South Yemen supported left-wing separatist guerrillas in the southern province of Dhofar, but the revolt was suppressed with military assistance from the UK.

PAKISTAN

Official name: Islami Jamhuria-e-Pakistan (Islamic Republic of Pakistan)

Member of: UN, Commonwealth

Area: 803 943 km² (310 403 sq mi), or 888 102 km² (333 897 sq mi), including the Pakistani-held areas of Kashmir (known as Azad Kashmir) and the disputed Northern Areas (Gilgit, Baltistan and Diamir)

Population: 126 406 000 (1990 est; including the Pakistani-held areas of Kashmir – Azad Kashmir – and the disputed Northern Areas)

Capital and major cities: Islamabad 266 000, Karachi 6 771 000, Lahore 3 850 000, Faisalabad 1 435 000, Rawal-

pindi 1 100 000, Hyderabad 1 041 000, Multan 999 000, Gujranwala 912 000 (all including suburbs; 1991 est)

Languages: Urdu (national; 20%), Punjabi (60%), Sindhi (12%), English, Pushto, Baluchi

Religions: Sunni Islam (official; 92%), Shia Islam (5%), Ismaili Muslim and Ahmadi minorities.

GOVERNMENT

The 87-member Senate (the upper house) comprises 19 senators elected for six years by each of the four provinces, plus 8 senators elected from the federally administered Tribal Areas and 3 senators chosen to represent the federal capital. The 237-member National Assembly comprises 207 members elected by universal adult suffrage for five years, 20 seats reserved for women and 10 members representing non-Islamic minorities. The President – who is chosen by the Federal Legislature – appoints a Prime Minister who commands a majority in the National Assembly. The PM, in turn, appoints a Cabinet of Ministers, responsible to the Assembly. The four provinces, Azad Kashmir and the Northern Areas have their own legislatures.

GEOGRAPHY

The Indus Valley divides Pakistan into a highland region in the W and a lowland region in the E. In Baluchistan – in the S – the highlands consist of ridges of hills and low mountains running NE to SW. In the N – in the North-West Frontier Province and the disputed territories – the mountain chains rise to over 7000 m (21 300 ft) and include the Karakoram, parts of the Himalaya and the Hindu Kush. The highest point is K2 (Mount Godwin Austen), at 8607 m (28 238 ft) the second highest peak in the world. The Indus Valley – and the valleys of its tributaries – form a major agricultural region and contain the majority of Pakistan's population. A continuation of the Indian Thar Desert occupies the E.

Principal rivers: Indus 2880 km (1790 mi), Sutlej 1450 km (900 mi)

Climate: The N and W of Pakistan are arid; the S and much of the E experience a form of the tropical monsoon. Temperatures vary dramatically by season and with altitude, from the hot tropical coast to the cold mountains of the far N.

ECONOMY

More than one half of the labour force is involved in subsistence farming, with wheat and rice as the main crops. Cotton is the main foreign-currency earner. The government is encouraging irrigation schemes, but over one half of the cultivated land is subject to either waterlogging or salinity. Although there is a wide range of mineral reserves – including coal, gold and copper – these resources have not been extensively developed.

Manufacturing is dominated by food processing, textiles and consumer goods. Unemployment and underemployment are major problems, and the country relies heavily upon foreign aid and money sent back by Pakistanis working abroad.

HISTORY

The Indus Valley was the seat of the ancient Harappan civilization (2300–1700 BC; see p. 384), but by 1500 BC the Ganges Basin had become the driving force in the subcontinent. The area was ruled by a succession of kingdoms and empires before the colonial age (see p. 385), and from the 8th century Pakistan was converted to Islam. From the 18th century the region came under British rule.

Pakistan as a nation was born in August 1947 when British India was partitioned as a result of demands by the Muslim League for an Islamic state in which Hindus would not be in a majority. Large numbers of Muslims moved to the new state and up to 1 000 000 people died in the bloodshed that accompanied partition. Pakistan had two 'wings' – West Pakistan (the present country) and East Pakistan (now Bangladesh) – separated by 1600 km (1000 mi) of Indian territory. A number of areas were disputed with India. Kashmir – the principal bone of contention – was effectively partitioned between the two nations, and in 1947–49 and 1965 tension over Kashmir led to war between India and Pakistan. The problem of Kashmir is unsolved with fighting continuing intermittently along parts of the cease-fire line. The Muslim League leader Muhammad Ali Jinnah (1876–1949) was the first Governor General, but Jinnah, who was regarded as 'father of the nation', died soon after independence. Pakistan – which became a republic in 1956 – suffered political instability and periods of military rule, including the administrations of General Muhammad Ayub Khan (from 1958 to 1969) and General Muhammad Yahya Khan (from 1969 to 1971). Although East Pakistan contained the majority of the population, from the beginning West Pakistan held political and military dominance. In elections in 1970, Shaikh Mujibur Rahman's Awami League won an overwhelming majority in East Pakistan, while the Pakistan People's Party (PPP) won most of the seats in West Pakistan. Mujibur Rahman seemed less interested in leading a new Pakistani government than in winning autonomy for the East. In March 1971, after abortive negotiations, the Pakistani army was sent from the West to East Pakistan, which promptly declared its independence as Bangladesh. Civil war broke out and India supported the new state, forcing the Pakistani army to surrender by the end of the year.

The leader of the PPP, Zulfiqar Ali Bhutto (PM 1972–77), was deposed in a military coup led by the Army Chief of Staff, Muhammad Zia al-Haq. Bhutto was imprisoned (1977) for allegedly ordering the murder of the father of a former political opponent, sentenced to death (1978) and, despite international protests, hanged (1979). In 1985 Zia lifted martial law and began to return Pakistan to civilian life. Zia was killed in a plane crash (1988). Following elections in 1988, Bhutto's daughter and the PPP's new leader, Benazir, became the first woman Prime Minister of an Islamic state. She was dismissed by the President in 1990, and subsequent elections were won by the Islamic Democratic Alliance.

PANAMA

Official name: La República de Panamá (The Republic of Panama)

Member of: UN, OAS

Area: 77 082 km² (29 762 sq mi)

Population: 2 329 000 (1990 census)

Capital and major cities: Panama City 828 000 (city 585 000), San Miguelito (part of the Panama City agglomeration) 243 000, Colón 141 000 (1990 census).

Language: Spanish (official)

Religion: Roman Catholic (85%)

GOVERNMENT

A 67-member Legislative Assembly and a President – who appoints a Cabinet of Ministers – are elected by universal adult suffrage for four years.

GEOGRAPHY

Panama is a heavily forested mountainous isthmus joining Central America to South America. The highest point is the extinct volcano Baru at 3475 m (11 467 ft).

Climate: Panama has a tropical climate with little seasonal change in temperature.

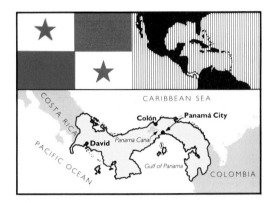

ECONOMY

Income from the Panama Canal is a major foreign-currency earner. Panama – which has a higher standard of living than its neighbours – has become an important 'offshore' banking centre. Major exports include bananas and shrimps.

HISTORY

Panama was discovered in 1501, and became part of Spanish New Granada (Colombia). In the 1880s a French attempt to construct a canal through Panama linking the Atlantic and Pacific Oceans proved unsuccessful. After Colombia rejected US proposals for completing the canal, Panama became independent (1903), sponsored by the USA. The canal eventually opened in 1914. From 1903 to 1979 the USA controlled land extending 8 km (5 mi) on either side of the canal – the Canal Zone. Panama will gain complete control of the canal itself in 2000. From 1983 to 1989 effective power was in the hands of General Manuel Noriega, who was deposed by a US invasion and taken to stand trial in the USA, where he was found guilty of criminal activities.

PAPUA NEW GUINEA

Official name: The Independent State of Papua New Guinea

Member of: UN, Commonwealth

Area: 462 840 km² (178 704 sq mi)

Population: 3 790 000 (1990 census)

Capital and major cities: Port Moresby 193 000 (city 174 000), Lae 81 000 (1990 census)

Languages: English (official), Pidgin English, Motu and over 700 local languages

Religions: Roman Catholic (33%), various Protestant Churches (nearly 60%)

GOVERNMENT

A 109-member Parliament is elected for five years by universal adult suffrage. The Governor General – the representative of the British Queen as sovereign of Papua New Guinea – appoints a Prime Minister who commands a majority in Parliament. The PM, in turn, appoints a Cabinet, which is responsible to Parliament.

GEOGRAPHY

Broad swampy plains surround New Guinea's mountainous interior, which rises to Mount Wilhelm at 4509 m (14 493 ft).

Climate: The country experiences a tropical climate with high temperatures and heavy monsoonal rainfall.

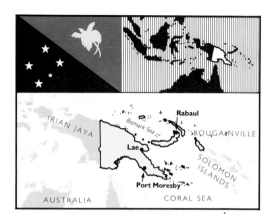

ECONOMIC ACTIVITY

Over 80% of the labour force is involved in agriculture – mainly subsistence farming – although agricultural exports include coffee, cocoa and coconuts. The mainstay of the economy is minerals, including large reserves of copper, gold and petroleum.

HISTORY

The first inhabitants of New Guinea came from Indonesia around 50 000 BC (see pp. 388–9). European colonization began in 1828 when the Dutch claimed W New Guinea. A British protectorate, established in the SE in 1884, was transferred to Australia (1906) and renamed Papua. NE New Guinea came under German administration in 1884, but was occupied by Australian forces in 1914. From 1942 to 1945 Japanese forces occupied New Guinea and part of Papua. In 1949 Australia combined the administration of the territories, which achieved independence as Papua New Guinea in 1975. Bougainville island, a major source of copper, attempted to secede (1990–92). Fighting on the island decreased in 1992 and peace talks began.

PARAGUAY

Official name: La República del Paraguay (The Republic of Paraguay)

Member of: UN, OAS, Mercosur, ALADI

Area: 406 752 km² (157 048 sq mi)

Population: 4 397 000 (1991 est)

Capital and major cities: Asunción 732 000 (city 608 000), San Lorenzo (part of the Asunción agglomeration) 124 000, Ciudad del Este 111 000 (1990 est)

Languages: Spanish (official), Guaraní (88%)

Religion: Roman Catholic (official; 97%)

GOVERNMENT

A 198-member Constituent Assembly was elected by universal adult suffrage in 1992 to draft a new constitution. The President currently serving was directly elected for five years.

GEOGRAPHY

The country W of the Paraguay River – the Chaco – is a flat semiarid plain. The region E of the river is a partly forested undulating plateau.

Principal rivers: Paraguay 2550 km (1584 mi), Paraná 4880 km (3032 mi)

Climate: The climate is subtropical with considerable variation in rainfall between the wet SE and the dry W.

ECONOMY

Agriculture – the main economic activity – is dominated by cattle ranching, cotton and soyabeans. Cheap hydro-electric power has greatly stimulated industry.

HISTORY

The Spanish reached the area in the 1520s. Jesuit missionaries to the Guaraní Indians dominated the country from 1609 until 1767, when they were expelled. Since independence in 1811, Paraguay has suffered many dictators, including General José Francia, who totally isolated Paraguay (1814–40). War against Argentina, Brazil and Uruguay (1865–70) cost Paraguay over one half of its people and much territory. Wars with Bolivia (1929-35) further weakened Paraguay. General Alfredo Stroessner gained power in 1954, ruling with increasing disregard for human rights until his overthrow in a military coup in 1989. Free elections for a constituent assembly were held in 1992.

PERU

Official name: República del Perú (Republic of Peru)

Member of: UN, OAS, Andean Pact, ALADI

Area: 1 285 216 km² (496 225 sq mi)

Population: 22 881 000 (1991 est)

Capital and major cities: Lima 6 405 000 (city 5 494 000), Arequipa 612 000, Callao (part of the Lima agglomeration) 515 000 (1990 est)

Languages: Spanish (68%), Quechua (27%), Aymara (3%) – all official

Religion: Roman Catholic (official; 91%)

GOVERNMENT

The President and the National Congress – comprising a 60-member Senate and a 180-member Chamber of Deputies – are elected by universal adult suffrage for five years. Former presidents serve as additional life members of the Senate. The President appoints a Council of Ministers headed by a Prime Minister.

GEOGRAPHY

The coastal plain is narrow and arid. The Andes – which are prone to earthquakes – run in three high parallel ridges from N to S, rising at Huascaran to 6768 m (22 205 ft). Nearly two thirds of Peru is tropical forest (the Selva) in the Amazon Basin.

Principal rivers: Amazon-Ucayali 6448 km (4007 mi)

Climate: A wide climatic variety includes semitropical desert – cooled by the Humboldt Current – on the coast, the very cold Alpine High Andes and the tropical Selva with a heavy rainfall.

ECONOMY

About one third of the labour force is involved in agriculture. Subsistence farming dominates in the interior; crops for export are more important near the coast. Major crops include coffee, sugarcane, cotton and potatoes, as well as coca for cocaine. Sheep, llamas, vicuñas and alpacas are kept for wool. Rich natural resources include silver, copper, coal, gold, iron ore, petroleum and phosphates. The fishing industry – once the world's largest – has declined since 1971. A combination of natural disasters, a very high birth rate, guerrilla warfare and the declining value of exports has severely damaged the economy.

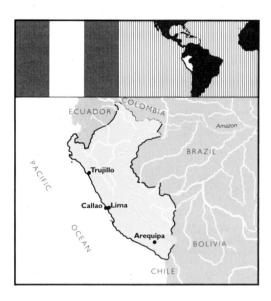

HISTORY
When the Spanish arrived in Peru in 1531 the Inca Empire was at its peak (see p. 390). Inca resistance was quickly subdued by Pizarro and Peru became one of Spain's most valuable possessions. Much of South America was governed from Lima as the Spanish Viceroyalty of Peru. Independence was proclaimed in 1821 after the Argentine San Martín took Lima, but Spanish forces did not leave until 1824. Independent Peru saw political domination by large landowners. Progress was made under General Ramon Castilla (1844–62) and civilian constitutional governments at the beginning of the 20th century, but instability and military coups have been common. War (1879–83) in alliance with Bolivia against Chile resulted in the loss of nitrate deposits in the S, while victory against Ecuador (1941) added Amazonian territory. From 1968 a reformist military government instituted land reform, attempting to benefit workers and the Indians, but faced with mounting economic problems the military swung to the right in 1975. In 1980 elections were held, but owing to the economic crisis and the growth of an extreme left-wing guerrilla movement – the Sendero Luminoso ('Shining Path') – Peru's democracy remained under threat. In 1992, the president effected a coup, suspending the constitution and detaining opposition leaders. Subsequent elections were boycotted by the principal opposition parties.

THE PHILIPPINES

Official name: Repúblika ñg Pilipinas (Republic of the Philippines)

Member of: UN, ASEAN

Area: 300 001 km² (115 831 sq mi)

Population: 62 354 000 (1991 est)

Capital and major cities: Manila 7 832 000 (city 1 599 000), Quezon City (part of the Manila agglomeration) 1 667 000, Davao City 850 000, Caloocan City (part of the Manila agglomeration) 761 000 (1990 census)

Languages: Pilipino (based on Tagalog; national; 55%), Tagalog (over 20%), Cebuano (24%), Ilocano (11%), English, Spanish and many local languages

Religions: Roman Catholic (84%), Aglipayan Church (4%), Sunni Islam (5%)

GOVERNMENT
The President and the 24-member Senate – the upper House of Congress – are elected by universal adult

suffrage for six years. The House of Representatives comprises 200 directly elected members and no more than 50 members appointed by the President from minority groups. The President appoints a Cabinet.

GEOGRAPHY
Some 2770 of the Philippines' 7000 islands are named. The two largest islands, Luzon and Mindanao, make up over two thirds of the country's area. Most of the archipelago is mountainous with restricted coastal plains, although Luzon has a large, densely populated central plain. Mount Apo, on Mindanao, is the highest point at 2954 m (9692 ft).

Climate: The climate is tropical maritime with high humidity, high temperatures and heavy rainfall. Typhoons are frequent.

ECONOMY
Almost one half of the labour force is involved in agriculture. Rice and maize are the principal subsistence crops, while coconuts, sugar cane, pineapples and bananas are grown for export. Deforestation is a problem as land is cleared for cultivation. Major industries include textiles, food processing, chemicals and electrical engineering. Mineral resources include copper (a major export), gold, petroleum and nickel. Money sent back by Filipinos working abroad is an important source of foreign currency.

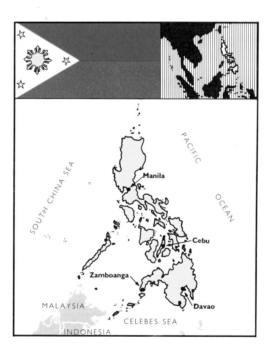

HISTORY
Magellan discovered the islands in 1521, naming them after Philip II of Spain. Spanish rule spread through the archipelago from the middle of the 16th century, but was harassed by the Dutch and by Moro pirates from Mindanao. The Spanish colonial regime was harsh, and although trade grew, economic growth was not matched by political development. The islands' administration was archaic and Jesuit influence was strong. Eventually a combination of rising nationalism and resentment at economic injustice led to an unsuccessful revolt (1896) against Spanish rule. The islands were ceded to the USA after the Spanish-American War (1898), but American rule had to be imposed by force and resistance continued until 1906. A powerful American presence had a profound effect on Filipino society, which bears the triple imprint of Asian culture, Spanish Catholicism and American capitalism. US policy in the Philippines wavered between accelerating and delaying Filipino self-rule. In 1935 the nationalist leader Manuel Quezon became president of the semi-independent 'Commonwealth' of the Philippines. The surprise Japanese inva-

sion of 1941 traumatized the islands' American and Filipino defenders. Japan set up a puppet 'Philippine Republic', but, after the American recapture of the archipelago, a fully independent Republic of the Philippines was established in 1946.

Between 1953 and 1957 President Ramon Magsaysay crushed and conciliated Communist-dominated Hukbalahap guerrillas, but his death ended a programme of land reforms. Coming to power in 1965, Ferdinand Marcos (1917–89) inaugurated flamboyant development projects, but his administration presided large-scale corruption. Marcos used the continuing guerrilla activity as a justification for his increasingly repressive rule. When he attempted to rig the result of presidential elections in 1986, Marcos was overthrown in a popular revolution in favour of Corazon Aquino. President Aquino is the widow of a leading opposition politician who had allegedly been murdered on Marcos' orders. Her government faced several attempted coups. Insurgency by groups including Communists and Islamic nationalists remains a problem.

POLAND

Official name: Polska Rzecpospolita (Republic of Poland)

Member of: UN, CSCE

Area: 312 683 km² (120 727 sq mi)

Population: 38 273 000 (1991 est)

Capital and major cities: Warsaw (Warszawa) 1 656 000, Lódź 848 000, Kraków 751 000, Wroclaw 643 000, Poznań 590 000, Gdańsk 465 000 (1990 est)

Language: Polish

Religion: Roman Catholic (93%)

GOVERNMENT
The 100-member Senate and the 460-member Sejm are elected for four years by universal adult suffrage. The President – who is also directly elected – appoints a Prime Minister who commands a majority in the Sejm. The PM, in turn, appoints a Council of Ministers.

GEOGRAPHY
Most of Poland consists of lowlands. In the N are the the Baltic lowlands and the Pomeranian and Mazurian lake districts. Central Poland is a region of plains. In the S are the hills of Little Poland and the Tatra Mountains, whose highest peak is Rysys at 2499 m (8199 ft).

Principal river: Vistula (Wisla) 1090 km (677 mi)

Climate: Poland's climate tends towards continental with short warm summers and longer cold winters.

ECONOMY
Polish agriculture remains predominantly small-scale and privately owned. Over 25% of the labour force is still involved in agriculture, growing potatoes, wheat, barley, sugar beet and fodder crops. The industrial sector is large-scale and, until the switch to a market economy began in 1990, centrally planned. Poland has major deposits of coal, as well as reserves of natural gas, copper and silver. Engineering, food processing, and the chemical, metallurgical and paper industries are important, but the economic situation has steadily deteriorated since the 1960s. To add to inflation and a rampant black market, Poland has crippling foreign debts. Privatization has been accelerated since 1991 but living standards have decreased.

HISTORY
Small Polish states united to form a single nation in the 11th century. Kings Wladyslaw I and Casimir III (the Great) strengthened Poland, encouraged trade, codified laws and founded the country's first university at Kraków. In 1386 Queen Jadwiga married Jagiello, the grand duke of Lithuania, uniting the two realms. The union of Lublin (1569) established full political ties between the two countries, and at its height the 'Commonwealth of Two Nations' extended from the Baltic to the Black Sea. In 1572 the last of the Jagiellons died, leaving no heir. The monarchy became elective,

and the power of both the sovereign and the Sejm declined. The country became involved in numerous wars – against Muscovites, Turks, Tartars, Cossacks and Swedes. Poland was too weak to prevent a partition of its territory in 1772 by Russia, Prussia and Austria. Two further partitions took place in 1793 and in 1795, when Poland disappeared from the map of Europe.

In the 19th century the greater part of Poland was within Imperial Russia, against which the Poles revolted unsuccessfully in 1830, 1848 and 1863. National feeling also grew in the areas ruled by Austria and Prussia. After World War I, Poland was restored to statehood (1919), but the country was unstable. Marshal Józef Piłsudski (1867–1935) staged a coup in 1926, and became a virtual dictator. During the 1930s relations with Hitler's Germany became strained (see p. 443). An alliance with Britain was not enough to deter Hitler from attacking Poland, and thus precipitating World War II (1939). Poland was partitioned once again, this time between Nazi Germany and the USSR. Occupied Poland lost one sixth of its population, including almost all the Jews, and casualties were high after the ill-fated Warsaw Rising (1944). Poland was liberated by the Red Army (1945), and a Communist state was established. The new Poland lost almost one half its territory in the E to the USSR, but was compensated in the N and W at the expense of Germany.

A political crisis in 1956 led to the emergence of a Communist leader who enjoyed a measure of popular support, Władysław Gomułka. In 1980, following the downfall of Gomułka's successor, Edward Gierek, a period of unrest led to the birth of the independent trade union Solidarity (Solidarność), led by Lech Wałęsa (1943–). Martial law was declared by General Wojciech Jaruzelski in 1981 in an attempt to restore Communist authority. Solidarity was banned and its leaders were detained, but public unrest and economic difficulties continued. In 1989 Solidarity was legalized and agreement was reached on political reform. Solidarity won free elections to the new Senate, and with the support of former allies of the Communists won enough seats to gain a majority in the Sejm, and to form a government. Solidarity leader Lech Wałęsa became President in 1990. Since multi-party elections for the Sejm were held in 1991, several short-lived coalition governments have held office.

PORTUGAL

Official name: A República Portuguesa (The Portuguese Republic)

Member of: UN, EC, NATO, CSCE, OECD

Area: 92 072 km² (33 549 sq mi) including Madeira and the Azores

Population: 10 421 000 (1991 est)

Capital and major cities: Lisbon (Lisboa) 2 131 000 (city 950 000), Oporto (Porto) 1 695 000 (city 450 000), Amadora (part of the Lisbon agglomeration) 100 000, Setúbal 80 000, Coímbra 75 000, Braga 67 000 (1990 est)

Language: Portuguese (official)

Religion: Roman Catholic (nearly 90%)

Portuguese overseas territory (with area, population and capital):
Macau – 17 km² (6.5 sq mi), 402 000 (1991 census), Macau.

GOVERNMENT
An executive President is elected for a five-year term by universal adult suffrage. The 250-member Assembly is directly elected for four years. The President appoints a Prime Minister who commands a majority in the Assembly. The PM, in turn, appoints a Council of Ministers (Cabinet), responsible to the Assembly. Madeira and the Azores have autonomous governments.

GEOGRAPHY
Behind a coastal plain, Portugal N of the River Tagus is a highland region at the centre of which is the mainland's principal mountain range, the Serra da Estrela, rising to 1993 m (6539 ft). A wide plateau in the NE is a continuation of the Spanish Meseta. Portugal S of the Tagus is mainly an undulating lowland. The Atlantic islands of Madeira and the Azores are respectively nearly 1000 km (620 mi) and 1200 km (745 mi) SW of the mainland. At 2315 m (7713 ft), Pico in the Azores is Portugal's highest peak.

Principal river: Tagus (Rio Tejo) 1007 km (626 mi).

Climate: Portugal has a mild and temperate climate which is wetter and more Atlantic in the N, and drier, hotter and more Mediterranean inland and in the S.

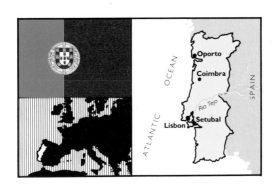

ECONOMY
Agriculture involves one fifth of the labour force, but lacks investment following land reforms in the 1970s, since when production has fallen. Major crops include wheat and maize, grapes (for wines such as port and Madeira), tomatoes, potatoes and cork trees. Portugal lacks natural resources. Manufacturing industry includes textiles and clothing (major exports), footwear, food processing, cork products, and, increasingly, electrical appliances and petrochemicals. Tourism and money sent back by Portuguese working abroad are major foreign-currency earners. Despite impressive recent economic development Portugal remains W Europe's poorest country.

HISTORY
The N of Portugal resisted the Muslim conquests in the Iberian peninsula in the 8th century. Reconquest of Portuguese territory from the Muslims was slow, but Portugal – a kingdom from 1139 – established its present boundaries in 1270. In the 15th century Portugal became a dynamic trading nation. Prince Henry the Navigator (1394–1460) became a leading patron of Portuguese exploration, which in the 15th century had mapped much of the West African coast (see p. 405). By the middle of the 16th century Portugal had laid the founda-

tions of a vast colonial empire in Brazil, Africa and Asia (see pp. 410–11).

On the extinction of the Aviz dynasty in 1580, the thrones of Spain and Portugal were united, until a revolution in 1640 led to the accession of the Portuguese Braganza family. In the 17th and 18th centuries Portuguese power declined, but the country retained major colonies. In 1807 the royal family fled to Brazil to escape a Napoleonic invasion. King John VI did not return from Brazil until 1821, and in his absence the Portuguese had established a liberal constitution. Dynastic problems began when John VI's son Pedro declared Brazil independent (1822), and they continued in a crippling civil war (1832–34) between liberal constitutionalists supporting Queen Maria II (Pedro's daughter) and absolutists under the rival King Miguel (Pedro's brother). Instability continued for much of the 19th century. Portugal's African empire was confirmed, although the country lacked the power to gain more territory in the scramble for Africa.

The monarchy was overthrown in 1910, but the Portuguese republic proved unstable and the military took power in 1926. From 1932 to 1968, under the dictatorship of Premier Antonio Salazar (1889–1970), stability was achieved but at great cost. Portugal became a one-party state, and expensive colonial wars dragged on as Portugal attempted to check independence movements in Angola and Mozambique. In 1974 there was a left-wing military coup whose leaders granted independence to the African colonies (1974–75), and initially attempted to impose Marxism on the country. However, elections in 1976 decisively rejected the far left. Civilian rule was restored as Portugal effected a transition from dictatorship to democracy, and simultaneously – through the loss of empire and membership of the EC – became more closely integrated with the rest of Europe.

QATAR

Official name: Dawlat Qatar (State of Qatar)

Member of: UN, Arab League, OPEC, GCC

Area: 11 437 km² (4416 sq mi)

Population: 458 000 (1991 est)

Capital: Doha 272 000 (city 217 000; 1986 est)

Language: Arabic

Religion: Wahhabi Sunni Islam (official; 98%)

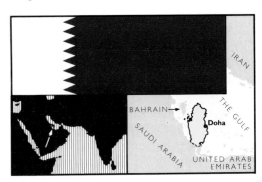

GOVERNMENT
Qatar is an absolute monarchy. The Amir – who is head of state and of government – appoints a Council of Ministers and a 30-member Advisory Council. There are no political parties.

GEOGRAPHY
Qatar is a low barren peninsula projecting into the Gulf.

Climate: Qatar is very hot in summer, but milder in winter. Rainfall averages 50 to 75 mm (2 to 3 in).

ECONOMY
The export of petroleum and natural gas give Qatar a high standard of living. The steel and cement industries have been developed in an attempt to diversify.

HISTORY

By the 8th century AD Qatar was Islamic and had developed as a trading centre. In the 1860s Britain intervened in a dispute between Qatar and its Bahraini rulers, installing a member of the Qatari ath-Thani family as sheik. Qatar was part of the Ottoman Empire from 1872 until 1914. Its ruler signed protection treaties with Britain in 1916 and 1934, and did not regain complete independence until 1971.

ROMANIA

Official name: Rômania

Member of: UN, CSCE

Area: 237 500 km² (91 699 sq mi)

Population: 22 749 000 (1992 census)

Capital and major cities: Bucharest (Bucuresti) 2 325 000, Brasov 352 000, Iasi 334 000, Timisoara 325 000, Cluj-Napoca 319 000, Constanta 313 000 (1990 est)

Languages: Romanian (official; 89%), Hungarian (10%), German

Religions: Orthodox (70%), Roman Catholic

GOVERNMENT

The President is elected by universal adult suffrage for five years. The 396-member National Assembly and 119-member Senate are directly elected under a modified system of proportional representation for 30 months. The President appoints a Prime Minister who, in turn, appoints a Council of Ministers.

GEOGRAPHY

The Carpathian Mountains run through the N, E and centre of Romania. The highest point is Moldoveanu at 2544 m (8346 ft). To the W of the Carpathians is the tableland of Transylvania and the Banat lowland. In the S the Danube Plain ends in a delta on the Black Sea.

Principal river: Danube (Dunăria) 2850 km (1770 mi)

Climate: Romania experiences cold snowy winters and hot summers. Rainfall is moderate in the lowlands but heavier in the Carpathians.

ECONOMY

State-owned industry – which employs nearly 40% of the labour force – includes mining, metallurgy, mechanical engineering and chemicals. Natural resources include petroleum and natural gas. Large forests support a timber and furniture industry. Major crops include maize, sugar beet, wheat, potatoes and grapes for wine, but agriculture has been neglected, and food supplies have fallen short of Romania's needs. Privatization of land began in 1990. Economic mismanagement under Ceausescu decreased low living standards, and Romania faces severe economic difficulties.

HISTORY

Romanians claim descent from the Dacians, a Thracian people, who were Romanized in the 2nd and 3rd centuries AD. They survived as a Latinate population by retreating to the highlands, and emerged to found the principalities of Walachia and Moldavia in the 14th century. Although compelled to accept Ottoman overlordship in the 15th century, they were never subjected to direct Turkish rule. Oppressive rule by Greek princes imposed by the Turks in the 18th century stimulated Romanian nationalism. Unity was achieved when Alexander Cuza was elected prince of both Walachia and Moldavia (1859). A German dynasty was chosen in 1866, and Romania's independence was internationally recognized in 1878.

When both the Russian and Austro-Hungarian Empires collapsed at the end of World War I, Romania won additional territory with substantial Romanian populations from both. 'Greater Romania' was beset with deep social and ethnic divisions, which found expression in the rise of the Fascist Iron Guard in the 1930s. King Carol II suppressed the Guard and substituted his own dictatorship, but he was forced by Germany to cede lands back to Hungary (1940), while the USSR retook considerable territories, including the present Moldavian Republic. Carol fled and Romania – under Marshal Ion Antonescu – joined the Axis powers (1941), fighting the USSR to regain lost territories. King Michael dismissed Antonescu and declared war on Germany as the Red Army invaded (1944), and a Soviet-dominated government was installed (1945). The monarchy was abolished in 1947. From 1952, under Gheorghe Gheorghiu-Dej (1901–65) and then under Nicolae Ceausescu (1918–89), Romania distanced itself from Soviet foreign policy while maintaining strict Communist orthodoxy at home. Ceausescu – and his wife Elena – impoverished Romania by their harsh, corrupt and nepotistic rule. When the secret police put down demonstrations in Timisoara (1989), a national revolt broke out. The army took power, executing Nicolae and Elena Ceausescu on charges of genocide and corruption. A National Salvation Front (NSF) was formed and the Communist Party was dissolved. An international team of monitors judged multi-party elections in 1990 to be 'flawed' but not fraudulent. The NSF has been returned in subsequent elections.

RUSSIA

Official name: Rossiyskaya Federativnaya Respublika (Republic of the Russian Federation) or Rossiya (Russia)

Member of: UN, CIS, CSCE

Area: 17 075 400 km² (6 592 800 sq mi)

Population: 148 543 000 (1991 est)

Capital and major cities: Moscow (Moskva) 8 967 000, St Petersburg (Sankt-Peterburg; formerly Leningrad) 5 020 000, Nizhny Novgorod (formerly Gorky) 1 438 000, Novosibirsk 1 436 000, Yekaterinburg (formerly Sverdlovsk) 1 367 000, Samara (formerly Kuybyshev) 1 257 000, Omsk 1 148 000, Chelyabinsk 1 143 000, Kazan 1 094 000, Perm 1 091 000, Ufa 1 083 000, Rostov 1 020 000, Volgograd 999 000, Krasnoyarsk 912 000 (1989 est)

Languages: Russian (83%), Tatar (4%), Ukrainian (3%), Chuvash (1%), plus more than 100 other languages

Religions: Orthodox (27%), with Sunni Islam, Jewish and other minorities

GOVERNMENT

Constitutional reform is expected in 1993. Under the proposed constitution, Russia would have a parliament of two houses elected for four years by universal adult suffrage – a lower house, comprising 300 representatives of constituencies elected on a system of proportional representation, and a smaller upper house, comprising delegates from each province, region and autonomous republic. An executive President – who will appoint a Council of Ministers – will also be directly elected. Under the terms of a new Russian Federal Treaty (1992),

varying degrees of self-government are exercised by the 20 autonomous republics and by autonomous regions. (Tatarstan and Chechenya did not sign the treaty).

GEOGRAPHY

Russia is the largest country in the world and covers over 10% of the total land area of the globe. Most of the land between the Baltic and the Ural Mountains is covered by the North European Plain, S of which the relatively low-lying Central Russian Uplands stretch from the Ukrainian border to N of Moscow. To the E of the Urals is the vast West Siberian Lowland, the greater part of which is occupied by the basin of the River Ob and its tributaries. The Central Siberian Plateau – between the Rivers Yenisey and Lena – rises to around 1700 m (5500 ft). Beyond the Lena are the mountains of E Siberia, including the Chersky Mountains and the Kamchatka Peninsula. Much of the S of Siberia is mountainous. The Yablonovy and Stanovoy Mountains rise inland from the Amur Basin, which drains to the Pacific coast. The Altai Mountains lie S of Lake Baikal and along the border with Mongolia. Between the Black and Caspian Seas are the high Caucasus Mountains which rise to Elbrus at 5642 m (18 510 ft) on the Georgian border. The Kaliningrad enclave between Poland and Lithuania on the Baltic is a detached part of Russia.

Climate: Russia has a wide range of climatic types, but most of the country is continental and experiences extremes of temperature. The Arctic N is a severe tundra region in which the subsoil is nearly always frozen. The forested taiga zone – to the S – has long hard winters and short summers. The steppes and the Central Russian Uplands have cold winters, but hot, dry summers. Between the Black and Caspian seas, conditions become almost Mediterranean. The Kaliningrad enclave has a more temperate climate than the rest of W Russia.

ECONOMY

Russia is one of the largest producers of coal, iron ore, steel, petroleum and cement. However, its economy is in crisis. The economic reforms (1985–91) of Mikhail Gorbachov introduced decentralization to a centrally-planned economy. Since 1991, reform has been accelerated through the introduction of free market prices and the encouragement of private enterprise. However, lack of motivation in the labour force affects all sectors of the economy and poor distribution has resulted in shortages of many basic goods. Inflation is rampant, reaching 2200% in 1992. Manufacturing involves one third of the labour force and includes the steel, chemical, textile and heavy machinery industries. The production of consumer goods is not highly developed. Agriculture is large-scale and organized either into state-owned farms or collective farms, although the right to own and farm land privately has been introduced. Despite mechanization and the world's largest fertilizer industry, Russia cannot produce enough grain for its needs, in part because of poor harvests, and poor storage and transport facilities. Major Russian crops include wheat, barley, oats, potatoes, sugar beet and fruit. Natural resources include the world's largest reserves of coal, nearly one third of the world's natural gas reserves, one third of the world's forests, major deposits of manganese, gold, potash, bauxite, nickel, lead, zinc and copper, as well as plentiful sites for hydroelectric power installations. Machinery, petroleum and petroleum products are Russia's major exports and the republic is self sufficient in energy. Russia has a large trade surplus with the other former Soviet republics.

HISTORY

The earliest known homeland of the Slavs is thought to lie in the N foothills of the Carpathians in Ukraine from whence the E Slavs migrated towards the Dneiper valley during the first millennium BC. The steppes to the N of the Black Sea were dominated by a series of nomadic peoples – Sarmatians, Scythians, Huns, Avars, Khazars, Pechenegs and Mongols. Rus' – centred on Kiev – was the ancestor of both Russia and Ukraine. It developed from the 9th century on the trade route linking the Baltic with the Black Sea. Its first princes were of Viking origin, though its population was largely E Slav. In AD 988, Grand Prince Volodymyr (Vladimir) of Kiev established Orthodox Christianity in Rus'. Kiev subsequently declined, but other powerful centres grew up including the mercantile republic of Novgorod (W Russia). In 1240, the principalities of Rus' were destroyed by Tatar invasions.

The city of Moscow (founded pre-1147) claimed the lands of Rus' and created the first state to use the name Rossiya (Russia). Ivan III (reigned 1462–1505) threw off the Tatar yoke and annexed Moscow's chief rival, Novgorod. He assumed the title of Tsar (Caesar). Claiming that Moscow was 'the Third Rome' – after Constantinople – he began a 500-year saga of imperial conquest unparalleled in European history. Ivan IV ('the Terrible'; reigned 1533–84) launched Russia's expansion into Siberia, and in 1589 created the first Patriarch of Moscow, thus formalizing the separate existence of the Russian Orthodox Church. The Romanov dynasty, which ruled until 1917, emerged from the wars of the Time of Troubles (1598–1613). In 1662, Muscovy annexed part of Ukraine from Poland. Peter I ('the Great'; reigned 1682–1725) proclaimed himself Emperor and turned Russia into a great power by his victories over Sweden in the Great Northern War, by social and administrative reforms, by founding a new capital on the Baltic (St Petersburg) and by welcoming Western influence (see p. 417).

In Russia's imperial history, perpetual military conquests interlace with repeated bouts of failed internal reform. Catherine II ('the Great'; reigned 1762–96) was responsible for the three partitions of Poland – which brought more land and population – and for increasing the privileges of the nobility and of the cities. Alexander I (reigned 1801–25) dabbled with constitutional ideas, but was absorbed with the struggle against Napoleon I, who occupied Moscow in 1812 (see pp. 426–7). Under Nicholas I (reigned 1825–55) – the champion of autocracy, Orthodoxy and Russian nationalism – a fierce reaction set in. Alexander II ('the Liberator'; reigned 1855–81) emancipated the serfs, but suppressed the Polish rising of 1863–64 with severity. Throughout the

19th century, the frontiers of the Russian Empire continued to expand – into Central Asia, the Caucasus and the Far East – and at the same time Russia attempted to increase its influence in SE Europe at the expense of the declining Turkish Empire. These imperial tendencies sometimes led to confrontation with Western European powers (see p. 429). Alexander III (reigned 1881–94) combined repression at home with restraint abroad. Under Nicholas II (reigned 1894–1917), Russia saw rapid industrialization, rising prosperity, and (after 1906) limited constitutional reform, but his reign was cut short by World War I and the two Revolutions of February and October 1917 (see pp. 436–7 and 438–9).

For details of the Russian Revolutions, the establishment of the USSR and the careers of Lenin and Stalin, see pp. 438–9.

In World War II – in which up to 20 million Soviet citizens may have died – the USSR at first concluded a pact with Hitler (1939), and invaded Poland, Finland, Romania and the Baltic states, annexing considerable territory. However, in 1941 the Germans invaded the USSR (see pp. 444–5). In victory the Soviet Union was confirmed as a world power, controlling a cordon of satellite states in Eastern Europe and challenging the West in the Cold War (see pp. 450–1). However, the economy stagnated and the country was drained by the burdens of an impoverished and overstretched empire. Leonid Brezhnev (leader 1964–82) reversed the brief thaw that had been experienced under Nikita Khruschev (leader 1956–64), and far-reaching reform had to await the policies of Mikhail Gorbachov (1931–) after 1985.

Faced with severe economic reforms, Gorbachov attempted to introduce reconstruction (perestroika) and greater openness (glasnost) by implementing social, economic and industrial reforms. The state of the economy also influenced the desire to reduce military spending by reaching agreements on arms reduction with the West (see pp. 289 and 451). Dissent was tolerated, a major reform of the constitution led to more

open elections, and the Communist Party gave up its leading role. Many hardliners in the Communist Party were defeated by reformers (many of them non-Communists) in elections in 1989. The abandonment of the Brezhnev Doctrine – the right of the USSR to intervene in the affairs of Warsaw Pact countries (as it had done militarily in Hungary in 1956 and Czechoslovakia in 1968) – prompted rapid change in Eastern Europe, where one after another the satellite states renounced Communism and began to implement multi-party rule.

From 1989 there were increased nationalistic stirrings within the USSR. In the Baltic republics popular movements called for a restoration of independence. Disturbances in the Caucasus – initially over the status of the Nagorno Karabakh region, which was disputed by Armenia and Azerbaijan – erupted into serious violence in 1990. In August 1991, an attempt by a group of Communist hardliners to depose Gorbachov was defeated by the resistance of Russian President Boris Yeltsin (1931–) and by the refusal of the army to take action against unarmed civilian protestors. The opposition of Yeltsin and the Russian parliament to the coup greatly enhanced the status and powers of Russia and the 14 other Union Republics. Fourteen of the 15 republics declared independence and the secession of the three Baltic republics was recognized internationally. The remaining republics began to renegotiate their relationship. Gorbachov suspended the Communist Party and – with Yeltsin – initiated far-reaching political and economic reforms. However, it was too late to save the Soviet Union, whose fate was sealed by the refusal of Ukraine, the second most important of the republics, to participate in the new looser Union proposed by Gorbachov. By the end of 1991 the initiative had passed from Gorbachov to Yeltsin, who was instrumental in establishing the Commonwealth of Independent States (CIS), a military and economic grouping of sovereign states that included all the former Union republics except Georgia and the Baltic states.

After Gorbachov resigned and the Soviet Union was dissolved (December 1991), Russia took over the international responsibilities of the USSR, including its seat on the UN Security Council. Externally, Russia faces potential territorial claims on other former Soviet republics. Internally, Russia faces a severe economic crisis, nationalist stirrings in several autonomous republics and a constitutional crisis as Communist hardliners in the Congress dispute power with President Yeltsin.

RWANDA

Official name La République rwandaise (French) or Republika y'u Rwanda (Kinyarwanda) (Republic of Rwanda)

Member of: UN, OAU

Area: 26 338 km² (10 169 sq mi)

Population: 7 491 000 (1991 est)

Capital: Kigali 300 000 (1990 est)

Languages: French and Kinyarwanda (both official)

Religions: Roman Catholic (63%), animist (21%)

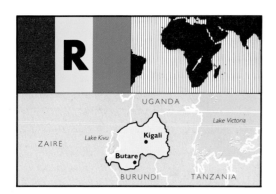

GOVERNMENT
The President – who appoints a Council of Ministers – and the 70-member National Development Council are elected for five years by universal adult suffrage.

GEOGRAPHY
Rwanda is a mountainous country rising to Mount Karisimbi at 4507 m (14 787 ft). Most of the western boundary is formed by Lake Kivu.

Climate: The climate is tropical with cooler temperatures in the mountains.

ECONOMY
Subsistence farming dominates Rwanda's economy. Coffee and tin are the main exports. There are major (unexploited) reserves of natural gas under Lake Kivu.

HISTORY
The kingdom of Rwanda was a German possession from 1890 until it was taken over by Belgium after World War I. The monarchy – of the dominant minority Tutsi people – was overthrown by the majority Hutu people shortly before independence in 1962. Tribal violence has continued intermittently. In 1990–91 an army of Tutsi refugees occupied much of the N. In 1991 the government conceded the principle of multi-party elections.

SAINT CHRISTOPHER AND NEVIS

Official name: The Federation of Saint Christopher and Nevis. St Christopher is popularly known as St Kitts.

Member of: UN, Commonwealth, OAS, CARICOM

Area: 262 km² (101 sq mi)

Population: 43 000 (1991 est)

Capital: Basseterre 18 500 (1986 est)

Language: English (official)

Religions: Anglican (36%), Methodist (32%)

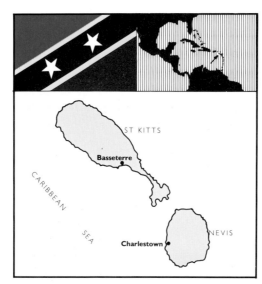

GOVERNMENT
The National Assembly consists of 11 members elected by universal adult suffrage for five years and 3 or 4 appointed members. The Governor General – the representative of the British Queen as sovereign of St Kitts – appoints a Prime Minister who commands a majority in the Assembly. The PM appoints a Cabinet responsible to the Assembly. Nevis has its own legislature.

GEOGRAPHY
St Kitts and Nevis are two well-watered mountainous islands, set 3 km (2 mi) apart.

Climate: The moist tropical climate is cooled by sea breezes.

ECONOMY
The economy is based on agriculture (mainly sugar cane) and tourism.

HISTORY
Both islands were discovered by Columbus in 1493, settled by the English early in the 17th century, but disputed by France in the 18th century. St Kitts was united with Nevis and the more distant small island of Anguilla in a single British colony, which gained internal self-government in 1967. When Anguilla – a reluctant partner – proclaimed independence, the British intervened, eventually restoring Anguilla to colonial rule while St Kitts-Nevis progressed to independence in 1983.

SAINT LUCIA

Member of: UN, Commonwealth, OAS, CARICOM

Area: 616 km² (238 sq mi)

Population: 151 000 (1990 census)

Capital: Castries 57 000 (1990 census)

Languages: English (official), French patois (majority)

Religion: Roman Catholic (over 80%)

GOVERNMENT
The 11-member Senate is appointed. The 17-member House of Assembly is elected by universal adult suffrage for five years. The Governor General – as representative of the British Queen as sovereign of St Lucia – appoints a Prime Minister who commands a majority in the House. The PM, in turn, appoints a Cabinet which is responsible to the House.

GEOGRAPHY
St Lucia is a forested mountainous island rising to Mount Gimie at 959 m (3145 ft).

Climate: St Lucia has a wet tropical climate. There is a dry season from January to April.

ECONOMY
The economy depends on agriculture, with bananas and coconuts as the main crops. Tourism is increasingly important.

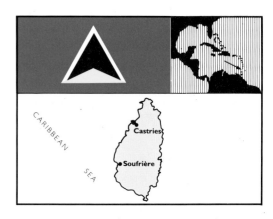

HISTORY
St Lucia was discovered early in the 16th century and was disputed between England and France throughout the 17th and 18th centuries, finally being confirmed as a British colony in 1814. Internal self-government was achieved in 1967 and independence in 1979.

SAINT VINCENT AND THE GRENADINES

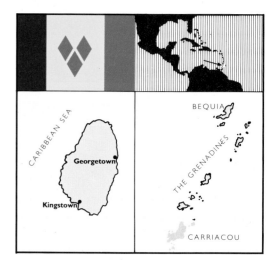

Member of: UN, OAS, Commonwealth, CARICOM

Area: 389 km² (150 sq mi)

Population: 108 000 (1991 census)

Capital: Kingstown 34 000 (city 19 000; 1989 est)

Language: English (official)

Religions: Anglican (42%), Methodist (21%)

GOVERNMENT
The single-chamber House of Assembly consists of six nominated senators and 15 representatives elected for five years by universal adult suffrage. The Governor General – who is the representative of the British Queen as sovereign of St Vincent – appoints a Prime Minister who commands a majority of the representatives. The PM in turn appoints a Cabinet responsible to the House.

GEOGRAPHY
The mountainous wooded island of St Vincent rises to Mount Soufrière – an active volcano – at 1234 m (4048 ft). The Grenadines – which include Bequia and Mustique – are a chain of small islands to the S of St Vincent.

Climate: The country experiences a tropical climate with heavy rainfall in the mountains.

ECONOMY
Bananas and arrowroot are the main crops of a largely agricultural economy.

HISTORY
St Vincent was discovered by Columbus in 1498, but resistance by the native Carib Indians delayed European settlement until the 18th century. The island became a British colony in 1763, gained internal self-government in 1969, and achieved independence in 1979.

SAN MARINO

Official name: Serenissima Reppublica di San Marino (Most Serene Republic of San Marino)

Member of: UN, CSCE

Area: 61 km² (23 sq mi)

Population: 23 700 (1991 est)

Capital and major cities: San Marino 9000 (city 4200), Seravalle 7300 (1991 est)

Language: Italian

Religion: Roman Catholic (official; 95%)

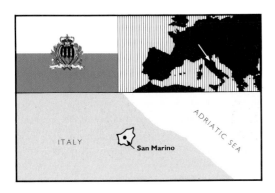

GOVERNMENT
The 60-member Great and General Council is elected by universal adult suffrage for five years. The Council elects two of its members to be Captains-Regent, who jointly hold office as heads of state and of government for six months. The Captains-Regent preside over a 10-member Congress of State – the equivalent of a Cabinet – which is elected by the Council for five years.

GEOGRAPHY
The country is dominated by the triple limestone peaks of Monte Titano at 739 m (2424 ft).

Climate: San Marino has a mild Mediterranean climate.

ECONOMY
Manufacturing and tourism – in particular visitors on excursions – are the mainstays of the economy.

HISTORY
Established as an independent commune by the 12th century, San Marino retained its autonomy because of its isolation and by playing off powerful neighbours against each other. Its independence was recognized by Napoleon (1797), the Congress of Vienna (1815) and the new Kingdom of Italy (1862). In 1957 a bloodless 'revolution' replaced the Communist-Socialist administration that had been in power since 1945.

SÃO TOMÉ E PRÍNCIPE

Official name: A República de São Tomé e Príncipe (Republic of São Tomé and Príncipe)

Member of: UN, OAU

Area: 964 km² (372 sq mi)

Population: 123 000 (1991 est)

Capital: São Tomé 35 000 (1989 est)

Language: Portuguese (official); Fang (90%)

Religion: Roman Catholic (90%)

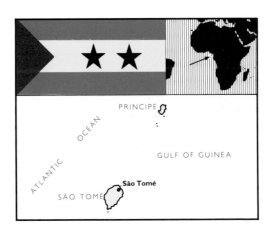

GOVERNMENT
The 55-member National Assembly is elected by universal adult suffrage for four years. The President – who appoints a Prime Minister and Council of Ministers – is also directly elected.

GEOGRAPHY
The republic consists of two mountainous islands about 144 km (90 mi) apart. São Tomé rises to 2024 m (6640 ft).

Climate: The climate is tropical. A wet season – with heavy rainfall – lasts from October to May.

ECONOMY
Cocoa is the mainstay of a largely agricultural economy. Most of the land is nationalized.

HISTORY
The islands were first settled as a convict colony by the Portuguese in the late 15th century, and became slave-trading centres. Early in the 20th century, the islands' plantations were notorious for forced labour. Independence was gained in 1975 as a one-party socialist state. The Marxist system was abandoned in 1990, and multi-party elections were held in 1991.

SAUDI ARABIA

Official name: Al-Mamlaka al-'Arabiya as-Sa'udiya (The Kingdom of Saudi Arabia)

Member of: UN, Arab League, OPEC, GCC

Area: 2 240 000 km² (864 869 sq mi)

Population: 14 691 000 (1991 est)

Capital and major cities: Riyadh (Ar Riyad) – the royal capital – 2 000 000, Jeddah (Jiddah) – the administrative capital – 1 400 000, Mecca (Makkah) 620 000, Medina (Al-Madinah) 500 000 (all including suburbs; 1986 est)

Language: Arabic (official)

Religion: Islam (official) – Sunni (mainly Wahhabi) 92%, Shia 8%

GOVERNMENT
Saudi Arabia is an absolute monarchy with neither formal political institutions nor parties. The King appoints a Council of Ministers and a 60-member consultative council.

GEOGRAPHY
Over 95% of the country is desert, including the Rub 'al-Khali ('The Empty Quarter') – the largest expanse of sand in the world. The Arabian plateau ends in the W in a steep escarpment overlooking a coastal plain beside the Red Sea. There are no permanent streams.

Climate: The country is very hot – with temperatures up to 54 °C (129 °F). The average rainfall is 100 mm (4 in), but many areas receive far less and may not experience any precipitation for years.

ECONOMY
Saudi Arabia's spectacular development and present prosperity are based almost entirely upon exploiting vast reserves of petroleum and natural gas. Industries include petroleum refining, petrochemicals and fertilizers. The country has developed major banking and commercial interests. Less than 1% of the land can be cultivated.

HISTORY
The Prophet Muhammad was born in the early 7th century AD in Mecca where he received revelations from God and proclaimed Islam (see p. 478). Arabia quickly became Muslim, but, following the Prophet's death, the political focus of Islam moved, first to Damascus, then to Baghdad. The unity of Muslim Arabia collapsed and gave way to tribal rivalries. Early in the 16th century the Ottoman Turks established their authority over much of the peninsula. In 1744 a Muslim preacher – Muhammad ibn abd al-Wahhab – and the ancestor of the country's present rulers, the Saudis, formed an alliance that was to spearhead the Wahhabi political-religious campaign. In the 20th century the Wahhabis united most of Arabia under Ibn Saud (1882–1953). In 1902 Ibn Saud took Riyadh and in 1906 defeated his rivals to control central Arabia (Nejd). Between 1912 and 1927 he added the E, the SW (Asir) and the area around Mecca (Hejaz).

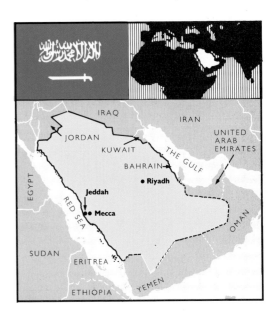

In 1932 these lands became the kingdom of Saudi Arabia. Although the country has been pro-Western, after the 1973 Arab-Israeli War (see p. 455), Saudi Arabia put pressure on the USA to encourage Israel to withdraw from the occupied territories of Palestine by cutting oil production. Saudi Arabia has not escaped problems caused by religious fundamentalism and the rivalry between Sunni and Shia Islam. Saudi Arabia found itself bound to support Iraq in its war with Shiite Iran (1980), but played a major role in the coalition against Iraq in the Second Gulf War (1991).

SENEGAL

Official name: La République du Sénégal (The Republic of Senegal)

Member of: UN, OAU, ECOWAS

Area: 196 722 km² (75 954 sq mi)

Population: 7 517 000 (1991 est)

Capital and major cities: Dakar 1 490 000, Thiès 185 000, St Louis 161 000 (1988 census)

Languages: French (official), Wolof (36%), Serer (19%)

Religions: Sunni Islam (94%), Roman Catholic

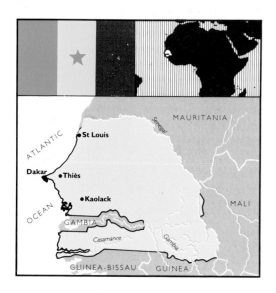

GOVERNMENT
Every five years the President and the 120-member National Assembly are elected by universal adult suffrage. The President appoints and leads a Cabinet which includes a Prime Minister.

GEOGRAPHY
Senegal is mostly low-lying and covered by savannah. The Fouta Djalon mountains in the S rise to Gounou Mountain at 1515 m (4970 ft).

Principal river: Sénégal 1641 km (1020 mi).

Climate: Senegal has a tropical climate with a dry season from October to June.

ECONOMY
Over three quarters of the labour force is involved in agriculture, growing groundnuts and cotton as cash crops, and rice, maize, millet and sorghum as subsistence crops. The manufacturing sector is one of the largest in West Africa, but unemployment is a major problem.

HISTORY
The region was part of the medieval empire of Mali. The coast was explored by the Portuguese in the 15th century and gradually came under French control from the 17th century. A national political awareness developed in the early 20th century, and the country contributed substantially to the nationalist awakening in French Africa. After independence in 1960 – under the poet, Léopold Sedar Senghor (1906–   ) – Senegal maintained close relations with France, and received substantial aid. Attempted federations with Mali

(1959–60) and Gambia (1981–89) were unsuccessful. Senghor retired in 1980, having re-introduced party politics.

SEYCHELLES

Official name: The Republic of Seychelles

Member of: UN, OAU, Commonwealth

Area: 454 km² (173 sq mi)

Population: 68 000 (1991 est)

Capital: Victoria 24 000 (1987 est)

Languages: Creole (95%), English, French – all official

Religion: Roman Catholic (92%)

GOVERNMENT
The President – who appoints a Council of Ministers – is elected for five years by universal adult suffrage. The National Assembly comprises 23 directly elected members and 2 members appointed by the President.

GEOGRAPHY
The Seychelles consist of 40 mountainous granitic islands and just over 50 smaller coral islands.

Climate: The islands have a pleasant tropical maritime climate with heavy rainfall.

ECONOMY
The economy depends heavily on tourism, which employs about one third of the labour force.

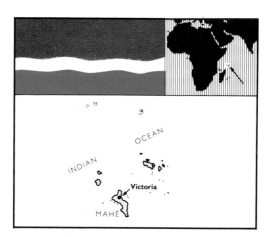

HISTORY
The islands became a French colony in the middle of the 18th century, were ceded to Britain in 1814 and gained independence in 1976. The PM – Albert René – led a coup against President James Mancham in 1977, and established a one-party socialist state. Attempts to overthrow René, including one involving South African mercenaries (1981) were unsuccessful. Multi-party elections were held in 1992.

SIERRA LEONE

Official name: The Republic of Sierra Leone

Member of: UN, OAU, Commonwealth, ECOWAS

Area: 71 740 km² (27 699 sq mi)

Population: 4 260 000 (1991 est)

Capital: Freetown 550 000 (city 470 000; 1985 census)

Languages: English (official), Krio, Mende (34%), Temne (31%)

Religions: Animist (52%), Sunni Islam (39%)

GOVERNMENT
There is constitutional provision for a President – who appoints a Cabinet – to be elected for seven years by universal adult suffrage and for a 124-member House of

Representatives to be directly elected for five years. Power is currently exercised by a military council.

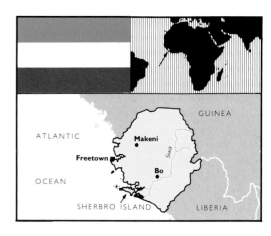

GEOGRAPHY
The savannah interior comprises plateaus and mountain ranges rising to Bintimani Peak at 1948 m (6390 ft). The swampy coastal plain is forested.

Climate: The climate is tropical with a dry season from November to June.

ECONOMY
Subsistence farming – mainly rice – involves the majority of the labour force. Rutile, bauxite and cocoa are major exports. The decline of diamond mining has added to severe economic problems.

HISTORY
Freetown was founded by British philanthropists (1787) as a settlement for former slaves and became a British colony in 1808. The interior was added in 1896. Independence was gained in 1961. A disputed election led to army intervention (1967), and Dr Siaka Stevens – who came to power in a coup in 1968 – introduced a one-party state. A military junta seized power in 1992.

SINGAPORE

Official name Hsing-chia p'o Kung-ho Kuo (Chinese) or Republik Singapura (Malay) or Republic of Singapore

Member of: UN, ASEAN, Commonwealth

Area: 623 km² (240 sq mi)

Population: 2 705 000 (1990 census)

Capital: Singapore 2 705 000 (1990 census)

Languages: Chinese (77%), Malay (14%), Tamil (5%), English – all official

Religions: Buddhist and Daoist (54%), Sunni Islam (15%), various Christian Churches (13%), Hindu

GOVERNMENT
The 81-member Parliament is elected by universal adult

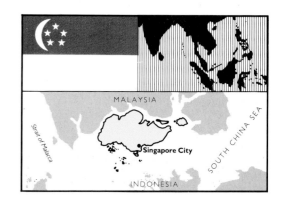

suffrage for five years. Additional non-voting members may be appointed. The President – who is elected by Parliament – appoints a Prime Minister who commands a parliamentary majority. The PM, in turn, appoints a Cabinet which is responsible to Parliament. In 1993 an executive President will be elected by universal adult suffrage for four years.

GEOGRAPHY
Singapore is a low-lying island – with 56 islets – joined to the Malay peninsula by causeway.

Climate: The climate is tropical with monsoon rains from December to March.

ECONOMY
Singapore relies on imports for its flourishing manufacturing industries (electronics, oil refining, rubber processing, food processing) and entrepôt trade. Finance and tourism are important. Singapore has the second highest standard of living in Asia.

HISTORY
Singapore was a trading centre until destroyed by the Javanese in the 14th century. The city was revived by Sir Stamford Raffles for the British East India Company (1819), and developed rapidly as a port for shipping Malaya's tin and rubber. It acquired a cosmopolitan population and became a strategic British base. Occupied by the Japanese (1942–45), it achieved self-government (1959), and joined (1963) and left (1965) the Federation of Malaysia. Since independence it has become wealthy under the strong rule of Prime Minister Lee Kuan Yew (1923– ; PM 1965–91).

SLOVAKIA

Official name: Republika Slovenská (Slovak Republic)

Member of: UN, CSCE

Area: 49 025 km² (18 929 sq mi)

Population: 5 269 000 (1991 census)

Capital and major cities: Bratislava 442 000, Kosice 235 000, Nitra 212 000 (including suburbs; 1991 census)

Languages: Slovak (87%), Hungarian (12%)

Religions: Roman Catholic (60%), Evangelical Churches (6%).

GOVERNMENT
The 150-member Assembly is elected by universal adult suffrage for five years. The Assembly elects a President who appoints a Prime Minister and a Council of Ministers, responsible to the Assembly.

GEOGRAPHY
Slovakia mainly comprises mountain ranges including the Tatra Mountains which rise to Gerlachovka 2655 m (8737 ft) on the Polish border. The only significant lowlands are in the South adjoining the River Danube.

Climate: The climate is continental with hot, relatively dry, summers and cold winters.

ECONOMY
Slovakia has a mainly agricultural economy into which heavy industry – particularly steel and chemicals – was introduced when the country was part of Communist Czechoslovakia. Wheat, maize, potatoes, barley and sheep are important. Varied natural resources include iron ore and brown coal. Slovakia has slowed the privatization of its uncompetitive out-of-date factories.

HISTORY
Slovakia was part of Hungary from the 11th century, although when most of Hungary fell to the Ottoman Turks in the 16th century, Slovakia remained in the hands of the Habsburgs. Slovak nationalism grew in the 19th century and increased Magyarization under the Austro-Hungarian Dual Monarchy (1867–1918) was greatly resented. On the collapse of the Habsburg Empire (1918), the Slovaks joined the Czechs to form Czechoslovakia. When Hitler's Germany dismembered Czechoslovakia in 1938, Slovakia became an Axis puppet state. A popular revolt against German rule (the

Slovak Uprising) took place in 1944. Following liberation (1945) Czechoslovakia was re-established.

After the Communist takeover in 1948, heavy industry was introduced into rural Slovakia. In 1968, moves by Party Secretary Alexander Dubček (a Slovak) to introduce political reforms met with Soviet disapproval, and invasion by Czechoslovakia's Warsaw Pact allies. The conservative wing of the Communist party regained control until 1989, when student demonstrations developed into a peaceful revolution. The Communist Party renounced its leading role. A new government, in which Communists were in a minority, was appointed. In 1990 free multi-party elections were held, Soviet troops were withdrawn and the foundations of a market economy were laid, but the pace of economic reform brought distress to Slovakia, whose old-fashioned industries were ill-equipped to face competition. Increased Slovak separatism led to the division of the country in 1993. Independent Slovakia faces possible tension concerning the large Hungarian minority.

SLOVENIA

Official name: Republika Slovenija (The Republic of Slovenia)

Member of: UN, CSCE

Area: 20 251 km² (7819 sq mi)

Population: 1 963 000 (1991 census)

Capital and major cities: Ljubljana 338 000 (city 286 000), Maribor 186 000 (city 105 000) (1991 census)

Languages: Slovene (91%), Serbo-Croat (5%)

Religion: Roman Catholic (over 90%)

GOVERNMENT
The 240-member Assembly and a President – who appoints a Prime Minister and Cabinet – are directly elected by universal adult suffrage for four years.

GEOGRAPHY
Most of Slovenia comprises mountains including the Karawanken Alps and Julian Alps, which rise to Triglav at 2864 m (9396 ft). In the E, hill country adjoins the Drava valley; in the W, Slovenia has a very short Adriatic coastline.

Climate: The S and W have a Mediterranean climate; the N and E are more continental.

ECONOMY
With a standard of living approaching that of West European countries, Slovenia was the most industrialized and economically developed part of Yugoslavia. Industries include iron and steel, textiles and coal mining. Agriculture specializes in livestock and fodder crops.

HISTORY
The Slovenes arrived in the W Balkans in the 6th and 7th centuries. In the 9th century, the area was divided between several German rulers and only the Slovenes in the S (Carniola) resisted Germanization. Carniola became a Habsburg (Austrian) province in 1335 and, although it remained under Habsburg rule almost continuously until 1918, the Slovenes managed to preserve their national identity. Official encouragement of the Slovene language under Napoleonic French rule (1809–14) gave impetus to a Slovene national revival in the 19th century. When the Habsburg Empire collapsed (1918), the Slovenes joined the Serbs, Croats and Montenegrins in the new state that was renamed Yugoslavia in 1929. When Yugoslavia became a Communist federal state in 1945, the Slovene lands were reorganized as the republic of Slovenia. After the death of Yugoslav President Tito (1980), the federation faltered in nationalist crises. Slovenia, the wealthiest part of Yugoslavia,

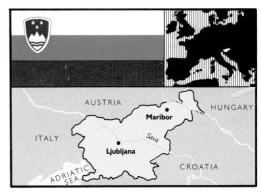

edged towards democracy. In free elections in 1990, nationalists gained a majority in the Slovene Assembly, which declared independence in June 1991. Following reverses in a short campaign, Yugoslav federal forces were withdrawn from Slovenia, whose independence gained widespread diplomatic recognition in 1992.

SOLOMON ISLANDS

Member of: UN, Commonwealth

Area: 27 556 km² (10 639 sq mi)

Population: 328 000 (1991 est)

Capital: Honiara 35 300 (1990 est)

Languages: English (official), Pidgin English, over 85 local (mainly Melanesian) languages

Religions: Anglican (34%), Roman Catholic (19%), other Christian Churches

GOVERNMENT
The 38-member National Parliament – which is elected

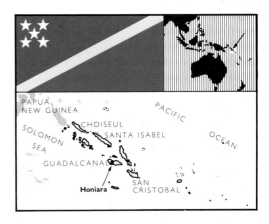

by universal adult suffrage for four years – elects a Prime Minister who appoints a Cabinet. A Governor General is the representative of the British Queen as sovereign of the islands. A federal republican constitution is to be adopted.

GEOGRAPHY
The mountainous volcanic Solomons rise to Mount Makarakomburu at 2447 m (8028 ft).

Climate: The climate is tropical with temperature and rainfall maximums from November to April.

ECONOMY
Most of the labour force is involved in subsistence farming, although copra and cocoa are exported. Fishing is a major industry.

HISTORY
Settled by Melanesians about 2500 BC (see p. 389), the islands were briefly colonized by Spain (1568–1606). The islanders were exploited as a workforce for plantations in other Pacific islands before Britain established a protectorate in 1893. Occupied by the Japanese (1942–45), the Solomons were the scene of fierce fighting, including a major battle for Guadalcanal (see p. 445). Independence was gained in 1978.

SOMALIA

Official name: Jamhuuriyadda Dimuqraadiga Soomaaliya (Somali Democratic Republic)

Member of: UN, Arab League, OAU

Area: 637 657 km² (246 201 sq mi)

Population: 7 691 000 (1991 est)

Capital: Mogadishu 1 000 000 (1986 est)

Languages: Somali (national), Arabic (official)

Religion: Sunni Islam (official)

GOVERNMENT
The constitution provides for the election of a 171-member Assembly and a President by universal adult suffrage. Since 1991 there has been no effective government.

GEOGRAPHY
Somalia occupies the 'Horn of Africa'. Low-lying plains cover most of the S, while semi-arid mountains in the N rise to Surud Ad at 2408 m (7900 ft).

Climate: Somalia is hot and largely dry with rainfall totals in the N as low as 330 mm (13 in).

ECONOMY
Nearly two thirds of the labour force are nomadic herdsmen or subsistence farmers. Bananas are grown for export in the S, but much of the country suffers drought. As a result of the civil war since 1991, much of the economic infrastructure of the country has been destroyed and widespread famine has occurred.

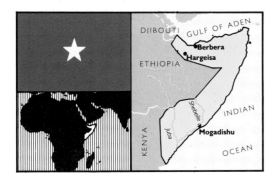

HISTORY
Muslim traders established trading posts along the Somali coast from the 7th century. In 1886 Britain established a protectorate in the N of the region, while

the Italians took the S. In World War II the Italians briefly occupied British Somaliland. In 1960 the British and Italian territories were united as an independent Somalia. In 1969 the president was assassinated and the army – under Major-General Muhammad Siad Barre – seized control. Barre's socialist Islamic Somalia became an ally of the USSR. In 1977 Somali guerrillas – with Somali military support – drove the Ethiopians out of the largely Somali-inhabited Ogaden. Somalia's Soviet alliance was ended when the USSR supported Ethiopia to regain the Ogaden. Barre was overthrown in 1991, but dissidents controlled the S and the former British N attempted to secede. Since 1991 the infrastructure of Somalia has collapsed in bitter civil war between several factions. In 1992, a US-led UN force intervened to relieve famine victims.

SOUTH AFRICA

Official name Republic of South Africa or Republiek van Suid-Afrika

Member of: UN

Area: 2 347 661 km² (906 437 sq mi) including Walvis Bay – 1124 km² (434 sq mi) – and the 'independent' homelands – 1 125 500 km² (434 558 sq mi)

Population: 33 140 000 (1991 est) including Walvis Bay – 21 000 (1981) – and the 'independent' homelands – 5 954 000 (1985)

Capital and major cities: Pretoria (administrative capital) 823 000 (city 443 000), Cape Town (legislative capital) 1 912 000 (city 777 000), Bloemfontein (judicial capital) 233 000 (city 104 000), Johannesburg 4 000 000 (city 632 000; 'Greater Johannesburg' 1 762 000), Durban 982 000 (city 634 000), Soweto (part of the Johannesburg agglomeration) 915 000, Port Elizabeth 652 000 (city 273 000) (1985 census)

Languages: Afrikaans and English (both official), Xhosa (21%), Zulu (16%)

Religions: Dutch Reformed Church, independent African Churches, with Anglican, Methodist, Roman Catholic, Hindu and Sunni Islam minorities

GOVERNMENT
A new power-sharing transitional government, including a collective presidency, and a multi-racial constituent assembly are under discussion. At the beginning of 1992, Parliament consisted of three chambers elected for five years – a House of Assembly elected by adult White suffrage, a House of Representatives elected by Coloured (mixed race) voters, and a House of Delegates elected by Indian voters. The State President – who appoints a Cabinet – was chosen by an electoral college of the three Houses. Blacks had no parliamentary vote, but elected the Legislative Assemblies of the ten homelands. Four homelands – Bophuthatswana, Ciskei, Transkei and Venda – had been granted 'independence', but this status was unrecognized internationally.

GEOGRAPHY
The Great Escarpment rises behind a discontinuous coastal plain and includes the Drakensberg Mountains, which reach 3408 m (11 1182 ft) at Injasuti. A vast plateau occupies the interior, undulating in the W and rising to over 2400 m (about 8000 ft) in the E. Much of the W is semi-desert, while the E is predominantly savannah grassland (veld). Walvis Bay is an enclave on the Namibian coast.

Principal rivers: Orange (Oranje) 2092 km (1300 mi), Limpopo 1770 km (1100 mi)

Climate: South Africa has a subtropical climate with considerable regional variations. The hottest period is between December and February. Rainfall is highest on the E coast but much of the country is dry.

ECONOMY
The country is the world's leading exporter of gold – which forms 35% of South African exports – and a major producer of uranium, diamonds, chromite, antimony, platinum and coal (which meets three quarters of the

country's energy needs). Industry includes chemicals, food processing, textiles, motor vehicles and electrical engineering. Agriculture supplies one third of South Africa's exports including fruit, wine, wool and maize. The highest standard of living in Africa is very unevenly distributed between Whites and Non-whites. The withdrawal of some foreign investors in the 1970s and 1980s increased the drive towards self-sufficiency.

HISTORY
Black African peoples were long established in what is now South Africa when White settlement began in the Dutch colony of Cape Town (1652). Slaves were imported, but the conquest of the local African societies – only completed late in the 19th century – provided an alternative source of labour. Britain acquired the Cape (1814), abolished slavery (1833), and annexed Natal (1843). The Boers (or Afrikaners) – of Dutch and French Huguenot descent – moved inland on the Great Trek (1835–37) to found the republics of the Transvaal and Orange Free State.

After the discovery of diamonds (1867) and gold (1886), the Boers – led by Paul Kruger (1825–1904), president of the Transvaal – resisted British attempts to annex their republics in which British settlers were denied political rights. This culminated in the Boer War (1899–1902). Despite their military superiority, the British initially suffered defeats and were beseiged in a number of towns, including Mafeking and Ladysmith. In 1900 the Boers were beaten in the field but began guerrilla action. The British responded by interning the families of the guerrillas, and more than 20 000 Boer women and children died of disease in internment camps. Although they lost the war, the Afrikaners were politically dominant when the Union of South Africa was formed (1910).

The creation of the African National Congress (ANC) in 1912 was a protest against White supremacy, and by the 1920s Black industrial protest was widespread. South Africa entered World War I as a British ally, taking German South West Africa (Namibia) after a short campaign (1914–15) – after the war, the territory came under South African administration. Despite strong Afrikaner opposition, South Africa – under General Jan Christiaan Smuts (1870–1950; PM 1919–24 and 1939–48) – joined the Allied cause in World War II.After the Afrikaner National Party came to power (1948), racial segregation was increased by the policy of apartheid ('separate development'), which deprived Blacks of civil rights, segregated facilities (such as schools and hospitals) and areas of residence by race, and confined black political rights to restricted homelands ('Bantustans'). Black opposition was crushed following a massacre of demonstrators at Sharpeville, and the ANC was banned (1960) by the government of Hendrik Verwoerd (1901–66; PM from 1958 to 1966, when he was assassinated).

International pressure against apartheid increased. In 1961 South Africa left the Commonwealth, the majority of whose members continue to press for economic sanctions against South Africa. In 1966 the UN cancelled South Africa's trusteeship of South West Africa (Namibia), but South Africa continued to block the territory's progress to independence.

Black opposition revived in the 1970s and 1980s and found expression in strikes, the Soweto uprising of 1976, sabotage and the rise of the Black consciousness movement. South African troops intervened in the Angolan civil war against the Marxist-Leninist government (1981) and were active in Namibia against SWAPO Black nationalist guerrillas. P.W. Botha (1916– ; PM 1978–1984 and president 1984–89) granted political rights to the Coloured and Indian communities, and implemented minor reforms for Blacks. However, in 1986 – in the face of continuing unrest – Botha introduced a state of emergency, under which the press was strictly censored, the meetings of many organizations were banned and the number of political detainees – including children – rose sharply. His successor F.W. de Klerk released some ANC prisoners, promised further reforms and agreed to UN-supervised elections in Namibia leading to independence for that territory. In 1990 de Klerk lifted the ban on the ANC and released its imprisoned leader Nelson Mandela (1918–). In 1990–91, negotiations between the government and Black leaders led to the dismantling of the legal structures of apartheid. Fighting between (mainly Xhosa) ANC and (mainly Zulu) Inkatha supporters in Black townships has caused concern, but negotiations concerning a new multi-racial power-sharing constitution continued intermittently. Elections for a constituent assembly are scheduled for 1993.

SPAIN

Official name: Reino de España (Kingdom of Spain)

Member of: UN, NATO, EC, OECD, CSCE

Area: 504 782 km² (194 897 sq mi) including the Canary Islands, Ceuta and Melilla

Population: 39 952 000 (1991 census)

Capital and major cities: Madrid 4 846 000 (city 3 121 000), Barcelona 3 400 000 (city 1 707 000), Valencia 777 000, Seville (Sevilla) 754 000 (city 684 000), Zaragoza 614 000, Málaga 525 000, Bilbao 477 000 (city 372 000), Las Palmas 348 000, Valladolid 345 000, Murcia 329 000, Palma de Mallorca 309 000, Córdoba 309 000 (1991 census)

Languages: Spanish or Castilian (official; as a first language over 70%), Catalan (as a first language over 20%), Basque (3%), Galician (4%)

Religion: Roman Catholic (98%)

GOVERNMENT

Spain is a constitutional monarchy. The Cortes (Parliament) comprises a Senate (Upper House) and a Chamber of Deputies (Lower House). The Senate consists of 208 senators – 4 from each province, 5 from the Balearic Islands, 6 from the Canary Islands and 2 each from Ceuta and Melilla – elected by universal adult suffrage for four years, plus 49 senators indirectly elected by the autonomous communities. The Congress of Deputies has 350 members directly elected for four years under a system of proportional representation. The King appoints a Prime Minister (President of the Council) who commands a majority in the Cortes. The PM, in turn, appoints a Council of Ministers (Cabinet) responsible to the Chamber of Deputies. Each of the 17 autonomous communities (regions) has its own legislature.

GEOGRAPHY

In the N of Spain a mountainous region stretches from the Pyrenees – dividing Spain from France – through the Cantabrian mountains to Galicia on the Atlantic coast. Much of the country is occupied by the central plateau, the Meseta. This is around 600 m (2000 ft) high, but rises to the higher Sistema Central in Castile, and ends in the S at the Sierra Morena. The Sierra Nevada range in Andalusia in the S contains Mulhacén, mainland Spain's highest peak at 3478 m (11 411 ft). The principal lowlands include the Ebro Valley in the NE, a coastal plain around Valencia in the E, and the valley of the Guadalquivir River in the S. The Balearic Islands in the Mediterranean comprise four main islands – Mallorca (Majorca), Menorca (Minorca), Ibiza and Formentera – with seven much smaller islands. The Canary Islands, off the coast of Morocco and the Western Sahara, comprise five large islands – Tenerife, Fuerteventura, Gran Canaria, Lanzarote and La Palma – plus two smaller islands and six islets. Pico del Tiede in the Canaries is Spain's highest peak at 3716 m (12 192 ft). The cities of Ceuta and Melilla are enclaves on the N coast of Morocco.

Principal rivers: Tagus (Tajo) 1007 km (626 mi), Ebro 910 km (565 mi)

Climate: The SE has a Mediterranean climate with hot summers and mild winters. The dry interior is continental with warm summers and cold winters. The high Pyrenees have a cold Alpine climate, while the NW (Galicia) has a wet Atlantic climate with cool summers.

ECONOMY

Over 10% of the labour force is involved in agriculture. The principal crops include barley, wheat, sugar beet, citrus fruit and grapes (for wine). Pastures for livestock occupy some 20% of the land. Manufacturing developed rapidly from the 1960s, and there are now major motor-vehicle, textile, plastics, metallurgical, shipbuilding, chemical and engineering industries. Spain now has the eighth largest economy in the world. Foreign investors have been encouraged to promote new industry, but unemployment remains high. Banking and commerce are important, and tourism is a major foreign-currency earner. Over 30 000 000 foreign tourists a year visit Spain, mainly staying at beach resorts on the Mediterranean, Balearic Islands and the Canaries.

HISTORY

In the 8th century BC Greek settlements were founded on the Mediterranean coast, and in the following century Celtic peoples settled in the Iberian peninsula. In the 6th century BC the Carthaginians founded colonies in Spain including Barcelona, Cartagena and Alicante, but from the time of the Second Punic War (218 BC) the Romans gradually annexed Iberia. Roman rule in Spain lasted until the Germanic invasions of the 5th century. By the 7th century almost all of the Iberian peninsula was controlled by the Visigoths and Christianity had been introduced. Muslim invaders from Morocco overran most of the peninsula rapidly (711–714) and a powerful emirate, later a caliphate, was established at Córdoba, which became one of the most important cities in the Islamic world (see p. 392). From the 11th century, a lengthy struggle began as small Christian kingdoms in the N of Spain began to expand S into

Muslim areas (the Reconquista; see p. 399). Asturias was the first Spanish Christian kingdom to defeat the Moors – at Covadonga (722) – but by 1035 Castile, Aragon and Navarre were the leaders of the reconquest. By the 13th century only Granada remained in Muslim hands.

Unity was achieved following the marriage in 1469 of Ferdinand II (1452–1516; king of Aragon after 1479) to Isabella I (1451–1504; queen of Castile after 1474). The new nation's domestic and international situation changed rapidly. Granada was reconquered from the Moors in 1492, and a dramatic expansion of Spanish power outside of Europe began almost immediately. The Spanish monarchs sponsored voyages of discovery and gained an empire in Central and South America (see p. 410). In 1516, Charles I (1500–58; after 1519 the Emperor Charles V) became king of Spain and brought Habsburg domination to Europe (see pp. 410–11). Control of such vast territories by one ruler proved impossible, and after Charles' abdication in 1555, the Habsburg realms were divided between what became the Austrian and Spanish branches of the family. The territories of the Spanish ruler were further diminished by the revolt and then the independence of the Netherlands (1568–1648). Many Spaniards played important roles in the Counter-Reformation of the 16th and 17th centuries (see p. 409). Philip II encouraged the Inquisition and sent the Armada against Protestant England, while Ignatius Loyola founded the Jesuits, and the example of Teresa of Avilá encouraged mysticism in Roman Catholicism.

Spanish power in the 17th and 18th centuries was probably overextended. The wealth of the Latin American possessions was not used to power economic development in Spain. The 17th-century Spanish Habsburgs were not as gifted as their ancestors and were unable to override strong provincial loyalties and institutions that hindered the development of a centralized state. In 1700, the Habsburg line ended and a grandson of Louis XIV of France, became the first Bourbon king of Spain as Philip V (1683–1746). In the subsequent War of the Spanish Succession (1701–14), Spain lost further possessions – including Belgium, Luxembourg, Lombardy, southern Italy and Sardinia – and ceded Gibraltar to Britain. However, Spain's Bourbon rulers brought a measure of reform and enlightenment to a deeply conservative country. In 1808 Napoleon placed his brother Joseph on the throne of Spain, but Spanish resistance was spirited and in 1814 the British and Spanish armies forced the evacuation of the French (see p. 427).

King Ferdinand VII (1784–1833) – restored in 1814 – was an absolutist who rejected a liberal constitution introduced in his absence. He lost the Latin American empire when the Spanish possessions in Central and South America made good use of Spain's weakness to take their independence. During the first half of the 19th century, Spain saw a series of struggles between liberal and monarchist elements, with radical republicans poised to intervene from the left and army officers from the right. In the Carlist Wars (1833–39, 1849 and 1872–76) the supporters of Queen Isabella II (1830–1904) – Ferdinand VII's daughter – countered the rival claims of her uncle Don Carlos and his descendants. Isabella was deposed in the revolution of 1868, which was followed by a short-lived liberal monarchy under an Italian prince (1870–73) and a brief republican experiment in 1873–4. In the last decades of the 19th century, the political situation became increasingly unstable, with the turmoil of labour disturbances, pressure for provincial autonomy, and growing anti-clericalism. As a result of the Spanish-American War of 1898 the last significant colonial possessions – Cuba, the Philippines, Guam and Puerto Rico – were lost. The end of Spain's empire inflicted a severe wound to Spanish pride and led to doubts as to whether the constitutional monarchy of Alfonso XIII (1886–1941) was capable of delivering the dynamic leadership that Spain was thought to require.

Spain remained neutral in World War I, during which social tensions increased. A growing disillusionment with parliamentary government and political parties led to a military coup in 1923 led by General Miguel Primo de Rivera (1870–1930). Primo was initially supported by Alfonso XIII, but in 1930 the King withdrew that support. However, the range of forces arrayed against the monarchy and the threat of civil war led Alfonso to abdicate (1931). The peace of the succeeding republic was short-lived. Neither of the political extremes – left nor right – was prepared to tolerate the perceived inefficiency and lack of authority of the Second Spanish Republic. In 1936, the army generals rose against a newly elected republican government. Nationalists – led by General Francisco Franco (1892–1975) and supported by Germany and Italy – fought the republicans in the bitter Spanish Civil War (see p. 443). Franco triumphed in 1939 to become ruler – Caudillo – of the neo-Fascist Spanish State. Political expression was restricted, and from 1942 to 1967 the Cortes (Parliament) was not directly elected. Spain remained neutral in World War II, although it was beholden to Germany. After 1945, Franco emphasized Spain's anti-Communism – a policy that brought his regime some international acceptance from the West during the Cold War.

In 1969, Franco named Alfonso XIII's grandson Juan Carlos (1938–) as his successor. The monarchy was restored on Franco's death (1975) and the King eased the transition to democracy through the establishment of a liberal constitution in 1978. In 1981 Juan Carlos played an important role in putting down an attempted army coup. In 1982 Spain joined NATO and elected a socialist government. Since 1986 the country has been a member of the EC. Despite the granting of regional autonomy (1978), Spain continues to be troubled by campaigns for provincial independence, for example in Catalonia, and by the violence of the Basque separatist movement ETA.

SRI LANKA

Official name: Sri Lanka Prajatantrika Samajawadi Janarajaya (Democratic Socialist Republic of Sri Lanka)

Member of: UN, Commonwealth

Area: 65 610 km² (25 332 sq mi)

Population: 17 219 000 (1991 est)

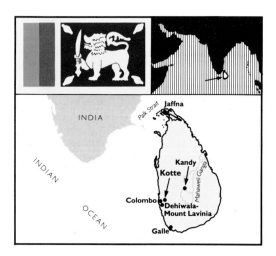

Joint capitals and major cities: Colombo – administrative capital – 1 446 000 (city 615 000), (Sri Jayewardenepura) Kotte – legislative capital – 109 000 (part of the Colombo agglomeration), Dehiwala-Mt Lavinia 196 000 and Moratuwa 170 000 are part of the Colombo agglomeration, Jaffna 138 000 (city 129 000) (1988 est)

Languages: Sinhala (72%), Tamil (21%), English – all official

Religions: Buddhist (69%), Hindu (15%), with Roman Catholic and Sunni Islam minorities

GOVERNMENT

The 225-member Parliament is elected for six years under a system of proportional representation by universal adult suffrage. The President – who is also directly elected for six years – appoints a Cabinet and a Prime Minister who are responsible to Parliament.

GEOGRAPHY

The central highlands of Sri Lanka rise to Pidurutalagala at 2527 m (8292 ft). Most of the rest of the island consists of forested lowlands which in the N are flat and fertile.

Climate: The island has a tropical climate modified by the monsoon. Rainfall totals vary between 5000 mm (20 in) in the SW and 1000 mm (40 in) in the NE.

ECONOMY

About 50% of the labour force is involved in agriculture, growing rice for domestic consumption, and tea, rubber and coconuts for export. Major irrigation and hydroelectric installations on the Mahaweli River are being constructed. Industries include food processing and textiles, but the economy – in particular tourism – has been damaged by guerrilla activity.

HISTORY

In the 6th century BC Sinhalese invaders from N India arrived in Ceylon – as Sri Lanka was known before 1972. They established a capital at Anuradhapura, which became a key centre of Buddhist learning (see p. 384). In the 12th century Tamil invaders from S India established a kingdom in the N where they displaced the Sinhalese. Spices drew Arab traders. Trading settlements were founded by the Portuguese in the 16th century, and then by the Dutch, who were invited by the king of Kandy to oust the Portuguese in the 17th century. From 1796 British rule replaced the Dutch, uniting the entire island for the first time.

Nationalist feeling grew from the beginning of the 20th century, leading to independence in 1948, and a republican constitution in 1972. The country has been bedevilled by Tamil-Sinhalese ethnic rivalry, which led to major disorders in 1958, 1961 and since 1977. In 1971 a Marxist rebellion was crushed after heavy fighting. Sri Lanka elected the world's first woman Prime Minister, Sirimavo Bandaranaike (1916– ; PM 1960–65 and 1970–77). In the 1980s separatist Tamil guerrillas fought for an independent homeland (Eelam). Fighting between rival Tamil guerrilla groups, Sinhalese extremists and government forces reduced the NE to near civil war. An Indian 'peace-keeping' force intervened (1987), but this aggravated an already complex situation. The Tamil NE is scheduled to achieve autonomy, under the dominant Tamil Tigers guerrillas who registered as a political party in 1989. Indian forces withdrew in 1990, but Tamil guerrilla activity continues in the NE.

SUDAN

Official name: Al Jumhuriyat as-Sûdân (The Republic of Sudan)

Member of: UN, Arab League, OAU

Area: 2 505 813 km² (967 500 sq mi)

Population: 29 129 000 (1991 est)

Capital and major cities: Khartoum 1 802 000 (city 476 000, Omdurman 526 000, Khartoum North 341 000), Port Sudan (Bûr Sûdân) 207 000 (1983 est)

Language: Arabic (over 50%; official)

Religions: Sunni Islam (70%), animist (22%), with various Christian Churches (8%)

GOVERNMENT

Since the military coup in June 1989, Sudan has been ruled by the 15-member Command Council of the Revolution of National Salvation, whose chairman is head of state and of government. A 300-member Transitional National Assembly was appointed in 1992. In future, the Assembly will comprise representatives from nine provincial councils, which, in turn, will consist of delegates from directly elected popular committees.

GEOGRAPHY

The Sahara Desert covers much of the N and W, but is crossed by the fertile Nile Valley. The southern plains are swampy. Highlands are confined to hills beside the Red Sea and mountains on the Ugandan border.

Principal river: Nile 6648 km (4132 mi)

Climate: The S is equatorial, but the N is dry with some areas receiving negligible rainfall.

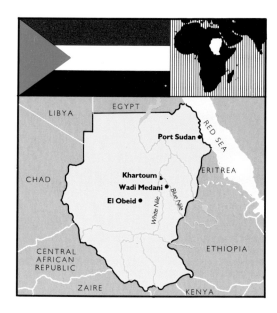

ECONOMY

Over 60% of the labour force is involved in agriculture, growing cotton for export and sorghum and millet for domestic consumption. Since the early 1980s Sudan has been severely affected by drought, civil war and famine.

HISTORY

Northern Sudan – once known as Nubia – was strongly influenced by Egypt, and was later the seat of the Kingdom of Kush (600 BC–AD350). Medieval Christian kingdoms fell to Muslim invaders from the 13th century. In 1820–21 Sudan was conquered by the Egyptians, who were challenged in the 1880s by an Islamic leader who claimed to be the Mahdi (see p. 479). The Mahdists took Khartoum, killed Sudan's Egyptian-appointed governor, General Charles George Gordon (1885), and created a theocratic state. Britain intervened, and from 1899 Sudan was administered jointly by Britain and Egypt. Nationalism developed strongly after World War I, but independence was only gained in 1956. Sudan remains politically unstable, alternating between civilian and military regimes. The civil war between the Muslim N and the animist-Christian S that began in 1955 remains unresolved. The military regime that came to power in 1989 has intensified the offensive against Christian rebels in the S, has encouraged Islamic fundamentalism and has led Sudan into international isolation through its backing for Iraq and Libya.

SURINAME

Official name: Republiek Suriname (Republic of Suriname)

Member of: UN, OAS

Area: 163 265 km² (63 037 sq mi)

Population: 417 000 (1991 est)

Capital: Paramaribo 246 000 (city 68 000; 1988 est)

Languages: Dutch (official; 30%), Sranang Togo (Creole; 31%), Hindi (30%), Javanese (15%), Chinese, English (official), Spanish (official – designate)

Religions: Hinduism (28%), Roman Catholic (22%), Sunni Islam (20%), Moravian (15%)

GOVERNMENT
The 51-member National Assembly is elected for five years by universal adult suffrage. A President and a Vice-President – who is also the Prime Minister – are elected by the Assembly. The President appoints a Cabinet. An appointed Council of State is empowered to overrule the National Assembly.

GEOGRAPHY
Suriname comprises a swampy coastal plain, a forested central plateau, and mountains in the S.

Climate: Suriname has a tropical climate with heavy rainfall.

ECONOMY
The extraction and refining of bauxite is the mainstay of the economy. Other exports include shrimps, sugar and oranges.

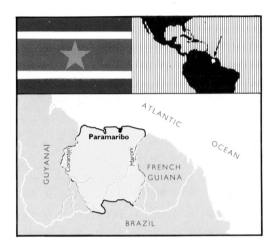

HISTORY
Dutch settlement began in 1602 and the area was confirmed as a Dutch colony in 1667. Suriname has a mixed population, including American Indians, and the descendants of African slaves and of Javanese, Chinese and Indian plantation workers. Since independence in 1975, racial tension has contributed to instability and there have been several coups.

SWAZILAND

Official name: Umbuso Weswatini (The Kingdom of Swaziland)

Member of: UN, Commonwealth, OAU

Area: 17 363 km² (6704 sq mi)

Population: 798 000 (1991 est)

Capital and major cities: Mbabane – administrative capital – 38 000, Lobamba – legislative capital – 6000, Manzini 52 000 (1986 census)

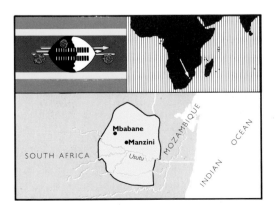

Languages: siSwati and English (both official)

Religions: Animist (majority), various Christian Churches

GOVERNMENT
Swaziland is a monarchy in which the King appoints a Prime Minister and Cabinet. The King is advised by the 20-member Senate and the 50-member House of Assembly, and appoints 10 members to both. Each of the 40 traditional tribal communities elect 2 members to the Electoral College, which chooses 10 of its members to sit in the Senate and 40 in the House. No political parties are permitted.

GEOGRAPHY
From the mountains of the W – which rise to 1869 m (6100 ft) – Swaziland descends in steps of savannah (veld) towards hill country in the E.

Climate: The veld is subtropical, while the highlands are temperate.

ECONOMY
The majority of Swazis are subsistence farmers. Cash crops include sugar cane (the main export).

HISTORY
The Swazi kingdom was formed early in the 19th century, and came under British rule in 1904. The country resisted annexation by the Boers in the 1890s and by South Africa during the colonial period. Following independence (1968), King Sobhuza II suspended the constitution in 1973 and restored much of the traditional royal authority. A bitter power struggle after his death (1982) lasted until King Mswati III was invested in 1986.

SWEDEN

Official name: Konungariket Sverige (Kingdom of Sweden)

Member of: UN, EFTA, OECD, CSCE

Area: 449 964 km² (173 732 sq mi)

Population: 8 586 000 (1990 census)

Capital and major cities: Stockholm 1 471 000 (city 679 000), Göteborg (Gothenburg) 720 000 (city 432 000), Malmö 466 000 (city 235 000), Uppsala 171 000 (city 168 000), Linköping 124 000, Orebro 122 000, Norrköping 121 000, Vasteras 120 000 (1990 census)

Languages: Swedish (official), small Lappish minority

Religion: Evangelical Lutheran Church of Sweden (over 85%)

GOVERNMENT
Sweden is a constitutional monarchy in which the King is ceremonial and representative head of state without any executive role. The 349-member Riksdag (Parliament) is elected for three years by universal adult suffrage under a system of proportional representation. The Speaker of the Riksdag nominates a Prime Minister who commands a parliamentary majority. The PM, in turn, appoints a Cabinet of Ministers who are responsible to the Riksdag.

GEOGRAPHY
The mountains of Norrland – along the border with Norway and in the N of Sweden – cover two thirds of the country, rising at Kebnekaise to 2123 m (6965 ft). Svealand – in the centre – is characterized by a large number of lakes. In the S are the low Smaland Highlands and the fertile lowland of Skane.

Climate: Sweden experiences long cold winters and warm summers, although the N – where snow remains on the mountains for eight months – is more severe than the S, where Skane has a relatively mild winter.

ECONOMY
Sweden's high standard of living has been based upon its neutrality in the two World Wars, its cheap and plentiful hydroelectric power and its mineral riches. The country has about 15% of the world's uranium deposits, and large reserves of iron ore that provide the basis of domestic heavy industry and important exports to West-

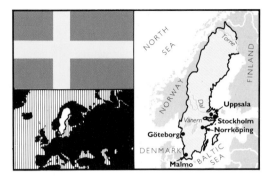

ern Europe. Agriculture – like the bulk of the population – is concentrated in the S. The principal products include dairy produce, meat, barley, sugar beet and potatoes. Vast coniferous forests are the basis of the paper, board and furniture industries, and large exports of timber. Heavy industries include motor vehicles (Saab and Volvo), aerospace and machinery, although the large shipbuilding industry has ceased to exist.

HISTORY
Sweden became Christian in the 10th and 11th centuries, and a stable monarchy dominated much of the Middle Ages. In 1397, the crowns of Sweden, Norway and Denmark were united, and for just over a century Sweden struggled for independence and then with Denmark for dominance of Scandinavia. Stability returned with the accession in 1523 of Gustaf I (reigned 1523–60), who founded the Vasa dynasty and confiscated Church lands, an act that led to the Reformation in Sweden. Under the Vasas, Sweden's role in Northern Europe expanded considerably, particularly during the reign of Gustaf II Adolf (better known as Gustavus Adolphus; reigned 1611–32) when Sweden played a major part on the Protestant side in the Thirty Years War (see p. 409). Gustavus Adolphus, a brilliant tactician, gained initial successes in Germany, and by the time of his death in battle at Lützen (1632), Sweden was a great power. His able chief minister Axel Oxenstierna (1583–1654) helped win a Baltic empire that by 1648 included Finland, Estonia, Latvia and parts of northern Germany.

The military adventures of Charles XII (reigned 1697–1718) in the Great Northern War (1700–21) ended in defeat. The Battle of Poltava (1709) was a turning point in European history and marked the rise of Russia to prominence at the expense of Sweden. Throughout the 18th century Sweden was troubled by internal struggles between the monarchy and the aristocracy. Involvement in the Napoleonic Wars was Sweden's last conflict, and since then the country has enjoyed neutrality. The founder of the present Swedish dynasty, the French marshal Jean-Baptiste Bernadotte, was elected crown prince to the childless king (1810), and succeeded in 1818. In 1814 Sweden lost Finland and the last possessions S of the Baltic, but gained Norway from Denmark in compensation. The union of Norway and Sweden was dissolved in 1905 when King Oscar II (reigned 1872–1907) gave up the Norwegian throne upon Norway's vote for separation. In the 20th century neutral Sweden has developed a comprehensive welfare state under social democratic governments. The country assumed a moral leadership on world issues but was jolted by the (unclaimed) assassination of PM Olof Palme (1986). In the 1990s economic necessity has obliged Sweden to dismantle aspects of the welfare system. The country has also become a candidate for EC membership.

SWITZERLAND

Official name: Schweizerische Eidgenossenschaft (German) or Confédération suisse (French) or Confederazione Svizzera (Italian) or Confederaziun Helvetica (Romansch); (Swiss Confederation)

Member of: EFTA, OECD, CSCE

Area: 41 293 km² (15 943 sq mi)

Population: 6 820 000 (1991 est)

Capital and major cities: Berne (Bern) 299 000 (city 134 000), Zürich 839 000 (city 343 000), Geneva (Genève) 389 000 (city 165 000), Basel 359 000 (city 170 000), Lausanne 263 000 (city 123 000), Luzern 161 000 (city 59 000), St Gallen 126 000 (city 73 000) (1990 est)

Languages: German (65% as a first language), French 18% (first language), Italian (10% first language), Romansch (under 1%) – all official

Religions: Roman Catholic (48%), various Protestant Churches (44%)

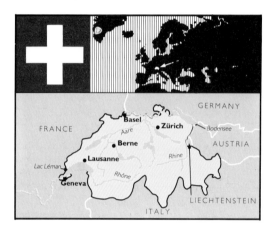

GOVERNMENT

Switzerland is a federal republic in which each of the 20 cantons and 6 half-cantons has its own government with very considerable powers. Federal matters are entrusted to the Federal Assembly comprising the 46-member Council of States and the 200-member National Council. The Council of States is directly elected for three or four years with two members from each canton and one from each half-canton. The National Council is elected for four years by universal adult suffrage under a system of proportional representation. The Federal Assembly elects a seven-member Federal Council – the equivalent of a Cabinet – for four years. The Federal Council appoints one of its members to be President for one year. All federal and cantonal constitutional amendments must be approved by a referendum.

GEOGRAPHY

The parallel ridges of the Jura Mountains lie in the NW on the French border. The S of the country is occupied by the Alps, which rise to Dufourspitze (Monte Rosa) at 4634 m (15 203 ft). Between the two mountain ranges is a central plateau that contains the greater part of Switzerland's population, agriculture and industry.

Principal rivers: Rhine (Rhein) 1320 km (820 mi), Rhône 812 km (505 mi)

Climate: Altitude and aspect modify Switzerland's temperate climate. Considerable differences in temperature and rainfall are experienced over relatively short distances; for instance, the cold Alpine climate around the St Gotthard Pass is only 50 km (just over 30 miles) from the Mediterranean climate of Lugano.

ECONOMY

Nearly two centuries of neutrality have allowed Switzerland to build a reputation as a secure financial centre. Zürich is one of the world's leading banking and commercial cities. The country enjoys one of the highest standards of living in the world. Industry – in part based upon cheap hydroelectric power – includes engineering (from turbines to watches), textiles, food processing (including cheese and chocolate), pharmaceuticals and chemicals. Dairying, grapes (for wine) and fodder crops are important in agriculture, and there is a significant timber industry. Tourism and the international organi-

zations based in Switzerland are major foreign-currency earners. Foreign workers – in particular Italians – help alleviate the country's labour shortage.

HISTORY

Switzerland occupies a strategic position, but the Swiss have used their remarkable position to withdraw from, rather than participate in, European power politics. In the 11th century, what is now Switzerland became part of the Holy Roman Empire. In 1291, three local territorial units – the 'Forest Cantons' of Schwyz (which gave its name to the country), Unterwalden and Uri – joined together in a League against the (Austrian) Habsburg Emperors. Other similar cantons joined the infant League throughout the later Middle Ages, and by 1513 the League included 13 cantons and a variety of dependent territories. Intense religious rivalries in the 16th century – with Zürich, Basel, Berne and Schaffhausen becoming Protestant – resulted in a civil war that tested but did not destroy the League. At the end of the Thirty Years War (1648), Switzerland's independence was finally recognized.

The French Revolutionary Wars saw the creation of a Helvetian Republic in 1798, but in 1803 Napoleon dismantled this unitary state and returned the country to a confederation. At the Congress of Vienna (1815) Swiss neutrality was recognized and the country gained its present boundaries. Continuing tensions in the early 19th century saw attempts by some cantons to secede and set up a new federation, but the compromises of a new constitution in 1848 – which is still the basis of Swiss government – balanced cantonal and central power. As a neutral country Switzerland proved the ideal base for the Red Cross (1863), the League of Nations (1920) and other world organizations, but Switzerland has avoided membership of any body it considers might compromise its neutrality – national referenda voted against Swiss membership of the UN (1986) and of the EEA (the combined trade block to be formed by ETFA and EC countries; 1992).

SYRIA

Official name: Al-Jumhuriya al-'Arabiya as-Suriya (The Syrian Arab Republic)

Member of: UN, Arab League

Area: 185 180 km² (71 498 sq mi) – including the Israeli-occupied Golan Heights

Population: 12 529 000 (1991 est)

Capital and major cities: Damascus 1 361 000, Halab (formerly Aleppo) 1 308 000 (1989 est)

Languages: Arabic (89%; official); Kurdish (6%)

Religions: Islam (official; Sunni 90%, Shia and Druze minorities), with various Orthodox and Roman Catholic minorities (9%)

GOVERNMENT

The 250-member National People's Assembly is elected by universal adult suffrage for four years. The President – who is directly elected for seven years – appoints a Prime Minister (to assist him in government) and a Council of Ministers. The National Progressive Front – including the ruling Ba'ath Party – has a leading role.

GEOGRAPHY

Behind a well-watered coastal plain, mountains run from N to S, rising to Jabal ash Shaik (Mount Hermon) at 2814 m (9232 ft). Inland, much of the country is occupied by the Syrian Desert.

Principal river: Euphrates (Al Furat) 2800 km (1740 mi)

Climate: The coast has a Mediterranean climate. The arid interior has hot summers and cool winters.

ECONOMY

Petroleum is the main export although Syria's petroleum reserves are small by Middle East standards. Agriculture involves 25% of the labour force, with farming concentrated in the coastal plain and irrigated land in the Euphrates Valley. Major crops include cotton, wheat and barley.

HISTORY

Syria was an important part of the Hittite, Assyrian and Persian empires (see pp. 364–5), before being conquered by Alexander the Great (332 BC). From 305 BC Syria was the centre of the Seleucid Empire (see pp. 372–3), and in 64 BC the area became a Roman province based on Antioch. The Byzantine Empire ruled the area (300–634) until the Muslim armies of Khaled ibn al-Walid invaded the country. Most Syrians accepted Islam rapidly. In 661 Mu'awiyya, the founder of the Umayyad dynasty (see p. 392), established his capital in Damascus, and the city reached the zenith of its power. When the Umayyads were overthrown by the Abbasid dynasty from Baghdad (750) Damascus' pre-eminence ended.

From the 12th to the 14th century parts of coastal Syria were ruled by Crusader principalities (see p. 398). The Mamluks – originally Turkish slaves – ruled Syria from the 13th century until 1516 when the area was annexed by the (Turkish) Ottoman Empire. Ottoman rule was not ended until 1917 when a combined British-Arab army was led into Damascus. In 1920 independence was declared, but the victors of World War I handed Syria to France (1920) as a trust territory. Since independence in 1946 Syria has suffered political instability. The pan-Arab, secular, socialist Ba'ath Party engineered Syria's unsuccessful union with Egypt (1958–61). Syria fought wars with Israel in 1948–49, 1967 and 1973 (see pp. 454–55), and in the 1967 Arab-Israeli War Israel captured the strategic Golan Heights from Syria. A pragmatic Ba'athist leader Hafiz Assad came to power in 1970 and allied Syria to the USSR. Assad's popularity has been challenged by Syria's increasing involvement in Lebanon since 1976 and by Shiite fundamentalism. After 1989–90, economic pressures lessened Syria's dependence upon the USSR. Syria's participation in the coalition against Iraq (1990–91) gained greater international acceptance for Syria, which had attracted criticism for sympathizing with terrorism.

TAJIKISTAN

Official name: Respublika i Tojikiston (Republic of Tajikistan)

Member of: UN, CIS, CSCE

Area: 143 100 km² (55 300 sq mi)

Population: 5 358 000 (1991 est)

Capital and major cities: Dushanbe 604 000, Khodzhent (formerly Leninabad) 157 000 (1989 census)

Language: Tajik (59%), Uzbek (23%), Russian (10%)

Religion: Sunni Islam majority

GOVERNMENT

A 230-member legislature and a President are elected for four years by universal adult suffrage. A new constitution is to be drafted.

GEOGRAPHY

The mountainous republic of Tajikistan lies within the

Tien Shan range and part of the Pamirs. The highest point at 7495 m (24 590 ft) is Mount Garmo, which was known as Pik Kommunizma (Communism Peak) when it was the highest mountain in the USSR. The most important lowland is the Fergana valley.

Climate: High altitude and the country's position deep in the interior of Asia combine to give most of Tajikistan a harsh continental climate. The Fergana valley has a subtropical climate.

ECONOMY
Cotton is the mainstay of the economy. Other agricultural interests include fruit, vegetables and raising cattle. Major natural resources include coal, natural gas, iron ore, oil, lead, zinc and hydroelectric-power potential. Industries include textiles and carpet-making. The economy remains centrally planned and largely state-owned.

HISTORY
The Tajiks, who are an Iranian people, were included in the Persian Empire until the 8th century AD when the Arabs extended their influence over the area. In the 13th century the Tajiks were overrun by the Mongols and became part of the empire of Tamerlane (Timur) and his dynasty. A period of Uzbek rule was ended when the Afghans invaded in the 18th century. In the 19th century most of the Tajiks owed allegiance to the (Uzbek) khan of Bukhara. The area was annexed by Tsarist Russia (1860–68). After the Russian Revolution (see p. 438), the area was reoccupied by the Soviet Red Army (1920), but Tajik revolts simmered from 1922 to 1931. Tajikistan became a Union Republic within the USSR in 1929, declared independence after the abortive coup by Communist hardliners in Moscow (September 1991), and was internationally recognized when the Soviet Union was dissolved (December 1991). Since independence the country has been wracked by civil war between former Communists and Islamic fundamentalists.

TANZANIA

Official name: Jamhuri ya Muungano wa Tanzania (Swahili) or The United Republic of Tanzania

Member of: UN, Commonwealth, OAU

Area: 945 087 km² (364 900 sq mi)

Population: 25 096 000 (1991 est)

Capital and major cities: Dodoma 204 000, Dar es Salaam 1 361 000, Mwanza 223 000, Zanzibar 158 000 (1988 census)

Languages: English and Swahili (90%; 9% as a first language) – both official

Religions: Animist (40%), Sunni Islam (33%), Roman Catholic (20%)

GOVERNMENT
The President is elected by universal adult suffrage for a five-year term. The President appoints a Cabinet of Ministers and two Vice Presidents – one President of Zanzibar, the other concurrently Prime Minister. The 244-member National Assembly comprises 119 members directly elected from the mainland, 50 members directly elected from Zanzibar, plus appointed and indirectly elected members. Zanzibar has its own legislature.

GEOGRAPHY
Zanzibar comprises three small islands. The mainland – formerly Tanganyika – comprises savannah plateaux divided by rift valleys and a N–S mountain chain rising to Kilimanjaro at 5894 m (19 340 ft), the highest point in Africa.

Climate: Tanzania has a tropical climate, although the mountains are cooler.

ECONOMIC ACTIVITY
Subsistence farming involves over 80% of the labour force. Cash crops include coffee and cotton. Mineral resources include diamonds and gold.

HISTORY
The coast was explored by Arabs from the 8th century and the Portuguese from the 16th century. Zanzibar was an Omani possession from the 18th century, became an independent sultanate in 1856 and then a British protectorate (1890–1963). After independence in 1963 the sultan of Zanzibar was deposed in a radical left-wing coup. The mainland became the colony of German East Africa in 1884, the British trust territory of Tanganyika in 1919 and an independent state in 1961. President Julius Nyerere's policies of self-reliance and egalitarian socialism were widely admired, but proved difficult to implement and were largely abandoned by the time he retired as President in 1985. In 1964 Tanganyika and Zanzibar united to form Tanzania. The country was effectively a one-party state from 1965 until 1992, when the principle of political pluralism was conceded.

THAILAND

Official name: Prathet Thai (Kingdom of Thailand)

Member of: UN, ASEAN

Area: 513 115 km² (198 115 sq mi)

Population: 57 150 000 (1991 est)

Capital and major cities: Bangkok 5 876 000, Nakhon Ratchasima 207 000, Songkhla 173 000 (1990 census)

Language: Thai (official)

Religions: Buddhism (95%), Sunni Islam (4%)

GOVERNMENT
Thailand is a constitutional monarchy. The National Assembly comprises a non-political Senate whose 270 members are appointed by the (military) National

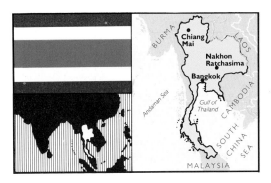

Peacekeeping Council and a 360-member House of Representatives elected by universal adult suffrage for four years. The King appoints a Prime Minister who commands a majority in the House. The PM appoints a Cabinet of Ministers responsible to the House.

GEOGRAPHY
Central Thailand is a densely populated fertile plain. The mountainous N rises to Doi Inthanon at 2595 m (8514 ft). The infertile Khorat Plateau occupies the NE, while the mountainous Isthmus of Kra joins southern Thailand to Malaysia.

Principal river: Mekong 4350 km (2702 mi)

Climate: Thailand has a subtropical climate with heavy monsoon rains from June to October, a cool season from October to March and a hot season from March to June.

ECONOMY
Two thirds of the labour force is involved in agriculture, mainly growing rice (a major export), tapioca and rubber. Tin and natural gas are the main natural resources. Manufacturing – based on cheap labour – is expanding and includes textiles, clothes, electrical and electronic engineering. Thailand achieved high economic growth rates throughout the 1980s and early 1990s. Tourism is a major foreign-currency earner.

HISTORY
Before 1939 Thailand was known as Siam. The Thais originated in Yunnan (China) and moved S after the Mongol destruction of their kingdom, Nanchao (1253). The Thais seized the Khmer (Cambodian) city Sukhotai, making it the centre of a new kingdom. After 1350 – based on the city of Ayutthaya – Thai rulers consolidated their hold on S Siam and the Malay peninsula. Centuries of warfare with Burma, Laos and Cambodia did not prevent Siam from becoming the most powerful state in SE Asia, and the adroit diplomacy of its rulers enabled it to remain free of European colonization. Rama I (reigned 1782–1809), founder of the present dynasty, moved the capital to Bangkok. His successors were forced to cede their claims over neighbouring lands to Britain and France.

A constitutional monarchy was established by a bloodless coup (1932), whose Westernized leaders (Pibul Songgram and Pridi Phanomyang) struggled for political dominance for the next quarter of a century. During World War II Thailand was forced into an alliance with Japan. Since then Thailand has made a decisive commitment to the US political camp, which has brought major benefits in military and technical aid. Despite continuing army interventions in politics, Thailand has prospered. However, the stability of the country was compromised by the wars in Vietnam (see pp. 452–3) and by the continuing Cambodian conflict (until 1991), as Cambodian refugees and guerrillas remained in Thai border regions. Under a revised constitution (1991) the military-dominated Senate assumed a leading role.

TOGO

Official name: La République togolaise (The Togolese Republic)

Member of: UN, OAU, ECOWAS

Area: 56 785 km² (21 925 sq mi)

Population: 3 531 000 (1990 est)

Capital: Lomé 366 000 (1983 est)

Languages: French, Ewe (47%), Kabiye (22%) – all official

Religions: Animist (50%), Roman Catholic (26%), Sunni Islam (15%), various Protestant Churches (9%)

GOVERNMENT

The President – who appoints a Prime Minister and a Council of Ministers – is elected by universal adult suffrage for seven years, while the 79-member National Assembly is directly elected for five years.

GEOGRAPHY

Inland from a narrow coastal plain is a series of plateaux rising in the N to the Chaine du Togo, including Pic Baumann at 983 m (3225 ft).

Climate: Togo has a hot and humid tropical climate, although the N is drier.

ECONOMY

The majority of the labour force is involved in subsistence farming, with yams and millet as the principal crops. Phosphates are the main export.

HISTORY

Colonized by Germany in 1884, Togoland was occupied by Franco-British forces in World War I, after which it was divided between them as trust territories. British Togoland became part of Ghana; the French section gained independence as Togo in 1960, and subsequently relations with Ghana have been strained. Togo has experienced great political instability and several coups. A multi-party system was restored in 1991.

TONGA

Official name: Pule'anga Fakatu'i'o Tonga (The Kingdom of Tonga)

Member of: Commonwealth

Area: 748 km² (289 sq mi)

Population: 97 000 (1991 est)

Capital: Nuku'alofa 28 900 (1986 est)

Languages: Tongan, English

Religions: Methodist (40%; official), Roman Catholic

GOVERNMENT

Tonga is a constitutional monarchy. The King appoints a Prime Minister and other Ministers to the Privy Council, which acts as a Cabinet. The 31-member Legislative Assembly comprises the King, the Privy Council, 9 hereditary nobles (chosen by their peers) and 9 representatives of the people elected for three years by universal adult suffrage. There are no political parties.

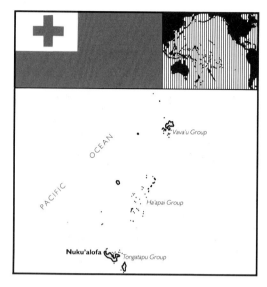

GEOGRAPHY

The 172 Tongan islands – 36 of which are inhabited – comprise a low limestone chain in the E and a higher volcanic chain in the W.

Climate: The climate is warm with heavy rainfall.

ECONOMY

Agriculture involves most Tongans with yams, cassava and taro being grown as subsistence crops. Coconut products are the main exports.

HISTORY

Inhabited by Polynesians for over 3000 years (see p. 389), Tonga has been ruled by kings since the 10th century. European intervention began when Captain Cook visited Tonga (1773–77). Civil war in the first half of the 19th century was ended by King George Tupou I (reigned 1845–93) who reunited Tonga, preserved its independence and gave it a modern constitution. From 1900 to 1970 Tonga was a British protectorate. Since 1987 pressure for constitutional reform has increased.

TRINIDAD AND TOBAGO

Official name: Republic of Trinidad and Tobago

Member of: UN, Commonwealth, OAS, CARICOM

Area: 5130 km² (1981 sq mi)

Population: 1 234 000 (1990 census)

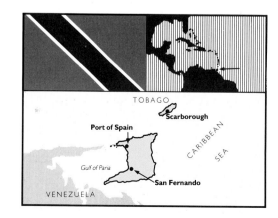

Capital: Port of Spain 51 000 (1990 census)

Languages: English (official), Hindu (25%)

Religions: Roman Catholic (34%), Hinduism (25%), Anglican (15%), Sunni Islam (6%)

GOVERNMENT

The 31-member Senate – the Upper House of Parliament – is appointed by the President, who is elected by a joint sitting of Parliament. The 36-member House of Representatives is elected for five years by universal adult suffrage. The President appoints a Prime Minister who commands a majority in the House. The PM, in turn, appoints a Cabinet, which is responsible to the House. Tobago has full internal self-government.

GEOGRAPHY

Trinidad is generally undulating, although the Northern Range rises to 940 m (3085 ft). Tobago is more mountainous.

Climate: Trinidad has a humid tropical climate, with a dry season from January to May.

ECONOMY

Petroleum and petrochemicals are the mainstay of the economy. Trinidad also has important reserves of natural gas and asphalt. Tourism is a major foreign-currency earner.

HISTORY

Trinidad was inhabited by Arawak Indians and Tobago by Carib Indians when Columbus discovered them in 1498. Trinidad was neglected by Spain and became British in 1797. Tobago was claimed by the Spanish, Dutch and French before being ceded to Britain in 1802. African slaves were imported to work sugar plantations, but after the abolition of slavery in the 1830s, labourers came from India. The islands merged as a single colony in 1899 and gained independence in 1962 under Dr Eric Williams. His moderate policies brought economic benefits but provoked a Black Power revolt and an army mutiny in 1970. The country has been a republic since 1976. In 1990 a small group of Islamic fundamentalists attempted a coup.

TUNISIA

Official name: Al-Jumhuriya at-Tunisiya (Republic of Tunisia)

Member of: UN, Arab League, OAU

Area: 163 610 km² (63 170 sq mi)

Population: 8 293 000 (1991 est)

Capital and major cities: Tunis 1 395 000 (city 597 000), Nabeul (part of the Tunis agglomeration) 335 000, Sfax 232 000, Bizerta 95 000 (1988 est)

Languages: Arabic (official), Berber minority

Religion: Sunni Islam (official; 99%)

GOVERNMENT

The President and the 141-member National Assembly are elected by universal adult suffrage for a five-year term. The President appoints a Cabinet, headed by a Prime Minister.

GEOGRAPHY

The Northern Tell and the High Tell mountains rise to 1544 m (5066 ft) at Jabal ash-Shanabi. Wide plateaux cover central Tunisia. The Sahara Desert lies S of a zone of shallow salt lakes.

Climate: The N has a Mediterranean climate with adequate rainfall. The S has a hot dry climate.

ECONOMY

Phosphates and petroleum are the mainstay of the economy. The main crops are wheat, barley and vegetables, plus olives and citrus fruit for export. Tourism is a major foreign-currency earner.

HISTORY

The Phoenicians founded Carthage (near Tunis) in the 8th century BC, and the city built up an empire dominating the Western Mediterranean. After the Punic Wars

(see p. 376) Rome ruled the region from 146 BC until it fell to the Byzantine Empire in 533 AD. In 647 an Arab invasion won Tunisia for the Islamic world and for over 900 years the area was disputed by a variety of Muslim dynasties. From 1574 to 1881 Tunisia was part of the (Turkish) Ottoman Empire. In 1881 France established a protectorate, although the bey (monarch) remained the nominal ruler. Nationalist sentiments grew in the 20th century. Tunisia was occupied by the Germans (1942–43). Independence was gained under Habib Bourguiba (1903–) in 1956 and the monarchy was abolished (1957). In the late 1980s the regime became increasingly unpopular and intolerant of opposition. Since Bourguiba was deposed by his PM (1988) – because of 'incapacity' – multi-party politics have been permitted.

TURKEY

Official name: Türkiye Cumhuriyeti (Republic of Turkey)

Member of: UN, NATO, OECD, CSCE

Area: 779 452 km² (300 948 sq mi)

Population: 58 376 000 (1991 est)

Capital and major cities: Ankara 2 560 000, Istanbul 6 620 000, Izmir 1 757 000, Adana 916 000, Bursa 835 000 (all including suburbs; 1990 census)

Languages: Turkish (official); Kurdish (20%)

Religion: Sunni Islam (67%), Shia Islam (30%)

GOVERNMENT
The 450-member National Assembly is elected by universal adult suffrage for five years. The President – who is elected by the Assembly for seven years – appoints a Prime Minister and a Cabinet commanding a majority in the Assembly.

GEOGRAPHY
Turkey W of the Dardenelles – 5% of the total area – is part of Europe. Asiatic Turkey consists of the central Anatolian Plateau and its basins, bordered to the N by the Pontic Mountains, to the S by the Taurus Mountains, and to the E by high ranges rising to Ağridaği (Mount Ararat) at 5185 m (17 011 ft).

Principal rivers: Euphrates (Firat) 1900 km (1180 mi), Tigris (Dicle) 2800 km (1740 mi)

Climate: The coastal regions have a Mediterranean climate. The interior is continental with hot, dry summers and cold, snowy winters.

ECONOMY
Agriculture involves one half of the labour force. Major crops include wheat, rice, tobacco, and cotton. Both tobacco and cotton have given rise to important processing industries, and textiles are Turkey's main export. Manufacturing – in particular the chemical and steel

industries – has grown rapidly. Natural resources include copper and coal. Unemployment is severe. Money sent back by the large number of Turks working in Western Europe is a major source of foreign currency. Tourism is increasingly important.

HISTORY
The Hittite empire was founded around 1650 BC (see p. 364), and quickly gained control of all of Anatolia (present-day Turkey), spread to N Syria and later came into conflict with the Egyptians. By the 6th century BC (Persian) Achaemenid power was expanding into Anatolia (see p. 365). However, in 334 BC Alexander the Great crossed into Asia and destroyed the Achaemenid Empire (see p. 372). Anatolia was divided into several Hellenistic states until the Roman Empire took control of the area (133 BC). In AD 330 Emperor Constantine established the new city of Constantinople (now Istanbul), which became capital of the Byzantine Empire (see pp. 381 and 394–5).

In the 11th century the Muslim Seljuk Turks occupied most of Anatolia. In the 13th century the Seljuks were replaced by the Ottoman Turks, who by the end of the 14th century had conquered most of the Balkans. In 1453 the Christian Byzantine Empire fell with the loss of Constantinople, which became the Ottoman capital. Under Suleiman the Magnificent (reigned 1520–66), the (Turkish) Ottoman Empire extended from the Danube to Aden and Eritrea, and from the Euphrates and the Crimea to Algiers (see p. 393). However, from that time the empire began a long decline in military and political might and in extent. The Ottoman Empire came to be regarded as 'the sick man of Europe', and the future of the empire and its Balkan territories troubled the 19th century as 'the Eastern Question' (see p. 429). In 1908 the Young Turks revolt attempted to stop the decline, but defeat in the Balkan Wars (1912–13) virtually expelled Turkey from Europe.

Alliance with Germany in World War I ended in defeat and the loss of all non-Turkish areas. The future of Turkey in Asia itself seemed in doubt when Greece took the area around Izmir and the Allies defined zones of influence. General Mustafa Kemal (1881–1938) – later known as Atatürk ('father of the Turks') – led forces of resistance in a civil war and went on to defeat Greece. Turkey's present boundaries were established in 1923 by the Treaty of Lausanne. With the abolition of the sultanate (1922) Turkey became a republic, which Atatürk transformed into a secular Westernized state. Islam was disestablished, Arabic script was replaced by the Latin alphabet, the Turkish language was revived, and women's veils were banned.

Soviet claims on Turkish territory in 1945 encouraged a pro-Western outlook, and in 1952 Turkey joined NATO. PM Adnan Menderes was overthrown by a military coup in 1960 and hanged on charges of corruption and unconstitutional rule. Civilian government was restored in 1961, but a pattern of violence and ineffective

government led to a further army takeover in 1980. In 1974, after President Makarios was overthrown in Cyprus by a Greek-sponsored coup, Turkey invaded the island and set up a Turkish administration in the N (1975). Differences with Greece over Cyprus have damaged the country's attempts to join the EC, as has the country's record on human rights. In 1983 civilian rule replaced the military government. Since then Turkey has drawn as close as possible to Western Europe, although the emergence of Islamic fundamentalism in the late 1980s has raised doubts concerning Turkey's European identity. Since the dissolution of the USSR (December 1991) Turkey has forged economic and cultural ties with the former Soviet republics of Central Asia, most of which are Turkic in language and tradition. Following the exodus of Iraqi Kurdish refugees into Turkey (1991), unrest among Turkey's ethnic Kurds intensified.

TURKMENISTAN

Official name: Tiurkmenostan (Turkmenistan)

Member of: UN, CIS, CSCE

Area: 488 100 km² (188 500 sq mi)

Population: 3 714 000 (1991 est)

Capital and major cities: Ashkabad 411 000, Chardzhou 166 000 (1989 census)

Languages: Turkmen (72%), Russian (9%), Uzbek (9%)

Religions: Sunni Islam majority

GOVERNMENT
A legislature and a President are elected by universal adult suffrage for four years. A new constitution is to be drafted.

GEOGRAPHY
The sandy Kara-Kum Desert occupies the centre of the republic, over 90% of which is desert. The Kopet Dag mountains form the border with Iran.

Climate: Turkmenistan has a continental climate characterized by hot summers, freezing winters and very low precipitation.

ECONOMY
Turkmenistan is rich in oil and natural gas. Industries include engineering, metal processing and textiles. Collective farms grow cotton under irrigation and raise sheep, camels and horses. The economy remains largely state-owned and centrally planned.

HISTORY
The Turkmens are a nomadic Turkic people who were nominally subject to Persia, or to the khans of Khiva and Bukhara (now both in Uzbekistan), before coming under Russian rule between 1869 and 1881. The Turkmens fiercely resisted the Russians and rose in revolt in 1916. An autonomous Transcaspian government was formed after the Russian Revolution (see p. 438), and the

area was not brought under Soviet control until the Red Army invaded in 1919. The Turkmen territories were reorganized as the Republic of Turkmenistan in 1924 and admitted to the USSR as a full Union Republic in 1925. Independence was declared following the abortive coup by Communist hardliners in Moscow (September 1991), and the republic received international recognition when the USSR was dissolved (December 1991).

TUVALU

Member of: Commonwealth (special member)

Area: 26 km² (10 sq mi)

Population: 9300 (1991 est)

Capital: Fongafale on Funafuti atoll 2800 (1985 est)

Languages: Tuvaluan and English

Religion: Protestant Church of Tuvalu (98%)

GOVERNMENT

The 12-member Parliament – which is elected by universal adult suffrage for four years – chooses a Prime Minister who appoints other Ministers. A Governor General represents the British Queen as sovereign of Tuvalu.

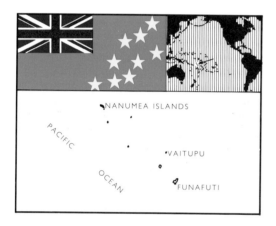

GEOGRAPHY

Tuvalu comprises nine small islands whose highest point is only 6 m (20 ft) above sea level.

Climate: Tuvalu experiences high temperatures and heavy rainfall – 3000–4000 mm (120–160 in).

ECONOMY

Subsistence farming – based on coconuts, pigs and poultry – involves most of the labour force. The only export is copra from coconuts.

HISTORY

Tuvalu was settled from Samoa or Tonga in the 14th century. Although the islands were sighted by 16th-century Spanish navigators, European settlement did not begin until the early 19th century. Claimed for Britain in 1892 as the Ellice Islands, the territory became linked administratively with the Gilbert Islands. A referendum in 1974 showed a majority of Polynesians in the Ellice Islands in favour of separation from the Micronesians of the Gilbert Islands (Kiribati). Independence was achieved as Tuvalu in 1978.

UGANDA

Official name: The Republic of Uganda

Member of: UN, Commonwealth, OAU

Area: 241 139 km² (93 104 sq mi)

Population: 16 583 000 (1991 census)

Capital and major cities: Kampala 773 000, Jinja 61 000, Mbale 54 000 (1991 census)

Languages: English and Swahili (both official), with local languages including Luganda

Religions: Roman Catholic (45%), Protestant Churches (17%), animist (32%), Sunni Islam (6%)

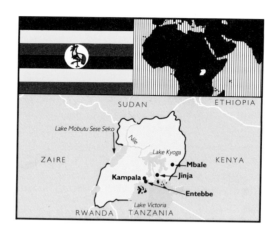

GOVERNMENT

The commander of the National Resistance Army – which took power in 1986 – is President. He appoints a Prime Minister and other Ministers. The advisory 278-member National Resistance Council comprises 210 indirectly elected members and 68 members appointed by the President.

GEOGRAPHY

Most of Uganda is a plateau. This ends in the W at the Great Rift Valley and the Ruwenzori Mountains, rising to Ngaliema at 5118 m (16 763 ft). Lake Victoria covers SE Uganda.

Principal river: Nile 6648 km (4132 mi)

Climate: Uganda's tropical climate is moderated by its altitude.

ECONOMY

Agriculture involves over 75% of the labour force; coffee accounts for 90% of Uganda's exports. Subsistence crops include plantains, cassava and sweet potatoes.

HISTORY

The British protectorate of Uganda – established in 1894 – was built around the powerful African kingdom of Buganda, whose continuing special status contributed to the disunity that has plagued the country since independence in 1962. Dr Milton Obote, who suppressed the Buganda monarchy in 1966, was overthrown in a coup by General Idi Amin in 1971. Amin earned international criticism when political and human rights were curtailed, opponents of the regime were murdered and the Asian population was expelled. The army took over in 1979, supported by Tanzanian troops. Obote was restored but was ousted in a military coup in 1985, since when instability and guerrilla action have continued.

UKRAINE

Official name: Ukraina (The Ukraine)

Member of: UN, CIS, CSCE

Area: 603 700 km² (233 100 sq mi)

Population: 51 944 000 (1991 est)

Capital and major cities: Kiev (Kyiv) 2 587 000, Kharkov (Kharkiv) 1 611 000, Dnepropetrovsk (Dnipropetrovske) 1 179 000, Odessa 1 141 000, Donetsk (Donetske) 1 110 000, Zaporozhye (Zaporizhia) 875 000, Lvov (Lviv) 767 000, Krivoy Rog (Kryvyi Rih) 698 000 (1989 census)

Languages: Ukrainian (73%), Russian (22%)

Religions: Ukrainian Uniat (Roman Catholic), Orthodox (Ukrainian Autocephalous and Russian)

GOVERNMENT

A 450-member legislature and a President – who appoints a Council of Ministers – are elected for four years by universal adult suffrage. A new constitution is to be drafted.

GEOGRAPHY

Most of Ukraine – after Russia, the largest country in Europe – comprises plains (steppes), interrupted by low plateaux and basins. The N includes part of the Pripet Marshes; the S is a coastal lowland beside the Black Sea and the Sea of Azov. Central Ukraine comprises the Dnepr Lowland and the Dnepr Plateau, the most extensive upland in the republic. Eastern Ukraine comprises the Don Valley and part of the Central Russian Upland. The most diverse scenery is in the W where an extensive lowland extends into Hungary and the Carpathian Mountains rise to 2061 m (6762 ft) at Mount Hoverla. The Crimean Peninsula consists of parallel mountain ridges and fertile valleys.

Climate: The Crimean Peninsula has a Mediterranean climate. The rest of Ukraine is temperate. Winters are milder and summers are cooler in the W. Snowfall is heaviest in the N and the Carpathians. Rainfall is moderate, usually with a summer maximum.

ECONOMY

Ukraine was known as the bread basket of the USSR. Large collectivized farms on the steppes grow cereals, fodder crops and vegetables. Potatoes and flax are important in the N; fruit farming (including grapes and market gardening) is widespread, particularly in the Crimea. Natural resources include iron ore, oil, manganese and rock salt, but the vast Donets coalfield is the principal base of Ukraine's industries. The Ukrainian iron and steel industry is almost as large as that of Russia. Other major industries include consumer goods, heavy engineering (railway locomotives, shipbuilding, generators), food processing, and chemicals and chemical equipment. Within the USSR, Ukraine had surpluses of electricity, cereals and many industrial goods. The first steps in privatization have been taken but the economy faces serious difficulties including rampant inflation and declining industries.

HISTORY

Greek colonies flourished on the Crimean coast from about the 7th century BC. The earliest known homeland of the Slavs is thought to be in the N foothills of the Carpathians in Ukraine from whence the E Slavs migrated towards the Dnepr valley during the first millennium BC. The state of Rus' – centred on Kiev – is the common ancestor of both Russia and Ukraine. It developed from the 9th century on the trade route linking the Baltic with the Black Sea. Its first princes were of Viking origin, though its population was largely E Slav. In AD 988, Grand Prince Volodymyr (Vladimir) of Kiev established Orthodox Christianity in Rus'. Kiev subsequently declined and was wrecked by the invasion of the Tatars (1237–41), but other powerful centres grew to the W in Galicia. These centres came under Polish rule in the 14th century when both Poland and Lithuania extended S and E into the steppes on their border (*u krajina*, on the border).

Polish influence increased in Ukraine, particularly after the formal union of Poland and Lithuania (1569), but Polish landowners and administrators were resented by the Ukrainians who were reduced to serfdom. In the 16th century, Poland encouraged the foundation in Ukraine of autonomous colonies of Cossacks – Slavic warrior-peasants who formed mercenary cavalry forces – to act as buffers against Tatar invasions. However, the Cossacks grew overstrong and challenged the Poles, most seriously in the 1648–51 rebellion when the Cossacks requested assistance from the Russian tsar. Two Russo-Polish wars followed and in 1660 Ukraine was partitioned between Poland and Russia. The Ottoman Turks occupied Polish Ukraine from 1672 to 1699. Tsarist Russia suppressed the autonomy of the Cossacks in 1775 and reunited most of Ukraine under Russian rule (1793) in the second partition of Poland. In 1876 Russia banned the use of the Ukrainian language in schools and in print. However, the Ukrainian nationalist movement continued in the more liberal atmosphere of Galicia in the W, which had been annexed by Austria in the first partition of Poland (1772). The Ukrainians in Russia took the opportunity afforded by World War I and the Russian Revolution to proclaim independence (January 1918), but a Ukrainian Soviet government was established in Kharkov. Ukraine united with Galicia when the Austro-Hungarian Empire collapsed (November 1918). The new state was invaded by Poland in pursuit of territorial claims and by the Soviet Red Army in support of the Kharkov Soviet. The Red Army prevailed and in 1922 Ukraine became one of the founding republics of the USSR, but the Lvov district of Galicia remained in Polish hands.

From 1928, Soviet leader Joseph Stalin instituted purges in Ukraine and a new programme of Russification. After World War II – when Ukraine was occupied by Nazi Germany – Soviet Ukraine was enlarged by the addition of Lvov (from Poland), Bukovina (from Romania), and Ruthenia (from Czechoslovakia), and, finally, Crimea (from Russia) in 1954. Ukrainian nationalism was spurred by the perceived Soviet indifference to Ukraine at the time of the nuclear accident at Chernobyl, N of Kiev, in 1986. Ukrainian politicians responded to the restructuring of the USSR in the late 1980s by seeking increased autonomy. The decision of the republic to declare independence following the abortive coup by Communist hardliners (September 1991) hastened the demise of the USSR. Ukraine gained international recognition in December 1991 when the Soviet Union was dissolved, but tension remained between Moscow and Kiev concerning the allegiance of Soviet forces in Ukraine, and the status of Crimea and the Black Sea fleet.

UNITED ARAB EMIRATES

Official name: Al-Imarat Al'Arabiya Al-Muttahida (The United Arab Emirates)

Member of: UN, Arab League, OPEC, GCC

Area: 77 700 km² (30 000 sq mi)

Population: 1 945 000 (1991 est)

Capital and major cities: Abu Dhabi 243 000, Dubai 266 000, Sharjah 125 000 (1985 census)

Languages: Arabic (official); English (commercial)

Religion: Sunni Islam (official)

Emirates: Abu Dhabi, Ajman, Dubai, Fujairah, Ras al-Khaimah, Sharjah, Umm al-Qaiwain

GOVERNMENT

The hereditary absolute rulers of the seven emirates form the Supreme Council of Rulers, which elects one of its members as President. The Prime Minister and Council of Ministers are appointed by the President. The Supreme Council appoints a 40-member advisory Federal National Council. There are no political parties.

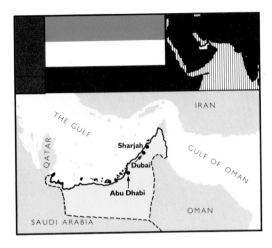

GEOGRAPHY

The country is a low-lying desert except in the E where the Jajar Mountains rise to 1189 m (3901 ft).

Climate: Summer temperatures exceed 40 °C (104 °F); winter temperatures are milder. Rainfall is very low.

ECONOMY

Based upon the export of offshore and onshore reserves of petroleum and natural gas, the country has one of the highest standards of living in the world. Dry docks, fertilizer factories, commercial banking interests, international airports and an entrepôt trade have been developed. Immigrants from the Indian subcontinent and Iran form the majority of the labour force. Agriculture is confined to oases and a few coastal sites irrigated by desalinated water.

HISTORY

The Gulf tribes were converted to Islam in the 7th century AD. When the Portuguese occupied some ports in the 16th century, the region was prosperous, but economic decline followed, coinciding with the (Turkish) Ottoman conquest. A political vacuum in the mid-18th century was filled by the British, who saw the region as a link in the trade route to India. Treaties ('truces') were signed with local rulers during the 19th century, bringing the Trucial States under British protection. In 1958 oil was discovered in Abu Dhabi. When the British withdrew in 1971 the Trucial States formed the United Arab Emirates.

UNITED KINGDOM

Official name: The United Kingdom of Great Britain and Northern Ireland

Member of: UN, EC, NATO, Commonwealth, G7, OECD, CSCE

Area: 244 103 km² (94 249 sq mi)

Population: 57 410 000 (1990 est)

Capital and major cities: London 7 797 000 (London Urban Area; Greater London 6 794 000), Birmingham 2 324 000 (West Midlands Urban Area; city 992 800), Manchester 2 310 000 (Greater Manchester Urban Area; city 446 700), Glasgow 1 650 000 (Central Clydeside Urban Area; city 689 200), Leeds-Bradford 1 547 000 (West Yorkshire Urban Area – Leeds 712 200, Bradford 468 800), Newcastle-upon-Tyne 762 000 (Tyneside Urban Area; city 277 800), Liverpool 659 000 (city 462 900), Sheffield 649 000 (city 525 800), Nottingham 615 000 (city 274 900), Bristol 530 000 (city 374 300), Edinburgh 523 000 (city 434 500), Brighton 471 000 (town 141 200), Ports-

mouth 453 000 (city 184 100), Belfast 441 000 (city 295 100), Leicester 407 000 (city 278 000), Stoke-on-Trent 371 000 (The Potteries Urban Area; city 246 700), Middlesbrough 368 000 (Teesside Urban Area; town 141 600), Bournemouth 353 000 (town 154 000), Coventry 333 000 (city 303 700), Cardiff 317 000 (city 287 200), Preston 316 000 (town 128 500), Hull 302 000 (city 245 300), Southampton 301 000 (city 197 400), Southend 291 000 (town 167 300), Swansea 284 000 (city 186 600), Blackpool 283 000 (town 139 100), Birkenhead 278 000 (town 99 000), Plymouth 253 000 (city 252 800), Rochester 244 000 (Medway Towns Urban Area; city 149 300), (figures are for urban areas – cities and their agglomerations – not for local government areas; 1990 est)

Languages: English, with Welsh and Gaelic minorities

Religions: Anglican (55% nominal; 4% practising), Roman Catholic (9%), Presbyterian (3%, including Church of Scotland), Methodist (2%), various other Christian Churches (4%), Sunni Islam (2%), Judaism (under 1%)

Countries of the United Kingdom (with areas, populations and capitals):
England – 130 441 km² (50 363 sq mi), 47 837 300 (1990 est), London.
Northern Ireland – 14 120 km² (5452 sq mi), 1 589 400 (1990 est), Belfast.
Scotland – 78 775 km² (30 415 sq mi), 5 102 400 (1990 est), Edinburgh.
Wales – 20 768 km² (8019 sq mi), 2 881 400 (1990 est), Cardiff.

Crown Dependencies associated with but not part of the UK (with areas, populations and capitals):
Guernsey and Dependencies (Alderney and Sark) – 75 km² (29 sq mi), 59 600 (1989 est), St Peter Port.
Isle of Man – 572 km² (221 sq mi), 70 000 (1991 census), Douglas.
Jersey – 116 km² (45 sq mi), 83 000 (1989 est), St Helier.

Dependencies (with areas, populations and capitals):
Anguilla – 96 km² (37 sq mi), 6900 (1989 est), The Valley.
Bermuda – 54 km² (21 sq mi), 60 000 (1990 est), Hamilton.
British Antarctic Territory – 1 810 000 km² (700 000 sq mi); no permanent population.
British Indian Ocean Territory – 60 km² (23 sq mi); no permanent civilian population.
British Virgin Islands – 153 km² (59 sq mi), 16 600 (1991 census), Road Town.
Cayman Islands – 259 km² (100 sq mi), 25 500 (1989 census), George Town.
Falkland Islands – 12 170 km² (4698 sq mi), 2100 (1991 census), Port Stanley.
Gibraltar – 6.5 km² (2.5 sq mi), 31 000 (1990 est), Gibraltar.
Hong Kong – 1045 km² (403 sq mi), 5 674 000 (1991 census), Victoria.
Montserrat – 98 km² (38 sq mi), 12 400 (1989 est), Plymouth.
Pitcairn Islands – 48 km² (18.5 sq mi), 52 (1990 est), Adamstown.
St Helena and Dependencies (Ascension and Tristan da Cunha) – 419 km² (162 sq mi), 7100 (1991 est), Jamestown.
South Georgia and South Sandwich Islands – 4091 km² (1580 sq mi), no permanent population.
Turks and Caicos Islands – 430 km² (166 sq mi), 12 400 (1990 census), Cockburn Town.

GOVERNMENT

The UK is a constitutional monarchy without a written constitution. The House of Lords – the Upper (non-elected) House of Parliament – comprises over 750 hereditary peers and peeresses, over 20 Lords of Appeal (non-hereditary peers), over 370 life peers, and 2 archbishops and 24 bishops of the Church of England. The House of Commons consists of 651 members elected for five years by universal adult suffrage. The sovereign appoints a Prime Minister who commands a majority in the Commons. (See also p. 267.)

GEOGRAPHY

The UK comprises the island of Great Britain, the NE part of Ireland plus over 4000 other islands. Lowland Britain occupies the S, E and centre of England. Clay valleys and river basins – including those of the Thames and the Trent – separate relatively low ridges of hills, including the limestone Cotswolds and Cleveland Hills, and the chalk North and South Downs and the Yorkshire and Lincolnshire Wolds. In the E, low-lying Fenland is largely reclaimed marshland. The flat landscape of East Anglia is covered by glacial soils. The NW coastal plain of Lancashire and Cheshire is the only other major lowland in England. A peninsula in the SW – Devon and Cornwall – contains granitic uplands, including Dartmoor and Exmoor. The limestone Pennines form a moorland backbone running through northern England. The Lake District (Cumbria) is a mountainous dome rising to Scafell Pike, the highest point in England at 978 m (3210 ft).

Wales is a highland block, formed by a series of plateaux above which rise the Brecon Beacons in the S, Cader Idris and the Berwyn range in the centre, and Snowdonia in the N, where Snowdon reaches 1085 m (3560 ft).

In Scotland, the Highlands in the N and the Southern Uplands are separated by the rift valley of the Central Lowlands, where the majority of Scotland's population, agriculture and industry are to be found. The Highlands are divided by the Great Glen in which lies Loch Ness. Although Ben Nevis is the highest point at 1392 m (4406 ft), the most prominent range of the Highlands is the Cairngorm Mountains. The Southern Uplands lie below 853 m (2800 ft). Scottish lowlands include Buchan in the NE, Caithness in the N and a coastal plain around the Moray Firth. To the W of Scotland are the many islands of the Inner and Outer Hebrides, while to the N are the Orkney and Shetland Islands.

Uplands in Northern Ireland include the Sperrin Mountains in the NW, the uplands in County Antrim, and the Mourne Mountains rising to Slieve Donard at 852 m

(2796 ft). Lough Neagh – at the centre of Northern Ireland – is the UK's largest lake.

Principal rivers: Severn 345 km (220 mi), Thames (with Churn) 346 km (215 mi), Trent-Humber 297 km (185 mi), Aire (with Ouse) 259 km (161 mi)

Climate: The temperate climate of the UK is warmed by the North Atlantic Drift. There is considerable local variety, particularly in rainfall totals, which range from just over 500 mm (20 in) in the SE to 5000 mm (200 in) in NW Scotland.

ECONOMIC ACTIVITY

About 20% of the British labour force is involved in manufacturing. The principal industries include iron and steel, motor vehicles, electronics and electrical engineering, textiles and clothing, and consumer goods. British industry relies heavily upon imports of raw materials. The UK is self-sufficient in petroleum (from the North Sea) and has important reserves of natural gas. The coal industry is declining as seams become uneconomic. As Britain is a major trading nation, London is one of the world's leading banking, financial and insurance centres, and the 'invisible earnings' from these services make an important contribution to exports. Tourism is another major foreign-currency earner. Agriculture involves about 2% of the labour force and is principally concerned with raising sheep and cattle. Arable farming is widespread in the E, where the main crops are barley, wheat, potatoes and sugar beet. Since the 1970s the UK has not experienced the same rate of economic growth as most other EC countries. Economic problems have included repeated crises of confidence in the value of the pound, credit squeezes and high rates of unemployment. Since 1980 most major nationalized industries have been privatized.

HISTORY

Pre-Roman Britain was inhabited by the Celts (see pp. 374–5). Julius Caesar invaded Britain in 55–54 BC, although wholesale conquest and Romanization did not occur until after AD 43. The Roman province of Britannia – covering the area S of Hadrian's Wall (see p. 378) – lasted until the 5th century AD. The Scots from NE Ireland invaded N Britain in the 5th and 6th centuries (see p. 396), and when their king also became king of the Picts (843) the foundations of a Scottish state were laid. From the 6th century Wales was divided into small kingdoms, which by the 12th century had been reduced to Gywnedd (in the N), Powys (centre) and Deheubarth (the S). The Anglo-Saxons first invaded England in the 5th century, and by the 7th and 8th centuries had established a fluctuating number of kingdoms (see pp. 396–7). Mercia and Northumbria were dominant until the rise of Wessex to supremacy in the 9th century, and in the 950s King Edgar of Wessex united England. However, from the 8th century Vikings raided the country (see p. 397), and, although partly repulsed by King Alfred in the 9th century, they established kingdoms in the E. After the short-lived Anglo-Danish kingdom of Cnut and his sons, the Normans invaded in 1066 (see p. 397).

The Normans established a strong centralized monarchy. At first England was just part of the Anglo-Norman state, but soon became the dominant force in an empire that included much of France. Throughout the Middle Ages England waged war to retain possessions in France (see pp. 400–401). Scotland came increasingly under English influence from the 11th century, and Edward I (reigned 1272–1307) attempted to dominate Scotland at a time of disputed succession. After the Battle of Bannockburn (1314), Scottish independence was asserted by Robert the Bruce (reigned 1306–29), whose grandson was the first Stewart (Stuart) king of Scotland. Henry II of England (reigned 1154–89) became overlord of Ireland in 1171, but English control of the N was limited until Protestant settlers arrived in great numbers in the 16th and 17th centuries. Wales was gradually absorbed by England, despite the attempt by Llywelyn II of Gwynedd to establish an independent Welsh nation in the 13th century.

In the Middle Ages succession to the English throne was often contested, most notably in the civil war between the Houses of York and Lancaster (the Wars of the Roses, 1455–85). The development of the English state was aided by the emergence of the Houses of Parliament, but conflicts between the Crown and overmighty nobles were common. In 1215 King John (reigned 1199–1216) was forced to grant considerable powers to the nobles. By the time Henry VII (reigned 1485–1509) seized the throne to establish the Tudor dynasty the numbers and strength of the nobility were diminished, and England was poised to emerge as a leading power. Under Henry VIII (reigned 1509–47) the English Reformation began (see p. 412). Under his daughter Elizabeth I (reigned 1558–1603) a religious settlement was achieved and the country's colonial history began when English explorers challenged Spain in the New World (see p. 413).

The succession of James VI of Scotland as James I of England in 1603 united the crowns of the two realms, although full integration did not occur until Scotland's Parliament was abolished by the Act of Union in 1707. Under Charles I (reigned 1625–49) the English Civil War (1640–60) was prompted by arguments over the precise nature of the Protestant religion to which his subjects should adhere, as much as by conflicts over parliamentary rights (see pp. 412–3). After the Commonwealth (1649–60), the restored Charles II (reigned 1660–85) attempted to establish an absolutist monarchy. The efforts of James II to reimpose Catholicism ended in his flight and the invasion of William (III) of Orange (reigned 1688–1702) in the Glorious Revolution (see p. 413). William III and his successor Queen Anne (reigned 1702–14) fought the ambitions of Louis XIV of France (see pp. 414–5), and an involvement in European wars continued after the (German) Hanoverian monarchs came to the throne in 1714. Colonial wars against the

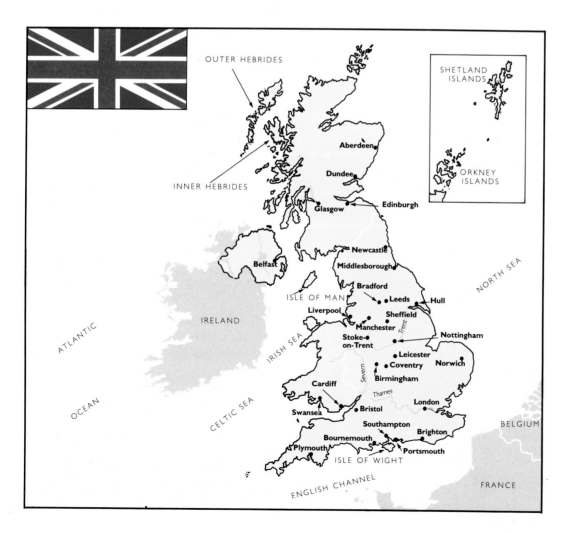

Dutch in the 17th century and the French in the 18th century (see p. 417) saw a notable expansion of the British Empire. The American colonies were lost in 1783 (see pp. 422–3), although Canada and West Indian islands were retained. As if to compensate for the loss, British interest turned almost simultaneously to India, where much of the subcontinent had come under the sway of the East India Company (see p. 417). The United Kingdom – formed in 1801 through the union of Great Britain and Ireland – fought almost continuous wars against Revolutionary and Napoleonic France (1789–1815; see pp. 426–7), and emerged from the wars with further colonial gains.

The reign of Queen Victoria (1837–1901) witnessed the height of British power. Britain – the first country to undergo an industrial revolution (see pp. 420–1) – dominated world trade. British statesmen – including PMs Sir Robert Peel (1788–1850), Lord Palmerston (1784–1865), William Ewart Gladstone (1809–98) and Benjamin Disraeli (1804–81) – dominated the world stage. The British Empire included much of Africa, the Indian subcontinent and Australasia (see pp. 432–3). Parliamentary democracy increased with the gradual extension of the right to vote, starting with the Reform Act of 1832. Representative government was granted to distant colonies, beginning with Canada and Australia, but was denied to Ireland, where nationalist sentiment was stirring. By 1900 Britain's economic dominance was being challenged by the USA and, more particularly, by Germany. Rivalry with Imperial Germany was but one factor contributing to the causes of World War I (see pp. 436–7). PM Herbert Asquith (1852–1928) led a reforming Liberal Government from 1908 to 1916 but – after criticism of his conduct of the war – he was replaced by David Lloyd George (1863–1945), who as Chancellor of the Exchequer had introduced health and unemployment insurance.

The 'old dominions' – Canada, Australia, New Zealand and South Africa – emerged from the war as autonomous countries, and their independent status was confirmed by the Statute of Westminster (1931). The Easter Rising in Ireland (1916) led to the partition of the island in 1922. Only Northern Ireland – the area with a Protestant majority – stayed within the United Kingdom, but in the 1970s and 1980s bitter conflict resurfaced in the province as Roman Catholic republicans – seeking unity with the Republic of Ireland – clashed with Protestant Loyalists intent upon preserving the link with Britain. British troops were stationed in Northern Ireland to keep order and to defeat the terrorist violence of the IRA.

In World War II (see pp. 444–5) Britain – led by PM Sir Winston Churchill (1874–1965), who had strenuously opposed appeasement in the 1930s (see p. 443) – played a major role in the defeat of the Axis powers, and from 1940 to 1941 the UK stood alone against an apparently invincible Germany. Following the war, the Labour government of Clement Attlee (1883–1967) established the 'welfare state'. At the same time, the British Empire began its transformation into a Commonwealth of some 50 independent states, starting with the independence of India in 1947 (see pp. 448–9). By the late 1980s Britain was no longer a world power, although a British nuclear deterrent was retained. By the 1970s the UK was involved in restructuring its domestic economy and, consequently, its welfare state – from 1979 to 1990 under the Conservative premiership of Margaret Thatcher (1925–). The country has also joined (1973) and has attempted to come to terms with the EC.

UNITED STATES OF AMERICA

Member of: UN, NATO, OAS, OECD, NAFTA, CSCE, G7, ANZUS

Area: 9 372 614 km² (3 618 770 sq mi)

Population: 252 177 000 (1991 est)

Capital and major cities: Washington D.C. 3 924 000 (city 598 000), New York 18 087 000 (city 7 323 000, Newark 275 000), Los Angeles 14 532 000 (city 3 485 000, Long Beach 429 000, Anaheim 266 000), Chicago 8 066 000 (city 2 784 000), San Francisco 6 253 000 (city 724 000, San Jose 782 000, Oakland 372 000), Philadelphia 5 899 000 (city 1 586 000), Detroit 4 665 000 (city 1 028 000), Boston 4 172 000 (city 574 000), Dallas 3 885 000 (city 1 007 000, Fort Worth 478 000), Houston 3 711 000 (city 1 631 000), Miami 3 193 000 (city 359 000), Atlanta 2 834 000 (city 394 000), Cleveland 2 760 000 (city 506 000), Seattle 2 559 000 (city 516 000), San Diego 2 498 000 (city 1 111 000), Minneapolis 2 464 000 (city 368 000, St Paul 272 000), St Louis 2 444 000 (city 397 000), Baltimore 2 382 000 (city 736 000), Pittsburgh 2 243 000 (city 370 000), Phoenix 2 122 000 (city 983 000), Tampa 2 068 000 (city 280 000), Denver 1 848 000 (city 468 000), Cincinnati 1 744 000 (city 364 000), Milwaukee 1 607 000 (city 628 000), Kansas City 1 566 000 (city 435 000), Sacramento 1 481 000 (city 369 000), Portland 1 478 000 (city 437 000), Norfolk 1 396 000 (city 261 000), Columbus 1 377 000 (city 633 000), San Antonio 1 302 000 (city 936 000), Indianapolis 1 250 000 (city 742 000), New Orleans 1 239 000 (city 497 000), Buffalo 1 189 000 (city 328 000), Charlotte 1 162 000 (city 396 000), Providence 1 142 000 (city 161 000), Hartford 1 086 000 (city 140 000), Orlando 1 073 000 (city 165 000), Salt Lake City 1 072 000 (city 160 000), Rochester 1 002 000 (city 232 000) (1990 census)

Languages: English (official), Spanish (6%, as a first language)

Religions: Roman Catholic (23%), Baptist (10%), Methodist (5%), Lutheran (3%), Judaism (2%)

US states (with areas, populations – 1991 est – and capitals):

Alabama – 133 915 km² (51 705 sq mi), 4 089 000, Montgomery.

Alaska – 1 530 693 km² (591 004 sq mi), 570 000, Juneau.

Arizona – 295 259 km² (114 000 sq mi), 3 750 000, Phoenix.

Arkansas – 137 754 km² (53 187 sq mi), 2 372 000, Little Rock.

California – 411 047 km² (158 706 sq mi), 30 380 000, Sacramento.

Colorado – 269 594 km² (104 091 sq mi), 3 377 000, Denver.

Connecticut – 12 997 km² (5018 sq mi), 3 291 000, Hartford.

Delaware – 5294 km² (2045 sq mi), 680 000, Dover.

Florida – 151 939 km² (58 664 sq mi), 13 277 000, Tallahassee.

Georgia – 152 576 km² (58 910 sq mi), 6 628 000, Atlanta.

Hawaii – 16 760 km² (6471 sq mi), 1 135 000, Honolulu.

Idaho – 216 430 km² (83 564 sq mi), 1 039 000, Boise.

Illinois – 149 885 km² (57 871 sq mi), 11 543 000, Springfield.

Indiana – 94 309 km² (36 413 sq mi), 5 610 000, Indianapolis.

Iowa – 145 752 km² (56 275 sq mi), 2 795 000, Des Moines.

Kansas – 213 096 km² (82 277 sq mi), 2 495 000, Topeka.

Kentucky – 104 659 km² (40 410 sq mi), 3 713 000, Frankfort.

Louisiana – 123 677 km² (47 752 sq mi), 4 252 000, Baton Rouge.

Maine – 86 156 km² (33 265 sq mi), 1 235 000, Augusta.

Maryland – 27 091 km² (10 460 sq mi), 4 860 000, Annapolis.

Massachusetts – 21 455 km² (8284 sq mi), 5 996 000, Boston.

Michigan – 251 493 km² (97 102 sq mi), 9 368 000, Lansing.

Minnesota – 224 329 km² (86 614 sq mi), 4 432 000, St Paul.

Mississippi – 123 514 km² (47 689 sq mi), 2 592 000, Jackson.

Missouri – 180 514 km² (69 697 sq mi), 5 158 000, Jefferson City.

Montana – 380 847 km² (147 046 sq mi), 808 000, Helena.

Nebraska – 200 349 km² (77 355 sq mi), 1 593 000, Lincoln.

Nevada – 286 352 km² (110 561 sq mi), 1 284 000, Carson City.

New Hampshire – 24 032 km² (9279 sq mi), 1 105 000, Concord.

New Jersey – 20 168 km² (7787 sq mi), 7 760 000, Trenton.

New Mexico – 314 924 km² (121 593 sq mi), 1 548 000, Santa Fe.

New York – 136 583 km² (52 735 sq mi), 18 058 000, Albany.

North Carolina – 136 412 km² (52 669 sq mi), 6 737 000, Rayleigh.

North Dakota – 183 117 km² (70 702 sq mi), 635 000, Bismarck.

Ohio – 115 998 km² (44 787 sq mi), 10 939 000, Columbus.

Oklahoma – 181 185 km² (69 956 sq mi), 3 175 000, Oklahoma City.

Oregon – 251 418 km² (97 073 sq mi), 2 922 000, Salem.

Pennsylvania – 119 251 km² (46 043 sq mi), 11 961 000, Harrisburg.

Rhode Island – 3139 km² (1212 sq mi), 1 004 000, Providence.

South Carolina – 80 582 km² (31 113 sq mi), 3 560 000, Columbia.

South Dakota – 199 730 km² (77 116 sq mi), 703 000, Pierre.

Tennessee – 109 152 km² (42 144 sq mi), 4 953 000, Nashville.

Texas – 691 027 km² (266 807 sq mi), 17 349 000, Austin.

Utah – 219 887 km² (84 899 sq mi), 1 770 000, Salt Lake City.

Vermont – 24 900 km² (9614 sq mi), 567 000, Montpelier.

Virginia – 105 586 km² (40 767 sq mi), 6 286 000, Richmond.

Washington – 176 479 km² (68 139 sq mi), 5 018 000, Olympia.

West Virginia – 62 758 km² (24 323 sq mi), 1 801 000, Charleston.

Wisconsin – 171 496 km² (66 215 sq mi), 4 955 000, Madison.

Wyoming – 253 324 km² (97 809 sq mi), 460 000, Cheyenne.

District of Columbia – 179 km² (69 sq mi), 598 000, Washington.

Commonwealth Territories in Association with the USA (with areas, populations and capitals):

North Mariana Islands – 471 km² (184 sq mi), 43 300 (1990 census), Chalan Kanoa on Saipan.

Puerto Rico – 9104 km² (3515 sq mi), 3 522 000 (1990 census), San Juan.

UN Trusteeship Territory

Palau (also known as Belau) – 497 km² (192 sq mi), 15 100 (1990 census), Koror.

External Territories

American Samoa – 197 km² (96 sq mi), 47 000 (1990 est), Pago Pago.

Guam – 541 km² (209 sq mi), 133 000 (1990 census), Agaña.

United States Virgin Islands – 352 km² (136 sq mi), 102 000 (1990 census), Charlotte Amalie.

Territories administered by US Department of Defense Johnston Atoll – 1.3 km² (0.5 sq mi), no permanent population.

Kingman Reef – 0.03 km² (0.01 sq mi), uninhabited.

Midway Islands – 5 km² (2 sq mi), no permanent population.

Wake Island – 8 km² (3 sq mi), no permanent population.

Howland, Baker and Jarvis Islands (administered by the US Fish and Wildlife Service) – 5 km² (2 sq mi), uninhabited.

GOVERNMENT

Congress comprises the Senate (the Upper House) and the House of Representatives (the Lower House). The Senate has 100 members – two from each state – elected by universal adult suffrage for six years, with one third of the senators retiring every two years. The 435-member House of Representatives is directly elected for a two-year term from single-member constituencies. Additional non-voting members of the House are returned by the District of Columbia, Guam, Puerto Rico, United States Virgin Islands and American Samoa. Executive federal power is vested in the President, who serves a maximum of two four-year terms. The President and Vice President are elected by an electoral college of delegates pledged to support individual presidential candidates – the college itself is elected by universal adult suffrage. Upon the approval of the Senate, the President appoints a Cabinet of Secretaries. Each of the

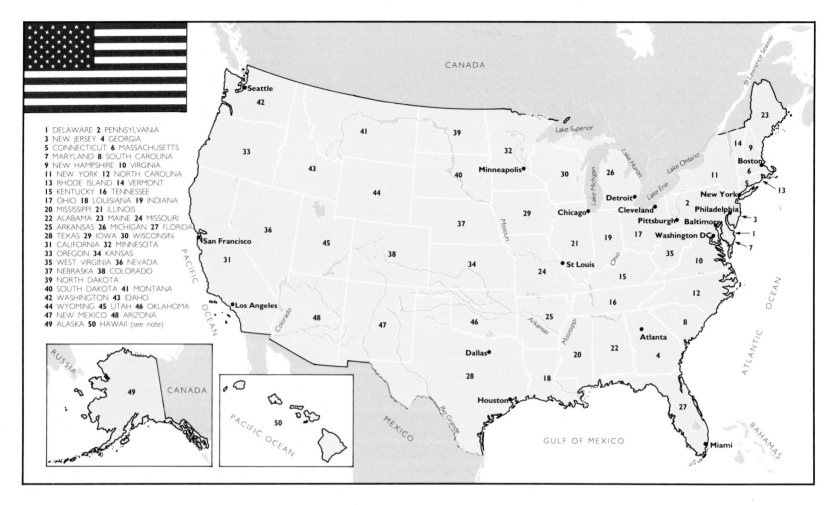

I DELAWARE 2 PENNSYLVANIA
3 NEW JERSEY 4 GEORGIA
5 CONNECTICUT 6 MASSACHUSETTS
7 MARYLAND 8 SOUTH CAROLINA
9 NEW HAMPSHIRE 10 VIRGINIA
11 NEW YORK 12 NORTH CAROLINA
13 RHODE ISLAND 14 VERMONT
15 KENTUCKY 16 TENNESSEE
17 OHIO 18 LOUISIANA 19 INDIANA
20 MISSISSIPPI 21 ILLINOIS
22 ALABAMA 23 MAINE 24 MISSOURI
25 ARKANSAS 26 MICHIGAN 27 FLORIDA
28 TEXAS 29 IOWA 30 WISCONSIN
31 CALIFORNIA 32 MINNESOTA
33 OREGON 34 KANSAS
35 WEST VIRGINIA 36 NEVADA
37 NEBRASKA 38 COLORADO
39 NORTH DAKOTA
40 SOUTH DAKOTA 41 MONTANA
42 WASHINGTON 43 IDAHO
44 WYOMING 45 UTAH 46 OKLAHOMA
47 NEW MEXICO 48 ARIZONA
49 ALASKA 50 HAWAII (see note)

50 states has a separate constitution and legislature with wide-ranging powers. Executive power in each state is held by a directly elected Governor.

GEOGRAPHY
The Atlantic coastal plain stretches along the entire E coast, including the lowland peninsula of Florida, and along the coast of the Gulf of Mexico, where it reaches up to 800 km (500 mi) inland. The Blue Ridge escarpment rises sharply to the W of the plain. This is the most easterly part of the forested Appalachian Mountains, which stretch for some 2400 km (1500 mi) and reach 2037 m (6684 ft) at Mount Mitchell. The largest physical region of the USA is a vast interior plain drained by the Mississippi and major tributaries, including the Missouri, Arkansas, Nebraska, Ohio and Red River. This lowland stretches from the Great Lakes in the N to the coastal plain in the S, and from the Rocky Mountains in the W to the Appalachians in the E. The Central Lowlands – the eastern part of the lowland – comprise the Cotton Belt in the S and the Corn (maize) Belt in the N. The Great Plains – the drier western part of the lowland – begin some 480 km (300 mi) W of the Mississippi. The W of the USA is the country's highest region and includes the Rocky Mountains in the E and the Cascades, the Sierra Nevada and the Coastal Ranges in the W. The mountains continue N into Alaska, where Mount McKinley – the highest peak in the USA – reaches 6194 m (20 320 ft). The western mountainous belt is prone to earthquakes, in particular along the line of the San Andreas Fault in California. Within the mountains are deserts – including the Mojave and the Arizona Deserts – and the large Intermontane Plateau containing the Great Basin, an area of internal drainage around the Great Salt Lake. The 20 islands of Hawaii are volcanic in origin and contain active volcanoes. The USA's natural vegetation ranges from tundra in Alaska to tropical vegetation in Hawaii, and includes coni-

ferous forest in the NW, Mediterranean scrub in S California, desert in the Intermontane Plateau, and prairie grasslands on the Great Plains.

Principal rivers: Mississippi (with Missouri and Red Rock) 6020 km (3741 mi), Rio Grande 3035 km (1885 mi), Yukon (with Nisutlin) 3185 km (1979 mi).

Climate: The mountains behind the Pacific NW coast are the wettest region of the USA. Coastal California has a warm Mediterranean climate. Desert or semidesert conditions prevail in mountain basins. The continental Great Plains receive 250–750 mm (10–30 in) of rain a year, while the Central Lowlands to the E are generally wetter. Extremes of temperature are experienced in the N of the continental interior. The E is generally temperate. The Appalachians and the E coastal plain are humid, with temperatures rising in the S where Florida is subtropical. Coastal Alaska has a cold maritime climate while the N and interior is polar. Hawaii has a Pacific climate with high temperatures and little seasonal variation.

ECONOMY
The position of the USA as the world's leading economic power is threatened by Japan. The USA is self-sufficient in most products apart from petroleum, chemicals, certain metals and manufactured machinery, and newsprint. Agriculture is heavily mechanized and produces considerable surpluses for export. The main crops include maize, wheat, soyabeans, sugar cane, barley, cotton, potatoes and a wide variety of fruit (including citrus fruit in Florida and California). More than 25% of the USA is pastureland, and cattle and sheep are important in the Great Plains. Forests cover over 30% of the country and are the basis of the world's second largest timber industry. The USA has great natural resources, including coal (mainly in the Appalachians), iron ore, petroleum and natural gas (mainly in Texas, Alaska and California), copper, bauxite, lead and silver,

and major rivers that have proved suitable for hydroelectric power plants. The industrial base of the USA is diverse. Principal industries include iron and steel, motor vehicles, electrical and electronic engineering, food processing, chemicals, cement, aluminium, aerospace industries, telecommunications, textiles and clothing, and consumer goods. Tourism is a major foreign-currency earner. Service industries involve over three quarters of the labour force. Finance, insurance and banking are important, and Wall Street (New York) is one of the world's major stock exchanges. US economic policy exerts an influence throughout the world, thus a revival of pressure for trade protectionism since the late 1980s has caused international concern.

HISTORY
The earliest human settlement in America was probably around 10 000 BC, when descendants of hunters from Siberia moved S. Nearly all the American Indians spring from this ancestry (see pp. 390–1). The Vikings may have reached Maine and even Cape Cod, but the first recorded European landing was by the Spaniard Juan Ponce de León in Florida (1513). After abortive attempts at colonization, continuous European settlement began in the 17th century. The Spanish settled in Florida (which they retained until the early 19th century); the French gradually took possession of a vast territory (Louisiana) stretching from New Orleans to the Great Lakes; Dutch colonists were active in New York (originally New Amsterdam); and a Swedish colony was founded in Delaware (1638–55). However, it was the British who gained mastery of the region.

The Virginia plantation, based on Jamestown, began in 1607, and in 1620 the Puritans (the Pilgrim Fathers) reached Cape Cod (see p. 422). By 1700 there were 13 British colonies on the eastern seaboard of what is now the USA. Throughout the 18th century discontent with British rule grew in the colonies, leading to the American War of Independence (1775–83). For details of the birth of the USA see pp. 422–3. The USA grew rapidly. The Louisiana Purchase (1803), from France, doubled the size of the country, taking its frontier deep into the Central Lowlands. Expansion to the W was part of the transformation of the USA from an underdeveloped rural nation into a world power stretching from the Atlantic to the Pacific (see pp. 430–1). As a result of wars against Mexico in the 1840s vast new territories were added to the Union – Texas, California, Arizona and New Mexico. Strains appeared between the increasingly industrial N and the plantation S over the issue of slavery. This led to the Civil War (see pp. 430–1) under the presidency of Abraham Lincoln (1809–65). The N was victorious, but after federal troops were withdrawn from the S (1877) racial segregation returned to the S until after World War II.

Between 1880 and 1900 the USA emerged as an industrial giant (see p. 431). At the same time, the population increased dramatically, as immigrants flocked to the New World, in particular from Germany, eastern Europe and Russia (see p. 431). Interest in world trade increased American involvement abroad. The Cuban revolt against Spanish rule led the USA into a war against Spain (1898) and brought US rule to the Philippines, Puerto Rico and Guam. American participation in World War I from 1917 hastened the Allied victory (see p. 437), but the idealistic principles favoured by President Woodrow Wilson (1856–1924) were compromised in the post-war settlement (see pp. 440–1). After the war the USA retreated into isolationism and protectionism in trade. The imposition of Prohibition (1919–33) increased smuggling and the activities of criminal gangs, but the 1920s were prosperous until the Depression began in 1929 with the collapse of the stock market (see p. 441). Federal investment and intervention brought relief through the New Deal programme of President Franklin Roosevelt (1882–1945). The Japanese attack on Pearl Harbor brought the USA into World War II (1941; see p. 444). American involvement in the European and Pacific theatres of war was decisive and committed the USA to a world role as a superpower in 1945. US assistance was instrumental in rebuilding Europe (through the Marshall Plan) and Japan.

From the late 1940s to the end of the 1980s, the USA confronted the Soviet Union's perceived global threat in the Cold War (see pp. 450–1). As the leader of the Western alliance, the USA established bases in Europe, the Far East and the Indian and Pacific Oceans, so encircling the Soviet bloc. The USA was involved in the Korean War (1950–53) against Chinese and North Korean forces (see p. 450), and in direct military intervention in Guatemala (1954), Lebanon (1958 and 1983–85), the Dominican Republic (1965), Panama (1968 and 1989) and Grenada (1983) (see pp. 450–1). The greatest commitment, however, was in Vietnam, where from 1964 to 1973 US forces attempted to hold back a Communist takeover of Indochina (see pp. 452–3), but a growing disenchantment with the war forced an American withdrawal.

From the 1950s the civil rights movement – led by Martin Luther King (1929–68) – campaigned for full political rights for Blacks and for desegregation of schools, hospitals, buses, etc. (see p. 291). In the early 1960s President John F. Kennedy (1917–63) made racial discrimination illegal. Kennedy supported the unsuccessful invasion of Cuba by right-wing exiles (1961) and was assassinated in 1963. Growing economic problems in the 1970s led to the election of a monetarist President, Ronald Reagan (1911–), in 1981. The USA continued to support movements and governments perceived as being in the Western interest – for example, backing Israel in the Middle East (see pp. 454–5), providing weapons to the UNITA guerrillas in Angola and the Contra guerrillas in Nicaragua, and leading the coalition against Saddam Husain's Iraq (1990–91). However, the increasing economic challenge from Japan, and the collapse of Communism in Eastern Europe (1989) and the USSR (1991), raised questions about the USA's future world role. From 1990–91 some overseas bases were closed and

stocks of nuclear weapons were cut. In 1992, American forces led relief efforts in Somalia.

URUGUAY

Official name: La República Oriental del Uruguay (The Eastern Republic of Uruguay)
Member of: UN, OAS, ALADI, Mercosur
Area: 176 215 km² (68 037 sq mi)
Population: 3 112 000 (1991 est)
Capital and major cities: Montevideo 1 312 000, Salto 80 000, Paysandú 76 000 (1985 census)
Language: Spanish (official)
Religions: Roman Catholic (58%), Protestant Churches

GOVERNMENT
The President and Congress – consisting of a 31-member Senate and a 99-member Chamber of Deputies – are elected for five years by universal adult suffrage. The President appoints a Council of Ministers.

GEOGRAPHY
Uruguay consists mainly of low plains and plateaux. Hills in the SE rise to over 500 m (1640 ft).
Climate: Uruguay has a temperate climate with warm summers and mild winters. Rainfall averages around 900 mm (35 in).

ECONOMY
Pastureland – for sheep and beef cattle – covers about 80% of the land. Meat, wool and hides are the leading exports. Despite a lack of natural resources, Uruguay has a high standard of living.

HISTORY
The Spanish landed in Uruguay in 1516, and for much of the colonial era Uruguay was disputed between Spain and Portugal. In 1808 independence was declared from Spain, but Uruguay had to repulse successive Brazilian and Argentinian armies (1811–27) before independence was achieved (1828). Until 1903 Uruguay was ruled by dictators and wracked by civil war. However, prosperity from cattle and wool, and the presidencies of the reformer José Battle (1903–7 and 1911–15), turned Uruguay into a democracy and an advanced welfare state. A military dictatorship held power during the Depression (see p. 441). By the late 1960s economic problems had ushered in a period of social and political turmoil, and urban guerrillas became active. In 1973 a coup installed a military dictatorship that made Uruguay notorious for abuses of human rights. In 1985 the country returned to democratic rule.

UZBEKISTAN

Official name: Ozbekiston (Uzbekistan)
Member of: UN, CIS, CSCE
Area: 447 400 km² (172 700 sq mi)
Population: 20 708 000 (1991 est)
Capital and major cities: Tashkent 2 079 000, Samarkand 388 000, Namangan 291 000 (1989 census)
Languages: Uzbek (71%), Russian (8%), Tajik (5%)
Religion: Sunni Islam majority

GOVERNMENT
A 500-member legislature and a President are elected for four years by universal adult suffrage. A new constitution is to be drafted.

GEOGRAPHY
Western Uzbekistan is flat and mainly desert. The mountainous E includes ridges of the Tien Shan and part of the Fergana valley.
Climate: Uzbekistan has a warm continental climate characterized by hot summers and low rainfall. Only the mountains receive over 500 mm (20 in) of rain a year.

ECONOMY
Uzbekistan is one the world's leading producers of cotton, but the extraction of irrigation from the Amu Darya and its tributaries has contributed to the gradual shrinkage of the Aral Sea. The republic has important reserves of natural gas and major machine and heavy engineering industries. The economy is still mainly state-owned and centrally planned.

HISTORY
The region was overrun by the Persians (6th century BC), the Arabs (8th century AD) and the Mongols (13th century), before becoming the centre of the empire of Tamerlane (Timur) and his descendants. The Uzbek khanates of Bukhara and Khiva were established in the 15th and 16th centuries respectively. Tsarist Russia first attempted to invade the region in 1717 but the Uzbeks did not finally come under Russian rule until the khans of Bukhara and Khiva became vassals of the Tsar (1868–73). After the Russian Revolution (see p. 438), the Basmachi revolt (1918–22) resisted Soviet rule, but the khans were eventually deposed (1920) and Soviet republics established (1923–4). Uzbekistan was created in 1924 when the boundaries of Soviet Central Asia were reorganized. Independence was declared after the abortive coup in Moscow by Communist hardliners (September 1991) and international recognition was achieved when the USSR was dissolved (December 1991).

VANUATU

Official name: The Republic of Vanuatu or La République de Vanuatu

Member of: UN, Commonwealth

Area: 12 189 km² (4706 sq mi)

Population: 150 000 (1991 est)

Capital: Port-Vila 19 000 (1989 census)

Languages: English (official; 60%), French (official;
40%), Bislama (national; 82%), 130 local dialects

Religions: Presbyterian (33%), Anglican (30%), animist

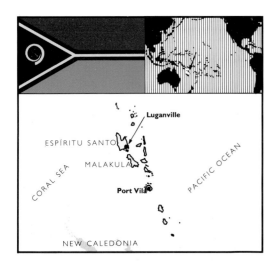

GOVERNMENT
The 46-member Parliament is elected for four years by
universal adult suffrage. It elects a Prime Minister who
appoints a Council of Ministers. The President is elected
for five years by Parliament and the Presidents of
Regional Councils.

GEOGRAPHY
Vanuatu comprises over 75 islands, some of which are
mountainous and include active volcanoes.

Climate: Vanuatu's tropical climate is moderated by SE
trade winds from May to October.

ECONOMY
Subsistence farming occupies the majority of the labour
force. The main exports include copra, fish and cocoa.
Tourism is increasingly important.

HISTORY
Vanuatu was settled by Melanesians around 2000 BC
(see p. 389). Discovered by the Portuguese in 1606, the
islands were charted in 1774 by Captain Cook, who
named the group the New Hebrides. British and French
commercial interests in the 19th century resulted in
joint control over the islands and the establishment of a
condominium in 1906. The islands gained independence
as Vanuatu in 1980, but have been troubled by attempted
secession and political unrest.

VATICAN CITY

Official name: Stato della Cittá del Vaticano (State of
the Vatican City). Also known as the Holy See.

Member of: CSCE

Area: 0.44 km² (0.17 sq mi)

Population: 750 (1989 est)

Languages: Italian and Latin (both official)

Religion: The Vatican is the headquarters of the Roman
Catholic Church.

GOVERNMENT
The Pope is elected Bishop of Rome and head of the

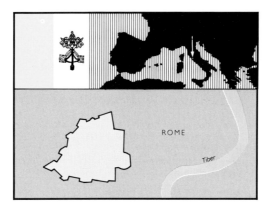

Roman Catholic Church for life by the Sacred College of
Cardinals. The Vatican City is administered by a Pon-
tifical Commission appointed by the Pope.

GEOGRAPHY
The state consists of the Vatican City, a walled enclave
in Rome, plus a number of churches in Rome (including
the cathedral of St John Lateran) and the papal villa at
Castelgandolfo.

HISTORY
The tiny Vatican City state is all that remains of the
once extensive Papal States. In 756 the Lombard king
ceded territory in central and N Italy to the Pope, who
became a temporal as well as a spiritual ruler. The Papal
States comprised Latium (the area around Rome),
Umbria, Marche and Romagna. The Papacy maintained
its temporal power despite numerous disputes with the
Holy Roman Emperors (see p. 399) through the Middle
Ages. For much of the 14th century the Popes resided at
Avignon in France, and from 1378 to 1417 – in the Great
Schism (see p. 399) – there were always two or three men
claiming to be the rightful Pope. The Papal States
reached their greatest extent under Pope Julius II
(reigned 1503–13), but by the 17th and 18th centuries the
Pope's temporal power was weak and his States were
poorly administered. During the Revolutionary and
Napoleonic Wars (see pp. 426–7), the Papal States were
variously annexed by neighbours and absorbed into the
French Empire (1798–1815). The Papal States were
restored in 1815, but all except Rome and Latium were
lost during Italian unification (1859–60; see p. 428).
When the French troops protecting the Pope were
withdrawn in 1870, Italian forces entered Rome, which
became the capital of the new kingdom of Italy. Pope
Pius IX (reigned 1846–78) protested at the loss of his
temporal power and retreated into the Vatican, from
which no Pope emerged until 1929, when the Lateran
Treaties provided for Italian recognition of the Vatican
City as an independent state. Since the 1960s the Papacy
has again played an important role in international
diplomacy, particularly under Popes Paul VI (reigned
1963–78) and John Paul II (1978–).

VENEZUELA

Official name: La República de Venezuela (Republic of
Venezuela)

Member of: UN, OAS, ALADI, Andean Pact

Area: 912 050 km² (352 144 sq mi)

Population: 20 226 000 (1991 est)

Capital and major cities: Caracas 3 436 000, Maracaibo
1 401 000, Valencia 1 274 000 (with suburbs; 1990 est)

Language: Spanish (official; 98%)

Religion: Roman Catholic (92%)

GOVERNMENT
The President and both Houses of the National Congress
are elected for five years by universal adult suffrage. The
Senate – the upper House – comprises 44 elected senators, plus former Presidents and additional senators to

represent minority parties. The Chamber of the Deputies
has 201 directly elected members. The President
appoints a Council of Ministers.

GEOGRAPHY
Mountains in the N – which include part of the Andes –
rise to Pico Bolivar at 5007 m (16 423 ft). Central
Venezuela comprises low-lying grassland plains (the
Llanos). The Guiana Highlands in the SE include many
high steep-sided plateaux.

Principal river: Orinoco 2736 km (1700 mi)

Climate: The tropical coast is arid. The cooler mountains and the tropical Llanos are wet, although the
latter has a dry season from December to March.

ECONOMY
As petroleum and natural gas account for 80% of export
earnings, the fall in petroleum prices in the 1980s
damaged Venezuela's economy. Agriculture is mainly
concerned with raising beef cattle, and growing sugar
cane and coffee for export; bananas, maize and rice are
grown as subsistence crops.

HISTORY
Venezuela was originally inhabited by Arawak and
Carib Indians. Although the first permanent Spanish
settlement was established in 1520, Spain did not Venezuela until the 17th century. In 1806 Francisco Miranda
(1752–1816) led a war of independence that was successfully concluded by Simón Bolívar (1783–1830) in 1823.
Initially united with Colombia and Ecuador, Venezuela
seceded in 1830. Independence was followed by a series of
military coups, revolts and dictators, including Juan
Vicente Gómez, whose harsh rule lasted from 1909 to
1935. Since General Marcos Peréz Jiménez was overthrown (1958), Venezuela has been a civilian democracy.
However, there have been two abortive coup attempts in
the 1990s as a result of economic uncertainty.

VIETNAM

Official name Công hoa xâ hôi chu nghia Viêt (The
Socialist Republic of Vietnam)

Member of: UN

Area: 329 566 km² (127 246 sq mi)

Population: 67 589 000 (1991 est)

Capital and major cities: Hanoi 3 057 000 (city
1 089 000), Ho Chi Minh City (formerly Saigon) 3 934 000
(city 3 169 000), Haiphong 1 448 000 (city 456 000) (1989
census)

Language: Vietnamese (official; 84%), Tay, Khmer

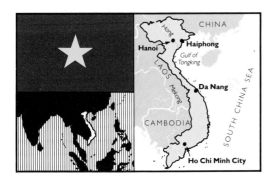

Religions: Buddhist (55%), Roman Catholic (7%), Cao Dai (3%), Buddhist minority

GOVERNMENT

The 496-member National Assembly is elected by universal adult suffrage for five years. The Assembly elects, from its own members, a Council of State – whose Chairman is head of state – and a Council of Ministers, headed by a Prime Minister. Effective power is in the hands of the Communist Party, the only legal party.

GEOGRAPHY

Plateaux, hill country and chains of mountains in Annam (central Vietnam) lie between the Mekong River delta in the S and the Red River (Hongha) delta in the N. The highest point is Fan si Pan (3142 m/10 308 ft).

Principal river: Mekong 4350 km (2702 mi)

Climate: Vietnam has a hot humid climate, although winters are cool in the N. Heavy rainfall comes mainly during the monsoon season from April to October.

ECONOMY

Over three quarters of the labour force is involved in agriculture, mainly cultivating rice. Other crops include cassava, maize and sweet potatoes for domestic consumption, and rubber, tea and coffee for export. Natural resources include coal, phosphates and tin, which are the basis of industries in the N. The wars in Vietnam, involvement in Cambodia and the loss of skilled workers through emigration have all had a serious effect on the economy. Despite aid from the USSR and the Eastern bloc up to the end of the 1980s, Vietnam remains underdeveloped. Attempts have been made to encourage Western investment since 1989–90.

HISTORY

Tonkin (the N of Vietnam) and Annam (the centre) broke free of Chinese rule in 939 and, apart from a brief reconquest (1407–28), these areas formed an independent Vietnamese state until 1757. In 1802 Nguyen Anh united Tonkin, Annam and Cochin-China (the S), and made himself emperor of Vietnam. The French intervened in the area from the 1860s, established a protectorate in Vietnam in 1883 and formed the Union of Indochina – including Cambodia and Laos – in 1887. Revolts against colonial rule in the 1930s marked the start of a period of war and occupation that lasted for over 40 years. For the history of the Japanese occupation during World War II, the war against French colonial forces (1946–54), the partition (1954) into a Communist state in the N and a pro-Western state in the S, the Vietnam War and US involvement (1964–73), see pp. 452–3. Since the Communist takeover of the S (1975) and the reunification of Vietnam, reconstruction has been hindered by a border war with China (1979) and the occupation of Cambodia (1979–89) by Vietnamese forces. Lack of Western aid and investment has hindered economic development, and this, combined with political repression, led to large numbers of refugees (the 'Boat People') fleeing Vietnam.

WESTERN SAMOA

Official name: The Independent State of Western Samoa

Member of: UN, Commonwealth

Area: 2831 km² (1093 sq mi)

Population: 160 000 (1991 census)

Capital: Apia 33 000 (1991 census)

Languages: English and Samoan (official)

Religions: Congregational (47%), Roman Catholic

GOVERNMENT

The Legislative Assembly comprises 45 members elected for three years by universal adult suffrage and 2 members elected by non-Samoan citizens. The current head of state is analogous to a constitutional monarch, but future heads of state will be elected for a five-year term by the Assembly. The head of state appoints a Prime Minister who, in turn, appoints a Council of Ministers.

GEOGRAPHY

The country consists of seven small islands and two larger and higher volcanic islands.

Climate: The islands have a tropical climate with high temperatures and very heavy rainfall.

ECONOMY

The majority of Samoans are involved in subsistence agriculture. Copra (from coconuts), cocoa and bananas are the main exports.

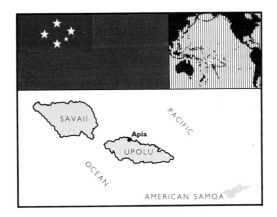

HISTORY

Samoa was settled by Polynesians about 300 BC (see p. 389). From the 1870s the USA, UK and Germany became active in Samoa. In 1899 the three rival powers divided the group, giving the western islands to Germany. New Zealand occupied the German islands in 1914, and administered Western Samoa until independence in 1962. A large proportion of the economically active population has emigrated to New Zealand.

YEMEN

Official name: Al-Jamhuriya al-Yamaniya (Republic of Yemen)

Member of: UN, Arab League

Area: 531 870 km² (205 360 sq mi)

Population: 11 843 000 (1991 est)

Capital and major cities: Sana'a 427 000, Aden 318 000, Taiz 178 000 (1986 est)

Language: Arabic (official)

Religions: Sunni Islam (54%), Shia Islam (46%)

GOVERNMENT

A transitional five-member Presidential Council holds office. A 301-member House of Representatives – comprising the parliaments of the former North and South Yemen plus additional members chosen by the Council – is drafting a new constitution.

GEOGRAPHY

The Yemen Highlands rise from a narrow coastal plain to 3760 m (12 336 ft) at Jebel Hadhar. An arid plateau in the E extends into the Arabian Desert.

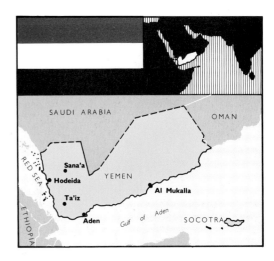

Climate: Most of the highlands have a temperate climate, but the rest of the country is hot and dry.

ECONOMY

Cereal crops, coffee and citrus fruit are grown under irrigation in the fertile highlands. In the S, subsistence farming and fishing occupy the majority of the labour force. Money sent back by Yemenis working in Saudi Arabia is an important source of revenue.

HISTORY

From the 8th to the 1st century BC the N was the home of the Sabaeans. In AD 628 the area became Islamic. The Ottoman Turks first occupied the area in 1517 and were not finally expelled from the N until 1911, when Imam Yahya secured Yemen's independence. Britain took Aden as a staging post to India (1839) and gradually established a protectorate over the S. In 1963 an armed rebellion began against British rule in the S, which gained independence in 1967 after a civil war between rival liberation movements. A republican revolution broke out in the N in 1962, and from 1963 until 1970 a civil war was fought, with President Nasser's Egypt supporting the victorious republicans and Saudi Arabia supporting the royalists. Relations between North Yemen and Marxist South Yemen were difficult. The collapse of South Yemen's Communist trading partners (1989–90) undermined the country's weak economy, and the two countries merged in May 1990.

YUGOSLAVIA

Official name: Federativna Republika Jugoslavija (The Federal Republic of Yugoslavia)

Member of: UN (suspended)

Area: 102 173 km² (39 449 sq mi)

Population: 10 407 000 (1991 census)

Capital and major cities: Belgrade (Beograd) 1 555 000 (city 1 500 000), Novi Sad 260 000 (city 179 000), Niš 230 000 (city 176 000), Pristina 210 000 (1991 census)

Languages: Serbo-Croat (including Montenegrin; 80%), Albanian (13%), Hungarian (3%)

Religions: Orthodox (over 75%), Sunni Islam (12%)

Republics (with areas, populations and capitals):
Montenegro – 13 812 km² (5333 sq mi), 615 000 (1991 census), Podgorica (formerly Titograd).
Serbia – 88 361 km² (34 116 sq mi), 9 791 000 (1991 census), Belgrade.

GOVERNMENT

Yugoslavia comprises two equal republics – Serbia and Montenegro. A Federal Assembly and a Federal President – who appoints a Premier and a Cabinet – are elected by universal adult suffrage for four years. The republics have their own legislatures and governments with very considerable powers – the Serbian presidency has virtually assumed sovereign powers.

GEOGRAPHY

Ridges of mountains occupy the greater part of the country. The N (Vojvodina) is occupied by plains drained by the rivers Danube and Tisa. The Yugoslav coastline is now confined to a short stretch on the Adriatic in Montenegro.

Principal river: Danube (Dunav) 2850 km (1770 mi)

Climate: Coastal Montenegro has a Mediterranean climate; inland there is a moderate continental climate.

ECONOMY

Agriculture involves over one quarter of the labour force. Most of the land is privately owned. Major crops include maize, wheat, sugar beet, potatoes, citrus fruit and fodder crops for sheep. Industry – which is mainly concentrated around Belgrade – includes food processing, textiles, metallurgy, motor vehicles and consumer goods. The country's economy was severely damaged by the wars that began in 1991, by rampant inflation (over 20 000% in 1992) and an international embargo on trade with Serbia and Montenegro.

HISTORY

The Slav ancestors of the Serbs arrived in the W Balkans in the 6th and 7th centuries AD. In the 12th century, the Serbs created a large state and in 1345 Stefan Dušan declared himself emperor. The Serbian empire was destroyed by (Turkish) Ottoman conquest, symbolized by the battle of Kosovo in 1389. Only mountainous Montenegro managed to preserve any autonomy. Led by Karadjordje, the Serbs rose against Turkish rule between 1804 and 1813. Under his rival Miloš Obrenović, the Serbs rose again in 1815 and became an autonomous principality, but Serbia was destabilized by rivalry between the Karadjordje and Obrenović dynasties. Both Serbia and Montenegro were recognized as independent in 1878 (see p. 429). By the beginning of the 19th century the Slavs within the Austro-Hungarian Habsburg Empire looked increasingly to Serbia to create a South ('Yugo') Slav state. After Serbia gained Macedonia in the Balkan Wars (1912–13; see p. 429), Austria grew wary of Serb ambitions. The assassination of the Habsburg heir (1914) by a Serb student provided Austria with an excuse to quash Serbian independence. This led directly to World War I (see p. 436) and the dissolution of the Habsburg Empire, whose South Slav peoples united with Serbia and Montenegro in 1918.

The interwar Kingdom of Serbs, Croats and Slovenes – renamed Yugoslavia in 1929 – was run as a highly centralized 'Greater Serbia'. The country was wracked by nationalist tensions, and Croat separatists murdered King Alexander in 1934. Yugoslavia was attacked and dismembered by Hitler in 1941, and Yugoslavs fought the Nazis and each other. The Communist-led partisans of Josip Broz Tito (1892–1980) emerged victorious in 1945,

and re-formed Yugoslavia on Soviet lines. Expelled by Stalin from the Soviet bloc in 1948 on account of their indiscipline, the Yugoslav Communists rejected the Soviet model, and pursued policies of decentralization, workers' self-management and non-alignment. However, after Tito's death in 1980, the Yugoslav experiment faltered in economic and nationalist crises.

In 1990 free elections were held throughout Yugoslavia. In June 1991 Slovenia and Croatia declared independence. Following reverses in a short campaign, federal forces were withdrawn from Slovenia, but Serb insurgents, backed by Yugoslav federal forces, occupied one third of Croatia including those areas with an ethnic Serb majority. In 1992 the fierce Serbo-Croat war came to an uneasy halt and a UN peace-keeping force was agreed. Croatia and Slovenia gained international recognition of their independence. When Bosnia-Herzegovina received similar recognition, Bosnian Serbs, encouraged by Serbia, seized 70% of Bosnia, killing or expelling Muslims and Croats in a campaign of 'ethnic cleansing'. Serbia was widely blamed for the continuation of the conflict and – with Montenegro – was subjected to UN sanctions. International efforts to end the conflict were attempted and humanitarian aid was supplied to Bosnian Muslims by the UN. Tension also rose in Kosovo province where Serbia forcefully resisted the separatist aspirations of ethnic Albanians.

Macedonia also declared sovereignty (1991). However, owing to Greek opposition to the use of the name Macedonia, it was unable to gain general recognition, although it is effectively independent (see below).

ZAIRE

Official name: La République du Zaïre (Republic of Zaïre)

Member of: UN, OAU

Area: 2 344 885 km² (905 365 sq mi)

Population: 34 964 000 (1991 est)

Capital and major cities: Kinshasa 3 741 000, Lubumbashi 710 000, Mbuji-Mayi 524 000, Kisangani 321 000, Kananga 303 000 (1991 est)

Languages: French (official); four national languages – Kiswahili, Tshiluba, Kikongo and Lingala

Religions: Roman Catholic (48%), various Protestant churches (28%), Kimbanguists (17%)

GOVERNMENT

The 222-member National Legislative Council is elected by compulsory universal suffrage for five years. The President – who is directly elected for seven years – appoints a Prime Minister and a Cabinet of Ministers.

GEOGRAPHY

Over 60% of the country comprises a basin of tropical rain forest, drained by the River Zaïre (Congo) and its tributaries. Plateaux and mountain ranges surrounding the basin include the Ruwenzori Massif in the E, rising to Mount Ngaliema at 5109 m (16 763 ft).

Principal river: Zaïre 4700 km (2920 mi)

Climate: Zaïre has a humid, tropical climate with little seasonal variation, although the N is drier from December to February.

ECONOMY

Over 65% of the labour force is involved in agriculture. Although subsistence farming predominates, coffee, tea and palm products are exported. Minerals are the mainstay of the economy, with copper, cobalt, zinc and diamonds accounting for about 60% of Zaïre's exports. Zaïre has one of the lowest standards of living in Africa.

HISTORY

The African Luba and Kuba kingdoms flourished from the 16th to the 18th centuries. The region was ravaged by the slave trade, and in 1885 became the personal possession of King Leopold II of the Belgians. However, international outrage at the brutality of the regime in the Congo Free State forced the king to grant the region to Belgium as a colony in 1908. As the Belgian Congo, the colony became a major exporter of minerals. The provision of social services, especially primary education, was relatively advanced, but the administration curbed almost all African political activity. As a result, the country was inadequately prepared when Belgium suddenly decolonized the Congo in 1960. Within days of independence, the army mutinied and the richest region – Katanga, under Moïse Tshombe – attempted to secede. The Congo invited the United Nations to intervene, but the UN force was only partly successful in overcoming continuing civil wars. Colonel Mobutu twice intervened and in 1965 made himself head of state. He renamed the country Zaïre, gradually restored the authority of the central government, and introduced a one-party state (1967). Mobutu's strong rule attracted international criticism. Following growing popular pressure, he was obliged to concede political pluralism and a national conference to bring democracy to Zaïre (1991). In 1992–93 conflicts erupted between Mobutu and the conference (represented by the PM), and law-and-order broke down in parts of the country.

ZAMBIA

Official name: The Republic of Zambia

Member of: UN, Commonwealth, OAU

Area: 752 614 km² (290 586 sq mi)

Population: 7 818 000 (1990 census)

Capital and major cities: Lusaka 870 000, Kitwe 472 000, Ndola 443 000 (1988 est)

Languages: English (official), Bemba (34%), Tonga

Religions: Various Protestant Churches (50%), animist (25%), Roman Catholic (20%)

GOVERNMENT

A President and the 150-member National Assembly are elected by universal adult suffrage for five years. The President appoints a Prime Minister and a Cabinet.

GEOGRAPHY

Zambia comprises plateaux some 1000 to 1500 m (3300 to 5000 ft) high, above which rise the Muchinga Mountains – reaching 2164 m (7100 ft) – and the Mufinga Hills.

Principal river: Zambezi 3540 km (2200 mi)

Climate: Zambia has a tropical climate with a wet season from November to April.

ECONOMY

Zambia's economy depends upon the mining and processing of copper, lead, zinc and cobalt. Agriculture is underdeveloped and many basic foodstuffs have to be imported. Maize and cassava are the main crops.

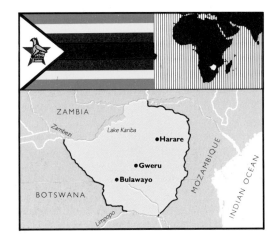

Member of: UN, Commonwealth, OAU

Area: 390 759 km² (150 873 sq mi)

Population: 9 619 000 (1991 est)

Capital and major cities: Harare (formerly Salisbury) 863 000, Bulawayo 495 000 (1989 est)

Languages: English (official), Chishona, Sindebele

Religions: Animist (42%), Anglican (30%), Roman Catholic (15%), Presbyterian

GOVERNMENT

The 150-member House of Assembly comprises 120 members elected by universal adult suffrage for six years plus 30 appointed and nominated members. The President – who is elected by Parliament for six years – appoints a Cabinet which is responsible to the Assembly.

GEOGRAPHY

Central Zimbabwe comprises the ridge of the Highveld, rising to between 1200 and 1500 m (about 4000 to 5000 ft). The Highveld is bounded on the SW and NE by the Middle Veld and the Lowveld plateaux. The highest point is Mount Inyangani at 2592 m (8504 ft).

Principal river: Zambezi 3540 km (2200 mi)

Climate: The climate is tropical in the lowlands and subtropical at altitude. There is a pronounced dry season from June to September.

ECONOMY

Agriculture involves over 65% of the labour force. Tobacco, sugar cane, cotton, wheat and maize are exported as well as being the basis of processing industries. Natural resources include coal, gold, asbestos and nickel.

HISTORY

The region was the location of the ancient Zimbabwe kingdom (see p. 388). The area was gradually penetrated by British and Boer hunters, missionaries and prospectors from the 1830s, and was occupied by the British South Africa Company of Cecil Rhodes in the 1890s. The highlands of what became Southern Rhodesia were settled by White farmers, who deprived Africans of land and reduced them to a cheap labour force. Britain took over the administration from the Company in 1923 and granted self-government to the White colonists. Immi-

HISTORY

The area was brought under the control of the British South Africa Company of Cecil Rhodes in the 1890s. In 1924 Britain took over the administration from the Company, but development of the colony (named Northern Rhodesia) was initially slow. Skilled mining jobs were reserved for white immigrants, and, fearing increased discrimination, Africans opposed inclusion in the Central African Federation, with Nyasaland (Malawi) and Southern Rhodesia (Zimbabwe) – in 1953. Against strong opposition from white settlers, Kenneth Kaunda (1924–) led Northern Rhodesia, renamed Zambia, to independence in 1964. Zambia was a one-party state from 1973 to 1990. In elections in 1991 Kaunda was defeated in the first democratic change of government in English-speaking Black Africa.

ZIMBABWE

Official name: The Republic of Zimbabwe

gration from Britain and South Africa increased after World War II, but the Whites remained outnumbered by the Africans by more than 20 to 1. Racial discrimination stimulated African nationalism, initially led by Joshua Nkomo (1917–). When the short-lived Central African Federation of South Rhodesia, North Rhodesia (Zambia) and Nyasaland (Malawi) was dissolved (1963), Britain refused the White South Rhodesian administration independence without progress to majority rule. The White government led by Ian Smith (1919–) unilaterally declared independence in 1965, renaming the country Rhodesia. Internal opposition was crushed and international economic sanctions were overcome, but guerrilla wars, mounted by African nationalists during the 1970s, became increasingly effective. In 1979 Smith had to accept majority rule, but the constitution he introduced was unacceptable either to the Zimbabwe African People's Union (ZAPU) of Joshua Nkomo or to the Zimbabwe African National Union (ZANU) of Robert Mugabe (1928–). All parties agreed to the brief reimposition of British rule to achieve a settlement. ZANU under Mugabe took the country to independence in 1980. In 1987 ZANU and ZAPU finally agreed to unite, effectively introducing a one-party state.

MACEDONIA (FORMER YUGOSLAV REPUBLIC OF)

Official name: (internal) Republika Makedonija; (temporary name for international use) The Former Yugoslav Republic of Macedonia

Member of: UN

Area: 25 713 km² (9928 sq mi)

Population: 2 034 000 (1991 census)

Capital and major cities: Skopje (Skoplje) 563 000, Bitola (Bitolj; formerly Monastir) 140 000 (all including suburbs; 1991 census)

Languages: Macedonian (67%), Albanian (20%), Turkish (4%)

Religions: Macedonian Orthodox (over 60%), Sunni Islam (nearly 25%)

GOVERNMENT

The 120-member Assembly and a President – who appoints a Cabinet and a Prime Minister – are directly elected for four years by universal adult suffrage.

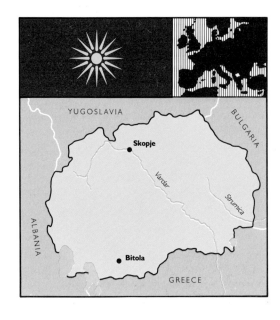

GEOGRAPHY

Macedonia is a plateau about 760 m (2500 ft) high, bordered by mountains including the Sar range which rises to 2753 m (9032 ft) at Korab. The central Vardar valley is the only major lowland.

Climate: The climate is almost continental, with warm summers and cold winters. There is heavy snowfall in winter.

ECONOMY

Macedonia was one of the least developed regions of Yugoslavia. The republic is largely agricultural, raising sheep and cattle and growing cereals and tobacco. Steel, chemical and textile industries rely, in part, upon local resources that include iron ore, lead and zinc. The economy has been severely damaged by a Greek economic blockade.

HISTORY

Macedonia is at a crossroads in SE Europe, between different peoples and religions. It has been disputed by its neighbours throughout much of its history and the problem of delineating boundaries through or around the region is known to historians and politicians alike as the Macedonian question. Ancient Macedonia – the kingdom of Philip of Macedon and Alexander the Great – was an Hellenic state whose centre was in northern Greece, although the southern part of the present republic was included in its boundaries.

The region came under Roman rule in 146 BC and became Christian in the 4th century AD. In the following centuries, the area was invaded by the Goths, Huns, Avars and Slavs. In the 8th and 9th centuries all of the present republic was overrun by Bulgarians and as part of Bulgaria for the most of the next 500 years it became thoroughly Slavic. Serbian intervention began in the 1280s but Serb rule was ended in 1371 by the (Turkish) Ottoman Empire. During Ottoman rule (1371–1912), Muslim Albanians settled in the W and the entire region suffered political and economic stagnation.

By the middle of the 19th century, nationalist stirrings in Macedonia's neighbours heralded the modern territorial dispute concerning the region. A revived Bulgaria claimed the entire region but Macedonia was partitioned following the First Balkan War (1912). Those areas with a Greek-speaking majority – the southern districts – were assigned to Greece and the remainder in the N was partitioned between Bulgaria and Serbia, the latter gaining the area comprising the present republic. Bulgaria continued to claim all Macedonia and occupied the region during World War I. In 1918 Serbian Macedonia – then called South Serbia – was incorporated within the new kingdom of Serbs, Croats and Slovenes, which was renamed Yugoslavia in 1929.

When Yugoslavia was reorganized on Soviet lines by Marshal Tito in 1945 a separate Macedonian republic was formed within the Communist federation. After Tito's death (1980), the Yugoslav experiment faltered and local nationalist movements arose. Following the secession of Slovenia and Croatia and the outbreak of the Yugoslav civil war (1991), Macedonia declared its own sovereignty. Despite fierce opposition from Greece, which objected to the use of the name 'Macedonia' and denied the existence of a 'Macedonian' people, the republic eventually gained international recognition in 1993.

INDEX

Notes:

1. Illustrations and maps are indicated by *italicized* numbers; there are also textual references on most of these pages.

2. When there are several page references for an entry, the major reference is shown in **bold** numbers, except where it is already italicized to show an illustration.

3. Sub-entries are in alphabetical order except where chronological order is more helpful.

4. The Countries of the World section (pages 660–739) has not been indexed in detail. Facts on history, geography, government and economy can be obtained by looking in this section.

5. Prefixes to Arabic names, such as el-, al- and ibn-, are ignored for purposes of alphabetization.

Aachen 394, 519
aardvark 145
aardwolf 153
abacus 65
Abbas I, Shah 511
Abbas, Abd Allah ibn 392
Abbasids 392, 510, 511, 616
abdomen 124, *126*
Abdullah, Amir 695
abiotic components 176
Aboriginals, Australian 389, 513
abortion 243, 293, 495
Aboukir Bay, battle of 426
Abraham 472, 478
absolutism 370, 379, **414–15**, **418–19**
    see also totalitarian regimes
absorption, wave 28
abstract art **549**, 554
absurd in literature 643, 644, 648
Abydos 507
abyssal plains *101*
abyssal zone *179*
Abyssinia see Ethiopia
Academies, French 60, 414, 596, 607, 626
acceleration 20, *21*, 22
accidents, industrial 244, 301, 305
accounting **282–3**
accumulators 36
acetate/acetone 320, 321
acetic acid 47, 52, 320, 321
Achaemenids 365, 367, 461, 506
achondroplasia 236
acid rain 49, 178, 300, 304
acids 36, 41, 47, 52, 320, 321
acorn worms 123
acoustics see sound
acoustic signals (animal) 166
Acropolis (Athens) 370, *509*
acrylic paint 501
actinium 42–3
Actium, battle of 373, 377, 378
Acts see law; statute law
acupuncture 250, 251
Adam 479, 625
Adam, Robert 535
Adams, Ansel 556
Adams, Eddie 654
Adams, John (b.1947) 581, 585
Adams, John Couch (b.1819) 15
Adams, Grantley 666
addax *161*
addiction 235, **246–7**
addition 64
additives, food *196*, **197**
Adenauer, Konrad 685
administration 267, 276
adolescence 294–5
    see also puberty
Adolphus, Gustavus 409, 723
adoration in prayer 480
adrenal gland/adrenaline *214*, 215, 232
Advent 475
advertising 246, 247, 554, 611
Aegean 505, 506, 571
aerobic bacteria 110
aerodynamics see flight
aeroplanes see aircraft
Aertsen, Pieter 527
Aeschylus 614
Aesculapius 462
Aesop *621*
aesthetics 492, 539, **640**, 641
aestivation 131, 132, 149, *171*
'affirmative action' 268

Afghanistan **660**
    history 366, 385, 429
        colonialism 385, 432, 433
        invaded by USSR 289, 299, 429, 451
    international relations 284, 285, 287
Africa
    agriculture 190–1
    animals 131, 135, 167, 170–1, *184*, *185*
        birds *113*, 138, *139*
        fish 128, 129
        mammals 140–1, 145, 148–61, 164, 165
    art and architecture 504, *509*, *516*, **517**, 547, 548
    climate and weather 103, *105*
    desert see Sahara
    and developed countries 298, 299
    diseases 236
    environment 300
    famine 296
    film 563
    fishing 194
    geology/geomorphology 78–9, 86, 87, 92, 93, 94, 95
    history
        Romans in 376, 381
        before colonial age 376, 381, **388–9**, 392, 394–5
        colonialism 389, 398, 405, 410, 416, 417, 432, 433, 637
        20th-Century 444, *445*, 448–9, *451*, 454
    human evolution 200–1
    industry 306, 310, *311*, 312, 313
    international relations 284, 287
    and Islam 478, 479
    language 608, 610
    law and crime 262
    in literature 649
    medicine 240, 249
    music 590, 592, 593, 595
    plants 184, 185, 187
    population 297
    religion 458, 459, 464, 465, 475, 477, 480, 481, *482–3*
    society 254, 255, 256, 259, *271*
    transport 346
    vegetation *104*
    women's suffrage 292
African Charter on Human and People's Rights 290
Aga Khan 479
age
    ageism 254
    mental 231
    roles and rites of passage **254–5**
    see also children; initiation; old people
agglutinative languages 602
Agincourt, battle of 401
Agra 511
agribusiness 189
agriculture **188–91**
    collectivized 439
    crops
        rotation 116, **188**, 189, 420
        see also cash crops; cereals; fruit
    and erosion 441
    failure see famine
    history
        ancient 374, 383, 386, 388, 389, 390
        Middle East 364, 366, *367*

    Neolithic 363, 382, 384, 389
    Medieval 403, *404*
    Revolution 188, **420–1**
    irrigation 95, *298*, 364, 366
    mechanized 420
    plantations *316*
    and plants 122, 182, 185
    and religion 462, 480
    subsistence 188, 296–7
    see also livestock; peasants
agoutis *150*
aid
    disaster 290
    foreign 286, 290, 297, 298–9, 450
    legal 265
AIDS 175, **213**, **239**, 245
Ainu people 386
air see atmosphere; oxygen; respiration
airborne infection 238, 239
aircraft **348–51**
    airships 48, *348*, 437
    carriers 343
    engines 309
    flying boat *349*
    hijackers *263*
    in wartime see under defence
Akbar, armies of *385*
Akhenaton 367, 460, 507
Akkadians 364, 460, 604, 612
ALADI 287
Alamein, battle of *445*
Alamogordo nuclear test 288
alanine 52
Alaric (Visigoth) 381, 693
Alaska 91, *154*, 163, 194, 300, 431
Albania 287, 603, **660**
    history 443, 450, *451*
albatrosses 136
Albee, Edward 645
Albers, Joseph 555
Albert, King of Belgium 667
Albert, Prince 539
Alberti, Leon Battista 525
Albigensians 398, 403
Albinoni, Tommaso 572
albumen 139
Alcaeus 614
alchemy 60, 470
Alcibiades 371
Alcock, Captain John 349
alcohol 40, 52, 196, 233, 321
    dependence **247**
    and disease 235, 237, 245
aldehydes 52
alders 181
Aldiss, Brian 651
Aldrin, Edwin 'Buzz' 18
Alea, Tomás Gutiérrez 563
Alemanni 380
Alexander the Great 365, 366, 367, **372–3**, 385, 462, 618, 737
    countries visited 660, 663, 686, 691, 727
Alexander I, II and III of Russia 715
Alexander, King of Yugoslavia 736
Alexander technique 251
Alexandria 341, 373, 509, 614, 679
Alexius I, emperor 398
Alfonso XIII of Spain 721
Alfred the Great 397, 606, 730
algae *110*, *118*, 145
    and symbiosis 99, 122, 123, 175
    see also lichen
algebra **64–5**, 392
Algeria 287, 449, **660–1**

Alhambra Palace 511
Ali (son of Muhammad) 392, 478–9
Ali, Mehemet 680
Ali, Tariq 295
alienation 642, 648, 649
alkalis 42
alkaloids 321
alkenes 52
allantois 134
allegory 509, 527, 620, **621**, 649
Allen, Woody 561
Allende, Salvador 673
allergies 238
Allies in World Wars see Britain; France; Russia (Soviet Union); United States
alligators 134–5
alliteration 620–1
allotropes 45
alloys 51, 305, 315
    see also bronze
alluvial mining 313
alluvium 87, 93
Almeida, Maria 596
almsgiving 478
alpaca 159, 190
alphabet see script
alpha–particles 39
Alpine ecosystems **186–7**
Alps 86, 87, 90, 141, *187*
    European 187
    history 362, 374, 376, 377, 378
Alsace 436, 440, 526
altarpieces 526, 527
Altdorfer, Albrecht 527
alternating current 36–7
alternative education 260, 261
alternative energy **306–7**
alternative family 237, 241
alternative medicine **250–1**
alternators 37
altitude 90
    altimeters 332
    and climate and temperature 77, 104, 105
    see also mountains
aluminium 42–3, 47, **50**, 54, 77, 300, 305, 312, 313
Amazon 94, 129, 131, 165, 482
ambiguities 225, 496
Ambrose of Milan, St 570
Amenophis III 507
American Samoa 731
American Sign Language 167
americium 42–3
Amerindians see Indians
Amiens, Peace of 427
Amin, Idi 728
amines and amides 52
amino acids 53, *110*, 116, 208, 209
Amish 477
ammonia 14, 15, **49**, 110, 116, 320
ammonites 123
ammonium sulphate 56
amnesia 223, 235
amnion 134
Amnesty International 291
amoeba *111*, 162, 174
    and diseases 210, 227, 238, 239
    in symbiosis 111, 174
    movement 172
Amorites 364, 612
Ampère, André 35, 61
amphetamines 246, **247**
amphibians **130–1**, 159, 169, 170, 173

migration 170
movement 173
amphisbaenids 134–5
ampicillin 57
amplifiers 329
amplitude 28, *29*
Amsterdam 533, 554
Anabaptists 477
anabolic steroids 215
anaemia 210, 236
anaesthetics 41, 56, 240, **241**, 247, *249*, 321
anal stage 232
analogue systems 26, 329
Analytical Cubism 548
anastomosis 240
Anatolia
    art and architecture **507**
    carpets 511
    history 364, *365*, 393
    languages 603
    literature 616
    modern see Turkey
    religion 461
anatomy 248, 249
    and evolution *112*
ancestors and religion 255, 464, 469, 470, 517
ancien régime *424*
Andean Pact 287
Anderson, Lindsay 562
Andes 86, 87, 186, *187*, 390
    Incas 391, 410, 516
Andorra **661**
Angelico, Fra 524
Angelopoulos, Theodor 562
angina 237, 241
angioplasty 241
angiosperms **120–1**
Angkor 384, 512
Angles 380, 396
Anglicanism 409, 412, 413, **475**, 477, 570
Anglo-Dutch Wars 416, 417
Anglo-Frisian languages 603
Anglo-Saxons 396, 519, 605, 606
Angola 287, 298, 432, 433, *451*, **661**
Angora goat 191
aorta 210, *211*
apartheid 259, 262, 291
Apelles 508
apes **165**, 167
aphasia 223, 227
Apollinaire, Guillaume 640
Appalachians 86, 185, 587
appeasement of Hitler 443
Appel, Karel 554
applications (computer programmes) 335
applied arts 538–9, 552–3
applied mathematics 62
Appomattox surrender 431
appreciation (economic) 279
Apuleius 615
aquatic environments 195
    see also freshwater; oceans; water
aquatint 502
aquifer 94
Aquinas, St Thomas 290, 487, *489*
Aquino, Corazon 267, 712
Arabia see Saudi Arabia
Arabic language 406, 478, 602, 609, **616**, 620
arable see agriculture

anion 44
ankylosaur *133*
Anne, Queen 413, 730
Anne Boleyn 412
annelid worms 122
annual plants 120
annulment of marriage 256
anodes 36, 37, 47, 50
Anschluss 443
Anselm, St 487, 489
antagonistic pairs 172
Antarctic 92
    animals 129, 131, 136, 137, 162, 171
    ice sheet 90
    ozone hole *301*
    plants *118*
anteaters 144
antechinus 143
antelope 141, 160, **161**, 171, 182, *184*
antenatal see pregnancy
anther *120*
Anthony, Susan B. 292
anthropoids 164
anthropology 254
antiballistics see missiles
antibiotics see under drugs
antibodies 211, **212–13**, 237, 238
anticyclones 103
antidepressants 235
antigens 212–13
Antigonid Empire 372
Antigua **661–2**
anti-imperialism see decolonization
anti-inflammatory drugs 207
antimony 42–3
Antioch 398, 509
antiparticles 4, 39
antirationalism 271
antisepsis 56, *241*, 249
antisubmarine warfare 289, 437
antlers **160**, 168
Antonescu, Ion 714
Antoninus Pius 378
Antonioni, Michelangelo 563
Antony, Mark 377
ants *126*, **127**, 166, 169, 175
anxiety 232, 233, **234**, 240, 250
Anzio, landing at 445
ANZUS Pact 287, *451*
animals 18, 93, 244, 306, 366
    amphibians **130–1**, 159, 169, 170, 173
    in art 504, *506*, 516, *517*, 521, 534
    arthropods **124–7**, 238
        see also insects
    biosphere 176–7
    classification 108–9
    communication **166–7**
    dinosaurs **132–3**, 140, 173
    domestic 151, 160, **190–1**, 244
    fibres from 125, 190–1, 318, 413, 416, 514
    migration 128, **170–1**, 181, 187
    primitive **122–3**
    territory and social organization 127, 139, 151, 153, 160, 166, **168–9**
    see also birds; ecosystems; evolution; fish; livestock; mammals; movement; parasitism; reptiles; reproduction; symbiosis
animated films 565
animism see spirits

Arabs 381
Arab League **287**
Arab-Israeli wars 287, 298, 451, *454*, 455
Empire *392*
and medicine 248
nationalism 448
revolt 437
ship *393*
see also Arabic; Islam; Middle East
arachnids **125**, 167, 172
Arafat, Yasser *287*, 455
Aragon 399, 410
Aramaeans 364–5
Aramaic language 475, 605
Arbenz, Jacob 688
Arbuckle, 'Fatty' 559
Arbus, Diane 557
archaeology 360, *361*, 362
archaeopteryx *133*, 136
Archilocus 614
Archimedes **23**, 60, **62**
architecture, history of
prehistoric 504–5
Middle East 506–7
Greek and Roman 508–9
Islamic 510–11
Southeast Asian, Australasian and Oceanic 512–13
Chinese and Japanese 514–15
American and African 516, 517
Medieval and Byzantine 518–19
Gothic 406, 522–3
Renaissance 524–5, 528–9
Baroque and Classicism 530–1
Rococo and Neoclassicism 534–5
see also art; cathedrals and churches; housing
Arctic 90, 517
animals 154, 160, 163, 171, 187
ecosystems 187
history 390, 391
people *see* Inuit
Arden, John 644
Argentina 185, **662**
animals 144, 158
dance 595
debt 299
film 563
fishing 195
human rights protests *291*
law 265
literature 649
argon *42–3*, 77
argument 494–5
aridity *see* deserts
Ariosto 625
Aristarchus of Samos 16, 60
aristocracy *see* nobility
Aristophanes 614
Aristotle
classification 108
literature 614, 624, 626, *652*
philosophy 372, 392, 487, 488, 489, 492
science/medicine 60, 248
arithmetic 64
Arkwright, Richard 318
Arlandes, Marquis d' 348
Armada, Spanish 411
armadillos 144
Arman (Fernandez) 555
Armat, Thomas 558
armed forces *see* armies; navies; wars; weapons
Armenia 603, **662–3**
history 372, 373, 395
religion 461, 477
armies
Akbar's *385*
American *423*, 431, 452–3
Assyrian *365*
British 401, 413, 422, *423*, 432, *436*, 436–7
Byzantine *394*
Cambodian 453
Chinese 446, 447
Chinese terracotta *382*, 514
Crusaders 398–9
Egyptian, ancient 367
English *see* British
French 401, 424, *426*, 427, 436–7
German 436, *437*, 440, 443
Greek 370, 373
Indian warrior caste 258
Japanese 387
knights *401*
Masai warriors 254
Mayan 391
Medieval *401*, 403
mercenary 396, 397, 449
Napoleonic *426*, 427
New Model 413
Norman *397*
Persian 365
Roman 376, 378, 380
Russian 417, 436–7
Saxon 396
Turkish *426*
United Nations 447, 449, 450
Vietnamese 452–3
armour *401*
arms (military) *see* armed forces; defence
arms (on body) *see* hands
Armstrong, Louis 588
Armstrong, Neil 18
Arnold, Matthew 652, *653*
Arnolto di Cambio 520
aromatherapy 250
aromatic compounds *52*
Arp, Jean (Hans) *550*
Arrest, Heinrich d' 15
Arretine pottery 509
arsenic *42–3*
Arsuf, battle of 399
art
and ballet 597
history **504–57**
Assyrian *365*
prehistoric 504–5
see also under caves
Middle East and Egypt 366, *367*, 506–7
Celts *374*, 375.
Greek and Roman 462, 508–9
Islamic 510–11
Southeast Asian, Australian and Oceanic 411, 512–13
Chinese and Japanese 382, 514–15
American and African *390*, 516–17
early Medieval and Byzantine 518–19
Gothic 520–1
Renaissance 524–5, 528–9
early Netherlandish and German 526–7
Baroque and Classicism 530–1
Dutch School 532–3
Rococo and Neoclassical 534–5, *626*
Romanticism 536–7, *632*, *633*
Realism 540–1, *634*, *635*
Impressionism and Neoimpressionism 542–3
Post-Impressionism 544–5
Symbolism, Sezession and Expressionism 546–7
Cubism and abstraction 548–9
Dada and Surrealism 550–1
movements since 1945 554–5
techniques **500–3**
therapy 235
see also applied arts; architecture; films; photography
Art Deco *553*
Art Informel 554
Art Nouveau 547, 552–3
Artaud, Antonin 643
arteries and veins 23, 207, 210, *211*, 237, 241, 242, 243
arthritis *207*, 213, 237, 240, 250
arthropods **124–7**, 238
see also insects
Arthur, King 396, *618*, 619
artificial insemination 190
artificial intelligence **336–7**, 609
artificial products *see* synthetic
artiodactyls 156, **158–61**
Arts and Crafts 539
Aruba 707
ARVN (Army of Republic of Vietnam) 452–3
Aryans 384, 467
asbestosis 237
Ascension Island 170, 731
Ascension of Jesus *475*
asceticism 466
ascidions 123
ascorbic acid 208, 244
ASEAN 287
asepsis 249
Ashanti *388*, 389, 432, 464
Ashcroft, Peggy *643*
ashes (trees) 189
Ashikaga family 386
Ashkenazi Judaism 473
Ashmore and Cartier Islands 663
Ashoka 385, 468, 512
Ashton, Frederick 596, 597
Ashur 364, *365*
Ashurbanipal 365
Asia
agriculture 191
animals 128, 129, 131, 138, *139*, *181*, *184*
mammals 140–2, 145, 146–7, 149–50, 163, 164
art and architecture *510*, 511, **512–15**
business organization 282
climate/weather 103, *105*
conflict 259
desert 186
economy 278
environment 300, 301
famine 296
film 562, 563
fishing 194, 195
food processing 196, 197
geology/geomorphology 78–9, 86, 87, *88*, *89*, 92, 93, *98–9*
health 245, *250*, 251
history
before colonial age 360–3, 366, **382–7**
colonialism 383, 385, 405, **410**, **416–17**, **432**, **433**
in 20th-Century *444*, 445, **446–7**, 448–9, 450, *451*, 452–4
human evolution 200–1
international relations 278, 284, 285, 287
law 263, 264
music 586, **590–1**, 592, 593, 599
nuclear weapons 288
plants 118, 180, 182
politics 268, 269
population 297
religion 458, 459, **466–71**, 475, 476–7, *480*
good and evil 484, *485*
primal 464
space and time 482, *483*
see also Buddhism; Confucianism; Daoism; Hinduism; Jainism; Shinto; Sikkhism
society 254, 255, 256, 258, 259
vegetation *104*
women's suffrage 292, 293
writing 604
see also individual countries
Asia Minor *see* Turkey
Asimov, Isaac 651
Asklepios 462
Asociación Latinoamericana de Integración *see* ALADI
aspirin *40*
Asquith, Herbert 731
ass 156, 191
Assad, Hafiz 724
assault 262
assemblies *see* National Assemblies
assets 279, 283
Assisi *476*, 521
association areas 223
Association of South East Asian Nations 287
associations
biological 174–5
social *see* international organizations
associative law 64
Assyria 16, 364, *365*, 367
art 506, 507
religion 460–1
Astaire, Fred 561, 595, 598
astatine *42–3*
asteroids 13, 14
asthenosphere *76*, **77**, *79*, 82
asthma 238
astrology 250
astronomy **4–19**
astronomical distances 5
history of **16–17**, *58*, 505
radio **332–3**
and scientific method 58
see also cosmology; planets; solar system; space exploration; stars; time
asylums *234*
Atatürk, Kemal 441, 727
Atget, Eugene 557
Athena 462, *508*, 509
Athens 266, 369, **370–1**
architecture *370*, *509*
education 260
literature 614
pollution 300
religion 462
see also Greece, ancient
athletes *see* exercise
athlete's foot 118, 175
Athos peninsula 509
Atlantic Ocean
animals 129, 137, 138, 162, 170–1
fishing *194*, 195
see also oceans
Atlantis 82
atmosphere
of Earth **23**, **77**, 102, 176, 300
see also climate
of planets 12, 13
pressure 23, 102
atomic bomb *see under* nuclear
atomic clock 7
atomic energy levels 26–7
atomic number 42
atoms 38–9
atonement 480
Attalos I and II of Pergamon 373
Attenborough, Richard 562
attenuation, wave 28
Attlee, Clement 731
Auden, W. H. 646
auditors 283
auditory *see* hearing
Augsburg settlement 408, 409
Augustan Age 535, **627**
Augustine, St (Canterbury) 396–7
Augustine, St (Hippo) 487
Augustulus, Romulus 381
Augustus, emperor 7, **377**, **378**, 463, 615, 627
'Auld Alliance' 400
Aung San Suu Kyi 706
Aurangzeb 385
Aurelian 380
Aurelius, Marcus 378
aurochs 161
aurora borealis and australis *11*
Auschwitz 445
Austen, Jane 632, 634, **636**
Austerlitz, battle of *427*
Austin, J. L. 497
Australia 286, **663–4**
Aboriginals 255, **389**, 482, **513**, 607
Antarctic Territory 663
agriculture 190–1
animals 129, 135, 138, *139*, 142–3, 146–8, 150, 158
art 504, **513**
climate *105*
dance 597
diseases 214
film 562
geology/geomorphology 78–9, 86, 89, 92, 93, 94, *97*, 99
government 267
history
early 363, **389**
colonialism 432, 433
20th-Century 437, 444, 449, *451*, 453
languages 603, *607*, 609
literature 649
plants 180, 181
religion 459, 464, 482
transport/travel 346, 347
vegetation *104*
weather 103
women's suffrage 292, 293
Australopithecus *200*, 362
Austria **664**
art and architecture 504, 546, 547, 552, 553, *578*
film 559
history
Crusades 403
Thirty Years War 409
and Spain 410
siege of Vienna *393*
Enlightenment 418
War of Succession 417
Napoleonic Wars 426–7
20th-Century 428, 441
see also Austria-Hungary
international relations 285, 286
literature 635, 641
music 585
Classical 574, 575
Romantic 576, 577
dance 594, 595, 596
Modernist 578, 579
transport/travel *340*
youth movements 294
Austria-Hungary (1867–1918) 394, 429, 436–7, 440, 441
see also Austria; Habsburgs; Hungary
Austronesian languages 602
authority 270
autocracy *see* totalitarian
autogyros 351
autoimmunity 207, *213*, 237
see also AIDS
automatic painters 551
automatism 554
automobiles *see* cars
autonomic muscle **207**, 221
autonomic nerves 221
autopsy 242
autotomy 135
autotrophs 110, 177
avalanches 87
avant garde
dance 598–9
literature 640–9
music 578–81
Avars 381, 395
Avataras 466
Aved, Jacques-André-Joseph *572*
Avercamp, Hendrik 532
Averroës 60, 392
Avery, Oswald 61, 114
Avicenna 60, 248, 392
Avignon 399, 403
avionics 349
avocat 265
axial tomography 332
axioms 62, 494
Axis powers 443, 444
axolotl *131*
Ayckbourn, Alan 644–5
aye-aye *164*
Ayer, A. J. 487, 489, 493
Azerbaijan **664–5**
Azores 715
Aztecs 316, **391**, 480, *516*

B cells **212**, 213, 238
Baader-Meinhof group 295
Baal *460*
Babangida, Ibrahim 709
Babbage, Charles 335
Babenberg family 664
Babenco, Hector 563
babies **202–3**, **204**, 233, 293
see also birth; milk; pregnancy
babirusa 158
baboons 165, 169
Babylonia 248, **364–5**, *365*, 367, 506
religion 460–1, 612
Bacchylides 614
Bach, Carl Philipp Emanuel 571, **573**
Bach, Johann Christian 571, **573**
Bach, Johann Sebastian 569, 570, 571, **572–3**, 574, 575, 577
bacilli 238
back problems 251
Bacon, Sir Francis (b.1561) 61
Bacon, Francis (b. 1909) 554
Bacon, Roger 60
bacteria *110*, *111*, 118, *174*
in digestive system *115*, 175, 209, 212, 238
and disease 110, 212, **238**, 239, 249
and genetic engineering 321
and immune system 212, 213
in soil 177
in symbiosis 111, *174*, 175, 212, 238
bacteriostats 238
Badem, Juan 563
Baden-Powell, Major-General Robert 294
badgers 155
'Badon, Mount', battle of 396
Baekeland, Leo 316
Baghdad 392, 510
Bahamas **665**
Bahrain **665**
Baird, John Logie *326*
bakelite 316
Bakst, Leon 597
Bakuba people 517
Balaclava, battle of 429
Balakirev, Mily 577
balance of payments 276, 278, **279**
balance of power 288–9
balance, sense of 224
balance sheet 283
balanced diet 208
Balanchine, George 597
Baldaccini, César 555
baleen 163
Balewa, Sir Abubakar T. B. 709
Balfour Declaration 454
Bali 592
Balkans, history of
ancient 362, 378, 381, 395, 505
recent 429, 436, 444, *445*
Ball, Hugo 550
Balla, Giacoma 548
Ballard, J. G. 651
ballet 578, 579, **596–7**, 598, 640
beginning of *593*, 596
ballistics 263, 288, 289
balloon angioplasty 241
balloons *348*
ballroom dancing 595
Baltic 417, 603
Balzac, Honoré de *634*, 639, 653
Bambara people 517
Band Aid 299
Banda, Hastings K. 701
Bandaranaika, Sirimavo 722
Bangkok *469*, 482, 725
Bangladesh *607*, **665–6**
banks **272**, 299, 404, 413
Bantus *388*, 389, *481*, 517, 602
baobabs 120
baptism 254, 255, *475*
baptisteries 518, 521, *524*
Baptists 475
bar mitzvah 255, 473, 480
Barbados **666**
barbarian invasions
of Britain *396–7*
of Rome 380, 381, 394
'Barbarossa' *see* Frederick I
barbiturates 247
Barbizon school 537, **540**
Barbuda **662**
Barca, Pedro de 622
Barcelona *552*
barium *42–3*
barley 188, **189**, 196
barnacles 124, 174
Barnard, Christian 240, 249
Baroque
art and architecture **530–1**, 539
music **572–3**, 574
literature 625
Barre, Muhammad S. 720
Barreto, Lima 563
barristers 265
Barrow, Errol 666
Barry, Charles 538
Barrymore, Lionel 559
barter 279
Barthes, Roland 610–11
Bartók, Béla 578–9, 586–7
Bartolommeo, Fra 528
Baryshnikov, Mikhail 597
basalt 77, 84
bases (chemical) 41, **47**
bases (numbers) 65
BASIC 334, 335
Basie, Count 589
Basil II, emperor 394
basilica *518*
basilisk 135
Basques 259, 603
bassoon 583
Bastille, storming of *424*
Batesian mimicry 167
batholith *85*
bathyal zone *179*
Batista, Fulgencio 677
bats 30, **146–7**, 171, 173, 175, 332
batteries *36*
battery hens *191*
Battle of Britain 332, **444**
Battle, José 733
battles *see* wars *and under* names of individual battles
Baudelaire, Charles 546, 631, **640**, 641
Bauhaus 553, 557
Bausch, Pina 599
Bavaria 428, *534*, *538*
Bay of Pigs 451
Bayer, Johann 17
beaches *96–7*
beaks 136, *137*, 139
beans 189
Beardsley, Aubrey 546
bearer stocks/shares 282–3
bears 141, 152, **154–5**, 169, 171, *187*
'Beat Generation' 295
beatific vision 480
Beatles *589*
Beatniks 295
Beauchamp, Charles Louis 596
Beaufort scale 103
Beaumarchais, Pierre-Augustin Caron de 627
Beaumont, Francis 623
beauty 536, 640
aesthetics 492
Beauvoir, Simone de 293
beavers *150*, 151
Beccaria, Cesare 418
Beckett, Samuel 641, *643*
Beckmann, Max 547
Becquerel, Henri 61

beeches 181
'Beer Hall Putsch' 442
Beerbohm, Max *639*
bees *121*, **125**, **126**, 127, 169, 171
communication 166, **167**
dance language 167
Beethoven, Ludwig van 569, 572, **574**, *575*, **576**, 580, 582, 583
opera 585
beetles 126–7
communication 167
behaviourism 491
Beiderbecke, Bix 588
Beijing (Peking) 673
architecture *470*, *471*, 514
history 383, 433, 446–7
massacre 295, 447
Beirut *263*, 455
Béjart, Maurice 598
Belarus **666**
el-Beled, Sheikh 507
belemnites 123
Belgian Congo see Congo; Zaïre
Belgium **666–7**
art and architecture 547, 552, 554
economy 278
government 267
history
17th to 19th centuries 421, 426, 433
20th-Century 436, 440, 444, *445*, 449
journalism 654, 655
Belgrade conference 287
belief 458
see also religion
Belisarius, General 394
Belize **667**
Bell, Alexander Graham 31, *330*
Bell family (Brontës) 636
Bellini, Giovanni **525**, 527, 529
Bellini, Vincenzo 585
Bellow, Saul 649
Belousov-Zhabotinsky reaction *47*
Belsen 445
Bembo, Pietro 624
Ben Bella, Ahmed 661
benefits see social security
Bengal 296, 603
Benin *388*, 389, *517*, 667
Benjedid, Colonel Chadli 661
Bennett, Arnold 637
Benois, Alexandre 597
Bentham, Jeremy 487, 493
Bentley, J. F. 539
Benz, Karl 352
benzodiazepines 235, **247**
Beowulf 618
Beqa'a Valley 455
Berbers *388*, 399
Berg, Alban **578**, 579, 585
Bergman, Ingmar 563
Berio, Luciano **580**, 585
Berkeley, Busby 561
Berkeley, George 487, 489
berkelium *42–3*
Berlanga, Luis Garcia 563
Berlin, Irving 588
Berlin
history *273*, 429, *445*, 450, *451*
Berliner, Emile 328
Berlioz, Hector *576*, 577, 580, 581, 582, 583
Bermuda 729
Bernadotte, Jean-Baptiste 723
Bernard of Clairvaux, St 399
Bernhardt, Sarah 559
Bernini, Gianlorenzo *531*
Bernstein, Leonard 588
Berri, Claude 562
Berry, Charles, Duc de 521
Berry, Chuck 589
Berryman, John 647
Bertolucci, Bernardo 563
Bertrand du Guesclin 401
beryllium *42–3*
Bessemer, Henry and process 315, 420, *421*
bestsellers 651
beta rays 39, 332
beta-blockers *57*
Beuys, Joseph 554
Bewick, Thomas *502*
Beyle, Marie-Henri 634
Bhagavadgita 466
Bhopal disaster 244
Bhutan **667–8**
Bhutto, Benazir 710
Bhutto, Zulfiqar Ali 713
Bible 364, 365, 408, **474–5**
and art 518, *533*, 537
Jewish *472*
myths 612, *613*
printed 322
Ten Commandments 262
translation **606**, 607
see also Christianity
biennial plants 120
big bang theory 4
big crunch theory 5
bilharzia see schistosomiasis
bills of exchange 272, 273
binary stars 9
binary system **65**, 334
Binchois, Gilles 570
Binet, Alfred 231
Bingham Canyon 312, *313*
binocular parallax 224
binomial classification 108
biodegradable plastics 317
biodiversity 301
biofeedback 251
biogas 306
biogeochemical cycles 177
biological weapons 289
biomass, energy from **306**
biopsy 241
biosphere **176–7**
Biot-Savart law 35
biotechnology 116, **320–1**
biotic components 176
bipedal movement 173
birches 180
birds **136–9**
communication 166, 167
early *133*, 140
in ecosystems *176*, 181, 185, 186, 187
evolution *113*
as food 146, 149, 363
migration 170, **171**
monogamous pairs *169*
movement 173
parasites on *174*
in symbiosis 175
territory, mating and reproduction 168–9
birds of paradise *139*
birth **202–3**, 207
control **203**, 213, 237, 292
religion and ritual 462, 473
birthmarks 241
Birtwistle, Harrison 585
Bishop, Maurice 686
Bismarck, Otto von **428**, 435, 685
bismuth *42–3*
bison 141, *161*, 185
bivalves 122
'Bizarre pottery' 553
Bizet, Georges 585
Black, Joseph 419
Black, James 57
Black Africa (history) *388*
Black Death *see* bubonic plague
black holes 8, 9
Black Panthers 291
black people 259, 291, 430, 431
see also slavery
Black Prince 401
black soils 185
Black Stone of Islam see Kaaba
Blackshirts 294, 442
Blake, William 537, *632*
Blanche, J. E. *641*
Blasis, Carlo 597
blasphemy 262
blast furnace *314*
Blaue Reiter, Der 547
bleach 320
Blériot, Louis 348
blind arcading 522
blindness 219
hysterical 235
'Blitz' 356, 444
Blok, Alexander 640, 647
blood **210–11**
cells 206, 210, *212*, 236
circulation 23, *210*, 211, 218, 241, 248
clotting 243, 321
and diet 208, 209
and disease 205, 236, 237, 238, 239
flukes 175
groups 240
and hormones 215
marrow 206, 212, 238
monitoring 242
and muscles 207
sucking 128, 147, 174
tests 245
transfusions and AIDS 213
blowouts, oil 310
Blücher, General von 427
Blue Mosque *510*
blue-green algae 110
blues **588–9**
boar, wild 158
'Boat people' 453
bobcat 153
Boccaccio, Giovanni 619, **620**, *621*, 624, 628
Boccioni, Umberto *548*
bodhisattvas 469, 485
body
language **228–9**
and mind 490–1
painting 504
scanning 30, 241, 242, *332*
see also diseases; humans, organism
Boeing *348*, 349
Boeotian Confederacy 371
Boers 389
Boer War 432, *433*
Boethius 615
Bogart, Humphrey 560
Böghazköy 364, 507
Bohdi Gaya 482
Bohemia 399, 403, 408, 409, 441
Bohr, Niels 38, 61
Bohras 479
Boileau, Nicolas 626, 652
Boise, Charles 200
Bokassa, Jean-Bédel 673
Boleyn, Anne 412
Bolívar, Simón 679, 734
Bolivia 246, 390, **668**
Böllstadt, Count von 60
Bologna University 248, 260, 406
Bolsheviks 268, 438, *439*
Bombay 689
Bomberg, David 549
bombers 289, *349*
bombing, aerial 443, 444–5
Bonaparte see Napoleon
Bond, Edward 644
Bondarchuk, Sergei 562
bonds (chemical) 40, **44–5**, 50
bonds (financial) 272
bones **172**, **206–7**, 215, *219*
amphibian 130
diseases and disorders 205, 206, *332*
evolution *112*
fish 128
minerals in 206, 208
tools 363
Bongo, Albert-Bernard 683
Bonnard, Pierre 544–5
books see literature
Boole, George 62
boreal forests 180–1
Borges, Jorge Luis 649
Borneo 690, 701
animals 147, 156, 165, 449
decolonization 449
Borobudur *512*
Borodino, battle of *427*
boron *42–3*
boroughs 404
Borromini, Francesco 531
Bosch, Hieronymous *526*, 551, 581
Bosnia-Herzegovina 429, 436, **668**
Boston 'Tea Party' 422
Boswell, James 627
Bosworth, battle of 412
Botany Bay 417, 664
Botha, P. W. 723
Botswana **668–9**
Botticelli, Sandro *501*, **525**
Boucher, François 535
Boudin, Eugène 541
Bougainville 711
Bougainville, Louis Antoine de 417
Boulez, Pierre 581
Boullée, Étienne-Louis 418
Boult, Sir Adrian 582
Boumédienne, Col. Houari 661
Bourbons 427
bourgeoisie see middle class
Bourges 401, 623
Bourguiba, Habib 726
Bournonville, August 596
Bouts, Dierick 526
Bouvet Island 711
bovids 160–1
'Bow Street Runners' 262
bowerbirds *139*
Boxer Rising 383, 433
Boy Scouts 294
Boyle, Richard, Earl of Burlington 535
Boyle, Robert 61
Boyne, battle of 413
Boys' Brigade 294
brachiosaur 132
Brahe, Tycho *16*, 17, 61
Brahmin caste 258
Brahms, Johannes 576, *577*, 587
brain 140, 206, **222–3**, 249
brainstem *221*, *222*
damage and disorder **223**, 235, 237, 491
development of 200, 201
glands in 214, 215, *222*
and learning **230**, 231
and mind 491
and muscles 207
section through *222*
and senses 216–17, 218, 223, 224, 226
and speech 226, *227*
Bramante, Donato 528
Brancusi, Constantin 549
Brando, Marlon 295, *561*
Brandt, Bill (photographer) 557
Brandt, Willy 299, 685
Braque, Georges *548*
Brasilia 553
brass instruments 583
Brassaï, André 557
Brassempouy 504
Braun, Wernher von 18, 309
Brazil **669**
art and architecture 553
debt 299
history 391, *410*, 416, 417, 432, 433
industry 306, 313
journalism 655
law 265
plants 193, 316
rubber 316
women's suffrage 292
see also Amazon
Brazza, Pierre de 676
break dance 593, 595, *599*
breasts 204, 214, 215
cancer 237, 245
breathing see respiration
Brecht, Bertolt *642*, 643, 644
breeding see reproduction
Brenton, Howard 644
Bresson, Robert 562
Brest-Litovsk 438
Brétigny, Treaty of 401
Breton, André 55
brewing *196*
Brezhnev, Leonid 715
bridges *341*
brit milah 254, 255
Britain **729–31**
animals 158, 191
art and architecture 527, 529
Medieval 519
Gothic 522–3
Baroque and Classicism 531
Rococo and Neoclassical 534–5
Romantic 536–7
19th-Century 538, *539*
Realism 541
Post-Impressionism 544
Symbolism 546
Cubism and abstraction 548–9
in 20th-Century 552, *553*
movements since 1945 554
business organization 282
calendar 7
economy/economics 272, *273*, 275, 276, 277, 278–9
fishing 195
geology/geomorphology 86, 87, 93, 99
government 266, **267**, 276, 277
health 245, 249
history
ancient 362, 363, 463
Romans in 378
invasions 396–7
Crusades 398, 399
Hundred Years War 400–1
14th-century crisis 402, 403
Medieval and Renaissance 404, 406, 407
Reformation 408, 409
and Armada 411
rise of 412–13
and Louis XIV 415
war with Holland *416*, 417
colonialism 389, **416–17**, 432, *433*
Asia 385, **432**, *433*, 447
and Industrial Revolution 420
language 607
and literature 637
North America 422, *433*
Civil War 413
Seven Years War 417
Enlightenment 418–19
Agricultural and Industrial Revolutions 420–1
wars with America 422–3, 430
Napoleonic Wars 426–7
Eastern Question 429
industrial society 434, 435
and Russian Revolutions 439
World War I 436–7
postwar settlement 440–1
and fascism 443
World War II 444, *445*
and decolonization 448, 449
in Cold War 450–1
and Middle East 454–5
human rights 290, 291
international relations 278–9, 285, 286, 287
journalism 654, *655*
language see English, Celtic
law *262*, 263, **264**, *265*, 291
literature
Medieval 618, 619, 620–1
Renaissance *622*, 623, 625
Neoclassical 626–7
novel, beginning of 628–9
Romanticism 632–3
Realism and Naturalism 635
novel in 19th-Century 636–7
Modernism 641
modern drama 644–5
modern poetry 646–7
modern novel 648–9
criticism 652
music 571, 573, 579, 580
dance *594*, 595, *596*, 597, 599
folk **587**, *594*, 595
opera 584–5
popular 588, *589*
nuclear weapons 288, *289*
politics 268, 270, 271
religion 408–9, 412–13, 463, 467, 475, 477
see also Anglicanism
society 254, 255, 256, 258, 259
education *260*, *261*
and Third World 298
women's movements 292–3
women's suffrage 292
youth movements 294, *295*
see also Ireland; Scotland; Wales
British Antarctic Territory 729
British Indian Ocean Territory 729
British Virgin Islands 729
British Museum *538*
Brittany 375, 401, 505, 603
Britten, Benjamin **579**, 580, 585, 587, 621
brittle stars 123
broadleaf forests 180–1
Broadway 588
Broca, Paul 223
Broca's area 226, 227
Broglie, Louis Victor de 26, 38
bromide 322
bromine *42–3*, 45, 47
bronchitis 237
bronchoscopy 241
Brontë, Charlotte, Anne and Emily 632, *636*
brontosaur 132
Bronze Age 312, **362, 363**, 369, 384, 391, 462, 463, *505*
bronze artwork 382, 502, *503*
American and African *517*
Chinese and Japanese *514*, 515
European 508, 521, 524
Middle Eastern 506, 507
Bronzino, Agnolo 528
Brook, Peter 643
Brooke, Sir James 701
Brooke, Rupert 646
Brooks, Cleanth 652
Broonzy, Big Bill 586
Brouwer, Adriaen *532*
Brown, Lieut. Arthur Whitten 349
Brown, Lancelot 'Capability' 534–5
Browne, Hablot K. see 'Phiz'
Browning, Robert and Elizabeth Barrett 633
Brücke, Die 547
Bruckner, Anton 577
Bruegel, Pieter, the Elder *527*, 581, *613*
Bruges 400, 404, 666
Brunei **669**
Brunel, Isambard Kingdom 341, 342–3
Brunelleschi, Filippo *524*, 525
Brunetière, Ferdinand 652
brushwork *501*
Brussels 286, 552
Brutus, Marcus Junius 377
bryophytes 119
Brythonic languages 603
bubonic plague (Black Death) 175, **239**
epidemics *238*, 394, **402**, 404, 436, 441, 450, 521
Bucephalus *372*, 373
Buchan, John 650
Buchenwald *445*
Büchner, Georg 635
buckminsterfullerene 45, 52
Buddha 385, 466, **468**, 469, 482
Buddhism 383, 384, 386, *458*, 459, **468–9**
and art and architecture 512, 513, 514, 515
countries practising 468–9, 470, **471**
good and evil 484–5
and literature 617
prayer 480
time and space 482–3
see also Zen
budget, government 276–7, 380
Buenos Aires 662
buffalo 161, **191**
buffer states 440
bufotoxins 131
building construction industry **338–9**
civil engineering **340–1**
see also architecture
building societies 272
bulbs (plant) 120
Bulgaria 261, 287, 477, 603, **670**
art 508
history 381, 395, 436, 441, 450, **670**
Bull, John 571
Bülow, Hans von 577
Bunker Hill, battle of *423*
Buñuel, Luis 558, 559, 563
Bunyan, John 621
Buonarroti see Michelangelo
buoyancy force 23
bureaucracy **267**, 380, 414
Burgundy 380, 394, 398, **401**, 526, 570
burial 255, 473
prehistoric and ancient 362–3, 369, *463*, 504–5
art in 369, 504, 505, 512
China *382*, 514
Egypt *366*, 460, 507
Burke, Edmund *270*, 271, 425
Burkina Faso **670**
Burlington, Earl of 535
Burma see Myanmar
Burne-Jones, Sir Edward 537, 546, *618*
burning see fire
Burns, Robert 632
Burundi *592*, **670**
bushbabies 164
Bush, George 733
Bushmen *388*, 517
business 282–3
Butler, Samuel 637
butterflies and moths 112, 113, **126–7**, 167, 169, *171*, 173
butterwort 121
Byelorussia *see* Belarus
Byrd, William 571
Byron, Lord, George Gordon 536, 631, *633*
bytes 334
Byzantine (Eastern) Empire **381**, **394–5**
capital of *see under* Constantinople
armies *394*
art and architecture 509, 510, 511, **518–19**, 520, 525
history
and Islam 392, 393
under Justinian 395–6
decline and fall 393, 395
literature 615
religion 476

cabinet government 267
cable television 326–7
Cabot, John *405*, 672
Cabral, Pedro 669
Cacoyannis, Michael 562
cacti *186*
cadmium *42–3*, 300
Ca'd'Oro 523
caecilians 130–1
Caesar see Julius Caesar
Caesar Octavian *see* Augustus
caesium *42–3*
caffeine 247
Cage, John 568, **580**
Cagney, James 560
Caillebotte, Gustave 541

Cain, James M. 650
Cairo 366, 399, 511, 679
Cakobau, Chief 681
Calatrava, knights of 399
calcium *42–3*, 51
in humans 206, 208, 215
in plants 116
in water 100, 178
calcium carbonate 84, 88–9
calculus 70–1
Calcutta 689
Calder, Alexander 555
Calder Hall 305
caldera *83*
Calderon 622
calendars **7**, 483
French Revolutionary 425
Islamic 478
Jewish 473
Meso-American 6, 391
see also festivals
californium *42–3*
Caligula, emperor 378
caliphs and caliphates 392
calligraphy *510*, 514
Callimachus 614
calories 24, 209
calotype process 324
Calvin, John and Calvinists **409**, 477
Camargo, La 596
Cambodia **670–1**
art and architecture 512, 513
history *384*, 385, *451*, 452, 453, **671**
religion 468
see also Indochina
Cambrian period *85*, *109*
Cambridge University 406, 652
Cambyses 367
camels **158–9**, *159*, **191**, *365*
cameras see photography
Cameron, Julia Margaret *556*
Cameroon 432, 433, **671**
Camoëns, Luis de 625
camouflage
animal 167
Camp David agreement 455
Campaign for Nuclear Disarmament *289*
Campbell, Colen 535
Campin, Robert *474*, **526**
Campion, Thomas 625
Camus, Albert 643, 648
Canaan 365, 460
Canada **671–2**
animals 151, 154, 171, *187*
economy 278
energy 305, 307
glaciation 90
history 390, 391, 417, 432, 433, 449
international relations 278, 286
journalism 655
plants 180, *192*, 193
separatism 259
transport/travel 341, 346
women's suffrage 292
Canaletto, Antonio 534
canals 340, **341**, 365, 420, 421, 430
cancer 236, **237**, 320
causes 213, 238, 247, 305
prevention 244, 245
scanning for *332*
treatment 241
Cancer, Tropic of 104, *105*
canine teeth 140, *152*
cannabis 246, **247**
canning 197
Cannizzaro, Stanislao 43
canopy, forest 182, *183*
Canova, Antonio 535
cantata 573
Canterbury 397
Canterbury Plains 185
Canterbury Tales 620
Cantor, Georg **62**, 69
Cao Xueqin 617
Cape Verde 405, **672**
Capetian dynasty 400
capillaries 210, *211*
capital 258–9, **273**, 279, 283
capital punishment 263, 264
capitals (architecture) *509*
capybara 150, 151
Caporetto, battle of 437
Capote, Truman 655
Capra, Frank 561
Capricorn, Tropic of 104, *105*
capuchin monkeys 165
carapace 124, 134
Caravaggio, Michelangelo Merisi da *530*, 532, 533
carbohydrates **208**, 209, 237
carbon 40, *42–3*, **45**
compounds *48*, 49, **52–3**, 320
see also carbon dioxide
in plants 117
in steel 314–15
carbon dioxide **48**
in atmosphere 13, 77
and greenhouse effect 182, **301**, 304
in industry 320
and life 110, *117*, 121, 176, 182, 210
molecule *48*
carbon monoxide *48*, **49**
Carbonari 428
carbonic acid 88
Carboniferous period *85*, *109*
plants 118, 119
carboxylic acid *52*, 53
Carchemish 365, 507
card games *72*
cardinality 69
cardiograph 249
cargo cults 465
cargoes see ships
Caribbean see Central America/Caribbean
caribou (reindeer) **160**, 170, 171, 181
caricature 541
CARICOM 287
Carissimi, Giacomo 573
Carlos, Don 721
Carlyle, Thomas 654
Carnac *363*
Carné, Marcel 562
Carnivores 152–5
carnivorous animals
birds 137, *138*
dinosaurs 132–3
in ecosystems *177*
fish *129*
mammals 140, 141, *146*, 147, **152–5**
marsupials 142, *143*
reptiles and amphibians 133, 135
carnivorous plants *121*
carnosaurs 132
Carnot, Sadi 25
Carol II of Romania 714
Carolingians 394, 519
Carothers, Wallace 317
Carpaccio, Vittorio 525
carpel *120*
carpets, Persian *511*
Carra, Carlo 548
Carracci, Agostino, Annibale and Ludovico 530
Carriera, Rosalba 501, 535
carrion eaters see scavengers
Carroll, Lewis *650*, 651
cars *51*, 311, 316, **352–5**
industry 278, *336*, 337
and pollution 300
semiology of *610*, 611
see also roads
cartels 287, 311
Carter, Elliott 580
Cartesian coordinates 70
Cartesian dualism 490
see also Descartes
Carthage 364, **376**, *377*
Cartier, Jacques 672
Cartier-Bresson, Henri *557*
cartilaginous fishes 128–9
cartoons (drawing) 500
cartoons (film) 565
Cartwright, Edmund 319, 420
Casavettes, John 561
cash crops 121, **188**, *316*, 318
cash flow 283
Cashmere goat 191
Casimir III of Poland 713
Cassatt, Mary 543
cassava 189
cassettes 328–9
Cassiopeia 17
Cassius Longinus, Gaius 377
cassowaries 138
castanets 583
caste system 258, *259*, 466
Castelvetro, Lodovico 626
Castiglione, Baldassare 406
Castile 399, 410, 411
Castilla, Ramon 712
casting (sculpture) 502, *503*
Castle, Irene and Vernon 595
castles see fortifications
Castner-Kellner process 320
castration 214, 232
Castro, Fidel *261*, 451, 677
'Cat and Mouse Act' 292
Catalan *603*
Catalonia 411
catalysts 47, 54–5, 313
see also enzymes
catalytic cracking 311, 320
cataracts in eye 219, 237
categorical imperative 493
Cathars 398, 403
cathedrals and churches 482
Byzantine *519*
Gothic 520–1, **522–3**
Renaissance *524*, 525
and mosques 510, 511
Baroque and Classical *531*
Rococo *534*
19th-century *539*
20th-century *552*
see also temples
Catherine of Aragon 412
Catherine de' Medici 408
Catherine the Great of Russia 417–18, 715
cathode-ray tube 35, 326, 332
cathodes **36**, *37*, 47, 50
Catholics see Roman Catholicism
cation 44
Catlin, George 391
cat, marsupial *140*
cat, sabre-toothed *141*
cats, domestic and large *141*, **152–3**, 168, 169, 173, *184*
CAT-scan 241, 242
cattle 141, 160, 161, *190*, **191**, 193, 462, 504
digestion *161*, 175
Catullus **615**, 625
Cauchy, Baron Augustin-Louis 62
Caudillo, El see Franco
caustic soda 320
cauterization 248
Cavalieri, Emilio de 584
cavalry, Hellenistic 373
caves **88–9**
animals in 88, 141, *147*
paintings in 141, 363, 389, 462, 500, *504*, *512*, 513, 516, *517*
cavies 150–1
Cavour, Count Camillo di 428, 693
Caxton, William **322**, 407, 606, 620
Cayman Islands 729
Ceausescu, Nicolae and Elena 714
Cefalu 519
celibacy 466, 468
Cellini, Benevenuto 528
cello 582, 583
cells, animal and human *111*
blood 206, 210, *212*, 236
cloning 175, 213
division 114
lymphocytes 212, *213*
memory 213
nerve see neurones
retina 139
single-celled organisms 110, 172
cells, electrical *36*
cells, plant *116*, *117*, 118
cells, solar 37, 306
celluloid 316
cellulose 118, 175
Celtic languages *603*
Celts 363, 369, **374–5**, 396–7, 463, 603
art *505*, 519
Cenozoic era *85*
censorship 563, 565, 648, 654
Centaurus A 8
centipedes **125**, 173
CENTO *451*
Central African Republic **672–3**
Central America/Caribbean 287
animals 128, 131, 135, 137, 171
mammals 144–7, 149, 150, 152, 155, 157–8, 161
art and architecture **516**
Caribbean Community 287
climate *105*
dance 592, 593, 595, 597
history
pre-Columbian **390–1**
discovery of *405*
Aztecs 6, 391, 410, 411
colonized 410, 416, 417
and decolonization 449
Cold War 450, *451*
language 609
politics 268, 269
religion *465*, 467, 475
society 255, 256
vegetation *104*, 121
volcanoes 82
women's suffrage 292
writing 604
youth culture 295
see also individual countries
central nervous system 220, *221*
central planning 276
Central Powers in World War I 436
see also Austro-Hungarian Empire; Germany
central processing unit *335*
centripetal acceleration 20, *21*
cephalochordates 123
cephalopods **122–3**, 195
ceramics/pottery 511, 553
history
ancient and prehistoric 504–5, 508, 509
Middle Eastern *506*, 507
Chinese and Japanese 388, *514*, 515
American and African 516, 517
history, industry in Britain 421
porcelain 514, 515, 534
cereals/grain 116, 120–1, 185, 188, **189**, 196, 366, 374, 402
cercariae 175
cerebral see brain
ceremonies see ritual
cerium *42–3*
certainty 488
Cervantes, Miguel de 411, **628**
cervix, cancer of 241, 245
César (Baldaccini) 555
cestodes 122
cetaceans 163
Ceylon see Sri Lanka
Cézanne, Paul 543, *544*, 548
CFCs 48, 301, 309
Chabrol, Claude 562
Chad **673**
Chadwick, John 369
chaetae 172
chaffinch 169
Chagall, Marc 558
Chaironeia, battle of 371, 372, *373*
Chalcolithic Age 363
Chaldaeans 365
chamber music 580
Chambers, William 535
Chambonnières, Jacques Champion de 573
chameleons *135*
chamois 161
Chamorro, Violeta 708
Chamoun, Camille 698
Champollion, Jean-François 366
chance 72–3
Chandler, Raymond 650
Chang Jiang see Yangtze
change
in mathematics 70–1
see also evolution
chanting 471
chaos theory 63
chaparral *104*
chapels see cathedrals and churches
Chaplin, Charlie *559*, 560
character in literature 629, 636, 648
charcoal 193
Chardin, Jean-Baptiste-Siméon 534, 535
charged-particle-beam weapons 289
charities 297, 299
Charlemagne ('Charles the Great') **394**, 518, 519, 683, 685, 693
Charles IV, emperor 394, 678
Charles V, emperor 394, 408, **410**, 412, 529, 664, 696, 721
Charles I of England **413**, 531, 623, 730
Charles I of Spain 721
Charles II of England 60, **413**, 627, 730
Charles V of France 401, 403
Charles VI of France 401
Charles VII of France 401
Charles IX of France 593
Charles XII of Sweden 723
Charles 'the Bold' **401**, 570
Charles of Anjou 399
Charles Augustus, Duke 685
Charles Edward Stuart, Prince 412, 413
Charles, Jacques 348
Charles' law 25
Charles Martel 394
Charpentier, Marc-Antoine 573
charters, town 404
Chartists *268*
Chartres cathedral 520, *522*
Chateaubriand, François René de 631
Chatilla massacre 455
Chaucer, Geoffrey 606, 619, *620*, 621
Chavin culture 516
cheetah 153, *173*
Chehel Situn 511
Chekhov, Anton **635**, 642
chelonians 134–5
chemicals/chemical
in agriculture 189, 191, 300
and disease 237, 248, 249
see also drugs
industry 244, 280, 311, 313, 316–17, **320**
pollution 177, **300**
sedimentary rocks 84
signals and animals *166*
see also pheromones
in weaponry 289
see also chemistry
chemistry **40–57**
bonds 44–5
classification of matter 40–1
elements and periodic table 42–3
in everyday life 56–7
history 60–1
materials 54–5
metals 50–1
molecules
organic 52–3
small 48–9
reactions 46–7
see also chemicals; science
chemoreceptors 124, 154
chemotherapy see drugs, therapeutic
Cheng Ho (Zheng He) *405*
Chernobyl 244, *301*, 305, 666
chernozem soils 185
Chesapeake Bay 422
Chesterton, G. K. 650
chestnuts 181
chevrotains 160
chi energy 250
Chiang Kai-shek see Jiang Jie Shi
chiaroscuro 530, 533
Chicago 731
chickenpox 239
chickens **191**
children and young people
adolescence 294–5
care of 293
childbirth see birth; pregnancy
disorders 219, *236*, 300
and family 257
growth and development *204–5*, 206
and immune deficiency disease *213*
initiation into adulthood 504, 592
intelligence 231, 232
and language 226, 603, 608, 609
and law 263
puberty 204–5
sexual development 204, 232
sleep 233
vaccination 244, *245*
working 294, 421, 434, *435*
youth movements 294–5, *447*
see also babies; education
Chile 180, 265, 312, **673**
history 390, 391, *451*
Chilembwe, John 702
chimpanzees **165**, 200
communication 167, 490, *491*
China **673–4**
acupuncture *250*, 251
animals 154–5, 160, 163
art and architecture 503, 510, **514–15**, 534, 538
calendar 7
dance 593
earthquakes 80
famine 296
film 563
fishing 194, 195
geology/geomorphology *88*, 89
history
before colonial age 362, **382–3**, 386, 387, 388, 392
colonialism *405*, 410, 432, 433
in 20th-Century 443, *444*, 445, **446–7**, 450, *451*, 453
human evolution 200, 201
industry 309, 318, 322, 323
language 602
law and crime 263
literature **616–17**
mathematics *65*
music 590
nuclear weapons 288
politics 268, 269
population *297*
religion 459, 468, **470**, *471*, 476, 477, 482, 485
see also Confucianism, Daoism
society 254, 255, 256, 259, 260
and UN 285
women's suffrage 292
writing 604
youth movements **295**
china (pottery) see ceramics
China, Republic of see Taiwan
chinchillas *150*
Ch'ing Ming festival 470
chinoiserie 534
chipmunk *150*
chirality *52*, 53
Chirico, Giorgio de 551
chiropractic 251
chitin 118
chivalry 407, 628
chlorine 40, *42–3*, 47, *321*
chlorine gas 289
chlorofluorocarbons 48, 301, 309
chlorophylls 117
chloroplasts 116, *117*
choice
mathematics 73
philosophy 491
cholera **239**, 244, 434
cholesterol 245
Chomsky, Noam 336, *608*, 609
Chopin, Frédéric 577
chordates 123
choreography 597, 598–9
Christ see Jesus
christening (baptism) *475*
Christensen, Benjamin 562
Christianity **474–7**
and architecture see cathedrals
and art 526–7
good and evil 484, 485, 622
history
ancient 379, 392, 396
Asia 383, 386–7
Roman Empire 379, **380–1**
and Islam and Crusades 392, **398–9**
Medieval and Renaissance 401, 403, 406, 407, 489
Reformation see Reformation
missionaries 432, 476–7
and education 260, 434
and human rights 290
and language 605, 606
and literature 622, 624–5, 635, 646
and music *see under* religion
philosophy **489**
pilgrimage 398, *481*, 519
prayer 480
rites of passage 254, 255
and social conflict 259
time and space 482–3
see also Bible; Orthodox; Protestantism; religion; Roman Catholicism
Christie, Agatha 650
Christmas 475
Christmas Island 663
Christo (Javacheff) *555*
Christophe, Henri 688
Christus, Petrus 526
chromaticism 570, 577, 578
chromium *42–3*, **313**, 315
chromosomes **114–15**, 236
chromosphere 10
chronometer 7
chrysalis *127*
Chuang Tzu (Zhuang Zi) 470
Chukrai, Grigori 562
Church see Christianity
Church of England see Anglicanism
churches see cathedrals and churches
Churchill, Caryl 644
Churchill, Sir Winston 444, 450, 731
Ciano, Count *443*
Cicero 260, 406, **615**
Cid, El *399*, 618
cilia *111*, 122, **172**, 212, 216
Cimabue 520, 521
cinema see films
circles, stone 505
circuitry, electrical *36*
circular motion 20
circulatory systems **210–11**
see also blood
circumcision 254, *255*, 480
cirque *86*, 87, *91*
cirrhosis 237
CIS see Commonwealth of Independent States
Cissé, Souleymane 563
cities
in art 532, 541
see also architecture
history
prehistoric 505
ancient 382, 384, 385, 386, *515*
Middle East 364, 365, 369–73, 376, 379, 511

Asia 382, 384, 386, *515*
South America 390, 391
Medieval and Renaissance 404, 406, 407, 524
and industrial society 420, 421, 434, 438
and literature 623
planning 553
see also individual cities
citric acid 321
City of London *360*, 413
city-states **370**, 372–3, 376
civets 153
civil law 264–5
civil rights *see* rights
civil service 267, 276
civil wars
China 447
Belgian Congo 449
Egypt, ancient 366
England 266, 401, **413**
France 414
America 421, 430, **431**, 435
Russia 438, 439
Spain **443**, *549*
worldwide during Cold War *451*
Yugoslav 736
see also wars
cladistics 108–9
Clair, René 559
clans *see* kinship; tribes
clarinet 583
Clark, Michael 598
Clarke, Arthur C. 651
class **258–9**
and economy 268, 269
in literature 636, 637
and politics 268, **269**
in Rome 379
struggle 259, 360
Classicism/Classical
art and architecture **508–9**, 525, **530–1**, **535**
music **574–5**
see also Neoclassicism; Renaissance
classifications
biological 108–9
chemical 40–1
Claude, Lorraine **531**, 532, 537, 540
Claudian 615
Claudius, emperor 378
clauses 608–9
clavichord 582
clavicle *206*
clay-humus complex 182
Cleisthenes 370
Clemenceau, Georges *440*
Clemens, Samuel L. 639
Cleopatra 373, 377
clergy 258
see also popes; priests; religion; shamans
Cliff, Clarice 553
climate **102–5**
and agriculture 188
changes 97, 363, 390
see also Ice Ages
classification 104
controls 104–5
desert 92–3
and ecosystems 176, 180, 181, 185, **186–7**
and lakes 95
and oceans 101, 178
and vegetation 105
regions *105*
see also drought; rainfall; snow; temperature; weather; wind
Clive, Robert 417
cloaca 130, 134, 135, 139
clocks 7
cloisonné 514
cloning 175, 189, 213
clothing *see* textiles
clouds *102*, 103
Clouet, François 529
clownfish *175*
clubmoss 119
CND *289*
Cnut 397, 678
coal
for electricity 300, **304**
and industry 314
mining **312**, 420, 421
Coalbrookdale 314
coasts **96–7**, *179*
ecosystems 178–9
cobalt *42–3*
COBE satellite *4*
COBOL 334, 335
Cobra (art movement) 554
cocaine *246*, **247**
cochlear implant 226, 240
Cocos (Keeling) Islands 663
Cocteau, Jean 559, 562, 640, 643
Code Napoléon 427
code/s 458, 610–11
Codrington family 662
coelacanth 128, 129, 173
coelenterates **123**, 172
coelurosaurs 132
coffee 196, 416, 432
cognition *see* learning; perception
cognitive science 609
Cohan, Robert 598
Cohn-Bendit, Daniel 295
cohorts, age 254
coinage 365, 508
coitus 202
coke 314
Colbert, Jean Baptiste 414–15
cold, climatic *102*, 103, *105*
cold, common 175, **239**, 250
Cold War 284, 289, 298, 299, 447, **450–1**
cold-blooded creatures *see* ectotherms
Coleman, Ornette 589
Coleridge, Samuel Taylor 631, **632–3**, 652
collage 548, 551, 557
collective bargaining 273
collective unconscious 232
collectivism 269
colleges 261
Collins, Michael 692
Collins, Wilkie 650
Collodi, Carlo 651
colloquial literature 615, 617, 621
Cologne 404, 523
Colombia 246, 390, 649, **675**
colonialism *see* empires
colour
of animals as camouflage *122*, 127, 167
and art **500–1**, 529, 534, 537, 555
Dutch school 532, 533
Impressionism 542, 543
Post-Impressionist 544, 545
blindness test *218*
subatomic particles 39
feathers 138–9
photography 325, 559
in printing *323*
recognition by birds 136
stained glass 522
and temperature of stars 9
colugos *147*
Columbus, Christopher 342, *405*, 410
countries visited 662, 665, 676, 677, 679, 688, 694, 708, 716, 717, 726
combat, trial by *264*
comedy/humour
in film 559
in literature 614, 615, 622–3, 626, 627, 636, 639, 644–5
see also satire
comets *11*
comic-strip art *554–5*
commensalism **174**, 175
Commodus, emperor 379
Common Agricultural Policy *279*
common law 264, 265, 291
common markets 279
see also European Community
commons (estate) 258
Commons, House of 267
Commonwealth 264, **287**, 449
Commonwealth of Independent States 715
communards 429
commune (social) 257
commune (political) **404**, 424, 429
communication/s
animals **166–7**
artificial intelligence 336–7, 609
hi-fi 318–19
language 608
semiology and signs 610
telecommunications 330–1
video 327
writing 604
see also computers; language; media; printing; radio; television; transport
communion, holy 475
Communism 268, **269**
Albanian 660
anti-Communism in USA 450, 645
and art 550, 551
Bulgarian 670
Cambodian 671
Chinese 269, 446–7, 470
Czech 678
and economy 268–9
German 685
government 267
history 269, 446–8, 450–3, 470
see also Russia, Revolutions
and human rights 291
and literature 617
and music 580
Polish 713
Soviet 715
and Third World 298–9
Vietnamese 452–3
and women's movement 293
youth movements 294–5
see also Eastern Europe; Marxism; socialism
community
ecological 176
policing 263
in religion 458
service as sentence 263
social 271
commutative law 64
Comoros **675**
animals 149, 158, 164
compact disc *329*, 334
companies 282, 404
Company Registrar 282
comparative advantage 278–9
compensation 263, 265
competition
in business 274–5
in education 261
in evolution 113
in political theory 270–1
complex numbers 65
composers *see* music
compounds 41
aromatic *52*
ionic *44*
compulsions 246
computers **334–5**
artificial intelligence 336–7, 609
behaviour of 490
and films *565*
'hacking' 262
and medicine 242
and music 581
perception 225
and printing 322
comsats 19
Conan Doyle, Sir Arthur 650
concentration camps 433, 442, *445*, 647
conceptual art 555, 557
concerto 572, **573**, 575, 576, 578, 581
Concorde 349
concrete 552–3
concrete poetry 640, *647*
Condamine, Charles de la 316
Condell, Henry 623
conditioning 221, 293
condom 213
condors 136
conductivity *25*, 35, 37, **50–1**, *55*
cones (of conifers) 119
Confederates (USA) 430, 431
Confederation, Articles of 422
Confederation of the Rhine 427
confirmation, Christian 255
conflict 257, 259
see also wars
Confucianism 383, 386, 459, **470**, 485
Confucius (Kongfuzi) 260, 383, **470**, 616
Congo **675–6**
Congo, Belgian 432, 433, *449*, 637
see also Zaïre
Congress of USA 430
Congress of Vienna 427, 428
Congreve, William 627
conies 151
conifers 118, **119**
forestry 192–3
forests 180–1
management 193
see also forests
Conquistadores 390, 410
Conrad III, emperor 399
Conrad, Joseph 637, 648
Conrad, marquis of Montferrat 399
conscience, right of 290
consciousness 490–1
lack of *see* unconscious
-raising 293
stream of 645
consent, government by 266, 290
conservation
of energy 24
of momentum 21
see also ecosystems
Conservatives 267, 270–1
Constable, John 537
Constance, council at 403
Constantine, emperor **380–1**, 509, 727
Constantine I and II of Greece 686
Constantinople (Istanbul) 381, 395
architecture *510*, *518*
history
attacked and besieged,
by Arabs 393
by Crusaders 394, 398–9
by Persians 394
by Turks 393, *395*, 511, 518–19, 615
by Vikings 397
as Byzantine capital 381, 393, 394, 395, 397, 398, 518, 615
as Roman capital 394, 509
constipation 237
constituency 267
constitutional monarchy **266–7**
constitutions 266–7, 291
of USA 264, 266, 422–3, 430, 654
Constructivism 549
consubstantiation 475
consuls 376
consumer organisms 177
consumerism 294
contagion 238, 239
container ships *344*
contamination 238, 239
contemplation 470
contemporary *see* modern
continental climates 92, *105*
Continental Congress of America 422
continental crust 76
continental drift **78**, *79*, 140, 390
continental margin/shelf *101*
continental plates *see* tectonic plates
Continental System 427
contingency fees 265
continuity hypothesis 361, 375
continuous variables 26
contraception **203**, 213, 237, 292
contract, law of 264–5
contraction, muscle *207*
'Contras' in Nicaragua 451
convection *25*
Conventional Forces in Europe 289
conventions
on Law of Sea 195
on rights *see* rights
convicts, transport of 417
see also prisons
Cook, Captain James 417, 664, 708, 726, 734
Cook Islands 707
Cooke, William 330
cooking 196–7
Cookson, Catherine 651
coolant in nuclear reactor 305
Cooper, James Fenimore 638
cooperation, biological 113, 154
coordinates, Cartesian 70
Copenhagen, battle of 426
copepods 124
Copernicus, Nikolaus 4, **16**, 60
Copland, Aaron 579
copper 40, 41, *42–3*, *50*, 312, *313*, 363, 366
compounds 47, 50
copperplate gravure 323
Coptic Church 477
coral *99*, *106–7*, **123**, 129
Coral Sea, battle of *444*
Coral Sea Island Territory 663
cor anglais 583
Corbusier, Le *552*, 553
Corday, Charlotte 425
Córdoba 510, *511*
co-regency 366–7
Corelli, Arcangelo 572, 573
Corinth, Lovis 547
Corinthian Order *509*
corms 120
corn (maize) 189
Corneille, Pierre 626, 629
cornet 583
Cornwall 307, 364, 375, *396*, *603*
Cornwallis, Charles, Marquis 422
corona, solar 10
coronary *see* heart
Corot, Camille *540*, 541
corporation tax 276
correctness (logic) 494–5
Correggio, Antonio 529
correspondence 68–9
corrie *86*, 87, *91*
corrosion *51*
cortex 216, *222*, 223, *227*
Cortez, Hernán 391, 410, **411**, 703
Cortona, Pietro da 531
Corvinus, Matthias 688
Cosimo I, grand duke 528
cosine 62–*3*, 71
Cosmic Background Explorer Satellite
see COBE satellite
cosmic rays 35
cosmic renewal rite 470
cosmic year 8
cosmogonies 612
cosmology **4–5**
Cossacks 728
Costa Rica **676**
'cost-push' inflation 276
Côte d'Ivoire 517, **676**
cotton 121, 188, *318*, 416, 420, 430, 432
see also textiles
cougars 153
coulomb 34
Coulomb, Charles Augustin 34, 61
Council of Europe 286
Council of Ministers 286
counterexamples 494
counterpoint 570, 572
Counter-Reformation 408, 409
countries, details about 660–739
Couperin, François 572, 573
Couperin, Louis 572
couple (physics) *22*
Courbet, Gustave *540*, 541
Courland 698
court (law) 262–6, 290, 606
court (royal) 593, 594, 623, 624–5
courtship 256, 594
animal 139, 166, **168**
covalent bonding 44
cow *see* cattle
Coward, Noel 627, 644
Cowell, Henry 579, 580
coyote 154
coypu *150*
Crabbe, George 627
crabs *124*, **125**, 167, 170, *175*, *178*, 195
migration 170
'crack' 247
craft guilds and unions 273, 404, 435, 621
Cranach, Lucas 409, *527*
Crane, Hart 580
Cranko, John 597
Crashaw, Richard 625
Crassus, Marcus 377
craters 13, *83*, 95
crawling 172
Creation 483
creativity 231
Crécy, battle of 401
creed 458
cremation 255, 467
Cretaceous period *85*, *109*
dinosaurs 133
mammals 140
plants 120
Crete 395, 444, *445*
cretinism 215
crevasses *91*
Crick, Francis 61, 114
crickets
communication 166
crime 246, **262–3**, 265, 294, 636
Crimea *429*, 445, 728
criticism, literary 627, **652–3**
Cro-Magnons 141, *200*, **201**, 362, 363
Croatia **676–7**
Croats 428
crocodiles 134–5
Croesus 508
Crompton, Samuel 318
Cromwell, Oliver 413, 627
Cromwell, Thomas 412
cross-fertilization 121
Crown *see* monarchy
Crown Court 265
cruelty, theatre of 643
Crusades 392, 395, **398–9**, 403
crust *see under* Earth
crustaceans **124–5**, 129, 137, 138, 195
crypsis 167
Crystal Palace 338, *434*, 539
crystals 55
liquid 54
CSCE 287
Cuba 287, **677**
and Angola 298
dance 597
education *261*
film 563
history *451*, **677**
politics 268, 269
Cubism 544, **548–9**, 550, 551, 556–7, 640
Cucuteni culture 505
cud, chewing 161
Culloden, battle of *412*
Cult of the Supreme Being 425, *459*
cults, religious 458, 462
Cultural Revolution 295, **447**
cultural rights 290
cuneiform script 364, 604
Cunningham, Merce 598
Curie, Marie *61*
Curie, Pierre 61
curium *42–3*, *50*
currencies 279
current account, national **279**
current, electrical 36–7
current, sea *see under* oceans
curriculum 260, 261
Curry, John 598
curves (maths) 70
Cushites 388
customs (frontiers) **279**, 428
cuticle 124
cuttlefish 122, *123*
Cuvier, Baron Georges 112
Cuyp, Aelbert 532
Cuza, Alexander 714
Cybele 379
cycads *119*
Cycladic art *505*
cycles
cosmic 5, 483
sleep *233*
cyclones 103, *104*
cyclothone 129
cyclosporin 240
cymbals 583
cynodonts 140
Cyprus 259, 285, 477, **677**
history 369, 395, 449
Cyril, St 605
Cyrillic writing 605
Cyrus 365
cystic fibrosis 236, 240
cysts 238
cytoplasm 111
cytotoxic T cells 213
Czechoslovakia 287
film 558, 562
history
Bohemia 399, 403, 408, 409, 441
Czechs 428, 429
invaded by Germany 443
20th-Century 287, 295, 441, 443, *445*, 450, *451*
literature 641, 653
music 577, 585
youth movements 295
see also Bohemia, Czech Republic, Slovakia
Czech Republic **677–8**
language *603*

D-Day invasions *444*, 445
Da Nang 452
Dachau 445
Dada 547, **550–1**, 554, 556, 578, 640
Daguerre, Louis 324, 556
daguerreotype 324, *556*, *634*
daily rhythm 232
daimyos 386, 387
dairy products 190–1, **196**
Dal Riada, kingdom of 396
Dalai Lama 447
Dali, Salvador *551*, 559
Dalton, John 38, 61
damages, legal 265
Damascus 399, 437, 510
dams *307*, 341
dance 465, 571, 572, **592–8**
bees 167
birds 139
classical ballet 593, **596–7**
folk and social 594–5
modern 597–8
see also music
Danelaw 397
Dante Alighieri 521, *619*, 624
Danton, Georges 425
'Danzig Corridor' 440
Daoism (Taoism) 459, **470**, *471*, 482, 485, 617
Dar-al-Islam 392
Darby, Abraham 314
Darius I of Persia 365, 508, 691
Darius III of Persia 365, 372

'Dark Ages' 406
dark reactions 117
Darwin, Charles 58, 61, 108, *112*, 113, 164
Social Darwinism 270
Dassin, Jules 562
database 335
data transmission 331
dating 89, 361, 362
Daubigny, Charles-François 540
Daumier, Honoré 502, **541**, *628*, *635*
Davenant, Sir William 623
David, King 365, 472, 593, 692, 695
David, Jacques-Louis 424, *535*, *626*
Davies, John 624
Davis, Miles *588*, 589
Davis, Peter Maxwell **580**, 585
Davy, Sir Humphrey 41
Day, Lucienne 553
days 6, 7, 463
DDT 113, 245
de Gaulle, Charles 287, 295, 449, 661, 683
de Klerk, F.W. 721
de la Tour, Maurice-Quentin 630
De Mille, Cecil 560
de Niro, Robert 564
De Stijl Movement 549
de Valera, Eamon 692
Dead Sea Scrolls 605
deaf people 226, **227**, 240, 608
deal (wood) 193
Dean, James 295, 561
death
penalty 263, 264
philosophy 491
ritual and religion 254, **255**, 460, 461, 463, 467, 469, 592
see also burial
debentures 272
debt/deficits 273, 277, 636
national 278, 279, 297, 299
debtors' prison 262
Debussy, Claude *578*, 579, 581, 585, 586, 597
decalomania 551
decapods 125
deceit, animal **167**
decibel 31
deciduous trees 181
Declarations *see* independence; rights
decolonization 299, **448–9**
decomposers 118, 176, 177
deconstruction 653
Decorated Gothic *522*
deduction 58, 59, 494, 495
deer *153*, **160**, 166, 168, 169, 181
defence
animals *129*, *131*, *135*, 166
camouflage *126*, *167*
colour *122*, 127, 167
human 276, 288–9
aircraft 332, **348–51**
ships *343*, *345*
see also armed forces; fortifications; wars; weapons
plants 182
deficiency *see under* diseases
deficits *see* debt
Defoe, Daniel **628**, 629, 634
Degas, Edgar 501, 541, *543*, 544, 556
Deinonychus 133
Deism 418, 459
see also God; religion
Delacroix, Eugène *536*, **537**, 540
Delaroche, Paul 556
Delaunay, Robert 548
Delhi *298*, 385
Delian League 371
delict, law of 265
delirium 235
Delius, Frederick 579
Delphi 462, 508
Delsarte, François 598
demand **274**, 275, 276, *279*
dementia 235, 236
Demilitarized Zones (DMZ) 440, 452–3
democracy 266, 268, 271
in Classical Greece 370–1
demonstrations for 295, *447*
Democrats (USA) 295, 430
Democritus 60
demons 484
demonstrations and riots 262, 289, *291*, 293, 295, *447*
see also peasants revolts; revolutions
Demosthenes 614
dendochronology 361
dendrites *220*
Deng Xiaoping 447
Denisov, Edison 581
Denmark **678**
art and architecture 505, 554
ballet 596
film 562
history
ancient 397, 463
18th-19th centuries 408, 426–7, 433
20th-Century 428, 440, 444
international relations 286
language *603*
women's suffrage 292
deoxyribonucleic acid *see* DNA
deposition *91*, 93, 96, 97, 98
depreciation 279
depression (climatic) 103
depression (economic) 279, 311, *441*, 442
depression (psychological) 232, 233, **234–5**, 250
Derain, André 544, *545*, 597
derivatives in calculus 71
dermatology 249
dermis *216*
Derrida, Jacques 653
dervish *510*
Descartes, René 58, 61, **62**, 70, **418**, 486, 487, **488**, *490*, 491
descriptions (in philosophy) 493, 496–7
desertion of spouse 256
deserts **92–3**, *104*, *105*, **186**
desertification 92, **186**, 187
design, computer-aided *337*
deskilling 259
despot *see* absolutism; enlightened despots; totalitarian
Desprès, Josquin 570
Dessalines, Jean-Jacques 688
detective stories 638, **650**
détente 451
detergent 23
determinism 486, 634
deuterium 4, *39*, 288, 305
devaluation 279
developed world 297
and Third World **298–9**
development *see* growth
deviance and crime **262–3**
Devlin, Bernadette 295
Devonian period *85*, *109*
plants 118
devolution 267
Dewey, John 487
dharma 466, 468, 484
dhole 154
diabetes 213, **214**, 236, 237, 241, 245, 321
diachronic linguistics 608
Diaghilev, Serge 579, **597**, 598, 640
diagonal theorem 69
dialect 606, 607, 608, *609*
dialysis 243
'Diamond' Buddhism 469
diamonds *313*
diaphragm *210*
Dias, Bartolomeu *405*
Díaz, Porfirio 703
Díaz de Vivar, Rodrigo *399*
Dickens, Charles 262, 616, 635, **636**, 637, 639, 650
Dickinson, Emily 639
dicotyledons 121
dictator *see* totalitarian
dictionaries 418, 606, 607, 627
dicynodonts 140
didacticism 614, 615
Diderot, Denis 418, 419, 629
Dien Bien Phu *452*
Diesel, Rudolf 309
diet of animals 116
arthropods 124, 125
birds 136–7
crustaceans 170
mammals 140, 141, 144, 147, 148–9, 158
whales 124, 163
reptiles and amphibians 130, 135, 170
see also carnivorous; herbivorous; insectivores
diet of humans *see* food
differentiation 71
diffraction *29*
digestion 207, *209*, 211
and bacteria 175
diseases 237, 241, 243, 250, 251
gut flora and fauna 161, 175, 212, 238
see also diet; ruminants
digital compact cassettes 329
digital systems 242, 329, 334
digoxin 250
dilation of time 27
Dine, Jim 554
dingo 154
Dinka people 255
dinosaurs **132–3**, 140, 173
Diocletian 380, 381
diodes *37*
diorite 84
diphtheria **239**, 245
diplodocus *133*
direct current 36–7
director, of films 564, 565
directors of companies 282
Directory (France) 424, 425
dirigibles 348
disaccharides 208
disarmament 440–1
disaster relief 290
discontinuities (in Earth) 76, 77
discourse analysis 609
discrete variables 26
discrimination 254, **258**, **259**, 262, 268, **291**
action against *see* rights
discs (records) *328–9*
discs (computer) 334
diseases and disorders, animal 143, 151, 195
diseases and disorders, human **234–9**
blood 205, 236, 237, 238, *239*
bones 205, 206, *332*
brain *223*, 235, 237, 491
causes and sources of infection
ageing 205, 207, 214, 219, 235, 240
amoeba 210, 227, 238, 239
animals 122, 149, 151, 244
bacteria 110, 212, **238**, 239, 249
drugs 213, 235, 238, 239, 245, **246–7**
fungi 118, 212, **238**, 239
germ theory 58, 240, 248
parasites 174, 175, **238**, 239, 244
pollution 300, 301
sexual activity 213, 235, 238, 239
see also viruses
control 296
deficiency *208*, *209*, 214, 215, 244
see also autoimmune response
degenerative 214
see also arthritis
digestive system 237, 241, 243, 250, 251
eyes 219, 237, 240, 241
hearing *see* deaf people
heart *see under* heart
history 402, 410, 411, 434
hormone system 213, 214–15, 245
immune system 212, 213, 237
infectious 211, 213, **238–9**
see also epidemics
learning problems 231
lymph system 175, **236**
malignant *see* cancer
mental **234–5**
nervous system 221, 227, 242
non-infectious **236–7**
old age *see* ageing *above*
prevention 213, 238, **244–5**
radioactivity 305
respiratory system 118, 237, 238, 239, 240, 244, 245, 247, 250
surgery **240–1**
technology **242–3**
see also drugs, therapeutic; epidemics; medicine; mental illness; *and* names of individual diseases and disorders
disinfectants 56
disks *see* discs
dispersal of seeds 182
displacement *20*
Disraeli, Benjamin 636, 637, 731
dissection 248
distances
astronomical *5*
perception of 224
distillation *311*, 320
distortions (in perception) *225*
distribution of goods *281*
distributive law 64
district heating 304, 306
divination 462
divinities *see* gods and goddesses
division, arithmetical 64–5
division of labour 278
Divisionism 548
divorce 256, 479
Djakarta 690
Djibouti **678–9**
Djoser, pharoah 366
Dmytryk, Edward 561
DNA (deoxyribonucleic acid) *53*, 110, 113, **114–15**, 200, 201, 263, 321
see also genetics
doctors *see* medicine
documentary photography 557
dodecaphony 578, 579
Doe, Samuel 699
Doge's Palace 523
Dogon people 482, 517
dogs 141, 152, **154**, 173, 190
Dolby, Ray 329
Dolin, Anton 597
dolphins 30, **163**, 166–7, 332
domain in mapping 68
Domenichino 530
domes (architectural) 511, 518
domes (geological) 310
domestic animals 151, 160, **190–1**, 244
Dominica **679**
Dominican Republic *451*, **679**
Domitian 378
Donatello *503*
Donizetti, Gaetano 585
donkey 156, 191
Donne, John 625
Doppler, C. J. 31
Doppler effect 5, **31**, 225, 242, 332
Dorians 369
Doric Order *509*
dormancy 181
dormice *150*, 171
Dostoevski, Fyodor *634*, **635**, 648
double bass 582–3
doubt 488
Dounreay 305
Dowell, Anthony *596*
Dowland, John 571, 625
Down's syndrome *236*
drag (drift) seines *194*
dragonfly 126
drainage *see* lakes; rivers
Drake, Colonel Edwin 310
Drake, Sir Francis 412
Drake, Frank: equation 17
drama *see* theatre
Draper, Ronald 647
Dravidians 384, 602
drawing 500
see also art
Drax power station *304*
dreams **232–3**, 551, 620–1, 632, 633
Dreiser, Theodore 635
Dreyer, Carl 562
drift mine *312*
drift seine *194*
drift velocity 37
drilling for oil *310*
Droeshont, Martin *623*
dromedaries *159*, 186
drought 181, 185, 187, 296, 441
see also famine
drugs
abuse **246–7**
and disorders 213, 235, 238, 239, 245, **246–7**
and law 262
and literature 632, 633
forensic identification 263
therapeutic **56–7**, 207, 211, 214, 242, **243**, 248
anti-inflammatory 207
antibiotics *57*, 118, 207, **238**, 239, 242, 249, 321
and bacterial infections 238, 239
and cancer 237
diseases resistant to 247
herbal 250
industry *320*
and mental disorder 234, 235, 241
pain-killers *40*, 207, 217, 247, 251
for sleep 233, 247
and surgery 240
druids 463
drums 583
drumlins *91*
dry climates *105*
dry ice *49*
Dryden, John 626, **627**
drying food 196
dry-plate process 324
Du Bartas, Guillaume 624
Du Bellay, Joachim 624
Du Fu 617
Du Pont 316
dualism, mind and body 490
duality, wave-particle 26
dubbing films 564
Dubček, Alexander 295, 678, 719
Duccio di Boninsegna 500, **520**
Duchamp, Marcel 550, 551
duck-billed dinosaurs 133
duck-billed platypus *142*
ducks 191
Dufay, Guillaume 570
Dufresnoy, Charles-Alphonse 492
Dufy, Raoul 545
dugong 162
Dumbarton Oaks 284
Duncan, Isadora *598*
dunnarts 142–3
Dunstable, John 570
Duras, Marguerite 649
Dürer, Albrecht *501*, 502, *527*
Durham Cathedral *519*
Dust Bowl 441
Dutch *see* Netherlands
Dutch East Indies *see* Indonesia
Dutschke, Rudi 295
duty 493
Duvalier, François and Jean-Claude 689
Dvořák, Antonín 577, 587
dwarfism *205*, 236
dyes, synthetic 320, *321*
dykes *85*
Dylan, Bob 589
dynamo *37*
dysentery 238, **239**
dyslexia 231
dysprosium *42–3*, *50*

E numbers 197
eagles *136*
Eakins, Thomas 541
Early English Gothic *522*
earnings *see* wages
ears *see* hearing
Earth *11*, **12**, **13**, 16, **76–9**
biosphere 176–7
crust **76–7**
see also geology/geomorphology; mining
interior heat 176–7, **307**
magnetic field 10, 77, 313
orbit 6, 7, 104
structure **76–7**
see also atmosphere; geography; geology
earthquakes *78*, **80–1**, 100, 369
earth-resources satellites 19
earthworms **122**, 148, 171, 172
East Germany (German Democratic Republic) 287, 603, 643, 685
history 450, *451*
East India Companies 385, *417*, 422, 432
East Indies *see* Indonesia
East Timor 690
Easter 475
Easter Island 389, 417, *513*
Eastern Empire *see* Byzantine
Eastern Europe 287
environment 301
music 587
Mutual Assistance Treaty *see* Warsaw Pact
politics 268, 269
women's suffrage 292, 293
youth movements 295
see also Albania; Bulgaria; Czechoslovakia; East Germany; Hungary; Poland; Romania
Eastman, George 325, 558
eavesdropping as crime 262
EC *see* European Community
echidnas 142
echinoderms 123
echocardiography 242
echolocation *see under* sound
eclipses 10, 16
Eco, Umberto *611*
ecology *see* ecosystems
Economic Community of West African states *see* ECOWAS
economics/economy **272–83**
business and accounting 282–3
capital and labour 273
and class 258–9
command economy 272
and government 268–71, 276–7
international 278–9
market 274–5
mixed economy 272
production 280–1
rights 290
of Rome 379, 380
Third World dominated 299
see also financial; industry; *and also under* individual countries *and* Countries of World section
ecosphere 110
ecosystems 105, 174, *176*, **178–87**
aquatic 178–9
extreme 186–7
model *176*
see also deserts; forests; grasslands
ECOWAS 287
ectoparasites 174
ectotherms 131, 134
see also fish; reptiles
Ecuador 287, 390, 391, **679**
ecumenical movement 477
edentates 144–5
Edinburgh 249, 419
Edison, Thomas *328*, 558
editing films 564
Edo (Tokyo) 386–7, *514*
EDSAC (computer) *334*, 335
education **260–1**, 276
and class 258
compulsory 294
for girls 292
and government 266, 267
health 245
history 370, 404, 406
17th–19th centuries 294, 409, 414, 418–19, 421, 432, 434, 448
literacy 370, 460
in literature 636, 637
see also universities
Edward the Confessor 397
Edward I of England 400–1, 523, 730
Edward III of England 400, 403
Edward IV of England 412
Edward VI of England 412
Edward, Prince of Wales ('the Black Prince') 401
eels 128, 129, **170**, 172
efferent neurones 220, 221
egg (plant) *120*
eggs (ova) 114, 139, *202*
in plants 118, 120
see also reproduction
ego 232
egoism 493
Egypt 287, **679–80**
history
ancient 364, *365*, **366–7**, 369, 372, 377, 379, 388
art and architecture 502, *506*, **507**, 509, 511, 538
medicine 248
religion *460*, **461**, 462, *612*
science 40
textiles 318
see also hieroglyphics
and Byzantine Empire 395
and Greeks 372, 373, 379
and Islam 392, 479
Crusades 398–9
Medieval 406
Napoleonic Wars 426, 427
colonialism 432, 433
20th-Century 444, 449, **454–5**
literature 616
religion *460*, **461**, 462, 477, *612*
women's movement 293
women's suffrage 292
Ehrlich, Paul 249
Eiffel Tower 539
Einstein, Albert 26, 27, 38, 61
einsteinium *42–3*, *50*
Eire *see* Ireland
Eisenhower, Dwight D. 445
Eisenstein, Sergei 559, 562
El Salvador *451*, **680**
El Greco *529*
Elamites 364, *365*
elands 161
elasmobranches 128
elasticity *23*
Elba 427
elderly *see* old people
Eleanor of Aquitaine 400, 619
elections *see* voting
elective surgery 240
electrical signals (in animals) 167, 220–1
electric-arc furnacing *314*, 315
electricity **34–7**
charges **34**
current, conductors and insulators **35**
first used in town 304
in fish 129, 167
generation 35, 300, **304–7**
see also nuclear power
in industry 421
static 34
transmission *304*

and transport *347*
electrocardiography (ECG) 242, 243
electrochemical series 51
electroconvulsive therapy *235*
electrodes 36, *37*, 47, 50
electroencephalograph 249
electrolysis 47, 320
electrolyte 36
electromagnetism *26*, 27, **34–5**
induction 35, 304
radiation 35, 39, 332, 333
spectrum 17, *35*
see also magnetism
electron/s **38–9, 42**
in electricity 34–7
emission 37
exchanges *330*
microscopy 38, *333*
transfer reaction 47
electronic funds transmission 331
electronics
in aircraft 349
and medicine 240
monitoring offenders 263
and music 580, 581
electroplating 47, 50
electrostatic precipitator 304
electrum 506
elementary education 260–1
elements **40–3**, 177, 248
elephant birds 138
elephant shrews 149
elephantiasis 122, 175, 238
elephants 30, 156, **157**, 171, 173, 182
in armies 373, 376, *377*
movement 173
elephant seals *168*
Eleusinian mystery 462
elevation *see* altitude
Elgar, Edward 579
Eliot, George 635, **637**, 639
Eliot, T. S. 580, **641**, 644, 646, 652
Elizabeth (Henry VII's wife) 412
Elizabeth I of England **412**, 621, 623, 625, 691, 730
elk **160**, 181
Ellington, Duke 589
elms 181
elvers 170
emancipation of slaves 416, 431
embalming 255, 460
embossing 505
embryos 109, 202, *203*
emergant trees 182, *183*
Emerson, Ralph Waldo 639
emigration
animal 170
see migration
emotions
and brain 223
in families 257
in novels 628–9
repressed 232
see also anxiety; depression
Empedocles 60, 248
emphysema 237
Empires
ancient Near East 364–5
see also Greece, ancient; Roman Empire
age of colonialism 268, **410–11**, **432–3**
see also decolonization *and under* Europe *and* individual countries
empiricism 58–9, 418, 488
employment *see* labour
Empson, William 652
EMS *see* European Monetary System
emulsion, film 324
enamelling 514, 515
enantiomers *52*, 53
enclosures, land 420, 627
encyclopedias 418
endocrine system *214*
see also hormones
endomorphins 251
endoparasites 174
endoscopy 33, 241
energy **24**, **304–7**
in alternative medicine 250, 251
alternative sources **306–7**
conservation of 24
from earthquakes 80
from food 209
from Sun 176, **306**
global policy suggested 299
transfer 28–9
see also coal; electricity; gas; nuclear power; oil
Engels, Friedrich 269
engines and machines 25, 37
agriculture *420*
industry *304*, *308–9*, 318–19, 420, *421*
see also steam; transport
England *see* Britain
Engle, Madeline L' 651
English language **602**, **603**, **606–7**, 608–9
dialect map *609*
origin of 396, 606
and semiotics 610
English literature
see Britain, literature
engraving *502*, 505, 526
enlightened despots 418
Enlightenment
Buddhist 470, 480
European 290, **418–19**, 424, 459, 629
Ennius 615
Ensor, James 547
entropy 25
environment
and literature 652
and mental disorder 236, 237
'nature versus nurture' **230–1**, 293
and plants 117
threats to **300–1**
environmental gradient *186*
enzymes **53**, 54, **110**, **196**, 208, 209, 243
Eocene epoch *85*
epicentre, earthquake 80, 81
epics 612, **614–5**, 616, **618–9**, 620, 625
epic theatre 642–3
Epidaurus *615*
epidemics 238, 244, 248, 434
see also bubonic plague; diseases
epidermis *216*
epiphytes 121
epistolary novels 628, 629
Epstein, Jacob 549
equality 268–9, 627
equator *see* tropics
equatorial forests **182–3**
Equatorial Guinea **680**
equilibrium
economic 274
evolutionary 113
in physics *22*
reaction 47
equinoxes 104
equities 272, 273
Erasmus, Desiderius 406, 407
Eratosthenes **16**, 60
erbium *42–3*, *50*
Erhard, Ludwig 685
Eric the Red 397
Ericcson, John 343
Erice, Victor 563
Eritrea 366, 432, 433, **681**
ERM 276
Ernst, Max 551
erosion 84, **87–9**, *91*, **93**, **96**, 98, 189, 297
eroticism *see* sexuality
Ershad, General 666
Eschenbach, Wolfram von 619
Escher, M. C. *224*
Eskimos *see* Inuit
Esoteric Buddhism 469
Esslin, Martin 643
estate system 258
Esterházy family 574
Estes, Richard 555
Estonia **680–1**
language 603
etching *502*
ethane 14, 311
ethanethiol *41*
ethanoic acid *see* acetic acid
ethanol *see* alcohol
Ethelred II 397
ethics 486, **492–3**
Ethiopia (Abyssinia) 287, **681**
and developed countries *298*, 299
famine *296*
history 366, 388, 389, 432, 433, *451*
politics *269*
religion 477
ethnicity 375
ethnomusicology 587
Etna 82, 83
Etruria *376*, 462, 509, 525
eucalyptus 120, 181, 193
eucharist 475
Euclid **62**, 486
eukaryote cell *111*
Euler, Leonhard **62**
Eumenes 373
eunuch *214*
Eupen 440
euphorbias 186
euphotic zone 179
Euphrates 364, *365*, 506
Euripides 614
Europe
agriculture 188–91
animals 112, 129, *130*, 131, 139, 170–1, *181*
mammals 140, 141, 147–8, *149*, 150–61 *passim*
art and architecture **504–9**, **518–57**
techniques 500–3
prehistoric 504–5
ancient 506–7
see also under Greece, ancient; Roman Empire
Medieval and Byzantine 518–19
Gothic 520–3
Renaissance 524–5, 528–9
Baroque and Classicism 530–1
Dutch School 532–3
Rococo and Neoclassical 534–5
Romantic 536–7
19th-century architecture 538–9
Realism 540–1
Impressionism 542–3
Post-Impressionism 544–5
Symbolism, Secession and Expressionism 546–7
Cubism and abstraction 548–9
Dada and Surrealism 550–1
20th-century architecture 552–3
movements since 1945 554–5
business organization 282
climate/weather 103, *105*
dance 592–9
economy 273, 278–9
environment 300–1
film 558–9, 562–3
fishing 194, 195
geology/geomorphology 78–9, *86*, 87, 89, 93, 94, 95, 96, 97, 99
glaciation 90, 91
government 266, 267
health 244, 245
history
prehistory 362–3
ancient 368–81
Celts 374–5
Islam 392, 393
barbarian invasions 380–1, 396–7
Crusades 398–9
Hundred Years War 400–1
14th-century crisis 402–3
Medieval and Renaissance 404–7
Reformation 408–9
France under Louis XIV 414–15
colonialism 383, 385, *387*, 391, **416–17**, 420, 426–9, **432–3**, 476
see also in particular Belgium; Britain; France; Germany; Portugal; Spain
Enlightenment 290, 418–19
Agricultural and Industrial Revolutions 260, 420–1
Revolutionary and Napoleonic Wars 426–7
nationalism 428–9
emigration to USA 431
Empires, peak of 432–3
World War I 436–7
industrial society 434–5
and Russian Revolutions 438–9
post-war settlement 440–1
fascism 442–3
World War II 444–5
decolonization 448–9
Cold War 450–1
and Middle East 454
human rights 290
international relations 278–9, 285, 286–7
journalism 654, 655
language 602–3
law 262, 264, 265
literature
Classical 614–15
Medieval 618–21
Renaissance 622–5
Neoclassical 626–7
Romanticism 630–1, 630–3
Realism and Naturalism 634–5
Symbolism, Aestheticism and Modernism 640–1
experimental theatre 642–3
novel 628–9, 634–7, 640–1, 648–51
criticism 652–3
medicine 248–9
music 570–89
nuclear weapons 288–9
photography 556–7
plants 180–1, *187*
politics 268, 269, 270–1
population 297
religion 462–3, 472–7
science 60–1
society 254, 256, 257, 258, 259, 260
and Third World 298–9
vegetation *104*
women's suffrage 292, 293
writing 604–5
youth movements 294–5
see also European Community; individual countries
European Atomic Energy Authority 286
European Coal and Steel Community 286
European Commission 286
European Community **286**
E numbers 197
government 267
and international economy 278, 279
law 264, 283, **286**
'single market' of 1992 278, 286
European Convention on Human Rights 286, 290, 291
European Court of Justice 286
European Economic Area 286
European Economic Community
see European Community
European Free Trade Association *284*, 286
European Monetary System 279
European Parliament 286
European Social Charter 290
europium *42–3*, *50*
eusocial insects 169
eustasy 97
eutrophication 179
eutrophic ecosystems 179
Evangelicals 477
Evans, Sir Arthur 368
Evans, Walker 557
'Eve hypothesis' 201
evergreen forest
tropical *105*, 182
see also coniferous
evergreen trees 180, 181
everyday life in art 532
evil 640
and good 484–5, 622
evolution 58, 108, 111, **112–13**, 176
of humans **200–1**, 362–3
of mammals 140–1
of plants 118–20
exaltone *41*
excavation (archaeology) *361*
exchange rate and controls **276**, 277, **279**, 297
Exchange Rate Mechanism *see* ERM
Exclusive Economic Zone 195
excretion/excrement 177, **209**, 211, 215, 306
urine 209, 211, 212, 214
see also sewage
executions *401*, *403*, *425*
executive government 266
executives *282*
exemplum 620
exercise and sport **210–11**, 215, 216
exhibitions, international 539, 541, 552, 553, 579
existentialism 491, 648
exorcism 480
exoskeleton 124, 126
exosphere 77
exotic species 193
expenditure *see* spending
experience 488–9
experiments 58–9
see also science
expert systems 336–7
expiation 480
explorers *405*, 417
explosives 320, 321, 356
exports *see* trade
Exposition Universelle 541
Expressionism
in art 544, 545, **547**, *554*, *555*
in literature 635, 642, 645
in music 578
extended family 169, *256*, 257
extinctions of animals **133**, 149, 162, 163, 195, 363
extraterrestrial life 17
extroverts 232
extrusion 197, 317
eye of storm 103
eyes *see* sight
fables *621*
Fabriano, Gentile da 521, 524
facial expressions 228–9
factor endowment 279
factories *see* industry
factors of production 282
see also capital; labour; resources
factory farming 190–1
factory fishing 194
facts and values 492–3
Faeroe Islands 678
Fairbanks, Douglas 560
faith 458, 472
see also religion
Falangists 443
Falconetti, Renée 559
Falkland Islands 195, 622, **729**
fallow land 188
families
animal 169
generations 254
human **256–7**, 293, 296
languages **602–3**
right to 290
see also genetics; home
famine/harvest failure **296–7**, 298, 299
history 415, 424, 432, 439
fan worms *122*
fantasy
in art 534, 536, 537, 546
in literature 632, 633, 634, 641, 649, 651
Fantin-Latour, Henri *640*
Far East *see* Asia
al-Farabi (Avicenna) 392
Faraday, Michael 35, 61, 304, 421
farce 634
farming *see* agriculture
Farouk, King 680
Farquhar, George 627
Fascism 294, **442–3**, 548, 563
Fashoda Incident 433
Fassbinder, Rainer Werner 563
fasting 478
Fathy, Hasan 511
Fatima 392
Fatimids 479, 511
fats, body 209, 215, 236, 237
fats and fatty acids **208**, 209, 217, 237, 245
Faulkner, William 648
faults, geological 78, 80, *85*, **86**, *87*, 88
Fauré, Gabriel 578
Fauvism 544, 545, 548
Fawcett, Millicent Garrett 292
fax 331
fears *see* anxiety
feathers 136
Federal Republic of Germany
see Germany
federalism 267
feelings *see* emotions
Fellini, Federico 563
feminism 292–3
femtosecond 7
Ferdinand I, grand duke 528
Ferdinand II, emperor 409
Ferdinand II and VII of Spain 721
Ferdinand of Aragon 399, 410
Ferguson, Adam 419
fermentation 196, 320–1
fermium *42–3*, *50*
Fernandez, Armand 555
ferns 119
fertility, human
and hormones 214
and ritual *374*, 462, *463*, 504, 516, 592, 593, 594
see also pregnancy; reproduction
fertility, soil/fertilizers 40, 56, 116, **177**, **182**, 189, 297, 300, 320, 321, 420
fertilization 114, 202
in plants 118–21
fertilizers 189
festivals, religious **467**, 469, 470, **473**, **475**, 480, 483
feudalism
in Europe 258, 404, 424
in Japan 386, 387, 515
in Russia 421
abolished 424
fibre in diet 237
fibre optics **33**, 241, *243*, *331*
fibres (textiles)
industry *see* textiles
man-made *see* synthetic
natural 125, 190–1, 318, 413, 416, 514
see also cotton
Fichte, J. G. 631
fiction, prose *see* novel; stories
fiefs 404
Fielding, Henry 628–9, 634
Fiji *389*, 432, 433, 467, 602, **681**
filament (plant) *120*
Fildes, Luke 541
file store *335*
filiariasis 175
Filippo Lippi, Fra 524
film, photographic 316, 320, 324–5
films **558–65**
Hollywood 559, **560–1**, 564–5, 610
international 562–3
making 564–5
and semiology *611*
silent 558–9
Surrealism in 550, 551
see also photography; theatre
'Final Solution' 445
financial system 262, **272–3**, 282, 283
see also banking
fingerprinting
conventional 263
genetic 115
Finland 286, **681–2**
history 363, *445*
language 602, *603*
music 579
women's suffrage 292
Finney, Albert *562*
Finno-Ugrian languages 602, *603*
Fiorentino, Rosso 529
Firdausi 616
fire
first use of 363
brigades 267
burning at stake *401*, *403*, 412
burns 250
of London 413
and plants 182, **184**, **185**
and religion 462, 466
firewood 306
firn and firnline 90
firs 180, 193
First World War *see under* wars
first-past-the-post system 267
first-person narrative 628, 629
fiscal policy 276–7
Fischer, Emil 249
Fischer, Karl 294
fish **128–9**, 167, 168, 169
in ecosystems 178, *179*
farming 195
as food 137, 163, 194, 195, 363
fishing **194–5**, 366, 389, 390, 391, 416
movement/migration 170, 171, 172–3
poisoned 300
in symbiosis 129, *175*
fission *see* nuclear
fissure volcanism 82, 83
Fitzgerald, Edward 616
Fitzgerald, F. Scott 648
Five Hundred, Council of 370, 371
Five K's *467*
Five-Year Plans 439
fixation point 230
fjords 91
flagellum 172
flamboyant style 522
flamingo *137*
Flanders/Flemish
art 474, 521, **526**, 527, 532, 534
history 400, 401, 402, 667
language *603*, 667
music 570, 571
flatfish 173
flatworms **122**, 172, 175, *238*, 238, **239**
Flaubert, Gustave 634
Flavian dynasty 378
flax 318, 366
fleas 173
Flémalle, Master of 526
Fleming, Sir Alexander 57, 249
Fleming, Ian 650
Flemish *see* Flanders
Fletcher, John 623
flies 126
flight 126, **127**, 131, *136*, *147*, *173*
see also aircraft
flightless birds 138
flint tools *362*
Flodden, battle of 412
flood 93, 366, 612
flood plains *94*, 95

Florence 404, 593
art and architecture 501, 520, 521, 523, *524*, 525
Floris, Frans 527
flowering plants 117, 119, **120–1**, 175, 250
fluids, forces affecting 22–3
flukes, blood 122, 175
fluorine 40, *42–3*, 44, 47
flute 583
flying see aircraft; flight
flying dragons/lizards 173
flying fish 173
flying foxes **146**, *173*
flying lemurs *147*
flying snakes 173
flying squirrels *147*, 150
Flyn, Tommy *587*
focus of earthquake 80
fodder 195, 420
foetus *203*
Fokine, Michel 597, 598
folds (geology) *85*, **86**, *87*
folic acid 208
folk music 577, 579, **586–7**, 589, 591, 617
dance 586, 593, **594**
Fontainbleau forest 540
Fontane, Theodor 635
Fonteyn, Margot 596
food **208–9**
agriculture 188–91
chain 118, 176, 177, 300
and disease 237, 245
fish 163, **194–5**, 363
food poisoning 174, **239**
global policy 299
main crops 189
and medicine 249
for plants 116
processing 196–7
as sacrifice 481
and semiology 611
see also agriculture; cereals; dairy; digestion; famine; fruit; hunger; meat; vegetables
Food and Agriculture Organization 192, 285, 297
force/s (physics) 20–3
Ford, Gerald 453
Ford, Henry 352
Ford, John 560, 561, 623
foreign aid see aid
foreign currencies 279
foreign exchange *see* exchange
forensic laboratory 263
forests *104*, 118, 119, **180–3**, **192–3**
animals *130*, 131, 140, *141–2*, 144, 148, 151, 154, *181*
cleared 182, 192
coniferous *104*, 118, 119, **180–3**, 192–3
cross section of tree trunk *116*
dating by tree rings 361
deciduous *104*, 180, *181*, 182, 192–3
ecosystems 180–1, 182–3
and environment *300*
firewood 306
forestry 180–1, 182, **192–3**, 306
timber 119, 121, 366, 416
wood pulp 323
temperate **180–1**, 182–3
tropical **182–3**
foretelling see predictions
Formalists 653
Forman, Milos 562
Forms, theory of 488
formula, chemical 40
Forster, E. M. 648
Forsyth, Bill 562
fortifications, history of
ancient Egypt 367
Iron Age 374, *375*
Inca 391, 516
Crusader's castle *398*
Medieval castles *407*
African 410
French 415
Gothic castles 523
see also wars
FORTRAN 334, 335
Fosse, Bob 561
fossils 200, *201*
fuels see coal; gas; oil
Foucault, Michel 653
Four Noble Truths 468, 469
Fourteen Points (Wilson) 440
Fowles, John 649
Fox Talbot, William 324
foxes 154, 187, 244
Fracastoro, Girolamo 248
fractional distillation *311*
fractures of bones 206
Fragonard, Jean-Honoré 534
frames, film 325
frames of reference 27
France **682–3**
art and architecture
prehistoric 504
Gothic 520, 521, **522–3**
Louis XIV 415
Renaissance 529
early Netherlandish and 527
Baroque and Classicism 531
Rococo and Neoclassical 534, 535
Romantic 536–7
19th-Century 538–9
Realism 540–1
Impressionism 542–3
Post-Impressionism 544–5
Symbolism 546
Cubism and abstraction 548, 549
Dada and Surrealism 551
in 20th century *552*, 553
movements since 1945 554–5
business organization 282
economy 273, 278
film 558, 559, 561, 562, *563*
government *266*, 267
health, disease prevention 245
history
prehistory 362, *363*
ancient 380, 385, 389, 394, 397
religion 462, 463
and Crusades 398, 399
Normans *397*, 401, 403
'Auld Alliance' with Scotland 400
Hundred Years War 400–1
14th century crisis 402–3
Reformation *408*, 409
and Spain 411
and Britain 412, 413
Louis XIV 414–15
colonialism 385, 389, 411, 416–17, 423, *432*, 433
Enlightenment 266, 418–19, 459
Industrial Revolution 421
expansion of USA 430
Revolutions 290, 419, **424–5**, 428, 435
and art 535
and literature 630, 632, 635
and politics 268, 270
and religion *459*
Revolutionary and Napoleonic Wars **426–7**, 428
Franco-Prussian War 428, *429*
nationalism 428, *429*
industrial society 421, 434, 435
and Russian Revolutions 439
World War I 436–7
and totalitarianism/fascism 443
postwar settlement 440–1
World War II 298, 444, *445*, 449
and decolonization 448, 449
Vietnam Wars *452*
and Middle East 454–5
human rights 290
industry 305, *307*, 319, *610*
international relations 278, 285, 286, 287
journalism 654, 655
language *see* French
law 262, 264, *265*
literature
Medieval 618, 619, 620, 621
Renaissance 635
Neoclassical 626–7
novel 629
Romanticism 630, 631
Realism and Naturalism 634–5
Symbolism, Aestheticism and Modernism 640–1
experimental theatre 642, 643
modern novel 648, 649
criticism 652, 653
medicine 243, 248, 249
music 570, 576, 578, 581, 584, 585
Baroque 572, 573
dance *593*, 594–5, 596, 597
folk 586, 587
nuclear weapons 288
photography *556*, *557*
politics 270
religion *459*, 462, 463, 481
science 60, *61*
education 261
and Third World 298
transport/travel 341, 342, *343*, *345*, *347*, 348, 349, 352
women's suffrage 292
youth movements *295–6*
Francesca, Piero della 524, **525**
Francesco, grand duke 528
Francia, José 711
Francis, St 476, *520*
Francis I of France 529
Francis II, emperor 664
francium *42–3*, *50*
Franco, Francisco 443, 722
Franco-Prussian War 428, *429*
Franconia 534, 603
Frank, Robert 557
Franks 380, 394, 397, 605
Franz Ferdinand, Archduke 429, 436
Fraser, Robert 554
fraternities 404
fraternity 269
Frauenlob, Heinrich *570*
Frederick I, emperor 399
Frederick II, emperor 398, 399, 685
Frederick the Great of Russia 417–18
Frederick William of Prussia 685
free association 641
free enterprise 419
free market 268
free trade **279**, 419
free verse 641
freedom 268, 491
artistic see Romanticism
political and social see rights
freemen 404
freezing 197
see also ice
Frege, Gottlob 67, 487, 496, 497
French Guiana see Guyane
French Polynesia 682
French Southern and Antarctic Territories 682
French language **602–3**, 604, 606, 609, 610, 626
Freon-12 309
frequency 28, 31, 72
fresco **500**, *501*, 509, 519, 520, *524*, 534
freshwater
animals 126, 128, 175, 176, 195
mammals 143, 148, 151, 153, 163
ecosystems 178, *179*
polluted 300, 321
see also lakes; rivers
Freud, Sigmund/Freudianism 58, *232*, 233, 645, 653
and art 550, 551
friction 22, *23*
Friedan, Betty 293
Friedlander, Lee 557
Friedman, Milton 277
Friedrich, Caspar David *536*, 536–7
Friendly Islands 417
see also Tonga
Friese-Greene, William 558
Frisians *396*, 603, 606
Frith, William Powell 541, *637*
Froberger, Johann Jacob 573
Froebel, Friedrich 260
frogs **130–1**, 146, 166, 170, *172*, 173
'Frondes' 414
fronts 102
Frost, Robert 647
frottage 551
fruit **120**, 139, 153, 182, 189, 196, 197, 366, 432
fruit bats **146**, *173*
Fry, Roger 544
fuel see energy
fugue 573
Fujiwara family 386
Fujiyama 83
fulmars 136
functional groups *52*, 53
functions in mathematics 70
Fundy, Bay of 307
funerals 254, **255**, 469
fungi **118**, *119*, 174, 175, 177
and disease 118, 212, **238**, 239
fungicides 56, 189
fur 140, 155, 162, 416
furniture *362*, 505, 534, 539, 553
Fuseli, Henry *233*, 537
fuses 36
fusion, linguistic 602
fusion, nuclear *see under* nuclear
Fust, Johann 322
Futabatei Shimei 617
future see predictions
Futurism 548, 556, 640
gabbro 77, 84
Gabin, Jean 562
Gabo, Naum 549
Gabon 287, **683**
Gabriel, Angel *474*, 478
Gabrieli, Andrea and Giovanni 571
Gaddafi, Moamar al 699
gadolinium *42–3*, *50*
Gaelic 413, 603, 606
Gagarin, Yuri 18
Gainsborough, Thomas 534, *535*
galagos 164
Galápagos Islands 112, 135
galaxies 4, *8–9*
Galen of Pergamum 248
Galileo Galilei 14, 17, 20, 58, 61
Galle, Johann 15
galleys **342**, 411
Gallipoli, attack on 437
gallium *42–3*, *50*
Galtieri, President 662
Gama, Vasco da *405*, 625
Gambia 607, **683–4**
gametes 114
gametophyte stage 119
gamma rays 17, *35*, 38, 237, *332*
Gamow, George 5
Gance, Abel 559
Gandhi, Indira 690
Gandhi, Mohandâs *449*, 467, 638, 690
Gandhi, Rajiv 690
Ganges river 163, 467, 481, 482
gannets 136, *137*
Garbo, Greta 563
gardens 511, 534–5, 536
Garibaldi, Giuseppe *428*, 693
Garland, Judy 561
Garrett see Anderson; Fawcett
Garrick, David 596
gas 40, *41*, 42, 77
abuse 246, **247**
natural 41, 49, 101, 306, **311**, 313, 332
poison, used in war 437
thermodynamics 24–5
see also anaesthetics; atmosphere
gas-turbine see jet
Gascony 400, 401, 403
Gaskell, Elizabeth 636, 637
'gasohol' 306, 321
gastrointestinal tract see digestion
gastropods 122
gastroscopy 241
GATT 278, 285
Gaudi, Antonio *552*
Gaudier-Brzeska, Henri 549
Gaugamela, battle of 372, 373
gauge, railway 347
Gauguin, Paul 543, *544*, 546, 547
Gaul 374, 376, 377, 380, 381, 603
Gauss, Carl Friedrich 62
Gautama, Prince see Buddha
Gautier, Théophile 576, 631, 640
gavial 134
Gay, John 621
gay people see homosexuality
Gaza 692
gazelles 161
Gdansk (Danzig) 440
geep 191
geese 191
Geldof, Bob 299
Gemini 9
gems **313**, 366, 514
gemsbok *161*
gender 606
discrimination see sexism
General Agreement on Tariffs and Trade 278, 285
General Assembly (UN) 284, 285
general theories 59
generations 254
genets 153
genetics/heredity **114–15**, 189
engineering 115, 189, 190, **321**
fingerprinting 115, 263
gene-replacement therapy 115
of hominids 200, 201
and intelligence 230–1
and mental disorder 235, 236
nature v. nurture **230–1**, 293
and unconscious 232
see also DNA
Geneva 290, 409, 452, 477
Genghis Khan 382, **383**, 393, 660, 705
genital stage 232
Gennep, Arnold van 254
genre painting 527, 532
Gentile da Fabriano 521, 524
Geoffrey of Monmouth 619
geography *see* geology and geomorphology; individual countries *and* Countries of World section *and also* climate
geology and geomorphology **76–101**, 176
coasts 96–7
deserts 92–3
Earth, structure of 76–7
earthquakes **80–1**, 369
and ecosystems 176
geological cycle *84*
geological time *85*
and industry 313, 420
islands 98–9
oceans 100–1
and oil 310, 311
rivers and lakes 94–5
rock formation 84–5
volcanoes **82–3**, 84, 85
see also caves; glaciation; mountains; tectonics
geometry **62–3**
and art 524–5, 553, 555
see also Cubism
geomorphology *see* geology
George I of England 413, 685
George III of England 234, 422, 580
George, Stefan 640
Georgia **684**
geostationary orbit 19
geothermal energy 307
Gerard of Cremona 60
Géricault, Théodore 536, 537
germ theory 58, 240, 248
German Democratic Republic see Germany
German measles see rubella
germanium *42–3*, *50*
Germany **684–5**
art and architecture 553
Gothic 520, 523
early 526, **527**
Rococo and Neoclassical 534
Romantic 536–7
19th-Century *538*
Realism 541
Symbolism, Secession and Expressionism 546–7
Dada and Surrealism 550–1
movements since 1945 554, 555
business organization 282
economy 273, 278
environment *300*
film 558, 559, 563
glaciation 90
government 267
history
prehistory 362, 363, 375
and Roman Empire 380, 381, 463
barbarian invasions from 396–7
Crusades 398–9, 403
colonialism 394, 432, 433
Medieval and Renaissance 404, 407
Reformation and Thirty Years War 408, 409, 628
Enlightenment 418
Industrial Revolution 420–1
Napoleonic Wars 427
unification 428, 429
emigration to USA 431
industrial society 434, 435
World War I 285, 436, *437*
postwar settlement 440–1
fascism 442–3
World War II 332, 439, 444, *445*
and decolonization 448
divided 450
reunification 686
international relations 278, 286, 287
journalism 654, 655
language 602, *603*, 606, 607
law and crime 262
literature
Medieval 618
Neoclassical 626–7
Romanticism 630–1
Realism and Naturalism 635
Symbolism, Aestheticism and Modernism 640–1
experimental theatre 642–3
modern novel 648
criticism 652
medicine 249
music, opera 584–5
music 570, *586*
Baroque 572–3
Classical 574–5
Romantic 576, 577, 579
dance 596, 597, 598, 599
new 580–1
popular 588
philosophy 629
photography 557
politics 270, 271
religion 463, 477
science *61*
society, education 260, 261
women's suffrage 292
youth movements 294, *295*
see also East Germany; Prussia
Gershwin, George 588
Gerstl, Richard *578*
Gestapo 442
gestures *228–9*, *611*
Gesualdo, Carlo 571
Ghana (Gold Coast) *607*, 608, **685–6**
history 388, 389, 410, 432, 433, *449*
gharial 134
al-Ghazali (Averroes) 392
Ghent 400, *526*
Gheorghiu-Dej, Gheorghe 714
Ghiberti, Lorenzo *524*
Ghirlandaio, Domenico 525
ghost stories 651
Giacometti, Alberto 554
Giambologna 528
giant molecules 45
giantism *205*
Gibbon, Edward 381
Gibbons, Orlando 571
gibbons 165
Gibraltar 729
Gide, André 648
Gierek, Edward 713
Giffard, Henri 348
Gigli, Beniamino 587
Gilbert, Thomas 696
Gilbert, W. S. (b. 1836) 588
Gilbert, William (b. 1540) 61
Gildas 396
gilding 508, *524*
Gillespie, Dizzy 589
gills 122, 126, **128**, 130, *131*
Giorgione 529
Giotto di Bondone 500, **520**, *520*, 521
giraffe 160
Girl guides 294
Girondins 425
Giscard d'Estaing, Valéry 683
Gish, Lillian and Dorothy 559
Giza 366, 507
glaciation *86*, 89, *90*, *91*, 94, 95
see also ice; Ice Ages
Gladstone, William Ewart 693, 731
glands see hormones
glandular fever **239**
Glasgow 294, 419, 552
glasnost 654, 715
glass 301, 320, 509, *522*, 553
Glass, Philip 581
glaucoma 219, 241
Glenn, John 18
gliders 350
gliding animals *147*, **173**
Glorious Revolution 290, 413, 415
glucagon 215
Gluck, Christoph Willibald von 584
glucose 117, 208, 209
glue sniffing 246, **247**
glycerol 208, 209, 321
glycogen 209
glyptodonts 140
gnomon 7
gnu see wildebeest
Goa *411*
goats **161**, 190, **191**, 366, *481*
Gobelins tapestry 415
Gobind Singh, Guru 467
God, concepts of 418, *459*, 461, 464, 465, **474**, 478, 480, 484, **489**
see also gods; religion
Godard, Jean-Luc 562, 611
Goddard, Robert 18
gods and goddesses 458, 459
ancient and primal 369, *374*, **461–3**, 464, 516, 612–13
Egypt 367, 379, *460*, **461**, 462, 507, 612–13
Asian 468, *471*
Hindu **468**, 469, *483*, 484, 613
days named after 7, 463
and good and evil 484, 485
see also God; religion
Goebbels, Josef 442, *443*
Goes, Hugo van der 526
Goethe, Johann Wolfgang von 536, 576, 628, *630*, 632
Gogol, Nikolai 634–5
Golan Heights 285, 455, **692**
gold *42–3*, **50–1**
artwork 363, 374, *508*, 509, 514, 515, 520
mining and trade 312, **313**, 366, 388, 389

Gold Coast *see* Ghana
golden moles 148–9
Golding, William 649
Goldsmith, Oliver 627
Gómez, Juan Vicente 734
Gomulka, Wladyslaw 713
gonads *see* ovaries; testes
Goncharova, Natalia 548
gonorrhoea 239
Gonzaga family 525
good 484–5, 493, 622
Good Hope, Cape of *405*
Goodman, Benny 589
Goodyear, Charles 316
gophers *150*
Gorbachov, Mikhail 289, 451, 715
Gordon, Charles George 722
Gordonstoun School 260
gorillas *165*
Gorki, Maxim 635
goshawk *137*
Gossaert, Jan (Mabuse) 527
Gothic
art and architecture 406, **522–3**, 524, 527
International 521, 526
revival 534, 536, *538*, 539
language 603
novels 632, 636
Goths 380, 394
Götterdämmerung 463
Gottsched, Johann Christoph 626
gouache 501
Goujon, Jean 529
government **266–7**
and economics 272, 275, **276–7**, 380
and education 260, 261
European Community **286**
history 370, 376, 378, 379, 380, 386, 387, 428
and politics 266–71
and religion 462–3, 471
and rights 290–1
subsidies to industry 279
and theatre 645
theories and philosophy of 266, 290
see also law; parliament; *and also under* Countries of World section
Gower, John 620
Gowon, Yakubu 709
Goya y Lucientes, Francisco de *537*, 537
graben (rift valley) 78, *86*
Gracchus, Tiberius and Gaius 376
gradualism 113
graduation 255
Graham, Martha 598
grains *see* cereals
grammar 604, 606, 607, 608–9
gramophone 328
Granada 399, 410, 511
Grand Canyon 94
Granikos, battle of 372, 373
granite 76–7, 84
Grant, General Ulysses S. 431
graphite 45, 52, 305
graphs *70–1*
grass 184
Grass, Günter 649
grasshoppers 173
grasslands **184–5**
and animals 140–1, 161
grazing 142, 160, *161*, 176, 182, 185, 190–1
Gravelines, battle of 412
Graves, Michael 553
Graves, Robert 646
Graves disease 215
gravimetric surveys 310, 313
gravitation 17, 21, 22, 100–1
Gray, Thomas 627
grazing *see under* grasslands
Great Exhibition *434*, 539
Great Fire of London 413
'Great Leap Forward' 447
Great Northern War 417
Great Purge 439
Great Schism 399, 403
Great Wall of China 382, *383*
grebes *139*
Greco, El *529*
Greece, ancient **368–73, 686**
art and architecture *505*, **508–9**, 512
dance 593, 596
government 266
and India 372, 385
and Rome 376
and Islam 392
influence on later ages 395, 406–7
art and architecture 534, 535, 538
literature 615, 624–7, 633, 652
religion 462
language *see* Greek
literature 462, **614–15**
major periods
prehistoric 363
Mycenaean **368–9**
Archaic and Classical 365, **370–1**, 508–9
Hellenistic Age and Alexander the Great **372–3**, 509
medicine 248
philosophy 248, 290, 407, 462, 476, 486–7, **492**, 652
religion 459, 461, *462*
science 60
society, education 260
Greece, modern **686**
art 519
astronomy 16
environment 300
film 562
Greeks in Cyprus 259
history
ancient *see* Greece, ancient
20th-Century 428, 429, *437*, 441, 444, *445*, *451*
international relations 286, 287
language *see* Greek
law 264
music 581
religion 477
society 254
volcanoes 82
Greek language 474, 476, **602**, **603**, 604, *605*, 607
Green politics 269, 301
Green Revolution 189
Greene, Graham 648–9
greenhouse effect **48**, 182, 301, 304
Greenland 171, 397, 405, **678**
ecology *118*, 187
geology/geomorphology 90, *91*, 98
Greenwich 7
Greer, Germaine 293
Gregorian calendar 7, 425
Gregorian chant 568
Gregorian reform 398
Gregory I, Pope 568
Gregory VII, Pope 398
Gregory XIII, Pope 7, 425
Grenada *451*, **686–7**
Grice, H. P. 497
Grieg, Edvard 577, 587
Grien, Hans Baldung 527
Grierson, John 562
Grieve, C. M. 647
Griffith, Arthur 692
Griffith, D. W. *558*, 559, 564
Grimm, Jacob and Wilhelm Carl 602
Grimmelshausen, J. J. C. von 628, 629
Gris, Juan 548
Gropius, Walter 553
gross domestic and national products 277, 296
Grosz, George 547, 550–1
groundsels 187
ground sloth *140*
ground state 26–7
groups, social 258–9
see also class; family; society
growth, economic 276, 277
growth, physical *116*, 191, **204–5**, 215
grunion 129
Guadalcanal *444*, 445
Guadeloupe 682
Guam 432, 433, *444*, **731**
guanaco 159
guano 147
Guardi, Gianantonio and Francesco 534
Guatemala *451*, **687**
Guernica 443
Guernsey 729
Guerrero, Vicente 703
guerrilla warfare 433, 452
Guesclin, Bertrand du 401
Guevara, 'Che' 295, 451
guilds 404, 621
Guimard, Hector 552
Guinea 167, 432, 433, *449*, **687**
Guinea Bissau *449*, **687**
guinea pigs *150*, 151
Guinness, Alec 562
Gulf Stream 99
Gulf War 455
gulls **136–7**, 168
Gundestrup Cauldron *374*
gundis *150*
Güney, Yilmaz 563
gunpowder 356
guns *see* weapons
Guomindang 446
Guptas 385, 512, 513
Guru Granth Sahib 467, 482
gurus 260, 466, 467, 482
Gustaf I of Sweden 723
Gustavus Adolphus of Sweden 409, 723
Gutenberg, Johannes 322, 407
Gutenberg discontinuity *76*, *77*
gut flora **175**
Guyana 467, *607*, **687–8**
Guyane (French Guiana) 682
gymnosperms **119**
Gypsies 445, 594, 603
gyptodont *141*
gyroplane 349

Haakon IV and VI of Norway 709
Haber, Fritz 320
Habeus Corpus Act 290
Habsburgs 394, 409, 410, 411, 418
see also Austria-Hungary
'hacking' computers 262
Hackworth, Timothy 347
Hadrian 378, *379*, *509*
Hadrian VI, Pope 527
haemodialysis 243
haemoglobin 139, 208, 210, 236
haemophiliacs 238
haemorrhoids 237
Hafiz 616
hafnium *42–3*, *50*
Hagia Sophia 394, 511, *518*
Hahn, Kurt 260
Hahn, Otto 288
Haicheng earthquake 80
haiku 617
hailstones 102
Haiti *465*, 592, **688**
half-life 39
halftone process *323*
Hall, G. Stanley 294
Haller, Albrecht von 249
Halley's Comet 11
Hallstatt art 374–5
hallucinations 224, **247**, 551, 632, 633, 635, 641
halogens 42, 47
Hals, Franz 533
Haly Abbas (al-Majri) 392
Hamilton, Alexander 430
Hamilton, Richard 554
Hamites 364, 388, 602
Hammerstein II, Oscar 588
Hammett, Dashiel 650
Hammurabi 248, 364
hamsters *150*
Han Empire 382, 383, 514, 617
Handel, George Frideric 572, *573*, 574, 575, **584**
Hannibal 376, 377
Hanoverians 413
Hanslick, Eduard 577
Happenings 554
al-Haq, Muhammad Zia 710
Harappans 384, 512
Harare meeting *287*
harbours *see* ports
Hardenberg, Friedrich Leopold von 631
hardware (computers) 334–7
hardwoods 192, *193*
hardwood forests 180–3
Hardy, Thomas 637, 646, 647, 648
Hare, David 644
Hare, Richard 493
Hare Krishna 459, 467
hares *151*
Hargreaves, James 318
Harijan caste 258, *259*
al-Hariri, Abu Muhammad al-Kasim *616*
harmony 470, 471, 534
harmonics *31*
Harold Godwinson, King 397
Harold Hardrada 397
harp 583
harpsichord *582*
Harrison, John 7
Harsha 385
Hartung, Hans 554
harvest 480
failure *see* famine
Harvey, William 210, 248
Hassan II of Morocco 705
Hassidic Judaism 473
Hastings, Warren 417
Hastings, battle of 397
Hattusas 364, 507
Hattusilis III 364
Hauptmann, Gerhart 635
Hausmann, Raoul 550–1
Havel, Vaclav 678
Hawaii
geology/geomorphology *82*, 83, 86, 89, *98*, 99
history 388, 417, 432, 433
Hawkins, Sir John 412
hawks 136, *137*
Hawksmoor, Nicholas 531
Haydn, Franz Joseph **574**, 575, 577, 580, 582
Hayek, Friedrich 271
health/healing *see* diseases; medicine
Heaney, Seamus 646
Heard and MacDonald Islands 663
hearing 139, **219**, 223, 224, 225, 240
see also deaf; sound
heart 207, **210–11**, 215
and circulation 210, *211*
disorders 57, 236, **242**, **243**, 245, 247, 250
surgery 240, 241, 249
Heartfield, John 551, 556–7
heat **24–5**
body 211
engines 308–9
heating 36, 304, 306
see also electricity
hot-spot volcanoes 83
and internal energy 24–5
transfer 25
wasted 304
within Earth 176–7, 307
see also temperature
heaven 461
heavy water 305
Hebrew 602, 603, 605
Hebrides 587
Heckel, Erich *547*
hedgehogs *149*, 171
Hedley, William 347
hedonism 493
Heemskerck, Maerten van 527
Hegel, G. W. F. 271, 487, 631
Heian period 386, 515, 616
Heidegger, Martin 487
heights, measuring *see* trigonometry
Heine, Heinrich 576, 631
Heisenberg, Werner Karl 21, 26
helicopters *349*, 351
helium 4, 9, 10, 14, 15, 40, **42**, *43*, 77, 305
hell 461, *485*
Hellenic languages 603
Hellenistic Age 372–3
Hell's Angels *294*
Helmholtz, Herman von 24
helots 370
Helsinki Conference 451
hemichordates 123
Heminges, John 623
Hemingway, Ernest 648
hemp 318
Hendrix, Jimi 589
Henri of Navarre 593
Henry I, emperor 394
Henry VI, emperor 399
Henry II of England 400, 619, 691, 731
Henry IV of France 683
Henry V of England 401, 403
Henry VII of England *405*, 412, 622, 731
Henry VIII of England 412, 527, 622
Henry, Joseph 35, 61
Henry the Navigator, Prince 398, *405*, 713
Henze, Hans Werner 581, 585, 596
hens 191
hepatitis 237, **239**
Hepworth, Barbara 549
Hepworth, Cecil 559
Heraclitus 487, 488
Heraclius, emperor 395
herb/herbaceous plants 120, 248, 250
Herbert, George 625
Herbert, Victor 588
herbicides *56*, 189, 321
herbivorous animals
in ecosystems *177*, 181, 184, *185*, 187
mammals 140, 142, 150, 154–62 *passim*, 177
reptiles and amphibians 132, 133, 135
Herculaneum 82, *462*, 509
Herder, Johann Gottfried 630
heredity *see* genetics
Hereros 432, 602
heresies 398–9, 403, 408, 409
Herkomer, Hubert 541
hermaphrodites 122
hermit crabs *175*
Herodotus 360, 366, 614
heroin 246, **247**
herpes 239
Herschel, Sir William 14
Hertz, Heinrich Rudolf 35, 61
Hertzsprung–Russell diagram *9*
Herzefelde *see* Heartfield
Herzegovina 429, 668
Herzl, Theodor 454
Herzog, Werner 563, *651*
Hesiod 614
Hess, Rudolf *443*
Hesyre 507
heterotrophs 110, 177
Hevelius, Johannes 12
Hewa men *256*
Heyer, Georgette 651
hibernation 135, 147, 149, 154, **171**, 181
hickories 181
Hideyoshi, Toyatomi 386
hierarchy 270–1 *see also* class
hieroglyphs *361*, 366, 391, 604, *605*
hi-fi 328–9
'High Art' 557
high-lift system 351
higher education 261
see also universities
high-pressure areas 103
high-speed photography *325*
hijackers *263*
Hijikata, Tatsumi 599
Hijra 478
Hilbert, David **62**, 68
Hildesheim Treasure 509
Hill, Geoffrey 646, 647
Hilliard, Nicolas 412
Himalaya 76, 86, 87, *187*, 190
animals 131, 141, 151, 153, 155, 158
Himmler, Heinrich 442, *443*
Hindenburg, Paul von 442
Hindenburg airship 48, *348*
Hindi 602, 603, 607
Hinduism **466–7**, 469, 484
and art 512
castes 258, *259*, 466
and dance 592
history 384, 392, 458, 459
myths 613
pilgrimage 481
prayer 480
time and space 482, *483*
and women 293
hip replacement 240
Hipparchus of Nicaea 60
hippies 295
Hippocrates/Hippocratic Oath 248
hippopotamuses **158–9**, *159*, *506*
Hiram of Tyre 507
Hirohito, emperor 471, 694
Hiroshige *471*
Hiroshima *288*, 445
Hispaniola 149
historical materialism 269
historical novels 632, 638
history **358–455**
major periods
prehistory 360–3
ancient world 364–81
Celts 374–5
Egypt 366–7
Greece 368–73
Minoans and Mycenaeans 368–9
Roman Empire 376–81
pre-colonial age 382–407
Africa, Australasia and Oceania 388–9
America 390–1
China 382–3
India and Southeast Asia 384–5
Japan 386–7
Islam, rise of 392–3
Holy Roman and Byzantine Empires 394–5
barbarian invasions 396–7
Crusades 398–9
Hundred Years War 400–1
14th-century crisis 402–3
Medieval and Renaissance 404–7
16th to 19th centuries 408–35
Reformation 408–9
colonialism 410–13, 416–17, 432–3
Louis XIV 414–15
Enlightenment 418–19
Agricultural and Industrial Revolutions 420–1
USA, development of 422–3, 430–1
French Revolution 424–5
Revolutionary and Napoleonic Wars 426–7
nationalism in Europe 428–9
industrial society 434–5
20th century 436–55
World War I 436–7
Russian Revolutions 438–9
postwar settlement 440–1
totalitarianism 442–3
World War II 444–5
China 446–7
decolonization 448–9
Cold War 450–1
Vietnam Wars 452–3
Middle East 454–5
of agriculture 188
of architecture *see* architecture
of art *see* art
of astronomy **16–17**, *58*, 505
of education 260
of government 266
of languages 602–3, 606–7
of literature *see* literature
of mathematics **63**, 365, 391, 392, 418
of medicine **248–9**, 292, 392, 406
of music *see* music
of philosophy 487
of religion *see* religion
of science *see under* science
of society 258
see also individual countries *and* Countries of World section
Hitchcock, Alfred 561, 562
hi-tech *553*
Hitler, Adolf 341, 439, 441, **442**, *443*, 444, 445, 678, 681, 685, 689, 698, 700, 713, 715, 719, 736
Hitler Youth 294
Hittites 364, 367, 461, 507, 603, 604
HIV 115, 175, **213**, 239, 247
Hizbollah 698
Ho Chi Minh 295, 452
Ho Chi Minh City (Saigon) *453*
hoatzin 138
Hobbema, Meindert 532
Hobbes, Thomas 266, 487, 488
Höch, Hannah *550*
Hockney, David 501, 554
Hodgkin's disease *236*
Hoffman, Abbie 295
Hoffman, Josef 552
Hoffmann, E. T. A. 651
Hogarth, William 534, 554, *629*
Hogmanay 254
Hohenheim, Theophrastus B. von *see* Paracelsus
Hohenstaufen dynasty 394, 399
Hokusai *515*
Holbein, Hans, the Younger 527
Hölderlin, Friedrich 631
Holiday, Billie 588
Holinshed, Raphael 360
holistic medicine 250
Holland, Henry 535
Holland *see* Netherlands
Hollerith, Herman 335
Holly, Buddy 589
Hollywood 559, **560–1**, 564–5, 610
Holman Hunt, William 537
holmium *42–3*, *50*
Holocene epoch *85*
holograms *33*
Holst, Gustav 579
Holstein 428
Holt, Victoria 651
Holy Land *see* Israel; Palestine
Holy Roman Empire 394, 410, 415, 519
Holy Spirit 475, 483
home/household
in art 527, 532, 545
and religion 462, 471
work in 293
see also families
Homer 369, 462, 614, 627, 641
Homer, Winslow *541*
hominids 200, *201*
Homo genus *108*, *200*, *201*, 362–3, 388
see also humans
homoeopathy 250, 251
homoiothermy 140
homologous structures *112*
homosexuality 262, 293, 371, 617

Honduras **688**
Honecker, Erich 685
Hong Kong 278, 453, 470, *607*, **729**
  film 562, 563
  history 433, *444*, 445, 447
Hongwe (Hung-Wu) 383
Honthorst, Gerard van 532
Hooch, Pieter de 532, 534
Hooke, Robert 23, 61
hookworms **122**, 238
Hopkins, Sir Frederick G. 249
Hopkins, Gerard Manley 646
hoplite warriors 370, *371*
Horace **615**, 624, 625, 626, 627
Horatii, Oath of *626*
horizontal-axis turbines 306, *307*
hormones 211, **214–15**, 237, 243, 251
  growth 116, 191, 204–5
  manufacture 321
  replacement therapy 205
  and reproduction 202
  and sleep 232
Horn, Cape *405*
horns **161**, 168
horror stories 632, 638, 651
horses 141, **156**, 157, 190, **191**, 391, *401*, 504
  movement 173
horsetails 118, *119*
horst *86*
Horta, Victor 552
Horthy, Miklás 689
horticulture 188, 189
Hoskins, Bob *565*
Hospitallers 399
hospitals 248, *249*
  history 392, 406
  mental *234*
  see also medicine
hosts (of parasites) 174
hot-metal printing 322
Houghton Hall 535
Houphouet-Boigny, Felix 676
household *see* families; home
Houses of Parliament 265, 267, 538
housing 244, 267, *298*, 553
  construction 338–9
  history of 434, *435*, 505
  see also architecture
hovercraft *344*
Howard of Effingham 412
Howland, Baker and Jarvis Islands 731
howler monkeys 165, 166
Hoxha, Enver 660
Hoyle, Sir Fred 5
Huang Gongwang *514*
Hubble, Edwin 4, **5**, 8, 19, 31
Hudson, Hugh 562
Hudson, Thomas *573*
Huelsenbeck, Richard 550
Huggins, Sir William 5
Hughes, Ted 646, 647
Hugo, Victor *631*, 640
Huguenots 409, 624
human immunodeficiency virus 213, 239, 247
humanism 406, 408, 458
humans
  development of *see Homo*
  and ecosystems 180, 182
  human capital 272
  organism
    diet 208–9
      see also food; digestion
    evolution 200–1
    glands and hormones 214–15
    immune system 212–13
    movement 206–7
    nervous system 220–1
    perception 224–5
    physical development 204–5
    reproduction 202–3
    respiratory and circulatory systems 210–11
    senses 216–19
    see also diseases and disorders; psychology
  parasites on and in 174–5
  prehistory 141, 360–1, **362–3**, 388
  in space 18, 19
  see also history; rights
Humayun 511
Humboldt, Wilhelm von *602*
Hume, David 59, 419, 487, **489**, *494*
hummingbirds 136, *137*, 171, 175
humour *see* comedy
humours in medicine 248
humus 182
Hunan 446
Hundred Years War **400–1**, 403, 412
Hung-Wu (Hongwe) 383
Hungary 287, **688–9**
  art and architecture 555
  history
    ancient 375
    Magyars 394
    Austria reconquers 417
    nationalism 428, 429
    and fascism 442
    postwar settlement 441
    World War II *445*
    Cold War 450, *451*
    uprising *450*, 450, *451*
    see also Austria-Hungary
  language 602, *603*
  law 265
  literature 652
  medicine 249
  music 577, 578, 579, 581, 586, 598
hunger *see* famine
Huns 380, 381
Hunt, Holman 537, 541
Hunter, John 249
hunting 163, 195, 201, 363, 366
  art *see* caves, paintings
  dances 592
  history 363, 366
    hunter-gatherers 386, 388, 389, 390–1, 504
  religion and ritual 462, 464
  whales 163, 195, *639*
Huntington's chorea 236
hurricanes 103, *104*
Hurt, John *564*
Hus, Jan *403*
Hussein, King of Jordan 455, 695
Hussein, Saddam 691
Husserl, Edmund 487
Hussites 399, 403, 408
hutias *150*
Hutton, James 61
Huxley, Aldous 651
Huxley, T. H. 112, 113
Huygens, Christiaan 7, 14, 29
Huysmans, Joris-Karl 641
Hyatt, John Wesley 316
hybridization 109, 189
hydrocarbons 52, 320
  see also gas; oil
hydroelectric power 95, **307**
hydrogen 4, **42**, *43*, **48**, 77
  bomb 288, 305
  bonds 40, 44, **45**, 47, *53*
  isotopes 305
  on planets 14, 15
  in stars 9, 10
hydroids 175
hydrological cycle *95*, 176
hydroponics *189*
hydrostatics 23
hyenas 152, *153*, 166, 168, 169
Hyksos kings 367
hyperglycaemia 214
hyphae 118
hypnotic drugs 233, 247
hypocentre of earthquake 80
hypostyle 507
hypothalamus 214, 215, 216, *222*
hypothesis testing 59
hyraxes 151
hysteria 232, 235

I Ching (Yijing) 470, 616
ibex 161
Ibsen, Henrik 635, 642, 644
ice 48, 87, 89, **90–1**, 96 102
  icebergs *100*
  see also freezing; glaciation
Ice Ages 99, *141*, 180, 362, 388, 390
  and human development 200, 201
  see also glaciation
Iceland 286, **689**
  energy 304, 307
  fishing 195
  geology/geomorphology 87, 89
  glaciation 90
  history 397, 463
  language *603*
  literature 618
ichthyosaur 132
icons/iconography *458*, 480, 518, 520
  iconoclasm 519
  in semiology 610
id 232
ideal gas 24, *25*
idealism/ideal 58–9, 470, 489, 628
ideas (philosophy) 488–9
identity *see* individual
ideology, political 276
idiot savant 231
Idris, King of Libya 699
Ieyasu, Tokugawa 386
Ife people *516*, 517
igneous rocks 84, *85*
iguanodon 133
Ihara Saikaku 617
Ikeda Daisuku 471
Il-Sung, Kim 295, 696
illness *see* diseases and disorders
illuminated manuscripts *519*, *521*
illusion *224*, **225**
  in art 525, 533
image
  intensifiers 333
  recognition 218–19
  of self 610, 611
imaginary numbers 65
imaging, medical 55, 241, 242, *243*, *332*
imams 478–9, 510
Imhotep 248, 366, 461, 507
immanence of God 480
immune system **212–13**, 237, 240, 249
immunization 213, 238, 239, **244–5**, 249
impala 161
imperialism *see* Empires
impermanence 468
impermeable and impervious rock *88*, *89*, 94, 310
imports *see* trade
Impressionism 537, 540, **542–3**, 548, 556
in vitro fertilization 215
Incas 391, 410, 516
incense 366
incest taboo 256
incisors 140, *152*
income 275
  tax 276
  see also wages
inconsistency (logic) 494, 495
incorporation 254, 255
independence
  American 417, 419, **422–3**, 424
  decolonization 448–9
'Index' of heretical books 409
index in semiology 610
India 191, 287, **689–90**
  animals 128, 139, 153, 154, 156–7, 161, 163
  art and architecture *510*, **511**, 538
  caste system 258, *259*, 466
  conflict 259
  and developed countries *298*
  film 562, 563
  health/medicine 245, 248
  history
    before colonial age 260, 365, 372, 373, **384–5**
    colonialism 383, 405, 410, 432, 433, 637
      East India Companies 385, *417*, 422, 432
    and Islam 392, 393, *479*
    20th-Century 447, *451*, 690–1
      independence/partition 259, 298, 448, 449
  journalism 655
  languages 602, **603**, *607*
  literature 616, 620, 649
  music 586, 590, *591*, *593*
  religion 458, 459, 461, **466–7**, 468, 476, 477, *480*, 482, 484
    see also Hinduism; Jainism; Sikhhism
  society 255, 260
  weather 103
  women's suffrage 292, 293
Indian Ocean area 301, *485*
  animals 128, 138, 146, 149, 158, 162, 163
  geology/geomorphology *99*, **100**
Indians, American
  North American **185**, 186, 214, 390, *391*, 465, 592, 602
  South American 410, 411
indium *42–3*, *50*
individual/person
  crimes against 262
  and economy 269
  identity 490–1
  in literature 632, 633, 634, 648, 649
  see also rights
Indo-Aryan 461, 603
Indochina 268, 269
  history 432, 433, 449, *451*, 452
  see also Cambodia; Laos; Vietnam
Indo-Europeans 462, 603
  languages **602–3**
  religion 461
Indonesia 82, 158, 287, 591, **690**
  animals 139, 164, 165
  geology/geomorphology 86, 99
  history 388, 393, 405, 417
    World War II *444*, 445
    decolonization *448*, 449
indri 164
induction (electromagnetic) **35**, 304
induction (philosophical) 59, 495
industry 280, **304–21**
  and art 543, 548, 555
  building construction 338–9
  chemicals and biotechnology 320–1
  crops for 121
  and disease 237
  electrochemistry *50*
  engines 308–9
  government subsidies to 279
  history
    Industrial Revolution 314, **420–1**
      and deforestation 193
    industrial society 434–5
  and international economy 278
  iron and steel 314–15
  labour 273
  in literature 636
  moles in 47
  nationalized 276
  oil and gas 310–11
  and plant crops 182
  privatized 276
  robotics in *336*, 337
  rubber and plastics 314–15
  safety and health hazards 244, 305
  tribunals 265
  see also communications; economics; energy; metals; mining; technology; textiles; trade unions; transport; weapons; *and under* Countries
inert gases *see* noble gases
inertia 21
inertial frames 27
infectious diseases 211, 213, **238–9**
inferences in science 58, 59
infinitesimals 70
infinity 68, 69
inflation 273, **276**, 279, 311, 441
inflectional language 602, 603, 606, 609
influenza 238, **239**
infrared waves 17, *35*, 333
infrasonic sounds 171
infrasound 171
infrastructure, economic 276
inhabited scroll 519
inheritance *53*, 112, 113, **114–15**, 394
initiation rites **254–5**, 470, 480, *481*, 504, 592
injunction 265
Inkerman, battle of 429
Innocent III, Pope 399
Innocent VIII, Pope *409*
inoculation *see* vaccination
input peripherals *335*
Inquisition 409
inquisitorial system of law 264, 265
insecticides *see* pesticides
insectivores 148–9
insects **126–7**, 172, 173, 181
  anatomy *126*
  communication 166
  disease transmission by 238, 239
  in ecosystems 186
  evolution 112, 113
  movement 173
  as parasites 174, 175
  as pollinators 121
  and symbiosis 175
  social organization 169
inshore fishing 194
instincts 223, 419
instruments, musical 31, *570*, 571, 572, **582–3**, 587, 590–1
insulation 307, *339*
insulator 35
insulin 115, 214, 215, 321
  lack of *see* diabetes
insurance **272**, 413, 434
intaglio 323, 502
integers 64
integration in calculus 71
intelligence **230**, *231*
  artifical **336–7**, 609
Intelsat 331
intensive care 242
interactionism 490
Inter-American Convention on Human Rights 290
interest rate 277
interference *26*, *29*
interferon 238
interludes 621
intermediate nuclear forces 289, 451
internal-combustion engine 308, *309*, *354–5*
internal energy 24–5
internal reflection, total *30*, *32*
International Atomic Energy Authority 285
International Court of Justice 285
International Covenants on Rights 290
International Gothic 521, 526
international language *see* English
International Monetary Fund 279, **299**
international music 590–1
international relations 269, **278–9**, **284–9**, **298–9**
  disease control 244
  division of labour 278
  economics **278–9**, 299
  environmental threats 300–1
  films 562–3
  human rights 290–1
  nuclear armament and disarmament 288–9
  organizations **284–7**, 298, **299**
  population and hunger 296–7
  rights 290–1
  Third and Developed Worlds 298–9
  women's movement 292–3
  see also history; trade;
    and also individual countries
intestines 209
Intifada 455
Intimists 544–5
intoxication 247
introverts 232
intuitionism 69
Inuit people 195, 390, 391, 464, 465, 517
invasions
  animal 170
  invasion hypothesis 361
  see also barbarian
invertebrates *see* arthropods; primitive animals
Investiture Contest 398
investment **272–3**, 279
invisible trade 279
iodine *42–3*, 47
Ionesco, Eugene 643
Ionic Order *509*
ionizing radiation 237
  see also radioactivity
ionosphere 77
ions/ionic compounds *44*
Iran (Persia before 1935) **690–1**
  history 454, 455
    ancient *see* Persia
  international relations 285, 287
  Iran–Iraq War 455
  language *see* Persian
  literature 616, 649
Iran–Iraq War 455
Iraq **692**
  Gulf War 455, 691
  history 285, 392, 441, 454, *455*, 479
    ancient *see* Mesopotamia
  Iran–Iraq War 455, 692
  international relations 284, 285, 287
Ireland **691–2**
  art and architecture 505
  history
    ancient 363, 375, 396, 397, 463
    and England 412, 413
    emigration from 420, 431
  international relations 284, 286
  language 602, 603, 605
  law and crime 262
  literature 641, 643, 644, **645**, 646
  music *587*, 595
  religion 463, 476, 477
  separatism 259
  society 256, 261
  women's suffrage 292
  see also Northern Ireland
iridium *42–3*, *50*, 133
iron 9, 40, 41, *42–3*, **50–1**, 383, 389
  in architecture 538–9
  mining 312, **313**
  organic 116, 208
  in rocks 77
  ships 342
  and steel industry **314–15**, 420
  see also Iron Age
Iron Age 312, **362–3**, 364–5, *374–5*, 388, *505*
Iron Bridge 539
Iron Curtain 450
  see also Eastern Europe
irony 634
irradiation of food *197*
irrational numbers 65
irrigation *see under* agriculture
Irving, Washington 638
Isabella I of Spain 399, 410, 721
Isabella II of Spain 721
Islam and Muslims **392–3**, **478–9**
  art and architecture **510–11**, 513
  calendar 7
  and Christianity 476, 477
  and dance 592
  education 261
  history
    and Africa 388–9
    rise of **392–3**
    and Byzantine Empire 395
    Crusades against **398–9**
    map of distribution *409*
    and decolonization 449
    and Arab-Israeli wars 455
    law 479
  human rights 290
  law 262, 264, 265, 479
  and literature 616, 649
  religion 299, 459, **478–9**, 480
    alcohol forbidden 246, 262
    good and evil 484, 485
    pilgrimage *see* Mecca
    Pillars of 478
    time and space 482–3
  science 60
  and social conflict 259
  society, family 256, 257
  and women 293
  see also Arabs; Shiite; Sunni
islands 83, **98–9**
  see also Atlantic; Indian Ocean; Pacific
Ismail and Ismailis 479
isobars 102, *103*
Isocrates 614
isolating languages 602
isometric contraction 207
isostasy 97
isotonic contraction 207
isotopes **39**, 43, 304–5
Israel **692**
  history
    ancient 363, 365
    and decolonization 449
    creation of 454–5
    Arab-Israeli wars 287, 298, 451, *454*, 455
  language *605*, *607*
  law and crime 263
  religion 476
  society 255
  see also Palestine
Issigonis, Sir Alexander 352, *353*
Issos, battle of *372*, 373
Istanbul 727
  see also Constantinople
Istria 441
Italic languages 602–3
Italy **692–3**
  art and architecture 553
    prehistoric 505
    Medieval and Byzantine *518*, 519
    Gothic 520–1, 523
    Renaissance 524–5, 528–9
    early Netherlandish and 526–7
    Baroque and Classicism **530–1**
    Dutch school 532
    Rococo and Neoclassical 534, 535
    19th-century 538, 539
    Realism 541
    Cubism and abstraction 548
  astronomy 17
  business organization 282
  economy 278
  environment 301
  film 559, 561, 562, 563, 564
  government 266, 267
  history
    ancient *see* Roman Empire
    barbarian invasions 381
    post-Roman Empire 394–5
    Crusades 399
    and crisis in Europe 403
    Reformation 408
    and Spain 411
    Enlightenment 418
    Medieval and Renaissance 404, 405, 406, 407
    Napoleonic Wars 426–7
    unification 428
    emigration from 431
    colonialism 432, 433
    World War I 436, 437
    fascism 442–3, 548
    postwar settlement 441
    society, education 260
    World War II 444, *445*

and decolonization 448
and Middle East 454
international relations 278, 286
language 603, 609, 611
law and crime 262
literature 631, 643
Medieval 618, *619*, 620, 621
Renaissance 622, 624–5
Realism and Naturalism 635
Symbolism and Aestheticism 640
modern novel 648, 649
medicine 248, 249
music 570, 571–3, 576, 580, 581, 584–5, 587
dance 593, 595, 597
photography 556
religion 476
society 256
education 260
volcanoes 82, 83
women's suffrage 292, 293
youth movements 294
Ivan III of Russia 715
Ivan IV of Russia 715
Ives, Charles 579, 580
ivory 157, 366, 388, *506*, 507, *508*, *515*
Ivory Coast *see* Côte d' Ivoire
Iwo Jima, battle of *444*, 445

jacana 169
jackal 154
Jackson, Andrew 430
Jackson, John Hughlings 223
Jacobeans 623
Jacobins 425
Jacobites 413
Jacquard, Joseph-Marie 319, 335
Jadwiga, Queen of Poland 700, 712
Jagger, Mick 554
Jagiello, grand duke 700, 712
jaguar 153
Jainism *458*, 459, 466, **467**, 484
meditation *480*
Jakobson, Roman 653
Jamaica 292, 595, 609, **694**
James, St 481
James I of England (VI of Scotland) 412–13, 606, 607, 623, 692, 730
James II of England 413, 693, 730
James VI of Scotland *see* James I
James Francis Edward Stuart, Prince ('Old Pretender') 413
James, Henry 639, 648
James, M. R. 651
James, William 487
Janáček, Leoš 585
Janesz, Willem de 663
Jansenists 415
Jansky, Karl 17, 332
Japan 98, 165, 286, **694**
art and architecture 515
business organization 282
dance 593, 597, 599
economy 273
environment 300
film 562, *563*
fishing 194, 195
history
before 20th century 383, **386–7**
colonialism 432, 433
Industrial Revolution 421
industrial society 434, 435
Russo-Japanese War 387, 421, 433, 438
and Russian Revolutions 439
navy in 1920s 441
totalitarianism 442–3
invasion of Manchuria (1931) 446
World War II *288*, *444*, 445, 446, 452
and China in 20th century 446
and decolonization 448
Cold War *451*
unions 435
language 602, 603
literature 616, **617**
music *591*
religion 386, 459, 468, 469, **470–1**, 485
society 258, 261
volcanoes 83
women's suffrage 292
writing 604
youth movements **295**
Jarry, Alfred *643*
Jaruzelski, Tadeusz 713
Java *513*
history 362, 385, 416
Java man 200
Javacheff, Christo *555*
Jawara, Dawda K. 684
Jawlensky, Alexej 547
Jayavarman II, King 671
jazz **588–9**, 593, 595
Jefferson, Thomas 422, 430
Jehovah's Witnesses 477
jellyfish *123*, 129, 172
Jena, battle of *427*
Jenner, Edward 249
jerboas *150*, 186
Jericho 365, 506
Jersey 729
Jerusalem 692
art and architecture 507, 510
history *365*, 392, 398, 399, 437, 621
pilgrimage to 481
religion 476, *482*
Temple destroyed 472, 480
Jesuits 409, 419
Jesus Christ **474–7**, 478, 480, 482
see also Christianity
jet lag 232
jets 308, *309*, 348, *349*
jewellery 506, 508, 514
Jews
discrimination against 291, 442, 445
history 365, 424, 442, 445
languages of 603
religion (Judaism) 7, 454, 459, 461, 466, **472–3**, 480
festivals **473**, 483
good and evil 484, 485
and human rights 290
myth 612
rites of passage 254, *255*, **472**, 480
see also Israel
Jiang Jie Shi 446, 447, 675
Jiangxi 446
jihad ('holy war') 392, 478
Jiménez, Marcos Peréz 734
Jimmu, emperor 694
Jin nomads 383
Jingdezhen 514
Jinn 484
Jinnah, Muhammad Ali 690, 710
Joan of Arc 235, *401*
João, Dom 669
Joffe, Roland 562
Johansson, Christian 597
John, St 482
John, St, Knights of 399
John the Baptist 475, *526*
John of England 400, 730
John I of Portugal *405*
John II of France 401
John VI of Portugal 713
John of Austria, Don 411
Johns, Jasper 554
John 'the Fearless' of Burgundy 401
John Paul II, Pope 476, 734
Johnson, Andrew 431
Johnson, Lyndon B. 452–3
Johnson, Dr Samuel 606, 625, **627**, 633, 652
Johnston Atoll 731
joint-stock company 282
Jolson, Al 560
Jonathan, Chief 699
Jones, Inigo 529, 531, 623
Jones, Jennifer *564*
Jones, Sir William 602
Jong-Il, Kim 696
Jonson, Ben 623
Jooss, Kurt 598
Joplin, Scott 588
Jordaens, Jacob 531
Jordan 292, 455, *509*, **694–5**
Jorn, Asger 554
Joseph II 418, *574*, 664
Josephine, empress 427
Joshua 365
joule 24
Joule, James 24, 25, 61
journalism 654–5
joust *407*
Joyce, James 39, 629, *641*, 648
Juan Carlos 721
Juárez, Benito 703
Judah 365
Judaism *see under* Jews
Judas Maccabeus 692
Judd, Donald 555
judgements, moral 493
judiciary *see* justice
Jugendstil 547
Julian the Apostate 381
Julian calendar 7
Julio-Claudian dynasty 378
Julius Caesar 7, **377**, 463, 615, 730
Julius II, Pope 528, 734
Jung, Carl Gustave **232**, 233, 526, 580
Jupiter *11*, *14*, **15**, 17, 19
Jurassic period *85*, *109*
dinosaurs 132–3
paramammals 140
justice/judicial system 264, 265, 266, 493
Justinian, emperor 394, 518
jute 121, 188, 318
Jutes 380, *396*, 606
Juvenal 615, 627

Kaaba *479*, 481, 482
Kabuki 617
Kadar, János 689
Kaddish 473
Kafka, Franz 581, **641**, 648
Kaiser, Georg 642
kakapo 138
Kalambo Falls 201
Kalatzov, Mikhail 562
Kalf, Willem *532*
Kamakura period 386, 515, 617
Kami 471, 485
Kampuchea *see* Cambodia
Kandinsky, Wassily 547, 549
kangaroo rats 186
kangaroos **142**, 173
Kansas-Nebraska Act 430
Kant, Immanuel 487, *489*, 493
Kapp Putsch 442
Karachi 710
karma 466, 468, 484
Karnak 367, 507
Karsavina, Tamara 597
karst *89*
Kaunda, Kenneth 737
Kavanagh, Patrick 646
Kazakhstan **695**
Kazan, Elia 561
Kazuo Ohno and Yoshito 599
Keaton, Buster 559
Keats, John 537, 633
Keller, Gottfried 635
Kellogg-Briand Pact 441
Kelly, Gene 561
Kelud, eruption of 82
Kelvin, Lord 24, 61
Kennedy, John F. 18, 291, 733
Kennedy-Fraser, Marjory 587
Kenneth MacAlpine, king of Scotland 396
Kent, William 534–5
Kent State University massacre 295
Kentucky 431
Kenya 89, 156, 292, *607*, **695–6**
history 201, 432, 433, *448*, 449
Kenyatta, Jomo *449*, 695
Kepler, Johann **17**, 61
keratin 134, 136, 139
Kerenski, Aleksandr F. 438
Kern, Jerome 588
Kerouac, Jack 295
Kertesz, André 557
keto-acids 214
kettledrums 583
keyboard instruments 582
keyhole surgery 241
Keynes, John Maynard *277*, 441
Keynes, Lydia *277*
al-Khalifa family 665
Khalistan 467
Khama, Sir Seretse 669
Khan, Muhammad Ayub 710
Khan, Muhammad Yahya 710
Khmer 384, 385, 453, 671
Khmer Rouge 453, 671
Khojas 479
Khomeini, Ayatollah Ruhollah *455*, 479, 649, 691
Khruschev, Nikita 298, 562, 715
al-Khwarizmi 392
kibbutz 257
kidneys *209*, 211, 215
disorders, treatment of *240*, 243, 249
Kiefer, Anselm *555*
Kierkegaard, Søren 487
Kiesinger, Georg 685
Kilauea-Iki, eruption of *82*
Kilimanjaro 187
kilocalorie 24
kilogram 20
al-Kindi 392
kinematic equations 20
Kinetic art 555
kinetic energy *24*
kinetic theory of gases 25
King, Martin Luther 290, 733
King, Stephen 651
Kingman Reef 731
kings *see* monarchy
kinkajou 155
kinship *see* families
Kipling, Rudyard 637
Kirchner, Ernst Ludwig 547
Kiribati **696**
Kirghizia *see* Kyrgyzstan
Kirov 439
'Kitchen Sink' drama 644
Kitz, Wolf *649*
kiwi 138, 139
Klee, Paul 549
Klein, Christian Felix 62
Kleist, Heinrich von 631
Klemperer, Otto 582
Klerk, F. W. de 721
Klimt, Gustav *547*
Kline, Franz 554
knights 399, *401*, 628
knitting *319*
Knossos, palace at *368*, 369
knowledge, philosophy of 225, **488–9**
see also learning
Knox, John 409
koala *143*
Kobayashi, Masaki 563
kob, Uganda 168
Koca Sinan 511
Koch, Robert 249
Kodály, Zoltán 586
Kodiak Island 154
Kohl, Helmut 685
Kokoschka, Oskar *547*
Komsomol 294
Kongfuzi *see* Confucius
Kooning, Willem de 554
Koran *see* Qur'an
Korda, Alexander 562
Korea **696–7**
economy 278
history 386
colonialism 383, 387, 433
20th-century 447
Korean War 349, *353*, 447, 450, *451*
religion 468
see also North Korea; South Korea
Kossuth, Lajos 689
Kotromanić dynasty 668
Koxinga, General 675
Kozintsev, Grigori 562
Krajina 676
Krak des Chevaliers *398*
Krakatau 86
krill **124**, 129, 163, 195
Kronstadt mutiny 439
Kropotkin, Prince Petr 113
Kruger, Paul 720
krypton 42, *43*, 77
Kshatriya caste 258
Ku Klux Klan *291*
Kublai Khan 383, *405*
Kukulcan *516*
kulaks 439
Kumamotu castle *386*
Kumbha Mela 481
Kun, Béla 689
Kuomintang 446
Kurds 289, 603, 691, 727
Kurosawa, Akira 563
Kursk, battle of 445
Kushans 385
Kuwait 285, 287, **697**
invasion of 455, 698
Kwagiutl people 517
kwashiorkor *209*
Kyd, Thomas 622
Kylian, Jiri 597
Kyrgyzstan **697**

la Condamine, Charles de 316
la Fayette, Madame de 629
La Fontaine, Jean de 621
La Rance *307*
La Tène art 375
Laban, Rudolph 598
labour 269, **272–3**, 275, 276, 278, 434
see also trade unions; wages; working class
Labour Party 267, 435
Labrador Current *105*
Labrunie, Gérard *see* Nerval
laccolith *83*, *85*
Laclos, Choderlos de 629
lacquer ware 514, 515
Laennec, René T. H. 249
Laetoli 200, 201
Laforgue, Jules 641
lagomorphs **151**
'Lake Poets' 632–3
lakes *83*, 87, *91*, **94–5**
ecosystems 178–9
polluted 300, 321
Lamarck, Jean-Baptiste 112
Lamartine, Alphonse de 631
lampreys 128, *174*
lampyrid beetle 167
lancelets 123
Land, Edwin 325
land
enclosures 420
reclamation 97
use and tenure *188*, 376, 379
see also agriculture
Lander, Harold 597
landforms *see* geology/geomorphology
landscapes in art *540*
Chinese and Japanese 515
Impressionists *542*, 543
Dutch School *532*, *533*
Rococo and Neoclassical 534, 535
Romanticism *536*, *537*
Post-Impressionist *544*, *545*
see also nature; pastoralism
Lang, Fritz 559, 563
Langland, William 620
language
of animals 167
of Bible 606
body 228–9
computers 334–5
of countries 364, 413, 466, **602–3**, *607*
see also under individual countries
discrimination 259
how it works 608–9
and numbers 65
perception of words 230, 231
and philosophy 491, 496–7
and religion 466, 476, 477, 606, 607
sign 167, 490, *491*, 608
of signs 610–11
see also speech; writing
Lanston, Tolbert 322
lanthanum *42–3*, *50*
Lao Zi (Lao-tzu) 470
Laos 287, 449, *451*, 452, 453, **698–9**
see also Indochina
laparotomy 241
lapis lazuli 366, 506
Lapps 602
larches **119**, 180
Larkin, Philip 646–7
Lartigue, Jacques-Henri 557
larval stage 122, 124, *126*, *127*
larynx **226–7**, 237
Lascaux caves 500, *504*
laser **33**
computers 335
medical 242, *243*, 249
scanning 322
weapons 19, 289, 357
Lassus, Roland de 570, 571
Late Gothic art 526–7
latency period 232
latent heat 25
Lateran Treaty 442
latex *316*
Latin America *see* Central America; South America
Latin Empire 395, 399
Latin language 108, 476, 477, **602–3**, 604, 605, 606, 607, 609, 615
Latvia **698**
Laud, Archbishop 413
laudanum 248
laughing gas *41*, 49, 56
Laurencin, Marie 597
Lausanne, Treaty of 441
Lauste, Eugene 559
Lautréamont, Comte de 551
lava *82*, 83, 84, *85*, 89
Lavoisier, Antoine 61
law
British *262*, 263, **264–5**, 434
civil and criminal 264–5
discrimination abolished 258, 291
drugs 246, 247
enforcement 262–3
European Community 264, 283, **286**
history
ancient to Medieval 248, 364, 365, 387, 394, 406
17th to 19th centuries 264, 418, 427, 434
Islamic 262, 264, 265, 479
and human rights 290–1
international 285, 290–1
and language 606
in literature 636
pollution 321
profession and women 292
protests about 295
religious 255, 262, 264, 265, 479, 484
reports 264
status 258
and women 292, 293
see also Acts
Lawrence, D. H. 646, 648
Lawrence, T. E. (b. 1888) 437
Lawrence, Thomas (b. 1769) 535
lawrencium *42–3*, *50*
lawyers 264–5
Le Brun, Charles 415
Le Carré, John 650
Le Fanu, J. S. 651
Le Guin, Ursula 651
Le Nôtre, André 415, 531
Le Vau, Louis 531
Le Verrier, Urbain 15
leaching 182
lead *42–3*, **50–1**, 237, 300, 313
League of Arab States 287
League of Nations 284, 440, **441**, **443**, 448, 454
Leakey, Dr Mary 201
Lean, David 562
leap years 7
learning **230–1**
leather 190
Léaud, Jean-Pierre *563*
Leavis, F. R. *652*
Lebanon **698**
history
ancient 364, *365*, 366
20th-century 259, *451*, 454, 455
religion 477
and UN *284*, 285
lebensraum 442
Leblanc, Nicolas 320
Lebrun, Charles 531
Lech, battle of the 394
Lee, Bruce 563
Lee Kuan Yew 719
Lee, Robert E. 431
leeches **122**, 172
Left, politics of the 268–9
Léger, Fernand 548
legionnaire's disease 239
legislation *see* law
Legislative Assembly (France) 425
legislature 264, 266
legs
anatomy *206*
ballet and dance 596, *597*
legumes 116, 175, 177
Leibl, William 541
Leibniz, Gottfried Wilhelm 70, 487, 488, 489, 629
Leif Eriksson 397
Leipzig, battle of *427*
lek 139, **168**
lemmings 151, 170
lemurs 164
'Lend-Lease' 444
length contraction 27
Lenin, Vladimir Ilyich 269, *438*, 559, 655
and Bolsheviks **438–9**
see also Marxism-Leninism
Leningrad *see* St. Petersburg
Lennon, John *589*
Lenoir, Étienne 308
lenses *32*, 33, 218, *324*
Lent 475
Leonardo da Vinci 60, *525*, 527
Leoncavallo, Ruggero 585
Léonin 570
leopard 152–3, *184*
Leopardi, Giacomo 631
Leopold II of Belgium 432, 667, 736
Leopold III of Belgium 667
Lepanto, battle of 342, 393, *411*
Lepidus, Marcus 377
leprosy *238*, **239**
Lermontov, Mikhail 631
Leroy, Louis 543
lesbianism 293
Lescot, Pierre 529
Lesotho **698–9**
Lessing, Gotthold Ephraim 626–7
letter novels 628, 629
Leucippus 60
leucotomy 240
Levant 366, 367
Lévi-Strauss, Claude 610, 611, 653
Lewes, G. H. 637
Lewis, C. S. 651
Lewis, Percy Wyndham 548–9, *641*

LeWitt, Sol 555
lexias *653*
Lexington 422
Leyden, Lucas van 527
Leyte Gulf, battle of *444*, 445
Li Bai 617
liabilities (financial) 282–3
libel 262
liberalism 268, 428
Liberia **699**
liberty 268, 269
library of Ashurbanipal *365*
Libya 287, **699**
  history 366, 376, 432, 433, 444, *445*
lichen *118*, **118–19**
Lichtenstein, Roy *554–5*
Liebermann, Max 547
Liebig, Justus von 61
Liechtenstein **699–700**
Lifar, Serge 597
life
  classification of 108–9
  extraterrestrial 17
  genetics and inheritance 114–15
  life cycle 254–5
    see also reproduction
  reproduction 202–3
  right to 290
  see also animals; humans; plants
Ligeti, Gyorgy 581
light 26–7
  in art 525, 532, 533, *534*, 537, 542, 543, 556
  invisible **332–3**
  pulses, time measured with 7
  reactions and plants 117
  speed of 27
  see also optics
Light Brigade 429
light year 5
light-water reactors 305
lighting, electrical 36
lightning *34*
lignin 120
Lima 711
limbic system 217, 223
Limbourg, Paul, Jean and Herman *521*
limestone 84, 85, *88–9*
limnetic zone *179*
limited-liability companies 282–3
limonene *52*, *53*
Lincoln, Abraham *225*, 430, *431*, 733
Lindbergh, Charles *348*
Lindisfarne Gospels *519*
Lindsay, Sir David 621
Linear B *see under* writing
linear model of time 483
linguistics *see* language
Linnaeus, Carl 61, 108
linocuts 502
Linotype machine 322
linsangs 153
Linz-Donawitz process 315
lions *152*, 168, 169
Lippershey, Hans 17
Lippi, Fra Filippo 524
liquefied natural gas 311, 344
liquid crystals *54*
Lister, Lord Joseph 249
listeria 239
Liszt, Franz *577*, 586
literacy 370, 406
literature
  and art 546
  history 364, 402, 419, **612–55**
    myths 463, **612–13**
    Classical 462, **614–15**
    Asian 616–17
    epics and romances 618–19
    tales, fables, mysteries and moralities 620–1
    Renaissance 622–4
    Neoclassical 626–7
    novel, beginning of 628–9
    Romanticism **630–3**, 636
    Realism and Naturalism 634–5
    Novel in 19th-century 636–7
    American 638–9
    Symbolism, Aestheticism and Modernism 640–1
    experimental theatre 642–3
    modern drama 644–5
    modern poetry 646–7
    modern novel 648–9
    popular literature 650–1
    critical theory 652–3
    journalism 654–5
    see also novels; poetry; theatre
  and music 576, 578, 590, 591, 642
  and semiology 611
  see also under philosophy
lithium *42–3*, **50**
lithography *322*, 323, 502, *635*
lithosphere 77, *79*, 82
Lithuania 603, **700**
litoptern *140*
liturgies 475
liver **209**, 211, 215, 237, 240
liverworts *119*
livestock farming **190–1**
  grazing 142, 160, *161*, 176, 182, 185, 190–1
  history 366, 374, 384, 420
Livingstone, David 701
Livonia 698
Livy 615
lizards 134–5
llama 159
Lloyd George, David *440*, 731
Llywelyn of Wales 730
Loach, Ken 562
Loan, Brigadier General *654*
loans *see* debt
lobelias 187
local government **267**, 276, 424, 429, 434
Locarno Treaties 441
Lochner, Steven 526
Locke, John 266, 271, 290, 418, 487, **488–9**, *496*
locusts 127, 170
logarithms 65
logging 192–3
logic 59, 67, 486, **494–5**
logographic scripts 604
Lollards 399, 403, 408
Lombards 395
London **413, 731**
  art and architecture 523, *531*, *538*, *539*, *553*, 554
  demonstrations *289*, 295
  disease 244
  Docklands *275*
  drama 644
  education *260*, *261*
  government 267
  Hell's Angels *294*
  history 244, *262*, *360*, *413*, *435*, *595*, 627
  law and crime 262, 263
  and literature 623, 636, 646
  music *595*, 596, 598
  police 262
  prison *262*
  slum *435*
  stock market 273, 282
  Thames barrier *341*
  University 292
  women's movement *292*
  youth movements *294*, 295
Long March 446
Longinus, Gaius Cassius 377
longitudinal wave *28*
Lope de Vega 622
Lopokova, Lydia (Keynes) 277
lopolith *85*
Lords, House of 265, 267
Lorenzetti, Ambrogio and Pietro 521
Lorenzo the Magnificent 528
lorises 164
Lorraine 393, 436, 440
Lorraine, Claude *see* Claude
Lorris, Guillaume de 619
Los Angeles *263*, 300, 598, 731
Losey, Joseph 562
lost-wax process 503
loudness 31
loudspeakers 329
Louis, St 399, 400
Louis Bonaparte 707
Louis the Pious, emperor 394
Louis VII of France 399
Louis IX of France (St Louis) 399, 400
Louis XIII of France 414
Louis XIV of France 413, **414–15**, 417, 683, 707, 721
  as patron of arts 531, 534, 584, *593*, 594, 596
  and science 60
Louis XV of France 415, 534, 535
Louis XVI of France 415, 424, *425*, 535
Louis XVIII of France 427
Louis Napoleon 683
Louis Philippe 541
Louisiana 422, 430, *431*
Louvois, Marquis de 414
love
  in literature 614, 615, 620, 640
  and religion 462
  romantic and courtly 257, 620, 625
Love wave *81*
Lovell telescope 17
Low Countries *see* Belgium; Flanders; Netherlands
Lowell, Robert 647
low-pressure areas 103
Loya Jirgha 660
Loyola, Ignatius 409, 721
LSD 247
Lucan 615
Lucas, George 611
Lucian 508
Lucretius 615
'Lucy' (hominid) 200
Luddites 420
Ludwig II of Bavaria 538
Lukács, Georg 652
Lully, Jean-Baptiste 415, 572, 584, 596
lumber *see* forests
Lumet, Sidney 564
Lumière, Auguste and Louis 558
lunar *see* Moon
Lunar Roving Vehicle (LRV) *18*
lungfish 128, 130, 171, 173
lungs 23, 206, **210–11**, 243
  diseases of 118, 237, 244, 245, 247
lute *583*
lutetium *42–3*, *50*
Lutfullah, Shaykh 51
Luther, Martin and Lutherans 408, *409*, 475, 477, 570, 572, 686
Lutoslawski, Witold 581
Lutyens, Edwin 539
Lützen, battle of 409
Luxembourg 278, 286, **700**
Lydia, art of 508
lymph system 175, 209, *212*, **236**
lynx 153
lyric poetry 625
Mabuse (Gossaert) 527
McAdam, John 340, 421
macaques 165
MacArthur, Gen. Douglas 445
Macau 713
Macaulay, Lord Thomas 360
macaw *137*
McCandless, Bruce *19*
McCarthy, Joseph 450, 561, 562
McCartney, Paul *589*
McColl, Ewan 587
MacDiarmid, Hugh 647
Macedon 371, 372, 373, 614
Macedonia **737–8**
Machaut, Guillaume de 570, 571
Machiavelli, Niccolò 266, 407
machine guns **356–7**, 437
machine code 334
Machu Pichu *390*
Macintosh, Charles 316
Macke, August 547
Mackintosh, Charles Rennie 552
Macmillan, Harold 449
Macmillan, Kenneth 597
MacNeice, Louis 646
macroeconomics 276–7
macroelements 177
Macronesia *389*
macro-nutrients 56
macroparasites 174, 175
macrophage 211, *212*
MAD 288–9
Madagascar **700–01**
  animals 138, 147, 149, 153, 158, 164
  history *388*, 432, 433
Madero, Francisco 703
Madison, James 422
Madox Brown, Ford 541
madrigal 571
Maeterlinck, Maurice 578
Mafeking, Siege of 294
Magdalha 385
Magellan, Ferdinand *405*, 625, 712
Maghreb 388
  see also Algeria; Morocco; Tunisia
magic 458, 592
Magic Realism 649
magistrates 265
magma *77*, 82
Magna Carta 290
magnesium *42–3*, 44, 47, **50–1**, 77, 100, 116, 178, 305, 312, 313
magnetism **34–5**
  maglev trains 55, *347*
  magnetic fields 10, *34*, *77*, 313
  magnetic resonance imaging 55, 241, 242, *243*
  magnetic surveys 310, 313
magnolia *120*
magnox reactor 305
Magnus, Albertus 60
Magritte, René 551
Magsaysay, Ramon 712
Magyars 394
Mahabharata 466, 613
Mahavira 467
Mahayana Buddhism **468–9**, 471
Mahdi 479
Mahendra, king of Nepal 707
Mahfuz, Najib 616
Mahler, Gustave **577**, 580
mahogany 193
Maiden Castle *375*
Mailer, Norman 655
Maimonides, Rabbi Moses 472
mainframe computer 334
Maistre, Joseph de 270
maize (corn) 188, **189**, 196, 390, 420
al-Majri (Haly Abbas) 392
Makarios, President 677, 727
Makarova, Natalia 597
make-up *564*
Makiguchi Tsunesaburo 471
malaria 149, 175, 238, **239**
  prevention 244, **245**
Malawi *607*, **701**
Malaya/Malaysia 182, 287, **701**
  animals 154, 157
  art and architecture 512, 513
  history 393, 432, 433
    20th-century *444*, 445, 449, *451*, 453
  language 609
Maldives 99, 301, **701–2**
Malebranche, Nicolas 490
Malevich, Kasimir 549
Mali 388, 389, *482–3*, 517, 702
malignancy *see* cancer
Mallarmé, Stéphane 578, 631, 640, 641
Malle, Louis 562
malnutrition *208*, *209*
Malory, Sir Thomas 546, 619
Malta 399, 444, *445*, 505, 702
Malthus, Thomas 296
Mamet, David 645
Mamluks 392, 398, 511, 616
mammals 140–65
  basic characteristics 140
mammoths *141*, 157, 390, 504
man *see* humans
Man, Isle of 729
mana 513
manatees *162*
Mancham, James 718
Manchu (Qing) dynasty 383
Manchuria 383, 387, 433, 443, 446–7
mandala *469*, 480
mandates, League of Nations 440, 441, 454
Mandela, Nelson 720
mandrills *164*
Manet, Edouard 541, *542*, 542, 543, 549
manganese *42–3*, *50*, 315
Mangbetu 517
mangrove swamps *178*
mania 234, 235
Manila 712
Manley, Michael 694
man-made *see* artificial; synthetic
Mann, Thomas 648, *649*
Mannerism 527, **528–9**, 532, 625
Mansart, François 531
Mansart, Jules Hardouin 415, 531
Mantegna, Andrea 508, 525
mantle of Earth *76*, *77*
mantra 469
manual classes *see* working class
manuscripts, illuminated *519*, *521*
Manzoni, Alessandro 631
Mao Zedong (Mao Tse-tung) 269, 295, *446*, 447
Maoris 185, 389
maples 181
Mappa Mundi 482
mappings *68*, *70*
Marat, Jean-Paul 425
marble 85, 508, 514
Marc, Franz 547
Marconi, Guglielmo 326
Marcos, Ferdinand 267, 714
Marengo, battle of 426, *427*
Marenzio, Luca 571
Marey, Etienne 558
Margrethe I of Denmark 678, 709
Mari 364, *365*, 506
Maria II of Portugal 713
Maria Theresa, Empress 418, *574*
Mariana Islands *444*, 445
Marie Antoinette 424, 425
marine *see* oceans
Marines, American 452–3
Marinetti, Filippo 548, 640
maritime climates *105*
Marius, Gaius 377
Marivaux, Pierre 626, 628, 629
Mark Antony 377, 615
market/s **274–5**
  and class 259
  colonies as 420
  common 278
    see also European Community
  free 268
  research 259
Markova, Alicia 597
Marlowe, Christopher 622
marmosets 164–5
marmots *150*, 151, 168
Marquet, Albert 544, 545
Marquez, Gabriel Garcia 649
marriage *254*, 255, 256, 462, 479
marrow, bone 206, *212*, 236, 238
Mars *11*, 12, *13*, 19, 110
Marshall Islands 99, *444*, 445, **702**
Marshall Plan 286, 450
marsupial cat *140*
marsupial mole 142
marsupials 140, *141*, **142–3**
Martial 615
Martin, John 537
Martini, Simone *521*
Martinique 682
martyria 518
Marvell, Andrew 625
Marx, Karl/Marxism-Leninism 268, **269**, **487**, 631
  and art 550
  in China 269, 470
  on class 258–9, 360
  and Cold War 450
  on drama 622
  and education 261
  and law 264
  and literature 640, 652
  on population 296
  portrait of Marx *269*
  and religion 458
  and revolution 259, 269, 438
  on science 58
  in Third World 298, 477
  see also Communists
Marx Brothers 561
Mary I of England 409, 412
Mary II of England 413
Mary, Queen of Scots 409, 412
Mary, Virgin *474*, 481
Masaccio *524*
Masai people 254
Mascagni, Pietro 585
masks *517*, 596
masques 593, 623
mass (music) 571
mass (physics) 21, 22
mass production 352, 420
massacres 295, *408*, 409, 447, 455, 593
Massine, Leonide 597
Massys, Quentin 527
Masters of Rolls 265
materialism 486, 490–1, 634
mathematics 62–73
  algebra 64–5
  applications 62–3
  and art 524–5
  and chaos theory 63
  correspondence, counting and infinity 68–9
  functions and graphs 70–1
  history 365, 391, 392, 418
  and music 581
  probability, chance and choice 72–3
  and scientific method 58
  sets and paradoxes **66–7**, 68–9, 254
  see also numbers; science
mating, animal **168**
  see also reproduction
Matisse, Henri 544, *545*, 597
matrix (archaeology) *361*
Matsuo Basho 617
Mau Mau *448*
Mauna Loa 83
Maupassant, Guy de 634, 637
Mauritania **702–3**
Mauritius 467, **703**
Maurya, Chandragupta and Mauryans 385, 468, 512
Maximian, emperor 380
Maximilian, Archduke 703
Maxwell, James Clerk 26, 35, 61
Mayan people 316, *390*, 391, 410, *516*, 604
Mayflower 422
Mayotte 682
Mazarin, Cardinal 414
Mazzini, Guiseppe 428
M'Ba, Léon 683
meaning/s 493, **496–7**, 609, 610
measles **239**, 245
meat 190–1, 196
Mecca 478, *479*, 480, 481, 482, 510
mechanical strength 51
mechanics 20–1, 27
Mechnikov, Ilya 196
Medes 365
media *see* communications
Medici family 528
  Catherine de' 408, 593
medicine and health care
  alternative 250–1
  and government 266, 276
  healing cults 462, 471, 480, 481
  history of 56–7, **248–9**, 292, 392, 406
  public 244, 434
  surgery **240–1**, 248, *249*
  technology **242–3**, 249
  women allowed to study 292
  women's access to 293
  see also diseases; drugs, therapeutic; hospitals
medieval *see* Middle Ages
Medina 478, 510
meditation 459, **468**, 469, 470, *480*
Mediterranean area *see* Greece; Italy; Middle East; Roman Empire; Spain; Turkey
meerkats *153*
megalithic monuments *363*, 505
Mehmed II, Sultan 393
Meiji 387
Meissner effect *55*
Melanchthon, Philip 409
Melanesia 464
melanoma 237, 245
Méliès, Georges 559, 565
meltwater, glacial *91*, 94
Melville, Herman 638–9
Memling, Hans 526
Memmi *521*
Memnon 507
memory cells 213
memory (computers) *335*
Menander 614
Mencius (Mengzi) 470
Mendel, Gregor 61, **114**
mendelevium *42–3*, *50*
Mendeleyev, Dmitri **43**, 61
Mendelssohn, Felix 572, 577
Menderes, Adnan 727
Menes of Egypt 366
menhirs *363*
meninges 222
meningitis 239
menopause 205
Mensheviks 438
menstruation 202, 204, 214
mental age 231
mental illness 232, 233, **234–5**, 240, 250, 257
  and drugs 234, 235, 241, 247
  in literature 635
Mentuhotep II, pharoah 366
Menzel, Adolph von 541
Menzel, Jiři 562
Mercalli scale *81*
mercantilism 416, 623
mercenaries 396, 397, 449
Mercia *396*, 397
mercury (metal) *42–3*, **50–1**, 237, 248, 300, 313
Mercury (planet) *11*, *12*, 59
Merenptah, pharoah 364
Mergenthaler, Ottmar 322
meridians (of body) 251
meridians (of Earth) 6, 7
Merovingian dynasty 394
Mesolithic 362, 363
  see also Stone Ages
Mesopotamia
  art and architecture 506
  history 362, 364, *365*, 373, 384, 392, 395, 437
    modern *see* Iraq
  myth 612
  religion 460, *461*
  writing 604
mesosphere 77
Mesozoic era *85*
Messiaen, Olivier 581, 585
Messina, Antonello da 525
metabolism 214, **215**
metals and metalworking **50–1**, 312, **313**
  in art *502*, 516, *517*
    see also bronze; copper; gold; silver

  chemistry 42, 47, **50–1**
  heavy metal poisoning 237
  history 50, 363, 374, 382, 383, 420
    see also Bronze Age; Iron Age
  hot-metal printing 322
  smelting 47, *314*, 420
  see also iron; mining
metamorphic rocks and metamorphism 84–5
metamorphosis (insects) 126, *127*
metamorphosis (musical) 577
metaphysical poets 625
metastases *237*
Metaxas, General Ioannis 686
meteorites 13, 133, 312
meteors/meteoroids 13
methane 14, 15, 41, *49*, 77, 110
  production 306, 310, 311
Method acting 642
Methodists 475
Methodius, St 605
Metternich, Prince Clemens L. W. 664
Meun, Jean de 619
Mexico **703**
  animals *131*, 135, 144, *147*, 161
  art and architecture 516
  debt 299
  earthquake *80*
  film 563
  history 390, 391, 410, 411, 430
  in literature 649
  society 255, 256
  volcanoes 83
  women's suffrage 292
Mexico City 703
mice 141, 142, **150–1**, 168, 171
Michael of Romania 714
Michelangelo Buonarroti 501, *528*, 625
Micheli, Andrea *411*
Michelin 316
Michelino, Domenico di *619*
Mickiewicz, Adam 631
microcomputer 334, *335*
microeconomics 274–5
microelements 177
Micronesia *389*, **703–4**
microorganisms *see* bacteria; fungi; parasites; viruses
microparasites *174*, 175
microphages 211
microphone 328
microprocessor 35, 334
microscope/microscopy *33*, 38, 238, 249, *333*
microwaves 4–5, 17, *35*, 331, 332
Midas 507
Middle Ages
  art and architecture 518–19, 536, 537
  culture 406–7
  economy and society 404–5
  literature 618–19
  medicine 248
  music 587, **593**
middle class/bourgeoisie 258, **259**, 424
  and art 515
  and children 294
  and economy 268, 269
  in literature 617, 636, 637, 645
  and youth movements 295
Middle East
  agriculture 190–1
  art and architecture 504, 505, **506–7**, 510–11
  conflict 259
  energy 310, *311*
  geology/geomorphology 92
  history **454–5**
    prehistory 361, 362, 363
    ancient **364–5**, 370, 388–9
    Silk Route 382
    World War I 437
    religions 460–1
    and decolonization 448, 449
    Arab-Israeli wars 451, *454*, 455
  international relations 284–5, 287
  law and crime 263
  literature 616
  medicine 248
  music, dance 593
  religion 459, **460–1**, 476, 477, 480, 481
    see also Jews; Islam
  women's suffrage 292, 293
  writing 604–5
  see also Arabs *and individual countries*
Middle English 606–7
middle way 468, 469
Middleton, Thomas 623
Midway Islands *444*, 445, **734**
Midway, battle of *444*, 445
migration
  animal 128, **170–1**, 181, 187
  human 420, *431*, 467
    see also refugees
Miguel, king of Portugal 713
Milan 394, 404, 596
  art and architecture 509, 539, 553, 623
Milhaud, Darius 578
military activities *see* aircraft; armies; defence, human; navies; weapons; wars
milk 214, 215
Milky Way 8, 17
Mill, John Stuart 292, 487, *493*
Millais, John Everett 537
Millar, John 419
Miller, Arthur 645
Miller, Glenn 589
Millet, Jean-François 540, *541*
millipedes **125**, 173
mills, water and wind 306–7
Milton, John 624, 625
mimicry, animal 139, **167**
minarets 511
minerals **208**, 215
  see also metals; mining
Ming dynasty 383, 514, 617
minicomputer 334, 335
mini discs 329
Minimalism 555, 557, 578, 580, **581**
mining *273*, **312–13**
  history 366, 420, 421, 440
mink 155
Minoans 82, **368–9**
Minos, King and Minotaur 368
Miocene epoch *85*
  mammals 140–1
miracidium 175
Miranda, Francisco 737
Miró, Joan *551*, 553
mirrors 33
Mishima Yukio 617
missiles 288, 289, 332, *357*, 451
missionaries 410, 432, 459, 476, 477
Mississippi 94, 390, 430
mistletoe 121
Mitannians 364, 461
mites 125
Mithraism 379, **462**
mitochondria 111, *117*, 201
mitosis 114, 116
Mitterand, François 684
mixed economies 276
mixtures 41
moas 185
mobility, social 258
  see also migration; movement
Mobuto Sése Séko 736
Mochica people 516
modelling (mathematical) 62
modelling (sculpture) 502, 503, 565
modem 331
moderator 305
Modernism/modern
  art and architecture 546–55
  dance 598–9
  literature and drama 640–9
  music 578–81
Modigliani, Amedeo 549
Mods 295
modulation *29*, 326
modulus 23
Moguls 385, 432, *510*, 511
Mohammed *see* Muhammad
Mohenjo Daro *384*, 512
Mohorovičić discontinuity 76, 77
Moi, Daniel arap 696
molars 140
Moldavia *see* Moldova
Moldova 429, **704**, 714
mole concept (chemistry) 47
molecular energy 24–5
molecular sieves 54
molecules **40–1**
  small 48–9
mole rats 169
moles *148*
Molière 415, 596, **626**, 627
molluscs **122–3**, 137, 138, 172, 175, 195
molybdenum *42–3*, *50*, 315
momentum conservation 21
Momoyama period 514
Monaco, James 611
Monaco, Lorenzo *500*, 521
Monaco **704**
monarchy
  absolute 266
  constitutional 266–7
  divine 471
  see also names of individual kings and queens
monasteries *see* monks
Mondrian, Piet *549*
Monet, Claude 541, *542*, 543, 578
monetarism 277
monetary policy 277
money 273, 277, 279, 365, 508
Mongolia/Mongols 287, 309, 602, **704–5**
  animals 153, 156
  art and architecture 510, 511, 514
  history *382*, 383, 392, 393, 616
mongooses 153
monitoring, medical 242–3
monkeys 164, **165**, 166, 169
monks and monasteries 406, 468, *469*, *480*
monochrome 501, 525
monocotyledons 120–1
monoculture 188
monogamy 256
  animal **168**, *169*
monomers 56
monophony 570
Monophysitism 476, 477
monopoly 275
monosaccharides 208
monosodium glutamate *196*
monotheism 388, 467
  see also Christianity; Islam; Jews; Sikhs
monotremes 140, **142**
Monotype machine 322
Monroe, James and Doctrine 431, 450
monsoons 103, *104*
Monte Cassino, battle of 445
Montenegro **735**, 736
Montesquieu 266, 267, 418
Montessori, Maria 260
Monteverdi, Claudio *571*, 572, 584
Montezuma 411
Montgolfier brothers *348*
Montgomery, Field Marshall Bernard 445
Montserrat 732
Moon *12*, *13*, 17, 58
  eclipse 16
  landings on 13, *18*
  moon-phase spawning 129
  and religion 462
  and tides 100–1
'Moonies' 459
moons and satellites of planets 12, 13, *14*, *15*, 17
  see also Moon
Moorcock, Michael 651
Moore, G. E. 493
Moore, Henry 503, 549
Moors 399, 410
moraines 87, *91*, 95
morality 492–3
  and crime 262
  and Enlightenment 418
  and literature 621, 636, 639, 648
  and person concept 490
  and philosophy 486
  and religion 485
Moravia 295, 441
Moreau, Gustave *546*
Morgagni, Giovanni B. 249
Morgan, Jeffrey *652*
Morgan, Thomas Hunt 61
Morisot, Berthe 543
Morley, Thomas 571
Mormons 477
Morocco 287, 411, 433, 590, 609, **705**
morphine 247
morphology (linguistic) 602, 608, 609
morphology (physical) 109
Morris, William 537, 539, **637**
Morrissey, Paul 561
Morse, Samuel and code 330
mortgage 273
Morton, William *249*
mosaics 506, *509*, *518*, 519
Moscow 714
Moses 255, 365, 472, 478
Moshoeshoe I 700
Moslems *see* Islam
mosques 478, 482, 510, *511*, 517
  see also temples
mosquitoes 113, 175, 245
mosses 119
moths *see* butterflies and moths
motion, laws of 17, **20–1**
motor neurones 221
motors *see* cars; engines
moulding 503
mountains
  agriculture 188
  climate 104, *105*, 176
  ecosystems *104*, 153, **186–7**
  formation 79, **86–7**
mouse *see* mice
movement
  animals 124, 125, 132, 135, 142, 145, 161, **172–3**
  human 206–7
movies *see* films
Mozambique 287, 299, **705**
  history 388, *410*, 432, 433, *449*, *451*
Mozart, Wolfgang Amadeus 572, 573, *574*, 580, 582, 583, 627
  Classicism **574**, 575
  opera 584–5
  Romanticism 576, 577
Mswati III, King 723
Mu'awiyya 724
mucus 212, 216
Mugabe, Robert 737
Muhammad, Prophet **392, 478**, 510, 616, 705, 717
Muir, Edwin 647
Mujibur Rahman, Shaikh 665, 710
mule 191
mullahs 478
Müllerian mimicry 167
multi-family households 257
multi-host life cycles 174, 175
multi-male groups 169
multimedia 335
multinational companies 273, **278**
multiple sclerosis 221, 227, 242
multiple stars 9
multiplexing 330–1
multiplication 64
mummification 255
mumps 239
Munch, Edvard *546*, 547
Munich 443, 534, 546, 547, 598
Murasaki Shikibu 617
murder 257, 262
Murdoch, Iris 649
Murnau, F. W. 559
Muromachi period *514*, 515, 617
Murray, Sir James *606*, 607
muscles 172, *206*, **207**, 210, 215, 218, 221
  animal 172
  diseases 250, 251
mushrooms 118
  hallucinogenic 247
music
  defined 568–9
  international 590–1
  and literature 617, 621, 627, 640
  major periods
    plainsong and polyphony 570–1
    Baroque 572–3
    Classical 574–5
    Romantics 576–7
    Modernist 578–9
    popular, rock and punk 294, *295*, **588–9**
    since 1945 580–1
  and religion 462, 466
  therapy 235
  see also dance; folk; instruments; opera; orchestra
musk ox 187
Muslims *see* Islam
Musorgsky, Modest 577
Mussadiq, Muhammad 691
Musset, Alfred de 631
Mussolini, Benito 294, 341, **442**, *443*, 563, 660, 693
mustard gas 289
mustelids 155
mutation 112–13, 114
Mutiny, Indian 432
Mutsuhito, emperor 387
mutual assured destruction 288–9
Mutual and Balanced Force Reduction 289
Muybridge, Eadweard 556, 558
Myanmar (*formerly* Burma) 512, **705–6**
  history
    colonialism 384, 385, 432, 433
    20th-Century 445, 449
Mycenaeans 363, **369**, 462
myriapods 124–5
mystery cult 462
mystery plays 621
mysticism 462, 616
  see also religion
myths **465**, 504, **612–13**, 645
myxomatosis 151

Nabokov, Vladimir 649
Nabonidas 365
Nadar 543, *634*
NAFTA 287
Nagasaki 288, 387, 445
Nagy, Imre 690
Nagy, László Moholy 557
names 496–7
Namibia *92*, 285, 432, 433, 517, 603, *607*, **706**
Nanak, Guru 467
Nanda dynasty 385
Nantes 295, 409, 415
Napirasu, Queen 506
Naples 426–7, 584
Napoleon Bonaparte (*later* Napoleon I) **425**, **426**, 538
  and arts 535, 576, 577, 631, 632
  empire *427*, 430, 683, 693, 717, 734
  Napoleonic Code 264, 427
Napoleon III 542
Napoleonic Wars 426–7, 428, 683
Nara period 386, 515, 617
NASA 333
Nash, John 538
Nasser, Gamal Abdel 287, *449*, 455, 680, 695, 735
National Assemblies **266**, 424, 425, 428, 429
national economy *see* economics
national grid (electricity) 304
national press 655
National Socialists *see* Nazis
nationalism
  history 426–7, **428–9**, 441, 443, 446, 448–9
  and Left 268, 269
  and literature 625, 631
  and music 577, 587
  and women's movement 293
nationalization 276, 439
NATO **287**, 450, *451*
natural gas *see under* gas
'natural law' 290
natural numbers **64**, 68
natural resources *see* resources
natural selection *see* evolution
natural vegetation *see* plants
naturalistic fallacy 493
nature
  in art 536–7
  in literature 627, 629, *633*, 638, 646
  and religion 460
  'versus nurture' debate 2**30–1**, 293
  see also landscapes
Naturalism
  in art 520, **521**, **541**
  in literature **634–5**, 642
  see also Realism
Nauru **706**
nautilus 122
Navarino Bay, battle of 429
navies
  Britain 401, 413, *416*, 422, 426, 436, 437, 441
  France 415, 426, 429
  Germany 436, 437
  Greece, ancient 371
  Netherlands *416*
  Russia 417
  Spain 411
  Turkey 411, 429
  USA 441
  Venice 411
  Washington Conference on 441
  see also ships and boats
navigation
  by animals 139, 146–7, 171
  by humans 332
Návpaktos 411
Nazarenes 537
Nazca people 516
Nazis 270, **442**, 547, 555, 647
  Nazi-Soviet Non-Aggression Pact 439, 444
  and theatre 642
  trials of *264*
  youth movements 294
  see also Hitler
Ndebele rebellion 432
Ne Win, General 706
Neanderthal man *200*, **201**, 362, 363
neap tides *101*
Near East *see* Middle East
Nebuchadnezzar 365
nebulae 8, 9
nectar **121**, *137*, 168
Nefertiti 367, *507*
Negroes *see* Black people
Nehru, Jawaharlal 287, *449*, 690
Neill, A. S. 260
Neithardt-Gothardt, Mathis 527
Nelson, Admiral Horatio 426–7, 538
nematodes 122
Neoclassicism
  in art and architecture 534, **535**, 536, 539
  in literature **626–7**, 652
neodymium *42–3*, *50*
Neo-Expressionism *555*
Neo-Georgian architecture 539
neo-imperialism 299
Neoimpressionism 542, **543**, 544
Neolithic **362**, **363**
  agriculture 363, 382, 384, 389
  houses *362*, 505
  megalithic monuments *363*, 505
  pottery and art 504–5, 514
  see also Stone Age
neon **42**, *42–3*, 44, 77
neo-Nazis *271*
Neoplatonism 525, 624
neoteny 130, **131**
Nepal 306, 432, 467, *607*, **706–7**
Neptune *11*, 14, *15*
neptunium *42–3*, *50*
neritic zone *179*
Nero, emperor 378
Nerva, emperor 378
Nerval, Gérard de 631
nerve gas 289
nervous system 218, 219, **220–1**, 232, 242, 249
  and hormones 214, 215
  and muscles 207
  and senses 216, 216–17, 217, 224
  see also brain
Nestorianism 476, 477
Netherlands **707**
  art and architecture 501, 525, 529, 531, 534
    Dutch School **532–3**
    early **526**, 527
    Post-Impressionism 544, 545
    De Stijl Movement 549
    movements since 1945 554
  economy 278
  geology/geomorphology 90, *97*
  history
    Medieval and Renaissance 404, 407
    colonialism 385, 387, 389, 411, 416, 433, 513
    trade 413
    Anglo-Dutch Wars *416*, 417
    Napoleonic Wars 426–7
    World War II 444, *445*, 449
    and decolonization *448*, 449
  international relations 278, 286
  language **602**, 603, 666
  medicine 249
  music *572*, 597
  plural society 259
  women's suffrage 292
Netherlands Antilles 707
Neto, Dr Agostinho 661
Neuilly, Treaty of 441
Neumann, Balthasar 534
Neumann, John von 335
neural computing 337
neurones *220*, 221, 223
neurosis 234, 235
neurotransmitters 220
neutrinos 4, 39
neutron star *9*
neutrons 4, **38**, 305
New Caledonia 388, 417, **682**
'New Cold War' 289
New Deal 441
New Economic Policy 439
New Guinea *see* Papua
New Hebrides 388, 417, 592–3
new middle class 259
New Model Army 413
New Realism in art 554, *555*
new religions 459, 465, 471
New York 731
  art and architecture 550, 554
  dance 598
  education 260
  film 558
  history 422
  photography 556
  stock market 273, 282
New Zealand 191, 286, 388, **707–8**
  animals 129, 134, 138, *139*, 148, 158
  climate *105*
  geology/geomorphology 94, 98
  history 363, **389**
    colonialism 417, 432, 433
    20th-Century 437, 449, *451*
  language *607*
  law and crime 263
  literature 513

plants 180, 181, 185
women's suffrage 292, 293
Newcomen, Thomas 308, 420
Newfoundland 171, 671
Newlands, John 43
'newly industrializing countries' 278
see also Hong Kong; South Korea; Taiwan
Newman, Barnett 554
news agencies 655
see also journalism
Newton, Sir Isaac 17, *20*, 26, 27, 40, 58–9, 61, **62**, 70, *418*
laws **20–1**, 22, 25, 35
newts 130–1
Ney, Marshall 427
Nguema, Francisco 680
Nguyen Anh 735
niacin 208
Nicaragua 287, *450*, *451*, **708**
niches, ecological *176*
Nichiren Buddhism 469, 470, **471**
Nicholas I of Russia 715
Nicholas II of Russia 438, 715
Nicholson, Ben 549
nickel *42–3*, *50*, 312, 313, 315
Nicopolis 398
nicotine *see* tobacco
nicotinic acid 208
nictitating membrane 130
Nielsen, Carl 579
Niepce, Nicéphore 324
Nietzsche, Friedrich 487, 640
Niger 190, **710**
Nigeria 287, *465*, 517, *607*, **708–9**
history 432, 433
Nightingale, Florence 249
'Night of the Long Knives 442
night sound 30
nightmare 233
Nihon University 295
Nijinsky, Bronislava 597
Nijinsky, Vaslav 597
Nile **94**, 95, 366, 367, 506
battle of 426
Niles, John Jacob 587
Nilo-Saharans *388*
Nimitz, Admiral Chester 445
Nimrud *506*
'Ninety-five Theses' 409
Nineveh *365*
niobium *42–3*, *50*
nirvana 468, 484
nitrogen 14, 15, 40, *42–3*, 45, **49**, 56
in atmosphere 13, 77
compounds *41*, **177**
nitrates 56, 116, 177, 320, 321
oxides *41*, *49*, 300, 304
cycle *177*
fixing 116, 177
and plants 116, 177, 321
Niue 707
Nixon, Richard 453, 655
Nkomo, Joshua 737
Nkrumah, Kwame *449*, 686
No theatre *617*
Nobel Prizes 61, 616
nobelium *42–3*, *50*
nobility/ruling class **258**, 268, 269
and dance 593, 594
history
ancient 367, 374
Japanese 386
French 397, 400, 414, 424
Medieval *406*
Noble Eightfold Path 468, 469
noble gases 42, 44
'noble man', ideal of 470
Nobunaga, Odo 386
Nok culture *388*, 517
Nolde, Emil 547
nomads/nomadism *190*
Non-aligned Movement 287
Nono, Luigi 585
non-vascular plants 118
non-verbal reasoning *231*
non-violence 291, 467, 468
noradrenaline 215, 220
Norfolk Island 663
Noriega, Manuel 711
Normandy/Normans
architecture *see* Romanesque
history 403, 425
invasions from *397*, 401, 519
D-Day invasions of *444*, 445
language 606
Norse *see* Vikings
North America *see* Canada; United States
North American Free Trade Agreement *see* NAFTA
North Atlantic Drift *105*
North Atlantic Treaty Organization *see* NATO
North Korea (Democratic People's Republic) 285, 295, 447, **696**
see also Korea
North Mariana Islands 731
North Sea 170, 194, *310*
North Vietnam 452–3
see also Vietnam
North Yemen *see* Yemen
Northcliffe, Lord 654
Northern Ireland 580, 609, **729**
conflict *259*, *291*, 295
northern lights *11*
'Northern Renaissance' art 526–7
Northern Rhodesia 432, 433
North–South issue 298–9
see also Third World
Northumbria *396*, 397
Northwest Passage 417
Norway *187*, **709**
environment 300
fishing 195
glaciation 90, 91
history 363, 397, 444, *445*, 463
international relations 285, 286
language 603
literature 635, 644
music 577, 581, 587
women's suffrage 292
nose **216–17**, *246*, 247
see also smell, sense of
notation, musical 568, *569*
notes, characteristics of 31
Notre Dame Cathedral 622
Nouveau Réalisme 554, *555*
Nouveau Roman 649
Novalis (Hardenberg) 631
novels, history of
beginning of 419, 607, 615, 616, 617, **628–9**
Romanticism 630–1, 632
Realism and Naturalism 634–5
in 19th century 636–7, 652
American 638–9
modern 641, 648–9
popular 650–1
criticism 653
see also stories
Noverre, Jean Georges 596
Nubia 366, 367, 388
nuclear family *256*, 257
nuclear reactions
fission 38, **39**, 288, **304–5**
fusion 10, 38, **39**, 288, **305**
power 236, 286, **304–5**, 311
accidents 244, 301, 305
weapons 19, 236
armament and disarmament **288–9**, 293, 451
used on Japan *288*, 445
tests 288, 447
use threatened in Korean War 450
see also missiles; submarines
see also radioactivity
nucleic acids *see* DNA; RNA
nucleus of cell 111
nudes in art *542*
nuée ardente 83
Nujoma, Sam 706
numbers **64–5**
Arabic 392
and correspondence 68–9
law of large numbers 72
numerical data and Venn diagrams *67*
see also mathematics
Nuremberg 264, 442
Nureyev, Rudolph 597
nurture *see* environment; nature versus nurture
nutrients *see* diet; food
Nuwas, Abu 616
NVA (North Vietnamese Army) 452–3
Nyasaland 432, 433, 701
Nyerere, Julius 725
nylon *56*, 317, 318
nymph (insect) 126

oaks 181
oases 93
oats 189
obesity *see* fat, body
oboe 583
Obote, Milton 728
Obrenović, Miloš 736
observation, scientific 59
obsessive-compulsion 234
O'Casey, Sean 645
occupation 258, **259**
Oceania *see* Pacific Ocean
oceans and seas
animals
arthropods 124, *125*
birds 136–7
fish 128–9
food chains 118
mammals *155*, **162–3**, *168*, 169, 171–3, 332
see also whales
parasitism and symbiosis *174*, *175*
primitive 122–3
and climate 101, 178
coasts **96–7**, *179*, 306–7
currents 90, 96, **101**, 104, *105*
ecosystems 178–9
energy from tides *307*
erosion 87
fishing 194–5
geology/geomorphology 76, 83, 89, 95, **100–1**
ridges 78, 79, 80, 82, 98, *101*
seamounts 83, *101*
see also islands
in literature 637, *638*
oil industry *310*, 311
pollution 179, 300
and religion 462, 463
sea-level changes **97**, 99, 301, 390
sound velocity 30
tides 96, **100–1**, 129, *307*
waves *100*, 306
see also navies; ships and boats
ocean deeps 179
Ockeghem, Johannes 570
Ockham's razor 60
O'Connell, Daniel 692
octaves 568–9
Octavian *see* Augustus
Octobrists 295
octodonts *150*
octopuses **122–3**, 163, 195
Odoacer (Goth) 381, 693
OECD *284*, **286**
Oedipus complex 232
Oersted, Hans Christiaan 35, 330
oesophagus **209**, 227, 237
oestrogen 204, 205, 215
Offenbach, Jacques 588
offset lithography 323, 502
O'Higgins, Bernardo 673
Ohm, Georg Simon/ohms 36
Ohno, Kazua and Yoshito 599
oil, mineral
and chemical industry 41, *280*, 320, *321*
for electricity 304
engines 308, *309*
'gasohol' as substitute for 306
industry and refining **310–11**, 320, 332
price shocks 278, 299, 311, 321
production 311
spills 300
tankers 344
see also OPEC
oil painting **501**, 525, 526
oil, vegetable 182, 188, 250, 306, 366
okapi *160*
Okinawa, battle of *444*, 445
Olaff II Haraldsson 709
Old English 539, 606
old people
ageing and disorders 205, 207, 214, 219, 235, 240
bones 205, 206
pensions 276, 277, 434
sleep 233
Oldcastle, Sir John 403
Olduvai Gorge 200
olfactory *see* nose; smell
oligarchy 370, 371
Oligocene epoch *85*
mammals 141
oligopoly 275
oligotrophic ecosystems 179
olingo 155
Olivier, Lawrence 562
Olmec people 516
Olympus, Mount *462*, 509
Oman 454, **709–10**
Omar Khayyám 616
ombudsman 267
oncology *see* cancer
Ondine 596
one-party government 267
O'Neill, Eugene 645
oneiric painters 551
Onnes, Heike Kamerlingh 37, 55
Oort Cloud 11
Op (optical) art *555*
OPEC 279, **287**, 311
opencast mining *312*, *313*
open-hearth process 315
opera 575, 576, **584–5**
beginning of 593
Baroque 572, 573
China 590, 617
and literature 621, 627, 629
modern 578, 579, 580–1
operating systems, computer 334
operations (surgical) 240, *241*, 248, *249*
operculum 128
opiates 246, **247**, 248, 250, 632, 633
Opium Wars 383, 433
opossums 142–3
opportunistic infection 213
opportunity, equal 268
optical illusions *225*
optical telescopes 17
optics **32–3**, 218, 241, *243*, 418
see also fibre optics
oracles 462
oral literature 614, 617
oral stage 232
orang-utan 165
oratorio 573, 580
orbits
of electrons 38
of planets 58, 59, 104
orchestra 574–5, *576*, 578, 579, **582–3**, 591
orchids 121
ordeal, trial by 264
orders, architectural *509*, 525
Ordovician period *85*, *109*
ores 47, **50**, 312, 314
Oresme, Nicole d' 60
organ 582
organelles *111*
organic chemical industry 320
organic chemistry 52–3
organic mental disorder 235
Organization of African Unity 287
Organization of American States 287
Organization for Economic Cooperation and Development *284*, **286**
Organization for European Economic Cooperation 286
Organization of Petroleum Exporting Countries *278*, 279, **287**, 311
organizations
voluntary *see* charities
international 284–7
origin, family of 257
Orkney Islands 306, *362*, 463, 505, 580
Orléans, battle at 401
ornithischian dinosaurs 132
ornithopods *132*
Ortega, Daniel 710
Orthodox Christianity *254*, 395, *409*, **476–7**, 480
Orton, Joe 644
Orwell, George 621, *649*, 651
oryxes 161
Osborne, John 644
Oscar II of Sweden 709, 723
Oscars 562
Oshima, Nagasi 563
osmium *42–3*, *50*
osprey 137
Ostade, Adriaen van *60*
osteopathy 251
osteoporosis 205
ostracism 370
ostrich *113*, 138
Ostrogoths 380, 394
otters 155
otter trawl *194*
Otto I, emperor ('the Great') 394, 686
Otto IV of Brandenburg *406*
Otto, Nikolaus August 308
Ottoman Empire *see under* Turkey
Ottonian dynasty 394
outout peripherals *335*
Ouverture, Toussaint l' 688
ova *115*, 139, **202**
ovary
of flower *120*
human 202, 204, 205, *214*, 215, *237*
overburden 312
overglaze painting 514
Overlord, Operation *444*
Ovid **615**, 625
ovoviviparity 131, 134
ovulation 202
ovule *120*
Owen, Robert 435
Owen, Wilfred 646
owls *138*
Oxenstierna, Axel 723
Oxford *260*, 406, 646
oxidization/oxidation 41, **47**, 116–17, 209, 509
oxygen **48**
in atmosphere 13, 77, 176
in blood 242
bonding 40, 41, 44–5, 47, *53*
and industry 315, *321*
with metals *see* ores
in oceans 178
and plants 116, *117*
in respiration 208, 210, 211, 243
in synthetics 54, 56
oxytocin 214, 215
Oyo *388*, 389
ozone 48–9, 77, 300
layer 177, *301*, 309
Ozu, Yasujiro 563

Pabst, Georg 559, 563
paca *150*
pacarana *150*
pacemaker 240
Pacific Ocean area
animals *124*, 129, 138, 162, 163, 170–1
dance 592–3
fishing 194, 195
geology/geomorphology 78–9, 80, 86, 87, *98*, 99, **100**
history **389**
colonialism *389*, 410, *417*, 432, 433
20th-Century *289*, *444*, 445, 446, 448, 449
languages 602
population 297
religion 459, 464, 465, 476
Padua 520, **525**
Paganini, Nicolo 581
paganism *see* gods and goddesses
Page, Ashley 599
pagodas 515
Pahlavi, Reza Khan 691
pain **216**, *217*, 418
treatment *see under* drugs
Paine, Thomas 290, 425
painting and paints 41, 320, **500–1**
see also art
Pakistan 191, 261, 603, *607*, **710**
history 200, 259, 385, 449, *451*, 479
Palach, Jan 295
palaeoanthropology 200–1
Palaeocene epoch *85*
Palaeolithic **362**, **363**, 462, 504
see also caves, paintings; Stone Ages
Palaeozoic era *85*
Palestine
art and architecture **506–7**
history
ancient 364, 365, 369
Crusades 398–9
20th-Century 437, 441, 449, 454–5
Palestine Liberation Organization **287**, 455
religion 461, 476
terrorism 263
see also Israel, West Bank
Palestrina, Giovanni 570, 571
Palladio, Andrea/Palladian 508, 529, 531, 534, **535**
palladium *42–3*, *50*
Palme, Olof 723
Palmer, Samuel 537
Palmerston, Lord 539, 731
Palau 734
Panama *451*, **710–11**
Canal 341, 432, 433
pampas 184, **185**
panchromatic film 325
pancreas 209, *214*, 215, 237
pandas 154–5
Pangaea 78, 79, 140
pangolins 145
Pankhurst, Christabel 292
Pankhurst, Emmeline *292*
panning 313
panthers 152–3
papacy *see* popes
Papal States 428, 734
paper 188, *323*, 366, 501
Papua New Guinea 98, 142, **711**
art 512, 513
birds 138, *139*
history 388, 389, 432, 433, 445
language 602
men of *256*
religion 465
papyrus 323, 366, 507, 605
Paracelsus 60, 248
paradigms 58
paradoxes 27, **67**, **68**, *224*, 225
Paraguay 158, **711**
parallax 5, 224
parallel connection *36*
paralysis, 'hysterical' 232, 235
paramammals 140
paramilitary parties 442–3
paranoia 247, 551
parasites/parasitism 118, 121, 122, 129, 139, **174–5**
and disease 174, 175, **238**, 239, 244
plant 121
parathyroid *214*, 215
paratyphoid 174
Paré, Ambroise 248
parents 256–7
Paricutín 83
Paris 682
art and architecture 531, 535, 539, 546
Gothic 622
Realism 540, 541
Impressionists 542
Dada and Surrealism 551
20th-century 552, 553, 554
film 558
history 406, *408*, 427, 428
commune 425, 429
20th-Century 435, 436, 440
law court *265*
literature 640–1
music 575, 579, 588, 596, 598
University 260, 406
Park Chung-Hee 697
Parker, Charlie *588*, 589
Parkinson's disease 227
parliament 266–7, 387
Britain 265, **267**, 412–13, 422
history 387, 412–13, 422
Parmenides 487, 488
Parmigianino 529
Parnell, Charles Stewart 692
parrots *137*, 138, 139
parsec 5
Parsis 255, 467
see also Zoroastrianism
Parson, Charles 308
Parthenon *370*, *509*
particles 26
partnership 282
parts of speech 609
Pasolini, Pier Paolo 563
Passchendaele 437
pastel 501
Pasternak, Boris 649
Pasteur, Louis 58, 196, *249*
pasteurization 196
pastoralism
agricultural **190–1**
literary *see under* nature
Patenir, Joachim 527
Pater, Walter 641
Pathet Lao 453
pathogens *see* bacteria; fungi; parasites; viruses
patinated silver 509
patricians 376
Patrick, St 692
patriotism *see* nationalism
patronage of arts 525, 528
see also Louis XIV
patterns 319
Paul, St 475
Paul VI, Pope 734
Pavarotti, Luciano 587
Pavlov, Ivan Petrovitch *221*
Pavlova, Anna 597
Pax Romana 379
Paxton, Joseph 539
pay *see* wages
Pearl Harbor 444
Pears, Peter 587
peas 189
peasants 258
in art 527, 540, *541*, 544
Revolts *402*, 403, 408, 420, 438
see also agriculture
peccaries 158
Pechstein, Max 547
Peck, Gregory *564*
Pedro II of Brazil 669
Pedro of Portugal 713
Peel, Sir Robert 262, 731
Peelers 262
Peirce, Charles Sanders 487, 610

Peisisratos 370
Peking *see* Beijing
Pelée, Mont 82
pelicans 137
Peloponnesia 370, 371, 614
penal systems *see* prisons
Penderecki, Krzysztof 581
penguins *136*, 137, 138, *139*, 173
penicillin **57**, 118, 242, 249, 321
pensions 266, 276, 277, 434
funds 272
Pentecost 475
Penzias, Arno 5
people *see* humans
Pepin the Short 394
pepsin 243
peptides 321
perception 224–5
percussion 582
perennial plants 120
perestroika 269
performance art 554, 557
Pergamon 373, 509
Peri, Jacopo 584
Pericles 370, 371
Periodic Table *42–3*, *50*, 51
perissodactyls 156–7
permafrost 187
Permian period *85*, *109*
Perón, Eva and Juan 662
Pérotin 570
Perov, Vassily Grigorievich *635*
Per-Ramesses 367
Perry, Commodore 387
Persepolis *365*, *506*
Persia/Persian Empire 363, **691**
map of *365*
art and architecture **506**, 508, 509, 510, **511**
and Egypt 366, 367
and Greece, wars with 370–1, 372, 535
religion 379, 461, 462
and India 385
and Islam 392, 478, 479
and Byzantine Empire 395
language 602, 603
literature **616**, 620
religion 477
after 1935 *see* Iran
Persian Gulf, war *455*
person *see* individual
Personal Computer (PC) 335
personal space 229
personality cult 295, 632
perspective in art 524, *525*, 526, 532
Peru 87, *187*, 194, 285, 516, **711–2**
history 390, *391*, 410, *451*
pesticides 56, 147, 189, 300–1, *321*
Pétain, Philippe 683
petal *120*
Peter, St 477
Peter I ('the Great') of Russia 417, 715
Peter I Island 709
pethidine 247
Petipa, Maurice 597
Petit, Roland 597
petition in prayer 480
Petra *509*
Petrarch 406, 521, 619, 624
petrels 136
petrochemicals *see* chemicals industry
Petrograd (St Petersburg)) 438, *439*
petroleum *see* oil, mineral
Petronius 615, 628
Petrus Christus 526
Petrus Peregrinus 60
Petrushka 597
Pettit-Smith, Francis 343
petty bourgeoisie 259
Pevsner, Antoine 549
phalanges *206*
phalanx 373
phallic stage 232
Phanomyang, Pridi 725
pharmaceuticals *see* drugs
Pharsalus, battle of 377
phencyclidine (PCP) 247
phenetic classification 108
phenol 320
phenothiazines 235
pheromones 126, 130, 134, 166, 217
Phidias *508*, 509
Philadelphia 731
Philip II of Macedon 371, 372, 737
Philip II of Spain 409–11, 412, 529, 712, 721
Philip IV ('the Fair') 399, 400
Philip V of Spain 721
Philip VI of France 400
Philip Augustus of France 400
Philip 'the Good', Duke 401, 570
Philippi, battle of 377
Philippine Sea, battle of *444*, 445
Philippines 98, 165, 287, **712**
government, uprising against *267*
history 389
colonialism 431, 432, 433
20th-Century *444*, 445, 449, *451*, 453
language *607*
women's suffrage 292
Philistines 364
Phillips, Thomas *633*
philology 602
philosophy
and art 525
of education 260–1
ethics 492–3
and government 266, 290
history and evolution of 392, 406, 407, 419, **486–7**
human rights 290
knowledge and reality 225, **488–9**
and language 491, **496–7**
and literature 629, **631**, 633, **635**, **640–1**, 643, 648, 649, 652
logic and argument 494–5
and medicine 248
mind and body 490–1
and perception 225
Philostratus 508
'Phiz' *636*
phobias 232, 234
Phoenicians 364, *506*, 604, 605
phonetics **226**, 608
'Phoney War' 444
phonograph 328
phonology 602–3
phosgene gas 289
phosphates 320
phosphorus 40, *42–3*, *53*, 56, 116, 208, 215, 320
photochemical smog 49, 300
photoelectric effect 37
photography **324–5**, **556–7**
early 324
as art 556–7
cameras 324, *325*, 326, 558
forensic 263
gamma ray 237, *332*
Kirlian *251*
photogravure *322*, 323
photolithography 502
photomicrography 263, 325
photomontage 551, 556–7
Photo-Realism 555
photo-screen printing 502
see also films
photons 4, 26, 27
photoperiod 117
photosphere 10
photosynthesis 110, 116, *117*, 123, 175, 177
phototropism 117
photovoltaic effect 37, 306
phrases 608–9
Phrygian religion 379, 461, 462
phylogenetic classification 108
physical development *see* growth
physics **20–39**
acoustics 30–1
atoms and subatomic particles 38–9
electricity in action 36–7
motion and force 20–1
as paradigm of science 58
quantum theory and relativity 26–7
statics and hydrostatics 22–3
thermodynamics 24–5
wave theory 28–9
see also electricity; electromagnetism; optics; science
physiology 109
see also humans, organism
physiotherapy 207
phytoplankton 179
piano 582
music for 575, 576, 577, 578, 579, 580, 582
Piano, Renzo 553
Picabia, Frances 550, 551
picaresque novel 628, 629
Picasso, Pablo *502*, 517, 544, **548**, *549*, 579, 597, 640
piccolo 583
pichiciegos 144
Pickford, Mary 559, 560
Picts *396*
picture plane 525
pictures *see* art; photography
picturesque 534, 536, 627
see also landscape; pastoralism
pidginized languages 602, 603
Piero della Francesca 524, **525**
Pietism 477
pigments 500
pigs **158**, 190, **191**
pikas 151
pilgrimages **480–1**
Christian 398, *481*, 519, 534
Islamic *see* Mecca
Pilon, Germaine 529
Pilsudski, Józef 713
Pindar 614
pineal organ 171, *222*
pines **119**, 180, 193
pinnipeds 162–3
Pinochet, General Augusto 673
Pinter, Harold 644, *645*
Pirandello, Luigi 643
Pisa 404, 520
Pisanello, Antonio 521, 524
Pisano, Giovanni *520*, 521
Pisano, Nicola 520
Piscator, Erwin 642
Pissarro, Camille 543
pistols *356*
Pitcairn Islands 729
pitch, musical 31, 568
pitcher plants 121
pituitary glands 171, *214*, 215, *222*
Pius IX, Pope 736
Pizarro, Francisco 391, 410, 712
place-names 606
placenta 140, 215
placental mammals 140, 144–65
plague *see* bubonic plague
plainsong 568, 570, 587
Planck, Max 26, 38, 61
plane, picture 525
plane surfaces *29*
planets 9, 10, *11*, *15*, 17, 19, 110
inner 12–13
orbits 58, 59, 104
outer 14–15
satellites *see* Moon; moons
see also Earth; solar system
planigale 143
plankton 99, **124**, 129, 137, 163, 170, 179
migration 170
planned economy 268–9
planographic techniques 502–3
Plantagenets 400
plantations *see* cash crops
plants **116–21**
agriculture **188–9**
and animals 140–1, 143, 147, 151, 168
see also herbivorous
in art 510, 521, 534
biosphere **176–7**
cells *116*, *117*, 118
classification 108–9
in deserts 93, 186
drugs from 246, 247, 250
ecosystems **178–87**
energy from 306
and fertilizers 320
flowering 120–1
forestry **192–3**
herbalism 250
and insects 121, **127**
non-flowering 118–19
non-vascular 118
parasitism and symbiosis 174–5
pests 122
physiology 116–17
reproduction 118–21
vascular 119
vegetation regions 93, **105**
see also ecosystems; forests; flowering plants; grasslands
plaque, arterial 241
plasma 210, 213
plastic flow *23*
plastics 41, 311, **316–17**, 320, *321*, 553
plastron 134
Plataea, battle of 371
plateaux 93
platelets 210
plates *see* tectonic plates
Plath, Sylvia 647
platinum *42–3*, *50*, 47, **313**
Plato 290, 407, **487**, *488*, **492**, 496, 614, 624
Platonic love 625
platypus 142
Plautus 615, 626
Playford, John 595
plebeians 376
plein air 540, *541*
Pleistocene epoch *85*
mammals 141
see also Ice Ages
plesiosaurs 132
Pliny the Elder 60
Pliocene epoch *85*
Plisetskaya, Maya 597
PLO **287**, 455
plural society 259, 269
Plutarch 615
Pluto *11*, 15
plutonium 39, *42–3*, *50*, 305
plywood *193*
pneumonia 238, *239*
Poe, Edgar Allan **638**, 650, 651
Poetic Realists 635
poetry
and art 546
history of
Classical 614–15
Asian 616–17
epics and romances 618–19
Renaissance 624–5
Neoclassical 627
Romanticism 630–3
American 638–9, 647
Medieval 620–1
Symbolism, Aestheticism and Modernism 640–1
modern 646–7
language 606, 607
and music 577, 578, 579, 591
and religion 462
criticism 652
pointwork in ballet 596–7
poisons
from animals 129, 131, 135, 148
food poisoning 174
forensic identification 263
gas used in war 437
heavy metal 237, 300
toxic wastes 321
Poitiers, battle of 394, 401, 403
Pol Pot 453, 671
Poland 287, **712–3**
film 562
history
and Islam/Crusades 393, 399
Reformation 409
witch craze 409
and Napoleonic Wars 427
partitioned 417, 439
nationalism 428, 429
World War I 436
and fascism 442
state created 440, 441
World War II 443, 444, *445*
Cold War 450
martial law *451*
language 603
literature 631
music 581
plants 181
science 60
women's suffrage 292
Polanski, Roman 562
polar areas 19, 92, *105*, **187**
ecosystems 187
see also Antarctic; Arctic
polar bear 154, *187*
police 262, 276, 442
poliomyelitis **239**, 245
polis 370
politics
discrimination 259
and economy 276
and government 266–71
human rights 290–1
Left 267, 268–9, 435
see also Communists; socialism
and literature 621, 632, 633, 634, 635, 637, 643, 648
participation 267
and pollution 301
Right 267, 270–1
Fascist 442–3
Pollaiuolo, Antonio 525
pollen and pollination *120*, 121, 137, 175
pollen tube 120
pollination *see* pollen
Pollock, Jackson 554
pollution **300–1**
and disease 236–7, 244
greenhouse effect 182, 301, 304
industrial wastes and accidents 95, 244, 275, 301, 304, 305, 306, 321
plastic 317
water 179, 244, **300**
Polo, Marco 404, *405*
polonium *42–3*, *50*
Polonnaruwa 384
polyandry 168–9, 256
Polycrates 508
polyculture 188
polygamy 256
animal 168
polygyny 256
animal 168
polymers (polythene, PVC etc) *56*, 311, 316, *317*, 320, *321*
Polynesia *389*
polyp 123
polyphony 570–1
polysaccharides 53, 208, 209
polytechnics 261
polytheism 459, 460
see also gods; Hinduism; primal religions
Pompadour, Marquise Jeanne de 534
Pompeii 82, 244, *372*, 509, *614*
Pompey (Gnaeus Pompeius) 377
Pompidou, Georges 683
Pontormo, Jacopo 528
Pop art 503, 554–5, 557
pop music *see under* music
Pope, Alexander 534, 626, **627**, 652
popes 476, **477**, 528
history
Gregorian reform 398
and German Empire 394, 399
anticlericalism 403, 415
and Reformation 408, 409
see also Roman Catholics; Vatican
Popper, Sir Karl *58*, 59, 489
popular sovereignty 266
population
growth 420, 431, 432
and hunger **296–7**
loss *see* bubonic plague
Poquelin, Jean-Baptiste *see* Molière
porcelain *see under* ceramics
porcupines 150, *151*
porpoises 163
Porter, Cole 588
Porter, Edwin 559
ports and harbours 420
see also ships
Portugal 342, **713**
dance 595
history
founded 399
colonialism 405, **410–11**, *433*, *625*
in Africa 389, 398, 405, 410, 417, 432
in Brazil 410, 417, 432
in India 385, 410, *411*, 417
Napoleonic Wars 426–7
and decolonization 448, 449
international relations 286
language 603
literature 625
positrons 4
postal systems 330, 365
Post-Impressionism 515
Post-Modernism 553, 649
post-structuralism 653
posture 228–9, 251
postwar settlement 440–1
potassium *42–3*, 46, *50*, 56, 100, 178, 208, 320
potassium chloride 44
potatoes 188, **189**, 390, 420
potential energy *24*
potential energy, electrical 34
potentizing 251
pottery *see* ceramics
pottos 164
Poulenc, Francis 578, 597
poultry 191
Pound, Ezra 548, 641, 646
Poussin, Nicolas *531*, 535, 540, 544
poverty 296–7
Powell, Anthony 649
Powell, Michael 562
power (energy) 176–7
stations *see* electricity
see also energy
pragmatics 609
Prague 295, 406, 653, 677
prairie dogs 151, 168, 185
prairie earth 185
prairies **184–5**
prawns 124–5
praseodymium *42–3*, *50*
praxinoscope *558*
prayer 467, 478, **480**
praying mantis *126*
Precambrian era *85*, *109*
precession 6
precious stones *see* gems
precipitation (chemical) 46, 47
precipitation (climatic) 102–3
see also rainfall; snow
predatory animals 123, 125, 143, 162
birds of prey *136*, *137*, *138*
see also carnivorous
preen gland 136
pregnancy **202–3**, 213, 214, 247, 255
monitoring 30, 131, *242*, 245, 249, 332
prehistory **362–3**
archaeology 360–2
religion 462–3
Preminger, Otto 561
Pre-Raphaelites **537**, 541, 546, 556
Presbyterians 413, 419
presidential systems 266
Presley, Elvis 295, 589
press *see* journalism
Pressburger, Emeric 562
presses, printing 323
pressure, atmospheric **23**, 102, *103*
pressurized-water reactors *305*
prestige *see* status
Prévost, Antoine-François 629
prey *see* predators
prices **274–5**, 276
Priestley, J. B. 644
Priestley, Joseph 61, 316
priests 465, 466, 475, 513
see also shamans
primal religions 458–9, 462–5
primary education 260–1
primary growth 116
primary producers 177
primary sources 360
primates 153, **164–5**, 166, 169, 200
early 140–1
and language 167, 490, *491*
see also humans
Primaticcio 529
prime ministers **266**, 413
prime numbers 64
primitive animals **122–3**
primitive plants 118
Prince, Jean-Baptiste le 502
Princip, Gavrilo 668
printing **322–3**
artistic 515, 527
history of 406, 407, 408, 607
invention of 248
printmaking **502–3**
textiles *318*, 319
prism **32**, *324*
prison *262*, 263, 418
in literature 636
rights in 290, 291
USSR labour camps 439
private enterprise 276
private property 268
privatization 276
probability **72–3**
probation 263
proboscis monkey 165
proconsul 200
procreation, family of 257
see also reproduction
production of films 564–5
professional class 259
profit-and-loss account 283
profundal zone *179*
progesterone 202, *215*
programme music 576–7
programs, computer 334–7
progressive education *261*
prohibition in USA *246*
projectors 325, 558
Prokofiev, Sergei 579, 597
Prokuratura 265
proletariat *see* working class
promethium *42–3*, *50*
pronghorn 161
proof 494
propaganda *437*, 442
propagation, wave 28
Propertius 615
property rights 262, 268, 271, 292
prophecy 462, 465
propitiation 480
proportional representation 267
Propylaea *370*
prose fiction *see* novels
prosecutions 262, 263
prosimians 164
prosthesis *240*
protactinium *42–3*, *50*
Protagoras 260
protectionism 279
Protectorate, Cromwell's 412, 627
proteins 53, *110*, 116, 200, 209, 321

in diet **208**, 209
protest *see* demonstrations; revolutions
Protestantism **477**
and art 527
and conflict 259, 291, 295
history 408–9, 411, 412, 415, 422, 424
and literature 624
and music 570
ritual 475
youth movements 294
see also Anglicanism; Christianity; Puritans; United Churches
protists *110–11*, 118, 174, 175
protons 4, 38
protoplasm 110, 116, 118, 178
protozoans 111, 238, 239
Proust, Marcel **641**, 652
Proxima Centauri 8
Prussia 603
history 399, 417, 418, 426–7, 428, *429*, 440
see also Germany
psychoanalysis **232**, 235, 551, 640
psychology **222–33**
body language 228–9
brain 222–3
disorders *see* mental illness
drug dependence 246, 247
and language 609
learning, creativity and intelligence 230–1
and muscle movement 207
perception 224–5
problems *see* mental illness
sleep, dreams and unconscious 232–3, 247
speech 226–7
unconscious 232
see also human organism
psychosis 234, 235, 247
psycho-surgery 240
psychotherapy 235
ptarmigan 187
pterodactyl *132*
pterosaurs 132
Ptolemaic dynasty 367, 372, 507
Ptolemy (Claudius Ptolemaeus) **16**, **60**, 624
puberty *204–5*, 255
see also adolescence
public goods 275
public health 244, 249, 434
public limited company 282
public sector borrowing requirement 277
public speaking 260
Puccini, Giacomo **585**, 629
Pucelle, Jean 521
Puerto Rico 17, 431, 432, 433, **731**
Pugin, A. W. N. 538–9
puja 466
pulp, wood *193*
pulsars 9, 333
pulse oximeter 242
pulse-code modulation 331
pulses (peas and beans) 116, **189**, 196–7, 366
Punic Wars 376
punishment 262–3
Punjab 432, 467, 603
punks *295*, 589, 595
pupal stage *127*
Purcell, Henry 573, 584
purdah 293
Pure Land Buddhism **469**, 470
pure mathematics 62
Purgatorius 140
Puritans 412, 422
purse seine *194*
'push-pull' concept 448, 449
Pushkin, Alexander 631, 634
P-waves *81*
pygmies *388*
pygmy animals 144, 147, 158, 159, 160
Pyle, Ernie 655
pylon *304*
Pylos 369
Pynchon, Thomas 649
pyramids *366*, 391, 460, 507, *516*
pyridoxine 208
pyroclasts 82
Pythagoras 60, **62**, 63, 65

Qaboos, Sultan 710
Qatar *287*, **713–14**
Qin dynasty 383, 514
Qing (Manchu) dynasty 383, 515
Qu Yuan 616–17
quadrant 17
quadripedal movement 173
Quakers 422
quantity theory 277
quantum theory **26–7**, 58
quarantine 244, 262
quarks 39
quartet **575**, 576, 579, 580, 581
quartz clock 7
quartzite 85
quasars 8–9, 333
Quaternary period *85*, *109*
Quebec 259, 417, **671**
Queen Maud Land 709
queens *see* monarchy
Quetzalcoatl 516
Quezon, Manuel 712
Quiller-Couch, Arthur 652
Quine, Willard van Orman 487
quintet 575
Quintilian 260
Quintus Fabius Maximus 376
Quisling, Vidkun 709
Quixote, Don 411, 628
quoll 143
quotas 279
Qur'an (Koran) 264, 392, *478*, 479, 510, 616

rabbits 151
rabies 244, 249
raccoons 155
race *see* ethnicity; racism
Racine, Jean 611, 627
racism 254, 259, 268
radar **332**, 335
Radcliffe, Mrs Ann 632
radiation *25*, 177, **332–3**
see also radioactivity
Radicals, Christian 477
radio *35*, **326**, 331, 654
astronomy 17, **332–3**
radioactivity **39**, 144, 289
radiograph 242
radioisotopes 332
radiotherapy *236*, 237
sickness 236, 301, 305
see also nuclear reactions
radiocarbon dating 361
radium *42–3*, *50*
radon *42–3*, *50*
Raeburn, Henry 535
RAF (Royal Air Force) 349, 444
Raffles, Sir Stamford 719
ragtime 588
railways 194, **346–7**
in art 541, 543
engines 308, *421*
history 420–1, 430, 432, 448
maglev trains 55, *347*
rain forest
tropical 104, **182–3**
temperate *180*
rainfall **102–3**, 104, 105
acid 49, 178, 300, 304
and caves 88
lack of *see* deserts
and plants 182
rain shadow 92, 105
and religion 516
and rivers 94
Rainier III, Prince 704
Rakhmaninov, Sergey 579
Rama I of Thailand 725
Ramadan 478
Rambert, Marie 597
ramblers 294
Rameau, Jean-Philippe *572*, 573, 584
Ramsay, Allan 535
Ramses II and III 364, 367, *507*
Rance, La *307*
Ransom, John Crowe 647, 652
Rapallo, Treaty of 439
Raphael 527, *528*, 529
al-Rashid, Harun 392
Rasputin, Grigori Efimovich 438
Ras Shamra 460, 605
Rastas 295
ratel 155
rats 150–1
and plague 402
rational choice 73
rational numbers **64–5**, 69
rationalism 269, **488**
Rauschenberg, Robert 503, 554, 557
Ravel, Maurice 578, 583
Ravenna *518*
Ravilious, Eric 502
Rawlings, Flt. Lieut. Jerry 686
Rawls, John 493
Ray, John 108
Ray, Man 550, 557
Ray, Satyajit 563
Rayleigh wave *81*
Rayonists 548
rayonnant style 522
rays (fish) 128–9, 173
rays (physics) *see* radiation
Razes (al-Rhazi) 248, 392
reactions, chemical 42, **46–7**
reactors *see* nuclear power
Reagan, Ronald 289, 451, 733
real numbers 69
Realism
in art and architecture **540–1**
Gothic 520, *521*
Renaissance 524
Netherlandish 526
modern 555
in literature 617, **634–5**
Neoclassical 626, 627
novels 628, 629, 637, 648, 649, 652
theatre 642
modern 641, 645, 646–9
see also Naturalism
reality
and knowledge **488–9**
rearmament 442–3
reason 269, 290, **488**
reasoning, non-verbal *231*
receptacle (plant) *120*
receptor *220*
recession *see* depression (economic)
reclamation, land 97
recombination 114–15
Reconquista 410
Reconstruction 430–1
recording sound *328–9*
rectum 209
Red Army faction (Japan) 295
Red Army (USSR) 438–9
red blood cells 206, 210, *212*, 236
Red Crescent 290
Red Cross 290, 291
Red Falcons 294
red giant 9
Red Guards 295, 447
Red Sea 162, 299, 365, 388
red shift 5
Redon, Odilon 544, 546
Redshirts 428
reduction (chemical) 47
Reed, Carol 562
reference (in philosophy) 496
referenda 267
refining *see under* oil, mineral
reflection 28, *29*, *32*
reflexology *251*
Reformation 407, **408–9**, 412, 477
and art and architecture 522, 526–7
and language 607
and literature 624
refracting telescopes 17
refraction 28, *29*, 30, *32*
refrigeration *309*
refugees *284*, 290, 453, 455
Refusés, Salon des 542
refuting theories 59
Regency architecture 538
regional novel **637**
Reich, Steve 581
Reichstag 442
Reimann, Aribert 585
reincarnation 483
reindeer (caribou) **160**, 170, 171, 181
Reinitzer, Friedrich 54
Reisz, Karel 562
relative chronology 362
relatives *see* families
relativism 418
relativity 27, **58–9**
relaxation *207*
relics 482
religion **458–83**
and art and architecture 507, 512–13, 526–8, 532, *533*
Native American and African 516, 517
see also cathedrals and churches; mosques; temples
and conflict 259
discrimination 259
and family 256
history of
ancient 460–3
primal 462–5
Minoan and Mycenaean 369
Celtic *374*, *375*
Roman 378, 379, 380–1
Asian 466–71
Persian 379
Mayan 391
Wars of 408, 409, 411
and French Revolution 424, 425
wars of, Islamic *see* jihad
and language 466, 476, 477, 606, 607
and literature 612–13, 616–17, 620–1, 622, 624–5, 635, 646
and music 568, 570–1, 575, 581, 592, 593, 594
scriptures *see* Bible; Qur'an; Vedas
youth movements 294
see also Buddhism; Christianity; Confucianism; Daoism; festivals; gods and goddesses; Islam; Jainism; Judaism; missionaries; ritual; Sikhs; *and under* individual countries
REM sleep 232, *233*
Rembrandt van Rijn 502, *533*, 549
Renaissance
art and architecture **524–5**, **528–9**
Northern 526–7
culture 406–7
economy and society 404–5
and English language 607
Man 406
René, Albert 718
renewable resources 306–7
Reni, Guido 530
Renoir, Auguste 541, 542, *543*
Renoir, Jean 561, 562
reparations for war 441
replication 114
repression of feelings 232
reproduction
animals 166, **168–9**, 177
arthropods 125, 126
asexual 123
birds 137, 139
fish **129**
mammals 143, 144, 147, 160, 162, 168
origins 111
parasites 174, *175*
reptiles and amphibians 130–1, 132, **134**, 134
scientific breeding 190, 374, 420
vegetative 120, 121, 184
viruses *110*
human **202–3**, 207
and hormones **214–15**
plants 118–21
vegetative 120, 121, 184
reproductive behaviour, animal **168**
reptiles **134–5**, 166, 167, 168, 170, 173, 186
dinosaurs **132–3**
movement 173
Republican Party (USA) 430, 431
republicanism 266, 376, 424–5
in Ireland 692
rescue archaeology 361
research and development 273
reservoir *307*
resistance, electrical 36, 55
resistance to disease 212–3
Resnais, Alain 562
resonatory system 226
resources 177, 272, 278
renewable *see* conservation; forests; water
respiration
human 176, 207, **210**, 211
supported 242–3
see also under diseases
plants 116, *117*, 176
and speech 226
in water 122, 126, *128*, 130, *131*
Restoration drama 627
retailers 281
Réunion 683
revaluation 279
revolutions
Agricultural and Industrial 188, 314, **420–1**
American 422
Chinese 446, 447
French 424–5
Glorious (English) 290, 413
Marxism and 259, 269, 438
Russian 438–9
see also demonstrations; *and under* France; peasants; Russia; United States
Reynolds, Joshua 535
Reza, Mohammed 691
Rhaetian languages 603
al-Rhazi (Razes) 248, 392
rheas *113*, 138
rhenium *42–3*, *50*
rhetoric 260
Rhineland 375, 427, 440, 443
rhinoceros **156–7**, *168*
woolly *141*
rhizomes *120*
Rhodes, Cecil 737
rhodium *42–3*, *50*
riboflavin 208
ribonucleic acid *see* RNA
ribosomes 111, 114
Ricardo, David 296
rice 188, **189**
Richard I of England 398, 399
Richard II of England 401, 403
Richard III of England 360, 412
Richards, I. A. 652
Richardson, Samuel 628, 629, 634
Richelieu, Cardinal 414
Richmond, George *636*
Richter scale 80
rickets *208*
Riefenstahl, Leni 563
rifles *356*, *357*
rift valley (graben) 78, *86*
Rig Veda 613
Rigaud, Hyacinthe 414
Right, politics of the 270–1
rights, property 262, 268, 271, 292
rights, human 254, 268, **290–1**
declarations, Covenants and Bills
England 290, 413
European 286, 290–1
France *290*, 424
United Nations 290
USA 290, 422–3
Riley, Terry 581
Rilke, Rainer Maria 641
Rimbaud, Arthur *640*
Rimsky-Korsakov, Nikolay 579
ringworm 118, 175, 238
Rio de Janeiro 669
riots *see* demonstrations
Risorgimento 428
Ritchie, Jean 587
rites of passage *see* ritual
ritual **470**, 475, **480**
and art 462, 504, 517
and dance *592*, 593, 594
and myths 612
rites of passage **254–5**, 470, **472**, 480, *481*, 504, 592
see also religion
Rivera, Primo de 722
rivers **94–5**
animals in 135, 163
see also freshwater animals
ecosystems 178–9
geology/geomorphology 93, **94–5**
navigable 420
polluted 300, 321
RNA (ribonucleic acid) *53*, 109, 114
roads 276, *317*, **340–1**
history 340–1, 391, 421, 432, 448
see also cars
Robbe-Grillet, Alain 649
Robbins, Harold 651
Robbins, Jerome 597
Robert brothers 348
Robert the Bruce 730
Robeson, Paul 588
Robespierre, Maximilien 425
robin 168, 169
Robinson, Bill 'Bojangles' 598
Robinson, Edward G. 560
robotics *336*, 337
Rocha, Glauber 563
rock art *see under* caves
rock music 294, *295*, *588*, **589**, 595
Rockers 295
rockets 18, *19*, 309, 357
see also missiles
Rockies 161, 185
rocks *see* geology
Rococo art **534**, 539
rodents 141, 146, **150–1**, 166, 168, 169, 244
in ecosystems 181, 186, 187
Rodgers, Richard 588
Rodin, Auguste *503*
Roehm, Ernest 442
Rogers, Richard *553*
rognons (nunataks) 90, *91*
Roh Tae Woo 697
Rohmer, Eric 562
Roi Soleil *see* Louis XIV
Roland 618, 625
Rolling Stones *294*, 589
Rollo (Viking) 397
Roman alphabet *605*
Roman Catholicism 476, **477**
and conflict 259, 291, 295
and family 256
history
map of distribution *409*
and Reformation 408–9
'Index' of heretical books 409
missionaries 410
and Louis XIV 415
in England 412, 413
and Enlightenment 418
and French Revolution 424–5
and Mussolini 442
and music 571
prayer and pilgrimage 480, 481
and trade unions 435
youth movements 294
see also Christianity; heresies; popes; religion
Roman Empire 376–81
prehistory and archaeology *360*, *361*, 363
rise of **376–7**
art and architecture **509**, 518
extent and influence 244, 363, 367, 374, 382, 406
education 260
literature 615, 652
maps of *377*, *380*
decline and barbarian invasions 375, **380–1**, 394, 448
dance 593
influence on later ages 525, 535, 538, 615, 624–7
language *see* Latin
law 264, 265
literature 614, **615**
medicine 248
philosophy 290
religion 461, *462*, 463, 476
science 60
transport/travel 340
see also Rome
romance (literary forms) 618–9, 623–4, 651, 652
Romance languages 603, 606, 607
Romanesque architecture *519*, *522*, 523
Romania 149, 287, 603, **714**
art and architecture 505, 549
history 378, 440, 442, *445*, 450
and Moldova 706
religion 477
Romano, Giulio 529
Romanticism
art and architecture 534, **536–7**
ballet 596–7
literature 629, **630–1**, **632–3**, 634, **636**, 640
music 576–7
and nationalism 428
as reaction against Enlightenment 419
Rome *379*, 692
art and architecture 518, 527, 528–9, 531, 532, 534, 535, 539
liberation of 445
Treaties of 286
see also Roman Empire; Vatican City
Rommel, General Erwin 444
Ronsard, Pierre de 624, 625
Röntgen, Wilhelm K. 61, 242, 249, 332
Roosevelt, Franklin Delano 284, 441, 444, 450, 733
roots, mathematical 65
roots of plants 120
rorquals 163
Rosa, Salvator 531
rosaries 480
Rosas, Juan Manuel de 662
Rosenberg, Isaac 646
Roses, Wars of the 401, 412
rosewood 193
Ross Dependency 707
Ross Ice Shelf 90
Rossellini, Roberto 563
Rossetti, Dante Gabriel 537, 546
Rossi, Franco 563
Rossini, Gioachino Antonio 585, 627
rotation, crop 116, **188**, 188–9, 420
rotation (physics) 22
Rothko, Mark 554
Rouault, Georges 544, 545
roulette *73*
Roumania *see* Romania
roundworms 175
Rousseau, Henri 544
Rousseau, Jean-Jacques 266, 290, 419, 487, 628, 629, *630*, **631**
Rousseau, Théodore 540
Rowley, William 623
royal academies *see* academies
Royal Air Force 349, 444
royal assent 267

Royal Society 60
royalty *see* monarchy
Rozier, François Pilâtre de 348
rubber **316**, 432
rubbish *see* wastes
rubella 145, 213, **239**, 244
Rubens, Peter Paul 501, 508, *530*, **531**, 533, 534
rubidium *42–3*, *50*
Rubin, Jerry 295
Rudies 295
Rudolf II of Habsburg 529, 664
Rudolph, Archduke 577
Ruggles, Carl 579
Ruhr 421, 441, 685
Ruisdael, Jacob van 532, *533*
ruling class *see* nobility
Rumania *see* Romania
Rumford, Count 61
ruminants 158, 160, *161*, 175
running *173*
Rupert of Bavaria 502
rural life *see* agriculture; peasants
ibn-Rushd *see* Averroës
Rushdie, Salman 649
Ruskin, John 538
Russell, Lord Bertrand **62**, 67, 68, 487, *495*, 496–7
Russell, Henry Norris 9
Russell, Ken 562
Russia **714–16**
art and architecture 541, 547, 548, 549
calendar 7
dance 597, 598
grassland 184
history
and Islam 393
and Byzantium 395
and Sweden 397, 417
as European power 417, 418
industrial revolution 421
Napoleonic Wars 426–7
nationalism 428
Alaska sold to USA 431
colonialism 432, 433
industrial society 434, 435
Russo-Japanese War 387, 421, 433, 438
World War I 436, 437, 438
revolutions 421, 437, **438–9**, 440, 446
and literature 635
after Revolution *see* Soviet Union
language 603, 609
literature 617, 631, 640, 653
music 577, 578–9
politics 268
religion 476, 477
space exploration 19
transport/travel 346
see also Soviet Union
rusts (fungi) 118
rut 160
ruthenium *42–3*, *50*
Rutherford, Ernest 38, 61
Rwanda **716**
Ryle, Gilbert 491

Saarland 440
Sabra camp massacre 455
sabre-toothed cat *141*
Sachs, Hans 625
sacraments 475
Sacred Way *see* Shinto
sacrifices, religious 462, 463, 465, **480**, *481*
Sadat, Anwar 680
Sadhus 246, *467*
Sa'di 616
Sadowa, battle of 428
Saenredam, Pieter 532
Safavids 511
sagas 618
sage grouse 168
Sagittarius 333
Sahara 92, 186, 389, 504, 517
Sahel *388*, 389
Sa'id, Ahmad ibn 710
Saigon *453*, 734
Sailendra, King 512
sailing 342, 343
St Christopher and Nevis **716**
St Denis, Ruth 598
St Germain, Treaty of 441
St Helena 729
St Helens, Mount 82
St Louis (USA) 552
St Lucia **716**
St Petersburg (*formerly* Leningrad) 438, *439*, *445*, 714
Saint Pierre, Bernardin de 629
St Pierre-et-Miquelon 682
St Vincent and Grenadines **716–17**
saints 401, 482
Saite kings 367
Saladin 398, 399, 511, *621*
salamanders 130, 131, 170
Salamis, battle of 371
salaries *see* wages
Salazar, Antonio 713
Salem witch trials 409, 645
Salians 394
salinity 178
Salisbury Cathedral 522, 523
Sallé, Marie 596
Sallust 615
salmon *170*
salmonella *174*, 239
SALT I and II 289, 451
salt/salinity 40, 41, 95, **178**, 208, 313, 320
water *see* oceans
saltations 139
salvation 483
Salzburg 574, 575, 576
Samanids 616
samarium *42–3*, *50*
Samoa *389*, 513, 592
Samos 508
samsara 466, 468, 484, 485
Samurai 386, *387*
San Andreas fault 78, 80
sandalwood 193
San Francisco 731
San people (Bushmen) 517
San Marino **717**
San Martín, José de 662, 673, 712
sand casting 503
sand dunes *92*, *93*
sandhoppers 170
Sandinistas 451
sandpipers 169, 171
sandstone 84, 85
Sandwich Islands *see* Hawaii
sangha 468
sans culottes 425
Sanskrit 466, 602, 603
Santiago 673
Santiago de Compostela *481*
Santorini, eruption of 82, 369
São Paulo 669
São Tomé e Príncipe **717**
Sappho *614*, 615
Saqqara *366*, 507
Saragossa 399
Sarajevo 429, 436
Saratoga, battle of 422
sarcoma 213
sarcomere 207
Sardinia 428
Sargasso Sea 170
Sargon of Akkad *364*
Sarto, Andrea del 528
sartorius *206*
Sartre, Jean-Paul 487, *491*, 648
Sassanids *see* Persian Empire
Sassoon, Siegfried 646
Satan 484, 625
satellites 18, 19
communication 273, 326–7, *331*
Landsat map *333*
military 345
of planets *see* moons and satellites
surveys 313
Satie, Erik 578, 597
satire 614, 615, 620, 626, 627, 633, 642
saturated fats 208, 209, 245
Saturn *11*, **14**, **15**, 19
Saud, Ibn 717
Saudi Arabia/Arabia 92, 261, 287, 590, **717–18**
architecture 510, 511
history 365, *410*
see also Mecca
Saul, King 365
saurischian dinosaurs 132
sauropods 132
Saur Revolution 660
Saussure, Ferdinand de *608*, 609, 610, 653
savannah *104*, 182, **184**, *185*
Savart, Félix 35
Savery, Captain Thomas 308, 420
Sax, Adolphe 583
Saxons and Saxony 380, 394, *396*, 603, 606
see also Anglo-Saxons
saxophone 583
Sayers, Dorothy L. 650
scales, musical 568, *569*
Scandinavia
languages 603, 606
literature 618, 619, 635
pollution in 300, 301
see also Denmark; Finland; Norway; Sweden
scandium *42–3*, *50*
scanning, body 30, 241, 242, *332*
scanning electron microscopy 38, *333*
Scarlatti, Alessandro 572, 573, 584
Scarlatti, Domenico 572
scarlet fever **239**
scavengers and carrion eaters 132, 137, *143*, 153, 154, 158
scent glands and marking 155, 168–9
Schelling, F. W. J. 631
Schiaparelli, Giovanni 12, 13
Schiele, Egon 547
Schiller, Johann Christoph Friedrich von 536, 585, 630
Schirrmann, Richard 294
schistosomiasis 122, 175, *238*, **239**
schizophrenia 224, 234, 235
Schlegel, August Wilhelm von 630
Schlegel, Friedrich von 630
Schleicher, August 602
Schleswig 428, 440
Schlieffen Plan 436
Schliemann, Heinrich 369
Schmidt, Helmut 686
Schmidt, Wilhelm 347
Schmidt-Rotluff, Karl 547
Schoenberg, Arnold 569, *578*, 579, 580
Schongauer, Martin 526
school leaving age 294
schooling *see* education
Schopenhauer, Arthur 487
Schrödinger, Erwin 26
Schubert, Franz **574**, 575, 576, 577
Schumann, Clara 577
Schumann, Robert **576**, 577, 579
Schütz, Heinrich 571, 572, 573
Schutzstaffel (SS) 442
Schwitters, Kurt 551
science
history **60–1**, 365
and Islam 392
Medieval 58, 406
under Louis XIV 414
and Enlightenment 418, 419
industrial revolution 421
scientific method **58–9**
see also astronomy; chemistry; physics; mathematics; technology
science fiction 632, 651
Scipio Africanus 376
Scorel, Jan van 527
scorpions 125
Scotland 729
art and architecture 505, 552
education 249, 260, 261, 419
folk music 587
geology/geomorphology 86, 87
government 267
health 245
history
ancient and prehistoric 363, 374, 375
invasions 396, 397
'Auld Alliance' with France 400
wars with English *396*, *400*, 412, 413
and 14th-century crisis 403, 404
Reformation 409
Stuarts 412, 413
industrial revolution 421
union with England 413, 416
Enlightenment 419
emigration from 420
Hogmanay 254
law 265
literature 621, 632, 647
religion 477
Scott, George Gilbert 538, 539
Scott, Sir Walter 536, 537, 585, 631, 632
Scouts 294
scrap steel 314, 315
scree *91*
screen printing 502
screening, health 245, *323*
script *see* writing
scriptures *see under* religion
scroll painting *514*, 515
scrubland *104*
sculpture **503**
ancient Greek and Roman *508*, *509*
prehistoric 504, *505*
Middle Eastern 506, *507*
Chinese and Japanese 514, 515
American and African *516*, 517
Gothic *520*, 521, 523
Renaissance 524, 525
early Netherlandish and German 526
Medieval 519
Rococo and Neoclassical 535
abstract 549
modern 554
scurvy 209, 244
Scythians 365
SDI 19, 289
sea *see* oceans and seas
sea anemone *175*
sea cows 162
sea cucumbers 123
sea lilies 123
sea lions 162–3
Sea Peoples 364, 367
sea squirts 123
sea stars 123
sea urchins 123
seals **162–3**, *168*, 171
movement 172–3
seasons **104**, *105*
SEATO *451*
seaweeds 118
sebaceous glands 212, *216*
Secession in art 546–7
second 6
Second World War *see under* wars
secondary education 261
secondary producers 177
secondary sexual characteristics 214–15
secondary sources (of historical material) 360
second-order activity (in philosophy) 486
Secretariat (UN) 285
section (archaeology) *361*
secularism 459
securities, financial 272, 273
security, right of 290
Security Council (UN) 284, 285
sedimentary rocks **84**, *85*, 310
seeds 116, 120, 139, 182
seeing *see* sight
segmented bodies 122, 124, 172
Sei Shonagon 617
seine nets *194*
seismic surveys *30*, 310, 313, 332
seismic waves 28, *76*, *77*, 80, *81*
Selassie, Haile 681
selection (in education) 261
selection, natural *see* evolution
selenium *42–3*, *50*
Seleucid Empire 372, 373, 662
self *see* individual
self-government *see* independence
Selim I, Sultan 393
Seljuks 392, 511, *616*
semantics 609
semiconductor 37
semiotics/semiology 610–11
Semites/Semitic 388, 461
languages 364, 602, 605
religions 459, 484
see also Christianity; Islam; Jews
Semmelweiss, Ignaz P. 249
Senate, Roman 376, 378, 379
Seneca 593, 615
Seneca Falls Convention 292
Senefelder, Aloys 322
Senegal 563, **718**
Senghor, Léopold Sedar 718
Sennedjem *367*
Sennet, Mack 559
senses/sense organs
animals 124, 125, 126, 128–9, 139, 155, **166–7**
human **216–19**, 223, 224
see also hearing; sight; smell; taste; touch
sentences (judicial) 263
sentences (language) 608–9
sentiment, novels of 628–9
Seoul 696
sepal *120*
separation of powers 266
separatism 259
Sephardic Jews 473, 603
sepia 501
Septuagint 474
sequoias 119
Serbia 428, 429, 436, 440, 505, **735**
Serbo-Croat 603
serfs 258, 402, 404, 438
series, electrical 36
Serlio, Sebastiano 529
serpent stars 123
service industries 273
setae 172
sets 66–7
Seurat, Georges 542, *543*, 544, 552
Sevastopol 429
Seven Weeks War 428
Seven Years War 413, 417, 422
Severn estuary 307
Severus, Alexander 379
Severus, Septimius 379
Seville 510
Sèvres porcelain 534
Sèvres, Treaty of 441
sewage 95, 244, 249, 300, 306, 434
see also excretion
sexism 254, 259, 268, 291
sexual/sexuality
in art 546, 547
in dance 593
development *204–5*, 214–15, **232**
discrimination *see* sexism
in literature 617, 620, 625, 627, 629, 645, 648, 649
and marriage 256, 257
see also reproduction
sexual intercourse 202
sexually transmitted diseases (venereal diseases) 207, **213**, 235, 238, **239**
Seychelles **718**
Seymour, Jane 412
Shaarawi, Huda 293
shaft graves 363, 369
shaft mine *312*
Shaftesbury, Lord 434
Shakespeare, William 615, 621, **622**, *623*, 625, 627, 631, 641, 643
and music 573, 585, 588
shamans **464**, 465, 470–1, 592, 617
Shang dynasty 382, *514*
Shanghai 673
Shankar, Ravi 581, *591*
shares/shareholders 272, 282–3
Sharia 392, 479
sharks 128, *129*
Sharp, Cecil 587
Shaw, George Bernard *644*
Shaw, R. Norman 539
Shawn, Ted 598
shearwaters 136, 171
sheep 153, **160–1**, 190, **191**, 321
Shelley, Mary Wollstonecraft 632
Shelley, Percy Bysshe 537, 633
shellfish *see* molluscs
Shepard, Sam 645
Sheridan, Richard 627
Sherman, William T. 431
Sherriff, R. C. 644
Shi Huangdi, emperor *382*, 383
Shiat Ali 479
Shiite (Shia) Islam 392, *455*, 478–9
shingles 239
Shinto 386, 459, **470–1**, 485
ships and boats **342–5**
in art 532
engines in *308*
and fishing 194, 195
history *342–3*
ancient *393*, *396*, 397
voyages of discovery 404, *405*, 417
slave *416*
Industrial Revolution 420–1
modern *344–5*
in literature 638–9
oil tankers 311
radar 332
see also navies; oceans; trade
Shirley, James 623
Shiva **466**, 467, *483*, 484, 593
Shklovski, Viktor 653
Shnitke, Alfred 581
shogunate 386–7, 515, 617
Sholokhov, Mikhail 649
Shona rebellion 432
Short brothers 348
Shostakovich, Dmitri 579, 581
shrews *148*
shrimps **124–5**, 129, 195
Shrivijaya 385
Siam *see* Thailand
Sibelius, Jean 579
Siberia 180, 390, 417, 464, 465
Sica, Vittorio de 563
Sicily
art and architecture *509*, 519
history 371, 376, 394, 428, *445*
Sickert, Walter 544
sickle cell disease 236
side effects of drugs 250
sidereal time 6, 7
sidewinder 135, 172
Sidney, Sir Philip *624*, 625
Siegen, Ludwig von 502
Siena 520–1
Sierra Leone 405, *607*, 718
sifaka *147*, 164
sight
of animals 124, 126, 128, 130, 133, 136, 139, 146
of humans 207, **218–19**, 223, **224**, **225**
disorders 219, 237, 240, 241
eye *218*
gaze 228
rapid eye movement sleep 232, *233*
visual fields 230
signalling with eyes 228, 229
visual neglect 223
see also light
Signac, Paul 542, 543, 544, 545
signs/signals
animals 166–7
sign language 167, 490, *491*, 608
see also semiotics
Sihanouk, Prince Norodom 453, 671
Sikhs/Sikhism 259, 432, 459, 466, **467**, 482–3, 484
Sikorsky, Igor *349*
silent films 558–9
Silesia 403, 417, 421
silicon/silicates *42–3*, *50*, 54, 77, 84, 306
silk 125, 318, 416, 514
Silk Route *382*, 405
sill *85*
Silurian period *85*, *109*
plants 119
silver *42–3*, *50*, 312, **313**, 366, 374
artwork *508*, 509, 515, 534
Simone Martini *521*
Simpson, Sir James Young 249
Sinai 366, 455
Sinan, Koca 511
Sind 385, 432
sine *62–3*, 71
Singapore 287, 432, 433, *444*, 445, **718–19**
Singing Sculpture 554
single market (EC) 278, 286
single-celled organisms **110–11**, 118, 172
single-parent family 257
Sinna, Ibn *see* Avicenna
sirenians 162
Sirius 9
Sisley, Alfred 543
sit-ins 295
sitatunga 161
situla art *505*
Sitwell, Edith 579
Six-Day War 455
Sizewell 305
Sjöberg, Alf 563
Skara Brae 505
skates 128, 129
skating 598
skeletons
animal 172
human *206*
see also bones
Skelton, John 621
skimmer (bird) *137*
skin 207, *216*
disorders 175, 236, 238, 239, 249, 250
cancer 213, 237, 245
as immune system 212
skinheads 295
Skryabin, Alexander 579
skulls *161*, *206*, *332*, *516*
skunks 155
Skylab space station 19
slash-and-burn 182, 188
slate 85
slavery
anti-slavery movements 290
and dance 595
history
in Roman Empire 376, 379
in medieval society 404
trade 388, 389, 410, *416*, 423
in America 422, 423, 430, 431
abolition of 416, 431
in literature 639
and religion 465
Slavs 395, 429, 436, 445, 476
Slavonic languages *603*
sleep 232, *233*
drugs for 233, 247
sleeping sickness 175
slide rule *65*

Slipher, Vesto 4
sloths 140, *141*, 144, *145*
Slovaks 429, 603
Slovakia **719**
Slovenia **719**
slugs **122**, 172
slump see depression (economic)
slums *298*, 434, *435*
Sluter, Claus 521, 526
Sluys, battle of 401
smallpox 244, *245*, 249, 411
Smeaton, John 340
smell 128, 139, 171, **216–17**, 224
in animal communication 166
in animal navigation 171
smelting 47, **50**, *314*, 420
Smetana, Bedřich 577
Smirke, Sir Robert 539
Smith, Adam 271, 275, 419
Smith, Bessie 588
Smith, Ian 737
Smith, Joseph 595
Smith, William Alexander 294
Smithson, Harriet 577
smog 49, 300
smoking see tobacco
Smollett, Tobias 629
Smuts, Jan Christiaan 720
Smythson, Robert 529
snails **122**, 172, 175
snakes 134, *135*, 153, 166, 172, *484*
in dances 592, 594
Snell, Willebrord **29**, 30, 32
Snider, Antonio 78
snow *45*, 90, 102
Soane, John 538
soap 320
Sobhuza II, King 723
Sobieski, Jan 393
social capital 272
social class see class
social contract 266
social dancing 593, **594–5**
social democrats 268, 269
social mobility 258
social organization
of animals 127, 151, 153, **169**
see also society
social security 276, 277
social services 266, 267
socialism 268–9, 435
law 264
and women's movement 293
and youth movements 294–5
see also Communists
socialist realism 617, 635
society **254–9**
and art see realism
family **256–7**
history
prehistoric 361, 363
of Rome 379
China, classical 382
India 385
Carolingian 394
Islamic *392*
and Enlightenment 418–19
reforms and industrial society 434
Western, in China 447
and literature 636–7
see also realism
social structures and groups **258–9**
see also rights; social *and under* economics; education; government; law
Society Islands 417
sociolinguistics 609
sociology *see* society
Socrates 371, 462, 487, 488, *492*
sodium *42–3*, 47, *50*, 56, 178, 208
compounds 44, 320
sodium chloride 40, 178, 313, 320
software 334–7
softwoods 119, **192–3**
soil 121, 122, 176, 182, 185, 297, 300
erosion 193
Sōka Gakkai 471
solar see Sun
Solar One *306*
solar system **10–15**
see also planets
soldiers see armies
sole proprietorship 282
solenodons 149
solicitors 265
Solomon, King 365, 507, 692, 695
Solomon Islands *444*, 445, **719–20**
Solon 370
solstices 104
solution 41
solvents 246, **247**, 320, *321*
Solzhenitsyn, Alexander 649
Somalia (Somaliland) **720**
history 366, *388*, 432, 433, 444, *445*
Somme, battle of 437
Somoza, Anastasio 708
sonar *see under* sound
sonata 572, **573**, 575, 576
sonata form 573, **575**
Sondheim, Stephen 588
Song dynasty 383, 514, 617
Songgram, Pibul 725
songs
birds **139**, 166, 168–9
human **570–1**, 576, 577, 578, **588–9**, 590, 591, 642
whales 163, 167
sonic booms *31*
sonnet 625
Sophocles 614
Sosigenes 7
Sottsass, Ettore 553
soul 466, 490
Soulages, Pierre 554
sound
acoustics **30–1**, 166
animals
birds 139, 168–9
signals and navigation 30, **146–7**, 163, 167, 168–9, 171, 194, 332
in film 559, 564, 565
recording *328–9*
sonar and echolocation 30, **146–7**, 163, 194, **332**
ultrasound 30, 171, 332
in medicine 241, 242, 249, 332
waves 28, 29, 30–1, 332
see also hearing; language; music; songs
South Africa **720–21**
and Angola and Mozambique 298, 299
apartheid 259, 262, 291
art 517
birds 137
fishing 194
history 389, 432, 433, 449
human evolution 200
language *607*
law and crime 262
mining 312, 313
politics 270, *271*
and UN 284
South America
agriculture 191, 316
animals *113*, 129, 131, 135, 138, 167, 170–1
mammals *140*, 143–5, 147–8, 150–5, 157–9, 161, 163, 165
art and architecture **516**, 553
climate *105*
cocaine trade 246
debt 299
destruction of rain forests 182, 193, 300
and developed countries *298*
ecosystems 180, 181, 182, 184, 185, *186*, 187
evolution 112, 113
film 563
fishing 194, 195
forestry 193
geology/geomorphology 78–9, 86, 87, 92, *94*
government 267
history
pre-Columbian 363, **390–1**
discovery of 405
colonialism *410*, 411, 416, 417, 432, 433
Cold War 450, *451*
human rights protests *291*
industry
chemicals 321
energy 306, 310, *311*
mining 312, 313
international relations 285, 287
law 265
literature 637, 649, 655
music, dance 595, 597
religion 458, 459, 464, 465, 475, 476, 477, 482
vegetation *104*
women's suffrage 292
see also individual countries
South Georgia and South Sandwich Islands 729
South Korea (Republic of Korea) 278, 284, 285, 447, 453, **696–7**
see also Korea
South Vietnam 452–3
see also Vietnam
Southeast Asia
agriculture 191, 316
animals 131, 142, 146–7, 149, 153–4, 156–8, 160, 164, 165
birds 138, *139*
fish 129
art and architecture 512–13
climate and weather 103, *105*
destruction of rain forests 182, 193, 300
geology/geomorphology 86, 99
history 392
prehistory 362
discovery of 405
before colonial age **384–5**
and decolonization 448–9
Cold War *451*
Vietnam Wars 452–3
human evolution 200
international relations 285, 287
music 591, *592*
religion 464, 468, 482
vegetation *104*
see also individual countries
southern lights 11
Southern Rhodesia 284, 432, 433, 737
Southey, Robert *41*, 632
South West Africa 432, 433
see also Namibia
South Yemen
see Yemen
sovereigns see monarchy
sovereignty, popular 266
Soviet Union
Afghanistan invaded 289, 429, *450*, *451*
withdrawal from *299*
animals 131, 148, 154
astronomy 17
economy 276, 278
education 261
energy industry 304, *311*
accidents 244, 305
film 559, 562
fishing 194, 195
forestry 193
government 267
grasslands 185
history
formed 439
postwar settlement 440
totalitarianism 443
World War II 439, 444, *445*, 450
and China 446, 447
Cold War 450, *451*
see also Afghanistan *above*
and Albania 660
and Angola 661
and Czechoslovakia 287, 295
and Middle East 455
see also Russia
human rights 291
international relations 278, 284, 285, 287
journalism 654, 655
language see Russian
law 265
literature 634–5, 642, 647, 649
music 581, 594, 598
nuclear accident at Chernobyl 300
nuclear weapons 288–9
plural society 259
politics 268, 269, 271
society 256, 259
space exploration 13, 18–19
and Third World 298–9
women's suffrage 292, 293
writing 605
youth movements 294–5
see also Russia
soyabean 189
space, exploration of **18–19**, 58, 301
landings on Moon 13, *18*
planets observed 12, 13, 14, 17
shuttles and stations 18, *19*
space, perception of 224
space, sacred 483–4
space-time 27
Spain **721–2**
animals *552*
art and architecture 500, 505, 526, 529, 531
Islamic 510, *511*
Cubism and abstraction 548, 549
divorce rate 256
film 561, 563
history
ancient and prehistory 363, 375, 378, 381
and Islam 392
Crusades 398, 399
Medieval and Renaissance 399, 410–11
and 14th-century crisis 403
Inquisition 409
Armada defeated *412*
colonialism *405*, **410–11**, 413, 431, *433*
in South and Central America 390, 391, 432
wars with France 415, 427
Spanish Succession, War of 411, 415
Civil War *443*, *549*
and decolonization 448, 449
Basque separatism 259
international relations 278, 286, 287
language *603*
literature 618, 622
music 570, 581, *587*, 594, 595
religion *481*
Spanish influenza 238
Spanish Sahara 449
Sparta 370, 371, 508
Spartacists 442
spawning 129, 130, *151*
special effects (cinema) 564, 565
spectra 5, 9, 17, *35*, 333
speech **226–7**, 608–9
freedom of 291
recognition by computers *336*
see also language
speed of light 27, 32, 35
Spender, Stephen 646
spending, government 276, 277, 295
Spenser, Edmund 621, 624, 625
sperm *202*, 205, 214
spermatophore 130
spice trade 410, 417
spicules, solar 10
spider monkeys *164*, 165
spiders **125**, 172
communication 167
spinal cord *206*, 251
spinnerets 125
spinning **318**, 420
Spinoza, Baruch 487, 488
spiny anteater 142
spiracle *126*
spire *523*
spirits **458**, 471, 480, 481, **482**, 517
and Asian religions 466, 468, 470
good and evil 484, 485
possession *485*
and primal religions 464, 465
spirochaetes 111, 238
spleen *212*, 236, *237*
spores 118, 119, 238
sport see exercise
spreadsheet 335
spring tides *101*, 129
springbok 161
springs 94
spruces **119**, 193
Sputnik 18, *19*
spying 19, 648, 650–1
squids **122–3**, 163, 173, 195
squirrels *147*, **150–1**, 171
Sri Lanka (Ceylon) **722**
animals 153, 154
art and architecture 512, *513*
fishing *195*
history 384, 385
languages 602, 603, *607*
mining 313
religion 468, 482
women's suffrage 292
SS (Schutzstaffel) 442
Staël, Madame de 631
Staël, Nicolas de 554
Stahl, Georg 61
stained glass *522*
stainless steel 315
stalactites *88*, 89
stalagmites *88*, 89
Stalin, Joseph 271, **439**, **444**, 450, 715
Stalingrad, battle of *445*
stamen *120*
Stamford Bridge, battle of 397
Stamitz, Johann and Karl 575
Standard Oil 431
standing stones *363*
standing waves 29
Stanislavsky, Constantin 642
Stanton, Elizabeth Cady 292
Star Wars (Strategic Defence Initiative) 19, 289
starch 116, *117*, 196
starfish 123
starlings 169
stars 4, 5, *8–9*, 333
see also Sun
START (Strategic Arms Reduction Talks) 289
state 266–7, 658
crimes against 262, 265
and economy 268–9, 276
see also government; laws
States-General (France) 425
statics 22
stationary waves 29
statues see sculpture
status, social 258, **259**, 480
statute law 264, 402
Sainte-Beuve, Charles Augustin 652
Ste Chapelle 622
steady-state theory 5
Stealth fighter *351*
steam engines and machines *304*, *308*, *309*, 419, *420* 421
transport 342, *343*, *346*
steel 40, *314–15*, *421*, 431, 552
Steen, Jan 532, *572*
stegosaur *133*
Steinbeck, John 561
stems of plants 120
Stendhal 634
Stephen, King of Hungary 688
Stephenson, George 346, 347
Stephenson, Robert 347, 421
steppes 184, **185**
stereophony 329
stereotyping (printing) 323
sterile health care 56, 241, 249
Sternberg, Josef von 560
Sterne, Laurence *68*, 628, *629*
steroids 214–15
stethoscope 249
Stevens, Siaka 718
Stevens, Wallace 647
Stevenson, Robert Louis 651
sticklebacks 168
Stieglitz, Alfred 556
Stifter, Adalbert 635
stigma (plants) *120*, 121
still life *532*
Stiller, Mauritz 563
stoat 155
stock exchanges and markets 272, 282–3
Stockhausen, Karlheinz *580*, 581, 585
stoichiometry 47
Stoker, Bram 651
Stolypin, Petr Arkadievich 438
stomach
human 209
ruminant *161*
stomata 117
Stone Age (Palaeolithic, Mesolithic and Neolithic) **362–3**
agriculture *see under* Neolithic
art 504–5, 514
see also caves, painting
dance 595
houses *362*, 505
human evolution 200, 201
monuments and temples *363*, 505
religion 462
stonefish *167*
Stonehenge 338, 363, 505
stop-action photography (cinema) 559
Stoppard, Tom 644–5
storage of information 336, *337*
storage of nutrients 209
stories and tales *616*, 617, 618–21, 638, 641, 650–1
see also novels
storks 171
Storm, Theodor 635
storms 103
Stormtroopers 437, 442
Stourhead 535
strain (physics) 23
Strand, Paul 556
Strassburg, Gottfried von 619
strata of rock *85*, *88–9*
Strategic Arms Limitation and Reduction Talks 289, 451
Strategic Defence Initiative (Star Wars) 19, 289
stratosphere 30, 77
Strauss, Johann 582, 588
Strauss, Richard 577, 585
Stravinsky, Igor 578, *579*, 582, 583, 597, 640
Strawson, Peter 489, 497
stream of consciousness 641, 645, 648
stress (physics) 23
stress (psychological) 235
strikes 295
Strindberg, August **635**, 642
stringed instruments 582–3
strip mines *312*
stroboscopy 325
Stroessner, Alfredo 711
Stroheim, Erich von 561
strokes 237
stromatolites *110*
Stromboli 83
strontium *42–3*, *50*
Strowger, Almon B. 330
structuralism *608*, 610–11, 653
structured query language 335
Stuarts 412, 413
stucco 510, 511
students *see* universities
stupas 512
style (plants) *120*
sub-atomic particles 4, 38–9
subcastes 258
subduction zones 79, 80, 82, 83, 84–5
subjective time 6
sublimation of sexuality 232
Sublime (in art) 534, 536
submarines *345*, *436*, 437, 444
and missiles 288, 289
submission *166*
subsets 66, 69
subsidies 279, 645
subsistence agriculture **188**, 296–7
subtraction 64
succession, vegetation 180
succulent plants 186
succussion 251
Sucre, Antonio José de 679
sucrose 116, 117, 208
Sudan **722**
history 366, 367, 432, 433, 722
religion 465
society 255
Sudetenland 441, 443
Sudra caste 258
Suez Canal 341
Suez Crisis 449, *454*, 455, 644
suffrage 291, 435
universal 435
women's 292
suffragettes *292*
Sufism 410, 432, 478, 616
sugar 196, 237, 306, 410, 603
for fuel 306
Suger, Abbot 522
suicide 257, 262
Sukarno, Achmed *449*, 691
Suleiman the Magnificent 393, 727
Sulla, Lucius 377
Sullivan, Arthur 588
sulphonamides 249
sulphur 40, *42–3*, 44, *45*, *50*, 116, 312, 313, 316
compounds **49**, 300, 304
sulphuric acid 13, 320
dilute see acid rain
Sumatra 156, 157, 165, 385, 512
Sumerians 364, *365*, 460–1, 612
Summerhill School 260
Sumter, Fort, battle of 430
Sun **10–11**
and cancer 237
as compass for migration 171
eclipse 10, 16
energy from 176, **306**
magnitude 9
mean, time systems and 6, 7
position in galaxy 9
as power source 176–7
and religion 462, 466, 471
and seasons 104, *105*
solar cells 37, 306
solar day 6, 7
solar flares 10
solar nebula 11
solar wind 10–11
sunlight in oceans 179
sunspots **10**
surface *10*
and tides 100–1
see also solar system
sun bear 154
sunbird 168
sundew *121*
Sun King *see* Louis XIV
Sun Zhong Shan (Sun Yat-sen) 446
sundial 7
sunflower oil (for fuel) 306
Sunni Islam 455, 478
supercomputer 334, 335
superconductivity 37, *55*
superego 232
supernatural (in literature) 632, 633, 636
see also spirits
supernova 9, 17, *27*
superphosphate 320
Suppiluliumas I 364
supply **274**, 275, 276, 277, *279*
Suprematism 549

Supreme Being *459*, 464, 465
surface tension 23
surgery **240–1**, 248, *249*
Suriname **722–3**
surplus 277, 279
Surrealism 233
in art **551**, 554, 557
in literature 635, 640, 641, 649
surveys 310, 313, 332
S-waves *81*
swallows 171
Swaziland **723**
sweat glands and pores *216*
Sweden **723**
film 562–3
history 397, 408, 409, 417, 463
international relations 285, 286
journalism 654
language *603*
law and crime 263
literature 635
pollution in 300
religion 477
sweet potatoes **189**
Swift, Jonathan 627, 628, 629
swifts 137
swim bladder *128*
swimming *128*, 138
see also fish
Swinburne, Algernon Charles 641
swing (music) 589
Switzerland **723–4**
art and architecture 550, 553, 554, 555
economy 278
government 267
history 375, 409, 426–7
international relations 278, 285, 286
journalism 655
language 608, 610
law 265
literature 635
medicine 240, 248, 249
religion 477
women's suffrage 292
syllabic scripts 604–5
symbionts 174
symbiosis 174, **175**
algae 99, 122, 123, 175
see also lichens
bacteria 111, 174, 175, 212, 238
in digestive systems 175, 212, 238
and pollination 137, 175
sea creatures 99, 122, 123, 129, *175*
symbiotes 174
symbol/Symbolism
in art 504, 544, **546**, 547
in literature 578, 635, 638, **640–1**, 645, 647, 652, 653
and logics 494
in semiology 610
sympathetic nervous system 221
symphony 573, **574–5**, 576, 578, 579, 580, 587
see also orchestra
synagogues 472–3
synapse *220*
synchronic linguistics 608
synchronous rotation 13
syncopation 588, 595
Synge, J. M. 645
Syngman Rhee 697
syntax 608–9
Synthetic Cubism 548
synthetic products **54–5**, 243
fibres 40, 41, *56*, 317, 318, 320
see also artificial
synthetic speech *227*, 609
syphilis 235, **239**, 640
Syria **724**
history
ancient 364, 366, 367, 369, 395, 605
art **506**, 509, 510
religion 462
Medieval 392, *398*, 406
20th-Century 454, 455
philosophy 476
religion 460, 461, 477, 612
systemic circulation 210

T cells 212, *213*
taboos 256, 513, 648
Tachism 554
Tacitus 615
tactile signals (animals) *167*
tadpole 130
Tadzhikistan *see* Tajikistan
TAGaMET *57*
Taglioni, Marie *597*
Taillefer 618
Taine, Hippolyte 652
Taiping movement 383
Taira Kiya mori 386
Taiwan (Republic of China) **674–5**
economy 278
history 285, 387, 433, 447, *451*, **675**
religion 470
Taj Mahal 385, 511
Tajikistan **724–5**
tales *see* novels; stories
talons 137
Tallis, Thomas 571
Talmud 472
tamarins 164–5
Tambora, eruption of 82
Tamerlane 393, 511, 660, 725, 733
Tamils 384, 602
Tang dynasty 383, *514*, 617
Tanganyika 432, 433, 725
tangent *62–3*
Tangshan earthquake 80
Tanis 366, 367
tank warfare *356*, 357
tankers, oil and gas 311, 343, *344*
tanks 437
Tannenberg battles 399, 436
tanning 190
tantalum *42–3, 50*
Tantric Buddhism 469
Tanzania *185*, 200, 201, 306, *607*, **725**
tapestries 520
tapetum 128
tapeworms 122, 238, **239**
tapirs *157*
tapping for latex *316*
Tarawa, battle of *444*
target tissues 211, 214–15, *220*
tariffs 279
Tariq Ali 295
Tarkington, Booth 560
Tarkovsky, Andrei 562
tarmacadam 340
tarnishing 51
Tarquin the Proud 376
tarsiers 164
Tarxien 505
Tasman, Abel 417, 663, 708
Tasmania 142, *143*, *180*, 417, 663
Tasmanian devil *143*
Tasmanian wolf *143*
Tasso, Torquato 624, 625
taste (intellectual) 492
taste (sense) 217
Tate, Allen 647
Tati, Jacques 562
Tatsumi Hijikata 599
Tatum, Art 589
taxation 268, 275, 276, 277
history 380, 381, 387, 395, 402–3, 414, 422, 424
taxonomy *see* classification
Taylor, Paul 598
Tchaikovsky, Pyotr Ilyich 577, 597
tea *281*, 432, 469, 515
teachers *see* education
teak 193
technetium *42–3, 50*
technology
history 419, 432, 447
and industry **302–57**
see also industry; science
medical **242–3**, 249
new 261, 262, 607
see also computers
tectonic plateaux 93
tectonic plates **78–9**, 80, 82, 83, 84–5
Teddy Boys 295
teenagers 294–5
teeth
mammals **140**
lack of 144–5
land 140, 142, 150, 152, 156, 157, 161
marine 162, 163
non-mammals 128, 129, 133
Tehran 690
telecommunications *see* communications
telegraphy 330, 421
Telemann, Georg Phillipp 573
teleosts 128
telephones 330–1
telescope 14, 17, *33*, 333
television 35, **326**, *327*, 561, 565, 654
telex 331
Telford, Thomas 340, 421
Tell-el-Amarna 367
tellurium *42–3, 50*
Telstar 331
tempera *500*
temperate climates **103**, *105*
temperate forests **180–1**
temperature
and animals 131
see also ectotherms; hibernation
climatic and atmospheric 77, 102, 104, 105
global warming 301
and colour of stars 9
and ecosystems 176
human body 211, 216, 223
of lava 83
of oceans **179**
and superconductivity 55
thermo-dynamics 24
see also cold; heat
Temple, Shirley 561
Temple Mound culture 390
temples 505, **512**, *516*, 593
Asian 467, *470*, 482, 514, 515
Middle Eastern 367, *461*, 472, 480, 482, 506, 507
see also cathedrals and churches; mosques; religion
Ten Commandments 262
Tenniel, Sir John *650*
Tennis Court Oath *424*
Tennyson, Alfred, Lord 633
Tenochtitlan 411
tenrecs 149
Teotihuacán 391, 516
Tepantitla *516*
terbium *42–3, 50*
Terborch, Gerard 532, 534
Terbrugghen, Hendrick 532
Terence **615**, 626
Teresa of Avilá 721
termites *127*, 145, *169*, 175
tern, arctic 171
terracotta *382*, *503*, 514, *516*, 517
terrestrial communities 176
terrestrial ecosystems *see* ecosystems
terrestrial planets **12–13**
territory, animal 168
terror *see* horror
Terror, Reign of 425
terrorism 263, 467
Tertiary period *85*, *109*
Tertullian 296
testes/testicles 205, *214*, 215
testosterone 205, *214*, 215
tests
blood 245
forensic 263
IQ 231
nuclear weapons 288, *289*, 447
Tet Offensive 453
tetanus **239**, 245
tetrarchy 380
Teutoburger Forest battle 378
Teutonic Order 399
Texas *431*, 731
textiles and clothing **318–19**
and applied arts *511*, 553
artificial fibres 56, 317
history 389, 400, 416, 420, 432, *511*, 515, 516
industry and trade **318–19**, 389, 416, 420
see also fibres
textual analysis 652, *653*
Thackeray, William Makepeace **634**, 635
Thailand 287, **725**
animals 146, 157
art and architecture 513
dance *592*
history 384, 385, 453
language 608
religion 468, *469*, 482
Thales of Miletus 16, 60
thallium *42–3, 50*
thanksgiving 480
Tharp, Twyla 598
Thatcher, Margaret *271*, 731
theatre and drama
and art 554
criticism 652
history
Classical 614
Asian 616, *617*
morality plays 621
Renaissance 622–3
Neoclassical 626–7
Romanticism 633
Realism 635
Expressionism 642
experimental 642–3
modern 640, 644–5
language 607
and music 591, 592
see also ballet; opera
therapy 235
see also films
Thebes (Egypt) 366, 367, 460, *507*
Thebes (Greece) 369, 371, 372, 373
thecodonts *132*
theism 493
Themistocles 371
Theocritus 614
Theodore of Samos 508
Thera, eruption at 82, 369
therapy, speech 227
Theresa, Maria 664
thermal isolation 25
thermals 102
thermionic emission 37
thermodynamics 24–5
thermonuclear bomb 288
thermoplastic 316
Thermopylae 371, *535*
thermosphere 77
theropods 132
thiamine 208
thiols *52*
Third Estate 424
Third International *439*
Third World 267, **296–7**, **298–9**, 449
and developed world **298–9**
see also Africa; Asia; Central America; South America
Thirty Tyrants 371
Thirty Years War **409**, 411, 628
Thirty-Nine Articles 412
Thomarists 477
Thomas Becket, St 398
Thomas, Dylan 647
Thomas, Edward 646
Thomas, R. S. 647
Thompson, Benjamin (Count Rumford) 61
Thompson, J. J. 38
Thomson, Virgil 579
Thomson, William (Lord Kelvin) 24, 61
thorax 124, *126*
Thoreau, Henry David 638
thorium *42–3, 50*
thought, limits of 489
Thrace 381, 508
three dimensions 224
Three Mile Island (nuclear accident) 301, 305
thrillers 650–1
Thucydides 614
thulium *42–3, 50*
thunder 463
thylacine *143*
thymus gland 212
thyroid gland *214*, 215
disease 213, 215, 237
thyroxine 215
Tiahuanaco 391
Tiberius, emperor 378
Tiberius Gracchus 376
Tibet 383, 447, *451*, *458*, 468, 469, 602, 674
Tibullus 615
ticks 125
tides 96, **100–1**, 129, *307*
Tientsin 674
Tiepolo, Giambattista 534
tiger 152, *153*
Tiglathpileser III 365
Tigray 681
Tigris 364, *365*, 506, 510
till, glacial 91
timber 192–3
Timbuktu *432*, 517
time **6–7**
in art 532
chart, geological 85
in literature 626, 641, 644
relative *27*
sacred 483
timing of migrations **171**
unity of (in drama) 626
timpani 583
Timur *see* Tamerlane
tin *42–3, 50*, **313**, 364
Tindle, David 500
Tinguely, Jean 555
Tintoretto, Jacopo 501, 529
Tippett, Sir Michael *580*, 585
Tischbein, J. H. W. *630*
titanium *42–3, 50*
Titian 501, *529*
Tito, Josip Broz 287, 668, 677, 719, 736, 738
toads **130**, *131*, 166, 167, 168, 170
toadstools **118**, *119*
tobacco 188, 237, 245, 246, **247**, 416, 422
Tobago *see* Trinidad
Toda Josei 471
Togo 432, 433, **725–26**
Tojo, Hideki 443
Tokelau 707
Tokugawa shogunate 386–7, 515, 617
Tokyo 282, 295, 300, 386–7, 434, 694
Toland, Gregg 561
tolerance, of pain *217*
tolerance, religious 41, 424
Tolkien, J. R. R. 651
Toller, Ernst 642
Tolpuddle Martyrs 435
Tolstoy, Leo 635, 648
Toltecs 391, 516
Tomkins, Thomas 571
tomography 332
tonality in music 568–9
tone, musical 31
tone languages 603
Tonga *389*, **726**
tongue 139, *217*
Tonkin, Gulf of 452
tonsils *212*, 212
tools, prehistoric 200, 201, *362*, 363
Torah 472, 473
Torch, Operation *445*
Tordesillas, Treaty of 410
torque *22*
Torre-Nilson, Leopoldo 563
tort, law of 265
tortoises 134–5
torture 418
total internal reflection *30*, *32*
totalitarian regimes 266, *269*, 294, 421, 424, **442–3**
Communist **438–9**
fascist 442, *443*, 444–5
growth of **442–3**
see also absolutism
totals in calculus 71
totems 504, 513, 517
toucan *137*
touch, sense of 216, 229
Toulouse Lautrec, Henri de 502, 544
Tour, Maurice-Quentin de la *630*
Touré, Sékou *449*, 687
towns *see* cities
toxicity *see* poisons
trade **278–9**
fish 195
forestry *193*
history
ancient 363, 364, 366
and empires **382**, 385, 386, 387, 410, 413, **416–17**, 432
Japan 386, 387
Islam 393
Medieval 402, 404–5
Agricultural and Industrial Revolutions 420–1
blockade (Continental System) 427
and peak of Empire 432
oil *279*, 311
see also ships; transport
trade unions 269, **273**, 434–5
trade winds 101
Trafalgar, battle of *427*
tragedy 614, 622–3, 626, 627, 634–5
training *see* education
trains *see* railways
Trajan, emperor 378, 509
trance, dance 592
tranquillizers 235
transcendence of God 480
transcendental idealism 489
Transcendental Meditation 459
Transcendentalists 638
transfer payments *see* social security
transfinite arithmetic 69
transform faults **78**, 80
transformation, social 255
transformers *37*
transfusions, blood 213
transistors 37
Transjordan 441, 454, 695
translation 603
transmigration of souls 466
transmission in cars 354
transplants, organ *240*, 249, 491
transport and travel **340–55**
aircraft 348–51
cars 354–5
civil engineering 340–1
and engines 308–9
history
ancient 365, 391, *393*, *396*, 397
voyages of discovery 404, *405*, 417
slaves *416*
in America 430
Industrial Revolution 420–1
in colonies 432, 448
see also aircraft; canals; cars; pilgrimages; railways; roads; ships and boats; space exploration; trade
transubstantiation 475
transverse wave *28*
travel *see* transport
trawling *194*
Treblinka 445
tree shrews 140, *141*
tree, world *see* Yggdrasil
trees *see* forests
Treuhandanstalt 684
trematodes 122
trench warfare 436–7, 646, *647*
Trent, Council of 409
Trevithick, Richard 308, 347
trials 262–5, 290
triangulation *62–3*
Triassic Period *85*, *109*
dinosaurs 132
paramammals and mammals 140
tribes 258, 504, *592*
see also Indians
triceratops *133*
Trier 509, 523
trigonometry *62–3*
Trinidad and Tobago 467, **726**
Trinity, Christian 474
trio 575
trio sonata 573
triodes *37*
tritium 288, 305
Trojan War 369
Trollope, Anthony 637
trombone 583
tropics/tropical/equatorial
climates/weather 103, *105*
forests *104*, **182–3**
storm 103
year 6
see also individual tropical countries
troposphere 30, 77
Trotsky, Leon 295, 439
Troyes, Chrétien de 619
Troyes, Treaty of 401
Truffaut, François 562
Trujillo, Rafael 679
Truman, Harry 288, 445, 450
Trumbull, John 423
trumpet 583
Trusteeship Council (UN) 284, 285
tsetse fly 175
Tshombe, Moïse 736
Tsiolkovsky, Konstantin 18
tsunami 80, 100
tuatara 134
tuberculosis **239**, 244, 245, 249
tubers 120
Tubman, William 699
Tucker, Christopher 564
tuco-tucos *150*
Tudors 412, 622
Tughluq, Muhammed bin 385
Tukhachevski, Marshal 439
Tull, Jethro 420
tundra 141, 187
tungsten *42–3, 50*
Tunguska disaster 11
Tunisia 376, 392, *445*, **726–7**
tunnels 341
Tupou I of Tonga 726
turbellarians 122
turbines *304*, 306, *307*, *308*
turbojet and turbofan *309*
turboprop engine 349
turbulence 23
Turgenev, Ivan 634
Turing, Alan 336
turkeys 191
Turkey **727**
Asian *see* Anatolia
film 563
Greeks in Cyprus 259
history (Ottoman Empire until 1922)
ancient 363, 364, *365*, 369, 370, 372, 373, 376, 381, 604
art and architecture 509, 511
religion 462
and Islam 392, *393*
and Byzantium 393, 394, *395*, 518–19
and Crusades 398
and 14th-century crisis 403
and Spain 393, *411*
Napoleonic Wars 426, 427
and Balkan nationalism 428, 429
World War I 436, 437

postwar settlement 440, 441
in CENTO *451*
see also Constantinople
international relations 286, 287
language 602, 603
music and dance 592
Turkmenistan **727–8**
Turks and Caicos Islands 729
Turner, Joseph Mallord William *537*, 537
turtles 134–5
migration 170
Tuvalu **728**
Twain, Mark 639
Twelvers 479
twins 230–1
tympanum 519
Tyndale, William 606
type, printing 322
typhoid 174, **239**, 244
typhoon 103
typhus 238, *239*
typological linguistics 602–3
typology 361
tyrannosaur *133*
tyrants 370
see also totalitarian
Tyrol 441, 594, 664
Tzara, Tristan 550, 551
Tz'u-hsi *446*

Ubaid period 506
U-boats *436*, 437, 444
Uccello, Paolo 524, 525
Uganda 168, 432, 433, *607*, **728**
Ugarit 460, 506, 605, 612
Ukraine 402, 437, 445, 477, 603, 715, **728–9**
Ulanova, Galina 597
Ulbricht, Walter 686
ulcers 57, 241, 243
Ulm, battle of *427*
ultrasound *see under* sound
ultraviolet waves 17, *35*, 179, 237, 301
Umayyad dynasty 392, 510–11
Umberto I of Italy 693
Uncertainty Principle 21, 26
unconscious **232**, 526
underglaze painting 514
understorey, forest *183*
unemployment 273, *276*, 277, 434
ungulates 156–61
odd-toed 156–7
even-toed 158–61
unicellular *see* single-celled
Unification Church 459
Union, Act of 413
Union Army 431
Union of Soviet Socialist Republics
see Soviet Union
unions *see* trade unions
Unitarianism 477
unitary government 267
United Arab Emirates 287, **729**
United Churches 475, 477
United Kingdom *see* Britain
United Nations **284–5**, 286
agencies and organizations 285
FAO 192, 297
UNICEF 297, 298
Convention on Law of Sea 195
history 284, 447, 449, 450, 454, 455
Universal Declaration of Human Rights 290
United States **731–3**
agriculture 188–91
animals 112, 129, 131, 134, 135, 139, 170–1, *181*, 187
mammals 141, 143–4, 147–8, 150–2, 154–5, 157–8, 160–3
anti-Communism 450, 645
art and architecture **517**, 541, 550
in 20th century 550, 552, 553, 554, 555
astronomy 17, 333
business organization 282
climate *105*
communications 326–7, 328–9, 330
desert 186
drought 296
economy 272, 273, 275, 278–9
ecosystems
coniferous and temperate forests 180, 181
grasslands 184–5
environmental damage 300–1
film 558, **559–61**, 564–5
fishing 194, 195
forestry193
geology/geomorphology 78–9, 80, 82, 86, *87*, 90, 92, 93, 94, *95*, 96, 99
government 266, 267
health and diseases *213*, 214, 238, 245
history
pre-Columbian 363, **390–1**
discovery of 397, 405
witch trials 409
Revolution and War of Independence 266, 290, 417, 419, **422–3**, 424, 638
Industrial Revolution 420–1
Constitution and Bill of Rights 264, 266, 422–3, 430, 636
expansion of 430–1
colonialism 410, 411, 416–17, 432, 433
Civil War 431
Napoleonic Wars 427
industrial society 434, *435*
and Russian Revolutions 439
World War I 437
postwar settlement 440–1
Depression and New Deal 441
World War II 444–5
and China in 20th century 447
and decolonization 449
Cold War 450, *451*
Vietnam Wars 452, *453*
and Middle East 455
human rights 290, **291**
industry
chemicals 321
energy 305, *306*, *307*, 310, *311*
mining 312, *313*
plastics 317
printing 322
international relations 278–9, 284, 285, 286, 287
journalism 654, 655
language *607*, 608, 609, 610
law and crime 262, *263*, 264, 265
literature 637, **638–9**, 645, 647
Realism and Naturalism 635
Modernism 641
experimental theatre 642
modern 645, 647, 648, 649
criticism 652, 653
medicine 240, 249
music 579, 580, 581, 585
dance 592, 594, 595, 597, 599
new 580, 581
folk 586, 587
popular *588*, 589
nuclear weapons 288–9
photography 325, 556, *557*
plural society 259
politics 270, 271
population 297
Prohibition *246*
racism *291*
religion 459, 464, 465, 467, 477
science 61
society 256, 259
education 260, 261
space exploration 12, 13, 18–19, 58, 333
states 731
and Third World 298–9
transport/travel
aircraft 348, 349
cars *352*, *353*
railways 346–7
ships 342, 343, *345*
space exploration 12, 13, 18–19, 58, 333
vegetation *104*
women's movement and suffrage 292–3
youth movements 294, *295*
unities (in drama) 626, 627
Universal Declaration of Human Rights 290
universal religions 459
see also Christianity; Islam
Universal Time (UT) 7
universe
and cosmology 4–5
time 6–7
see also planets; solar system; stars
universities 248, 249, *260*, **261**, 295
history *260*, 406, 419, *479*
see also education
unnilenium *42–3*, *50*
unnilhexium *42–3*, *50*
unniloctium *42–3*, *50*
unnilpentium *42–3*, *50*
unnilquadium *42–3*, *50*
unnilseptium *42–3*, *50*
untouchables 258, *259*
Upanishads 613
upwarped mountains 86, *87*
Ur 364, *365*, 506, 612
uranium 39, *42–3*, *50*, 288, 304–5, 313
Uranus *11*, 14, 15
urban areas *see* cities
Urban II, Pope 398
Urdu language 603, 607
Urgel, bishop of 661
urine *see* excretion
urostyle 130
Uruguay 185, **733**
Uruk 364, 506, 612
USSR *see* Soviet Union
uterus 204, 207, 214, 215
utilitarianism 493
Utopianism 557, 622, 633
Uzbekistan **733**

V2 rocket *19*, 309, 357
vaccination and vaccines 213, 244, *245*, 249
vacuole *117*
vagina 202, 212
Vail, Alfred 330
Vaishya caste 258
Valdivia, Pedro de 673
Valerian, emperor 380
Valéry, Paul 641
Valhalla 463
validity (logic) 66, 494–5
Valkyries 463
Valley of Kings 367, 507
Valois, Ninette de 597
value added tax (VAT) 276
values (ethics) 492–3
vanadium *42–3*, *50*
Van Allen Zones 10–11
van de Velde, Willem 416
van Dongen, Kees 545
Van Dyck, Anthony 531, 534
Van Eyck, Jan and Hubert 500, *526*
Van Gogh, Vincent 234, 501, 540, 544, *545*, 547
van Leeuwenhoek, Anton 249
Vanbrugh, Sir John 531, 627
Vandals 380
vanishing point *525*
Vanuatu **734**
Varanasi (Benares) 467
Varda, Agnès 562
Varèse, Edgard 579
Vargas, Getúlio 669
Vasarély, Victor *555*
Vasari, Giorgio 524, 527, **528**
VAT 276
Vatican City 428, 527, **734**
Vatican Council 477
Vaughan, Henry 625
Vaughan Williams, Ralph 579
Vauxcelles, Louis 545
Vauxhall Gardens *595*
vector quantity 20
Vedas 248, 461, 466, 467
vegetables 189, 196–7, 366
vegetation 116–21, 176-89
and climate 105
zones *105*
see also plants
vegetative reproduction **120**, 184
vehicles *see* transport
veins *see* arteries and veins
Velasquez, Diego *530*, 531
veld 185
Velde, Willem van der 416, 532
velocity *20*, 30, 37, **70–1**
venereal diseases *see under* sexuality
Venezuela 287, 390, **734**
Venice 301, 571
art and architecture 501, 519, 521, 523, **525**, 527, 529, 534
history 244, 398, 404, 411, 426, 427
Venizélos, Eleuthérios 686
Venn diagrams *66*, *67*
venom 135
ventilators, medical 242–3
ventricle 210, *211*
Ventris, Michael 369
Venus 9, *11*, **12–13**, 19, 110
Venus flytrap 121
verbal *see* language
Verdi, Giuseppe 571, 576, **585**
Verdun, battle of 437
Verga, Giovanni 635
Verlaine, Paul *640*
Vermeer, Jan 532, *533*
vernalization 117
Verne, Jules 651
Verner, Karl 602
Verona 521
Veronese, Paolo 529
Verrocchio, Andrea 525
Versailles 414, *415*, 424, 425, 531, 534
Treaty of 415, *440*, 441, 442
verse drama 633, 644
see also poetry; theatre
vertebrates *see* amphibians; birds; fish; mammals; reptiles
vertical take-off *349*
Verwoerd, Hendrik 720
Vesalius, Andreas *248*
Vespasian 378
vestigial structures *113*
Vestris, Gaetano 596
Vesuvius 82, 83, 86, 462
vibration signals 167
Vichy 444
Victor Emmanuel II of Italy 693
Victor Emmanuel III of Italy 442, *443*
Victoria, Queen 541, 731
Victoria, Luis de 570, 571
vicuna 159, 190
video 327
Vidor, King 560, 564
Vienna 249, 547, 596, 644
Congress of 427, 428
history *393*, 427, 428
music 574, 575, 576, 578, 579, 588
Viet Cong 452–3
Viet Minh 452
Vietnam 157, 287, 512, 602, **734–5**
art and architecture 512
history 383, 447, 449, **452–3**
wars 295, 449, *451*, **452–3**
Vietnamization 453
see also Indochina
Vignola, Giacomo 529
Vigny, Alfred de 631
Vijayanaga 385
Vikings 342, 394, *396*, *397*, 463, 603, 606
Villa, Pancho 703
villages 374, 388, *594*
villeins 404
Villon, François 620
Vinca culture 505
Vinland 397
violence 257, 259, 293, 295
see also wars
viola 582–3
violin 582
viols 582
Viollet-le-Duc, Eugene 538
Virgil 615, 619, 625, 627
Virginia 143, 422, 431
Virgin Islands 731
viruses **238**, 239
and AIDS (HIV) *213*, 239, 247
and diabetes 214
and immune system 212, 213
as parasites 174, 175
reproduction *110*
Visconti, Luchino 563
viscosity 23
Vishnu *466*, 467, 484
Visigoths 380, 381, 394
vision *see* sight
visual imagery 230
visual signals (animal) *167*
vitamins 138, **208–9**, 215, 238, 244, 249
Vitoria, battle of *427*
vitrification 301
Vitruvius 508, 527, 529
Vittorio Veneto, battle of 437
Vivaldi, Antonio 572
viverrids 153
viviparity 134
Vladivostok 289
Vlaminck, Maurice de 544, 545
vocabulary 608–9
vocals *see* speech
voice 226
volcanoes *78*, **82–3**, 84, *85*, *98*, 99, 100, 176, 462
landforms **86**, *87*, 93, 95, **98**
Voldemaras, Augustinas 700
voles 151, 170
Volgograd *see* Stalingrad
Volodymyr, Prince 714, 728
Volta, Alessandro 34, 36, 61
voltage 35, 36
Voltaire 418, *419*, 629
voluntary organizations 297, 299
voodoo *465*, 592, 688
Vorticism 548–9
voting **266–7**, 286, 291, 292, 370, 435
refused in Vietnam 452
rights 291, *292*, 431, 435
voyages of discovery *405*, 417
Voysey, C. F. A. 539
Vuillard, Edouard 545
vulcanization, rubber 316

Waddaulah, Hassanal Bolkiah Mu'izzudin 669
Wadlow, Robert *205*
wages 273, 276, 402, 404
Wagner, Cosima *577*
Wagner, Richard 538, 569, **576**, *577*, 578, 579, 580, 583, 584, 585, 641
wagon train *430*
al-Wahhab, Muhammad ibn abd 717
al-Wahid Wakil, Abd 511
Wailing Wall *482*
Wajda, Andrzej 562
Wake Island 731
Wales 729
art and architecture 523
government 267
history 375, *396*, 397, 412, 421
language 603, 606
law 265
literature 647
Walesa, Lech 713
al-Walid, Khaled ibn 510
Wallis and Futuna Islands 682
walking 173
Wall Street Crash 441, 443
Wallace, Alfred Russel 112
Walpole, Horace 632
Walpole, Robert 413
walrus *162*, 162–3, 172–3
Walton, William 579
Wang Shifu 617
Warhol, Andy 503, 554, 557, 561
warm front/occlusion *102*, 103
warm-blooded animals *see* mammals
warriors *see* armies
wars
Afghanistan 451, 660
Algeria 448, 660
American Civil 431
American Independence 266, 290, 417, 419, **422–3**, 424
Anglo-Dutch *416*, 417
Angola 298, *451*
Arab-Israeli 287, 298, 451, **454–5**
and art 516, *647*
Austrian Succession 417
Balkan 429
Boer 294, 432, *433*
British 396–401. 412–13, *416*, 417
with America 422–3, 430
English Civil 266, 413, 623
in India 432
Cambodia *451*, 452, 453
Chinese Civil 447, *451*
Cold War 450–1
Crimean *429*
Crusades 392, 395, **398–9**, 403
Egypt, ancient 366
First World *see* World War I *below*
France
with England 400–1
religious 409
Civil 414
of Louis XIV *415*
Napoleonic 426–7
Franco-Prussian 428, *429*
see also Louis XIV *and* Religion; Revolutionary *below*
Great Northern 417
Greece, ancient 360, 371
Gulf *455*
Hundred Years **400–1**, 403, 412
Islamic jihad 392, 478
Japan and Russia 387, 421, 433, 438
Korean 349, *353*, 447, 450, *451*
Lebanon 455
and literature 628, 638, 646
Malaysia *451*
Maori 389
Mexico and USA 430
Mozambique 299
Napoleonic *see* Revolutionary *below*
Netherlands *416*, 417
Opium 383, 433
Peloponnesian 371
Persian 370–1, 372
Punic 376
of Religion 408, 409, 411
Revolutionary and Napoleonic 426–7, 428
Roman Empire 376–7, 378, 379, 380–1
of the Roses 401, 412
Russian Civil 438, 439
Russo-Japanese 387, 421, 433, 438
Second World War *see* World War II *below*
Seven Weeks 428
Seven Years 413, **417**, 422
Six Day 455
Spanish Civil 443
Spanish Succession 411, 415
Suez Crisis 449, *454*, 455, 644
and technology 332, 333, 342–3, 345, 348–9, 351, *353*, 356–7
Thirty Years **409**, 411, 628
Trojan 369, 614
USA
with Mexico 430
see also American *above*
Vietnam 295, *299*, 449, *451*, **452–3**
World War I **436–7**
art 547, *647*
poetry 646, *647*
transport 348, *356*
see also under individual countries
World War II **444–5**, 446, 448–9, 450
aircraft 309, 348, *349*, 351
atom bomb *293*, 445
costs 298, 450
radar 332
women's labour *293*
Yom Kippur 455
see also armies; arms; civil wars; fortifications; navies; weapons; *and also under* names of individual countries
Yugoslav Civil 738–9
Warsaw Pact 450, *451*
wart hog *152*, **158**
Washington Conference 441
Washington, George 422, *423*
wasps 126
wastes
bodily *see* excretion
energy from 306
industrial 95, 244, 301, 304, 306, 321
Wat Phai Lom 482
watches 7
water
aquatic ecosystems 178–9
see also freshwater; oceans
in body 211
chemistry of 41, 44, 45, **48**
as climatic control 104–5
on Earth 13, 110
and ecosystems 176, **178–9**
energy from 306–7
erosion 87
hydrological cycle 176
and life 110, 117, 118, 119, 211
movement in 172–3
and nuclear reactors 304, 305
physics (hydrostatics) 23
pollution 179, 244, **300–1**
power from 95, **307**
supply 238, 244, 434
waves 28, 96, 100
see also freshwater; lakes; oceans; rainfall; rivers
water boatmen 173
water buffalo 191
water frame 420
water strider 167
water vapour 176
see also precipitation
watercolour 501
waterfalls *95*
Watergate scandal 453, 655
Waterloo, battle of *427*, 636
waterproofing 316, 317
watersheds 94
Watson, James 61, 114
Watt, James 36, 308, 419, 420
Watteau, Antoine *534*, 535
watts 36
Waugh, Evelyn 648
wave/s
electromagnetic *35*
ocean *100*, 306
seismic 28, *76*, 80, *81*
theory 28–9
wave-particle duality 26, 38
Wayne, John *560*
weapons **356–7**
and criminals 263
history 309, 349, 356–7, 373, 374, 389, 391, 407, 437, 505
and police 262
trade 389
see also nuclear weapons; missiles; rockets; wars
weasels 155
weather 19, **102–3**, 176, 301, 310
see also climate
weathering 87
weaving *319*, 420

Weber, Carl Maria von 585
Weber, Max 258, 259, 267
Webern, Anton 578
Webster, John 623
wedding see marriage
Wedgwood, Josiah 421
Weelkes, Thomas 571
weever (fish) 129
Wegener, Alfred 78
weight 21
weightlessness 19
Weill, Kurt 642
Weimar Republic 442, 547
Weine, Robert 559
Weir, Peter 562
welfare state 266, 268, 270, 434
  see also social security
Wells Cathedral 523
Welles, Orson 560, 561
Wellington, Duke of 427
Wells, H. G. 651
Wells, Horace 249
Wenders, Wim 563
Wernicke's area 226, 227
Wesker, Arnold 644
Wessex 396, 397
West Bank 455, 692
West Germany see Germany
West Indies see Central
  America/Caribbean
westerlies 101
Western Sahara 705
Western Samoa 735
Westminster Cathedral 539, 622
Weston, Edward 556, 557
Westphalia, Peace of 409
Weyden, Rogier van der 526
whales 162, 163, 171, 172, 332
  communication 30, 166–7
  hunting 195, 639
  migration 171
wheat 188, 189, 196
Wheatley, Dennis 651
Wheatstone, Sir Charles 330

wheels 364
white blood cells 210, 212
white dwarf 9
white of egg 139
White, Patrick 649
Whitehead, A. N. 495
Whitman, Walt 639
Whitney, Eli 430
Whittle, Frank 309
wholesalers 280–1
whooping cough 239, 245
Wieskirche 534
Wigman, Mary 598
Wilberforce, William 416
Wilbye, John 571
wild boar 158
Wilde, Oscar 546, 627, 641, 644
wildebeest 153, 161, 170, 171, 185
Wilder, Billy 560
Wilhelm I of Germany (Kaiser) 415, 428
Wilkins, Maurice 61
Will of Heaven see Confucianism
William I (the Conqueror) 397, 400
William II, emperor 685
William III of England (of Orange,
  b.1650) 413, 692, 707, 730
William of Ockham 60
William of Orange (b. 1533) 709
  see also William III
William of Tyre 398
Williams, Eric 726
Williams, Tennessee 645
Williams, William Carlos 647
willows 180
willy-willies 104
Wilson, Richard 633
Wilson, Robert 5
Wilson, Woodrow 440, 733
wind 87, 93, 101, 103, 306, 307
wine 196
wings see flight
witches 409, 645
Wittgenstein, Ludwig 487, 489, 497
Witz, Konrad 526

Wladyslaw I of Poland 712
Wodaabe people 190
Wolfe, General James 417, 672
Wollstonecraft, Mary 292
Wolsey, Cardinal Thomas 412
wolverine 155
wolves 154, 166, 168, 181
wombat 142
women
  and Islam 478
  and ordination 476
  the women's movement 292–3
  working 273, 292–3, 434
  see also humans; menstruation;
    pregnancy; sexism
wood artwork 502, 503
  see also forests
woodlice 124, 125
wood production 192–3
woodwind 583
wool 190–1, 318, 413
Woolf, Virginia 641, 648
woolly monkeys 165
words 603, 608–9
  see also language
Wordsworth, William 41, 537, 631,
  632–3
work 24
  see also labour
working class 259, 268, 269, 540, 636,
  637
World Bank (IBRD) 285, 299
World Council of Churches 477
World Health Organization (WHO)
  244, 245, 285
world map 625
world music 586
world tree see Yggdrasil
World War I 436–7
  art 547, 647
  poetry 646, 647
  transport 348, 356
  see also under individual countries
World War II 444–5, 446, 448–9, 450

aircraft 309, 348, 349, 351
atom bomb 293, 445
  costs 298, 450
  radar 332
  women's labour 293
worms 122, 148, 171, 172, 174, 175
  and diseases 238, 239, 244
worry see anxiety
worship 472–3, 480
  see also religion
Wren, Sir Christopher 260, 531
Wright, Frank Lloyd 552
Wright, Joseph 486
Wright, Wilbur and Orville 348
writing 604–5, 608
  alphabet invented 364, 605
  calligraphy 510, 514
  Chinese 382, 386, 604
  cuneiform 604
  hieroglyphic 361, 366, 391, 604, 605
  Japanese 604
  Linear B 369, 462, 604, 614
  see also script
Wuppertal Company 599
Wycherley, William 627
Wycliffe, John 403, 606
Wyeth, Andrew 500
Wyler, William 561
Wyndham, John 651
Wyndham Lewis, Percy 548–9, 641

X, Planet 11
xenon 42–3, 50
xeromorphic features 187
Xerxes 365, 370, 372
Xia dynasty 382
Xian dynasty 382, 514
X-rays 17, 35, 144, 197, 236, 237, 242,
  249, 332, 333

Yahya, Imam 738
yak 161, 190

Yalta Conference 450
Yangtze River 382, 383
al-Yaqubi 392
Yasovarman 512
Yeager, Captain Charles 349
year 6, 8, 483
yeast 320
Yeats, John Butler 646
Yeats, W. B. 641, 645, 646
Yeltsin, Boris 715–16
Yemen 287, 454, 479, 735
Yggdrasil 463
Yiddish language 603
Yijing (I Ching) 470, 616
Yin/Yang 470, 471
Yippies 295
yoga 480
yoghurt 196
yolk (egg) 139
Yom Kippur War 455
Yorimoto 386
York
  House of 401, 412
  mystery plays 621
Yoruba people 464, 517
Young, Lester 589
Young, Thomas 29
young people see children and young
  people
youth hostels 294
youth movements 294–5
Ypres 400, 437
ytterbium 42–3, 50
yttrium 42–3, 50
'Yuaikai' 435
Yuan dynasty 383, 514, 617
Yucatán 390, 391, 410, 516
yucca 121
Yugoslavia 668, 677, 719, 735–6, 738
  art and architecture 505, 519
  geology/geomorphology 89
  history 441, 442, 445, 450, 451
  international relations 285, 286, 287,
    660

law 265
religion 477, 481

Zaidis 479
Zaïre 160, 165, 517, 736
Zama, battle of 376
Zambia 607, 736–7
Zanzibar 725
Zarathustra 461
zazen 468
zebra 153, 156, 156, 169, 171, 182
Zen Buddhism 468, 469, 470, 515,
  599, 617
zeolites 54–5
Zeppelin, Count Ferdinand von and
  Zeppelins 348, 437
Zeuxis 508
Zheng He (Cheng Ho) 405
Zhivkov, Todor 670
Zhou dynasty 382–3, 514, 616
Zhuang Zi (Chuang Tzu) 470
Zhukov, Marshal Georgi 445
Zi Xi 446
Zia-ur-Rahman, General 666
ziggurats 461, 506, 613
Zimbabwe 287, 388, 389, 517, 607,
  737
Zimmermann, Bern-Alois 585
zinc 42–3, 50, 208, 300, 313
Zionists 454
zirconium 42–3, 50
Zola, Émile 616, 635, 642
zooplankton 179
zorilla 155
Zoroastrianism 461, 467, 484
  see also Parsis
Zukor, Adolph 559
Zulus 602
Zurich dada 550
Zuse, Konrad 335
Zworykin, Vladimir 326
zygotes 114, 118, 202